From the knowledge leader since 1768

# ENCYCLOPÆDIA
# Britannica
# ALMANAC
# 2004

ENCYCLOPÆDIA
## Britannica®

Jacob E. Safra, *Chairman of the Board*
Jorge Cauz, *President*

Chicago · London · New Delhi · Paris · Seoul · Sydney · Taipei · Tokyo

## Bush, Iraq, and the World

*by Strobe Talbott*

From the moment that the first explosions lit up the night sky over Baghdad, this war was personal. Four huge bombs and about forty cruise missiles slammed into a heavily fortified VIP compound near the Tigris River. The opening salvo was intended not just to inspire "shock and awe" among the Iraqi people but to kill their leader, Saddam Hussein. "Selected targets of military importance," said Pres. George W. Bush when he went on national television half an hour later. "A target of opportunity," added White House and Pentagon sources in the hours that followed. They left no doubt who was in the crosshairs.

Bush came by his animus honestly. The greatest triumph of the presidency of his father, George H.W. Bush, had been to end Saddam's occupation of Kuwait in the Gulf War of 1991. But that victory had been incomplete. Saddam survived, and two years later he plotted to assassinate the senior Bush, who was then out of office, during a visit to Kuwait.

No wonder the second President Bush felt he had a score to settle. He also had objective reasons to wish for Saddam's demise, as did the whole world. The Iraqi dictator was an affront to the very idea of an international community. He had spent the 1990s intimidating his neighbors, brutalizing his own people, engaging in genocidal repression of Iraq's Marsh Arabs and Kurds, and systematically flouting the terms of probation that the UN had imposed on him after his eviction from Kuwait. Saddam played cat-and-mouse with the UN as it tried to make sure he was not illicitly developing chemical, biological, and nuclear weapons. In 1998 the UN withdrew its arms inspectors in the face of Iraqi deceit, defiance, and obstruction.

So, in addition to its being personal for President Bush, this was a war waiting to happen. Whenever it had occurred and however it was explained from the bully pulpit in Washington, it would have set off a wave of criticism and second-guessing around the world. For at least half a century the emergence of the US as the strongest nation in history had aroused a combination of ambivalence and resentment in other countries, including friends and allies of the US. They counted on the strength of the American economy to boost their own, admired the US for its political values and the dynamism of its culture and society, and looked to Washington for protection. However, when American presidents—in disregard of John Quincy Adams's famous advice—went abroad in search of monsters to destroy, the foreign reaction to success was two cheers, not three, and the reaction to failure was varying degrees of schadenfreude.

Pres. John F. Kennedy took his lumps abroad as well as at home for botching an attempt to eliminate Fidel Castro in Cuba. Lyndon Johnson's debacle in Vietnam was seen internationally as Goliath meeting his match. Ronald Reagan made quick work of tiny Grenada in 1983, but the pretext for the invasion—the rescue of American students at a beachfront medical school—struck many as implausible and unjustified. In addition to his own showdown with Saddam Hussein, George H.W. Bush went into Panama with guns blazing, kicked down the door, and dragged the country's strongman, Manuel Noriega, off to an American jail. By what right? asked many, especially in Latin America, which has had long experience with "Tio Sam" armed with a pistol and a "Wanted Dead or Alive" poster.

Under Pres. Bill Clinton, the US resorted to force on a significant scale three times: in 1994, when it replaced a military junta in Haiti with the democratically elected president, and in 1995 and 1999, when it conducted bombing campaigns to stop Slobodan Milosevic's rampages of ethnic cleansing in the Balkans. Once again the reaction abroad to America's actions was a mixture of astonishment (sometimes tinged with anxiety) at US military prowess, gratitude (sometimes grudging) for American leadership, and unease at the unprecedented, unrivaled, and unregulated extent of American power. When in 1999 French Foreign Minister Hubert Védrine labeled the US *l'hyperpuissance*, or "the hyperpower," he did not mean it as a compliment, and he had in mind the foreign policy of the arch-multilateralist Clinton.

It was against this backdrop that George W. Bush became the custodian of all that power in January 2001. Yes, he had a glint of vengeance in his eye on the subject of Saddam, and yes, he slipped naturally into the Gary Cooper role as the marshal in *High Noon*—facing down the bad guys while the frightened townspeople disappear from the streets, duck behind closed doors, and peek out through drawn blinds. But he also had a strong case, and plenty of precedent, for making the downfall of an international outlaw a priority of his foreign policy.

However, the second gulf war as waged by the second President Bush proved to be more controversial abroad than any American military adventure since Vietnam—which is all the more extraordinary in that it took only six weeks and relatively little death and destruction for the US to accomplish its immediate objective. The war was seen as dramatic evidence of what many had feared for over two years. From virtually the day he took office, Bush had put the world on notice that the executive branch of the US government was operating under a new concept of the American mission and how to accomplish it. Previously, the assumption had been: "Together if we can,

> " *[Bush] had objective reasons to wish for Saddam's demise, as did the whole world.* "

alone if we must." "Together" meant a preference for working with allies, with regional security organizations, and with the authorization of UN Security Council resolutions. The Bush administration stood the formula on its head: "Alone if we can, together if we must."

In one respect, this shift was unabashedly political. Spokesmen for the new administration claimed that Democrats—particularly the one who occupied the presidency between the two Bushes—had diluted America's power, squandered the nation's resources, and emboldened its enemies. They had done so through misplaced idealism about the nature of the world, a naive belief in the illusory if not oxymoronic concept of international law, excessive deference to the sensibilities of other countries (notably including allies), a foolish reliance on feckless international organizations, and a timidity about the decisive use of US force.

While this critique was directed primarily against Clinton, it was, ironically though inescapably, also a tacit putdown of the elder Bush's concept, enunciated in 1991, that the end of the Cold War made possible a "new world order," led by the US but based on collaboration with old friends and new partners and the strengthening of international institutions.

During the first nine months of 2001, the administration made statements and took actions intended to demonstrate a new self-reliance and assertiveness and, accordingly, a new resistance to agreements and arrangements that limited America's freedom of action. The US renounced, "unsigned," weakened, disdained, or ignored more than a dozen treaties and diplomatic works in progress that it had inherited from its predecessors, Republican as well as Democratic. These included the Kyoto Protocol on climate change, the International Criminal Court, the Treaty on Anti-Ballistic Missile Systems, the land mine ban treaty, and an array of conventions designed to protect the rights of children, stop torture, curb discrimination by race and gender, end the production of biological weapons, prevent money laundering, and limit trafficking in small arms. Earlier administrations had had objections to some features of many of these accords but sought to improve them; the Bush administration seemed to want nothing to do with agreements of this kind.

The new US leadership also downgraded the importance it attached to diplomacy, since that is an exercise in compromise, and the Bush team was not in a compromising mood. The US suspended the Middle East peace process and the dialogue with North Korea.

By the late summer of 2001 there was more grumbling than ever from those around the world who were prepared to follow the US president as a leader but less inclined to take orders from him as a boss. Vice Pres. Richard Cheney and Secretary of Defense

Donald Rumsfeld quickly established themselves as the advocates, in public and in the councils of the administration, of unilateralism without apologies. Secretary of State Colin Powell seemed to be alone in voicing a more traditional, cooperative, and institutional approach. He lost one battle after another, and his imminent resignation was frequently rumored.

Then came 11 September. The immediate effect of the attacks was to galvanize international sympathy for the US. There was a sudden burst of approval for President Bush as a righteous lawman, and the world became one big posse. The normally *hyperpuissance*-bashing Paris daily *Le Monde* ran a banner headline proclaiming, "We are all Americans now."

Secretary Powell went from being the odd man out to being the man of the hour. He assembled an international coalition of unprecedented breadth to back the US as it prepared for retribution against Afghanistan, which had become a breeding ground for radical Islamists and a sanctuary for Osama bin Laden and his al-Qaeda terrorist network.

The Bush administration was glad to have good wishes and political support from abroad. But when NATO, for the first time in its history, invoked Article V of its charter, proclaiming that the assaults against the World Trade Center and the Pentagon constituted an attack on all member states, the US said, in effect, "Thanks very much, now please stay out of the way while we take care of this." As a result, the alliance was largely sidelined during the military action in Afghanistan.

> " *Before the terror attacks, the phrase 'national security' had been an abstraction for many Americans. Afterward, it had new, concrete meaning virtually synonymous with personal safety.* "

Only when the Afghan Taliban were driven from power and the US turned to the hard work of reconstruction did it welcome international participation. One reason was that the Bush administration saw itself as doing regime-change but not nation-building. Another was that it wanted, as quickly as possible, to get on with changing another regime—in Iraq. The day after 11 September, Paul Wolfowitz, Rumsfeld's intellectually formidable and politically powerful deputy, made the case in a meeting with the president that once the US had taken care of Target Kabul it should turn to Target Baghdad.

The willingness of the American people to support military action in Iraq increased because of 11 September. Before the terror attacks, the phrase "national security" had been an abstraction for many Americans. Afterward, it had new, concrete meaning virtually synonymous with personal safety. The world was a place where bad people—"evildoers," in the president's phrase—were looking for ways to kill Americans on America's own territory. It was easier than it would have been otherwise for the administration to convince Americans that Saddam Hussein, too, was an evildoer who would kill Americans if he could and that therefore the US had to kill him first. That was the subtext of the doctrine that the administration promulgated a year after 11 September in a presidential document identifying preemptive and preventive war as vital tools for the defense of the homeland.

In a speech to the Veterans of Foreign Wars in August 2002, Vice President Cheney set the stage for applying the new doctrine to Iraq. "We must take the battle to the enemy," he said. "We" meant the US; the United Nations, Cheney made clear, had disqualified itself and should step aside.

In a phrase that had gained currency since 11 September, the administration set about "connecting the dots" between Saddam Hussein on the one hand and weapons of mass destruction and the forces of international terrorism on the other. Since Saddam was trying to acquire WMD and might give them to terrorists, the US should bring him down. Embedded in this syllogism was a major weakness in the administration's case for war. In his effort to build domestic and international support for military action, Bush was driven to assert—and, as it turned out, exaggerate—the extent of Saddam's WMD programs and his ties to terrorists.

The most vocal skeptics about the logic of the administration's argument were Republicans associated with the first President Bush, particularly former national security adviser Brent Scowcroft and former secretary of state James Baker. Whatever the misgivings of prominent Democrats, they were reluctant to tackle a president who was riding high largely because of his robust response to 11 September. Within the administration, Powell continued to be a force for moderation. He persuaded Bush to address the UN and give multilateralism one more chance. The president dared the UN to prove itself relevant but, unlike Cheney, did not dismiss its ability to do so. The challenge led directly to the unanimous passage of Security Council Resolution 1441, which warned of "serious consequences" if Iraq did not comply with tough new inspections. Saddam immediately adopted his familiar practice of dodging and weaving, but it looked as though the US might finally have laid the basis for a UN-authorized, US-led military action.

Had it worked out that way, Gulf War II would have been part of the continuum going back to Gulf War I and the Clinton administration's use of force in Haiti and the Balkans. Not only would Bush have prevailed over Saddam, but he would have had the much-vaunted international community largely behind him—and, indeed, with him on the ground in large and diverse numbers.

Instead, the juggernaut that Bush and Powell had put in motion turned into a train wreck, primarily between the US and France. Pres. Jacques Chirac

> " *The war ... heightened anxieties that American power ... was a problem for virtually every other country on Earth.* "

shares the blame. In an interview on 10 Mar 2003 he warned that France would veto a new resolution authorizing force under any circumstances. Russia and China, which were prepared to go along with France in either direction, took a similar position. Chirac's obstinacy and grandstanding cut the legs out from under Powell and strengthened those in the administration who had warned that by going to the UN in the first place, the president had fallen into a trap. Now the US was, in the eyes of the unilateralists, free to do the job right, with a "coalition" that included, in its military dimension, Great Britain, Australia, and Poland as well as some crucial logistical support from the smaller gulf states.

Operation Iraqi Freedom produced two positive results. First, it rid Iraq, the region, and the world of a scourge; and, second, in part because of an understanding he had with British Prime Minister Tony Blair, his staunchest ally, Bush relaunched the Middle East peace process.

On the other hand, the war did profound damage to American relations with a wide array of countries and several international institutions, principally the UN and NATO, which was further marginalized. More generally, it heightened anxieties that American power, benevolent though its motivations might be, was a problem for virtually every other country on Earth, especially if the victory in Iraq vindicated the unilateralists and ensured their continued ascendancy in the US. As American and British troops were tearing down Saddam's statues and scouring the country for the man himself, many around the world (and in the US as well) feared that the "Iraq model" would serve as a template for changing two other regimes that Bush had named as part of the "axis of evil," Iran and North Korea, since both had nuclear weapons programs far more advanced than Iraq's.

It was not that simple, however. In the second half of 2003 the US military had its hands full in Iraq and Afghanistan, both of which were far from stabilized. Partly for that reason, and also because the US needed as much international help as possible for the jobs ahead in those two countries, the administration put its six-shooter back in its holster and resorted to multilateral diplomacy in trying to deal with Iran and North Korea. Just as it quickly became apparent that the Iraq war would have a long, messy, and uncertain aftermath, so the struggle to define the future of American foreign policy was far from over. What was already being called the Bush revolution in US foreign policy might yet give way to a restoration of traditional American internationalism.

*Strobe Talbott is a former journalist for Time and deputy secretary of state (1994–2001) and now president of The Brookings Institution, Washington DC. His latest book is The Russia Hand: A Memoir of Presidential Diplomacy (Random House, 2002).*

## ETHNIC AND RELIGIOUS GROUPS IN IRAQ AND VICINITY

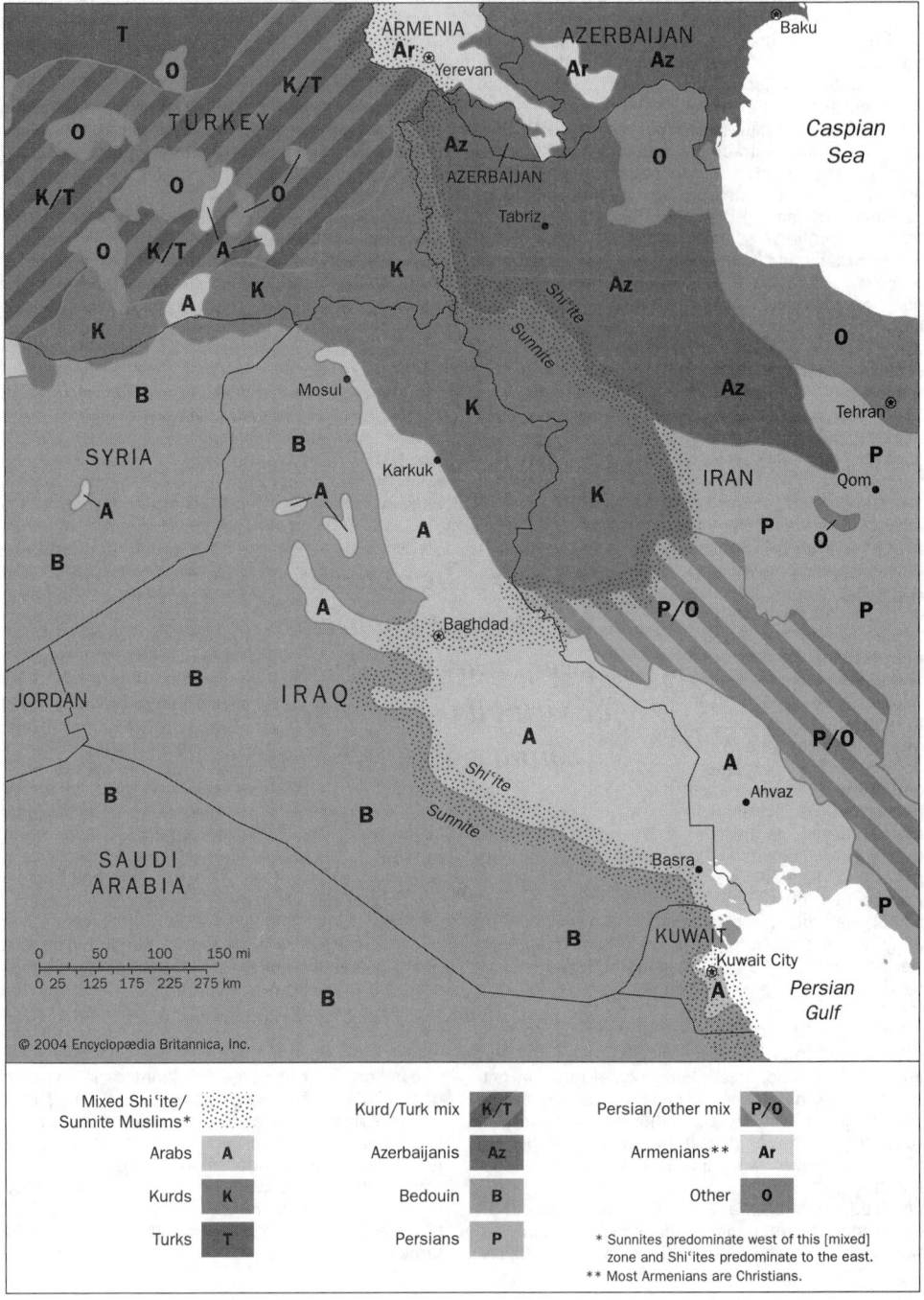

© 2004 Encyclopædia Britannica, Inc.

| | | |
|---|---|---|
| Mixed Shiʻite/Sunnite Muslims* | Kurd/Turk mix **K/T** | Persian/other mix **P/O** |
| Arabs **A** | Azerbaijanis **Az** | Armenians** **Ar** |
| Kurds **K** | Bedouin **B** | Other **O** |
| Turks **T** | Persians **P** | |

\* Sunnites predominate west of this [mixed] zone and Shiʻites predominate to the east.
\** Most Armenians are Christians.

# SARS (Severe Acute Respiratory Syndrome)

The viral infection that came to be known as SARS is believed to have emerged in southern China in November 2002. Those who contract the disease experience pneumonia-like symptoms, including respiratory distress, fever, and achiness, and in about 15% of cases, death ensues. SARS spread across China and to other areas of Southeast Asia as well as to Toronto in February and early March 2003. By July the disease had claimed 810 lives and affected thousands in 33 countries. The World Health Organization (WHO) and the US Centers for Disease Control and Prevention issued travel advisories, and governments in the affected countries closed schools and other institutions and issued quarantine orders to stem the spread of the disease. Eventually, researchers in Hong Kong established a tentative link between the SARS outbreak in humans and the consumption of civets, considered a delicacy by some. The outbreak was devastating to tourism and to economies generally in the affected areas, but WHO declared the outbreak contained in July 2003.

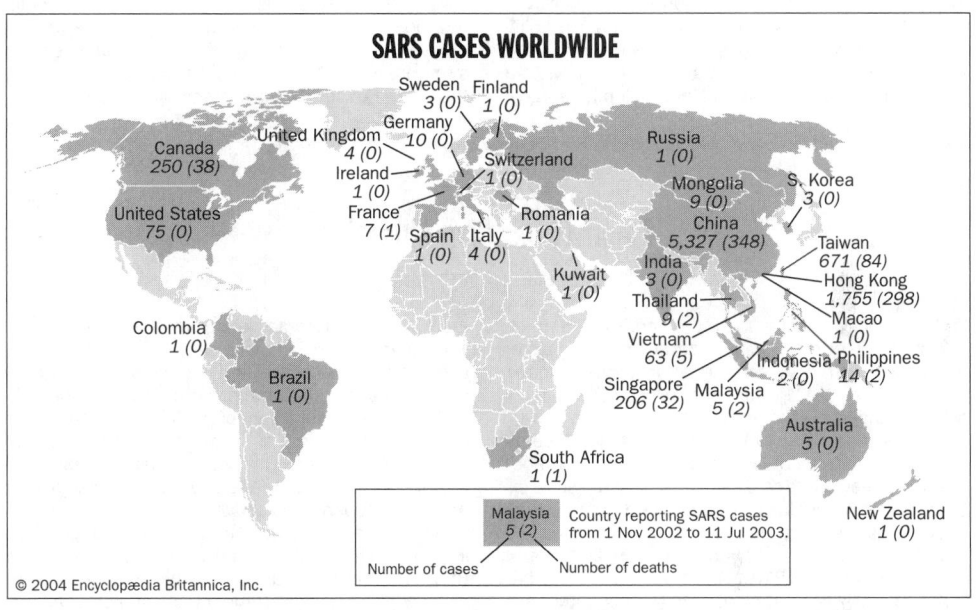

**SARS CASES WORLDWIDE**

Sweden 3 (0)
Finland 1 (0)
Germany 10 (0)
United Kingdom 4 (0)
Canada 250 (38)
Ireland 1 (0)
Switzerland 1 (0)
Russia 1 (0)
Mongolia 9 (0)
S. Korea 3 (0)
United States 75 (0)
France 7 (1)
Spain 1 (0)
Italy 4 (0)
Romania 1 (0)
China 5,327 (348)
Taiwan 671 (84)
India 3 (0)
Kuwait 1 (0)
Hong Kong 1,755 (298)
Thailand 9 (2)
Macao 1 (0)
Colombia 1 (0)
Vietnam 63 (5)
Indonesia 2 (0)
Philippines 14 (2)
Brazil 1 (0)
Singapore 206 (32)
Malaysia 5 (2)
Australia 5 (0)
South Africa 1 (1)
New Zealand 1 (0)

Malaysia 5 (2) — Country reporting SARS cases from 1 Nov 2002 to 11 Jul 2003.
Number of cases — Number of deaths

© 2004 Encyclopædia Britannica, Inc.

# The US 2002 Midterm Elections

*by David C. Beckwith*

The 2002 midterm elections proved that no generality in American politics was absolute. Although a first-term president's party had not gained ground in midterm elections since 1934, Republicans in 2002 increased their narrow margins in the US House and regained control of the US Senate with Pres. George W. Bush taking the point.

Though Democrats were perceived to have had the advantage early in the year as concerns over the sluggish national economy and a declining stock market unsettled voters, Bush's conduct regarding the "war on terrorism" was widely supported. Democrats were generally supportive of that effort and had attempted to remove security as an issue by focusing public attention on domestic issues, such as the establishment of a prescription drug benefit for senior citizens, the provision of additional federal help for education, and a slower phase-in period for Bush's 2001 tax-cut plan.

With control of the White House "bully pulpit," however, Republicans kept the focus on support for the popular president. During the year the Republican-controlled House passed dozens of Bush-approved bills, only to see them die in the Senate. When Bush attempted to set up a new umbrella Department of Homeland Security to coordinate domestic anti-terrorism efforts, Democrats objected because the proposal allowed the administration to bypass civil-service protections for department employees. By accident or design the controversy was not settled before the election, and Democrats were widely criticized for blocking security efforts.

At one point Republicans appeared poised to replace a rising Democratic star, Sen. Robert Torricelli

> " *A first-term president's party had not gained ground in midterm elections since 1934.* "

of New Jersey, who was admonished by his Senate colleagues following an ethics investigation into his campaign contributions and acceptance of personal gifts. Torricelli fell more than 10 points behind an inexperienced GOP challenger and abruptly quit the race only five weeks before the election. Democrats, however, were able to replace him with former senator Frank Lautenberg, 78, who won the seat handily.

Then, in late October, Sen. Paul Wellstone, a liberal Democrat who was expected to win a third term, was killed when his light plane crashed in northern Minnesota. Democrats quickly settled on replacement candidate Walter Mondale, 74, a popular former senator and US vice president. A nationally televised memorial service for Wellstone turned ugly, however, when Wellstone partisans booed conservative politicians in attendance, and Democrats were perceived to have turned the occasion into a political rally. As a result, support for Republican Norm Coleman surged.

Bush was unusually active on the campaign trail, barnstorming the country and effectively transforming local elections into referenda on his stewardship. By contrast, Democrats had difficulty settling on a common message. A notable split developed among prominent Democrats over scrapping the tax cuts to balance the federal budget; another appeared over challenging Bush's aggressive stance against Iraq.

On election day Republicans expanded their advantage in the House by six seats to 229–205 (plus one independent). More important, the GOP recorded a net gain of two Senate slots, to take control of that body. Sen. Mary Landrieu of Louisiana won a competitive runoff in December to retain her seat, which allowed Democrats to finish the year on an upbeat note. As a practical matter, however, the two parties were at parity across the country when the new Congress was sworn in in 2003, but Republicans enjoyed control of the White House and both chambers of Congress.

*David C. Beckwith is the president of the National Cable Television Association.*

# Security vs. Civil Liberties

*by Stephen J. Phillips*

Technology has been at the forefront of international efforts to fight terrorism and bolster security in the wake of the terrorist attacks in the US on 11 Sep 2001. The rush to deploy new technologies and to give law-enforcement officials new investigative powers in cyberspace sparked concerns for the civil liberties of law-abiding citizens. For other observers, however, the threat posed by religious extremists and other shadowy groups bent on mass destruction gave security precedence over freedom.

In the US, debate continued on the implications of the antiterrorist USA PATRIOT Act adopted in October 2001. The new law, aimed at empowering authorities to move more nimbly against terrorist threats, relaxed legal checks on surveillance, granting the CIA and the FBI a freer hand to gather data electronically on citizens and resident foreigners. The legislation, approved by a sweeping majority in Congress, reduced the need for subpoenas, court orders, or warrants for eavesdropping on Internet communications, monitoring financial transactions, and obtaining individuals' electronic records. As part of criminal investigations, law-enforcement and intelligence agencies were authorized to track the Web sites that suspects visited and identify those to whom they sent e-mail. Internet service providers were required to turn over data on customers' Web-surfing habits to authorities on demand.

Many of the measures were hailed as necessary revisions of surveillance laws to keep increasingly sophisticated and determined terrorists at bay. Civil liberties advocates, however, worried that the PATRIOT Act's easing of judicial oversight and vague definition of legitimate subjects for electronic surveillance opened it to abuse and could cast the legal dragnet too wide in the search for incriminating evidence. The legislation paved the way for wider deployment of the controversial FBI program formerly known as Carnivore—renamed, less menacingly, DCS 1000—which sifts e-mail for particular addresses or specific text strings (sequences of characters). In December 2001 it was reported that the FBI had developed "Magic Lantern," a so-called Trojan horse pro-

gram designed to crack encrypted files and e-mails. The program could implant itself surreptitiously in a suspect's computer via an e-mail message and then record keystrokes to obtain the user's passwords. In mid-2002 the Department of Justice (DOJ) announced Operation TIPS (Terrorism Information and Prevention System), a plan to recruit workers such as mail carriers and utility-meter readers as informants to spot and report "suspicious activity."

Concerns about government access to personal information were not limited to the US. In June the British government, amid a public outcry, shelved plans to give local government units and other administrative bodies the right to access an individual's telephone and e-mail records. Such privileges were given only to police, tax authorities, and security agencies. Across the world, debate raged over national identity cards to verify people's identity and to screen access to potential terrorist targets. Compulsory identification schemes, based on laminated ID cards, had been long-standing in countries as diverse as China, Argentina, Germany, and Spain. The latest proposals, however, were based on cards bearing unique biological identifiers—such as an iris scan or a digitized thumbprint—known as biometrics, as well as a microchip programmed with additional personal details. In September 2001 Malaysia mandated such a "smart card," dubbed the Mykad, for all citizens over the age of 12. Meanwhile, Hong Kong geared up to overhaul its compulsory ID system with smart cards for its 6.8 million inhabitants in 2003. Officials hoped to crack down on illegal immigrants while easing bottlenecks at the territory's border with China. Border crossers would have their thumbprints scanned by an optical reader and—instead of waiting hours for their papers to be read—could pass through the checkpoint in a matter of seconds if the print matched the digital replica on their card.

In July 2002 British ministers began a six-month public consultation to determine how an ID card scheme could be administered. The measure faced opposition from various quarters, ranging from civil libertarians objecting to citizens' being treated as suspects to individuals concerned about bureaucratic overheads. Such a scheme would not come cheap either. The cost of issuing biometrics cards to the 60.2 million population was put at £3.1 billion (about $4.8 billion). Belgium planned to issue ID cards with embedded digital signatures.

Identity-authentication proposals were also contentious in the US. As an alternative to building an infrastructure from scratch, driver's licenses held by up to 200 million Americans—more than 87% of the adult population—offered an obvious starting point for a de facto national scheme. The Driver's License Modernization Act of 2002, proposed in May, sought to set nationwide standards for licenses issued by each of the 50 states that would include embedded chips and biometrics data. Under the plan the cards would be linked to networked databases, allowing officials to check out any suspicious activity quickly.

Others were disquieted by the specter of Big Brother. They feared that cards linked to databases would turn into internal passports to monitor citizens' movements. Privacy groups called for the US government at the very least to spell out the uses to which data gleaned from credential checks could be put—anticipating "function creep," the tendency for information to be used for purposes beyond those originally envisaged. Public support for a national identity scheme also appeared to cool as the memory of 11 September receded. A Pew Research Center poll conducted immediately after the attacks returned a 70% approval rating for such a scheme, but support had dwindled to 26% by March 2002, according to a survey by Gartner Group.

The Enhanced Border Security and Visa Entry Reform Act mandated that by 26 Oct 2003, all US visas, as well as passports issued by visa-waiver countries, such as Australia, must be machine-readable and tamper-resistant and must incorporate biometric identifiers. In October 2002 the Immigration and Naturalization Service began fingerprinting foreign visitors on arrival from designated, mainly Middle Eastern, countries.

Other technologies under consideration included scanners—tested at Orlando Sanford International Airport in Florida—that deployed low-level X-rays to subject airline passengers to virtual strip searches. Supporters said such drastic measures were necessary to deal with suicide bombers prepared to conceal explosives in body cavities, but critics branded them invasive. Another biometrics application put through its paces was facial-recognition cameras, or "facecams." Such technology uses software to map facial characteristics, sounding an alarm if a certain proportion of features picked up by a camera match those of police mugshots. It has been used in London to collar criminals since 1998. In 2002 such cameras were installed in several American cities and airports. The systems, also condemned by civil libertarians as intrusive, proved unreliable. Cameras tested at Palm Beach (FL) International Airport failed more than half the time to identify employees whose features were programmed into the database, while a trial in nearby Tampa did not make a single match in six months of use. Moreover, biometrics are only as effective as the comprehensiveness of the background-information archives they scrutinize. Technologically sophisticated face scans or thumbprint matching probably would not have identified, much less foiled, the 11 September hijackers, as only 2 of the 19 were on the CIA's "watch list."

While no security panacea, technology puts some powerful counterterrorism tools at the disposal of governments, but the debate in 2002 showed that leaders must plot a judicious path to ensure that new techniques do not undermine the freedoms they are intended to protect.

> " *Leaders must plot a judicious path to ensure that new techniques do not undermine the freedoms they are intended to protect.* "

*Stephen J. Phillips is a freelance journalist and a US-based information technology writer for the* Financial Times.

## Strangers at the Gates: The Immigration Backlash

*by Bob Birrell*

Immigration has emerged as a key issue in many developed nations of the world. The determination of governments to control the flow of immigrants to their nations' shores has been the focus of intense debate and, increasingly, the subject of controversy. In an incident that captured worldwide attention in August 2001, Australian authorities intercepted the Norwegian freighter *Tampa* and refused to allow the 433 asylum seekers who had been picked up by the vessel to set foot on Australian soil. These asylum seekers—mostly Afghans and Iraqis—were subsequently transported to Nauru while their claims for refugee status were processed. Meanwhile, the Australian government hastened to pass legislation toughening the country's asylum laws, and the United Nations High Commissioner for Refugees (UNHCR) eventually ruled that most of the asylum seekers did not qualify for refugee protection visas.

Despite international protests over the treatment of the *Tampa* "boat people," the hard-line stance taken by the government of Australian Prime Minister John Howard was consistent with a recent trend toward the tightening of immigration policies around the globe. This trend was particularly evident in Europe during 2002. Under new rules announced in Britain, for example, immigrants could be deported even before their appeals regarding refugee status had been heard. Legislation was introduced in the Italian parliament that would facilitate expulsions from the country and impose stiff fines and prison sentences on those involved in human trafficking. It was Denmark, however, that enacted the strictest asylum laws on the continent; a new immigration package that went into effect in July denied immigrants a residence permit until they had lived in the country for at least seven years and curbed the rights of immigrants to bring their families into the country.

While foreign workers often play vital roles in helping developed nations maintain their economies, illegal immigration and the difficulty in reconciling cultural differences between various ethnic groups can pose major problems. By 2002, 300,000 to 500,000 illegal immigrants were believed to be arriving in Europe each year. Tightening border controls was a response that appealed to many voters, as evidenced by the recent rise in popularity of anti-immigrant political groups. In Austria the far-right Freedom Party—led by Jörg Haider, who virulently denounced immigration—joined the country's ruling coalition in 2000. In Portugal a right-wing coalition that included the anti-immigrant Popular Party came into power in 2002, while in France, Norway, Switzerland, and The Netherlands, anti-immigrant parties began to exert considerable influence on mainstream politics.

> " *While foreign workers often play vital roles in helping developed nations maintain their economies, illegal immigration and the difficulty in reconciling cultural differences between various ethnic groups can pose major problems.* "

In Australia evidence that many citizens were prepared to vote on the basis of immigration issues was made clear when Pauline Hanson's One Nation party won 8% of first preference votes in the House of Representatives in the 1998 federal election, primarily owing to the party's strident anti-immigration and anti-multicultural platform. Hanson had rapidly raised her party's profile by warning that the country was in danger of being overrun by Asian immigrants—who, she claimed, took jobs from Australian citizens and made no effort to assimilate into Australian society—and by calling for a short-term halt to Asian immigration.

This atmosphere shaped the response of Howard's government to the *Tampa*'s arrival in Australian waters. At the time, the country's detention camps were bulging. The government could not even return the minority of claimants who had been denied refugee status to their countries of origin because most states would not accept them. There had been dramatic protests within these camps, including hunger strikes and riots; in one incident 58 detainees at a remote camp north of Adelaide sewed up their lips to protest delays in processing their visa applications. These protests polarized public opinion. For liberals detention was a deep stain on Australia's reputation. Although the country had no tradition of welcoming "tired and huddled masses," it had witnessed the relatively trouble-free settlement of a large influx of people from southern and eastern Europe in the 1950s and '60s and from Asia and the Middle East during the 1980s and much of the '90s. In 1999–2000, however, the arrival of unauthorized boat people—most of them Muslims from Afghanistan, Iraq, and Iran—increased fourfold from the year before, to 4,175. This led to widespread frustration over the government's apparent inability to stop an unwelcome influx.

The government was in a difficult situation because, once they were in Australia, most unauthorized claimants were being determined to be refugees according to the requirements of the 1951 UN Convention Relating to the Status of Refugees. As outlined by the convention, a person is considered a refugee who, "owing to a well-founded fear of being persecuted for reasons of race, religion, nationality, embership in a particular social group, or political opinion, is outside the country of his nationality, and is unable or, owing to such fear, is unwilling to avail himself of the protection of that country." In many cases it was not possible to put asylum claims to any empirical test, because there was a lack of access to relevant information in states where the alleged persecution occurred. Nevertheless, the various review tribunals, as well as the Australian federal and high-court judges hearing the appeals of those rejected, tended to give claimants the benefit of the doubt. The government feared that Australia was turning itself into a beacon, virtually inviting human traffickers to look to it as a destination for their clients.

The *Tampa* incident brought these matters to a head. A federal election campaign was in progress at the time, with neither major party assured of victory. The coalition government's decisive actions, which, besides transporting the asylum seekers to Nauru, also included denying the Australian courts any jurisdiction over their cases, effectively prevented any further unauthorized boat people from making asylum claims in the country. These actions were condemned by many observers as violations of the spirit of the 1951 convention, to which Australia is a signatory. The political consequence in Australia, however, was a surge in Howard's popularity, which carried through to an electoral victory in November 2001.

The problem remains of what to do with those asylum seekers who fail in their refugee claims. Many who have been denied Australian visas have resisted repatriation and languish in processing camps at considerable expense to taxpayers. Still, most voters continue to support the government's tough control measures. Meanwhile, other countries appeared to be moving toward the adoption of common policies for the treatment of asylum seekers. In June 2002 leaders of the 15 European Union nations grappled with immigration issues at a summit held in Seville, Spain. The leaders agreed to work on visa regulations that would apply in every EU country, to speed up the repatriations of those immigrants who do not qualify, and to ensure closer cooperation on border controls.

*Bob Birrell is Director of the Centre for Population and Urban Research at Monash University, Clayton, Victoria, Australia.*

# The Wireless Revolution

*by Fiona Harvey*

In Helsinki, Finland, gamblers are getting their national lottery tickets by mobile telephone. In Hull, England, drivers are paying for their parking spaces with their mobile phones. In Tokyo people are using their phones to make home movies. In Toronto, ads for Fido cell phones show students using instant text messaging to cheat on an exam. Welcome to the wireless revolution.

The mobile phone has truly taken hold of consumers in the past few years, and in most wealthy nations the technology is virtually ubiquitous. There are now about a billion mobile phones in the world, and the increase in users shows little sign of abating as the technology gathers pace in less-developed countries too. Not only are more people getting mobile connections, but as the phones themselves become more advanced people are using them for much more than mere phone calls.

The simple usefulness of the mobile phone has been the secret of its success. People are no longer tethered to fixed telephone lines or left scrabbling for loose change to feed public phones. Being able to communicate with friends, family, or business colleagues at any time from any place frees individuals to work or plan their social lives while on the move. Mobile phones can increase safety, as people monitor each other by staying in touch or phone for help from the scene of an accident. Emergency services can even use phones to trace the whereabouts of those calling for help. Indeed, a survey in the UK found that 7 out of 10 people would rather lose their wallet than their mobile phone.

Phones, however, are only part of the wireless revolution. Laptop and hand-held computers with wireless connections, as well as the increasingly common personal digital assistants (PDAs), have given rise to a generation of mobile workers. The average office worker is estimated to have about 15 m (about 50 ft) of cabling in his or her desk area. All of that could be eliminated with two technologies: Bluetooth and 802.11, sometimes known as Wi-Fi (for wireless fidelity). These two standards allow data to be sent across short distances without wires. In the UK Bluetooth networks are being set up in railway stations so that passengers can read their e-mail while waiting for the train. In the US Wi-Fi networks are appearing in cafes, allowing patrons to log on while they drink their coffee.

Radio and television are also being reinvigorated by new digital wireless technologies that will allow radios to convert binary data into text and pictures on tiny screens and enable viewers to "talk back" to the TV with interactive programs. (Interactive programming already enables viewers to change the camera angle on some sports matches.) Wireless technology can also be used to generate broadband Internet connections, which allow surfers to send and receive large quantities of data, such as live full-motion video broadcasts, from their personal computers, and could potentially turn PCs into TVs.

The wireless revolution already has reached the farthest corners of the globe—where global positioning system (GPS) devices guide soldiers, mountaineers, sailors, and even drivers. These devices can communicate with the network of 24 global positioning satellites placed in the sky by the US government, triangulating between the GPS satellites to work out the device's exact location to within about 5 m (about 15 ft) in good conditions. The revolution is even reaching inside our bodies; Medtronic, Inc., for example, has developed technology that allows information from a patient's pacemaker to be transmitted to a physician over the Internet.

> *" In 2001 China overtook the US as the world's largest mobile phone market and now boasts more than 120 million mobile phone users. "*

Two factors have been central to the success of wireless technology: the digitization of data and the increasing understanding of how to make use of the electromagnetic spectrum. When modern mobile phones were first introduced in the 1970s, they used analog technology, in which a modulated wave is transmitted across the airwaves. Analog phones, however, can be used only for making voice calls. With digital phone technology, which renders data into binary form and transmits a discrete series of zeros and ones, it is possible to squeeze much more usage from the electromagnetic spectrum. This enables mobile phone operators to take on far more users and charge them less, allows the sending and receiving of text messages, and makes possible much more advanced services, such as Internet access through phones.

These advanced services will become even more widespread with so-called third-generation (3G) mobile-phone networks. Most digital mobile phones can send and receive about 9.6 Kbps (kilobits per second), which is enough for calls and exchanging text messages. Using 3G, it will be possible to send and receive perhaps 144 Kbps or 344 Kbps, enough for sending and receiving video clips, Web pages, e-mails, and more. Consumers in Japan can send each other animations with NTT DoCoMo Inc.'s i-mode phone, which was introduced in 1999 and boasts 3G-like features. T-Mobile and Vodafone, among others, offer European consumers camera phones that can take and exchange snapshots with compatible mobiles. With 3G, mobile phones will become even more like PCs, combining the ability to take digital pictures and video, send and receive e-mail, surf the Internet, and download music. The only question is how many of these services the network operators choose to provide. In most developed countries, 3G networks are expected to enter into operation within the next three years or so, though ongoing problems in the telecommunications industry and the high cost of buying spectrum licenses are delaying their introduction in some areas.

One of the most intriguing features of 3G phones will be more precise location-finding capabilities. In 2002 the Pinpoint Co., based in Hong Kong, already allowed subscribing companies to track employees to within about 200 m through their company-issued phones. One technology built into 3G handsets and networks, however, will make it possible to trace the position of the handsets to within about 5 m or less. This technology raises privacy issues, as bosses will be able to keep tabs on employees, parents monitor children, and suspicious spouses spy on one another. In light of increased security following the terrorist attacks in the US on 11 Sep 2001, law-enforcement agencies may employ these capabilities to increase their surveillance of citizens, which thus raises concerns over civil liberties. (See feature "Security vs. Civil Liberties".)

To take advantage of these new services, very different phone handsets will be developed, and the distinction between phones and PDAs will likely blur

or disappear. Handsets will need much bigger screens and may have keyboards or handwriting recognition. Some may have voice-recognition software, which will turn speech into text. Using Bluetooth technology, the handset can be separated from the headset, so a user can wear a tiny microphone in his or her ear while tapping on the handset's screen.

For less-developed countries, wireless technology holds out a tantalizing possibility. Huge swathes of the globe lack telephone lines, and this inhibits economic growth. According to the International Telecommunications Union, many of these countries are abandoning the idea of fixed phone lines and moving straight to wireless technology, which is easier to introduce, as it requires the setting up of widely spaced base stations rather than extensive cabling. Already, less-developed nations are catching up. In 2001 China overtook the US as the world's largest mobile phone market and now boasts more than 120 million mobile phone users.

*Fiona Harvey is a technology writer for the* Financial Times.

# Blogs Mix Up the Media

*by Alan Stewart*

Web logs are not new, but as a forum for personal expression they are sprouting prodigiously on the Internet, capturing new audiences, and drawing intensified attention in the media. Web logs (usually abbreviated to "blogs") originated in the US in 1997 as on-line journals, often with links to news items on the World Wide Web plus brief, personal comments on those items by the originators-editors ("bloggers"), as well as responses from readers. By mid-2002 the number of blogs had grown from only 23 (by one count) at the start of 1999 to as many as 500,000 globally. This growth was fueled by the spread of free blog-creation software (such as Blogger, Pitas, Movable Type, and Radio UserLand), which removed the need for the blogger to be skilled in computer programming.

In the wake of the terrorist attacks in the US on 11 Sep 2001, a new type of Web log was born: the "war blog." The generally better quality of writing and the political stance of the blogger (often right-wing) distinguished the war blogs from the on-line diaries. War bloggers included Andrew Sullivan, former editor of *The New Republic*, whose blog has reportedly received more than 800,000 visits in one month from more than 200,000 individual readers. Glenn Reynolds, a University of Tennessee law professor, drew around 43,000 visits in a single day to his InstaPundit site. *The Jerusalem Post* also reported in 2002 that Israeli and Palestinian bloggers were writing Web logs as a way to let the outside world see their respective sides of the ongoing Middle East conflict.

Alex Beam, a columnist at the *Boston Globe*, scathingly referred to blogs as an "infinite echo chamber of self-regard." Web logs' high site-visit figures made the mainstream media jumpy, however, especially as some of the new bloggers carried on their sites detailed criticism of stories in newspapers such as the *New York Times* and the *Los Angeles Times*. A number of mainstream media outlets even added blogs to their Web sites, notably the British daily *The Guardian*, which ran a competition for the UK's best blog. The on-line magazine *Slate* embraced a preexisting blog by Mickey Kaus, a former *Newsweek* magazine reporter.

In 2001 John Robb, president and chief operating officer of blogging-software developer UserLand, put forward a business use for Web logs, in which workers would use blogs as a collaborative medium to record and disseminate their thoughts. In 2002, however, the Web log came of age; the University of California, Berkeley, Graduate School of Journalism began offering a class in blogging, in which students created a blog on copyright issues. The course tutors were John Battelle, a cofounder of *Wired* magazine, and Paul Grabowicz, media program director at the school.

While veteran bloggers might object to the new, more politicized Web logs, blogging as an expanding form of on-line communication seems to be here to stay.

> " *By mid-2002 the number of blogs had grown from only 23 (by one count) at the start of 1999 to as many as 500,000 globally.* "

*Alan Stewart is a freelance journalist and author of* How to Make it in IT.

# Chronology, July 2002–June 2003

*A day-by-day listing of important and interesting events, adapted from Britannica Book of the Year. See also Disasters.*

## July 2002

**1 Jul** US fighter airplanes strike a wedding party in Oruzgan province in Afghanistan, killing some 48 civilians; the following day, for the first time in the war, the government of Afghanistan demands an explanation.

▸ A new legal code, enshrining rights guaranteed in Western countries, goes into effect in Russia; it replaces a code written in 1960.

▸ New rules designed to make immigration considerably more difficult go into effect in Denmark.

**2 Jul** Adventurer Steve Fossett succeeds in becoming the first person to fly a balloon solo around the world when he crosses longitude 117° E off the south coast of Western Australia, where he had started 13 days previously; it is his sixth attempt at the goal, and he traveled some 31,220 km (19,400 mi; [the circumference of the Earth at the Equator is about 40,070 km, or 24,900 mi]).

▸ The United Nations releases a report ahead of the 14th International AIDS Conference that says that earlier analyses underestimated the spread of the disease and that it is now projected that the number of deaths from AIDS between 2000 and 2020 will reach 68 million.

▸ Former Mexican president Luis Echeverría is called before a special prosecutor to face questions about the government violence in the 1960s and '70s; it is the first time that a former head of state has been called to account in Mexico.

**3 Jul** NASA launches a probe that constitutes the Comet Nucleus Tour (CONTOUR) mission; it is intended to intercept and probe, with cameras and chemical-measuring instruments, two nearby comets over the next four years. (See 15 August.)

▸ Texas Gov. Rick Perry declares 29 counties in central Texas a disaster area; 41 cm (16 in) of rain had fallen during the previous weekend in San Antonio, which normally sees 5 cm (2 in) of rain in the entire month of July.

**4 Jul** A man armed with two handguns opens fire at the El Al Airlines ticket counter at the Los Angeles International Airport and kills two people before being killed himself by a security guard.

▸ Greek police announce that they have in custody a member of the terrorist organization November 17 for the first time in the 27 years the group has been active. (See 26 July.)

▸ In Bangui, Central African Rep., a Boeing 707 carrying a cargo of vegetables and a few passengers crashes in a sparsely populated neighborhood; 2 of the 25 aboard survive.

**5 Jul** Dozens of people are killed when bombs explode in several areas where Algerians are celebrating the 40th anniversary of the country's independence; it is believed that Islamist rebels are behind the carnage.

▸ The Constitutional Court in South Africa orders the government to provide nevirapine to HIV-infected pregnant women in state hospitals; though the drug had been shown greatly to reduce transmission of HIV to newborns, the South African government held that preventing HIV transmission would not prevent AIDS.

▸ A new branch of the Imperial War Museum, the Imperial War Museum North, opens in Manchester, England, in a building designed by Daniel Libeskind and meant to echo the museum's theme—war and conflict in the 20th and 21st centuries.

▸ The ceremonial reopening of the White Mosque takes place in Srebrenica, Bosnia and Herzegovina; it replaces an Ottoman mosque that was destroyed during the 1992–95 war.

**6 Jul** Haji Abdul Qadir, a vice president of Afghanistan and one of the few Pashtun members of the interim government, is assassinated.

▸ American tennis star Serena Williams defeats her sister, Venus, to win her first Wimbledon title; the following day Australian Lleyton Hewitt defeats David Nalbandian of Argentina to win the men's title in the most lopsided final at Wimbledon since 1984.

▸ The Museum of Glass opens in Tacoma WA featuring contemporary glass art and a glassblowing studio.

▸ American Juli Inkster wins her seventh major golf tournament when she defeats Annika Sörenstam of Sweden by two strokes to win the US Women's Open; on the same day, Jerry Kelly defeats fellow American Davis Love III by two strokes to win the Western Open golf tournament.

**8 Jul** The large German engineering company Babcock Borsig's attempt to avoid insolvency is unsuccessful, and the company becomes the fourth major enterprise in Germany to fail in 2002.

▸ The on-line auction house eBay Inc. announces plans to buy PayPal, Inc., the most successful online payment service.

**9 Jul** Bands, dancers, and military displays attend the inauguration of the African Union, the new international organization that replaces the Organization of African Unity, in Durban, South Africa.

▸ Celebrations of Argentina's Independence Day turn into one of the largest protests to date against the continuing economic crisis.

▸ The first long-term, large-scale study of the effects of hormone-replacement therapy for women in the US is halted because the hormones have been shown to cause a small but significant increase in the risk of developing invasive breast cancer.

▸ US baseball commissioner Bud Selig disappoints fans when he stops the All-Star Game after 11 innings, though the score is tied at 7–7; the teams' managers were concerned that they did not have enough substitute players, especially pitchers, to continue.

▸ Standard & Poor's surprises the financial community by replacing seven non-American companies on its benchmark 500 index: Royal Dutch Petroleum, Unilever NV, Nortel Networks, Alcan Inc., Barrick Gold Corp., Placer Dome Inc., and Inco Ltd. are replaced by US-based companies Goldman Sachs, United Parcel Service, Principal Financial Group, Prudential Financial, eBay Inc., Electronic Arts, and SunGard Data Systems.

**10 Jul** The Nasdaq composite stock index closes at 1,346.01, its lowest close since 19 May 1997.

▸ US Navy officials confirm that marine archaeologist

Robert D. Ballard has likely found *PT 109*, the patrol torpedo boat commanded by John F. Kennedy, in the Solomon Islands; the vessel was sunk by a Japanese destroyer in 1943.

**11 Jul** *Nature* magazine publishes a paper that describes the finding in Chad of a hominid skull with a mix of hominid and apelike characteristics that is believed to be an astonishing six million to seven million years old.

▸ Moroccan soldiers seize the uninhabited islet of Perejil, claimed by Spain since 1668.

▸ The Italian Parliament lifts the constitutional ban that since 1948 had prevented male members of the house of Savoy from entering Italy; the former ruling family of Italy lives in exile in Switzerland.

▸ Criminal pornography charges are filed against Russian avant-garde writer Vladimir Sorokin; sales of his books soar over the next few weeks.

**12 Jul** After weeks of confrontation and negotiations, the UN Security Council effectively permits UN peacekeeping troops from the US to be immune from prosecution by the International Criminal Court for a period of one year, and the mandates for the peacekeeping missions in Bosnia and Herzegovina and the Prevlaka peninsula in Croatia are then renewed.

▸ Vladimir Spidla is appointed by Pres. Vaclav Havel as prime minister of the Czech Republic.

▸ The Superior Court of Ontario rules that the province must register the marriages of two gay couples who married in a joint church ceremony in Toronto in January 2001.

**13 Jul** In the city of Jammu in the Indian-administered part of Kashmir, a number of men invade a Hindu shantytown and, with automatic weapons and grenades, kill at least 27 people.

▸ A wildfire begins in the Coast Ranges of southwestern Oregon and over the next few weeks grows to become one of the largest wildfires in the state's history, the Biscuit Fire.

**14 Jul** Just before the annual Bastille Day military parade in Paris, a gunman attempts to assassinate French Pres. Jacques Chirac; no one is hurt.

**15 Jul** The giant drug company Pfizer Inc. announces that it will buy Pharmacia Corp.; the combined company will be the largest pharmaceutical company in the world.

▸ In Hyderabad, Pakistan, under extremely tight security, Ahmed Omar Saeed Sheikh is sentenced to death for the kidnapping and murder of American reporter Daniel Pearl.

▸ In a plea agreement that surprises observers, John Walker Lindh, the American who was captured with Taliban forces in late 2001, pleads guilty to two charges and agrees to a 20-year prison term.

▸ In the face of nationwide protests over the economy, in which two people were killed, Paraguayan Pres. Luis González Macchi declares a state of emergency.

▸ The third annual Cain Prize for African Writing, given to a short story by an African writer working in English and intended to increase the audience for African literature, is won by "Discovering Home," by Kenyan food journalist Binyavanga Wainaina.

**16 Jul** The Irish Republican Army publishes a full apology to the families of those killed by IRA activities, in particular noncombatants; the apology comes just before the 30th anniversary of Bloody Friday, when a series of 22 IRA bombs killed 9 people and injured 130.

▸ The Irish Hunger Memorial, a 0.2-ha (0.5-ac) artistic reproduction of an Irish hillside with a potato field and a fieldstone cottage, opens in New York City.

▸ After nearly a month of relative quiet, a bus approaching a Jewish settlement in the West Bank is ambushed, and nine people are killed; the Palestinian Authority immediately condemns the violence, while Israel says it plans no retaliation.

**17 Jul** Spanish special forces, with backing from air and sea, retake the islet of Perejil from the occupying force of six Moroccan soldiers.

> **QUOTE OF THE MONTH**
>
> " *Spain has been attacked by force in a sensitive part of its geography.* "
>
> —Spanish Defense Minister Federico Trillo, justifying Spain's retaking of Perejil islet, 17 July

▸ Two suicide bombers strike in a low-income immigrant neighbourhood in Tel Aviv, killing five people in addition to themselves.

▸ Temperatures reach 30 °C (86 °F) in Buffalo NY where 100 years earlier Willis Haviland Carrier invented the first air conditioner; Carrier developed his device to stabilize lithographs at a printing company.

**18 Jul** National and state legislators in India elect a new president, A.P.J. Abdul Kalam, a nuclear scientist and a Muslim.

▸ Robert W. Pittman, one of the architects of America Online and a leading voice in favor of the merger of AOL with Time Warner, resigns as chief operating officer of AOL Time Warner in a major reorganization that sees almost all the top positions filled by Time Warner old-media veterans.

**19 Jul** The findings of a yearlong inquiry into the activities of convicted mass murderer Harold Shipman are published by the leader of the investigation, Dame Janet Smith; she believes that Shipman, a doctor in Hyde, England, murdered at least 215 of his patients.

▸ A panel of scientists studying the problem of how to prevent the northern snakehead, a voracious Chinese fish that has become established in a pond near Annapolis MD from spreading into rivers and streams recommends poisoning all the fish in the pond and then reestablishing the native populations.

▸ The US Department of Agriculture announces a recall of 8.6 million kg (19 million lb) of ground beef produced in a ConAgra Beef Co. plant in Greeley CO; 19 people in six states had become ill from eating the meat, which was contaminated with *Escherichia coli* bacteria.

▸ The International Spy Museum, featuring interactive exhibits and high-tech gadgets, opens in Washington DC.

**20 Jul** A preliminary peace agreement between the government of The Sudan and the Sudanese People's Liberation Army is signed after five weeks of negotiations; a week later Pres. Omar Hassan al-Bashir meets with rebel leader John Garang in Kampala, Uganda.

▸ Under a deal brokered by the US, Spanish soldiers withdraw from the islet of Perejil and the status quo ante is restored.

**21 Jul** The communications company WorldCom files for bankruptcy; at $107 billion, it by far surpasses Enron's ($63 billion) as the biggest bankruptcy filing in American history.

▸ German race-car driver Michael Schumacher wins the French Grand Prix and secures the title for the season; he is the second person ever to win five Formula One world drivers titles.

▸ Ernie Els of South Africa emerges the winner in the first four-man play-off in the history of the British Open golf tournament, defeating Australians Steve Elkington and Stuart Appleby and Thomas Levet of France.

▸ The Museum of Spanish Colonial Art holds its grand opening in Santa Fe NM; the inaugural exhibit, "Conexiones: Connections in Spanish Colonial Art," features some 500 objects from the new museum's permanent collection.

**22 Jul** Officials in Africa announce that a tentative agreement between Rwanda and the Democratic Republic of the Congo has been reached whereby Congo will demobilize guerrillas who threaten Rwanda, and Rwanda will withdraw its troops from the eastern portion of Congo; Pres. Paul Kagame of Rwanda and Pres. Joseph Kabila of Congo sign the agreement on 30 July.

▸ The US government chooses to withhold previously approved funding for the UN Population Fund on the basis that it believes that the international organization condones the practice of mandatory abortions in China, in spite of the fact that its own investigative team found no evidence to support the contention.

**23 Jul** US Pres. George W. Bush signs a resolution approving the creation of a repository for radioactive by-products of the country's nuclear energy reactors under Yucca Mountain in Nevada, ending 20 years of discussion and debate over the best place to store such materials; they are currently housed in 131 temporary sites in 39 states.

▸ An Israeli warplane fires a missile into the home of Hamas leader Sheikh Salah Shehada in Gaza City, killing at least 14 people, several of them children, in addition to Shehada; US Pres. George W. Bush criticizes the strike as being "heavy-handed."

▸ Britain announces that Rowan Williams, a Welsh churchman of a notably liberal bent, will succeed George Carey as archbishop of Canterbury when Carey retires in October.

▸ Pope John Paul II arrives in Toronto for the week-long World Youth Day festival, which he addresses on 25 July.

**24 Jul** After falling for several weeks, the Dow Jones Industrial Average posts its second largest one-day point gain (488.95 points) since the recovery from the market crash of 1987.

▸ John Rigas, the founder and former CEO of Adelphia Communications Corp., and his sons Timothy and Michael are arrested on charges of embezzlement of hundreds of millions of dollars from the company, which filed for bankruptcy in June.

▸ The UN Development Programme releases its annual Human Development Report, in which it ranks Norway as the most developed and Sierra Leone as the least developed countries in the world.

**25 Jul** A group of American investors, led by the Texas Pacific Group, agrees to buy Burger King from the British liquor concern Diageo PLC.

▸ In San Juan PR thousands gather to commemorate the 50th anniversary of the island's becoming a US commonwealth, while a similarly large group of independence advocates protest the same event.

**26 Jul** In Indonesia Tommy Suharto (Hutomo Mandala Putra), the son of former president Suharto, is convicted of murder and sentenced to 15 years in prison for having hired assassins to kill a judge who had sentenced him to prison for corruption.

▸ Police in Greece arrest Nikos Papanastasiou, who is believed to be one of the founders of the November 17 terrorist group. (See 4 July.)

**27 Jul** At an air show near Lviv, Ukraine, a Ukrainian air force Sukhoi Su-27 fighter jet performing an acrobatic stunt crashes and skids into the crowd, killing 85 spectators in the world's most deadly air show accident to date.

**28 Jul** After days of frantic efforts all nine miners trapped in a coal mine in Quecreek PA after a wall leading into a flooded abandoned mine was breached on 25 July are rescued.

▸ Thomas Middelhoff, the chairman and CEO of the German media conglomerate Bertelsmann AG, is forced out; Gunter Thielen is named as his replacement.

▸ Qwest Communications International Inc., the dominant local phone service provider in 14 western US states, announces that it incorrectly accounted for $1.16 billion in transactions between 1999 and 2001.

▸ American Lance Armstrong coasts to his fourth consecutive victory in the Tour de France bicycle race.

**29 Jul** A pod of 56 pilot whales strands itself on a Cape Cod Bay, Massachusetts, beach; rescuers drive 46 of them back to sea, but the following day they wash up 40 km (25 mi) north, and volunteers are unable to save them.

▸ Workers at the Edenhurst Gallery in Los Angeles discover that during the previous night two valuable Maxfield Parrish murals were stolen.

**30 Jul** US Pres. George W. Bush signs into law a broad new act intended to crack down on corporate fraud; it is believed to be the most far-reaching change in business regulation since the 1930s.

▸ Vanguard Airlines Inc., which operates 70 flights a day in 18 cities and is based in Kansas City MO, announces that it is filing for bankruptcy and ceasing operations. (See 11 August.)

▸ Uruguay closes its banks to prevent a run, and the following day it is announced that the banks will remain closed for the rest of the week; Uruguay's economy has been badly affected by the crisis in Argentina and turmoil in Brazil. (See 4 August.)

▸ In Guatemala City, Guatemala, Pope John Paul II canonizes Pedro de San José Betancur, a 17th-century Spanish missionary and the first person from Central America to be canonized; the following day in Mexico City, the pontiff canonizes Juan Diego, an Aztec who is said to have received a vision of the Virgin of Guadalupe in 1531 but who is not universally believed to have actually lived.

**31 Jul** A bomb explodes in the cafeteria at the Frank Sinatra International Student Center of the Hebrew University of Jerusalem, killing nine people, five of them Americans, and wounding dozens, among them a number of Israeli Arabs.

▸ A clerk in the Ministry of Education in Beirut, Lebanon, guns down eight coworkers before running out of ammunition; it is thought that financial difficulties drove him over the edge.

▶ Albania's legislature approves Socialist Party leader Fatos Nano as prime minister.

▶ An Uzbek man believed to be a member of Russian organized crime is arrested in Italy on suspicion of having conspired to rig the outcomes of the pairs figure-skating and ice-dancing competitions at the Olympic Winter Games in Salt Lake City UT.

# August 2002

**1 Aug** WorldCom's former chief financial officer, Scott D. Sullivan, and its former controller, David F. Myers, are publicly escorted in handcuffs to a federal courthouse in New York City to face fraud charges. (See 21 July.)

▶ As it increasingly appears that the US is making plans to invade Iraq, the Iraqi government for the first time since 1998 requests that the head of the UN team that is charged with inspecting Iraq for weapons violations go to Baghdad for negotiations.

▶ The Education Ministry in Iran decrees that, for the first time since 1979, teachers and students in girls' schools in Tehran are permitted to remove their veils in the classroom.

**2 Aug** Representatives of the Angolan government and of the UNITA rebels declare that the war between them, which began in 1975, is officially over.

▶ In response to the attack at the Hebrew University of Jerusalem on 31 July, Israeli forces conduct a house-to-house search for explosives laboratories and suspected terrorists in the old city of Nabulus in the West Bank.

▶ Health officials in the US state of Louisiana report that a recent outbreak of West Nile virus has left 4 people dead and 58 people sick; with additional cases reported in Texas and Mississippi, it is the largest outbreak of the disease since it was first detected in the US in 1999.

**3 Aug** The Turkish Grand National Assembly passes a package of reforms that among other things abolishes the death penalty in peacetime and permits radio and television broadcasting in the Kurdish language; the hotly debated reforms are made with an eye toward Turkey's joining the European Union.

▶ Chip Chip Hooray wins the Hambletonian final at the Meadowlands Racetrack in New Jersey; the same day Victory Tilly wins the Nat Ray final on the same track in 1 min 50.4 sec, a world trotting record.

**4 Aug** The National Congress in Bolivia elects the political centrist Gonzalo Sánchez de Lozada president by a vote of 84–43 over the radical Indian coca champion Evo Morales; a close popular vote in June had thrown the election to the National Congress.

▶ A bomb that kills 9 people on an Israeli commuter bus in Galilee inaugurates a series of Palestinian attacks over the next several hours that include a shootout and three ambushes, with a total death toll of 14.

▶ The US government announces that it will make a short-term loan of as much as $1.5 billion to enable Uruguay to reopen its banks, in spite of the assertion of the administration of Pres. George W. Bush that lending money to countries with weak economies is counterproductive.

**5 Aug** The newly elected legislature in Papua New Guinea unanimously chooses Sir Michael Somare to be the new prime minister; he is a founding father of independent Papua New Guinea.

▶ Armed Pakistani militants attack a boarding school for children of Christian missionaries in the Himalayan foothills northeast of Islamabad; six Pakistani adults are killed on school grounds, but the attackers are unable to penetrate the school itself, and no children are hurt.

**6 Aug** US Pres. George W. Bush signs into law a measure that gives to the president sole authority to negotiate international trade agreements; presidents from 1975 to 1994 enjoyed this power, once known as "fast track."

▶ Doctors at Mattel Children's Hospital at the University of California, Los Angeles, successfully complete the surgical separation of conjoined twins María Teresa and María de Jesús Quiej Álvarez, who were born joined at the top of the head on 25 Jul 2001 in Guatemala.

▶ The large mining company Anglo American PLC announces that it will offer free drug treatment to its employees in South Africa who are infected with HIV; such employees constitute nearly a quarter of the company's workforce.

**7 Aug** As Álvaro Uribe Vélez is sworn in as president of Colombia, scattered mortar shells fall in various places in Bogotá, killing 21 people and wounding at least 60; it is assumed that FARC guerrillas are behind the carnage.

▶ Construction begins on the foundation of a light-water nuclear reactor in North Korea; the reactor is being built by an international consortium led by the US under the terms of a 1994 agreement that also calls for North Korea to dismantle its graphite reactors and place its plutonium under international supervision.

▶ The IMF agrees to loan $30 billion to Brazil in hopes of rescuing its flailing economy; the loan is nearly twice what analysts in Brazil had expected.

▶ Jordan shuts down the local office of the Qatar-based satellite television network al-Jazeera the day after the network broadcast a program that criticized the late kings Hussein and Abdullah I as being too sympathetic to Israel.

**8 Aug** In Zimbabwe 2,900 white farmers are ordered to vacate their farms by midnight, but nearly two-thirds defy the deadline.

▶ After the successful July blockading of ChevronTexaco plants by unarmed women in southern Nigeria in order to force community development concessions from the oil company, hundreds more unarmed women blockade ChevronTexaco and Shell offices in southern Nigeria; order is restored by the following day.

▶ Turkmen Pres. Saparmurad Niyazov announces plans to rename the months of the year for Turkmen heroes and symbols, beginning the year with a month named for himself.

**9 Aug** A powerful explosion takes place outside a road-construction warehouse a few hundred meters from a major hydroelectric dam in Jalalabad, Afghanistan; at least 11 people are killed.

▶ Pres. Denis Sassou-Nguesso of the Republic of the Congo announces that the transitional government has succeeded and democratic rule has been restored; the country's new constitution is to take effect at midnight.

▸ *Science* magazine publishes a report by researchers at the University of Oxford who were astonished when a New Caledonian crow they were studying bent a piece of wire in order to retrieve food; an animal's purposeful modification of an object to make a tool in the absence of considerable past experience is virtually unknown.

**10 Aug** On the second day of meetings in Washington DC between Iraqi opposition leaders and US government officials, Vice Pres. Dick Cheney is reported to have said via videoconference that the US government intends to replace Iraqi ruler Saddam Hussein with a democratic government.

**11 Aug** In Indonesia the People's Consultative Assembly approves constitutional amendments that provide for direct election of the president and eliminate reserved places in government for the military; in addition, the assembly rejects the proposed imposition of Islamic law (Shari'ah).

▸ US Airways, the sixth largest carrier in the US, files for Chapter 11 bankruptcy protection but says it intends to continue operations. (See 30 July.)

▸ Australian golfer Karrie Webb wins the Women's British Open tournament in Ayrshire, Scot.

**12 Aug** As heavy rains continue to fall in the Czech Republic, 50,000 residents of Prague are ordered evacuated to avoid flooding—the worst in over a century—which has killed more than 70 people as rivers in southeastern Russia and Eastern and Central Europe overflow.

▸ Meteorologists in India say the August monsoon is unlikely to be able to compensate for the driest July in India's history.

**13 Aug** Members of the militant Palestinian organizations Hamas and Islamic Jihad refuse to sign on to an agreement supported by Palestinian leader Yasir Arafat to stop attacks on civilians.

▸ US officials react with annoyance to reports that the European Union is urging aspiring members not to sign bilateral agreements with the US to refrain from bringing any Americans before the new International Criminal Court. (See 12 July.)

▸ The US Food and Drug Administration orders CryoLife, Inc., which processes donated human tissue, to recall and destroy all tissues processed since 3 Oct 2001 on the basis that they may be contaminated with harmful bacteria and fungi.

**14 Aug** Pres. Alyaksandr Lukashenka of Belarus rejects the plan put forward by Russian Pres. Vladimir Putin for a union of Belarus and Russia in which Belarus would essentially be absorbed by Russia.

▸ Javier Suárez Medina, a Mexican national who had been found guilty of having murdered an undercover narcotics officer in 1988, is executed in Texas over Mexico's strenuous objections.

▸ The last major regional chain of discount department stores in the US, Ames Department Stores, Inc., based in the northeastern US, announces that it is going out of business and closing its 327 stores.

▸ *Nature* magazine publishes a study on-line showing that a gene connected to language acquisition underwent mutation and quickly became fixed in hominid populations about 200,000 years ago.

**15 Aug** NASA announces that it has lost contact with its new Comet Nucleus Tour (CONTOUR) spacecraft; it is later found that the spacecraft may have broken apart.

▸ The stage musical version of the 1988 John Waters movie *Hairspray*, starring Marissa Jaret Winokur and Harvey Fierstein, opens to rave reviews in the Neil Simon Theatre in New York City.

**16 Aug** Pope John Paul II begins a three-day visit to his home country of Poland and celebrates an enormous open-air mass in Krakow on 18 August.

▸ After finding cracks in locomotives, Amtrak cancels all its high-speed Acela Express trains as well as a number of other trains, amounting to close to 20% of its service in the northeastern US.

▸ The government of Zambia announces that it will not accept donations of genetically modified corn (maize) from the US in spite of the danger of famine.

**17 Aug** The Charles M. Schulz Museum and Research Center, which features exhibits devoted to the cartoonist and his *Peanuts* comic strip, opens in Santa Rosa CA.

▸ David McVicar's production of Bizet's *Carmen* at the Glyndebourne Opera Festival in England features a live BBC satellite relay of the show to the Somerset House Courtyard in London; it is the first time that a production at the festival has been broadcast to audiences elsewhere.

▸ The bodies of two 10-year-old girls, missing from near their homes in the town of Soham, Cambridgeshire, England, since 4 August, are found buried in a wooded area a few kilometers outside town; the search for the girls had riveted Britain.

**18 Aug** The relatively unknown American golfer Rich Beem defeats Tiger Woods by one stroke, winning the Professional Golfers' Association of America championship.

▸ Israeli and Palestinian negotiators agree on a plan for Israeli forces to begin a withdrawal from the Gaza Strip and Bethlehem, provided Palestinian forces can maintain order.

▸ CNN begins broadcasting portions of videotapes from a library of tapes made and maintained by al-Qaeda and acquired by a CNN reporter in Afghanistan; the broadcast tapes show, among other things, the apparent testing of chemical weapons.

▸ The 43rd Edward MacDowell Medal, for outstanding contribution to the arts, is awarded to the photographer Robert Frank at the MacDowell Colony in Peterborough NH.

▸ The *New York Times* announces that beginning in September it will include coverage of commitment ceremonies of gay and lesbian couples in the renamed "Weddings/Celebrations" portion of its Sunday Styles section.

**19 Aug** A Palestinian newspaper reports that Abu Nidal, who was believed to have been behind many of the more notorious terrorist attacks from the early 1970s to the early 1990s, has been found dead in his home in Baghdad, Iraq.

▸ A large Russian military helicopter, carrying 147 people, crashes in a minefield near the main military base in Chechnya; the death toll is well over 100.

▸ The global mining conglomerate Anglo American PLC says that it has pulled out of the Zambian copper industry, finding it unlikely that it would profit from Zambia's copper mines.

▸ Pakistan's Federal Shari'ah Court (the top religious court) publishes its ruling that victims of rape or coerced adultery should not face trial for adultery and that pregnancy alone is not evidence of adultery.

**20 Aug** Members of the Abu Sayyaf guerrilla group in the Philippines kidnap six Jehovah's Witnesses and two Muslims from the town of Patikul on the island of Jolo; two days later it is found that they have beheaded two of their captives.

▸ George Pell, the Roman Catholic archbishop of Sydney, Australia, takes a temporary leave of office while investigators look into allegations of child sex abuse made against him; he is cleared of the charges in October.

**21 Aug** Pakistani Pres. Pervez Musharraf unilaterally imposes 29 amendments to the country's constitution; they have the effect of increasing the power of the presidency and the military at the expense of the legislature.

▸ Former Enron financial executive Michael J. Kopper enters a guilty plea in federal court and agrees to cooperate with investigators; he subsequently tells a federal judge that he paid large kickbacks to Andrew Fastow when Fastow was chief financial officer. (See 2 October.)

▸ Canadian Prime Minister Jean Chrétien announces his plans to step down from office in 2004.

**22 Aug** The US government's September 11th Victim Compensation Fund announces its first awards to 25 families of people killed in the terrorist attacks in 2001.

▸ The US government exempts nearly 200 imported steel products from the steel tariffs it imposed in the spring.

▸ Brazilian Pres. Fernando Henrique Cardoso decrees the creation of the Tumuc-Humac Mountains National Park, 3.9 million ha (9.6 million ac) of mostly virgin rainforest on Brazil's northern border with French Guiana and Suriname; the new national park, containing at least 8 primate species and 350 bird species, is the biggest tropical national park in the world.

▸ A statue honoring Irish independence hero Michael Collins is unveiled in his home village of Clonakilty in West Cork; more than 5,000 people attend the ceremony, which takes place on the 80th anniversary of his assassination.

▸ Controversial German filmmaker Leni Riefenstahl celebrates her 100th birthday; one week earlier her first movie in half a century, the documentary *Underwater Impressions*, had been broadcast on German TV.

**23 Aug** Georgian security forces move against Chechen guerrillas in Georgia's Pankisi Gorge as Georgian Pres. Eduard Shevardnadze accuses Russia of making raids in Georgian territory.

▸ US District Court Judge Miriam Goldman Cedarbaum rules that the rights to the majority of Martha Graham's dances belong to the Martha Graham Center of Contemporary Dance and not to her heir, Ronald Protas.

▸ *Science* magazine publishes a report describing evidence that an asteroid hit the Earth some 3.5 billion years ago with 10 to 100 times the impact of the one believed to have ended the age of dinosaurs 65 million years ago.

**24 Aug** The Carolina Courage wins the Women's United Soccer Association championship when it defeats the Washington Freedom 3–2 and takes home the Founders Cup; Birgit Prinz is named Most Valuable Player.

▸ Saud A.S. al-Rasheed, age 21, surrenders to authorities in Saudi Arabia after the US Federal Bureau of Investigation had put out a worldwide alert for him, believing him to have connections with the hijackers of 11 Sep 2001; Rasheed says he is wholly innocent and is later released.

**25 Aug** The two leading candidates for chancellor of Germany, incumbent Gerhard Schröder and Edmund Stoiber, engage in a televised debate that is watched by eight million viewers; it is the first televised debate between political candidates ever held in Germany.

▸ The Valley Sports American Little League team from Louisville KY representing the US Great Lakes, becomes the 56th Little League world champion when it defeats the team from Sendai, Japan, representing Asia, 1–0.

**26 Aug** The 10-day UN World Summit on Sustainable Development opens in Johannesburg, South Africa.

▸ A judge in Spain bans the Basque political party Batasuna, accusing it of involvement in the terrorist activities of the separatist organization ETA.

▸ The US Court of Appeals for the 6th Circuit rules that the secret deportation hearings that took place in the wake of the terrorist attacks of 11 Sep 2001, were unconstitutional, stating, "Democracies die behind closed doors."

---

**QUOTE OF THE MONTH**

❝ *The devastation caused by the flood offers much opportunity to build better, more sensibly, in a more intelligent manner. To build more beautiful buildings than some of those that have been destroyed.* ❞

—Czech Rep. Pres. Vaclav Havel, speaking to reporters on the aftermath of catastrophic flooding, 27 August

---

**27 Aug** A district court in Tokyo acknowledges for the first time that Japan engaged in germ warfare against China before and during World War II.

▸ Archaeologists working in the ancient town of Butrint in Albania announce their discovery of a large marble statue, possibly depicting the Roman goddess Minerva, believed to date to the time of the Roman emperor Caesar Augustus; it is the first major find at the site, which is a UNESCO World Heritage site and a national park.

**28 Aug** A federal grand jury indicts a group of five men arrested near Detroit who the US government believes are a terrorist "sleeper cell" associated with Salafiyya, an Islamic extremist movement.

▸ Transparency International, based in Berlin, releases its Corruption Perceptions Index 2002, on which Bangladesh rates as the world's most corrupt country and Finland as the least.

▸ A research team working in the vicinity of Pearl Harbor in Hawaii finds the Japanese midget submarine that was sunk by the American destroyer *Ward* about an hour before the air attacks of 7 Dec 1941; heretofore there had been no proof that the sinking had occurred.

**29 Aug** Authorities in Germany say that investigators have found that the al-Qaeda cell based in Hamburg began planning the terrorist attacks of 11 Sep 2001, as long ago as 1999.

**30 Aug** The World Trade Organization rules that a tax break in the US that is intended to promote exports is in violation of international trade treaties and that the European Union is entitled to penalize the US as much as $4 billion.

▶ German Defense Minister Peter Struck says that if the US unilaterally attacks Iraq, Germany will withdraw from Kuwait its specialized unit dedicated to detecting biological, chemical, and nuclear weapons; the unit had been sent out in support of the campaign against al-Qaeda and the Taliban in Afghanistan.

▶ Major League Baseball players and owners reach an agreement just a few hours short of a strike deadline; it is the first time in more than 30 years that a new labor contract has been signed in baseball without a strike.

**31 Aug** Chechen fighters shoot down a Russian helicopter gunship, killing both pilots; it had recently been revealed that the large transport helicopter that crashed on 19 August was brought down by a shoulder-launched missile.

▶ The Los Angeles Sparks defeat the New York Liberty 69–66 to win the Women's National Basketball Association championship for the second consecutive year.

▶ The US-based search engine Google becomes unavailable to Internet users in China; it is believed that the Chinese government is blocking access to the search engine.

# September 2002

**1 Sep** At the UN World Summit on Sustainable Development in Johannesburg, South Africa, Israel and Jordan announce a plan to build a joint pipeline to pump water from the Red Sea into the rapidly shrinking Dead Sea in an effort to prevent the Dead Sea from drying up.

▶ A fire starts in the Angeles National Forest in California and rapidly consumes about 4,450 ha (11,000 acres), forcing the immediate evacuation of at least 7,000 recreationists; it is one of three large fires in the Los Angeles area.

▶ For the second day Typhoon Rusa batters South Korea, causing the most damage in Kangnung; the worst storm in South Korea since 1959, Rusa kills at least 120 people.

**2 Sep** In the face of a governmental investigation into possible falsification of repair reports at nuclear plants in the late 1980s and '90s, the president and other top executives of the Tokyo Electric Power Co., Japan's biggest electric utility, admit that the company has falsified such reports and immediately announce their resignations.

▶ Consolidated Freightways Corp., one of the biggest trucking companies in the US, announces that it will immediately shut down almost all of its operations and will file for bankruptcy protection.

▶ In Los Angeles the new $195 million Cathedral of Our Lady of the Angels, conceived by Spanish architect José Rafael Moneo, is dedicated with a three-hour mass and a procession of 565 cardinals, bishops, archbishops, and priests.

**3 Sep** Japan's main stock index falls to its lowest point in nearly 19 years, which raises fears of a banking crisis; banks in Japan typically hold a great deal of stock in their clients.

▶ The first of four High Energy Stereoscopic System (HESS) telescopes, the most sensitive gamma-ray telescopes to be built so far, is inaugurated in Namibia; the telescope array is a joint European-African project.

**4 Sep** Delegates at the World Summit on Sustainable Development agree on a plan that sets broadly drawn goals intended to reduce global poverty and preserve natural resources; the previous day Russia had announced that it will ratify the Kyoto Protocol.

▶ The Organization of American States passes a resolution supporting the holding of legislative and local elections in 2003 in Haiti and the unblocking of foreign aid, despite the fact that no settlement has been reached with the opposition coalition in the country.

▶ On the Fox television show *American Idol*, a summerlong singing competition that was the most-watched television show of the summer, the winner is Kelly Clarkson; the voters, viewers of the show, voted via telephone.

**5 Sep** In Kandahar, Afghanistan, an assassination attempt on Pres. Hamid Karzai narrowly fails, and a car bomb explodes in Kabul, killing at least 26 people.

▶ An enormous bomb is intercepted as it is being transported from the West Bank into Israel, and another bomb destroys an Israeli tank in Gaza; the Jewish High Holy Days begin at sundown the following day.

▶ In Oakland CA the Oakland Athletics beat the Kansas City Royals 12–11 to win their 20th consecutive baseball game, the longest winning streak in the history of the American League.

**6 Sep** In Luanda, Angola, Pres. Yoweri Museveni of Uganda and Pres. Joseph Kabila of the Democratic Republic of the Congo sign a peace agreement that calls for Uganda to remove its troops from Congo and for Congo to take action against rebels who are hostile to the government in Uganda.

▶ A grenade attack wounds a senior government official outside his home in Bishkek, Kyrgyzstan; opposition to the rule of Pres. Askar Akayev has been growing since March, and civil war seems to be a threat.

▶ The US Bureau of Labor Statistics reports that the number of long-term unemployed people in the US rose by more than 50% over the past year.

**7 Sep** Winning her third straight major championship, Serena Williams defeats her older sister, Venus, to win the US Open tennis tournament; the following day Pete Sampras defeats Andre Agassi to win the men's championship.

▶ Sir Simon Rattle conducts his first concert as chief conductor and artistic director of the Berlin Philharmonic.

**8 Sep** Metropolitan Herman is installed as the third primate of the Orthodox Church in America in a ceremony in Washington DC.

▶ In Indianapolis Yugoslavia defeats Argentina to win the men's world basketball championship; on 25 September the US beats Russia in the women's final in Nanjing, China.

**9 Sep** Martin Strel of Slovenia beats his own record for the longest swim when he becomes the first person to have swum the entire length of the Mississippi River; he began the 3,780-km (2,350-mi) swim on 4 July.

**10 Sep** Switzerland joins the United Nations as its 190th member.

▶ After days of severe storms that sparked flash floods that killed at least 21 people, rains in southeastern France ease; a day earlier a dam had given way, inundating the village of Aramon and leaving thousands without electricity or telephone service.

▸ TRW Inc. announces that it has won the contract to build the James Webb Space Telescope for NASA; the new telescope will have a light-gathering area six times larger than that of the Hubble Space Telescope, which it is scheduled to replace in 2010.

▸ US government officials move the terrorism alert level up one step, from yellow (elevated) to orange (high); US embassies around the world are closed, and Vice Pres. Dick Cheney is whisked to an undisclosed location.

▸ It is revealed that the actor Christopher Reeve, who became quadriplegic in 1995, has, after extensive therapy involving electrical stimulation of his muscles, regained the ability to move some of his fingers and joints as well as sensation on most of his body; this degree of improvement is unprecedented.

▸ The government of Argentina orders banks to allow customers, starting in October, to make withdrawals from savings accounts, which have been frozen since the end of 2001.

**11 Sep** Meeting in Ram Allah in the West Bank, the Palestinian Legislative Council, in an unprecedented show of strength, forces Palestinian leader Yasir Arafat to accept the resignation of his entire cabinet and schedule elections for 20 Jan 2003.

▸ A great variety of solemn observances of the one-year anniversary of the 11 September terrorist attacks in the US are held throughout the world.

**12 Sep** US Pres. George W. Bush addresses the General Assembly of the United Nations, enjoining the member nations to act quickly to force Iraq to disarm under threat of force and implying that the US will act on its own if the UN does not do so.

---

**QUOTE OF THE MONTH**

" *But the purposes of the United States should not be doubted. The Security Council resolutions will be enforced. The just demands of peace and security will be met, or action will be unavoidable.* "

—US Pres. George W. Bush, in his address to the UN General Assembly, 12 September

---

▸ L. Dennis Kozlowski, the former CEO of Tyco International Ltd., and Tyco's former chief financial officer, Mark H. Swartz, are indicted for fraud and racketeering, accused of having acquired $600 million in ill-gotten gains.

▸ Archaeologists report their discovery in Vilnius, Lithuania, of some 100 skeletons believed to be remnants of Napoleon's Grand Army, almost the entirety of which likely died of cold and starvation in December 1812; nearly 2,000 skeletons had been discovered in the area in 2001.

▸ In North Korea the Supreme People's Assembly issues a decree establishing an autonomous capitalist investment zone in the city of Sinuiju, on the Chinese border; the Sinuiju Special Administrative Region is to be run by Chinese agricultural and industrial magnate Yang Bin.

**13 Sep** American officials report that Ramzi ibn al-Shibh, believed to be a high-ranking al-Qaeda official and to have been closely involved with the 11 Sep 2001 hijackers, has been captured and is in custody in Karachi, Pakistan.

▸ Federal agents arrest five men in Lackawanna NY believing that they have ties to a terrorist group operating in the US.

**14 Sep** In Las Vegas NV Oscar de la Hoya defeats Fernando Vargas by technical knockout to add the World Boxing Association super welterweight (junior middleweight) title to the World Boxing Council title that he already holds.

▸ At the 18th International Association of Athletics Federations Grand Prix final in Paris, American sprinter Tim Montgomery runs the 100-m race in 9.78 sec, beating Maurice Green's three-year-old world record by one one-hundredth of a second.

▸ In Uganda members of the Lord's Resistance Army, a rebel group that wants to replace the government with a theocracy based on the Ten Commandments, raids a Roman Catholic mission, kidnapping 2 priests and 45 civilians, and attacks a World Food Programme truck, killing the driver.

**15 Sep** Elections in Sweden keep the center-left Social Democrats, led by Prime Minister Göran Persson, in power.

▸ In parliamentary elections in Macedonia, the ruling party is decisively defeated by a coalition led by the opposition Social Democratic Union, headed by Branko Crvenkovski.

▸ Brazil closes down São Paulo's Casa de Detenção, the largest prison in Latin America, which was the center of 2001's enormous prison uprising and, in 1992, the site of Brazil's biggest prison massacre.

**16 Sep** Iraq notifies the United Nations that it is willing to allow UN weapons inspectors to return to the country "without conditions."

▸ In major cities throughout Ukraine, demonstrators rally to demand the resignation of Pres. Leonid Kuchma.

▸ Peace talks between the government of Sri Lanka and the rebel Liberation Tigers of Tamil Eelam open at a naval base in Sattahip, Thailand; the cease-fire signed in February still holds.

▸ The Pinakothek der Moderne, the largest museum of modern art in Germany, opens in Munich.

▸ The first of four phases of Indian elections in Jammu and Kashmir takes place; many voters must contend with Indian soldiers ordering them to vote and Muslim militants ordering them not to vote.

**17 Sep** A Burundi government official says that gunmen massacred at least 183 people, 112 of them civilians, in Itaba commune in Gitega province on 9 September; the number of dead is later reduced to some 173, and all are reported to have been unarmed civilians.

▸ In Pyongyang, North Korea, Japanese Prime Minister Junichiro Koizumi and North Korean leader Kim Jong Il agree to begin normalizing relations, and North Korea admits that its agents kidnapped 11 people from Japan during the late 1970s and early '80s.

▸ NASA astronomers announce that the Hubble Space Telescope has detected clear evidence of medium-mass black holes, the existence of which was hinted at by data from the Chandra X-Ray and Roentgen Satellite (ROSAT) observatories; it is believed that this new type of black hole, found in the cores of globular star clusters, may provide information on how galaxies and globular clusters formed.

**18 Sep** *Nature* magazine publishes a paper on-line in which physicists working at CERN in Switzerland announce that they have created atoms of antimatter—specifically, antihydrogen; the researchers hope to test theories that antimatter should look and behave exactly like ordinary matter.

▸ Ground-breaking ceremonies kick off the construction of a pipeline designed to carry oil from the Sangachal terminal in Azerbaijan to the port of Ceyhan in Turkey, traveling through Georgia and bypassing Russia and Iran; the pipeline is expected to start carrying oil in 2005.

▸ Abu Salem, suspected of having been behind a series of high-profile murders and other terror attacks in India, including the worst bombings in the country's history, in 1993, is arrested in Portugal.

**19 Sep** A coup is attempted in Côte d'Ivoire while Pres. Laurent Gbagbo is out of the country; Robert Guei, who had become the military ruler of the country in a coup in 1999 but been forced out in 2000, is killed in the fighting.

▸ In the second bombing in 24 hours, a suicide bomber detonates his weapons on a bus in Tel Aviv, Israel, outside the main synagogue, killing six passengers; the bombings mark the end of a period of 45 days with no attacks with Israel.

▸ *On the Transmigration of Souls*, an orchestral and choral work commissioned from John Adams to commemorate the terrorist attacks of 11 Sep 2001, premieres in New York City, conducted by Lorin Maazel. (See 7 Apr.)

**20 Sep** The Israeli army demolishes all but a single building in the compound of Palestinian leader Yasir Arafat and imprisons him within the remaining building.

▸ After months of resisting, the administration of US Pres. George W. Bush accedes to Congress's demands for an independent investigation into possible intelligence failures in the period leading up to the terrorist attacks of 11 Sep 2001.

▸ A glacier in the Caucasus Mountains calves an enormous chunk of ice, which triggers mud slides that bury a village and tourist centers in Russia's republic of North Ossetia; among the missing is Sergey Bodrov, Jr., the star of a popular series of action movies.

▸ Nearly four weeks after his arrest, which caused an international outcry, AIDS activist Wan Yanhai is released from custody by Chinese authorities, apparently without restrictions.

**21 Sep** The party of Prime Minister Mikulas Dzurinda, the Slovak Democratic and Christian Union, comes in only second best in parliamentary elections in Slovakia; Dzurinda is nonetheless reappointed prime minister on 15 October.

▸ The winners of the 2002 Albert Lasker Medical Research Awards are announced; they are James E. Rothman and Randy W. Schekman for basic medical research, Willem J. Kolff and Belding H. Scribner for clinical research, and James E. Darnell for special achievement.

▸ Among the 16 people being inducted into the National Inventors Hall of Fame is Nils Bohlin, inventor of the three-point seat belt; he dies the same day in his native Sweden.

▸ Miss Illinois, Erika Harold, is crowned Miss America in Atlantic City NJ.

**22 Sep** Elections in Germany keep Chancellor Gerhard Schröder in power.

▸ The Emmy Awards are presented in Los Angeles, hosted by Conan O'Brien; winners include the television series *Friends* and *The West Wing* and the actors Ray Romano, Michael Chiklis, Jennifer Aniston, Allison Janney, Brad Garrett, John Spencer, Doris Roberts, and Stockard Channing.

▸ Hundreds of thousands of rural protesters converge on London to demonstrate in favor of fox hunting (under partial ban in Scotland and under review in England) and to protest the lack of services in the countryside.

▸ Germany defeats Chivas Regal (an international team) 8–6 to win Thailand's second annual King's Cup Elephant Polo Tournament; the game, first played in Mughal India but reinvented in Nepal in 1982, involves three players, each on an elephant with a mahout (handler), on each team and lasts 20 minutes.

**23 Sep** US officials issue a detailed plan to states on quick mass inoculation in the event of a biological attack involving smallpox; the states are instructed to prepare to vaccinate the entire population.

▸ Russian Pres. Vladimir Putin and Azerbaijani Pres. Heydar Aliyev sign an agreement establishing the two countries' borders in the Caspian Sea and thus divide energy resources in the sea.

**24 Sep** Argentina's economy minister, Roberto Lavagna, announces that Argentina will not use its foreign reserves to repay loans from the IMF and other multilateral lenders; Argentina has been complaining that the demands of the IMF are too burdensome.

▸ Men with grenades and automatic weapons open fire in a Hindu temple complex in Gandhinagar, in Gujarat state in India, killing at least 30 people and wounding 74 before being killed themselves.

▸ Oksana Fyodorova of Russia, who was crowned Miss Universe in May, is forced by the pageant to step down because it is believed that she is married and pregnant; Miss Panama, Justine Pasek, takes her place as Miss Universe.

**25 Sep** As a rebellion in the interior of Côte d'Ivoire continues unabated, French troops rescue trapped students from the International Christian Academy in Bouaké, a school for the children of foreign missionaries in West Africa.

▸ Armed men enter the offices of the Institute for Peace and Justice, a Christian charity, in Karachi, Pakistan, and tie up and murder seven employees; an eighth employee survives a gunshot to the head.

▸ Jan Hendrik Schön, a star research physicist, is fired by Bell Labs, Murray Hill NJ, for scientific misconduct; Schön, whose revolutionary work had been the object of keen excitement in scientific circles, is accused of having falsified data in 16 of the 24 suspect scientific papers he published in top journals from 1998 to 2001 and has shaken faith in the peer-review system for publishing.

**26 Sep** Chechen fighters and Russian military forces engage in the biggest battle of 2002 in the Caucasus in the Russian republic of Ingushetia, leaving dozens dead.

▸ US Federal Reserve Board Chairman Alan Greenspan is given an honorary knighthood by the UK's Queen Elizabeth II.

▸ Federal prosecutors admit in a court document that they mistakenly turned 48 classified FBI reports over to accused terrorist Zacarias Moussaoui, who is conducting his own defense.

▸ The son-in-law and three grandsons of former strongman U Ne Win are sentenced to death in Myanmar (Burma) for having plotted a coup against the government; the sentences are regarded as shockingly harsh.

▶ SBC Communications Inc., the second biggest local telephone company in the US, says it has to lay off 11,000 employees, claiming that regulations that require it to sell access to its lines to competitors at low prices are contributing to its financial difficulties.

**27 Sep** East Timor becomes the 191st member of the United Nations just four months after becoming independent.

▶ The Naismith Memorial Basketball Hall of Fame inducts players Earvin ("Magic") Johnson and Drazen Petrovic, coaches Larry Brown, Lute Olsen, and Kay Yow, and the Harlem Globetrotters; the following day the Hall of Fame's state-of-the-art basketball-shaped new home opens to the delighted public in Springfield MA.

▶ The acquisition of the Pennzoil-Quaker State Co. by the Shell Oil Co. is approved by the Federal Trade Commission in the US.

▶ A federal judge in Australia ceremonially delivers a 136,000-sq-km (52,500-sq-mi) tract of land in Western Australia to the Martu Aboriginal tribe, which had traditionally occupied the land before they were removed during the 1950s by the British government, which used the land as a missile test range.

**28 Sep** Two bombs explode in a crowded movie theater in Satkhira, Bangladesh, and shortly thereafter two more bombs explode at a circus in the same town; three people are killed and many more seriously wounded, and it is not clear who set the bombs.

▶ The inaugural Maazel/Vilar Conductors' Competition—with a prize that includes $45,000, a conducting fellowship directed by Lorin Maazel, and a series of symphonic engagements—concludes after 20 months and 362 contestants, with two winners: Xian Zhang, from China, and Bundit Ungrangsee, from Thailand.

**29 Sep** The National Gallery of Art in Washington DC opens to the public its new sculpture galleries, showcasing 900 works from the Middle Ages to the early 20th century.

▶ West African leaders hold an emergency meeting in Ghana to discuss how to end the civil war in Côte d'Ivoire as American and French forces continue to evacuate foreigners from harm's way.

▶ Israeli forces pull out of the largely destroyed compound of Palestinian leader Yasir Arafat, who emerges to the cheers of supporters.

▶ The 34th Ryder Cup golf tournament, delayed for one year by the terrorist attacks of 11 Sep 2001 concludes in Sutton Coldfield, England, with the European team defeating the heavily favored Americans.

▶ Port operators shut down 29 US ports from Seattle WA to San Diego CA maintaining that longshoremen have been staging a work slowdown.

**30 Sep** The European Union agrees to exempt US soldiers from prosecution before the International Criminal Court, provided that accused Americans are tried in a US court.

▶ In an attempt to turn Japan's troubled economy around, Prime Minister Junichiro Koizumi replaces the country's conservative financial services minister with the reform-minded economic and fiscal policy minister, Heizo Takenaka.

# October 2002

**1 Oct** Croatian Pres. Stipe Mesic appears before the international war crimes tribunal in The Hague to testify against former Serbian leader Slobodan Milosevic; it is the first time that a sitting head of state has testified before the war crimes tribunal, and it is regarded as an important precedent in international law.

▶ The US Northern Command, charged with the military protection of the entire US and its territories as well as Canada and Mexico, opens near Colorado Springs CO; it is the first time since the Revolutionary War that a single command center has controlled the whole country's defense.

▶ Reports say census takers in Russia's Taymyr autonomous *okrug* (district) have found a new ethnic group in northern Siberia, the Chalymtsy, who number about 130 and engage in hunting and subsistence agriculture.

**2 Oct** The former chief financial officer of the defunct energy giant Enron, Andrew S. Fastow, is arrested and charged in federal court with fraud, money laundering, and conspiracy. (See 21 August.)

▶ American and British scientists jointly announce that in separate projects, published in *Nature* and *Science*, they have sequenced the genome of the parasite that causes malaria as well as that of the *Anopheles gambiae* mosquito, which carries and transmits the disease.

**3 Oct** Five people are randomly killed by a sniper in the suburbs of Washington DC after another person had been killed the previous evening; the next day a seventh person is wounded.

▶ Hurricane Lili weakens as it moves ashore in Louisiana; the previous day Russia's Mission Control Center (MCC), near Moscow, had taken temporary control of the International Space Station while Lili threatened the MCC in Houston TX.

▶ At a meeting in Bouaké, Côte d'Ivoire, with mediators from five West African countries, rebels who had begun a civil war 14 days earlier agree to a cease-fire; fighting later resumes, however.

**4 Oct** King Gyanendra of Nepal dismisses Prime Minister Sher Bahadur Deuba and assumes direct power after Deuba recommends delaying parliamentary elections for a year; Deuba argues that the constitution does not give the king the power to fire an elected prime minister. (See 11 October.)

▶ As rhetoric between Pakistan and India again heats up, Pakistan test-fires a nuclear-capable medium-range missile.

**5 Oct** Countrywide elections are held in Bosnia and Herzegovina; they are the first elections since the 1992–95 war that are run by the country rather than by the Organization for Security and Co-operation in Europe, and the nationalist parties are the biggest winners.

▶ South Korea's National Assembly overwhelmingly approves Kim Suk Soo as prime minister after having rejected Pres. Kim Dae Jung's first two choices earlier in the year.

▸ Venezuelan Pres. Hugo Chávez announces that his government has foiled another attempted coup.

▸ A much-anticipated new museum, the Museum of Sex, opens in New York City in what organizers suspect is a former brothel.

**6 Oct** An explosion causes a fire and massive oil leak on the French oil tanker *Limburg* off the southeastern coast of Yemen; it is later determined that a terrorist attack caused the disaster.

▸ Presidential elections held in Brazil result in no candidate's getting more than 50% of the vote, and a runoff becomes necessary, though leftist candidate Lula (Luiz Inácio da Silva) has a commanding lead. (See 27 October.)

▸ Pope John Paul II canonizes Josemaría Escrivá de Balaguer y Albás, the founder of the conservative Roman Catholic lay organization Opus Dei.

**7 Oct** The Nobel Prize for Physiology or Medicine is awarded to Sydney Brenner, H. Robert Horvitz, and John E. Sulston for their discoveries regarding genetic regulation of organ development and the process of apoptosis, or programmed cell death.

▸ Wolfgang Clement, the premier of North Rhine-Westphalia, is named head of Germany's new "superministry" for the economy and employment.

▸ The American Astronomical Society announces that on 4 June researchers Michael Brown and Chadwick Trujillo discovered a Sun-orbiting object, which they named Quaoar, that is the largest body found in the Earth's solar system since Pluto was discovered in 1930; it is seen as strengthening the case that Pluto should be classified, like Quaoar, as a Kuiper Belt object rather than as a planet.

**8 Oct** US Pres. George W. Bush invokes the Taft-Hartley Act, last employed in 1971, to persuade a federal judge to issue an injunction temporarily halting the lockout of longshoremen that has shut down 29 West Coast ports for 10 days.

▸ The Nobel Prize for Physics is awarded to Raymond Davis, Jr., and Masatoshi Koshiba for their detection of cosmic neutrinos and to Riccardo Giacconi for his discovery of sources of cosmic X-rays.

▸ Two men open fire on US marines engaging in training exercises in Kuwait, killing one soldier and wounding another before being killed themselves.

**9 Oct** The US Department of Justice indicts Enaam M. Arnaout on conspiracy, fraud, money-laundering, and racketeering charges, maintaining that the Chicago-based Benevolence International Foundation, a charity organization headed by Arnaout, contributed funds to support al-Qaeda.

▸ The Nobel Prize for Economics is awarded to Daniel Kahneman and Vernon L. Smith, while the Nobel Prize for Chemistry goes to John B. Fenn, Koichi Tanaka, and Kurt Wüthrich for their work in developing techniques for identifying and mapping large biological molecules.

**10 Oct** The Nobel Prize for Literature is awarded to the Hungarian writer Imre Kertész.

▸ The International Court of Justice rules that the Bakassi Peninsula in the Gulf of Guinea between Nigeria and Cameroon belongs to Cameroon; the peninsula is believed to contain rich oil deposits.

▸ KazMunayGaz, the national oil and gas company of Kazakhstan, announces that it has discovered economically significant new oil reserves in the Caspian Sea.

**11 Oct** The Nobel Peace Prize is awarded to former US president Jimmy Carter.

▸ The US Congress passes a bill by a wide margin granting US Pres. George W. Bush broad authority to use force against Iraq.

▸ King Gyanendra of Nepal names Lokendra Bahadur Chand prime minister and appoints a nine-member cabinet as thousands of people demonstrate against the firing of the elected prime minister, Sher Bahadur Deuba. (See 4 October.)

▸ In Sholapur, India, five people are killed in riots that break out after a local newspaper reports that religious commentator Jerry Falwell on the television show *60 Minutes* characterized the Prophet Muhammad as a terrorist and a violent man.

▸ The executive committee of New York City's Metropolitan Opera announces its appointment of opera star Beverly Sills as the Met's next chairman.

**12 Oct** A car bomb explodes outside two nightclubs popular with foreigners on Bali, Indonesia; at least 183 people, most of them Australian tourists, are killed. (See 21 November.)

▸ A large and distinctive new national performing arts center, the Esplanade–Theaters on the Bay, puts on a gala opening in Singapore.

**13 Oct** Wampler Foods recalls a record 12.4 million kg (27.4 million lb) of poultry, all the cooked deli products produced in a plant in Franconia PA since May; the poultry may be contaminated with *Listeria monocytogenes* bacteria.

▸ Michael Schumacher wins the Japan Grand Prix auto race, his 11th victory for the year. (See 21 July.)

▸ During the Frankfurt (Germany) Book Fair, Nigerian writer Chinua Achebe is awarded the Peace Prize of the German Book Trade; the prize, currently valued at €15,000 (about $15,000) has been awarded annually since 1950.

**14 Oct** John Reid, the British secretary for Northern Ireland, announces that the British government is suspending home rule and taking over the government of Northern Ireland for the fourth time in less than three years.

▸ Kenya's ruling party, Kenya African National Union, chooses Uhuru Kenyatta, son of the country's founding president, Jomo Kenyatta, as its candidate in elections to replace retiring Pres. Daniel arap Moi. (See 27 December.)

▸ Workers in Denison IA are horrified when they open a Union Pacific railcar to find that it contains the remains of 11 would-be emigrants from Mexico.

▸ A new university, the Bulgarian-Romanian Interuniversity Europe Center, supported by the German Federal Ministry of Education and Research and the association of German universities, opens its twin campuses in the Danube port cities of Ruse, Bulgaria, and Giurgiu, Romania.

▸ The European Commission rules that only cheese made in Greece may be called feta; cheeses made in imitation of that cheese in other countries must within five years be marketed under a different name.

**15 Oct** A presidential election is held in Iraq in which the only candidate is Pres. Saddam Hussein; the following day it is announced that 100% of the electorate voted to retain him for another seven-year term.

▸ In peace negotiations taking place in Machakos, Kenya, the government of The Sudan agrees to a temporary cease-fire with the Sudanese People's Liberation Army.

**16 Oct** Dutch Prime Minister Jan Peter Balkenende resigns just three months after taking office as squabbling among the politically inexperienced members of coalition partner List Pim Fortuyn causes the collapse of the government.

▸ The US State Department announces that North Korea has admitted that it has been secretly developing a nuclear weapons program for several years, in violation of a 1994 agreement with the US. (*See* 20 October.)

▸ India announces that it will pull back its troops from the Pakistani border, where they have been deployed since shortly after the attack on the Indian Parliament building on 13 Dec 2001; the following day Pakistan announces that it will follow suit.

▸ The ruling People's National Party wins general elections in Jamaica, giving Prime Minister Percival J. Patterson an unprecedented third consecutive term of office.

▸ The Bibliotheca Alexandrina, the successor to the fabled library of Alexandria, is officially dedicated by Egyptian Pres. Hosni Mubarak.

**17 Oct** Officials representing the rebels in Côte d'Ivoire sign a truce agreement with West African mediators in Bouaké.

▸ More than 20 years after he fled the country following his arrest for the murder of his former girlfriend Holly Maddux, onetime counterculture star Ira Einhorn is convicted of the 1977 murder in Philadelphia.

▸ *Le Monde* publishes an interview with Romano Prodi, president of the European Commission, in which he characterizes the 1997 Stability and Growth Pact, which is the framework for the European single currency and which the European Commission is empowered to enforce, as "stupid"; shock waves reverberate throughout Europe.

**18 Oct** The Vatican rejects the policy drawn up by American bishops to address the problem of sexual abuse of minors by priests, indicating that the policy fails to safeguard the rights of accused priests.

▸ The last major shirt-making factory in the US, a C.F. Hathaway Co. unit in Waterville ME closes for good after 165 years of production.

▸ The poet Quincy Troupe, who had become California's first official poet laureate on 11 June, resigns after admitting that he had claimed on his résumé to have graduated from college, whereas he only attended.

▸ American Ballet Theater premieres a new production, *A Tribute to George Harrison*, in New York City.

**19 Oct** The Treaty of Nice, which permits the European Union to add 10 new members, passes in a referendum in Ireland; the terms of the treaty required unanimous agreement by the member states, and Ireland had been the last holdout.

▸ The first segment of the new Copenhagen Metro, featuring both subway and elevated train service, opens; Queen Margrethe II of Denmark is among the first passengers.

**20 Oct** The US announces that it considers a 1994 agreement under which it provided help to North Korea in building an energy infrastructure in return for North Korea's refraining from attempting to develop nuclear weapons to be effectively "nullified." (*See* 16 October and 22 December.)

▸ Iraqi Pres. Saddam Hussein announces an unprecedented amnesty of nearly all prisoners in the country, and as crowds mob the prisons, tens of thousands are released; some are killed in the crush.

▸ Blue Stream, the deepest underwater pipeline in the world and a joint venture between Russia and Turkey, opens.

**21 Oct** The UN Food and Agriculture Organization appeals for immediate food and agricultural aid, saying that more than 14 million people in sub-Saharan Africa are in danger of starvation and that famine also threatens in Afghanistan.

▸ A three-tiered system of labels for organic foods denoting standards set by the US Department of Agriculture goes into effect in grocery stores.

▸ The *Biblical Archaeological Review* announces the discovery of a stone ossuary with an ancient Aramaic inscription reading "James, son of Joseph, brother of Jesus"; some believe this is the first mention of Jesus Christ outside the Bible. (*See* 18 June.)

**22 Oct** The New York Times Co. announces that it is buying out the Washington Post Co.'s share of the *International Herald Tribune*; the rival companies had co-owned the respected international newspaper for 35 years.

▸ The Man Booker Prize for Fiction, Great Britain's top literary award, goes to Canadian writer Yann Martel for his novel *Life of Pi*.

▸ The Royal Canadian Mounted Police file fraud charges against Garth Drabinsky and Myron Gottlieb, the founders of Livent Inc., one of North America's largest theater companies from the late 1980s until its demise in 1998; the two are charged with having defrauded creditors and investors of nearly $320 million.

▸ Lithuania's legislature votes to adopt new rules that permit the use of the euro as legal tender in the country.

**23 Oct** During a production of the popular musical *Nord-Ost* in a theater in Moscow, more than 50 Chechen guerrillas storm the stage and take the actors and audience hostage. (*See* 26 October.)

---

### QUOTE OF THE MONTH

" *We will start killing them, the people who are here. One by one we will kill them—all of them. We didn't come here to go home again; we came here to die.* "

—Abusaid, Chechen hostage taker, in a phone call to the BBC, 23 October

---

▸ In a ceremony in Tokyo, the winners of the 2002 Praemium Imperiale Awards are presented with their medals for global achievement in the arts: Jean-Luc Godard in theater/film, Norman Foster in architecture, Dietrich Fischer-Dieskau in music, Sigmar Polke in painting, and Giuliano Vangi in sculpture.

**24 Oct** A man and a teenage boy, John Allen Muhammad and John Lee Malvo, are arrested near Myersville MD for the sniper killings that have left 10 people dead and 3 wounded and have terrified the area around Washington DC since 2 October. (*See* 3 October.)

▸ In a ceremony in Ames, Iowa, soil scientist Pedro Sanchez is presented with the World Food Prize for having developed a low-tech, sustainable way for impoverished Africans to as much as quadruple their crop yields without exhausting the soil.

▶ Police in Ireland set up a special unit to investigate charges of sexual abuse made against priests; the public is increasingly angry over the appearance that the hierarchy of the Roman Catholic Church has protected priests who have abused minors.

▶ Elections are held in Bahrain to choose its first parliament since 1973, and for the first time anywhere in the Persian Gulf, women are allowed to vote and run for office in a national election.

▶ *Science* magazine publishes a paper on-line that describes an experiment in which scientists manipulated molecules to make a working logic circuit that is some 260,000 times smaller than the most advanced silicon circuitry.

**25 Oct** Minnesota Sen. Paul Wellstone is killed when his campaign airplane crashes in northern Minnesota; the tragedy takes place less than two weeks before the election in which the prominent and outspoken liberal was expected to be returned to office.

▶ Koki Ishii, a member of the Diet (parliament) who is head of an anticorruption task force in the Democratic Party of Japan, is stabbed to death as he is leaving his house to go to work; the following day a right-wing extremist admits to the assassination and turns himself in to police.

▶ A year after the announcement of a planned merger between P&O Princess Cruises and Royal Caribbean Cruises, Carnival Corp. announces that it has reached an agreement to buy P&O Princess; Carnival is the world's largest cruise ship company.

**26 Oct** Russian troops pump a gas intended to render people unconscious into the Moscow theater in which Chechen guerrillas are holding the audience and performers hostage and then storm the theater, freeing most of the 750 people, but at least 127 are killed by the disabling gas. (See 23 October.)

▶ Tens of thousands of people march in Washington DC and in other cities across the US to express their opposition to a possible war with Iraq.

▶ The Breeders' Cup Classic Thoroughbred race is run at Arlington Park racetrack in Illinois, the winner is 43.5–1 long shot Volponi.

**27 Oct** In Brazil's runoff presidential election, Workers' Party politician Lula (Luiz Inácio da Silva) wins by the largest margin of victory in the country's history.

▶ In their first appearance in the World Series in their 42-year history, the Anaheim Angels defeat the San Francisco Giants in the seventh game to win the major league baseball championship in Anaheim CA.

**28 Oct** The committee headed by Valéry Giscard d'Estaing unveils a draft constitution for the European Union; the document proposes a larger role in international affairs for the union.

▶ Laurence Foley, a senior US diplomat, is assassinated outside his home in Amman, Jordan; the attack is regarded as part of the worldwide terror campaign against Western targets.

▶ Italian Prime Minister Silvio Berlusconi meets with Libyan leader Muammar al-Qaddafi in Bab al-Aziziyah; Berlusconi is one of only a few top European officials to have visited Libya in two decades.

▶ The Prix Goncourt, France's top literary prize, is awarded to Pascal Quignard for *Les Ombres errantes*.

**29 Oct** The Palestinian Legislative Council approves a new cabinet appointed by Yasir Arafat with two fewer ministers than the old.

▶ The fifth annual Mark Twain Prize for American Humor is presented to Bob Newhart in a ceremony in the Kennedy Center in Washington DC.

▶ A fire destroys the International Trade Center building in downtown Ho Chi Minh City, Vietnam, killing dozens of people.

**30 Oct** Labour Party ministers in the coalition government of Israel resign, leaving Prime Minister Ariel Sharon without a majority; the ministers object to a budget that they see as favoring Israeli settlers in Palestinian regions over the poor of Israel.

▶ Nine bombs go off in various places in Soweto, South Africa's largest black township; the bombings are blamed on white extremists.

▶ The government of the Central African Republic announces that it has retaken the capital, Bangui, from rebels who had seized the city nearly a week earlier.

▶ Jam Master Jay, a deejay for the seminal rap group Run-D.M.C., is shot to death in his recording studio in Queens NY; friends and authorities are baffled.

**31 Oct** George Carey retires as the archbishop of Canterbury, a position that he held for more than 11 years.

# November 2002

**1 Nov** US District Court Judge Colleen Kollar-Kotelly approves the antitrust settlement reached between the Department of Justice and Microsoft Corp., dismissing almost all the additional sanctions sought by the nine states that had not signed on to the proposed settlement.

▶ In London, charges of robbery against Paul Burrell, who had been the butler of Diana, princess of Wales, are dropped after Queen Elizabeth II unexpectedly lets it be known that Burrell had told her that he was taking the princess's belongings for safekeeping after her death.

▶ Uniformed officers in Tokyo begin to fine violators of a ban on smoking in designated public areas; the ordinance, which went into effect on 1 October, was introduced in response to complaints that people had been holding lit cigarettes at the same level as children's faces in crowded areas.

**2 Nov** In Norwegian-brokered peace negotiations held in Thailand, the government of Sri Lanka and the Liberation Tigers of Tamil Eelam agree to set up a panel to discuss ways to share power.

▶ A new moderate coalition government takes office in the Indian state of Jammu and Kashmir, in spite of several attacks by Islamic militants.

▶ In elections that began the previous day, the ruling coalition in the Czech Republic loses its majority in the Senate.

▶ Police in London arrest five people they believe were planning to kidnap Victoria Beckham, wife of association football star David Beckham and former member of the Spice Girls; four additional suspects are arrested overnight but are later cleared of connection with the conspiracy.

**3 Nov** Legislative elections in Turkey result in a resounding victory for the opposition Justice and Development Party; the party's leader, former Islamist Recep Tayyip Erdogan, has been barred from holding office, however.

▶ A major earthquake, measuring an astonishing 7.9 in magnitude, occurs in Alaska; because its epicenter is in the state's sparsely populated interior, however, there are no casualties.

▶ The Reventador volcano in Ecuador erupts, leaving the city of Quito covered with a thick layer of ash; residents are warned to remain indoors.

▶ In the New York City Marathon, Rodgers Rop of Kenya wins with a time of 2 hr 8 min 7 sec; the fastest woman is Joyce Chepchumba, also from Kenya, who comes in at 2 hr 25 min 56 sec.

▶ A missile fired by an unmanned US Predator aircraft in Yemen kills six people, including a man known as Abu Ali, a top al-Qaeda figure.

**4 Nov** Construction workers in Switzerland go on strike to protest the employers group's refusal to sign a negotiated contract; the last strike in Switzerland, also by construction workers, took place in 1947.

▶ In Phnom Penh, Cambodia, Premier Zhu Rongji of China signs a framework agreement with the members of the Association of Southeast Asian Nations to set up a common free-trade area within the next decade.

**5 Nov** In midterm congressional elections in the US, the Republican Party increases its majority in the House of Representatives and gains a majority in the Senate.

▶ Harvey L. Pitt resigns as chairman of the US Securities and Exchange Commission.

▶ The European Court of Justice finds that bilateral aviation treaties between the US and eight European countries violate European Union law.

▶ Brazil's National Institute for Space Research releases the results of a satellite-data study of lightning incidence; it found that Brazil has more lightning strikes than any other country in the world.

**6 Nov** In France's worst rail accident in five years, a train just outside a station in Nancy is engulfed in flames that are later determined to have been sparked by a kitchenette hot plate; 12 people die.

▶ At the 36th annual Country Music Association Awards, musician Alan Jackson becomes only the third person to win five awards, including Entertainer of the Year and Single of the Year for his song "Where Were You (When the World Stopped Turning)."

**7 Nov** The legislature of Latvia approves a new center-right coalition government headed by Einars Repse.

▶ The US Food and Drug Administration approves a highly accurate test that can reveal in as little as 20 minutes whether a subject is infected with HIV; standard HIV testing usually requires a minimum two-day wait for results.

▶ The University of Michigan announces that, having found that more than $600,000 in loans had been made to four university basketball players in violation of NCAA rules, it is imposing severe penalties on itself, including forfeiting all games in which those players were improperly involved and excluding itself from championship play for the coming season.

**8 Nov** The UN Security Council unanimously approves a resolution sponsored by the US and the UK requiring Iraq to submit to stringent weapons inspections, with deadlines for various related activities, or face "serious consequences."

▶ Officials in Ecuador say that more than 1,000 people in the city of Ibarra have been made sick by contaminated municipal water after broken water pipes allowed purification systems to be overwhelmed by farm runoff after a storm.

**9 Nov** In Dresden, Germany, the Zwinger Palace Museum's Old Masters Picture Gallery and the Semper Opera reopen for the first time since the summer floods.

**10 Nov** The Arab League, meeting in Cairo, passes a resolution expressing support for weapons inspections in Iraq.

▶ Police in Jordan begin a five-day siege of the city of Maan, looking for Islamic militants who have been terrorizing the country; firefights during the siege kill at least four people.

▶ The constitutional ban on the return to Italy of members of the house of Savoy, Italy's former royal family, expires.

**11 Nov** The UN presents a plan to both Greek and Turkish Cyprus, as well as Greece, Turkey, and the UK, for reunification of Cyprus with a structure similar to that of Switzerland; acceptance of the plan is seen as vital to the island country's being invited to join the European Union. (See 1 Apr 2003.)

▶ Microsoft chairman Bill Gates pledges to donate $100 million from the Bill & Melinda Gates Foundation to combat the spread of HIV/AIDS in India.

**12 Nov** The Qatar-based satellite television station al-Jazeera broadcasts a new audio tape that it says was made by Osama bin Laden and in which he praises recent terrorist attacks and threatens additional assaults; on 18 November, US intelligence officials say that they are convinced that the voice on the tape is indeed that of Bin Laden.

▶ In a meaningless show of defiance, Iraq's National Assembly rejects the UN resolution on weapons inspections but authorizes Pres. Saddam Hussein to make the final decision; the following day a letter is sent from Iraq accepting the resolution.

▶ The United Nations Convention on International Trade in Endangered Species of Wild Fauna and Flora agrees to allow Botswana, Namibia, and South Africa each to hold a one-time sale of legal ivory mostly collected from elephants that died of natural causes; the sales are to take place after May 2004 if enough information on elephant populations and poaching levels has been gathered and if it has been determined that ivory-buying countries can control the domestic ivory trade.

▶ The *Kenyon Review* literary magazine bestows its first Kenyon Review Award for Literary Achievement to American novelist E.L. Doctorow.

▶ The British governmental organization English Nature designates Sherwood Forest, the legendary home of Robin Hood, a national nature reserve.

**13 Nov** An aging single-hulled Bahamian-flagged tanker, the *Prestige*, which is carrying 77,000 metric tons of oil, begins to sink off the coast of Galicia, Spain; rescue workers frantically attempt to tow the leaking ship as far from the coast as possible. (*See* 19 November.)

▶ Great Britain's 50,000 full-time firefighters begin a 48-hour strike for higher pay; it is the first nationwide firefighter strike in 25 years.

**14 Nov** Nancy Pelosi of California is elected to succeed Richard Gephardt, who chose to step down, as leader of the Democratic Party in the US House of Representatives; she is the first woman to be named leader of either party in either house of Congress.

▸ Pres. Eduardo Duhalde of Argentina says that the country will be unable to meet the $805 million loan installment due today to the World Bank until the IMF restores a line of credit that it cut off almost a year ago.

▸ Kai-Uwe Ricke, a top communications executive, is named to head Deutsche Telekom, Germany's telecommunications company.

**15 Nov** At the end of the 16th Communist Party Congress in China, Hu Jintao is named the new leader of the Communist Party of China, replacing Pres. Jiang Zemin, who nevertheless will retain power behind the scenes.

▸ Palestinian snipers kill nine Israeli soldiers and three civilians from an emergency response team in an ambush in the West Bank city of Hebron.

▸ Joseph Parisi, editor of *Poetry*, announces that philanthropist Ruth Lilly has given the distinguished small journal a bequest that is likely to be worth at least $100 million and that makes it suddenly one of the world's richest publications.

**16 Nov** Abdullah Gul, of the Justice and Development Party, is named prime minister of Turkey.

▸ Unable to secure enough support in the parliament to carry out his policies, Pres. Leonid Kuchma of Ukraine dismisses the government of Prime Minister Anatoly Kinakh and names Viktor Yanukovich prime minister in his place.

▸ Police in Bishkek, the capital of Kyrgyzstan, detain more than 100 people and crush a protest calling for the resignation of Pres. Askar Akayev; regardless of concessions made by Akayev, protesters have been implacable since the killing of five protesters in March.

**17 Nov** Voters in Peru, electing 25 new regional governments, choose the opposition party or independent parties over the party of Pres. Alejandro Toledo in almost every case.

▸ An appeals court in Italy overturns the acquittal of former prime minister Giulio Andreotti on charges of complicity with the Mafia in the 1979 murder of a journalist and sentences him to 24 years in prison; politicians of all political bents condemn the development.

**18 Nov** The European Union sets a tentative date of 1 May 2004 for 10 countries to become new members.

▸ An advance team of UN weapons inspectors arrives in Baghdad, Iraq.

**19 Nov** The US Senate overwhelmingly approves the creation of a new cabinet department, the Department of Homeland Security, which will have a workforce of about 170,000; the House of Representatives had approved it the previous week.

▸ Holland America Line announces that it is taking the cruise ship *Amsterdam* out of service for 10 days for disinfection as soon as it docks at Fort Lauderdale FL; on the past four cruises, more than 500 people on the ship have come down with the Norwalk virus.

▸ Astronomers at NASA say they have detected in the galaxy NGC 6240 two supermassive black holes that in several hundred million years will merge in a collision, the effects of which will be felt throughout the universe.

▸ The leaking oil tanker *Prestige*, being towed out to sea by order of the Spanish government, splits in two and sinks; the oil spill is believed to be among the worst in history. (See 13 November.)

**20 Nov** The National Book Awards are presented to Julia Glass for her first novel, *Three Junes*, Robert A. Caro for his nonfiction book *The Years of Lyndon Johnson: Master of the Senate*, Ruth Stone for her poetry collection *In the Next Galaxy*, and Nancy Farmer for her young-adult book *The House of the Scorpion*; novelist Philip Roth is given the Medal for Distinguished Contribution to American Letters.

▸ The broadcasting authority in Turkey authorizes state radio and television stations to present a limited number of programs in Kurdish.

▸ Major League Baseball commissioner Bud Selig announces that the Montreal Expos will play some of next season's "home" games in San Juan PR.

**21 Nov** At a summit meeting in Prague, NATO extends an official invitation to Bulgaria, Estonia, Latvia, Lithuania, Romania, Slovakia, and Slovenia to become new alliance members; they are expected to join in May 2004.

▸ Zafarullah Khan Jamali is chosen by a narrow margin in Pakistan's Parliament to be prime minister; Jamali's name had been put forward by Pres. Pervez Musharraf, and he was chosen over Islamist candidate Fazlur Rahman.

▸ Authorities in Indonesia arrest Imam Samudra, who they believed played a leading role in the Bali nightclub bombing. (See 12 October.)

▸ American missionary Bonnie Witherall is shot to death in Sidon, Lebanon; it is the first time in over 10 years that an American has been murdered in Lebanon.

**22 Nov** Following a summit meeting between US Pres. George W. Bush and Russian Pres. Vladimir Putin in St. Petersburg, both leaders promise to cooperate in matters of international terrorism and energy.

▸ After the US responds to news of North Korea's secret nuclear-weapons-development project by cutting off delivery of fuel supplies to North Korea, the Pyongyang regime says that it will not permit foreign inspectors to enter the country to verify that fuel supplies are being used for peaceful purposes.

▸ Organizers of the Miss World beauty contest scheduled to be held on 7 December announce that the pageant will be moved from Abuja, Nigeria, to London; the decision came after more than 200 people were killed in violence touched off by a newspaper article expressing the opinion that the Prophet Muhammad would have approved of the contest.

▸ *Science* magazine publishes three studies on dogs; one of them uses variations in mitochondrial DNA sequences to suggest that all dogs are descended from a population of wolves that lived in East Asia between 15,000 and 40,000 years ago.

**23 Nov** Negotiators for dockworkers and terminal operators at the 29 ports on the US West Coast that had closed in a contract dispute in October reach an agreement on a six-year contract.

▸ After two weeks of delays caused by technical difficulties and bad weather, the space shuttle *Endeavour* finally blasts off, carrying a replacement crew for the International Space Station and the first Native American astronaut, John B. Herrington, a registered member of the Chickasaw Nation.

**24 Nov** Lucio Gutiérrez Borbúa, a leftist military man with virtually no previous political experience, is elected president of Ecuador in a runoff election.

▸ Elections in Austria keep Chancellor Wolfgang Schüssel in office; only 10% of the popular vote goes to the far-right Freedom Party.

▸ The Montreal Alouettes defeat the Edmonton Eskimos 25–16 in the Canadian Football League Grey Cup; it is Montreal's first CFL championship since 1977.

**25 Nov** US Pres. George W. Bush names Tom Ridge to be secretary of the new Department of Homeland Security.

▸ Turkmenistan's Pres. Saparmurad Niyazov announces an amnesty for almost half the prisoners in the country; later he survives an assassination attempt when a man opens fire on his motorcade.

▸ New York City authorities say they have broken up a credit-theft ring that has stolen the identities of more than 30,000 people.

**26 Nov** The UN announces that for the first time half of all people with HIV infections are women and that some 42 million people worldwide have been infected.

▸ Canadian Prime Minister Jean Chrétien accepts the resignation of Françoise Ducros, his communications director, as a result of controversy that erupted over her off-the-record characterization of US Pres. George W. Bush as "a moron."

▸ The US-based group Nature Conservancy announces that it believes that it has found evidence of a previously unknown population of orangutans in Kalimantan Timur on the island of Borneo in Indonesia; if confirmed, the discovery will increase the known number of orangutans in the world by approximately 10%.

**27 Nov** UN weapons inspectors begin their work in Iraq under the new UN mandate; weapons inspectors under the previous mandate had left Iraq in 1998 because of the lack of cooperation of the Iraqi regime.

▸ US Pres. George W. Bush surprises observers by naming Henry Kissinger head of the independent investigation into the terrorist attacks of 11 Sep 2001. (See 16 December.)

**28 Nov** Suicide bombers attack an Israeli resort hotel in Mombasa, Kenya, killing 16 people, including themselves and members of a Kenyan dance troupe; at nearly the same time, shoulder-launched missiles are fired at an Israeli passenger jet leaving Mombasa, but this attack fails.

▸ Javier Solana, secretary-general of the Council of the European Union, announces that the leaders of Serbia and Montenegro have agreed on the constitutional charter of the future union of Serbia and Montenegro.

**29 Nov** The government of Italy releases the first of the money for the creation of the Moses Project, a plan to build barriers in the Adriatic seabed to protect Venice from tidal waters.

**30 Nov** Turkey lifts a state of emergency that has been in place for 15 years in the largely Kurdish southeastern part of the country.

▸ French romantic novelist Alexandre Dumas, who died in 1870, is reburied in the crypt of the Panthéon, France's official tomb of honor.

# December 2002

**1 Dec** Prime Minister Janez Drnovsek of Slovenia wins a runoff election for president; he will take office on 23 December, and Anton Rop replaces him as prime minister on 11 December.

▸ In the final set of the final match of the Davis Cup team tennis tournament, Mikhail Yuzhny of Russia defeats Paul-Henri Mathieu of France to bring Russia its first-ever Davis Cup victory.

**2 Dec** An open-ended general strike, intended to force Pres. Hugo Chávez into calling early elections, begins in Venezuela.

▸ The health ministers of the members of the European Union approve a new rule that will ban tobacco advertising in magazines and newspapers as well as on the radio and the Internet and also prohibit tobacco-company sponsorship of major public events.

▸ Afghan Pres. Hamid Karzai announces plans to establish a professional national army of up to 70,000 troops under civilian control.

**3 Dec** Rowan Williams is formally installed as the 104th archbishop of Canterbury in an ancient ceremony at St. Paul's Cathedral in London.

▸ United Nations weapons inspectors in Iraq engage in the previously unthinkable act of entering and searching one of Saddam Hussein's presidential palaces.

▸ The finance ministers of the members of the European Union approve a law making insider trading illegal, but they are unable to achieve an agreement on detecting tax evasion because Switzerland will not agree to loosen its laws on bank secrecy.

▸ *De Organizer*, a one-act blues opera by James P. Johnston and Langston Hughes, is performed in Orchestra Hall in Detroit for the first time since its single performance at a convention of the International Ladies' Garment Workers' Union in 1940.

**4 Dec** The US Air Transportation Stabilization Board rejects a plea by United Airlines for $1.8 billion in loan guarantees, saying the business plan submitted by the company is unsound.

▸ Balkan Air Tour, the new national airline of Bulgaria, begins operations; it replaces the state-owned Balkan Airlines, which went bankrupt earlier in the year.

**5 Dec** Negotiators for the government of Sri Lanka and the Liberation Tigers of Tamil Eelam announce an agreement to explore the creation of a united Sri Lanka with a federal structure.

▸ US Sen. Strom Thurmond celebrates his 100th birthday; he is the oldest person ever to have served in Congress and has been a member of the Senate longer than anyone else in history.

**6 Dec** US Pres. George W. Bush demands the resignations of Paul O'Neill as secretary of the treasury and Lawrence Lindsey as director of the National Economic Council.

---

**QUOTE OF THE MONTH**

❝ *I want to say this about my state: When Strom Thurmond ran for president, we voted for him. We're proud of it. And if the rest of the country had followed our lead, we wouldn't have had all these problems over all these years, either.* ❞

—US Senate Republican leader Trent Lott, at the centennial birthday celebration for Sen. Strom Thurmond, 5 December

---

▶ The governments of Yugoslavia's constituent republics of Serbia and Montenegro accept a constitutional charter for a new state to be called Serbia and Montenegro; if accepted by the legislature of each republic, the new entity will become a reality.

▶ The US government releases figures showing that the unemployment rate rose to 6% in November, a level of joblessness last seen in 1994.

▶ *Science* magazine publishes an article saying that archaeologists at Florida State University believe they have found evidence of writing in pre-Columbian Mexico in Olmec artifacts dating to 650 BC; it had been believed that the earliest writing in Mexico was by the Zapotec culture in about 300 BC.

▶ Researchers at the Information Technology Center of the University of Tokyo announce that in September they calculated the value of pi to 1.24 trillion places, using a Hitachi supercomputer for over 400 hours to achieve the record-breaking feat.

**7 Dec** One day ahead of the Security Council deadline, Iraq delivers to the UN a 12,000-page declaration of its weapons-development programs.

▶ Bombs go off almost simultaneously in four movie theaters in and around Mymensingh, Bangladesh, killing at least 15 people and wounding about 200; the movie houses were crowded with people celebrating the three-day Eid al-Fitr.

▶ Two early paintings by Vincent van Gogh, *Congregation Leaving the Reformed Church in Nuenen* and *View of the Sea at Scheveningen*, are stolen from the Van Gogh Museum in Amsterdam.

▶ The Miss World contest, beset by controversy after religious violence led it to relocate to London from its planned venue in Nigeria, is won by Miss Turkey, Azra Akin. (See 22 November.)

**8 Dec** Serbia's third attempt to elect a new president again fails, with a turnout of 45%; the speaker of the parliament becomes acting president on 30 December, while changes to the constitution are considered.

▶ The annual Kennedy Center Honors are presented at the John F. Kennedy Center for the Performing Arts in Washington DC in celebration of the artistic achievements of actor James Earl Jones, conductor James Levine, musical theater star Chita Rivera, singer-songwriter Paul Simon, and movie star Elizabeth Taylor.

▶ Conceptual artist Keith Tyson is awarded the Turner Prize, administered by Tate Britain in London; the work for which he won is entitled *The Thinker* and consists of a large block filled with computer parts.

▶ *The Times* of London publishes a letter signed by directors of 18 major museums around the world asserting the right of museums to continue to hold antiquities that they have held for many years, even when they came from other countries.

**9 Dec** United Airlines, the world's second largest airline, files for bankruptcy protection but continues operating. (See 11 August.)

▶ US Senate Majority Leader Trent Lott issues an apology for remarks he made at Sen. Strom Thurmond's 100th birthday party (see 5 December) in which he indicated continuing support for Thurmond's presidential candidacy in 1948, when Thurmond ran on a segregationist platform.

▶ Representatives of the Indonesian government and of the Free Aceh Movement sign a peace treaty in Geneva providing autonomy and regional legislative elections for the district of Aceh on Sumatra and for negotiations on demilitarization.

▶ The Right Livelihood Awards are presented in Stockholm to the Center Jeunes Kamenge, a young people's center in Burundi; Kvinna till Kvinna (Woman to Woman), a Swedish organization that works against ethnic hatred; Martin Almada, a Paraguayan human rights champion; and Martin Green, an Australian professor who specializes in the harnessing of solar energy.

▶ Pres. Thabo Mbeki of South Africa, Pres. Robert Mugabe of Zimbabwe, and Pres. Joaquim Chissano of Mozambique officially launch the Great Limpopo Transfrontier Park, the largest game reserve in the world.

**10 Dec** US government officials report that Spanish warships the previous day had stopped a North Korean vessel flying no flag some 1,000 km (600 mi) off the coast of Yemen and found it to be carrying Scud missiles hidden under sacks of cement; the following day the shipment is released to Yemen, which maintains that it had legally bought the weapons.

▶ Former US president Jimmy Carter accepts his Nobel Peace Prize in a ceremony in Oslo.

▶ US Pres. George W. Bush selects a former head of the New York Stock Exchange, William Donaldson, to replace Harvey Pitt as head of the Securities and Exchange Commission and, in a policy change, promises to increase funding for the agency.

**11 Dec** A joint congressional panel in the US releases its final report on the 11 Sep 2001 terrorist attacks; it recommends the creation of a new cabinet-level "director of national intelligence" to remedy the lack of coordination between the various intelligence agencies.

▶ The US reaches a free-trade agreement with Chile that, if approved, will immediately remove tariffs on the vast majority of items traded between the two countries.

**12 Dec** A week after Congress decided to begin impeachment hearings against him, Paraguayan Pres. Luis González Macchi offers to leave office immediately after elections scheduled for April 2003 rather than wait for a further three months, as is customary.

▶ The on-line search engine Google launches a new shopping site, different from other shopping sites in that it does not charge merchants to be listed; the new site is called Froogle.

**13 Dec** US Pres. George W. Bush announces a precautionary plan to give 500,000 military personnel smallpox vaccinations, to be followed by inoculations for as many as 10 million health care and emergency service workers; the general public is urged not to have vaccinations.

▶ Pope John Paul II accepts the resignation of Bernard Cardinal Law, archbishop of the Boston archdiocese and the senior Roman Catholic prelate in the US.

▶ Former secretary of state Henry Kissinger surprises US Pres. George W. Bush by resigning as head of the commission created to look into possible intelligence failures surrounding the terror attacks of 11 Sep 2001; Kissinger says he cannot serve if he has to reveal the clients of his consulting firm.

**14 Dec** The Norwegian-registered *Tricolor*, carrying nearly 3,000 luxury cars, collides with a container ship and sinks in the North Sea, at the entrance to the Dover Strait between Great Britain and France.

▶ Association football (soccer) star Ronaldo is named the male FIFA World Player of the Year for the third time in his career; two days later he is named European Player of the Year by *France Football* magazine.

**15 Dec** Former US vice president Al Gore says that he will not be a candidate for president in the elections of 2004.

▶ In elections in the religiously polarized state of Gujarat in India, the Hindu nationalist Bharatiya Janata Party wins in a landslide over the secularist Congress Party.

**16 Dec** Election officials in Equatorial Guinea announce that the winner of the previous day's presidential election was Pres. Teodoro Obiang Nguema Mbasogo, with more than 97% of the votes; the four opposition candidates, who had withdrawn on election day, citing voting irregularities and fraud, release a statement characterizing the election as invalid.

▶ US Pres. George W. Bush names Thomas Kean, a former governor of New Jersey, to head the commission to inquire into possible intelligence failures in the US prior to the 11 Sep 2001 terrorist attacks.

**17 Dec** In Pretoria, South Africa, an agreement is reached between Pres. Joseph Kabila of the Democratic Republic of the Congo and representatives of the two main rebel groups and the unarmed opposition whereby Kabila will be head of an 18-month transitional government, with each group contributing one vice president, at the end of which democratic elections will be held.

▶ US Pres. George W. Bush orders the Pentagon to have an antimissile shield system in place by the end of 2004.

▶ Six members of the board of directors of WorldCom resign, leaving only three members, all recently appointed.

▶ Australian surfer Layne Beachley wins her fifth consecutive world surfing championship in Maui, Hawaii, becoming the most successful female surfer in history.

**18 Dec** The insurance holding company Conseco files for bankruptcy protection; it is the third largest bankruptcy filing in US history, behind WorldCom and Enron.

▶ Robert L. Johnson, founder of Black Entertainment Television, is awarded a new basketball franchise to be established in Charlotte NC and thereby becomes the first African American majority owner in the National Basketball Association.

**19 Dec** In presidential elections in South Korea the winner is Roh Moo Hyun, of the governing Millennium Democratic Party.

▶ The Supreme Court of Venezuela orders the state-owned oil company, Petróleos de Venezuela, to cease striking and return to work; the order has no effect on the continuation of the general strike, now in its 18th day.

**20 Dec** US Sen. Trent Lott, unable to quell the furor over his remarks at the 100th birthday celebration of Sen. Strom Thurmond, announces that he will step down as leader of the Republican Party in the Senate, though he will retain his seat; on 23 December Sen. Bill Frist is chosen to replace him as majority leader.

▶ The US, the European Union, the United Nations, and Russia call for a Palestinian state to be created in three years; alone among the partners, however, the US does not want a timetable for statehood to be set out at this time.

▶ Pope John Paul II grants official recognition to a posthumous miracle attributed to Mother Teresa, the curing of cancer for a woman in India, and thus makes her eligible for beatification.

▶ A court in France, after a 14-year investigation, finds American financier George Soros guilty of insider trading and fines him €2.2 million (about $2.3 million).

**21 Dec** A helicopter carrying German peacekeepers crashes in Kabul, Afghanistan, killing all seven aboard as well as two Afghani children on the ground.

▶ After fighting extradition from Brazil for three years, Mexican pop star Gloria Trevi returns to Mexico to face charges of sex crimes against a girl; she and her manager, Sergio Andrade, have been publicly accused of having held young women for purposes of sexual exploitation.

**22 Dec** North Korea announces that it has removed monitoring equipment installed by international inspectors to ensure that its supply of plutonium was not used in weapons production; the previous day it had begun removing monitoring equipment from a nuclear reactor.

▶ In presidential elections in Lithuania, none of the candidates receives an absolute majority; a runoff between the top two finishers, Pres. Valdas Adamkus and Rolandas Paksas, will be held on 5 Jan 2003.

▶ In presidential elections in the Yugoslav republic of Montenegro, as in Serbia, the voter turnout is below 50%, which invalidates the election; the election will be held again in January 2003.

▶ North Korea breaks seals on and disables surveillance equipment at a plutonium-reprocessing facility and a fuel-rod-fabrication plant in what the International Atomic Energy Agency says is the most dangerous step it has yet taken.

**24 Dec** One week after the US made pleas on his behalf, China releases from prison Xu Wenli, its best-known pro-democracy prisoner; he immediately moves to the US.

▶ A new Metro railway system is ceremonially opened in Delhi, India; the following day, its first day of operation, the system is swamped by more than a million people who want to be first to ride the new trains.

▸ Many of the 12,000 US troops stationed in Kuwait awaiting a possible war against Iraq celebrate Christmas Eve with carols, donated gifts, and a visit from Santa Claus.

**25 Dec** Russia and Iran agree to speed up completion of a nuclear power plant; the US opposes this cooperation, fearing that Iran will use the plant to develop nuclear weapons.

**26 Dec** In response to a request from Venezuelan Pres. Hugo Chávez, Brazil sends an emergency shipment of 520,000 bbl of gasoline to Venezuela, which is suffering shortages because of the nationwide general strike.

▸ Millionaire Andrew J. Whittaker, Jr., is announced as the winner of the $314.9 million Christmas Day Powerball prize in West Virginia, the biggest undivided lottery jackpot ever; he plans to tithe the windfall to three churches.

**27 Dec** In elections that are far from flawless but are far closer to free and fair than those in 1992 and 1997, Kenyans elect as their new president Mwai Kibaki of the National Rainbow Coalition, a collection of opposition parties.

▸ North Korea announces that it will expel all international nuclear inspectors; unless North Korea "cooperates, and cooperates fully," with International Atomic Energy Agency demands, the IAEA plans to declare before the UN Security Council that the country is in violation of international agreements.

▸ Suicide bombers drive two explosives-laden vehicles into the headquarters of the pro-Russian government in Grozny, the capital of the Russian republic of Chechnya, destroying the building and killing 72 people.

▸ Russia announces that it is withdrawing from the Peace Corps agreement, saying that Peace Corps volunteers have been spying for the US and that the Peace Corps no longer serves Russia's needs.

▸ Brigitte Boisselier, the CEO of Clonaid, a company founded by the Raelians, a religious group that believes that all humans were cloned from space travelers 25,000 years ago, announces that a cloned human baby has been born; the skepticism and condemnation that greet the announcement are later compounded by the group's failure to provide proof of the cloning by year's end.

**28 Dec** Hundreds of French troops arrive in Côte d'Ivoire to reinforce the government forces in their civil war against three rebel groups.

▸ As expected, the 27-m (90-ft) Australian yacht *Alfa Romeo* wins the annual Sydney–Hobart Race down the east coast of Australia.

▸ Cyclone Zoe slams into the relatively inaccessible islands of Tikopia, Fataka, and Anuta in the Solomon Islands; Zoe is one of the most powerful cyclones ever recorded in the Pacific, and it will take days for relief ships to reach the remote islands.

**29 Dec** The FBI issues an alert to the public and to law-enforcement agencies around the US and throughout the world to help find five men from the Middle East who are believed to have entered the US illegally in the past few days; it is later learned that the alert was based on false information.

**30 Dec** Gary Winnick announces that the following day he will resign as chairman of Global Crossing Ltd.; the bankrupt company's assets have been sold to Hutchison Telecommunications Ltd. of Hong Kong and Singapore Technologies Telemedia.

▸ Tyco International Ltd. announces that an internal investigation has found no systemic fraud but has revealed that for years, contrary to previous claims, the company engaged in accounting trickery to inflate its stated earnings.

**31 Dec** A trial run of a new maglev (magnetic levitation) train, linking downtown Shanghai with Pudong International Airport, is enjoyed by Chinese Premier Zhu Rongji and German Chancellor Gerhard Schröder; afterward Schröder announces that China has awarded Germany a contract to expand the maglev rail system in the Shanghai area.

▸ The stock market ends a year in which stock prices in the US fell precipitously, the third consecutive year of decline on Wall Street.

# January 2003

**1 Jan** The Socialist Lula (Luiz Inácio Lula da Silva) takes office as president of Brazil.

---

**QUOTE OF THE MONTH**

" *So long as there is a single Brazilian brother or sister going hungry, we have ample reason to be ashamed of ourselves.* "

—Lula, in his inaugural address as president of Brazil, 1 January

---

▸ The American Academy of Arts and Letters awards Strauss Livings to writers Gish Jen and Claire Messud; the prizes, for $250,000, are given out every five years.

**2 Jan** *Nature* magazine publishes two studies showing that global warming is causing many different species of plants and animals to change their ranges or alter their reproductive habits; the scientists are alarmed at the extent of the change given the small amount of warming that has taken place and the greater amount that is predicted.

▸ Officials of Los Alamos National Laboratory in New Mexico announce the resignation of John C. Browne as director; the nuclear weapons laboratory has been under investigation because of apparent corruption and missing equipment.

**3 Jan** In Caracas a peaceful protest against the administration of Venezuelan Pres. Hugo Chávez is intercepted by pro-government demonstrators and a great street fight ensues, leaving at least two people dead; an antigovernment strike began 33 days earlier.

▸ Brazil suspends the planned purchase of 12 new fighter jets, intending to devote the money to alleviating hunger instead.

▸ Peru's Supreme Court issues a ruling invalidating some of the antiterrorism laws passed under former president Alberto K. Fujimori; there are expected to be a large number of retrials as a result.

▸ In the annual post-season Fiesta Bowl, Ohio State University defeats the University of Miami (Florida)

31–24 in double overtime to win the national college football Division I-A Championship.

**4 Jan** India announces that it has created a nuclear command authority, headed by the prime minister; Pakistan already had such an entity, and the countries spent much of 2002 at loggerheads.

▸ The National Society of Film Critics chooses *The Pianist* as the best film of 2002.

**5 Jan** A man steals a small private airplane and threatens to crash it into the European Central Bank building in Frankfurt am Main, Germany; much of downtown is evacuated and the city is paralyzed for several hours until the man is talked down, saying he wished to commemorate the American astronaut Judith Resnick, who died in the *Challenger* explosion in 1986.

▸ Two suicide bombers set off their bombs in downtown Tel Aviv, Israel, killing 23 people in addition to themselves and injuring scores.

▸ In the runoff presidential election in Lithuania the right-wing candidate Rolandas Paksas unexpectedly defeats incumbent Valdas Adamkus, who held the lead in the first round of voting.

**6 Jan** The International Atomic Energy Agency passes a resolution demanding that North Korea readmit IAEA inspectors lest the agency be required to refer the matter to the UN Security Council.

▸ Kenyan Pres. Mwai Kibaki's new cabinet is sworn in; it is the first non-KANU cabinet in 39 years.

▸ The city of Louisville KY merges with surrounding Jefferson county, putting it for the first time among the top 20 US cities in population; other cities are considering similar changes because the metropolitan areas are finding that city and suburbs increasingly have common interests.

▸ Uttar Pradesh, the most populous state in India, bans the slaughter of cows, which are held to be sacred by Hindus.

▸ A large statue of the Hindu deity Krishna, under construction for the past six years and nearly complete, collapses and kills three workers outside New Delhi, India.

**7 Jan** Great Britain mobilizes 1,500 reservists in support of a possible war against Iraq.

▸ For the first time, under a presidential decree, Christmas (today on the Coptic Christian calendar) is celebrated as a national holiday in Egypt, an almost entirely Muslim country.

▸ Shlomo Koves becomes the first Orthodox Jewish rabbi inaugurated in Hungary since before the Holocaust.

▸ The Danish Committees on Scientific Dishonesty rebukes Bjørn Lomborg for his book *The Skeptical Environmentalist,* finding that it is "clearly contrary to the standards of good scientific practice."

▸ Catcher Gary Carter and switch-hitter Eddie Murray are elected to the National Baseball Hall of Fame.

**8 Jan** A US court of appeals rules that the government during wartime may detain indefinitely a US citizen captured as an enemy combatant and deny him access to a lawyer.

▸ The United States Sentencing Commission approves a plan to lengthen prison sentences for people convicted of corporate crimes, such as securities fraud.

▸ The US opens talks intended to lead to a free-trade agreement with Nicaragua, El Salvador, Costa Rica, Guatemala, and Honduras.

**9 Jan** Chief UN weapons inspector Hans Blix and IAEA head Mohamed El Baradei report to the UN Security Council that Iraq's disclosure of weapons programs was insufficiently informative but that inspectors have found no evidence of weapons or programs.

▸ Astronomers announce that they have found 26 galaxies and 3 quasars approximately 13 billion light-years away, which means they date from early in the period that light first appeared in the universe.

**10 Jan** North Korea announces that it is withdrawing from the Nuclear Non-proliferation Treaty; the following day one million people rally in Pyongyang in support of the decision.

▸ Mexico's foreign minister, Jorge G. Castañeda, resigns, apparently as a result of his failure to achieve goals regarding relations with the US; Luis Ernesto Derbéz is named as his replacement.

▸ Russian Pres. Vladimir Putin and Japanese Prime Minister Junichiro Koizumi sign an agreement to improve trade relations and seek a resolution to their long-standing dispute over ownership of the Kuril Islands.

▸ The Sony Corporation of America names Andrew Lack as head of Sony Music Entertainment, replacing Thomas Mottola, who is a top power in the music industry.

**11 Jan** In the last two days of his term of office, Illinois Gov. George Ryan commutes the death sentences of all 167 people on Death Row in Illinois, saying that the system is flawed.

**12 Jan** Stephen M. Case resigns as chairman of the media conglomerate AOL Time Warner; on 16 January Richard D. Parsons, the CEO of the company, is named to succeed him.

▸ The ceremonial groundbreaking for Hong Kong Disneyland, a new theme park to be located on Lantau Island, takes place, led by Michael Eisner, CEO of Walt Disney.

**13 Jan** The Harvard-Smithsonian Center for Astrophysics reports that astronomers at the Cerro-Tololo Inter-American Observatory in Chile and in Hawaii have detected three new moons orbiting Neptune, bringing the total number of the planet's known satellites to 11.

▸ FAO Inc., which owns the high-end toy store chains F.A.O. Schwarz, Zany Brainy, and Right Start, files for bankruptcy protection.

▸ The Voter News Service, owned by NBC, ABC, CBS, CNN, Fox News Channel, and the Associated Press and its subscribers, goes out of business; the networks plan to have a new system in place in time for the US presidential election in 2004.

**14 Jan** Representatives of a newly created Islamic council in France are officially welcomed to a New Year's reception by Pres. Jacques Chirac; the new council will help put Muslims in France on a more equal footing with members of other religions, which have long had their own councils.

▸ The US Food and Drug Administration suspends 27 gene therapy trials after a second child in a gene therapy trial in France developed a leukemia-like disease.

▸ General Electric employees nationwide begin a 48-hour strike to protest a company decision to raise employee health care costs; it is the first nationwide strike at the company since 1969.

**15 Jan** In Paris, French Foreign Minister Dominique de Villepin opens peace talks between the various factions in the civil war in Côte d'Ivoire.

▸ A UN investigative team says that rebel groups in the Ituri region of the Democratic Republic of the

Congo last year carried out systematic atrocities, including torture, rape, and cannibalism.

▶ In a televised address, US Pres. George W. Bush denounces the use of racial preferences in university admission and describes plans to file a brief with the Supreme Court asking that the admissions policies at the University of Michigan, in which race is one of a number of factors considered, be found unconstitutional.

**16 Jan** The space shuttle *Columbia* lifts off for a 16-day mission that is the first in three years not connected to the International Space Station or the Hubble Space Telescope; among its crew members is Ilan Ramon, the first Israeli astronaut in space.

▶ Random House Inc. announces that it is merging two of its units, the Random House Trade Group, known for publishing literature, and Ballantine Books, known for mass-market paperbacks; Ann Godoff, the influential head of the former group, is forced out, and Gina Centrello, the head of the latter, becomes the head of the Random House Ballantine Publishing group.

▶ UN weapons inspectors in Iraq discover at a storage bunker 11 empty chemical warheads and a 12th that requires further testing.

**17 Jan** The IMF agrees to allow Argentina to postpone a $1 billion debt payment until August in return for which Argentina agrees to a program of fiscal policies supplied by the IMF.

▶ The American financier Boris Jordan is fired as CEO of Gazprom Media in Russia and as director general of the popular television station NTV.

**18 Jan** Tens of thousands of people in cities across the US demonstrate against the US government's threat of war on the Iraqi regime; the biggest demonstration takes place in Washington DC.

▶ Wildfires burning outside the city of Canberra in Australia spread into town and destroy 402 homes; firefighters are unable to make headway against the fires.

▶ In an exceptionally mistake-filled US Figure Skating Championship competition, Michelle Kwan wins for the sixth consecutive time in the women's competition, and Michael Weiss wins the men's competition.

▶ With their 55th consecutive win, the University of Connecticut Huskies set a new record for women's college basketball.

▶ Emperor Akihito of Japan undergoes prostate surgery; the open reporting on the subject is a first for the Imperial Household Agency.

**19 Jan** The Yuzhengong Palace in Hubei province in China burns to the ground; designated a UN World Heritage Site in 1994, it exemplified a millennium of artistic and architectural achievement during the Yuan, Ming, and Qing dynasties.

▶ At the Golden Globe Awards in Beverly Hills, Calif., best picture honors go to *The Hours* and *Chicago;* best director goes to Martin Scorsese for *Gangs of New York;* and the screenplay award goes to Alexander Payne and Jim Taylor for *About Schmidt.*

**20 Jan** Iraq makes 10 specific commitments to the UN inspectors in response to their demands; key among them is the promise to press scientists to agree to private interviews with inspectors.

▶ France announces that it will not support a UN resolution permitting military action against the Iraqi regime, should one be proposed.

▶ In Geneva at a meeting of the UN Commission on Human Rights, the US insists on a vote for the chairmanship; for the first time in the committee's

history and contrary to the desires of the US, Libya is elected.

**21 Jan** The US Census Bureau announces that the Hispanic population of the US has grown to surpass that of the black population as a percentage of the total; at close to 13%, Hispanics are now the largest minority in the US.

▶ Pres. Ismail Omar Guelleh of Djibouti visits US Pres. George W. Bush in Washington DC and is greeted with red-carpet treatment; Djibouti has become a staging area for US troops in the Middle East.

▶ North Korean representatives arrive in Seoul in order to resume high-level talks with their South Korean counterparts.

**22 Jan** In elections in The Netherlands, the conservative Christian Democratic Party of Prime Minister Jan Peter Balkenende comes in with the most votes, followed by the Labour Party, with the Pim Fortuyn List a distant fifth.

▶ The US deploys a system called Bio-Watch that uses Environmental Protection Agency air-quality monitoring systems to also check for the presence of germs related to biological warfare.

▶ Researchers in China announce the discovery of a small feathered dinosaur with four wings and a plumed tail; about 76 cm (30 in.) long, the dragon-like animal has been named *Microraptor gui.*

**23 Jan** Australian forces begin heading for the Persian Gulf in support of a possible US-led war against Iraq.

▶ McDonald's Corp., the biggest restaurant chain in the world, reports that in the last quarter of 2002 it posted a loss for the first time in its history.

▶ It is reported that some 40 librettos of operas by Joseph Haydn dating from his lifetime were serendipitously discovered in a second-hand bookstore in Budapest; these librettos were believed to have been destroyed in bombings during World War II.

**24 Jan** Representatives of a number of Palestinian groups meet in Cairo under the guidance of Omar Suleiman, the head of Egyptian intelligence, to discuss a possible Palestinian cease-fire.

▶ The US plan to inoculate 500,000 health care workers against smallpox gets under way with the vaccination of four doctors in Connecticut.

▶ A chartered plane carrying members of Kenya's new government crashes on takeoff from the airport at Busia, killing the minister of labor and two others.

**25 Jan** West African leaders meet in Paris to discuss the peace agreed to by the parties in Côte d'Ivoire, and Ivoirian Pres. Laurent Gbagbo accepts the appointment of Seydou Diarra as prime minister to lead the reconciliation government.

▶ Serena Williams defeats her sister Venus to win the Australian Open tennis tournament in her fourth straight victory in a major tournament; the following day Andre Agassi defeats Rainer Schüttler to win the men's title.

**26 Jan** In San Diego, the Tampa Bay Buccaneers convincingly defeat the Oakland Raiders 48–21 to win Super Bowl XXXVII.

▶ Winning films at the Sundance Film Festival awards ceremony in Park City UT include *Capturing the Friedmans, American Splendor, My Flesh and Blood,* and *The Station Agent.*

**27 Jan** Hans Blix, the head of the UN weapons inspectors in Iraq, reports to the UN Security Council that the Iraqi regime has been insufficiently cooperative and does not appear to accept the need to disarm. (See 9 January.)

▸ Kazakhstan reaches an agreement with a consortium led by ChevronTexaco that allows the consortium to run an expansion of the Tengiz oil field.

▸ A retailing group consisting of Best Buy, Tower Records, Virgin Entertainment Group, Wherehouse Entertainment, Hastings Entertainment, and Trans World Entertainment announces plans to sell music to be downloaded from the Internet.

▸ In horse racing's 2002 Eclipse Awards, the filly Azeri, trained by Laura De Seroux, is named Horse of the Year.

**28 Jan** In elections in Israel, there is no significant opposition to Ariel Sharon, and he retains his post as prime minister with a strong showing by Likud, his party.

▸ US Pres. George W. Bush delivers his second state of the union address; he stresses plans to revive the economy and his intentions to address what he portrays as the intolerable threat represented by Pres. Saddam Hussein of Iraq, and he pledges $15 billion to combat AIDS in Africa and the Caribbean.

▸ A South Korean epidemiologist and expert on diseases associated with poverty, Jong Wook Lee, is named director general of the World Health Organization.

▸ Claire Tomalin wins the 2002 Whitbread Book of the Year Award—given for books published in the UK—for her biography Samuel Pepys: The Unequalled Self; one of the other books in contention for the prize was the novel Spies, by Tomalin's husband, Michael Frayn.

▸ Norio Ohga, a longtime driving force behind the company, announces that he is retiring as chairman of Sony Corp.; simultaneously, the company says that it will adopt American-style auditing arrangements.

**29 Jan** AOL Time Warner announces that CNN founder Ted Turner has resigned as vice chairman and that for the first time the number of people subscribing to AOL's services has declined.

▸ Ukrainian Pres. Leonid Kuchma is elected chairman of the Commonwealth of Independent States; it is the first time since the alliance was created in 1991 that someone other than a Russian has held the post.

▸ A French court of appeals overturns the conviction for corruption of former foreign minister Roland Dumas; he was convicted as part of the enormous Elf Aquitaine scandal.

▸ The government of Nepal and Maoist rebels unexpectedly agree to a cease-fire.

**30 Jan** The World Food Programme says that the food crisis in sub-Saharan Africa has eased everywhere except Zimbabwe, where conditions continue to deteriorate.

▸ In Boston, Richard Reid, who pleaded guilty in a trial for having attempted to blow up an airplane with a bomb concealed in his shoe, is sentenced to life in prison.

▸ Irish Minister of Health Michael Martin announces that, beginning next year, smoking will be banned in all places of employment, including restaurants and pubs.

**31 Jan** A mob of 5,000 people throwing stones invades the airport at Port-Bouët in Côte d'Ivoire, terrorizing hundreds of French residents trying to flee the war-torn country.

▸ The American Red Cross quarantines almost all of its blood supply for the state of Georgia and some of South Carolina because of unidentified white particles that have been found in some bags of donated blood.

# February 2003

**1 Feb** In New York City's Chinatown, the first day of the Year of the Goat, 4701, is greeted with firecrackers; it is the first time in seven years that the city has allowed the traditional use of firecrackers in the New Year's festival.

---

**QUOTE OF THE MONTH**

❝ *The crew of the shuttle* Columbia *did not return safely to Earth. Yet we can pray that all are safely home.* ❞

—US Pres. George W. Bush, announcing the loss of the space shuttle *Columbia*, 1 February

---

▸ The space shuttle *Columbia* overheats and burns up on its reentry in the Earth's atmosphere, spreading debris across Texas and Louisiana and killing all seven astronauts aboard.

**2 Feb** After 13 years as president of Czechoslovakia and then of the Czech Republic, Vaclav Havel gives his farewell address.

**3 Feb** Shops and factories in Venezuela begin reopening after opponents of Pres. Hugo Chávez decide to largely end the national strike that began on 2 Dec 2002; oil workers continue to strike.

▸ The trial for treason of opposition leader Morgan Tsvangirai begins in Zimbabwe; many believe that Pres. Robert Mugabe stole the 2002 presidential election from Tsvangirai.

▸ Legendary rock-and-roll producer Phil Spector is arrested for the murder of a woman found dead in his home in Alhambra CA.

**4 Feb** The legislature votes Yugoslavia out of existence as the country officially becomes Serbia and Montenegro.

▸ The new African Union concludes its first meeting, in Addis Ababa, Ethiopia, with plans to create a new peace and security council and plans to send peacekeeping troops to Burundi.

▸ Marty Mankamyer, the president of the US Olympic Committee, resigns; the committee has been split by bitter infighting since an inquiry early in the year into conflict-of-interest charges against the CEO of the committee.

**5 Feb** US Secretary of State Colin Powell appears before the UN Security Council to present photographs, recordings, and other material as evidence that Iraq possesses forbidden chemical and biological weapons as well as weapons of mass destruction and that therefore the country poses an imminent danger.

▸ The rebel group Liberians United for Reconciliation and Democracy advances to within 15 miles of Monrovia, Liberia's capital; Pres. Charles Taylor proposes peace talks and suggests the rebels lay down their arms and run in the presidential election scheduled for October.

▶ Pres. Pervez Musharraf of Pakistan meets with Pres. Vladimir Putin of Russia in Moscow; it is the first time in 33 years that the leaders of Pakistan and Russia have met.

▶ Activists, including the first ladies of several African countries, gather in Addis Ababa, Ethiopia, for a conference seeking the end of female genital mutilation, practiced in some 28 countries.

**6 Feb** Brazil's flagship airline, Varig, announces plans to merge with its main competitor, TAM Linhas Aéreas, to form the biggest airline in Latin America.

▶ A small private airplane carrying the Colombian minister of social welfare, Juan Luís Londoño, crashes in the Andes Mountains, killing him.

▶ The Freedom Forum announces that Myanmar activist Aung San Suu Kyi is the winner of its annual Al Neuharth Free Spirit of the Year Award.

**7 Feb** China and France indicate that they would not support a new security resolution authorizing the use of force against Iraq; both governments say they believe UN weapons inspectors should be given more time.

▶ The US government raises the official terror-alert level from yellow (elevated) to orange (high).

▶ NASA makes its final and futile attempt to contact Pioneer 10, last heard from on January 22; Pioneer 10 was launched in 1972 and left the solar system in 1983.

▶ In New York City, Russian chess grandmaster Garry Kasparov and the IBM computer Deep Junior agree to a draw in the final game of their six-game series, closing out the competition at a tie (one win each and four draws).

**8 Feb** Members of the Islamist group Ansar al-Islam assassinate a Kurdish government minister and two other government officials as well as three civilians in Qamesh Tapa in northern Iraq.

▶ The biggest Winter Asian Games to date come to a close in Aomori, Japan; athletes from 29 countries competed for eight days, with Japan, South Korea, and China winning the most gold medals.

**9 Feb** Recently reelected Israeli Prime Minister Ariel Sharon officially accepts the task of forming a new government.

▶ India begins the biggest mass immunization campaign in its history in an effort to put an end to a polio epidemic in Uttar Pradesh state.

**10 Feb** France, Germany, and Belgium block efforts led by the US for NATO to begin planning the defense of Turkey in the event that a US-led war against Iraq should make such a defense necessary.

▶ Seydou Diarra is installed as prime minister of Côte d'Ivoire, as specified in the peace agreement signed the previous month in Paris. (See 25 January.)

▶ Israel completely closes its borders with the West Bank and the Gaza Strip, stopping Palestinian travel during the Eid al-Adha holiday.

▶ Scientists announce the discovery of the first asteroid with a solar orbit between the Earth and the Sun.

**11 Feb** Philippine Pres. Gloria Macapagal Arroyo announces a suspension in the government offensive against Muslim separatists in deference to the Eid al-Adha holiday; the following day fighting erupts again.

▶ The giant oil company BP agrees to a deal with the Russian oil company Sidanco and others to form a new Russian oil company in which BP will have a 50% stake.

▶ A US bombing raid is called in by forces under rebel ambush in the mountains of southern Afghanistan; 17 Afghani civilians are killed.

▶ The English cricket team announces that it will not participate in its first World Cup game, scheduled to take place in Harare, Zimbabwe; it is the first time ever that a team has boycotted a venue in World Cup cricket.

▶ The Kerry Blue Terrier Torums Scarf Michael, who had been favored to win in the previous two years, is finally named Best in Show at the Westminster Kennel Club Dog Show.

**12 Feb** India successfully test fires a short-range cruise missile from a naval destroyer, raising the already high tension with Pakistan.

▶ Protests against a government plan to introduce a graduated income tax explode into riots in La Paz, Bolivia; by the following day 27 people have been killed.

▶ The album *Get Rich or Die Trying* by the gangsta rapper 50 Cent sells 872,000 copies in its first four days; it is believed to be the fastest selling first album on a major label ever.

▶ Scientists studying the monarch butterfly announce that they have found, to their surprise, that the population of the monarch butterfly appears to have nearly fully recovered from the enormous die-off that occurred in winter 2002.

▶ Adrienne Rich is named the winner of the biennial Bollingen Prize in American Poetry.

**13 Feb** The board charged with investigating the *Columbia* disaster releases preliminary findings that a breach in the skin of the space shuttle allowed superheated gases to enter the left wing, causing the breakup; the cause of the breach has not been determined.

▶ A US government plane carrying four Americans and a Colombian crashes in an area of Colombia controlled by the Revolutionary Armed Forces of Colombia (FARC); three Americans are kidnapped and the other two passengers shot to death.

▶ American microbiologist Carl R. Woese is named winner of the Crafoord Prize for demonstrating that the single-celled organisms now called archaea qualify as a separate major domain of life in addition to bacteria and eukaryotes.

▶ The city council of New York City approves a ban on the use of mobile telephones in such public places as theaters and museums.

**14 Feb** Palestinian leader Yasir Arafat announces that he will appoint a prime minister.

▶ As UN weapons inspectors Hans Blix and Mohamed El Baradei report increasing cooperation from Iraq, several members of the Security Council agree with France's proposal to allow the inspectors more time.

▶ Dolly the sheep, the first cloned mammal, is euthanized by veterinarians after being found to be suffering from progressive lung disease.

▶ In London, Sam Mendes wins three Laurence Olivier Awards: best director, for *Twelfth Night,* best revival, for *Uncle Vanya,* and special achievement, for his leadership of the Donmar Warehouse Theatre.

**15 Feb** Millions of people in more than 350 cities throughout the world rally and march against the threatened US invasion of Iraq.

▸ The Vatican opens archives relating to the activities of Pope Pius XII in the Vatican Secretariat of State in the years 1922 to 1939, before his papacy, in hopes of showing that he did not shirk responsibilities to protect Jews and Roman Catholics during the rise of Nazism in Germany.

▸ At the Berlin International Film Festival, the Golden Bear goes to the British film *In This World,* and the Silver Bear is won by the American movie *Adaptation.*

▸ It is reported that the Internet search engine Google has bought Pyra Labs, which deals in software for creating Web logs, or blogs; it is believed that this will vastly increase the audience for Web logs.

**16 Feb** Greek Cypriot opposition leader Tassos Papadopoulos handily and unexpectedly defeats the incumbent president, Glafcos Clerides.

▸ On a rainy day in Daytona Beach FL the shortest Daytona 500 NASCAR race in history (109 of 200 laps), called because of rain, is won by Michael Waltrip.

**17 Feb** Twenty-one people die in a stampede during a fire at a Chicago nightclub. (See Disasters.)

▸ Uri Lupolianski, a member of Israel's most Orthodox Jewish community, becomes acting mayor of Jerusalem.

▸ Beginning this day, anyone driving a private vehicle into a demarcated area of central London between the hours of 7:00 AM and 6:30 PM on weekdays must pay a £5 fee for the privilege.

▸ Workers in the diamond district in Antwerp, Belgium, discover that the largest safe-deposit box robbery as well as the largest jewel theft in Belgian history—$100 million worth of gems—have taken place over the previous two days.

**18 Feb** On a rush-hour subway train in Taegu, South Korea, a man attempts suicide by fire, igniting the train and killing at least 198 people.

▸ In North Korea, the Korean People's Army releases a statement saying that if the US should impose penalties against North Korea for its suspected illegal nuclear arms program, the North Korean military would no longer feel bound by the 1953 armistice agreement ending hostilities in the Korean War.

▸ The US National Academy of Engineering awards its Draper Prize to Bradford Parkinson and Ivan Getting for their work in developing the Global Positioning System satellites, and its Russ Prize to Willem Kolff for his invention of the artificial kidney dialysis machine.

**19 Feb** A Russian-made Ilyushin airliner, flying from Zahedan to Kerman in Iran and carrying 302 people, mostly members of the Revolutionary Guards, crashes near Shahdad, killing all aboard; it is the worst air disaster in Iran's history.

▸ In a trial in Hamburg, Germany, the first person is convicted in relation to the terrorist attacks of 11 Sep 2001; Mounir al-Motassadeq is found guilty of 3,066 counts of accessory to murder and is sentenced to 15 years in prison.

▸ It is announced at a NASA briefing that erosional gullies on the Martian surface, revealed in photographs from the Mars Odyssey spacecraft, may be the result of snowmelt running underneath a thick snow covering; the previous week it was reported that both polar icecaps on Mars could contain much more water than previously thought.

▸ It is reported that the human remains in the Lake Mungo region of Australia, previously dated as 62,000 years old, are in fact only 42,000 years old and thus in line with theories that the great human migration out of Africa began 50,000 years ago.

**20 Feb** More than 100 people die in a stampede during a nightclub fire in West Warwick RI. (See Disasters.)

▸ In the midst of a period of violence between Israelis and Palestinians, Israel divides the Gaza Strip into three separate security zones, leading to fears among Palestinians of a complete takeover.

▸ A new pan-Arab television news channel, al-Arabiyah, owned by the satellite television station MBC, goes on the air in the United Arab Emirates.

▸ US officials announce plans to send some 1,700 troops to the southern Philippines to combat the Muslim terrorist group Abu Sayyaf.

▸ The US government brings charges against eight people, including Sami al-Arian, a professor at the University of South Florida, accusing them of sending financial and logistical support to Palestinian terrorists in the West Bank and the Gaza Strip.

**21 Feb** US Secretary of State Colin Powell begins a five-day trip to Asia to persuade the leaders of South Korea, China, and Japan to go along with the US approach to North Korea.

▸ UN weapons inspector Hans Blix orders Iraq to dismantle its al-Samoud 2 missiles, which have a range that exceeds UN-imposed limits, by the end of the month; on 27 February Iraq agrees to do so.

▸ The World Health Organization suggests an increase in preparedness in response to reports that two family members in Hong Kong have contracted avian flu and one has died, though human-to-human transmission of the flu is believed to be rare and difficult.

**22 Feb** The main Protestant paramilitary group in Northern Ireland, the Ulster Defense Association, declares a 12-month cease-fire and agrees to cooperate with an organization charged with monitoring disarmament of paramilitary groups.

▸ In Karachi, Pakistan, gunmen open fire inside a Shi'ite mosque, killing nine people, in the first major sectarian attack since June 2002.

▸ Sporting a new tattoo covering the left side of his face, Mike Tyson knocks out Clifford Etienne 49 seconds into the heavyweight fight in Memphis TN.

**23 Feb** The first large-scale trial of an AIDS vaccine results in findings that the vaccine is largely ineffective, though it appears to have some small efficacy among African Americans and Asians.

▸ At the Grammy Awards, which are held in New York City for the first time since 1998, the top winner is Norah Jones, who wins five Grammys, including Record of the Year ("Don't Know Why"), Album of the Year (*Come Away with Me*), and best new artist; the Song of the Year goes to her recording of "Don't Know Why," written by Jesse Harris.

**24 Feb** The US, Great Britain, and Spain request that the UN Security Council declare that Iraq has failed to disarm as required, while France, Germany, and Russia ask the council to give inspectors greater powers and more time.

▸ In Washington DC the National Governors Association, which pleads that the states are facing their worst financial crisis since World War II, is told by Pres. George W. Bush that the federal government will be unable to provide fiscal assistance to them.

▸ Frederick Chiluba, who was president of Zambia in 1991–2002, is arrested and accused of stealing from the state treasury.

▶ The Serbian nationalist paramilitary leader Vojislav Seselj voluntarily surrenders to the UN war crimes tribunal in The Hague.

**25 Feb** Roh Moo Hyun is inaugurated as president of South Korea; the US is represented by Secretary of State Colin Powell.

▶ Two months after deliveries of food aid to North Korea had been halted, the US announces that it will resume the shipments but at a reduced level.

▶ A US Army Black Hawk helicopter crashes in a sandstorm in Kuwait, killing all four crew members; the vehicle and crew were part of a troop buildup going on in Kuwait in anticipation of a war against Iraq.

▶ The Conference Board, a private business association, reports that consumer confidence in the US fell 15 points in February to its lowest level since 1993.

▶ The Credit Suisse Group reports a loss of $2.4 billion in 2002, the largest one-year deficit in the bank's history.

**26 Feb** In a nationally televised address, US Pres. George W. Bush asserts that removing Saddam Hussein as president of Iraq would increase stability in the Middle East and could lead to the creation of a Palestinian state living in peace with Israel; he also suggests that a failure to confront Iraq on the part of the UN Security Council would weaken the authority of the United Nations.

▶ US intelligence officials say that North Korea has restarted a reactor at its main nuclear complex.

▶ Israeli Prime Minister Ariel Sharon surprises analysts by replacing Benjamin Netanyahu as foreign minister with economist Silvan Shalom.

▶ It is reported that the personal art collection of Pierre Matisse, a son of the artist Henri Matisse, has been donated to New York City's Metropolitan Museum of Art; the collection contains more than 100 pieces by the most prominent artists of the 20th century.

**27 Feb** The US government lowers the terror-alert level to yellow (elevated).

▶ Archbishop Rowan Williams is enthroned as archbishop of Canterbury, the head of the Anglican Communion.

▶ Biljana Plavsic, who served two years as president of the self-proclaimed Republika Srpska in Bosnia and Herzegovina, is sentenced to 11 years in prison by the international war crimes tribunal for crimes against humanity.

▶ Officials in New York City announce that the design submitted by Studio Daniel Libeskind has been chosen for rebuilding on the site of the World Trade Center, destroyed on 11 Sep 2001.

**28 Feb** Vaclav Klaus is elected president of the Czech Republic.

▶ The Ninth Circuit Court of Appeals refuses a request from the US government that it reconsider its ruling that requiring children in public schools to recite the Pledge of Allegiance is unconstitutional because the pledge contains the words "under God."

# March 2003

**1 Mar** Authorities in Pakistan arrest Khalid Shaikh Mohammed, who is believed to be one of the top members of al-Qaeda and who is thought to have planned the terrorist attacks of 11 Sep 2001.

▶ Iraqi workers begin destroying the illegal al-Samoud 2 missiles under the supervision of UN weapons inspectors.

▶ Turkey's Grand National Assembly rejects the agreement made by government officials to allow the US to base troops in Turkey in order to wage war in northern Iraq.

▶ The World Health Organization adopts the final text for the Framework Convention on Tobacco Control, aimed at curtailing the use of tobacco products.

**2 Mar** Tens of thousands of people, mostly militant Muslims, in Islamabad, Pakistan, demonstrate their opposition to a US war against Iraq and the possibility of Pres. Pervez Musharraf's cooperating with such an action.

▶ French Pres. Jacques Chirac arrives in Algiers in the first state visit by the leader of France to Algeria since the former French colony became independent in 1962.

▶ The Swiss team Alinghi, led by Russell Coutts, defeats Team New Zealand to win the America's Cup, the world's most prestigious yacht race; it is Coutts's third consecutive victory, in two of which he served as the skipper for New Zealand.

▶ **3 Mar** The legislative body of the new country of Serbia and Montenegro holds its first session, in Belgrade, the capital; the body consists of 91 deputies from Serbia and 35 deputies from Montenegro.

▶ A radio announcer in North Korea reads a statement from leader Kim Jong Il to the effect that an attack on North Korea by the US would lead to nuclear war.

▶ On about 900 stages of all sizes and sorts in many countries, a reading of Aristophanes' play *Lysistrata* takes place as an organized, worldwide antiwar protest.

▶ A design by Julie Beckman and Keith Kaseman, featuring 184 benches with trees and reflecting pools, is chosen to memorialize the 11 Sep 2001 terrorist attack on the Pentagon in Washington DC.

**4 Mar** A bomb explodes at the international airport in Davao City, Philippines, killing at least 21 people and wounding 170 more. (See 2 April.)

**5 Mar** The foreign ministers of France, Russia, and Germany issue a statement that they would not permit passage of a UN Security Council resolution to authorize the use of force in Iraq, adding that France and Russia, permanent members of the council, would veto such a resolution.

▶ An emergency meeting of the Organization of the Islamic Conference in Doha, Qatar, which was called to try to find a way to avert a US war against the Iraqi regime, breaks up in acrimony and insults.

▶ A bomb destroys a city bus in Haifa, Israel, killing at least 15 passengers in the first deadly suicide attack in Israel in two months; the following day Israeli forces attack a refugee camp in the Gaza Strip, leaving 11 dead.

▶ The US Supreme Court upholds the constitutionality of California's "three strikes" law, which mandates lengthy prison terms for anyone who is convicted of the same type of crime three times, regardless of the severity of the crime.

‣ The Supreme Court of Argentina declares unconstitutional a presidential decree converting all dollars deposited in banks into pesos; the decree was promulgated a year earlier in an effort to bring stability to the Argentine economy.

**6 Mar** In his first formal White House news conference in almost 18 months, US Pres. George W. Bush says that Iraqi Pres. Saddam Hussein poses a direct threat to the US and that Washington will not be deterred by UN opposition from attacking Iraq.

‣ US Pres. George W. Bush and first lady Laura Bush award the 2002 National Medal of Arts to designer and architect Florence Knoll Bassett, dancer and choreographer Trisha Brown, museum director Philippe de Montebello, actress and educator Uta Hagen, architect and environmental planner Lawrence Halprin, cartoonist Al Hirschfeld (recently deceased), country singer and songwriter George Jones, painter and stage designer Ming Cho Lee, and singer-songwriter Smokey Robinson.

**7 Mar** US Pres. George W. Bush announces economic sanctions against the leaders of Zimbabwe's government, forbidding Americans to do business with them; the European Union had previously imposed similar measures.

‣ The legislature of Serbia and Montenegro elects Svetozar Marovic as president of the country; Marovic, who also holds the position of prime minister, had been an official in Montenegro's government.

‣ Almost all of Broadway goes dark as stage musicians in New York City go on strike and actors and stagehands honor the strike, causing nearly all musicals to cancel performances; at issue is the minimum number of musicians a production must employ.

**8 Mar** Meeting in Accra, Ghana, representatives of the warring parties in Côte d'Ivoire agree to the composition of a national reconciliation government, but fighting breaks out anew in the western region of the country.

‣ Citizens of Malta approve membership in the European Union; the national referendum is the first among the proposed new members of the EU, so the vote was watched with considerable interest.

‣ A judge in Argentina issues arrest warrants for four officials of the Iranian government, charging them with responsibility for the bombing of a Jewish community center in Buenos Aires on 18 Jul 1994 that killed 85 people.

**9 Mar** Israeli forces kill Ibrahim al-Makadmah, a leader of the Palestinian separatist group Hamas.

‣ In the biggest demonstrations since 1991, tens of thousands of protesters march in the Ukrainian capital, Kiev, to demand the resignation of Pres. Leonid Kuchma.

**10 Mar** Deutsche Telekom, the German telecommunications company, announces losses in 2002 of about $27.1 billion, the biggest shortfall in European corporate history.

‣ The Rock and Roll Hall of Fame in Cleveland inducts AC/DC, the Clash, Elvis Costello and the Attractions, the Police, and the Righteous Brothers.

**11 Mar** The new International Criminal Court holds its inaugural session in The Hague, attended by UN Secretary-General Kofi Annan and hundreds of other high-ranking officials.

‣ Turkish Pres. Ahmet Necdet Sezer asks Recep Tayyip Erdogan, the head of the ruling Justice and

Development Party, to form a government after Prime Minister Abdullah Gül resigns.

‣ In a small ribbon-cutting ceremony, the European Union opens its first diplomatic office in Cuba, in Havana; the EU is Cuba's biggest trading partner.

‣ The head of the US House Administration Committee orders that henceforth the cafeteria in the House of Representatives will serve "freedom fries" and "freedom toast" rather than French fries and French toast; the move is intended to showcase political frustration with the French position against a US-led war in Iraq.

‣ In NCAA women's basketball, the Villanova University Wildcats defeat the University of Connecticut Huskies in the Big East division championship, snapping the Huskies' record winning streak of 70 games.

**12 Mar** Serbian Prime Minister Zoran Djindjic is assassinated by snipers in downtown Belgrade; officials believe the killing is a response to Djindjic's crackdown on organized crime.

‣ Elizabeth Smart, who was kidnapped from her home in Salt Lake City UT in June 2002, is found with her kidnappers alive but apparently having been sexually abused.

**13 Mar** A bomb explodes on a rush-hour train at a station in Mulund, India, a suburb of Mumbai, killing 10 people and injuring 75.

‣ Robert Sorlie of Norway wins the Iditarod Trail Sled Dog Race; unusual weather had forced the organizers to include a detour that added 70 miles to the race and to cut the final 50 miles to the finish line in Nome AK.

**14 Mar** US Pres. George W. Bush says that he will adopt a peace plan, referred to as a "road map," for Israel and Palestine and will work for its acceptance as soon as Palestine has a new prime minister; he had previously said that he would not address that issue until the situation in Iraq had been resolved to his satisfaction.

‣ Admitting for the first time that the weakness of Germany's economy is partially due to structural flaws, Chancellor Gerhard Schröder introduces a major reform program.

‣ *Stancliffe's Hotel,* a novella written by Charlotte Brontë in 1838, appears in print for the first time, published in its entirety in *The Times* of London.

**15 Mar** The World Health Organization issues its first worldwide health alert in a decade, regarding a mysterious respiratory illness, Severe Acute Respiratory Syndrome, or SARS, that has struck hundreds of people in China, Hong Kong, and Vietnam and has been reported in Canada.

‣ Hu Jintao is ceremonially named as China's new president, replacing Jiang Zemin, who remains head of the People's Liberation Army; the following day Wen Jiabao is named prime minister, replacing Zhu Rongji.

‣ Opponents of war in Iraq lead large protests in several major American cities.

**16 Mar** Legislative elections in Finland result in a victory for the conservative Centre Party, led by Anneli Jäätteenmäki, over Prime Minister Paavo Lipponen's Social Democratic Party. (See 18 June).

‣ A referendum in Liechtenstein increases the already unusually great powers of Prince Hans-Adam II, who had said he would leave the country and move to Vienna if the referendum did not pass.

‣ Zoran Zivkovic is nominated to replace the assassinated Zoran Djindjic as prime minister of Serbia; Zivkovic was a key ally of Djindjic's.

**17 Mar** US Pres. George W. Bush, in a nationally televised address, declares that Saddam Hussein and his sons must abandon Iraq within 48 hours or suffer a military attack; the US government raises the terror-alert level from yellow, or "elevated," to orange, or "high."

---

**QUOTE OF THE MONTH**

" *Intelligence gathered by this and other governments leaves no doubt that the Iraqi regime continues to possess and conceal some of the most lethal weapons ever devised.* "

—US Pres. George W. Bush,
in his TV address, 17 March

---

▸ After a weekend coup in the Central African Republic, rebel leader François Bozize declares himself president; French citizens flee the country.
▸ Spain's Supreme Court bans the militant Basque political party Batasuna; it is the first time since the death of dictator Francisco Franco in 1975 that a political party has been outlawed in Spain.
**18 Mar** The aluminum-producing company Alcoa reaches an agreement with Iceland to build an aluminum smelter in Reyðarfjörður; the smelter is to be the sole customer for an enormous and controversial hydroelectric project in the wilderness area being undertaken by Landsvirkjun, Iceland's national power company.
▸ An Egyptian court dismisses all charges against democracy advocate Saad Eddin Ibrahim, whose conviction and imprisonment on the same charges in 2002 evoked international protests.
**19 Mar** The US begins air strikes against Baghdad, the capital of Iraq; the first target is a complex in which Saddam Hussein was believed to be holding a meeting; even months later, however, Hussein's fate is unknown.
▸ Palestinian leader Yasir Arafat names Mahmoud Abbas to the new position of prime minister.
▸ Holmes Rolston III, a Presbyterian minister and professor of philosophy known as a founder of environmental ethics, is named the winner of the Templeton Prize for Progress Toward Research or Discoveries About Spiritual Realities.
**20 Mar** US and British forces push into Iraq from Kuwait, and cruise missiles are directed into Baghdad; the first coalition casualties are reported as the result of a helicopter crash in Kuwait.
▸ Hundreds of thousands of people in cities throughout the world demonstrate against the US-led invasion of Iraq; the biggest protests take place outside the US.
**21 Mar** Avianca, Colombia's flagship carrier and the oldest airline in Latin America, files for bankruptcy protection in a US court; the company plans to continue operating, however.
▸ South Africa's Truth and Reconciliation Commission concludes its work, and commission head Bishop Desmond Tutu delivers its multivolume report to Pres. Thabo Mbeki.
**22 Mar** The French petroleum company TotalFinaElf announces that it is shutting its oil facilities in western Nigeria and evacuating its employees because of increasing ethnic violence; workers at a ChevronTexaco terminal have been stranded by the vio-

lence, and ChevronTexaco and Shell have already shut down operations in the area.
**23 Mar** A US soldier with the 101st Airborne Division in Kuwait allegedly attacks command tents with small-arms fire and grenades, killing two people and wounding 14.
▸ The Academy Awards ceremony is only slightly overshadowed by the war in Iraq; the gala is hosted by Steve Martin, and Oscars are won by, among others, *Chicago*, director Roman Polanski, and actors Adrien Brody, Nicole Kidman, Chris Cooper, and Catherine Zeta-Jones.
▸ In two referenda in Slovenia, citizens vote strongly in favor of their country joining both NATO and the European Union.
▸ A Russian-sponsored referendum on a new constitution is held in Chechnya; reported results are 96% in favor of the proposal, which envisions an elected government and a continuation of the republic's status as part of Russia.
▸ Australia defeats India by 125 runs to win a record third Cricket World Cup; Australia's score of 359 for 2 was that country's highest ever one-day total.
▸ At the close of the Third World Water Forum in Japan, UNESCO announces the creation of the Water Cooperation Facility in partnership with the World Water Council; the new organization will promote mechanisms for sustainable water development and will mediate disputes over international access to fresh water.
**24 Mar** US forces enter and fight for control of the Iraqi city of Al-Nasiriyah.
▸ The Qatar-based television network al-Jazeera launches an English-language Web site, starting with coverage of the war in Iraq; the site is almost immediately hijacked by hackers.
▸ In India, gunmen enter the Kashmiri village of Nadi Marg, spraying gunfire; 24 Hindu civilians are killed.
**25 Mar** Officials of the World Health Organization say that China has not allowed its team of investigators to enter Guangdong province, where the SARS epidemic is believed to have begun; China says the outbreak in that province has already died out.
▸ Boris Berezovsky, once one of the most influential people in Russia and now an expatriate billionaire in Great Britain, is arrested by British authorities for possible extradition to Russia on fraud charges.
▸ The US Air Force announces that the top four commanders of the US Air Force Academy in Colorado Springs CO will be replaced; the action comes after months of complaints by female cadets who reported being sexually harassed or abused and claimed they themselves, rather than their alleged attackers, were investigated.
▸ A group of figure-skating professionals, including coaches, judges, and skaters, announce the formation of the World Skating Federation; the new organization hopes to replace the International Skating Union as the governing body of the sport, believing the older organization to be hopelessly corrupt.
**26 Mar** US forces fighting in Iraq open a northern front with 1,000 paratroopers.
▸ Health officials in China double their estimate of the number of cases and deaths from SARS in Guangdong province as of the end of February; there are widespread complaints about the cooperation of Chinese officials in sharing information about the disease, about which almost nothing is known.

▸ The World Trade Organization rules that the steel tariffs imposed by the US in early 2002 are illegal under the agreements made by the organization's members.

**27 Mar** Amnesty International reports escalating violence on the part of the government of Zimbabwe against opposition figures; hundreds have been arrested, and there is evidence of torture.

**28 Mar** Japan launches a rocket to place into orbit two spy satellites; the move evokes strenuous objections from North Korea, whose recent bellicose policies were likely one factor behind the launching.

▸ The UN Security Council places UN Secretary-General Kofi Annan in charge of Iraq's oil-for-food program for the time being; some 60% of Iraq depends on this program.

▸ Argentina's government announces that it will lift the freeze on savings accounts in banks over the next three months and that depositors will get back some 80% of their assets; the freeze has been in place since 2001.

**29 Mar** In Washington DC, Michelle Kwan wins her fifth World Figure Skating Championship.

▸ Moon Ballad, owned by Sheikh Muhammad al-Maktoum and ridden by Frankie Dettori, wins the Dubai World Cup, the richest horse race in the world.

**30 Mar** A law banning cigarette smoking in all places of employment, including restaurants and bars, goes into effect in New York City.

▸ Tens of thousands of people attend opening ceremonies for the Sri Guru Singh Sabha Gurdwara in London; it is the largest Sikh temple outside India, with a capacity of 3,000 people.

▸ Susan Gibson, a chemist at King's College, London, is named the first recipient of the Rosalind Franklin Award, established by the British government to honor exemplary women in science.

**31 Mar** The parliament of the Czech Republic approves the treaty permitting the country to become a member of the European Union.

▸ Some 100,000 city workers in Jerusalem go on strike, joining national-government employees who are staging a work slowdown to protest layoffs and salary cuts promulgated by Finance Minister Benjamin Netanyahu.

▸ Chicagoans are stunned to find that during the night city crews have dug up the runways of the city's Meigs Airport; Mayor Richard M. Daley says the move was necessary to prevent small planes from flying over downtown in a time when the threat of terrorism is omnipresent.

▸ The Calder Hall nuclear reactor in Cumbria, England, ceases the production of electricity after 47 years of operation.

# April 2003

**1 Apr** American forces advance to within 80 km (50 mi) of Baghdad, Iraq.

▸ Prime Minister Recep Tayyip Erdogan of Turkey announces a new initiative to reunite Cyprus, which is seen as necessary not only to all of Cyprus joining the European Union but also to Turkey's ability to join the union.

▸ Air Canada files for bankruptcy protection, though it continues to operate.

**2 Apr** A peace accord is signed by the government of the Democratic Republic of the Congo and Congolese rebel groups in Sun City, South Africa.

▸ China acknowledges that it has almost 400 more suspected cases of and 12 more deaths from SARS than it had said; for the first time Beijing allows World Health Organization workers into Guangdong province, the epicenter of the disease.

▸ In Davao City, Philippines, a bomb explodes in a waiting area near a ferry terminal, killing at least 16 people and wounding dozens more; the following day, bombs go off at three of the city's mosques. (See 4 March.)

▸ US forces take custody of Jessica Lynch, a 19-year-old army private, who had been captured on March 23 with 14 others after the vehicle in which they were traveling made a wrong turn.

**3 Apr** The bodies of 26 villagers who had been kidnapped and executed are found in Assam state in northeastern India; the killings are believed to be part of an ongoing struggle for power in the area between the Dimasa and Hmar peoples.

**4 Apr** The Ituri Pacification Commission, bringing together representatives of all the groups that have tried to gain control over the northeastern district of the Democratic Republic of the Congo, is ceremonially inaugurated; three days later Pres. Joseph Kabila assumes power as interim head of state under the peace accord signed in Sun City, South Africa.

▸ As violence subsides in the western Niger Delta, two of the three oil companies that shut down operations in the previous months announce plans to return gradually to their previous levels of production.

▸ Authorities in Serbia and Montenegro announce that an arrest warrant for Mirjana Markovic, wife of former Yugoslav president Slobodan Milosevic, will be issued as part of the crackdown on organized crime that has been part of the response to the assassination of Serbian Prime Minister Zoran Djindjic.

▸ Macedonia becomes the 146th member of the World Trade Organization.

**5 Apr** US forces strike Baghdad, Iraq.

▸ A fistfight between rival gang members in a prison in Honduras soon escalates into riots that leave 86 inmates dead.

**6 Apr** UN officials say that attacks in the Ituri province of the Democratic Republic of the Congo during the previous week left some 966 people dead.

▸ In the worst "friendly fire" incident of the war in Iraq so far, US forces mistakenly bomb a convoy of American and Kurdish soldiers and journalists, killing 18 Kurds.

▸ David Hempleman-Adams becomes the first person to walk alone and unaided to the geomagnetic North Pole.

**7 Apr** In Iraq, US forces bomb a compound in Baghdad where they believe Pres. Saddam Hussein may be meeting with his advisers; British forces report that they have taken control of the city of Basra, Iraq.

▸ In New York City the winners of the 2003 Pulitzer Prizes are announced: journalistic awards go to, among others, the *Washington Post* and the *Los Angeles Times,* and winners in arts and letters include Robert Caro in biography and John Adams in music.

▶ Danish architect Jørn Utzon, famed for his design of the Sydney Opera House in Australia, is named the winner of the 2003 Pritzker Architecture Prize.

▶ The National Collegiate Athletic Association Championship in men's basketball is won by Syracuse (NY) University, which defeats the University of Kansas 81–78; in the women's final on the following day, the University of Connecticut defeats the University of Tennessee 73–68 for its second consecutive championship.

**8 Apr** *The Caprices,* a collection of stories by Sabina Murray, wins the 2003 PEN/Faulkner Award for fiction.

▶ It is reported that studies of mitochondrial DNA show that springtails (class Collembola) are not the ancestors of insects but rather arose as a separate group before the crustaceans and insects diverged.

**9 Apr** US-led forces in Iraq effectively take control of Baghdad.

---

### QUOTE OF THE MONTH

" *I now inform you that you are too far from reality.* "

—Iraqi Information Minister Muhammad Said al-Sahhaf, after weeks of steadfastly insisting that Iraq was routing the invaders, just before the fall of Baghdad, 9 April

---

▶ Negotiators for the US and South Korea agree that the headquarters of the US Army in South Korea should be moved out of Seoul as soon as it is feasible.

▶ The News Corporation, owned by Rupert Murdoch, agrees to buy the satellite-television distributor DirecTV from General Motors; the News Corporation owns the Fox Network and the Fox News Channel.

▶ It is reported that in India Satyabhama Mahapatra, age 65, has given birth to a son, making her the oldest woman in the world to give birth; the previous record holder was 62 years old.

**10 Apr** Kurdish militiamen take over the city of Kirkuk in northern Iraq.

▶ British Airways and Air France announce that they will both retire their fleets of Concorde supersonic jets this year; the Concorde first flew in commercial service in January 1976.

▶ Haiti officially recognizes voodoo as a religion; henceforth the state will accept as legal baptisms, marriages, and other sacraments.

**11 Apr** The World Health Organization issues a statement saying that the SARS outbreak appears to be under control, though it cautions that not enough is known about its spread in China; the causative agent has not been determined but is believed to be a coronavirus.

▶ Ten men being held on suspicion of belonging to al-Qaeda, including two of those believed responsible for the 2000 bombing of the USS *Cole,* escape from the facility where they were imprisoned in Aden, Yemen.

**12 Apr** As a three-day looting spree in Baghdad abates, it appears that the National Museum of Iraq has been thoroughly and catastrophically plundered; by the end of the month, however, it is clear that the damage is far less extensive than originally feared.

▶ China allows a team of World Health Organization investigators to visit hospitals in Beijing for the first time; on 16 April the investigators announce that the prevalence of SARS in Beijing has been significantly underreported.

▶ In legislative elections in Malta, the governing party, led by Prime Minister Eddie Fenech Adami, is reelected.

▶ In Brussels, Prince Laurent of Belgium marries Claire Coombs, a British-born surveyor.

**13 Apr** Rebel spokesmen say that five of the nine ministers who have been approved for Côte d'Ivoire's new coalition government have gone to the capital, Abidjan, to take up their posts; violence in the West African country continues, however.

▶ As US Marines approach the Iraqi city of Tikrit, Iraqi soldiers abandoned by their commanding officers lead Americans to seven American prisoners of war; no other Americans are believed to have been captured.

▶ The left-handed Canadian golfer Mike Weir comes from behind to win the Masters golf tournament in Augusta GA.

▶ British runner Paula Radcliffe smashes her own world record as she finishes first among the women at the London Marathon with a time of 2 hr 15 min 25 sec; the fastest man there is Ethiopian champion Gezahegne Abera, with a time of 2 hr 7 min 56 sec.

▶ Cypress Gardens, a theme park in Florida that first opened in 1936 and was best known for its water-skiing shows, closes for the last time.

**14 Apr** After US forces take control of Tikrit, Iraq, the Pentagon declares that major combat operations in the country have been concluded; at the same time US government officials accuse Syria of harboring terrorists and biological and chemical weapons.

▶ The Association of Computing Machinery announces that the winners of the A.M. Turing Award are Ronald L. Rivest, Adi Shamir, and Leonard M. Adleman, for their work in public-key cryptography.

▶ In San Francisco, the Goldman Environmental Prize is presented to Nigerian forest activist Odigha Odigha, Filipino air-pollution activist Von Hernández, Peruvian community activist María Elena Foronda Farro, Spanish physicist and economist Pedro Arrojo-Agudo, Australian Aboriginal elders Eileen Kampakuta Brown and Eileen Wani Wingfield, and American environmental activist Julia Bonds.

▶ The German radio and television manufacturer Grundig files for bankruptcy protection.

▶ Scientists from laboratories in China, France, Germany, Great Britain, Japan, and the US announce that they have now fully sequenced the human genome to an accuracy of 99.999% and that the work of the Human Genome Project has been completed.

**15 Apr** US Pres. George W. Bush declares that the government of Saddam Hussein in Iraq has fallen; the following day he calls on the UN to lift sanctions against Iraq that have been in place since 1991.

▶ US forces in Baghdad capture Abu Abbas, the leader of the faction of the Palestine Liberation Front that attacked the Italian cruise ship *Achille Lauro* in 1985.

▸ The Walt Disney Company agrees to sell its Major League Baseball championship team, the Anaheim Angels, to Arturo Moreno, a businessman from Arizona.

**16 Apr** The World Health Organization confirms that the causative agent of SARS is a new coronavirus first detected in Hong Kong on 21 March; the agent is to be called the SARS virus, and already the genome of the virus has been mapped.

▸ The US government lowers the terror-alert level from orange (high) to yellow (elevated).

▸ At the European Union summit meeting in Athens, the leaders of the 10 member states slated to join the EU in 2004 ceremonially sign accession treaties.

▸ *Partisan Review,* a respected and influential political and literary journal first published in 1934, announces it is ceasing publication.

▸ At the age of 40, Michael Jordan, widely regarded as the best player in the history of basketball, plays his last game with the Washington Wizards and retires for the third time in his career.

▸ The Bayer pharmaceutical company pleads guilty to engaging in a plot to overcharge Medicaid for the antibiotic Cipro and agrees to pay $257 million, a record Medicaid fraud settlement.

**17 Apr** The first major contract for the postwar rebuilding of Iraq is granted to the Bechtel Group by the US government.

▸ US forces in Baghdad, Iraq, capture Barzan Ibrahim al-Tikriti, a half brother of Saddam Hussein.

▸ Anneli Jäätteenmäki is sworn in as prime minister of Finland leading a center-left coalition government; Finland joins New Zealand as the first countries to have women heads of both state and government.

▸ Carnival Corporation takes over P&O Princess Cruises; P&O Princess had spent years fending off advances from Carnival.

▸ The personal art collection of Surrealist André Breton is sold at auction in Paris, many pieces for record-breaking prices; the government of France, which had declined to procure the collection outright, purchased pieces for 33 museums.

**18 Apr** Poland signs a deal to buy Lockheed Martin F-16s to upgrade its forces to a standard acceptable to NATO, which Poland joined in 1999.

▸ The world premiere of Pulitzer Prize-winning playwright August Wilson's *Gem of the Ocean* takes place at the Goodman Theatre in Chicago.

**19 Apr** In presidential elections in Nigeria, Pres. Olusegun Obasanjo is reelected, defeating some 19 opposition candidates.

▸ Some 3.5 million Belarusians participate in a day of voluntary unpaid work mandated by the government in order to raise money to build a new wing for the National Library of Belarus.

**20 Apr** The government of China admits that the incidence of SARS in the country is much greater than reported and dismisses the health minister and the mayor of Beijing.

**21 Apr** Jay Garner, who has been appointed US administrator of Iraq, arrives in Baghdad.

▸ Hundreds of thousands of Shi'ite Muslims make pilgrimage to Karbala, Iraq, to observe an important religious holiday on the Shi'ite calendar; it is the first time in a quarter century that they have been allowed to make this pilgrimage.

▸ Azerbaijani Pres. Heydar Aliyev collapses twice while giving a televised speech; he comes back

each time and finishes the speech, however, and returns to work the following day.

▸ The 107th Boston Marathon is won by Robert Kipkoech Cheruiyot of Kenya, with a time of 2 hr 10 min 11 sec; the winning woman is Svetlana Zakharova of Russia, with a time of 2 hr 25 min 20 sec.

▸ The 46th annual *Dance Magazine* Awards are presented to the choreographer William Forsythe, the dancers Susan Jaffe and Jock Soto, and the festival directors Charles and Stephanie Reinhart.

**22 Apr** France's ambassador to the UN proposes that UN sanctions against Iraq be dropped.

▸ The Yukos Oil Co., the biggest oil producer in Russia, announces that it will purchase the fifth largest company, Sibneft; YukosSibneft will be the fifth largest publicly traded oil company in the world.

▸ A subtropical storm in the open waters of the Atlantic Ocean develops into a tropical storm; dubbed Ana, this is the first tropical storm to occur in April since record-keeping began.

**23 Apr** On the authorization of Turkish Cypriot leader Rauf Denktash, checkpoints in the divided city of Nicosia, capital of Cyprus, open for the first time since 1974; thousands of people immediately line up at both sides of the border, and the flow of visitors continues for days.

▸ Alan Greenspan accepts a fifth term as chairman of the US Federal Reserve Board; he has served in that position for nearly 16 years.

▸ The World Health Organization adds Beijing and Toronto to its list of places that travelers should avoid because of the SARS outbreak.

▸ A three-day general strike is called for by labor unions in Zimbabwe, and most major stores and factories close.

**24 Apr** China imposes quarantines on thousands of people in the Beijing area in order to combat the spread of SARS, sealing a hospital complex with 2,000 workers and patients inside; the following day it broadens the quarantine dramatically.

▸ North Korean officials tell US diplomats that the country has nuclear weapons and is making bomb-grade plutonium.

▸ Iraqi Deputy Prime Minister Tariq Aziz surrenders to US forces in Baghdad.

▸ A group of Japanese researchers announce that the substance pyrroloquinoline quinone (PQQ), discovered in 1979, plays a role in fertility in mice and is probably a B vitamin; it is the first new vitamin to be identified in more than 50 years.

**25 Apr** Representatives of 11 Iraqi opposition groups meet in Madrid to discuss how to create a new government for Iraq.

▸ The John Bates Clark Medal of the American Economic Association, given out every two years to the leading US economist under the age of 40, is awarded to University of Chicago professor Steven D. Levitt.

**26 Apr** At a cache of munitions collected and guarded by US soldiers on the outskirts of Baghdad, Iraq, an explosion evidently set off by a flare fired into the dump kills at least six Iraqi civilians and wounds dozens more.

▸ Rome inaugurates a water-taxi service on the Tiber River, which had not been navigated in nearly a century.

**27 Apr** Nicanor Duarte Frutos, of the ruling Colorado Party, is elected president of Paraguay; he will take office on August 15.

▶ Presidential elections in Argentina result in a near tie between Néstor Kirchner and Carlos Menem, leading a field of 18 candidates; a runoff is scheduled for May.

▶ US forces in Iraq arrest Muhammad Mohsen Zobeidi, who had placed himself in charge of Baghdad, in order to make clear that challenges to US authority will not be tolerated.

▶ US military officials announce that the headquarters of US air operations in the Middle East will be moved from Riyadh, Saudi Arabia, to an air base in Qatar.

▶ A week after they were originally scheduled, talks open between the government of Nepal and the leaders of the Maoist insurgency.

▶ In Washington, DC, trombonist Andre Hayward wins the annual Thelonious Monk International Jazz Competition; the competition focuses on a different instrument each year.

**28 Apr** Some 15 people are killed by US forces during an anti-American rally in Falluja, Iraq; the occasion is the birthday of Saddam Hussein, which had traditionally been celebrated as a holiday in Iraq.

▶ Armenia, Belarus, Kazakhstan, Kyrgyzstan, Russia, and Tajikistan hold a summit meeting in Dushanbe, Tajikistan, to create the Collective Security Treaty Organization, which is intended to help address terrorism and narcotics issues affecting all the states.

▶ It is reported that, for the first time since magazines began being published on the World Wide Web, a Web-based magazine, *Slate*, has made more money than it spent.

**29 Apr** In Qatar a new constitution that provides for an elected legislature is overwhelmingly approved in a referendum.

▶ The US announces that it will withdraw all its combat forces from Saudi Arabia over the summer; the forces had been there since the Persian Gulf War in 1991 in order to contain Iraq.

▶ Police in Serbia and Montenegro charge 45 people with conspiracy in the assassination of Serbian Prime Minister Zoran Djindjic.

**30 Apr** The US, Russia, the UN, and the European Union present to leaders of Israel and Palestine the "road map" for peace, a document that contains detailed steps to be taken by each entity.

▶ An open-ended general strike begins in Israel, prompted by austerity measures taken by Finance Minister Benjamin Netanyahu.

▶ The presidency of Burundi is transferred from the Tutsi Pierre Buyoya to the Hutu Domitien Ndayizeye, as called for by the Arusha accords signed in 2000.

▶ The government of Libya formally accepts responsibility for having caused the 1988 bombing of Pan Am Flight 103 over Lockerbie, Scot.; this is a step toward the ending of UN sanctions against Libya.

# May 2003

**1 May** Trade unionists, communists, anarchists, and various protesters march in cities throughout Europe to mark May Day, the international labor day; this is usually the biggest holiday of the year in Beijing, but fear of SARS in addition to quarantines already in effect keeps the streets and subways almost empty.

▶ US Pres. George W. Bush announces that the military phase of the Iraq war has ended, referring to it as "one victory in a war on terror"; on the same day, US Secretary of Defense Donald Rumsfeld and Afghani Pres. Hamid Karzai announce that major combat operations in Afghanistan are over.

▶ Côte d'Ivoire signs a comprehensive cease-fire agreement with rebels and representatives of Liberia, including an agreement for a joint Ivoirian-Liberian patrol along the border between the two countries.

▶ After questions are raised about the integrity of his writing, Jayson Blair, a *New York Times* reporter whose work has been featured prominently in the newspaper, resigns. (*See* 28 May.)

**2 May** Indian Prime Minister Atal Bihari Vajpayee announces that India will restore diplomatic relations with Pakistan, broken off in December 2001 after an attack on Parliament; within hours Pakistani officials say that Pakistan will also restore normal diplomatic relations with India.

▶ Nigerian oil workers on strike release the first of the 250 foreign oil workers they have held hostage on oil rigs since 19 April; they agree to release all hostages.

**3 May** It is agreed by the leadership of the World Health Organization, which includes mainland China, that WHO inspectors will be permitted to visit Taiwan to fight the outbreak of SARS there.

▶ FIFA, the association football (soccer) governing authority, withdraws the Women's World Cup tournament from China, where it was to have been played in the fall, because of the SARS epidemic. (*See* 26 May.)

▶ Pope John Paul II, in a visit to Spain, makes a moving plea for peace to the half million people gathered to hear him speak; the following day at an open-air Mass in Madrid, he names five new saints.

▶ In the 129th running of the Kentucky Derby, the gelding Funny Cide, a long shot, outruns favorite Empire Maker by 1¾ lengths to win.

▶ It is found that the Old Man of the Mountain, a famous natural granite formation on Cannon Mountain in New Hampshire, has fallen; the formation resembled a face and had been an icon of the state.

**4 May** The astronauts who had been stranded in the International Space Station by the grounding of the US space shuttle fleet return to Earth in a Russian *Soyuz* capsule.

**5 May** When Colombian troops try to rescue hostages held by FARC guerrillas, the guerrillas execute 10 of the hostages, including a provincial governor and a former cabinet member.

▶ Italian Prime Minister Silvio Berlusconi testifies in his own defense in a courtroom where he is being tried on charges of bribery; it is the first time that a sitting Italian prime minister has ever testified as a criminal defendant.

▶ US and Iraqi officials say that just before the US invasion of Iraq, one of Iraqi Pres. Saddam Hussein's sons and an adviser removed some $1 billion in cash from the central bank.

**6 May** US Pres. George W. Bush makes L. Paul Bremer III the chief US administrator of Iraq, supplanting Jay Garner.

▶ The discount retail chain Kmart Corp. (now Kmart Holding Corp.) emerges from bankruptcy, minus 600 stores and with a new management team.

▶ A spokesman for Liberian Pres. Charles Taylor says that Liberian forces have killed Sam Bockarie, one of West Africa's most notorious warlords.

▸ A new passenger terminal combining traditional Khmer and modern styles opens at Pochentong international airport near Phnom Penh, Cambodia.

▸ Avery Fisher career grants are awarded to violinists Colin Jacobsen and Giora Schmidt, violinist and violist Scott St. John, flutist Demarre McGill, and pianist Natalie Zhu.

**7 May** US officials say that the government is asking members of the International Atomic Energy Agency to declare Iran to be in violation of the Nuclear Non-proliferation Treaty.

▸ Michael Jordan, who had planned to return to his former job as president of basketball operations for the NBA team the Washington Wizards after retiring as a player, is fired by team owner Abe Pollin.

▸ At the National Magazine Awards ceremony, the surprise big winner is *Parenting*; other awards for general excellence go to *ESPN the Magazine, The Atlantic Monthly, Texas Monthly, Architectural Record,* and *Foreign Policy.*

**8 May** In Morocco, Princess Salma Bennani, wife of King Muhammad VI, gives birth to a son, Hassan, who will be the chief heir to the throne.

▸ Georgia's new state flag, featuring the Star and Bars of the Confederacy, which is viewed as less inflammatory than the Confederate battle flag featured on the previous two flags, flies over the capitol building for the first time.

▸ In an extremely rare double birth, a woman in Cariacica, Brazil, who has two wombs produces a boy and a girl, one from each womb.

**9 May** William W. Parsons is appointed to take over management of the space shuttle program for NASA and to get the three remaining shuttles back in service; he replaces Ron D. Dittemore, who announced his resignation in April.

▸ Officials in Saudi Arabia announce publicly that, after a shootout during a raid on a building in Riyadh that contained a very large cache of arms, they are seeking 19 militants who are believed to be connected to al-Qaeda and to have been planning a major attack.

**10 May** The Russian play *Nord-Ost,* which was playing to packed houses in Moscow before Chechen terrorists took over the theater in October 2002, closes after reopening in February; audiences were staying away from the theater.

**11 May** In the third round of voting, after the abolishment of the 50% threshold that invalidated two earlier elections, Filip Vojanovic is elected president of Montenegro.

▸ The incomparable *Saliera,* a sculptured golden saltcellar by Benvenuto Cellini, is stolen from the Kunsthistorisches Museum in Vienna.

▸ In Racine WI, the new Racine Art Museum, housing an internationally recognized collection of contemporary crafts, opens with an installation of baskets by glass artist Dale Chihuly.

**12 May** A truck bomb blows up a residential complex in the town of Znamenskoye in the Russian republic of Chechnya, killing at least 59 people.

▸ Suicide bombers strike three residential compounds in Riyadh, Saudi Arabia, killing 35 people from a variety of countries and injuring more than 200.

▸ Clare Short, secretary for international development, becomes the second member of the British cabinet to resign because of Prime Minister Tony Blair's unstinting support of US policy toward Iraq.

**13 May** An interview with Israeli Prime Minister Ariel Sharon is published in which Sharon says the dismantling of Israeli settlements in Palestinian territory is not being contemplated; dismantling settlements built after March 2001 is one step on the road map for peace.

▸ France is paralyzed as more than one million people walk off their jobs and march in the streets to demonstrate their disagreement with proposed reforms to the state pension system.

▸ The US declares 14 Cuban diplomats personae non gratae; it is one of the largest diplomatic expulsions ever ordered by the US.

▸ The US Treasury Department unveils a new design for the $20 bill, featuring colors other than green in the background.

---

**QUOTE OF THE MONTH**

❝ *If those murderers believe that their bloody crimes will shake even one hair on the body of this nation and its unity, they are deceiving themselves.* ❞

—Saudi Arabian Crown Prince Abdullah, addressing the nation on 13 May, a day after the terrorist bombings in Riyadh

---

**14 May** A suicide bomber detonates her weapon at a religious festival in Iliskhan-Yurt in the Russian republic of Chechnya in an apparent attempt to assassinate the pro-Russian regional administrator, Akhmad Kadyrov; at least 15 people are killed.

▸ Taiwan's top hospital, the National Taiwan University Hospital, utterly overwhelmed by an outbreak of SARS, shuts down as thousands are quarantined; three weeks after the last reported case of SARS in Toronto, the World Health Organization removes that city from its travel advisory list.

▸ Three top executives of Banco Intercontinental, the Dominican Republic's second biggest commercial bank, are arrested after the discovery of a scheme that resulted in the embezzlement of $2.2 billion.

▸ Italian Prime Minister Silvio Berlusconi officially lays the first foundation stone for the massive Venice dike project, scheduled to be completed by 2011 in order to save the low-lying city from flooding.

**15 May** As part of an effort to make it clear that China is serious about stopping the spread of SARS, the country temporarily suspends almost all foreign adoptions; China is a major provider of adopted babies to Westerners.

▸ British forces in Iraq formally turn over control of the port city of Umm Qasr to a council made up of Iraqi volunteers.

▸ France lodges a formal complaint with the US government against what it sees as a formal campaign of false and hurtful information against the French being published in US news sources and frequently attributed to anonymous administration sources.

**16 May** Japan's House of Representatives passes three bills intended to strengthen the military; though Japan renounced the right to wage war in 1947, the perceived threat from North Korea has impelled lawmakers to improve Japan's defensive capabilities.

▸ Suicide bombings occur at five different places nearly simultaneously in Casablanca, Morocco, killing at least 41 people, including many foreigners.

**17 May** The Vatican acknowledges for the first time that Pope John Paul II has Parkinson disease.

▸ Peace talks between representatives of the government of Indonesia and separatist groups in the breakaway Indonesian province of Aceh open in Tokyo in an effort to salvage the peace agreement made in December 2002.

▸ The referendum on joining the European Union passes comfortably in Slovakia.

▸ Funny Cide, the Kentucky Derby winner, wins the Preakness Stakes by 9¾ lengths.

**18 May** Four attacks by Palestinians kill nine Israelis; Israeli Prime Minister Ariel Sharon cancels a trip to the US and indicates that the simultaneous concessions by each side called for by the road map for peace will be impossible.

▸ Indonesian Pres. Megawati Sukarnoputri puts Aceh province under martial law; the following day the national government begins a major military offensive in the area.

▸ The curtain falls for the final time after the 6,680th performance of *Les Misérables* on Broadway; the show, which opened in March 1987, was Broadway's second longest-running show, after *Cats*.

**19 May** Thousands of Shi'ites march in downtown Baghdad in opposition to the US occupation of Iraq; a number of other groups feel that change is coming too slowly.

▸ MCI, as WorldCom has now been renamed, agrees to a settlement of fraud charges brought by the US Securities and Exchange Commission; the telecommunications company will pay $500 million.

▸ The Annual International IMPAC Dublin Literary Award goes to *My Name Is Red*; the prize will be split between the Turkish author, Orhan Pamuk, and his translator, Erdag Goknar.

▸ Ari Fleischer, US Pres. George W. Bush's press secretary, announces that he is stepping down.

**20 May** Mad cow disease is diagnosed in a cow in Canada; a ban on all beef imports from Canada is immediately imposed in the US.

▸ The US government raises the terror-alert level from yellow (elevated) to orange (high).

**21 May** The Framework Convention on Tobacco Control is unanimously adopted by the World Health Organization, committing all 192 member countries to strict limits on the advertising and sale of tobacco products; the convention will come into force once it is ratified by 40 of those countries.

▸ The European Commission fines Deutsche Telekom €12.6 million (about $14 million) for charging competitors higher prices for access to its telecommunications lines than it charged customers; though the German phone industry was deregulated five years ago, Deutsche Telekom still holds 95% of the market.

▸ Jong-Wook Lee, an epidemiologist and expert on vaccines, is elected director general of the World Health Organization, replacing Gro Harlem Brundtland; he will take office on 21 July.

▸ Christine Todd Whitman announces her resignation as head of the US Environmental Protection Agency.

**22 May** The UN Security Council passes a resolution granting to the US-led coalition the military occupation and administration of Iraq and abolishing economic sanctions against Iraq; an interim administration is to be set up by the Iraqi people.

▸ The results of two studies published in *The New England Journal of Medicine* show that people on the low-carbohydrate Atkins diet for several months lower their triglycerides, blood fats that tend to clog arteries, and raise their HDL, or good cholesterol; researchers are surprised by these findings.

▸ Annika Sörenstam becomes the first woman to play in a PGA Tour event since Babe Didrikson Zaharias in 1945 when she starts at the Colonial golf tournament; she fails to make the cut for the final two rounds, however.

**23 May** Negotiators for the government and the opposition in Venezuela reach an agreement to hold a referendum on the presidency of Hugo Chávez after 19 August in an attempt to curtail the conflict that has been going on since last year.

▸ Researchers in Hong Kong and at the World Health Organization say they have identified a virus that is at least very similar to the SARS virus in palm civets, which are eaten in Asia, and in a raccoon dog and a badger; meanwhile, WHO lifts its travel advisory for Hong Kong and for Guangdong province in China, but the US Centers for Disease Control and Prevention reinstates the advisory for Toronto.

▸ Georgian Pres. Eduard Shevardnadze ceremonially lays the first section of the Baku-Tbilisi-Ceyhan oil pipeline.

**24 May** Tens of thousands of trade union members march in Berlin to protest government plans to cut unemployment benefits and loosen job protections.

▸ At the annual Eurovision song competition, held this year in Riga, Latvia, the Turkish singer Sertab Erener wins first place with her song "Every Way That I Can."

**25 May** Néstor Kirchner is sworn in as president of Argentina.

▸ Controversial legislative elections in Armenia result in a win for Prime Minister Andranik Markaryan's Republican Party of Armenia.

▸ The cabinet in Israel gives its qualified approval for Prime Minister Ariel Sharon to pursue the steps of the road map for peace, which calls eventually for the creation of a Palestinian state.

▸ At the Cannes International Film Festival, American director Gus Van Sant's film *Elephant* wins the Palme d'Or, and the Grand Prix goes to Turkish director Nuri Bilge Ceylan for *Uzak (Distant)*.

▸ Brazilian Gil de Ferran wins the Indianapolis 500 auto race by 0.2990 sec over his teammate Helio Castroneves, who was trying to win an unprecedented third consecutive Indy.

**26 May** FIFA chooses the US to host the 2003 Women's World Cup in association football (soccer); officials believe it will still be possible to hold the tournament within the original time frame. (See 3 May.)

**27 May** Belgium, France, Great Britain, Germany, Luxembourg, Spain, and Turkey join forces to acquire 180 military transport planes from Airbus in one of Europe's biggest military projects.

▸ The official celebration of the 300th anniversary of St. Petersburg, Russia, begins with fireworks, a laser show, and balloons; it continues with lavish parties attended by the leaders of the world's countries.

**28 May** A new tax law is signed by US Pres. George W. Bush in which a last-minute revision prevents low-income parents from taking the child-tax credit.

▸ Health authorities in Toronto quarantine some 2,000 students and staff of a parochial school where a student attended classes for two days while she had symptoms of SARS.

▸ Pres. Alejandro Toledo declares a state of emergency in Peru as strikes and protests spread throughout the country.

▶ A second reporter for the *New York Times,* Rick Bragg, resigns after a controversy arises over the extent of his reliance on a freelance journalist for his reporting of a story. (*See* 1 May.)

▶ AC Milan defeats Juventus Turin by a score of 3–2 in the final match in Manchester, England, to win the association football (soccer) Champions League competition.

▶ Krispy Kreme Doughnuts announces that its first-quarter profit grew an astonishing 48% compared with the first quarter of the previous year.

**29 May** Scientists announce that for the first time an equine has been cloned; the baby mule, born 4 May, has been dubbed Idaho Gem.

▶ A gala dinner in Kathmandu attended by Sir Edmund Hillary is only one of many celebrations taking place in Nepal and elsewhere in commemoration of the 50th anniversary of the first successful ascent of Mt. Everest, by Hillary and Tenzing Norgay.

▶ In the Scripps-Howard National Spelling Bee, Sai R. Gunturi of Dallas spells *pococurante* correctly to win the prize.

**30 May** The US government lowers the terror-alert level from orange (high) to yellow (elevated).

▶ The US opens a new embassy in Beirut, Lebanon; there has not been a US consulate there since the old US embassy was blown up in 1983.

**31 May** Eric Rudolph, sought since 1996 in connection with a bombing at the Olympic Games in Atlanta that year, is caught in Murphy NC.

▶ The pioneering Menninger Clinic, which opened in Topeka KS in 1925, closes its doors; it will reopen in Houston in partnership with the Baylor College of Medicine and the Methodist Hospital.

▶ The world premiere of the opera *The Little Prince,* based on the book by Antoine de Saint-Exupéry and scored by Rachel Portman, opens at the Houston Grand Opera.

# June 2003

**1 Jun** A second attempt by British forces occupying Basra, Iraq, to install a governing council is thwarted by protesters incensed that the council was chosen by the British and by disagreements between members of the council.

▶ The sluice gates of the Three Gorges Dam on the Yangtze River in China are closed, and the water level quickly rises.

**2 Jun** The European Space Agency successfully launches the Mars Express orbiter and the Beagle 2, a landing vehicle, from the Baikonur Cosmodrome in Kazakhstan; the vehicles are expected to reach Mars in December.

▶ Authorities in Zimbabwe arrest Morgan Tsvangirai, the opposition leader, charging him with contempt of court for planning antigovernment demonstrations; after being released, he is taken into custody again on 6 June.

▶ Jonathan Ive, the designer of Apple Computers' iMac personal computer, wins the Design Museum of London's first Designer of the Year award.

**3 Jun** Most of Zimbabwe is shut down by a general strike that is an attempt to force Pres. Robert Mugabe to resign, but security forces effectively prevent demonstrations from taking place.

▶ A wave of strikes takes place in cities in France, Austria, Italy, and Germany; workers object to government proposals to cut back on retirement benefits.

▶ Sammy Sosa, the only Major League Baseball player ever to hit 60 home runs in three different seasons, is ejected from a game when his bat breaks and reveals the presence of cork inside it; cork is thought to enhance batter performance, and its use is prohibited.

**4 Jun** After a meeting with US Pres. George W. Bush in Aqaba, Jordan, Israeli Prime Minister Ariel Sharon agrees to dismantle some unauthorized outposts of Israeli settlements in Palestinian areas; Palestinian Prime Minister Mahmoud Abbas agrees that the armed uprising on the part of Palestinians must end.

▶ A UN Special Court in Sierra Leone announces that it has indicted Liberian Pres. Charles Taylor for war crimes.

▶ The European Union agrees to send a force of peacekeepers, under France's leadership, to the Democratic Republic of the Congo; it is the first

time the union has martialed a force on its own to operate outside Europe.

▶ In a televised speech to the country, Argentine Pres. Néstor Kirchner calls for the impeachment of the Supreme Court.

▶ Good-living advocate Martha Stewart is indicted by the US federal government on charges of conspiracy, obstruction of justice, and securities fraud; she resigns as chairman and CEO of her company, Martha Stewart Living Omnimedia.

**5 Jun** A suicide bomber kills at least 18 people in addition to herself on a bus carrying military and civilian workers to a Russian air base just outside the republic of Chechnya.

▶ The UN Security Council lifts sanctions against the import of diamonds from Sierra Leone, in the belief that Sierra Leone has taken the steps necessary to ensure that diamonds exported from the country have not been sold to finance guerrilla military activity.

▶ Pope John Paul II arrives in Croatia for a five-day visit on the 100th trip of his papacy. (*See* 22 June.)

**6 Jun** The US and Chile sign a free-trade agreement, the first such accord ever signed between the US and a country in South America.

▶ Leaders of Hamas, a Palestinian militia, break off cease-fire talks with Palestinian Prime Minister Mahmoud Abbas, feeling that Abbas had become too supportive of Israel.

▶ Volkswagen announces that the company will cease production of the original Beetle by summer's end; the classic car, first produced in 1934, is now made at one plant, located in Puebla, Mexico.

**7 Jun** A car bomb strikes a bus carrying German troops from an international security force in Kabul, Afghanistan, killing at least 4 soldiers and injuring 29 others.

▶ An amnesty goes into effect in Russia's separatist republic of Chechnya; rebels who turn in their weapons will be guaranteed freedom from prosecution.

▶ Justine Henin-Hardenne of Belgium defeats her countrywoman Kim Clijsters to win the women's French Open tennis title; the following day Juan Carlos Ferrero of Spain defeats Martin Verkerk of The Netherlands to win the men's title.

▶ Empire Maker surprises observers by winning the

Belmont Stakes horse race on a wet and sloppy track; Kentucky Derby and Preakness winner Funny Cide runs third.

▸ The two-day referendum on joining the European Union gets under way in Poland; the results are a resounding yes to membership.

**8 Jun** The 57th annual Tony Awards are presented in Radio City Music Hall in New York City; winners include the plays *Take Me Out, Hairspray, Long Day's Journey into Night,* and *Nine* and the actors Brian Dennehy, Vanessa Redgrave, Harvey Fierstein, and Marissa Jaret Winokur.

▸ Annika Sörenstam of Sweden wins the Ladies Professional Golf Association championship on the first play-off hole, defeating Grace Park of South Korea.

**9 Jun** Mexican Pres. Vicente Fox signs a bill that outlaws discrimination based on race, sex, age, or religion in all sectors of society.

▸ During an investigation into questionable accounting practices at Freddie Mac, the federal mortgage insurer that is crucial to the housing market, David Glenn, the company president, is suddenly fired, and the chairman and CEO and the chief financial officer resign.

▸ French forces land in Monrovia, Liberia, to evacuate hundreds of foreigners as the rebel group Liberians United for Reconciliation and Democracy continues a battle for the northern suburbs of the capital.

▸ After two days of fighting in Nouakchott that followed a crackdown on Muslim extremists, the government of Mauritanian Pres. Maaouya Ould Sidi Ahmad Taya succeeds in averting an attempted coup.

▸ The US Centers for Disease Control and Prevention announces that the number of cases in an outbreak of monkeypox, the first ever in the Western Hemisphere, in the Midwest, has risen to 33, with most cases occurring in Wisconsin.

▸ The New Jersey Devils defeat the Anaheim Mighty Ducks to win the Stanley Cup, the National Hockey League championship; the score of the final game is 3–0.

▸ With much hoopla, *Living History,* an autobiography of US Sen. Hillary Clinton, goes on sale; some 200,000 copies are sold the first day.

**10 Jun** Israel fires missiles into Gaza in an attempt to kill Hamas leader Abdel Aziz Rantisi; the US government views the move as undermining attempts at peace.

▸ In Santiago, Chile, the members of the Organization of American States vote to deny the US a representative on the Inter-American Commission on Human Rights.

▸ A rocket takes off from Cape Canaveral FL carrying a robotic probe called *Spirit* to Mars; the robot will be looking for evidence of water.

**11 Jun** A Hamas suicide bomber blows up a rush-hour bus in Jerusalem, killing 16 people in addition to himself and wounding nearly 100 others; meanwhile, Israeli helicopter strikes in Gaza kill 10 Palestinians.

▸ At a press conference in Ethiopia, it is revealed that three skulls found in the Afar region of the country and dated at 160,000 years old are the oldest known fossils of *Homo sapiens.*

▸ Four UN monitors arrive in Tbilisi, Georgia, after being released by their kidnappers in the Kodori Gorge area some six days after they were kidnapped for ransom.

**12 Jun** British Prime Minister Tony Blair abolishes the post of lord chancellor, a position that existed for 1,400 years.

▸ In the first major battle since the end of the war in Iraq was announced, US forces attack a site believed to be a training ground for the Iraqi resistance in an area about 145 km (90 mi) northwest of Baghdad.

▸ Several items taken from the collections of the Iraqi National Museum are returned by unidentified men; the items include the Warka Vase, a particularly important artifact dating from some 5,000 years ago that depicts scenes of everyday life in ancient Uruk.

▸ Investigators say that a mass grave containing the remains of hundreds of people has been uncovered at a construction site at Ulaanbaatar, Mongolia, dating from the 1930s, when Stalinist purges killed some 30,000 people in Mongolia.

▸ A five-day celebration of the 100th anniversary of the Ford Motor Co. gets under way in Dearborn MI.

**13 Jun** In Brussels, Valéry Giscard d'Estaing, head of the Convention on the Future of Europe, announces that a first draft of a constitution for the European Union has been adopted by the convention.

▸ *Science* magazine publishes a report by geologists detailing evidence for what they believe was a major meteor impact on the Earth some 380 million years ago that may have caused a mass extinction of fishes.

**14 Jun** A railroad linking North and South Korea is ceremonially reopened; the connection had been severed after the Korean War.

▸ Sheikh Khalid ibn Saqr al-Qassami is deposed as crown prince of Ra's al-Khaymah in the United Arab Emirates in favor of his younger brother.

▸ British Queen Elizabeth II publishes the list of those appointed Officers of the Order of the British Empire; they are association football (soccer) star David Beckham, musicians Sting and David Gilmour, actors Helen Mirren and Roger Moore, and fashion designer Alexander McQueen.

▸ Somewhat to the surprise of their leaders, voters in the Czech Republic firmly vote in favor of joining the European Union in a binding referendum.

**15 Jun** The top investigator of the UN Special Court in Sierra Leone announces that Johnny Paul Koroma, a former ruler of Sierra Leone who had been indicted for war crimes by the court, has been killed in Liberia.

▸ The San Antonio Spurs defeat the New Jersey Nets 88–77 to win the National Basketball Association championship; Tim Duncan of the Spurs is named Most Valuable Player of the finals.

▸ At the US Open golf tournament at Olympia Fields Country Club in Illinois, Jim Furyk emerges as the winner as he ties the scoring record for the tournament.

▸ At the Baden-Baden Pentecost music festival in Germany, violinist Anne-Sophie Mutter is awarded the first Herbert von Karajan Award for outstanding contemporary musicians.

**16 Jun** The death of a black motorcyclist in a high-speed police chase touches off two days of rioting in the small, mostly African American, and desperately poor town of Benton Harbor MI.

▸ The world's first offshore tidal-energy turbine is launched off the coast of Devon in England; the turbine works on the principle of a windmill but uses water currents to generate energy.

▸ At the Paris Air Show, Emirates Airline agrees to buy 41 new airplanes, among them 21 giant A380s, from Airbus Industrie; it is among the largest civil aircraft orders ever placed.

**17 Jun** The government of Liberia and representatives of a rebel group sign a cease-fire agreement in which Pres. Charles Taylor promises to yield power.

▸ Britons are aghast to learn that association football (soccer) sensation David Beckham is leaving Manchester United to play for Spain's Real Madrid.

**18 Jun** Military officials announce that US forces in Iraq have captured Abid Hamid Mahmoud al-Tikriti, believed to be Saddam Hussein's top aide.

▸ The Italian Parliament passes a law making the top five government officials immune from prosecution while they hold office, effectively stopping the corruption trial of Prime Minister Silvio Berlusconi.

▸ Israel's Antiquities Authority announces that the Aramaic inscription on a 2,000-year-old stone box made public in October 2002 suggesting that it might be the ossuary of James, the brother of Jesus, is a modern forgery.

**19 Jun** The government of the Democratic Republic of the Congo signs a cease-fire agreement in Burundi with two rebel groups backed by the government of Rwanda.

▸ McDonald's Corp. announces that it will instruct its meat suppliers throughout the world to reduce their use of antibiotics in stock raising; because the fast-food chain is one of the world's largest meat purchasers, this decision is expected to cause widespread change in farming practices.

**20 Jun** Pres. Nursultan Nazarbayev of Kazakhstan signs into law a controversial reform measure that for the first time permits the private ownership of land.

▸ The US Food and Drug Administration approves the over-the-counter sale of the top-selling prescription medicine Prilosec, which is used for heartburn and ulcers.

**21 Jun** The long-awaited and closely guarded novel *Harry Potter and the Order of the Phoenix* goes on sale; by the end of the day a record five million copies have been sold.

▸ The World Economic Forum, which prior to 2002 held its annual conference in Davos, Switzerland, convenes in Suweima, Jordan.

▸ After months of work to dress Paris's Eiffel Tower in 20,000 new lights, the lights are switched on in a festive ceremony; the light show will be played on the tower every night.

**22 Jun** At an open-air Mass in Banja Luka, Bosnia and Herzegovina, Pope John Paul II apologizes for crimes committed by Roman Catholics in the lands of the former Yugoslavia and exhorts his listeners to forgiveness and reconciliation in order to bring healing to the country. (See 5 June.)

▸ Voters in Tajikistan approve a number of changes to the constitution, including one that will permit Pres. Imomali Rakhmonov to serve two more seven-year terms.

▸ A law goes into effect in Turkmenistan preventing people from holding both Russian and Turkmen passports; panicky Russians have been fleeing Turkmenistan for weeks.

**23 Jun** In a pair of landmark decisions, the US Supreme Court rules that it is constitutional for universities to consider race in deciding admissions but that the numerical weighting of "underrepresented" races is too mechanistic and therefore not permissible. (See 26 June.)

**24 Jun** Matti Vanhanen is chosen by the Finnish legislature as the new prime minister, replacing Anneli Jäätteenmäki, who resigned on 18 June after a scant two months in office.

▸ During a visit of Indian Prime Minister Atal Behari Vajpayee to Beijing, it is announced that India and China have agreed to reopen a border crossing between India's Sikkim state and the Tibet Autonomous Region of China that had been closed since 1962; China does not recognize India's sovereignty over Sikkim.

**25 Jun** The US Federal Reserve Board lowers short-term interest rates by one-quarter of a percentage point, to 1%; rates have not been this low since 1958.

▸ The US Internal Revenue Service releases a report showing that the 400 wealthiest taxpayers more than doubled their share of the nation's wealth over the past eight years, while the percentage of their income that they paid in taxes dropped significantly.

▸ Battles break out in the streets of Monrovia, the capital of Liberia, as rebel troops intent on overthrowing Pres. Charles Taylor attack the city.

▸ The Indian Memorial at the Little Bighorn Battlefield National Monument in Montana is dedicated in ceremonies that attract thousands of Native Americans; the memorial commemorates for the first time the Indian warriors who died in the 1876 Battle of Little Bighorn, in which Lieut. Col. George A. Custer and all his men perished.

**26 Jun** In another landmark decision (*see* 23 June), the US Supreme Court rules that states may not forbid private homosexual conduct, overturning the precedent set in 1986.

▸ Authorities in Saudi Arabia arrest Ali Abd al-Rahman al-Faqasi al-Ghamdi, believed to be the top al-Qaeda operative in the country and also thought to be behind the bombings in Riyadh in May.

**27 Jun** The day after US Pres. George W. Bush called on him to step down, Liberian Pres. Charles Taylor gives a radio address in which he asks for international help and declares that he will not resign, stressing his commitment to peace and security; the following day UN Secretary-General Kofi Annan calls for a peacekeeping force to be sent to Liberia.

---

**QUOTE OF THE MONTH**

*" We ask the international community, most specifically the United States, to do everything within its power to help Liberia and Liberians out of this mess. "*

—Liberian Pres. Charles Taylor, in a radio address to the country, 27 June

---

▸ A national registry for people who wish not to receive telemarketing calls opens in the US; the registry is immediately overwhelmed by the volume of requests.

▸ Negotiators for Israel and Palestine reach an agreement whereby Palestinian leaders will attempt to prevent attacks and Israel will begin withdrawing its troops from the Gaza Strip.

**28 Jun** At a party in a three-story apartment building in Chicago, the overcrowded back decks collapse, killing 13 people.

▸ Two men enter an Indian army barracks outside the city of Jammu in the state of Jammu and Kashmir and launch an attack with assault rifles and grenades; 12 unarmed Indian soldiers are killed and 7 wounded.

**29 Jun** Hamas and Islamic Jihad declare a three-month cease-fire, and al-Fatah follows suit with a six-month moratorium; in response, Israeli troops begin pulling back from the Gaza Strip.

▸ China and Hong Kong conclude an economic partnership agreement in which China agrees to open its markets to a wide variety of goods from Hong Kong.

▸ France defeats Cameroon 1–0 to win the Confederations Cup in association football (soccer), in Saint-Denis, France; the occasion is overshadowed, however, by the death the previous week of Cameroon's Marc-Vivien Foe during a semifinal game against Colombia.

**30 Jun** It is reported that particle physicists in Japan researching mesons may have produced subatomic particles containing five quarks; such particles are theoretically possible but have up to now not been detected.

▸ The 50th anniversary of the iconic Corvette sports car is observed.

# Disasters

*Listed here are major disasters between July 2002 and June 2003. The list includes natural and nonmilitary mechanical disasters that claimed 15 or more lives and/or resulted in significant damage to property.*

## July 2002

**1 Jul** Near Lake Constance, Germany. A midair collision between a Boeing 757 cargo plane and a Russian airliner in Baden-Württemberg state on the German-Swiss border claims the lives of all 71 persons aboard the two aircraft.

**2 Jul** Chuuk state, Federated States of Micronesia. Tropical Storm Chata'an wreaks havoc in the tiny Pacific island nation; strong winds, rain, and landslides claim the lives of 47 persons.

**4 Jul** Bangui, Central African Republic. A cargo plane goes down in a residential area while attempting to land because of mechanical problems; 23 of the 25 persons aboard are killed, but no one on the ground appears to have been injured.

**7 Jul** Palembang, Indonesia. A fire, which was reportedly caused by an electrical short circuit, destroys a five-story karaoke bar, killing at least 46 persons; the bar lacked emergency exits and other safety features.

**July** Donbas region, Ukraine. Three separate mining disasters occur during a roughly three-week period. On 7 July in Donetsk, 35 miners die from smoke inhalation after a fire breaks out in their mine. On 21 July in the Dnepropetrovsk province, a methane-gas explosion claims the lives of 6 miners, and another 28 are missing. At another mine in Donetsk on 31 July, a gas explosion claims the lives of 20 miners.

**18 Jul** Lutoto, western Uganda. A collision between a runaway fuel truck and a passenger bus claims the lives of at least 60 persons.

**19 Jul** Henan province, China. A storm produces high winds and egg-size hailstones that batter the province; a number of buildings collapse, and power is temporarily cut off; 16 persons die and some 200 are injured.

**20 Jul** Lima, Peru. A blaze starts in an illegally operated disco after a bartender's fire-eating stunt goes awry; at least 30 persons die.

**21–22 Jul** Eastern South Africa. Snowstorms dump up to 1 m (3.3 ft) of snow on parts of Eastern Cape and KwaZulu/Natal provinces; thousands of homes and other buildings are damaged and 22 persons die.

**23 Jul** Mhondoro, Zimbabwe. A shaft caves in at an abandoned gold mine, killing at least 15 persons who are mining illegally at the site.

**27 Jul** Lviv, Ukraine. A fighter jet plane crashes into a crowd of spectators during an air show; 76 persons die and more than 100 are injured; the jet was performing a low-altitude stunt when one of its wings hit the runway, causing the jet to cartwheel into the crowd.

**28 Jul** Moscow, Russia. Shortly after takeoff from Sheremetyevo Airport, a cargo plane crashes in a forest, killing 15 persons.

## August 2002

**6 Aug** Near Zinapecuaro, Mexico. A bus crashes into a bridge after its brakes fail; 33 persons die.

**7 Aug** Dasht, Tajikistan. A mud slide destroys some 56 homes in the village located in the Gorno-Badakhshan region; at least 20 persons die.

**11 Aug** Uttaranchal state, India. Flash floods and mud slides wreak havoc in several villages as homes are swept away after heavy monsoonal rains; at least 43 persons perish.

**18 Aug** Yantikovo, Russia. Brake failure causes the driver of a bus to lose control of the vehicle; 24 persons die as the bus plummets into a ravine near the central Russian village.

**22 Aug** Near Pokhara, Nepal. A small plane flying in bad weather slams into a mountain about 200 km

(125 mi) west of Kathmandu; the 15 foreign tourists and 3 Nepalese crew members aboard are killed.

**22 Aug** Western Nepal. A bus, while attempting to pass another vehicle, runs off the road and falls into the Trishuli River; 45 persons are believed to be dead.

**31 Aug–1 Sep** Korea. The strongest storm to hit the peninsula in 40 years claims the lives of at least 113 persons in South Korea. Typhoon Rusa, moving across the southern part of the peninsula, brings extensive flooding and winds exceeding 200 km/hr (125 mph).

# September 2002

**9 Sep** Near Rafiganj, Bihar state, India. The Rajdhani Express train, while en route from Kolkata (Calcutta) to New Delhi, derails on a bridge and plunges into the rain-swollen Dhavi River; at least 106 persons die. There is some speculation that sabotage was involved, but local officials cite problems with the maintenance of the bridge.

**12 Sep** El Porvenir, Guatemala. A landslide that occurs following heavy rains buries the mountain village some 120 km (75 mi) south of Guatemala City; 26 persons are killed and 7 are missing.

**15 Sep** Mediterranean Sea, off the coast of Sicily. A Tunisian-registered fishing boat carrying some 130 illegal immigrants from Liberia to Italy capsizes in a storm and sinks; at least 36 persons die.

**15 Sep** Near Catamarca, Argentina. A bus loses its brakes on a mountain road and plunges into a gorge; at least 50 persons are killed and 25 injured.

**20 Sep** North Ossetia, Russia. An immense glacier-borne landslide occurs in the Caucasus Mountains; 16 deaths are confirmed, but according to officials 132 are missing, including Russian action-film star Sergey Bodrov, Jr., who was making a movie in the area.

**24 Sep** Fangzhen, China. A guardrail in an unlighted stairwell at a middle school collapses as students are leaving for the day; 21 students die.

**26 Sep** Off the coast of The Gambia. In what is described as Africa's deadliest disaster at sea, a Senegalese ferry carrying more than twice its 550-passenger capacity capsizes in stormy weather on the Atlantic Ocean; an estimated 1,200 persons die, according to the head of an official inquiry into the incident.

**28 Sep** Lucknow, India. A stampede occurs at a railway station where thousands of people are in the process of returning home after having attended a political rally; at least 16 persons are killed and 44 are injured.

# October 2002

**1 Oct** Near Panaji, India. A midair collision between navy transport planes during an air show in Goa state kills all 12 persons aboard both planes and 5 persons on the ground.

**2 Oct** Northern Syria. A landslide causes several buildings to collapse; at least 20 persons are killed and 30 are injured.

**22 Oct** Caspian Sea. An Azerbaijani-owned Caspian Sea ferry en route from Aqtau, Kazakhstan, to Azerbaijan's capital, Baku, capsizes and sinks in stormy seas hours after sending a distress signal; of the 51 persons aboard, only 9 are rescued, and one of the survivors later dies in a hospital.

**26–27 Oct** Northern Europe. A powerful storm rages, killing 7 in Great Britain, 6 in France, at least 10 in Germany, 5 in Belgium, 4 in The Netherlands, and 1 in Denmark.

**29 Oct** Ho Chi Minh City, Vietnam. Fire engulfs a six-story office building, killing more than 100 persons; the fire is reported to have started in the kitchen of a nightclub on the building's second floor.

**29 Oct** Nanning, Guangxi province, China. A fire at a coal mine claims the lives of 30 miners.

**29 Oct** Montecristo, Colombia. A mud slide brought on by heavy rains sweeps through the northern village in the San Lucas Mountains; 6 deaths are confirmed, and at least 60 persons are missing and feared dead.

**31 Oct** Molise region, central Italy. A severe earthquake shakes the mountainous region northeast of Naples; in the town of San Giuliano di Puglia, 26 children and a teacher are killed when their school collapses. Some 11,000 in surrounding areas are left homeless.

# November 2002

**1 Nov** El Jadida, Morocco. An electrical short circuit apparently is the cause of a blaze at an overcrowded prison; at least 49 inmates are killed, most by smoke inhalation or in the stampede of prisoners attempting to escape the blaze.

**3 Nov** Near Gilgit, Jammu and Kashmir. A magnitude-4.5 earthquake rocks several mountain villages in the Pakistan-administered areas, killing at least 17 persons, injuring 65, and leaving some 1,600 families homeless.

**6 Nov** Luxembourg. A twin-engine passenger plane crashes in thick fog near Luxembourg's international airport, killing 18 of the 22 persons aboard the craft.

**9–11 Nov** United States. A storm front that produces nearly 90 tornadoes cuts a broad swath of destruction extending from the Gulf of Mexico to the Great Lakes. The highest death toll is in Tennessee, where 17 persons are killed; 12 persons die in Alabama, 5 in Ohio, and 1 each in Mississippi and Pennsylvania. More than 200 persons are injured, and tens of thousands of people are left without power.

**11 Nov** Near Manila, Philippines. A twin-engine commuter plane goes down in Manila Bay shortly after takeoff, killing 19 of the 34 persons aboard; engine failure is the suspected cause of the crash.

**13 Nov** Bay of Bengal. A cyclone strikes, and scores of fishing boats sink off the coast of West Bengal state, India, during the storm; 10 deaths are confirmed, and at least 150 other fishermen are missing and feared dead.

**17–25 Nov** Central Morocco. Unusually heavy rain triggers flash floods that claim the lives of at least 25 persons.

**20 Nov** Near Jabalpur, India. A bus overturns, and two gasoline-filled containers on board ignite a fire; 30 persons are killed and 26 are injured.

**24 Nov** Quezon province, Philippines. While rounding a sharp downhill curve, a bus crashes through a railing and plunges into a ravine; at least 33 persons perish.

**30 Nov** Caracas, Venezuela. Flames engulf a crowded nightclub in the basement of a downtown hotel; at least 50 persons perish, according to official figures.

# December 2002

**1 Dec** Mediterranean Sea. A fishing trawler with more than 100 illegal immigrants bound for Italy on board sinks in bad weather off the coast of Libya; 11 deaths are confirmed, and at least 50 are missing and feared dead.

**1 Dec** Gaibandha, Bangladesh. A crowd of more than 10,000 people stampedes as guards open the gates of a mill where clothes donated by a charitable businessman are to be distributed; at least 30 persons die.

**2 Dec** Chiapas state, Mexico. A bus crashes on a mountain road near San Cristóbal de las Casas; 21 persons die.

**4–5 Dec** The Carolinas, eastern US. In one of the worst ice storms to strike the area, widespread power outages leave some 1.8 million customers without electricity; the storm, which brings heavy snow as well as ice to some areas, is blamed for at least 22 deaths.

**6 Dec** Near Taonan, Jilin province, China. A fire at the Wanbao coal mine kills at least 25 miners.

**8–9 Dec** Angra dos Reis, Brazil. Mud slides brought on by torrential rains bury numerous hillside houses; at least 34 persons are dead and 40 are missing.

**14 Dec** Mofa River, Liberia. An overcrowded ferryboat capsizes near the coastal city of Robertsport in northwestern Liberia; more than 100 persons are feared drowned.

**mid-Dec–late Jan** South Asia. A winter that brings record cold temperatures to India, Bangladesh, and Nepal leaves more than 1,900 people dead.

**18 Dec** Pará River, Brazil. A ferryboat carrying more than twice its 150-passenger capacity capsizes near the town of Barcarena; at least 80 persons are missing and feared drowned.

**23 Dec** Near Isfahan, Iran. A Ukrainian passenger plane en route from Kharkiv to Isfahan crashes while preparing to land; all 46 persons aboard the plane—mostly Ukrainian and Russian aerospace scientists who were traveling to Iran to test a new airplane—are killed.

**29 Dec** Gorgan, Iran. A fire at a prison in the northern Iranian town claims the lives of at least 27 inmates and injures some 50 others; an electrical fault reportedly caused the fire.

**31 Dec** Veracruz, Mexico. An explosion of illegal fireworks and resulting fire engulfs an outdoor market and nearby buildings and cars; at least 28 persons die.

**31 Dec** Indian Ocean. An overloaded ferryboat capsizes off the coast of Tanzania, reportedly during a storm; up to 40 persons are missing and feared dead.

# January 2003

**early–late Jan** Madagascar. Weeks of unusually heavy rains leave 2,218 people homeless and at least 13 dead, mostly in Antananarivo and Fianarantsoa provinces.

**3 Jan** Indian Ocean, off Tanzania. A boat capsizes shortly after leaving port; some 40 passengers are drowned.

**3 Jan** Near Parli, India. An express passenger train hits a stationary freight train that should not have been on the passenger track; 18 passengers are killed.

**5 Jan** Lake Victoria, Tanzania. A boat capsizes in strong winds; although 4 people are rescued, it is feared that more than 30 people have lost their lives.

**6 Jan** Zacatecas state, Mexico. A bus goes off a mountain road when its brakes fail as it is trying to make a sharp bend and plunges into the valley below, leaving at least 18 of its passengers dead.

**8 Jan** Diyarbakir, Turkey. A Turkish Airlines plane crashes as it is attempting to land in heavy fog at the municipal airport; 5 people survive, but 75 are killed.

**8 Jan** Charlotte NC. A commuter plane, a Beech 1900 twin-engine turboprop operated by US Airways Express, crashes into a hangar on takeoff, killing 21 passengers and crew members; the cause of the crash is believed to be excessive weight, and the Federal Aviation Administration responds by changing the rules on estimation of weight for such flights.

**9 Jan** Near Chachapoyas, Peru. A Trans Peru Fokker F-28 crashes in a jungle in the Andes Mountains, killing all 46 people aboard; the wreckage of the plane is not found until January 11.

**11 Jan** Harbin, Heilongjiang province, China. A predawn explosion in the Boaxing coal mine kills 34 miners; on the previous day 8 miners were killed in a blast in a coal mine at Baishan, in Jilin province.

**16 Jan** Minas Gerais state, Brazil. Mud slides occasioned by heavy rains kill at least 14 people, most of them in Belo Horizonte.

**18 Jan** Near Cochabamba, Bolivia. A bus crashes into a hill in heavy rainfall; at least 20 people are killed.

**20 Jan** Jixi, Heilongjiang province, China. A gas explosion blasts through Lishu Coal Mine No. 7, killing 16 of the 97 miners at work at the time.

**21 Jan** Colima state, Mexico. An earthquake of at least magnitude 7.6 strikes, collapsing scores of buildings and killing at least 29 people.

**21 Jan** Eastern Egypt. A tourist bus traveling between resorts overturns, killing at least 20 passengers.

**24 Jan** Slawi, Java, Indonesia. A bus goes out of control, possibly after bursting a tire; it runs into oil drums and houses and erupts in flames; at least 17 people are killed in the incident.

**26 Jan** Ebomey, Cameroon. A bus veers into oncoming traffic and crashes into a second bus; three cars then collide with the wrecked buses; a total of more than 70 people die in the incident, which is blamed on recklessness and driving at excessive speed.

**26 Jan** Near Devpur, Nepal. A bus plunges off the road, killing at least 20 people and injuring another 25.

**28 Jan** Near Uluberia, India. A tourist bus runs head-on into a truck carrying paint; at least 40 passengers are burned to death.

**31 Jan** Kandahar, Afghanistan. An antitank mine blows up a minibus crossing a bridge, killing at least 16 Afghanis, including several women and children; it is not certain whether the bus or a military vehicle was the target.

# February 2003

**1 Feb** Near Dete, Zimbabwe. A passenger train traveling in the predawn hours collides with a freight train carrying flammable substances; at least 46 people lose their lives.

**2 Feb** Lagos, Nigeria. An explosion destroys a bank and the apartment complex above it in the commercial center, killing at least 40 people and setting off fighting and looting; authorities believe the disaster to be the result of an accident.

**2 Feb** Harbin, China. A fire breaks out at a hotel during celebrations of the Chinese New Year, leaving 33 people dead.

**2 Feb** Bandundu province, Dem. Rep. of the Congo. A tornado roars through the province in the area of the town of Yumbi, leaving 17 people dead and injuring hundreds more as well as leaving crops destroyed.

**4 Feb** Sialkot, Pakistan. Shipping containers packed with fireworks explode at a depot next to a school, killing at least 17 people; the containers had been labeled as containing plastic toys.

**7 Feb** Bogotá, Colombia. A bomb goes off in a fashionable nightclub; at least 32 people are killed in the blast and the ensuing fire.

**11 Feb** Mecca, Saudi Arabia. During the "stoning of the devil," the final ritual of the five-day hajj, 14 people are accidentally trampled to death on one day and 21 people suffer the same fate on the succeeding day.

**mid-Feb** Eastern seaboard of the US. A record-breaking snowstorm covers the area with some 0.6 m (2 ft) of snow; 59 people in several states are killed.

**mid-Feb** Northern Mozambique. Heavy flooding in Nampula province kills at least 47 people, destroys some 6,000 homes, and ruins an estimated 13,600 acres of crops.

**16 Feb** Masnaa, Lebanon. The brakes fail on a Syrian military truck approaching a border crossing; the truck hits the immigration office and overturns onto several cars, catching fire; at least 17 people are killed.

**17 Feb** Southern Pakistan, Kashmir, Afghanistan. In Pakistan heavy rains cause flooding and the collapse of several houses and a bridge, from which a bus is swept away; at least 16 people are killed, while in Kashmir snowstorms kill at least 8 more people; the final death toll from the storms exceeds 86 people.

**17 Feb** Chicago. At a crowded nightclub on the second floor of a restaurant, pepper spray is used by a security guard in a misguided effort to stop a fight, causing panic among the 1,500 patrons, who attempt to flee; the ensuing stampede leaves 21 people dead.

**18 Feb** Taegu, South Korea. A man attempting to set himself on fire with paint thinner on a rush-hour subway train ignites both the train on which he is riding and a second train that pulls in next to the burning train and briefly opens its doors; most of the estimated 198 people who die are on the second train.

**19 Feb** Near Shahdad, Iran. An Ilyushin airliner transporting Revolutionary Guards from Zahedon to Kerman crashes, killing all 302 aboard, in the worst air disaster ever to occur in Iran.

**20 Feb** Near Kohat, Pakistan. Minutes before it was to land, a Fokker-27 aircraft carrying the head of Pakistan's air force, Mushaf Ali Mir, and 16 others crashes into the low hills outside the town; all aboard perish.

**20 Feb** West Warwick RI. Pyrotechnics used by the hard-rock band Great White ignite soundproofing foam on the stage of the Station, a nightclub, and the club goes up in flames; some 100 people, including a musician in the band, perish.

**24 Feb** China. At least 49 miners die in three separate incidents: some 35 are killed in a gas explosion at the Muchonggou coal mine in Liupanshui, Guizhou province, the same mine where 162 miners died in 2001; 6 miners are killed in an explosion in a mine in Jixi, Heilongjiang province; and 14 miners are killed when a cable lowering them into a mine snaps in Shanxi province.

**24 Feb** Xinjiang region, China. An earthquake measured at 6.8 strikes the region, leaving 268 people dead and more than 4,000 injured in the worst earthquake in 50 years in the area; tens of thousands of buildings are destroyed as well.

# March 2003

**1 Mar** Niger River, Nigeria. A boat carrying about 100 people strikes a rock and sinks; some 80 people are believed drowned.

**1 Mar** Chiayi county, Taiwan. The brakes of a train descending Alishan mountain fail, and the train derails, crashing into a ravine; 17 people are killed and 173 injured.

**6 Mar** Near Tamanrasset, Algeria. In what is believed to be the first accident in the history of Algeria's national airline, Air Algerie Flight 6239 crashes in the Sahara shortly after takeoff, killing 102 people of the 103 aboard.

**7 Mar** Kashmir. Avalanches caused by heavy snow kill at least 17 people in the area of the cease-fire line between the India- and Pakistan-controlled portions of the disputed region.

**9 Mar** Near Kaplice, Czech Rep. A bus carrying tourists home from a vacation in Austria goes off the road and falls some 8 m (25 ft), killing at least 19 passengers.

**12 Mar** The Sudan. A bus carrying members of the Al-Merreikh association football (soccer) team back from a match crashes, killing 25 people, among them the team's coach.

**17 Mar** Yunnan province, China. A truck illegally carrying passengers goes off a mountain road, falling into a gorge; at least 21 of the more than 40 people in the truck are killed.

**22 Mar** Lake Tanganyika, Dem. Rep. of the Congo. A ferry traveling between the towns of Kalemie and Uvira sinks, drowning at least 111 people; 41 are rescued.

**23 Mar** Shanxi province, China. A powerful gas explosion kills at least 64 of the 87 miners working in the Mengnanzhuang coal mine, with 8 others missing and likely dead.

**24 Mar** Xiaoyi, Shanxi province, China. A gas explosion kills at least 50, and possibly as many as 72, people in the Mengnanzhuang coal mine.

**27 Mar** Southeastern Kyrgyzstan. A double-decker

bus headed for China is set upon by bandits, who kill the 21 passengers and set the bus on fire; investigators at first believe the bus was driven over a cliff.

**30 Mar** Liaoning province, China. At least 16 coal miners are killed, with 10 others missing, after an explosion in the Mengjiagou coal mine; there were more than 40 workers in the mine at the time of the incident.

**31 Mar** Chima, Larecaja province, Bolivia. A gold-mining town is engulfed by a huge mud slide triggered by days of heavy rain; at least 14 people are killed and hundreds are missing.

## April 2003

**1 Apr** Flores Island, Indonesia. Flash floods and mud slides wash away 17 houses and damage hundreds of others; at least 29 people lose their lives.

**3 Apr** Narmada River, Gujarat state, India. A passenger ship carrying people to a religious ceremony where the river meets the sea capsizes in strong winds; 16 bodies are recovered.

**4 Apr** Surma River, Bangladesh. A boat carrying seasonal quarry workers and their families collides with a cargo ship in the dark and sinks, killing more than 70 passengers, most of them women and children.

**5 Apr** Shandong province, China. A fire breaks out during the night shift at a food-processing plant; at least 21 of the 500 employees die, and the building collapses.

**7 Apr** Sydybal, Yakutia, Russia. Fire breaks out in the cloakroom of a wooden schoolhouse, blocking the only exit; 22 children die.

**10 Apr** Makhachkala, Dagestan, Russia. A school for deaf boys goes up in flames, killing at least 28 sleeping students and injuring more than 100; teachers had to wake the children, as they were unable to hear the alarms.

**11 Apr** Thailand. In the first three days of the Songkran festival, which is Thailand's biggest public holiday, more than 359 people die in traffic accidents; many of the accidents are due to drunken driving.

**12 Apr** Nakchinee River, Bangladesh. A ferry is caught in a storm and sinks, killing at least 22 people, with a further 100 unaccounted for.

**13 Apr** Near Larissa, Greece. A tour bus collides with a truck carrying a load of plywood on a narrow stretch of mountainous road; 21 schoolchildren are killed.

**15 Apr** Cayo Arena, Dominican Republic. A boat carrying more than 150 Haitians capsizes near the northwest coast, with six passengers reported dead and dozens missing.

**19 Apr** Off Cabo Frio, Brazil. A tourist schooner returning from a day trip to Paris Island is swamped by a large wave shortly after resuming its journey following a break for passengers to swim and snorkel; it overturns and at least 15 passengers die.

**20 Apr** Kurbu-Tash, Kyrgyzstan. A mud slide destroys the town in the Uzgen district, killing at least 38 residents; the site is declared a common grave, as recovery of the victims is essentially impossible.

**21 Apr** Bangladesh. An overloaded ferry sinks in a storm in the Buriganga River, near Dhaka, killing at least 140 passengers; later, another ferry, carrying a bridal party, also goes down in a storm, in the Meghna River in Kishoreganj district.

**22 Apr** Assam, India. Thunderstorms leave at least 33 people dead and thousands more homeless; most of the damage is concentrated in the Dhubri district.

**23 Apr** Chichicaste, Guatemala. An eroded mountain slides downhill, burying a village and killing 23 people.

**26 Apr** Jammu and Kashmir, India. A boat carrying children capsizes while crossing a stream; 20 children are lost.

**late Apr–early May** Kenya. Nearly two weeks of rain and torrential storms destroy water-purification systems, force thousands of people to evacuate their homes, and leave at least 30 people dead.

## May 2003

**early May** Southern Ethiopia. Catastrophic flooding in the drought-stricken region destroys health centers and schools and forces 96,000 people to flee to higher ground.

**early–mid May** Horn of Africa. Days of heavy rain create havoc in several African countries: in Ethiopia 117 people are killed and some 100,000 more left homeless; in Kenya 47 die and 60,000 are displaced; and thousands more are displaced in Somalia.

**1 May** Bingol, Turkey. An earthquake measuring 6.4 strikes in the predawn hours, causing a boarding school to collapse and killing 167 people.

**1 May** Near Bethlehem, South Africa. A bus carrying trade-union members to a May Day rally falls into a reservoir after the driver becomes confused and drives onto a track leading to a dam; some 80 people are believed killed.

**2 May** Bac Ninh, Vietnam. An explosion on a bus as it is stopping at a market to pick up passengers kills at least 19 people and seriously wounds a further 19; the cause is believed to be the ignition of explosives being carried on the bus.

**2 May** Yellow Sea, China. China reports a "recent" submarine accident involving a diesel-powered submarine that killed all 70 aboard; the timing and nature of the accident are not disclosed.

**4–12 May** US Midwest and South. More than 300 tornadoes and other severe storms rake through several states, destroying entire towns, damaging hundreds of homes, and killing 42 people.

**4 May** Noabadi, Bangladesh. Tropical storms cause a landslide that buries a village, killing at least 23 people; 31 people have been killed and more than 100 injured in the storms.

**4 May** Cotonou, Benin. At a concert by the popular Congolese musician Kofi Olomide in Friendship Stadium, 15 people are crushed to death when the capacity crowd surges forward to get closer to the stage.

**8 May** Dem. Rep. of the Congo. On an Ilyushin-76 cargo plane crammed with passengers flying from

Kinshasa to Lubumbashi, a door opens and dozens of people fall out to their deaths; the death toll is later estimated to be about 160.

**8 May** Siofok, Hungary. In one of Hungary's worst-ever accidents, an express train runs into a double-decker bus on the tracks, killing 33 elderly German tourists.

**9 May** Near Shorkot, Pakistan. A passenger bus and an oil tanker crash in a head-on collision after the bus driver loses control of his vehicle; at least 24 people perish.

**13 May** Hefei, Anhui province, China. An underground gas explosion in the Luling coal mine kills at least 81 miners with 5 others missing.

**13 May** Wanshui, Hunan province, China. Flash floods and mud slides wash away a number of carpet factories and bury the living quarters of coal miners; at least 12 are killed and more than 20 cannot be found.

**14 May** Victoria TX. At a truck stop, a container truck is discovered loaded with would-be undocumented immigrants, most from Mexico; at least 18 of them have suffocated to death owing to excessively high heat.

**15 May** Ludhiana, Punjab state, India. Fire sweeps through three cars of a Mumbai (Bombay)–Amritsar train that had pulled out of the station just minutes previously; the fire, which began in a restroom on one of the cars, leaves some 39 people dead and 20 injured.

**15 May** Mecca, Saudi Arabia. A fire breaks out in a building housing 270 pilgrims making the hajj; at least 14 people die of smoke inhalation and 43 are injured.

**mid-May–10 Jun** South Asia. A monthlong heat wave and drought across India that ends only with the unusually late arrival of the monsoon creates an acute shortage of drinking water in Karnataka state and leaves 1,522 people dead, 1,040 of them in Andhra Pradesh; in addition, more than 60 people in Bangladesh and 40 people in Pakistan have succumbed.

**17 May** Southern Sri Lanka. After several days of heavy rain, floods and landslides kill some 300 people, with a further 500 unaccounted for.

**17 May** Near Lyon, France. A bus carrying German tourists to Spain apparently skids on wet pavement and leaves the road, falling down an embankment; at least 28 passengers are killed.

**19 May** Quang Nam province, Vietnam. A ferry designed to carry 20 people but loaded with 40 passengers, most of them children returning home from school, founders in rough waters; 18 children perish.

**21 May** Thenia, Algeria. A magnitude-6.8 earthquake shakes a densely populated area, killing more than 1,600 people and injuring close to 2,500; the capital, Algiers, sustains particularly heavy damage.

**21 May** Sri Lanka. Flash floods lead to the demise of 256 people.

**25 May** Philippines. Two passenger ferries collide in rough waters off the coast of Corregidor and Limbones islands, and at least 28 people drown in the accident; 203 are rescued.

**26 May** Macka, near Trabzon, Turkey. An airplane carrying 62 Spanish peacekeepers home from a four-month tour of duty in Afghanistan crashes into a mountain while attempting to land in bad weather for refueling, killing all 75 aboard.

**27 May** Luzon, Philippines. Tropical Storm Linfa brings torrential rains, relieving a drought but also causing hundreds of thousands of dollars of damage and killing some 25 people, with 12 people reported missing.

# June 2003

**3 Jun** Chinchilla, Spain. On a stretch of single-track rail in Albacete province, a passenger train meets a freight train in a head-on collision; at least 19 people are killed.

**7 Jun** Near Erzincan, Turkey. A bus crashes into a tunnel wall, killing 27 passengers and injuring 33 more; it is suspected that the driver fell asleep.

**16 Jun** Off Lampedusa, Italy. A boat loaded with illegal immigrants sinks, killing as many as 70 people.

**16 Jun** Andhra Pradesh, India. In Karimnagar district, water bursts through the wall of a coal mine, trapping miners underground; the bodies of 17 men are found after two days are spent pumping water out of the mine.

**16 Jun** Near Sragen, Java, Indonesia. A train hits a bus carrying a wedding party and drags it for hundreds of meters; 15 of the 22 aboard the bus, including the bride and groom, are killed.

**19 Jun** Onicha Amiyi-Uhu, Nigeria. As villagers steal crude oil from a vandalized pipeline, a spark from a motorcycle ignites the fuel, causing an explosion; some 105 people are killed.

**20 Jun** Off the coast of Tunisia. A boat carrying illegal immigrants and believed to have started from Libya bound for Italy sinks; it is feared that up to 190 people may have drowned.

**22 Jun** Vaibhyavadi, India. A passenger train traveling from Karwar to Mumbai (Bombay) strikes a boulder left on the tracks after a landslide caused by monsoon rains; four of the cars derail and plunge into a river, killing 51 passengers.

**25 Jun** Madhya Pradesh state, India. A bus crossing a small bridge falls into the river below and is swept away; at least 40 people are missing.

**26 Jun** Southeastern Bangladesh. Unusually heavy pre-monsoon rains, amounting to as much as 120 mm (4.5 in) in 24 hours, cause flash flooding and landslides, fatally sweeping away or burying at least 31 people.

**30 Jun** Blida, Algeria. A Hercules C-130 military transport plane crashes into a row of houses shortly after takeoff; at least 17 people are killed and a further 20 injured.

# Personalities

## Celebrities & Newsmakers

These mini-biographies are intended to provide background information about people in the news. See also the Obituaries (below) for recently deceased persons as well as the presidential biographies and the Britannica lists elsewhere in the *Britannica Almanac*.

**Magdalena Abakanowicz** (20 Jun 1930, Falenty, Poland), Polish artist known for her innovative metal sculptures of human and animal figures, usually presented in groups.

**Claudio Abbado** (26 Jun 1933, Milan, Italy), Italian orchestra conductor; principal conductor and artistic director of the Berlin Philharmonic, 1990–91 through 2001–02 seasons.

**Mahmoud (Ridha) Abbas** (nom de guerre, Abu Mazen; 1935, Zefat, Palestine), Palestinian politician; secretary general of the PLO executive committee and cofounder of the Fatah movement; he was named the first prime minister of the Palestine Authority, March 2003.

**A.P.J. Abdul Kalam** (Avul Pakir Jainulabdeen Abdul Kalam; 15 Oct 1931, Rameswaram, Tamil Nadu state, British India), Indian aeronautical engineer; president of India from 25 Jul 2002.

**Crown Prince Abdullah** ('Abdallah ibn 'Abd al-'Aziz Al Saud; 1923, Riyadh, Saudi Arabia), heir to the Saudi Arabian throne and de facto ruler from 1995.

**King Abdullah II** (Abdallah ibn al-Hussein al-Hashimi; 30 Jan 1962, Amman, Jordan), king of Jordan from 1999.

**John (Philip) Abizaid** (1 Apr 1951, Coleville CA), American military officer (lieutenant general, US Army) who was named commander-in-chief of the US Central Command and supreme commander of occupation forces in Iraq as of 7 Jul 2003.

**Rabih Abou-Khalil** (Beirut, Lebanon), Lebanese-born German oud player and flutist, composer, and arranger who has integrated Arabic music with Western jazz and world music; his recordings have won five German Phono Academy Awards.

**Spencer Abraham** (12 Jun 1952, East Lansing MI), American government official; US secretary of energy from January 2001.

**Roman (Arkadyevich) Abramovich** (24 Oct 1966, Saratov, Russian SFSR, USSR [now Russia]), Russian businessman, reportedly the second richest man in Russia in 2003; he is the owner of the Sib-Neft petroleum company and part owner of Russian Aluminum Co.; he is also the governor of Chukhotka province. In 2003 he purchased the Chelsea Football Club in London.

**Nasr Hamid Abu Zayd** (7 Oct 1943, Tanta, Egypt), Egyptian scholar and religious reformer.

**Salvatore Accardo** (26 Sep 1941, Turin, Italy), Italian violinist and conductor.

**Chinua Achebe** (Albert Chinualumogu Achebe; 16 Nov 1930, Ogidi, Nigeria), Nigerian novelist acclaimed for his unsentimental depictions of the social and psychological disorientation accompanying the imposition of Western customs and values upon traditional African society.

**Josef ("Joe") Ackermann** (7 Feb 1948, Mels, Sankt Gallen, Switzerland), Swiss corporate executive; CEO of Deutsche Bank AG from 1997.

**Eddie Fenech Adami** (7 Feb 1934, Birkirkara, Malta), Maltese politician and prime minister of Malta, 1987–96, and again from 1998.

**Bryan (Guy) Adams** (5 Nov 1959, Kingston, ON, Canada), Canadian rock musician.

**Gerry Adams** (Gerard Adams; 6 Oct 1948, Belfast, Northern Ireland), Northern Irish resistance leader; president of Sinn Féin, the political wing of the Irish Republican Army.

**John Coolidge Adams** (15 Feb 1947, Worcester MA), American composer who works in a wide range of genres and is noted for the operas *Nixon in China* (1987) and *The Death of Klinghoffer* (1991); he won the 2003 Pulitzer Prize for Music for *On the Transmigration of Souls,* written to commemorate the 11 Sep 2001 terrorist attacks.

**Scott Adams** (8 Jun 1957, Windham NY), American cartoonist, creator of *Dilbert.*

**Thomas Adès** (27 Jun 1971, London, England), English composer, pianist, and conductor; his compositions are known for their wit and wide-ranging styles.

**Trace Adkins** (13 Jan 1962, Sarepta LA), American country singer whose 1996 debut album *Dreamin' Out Loud* was an immediate hit and led to his winning the Academy of Country Music Top New Male Vocalist for 1996.

**Ben Affleck** (Benjamin Geza Affleck; 15 Aug 1972, Berkeley CA), American actor, director, and writer known for commercially successful films such as *Good Will Hunting* (1997).

**Isaias Afwerki** (2 Feb 1946, Asmara, Ethiopia [now in Eritrea]), Eritrean independence leader, secretary-general of the Provisional Government and first president of Eritrea (from 1993).

**Andre (Kirk) Agassi** (29 Apr 1970, Las Vegas NV), American tennis player who won Wimbledon (1992), the US Open (1994, 1999), the Australian Open (1995, 2000, 2001, 2003), the French Open (1999), and an Olympic gold medal (1996).

**Mehmet Ali Agca** (9 Jan 1958, Guzelyurt, Turkey), Turkish assassin; in 2003 he was serving time in jail in Turkey for a murder committed before his attempt to assassinate Pope John Paul II in 1981.

**Umberto Agnelli** (1 Nov 1934, Lausanne, Switzerland), Italian automotive executive who took over the family company, Fiat SpA, after the death of his older brother, Gianni Agnelli, in January 2003.

**Christina (Maria) Aguilera** (18 Dec 1980, Staten Island NY), American pop singer who won the Grammy for best new artist in 1999; the adult content of her 2002 album *Stripped* marked a change from her former teen-oriented material; in 2003 she was selected to represent the fashion house Versace.

**Bertie Ahern** (Bartholomew Patrick Ahern; 12 Sep 1951, Dublin, Ireland), Irish politician; prime minister (*taoiseach*) of Ireland from 1997.

**Iajuddin Ahmed** (1 Feb 1931, Nayagaon, Bengal state, British India [now in Bangladesh]), Bangladeshi scientist and educator; president of Bangladesh from 6 Sep 2002.

**Martti Ahtisaari** (23 Jun 1937, Viipuri, Finland [now Vyborg, Russia]), Finnish statesman and diplomat; president of Finland, 1994–2000.

**Askar Akayev** (10 Nov 1944, Kyzyl-Bairak, Kirghiz SSR, USSR [now Kyrgyzstan]), Kyrgyz politician; president of Kyrgyzstan from 1990.

**Emperor Akihito** (original name Tsugu Akihito; era name Heisei; 23 Dec 1933, Tokyo, Japan), emperor of Japan from 1989.

**Akil Akilov** (1944, Tajikistan?), Tajik politician; prime minister of Tajikistan from 1999.

**Vasily Pavlovich Aksyonov** (20 Aug 1932, Kazan, Tatar ASSR, USSR [now in Tatarstan, Russia]), Russian novelist and short-story writer, one of the leading literary spokesmen for the generation of Soviets who reached maturity after World War II.

**Roberto Alagna** (7 Jun 1963, Clichy-sur-Bois, France), French operatic tenor, mostly self-taught, who has been hailed as the first of the new generation of lyric tenors; he is especially known for his appearances with his wife, soprano Angela Gheorghiu.

**Azzedine Alaïa** (1940, Tunis, Tunisia), Tunisian-born French fashion designer known for using unusual fabrics to create body-hugging dresses.

**Edward Albee** (12 Mar 1928, Washington DC), American dramatist and three-time Pulitzer Prize winner; his best-known works include *The Zoo Story* (1959) and *Who's Afraid of Virginia Woolf?* (1962).

**Prince Albert** (Albert Alexandre Louis Pierre; 14 Mar 1958, Monaco), heir to the throne of Monaco.

**Albert II** (Albert Félix Humbert Théodore Christian Eugène Marie of Saxe-Coburg-Gotha; 6 Jun 1934, Brussels, Belgium), king of Belgium from 1993.

**Bruce (Michael) Alberts** (14 Apr 1938, Chicago IL), American molecular biologist; president of the US National Academy of Sciences from 1993.

**Alan Alda** (Alphonso Joseph D'Abruzzo; 28 Jan 1936, New York NY), American film and TV actor, best known for playing Hawkeye Pierce in the TV version of *M*A*S*H.*

**Vagit Yusufovich Alekperov** (1 Sep 1950, Baku, Azerbaijani SSR, USSR [now Azerbaijan]), Russian businessman, one of the "seven oligarchs" who allegedly rule Russia; founder and president since 1991 of Lukoil petroleum company.

**Jason Alexander** (Jay Scott Greenspan; 23 Sep 1959, Newark NJ), American film, TV, and theater actor, best known for playing George on *Seinfeld.*

**Princess Alexandra** (25 Dec 1936, London, England), British royal.

**Sherman J. Alexie, Jr.** (7 Oct 1966, Wellpinit, Spokane Indian Reservation, Washington), American poet and novelist who writes of his Native American upbringing.

**Alexis II** (Aleksey Mikhaylovich Ridiger; 23 Feb 1929, Tallinn, Estonia), Russian religious leader; Orthodox Patriarch of Moscow and All Russia, the 15th primate of Russia, from 1990.

**Laila Ali** (30 Dec 1977, Los Angeles CA), American professional boxer; daughter of Muhammad Ali.

**Muhammad Ali** (Cassius Marcellus Clay, Jr., until 1964; 17 Jan 1942, Louisville KY), American boxer, the first to win the heavyweight championship three separate times. Ali's quick reflexes and defensive speed in the ring, combined with his engaging (sometimes outrageous) personality and his refusal on religious grounds to be inducted into the army made him a cultural icon during his 20-year career and long after his final retirement.

**Heydar Aliyev** (Geidar Ali Reza ogly Aliev; 10 May 1923, Nakhichevan, Khanate of Nakhichevan [now part of Azerbaijan]), Azerbaijani politician; first president of independent Azerbaijan (from 1993).

**Ilham Aliyev** (Ilham Geidar ogli Aliev; 24 Dec 1961, Baku, Azerbaijani SSR, USSR [now in Azerbaijan]), Azerbaijani politician and son of Pres. Heydar Aliyev; he was named prime minister of Azerbaijan on 4 Aug 2003.

**Mari Alkatiri** (26 Nov 1946, Dili, East Timor), Timorese politician; first prime minister of independent East Timor (from 20 May 2002).

**Paul G. Allan** (21 Jan 1953, Mercer Island WA), American businessman; cofounder of Microsoft Corp. (1975) and founder and CEO of Vulcan Ventures (1986).

**Thomas (Boaz) Allen** (10 Sep 1944, Seaham Harbour, Durham, England), British operatic baritone.

**Tim Allen** (Timothy Allen Dick; 13 Jun 1953, Denver CO), American TV and film actor and comedian best known as Tim "The Toolman" Taylor on TV's *Home Improvement.*

**Woody Allen** (Allen Stewart Konigsberg; 1 Dec 1935, Brooklyn NY), American filmmaker, actor, and comedian best known for absurdly comic but sympathetic works; he won Academy Awards for direction (*Annie Hall,* 1977) and best original screenplay (*Hannah and Her Sisters,* 1986).

**Isabel Allende** (2 Aug 1942, Lima, Peru), Chilean writer in the magic realist tradition who is considered one of the first successful women novelists in Latin America.

**Mose Allison** (Mose John Allison, Jr.; 11 Nov 1927, Tippo MS), American jazz pianist, singer, and composer.

**Pedro Almodóvar** (24 Sep 1949, Calzada de Calatrava, Spain), Spanish film director specializing in film noir; his first success was *Women on the Verge of a Nervous Breakdown* (1988).

**Lincoln Almond** (16 Jun 1936, Central Falls RI), American Republican politician; governor of Rhode Island, 1995–2003.

**Marin Alsop** (1957?, New York NY), American conductor, the first woman to lead a major British orchestra when she was appointed principal conductor of the Bournemouth Symphony Orchestra from the 2002–03 season.

**Robert Altman** (20 Feb 1925, Kansas City MO), American filmmaker noted for his unconventional and independent style.

**Julia Alvarez** (27 Mar 1950, New York NY), American poet and novelist who grew up in the Dominican Republic and who wrote about her experiences in novels such as *How the García Girls Lost Their Accents* (1991) and In the *Time of the Butterflies* (1994); she has also published several collections of poetry and works for children.

**Christiane Amanpour** (1958, London, England), American TV news reporter.

**Lauren Ambrose** (Lauren Anne D'Ambruoso; 16 Nov 1978, New Haven CT), American TV actor starring as Claire Fisher on HBO's series *Six Feet Under.*

**Aldrich (Hazen) Ames** (26 Jun 1941, River Falls WI), American CIA employee who, together with his Colombian-born wife, Rosario, was convicted of selling intelligence to the USSR beginning in 1985; he was arrested and imprisoned for life in 1994.

**Martin (Louis) Amis** (25 Aug 1949, Oxford, England), English satirist known for his virtuoso storytelling technique and his dark views of 20th-century English society.

**Tori Amos** (Myra Ellen Amos; 22 Aug 1963, Newton NC), American pop and rock singer and songwriter known for the heavy sexuality of her lyrics.

**Viswanathan Anand** ("Vishy"; 11 Dec 1969, Madras [now Chennai], Tamil Nadu state, British India), Indian chess grand master who won the FIDE world championship in 2000.

**Gillian Anderson** (9 Aug 1968, Chicago IL), American TV and film actress, best known as Agent Dana Scully on TV's *The X-Files,* for which role she won an Emmy Award in 1997.

**Pamela (Denise) Anderson** (1 Jul 1967, Ladysmith, BC, Canada), Canadian-born model and actress who has appeared nine times on the cover of *Playboy* magazine.

**Reid Anderson** (New Westminster, BC, Canada), Canadian dancer, choreographer, and director who danced for 17 years with the Stuttgart Ballet under its founder, John Cranko, and later served as artistic director of the National Ballet of Canada (1989–96) and of the Stuttgart Ballet (from 1996).

**Rocky Anderson** (1951, Logan UT), American Democratic politician; mayor of Salt Lake City UT from 2000.

**Wes Anderson** (1 May 1969, Houston TX), American film director whose successes include *Rushmore* (1998) and *The Royal Tenenbaums* (2001).

**Piotr Anderszewski** (4 Apr 1969, Warsaw, Poland), Polish pianist known especially for his playing of Beethoven's *Diabelli Variations* and for his duo work with Russian violinist Victoria Mullova.

**Tadao Ando** (1941, Osaka, Japan), Japanese architect; winner of the 1995 Pritzker Prize.

**Marc Andreessen** (July 1971, New Lisbon WI), American computer innovator, cofounder (1994) of Mosaic Communications Corp., and developer of Netscape, a software system for browsing the Internet.

**Prince Andrew** (19 Feb 1960, Buckingham Palace, London, England), British royal; Duke of York; second son of Queen Elizabeth II and Prince Philip, Duke of Edinburgh.

**Jessica Andrews** (29 Dec 1983, Huntingdon TN), American country-and-western singer who won the Academy of Country Music Top New Female Vocalist award in 1999 and had her first No. 1 hit in 2001 with "Who I Am."

**Leif Ove Andsnes** (7 Apr 1970, Karmøy, Norway), Norwegian pianist who has won international acclaim for his concerts and his prize-winning recordings of works by Leos Janacek and Robert Schumann.

**Maya Angelou** (Marguerite Annie Johnson; 4 Apr 1928, St. Louis MO), American poet whose several volumes of autobiography explore the themes of economic, racial, and sexual oppression.

**Jennifer Aniston** (Jennifer Linn Anistassakis; 11 Feb 1969, Sherman Oaks CA), American TV and film actress who stars as Rachel Green on TV's *Friends* (from 1994).

**Paul Anka** (30 Jul 1941, Ottawa, ON, Canada), Canadian pop singer and composer.

**Kofi (Atta) Annan** (18 Apr 1938, Kumasi, Gold Coast [now Ghana]), Ghanaian diplomat; UN secretary-general from 1997; cowinner, with the UN, of the 2001 Nobel Peace Prize.

**Princess Anne** (15 Aug 1950, Clarence House, London, England), the Princess Royal; daughter of Queen Elizabeth II and Prince Philip, Duke of Edinburgh.

**Kenny D. Anthony** (8 Jan 1951, Saint Lucia), West Indian politician; prime minister of Saint Lucia from 1997.

**Marc Anthony** (Marco Antonio Muñiz; 16 Sep 1968, Spanish Harlem, New York NY), American salsa singer.

**Severino Antinori** (c. 1945, Rome, Italy), Italian gynecologist and specialist in human fertility; leader of a project to clone humans.

**Christina Applegate** (25 Nov 1971, Los Angeles CA), American TV and film actress, best known for playing Kelly on TV's *Married...with Children* (1987–97).

**(Maria) Corazon Aquino** (25 Jan 1933, Manila, Philippines), Philippine political leader and president of the Philippines, 1986–92.

**Yasir 'Arafat** (Muhammad 'Abd ar-Ra'uf al-Qudwah al-Husayni 'Arafat; 24? Aug 1929, Cairo, Egypt?), Palestinian statesman; president of the Palestinian Authority from 1996; cowinner of the 1994 Nobel Peace Prize.

**Vladislav Ardzinba** (1945, Abkhazia?, Georgian SSR, USSR [now Georgia]), Georgian politician; chairman of parliament of Georgia's secessionist republic of Abkhazia from 1990.

**Martha Argerich** (5 Jun 1941, Buenos Aires, Argentina), Argentine concert pianist.

**Jean-Bertrand Aristide** (15 Jul 1953, Port Salut, Haiti), Haitian politician; president of Haiti, 1991, 1993–94 (in exile), 1994–96, and again from 2001.

**Alan Arkin** (26 Mar 1934, New York NY), American wry, deadpan actor, whose breakthrough came in *The Russians Are Coming, The Russians Are Coming* (1966); he has recently starred in TV's *100 Centre Street* (from 2001).

**Giorgio Armani** (11 Jul 1934, Piacenza, Italy), Italian fashion designer whose signature style is relaxed yet luxurious ready-to-wear and elegant evening wear.

**Richard K. Armey** (7 Jul 1940, Cando ND), American politician and congressman; House majority leader.

**C. Michael Armstrong** (18 Oct 1938, Detroit MI), American corporate executive; CEO of AT&T, 1997–2002; head of AT&T Comcast Corp. from 2002.

**Garner Ted Armstrong** (9 Feb 1930, Portland OR), American radio and TV evangelist who rose in the Worldwide Church of God, founded by his father, Herbert W. Armstrong, before breaking with him in the 1970s and forming his own, less dogmatic group, the Church of God International and, after his expulsion from that body, the Intercontinental Church of God.

**Lance Armstrong** (18 Sep 1971, Plano TX), American cyclist; he won the Tour de France five years in succession (1999–2003) after recovering from cancer in the mid-1990s.

**Neil (Alden) Armstrong** (5 Aug 1930, Wapakoneta OH), American astronaut, the commander of the Apollo 11 mission and the first man to set foot on the moon (July 1969).

**Courteney Cox Arquette** (15 Jun 1964, Birmingham AL), American TV and film actress who is featured as Monica Geller Bing on TV's *Friends* (from 1994).

**Beatrice Arthur** (Bernice Frankel; 13 May 1926, New York NY), American film and TV actress, known especially for the TV sitcoms *Maude* and *The Golden Girls.*

**Owen Seymour Arthur** (17 Oct 1949, Barbados), West Indian politician; prime minister of Barbados from 1994.

**Asashoryu** (Dolgorsuren Dagvadorj; 27 Sep 1980, Ulaanbaatar, Mongolia), Mongolian-born sumo wrestler, only the third foreign-born *yokozuna* (from January 2003); he won four of the six top contests in the first half of 2003 (Aki, Kyushu, Hatsu, and Natsu bashos).

**Ashanti** (Ashanti S. Douglas; 1980, Glen Cove NY), American hip-hop singer who had the distinction of having three songs in the top 10 of *Billboard* magazine's Hot 100 in spring 2003.

**John (Lawrence) Ashbery** (28 Jul 1927, Rochester NY), American poet noted for the elegance, originality, and obscurity of his poetry.

**John (David) Ashcroft** (9 May 1942, Chicago IL), American government official; US attorney general from 2001.

**Paddy Ashdown** (Jeremy John Durham Ashdown; Baron Ashdown of Norton-sub-Hamdon in the County of Somerset; 27 Feb 1941, New Delhi, British India), British politician and diplomat; first chairman of the Liberal Democratic Party (1988–99) and international high representative in Bosnia and Herzegovina from 27 May 2002.

**Vladimir (Davidovich) Ashkenazy** (6 Jul 1937, Gorky, Russian SFSR, USSR [now Nizhny Novgorod, Russia]), Russian-born Icelandic pianist and conductor.

**Hanan Ashrawi** (8 Oct 1946, Ram Allah, Palestine), Palestinian academic and spokeswoman for Palestine.

**Bashar al-Assad** (11 Sep 1965, Damascus, Syria), Syrian statesman; president of Syria from 2000.

**Azali Assoumani** (1959, Grand Comoro Island, Comoros), Comoran politician; president of Comoros, 1999–January 2002, and again from 26 May 2002.

**Richard C. Atkinson** (19 Mar 1929, Oak Park IL), American psychologist, a specialist on cognition and memory. He served as director of the National Science Foundation, 1977–80; chancellor of the University of California, San Diego, 1980–95; and president of the University of California from 1995.

**Rick Atkinson** (1952, Munich, West Germany [now in Germany]), American journalist and military historian; he won a Pulitzer Prize for national reporting in 1982, a second, for public service, in 1999, and a third, for history, in 2003 for *An Army at Dawn: The War in North Africa, 1942–1943.*

**Rowan (Sebastian) Atkinson** (6 Jan 1955, Consett, Durham, England), British comedian and actor who starred in the "Blackadder" series on British TV and later played the popular character Mr. Bean; in 2003 he starred in *Johnny English,* a James Bond spoof.

**Abdul Rahman ibn Hamad al-Attiyah** (1950, Qatar), Qatari international official; secretary-general of the Gulf Cooperation Council from March 2002.

**Margaret (Eleanor) Atwood** (18 Nov 1939, Ottawa, ON, Canada), Canadian poet, novelist, and critic, noted for her Canadian nationalism and her feminism.

**Daw Aung San Suu Kyi** (19 Jun 1945, Rangoon, Burma [now Yangon, Myanmar]), Myanmar (Burmese) opposition leader; winner of the 1991 Nobel Peace Prize.

**Patti Austin** (10 Aug 1948, New York NY), American rock singer, a durable performer who has been on the charts since the 1960s.

**Frankie Avalon** (18 Sep 1940, Philadelphia PA), American singer and film actor.

**Pyotr Olegovich Aven** (16 Mar 1955, Moscow, USSR [now in Russia]), Russian business tycoon, president of AlfaBank and director-general of the financial corporation FinPa.

**Emanuel Ax** (8 Jun 1949, Lvov, Ukrainian SSR, USSR [now Lviv, Ukraine]), Ukrainian concert pianist known for his lyricism and technique; he has specialized in the 19th-century repertoire.

**Dan Aykroyd** (1 Jul 1952, Ottawa, ON, Canada), Canadian-born comic actor best known for TV's *Saturday Night Live* (1975–79) and the film *The Blues Brothers* (1980).

**Hank Azaria** (25 Apr 1964, Forest Hills NY), American actor best known for comic film roles and for providing voices for TV's *The Simpsons.*

**José María Aznar López** (25 Feb 1953, Madrid, Spain), Spanish politician; prime minister from 1996.

**B-Real** (Louis Freese; 2 Jun 1970, Los Angeles CA), American Latino rap artist (of Cypress Hill).

**'Abd al-Qadir al-Ba Jamal** (1946, Yemen?), Yemeni politician; prime minister of Yemen from 2001.

**Juan N. Babauta** (7 Sep 1953, Tanapag, Saipan, Northern Mariana Islands), American Republican politician; governor of the Northern Mariana Islands from January 2002.

**Susana Baca** (1944, Chorrillos, Peru), Peruvian singer in the Afro-Peruvian tradition who came to prominence with her 1996 single "Maria Lando."

**Amitabh Bachchan** (11 Oct 1942, Allahabad, United Provinces [now Uttar Pradesh state], British India), Indian film actor and host of the Indian TV version of *Who Wants To Be a Millionaire?*

**Kevin Bacon** (8 Jul 1958, Philadelphia PA), American film and theater actor best known for his breakthrough role in *Footloose* (1984).

**Abdullah Ahmad Badawi** (26 Nov 1939, Penang state, Malaysia), Malaysian politician and deputy prime minister who was designated to succeed Mahathir bin Mohamad as prime minister of Malaysia in October 2003.

**Mark Badgley** (12 Jan 1961, East St. Louis IL), American fashion designer who, with James Mischka, produces the Badgley Mischka line of beaded evening gowns.

**Erykah Badu** (Erica Wright; 26 Feb 1972, Dallas TX), American singer-songwriter appreciated for the phrasing and emotive qualities of her smooth, jazz-inflected vocals.

**Bob Baffert** (13 Jan 1953, Nogales AZ), American trainer of Thoroughbred horses, including winners of the Preakness Stakes four times, the Kentucky Derby three times, and the Belmont Stakes once.

**Natsagiyn Bagabandi** (22 Apr 1950, Yaruu Soum, Mongolia), Mongolian politician; president of Mongolia from 1997.

**F(rancis) Lee Bailey** (10 Jun 1933, Waltham MA), American attorney famous for his defenses of celebrities including Dr. Sam Sheppard, Patty Hearst, and O.J. Simpson.

**Jerry D. Bailey** (29 Aug 1957, Dallas TX), American jockey, twice winner of the Kentucky Derby (1993, 1996) and twice the Preakness Stakes (1991, 2000); he was five times North America's leading jockey.

**John Elias Baldacci** (30 Jan 1955, Bangor ME), American Democratic politician; governor of Maine from 8 Jan 2003.

Jan Peter Balkenende (7 May 1956, Kapelle, The Netherlands), Dutch Christian-Democratic politician; prime minister of The Netherlands from July 2002.

Alan Ball (1957, Atlanta GA), American TV director, screenwriter, and producer noted for his film *American Beauty* (1999) and the HBO TV series *Six Feet Under*.

Robert Duane Ballard (30 Jun 1942, Wichita KS), American oceanographer, underwater explorer, and educator best known for discovering several of history's most famous shipwrecks, including the *Titanic* in 1985, the *Bismarck* in 1989, and John F. Kennedy's *P.T. 109* in 2002.

Steven A. Ballmer (24 Mar 1956, Detroit? MI), American corporate executive; CEO of Microsoft Corp. from 2000.

Ed(ward) Balls (25 Feb 1967, Norwich, England), British public official; chief economic adviser to the treasury.

David Baltimore (7 Mar 1938, New York NY), American microbiologist who was awarded (with Renato Dulbecco and Howard M. Temin) the 1975 Nobel Prize in Physiology or Medicine for research on how certain viruses affect the genes of cancer cells. He received a National Medal of Science in 1999 and has been president of the California Institute of Technology since 1997.

Shigeru Ban (5 Aug 1957, Tokyo, Japan), Japanese architect known for his practical solutions and assistance with the reconstruction of Kobe, Japan, following the 1995 earthquake.

Enric Banda (1948, Girona, Spain), Catalan geophysicist; secretary general of the European Science Foundation from 1998.

Antonio Banderas (José António Domínguez Banderas; 10 Oct 1960, Málaga, Spain), Spanish actor and director who successfully crossed over to American films in the 1990s.

John Bennett Bani (1940, Pentecost Island, New Hebrides [now Vanuatu]), Anglican priest; president of Vanuatu from 1999.

Russell Banks (28 Mar 1940, Newton MA), American novelist known for his portrayals of the interior lives of characters at odds with economic and social forces.

Tyra Banks (4 Dec 1973, Los Angeles CA), American model and actress best known for Victoria's Secret ads; she is host of the TV show *America's Next Top Model* (2003).

Fiona Banner (1966, Merseyside, England), British artist who created "wordscapes," installations, and later porn art; she was nominated for the Turner Prize in 2002.

Jill E. Barad (Jill Elikann; 23 May 1951, New York NY), American corporate executive; CEO of Mattel, Inc. from 1997.

Ehud Barak (Ehud Brog; 12 Feb 1942, Mishmar HaSharon kibbutz, Palestine), Israeli politician; prime minister of Israel, 1999–2001.

Amiri Baraka (Everett LeRoi Jones; also known as Imamu Amiri Baraka; 7 Oct 1934, Newark NJ), American playwright, poet, novelist, essayist, black nationalist, and self-professed Third World Marxist; while poet laureate of New Jersey Baraka brought on a raging controversy with his poem "Somebody Blew Up America," which suggests that Israelis knew about the 11 Sep 2001 terrorist attacks in advance.

Patricia Barber (8 Nov 1955, Lisle IL), American jazz singer and pianist.

Daniel Barenboim (15 Nov 1942, Buenos Aires, Argentina), Israeli pianist and conductor; music director of the Chicago Symphony Orchestra from 1989.

Roy Barnes (11 Mar 1948, Mableton GA), American Democratic politician; governor of Georgia, 1999–2003.

Hector V. Barreto, Jr. (Kansas City MO), American government official; head of the US Small Business Administration from 2001.

Craig R. Barrett (29 Aug 1939, San Francisco CA), American materials scientist and corporate executive; CEO of Intel Corp. from 1997.

Kenny Barron (9 Jun 1943, Philadelphia PA), American jazz pianist and composer.

Dave Barry (3 Jul 1947, Armonk NY), American humorist, syndicated newspaper columnist, and author of multiple best-sellers.

Drew (Blythe) Barrymore (22 Feb 1975, Culver City CA), American film actress successful both as a child star (*E.T.–the Extra-Terrestrial*; 1982) and as an adult in such films as *Boys on the Side* (1995), *The Wedding Singer* (1998), *Never Been Kissed* (1999), and two *Charlie's Angels* pictures (2000, 2003).

Cecilia Bartoli (4 Jun 1966, Rome, Italy), Italian operatic mezzo-soprano praised for her supple voice, with its wide, even range, and for her vivaciousness as an actress in comic roles.

Omar Hassan Ahmad al-Bashir (1944, Hosh Bannaga, Anglo-Egyptian Sudan [now The Sudan]), Sudanese military leader; president of The Sudan from 1989.

Yury Bashmet (24 Jan 1953, Rostov-on-Don, Russian SFSR, USSR [now Russia]), Russian violist and leader of the Moscow Soloists (from 1992).

Kim Basinger (8 Dec 1953, Athens GA), American motion-picture actress most acclaimed for *L.A. Confidential* (1997; Academy Award).

Kathy Bates (Kathleen Doyle Bates; 28 Jun 1948, Memphis TN), American film actress most famous for *Misery* (1990; Academy Award).

Jorge Batlle Ibáñez (25 Oct 1927, Uruguay?), Uruguayan politician; president of Uruguay from 2000.

Kathleen Battle (Kathleen Deanne Battle; 13 Aug 1948, Portsmouth OH), American operatic soprano, among the finest coloraturas of her time; her roles included Susanna in *The Marriage of Figaro*, Rosina in *The Barber of Seville*, and Sophie in *Der Rosenkavalier*.

Beatrice Elizabeth Mary, Princess of York (8 Aug 1988, London, England), daughter of Prince Andrew and Sarah Ferguson.

Queen Beatrix (31 Jan 1938, Soestdijk, The Netherlands), queen of The Netherlands from 1980.

(Henry) Warren Beatty (30 Mar 1937, Richmond VA), American film actor and director best known for politically charged portrayals.

Beck (Beck Hansen; 8 Jul 1970, Los Angeles CA), American singer and songwriter who won Grammys for best male rock vocal performance in 1996 with "Where It's At" and for best alternative music album with *Odelay* (1996) and *Mutations* (1999).

Margaret Beckett (15 Jan 1943, Ashton-under-Lyne, Lancashire, England), British environment secretary in 2002.

David Beckham (2 May 1975, Leytonstone, East London, England), British association football (soccer) player, star midfielder for Manchester United, and captain of England's national team in the 2002 World Cup; he was also known for his celebrity marriage to Victoria Adams (of the Spice Girls). He was made OBE in 2003, a few days before he agonized fans by being traded to the Real Madrid football club.

**Victoria (Caroline) Adams Beckham** (7 Apr 1975, Goff's Oak, Hertfordshire, England), British pop singer ("Posh Spice" of the Spice Girls); also known for her marriage to David Beckham.

**Bei Dao** (original name Zhao Zhenkai; 2 Aug 1949, Beijing, China), Chinese poet and writer of fiction whose works were published underground for most of his career.

**Kenenisa Bekele** (20 Jun 1982, Ethiopia), Ethiopian cross-country runner; world champion in the short and long races in 2002 and 2003.

**Harry Belafonte** (Harold George Belafonte, Jr.; 1 Mar 1927, New York NY), American pop singer and actor who was a key figure in the 1950s popularity of folk music.

**Angela M. Belcher** (1967? TX), American materials scientist, a specialist in biomaterials, who uses viruses to grow semiconductors and other materials with applications in microsensor and computer technology.

**Abdelwahed Belkeziz** (5 Jul 1939, Marakech, Morocco), Moroccan international official; secretary-general of the Organization of the Islamic Conference from 2001.

**Derrick Albert Bell, Jr.** (6 Nov 1930, Pittsburgh PA), American legal scholar; civil-rights activist.

**Joshua Bell** (9 Dec 1967, Bloomington IN), American violinist; he won a Grammy for his world premiere recording of Nicholas Maw's *Concerto for Violin* (2001).

**John B. Bellinger, III** (1960?), American attorney; senior associate counsel to the president and legal adviser to the National Security Council from 2001.

**Saul Bellow** (10 Jun 1915, Lachnine, QC, Canada), Canadian-born American novelist renowned for his characterizations of modern urban man, disaffected by society but not destroyed in spirit; he won the 1976 Nobel Prize for Literature.

**Arden L. Bement, Jr.** (22 May 1932, Pittsburgh PA), American materials scientist; director of the National Institute of Standards and Technology from 2001.

**Zine al-Abidine Ben Ali** (3 Sep 1936, Hammam-Sousse, Tunisia), Tunisian politician; president of Tunisia from 1987.

**Binyamin (Fuad) Ben-Eliezer** (1936, Iraq), Israeli politician; leader of the Labor Party and Minister of Defense 2001–02.

**Luciano Benetton** (13 May 1935, Treviso, Italy), Italian retailer and cofounder (1965) of the Benetton company noted for sportswear and provocative advertisements.

**Roberto Benigni** (27 Oct 1952, Misericordia, Italy), Italian actor, comic, and screenwriter best known in America for *La vita è bella* (*Life Is Beautiful*; 1998) for which he won the Academy Award for best actor.

**Annette Bening** (29 May 1958, Topeka KS), American film actress who won critical acclaim for *American Beauty* (1999).

**Tony Bennett** (Anthony Dominick Benedetto; 3 Aug 1926, Astoria, Queens NY), American pop and jazz singer, one of the most enduring of the crooners, who won his first Grammy in 1962 ("I Left My Heart in San Francisco").

**Craig Benson** (8 Oct 1954, New York NY), American businessman and Republican politician; governor of New Hampshire from 9 Jan 2003.

**George Benson** (22 Mar 1943, Pittsburgh PA), American jazz and pop guitarist and vocalist.

**Yelena Berezhnaya** (11 Oct 1977, Nevinnomyssk, Russian SFSR, USSR [now Russia]), Russian pairs skater (with Anton Sikharulidze); shared the 2002 Olympic gold medal with Canadians Jamie Salé and David Pelletier.

**Boris (Abramovich) Berezovsky** (23 Jan 1946, Moscow, USSR [now in Russia]), Russian businessman and oligarch; former owner of Russian Public Television (ORT) and Aeroflot, the Russian airline, among other holdings; in 2003 he was in the UK facing extradition to Russia on a number of criminal charges.

**Maarten van den Bergh** (19 Apr 1942, New York state), Dutch corporate executive; chairman of Lloyds TSB.

**(Ernst) Ingmar Bergman** (14 Jul 1918, Uppsala, Sweden), Swedish film writer-director noted for his versatile camera work and fragmented narrative style; works include *The Seventh Seal* (1958), *Wild Strawberries* (1959), *Through a Glass Darkly* (1962), and *Fanny and Alexander* (1983).

**David Berkowitz** (1 Jun 1953), American serial killer convicted as "The Son of Sam."

**Silvio Berlusconi** (29 Sep 1936, Milan, Italy), Italian businessman and politician; prime minister of Italy, 1994–95, and again from 2001.

**Tim Berners-Lee** (8 Jun 1955, London, England), British inventor of the World Wide Web and director, from 1994, of the World Wide Web Consortium (W3C) at the MIT Laboratory for Computer Science.

**Chuck Berry** (Charles Edward Anderson Berry; 18 Oct 1926, St. Louis MO), American singer, songwriter, and guitarist who was one of the most popular and influential performers in rhythm-and-blues and rock-and-roll music in the 1950s, '60s, and '70s.

**Halle (Maria) Berry** (14 Aug 1968, Cleveland OH), American actress and model who received an Academy Award in 2001 for her role in *Monster's Ball* and much publicity for starring in the James Bond film *Die Another Day* (2002).

**Bernardo Bertolucci** (16 Mar 1940, Parma, Italy), Italian film director, whose erotically charged *Last Tango in Paris* (1972) created an international sensation.

**Jeffrey P. Bezos** (12 Jan 1964, Albuquerque NM), American corporate executive; founder and CEO of Amazon.com from 1995.

**Manjul Bhargava** (8 Aug 1974, Hamilton, ON, Canada), Canadian-born American mathematician and tabla player, a specialist in algebraic number theory who devised an elegant proof of the Fifteen Theorem.

**King Bhumibol Adulyadej** (Rama IX; 5 Dec 1927, Cambridge MA), king of Thailand, ninth of the Chakkri dynasty.

**Benazir Bhutto** (21 Jun 1953, Karachi, Pakistan), Pakistani politician, prime minister 1988–90 and 1993–96, and the first woman leader of a predominantly Muslim nation in modern history.

**Joseph R(obinette) Biden, Jr.** (20 Nov 1942, Scranton PA), American Democratic politician; senator from Delaware.

**James Hadley Billington** (1 Jun 1929, Bryn Mawr PA), American cultural historian; librarian of Congress from 1987.

**Osama bin Laden** (also spelled Usamah ibn Ladin; 10 Mar 1957, Riyadh, Saudi Arabia), Saudi Arabian–born terrorist leader, alleged mastermind of the 1993 bombing of the World Trade Center and the 11 Sep 2001 attacks on the World Trade Center and the Pentagon; his al-Qaeda network has been linked to many international terrorist acts since 2001 as well.

**Pat Binns** (8 Oct 1948, Weyburn, SK, Canada), Canadian politician; premier of Prince Edward Island from 1996.

**Juliette Binoche** (9 Mar 1964, Paris, France), French film actress famous for complex characterizations; her breakthrough performance was in *The English Patient* (1996; Academy Award for best supporting actress).

**Lester Bryant Bird** (21 Feb 1938, Antigua), West Indian politician; prime minister of Antigua and Barbuda from 1994.

**Harrison Birtwistle** (15 Jul 1934, Accrington, Lancashire, England), British composer of operas, chamber music, and orchestral music in a contemporary, avant-garde style.

**Paul Biya** (13 Feb 1933, Mvomeka'a, Cameroon), Cameroonian politician; president of Cameroon from 1982.

**Björk** (Björk Gudmundsdottir; 21 Nov 1965, Reykjavík, Iceland), Icelandic singer and actress who won the best actress award at the 2000 Cannes Film Festival for *Dancer in the Dark.*

**Jonas Bjorkman** (23 Mar 1972, Vaxjo, Sweden), Swedish tennis player best known for doubles play; he won the doubles championships in the Australian Open in 1998, 1999, and 2001 and at Wimbledon in 2002 and 2003.

**Ole Einar Bjørndalen** (27 Jan 1974, Drammen, Norway), Norwegian biathlete and cross-country skier who swept the Olympic biathlon (four golds in 2002).

**Conrad (Moffat) Black** (25 Aug 1944, Montreal, QC, Canada), Canadian financier and press baron, an icon of capitalism in Canada who built a media empire of almost 250 newspapers worldwide. Among other newspapers, Black controlled the London *Daily Telegraph,* the Fairfax Group in Australia, the *Jerusalem Post,* Southam Press in Canada, and nearly 100 local dailies in the US.

**Rubén Blades** (16 Jul 1948, Panama City, Panama), Panamanian salsa singer and songwriter, actor, and politician.

**Rod R. Blagojevich** (10 Dec 1956, Chicago IL), American Democratic politician; governor of Illinois from 13 Jan 2003.

**Manolo Blahnik** (27 Nov 1942, Santa Cruz, Canary Islands, Spain), Spanish shoe designer and maker whose elegant, stylish creations are characterized by high stiletto heels.

**Tony Blair** (Anthony Charles Lynton Blair; 6 May 1953, Edinburgh, Scotland), British politician; Labour Party leader and prime minister of the UK from 1997.

**Robert Blake** (Michael James Vijencio Gubitosi; 18 Sep 1933, Nutley NJ), American film and TV actor best known for the 1970s cop show *Baretta;* he was arrested in 2002 and charged with the 2001 murder of his wife.

**Cate Blanchett** (Catherine Elise Blanchett; 14 May 1969, Melbourne, VIC, Australia), Australian film actress known for serious roles, including *Elizabeth* (1998) and *The Talented Mr. Ripley* (1999).

**Sir Christopher Bland** (29 May 1938, Japan), British corporate executive; chairman of British Telecom from 2001.

**Billy Blanks** (1 Sep 1955, Erie PA), American physical fitness expert and developer of the Tae Bo system of fitness training.

**Carla Bley** (Carla Borg; 11 May 1938, Oakland CA), American jazz bandleader, arranger, and multi-instrumentalist known for her experimental, avant-garde creations and her wide-ranging collaborations.

**Paul Bley** (10 Nov 1932, Montreal, QC, Canada), Canadian jazz pianist and composer known for his intellectual approach, avant-garde ideas, and large output of albums.

**Mary J. Blige** (11 Jan 1971, New York NY), American hip-hop soul singer.

**Hans Blix** (28 Jun 1928, Uppsala, Sweden), Swedish diplomat and international official; director general of the International Atomic Energy Agency, 1981–97, and executive chairman of the United Nations Monitoring, Verification and Inspection Commission (UNMOVIC) from 2000 to June 2003.

**Herbert Blomstedt** (11 Jul 1927, Springfield MA), American-born Swedish conductor; music director of the Leipzig Gewandhaus Orchestra from 1998.

**Harold Irving Bloom** (11 Jul 1930, New York NY), American literary critic known for his innovative interpretations of literary history and of the creation of literature, and for his unconventional approach to writing as in, for example, *The Western Canon* (1994).

**Michael R. Bloomberg** (14 Feb 1942, Medford MA), American businessman and Republican politician; mayor of New York City from 1 Jan 2002.

**Judy Blume** (Judy Sussman; 12 Feb 1938, Elizabeth NJ), American author of popular books for children and adolescents.

**David Blunkett** (6 Jun 1947, Sheffield, England), British politician, blind from birth; British home secretary from 2001.

**James Blyth, Lord Blyth of Rowington** (8 May 1940, Scotland), British corporate executive; chairman of beverage maker Diageo PLC from 2000.

**Andrea Bocelli** (22 Sep 1958, Lajatico, Italy), Italian operatic tenor, blind from age 12.

**Enrique Bolaños Geyer** (13 May 1928, Masaya, Nicaragua), Nicaraguan politician; president of Nicaragua from 10 Jan 2002.

**William Bolcom** (26 May 1938, Seattle WA), American composer, pianist, and teacher.

**Sir Haji Hassanal Bolkiah Mu'izzadin Waddaulah** (15 Jul 1946, Brunei Town [now Bandar Seri Begawan], Brunei), 29th sultan of Brunei, from 1967.

**Timo Boll** (8 Mar 1981, Erbach, West Germany [now in Germany]), German table tennis player; the top-ranked male player as of August 2003.

**Joshua B. Bolten** (6 Aug 1954, Washington DC?), American international lawyer and government official in the presidential administrations of George H.W. Bush and George W. Bush; director of the Office of Management and Budget from June 2003.

**Jon Bon Jovi** (John Bongiovi; 2 Mar 1962, Perth Amboy NJ), American singer, musician, and songwriter.

**Julian Bond** (14 Jan 1940, Nashville TN), American civil rights leader.

**Kjell Magne Bondevik** (3 Sep 1947, Molde, Norway), Norwegian politician; prime minister of Norway, 1997–2000, and again from 2001.

**Barry (Lamar) Bonds** (24 Jul 1964, Riverside CA), American baseball player who hit a record 73 home runs and 177 walks in 2001; only five-time National League MVP (1990, 1992, 1993, 2001, 2002) and the only player with more than 500 home runs and 500 stolen bases.

**Omar Bongo** (Albert-Bernard Bongo; 30 Dec 1935, Lewai, Gabon), Gabonese politician; president of Gabon from 1967.

**Helena Bonham Carter** (26 May 1966, Golders Green, London, England), British actress known for serious dramatic and period pieces, often based on novels by E.M. Forster.

**Bono** (Paul David Hewson; also known as Bono Vox; 10 May 1960, Dublin, Ireland), Irish rock guitarist and vocalist (of U2); activist and mediator.

**Cherie Booth** (23 Sep 1954, Bury, Lancashire, England), British barrister; wife of prime minister Tony Blair.

**Umberto Bossi** (19 Sep 1941, Cassano Magnano, Italy), Italian politician and leader of the separatist Northern League from 1991.

**Ian (Charles) Bostridge** (25 Dec 1964, London, England), English operatic tenor and author whose work includes recent recordings of Benjamin Britten's *The Turn of the Screw* and *Canticles,* Claudio Monteverdi's *L'Orfeo,* and a collection of Noël Coward songs.

**Fernando Botero** (19 Apr 1932, Medellín, Colombia), Colombian painter and sculptor of monumental bronze pieces known for his exaggerated representations of human and animal forms.

**Lucien Bouchard** (22 Dec 1938, Saint-Coeur-de-Marie, QC, Canada), French Canadian politician, an advocate of the separation of Quebec from the rest of Canada.

**Pierre Boulez** (26 Mar 1925, Montbrison, France), French composer, conductor, and music theorist whose complex, serialist music is marked by a sensitivity to the nuances of instrumental texture and color.

**Matthew Bourne** (13 Jan 1950, Hackney, London, England), British choreographer known for his radical reinterpretations of the classical ballet repertory.

**Ray Bourque** (28 Dec 1960, Montreal, QC, Canada), American ice hockey defenseman; five-time James Norris Trophy winner.

**Raphael Bousso** (31 May 1971, Israel), Israeli-born American mathematical physicist, a leading proponent of the holographic principle, which holds that our universe is possibly a shadow of a higher-dimensional world.

**Abdelaziz Bouteflika** (2 Mar 1937, Tlemcen, Algeria), Algerian politician and diplomat; president of Algeria from 1999.

**David Bowie** (David Robert Jones; 8 Jan 1947, Brixton, London, England), British rock singer and actor who was most prominent in the 1970s and best known for his shifting personae and musical genre hopping.

**Mame Madior Boye** (1940, French West Africa [now in Senegal]), Senegalese politician; prime minister of Senegal from 2001.

**Ray (Douglas) Bradbury** (22 Aug 1920, Waukegan IL), American author of science-fiction short stories and novels, nostalgic tales, poetry, radio drama, and television and motion-picture screenplays.

**Ed Bradley** (22 Jun 1941, Philadelphia PA), American TV journalist.

**Kenneth (Charles) Branagh** (10 Dec 1960, Belfast, Northern Ireland), British theater and film actor, director, and writer best known for screen adaptations of Shakespearean plays.

**Marlon Brando (Jr.)** (3 Apr 1924, Omaha NE), American motion-picture and stage actor known for visceral, brooding characterizations; well-respected films include *A Streetcar Named Desire* (1951), *On the Waterfront* (1954), and *The Godfather* (1972).

**Brandy** (Brandy Norwood; 11 Feb 1979, McComb MS), American rhythm-and-blues singer and actress.

**Richard (Charles Nicholas) Branson** (18 Jul 1950, Blackheath, London, England), British entrepreneur; founder of the Virgin empire in 1973.

**Benjamin Bratt** (16 Dec 1963, San Francisco CA), American TV and motion-picture actor; he first gained fame on TV's *Law & Order.*

**Rose Marie Bravo** (1951?, Bronx NY), American executive; president of Saks Fifth Avenue, 1992–97, and CEO of Burberry's from 1997.

**Anthony Braxton** (4 Jun 1945, Chicago IL), American reed player and composer whose idiosyncratic style partook of the classical avant-garde (composers such as Karlheinz Stockhausen and John Cage) as well as the classical jazz saxophone repertory and confounded exponents of both styles.

**Algirdas Mykolas Brazauskas** (22 Sep 1932, Rokiskis, Lithuanian SSR, USSR [now Lithuania]), Lithuanian politician; president of Lithuania, 1992–98, and prime minister from 2001.

**Phil Bredesen** (Philip Norman Bredesen; 21 Nov 1943, Oceanport NJ), American Democratic politician and mayor of Nashville TN; governor of Tennessee from 18 Jan 2003.

**Jerry Bremer** (L. Paul Bremer III; 30 Sep 1941, Hartford CT), American diplomat; US ambassador to The Netherlands (1983–86) and ambassador-at-large for counterterrorism (1986–89; he was appointed [6 May 2003] to replace Jay Garner as chief administrator following the coalition occupation of Iraq).

**Amy Brenneman** (22 Jun 1964, New London CT), American TV actress and producer, known for her role in TV's *Judging Amy.*

**Sydney Brenner** (13 Jan 1927, Germiston, South Africa), British cowinner of the 2002 Nobel Prize for Physiology or Medicine for his work on the life of a cell.

**Thierry Breton** (15 Jan 1955, Paris, France), French corporate executive; executive chairman of Thompson Multimedia to 2002, and executive chairman of France Télécom from 2002.

**Stephen Breyer** (15 Aug 1938, San Francisco CA), American jurist; associate justice of the US Supreme Court from 1994.

**Beau Bridges** (Lloyd Vernet Bridges III; 9 Dec 1941, Los Angeles CA), American film and TV actor.

**Jeff Bridges** (4 Dec 1949, Los Angeles CA), American actor whose breakthrough performance came in *The Last Picture Show* (1971) and who starred in *Seabiscuit* (2003).

**Sarah Brightman** (14 Aug 1960, Berkhampstead, England), British soprano who made her reputation appearing in stage musicals such as *The Phantom of the Opera* and *Cats* and has gone on to issue successful light classical albums.

**Matthew Broderick** (21 Mar 1962, New York NY), American comic actor of stage and screen who gained widespread fame following the film *Ferris Bueller's Day Off* (1986).

**Sir Alec N. Broers** (17 Sep 1938, Calcutta [now Kolkata], British India), British electronics engineer and vice chancellor of the University of Cambridge, 1996–2003.

**Tom Brokaw** (Thomas John Brokaw; 6 Feb 1940, Webster SD), American TV news anchorman.

**Edgar M. Bronfman** (20 Jun 1929, Montreal, QC, Canada), Canadian-born American businessman; he was chairman of The Seagram Co. Ltd. and, following that company's merger with Vivendi Universal, served on the board of Vivendi; he is equally well known as president of the World Jewish Congress (from 1979) and officer of other Jewish organizations.

**Yefim Bronfman** (10 Apr 1958, Tashkent, Uzbek SSR, USSR [now Uzbekistan]), Soviet-born American pianist; winner of the Avery Fisher Prize in 1991 and a Grammy Award in 1997 for his recording of the Bartok piano concertos.

**Garth Brooks** (Troyal Garth Brooks; 7 Feb 1962, Tulsa OK), American country-and-western singer known for his cowboy hats and commercialism (and great commercial success) of his music from the early 1980s.

**James F. Brooks** (1955, Colorado?), American historian and director of the School of American Research in Santa Fe NM; his 2002 book, *Captives & Cousins: Slavery, Kinship, and Community in the Southwest Borderlands,* won three top awards for American history.

**James L. Brooks** (9 May 1940, Brooklyn NY), American motion-picture and TV director, writer, and producer.

**Kix Brooks** (12 May 1955, Shreveport LA), American country-and-western singer, of Brooks & Dunn (Academy of Country Music Entertainer of the Year, 1995, 1996, 2001; Country Music Association Entertainer of the Year, 1996, and Vocal Duo of the Year, 2002).

**Mel Brooks** (Melvin Kaminsky; 28 Jun 1926, Brooklyn NY), American comedian, actor, producer, and director; an offbeat comic genius.

**Pierce (Brendan) Brosnan** (16 May 1953, Navan, County Meath, Ireland), Irish actor known for portrayal of handsome, suave leading men, including Remington Steele and James Bond.

**Clarence ("Gatemouth") Brown** (18 Apr 1924, Vinton LA), American blues singer and guitarist.

**Dan Brown** (22 Jun 1964, Exeter NH), American novelist, author of the number-one best-selling work of fiction, *The Da Vinci Code.*

**Gordon Brown** (20 Feb 1951, Glasgow, Scotland), British politician and chancellor of the exchequer from 1997.

**James Brown** (3 May 1933, Barnwell SC), American singer, songwriter, arranger, and dancer.

**Jerry Brown** (Edmund Gerald Brown, Jr.; 7 Apr 1938, San Francisco CA), American politician, governor of California, 1975–83; mayor of Oakland CA from 1998; and presidential candidate.

**Lee P. Brown** (4 Oct 1937, Wewoka OK), American Democratic politician; mayor of Houston from 1998.

**Willie L. Brown, Jr.** (20 Mar 1934, Mineola TX), American Democratic politician; mayor of San Francisco from 1996.

**Sir John Browne** (Edmund John Phillip Browne; Lord Browne of Maddingly; 20 Feb 1948, Hamburg, West Germany [now in Germany]), British corporate executive; group CEO of British Petroleum/Amoco from 1998.

**Dave Brubeck** (David Warren Brubeck; 6 Dec 1920, Concord CA), American pianist-composer who brought elements of classical music into jazz.

**Jerry Bruckheimer** (21 Sep 1945, Detroit MI), American film and TV producer who scored big hits with two *CSI* (Crime Scene Investigation) TV series (from 2000), the series *Without a Trace* (2002), *Cold Case* (2003), and others, as well as films that included *Beverly Hills Cop* (1984), *Pearl Harbor* (2001), and *Black Hawk Down* (2001).

**Gro Harlem Brundtland** (20 Apr 1939, Oslo, Norway), Norwegian politician and international official; prime minister of Norway, 1981, 1986–89, and again 1990–96; director-general of the World Health Organization, 1998–2003.

**Kobe Bryant** (23 Aug 1978, Philadelphia PA), American basketball player who won three straight NBA titles (2000–02) with the Los Angeles Lakers; four-time NBA all star.

**Bill Bryson** (1951, Des Moines IA), British journalist and travel writer whose 1996 *Notes from a Small Island* was voted in a 2003 World Book Day poll in Great Britain as the book that best represents Britain.

**Chico Buarque (de Hollanda)** (1944, Rio de Janeiro, Brazil), Brazilian singer and pop star.

**Patrick J. Buchanan** (2 Nov 1938, Washington DC), American journalist and newspaper columnist; presidential candidate.

**William F. Buckley, Jr.** (24 Nov 1925, New York NY), American magazine editor and columnist, author, and noted conservative.

**Jimmy Buffett** (25 Dec 1946, Pascagoula MS), American rock singer and songwriter who made the world of his song "Margaritaville" a way of life on the Gulf Coast.

**Warren (Edward) Buffett** (30 Aug 1930, Omaha NE), American investor; CEO of Berkshire Hathaway Inc. since 1965 and chairman of the board of Salomon Brothers Inc. from 1991.

**Sandra (Annette) Bullock** (26 Jul 1964, Arlington VA), American film actress who achieved fame after her performance in *Speed* (1994) and became a top box office draw; recent films include *Miss Congeniality* (2000), *Murder by Numbers* (2002), and *Divine Secrets of the Ya-Ya Sisterhood* (2002).

**Gisele Bündchen** (Gisele Caroline Nonnenmacher Bündchen; 20 Jul 1980, Horizontina, Rio Grande do Sul state, Brazil), Brazilian fashion model.

**Brooke Burke** (8 Sep 1971, Tucson AZ), American model and host of E! channel's television series *Wild On.*

**Ken Burns** (Kenneth Lauren Burns; 29 Jul 1953, Brooklyn NY), American documentary filmmaker who directed and cowrote the TV miniseries *The Civil War, Baseball,* and *Jazz,* among others.

**Kenny Burrell** (31 Jul 1931, Detroit MI), American jazz guitarist and composer.

**Ellen Burstyn** (Edna Rae Gillooley; 7 Dec 1932, Detroit MI), American motion-picture and stage actress of great depth.

**Gary Burton** (23 Jan 1943, Anderson IN), American jazz vibraphonist and composer.

**Tim Burton** (Timothy William Burton; 25 Aug 1958, Burbank CA), American director and writer known for offbeat, imaginative films.

**Barbara Bush** (Barbara Pierce; 8 Jun 1925, Rye NY), American first lady; wife of Pres. George H.W. Bush (married 6 Jan 1945).

**Barbara Bush** (25 Nov 1981, Dallas TX), American personality; daughter of Pres. George W. Bush.

**George Herbert Walker Bush** (12 Jun 1924, Milton MA), American statesman; vice president of the US, 1981–89, and 41st president of the US, 1989–93 (see full biography at Presidents).

**George Walker Bush** (6 Jul 1946, New Haven CT), American statesman; 43rd president of the US from 2001 (see full biography at Presidents).

**Jeb Bush** (John Ellis Bush; 11 Feb 1953, Midland TX), American Republican politician; governor of Florida from 1999.

**Jenna Bush** (25 Nov 1981, Dallas TX), American personality; daughter of Pres. George W. Bush.

**Kate Bush** (30 Jul 1958, Bexleyheath, England), British singer and songwriter.

**Laura Bush** (Laura Lane Welch; 4 Nov 1946, Midland TX), American first lady; wife of Pres. George W. Bush (married 5 Nov 1977).

**Darcey (Andrea) Bussell** (1969, London, England), British ballerina who has been a principal dancer with the Royal Ballet from 1989.

**Chief Mangosuthu Gatsha Buthelezi** (27 Aug 1928, Mahlabatini, Natal, South Africa), South African Zulu chief, the head (1972–94) of the nonindependent black South African state of KwaZulu, and leader of the Inkatha Freedom Party.

**Jerry "the Iceman" Butler** (8 Dec 1939, Sunflower county MS), American soul singer and politician.

**Pierre Buyoya** (14 Nov 1949, Rutovu, Belgian Rwanda-Urundi [now Burundi]), Burundian Tutsi politician; president of Burundi, 1987–93, and again 1996–2003.

**Donald Byrd** (Donaldson Toussaint L'Ouverture II; 9 Dec 1932, Detroit MI), American jazz trumpeter and flügelhornist.

**Michel Cadot** (1954), West Indian politician; prefect of Martinique from 2000.

**Nicolas Cage** (Nicholas Coppola; 7 Jan 1964, Long Beach CA), American versatile film star who garnered critical acclaim for his performance in Leaving Las Vegas (1995).

**Sila María Calderón** (23 Sep 1942, San Juan, Puerto Rico), Puerto Rican politician; governor of Puerto Rico from 2001.

**Lorne Calvert** (24 Dec 1952, Moose Jaw, SK, Canada), Canadian politician; premier of Saskatchewan from 8 Feb 2001.

**Félix Pérez Camacho** (30 Oct 1957, Camp Zama, Japan), American Republican politician; governor of Guam from 6 Jan 2003.

**James Cameron** (16 Aug 1954, Kapuskasing, ON, Canada), Canadian director and producer whose credits include some of the top-grossing movies of all time, including Titanic (1997; Academy Award for directing).

**Louis C. Camilleri** (1955, Alexandria, Egypt), American corporate executive; president and CEO of Philip Morris Companies Inc. from 2002.

**Gordon Campbell** (12 Jan 1948, Vancouver, BC, Canada), Canadian politician; premier of British Columbia from 2001.

**Naomi Campbell** (22 May 1970, London, England), British runway and photographic model.

**Jennifer Capriati** (29 Mar 1976, New York NY), American tennis player; youngest US player to turn professional (1989, at age 13); she won the Australian Open in 2001 and 2002 and the French Open in 2001.

**Don Carcieri** (16 Dec 1942, East Greenwich RI), American banker and Republican politician; governor of Rhode Island from 7 Jan 2003.

**Andrew H. Card, Jr.** (10 May 1947, Brockton MA), American government official; White House chief of staff from 2001.

**Drew (Allison) Carey** (23 May 1958, Cleveland OH), American comic TV actor known for his everyman portrayal in The Drew Carey Show (from 1995) and improvisational skills on Whose Line Is It Anyway? (from 1998).

**Mariah Carey** (27 Mar 1970, Greenlawn, Long Island NY), American pop singer.

**Peter (Philip) Carey** (7 May 1943, Bacchus Marsh, VIC, Australia), Australian author; winner of the Booker Prize in 1988 (Oscar and Lucinda) and 2001 (True History of the Kelly Gang).

**King Carl XVI Gustaf** (Carl Gustaf Folke Hubertus; 30 Apr 1946, Stockholm, Sweden), king of Sweden from 1973.

**George Carlin** (12 May 1937, New York NY), American comedian and TV actor famous for subversive material.

**Tucker Carlson** (16 May 1969, San Francisco CA), American journalist, TV commentator and cohost of CNN's Crossfire.

**Richard H. Carmona** (22 Nov 1949, Harlem NY), American physician; surgeon general of the US from 23 Jul 2002.

**Robert A. Caro** (30 Oct 1935, New York NY), American biographer who won Pulitzer Prizes in 1975 and 2003, respectively, for The Power Broker, about New York City politician Robert Moses, and Master of the Senate, the third of a planned four-volume biography of Lyndon B. Johnson.

**Princess Caroline** (Caroline Louise Margaret Grimaldi; 23 Jan 1957, Monte Carlo, Monaco), Monegasque royal; daughter of Prince Rainier III and Princess Grace (the former Grace Kelly).

**Mary Chapin Carpenter** (21 Feb 1958, Princeton NJ), American country music singer and songwriter.

**José Carreras** (5 Dec 1946, Barcelona, Spain), Spanish operatic tenor, one of the popular "Three Tenors" (with Luciano Pavarotti and Plácido Domingo).

**Jim Carrey** (James Eugene Carrey; 17 Jan 1962, Newmarket, ON, Canada), Canadian actor originally known for his rubber-faced visual comedy, he graduated to more serious roles.

**Edwin W. Carrington** (1938, Tobago), Trinidadian international official; secretary-general of the Caribbean Community (CARICOM) from 1992.

**Chris Carter** (13 Oct 1957, Bellflower CA), American writer and TV producer, creator of The X-Files.

**E(dward) Graydon Carter** (14 Jul 1949, Canada), Canadian magazine and newspaper publisher (Spy, Observer, Vanity Fair).

**Elliott Carter** (Elliott Cook Carter, Jr.; 11 Dec 1908, New York NY), American composer whose erudite style and novel principles of polyrhythm, called metrical modulation, won worldwide attention.

**James Carter** (3 Jan 1969, Detroit MI), American jazz saxophonist.

**Jimmy Carter** (James Earl Carter, Jr.; 1 Oct 1924, Plains GA), American statesman; 39th president of the US, 1977–81; winner of the Nobel Prize for Peace, 2002 (see full biography at Presidents).

**Ron Carter** (4 May 1937, Ferndale MI), American jazz bassist.

**Rosalynn Carter** (Eleanor Rosalynn Smith; 18 Aug 1927, Plains GA), American first lady (1977–81), the wife of Pres. Jimmy Carter, and mental health advocate.

**Stephen L. Carter** (26 Oct 1954, Washington DC), American law professor, political commentator, and author.

**Dame Silvia Cartwright** (1943, Dunedin, New Zealand), New Zealand governor-general from 2001.

**Dana (Thomas) Carvey** (2 Apr 1955, Missoula MT), American comedian and film and TV actor best known for his roles on Saturday Night Live and in the Wayne's World movies.

**James Carville, Jr.** (25 Oct 1944, Fort Benning GA), American political strategist and commentator; guided Bill Clinton's presidential campaign in 1992.

**Steve Case** (Stephen McDonnell Case; 21 Aug 1958, Honolulu HI), American corporate executive; founder (1991) and CEO of America Online and chairman of AOL Time Warner, 2001–May 2003.

**Johnny Cash** (J.R. Cash; 26 Feb 1932, Kingsland AR), American singer and songwriter whose work sparked a revival of American country-and-western music.

**Rosanne Cash** (24 May 1955, Memphis TN), American country-and-western singer and songwriter, the daughter of Johnny Cash.

**David Cassidy** (12 Apr 1950, New York NY), American pop and rock singer and TV actor.

**Shaun Cassidy** (27 Sep 1958, Los Angeles CA), American singer and TV actor.

**Laetitia (Marie Laure) Casta** (11 May 1978, Pont-Audemer, France), French fashion model known for advertisements for GUESS? clothing.

**Fidel Castro Ruz** (13 Aug 1926, near Birán, Cuba), Cuban revolutionary and leader of Cuba from 1959, who became a symbol of communist revolution in Latin America.

**Helio Castroneves** (10 May 1975, São Paulo, Brazil), Brazilian race-car driver who won the Indy 500 in 2001 and 2002 and came in second in 2003.

**Kim Cattrall** (21 Aug 1956, Liverpool, England), British film actress of the 1980s who made a comeback in the 1990s as Samantha Jones on TV's *Sex and the City* (from 1998).

**Ch'en Shui-bian** (18 Feb 1951, Hsichuang village, Taiwan), Taiwanese politician; president of Taiwan from 2000.

**Claude Chabrol** (24 Jun 1930, Paris, France), French motion-picture director, scenarist, and producer who was France's master of the mystery thriller.

**Riccardo Chailly** (20 Feb 1953, Milan, Italy), Italian orchestra conductor; chief conductor of the Royal Concertgebouw Orchestra of Amsterdam 1989–2004, after which he will become music director of the Leipzig (Germany) Opera.

**Hussein Chalayan** (Huseyin Chaglayan; 12 Aug 1970, Nicosia, Cyprus), Cypriot-born British fashion designer whose experimental creations display an intellectual and artistic flavor.

**(George) Richard Chamberlain** (31 Mar 1934, Beverly Hills CA), American film and TV actor, the handsome leading man in TV's *Dr. Kildare* medical series (1961–66) and the miniseries *The Thorn Birds* (1983).

**John T. Chambers** (23 Aug 1949, Cleveland OH), American corporate executive; president and CEO of Cisco Systems, Inc. from 1997.

**Jackie Chan** (Chan Kwong-Sang; 7 Apr 1954, Hong Kong), Chinese actor and director whose martial arts and acrobatic skills have made him an international movie star.

**Stockard Channing** (Susan Antonia Williams Stockard; 13 Feb 1944, New York NY), American motion-picture and TV actress; currently stars as the first lady on TV's *The West Wing*.

**Elaine Chao** (26 Mar 1953, Taipei, Taiwan), American government official; US secretary of labor from 2001.

**Manu Chao** (Oscar Tramor; 26 Jun 1961, Paris, France), French-born Spanish international rock musician noted for his politics and his unstructured approach to the business side of music.

**Jean Charest** (John James Charest; 24 Jun 1958, Sherbrooke, QC, Canada), French Canadian politician; leader of the Quebec Liberal Party from 1998.

**Pierre Charles** (30 Jun 1954, Dominica), Dominican politician; prime minister of Dominica from 2000.

**Ray Charles** (Ray Charles Robinson; 23 Sep 1930, Albany GA), American blues and pop singer, pianist, and composer.

**Charles, Prince of Wales** (14 Nov 1948, Buckingham Palace, London, England), heir apparent to the British throne; eldest son of Queen Elizabeth II and Prince Philip, Duke of Edinburgh.

**David Chase** (David DeCesare; 22 Aug 1945, Mount Vernon NY), American TV writer, producer, and director known especially for his award-winning series on cable TV, *The Sopranos* (from 1999).

**Praveen Chaudhari** (India), Indian-born American materials scientist specializing in electronic materials; director of Brookhaven National Laboratory from 1 Apr 2003.

**Hugo Chávez Frías** (28 Jul 1954, Sabaneta, Venezuela), Venezuelan military leader and politician; president of Venezuela from 1999 (with a one-day interruption in April 2002).

**Chayanne** (Elmer Figueroa Alce; 28 Jun 1968, Río Piedras, Puerto Rico), Puerto Rican singer and star of Mexican and Puerto Rican soap operas.

**Chen Kaige** (12 Aug 1952, Beijing, China), Chinese film director known in the West for his *Farewell, My Concubine* (1993).

**Dick Cheney** (Richard Bruce Cheney; 30 Jan 1941, Lincoln NE), American politician; US secretary of defense, 1989–93; vice president of the US from 2001.

**Lynne V. Cheney** (Lynne Ann Vincent; 14 Aug 1941, Casper WY), American political commentator; wife of Vice Pres. Dick Cheney (married 1964).

**Cher** (Cherilyn Sarkasian LaPier; 20 May 1946, El Centro CA), American pop singer and motion-picture actress; she won an Academy Award for best actress in 1987 (*Moonstruck*).

**Taïeb Chérif** (29 Dec 1941, Kasr El Boukhari, Algeria), Algerian international official; secretary-general of the International Civil Aviation Organization (ICAO) from 1 Aug 2003.

**Judy Chicago** (Judy Cohen; 20 Jul 1939, Chicago IL), American artist and feminist; creator (with Miriam Schapiro) of the controversial installation *Womanhouse*, 1972; Chicago is especially well known for her triangular multimedia installation *The Dinner Party* (1979) with "place settings" for historical women.

**Dale Chihuly** (20 Sep 1941, Tacoma WA), American glassblower and glass artist known for his vibrantly colored organic sculptures designed for large spaces.

**Michael Chiklis** (30 Aug 1963, Lowell MA), American TV actor; star of the award-winning cable TV series *The Shield* from 2002.

**Julia Child** (Julia McWilliams; 15 Aug 1912, Pasadena CA), American cooking expert, author, and TV personality noted for her promotion of traditional French cuisine.

**Frederick Jacob Titus Chiluba** (30 Apr 1943, Kitwe, British Northern Rhodesia [now Zambia]), Zambian statesman; president of Zambia, 1991–2002.

**Tadao Chino** (1934, Shizuoka prefecture, Japan), Japanese banker; president of the Asian Development Bank from 1999.

**Jacques (René) Chirac** (29 Nov 1932, Paris, France), French politician; prime minister of France, 1974–76 and 1986–88, and president from 1995.

**Joaquim (Alberto) Chissanó** (22 Oct 1939, Malehice, Mozambique), Mozambican politician; president of Mozambique from 1986.

**Chiyotaikai** (Yuji Hiroshima; 29 Apr 1976, Chitose, Hokkaido, Japan), Japanese sumo wrestler with the rank of *ozeki* (champion); he was the winner of the Nagoya Basho (July 2002) and the 2003 Haru Basho (March 2003).

**Fujio Cho** (1937, Tokyo, Japan), Japanese corporate executive; president of Toyota Motor Corp. from 1999.

**Margaret Cho** (Moran Cho; 5 Dec 1968, San Francisco CA), Korean American actress and comedian known for autobiographical material.

**(Avram) Noam Chomsky** (7 Dec 1928, Philadelphia PA), American linguist, writer, educator, and political activist, one of the founders of transformational, or generative, grammar.

**Chow Yun-Fat** (Zhou Runfa; 18 May 1955, Lamma Island, Hong Kong), Hong Kong actor wildly popular in Hong Kong; famous in the West for films such as *Crouching Tiger, Hidden Dragon* (2000).

**Jean Chrétien** (Joseph Jacques Jean Chrétien; 11 Jan 1934, Shawinigan, QC, Canada), Canadian lawyer, Liberal Party politician, and prime minister from 1993.

**Perry (Gladstone) Christie** (1943, The Bahamas?), Bahamian politician; prime minister of The Bahamas from 3 May 2002.

**Christo** (Khristo Yavachev; 13 Jun 1935, Gabrovo, Bulgaria), Bulgarian conceptual artist and "environmental sculptor."

**Connie Chung** (20 Aug 1946, Washington DC), American TV journalist and anchorwoman.

**Kyung-Wha Chung** (26 Mar 1948, Seoul, Korea [now in South Korea]), Korean violinist.

**Myung-Whun Chung** (22 Jan 1953, Seoul, South Korea), Korean pianist and conductor.

**Chung Mong Joon** (17 Oct 1951, Seoul, South Korea), Korean businessman and politician, CEO of the Hyundai Group from 1987, and cochairman of the Korean Organizing Committee for the 2002 FIFA World Cup.

**Charlotte Church** (21 Feb 1986, Llandaff, Cardiff, Wales), Welsh soprano who issued a best-selling album, *Voice of an Angel,* in 1998 when she was just 13.

**Carlo Azeglio Ciampi** (9 Dec 1920, Livorno, Italy), Italian politician; prime minister of Italy, 1993–94, and president from 1999.

**Tom Clancy** (Thomas L. Clancy, Jr.; 12 Apr 1947, Baltimore MD), American best-selling novelist who enjoyed yet another success in 2002 with his novel *Red Rabbit.*

**Eric Clapton** (Eric Patrick Clapp; 30 Mar 1945, Ripley, Surrey, England), British guitarist, singer, and songwriter.

**Dick Clark** (Richard Wagstaff Clark; 30 Nov 1929, Mount Vernon NY), American TV host and producer whose shows have included *American Bandstand* and *The $10,000 Pyramid.*

**Helen Clark** (26 Feb 1950, Hamilton, New Zealand), New Zealand Labour politician; prime minister of New Zealand from 1999.

**Mary Higgins Clark** (24 Dec 1931, New York NY), American writer of best-selling books, usually stories of suspense or historical novels.

**Vern Clark** (7 Sep 1944, Sioux City IA), American military official; chief of naval operations, US Navy, from 2000.

**Wesley Clark** (Wesley Kanne; 23 Dec 1944, Chicago IL), American general who served as Supreme Allied Commander of NATO (1997–2000) and Commander-in-Chief for the United States European Command.

**Adrienne Clarkson** (10 Feb 1939, Hong Kong), Canadian journalist, publisher, and governor-general of Canada from 1999.

**Kelly Clarkson** (24 Apr 1982, Burleson TX), American celebrity; winner of Fox TV's *American Idol: The Search for a Superstar* competition in 2002.

**John (Marwood) Cleese** (27 Oct 1939, Weston-super-Mare, England), British comic actor best known for his TV work on *Monty Python's Flying Circus* and *Fawlty Towers.*

**(William) Roger Clemens** (4 Aug 1962, Dayton OH), American professional baseball pitcher; six-time Cy Young winner (1986, 1987, 1991, 1997, 1998, 2001).

**Kim Clijsters** (8 Jun 1983, Bilzen, Belgium), Belgian tennis player who was a finalist in the French Open in 2001 and 2003, won the women's doubles at Wimbledon in 2003, and was ranked number 2 in the world in mid-2003.

**Bill Clinton** (William Jefferson Blythe IV; 19 Aug 1946, Hope AR), American statesman; 42nd president of the US, 1992–2000 (see full biography at Presidents).

**Chelsea (Victoria) Clinton** (27 Feb 1980, Little Rock AR), American personality; daughter of former president Bill Clinton and Sen. Hillary Rodham Clinton.

**Hillary Rodham Clinton** (Hillary Diane Rodham; 26 Oct 1947, Chicago IL), American politician; wife of Pres. Bill Clinton; Democratic senator from New York from 2000.

**George Clooney** (6 May 1961, Lexington KY), American film and TV actor who achieved widespread fame with his TV role on *ER.*

**Chuck (Thomas) Close** (Charles Thomas Close; 5 Jul 1940, Monroe WA), American painter noted for his highly inventive techniques used to paint the human face. He is best known for his large-scale, Photo-Realist portraits.

**Glenn Close** (19 Mar 1947, Greenwich CT), American actress perhaps best known for her motion pictures *The Big Chill* and *Fatal Attraction;* she won a Tony Award in 1995 for *Sunset Boulevard.*

**Johnnie L. Cochran, Jr.** (2 Oct 1937, Shreveport LA), American attorney known for his successful defense of O.J. Simpson in his 1995 murder trial.

**Joe Cocker** (John Robert Cocker; 20 May 1944, Sheffield, England), British rock singer.

**Andrei Codrescu** (20 Dec 1946, Sibiu, Romania), Romanian-born American poet, writer, radio commentator, and professor who is editor of the Web journal *Exquisite Corpse* and commentator on literary matters for National Public Radio.

**Paulo Coelho** (August 1947, Rio de Janeiro, Brazil), Brazilian author of best-selling novels, including *The Alchemist* (1988).

**Ethan Coen** (21 Sep 1958, St. Louis Park MN) and **Joel Coen** (29 Nov 1955, St. Louis Park MN), American filmmakers who are known for off-center creations such as *Raising Arizona* (1987), *Fargo* (1996), and *O Brother, Where Art Thou?* (2000).

**Leonard Cohen** (21 Sep 1934, Montreal, QC, Canada), Canadian singer and songwriter.

**Bruce Cole** (1939?, Cleveland OH), American historian of Renaissance art and chairman of the National Endowment for the Humanities from 2001.

**Kenneth Cole** (New York NY), American fashion designer of shoes, accessories, and apparel who is known for socially conscious advertisements.

**Natalie (Maria) Cole** (6 Feb 1950, Los Angeles CA), American pop singer.

**Eoin Colfer** (1965, Wexford, Ireland), Irish best-selling author of novels for children and adults.

**Billy Collins** (1941, New York NY), American poet; 11th poet laureate of the US, from 2001.

**Francis Sellers Collins** (14 Apr 1950, Staunton VA), American geneticist, one of the leaders in the project to sequence the human genome.

**Phil Collins** (31 Jan 1951, Chiswick, England), British rock vocalist and percussionist (of Genesis, etc.).

**Rita Rossi Colwell** (23 Nov 1934, Beverly MA), American marine microbiologist and epidemiologist; director of the National Science Foundation from 1998.

**Sean Combs** (Puffy; Puff Daddy; P. Diddy; 4 Nov 1970, New York NY), American rap artist and impresario.

**Blaise Compaoré** (1951, Ziniane, Upper Volta [now Burkina Faso]), Burkinabe politician; president of Burkina Faso from 1987.

**Philip M. Condit** (2 Aug 1941, Berkeley CA), American aerospace engineer and corporate executive; chairman and CEO of the Boeing Co. from 1996.

**Jennifer Connelly** (12 Dec 1970, Catskill Mountains NY), American fashion model and film actress; she won an Academy Award for best supporting actress in 2001 (*A Beautiful Mind*).

**Ward Connerty** (15 Jun 1939, Leesville LA), American anti-affirmative action activist.

**Sir Sean Connery** (Thomas Connery; 25 Aug 1930, Edinburgh, Scotland), Scottish film actor of enduring attraction who is known for portrayals of rugged leading men, including James Bond; also active in Scottish nationalist politics.

**Alain Connes** (1 Apr 1947, Draguignan, France), French mathematician, 1983 Fields medallist, and winner of the 2001 Crafoord Prize "for penetrating work on the theory of operator algebras and for having been a founder of the non-commutative geometry."

**Frances Conroy** (13 Nov 1953, Monroe GA), American stage and TV actress starring as Ruth Fisher on HBO's series *Six Feet Under*.

**King Constantine II** (2 Jun 1940, Psikhikó, Greece), king of Greece, 1964–74.

**Lansana Conté** (1934, Moussayah Loumbaya, French West Africa [now in Guinea]), Guinean military leader; president of Guinea from 1984.

**Paolo Conte** (6 Jan 1937, Asti, Italy), Italian songwriter, singer, and pianist.

**Ry Cooder** (Ryland Peter Cooder; 15 Mar 1947, Los Angeles CA), American musician and musicologist whose wide-ranging musical curiosity has led to the popularity of overlooked idioms, most recently traditional Cuban *son* music via the Buena Vista Social Club project.

**Coolio** (Artis Ivey, Jr.; 1 Aug 1963, Compton CA), American rap performer.

**Cynthia Cooper** (14 Apr 1963, Chicago IL), American collegiate, Olympic, and professional basketball player and coach.

**Stephen F. Cooper** (23 Oct 1946), American corporate executive and turnaround specialist; CEO of Enron from 2002.

**John Corbett** (9 May 1961, Wheeling WV), American actor who attracted attention for the TV series *Northern Exposure* (1990–95) and *Sex and the City* (1998) and the film *My Big Fat Greek Wedding* (2002).

**Chick Corea** (Armando Anthony Corea; 12 Jun 1941, Chelsea MA), American jazz pianist and composer; classically trained American jazz pianist, composer, and bandleader whose piano style and tunes were extensively imitated during the 1970s and '80s.

**John Corigliano** (16 Feb 1938, New York NY), American composer of lyrical, tonal, expressive works in orchestral music, opera, chamber music, and film scores.

**Karen Corr** (10 Nov 1969, Ballymoney, Northern Ireland), Northern Ireland-born billiards player; WPBA national champion in 2002 and number-two ranked player (after Allison Fisher) at the start of 2003.

**Larry Coryell** (2 Apr 1943, Galveston TX), American jazz and rock guitarist and singer.

**Bill Cosby** (William Henry Cosby, Jr.; 12 Jul 1937, Philadelphia PA), American comedian and actor beloved for the groundbreaking 1980s TV series *The Cosby Show*.

**Albert Costa** (25 Jun 1975, Lérida, Spain), Spanish tennis player; winner of the 2002 French Open.

**Gabriel Costa** (11 Dec 1954, São Tomé and Príncipe politician; prime minister of São Tomé and Príncipe from March to October 2002.

**Renato Cláudio Costa Pereira** (30 Nov 1936, Brazil), Brazilian international official; secretary-general of the International Civil Aviation Organization (ICAO), 1997–2003.

**Bob Costas** (Robert Quinlan Costas; 22 Mar 1952, New York NY), American TV sportscaster and host.

**Elvis Costello** (Declan Patrick MacManus; 25 Aug 1954, Liverpool, England), British songwriter and performer.

**Kevin Costner** (18 Jan 1955, Compton CA), American motion-picture actor and director most acclaimed for *Dances with Wolves* (1990).

**Pascal Couchepin** (5 Apr 1942, Martigny, Switzerland), Swiss president in 2003.

**David Coulthard** (27 Mar 1971, Twynholm, Scotland), Scottish Formula One race-car driver; winner of the Monte Carlo Grand Prix, 2002.

**Katie Couric** (7 Jan 1957, Arlington VA), American TV talk-show host (*Today*).

**Russell Coutts** (1 Mar 1962, New Zealand), New Zealand yachtsman; first New Zealander and second non-American to win the America's Cup (1995); he and his crewmates successfully defended it in 2000.

**Cindy Crawford** (20 Feb 1966, De Kalb IL), American fashion model.

**Martin Creed** (1968, Wakefield, West Yorkshire, England), British installation artist who won the Turner Prize in 2001.

**(John) Michael Crichton** (23 Oct 1942, Chicago IL), American best-selling writer and director specializing in novels on scientific themes.

**Walter (Leland) Cronkite, Jr.** (4 Nov 1916, St. Joseph MO), American TV journalist, commentator, and TV news anchor.

**David Crosby** (David Van Cortland; 14 Aug 1941, Los Angeles CA), American singer and songwriter with Crosby, Stills & Nash and The Byrds.

**Sheryl Crow** (11 Feb 1962, Kennett MO), American pop-rock singer-songwriter.

**Cameron B. Crowe** (13 Jul 1957, Palm Springs CA), American motion-picture director and writer acclaimed for the autobiographical *Almost Famous* (2000).

**Russell (Ira) Crowe** (7 Apr 1964, Wellington, New Zealand), New Zealand–Australian motion-picture actor famous for *Gladiator* (2000; Academy Award for best actor) and *A Beautiful Mind* (2001).

**Rodney Crowell** (7 Aug 1950, Houston TX), American country and rock singer and songwriter.

**Tom Cruise** (Thomas Cruise Mapother IV; 3 Jul 1962, Syracuse NY), American actor, one of the highest paid film stars of the late 1990s and early 2000s; his breakthrough performance occurred in *Risky Business* (1983), and he followed with *Top Gun* (1986), *Born on the Fourth of July* (1989), and three *Mission: Impossible* films (1996, 2000, and one slated for 2004 release).

**George (Henry) Crumb** (24 Oct 1929, Charleston WV), American composer known for his innovative techniques in the use of vivid sonorities obtained from a wide range of instrumental and vocal effects.

**Nilo Cruz** (1962?, Matanzas, Cuba), Cuban-born American playwright who won the 2003 Pulitzer Prize for *Drama for his Anna in the Tropics*.

**Penélope Cruz (Sánchez)** (28 Apr 1974, Madrid, Spain), Spanish actress who achieved international fame in the late 1990s.

**Branko Crvenkovski** (12 Oct 1962, Sarajevo, Yugoslavia [now in Bosnia and Herzegovina]), Macedonian politician; prime minister of Macedonia, 1992–98, and again from 1 Nov 2002.

**Billy Crystal** (14 Mar 1947, Long Beach NY), American comedic actor popular for light dramatic comedies.

**Kieran Culkin** (30 Sep 1982, New York NY), American actor who won the Newcomer Award at the 2002 VH1/Vogue Fashion Awards.

**John Currin** (1962, Boulder CO), American artist known for his synthesis of classical and modern styles and his nudes.

**Ben Curtis** (26 May 1977, Ostrander OH), American golfer who amazed the public when, as a rookie, he won the 2003 British Open.

**Christopher Paul Curtis** (10 May 1954, Flint MI), American author of children's books.

**Jamie Lee Curtis** (22 Nov 1958, Los Angeles CA), American film and TV actress.

**D.M.C.** (Darryl McDaniels; 31 May 1964, Hollis, Queens NY), American hip-hop pioneer (of Run-D.M.C.).

**Vincent D'Onofrio** (30 Jul 1959, Brooklyn NY), American TV actor starring in *Law & Order: Criminal Intent* from 2001.

**Paquito D'Rivera** (4 Jun 1948, Havana, Cuba), Cuban-born American jazz reed player and Afro-Cuban bandleader.

**Bjørn Dæhlie** (19 Jun 1967, Råholt, Norway), Norwegian cross-country skier who owns the Winter Olympic records for the most medals won (12) and the most golds (8).

**Willem Dafoe** (William Dafoe, Jr.; 22 Jul 1955, Appleton WI), American actor known for his complex, passionate portrayals; his films include *Platoon* (1986), *The Last Temptation of Christ* (1988), *The English Patient* (1996), and *Spider-Man* (2002).

**Douglas N. Daft** (Australia), American corporate executive; chairman and CEO of the Coca-Cola Co. from 2000.

**Arne Dahl** (Jan Arnald; 1963, Sweden), Swedish writer best known for the "A-Team" series of crime novels (six of the planned 10 had appeared by 2003).

**Dalai Lama** (the 14th Dalai Lama, Tenzin Gyatso, birth name Lhamo Dhondrub; 6 Jul 1935, Takster, Amdo province, Tibet [now Tsinghai province, China]), Tibetan spiritual leader (enthroned in 1940) and ruler-in-exile; head of the Tibetan Buddhists, who recognize him as a manifestation of the Bodhisattva of Compassion and the reincarnation of the previous Dalai Lama. He has led the Tibetan government-in-exile from India since 1959, and won the 1989 Nobel Peace Prize.

**Richard M. Daley** (24 Apr 1942, Chicago IL), American Democratic politician; mayor of Chicago from 1989.

**Carson Daly** (22 Jun 1973, Santa Monica CA), American MTV VJ and host of NBC's *Last Call*.

**Matt(hew Paige) Damon** (8 Oct 1970, Cambridge MA), American actor, screenwriter; his performance in *Good Will Hunting* (1997) made him a top box-office draw.

**Charlie Daniels** (28 Oct 1936, Wilmington NC), American country fiddler and singer.

**Jeff Daniels** (19 Feb 1955, Athens GA), American actor who costarred in the 1994 film *Dumb and Dumber* with comic Jim Carrey.

**Mitchell E. Daniels, Jr.** (7 Apr 1949, Monongahela PA), American businessman and politician; director of the Office of Management and Budget, 2001–03.

**Ted Danson** (Edward Bridge Danson III; 29 Dec 1947, San Diego CA), American film and TV actor best known for playing Sam "Mayday" Malone on the TV series *Cheers* (1982–93) and Dr. John Becker on *Becker* (from 1998).

**Edwidge Danticat** (19 Jan 1969, Port-au-Prince, Haiti), Haitian-born American author whose works focus on the lives of women and their relationships; she also addressed issues of power, injustice, and poverty.

**Mahmoud Darwish** (13 Mar 1942, Birwa, Palestine), Palestinian nationalist poet, probably the most acclaimed poet of the Arab world; his *Halat hisar* (2002; "A State of Seige") dealt with the ordeal of the people of the city of Ram Allah.

**Thomas Andrew Daschle** (9 Dec 1947, Aberdeen SD), American Democratic politician; senator from South Dakota; Senate majority leader (2002–03) and minority leader from 2003.

**Lindsay Davenport** (8 Jun 1976, Palos Verdes CA), American tennis player; won an Olympic gold medal (1996), the US Open (1998), Wimbledon (1999), and the Australian Open (2000).

**Craig David** (5 May 1981, Southampton, Hampshire, England), British rhythm-and-blues and rap performer.

**Sir Colin (Rex) Davis** (25 Sep 1927, Weybridge, Surrey, England), English conductor; principal conductor of the London Symphony Orchestra from 1995.

**Gray Davis** (26 Dec 1942, New York NY), American Democratic politician; governor of California from 1999; in the summer of 2003 a powerful campaign to recall him from the governorship was mounted.

**Raymond Davis, Jr.** (14 Oct 1914, Washington DC), American astronomer; cowinner of the 2002 Nobel Prize for Physics for his study of neutrinos, which he studied by building a huge neutrino detector in a gold mine in South Dakota.

**Patrick Day** (13 Oct 1953, Brush CO), American jockey; all-time top North American money winner with more than 7,000 career victories.

**Stockwell Day** (16 Aug 1950, Barrie, ON, Canada), Canadian politician; leader of the opposition from September 2000.

**Daniel Day-Lewis** (29 Apr 1957, London, England), British motion-picture actor usually cast in serious and compelling roles.

**Inge De Bruijn** (24 Aug 1973, Barendrecht, The Netherlands), Dutch swimmer; she set numerous world records after returning from retirement in mid-1990s and won three Olympic golds (and set three world records) and one silver in 2000.

**Jaap de Hoop Scheffer** (Jakob Gijsbert de Hoop Scheffer; 3 Apr 1948, Amsterdam, The Netherlands), Dutch chairman-in-office of the Organization for Security and Cooperation in Europe from 1 Jan 2003.

**F(rederik) W(illem) de Klerk** (18 Mar 1936, Johannesburg, South Africa), South African politician who as president of South Africa (1989–94) brought apartheid to an end and negotiated a transition to majority rule; shared (with Nelson Mandela) the 1993 Nobel Peace Prize.

**Oscar De La Hoya** (4 Feb 1973, Los Angeles CA), American boxer; he held professional titles in five weight classes: junior lightweight, 1994; lightweight, 1995; super lightweight, 1996; welterweight, 1997 (lost 1999, recovered 2000); and super welterweight, 2001.

**Oscar de la Renta** (22 Jul 1932, Santo Domingo, Dominican Republic), Dominican-born American fashion designer who blended European luxury with American ease to define standards of elegant dressing.

**Robert De Niro** (17 Aug 1943, New York NY), American film actor known for his uncompromising portrayals of violent and abrasive characters.

**Howard Dean** (17 Nov 1948, New York NY), American physician and Democratic politician; governor of Vermont, 1991–2003.

**Idriss Déby** (1952, Fada, Chad), Chadian politician; president of Chad from 1990.

**Ellen DeGeneres** (26 Jan 1958, Metairie LA), American comedienne and TV personality best known for her TV series *Ellen.*

**Jack DeJohnette** (9 Aug 1942, Chicago IL), American jazz drummer and composer.

**Benicio Del Toro** (19 Feb 1967, San Turce, Puerto Rico), American motion-picture actor who won an Academy Award for best supporting actor in 2000 for *Traffic.*

**David Del Tredici** (16 Mar 1937, Cloverdale CA), American composer.

**Bertrand Delanoë** (30 May 1950, Tunis, Tunisia), French politician; mayor of Paris from 2001.

**Michael S. Dell** (23 Feb 1965, Houston TX), American businessman; founder and CEO of Dell Computer Corp. from 1984; he is believed, as of summer 2003, to receive the highest compensation of any US executive.

**Iris Dement** (5 Jan 1961, Paragould AR), American contemporary folk and country singer and songwriter.

**Ann Demeulemeester** (1959, Kortrijk, Belgium), Belgian fashion designer noted for her modernist long coats and unusual fabrics.

**Jonathan Demme** (22 Feb 1944, Baldwin, Long Island NY), American motion-picture director; he won an Academy Award for directing in 1991 (*The Silence of the Lambs*); he later made *Philadelphia* (1993) and *The Truth about Charlie,* a remake of *Charade* (2002).

**Dame Judi Dench** (Judith Olivia Dench; 9 Dec 1934, York, England), British actress known for her powerful stage, TV, and screen roles; she won an Academy Award for best supporting actress in 1998 (*Shakespeare in Love*).

**Rauf Denktash** (1924, Baf [Paphos], Cyprus), Turkish Cypriot politician; president of Turkish Cyprus from 1975.

**Brian Dennehy** (9 Jul 1938, Bridgeport CT), American TV, film, and stage actor known for serious dramatic roles; he won the 2003 Tony Award for best actor in a play for his role in *Long Day's Journey into Night.*

**Gérard Depardieu** (27 Dec 1948, Châteauroux, France), French motion-picture actor.

**Johnny Depp** (John Christopher Depp III; 9 Jun 1963, Owensboro KY), American film and TV actor known for eccentric, brooding roles; he starred in *Edward Scissorhands* (1990), *What's Eating Gilbert Grape* (1993), *Chocolat* (2000), and *Pirates of the Caribbean: The Curse of the Black Pearl* (2003).

**Luis Ernesto Derbez** (1 Apr 1947, Mexico City, Mexico), Mexican foreign minister from 15 Jan 2003.

**Jacques Derrida** (15 Jul 1930, El Biar, Algeria), French philosopher whose critique of Western philosophy and analyses of the nature of language, writing, and meaning were highly controversial yet immensely influential in much of the intellectual world in the late 20th century. He is most celebrated as the principal exponent of deconstruction.

**Alan Dershowitz** (1 Sep 1938, Brooklyn NY), American attorney and legal commentator.

**Thierry Desmarest** (1945), French corporate executive; CEO of TotalFinaElf SA from 1995.

**Frankie Dettori** (Lanfranco Dettori; 15 Dec 1970, Milan, Italy), Italian-born English jockey; winner of more than 2,000 flat races in England and Europe since the mid-1980s.

**Danny DeVito** (Daniel Michaeli; 17 Nov 1944, Neptune NJ), American actor, director, and producer specializing in supporting comic roles.

**Ani Di Franco** (23 Sep 1970, Buffalo NY), American singer and songwriter.

**Neil Diamond** (24 Jan 1941, Brooklyn NY), American pop singer and songwriter who first reached fame in the mid-1960s with the songs "Cherry Cherry" and "I'm a Believer" and continued to write and perform hits into the 1980s; he came back with an album, *Tennessee Moon,* in 1996.

**Cameron M. Diaz** (30 Aug 1972, San Diego CA), American model and actress whose roles have included the hit comedy *There's Something about Mary* (1998), *Being John Malkovich* (1999), *Gangs of New York* (2002), and two Charlie's Angels films (2000, 2003).

**Leonardo Wilhelm DiCaprio** (11 Nov 1974, Los Angeles CA), American actor and heartthrob who achieved box-office success with *Titanic* (1997).

**Bo Diddley** (Ellas Bates; 30 Dec 1928, McComb MS), American singer, songwriter, and musician.

**Dido** (Florian Cloude De Bourneville Armstrong; 25 Dec 1971, London, England), British pop singer.

**Vin Diesel** (Mark Vincent; 18 Jul 1967, New York NY), American film actor; *The Fast and the Furious* (2001) was his first big hit, and in 2003 he starred in *A Man Apart.*

**Barry Diller** (2 Feb 1942, San Francisco CA), American corporate executive; CEO of USA Interactive and Vivendi Universal Entertainment to 2003.

**Matt Dillon** (18 Feb 1964, New Rochelle NY), American actor first known as a teen heartthrob; he often plays alienated, dark characters.

**Jim Dine** (16 Jun 1935, Cincinnati OH), American painter, graphic artist, sculptor, and poet.

**Céline Dion** (30 Mar 1968, Charlemagne, QC, Canada), French Canadian pop singer.

**Jacques Diouf** (1 Aug 1938, Saint-Louis, French West Africa [now in Senegal]), Senegalese international civil servant; director-general of the Food and Agriculture Organization of the UN from 1994.

**Waris Dirie** (c. 1967, Somalia), Somali supermodel and women's rights activist.

**Milo Djukanovic** (15 Feb 1962, Niksic, Yugoslavia [now Serbia and Montenegro]), Yugoslavian politician; president of the Yugoslav Republic of Montenegro from 1998.

**E(dgar) L(aurence) Doctorow** (6 Jan 1931, New York NY), American novelist known for his skillful manipulation of traditional genres; his novels often take place in 1930's New York City. *Ragtime* (1975) and *Billy Bathgate* (1989) both won multiple literary awards. *City of God* (2002) is his most recent novel.

**Gary Doer** (31 Mar 1948, Winnipeg, MB, Canada), Canadian politician; premier of Manitoba from 1999.

**Christoph von Dohnányi** (8 Sep 1929, Berlin, Germany), German conductor; principal conductor of the London Symphony Orchestra from 1996.

**Domenico Dolce** (13 Aug 1958, Polizzi Generosa, near Palermo, Italy), Italian fashion designer, along with partner Stefano Gabbana, whose designs are inspired by the Mediterranean region.

**Plácido Domingo** (21 Jan 1941, Madrid, Spain), Spanish-born Mexican operatic tenor, one of the most popular tenors of the second half of the 20th century.

**Fats Domino** (Antoine Domino, Jr.; 26 Feb 1928, New Orleans LA), American rhythm-and-blues musician who became one of the first rock-and-roll stars.

**Sam Donaldson** (11 Mar 1934, El Paso TX), American TV news correspondent.

**William Henry Donaldson** (1931, Buffalo NY), American banker and corporate executive; chairman of the New York Stock Exchange (1990–95); chairman of the Security and Exchanges Commission from 18 Feb 2003.

**David W. Dorman** (c. 1955), American corporate executive; chairman and CEO of AT&T Corp. from July 2002.

**José Eduardo dos Santos** (28 Aug 1942, Luanda, Angola), Angolan statesman; president of Angola from 1979.

**Abdul Rashid Dostum** (1954, Juzjian province, Afghanistan), Afghani Uzbek military leader who worked with the Northern Alliance against the Taliban.

**Michael Doucet** (14 Feb 1951, Scott LA), American Cajun musician.

**Denzil L. Douglas** (14 Jan 1953, St. Paul's, St. Kitts and Nevis), West Indian politician; prime minister of Saint Kitts and Nevis from 1995.

**James H. Douglas** (21 Jun 1951, Springfield MA), American Republican politician; governor of Vermont from 9 Jan 2003.

**Michael Douglas** (25 Sep 1944, New Brunswick NJ), American film actor and producer who is best known for his intense portrayals of flawed heroes.

**Rita (Frances) Dove** (28 Aug 1952, Akron OH), American writer and teacher who was poet laureate of the US in 1993–95.

**Alexander (John Gosse) Downer** (9 Sep 1951, Adelaide, SA, Australia), Australian politician; foreign minister from 1996.

**Robert Downey, Jr.** (4 Apr 1965, New York NY), American troubled film and TV actor of substance and intelligence; he achieved critical success for the film *Chaplin* (1992).

**Jim Doyle** (23 Nov 1945, Washington DC), American attorney and Democratic politician; governor of Wisconsin from 6 Jan 2003.

**Dr. Dre** (Andre Young; 18 Feb 1965, Los Angeles CA), American rap musician and impresario, considered the pioneer of gangsta rap.

**Stacy Dragila** (25 Mar 1971, Auburn CA), American pole vaulter; she won the gold medal in the first-ever Olympic women's pole vault, 2000.

**E. Linn Draper, Jr.**, American energy engineer and corporate executive; chairman, president, and CEO of American Electric Power, Inc. from 1992.

**Heike Drechsler** (16 Dec 1964, Gera, East Germany [now in Germany]), German long jumper; she is a world-record holder who won a gold medal at the 1983 world championships and made a big comeback to win again at the 1993 worlds and at the 1992 and 2000 Olympics.

**Elizabeth Drew** (16 Nov 1935, Cincinnati OH), American journalist.

**Janez Drnovsek** (17 May 1950, Celje, Yugoslavia [now Slovenia]), Slovene politician; prime minister of Slovenia from 1992–2000 and again 2000–02 and president thereafter.

**Matt Drudge** (27 Oct 1967 Maryland), American Internet journalist.

**Nicanor Duarte Frutos** (c. 1957, Coronel Oviedo, Paraguay), Paraguayan politician; president of Paraguay from 15 Aug 2003.

**David Duchovny** (David William Ducovny; 7 Aug 1960, New York NY), American TV and film actor, best known as Fox Mulder on *The X-Files*.

**Wim Duisenberg** (Willem Frederik Duisenberg; 9 Jul 1935, Heerenveen, The Netherlands), Dutch banker and first president of the European Central Bank, from 1998 to July 2003.

**Olympia Dukakis** (20 Jun 1931, Lowell MA), American film actress and theatrical director.

**Candy Dulfer** (19 Sep 1969, near Amsterdam, The Netherlands), Dutch jazz and pop saxophonist.

**Faye Dunaway** (Dorothy Faye; 14 Jan 1941, Bascom FL), American film actress known for tense, absorbing performances.

**Iain Duncan Smith** (9 Apr 1954, Edinburgh, Scotland), British politician; leader of the Conservative Party from 2001.

**Ronnie Dunn** (1 Jun 1953, Coleman TX), American country-and-western singer; member of the popular vocal duo Brooks & Dunn (Academy of Country Music Entertainer of the Year, 1995, 1996, 2001; Country Music Association Entertainer of the Year, 1996, and Vocal Duo of the Year, 2002).

**Kirsten Dunst** (30 Apr 1982, Point Pleasant NJ), American film actress who has appeared in a string of successful movies including *Spider-Man* (2002).

**José Manuel Durão Barroso** (1956, Portugal?), Portuguese politician; prime minister of Portugal from 6 Apr 2001.

**Charles Dutoit** (7 Oct 1936, Lausanne, Switzerland), Swiss conductor; music director of the Montreal Symphony Orchestra from 1977 until April 2002, when he resigned over a labor dispute; he was music director of the NHK Symphony Orchestra in Tokyo from 1996.

**Sanjay Dutt** (29 Jul 1959, India), Indian film actor whose work in *Vaastav* (1999) and *Kaante* (2002) was particularly appreciated.

**David Duval** (9 Nov 1971, Jacksonville FL), American golfer who won the 2001 British Open.

**Jean-Claude Duvalier** (3 Jul 1951, Port-au-Prince, Haiti), Haitian president of Haiti, 1971–86, who later lived in exile in France.

**Robert Duvall** (5 Jan 1931, San Diego CA), American actor, producer, and screenwriter noted for portrayals of average working people.

**Ronald Dworkin** (1931, Worcester MA), American legal theorist; best known for *Law's Empire*.

**Greg Dyke** (20 May 1947, London, England), British TV executive and head of the BBC from 1999.

**Bob Dylan** (Robert Allen Zimmerman; 24 May 1941, Duluth MN), American singer and songwriter who moved from folk to rock music in the 1960s, infusing the lyrics of rock and roll—which had previously been concerned mostly with boy-girl romantic innuendo—with the intellectualism of classic literature and poetry.

**Esther Dyson** (14 Jul 1951, Zürich, Switzerland), American economist and journalist specializing in computer and cyberspace issues.

**Mikulas Dzurinda** (4 Feb 1955, Spissky Stvrtok, Czechoslovakia [now in Slovakia]), Slovak politician; prime minister of Slovakia from 1998.

**Michael F. Easley** (23 Mar 1950, Nash county NC), American Democratic politician; governor of North Carolina from January 2001.

**Clint Eastwood** (31 May 1930, San Francisco CA), American enduring film actor and moviemaker, originally famous for tough guy roles such as Dirty Harry.

**Bernard J. Ebbers** (27 Aug 1941, Edmonton, AB, Canada), Canadian-born American corporate executive; CEO of WorldCom Group until his resignation in 2002.

**Atef Mohamed Ebeid** (14 Apr 1932, Gharbiya, Egypt), Egyptian politician; prime minister of Egypt from 1999.

**Roger Ebert** (18 Jun 1942, Urbana IL), American film critic, one of America's leading tastemakers for his newspaper columns and TV programs; he is best known for his work with fellow critics Gene Siskel (until Siskel's death in 1999) and Richard Roeper thereafter.

**Rolf Eckrodt** (25 Jun 1942, Gronau, Germany), German business executive; CEO of Mitsubishi Motors Corp. from 2001.

**Umberto Eco** (5 Jan 1932, Alessandria, Italy), Italian literary critic, novelist, and semiotician.

**Marian Wright Edelman** (6 Jun 1939, Bennettsville SC), American attorney and civil rights advocate; founder of the Children's Defense Fund.

**The Edge** (Dave Evans; 8 Aug 1961, Barking, Essex, England), British rock musician (with U2).

**Prince Edward** (Edward Anthony Richard Louis, Earl of Wessex; 10 Mar 1964, Buckingham Palace, London, England), third son of Queen Elizabeth II.

**John Edwards** (10 Jun 1953, Seneca SC), American Democratic politician; senator from North Carolina from 1999.

**Edward Egan** (2 Apr 1932, Oak Park IL), American church leader; Roman Catholic cardinal archbishop of New York.

**Atom Egoyan** (19 Jul 1960, Cairo, Egypt), Armenian Canadian film director, producer, and writer.

**Robert L. Ehrlich, Jr.** (25 Nov 1957, Arbutus MD), American Republican politician; governor of Maryland from 15 Jan 2003.

**Michael D(ammann) Eisner** (7 Mar 1942, Mount Kisco NY), American corporate executive; CEO of the Walt Disney Co. from 1984.

**Hicham El Guerrouj** (14 Sep 1974, Berkane, Morocco), Moroccan runner who set world records in the 1,500-m, 2,000-m, and 1-mile races.

**Queen Elizabeth II** (21 Apr 1926, London, England), queen of the United Kingdom of Great Britain and Northern Ireland from 1952.

**Lawrence J. Ellison** (17 Aug 1944, Chicago IL), American corporate executive; founder and CEO of Oracle Corp. from 1977.

**James Ellroy** (Lee Earle Ellroy; 4 Mar 1948, Los Angeles CA), American mystery writer.

**Ernie Els** (Theodore Ernest Els; 17 Oct 1969, Johannesburg, South Africa), South African golfer who won the US Open (1994, 1997), the British Open (2002), and numerous other tournaments.

**John Elway** (28 Jun 1960, Port Angeles WA), American football player, quarterback who led the Denver Broncos to victory in Super Bowl XXXII in 1998 and XXXIII in 1999.

**John Hart Ely** (3 Dev 1938, New York NY), American legal scholar whose book *Democracy and Distrust* is among the most-cited sources in American law.

**Eminem** (Marshall Bruce Mathers III; 17 Oct 1973, St. Joseph MO), American entertainer, hip-hop artist.

**Emme** (Melissa Miller; New York NY), American fashion model and TV host.

**John Engler** (12 Oct 1948, Mount Pleasant MI), American Republican politician; governor of Michigan, 1991–2003.

**Nambaryn Enkhbayar** (1 Jun 1958, Ulaanbaatar, Mongolia), Mongolian politician; prime minister of Mongolia from 2000.

**Hans Enoksen** (1956), Greenland politician; prime minister from 14 Dec 2002.

**Okwui Enwezor** (1963, Calabar, Nigeria), Nigerian poet and art critic; art museum curator; director of Documenta 11, a contemporary art festival in Kassel, Germany.

**Enya** (Eithne Ní Bhraonáin; 17 May 1961, Gweedore, Ireland), Irish singer of Celtic music.

**Nora Ephron** (19 May 1941, New York NY), American novelist, screenwriter, and director known for romantic comedies.

**Recep Tayyip Erdogan** (26 Feb 1954, Rize, Turkey), Turkish politician; he is the leader of the Justice and Development Party and prime minister from 14 Mar 2003.

**Christoph Eschenbach** (20 Feb 1940, Wroclaw, Poland), Polish-born pianist and conductor; he was named music director of the Philadelphia Orchestra beginning in 2003.

**Adolfo Pérez Esquivel** (26 Nov 1931, Buenos Aires, Argentina), Argentine sculptor and architect who became a champion of human rights and nonviolent reform in Latin America.

**Laura Esquivel** (1951, Mexico City, Mexico), Mexican novelist whose *Como agua para chocolate* (1989; *Like Water for Chocolate*) and *La ley del amor* (1996; *The Law of Love*) were popular successes.

**Amara Essy** (20 Dec 1944, Bouaké, Côte d'Ivoire), Ivoirian diplomat; secretary general of the Organization of African Unity from 2001 and of its successor organization, the African Union, from 2002.

**Gloria Estefan** (Gloria Fajardo; 1 Sep 1957, Havana, Cuba), Cuban-born American salsa singer and lyricist.

**Joseph Estrada** (Joseph Ejercito; "Erap"; 19 Apr 1937, Manila, Philippines), Philippine actor and politician; president of the Philippines, 1998–2001.

**Melissa Etheridge** (29 May 1961, Leavenworth KS), American rock singer and songwriter.

**Kevin (Tyrone) Eubanks** (15 Nov 1957, Philadelphia PA), American jazz guitarist and leader of the Tonight Show Band on TV.

**Robin Eubanks** (25 Oct 1955, Philadelphia PA), American jazz trombone player.

**Jeffrey Eugenides** (1960, Detroit MI), American novelist, author of *The Virgin Suicides* (1993) and *Middlesex,* which won the 2003 Pulitzer Prize for Fiction.

**Donald Evans** (27 Jul 1946, Houston TX), American government official; US secretary of commerce from January 2001.

**Faith Evans** (10 Jun 1973, Lakeland FL), American soul singer.

**Eve** (Eve Jihan Jeffers; Eve of Destruction; Rapper Eve; 10 Nov 1979, Philadelphia PA), American rap singer; won the Breakthrough Style award at the VH1/Vogue Fashion Awards, 2002.

**Ernie Eves** (1946, Windsor, ON, Canada), Canadian politician; premier of Ontario from 15 Apr 2002.

**Cesaria Evora** (1941, Mindelo, Cape Verde), Cape Verdean singer of *mornas.*

**Patrick Ewing** (5 Aug 1962, Kingston, Jamaica), American basketball player with the New York Knicks who was among the top 15 all-time scorers in the NBA and was voted NBA All-Star 11 times.

**(Étienne) Gnassingbe Eyadema** (26 Dec 1937, Pya village, Togoland [now Togo]), Togolese soldier; president of Togo from 1967.

**Fabio (Lanzoni)** (15 Mar 1961, Milan, Italy), Italian model and actor known for appearances on romance novel covers, in TV commercials, and in brief movie cameos.

**Fahd ibn 'Abd al-'Aziz al-Sa'ud** (1923, Riyadh, Arabia [now Saudi Arabia]), king of Saudi Arabia from 1982.

**Richard D. Fairbank** (18 Sep 1950, Menlo Park CA), American corporate executive; founder, chairman, and CEO of Capital One Financial Corp. from 1988.

**Leo Amy Falcam** (20 Nov 1935, Pohnpei Island, Micronesia), Micronesian politician; president of the Federated States of Micronesia, 1999–2003.

**Edie Falco** (Edith Falco; 5 Jul 1963, Brooklyn NY), American film and TV actress; star of the TV drama *The Sopranos.*

**Nuruddin Farah** (24 Nov 1945, Baydhabo, Somaliland [now in Somalia]), Somali writer in English known for his rich imagination and refreshing and often fortuitous use of his adopted language; winner of the Neustadt Prize in 1998.

**Louis (Abdul) Farrakhan** (Louis Eugene Walcott; 11 May 1933, Bronx NY), American leader of the Nation of Islam (Black Muslims) from 1978.

**Colin (James) Farrell** (31 May 1976, Dublin, Ireland), Irish actor who has had lead roles in *Phone Booth* (2002), *Hart's War* (2002), and *S.W.A.T.* (2003).

**Mia Farrow** (Maria de Lourdes Villiers Farrow; 9 Feb 1945, Los Angeles CA), American film actress famous for *Rosemary's Baby* (1968), for her stormy relations with director Woody Allen, and as UNICEF special representative from 2000.

**Mohamed al-Fayed** (27 Jan 1933, Alexandria, Egypt), Egyptian businessman; owner of Harrods department store in London from 1985.

**Roger Federer** (8 Aug 1981, Basel, Switzerland), Swiss tennis player who won the British (Wimbledon) men's title in 2003.

**Dianne (Goldman Berman) Feinstein** (22 Jun 1933, San Francisco CA), American Democratic politician; mayor of San Francisco, 1978–88; US senator from 1992.

**Douglas J. Feith** (Philadelphia PA?), American defense official who served in the Pentagon as undersecretary of defense for policy from 2001.

**Prince Felipe** (Felipe de Borbón y Grecia; 30 Jan 1968, Madrid, Spain), prince of Asturias; heir to the throne of Spain.

**John B. Fenn** (15 Jun 1917, New York NY), American chemist; cowinner of the 2002 Nobel Prize for Chemistry for his work in the study of macromolecules.

**Svetlana Feofanova** (16 Jul 1980, Moscow, USSR [now in Russia]), Russian pole vaulter; European champion and worldwide leader, set several European records in succession in 2002.

**Sarah (Margaret) Ferguson** (15 Oct 1959, London, England), duchess of York after her marriage (23 Jul 1986) to Prince Andrew; they separated in 1992 and divorced in 1996.

**Lawrence Ferlinghetti** (24 Mar 1919, Yonkers NY), American poet, one of the founders of the Beat movement and cofounder (1953) of the City Lights bookstore, a San Francisco cultural landmark.

**Roberto Fernández Retamar** (9 Jun 1930, Havana, Cuba), Cuban poet, essayist, and literary critic and cultural spokesman for the regime of Fidel Castro.

**Gil de Ferran** (11 Nov 1967, Paris, France), French-born Brazilian race-car driver; CART (Indy Car) champion, 2000 and 2001, and winner of the Indy 500 in 2003.

**Gianfranco Ferré** (15 Aug 1944, Legnano, Italy), Italian fashion designer especially noted for his white dress shirts.

**Will Ferrell** (16 Jul 1967, Irvine CA), American comedian and actor; member of the cast of TV's *Saturday Night Live* (1995–2002).

**Alberta Ferretti** (1950, Riccione, Italy), Italian clothes designer and manufacturer, a leader of the Italian fashion industry.

**Cy Feuer** (15 Jan 1911, Brooklyn NY), American stage and film producer who received a special award for lifetime achievement at the 2003 Tony Awards presentation.

**Sally Field** (Sally Mahoney; 6 Nov 1946, Pasadena CA), American endearing comic and dramatic actress known for her versatility.

**Ralph (Nathaniel) Fiennes** (22 Dec 1962, Suffolk, England), British dramatic actor known for intense roles.

**Harvey (Forbes) Fierstein** (6 Jun 1954, Brooklyn NY), American playwright (*La Cage aux Folles, Torch Song Trilogy*) and performer; he won the 2003 Tony award for best actor in a musical for his role in *Hairspray.*

**50 Cent** (Curtis Jackson; 6 Jul 1976, Jamaica, Queens NY), American hardcore rapper with a troubled upbringing whose *Get Rich or Die Tryin'* (2003) was the fastest-selling album in history.

**Luis Figo** (4 Nov 1972, Almada, Portugal), Portuguese association football (soccer) player; FIFA player of the year, 2001.

**Harvey V. Fineberg** (15 Sep 1945, Pittsburgh PA), American public-health physician and medical administrator; president of the Institute of Medicine from 2002.

**Carly Fiorina** (Cara Carleton Sneed; 6 Sep 1954, Austin TX), American corporate executive; chairman and CEO of Hewlett-Packard Co. and Compaq Computer (which merged in 2002).

**Colin Firth** (10 Sep 1960, Grayshott, Hampshire, England), British film, stage, and TV actor famous for reserved but likeable characters.

**Joschka Fischer** (Joseph Martin Fischer; 12 Apr 1948, Gerabronn, West Germany [now in Germany]), German politician and Green/Alliance 90 leader; foreign minister of Germany from 1998.

**Dietrich Fischer-Dieskau** (28 May 1925, Berlin, Germany), German operatic baritone and lieder singer, distinguished for his lyrical voice, commanding presence, and superb artistry; he won a Japanese Praemium Imperiale Award for excellence in arts in 2002.

**Laurence Fishburne** (30 Jul 1961, Augusta GA), American stage and film actor who achieved lead status with the films *Boyz N the Hood* (1991), *What's Love Got to Do with It* (1993), and The Matrix movie series.

**Allison Fisher** (24 Feb 1968, Cheshunt, Hertfordshire, England), British pocket billiards champion; she won the WPA nine-ball world championships in 1996, 1997, 1998, and 2001.

**Sarah Fitz-Gerald** (1 Dec 1968, Melbourne, VIC, Australia), Australian squash rackets champion; World Open champion, 1996–98, 2001, and 2002; won the British Open, 2001 and 2002, and the Commonwealth Games gold medal, 2002; top-ranking world player from 2001.

**Michael Flatley** (16 Jul 1958, Chicago IL), American dancer and popularizer of Celtic folk dancing.

**Bela Fleck** (10 Jul 1958, New York NY), American banjo player who has made a career of pushing the limits of his instrument beyond mountain music and bluegrass into the realms of classical music and progressive jazz.

**Mick Fleetwood** (24 Jun 1947, Redruth, Cornwall, England), British rock percussionist (of Fleetwood Mac).

**Heidi Fleiss** (30 Dec 1965 California), American socialite, known as the "Hollywood Madam," who was arrested in 1993 and convicted in 1997 for involvement in a prostitution ring with many high-profile clients.

**Osbourne Berlington Fleming** (18 Feb 1940, East End, Anguilla), West Indian politician; chief minister of Anguilla from 2000.

**Renée Fleming** (14 Feb 1959, Indiana PA), American operatic soprano.

**Calista (Kay) Flockhart** (11 Nov 1964, Freeport IL), American stage, film, and TV actress; star of TV's *Ally McBeal* (1997–2002).

**Francisco Flores Pérez** (19 Oct 1959, El Salvador?), Salvadoran politician; president of El Salvador from 1999.

**Juan Diego Flórez** (13 Jan 1973, Lima, Peru), Peruvian operatic tenor especially admired for his interpretations of Rossini heroes.

**Gaston Flosse** (24 Jun 1931, Rikitea, Gambier Islands, French Polynesia), French Polynesian politician; president of French Polynesia, 1984–87, and again from 1991.

**Larry (Claxton) Flynt** (1 Nov 1942, Magoffin county KY), American publisher of *Hustler Magazine* and freedom of the press advocate.

**Ken Follett** (also published as Zachary Stone and Simon Myles; 5 Jun 1949, Cardiff, Wales), Welsh author of political thrillers; his first novel, *Eye of the Needle,* was a best-seller and won the Mystery Writers of America's Edgar Award.

**Jean-Martin Folz** (11 Jan 1947, Strasbourg, France), French corporate executive; CEO of PSA Peugeot Citroën, Europe's second-largest automaker, from 1997.

**Steve Forbes** (Malcolm Forbes, Jr.; 18 Jul 1947, Morristown NJ), American publisher of *Fortune* magazine and one-time presidential contender.

**Carolyn Forché** (28 Apr 1950, Detroit MI), American poet noted for her concern for human rights.

**Betty Ford** (Elizabeth Anne Bloomer Warren; 8 Apr 1918, Chicago IL), American first lady; wife of Pres. Gerald R. Ford.

**Gerald Rudolph Ford** (Leslie Lynch King, Jr.; 14 Jul 1913, Omaha NE), American statesman; 38th president of the US, 1974–77 (see full biography at Presidents).

**Harrison Ford** (13 Jul 1942, Chicago IL), American film actor, a strong leading man, known especially for his work in action films; he achieved immense popularity for playing Han Solo in the *Star Wars* film series (1977, 1980, 1983) and Indiana Jones in the film series of the same name (1981, 1984, 1989, and another scheduled for 2005).

**Tom Ford** (27 Aug 1961, Austin TX), American fashion designer who revamped the image of the house of Gucci in the 1990s; he won Designer of the Year at the Vogue Fashion Awards, 2002.

**William Clay Ford, Jr.** (3 May 1957, Detroit MI), American corporate executive; chairman and CEO of Ford Motor Co. from 2001.

**George Foreman** (10 Jan 1949, Marshall TX), American heavyweight boxing champion, 1973–74 and 1994–95.

**Marc Forné Molné** (1946), Andorran politician; head of government of Andorra from 1994.

**Frederick Forsyth** (25 Aug 1938, Ashford, Kent, England), British journalist and author of best-selling thrillers that include *The Day of the Jackal* (1971) and *The Dogs of War* (1974); a new novel, *Avenger,* appeared in 2003.

**Steve Fossett** (22 Apr 1944, Jackson TN), American commodities trader and adventurer; the first to circle the globe solo in a hot-air balloon (2002).

**Jodie Foster** (Alicia Christian Foster; 19 Nov 1962, Los Angeles CA), American actress widely respected for her intense performances; her breakthrough came at age 13 in the film *Taxi Driver* (1976); she won Academy Awards for best actress in 1988 (*The Accused*) and 1991 (*The Silence of the Lambs*).

**Mike Foster** (Murphy James Foster, Jr.; 11 Jul 1930, Shreveport LA), American Republican politician; governor of Louisiana from 1996.

**Sir Norman (Robert) Foster** (1 Jun 1935, near Manchester, England), British architect who is noted for his conceptual work in corporate, institutional, and transportation structures, such as the Hong Kong Airport; he won the 1999 Pritzker Prize and a Japanese Praemium Imperiale Award for excellence in arts in 2002.

**Jean-René Fourtou** (20 Jun 1939, Libourne, France), French corporate executive; chairman and CEO of Vivendi Universal from July 2002, who in March 2003 also took over VUE, the entertainment operations previously headed by Barry Diller.

**Michael J. Fox** (Michael Andrew Fox; 9 Jun 1961, Edmonton, AB, Canada), Canadian-born American film and TV actor and lobbyist for funding for Parkinson disease research.

**Vicente Fox Quesada** (2 Jul 1942, Mexico City, Mexico), Mexican politician and businessman; president of Mexico from 2000.

**Don Francisco** (Mario Kreutzberger; 28 Dec 1940, Talca, Chile), Chilean-born American TV personality;

host of the popular show *Sábado Gigante,* which celebrated its 40th anniversary on the air in 2002, by far the longest-running TV show with the same host.

**Al Franken** (21 May 1951, New York NY), American comedian and writer who worked for more than a decade on TV's *Saturday Night Live* and later made a career with his liberal political comedy and best-selling books such as *Rush Limbaugh Is a Big Fat Idiot and Other Observations* (1996) and *Oh, the Things I Know: A Guide to Success, or, Failing That, Happiness* (2002).

**Helen Frankenthaler** (12 Dec 1928, New York NY), American Abstract Expressionist painter whose brilliantly colored canvases have been much admired for their lyric qualities.

**Aretha Franklin** (25 Mar 1942, Memphis TN), American gospel and blues singer-composer.

**Tommy R. Franks** (17 Jun 1945, Wynnewood OK), American four-star general in the US Army; as commander-in-chief of the US Central Command from 2000 to July 2003 he was in charge of US operations in Afghanistan, against al-Qaeda, and in Iraq.

**Dennis Franz** (Dennis Schlachta; 28 Oct 1944, Maywood IL), American TV actor famous for police dramas, notably *NYPD Blue.*

**Jonathan Franzen** (1959, Western Springs IL), American author whose The *Corrections* won a National Book Award in 2001.

**Franco Frattini** (14 Mar 1957, Rome, Italy), Italian foreign minister from 2002.

**Cathy Freeman** (Catherine Astrid Salome Freeman; 16 Feb 1973, Mackay, QLD, Australia), Australian Aboriginal sprinter; won the Olympic gold medal in the 400-m race in 2000.

**Morgan Freeman** (1 Jun 1937, Memphis TN), American prolific theater and film actor most famous for the films *Driving Miss Daisy* (1989) and *The Shawshank Redemption* (1994); he starred in *Bruce Almighty* in 2003.

**Dawn French** (11 Oct 1957, Holyhead, Wales), British actress, comedian, and writer known for her work in the TV series *French & Saunders* (with Jennifer Saunders) and *The Vicar of Dibley.*

**Dave Freudenthal** (12 Oct 1950, Thermopolis WY), American attorney and Democratic politician; governor of Wyoming from 6 Jan 2003.

**Mikhail M. Fridman** (21 Apr 1964, Lvov, Ukrainian SSR, USSR [now Lviv, Ukraine]), Russian business tycoon and chairman of the board of the Alfa Group, a financial and management company with interests in banking, insurance, and oil.

**Stephen E. Friedman** (c. 1939), American financier and economist who was named assistant to the president and director of the National Economic Council (chief economic adviser) on 12 Dec 2002.

**Thomas L. Friedman** (20 Jul 1953, Minneapolis MN), American newspaper columnist and author, prominent foreign affairs columnist for the *New York Times.*

**Bill Frisell** (18 Mar 1951, Baltimore MD), American jazz guitarist who has worked in a variety of genres—most recently country and world music—both as a soloist and with acclaimed bands; he has a unique, heavily electrified synthesizer-like sound.

**Bill Frist** (22 Feb 1952, Nashville TN), American cardiac surgeon and politician; Republican senator from Tennessee; Senate majority leader from January 2003.

**Pierre Frogier** (16 Nov 1950, Nouméa, New Caledonia), New Caledonian politician; president of New Caledonia from 2001.

**Fu Mingxia** (16 Aug 1978, Wuhan?, Hubei province, China), Chinese diver; she became youngest world champion diver (1991, at 12) and Olympic champion (1992, at 13, for 10-m platform); gold medalist in 1996 and 2000 Olympics.

**Carlos Fuentes** (11 Nov 1928, Mexico City, Mexico), Mexican novelist, short-story writer, playwright, critic, and diplomat; winner of the Cervantes Prize in 1987.

**Takeo Fukui** (28 Nov 1944, Tokyo, Japan), Japanese corporate executive; president and CEO of Honda Motor Co., Ltd., from June 2003.

**Toshihiko Fukui** (7 Sep 1935, Japan), Japanese banker; governor of the Bank of Japan from 19 March 2003.

**Francis Fukuyama** (27 Oct 1952, Chicago IL), American scholar, newspaper columnist, and author, most notably of *The End of History and the Last Man* (1992).

**Richard S. Fuld, Jr.** (26 Apr 1946), American corporate executive; CEO of Lehman Brothers Holdings from 1993.

**Nelly (Kim) Furtado** (2 Dec 1978, Victoria, BC, Canada), Canadian singer and songwriter.

**Oksana Fyodorova** (1978?, Pskov, Russian SFSR, USSR [now Russia]), Russian police officer selected as Miss Universe in May 2002 but stripped of her title four months later.

**Diana Gabaldon** (11 Jan 1952, Flagstaff AZ), American romance novelist, best-selling author of the Outlander series.

**Stefano Gabbana** (14 Nov 1962, Milan, Italy), Italian fashion designer, along with partner Domenico Dolce, whose designs are inspired by the Mediterranean region.

**Peter Gabriel** (13 Feb 1950, Woking, Surrey, England), British rock and pop singer.

**Neil (Richard) Gaiman** (10 Nov 1960, Portchester, England), British author of the multiple-award-winning adult comic strip Sandman series and other "graphic novels."

**John (Charles) Galliano** (28 Nov 1960, Gibraltar), British fashion designer and designer-in-chief at Christian Dior.

**Frank Gallo** (13 Jan 1933, Toledo OH), American artist and sculptor.

**Christopher B. Galvin** (21 Mar 1950, Chicago IL), American corporate executive; CEO of the Motorola Corp. from 1997.

**James Galway** (8 Dec 1939, Belfast, Northern Ireland), Irish classical flutist.

**Sonia Gandhi** (née Sonia Maino; 9 Dec 1947, Turin, Italy), Italian-born widow of Rajiv Gandhi and political force in India.

**James Gandolfini** (18 Sep 1961, Westwood NJ), American TV and film actor, star of the TV series *The Sopranos.*

**Jan Garbarek** (4 Mar 1947, Mysen, Norway), Norwegian jazz saxophonist and flutist.

**Gael García Bernal** (30 Oct 1978, Guadalajara, Jalisco, Mexico), Mexican actor who scored film hits in three successive years, *Amores perros* (2000), *Y tu mamá también* (2001), and *El crimen del padre Amaro* (2002).

**Gabriel García Márquez** (6 Mar 1928, Aracataca, Columbia), Colombian novelist and short-story writer, a central figure in the magic realism movement in Latin-American literature; he won the 1972 Neustadt Prize and the 1982 Nobel Prize for Literature.

**Rulon Gardner** (16 Aug 1971, Afton WY), American Greco-Roman wrestler who won the Olympic gold medal in 2000.

**Art Garfunkel** (Arthur Garfunkel; 5 Nov 1941, Forest Hills NY), American singer and actor who made his name with his folk-rock work with Paul Simon and later as a soloist and film actor.

**Jay M(ontgomery) Garner** (15 Apr 1938, Arcadia FL), American military officer, a lieutenant general (ret.) in the US Army who served briefly (March–May 2003) as military governor of Iraq following the coalition occupation.

**Jennifer (Anne) Garner** (17 Apr 1972, Houston TX), American TV actress, star of the series *Alias* (from 2001).

**Jean-Pierre Garnier** (31 Oct 1947, France), Swiss corporate executive; head of GlaxoSmithKline PLC from 2000.

**Julie Garwood** (Kansas City MO), American author of romantic fiction whose best-sellers include *For the Roses* (1995) and *Killjoy* (2002).

**Ed Garza** (30 Jan 1969, San Antonio TX), American Democratic politician; mayor of San Antonio TX from 2001.

**Bill Gates** (William Henry Gates III; 28 Oct 1955, Seattle WA), American computer programmer and businessman who cofounded the Microsoft Corp.

**Henry Louis Gates, Jr.** (16 Sep 1950, Keyser VA), American scholar of African American studies.

**Daniele Gatti** (1960, Milan, Italy), Italian conductor of the Royal Philharmonic Orchestra.

**Jean-Paul Gaultier** (24 Apr 1952, Arcueil, France), French fashion designer known for his unusual and extravagant creations.

**Maumoon Abdul Gayoom** (29 Dec 1937, Malé, Maldives), Maldive politician; president of Maldives from 1978.

**Laurent Gbagbo** (31 May 1945, Gagnoa, French West Africa [now in Côte d'Ivoire]), Ivoirian politician; president of Côte d'Ivoire from 2000.

**Haile Gebrselassie** (18 Apr 1973, Assela, Ethiopia), Ethiopian runner; world record holder in the 5,000-m and 10,000-m distances.

**Frank O(wen) Gehry** (28 Feb 1929, Toronto, ON, Canada), Canadian-born American architect and designer whose original, sculptural, often audacious work won him worldwide renown; awarded the Pritzker Prize in 1989.

**Sir Bob Geldof** (5 Oct 1954, Dublin, Ireland), Irish musician (of The Boomtown Rats) who was knighted for his humanitarian work.

**Sarah Michelle Gellar** (14 Apr 1977, New York NY), American TV actress, star of *Buffy the Vampire Slayer*.

**Sir Edward ("Eddie") George** (1938), British financial official; governor of the Bank of England 1993 until his retirement in June 2003.

**(Susan) Elizabeth George** (26 Feb 1949, Warren OH), American mystery writer who has found great success with her novels set in England beginning with *A Great Deliverance* (1988), which was filmed for British TV in 2000; her latest novel is *A Place of Hiding* (2003).

**Ljubco Georgievski** (17 Jan 1966, Stip, Yugoslavia [now in Macedonia]), Macedonian politician; prime minister of Macedonia, 30 Nov 1998–1 Nov 2002.

**Richard Gephardt** (31 Jan 1941, St. Louis MO), American politician; Democratic congressman from Missouri from 1977; House minority leader from 1989.

**Julie Louise Gerberding** (1956?), American physician and public-health specialist; director of the Centers for Disease Control from 3 Jul 2002.

**Richard (Tiffany) Gere** (31 Aug 1949, Philadelphia PA), American film actor made famous for his performances in *American Gigolo* (1980), *An Officer and a Gentleman* (1982), and *Pretty Woman* (1990); his most recent hit was *Chicago* (2002); also known for his work for Tibetan cultural and Buddhist causes.

**Valery Gergiev** (2 May 1953, Moscow, USSR [now in Russia]), Russian conductor; director of the Kirov Opera from 1998.

**Jim Geringer** (24 Apr 1944, Wheatland WY), American Republican politician; governor of Wyoming, 1995–2003.

**Louis Gerstner** (1 Mar 1942, Mineola NY), American corporate executive; president of the IBM Corp. from 1993.

**Mark Getty**, Irish businessman, son of billionaire J. Paul Getty, Jr., and owner of Getty Images, one of the largest photo archives in the world.

**Mohamed Ghannouchi** (1941), Tunisian politician; prime minister of Tunisia from 1999.

**Angela Gheorghiu** (7 Sep 1965, Adjud, Romania), Romanian operatic soprano.

**Nicolas Ghesquiere** (9 May 1971, Loudun, France), French fashion designer, creative director of the house of Balenciaga since 1997; named International Designer of the Year at the 2001 Fashion Designers of America awards.

**Riccardo Giacconi** (6 Oct 1931, Genoa, Italy), Italian-born American X-ray astronomer; cowinner of the 2002 Nobel Prize for Physics for his studies of solar X-ray radiation using rocketry and telescopes and, later, the Chandra X-Ray Observatory.

**Mossimo Giannulli** (4 Jun 1963, California), American fashion designer known for his Mossimo line of sportswear and casual clothing for Target stores.

**Mel Gibson** (Mel Columcille Gerard Gibson; 3 Jan 1956, Peekskill NY), Australian-American actor, producer, and director; one of Hollywood's biggest box-office draws in films that include *The Year of Living Dangerously* (1982), the "Lethal Weapon" trilogy, *Braveheart* (1995), *The Patriot* (2000), and *We Were Soldiers* (2002).

**Romeo Gigli** (1950, Faenza, Italy), Italian fashion designer whose soft, fluid creations exhibit rich fabrics and detailing.

**Gilberto Gil** (Gilberto Passos Gil Moreira; 26 Jun 1942, Salvador, Bahia state, Brazil), Brazilian pop singer and songwriter.

**Melissa Gilbert** (8 May 1964, Los Angeles CA), American film and TV actress beloved for her role as Laura on TV's *Little House on the Prairie*; president of the Screen Actors Guild from 2002.

**João Gilberto (do Prado Pereira de Oliveira)** (10 Jun 1931, Juazeiro, Bahia state, Brazil), Brazilian bossa-nova songwriter, guitarist, and pianist.

**Vince Gill** (Vincent Grant Gill; 12 Apr 1957, Norman OK), American country and progressive-bluegrass instrumentalist and singer who steadily won Nashville's top music awards through the 1990s.

**Liam Gillick** (1964, Aylesbury, Buckinghamshire, England), British installation artist who uses materials such as Plexiglas, aluminum, and wood in his environmentally challenging work; nominated for the Turner Prize in 2002.

**Raymond V. Gilmartin** (Sayville NY), American corporate executive; CEO of Merck & Co. from 1994.

**David Gilmour** (6 Mar 1944, Cambridge, England), British rock guitarist, vocalist, and keyboardist (of Pink Floyd); he was made CBE in 2003.

**Ruth Bader Ginsburg** (15 Mar 1933, Brooklyn NY), American jurist; associate justice of the US Supreme Court from 1993.

**Dana Gioia** (1950, Los Angeles CA), American poet and critic; chairman of the US National Endowment for the Arts from 29 Jan 2003.

**Rudy Giuliani** (Rudolph William Giuliani; 28 May 1944, Brooklyn NY), American Republican politician; mayor of New York City, 1994–2002.

**Hubert de Givenchy** (21 Feb 1927, Beauvais, France), French fashion designer noted for his elegant, classic designs for separates (blouses, skirts, and pants).

**Ira Glass** (3 Mar 1959, Baltimore MD), American radio broadcaster, creator and host of the innovative show *This American Life* (from 1995) on National Public Radio.

**Philip Glass** (31 Jan 1937, Baltimore MD), American composer of innovative minimalist instrumental, vocal, and operatic music.

**Parris N. Glendening** (11 Jun 1942, Bronx NY), American Democratic politician; governor of Maryland, 1995–2003.

**John H(erschel) Glenn, Jr.** (18 Jul 1921, Cambridge OH), American astronaut, the first American to orbit the Earth; he later served as US senator from Ohio.

**Duchess of Gloucester** (Birgitte Eva van Deurs; 20 Jun 1946, Odense, Denmark), British royal; wife of the Duke of Gloucester.

**Duke of Gloucester** (Prince Richard; 26 Aug 1944), British royal.

**Danny (Lebern) Glover** (22 Jul 1947, San Francisco CA), American film and TV actor mostly cast in supporting roles.

**Louise (Elisabeth) Glück** (22 Apr 1943, New York NY), American poet whose willingness to confront the horrible, the difficult, and the painful has resulted in a body of work characterized by insightfulness and a severe lyricism.

**Jean-Luc Godard** (3 Dec 1930, Paris, France), French film director who came to prominence with the New Wave group in France during the late 1950s and the 1960s; he won a Japanese Praemium Imperiale Award for excellence in arts in 2002.

**Goh Chok Tong** (20 May 1941, Singapore), Singaporean politician; prime minister of Singapore from 1990.

**Goh Kun** (1938, Seoul, Korea [now in South Korea]), Korean politician; prime minister of the Republic of Korea, 1997–98, and again from 26 Feb 2003.

**Jacqueline Gold** (1960?), British chief executive of Ann Summers, a chain of 80 lingerie and sex shops in Great Britain.

**Whoopi Goldberg** (Caryn Elaine Johnson; 13 Nov 1955, New York NY), American comedienne and established film actress.

**Osvaldo Golijov** (5 Dec 1960, La Plata, Argentina), Argentine composer of Eastern European Jewish heritage who has found success with his passionate and expressive music.

**Gong Li** (31 Dec 1965, Shenyang, Liaoning province, China), Chinese film actress; she starred in Zhang Yimou's film *Hong gao liang* (1987; *Red Sorghum*), *Ba wang bie ji* (1993; *Farewell My Concubine*), and many others; recently she appeared in *Zhou Yu de huo che* (2002; *Zhou Yu's Train*).

**Ralph E. Gonsalves** (8 Aug 1946, Colonarie, Saint Vincent and the Grenadines), West Indian politician; prime minister of Saint Vincent and the Grenadines from 2001.

**Luis Ángel González Macchi** (13 Dec 1947, Asunción, Paraguay), Paraguayan politician; president of Paraguay from 28 Mar 1999 to 15 Aug 2003.

**Jane Goodall** (3 Apr 1934, London, England), British ethologist known for her exceptionally detailed and long-term research on chimpanzees.

**Cuba Gooding, Jr.** (2 Jan 1968, Bronx NY), American film actor made famous by his supporting role in *Jerry Maguire* (1996).

**Ellen Goodman** (11 Apr 1941, Newton MA), American political columnist.

**John Goodman** (20 Jun 1952, Affton MO), American film and TV actor who broke through with the TV comedy *Roseanne* (1988–97) and has played numerous and widely varied roles in major films including voice work in animated films such as *Monsters, Inc.* (2001) and *Jungle Book 2* (2003).

**Doris Kearns Goodwin** (4 Jan 1943, Rockville Centre NY), American historian, biographer, and TV commentator.

**Googoosh** (Faegheh Atashin; 1950, Tehran, Iran), Iranian popular singer.

**Mikhail Sergeyevich Gorbachev** (2 Mar 1931, Privolye, Russian SFSR, USSR [now Russia]), Soviet Russian official; general secretary of the Communist Party of the Soviet Union (1985–1991) and president of the Soviet Union (1990–91); presided over the political and economic liberalization that led to the downfall of Soviet communism and the breakup of the USSR in 1991; was awarded the 1990 Nobel Peace Prize.

**Jeff Gordon** (4 Aug 1971, Vallejo CA), American racecar driver; NASCAR Winston Cup champion, 1995, 1997, 1998, 2001.

**Albert A. Gore, Jr.** (31 Mar 1948, Washington DC), American Democratic politician; vice president of the US, 1993–2001; presidential candidate, 2000.

**Tipper Gore** (Mary Elizabeth Aitcheson; 19 Aug 1948, Washington DC), American personality; wife of Vice Pres. Al Gore (married 19 May 1966).

**Henryk (Mikolaj) Gorecki** (6 Dec 1933, Czernica, Poland), Polish composer whose often atonal early compositions gave way to works characterized by folk songs, medieval music, and Roman Catholicism.

**Louis Gossett, Jr.** (27 May 1936, Brooklyn NY), American film, stage, and TV actor of repute; roles in *An Officer and a Gentleman* (1982), *Iron Eagle* (1986), and *Return to Lonesome Dove* (1993).

**Memo Gracida** (Guillermo Gracida, Jr.; 25 Jul 1956, Mexico City, Mexico), Mexican polo player, leader of the Isla Carroll team, who held a 10–goal handicap for 20 years.

**Steffi Graf** (Stephanie Maria Graf; 14 Jun 1969, Brühl, West Germany [now in Germany]), German tennis player who dominated the sport during the late 1980s and '90s with her intensity, speed, and powerful forehand.

**Bill Graham** (1939, Montreal, QC, Canada), Canadian politician; foreign minister from 2002.

**Billy Graham** (William Franklin Graham; 7 Nov 1918, Charlotte NC), American evangelist whose large-scale preaching tours, known as crusades, and friendship with numerous US presidents brought him to international prominence.

**Bob Graham** (9 Nov 1936, Coral Gables FL), American Democratic politician; senator from Florida from 1986.

**Jorie Graham** (9 May 1951, New York NY), American poet whose abstract, intellectual verse is known for its visual imagery, complex metaphors, and philosophical content.

**(Allen) Kelsey Grammer** (21 Feb 1955, St. Thomas, Virgin Islands), American TV actor, writer, and producer especially known for the TV series *Frasier*.

Jennifer Granholm (5 Feb 1959, Vancouver, BC, Canada), Canadian-born American attorney and Democratic politician; governor of Michigan from 1 Jan 2003.

Amy Grant (25 Nov 1960, Augusta GA), American pop singer.

Hugh Grant (9 Sep 1960, London, England), British-born versatile film actor whose characters range from awkward to sexy.

Günter (Wilhelm) Grass (16 Oct 1927, Danzig, Germany [now Gdansk, Poland]), German poet, novelist, playwright, sculptor, and printmaker who became a literary spokesman for the German generation that grew up in the Nazi era and survived the war; he won the 1999 Nobel Prize for Literature.

Bill Graves (9 Jan 1953, Salina KS), American Republican politician; governor of Kansas, 1995–2003.

Michael Graves (9 July 1934, Indianapolis IN), American architect and housewares designer in the Postmodernist style, known for his signature creations for Target stores.

Macy Gray (Natalie McIntyre; 9 Sep 1970, Canton OH), American rhythm-and-blues singer.

Spalding Gray (5 Jun 1941, Barrington RI), American performance artist, actor, and writer.

Brian Grazer (12 Jul 1951, Los Angeles CA), American film producer, considered one of the most influential in Hollywood, whose A Beautiful Mind won the 2002 best-picture Oscar; his other films include Splash (1984), Apollo 13 (1995), and 8 Mile (2002).

Sir Guy (Stephen Montague) Green (26 Jul 1937, Launceston, TAS, Australia), Australian attorney, jurist, and statesman; served as administrator of the Commonwealth for Australia from 15 May 2003.

Philip Green (15 Mar 1952, London, England), British entrepreneur, owner of the Bhs retail chain.

Richard Greenberg (1958, Long Island NY), American playwright whose Take Me Out won the 2003 Tony Award for best play.

Bob Greene (10 Mar 1947, Columbus OH), American journalist and syndicated columnist.

Mo Greene (Maurice Greene; 23 Jul 1974, Kansas City KS), American sprinter who won the 100-m world championship, 1997, 1999, and 2001; set the 100-m world record, 1999; and won Olympic gold medals in the 100 m and the 4 x 100-m relay, 2000.

Jeff Greenfield (10 Jun 1943, New York NY), American TV journalist.

Alan Greenspan (6 Mar 1926, New York NY), American monetary policymaker; chairman of the US Federal Reserve Bank from 1987.

Bettina Gregory (4 Jun 1946, New York NY), American journalist who for more than 25 years was a correspondent for ABC TV and radio news and later host of The American Family on the Goodlife TV network.

Merv Griffin (6 Jul 1925, San Mateo CA), American TV host and business executive.

Linda G. Griffith (1960?), American bioengineer; a specialist in tissue engineering who developed a chip that mimics the liver.

Nanci Griffith (6 Jul 1954, Seguin TX), American country-folk singer and songwriter.

Roger Grimes (1950, Grand Falls-Windsor, NL, Canada), Canadian politician; premier of Newfoundland and Labrador from 2001.

Ólafur Ragnar Grímsson (14 May 1943, Ísafjörður, Iceland), Icelandic politician; president of Iceland from 1996.

John Grisham (8 Feb 1955, Jonesboro AR), American lawyer and best-selling novelist.

Matt Groening (15 Feb 1954, Portland OR), American cartoonist, creator of TV's The Simpsons.

Herbert Grönemeyer (12 Apr 1956, Göttingen, West Germany [now in Germany]), German pop singer, songwriter, and actor.

Andrew S. Grove (Andras Grof; 2 Sep 1936, Budapest, Hungary), American corporate executive; CEO of Intel Corp. from 1997.

Sofia (Asgatovna) Gubaidulina (24 Oct 1931, Chistopol, Tatar ASSR, USSR [now Tatarstan, Russia]), Russian Tatar composer whose works are polytonal and characterized by dualities and strongly accented rhythms but also employ traditional genres.

Ismail Omar Guelleh (27 Nov 1947, Diré-Dawa, Ethiopia), Djibouti politician; president of Djibouti from 1999.

Gilbert Guillaume (4 Dec 1930, Bois-Colombes, France), French jurist; president of the International Court of Justice from 2000.

Sylvie Guillem (25 Feb 1965, Paris, France), French ballerina; principal dancer with the Royal Ballet.

Kenny C. Guinn (24 Aug 1936, Garland AK), American Republican politician; governor of Nevada from 1999.

Vladimir (Aleksandrovich) Gusinsky (6 Oct 1952, Moscow, USSR [now in Russia]), Russian media mogul and founder of the MOST Group, the owner of several key newspapers, magazines, and broadcast media; he was one of Russia's richest men and one of the "seven oligarchs" who allegedly ruled the country, until government pressure forced him into exile in 2001 and he lost control of MOST.

José Alexandre ("Xanana") Gusmão (20 Jun 1946, Laleia, [Portuguese] East Timor), Timorese independence leader; first president of independent East Timor from 20 May 2002.

David Guterson (4 May 1956, Seattle WA), American novelist who followed his best-selling Snow Falling on Cedars (1994; PEN/Faulkner Award) and East of the Mountains (1999) with Our Lady of the Forest (2003).

Alan H. Guth (27 Feb 1947, New Brunswick NJ), American physicist who developed the theory of inflationary cosmology.

Arlo Guthrie (10 Jul 1947, Coney Island, Brooklyn NY), American folk singer and songwriter.

Carl T.C. Gutierrez (15 Oct 1941, Agana Heights, Guam), American Democratic politician; governor of Guam, 1995–2003.

Lucio Gutiérrez Borbúa (23 Mar 1957, Quito, Ecuador), Ecuadorian politician; president of Ecuador from 15 Jan 2003.

Buddy Guy (30 Jul 1936, Lettsworth LA), American blues guitarist and singer.

King Gyanendra, Bir Bikram Shah Deva (7 Jul 1947, Kathmandu, Nepal), Nepalese king, 1950–51, and again from 2001.

Crown Prince Haakon (Haakon Magnus; 20 Jul 1973, Oslo, Norway), Norwegian crown prince.

Gene Hackman (30 Jan 1930, San Bernardino CA), American motion-picture actor known for emotionally honest and natural performances.

Michael W. Hagee (1945, Hampton VA), American US Marine Corps general; commandant of the USMC from 13 Jan 2003.

Merle Haggard (6 Apr 1937, Bakersfield CA), American country-and-western singer and songwriter; one of the most popular country-music performers of the late 20th century.

**James K. Hahn** (3 Jul 1950, Los Angeles CA), American Democratic politician; mayor of Los Angeles from 1 Jul 2001.

**Jörg Haider** (26 Jan 1950, Bad Giosern, Austria), Austrian ultra-right-wing politician.

**Zoltán Haiman** (8 May 1971, Budapest, Hungary), Hungarian-born American cosmologist working on the early history of the universe, especially the development of dark matter and galaxies that consist of a few very large stars.

**Mika (Pauli) Häkkinen** (28 Sep 1968, Vantaa, Finland), Finnish Formula One race-car driver; Grand Prix world champion in 1998 and 1999.

**Lasse Hallström** (2 Jun 1946, Stockholm, Sweden), Swedish film director and screenwriter who reached international fame (and garnered Academy Award nominations) for *My Life as a Dog* (1986) and *The Cider House Rules* (1999); more recent successes include *Chocolat* (2000) and *The Shipping News* (2001).

**Tarja (Kaarina) Halonen** (24 Dec 1943, Helsinki, Finland), Finnish politician; president of Finland from 2000.

**Pete Hamill** (24 Jun 1935, Brooklyn NY), American journalist and author.

**Sam Hamill** (1943, northern California?), American poet, editor, translator, and essayist; founder of Copper Canyon Press and catalyst of the Poets Against the War movement in 2003.

**John Hamm** (8 Apr 1938, New Glasgow, NS, Canada), Canadian politician; premier of Nova Scotia from 1999.

**Mia Hamm** (Mariel Margaret Hamm; 17 Mar 1972, Selma AL), American association football (soccer) player who led the US women's team to an Olympic gold medal in 1996, the world championship in 1991, and the Women's World Cup in 1999.

**Hammer** (Stanley Kirk Burrell; also known as M.C. Hammer; 30 Mar 1963, Oakland CA), American rap musician.

**Herbie Hancock** (Herbert Jeffrey Hancock; 12 Apr 1940, Chicago IL), American jazz keyboardist and composer.

**Daniel Handler** (nom de plume Lemony Snicket; 28 Feb 1970, San Francisco CA), American children's book author.

**Tom Hanks** (9 Jul 1956, Concord CA), American film actor and director who won an Academy Award for best actor in 1993 (*Philadelphia*) and 1994 (*Forrest Gump*).

**Prince Hans Adam II** (14 Feb 1945, Vaduz, Liechtenstein), prince of Liechtenstein since 1989.

**Pauline Lee Hanson** (27 May 1954, Brisbane, QLD, Australia), Australian politician; leader of the One Nation party and independent member of Parliament.

**Robert Philip Hanssen** (18 Apr 1944, Chicago IL), American counterintelligence agent for the FBI; arrested in February 2001 for having spied for the USSR for some 15 years and sentenced in May 2002 to life in prison.

**King Harald V** (21 Feb 1937, Skaugum, Norway), king of Norway from 1991.

**John Harbison** (20 Dec 1938, Orange NJ), American composer of expressive music in a wide range of forms; he won the Pulitzer Prize in 1987 for his cantata *The Flight into Egypt*.

**Marcia Gay Harden** (14 Aug 1959, La Jolla CA), American motion-picture actress; she gained acclaim for *Pollock* (2000).

**Roy Hargrove** (16 Oct 1969, Waco TX), American jazz trumpeter.

**Rafiq al-Hariri** (November 1944, Sidon, Lebanon), Lebanese politician; prime minister of Lebanon, 1992–98, and again from 2000.

**Katie Marie Harman** (1981?, Gresham OR), American beauty pageant contestant selected as Miss America, 2002.

**Ofra Harnoy** (31 Jan 1965, Hadera, Israel), Israeli-born Canadian cellist who has appeared in concerts and recorded widely; she has performed important new concertos for the cello by Giovanni Batista Viotti and Sir Arthur Bliss as well as works by Vivaldi and Offenbach.

**Lynn Harrell** (30 Jan 1944, New York NY), American cellist.

**Tom Harrell** (16 Jun 1946, Urbana IL), American jazz trumpeter.

**Woody Harrelson** (Woodrow Tracy Harrelson; 23 Jul 1961, Midland TX), American actor, first noticed for his role as Woody on TV's *Cheers.*

**Ed Harris** (28 Nov 1950, Englewood NJ), American film actor known for the range and depth of his work, especially in *Pollock* (2000).

**Emmylou Harris** (2 Apr 1947, Birmingham AL), American folk and country singer who ranged effortlessly among folk, pop, rock, and country-and-western styles and established herself as "the queen of country rock."

**Lou Harris** (Louis Harris; 6 Jan 1921, New Haven CT), American pollster and public opinion analyst.

**René Harris** (1948), Nauruan politician; four-time president of Nauru, most recently from 8 Aug 2003.

**Thomas Harris** (1940, Jackson TN), American writer, author of the Hannibal Lecter novels, including *The Silence of the Lambs* (1988), which have been made into acclaimed movies.

**William B. Harrison, Jr.** (1943, Rocky Mount NC), American corporate executive; CEO of J.P. Morgan Chase & Co. from 2001.

**Prince Harry** (Henry Charles Albert David; 15 Sep 1984, London, England), son of Charles and Diana, Prince and Princess of Wales, and third in line to the British throne.

**Paul Harvey** (Paul Harvey Aurandt; 4 Sep 1918, Tulsa OK), American radio news broadcaster and commentator.

**Dominik Hasek** (29 Jan 1965, Pardubice, Czechoslovakia [now in the Czech Republic]), Czech ice hockey goalie; two-time NHL MVP and five-time all star; he led the NHL in saves for six seasons and won the 2002 Stanley Cup with the Detroit Red Wings.

**Robert Hass** (1 Mar 1941, San Francisco CA), American poet and translator; US poet laureate consultant in poetry, 1995–97.

**Abdiqasim Salad Hassan** (1942, Somaliland?), Somali politician; head of the Transitional National Government of Somalia.

**Vaclav Havel** (5 Oct 1936, Prague, Czechoslovakia [now in the Czech Republic]), Czech playwright, poet, and political dissident; he served as president of Czechoslovakia, 1989–92, and president of the Czech Republic, 1993–2003.

**Ethan Hawke** (6 Nov 1970, Austin TX), American film actor who first gained recognition for *Dead Poets Society* (1989).

**Stephen W. Hawking** (8 Jan 1942, Oxford, England), British theoretical physicist, a specialist in cosmology and quantum gravity. Although severely disabled by ALS (amyotrophic lateral sclerosis, or Lou Gehrig's disease), Hawking remains active in science, publishing theoretical papers, and explaining complex phenomena to lay persons in such best-selling books as *A Brief History of Time* (1988) and *The Universe in a Nutshell* (2001).

**Goldie Hawn** (21 Nov 1945, Washington DC), American TV and film actress known for free-spirited, feisty performances.

**Maseru Hayami** (24 Mar 1925, Kobe, Japan), Japanese banking executive, governor of the Bank of Japan, 1998–2003.

**Issa Hayatou** (9 Aug 1945, Garoua, [French] Cameroun [now Cameroon]), Cameroonian sports executive; president of African Football Confederation and vice president of FIFA from 1988, and member of the IOC from 2001.

**Salma Hayek** (Salma Hayek-Jiménez; 2 Sep 1966, Coatzacoalcos, Veracruz, Mexico), Mexican-born actress who started her career in Mexican TV soap operas before she went to Hollywood; she starred as her countrywoman, the artist Frida Kahlo, in the 2002 film *Frida.*

**Isaac Hayes** (20 Aug 1942, Covington TN), American musician, singer, and songwriter.

**Seamus (Justin) Heaney** (13 Apr 1939, near Castledawson, Northern Ireland), Irish poet whose works evoke events in Irish history and allude to Irish myths; he won the 1995 Nobel Prize for Literature.

**Hugh M. Hefner** (9 Apr 1926, Chicago IL), American publisher and founder of *Playboy* magazine (1953).

**Heloise** (Pónce Kiah Marchelle Heloise Cruse; 15 Apr 1951, Waco TX), American advice columnist.

**Justine Henin-Hardenne** (1 Jun 1982, Liège, Belgium), Belgian tennis player who won the women's singles in the French Open in 2003.

**Jill Hennessy** (Jillian Hennessy; 25 Nov 1969, Edmondton, AB, Canada), Canadian-born American TV actress starring in *Crossing Jordan* from 2001.

**John L. Hennessy** (22 Sep 1952, New York NY), American computer scientist who specializes in computer architecture, especially RISC (reduced instruction set computer); he led Stanford University's Computer Systems Laboratory from 1983 to 1993 and has been president of the university since 2000.

**Grand Duke Henri** (16 Apr 1955, Château de Betzdorf, Luxembourg), grand duke of Luxembourg from 2000.

**Brad Henry** (10 Jun 1963, Shawnee OK), American attorney and Democratic politician; governor of Oklahoma from 13 Jan 2003.

**Hans Werner Henze** (1 Jul 1926, Gütersloh, Germany), German composer whose operas, ballets, symphonies, and other works are marked by an individual and advanced style within traditional forms.

**Orlando Hernández** (byname El Duque; 11 Oct 1969, Villa Clara, Cuba), Cuban baseball player; pitcher for the Cuban national team who later won three World Series titles with the New York Yankees, 1998–2000.

**Carolina Herrera** (María Carolina Josefina Pacanins y Niño; 8 Jan 1939, Caracas, Venezuela), Venezuelan-born American fashion designer and perfume creator whose designs exhibit simple elegance.

**Jacques Herzog** (19 Apr 1950, Basel, Switzerland), Swiss architect; cowinner, with Pierre de Meuron, of the 2001 Pritzker Prize.

**Charlton Heston** (John Charlton Carter; 4 Oct 1924, Evanston IL), American enduring film actor known for historical and literary roles, as in, notably, *Ben-Hur* (1959); he was also president of the Screen Actors Guild, 1966–71, and of the National Rifle Association, 1998–2003.

**Hevia** (José Angel Hevia; 1967, Villaviciosa, Spain), Spanish pop/folk musician, master of the *gaita,* an Asturian bagpipe; his 2000 album *Tierra de Nadie* sold well over a million copies.

**Angela Hewitt** (26 Jul 1958, Ottawa, ON, Canada), Canadian-born British pianist who won the International Bach Competition in 1985 and who has been especially appreciated for her interpretations of that composer; in 2002 she performed the world premiere of Dominic Muldowney's Second Piano Concerto.

**Lleyton Hewitt** (24 Feb 1981, Adelaide, SA, Australia), Australian tennis player who won the 2001 US Open and Wimbledon in 2002; he was the top-ranked men's player in 2001 and 2002.

**Wolfgang Hilbig** (31 Aug 1941, Meuselwitz, Germany), German poet and prose writer known for his dark images and moods; winner of the 2002 Georg Büchner Prize.

**Tommy Hilfiger** (Thomas Jacob Hilfiger; 24 Mar 1951, Elmira NY), American fashion designer whose sportswear and jeans collections express an all-American theme.

**Faith Hill** (Audrey Faith Perry; 21 Sep 1967, Jackson MS), American country singer.

**Julia "Butterfly" Hill** (18 Feb 1974, Mount Vernon MO), American environmental activist.

**Lauryn Hill** (26 May 1975, South Orange NJ), American hip-hop singer and actress.

**Sir Edmund (Percival) Hillary** (20 Jul 1919, Auckland, New Zealand), New Zealand mountain climber and Antarctic explorer who, with Tenzing Norgay, was the first person to set foot on the summit of Mount Everest (29 May 1953).

**Laura Hillenbrand** (1968, Fairfax VA), American writer about horses, winner of the 1998 Eclipse Award for Magazine Writing, and author of the runaway best-seller *Seabiscuit* (2001; film version, 2003), the story of the fabled Thoroughbred, with almost four million copies in print by mid-2003.

**Stephen Hillenburg** (21 Aug 1961, Fort Sill OK), American animator, the creator and executive producer of Nickelodeon TV's *SpongeBob Square Pants* (from 1999).

**Tony Hillerman** (27 May 1925, Sacred Heart OK), American mystery writer whose best-selling novels usually take place in and around the Navajo Reservation.

**Gordon B. Hinckley** (23 Jun 1910, Salt Lake City UT), American church official; president of the Church of Jesus Christ of Latter-day Saints from 12 Mar 1995.

**John (Warnock) Hinckley, Jr.** (29 May 1955, Ardmore OK), American assassin; convicted for shooting (30 Mar 1981) US Pres. Ronald Reagan and others; confined to St. Elizabeth's Hospital in Washington DC in 1982.

**Sam Hinds** (1943), Guyanese politician; president of Guyana in 1997, prime minister 1992–97, 1997–99, and again from 1999.

**Ludwig Hirsch** (28 Feb 1948, Weinberg, Austria), Austrian songwriter and singer.

**Damien Hirst** (1965, Bristol, England), British artist.

**Christopher Hitchens** (13 Apr 1949, Portsmouth, England), American cultural and political critic and journalist.

**Eric Hobsbawm** (9 Jun 1917, Alexandria, Egypt), British historian of the 19th and 20th centuries in volumes such as *The Age of Revolution* (1962), *The*

*Age of Capital* (1975), *The Age of Empire* (1987), and *The Age of Extremes* (1994) and keen observer of contemporary life and society; his memoir, *Interesting Times: A Twentieth-Century Life,* was published in 2002.

**David Hockney** (9 Jul 1937, Bradford, Yorkshire, England), British painter, draftsman, printmaker, photographer, and stage designer whose works are characterized by economy of technique, a preoccupation with light, and a frank, mundane realism derived from Pop art and photography.

**Jim Hodges** (19 Nov 1956, Lancaster SC), American Democratic politician; governor of South Carolina, 1999–2003.

**John Hoeven** (13 Mar 1957, Bismarck ND), American Republican politician; governor of North Dakota from 2001.

**James P. Hoffa** (19 May 1941, Detroit MI), American labor leader; head of the International Brotherhood of Teamsters from 1999.

**Dustin Hoffman** (8 Aug 1937, Los Angeles CA), American motion-picture actor of great range and endurance; major films include *The Graduate* (1967) and *All the President's Men* (1976); he won best-actor Academy Awards for *Kramer vs. Kramer* (1979) and *Rain Man* (1988).

**Christopher (Jarvis Haley) Hogwood** (10 Sep 1941, Nottingham, England), British harpsichordist.

**Richard (Charles Albert) Holbrooke** (24 Apr 1941, New York NY), American diplomat; US permanent representative to the UN, 1999–2001.

**Bob Holden** (24 Aug 1949, Kansas City MO), American Democratic politician; governor of Missouri from 2001.

**Chamique Holdsclaw** (9 Aug 1977, Flushing NY), American basketball player; 1999 WNBA Rookie of the Year; three-time WNBA All Star; twice national player of the year; she led the University of Tennessee to three NCAA titles, 1996–98.

**Dave Holland** (1 Oct 1946, Wolverhampton, England), English-born American jazz bassist.

**Peter Hollingworth** (10 Apr 1935, Adelaide, SA, Australia), Australian church leader and statesman; he served as Anglican archbishop of Brisbane (1990–2001) before being named governor-general of Australia, a post he held from 2001 to 2003.

**Evander Holyfield** (19 Oct 1962, Atmore AL), American boxer; four-time heavyweight champion, 1990–92 (WBA, WBC, IBF), 1993–94 (WBA, IBF), 1996–99 (WBA, IBF from 1997), 2000–01 (WBA).

**bell hooks** (Gloria Jean Watkins; 25 Sep 1952, Hopkinsville KY), American feminist scholar.

**Sir Anthony Hopkins** (31 Dec 1937, Port Talbot, West Glamorgan, Wales), British intense, gifted film and stage actor.

**Bernard Hopkins** (15 Jan 1965, Philadelphia PA), American middleweight boxer who won the unified title in 2001 by defeating favored Félix Trinidad.

**Dennis Hopper** (17 May 1936, Dodge City KS), American film actor.

**H. Robert Horvitz** (8 May 1947, Chicago IL), American cell biologist; cowinner of the 2002 Nobel Prize for Physiology or Medicine for his work on the life of a cell.

**Whitney (Elizabeth) Houston** (9 Aug 1963, Newark NJ), American pop singer and film actress.

**John Winston Howard** (26 Jul 1939, Sydney, NSW, Australia), Australian politician; Liberal Party chairman, and prime minister of Australia from 1996.

**Michael Howard** (7 Jul 1941, England), British Conservative politician who served as home secretary (1993–97) and was shadow chancellor from 2001.

**Ron Howard** (1 Mar 1954, Duncan OK), American TV and film actor famous for his role on TV's *Happy Days* and as an acclaimed movie director; he won an Oscar in 2002 for best director (*A Beautiful Mind*).

**Hu Jintao** (Dec 1942, Jixi, Anhui province, China), Chinese statesman; general secretary of the Communist Party of China, president of China, and vice chairman of the Military Commission.

**Mike Huckabee** (24 Aug 1955, Hope AR), American Republican politician; governor of Arkansas from 1996.

**Kate (Garry) Hudson** (19 Apr 1979, Los Angeles CA), American film actress who starred in *Almost Famous* (2000) and *Le Divorce* (2003).

**Robert (Studley Forrest) Hughes** (28 Jul 1938, Sydney, NSW, Australia), Australian art critic and author.

**Sarah Hughes** (2 May 1985, Great Neck NY), American figure skater; gold medalist at the 2002 Winter Olympic Games.

**Jane Dee Hull** (8 Aug 1935, Kansas City MO), American Republican politician; governor of Arizona, 1997–2003.

**John Hume** (18 Jan 1937, Londonderry, Northern Ireland), Northern Ireland politician; cowinner of the Nobel Peace Prize in 1998 and winner of the Gandhi Peace Prize in 2002.

**Hun Sen** (4 Apr 1951, Kompong Chom province, Cambodia), Cambodian politician and leader of the government from 1985.

**Helen Hunt** (15 Jun 1963, Culver City CA), American film and TV actress made popular by the series *Mad About You,* she has gone on to star in major films, including *As Good As It Gets* (1997; Academy Award) and *What Women Want* (2000).

**(Nelson) Bunker Hunt** (22 Feb 1926, El Dorado TX), American business executive, oil heir, and speculator.

**Charlayne Hunter-Gault** (27 Feb 1942, Due West SC), American TV journalist especially noted for her work with *The MacNeil/Lehrer Report.*

**Elizabeth Hurley** (10 Jun 1965, Hampshire, England), British actress, dancer, and model known for glamorous leading roles; her films include *Austin Powers* (1999), *Bedazzled* (2000), and *Serving Sara* (2002).

**William Hurt** (20 Mar 1950, Washington DC), American actor known for his cerebral, diverse characters.

**Saddam Hussein** (in full Saddam Hussein Al-Tikriti; 28 Apr 1937, Tikrit district, Iraq), Iraqi military leader and politician; president of Iraq from 1979 until 2003, when he was deposed by the invasion of Iraq by US-UK coalition forces.

**Anjelica Huston** (8 Jul 1951, Santa Monica CA), American original film actress whose work has spanned many decades.

**Kumba Ialá** (1952), Guinea-Bissau politician; president of Guinea-Bissau from 2000.

**Ice Cube** (O'shea Jackson; 15 Jun 1969), American rap singer, songwriter, and actor.

**Nobuyuki Idei** (22 Nov 1937, Tokyo, Japan), Japanese corporate executive; CEO of Sony Corp. from 1998 and chairman from 2000.

**Eric Idle** (29 Mar 1943, South Shields, Durham, England), British TV actor and author, a founding member of the Monty Python Flying Circus troupe.

**Enrique Iglesias** (1931, Spain), Uruguayan international banker; president of the Inter-American Development Bank from 1988.

**Enrique Iglesias** (8 May 1975, Madrid, Spain), Spanish pop singer; son of Julio Iglesias.

**Julio Iglesias** (Julio José Iglesia de la Cueva; 23 Sep 1943, Madrid, Spain), Spanish pop singer.

**Ion Iliescu** (3 Mar 1930, Oltenita, Romania), Romanian politician; president of Romania, 1989–96, and again from 2000.

**Ratu Josefa Iloilo** (1920), Fijian politician; president of Fiji from 2000.

**Im Kwon-taek** (2 May 1936, Jansung, Korea [now in South Korea]), Korean film director, winner of the best director award at the Cannes Film Festival in 2002 for his *Chihwaseon*.

**Iman** (Iman Mohamed Abdulmajid; 25 Jul 1955, Mogadishu, Somalia), Somali fashion model of the 1970s and '80s, actress, and cosmetics executive.

**Natalie Imbruglia** (4 Feb 1975, Sydney, NSW, Australia), Australian pop singer who scored a huge success in the UK with her first single, "Torn" (1997), and followed with a well-received album, *Left of the Middle,* in 1998.

**Jeffrey R. Immelt** (19 Feb 1956, Cincinnati OH), American corporate executive; CEO of the General Electric Co. from 2001.

**Don Imus** (23 Jul 1940, Riverside CA), American radio talk-show host.

**India.Arie** (India Arie Simpson; 3 Oct 1976, Denver CO), American singer and songwriter; her debut album, *Acoustic Soul* (2001), received seven Grammy nominations.

**Juli Inkster** (Juli Simpson; 24 Jun 1960, Santa Cruz CA), American golfer who won the US Women's Open in 1999 and 2002 and the LPGA championship in 1999 and 2000.

**Kathy Ireland** (8 Mar 1963, Glendale CA), American fashion model, designer, and actress whose clothing and home-furnishings collections are noted for their affordability.

**Steve Irwin** (Stephen Robert Irwin; 22 Feb 1962, Melbourne, VIC, Australia), Australian television nature-show host.

**Walter Isaacson** (20 May 1952, New Orleans LA), American corporate executive; chairman and CEO of the Cable News Network (CNN) from 2001.

**Eugene M. Isenberg** (Chelsea MA), American corporate executive; CEO of Nabors Industries, Inc. from 1987.

**Yusuf Islam** (Steven Georgiou; Cat Stevens; 21 Jul 1947, London, England), British pop singer, songwriter, and pianist.

**Goran Ivanisevic** (13 Sep 1971, Split, Yugoslavia [now in Croatia]), Croatian tennis player; he won the Wimbledon singles in 2001, the first wild-card choice to win the title in the history of the tournament.

**Igor Sergeyevich Ivanov** (1945, Moscow, USSR [now in Russia]), Russian foreign minister from 1998.

**Allen (Ezail) Iverson** (7 Jun 1975, Hampton VA), American basketball player; 2001 all-star and NBA MVP; he led the NBA in points per game and steals per game in 2001–02.

**Molly Ivins** (30 Aug 1944, Monterey CA), American political commentator and columnist.

**James (Francis) Ivory** (7 Jun 1928, Berkeley CA), American film director famous for his collaboration with producer Ismail Merchant on many period pieces, including *A Room with a View* (1986), *Howards End* (1992), and *The Remains of the Day* (1993).

**B.K.S. Iyengar** (14 Dec 1918, Bellur, Karnataka state, British India), Indian teacher, practitioner, and popularizer of yoga.

**Ja Rule** (Jeff Atkins; 29 Feb 1976, Queens NY), American rap performer.

**Anneli Jäätteenmäki** (11 Feb 1955, Lappo, Finland), Finnish politician; prime minister of Finland, 17 April–19 Jun 2003.

**Alan (Eugene) Jackson** (17 Oct 1958, Newnan GA), American country music singer and guitarist; CMA Entertainer of the Year in 1995 and 2002.

**Janet Jackson** (16 May 1966, Gary IN), American singer and film and TV actress.

**Jesse (Louis) Jackson** (8 Oct 1941, Greenville SC), American civil-rights leader, Baptist minister, and politician, the first African American to make a serious bid for the US presidency (in the Democratic Party's nomination races in 1983–84 and 1987–88).

**Michael (Joseph) Jackson** (29 Aug 1958, Gary IN), American singer, songwriter, and dancer who was the most popular entertainer in the world in the early and mid-1980s.

**Peter Jackson** (31 Oct 1961, Pukerua Bay, New Zealand), New Zealand film director and producer who directed "The Lord of the Rings" trilogy (from 2001).

**Phil Jackson** (Philip Douglas Jackson; 17 Sep 1945, Deer Lodge MT), American basketball player and coach; as coach, he won nine NBA titles with the Chicago Bulls (1991–93, 1996–98) and the Los Angeles Lakers (2000–02); he holds the record for most NBA playoff coaching wins (156).

**Samuel L. Jackson** (21 Dec 1948, Washington DC), American film actor whose breakthrough performance in *Jungle Fever* (1991) launched a successful career.

**Marc Jacobs** (9 Apr 1963, New York NY), American fashion designer, creator of his own signature lines and artistic director for Louis Vuitton.

**Christian Jacq** (1947, Paris, France), French Egyptologist and author.

**Bharrat Jagdeo** (23 Jan 1964, Unity village, Demarara, Guyana), Guyanese politician and president from 1999.

**Mick Jagger** (Michael Philip Jagger; 26 Jul 1943, Dartford, Kent, England), British rock musician and lead singer of the Rolling Stones.

**Jaromír Jagr** (15 Feb 1972, Kladno, Czechoslovakia [now in the Czech Republic]), Czech hockey player; NHL MVP in 1999; he won the Art Ross Trophy (leading scorer) 1995, 1998–2001.

**Helmut Jahn** (4 Jan 1940, Nürnberg, Germany), German-born architect known especially for his use of light and color.

**Ahmad Jamal** (2 Jul 1930, Pittsburgh PA), American jazz pianist and composer.

**Etta James** (Jamesetta Hawkins; 25 Jan 1938, Los Angeles CA), American rhythm-and-blues entertainer who later became a successful ballad singer.

**P.D. James** (3 Aug 1920, Oxford, Oxfordshire, England), British mystery novelist.

**Yahya Jammeh** (Alphonse Jamus Jebulai Jammeh; 25 May 1965, Kanilai village, The Gambia), Gambian politician; president of The Gambia from 1994.

**William J. Janklow** (13 Sep 1939, Chicago IL), American Republican politician; governor of South Dakota, 1995–2003.

**Mariss Jansons** (1943, Riga, Latvian SSR, USSR [now Latvia]), Latvian-born American conductor; music director of the Pittsburgh Symphony Orchestra from 1997; he was named in 2002 to become music director of the Royal Concertgebouw Orchestra of Amsterdam in 2004.

**Jim Jarmusch** (22 Jan 1953, Akron OH), American avant-garde filmmaker.

**Keith Jarrett** (8 May 1945, Allentown PA), American jazz pianist, composer, and saxophonist.

**Tom Jarriel** (Thomas Edwin Jarriel; 29 Dec 1934, La-Grange GA), American broadcast journalist, long-time reporter and anchor on ABC TV newscasts and news journals, notably *20/20.*

**Neeme Järvi** (7 Jun 1937, Tallinn, Estonia), Estonian conductor; music director of the Detroit Symphony Orchestra from 1990.

**Jay-Z** (Shawn Carter; 4 Dec 1970, Brooklyn NY), American rap performer.

**Mae C. Jemison** (17 Oct 1956, Decatur AL), American physician and the first African American woman to become an astronaut (1992).

**Peter (Charles) Jennings** (29 Jul 1938, Toronto, ON, Canada), Canadian-born American broadcast journalist and news anchor of *ABC World News Tonight with Peter Jennings* from 1983.

**Siegfried Jerusalem** (17 Apr 1940, Oberhausen, Germany), German operatic tenor.

**Derek Jeter** (26 Jun 1974, Pequannock NJ), American baseball player; shortstop for the New York Yankees (from 1995) during four World Series-winning seasons (1996, 1998–2000).

**Jean-Pierre Jeunet** (3 Sep 1953, Roanne, France), French film director whose work includes *Delicatessen* (1991), which won four Césars, *La Cité des enfants perdus* (1995; *City of Lost Children*), and *La Fabuleux destin d'Amélie Poulain* (2001; *Amélie*).

**Jewel** (Jewel Kilcher; 23 May 1974, Payson UT), American pop singer and songwriter.

**Ruth Prawer Jhabvala** (7 May 1927, Cologne, Germany), German-born writer of short stories and novels especially known for her collaboration as screenwriter with filmmakers Ismail Merchant and James Ivory; her novel *Heat and Dust* won the Booker Prize in 1975, and she won Academy Awards for her screen adaptations of E.M. Forster's novels *A Room with a View* (1986) and *Howards End* (1992).

**Jiang Zemin** (17 Aug 1926, Yangzhou, Jiangsu province, China), Chinese politician; general secretary of the Communist Party, and president of China, 1993–2003; he became powerful following the Tiananmen Square massacre and promoted an "open door" economic policy for China.

**Ha Jin** (Xuefei Jin; 21 Feb 1956, Jinzhou, Liaoning province, China), Chinese American writer whose novel *Waiting* won the 1999 National Book Award and the PEN/Faulkner Award for fiction in 2000.

**Sumi Jo** (1962, Seoul, South Korea), Korean operatic soprano.

**Steven Paul Jobs** (24 Feb 1955, San Francisco CA), American corporate executive; cofounder of Apple Computer, and CEO of Apple Computer, Inc. from 1997.

**Billy Joel** (William Martin Joel; 9 May 1949, Hicksville NY), American pop singer, pianist, and songwriter.

**Mike Johanns** (18 Jun 1950, Osage IA), American Republican politician; governor of Nebraska from 1999.

**Thomas Johansson** (24 Mar 1975, Linkoping, Sweden), Swedish tennis player, winner of the 2002 Australian Open.

**Elton John** (Reginald Kenneth Dwight; 25 Mar 1947, Pinner, Middlesex, England), British singer, composer, and pianist who was one of the most popular and enduring entertainers of the late 20th century.

**John Paul II** (Latin Ioannes Paulus, original name Karol Jozef Wojtyla; 18 May 1920, Wadowice, Poland), Polish-born pope (from 1978); the first non-Italian pope in 455 years and the first ever from a Slavic country.

**Jasper Johns** (15 May 1930, Augusta GA), American painter and graphic artist, a pioneer of Pop art; he raised commonplace subjects (such as numbers, letters, flags) to status of icons by rendering them in simple colors and with purposeful, ironic banality.

**Betsey Johnson** (10 Aug 1942, Wethersfield CT), American fashion designer whose rock-star personality is exhibited in whimsical creations meant to make fashion fun.

**Boris Johnson** (Alexander Boris de Pfeffel Johnson; 19 Jun 1964, New York NY), American-born British journalist, editor of *The Spectator,* and Conservative member of Parliament.

**Gary E. Johnson** (1 Jan 1953, Minot ND), American Republican politician; governor of New Mexico, 1995–2003.

**Lady Bird Johnson** (Claudia Alta Taylor; 22 Dec 1912, Karnack TX), American first lady; widow of Pres. Lyndon B. Johnson.

**Angelina Jolie** (Angelina Jolie Voight; 4 Jun 1975, Los Angeles CA), American film actress with a knack for keeping her name in the headlines; she is best known for the starring role in *Lara Croft: Tomb Raider* (2001, with a sequel released in 2003) and her work in *Girl, Interrupted* (1999; Academy Award for best supporting actress).

**George Jones** (12 Sep 1931, Saratoga TX), American honky-tonk performer and balladeer considered to be one of the greatest country singers of all time.

**James Earl Jones** (17 Jan 1931, Arkabutla MS), American actor best known for his leading roles in Shakespeare's *Othello* and in *The Great White Hope*; also the famous voice of Darth Vader in the Star Wars trilogy.

**James L. Jones** (19 Dec 1943, Kansas City MO), American Supreme Allied Commander, Europe (SACEUR) and the Commander of the United States European Command (COMUSEUCOM) from January 2003.

**Marion Jones** (12 Oct 1975, Los Angeles CA), American sprinter and long-jumper; she was Olympic gold medalist (2000) in three running events and won bronzes in two other events, the most medals ever won by a woman in track and field in one Olympic Games.

**Norah Jones** (30 Mar 1979, New York NY), American jazz-pop vocalist and pianist who won five Grammy Awards for her 2002 debut album, *Come Away with Me,* and her song "Don't Know Why."

**Quincy Jones** (Quincy Delight Jones, Jr.; 14 Mar 1933, Chicago IL), American arranger, composer, and producer.

**Rickie Lee Jones** (8 Nov 1954, Chicago IL), American pop singer.

**Roy Jones, Jr.** (16 Jan 1969, Pensacola FL), American boxer; the undisputed light-heavyweight champion from 1999 and WBA heavyweight champ with his victory over John Ruiz on 1 Mar 2003.

**Tom Jones** (Thomas Jones Woodward; 7 Jun 1940, Pontypridd, Wales), Welsh pop singer, a durable crooner and sex symbol who has enjoyed a great number of hits, including "It's Not Unusual" and "What's New Pussycat?" (1965), and "Delilah" (1968).

**Tommy Lee Jones** (15 Sep 1946, San Saba TX), American actor whose films include *Coal Miner's Daughter* (1980), *The Executioner's Song* (TV, 1982), *The Fugitive* (1993; Academy Award), and the popular Men in Black (1997 and 2002) movies.

**Michael (Jeffrey) Jordan** (17 Feb 1963, Brooklyn NY), American basketball player; playing for the Chicago Bulls, he led NBA in scoring, 1987–93, 1996–98; he was MVP in 1988, 1991–92, 1996, 1998; he was voted ESPN's Athlete of the Century and is believed by many to be the best basketball player in the history of the sport.

**King Juan Carlos I** (Juan Carlos Alfonso Victor María de Borbón y Borbón; 5 Jan 1938, Rome, Italy), king of Spain from 1975.

**Juanes** (Juan Esteban Aristizabal; Medellín, Colombia), Colombian singer, songwriter, and guitarist whose first album, *Fíjate bien,* and a later single, "A Dios le pido," won several Latin Grammy awards and spent a year on the top of the Latin pop charts.

**Naomi Judd** (Diana Ellen Judd; 11 Jan 1946, Ashland KY), American country-and-western singer.

**Wynonna Judd** (Christina Claire Ciminella; 30 May 1964, Ashland KY), American country-and-western singer.

**Sir Anerood Jugnauth** (29 Mar 1930), Mauritian politician; prime minister of Mauritius, 1982–95, and again from 2000.

**John P. Jumper** (4 Feb 1945, Paris TX), American military official; chief of staff of the US Air Force from 2001.

**Jean-Claude Juncker** (9 Dec 1954, Rédange-sur-Attert, Luxembourg), Luxembourgian politician; prime minister of Luxembourg from 1995.

**Andrea Jung** (1959, Toronto, ON, Canada), Canadian-born American business executive; CEO of Avon Products, Inc. from 1999.

**Ahmad Tejan Kabbah** (16 Feb 1932, Pendembu, Sierra Leone), Sierra Leonean politician; president of Sierra Leone, 1996–97, and again from 1998.

**Joseph Kabila** (4 Jun 1971, Sud-Kivu province, Dem. Rep. of the Congo), Congolese politician; president of the Dem. Rep. of the Congo from 17 Jan 2001.

**Ismail Kadare** (28 Jan 1938, Gjirokastër, Albania), Albanian novelist and poet, renowned in Albania for his poetry and internationally for his fiction.

**Paul Kagame** (1957?, Gitarama, Ruanda-Urundi [now Rwanda]), Rwandan politician; president of Rwanda from 2000.

**Dahir Riyale Kahin** (1952), Somali politician; president of the secessionist Republic of Somaliland from 3 May 2002.

**Oliver Kahn** (15 Jun 1969, Karlsruhe, West Germany [now in Germany]), German association football (soccer) goalie for the second-place German national team at the 2002 World Cup.

**Daniel Kahneman** (5 Mar 1934, Tel Aviv, British Palestine [now in Israel]), American economist; cowinner of the 2002 Nobel Prize for Economics for his work in integrating psychology and economic theory.

**Stephen Kakfwi** (1950, near Fort Good Hope, NWT, Canada), Canadian politician; premier of Northwest Territories from 17 Jan 2000.

**Siim Kallas** (2 Oct 1948, Tallinn, Estonian SSR, USSR [now Estonia]), Estonian politician; prime minister of Estonia from 2002.

**Anfinn Kallsberg** (1947), Faroese politician; prime minister of the Faroe Islands from 1998.

**Dean Kamen** (1951, Rockville Centre NY), American engineer and inventor of the Segway Human Transporter (unveiled in December 2001).

**Giya Kancheli** (10 Aug 1935, Tbilisi, Georgian SSR, USSR [now Georgia]), Georgian composer of deeply spiritual music, mostly in symphonic and theatrical forms.

**Aleksandr Kantorov** (1947, Leningrad, USSR [now St. Petersburg, Russia]), Russian artistic director and principal conductor of the St. Petersburg State Symphony Orchestra.

**Anish Kapoor** (1954, Bombay [now Mumbai], India), Indian-born British sculptor and installation artist.

**Radovan Karadzic** (19 Jun 1945, Petnjica, Yugoslavia [now in Serbia and Montenegro]), Bosnian Serb politician; president of Republika Srpska (Bosnia and Herzegovina), 1992–96; he was wanted as a war criminal and was at large in 2003.

**Donna Karan** (Donna Faske; 2 Oct 1948, Forest Hills NY), American fashion designer known for the simplicity of her predominately black- and neutral-colored designs.

**Aleksandr Karelin** (19 Sep 1967, Novosibirsk, Russian SFSR, USSR [now Russia]), Russian Greco-Roman wrestler revered for his extraordinary strength and unprecedented success in international competition. Beginning in 1988 he won 12 consecutive world championships and 3 Olympic gold medals until he was defeated in the final at the 2000 Olympics by Rulon Gardner.

**Islam Karimov** (30 Jan 1938, Samarkand, Uzbek SSR, USSR [now Uzbekistan]), Uzbek politician; president of Uzbekistan from 1990.

**Hamid Karzai** (24 Dec 1957, Karz, Afghanistan), Afghani statesman; head of the interim administration of Afghanistan following the ousting of the Taliban; president of Afghanistan from 22 Dec 2001.

**Garry Kasparov** (Garri Kimovich Kasparov, original name Garri Weinstein or Harry Weinstein; 13 Apr 1963, Baku, Azerbaijani SSR, USSR [now Azerbaijan]), Azerbaijani-born Russian chess champion of the world from 1985 to 2000.

**Mikhail Mikhaylovich Kasyanov** (8 Dec 1957, Solntsevo, Russian SFSR, USSR [now Russia]), Russian politician; prime minister of Russia from 2000.

**Moshe Katsav** (1945, Iran), Iranian-born Israeli politician; president of Israel from 2000.

**Kurt Kauper** (1966, Indianapolis IN), American figurative artist.

**Lydia E. Kavraki** (1967?, Crete, Greece), Greek-born American computer scientist, a specialist in bioinformatics and robotics whose work has revolutionized the study of robot navigation.

**Yoriko Kawaguchi** (14 Jan 1941, Tokyo, Japan), Japanese politician; foreign minister of Japan from 2002.

**Nobuhiko Kawamoto** (3 Mar 1936, Tokyo, Japan), Japanese corporate executive, president of Honda Motor Co. Ltd. from 1990.

**Andrey I. Kazmin** (25 Jun 1958, Moscow, USSR [now in Russia]), Russian chairman and CEO of Sberbank who, as a former finance ministry official, has close ties to the government; he is one of the "seven oligarchs" who allegedly run Russia.

**Frank Keating** (10 Feb 1944, St. Louis MO), American Republican politician; governor of Oklahoma, 1995–2003.

**Liya Kebede** (13 Jan 1980, Addis Ababa, Ethiopia), Ethiopian-born American fashion model, named in 2003 to represent the Estée Lauder brand, the first black woman to be so selected.

**Garrison Keillor** (Gary Edward Keillor; 7 Aug 1942, Anoka MN), American humorist and writer best known for his long-running radio variety show, *A*

*Prairie Home Companion*; his latest book, *Love Me,* appeared in 2003.

**Salif Keita** (1949, Djoliba, French West Africa [now in Mali]), Malian folk and pop musician.

**Toby Keith** (Toby Keith Covel; 8 Jul 1961, Clinton OK), American country musician.

**Jakob Kellenberger** (1944, Heiden, Switzerland), Swiss international official; president of the International Committee of the Red Cross from 2000.

**Bill Keller** (18 Jan 1949), American journalist; served as managing editor of the *New York Times* from 1997 to 2001 and was appointed executive editor in mid-June 2003.

**David E. Kelley** (4 Apr 1956, Waterville ME), American screenwriter who created the hit TV series *The Practice* and *Ally McBeal.*

**Ellsworth Kelly** (31 May 1923, Newburgh NY), American painter and sculptor who was a leading exponent of the hard-edge style, in which abstract contours are sharply and precisely defined.

**Jim Kelly** (14 Feb 1960, Pittsburgh PA), American football player; Kelly passed for more than 3,000 yd in 8 of 11 seasons as quarterback for the Buffalo Bills.

**R. Kelly** (Robert S. Kelly; 8 Jan 1969, Chicago IL), American rhythm-and-blues performer.

**Sir Allan Kemakeza** (1951, Panueli village, Savo Island, Solomon Islands), Solomon Islands politician; prime minister of the Solomon Islands from 2001.

**Yashar Kemal** (Kemal Sadik Göğçeli; 1922, Hemite, Turkey), Turkish novelist of Kurdish descent best known for his stories of village life and for his outspoken advocacy on behalf of the dispossessed.

**Dirk Kempthorne** (29 Oct 1951, San Diego CA), American Republican politician; governor of Idaho from 1999.

**Thomas (Michael) Keneally** (also published as Willam Coyle; 7 Oct 1935, Sydney, NSW, Australia), Australian novelist who was shortlisted for the Booker Prize four times before he won in 1982 with his journalistic novel *Schindler's Ark,* later made into the award-winning film *Schindler's List.*

**Anthony Kennedy** (23 Jul 1936, Sacramento CA), American jurist; associate justice of the US Supreme Court from 1988.

**Charles Kennedy** (25 Nov 1959, Inverness, Scotland), British politician; leader of the Liberal Democratic Party from 1999.

**Edward M(oore) Kennedy** (22 Feb 1932, Brookline MA), American Democratic politician; senator from Massachusetts from 1963.

**Charles F. Kennel** (Cambridge MA), American physicist and director of the Scripps Institution of Oceanography of the University of California, San Diego, from 1998.

**Kenny G.** (Kenneth Gorelick; 5 Jun 1956, Seattle WA), American jazz-pop instrumentalist.

**Duchess of Kent** (Katharine Worsley; 22 Feb 1933, Yorkshire, England), British royal; wife of the Duke of Kent (married 1961).

**Duke of Kent** (Edward George Nicholas Paul Patrick Windsor; 9 Sep 1935, London, England), British royal, the head of the English Freemasonry movement, and, with the Duchess of Kent, presenter of the trophies at the Wimbledon tennis tournament each year.

**Prince Michael of Kent** (Michael George Charles Franklin; 4 Jul 1942, Iver, Buckinghamshire, England), British royal.

**Mathieu Kérékou** (2 Sep 1933, Kouarfa, Dahomey [now Benin]), Beninese politician; president of Benin, 1972–91, and again from 1996.

**Sir Frank Kermode** (1919, Isle of Man), British literary critic and author; his *Pieces of My Mind: Essays and Criticism 1958–2002* was published in 2003.

**Bob Kerrey** (Joseph Robert Kerrey; 27 Aug 1943, Lincoln NE), American businessman and Democratic politician; governor of Nebraska, 1983–87, and senator from Nebraska, 1989–2001.

**John F. Kerry** (11 Dec 1943, Denver CO), American Democratic politician; senator from Massachusetts from 1985.

**Imre Kertész** (9 Nov 1929, Budapest, Hungary), Hungarian writer; winner of the 2002 Nobel Prize for Literature for work that "upholds the fragile experience of the individual against the barbaric arbitrariness of history."

**Jack Kevorkian** (26 May 1928, Pontiac MI), American physician and assisted-suicide activist.

**Alicia Keys** (Alicia Augello Cook; 25 Jan 1981, New York NY), American rhythm-and-blues singer; winner of five Grammy Awards in 2002.

**Cheb Khaled** (Khaled Hadj Brahim; 29 Feb 1960, Sidi-El-Houri, near Oran, Algeria), Algerian rai performer.

**Sheikh Hamad ibn Isa al-Khalifah** (28 Jan 1950, Bahrain), Bahraini emir and chief of state from 1999; he proclaimed himself king on 14 Feb 2002.

**Hojatolislam Sayyed Ali Khamenei** (1939, Mashad, Iran), Iranian religious leader; supreme political and religious authority in Iran from 1989.

**Khamtai Siphandon** (8 Feb 1924, Champassak province, Laos), Laotian politician; general secretary of the Lao People's Revolutionary Party from 1992 and president of Laos from 1998.

**Ismail Khan** (1946, Farah province, Afghanistan), Afghani military leader, a warlord with a large following among Afghanistan's Tajik minority; he was involved in the fighting against the Russians in the 1980s and escaped from imprisonment by the Taliban regime in 2000 and was a key member of the anti-Taliban Northern Alliance.

**Khalid Khannouchi** (22 Dec 1971, Meknes, Morocco), Moroccan-American marathon runner who broke his own world record with a time of 2 hr 5.38 min in the 2002 London Marathon.

**Hojatoleslam Mohammad Khatami** (1943, Ardakan, Iran), Iranian politician; president of Iran from 1997.

**Mikhail Borisovich Khodorkovsky** (1963, Moscow, USSR [now in Russia]), Russian billionaire head of Yukos Oil Company and the richest man in Russia.

**Cheikh El Afia Ould Mohamed Khouna** (1956, Mauritania), Mauritanian politician; prime minister of Mauritania, 1996–97, and again from 1998.

**Mwai Kibaki** (15 Nov 1931, Gatuyaini village, Central province, Kenya), Kenyan politician; president from 30 Dec 2002.

**Angelique Kidjo** (14 Jul 1960, Ouidah, Dahomey [now Benin]), Beninese pop singer who won international acclaim with her blend of musical styles from Africa, Europe, and the Americas.

**Nicole Kidman** (20 Jun 1967, Honolulu HI), American-born Australian actress who in recent years has risen to become one of Hollywood's most popular stars; she won the 2003 Academy Award for best actress for her work in *The Hours* and was given the 2003 Fashion Icon Award by the Council of Fashion Designers America.

**Anselm Kiefer** (8 Mar 1945, Donaueschingen, Germany), German painter in the Neo-Expressionist movement, known for works that deal ironically with 20th-century German history.

**Kwame M. Kilpatrick** (8 Jun 1970, Detroit MI), American Democratic politician; mayor of Detroit from 4 Jan 2002.

**Kim Jong Il** (16 Feb 1941, near Khabarovsk, Russian SFSR, USSR [now Russia]), Korean politician; general secretary of the Central Committee of the Worker's Party of Korea (i.e., North Korea) from 1997.

**Kim Woo Choong** (19 Dec 1936, Taegu, Korea [now in South Korea]), Korean businessman; founder and chairman of the Daewoo Group; chairman of the Federation of Korean Industries from 1998.

**Jimmy Kimmel** (13 Nov 1967, Brooklyn NY), American comedian and TV talk show host, anchor of Comedy Central's *The Man Show* (from 1999) and of the late-night *Jimmy Kimmel Show* on ABC (from 2002).

**Angus S. King, Jr.** (31 Mar 1944, Alexandria VA), American politician; Independent governor of Maine, 1995–2003.

**B.B. King** (Riley B. King; 16 Sep 1925, Itta Bena MS), American guitarist and singer, a principal figure in the development of blues and from whose style leading popular musicians have drawn inspiration.

**Stephen (Edward) King** (21 Sep 1947, Portland ME), American writer; author of novels combining horror, fantasy, and science fiction; his best-sellers include *Carrie, The Shining*, and *Misery*.

**Greg Kinnear** (17 Jun 1963, Logansport IN), American actor, gained fame as the first host of TV's *Talk Soup*.

**Neil Gordon Kinnock** (28 Mar 1942, Tredegar, Wales), British politician and Labour Party leader.

**Michael Kinsley** (9 Mar 1951, Detroit MI), American political commentator and editor; originator (1996) of the on-line magazine *Slate* and its editor 1996–2002.

**Bodo Kirchhoff** (6 Jul 1948, Hamburg, West Germany [now in Germany]), German novelist; his best-received works include *Parlando* (2001) and *Schundroman* (2002).

**Néstor Kirchner** (25 Feb 1950, Río Gallegos, Argentina), Argentine politician; president of Argentina from 25 May 2003.

**Yevgeny Kissin** (10 Oct 1971, Moscow, USSR [now in Russia]), Russian concert pianist.

**Henry A(lfred) Kissinger** (27 May 1923, Fürth, Germany), German-born American political scientist, adviser for national security affairs, and secretary of state (1973–76) under presidents Richard Nixon and Gerald Ford; he was awarded the 1973 Nobel Peace Prize jointly with Le Duc Tho of North Vietnam for their efforts toward ending the Vietnam War.

**Ewald Kist**, Dutch corporate executive; chairman of ING Group from 2000.

**R(onald) B(rooks) Kitaj** (29 Oct 1932, Chagrin Falls OH), American-born Pop art painter.

**Kitaro** (Masanori Takahashi; 1953, Japan), Japanese New Age electronic musician.

**John A. Kitzhaber** (5 Mar 1947, Colfax WA), American physician and Democratic politician; governor of Oregon, 1995–2003.

**Calvin (Richard) Klein** (19 Nov 1942, Bronx NY), American fashion designer noted for his classic, elegant, and easy-to-wear clothing.

**Ralph Klein** (1 Nov 1942, Calgary, AB, Canada), Canadian politician; premier of Alberta from 1992.

**Thomas Klestil** (4 Nov 1932, Vienna, Austria), Austrian statesman; president of Austria from 1992.

**Kevin Kline** (24 Oct 1947, St. Louis MO), American comic and dramatic actor who excelled in such works as *Sophie's Choice* (1982) and *A Fish Called Wanda* (1988); his most recent film *The Emperor's Club* (2002).

**Vitali Klitschko** (Vitaly Klichko; 19 Jul 1971, Belovodsk, Kirghiz SSR, USSR [now Kyrgyzstan]), Ukrainian heavyweight boxer who lost, in a controversial decision, to world champion Lennox Lewis in June 2003.

**Wladimir Klitschko** (Vladimir Klichko; 25 Mar 1976, Semipalatinsk, Kazakh SSR, USSR [now Kazakhstan]), Ukrainian heavyweight boxer who in 2003 was the WBO world champion; he is the brother of Vitali Klitschko.

**Yana Klochkova** (7 Aug 1982, Simferopol, Ukrainian SSR, USSR [now Ukraine]), Ukrainian swimmer who broke the world record in 400-m individual medley in 2002.

**Gladys Knight** (28 May 1944, Atlanta GA), American rhythm-and-blues singer (of Gladys Knight and the Pips).

**Philip H. Knight** (24 Feb 1938, Portland OR), American business executive; CEO of Nike.

**Suge Knight** (Marion Knight; 19 Apr 1966, Compton, Los Angeles CA), American gangsta rap music producer and impresario, the controversial head of Death Row Records.

**Keira Knightley** (22 Mar 1985, Teddington, London, England), British film actress who appeared in *Bend It Like Beckham* (2002) and *Pirates of the Caribbean: The Curse of the Black Pearl* (2003).

**Mark Knopfler** (12 Aug 1949, Glasgow, Scotland), British rock vocalist/guitarist (of Dire Straits).

**Beyoncé Knowles** (4 Sep 1981, Houston TX), American pop singer formerly of the group Destiny's Child and from 2003 a successful solo act.

**Tony Knowles** (1 Jan 1943, Tulsa OK), American Democratic politician; governor of Alaska, 1994–2002.

**Robert (Sedraki) Kocharyan** (31 Aug 1954, Stepanakert, Nagorno-Karabakh, Azerbaijani SSR, USSR [now Azerbaijan]), Armenian politician; president of Armenia from 1998.

**Horst Köhler** (22 Feb 1943, Skierbieszow, Poland), German banker; managing director of the International Monetary Fund from 2000.

**Junichiro Koizumi** (8 Jan 1942, Yokosuka, Kanagawa prefecture, Japan), Japanese politician; prime minister of Japan from 2001.

**Willem ("Wim") Kok** (29 Sep 1938, Bergambacht, The Netherlands), Dutch politician; prime minister of The Netherlands, 1994–2002.

**Tim Koogle** (1951?, Alexandria VA), American corporate executive; CEO of Yahoo! Inc. from 1995.

**Rem Koolhaas** (1944, Rotterdam, The Netherlands), Dutch architect known especially for his concepts of large-scale structures; he was awarded the 2000 Pritzker Prize.

**Jeff Koons** (21 Jan 1955, York PA), American Pop-art painter and sculptor.

**Dean (Ray) Koontz** (9 Jul 1945, Everett PA), American writer of novels often with a grotesque or science-fiction atmosphere; seven of his books have been on the *New York Times* best-seller list.

**Ted Koppel** (Edward James Koppel; 8 Feb 1940, Lancashire, England), British-born American TV news broadcaster and anchor of the news analysis show *Nightline* from 1980.

**Michael Kors** (Karl Anderson, Jr.; Michael David Kors; 1959, Merrick, Long Island NY), American fashion designer, creator of his own signature lines and artistic director for Celine.

**Masatoshi Koshiba** (19 Sep 1926, Toyohashi, Japan), Japanese astronomer; cowinner of the 2002 Nobel Prize for Physics for his study of neutrinos using a large detector called Kamiokande II that he set up in a zinc mine in Japan.

**Janica Kostelic** ("The Croatian Sensation"; 5 Jan 1982, Zagreb, Yugoslavia [now in Croatia]), Croatian Alpine skier who won three gold medals and one silver at the 2002 Winter Olympic Games.

**Vojislav Kostunica** (24 Mar 1944, Belgrade, Yugoslavia [now Serbia and Montenegro]), Yugoslavian politician and president of Yugoslavia from 2000 until that country's dissolution, 7 Mar 2003.

**Anna Kournikova** (Anna Sergeyevna Kurnikova; 7 Jun 1981, Moscow, USSR [now in Russia]), Russian-born fashion model and tennis player.

**Magdalena Kozena** (1973, Brno, Czechoslovakia [now in the Czech Republic]), Czech mezzo-soprano.

**Diana Krall** (16 Nov 1964, Nanaimo, BC, Canada), Canadian jazz pianist and singer.

**Larry Kramer** (25 Jun 1935, Bridgeport CT), American writer and AIDS activist.

**Vladimir Kramnik** (25 Jun 1975, Tuapse, Russian SFSR, USSR [now Russia]), Russian chess grand master who defeated Garry Kasparov to become world chess champion in 2000.

**Peter Krause** (12 Aug 1965, Alexandria MN), American TV actor starring as Nate Fisher on HBO's series *Six Feet Under*.

**Alison Krauss** (23 Jul 1971, Decatur IL), American bluegrass fiddle player and singer.

**Lenny Kravitz** (26 May 1964, Brooklyn NY), American rock performer.

**Gidon Kremer** (27 Feb 1947, Riga, Latvian SSR, USSR [now Latvia]), Latvian-born violinist and conductor known for his explorations of the far reaches of the violin repertory, promotion of contemporary music, and his work with chamber orchestras.

**Kris Kristofferson** (22 Jun 1936, Brownsville TX), American country-rock singer and songwriter and actor.

**Irving Kristol** (Irving Horenstein; 1920, New York NY), American essayist and columnist; editor of *The Public Interest* from 1965.

**William Kristol** (23 Dec 1952, New York NY), American editor and columnist.

**Leonid Danylovych Kuchma** (9 Aug 1938, Chaykyne, Ukrainian SSR, USSR [now Ukraine]), Ukrainian engineer, politician; prime minister of Ukraine, 1992–93, and president from 1994.

**Dennis J. Kucinich** (8 Oct 1946, Cleveland OH), American Democratic politician; Cleveland mayor (1977–79); congressman from Ohio.

**Lisa Kudrow** (30 Jul 1963, Encino CA), American TV and film actress who stars as Phoebe Buffay on the TV sitcom *Friends* (from 1994).

**Gustavo Kuerten** (10 Sep 1976, Florianópolis, Santa Catarina state, Brazil), Brazilian tennis player, three-time winner of the French Open (1997, 2000, 2001).

**John (Kofi Agyekum) Kufuor** (8 Dec 1938, Kumisi, Gold Coast [now Ghana]), Ghanaian politician; president of Ghana from 2001.

**Ted Kulongoski** (5 Nov 1940 Missouri), American Democratic politician; governor of Oregon from 13 Jan 2003.

**Chandrika (Bandaranaike) Kumaratunga** (29 Jun 1945, Colombo, Ceylon [now Sri Lanka]), Sri Lankan politician; president of Sri Lanka from 1994.

**Karolina Kurkova** (28 Feb 1984, Pardubice, Czechoslovakia [now in the Czech Republic]), Czech fashion model; won Model of the Year at the 2002 VH1/Vogue Fashion Awards.

**Raymond Kurzweil** (12 Feb 1948, Queens NY), American computer scientist and visionary, a specialist in pattern recognition, whose work resulted in inventions of flatbed scanners, speech-recognition devices, and reading machines for the blind.

**Tony Kushner** (July 1956, New York NY), American playwright; author of a series of unconventional but highly regarded plays, including *Millennium Approaches, Angels in America,* and *Perestroika*.

**Michelle Kwan** (Kwan Shan Wing; 7 Jul 1980, Torrance CA), American figure skater; US (1996, 1998–2003), world (1996, 1998, 2000, 2001, 2003), and Olympic medalist champion (silver medal in 1998 and bronze in 2002).

**Aleksander Kwasniewski** (15 Nov 1954, Dojlidy, Poland), Polish politician; president of Poland from 1995.

**Patti LaBelle** (Patricia Louise Holt; 4 Oct 1944, Philadelphia PA), American soul and rock singer.

**Christian Lacroix** (17 May 1951, Arles, France), French fashion designer known for his ostentatious, extravagant, and colorful creations.

**Emeril (John) Lagasse** (15 Oct 1959, Fall River MA), American chef, restaurateur, and media personality known for his energetic TV cooking shows.

**Karl Lagerfeld** (10 Sep 1938, Hamburg, Germany), German-born French fashion designer known for his highly feminine creations for the houses of Chloé and Chanel.

**Émile Jamil Lahoud** (12 Jan 1936, Baabdat, Lebanon), Lebanese politician; president of Lebanon from 1998.

**Princess Lalla Salma** (Lalla Salma Bennani; 10 May 1978, Fes, Morocco), consort of King Muhammad VI of Morocco (married 21 Mar 2002).

**Rachael Lampa** (8 Jan 1985, Ann Arbor MI), American pop singer.

**Bernard Landry** (9 Mar 1937, Saint-Jacques-de-Montcalm, QC, Canada), Canadian politician; premier of Quebec from 2001.

**Nathan Lane** (Joseph Lane; 3 Feb 1956, Jersey City NJ), American comedic actor of stage and screen; recently starred in *The Producers* on Broadway.

**Helmut Lang** (10 Mar 1956, Vienna, Austria), Austrian fashion designer whose simple creations are changed very little from season to season.

**kd lang** (Kathryn Dawn Lang; 2 Nov 1961, Consort, AB, Canada), Canadian singer and songwriter, originally in the country-rock style, but later (after her album *Ingenue* [1992]) in the adult contemporary style.

**Angela Lansbury** (16 Oct 1925, London, England), British character actress best known to TV audiences as Jessica Fletcher on *Murder, She Wrote*.

**Anthony M. LaPaglia** (31 Jan 1959, Adelaide, SA, Australia), Australian film and TV actor who appeared in the film *Lantana* (2001) and starred on TV's *Without a Trace* (from 2002).

**Lyndon Hermyle LaRouche, Jr.** (8 Sep 1922, Rochester NH), American economist and populist politician; frequent candidate for president.

**Marit (Elisabeth) Larsen** (1 Jul 1983, Lørenskog, Norway), Norwegian pop musician and composer (of M2M).

**Queen Latifah** (Dana Owens; 18 Mar 1970, Newark NJ), American rap musician, film actress, and TV personality noted for her performance in the film *Chicago* (2002).

**Matt(hew Todd) Lauer** (30 Dec 1957, New York NY), American TV journalist; host of the *Today* show from 1994.

**Cyndi Lauper** (Cynthia Anne Stephanie Lauper; 22 Jun 1953, Queens NY), American pop singer.

**Ralph Lauren** (Ralph Lipschitz; 14 Oct 1939, New York NY), American fashion designer known for his ready-to-wear collections and his use of unconventional materials.

**Avril Lavigne** (27 Sep 1984, Napanee, ON, Canada), Canadian pop singer; her first album, *Let Go,* sold more than six million copies.

**Cardinal Bernard Law** (4 Nov 1931, Torreón, Mexico), American clergyman, Roman Catholic cardinal archbishop of Boston and senior Catholic leader in the US; he resigned in December 2002.

**Jude Law** (29 Dec 1972, Blackheath, London, England), British stage and screen actor who rose to prominence after appearing in the film *The Talented Mr. Ripley* (1999).

**Martin Lawrence** (16 Apr 1965, Frankfurt am Main, West Germany [now in Germany]), American TV and film actor and comedian, star of the TV series *Martin* (from 1992).

**Nigella (Lucy) Lawson** (6 Jan 1960), British cook and author of food-related books such as *How to Be a Domestic Goddess* (2000) and *Nigella Bites* (2002) as well as hostess of the TV show *Nigella Bites*.

**John Le Carré** (David John Moore Cornwell; 19 Oct 1931, Poole, Dorset, England), English novelist who created suspenseful, realistic spy novels based on a wide knowledge of international espionage.

**Jean-Marie Le Pen** (20 Jun 1928, La Trinité-sur-Mer, France), French politician, president of the Front National, a right-wing extremist party that surprised pundits in the 2002 French presidential elections by outpolling the Socialists and coming in second to the incumbent, Jacques Chirac.

**Richard (Erskine Frere) Leakey** (19 Dec 1944, Nairobi, Kenya), Kenyan physical anthropologist, paleontologist, conservationist, and politician.

**Michael O. Leavitt** (11 Feb 1951, Cedar City UT), American Republican politician; governor of Utah from 1993; in August 2003 he was named to head the US Environmental Protection Agency.

**Matt LeBlanc** (25 Jul 1967, Newton MA), American TV actor who plays Joey Tribbiani on the TV sitcom *Friends* (from 1994).

**Ang Lee** (23 Oct 1954, P'ing-Tung county, Taiwan), Taiwanese-born film director of extraordinary versatility most famous for *Crouching Tiger, Hidden Dragon* (2000).

**Spike Lee** (Shelton Lee; 20 Mar 1957, Atlanta GA), American filmmaker known for his uncompromising, provocative approach to controversial subject matter; his works include *Do the Right Thing* (1989), *Mo' Better Blues* (1990), and *Malcolm X* (1992).

**Stan Lee** (Stanley Lieber; 1922, New York NY), American comic-book artist and creator of *Spider-Man* and *Stripperella.*

**Lee Kun Hee** (9 Jan 1942, Uiryung, Korea [now in South Korea]), Korean corporate executive; chairman of the Samsung Group from 1987.

**John Leguizamo** (22 Jul 1964, Bogotá, Colombia), Colombian-born American comedian and actor.

**Jim Lehrer** (James Lehrer; 19 May 1934, Wichita KS), American TV journalist and author, cohost with Robert MacNeil of *The MacNeil/Lehrer Report* from 1975 and, after MacNeil's retirement in 1995, the host of *The NewsHour with Jim Lehrer.*

**Annie Leibovitz** (Anna-Lou Leibovitz; 2 Oct 1949, Westbury CT), American photographer and photojournalist known for her intense, often intimate portraits of celebrities.

**Jean Lemierre** (6 Jun 1950, Sainte Adresse, France), French international banking executive; president of the European Bank for Reconstruction and Development from 2000.

**Greg LeMond** (Gregory James LeMond; 26 Jun 1961, Lakewood CA), American cyclist who was the first non-European rider to win the Tour de France. In his career he won that tour three times (1986, 1989, 1990) and twice won the World Road Race Championship (1983, 1989).

**Ute Lemper** (4 Jul 1963, Münster, West Germany [now in Germany]), German cabaret singer.

**Annie Lennox** (25 Dec 1954, Aberdeen, Scotland), British pop singer (solo and with Eurythmics).

**Jay Leno** (James Douglas Muir Leno; 28 Apr 1950, Short Hills NJ), American comedian; host of *The Tonight Show* from 1992.

**Aleksey Arkhipovich Leonov** (30 May 1934, near Kemerovo, Russian SFSR, USSR [now Russia]), Soviet Russian cosmonaut, the first man to climb out of a spacecraft in space.

**Lisa Leslie** (7 Jul 1972), American professional basketball player; in 2001 she was named MVP for the regular season, the WNBA championship, and the All-Star Game—the first player to win all three awards in a single year.

**King Letsie III** (David Mohato; 17 Jul 1963, Morija, Lesotho), king of Lesotho, 1990–95, and again from 1996.

**David (Michael) Letterman** (12 Apr 1947, Indianapolis IN), American TV personality; host of the *Late Show with David Letterman* from 1993.

**Richard C. Levin** (1947, San Francisco CA), American economist, a specialist on technological change; he was elected president of Yale University in 1993.

**James Levine** (23 Jun 1943, Cincinnati OH), American conductor and pianist, especially noted for his work with the Metropolitan Opera of New York City; principal conductor of the Boston Symphony Orchestra from 2004.

**Monica Lewinsky** (23 Jul 1973, San Francisco CA), American personality; former White House intern, key figure in the Clinton presidential scandal; TV hostess from 2003.

**Jerry Lewis** (Jerome Levitch; 16 Mar 1926, Newark NJ), American comedian, actor, and humanitarian often partnered with crooner Dean Martin.

**Jerry Lee Lewis** (29 Sep 1935, Ferriday LA), American singer and pianist whose virtuosity, ecstatic performances, and colorful personality made him a legendary rock music pioneer.

**Kenneth D. Lewis** (9 Apr 1947, Meridian MS), American corporate executive; CEO of the Bank of America Corp. from 1999.

**Lennox (Claudius) Lewis** (2 Sep 1965, West Ham, London, England), British boxer, world heavyweight champion in the WBC from 1997 and the IBF from 1999.

**Sol LeWitt** (9 Sep 1928, Hartford CT), American sculptor, printmaker, and draftsman of the Minimalist school, noted for his constructions and drawings featuring basic geometric forms.

**Li Hongzhi** (7 Jul 1952, Jilin province, China), Chinese religious leader who developed the Falun Dafa system, a cultivation of five meditation exercises (known as Falun Gong).

**Li Ka-shing** (13 Jun 1928, Chaozhou, Guangdong province, China), Chinese (Hong Kong) corporate executive; chairman of Hutchison Whampoa Ltd. and Cheung Kong Holdings.

**Li Zhaoxing** (October 1940, Shandong province, China), Chinese politician; foreign minister from 2003.

**Daniel Libeskind** (12 May 1946, Lodz, Poland), Polish-born Israeli-American architect noted for his design of the Jewish Museum in Berlin; tapped in February 2003 to design the rebuilt World Trade Center complex in New York City.

**Joseph I. Lieberman** (24 Feb 1942, Stamford CT), American Democratic politician; US senator from Connecticut; vice-presidential candidate in 2002.

**Lil' Kim** (Kimberly Denise Jones; 11 Jul 1975, Bedford-Stuyvesant, Brooklyn NY), American hip hop performer.

**Rush Limbaugh** (12 Jan 1951, Cape Girardeau MO), American radio talk-show host and conservative commentator.

**Maya Lin** (5 Oct 1959, Athens OH), American architect and sculptor who is best known for her design of the Vietnam Veterans Memorial in Washington DC.

**Abbey Lincoln** (later Aminata Moseka; 6 Aug 1930, Chicago IL), American jazz singer.

**Linda Lingle** (4 Jun 1953, St. Louis MO), American Republican politician; mayor of Maui county and governor of Hawaii from 3 Dec 2002.

**Tara (Kristen) Lipinski** (10 Jun 1982, Philadelphia PA), American figure skater, the youngest ever to win US and world championships (1997) and the youngest individual gold medalist in the Winter Olympics, in 1998.

**Paavo (Tapio) Lipponen** (23 Apr 1941, Turtola [now Pello], Finland), Finnish politician; prime minister of Finland, 1995–2003.

**John Lithgow** (19 Oct 1945, Rochester NY), American film and TV actor known for his skill at comic and dramatic roles; he won multiple awards for his work on the TV sitcom *3rd Rock from the Sun.*

**Little Richard** (Richard Wayne Penniman; 5 Dec 1935, Macon GA), American singer and pianist.

**Lucy (Alexis) Liu** (2 Dec 1968, Jackson Heights, Queens NY), American TV and film actress who gained fame for playing Ling on TV's *Ally McBeal* and for her role in two *Charlie's Angels* films.

**Liu Xiaoqing** (31 Oct 1951, Peilin, Sichuan province, China), Chinese actress, film producer, and businesswoman who claimed to the richest woman in China and the country's first female yuan billionaire; she was arrested in 2002 for tax evasion.

**Kenneth Livingstone** (17 Jun 1945, Lambeth, London, England), British politician; Labour mayor of London from 2000.

**LL Cool J** (James Todd Smith; 16 Aug 1969, Queens NY), American hip-hop artist and actor.

**Christopher Lloyd** (22 Oct 1938, Stamford CT), American film and TV actor.

**Sir Andrew Lloyd Webber** (22 Mar 1948, London, England), British composer whose eclectic stage musicals such as *Jesus Christ Superstar, Evita, Cats,* and *The Phantom of the Opera,* blended pop, rock, and classical forms and helped revitalize musical theater.

**Gary Locke** (21 Jan 1950, Seattle WA), American Democratic politician; governor of Washington from 1997.

**Keith Alan Lockhart** (7 Nov 1959, Poughkeepsie NY), American conductor of the Boston Pops from 1993.

**Heather Locklear** (25 Sep 1961, Westwood CA), American TV actress best known for her work on *Melrose Place* and *Spin City.*

**Bjørn Lomborg** (6 Jan 1965, Denmark), Danish statistician and controversial environmentalist, author of *The Skeptical Environmentalist* (2001) and director of Denmark's Environmental Assessment Institute (from 2002).

**Jonah Tali Lomu** (12 May 1975, Auckland, New Zealand), New Zealand rugby winger of Tongan heritage; perhaps the most famous rugby player in the world.

**Jeannie Longo** (Jeannie Longo-Ciprelli; 31 Oct 1958, Saint-Gervais, France), French cyclist who was world champion 12 times and broke the women's record for distance traveled in one hour (44.767 km) in 2000.

**George Lopez** (23 Apr 1961), American TV actor and star of *The George Lopez Show* from 2002.

**Jennifer Lopez** (24 Jul 1970, Bronx NY), American pop singer, actress, and fashion designer; she won Most Influential award at the Vogue Fashion Awards, 2002.

**Bernard Lord** (27 Sep 1965, Moncton?, NB, Canada), Canadian politician; premier of New Brunswick from 21 Jun 1999.

**Traci Lords** (Nora Louise Kuzma; 7 May 1968, Steubenville OH), American actress and pornographic movie star of the 1980s; her autobiography, *Underneath It All,* was published in 2003.

**Trent Lott** (9 Oct 1941, Grenada MS), American Republican politician; senator from Mississippi from 1989, and Senate minority leader to 2003.

**Dame (Calliopa) Pearlette Louisy** (1946, Laborie, Saint Lucia), West Indian government official; governor-general of Saint Lucia from 1997.

**Courtney Love** (Love Michelle Harrison; 9 Jul 1964, San Francisco CA), American pop-punk singer, actress.

**Lyle (Pierce) Lovett** (1 Nov 1957, Klein TX), American country-music singer.

**Rob Lowe** (17 Mar 1964, Charlottesville VA), American actor and heartthrob of the 1980s whose career was revitalized by his role on TV's *The West Wing* (1999–2003).

**Henri Loyrette** (31 May 1952, Neuilly-sur-Seine, France), French director of the Louvre museum in Paris from 2001.

**Niko Lozancic** (1957, Kakanj, Yugoslavia [now in Bosnia and Herzegovina]), Bosnian Croat politician; president of the tripartite presidency of Bosnia and Herzegovina for 2003.

**Lu Yongxiang** (1942, Ningbo, Zhejiang province, China), Chinese mechanical engineer, president of Zhejiang University, 1988–95, and president of the Chinese Academy of Sciences from 1997.

**Ruud Lubbers** (Rudolphus Franciscus Marie Lubbers; 7 May 1939, Rotterdam, The Netherlands), Dutch politician; prime minister of The Netherlands, 1982–94, and UN High Commissioner for Refugees from 2001.

**Jane Lubchenco** (4 Dec 1947, Denver CO), American marine ecologist and science administrator; president of the American Association for the Advancement of Science, 1996–97; president of the International Council of Scientific Unions from 2002.

**George Lucas** (George Walton Lucas, Jr.; 14 May 1944, Modesto CA), American motion-picture producer and director best known for the Star Wars blockbusters; he was the founder of Lucasfilm (1971), which became five companies involved in film production; he is thought to be the richest man in Hollywood.

**Paco de Lucia** (Francisco Sánchez Gómez; 21 Dec 1947, Algeciras, Spain), Spanish flamenco guitarist.

**Baz Luhrmann** (Bazmark Anthony Luhrmann; 17 Sep 1962, near Sydney, NSW, Australia), Australian film and stage director and producer known for his showy spectacles, often rewrites of theatrical classics in 20th-century terms; he was much acclaimed for his 2001 film, *Moulin Rouge.*

**Alyaksandr (Hrygorevich) Lukashenka** (30 Aug 1954, Kopys, Belorussian SSR, USSR [now Belarus]), Belarusian politician; president of Belarus from 1994.

**Luiz Inácio Lula da Silva** ("Lula"; 27 Oct 1945, Garanhuns, Pernambuco state, Brazil), Brazilian labor leader and socialist politician; he helped found the Workers Party in 1980 and was elected president of Brazil in 2002.

**Sidney Lumet** (25 Jun 1924, Philadelphia PA), American motion-picture, TV, and stage director whose urban, gritty films often take place in New York City; his film credits include *The Pawnbroker* (1964), *Serpico* (1973), *Dog Day Afternoon* (1975), and *Prince of the City* (1981).

**Luo Gan** (1935, Jinan, Shandong province, China), Chinese police official; member of the Politburo of the Communist Party of China and of the Central Committee from 1997, secretary of the CPC Political and Legal Affairs Committee, and Politburo Standing Committee member from 2002.

**Luo Xuejuan** (26 Jan 1984, Hangzhou, Zhejiang province, China), Chinese swimmer who broke the world record in the 50-m breaststroke in 2002.

**Yury (Mikhaylovich) Luzhkov** (21 Sep 1936, Moscow, USSR [now in Russia]), Russian politician; mayor of Moscow from 1992.

**David Lynch** (20 Jan 1946, Missoula MT), American avant-garde TV and motion-picture director famous for the TV series *Twin Peaks* (1990–91) and the film *Mulholland Dr.* (2001).

**Jessica Lynch** (26 Apr 1983, Palestine WV), American US Army private and celebrity figure of Operation Iraqi Freedom who, after sustaining two broken bones and a dislocated ankle in an apparent wreck of her military vehicle, was taken into custody and treated at a hospital in Nasiriya, Iraq; on 1 Apr 2003 she was released or rescued by US special forces while the operation was being videotaped.

**Loretta Lynn** (Loretta Webb; 14 Apr 1935, Butcher Hollow KY), American country-and-western singer, a pioneer among women in country music and one of the greatest stars ever; she was inducted into the Country Music Hall of Fame in 1988.

**Yo-Yo Ma** (7 Oct 1955, Paris, France), French-born American cellist noted for impeccable technique, fine interpretations of the classical repertoire, the large number of commissions of new works he has attracted, and the breadth of his musical interests.

**Lorin Maazel** (6 Mar 1930, Neuilly, France), French-born American conductor and violinist; music director of the Cleveland Orchestra, 1972–82, and of the New York Philharmonic from 2002.

**Bernie Mac** (Bernard Jeffrey McCollough; 5 Oct 1958, Chicago IL), American TV and film entertainer; star of TV's *Bernie Mac Show* (from 2001) and the film *Charlie's Angels: Full Throttle* (2003).

**Gloria (Macaraeg) Macapagal-Arroyo** (5 Apr 1947, San Juan, Philippines), Philippine politician; president of the Philippines from 2001.

**Julien MacDonald** (19 Mar 1972, Merthyr, Tydfyl, Wales), Welsh fashion designer.

**Bob Mackie** (Robert Gordon Mackie; 24 Mar 1940, Monterey Park CA), American fashion and costume designer noted for his glamorous and daring evening dresses.

**Catharine A(lice) MacKinnon** (7 Oct 1946, Minneapolis MN), American legal scholar; helped develop legal theory for hostile work environment and sexual harassment.

**Alistair MacLeod** (1936, North Batteford, SK, Canada), Canadian writer who won the Dublin IMPAC award in 2001 for his novel *No Great Mischief.*

**Elle Macpherson** (Eleanor Gow; 29 Mar 1964, Cronulla, Sydney, NSW, Australia), Australian fashion model, actress, and lingerie designer.

**Ferenc Mádl** (29 Jan 1931, Hungary), Hungarian politician; president of Hungary from 2000.

**Madonna** (Madonna Louise Veronica Ciccone; 16 Aug 1958, Bay City MI), American singer, songwriter, actress, and entrepreneur whose immense popularity in the 1980s and '90s allowed her to achieve levels of power and control unprecedented for a woman in the entertainment industry.

**Ricardo Maduro** (20 Apr 1946, Panama), Panamanian-born Honduran politician; president of Honduras from 27 Jan 2002.

**João Magueijo** (1967?, Portugal), Portuguese-born cosmologist who developed a controversial theory that in the first instant of the creation of the Universe light must have traveled at a speed much faster than that generally accepted by physicists.

**Tobey Maguire** (27 Jun 1975, Santa Monica CA), American film star known for playing unconventional leads.

**Taj Mahal** (Henry Saint Clair Fredericks; 17 May 1942, New York NY), American singer, guitarist, songwriter, and one of the pioneers of what has come to be called world music.

**Datuk Seri Mahatir bin Mohamad** (20 Dec 1925, Alor Setar, Malaya [now Malaysia]), Malaysian politician; prime minister of Malaysia from 1981.

**Bill Maher** (20 Jan 1956, New York NY), American TV comedian and personality, host of TV's *Politically Incorrect* (canceled in 2002 after Maher's politically incorrect observations on September 11); host of weekly TV show *Real Time with Bill Maher* on HBO from February 2003.

**Maharishi Mahesh Yogi** (Mahesh Varma; 18 Oct 1911, Allahabad, United Provinces, British India [now Uttar Pradesh state, India]), Hindu religious leader who inaugurated the Spiritual Regeneration Movement (1957) in India and was responsible for bringing transcendental meditation (TM), a method of achieving a higher state of consciousness, to the West.

**Naguib Mahfouz** (11 Dec 1911, Cairo, Egypt), Egyptian novelist and screenplay writer noted for works dealing with social issues involving women and political prisoners; awarded the 1988 Nobel Prize for Literature, the first Arabic writer to be so honored.

**Norman Mailer** (31 Jan 1923, Long Branch NJ), American novelist and journalist whose fiction and nonfiction made a radical critique of the totalitarianism he believed inherent in the centralized power structure of 20th-century America.

**Natalie Maines** (14 Oct 1974, Lubbock TX), American country musician; member of the Dixie Chicks.

**Miriam Makeba** (4 Mar 1932, Prospect Township, South Africa), South African–born pop singer;

recipient of the 2002 Polar Music Prize of the Royal Swedish Academy of Music.

**Tommi Mäkinen** (26 Jun 1964, Puuppola, Finland), Finnish rally race-car driver who won the Monte-Carlo Rally, 1999–2001.

**Sheikh Maktum ibn Rashid al-Maktum** (1943?, Dubai [now in United Arab Emirates]), prime minister of the UAE, 1971–79, and again from 1990.

**Sheikh Mohammed ibn Rashid al-Maktum** (1949, Dubai? [now in United Arab Emirates]), crown prince of Dubai from 1995; he is also a noted horse breeder and runs Godolphin Stables with his brothers.

**Tuilaepa Sailele Malielegaoi** (14 Apr 1945, Lepa, Samoa), Samoan politician; prime minister of Samoa from 1998.

**Karl Malone** (24 Jul 1963, Summerfield LA), American basketball player, forward for the Utah Jazz; he was the NBA MVP in 1997 and 1999 and an all-star 11 times.

**David (George Joseph) Malouf** (20 Mar 1934, Brisbane, QLD, Australia), Australian author; winner of the 2000 Neustadt Prize.

**Tandja Mamadou** (1938), Nigerois politician; president of Niger from 1999.

**David (Alan) Mamet** (30 Nov 1947, Chicago IL), American playwright, director, and screenwriter noted for his often desperate working-class characters and for his distinctive and colloquial dialogue that is frequently profane.

**Cheb Mami** (11 Jul 1956, Saida, Algeria), Algerian *rai* singer.

**Ange Mancini** (15 Jun 1944, Beausoleil, France), French Guianan politician; prefect of French Guiana from 31 Jul 2002.

**Nelson (Rolihlahla) Mandela** (18 Jul 1918, Umtata, Cape of Good Hope, South Africa), South African nationalist leader and statesman; political prisoner 1962–90, president of South Africa (1994–99); corecipient of the 1993 Nobel Peace Prize.

**Winnie Madikizela Mandela** (original name Nomzamo Winifred, original Xhosa name Nkosikazi Nobandle Nomzamo Madikizela; 26 Sep 1934/36, Transkei, South Africa), South African social worker and black nationalist leader; second wife of Nelson Mandela; in April 2003 she was sentenced to five years in prison on charges of fraud and theft from a women's political organization.

**Barry Manilow** (Barry Alan Pincus; 17 Jun 1946, Brooklyn NY), American pop singer and songwriter.

**Henning Mankell** (3 Feb 1948, Härjedalen, Sweden), Swedish detective novelist whose *Die Rückkehr des Tanzlehrers* ("The Return of the Dance Teacher") shot to the top of the German best-seller list in October 2002.

**John Manley** (5 Jan 1950, Ottawa, ON, Canada), Canadian politician who became minister of finance in 2002 and was tipped as the likely successor to Prime Minister Jean Chrétien.

**Herbie Mann** (Herbert Jay Solomon; 16 Apr 1930, Brooklyn NY), American jazz flutist and composer.

**Patrick (Augustus Merving) Manning** (17 Aug 1946, San Fernando, Trinidad), West Indian politician; prime minister of Trinidad and Tobago, 1991–95, and again from 2001.

**Preston Manning** (10 Jun 1942, Edmonton, AB, Canada), Canadian politician; leader of the Reform Party.

**Charles (Milles) Manson** (11 Nov 1934, Cincinnati OH), American cult leader and multiple murderer; incarcerated from 1970.

**Marilyn Manson** (Brian Warner; 5 Jan 1969, Canton OH), American rock singer.

**Joe Mantello** (27 Dec 1962, Rockford IL), American stage actor and director; he won the 2003 Tony award for best direction of a play for *Take Me Out*.

**John H. Marburger, III** (Staten Island NY), American physicist; presidential science adviser and head of the Office of Science and Technology Policy from 2001.

**Geoffrey W. Marcy** (29 Sep 1954, St. Clair Shores MI), American astronomer; discoverer of planetary systems outside the solar system.

**Brice Marden** (15 Oct 1938, Bronxville NY), American painter and printmaker who combined the techniques of Abstract Expressionism with the philosophies of Minimalism.

**Cindy Margolis** (1 Oct 1968, Los Angeles CA), American model and actress whose Internet image has reached cult status.

**Queen Margrethe II** (Margrethe Alexandrine Thorhildur Ingrid; 16 Apr 1940, Copenhagen, Denmark), queen of Denmark from 1972.

**Dan Marino** (Daniel Constantine Marino, Jr.; 15 Sep 1961, Pittsburgh PA), American professional football quarterback who holds the NFL record for passing (5,084 yd and 48 touchdowns).

**Marisol (Escobar)** (22 May 1930, Paris, France), American sculptor of boxlike figurative works combining wood and other materials and often grouped as tableaux.

**Andranik Markaryan** (12 Jun 1951, Yerevan, Armenia), Armenian politician; prime minister of Armenia from 12 May 2000.

**Ziggy Marley** (David Marley; 17 Oct 1968, Kingston, Jamaica), Jamaican reggae performer.

**Monika Maron** (4 Jun 1941, Berlin, Germany), German novelist from the former GDR; her works include *Pawels Briefe* (1999; "Pawel's Letters") and *Endmoränen* (2002; "Terminal Moraines").

**Branford Marsalis** (26 Aug 1960, Breaux Bridge LA), American jazz saxophonist and bandleader.

**Wynton Marsalis** (18 Oct 1961, New Orleans LA), American jazz trumpeter.

**Penny Marshall** (Carole Penelope Masciarelli; 15 Oct 1942, Bronx NY), American film and TV director, actress, and producer first famous for playing Laverne in the TV series *Laverne & Shirley*.

**Yann Martel** (1963, Spain), Spanish-born Canadian novelist whose *The Life of Pi* won the 2002 Booker Prize.

**Ricky Martin** (Enrique Martin Morales; 24 Dec 1971, San Juan, Puerto Rico), American Latin music singer.

**Steve Martin** (14 Aug 1945, Waco TX), American comedic actor and author known for many popular films.

**Melquiades ("Mel") Martinez** (23 Oct 1946, Sagua la Grande, Cuba), Cuban-born American government official; US secretary of housing and urban development from 2001.

**Tomás Eloy Martínez** (16 Jul 1934, Tucumán, Argentina), Argentine writer and journalist, winner of the 2002 Alfaguara Prize for his novel *El vuelo de la reina*.

**Antônio Martins da Cruz** (1946, Portugal), Portuguese chairman-in-office of the Organization for Security and Cooperation in Europe, April–December 2002.

**Judy Martz** (28 Jul 1943, Big Timber MT), American Republican politician; governor of Montana from 2001.

**Princess Masako** (Masako Owada; 9 Dec 1963, Tokyo, Japan), consort of Japanese Crown Prince Naruhito.

**Aslan Maskhadov** (1951, Kazakh SSR, USSR [now Kazakhstan]), Chechen politician; president of the Russian Republic of Chechnya from 1997.

**Janet Maslin** (12 Aug 1949, New York NY), American film critic, author.

**Master P** (Percy Miller; 29 Apr 1970, New Orleans LA), American gangsta rap performer and producer.

**Kurt Masur** (18 Jul 1927, Brieg, Germany [now Brzeg, Poland]), German-born conductor; music director of the New York Philharmonic, 1991–2002, and of the London Philharmonic from 2002.

**Mary Matalin** (19 Aug 1953, Chicago IL), American political commentator.

**Princess Mathilde** (Mathilde d'Udekem d'Acoz; 21 Jan 1973, Uccle, Belgium), consort of Prince Philippe, the heir to the Belgian throne.

**Hideki Matsui** (12 Jun 1974, Ishikawa prefecture, Japan), Japanese baseball outfielder known for his hitting; he led Japan's Central League in the 2002 season in home runs (50) and RBIs (107); he joined the New York Yankees in 2003.

**Koichiro Matsuura** (1937, Tokyo, Japan), Japanese international official; director-general of UNESCO from 1999.

**Chris Matthews** (1945, Philadelphia PA), American TV and newspaper journalist, host of cable TV's *Hardball*.

**Dave Matthews** (9 Jan 1967, Johannesburg, South Africa), South African–born American rock musician, songwriter.

**Princess Máxima** (Máxima Zorreguieta Cerruti; 17 May 1971, Buenos Aires, Argentina), Argentine-born Dutch investment banker; she married Crown Prince Willem-Alexander of The Netherlands (2 Feb 2002).

**Maxwell** (23 May 1973, Brooklyn NY), American rhythm-and-blues and soul singer.

**Willie (Howard) Mays** (6 May 1931, Westfield AL), American baseball player who was considered one of the game's finest all-around players, notable for both his batting and his fielding; his 660 career home runs place him third on the all-time list, behind Hank Aaron (755) and Babe Ruth (714).

**Thabo (Mvuyelwa) Mbeki** (18 Jun 1942, Idutywa, South Africa), South African politician; president of South Africa from 1999.

**Mary Patricia McAleese** (27 Jun 1951, Belfast, Northern Ireland), Irish politician; president of Ireland from 1997.

**Martina McBride** (Martina Maria Schiff; 29 Jul 1966, Sharon KS), American country singer; voted Country Music Association Female Vocalist of the Year in 1999 and 2002; Academy of Country Music Top Female Vocalist, 2001.

**John McCain** (John Sidney McCain III; 29 Aug 1936, Panama Canal Zone), American Republican politician; senator from Arizona.

**Chris McCarron** (27 Mar 1955, Dorchester MA), American jockey who has won the Kentucky Derby, Preakness Stakes, and Belmont Stakes each two times and who has been the leading jockey in earnings in four seasons.

**Cormac McCarthy** (Charles McCarthy, Jr.; 20 Jul 1933, Providence RI), American writer in the Southern gothic tradition whose novels about wayward characters in the rural American South and Southwest are noted for their dark violence.

**Sir Paul McCartney** (James Paul McCartney; 18 Jun 1942, Liverpool, England), British singer, song-writer; member of the Beatles.

**Stella (Nina) McCartney** (13 Sep 1971, London, England), British fashion designer who gained fame at a young age as a designer for Chloé and for her own signature line.

**Delbert McClinton** (4 Nov 1940, Lubbock TX), American country-and-western singer and harmonica player, a pioneer of the Texas roots music revival.

**Matthew McConaughey** (4 Nov 1969, Uvalde TX), American film actor made famous by *A Time to Kill* (1996).

**Jack McConnell** (1960, Irvine, Ayrshire, Scotland), Scottish politician; first minister of Scotland from 2001.

**Mitch McConnell** (20 Feb 1942, Sheffield AL), American Republican politician; senator from Kentucky; Senate majority whip from 12 Nov 2002.

**Frank McCourt** (1930, Brooklyn NY), American novelist who wrote highly successful stories about growing up poor in Ireland; his books include *Angela's Ashes* (1996) and *'Tis* (1999).

**David McCullough** (1933, Pittsburgh PA), American biographer and historian, author of best-selling books such as *Truman* (1992) and *John Adams* (2001).

**Dylan McDermott** (26 Oct 1961, Waterbury CT), American TV and film actor who played Bobby Donnell on TV's *The Practice* (1997–2003).

**Frances McDormand** (23 Jun 1957, IL), American versatile film actress first famous for *Fargo* (1996).

**John McEnroe** (John Patrick McEnroe, Jr.; 16 Feb 1959, Wiesbaden, West Germany [now in Germany]), American tennis player, a leading competitor in the late 1970s and the '80s, and sports broadcaster.

**Reba McEntire** (28 Mar 1954, McAlester OK), American country singer and TV and film actress.

**Bobby McFerrin** (11 Mar 1950, New York NY), American jazz and pop vocalist.

**Tim McGraw** (Samuel Timothy McGraw; 1 May 1967, Delhi LA), American country music singer.

**James E. McGreevey** (6 Aug 1957, Jersey City NJ), American Democratic politician; governor of New Jersey from 2002.

**Sir Ian (Murray) McKellen** (25 May 1939, Burnley, Lancashire, England), British stage and film actor famous for his Shakespearian characterizations.

**Dan Peter McKenzie** (21 Feb 1942, Cheltenham, England), British geophysicist; winner of the 2002 Crafoord Prize "for fundamental contributions to the understanding of the dynamics of the lithosphere, particularly plate tectonics, sedimentary basin formation and mantle melting."

**Kevin McKenzie** (29 Apr 1954, Burlington VT), American ballet dancer, choreographer, and director who danced with the American Ballet Theatre (1979–91) and became its artistic director in October 1992.

**Donald Charles ("Don") McKinnon** (27 Feb 1939, Greenwich, England), New Zealand international official; secretary-general of the Commonwealth from 2000.

**Sarah McLachlan** (28 Jan 1968, Halifax, NS, Canada), Canadian singer and songwriter; organizer and headliner of the Lilith Fair, a traveling summer concert tour featuring female performers.

**Beverley McLachlin** (7 Sep 1943, Pincher Creek, AB, Canada), Canadian Supreme Court justice from 1989; chief justice from 2000.

**Larry McMurtry** (3 Jun 1936, Wichita Falls TX), American writer noted for his novels set on the frontier, in contemporary small towns, and in increasingly urbanized and industrial areas of Texas.

**Marian McPartland** (Margaret Marian Turner; 20 Mar 1918, Slough, England), British-born jazz pianist and composer, host of *Piano Jazz*, a weekly music and talk show on America's National Public Radio (from 1978).

**Alexander McQueen** (Lee McQueen; 1969, London, England), British fashion designer known for his rebellious style and his extravagant runway shows.

**Russell Charles Means** (10 Nov 1940, Pine Ridge SD), American Native American rights activist.

**Meat Loaf** (Marvin Lee Aday; 27 Sep 1947, Dallas TX), American rock performer and actor.

**Péter Medgyessy** (1942, Budapest, Hungary), Hungarian politician; prime minister of Hungary from 27 May 2002.

**Zubin Mehta** (29 Apr 1936, Bombay [now Mumbai], British India), Indian-born orchestral conductor; music director of the Los Angeles Philharmonic, 1962–78, the New York Philharmonic, 1978–91, and the Israel Philharmonic from 1968.

**Rafael Hipólito Mejía Domínguez** (22 Feb 1941, Gurabo, Dominican Republic), Dominican politician; president of Dominican Republic from 2000.

**John Mellencamp** (also known as John Cougar and John Cougar Mellencamp; 7 Oct 1951, Seymour IN), American rock singer and songwriter.

**Sam Mendes** (Samuel Alexander Mendes; 1 Aug 1965, Reading, England), British motion-picture director who won an Academy Award for directing in 1999 (*American Beauty*).

**Fradique de Menezes** (1942), São Tomé and Príncipe politician; president of São Tomé and Príncipe from 2001.

**Thomas M. Menino** (27 Dec 1942), American Democratic politician; mayor of Boston from 1993.

**Gian Carlo Menotti** (7 Jul 1911, Cadegliano, Italy), Italian composer of operas of great popular appeal; he is best known for TV opera *Amahl and the Night Visitors* and for Pulitzer Prize–winning operas *Amelia Goes to the Ball* and *The Consul*.

**Ismail (Noormohamed) Merchant** (25 Dec 1936, Bombay [now Mumbai], British India), Indian-born British film producer famous for his collaboration with James Ivory on many period pieces, including *A Room with a View* (1986), *Howards End* (1992), and *The Remains of the Day* (1993).

**Angela Merkel** (Angela Dorothea Kasner; 17 Jul 1954, Hamburg, West Germany [now in Germany]), German politician; leader of the Christian Democratic Union and parliament leader.

**Stipe Mesic** (Stjepan Mesic; 24 Dec 1934, Orahovica, Yugoslavia [now in Croatia]), Croatian politician; president of Croatia from 18 Feb 2000.

**Jean-Marie Messier** (13 Dec 1956, Grenoble, France), French corporate executive; chairman and CEO of Vivendi Universal from 1996 to July 2002.

**Jo Dee Messina** (25 Aug 1970, Holliston MA), American country-and-western singer.

**Debra Messing** (15 Aug 1968, Brooklyn NY), American TV actress who plays Grace Adler on *Will & Grace* (from 1998).

**Pat Metheny** (12 Aug 1954, Lee's Summit MO), American jazz guitarist.

**Princess Mette-Marit** (Mette-Marit Tjessem Høiby; 19 Aug 1973, Kristiansand, Norway), consort of Crown Prince Haakon of Norway.

**Pierre de Meuron** (8 May 1950, Basel, Switzerland), Swiss architect; cowinner, with Jacques Herzog, of the 2001 Pritzker Prize.

**Kweisi Mfume** (Frizzell Gray; Frizzell Gerard Tate; 24 Oct 1948, Baltimore MD), American civil-rights leader, former US congressman; chairman of the National Association for the Advancement of Colored People (NAACP) from 1996.

**King Michael** (Michael Hohenzollern-Sigmaringen; ruled as Mihai I; 25 Oct 1921, Sinaia, Romania), king of Romania, 1927–30 and 1940–47.

**George Michael** (Georgios Kyriakos Panayiotou; 25 Jun 1963, London, England), British pop singer.

**Lorne Michaels** (Lorne Michael Lipowitz; 17 Nov 1944, Toronto, ON, Canada), Canadian-born TV and film producer; originator and executive producer of TV's *Saturday Night Live* from its inception in 1975 (except for 1980–85) and executive producer of *Late Night with Conan O'Brien* from 1993.

**Kate Michelman** (4 Aug 1942 New Jersey), American activist; president of NARAL Pro-Choice America (formerly National Abortion and Reproductive Rights Action League) from 1985.

**Empress Michiko** (Michiko Shoda; 20 Oct 1934, Tokyo, Japan), consort of Emperor Akihito of Japan.

**Midori** (25 Oct? 1971, Osaka, Japan), Japanese-born American violinist.

**Arthur Miller** (17 Oct 1915, New York NY), American playwright, one of the leading figures of post–World War II drama, whose works combine social awareness with a searching concern for his characters' inner lives; best known for *Death of a Salesman* (1949) and *The Crucible* (1953).

**Laura Miller** (18 Nov 1958, Baltimore MD), American journalist and Democratic politician; mayor of Dallas from 20 Feb 2002.

**Leszek Miller** (3 Jul 1946, Zyrardow, near Warsaw, Poland), Polish politician; prime minister of Poland from 2001.

**Slobodan Milosevic** (29 Aug 1941, Pozarevac, Yugoslavia [now in Serbia and Montenegro]), Serbian nationalist leader, president of Serbia, 1989–97, and of Yugoslavia, 1997–2000.

**Czeslaw Milosz** (30 Jun 1911, Sateiniai, Lithuania, Russian Empire [now Lithuania]), Polish-American author, translator, and critic noted for his classical style and preoccupation with philosophical and political issues; he won the 1978 Neustadt Prize and the 1980 Nobel Prize for Literature.

**Norman (Yoshio) Mineta** (12 Nov 1931, San Jose CA), American government official; former US secretary of commerce, 2000–01; US secretary of transportation from 2001.

**Ruth Ann Minner** (17 Jan 1935, Milford DE), American Democratic politician; governor of Delaware from 2001.

**Kylie Minogue** (28 May 1968, Melbourne, VIC, Australia), Australian pop singer.

**Dame Helen Mirren** (Ilyena Lydia Mironoff; 26 Jul 1945, Chiswick, London, England), British stage and film actress best known for the TV series *Prime Suspect*.

**James Mischka** (23 Dec 1960, Burlington WI), American fashion designer who, with Mark Badgley, produces the Badgley Mischka line of beaded evening gowns.

**Rohinton Mistry** (3 Jul 1952, Bombay [now Mumbai], India), Indian-born Canadian novelist whose stories often evoke the lives of lower-middle-class people of metropolitan Mumbai's Parsi community; his *Family Matters* was short-listed for the 2002 Booker Prize.

**Joni Mitchell** (Roberta Joan Anderson; 7 Nov 1943, Fort MacLeod, AB, Canada), Canadian pop singer and songwriter.

**Keith Claudius Mitchell** (12 Nov 1946, Grenada), West Indian politician; prime minister of Grenada from 1995.

**Issey Miyake** (22 Apr 1938, Hiroshima, Japan), Japanese fashion designer whose creations are a blend of Eastern and Western themes.

**Hayao Miyazaki** (5 Jan 1941, Tokyo, Japan), Japanese animation film director whose *Sen to chihiro no kamikakushi* (2002; *Spirited Away*) captured the top prize at the Berlin Film Festival and was a surprise winner of the Academy Award for animated films in 2003.

**Jun'ichiro Miyazu**, Japanese corporate executive; CEO of Nippon Telephone & Telegraph from 2002.

**Isaac Mizrahi** (14 Oct 1961, Brooklyn NY), American fashion designer and TV personality who was the subject of a 1995 documentary film, *Unzipped*.

**Benjamin (William) Mkapa** (12 Nov 1938, Masasi, Tanganyika [now Tanzania]), Tanzanian politician; president of Tanzania from 1995.

**Moby** (Richard Melville Hall; 11 Sep 1965, Darien CT), American techno musician.

**Festus (Gontebanye) Mogae** (23 Jul 1939, Kanye, Botswana), Botswanan politician; president of Botswana from 1998.

**Alfred Moisiu** (1 Dec 1929, Shkodër, Albania), Albanian politician; president of Albania from 24 Jul 2002.

**N. Scott Momaday** (27 Feb 1934, Lawton OK), American author of many works centered on his Kiowa (Native American) heritage.

**Meredith (Jane) Monk** (20 Nov 1942, Lima, Peru), American performance artist, a pioneer in the avant-garde, whose work integrates diverse disciplines and media, including singing, filmmaking, choreography, and acting.

**Tim Montgomery** (25 Jan 1975, Gaffney SC), American sprinter who set a world record for the 100 m, 9.78 sec, at the IAAF Grand Prix final in Paris on 14 Sep 2002.

**Juan Pablo Montoya** (20 Sep 1975, Bogotá, Colombia), Colombian Formula One race-car driver and IndyCar Champion in 1999.

**Sir Mark Moody-Stuart** (1941, Antigua, West Indies), British corporate executive; CEO of the Royal Dutch/Shell Group (UK).

**Robert Moog** (23 May 1934, Flushing, Queens NY), American inventor of the first commercially viable keyboard synthesizer.

**Demi Moore** (Demetria Gene Guynes; 11 Nov 1962, Roswell NM), American actress and star of commercially successful films.

**Julianne Moore** (Julie Smith; 3 Dec 1960, Fayetteville NC), American film actress whose recent works include *The End of the Affair* (1999), *Magnolia* (1999), *Far from Heaven* (2002), and *The Hours* (2002).

**Mandy Moore** (Amanda Leigh Moore; 10 Apr 1984, Nashua NH), American pop singer and actress.

**Mary Tyler Moore** (29 Dec 1936, Brooklyn NY), American film and TV actress known for her work on *The Dick Van Dyke Show* and *The Mary Tyler Moore Show* series.

**Michael Moore** (23 Apr 1954, Davison MI), American film director and author; his book *Stupid White Men ... and Other Sorry Excuses for the State of the Nation!* (2002) topped the nonfiction best-seller lists in 2002, and his film *Bowling for Columbine* won an Academy Award for best documentary in 2003.

**Jason Moran** (21 Jan 1975, Houston TX), American jazz pianist and bandleader who was named *Downbeat Magazine*'s jazz artist rising star in 2003.

**Airto Moreira** (5 Aug 1941, Itaiopolis, Santa Catarina state, Brazil), Brazilian jazz percussionist.

**Nanni Moretti** (Giovanni Moretti; 19 Aug 1953, Brunico, Italy), Italian film director who first tasted success with his 1978 film *Ecce Bombo*; his *La stanza del figlio* (*The Son's Room*) won the Palme d'Or at the Cannes Film Festival in 2001.

**Lorrie Morgan** (Loretta Lynn Morgan; 27 Jun 1959, Nashville TN), American country singer popular from the 1980s; in 1984 she was the youngest singer ever to be invited to join the Grand Ole Opry.

**Rhodri Morgan** (29 Sep 1939, Cardiff, Wales), Welsh Labour politician and first minister of Wales from 2000.

**Yasumasa Morimura** (1951, Osaka, Japan), Japanese photographer especially known for his large-scale self-portraits.

**Alanis Morissette** (1 Jun 1974, Ottawa, ON, Canada), Canadian pop singer and songwriter.

**Giorgio Moroder** (26 Apr 1940, Ortisei, Italy), Italian-born German pop music producer and songwriter.

**Toni Morrison** (Chloe Anthony Wofford; 18 Feb 1931, Lorain OH), American novelist noted for her examination of black experience (particularly black female experience) within the African American community; she won the 1993 Nobel Prize for Literature.

**Van Morrison** (George Ivan Morrison; 31 Aug 1945, Belfast, Northern Ireland), British rock singer/songwriter.

**Morrissey** (Steven Patrick Morrissey; 22 May 1959, Manchester, England), British rock singer and songwriter.

**Mireya Elisa Moscoso de Gruber** (1 Jul 1946, Pedasí, Panama), Panamanian politician; president from 1999.

**Carol Moseley-Braun** (16 Aug 1947, Chicago IL), American lawyer and Democratic politician; she served as US senator from Illinois, 1992–98, and US ambassador to New Zealand, 1999–2001.

**Andrew Motion** (26 Oct 1952, London, England), British poet, teacher, editor, and biographer; poet laureate of England from 1999; his biography of Philip Larkin won the 1994 Whitbread Prize.

**Mohammed Mourhit** (10 Oct 1970, Morocco), Moroccan-born Belgian cross-country runner; world champion in 2000–01.

**Amr Muhammad Moussa** (3 Oct 1936, Cairo, Egypt), Egyptian diplomat; secretary-general of the League of Arab States from 2001.

**Bill Moyers** (6 Jun 1934, Hugo OK), American TV journalist, government official, and author.

**George Mraz** (Jiri Mraz; 9 Sep 1944, Písek, Czechoslovakia [now in the Czech Republic]), Czech jazz bassist.

**Ms. Dynamite** (Niomi McLean-Daley; 1982, London, England), British rhythm-and-blues singer, the first black female artist to win a Mercury Music Prize (2002); she also won the 2003 Brit Award for female solo artist.

**King Mswati III** (19 Apr 1968, Swaziland), king of Swaziland from 1986.

**Cándido Muatetema Rivas** (1961, Equatorial Guinea?), Equatorial Guinean politician; prime minister of Equatorial Guinea from 2001.

**Muhammed Hosni Mubarak** (4 May 1928, Al-Minufiyah governorate, Egypt), Egyptian politician; president of Egypt from 1981.

**Robert S(wan) Mueller III** (7 Aug 1944, New York NY), American government official; FBI director from 2001.

**Robert (Gabriel) Mugabe** (21 Feb 1924, Kutama, Southern Rhodesia [now Zimbabwe]), Zimbabwean politician; first prime minister (1980–87) of the reconstituted state of Zimbabwe, and president from 1987.

**Thierry Mugler** (1948, Strasbourg, France), French fashion designer known for his varied, innovative style and theatrical fashion shows.

**King Muhammad VI** (Muhammad ibn al-Hassan; 21 Aug 1963, Rabat, Morocco), king of Morocco from 1999.

**Paul Muldoon** (20 Jun 1951, Portadown, Northern Ireland), Northern Irish poet known for his ingenious verses and flashy wordplay; he won the 2003 Pulitzer Prize for Poetry for his *Moy Sand and Gravel*.

**Viktoria Mullova** (27 Nov 1959, Moscow, USSR [now in Russia]), Russian-born violinist who specializes in chamber music and founded (1994) the Mullova Chamber Ensemble but has explored music from the Baroque to modern jazz.

**Bakili Muluzi** (17 Mar 1943, Machinga, Nyasaland [now Malawi]), Malawian politician; president of Malawi from 1994.

**Alice Munro** (10 Jul 1931, Wingham, ON, Canada), Canadian short-story writer who gained international recognition with her exquisitely drawn stories, usually set in southwestern Ontario, peopled by characters of Scotch-Irish stock.

**Glenn Murcutt** (25 Jul 1936, London, England), Australian modernist architect noted for his devotion to ecological designs; winner of the 2002 Pritzker Prize.

**(Keith) Rupert Murdoch** (11 Mar 1931, Melbourne, VIC, Australia), Australian-born British corporate executive and media mogul.

**Frank Hughes Murkowski** (28 Mar 1933, Seattle WA), American Republican politician; four-term senator from Alaska and governor of Alaska from 2 Dec 2002.

**Eddie Murphy** (3 Apr 1961, Brooklyn NY), American enduring comedian and film actor from the *Saturday Night Live* cast and later in a string of highly successful film comedies.

**Richard ("Dick") Murphy** (c. 1943), American Republican politician; mayor of San Diego from December 2000.

**Cormac Murphy-O'Connor** (24 Aug 1932, Reading, Berkshire, England), British church leader; archbishop of Westminster and head of the Roman Catholic church in the UK; named cardinal in 2001.

**Bill Murray** (21 Sep 1950, Wilmette IL), American comedian and film actor known for eccentric characterizations; he was a cast member of TV's *Saturday Night Live* (1977–80); his films include *Caddyshack* (1980), *What About Bob?* (1991), *Rushmore* (1998), and *The Royal Tenenbaums* (2001).

**Said Wilbert Musa** (19 Mar 1944, San Ignacio, British Honduras [now Belize]), Belizean politician; prime minister of Belize from 1998.

**Musashimaru** (Fiamalu [Fia] Penitani; 2 May 1971, Samoa), Samoan-born sumo wrestler; Japan's second (after Akebono) foreign-born *yokozuna* (grand champion), from 1999.

**Yoweri Kaguta Museveni** (1944, Mbarra district, Uganda), Ugandan politician; president of Uganda from 1986.

**Ronnie Musgrove** (29 Jul 1956, Tocowa MS), American Democratic politician; governor of Mississippi from 2000.

**Pervez Musharraf** (11 Aug 1943, New Delhi, British India), Pakistani military leader and politician; head of Pakistan's government, 1999–2001, and president from 2001.

**Musiq Soulchild** (Taalib Johnson; Philadelphia PA), American soul singer and songwriter.

**Riccardo Muti** (28 Jul 1941, Naples, Italy), Italian conductor of both opera and the symphonic repertory; music director of the Philadelphia Orchestra, 1980–92.

**Álvaro Mutis** (25 Aug 1923, Bogotá, Colombia), Colombian writer; winner of the Cervantes Prize in 2001 and the Neustadt Prize in 2002.

**Halil Mutlu** (Huben Hubenov; "Little Dynamo"; 14 Jul 1973, Postnik, Bulgaria), Bulgarian-born Turkish weightlifter in the 54-kg class who has set more than 20 world records during his career; gold medalist at the 1999 world championships, the 2000 European championships, and the 2000 Olympic Games.

**Anne-Sophie Mutter** (29 Jun 1963, Rheinfelden, West Germany [now in Germany]), German violinist known for her striking onstage appearance, impeccable technique, and idiosyncratic interpretations of the standard repertoire.

**Levy Patrick Mwanawasa** (3 Sep 1948, Mufulira, Southern Rhodesia [now Zambia]), Zambian politician; president of Zambia from 2 Jan 2002.

**Mike Myers** (25 May 1963, Scarborough, ON, Canada), Canadian comedian and actor famous for offbeat comedy; he is best known for the *Austin Powers* film series.

**Richard B. Myers** (1 Mar 1942, Kansas City MO), American military official, general in the US Air Force, and chairman of the Joint Chiefs of Staff from 2001.

**Youssou N'Dour** (1959, Dakar, Senegal), Senegalese singer and songwriter.

**James Nachtwey** (14 Mar 1948, Syracuse NY), American photojournalist known especially for his award-winning work typically in zones of war and other turmoil.

**Ralph Nader** (27 Feb 1934, Winsted CT), American social activist and politician; presidential candidate in 2000.

**Sheikh Zaid ibn Sultan al-Nahayan** (1918), United Arab Emirates ruler of Abu Dhabi from 1966 and president of the United Arab Emirates from 1971.

**V.S. Naipaul** (Vidiadhar Surajprasad Naipaul; 17 Aug 1932, Chaguanas, Trinidad), Trinidadian-born British writer known for his pessimistic novels set in the Third World nations; he won the 2001 Nobel Prize for Literature.

**Mira Nair** (15 Oct 1957, Bhubaneshwar, Orissa state, India), Indian film director and screenwriter known for controversial documentary and feature films, including *Kama Sutra: A Tale of Love* (1996) and *Monsoon Wedding* (2001).

**Michie Nakamura** (24 Jul 1960, Shimodate, Ibaraki prefecture, Japan), Japanese operatic soprano.

**Fatos Nano** (September 1952, Tirana, Albania), Albanian politician; prime minister of Albania in 1991, 1997–98, and again from 31 Jul 2002.

**Janet Napolitano** (29 Nov 1957, New York NY), American Democratic politician; governor of Arizona from 6 Jan 2003.

**Robert Louis Nardelli** (17 May 1948, Old Forge PA), American corporate executive; CEO of The Home Depot, Inc. from 2000.

**Prince Naruhito** (23 Feb 1960, Tokyo, Japan), crown prince of Japan.

**Milton Nascimento** (1942, Rio de Janeiro, Brazil), Brazilian pop singer and songwriter.

**Graham Nash** (2 Feb 1942, Blackpool, England), British rock guitarist, vocalist, and keyboardist.

**John Forbes Nash, Jr.** (13 Jun 1928, Bluefield VA), American mathematician who was awarded the 1994 Nobel Prize for Economics for his work on the mathematics of game theory.

**Taslima Nasrin** (25 Aug 1962, Mymensigh, Bangladesh), Bangladeshi Islamic feminist writer.

**Adrian Nastase** (22 Jun 1950, Bucharest, Romania), Romanian politician; prime minister of Romania from 2000.

**Edward Natapei** (1954), Vanuatu politician; acting president of Vanuatu, 1999, and prime minister from 2001.

**Henadz Navitski** (1949, Belorussian SSR, USSR [now Belarus]), Belarusian politician; prime minister of Belarus from 2001.

**Martina Navratilova** (18 Oct 1956, Prague, Czechoslovakia [now in the Czech Republic]), Czech-born American tennis player who dominated her sport from 1973 to 1995; she was the most prolific winner of the modern open era and won a record 168 titles; with her victory in the mixed doubles in 2003 she tied Billie Jean King's record of 20 wins at Wimbledon.

**Nursultan Nazarbayev** (6 Jul 1940, Chemolgan, Kazakh SSR, USSR [now Kazakhstan]), Kazakh statesman; president of Kazakhstan from 1990.

**Catherine Ndereba** (c. 1972, Kenya), Kenyan runner who twice in 2001 set record times for the marathon, in Boston and Chicago.

**Liam Neeson** (William Neeson; 7 Jun 1952, Ballymena, Northern Ireland), British film actor respected for his lead role in *Schindler's List* (1993).

**John D(imitri) Negroponte** (21 Jul 1939, London, England), British-born American diplomat; US representative to the United Nations from 2001.

**Nelly** (Cornell Haynes, Jr.; 2 Nov 1980, Austin TX), American rap artist.

**Willie (Hugh) Nelson** (30 Apr 1933, Fort Worth TX), American songwriter and guitarist, one of the most popular country-music singers of the late 20th century.

**Benjamin Netanyahu** (21 Oct 1949, Tel Aviv, Israel), Israeli politician (head of the Likud Party); prime minister of Israel, 1996–99, and later foreign minister and finance minister.

**Anna Netrebko** (1971, Krasnodar, Russian SFSR, USSR [now Russia]), Russian operatic soprano.

**José Maria Neves** (1960), Cape Verdean politician; prime minister of Cape Verde from 2001.

**Bob Newhart** (5 Sep 1929, Oak Park IL), American comedian and TV actor; he won the Kennedy Center's Mark Twain Award in 2002.

**Paul Newman** (26 Jan 1925, Cleveland OH), American film actor and director with a long career of critical and box-office successes.

**Randy Newman** (Randall Stuart Newman; 28 Nov 1943, Los Angeles CA), American singer, songwriter, and composer.

**(Carson) Wayne Newton** (3 Apr 1942, Roanoke VA), American pop singer.

**Teodoro Obiang Nguema Mbasogo** (1942, Acoacan, Río Muni [now Equatorial Guinea]), Equatorial Guinean politician; president of Equatorial Guinea from 1979.

**Mike Nichols** (Michael Igor Peschowsky; 6 Nov 1931, Berlin, Germany), American motion-picture and stage director whose productions focus on the absurdities and horrors of modern life as revealed in personal relationships.

**Jack Nicholson** (John Joseph Nicholson; 22 Apr 1937, Neptune NJ), American film actor; he won Academy Awards for best actor in 1975 (*One Flew over the Cuckoo's Nest*) and 1997 (*As Good As It Gets*) and for best supporting actor in 1983 (*Terms of Endearment*).

**Stevie Nicks** (Stephanie Lynn Nicks; 26 May 1948, Phoenix AZ), American singer and songwriter (of Fleetwood Mac).

**Peter Franz Nicol** (5 Apr 1973, Inverurie, Scotland), British squash player, the world top-ranked male player in 2003.

**Uichiro Niwa** (c. 1941, Aichi prefecture, Japan), Japanese corporate executive; CEO and president of Itochu Corp. from 1998.

**Saparmurad Niyazov** ("Turkmenbashi"; 19 Feb 1940, Askhabad, Turkmen SSR, USSR [now Ashgabat, Turkmenistan]), Turkmenistani politician; president of Turkmenistan from 1990.

**Ronald K(enneth) Noble** (1957?, New Jersey?), American law professor and government official; secretary-general of Interpol from 2000.

**Christopher (Jonathan James) Nolan** (30 Jul 1970, London, England), British film director known for his psychologically challenging pictures *Following* (1998), *Memento* (2000) and *Insomnia* (2002).

**Queen Noor (al-Hussein)** (Lisa Najeeb Halaby; 23 Aug 1951), American-born widow of King Hussein of Jordan (married 15 June 1978); she is active in civic and cultural affairs in Jordan.

**Jessye Norman** (15 Sep 1945, Augusta GA), American operatic and concert soprano.

**Norodom Sihanouk** (Preah Baht Samdach Preah Norodom Sihanuk Varman; 31 Oct 1922, Phnom Penh, Cambodia), king of Cambodia from 1941 to 1955, and again from 1993, and head of state, 1960–70, and again in 1991–93.

**Gale Norton** (11 Mar 1954, Wichita KS), American government official; US secretary of the interior from 2001.

**Kessai H. Note** (1950, Ailinglaplap atoll, Marshall Islands), Marshallese politician; president of the Marshall Islands from 2000.

**Richard C. Notebaert** (1948?, Wisconsin?), American corporate executive; chairman and CEO of Ameritech Corp., 1993–99, and of Qwest Communications International Inc. from 17 Jun 2002.

**Dries van Noten** (1958, Antwerp, Belgium), Belgian fashion designer who mixes opposing elements, such as classic and contemporary, within a single creation.

**Robert Novak** (26 Feb 1931, Joliet IL), American newspaper and TV journalist.

**Jean-François Ntoutoume-Emane** (1939, Gabon?), Gabonese politician; prime minister of Gabon from 1999.

**Sam Nujoma** (Samuel Daniel Shafiishuna Nujoma; 12 May 1929, Owambo, South West Africa [now Namibia]), Namibian independence leader and president of Namibia from 1990.

**Martha Nussbaum** (6 May 1947, New York NY), American moral philosopher; professor of law and ethics, and political activist.

**Frank O'Bannon** (30 Jan 1930, Louisville KY), American Democratic politician; governor of Indiana from 1997.

**Conan O'Brien** (18 Apr 1963, Brookline MA), American TV personality; host of *Late Night with Conan O'Brien* (from 1993).

**Jack O'Brien** (c. 1940), American stage director, artistic director of the Old Globe Theatre, San Diego CA (from 1981); he won the 2003 Tony Award for best direction of a musical for *Hairspray.*

**Mark O'Connor** (5 Aug 1961, Seattle WA), American country fiddle player whose *Folk Mass* debuted in 2003.

**Sandra Day O'Connor** (26 Mar 1930, El Paso TX), American jurist; associate justice of the US Supreme Court from 1981 and the first woman appointed to the Court.

**Sineád O'Connor** (8 Dec 1966, Dublin, Ireland), Irish singer and songwriter.

**Rosie O'Donnell** (Roseanne O'Donnell; 21 Mar 1962, Commack NY), American TV personality; host of *The Rosie O'Donnell Show,* 1996–2002.

**Sean O'Keefe**, American public official; administrator of NASA from 1 Dec 2001.

**Sean Patrick O'Malley** (29 Jun 1944, Lakewood OH), American Roman Catholic churchman; archbishop of Boston from 1 Jul 2003.

**Shaquille (Rashaun) O'Neal** (6 Mar 1972, Newark NJ), American professional basketball center who led the Los Angeles Lakers to NBA titles in 2000, 2001, and 2002; he was only the third player in history to be named MVP of the regular season, the all-star game, and the finals in the same season (2000).

**Paul H. O'Neill** (4 Dec 1935, St. Louis MO), American corporate executive; chairman of Alcoa, Inc., 1987–2000; secretary of the treasury, 2001–2003.

**David J. O'Reilly** (January 1947, Dublin, Ireland), Irish-born American corporate executive; chairman and CEO of ChevronTexaco Corp. from 2001.

**P.J. O'Rourke** (Patrick Jake O'Rourke; 14 Nov 1947, Toledo OH), American political satirist.

**John O'Sullivan** (1942, England), British journalist, commentator, and political adviser; editor-in-chief of United Press International from 1998 until his resignation in July 2003.

**Peter O'Toole** (2 Aug 1932, Connemara, County Galway, Ireland), British stage and film actor of great range famous for Shakespearean roles and the film *Lawrence of Arabia* (1962).

**Joyce Carol Oates** (16 Jun 1938, Lockport NY), American novelist, short-story writer, and essayist noted for her depictions of violence and evil in modern society.

**Thoraya Obaid** (2 Mar 1945, Baghdad, Iraq), Iraqi-born Saudi Arabian civil servant; executive director of the UN Population Fund from 2001.

**Olusegun Obasanjo** (5 Mar 1937, Abeokuta, Nigeria), Nigerian military leader and politician; president of Nigeria from 1999.

**Abdullah Ocalan** (1948?, Omerli, Turkey), Turkishborn leader of the independence movement for Turkey's Kurdish minority; in prison in Turkey in 2003.

**David Oddson** (17 Jan 1948, Reykjavík, Iceland), Icelandic politician; prime minister of Iceland from 1991.

**Nelson O. Oduber** (1947), West Indian politician; prime minister of Aruba, 1989–94, and again from 2001.

**Kenzaburo Oe** (31 Jan 1935, Ose, Ehime prefecture, Japan), Japanese novelist whose works express the disillusionment and rebellion of his post-World War II generation; he won the 1994 Nobel Prize for Literature.

**Karl Aguste Offman** (1940), Mauritian politician; president of Mauritius from 25 Feb 2002.

**Norio Oga** (29 Jan 1930, Shizuoka prefecture, Japan), Japanese president, chairman, and CEO of Sony Corp. from 1995.

**Garrick Ohlsson** (3 Apr 1948, Bronxville NY), American concert pianist.

**Chukwuemeka Odumegwu Ojukwu** (4 Nov 1933, Nnewi, Nigeria), Nigerian military leader and head of the secessionist state of Biafra (1967–70), who ran as a candidate in the 2003 presidential election.

**Motoyuki Oka**, Japanese corporate executive; CEO of the Sumitomo Group.

**Paul Okalik** (26 May 1964, Pangnirtung, NWT [now in Nunavut], Canada), Canadian politician; premier of Nunavut from 1999.

**Claes (Thure) Oldenburg** (28 Jan 1929, Stockholm, Sweden), Swedish-born Pop-art sculptor, best known for his giant soft sculptures of everyday objects.

**Todd Oldham** (1960, Corpus Christi TX), American fashion designer known for his bright and bold colors and patterns.

**Sharon Olds** (19 Nov 1942, San Francisco CA), American poet best known for her powerful, often erotic, imagery of the body and her examination of the family.

**Pat Oliphant** (24 Jul 1935, Adelaide, SA, Australia), Australian-born political cartoonist.

**Eric Christian Olsen** (31 May 1977, Eugene OR), American actor who costarred (with Derek Richardson) in the 2003 hit film *Dumb and Dumberer: When Harry Met Lloyd.*

**(Philip) Michael Ondaatje** (12 Sep 1943, Colombo, Ceylon [now Sri Lanka]), Canadian novelist and poet whose musical prose and poetry are created from a blend of myth, history, jazz, memoirs, and other forms.

**Yoko Ono** (18 Feb 1933, Tokyo, Japan), Japanese-born artist and musician; widow of Beatle John Lennon.

**Suze Orman** (5 Jun 1951, Chicago IL), American financial adviser and best-selling author.

**Stacie Orrico** (1986?, Seattle WA), American gospel singer.

**Amancio Ortega** (March 1936, León, Spain), Spanish fashion and textile tycoon; reportedly one of Europe's richest men.

**John Alfred Osborne** (27 May 1936), West Indian politician; chief minister of Montserrat from 2001.

**Ozzy Osbourne** (John Michael Osbourne; 3 Dec 1948, Birmingham, England), British singer and songwriter, originally the lead singer of Black Sabbath; he and his family are featured in the popular reality TV series, *The Osbournes,* from the 2002 season.

**Yury (Sergeyevich) Osipov** (7 Jul 1936, Tobolsk, Russian SFSR, USSR [now Russia]), Russian mathematician and computer scientist; president of the Russian Academy of Sciences from 1991.

**Albert Osterhaus** (c. 1949, The Netherlands), Dutch virologist famed for his knack for isolating and identifying pathogenic human and animal viruses, including, in March-April 2003, the SARS (severe acute respiratory syndrome) virus.

**Anne Sofie von Otter** (9 May 1955, Stockholm, Sweden), Swedish mezzo-soprano.

**Ahmed Ouyahia** (1952), Algerian politician; prime minister of Algeria, 1995–98, and again from 5 May 2003.

**Michael Ovitz** (14 Dec 1946, Encino CA), American entertainment executive; cofounder of the Creative Artists Agency (1975).

**Bill Owens** (22 Oct 1950, Fort Worth TX), American Republican politician; governor of Colorado from 1999.

**Amos Oz** (4 May 1939, Jerusalem, Palestine), Israeli novelist, short-story writer, and essayist.

**Seiji Ozawa** (1 Sep 1935, Hoten, Manchukuo [now in China]), Japanese-born American conductor, notably of the Boston Symphony Orchestra.

**Makoto Ozone** (25 Mar 1961, Kobe, Japan), Japanese jazz pianist known for his performances with vibraphonist Gary Burton as well as his solo work.

**Rajendra K. Pachauri** (20 Aug 1940, Nainital, Uttar Pradesh [now in Uttaranchal] state, British India), Indian businessman; head of the Intergovernmental Panel on Climate Change from 2002.

**Abel Pacheco de la Espriella** (22 Dec 1933, San José, Costa Rica), Costa Rican politician; president of Costa Rica from 8 May 2002.

**Al Pacino** (25 Apr 1940, New York NY), American film actor known for intense, explosive roles; he won an Academy Award for best actor in 1992 (*Scent of a Woman*).

**Bohdan Paczynski** (8 Feb 1940, Wilno, Poland [now Vilnius, Lithuania]), Polish-born American astronomer, a specialist in various aspects of astronomy, including stellar evolution, accretion disks around compact stars and in binary star systems, and gamma ray bursters; he was the recipient of the Bruce Medal in 2002.

**Elaine (Hiesey) Pagels** (13 Feb 1943, Palo Alto CA), American religious historian and author of scholarly and popular books about early Christianity and gnosticism; her *Beyond Belief: The Secret Gospel of Thomas* was on the best-seller list in 2003.

**Camille Paglia** (2 Apr 1947, Endicott NY), American scholar, author, and controversial feminist.

**Roderick R. Paige** (17 Jun 1933, Monticello MS), American government official; US secretary of education from 2001.

**Nam June Paik** (20 Jul 1932, Seoul, Korea [now in South Korea]), Korean-born German sculptor and performance artist who is called the father of video art.

**Rolandas Paksas** (10 Jun 1956, Telsiai, Lithuanian SSR, USSR [now Lithuania]), Lithuanian politician; president of Lithuania from 26 Feb 2003.

**Michael Palin** (5 May 1943, Yorkshire, England), British comedian and film and TV actor; a founding member of the Monty Python's Flying Circus comedy troupe.

**Dan M. Palmer**, American corporate executive; founder and CEO of Concord EFS, Inc., from 1982.

**Robert Palmer** (Alan Palmer; 19 Jan 1949, Batley, Yorkshire, England), British soul and rhythm-and-blues vocalist.

**Samuel J. Palmisano**, American corporate executive; president and CEO of the International Business Machines (IBM) Corp. from 2002.

**Gwyneth Paltrow** (28 Sep 1972, Los Angeles CA), American motion-picture and stage actress who gained acclaim for the film *Shakespeare in Love* (1998).

**Orhan Pamuk** (7 Jun 1952, Istanbul, Turkey), Turkish novelist, a prize-winning and best-selling author in his own country and abroad; his recent works include *Benim adim kirmiz* (1998; *My Name Is Red*), a historical murder mystery.

**Anna (Helene) Paquin** (24 Jul 1982, Winnipeg, MB, Canada), New Zealand film actress whose work includes *The Piano* (1993; Academy Award), *Jane Eyre* (1996), and *Fly Away Home* (1996).

**Joseph Parisi**, American poet, scholar, and editor of *Poetry* magazine from 1983; he was named executive director of publications and programs for The Poetry Foundation effective June 2003.

**Eugene Newman Parker** (10 Jun 1927, Houghton MI), American physicist and astronomer who was awarded the 2003 Kyoto Prize in the basic science section for his prediction of the existence of the solar wind; he received a National Medal of Science in 1989.

**Robert M. Parker, Jr.** (23 Jul 1947, Baltimore MD), American lawyer and wine authority; founder (1978) and editor of *The Wine Advocate,* a highly influential bimonthly wine periodical.

**Sarah Jessica Parker** (25 Mar 1965, Nelsonville OH), American TV and film actress popular since the 1980s, she reestablished her reputation as star of TV's *Sex and the City*.

**Camilla Parker Bowles** (née Camilla Shand; 17 Jul 1947, London, England), English personality, friend of Prince Charles.

**Derek Parra** (15 Mar 1970, San Bernardino CA), American speed skater; 2002 Olympic gold medalist in the 1,500-m race in world-record time.

**Richard D. Parsons** (4 Apr 1949, Brooklyn NY), American corporate executive; CEO of AOL Time Warner from 2002.

**Arvo Pärt** (11 Sep 1935, Paide, Estonia), Estonian composer whose works display a simplicity and a medieval liturgical sound.

**Dolly (Rebecca) Parton** (19 Jan 1946, Locust Ridge TN), American country singer, songwriter, and actress.

**Justine Pasek** (29 Aug 1979, Ukrainian SSR, USSR [now Ukraine]), Ukrainian-born Panamanian beauty queen; named Miss Panama, she was crowned Miss Universe after the dethronement of Miss Russia, Oksana Fyodorova, in September 2002.

**George E. Pataki** (24 Jun 1945, Peekskill NY), American Republican politician; governor of New York from 1995.

**Ange-Félix Patassé** (1937, Paoua, Ubangi-Shari [now Central African Republic]), Central African Republic politician; president of the Central African Republic from 1993 to 15 Mar 2003.

**Ann Patchett** (2 Dec 1963, Los Angeles CA), American novelist whose *Bel Canto* won the PEN/Faulkner Award and the Orange Prize in 2002.

**Joe Paterno** (Joseph Vincent Paterno; 21 Dec 1926, Brooklyn NY), American football coach for Pennsylvania State University, the winningest coach in history (336 wins at the end of the 2002 season).

**Mandy Patinkin** (30 Nov 1952, Chicago IL), American film, stage, and TV actor recognized for playing Che Guevara in the Broadway play *Evita* (Tony Award, 1980) and his role on the TV series *Chicago Hope* (Emmy Award, 1995).

**Christopher Francis Patten** (12 May 1944, Lancashire, England), British diplomat; last governor general of Hong Kong, 1992–97; chancellor of Newcastle University from 1999 and EC Commissioner for External Relations from 1999.

**Percival (Noel James) Patterson** (10 Apr 1935, Goodwill, Jamaica), Jamaican politician; prime minister of Jamaica from 1992.

**Paul E. Patton** (26 May 1937, Fallsburg KY), American Democratic politician; governor of Kentucky from 1995.

**Sean Paul** (Sean Paul Henriques; 8 Jan 1973, St. Andrew, Jamaica), Jamaican musician who first became a hit with his reggae music in Jamaica and scored in the American market beginning in 1999 with his rap single "Hot Gal Today."

**(Margaret) Jane Pauley** (31 Oct 1950, Indianapolis IN), American TV personality, coanchor of the *Today* show from 1976 to 1989 and host of *Dateline NBC* to 2003.

**Laura Pausini** (16 May 1974, Solarolo, Italy), Italian singer; won the San Remo Song festival in 1993 and won international acclaim for her songs in Italian and Spanish; her English-language album, *From the Inside,* debuted in 2002.

**Luciano Pavarotti** (12 Oct 1935, Modena, Italy), Italian tenor who performed in operatic houses and concert halls worldwide; he is celebrated for the purity of his voice and his ability to reach the highest notes in a tenor's range.

**Tim Pawlenty** (Timothy James Pawlenty; 21 Nov 1960, St. Paul MN), American Republican politician; governor of Minnesota from 6 Jan 2003.

**Tom Paxton** (31 Oct 1937, Chicago IL), American folk singer and songwriter.

**Claudia Pechstein** (22 Feb 1972, East Berlin, East Germany [now Berlin, Germany]), German speed skater; 2002 Olympic gold medalist in the 3,000-m and 5,000-m races, and winner of the latter race in the two previous Olympics as well (and the bronze in 1992).

**Niels-Henning Ørsted Pedersen** (27 May 1946, Osted, Denmark), Danish jazz bassist.

**I.M. Pei** (Ieoh Ming Pei; 26 Apr 1917, Canton [Guangzhou], China), Chinese-born American architect noted for his large but elegantly designed urban buildings and complexes, such as the John Hancock Tower in Boston and the glass pyramids at the Louvre, Paris; winner of the 1983 Pritzker Architecture Prize and the 1988 National Medal of the Arts.

**Viktor (Olegovich) Pelevin** (22 Nov 1962, Moscow, USSR [now in Russia]), Russian novelist especially popular among young readers.

**David Pelletier** (22 Nov 1974, Sayabec, QC, Canada), Canadian pairs skater (with Jamie Salé); shared the 2002 Olympic gold medal with Russians Yelena Berezhnaya and Anton Sikharulidze.

**Krzysztof Penderecki** (23 Nov 1933, Debica, Poland), Polish composer, a leader of the European avant-garde whose works exhibit a novel and masterful treatment of orchestration.

**Jacques Pépin** (Bourg-en-Bresse, France), French-born American chef, host of PBS's cooking show *Today's Gourmet,* and author of the popular cookbooks *La technique* and *The Art of Cooking.*

**Murray Perahia** (19 Apr 1947, New York NY), American concert pianist who returned to the concert stage and recording studio after an hand injury and has been impressing critics and fans with a series of outstanding recordings, notably of the music of J.S. Bach.

**Sonny Perdue** (20 Dec 1946, Perry GA), American agrobusinessman and Republican politician; governor of Georgia from 13 Jan 2003.

**Arturo Pérez Reverte** (24 Nov 1951, Cartagena, Spain), Spanish TV journalist and novelist who has won an international audience for his novels, often historical mysteries; his *La reina del sur* was a bestseller in Spain and Latin America in 2002.

**Kieran Perkins** (14 Aug 1973, Brisbane, QLD, Australia), Australian swimmer who held 12 world records in distance freestyle events.

**Richard N. Perle** (New York NY), American defense and intelligence analyst and official; resigned as chairman of the Defense Policy Board Advisory Committee, a key advisory group to the Pentagon, in March 2003.

**Itzhak Perlman** (31 Aug 1945, Tel Aviv, Palestine [now Tel Aviv-Yafo, Israel]), Israeli-born American violinist.

**Rhea Perlman** (31 Mar 1948, Brooklyn NY), American film and TV actress best remembered as Carla Maria Victoria Angelina Teresa Apollonia Lozupone Tortelli LeBec on the TV series *Cheers* (1982–93).

**Matthew Perry** (19 Aug 1969, Williamstown MA), American TV actor who appears as Chandler Bing on the hit TV sitcom *Friends* (from 1994).

**Rick Perry** (4 Mar 1950, West Texas TX), American Republican politician; governor of Texas from 2000.

**Göran Persson** (20 Jan 1949, Vingaker, Sweden), Swedish politician; prime minister of Sweden from 1996.

**Joe Pesci** (9 Feb 1943, Newark NJ), American motion-picture actor best known for roles in gangster movies and comedies.

**Dragisa Pesic** (8 Aug 1954, Danilovgrad, Yugoslavia [now in Serbia and Montenegro]), Yugoslavian politician; the last prime minister of Yugoslavia (2001–03) before it became Serbia and Montenegro.

**Bernadette Peters** (Bernadette Lazzaro; 28 Feb 1948, Queens NY), American singer and actress on Broadway, TV, and in films.

**Oscar (Emanuel) Peterson** (15 Aug 1925, Montreal, QC, Canada), Canadian jazz pianist.

**Tom Petty** (20 Oct 1953, Gainesville FL), American singer and songwriter whose roots-oriented guitar rock arose from the new-wave movement of the late 1970s and resulted in a string of hit singles and albums.

**Michelle Pfeiffer** (29 Apr 1958, Santa Ana CA), American leading actress of great talent and beauty.

**Liz Phair** (Elizabeth Clark Phair; 17 Apr 1967, New Haven CT), American indie rock star first noticed for her debut album, *Exile in Guyville* (1993).

**Phan Van Khai** (25 Dec 1933, Tan Thong Hoi village, near Saigon, French Indochina [now Ho Chi Minh City, Vietnam]), Vietnamese politician; prime minister of Vietnam from 1997.

**Michael Phelps** (30 Jun 1985, Baltimore MD), American swimmer who won three gold medals and one silver medal (including firsts in three different strokes, a record) at the 2003 US nationals and set five world records (itself a record) at the 2003 FINA World Championships.

**Regis (Francis Xavier) Philbin** (25 Aug 1934, New York NY), American TV personality, host of *Live with Regis and Kelly* and *Who Wants To Be a Millionaire?*

**Prince Philip, Duke of Edinburgh** (10 Jun 1921, Corfu, Greece), husband of Queen Elizabeth II.

**Crown Prince Philippe** (Philippe Leopold Louis Marie; 15 Apr 1960, Brussels, Belgium), duke of Brabant and prince of Belgium.

**Mark Philippoussis** (7 Nov 1976, Melbourne, VIC, Australia), Australian tennis player; a strong contender in Grand Slam play; he lost to Roger Federer in the 2003 Wimbledon finals.

**Renzo Piano** (14 Sep 1937, Genoa, Italy), Italian architect; winner of the 1998 Pritzker Prize and the 2002 UIA Gold Medal for Architecture.

**Joseph A. Pichler,** American corporate executive; chairman and CEO of the Kroger Co. from 1990.

**Heinrich von Pierer** (26 Jan 1941, Erlangen, Germany), German corporate executive; CEO of Siemens AG from 1992.

**Rosamund Pike** (27 Jan 1979, London, England), British film actress who starred in the James Bond motion picture *Die Another Day* (2002).

**Pink** (Alecia Moore; 8 Sep 1979, Doylestown PA), American pop vocalist.

**Steven Pinker** (18 Sep 1954, Montreal, QC, Canada), Canadian-born American experimental psychologist and author of scholarly and popular books of language.

**Trevor Pinnock** (16 Dec 1946, Canterbury, England), English harpsichordist and conductor.

**Augusto Pinochet (Ugarte)** (25 Nov 1915, Valparaíso, Chile), Chilean leader of the military junta that overthrew Pres. Salvador Allende and head of Chile's military government (1974–90).

**Robert Pinsky** (20 Oct 1940, Long Branch NJ), American poet and critic whose poems searched for the significance underlying everyday acts; poet laureate of the US, 1997–2000.

**Harold Pinter** (10 Oct 1930, London, England), English playwright regarded as one of the most complex and challenging post–World War II dramatists. His plays are noted for their use of understatement, small talk, reticence, and even silence to convey the substance of their characters.

**Billie Piper** (22 Sep 1982, Swindon, England), British pop singer.

**Scottie Pippen** (25 Sep 1965, Hamburg AR), American basketball player with the winning Chicago Bulls teams of the 1990s.

**Pedro Verona Rodrigues Pires** (April 1934, Ilha do Fogo, Cape Verde), Cape Verdean politician; president of Cape Verde from 2001.

**Bernd Pischetsrieder** (15 Feb 1948, Munich, West Germany [now in Germany]), German corporate executive; CEO of Volkswagen AG from September 2001.

**Joe Piscopo** (17 Jun 1951, Passaic NJ), American comedian and film and TV actor.

**Brad Pitt** (William Bradley Pitt; 18 Dec 1963, Shawnee OK), American actor, one of the biggest box-office draws; his films include *A River Runs Through It* (1992), *Interview with the Vampire* (1994), and *Ocean's Eleven* (2001).

**Robert Plant** (20 Aug 1948, West Bromwich, England), British singer and songwriter.

**Mikhail Pletnev** (14 Apr 1957, Arkhangelsk, Russian SFSR, USSR [now Russia]), Russian pianist and conductor.

**Sylvia Poggioli** (Providence RI), American foreign correspondent for National Public Radio.

**Sidney Poitier** (20 Feb 1927?, Miami FL), Bahamian-American motion-picture actor and director; won an Academy Award for best actor in 1963 (*Lilies of the Field*).

**Roman Polanski** (Raimund Liebling; 18 Aug 1933, Paris, France), Polish film director, scriptwriter, and actor; his *The Pianist* (2002) won a French César award, a British BAFTA, and the Palme d'Or at the 2002 Cannes Film Festival, and brought Polanski a best director Oscar.

**Judit Polgar** (23 Jul 1976, Budapest, Hungary), Hungarian chess player, the youngest of the three chess-playing Polgar sisters; she achieved the rank among male chess players of grandmaster in December 1991 at the age of 15.

**Sigmar Polke** (13 Feb 1941, Oels, Germany [now Olesnica, Poland]), German painter who was one of the founders of Capitalist Realism, a movement that depicts popular and mundane cultural artifacts with ironic seriousness; he won a Japanese Praemium Imperiale Award for excellence in arts in 2002.

**John (Charlton) Polkinghorne** (16 Oct 1930, Weston-super-Mare, England), British Anglican priest and particle physicist; winner of the 2002 Templeton Prize.

**Sydney Pollack** (1 Jul 1934, Lafayette IN), American film producer, director, and actor who won an Academy Award for directing in 1985 (*Out of Africa*); his recent production credits include *The Talented Mr. Ripley* (1999), *Iris* (2001), and *The Quiet American* (2002).

**Jonathan Jay Pollard** (7 Aug 1954, Galveston TX), American naval-intelligence officer who was arrested in 1985 for passing classified US information to Israel; he was sentenced to life in prison.

**Ruslan Ponomaryov** (11 Oct 1983, Gorlovka, Ukrainian SSR, USSR [now Horlivka, Ukraine]), Ukrainian chess master; winner of the FIDE world chess championship, 2002.

**Alfonso Antonio Portillo Cabrera** (24 Sep 1951, Zacapa department, Guatemala), Guatemalan politician; president of Guatemala from 2000.

**Natalie Portman** (Natalie Hershlag; 9 Jun 1981, Jerusalem, Israel), Israeli-born American motion-picture actress who appeared in *Star Wars Episode I* (1999), *II* (2002), and *III* (2005).

**Zac Posen** (Zachary E. Posen; 24 Oct 1980, New York NY), American fashion designer whose first independent show in February 2002 featured 1930s-inspired fashions.

**Vladimir Olegovich Potanin** (3 Jan 1961, Moscow, USSR [now in Russia]), Russian tycoon and financial expert; he was a cofounder of Oneksimbank (1993) and major stockholder in a number of large corporations; he has also held a number of important government posts.

**John E. Potter** (195?), American corporate executive; CEO and postmaster general of the US Postal Service from 2001.

**Colin (Luther) Powell** (5 Apr 1937, New York NY), American military officer and government official; chairman of the Joint Chiefs of Staff, 1989–93; national security adviser, 1987–89; and US secretary of state from 2001.

**Earl A. ("Rusty") Powell** (24 Oct 1943, Spartanburg SC), American museum official; director of the National Gallery of Art in Washington DC from 1992.

**Samantha Power** (1970, Ireland), Irish-born American writer; author of *A Problem from Hell*, a study of US inaction against genocide in the 20th century, which won the 2003 Pulitzer Prize for General Nonfiction.

**Velupillai Prabhakaran** (26 Nov 1954, Jaffna, Sri Lanka), Sri Lankan secessionist; founder and leader of Liberation Tigers of Tamil Eelam (Tamil Tigers) from the early 1970s.

**Miuccia Prada** (1949, Milan, Italy), Italian fashion designer whose clothing, footwear, and accessories designs are characterized by casual luxury.

**Azim Hasham Premji** (24 Jul 1945, Bombay [now Mumbai], British India), Indian corporate executive; chairman of the Wipro Corp. of Bangalore, India from 1977.

**André (George) Previn** (6 Apr 1929, Berlin, Germany), German-born American pianist, composer, and conductor; music director of the Los Angeles Philharmonic, 1985–89, and the Oslo Symphony Orchestra from 2002.

**Prince** (Prince Rogers Nelson; 7 Jun 1958, Minneapolis MN), American singer and songwriter who was among the most talented American musicians of his generation.

**Anthony Principi** (16 Apr 1944, Bronx NY), American government official; US secretary of veterans affairs from 2001.

**Richard B. Priory** (15 May 1946, Lakehurst NJ), American energy engineer and corporate executive; CEO of Duke Energy from 1997.

**Romano Prodi** (9 Aug 1939, Scandiano, Italy), Italian politician; prime minister of Italy, 1996–98, and president of the European Commission from 1999.

**E(dna) Annie Proulx** (22 Aug 1935, Norwich CT), American writer whose darkly comic yet sad fiction is peopled with quirky, memorable individuals and unconventional families.

**Paul Prudhomme** (13 Jul 1940, near Opelousas LA), American chef and restaurateur who popularized Louisiana Cajun cooking through his TV appearances and cookbooks.

**Georgi Purvanov** (28 Jun 1957, Kovachevtsi, Bulgaria), Bulgarian politician; president of Bulgaria from 22 Jan 2002.

**Vladimir Vladimirovich Putin** (7 Oct 1952, Leningrad, USSR [now St. Petersburg, Russia]), Russian intelligence officer and politician; president of Russia from 1999.

**Thomas Pynchon** (8 May 1937, Glen Cove, Long Island NY), American novelist and short-story writer.

**Muammar al-Qaddafi** (also spelled Muammar Khadafy, Moammar Gadhafi, or Mu'ammar al-Qadhdhafi; 1942, near Surt, Libya), Libyan military leader; de facto chief of state of Libya from 1969; controversial Arab statesman.

**Laisenia Qarase** (1941), Fijian politician; prime minister of Fiji, 2000–01, and again from 2001.

**Anna Quindlen** (8 Jul 1953, Philadelphia PA), American political commentator and author whose *Blessings* was a best-seller in 2002.

**Ivica Racan** (24 Feb 1944, Ebersbach, Germany), Croatian politician; prime minister of Croatia from 27 Jan 2000.

**Daniel Radcliffe** (23 July 1989, London, England), British actor who plays Harry Potter in the highly successful series of films (from 2001).

**Paula Radcliffe** (17 Dec 1973, Northwich, Cheshire, England), British long-distance runner; the world cross-country champion in 2001 and 2002, she set a world women's record—2 h 17 min 18 sec—at the 2002 Chicago Marathon and shaved almost two minutes from her record in the London Marathon in April 2003.

**Raël** (Claude Vorilhon; 30 Sep 1946, Vichy, France), French journalist, founder of the Raelian Movement, which teaches that life on Earth was created (i.e., cloned) by extraterrestrial scientists and that the Movement must prepare the Earth for their return; the sect was in the news when they announced the birth of the first cloned human baby, on 26 Dec 2002.

**Jean-Pierre Raffarin** (3 Aug 1948, Poitiers, France), French politician; prime minister of France from 6 May 2002.

**Franklin D. Raines** (14 Jan 1949, Seattle WA), American corporate executive; CEO of Fannie Mae from 1999.

**Prince Rainier III** (Rainier-Louis-Henri-Maxence-Bertrand de Grimaldi; 31 May 1933, Monaco), prince of Monaco from 1949.

**Konrad Raiser** (25 Jan 1938, Magdeburg, Germany), German church official; general secretary of the World Council of Churches from 1 Jan 1993.

**Bonnie Raitt** (8 Nov 1949, Burbank CA), American singer and bottleneck guitarist remarkable for her gutsy blend of blues and rhythm-and-blues styles.

**Imomali Rakhmonov** (5 Oct 1952, Dangara, Tadzhik SSR, USSR [now Tajikistan]), Tajik politician; president of Tajikistan from 1992.

**Joseph W. Ralston** (4 Nov 1943, Hopkinsville KY), American military officer, USAF general; head of the US European Command, 2000–03.

**Samuel Ramey** (28 Mar 1942, Colby KS), American bass, one of the operatic stars of his generation, known for his mastery of the repertory and commanding stage presence.

**Queen Rania, al-Abdullah** (Rania al-Yaseen; 31 Aug 1970, Kuwait), Kuwaiti-born consort of King Abdullah II of Jordan.

**Raphael I Bidawid** (1922, Mosul, Iraq), Iraqi religious leader; patriarch of the Chaldean Catholic Church from 1989.

**Anders Fogh Rasmussen** (26 Jan 1953, Ginnerup, Denmark), Danish politician; prime minister of Denmark from 2001.

**Dan Rather** (31 Oct 1931, Wharton TX), American TV journalist and news anchor.

**Aleksey Ratmansky** (1968, Leningrad, USSR [now St. Petersburg, Russia]), Russian dancer, choreographer, and director who was named artistic director of the Bolshoi Ballet in May 2003.

**Sir Simon (Denis) Rattle** (19 Jan 1955, Liverpool, England), British orchestra conductor; principal conductor and artistic director of the Berlin Philharmonic from the 2002-03 season.

**Johannes Rau** (16 Jan 1931, Wuppertal-Barmen, Germany), German politician; president of Germany from 1999.

**Robert Rauschenberg** (22 Oct 1925, Port Arthur TX), American painter and graphic artist whose works incorporate a wide range of trash and debris with splashes of paint in collages and "combines"; his early works anticipated the Pop-art movement.

**Marc Ravalomanana** (1949, near Atananarivo, [French] Madagascar), Malagasy politician; president of Madagascar from 22 Feb 2002.

**Lee R. Raymond** (1938, Waterstown SD), American corporate executive; chairman and CEO of Exxon Mobil Corp. from 1994.

**Chris Rea** (4 Mar 1951, Middlesborough, England), British pop singer.

**Nancy Davis Reagan** (Anne Frances Robbins; 6 Jul 1921, New York NY), American first lady; second wife of Pres. Ronald Reagan.

**Ronald (Wilson) Reagan** (6 Feb 1911, Tampico IL), American film actor and statesman; 40th president of the US, 1981–89 (see full biography at Presidents).

**Robert Redford** (18 Aug 1937, Santa Monica CA), American film actor and director; founder of the Sundance Institute and Film Festival.

**Lynn Redgrave** (8 Mar 1943, London, England), British stage, screen, and TV actress whose breakthrough came in the film *Georgy Girl* (1966).

**Vanessa Redgrave** (30 Jan 1937, London, England), British actress and political activist; she won the 2003 Tony Award for best actress in a play for her role in *Long Day's Journey into Night*.

**Joshua Redman** (1 Feb 1969, Berkeley CA), American jazz-saxophone player.

**Sumner Redstone** (Sumner Rothstein; 27 May 1923, Boston MA), American corporate executive; chairman of the board (from 1987) and CEO (from 1996) of Viacom Inc.

Lou Reed (2 Mar 1942, Brooklyn NY), American rock singer and songwriter.

Ralph Eugene Reed, Jr. (24 Jun 1961, Portsmouth VA), American activist; executive director of the Christian Coalition.

Rex Reed (2 Oct 1938, Fort Worth TX), American film critic.

Christopher Reeve (25 Sep 1952, New York NY), American film actor best known for playing Superman; following a severe injury in a horse-riding accident he became a crusader for spinal-cord-injury research.

Keanu Reeves (2 Sep 1964, Beirut, Lebanon), American actor known for many popular films.

Martha Reeves (18 Jul 1941, Eufala AL), American musician, lead singer of Martha and The Vandellas.

William Hubbs Rehnquist (1 Oct 1924, Milwaukee WI), American jurist; associate justice of the US Supreme Court from 1972 and chief justice from 1986.

Robert Bernard Reich (24 Jun 1946, Scranton PA), American political economist and government official who served as US secretary of labor (1993–97); he is also a university professor and political commentator.

Steve Reich (Stephen Michael Reich; 3 Oct 1936, New York NY), American minimalist composer.

Marcel Reich-Ranicki (2 Jun 1920, Wroclawek, Poland), Polish-born German literary critic, author, and TV host; winner of the Goethe Prize in 2002.

Harry Reid (2 Dec 1939, Searchlight NV), American Democratic politician; senator from Nevada and Senate minority whip from 1998.

Rob Reiner (6 Mar 1947, Bronx NY), American actor, director, writer, and producer of critical and commercially successful films.

Thomas Esang Remengesau, Jr. (1956), Palauan politician; president of Palau from 2001.

Edward Gene Rendell (5 Jan 1944, New York NY), American Democratic politician; mayor of Philadelphia 1992–2000 and governor of Pennsylvania from 21 Jan 2003.

France-Albert René (16 Nov 1935, Mahé, Seychelles), Seychelles politician; president of Seychelles from 1977.

Einars Repse (9 Dec 1961, Jelgava, Latvian SSR, USSR [now Latvia]), Latvian politician; prime minister of Latvia from 7 Nov 2002.

Yasmina Reza (1 May 1959, Paris, France), French playwright of international acclaim, best known for her play Art.

Manon Rheaume (24 Feb 1972, Lac Beauport, QC, Canada), Canadian ice-hockey goalie who is the only woman to play in the NHL.

Busta Rhymes (Trevor Smith, Jr.; 20 May 1972, Brooklyn NY), American rap performer.

Anne Rice (Howard Allen O'Brien; noms de plume, A.N. Roquelaure and Anne Rampling; 4 Oct 1941, New Orleans LA), American gothic novelist known especially for her six-volume Vampire Chronicles.

Condoleezza Rice (14 Nov 1954, Birmingham AL), American academic and government official; national security adviser from 2001.

Tim Rice (10 Nov 1944, Amersham, Buckinghamshire, England), British lyricist who collaborated with Andrew Lloyd Webber on a number of hit stage musicals.

Adrienne (Cecile) Rich (16 May 1929, Baltimore MD), American poet, scholar, teacher, and critic; recipient of the 2003 Bollingen Prize for American Poetry.

Keith Richards (18 Dec 1943, Dartford, Kent, England), British guitarist and singer with the Rolling Stones.

Bill Richardson (15 Nov 1947, Pasadena CA), American government official; US secretary of energy, ambassador to the UN, congressman, and governor of New Mexico from 1 Jan 2003.

Derek Richardson, American actor who costarred (with Eric Christian Olsen) in the 2003 hit film Dumb and Dumberer: When Harry Met Lloyd.

Lionel B. Richie, Jr. (20 Jun 1949, Tuskegee AL), American rhythm-and-blues songwriter and singer.

Gerhard Richter (9 Feb 1932, Dresden, Germany), German artist and cofounder of the movement known as Capitalist Realism, in which ordinary objects such as furniture and food, and sometimes the artists themselves, are depicted as art.

Kai-Uwe Ricke (Oct 1961, Krefeld, West Germany [now in Germany]), German corporate executive; CEO of Deutsche Telekom from 15 Nov 2002.

Sally K(risten) Ride (26 May 1951, Encino CA), American astronaut and astrophysicist who was the first American woman in space (1983).

Thomas Joseph Ridge (26 Aug 1945, Munhall PA), American government official; he was designated in 2002 to be secretary of homeland security, a new cabinet-level office.

Leni Riefenstahl (22 Aug 1902, Berlin, Germany), German filmmaker both praised and reviled for documentary films of the 1930s dramatizing the Nazi movement.

Klaus (Thorvald) Rifbjerg (15 Dec 1931, Copenhagen, Denmark), Danish poet, novelist, playwright, and editor.

Leonard S. Riggio (28 Feb 1941, Bronx NY), American corporate executive; founder and chairman of Barnes & Noble, Inc., from 1971.

Bridget Riley (24 Apr 1931, London, England), English Op-art painter.

Robert R. Riley (3 Oct 1944, Ashland AL), American Republican politician; governor of Alabama from 20 Jan 2003.

LeAnn Rimes (28 Aug 1982, Jackson MS), American country-and-western singer.

Anton E. ("Skip") Rimsza (31 Mar 1955, Chicago IL), American Republican politician; mayor of Phoenix from 1994.

Faith Ringgold (8 Oct 1930, New York NY), American artist and author who became famous for innovative, quilted narrations that communicate her political beliefs.

Kelly Ripa (2 Oct 1970, Stratford NJ), American talk-show host and actress on daytime TV.

Pipilotti Rist (Charlotte Rist; 21 Jun 1962, Grabs, Switzerland), Swiss video-installation artist.

Rivaldo (Vitor Borba Ferreira; 19 Apr 1972, Recife, Brazil), Brazilian association football (soccer) player; he was named FIFA World Footballer of the Year in 1999 and was a key player on the Brazilian national team in the 1998 and 2002 World Cup competitions.

Geraldo Rivera (4 Jul 1943, New York NY), American TV journalist and talk-show host.

Tim Robbins (16 Oct 1958, West Covina CA), American actor whose films include Bull Durham (1988), The Player (1992), The Shawshank Redemption (1994), and Mystic River (2003).

Cecil E(dward) Roberts, Jr. (31 Oct 1946, Kanawha county WV), American labor leader; president of the United Mine Workers of America from 1995.

**Cokie Roberts** (Mary Martha Corinne Morrison Claiborne Boggs; 27 Dec 1943, New Orleans LA), American radio and TV journalist and commentator.

**Julia Roberts** (28 Oct 1967, Smyrna GA), American actress, one of the biggest names in Hollywood since her performance in the film *Pretty Woman* (1990).

**George (Islay MacNeill) Robertson** (Baron Robertson of Port Ellen; 1946, Port Ellen, Isle of Islay, Scotland), British military leader; secretary-general of NATO from 1999; he was expected to step down at the end of 2003.

**Pat Robertson** (22 Mar 1930, Lexington VA), American TV evangelist and broadcasting executive, one-time presidential contender and president of the Christian Coalition (to 2001).

**Robbie Robertson** (Jaime Roberts; 5 Jul 1944, Toronto, ON, Canada), Canadian rock musician (guitarist with The Band).

**(Michael) Duke Robillard** (4 Oct 1948, Woonsockett RI), American blues guitarist, singer, and songwriter.

**David (Maurice) Robinson** (6 Aug 1965, Key West FL), American basketball player; he was a center who led the San Antonio Spurs to NBA championships in 1999 and 2003.

**Mary Robinson** (21 May 1944, Ballina, Ireland), Irish statesman; president of Ireland, 1990–97; United Nations High Commissioner for Human Rights, 1997–2003.

**Smokey Robinson** (William Robinson, Jr.; 19 Feb 1940, Detroit MI), American rhythm-and-blues singer and songwriter.

**Emily Robison** (16 Aug 1972, Pittsfield MA), American country musician; member of the Dixie Chicks (Academy of Country Music Entertainers of the Year, 2000).

**Robyn** (Robyn Carlsson; 12 Jun 1979, Stockholm, Sweden), Swedish pop singer.

**Chris Rock** (7 Feb 1966, Georgetown SC), American stand-up performer and actor known for his brash style.

**Kid Rock** (Robert James Ritchie; 17 Jan 1971, Romeo MI), American rap-rock artist.

**The Rock** (Dwayne Douglas Johnson; 2 May 1972 California), American wrestler turned actor.

**Anita (Lucia) Roddick** (23 Oct 1942, Littlehampton, England), British businesswoman; cofounder of The Body Shop in 1976.

**Judith Rodin** (9 Sep 1944, Philadelphia PA), American psychologist and educator; president of the University of Pennsylvania from 1994, the first woman president of an Ivy League college.

**Dennis (Keith) Rodman** (13 May 1961, Trenton NJ), American basketball forward who led the NBA in rebounding 1991–98 and who was known for his eccentric behavior on and off the court.

**Alex Rodriguez** (27 Jul 1975, New York NY), American baseball player; he is a shortstop known as a fine all-around player who signed the largest salary deal in history ($252 million over 10 years) in 2000.

**Narciso Rodríguez** (1961, New Jersey), American fashion designer who rose quickly to fame when he designed Carolyn Bessette's dress for her 1996 wedding to John F. Kennedy, Jr.; he was named the best women's wear designer by the Council of Fashion Designers of America in 2002 and 2003.

**Kenny Rogers** (Kenneth Donald Rogers; 21 Aug 1938, Houston TX), American country-and-western and pop singer.

**Jacques Rogge** (2 May 1942, Ghent, Belgium), Belgian Olympic yachtsman, surgeon, and sports executive; he has been president of the International Olympic Committee from 2001.

**Roh Moo Hyun** (6 Aug 1946, near Pusan, Korea [now in South Korea]), Korean politician; president of the Republic of Korea from 25 Feb 2003.

**Sonny Rollins** (Theodore Walter Rollins; 7 Sep 1930, Harlem, New York NY), American jazz tenor and soprano saxophonist.

**Holmes Rolston, III** (19 Nov 1932, Staunton VA), American Presbyterian minister and environmental ethicist; leading scholar of the philosophical, scientific, and religious conceptions of nature and founder of the journal *Environmental Ethics* (1979); winner of the 2003 Templeton Prize.

**Ray Romano** (21 Dec 1957, Queens NY), American comic actor best known for the prizewinning TV series *Everybody Loves Raymond*.

**Mitt Romney** (12 Mar 1947, Bloomfield MI), American businessman, sports executive (CEO of the group that organized the 2002 Winter Olympics in Salt Lake City), and Republican governor of Massachusetts from 2 Jan 2003.

**Ronaldo** (Ronaldo Luiz Nazario de Lima; 22 Sep 1976, Itaguai, Rio de Janeiro state, Brazil), Brazilian association football (soccer) player; FIFA Player of the Year in 1996 and 1997 and star of Brazil's national team in the 2002 World Cup.

**Linda (Marie) Ronstadt** (15 Jul 1946, Tucson AZ), American pop singer.

**Andy Rooney** (14 Jan 1919, Albany NY), American TV commentator.

**Anton Rop** (27 Dec 1960, Ljubljana, Yugoslavia [now in Slovenia]), Slovene politician; prime minister from 11 Dec 2002.

**Axl Rose** (William Bailey; 6 Feb 1962, Lafayette IN), American rock vocalist (of Guns N' Roses).

**Charlie Rose** (5 Jan 1942, Henderson NC), American TV journalist and interviewer.

**Roseanne** (also known as Roseanne Barr and Roseanne Arnold; 3 Nov 1953, Salt Lake City UT), American TV and night club personality who is best known for her TV series *Roseanne*.

**Diana Ross** (Diane Earle; 26 Mar 1944, Detroit MI), American rhythm-and-blues singer and actress.

**Mstislav (Leopoldovich) Rostropovich** (27 Mar 1927, Baku, Transcaucasian SFSR, USSR [now in Azerbaijan]), Russian-born cellist, conductor, and pianist; he was music director of the National Symphony Orchestra, 1977–94.

**Philip (Milton) Roth** (19 Mar 1933, Newark NJ), American novelist and short-story writer whose works are characterized by an acute ear for dialogue, a concern with Jewish middle-class life, and the painful entanglements of sexual and familial love.

**Sister Elaine Roulet** (1930, Maspath NY), American activist, called the "Prison Angel," who has concerned with the protection and care of the children of women in prison.

**Mike Rounds** (24 Oct 1954, Huron SD), American Republican politician; governor of South Dakota from 7 Jan 2003.

**Karl Rove** (25 Dec 1950, Denver CO), American political consultant; chief strategist for Pres. George W. Bush.

**John G. Rowland** (24 May 1957, Waterbury CT), American Republican politician; governor of Connecticut from 1995.

**Kelly Rowland** (Kelendria Rowland; 11 Feb 1981, Atlanta GA), American rhythm-and-blues singer, a member of the popular female vocal group Destiny's Child, who issued her first solo album, *Simply Deep*, in 2002.

**Landon H. Rowland**, American corporate executive; chairman and CEO of Stilwell Financial Inc.

**J.K. Rowling** (Joanne Kathleen Rowling; 31 Jul 1965, Chipping Sodbury, England), British author, creator of the popular and critically acclaimed Harry Potter series about a young sorcerer in training.

**Arundhati Roy** (24 Nov 1961, Shillong, Bengal state, India), Indian novelist who won the Booker Prize in 1998 for *The God of Small Things*.

**Patrick Roy** (5 Oct 1965, Quebec City, QC, Canada), Canadian ice-hockey goalie; he is the only three-time NHL playoffs MVP, winning the Conn Smythe Trophy in 1986, 1993, and 2001.

**Paulina Rubio** (17 Jun 1971, Mexico City, Mexico), Mexican-born singer, dancer, and actress whose collection *Paulina* was Billboard's No. 1 Latin album of 2001.

**Ibragim Rugova** (1944, Kosovo?, Yugoslavia [now in Serbia and Montenegro]), Kosovar (Albanian) nationalist leader and officer in the opposition government of Kosovo.

**Louis Rukeyser** (30 Jan 1933, New York NY), American TV journalist and financial analyst.

**Donald (Henry) Rumsfeld** (9 Jul 1932, Chicago IL), American government official; US secretary of defense, 1975–77, and again from 2001.

**(Ahmed) Salman Rushdie** (19 Jun 1947, Bombay [now Mumbai], India), Anglo-Indian novelist who was condemned to death by leading Iranian Muslim clerics in 1989 for allegedly having blasphemed Islam in his novel *The Satanic Verses*.

**Leon Russell** (Claude Russell Bridges; 2 Apr 1941, Lawton OK), American rock pianist, instrumentalist, and singer.

**Patricia F. Russo** (Trenton NJ), American business executive; CEO of Lucent Technologies from 2002.

**Edward B. Rust, Jr.** (Illinois), American corporate executive; president and CEO of State Farm Insurance from 1985.

**John Rutter** (24 Sep 1945, London, England), British composer and conductor; he is the founder (1981) and leader of the Cambridge Singers, a professional chamber choir.

**Arnold Rüütel** (10 May 1928, Saaremaa, Estonia), Estonian politician; chairman of the Supreme Council of Estonia, 1990–92, and president from 2001.

**George H. Ryan** (24 Feb 1934, Maquoketa IA), American Republican politician; governor of Illinois, 1999–2003.

**Meg Ryan** (Margaret Mary Emily Anne Hyra; 19 Nov 1961, Fairfield CT), American film star of great popularity known mostly for upbeat romantic comedies.

**Winona Ryder** (Winona Laura Horowitz; 29 Oct 1971, Winona MN), American film actress noticed for her roles in *The Age of Innocence* (1993) and *Little Women* (1994).

**Sa'd ad-din Ibrahim** (3 Dec 1938, near Mansurah, Egypt), Egyptian political sociologist and government critic.

**Prince al-Walid ibn Talal ibn Abdulaziz as-Sa'ud** (1954, Riyadh, Saudi Arabia), Saudi Arabian businessman who saved EuroDisney; a majority stockholder in CitiGroup, he is listed fifth on Forbes magazine's 2003 list of influential billionaires.

**Charles Saatchi** (9 Jun 1943, Baghdad, Iraq), Iraqi-born British advertising executive and art collector and patron of British art.

**Sheikh Jabir al-Ahmad al-Jabir Al Sabah** (29 Jun 1928, Kuwait), emir of Kuwait from 1977.

**Sheikh Sabah al-Ahmad al-Jabir Al Sabah** (1929?, Kuwait), prime minister of Kuwait from 13 Jul 2003.

**Sade** (Helen Folasade Adu; 16 Jan 1959, Ibadan, Nigeria), Nigerian-born British singer and songwriter.

**Morley Safer** (8 Nov 1931, Toronto, ON, Canada), Canadian TV journalist.

**Carole Bayer Sager** (8 Mar 1946, New York NY), American song lyricist and singer who has written scores for plays and films as well as a string of successful and enduring pop songs, some in conjunction with Marvin Hamlisch and Burt Bacharach, to both of whom she has been married.

**Edward Said** (1 Nov 1935, Jerusalem, Palestine), Palestinian-born American scholar and a noted postcolonial cultural and literary critic.

**Sayyid Qaboos ibn Said Al Saidi** (18 Nov 1940, Salalah, Oman), sultan of Oman from 1970.

**Yves Saint Laurent** (Yves-Henri-Donat-Mathieu Saint Laurent; 1 Aug 1936, Oran, Algeria), French fashion designer noted for his popularization of women's trousers for all occasions.

**Ryuichi Sakamoto** (17 Jan 1952, Tokyo, Japan), Japanese composer of electronic music.

**Jamie Salé** (21 Apr 1977, Calgary, AB, Canada), Canadian pairs skater (with David Pelletier); shared the 2002 Olympic gold medal with Russians Yelena Berezhnaya and Anton Sikharulidze.

**Sebastião Salgado** (8 Feb 1944, Aimorés, Minas Gerais state, Brazil), Brazilian photographer whose work powerfully expresses the suffering of the homeless and downtrodden.

**'Ali 'Abdullah Salih** (1942), Yemeni politician; president of the unified Yemen from 1990.

**Esa-Pekka Salonen** (30 Jun 1958, Helsinki, Finland), Finnish conductor; musical director of the Los Angeles Philharmonic from 1992.

**Jorge (Fernando Branco de) Sampaio** (18 Sep 1939, Lisbon, Portugal), Portuguese politician; president of Portugal from 1996.

**Pete Sampras** (12 Aug 1971, Washington DC), American tennis player who holds the record for most career Grand Slam wins (14).

**Pedro A. Sanchez** (1940, Havana, Cuba), Cuban-born American soil scientist who was awarded the 2002 World Food Prize; he is chair of the UN Millennium Project Task Force on World Hunger.

**Gonzalo Sánchez de Lozada Bustamante** (1 Jul 1930, La Paz, Bolivia), Bolivian politician; president of Bolivia, 1993–97, and again from 6 Aug 2002.

**Jil Sander** (Heidemarie Jiline Sander; 27 Nov 1943, Wesselburen, Germany), German fashion designer known for simple, sophisticated, classic creations.

**Adam Sandler** (9 Sep 1966, Brooklyn NY), American comic actor and former *Saturday Night Live* cast member (1991–95) known for playing flawed but endearing comic characters.

**Arturo Sandoval** (6 Nov 1949, Artemisa, Cuba), Cuban-born American jazz-trumpet player who won solo Grammy Awards in 1994 and 1998.

**Mark Sanford** (15 Jan 1960, Fort Lauderdale FL), American Republican politician; governor of South Carolina from 15 Jan 2003.

**Carlos Santana** (20 Jul 1947, Autlán de Navarro, Mexico), Mexican-born American guitarist and bandleader.

**Alejandro Sanz** (Alejandro Sánchez Pizarro; 18 Dec 1968, Madrid, Spain), Spanish pop singer-songwriter and "flamenco-pop" artist who won multiple Latin Grammy awards in 2001 and 2002.

Cristina Saralegui (29 Jan 1948, Havana, Cuba), Cuban-born American Spanish-language TV talk-show host.

Susan Sarandon (Susan Abigail Tomalin; 4 Oct 1946, New York NY), American film actress who won an Academy Award for best actress in 1995 (*Dead Man Walking*) and whose works include *Thelma & Louise* (1991) and *Anywhere but Here* (1999).

Mikio Sasaki, Japanese corporate executive; president and CEO of Mitsubishi Motors Corp. from 1998.

Sasha (Sasha Schmitz; 5 Jan 1972, Soest, West Germany [now in Germany]), German pop singer.

Vidal Sassoon (17 Jan 1928, London, England), British hairstylist who pioneered the idea of simple haircuts that require little styling and who created his own hair product line.

Denis Sassou-Nguesso (1943, Edou, French Equatorial Africa [now in the Republic of the Congo]), Congolese politician; president of the Republic of the Congo, 1979–92, and again from 1997.

Jennifer Saunders (6 Jul 1958, Sleaford, Lincolnshire, England), British TV actress and comedian, best known for her work in the TV series *French & Saunders* (with Dawn French) and *Absolutely Fabulous*.

Diane K. Sawyer (22 Dec 1945, Glasgow KY), American TV reporter.

Simeon Saxecoburggotski (16 Jun 1937, Sofia, Bulgaria), the last king of Bulgaria (Simeon II, 1943–46) and prime minister of the country from 2001.

Antonin Scalia (11 Mar 1936, Trenton NJ), American jurist; associate justice of the US Supreme Court from 1986.

Peter Schickele (17 Jul 1935, Ames IA), American composer, radio personality, and creator and impersonator of P.D.Q. Bach, an imaginary son of Johann Sebastian Bach.

Claudia Schiffer (25 Aug 1970, Düsseldorf, West Germany [now in Germany]), German fashion model who appeared on hundreds of magazine covers and in advertisements.

Phyllis Stewart Schlafly (15 Aug 1924, St. Louis MO), American antiabortion activist, commentator, and author.

Daniel Schorr (31 Aug 1916, New York NY), American TV and radio journalist and political commentator.

Jürgen Schrempp (14 Sep 1944, Freiburg im Breisgau, Germany), German executive; chairman of DaimlerChrysler from 1998.

Gerhard Schröder (7 Apr 1944, Mossenberg, Lower Saxony, Germany), German Socialist politician who served as defense minister and, from 1998, as chancellor.

Gunther Schuller (11 Nov 1925, Jackson Heights, Queens NY), American classical and jazz composer and conductor.

Dieter Schulte (13 Jan 1940, Duisberg, Germany), German labor leader and head of the German Trade Union Federation from 1994.

Henning Schulte-Noelle (26 Aug 1942, Essen, Germany), German corporate executive; CEO of Allianz AG from 1991.

Michael Schumacher (3 Jan 1969, Hürth-Hermülheim, West Germany [now in Germany]), German Formula One race-car driver who dominated Grand Prix racing in the early 2000s and whose sports winnings, approaching $1 billion, were reportedly the highest of any athlete.

Wolfgang Schüssel (7 Jun 1945, Vienna, Austria), Austrian politician; chancellor of Austria from 2000.

Rudolf Schuster (4 Jan 1934, Kosice, Czechoslovakia [now Slovakia]), Slovak politician; president of Slovakia from 1999.

Arnold Schwarzenegger (30 Jul 1947, Graz, Austria), Austrian-born American bodybuilder, film actor, and politician; he is known for tough-guy leading roles as in the Terminator films and in *True Lies* (1994); in the summer of 2003 he declared himself a candidate to replace Gray Davis as governor of California.

Mark S. Schweiker (31 Jan 1953, Levittown PA), American Republican politician; governor of Pennsylvania, 2001–2003.

David Schwimmer (2 Nov 1966, Astoria, Queens NY), American TV and film actor best known for his portrayal of Ross Geller on the hit TV comedy *Friends* (from 1994).

Walter Schwimmer (16 Jun 1942, Vienna, Austria), Austrian international executive; secretary-general of the Council of Europe from 1999.

Martin Scorsese (17 Nov 1942, Flushing, Long Island NY), American motion-picture director, writer, and producer known for harsh, violent depictions; his works include *Taxi Driver* (1976), *Raging Bull* (1980), *Goodfellas* (1990), and *Gangs of New York* (2002).

H. Lee Scott, Jr., American corporate executive; CEO of Wal-Mart Stores from 2000.

Jill Scott (Philadelphia PA), American soul singer and songwriter.

Sir Ridley Scott (30 Nov 1937, South Shields, England), British film director and producer known for visual style and rich details; his films include *Alien* (1979), *Blade Runner* (1982), *Thelma & Louise* (1991), and *Gladiator* (2000).

Kristin Scott Thomas (24 May 1960, Redruth, Cornwall, England), British actress whose film credits include *The English Patient* (1996), *The Horse Whisperer* (1998), *Life as a House* (2001), and *Gosford Park* (2001). She was made OBE in 2003.

Gil Scott-Heron (1 Apr 1949, Chicago IL), American pop singer and songwriter.

Earl (Eugene) Scruggs (6 Jan 1924, Flint Hill NC), American bluegrass banjo player who developed a unique instrumental style that helped to popularize the five-string banjo.

Se Ri Pak (28 Sep 1977, Daejon, South Korea), Korean golfer who, in her first year on the LPGA circuit (1998), won two major tournaments, became the second highest money winner on the tour, and carded the lowest 18- and 72-hole scores in LPGA history.

Son Seals (13 Aug 1942, Osceola AR), American blues singer.

Kathleen Sebelius (15 May 1948, Cincinnati OH), American Democratic politician; governor of Kansas from 13 Jan 2003.

Alice Sebold (1963, Madison WI), American author whose first published novel, *The Lovely Bones* (2002), was a best-seller in 2002.

David Sedaris (26 Dec 1956, Binghamton NY), American writer and humorist.

Pete Seeger (3 May 1919, New York NY), American singer who sustained the folk-music tradition and who was the principal inspiration for younger performers in the folk revival of the 1960s.

Bob Seger (6 May 1945, Ann Arbor MI), American musician and singer.

**Martie Seidel** (12 Oct 1969, York PA), American country musician; member of the Dixie Chicks (Academy of Country Music Entertainers of the Year, 2000).

**Ivan G. Seidenberg** (New York NY), American corporate executive; CEO of Verizon Communications from 2002.

**Jerry Seinfeld** (29 Apr 1954, Brooklyn NY), American comic and TV personality made famous by his hit series *Seinfeld*.

**Monica Seles** (2 Dec 1973, Novi Sad, Yugoslavia [now in Serbia and Montenegro]), Yugoslav-born tennis player who holds nine Grand Slam titles.

**Bud Selig** (Allan H. Selig; 30 Jul 1934, Milwaukee WI), American sports executive; Major League Baseball commissioner from 1998 (and de facto commissioner for six years before that).

**Paul Sereno** (11 Oct 1957, Aurora IL), American paleontologist credited with a number of significant dinosaur finds.

**Richard Serra** (2 Nov 1939, San Francisco CA), American sculptor known for large, powerful outdoor works.

**Jean-Pierre Serre** (15 Sep 1926, Bages, France), French mathematician, specialist in algebraic topology; 1954 Fields medallist, and first winner (2003) of the Abel Prize.

**Vikram Seth** (20 Jun 1952, Calcutta [now Kolkata], India), Indian poet, novelist, and travel writer known for his verse novel *The Golden Gate* (1986) and his epic novel *A Suitable Boy* (1993).

**Rodolfo C. Severino** (1936, Philippines), Philippine international official; secretary-general of ASEAN (the Association of Southeast Asian Nations), 1998–2003.

**Ahmed Necdet Sezer** (13 Sep 1941, Ayfon, Turkey), Turkish politician; president of Turkey from 2000.

**Shaggy** (Orville Richard Burrell; 22 Oct 1968, St. Andrews, Jamaica), Jamaican reggae artist.

**Gil Shaham** (19 Feb 1971, Champaign-Urbana IL), American violinist often heard in concerts and recordings; he is known for his musicianship and broad repertory.

**Jeanne Shaheen** (28 Jan 1947, St. Charles MO), American Democratic politician; governor of New Hampshire, 1997–2003.

**Shakira** (Shakira Isabel Meberak Ripoll; 2 Feb 1977, Barranquilla, Colombia), Colombian-born pop singer.

**Silvan Shalom** (1958, Tunisia), Tunisian-born Israeli foreign minister from 2003.

**Garry Shandling** (29 Nov 1949, Chicago IL), American actor and talk-show host who was the star of *It's Garry Shandling's Show* (1986–90) and *The Larry Sanders Show* (1992–98).

**Ravi Shankar** (7 Apr 1920, Benares, Varanasi state, British India [now Varanasi, Uttar Pradesh state]), Indian sitar player, composer, and founder of the National Orchestra of India.

**Omar Sharif** (Michael Shalhoub; 10 Apr 1932, Alexandria, Egypt), Egyptian-born American film star famous for exotic leading roles; he is also a contract-bridge expert.

**Ariel Sharon** (Ariel Sheinerman; 26 Feb 1928, Kefar Malal, Palestine), Israeli politician; prime minister of Israel from 2001.

**Al Sharpton** (3 Oct 1954, New York NY), American political activist; civil-rights leader.

**William Shatner** (22 Mar 1931, Montreal, QC, Canada), Canadian TV actor, author, and personality famous as Captain Kirk in the *Star Trek* TV series and films.

**Bernard Shaw** (22 May 1940, Chicago IL), American TV journalist and newsman.

**Vernon Shaw** (13 May 1930, Dominica), West Indian politician; president of Dominica from 1998.

**Jim Shea, Jr.** (10 Jun 1968, Hartford CT), American skeleton slider and third-generation Olympic competitor; he won the gold medal in the 2002 Winter Games.

**Charlie Sheen** (Carlos Irwin Estevez; 3 Sep 1965, New York NY), American film and TV actor.

**Martin Sheen** (Ramon Estevez; 3 Aug 1940, Dayton OH), American stage, film, and TV actor who plays the president in the award-winning TV series *The West Wing* (from 1999).

**Judith Sheindlin** (21 Oct 1942, Brooklyn NY), American TV judge (*Judge Judy*).

**Sam Shepard** (Samuel Shepard Rogers; 5 Nov 1943, Fort Sheridan IL), American playwright and actor whose plays adroitly blend images of the American West, Pop motifs, science fiction, and other elements of popular and youth culture.

**Cindy Sherman** (Cynthia Morris Sherman; 19 Jan 1954, Glen Ridge NJ), American photographer who is known for her elaborately "disguised" self-portraits that comment on social role-playing and sexual stereotypes.

**Eduard (Amvrosiyevich) Shevardnadze** (25 Jan 1928, Mamati, Transcaucasian SFSR, USSR [now in Georgia]), Georgian politician; foreign minister of the Soviet Union (1985-90, 1991) and president of Georgia from 1992.

**Brooke (Christa) Shields** (31 May 1965, New York NY), American actress famous for childhood and teenage roles in films; she also starred in a TV sitcom, *Suddenly Susan* (1996–2000).

**Shinjiro Shimizu**, Japanese corporate executive; CEO of Mitsui & Co. from 2000.

**Eric K. Shinseki** (28 Nov 1942, Lihue HI), American military official; chief of staff of the US Army from 22 Jun 1999.

**Vandana Shiva** (1952, Dehra Dun, Uttar Pradesh [now in Uttaranchal] state, India), Indian biologist and social activist against the "biological theft" of the resources of poor countries by the richer ones; director of the Research Foundation on Science, Technology, and Ecology in India.

**Bobby Short** (Robert Waltrip Short; 15 Sep 1926, Danville IL), American jazz singer and pianist.

**Martin Short** (26 Mar 1950, Hamilton, ON, Canada), Canadian actor and comedian.

**Will Shortz** (1952), American "enigmatologist" and "puzzlemaster"; crossword-puzzle editor at the *New York Times*.

**Elaine Showalter** (21 Jan 1941, Cambridge MA), American feminist literary critic and teacher.

**Etsuhiko Shoyama** (c. 1937), Japanese corporate executive; CEO of Hitachi, Ltd. from 1999.

**Than Shwe** (1933, Kyaukse, Burma [now Myanmar]), Burmese military leader; head of state and government of Myanmar from 23 Apr 1992.

**M. Night Shyamalan** (6 Aug 1970, Pondicherry, India), Indian-born film director and screenwriter made famous by *The Sixth Sense* (1999) and *Signs* (2001).

**John W. Sidgmore** (1950?), American corporate executive; CEO of WorldCom, Inc. from 2002.

**Thomas M. Siebel** (February 1953, Chicago IL), American corporate executive; founder and CEO of Siebel Systems from 1993.

**Don Siegelman** (24 Feb 1946, Mobile AL), American Democratic politician; governor of Alabama, 1999–2003.

**Anton Sikharulidze** (25 Oct 1976, Leningrad, USSR [now St. Petersburg, Russia]), Russian pairs skater (with Yelena Berezhnaya); shared the 2002 Olympic gold medal with Canadians Salé and Pelletier.

**Álvaro Silva Calderón** (9 Jun 1929, Teresén, Venezuela), Venezuelan international official; secretary-general of the Organization of the Petroleum Exporting Countries from 2002.

**Horace Silver** (Horace Ward Martin Tavares Silver; 2 Sep 1928, Norwalk CT), American jazz pianist, composer, and bandleader.

**Queen Silvia** (Silvia Renate Sommerlath; 23 Dec 1943, Heidelberg, Germany), queen consort of King Carl XVI Gustaf of Sweden and social activist.

**Charles Simic** (9 May 1938, Belgrade, Yugoslavia [now in Serbia and Montenegro]), Yugoslav-born American poet noted for his poetic commentaries on the dearth of spirituality in contemporary life.

**Kostas Simitis** (Konstantinos Georgiou Simitis; 23 Jun 1936, Athens, Greece), Greek politician; prime minister of Greece from 1996.

**(Marvin) Neil Simon** (4 Jul 1927, New York NY), American playwright, screenwriter, television writer, and librettist who was one of the most popular playwrights in the history of the American theater.

**Paul Simon** (13 Oct 1941, Newark NJ), American singer and songwriter known first for his folk-rock albums with partner Art Garfunkel and later for his solo work.

**Jessica Simpson** (10 Jul 1980, Dallas TX), American dance-pop singer.

**O.J. Simpson** (Orenthal James Simpson; 9 Jul 1947, San Francisco CA), American collegiate and professional football player who was a premier running back known for his speed and evasiveness; he was the defendant in highly publicized criminal and civil suits over the 1994 murder of Simpson's ex-wife and a friend.

**Yashwant Sinha** (6 Nov 1937, Patna, Bihar state, India), Indian politician; foreign minister from 2002.

**Sirhan Bishara Sirhan** (19 Mar 1944, Jerusalem, Palestine), Palestinian assassin; convicted of the fatal shooting of Sen. Robert F. Kennedy (5 Jun 1968); incarcerated in the California State Prison, Corcoran.

**Tom Sizemore** (Thomas Edward Sizemore, Jr.; 29 Sep 1961, Detroit MI), American film actor, usually in tough-guy roles, whose credits include *The Relic* (1997), *Saving Private Ryan* (1998), and *Black Hawk Down* (2001).

**Ricky Skaggs** (18 Jul 1954, Cordell KY), American bluegrass and country musician, a top award-winner and concert draw in the 1980s and '90s.

**Matz Skoog** (1957, Stockholm, Sweden), Swedish ballet dancer and director; he danced with the Royal Swedish Ballet (1973–79) and the London Festival Ballet (renamed the English National Ballet; 1979–91) and became artistic director of the English National Ballet in 2001.

**Slash** (Saul Hudson; 23 Jul 1965, Stoke-on-Trent, Staffordshire, England), British rock guitarist (of Guns N' Roses).

**Leonard Slatkin** (1 Sep 1944, Los Angeles CA), American conductor; music director of the National Symphony Orchestra from 1996.

**Carlos Slim Helu** (c. 1940, Mexico?), Mexican investor; head of Grupo Carso and reportedly the richest man in Latin America.

**Lawrence M. Small** (14 Sep 1941, New York NY), American businessman; president and COO of Fannie Mae, the housing finance company; secretary of the Smithsonian Institution from 2000.

**Eleanor (Marie Cutri) Smeal** (30 Jul 1939, Ashtabula OH), American feminist; president of the National Organization of Women (NOW; 1977–82 and 1985–87) and cofounder and president of the Feminist Majority Foundation (from 1987).

**Anna Nicole Smith** (Vickie Lynn Hogan; 28 Nov 1967, Mexia TX), American model, *Playboy* magazine's Playmate of the Year 1993; known for her marriage to billionaire J. Howard Marshall and her reality-based TV series from 2002.

**Emmitt Smith** (Emmitt James Smith III; 15 May 1969, Pensacola FL), American football player; Dallas Cowboys running back who on 27 Oct 2002 surpassed Walter Payton's record 16,726 yd rushing.

**Gregg Smith** (21 Aug 1931, Chicago IL), American choral conductor.

**Jennifer M. Smith** (1947, Bermuda?), Bermudan politician; premier of Bermuda from 1998.

**Marc (Kelly) Smith** ("Slampapi"; 195?, Chicago IL), American poet and originator of the "poetry slam"—performance-poetry competitions—in the mid-1980s.

**Patti Smith** (30 Dec 1946, Chicago IL), American musician; poet; visual artist.

**Vernon L. Smith** (1 Jan 1927, Wichita KS), American economist; cowinner of the 2002 Nobel Prize for Economics for developing experimental methods that have been key to empirical economic analysis.

**Will Smith** (Willard Christopher Smith, Jr.; 25 Sep 1968, Philadelphia PA), American rap singer and actor on TV (*The Fresh Prince of Bel Air*, 1990–96) and in films, such as *Men in Black I* (1997) and *II* (2002).

**Zadie Smith** (1975, Willesden Green, London, England), British novelist; her *White Teeth* (2000) won the Whitbread First Novel Award.

**Aleksandr Pavlovich Smolensky** (1954), Russian banker and president of Stolichny Bank Sberezhny (SBS; now SBS-Agro); he is one of the "seven oligarchs" who allegedly run Russia.

**John W. Snow** (2 Aug 1939, Toledo OH), American businessman and government official; secretary of the treasury from 3 Feb 2003.

**Phoebe Snow** (Phoebe Laub; 17 Jul 1952, Teaneck NJ), American jazz singer and composer.

**Gary (Sherman) Snyder** (8 May 1930, San Francisco CA), American poet early identified with the Beat movement and, from the late 1960s, an important spokesman for the concerns of communal living and ecological activism.

**Cardinal Angelo Sodano** (23 Nov 1927, Isola d'Asto, Italy), Italian Roman Catholic churchman; secretary of state of the Vatican from 1990; cardinal from 1991.

**Steven Soderbergh** (14 Jan 1963, Atlanta GA), American film director who has won commercial success and critical acclaim; he received an Academy Award for directing *Traffic* in 2000.

**Queen Sofia** (Princess Sophie of Greece; Sofia de Grecia y Hannover; 2 Nov 1938, Athens, Greece), queen consort of King Juan Carlos of Spain.

**Tugan Sokhiev** (21 Oct 1977, Vladikavkaz, North Ossetian Autonomous Oblast, USSR [now in Russia]), Russian-born conductor; director of the Welsh National Opera from January 2003.

**Javier Solana Madariaga** (14 Jul 1942, Madrid, Spain), Spanish politician; NATO secretary-general, 1995–99 and secretary-general of the Western European Union from 1999.

**Howard Solomon** (12 Aug 1927, New York NY), American corporate executive; CEO of Forest Laboratories, Inc., from 1977.

**Susan Solomon** (19 Jan 1956, Chicago IL), American photochemist specializing in the chemistry of the stratosphere, especially the science of the Antarctic ozone hole; recipient of a National Medal of Science in 2000 and the 2002 Weizmann Women & Science Award.

**Aleksandr (Isayevich) Solzhenitsyn** (11 Dec 1918, Kislovodsk, Russia), Russian novelist and historian who led the struggle for open expression in literature in the USSR beginning in the 1960s and was eventually expelled by the Communist regime; he was awarded the 1970 Nobel Prize for Literature.

**Sir Michael (Thomas) Somare** (9 Apr 1936, Rabaul, [Australian-mandated] New Guinea [now Papua New Guinea]), Papua New Guinean politician; the first prime minister of independent Papua New Guinea, 1975–80, a second time in 1982–85, and again from 5 Aug 2002.

**Juan Octavio Somavia** (21 Apr 1941, Chile), Chilean international official; director-general of the International Labour Organization from 1999.

**Ron Sommer** (29 Jul 1949, Haifa, Israel), Israeli-born German corporate executive; CEO of Deutsche Telekom AG, 1995–June 2002.

**Stephen (Joshua) Sondheim** (22 Mar 1930, New York NY), American composer and lyricist for musical theater whose name is almost synonymous with Broadway; he has won eight Tony Awards.

**Queen Sonja** (Sonja Haraldsen; 4 Jul 1937, Oslo, Norway), queen consort of King Harald V of Norway.

**Susan Sontag** (16 Jan 1933, New York NY), American intellectual and writer best known for her essays on modern culture; 2001 Jerusalem Prize winner.

**Saufatu Sopoanga** (Tuvalu), Tuvalu politician; prime minister of Tuvalu from 2 Aug 2002.

**Annika Sörenstam** (9 Oct 1970, Stockholm, Sweden), Swedish golfer who was the LPGA top golfer in 2001 and 2002; she completed a career grand slam on 4 Aug 2003 by winning the British Open, having previously won the US Open (2002), the LPGA championship (2003), and the Kraft Nabisco competition (2001). In 2003 she also competed in a PGA (normally all-men) Tour event, the first woman in 58 years to do so.

**George Soros** (12 Aug 1930, Budapest, Hungary), Hungarian-born American financier and philanthropist; he established the Quantum fund in 1969 and made a fortune through daring investment decisions and shrewd currency trading. He began philanthropic activity in 1979, and as the Cold War ended and the Soviet regime collapsed, set up foundations in Poland, Czechoslovakia, Yugoslavia, and Russia.

**Sammy Sosa** (Samuel Sosa Peralta; 12 Nov 1968, San Pedro de Macoris, Dominican Republic), Dominican baseball outfielder for the Chicago Cubs and home-run hitter; the only player to hit more than 60 homers three times (1998, 1999, 2001).

**David H(ackett) Souter** (17 Sep 1939, Melrose MA), American jurist; associate justice of the US Supreme Court from 1990.

**Kevin Spacey** (Kevin Matthew Fowler; 26 Jul 1959, South Orange NJ), American stage and film actor who became a popular leading man in *American Beauty* (1999).

**David Spade** (22 Jul 1964, Birmingham MI), American comedian and actor; a member of the cast of *Saturday Night Live* (1991–95) and star of TV's *Just Shoot Me!* (1997–2003).

**James (Todd) Spader** (7 Feb 1960, Boston MA), American film and TV actor who won a best-actor award at the Cannes Film Festival in 1989 for his work in *Sex, Lies, and Videotape*; he joined the cast of the TV series *The Practice* in 2003.

**Nicholas Sparks** (31 Dec 1965, Omaha NE), American author of best-selling novels including *Nights in Rodanthe* (2002) and *The Guardian* (2003).

**Britney (Jean) Spears** (2 Dec 1981, Kentwood LA), American pop singer, film star, and teen idol.

**Phil Spector** (26 Dec 1940, New York NY), American music producer.

**Aaron Spelling** (22 Apr 1923, Dallas TX), American TV producer.

**Vladimir Spidla** (22 Apr 1951, Prague, Czechoslovakia [now in the Czech Republic]), Czech politician; prime minister of the Czech Republic from 12 Jul 2002.

**Steven Spielberg** (18 Dec 1947, Cincinnati OH), American motion-picture director and producer, one of the foremost of all time; he won Academy Awards for directing in 1993 (*Schindler's List*) and 1998 (*Saving Private Ryan*); his other works include *Jaws* (1975), *E.T. the Extra-Terrestrial* (1982), *The Color Purple* (1985), and *Catch Me If You Can* (2002).

**Jerry Springer** (Gerald N. Springer; 13 Feb 1944, London, England), British-born American politician and TV personality; he served as mayor of Cincinnati OH (1977–78) and ran in the primary race for governor of Ohio before becoming a TV journalist and commentator in 1982; he launched the sensationalist and often physical *The Jerry Springer Show* on TV in 1991.

**Bruce Springsteen** (23 Sep 1949, Freehold NJ), American rock singer and songwriter who became the archetypal rock performer of the 1970s and '80s and who enjoyed a new surge of popularity in 2002 with a concert tour and a new album, *The Rising*, that treated the aftermath of 11 September.

**Ralph (Edmond) Stanley** (25 Feb 1927, Stratton VA), American bluegrass songwriter, singer, and banjo player.

**Kenneth W. Starr** (21 Jul 1946, Vernon TX), American lawyer; independent counsel in the Clinton-era Whitewater investigation.

**Ringo Starr** (Richard Starkey, Jr.; 7 Jul 1940, Liverpool, England), British singer and drummer, former member of the Beatles.

**Danielle Steel** (Danielle Fernande Schuelein-Steel; 14 Aug 1947, New York NY), American romance novelist.

**Shelby Steele** (1 Jan 1946, Chicago IL), American critic and scholar of race issues who has opposed quota-based affirmative action.

**Konstantinos Dimitriou ("Kostis") Stefanopoulos** (15 Aug 1926, Patras, Greece), Greek politician; president of Greece from 1995.

**Gloria Steinem** (25 Mar 1934, Toledo OH), American feminist, political activist, and editor.

**Frank P(hilip) Stella** (12 May 1936, Malden MA), American painter, a leading figure in the Minimal art movement, known especially for paintings that were austere yet monumental in the simplicity of their design.

**George Stephanopoulos** (10 Feb 1961, Fall River MA), American journalist, former presidential adviser.

**Howard Stern** (12 Jan 1954, Roosevelt NY), American radio and TV "shock jock," actor, and author.

**John Paul Stevens** (20 Apr 1920, Chicago IL), American jurist; associate justice of the US Supreme Court from 1975.

**Ted Stevens** (18 Nov 1923, Indianapolis IN), American Republican politician; senator from Alaska and president pro tempore of the Senate from January 2003.

**Jon Stewart** (Jonathan Stewart Leibowitz; 28 Nov 1962, New York NY), American actor, writer, and comedian; anchor of TV's *The Daily Show* from 1999.

**Martha Stewart** (Martha Helen Kostyra; 3 Aug 1941, Nutley NJ), American homemaking adviser, TV personality, and entrepreneur.

**Rod Stewart** (Roderick David Stewart; 10 Jan 1945, London, England), British singer whose soulful, raspy voice has graced rock and pop hits since the late 1960s.

**Ben Stiller** (30 Nov 1965, New York NY), American comedian, actor, and film director.

**Stephen Stills** (3 Jan 1945, Dallas TX), American rock and pop singer and guitarist.

**R.L. Stine** (Robert Lawrence Stine; 8 Oct 1943, Columbus OH), American author of children's books.

**Sting** (Gordon Matthew Sumner; 2 Oct 1951, Newcastle upon Tyne, England), British musician, singer, songwriter, and actor; he was made CBE in 2003.

**Edmund Stoiber** (28 Sep 1941, Oberaudorf, Bavaria, Germany), German politician and Christian Socialist Union party leader; premier of Bavaria and unsuccessful candidate for the German chancellorship in 2002.

**Oliver Stone** (15 Sep 1946, New York NY), American director, writer, and producer of films with often controversial content; he has won Academy Awards for directing in 1986 (*Platoon*) and 1989 (*Born on the Fourth of July*).

**Sharon Stone** (10 Mar 1958, Meadville PA), American actress and model made famous by the film *Basic Instinct* (1992).

**Sly Stone** (Sylvester Stewart; 15 Mar 1944, Denton TX), American soul singer and musician.

**Sir Tom Stoppard** (Tomas Straussler; 3 Jul 1937, Zlin, Czechoslovakia [now in the Czech Republic]), Czech-born British playwright and screenplay writer whose work is marked by verbal brilliance, ingenious action, and structural dexterity.

**George Strait** (18 May 1952, Pearsall TX), American singer known for his traditional approach to country music and one of the most influential and popular country-music stars of his generation.

**Mark Strand** (11 Apr 1934, Summerside, PE, Canada), Canadian writer whose poetry, noted for its surreal quality, explores the boundaries of the self and the external world.

**Jozef Straus** (1946, Velke Kapusany, Czechoslovakia [now in Slovakia]), Czechoslovakian-born American corporate executive; CEO of JDS Uniphase, Inc. from 1999.

**Jack Straw** (3 Aug 1946, Essex, England), British politician; foreign secretary from 2001.

**Meryl Streep** (Mary Louise Streep; 22 Jun 1949, Summit NJ), American film actress in serious roles who won Academy Awards for best supporting actress in 1979 (*Kramer vs. Kramer*) and best actress in 1982 (*Sophie's Choice*).

**John F. Street** (15 Oct 1943, Norristown PA), American Democratic politician; mayor of Philadelphia from 3 Jan 2000.

**Barbra Streisand** (Barbara Joan Streisand; 24 Apr 1942, Brooklyn NY), American singer, actress, and film director.

**Susan Stroman** (17 Oct 1954, Wilmington DE), American theater director, winner of two Tony Awards in 2001 for *The Producers*.

**(Christopher) Ruben Studdard** (12 Sep 1978, Frankfurt am Main, West Germany [now in Germany]), American singer, the winner on the 2003 television show *American Idol*.

**Juan Manuel Suárez del Toro Rivero** (1952, Spain), Spanish international official; president of the International Federation of Red Cross and Red Crescent Societies from 2001.

**Hiroshi Sugimoto** (1948, Tokyo, Japan), Japanese photographer who achieved a striking, meditative quality in his very-long-exposure black-and-white photographs of architectural subjects and in his portraits of wax models.

**Anna Sui** (1955, Dearborn MI), American fashion designer whose clothing and cosmetics reflect a rock-music style mixed with vintage-inspired designs.

**Megawati Sukarnoputri** (23 Jan 1947, Jakarta, Indonesia), Indonesian politician; president of Indonesia from 23 Jul 2001; she is the daughter of Sukarno, the founder of independent Indonesia.

**Naim Suleymanoglu** (original name Naim Suleimanov, Bulgarian Naum Shalamanov; "Pocket Hercules"; 23 Jan 1967, Ptichar, Bulgaria), Bulgarian-born Turkish weight lifter who went 8 $1/2$ years without a loss, set numerous world records, and won three Olympic gold medals (1988, 1992, 1996).

**Andrew Sullivan** (10 Aug 1963, South Godstone, England), English-born American journalist, political commentator, editor of *The New Republic* (1991–96), and publishes of one of the more widely read blogs (Web logs).

**John E. Sulston** (27 Mar 1942, Cambridge, England), British cell biologist; cowinner of the 2002 Nobel Prize for Physiology or Medicine for his work on the life of a cell.

**Arthur Ochs Sulzberger** (5 Feb 1926, New York NY), American newspaper executive, publisher of the *New York Times* from 1963.

**Frederick Sumaye** (29 May 1950, Hanang district, Tanganyika [now Tanzania]), Tanzanian politician; prime minister of Tanzania from 1995.

**Lawrence H. Summers** (30 Nov 1954, New Haven CT), American university and government official; US secretary of the treasury, 1999–2001, and president of Harvard University from 2001.

**Sun Myung Moon** (6 Jan 1920, Kwangju Sangsa Ri, Korea [now in North Korea]), Korean evangelist and founder of the Unification Church.

**Don Sundquist** (15 Mar 1936, Moline IL), American Republican politician; governor of Tennessee, 1995–2003.

**Cass R. Sunstein** (1954), American constitutional scholar and law professor.

**(Lucia Francisca) Susi Susanti** (11 Feb 1971, Tasikmalaya, Indonesia), Indonesian badminton player.

**Ichiro Suzuki** (22 Oct 1973, Aichi, Japan), Japanese baseball player, right fielder for the Orix BlueWave of Japan's Pacific League, who moved to the US to play with the Seattle Mariners in 2000 and was named American League MVP and Rookie of the Year in 2001.

**Koji Suzuki** (13 May 1957, Hamamatsu, Shizuoka prefecture, Japan), Japanese novelist, creator of the Ring series of psycho-thriller books and films (from 1998).

**Hilary Swank** (30 Jul 1974, Lincoln NE), American film actress most noted for her Academy Award-winning performance for best actress in *Boys Don't Cry* (1999).

**John J. Sweeney** (5 May 1934, New York NY), American labor leader; president of the AFL-CIO from 1995.

**Tuanku Syed Sirajuddin ibni al-Marhum Syed Putra Jamalullail** (16 May 1943, Arau, British Malaya [now Malaysia]), *yang di-pertuan agong* (paramount ruler) of Malaysia from 2001.

**Wislawa Szymborska** (2 Jul 1923, Bnin [now in Kornik], Poland), Polish poet known for works that explore philosophical, moral, and ethical issues with intelligence and empathy; in 1996 she received the Nobel Prize for Literature.

**Azadeh Tabazadeh** (1965?, Iran), Iranian-born American atmospheric scientist whose work was instrumental in proving that naturally produced materials cannot be responsible for the degradation of the Earth's ozone layer.

**Bob Taft** (8 Jan 1942, Boston MA), American Republican politician; governor of Ohio from 1999.

**Paul Tagliabue** (24 Nov 1940, Jersey City NJ), American sports executive; commissioner of the National Football League from 1989.

**Vivienne Tam** (Canton [Guangzhou], China), Chinese fashion designer who combines Eastern and Western style and traditional and contemporary style in her work.

**Koichi Tanaka** (3 Aug 1959, Toyama City, Japan), Japanese chemist; cowinner of the 2002 Nobel Prize for Chemistry for his work in the study of macromolecules.

**Yoshio Taniguchi** (17 Oct 1937, Tokyo, Japan), Japanese architect who became internationally prominent in 1997 when his design for the planned expansion of the Museum of Modern Art in New York City was selected in a competition.

**Malietoa Tanumafili II** (4 Jan 1913, Apia, Western Samoa [now Samoa]), *O le Ao o le Malo* (elective monarch) of Samoa from 1963.

**Vasile Tarlev** (9 Oct 1963, Bascalia, Moldavian SSR, USSR [now Moldova]), Moldovan politician; prime minister of Moldova from 2001.

**Brandon Tartikoff** (13 Jan 1949, Long Island NY), American TV executive.

**King Taufa'ahau Tupou IV** (4 Jul 1918, Nuku'alofa, Tonga), king of Tonga from 1965.

**Sir John Tavener** (28 Jan 1944, London, England), British composer whose works were inspired by sacred and spiritual texts and drew from Russian, Byzantine, and Greek influences.

**Maaouya Ould Sidi Ahmed Taya** (1941, Atar, Mauritania), Mauritanian politician; president of Mauritania from 1992.

**Cecil (Percival) Taylor** (15 Mar 1933, New York NY), American jazz pianist and composer; a leading exponent of free jazz.

**Charles (McArthur Ghankay) Taylor** (27 Jan 1948, Athington, Liberia), Liberian coup leader and president of Liberia from 1997 until 12 Aug 2003, when he stepped down and went into exile.

**Elizabeth Taylor** (27 Feb 1932, London, England), American film actress of great distinction noted for emotionally volatile characters; she won Academy Awards for best actress in 1960 (*Butterfield 8*) and 1966 (*Who's Afraid of Virginia Woolf?*).

**James (Vernon) Taylor** (12 Mar 1948, Boston MA), American pop singer and songwriter.

**Dame Kiri (Janette) Te Kanawa** (6 Mar 1944, Gisborne, North Island, New Zealand), New Zealand operatic soprano.

**Te Ata-i Rangi-Kahu Koroki Te Rata Mahuta Tawhiao Potatau Te Wherowhero** (1931), queen of New Zealand's Maori community from 1966.

**Edward Teller** (Ede Teller; 15 Jan 1908, Budapest, Hungary, Austria-Hungary), Hungarian-born American nuclear physicist who participated in the production of the first atomic bomb (1945) and who led the development of the world's first thermonuclear weapon, the hydrogen bomb.

**Sachin Ramesh Tendulkar** (24 Apr 1973, Bombay [now Mumbai], India), Indian cricket batsman who scored 673 runs in the 2003 World Cup, breaking his own world record or the tournament.

**George John Tenet** (5 Jan 1953, Queens NY), American government official; Director of Central Intelligence and CIA director from 1997.

**Valentina (Vladimirovna) Tereshkova** (6 Mar 1937, Maslennikovo, Russian SFSR, USSR [now Russia]), Soviet cosmonaut, the first woman to travel into space (1963).

**Bryn Terfel** (Jones; 9 Nov 1965, near Pant Glas, Wales), Welsh operatic bass-baritone.

**Studs Terkel** (Louis Terkel; 16 May 1912, New York NY), American author, radio host, and oral historian.

**Thaksin Shinawatra** (26 Jul 1949, Chiangmai, Thailand), Thai politician; prime minister of Thailand from 2001.

**Thalia** (Ariadne Thalia Sodi y Miranda; 26 Aug 1971, Mexico City, Mexico), Mexican pop singer and TV actress.

**Sheikh Hamad ibn Khalifah ath-Thani** (1950, Doha, Qatar), emir of Qatar from 1995.

**Dame Margaret Thatcher** (Margaret Hilda Roberts; 13 Oct 1925, Grantham, Lincolnshire, England), British Conservative politician and prime minister (1979–90); Europe's first woman prime minister.

**Mikis Theodorakis** (29 July 1925, Chios, Greece), Greek composer and political activist whose film scores and dramatic music often deal with Greek themes.

**Thich Nhat Hanh** (1926, central Vietnam), Vietnamese Buddhist monk, pacifist, and teacher.

**Clarence Thomas** (23 Jun 1948, Pinpoint community, near Savannah GA), American jurist; associate justice of the US Supreme Court from 1991.

**Michael Tilson Thomas** (21 Dec 1944, Hollywood CA), American conductor and composer; music director of the San Francisco Symphony from 1995.

**Emma Thompson** (15 Apr 1959, London, England), American motion-picture actress known for heavy dramatic roles and period pieces.

**Jenny Thompson** (26 Feb 1973, Dover NH), American swimmer; 10-time Olympic medalist (eight gold) in the 1992, 1996, and 2000 Games.

**Tommy G. Thompson** (19 Nov 1941, Elroy WI), American government official; Wisconsin governor, 1987–2001; US secretary of health and human services from 2001.

**James Thomson** (20 Dec 1958, Chicago IL), American cell biologist and stem-cell researcher, the first person to isolate stem cells from human embryos.

**Robert Thomson** (11 Mar 1961, Echuca, VIC, Australia), Australian journalist; editor of *The Times* of London from February 2002 and the first non-Briton ever to hold the post.

**Billy Bob Thornton** (4 Aug 1955, Hot Springs AR), American director and actor whose work includes *Sling Blade* (1996), *Monster's Ball* (2001), and *Levity* (2003).

**Ian Thorpe** ("The Thorpedo"; 13 Oct 1982, Sydney, NSW, Australia), Australian swimmer; won three gold and one silver medal in the 2000 Games, then won six gold medals and set four world records in the 2001 world championships.

**Uma Thurman** (29 Apr 1970, Boston MA), American film actress in lead and supporting roles.

**Tiffany** (Tiffany Darwisch; 2 Oct 1971, Norwalk CA), American pop singer.

**Justin (Randall) Timberlake** (31 Jan 1981, Memphis TN), American singer at the forefront of the teen pop movement of the 1990s; he was a member of the group *NSYNC and, after 2001, performed as a solo artist and released a successful solo album, *Justified* (2002).

**Alejandro Toledo (Manrique)** (28 Mar 1946, Cabana, Peru), Peruvian politician; president of Peru from 2001.

**Tomatito** (José Fernández Torres; 1958, Almería, Spain), Spanish flamenco guitarist.

**Anote Tong**, Kiribati politician; president from 10 Jul 2003.

**Linus (Benedict) Torvalds** (28 Dec 1969, Helsinki, Finland), Finnish-born computer scientist who developed the Linux operating system.

**Princess Toshi** (Toshi no miya Aiko Naishinno; 1 Dec 2001, Tokyo, Japan), daughter of Crown Prince Naruhito and Crown Princess Masako.

**Amadou Toumani Touré** (1948, Mpoti, French Sudan [now in Mali]), Malian politician; president of Mali, 1991–92, and again from 8 Jun 2002.

**Emanuel Tov** (1941, Amsterdam, The Netherlands), Dutch classical scholar; director of the Dead Sea Scrolls project.

**James Anthony Traficant, Jr.** (8 May 1941, Youngstown OH), American Democratic politician; US representative from Ohio; convicted on several charges in April 2002, including bribery, and expelled from the House of Representatives.

**Boris Trajkovski** (25 Jun 1956, Strumica, Yugoslavia [now in Macedonia]), Macedonian politician; president of Macedonia from 1999.

**Tran Duc Luong** (5 May 1937, Quang Ngai province, French Indochina [now in Vietnam]), Vietnamese politician; president of Vietnam from 1997.

**Tomas Tranströmer** (15 Apr 1931, Stockholm, Sweden), Swedish lyrical poet noted for his resonant and strangely suggestive imagery.

**Jean-Claude Trichet** (20 Dec 1942, Lyons, France), French banker; governor of the Banque de France from 1993; tapped to take over the presidency of the European Central Bank in the fall of 2003.

**Lars von Trier** (30 Apr 1956, Copenhagen, Denmark), Danish film director and cinematographer known for his avant-garde approach to filmmaking.

**Calvin Trillin** (5 Dec 1935, Kansas City MO), American author, commentator, and occasional poet.

**David Trimble** (15 Oct 1944, Belfast, Northern Ireland), British (Northern Ireland) politician and first minister of Northern Ireland from 1998 (with a three-week interruption in October-November 2001); cowinner of the 1998 Nobel Peace Prize.

**Travis Tritt** (9 Feb 1963, Marietta GA), American country singer who found great success from 1990 onward with a blues- and rock-tinged style.

**Quincy (Thomas) Troupe, Jr.** (1943, New York NY), American poet, performer, and music journalist associated with Los Angeles's Watts Writers' Movement and winner of the American Book Award in 1980 and 1990.

**Garry Trudeau** (21 Jul 1948, New York NY), American cartoonist, creator of the durable *Doonesbury* syndicated comic strip.

**Donald (John) Trump** (14 Jun 1946, New York NY), American real-estate developer known for his high-profile real estate developments, including New York City's Trump Tower and Atlantic City's Trump Taj Mahal casino.

**Tohru Tsuji**, Japanese corporate executive; president and CEO of Marubeni Corp. from 1999.

**Tanya (Denise) Tucker** (10 Oct 1958, Seminole TX), American country-and-western singer.

**Togiola Tulafono** (28 Feb 1947, American Samoa), American Democratic politician; governor of American Samoa from 26 Mar 2003.

**Tung Chee-hwa** (29 May 1937, Shanghai, China), Chinese businessman and chief executive of Hong Kong (now the Hong Kong Special Administrative Region of China) from 1997.

**Christy Turlington** (2 Jan 1969, Oakland CA), American fashion model.

**Charles Wesley Turnbull** (5 Feb 1935, St. Thomas, Virgin Islands), American Democratic politician; governor of the Virgin Islands from 1999.

**Ted Turner** (Robert Edward Turner III; 19 Nov 1938, Cincinnati OH), American TV executive, the founder of Turner Broadcasting System and owner of Cable News Network (CNN), a pioneer in the use of satellite and cable technology. Turner is also a sports club owner (Atlanta Braves and others), a noted yachtsman, and philanthropist.

**Tina Turner** (Anna Mae Bullock; 26 Nov 1939, Nutbush TN), American rock performer of international appeal and fame, first known for her work with her then husband, Ike Turner, and later as an enduring top solo act.

**Scott Turow** (12 Apr 1949, Chicago IL), American best-selling novelist, the creator of a genre of crime and suspense novels dealing with law and the legal profession.

**Steve Turre** (12 Sep 1948, Omaha NE), American jazz trombone and conch-shell player and arranger.

**Desmond (Mpilo) Tutu** (7 Oct 1931, Klerksdorp, South Africa), South African Anglican cleric who in 1984 received the Nobel Peace Prize for his role in the opposition to apartheid in South Africa.

**Shania Twain** (Eileen Regina Edwards; 28 Aug 1965, Windsor, ON, Canada), Canadian country singer; Academy of Country Music Top New Female Vocalist, 1995, and Entertainer of the Year; Country Music Association Entertainer of the Year, 1999.

**Jeff Tweedy** (1968, Belleville IL?), American rock musician, of Uncle Tupelo and Wilco.

**Cy Twombly** (Edwin Parker Twombly, Jr.; 25 Apr 1928, Lexington VA), American artist and sculptor.

**Anne Tyler** (25 Oct 1941, Minneapolis MN), American novelist and short-story writer whose comedies of manners are marked by compassionate wit and precise details of domestic life.

**Richard Tyler** (22 Sep 1950, Melbourne, VIC, Australia), Australian fashion designer noted for his evening gowns.

**Steven Tyler** (Steven Tallarico; 26 Mar 1948, New York NY), American rock vocalist (of Aerosmith).

**(Alfred) McCoy Tyner** (later Sulaimon Saud; 11 Dec 1938, Philadelphia PA), American jazz pianist and composer.

**Cicely Tyson** (19 Dec 1939, New York NY), American film actress.

**Keith Tyson** (1969, Ulverson, Cumbria, England), British artist and sculptor who is fascinated by science and who uses technological and mechanical principles in his work; winner of the 2002 Turner Prize.

**Mike Tyson** (Michael Gerard Tyson; 30 Jun 1966, New York NY), American boxer; undisputed heavyweight champion, 1987–90.

**Alex Ubago** (1982, San Sebastián, Spain), Spanish pop singer whose first album, *¿Qué pides tú?*, put him on the charts.

**João Ubaldo Ribeiro** (João Ubaldo Osório Pimentel Ribeiro; 23 Jan 1941, Itaparica, Bahia state, Brazil), Brazilian novelist whose *Diário do farol*—about a morally corrupt priest—was a best-seller in 2002.

**Shungiku Uchida** (7 Aug 1959, Nagasaki, Japan), Japanese novelist and short-story writer, *manga* cartoonist, and singer.

**Shigeji Ueshima** (25 Aug 1931), Japanese corporate executive; CEO of Mitsui & Co. Ltd. from 1996.

**Liv (Johanne) Ullmann** (16 Dec 1939, Tokyo, Japan), Norwegian film actress and director.

**Robert J. Ulrich** (Minneapolis MN), American corporate executive; CEO of Target Corp. from 1994.

**Blair Underwood** (25 Aug 1964, Tacoma WA), American actor who starred in the TV series *L.A. Law* (1987–94) and *City of Angels* (from 2000) and in the film *Full Frontal* (2002).

**Emanuel Ungaro** (13 Feb 1933, Aix-en-Provence, France), French fashion designer whose creations are characterized by mixtures of bold patterns.

**John (Hoyer) Updike** (18 Mar 1932, Shillington PA), American writer of novels, short stories, and poetry, known for his careful craftsmanship and realistic but subtle depiction of American, Protestant, small-town, middle-class life.

**Dawn Upshaw** (17 Jul 1960, Nashville TN), American concert soprano.

**Álvaro Uribe Vélez** (4 Jul 1952, Medellín, Colombia), Colombian politician; president of Colombia from 7 Aug 2002.

**Joseph J. Urusemal** (19 Mar 1952, Woleai, Yap, Trust Territory of the Pacific Islands [now in the Federated States of Micronesia]), Micronesian politician; president of the Federated States of Micronesia from 11 May 2003.

**Usher** (Usher Raymond IV; 14 Oct 1978, Chattanooga TN), American rhythm-and-blues singer.

**Yoshio Utsumi** (14 Aug 1942, Shikoku island, Japan), Japanese international official; secretary-general of the International Telecommunication Union from 1999.

**Jørn Utzon** (9 Apr 1918, Copenhagen, Denmark), Danish architect best known for his design for the Sydney Opera House, Australia; winner of the 2003 Pritzker Prize.

**Jochem Uytdehaage** (9 Jul 1976, Utrecht, The Netherlands), Dutch speed skater; Olympic gold medalist in the 5,000-m race, 2002.

**Atal Bihari Vajpayee** (25 Dec 1924, Gwalior, Madhya Pradesh state, British India), Indian politician; prime minister of India in 1996, and again from 1998.

**Valentino** (Valentino Garavani; 11 May 1932, Voghera, Italy), Italian fashion designer known for his elegant and classic evening gowns.

**Abigail Van Buren** (Pauline Esther Friedman; 4 Jul 1918, Sioux City IA), American advice columnist.

**Dick Van Dyke** (13 Dec 1925, West Plains MO), American actor and comedian best remembered as the star of the TV series *The Dick Van Dyke Show* and *Diagnosis Murder*.

**Eddie Van Halen** (Edward van Halen; 26 Jan 1957, Nijmegen, The Netherlands), American rock guitarist (of Van Halen).

**Gus van Sant** (24 Jul 1952, Louisville KY), American film director whose recent work includes the films *Finding Forrester* (2002) and *Elephant* (2003).

**Luther Vandross** (20 Apr 1951, New York NY), American rhythm-and-blues singer and songwriter.

**Giuliano Vangi** (1931, Barberino di Mugello, Italy), Italian sculptor known for his sculptures of human forms and his inventive use of natural materials alone in in combination; he won a Japanese Praemium Imperiale Award for excellence in arts in 2002.

**Matti Vanhanen** (4 Nov 1955, Jyväskylä, Finland), Finnish politician; prime minister of Finland from 24 Jun 2003.

**(Jorge) Mario (Pedro) Vargas Llosa** (28 Mar 1936, Arequipa, Peru), Peruvian novelist and presidential candidate.

**Naná Vasconcelos** (2 Aug 1944, Recife, Brazil), Brazilian jazz percussionist and virtuoso player of the berimbau.

**Daniel Lucius Vasella** (1953, Fribourg?, Switzerland), Swiss corporate executive and CEO of the Novartis Group (from merger, 1996).

**Jeroen van der Veer** (1947, Utrecht, The Netherlands), Dutch corporate executive; CEO of Royal Dutch Shell Group (Netherlands).

**Amelia Vega** (1985?, Dominican Republic?), Dominican beauty queen selected as Miss Universe 2003.

**Suzanne Vega** (11 Jul 1959, Santa Monica CA), American pop songwriter and singer.

**Caetano Veloso** (1942, Santo Amaro da Purificacão, Bahia state, Brazil), Brazilian singer and one of the originators of the "tropicália" movement in Brazilian popular music.

**Helen (Hennessy) Vendler** (1933, Boston MA), American university professor and influential poetry critic.

**Ann M. Veneman** (29 Jun 1949, Modesto CA), American government official; US secretary of agriculture from 2001.

**(Runaldo) Ronald Venetiaan** (18 Jun 1936, Paramaribo, Dutch Guiana [now Suriname]), Surinamese politician; president of Suriname, 1991–96, and again from 2000.

**Maxim Vengerov** (20 Aug 1974, Novosibirsk, Russian SFSR, USSR [now Russia]), Russian-born concert violinist known for his mastery of technique and ardent, lyrical playing.

**J. Craig Venter** (14 Oct 1946, Salt Lake City UT), American geneticist and researcher into the human genome; founder of Celera Genomics.

**Jesse Ventura** (Jesse George Janos; "The Body"; 15 Jul 1951, Minneapolis MN), American professional wrestler and Independent politician; governor of Minnesota, 1999–2003.

**Guy Verhofstadt** (11 Apr 1953, Dendermonde, Belgium), Belgian politician; prime minister of Belgium from 1999.

**Luis Fernando Verissimo** (26 Sep 1936, Porto Alegre, Rio Grande do Sul state, Brazil), Brazilian best-selling author, whose novel *O analista de Bagé* is the top-selling literary work in Brazilian history; he is probably best known in the US for his *O Clube dos anjos* (1998; *The Club of Angels*, 2001).

**Donatella Versace** (2 May 1955, Reggio di Calabria, Italy), Italian fashion designer who took over as creative director at her brother Gianni Versace's design house after he was murdered in 1997.

**Ben Verwaayen** (Feb 1952), Dutch corporate executive; CEO of British Telecommunications PLC from 2002.

**Charles M. Vest** (9 Sep 1941, Morgantown WV), American mechanical engineer, a specialist in thermal sciences and the application of lasers and coherent optics; he has been president of the Massachusetts Institute of Technology since 1990.

**Angela Vía** (29 Dec 1981, Raymondville TX), American pop singer.

**Dominique Vian** (1944), West Indian politician; prefect of Guadeloupe from 6 Aug 2002.

**Princess Victoria** (Victoria Ingrid Alice Desiree; 14 Jul 1977, Stockholm, Sweden), heiress to the throne of Sweden.

**Gore Vidal** (Eugene Luther Vidal; 3 Oct 1925, West Point NY), American novelist, playwright, and essayist known for his irreverent and intellectually adroit works, some of which vividly recreate prominent figures and events in American history.

**Vaira Vike-Freiberga** (1 Dec 1937, Riga, Latvia), Canadian-Latvian folklorist and politician; president of Latvia from 1999.

**Dominique (Galouzeau) de Villepin** (14 Nov 1953, Rabat, Morocco), French politician; foreign minister from 2002.

**Kaspar Villiger** (5 Feb 1941, Sins, Switzerland), Swiss politician; president of Switzerland, 1995 and 2002.

**Tom Vilsack** (13 Dec 1950, Pittsburgh PA), American Democratic politician; governor of Iowa from 1999.

**Oleg Vinogradov** (1937, Leningrad, USSR [now St. Petersburg, Russia]), Russian choreographer and director; artistic director of the Kirov Ballet from 1977 (renamed Mariinsky Ballet in 1997).

**Vladimir Viktorovich Vinogradov** (1955, Ufa, Bashkir ASSR, USSR [now Bashkortostan, Russia]), Russian industrialist and banker; chairman of the Moscow Banking Union.

**Miroslav Ladislav Vitous** (6 Dec 1947, Prague, Czechoslovakia [now in the Czech Republic]), Czech jazz bassist.

**Nora D. Volkow** (c. 1956, Mexico City, Mexico), American biochemist and specialist in the use of PET imaging to record the biochemical effects of drugs on the brain; she is director of the National Institute for Drug Addiction, part of the National Institutes of Health, from 15 Apr 2003.

**Diane von Furstenberg** (Diane Simone Michelle Halfin; 31 Dec 1946, Brussels, Belgium), Belgian-born American fashion designer who made her name in the 1970s with the wrap dress and successfully relaunched it in the '90s.

**Vladimir Voronin** (25 May 1941, Corjova, Moldavian SSR, USSR [now Moldova]), Moldovan politician; president of Moldova from 2001.

**Rem Ivanovich Vyakhirev** (23 Aug 1934, Bolshaya Chernigovka, Russian SFSR, USSR [now Russia]), Russian billionaire head (1992–2001) of Gazprom, the largest company in Russia, with interests chiefly in petroleum and the media, and chairman (from 1996) of Siberia Oil Co..

**Linda Wachner** (3 Feb 1946, New York NY), American apparel industry executive; chairwoman (from 1991) and CEO (from 1987) of Warnaco Group, Inc. and Authentic Fitness Corp. until November 2001; the first woman to lead a Fortune 500 company.

**Norio Wada**, Japanese corporate executive; CEO of Nippon Telegraph & Telephone from 2002.

**Abdoulaye Wade** (29 May 1926, Kébémer, Senegal), Senegalese politician; president of Senegal from 2000.

**G. Richard Wagoner, Jr.** (9 Feb 1953, Wilmington DE), American corporate executive; CEO of General Motors Corp. from 2000.

**Tom Waits** (Thomas Alan Waits; 7 Dec 1949, Pomona CA), American singer, songwriter, and film actor.

**Christopher Walken** (31 Mar 1943, Queens NY), American actor famous for playing menacing villains.

**Catherine Walker** (27 Jun 1945, France), French-born British fashion designer, a favorite of the late Diana, Princess of Wales, and other members of high society.

**Mark J. Walport** (1953, England), British immunologist and specialist in lupus and other autoimmune diseases; director of The Wellcome Trust from 1 June 2003.

**Martin Walser** (24 Mar 1927, Wasserburg, Germany), German novelist and winner of the 1981 Georg Büchner Prize; his 2002 novel *Der Tod eines Kritikers* (*The Death of a Critic*), was so controversial that the influential newspaper *Frankfurter Allgemeine Zeitung* abandoned plans to serialize it.

**Courtney (Andrew) Walsh** (30 Oct 1962, Kingston, Jamaica), Jamaican cricket bowler who in 2000 became the highest wicket-taker in Test history.

**Robert D. Walter** (Columbus OH), American corporate executive; founder and CEO of Cardinal Health, Inc. from 1971.

**Barbara Walters** (25 Sep 1931, Boston MA), American broadcast journalist known especially as an interviewer, first on television's *Today* show, then on the *Barbara Walters Special;* in 1976 she became the first woman to anchor a network news program (*ABC Evening News*).

**John P. Walters**, American civic and government official; director of the White House Office of National Drug Control Policy from 2001.

**Alice L. Walton** (c. 1949), American heiress of part of the Wal-Mart fortune; listed seventh on *Forbes* magazine's 2003 list of the world's richest persons.

**Helen R. Walton** (c. 1920), American heiress of part of the Wal-Mart fortune of her husband, Sam Walton, who died in 1992; listed eighth on *Forbes* magazine's 2003 list of the world's richest persons.

**Jim C. Walton** (c. 1948), American business executive; listed ninth on *Forbes* magazine's 2003 list of the world's richest persons; chairman and CEO of the Arvest Group.

**John T. Walton** (c. 1946), American heir of part of the Wal-Mart fortune of Sam Walton; listed 10th on *Forbes* magazine's 2003 list of the world's richest persons.

**Vera Wang** (27 June 1949, New York NY), American fashion designer known for her elegant and luxurious wedding gowns.

**Wang Nan** (23 Oct 1978, Liaoning province, China), Chinese table tennis player, the second-ranked woman player in August 2003.

**Jigme Singye Wangchuk** (11 Nov 1955, Dechencholing Palace, Thimphu, Bhutan), king of Bhutan from 1972.

**Lloyd Ward** (1949, Romulus MI), American corporate executive; CEO of Maytag Co. from 1999; CEO of the US Olympic Commission from 2001.

**Sela (Ann) Ward** (11 Jul 1956, Meridian MS), American actress who got her break in Hollywood in

1983 in *The Man Who Loved Women* and was the popular star of the TV series *Sisters* for six seasons (1991–96).

**Shane Keith Warne** (13 Sep 1969, Ferntree Gully, VIC, Australia), Australian cricketer, a spin bowler named one of Wisden's Five Cricketers of the Century.

**Mark R. Warner** (15 Dec 1954, Indianapolis IN), American Democratic politician; governor of Virginia from 2002.

**Rick Warren** (San Jose CA), American evangelist minister whose Saddleback Church in Lake Forest CA (established in 1980) enjoys a membership of 50,000, reportedly the largest church in the Southern Baptist Convention and possibly the fastest growing congregation anywhere.

**Denzel Washington** (28 Dec 1954, Mount Vernon NY), American motion-picture and TV actor who won Academy Awards for best supporting actor in 1989 (*Glory*) and best actor in 2001 (*Training Day*).

**(Chaudhry) Wasim Akram** (3 Jun 1966, Lahore, Pakistan), Pakistani cricketer, called the greatest left-handed fast bowler, pioneer of "reverse swing" bowling.

**John Waters** (29 Apr 1946, Baltimore MD), American filmmaker who first transcended his Baltimore upbringing in 1972 with the celluloid monument to bad taste, *Pink Flamingos,* and went on to write, direct, and produce mainstream film successes such as *Hairspray* (1988; made into a Tony-winning Broadway musical in 2002), *Cry-Baby* (1990), and *Cecil B. Demented* (2000).

**Sam Waterston** (15 Nov 1940, Cambridge MA), American film and TV actor most recognized for his role on TV's *Law & Order.*

**Doc Watson** (Arthel L. Watson; 2 Mar 1923, Deep Gap NC), American guitarist, singer, and songwriter, an authentic point of reference for younger musicians during the folk-music boom of the 1960s and a durable presence at bluegrass festivals and in recording studios since then.

**James Watson** (6 Apr 1928, Chicago IL), American geneticist and biophysicist; corecipient of the 1962 Nobel Prize for Physiology or Medicine for determination of the molecular structure of deoxyribonucleic acid (DNA).

**Faye Wattleton** (8 Jul 1943, St. Louis MO), American reproductive rights activist, president of the Planned Parenthood Federation of America (1978-92), and president of the Center for Gender Equality (from 1995).

**André Watts** (20 Jun 1946, Nürnberg, West Germany [now in Germany]), American pianist.

**Charlie Watts** (2 Jun 1941, Islington, England), British rock drummer (of the Rolling Stones).

**Philip B. Watts,** American corporate executive; director of Royal Dutch/Shell Group from 1997.

**Damon Wayans** (4 Sep 1960, New York NY), American TV and film actor, the star of the TV comedy series *My Wife and Kids* (from 2001).

**Keenen Ivory Wayans** (8 Jun 1958, New York NY), American TV and film actor, the host of *The Keenen Ivory Wayans Show* (1997–98).

**George Weah** (George Manneh Oppong Ousman Weah; 1 Oct 1966, Monrovia, Liberia), Liberian-born association football (soccer) star who in 1995–96 achieved the triple honor of being elected European, African, and FIFA World Footballer of the Year, the first player ever to win three such titles in one year. In 1996 Weah was named Commonwealth Sportsman of the Year and in 1998 African Player of the Century.

**Sigourney Weaver** (8 Oct 1949, New York NY), American strong leading lady most recognized for the *Alien* films.

**Karrie Webb** (21 Dec 1974, Ayr, QLD, Australia), Australian golfer who won the Women's British Open in 2002, completing a round of wins in the top six major women's tournaments.

**Andrew Thomas Weil** (8 Jun 1942, Philadelphia PA), American physician and champion of alternative medicine.

**Sandy Weill** (Sanford Weill; 16 Mar 1933, Brooklyn NY), American corporate executive; CEO of Travelers Group and, after its merger in 1998 with Citicorp, CEO of Citigroup.

**Stanford I. Weill** (16 Mar 1933), American corporate executive; CEO of Citigroup from 2000.

**Harvey Weinstein** (19 Mar 1952, Queens NY), American motion-picture executive, cochairman (with his brother Bob) of Miramax Films from 1979; in 2003 Miramax movies garnered 40 Academy Award nominations and won 9 Oscars, including best picture, for *Chicago.*

**Jacob Weisberg,** American journalist; editor of the Internet magazine *Slate* from April 2002.

**Alek Wek** (1977, Wau, The Sudan), Sudanese-born fashion model.

**John Francis ("Jack") Welch, Jr.** (19 Nov 1935, Salem MA), American chairman and CEO of General Electric Co., 1981–2001; a legendary success among top corporate managers.

**Franz Welser-Möst** (16 Aug 1960, Linz, Austria), Austrian conductor; music director of the Cleveland Orchestra from 2002.

**Wen Jiabao** (September 1942, Tianjin, China), Chinese geologist and party and state official; he was a member of the Communist Party of China Politburo from 1997 and full member of the Secretariat from 1993; he became premier of China on 16 Mar 2003.

**Jann S. Wenner** (7 Jan 1946, New York NY), American journalist and originator (1967) and publisher of *Rolling Stone* magazine and other periodicals.

**Sophie, Countess of Wessex** (Sophie Helen Rhys-Jones; 20 Jan 1965, Oxford, England), wife of Prince Edward, Earl of Wessex.

**Cornel (Ronald) West** (2 Jun 1953, Tulsa OK), American scholar, critic, and African American intellectual.

**Randy Weston** (Randolph Edward Weston; 6 Apr 1926, Brooklyn NY), American jazz pianist and composer.

**Vivienne Westwood** (Vivienne Swire; 8 Apr 1941, Tintwistle, Derbyshire, England), British fashion designer whose radical, antiestablishment creations started the 1970s punk fashion trend.

**Christopher Wheeldon** (22 Mar 1973, Yeovil, Somerset, England), British dancer and choreographer with the New York City Ballet.

**George McClelland Whitesides** (3 Aug 1939, Louisville KY), American chemist who won the 2003 Kyoto Prize in the advanced technology section for "pioneering a technique of organic molecular self-assembly and its application to nanomaterials science," which has added new dimensions to materials science; he was awarded the National Medal of Science in 1998.

**Christine Todd Whitman** (26 Sep 1946, New York NY), American Republican politician and public official; governor of New Jersey; Administrator of the Environmental Protection Agency from 2001 until her resignation, effective 27 Jun 2003.

**Meg Whitman** (Margaret C. Whitman; 4 Aug 1956, Cold Spring Harbor? NY), American corporate executive; president and CEO of eBay, the Internet auction house, from 1998.

**Ranil Wickremesinghe** (24 Mar 1949), Sri Lankan politician; prime minister of Sri Lanka, 1993–94, and again from 2001.

**Elie Wiesel** (Eliezer Wiesel; 30 Sep 1928, Sighet, Romania), Romanian-born American scholar and author whose works provide a sober yet passionate testament of the destruction of European Jewry during World War II; he received the 1986 Nobel Peace Prize.

**Simon Wiesenthal** (31 Dec 1908, Buczacz, Austria-Hungary), Austrian founder and head (since 1961) of the Jewish Documentation Center in Vienna, which documents the Holocaust and locates war criminals.

**Andrew John Wiles** (11 Apr 1953, Cambridge, England), British mathematician who proved Fermat's last theorem.

**Bruce Wilkinson** (New Jersey), American author of best-selling Christian books, including *The Prayer of Jabez* (2001).

**Tom Wilkinson** (12 Dec 1948, Leeds, England), British character actor and star of *In the Bedroom* (2001).

**George F. Will** (4 May 1941, Champaign IL), American political commentator and columnist.

**Crown Prince Willem-Alexander** (27 Apr 1967, Utrecht, The Netherlands), heir to the throne of The Netherlands.

**Prince William** (William Arthur Philip Louis; 21 Jun 1982, London, England), son of Charles and Diana, Prince and Princess of Wales; second in line to the British throne.

**Anthony A. Williams** (28 Jul 1951, Los Angeles CA), American Democratic politician; mayor of Washington DC from 1999.

**Hank Williams, Jr.** (Randall Hank Williams, Jr.; 26 May 1949, Shreveport LA), American country-and-western singer.

**John Williams** (8 Feb 1932, New York NY), American conductor and composer, especially of film scores; director of the Boston Pops orchestra, 1980–93.

**John Williams** (24 Apr 1941, Melbourne, VIC, Australia), Australian-born classical guitarist.

**Lucinda Williams** (26 Jan 1953, Lake Charles LA), American contemporary folk and country singer and songwriter.

**Montel Williams** (3 Jul 1956), American TV talk-show host.

**Robin Williams** (21 Jul 1952, Chicago IL), American comedian and actor known for his eccentricity, rapid-fire wit, and energy; his works include the TV series *Mork and Mindy* (1978–82) and the films *Good Morning, Vietnam* (1987), *Dead Poets Society* (1989), *Good Will Hunting* (1997; Academy Award for best supporting actor), and *Insomnia* (2002).

**Rowan Williams** (14 Jun 1950, Swansea, Wales), Welsh-born Anglican clergyman who was enthroned as the 104th archbishop of Canterbury on 27 Feb 2003.

**Serena Williams** (26 Sep 1981, Saginaw MI), American tennis player and sister of Venus Williams; Olympic and Grand Slam champion; she won Wimbledon in 2002 and 2003 and the Australian Open in 2003.

**Treat Williams** (Richard Williams; 1 Dec 1951, Rowayton CT), American TV and film actor who starred in the TV series *Everwood* from 2002.

**Venus Williams** (17 Jun 1980, Lynwood CA), American tennis player who won both the US Open and Wimbledon in 2000 and 2001; she was no. 4 in the WTA rankings in mid-2003; sister of Serena Williams.

**Walter Ray Williams, Jr.** (6 Oct 1959, San Jose CA), American bowler; bowled four perfect games in one tournament and was five-time PBA Bowler of the Year.

**Bruce Willis** (Walter Willison; 19 Mar 1955, Idar-Oberstein, West Germany [now in Germany]), American actor first famous as the star of TV's *Moonlighting*; popular for the Die Hard movies and *The Sixth Sense* (1999).

**August Wilson** (27 Apr 1945, Pittsburgh PA), American playwright who created a cycle of plays, each set in a different decade of the 20th century, about black American life. He won Pulitzer Prizes for *Fences* (1986) and *The Piano Lesson* (1990).

**Cassandra Wilson** (4 Dec 1955, Jackson MS), American jazz singer who applies her wide-ranging "smoky contralto" voice to jazz standards, folk songs, Delta blues, and pop classics as well as many original numbers that defy categorization.

**Nancy Wilson** (20 Feb 1937, Chillicothe OH), American pop and jazz singer.

**Owen (Cunningham) Wilson** (18 Nov 1968, Dallas TX), American film actor who often teamed with director and producer Wes Anderson, as in *Rushmore* (1998) and *The Royal Tenenbaums* (2001).

**Robert Wilson** (4 Oct 1941, Waco TX), American avant-garde theater director.

**Oprah Winfrey** (29 Jan 1954, Kosciusko MS), American TV personality; host and producer of *The Oprah Winfrey Show* from 1985.

**Marissa Jaret Winokur** (2 Feb 1973, New York NY), American stage actress who starred in *Grease* on Broadway (1994–99) and won the 2003 Tony Award for best actress in a musical for her role in *Hairspray*.

**Kate Winslet** (5 Oct 1975, Reading, England), British film actress made famous by her performance in *Titanic* (1997).

**Paul (Theodore) Winter, Jr.** (31 Aug 1939, Altoona PA), American jazz and pop saxophonist and composer; formed the Paul Winter Consort in 1967.

**Anna Wintour** (3 Nov 1949, London, England), British-born fashion magazine editor, editor in chief of *American Vogue* from 1988.

**Steve Winwood** (Stephen Lawrence Winwood; 12 May 1948, Birmingham, England), British rhythm-and-blues and pop performer.

**Bob Wise** (6 Jan 1948, Washington DC), American Democratic politician; governor of West Virginia from 2001.

**Reese Witherspoon** (Laura Jean Reese Witherspoon; 22 Mar 1976, Nashville TN), American film actress whose credits include *Pleasantville, Election*, two *Legally Blonde* films, and *The Importance of Being Earnest*.

**Katarina Witt** (3 Dec 1965, Karl-Marx-Stadt, East Germany [now in Germany]), German figure skater; two-time Olympic gold medalist and four-time world champion for East Germany in the 1980s.

**Girma Wolde-Giorgis** (December 1924, Addis Ababa, Ethiopia), Ethiopian military officer; president of Ethiopia from 2001.

**Christa Wolf** (Christa Ihlenfeld; 18 Mar 1929, Landsberg an der Warthe, Germany [now Gorzow Wielkopolski, Poland]), German novelist, essayist, and screenwriter who writes about life in East

Germany and the problems of reunification, as, for example, in her 2002 novel *Liebhaftig*.

**Tom Wolfe** (Thomas Kennerly Wolfe, Jr.; 2 Mar 1930, Richmond VA), American novelist and social commentator who is a leading critic of contemporary life and a proponent of New Journalism (the application of fiction-writing techniques to journalism).

**James D. Wolfensohn** (1 Dec 1933, Sydney, NSW, Australia), Australian-born American banker; president of the World Bank from 1995.

**Paul Wolfowitz** (22 Dec 1943, New York NY), American scholar and government official; US deputy secretary of defense from March 2001.

**Stephen Wolfram** (29 Aug 1959, London, England), British-born American physicist whose book *A New Kind of Science* (2002) suggested the inadequacy of math-based science and proposed "cellular automata" as a better key to understanding the patterns of nature.

**Lee Ann Womack** (19 Aug 1966, Jacksonville TX), American country singer.

**Stevie Wonder** (Steveland Judkins, later Steveland Morris; 13 May 1950, Saginaw MI), American pop composer, singer, and pianist.

**Ron Wood** (1 Jun 1947, London, England), British rock guitarist (of the Rolling Stones).

**Alfre Woodard** (8 Nov 1953, Tulsa OK), American Broadway, film, and TV actress.

**Todd Woodbridge** (2 Apr 1971, Sydney, NSW, Australia), Australian tennis player best known for doubles play; he won the doubles competition in the Australian Open in 1992, 1997, and 2001; the French Open in 2000; Wimbledon in 1993–97, 2000, and 2002–03; and the US Open in 1995 and 1996.

**Eldrick ("Tiger") Woods** (30 Dec 1975, Cypress CA), American golfer, perhaps the greatest of all time; among his many honors, in 2001 he was the first to hold all four major golf championships at the same time.

**Bob Woodward** (26 Mar 1943, Geneva IL), American journalist and author; he joined the Washington Post newspaper in 1971 and covered the Watergate scandal (1972–74). His reportage with fellow Post reporter Carl Bernstein earned them a Pulitzer Prize in 1973, and *All the President's Men* (1974) and The Final Days (1976), their books about the Nixon years, were national best-sellers.

**Stephen Wozniak** (11 Aug 1950, San Jose CA), American electrical engineer; cofounder of Apple Computer Corp., and youth leader.

**Wu Bangguo** (Jul 1941, Feidong, Anhui province, China), Chinese Communist Party official, Politburo member from 1992; chairman of the National People's Congress Standing Committee from March 2003.

**William A. Wulf** (8 Dec 1939, Chicago IL), American computer scientist; president of the National Academy of Engineering from 1997.

**Charles Wuorinen** (9 Jun 1938, New York NY), American composer whose contemporary, serialist works were created using his own "time-point system."

**Kurt Wüthrich** (4 Oct 1938, Aarberg, Switzerland), Swiss chemist; cowinner of the 2002 Nobel Prize for Chemistry for his work in the study of macromolecules.

**Andrew (Newell) Wyeth** (12 Jul 1917, Chadds Ford PA), American watercolorist and worker in tempera noted primarily for his realistic depictions of the buildings, fields, hills, and people of his private world.

**Bill Wyman** (William Perks; 24 Oct 1936, London, England), British rock bassist (of the Rolling Stones).

**Xie Jun** (30 Oct 1970, Baoding, Hebei province, China), Chinese women's chess champion of the world, 1991–96 and 1999–2001.

**Xuxa** (Maria da Graça Xuxa Meneghel; 27 Mar 1963, Santa Rosa, Rio Grande do Sul state, Brazil), Brazilian television hostess, actress, singer, and model.

**Aleksey (Konstantinovich) Yagudin** (18 Mar 1980, Leningrad, USSR [now St. Petersburg, Russia]), Russian figure skater; four-time world champion and 2002 Olympic gold medalist.

**Yohji Yamamoto** (3 Oct 1943, Tokyo, Japan), Japanese fashion designer known for his simple and sophisticated creations.

**Ryuzo Yanagimachi** (27 Aug 1928, Sapporo, Japan), Japanese reproductive biologist; first to clone an adult male mammal (a mouse, in 1999).

**Yang Bin** (c. 1963, Nanjing, China), Chinese-born Dutch flower tycoon; once reported to be the second richest man in China, he was arrested in October 2002.

**Yang Yang (A**; 24 Aug 1976, Heilongjiang province, China), Chinese short-track speed skater; five-time world champion.

**Alfred ("Weird Al") Yankovic** (23 Oct 1959, Lynwood CA), American satirical singer and songwriter.

**Yanni** (Yannis Khrisomalis; 14 Nov 1954, Kalamata, Greece), Greek-born New Age orchestra leader and arranger.

**Viktor Yanukovych** (1950, Yenakiyevo, Ukrainian SSR, USSR [now Ukraine]), Ukrainian politician; prime minister of Ukraine from 21 Nov 2002.

**Yao Ming** (12 Sep 1980, Shanghai, China), Chinese basketball player, 7 ft 5 in (2.26 m) tall, who starred with the Shanghai Sharks from 1997–2002; 1st overall pick in the 2002 NBA draft (by the Houston Rockets).

**Yury (Fyodorvich) Yarov** (2 Apr 1942, Leningrad, USSR [now St. Petersburg, Russia]), Russian international official; executive secretary of the Commonwealth of Independent States from 1999.

**Catherine Yass** (1963, London, England), British photographic artist whose work often combines positive and negative photographic images to eerie effect; nominated for the Turner Prize in 2002.

**Shayk Ahmed Yassin** (1936–38?, al-Jura, Palestine), Palestinian founder and spiritual leader of the Islamic Resistance Movement in Palestine (Hamas).

**Trisha Yearwood** (Patricia Lynn Yearwood; 19 Sep 1964, Monticello GA), American country singer.

**Boris Nikolayevich Yeltsin** (1 Feb 1931, Sverdlovsk, Russian SFSR, USSR [now Yekaterinburg, Russia]), Soviet Russian politician; president of Russia, 1991–99.

**Gloria Yerkovich** (1942), American founder of CHILDFIND, a nationwide organization that helps locate missing children.

**Yevgeny (Aleksandrovich) Yevtushenko** (18 Jul 1933, Zima, Irkutsk oblast, Russian SFSR, USSR [now Russia]), Russian poet and spokesman for the post-Stalin generation of Russian youth.

**Frances Yip** (Lai Yee; 1948, Hong Kong), Hong Kong popular singer.

**Dwight (David) Yoakam** (23 Oct 1956, Pikesville KY), American country-and-western singer, songwriter, and actor.

**Tamao Yoshida** (Sueichi Ueda; 7 Jan 1919, Osaka, Japan), Japanese puppeteer, his generation's foremost exponent of Bunraku, the classical art of

Japanese puppetry; Yoshida was awarded the 2003 Kyoto Prize in the arts and philosophy category.

**Banana Yoshimoto** (24 Jul 1964, Tokyo, Japan), Japanese writer of best-selling fiction.

**Hiroyuki Yoshino** (1939, Fukui, Japan), Japanese corporate executive; president and CEO of Honda Motor Co., Ltd., 1998–2003.

**Andrew (Jackson) Young, Jr.** (12 Mar 1932, New Orleans LA), American politician, civil rights leader, and clergyman; he was a leader in the Southern Christian Leadership Conference with Martin Luther King, Jr. and served as US ambassador to the United Nations (1977–79).

**Neil Young** (12 Nov 1945, Toronto, ON, Canada), Canadian rock and pop singer and songwriter.

**Will Young** (William Robert Young; 20 Jan 1979, Hungerford, Berkshire, England), British rock singer who won the 2002 Pop Idol contest and whose 2002 single "Anything Is Possible/Evergreen" was the fastest-selling record in British history.

**Étienne Ys** (Curaçao, Netherlands Antilles?), West Indian politician; prime minister of the Netherlands Antilles from 3 Jun 2002.

**Yu Miri** (22 Jun 1968, Yokohama, Japan), Japanese writer of Korean ancestry who won the Akutagawa Prize in 1997 for her novel *Kazoku shinema* (1996; "Family Cinema").

**Yu Shyi-kun** (25 Apr 1948, Taiho, Taiwan), Taiwanese politician; prime minister of Taiwan from 1 Feb 2002.

**Raúl Yzaguirre** (south Texas), American Hispanic rights activist; president of the National Council of La Raza.

**Peter Zadek** (19 May 1926, Berlin, Germany), German theater, opera, and film director especially known for his imaginative restagings of the works of Shakespeare, Chekov, and Ibsen.

**Mohammad Zahir Shah** (15 Oct 1914, Kabul, Afghanistan), king of Afghanistan, 1933-73.

**Paula Zahn** (24 Feb 1956, Omaha NE), American TV anchorwoman and journalist, host of CNN's prime-time evening program *Live from the Headlines* and *People in the News.*

**Joe Zawinul** (7 Jul 1932, Vienna, Austria), Austrian-born jazz pianist and composer.

**Ernesto Zedillo Ponce de León** (27 Dec 1951, Mexico City, Mexico), Mexican politician; president of Mexico, 1994–2000.

**Franco Zeffirelli** (Gianfranco Corsi; 12 Feb 1923, Florence, Italy), Italian opera, film, and theater director; noted for the authentic detail and opulence of his productions including the opera *La traviata* and the films *The Taming of the Shrew* and *Romeo and Juliet.*

**Renée Zellweger** (25 Apr 1969, Katy TX), American actress first famous for her role in *Jerry Maguire* (1996).

**Robert Zemeckis** (14 May 1952, Chicago IL), American director, producer of popular mainstream films, including *Forrest Gump* (1994).

**Meles Zenawi** (8 May 1955, Adoua, Ethiopia), Ethiopian politician; prime minister of Ethiopia from 1995.

**Zeng Qinghong** (Jul 1939, Jian, Jiangxi province, China), Chinese Communist Party official; director of the Organization Department of the CPC Central Committee from 1999.

**Elias (Adam) Zerhouni** (1 Apr 1951, Nedroma, Algeria), Algerian-born American radiologist and medical administrator; director of the National Institutes of Health from 2002.

**Catherine Zeta-Jones** (25 Sep 1969, Swansea, West Glamorgan, Wales), British-born American actress first recognized in *The Mask of Zorro* (1998); her other films include *Entrapment* (1999), *Traffic* (2000), *America's Sweethearts* (2001), and *Chicago* (2002).

**Zhang Yimou** (14 Nov 1951, Xi'an, Shaanxi province, China), Chinese film director of international reputation who made such films as *Red Sorghum* (1987), *The Story of Qiu Ju* (1992), and *Hero* (2002).

**Zhang Yining** (5 Oct 1982, China), Chinese table tennis player; the top-ranked woman player in August 2003.

**Zhang Ziyi** (9 Feb 1980, Beijing, China), Chinese actress who came to international fame in the film *Crouching Tiger, Hidden Dragon* (2000).

**Zhou Guangzhao** (May 1929, Changsha, Hunan province, China), Chinese mechanical engineer; president of the Chinese Academy of Sciences, 1987–97, and chairman of the China Association of Science and Technology from 1996.

**Zhu Chen** (16 Mar 1976, China), Chinese chess grandmaster; women's world champion from 2001.

**Zhu Rongji** (1 Oct 1928, Changsha, Hunan province, China), Chinese politician; premier of China from 1998 to 16 Mar 2003.

**Khaleda Zia** (Khaleda Majumdar; 15 Aug 1945, Dinajpur, West Bengal state, British India [now in Bangladesh]), Bangladeshi politician; prime minister of Bangladesh, 1991–96, and again from 2001.

**Zinedine Zidane** (23 Jun 1972, Marseille, France), French association football (soccer) player, star of the French team that won the FIFA World Cup in 1998; FIFA world footballer of the year, 1998 and 2000.

**Krystian Zimerman** (1956, Zabrze, Poland), Polish concert pianist.

**Mary Zimmerman** (23 Aug 1960, Lincoln NE), American stage director who won a Tony Award for best director in 2002 for her Metamorphoses; she contributed the libretto to the opera *Galileo Galilei,* which opened in Chicago in June 2002.

**Anthony C. Zinni** (17 Sep 1943, Conshohocken PA), American military leader (lieutenant general, US Marine Corps) and diplomat; he saw action in Vietnam and Somalia and served as the commander of the Central Command leading US forces in the Middle East (1997–2000) and, following his retirement from the military, as US special envoy to the Middle East.

**Robert B. Zoellick** (25 Jul 1953, Evergreen Park IL), American businessman and government official; US Trade Representative from 7 Feb 2001.

**Armin Zöggeler** (4 Jan 1974, Merano?, Italy), Italian luger and World Cup champion.

**Mortimer B. Zuckerman** (4 Jun 1937, Montreal, QC, Canada), Canadian-born American publisher, columnist, and editor in chief of *U.S. News & World Report.*

**Pinchas Zukerman** (16 Jul 1948, Tel Aviv, Israel), Israeli-born American violinist, violist, and conductor.

**Klaus Zwickel** (31 May 1939, Heilbronn, Germany), German trade union leader; head of the IG Metall metal and engineering union, 1993–2003.

**Ellen Taaffe Zwilich** (30 Apr 1939, Miami FL), American composer whose works display both technical expertise and wide audience appeal.

# Obituaries

*Deaths of notable people since 1 Jul 2002.*

## Astronauts Who Died Aboard the US Space Shuttle *Columbia*

▶ **Michael P. Anderson** (25 Dec 1959, Plattsburgh NY–1 Feb 2003, over Texas), American payload commander and mission specialist. He was educated at the University of Washington and at Creighton University (Omaha NE), where he earned a master's degree in physics. In 1991–95 he served in the US Air Force as an instructor pilot and tactical officer, and in 1998 he flew on a mission in the space shuttle *Endeavour* to the Russian space station Mir.

▶ **David M. Brown** (16 Apr 1956, Arlington VA–1 Feb 2003, over Texas), American mission specialist and flight surgeon. Brown was educated at the College of William and Mary (Williamsburg VA) and at Eastern Virginia Medical School, where he earned a doctorate in medicine in 1982. He was director of medical services at the Navy Branch Hospital in Adak AK and served on an aircraft carrier before beginning pilot training in 1988; he was chosen for the astronaut program in 1996.

▶ **Kalpana Chawla** (1 Jul 1961, Karnal, Haryana state, India–1 Feb 2003, over Texas), Indian-born American mission specialist. Chawla was the first woman to study aeronautical engineering at Punjab Engineering College; she continued her education at the University of Texas at Arlington and the University of Colorado at Boulder, where she earned a doctorate in aeronautical engineering (1988). She first flew on the *Columbia* in 1997 as a mission specialist and primary robotic arm operator.

▶ **Laurel Blair Salton Clark** (10 Mar 1961, Ames IA–1 Feb 2003, over Texas), American mission specialist and flight surgeon. She was educated at the University of Wisconsin at Madison, where she earned a medical doctorate in 1987. In the US Navy she served as a diving medical officer and headed a submarine squadron medical SEAL unit before becoming a flight surgeon; she was chosen for the astronaut program in 1996.

▶ **Rick D. Husband** (12 Jul 1957, Amarillo TX–1 Feb 2003, over Texas), American commander. Husband was educated at Texas Tech University and at California State University at Fresno, where he earned a master's degree in 1990. He joined the US Air Force in 1980. In 1999 he flew on the *Discovery* on the first space shuttle mission to dock with the International Space Station.

▶ **William C. McCool** (23 Sep 1961, San Diego CA–1 Feb 2003, over Texas), American captain and pilot. McCool was educated at the US Naval Academy; he earned a master's degree in computer science from the University of Maryland in 1985 and another in aeronautical engineering from the US Naval Postgraduate School in 1992. He became a pilot for the US Navy in 1986 and was chosen for the astronaut program in 1996.

▶ **Ilan Ramon** (20 Jun 1954, Tel Aviv, Israel–1 Feb 2003, over Texas), Israeli payload specialist. Ramon received a bachelor of science degree in electronics and computer engineering from the University of Tel Aviv in 1987 and later graduated from the Israel Air Force Flight School. He was selected for the US astronaut program in 1998.

**'Abu Nidal** (nom de guerre of Sabri al-Banna; May 1937, Jaffa, British Palestine [now Tel Aviv-Yafo, Israel]–16? Aug 2002, Baghdad, Iraq), Palestinian militant who was believed to have masterminded countless deadly attacks for nearly two decades, from the early 1970s to the 1990s.

**Gianni Agnelli** (Giovanni Agnelli; 12 Mar 1921, Turin, Piedmont, Italy–24 Jan 2003, Turin, Italy), Italian chairman of the automobile-manufacturing company Fiat SpA, Italy's largest employer, from 1966 to 1996 and honorary chairman until his death.

**Gabriel A(braham) Almond** (12 Jan 1911, Rock Island IL–25 Dec 2002, Pacific Grove CA), American political scientist noted for his comparative studies of political systems and his analysis of political development.

**Manuel Álvarez Bravo** (4 Feb 1902, Mexico City, Mexico–19 Oct 2002, Mexico City, Mexico), Mexican photographer whose photography depicted both urban scenes and rural areas, with folkways, industrial development, and politics among the subjects.

**Dhirubhai Ambani** (Dhirajlal Hirachand Ambani; 28 Dec 1932, Chorwad, Gujarat state, British India–6 Jul 2002, Mumbai [Bombay], India), Indian industrialist, the founder and chairman of Reliance Industries, a $13.5-billion petrochemicals, communications, power, and textiles conglomerate and the only privately owned Indian company on the Fortune 500.

**Stephen Edward Ambrose** (10 Jan 1936, Decatur IL–13 Oct 2002, Bay St. Louis MS), American biographer and historian who wrote some three dozen books on US history. His later works were populist in tone, celebrating the achievements of ordinary people. In 2002 he was accused of plagiarism, but in his defense he argued that he had cited sources for his material. Ambrose founded the Eisenhower Center for American Studies and the National D-Day Museum, both in New Orleans.

**Sir (Edwin) Hardy Amies** (17 Jul 1909, London, England–5 Mar 2003, Langford, Oxfordshire, England), British couturier who dressed Queen Elizabeth II of England for half a century and is credited with having been a major influence on the menswear fashion revolution of the 1960s.

**Per Johan Valentin Anger** (7 Dec 1913, Göteborg, Sweden–25 Aug 2002, Stockholm, Sweden), Swedish diplomat who, with Raoul Wallenberg, was instrumental in saving tens of thousands of Jews from being sent to concentration camps during World War II and who devoted his subsequent diplomatic career to trying to find out the fate of Wallenberg, who disappeared in the USSR in 1945.

**Walter Hubert Annenberg** (13 Mar 1908, Milwaukee WI–1 Oct 2002, Wynnewood PA), American publisher and philanthropist who used his wealth to promote conservative political causes and to support education and the arts. He bought radio and television stations, began *Seventeen* magazine in 1944, and in 1953 launched *TV Guide.* As publisher and editor of the *Philadelphia Inquirer,* he promoted local reforms but also used the paper to advance partisan causes. A supporter of Richard M. Nixon and Ronald Reagan, he was ambassador to Britain from 1969 to 1974. He established the Annenberg School for Communication at the University of Pennsylvania (1958) and at the University of Southern California (1971).

**Herbert Aptheker** (31 Jul 1915, Brooklyn NY—17 Mar 2003, Mountain View CA), American historian who wrote and lectured extensively on African American history and on his Marxist political views. He worked as an editor of various left-wing publications and served as executive director of the American Institute of Marxist Studies (1962–85).

**Roone Pinckney Arledge** (8 Jul 1931, Forest Hills NY—5 Dec 2002, New York NY), American television executive who transformed television sports broadcasting in the 1960s and '70s by introducing an array of technical innovations and by creating popular programs such as *Wide World of Sports* and *Monday Night Football*; later in his career he became one of the most influential figures in television news.

**Ted Ashley** (Theodore Assofsky; 3 Aug 1922, New York NY—24 Aug 2002, New York NY), American business executive who revived Warner Brothers studios during his tenure as chairman and CEO (1969–80) with films such as *A Clockwork Orange* (1971), *The Exorcist* (1973), *Blazing Saddles* (1974), *All the President's Men* (1976), and *Superman* (1978).

**Cholly Atkins** (Charles Sylvan Atkinson; 13 Sep 1913, Pratt City AL—19 Apr 2003, Las Vegas NV), American dancer and choreographer who created the synchronized moves that characterized many of the Motown acts of the 1950s and '60s, including the Temptations, Gladys Knight and the Pips, the Supremes, the Shirelles, Martha and the Vandellas, and Smokey Robinson and the Miracles. He later shared a Tony Award for his work on the 1988 Broadway revue *Black and Blue.*

**Robert Coleman Atkins** (17 Oct 1930, Columbus OH—17 Apr 2003, New York NY), American cardiologist and nutritionist who wrote seven best-selling diet books—beginning in 1972 with *Dr. Atkins' Diet Revolution*—advocating that dieters adopt his controversial weight-loss plan that counseled them to consume large amounts of fats and protein and to minimize their intake of carbohydrates. Although for many years a large number of health experts deemed that diet potentially dangerous, some later studies showed it to be effective and nondetrimental to health.

**Rudolf Karl Augstein** (5 Nov 1923, Hanover, Germany—7 Nov 2002, Hamburg, Germany), German publisher, editor (until 1995), and chief editorial writer of *Der Spiegel,* the influential weekly newsmagazine that he founded in January 1947 and guided until the day of his death.

**George Axelrod** (9 Jun 1922, New York NY—21 Jun 2003, Los Angeles CA), American playwright and screenwriter, as well as a film producer and director, known for his biting sex comedies, the most famous of which was probably the play *The Seven Year Itch,* which played on Broadway for three years (1952–55) before being made into a popular film (1955) based on his screenplay. His other original hit plays were *Will Success Spoil Rock Hunter*

(1955) and *Goodbye Charlie* (1959). Axelrod's screenplays and adaptations included *Phffft!* (1954), *Bus Stop* (1956), *Breakfast at Tiffany's* (1961), and *The Manchurian Candidate* (1962).

**Harivansh Rai Bachchan** (27 Nov 1907, Allahabad, United Provinces [now Uttar Pradesh state], British India—18 Jan 2003, Mumbai [Bombay], Maharashtra state, India), Indian writer who was one of the most acclaimed Hindi-language poets of the 20th century.

**Abdel Rahman Badawi** (17 Feb 1917, Sharabass, Egypt—25 Jul 2002, Cairo, Egypt), Egyptian philosopher and academic who was generally regarded as Egypt's first and foremost existential philosopher.

**Joaquín Vidella Balaguer y Ricardo** (1 Sep 1907, Villa Navarrete [now Villa Bisonó], Dominican Republic—14 Jul 2002, Santo Domingo, Dominican Republic), Dominican lawyer, politician, and writer; populist but autocratic president of the Dominican Republic, 1960–62, 1966–78, and 1986–96.

**Hank Ballard** (John H. Kendricks; 18 Nov 1936, Detroit MI—2 Mar 2003, Los Angeles CA), American singer and songwriter who lit up the rhythm-and-blues charts in the 1950s with a series of earthy, blues-inspired songs and who wrote the dance hit "The Twist."

**Edward Latimer Beach, Jr.** (20 Apr 1918, New York NY—1 Dec 2002, Washington DC), American submariner and writer who was commander of the nuclear-powered submarine *Triton* when it made the first underwater circumnavigation of the globe in 1960. To the general public, though, he was better known as the author of the war novel *Run Silent, Run Deep* (1955).

**(George) Derek Fleetwood Bell** (21 Oct 1935, Belfast, Northern Ireland—17 Oct 2002, Phoenix AZ), Irish musician and composer who brought a classical music background to the popular Irish folk group the Chieftains when he joined them as harpist in 1972.

**Benyoussef Ben Khedda** (23 Feb 1920, Berrouaghia, Algeria—4 Feb 2003, Algiers, Algeria), Algerian independence leader who negotiated Algeria's independence from France in 1962 but was forced from power shortly thereafter.

**Luciano Berio** (24 Oct 1925, Oneglia, Italy—27 May 2003, Rome, Italy), Italian composer who drew on serialism, aleatoric practices, electronic sounds, *musique concrète,* and other sources to create a complex music language. In the mid-1950s, with the composer Bruno Maderna, he founded an electronic music studio in Milan and during that time also published the journal *Incontri Musicali.* Berio spent much of the 1960s teaching and conducting in the US. Berio wrote in many forms, from solo pieces to chamber and orchestral works to operas. He also wrote several early works for solo voice that were intended to be performed by his first wife, Cathy Berberian.

**Philip Francis Berrigan** (5 Oct 1923, Two Harbors MI—6 Dec 2002, Baltimore MD), American peace activist and former Roman Catholic priest. During the Vietnam War he and his brother, the Rev. Daniel J. Berrigan, engaged in numerous protest activities, were repeatedly imprisoned for their deeds, and served as inspiration for the peace activists of the era.

**Julian Himely Bigelow** (19 Mar 1913, Nutley NJ—17 Feb 2003, Princeton NJ), American engineer and mathematician who engineered one of the earliest computers, which was built in the late 1940s and came to be known as the IAS. The basic design of the IAS is the template for the modern computer.

**Rupert Everett Billingham** (15 Oct 1921, Warminster, England–16 Nov 2002, Boston MA), British-born American immunologist and transplant researcher. Under his mentor, zoologist Peter B. Medawar, Billingham helped conduct a series of groundbreaking experiments involving skin grafts on animals that proved the theory of acquired immunologic tolerance—the concept on which tissue transplantation was founded. Medawar was awarded the Nobel Prize for Physiology or Medicine in 1960 and shared the prize money with Billingham.

**Prince Ahmed Bin Salman** (Prince Ahmed ibn Salman ibn Abd al-Aziz; 17 Nov 1958, Riyadh, Saudi Arabia–22 Jul 2002, Riyadh, Saudi Arabia), Saudi Arabian businessman and racehorse owner whose horses included Spain, the greatest female money winner in Thoroughbred racing history, Point Given, who won the Preakness and Belmont stakes in 2001, and War Emblem, who won the 2002 Kentucky Derby.

**Anil Biswas** (7 Jul 1914, Barisal, East Bengal state, India [now in Bangladesh]–31 May 2003, New Delhi, India), Indian composer and singer who introduced orchestral music, often with native classical or folk elements, into popular Indian cinema. Biswas wrote music for some 100 films between 1935 and 1965, when he retired from the movie industry to take over as director of the national orchestra on All India Radio.

**Maria Bjørnson** (Maria Elena Proden; 16 Feb 1949, Paris, France–13 Dec 2002, London, England), British costume and set designer who created imaginative and innovative designs for more than 125 opera, ballet, and theater productions in a career that spanned 32 years. She was most acclaimed for her work on Andrew Lloyd Webber's *Phantom of the Opera* (1986).

**Maurice Blanchot** (27 Sep 1907, Quain, France–20 Feb 2003, Le Mesnil-Saint-Denis, France), French novelist and critic, a reclusive intellectual who influenced postmodernist thinkers such as Jacques Derrida, Michel Foucault, and Roland Barthes; he was also a supporter of new writers such as Samuel Beckett and Alain Robbe-Grillet. He was involved with Jean-Paul Sartre on *Les Temps modernes* and wrote a monthly column for *La Nouvelle Revue française* (1953–68).

**Janko Bobetko** (10 Jan 1919, Crnac, Kingdom of Serbs, Croats, and Slovenes [now in Croatia]–29 Apr 2003, Zagreb, Croatia), Croatian army chief who was regarded as a hero of Croatia's independence. In 1991 Bobetko assumed command of the new Croatian Defense Forces, which he led into battle in 1993 and 1995 to retake Croatian territory that had been conquered by Serbian forces. In September 2002 the International Criminal Tribunal for the former Yugoslavia ordered him to stand trial in The Hague for engaging in "ethnic cleansing" during the fighting.

**Nils Bohlin** (17 Jul 1920, Härnösand, Sweden–21 Sep 2002, Tranas, Sweden), Swedish safety engineer who invented the three-point seat belt in the 1950s while working for the Volvo Car Corp.

**Robert Borkenstein** (31 Aug 1912, Fort Wayne IN–10 Aug 2002, Bloomington IN), American inventor who patented the Breathalyzer, the innovative device used for decades by police to determine a driver's level of intoxication.

**Lyle Benjamin Borst** (24 Nov 1912, Chicago IL–30 Jul 2002, Williamsville NY), American nuclear physicist who supervised the construction of the nation's largest atomic reactor at Brookhaven National Laboratory in 1950.

**Pierre Bourgault** (23 Jan 1934, East Angus, QC, Canada–16 Jun 2003, Montreal, QC, Canada), Canadian politician and journalist, a fiery orator with a firm resolve to see Quebec gain national and cultural respect. He was among the founding members of the Rassemblement pour l'Indépendance (RIN) and became its leader in 1964. The party merged into the Parti Québécois in 1968. Bourgault assumed credit for organizing the Saint-Jean Baptiste riot in Montreal in June 1968 in which pro-independence forces sought to embarrass Pierre Elliott Trudeau, then running for prime minister of Canada, with a show of violence.

**Eddie Bracken** (Edward Vincent Bracken; 7 Feb 1915/20, Astoria NY–14 Nov 2002, Montclair NJ), American stage and film comedian and character actor who had a 70-year career highlighted by roles in two 1944 Preston Sturges movies, *The Miracle of Morgan's Creek* and *Hail the Conquering Hero,* and by his Tony Award-nominated role as Horace Vandergelder opposite Carol Channing in a Broadway revival of *Hello, Dolly!* (1978).

**Linda Schreiber Braidwood** (9 Oct 1909, Grand Rapids MI–15 Jan 2003, Chicago IL), American archaeologist [see Robert J. Braidwood, following].

**Robert John Braidwood** (29 Jul 1907, Detroit MI–15 Jan 2003, Chicago IL), American archaeologist, investigated the beginnings of settled farming communities, developed interdisciplinary methods of field research, and helped to establish Middle Eastern prehistory as a disciplined field of scholarship. In 1937 Robert and Linda Braidwood married, and thereafter they collaborated in their work.

**Stan Brakhage** (James Stanley Brakhage; 14 Jan 1933, Kansas City MO–9 Mar 2003, Victoria, BC, Canada), American experimental filmmaker whose goal was to free the act of seeing from the constraints of representation and expectation. He used a variety of methods, creating films from a few seconds to several hours in length, and showed visions ranging from those produced by cinematography to those made by gluing objects to the celluloid and scratching and painting the film.

**Chris Brasher** (Christopher William Brasher; 21 Aug 1928, Georgetown, British Guiana [now Guyana]–28 Feb 2003, Chaddleworth, Berkshire, England), British athlete, journalist, and businessman who on 6 May 1954 set the pace for the first two laps of Roger Bannister's historic race breaking the four-minute mile; he later cofounded the London Marathon.

**David Brinkley** (10 Jul 1920, Wilmington NC–11 Jun 2003, Houston TX), American TV journalist and commentator who achieved iconic status first as coanchor (with Chet Huntley) of the NBC nightly news program *The Huntley-Brinkley Report* (1956–70) and later as the anchor of the ABC interview and analysis program *This Week with David Brinkley* (1981–96).

**Dee Brown** (Dorris Alexander Brown; 29 Feb 1908, near Alberta LA–12 Dec 2002, Little Rock AR), American writer and academic who, while serving as a librarian at the University of Illinois, began writing books—a number of them for children—and ultimately published some 30, including 11 novels. His best-known work was *Bury My Heart at Wounded*

*Knee* (1970), a chronicle of the brutal treatment and conquest of Native Americans that ended in the massacre of 300 Sioux at Wounded Knee Creek in South Dakota in 1890.

**Earle Brown** (26 Dec 1926, Lunenburg MA—2 Jul 2002, Rye NY), American composer, one of the leading American exponents of avant-garde music, best known for his development of graphic notation and the open-form system of composition.

**Norman O(liver) Brown** (25 Sep 1913, El Oro, Mexico—2 Oct 2002, Santa Cruz CA), American philosopher and intellectual historian, whose books *Life Against Death: The Psychoanalytical Meaning of History* (1959) and *Love's Body* (1966) were influential among youth in the 1960s and '70s.

**Ray Brown** (Raymond Matthews Brown; 13 Oct 1926, Pittsburgh PA—2 Jul 2002, Indianapolis IN), American jazz bassist who played with a long parade of swing- and bop-era greats on more than 2,000 recordings, on worldwide Jazz at the Philharmonic (JATP) concert tours, as a member of the Oscar Peterson Trio, and then as leader or coleader of small and large ensembles.

**Valery (Nikolayevich) Brumel** (14 Apr 1942, Tolbuzhino, Siberia, USSR—26 Jan 2003, Moscow, Russia), Soviet Russian track and field athlete who dominated the sport of high jumping in the early 1960s, winning two Olympic medals (silver in 1960 and gold in 1964) and setting six consecutive outdoor world records between 1961 and 1963. His final record, 2.28 m (7 ft 5¾ in), was not broken officially until 1971.

**Cécile de Brunhoff** (Cécile Sabouraud; 16 Oct 1903, Paris, France—7 Apr 2003, Paris, France), French pianist and teacher who invented the character of Babar the Elephant and his original adventure in 1930 in a bedtime story for her two sons. *Histoire de Babar, le petit éléphant* (1931; *The Story of Babar, the Little Elephant,* 1933) became a worldwide children's favorite.

**Felice Bryant** (Matilda Genevieve Scaduto; 7 Aug 1925, Milwaukee WI—22 Apr 2003, Gatlinburg TN), American songwriter who, with her husband, Boudleaux Bryant, formed one of the most successful and prolific songwriting teams in history. Their more than 800 songs included most of the hits of the Everly Brothers, as well as the bluegrass standard "Rocky Top."

**Horst Buchholz** (4 Dec 1933, Berlin, Germany—3 Mar 2003, Berlin), German film actor who enjoyed a lengthy career in several countries. The best of his several Hollywood films were *The Magnificent Seven* (1960) and the Billy Wilder farce *One, Two, Three* (1961). In 1997 he appeared as a Nazi doctor in the Academy Award-winning film *La vita è bella* (*Life Is Beautiful*).

**Barry Bucknell** (Robert Barraby Bucknell; 26 Jan 1912, London, England—21 Feb 2003, St. Mawes, Cornwall, England), British TV show host who inspired do-it-yourself fans with his popular home-renovation shows in the 1950s and '60s.

**Angelo Buono, Jr.** (5 Oct 1934, Rochester NY—21 Sep 2002, Calipatria CA), American crime figure who, together with his cousin Kenneth Bianchi, was known as the "Hillside Strangler"; both were convicted in 1983 of murdering nine women in Los Angeles and disposing of their naked bodies on hillsides.

**Charles Robert Burton** (13 Dec 1942, Cape Town, South Africa—15 Jul 2002, Framfield, East Sussex, England), British explorer who was part of the first team to circumnavigate the globe from pole to pole along the Greenwich meridian (1979–82).

**Vasil Bykau** (Vasily Bykov; 19 Jun 1924, Bychki, Belorussian SSR, USSR [now Belarus]—22 Jun 2003, Minsk, Belarus), Belarusian novelist who explored the psychology of individuals struggling with the moral dilemmas of wartime. A fierce critic of Pres. Alyaksandr Lukashenka's pro-Russian regime, Bykau lived in exile from 1998 until shortly before his death.

**Phyllis Calvert** (Phyllis Bickle; 18 Feb 1915, London, England—8 Oct 2002, London, England), British stage actress who gained renown in such popular films as *The Man in Grey* (1943), *Fanny by Gaslight* (1944), and *Madonna of the Seven Moons* (1944). Her last film was *Mrs. Dalloway* (1997).

**Vinnette Carroll** (11 Mar 1922, New York NY—5 Nov 2002, Lauderhill FL), American stage director and actress who was the first African American woman to direct on Broadway. In 1962 she won an Obie Award for *Moon on a Rainbow Shawl,* and in 1964 she received an Emmy Award for *Beyond the Blues.*

**Benny Carter** (Bennett Lester Carter; 8 Aug 1907, New York NY—12 Jul 2003, Los Angeles CA), American jazz musician, one of the most original and influential alto saxophonists, who was also a masterly composer and arranger and an important bandleader, trumpeter, and clarinetist.

**Nell Carter** (Nell Hardy; 13 Sep 1948, Birmingham AL—23 Jan 2003, Beverly Hills CA), American singer and actress who won a Tony Award in 1978 for her exuberant performance in the Broadway musical revue *Ain't Misbehavin'* and in 1982 won an Emmy Award for a TV presentation of that show. She later achieved acclaim for her role as a sassy housekeeper in the 1980s TV sitcom *Gimme a Break!*

**June Carter Cash** (23 Jun 1929, Maces Spring VA—15 May 2003, Nashville TN), American singer, songwriter, and actress who first performed as a member of the legendary Carter Family, who were paramount in leading country music into the mainstream. In 1963 she cowrote her best-known song, "Ring of Fire," to describe her feelings about singer Johnny Cash, whom she later (1968) married.

**Achille Castiglioni** (16 Feb 1918, Milan, Italy—2 Dec 2002, Milan, Italy), Italian architect and interior designer who produced modern furnishings and accessories that were noted for their functional nature and witty styling. Castiglioni won the Golden Compass, Italy's top prize for industrial design, nine times. In 1997 the Museum of Modern Art in New York City held an exhibition of his work.

**Lynn Russell Chadwick** (24 Nov 1914, London, England—25 Apr 2003, Stroud, Gloucestershire, England), British sculptor who was renowned for his skeletal iron and bronze armatures, notably animal- and humanlike forms of great emotional power.

**Henry Chauncey** (9 Feb 1905, New York NY—3 Dec 2002, Shelburne VT), American educator who was an assistant dean at Harvard University when he began the quest for a meritocratic means of assessing applicants for admission to the university. In 1947, with Harvard president James Bryant Conant, he founded the Educational Testing Service (ETS) to encourage standardized testing in college admissions.

**Leslie Cheung** (Cheung Kwok-Wing; 12 Sep 1956, British Hong Kong—1 Apr 2003, Hong Kong, China), Hong Kong pop singer and popular Cantonese actor known first for his bad-boy image and later for his androgynous roles as, for example, in the world-wide hit, Chen Khaige's *Farewell My Concubine* (1993). In his last film, *Inner Senses* (2002), Cheung plays a man who is lured into committing suicide by his personal spirits; Cheung in fact killed himself by jumping from a hotel window.

**Eduardo Chillida Juantegui** (10 Jan 1924, San Sebastián, Spain—19 Aug 2002, near San Sebastián, Spain), Spanish Basque sculptor whose works are characterized by his craftsman's respect for materials, both in his small iron pieces and in his later, monumental works in granite.

**Cho Choong Hoon** (11 Feb 1920, Seoul, Korea [now in South Korea]—17 Nov 2002, Seoul, South Korea), Korean businessman who founded the Hanjin Group, which became the eighth largest conglomerate in the country and included 21 companies, including Korean Air Lines, for which he served as chairman from 1969 to 1999.

**Prince Claus** (Claus Georg Wilhelm Otto Friedrich Gerd, Jonkheer von Amsberg; 6 Sep 1926, Dötzingen, Germany—6 Oct 2002, Amsterdam, Netherlands), German-born Dutch royal, consort of Queen Beatrix of The Netherlands, who worked for development and regional planning, historic preservation, and environmental conservation.

**James Coburn** (31 Aug 1928, Laurel NE—18 Nov 2002, Beverly Hills CA), American actor who had a powerful screen presence that was made more commanding by his deep voice, wry delivery, toothy grin, and satanic laugh. His more than 70 films ranged from the one that brought him public attention, *The Magnificent Seven* (1960), to *The Great Escape* (1963), *Charade* (1963), the James Bond spoofs *Our Man Flint* (1966) and *In Like Flint* (1967), the satiric *The President's Analyst* (1967), and *Pat Garrett and Billy the Kid* (1973); he won a best-supporting-actor Oscar for his role in *Affliction* (1997).

**Ted Codd** (Edgar Frank Codd; 23 Aug 1923, Portland, Dorset, England—18 Apr 2003, Williams Island FL), British-born American computer scientist and mathematician who devised the "relational" data model, which led to the creation of the relational database, a standard method of retrieving and storing computer data. He also invented the technique of "multiprogramming," allowing several programs to run at once. In 1981 Codd received the Turing Award, the highest honor for computer science.

**Janet Collins** (7 Mar 1917, New Orleans LA—28 May 2003, Fort Worth TX), American ballet dancer and choreographer who was acclaimed for the beauty of her dancing on the Broadway stage—notably in *Out of This World* (1950)—as well as in film and on television but was best known for having become (1951) the first African American performer to appear on the stage of the Metropolitan Opera House.

**Francisco Coloane** (19 Jul 1910, Quemchi, Chile—5 Aug 2002, Santiago, Chile), Chilean author who penned seafaring adventure tales that were wildly popular and critically praised. His stories drew on local legends and reflected the landscape of the harsh Chilean coast, particularly Tierra del Fuego.

**Ray Conniff** (6 Nov 1916, Attleboro MA—12 Oct 2002, Escondido CA), American arranger, composer, and bandleader who became identified with easy-listening pop. He won a Grammy Award in 1966 for "Somewhere My Love," an adaptation of Maurice Jarre's "Lara's Theme" from the film *Dr. Zhivago* (1965). In all he recorded more than 100 albums that sold in the tens of millions of copies and won numerous awards.

**George (Leo) Connor** (21 Jan 1925, Chicago IL—31 Mar 2003, Evanston IL), American collegiate and professional football player who played for the University of Notre Dame and the NFL Chicago Bears and was later a coach and sports broadcaster.

**Art Cooper** (15 Oct 1935, Berwick PA—9 Jun 2003, New York NY), American magazine editor; he was the longtime (1983–2003) editor of Condé Nast's *GQ* (*Gentlemen's Quarterly*).

**Joseph Coors** (12 Nov 1917, Golden CO—15 Mar 2003, Rancho Mirage CA), American businessman who, with his brother William, expanded the brewery of the Adolph Coors Co. from being the producer of a local Western beer to becoming the third largest brewer in the US and was a founder in 1973 of the Heritage Foundation, a prominent conservative think tank.

**Jeff Corey** (10 Aug 1914, New York NY—16 Aug 2002, Santa Monica CA), American actor in character roles; he was blacklisted during the Communist "witch-hunts" in Hollywood during the 1950s.

**H(arold) S(cott) M(acdonald) Coxeter** (9 Feb 1907, London, England—31 Mar 2003, Toronto, ON, Canada), British-born Canadian geometer, a leader in the understanding of non-Euclidean geometries, reflection patterns, and polytopes (higher-dimensional analogs of three-dimensional polyhedra). His work served as an inspiration for R. Buckminster Fuller's concept of the geodesic dome and for the intricate geometrical designs of Dutch graphic artist M.C. Escher.

**José Craveirinha** (José G. Vetrinha; 28 May 1922, Lourenço Marques, Portuguese East Africa [now Maputo, Mozambique]—6 Feb 2003, South Africa), Mozambican writer who was generally considered Mozambique's greatest poet as well as one of the best contemporary poets writing in Portuguese.

**Richard Donald Crenna** (30 Nov 1927, Los Angeles CA—17 Jan 2003, Los Angeles CA), American radio, TV, and film actor who starred in *The Real McCoys* (1957–63) as well as in a number of other TV series and films that included *The Sand Pebbles* (1966), *Wait Until Dark* (1967), *Body Heat* (1981), and the "Rambo" movies (from 1982).

**James Hardesty Critchfield** (30 Jan 1917, Hunter ND—22 Apr 2003, Williamsburg VA), American spymaster who acted as liaison officer with the Gehlen Organization, a group of German ex-Nazi officials, led by Hitler's anti-Soviet espionage chief, who were forming the West German defense-intelligence system. Later Critchfield was CIA division chief for the Middle East and was among those who in the early 1960s recommended that the US support the Iraqi Ba'th Party to oppose the threat of communism in that country.

**Hume Cronyn** (Hume Blake; 18 Jul 1911, London, ON, Canada—15 Jun 2003, Fairfield CT), Canadian-born American actor and director who often appeared onstage with his wife, Jessica Tandy, starring in plays such as *The Fourposter* (1951), *A Delicate Balance* (1966), and *The Gin Game* (1977) and in films (*Cocoon* [1985]). He was awarded the National Medal of the Arts in 1990.

**John O'Hea Crosby** (12 Jul 1926, New York NY—15 Dec 2002, Rancho Mirage CA), American impresario who was the founder, in 1957, of the Santa Fe (NM) Opera and served as its general director until he stepped down in 2000.

**Celia Cruz** (21 Oct 1929?, Santa Suárez, Havana, Cuba—16 Jul 2003, Fort Lee NJ), Cuban American singer, called the "Queen of Salsa Music," who became a hit in the 1950s during the mambo dance craze and then again, beginning in 1973, as a singer of salsa music; she won five Grammy Awards in her career and was awarded the National Medal of the Arts in 1994.

**Derek Gwyn Davies** (9 Mar 1931, London, England—15 Sep 2002, Antibes, France), British journalist and editor of the *Far Eastern Economic Review*, 1962–89.

**Benjamin Oliver Davis, Jr.** (18 Dec 1912, Washington DC—4 Jul 2002, Washington DC), American military leader, the first African American general in the US Air Force, who led the Tuskegee Airmen, an all-black combat squadron, in World War II; he was awarded a fourth star after retirement in 1998.

**Jan de Hartog** (22 Apr 1914, Haarlem, Netherlands—22 Sep 2002, Houston TX), Dutch-American novelist and playwright who was the author of adventure tales and works for the theater, including the long-running hit *The Fourposter*, as well as of nonfiction.

**Andre De Toth** (Endre Antal Mihaly Sasvari Farkasfalvi Tothfalusi Toth; 15 May 1912, Mako, Hungary, Austro-Hungarian Empire—27 Oct 2002, Burbank CA), Hungarian-born American film director who made a number of raw, violent, and psychologically disturbing B movies as well as *House of Wax* (1953), considered the best of the 3-D films.

**Felix (George) de Weldon** (12 Apr 1907, Vienna, Austria—3 Jun 2003, Woodstock VA), Austrian-born American sculptor best known for his monumental and historical work. His most famous work is probably the Iwo Jima monument installed in 1954 above Arlington National Cemetery, near Washington DC. De Weldon was also commissioned to create busts of presidents Harry S. Truman, Dwight D. Eisenhower, and John F. Kennedy, as well as a wide variety of others including South American independence leader Simon Bolívar and a statue of Elvis Presley that is on display at Graceland, Presley's mansion, in Memphis TN.

**Dave DeBusschere** (David Albert DeBusschere; 16 Oct 1940, Detroit MI—14 May 2003, New York NY), American basketball player. During six seasons with the New York Knicks the 198-cm (6-ft 6-in) DeBusschere became a basketball great, providing tenacious defense and sturdy rebounding as his team won NBA championships in 1970 and 1973. After retiring in 1974, he became general manager of the New York Nets, in the young American Basketball Association; the next year he became the ABA's commissioner, and he was instrumental in the league's merger with the NBA in 1976.

**André Delvaux** (21 Mar 1926, Heverlee, Belgium—4 Oct 2002, Valencia, Spain), Belgian filmmaker who was widely regarded as the founder of the Belgian national cinema. In 1991 he received the Plateau Life Achievement Award at the International Film Festival in Ghent.

**Alejandro DeTomaso** (10 Jul 1928, Buenos Aires, Argentina—21 May 2003, Modena, Italy), Argentine industrialist who raced cars in Modena, Italy, before founding (1959) DeTomaso Automobili with his wife, Isabelle Haskell, and producing a line of sports cars and a number of limited-edition cars, including the Vallelunga, the Mangusta, and the Pantera, for public roads during the 1960s.

**Martin Deutsch** (29 Jan 1917, Vienna, Austria—16 Aug 2002, Cambridge MA), Austrian-born American physicist who discovered positronium, a fleeting hydrogen-like atom that contains a particle of antimatter; his work confirmed Einstein's theory that matter could be converted entirely into energy and further substantiated the theory of quantum electrodynamics for a two-particle system.

**Mohammed Dib** (21 Jul 1920, Tlemcen, Algeria—2 May 2003, La Celle-Saint-Cloud, France), Algerian novelist and poet, the author of some 30 books in French of fiction, poetry, and essays, many of which closely examined contemporary life in Algeria. Widely regarded as Algeria's foremost writer, Dib was best known for an early trilogy of novels—*La Grande maison* (1952; "The Big House"), *L'Incendie* (1954; "The Fire"), and *Le Métier à tisser* (1957; "The Loom")—that offered a starkly realistic portrayal of Algerian peasants and workers in the years preceding World War II.

**Edsger Wybe Dijkstra** (11 May 1930, Rotterdam, Netherlands—6 Aug 2002, Nuenen, Netherlands), Dutch computer scientist who provided the mathematical foundation for "structured programming"; his idea, which came to be called Dijkstra's algorithm, established the "shortest-path" concept of logically structured sets and subsets of computer commands in place of the excessively complex and disorganized commands often written by early programmers. This concept later found application in everything from electronic circuit design to graphic image processing to voice recognition.

**C(larence) Douglas Dillon** (21 Aug 1909, Geneva, Switzerland—10 Jan 2003, New York NY), American financier, politician, and arts patron who, though a Republican, served as secretary of the treasury (1961–65) under Democratic presidents John F. Kennedy and Lyndon B. Johnson; Dillon's policies are given credit for the long peacetime economic expansion of those years.

**Zoran Djindjic** (1 Aug 1952, Bosanski Samac, Bosnia, Yugoslavia [now in Bosnia and Herzegovina]—12 Mar 2003, Belgrade, Serbia and Montenegro), Yugoslav politician who, as the boldly pragmatic prime minister of Serbia, reformed the economy and brought former strongman Slobodan Milosevic before the UN war crimes tribunal. Djindjic was gunned down by multiple assailants in downtown Belgrade.

**Larry Doby** (Lawrence Eugene Doby; 13 Dec 1923, Camden SC—18 Jun 2003, Montclair NJ), American baseball player who became the second African American player in the major leagues and the first in the American League when he joined the Cleveland Indians in 1947. The next year he starred as the Indians' center fielder, batting .301, and his home run won a World Series game. A power hitter, Doby was an all-star for seven years, after his playing career ended, he coached baseball and, for half a season in 1978, managed the Chicago White Sox.

**Lonnie Donegan** (Anthony James Donegan; 29 Apr 1931, Glasgow, Scotland—3 Nov 2002, Peterborough, Cambridgeshire, England), Scottish musician who became known as the king of skiffle—a blend of music styles that encompassed folk, country, jazz, blues, and jug band—and in the process served as the inspiration for the British rock and roll musicians who followed in the 1960s, including Paul McCartney, John Lennon, Pete Townshend, and Van Morrison.

**Bernard Dowiyogo** (14 Feb 1946, Nauru—9 Mar 2003, Washington DC), Nauruan politician who served seven times (1976–78, 1989–95, 1996, 1998–99, 2000–01, and twice in 2003) as president of the Pacific islet nation of Nauru.

**Natalya Mikhaylovna Dudinskaya** (21 Aug 1912, Kharkiv, Ukraine, Russian Empire—29 Jan 2003, St. Petersburg, Russia), Russian prima ballerina of the Kirov (now Mariinsky) Ballet who was celebrated for her virtuosity and her pure classical technique during her performing career from the 1930s to the early 1960s; she went on to renown as a cherished and highly respected teacher.

**Abba Eban** (Aubrey Solomon Meir; 2 Feb 1915, Cape Town, South Africa—17 Nov 2002, Jerusalem, Israel), Israeli politician and diplomat who was a key figure in the founding of the state of Israel and served as that country's first permanent representative to the UN (1949–59), first ambassador to the US (1950–59), and longest-serving foreign minister (1966–74).

**Buddy Ebsen** (Christian Rudolph Ebsen, Jr.; 2 Apr 1908, Belleville IL—6 Jul 2003, Torrance CA), American dancer and actor who starred in the TV series *The Beverly Hillbillies* and *Barnaby Jones.*

**Sir George Robert Edwards** (9 Jul 1908, Chingford, Essex, England—2 Mar 2003, Guildford, Surrey, England), British aircraft designer whose work includes notably the Viscount turboprop airliner; in the 1970s Edwards was instrumental in persuading French and English politicians and aircraft designers to bring the supersonic Concorde project to fruition.

**Manfred Ewald** (17 May 1926, Podejuch, Germany [now Podjuchy, Poland]—21 Oct 2002, Damsdorf, Germany), German sports official who formed a powerhouse Olympic team but was discredited when it was discovered that his athletes' success was based in part on the use of performance-enhancing drugs. In 2000 he was convicted of having caused bodily harm to 142 female athletes.

**Adam Faith** (Terence Nelhams; 23 Jun 1940, London, England—8 Mar 2003, Stoke-on-Trent, Staffordshire, England), British pop singer, actor, and businessman who held the public eye through a succession of overlapping careers, beginning as a teen pop idol in the early 1960s. Faith had number-one singles in "What Do You Want" (1959) and "Poor Me" (1960). He also began appearing in movies and TV series. In the 1980s he reinvented himself as a financial guru and wrote newspaper columns on investing.

**Howard Melvin Fast** (11 Nov 1914, New York NY—12 Mar 2003, Old Greenwich CT), American writer, the prolific author of, most notably, popular historical novels on themes of human rights and social justice. Fast, who was well known for his leftist political beliefs, wrote more than 80 books in addition to poetry, screenplays, and newspaper articles.

**Leslie Aaron Fiedler** (8 Mar 1917, Newark NJ—29 Jan 2003, Buffalo NY), American literary critic known for his influential book *Love and Death in the American Novel* (1960), which examined underlying themes of race and sex in classic American novels and roused the ire of many commentators.

**Charles Henri Ford** (Charles Henry Ford; 10 Feb 1908, Hazelhurst MS—27 Sep 2002, New York NY), American poet, writer, and artist who lived and worked among the bohemian avant-garde. In all he published 16 books of poetry, most of it in a Surrealist vein. His artwork included paintings, drawings, collages, and photographs.

**Robert Lull Forward** (15 Aug 1932, Geneva NY—21 Sep 2002, Seattle WA), American physicist and science-fiction writer who utilized his knowledge of gravitational physics and advanced space propulsion to create finely crafted, scientifically feasible worlds for his readers.

**John Paul Frank** (10 Nov 1917, Appleton WI—7 Sep 2002, Scottsdale AZ), American lawyer who was involved in two of the most important US Supreme Court cases of the second half of the 20th century: *Brown* v. *Board of Education of Topeka* (1954), in which school segregation was declared unconstitutional, and *Miranda* v. *Arizona* (1966), which established police procedures for handling criminal suspects. In addition, Frank took on several political causes, which included opposing the confirmation of Robert H. Bork as a Supreme Court justice in 1987 and advising Anita Hill in her testimony in 1991 against another court nominee, Clarence Thomas.

**John (Michael) Frankenheimer** (19 Feb 1930, Queens NY—6 Jul 2002, Los Angeles CA), American television and film director early considered one of the most important and creatively gifted directors of the 1950s and early '60s and who enjoyed a second surge of success in the 1990s when he produced a number of outstanding films for cable TV.

**Vincent Freda** (16 Dec 1927, New Haven CT—7 May 2003, New York NY), American obstetrician who shared the 1980 Albert Lasker Award for clinical research for his pioneering work in developing a vaccine (Rhogam) that saved Rh-positive infants born to mothers with a Rh-negative blood factor from a potentially fatal condition, hemolytic disease.

**Orville Lothrop Freeman** (9 May 1918, Minneapolis MN—20 Feb 2003, Minneapolis MN), American government official who served three terms as governor of Minnesota (1955–61) and as US secretary of agriculture (1961–69) under presidents John F. Kennedy and Lyndon B. Johnson.

**Kinji Fukasaku** (3 Jul 1930, Mito, Japan—12 Jan 2003, Tokyo, Japan), Japanese filmmaker who created a series of increasingly violent and well-received *yakuza* (gangster) movies. Standouts among the more than 60 films that he directed are *Kurotokage* (1968; *Black Lizard*), *Gunki hatameku motoni* (1972; *Under the Flag of the Rising Sun*), and *Jingi naka tatakai* (1973). Fukasaku was probably best known to Americans for his direction of the Japanese sequences of *Tora! Tora! Tora!* (1970).

**Uziel Gal** (15 Dec 1923, Germany—7 Sep 2002, North Wales PA), Israeli army officer and inventor who designed the Uzi submachine gun, a compact automatic weapon used throughout the world as a police and special-forces firearm.

**Leopoldo Fortunato Galtieri** (15 Jul 1926, Caseros, Argentina—12 Jan 2003, Buenos Aires, Argentina), Argentine military ruler who, during his brief period as the head of the junta that ruled Argentina in 1976–83, initiated the disastrous (for Argentina) 1982 war with Britain over the Falkland Islands/Islas Malvinas.

**Kid Gavilan** (Gerardo González; 6 Jan 1926, Camagüey, Cuba—13 Feb 2003, Miami FL), Cuban-born American boxer who was one of the most popular attractions of the 1950s. Known for his colorful boxing style, he was world welterweight champion from 1951 to 1954.

**Jack Gelber** (12 Apr 1932, Chicago IL—9 May 2003, New York NY), American playwright who broke new theatrical ground in 1959 with his controversially raw and realistic play about drug addiction, *The Connection.* He later had a successful career as a director and teacher.

**Sir J(ohn) Paul Getty, Jr.** (7 Sep 1932, Italy—17 Apr 2003, London, England), British philanthropist who, after years of bohemian dissipation, devoted his later life to doing good works with his inherited fortune. He donated millions to the National Gallery and the British Film Institute and stepped in several times to prevent art treasures from being sold to American institutions. He gave smaller sums to other causes that struck him as deserving.

**Maurice Gibb** (22 Dec 1949, Douglas, Isle of Man—12 Jan 2003, Miami FL), British singer, musician, and composer; he joined with his brothers to form a pop music trio, who, while living in Australia, became popular as the Bee Gees (from Brothers Gibb); they went on to be one of the most successful British groups ever.

**Sid Gillman** (26 Oct 1911, Minneapolis MN—3 Jan 2003, Los Angeles CA), American football coach who was regarded as the progenitor of the modern passing game. His career included positions at Miami University in Oxford OH, the University of Cincinnati, the NFL Los Angeles Rams, the AFL Los Angeles (later San Diego) Chargers, and the Houston Oilers.

**Harold Samuel Ginsberg** (27 May 1917, Daytona Beach FL—2 Feb 2003, Woods Hole MA), American microbiologist who did pioneering work in virology; his research into adenoviruses showed how viral genes function in cells and how the viruses cause disease.

**Aleksandr Ilich Ginzburg** (21 Nov 1936, Moscow, USSR—19 Jul 2002, Paris, France), Russian journalist, dissident, and human rights advocate who edited the literary journal *Sintaksis* ("Syntax"), often said to have been the first *samizdat*—a self-published underground work that circulated among opponents of the Soviet government. He was repeatedly arrested and jailed and became a symbol in the West of resistance to Soviet rule.

**José María Gironella Pous** (31 Dec 1917, Darníus, Gerona, Spain—3 Jan 2003, Arenys de Mar, Spain), Spanish novelist who wrote the first best-selling novel published in Spain, *Los cipreses creen en Dios* (1953; *The Cypresses Believe in God* [1955]), set in the years immediately preceding the Spanish Civil War (1936–39).

**Françoise Giroud** (France Gourdji; 21 Sep 1916, Geneva, Switzerland—19 Jan 2003, Neuilly-sur-Seine, France), Swiss-born French journalist and government official; she served as editor in chief of the magazine *Elle* and was a founder of the weekly *L'Express;* she served as secretary of state for women (1974–76) and minister of culture (1976–77).

**Robert Alan Good** (21 May 1922, Crosby MN—13 Jun 2003, St. Petersburg FL), American microbiologist and pathologist who was considered a founder of modern immunology and a pioneer in bone-marrow transplantation. He first attracted recognition for a seminal paper that established the importance of the thymus gland in the body's defense mechanisms. His research on the tonsils demonstrated that they play an important role in the infection-fighting abilities of young children. Good also was a leading researcher in bone-marrow transplants and performed the first such procedure in 1968.

**Adolph Green** (2 Dec 1915, Bronx NY—23 Oct 2002, New York NY), American lyricist, screenwriter, and actor who enjoyed a six-decade-long creative collaboration with Betty Comden. They wrote the book and lyrics for Broadway hits such as *On the Town* (1944; filmed 1949), *Wonderful Town* (1953), *Peter Pan* (1954), and *Bells Are Ringing* (1956; filmed 1960), and their screenplays included those for *Singin' in the Rain* (1952), *The Band Wagon* (1953), *It's Always Fair Weather* (1955), and *Auntie Mame* (1958).

**Cecil Howard Green** (6 Aug 1900, Manchester, England—12 Apr 2003, La Jolla CA), British-born American seismographic engineer and philanthropist who cofounded in 1941 the company that became known as Texas Instruments Inc., the semiconductor firm that developed the first pocket-sized transistor radio (1954) and the integrated circuit board (1958).

**Martha Griffiths** (Martha Edna Wright; 29 Jan 1912, Pierce City MO—22 Apr 2003, Armada MI), American Democratic politician and women's rights advocate who successfully lobbied to include women on the list of those protected by the 1964 Civil Rights Act and nearly made the Equal Rights Amendment (prohibiting sex discrimination) a part of the US Constitution while serving (1955–75) in the US House of Representatives.

**Robert Gueï** (16 Mar 1941, Kabakouma, French West Africa—19 Sep 2002, Abidjan, Côte d'Ivoire), Ivorian military leader who mounted in 1999 the first successful coup d'état in his native country. His rule lasted only 10 months, but it marked the beginning of years of conflict in Côte d'Ivoire, which had been known as a haven of stability in West Africa.

**Charles Eli Guggenheim** (31 Mar 1924, Cincinnati OH—9 Oct 2002, Washington DC), American film producer and director who made more than 100 documentaries during a half-century-long career. He was nominated for 12 Academy Awards and won 4—for *Nine from Little Rock* (1964), *Robert Kennedy Remembered* (1968), *The Johnstown Flood* (1989), and *A Time for Justice* (1994).

**Billy Guy** (Frank Phillips, Jr.; 20 Jun 1936, Itasca TX—12 Nov 2002, Las Vegas NV), American pop singer who was one of the original members of the Coasters, a rock and roll group popular in the late 1950s. A baritone, he sang the lead on one of the quartet's biggest hits, "Searchin'" (1957).

**Arthur Clay Guyton** (8 Sep 1919, Oxford MS—3 Apr 2003, Jackson MS), American medical researcher and educator who wrote one of the most widely used medical textbooks in the world, *Textbook of Medical Physiology* (1956), which is now in its 10th edition and has been translated into 15 languages. He also contributed greatly to the understanding of hypertension.

**Buddy Hackett** (Leonard Hacker; 31 Aug 1924, Brooklyn NY—30 Jun 2003, Malibu CA), American comedian and film actor who began his career as a standup comedian and later moved to southern California and became a popular act in nightclubs. Hackett's routines were risqué for the time, and his appearances were sometimes labeled "For Mature Audiences." He was also a frequent guest on TV late-night shows. Hackett appeared in a few stage shows and did two short stints on TV sitcoms, as well as giving memorable performances in motion pictures that included the animated "Little Mermaid" films (1989 and 2002) as the voice of Scuttle.

**Sue Sally Hale** (23 Aug 1937, Los Angeles CA—29 Apr 2003, Coachella Valley CA), American polo player who for nearly 20 years played in polo tournaments disguised as a man, under the name "A. Jones," because the United States Polo Association would not admit women. In 1972 the association was pressured into relenting, however, and she became the first woman to be granted membership.

**Conrad L. Hall** (21 Jun 1926, Papeete, Tahiti, French Polynesia–4 Jan 2003, Santa Monica CA), American cinematographer who gained renown as a master of the use of light to create the desired mood of a film; among his numerous honors were three Academy Awards–for *Butch Cassidy and the Sundance Kid* (1969), *American Beauty* (1999), and *Road to Perdition* (2002), the last awarded posthumously.

**Lionel (Leo) Hampton** ("Hamp"; 20 Apr 1908 [?], Louisville KY–31 Aug 2002, New York NY), American musician who was one of the first jazz vibraphonists; he became a star during the swing era and then led bands with endless, infectious energy for over 50 years.

**Sir Roland Pembroke Hanna** (10 Feb 1932, Detroit MI–13 Nov 2002, Harris NY), American jazz pianist who fused classical music bravura and bop-era sophistication as a versatile accompanist, leader, and soloist. Besides serving as a music teacher, he composed both jazz and classical works; in 1970, during a benefit concert tour, he was knighted by the government of Liberia.

**James Daniel Hardy** (14 May 1918, Newala AL–19 Feb 2003, Madison MS), American transplant surgeon who performed the first lung transplant (1963) and other path-breaking operations.

**Isser Harel** (Isser Halperin; 1912, Vitebsk, Belorussia, Russian Empire [now in Belarus]–18 Feb 2003, Petah Tiqwa, Israel), Israeli spymaster who directed the abduction from Argentina of Adolf Eichmann, the Nazi official responsible for carrying out the "final solution," the extermination of Jews in Europe.

**Richard St. John Harris** (1 Oct 1930, Limerick, Ireland–25 Oct 2002, London, England), Irish actor who had a sometimes-uneven career notable not only for his formidable talent in portraying the intense, volatile, and rebellious hell-raising characters that established his image but also for conducting his real life in a similar manner for a number of years. Near the end of his life, though, he became known as the lovable though curmudgeonly Professor Albus Dumbledore in the first two Harry Potter movies.

**Lou (Silver) Harrison** (14 May 1917, Portland OR–2 Feb 2003, Lafayette IN), American composer, a tireless experimenter who created memorable melodies as he fused the classical tradition of the West with idioms from around the world, especially music from Asia; elements of Navajo, Korean, Indian, Javanese gamelan, African, medieval European, and Baroque music appeared in his four symphonies and many other instrumental and vocal works.

**Leon Hart** (2 Nov 1928, Turtle Creek PA–24 Sep 2002, South Bend IN), American football player who in 1949 became the second of the only two linemen to have won the Heisman Trophy, the highest honor in college football. In his four seasons (1946–49) on the University of Notre Dame team, he played both offensive and defensive end on a squad that, while never losing a game, captured national titles three times and once finished second (1948).

**Harry Hay** (Henry Hay, Jr.; 7 Apr 1912, Worthing, England–24 Oct 2002, San Francisco CA), American gay-rights activist who believed that homosexuals should see themselves as an oppressed minority entitled to equal rights. He acted on his convictions and in large measure prompted the dramatic changes in the status of homosexuals that took place in the US in the second half of the 20th century.

**Bob Hayes** (Robert Lee Hayes; 20 Dec 1942, Jacksonville FL–18 Sep 2002, Jacksonville FL), American sprinter and football player who commanded an incredible speed that not only helped him set records in track and field but also fundamentally changed professional football when opposing teams, finding that they could not match his speed man-to-man, adopted defensive-zone coverages to contain him.

**Chick Hearn** (Francis Dayle Hearn; 27 Nov 1916, Buda IL–5 Aug 2002, Los Angeles CA), American sports broadcaster who was for more than 40 years the play-by-play radio and television announcer for the Los Angeles Lakers of the National Basketball Association. Witty and sincere, he was credited with the coining of several sporting terms, including "air ball" and "slam dunk."

**Richard McGarrah Helms** (30 Mar 1913, St. Davids PA–22 Oct 2002, Washington DC), American intelligence official and diplomat who headed the Central Intelligence Agency from 1966 to 1973; to supporters he was a patriot who upheld the security of the country above all else, while to critics he typified the worst faults of the CIA.

**Katharine Hepburn** (12 May 1907, Hartford CT–29 Jun 2003, Old Saybrook CT), American stage and motion-picture actress known especially for her roles as strong-willed women and for her incandescent work opposite actor Spencer Tracy. Her first film was *A Bill of Divorcement* (1932) with John Barrymore, and for her performance in her third film, *Morning Glory* (1933), she won an Academy Award for best actress. She received three more best-actress Oscars–a record–for *Guess Who's Coming to Dinner* (1967) with Tracy, *The Lion in Winter* (1968), and *On Golden Pond* (1981), and her 12 best-actress nominations were also a record until 2003.

**Orvan Walter Hess** (18 Jun 1906, Margaretville NY–6 Sep 2002, New Haven CT), American obstetrician and gynecologist who developed the first fetal heart monitor, at the Yale University Medical School, in 1957. The device, which allowed monitoring to continue during labor, became, except for ultrasound, the most-used technique in obstetrics.

**Dorothy Coade Hewett** (21 May 1923, Perth, WA, Australia–25 Aug 2002, Springwood, NSW, Australia), Australian writer who rebelled against the comforts of a conventional lifestyle to embrace progressivist causes in her life and her work. A self-styled "modern Romantic," Hewett crossed genres, composing poetry, plays, novels, and stories.

**José Hierro** (3 Apr 1922, Madrid, Spain–20 Dec 2002, Madrid, Spain), Spanish poet who was one of Spain's most recognizable and beloved contemporary literary figures. Although he was not a prolific poet, his intense, concise verse drew critical and commercial attention.

**George Roy Hill** (20 Dec 1922, Minneapolis MI–27 Dec 2002, New York NY), American director, writer, and actor who enjoyed for a time the distinction of being the only director to have two films on the list of the top 10 moneymakers–*Butch Cassidy and the Sundance Kid* (1969) and *The Sting* (1973)

**(John Edward) Christopher Hill** (6 Feb 1912, York, England–23 Feb 2003, Oxfordshire, England),

British historian who changed the way generations of students understood the history of 17th-century England through his Marxist interpretations of the period of the English Civil Wars (1642–51) and their aftermath. Hill wrote more than 20 books upholding his belief that the mid-17th century in England saw a profound revolution that opened the way for the establishment of capitalism.

**Dame Wendy Hiller** (Wendy Margaret Watkin; 15 Aug 1912, Bramhall, Cheshire, England—14 May 2003, Beaconsfield, Buckinghamshire, England), British actress celebrated for her performances of strong, spirited women and for the slightly quavering voice in which she carefully enunciated those characters' lines. She was especially noted for being one of George Bernard Shaw's favorite leading ladies and created two of his most memorable roles, Eliza Doolittle in *Pygmalion* and the title character in *Major Barbara,* first onstage and later in the film versions.

**Myra Hindley** (23 Jul 1942, Manchester, England—15 Nov 2002, Bury St. Edmunds, Suffolk, England), British serial killer who was convicted in 1966 of the torture and murder of two children and of having been the accessory in the murder of a third. As England's first convicted female serial killer, Hindley became a cause célèbre—considered a sadistic murderer by some but seen by others as a weak young woman brutalized into helping her homicidal lover.

**Gregory Hines** (14 Feb 1946, New York NY—9 Aug 2003, Los Angeles CA), American dancer who came to prominence as a child performer, achieved stardom in an act with his father, Maurice Hines, and his brother Maurice Hines, Jr., and later became a successful film and TV actor; he won a Tony Award for his work in *Jelly's Last Jam* and starred in his own TV show, *The Gregory Hines Show,* in 1997.

**Jerome Hines** (Jerome Albert Link Heinz; 8 Nov 1921, Hollywood CA—4 Feb 2003, New York NY), American operatic bass who sang for 41 years at the Metropolitan Opera in New York City; he was known for his rich and flexible voice as well as his imposing stage presence.

**Al(bert) Hirschfeld** (21 Jun 1903, St. Louis MO—20 Jan 2003, New York NY), American caricaturist who needed only a few strokes of his pen to capture the likenesses and the essences of the personalities of his subjects—mostly show-business celebrities but also political and governmental leaders. He was internationally acclaimed for having created a visual history of the 20th-century Broadway stage. In 1996 Hirschfeld was declared an official Living New York City Landmark.

**Ramon John Hnatyshyn** (Ray; 16 Mar 1934, Saskatoon, SK, Canada—18 Dec 2002, Ottawa, ON, Canada), Canadian politician who served as a Conservative in the House of Commons for 14 years (1974–88) before being named governor-general of Canada, a post he held from 1990 to 1995. At the time of his death, he was chancellor of Carleton University, Ottawa.

**Bob Hope** (Leslie Townes Hope; 29 May 1903, Eltham, England—27 Jul 2003, Toluca Lake CA), British-born American comedian and film actor, most noted for his entertainment of American military troops overseas throughout World War II, the Korean War, the Vietnam War, and the Persian Gulf War. He appeared in about 60 films, including, with Dorothy Lamour and Bing Crosby, *The Cat and the Canary* (1939), *Road to Singapore* (1940), *Road to Zanzibar* (1941), *Road to Utopia* (1946), *Road to Rio* (1947), and *Road to Bali* (1952). His sharp wit and mastery of repartee made him an American icon and an enduring star.

**Robert Guy Hoyt** (30 Jan 1922, Clinton IA—10 Apr 2003, New York NY), American editor who transformed Roman Catholic journalism with the creation of the *National Catholic Reporter,* the first Roman Catholic newspaper to use the standards of secular journalism. Hoyt was later editor in chief of *Christianity & Crisis* (1977–85) and a senior editor at *Commonweal* (1989–2002).

**(Hugh) Desmond Hoyte** (9 Mar 1929, Georgetown, Guyana—22 Dec 2002, Georgetown, Guyana), Guyanese politician who became president of Guyana after the death of Forbes Burnham in 1985 and soon thereafter began dismantling Burnham's socialist framework.

**Kim Hunter** (Janet Cole; 12 Nov 1922, Detroit MI—11 Sep 2002, New York NY), American stage, film, and TV actress who won an Academy Award for best supporting actress for her portrayal of Stella Kowalski in the 1951 film *A Streetcar Named Desire* after having originated the role on Broadway (1947).

**Saburo Ienaga** (3 Sep 1913, Nagoya, Japan—29 Nov 2002, Tokyo, Japan), Japanese historian who waged a long-running battle with the Japanese Ministry of Education over his depiction in history textbooks of wartime atrocities committed by the Japanese.

**Maynard (Holbrook) Jackson, Jr.** (23 Mar 1938, Dallas TX—23 Jun 2003, Arlington VA), American Democratic politician, the first African American to serve as mayor of a large southern US city (1974–82 and 1990–94). His accomplishments in his three terms as mayor included the planning for the Hartsfield International Airport, the practice of earmarking a portion of contract funds for minority businesses, and the city's successful bid for the Olympic Games in 1996.

**Jam Master Jay** (Jason Mizell; 21 Jan 1965, New York NY—30 Oct 2002, New York NY), American rap musician and producer who was a member of Run-D.M.C., the first rap group to attract a worldwide audience. He was shot dead at his recording studio in New York City.

**Elliott Jaques** (18 Jan 1917, Toronto, ON, Canada—8 Mar 2003, Gloucester MA), Canadian-born psychologist and social analyst who developed the concept of corporate culture and coined the phrase "midlife crisis." His ideas were widely used by consultancies and other organizations.

**Roy Jenkins** (Roy Harris Jenkins, Baron Jenkins of Hillhead; 11 Dec 1920, Abersychan, Monmouthshire, England—5 Jan 2003, East Hundred, Oxfordshire, England), British politician and author, a leading figure in the Labour Party for decades before breaking away in 1981 to help form the centrist Social Democratic Party (SDP); he was instrumental in liberalizing British society and in stabilizing the budget, promoting European monetary union, and championing British membership in the European Economic Community (EEC).

**Katy Jurado** (María Cristina Estella Marcella Jurado García; 16 Jan 1924, Guadalajara, Mexico—5 Jul 2002, Cuernavaca, Mexico), Mexican film actress who projected a smoldering sensuality and vitality that captured audiences' attention first in Mexico and later in the US, where she was one of the first Latina actresses to find success in Hollywood.

**Martin David Kamen** (27 Aug 1913, Toronto, ON, Canada–31 Aug 2002, Santa Barbara CA), Canadian-born American chemist known for his work on cytochromes; he received the 1995 Enrico Fermi Award for lifetime achievement in energy research.

**Krishan Kant** (28 Feb 1927, Kot Mohammad Khan, Punjab, British India–27 Jul 2002, New Delhi, India), Indian politician who devoted his entire life to Indian freedom, social welfare, and civil liberties and rose to become vice president in 1997.

**Yousuf Karsh** (23 Dec 1908, Mardin, Turkey–13 Jul 2002, Boston MA), Turkish-born Canadian photographer, who achieved international renown for his portraits of political, military, artistic, and business leaders including, most famously, his iconic photograph of Winston Churchill.

**Sir Bernard Katz** (26 Mar 1911, Leipzig, Germany–23 Apr 2003, London, England), German-born British biophysicist who was awarded (with J. Axelrod and U.S. von Euler) the 1970 Nobel Prize for Physiology or Medicine for discoveries in the role of certain chemicals in transmitting nerve impulses.

**Michael Kelly** (17 Mar 1957, Washington DC–3 Apr 2003, south of Baghdad, Iraq), American journalist who was a fierce and courageous reporter, editor, and columnist. In the 1990s he wrote for the *New York Times* and *The New Yorker* magazine. He was ferociously opposed to the administration of Pres. Bill Clinton, and his columns exuberantly expressed that opposition. He became editor of *The New Republic* in 1996 and soon thereafter editor of *The Atlantic Monthly*.

**Rachel Kempson** (Lady Redgrave; 28 May 1910, Dartmouth, Devon, England–24 May 2003, Millbrook NY), British actress who had a distinguished stage, film, and television career in Great Britain but, especially in the US, became better known as the matriarch of the Redgrave acting family—the wife of Sir Michael Redgrave, the mother of Vanessa, Corin, and Lynn Redgrave, and the grandmother of Natasha and Joely Richardson.

**Kerim (Aliyevich) Kerimov** (14/17 Nov 1917, Baku, Azerbaijan, Russian Empire [now Azerbaijan]–29 Mar 2003, Moscow, Russia), Soviet rocket scientist who was for many years a central figure in the Soviet space program, though his name was kept secret from the public. Kerimov worked with military rockets then joined the space program and worked toward the launch of Sputnik, the first satellite, in 1957. In 1966 Kerimov was put in charge of the state commission for testing of the Soyuz manned-spacecraft program, intended to lead to a Moon landing.

**Jean Kerr** (Bridget Jean Collins; 10 Jul 1922, Scranton PA–5 Jan 2003, White Plains NY), American playwright and author whose anecdotal book *Please Don't Eat the Daisies* (1957) was a bestseller that went on to become the basis of a 1960 movie and a mid-'60s TV sitcom; she followed up with such successes as the book *The Snake Has All the Lines* (1960) and the plays *Mary, Mary* (1961; filmed 1963) and *Finishing Touches* (1973).

**Ward Kimball** (4 Mar 1914, Minneapolis MN–8 Jul 2002, Arcadia CA), American animator who was among the "Nine Old Men" who made the Walt Disney Studios the leader of film cartoons by drawing, directing the animation of classic features and shorts (including *Dumbo, Fantasia, Peter Pan, Alice in Wonderland, Cinderella,* and *Three Caballeros*), and creating television shows for Disney for 39 years.

**Earl King** (Earl Silas Johnson IV; 7 Feb 1934, New Orleans LA–17 Apr 2003, New Orleans LA), American blues musician and songwriter who played an incandescent guitar and wrote a number of songs that became standards of the genre, including "Trick Bag," "Big Chief," and "Come On (Let the Good Times Roll)."

**Ernst Kitzinger** (27 Dec 1912, Munich, Germany–22 Jan 2003, Poughkeepsie NY), German-born American historian and scholar of Byzantine, early Christian, and early medieval art, considered one of the last great exponents of Kunstwissenschaft, or art-historical method, by which intensive visual studies are used as a point of access to the thought and culture of past years.

**Frederick Major Paul Knott** (28 Aug 1916, Hankow [Hankou], China–17 Dec 2002, New York NY), British playwright who wrote only three plays, but two of them—*Dial M for Murder* (1952) and *Wait Until Dark* (1966)—met with enormous success.

**Kenneth (Jay) Koch** (27 Feb 1925, Cincinnati OH–6 Jul 2002, New York NY), American poet, writer, and teacher who was known for verse that combined modernism with lyricism and that conveyed a sense of enthusiasm and fun.

**Jiri Kolar** (24 Sep 1914, Protivin, Bohemia, Austria-Hungary–11 Aug 2002, Prague, Czech Rep.), Czech artist and writer who excelled in both poetry and collage, but his works embodied independence and originality at a time when communist cultural repression made such qualities liabilities, and he suffered oppression and imprisonment in his native country.

**Sam Lacy** (Samuel Harold Lacy; 23 Oct 1903, Mystic CT–8 May 2003, Washington DC), American sportswriter who was an editor and columnist for the Afro-American Newspapers in Baltimore MD from 1943 until shortly before his death and in that position was an influential crusader for racial integration in the major leagues. He was (1948) the first African American to be accepted as a member of the Baseball Writers Association of America.

**Jean-Luc Lagardère** (10 Feb 1928, Aubiet, France–14 Mar 2003, Paris, France), French entrepreneur who created one of France's largest industrial empires and was instrumental in the creation of the European Aeronautic Defense and Space company (EADS), the trans-European aerospace behemoth and manufacturer of the Airbus aircraft. In 1980 Lagardère acquired the publishing company Hachette, which he built into one of the world's biggest magazine publishers; among its titles are *Paris Match, Elle, Woman's Day,* and *Car and Driver.*

**John S. Latsis** (Ioannis Spyridon Latsis; 14 Sep 1910, Katakolo, Greece–17 Apr 2003, Athens, Greece), Greek shipping and oil magnate, a bold and surefooted businessman who became one of the richest men in the world. In his later years he used his wealth for philanthropic projects.

**Colin Legum** (3 Jan 1919, Kestell, Orange Free State [now in South Africa]–8 Jun 2003, Cape Town, South Africa), South African journalist and one of the most respected African affairs analysts. His work as the Commonwealth correspondent (1951–81) for *The Observer* newspaper and as editor (from 1968) of the *Africa Contemporary Record* led him to develop friendly personal relations with most of the top African leaders, including Julius Nyerere, Jomo Kenyatta, and Oliver Tambo.

**J(ohn) Hugh Liedtke** (10 Feb 1922, Tulsa OK—28 Mar 2003, Houston TX), American business executive who, as longtime CEO of Pennzoil Co., became known as a takeover artist and won billions of dollars from Texaco Inc. in a legal settlement over the acquisition of Getty Oil. In 1953 Liedtke and his brother William, in partnership with future US president George H.W. Bush, formed the Zapata Petroleum Corp. and drilled a string of 127 successful oil wells in West Texas. The following decade the Liedtke brothers took over the South Penn Oil Co. and named the combined company Pennzoil.

**Felice Marks Lippert** (1929, New York NY—22 Feb 2003, Manhasset NY), American businesswoman who in 1963, with her husband and Jean Nidetch, cofounded Weight Watchers, one of the most successful weight-loss organizations in the world.

**Little Eva** (Eva Narcissus Boyd; 29 Jun 1943, Belhaven NC—10 Apr 2003, Kinston NC), American pop singer who achieved timeless popularity in 1962 with her number one hit "Loco-Motion."

**Joan Maud Littlewood** (5/6 Oct 1914, Stockwell, England—20 Sep 2002, London, England), English director and writer who was a pioneer of radical theater whose experimental productions, often performed by and devoted to the working class, helped bring about a revolution on the British stage in the 1950s and '60s.

**Bernard Daniel Jacques Loiseau** (13 Jan 1951, Chamalières, France—24 Feb 2003, Saulieu, France), French master chef who created a light, flavorful cuisine that was regarded as among the best in Europe; he was only the second chef ever to be awarded the Legion of Honor (1995) and the first to put his company on the French stock exchange (1998). In 1975 Loiseau began working at La Côte d'Or in Burgundy. By 1991 he had earned three stars from the Michelin guide. Louiseau opened three restaurants in Paris in the late 1990s, established a line of frozen foods, and wrote a number of cookbooks.

**Alan Lomax** (15 Jan 1915, Austin TX—19 Jul 2002, Safety Harbor FL), American ethnomusicologist, one of the most dedicated and knowledgeable folk-music scholars of the 20th century; he spent a lifetime crisscrossing America to document the nation's traditional songs and singers and was instrumental in "discovering" musicians such as Leadbelly (Huddie Ledbetter), Woody Guthrie, Muddy Waters, Josh White, and Burl Ives.

**Russell Billiu Long** (3 Nov 1918, Shreveport LA—9 May 2003, Washington DC), American politician who had a major influence on US tax laws while he served (1948–87) as a Democratic US senator from Louisiana. As the powerful chairman (1969–80) of the Senate Finance Committee, he favored tax breaks for business and industry. He also spearheaded the creation of popular legislation that resulted in the earned-income tax credit, expansion of social security, federal health insurance, and the massive 1986 revision and simplification of the tax laws.

**Johnny Longden** (John Eric Longden; 14 Feb 1907, Wakefield, Yorkshire, England—14 Feb 2003, Banning CA), British-born American jockey and horse trainer who won the Triple Crown aboard Count Fleet in 1943 and was the only person to both ride and train a Kentucky Derby winner.

**Elizabeth Harman Pakenham, Countess of Longford** (30 Aug 1906, London, England—23 Oct 2002, Hurst Green, East Sussex, England), British historian and biographer who was an acclaimed author and the matriarch of one of England's most brilliant literary families—her eight children included biographer Lady Antonia Fraser, writer Thomas Pakenham, novelist Rachel Billington, and poet Judith Kazantzis.

**Franco Lucentini** (24 Dec 1920, Rome, Italy—5 Aug 2002, Turin, Italy), Italian novelist who achieved fame with Carlo Fruttero in a remarkable, if unconventional, literary partnership. The two were best known for their mystery thrillers, which were composed in a strangely businesslike manner. After choosing a subject, they worked in ping-pong fashion, one composing, the other editing and recomposing, until a novel was complete.

**Hank Luisetti** (Angelo Enrico Luisetti; 16 Jun 1916, San Francisco CA—17 Dec 2002, San Mateo CA), American collegiate basketball player who revolutionized the sport of basketball by introducing the running one-handed shot.

**Joseph Marie Antoine Hubert Luns** (28 Aug 1911, Rotterdam, The Netherlands—17 Jul 2002, Brussels, Belgium), Dutch international official who served as foreign minister of The Netherlands for 19 years before becoming secretary-general of NATO (1971–84).

**Lester Garfield Maddox** (30 Sep 1915, Atlanta GA—25 Jun 2003, Atlanta GA), American restaurateur who made national news in the 1960s when he refused to admit African Americans to his Pickrick fried-chicken restaurant in Atlanta and, on one well-publicized occasion, stood with a number of white diners and wielded pick handles to disincline blacks from entering. Maddox served as governor of Georgia (1967–71) after being elected on a technicality; he later served as lieutenant governor under Jimmy Carter.

**Luis Marden** (Annibale Luigi Paragallo; 25 Jan 1913, Chelsea MA—3 Mar 2003, Arlington VA), American photographer, writer, and explorer who discovered the wreck of HMS *Bounty*, retraced the voyages of Christopher Columbus to the New World, and revolutionized underwater color photography; he also discovered a new species of orchid and a new species of sea flea, both of which were named for him.

**Michael Marmarosa** ("Dodo"; 12 Dec 1925, Pittsburgh PA—17 Sep 2002, Pittsburgh PA), American jazz pianist who was a teenage musician in top swing bands (Gene Krupa, Charlie Barnet, and Artie Shaw) before he became one of the first pianists to master the complexities of bebop.

**Burke Marshall** (1 Oct 1922, Plainfield NJ—2 Jun 2003, Newtown CT), American lawyer who served as assistant attorney general and head of the Civil Rights Division of the US Department of Justice in the early 1960s under Robert F. Kennedy and in that position crafted the Civil Rights Act of 1964; this law banned discrimination in employment and in all public facilities and is the cornerstone of racial desegregation and of progress in equal rights since.

**A(rcher) J(ohn) P(orter) Martin** (1 Mar 1910, London, England—28 Jul 2002, Llangarron, Herefordshire, England), British biochemist who in 1952 shared the Nobel Prize in Chemistry with R.L.M. Synge for their development of partition chromatography, a sophisticated analytic technique by which samples of a mixture of closely related chemicals such as amino acids can be separated for identification and further study.

**Kohei Matsuda** (28 Jan 1922, Hiroshima, Japan—10 Jul 2002, Tokyo, Japan), Japanese corporate executive who served as president (1970–77) and chairman (1977–80) of the Mazda Motor Corp. and from 1970 owned and managed the Hiroshima Toyo Carp professional baseball team.

**Roberto Matta** (Roberto Sebastián Antonio Matta Echuarren; 11 Nov 1911, Santiago, Chile—23 Nov 2002, Civitavecchia, Italy), Chilean-born artist who referred to his paintings, which were huge and often mural-like, as "inscapes," the transference of psychic states to canvas—hence, the description of his art as hallucinatory, nightmarish, and fantastic.

**Bill Mauldin** (William Henry Mauldin; 29 Oct 1921, Mountain Park NM—23 Jan 2003, Newport Beach CA), American cartoonist who created Willie and Joe—two "everyman" dogfaces whose weary struggles against incompetent officers in addition to battles against the enemy made them inspiring symbols—and through them captured the reality of war and the way the infantrymen on the World War II battlefields experienced it; in 1945 these depictions won Mauldin the first of his two Pulitzer Prizes.

**Mauro** (Mauro Ramos de Oliveira; 30 Aug 1930, Pocos de Caldas, Minas Gerais state, Brazil—18 Sep 2002, Pocos de Caldas, Minas Gerais state, Brazil), Brazilian association football (soccer) player who was a center-half for Brazil in 23 international matches between 1949 and 1965; his career peaked in 1962 when he applied his defensive skills and cunning tactics as captain of the World Cup champion team.

**Val Irvine McCalla** (3 Oct 1943, Kingston, Jamaica—22 Aug 2002, Seaford, East Sussex, England), Jamaican-born British publisher who founded *The Voice,* a highly successful British newspaper centered on black issues and interest; he also owned *Chic* and *Pride* magazines.

**Sarah Newcomb McClendon** (8 Jul 1910, Tyler TX—8 Jan 2003, Washington DC), American journalist who became a Washington institution during her more than 50 years of service as White House correspondent for a group of Texas newspapers; known for her direct, pointed questions, she had pitched them to every US president since Franklin D. Roosevelt.

**Robert McCloskey** (14 Sep 1914, Hamilton OH—30 Jun 2003, Deer Isle ME), American writer and illustrator who delighted children with a series of books noted for their detailed illustrations and universal themes. *Make Way for Ducklings* (1941), perhaps his best-known work, follows a mallard family's journey through the streets of Boston. He was the recipient of two Caldecott Medals.

**Mark McCormack** (6 Nov 1930, Chicago IL—16 May 2003, New York NY), American sports marketing entrepreneur who began in 1960 with a handshake agreement to represent golfer Arnold Palmer as his business agent and built his enterprise into IMG (formerly International Management Group), which pioneered the idea of gaining lucrative product-endorsement deals for its clients and came to include many of the world's top sports and entertainment figures in its roster.

**Walter C. McCrone, Jr.** (9 Jun 1916, Wilmington DE—10 Jul 2002, Chicago IL), American scientist who used chemical microscopy to debunk historical myths and forgeries, disproving that the Shroud of Turin was the burial cloth of Jesus, that the celebrated Vinland Map existed before Columbus's voyages, and that Napoleon died from poisoning.

**Kathleen McGrath** (4 Jun 1952, Columbus OH—26 Sep 2002, Bethesda MD), American naval officer who was appointed captain of the guided-missile frigate USS *Jarrett* in 1998 and thereby became the first woman to command a navy warship.

**Leo McKern** (Reginald McKern; 16 Mar 1920, Sydney, Australia—23 Jul 2002, Bath, England), Australian-born British actor who gained international recognition as the irascible, henpecked, claret-swilling, deceptively crafty English barrister Horace P. Rumpole in the 44-episode TV series *Rumpole of the Bailey* (1975–92).

**Dave McNally** (David Arthur McNally; 31 Oct 1942, Billings MT—1 Dec 2002, Billings MT), American professional baseball player who was a phenomenal left-handed pitcher for the Baltimore Orioles; he completed four consecutive 20-win seasons between 1968 and 1971, appeared in three All-Star games (1969, 1970, and 1972), and helped his team win World Series titles in 1966 and 1970.

**Robert King Merton** (Meyer R. Schkolnick; 4 Jul 1910, Philadelphia PA—23 Feb 2003, New York NY), American sociologist who made wide-ranging contributions to the field, especially the sociology of science; he coined such expressions as "self-fulfilling prophecy," "role model," "unanticipated consequences," "theories of the middle range," "opportunity structure," and "focused interview" (whence "focus group"). Merton served as president of the American Sociological Association in 1957 and was the first sociologist to receive a National Medal of Science (1994).

**Leonard Michaels** (22 Jan 1933, New York NY—10 May 2003, Berkeley CA), American short-story writer who taught English literature at the University of California, Berkeley, for 24 years while writing darkly humorous stories and novels, the best known of which was probably *The Men's Club* (1981; filmed 1986).

**Patsy Mink** (Patsy Takemoto; 6 Dec 1927, Paia, Hawaii Territory—28 Sep 2002, Honolulu HI), American Democratic politician, the first Asian American woman elected to the US Congress. She served 12 terms as representative from Hawaii, 1965–77 and again from 1990, and she had just won election to another term when she died.

**Tanya Moiseiwitsch** (3 Dec 1914, London, England—19 Feb 2003, London, England), British theater designer renowned for her visionary stage designs, including the influential thrust stage at Stratford ON, and for her fruitful collaboration with director Tyrone Guthrie.

**Jürgen W. Möllemann** (15 Jul 1945, Augsburg, Germany—5 Jun 2003, Marl, Germany), German politician who held several cabinet posts from 1982, but in 1993, after only a few months in office, resigned as vice-chancellor amid accusations of corruption. During the 2002 federal election campaign, Möllemann drew sharp criticism for remarks that were perceived as anti-Semitic. He was under investigation for alleged fraud and other financial irregularities when he died in a recreational parachute jump.

**Mickie Most** (Michael Peter Hayes; 20 Jun 1938, Aldershot, Hampshire, England—30 May 2003, London, England), British pop-music producer from the mid-1960s to the mid-'80s in Great Britain; he enjoyed some 37 number-one hits (more, he claimed, than any other producer) for acts that included Donovan, Lulu, the Animals, Herman's Hermits, and Hot Chocolate and sold some 400 million records.

**Guy Reginald Mountfort** (4 Dec 1905, London, England–23 Apr 2003, Bournemouth, Dorset, England), British advertising executive, ornithologist, and conservationist who cowrote *A Field Guide to the Birds of Britain and Europe* (1954), with Roger Tory Peterson and Philip Hollom; cofounded (1961) the World Wildlife Fund (now WWF), with Peter Scott, Julian Huxley, and Max Nicholson (q.v.); and spearheaded WWF's Operation Tiger to save that species from what appeared to be imminent extinction.

**Daniel Patrick Moynihan** (16 Mar 1927, Tulsa OK–26 Mar 2003, Washington DC), American scholar and Democratic neoconservative politician who served as US senator from New York state (1977–2001). While working in the US Department of Labor in the 1960s, Moynihan co-wrote *The Negro Family: The Case for National Action,* popularly called the Moynihan Report, which held that many of the educational problems of African Americans resulted from the instability of black urban families. The report caused a storm of controversy and made Moynihan famous. He became a professor at Harvard in 1966, held advisory posts in the administration of Pres. Richard M. Nixon, and served as US ambassador to India (1973–75) and permanent representative to the UN (1975–76).

**U Ne Win** (Shu Maung; 24 May 1911, Paungdale, Burma [now Myanmar]–5 Dec 2002, Yangon [Rangoon], Myanmar), Burmese general and dictator who ruled at the head of a repressive dictatorship from March 1962, when he overthrew the elected government of Prime Minister U Nu, until he resigned in 1988.

**Roger Michael Needham** (9 Feb 1935, Sheffield, England–28 Feb 2003, Cambridge, England), British engineer and computer scientist who devised a secure way of encrypting computer password files that is the basis for all systems used today.

**Zara Nelsova** (Sara Nelson; 24 Dec 1917, Winnipeg, MB, Canada–10 Oct 2002, New York NY), Canadian-born American cellist who had a long career, beginning as a child prodigy. Called the "queen of cellists," she was known particularly for performing contemporary works, including *Schelomo* and other music by Ernest Bloch.

**Lucas Moreira Cardinal Neves** (16 Sep 1925, São João del Rei, Minas Gerais state, Brazil–8 Sep 2002, Rome, Italy), Brazilian-born Roman Catholic prelate who served in key Vatican posts (1974–87) and as archbishop (1987–98) of São Salvador da Bahia, where he spurred construction of a refuge for children and supported the Landless Workers Movement.

**Mickey Newbury** (Milton Sim Newbury; 19 May 1940, Houston TX–29 Sep 2002, Springfield OR), American songwriter and musician who wrote more than 500 songs. More literate and reflective than much of the music of the time, they were performed primarily by country singers but also by rhythm-and-blues artists and by mainstream musicians.

**François Xavier Cardinal Nguyen Van Thuan** (17 Apr 1928, Phu Cam, French Indochina–16 Sep 2002, Rome, Italy), Vietnamese Roman Catholic prelate who maintained his strong faith during 13 years of imprisonment in his homeland. In 1998 Thuan was named president of the Pontifical Commission for Justice and Peace, and in 2001 he was appointed cardinal.

**(Edward) Max Nicholson** (12 July 1904, Kiltenan, County Dublin, Ireland–26 Apr 2003, London, England), British ornithologist, environmentalist, and civil servant who cofounded (1961), with Julian Huxley, Peter Scott, and Guy Mountfort (q.v.), the World Wildlife Fund (now WWF) and was instrumental in the creation of the government-sponsored Nature Conservancy (now English Nature), of which he was director-general (1952–66).

**Alan Nunn May** (2 May 1911, Birmingham, England–12 Jan 2003, Cambridge, England), British nuclear physicist and one of the first Cold War atomic spies for the Soviet Union.

**Kristen Nygaard** (27 Aug 1926, Oslo, Norway–10 Aug 2002, Oslo, Norway), Norwegian mathematician and computer scientist who invented, with his coworker Ole-Johan Dahl, the computer programming language SIMULA, and they shared both the 2001 A.M. Turing Award and the IEEE 2002 John von Neumann Medal.

**Thomas Risley Odhiambo** (4 Feb 1931, Alego, Nyanza province, Kenya Colony–26 May 2003, Nairobi, Kenya), Kenyan entomologist; he was renowned for his research into nonchemical methods of agricultural insect control and was a pioneer in the promotion of indigenous African scientific education and research. He was the founding director general (1970–94) of the multidisciplinary, Nairobi-based International Centre of Insect Physiology and Ecology, the first dean (from 1970) of the University of Nairobi's department of agriculture, and founding president (1986–99) of the African Academy of Sciences.

**Eugene Pleasants Odum** (17 Sep 1913, Lake Sunapee NH–10 Aug 2002, Athens GA), American ecologist who brought prestige to the little-known field of ecology, helping to transform it from a subdivision of biology into a widely taught discipline of its own; he and his brother Howard Thomas Odum (q.v.), also an ecologist, were awarded the Crafoord Prize in 1987 "for pioneering contributions within the field of ecosystem ecology."

**Howard Thomas Odum** (1 Sep 1924, Durham NC–11 Sep 2002, Gainesville FL), American ecologist who often collaborated with his older brother, Eugene (q.v.); his research and advocacy in southern Florida were a boost to the preservation of the Everglades.

**Babatunde Olatunji** (1927, Ajido, Nigeria–6 Apr 2003, Salinas CA), Nigerian-born drummer who brought the sound of African drumming to an American audience and influenced a number of jazz and rock musicians. His seminal album, *Drums of Passion* (1959), was credited with sparking a vogue for Afro-jazz-fusion music in the 1960s.

**Suliman Saleh Olayan** (5 Nov 1918, Unayzah, [Saudi] Arabia–4 Jul 2002, New York NY), Saudi businessman, the founder of the Olayan Group, one of the largest and most successful corporations in Saudi Arabia; in 2001 Olayan with included on *Forbes* magazine's list of the world's richest people.

**Sydney Omarr** (Sidney Kimmelman; 5 Aug 1926, Philadelphia PA–2 Jan 2003, Santa Monica CA), American astrologer who became the most widely read horoscope writer in the world; he wrote 13 books a year; his columns were published in more than 200 newspapers; and he served as consultant to a number of celebrities.

**Adam Osborne** (6 Mar 1939, Thailand–18 Mar 2003, Kodaikanal, India), American computer engineer who originated the idea of a portable computer and, with Lee Felsenstein, cofounded (1981) the Osborne Computer Corp., to manufacture the

$1,800 11 kg (25 lb) machine with a 4MHz CPU, 64KB of RAM, and a 5-in built-in monochrome monitor. The company went bankrupt in 1983. Osborne started a software company, Paperback Software, which also went under following a law suit by the Lotus Development Corp. in 1987.

**Jorge Oteiza Embil** (21 Oct 1908, Orio, Spain–9 Apr 2003, San Sebastián, Spain), Spanish Basque sculptor who examined the nature of space and emptiness in monumental, minimalist sculptures that were influential in the art world of the mid-20th century. Oteiza won the grand prize for sculpture at the 1957 São Paulo (Brazil) Biennale, the Spanish Medal of Fine Arts (1985), the Prince of Asturias Art Prize (1988), and the Gold Medal of Navarre (1992).

**Ludek Pachman** (11 May 1924, Bela pod Bezdezem, Czechoslovakia [now in Czech Republic]–6 Mar 2003, Passau, Germany), Czech chess grand master who had a distinguished chess career, wrote respected books on the game, and vociferously criticized the Communist government of Czechoslovakia.

**Nani Adeshir Palkhivala** (16 Jan 1920, Bombay [now Mumbai], British India–11 Dec 2002, Mumbai, India), Indian jurist and civil rights activist who was revered in India as a top authority on constitutional law and government finance.

**Bruce Paltrow** (26 Nov 1943, Brooklyn NY–3 Oct 2002, Rome, Italy), American TV producer and director who earned critical acclaim as the genius behind the 1980s hit medical series *St. Elsewhere.* Previously, he had directed, written, and produced *The White Shadow.*

**Suzy Parker** (Cecilia Ann Renee Parker; married name Dillman; 28 Oct 1933, Long Island City NY–3 May 2003, Montecito CA), American model and actress who had a beauty and sophistication that led to her paving the way for future supermodels by becoming the first model to make more than $100 an hour and $100,000 a year.

**Valentin Sergeyevich Pavlov** (26 Sep 1937, Moscow, USSR–30 Mar 2003, Moscow, Russia), Soviet politician who was briefly prime minister of the USSR; he participated in the failed coup of August 1991 against Soviet Pres. Mikhail Gorbachev.

**Johnny PayCheck** (Donald Eugene Lytle; 31 May 1938, Greenfield OH–18 Feb 2003, Nashville TN), American country musician, a hard-living honky-tonk singer and songwriter who recorded 70 albums and had dozens of hit singles, but he was most widely recognized for his phenomenally popular 1977 cover of David Allan Coe's workingman anthem "Take This Job and Shove It."

**(Eldred) Gregory Peck** (5 Apr 1916, La Jolla CA–12 Jun 2003, Los Angeles CA), American film actor known for playing characters of integrity—for example, Atticus Finch in *To Kill a Mockingbird* (1962; Academy Award for best actor). Peck's film credits were legion from his first film, *Days of Glory* (1944), and included Alfred Hitchcock's *Spellbound* (1945), *Gentleman's Agreement* (1947; Academy Award for best picture), *Captain Horatio Hornblower* (1951), *Roman Holiday* (1953; Academy Award for Peck's costar, Audrey Hepburn), *The Guns of Navarone* (1961), and *The Boys from Brazil* (1978), in which he played Nazi doctor Joseph Mengele. Peck's last appearance was a cameo role in a 1998 TV version of *Moby Dick*; he had starred as Captain Ahab in the 1956 film version.

**Vladislas ("Vlado") Perlemuter** (26 May 1904, Kovno, Lithuania, Russian Empire [now Kaunas, Lithuania]–4 Sep 2002, Paris, France), Lithuanian-born French pianist who became one of the 20th century's foremost interpreters of the works of Ravel and Chopin, avoiding grandiose showmanship and theatrics for tonal sonority and rhythmic subtlety.

**Goffredo Petrassi** (16 Jul 1904, Zagarolo, Italy–2 Mar 2003, Rome, Italy), Italian composer who was one of the leading creators of Italian modernist music. His progressive exploration of compositional styles was exemplified in his eight concertos for orchestra. His last major work was the large choral piece *Orationes Christi* (1974–75).

**William Phillips** (14 Nov 1907, New York NY–13 Sep 2002, New York NY), American editor who was the cofounder of *Partisan Review,* an influential magazine of politics, literature, and culture.

**Maurice Pialat** (31 Aug 1925, Cunlhat, France–11 Jan 2003, Paris, France), French film director who created a body of work that is considered among the best of modern French cinema; his movies painted domestic desperation and were notable for their immediacy and difficulty.

**George Porter, Baron Porter of Luddenham** (6 Dec 1920, Stainforth, Yorkshire, England–31 Aug 2002, Canterbury, England), British chemist who was corecipient with Ronald G.W. Norrish and Manfred Eigen of the 1967 Nobel Prize for Chemistry for their studies in flash photolysis, a technique for observing the intermediate stages of very fast chemical reactions by subjecting a gas or liquid to short bursts of light that disturb its molecular equilibrium and allow the resulting intermediates to be analyzed spectroscopically.

**Chaim Potok** (Herman Harold Potok; 17 Feb 1929, New York NY–23 Jul 2002, Merion PA), American writer who explored the conflict between Jewish religious traditions and the secular world in such novels as *The Chosen* (1967), *The Promise* (1969), *My Name Is Asher Lev* (1972), and *The Gift of Asher Lev* (1990).

**Richard (Hooper) Pough** (19 Apr 1904, Brooklyn NY–24 Jun 2003, Chilmark MA), American ornithologist and conservationist who served as the founding president (1954–56) of the Nature Conservancy (formerly known as the Ecologists Union), which became one of the world's leading land-conservation organizations.

**Sir (Arnold Joseph) Philip Powell** (15 Mar 1921, Bedford, Bedfordshire, England–5 May 2003, London, England), British architect who, with his longtime partner, Hidalgo Moya, designed the Skylon "vertical feature" at the 1951 Festival of Britain; the award-winning Bauhaus-influenced Churchill Gardens in Pimlico, West London; Wolfson College, Oxford; the Chichester Festival Theatre; and the Museum of London.

**Ilya Prigogine** (25 Jan 1917, Moscow, Russia–28 May 2003, Brussels, Belgium), Russian-born Belgian physical chemist who was awarded the 1977 Nobel Prize for Chemistry for contributions to the understanding of nonequilibrium thermodynamics. In particular, Prigogine helped explain how complex systems, including living organisms, could arise spontaneously from less-ordered states and maintain themselves in apparent defiance of the classical laws of physics. His work was influential in a wide variety of fields, from physical chemistry to biology, and he was considered the "grandfather" of the new discipline of chaos theory.

**Abdul Qadir** (1954?, Sorkh Rod, Afghanistan—6 Jul 2002, Kabul, Afghanistan), Afghan warlord and political official, a Pashtun with a power base in Nangarhar province, who was assassinated less than three weeks after he had assumed the post of one of the country's new vice presidents.

**John Bordley Rawls** (21 Feb 1921, Baltimore MD—24 Nov 2002, Lexington MA), American philosopher who was among the most influential political thinkers of the 20th century.

**Grote Reber** (22 Dec 1911, Wheaton IL—20 Dec 2002, Tasmania, Australia), American astronomer and radio engineer who was widely regarded as the father of radio astronomy. In 1937 he constructed the world's first radio telescope—a bowl-shaped antenna 9.4 m (31 ft) in diameter—in the backyard of his home.

**Leighton Thomas Rees** (17 Jan 1940, Ynysybwl, Wales—8 Jun 2003, Pontypridd, Wales), Welsh darts player; was the first Embassy world professional darts champion (1978) and helped to popularize darts as a television spectator sport throughout the UK. Rees was Welsh champion in 1970, 1974, and 1976 and represented Wales 77 times in international darts competitions.

**Donald (Thomas) Regan** (21 Dec 1918, Cambridge MA—10 Jun 2003, Williamsburg VA), American businessman and politician who was the innovative chairman of Merrill Lynch & Co. (1971–80) before becoming a top aide to Pres. Ronald Reagan, serving as treasury secretary (1981–85) and chief of staff (1985–87). Regan first attracted national attention after transforming Merrill Lynch from a brokerage firm into a full-service financial company with activities in consulting, real estate, credit cards, and checking. After joining the Reagan administration, Regan came to wield great power and in 1986 helped implement a landmark tax reform. The Iran-Contra scandal and a growing feud with First Lady Nancy Reagan, however, forced Regan out of office in 1987.

**Karel Reisz** (21 Jul 1926, Ostrava, Czechoslovakia [now in the Czech Republic]—25 Nov 2002, London, England), Czech-born British film and stage director who made only 11 movies during his career but was instrumental in the creation of British new wave cinema in the 1960s.

**George Rickey** (6 Jun 1907, South Bend IN—17 Jul 2002, St. Paul MN), American sculptor who combined engineered exactness and visual minimalism to create stainless steel forms that, powered only by gravitation and natural wind patterns, teetered between equilibrium and motion; his work culminated with a 17.3-m (57-ft) sculpture that was installed in the Hyogo Museum, Japan, in March 2002.

**Aileen Riggin** (Aileen Riggin Soule; 2 May 1906, Newport RI—17 Oct 2002, Honolulu HI), American swimmer and diver who was the youngest American to win an Olympic gold medal and the first Olympic competitor to win medals in both swimming and diving at the same Games (in 1924).

**Herb Ritts** (Herbert Ritts, Jr.; August 1952, Los Angeles CA—26 Dec 2002, Los Angeles CA), American photographer who excelled in capturing images that celebrated the beauty of the human body—especially the male body—and in creating stylish, unorthodox portraits of celebrities; his efforts gained him such renown that he achieved nearly as much fame as his subjects.

**Larry Rivers** (Yitzroch Loiza Grossberg; 17 Aug 1923, New York NY—14 Aug 2002, Southampton NY), American painter whose works frequently combined the vigorous, painterly brushstrokes of Abstract Expressionism with the commercial images of the Pop art movement.

**J(ohn) M(orris) Roberts** (14 Apr 1928, Bath, Somerset, England—30 May 2003, Roadwater, Somerset, England), British historian who not only was a respected academician, scholar, and writer, but captured the viewing public's fancy as the presenter of *The Triumph of the West* (1985), a 13-part television series in which he analyzed how Western civilization came to dominate the modern world. In addition to writing several histories of Western civilization, he was editor (1967–77) of *The English Historical Review* and general editor of *Purnell's History of the 20th Century, Short Oxford History of the Modern World,* and *New Oxford History of England.*

**Roberto Rocca** (February 1922, Milan, Italy—10 Jun 2003, Milan, Italy), Italian-born Argentine industrialist who from 1978 was chairman of Techint, the enterprise his father, an Italian immigrant to Argentina, founded in 1945 to manufacture steel pipe. The holding company, Techint, based in Buenos Aires, Argentina, and Milan, Italy, grew to embrace more than 100 manufacturing, engineering, and construction companies, with 50,000 employees and revenues of $7.5 billion. In 2002, following a series of mergers, the seamless-steel-tube manufacturing activity was consolidated into a company named Tenaris, which is listed on the New York and Buenos Aires stock exchanges.

**Fred (McFeely) Rogers** (20 Mar 1928, Latrobe PA—27 Feb 2003, Pittsburgh PA), American television producer, writer, and actor who was the friend of millions of children for his empathy for the emotions they experienced and for the way he taught them how to get along with others, feel good about themselves, and cope with their fears. Singing the familiar "It's a beautiful day in the neighborhood" theme and putting on his sneakers and trademark zippered cardigan, he would open his public television program, *Mr. Rogers' Neighborhood,* and settle in with his viewers to begin the topic of the day; besides producing, writing the scripts, and serving as host, he wrote about 200 songs for the program, some 1,000 episodes of which were broadcast on PBS between 1968 and 2001.

**Henri Rol-Tanguy** (Henri Tanguy; 12 Jun 1908, Morlaix, France—8 Sep 2002, Monteaux?, France), French World War II Resistance leader who commanded the Resistance forces during the Parisian uprising against German occupation; he helped liberate Paris in August 1944 and was one of those who signed the document accepting Germany's surrender of the city.

**Bud Roper** (Burns Worthington Roper; 26 Feb 1925, Creston IA—20 Jan 2003, Bourne MA), American pollster, for decades chairman (1946–93) of the polling organization founded by his father and now known as RoperASW and chairman (1970–94) of the Roper Center for Public Opinion Research at the University of Connecticut.

**William Rosenberg** (10 Jun 1916, Boston MA—20 Sep 2002, Mashpee MA), American entrepreneur who founded the iconic Dunkin' Donuts chain, the largest coffee and pastry chain in the world.

**Manuel Rosenthal** (18 Jun 1904, Paris, France—5 Jun 2003, Paris, France), French composer and conductor; he championed modern French composers, notably Jacques Offenbach, Igor Stravinsky,

Olivier Messiaen, and Maurice Ravel, who took on Rosenthal as his third and last composition student in 1926 and who remained a close friend. Rosenthal was principal conductor of the French National Orchestra (1944–47), the Seattle Symphony (1948–51), and the Liège Symphony Orchestra (1964–67) and was professor of conducting (1962–74) at the Paris Conservatory. His best-known work, *Gaîté Parisienne* (1938), was a ballet suite based on music by Offenbach.

**Bertram Ross** (13 Nov 1920, Brooklyn NY—20 Apr 2003, New York NY), American dancer, choreographer, and cabaret singer who for 20 years (1953–73) was partnered with Martha Graham and was a custodian of her art, before beginning a successful career as a cabaret performer. He created dozens of roles with Graham, among them St. Michael in *Seraphic Dialogue* (1955), Agamemnon and Orestes in *Clytemnestra* (1958), and Adam in *Embattled Garden* (1958).

**Walt Whitman Rostow** (7 Oct 1916, New York NY—13 Feb 2003, Austin TX), American economic historian and government official who, as an adviser to presidents John F. Kennedy and Lyndon Johnson, advocated ever-increasing American commitment to the Vietnam War (1955–75), even after most other government officials had become convinced that the war was unwinnable.

**Galen Rowell** (23 Aug 1940, Berkeley CA—11 Aug 2002, near Bishop CA), American landscape photographer who captured breathtaking images of some of the remotest parts of the world. He used his work to further conservation awareness in an attempt to preserve the delicate regions he photographed. He and his wife, Barbara—an acclaimed writer, photographer, and pilot—died in a plane crash.

**Nikolay (Nikolayevich) Rukavishnikov** (18 Sep 1932, Tomsk, Siberia, USSR—19 Oct 2002, Moscow, Russia), Russian cosmonaut who, on his third trip into space, became the first cosmonaut to land a spacecraft manually.

**Prince Sadruddin Aga Khan** (17 Jan 1933, Paris, France—12 May 2003, Boston MA), international official; as the longest serving UN High Commissioner for Refugees (1965–77) he coordinated relief and resettlement efforts throughout the world, including in Bangladesh, Uganda, Vietnam, Angola, The Sudan, Burundi, Algeria, Chile, Cyprus, and the Middle East. He also worked with UNESCO, headed two environmental foundations, was humanitarian envoy to Afghanistan in the late 1980s, and, from 1992, served as UN chargé de mission. Prince Sadruddin was the younger son of Sir Sultan Mohammed Shah, the Aga Khan III, imam of the Nizari Isma'ilite Shi'ite Muslim sect, and was the uncle of the Aga Khan IV.

**Fidel Sánchez Hernández** (7 Jul 1917, El Divisadero, El Salvador—28 Feb 2003, San Salvador, El Salvador), El Salvadoran politician and military man who, as president of El Salvador (1967–72), led the country into the so-called Soccer War. In 1969 El Salvador and Honduras were experiencing tension over a border dispute and a plan by Honduras forcibly to repatriate hundreds of thousands of El Salvadorans. In this climate, a disputed World Cup association football (soccer) qualifying match touched off rioting, and El Salvador invaded Honduras on 14 July. Less than two weeks later, the Organization of American States stepped in to halt the war.

**Mongo Santamaria** (Ramón Santamaria; 7 Apr 1922, Havana, Cuba—1 Feb 2003, Miami FL), Cuban-born American conga drummer who played for years with mambo stars such as Perez Prado, Tito Puente, and Cal Tjader before forming his own bands and becoming a Latin jazz giant himself; in 1959 he composed the jazz standard "Afro Blue" and recorded several hits, notably "Watermelon Man" (1963).

**John Patrick Savage** (28 May 1932, Newport, Wales—13 May 2003, Nova Scotia, Canada), British-born Canadian politician and physician; he ended 17 years of Progressive Conservative rule in Nova Scotia when he was elected the Liberal premier of the province in 1993. Savage was the first premier of the province since Confederation who was not born in Canada. Savage's tenure was marked by turbulence; he slashed government spending and jobs and faced opposition within his own party when he refused to approve patronage jobs. When he resigned in 1997, following an opinion poll that showed that he had only a 19% approval rating among Nova Scotians, he returned to medicine and was instrumental in establishing medical centers and educational programs in Africa.

**Boris Schapiro** (22 Aug [9 Aug old style] 1909, Riga, Latvia, Russian Empire—1 Dec 2002, Long Crendon, Buckinghamshire, England), British contract bridge player who represented Great Britain in numerous international contract bridge tournaments and was a member of the national team that was victorious at the 1955 Bermuda Bowl world championship. He wrote the contract bridge column for *The Sunday Times* from 1966.

**John Schlesinger** (16 Feb 1926, London, England—25 Jul 2003, Palm Springs CA), English director known for sensitively told stories, including *Far from the Madding Crowd* (1967), *Midnight Cowboy* (1969; Academy Award for direction), and *Cold Comfort Farm* (1995).

**Laurent-Moïse Schwartz** (5 Mar 1915, Paris, France—4 Jul 2002, Paris, France), French mathematician who was awarded the Fields Medal in 1950 for his work on the theory of distributions.

**Martha (Ellen) Scott** (22 Sep 1914, Jamesport MO—28 May 2003, Van Nuys CA), American actress who made her Broadway debut as Emily in 1938 in the original production of Thornton Wilder's *Our Town,* made her film debut in the same role two years later, and over the next 60 years appeared in some 20 other motion pictures, about the same number of Broadway productions, and numerous television programs, in addition to serving as producer of several plays.

**Belding H(ibbard) Scribner** (18 Jan 1921, Chicago IL—19 Jun 2003, Seattle WA), American physician who revolutionized kidney dialysis by creating in 1960 the Scribner shunt, a device that allowed patients to receive long-term dialysis. Sewn into arteries and veins, the shunt eliminated the progressive damage caused by repeatedly inserting tubes from the dialysis machine directly into blood vessels, the method previously used. Scribner also oversaw the creation of committees to determine which patients would receive dialysis, thereby laying the foundations for bioethics committees. In 2002 he was awarded the Albert Lasker Award for Clinical Medical Research.

**Compay Segundo** (Máximo Francisco Repilado Muñoz; 18 Nov 1907, Siboney, Cuba—13 Jul 2003,

Havana, Cuba), Cuban musician, player of the *tres* (a kind of guitar) and clarinet, who was an important player of *son* music from the 1930s through the '50s; he was made famous a second time by the Buena Vista Social Club project; he won a Grammy Award in 1997.

**Barry Sheene** (11 Sep 1950, London, England—10 Mar 2003, Gold Coast, QLD, Australia), British motorcycle racer who brought widespread popularity to the sport, with his irreverent, playboy reputation and seeming indestructibility; he won two 500cc world championships (1976 and 1977) racing for Suzuki.

**Salah Mustafa Shehada** (1953, Beit Hanoun, Gaza Strip—22 Jul 2002, Gaza City, Gaza Strip), Palestinian guerrilla leader who was the commander of Izz al-Din al-Qassam, the military wing of the anti-Israeli Hamas (Islamic Resistance Movement); he was killed in an Israeli air strike against his home.

**Robert Marvin Shelton, Jr.** (12 Jun 1929, Tuscaloosa AL—17 Mar 2003, Tuscaloosa AL), American imperial wizard (1961–2003) of the United Klans of America, Inc., Knights of the Ku Klux Klan, a group associated with some of the most virulent and violent racist acts, particularly during the 1960s; Shelton spent nine months in jail in 1969–70 for contempt of Congress.

**Carol Shields** (Carol Warner; 2 Jun 1935, Oak Park IL—16 Jul 2003, Victoria, BC, Canada), American-born Canadian novelist who wrote stories about women's friendships and their inner moral and intellectual lives. In 1995 *The Stone Diaries* (1993) was awarded the Pulitzer Prize for Fiction after having won the 1993 Canadian Governor General's Literary Award and the 1994 National Book Critics Circle Award for fiction; Shields's *Unless* was short-listed for the Booker Prize in 2002.

**Richard W. Simmons** (19 Aug 1913, St. Paul MN—11 Jan 2003, Oceanside CA), American actor who appeared in numerous movies and television series during his 40-year career, most notably the 1950s TV series *Sergeant Preston of the Yukon*.

**Nina Simone** (Eunice Kathleen Waymon; 21 Feb 1933, Tryon NC—21 Apr 2003, Carry-le-Rouet, France), American singer who created urgent emotional intensity by singing songs of love, protest, and black empowerment in a dramatic style, with a rough-edged voice. Originally noted as a jazz singer, she became a prominent voice of the 1960s civil rights movement with recordings such as "Mississippi Goddam!" and "Old Jim Crow." Her best-known composition was "To Be Young, Gifted, and Black"; she also recorded songs by rock and pop songwriters.

**Sandman Sims** (Howard Sims; 24 Jan 1917, Fort Smith AR—20 May 2003, Bronx NY), American tap dancer who got his nickname from dancing on sand to achieve a unique soft brushing sound. In addition to dancing, he taught footwork to such dancers as Gregory Hines and Ben Vereen as well as to boxers, including Muhammad Ali, and off and on for three decades served Harlem's Apollo Theater in New York City as its "executioner" on amateur nights, ridding the stage of unpopular acts.

**Walter Max Ulyate Sisulu** (18 May 1912, Engcobo, South Africa—5 May 2003, Johannesburg, South Africa), South African political activist and a prominent African National Congress (ANC) member who helped lead the battle against apartheid. Before joining the ANC in 1940, he had been involved in trade union activism for some years. Sisulu met Nelson Mandela in 1941 and recruited him into the ANC. Under the leadership of Sisulu, Mandela, Oliver Tambo, and Albert Luthuli, the ANC and its Youth League sponsored nonviolent demonstrations, strikes, and boycotts to protest apartheid in the 1940s and '50s. Along with Mandela and 154 others, Sisulu was arrested for treason in 1956 but was acquitted after a four-year trial. He was arrested again with other top ANC leaders in 1963 and remained in prison until October 1989. After his release, Sisulu served as deputy president of the ANC and remained one of Mandela's closest confidants.

**Enos Bradsher Slaughter** ("Country"; 27 Apr 1916, Roxboro NC—12 Aug 2002, Durham NC), American baseball player who had a lifetime .300 batting average and was a hero of the St. Louis Cardinals, for whom he played 13 of his 19 major league seasons. He was a hard-hitting outfielder who led the National League in hits in 1942 and in runs batted in 1946; he played in 10 All-Star games and was elected in 1985 to the Baseball Hall of Fame.

**Mia Slavenska** (Mia Corak; 20 Feb 1914 [or 1916], Brodna Savi [now Slavonski Brod], Croatia—5 Oct 2002, Westwood CA), Croatian-born American ballerina and teacher who was celebrated for her powerful stage presence, enhanced by her dazzling virtuoso technique and dramatic flair, as well as the beauty of her face and red hair.

**Peter Denham Smithson** (18 Sep 1923, Stockton-on-Tees, Durham, England—3 Mar 2003, London, England), British architect who, with his wife, Alison, was among the foremost proponents of the New Brutalism style of architecture, which signified a new respect for the functionality of materials. Perhaps the most successful of the Smithson team's buildings was the Economist Building Group in St. James's, Westminster, in London (completed 1964), a miniaturized high-rise complex that is integrated into the fabric of the surrounding neighborhood.

**Alberto Sordi** (15 Jun 1919?, Rome, Italy—24 Feb 2003, Rome, Italy), Italian film actor who depicted the vices, virtues, and foibles of post–World War II Italy in a long career of mostly comic films; he was regarded as a national icon.

**Robert Stack** (Robert Longford Modini; 13 Jan 1919, Los Angeles CA—14 May 2003, Los Angeles CA), American actor who had a notable six-decade career that saw him go from giving former child star Deanna Durbin her first screen kiss in *First Love* (1939) to portraying more substantial characters in films that included *The High and the Mighty* (1954) and *Written on the Wind* (1956). The role that cemented his fame, however, was that of crime fighter Eliot Ness in the television series *The Untouchables* (1959–63), for which he won an Emmy Award in 1960. He parodied his stalwart-character type in the disaster spoof *Airplane* (1980) but later returned to it to be the serious host and narrator of the TV series *Unsolved Mysteries* (1988–2002).

**Edwin Starr** (Charles Edwin Hatcher; 21 Jan 1942, Nashville TN—2 Apr 2003, Bramcote, Nottinghamshire, England), American musician who achieved enduring popularity with his classic 1970 recording of the antiwar protest song "War," which remained on the pop charts for 13 weeks.

**Rod Steiger** (Rodney Steven Steiger; 14 Apr 1925, Westhampton NY—9 Jul 2002, Los Angeles CA), American film actor of great intensity whose works include *On the Waterfront* (1954), *Oklahoma!*

(1955), *The Pawnbroker* (1964), and *In the Heat of the Night* (1967).

**Alexander Rawson Stokes** (27 Jun 1919, Macclesfield, Cheshire, England–5 Feb 2003, Welwyn Garden City, near London, England), British mathematical physicist who demonstrated mathematically that DNA has a helical molecular structure, thus providing the foundation for the 1953 discovery of DNA's double helix by Francis Crick and James Watson.

**Peter Stone** (27 Feb 1930, Los Angeles CA–26 Apr 2003, New York NY), American screenwriter and librettist who was the first writer to win the Emmy, Oscar, and Tony awards. He won his first award, an Emmy, for *The Defenders* in the early 1960s. His first movie script was *Charade* (1963); other notable films included *Father Goose* (1964), for which he won an Oscar for best original screenplay, *Sweet Charity* (1969), and *The Taking of Pelham One Two Three* (1974). His first Broadway success was the book for the 1969 musical *1776*; the play won that year's Tony Award for best musical. He won Tony Awards for his books for *Woman of the Year* in 1981 and *Titanic* in 1997.

**W(illiam) Clement Stone** (4 May 1902, Chicago IL–3 Sep 2002, Evanston IL), American businessman and philanthropist who made a fortune in insurance but became better known for promoting his philosophy of success and for his support of political and social causes. He espoused what he called P.M.A. (positive mental attitude) as the key to achievement and wealth.

**Joe Strummer** (John Graham Mellor; 21 Aug 1952, Ankara, Turkey–22 Dec 2002, Broomfield, Somerset, England), British punk rock star who gave voice to a generation of unrest as leader of the Clash, and the band's passionate, politicized sounds were due in large part to Strummer's commitment to a populist ideology. The Clash was inducted into the Rock and Roll Hall of Fame in 2003.

**F(rederick) William Sunderman** (23 Oct 1898, Juniata PA–9 Mar 2003, Philadelphia PA), American scientist, physician, editor, and musician who was honored as the nation's oldest worker in 1998, when he reached 100 years old; he continued working into 2003. Sunderman was one of the first doctors to treat a diabetic coma patient with insulin. He invented a widely used instrument for testing glucose levels in blood and developed quality-control methods for medical laboratories that served as the standard for 36 years. He was medical director for the Manhattan Project at Los Alamos NM and later worked for the Centers for Disease Control.

**Tauese P.F. Sunia** (29 Aug 1941, Fagatogo, American Samoa–26 Mar 2003, en route to Honolulu HI), American politician; a Democrat, he served as governor of American Samoa from 1997 to 2003.

**Roman Tam** (Tam Pak-sin; 1949, Guangxi province [now Guangxi Zhuang Autonomous Region], China–18 Oct 2002, Hong Kong), Chinese pop musician; he was a flamboyant showman with an androgynous persona and a campy style, and was a star for three decades; because of his influence on younger musicians, he became known as the "godfather" of Hong Kong music.

**Sir Denis Thatcher** (10 May 1915, London, England–26 Jun 2003, London, England), British businessman and political spouse; as the devoted husband and confidant of British Prime Minister Margaret Thatcher, he was the object of public criticism and political satire, but he endured his seemingly thankless job with great style and self-deprecating good humor. Thatcher was a wealthy chemical executive when he married Margaret Roberts in 1951, and he served as a corporate director after his business was taken over by Burmah Oil in 1965. He was made a Member of the British Empire in his own right in 1944 and a hereditary baronet in 1991 shortly after his wife resigned from office.

**Lynne Thigpen** (22 Dec 1948, Joliet IL–12 Mar 2003, Los Angeles CA), American character actress on stage, screen, and television. In 1971 she was cast in the original production of *Godspell,* and in 1973 her first movie appearance was also in *Godspell.* She won a Tony Award for her role in *An American Daughter.* She was best known for her TV roles, however, which included a regular part on the soap opera *All My Children* (1993–2000), and a costarring role in the series *The District,* beginning in 2000.

**René Frédéric Thom** (2 Sep 1923, Montbéliard, France–25 Oct 2002, Bures-sur-Yvette, France), French mathematical philosopher who was awarded the Fields Medal in 1958 for his work in topology, notably for his introduction of the concept of cobordism for classifying differentiable manifolds. He was better known, however, for his development of catastrophe theory, which he introduced in 1972 to explain biological growth and differentiation—in particular, how slow, continuous growth may lead to a sudden ("catastrophic") change in form.

**Benjamin C. Thompson** (3 Jul 1918, St. Paul MN–17 Aug 2002, Cambridge MA), American architect, known for his designs of "festival marketplaces" in US cities, such as those at Faneuil Hall in Boston (1976) and Harborplace in Baltimore (1980).

**J(ohn) Lee Thompson** (1 Aug 1914, Bristol, Gloucestershire, England–30 Aug 2002, Sooke, BC, Canada), British-born film director who achieved international fame with *The Guns of Navarone* (1961), which exemplified his acute visual style and use of suspenseful narrative.

**(James) Strom Thurmond** (5 Dec 1902, Edgefield SC–26 Jun 2003, Edgefield SC), American politician who was the longest-serving senator (1954–2003) in US history and came to personify the changing political landscape of the South. Elected governor of South Carolina in 1946, Thurmond supported a number of progressive measures, including the improvement of African American schools and equal pay for women. In 1948 he gained national attention as the leader of a group of Southern democrats who broke with the Democratic Party over civil rights. They formed the States' Rights Democratic Party—popularly known as the Dixiecrats—and adopted a segregation platform with Thurmond as their presidential candidate. Thurmond lost, but the election marked the beginning of the decline in Southern white voters' support of the Democratic Party. In 1954 Thurmond became the first person elected to the US Senate as a write-in candidate. He quickly aligned himself with other Southern conservatives, supporting increased military spending and denouncing civil-rights legislation. After the enactment of the Civil Rights Act (1964), an angered Thurmond switched to the Republican Party. By the early 1970s, however, as integration and civil rights became inevitable, Thurmond changed his stance. In 1996 he became the oldest person to serve in the Senate, but failing health forced him to retire in 2003.

**To Huu** (Nguyen Kim Thanh; 1920, Hue, Vietnam, French Indochina—9 Dec 2002, Hanoi, Vietnam), Vietnamese poet and politician who was hailed as North Vietnam's poet laureate and inspired generations of fellow Communist Party members with his popular propagandistic verse.

**Sir (Reginald Stephen) Garfield Todd** (13 Jul 1908, Invercargill, New Zealand—13 Oct 2002, Bulawayo, Zimbabwe), New Zealand–born Zimbabwean politician who served from 1953 to 1958 as prime minister of the Federation of Rhodesia and Nyasaland (now divided into Zimbabwe, Zambia, and Malawi).

**Youssouf Togoimi** (1953?—24 Sep 2002, Tripoli, Libya), Chadian defense minister and later a rebel leader, the founder (in 1998) of the Movement for Democracy and Justice in Chad that carried on a guerrilla war in the Tibesti region against the central government.

**Beatriz Mariana Torres** (Lolita; 26 Mar 1930, Avellaneda, Argentina—14 Sep 2002, Buenos Aires, Argentina), Argentine actress who gained renown and the admiration of international audiences for her roles in musical comedies, which showcased her fine singing voice. Her popularity was due in part to the balance of tradition and independence in her roles that appealed to a changing Argentine society.

**H.R. Trevor-Roper** (Hugh Redwald Trevor-Roper, Baron Dacre of Glanton; 15 Jan 1914, Glanton, Northumberland, England—26 Jan 2003, Oxford, England), British historian and scholar noted for his works on aspects of World War II and Elizabethan history; he was catapulted into the public eye in an unfortunate way in 1983, when he authenticated as genuine some 60 volumes of diaries purported to be those of Adolf Hitler (and said to have been found by the German newsmagazine *Stern*); they proved to be a forgery, and he had to issue a public apology.

**José Trías Monge** (5 May 1920, San Juan PR—24 Jun 2003, Boston MA), Puerto Rican government official and judge who was heavily involved with drafting the Puerto Rican constitution, which took effect in 1952. Under its terms Puerto Rico bound itself to the US and acquired approximately the same level of self-government as the 50 US states. Later, Trías Monge, who served as attorney general (1953–57) and chief justice (1974–85) of Puerto Rico, decried the status of the island in the book *Puerto Rico: The Trials of the Oldest Colony in the World* (1997).

**Bobbi Trout** (Evelyn Trout; 7 Jan 1906, Greenup IL—24 Jan 2003, La Jolla CA), American aviator, the first woman to fly an all-night route and holder of many women's flight endurance and altitude records. She was the last survivor of the pilots who in 1929 took part in the first National Women's Air Derby, which Will Rogers dubbed the "Powder Puff Derby."

**Johnny Unitas** (John Constantine Unitas; 7 May 1933, Pittsburgh PA—11 Sep 2002, Timonium MD), American football player who was considered one of the greatest quarterbacks in the National Football League. His impressive career statistics (2,830 of 5,186 passing completions for 40,239 yards and 290 touchdowns) signaled the beginning of a new era in football as the focus switched from running to passing.

**Siegfried Unseld** (28 Sep 1924, Ulm, Germany—26 Oct 2002, Frankfurt, Germany), German publisher who headed the literary giant Suhrkamp Verlag.

**Carlo Urbani** (19 Oct 1956, Castelplanio, Italy—29 Mar 2003, Bangkok, Thailand), Italian epidemiologist who recognized that the SARS (severe acute respiratory syndrome ) outbreak was an epidemic and raised the alarm, allowing the disease to be somewhat contained, before dying himself of SARS.

**Leon (Marcus) Uris** (3 Aug 1924, Baltimore MD—21 Jun 2003, Shelter Island NY), American writer who wrote a number of best-sellers, many of which—including *Battle Cry* (1953), *Exodus,* his biggest success (1958), *Mila 18* (1961), *Topaz* (1967), and *Trinity* (1976)—were based on events of modern history. He also wrote the screenplays for such movies as *Battle Cry* (1955) and *Gunfight at the OK Corral* (1957).

**Raffaele Vallone** (Raf; 17 Feb 1916, Tropea, Italy—31 Oct 2002, Rome, Italy), Italian actor who was one of the leading stars of Italian Neorealist films of the 1940s.

**Rik Van Steenbergen** (Hendrik Van Steenbergen; 9 Oct 1924, Arendonk, Belgium—15 May 2003, Antwerp, Belgium), Belgian cyclist who, during a 23-year career (1943–66), won more than 900 professional races, including three world road-racing championships (1949, 1956, 1957) and eight classics—the Tour of Flanders (1944, 1946), Paris-Roubaix (1948, 1952), Flèche Wallonne (1949, 1958), Paris-Brussels (1950), and Milan–San Remo (1954). An indefatigable all-rounder, Van Steenbergen also won 25 grand tour stages, finished second in the 1951 Giro d'Italia, and won 40 six-day track races.

**Orlando Villas Bôas** (12 Jan 1914, near Botucatu, São Paulo state, Brazil—12 Dec 2002, São Paulo, Brazil), Brazilian explorer who was a leading advocate of the rights of indigenous Brazilians. With his brother Claudio, Villas Bôas wrote 12 books, and the two were nominated for the Nobel Prize for Peace in 1971 and again in 1975. Villas Bôas also received the Medal of the Royal Geographical Society in 1967.

**Meir Vilner(-Kovner)** (Ber Kovner; 27 Oct 1918, Vilnius, Lithuania—5 Jun 2003, Tel Aviv, Israel), Lithuanian-born Israeli politician, a member of the Israeli Knesset (parliament) for nearly 42 years (1949–90), secretary general (1965–90) and chairman (1990–93) of the Communist Party of Israel, and the last surviving signatory of the Declaration of the Establishment of the State of Israel (14 May 1948). Vilner fled to British Palestine as a refugee in 1938. He represented the Communists on the 37-member Provisional Council of State in 1948 and was, at age 29, the declaration's youngest signer.

**Vu Ngoc Nha** (1924, Thai Binh, French Indochina—7 Aug 2002, Ho Chi Minh City, Vietnam), Vietnamese spy who served as a trusted adviser to two presidents of South Vietnam while simultaneously leaking information to the Viet Cong and their communist allies in the north.

**Mal Waldron** (Malcolm Earl Waldron; 16 Aug 1925, New York NY—2 Dec 2002, Brussels, Belgium), American jazz musician who played piano in a rhythmically intense style that focused tightly on subtle thematic development, using spare, blues-oriented harmonies and ingeniously spaced phrases.

**John Paul Wallach** (18 Jun 1943, Scarsdale NY—9 Jul 2002, New York NY), American journalist and peace activist who worked for Hearst Newspapers from 1968 to 1995—the last 26 of those years as foreign editor—and who is best known for founding (1993) Seeds of Peace, a summer camp to gather teenagers from areas of conflict so that they could learn to live together harmoniously.

**William Caesar Warfield** (22 Jan 1920, West Helena AR–25 Aug 2002, Chicago IL), American concert and opera singer who had a powerful warm and elegant bass-baritone voice that he employed to dramatic effect in the concert hall, on the opera and musical theater stage, on recordings, on television, and in film. He was best known for his portrayal of Porgy in countless productions of *Porgy and Bess* and for his heartfelt rendition of "Ol' Man River" in the film *Show Boat* (1951), a song that became his trademark.

**Zerach Warhaftig** (2 Feb 1906, Volkovysk, Russian Empire [now in Belarus]–26 Sep 2002, Jerusalem, Israel), Israeli rabbi, lawyer, and politician who was one of the 37 signatories to the Israeli Declaration of Independence in 1948 and founder (1956) of the National Religious Party.

**Mike Webster** (Michael Lewis Webster; 18 Mar 1952, Tomahawk WI–24 Sep 2002, Pittsburgh PA), American football player who anchored a formidable offensive line that helped the Pittsburgh Steelers win four Super Bowl championships in the 1970s; he was inducted into the Pro Football Hall of Fame in 1997.

**Arnold Weinstock, Baron Weinstock of Bowden** (29 Jul 1924, London, England–23 Jul 2002, Bowden Hill, Wiltshire, England), British industrialist who led the UK's General Electric Co. (GEC) as managing director from 1963 to 1996; his stern management and conservative tactics evoked strong praise as well as fierce criticism.

**Theodore Russell Weiss** (16 Dec 1916, Reading PA–15 Apr 2003, Princeton NJ), American poet and editor who was the founding editor in 1943 (with Warren Carrier) of the *Quarterly Review of Literature*, which published works by poets William Carlos Williams, E.E. Cummings, and Ezra Pound, as well as those of little-known poets, non-English-language writers, and especially women, including the then-unknown writers Anne Sexton, Sylvia Plath, and Joyce Carol Oates. Weiss was on the faculty of Princeton University for 20 years and released more than a dozen volumes of his own poetry, mostly narrative verse.

**John Weitz** (Hans Werner Weitz; 25 May 1923, Berlin, Germany–3 Oct 2002, Bridgehampton NY), German-born American fashion designer, novelist, and historian who enhanced his renown as a menswear designer—and greatly increased his income—when he became one of the first to lend his name to the licensing of products. The wide variety of items sold under his name included men's cologne, neckties, umbrellas, sunglasses, sweaters, and socks.

**Paul David Wellstone** (21 Jul 1944, Washington DC–25 Oct 2002, near Eveleth MN), American Democratic politician who was a US senator from Minnesota from 1991 to his death. Often referred to as the most liberal member of the Senate, he was respected as a man of principle who did not forsake his convictions for political expediency. Along with his wife, daughter, three campaign aides, and two pilots, he was killed in a plane crash 11 days before the 2002 election.

**(James) Hoyt Wilhelm** (26 Jul 1923, Huntersville NC–23 Aug 2002, Sarasota FL), American baseball player who pitched knuckleballs that fluttered over the plate, baffling major league batters for 21 seasons. Altogether he pitched in 1,070 games—a record when he retired at the age of 48—and had

an outstanding lifetime 2.52 earned run average, with 143 wins, 122 losses, and 227 saves.

**Sir Bernard Arthur Owen Williams** (21 Sep 1929, Westcliff-on-Sea, Essex, England–10 Jun 2003, Rome, Italy), British philosopher who sought to revitalize moral philosophy and served on several public commissions investigating gambling, drug abuse, social justice, public schools, and obscenity and censorship. In opposition to the positivist and analytical approach to moral philosophy, which held that philosophers have no substantive contribution to make to ethics, Williams adopted a naturalistic position in which he attempted to embed ethics in history and culture. He opposed both Kantianism and utilitarianism, which both assert that there is a single valid principle of morality, arguing instead that moral life should be investigated as it is experienced rather than in terms of abstract theories.

**Ted Williams** (Theodore Samuel Williams; "The Splendid Splinter"; 30 Aug 1918, San Diego CA–5 Jul 2002, Inverness FL), American baseball player who compiled a lifetime batting average of .344 as a left-handed hitting outfielder with the Boston Red Sox from 1939 to 1960. He was the last .400 hitter (.406 in 1941) in the 20th century.

**Malcolm Benjamin Graham Christopher Williamson** (21 Nov 1931, Sydney, Australia–2 Mar 2003, Cambridge, England), Australian-born composer as well as the first non-Briton to become (1975) Master of the Queen's Music. His body of work, which juxtaposed a deep mysticism with popular idioms, includes 7 symphonies, 11 operas, 4 masses, and a large number of other choral and orchestral pieces.

**Kemmons Wilson** (Charles Kemmons Wilson, Jr.; 5 Jan 1913, Osceola AR–12 Feb 2003, Memphis TN), American businessman who transformed the motel industry when, in 1952, he founded the Holiday Inn chain of motels, which once advertised itself as "the nation's innkeeper."

**Sir Robert Wilson** (16 Apr 1927, South Shields, Durham, England–2 Sep 2002, Chelmsford, Essex, England), British astrophysicist who developed the International Ultraviolet Explorer that was launched in 1978 to detect invisible radiation from stars and was considered the forerunner of the Hubble Space Telescope.

**Sloan Wilson** (8 May 1920, Westport CT–25 May 2003, Colonial Beach VA), American novelist who launched a catchphrase with the title of his best-selling novel *The Man in the Gray Flannel Suit* (1955; filmed 1956), which captured the mood of the post–World War II suburban families dealing with the conformity and the sacrifice of family life seemingly necessary for the achievement of upward mobility in business and social position. Another of his successes was *A Summer Place* (1958; filmed 1959).

**Kathleen Winsor** (16 Oct 1919, Olivia MN–26 May 2003, New York NY), American novelist who achieved almost instant notoriety in 1944 with *Forever Amber,* her historical saga of a sexually adventurous young woman in Restoration England, which sold 100,000 copies its first week and paved the way for the many romantic "bodice-rippers" that followed. Although it contained no explicit sex scenes, it was extremely racy for its time, and it was widely condemned.

**Monique Wittig** (13 Jul 1935, Dannemarie, Haut-Rhin, Alsace, France–3 Jan 2003, Tucson AZ),

French avant-garde feminist writer who used an experimental approach to language and subject in an attempt to break down definitions and create a language and world free of the dictates of heterosexual society.

**G(eorg) H(enrik) von Wright** (14 Jun 1916, Helsinki, Finland–16 Jun 2003, Helsinki, Finland), Finnish analytical philosopher who was the successor to Ludwig Wittgenstein's chair of philosophy at the University of Cambridge (1948-51) and one of Wittgenstein's literary executors. He worked principally in inductive logic, modal logic, of which he founded a branch that he called deontic logic, and the theory of action.

**John Baptist Cardinal Wu Cheng-chung** (26 Mar 1925, Shui-tsai, Guangdong province, China–23 Sep 2002, Hong Kong), Chinese-born Roman Catholic prelate who capably maneuvered the Roman Catholic Church through the transition period when Hong Kong was handed from British to Chinese control in 1997. Although Hong Kong's Chinese clergy balked at his appointment, his discretion and dedication aided the church's independence from Beijing authorities.

**Zal Yanovsky** (Zalman Yanovsky; 19 Dec 1944, Toronto, ON, Canada–13 Dec 2002, Kingston, ON, Canada), Canadian musician who was the extroverted lead guitarist of the popular 1960s rock group the Lovin' Spoonful, whose hits included "Do You Believe in Magic" (1965) and "Summer in the City" (1966).

**Philip Yordan** (1 Apr 1914, Chicago IL–24 Mar 2003, La Jolla CA), American playwright and screenwriter who first achieved notice for his play Anna Lucasta (produced with an all-black cast on Broadway in 1944) and later, after he had moved to Paris during the McCarthy era, lent his name to materials written by blacklisted Hollywood screenwriters; he won an Academy Award in 1955 for his screenplay of Broken Lance.

**Janet Mary Baker Young, Baroness Young of Farnworth** (23 Oct 1926, Widnes, Lancashire, England–6 Sep 2002, Oxford, England), British politician who was the first woman to serve as leader of the House of Lords; a committed conservative, she was perhaps best known for her zealous dedication to traditional family values and sexual morality, a stance that brought her heated criticism, especially from gay rights groups, late in her career.

**Sharif Zaid ibn Shaker** (4 Sep 1934, Amman, Jordan–30 Aug 2002, Amman, Jordan), Jordanian military officer and government official who held the top three appointed posts in his country—commander of the armed forces (1976–88), chief of the royal court (1988, 1989, and 1993), and prime minister (1989, 1991–93, and 1995–96).

**Ron Ziegler** (Ronald Lewis Ziegler; 12 May 1939, Covington KY–10 Feb 2003, Coronado CA), American government official who, as press secretary for Pres. Richard Nixon, is best remembered for steadfastly holding the president's line as the Watergate scandal unraveled the administration, from the first news of the break-in in 1972 until Nixon's resignation in 1974. As Nixon's press secretary, he characterized the break-in at Democratic Party headquarters as a "third-rate burglary."

**Armand Zildjian** (1921, Milton MA–26 Dec 2002, Scottsdale AZ), American businessman who headed Avedis Zildjian Co., the world's most famous cymbal company.

**John Gerald Zimmerman** (30 Oct 1927, Pacoima CA–3 Aug 2002, Monterey CA), American sports photographer who helped develop modern sports photojournalism. He was a pioneer in the use of lighting at indoor arenas and was the first to use remote-controlled cameras to capture the action of a sporting event.

**Paul Zindel** (15 May 1936, New York NY–27 Mar 2003, New York NY), American writer of fiction for children and plays for adults, the latter including *The Effect of Gamma Rays on Man-in-the-Moon Marigolds*, which won the 1971 Pulitzer Prize for Drama.

**Vera Zorina** (Eva Brigitta Hartwig; 2 Jan 1917, Berlin, Germany–9 Apr 2003, Santa Fe NM), German-born dancer and actress who was a ballerina with the Ballet Russe de Monte Carlo for three years before attracting greater notice in 1936 as the star of the London production of *On Your Toes*. She went on to star in such other productions as the Hollywood film *The Goldwyn Follies* and the Broadway musical *I Married an Angel*, both in 1938. She was married for eight years to choreographer George Balanchine.

# Awards

## The Nobel Prizes

The Alfred B. Nobel Prizes are widely regarded as the world's most prestigious awards given for intellectual achievement. They are awarded annually from a fund bequeathed for that purpose by the Swedish inventor and industrialist Alfred Bernhard Nobel and administered by the Nobel Foundation. Nobel's 1895 will established five of the six prizes: those for physics, chemistry, literature, physiology or medicine, and peace. The prize for economic sciences was added in 1969. Country given is the citizenship of recipient at the time award was made. Prizes may be withheld or not awarded in years when no worthy recipient can be found or when the world situation (e.g., World Wars I and II) prevents the gathering of information needed to reach a decision. Prizes are announced in mid-October and awarded in December in Stockholm and Oslo. Web site: <www.nobel.se>

### Physics

| YEAR | WINNER(S) | COUNTRY | ACHIEVEMENT |
|---|---|---|---|
| 1901 | Wilhelm Conrad Röntgen | Germany | discovery of X rays |
| 1902 | Hendrik Antoon Lorentz | Neth. | investigation of the influence |
|  | Pieter Zeeman | Neth. | of magnetism on radiation |
| 1903 | Henri Becquerel | France | discovery of spontaneous radioactivity |
|  | Marie Curie | France | investigations of radiation phenomena |
|  | Pierre Curie | France | discovered by Becquerel |
| 1904 | John William Strutt, 3rd Baron Rayleigh (of Terling Place) | UK | discovery of argon |
| 1905 | Philipp Lenard | Germany | research on cathode rays |
| 1906 | Sir J.J. Thomson | UK | researches into electrical conductivity of gases |
| 1907 | A.A. Michelson | US | spectroscopic and metrological investigations |
| 1908 | Gabriel Lippmann | France | photographic reproduction of colors |
| 1909 | Ferdinand Braun | Germany | development of |
|  | Guglielmo Marconi | Italy | wireless telegraphy |
| 1910 | Johannes Diederik van der Waals | Neth. | research concerning the equation of state of gases and liquids |
| 1911 | Wilhelm Wien | Germany | discoveries regarding laws governing heat radiation |
| 1912 | Nils Dalén | Sweden | invention of automatic regulators for lighting coastal beacons and light buoys |
| 1913 | Heike Kamerlingh Onnes | Neth. | investigation into the properties of matter at low temperatures; production of liquid helium |
| 1914 | Max von Laue | Germany | discovery of diffraction of X rays by crystals |
| 1915 | Sir Lawrence Bragg | UK | analysis of crystal structure |
|  | Sir William Bragg | UK | by means of X rays |
| 1917 | Charles Glover Barkla | UK | discovery of characteristic X-radiation of elements |
| 1918 | Max Planck | Germany | discovery of the elemental quanta |
| 1919 | Johannes Stark | Germany | discovery of Doppler effect in positive ion rays and division of spectral lines in electric field |
| 1920 | Charles Édouard Guillaume | Switz. | discovery of anomalies in alloys |
| 1921 | Albert Einstein | Switz. | work in theoretical physics |
| 1922 | Niels Bohr | Denmark | investigation of atomic structure and radiation |
| 1923 | Robert Andrews Millikan | US | work on elementary electric charge and the photoelectric effect |
| 1924 | Karl Manne Georg Siegbahn | Sweden | work in X-ray spectroscopy |
| 1925 | James Franck | Germany | discovery of the laws governing the |
|  | Gustav Hertz | Germany | impact of an electron upon an atom |
| 1926 | Jean Perrin | France | work on discontinuous structure of matter |
| 1927 | Arthur Holly Compton | US | discovery of wavelength change in diffused X rays |
|  | C.T.R. Wilson | UK | method of making visible the paths of electrically charged particles |
| 1928 | Sir Owen Willans Richardson | UK | work on electron emission by hot metals |
| 1929 | Louis-Victor, 7e duc (duke) de Broglie | France | discovery of the wave nature of electrons |

## Physics (continued)

| YEAR | WINNER(S) | COUNTRY | ACHIEVEMENT |
|------|-----------|---------|-------------|
| 1930 | Sir Chandrasekhara Venkata Raman | India | work on light diffusion; discovery of Raman effect, light wavelength variation that occurs when a light beam is deflected by molecules |
| 1932 | Werner Heisenberg | Germany | creation of quantum mechanics |
| 1933 | P.A.M. Dirac | UK | ⎫ introduction of wave equations |
|      | Erwin Schrödinger | Austria | ⎬ in quantum mechanics |
| 1935 | Sir James Chadwick | UK | discovery of the neutron |
| 1936 | Carl David Anderson | US | discovery of the positron |
|      | Victor Francis Hess | Austria | discovery of cosmic radiation |
| 1937 | Clinton Joseph Davisson | US | ⎫ experimental demonstration of the interference |
|      | Sir George Paget Thomson | UK | ⎬ phenomenon in crystals irradiated by electrons |
| 1938 | Enrico Fermi | Italy | disclosure of artificial radioactive elements produced by neutron irradiation |
| 1939 | Ernest Orlando Lawrence | US | invention of the cyclotron |
| 1943 | Otto Stern | US | discovery of the magnetic moment of the proton |
| 1944 | Isidor Isaac Rabi | US | resonance method for registration of various properties of atomic nuclei |
| 1945 | Wolfgang Pauli | Austria | discovery of the exclusion principle of electrons |
| 1946 | Percy Williams Bridgman | US | discoveries in the domain of high-pressure physics |
| 1947 | Sir Edward V. Appleton | UK | discovery of Appleton layer in upper atmosphere |
| 1948 | Patrick M.S. Blackett | UK | discoveries in the domain of nuclear physics and cosmic radiation |
| 1949 | Yukawa Hideki | Japan | prediction of the existence of mesons |
| 1950 | Cecil Frank Powell | UK | photographic method of studying nuclear processes; discoveries concerning mesons |
| 1951 | Sir John D. Cockcroft | UK | ⎫ work on transmutation of atomic nuclei |
|      | Ernest T.S. Walton | Ireland | ⎬ by accelerated particles |
| 1952 | Felix Bloch | US | ⎫ discovery of nuclear magnetic |
|      | E.M. Purcell | US | ⎬ resonance in solids |
| 1953 | Frits Zernike | Neth. | method of phase-contrast microscopy |
| 1954 | Max Born | UK | statistical studies of atomic wave functions |
|      | Walther Bothe | W.Ger. | invention of coincidence method |
| 1955 | Polykarp Kusch | US | measurement of magnetic moment of electron |
|      | Willis Eugene Lamb, Jr. | US | discoveries in the hydrogen spectrum |
| 1956 | John Bardeen | US | ⎫ investigations on |
|      | Walter H. Brattain | US | ⎬ semiconductors and |
|      | William B. Shockley | US | ⎭ invention of the transistor |
| 1957 | Tsung-Dao Lee | China | ⎫ discovery of violations of the principle of parity, the |
|      | Chen Ning Yang | China | ⎬ symmetry between phenomena in coordinate systems |
| 1958 | Pavel Alexeyevich Cherenkov | USSR | ⎫ discovery and interpretation of the Cherenkov effect, |
|      | Ilya Mikhaylovich Frank | USSR | ⎬ which indicates that electrons emit light as they pass through a transparent medium at a speed |
|      | Igor Yevgenyevich Tamm | USSR | ⎭ higher than the speed of light in that medium |
| 1959 | Owen Chamberlain | US | ⎫ confirmation of the existence |
|      | Emilio Segrè | US | ⎬ of the antiproton |
| 1960 | Donald A. Glaser | US | development of the bubble chamber |
| 1961 | Robert Hofstadter | US | determination of shape and size of atomic nucleons |
|      | Rudolf Ludwig Mössbauer | W.Ger. | discovery of the Mössbauer effect, a nuclear process permitting the resonance absorption of gamma rays |
| 1962 | Lev Davidovich Landau | USSR | contributions to the understanding of condensed states of matter |
| 1963 | J. Hans D. Jensen | W.Ger. | ⎫ development of shell model theory of |
|      | Maria Goeppert Mayer | US | ⎬ the structure of the atomic nuclei |
|      | Eugene Paul Wigner | US | principles governing interaction of protons and neutrons in the nucleus |
| 1964 | Nikolay G. Basov | USSR | ⎫ work in quantum electronics leading to |
|      | Aleksandr M. Prokhorov | USSR | ⎬ construction of instruments based on |
|      | Charles Hard Townes | US | ⎭ maser-laser principles |
| 1965 | Richard P. Feynman | US | ⎫ basic principles of quantum electrodynamics, which |
|      | Julian Seymour Schwinger | US | ⎬ describes mathematically all interactions of light with |
|      | Tomonaga Shin'ichiro | Japan | ⎭ matter and of charged particles with one another |
| 1966 | Alfred Kastler | France | discovery of optical methods for studying Hertzian resonances in atoms |
| 1967 | Hans Albrecht Bethe | US | discoveries concerning the energy production of stars |
| 1968 | Luis W. Alvarez | US | work with elementary particles, discovery of resonance states |
| 1969 | Murray Gell-Mann | US | classification of elementary particles and their interactions |

# Physics (continued)

| YEAR | WINNER(S) | COUNTRY | ACHIEVEMENT |
|------|-----------|---------|-------------|
| 1970 | Hannes Alfvén | Sweden | work in magnetohydrodynamics and |
|      | Louis-Eugène-Félix Néel | France | in antiferromagnetism and ferrimagnetism |
| 1971 | Dennis Gabor | UK | invention of holography |
| 1972 | John Bardeen | US | development of thetheory of superconductivity, the |
|      | Leon N. Cooper | US | disappearance of electrical resistancein various |
|      | John Robert Schrieffer | US | solids when they are cooled below certain temperature |
| 1973 | Leo Esaki | Japan | experimental disoveries in tunneling in |
|      | Ivar Giaever | US | semiconductors and superconductors |
|      | Brian D. Josephson | UK | predictions of supercurrent properties through a tunnel barrier |
| 1974 | Antony Hewish | UK | work in radio |
|      | Sir Martin Ryle | UK | astronomy |
| 1975 | Aage N. Bohr | Denmark | work on the atomic nucleus |
|      | Ben R. Mottelson | Denmark | that paved the way for nuclear |
|      | James Rainwater | US | fusion |
| 1976 | Burton Richter | US | discovery of new class of |
|      | Samuel C.C. Ting | US | elementary particles (psi, or J) |
| 1977 | Philip W. Anderson | US | contributions to understanding the |
|      | Sir Nevill F. Mott | UK | behavior of electrons in |
|      | John H. Van Vleck | US | magnetic, noncrystalline solids |
| 1978 | Pyotr L. Kapitsa | USSR | research in magnetism and low-temperature physics |
|      | Arno Penzias | US | discovery of cosmic microwave background |
|      | Robert Woodrow Wilson | US | radiation, providing support for the big-bang theory |
| 1979 | Sheldon Lee Glashow | US | unification of electromagnetism and |
|      | Abdus Salam | Pakistan | the weak interactions of |
|      | Steven Weinberg | US | subatomic particles |
| 1980 | James Watson Cronin | US | demonstration of simultaneous violation of both |
|      | Val Logsdon Fitch | US | charge-conjugation and parity-inversion symmetries |
| 1981 | Nicolaas Bloembergen | US | applications of lasers |
|      | Arthur L. Schawlow | US | in spectroscopy |
|      | Kai M. B. Siegbahn | Sweden | electron spectroscopy for chemical analysis |
| 1982 | Kenneth G. Wilson | US | analysis of continuous phase transitions |
| 1983 | Subrahmanyan Chandrasekhar | US | contributions to understanding the evolution and devolution of stars |
|      | William A. Fowler | US | studies of nuclear reactions key to the formation of chemical elements |
| 1984 | Simon van der Meer | Neth. | discovery of subatomic particles W and Z |
|      | Carlo Rubbia | Italy | which supports the electroweak theory |
| 1985 | Klaus von Klitzing | W.Ger. | discovery of the quantized Hall effect, permitting exact measurements of electrical resistance |
| 1986 | Gerd Binnig | W.Ger. | development of the scanning tunnelling |
|      | Heinrich Rohrer | Switz. | electron microscopes |
|      | Ernst Ruska | W.Ger. | development of the electron microscope |
| 1987 | J. Georg Bednorz | W.Ger. | discoveries of superconductivity in |
|      | Karl Alex Müller | Switz. | ceramic materials |
| 1988 | Leon Max Lederman | US | research in |
|      | Melvin Schwartz | US | subatomic |
|      | Jack Steinberger | US | particles |
| 1989 | Hans Georg Dehmelt | US | development of methods to isolate atoms |
|      | Wolfgang Paul | W.Ger. | and subatomic particles for study |
|      | Norman Foster Ramsey | US | development of the atomic clock |
| 1990 | Jerome Isaac Friedman | US | discovery of |
|      | Henry Way Kendall | US | atomic |
|      | Richard E. Taylor | Canada | quarks |
| 1991 | Pierre-Gilles de Gennes | France | discovery of general rules for behavior of molecules |
| 1992 | Georges Charpak | France | inventor of detector that traces subatomic particles |
| 1993 | Russell Alan Hulse | US | identifying |
|      | Joseph H. Taylor, Jr. | US | binary pulsars |
| 1994 | Bertram N. Brockhouse | Canada | development of |
|      | Clifford G. Shull | US | neutron-scattering techniques |
| 1995 | Martin Lewis Perl | US | discovery of tau subatomic particle |
|      | Frederick Reines | US | discovery of neutrino subatomic particle |
| 1996 | David M. Lee | US | discovery of |
|      | Douglas D. Osheroff | US | superfluidity in |
|      | Robert C. Richardson | US | isotope helium-3 |

## Physics (continued)

| YEAR | WINNER(S) | COUNTRY | ACHIEVEMENT |
|------|-----------|---------|-------------|
| 1997 | Steven Chu | US | } process of |
|      | Claude Cohen-Tannoudji | France | cooling and trapping atoms with |
|      | William D. Phillips | US | laser light |
| 1998 | Robert B. Laughlin | US | discovery of fractional quantum Hall effect,demonstra- |
|      | Horst L. Störmer | US | ting that electrons in a powerful low-temperature |
|      | Daniel C. Tsui | US | magnetic field can form a quantum fluid whose |
|      |  |  | particles have fractional electric charges |
| 1999 | Gerardus 't Hooft | Neth. | study of quantum structure |
|      | Martinus J.G. Veltman | Neth. | of electroweak interactions |
| 2000 | Zhores I. Alferov | Russia | development of fast semiconductors |
|      | Herbert Kroemer | Germany | for use in microelectronics |
|      | Jack S. Kilby | US | development of the integrated circuit (microchip) |
| 2001 | Eric A. Cornell | US | achievement of Bose-Einstein condensation in dilute |
|      | Wolfgang Ketterle | Germany | gases of alkali atoms, and for early fundamental |
|      | Carl E. Wieman | US | studies of the properties of the condensates |
| 2002 | Raymond Davis, Jr. | US | for pioneering contributions to astrophysics, |
|      | Masatoshi Koshiba | Japan | in particular for the detection of cosmic neutrinos |
|      | Riccardo Giacconi | US | for pioneering contributions to astrophysics, which |
|      |  |  | have led to the discovery of cosmic X-ray sources |

## Chemistry

| YEAR | WINNER(S) | COUNTRY | ACHIEVEMENT |
|------|-----------|---------|-------------|
| 1901 | Jacobus H. van 't Hoff | Neth. | laws of chemical dynamics and osmotic pressure |
| 1902 | Emil Fischer | Germany | work on sugar and purine syntheses |
| 1903 | Svante Arrhenius | Sweden | theory of electrolytic dissociation |
| 1904 | Sir William Ramsay | UK | discovery of inert gas elements and their |
|      |  |  | places in the periodic system |
| 1905 | Adolf von Baeyer | Germany | work on organic dyes, hydroaromatic compounds |
| 1906 | Henri Moissan | France | isolation of fluorine; introduction of Moissan furnace |
| 1907 | Eduard Buchner | Germany | discovery of noncellular fermentation |
| 1908 | Ernest Rutherford | UK | investigations into the disintegration of elements |
|      |  |  | and the chemistry of radioactive substances |
| 1909 | Wilhelm Ostwald | Germany | pioneer work on catalysis, chemical |
|      |  |  | equilibrium, and reaction velocities |
| 1910 | Otto Wallach | Germany | pioneer work in alicyclic combinations |
| 1911 | Marie Curie | France | discovery of radium and polonium; isolation of radium |
| 1912 | Victor Grignard | France | discovery of the Grignard reagents |
|      | Paul Sabatier | France | method of hydrogenating organic compounds |
| 1913 | Alfred Werner | Switz. | work on the linkage of atoms in molecules |
| 1914 | Theodore W. Richards | US | accurate determination of the atomic weights |
|      |  |  | of numerous elements |
| 1915 | Richard Willstätter | Germany | research in plant pigments, especially chlorophyll |
| 1918 | Fritz Haber | Germany | synthesis of ammonia |
| 1920 | Walther Hermann Nernst | Germany | work in thermochemistry |
| 1921 | Frederick Soddy | UK | chemistry of radioactive substances; |
|      |  |  | occurrence and nature of isotopes |
| 1922 | Francis William Aston | UK | work with mass spectrograph; whole-number rule |
| 1923 | Fritz Pregl | Austria | method of microanalysis of organic substances |
| 1925 | Richard Zsigmondy | Austria | elucidation of the heterogeneous nature of |
|      |  |  | colloidal solutions |
| 1926 | Theodor H.E. Svedberg | Sweden | work on disperse systems |
| 1927 | Heinrich Otto Wieland | Germany | researches into the constitution of bile acids |
| 1928 | Adolf Windaus | Germany | constitution of sterols and their connection |
|      |  |  | with vitamins |
| 1929 | Hans von Euler-Chelpin | Sweden | investigations in the fermentation of sugars |
|      | Sir Arthur Harden | UK | and the enzyme action involved |
| 1930 | Hans Fischer | Germany | hemin, chlorophyll research; synthesis of hemin |
| 1931 | Friedrich Bergius | Germany | invention and development of |
|      | Carl Bosch | Germany | chemical high-pressure methods |
| 1932 | Irving Langmuir | US | discoveries and investigations in surface chemistry |
| 1934 | Harold C. Urey | US | discovery of heavy hydrogen |
| 1935 | Frédéric and Irène | France | synthesis of new radioactive elements |
|      | Joliot-Curie |  |  |
| 1936 | Peter Debye | Neth. | work on dipole moments and diffraction of X rays |
|      |  |  | and  electrons in gases |

# Chemistry (continued)

| YEAR | WINNER(S) | COUNTRY | ACHIEVEMENT |
|---|---|---|---|
| 1937 | Sir Norman Haworth | UK | research on carbohydrates and vitamin C |
|  | Paul Karrer | Switz. | research on carotenoids, flavins, and vitamins |
| 1938 | Richard Kuhn (declined) | Germany | carotenoid and vitamin research |
| 1939 | Adolf Butenandt (declined) | Germany | work on sexual hormones |
|  | Leopold Ruzicka | Switz. | work on polymethylenes and higher terpenes |
| 1943 | Georg Charles von Hevesy | Hungary | use of isotopes as tracers in chemical research |
| 1944 | Otto Hahn | Germany | discovery of the fission of heavy nuclei |
| 1945 | Artturi Ilmari Virtanen | Finland | invention of fodder preservation method |
| 1946 | John Howard Northrop | US | } preparation of enzymes and |
|  | Wendell M. Stanley | US | } virus proteins in pure form |
|  | James B. Sumner | US | discovery of enzyme crystallization |
| 1947 | Sir Robert Robinson | UK | investigation of alkaloids and other plant products |
| 1948 | Arne Tiselius | Sweden | researches in electrophoresis and adsorption analysis; serum proteins |
| 1949 | William Francis Giauque | US | behavior of substances at extremely low temperatures |
| 1950 | Kurt Alder | W.Ger. | } discovery and development of |
|  | Otto Paul Hermann Diels | W.Ger. | } diene synthesis |
| 1951 | Edwin M. McMillan | US | } discovery of and research on |
|  | Glenn T. Seaborg | US | } transuranium elements |
| 1952 | A.J.P. Martin | UK | } development of partition |
|  | R.L.M. Synge | UK | } chromatography |
| 1953 | Hermann Staudinger | W.Ger. | work on macromolecules |
| 1954 | Linus Pauling | US | study of the nature of the chemical bond |
| 1955 | Vincent du Vigneaud | US | first synthesis of a polypeptide hormone |
| 1956 | Sir Cyril N. Hinshelwood | UK | } work on the kinetics of |
|  | Nikolay N. Semyonov | USSR | } chemical reactions |
| 1957 | Alexander Robertus Todd, Baron Todd (of Trumpington) | UK | work on nucleotides and nucleotide coenzymes |
| 1958 | Frederick Sanger | UK | determination of the structure of the insulin molecule |
| 1959 | Jaroslav Heyrovsky | Czechoslovakia | discovery and development of polarography |
| 1960 | Willard Frank Libby | US | development of radiocarbon dating |
| 1961 | Melvin Calvin | US | study of chemical steps that take place during photosynthesis |
| 1962 | Sir John C. Kendrew | UK | } determination of the structure of |
|  | Max Ferdinand Perutz | UK | } hemoproteins |
| 1963 | Giulio Natta | Italy | } structure and synthesis of polymers |
|  | Karl Ziegler | W.Ger. | } in the field of plastics |
| 1964 | Dorothy M.C. Hodgkin | UK | determining the structure of biochemical compounds essential in combating pernicious anemia |
| 1965 | R.B. Woodward | US | synthesis of sterols, chlorophyll, and other substances |
| 1966 | Robert S. Mulliken | US | work concerning chemical bonds and the electronic structure of molecules |
| 1967 | Manfred Eigen | W.Ger. | studies of extremely fast chemical reactions |
|  | Ronald G. W. Norrish | UK | } studies of extremely fast |
|  | Sir George Porter | UK | } chemical reactions |
| 1968 | Lars Onsager | US | work on theory of thermodynamics of irreversible processes |
| 1969 | Sir Derek H.R. Barton | UK | } work in determining actual |
|  | Odd Hassel | Norway | } three-dimensional shape of molecules |
| 1970 | Luis Federico Leloir | Argentina | discovery of sugar nucleotides and their role in the biosynthesis of carbohydrates |
| 1971 | Gerhard Herzberg | Canada | research in the structure of molecules |
| 1972 | Christian B. Anfinsen | US | fundamental contributions to enzyme chemistry |
|  | Stanford Moore | US | } fundamental contributions |
|  | William H. Stein | US | } to enzyme chemistry |
| 1973 | Ernst Otto Fischer | W.Ger. | } organometallic |
|  | Sir Geoffrey Wilkinson | UK | } chemistry |
| 1974 | Paul J. Flory | US | studies of long-chain molecules |
| 1975 | Sir John W. Cornforth | UK | } work in |
|  | Vladimir Prelog | Switz. | } stereochemistry |
| 1976 | William N. Lipscomb, Jr. | US | structure of boranes |
| 1977 | Ilya Prigogine | Belgium | widening the scope of thermodynamics |
| 1978 | Peter Dennis Mitchell | UK | formulation of a theory of energy transfer processes in biological systems |

# Chemistry (continued)

| YEAR | WINNER(S) | COUNTRY | ACHIEVEMENT |
|---|---|---|---|
| 1979 | Herbert Charles Brown | US | introduction of compounds of boron and phosphorus in the synthesis of organic substances |
|  | Georg Wittig | W.Ger. | introduction of compounds of boron and phosphorus in the synthesis of organic substances |
| 1980 | Paul Berg | US | first preparation of a hybrid DNA |
|  | Walter Gilbert | US | development of chemical and |
|  | Frederick Sanger | UK | biological analyses of DNA structure |
| 1981 | Fukui Kenichi | Japan | orbital symmetry interpretation |
|  | Roald Hoffmann | US | of chemical reactions |
| 1982 | Aaron Klug | UK | determination of structure of biological substances |
| 1983 | Henry Taube | US | study of electron transfer reactions |
| 1984 | Bruce Merrifield | US | development of a method of polypeptide synthesis |
| 1985 | Herbert A. Hauptman | US | development of a way to map the |
|  | Jerome Karle | US | chemical structure of small molecules |
| 1986 | Dudley R. Herschbach | US | development of methods |
|  | Yuan T. Lee | US | for analyzing basic |
|  | John C. Polanyi | Canada | chemical reactions |
| 1987 | Donald J. Cram | US | development of molecules |
|  | Jean-Marie Lehn | France | that can link with |
|  | Charles J. Pedersen | US | other molecules |
| 1988 | Johann Deisenhofer | W.Ger. | discovery of structure |
|  | Robert Huber | W.Ger. | proteins needed |
|  | Hartmut Michel | W.Ger. | in photosynthesis |
| 1989 | Sidney Altman | US | discovery of certain |
|  | Thomas Robert Cech | US | basic properties of RNA |
| 1990 | Elias James Corey | US | development of retrosynthetic analysis for synthesis of complex molecules |
| 1991 | Richard R. Ernst | Switz. | improvements in nuclear magnetic resonance spectroscopy |
| 1992 | Rudolph A. Marcus | US | explanation of how electrons transfer between molecules |
| 1993 | Kary B. Mullis | US | inventors of techniques for |
|  | Michael Smith | Canada | gene study and manipulation |
| 1994 | George A. Olah | US | development of techniques to study hydrocarbon molecules |
| 1995 | Paul Crutzen | Neth. | explanation of processes |
|  | Mario Molina | US | that deplete Earth's |
|  | F. Sherwood Rowland | US | ozone layer |
| 1996 | Robert F. Curl, Jr. | US | discovery of new |
|  | Sir Harold W. Kroto | UK | carbon compounds |
|  | Richard E. Smalley | US | called fullerenes |
| 1997 | Paul D. Boyer | US | explanation of the enzymatic conversion of |
|  | John E. Walker | UK | conversion of adenosine triphosphate |
|  | Jens C. Skou | Denmark | discovery of sodium-potassium-activated adenosine triphosphatase |
| 1998 | Walter Kohn | US | development of the density-functional theory |
|  | John A. Pople | UK | development of computational methods in quantum chemistry |
| 1999 | Ahmed H. Zewail | Egypt/US | study of the transition states of chemical reactions using femtosecond spectroscopy |
| 2000 | Alan J. Heeger | US | discovery of plastics |
|  | Alan G. MacDiarmid | US | that conduct |
|  | Shirakawa Hideki | Japan | electricity |
| 2001 | William S. Knowles | US | work on chirally catalyzed |
|  | Ryoji Noyori | Japan | hydrogenation reactions |
|  | K. Barry Sharpless | US | work on chirally catalyzed oxidation reactions |
| 2002 | John B. Fenn | US | development of soft desorption ionization methods |
|  | Koichi Tanaka | Japan | for mass spectrometric analyses of biological macromolecules |
|  | Kurt Wüthrich | Switz. | development of nuclear magnetic resonance spectroscopy for determining the three-dimensional structure of biological macromolecules in solution |

# Physiology or Medicine

| YEAR | WINNER(S) | COUNTRY | ACHIEVEMENT |
|---|---|---|---|
| 1901 | Emil von Behring | Germany | work on serum therapy |
| 1902 | Sir Ronald Ross | UK | discovery of how malaria enters an organism |
| 1903 | Niels Ryberg Finsen | Denmark | treatment of skin diseases with light |
| 1904 | Ivan Petrovich Pavlov | Russia | work on the physiology of digestion |
| 1905 | Robert Koch | Germany | tuberculosis research |
| 1906 | Camillo Golgi | Italy | work on the structure |
| 1906 | Santiago Ramón y Cajal | Spain | of the nervous system |
| 1907 | Alphonse Laveran | France | discovery of the role of protozoa in diseases |
| 1908 | Paul Ehrlich | Germany | work on |
| 1908 | Élie Metchnikoff | Russia | immunity |
| 1909 | Emil Theodor Kocher | Switzerland | physiology, pathology, and surgery of the thyroid gland |
| 1910 | Albrecht Kossel | Germany | researches in cellular chemistry |
| 1911 | Allvar Gullstrand | Sweden | work on dioptrics of the eye |
| 1912 | Alexis Carrel | France | work on vascular suture; transplantation of organs |
| 1913 | Charles Richet | France | work on anaphylaxis |
| 1914 | Robert Bárány | Austria-Hungary | work on vestibular apparatus |
| 1919 | Jules Bordet | Belgium | work on immunity factors in blood serum |
| 1920 | August Krogh | Denmark | discovery of capillary motor-regulating mechanism |
| 1922 | A.V. Hill | UK | discoveries concerning heat production in muscles |
|  | Otto Meyerhof | Germany | work on metabolism of lactic acid in muscles |
| 1923 | Sir Frederick G. Banting | Canada | discovery of |
|  | J.J.R. Macleod | UK | insulin |
| 1924 | Willem Einthoven | Neth. | discovery of electrocardiogram mechanism |
| 1926 | Johannes Fibiger | Denmark | contributions to cancer research |
| 1927 | Julius Wagner-Jauregg | Austria | work on malaria inoculation in dementia paralytica |
| 1928 | Charles-Jules-Henri Nicolle | France | work on typhus |
| 1929 | Christiaan Eijkman | Neth. | discovery of antineuritic vitamin |
|  | Sir Frederick Gowland Hopkins | UK | discovery of growth-stimulating vitamins |
| 1930 | Karl Landsteiner | US | grouping of human blood |
| 1931 | Otto Warburg | Germany | discovery of nature and action of respiratory enzyme |
| 1932 | Edgar Douglas Adrian, 1st Baron Adrian (of Cambridge) | UK | discoveries regarding function of neurons |
|  | Sir Charles Scott Sherrington | UK | discoveries regarding function of neurons |
| 1933 | Thomas Hunt Morgan | US | heredity transmission functions of chromosomes |
| 1934 | George Richards Minot | US | discoveries concerning |
|  | William P. Murphy | US | liver treatment |
|  | George H. Whipple | US | for anemia |
| 1935 | Hans Spemann | Germany | organizer effect in embryo |
| 1936 | Sir Henry Dale | UK | work on chemical |
|  | Otto Loewi | Germany | transmission of nerve impulses |
| 1937 | Albert Szent-Gyorgyi | Hungary | work on biological combustion |
| 1938 | Corneille Heymans | Belgium | discovery of role of sinus and aortic mechanisms in respiration regulation |
| 1939 | Gerhard Domagk (declined) | Germany | antibacterial effect of Prontosil |
| 1943 | Henrik Dam | Denmark | discovery of vitamin K |
|  | Edward Adelbert Doisy | US | discovery of chemical nature of vitamin K |
| 1944 | Joseph Erlanger | US | researches on differentiated |
|  | Herbert S. Gasser | US | functions of nerve fibers |
| 1945 | Sir Ernst Boris Chain | UK | discovery of penicillin |
|  | Sir Alexander Fleming | UK | and its curative value |
|  | Howard Walter Florey, Baron Florey | Australia | discovery of penicillin and its curative value |
| 1946 | Hermann Joseph Muller | US | production of mutations by X-ray irradiation |
| 1947 | Carl and Gerty Cori | US | discovery of how glycogen is catalytically converted |
|  | Bernardo A. Houssay | Argentina | pituitary hormone function in sugar metabolism |
| 1948 | Paul Hermann Müller | Switz. | properties of DDT |
| 1949 | António Egas Moniz | Portugal | therapeutic value of leucotomy in psychoses |
|  | Walter Rudolf Hess | Switz. | discovery of function of interbrain |
| 1950 | Philip Showalter Hench | US | research on adrenal cortex |
|  | Edward Calvin Kendall | US | hormones, their structure and |
|  | Tadeus Reichstein | Switz. | biological effects |

# Physiology or Medicine (continued)

| YEAR | WINNER(S) | COUNTRY | ACHIEVEMENT |
|---|---|---|---|
| 1951 | Max Theiler | South Africa | yellow fever discoveries |
| 1952 | Selman A. Waksman | US | discovery of streptomycin |
| 1953 | Sir Hans Adolf Krebs | UK | discovery of coenzyme A citric acid cycle in |
|  | Fritz Albert Lipmann | US | metabolism of carbohydrates |
| 1954 | John Franklin Enders | US | cultivation of the |
|  | Frederick C. Robbins | US | poliomyelitis virus in |
|  | Thomas H. Weller | US | tissue cultures |
| 1955 | Axel H.T. Theorell | Sweden | nature and mode of action of oxidation enzymes |
| 1956 | André F. Cournand | US | discoveries concerning |
|  | Werner Forssmann | W.Ger. | heart catheterization and |
|  | Dickinson W. Richards | US | circulatory changes |
| 1957 | Daniel Bovet | Italy | production of synthetic curare |
| 1958 | George Wells Beadle | US | genetic regulation of |
|  | Edward L. Tatum | US | chemical processes |
|  | Joshua Lederberg | US | genetic recombination |
| 1959 | Arthur Kornberg | US | work on producing nucleic |
|  | Severo Ochoa | US | acids artificially |
| 1960 | Sir Macfarlane Burnet | Australia | acquired immunity to |
|  | Sir Peter B. Medawar | UK | tissue transplants |
| 1961 | Georg von Békésy | US | functions of the inner ear |
| 1962 | Francis H.C. Crick | UK | discoveries concerning |
|  | James Dewey Watson | US | the molecular structure |
|  | Maurice Wilkins | UK | of DNA |
| 1963 | Sir John Carew Eccles | Australia | study of the transmission |
|  | Sir Alan Hodgkin | UK | of impulses along |
|  | Sir Andrew F. Huxley | UK | a nerve fiber |
| 1964 | Konrad Bloch | US | discoveries concerning |
|  | Feodor Lynen | W.Ger. | cholesterol and fatty-acid metabolism |
| 1965 | François Jacob | France | discoveries concerning |
|  | André Lwoff | France | regulatory activities |
|  | Jacques Monod | France | of the body cells |
| 1966 | Charles B. Huggins | US | research on causes and |
|  | Peyton Rous | US | treatment of cancer |
| 1967 | Ragnar Arthur Granit | Sweden | discoveries about chemical |
|  | Haldan Keffer Hartline | US | and physiological visual |
|  | George Wald | US | processes in the eye |
| 1968 | Robert William Holley | US | deciphering |
|  | Har Gobind Khorana | US | of the |
|  | Marshall W. Nirenberg | US | genetic code |
| 1969 | Max Delbrück | US | research and discoveries |
|  | A.D. Hershey | US | concerning viruses and |
|  | Salvador Luria | US | viral diseases |
| 1970 | Julius Axelrod | US | discoveries concerning |
|  | Ulf von Euler | Sweden | the chemistry of |
|  | Sir Bernard Katz | UK | nerve transmission |
| 1971 | Earl W. Sutherland, Jr. | US | action of hormones |
| 1972 | Gerald M. Edelman | US | research on the chemical |
|  | Rodney Robert Porter | UK | structure of antibodies |
| 1973 | Karl von Frisch | Austria | discoveries in |
|  | Konrad Lorenz | Austria | animal behavior |
|  | Nikolaas Tinbergen | UK | patterns |
| 1974 | Albert Claude | US | research on structural |
|  | Christian René de Duve | Belgium | and functional organization |
|  | George E. Palade | US | of cells |
| 1975 | David Baltimore | US | interaction between |
|  | Renato Dulbecco | US | tumor viruses and the genetic |
|  | Howard Martin Temin | US | material of the cell |
| 1976 | Baruch S. Blumberg | US | studies of origin and |
|  | D. Carleton Gajdusek | US | spread of infectious diseases |
| 1977 | Roger C.L. Guillemin | US | research on pituitary |
|  | Andrew Victor Schally | US | hormones |
|  | Rosalyn S. Yalow | US | development of radioimmunoassay |
| 1978 | Werner Arber | Switz. | discovery and application |
|  | Daniel Nathans | US | of enzymes that |
|  | Hamilton O. Smith | US | fragment DNA |
| 1979 | Allan M. Cormack | US | development of |
|  | Sir Godfrey N. Hounsfield | UK | the CAT scan |

## Physiology or Medicine (continued)

| YEAR | WINNER(S) | COUNTRY | ACHIEVEMENT |
|------|-----------|---------|-------------|
| 1980 | Baruj Benacerraf | US | investigations of genetic |
| | Jean-Baptiste-Gabriel- | France | control of the response of the |
| | George Davis Snell | US | immune system to foreign substances |
| 1981 | David Hunter Hubel | US | processing of visual |
| | Torsten Nils Wiesel | Sweden | information by the brain |
| | Roger Wolcott Sperry | US | functions of the cerebral hemispheres |
| 1982 | Sune K. Bergström | Sweden | biochemistry and |
| | Bengt I. Samuelsson | Sweden | physiology of |
| | John Robert Vane | UK | prostaglandins |
| 1983 | Barbara McClintock | US | discovery of mobile plant genes that affect heredity |
| 1984 | Niels K. Jerne | Denmark | theory and development |
| | Georges J.F. Köhler | W.Ger. | of a technique |
| | César Milstein | UK- | for producing |
| | | Argentina | monoclonal antibodies |
| 1985 | Michael S. Brown | US | discovery of cell receptors relating to |
| | Joseph L. Goldstein | US | cholesterol metabolism |
| 1986 | Stanley Cohen | US | discovery of chemical agents |
| | Rita Levi-Montalcini | Italy | that help regulate the growth of cells |
| 1987 | Tonegawa Susumu | Japan | study of genetic aspects of antibodies |
| 1988 | Sir James Black | UK | development of new |
| | Gertrude Belle Elion | US | classes of drugs for |
| | George H. Hitchings | US | combating disease |
| 1989 | J. Michael Bishop | US | study of cancer-causing |
| | Harold Varmus | US | genes called oncogenes |
| 1990 | Joseph E. Murray | US | development of kidney and |
| | E. Donnall Thomas | US | bone-marrow transplants |
| 1991 | Erwin Neher | Germany | discovery of how cells |
| | Bert Sakmann | Germany | communicate, as related to diseases |
| 1992 | Edmond H. Fischer | US | discovery of class of enzymes |
| | Edwin Gerhard Krebs | US | called protein kinases |
| 1993 | Richard J. Roberts | UK | discovery of "split," or |
| | Phillip A. Sharp | US | interrupted, genetic structure |
| 1994 | Alfred G. Gilman | US | discovery of cell signalers |
| | Martin Rodbell | US | called G-proteins |
| 1995 | Edward B. Lewis | US | identification of genes |
| | Christiane | Germany | that control the body's |
| | Nüsslein-Volhard | | early structural |
| | Eric F. Wieschaus | US | development |
| 1996 | Peter C. Doherty | Australia | discovery of how the immune |
| | Rolf M. Zinkernagel | Switz. | system recognizes virus-infected cells |
| 1997 | Stanley B. Prusiner | US | discovery of the prion, a type of disease-causing protein |
| 1998 | Robert F. Furchgott | US | discovery that nitric oxide (NO) |
| | Louis J. Ignarro | US | acts as a signaling molecule in |
| | Ferid Murad | US | the cardiovascular system |
| 1999 | Günter Blobel | US | discovery that proteins have signals governing cellular organization |
| 2000 | Arvid Carlsson | Sweden | discovery of how signals |
| | Paul Greengard | US | are transmitted between nerve |
| | Eric Kandel | US | cells in the brain |
| 2001 | Leland H. Hartwell | US | discovery of key |
| | R. Timothy Hunt | UK | regulators of |
| | Sir Paul M. Nurse | UK | the cell cycle |
| 2002 | Sydney Brenner | UK | discoveries concerning how genes |
| | H. Robert Horvitz | US | regulate and program organ |
| | John E. Sulston | UK | development and cell death |

**Did you know?** The first degree of doctor of civil law was awarded by the University of Bologna in the second half of the 12th century.

# Literature

| YEAR | WINNER(S) | COUNTRY | FIELD |
|------|-----------|---------|-------|
| 1901 | Sully Prudhomme | France | poetry |
| 1902 | Theodor Mommsen | Germany | history |
| 1903 | Bjørnstjerne Martinus Bjørnson | Norway | prose fiction, poetry, drama |
| 1904 | José Echegaray y Eizaguirre | Spain | drama |
|      | Frédéric Mistral | France | poetry |
| 1905 | Henryk Sienkiewicz | Poland | prose fiction |
| 1906 | Giosuè Carducci | Italy | poetry |
| 1907 | Rudyard Kipling | UK | poetry, prose fiction |
| 1908 | Rudolf Christoph Eucken | Germany | philosophey |
| 1909 | Selma Lagerlöf | Sweden | prose fiction |
| 1910 | Paul Johann Ludwig von Heyse | Germany | poetry, prose fiction, dramat |
| 1911 | Maurice Maeterlinck | Belgium | drama |
| 1912 | Gerhart Hauptmann | Germany | drama |
| 1913 | Rabindranath Tagore | India | poetry |
| 1915 | Romain Rolland | France | prose fiction |
| 1916 | Verner von Heidenstam | Sweden | poetry |
| 1917 | Karl Gjellerup | Denmark | prose fiction |
|      | Henrik Pontoppidan | Denmark | prose fiction |
| 1918 | Erik Axel Karlfeldt (declined) | Sweden | poetry |
| 1919 | Carl Spitteler | Switz. | poetry, prose fiction |
| 1920 | Knut Hamsun | Norway | prose fiction |
| 1921 | Anatole France | France | prose fiction |
| 1922 | Jacinto Benavente y Martínez | Spain | drama |
| 1923 | William Butler Yeats | Ireland | poetry |
| 1924 | Wladyslaw Stanislaw Reymont | Poland | prose fiction |
| 1925 | George Bernard Shaw | Ireland | drama |
| 1926 | Grazia Deledda | Italy | prose fiction |
| 1927 | Henri Bergson | France | philosophy |
| 1928 | Sigrid Undset | Norway | prose fiction |
| 1929 | Thomas Mann | Germany | prose fiction |
| 1930 | Sinclair Lewis | US | prose fiction |
| 1931 | Erik Axel Karlfeldt (posthumous award) | Sweden | poetry |
| 1932 | John Galsworthy | UK | prose fiction |
| 1933 | Ivan Alekseyevich Bunin | USSR | poetry, prose fiction |
| 1934 | Luigi Pirandello | Italy | drama |
| 1936 | Eugene O'Neill | US | drama |
| 1937 | Roger Martin du Gard | France | prose fiction |
| 1938 | Pearl Buck | US | prose fiction |
| 1939 | Frans Eemil Sillanpää | Finland | prose fiction |
| 1944 | Johannes V. Jensen | Denmark | prose fiction |
| 1945 | Gabriela Mistral | Chile | poetry |
| 1946 | Hermann Hesse | Switz. | prose fiction |
| 1947 | André Gide | France | prose |
| 1948 | T.S. Eliot | UK | poetry, criticism |
| 1949 | William Faulkner | US | prose fiction |
| 1950 | Bertrand Russell | UK | philosophy |
| 1951 | Pär Lagerkvist | Sweden | prose fiction |
| 1952 | François Mauriac | France | poetry, prose fiction, drama |
| 1953 | Sir Winston Churchill | UK | history, oration |
| 1954 | Ernest Hemingway | US | prose fiction |
| 1955 | Halldór Laxness | Iceland | prose fiction |
| 1956 | Juan Ramón Jiménez | Spain | poetry |
| 1957 | Albert Camus | France | prose fiction, drama |
| 1958 | Boris L. Pasternak (declined) | USSR | prose fiction, poetry |
| 1959 | Salvatore Quasimodo | Italy | poetry |
| 1960 | Saint-John Perse | France | poetry |
| 1961 | Ivo Andric | Yugoslavia | prose fiction |
| 1962 | John Steinbeck | US | prose fiction |
| 1963 | George Seferis | Greece | poetry |
| 1964 | Jean-Paul Sartre (declined) | France | philosophy, drama |
| 1965 | Mikhail A. Sholokhov | USSR | prose fiction |
| 1966 | S.Y. Agnon | Israel | prose fiction |
|      | Nelly Sachs | Sweden | poetry |
| 1967 | Miguel Ángel Asturias | Guatemala | prose fiction |

## Literature (continued)

| YEAR | WINNER(S) | COUNTRY | FIELD |
|------|-----------|---------|-------|
| 1968 | Kawabata Yasunari | Japan | prose fiction |
| 1969 | Samuel Beckett | Ireland | prose fiction, drama |
| 1970 | Aleksandr I. Solzhenitsyn | USSR | prose fiction |
| 1971 | Pablo Neruda | Chile | poetry |
| 1972 | Heinrich Böll | W.Ger. | prose fiction |
| 1973 | Patrick White | Australia | prose fiction |
| 1974 | Eyvind Johnson | Sweden | prose fiction |
|      | Harry Martinson | Sweden | prose fiction, poetry |
| 1975 | Eugenio Montale | Italy | poetry |
| 1976 | Saul Bellow | US | prose fiction |
| 1977 | Vicente Aleixandre | Spain | poetry |
| 1978 | Isaac Bashevis Singer | US | prose fiction |
| 1979 | Odysseus Elytis | Greece | poetry |
| 1980 | Czeslaw Milosz | US | poetry |
| 1981 | Elias Canetti | Bulgaria | prose |
| 1982 | Gabriel García Márquez | Colombia | prose fiction, journalism, social criticism |
| 1983 | Sir William Golding | UK | prose fiction |
| 1984 | Jaroslav Seifert | Czechoslovakia | poetry |
| 1985 | Claude Simon | France | prose fiction |
| 1986 | Wole Soyinka | Nigeria | drama, poetry |
| 1987 | Joseph Brodsky | US | poetry, prose |
| 1988 | Naguib Mahfouz | Egypt | prose fiction |
| 1989 | Camilo José Cela | Spain | prose fiction |
| 1990 | Octavio Paz | Mexico | poetry, prose |
| 1991 | Nadine Gordimer | South Africa | prose fiction |
| 1992 | Derek Walcott | St. Lucia | poetry |
| 1993 | Toni Morrison | US | prose fiction |
| 1994 | Kenzaburo Oe | Japan | prose fiction |
| 1995 | Seamus Heaney | Ireland | poetry |
| 1996 | Wislawa Szymborska | Poland | poetry |
| 1997 | Dario Fo | Italy | drama |
| 1998 | José Saramago | Portugal | prose fiction |
| 1999 | Günter Grass | Germany | prose fiction |
| 2000 | Gao Xingjian | France | prose fiction, drama |
| 2001 | Sir V.S. Naipaul | UK | prose fiction |
| 2002 | Imre Kertész | Hungary | prose fiction |

**Did you know?** The world's first novel, *Genji monogatari* (*The Tale of Genji*), was written in about 1010 and is also considered the greatest work of Japanese literature.

## Peace

| YEAR | WINNER(S) | COUNTRY | YEAR | WINNER(S) | COUNTRY |
|------|-----------|---------|------|-----------|---------|
| 1901 | Henri Dunant | Switz. | 1909 | Auguste-Marie-François Beernaert | Belgium |
|      | Frédéric Passy | France |      | Paul-H.-B. d'Estournelles de Constant | France |
| 1902 | Élie Ducommun | Switz. |      | | |
|      | Charles-Albert Gobat | Switz. | 1910 | International Peace Bureau | (founded 1891) |
| 1903 | Sir Randal Cremer | UK | 1911 | Tobias Michael Carel Asser | Neth. |
| 1904 | Institute of International Law | (founded 1873) |      | Alfred Hermann Fried | Austria-Hungary |
| 1905 | Bertha, Freifrau von Suttner | Austria-Hungary | 1912 | Elihu Root | US |
| 1906 | Theodore Roosevelt | US | 1913 | Henri-Marie Lafontaine | Belgium |
| 1907 | Ernesto Teodoro Moneta | Italy | 1917 | International Committee of the Red Cross | (founded 1863) |
|      | Louis Renault | France |      | | |
| 1908 | Klas Pontus Arnoldson | Sweden | 1919 | Woodrow Wilson | US |
|      | Fredrik Bajer | Denmark | 1920 | Léon Bourgeois | France |

# Peace (continued)

| YEAR | WINNER(S) | COUNTRY | YEAR | WINNER(S) | COUNTRY |
|------|-----------|---------|------|-----------|---------|
| 1921 | Karl Hjalmar Branting | Sweden | 1970 | Norman Ernest Borlaug | US |
| | Christian Lous Lange | Norway | 1971 | Willy Brandt | W.Ger. |
| 1922 | Fridtjof Nansen | Norway | 1973 | Henry Kissinger | US |
| 1925 | Sir Austen Chamberlain | UK | | Le Duc Tho | North Vietnam |
| | Charles G. Dawes | US | | (declined) | |
| 1926 | Aristide Briand | France | 1974 | Seán MacBride | Ireland |
| | Gustav Stresemann | Germany | | Sato Eisaku | Japan |
| 1927 | Ferdinand-Édouard Buisson | France | 1975 | Andrey Dmitriyevich | USSR |
| | Ludwig Quidde | Germany | | Sakharov | |
| 1929 | Frank B. Kellogg | US | 1976 | Mairéad Corrigan | Northern |
| 1930 | Nathan Söderblom | Sweden | | | Ireland |
| 1931 | Jane Addams | US | | Betty Williams | Northern |
| | Nicholas Murray Butler | US | | | Ireland |
| 1933 | Sir Norman Angell | UK | 1977 | Amnesty International | (founded 1961) |
| 1934 | Arthur Henderson | UK | 1978 | Menachem Begin | Israel |
| 1935 | Carl von Ossietzky | Germany | | Anwar el-Sadat | Egypt |
| 1936 | Carlos Saavedra Lamas | Argentina | 1979 | Mother Teresa | India |
| 1937 | Robert Gascoyne-Cecil, | UK | 1980 | Adolfo Pérez Esquivel | Argentina |
| | 1st Viscount Cecil | | 1981 | Office of the United Nations | (founded 1951) |
| | (of Chelwood) | | | High Commissioner for | |
| 1938 | Nansen International Office | (founded 1931) | | Refugees | |
| | for Refugees | | 1982 | Alfonso García Robles | Mexico |
| 1944 | International Committee of | (founded 1863) | | Alva Myrdal | Sweden |
| | the Red Cross | | 1983 | Lech Walesa | Poland |
| 1945 | Cordell Hull | US | 1984 | Desmond Tutu | South Africa |
| 1946 | Emily Greene Balch | US | 1985 | International Physicians for | (founded 1980) |
| | John R. Mott | US | | the Prevention of Nuclear | |
| 1947 | American Friends Service | US | | War | |
| | Committee | | 1986 | Elie Wiesel | US |
| | Friends Service Council | UK | 1987 | Oscar Arias Sánchez | Costa Rica |
| | (FSC) | | 1988 | United Nations Peace- | |
| 1949 | John Boyd Orr, Baron Boyd- | UK | | keeping Forces | |
| | Orr of Brechin Mearns | | 1989 | Dalai Lama | Tibet |
| 1950 | Ralph Bunche | US | 1990 | Mikhail Gorbachev | USSR |
| 1951 | Léon Jouhaux | France | 1991 | Aung San Suu Kyi | Myanmar |
| 1952 | Albert Schweitzer | Alsace | 1992 | Rigoberta Menchú | Guatemala |
| 1953 | George C. Marshall | US | 1993 | F.W. de Klerk | South Africa |
| 1954 | Office of the United Nations | (founded 1951) | | Nelson Mandela | South Africa |
| | High Commissioner for | | 1994 | Yasir 'Arafat | Palestinian |
| | Refugees | | | Shimon Peres | Israel |
| 1957 | Lester B. Pearson | Canada | | Yitzhak Rabin | Israel |
| 1958 | Dominique Pire | Belgium | 1995 | Pugwash Conferences | (founded 1957) |
| 1959 | Philip John Noel-Baker, | UK | | Joseph Rotblat | UK |
| | Baron Noel-Baker (of the | | 1996 | Carlos Filipe Ximenes Belo | Timorese |
| | City of Derby) | | | José Ramos-Horta | Timorese |
| 1960 | Albert John Luthuli | South Africa | 1997 | International Campaign to | (founded 1992) |
| 1961 | Dag Hammarskjöld | Sweden | | Ban Landmines | |
| 1962 | Linus Pauling | US | | Jody Williams | US |
| 1963 | International Committee of | (founded 1863) | 1998 | John Hume | Northern |
| | the Red Cross | | | | Ireland |
| | League of Red Cross | | | David Trimble | Northern |
| | Societies | | | | Ireland |
| 1964 | Martin Luther King, Jr. | US | 1999 | Doctors Without Borders | (founded 1971) |
| 1965 | United Nations Children's | (founded 1946) | 2000 | Kim Dae Jung | South Korea |
| | Fund | | 2001 | Kofi Annan | Ghana |
| 1968 | René Cassin | France | 2002 | Jimmy Carter | US |
| 1969 | International Labour Organi- | (founded 1919) | | | |
| | sation | | | | |

# Economics

| YEAR | WINNER(S) | COUNTRY | ACHIEVEMENT |
|---|---|---|---|
| 1969 | Ragnar Frisch | Norway | } work in |
| | Jan Tinbergen | Neth. | econometrics |
| 1970 | Paul Samuelson | US | work in scientific analysis of economic theory |
| 1971 | Simon Kuznets | US | extensive research on the economic growth of nations |
| 1972 | Kenneth J. Arrow | US | } contributions to general economic |
| | Sir John R. Hicks | UK | equilibrium theory and welfare theory |
| 1973 | Wassily Leontief | US | input-output analysis |
| 1974 | Friedrich von Hayek | UK | } pioneering analysis of the interdependence of |
| | Gunnar Myrdal | Sweden | economic, social, and institutional phenomena |
| 1975 | Leonid V. Kantorovich | USSR | } contributions to the theory of |
| | Tjalling C. Koopmans | US | optimum allocation of resources |
| 1976 | Milton Friedman | US | consumption analysis, monetary theory, and economic stabilization |
| 1977 | James Edward Meade | UK | } contributions to theory |
| | Bertil Ohlin | Sweden | of international trade |
| 1978 | Herbert A. Simon | US | decision-making processes in economic organizations |
| 1979 | Sir Arthur Lewis | UK | } analyses of economic processes |
| | Theodore W. Schultz | US | in developing nations |
| 1980 | Lawrence Robert Klein | US | development and analysis of empirical models of business fluctuations |
| 1981 | James Tobin | US | portfolio selection theory of investment |
| 1982 | George J. Stigler | US | economic effects of governmental regulation |
| 1983 | Gerard Debreu | US | mathematical proof of supply and demand theory |
| 1984 | Sir Richard Stone | UK | development of national income accounting system |
| 1985 | Franco Modigliani | US | analyses of household savings and financial markets |
| 1986 | James M. Buchanan | US | public-choice theory bridging economics and political science |
| 1987 | Robert Merton Solow | US | contributions to the theory of economic growth |
| 1988 | Maurice Allais | France | contributions to the theory of markets and efficient use of resources |
| 1989 | Trygve Haavelmo | Norway | development of statistical techniques for economic forecasting |
| 1990 | Harry M. Markowitz | US | ⎫ study of financial |
| | Merton H. Miller | US | } markets and investment |
| | William F. Sharpe | US | ⎭ decision making |
| 1991 | Ronald Coase | US | application of economic principles to the study of law |
| 1992 | Gary S. Becker | US | application of economic theory to social sciences |
| 1993 | Robert William Fogel | US | } contributions to |
| | Douglass C. North | US | economic history |
| 1994 | John C. Harsanyi | US | ⎫ development |
| | John F. Nash | US | } of game |
| | Reinhard Selten | Germany | ⎭ theory |
| 1995 | Robert E. Lucas, Jr. | US | incorporation of rational expectations in macroeconomic theory |
| 1996 | James A. Mirrlees | UK | } contributions to theory of incentives under |
| | William Vickrey | US | conditions of asymmetric information |
| 1997 | Robert C. Merton | US | } method for determining the value of |
| | Myron S. Scholes | US | stock options and other derivatives |
| 1998 | Amartya Sen | India | contribution to welfare economics |
| 1999 | Robert A. Mundell | Canada | analysis of optimum currency areas and of policy under different exchange rate regimes |
| 2000 | James J. Heckman | US | } development of methods of statistical |
| | Daniel L. McFadden | US | analysis of individual and household behavior |
| 2001 | George A. Akerlof | US | ⎫ analyses of |
| | A. Michael Spence | US | } markets with |
| | Joseph E. Stiglitz | US | ⎭ information |
| 2002 | Daniel Kahneman | US, Israel | integration of psychological research into economics, particularly concerning decision-making under circumstances of uncertainty |
| | Vernon L. Smith | US | establishment of laboratory experiments for empirical economic analysis, particularly in the area of alternative market mechanisms |

# Special Achievement Awards

## Templeton Prize Winners

Formerly the Templeton Prize for Progress in Religion, the Templeton Prize for Progress Toward Research or Discoveries about Spiritual Realities was established in 1972 by American-born British businessman and philanthropist Sir John Templeton. It recognizes the diversity of and rewards advancement in the ideas and perceptions of divinity. Each year a group of international, interfaith judges chooses a winner from any of the world's religions. Award amount: £700,000 (about $1.2 million). Templeton Prize Web site: <www.templetonprize.org>

| YEAR | NAME | FIELD |
|---|---|---|
| 1973 | Mother Teresa | founder, Missionaries of Charity |
| 1974 | Brother Roger | founder, Taizé Community |
| 1975 | Sir Sarvepalli Radhakrishnan | president of India, 1962–67 |
| 1976 | Leon Joseph Cardinal Suenens | pioneer, Charismatic Renewal Movement |
| 1977 | Chiara Lubich | founder, Focolare Movement |
| 1978 | Thomas F. Torrance | educator, writer on religion and science |
| 1979 | Nikkyo Niwano | founder, Rissho Kosei-Kai |
| 1980 | Ralph Wendell Burhoe | founder and editor, Zygon, Journal of Religion and Science |
| 1981 | Dame Cicely Saunders | founder, Hospice and Palliative Care Movement |
| 1982 | Billy Graham | Christian evangelist |
| 1983 | Aleksandr Solzhenitsyn | writer, dissident |
| 1984 | Michael Bourdeaux | scholar, religious freedom activist |
| 1985 | Sir Alister Hardy | scientist, educator |
| 1986 | James McCord | chancellor, Center of Theological Inquiry; president, Princeton Theological Seminary |
| 1987 | Stanley L. Jaki | Benedictine monk, professor of astrophysics |
| 1988 | Inamullah Khan | interfaith peace activist; founder, Modern World Muslim Congress |
| 1989 | Lord George MacLeod | founder, Iona Community |
| | Carl Friedrich von Weizsäcker | physics and theology scholar |
| 1990 | Baba Amte | social activist, philanthropist |
| | L. Charles Birch | natural scientist |
| 1991 | Lord Immanuel Jakobovits | Chief Rabbi of Great Britain and the Commonwealth, 1967–91 |
| 1992 | Kyung-Chik Han | founder, Young Nak Presbyterian Church |
| 1993 | Charles W. Colson | prison ministry founder |
| 1994 | Michael Novak | theologian, writer on theology and economics |
| 1995 | Paul Charles William Davies | mathematical physicist |
| 1996 | William R. Bright | founder, Campus Crusade for Christ |
| 1997 | Pandurang Shastri Athavale | founder, swadhyaya self-study |
| 1998 | Sir Sigmund Sternberg | philanthropist, businessman |
| 1999 | Ian Graeme Barbour | technology ethicist |
| 2000 | Freeman J. Dyson | physicist, social activist |
| 2001 | Arthur Peacocke | founder, Society of Ordained Scientists |
| 2002 | John C. Polkinghorne | Anglican priest, mathematical physicist |
| 2003 | Holmes Rolston III | Presbyterian minister, environmental ethicist |

 **Did you know?** One in 20 Pingelap islanders suffers from a rare type of total color-blindness. The color-blindness is a legacy of a violent storm that in 1775 killed all but 20 of the islanders on Pingelap atoll.

## Congressional Gold Medal

Individuals, institutions, or events of distinguished achievement are honored by the Congressional Gold Medal. First awarded in 1776, 128 medals have since been given out. Early medals went primarily to military figures; beginning in the mid-19th century, they were given to a wide variety of people. Past recipients include George Washington, Andrew Jackson, rocketry inventor Robert H. Goddard, Richard E. Byrd's Antarctic expedition, composer Aaron Copland, poet Robert Frost, baseball legend Roberto Clemente, first lady Lady Bird Johnson, Gen. Colin Powell, Simon Wiesenthal, the "Little Rock Nine," and the Navajo Code Talkers of World War II. In 2003 the Congress awarded the medal to British Prime Minister Tony Blair in recognition of Blair's support of the war in Iraq. Blair is the first Briton since Winston Churchill to receive the honor.

# The Kennedy Center Honors

The Kennedy Center Honors are bestowed annually by the John F. Kennedy Center for the Performing Arts in Washington DC. First conferred in 1978, the honors salute five artists each year for lifetime achievement in the performing arts and are celebrated by a televised gala in December. Web site: <www.kennedy-center.org/programs/specialevents/honors/>.

| YEAR | NAME | FIELD |
|---|---|---|
| 1978 | Marian Anderson | opera singer |
| | Fred Astaire | dancer, actor |
| | George Balanchine | choreographer |
| | Richard Rodgers | composer |
| | Arthur Rubenstein | pianist |
| 1979 | Aaron Copland | composer |
| | Ella Fitzgerald | singer |
| | Henry Fonda | actor |
| | Martha Graham | dancer, choreographer |
| | Tennessee Williams | playwright |
| 1980 | Leonard Bernstein | conductor |
| | James Cagney | actor |
| | Agnes de Mille | dancer, choreographer |
| | Lynn Fontanne | actress |
| | Leontyne Price | opera singer |
| 1981 | Count Basie | jazz pianist |
| | Cary Grant | actor |
| | Helen Hayes | actress |
| | Jerome Robbins | dancer, choreographer |
| | Rudolf Serkin | pianist |
| 1982 | George Abbott | theater producer, director, writer |
| | Lillian Gish | actress |
| | Benny Goodman | swing musician |
| | Gene Kelly | dancer, actor |
| | Eugene Ormandy | conductor |
| 1983 | Katherine Dunham | dancer, choreographer |
| | Elia Kazan | theater and film director |
| | Frank Sinatra | singer, actor |
| | James Stewart | actor |
| | Virgil Thomson | composer, music critic |
| 1984 | Lena Horne | singer, actress |
| | Danny Kaye | actor, comedian |
| | Gian Carlo Menotti | composer |
| | Arthur Miller | playwright |
| | Isaac Stern | violinist |
| 1985 | Merce Cunningham | dancer, choreographer |
| | Irene Dunne | actress |
| | Bob Hope | entertainer, actor |
| | Alan Jay Lerner | playwright, lyricist |
| | Frederick Loewe | composer |
| | Beverly Sills | opera singer |
| 1986 | Lucille Ball | actress |
| | Ray Charles | soul musician |
| | Hume Cronyn | actor |
| | Jessica Tandy | actress |
| | Yehudi Menuhin | violinist |
| | Antony Tudor | choreographer |
| 1987 | Perry Como | singer |
| | Bette Davis | actress |
| | Sammy Davis, Jr. | singer, dancer, entertainer |
| | Nathan Milstein | violinist |
| | Alwin Nikolais | choreographer |
| 1988 | Alvin Ailey | dancer, choreographer |
| | George Burns | actor, comedian |
| | Myrna Loy | actress |
| | Alexander Schneider | violinist, conductor |
| | Roger L. Stevens | arts administrator |
| 1989 | Harry Belafonte | folk singer, actor |
| | Claudette Colbert | actress |

| YEAR | NAME | FIELD |
|---|---|---|
| | Alexandra Danilova | ballet dancer |
| | Mary Martin | actress, singer |
| | William Schuman | composer |
| 1990 | Dizzy Gillespie | jazz musician |
| | Katharine Hepburn | actress |
| | Risë Stevens | opera singer |
| | Jule Styne | composer |
| | Billy Wilder | film director |
| 1991 | Roy Acuff | country musician |
| | Betty Comden | theater and film writer |
| | Adolph Green | theater and film writer |
| | Fayard Nicholas | dancer |
| | Harold Nicholas | dancer |
| | Gregory Peck | actor |
| | Robert Shaw | choral and orchestral conductor |
| 1992 | Lionel Hampton | swing musician |
| | Paul Newman | actor |
| | Joanne Woodward | actress |
| | Ginger Rogers | dancer, actress |
| | Mstislav Rostropovich | musician, conductor |
| | Paul Taylor | dancer, choreographer |
| 1993 | Johnny Carson | television entertainer |
| | Arthur Mitchell | dancer, choreographer |
| | George Solti | conductor |
| | Stephen Sondheim | composer, lyricist |
| | Marion Williams | gospel singer |
| 1994 | Kirk Douglas | actor |
| | Aretha Franklin | soul singer |
| | Morton Gould | composer |
| | Harold Prince | theater director, producer |
| | Pete Seeger | folk musician |
| 1995 | Jacques d'Amboise | dancer, choreographer |
| | Marilyn Horne | opera singer |
| | B.B. King | blues musician |
| | Sidney Poitier | actor |
| | Neil Simon | playwright |
| 1996 | Edward Albee | playwright |
| | Benny Carter | jazz musician |
| | Johnny Cash | country musician |
| | Jack Lemmon | actor |
| | Maria Tallchief | ballet dancer |
| 1997 | Lauren Bacall | actress |
| | Bob Dylan | singer, songwriter |
| | Charlton Heston | actor |
| | Jessye Norman | opera singer |
| | Edward Villella | dancer, choreographer |
| 1998 | Bill Cosby | actor, comedian |
| | Fred Ebb and John Kander | lyricist and composer |
| | Willie Nelson | country musician |
| | André Previn | pianist, composer, conductor |
| | Shirley Temple Black | actress |
| 1999 | Victor Borge | pianist, comedian |
| | Sean Connery | actor |
| | Judith Jamison | dancer, choreographer |
| | Jason Robards | actor |
| | Stevie Wonder | musician |
| 2000 | Mikhail Baryshnikov | dancer |

# The Kennedy Center Honors (continued)

| YEAR | NAME | FIELD |
|------|------|-------|
| | Chuck Berry | musician |
| | Plácido Domingo | opera singer |
| | Clint Eastwood | actor, director |
| | Angela Lansbury | actress |
| 2001 | Julie Andrews | actress |
| | Van Cliburn | pianist |
| | Quincy Jones | music producer, composer |
| | Jack Nicholson | actor |
| | Luciano Pavarotti | opera singer |

| YEAR | NAME | FIELD |
|------|------|-------|
| 2002 | James Earl Jones | actor |
| | James Levine | conductor |
| | Chita Rivera | musical theater performer |
| | Paul Simon | singer |
| | Elizabeth Taylor | actress |
| | Chuck Berry | musician |
| | Plácido Domingo | opera singer |
| | Clint Eastwood | actor, director |
| | Angela Lansbury | actress |

**Did you know?** Henri Matisse's painting *Le Bateau* (*The Boat*) was accidentally hung upside-down in New York's Museum of Modern art for 47 days in 1961. None among the 116,000 visitors during that time noticed it.

# The National Medal of Arts

The National Medal of Arts, awarded annually since 1985 by the National Endowment for the Arts (NEA) and the president of the United States, honors artists and art patrons for remarkable contributions to American arts. As many as 12 medals may be given out each year. Both the NEA and the president choose candidates for the award, and the winners are selected by the president. Web site: <www.arts.gov/honors/medals/allmedalists.html>.

| YEAR | NAME | FIELD |
|------|------|-------|
| 1985 | Elliott Carter, Jr. | composer |
| | Ralph Ellison | writer |
| | José Ferrer | actor |
| | Martha Graham | dancer, choreographer |
| | Louise Nevelson | sculptor |
| | Georgia O'Keeffe | painter |
| | Leontyne Price | opera singer |
| | Dorothy Buffum Chandler | patron |
| | Lincoln Kirstein | patron |
| | Paul Mellon | patron |
| | Alice Tully | patron |
| | Hallmark Cards, Inc. | patron |
| 1986 | Marian Anderson | opera singer |
| | Frank Capra | film director |
| | Aaron Copland | composer |
| | Willem de Kooning | painter |
| | Agnes de Mille | dancer, choreographer |
| | Eva Le Gallienne | actress, theater producer |
| | Alan Lomax | ethnomusicologist |
| | Lewis Mumford | architectural critic, historian |
| | Eudora Welty | writer |
| | Dominique de Menil | patron |
| | Exxon Corporation | patron |
| | Seymour H. Knox | patron |
| 1987 | Romare Bearden | painter |
| | Ella Fitzgerald | singer |
| | Howard Nemerov | writer, scholar |
| | Alwin Nikolais | choreographer |
| | Isamu Noguchi | sculptor |
| | William Schuman | composer |
| | Robert Penn Warren | writer |
| | J.W. Fisher | patron |
| | Armand Hammer | patron |
| | Sydney and Frances Lewis | patrons |

| YEAR | NAME | FIELD |
|------|------|-------|
| 1988 | Saul Bellow | writer |
| | Helen Hayes | actress |
| | Gordon Parks | photographer, writer |
| | I.M. Pei | architect |
| | Jerome Robbins | dancer, choreographer |
| | Rudolf Serkin | pianist |
| | Virgil Thomson | composer, music critic |
| | Sydney J. Freedberg | art historian, museum curator |
| | Roger L. Stevens | arts administrator |
| | Brooke Astor | patron |
| | Francis Goelet | patron |
| | Obert C. Tanner | patron |
| 1989 | Leopold Adler | historic preservationist, civic leader |
| | Katherine Dunham | dancer, choreographer |
| | Alfred Eisenstaedt | photojournalist |
| | Martin Friedman | museum director |
| | Leigh Gerdine | civic leader, patron |
| | Dizzy Gillespie | jazz musician |
| | Walker Kirtland Hancock | sculptor |
| | Vladimir Horowitz* | pianist |
| | Czelaw Milosz | writer |
| | Robert Motherwell | painter |
| | John Updike | writer |
| | Dayton Hudson Corporation | patron |
| 1990 | George Abbott | theater producer, director, writer |
| | Hume Cronyn | actor, director |
| | Jessica Tandy | actress |
| | Merce Cunningham | dancer, choreographer |
| | Jasper Johns | painter, sculptor |
| | Jacob Lawrence | painter |
| | B.B. King | blues musician |
| | Beverly Sills | opera singer |
| | Ian McHarg | landscape architect |

## The National Medal of Arts (continued)

| YEAR | NAME | FIELD |
|---|---|---|
| | Harris & Carroll Sterling Masterson | patrons |
| | David Lloyd Kreeger | patron |
| | Southeastern Bell Corporation | patron |
| 1991 | Maurice Abravanel | conductor, music director |
| | Roy Acuff | country musician |
| | Pietro Belluschi | architect |
| | J. Carter Brown | museum director |
| | Charles "Honi" Coles | tap dancer |
| | John O. Crosby | opera director, conductor |
| | Richard Diebenkorn | painter |
| | Isaac Stern | violinist |
| | Kitty Carlisle Hart | actress, singer, arts administrator |
| | R. Philip Hanes, Jr. | patron |
| | Pearl Primus | choreographer, anthropologist |
| | Texaco Inc. | patron |
| 1992 | Marilyn Horne | opera singer |
| | James Earl Jones | actor |
| | Allan Houser | sculptor |
| | Minnie Pearl | Grand Ole Opry performer |
| | Robert Saudek | television producer, museum director |
| | Earl Scruggs | banjo player |
| | Robert Shaw | choral and orchestral conductor |
| | Billy Taylor | jazz pianist |
| | Robert Venturi and Denise Scott Brown | architects |
| | Robert Wise | film director |
| | AT&T | patron |
| | Lila Wallace-Reader's Digest Fund | patron |
| 1993 | Cabell "Cab" Calloway | jazz musician |
| | Ray Charles | soul musician |
| | Bess Lomax Hawes | folklorist, musician |
| | Stanley Kunitz | poet |
| | Robert Merrill | opera singer |
| | Arthur Miller | playwright |
| | Robert Rauschenberg | painter |
| | Lloyd Richards | theater director |
| | William Styron | writer |
| | Paul Taylor | dancer, choreographer |
| | Billy Wilder | film director, producer, writer |
| | Walter and Leonore Annenberg | patrons |
| 1994 | Harry Belafonte | folk singer, actor |
| | Dave Brubeck | jazz musician |
| | Celia Cruz | salsa singer |
| | Dorothy DeLay | violin instructor |
| | Julie Harris | actress |
| | Erick Hawkins | dancer, choreographer |
| | Gene Kelly | dancer, actor |
| | Pete Seeger | folk musician |
| | Wayne Thiebaud | painter |
| | Richard Wilbur | poet |

| YEAR | NAME | FIELD |
|---|---|---|
| | Young Audiences | arts organization |
| | Catherine Filene Shouse | patron |
| 1995 | Licia Albanese | opera singer |
| | Gwendolyn Brooks | poet |
| | Ossie Davis and Ruby Dee | actors |
| | David Diamond | composer |
| | James Ingo Freed | architect |
| | Bob Hope | entertainer |
| | Roy Lichtenstein | painter |
| | Arthur Mitchell | dancer, choreographer |
| | William S. Monroe | bluegrass musician |
| | Urban Gateways | arts education organization |
| | B. Gerald and Iris Cantor | patrons |
| 1996 | Edward Albee | playwright |
| | Sarah Caldwell | opera conductor, producer |
| | Harry Callahan | photographer |
| | Zelda Fichandler | theater founder, director |
| | Eduardo "Lalo" Guerrero | Chicano musician |
| | Lionel Hampton | swing musician |
| | Bella Lewitzky | dancer, choreographer |
| | Robert Redford | actor, film director |
| | Maurice Sendak | illustrator, writer |
| | Stephen Sondheim | composer, lyricist |
| | Boys Choir of Harlem | youth performance group |
| | Vera List | patron |
| 1997 | Louise Bourgeois | sculptor |
| | Betty Carter | jazz singer |
| | Daniel Urban Kiley | landscape architect |
| | Angela Lansbury | actress |
| | James Levine | opera conductor, pianist |
| | Tito Puente | jazz and mambo musician |
| | Jason Robards | actor |
| | Edward Villella | dancer, choreographer |
| | Doc Watson | folk and country musician |
| | MacDowell Colony | artists' colony |
| | Agnes Gund | patron |
| 1998 | Jacques d'Amboise | dancer, choreographer |
| | Antoine "Fats" Domino | rock-and-roll musician |
| | Ramblin' Jack Elliott | folk musician |
| | Frank O. Gehry | architect |
| | Agnes Martin | painter |
| | Gregory Peck | actor |
| | Roberta Peters | opera singer |
| | Philip Roth | writer |
| | Gwen Verdon | actress, dancer |
| | Steppenwolf Theatre Company | arts organization |
| | Sara Lee Corporation | patron |
| | Barbara Handman | patron |
| 1999 | Aretha Franklin | soul singer |
| | Michael Graves | architect, designer |

## The National Medal of Arts (continued)

| YEAR | NAME | FIELD |
|---|---|---|
| | Odetta | folk singer |
| | Norman Lear | television producer, writer |
| | Rosetta LeNoire | actress, theater founder |
| | Harvey Lichtenstein | arts administrator |
| | Lydia Mendoza | Tejano musician |
| | George Segal | sculptor |
| | Maria Tallchief | ballet dancer |
| | The Julliard School | performing arts school |
| | Irene Diamond | patron |
| 2000 | Maya Angelou | poet, writer |
| | Eddy Arnold | country musician |
| | Mikhail Baryshnikov | dancer, dance company director |
| | Benny Carter | jazz musician |
| | Chuck Close | painter |
| | Horton Foote | dramatist |
| | Claes Oldenburg | sculptor |
| | Itzhak Perlman | violinist |
| | Harold Prince | theater director, producer |
| | Barbra Streisand | singer, actress, film director |
| | Lewis Manilow | patron |

| YEAR | NAME | FIELD |
|---|---|---|
| | NPR Cultural Pro–gramming Division | broadcaster |
| 2001 | Alvin Ailey Dance Foundation | modern dance company and school |
| | Rudolfo Anaya | writer |
| | Johnny Cash | country musician |
| | Kirk Douglas | actor |
| | Helen Frankenthaler | painter |
| | Judith Jamison | dancer, choreographer |
| | Yo-Yo Ma | cellist |
| | Mike Nichols | theater and film director |
| 2002 | Florence Knoll Bassett | designer, architect |
| | Trisha Brown | dancer, choreographer |
| | Philippe de Montebello | museum director |
| | Uta Hagen | actress, educator |
| | Lawrence Halprin | landscape architect |
| | Al Hirschfeld* | artist, caricaturist |
| | George Jones | singer, songwriter |
| | Ming Cho Lee | painter, stage designer |
| | William "Smokey" Robinson, Jr. | singer, songwriter |

*Awarded posthumously.*

## American Academy of Arts and Letters Awards, 2003

Each year the American Academy of Arts and Letters, a 250-member organization founded in 1898, confers some two dozen awards for excellence in the fields of art, music, literature, and architecture. Of the prizes, the Academy Awards in each field are the most prestigious. Winners receive $7,500; music winners receive an additional $7,500 to be used for the recording of a musical piece. The recipients for 2003 were as follows: ▶ **Architecture**, Greg Lynn, Guy Nordenson, and Andrew Zago; ▶ **Art**, R. Crumb, Robert Lazzarini, Nancy Rubins, Gary Stephan, and Richard Tuttle; ▶ **Literature**, Andrea Barrett, Clark Blaise, Percival Everett, Hilary Masters, Lynne McMahon, Gregory Orr, Tom Sleigh, and Anne Winters; ▶ **Music**, Eric Chasalow, Zhou Long, Jeffrey Mumford, and Roberto Sierra.

## National Humanities Medal

The National Humanities Medal (originally known as the Charles Frankel Prize, 1988–96) is awarded by the National Endowment for the Humanities for notable contributions to Americans' understanding of and involvement with the humanities. As many as 12 medals may be conferred each year. The recipients for 2002 were stage producer Frankie Hewitt, the Iowa Writers' Workshop, classics professor Donald Kagan, C-SPAN executive Brian Lamb, comedian Art Linkletter, children's writer Patricia MacLachlan, the Mount Vernon Ladies' Association, and social policy thinker Thomas Sowell.

Web site: <www.neh.gov/whoweare/awards.html>

Bob Hope was the fifth of seven sons of a stonemason and a former Welsh concert singer; his family immigrated to the US when he was four years old. He grew up in Cleveland OH, manifesting the first signs of his vocation at age 10 when he won a Charlie Chaplin imitation contest.

# The Spingarn Medal

*The National Association for the Advancement of Colored People (NAACP) presents the medal for distinguished achievement among African Americans. The medal is named for early NAACP activist Joel E. Spingarn.*

| YEAR | NAME | FIELD |
|---|---|---|
| 1915 | Ernest Everett Just | zoologist, marine biologist |
| 1916 | Charles Young | army officer |
| 1917 | Harry Thacker Burleigh | singer, composer |
| 1918 | William Stanley Braithwaite | poet, literary critic |
| 1919 | Archibald Henry Grimké | lawyer, diplomat, social activist |
| 1920 | W.E.B. Du Bois (William Edward Burghardt Du Bois) | sociologist, social activist |
| 1921 | Charles S. Gilpin | actor |
| 1922 | Mary Burnett Talbert | civil rights activist |
| 1923 | George Washington Carver | agricultural chemist |
| 1924 | Roland Hayes | singer, composer |
| 1925 | James Weldon Johnson | writer, diplomat, anthologist |
| 1926 | Carter G. Woodson | historian |
| 1927 | Anthony Overton | businessman |
| 1928 | Charles W. Chesnutt | writer |
| 1929 | Mordecai W. Johnson | minister, university president |
| 1930 | Henry Alexander Hunt | educator, government official |
| 1931 | Richard B. Harrison | actor |
| 1932 | Robert Russa Moton | educator, civil rights leader |
| 1933 | Max Yergan | civil rights leader |
| 1934 | William T.B. Williams | educator |
| 1935 | Mary McLeod Bethune | educator, social activist |
| 1936 | John Hope | educator |
| 1937 | Walter White | civil rights leader |
| 1938 | *no medal awarded* | |
| 1939 | Marian Anderson | opera singer |
| 1940 | Louis T. Wright | surgeon, civil rights leader |
| 1941 | Richard Wright | writer |
| 1942 | A. Philip Randolph | labor and civil rights leader |
| 1943 | William H. Hastie | lawyer, judge |
| 1944 | Charles Richard Drew | surgeon, research scientist |
| 1945 | Paul Robeson | actor, singer, social activist |
| 1946 | Thurgood Marshall | lawyer, US Supreme Court justice |
| 1947 | Percy L. Julian | chemist |
| 1948 | Channing H. Tobias | civil rights leader |
| 1949 | Ralph Bunche | diplomat, scholar |
| 1950 | Charles Hamilton Houston | lawyer |
| 1951 | Mabel Keaton Staupers | nurse, social activist |
| 1952 | Harry T. Moore | civil rights activist, educator |
| 1953 | Paul R. Williams | architect |
| 1954 | Theodore K. Lawless | dermatologist, philanthropist |
| 1955 | Carl Murphy | journalist, civil rights activist |
| 1956 | Jackie Robinson (Jack Roosevelt Robinson) | baseball player |
| 1957 | Martin Luther King, Jr. | civil rights leader |
| 1958 | Daisy Bates and the Little Rock Nine | school integration activists |
| 1959 | Duke Ellington (Edward Kennedy Ellington) | jazz musician |
| 1960 | Langston Hughes | writer |
| 1961 | Kenneth Bancroft Clark | educator |
| 1962 | Robert C. Weaver | economist, government official |
| 1963 | Medgar Evers | civil rights activist |
| 1964 | Roy Wilkins | civil rights leader |
| 1965 | Leontyne Price | opera singer |
| 1966 | John H. Johnson | publisher |
| 1967 | Edward W. Brooke III | lawyer, US senator |
| 1968 | Sammy Davis, Jr. | singer, dancer, entertainer |
| 1969 | Clarence M. Mitchell, Jr. | civil rights lobbyist |
| 1970 | Jacob Lawrence | painter |
| 1971 | Leon H. Sullivan | minister, civil rights activist |
| 1972 | Gordon Parks | photographer, writer |
| 1973 | Wilson C. Riles | educator |
| 1974 | Damon Keith | lawyer, judge |
| 1975 | Hank Aaron | baseball player |
| 1976 | Alvin Ailey | dancer, choreographer |
| 1977 | Alex Haley | writer |
| 1978 | Andrew Young | politician, civil rights leader |
| 1979 | Rosa Parks | civil rights activist |
| 1980 | Rayford W. Logan | educator, writer |
| 1981 | Coleman A. Young | labor activist, politician |
| 1982 | Benjamin E. Mays | educator, minister |
| 1983 | Lena Horne | singer, actress |
| 1984 | Thomas Bradley | politician |
| 1985 | Bill Cosby | actor, comedian |
| 1986 | Benjamin L. Hooks | civil rights leader, government official |
| 1987 | Percy Ellis Sutton | civil rights activist, politician |
| 1988 | Frederick Douglass Patterson | educator |
| 1989 | Jesse Jackson | minister, politician, civil rights leader |
| 1990 | L. Douglas Wilder | politician |
| 1991 | Colin Powell | army general, government official |
| 1992 | Barbara Jordan | lawyer, politician |
| 1993 | Dorothy I. Height | social activist |
| 1994 | Maya Angelou | poet |
| 1995 | John Hope Franklin | historian, educator |
| 1996 | A. Leon Higginbotham | lawyer, judge, scholar |
| 1997 | Carl T. Rowan | journalist, commentator |
| 1998 | Myrlie Evers-Williams | civil rights activist |

## The Spingarn Medal (continued)

| YEAR | NAME | FIELD | YEAR | NAME | FIELD |
|------|------|-------|------|------|-------|
| 1999 | Earl G. Graves | publisher | 2002 | John Lewis | politician, civil rights activist |
| 2000 | Oprah Winfrey | television host, media personality | 2003 | Constance Baker Motley | judge, lawyer, civil rights activist |
| 2001 | Vernon E. Jordan, Jr. | lawyer, civil rights activist | | | |

# Science Honors

## Fields Medal

The Fields Medal, officially known as the International Medal for Outstanding Discoveries in Mathematics, is granted every four years to between two and four mathematicians for outstanding or groundbreaking research. It is traditionally given to mathematicians under the age of 40. Prize: $1,500.

| YEAR | NAME | BIRTHPLACE | PRIMARY RESEARCH |
|------|------|------------|------------------|
| 1936 | Lars Ahlfors | Helsinki, Finland | Riemann surfaces |
| 1936 | Jesse Douglas | New York NY | Plateau problem |
| 1950 | Laurent Schwartz | Paris, France | functional analysis |
| 1950 | Atle Selberg | Langesund, Norway | number theory |
| 1954 | Kunihiko Kodaira | Tokyo, Japan | algebraic geometry |
| 1954 | Jean-Pierre Serre | Bages, France | algebraic topology |
| 1958 | Klaus Roth | Breslau, Germany | number theory |
| 1958 | René Thom | Montbéliard, France | topology |
| 1962 | Lars Hörmander | Mjällby, Sweden | partial differential equations |
| 1962 | John Milnor | Orange NJ | differential topology |
| 1966 | Michael Atiyah | London, England | topology |
| 1966 | Paul Cohen | Long Branch NJ | set theory |
| 1966 | Alexandre Grothendieck | Berlin, Germany | algebraic geometry |
| 1966 | Stephen Smale | Flint MI | topology |
| 1970 | Alan Baker | London, England | number theory |
| 1970 | Heisuke Hironaka | Yamaguchi prefecture, Japan | algebraic geometry |
| 1970 | Sergey Novikov | Gorky, Russia | topology |
| 1970 | John Thompson | Ottawa KS | group theory |
| 1974 | Enrico Bombieri | Milan, Italy | number theory |
| 1974 | David Mumford | Worth, Sussex, UK | algebraic geometry |
| 1978 | Pierre Deligne | Brussels, Belgium | algebraic geometry |
| 1978 | Charles Fefferman | Washington DC | classical analysis |
| 1978 | Gregory Margulis | Moscow, Russia | Lie groups |
| 1978 | Daniel Quillen | Orange NJ | algebraic $K$-theory |
| 1983 | Alain Connes | Darguignan, France | operator theory |
| 1983 | William Thurston | Washington DC | topology |
| 1983 | Shing-Tung Yau | Swatow, China | differential geometry |
| 1986 | Simon Donaldson | Cambridge, UK | topology |
| 1986 | Gerd Faltings | Gelsenkirchen, West Germany | Mordell conjecture |
| 1986 | Michael Freedman | Los Angeles CA | Poincaré conjecture |
| 1990 | Vladimir Drinfeld | Kharkov, Ukraine | algebraic geometry |
| 1990 | Vaughan Jones | Gisborne, New Zealand | knot theory |
| 1990 | Shigefumi Mori | Nagoya, Japan | algebraic geometry |
| 1990 | Edward Witten | Baltimore MD | superstring theory |
| 1994 | Jean Bourgain | Ostend, Belgium | analysis |
| 1994 | Pierre-Louis Lions | Grasse, France | partial differential equations |
| 1994 | Jean-Christophe Yoccoz | France | dynamical systems |
| 1994 | Yefim Zelmanov | Khabarovsk, Russia | group theory |
| 1998 | Richard Borcherds | Cape Town, South Africa | mathematical physics |
| 1998 | William Gowers | Marlborough, Wiltshire, UK | functional analysis |
| 1998 | Maksim Kontsevich | Khimki, Russia | mathematical physics |
| 1998 | Curt McMullen | Berkeley CA | chaos theory |
| 2002 | Laurent Lafforgue | Antony, France | number theory and analysis |
| 2002 | Vladimir Voevodsky | Russia | algebraic geometry |

# Japan Prize

The Science and Technology Foundation of Japan awards the Japan Prize annually to living individuals or small groups whose achievements in science and technology have advanced knowledge and promoted human peace and prosperity. A cash award of ¥50 million (about $415,000), a certificate of merit, and a commemorative medal are also given for each prize category. Web site: <www.japanprize.jp>.

| YEAR | LAUREATE | COUNTRY | AREA OF ACHIEVEMENT |
|------|----------|---------|---------------------|
| 1985 | John R. Pierce | US | electronics and communications technologies |
|      | Ephraim Katchalski-Katzir | Israel | basic theory of immobilized enzymes |
| 1986 | David Turnbull | US | new materials technology such as amorphous solids |
|      | Willem J. Kolff | US | artificial organs |
| 1987 | Henry M. Beachell | US | high-yield rice |
|      | Gurdev S. Khush | India | hardy rice |
|      | Theodore H. Maiman | US | lasers |
| 1988 | Georges Vendryes | France | fast breeder reactor technology |
|      | Donald A. Henderson | US | } |
|      | Isao Arita | Japan | } eradication of smallpox |
|      | Frank Fenner | Australia | } |
|      | Luc Montagnier | France | discovery of HIV |
|      | Robert C. Gallo | US | isolation of HIV and development of AZT |
| 1989 | Frank Sherwood Rowland | US | stratospheric ozone depletion by chlorofluorocarbons |
|      | Elias James Corey | US | syntheses of prostaglandins and related compounds |
| 1990 | Marvin Minsky | US | Artificial Intelligence |
|      | William Jason Morgan | US | } |
|      | Dan Peter Mckenzie | UK | } plate tectonics |
|      | Xavier Le Pichon | France | } |
| 1991 | Jacques-Louis Lions | France | analysis and control of distributed systems, applied analysis |
|      | John Julian Wild | US | ultrasound imaging |
| 1992 | Gerhard Ertl | Germany | chemistry and physics of solid surfaces |
|      | Ernest John Christopher Polge | UK | cryopreservation of semen and embryos in farm animals |
| 1993 | Frank Press | US | seismology and disaster science |
|      | Kary B. Mullis | US | polymerase chain reaction |
| 1994 | William Hayward Pickering | US | space travel and unmanned space exploration |
|      | Arvid Carlsson | Sweden | dopamine's role in mental and motor functions |
| 1995 | Nick Holonyak, Jr. | US | light emitting diodes and lasers |
|      | Edward F. Knipling | US | pest management |
| 1996 | Charles K. Kao | Hong Kong | wide-band, low-loss optical fiber communications |
|      | Masao Ito | Japan | cerebellum function |
| 1997 | Takashi Sugimura | Japan | } cancer |
|      | Bruce N. Ames | US | } |
|      | Joseph F. Engelberger | US | } robotics |
|      | Hiroyuki Yoshikawa | Japan | } |
| 1998 | Leo Esaki | Japan | man-made superlattice crystals |
|      | Jozef S. Schell | Belgium | } transgenic plants |
|      | Marc C. E. Van Montagu | Belgium | } |
| 1999 | W. Wesley Peterson | US | algebraic coding theory |
|      | Jack L. Strominger | US | } human histocompatibility |
|      | Don C. Wiley | US | } antigens and their bound peptides |
| 2000 | Ian L. McHarg | US | ecological city planning and land use evaluation |
|      | Kimishige Ishizaka | Japan | Immunoglobulin E and IgE-mediated allergic reactions |
| 2001 | John B. Goodenough | US | environmentally benign electrode materials for rechargeable lithium batteries |
|      | Timothy R. Parsons | Canada | fishery resources and marine environment conservation |
| 2002 | Timothy John Berners-Lee | UK | World Wide Web |
|      | Anne McLaren | UK | } study and manipulation of early- |
|      | Andrzej K. Tarkowski | Poland | } stage mammalian embryos |
| 2003 | Benoit B. Mandelbrot | France | fractals |
|      | James A. Yorke | US | concept of chaos in complex systems |
|      | Seiji Ogawa | Japan | magnetic resonance imaging |

# National Medal of Science

The National Medal of Science was established by Congress in 1959. Awarded annually since 1962 by the National Science Foundation and the president of the United States, it recognizes notable achievements in mathematics, engineering, and the physical, natural, and social sciences. A presidentially-appointed committee selects the winners from a pool of nominees. For more information, see the National Science Foundation Web site at <www.nsf.gov/nsb/ awards/nms/start.htm>

| YEAR | NAME | FIELD |
|------|------|-------|
| 1962 | Theodore von Karman | aerospace engineering |
| 1963 | Luis W. Alvarez | physics |
| | Vannevar Bush | electrical engineering |
| | John Robinson Pierce | communications engineering |
| | Cornelius Barnardus van Niel | biology |
| | Norbert Wiener | mathematics |
| 1964 | Roger Adams | chemistry |
| | Othmar Herman Ammann | bridge design engineering |
| | Theodosius Dobzhansky | genetics |
| | Charles Stark Draper | aerospace engineering |
| | Solomon Lefschetz | mathematics |
| | Neal Elgar Miller | psychology |
| | H. Marston Morse | mathematics |
| | Marshall Warren Nirenberg | biochemistry |
| | Julian Seymour Schwinger | physics |
| | Harold C. Urey | chemistry |
| | Robert Burns Woodward | chemistry |
| 1965 | John Bardeen | physics |
| | Peter J.W. Debye | physical chemistry |
| | Hugh L. Dryden | physics |
| | Clarence L. Johnson | aerospace engineering |
| | Leon M. Lederman | physics |
| | Warren K. Lewis | chemical engineering |
| | Francis Peyton Rous | pathology |
| | William W. Rubey | geology |
| | George Gaylord Simpson | paleontology |
| | Donald D. Van Slyke | chemistry |
| | Oscar Zariski | mathematics |
| 1966 | Jacob A.B. Bjerknes | meteorology |
| | Subrahmanyan Chandrasekhar | astrophysics |
| | Henry Eyring | chemistry |
| | Edward F. Knipling | entomology |
| | Fritz Albert Lipmann | biochemistry |
| | John Willard Milnor | mathematics |
| | William C. Rose | biochemistry |
| | Claude E. Shannon | mathematics, electrical engineering |
| | John H. Van Vleck | physics |
| | Sewall Wright | genetics |
| | Vladimir Kosma Zworykin | electrical engineering |
| 1967 | Jesse W. Beams | physics |
| | Francis Birch | geophysics |
| | Gregory Breit | physics |
| | Paul Joseph Cohen | mathematics |
| | Kenneth S. Cole | biophysics |
| | Louis P. Hammett | chemistry |

| YEAR | NAME | FIELD |
|------|------|-------|
| | Harry F. Harlow | psychology |
| | Michael Heidelberger | immunology |
| | George B. Kistiakowsky | chemistry |
| | Edwin Herbert Land | physics |
| | Igor I. Sikorsky | aircraft design |
| | Alfred H. Sturtevant | genetics |
| 1968 | Horace A. Barker | biochemistry |
| | Paul D. Bartlett | chemistry |
| | Bernard B. Brodie | pharmacology |
| | Detlev W. Bronk | biophysics |
| | J. Presper Eckert, Jr. | engineering, computer science |
| | Herbert Friedman | astrophysics |
| | Jay L. Lush | livestock genetics |
| | Nathan M. Newmark | civil engineering |
| | Jerzy Neyman | mathematics, statistics |
| | Lars Onsager | chemistry |
| | B.F. Skinner | psychology |
| | Eugene Paul Wigner | mathematical physics |
| 1969 | Herbert C. Brown | chemistry |
| | William Feller | mathematics |
| | Robert J. Huebner | virology |
| | Jack Kilby | electrical engineering |
| | Ernst Mayr | biology |
| | Wolfgang K.H. Panofsky | physics |
| 1970 | Richard Dagobert Brauer | mathematics |
| | Robert H. Dicke | physics |
| | Barbara McClintock | genetics |
| | George E. Mueller | physics |
| | Albert Bruce Sabin | medicine, vaccine development |
| | Allan R. Sandage | astronomy |
| | John C. Slater | physics |
| | John Archibald Wheeler | physics |
| | Saul Winstein | chemistry |
| 1971 | *no awards given* | |
| 1972 | *no awards given* | |
| 1973 | Daniel I. Arnon | biochemistry |
| | Carl Djerassi | chemistry |
| | Harold E. Edgerton | electrical engineering, photography |
| | Maurice Ewing | geophysics |
| | Arie Jan Haagen-Smit | biochemistry |
| | Vladimir Haensel | chemical engineering |
| | Frederick Seitz | physics |
| | Earl W. Sutherland, Jr. | biochemistry |
| | John Wilder Tukey | statistics |
| | Richard T. Whitcomb | aerospace engineering |
| | Robert Rathbun Wilson | particle physics |
| 1974 | Nicolaas Bloembergen | physics |
| | Britton Chance | biophysics |

# National Medal of Science (continued)

| YEAR | NAME | FIELD | YEAR | NAME | FIELD |
|------|------|-------|------|------|-------|
| | Erwin Chargaff | biochemistry | | Herman F. Mark | chemistry |
| | Paul J. Flory | physical chemistry | | Raymond D. Mindlin | mechanical engineering |
| | William A. Fowler | nuclear astrophysics | | | |
| | Kurt Gödel | mathematics | | Robert N. Noyce | computer science |
| | Rudolf Kompfner | physics | | Severo Ochoa | biochemistry |
| | James Van Gundia Neel | genetics | | Earl R. Parker | materials science |
| | | | | Edward M. Purcell | physics |
| | Linus Pauling | chemistry | | Simon Ramo | electrical engineering |
| | Ralph Brazelton Peck | geotechnical engineering | | John H. Sinfelt | chemical engineering |
| | | | | Lyman Spitzer, Jr. | astrophysics |
| | Kenneth Sanborn Pitzer | physical chemistry | | Earl Reece Stadtman | biochemistry |
| | | | | George Ledyard Stebbins | botany, genetics |
| | James Augustine Shannon | physiology | | | |
| | | | | Victor F. Weisskopf | physics |
| | Abel Wolman | sanitary engineering | | Paul Alfred Weiss | biology |
| 1975 | John W. Backus | computer science | 1980 | *no awards given* | |
| | Manson Benedict | nuclear engineering | 1981 | Philip Handler | biochemistry |
| | Hans Albrecht Bethe | theoretical physics | 1982 | Philip W. Anderson | physics |
| | Shiing-shen Chern | mathematics | | Seymour Benzer | molecular biology |
| | George B. Dantzig | mathematics | | Glenn W. Burton | genetics |
| | Hallowell Davis | physiology | | Mildred Cohn | biochemistry |
| | Paul Gyorgy | medicine, vitamin research | | F. Albert Cotton | chemistry |
| | | | | Edward H. Heinemann | aerospace engineering |
| | Sterling Brown Hendricks | chemistry | | | |
| | | | | Donald L. Katz | chemical engineering |
| | Joseph O. Hirschfelder | chemistry | | Yoichiro Nambu | theoretical physics |
| | William Hayward Pickering | physics | | Marshall H. Stone | mathematics |
| | | | | Gilbert Stork | organic chemistry |
| | Lewis H. Sarett | chemistry | | Edward Teller | nuclear physics |
| | Frederick Emmons Terman | electrical engineering | | Charles Hard Townes | physics |
| | Orville Alvin Vogel | research agronomy | 1983 | Howard L. Bachrach | biochemistry |
| | Wernher von Braun | aerospace engineering | | Paul Berg | biochemistry |
| | | | | E. Margaret Burbidge | astronomy |
| | E. Bright Wilson, Jr. | chemistry | | Maurice Goldhaber | physics |
| | Chien-Shiung Wu | physics | | Herman H. Goldstine | computer science |
| 1976 | Morris Cohen | materials science | | William R. Hewlett | electrical engineering |
| | Kurt Otto Friedrichs | mathematics | | Roald Hoffmann | chemistry |
| | Peter C. Goldmark | communications engineering | | Helmut E. Landsberg | climatology |
| | | | | George M. Low | aerospace engineering |
| | Samuel Abraham Goudsmit | physics | | | |
| | | | | Walter H. Munk | oceanography |
| | Roger Charles Louis Guillemin | physiology | | George C. Pimentel | chemistry |
| | | | | Frederick Reines | physics |
| | Herbert S. Gutowsky | chemistry | | Wendell L. Roelofs | chemistry, entomology |
| | Erwin W. Mueller | physics | | | |
| | Keith Roberts Porter | cell biology | | Bruno B. Rossi | astrophysics |
| | Efraim Racker | biochemistry | | Berta V. Scharrer | neuroscience |
| | Frederick D. Rossini | chemistry | | John Robert Schrieffer | physics |
| | Verner E. Suomi | meteorology | | Isadore M. Singer | mathematics |
| | Henry Taube | chemistry | | John G. Trump | electrical engineering |
| | George Eugene Uhlenbeck | physics | | Richard N. Zare | chemistry |
| | Hassler Whitney | mathematics | 1984 | *no awards given* | |
| | Edward O. Wilson | biology | 1985 | *no awards given* | |
| 1977 | *no awards given* | | 1986 | Solomon J. Buchsbaum | physics |
| 1978 | *no awards given* | | | Stanley Cohen | biochemistry |
| 1979 | Robert H. Burris | biochemistry | | Horace R. Crane | physics |
| | Elizabeth C. Crosby | neuroanatomy | | Herman Feshbach | physics |
| | Joseph L. Doob | mathematics | | Harry Gray | chemistry |
| | Richard P. Feynman | theoretical physics | | Donald A. Henderson | medicine, public health |
| | Donald E. Knuth | computer science | | | |
| | Arthur Kornberg | biochemistry | | Robert Hofstadter | physics |
| | Emmett N. Leith | electrical engineering | | Peter D. Lax | mathematics |
| | | | | Yuan Tseh Lee | chemistry |

## National Medal of Science (continued)

| YEAR | NAME | FIELD | YEAR | NAME | FIELD |
|---|---|---|---|---|---|
| | Hans Wolfgang Liepmann | aerospace engineering | | Katherine Esau | botany |
| | T.Y. Lin | civil engineering | | Herbert E. Grier | aerospace engineering |
| | Carl S. Marvel | chemistry | | Viktor Hamburger | biology |
| | Vernon B. Mountcastle | neurophysiology | | Samuel Karlin | mathematics |
| | | | | Philip Leder | genetics |
| | Bernard M. Oliver | electrical engineering | | Joshua Lederberg | genetics |
| | George Emil Palade | cell biology | | Saunders Mac Lane | mathematics |
| | Herbert A. Simon | social science | | Rudolph A. Marcus | chemistry |
| | Joan A. Steitz | molecular biology | | Harden M. McConnell | chemistry |
| | Frank H. Westheimer | chemistry | | Eugene N. Parker | theoretical astrophysics |
| | Chen Ning Yang | theoretical physics | | | |
| | Antoni Zygmund | mathematics | | Robert P. Sharp | geology |
| 1987 | Philip Hauge Abelson | physical chemistry | | Donald C. Spencer | mathematics |
| | Anne Anastasi | psychology | | Roger Wolcott Sperry | neurobiology |
| | Robert Byron Bird | chemical engineering | | Henry M. Stommel | oceanography |
| | Raoul Bott | mathematics | | Harland G. Wood | biochemistry |
| | Michael E. DeBakey | heart surgery | 1990 | Baruj Benacerraf | pathology, immunology |
| | Theodor O. Diener | plant pathology | | | |
| | Harry Eagle | cell biology | | Elkan R. Blout | chemistry |
| | Walter M. Elsasser | physics | | Herbert W. Boyer | biochemistry, genetics |
| | Michael H. Freedman | mathematics | | | |
| | William S. Johnson | chemistry | | George F. Carrier | mathematics |
| | Har Gobind Khorana | biochemistry | | Allan MacLeod Cormack | physics |
| | Paul C. Lauterbur | chemistry | | | |
| | Rita Levi-Montalcini | neurology | | Mildred S. Dresselhaus | physics |
| | George E. Pake | research, physics | | | |
| | H. Bolton Seed | civil engineering | | Karl August Folkers | chemistry |
| | George J. Stigler | economics | | Nick Holonyak, Jr. | electrical engineering |
| | Walter H. Stockmayer | chemistry | | Leonid Hurwicz | economics |
| | Max Tishler | chemistry | | Stephen Cole Kleene | mathematics |
| | James Alfred Van Allen | physics | | Daniel E. Koshland, Jr. | biochemistry |
| | Ernst Weber | electrical engineering | | Edward B. Lewis | developmental genetics |
| 1988 | William O. Baker | chemistry | | | |
| | Konrad E. Bloch | biochemistry | | John McCarthy | computer science |
| | David Allan Bromley | physics | | Edwin Mattison McMillan | nuclear physics |
| | Michael S. Brown | molecular genetics | | | |
| | Paul C.W. Chu | physics | | David G. Nathan | pediatrics |
| | Stanley N. Cohen | genetics | | Robert V. Pound | physics |
| | Elias James Corey | chemistry | | Roger R.D. Revelle | oceanography |
| | Daniel C. Drucker | engineering education | | John D. Roberts | chemistry |
| | Milton Friedman | economics | | Patrick Suppes | philosophy and statistics education |
| | Joseph L. Goldstein | molecular genetics | | | |
| | Ralph E. Gomory | mathematics, research | | E. Donnall Thomas | medicine |
| | | | 1991 | Mary Ellen Avery | pediatrics |
| | Willis M. Hawkins | aerospace engineering | | Ronald Breslow | chemistry |
| | | | | Alberto P. Calderon | mathematics |
| | Maurice R. Hilleman | vaccine research | | Gertrude B. Elion | pharmacology |
| | George W. Housner | earthquake engineering | | George H. Heilmeier | electrical engineering |
| | | | | Dudley R. Herschbach | chemistry |
| | Eric Kandel | neurobiology | | | |
| | Joseph B. Keller | mathematics | | G. Evelyn Hutchinson | zoology |
| | Walter Kohn | physics | | Elvin A. Kabat | immunology |
| | Norman Foster Ramsey | physics | | Robert W. Kates | geography |
| | | | | Luna B. Leopold | hydrology, geology |
| | Jack Steinberger | physics | | Salvador Luria | biology |
| | Rosalyn S. Yalow | medical physics | | Paul A. Marks | hematology, cancer research |
| 1989 | Arnold O. Beckman | chemistry | | | |
| | Richard B. Bernstein | chemistry | | George A. Miller | psychology |
| | Melvin Calvin | biochemistry | | Arthur L. Schawlow | physics |
| | Harry G. Drickamer | chemistry, physics | | Glenn T. Seaborg | nuclear chemistry |
| | | | | Folke K. Skoog | botany |

# National Medal of Science (continued)

| YEAR | NAME | FIELD | YEAR | NAME | FIELD |
|------|------|-------|------|------|-------|
| | H. Guyford Stever | aerospace engineering | 1998 | Bruce N. Ames | biochemistry, cancer research |
| | Edward C. Stone | physics | | Don L. Anderson | geophysics |
| | Steven Weinberg | nuclear physics | | John N. Bahcall | astrophysics |
| | Paul C. Zamecnik | molecular biology | | John W. Cahn | materials science |
| 1992 | Eleanor J. Gibson | psychology | | Cathleen Synge Morawetz | mathematics |
| | Allen Newell | computer science | | | |
| | Calvin F. Quate | electrical engineering | | Janet D. Rowley | medicine, cancer research |
| | Eugene M. Shoemaker | planetary geology | | | |
| | | | | Eli Ruckenstein | chemical engineering |
| | Howard E. Simmons, Jr. | chemistry | | George M. Whitesides | chemistry |
| | | | | William Julius Wilson | sociology |
| | Maxine F. Singer | biochemistry, administration | 1999 | David Baltimore | virology, administration |
| | Howard Martin Temin | virology | | Felix E. Browder | mathematics |
| | John Roy Whinnery | electrical engineering | | Ronald R. Coifman | mathematics |
| 1993 | Alfred Y. Cho | electrical engineering | | James Watson Cronin | particle physics |
| | Donald J. Cram | chemistry | | Jared Diamond | physiology |
| | Val Logsdon Fitch | particle physics | | Leo P. Kadanoff | theoretical physics |
| | Norman Hackerman | chemistry | | Lynn Margulis | microbiology |
| | Martin D. Kruskal | mathematics | | Stuart A. Rice | chemistry |
| | Daniel Nathans | microbiology | | John Ross | chemistry |
| | Vera C. Rubin | astronomy | | Susan Solomon | atmospheric science |
| | Salome G. Waelsch | molecular genetics | | Robert M. Solow | economics |
| 1994 | Ray W. Clough | civil engineering | | Kenneth N. Stevens | electrical engineering, speech |
| | John Cocke | computer science | | | |
| | Thomas Eisner | chemical ecology | 2000 | Nancy C. Andreasen | psychiatry |
| | George S. Hammond | chemistry | | John D. Baldeschwieler | chemistry |
| | Robert K. Merton | sociology | | | |
| | Elizabeth F. Neufeld | biochemistry | | Gary S. Becker | economics |
| | Albert W. Overhauser | physics | | Yuan-Cheng B. Fung | bioengineering |
| | Frank Press | geophysics, administration | | Ralph F. Hirschmann | chemistry |
| | | | | Willis Eugene Lamb, Jr. | physics |
| 1995 | Thomas Robert Cech | biochemistry | | | |
| | Hans Georg Dehmelt | physics | | Jeremiah P. Ostriker | astrophysics |
| | Peter M. Goldreich | astrophysics | | Peter H. Raven | botany |
| | Hermann A. Haus | electrical engineering | | John Griggs Thompson | mathematics |
| | Isabella L. Karle | chemistry | | | |
| | Louis Nirenberg | mathematics | | Karen K. Uhlenbeck | mathematics |
| | Alexander Rich | molecular biology | | Gilbert F. White | geography |
| | Roger N. Shepard | psychology | | Carl R. Woese | microbiology |
| 1996 | Wallace S. Broecker | geochemistry | 2001 | Andreas Acrivos | chemical engineering |
| | Norman Davidson | chemistry, molecular biology | | Francisco J. Ayala | molecular biology |
| | | | | George F. Bass | nautical archaeology |
| | James L. Flanagan | electrical engineering | | Mario R. Capecchi | genetics |
| | Richard M. Karp | computer science | | Marvin L. Cohen | materials science |
| | C. Kumar N. Patel | electrical engineering | | Ernest R. Davidson | chemistry |
| | Ruth Patrick | limnology | | Raymond Davis, Jr. | chemistry, astrophysics |
| | Paul Samuelson | economics | | | |
| | Stephen Smale | mathematics | | Ann M. Graybiel | neuroscience |
| 1997 | William K. Estes | psychology | | Charles D. Keeling | oceanography |
| | Darleane C. Hoffman | chemistry | | Gene E. Likens | ecology |
| | Harold S. Johnston | chemistry | | Victor A. McKusick | medical genetics |
| | Marshall N. Rosenbluth | theoretical plasma physics | | Calyampudi R. Rao | mathematics, statistics |
| | Martin Schwarzschild | astrophysics | | Gabor A. Somorjai | chemistry |
| | James Dewey Watson | genetics, biophysics | | Elias M. Stein | mathematics |
| | Robert A. Weinberg | biology, cancer research | | Harold Varmus | virology, administration |
| | George W. Wetherill | planetary science | | | |
| | Shing-Tung Yau | mathematics | | | |

## The National Inventor of the Year Award

The National Inventor of the Year Award is given by the Intellectual Property Owners Association, a trade organization established in 1972. Patented American inventions from the preceding four years are eligible for nomination annually; runners-up receive recognition as Distinguished Inventors. The winners for 2003 were Dr. Warren M. Zapol, Chief of Anesthesia and Critical Care at Massachu-setts General Hospital, and Dr. Claes Frostell, Head of Karolinska Institutet Danderyd Hospital in Sweden. They invented a system for delivering gaseous nitric oxide to treat patients suffering from respiratory failure associated with pulmonary hypertension. Award amount: $5,000. Web site: <www.ipo.org/IOY.html>.

## Intel Science Talent Search

The Intel Science Talent Search encourages American high school seniors to pursue careers in the sciences by awarding scholarships for outstanding science projects. Created in 1942 by Science Service, a nonprofit organization devoted to public appreciation of science, and Westinghouse Electric Corporation, the contest brings 40 finalists each year to exhibit their projects at the Science Talent Institute in Washington DC and compete for the top prizes. Since 1998 the talent search has been sponsored by Intel Corp. The highest-place winners for 2003 were **Jamie Rubin** of Fort Myers FL (first prize, $100,000), **Tianhui "Michael" Li** of Portland OR (second prize, $75,000), and **Anatoly Preygel** of Germantown MD (third prize, $50,000).

Rubin designed an agent that holds promise in treating infections caused by the yeast *Candida albicans*, which can pose a severe threat to individuals with compromised immune systems, such as AIDS and cancer patients. Li conducted a 3-year study of inertial-electrostatic confinement (IEC), a method of confining nuclear fusion that costs significantly less than conventional systems. Preygel developed a method of computing quandle cocycle knot invariants within knot theory, an area of mathematics that centers on closed curves in three-dimensional space. Web site: <www.sciserv.org/sts>.

**Did you know?**

The preeminent early stunt flyer was Lincoln Beachley, who started in balloons and switched to planes. Working to get publicity for aviation inventor Glenn Curtiss, Beachley barnstormed throughout the US. Before 150,000 observers he piloted his plane into the gorge at Niagara Falls and flew under the International Bridge. Beachley also set early altitude and distance records. He died in 1915 when he failed to pull out of a dive over Oakland Bay CA.

# Nature, Science, Medicine & Technology

## Time

### Measuring Time

The measurement of time is an ancient science, though many of its discoveries are relatively recent. The **Cro-Magnons** recorded the phases of the Moon some 30,000 years ago—but the first minutes were counted accurately only 400 years ago, and the atomic clocks that allow us to track time to the billionth of a second are less than 50 years old. Timekeeping has been both a lens through which humanity has observed the heavens and a mirror reflecting the progress of science and civilization.

Our millennia-long struggle to **define and calibrate** time through calendars and clocks has meant trying to bring the register of human affairs in line with natural cycles—of the Earth, Sun, Moon, and stars, of the physics of matter—but always, cycles. What vary are the cultural values and goals that dictate which cycles are significant.

With a religious culture dominated by gods of the Sun and sky, and a civilization dependent on the annual cycle of a river, the **ancient Egyptians** were expert astronomers who studied the Sun's recurrent movements and their effects on the Earth very closely. By plotting the beginning of the Nile's flood each year, a reliable harbinger of seasonal change, they measured a cycle 365 days long—a reasonable approximation of the duration of the tropical solar year. Observations of the star Sirius eventually allowed Egyptian astronomers to adjust the solar year to 365.25 days.

About 127 BC the **Greek astronomer Hipparchus** further refined the year. His adjustments centered on the equinoxes—which he discovered to be shifting to the west at the barely perceptible rate of two degrees in 150 years. Because of this discovery Hipparchus realized that the solar year was slightly shorter than the accepted 365.25 days. His calculation of 365.242 days was remarkably close to the present calculation of 365.242199 days.

Unfortunately for civic and religious leaders of the next 1,600 years, Hipparchus's discoveries were virtually ignored by calendar makers. **Julius Caesar**'s calendrical reforms in 46 BC left the calendar year at 365.25 days—more than 11 minutes too long. By the 1500s the Julian calendar was 10 days behind the solar year. The shortfall alarmed Christian religious leaders because it meant that holy days, including Easter, were being observed at the wrong times. In 1582, **Pope Gregory XIII** officially revised the accepted length of the year to 365.2422 days, adjusted the leap-year rule, and lopped off the 10 extra days, creating in the process the calendar in most widespread use today.

Meanwhile, the quest to measure time accurately on a much smaller scale was still in its early phases. The invention of the **weight-driven mechanical clock** some 200 years earlier had revolutionized timekeeping, making it possible to count equal units of time.

This leap forward in precision radically changed the way people thought about time and the best ways to measure it.

Calendars are deemed accurate according to how well they accommodate the variations in larger celestial cycles. Clocks, on the other hand, have historically been judged accurate in relation to the average duration of the Earth's rotation around the Sun—that is, by how well they keep **"mean time."** While calendrical standards have remained fairly stable, however, the clock's units of measure have gradually shifted away from using the Earth-Sun relationship as a norm. With the introduction of mechanical clocks in the late 13th or early 14th century, clock time became increasingly removed from cyclical events in the sky, for the cycles on which mechanical clocks base their measures are independent of Earth and Sun. A pendulum clock, for example, measures only the beat of its pendulum, not any part of a "real" day.

The **pendulum clock** kicked off the modern search for the perfect clock, a timepiece governed by a naturally cycling period—like a pendulum's—that operated free from mechanical friction and fatigue. Another 300 years would pass before any clock came close. In 1927 W.A. Marrison invented a clock that operated via a tiny **quartz crystal**. The crystal vibrated at an ultrasonic frequency when exposed to an electric field. These vibrations were constant and delivered a virtually frictionless beat to the counting mechanism of the clock. Accurate to thousandths of a second, quartz clocks led scientists to make the belated discovery that the Earth was not a reliable clock to begin with. Disparities between the measurements of quartz clocks and the rotation of the Earth revealed unpredictable irregularities in the rotation, which had to that point defined the duration of a second (1/86,400 of the mean solar day).

In 1967 the **definition of a second** was officially divorced from the Earth's rotation. That year, the 13th General Conference of Weights and Measures redefined the second as "9,192,631,770 periods of the radiation corresponding to the transition between the two hyperfine levels of the ground state of the cesium-133 atom." **Cesium atoms** are superior to quartz crystals because they do not wear out. These atoms have cycles that comprise oscillations between precisely defined energy states; these cycles can oscillate forever without any distortion whatsoever. Furthermore, each atom of cesium oscillates at exactly the same frequency as all others, making each one a perfect timekeeper—too perfect, even. To keep solar time and atomic time from drifting too far apart, the two were combined in 1964 to form **Coordinated Universal Time**, which is based on the atomic second and kept within 0.9 second of solar time by adding a leap second as needed.

## Time Zone Map

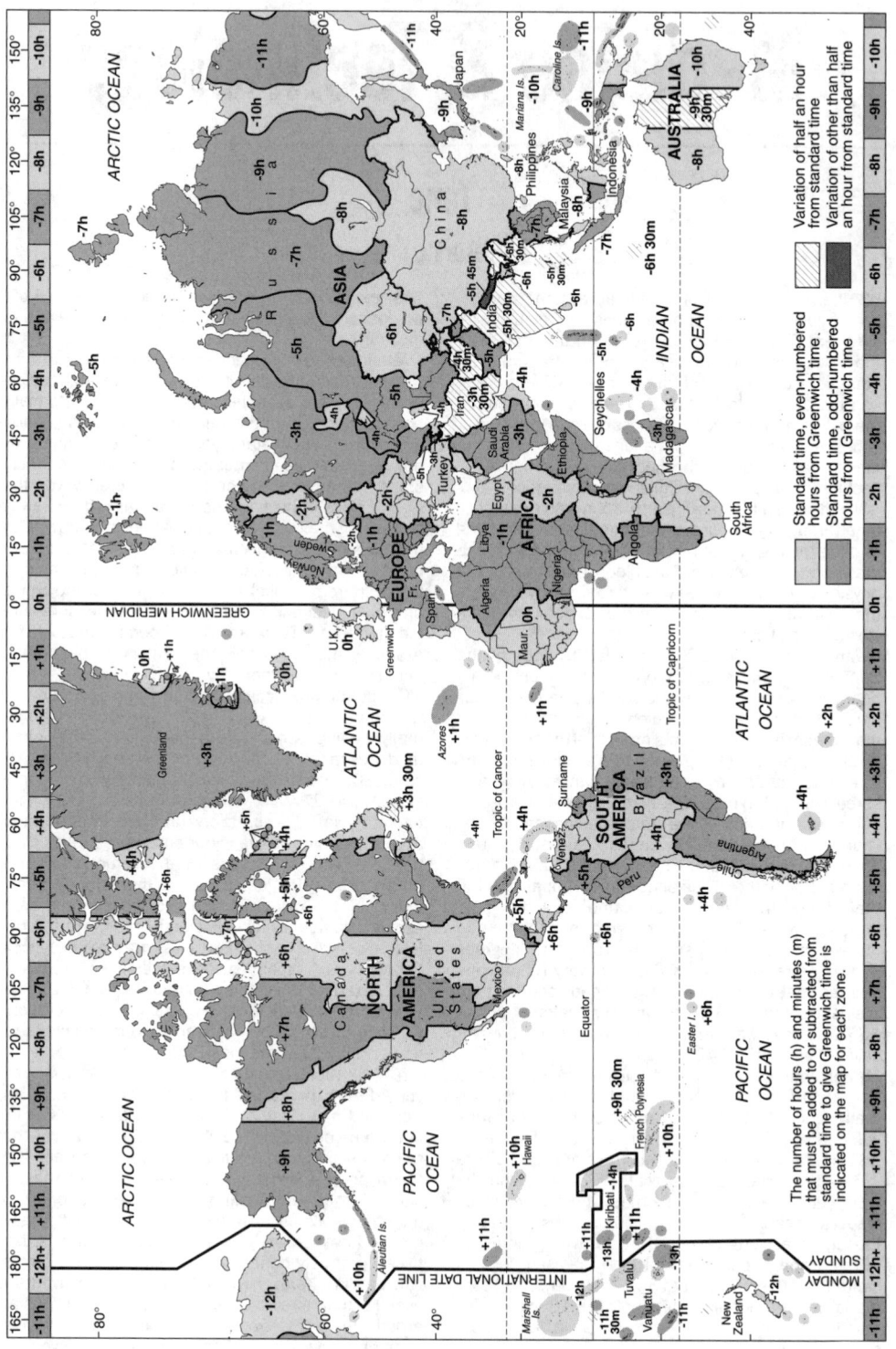

## Daylight Saving Time

Also called **summer time, daylight saving time** is a system for uniformly advancing clocks, especially in summer, so as to extend daylight hours during conventional waking time. In the Northern Hemisphere, clocks are usually set ahead one hour in late March or in April and are set back one hour in late September or in October.

The practice was first suggested in a whimsical essay by **Benjamin Franklin** in 1784. In 1907 an Englishman, William Willett, campaigned for setting the clock ahead by 80 minutes in four moves of 20 minutes each during the spring and summer months. In 1908 the House of Commons rejected a bill to advance the clock by one hour in the spring and return to Greenwich Mean (standard) Time in the autumn.

Several countries, including Australia, Great Britain, Germany, and the United States, adopted **summer daylight saving time** during World War I to conserve fuel by reducing the need for artificial light. During World War II, clocks were kept continuously advanced by an hour in some nations—e.g., in the United States from 9 Feb 1942 to 30 Sep 1945; and England used "double summer time" during part of the year, advancing clocks two hours from the standard time during the summer and one hour during the winter months.

In the US, daylight saving time formerly began on the last Sunday in April and ended on the last Sunday in October. In 1986 the US Congress passed a law moving up the start of daylight saving time to the first Sunday in April, while keeping its end date the same. In most of the countries of Western Europe, daylight saving time starts on the last Sunday in March and ends on the last Sunday in September. In Britain and many other countries worldwide, it lasts from 30 March to 26 October.

## Julian and Gregorian Calendars

The **Julian calendar**, also called the Old Style calendar, is a dating system established by Julius Caesar as a reform of the Roman republican calendar. Caesar, advised by the Alexandrian astronomer Sosigenes, made the new calendar solar, not lunar, and he took the length of the solar year as 365¼ days. The year was divided into 12 months, all of which had either 30 or 31 days except February, which contained 28 days in common (365-day) years and 29 in every fourth year (a leap year, of 366 days). Because of misunderstandings, the calendar was not established in smooth operation until AD 8. Further, Sosigenes had overestimated the length of the year by 11 minutes 14 seconds, and by the mid-1500s, the cumulative effect of this error had shifted the dates of the seasons by about 10 days from Caesar's time.

This inaccuracy led **Pope Gregory XIII** to reform the Julian calendar. His **Gregorian calendar**, also called the **New Style calendar**, is still in general use. Gregory's proclamation in 1582 restored the calendar to the seasonal dates of AD 325, an adjustment of 10 days. Although the amount of regression was some 14 days by Pope Gregory's time, Gregory based his reform on restoration of the vernal equinox, then falling on 11 March, to the date (21 March) it had in AD 325, the time of the Council of Nicaea. Advancing the calendar 10 days after 4 Oct 1582, the day following being reckoned as 15 October, effected the change.

The Gregorian calendar differs from the Julian only in that no century year is a leap year unless it is exactly divisible by 400 (e.g., 1600, 2000). A further refinement, the designation of years evenly divisible by 4,000 as common (not leap) years, will keep the Gregorian calendar accurate to within one day in 20,000 years.

## Jewish Calendar

The **Jewish calendar** is **lunisolar**—i.e., regulated by the positions of both the Moon and the Sun. It consists usually of 12 alternating lunar months of 29 and 30 days each (except for Heshvan and Kislev, which sometimes have either 29 or 30 days), and totals 353, 354, or 355 days per year. The average lunar year (354 days) is adjusted to the solar year (365¼ days) by the periodic introduction of leap years in order to assure that the major festivals fall in their proper season. The leap year consists of an additional 30-day month called **First Adar**, which always precedes the month of (Second) Adar. (During leap year, the Adar holidays are postponed to Second Adar.) A leap year consists of either 383, 384, or 385 days and occurs seven times during every 19-year period (the so-called Metonic cycle). Among the consequences of the lunisolar structure are these: (1) The number of days in a year may vary considerably, from 353 to 385 days. (2) The first day of a month can fall on any day of the week, that day varying from year to year. Consequently, the days of the week upon which an annual Jewish festival falls vary from year to year despite the festival's fixed position in the Jewish month. The months of the Jewish calendar and their Gregorian equivalents are as follows:

| JEWISH MONTH | GREGORIAN MONTH(S) | JEWISH MONTH | GREGORIAN MONTH(S) |
|---|---|---|---|
| Tishri | September–October | Nisan | March–April |
| Heshvan, or Marheshvan | October–November | Iyyar | April–May |
| Kislev | November–December | Sivan | May–June |
| Tevet | December–January | Tammuz | June–July |
| Shevat | January–February | Av | July–August |
| Adar | February–March | Elul | August–September |

## Muslim Calendar

The **Muslim calendar** (also called the **Islamic calendar**, or **Hijrah**) is a dating system used in the Muslim world that is based on a year of 12 months. Each month begins approximately at the time of the New Moon. The **months** of the Muslim calendar are: Muharram, Safar, Rabi I, Rabi II, Jumada I, Jumada II, Rajab, Sha'ban, Ramadan, Shawwal, Dhu al-Qa'dah, and Dhu al-Hijjah.

In the standard Muslim calendar the months are alternately 30 and 29 days long except for the 12th month, Dhu al-Hijjah, the length of which is varied in a 30-year cycle intended to keep the calendar in step with the true phases of the Moon. In 11 years of this cycle, Dhu al-Hijjah has 30 days, and in the other 19 years it has 29. Thus the year has either 354 or 355 days. No months are intercalated, so that the named months do not remain in the same seasons but retrogress through the entire solar, or seasonal, year (of about 365.25 days) every 32.5 solar years.

There are some exceptions to this calendar in the Muslim world. **Turkey** uses the Gregorian calendar, while the **Iranian Muslim calendar** is based on a solar year. The Iranian calendar still begins from the same dating point as other Muslim calendars (that is, some 10 years prior to the death of Muhammad in AD 632). Thus, the Gregorian year AD 2000 corresponded to the Hijrah year of AH 1420/1421.

## Chinese Calendar

The **Chinese calendar** is a dating system used concurrently with the Gregorian (Western) calendar in China and Taiwan and in neighboring countries (e.g., Japan). The calendar consists of 12 months of alternately 29 and 30 days, equal to 354 or 355 days, or approximately 12 full lunar cycles. Intercalary months have been inserted to keep the calendar year in step with the solar year of about 365 days. **Months** have no name but are instead referred to by number within a year and sometimes also by a series of 12 animal names that from ancient times have been attached to years and to hours of the day.

The calendar also incorporates a **meteorological cycle** that contains 24 points, each beginning one of the periods named. The establishment of this cycle required a fair amount of astronomical understanding of the Earth as a celestial body. Modern scholars acknowledge the superiority of pre-Sung **Chinese astronomy** (at least until about the 13th century AD) over that of other, contemporary nations.

The **24 points** within the meteorological cycle coincide with points 15° apart on the ecliptic (the plane of the Earth's yearly journey around the Sun or, if it is thought that the Sun turns around the Earth, the apparent journey of the Sun against the stars). It takes about 15.2 days for the Sun to travel from one of these points to another (because the ecliptic is a complete circle of 360°), and the Sun needs 365¼ days to finish its journey in this cycle. Supposedly, each of the 12 months of the year contains two points, but, because a lunar month has only 29½ days and the two points share about 30.4 days, there is always the chance that a lunar month will fail to contain both points, though the distance between any two given points is only 15°. If such an occasion occurs, the intercalation of an extra month takes place. For instance, one may find a year with two "Julys" or with two "Augusts" in the Chinese calendar. In fact, the exact length of the month in the Chinese calendar is either 30 days or 29 days—a phenomenon that reflects its lunar origin.

| SOLAR MONTHS—CHINESE (ENGLISH EQUIVALENTS) | GREGORIAN DATE (APPROXIMATE) | LUNAR MONTH (CORRESPONDENCE OF LUNAR AND SOLAR MONTHS APPROXIMATE) |
|---|---|---|
| Lichun (spring begins) | 5 February | 1—tiger |
| Yushui (rain water) | 19 February | |
| Jingzhe (excited insects) | 5 March | 2—rabbit/hare |
| Chunfen (vernal equinox) | 20 March | |
| Qingming (clear and bright) | 5 April | 3—dragon |
| Guyu (grain rains) | 20 April | |
| Lixia (summer begins) | 5 May | 4—snake |
| Xiaoman (grain fills) | 21 May | |
| Mangzhong (grain in ear) | 6 June | 5—horse |
| Xiazhi (summer solstice) | 21 June | |
| Xiaoshu (slight heat) | 7 July | 6—sheep/ram |
| Dashu (great heat) | 23 July | |
| Liqiu (autumn begins) | 7 August | 7—monkey |
| Chushu (limit of heat) | 23 August | |
| Bailu (white dew) | 8 September | 8—chicken/rooster |
| Qiufen (autumn equinox) | 23 September | |
| Hanlu (cold dew) | 8 October | 9—dog |
| Shuangjiang (hoar frost descends) | 24 October | |
| Lidong (winter begins) | 8 November | 10—pig/boar |
| Xiaoxue (little snow) | 22 November | |
| Daxue (heavy snow) | 7 December | 11—rat |
| Dongzhi (winter solstice) | 22 December | |
| Xiaohan (little cold) | 6 January | 12—cow/ox |
| Dahan (severe cold) | 20 January | |

## Chinese Calendar (continued)

| CHINESE NEW YEAR | GREGORIAN DATE | ANIMAL | CHINESE NEW YEAR | GREGORIAN DATE | ANIMAL |
|---|---|---|---|---|---|
| 4697 | 16 Feb 1999 | rabbit/hare | 4704 | 29 Jan 2006 | dog |
| 4698 | 5 Feb 2000 | dragon | 4705 | 18 Feb 2007 | pig/boar |
| 4699 | 24 Jan 2001 | snake | 4706 | 7 Feb 2008 | rat |
| 4700 | 12 Feb 2002 | horse | 4707 | 26 Jan 2009 | cow/ox |
| 4701 | 1 Feb 2003 | sheep/ram | 4708 | 14 Feb 2010 | tiger |
| 4702 | 22 Jan 2004 | monkey | 4709 | 3 Feb 2011 | rabbit/hare |
| 4703 | 9 Feb 2005 | chicken/rooster | | | |

 An atomic clock is accurate to within one second in 1.7 million years.

## Religious and Traditional Holidays

The word holiday comes from "holy day," and it was originally a day of dedication to religious observance; in modern times a holiday may be of either religious or secular commemoration. All dates in this article are Gregorian.

**Jewish holidays**—The major holidays are the Pilgrim Festivals: **Pesach** (Passover), **Shavuot** (Feast of Weeks, or Pentecost), and **Sukkot** (Tabernacles); and the High Holidays: **Rosh Hashana** (New Year) and **Yom Kippur** (Day of Atonement).

**Pesach** commemorates the Exodus from Egypt and the servitude that preceded it. As such it is the most significant of the commemorative holidays, for it celebrates the very inception of the Jewish people—i.e., the event that provided the basis for the covenant between God and Israel. The term Pesach refers originally to the paschal (Passover) lamb sacrificed on the eve of the Exodus, the blood of which marked the Jewish homes to be spared from God's plague. Leaven (se'or) and foods containing leaven (hametz) are neither to be owned nor consumed during Pesach. Aside from meats, fresh fruits, and vegetables, it is customary to consume only those foods prepared under rabbinic supervision and labeled "kosher for Passover." The unleavened bread (matzo) consists entirely of flour and water. On the eve of Pesach families partake of the Seder, an elaborate festival meal. The table is bedecked with an assortment of foods symbolizing the passage from slavery (e.g., bitter herbs) into freedom (e.g., wine). Pesach will begin at sundown on 5 April and end on 13 April in 2004. (All Jewish holidays begin at sundown.)

The most distinctive **Rosh Hashana** observance is the sounding of the ram's horn (shofar) at the synagogue service. Symbolic ceremonies, such as eating bread and apples dipped in honey, accompanied by prayers for a "sweet" and propitious year, are performed at the festive meals. Rosh Hashana will begin at sundown on 15 September and will end on 17 September of 2004. **Yom Kippur** is a day when sins are confessed and expiated and man and God are reconciled. It is the holiest and most solemn day of the Jewish year. It is marked by fasting, penitence, and prayer. Working, eating, drinking, washing, anointing one's body, engaging in sexual intercourse, and donning leather shoes are all forbidden. Yom Kippur begins on 24 September in 2004.

Though not as important theologically, the feast of **Hanukka** has become socially significant, especially in western cultures. Hanukka commemorates the rededication (164 BCE) of the Second Temple of Jerusalem after its desecration three years earlier. Though modern Israel tends to emphasize the military victory of the general Judas Maccabeus, the distinctive rite of lighting the menorah also recalls the Talmud story of how the small supply of nondesecrated oil—enough for one day—miraculously burned in the Temple for eight full days until new oil could be obtained. During Hanukka, in addition to the lighting of the ceremonial candles, gifts are exchanged and children play holiday games. The festival spans 20 through 27 December in 2003 and 7 through 15 December in 2004.

**Christian holidays**—The major holidays celebrated by nearly all Christians are **Easter** and **Christmas**.

**Easter** celebrates the Resurrection of Jesus on the third day after his Crucifixion. In the Christian liturgical year, Easter is preceded by the period of **Lent**, the 40 days (not counting Sundays) before Easter, which traditionally were observed as a period of penance and fasting. Lent begins on **Ash Wednesday**; a day devoted to penitence. Holy Week precedes **Easter Sunday** and includes **Maundy Thursday**, the commemoration of Jesus' last supper with his disciples; **Good Friday**, the day of his Crucifixion; and **Holy Saturday**, the transition between Crucifixion and Resurrection. Easter shares with Christmas the presence of numerous customs, some of which have little to do with the Christian celebration of the resurrection but clearly derive from folk customs. In 2004 the western churches (nearly all Christian denominations) will observe Ash Wednesday on 25 February and Easter on 11 April. For Eastern Orthodox Christians, Lent begins on 23 February and Easter will be observed on 11 Apr 2004.

**Christmas** commemorates the birth of Jesus Christ. Since the early part of the 20th century, Christmas has also become a secular family holiday, observed by non-Christians, devoid of Christian elements, and marked by an increasingly elaborate exchange of gifts. In this secular Christmas celebration, a mythical figure named Santa Claus plays the pivotal role. Christmas is held on 25 December in most Christian cultures, but will occur on 7 Jan 2004 for the Eastern Orthodox faith.

**Islamic holidays**—**Ramadan** is the holy month of fasting for Muslims. The Islamic ordinance prescribes abstention from evil thoughts and deeds as well as from food, drink, and sexual intercourse from dawn until dusk throughout the month. The beginning and end of Ramadan are announced when one trustworthy witness testifies before the authorities that the new moon has been sighted; a cloudy sky may, therefore, delay or prolong the fast. The end of the fast is celebrated as the feast of '**Id al-Fitr**. Ramadan begins on 15 October in 2004 and 'Id al-Fitr falls on 14 November of that year (all Islamic holidays begin at sundown). The Muslim New Year, **Hijra**, is on 22 February in 2004.

After 'Id al-Fitr, the second major Islamic festival is '**Id al-Adha**. Throughout the Muslim world, all who can sacrifice sheep, goats, camels, or cattle and then divide the flesh equally among themselves, the poor, and friends and neighbors, to commemorate the ransom of Ishmael with a ram. This festival falls at the end of the hajj, the pilgrimage to the holy city of Mecca in Saudi Arabia, which every adult Muslim of either sex must make at least once in his or her lifetime. 'Id al-Adha will be observed on 2 February in 2004.

**Ashura** was originally designated in AD 622 by Muhammad as a day of fasting from sunset to sunset, probably patterned on the Jewish Day of Atonement, Yom Kippur. Among the Shi'ites, Ashura is a major festival that commemorates the death of Husayn (Hussein), son of Ali and grandson of Muhammad. It is a period of expressions of grief and of pilgrimage to Karbala (the site of Husayn's death, now in present-day Iraq). Ashura is on 2 March in 2004.

**Buddhist holidays**—Holidays practiced by a large number of Buddhists are *uposatha* days and days that commemorate events in the life of the Buddha.

The four monthly holy days of ancient Buddhism continue to be observed in the Theravada countries of Southeast Asia. These *uposatha* days—the new moon and full moon days of each lunar month and the eighth day following the new and full moons—have their origin, according to some scholars, in the fast days that preceded the Vedic soma sacrifices.

The three major events of the Buddha's life—his birth, Enlightenment, and entrance into final nirvana—are commemorated in all Buddhist countries but not everywhere on the same day. In the Theravada countries the three events are all observed together on **Vesak**, the full moon day of the sixth lunar month, which usually occurs in May. In Japan and other Mahayana countries, the three anniversaries of the Buddha are observed on separate days (in some countries the birth date is 8 April, the Enlightenment date is 8 December, and the death date is 15 February).

**Chinese holidays**—The **Chinese New Year** is celebrated with a big family meal and presents of cash are given to children in red envelopes. In 2004 the Chinese New Year will be on 22 January.

During the **Chinese Moon Festival**, on the 15th day of the 8th month of the lunar calendar, people return to their homes to visit with their family. The traditional food is moon cakes, round pastries stuffed with food such as red bean paste. The Moon Festival will occur on 28 September in 2004.

**Japanese holidays**—The Japanese celebrate **3-5-7 day** (Shichigosan no hi) in which parents bring children of those ages to the Shinto shrine to pray for their continued health. This day is held on 15 November.

In mid-July (or mid-August, in some areas) the Japanese celebrate **Obon** (also known as Bon Matsuri, or Urabon). The festival honors the spirits of deceased householders and of the dead generally. Memorial stones are cleaned, community dances are performed, and paper lanterns and fires are lit to welcome the dead and to bid them farewell at the end of their visit. The Shinto New Year, **Gantan-sai**, is celebrated on 31 December–1 January.

**Hindu holidays**—**Dussehra** celebrates the victory of Rama over Ravana, the symbol of evil on earth. In 2004 Dussehra falls on 22 October. **Diwali** is a festival of lights devoted to Laksmi, the goddess of wealth. During the festival, small earthenware lamps filled with oil are lighted and placed in rows along the parapets of temples and houses and set adrift on rivers and streams. Diwali is on 24 November in 2004. **Sivaratri**, the most important sectarian festival of the year for devotees of the Hindu god Shiva, occurs on 18 February in 2004. **Holi** is a spring festival, probably of ancient origin. Participants throw colored waters and powders on one another, and, on this day, the usual restrictions of caste, sex, status, and age are disregarded. It will be on 6 March in 2004.

**Sikh holidays**—Sikhs observe all festivals celebrated by the Hindus of northern India. In addition, they celebrate the birthdays of the first and the last Gurus and the martyrdom of the fifth (Arjun) and the ninth (Tegh Bahadur). In 2003–04 **Guru Nanak Dev Sahib's birthday** is celebrated on 26 November, and that of **Guru Gobind Singh Sahib** is celebrated on 5 January. On 16 June **Arjun's martyrdom** is observed. *Kachi lassi* (sweetened milk) is offered to passersby to commemorate his death. On 24 November the **martyrdom of Tegh Bahadur** is observed.

**Baha'i holidays**—The Baha'i New Year (**Naw Ruz**) in 2004 will fall on 21 March. Other important observances include the **declaration of the Bab** on 23 May, the **Baha 'Ullah's birth** (12 November), and **Ascension** (29 May).

**Zoroastrian holidays**—Noruz (New Day) is on 21 March for 2004 and the 26th of that month is **Khordad Sal**, the birth of the prophet Zarathustra.

The **African American holiday** of **Kwanzaa** (Swahili for "First Fruits") is celebrated each year from 26 December to 1 January and is patterned after various African harvest festivals. Maulana Karenga, a black-studies professor, created Kwanzaa in 1966 as a nonreligious celebration of family and social values. Each day of Kwanzaa is dedicated to one of seven principles: unity (*umoja*), self-determination (*kuji chagulia*), collective responsibility (*ujima*), cooperative economics (*ujamaa*), purpose (*nia*), creativity (*kuumba*), and faith (*imani*).

# Perpetual Calendar

The perpetual calendar is a type of dating system that makes it possible to find the correct day of the week for any date over a wide range of years. Aspects of the perpetual calendar can be found in the Jewish religious and the Julian calendars, and some form of it has appeared in many proposed calendar reforms.

To find the day of the week for any Gregorian or Julian date in the perpetual calendar provided in this table, first find the proper dominical letter (one of the letters A through G) for the year in the upper table. Leap years have two dominical letters, the first applicable to dates in January and February, the second to dates in the remaining months. Then find the same dominical letter in the lower table, in whichever column it appears opposite the month in question. The days then fall as given in the lowest section of the column.

| YEAR | | | | CENTURY | | | | | | | | | | | | |
|---|---|---|---|---|---|---|---|---|---|---|---|---|---|---|---|---|
| | | | | JULIAN CALENDAR | | | | | | | | GREGORIAN CALENDAR | | | | |
| | | | | 0 | 100 | 200 | 300 | 400 | 500 | 600 | 1500** | 1600 | 1700 | 1800 | 1900 |
| | | | | 700 | 800 | 900 | 1000 | 1100 | 1200 | 1300 | | 2000 | 2100 | 2200 | 2300 |
| | | | | 1400 | 1500* | | | | | | | | | | |
| 0 | | | | DC | ED | FE | GF | AG | BA | CB | ... | BA | C | E | G |
| 1 | 29 | 57 | 85 | B | C | D | E | F | G | A | F | G | B | D | F |
| 2 | 30 | 58 | 86 | A | B | C | D | E | F | G | E | F | A | C | E |
| 3 | 31 | 59 | 87 | G | A | B | C | D | E | F | D | E | G | B | D |
| 4 | 32 | 60 | 88 | FE | GF | AG | BA | CB | DC | ED | CB | DC | FE | AG | CB |
| 5 | 33 | 61 | 89 | D | E | F | G | A | B | C | A | B | D | F | A |
| 6 | 34 | 62 | 90 | C | D | E | F | G | A | B | G | A | C | E | G |
| 7 | 35 | 63 | 91 | B | C | D | E | F | G | A | F | G | B | D | F |
| 8 | 36 | 64 | 92 | AG | BA | CB | DC | ED | FE | GF | ED | FE | AG | CB | ED |
| 9 | 37 | 65 | 93 | F | G | A | B | C | D | E | C | D | F | A | C |
| 10 | 38 | 66 | 94 | E | F | G | A | B | C | D | B | C | E | G | B |
| 11 | 39 | 67 | 95 | D | E | F | G | A | B | C | A | B | D | F | A |
| 12 | 40 | 68 | 96 | CB | DC | ED | FE | GF | AG | BA | GF | AG | CB | ED | GF |
| 13 | 41 | 69 | 97 | A | B | C | D | E | F | G | E | F | A | C | E |
| 14 | 42 | 70 | 98 | G | A | B | C | D | E | F | D | E | G | B | D |
| 15 | 43 | 71 | 99 | F | G | A | B | C | D | E | C | D | F | A | C |
| 16 | 44 | 72 | | ED | FE | GF | AG | BA | CB | DC | ... | CB | ED | GF | BA |
| 17 | 45 | 73 | | C | D | E | F | G | A | B | ... | A | C | E | G |
| 18 | 46 | 74 | | B | C | D | E | F | G | A | ... | G | B | D | F |
| 19 | 47 | 75 | | A | B | C | D | E | F | G | ... | F | A | C | E |
| 20 | 48 | 76 | | GF | AG | BA | CB | DC | ED | FE | ... | ED | GF | BA | DC |
| 21 | 49 | 77 | | E | F | G | A | B | C | D | ... | C | E | G | B |
| 22 | 50 | 78 | | D | E | F | G | A | B | C | ... | B | D | F | A |
| 23 | 51 | 79 | | C | D | E | F | G | A | B | ... | A | C | E | G |
| 24 | 52 | 80 | | BA | CB | DC | ED | FE | GF | AG | ... | GF | BA | DC | FE |
| 25 | 53 | 81 | | G | A | B | C | D | E | F | ... | E | G | B | D |
| 26 | 54 | 82 | | F | G | A | B | C | D | E | C | D | F | A | C |
| 27 | 55 | 83 | | E | F | G | A | B | C | D | B | C | E | G | B |
| 28 | 56 | 84 | | DC | ED | FE | GF | AG | BA | CB | AG | BA | DC | FE | AG |

| MONTH | DOMINICAL LETTER | | | | | | |
|---|---|---|---|---|---|---|---|
| January, October | A | B | C | D | E | F | G |
| February, March, November | D | E | F | G | A | B | C |
| April, July | G | A | B | C | D | E | F |
| May | B | C | D | E | F | G | A |
| June | E | F | G | A | B | C | D |
| August | C | D | E | F | G | A | B |
| September, December | F | G | A | B | C | D | E |
| 1  8 15 22 29 | Sunday | Saturday | Friday | Thursday | Wednesday | Tuesday | Monday |
| 2  9 16 23 30 | Monday | Sunday | Saturday | Friday | Thursday | Wednesday | Tuesday |
| 3 10 17 24 31 | Tuesday | Monday | Sunday | Saturday | Friday | Thursday | Wednesday |
| 4 11 18 25 | Wednesday | Tuesday | Monday | Sunday | Saturday | Friday | Thursday |
| 5 12 19 26 | Thursday | Wednesday | Tuesday | Monday | Sunday | Saturday | Friday |
| 6 13 20 27 | Friday | Thursday | Wednesday | Tuesday | Monday | Sunday | Saturday |
| 7 14 21 28 | Saturday | Friday | Thursday | Wednesday | Tuesday | Monday | Sunday |

*On and before 1582, 4 October only.    **On and after 1582, 15 October only.
Source: Smithsonian Physical Tables, 9th edition, rev. 1956.

# Civil Holidays

| DAY | EVENT |
| --- | --- |
| 1 January | New Year's Day, the first day of the modern calendar (various countries) |
| 20 January | Inauguration Day, for quadrennial inauguration of US president |
| 26 January | Australia Day, commemorates the establishment of the first British settlement in Australia |
| 3rd Monday in January | Martin Luther King Day, for birth of US civil-rights leader |
| 2nd new moon after winter solstice (at the earliest 21 January and at the latest 19 February) | New Year, for Chinese lunar year, inaugurating a 15-day celebration |
| 6 February | Waitangi Day, for Treaty of Waitangi, granting British sovereignty (New Zealand) |
| 6 February | National Foundation Day, for founding by first emperor (Japan) |
| 14 February | St. Valentine's Day, celebrating the exchange of love messages and named for either of two 3rd-century Christian martyrs (various) |
| 3rd Monday in February | Presidents' Day, Washington-Lincoln Day, or Washington's Birthday, for birthdays of US Presidents George Washington and Abraham Lincoln |
| 8 March | International Women's Day, celebration of the women's liberation movement |
| 17 March | St. Patrick's Day, for patron saint of Ireland (Ireland and various) |
| 21 or 22 March | Vernal Equinox Day, for beginning of spring (Japan) |
| 25 March | Independence Day, for proclamation of independence from the Ottoman Empire (Greece) |
| 4th Sunday in Lent | Mothering Day (UK) |
| 1 April | April Fools' Day, or All Fools' Day, day for playing jokes, falling one week after the old New Year's Day of 25 March (various) |
| 5 April | Ching Ming (Qingming), for sweeping tombs and honoring the dead (China) |
| 7 April | World Health Day, for founding of World Health Organization |
| 21/22 April | Earth Day, for conservation and reclaiming of the natural environment (various) |
| 25 April | ANZAC Day, for landing at Gallipoli (Australia/New Zealand/Samoa/Tonga) |
| 30 April | Queen's Birthday, for Queen Beatrix's investiture and former queen Juliana's birthday (The Netherlands) |
| 1 May | May Day, celebrated as labor day or as festival of flowers (various) |
| 3 May | Constitution Memorial Day, for establishment of democratic government (Japan) |
| 5 May | Children's Day, honoring children (Japan/South Korea) |
| 5 May | Cinco de Mayo, anniversary of Mexico's victory over France in the Battle of Puebla (Mexico) |
| 8/9 May | V-E Day, or Liberation Day, for end of World War II in Europe (various) |
| 2nd Sunday in May | Mother's Day, honoring mothers (US) |
| Monday on or preceding 25 May | Victoria Day, for Queen Victoria's birthday (Canada) |
| 30 or last Monday in May | Memorial Day, or Decoration Day, in honor of the deceased, especially the war dead (US) |
| 2 June | Anniversary of the Republic, for referendum establishing republic (Italy) |
| 5 June | Constitution Day (Denmark) |
| 6 June | National Day, for Gustav I Vasa's ascension to the throne and adoption of Constitution (Sweden) |
| 10 June | Portugal's Day, or Camões Memorial Day, anniversary of Luis de Camões's death |
| 14 June | Flag Day, honoring flag (US) |
| 3rd Saturday in June | Queen's Official Birthday, for Queen Elizabeth II (UK/New Zealand) |
| 3rd Sunday in June | Father's Day, honoring fathers (US) |
| 23 June | National Day, for Grand Duke Jean's official birthday (Luxembourg) |
| 23–24 June | Midsummer Eve and Midsummer Day, celebrating the return of summer (various European) |
| last Sunday in June | Gay and Lesbian Pride Day, final day of weeklong advocacy of rights of homosexuals (international) |
| 1 July | Canada Day (formerly Dominion Day), for establishment of dominion |
| 4 July | Independence Day, for Declaration of Independence from Britain (US) |
| 12 July | Orangemen's Day, or Orange Day, anniversary of the Battle of the Boyne (Northern Ireland) |
| 14 July | Bastille Day, for fall of the Bastille and onset of French Revolution (France) |
| 21 July | National Day, for separation from The Netherlands (Belgium) |
| 1 August | National Day, anniversary of the founding of the Swiss Confederation (Switzerland) |
| 6 August | Hiroshima Day, for dropping of atomic bomb (Japan) |
| full-moon day of 8th lunar month | Chusok, harvest festival (Korea) |
| 1st Monday in September | Labor Day, tribute to workers (US/Canada) |
| 15 September | Respect-for-the-Aged Day, for the elderly (Japan) |
| 16 September | Independence Day, for independence from Spain (Mexico) |
| 23 or 24 September | Autumnal Equinox Day, for beginning of autumn; in honor of ancestors (Japan) |

## Civil Holidays (continued)

| DAY | EVENT |
|---|---|
| two weeks ending on 1st Sunday in October | Oktoberfest, festival of food and drink, formerly commemorating marriage of King Louis (Ludwig) I (Germany) |
| 3 October | Day of German Unity, for reunification of Germany |
| 5 October | Republic Day, for founding of the republic (Portugal) |
| 12 or 2nd Monday in October | Hispanic Day, Columbus Day, Discovery Day, or Day of the Race, for Christopher Columbus's discovery of the New World on behalf of Spain (Spain and various) |
| 2nd Monday in October | Thanksgiving Day, harvest festival (Canada) |
| 24 October | United Nations Day, for effective date of UN Charter (international) |
| 26 October | National Day, for end of postwar occupation and return of sovereignty (Austria) |
| 31 October | Halloween, or All Hallows' Eve, festive celebration of ghosts and spirits, on eve of All Saints' Day (various) |
| 5 November | Guy Fawkes Day, anniversary of the Gunpowder Plot to blow up the king and Parliament (UK) |
| 11 November | Armistice Day, Remembrance Day, or Veterans' Day, honoring participants in past wars and recalling the Armistice of World War I (various) |
| 23 November | Labor Thanksgiving Day, honoring workers (Japan) |
| 4th Thursday in November | Thanksgiving Day, harvest festival (US) |
| 16 December | Day of Reconciliation, for promoting national unity (South Africa) |
| 23 December | Emperor's Birthday, for birthday of Emperor Akihito (Japan) |
| 26 December | Boxing Day, second day of Christmas, for giving presents to service people (various) |
| 31 December | New Year's Eve, celebration ushering out the old year and in the new year (various) |

# The Universe

## Cosmogony (Theories of the Origin of the Universe)

Three great ages of scientific thinking about the universe can be distinguished. The first began in Greece in the 6th century BC when the **Pythagoreans** introduced the concept of a **spherical Earth** and postulated a universe in which the motions of heavenly bodies were governed by natural laws. The **infinite atomist universe** of Leucippus and Democritus followed, wherein countless worlds, teeming with life, were the result of chance aggregations of atoms. The **geocentric Aristotelian universe** arose in the 4th century BC. It consisted of a central Earth surrounded by revolving, translucent spheres to which were attached the Sun and the planets; the outermost sphere supported the fixed stars.

The **Copernican revolution** ushered in the second great age. In the 16th century, Nicolaus Copernicus revived ancient ideas and proposed a heliocentric universe, which during the following century was transformed into the mechanistic, infinite **Newtonian universe** that flourished until the early 1900s. In the mid-18th century, Thomas Wright proposed the influential notion of a universe composed of numerous **galaxies**, and William Herschel, followed by many other astronomers, made rapid strides in the study of stars and of the Milky Way Galaxy, of which the Earth is a component.

The third great age began in the early years of the 20th century, with the discovery of **special relativity** and its development into **general relativity** by **Albert Einstein**. These years also saw momentous developments in astronomy: extragalactic redshifts were detected by Vesto Slipher; extragalactic nebulae were shown to be galaxies comparable with the Milky Way; and **Edwin Hubble** began to estimate the distances of these galactic systems. Such discoveries and the application of general relativity to cosmology eventually gave rise to the view that the **universe is expanding**. The basic premise of modern thinking on the universe is the principle that asserts that the universe is homogeneous in space (on the average all places are alike at any time) and that the laws of physics are everywhere the same.

Two theories of the origin of the universe have been the most influential during the last century—the steady state theory and the big bang theory. The **steady state theory** posits that the universe is always expanding but maintains a constant average density, matter being continuously created to form new stars and galaxies at the same rate that old ones become unobservable as a consequence of their increasing distance and velocity of recession. A steady-state universe has no beginning or end in time; and from any point within it the view on the grand scale—i.e., the average density and arrangement of galaxies—is the same. Galaxies of all possible ages are intermingled. Observations since the 1950s have produced much evidence contradictory to the steady-state picture and supportive of the big-bang model.

The essential feature of the widely-held **big bang theory** is the emergence of the universe from a state of extremely high temperature and density—the so-called big bang that occurred at least 10,000,000,000 years ago. Although this type of universe was proposed by Alexander Friedmann and Abbé Georges Lemaître in the 1920s, the modern version was developed by George Gamow and colleagues in the 1940s.

One current problem that scientists are studying is the **amount of matter in the universe**. Based upon such things as the rate of the motion of galaxies, scientists realized that there is some 90% more matter in the universe than can be seen. Scientists refer to the matter that can be observed as **"bright matter"** and this other 90% is called **"dark matter."** Whether dark matter is of a different and exotic nature from the matter with which we are familiar, or whether dark matter is just like luminous matter (and for some reason we cannot detect it), is something a large number of scientists are studying.

# Astronomical Constants

| QUANTITY | SYMBOL | VALUE |
|---|---|---|
| astronomical unit | AU | length of the semi-major axis of the Earth to the Sun—149,597,870 km (92,955,808 mi) |

measures large distances in space; equals the average distance from the Earth to the Sun

| parsec | pc | one parsec equals 3.26 light years |
|---|---|---|

measures the distance at which the radius of the Earth's orbit subtends an angle of one second of arc

| light-year | ly | $9.46089 \times 10^{12}$ km ($5.8787 \times 10^{12}$ mi) |
|---|---|---|

measures the distance traveled by light moving in a vacuum in the course of one year

| solar parallax | | 8.79414″ |
|---|---|---|

quantifies the angular difference in direction of the Sun as measured from two points on the Earth's orbit

| lunar parallax | | 57′ 02.608″ |
|---|---|---|

quantifies the angular difference in direction of the Moon as measured from two points on Earth's orbit

| general precession | | 50.29 arc seconds per year |
|---|---|---|

measures the cyclic wobbling in the orientation of the Earth's axis of rotation with a period of almost 26,000 years

| constant of aberration | | about 20.49″ of arc |
|---|---|---|

the maximum amount of the apparent yearly aberrational displacement of a star or other celestial body, resulting from the Earth's orbital motion around the Sun

| constant of nutation | | 9.202″ |
|---|---|---|

a small irregularity in the precession of the equinoxes that occurs over a period of 18.6 years

| speed of light (in a vacuum) | $c$ | $2.99792458 \times 10^{10}$ cm per sec (186,282 mi per sec) |
|---|---|---|

| radius of the Sun | Sun $R$ | $6.96 \times 10^{8}$ m (109 times the radius of Earth) |
|---|---|---|

| mass of the Sun | Sun $M$ | $1.989 \times 10^{30}$ kg (330,000 times the mass of the Earth) |
|---|---|---|

| Earth's mean radius | | 6,378 km (3,963 mi) |
|---|---|---|

| sidereal day (on Earth) | | 23 h 56 min 4.10 sec of mean solar time |
|---|---|---|

defined by the period between two passages of a star across the meridian

| mean solar day (on Earth) | | 24 h 3 min 56.55 sec duration |
|---|---|---|

the interval between two passages of the Sun across the meridian is a solar day; in practice, since the rate of the Sun's motion varies with the seasons, use is made of a fictitious Sun that always moves across the sky at an even rate

| tropical year (on Earth) | | 365.242191 days (for 2004) |
|---|---|---|

the rotation period it takes for the Earth to return the Sun to the spring equinoctial point

| sidereal year (on Earth) | | 365.256363 days (for 2004) |
|---|---|---|

the rotation period it takes for the Earth to return to the longitude of a fixed star

| synodic month (on Earth) | | 29.530588 days (for 2004) |
|---|---|---|

rotation period between two successive full moons

| sidereal month (on Earth) | | 27.321660 days (for 2004) |
|---|---|---|

rotation period it takes the Moon to return to a set place in relation to the stars

**Did you know?** Communications satellites comprising a network or system are nearly always launched to a distance of 35,890 km (22,300 mi) above the Earth. At this altitude, the motion of a satellite becomes synchronized with the Earth's rotation, causing the craft to remain fixed over a single location. If properly positioned, three communications satellites traveling in such a synchronous orbit can relay signals between stations around the world.

# Definitions of Astronomical Positions

A conjunction is an apparent meeting or passing of two or more celestial bodies. For example, the Moon is in conjunction with the Sun at the phase of new Moon, when it moves between the Earth and Sun and the side turned toward the Earth is dark. Inferior planets—those with orbits smaller than the Earth's (namely, Venus and Mercury)—have two kinds of conjunctions with the Sun. An **inferior conjunction** occurs when the planet passes approximately between Earth and Sun; if it passes exactly between them, moving across the Sun's face as seen from Earth, it is said to be in transit (*see below*). A **superior conjunction** occurs when Earth and the other planet are on opposite sides of the Sun, but all three bodies are again nearly in a straight line. Superior planets, those having orbits larger than the Earth's can have only superior conjunctions with the Sun.

When celestial bodies appear in opposite directions in the sky they are said to be in **opposition**. The Moon, when full, is said to be in opposition to the Sun (the Earth is then approximately between them). A superior planet (one with an orbit farther from the Sun than Earth's) is in opposition when Earth passes between it and the Sun. The opposition of a planet is a good time to observe it, because the planet is then at its nearest point to the Earth and in its full phase. The inferior planets, Venus and Mercury, can never be in opposition to the Sun.

When a celestial body as seen from the Earth makes a right angle with the direction of the Sun it is said to be in **quadrature**. The Moon at first or last quarter is said to be at east or west quadrature, respectively. A superior planet is at west quadrature when its position is 90° west of the Sun.

The east–west coordinate by which the position of a celestial body is ordinarily measured is known as **right ascension**. Right ascension in combination with **declination** defines the position of a celestial object. Declination is the angular distance of a body north or south of the celestial equator. North declination is considered positive and south, negative. Thus, +90° declination marks the north celestial pole, 0° the celestial equator, and −90° the south celestial pole. The symbol for right ascension is the Greek letter α (alpha) and for declination the lowercase Greek letter Δ (delta).

The angular distance in celestial longitude separating the Moon or a planet from the Sun is known as **elongation**. The greatest elongation possible for the two inferior planets is about 48° in the case of Venus and about 28° in that of Mercury. Elongation may also refer to the angular distance of any celestial body from another around which it revolves or from a particular point in the sky; e.g., the extreme east or west position of a star with reference to the north celestial pole.

The point at which a planet is closest to the Sun is called the **perihelion**, and the most distant point in that planet's orbit is the **aphelion**. The term helion refers specifically to the Sun as the primary body about which the planet is orbiting.

**Occultation** refers to the obscuring of the light of an astronomical body, most commonly a star, by another astronomical body, such as a planet or a satellite. Hence, a solar eclipse is the occultation of the Sun by the Moon. From occultations of stars by planets, asteroids, and satellites, astronomers are able to determine the precise sizes and shapes of the latter bodies in addition to the temperatures of planetary atmospheres. For example, astronomers unexpectedly discovered the rings of Uranus during a stellar occultation on 10 Mar 1977.

A complete or partial obscuring of a celestial body by another is an **eclipse**; these occur when three celestial objects become aligned. The Sun is eclipsed when the Moon comes between it and the Earth; the Moon is eclipsed when it moves into the shadow of the Earth cast by the Sun. Eclipses of natural or artificial satellites of a planet occur as the satellites move into the planet's shadow. When the apparent size of the eclipsed body is much smaller than that of the eclipsing body, the phenomenon is known as an **occultation** (*see above*). Examples are the disappearance of a star, nebula, or planet behind the Moon, or the vanishing of a natural satellite or space probe behind some body of the solar system. A **transit** (*see above*) occurs when, as viewed from the Earth, a relatively small body passes across the disk of a larger body, usually the Sun or a planet, eclipsing only a very small area: Mercury and Venus periodically transit the Sun, and a satellite may transit its planet.

When an object orbiting the Earth is at the point in its orbit that is the greatest distance from the center of the Earth, this point is known as **apogee**; the term is also used to describe the point farthest from a planet or a satellite (as the Moon) reached by an object orbiting it. **Perigee** is the opposite of apogee.

The difference in direction of a celestial object as seen by an observer from two widely separated points is termed **parallax**. The measurement of parallax is used directly to find the distance of the body from the Earth (geocentric parallax) and from the Sun (heliocentric parallax). The two positions of the observer and the position of the object form a triangle; if the base line between the two observing points is known and the direction of the object as seen from each has been measured, the apex angle (the parallax) and the distance of the object from the observer can be determined.

An **hour angle** is the angle between an observer's meridian (a great circle passing over his head and through the celestial poles) and the hour circle (any other great circle passing through the poles) on which some celestial body lies. This angle, when expressed in hours and minutes, is the time elapsed since the celestial body's last transit of the observer's meridian. The hour angle can also be expressed in degrees, 15° of arc being equal to one hour.

# Constellations

Constellations are certain groupings of stars that were imagined—at least by those who named them—to form conspicuous configurations of objects or creatures in the sky. Constellations are useful in tracking artificial satellites and in assisting astronomers and navigators to locate certain stars.

From the earliest times the star groups known as constellations, the smaller groups (parts of constellations) known as **asterisms**, and, also, **individual stars** have received names connoting some meteorological phenomena or symbolizing religious or mythological beliefs. At one time it was held that the constellation

## Constellations (continued)

names and myths were of Greek origin; this view has now been disproved. It is now thought that the Greek constellation system and the cognate legends are primarily of Semitic or even pre-Semitic origin and that they came to the Greeks through the Phoenicians.

The Alexandrian astronomer **Ptolemy** lists the names and orientation of the 48 constellations in his *Almagest*, and, with but few exceptions, they are identical with those used at the present time. The majority of the remaining 40 constellations that are now accepted were added by European astronomers in the 17th and 18th centuries. In the 20th century the delineation of precise boundaries for all the 88 constellations was undertaken by a committee of the International Astronomical Union. By 1930 it was possible to assign any star to a constellation.

| NAME | GENITIVE | MEANING | NOTES |
|---|---|---|---|
| **Constellations described by Ptolemy: the zodiac** | | | (First-magnitude stars are given in italics in this column) |
| Aries | Arietis | Ram | |
| Taurus | Tauri | Bull | *Aldebaran* is the constellation's brightest star. Taurus also contains the Pleiades star cluster and the Crab Nebula. |
| Gemini | Geminorum | Twins | The brightest stars in Gemini are Castor and *Pollux*. |
| Cancer | Cancri | Crab | Cancer contains the well-known star cluster Praesepe. |
| Leo | Leonis | Lion | *Regulus* is the brightest star in Leo. |
| Virgo | Virginis | Virgin | *Spica* is the brightest star in Virgo. |
| Libra | Librae | Balance | |
| Scorpius | Scorpii | Scorpion | *Antares* is the brightest star of Scorpius, which also contains many star clusters. |
| Sagittarius | Sagittarii | Archer | The center of the Milky Way Galaxy lies in Sagittarius, with the densest star clouds of the galaxy. |
| Capricornus | Capricorni | Sea-goat | |
| Aquarius | Aquarii | Water-bearer | |
| Pisces | Piscium | Fishes | |
| **Other Ptolemaic constellations** | | | |
| Andromeda | Andromedae | Andromeda (an Ethiopian princess of Greek legend, daughter of Cepheus and Cassiopeia) | The constellation's most notable feature is the great spiral galaxy Andromeda (also called M31). |
| Aquila | Aquilae | Eagle | The brightest star in Aquila is *Altair*. |
| Ara | Arae | Altar | |
| Argo Navis | Argus Navis | the ship *Argo* | Argo Navis is now divided into smaller constellations that include Carina, Puppis, Pyxis, and Vela. |
| Auriga | Aurigae | Charioteer | The brightest star in Auriga is *Capella*. The constellation also contains open star clusters M36, M37, and M38. |
| Boötes | Boötis | Herdsman | *Arcturus* is the brightest star in Boötes. |
| Canis Major | Canis Majoris | Greater Dog | *Sirius* is the brightest star in Canis Major. |
| Canis Minor | Canis Minoris | Smaller Dog | *Procyon* is the brightest star in Canis Minor. |
| Cassiopeia | Cassiopeiae | Cassiopeia was a legendary queen of Ethiopia | Tycho's nova, one of the few recorded supernovae in the Galaxy, appeared in Cassiopeia in 1572. |
| Centaurus | Centauri | Centaur (possibly represents Chiron) | *Alpha Centauri* in Centaurus contains Proxima, the nearest star to the Sun. |
| Cepheus | Cephei | Cepheus (legendary king of Ethiopia) | Delta Cephei was the prototype for cepheid variables (a class of variable stars). |
| Cetus | Ceti | Whale | Mira Ceti was the first recognized variable star. |
| Corona Austrina | Coronae Austrinae | Southern Crown | |
| Corona Borealis | Coronae Borealis | Northern Crown | |
| Corvus | Corvi | Raven | |
| Crater | Crateris | Cup | |
| Cygnus | Cygni | Swan | Cygnus contains the asterism (grouping of stars) known as the Northern Cross; the constellation's brightest star is *Deneb*. |
| Delphinus | Delphini | Dolphin | Delphinus contains the asterism known as Job's Coffin. |
| Draco | Draconis | Dragon | Drac contains the star Thuban, which was the polestar in 3000 BC. |

# Constellations (continued)

| NAME | GENITIVE | MEANING | NOTES |
|------|----------|---------|-------|
| **Other Ptolemaic constellations (continued)** | | | |
| Equuleus | Equulei | Little Horse | |
| Eridanus | Eridani | River Eridanus or river god | *Achernar* is the brightest star in Eridanus. |
| Hercules | Herculis | Hercules (Greek hero) | Hercules contains the great globular star cluster M13. |
| Hydra | Hydrae | Water Snake | |
| Lepus | Leporis | Hare | |
| Lupus | Lupi | Wolf | |
| Lyra | Lyrae | Lyre | The brightest star in Lyra is *Vega*. In some 10,000 years, *Vega* will become the polestar. Lyra also contains the Ring Nebula (M57). |
| Ophiuchus | Ophiuchi | Serpent-bearer | When the Zodiac was conceived of, Ophiuchus was not in the Sun's path, but the Sun does now pass through Ophiuchus each December. |
| Orion | Orionis | Hunter | *Rigel* is the brightest star in Orion, followed closely by *Betelgeuse;* M42 (the Great Nebula) resides in Orion. |
| Pegasus | Pegasi | Pegasus (winged horse) | The constellation contains stars of the Great Square of Pegasus. |
| Perseus | Persei | Perseus (legendary Greek hero) | |
| Piscis Austrinus | Piscis Austrini | Southern Fish | The brightest star in Piscis Austrinus is *Fomalhaut*. |
| Sagitta | Sagittae | Arrow | |
| Serpens | Serpentis | Serpent | |
| Triangulum | Trianguli | Triangle | The constellation contains M33, a nearby spiral galaxy. |
| Ursa Major | Ursae Majoris | Great Bear | The seven brightest stars of this constellation are the Big Dipper (also called the Plough). |
| Ursa Minor | Ursae Minoris | Lesser Bear | Ursa Minor contains Polaris (the north polestar). |
| **Southern constellations, added c. 1600** | | | |
| Apus | Apodis | Bird of Paradise | |
| Chamaeleon | Chamaeleontis | Chameleon | |
| Dorado | Doradus | Swordfish | The most notable object in Dorado is the Large Magellanic Cloud. |
| Grus | Gruis | Crane | |
| Hydrus | Hydri | Water Snake | |
| Indus | Indi | Indian | |
| Musca | Muscae | Fly | |
| Pavo | Pavonis | Peacock | |
| Phoenix | Phoenicis | Phoenix (mythical bird) | |
| Triangulum Australe | Trianguli Australis | Southern Triangle | |
| Tucana | Tucanae | Toucan | The most notable object in Tucana is the Small Magellanic Cloud. |
| Volans | Volantis | Flying Fish | |
| **Constellations of Bartsch, 1624** | | | |
| Camelopardalis | Camelopardalis | Giraffe | |
| Columba | Columbae | Dove | This constellation was formed by Petrus Plancius in the early 1600s. |
| Monoceros | Monocerotis | Unicorn | |
| **Constellations of Hevelius, 1687** | | | |
| Canes Venatici | Canum Venaticorum | Hunting Dogs | The constellation contains M51 (the Whirlpool Galaxy). |
| Lacerta | Lacertae | Lizard | |
| Leo Minor | Leonis Minoris | Lesser Lion | |
| Lynx | Lyncis | Lynx | |
| Scutum | Scuti | Shield | Scutum contains the Scutim star cloud in the Milky Way. |
| Sextans | Sextantis | Sextant | |
| Vulpecula | Vulpeculae | Fox | Vulpecula contains M27 (the Dumbbell Nebula). |

## Constellations (continued)

| NAME | GENITIVE | MEANING | NOTES |
|---|---|---|---|
| Ancient asterisms that are now separate constellations | | | |
| Carina | Carinae | Keel [of the legendary ship the *Argo*] | The brightest star in Carina is *Canopus*. |
| Coma Berenices | Comae Berenices | Berenice's Hair | The constellation contains both a coma (star cluster) and the north galactic pole (a point that lies perpendicular to the Milky Way). |
| Crux | Crucis | [Southern] Cross | |
| Puppis | Puppis | Stern [of the *Argo*] | |
| Pyxis | Pyxidis | Compass [of the *Argo*] | |
| Vela | Velorum | Sails [of the *Argo*] | |
| | | | |
| Southern constellations of Lacaille, c. 1750 | | | |
| Antlia | Antliae | Pump | |
| Caelum | Caeli | [Sculptor's] Chisel | |
| Circinus | Circini | Drawing Compasses | |
| Fornax | Fornacis | [Chemical] Furnace | |
| Horologium | Horologii | Clock | |
| Mensa | Mensae | Table [Mountain] | |
| Microscopium | Microscopii | Microscope | |
| Norma | Normae | Square | |
| Octans | Octantis | Octant | Octans contains the south celestial pole. |
| Pictor | Pictoris | Painter's [Easel] | |
| Reticulum | Reticuli | Reticle | |
| Sculptor | Sculptoris | Sculptor's [Workshop] | Sculptor contains the south galactic pole. |
| Telescopium | Telescopii | Telescope | |

## Astrology: The Zodiac

*Signs of the zodiac are popularly used for divination as well as for designation of constellations.*

| NAME | SYMBOL | DATES | SEX/NATURE | TRIPLICITY | HOUSE | EXALTATION |
|---|---|---|---|---|---|---|
| Aries the Ram | ♈ | 21 Mar–19 Apr | masculine/moving | fire | Mars | Sun (19°) |
| Taurus the Bull | ♉ | 20 Apr–20 May | feminine/fixed | earth | Venus | Moon (3°) |
| Gemini the Twins | ♊ | 21 May–21 Jun | masculine/common | air | Mercury | |
| Cancer the Crab | ♋ | 22 Jun–22 Jul | feminine/moving | water | Moon | Jupiter (15°) |
| Leo the Lion | ♌ | 23 Jul–22 Aug | masculine/fixed | fire | Sun | |
| Virgo the Virgin | ♍ | 23 Aug–22 Sep | feminine/common | earth | Mercury | Mercury (15°) |
| Libra the Balance | ♎ | 23 Sep–23 Oct | masculine/moving | air | Venus | Saturn (21°) |
| Scorpius the Scorpion | ♏ | 24 Oct–21 Nov | feminine/fixed | water | Mars | |
| Sagittarius the Archer | ♐ | 22 Nov–21 Dec | masculine/common | fire | Jupiter | |
| Capricorn the Goat | ♑ | 22 Dec–19 Jan | feminine/moving | earth | Saturn | Mars (28°) |
| Aquarius the Water Bearer | ♒ | 20 Jan–18 Feb | masculine/fixed | air | Saturn | |
| Pisces the Fish | ♓ | 19 Feb–20 Mar | feminine/common | water | Jupiter | Venus (27°) |

## Classification of Stars

The spectral sequence O–M represents stars of essentially the same chemical composition but of different temperatures and atmospheric pressures. Stars belonging to other, more rare types of spectral classifications differ in chemical composition from O–M stars.

Each spectral class is additionally subdivided into 10 spectral types. For example, spectral class A is subdivided into spectral types A0–A9 with 0 being the hottest and 9 the coolest. (Spectral class O is unusual in that it is subdivided into O4–O9.) Between two stars of the same spectral type, the more luminous star will also be larger in diameter. Thus the Yerkes system of luminosity also tells something of a star's radius, with Ia being the largest and V the smallest. Approximately 90% of all stars are main sequence, or type V, stars.

Based upon these systems, the Sun would be a G2 V star (a yellow, relatively hot dwarf star).

| SPECTRAL CLASS | COLOR | APPROXIMATE SURFACE TEMP (°C) | EXAMPLES |
|---|---|---|---|
| O | blue | 30,000 or greater | These stars are relatively rare |
| B | blue-white | 20,000 to 30,000 | Rigel, Alpha Crucis, Beta Crucis |
| A | white | 10,000 to 20,000 | Sirius, Vega, Fomalhaut |
| F | yellow-white | 7,000 to 10,000 | Canopus, Procyon |

# Classification of Stars (continued)

| SPECTRAL CLASS | COLOR | APPROXIMATE SURFACE TEMP (°C) | EXAMPLES |
|---|---|---|---|
| G | yellow | 6,000 to 7,000 | Sun |
| K | orange | 4,500 to 6,000 | Arcturus, Aldebaran |
| M | red | 3,000 to 4,500 | Betelgeuse, Antares |

LUMINOSITY CLASSES (BASED UPON THE YERKES SYSTEM)

| | |
|---|---|
| Ia | most luminous supergiants |
| Ib | luminous supergiants |
| II | bright giants |
| III | normal giants |
| IV | subgiants |
| V | main sequence stars (dwarfs) |

# The 20 Brightest Stars in the Night Sky

This table lists the stars in descending order from brightest to less bright, based on apparent visual magnitude. Formal names of stars, such as Alpha Carinae, refer to the constellation in which the star appears (Carina) and to which star appears the brightest in that constellation; the second highest would be designated Beta, etc. Some anomalies exist within the naming convention: Betelgeuse, for example, is the Alpha star of Orion, though Rigel appears brighter.

On the scale of brightness, negative magnitudes are brightest, and one magnitude difference corresponds to a difference in brightness of 2.5 times; e.g., a star of magnitude −1 is 10 times brighter than one of magnitude +1.5.

Apparent magnitude is a measure of how bright a star appears to a viewer on Earth. Absolute magnitude is the brightness one would perceive if all stars were at the same distance from Earth. The distance from Earth that scientists assume when computing absolute magnitude is 10 parsecs (about 32.6 light-years; one light-year equals about $9.46 \times 10^{12}$ km). With absolute magnitude a comparison can be made between a star such as Rigel, which is very bright but very distant, and a star such as Sirius, which is less bright but is fairly close to Earth. The Sun, for purposes of comparison with the stars in the table, has an apparent magnitude of −26.8 and an actual magnitude of +4.8; it is a yellow dwarf star that is 8.3 light-minutes from Earth.

| STAR | APPARENT VISUAL MAGNITUDE/ABSOLUTE VISUAL MAGNITUDE | DISTANCE FROM THE SOLAR SYSTEM (LIGHT-YEARS) | CONSTELLATION |
|---|---|---|---|
| Sirius (Alpha Canis Majoris, or Dog Star) | −1.46/+1.43 | 8.6 | Canis Major |

Sirius is a blue-white dwarf with a white-dwarf companion; among the ancient Romans, the hottest part of the year was associated with the time in which the Dog Star rose just before dawn; this connection survives in the expression "dog days."

| | | | |
|---|---|---|---|
| Canopus (Alpha Carinae) | −0.72/around −3.1 (reported values vary) | 74 (reported values vary) | Carina |

A yellow-white supergiant, Canopus is sometimes used as a guide in the attitude control of spacecraft because of its angular distance from the Sun and the contrast of its brightness among nearby celestial objects.

| | | | |
|---|---|---|---|
| Alpha Centauri (Rigel Kentaurus) | −0.01/+4.5 | 4.3 | Centaurus |

Alpha Centauri is a triple star—a binary yellow dwarf circled by a red dwarf with a much smaller red dwarf; the faintest of Alpha Centauri's three stars, Proxima, is the star closest to the Sun.

| | | | |
|---|---|---|---|
| Arcturus (Alpha Boötis) | −0.04/−0.3 | 34 | Boötes |

An orange-colored giant, Arcturus lies in an almost direct line with the tail of Ursa Major (the Great Bear); hence its name, derived from the Greek words for "bear guard."

| | | | |
|---|---|---|---|
| Vega (Alpha Lyrae) | +0.03/+0.58 | 25.3 | Lyra |

A blue dwarf, Vega will become the northern polestar by about AD 14,000 because of the precession of the equinoxes.

| | | | |
|---|---|---|---|
| Capella (Alpha Aurigae) | +0.08/−0.48 | 41 | Auriga |

Capella is actually four stars, two yellow giants and two red-dwarf companion stars. Scientists are studying Capella to determine why it emits more X-rays than other stars of its type.

| | | | |
|---|---|---|---|
| Rigel (Beta Orionis) | +0.12 (variable)/−6.4 | 815 | Orion |

Rigel is a blue-white supergiant with two smaller companion stars. The name Rigel derives from an Arabic term meaning "the left leg of the giant," referring to the figure of Orion.

# The 20 Brightest Stars in the Night Sky (continued)

| STAR | APPARENT VISUAL MAGNITUDE/ABSOLUTE VISUAL MAGNITUDE | DISTANCE FROM THE SOLAR SYSTEM (LIGHT-YEARS) | CONSTELLATION |
|---|---|---|---|
| Procyon (Alpha Canis Minoris) | +0.38/+2.7 | 11.4 | Canis Minor |

Procyon is a yellow-white subgiant with a faint white-dwarf companion. The name Procyon apparently derives from Greek words for "before the dog," as in northern latitudes the star rises just before Sirius, the Dog Star.

**Achernar** (Alpha Eridani) +0.46/−2.6 — 69 — Eridanus
Achernar is a blue dwarf. The name Achernar probably derives from an Arabic phrase meaning "the end of the river," in which the river referred to is the constellation.

**Betelgeuse** (Alpha Orionis) +0.50 (variable)/−5.1 — 650 — Orion
A red supergiant, Betelgeuse has a diameter that varies between 430 and 625 times the diameter of the Sun over a period of 5.8 years.

**Beta Centauri** (Hadar) +0.61/−3.1 — 320 — Centaurus
Beta Centauri is a blue-white supergiant with two smaller companion stars; the constellation Centaurus most likely is meant to represent the centaur Chiron. In Greek mythology Chiron was renowned for his wisdom and knowledge of medicine. He renounced his immortality to escape a painful wound, and Zeus placed him in the Southern sky.

**Altair** (Alpha Aquilae) +0.77/+2.2 — 16.8 — Aquila
A blue dwarf, Altair spins nearly 470,000 mph, as compared with Earth, which spins some 1,000 mph. This rapid spinning flattens Altair from a spherical into an oblate shape.

**Aldebaran** (Alpha Tauri) +0.85/−0.63 — 60 — Taurus
A red giant, Aldebaran has a name derived from the Arabic for "the follower," perhaps because it rises after the Pleiades cluster of stars.

**Antares** (Alpha Scorpii) +0.96/−5.28 — 425 — Scorpio
Antares is a red supergiant. The name Antares seems to come from a Greek phrase meaning "rival of Ares" (i.e., rival of the planet Mars) and was probably given because of the star's color and brightness.

**Spica** (Alpha Virginis) +0.98/−3.55 — 220 — Virgo
A binary blue-white dwarf with a nonvisible companion, Spica has a name derived from the Latin for "ear of wheat"; the star is said to represent the wheat being held by the Virgin.

**Pollux** (Beta Geminorum) +1.14/+1.09 — 40 — Gemini
A red giant, Pollux is named for one of the twins of ancient Greek mythology (the other is Castor).

**Fomalhaut** (Alpha Piscis Austrini) +1.16/+1.74 — 22 — Piscis Austrinus
The blue-white dwarf Fomalhaut's name is derived from the Arabic for "mouth of the fish."

**Deneb** (Alpha Cygni) +1.25/−8.73 — 1,630 — Cygnus
A blue-white supergiant, Deneb gained its name from an Arabic word meaning "tail," as it is considered the tail of the swan Cygnus.

**Becrux** (Beta Crucis, or Mimosa) +1.25/−3.92 — 460 — Crux (The Southern Cross)
A blue-white giant, Becrux forms the eastern tip of the Southern Cross.

**Regulus** (Alpha Leo) +1.35/−0.3 — 69 — Leo
Regulus is a blue-white main sequence star; its name is the diminutive form of the Latin *rex* ("king").

*Data for apparent visual magnitudes taken from The Astronomical Almanac for 2003, issued jointly by the Nautical Almanac Office of the United States Naval Observatory and Her Majesty's Nautical Almanac Office of the United Kingdom.*

---

The international space endurance record is held by Russian cosmonaut Valery V. Polyakov. A physician, Polyakov spent 437.75 days in Earth orbit in 1994-95, most of the time aboard the Russian space station Mir.

# Astronomical Phenomena for 2004

*Source:* The Astronomical Almanac 2004.

| MONTH | DAY | HOUR (GMT) | EVENT | MONTH | DAY | HOUR (GMT) | EVENT |
|---|---|---|---|---|---|---|---|
| January | 3 | 20 | Moon at apogee | March | 29 | 17 | Venus greatest elongation E (46°) |
| | 4 | 15 | Jupiter stationary | | | | |
| | 4 | 18 | Earth at perihelion | April | 2 | 19 | Jupiter 3° S of Moon |
| | 6 | 14 | Mercury stationary | | 5 | 11 | full Moon |
| | 7 | 00 | Saturn 5° S of Moon | | 6 | 21 | Mercury stationary |
| | 7 | 16 | full Moon | | 7 | 05 | Mars 7° N of Aldebaran |
| | 9 | 14 | Ceres at opposition | | | | |
| | 12 | 11 | Jupiter 3° S of Moon | | 8 | 02 | Moon at perigee |
| | 15 | 01 | Venus 0°.9 S of Uranus | | 12 | 04 | last quarter |
| | 15 | 05 | last quarter | | 13 | 16 | Neptune 5° N of Moon |
| | 17 | 10 | Mercury greatest elong. W (24°) | | 15 | 04 | Uranus 4° N of Moon |
| | 19 | 19 | Moon at perigee | | 16 | 10 | Venus 10° N of Aldebaran |
| | 20 | 03 | Mercury 5° N of Moon | | | | |
| | 21 | 21 | new Moon | | 17 | 01 | Mercury in inferior conjunction |
| | 23 | 21 | Uranus 4° N of Moon | | | | |
| | 24 | 16 | Venus 4° N of Moon | | 19 | 13 | new Moon[2] |
| | 28 | 03 | Mars 3° N of Moon | | 23 | 10 | Venus 1°.5 N of Moon |
| | 29 | 06 | first quarter | | 23 | 21 | Mars 2° S of Moon |
| | 31 | 14 | Moon at apogee | | 24 | 00 | Moon at apogee |
| | | | | | 25 | 06 | Saturn 5° S of Moon |
| February | 2 | 09 | Neptune in conjunction with Sun | | 27 | 18 | first quarter |
| | | | | | 29 | 10 | Mercury stationary |
| | 3 | 04 | Saturn 4° S of Moon | | 30 | 02 | Jupiter 4° S of Moon |
| | 6 | 09 | full Moon | | | | |
| | 8 | 14 | Jupiter 3° S of Moon | May | 2 | 08 | Venus greatest brilliancy |
| | 13 | 14 | last quarter | | | | |
| | 15 | 09 | Mercury 2° S of Neptune | | 4 | 21 | full Moon[2] |
| | 16 | 08 | Moon at perigee | | 5 | 13 | Jupiter stationary |
| | 19 | 01 | Neptune 5° N of Moon | | 6 | 05 | Moon at perigee |
| | | | | | 10 | 22 | Neptune 5° N of Moon |
| | 20 | 09 | new Moon | | | | |
| | 22 | 02 | Uranus in conjunction with Sun | | 11 | 11 | last quarter |
| | | | | | 12 | 12 | Uranus 4° N of Moon |
| | 23 | 19 | Venus 3° N of Moon | | 12 | 22 | Vesta 1°.1 N of Moon[1] |
| | 25 | 20 | Ceres stationary | | 14 | 21 | Mercury greatest elongation W (26°) |
| | 26 | 02 | Mars 0°.9 N of Moon[1] | | | | |
| | 28 | 03 | first quarter | | 15 | 08 | Juno stationary |
| | 28 | 11 | Moon at apogee | | 16 | 23 | Mercury 3° S of Moon |
| | | | | | 17 | 15 | Neptune stationary |
| March | 1 | 10 | Saturn 5° S of Moon | | 18 | 00 | Venus stationary |
| | 4 | 02 | Mercury in superior conjunction | | 19 | 05 | new Moon |
| | | | | | 21 | 12 | Moon at apogee |
| | 4 | 05 | Jupiter at opposition | | 21 | 12 | Venus 0°.3 S of Moon[1] |
| | 6 | 16 | Jupiter 3° S of Moon | | 22 | 16 | Mars 3° S of Moon |
| | 6 | 23 | full Moon | | 22 | 18 | Saturn 5° S of Moon |
| | 7 | 15 | Saturn stationary | | 24 | 23 | Mars 1°.6 N of Saturn |
| | 12 | 04 | Moon at perigee | | 27 | 08 | first quarter |
| | 13 | 21 | last quarter | | 27 | 12 | Jupiter 4° S of Moon |
| | 17 | 09 | Neptune 5° N of Moon | | | | |
| | 18 | 20 | Uranus 4° N of Moon | June | 3 | 04 | full Moon |
| | 20 | 07 | Equinox | | 3 | 13 | Moon at perigee |
| | 20 | 23 | new Moon | | 7 | 06 | Neptune 5° N of Moon |
| | 22 | 05 | Mercury 4° N of Moon | | | | |
| | 24 | 21 | Venus 2° N of Moon | | 8 | 09 | Venus in inferior conjunction, transit over Sun |
| | 24 | 23 | Pluto stationary | | | | |
| | 26 | 00 | Mars 0°.8 S of Moon[1] | | 8 | 19 | Uranus 4° N of Moon |
| | 27 | 07 | Moon at apogee | | 9 | 20 | last quarter |
| | 28 | 19 | Saturn 5° S of Moon | | 9 | 23 | Vesta 1°.2 S of Moon[1] |
| | 29 | 00 | first quarter | | 11 | 00 | Uranus stationary |
| | 29 | 12 | Mercury greatest elongation E (19°) | | 11 | 12 | Pluto at opposition |
| | | | | | 14 | 18 | Mars 6° S of Pollux |
| | | | | | 17 | 16 | Moon at apogee |

# Astronomical Phenomena for 2004 (continued)

| MONTH | DAY | HOUR (GMT) | EVENT | MONTH | DAY | HOUR (GMT) | EVENT |
|---|---|---|---|---|---|---|---|
| June | 17 | 20 | new Moon | September | 1 | 01 | Venus 1°9 S of Saturn |
| | 18 | 21 | Mercury in superior conjunction | | 1 | 18 | Mercury stationary |
| | 19 | 07 | Saturn 5° S of Moon | | 2 | 02 | Venus 9° S of Pollux |
| | 20 | 09 | Mars 4° S of Moon | | 6 | 15 | last quarter |
| | 21 | 01 | solstice | | 8 | 03 | Moon at apogee |
| | 23 | 23 | Jupiter 3° S of Moon | | 9 | 14 | Mercury greatest elongation W (18°) |
| | 24 | 21 | Venus 2° N of Aldebaran | | 9 | 22 | Saturn 5° S of Moon |
| | 25 | 19 | first quarter | | 10 | 05 | Mercury 0°06 S of Regulus |
| | 29 | 14 | Venus stationary | | 10 | 16 | Venus 7° S of Moon |
| | 30 | 20 | Pallas in conjunction with Sun | | 12 | 04 | Saturn 7° S of Pollux |
| July | 1 | 11 | Mercury 5° S of Pollux | | 13 | 01 | Mercury 4° S of Moon |
| | 1 | 23 | Moon at perigee | | 13 | 05 | Ceres in conjunction with Sun |
| | 2 | 11 | full Moon | | 13 | 07 | Vesta at opposition |
| | 4 | 10 | Venus 1°1 N of Aldebaran | | 14 | 14 | new Moon |
| | 4 | 15 | Neptune 5° N of Moon | | 15 | 13 | Mars in conjunction with Sun |
| July | 5 | 11 | Earth at aphelion | | 21 | 16 | first quarter |
| | 6 | 03 | Uranus 4° N of Moon | | 22 | 00 | Jupiter in conjunction with Sun |
| | 8 | 17 | Saturn in conjunction with Sun | | 22 | 16 | Equinox |
| | 9 | 04 | Juno at opposition | | 22 | 21 | Moon at perigee |
| | 9 | 08 | last quarter | | 24 | 15 | Neptune 5° N of Moon |
| | 10 | 23 | Mercury 0°2 N of Mars | | 26 | 03 | Uranus 4° N of Moon |
| | 14 | 00 | Venus 8° S of Moon | | 28 | 13 | full Moon |
| | 14 | 21 | Moon at apogee | October | 3 | 16 | Venus 0°2 S of Regulus |
| | 15 | 01 | Venus greatest brilliancy | | 5 | 19 | Mercury in superior conjunction |
| | 17 | 11 | new Moon | | 5 | 22 | Moon at apogee |
| | 19 | 02 | Mars 4° S of Moon | | 6 | 10 | last quarter |
| | 19 | 15 | Mercury 5° S of Moon | | 7 | 10 | Saturn 5° S of Moon |
| | 21 | 13 | Jupiter 3° S of Moon | | 10 | 19 | Venus 4° S of Moon |
| | 25 | 04 | first quarter | | 12 | 19 | Jupiter 1°6 S of Moon |
| | 26 | 00 | Mercury 1°5 S of Regulus | | 14 | 03 | new Moon[2] |
| | 27 | 03 | Mercury greatest elongation E (27°) | | 18 | 00 | Moon at perigee |
| | 30 | 06 | Moon at perigee | | 20 | 22 | first quarter |
| | 31 | 18 | full Moon | | 21 | 21 | Neptune 5° N of Moon |
| August | 1 | 00 | Neptune 5° N of Moon | | 23 | 08 | Uranus 4° N of Moon |
| | 1 | 17 | Vesta stationary | | 24 | 10 | Neptune stationary |
| | 2 | 12 | Uranus 4° N of Moon | | 28 | 03 | full Moon[2] |
| | 6 | 03 | Neptune at opposition | | 31 | 08 | Mars 3° N of Spica |
| | 7 | 22 | last quarter | | 31 | 11 | Vesta stationary |
| | 9 | 05 | Mercury stationary | November | 2 | 18 | Moon at apogee |
| | 11 | 10 | Moon at apogee | | 3 | 20 | Saturn 5° S of Moon |
| | 11 | 23 | Venus 8° S of Moon | | 4 | 21 | Venus 0°6 N of Jupiter |
| | 13 | 09 | Saturn 5° S of Moon | | 5 | 06 | last quarter |
| | 16 | 01 | new Moon | | 8 | 11 | Saturn stationary |
| | 17 | 03 | Mercury 6° S of Mars | | 9 | 16 | Jupiter 1°0 S of Moon[1] |
| | 17 | 19 | Venus greatest elongation W (46°) | | 10 | 02 | Venus 0°2 N of Moon[1] |
| | 18 | 05 | Jupiter 3° S of Moon | | 11 | 04 | Mars 0°5 N of Moon[1] |
| | 23 | 10 | first quarter | | 11 | 10 | Mercury 2° N of Antares |
| | 23 | 21 | Mercury in inferior conjunction | | 12 | 02 | Uranus stationary |
| | 27 | 06 | Moon at perigee | | 12 | 14 | new Moon |
| | 27 | 19 | Uranus at opposition | | 14 | 03 | Mercury 0°9 N of Moon[1] |
| | 28 | 09 | Neptune 5° N of Moon | | 14 | 14 | Moon at perigee |
| | 29 | 20 | Uranus 4° N of Moon | | 16 | 09 | Venus 4° N of Spica |
| | 30 | 02 | full Moon | | 18 | 03 | Neptune 5° N of Moon |
| | 31 | 14 | Juno stationary | | 19 | 06 | first quarter |
| | 31 | 17 | Pluto stationary | | 19 | 13 | Uranus 4° N of Moon |

# Astronomical Phenomena for 2004 (continued)

| MONTH | DAY | HOUR (GMT) | EVENT | MONTH | DAY | HOUR (GMT) | EVENT |
|---|---|---|---|---|---|---|---|
| November | 21 | 01 | Mercury greatest elongation E (22°) | December | 12 | 21 | Moon at perigee |
| | 26 | 20 | full Moon | | 13 | 17 | Pluto in conjunction with Sun |
| | 30 | 11 | Moon at apogee | | 15 | 11 | Neptune 5° N of Moon |
| | 30 | 13 | Mercury stationary | | 16 | 21 | Uranus 4° N of Moon |
| December | 1 | 02 | Saturn 5° S of Moon | | 18 | 17 | first quarter |
| | 5 | 01 | last quarter | | 20 | 07 | Mercury stationary |
| | 5 | 07 | Venus 1°3 N of Mars | | 21 | 13 | Solstice |
| | 7 | 11 | Jupiter 0°3 S of Moon[1] | | 23 | 21 | Venus 6° N of Antares |
| | 10 | 00 | Mars 2° N of Moon | | 26 | 15 | full Moon |
| | 10 | 05 | Venus 4° N of Moon | | 27 | 19 | Moon at apogee |
| | 10 | 08 | Mercury in inferior conjunction | | 28 | 06 | Saturn 5° S of Moon |
| | 12 | 01 | new Moon | | 29 | 05 | Mercury 1°2 S of Venus |
| | | | | | 29 | 21 | Mercury greatest elongation W (22°) |

[1]Occultation.  [2]Eclipse.

# Morning and Evening Stars

This table gives the morning and evening stars for autumn 2003 through 2004. The morning and evening stars are actually planets visible to the naked eye during the early morning and at evening twilight.

| PLANET | MORNING STAR | EVENING STAR |
|---|---|---|
| Mercury | mid-September through mid-October 2003 2 January–21 February, 26 April–11 June, 1–25 September, and 16–31 December 2004 | 10 November–21 December 2003 14 March–9 April, 26 June–17 August, and 20 October–4 December 2004 |
| Venus | mid-June through December 2004 | 25 September 2003–2 June 2004 |
| Mars | 30 October through December 2004 | October 2003 through July 2004 |
| Jupiter | September 2003–4 March 2004 5 October through December 2004 | 4 March–8 September 2004 |
| Saturn | September through December 2003 27 July through December 2004 | 1 January–20 June 2004 |
| Uranus | September through late November 2003 mid-March through November 2004 | September 2003 through January 2004, December 2004 |
| Neptune | late February–early November 2004 | November 2003–early January 2004, November 2004 |

# Meteors, Meteorites, and Meteor Showers

A meteor (also called a **shooting star** or **falling star**) is a streak of light in the sky that results when a particle or small chunk of stony or metallic matter enters the Earth's atmosphere and vaporizes. The term is sometimes applied to the falling object itself, but the latter is properly called a **meteoroid**. The vast majority of meteoroids burn up in the upper atmosphere, but occasionally one of relatively large mass survives its fiery plunge and reaches the surface as a solid body. Such an object is known as a **meteorite**.

On any clear night in the countryside beyond the bright lights of cities, one can observe with the naked eye several meteors per hour as they streak through the sky. Quite often they vary in brightness along the path of their flight, appear to emit "sparks" or flares, and sometimes leave a luminous train that lingers after their flight has ended. These meteors are the result of the high-velocity collision of meteoroids with the Earth's atmosphere. Nearly all such interplanetary bodies are small fragments derived from comets or asteroids.

The brightest meteor (possibly of cometary origin) for which historical documentation exists—called the **Tunguska event**—struck on 30 Jun 1908, in central Siberia and rivaled the Sun in brightness. The energy delivered to the atmosphere by this impact was roughly equivalent to that of a 10-megaton thermonuclear explosion and caused the destruction of forest over an area of about 2,000 sq km (772.2 sq mi). The geologic record of cratering attests to the impact of much more massive meteoroids. Fortunately, impacts of this magnitude occur only once or twice every 100 million years. It is hypothesized that large impacts of this kind may have played a major role in determining the course of biological evolution by causing simultaneous **mass extinctions** of many species of organisms, possibly including the dinosaurs some 65 million years ago. If so, the replacement of reptiles by mammals as the dominant land animals, the eventual consequence of which was the rise of the human species, would be the result of a grand example of a phenomenon observable every clear night.

The **visibility of meteors** is a consequence of the high velocity of meteoroids in interplanetary space. Before entering the region of the Earth's gravitational influence, their **velocities** range from a few kilometers per second up to as high as 72 km (44.7 mi) per second. As they approach the Earth, the Earth's gravitational field accelerates them to even higher velocities. This great release of energy destroys meteoroids of small mass—particularly those with relatively high velocities—very quickly. Numerous meteors end their observed flight at altitudes above 80 km (49.7 mi), and penetration to as low as 50 km (31 mi) is unusual.

"**Showers**" of meteors have been known since ancient times. On rare occasions, these showers are very dramatic, with thousands of meteors falling per hour. More often, the background hourly rate of roughly 5 observed meteors increases up to about 10–50. Some of the best-known meteor showers are listed below, with their average date of maximum strength and associated comet, if known:
**Quadrantid** (3 January); **Lyrid** (22 April; 1861 I [Thatcher]); **Eta Aquarid** (3 May; Halley); **S. Delta Aquarid** (29 July); **Capricornid** (30 July); **Perseid** (12 August; Swift-Tuttle); **Andromedid** (3 October; Biela); **Draconid** (9 October; Giacobini-Zinner); **Orionid** (21 October; Halley); **Taurid** (8 November; Encke); **Leonid** (17 November; Temple-Tuttle); **Germinid** (14 December; 3200 Phaeton [this body exhibits no cometary activity and may be of asteroidal rather than cometary origin]).

## Auroras

Auroras are **luminous phenomena** of the upper atmosphere that occur primarily in high latitudes of both hemispheres; auroras in the Northern Hemisphere are called **aurora borealis**, or **northern lights**; in the Southern Hemisphere, **aurora australis**, or **southern lights**.

Auroras are caused by the interaction of energetic particles (electrons and protons) from outside the atmosphere with atoms of the upper atmosphere. Such interaction occurs in zones surrounding the Earth's magnetic poles. During periods of intense solar activity, auroras occasionally extend to the middle latitudes; for example, the aurora borealis has been seen at latitudes as far south as 40° in the US.

Auroras take many **forms**, including luminous curtains, arcs, bands, and patches. The uniform arc is the most stable form of aurora, sometimes persisting for hours without noticeable variation. In a great display, however, other forms appear, commonly undergoing dramatic variation. The lower edges of the arcs and folds are usually much more sharply defined than the upper parts. Greenish rays may cover most of the sky poleward of the magnetic zenith, ending in an arc that is usually folded and sometimes edged with a lower red border that may ripple like drapery. The display ends with a poleward retreat of the auroral forms, the rays gradually degenerating into diffuse areas of white light.

The **mechanisms** that produce auroral displays are not completely understood. It is known, however, that charged particles arriving in the vicinity of Earth as part of the solar wind are captured by the Earth's magnetic field and conducted downward toward the magnetic poles. They collide with oxygen and nitrogen atoms, knocking away electrons to leave ions in excited states. These ions emit radiation at various wavelengths, creating the characteristic colors (red or greenish blue) of the aurora.

## Eclipses

An **eclipse** is a complete or partial obscuring of one celestial body by another; this event occurs when three celestial objects become aligned.

The Sun is eclipsed when the Moon comes between it and the Earth. (Hence, a **solar eclipse** can only occur during a new moon.) The Moon's shadow sweeps across the Earth, darkening the sky, while the Moon blocks out some portion of the view of the Sun. During a total eclipse of the Sun, the Moon's elliptical orbit brings the satellite closer to Earth and causes it to appear larger than the Sun. When the Moon's orbit places it at its farthest distance from Earth, the Moon appears smaller than the Sun and the eclipse will appear as a ring or "annulus" of bright sunlight around the Moon.

A **lunar eclipse** occurs when the Moon moves into the shadow of the Earth cast by the Sun. A lunar eclipse can only occur during a full moon. Lunar eclipses can be penumbral, partial, or total. The first type is of interest to astronomers but is difficult to detect. With the next two types either a portion of the Moon or the entire Moon passes through Earth's umbral shadow.

It is safe to watch a lunar eclipse, but solar eclipses must be viewed via a projection onto another surface or through protective filters designed specially for eclipses.

The eclipses for 2004 are given in the table below.

|  | DATE | TYPE | VISIBLE IN |
|---|---|---|---|
| **Solar eclipses** | 19 April | partial eclipse | southern Africa, Antarctica |
|  | 14 October | partial eclipse | northeastern Asia, Alaska |
| **Lunar eclipses** | 4 May | total eclipse | South America, Europe, Asia, Antarctica, Oceania, and Africa |
|  | 28 October | total eclipse | North America, South America, Europe, Africa, Asia |

# Characteristics of Celestial Bodies

*Mean orbital velocity* indicates the speed with which a planet orbits the Sun unless otherwise specified. *Inclination of orbit to ecliptic* indicates the angle of tilt between a planet's orbit and the plane at which the solar system lies (in degrees). *Orbital period* indicates the planet's year (in Earth days except where noted). *Rotation period* indicates the planet's day (in Earth days except where noted). *Inclination of equator to orbit* indicates the angle of tilt between a planet's orbit and its equator (in degrees). *Gravitational acceleration* measures the body's effect on other objects. *Escape velocity* measures the speed needed at the surface to escape the planet's gravitational pull.

## Sun

diameter (at equator): 1,390,000 km (863,705 mi)
mass (in $10^{20}$ kg): 19.8 billion
density (mass/volume, in kg/m$^3$): 1,408
eccentricity of orbit*: near 0
mean orbital velocity: the Sun orbits the galactic center at around 220 km/sec (136.7 mi/sec)
orbital period: the Sun takes approximately 250 million Earth years to complete its orbit around the Milky Way's galactic center
rotation period: 25–36 Earth days
inclination of equator to orbit: 7.25°
gravitational acceleration: 275 m/sec$^2$ (902.2 ft/sec$^2$)
escape velocity: 618.02 km/sec (384.01 mi/sec)
mean temperature at surface†: 5527 °C (9980 °F)
satellites: all planets in solar system
probes and space missions: (US) NASA–Pioneer 5-9, launched 1959–1987; Skylab, launched 1973; Ulysses, 1990. European Space Agency (ESA)–SOHO, 1995.

## Mercury

average distance from Sun: 58 million km (36 million mi)
diameter (at equator): 4,879 km (3,032 mi)
mass (in $10^{20}$ kg): 3,300
density (mass/volume, in kg/m$^3$): 5,427
eccentricity of orbit*: 0.205
mean orbital velocity: 47.9 km/sec (29.7 mi/sec)
inclination of orbit to ecliptic: 7.0°
orbital period: 88 Earth days
rotation period: 176 Earth days
inclination of equator to orbit: .001°
gravitational acceleration: 3.7 m/sec$^2$ (12.1 ft/sec$^2$)
escape velocity: 4.3 km/sec (2.7 mi/sec)
mean temperature at surface†: 167 °C (333 °F)
satellites: none
probes and space missions: NASA–Mariner 10, 1973; Messenger, 2004.

## Venus

average distance from Sun: 108.2 million km (67.2 million mi)
diameter (at equator): 12,104 km (7,521 mi)
mass (in $10^{20}$ kg): 48,700
density (mass/volume, in kg/m$^3$): 5,243
eccentricity of orbit*: 0.007
mean orbital velocity: 35.0 km/sec (21.8 mi/sec)
inclination of orbit to ecliptic: 3.4°
orbital period: 224.7 Earth days
rotation period: 243.0 (retrograde)
inclination of equator to orbit: 177.4°
gravitational acceleration: 8.9 m/sec$^2$ (29.1 ft/sec$^2$)
escape velocity: 10.4 km/sec (6.4 mi/sec)
mean temperature at surface†: 464 °C (867 °F)
satellites: none
probes and space missions: USSR–Venera 1–10, 1961–1975; Vega 1 and 2, 1984; NASA–Mariner 2, 5, and 10, 1962, 1967, and 1973; Galileo, 1989; Magellan, 1989.

## Earth

average distance from Sun: 149.6 million km (93 million mi)
diameter (at equator): 12,756 km (7,926 mi)
mass (in $10^{20}$ kg): 59,700
density (mass/volume, in kg/m$^3$): 5,515
eccentricity of orbit*: 0.017
mean orbital velocity: 29.8 km/sec (18.5 mi/sec)
inclination of orbit to ecliptic: 0.00°
orbital period: 365.25 mean solar days
rotation period: 23 hours, 56 minutes, and 4 seconds
inclination of equator to orbit: 23.5°
gravitational acceleration: 9.8 m/sec$^2$ (32.1 ft/sec$^2$)
escape velocity: 11.2 km/sec (7.0 mi/sec)
mean temperature at surface†: 15 °C (59 °F)
satellites: 1–the Moon.

## Moon (of Earth)

average distance from Earth: 384,401 km (238,855.7 mi)
diameter (at equator): 3,475 km (2,159 mi)
mass (in $10^{20}$ kg): 730
density (mass/volume, in kg/m$^3$): 3,340
eccentricity of orbit*: orbital eccentricity of Moon around Earth is 0.055
mean orbital velocity: the Moon orbits Earth at 1.0 km/sec (0.64 mi/sec)
inclination of orbit to ecliptic: 5.1°
orbital period: the Moon revolves around the Earth in 27.3 Earth days
rotation period: the Moon rotates on its axis every 27.32 Earth days
inclination of equator to orbit: 6.7°
gravitational acceleration: 1.6 m/sec$^2$ (5.3 ft/sec$^2$)
escape velocity: 2.4 km/sec (1.5 mi/sec)
mean temperature at surface†: daytime: 107 °C (224.6 °F); nighttime: –153 °C (–243.4 °F)
probes and space missions: On July 20, 1969, the first men stepped foot on the Moon, from NASA's Apollo 11. NASA–Pioneer 0-4, 1958–59; USSR Luna 1–24 1959–76.

## Mars

average distance from Sun: 227.9 million km (141.6 million mi)
diameter (at equator): 6,794 km (4,222 mi)
mass (in $10^{20}$ kg): 6,420
density (mass/volume, in kg/m$^3$): 3,933
eccentricity of orbit*: 0.094
mean orbital velocity: 24.1 km/sec (15 mi/sec)
inclination of orbit to ecliptic: 1.9°
orbital period: 687 Earth days (1.88 Earth years)
rotation period: 24.6 hours
inclination of equator to orbit: 25.2°
gravitational acceleration: 3.7 m/sec$^2$ (12.1 ft/sec$^2$)
escape velocity: 5.0 km/sec (3.1 mi/sec)
mean temperature at surface†: –65 °C (–85 °F)
satellites: 2–Phobos and Deimos
probes and space missions: NASA–Mariner 3-8, 1964–71; Viking 1 and 2, 1975; Mars Pathfinder,

1996; 2001 Mars Odyssey, 2001. USSR–Phobos 1 and 2, 1988.

## Jupiter

average distance from Sun: 778.6 million km (483.8 million mi)
diameter (at equator): 142,984 km (88,846 mi)
mass (in $10^{20}$ kg): 18,990,000
density (mass/volume, in kg/m³): 1,326
eccentricity of orbit*: 0.049
mean orbital velocity: 13.1 km/sec (8.1 mi/sec)
inclination of orbit to ecliptic: 1.3°
orbital period: 11.86 Earth years
rotation period: 9.9 hours
inclination of equator to orbit: 3.1°
gravitational acceleration: 23.1 m/sec² (75.9 ft/sec²)
escape velocity: 59.5 km/sec (37.0 mi/sec)
mean temperature at surface†:–110 °C (–166 °F)
satellites: 61 moons—including Callisto, Ganymede, Europa, and Io, plus rings
probes and space missions: NASA–Pioneer 10 and 11, 1972–73; Voyager 1 and 2, 1977; Ulysses, 1990; Galileo, 1989.

## Saturn

average distance from Sun: 1.433 billion km (890.8 million mi)
diameter (at equator): 120,536 km (74,897 mi)
mass (in $10^{20}$ kg): 5,680,000
density (mass/volume, in kg/m³): 687
eccentricity of orbit*: 0.057
mean orbital velocity: 9.7 km/sec (6 mi/sec)
inclination of orbit to ecliptic: 2.5°
orbital period: 29.43 Earth years
rotation period: 10.7 hours
inclination of equator to orbit: 26.7°
gravitational acceleration: 9.0 m/sec² (29.4 ft/sec²)
escape velocity: 35.5 km/sec (22.1 mi/sec)
mean temperature at surface†: –140 °C (–220 °F)
satellites: 31 moons, plus rings
probes and space missions: NASA–Pioneer 11, 1973; Voyager 1 and 2, 1977. NASA and ESA–Cassini/Huygens, 1997.

## Uranus

average distance from Sun: 2.872 billion km (1.784 billion miles)
diameter (at equator): 51,118 km (31,763 mi)
mass (in $10^{20}$ kg): 868,000
density (mass/volume, in kg/m³): 1,270
eccentricity of orbit*: 0.046
mean orbital velocity: 6.8 km/sec (4.2 mi/sec)
inclination of orbit to ecliptic: 0.8°
orbital period: 83.76 Earth years
rotation period: 17.2 hours (retrograde)
inclination of equator to orbit: 97.8°
gravitational acceleration: 8.7 m/sec² (28.5 ft/sec²)
escape velocity: 21.3 km/sec ( 13.2 mi/sec)
mean temperature at surface†: –195 °C (–320 °F)
satellites: 21 moons, plus rings
probes and space missions: NASA–Voyager 2, 1986.

## Neptune

average distance from Sun: 4.495 billion km (2.793 billion mi)
diameter (at equator): 49,528 km (30,775 mi)
mass (in $10^{20}$ kg): 1,020,000
density (mass/volume, in kg/m³): 1,638
eccentricity of orbit*: 0.011
mean orbital velocity: 5.4 km/sec (3.4 mi/sec)
inclination of orbit to ecliptic: 1.8°

orbital period: 163.75 Earth years
rotation period: 16.1 hours
inclination of equator to orbit: 28.3°
gravitational acceleration: 11.0 m/sec² (36.0 ft/sec²)
escape velocity: 23.5 km/sec (14.6 mi/sec)
mean temperature at surface†: –200 °C (–330 °F)
satellites: 11 moons, plus rings
probes and space missions: NASA–Voyager 2, 1989.

## Pluto

average distance from Sun: 5.870 billion km (3.647 billion mi)
diameter (at equator): 2,390 km (1,485 mi)
mass (in $10^{20}$ kg): 125
density (mass/volume, in kg/m³): 1,750
eccentricity of orbit*: 0.244
mean orbital velocity: 4.72 km/sec (2.93 mi/sec)
inclination of orbit to ecliptic: 17.2°
orbital period: 248 Earth years
rotation period: 6.38 Earth days (retrograde)
inclination of equator to orbit: 122.5°
gravitational acceleration: 0.6 m/sec² (1.9 ft/sec²)
escape velocity: 1.1 km/sec (0.7 mi/sec)
mean temperature at surface†: –225 °C (–375 °F)
satellites: 1–Charon.

## Charon (moon of Pluto)

average distance from Pluto: 19,600 km (12,178.8 mi)
diameter (at equator): 1,186 km (736.9 mi)
mass (in $10^{20}$ kg): 19
density (mass/volume, in kg/m³): 2,000
eccentricity of orbit*: 0
mean orbital velocity: Charon orbits Pluto at 0.23 km/sec (0.142 mi/min)
inclination of orbit to ecliptic: 98.8°
orbital period: 6.38725 Earth days
rotation period: 6.38725 Earth days
inclination of equator to orbit: 98.9°
gravitational acceleration: 0.21 m/s² (0.69 ft/s²)
escape velocity: 0.58 km/sec (0.36 mi/sec)
mean temperature at surface†: as low as –240 °C (–400 °F).

## Comet 1P Halley

average distance from Sun at closest point is 87.8 million km (54 million mi). Farthest distance from the Sun is 5.2 billion km (3.2 billion mi).
diameter (at equator): 16 x 8 x 8 km (9.9 x 4.9 x 4.9 mi)
mass (in $10^{20}$ kg): unknown
density (mass/volume, in kg/m³): 1
eccentricity of orbit*: 0.967
inclination of orbit to ecliptic: 18°
orbital period: 76.1 to 79.3 years. The next appearance will be 2061. The comet's orbit is retrograde.
rotation period: 52 hours
probes and space missions: ESA–Giotto, 1985; USSR–Vega, 1985.

## Comet 2P Encke

average distance from Sun at closest point is 50 million km (31 million mi). Farthest distance from the Sun is 658 million km (408 million mi).
eccentricity of orbit*: 0.847
orbital period: 3.3 years; visible on Earth 28 Dec 2003.

## Comet 81P Wild 2

average distance from Sun at closest point is 236.8 million km (147.1 million mi). Farthest distance from the Sun is 10 billion km (6.2 billion mi).

eccentricity of orbit*: 0.54

orbital period: 6.39 years; visible from Earth in February 2010.

**Comet Hale-Bopp**

average distance from Sun at closest point is 136 million km (84.5 million mi). Farthest distance from the Sun is 74.7 billion km (46.4 billion mi).

eccentricity of orbit*: 0.995

orbital period: 4,000 years, last appearance from Earth was 31 Mar 1997.

**Comet Hyakutake**

average distance from Sun at closest point is 34 million km (0.230 AU). Farthest distance from the Sun is 344 billion km (2300 AU).

eccentricity of orbit*: 0.9998

orbital period: ~40,000 years, last appearance from Earth was 1 May 1996.

**Kuiper Belt**

(a huge belt located beyond Neptune containing residual material left over from the formation of the planets)

average distance from Sun: 4.742 billion km (2.946 billion mi) to 7.120 billion km (4.424 billion mi)

diameter (at equator): asteroids in the Kuiper Belt have a general range from between 100–1200 km (62.1 mi–745.6 mi)

mass (in $10^{20}$ kg): Scientists estimate there may be as many as 70,000 asteroids of a size greater than 100 km in the Kuiper Belt, the belt is theorized to have a mass of 6000 x $10^{20}$ kg.

density: not known

eccentricity of orbit*: not known

mean orbital velocity: not known for the majority of objects

inclination of orbit to ecliptic: varies

orbital period: typically these objects have orbital periods of less than 200 years

rotation period: not known

inclination of equator to orbit: not known

gravitational acceleration: not known

escape velocity: not known

**Oort cloud**

(information about the Oort cloud is based on inference, as scientists cannot observe this phenomenon)

average distance from Sun: 30 trillion km (18.6 trillion mi)

diameter (at equator): spherical cloud of comets that extends some 3 light-years out at the edge of the solar system.

mass (in $10^{20}$ kg): some 1 to 6 trillion icy objects have an estimated density of not more than 2.4 million and not less than 700,000 x $10^{20}$ kg

**Milky Way Galaxy**

diameter (at equator): 100,000 light-years in diameter by 2,000 light-years in width

mass (in $10^{20}$ kg): The Milky Way is thought to contain enough mass to equal the mass of one trillion of the earth's Sun. Most of this mass cannot be accounted for and is thought to reside in dark matter.

mean orbital velocity: Galaxies do not travel; however, because space is expanding in all directions, the galaxy is moving along with the space containing it at a rate of around 300 km per second.

**Visible universe**

diameter (at equator): 30 billion light-years in diameter

mass (in $10^{20}$ kg): difficult to know; approximately $10^{52}$ kg

density: The density of the universe has not been ascertained. However, whether the universe will continue to expand forever, will instead begin to contract at a certain point, or whether it is balanced and stop expanding but never contract, depends on its density.

mean orbital velocity: Somewhere around 40 to 90 km/sec/megaparsec (3.26 million light-years). Thus, for every 3.26 million light-years between two galaxies, they're moving away at between 40 and 90 km/sec. (The rate at which the universe is expanding is known as the Hubble constant.)

mean temperature at surface†: The temperature of the cosmic background radiation is 2.735° above absolute zero (–273 °C and –459 °F).

*eccentricity of orbit measures circularity or elongation of an orbit; 0 indicates circular orbits, and closer to 1 more elliptical ones

†for planets with no surface, temperature given is at a level in the atmosphere = to 1 bar of pressure.

## Solar System Superlatives

**Largest planet in solar system:** Jupiter (142,984 km [88,846 mi] diameter); all of the other planets in the solar system could fit inside Jupiter.

**Largest moon in the solar system:** Jupiter's moon Ganymede (5,268 km [3,270 mi]), which also is likely to have an ocean beneath its icy crust.

**Smallest planet in solar system:** Pluto (2,390 km [1,485 mi] diameter).

**Smallest moon in the solar system:** Saturn and Jupiter both have numerous satellites that are smaller than 10 km (6 mi) in diameter.

**Planet closest to the Sun:** Mercury (average distance from the Sun 58,000,000 km [36,000,000 mi]).

**Planet farthest from the Sun:** usually Pluto (average distance from the Sun 5.870 billion km [3.647 billion mi]); every 248 years Neptune crosses Pluto's orbit and then spends about 20 years as the planet farthest from the Sun.

**Planet with the most eccentric (least circular) orbit:** Pluto (eccentricity of 0.248).

**Moon with the most eccentric orbit:** Neptune's moon Nereid (eccentricity of 0.75).

**Planet with the least eccentric orbit:** Venus (eccentricity of 0.007).

**Moon with the least eccentric orbit:** Plato's moon, Charon (eccentricity of 0.0).

**Planet most tilted on its axis:** Uranus (axial tilt of 98°).

**Planet with the most moons:** Jupiter (58).

**Planet with the fewest moons:** Mercury and Venus (no moons).

**Planet with the longest day:** Mercury (1 day on Mercury equals 176 Earth days).

**Planet with the shortest day:** Jupiter (1 day on Jupiter equals 9.9 Earth hours).

**Planet with the longest year:** Pluto (1 year on Pluto takes 248 Earth years).

**Planet with the shortest year:** Mercury (1 year on Mercury takes 88 Earth days).

**Fastest orbiting planet in the solar system:** Mercury (47.87 km per second [29.75 mi per second] average orbital speed).

**Slowest orbiting planet in the solar system:** Pluto (4.72 km per second [2.93 mi per second] average orbital speed).

**Hottest planet in solar system:** Venus (464 °C [867 °F] average temperature); although Mercury is closer to the Sun, Venus is hotter because Mercury has no atmosphere, whereas the atmosphere of Venus traps heat and causes higher temperatures.

**Coldest planet in the solar system:** Pluto (−223 °C [−369 °F] average temperature).

**Brightest visible star in the night sky:** Sirius (−1.46 apparent visual magnitude).

**Brightest planet in solar system:** Venus (apparent visual magnitude −4.5 to −3.77).

**Densest planet:** Earth (density of 5,515 kg/m³).

**Least dense planet:** Saturn (density of 687 kg/m³).

**Planet with most gravity:** Jupiter (more than twice the gravitational force of Earth).

**Planet with least gravity:** Pluto (about 1/17 the gravitational force of Earth).

**Planet with the largest mountain:** Mars (Olympus Mons, an extinct volcano, is some 27 km [17 mi] tall and 520 km [320 mi] across).

**Planet with deepest valley:** Mars (Valles Marineris, a system of canyons is some 4,000 km [2,500 mi] long and from about 2 to 7 km [1 to 5 mi] deep).

**Largest known impact crater:** Valhalla, a crater on Jupiter's moon Callisto, has a bright central area that is about 600 km (370 mi) across with sets of concentric ridges extending about 1,500 km (900 mi) from the center. For contrast, the largest known impact crater on Earth is the Barringer Crater in Arizona, which is about 1.2 km (0.8 mi) wide.

# The Sun

The Sun is the star around which the Earth and the other components of the solar system revolve. It is the dominant body of the system, constituting more than 99% of the system's entire mass. The Sun is the source of an enormous amount of energy, a portion of which provides the Earth with the light and heat necessary to support life. The geologic record of the Earth and Moon reveals that the Sun was formed about 4.5 billion years ago. The energy radiated by the Sun is produced during the conversion of hydrogen atoms to helium. The Sun is at least 90% hydrogen by number of atoms, so the fuel is readily available.

The Sun is classified as a G2 V star, where G2 stands for the second hottest stars of the yellow G class—of surface temperature about 5,500 °C (10,000 °F)—and V represents a main sequence, or dwarf, star, the typical star for this temperature class (see also "Classification of Stars"). The Sun exists in the outer part of the Milky Way Galaxy and was formed from material that had been processed inside a supernova.

The mass of the Sun is 743 times the total mass of all the planets in the solar system and 330,000 times that of the Earth. All the interesting planetary and interplanetary gravitational phenomena are negligible effects in comparison to the force exerted by the Sun. Under the force of gravity, the great mass of the Sun presses inward, and to keep the star from collapsing, the central pressure outward must be great enough to support its weight. The Sun's core, which occupies approximately 25% of the star's radius, has a density about 100 times that of water (roughly 6 times that at the center of the Earth), but the temperature at the core is at least 15,000,000 °C (27,000,000 °F), so the central pressure is at least 10,000 times greater than that at the center of the Earth. In this environ-

ment the nuclei of atoms are completely stripped of their electrons, and at this high temperature they collide to produce the nuclear reactions that are responsible for generating the energy vital to life on Earth.

The temperature of the Sun's surface is so high that no solid or liquid can exist; the constituent materials are predominantly gaseous atoms, with a very small number of molecules. As a result, there is no fixed surface. The surface viewed from Earth, the photosphere, is approximately 400 km (250 mi) thick and is the layer from which most of the radiation reaches us; the radiation from below the photosphere is absorbed and reradiated, while the emission from overlying layers drops sharply, by about a factor of six every 200 km (124 mi).

While the temperature of the Sun drops from 15,000,000 °C (27,000,000 °F) at the core to around 5,500 °C (10,000 °F) at the photosphere, a surprising reversal occurs above that point; the temperature begins to rise in the chromosphere, a layer several thousand kilometers thick. Temperatures there range from 4,200 °C (7,600 °F) to 100,000 °C (180,000 °F). Above the chromosphere is a dim, extended halo called the corona, which has a temperature of 1,000,000 °C (1,800,000 °F) and reaches far past the planets. Beyond a distance of around 3,500,000 km (2,200,000 mi) from the Sun, the corona flows outward at a speed (near the Earth) of 400 km/sec (250 mi/sec); this flow of charged particles is called the solar wind.

The Sun is a very stable source of energy. Superposed on this stable star, however, is an interesting 11-year cycle of magnetic activity manifested by regions of transient strong magnetic fields called sunspots. Sunspots, the largest of which can be seen even without a telescope, are regions of extremely strong magnetic field found on the Sun's surface.

# Mercury

Mercury is the planet closest to the Sun, revolving around it at an average distance of 58 million km (36 million mi). In Sumerian times, some 5,000 years ago, it was already known to be a planet. In classical Greece the planet was called Apollo when it appeared as a morning star and Hermes, for the Greek equivalent of the Roman god Mercury, when it appeared as an evening star.

Mercury's orbit lies inside the orbit of the Earth and is more elliptical than those of most of the other planets. At its closest approach (perihelion), Mercury is only 46 million km (28.5 million mi) from the Sun, while its greatest distance (aphelion) approaches 70 million km (43.5 million mi). Mercury orbits the Sun in 88 Earth days at an average speed of 48 km per second (29.8 mi per sec), allowing it to overtake and pass Earth every 116 Earth days (synodic period).

Because of its proximity to the Sun, the surface of Mercury can become extremely hot. High temperatures at "noon" may reach 400 °C (755 °F) while the "predawn" lowest temperature is –173 °C (–280 °F). Mercury's equator is almost exactly in its orbital plane (its spin axis inclination is nearly zero), and thus Mercury does not have seasons as does the Earth. Because of its elliptical orbit and a peculiarity of its rotational period (see below), however, certain longitudes experience cyclical variations in temperatures on a "yearly" as well as on a "diurnal" basis.

Mercury is about 4,878 km (3031 mi) in diameter, smaller than any other planet with the exception of Pluto. Mercury is only a bit larger than the Moon. Its mass, measured by the gravitational perturbation of the path of the Mariner 10 spacecraft during close fly-bys in 1974 and 1975 is about one-eighteenth of the mass of the Earth. Escape velocity, the speed needed to escape from a planet's gravitational field, is about 4.25 km per second (2.64 mi per second)—compared with 11.2 km per sec (7 mi per sec) for the Earth.

The mean density of Mercury, calculated from its mass and radius, is about 5.44 grams per cubic cm (0.48 ounce per inch), nearly the same as that of the Earth (5.5 grams per cubic cm, or 0.49 ounce per inch).

Photographs relayed by the Mariner 10 spacecraft showed that Mercury spins on its axis (rotates) once every 58.646 Earth days, exactly two-thirds of the orbital period of 87.9694 Earth days. This observation confirmed that Mercury is in a 3:2 spin-orbit tidal resonance—i.e., that tides raised on Mercury by the Sun have forced it into a condition that causes it to rotate three times on its axis in the same time it takes to revolve around the Sun twice.

The 3:2 spin-orbit coupling combines with Mercury's eccentric orbit to create very unusual temperature effects. Although it rotates on its axis once every 59 Earth days, one rotation does not bring the Sun back to the same part of the sky, because during that time Mercury has moved partway around the Sun. A solar day on Mercury (for example, from one sunrise to another, or one noon to another) is 176 Earth days (exactly two Mercurian years).

Mercury's low escape velocity and high surface temperatures do not permit it to retain a significant atmosphere.

## Venus

Venus is the second planet from the Sun and the planet whose orbit is closest to that of the Earth. When visible, Venus is the brightest planet in the sky. Viewed through a telescope, it presents a brilliant, yellow-white, essentially featureless face to the observer. The obscured appearance results because the surface of the planet is hidden from sight by a continuous and permanent cover of clouds.

Venus' orbit is the most nearly circular of that of any planet, with a deviation from perfect circularity of only about 1 part in 150. The period of the orbit—that is, the length of the Venusian year—is 224.7 Earth days. The rotation of Venus is unusual in both its direction and speed. Most of the planets in the solar system rotate in a counterclockwise direction when viewed from above their north poles; Venus, however, rotates in the opposite, or retrograde, direction. Were it not for the planet's clouds, an observer on Venus' surface would see the Sun rise in the west and set in the east.

Venus spins on its axis very slowly, taking 243 Earth days to complete one rotation. Venus' spin and orbital periods are synchronized with the Earth's orbit such that Venus always presents the same face toward the Earth when the two planets are at their closest approach.

Venus is nearly the Earth's twin in terms of size and mass. Venus' diameter is about 95% of the Earth's diameter at the Equator, while its mass is 81.5% that of the Earth. The similarities to the Earth in size and mass also produce a similarity in density; Venus' density is 5.24 grams per cubic centimeter, as compared with 5.52 for the Earth.

In terms of its shape, Venus is more nearly a perfect sphere than are most planets. A planet's rotation generally causes a slight flattening at the poles and bulging at the equator, but Venus' very slow rotation rate allows it to maintain its highly spherical shape.

Venus has the most massive atmosphere of all the terrestrial planets. Its atmosphere is composed of 96.5% carbon dioxide and 3.5% nitrogen. The atmospheric pressure at the planet's surface varies with the surface elevation but averages about 90 bars, or 90 times the atmospheric pressure at the Earth's surface. This is the same pressure found at a depth of about one kilometer in the Earth's oceans. Temperatures range between a minimum temperature of –45 °C (–49 °F) and a maximum temperature of 500 °C (932 °F); the average temperature is 464 °C (867.2 °F).

## Earth

The Earth is the third planet in distance outward from the Sun. It is the only planetary body in the solar system that has conditions suitable for life, at least as known to modern science.

The average distance of the Earth from the Sun—149.9 million km (93 million mi)—was designated as the distance of the unit of measurement known as the AU (astronomical unit). The Earth orbits the Sun at a speed of 29.8 km (18.5 mi) per second, making one complete revolution in 365.25 days. As it revolves around the Sun, the Earth spins on its axis and rotates completely once every 23 h 56 min 4 sec. The Earth has a single natural satellite, the Moon.

The fifth largest planet of the solar system, the Earth has a total surface area of roughly 509,600,000 sq km (197,000,000 sq mi), of which about 29%, or 148,000,000 square km (57,000,000 square mi), is land. Oceans and smaller seas cover the balance of the surface. The Earth is the only planet known to have liquid water. Together with ice, the liquid water constitutes the hydrosphere. Seawater makes up more than 98% of the total mass of the hydrosphere and covers about 71% of the Earth's surface. Significantly, seawater constituted the environment of the earliest terrestrial life forms. The Earth's surface is subdivided into continental masses, of which there are seven: Europe, Asia, Africa, Australia, North America, South

America, and Antarctica. These continents are surrounded by the so-called World Ocean, which is commonly broken down into three major bodies—namely, the Atlantic, Pacific, and Indian oceans.

The centrifugal force of the Earth's rotation makes the planet bulge at the Equator. Because of this, the Earth has the shape of an oblate spheroid, being flatter near the poles than near the Equator. The gravitational field, or gravity, of the Earth is manifested as the force acting upon a free, unsupported body causing it to move in the general direction of the center of the planet. The Earth's gravity is not fixed, but rather varies from place to place on the surface, with the main variation occurring with latitude. It averages approximately 983.22 cm (32.26 ft) per second per second at the poles, which is somewhat higher than at the Equator, where it is only about 973.03 cm (31.92 ft) per second per second.

The Earth's atmosphere consists of a mixture of gases, chiefly nitrogen (78%) and oxygen (21%). Argon makes up much of the remainder of the gaseous envelope, with trace amounts of water vapor, carbon dioxide, and various other gases also present.

The Earth is surrounded by a magnetosphere, a region of strong magnetic forces that extends upward from about 140 km (90 mi) in the upper atmosphere. In the magnetosphere, the magnetic field of the Earth traps rapidly moving charged particles (e.g., electrons and high-energy protons), the majority of which appear to be emitted by the Sun during periods of intense activity. If it were not for this shielding effect, such particles would bombard the terrestrial surface and destroy life. High concentrations of the trapped particles make up two doughnut-shaped zones called the Van Allen radiation belts. These belts play a key role in several geophysical phenomena, as, for example, auroras.

## The Moon

The Moon is the sole natural satellite of the Earth. It revolves around the planet from west to east at a mean distance of about 384,400 km (239,900 mi). The Moon is less than one-third the size of the Earth, having a diameter of only about 3,476 km (2,160 mi) at its equator. The Moon shines by reflected sunlight, but its albedo—i.e., the fraction of light received that is reflected—is only 0.073.

The Moon rotates about its own axis in about 29½ days, which is virtually identical to the time it takes to complete its orbit around the Earth. As a result, the Moon always presents nearly the same face to the Earth. The rate of actual rotation is uniform, but the arc through which the Moon moves from day to day varies somewhat, causing the lunar globe (as seen by a terrestrial observer) to oscillate slightly over a period nearly equal to that of revolution.

The surface of the Moon has been a subject of continuous telescopic study from the time of Galileo's first observation in 1609. The Italian Jesuit astronomer Giovanni B. Riccioli designated the dark areas on the Moon as seas, with such fanciful names as Mare Imbrium ("Sea of Showers") and Mare Nectaris ("Sea of Nectar"). This nomenclature continues to be used even though it is now known that the Moon is completely devoid of surface water. During the centuries that followed the publication of these early works, more detailed maps and eventually photographs were produced. A Soviet space probe photographed the side of the Moon facing away from the Earth in 1959. By the late 1960s the US Lunar Orbiter missions had yielded close-up photographs of the entire lunar surface, including both the visible and far sides. On 20 Jul 1969, Apollo 11 astronauts Neil Armstrong and Edwin ("Buzz") Aldrin set foot on the Moon.

The most striking formations on the Moon are its craters. These features, which measure up to about 200 km (320 mi) or more in diameter, are scattered over the surface in great profusion and often overlap one another. Meteorites hitting the lunar surface at high velocity produced most of the large craters. Many of the smaller ones—those measuring less than 1 km (0.6 mi) across—could have been formed by explosive volcanic activity, however. The darker areas of the Moon, known as maria, have relatively few craters. They are thought to be huge lava flows that spread over an area after most of the craters had already been formed.

Various theories for the Moon's origin have been proposed. At the end of the 19th century the English astronomer Sir George H. Darwin advanced a hypothesis the Moon had been originally part of the Earth but was broken away by tidal gravitational action and receded from the planet. This was proved unlikely in the 1930s. Another theory that arose during the 1950s postulated that the Moon formed elsewhere in the solar system and was then later captured by the Earth. This idea was also proved to be physically implausible and was dismissed. Today, most investigators favor an explanation known as the giant-impact hypothesis, which postulates that a Mars-sized body struck the proto-Earth early in the history of the solar system. As a result, a cloud of fragments was ejected into orbit around the Earth, and these later accreted into the Moon.

## Moon's Apogee and Perigee, 2004

The distance between the centers of mass of the Earth and the Moon varies rather widely due to the combined gravity of the Earth, the Sun, and the planets. For example, during the period 1969–2000, apogee (when the Moon is at the greatest distance from Earth) varied from 404,063 to 406,711 km (251,073 to 252,719 mi), while perigee (when the Moon is closest to Earth) varied from 356,517 to 370,354 km (221,529 to 230,127 mi). Tidal interactions have braked the Moon's spin so that presently the same side always faces the Earth.

| MOON AT APOGEE | |
| --- | --- |
| DATE | NEAREST PHASE OF MOON |
| 3 January | between first quarter and full moon |
| 31 January | first quarter |
| 28 February | first quarter |

| MOON AT PERIGEE | |
| --- | --- |
| DATE | NEAREST PHASE OF MOON |
| 19 January | new moon |
| 16 February | between last quarter and new moon |
| 12 March | last quarter |

**16 Jan 2003, Cape Canaveral FL:** the crew of the space shuttle *Columbia* departs for liftoff. *Columbia* broke apart upon reentry over Texas on 1 February, killing all seven astronauts just 16 minutes before the scheduled landing.

PLATE 2                                    THE WAR IN IRAQ

© AFP 2003, by Ramzi Haidar

**21 Mar 2003, Baghdad, Iraq:** *(above)* smoke rises from the Iraqi presidential palace during a US-led air raid.

**5 Jun 2003, Doha, Qatar:** *(right)* US Pres. George W. Bush greets service members at Camp As Sayliyah.

**29 Mar 2003, Basra, Iraq:** *(below)* Iraqi sisters wait for their mother to bring food.

AP/Wide World Photos

© Jerry Lampen/Reuters 2003

**18 Apr 2003, Baghdad, Iraq:** Iraqis batter a statue of Saddam Hussein with their shoes, a traditional display of contempt.

PLATE 4                    **PROTEST**

AP/Wide World Photos

**20 Mar 2003, Chicago:**
*(above)* Christin
Hinojosa and John
Didion lead a group of
protesters in antiwar
guerrilla theater.

**23 Apr 2003, Istanbul,
Turkey:** *(left)* a child
wearing traditional
Kurdish colors demon-
strates against the US-
led war on Iraq.

© AFP/Corbis

© Baring Witness 2003

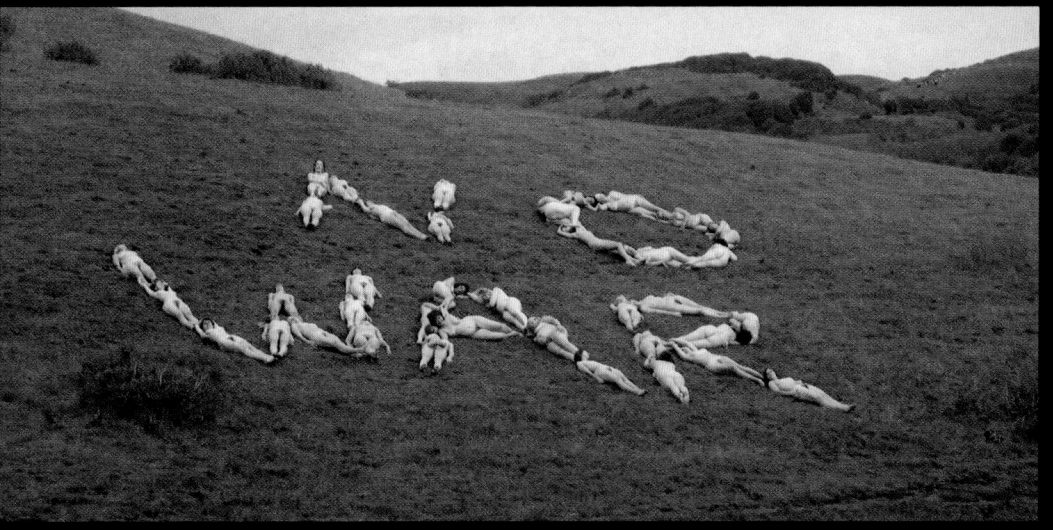

**4 Jan 2003, West Marin County, CA:** *(above)* 40 nude women register their opposition to the war in Iraq, spelling "No War" on a ranch hillside.

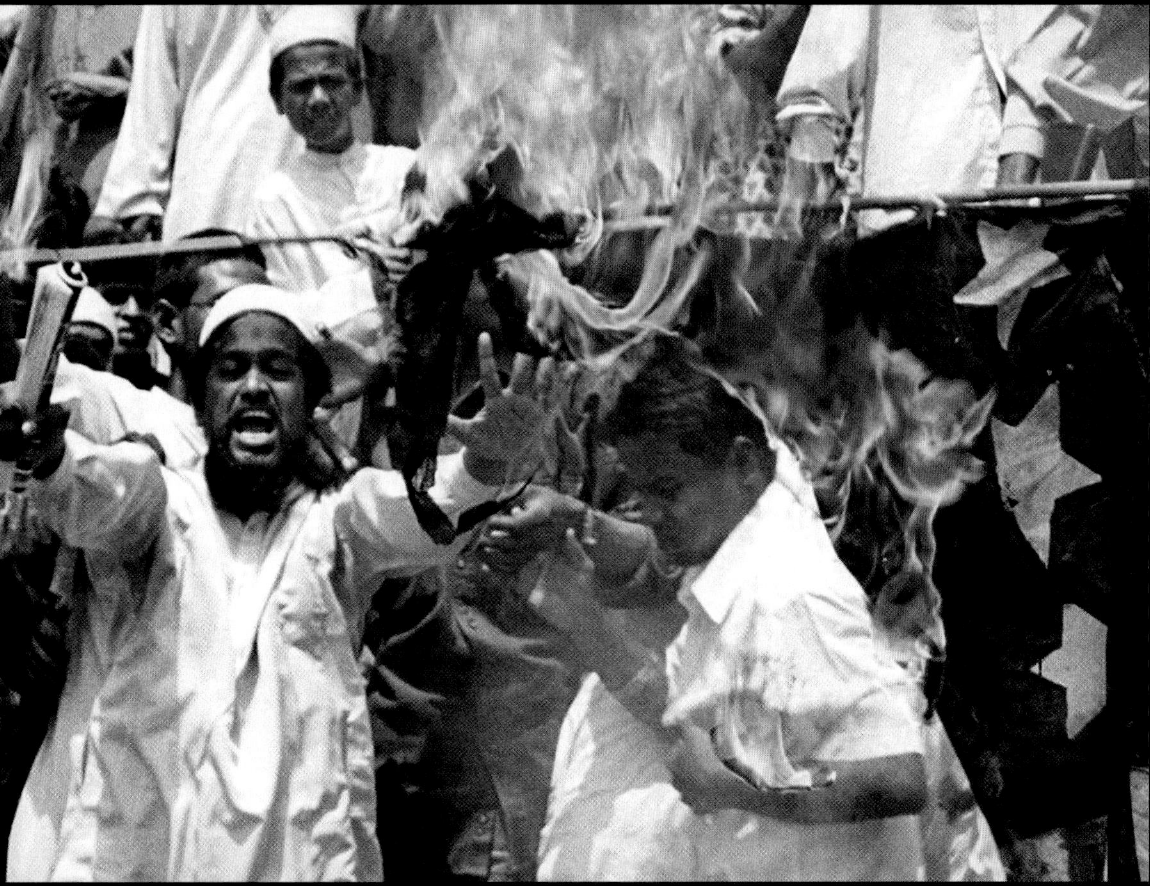

© AFP/Corbis

**6 Apr 2003, Dhaka, Bangladesh:** *(above)* demonstrators burn a US flag.

PLATE 6 WORLD EVENTS

**18 May 2003, Bunia, Dem. Rep. of Congo:** *(above)* a woman flees from an armed 10-year-old Hema militia member.

AP/Wide World Photos

**26 Oct 2002, Moscow:** Russian special forces evacuate patrons from the Dubrovka Theater after gassing it to regain control from Chechen guerrillas.

**17 Sep 2002, Asunción, Paraguay:** *(above)* riot police confront supporters of the exiled former general Lino Oviedo.

© Reuters 2002

AP/Wide World Photos

**20 Feb 2003, West Warwick RI:** *(above)* rescue workers struggle to contain a fire at the Station night-club that killed 100 and injured dozens of others.

**20 Oct 2002, Sydney:** *(left)* members of the Coogee Dolphins rugby club mourn six of their teammates who were killed in a bomb attack on a nightclub in Bali.

PLATE 8 WORLD EVENTS

AP/Wide World Photos

**17 Nov 2002, Calabar, Nigeria:** *(above)* a security forces member guards Miss World competitors. Organizers later had to move the pageant to London because of violent sectarian reaction in Nigeria to an editorialist's comment that the Prophet Muhammad would have chosen a Miss World contestant for a wife.

**4 Jun 2003, New York City:** *(right)* Martha Stewart leaves federal court after pleading innocent to insider trading charges.

Chris Hondros/Getty Images

**4 Jun 2003, Aqaba, Jordan:** *(left)* US Pres. George W. Bush holds talks with Israeli Prime Minister Ariel Sharon (left) and Palestinian Prime Minister Mahmoud Abbas (right).

AP/Wide World Photos

**27 Oct 2002, São Paolo, Brazil:** Brazilian President-elect Lula acknowledges supporters during his victory speech.

AP/Wide World Photos

AP/Wide World Photos

**9 Jun 2003, Zadar, Croatia:** Pope John Paul II waves to the crowd at the end of a five-day visit to Croatia.

AP/Wide World Photos

**14 May 2003, Noida, India:** Nisha Sharma, 21, sits in front of appliances bought as dowry for her marriage to Munish Dalal. Sharma refused to marry Dalal when she learned that his family had abused her father and demanded additional cash just prior to the wedding ceremony.

PLATE 10

# DISASTERS

**10 Sep 2002, South Africa:** a helicopter evacuates a crew member of the *Jolly Rubino* after the ship ran

© Reuters 2003

AP/Wide World Photos

**23 May 2003, Corso, Algeria:** *(above)* a Spanish volunteer with Firemen Without Borders lifts Emilie Kaidi, 2, to safety. She survived for two days after an earthquake leveled her house; her parents escaped major injury, but nearly 1,800 people died and thousands were wounded.

**6 May 2003, Kansas City KS:** *(left)* Helen Henderson, 82, surveys the remains of her home, which was destroyed by a tornado on 4 May.

© AFP 2003

**18 Feb 2003, Daegu, South Korea:** *(above)* firefighters walk through the charred wreckage of a subway train after a mentally ill passenger set fire to it. More than 190 people died and scores of others suffered serious injuries.

PLATE 12 SPORTS

© AFP 2003, by Jean-Loup Gautreau

**30 May 2003, Paris, France:** Serena Williams returns the ball to Barbara Schett during their third-round match in the French Open.

© Albert Gea/Reuters 2003

**2 Feb 2003, Barcelona, Spain:** Real Madrid's Zinedine Zidane (left) and Español's Doumoraud battle for the ball.

© AFP 2003, by Jacques Demarthon

**25 May 2003, Paris, France:** table tennis world champions Wang Nan (left) and Zhang Yining return the ball during the women's doubles final.

AP/Wide World Photos

**7 Jun 2003, Belmont Park in Elmont NY:** Triple Crown contender Funny Cide (second from right), with jockey José Santos up, leads the field of six horses in the back stretch, but Empire Maker (third from left), with Jerry Bailey up, won the Belmont Stakes.

AP/Wide World Photos

**2 May 2003, Boston MA:** Stacy Dragila clears the bar at 15 ft, 8¼ in, the new indoor women's pole vault record.

© Reuters NewMedia Inc./Corbis

**12 Dec 2002, Cleveland OH:** The NBA's no. 1 draft pick, high school phenom Lebron James, goes up for two points.

AP/Wide World Photos

**23 May 2003, Fort Worth TX:** Annika Sörenstam makes par hitting from a sand trap during the second round of the Colonial Golf Tournament.

PLATE 14        **SARS**

© Kin Cheung/Reuters 2003

**22 Apr 2003, Hong Kong:** *(above)* students at Ho Lap College stand in line to return to school after classes were suspended for three weeks owing to the outbreak of SARS.

**23 May 2003, Hong Kong:**
*(right)* a report indicates
that the virus that causes
SARS likely jumped to
humans from civets, considered a delicacy by many in
southern China.

© Reuters 2003

Scott Gries/Getty Images

**23 Feb 2003, New York City:** *(above)* singer Norah Jones drops one of the five Grammy statues she won for her album *Come Away with Me.*

Guy Ferrandis/H&K/CPI

*(above)* Director Roman Polanski with actor Adrien Brody during the filming of *The Pianist,* for which both won Academy Awards.

Ronald Asadorian/Splash

**1 May 2003, New York City:** *(above)* Diana Krall and Elvis Costello attend a film festival shortly before their wedding.

AP/Wide World Photos

**9 Jun 2003, New York City:** *(above)* Sen. Hillary Rodham Clinton (D-NY), signs copies of her memoir, *Living History.*

AP/Wide World Photos

**21 May 2003, Universal City CA:** *(above)* Ruben Studdard (right) gets congratulatory hug from Clay Aiken (left) after winning the American Idol competition.

*(left)* Carrie-Anne Moss, Laurence Fishburne, and Keanu Reeves star as Trinity, Morpheus, and Neo in *The Matrix: Reloaded.*

© AFP 2003/Eyepress, by Sunny Mok

PLATE 16        **OBITUARIES**

Katharine Hepburn, actress     © Bettmann/Corbis

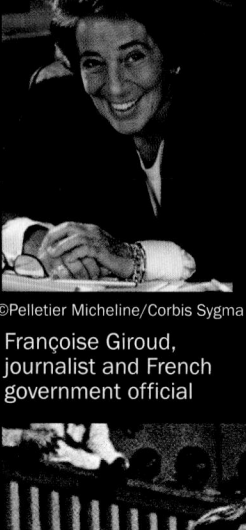

©Pelletier Micheline/Corbis Sygma

Françoise Giroud,
journalist and French
government official

AP/Wide World Photos

Sen. Strom Thurmond
(R-SC)

M. Fresco/Hulton-Deutsch/Corbis

Nina Simone, jazz singer

AP/Wide World Photos

Suzy Parker, model

Universal Studios/Getty Images

Gregory Peck, actor, as Atticus Finch in *To Kill a Mockingbird*

© Kevin Lamarque/Reuters 2003

Sen. Paul Wellstone
(D-MN)

© Reuters NewMedia Inc./Corbis

Laden (left) and
Laleh Bijani, Iranian

The Kobal Collection

Bob Hope, entertainer

AP/Wide World Photos

Barry White, soul singer

AP/Wide World Photos

Fred Rogers, television
personality

## Moon's Apogee and Perigee, 2004 (continued)

| MOON AT APOGEE | | MOON AT PERIGEE | |
|---|---|---|---|
| DATE | NEAREST PHASE OF MOON | DATE | NEAREST PHASE OF MOON |
| 27 March | first quarter | 8 April | between full moon and last quarter |
| 24 April | first quarter | 6 May | full moon |
| 21 May | new moon | 3 June | full moon |
| 17 June | new moon | 1 July | full moon |
| 14 July | new moon | 30 July | full moon |
| 11 August | between last quarter and new moon | 27 August | between first quarter and full moon |
| 8 September | last quarter | 22 September | first quarter |
| 5 October | last quarter | 18 October | first quarter |
| 2 November | last quarter | 14 November | new moon |
| 30 November | between full moon and last quarter | 12 December | new moon |
| 27 December | full moon | | |

## Moon Phases, 2003–2004

As the Moon orbits the Earth, more or less of the half of the Moon illuminated by the Sun is visible on Earth. During the lunar month the Moon's appearance changes from dark (the new moon) to being illuminated more and more on the right side (waxing crescent, first quarter, and waxing gibbous) to the full disc being illuminated (the full moon). The phases of the moon are completed by the Moon being illuminated less and less on the left side (waning gibbous, last quarter, and waning crescent) and ends with another new moon. The cycle of the moon takes place over a period of around 29 days; the time from new moon to new moon is referred to as a lunation.

The phases of the moon are caused by the positions of the Sun in relationship to the Moon. Thus, when the Sun and Moon are close in the sky a dark new moon is the result (the Sun is lighting the half of the Moon not visible to Earth). When the Sun and Moon are at opposition (in opposite parts of the sky) the full moon occurs (the Sun illuminates fully the half of the Moon seen on Earth). When the Sun and Moon are at about a 90-degree angle, one sees either a first quarter or last quarter moon.

The dates for the new moon, first quarter, full moon, and last quarter for July 2003–December 2004 are given in the table below.

| | NEW MOON | FIRST QUARTER | FULL MOON | LAST QUARTER |
|---|---|---|---|---|
| July 2003 | (29 June) | 7 | 13 | 21 |
| August 2003 | (29 July) | 5 | 12 | 20 |
| September 2003 | (27 August) | 3 | 10 | 18 |
| October 2003 | (26 September) | 2 | 10 | 18 |
| November 2003 | (25 October) | 1 | 9 | 17 |
| December 2003 | (23 November) | (30 November) | 8 | 16 |
| | (23 December) | (30 December) | (7 January) | (15 January) |
| January 2004 | 21 | 29 | (6 February) | (13 February) |
| February 2004 | 20 | 28 | (6 March) | (13 March) |
| March 2004 | 20 | 28 | (5 April) | (12 April) |
| April 2004 | 19 | 27 | (4 May) | (11 May) |
| May 2004 | 19 | 27 | (3 June) | (9 June) |
| June 2004 | 17 | 25 | (2 July) | (9 July) |
| July 2004 | 17 | 25 | 31 | (7 August) |
| August 2004 | 16 | 23 | 30 | (6 September) |
| September 2004 | 14 | 21 | 28 | (6 October) |
| October 2004 | 14 | 20 | 28 | (5 November) |
| November 2004 | 12 | 19 | 26 | (5 December) |
| December 2004 | 12 | 18 | 26 | (3 January) |

## Mars

Mars is the fourth planet in order of distance from the Sun and the seventh in order of diminishing size and mass. It orbits the Sun once in 687 Earth days and spins on its axis once every 24 h and 37 min.

Owing to its blood-red color, Mars has often been associated with the gods of war. It is named for the Roman god of war; as far back as 3,000 years ago, Babylonian astronomer-astrologers called the planet Nergal for their god of death and pestilence. The Greeks called it Ares for their god of battle: the plan-

et's two satellites, Phobos (Fear) and Deimos (Terror), were named for the two sons of Ares and Aphrodite.

Mars moves around the Sun at a mean distance of approximately 1.52 times that of the Earth from the Sun. Because the orbit of Mars is highly elliptical, the distance between Mars and the Sun varies from 206.6 to 249.2 million km (128.4 to 154.8 million mi). Mars completes a single orbit in roughly the time in which the Earth completes two. At its closest approach, Mars is less than 56 million km (34.8 million mi) from the Earth, but it recedes to almost 400 million km (248.5 million mi). Mars is a small planet. Its equatorial radius is about half that of Earth, and its mass is only one-tenth the terrestrial value.

The axis of rotation is inclined to the orbital plane at an angle of 24.935°, and, as for the Earth, the tilt gives rise to the seasons on Mars. The Martian year consists of 668.6 Martian solar days (called sols). The orientation and eccentricity of the orbit (eccentricity denotes how circular or elliptical the orbit is, the more elliptical the more eccentric) leads to seasons that are quite uneven in length.

The Martian atmosphere is composed mainly of carbon dioxide. It is very thin (less than 1% of the Earth's atmospheric pressure). Evidence suggests that the atmosphere was much denser in the remote past and that water was once much more abundant at the surface. Only small amounts of water are found in the lower atmosphere today, occasionally forming thin ice clouds at high altitudes and, in several localities, morning ice fogs.

The characteristic temperature in the lower atmosphere is about –73.15 °C (–99.67 °F). Unlike that of Earth, the total mass (and pressure) of the atmosphere experiences large seasonal variations, as carbon dioxide "snows out" at the winter pole.

The two satellites of Mars, Phobos and Deimos, were discovered in 1877 by Asaph Hall of the United States Naval Observatory. Little was known about these bodies until observations were sent from orbiting spacecraft a century later.

The orbit of Phobos is exceptionally close to Mars. At a mean distance of 2.8 planetary radii from the center of Mars, it is so close that, without internal strength, it would have been torn apart by gravitational (tidal) forces. These gravitational forces also slow the motion of Phobos and may ultimately cause the satellite to fall onto the surface of Mars, possibly in less than 100 million years. The orbit of Deimos suffers an opposite fate, for it moves in a more distant orbit, and tidal forces cause it to recede from the planet. The orbital period of Phobos around Mars is 7 hours and 39 minutes. This short period means that an observer at a suitable point on the planet would see Phobos rise and set twice in a sol. The moons of Mars cannot be seen from all locations on the planet because of their small size, proximity to the planet, and near-equatorial orbits.

## Small Celestial Bodies

Small bodies are defined as all the natural objects in the solar system other than the major planets and their satellites. The solar system is populated by vast numbers of these small bodies, which can be grouped as asteroids, comets, and meteoroids (at times, however, the distinctions between these groupings can be somewhat blurred).

Small bodies are found in several regions of the solar system. Most asteroids reside in the belt between Mars and Jupiter at approximately 330–508 million km (204–316 million mi). For example, the Trojan asteroids are found between Mars and Jupiter.

The trans-Neptunian objects (considered comets) are located outside the orbit of Neptune, located from around 4.4 billion km (2.7 billion mi) to 7.4 billion km (4.6 billion mi) in the area known as the Kuiper belt. A spherical cloud known as the Oort cloud also contains comets at a distance of some 3–15 trillion km (1.8–9 trillion mi).

Other small bodies travel in unstable paths which cross planetary orbits. These include: 1) all observable comets, 2) near-Earth objects, including asteroids classed as Atens, Apollos, and Amors, and 3) other planet-crossing objects (a mixture of both asteroids and comets). All objects on planet-crossing orbits will eventually collide with the Sun (or a planet) or be permanently ejected from the solar system, although many of these objects do survive for long periods of time due to stabilizing orbital resonances.

Comets originated, and most are still located, in the Kuiper belt and Oort cloud. Even though comets are brief visitors to the inner solar system, their population is constantly replenished through perturbations of the comets in these areas.

There are several characteristics that distinguish asteroids, comets, and meteoroids. These are based upon origin, orbital, and physical differences. An object is classified as a comet when it displays a coma or tail (or any evidence of gas or dust coming from it). In addition, objects found in the Kuiper belt (and the Oort cloud, though none of these are observable) are also considered to be comets. They are defined as comets even though they may not have originated in their present location and they do not display cometary activity (because of their great distance from the Sun). Nevertheless, they are believed to be made up of low-volatility material—primarily water and carbon dioxide—and it is the presence of these volatiles on the surface that is responsible for cometary activity. Finally, objects on parabolic or hyperbolic orbits are generally considered to be comets.

Meteoroids are defined as any object that moves in space and is larger than a molecule but smaller than around 1 km (the light that emanates from this phenomena is a meteor). Should any part of a meteoroid enter Earth's atmosphere without being completely vaporized, that object is termed a meteorite. Asteroids are objects usually larger than 1 km and are frequently made of the same materials that formed the planets.

## Asteroids and the Asteroid Belt

Asteroids are any of a host of small rocky bodies, about 1,000 km (620 mi) or less in diameter, that orbit the Sun. About 95% of the known asteroids move in orbits between those of Mars and Jupiter in an area known as the **asteroid belt**. The orbits of the asteroids, however, are not uniformly distributed within the asteroid belt, but exhibit "gaps." Known as **Kirkwood gaps**, these asteroid-less areas were created by the gravitational force exerted by Jupiter upon asteroids in certain orbits.

The vast majority of asteroids have **orbital periods** between three years and six years—i.e., between one-fourth and one-half of Jupiter's orbital period. These asteroids are said to be **main-belt asteroids**. Within the main belt are asteroids that share certain traits. Known as families, about 40% of all known asteroids belong to such groupings. Families are usually assigned the name of the lowest numbered asteroid in the family. The three largest families (Eos, Koronis, and Themis) have been determined to be compositionally homogeneous.

Besides the few asteroids in highly unusual orbits, there are a number of groups that fall outside the main belt. Those that have orbital periods greater than one-half that of Jupiter are called **outer-belt asteroids**. There are four such groups: the Cybeles, Hildas, and Thule, as well as the Trojan group, so called because all its members are named after characters from Homer's epic work about the Trojan War, the *Iliad*.

There is only one known group of **inner-belt asteroids**—namely, the Hungarias. The Hungaria asteroids have orbital periods that are less than one-fourth that of Jupiter. Finally, Asteroids that can pass inside the orbit of Mars are said to be near-Earth asteroids. There are two groups of **near-Earth asteroids** that deeply cross the Earth's orbit on an almost continuous basis. The first of these to be discovered were the

**Apollo asteroids**. The other group of Earth-crossing asteroids is named Atens.

Asteroids are thought to have been created from the same **material** that formed the planets. Scientists believe that at the time the planets were forming from the low-velocity collisions among asteroid-size planetesimals (small celestial bodies thought to have existed at an early stage in the development of the solar system), one of them grew at a high rate and to a size larger than the others. This large planetesimal became Jupiter. The gravity of Jupiter scattered other large planetesimals, some of which may have been as massive as the Earth is today. These planetesimals were eventually either captured by Jupiter or another of the trans-Jovian planets (Saturn, Uranus, and Neptune) or ejected from the solar system. While they were passing through the inner solar system, however, such large planetesimals strongly perturbed the orbits of the planetesimals in the region of the asteroid belt, raising their mutual velocities to the average 5 km per second (3.1 mi per second) they exhibit today.

## Jupiter

Jupiter is the most massive of the planets, and is fifth in distance from the Sun. When ancient astronomers named the planet Jupiter for the ruler of the gods in the Greco-Roman pantheon, they had no idea of the planet's true dimensions, but the name is appropriate, for Jupiter is larger than all the other planets combined. It has a narrow ring system and 61 known satellites, 3 larger than the Earth's Moon. Jupiter also has an internal heat source—i.e., it emits more energy than it receives from the Sun. This giant has the strongest magnetic field of any planet, with a magnetosphere so large that, if it could be seen from Earth, its apparent diameter would exceed that of the Moon. Jupiter's system is the source of intense bursts of radio noise, at some frequencies occasionally radiating more energy than the Sun.

Of special interest concerning Jupiter's physical properties is the low mean density of 1.33 grams per cubic cm—in contrast with Earth's 5.52 grams/cm$^3$—coupled with the large dimensions and mass and the short rotational period. The low density and large mass indicate that Jupiter's composition and structure are quite unlike those of the Earth and the other inner planets, a deduction that is supported by detailed investigations of the giant planet's atmosphere and interior.

Jupiter has no solid surface; the transition from the atmosphere to the core occurs gradually at great depths. The close-up views of Jupiter from the Voyager spacecraft revealed a variety of cloud forms, with a predominance of elliptical features reminiscent of cyclonic and anticyclonic storm systems on the Earth. All these systems are in motion, appearing and disappearing on time scales dependent on their sizes and locations. Also observed to vary are the

pastel shades of various colors present in the cloud layers—from the tawny yellow that seems to characterize the main layer, through browns and blue-grays, to the well-known salmon-colored Great Red Spot, Jupiter's largest, most prominent, and longest-lived feature.

Because Jupiter has no solid surface it has no topographic features, and latitudinal currents dominate the planet's large-scale circulation. The lack of a solid surface with physical boundaries and regions with different heat capacities makes the persistence of these currents and their associated cloud patterns all the more remarkable. The Great Red Spot, for example, moves in longitude with respect to all three of the rotation systems, yet it does not move in latitude.

The first Voyager spacecraft verified the existence of a ring system surrounding Jupiter when it crossed the planet's equatorial plane. The ring system is comprised of large numbers of micrometer-sized particles that produce strong forward scattering of incident sunlight. Submicrometric dust is also present. The presence of such small particles requires a source. Indeed, the finest material extends all the way into the planet itself. It seems likely that the source of this material is large boulders, or small moonlets, within the ring. Visible examples of what are presumably among the largest of such objects are satellites Thebe and Metis. The ring particles are generated by impacts of micrometeoroids, cometary debris, and possibly volcanically produced material from Io. It seems plausible that the orbit of one of these moonlets defines the inner edge of Jupiter's ring, even as the outer edge appears to be defined by the satellite Thebe.

---

**Did you know?** Voyager 1 and Voyager 2, twin spacecraft that were launched by NASA in 1977 to explore the planets of the outer solar system, are still returning information even though they are well past the orbit of Pluto. In 1998 Voyager 1 overtook Pioneer 10 to become the most distant human-made object in space.

# Jovian Moons

The satellites orbiting Jupiter are numerous; there are 61 known Jovian moons and likely more to be discovered.

The first objects in the solar system discovered by means of a telescope (by Galileo in 1610) were the four brightest moons of Jupiter. Now known as the Galilean satellites, they are (in order of increasing distance from Jupiter) Io, Europa, Ganymede, and Callisto. Each is a unique world in its own right. Callisto and Ganymede, for example, are as large or larger than the planet Mercury, but, while Callisto's icy surface is ancient and heavily cratered from impacts, Ganymede's appears to have been extensively modified by internal activity. Europa may still be geologically active and may harbor an ocean of liquid water, and possibly even life, beneath its frozen surface. Io is the most volcanically active body in the solar system; its suface is a vividly colored landscape of erupting vents, pools and solidified flows of lava, and sulfurous deposits.

Data for the first 16 known Jovian moons (discovered 1610–1979) are summarized below. The orbits of the inner eight satellites have low inclinations (they are not tilted relative to the planet's equator) and low eccentricities (their orbits are relatively circular). The orbits of the outer eight have much higher inclinations and eccentricities, and four of them are retrograde (they are opposite to Jupiter's spin and orbital motion around the Sun). The innermost four satellites are thought to be intimately associated with Jupiter's ring and are the sources of the fine particles within the ring itself.

Between 1999 and mid-2003, 45 tiny moons (including one seen in 1975 and then lost) were discovered photographically in observations from Earth. All have high orbital eccentricities and inclinations and large orbital radii; nearly all of the orbits are retrograde. Rough size estimates based on their brightness place them between 2 and 8 km (1.2 and 5 mi) in diameter. They were assigned provisional numerical designations on discovery; many also have received official names.

In the table, "sync" denotes that the orbital period and rotational period are the same, or synchronous; hence, the moon always keeps the same face toward Jupiter. "R" following the orbital period indicates a retrograde orbit. Unspecified quantities are unknown.

| NAME (DESIGNATION) | MEAN DISTANCE FROM JUPITER | DIAMETER | MASS ($10^{20}$ KG) | ORBITAL PERIOD (EARTH DAYS) | ROTATIONAL PERIOD (EARTH DAYS) |
|---|---|---|---|---|---|
| Metis (JXVI) | 128,000 km (79,500 mi) | 40 km (25 mi) | 0.001 | 0.295 | sync |
| Adrastea (JXV) | 129,000 km (80,000 mi) | 20 km (12 mi) | 0.0002 | 0.298 | sync |
| Amalthea (JV)* | 181,000 km (112,500 mi) | 189 km (117 mi) | 0.075 | 0.498 | sync |
| Thebe (JXIV) | 222,000 km (138,000 mi) | 100 km (62 mi) | 0.008 | 0.675 | |
| Io (JI)* | 422,000 km (262,000 mi) | 3,630 km (2,256 mi) | 893.2 | 1.769 | sync |
| Europa (JII)* | 671,000 km (417,000 mi) | 3,130 km (1,945 mi) | 480.0 | 3.551 | sync |
| Ganymede (JIII)* | 1,070,000 km (665,000 mi) | 5,268 km (3,273 mi) | 1,481.9 | 7.155 | sync |
| Callisto (JIV)* | 1,883,000 km (1,170,000 mi) | 4,806 km (2,986 mi) | 1,075.9 | 16.689 | sync |
| Leda (JXIII) | 11,094,000 km (6,893,500 mi) | 10 km (6 mi) | 0.00006 | 238.72 | |
| Himalia (JVI) | 11,480,000 km (7,133,000 mi) | 170 km (106 mi) | 0.095 | 250.57 | 0.4 |
| Lysithea (JX) | 11,720,000 km (7,282,500 mi) | 24 km (15 mi) | 0.0008 | 259.22 | |
| Elara (JVII) | 11,737,000 km (7,293,000 mi) | 80 km (50 mi) | 0.008 | 259.65 | 0.5 |
| Ananke (JXII) | 21,200,000 km (13,173,000 mi) | 20 km (12.5 mi) | 0.0004 | 631 R | |
| Carme (JXI) | 22,600,000 km (14,043,000 mi) | 30 km (18.6 mi) | 0.001 | 692 R | |
| Pasiphae (JVIII) | 23,500,000 km (14,602,000 mi) | 36 km (22.3 mi) | 0.003 | 735 R | |
| Sinope (JIX) | 23,700,000 km (14,726,500 mi) | 28 km (17.3 mi) | 0.0008 | 758 R | |

*Densities are known for these moons. They are: Amalthea (3.10 grams/cm³), Io (3.55 grams/cm³), Europa (3.04 grams/cm³), Ganymede (1.93 grams/cm³), Callisto (1.83 grams/cm³).

## Jovian Ring

Jupiter's complex ring was discovered and first studied by the twin Voyager spacecraft during their flybys of the giant planet in 1979. It is now known to consist of four main components: an outer gossamer ring, whose outer radius coincides with the orbital radius of the Jovian moon Thebe (222,000 km; 138,000 mi); an inner gossamer ring bounded on its outer edge by the orbit of Amalthea (181,000 km; 112,500 mi); the main ring, extending inward some 6,000 km (3,700 mi) from the orbits of Adrastea (129,000 km; 80,000 mi) and Metis (128,000 km; 79,500 mi); and a halo of particles with a thickness of 25,000 km (15,500 mi) that extends from the main ring inward to a radius of about 95,000 km (59,000 mi). For comparison, Jupiter's visible surface lies at a radius of about 71,500 km (44,400 mi) from its center. The four moons involved with the ring are believed to supply the fine particles that compose it.

## Saturn

Saturn is the sixth planet in order of distance from the Sun and the second largest of the planets in mass and size. Its dimensions are almost equal to those of Jupiter, while its mass is about three times smaller; it has the lowest mean density of any object in the solar system.

Both Saturn and Jupiter resemble stellar bodies in that the light gas hydrogen dominates their bulk **chemical composition**. Saturn's atmosphere is 91% hydrogen by mass and is thus the most hydrogen-rich atmosphere in the solar system. Saturn's structure and **evolutionary history**, however, differ significantly from those of its larger counterpart. Like the other giant planets Jupiter, Uranus, and Neptune, Saturn has an extensive satellite and ring system, which may provide clues to its origin and evolution. Saturn's satellites have, with the exception of the outermost moons, prograde, low-inclination, and low-eccentricity orbits with respect to the planet. Saturn's dense and extended rings, which lie in its equatorial plane, are currently the most impressive in the solar system.

Saturn has no single **rotation period**. Cloud motions in its massive upper atmosphere can be used to trace out a variety of rotation periods, with periods as short as about 10 hours, 10 minutes near the equator and increasing with some oscillation to about 30 minutes longer at latitudes higher than 40°. The rotation period of Saturn's deep interior can be determined from the rotation period of the magnetic field, which is presumed to be rooted in a metallic outer core. The "surface" of Saturn that is seen through telescopes and in spacecraft images is actually a complex layer of clouds.

The **atmosphere** of Saturn shows many smaller-scale time-variable features similar to those found in Jupiter, such as red, brown, and white spots, bands, eddies, and vortices. The atmosphere generally has a much blander appearance than Jupiter's, however, and is less active on a small scale. A spectacular exception occurred during September–November 1990, when a large white spot appeared near the equator, expanded to a size exceeding 20,000 km (12,400 mi), and eventually spread around the equator before fading.

## Saturnian Moons

Thirty-one natural satellites have been discovered circling the planet Saturn. Data for the first 18 Saturnian moons (discovered 1655–1990) are summarized below. As with the other giant planets, those satellites closest to Saturn are mostly regular, meaning that their orbits are fairly circular and not greatly inclined (tilted) with respect to the planet's equator. All of the satellites in the table except distant Phoebe are regular.

**Titan** is Saturn's largest moon and the only satellite in the solar system known to have clouds and a dense atmosphere (composed mostly of nitrogen and methane). The moon is also enveloped in a reddish haze, which is thought to be composed of complex organic compounds that are produced by the action of sunlight on its clouds and atmosphere. That organic molecules may have been settling out of the haze onto Titan's surface for much of its history, has encouraged some scientists to speculate on the possibility that life may have evolved there. Saturn's sec-

ond largest moon is **Rhea**, followed by **Iapetus** and **Dione**.

An unusual Saturnian satellite is **Hyperion**. Owing to its highly irregular shape and eccentric orbit, it does not rotate stably about a fixed axis. Unlike any other known object in the solar system, Hyperion rotates chaotically, alternating unpredictably between periods of tumbling and seemingly regular rotation.

In 2000 and 2003 a total of 13 additional tiny moons occupying distant orbits were discovered in Earth-based photographic observations. Like the numerous outer moons of Jupiter, the recent finds around Saturn belong to the irregular class, meaning that their orbits are highly inclined and elliptical. Six of them, plus Phoebe, are in retrograde orbits (they move opposite to Saturn's spin and orbital motion around the Sun).

In the table, "sync" denotes that the orbital period and rotational period are the same, or synchronous. Unspecified quantities are unknown.

| NAME (DESIGNATION) | MEAN DISTANCE FROM SATURN | DIAMETER | MASS ($10^{20}$ KG) | DENSITY (GRAMS/CM$^3$) | ORBITAL PERIOD (EARTH DAYS) | ROTATIONAL PERIOD (EARTH DAYS) |
|---|---|---|---|---|---|---|
| Pan (SXVIII) | 133,580 km (83,000 mi) | 20 km (12 mi) | 0.00003 | 0.63 | 0.5750 | |
| Atlas (SXV) | 137,670 km (85,540 mi) | 28 km (17 mi) | 0.0001 | 0.63 | 0.6019 | |
| Prometheus (SXVI) | 139,350 km (86,590 mi) | 92 km (57 mi) | 0.0033 | 0.63 | 0.6130 | |

## Saturnian Moons (continued)

| NAME (DESIGNATION) | MEAN DISTANCE FROM SATURN | DIAMETER | MASS ($10^{20}$ KG) | DENSITY (GRAMS/CM³) | ORBITAL PERIOD (EARTH DAYS) | ROTATIONAL PERIOD (EARTH DAYS) |
|---|---|---|---|---|---|---|
| Pandora (SXVII) | 141,700 km (88,050 mi) | 92 km (57 mi) | 0.002 | 0.63 | 0.6285 | |
| Epimetheus (SXI) | 151,420 km (94,090 mi) | 114 km (71 mi) | 0.0054 | 0.60 | 0.6942 | sync |
| Janus (SX) | 151,470 km (94,120 mi) | 178 km (111 mi) | 0.0192 | 0.65 | 0.6945 | sync |
| Mimas (SI) | 185,520 km (115,280 mi) | 392 km (244 mi) | 0.375 | 1.14 | 0.94 | sync |
| Enceladus (SII) | 238,020 km (147,900 mi) | 520 km (323 mi) | 0.7 | 1.0 | 1.37 | sync |
| Tethys (SIII) | 294,660 km (183,090 mi) | 1,060 km (659 mi) | 6.27 | 1.0 | 1.88 | sync |
| Telesto (SXIII)* | 294,660 km (183,090 mi) | 30 km (19 mi) | 0.00007 | 1.0 | 1.88 | |
| Calypso (SXIV)* | 294,660 km (183,090 mi) | 26 km (16 mi) | 0.00004 | 1.0 | 1.88 | |
| Dione (SIV) | 377,400 km (234,510 mi) | 1,120 km (696 mi) | 11 | 1.5 | 2.73 | sync |
| Helene (SXII)† | 377,400 km (234,510 mi) | 32 km (20 mi) | 0.0003 | 1.5 | 2.73 | |
| Rhea (SV) | 527,040 km (327,490 mi) | 1,530 km (951 mi) | 23.1 | 1.24 | 4.51 | sync |
| Titan (SVI) | 1,221,830 km (759,210 mi) | 5,150 km (3,200 mi) | 1,350 | 1.881 | 15.94 | sync |
| Hyperion (SVII) | 1,481,100 km (920,310 mi) | 286 km (178 mi) | 0.2 | 1.50 | 21.27 | chaotic |
| Iapetus (SVIII) | 3,561,300 km (2,212,890 mi) | 1,460 km (907 mi) | 16 | 1.02 | 79.33 | sync |
| Phoebe (SIX) | 12,952,000 km (8,048,000 mi) | 220 km (137 mi) | 0.004 | 1.3 | 550.5 (retrograde) | 0.4 |

*Telesto and Calypso occupy the same orbit as Tethys but about 60° ahead and behind, respectively.
†Helene occupies the same orbit as Dione but about 60° behind.

## Saturnian Rings

Saturn's rings rank among the most spectacular phenomena in the solar system. They have intrigued astronomers ever since they were discovered telescopically by Galileo in 1610, and their mysteries have only deepened since they were photographed and studied by Voyagers 1 and 2 in the early 1980s. The **particles** that make up the rings are composed primarily of water ice and range from dust specks to car- and house-sized chunks. The rings exhibit a great amount of structure on many scales, from the broad **A, B, and C rings** visible from Earth down to myriad narrow component ringlets. Odd structures resembling spokes, braids, and spiral waves are also present. Some of this detail is explained by gravitational interaction with a number of Saturn's many moons (the orbits of 13 known moons, from Pan to Dione and Helene, lie within the rings), but much of it remains unaccounted for.

Numerous divisions or **gaps** are seen in the major ring regions. A few of the more prominent ones are named for famous astronomers who were associated with studies of Saturn.

The major rings and gaps, listed outward from Saturn, are given below. For comparison, Saturn's visible surface lies at a radius of about 60,300 km (37,500 mi).

| RING (OR DIVISION) | RADIUS OF RING'S INNER EDGE | WIDTH | COMMENTS |
|---|---|---|---|
| D ring | 66,900 km (41,600 mi) | 7,500 km (4,700 mi) | faint, visible only in reflected light |
| (Guerin division) | | | |
| C ring | 74,500 km (46,300 mi) | 17,500 km (10,900 mi) | also called Crepe ring |
| (Maxwell division) | | | |
| B ring | 92,000 km (57,200 mi) | 25,500 km (15,800 mi) | brightest ring |
| (Cassini division, Huygens gap) | | | Cassini division is the largest ring gap |
| A ring | 122,200 km (75,900 mi) | 14,600 km (9,100 mi) | the outermost ring visible from Earth |
| (Encke division) | | | located within the A ring, near its outer edge |

## Saturnian Rings (continued)

| RING (OR DIVISION) | RADIUS OF RING'S INNER EDGE | WIDTH | COMMENTS |
|---|---|---|---|
| F ring | 140,200 km (87,100 mi) | 30–500 km (20–300 mi) | faint, narrowest major ring |
| G ring | 165,800 km (103,000 mi) | 8,000 km (5,000 mi) | faint |
| E ring | 180,000 km (111,800 mi) | 300,000 km (186,400 mi) | faint |

## Uranus

Uranus is the seventh planet in order of distance from the Sun. Its low density and large size place it among the four giant planets, all of which are composed primarily of hydrogen, helium, water, and other volatile compounds and which thus are without solid surfaces. Absorption of red light by methane gas gives the planet a blue-green color. The planet has more than 21 known satellites, ranging up to 789 km (490 mi) in radius, and 11 narrow rings.

Uranus spins on its side; its **rotation axis** is tipped at an angle of 98° relative to its orbit axis. The 98° tilt is thought to have arisen during the final stages of planetary accretion when bodies comparable in size to the present planets collided in a series of violent events that knocked Uranus onto its side.

Although Uranus is nearly featureless, extreme contrast enhancement of the Voyager images reveals faint bands oriented parallel to circles of constant latitude. Apparently the rotation of the planet and not the distribution of absorbed sunlight controls the cloud patterns.

**Wind** is the motion of the atmosphere relative to the rotating planet. At high latitudes on Uranus, as on the Earth, this relative motion is in the direction of the planet's rotation. At low (that is, equatorial) latitudes, the relative motion is in the opposite direction. On the Earth these directions are called east and west, respectively, but the more general terms are prograde and retrograde. The winds that exist on Uranus are several times stronger than are those of the Earth. The wind is 200 m (656 ft) per second (prograde) at a latitude of −55° and 110 m (360.8 ft) per second (retrograde) at the equator. Neptune's equatorial winds are also retrograde, although those of Jupiter and Saturn are prograde. No satisfactory theory exists to explain these differences.

Uranus has no large **spots** like the Great Red Spot of Jupiter or the Great Dark Spot of Neptune. Since the giant planets have no solid surfaces, the spots represent atmospheric storms. For reasons that are not clear, Uranus seems to have the smallest number of storms of any of the giant planets.

Uranus was discovered in 1781 by the English astronomer **William Herschel**, who had undertaken a survey of all stars down to eighth magnitude—i.e., those about five times fainter than stars visible to the naked eye. Herschel suggested naming the new planet the Georgian Planet after his patron, King George III of England, but the planet was eventually named according to the tradition of naming planets for the gods of Greek and Roman mythology; Uranus is the father of Saturn, who is in turn the father of Jupiter.

After the discovery, Herschel continued to observe the planet with larger and better telescopes and eventually discovered the outer two **satellites**, Titania and Oberon, in 1787. Two more satellites, Ariel and Umbriel, were discovered by the British astronomer William Lassell in 1851. The names of the four satellites come from English literature, three taken from Shakespeare, and were proposed by Herschel's son, John Herschel. A fifth satellite, Miranda, was discovered by Gerard P. Kuiper in 1948. The tradition of naming the satellites after characters in Shakespeare's plays continues to the present.

## Uranian Moons and Rings

Uranus has 21 known **satellites** forming three distinct groups: 10 small moons orbiting quite close to the planet, 5 large moons located somewhat farther out, and finally another 6 small and much more distant moons. All but the 6 outermost bodies are in nearly circular orbits with low inclinations with respect to the planet.

The densities of the 4 largest satellites, **Ariel, Umbriel, Titania,** and **Oberon**, suggest that they are about half (or more) water ice and the rest rock. Oberon and Umbriel are heavily scarred with large impact craters dating back to the very early history of the solar system, evidence that their surfaces probably have been stable since their formation. In contrast, Titania and Ariel have far fewer large craters, indicating relatively young surfaces shaped over time by internal geological activity. Miranda, though small compared with the other major moons, has a unique jumbled patchwork of varied surface terrain revealing surprisingly extensive past activity. Data for the major satellites are summarized below.

The five major moons were **discovered** telescopically from Earth between 1787 and 1948. The 10 innermost moons, with diameters of about 40–160 km (25–100 mi), were all found by Voyager 2 when it flew by Uranus in 1986. The 6 outermost, with diameters of 20–200 km (12–120 mi), were detected in Earth-based observations between 1997 and 2001; their orbital motion is retrograde (opposite to the direction of Uranus's spin and revolution around the Sun).

Eleven very narrow **rings** are known to encircle Uranus, with radii from 41,800 to 51,100 km (26,000 to 31,800 mi), for the most part within the orbits of the innermost moons. For comparison, Uranus's visible surface lies at a radius of about 25,600 km (15,900 mi). The ring system was first detected in 1977 during Earth-based observations of Uranus when the planet was passing in front of a star. Subsequent observations from Earth and images from Voyager 2 clarified the number and other features of the rings.

## Uranian Moons and Rings (continued)

| NAME (DESIGNATION) | MEAN DISTANCE FROM URANUS | DIAMETER | MASS ($10^{20}$ KG) | DENSITY (GRAMS/CM³) | ORBITAL PERIOD/ ROTATIONAL PERIOD (EARTH DAYS)* |
|---|---|---|---|---|---|
| Miranda (V) | 129,390 km (80,400 mi) | 472 km (293 mi) | 0.66 | 1.2 | 1.41 |
| Ariel (I) | 191,020 km (118,690 mi) | 1,158 km (720 mi) | 13.5 | 1.67 | 2.52 |
| Umbriel (II) | 266,300 km (165,470 mi) | 1,169 km (726 mi) | 11.7 | 1.4 | 4.14 |
| Titania (III) | 435,910 km (270,860 mi) | 1,578 km (981 mi) | 35.2 | 1.71 | 8.70 |
| Oberon (IV) | 583,520 km (362,580 mi) | 1,523 km (946 mi) | 30.1 | 1.63 | 13.46 |

*The orbital period and rotational period are the same, or synchronous, for the listed moons.

## Neptune

Neptune is the eighth planet in average distance from the Sun. It was named for the Roman god of the sea. The sea-god's three-pronged trident serves as the planet's astronomical symbol.

Neptune's **distance** from the Sun varies between 29.8 and 30.4 astronomical units (AUs). Its **diameter** is nearly four times that of the Earth, but because of its great distance Neptune cannot be seen from the Earth without the aid of a telescope. Neptune's deep blue **color** is due to the absorption of red light by methane gas in its atmosphere. It receives less than half as much sunlight as Uranus, but heat escaping from its interior makes Neptune slightly warmer than the latter. The heat released may also be responsible for Neptune's stormier **atmosphere**, which exhibits the fastest winds seen on any planet in the solar system.

Neptune's **orbital period** is 163.7 Earth years. It has not completely circled the Sun since its discovery in 1846, so some refinements in its orbital size and shape are still expected. The planet's orbital eccentricity of 0.009 means that its orbit is very nearly circular; among the nine planets in the solar system, only Venus has a smaller eccentricity. Neptune's seasons (and the seasons of its moons) are therefore of nearly equal length, each more than 41 Earth years in duration. The length of Neptune's day, as determined by Voyager 2, is 16.11 hr.

As with the other giant planets of the outer solar system, Neptune's atmosphere is composed predominantly of hydrogen and helium. The **temperature** of Neptune's atmosphere varies with altitude. A minimum temperature of about –223.15 °C (–369.67 °F) occurs at pressure near 0.1 bar. The temperature increases with altitude to about 476.85 °C (890.33 °F) at 2,000 km (1,240 mi, which corresponds to a pressure of 10–11 bars) and remains uniform above that altitude.

As with the other giant planets of the outer solar system, the **winds** on Neptune are constrained to blow generally along lines of constant latitude and are relatively invariable with time. Winds on Neptune vary from about 100 m/sec (328 ft/sec) in an easterly (prograde) direction near latitude 70° S to as high as 700 m/sec (2,300 ft/sec) in a westerly (retrograde) direction near latitude 20° S.

The high winds and relatively large contribution of escaping internal heat may be responsible for the observed turbulence in Neptune's visible atmosphere. Two large dark ovals are clearly visible in images of Neptune's southern hemisphere taken by Voyager 2. The largest, called the **"Great Dark Spot"** because of its similarity in latitude and shape to Jupiter's Great Red Spot, is comparable to the entire Earth in size. It is near this Great Dark Spot that the highest wind speeds were measured. A somewhat smaller "Small Dark Spot" circles the planet near latitude 55° S. These two atmospheric storms may be centers where strong upwelling of gases from the interior takes place.

Neptune's mean **density** is slightly less than 30% that of the Earth; nevertheless, it is the densest of the giant planets. Neptune's greater density implies that a larger percentage of its interior is composed of melted ices and molten rocky materials than is the case for the other gas giants.

## Neptunian Moons and Rings

Neptune has 11 known natural **satellites**, but Earth-based observations had found only 2 of them, Triton in 1847 and Nereid in 1949, before Voyager 2 made its flyby of the planet in 1989. The spacecraft observed 5 small moons orbiting close to Neptune and verified the existence of a 6th that had been detected from Earth in 1981. Data for these 8 moons are summarized in the table below; unspecified quantities are unknown. In 2002, 3 additional small moons (diameters roughly 40 km, or 25 mi) were discovered telescopically from Earth; they all occupy highly inclined and elliptical orbits that are comparatively far from Neptune.

Triton is Neptune's only large moon and the only large satellite in the solar system to orbit its planet in the retrograde direction (opposite the planet's rotation and orbital motion around the Sun). Thus, as is also suspected of the solar system's other retrograde moons, Triton likely was captured by its planet rather than having formed in orbit with its planet from the solar nebula. Its density (2 grams/cm³) suggests that it is about 25% water ice and the rest rock. Triton has a tenuous atmosphere, mostly of nitrogen. Its varied icy surface, imaged by Voyager 2, contains giant faults and dark markings that have been interpreted as the product of geyserlike "ice volcanoes" in which

## Neptunian Moons and Rings (continued)

the eruptive material may be gaseous nitrogen and methane. Nereid has the most elliptical orbit of any planet or moon in the solar system; it also is probably a captured object.

Neptune's system of 5 faint **rings**, with radii from about 42,000 to 63,000 km (26,000–39,000 mi), straddles the orbits of its 4 innermost moons. (Neptune's visible surface lies at a radius of 24,800 km, or 15,400 mi.) The outermost ring, named Adams, is

unusual in that it contains several clumps, or concentrations of material, that before Voyager 2's visit had been interpreted incorrectly as independent ring arcs. What created and has maintained this structure has not yet been fully explained; it has been suggested that the clumps resulted from the relatively recent breakup of a small moon and are being temporarily held together by the gravitational effects of the nearby moon Galatea.

| NAME (DESIGNATION) | MEAN DISTANCE FROM NEPTUNE | DIAMETER | MASS ($10^{20}$ KG) | ORBITAL PERIOD (EARTH DAYS) |
|---|---|---|---|---|
| Naiad (III) | 48,230 km (29,970 mi) | 58 km (36 mi) | | 0.294 |
| Thalassa (IV) | 50,070 km (31,110 mi) | 80 km (50 mi) | | 0.311 |
| Despina (V) | 52,530 km (32,640 mi) | 148 km (92 mi) | | 0.335 |
| Galatea (VI) | 61,950 km (38,490 mi) | 158 km (98 mi) | | 0.429 |
| Larissa (VII) | 73,550 km (45,700 mi) | 192 km (119 mi) | | 0.555 |
| Proteus (VIII) | 117,640 km (73,100 mi) | 416 km (258 mi) | | 1.122 |
| Triton (I)* | 354,800 km (220,460 mi) | 2,700 km (1,678 mi) | 214 | 5.877 (retrograde) |
| Nereid (II) | 5,509,100 km (3,423,200 mi) | 340 km (211 mi) | 0.2 | 359.632 |

*Among the rotational periods of Neptune's moons, only Triton's has been established; it is the same as (synchronous with) the orbital period.

## Pluto

Pluto is the planet normally farthest from the Sun. It is named for the god of the underworld in Roman mythology (Greek: Hades). Pluto has a single natural satellite, Charon. Because their dimensions are sufficiently similar and they orbit around a common center of gravity, it has become common to speak of the Pluto-Charon system as a double planet.

Pluto was the third planet to be discovered, as opposed to the six planets that had been visible in the sky to the naked eye since ancient times. Pluto is so distant that sunlight traveling at 299,792 km/sec (186,282.1 mi/sec) takes more than five hours to reach the planet. An observer standing on the planet's surface would see the Sun as an extremely bright star in the dark sky, providing Pluto with only 1/1600 the amount of sunlight reaching the Earth.

Pluto's average **distance** from the Sun (39.6 astronomical units, or AU), as well as its orbital eccentricity (0.244) and inclination (17.2°), are the greatest of any of the planets in the solar system. In traveling in its highly eccentric orbit, Pluto varies in distance from the Sun from 29.7 AU at perihelion to 49.5 AU at aphelion. Therefore, Pluto at times is actually closer to the Sun than Neptune, which has a nearly circular orbit at approximately 30 AU. A 3:2 resonance between the orbital periods of Neptune and Pluto prevents the two planets from ever passing closer than about 17 AU to one another. The most recent perihelion of Pluto occurred on 5 Sep 1989, so that Neptune was the most distant planet from the Sun from 1979 through 1999.

Pluto is by far the smallest planet, having a **diameter** less than half that of Mercury; it is about two-thirds the size of the Moon. Pluto's physical characteristics are unlike those of any other planet. Pluto

resembles most closely Neptune's icy satellite Triton, which implies a similar origin for these two bodies.

Observations of Pluto show that its **color** is slightly reddish, although not as red as Mars or Io. Thus, the surface of Pluto cannot be composed simply of pure ices. Its overall reflectivity, or albedo, ranges from 0.3 to 0.5, as compared with 0.1 for the Moon and 0.8 for Triton.

The surface **temperature** of Pluto has proved very difficult to measure. Observations made from the Infrared Astronomical Satellite suggest values in the range of –228.1 to –215.1 °C (–378.5 to –355.1 °F), whereas measurements at radio wavelengths imply a range of –238.1 to –223.1 °C (–396.5 to –369.5 °F). The temperature certainly must vary over the surface, depending on the local reflectivity and solar zenith angle. There is also expected to be a seasonal decrease in incident solar energy by a factor of roughly three as Pluto moves from perihelion to aphelion.

The detection of methane ice on the planet's surface made scientists confident that Pluto had an **atmosphere** before one was actually discovered. The atmosphere was finally detected in 1988 when Pluto passed in front of a star as observed from the Earth. The light of the star was dimmed before disappearing entirely behind the planet during the occultation. This proved that a thin, greatly distended atmosphere was present. Because Pluto's atmosphere must consist of vapors in equilibrium with their ices, small changes in temperature will have a large effect on the amount of gas in the atmosphere.

Pluto's only known **satellite** was discovered as a small bump on images of the planet that were recorded photographically at the US Naval Observatory in Flagstaff AZ less than six km from the site of

## Pluto (continued)

Pluto's discovery nearly 50 years earlier. The new satellite was named **Charon**, after the boatman who ferries dead souls across the River Styx to the underworld in Greek mythology. Subsequent observations showed that Charon's period of revolution around Pluto is exactly equal to the period of rotation of the planet itself. In other words, Pluto is the only planet in the solar system with a natural satellite in a synchronous orbit. As a result, Charon is only visible from one hemisphere of Pluto. In addition, as with most planetary satellites, Charon is in a state of synchronous rotation—i.e., it always presents the same face to its primary planet.

## Comets

Comets are a class of small celestial objects orbiting the Sun and developing diffuse gaseous envelopes. They also often form long luminous tails when near the Sun. The comet makes a transient appearance in the sky and is often said to have a "hairy" tail. In fact, the word comes from the Greek *kometes,* meaning "hairy one," a description that fits the bright comets noticed by the ancients.

Despite their name, many comets do not develop tails. Moreover, a comet is not surrounded by nebulosity during most of its lifetime. The only permanent feature of a comet is its **nucleus**, which is a small body that may be seen as a stellar image in large telescopes when tail and nebulosity do not exist, particularly when the comet is still far away from the Sun. Two characteristics differentiate the cometary nucleus from a very small asteroid—its orbit and its chemical nature. A comet's **orbit** is more eccentric (less circular); therefore, its distance to the Sun varies considerably. Its material is more volatile. When far from the Sun, however, a comet remains in its pristine state for eons without losing any volatile components because of the deep cold of space. For this reason, astronomers believe that pristine cometary nuclei may represent the oldest and best-preserved material in the solar system.

During a close passage near the Sun, the nucleus of a comet loses water vapor and other more volatile compounds, as well as dust dragged away by the sublimating gases. It is then surrounded by a transient dusty "atmosphere" that is steadily lost to space. This feature is the **coma**, which gives a comet its nebulous appearance.

The astronomer **Edmond Halley**, a friend of Isaac Newton, endeavored to compute the orbits of 24 comets for which he had found fairly accurate historical documents. Applying a method Newton had developed, Halley predicted that the comet that now bears his name would return to Earth in 1758, and that proved correct. Since its prediction by astronomers and its appearance in 1758/59, Comet Halley has reappeared three more times—in 1835, 1910, and 1986.

Each century, a score of comets brighter than Comet Halley have been discovered. Many are **periodic comets** like Comet Halley, but their periods are extremely long (millennia or even scores or hundreds of millennia), and they have not left any identifiable trace in prehistory. Bright Comet Bennett 1970 II will return in 17 centuries, whereas the spectacular Comet West 1976 VI will reappear in about 500,000 years. Among the comets that can easily be seen with the unaided eye, Comet Halley is the only one that returns in a single lifetime. Approximately 100 comets whose periods are between 3 and 200 years are known, however. Unfortunately, they are or have become too faint to be readily seen without the aid of telescopes.

For faraway objects that contain volatile ices, the distinction between **asteroids and comets** becomes a matter of semantics because many orbits are unstable; an asteroid that comes closer to the Sun than usual may become a comet by producing a transient atmosphere that gives it a fuzzy appearance and that may develop into a tail. Some objects have been reclassified as a result of such occurrences. For example, asteroid 1990 UL3, which crosses the orbit of Jupiter, was reclassified as Comet P/Shoemaker-Levy 2 late in 1990. Conversely, it is suspected that some of the Earth-approaching asteroids (Amors, Apollos, and Atens) could be the extinct nuclei of comets that have now lost most of their volatile ices.

# Measurements and Numbers

## The International System of Units (SI)

Rapid advances in science and technology in the 19th and 20th centuries fostered the development of several overlapping systems of units of measurements as scientists improvised to meet the practical needs of their disciplines. The **General Conference on Weights and Measures** was chartered by international convention in 1875 to produce standards of physical measurement based upon an earlier international standard, the meter-kilogram-second (MKS) system. The convention calls for regular General Conference meetings to consider improvements or modifications in standards, an International Committee of Weights and Measures elected by the Conference (meets annually), and several consultative committees. **The International Bureau of Weights and Measures** (Bureau International des Poids et Mesures) at Sèvres, France, serves as a depository for the primary international standards and as a laboratory for certification and intercomparison of national standard copies.

The 1960 **International System** (universally abbreviated as **SI**, from *système international*) builds upon the MKS system. Its **seven basic units**, from which other units are derived, are currently defined as follows: the **meter**, defined as the distance traveled by light in a vacuum in 1/299,792,458 second; the

# The International System of Units (SI) (continued)

kilogram (about 2.2 pounds avoirdupois), which equals 1,000 grams as defined by the international prototype kilogram of platinum-iridium in the keeping of the International Bureau of Weights and Measures; the **second**, the duration of 9,192,631,770 periods of radiation associated with a specified transition of the cesium-133 atom; the **ampere**, which is the current that, if maintained in two wires placed one meter apart in a vacuum, would produce a force of $2 \times 10^{-7}$ newton per meter of length; the **candela**, defined as the intensity in a given direction of a source emitting radiation of frequency $540 \times 10^{12}$ hertz and that has a radiant intensity in that direction of 1/683 watt per steradian; the **mole**, defined as containing as many elementary entities of a substance as there are atoms in 0.012 kilogram of carbon-12; and the **kelvin**, which is 1/273.16 of the thermodynamic temperature of the triple point (equilibrium among the solid, liquid, and gaseous phases) of pure water.

International Bureau of Weights and Measures Web site: <www.bipm.fr>.

## Elemental and Derived SI Units and Symbols

| Quantity | SI Units | | |
| --- | --- | --- | --- |
| | UNIT | FORMULA/EXPRESSION IN BASE UNITS | SYMBOL |
| **elemental units** | | | |
| length | meter | — | m |
| mass | kilogram | — | kg |
| time | second | — | s |
| electric current | ampere | — | A |
| luminous intensity | candela | — | cd |
| amount of substance | mole | — | mol |
| thermodynamic temperature | kelvin | — | K |
| | | | |
| **derived units** | | | |
| acceleration | meter/second squared | $m/s^2$ | |
| area | square meter | $m^2$ | |
| capacitance | farad | $A \times s/V$ | F |
| charge | coulomb | $A \times s$ | C |
| Celsius temperature | degree Celsius | K | °C |
| density | kilogram/cubic meter | $kg/m^3$ | |
| electric field strength | volt/meter | $V/m$ | |
| electrical potential | volt | $W/A$ | V |
| energy | joule | $N \times m$ | J |
| force | newton | $kg \times m/s^2$ | N |
| frequency | hertz | $s^{-1}$ | Hz |
| illumination | lux | $lm/m^2$ | lx |
| inductance | henry | $V \times s/A$ | H |
| kinematic viscosity | square meter/second | $m^2/s$ | |
| luminance | candela/square meter | $cd/m^2$ | |
| luminous flux | lumen | $cd \times sr$ | lm |
| magnetic field strength | ampere/meter | $A/m$ | |
| magnetic flux | weber | $V \times s$ | Wb |
| magnetic flux density | tesla | $Wb/m^2$ | T |
| plane angle | radian | $m \times m^{-1}=1$ | rad |
| power | watt | $J/s$ | W |
| pressure | pascal (newton/square meter) | $N/m^2$ | Pa |
| resistance | ohm | $V/A$ | Ω |
| solid angle | steradian | $m^2 \times m^{-2}=1$ | sr |
| stress | pascal (newton/square meter) | $N/m^2$ | Pa |
| velocity | meter/second | $m/s$ | |
| viscosity | newton-second/square meter | $N \times s/m^2$ | |
| volume | cubic meter | $m^3$ | |

**Did you know?** It takes about 40 minutes to hard-boil an ostrich egg.

# Conversion of Metric Weights and Measures

*The International System of Units is a decimal system of weights and measures derived from and extending the metric system of units. Adopted by the 11th General Conference on Weights and Measures in 1960, it is abbreviated "SI" in all languages.*
  *Below are common equivalents and conversion factors for US customary and SI systems.*

| approximate common equivalents | | conversions accurate within 10 parts per million | |
|---|---|---|---|
| 1 inch | = 25 millimeters | inches × 25.4[1] | = millimeters |
| 1 foot | = 0.3 meter | feet × 0.3048[1] | = meters |
| 1 yard | = 0.9 meter | yards × 0.9144[1] | = meters |
| 1 mile | = 1.6 kilometers | miles × 1.60934 | = kilometers |
| 1 square inch | = 6.5 sq. centimeters | square inches × 6.4516[1] | = square centimeters |
| 1 square foot | = 0.09 square meter | square feet × 0.0929030 | = square meters |
| 1 square yard | = 0.8 square meter | square yards × 0.836127 | = square meters |
| 1 acre | = 0.4 hectare[2] | acres × 0.404686 | = hectares |
| 1 cubic inch | = 16 cubic centimeters | cubic inches × 16.3871 | = cubic centimeters |
| 1 cubic foot | = 0.03 cubic meter | cubic feet × 0.0283168 | = cubic meters |
| 1 cubic yard | = 0.8 cubic meter | cubic yards × 0.764555 | = cubic meters |
| 1 quart (liq) | = 1 liter[2] | quarts (liquid) × 0.946353 | = liters |
| 1 gallon | = 0.004 cubic meter | gallons × 0.00378541 | = cubic meters |
| 1 ounce (avdp)[3] | = 28 grams | ounces (avdp)[3] × 28.3495 | = grams |
| 1 pound (avdp)[3] | = 0.45 kilogram | pounds (avdp)[3] × 0.453592 | = kilograms |
| 1 horsepower | = 0.75 kilowatt | horsepower × 0.745700 | = kilowatts |
| 1 millimeter | = 0.04 inch | millimeters × 0.0393701 | = inches |
| 1 meter | = 3.3 feet | meters × 3.28084 | = feet |
| 1 meter | = 1.1 yards | meters × 1.09361 | = yards |
| 1 kilometer | = 0.6 mile (statute) | kilometers × 0.621371 | = miles (statute) |
| 1 square centimeter | = 0.16 square inch | square centimeters × 0.155000 | = square inches |
| 1 square meter | = 11 square feet | square meters × 10.7639 | = square feet |
| 1 square meter | = 1.2 square yards | square meters × 1.19599 | = square yards |
| 1 hectare[2] | = 2.5 acres | hectares × 2.47105 | = acres |
| 1 cubic centimeter | = 0.06 cubic inch | cubic centimeters × 0.0610237 | = cubic inches |
| 1 cubic meter | = 35 cubic feet | cubic meters × 35.3147 | = cubic feet |
| 1 cubic meter | = 1.3 cubic yards | cubic meters × 1.30795 | = cubic yards |
| 1 liter[2] | = 1 quart (liq) | liters × 1.05669 | = quarts (liq) |
| 1 cubic meter | = 264 gallons | cubic meters × 264.172 | = gallons |
| 1 gram | = 0.035 ounce (avdp)[3] | grams × 0.0352740 | = ounces (avdp)[3] |
| 1 kilogram | = 2.2 pounds (avdp)[3] | kilograms × 2.20462 | = pounds (avdp)[3] |
| 1 kilowatt | = 1.3 horsepower | kilowatts × 1.34102 | = horsepower |

[1]*Exact.*    [2]*Common term not used in SI.*    [3]*avdp = avoirdupois.*
  *Source: National Institute of Standards and Technology.*

# British/US System (ft-lb-second, fps)

**length**

| | | | | |
|---|---|---|---|---|
| 1 statute mi | = 5,280 ft | = 1,760 yd | = 320 rods | = 8 furlongs |
| 1 nautical mi | = 6,076 ft | = 1.151 mi | | |
| 1 furlong | = 660 ft | = 220 yd | = 40 rods | = 1/8 mi |
| 1 chain (Gunter's) | = 66 ft | = 22 yd | = 100 links | = 4 rods |
| 1 rod | = 16.5 ft | = 5.5 yd | = 25 links | |
| 1 fathom | = 6 ft | = 72 in | | |
| 1 yd | = 3 ft | = 36 in | | |
| 1 ft | = 12 in | | | |
| 1 link (Gunter's) | = 0.66 ft | = 7.92 in | | |
| 1 hand | = 4 in | | | |
| 1 mil | = 0.001 in | | | |

**area**

| | | | | |
|---|---|---|---|---|
| 1 sq mi | = 640 acres | = 102,400 sq rods | = 3,097,600 sq yd | = 27,878,400 sq ft |
| 1 acre | = 10 sq chains | = 160 sq rods | = 4,840 sq yd | = 43,560 sq ft |
| 1 sq ft | = 144 sq in | | | |

**volume**

| | | | |
|---|---|---|---|
| 1 cu ft | = 1/27 cu yd | = 12 board ft | = 1,728 cu in |
| 1 cu in | = 1/46,656 cu yd | = 1/1,728 cu ft | |
| 1 acre-ft | = 43,560 cu ft | = 1,613 cu yd | |

## British/US system (ft-lb-second, fps) (continued)

**volume (continued)**

| | | |
|---|---|---|
| 1 board ft | = 144 cu in | = 1/12 cu ft | = 1 super ft (lumber) |
| 1 cord (US) | = 128 cu ft | | |

**capacity**

| | | |
|---|---|---|
| 1 cu ft | = 7.481 gal (US) | = 6.229 gal (British) |

**liquid measure (US)**

| | | | |
|---|---|---|---|
| 1 barrel, oil | = 42 gal (US) | = 34.97 gal (British) | | |
| 1 gal | = 0.833 gal (British) | = 4 quarts | = 231.00 cu in | = 128 fl oz |
| 1 quart | = 1/4 gal | = 2 pints | = 57.75 cu in | = 32 fl oz |
| 1 pint | = 1/8 gal | = 1/2 quart | = 28.88 cu in | = 16 fl oz |
| 1 gill | = 1/32 gal | = 1/4 pint | = 7.22 cu in | = 4 fl oz |
| 1 fl oz | = 1/128 gal | = 1/16 pint | = 1.80 cu in | |

**dry measure (US)**

| | | | | |
|---|---|---|---|---|
| 1 bushel | = 0.97 bushel (British) | = 4 pecks | = 2,150.4 cu in | = 1.24 cu ft |
| 1 peck | = 1/4 bushel | = 8 quarts | = 537.6 cu in | = 0.31 cu ft |
| 1 quart | = 1/32 bushel | = 2 pints | = 67.2 cu in | = 1/8 peck |
| 1 pint | = 1/64 bushel | = 1/2 quart | = 33.6 cu in | |

**liquid and dry measure (British)**

| | | | | | |
|---|---|---|---|---|---|
| 1 bushel | = 1.03 bushels (US) | = 8 gal | = 4 pecks | = 2,219.36 cu in | = 1.284 cu ft |
| 1 peck | = 0.25 bushel | = 2 gal | = 8 quarts | = 554.84 cu in | |
| 1 gal | = 1.20 gal (US) | = 4 quarts | | = 277.42 cu in | |
| 1 quart | = 0.30 gal | = 2 pints | = 1/8 peck | = 69.36 cu in | |
| 1 pint | = 4.80 gills (US) | = 4 gills | | = 34.68 cu in | = 20 fl oz |
| 1 gill | = 1.20 gills (US) | | | = 8.67 cu in | = 5 fl oz |
| 1 fl oz | = 0.96 fl oz (US) | | | = 1.73 cu in | |

**weight**

| | | | |
|---|---|---|---|
| 1 short ton (US) | = 0.89 long ton | = 2,000 lbs | = 20 short cwt* |
| 1 long ton (British) | = 1.12 short tons | = 2,240 lbs | = 22.4 short cwt* |
| 1 short cwt* (US) | = 0.05 short ton | = 100 lbs | |
| 1 long cwt* (British) | = 0.05 long ton | = 112 lbs | |
| 1 stone (person) | = 0.14 short cwt* | = 14 lbs | |
| 1 lb | = 0.07 stone (British) | | |
| 1 oz avdp† | = 437.50 grains | = 1/16 lb | = 0.911 oz troy |
| 1 oz troy | = 480.00 grains | = 1/12 lb | = 1.097 oz |
| 1 grain | | = 0.0023 oz | = 0.0021 oz troy |

*cwt = hundredweight.    †avdp = avoirdupois.

Did you know? There are 31,557,600 seconds in a year.

## Tables of Equivalents: Metric System Units and Prefixes

**base unit***

| QUANTITY | NAME OF UNIT | SYMBOL |
|---|---|---|
| length | meter | m |
| area | square meter | square m, or m² |
| | are (100 square meters) | a |
| volume | cubic meter | cubic m, or m³ |
| | stere (1 cubic meter) | s |
| mass | gram | g |
| | metric ton (1,000,000 grams) | t |
| capacity | liter | l |
| temperature | degree Celsius | °C |

## Tables of Equivalents: Metric System Units and Prefixes (continued)

prefixes designating multiples and submultiples

| PREFIX | SYMBOL | FACTOR BY WHICH UNIT IS MULTIPLIED | | EXAMPLES |
|---|---|---|---|---|
| exa- | E | $10^{18}$ | = 1,000,000,000,000,000,000 | |
| peta- | P | $10^{15}$ | = 1,000,000,000,000,000 | |
| tera- | T | $10^{12}$ | = 1,000,000,000,000 | |
| giga- | G | $10^{9}$ | = 1,000,000,000 | |
| mega- | M | $10^{6}$ | = 1,000,000 | megaton (Mt) |
| kilo- | k | $10^{3}$ | = 1,000 | kilometer (km) |
| hecto-, hect- | h | $10^{2}$ | = 100 | hectare (ha) |
| deca- dec- | da | 10 | = 10 | decastere (das) |
| | | | 1 | |
| deci- | d | $10^{-1}$ | = 0.1 | decigram (dg) |
| centi-, cent- | c | $10^{-2}$ | = 0.01 | centimeter (cm) |
| milli- | m | $10^{-3}$ | = 0.001 | milliliter (ml) |
| micro-, micr- | µ | $10^{-6}$ | = 0.000001 | microgram (µg) |
| nano- | n | $10^{-9}$ | = 0.000000001 | |
| pico- | p | $10^{-12}$ | = 0.000000000001 | |
| femto- | f | $10^{-15}$ | = 0.000000000000001 | |
| atto- | a | $10^{-18}$ | = 0.000000000000000001 | |

*The metric system of bases and prefixes has been applied to many other units, such as decibel (0.1 bel), kilowatt (1,000 watts), and microhm (one-millionth of an ohm).*

## Electrical Units

| UNIT | SYMBOL | ATTRIBUTE MEASURED | EXPRESSION IN OTHER UNITS |
|---|---|---|---|
| ampere | A | current | C/s* or V/Ω |

the basic electrical unit of the International System of Units (SI), since 1948 defined by the International Bureau of Weights and Measures as the constant current which, if maintained in two straight parallel conductors of infinite length, of negligible circular cross section, and placed one meter apart in a vacuum, would produce between these conductors a force equal to $2 \times 10^{-7}$ newton per meter of length. One ampere is equal to a flow of one coulomb of electricity per second; or, the flow produced in a conductor with a resistance of one ohm by a potential difference of one volt.

| farad | F | capacitance (ability to hold a charge) | A × s/V or C/V |
|---|---|---|---|

the ability of two parallel, oppositely charged plates (a capacitor) to hold an electric charge equals one farad when one coulomb of electricity changes the potential between the plates by one volt.

| coulomb | C | charge | A × s |
|---|---|---|---|

the quantity of electricity transported in one second by a current of one ampere. Approximately equal to $6.24 \times 10^{18}$ electrons.

| watt | W | power | J/s or V × A |
|---|---|---|---|

one joule of work performed per second; or, the power dissipated in an electrical conductor carrying one ampere current between points at one volt potential difference.

| ohm | Ω | resistance | V/A or W/A² |
|---|---|---|---|

resistance of a circuit in which a potential difference of one volt produces a current of one ampere; or, the resistance in which one watt of power is dissipated when one ampere flows through it.

| volt | V | potential | W/A or A × Ω |
|---|---|---|---|

the difference in potential between two points in a conductor carrying one ampere current when the power dissipated between the points is one watt; or, the difference in potential between two points in a conductor across a resistance of one ohm when one ampere is flowing through it.

*s = second.*

A small-scale climatic stage that affected most part of the world and lasted roughly from the beginning of the 16th century until the mid-19th century is known as the Little Ice Age. The harsh winters, moist, cool summers, and advancing ice sheets that characterized the Little Ice Age led to crop failures and the abandonment of the northern villages, and it necessitated the altering of oceanic sailing routes.

## Temperature Equivalents

Instructions for converting °F into °C or K*, and °C into °F: Find the figure you wish to convert in the second column. If this figure is in °F, the corresponding temperature in °C and K will be found in the third and fourth columns; if the figure is in °C, the corresponding temperature in °F will be found in the first column. To convert a temperature range between two scales, rather than finding equivalent temperatures, see the temperature conversion instructions, below.

| °FAHRENHEIT (°F) | FIGURE TO BE CONVERTED | °CELSIUS (°CENTIGRADE) (°C) | KELVIN (K) | °FAHRENHEIT (°F) | FIGURE TO BE CONVERTED | °CELSIUS (°CENTIGRADE) (°C) | KELVIN (K) |
|---|---|---|---|---|---|---|---|
| ... | −459.67 | −273.15 | 0 | +46.4 | +8 | −13.33 | +259.82 |
| | | | | +48.2 | +9 | −12.78 | +260.37 |
| ... | −400 | −240.00 | +33.15 | | | | |
| ... | −300 | −184.44 | +88.71 | +50.0 | +10 | −12.22 | +260.93 |
| −459.67 | −273.15 | −169.53 | +103.62 | +68.0 | +20 | −6.67 | +266.48 |
| | | | | +86.0 | +30 | −1.11 | +272.04 |
| −328.0 | −200 | −128.89 | +144.26 | +89.6 | +32 | 0.00 | +273.15 |
| −148.0 | −100 | −73.33 | +199.82 | +104.0 | +40 | +4.44 | +277.59 |
| | | | | +122.0 | +50 | +10.00 | +283.15 |
| −130.0 | −90 | −67.78 | +205.37 | +140.0 | +60 | +15.56 | +288.71 |
| −112.0 | −80 | −62.22 | +210.93 | +158.0 | +70 | +21.11 | +294.26 |
| −94.0 | −70 | −56.67 | +216.48 | +176.0 | +80 | +26.67 | +299.82 |
| −76.9 | −60 | −51.11 | +222.04 | +194.0 | +90 | +32.22 | +305.37 |
| −58.0 | −50 | −45.56 | +227.59 | | | | |
| −40.0 | −40 | −40.00 | +233.15 | +212.0 | +100 | +37.78 | +310.93 |
| −22.0 | −30 | −34.44 | +238.71 | +392.0 | +200 | +93.33 | +366.48 |
| −4.0 | −20 | −28.89 | +244.26 | +572.0 | +300 | +148.89 | +422.04 |
| +14.0 | −10 | −23.33 | +249.82 | +752.0 | +400 | +204.44 | +477.59 |
| | | | | +932.0 | +500 | +260.00 | +533.15 |
| +32.0 | 0 | −17.78 | +255.37 | +1112.0 | +600 | +315.56 | +588.71 |
| +33.8 | +1 | −17.22 | +255.93 | +1292.0 | +700 | +371.11 | +644.26 |
| +35.6 | +2 | −16.67 | +256.48 | +1472.0 | +800 | +426.67 | +699.82 |
| +37.4 | +3 | −16.11 | +257.04 | +1652.0 | +900 | +482.22 | +755.37 |
| +39.2 | +4 | −15.56 | +257.59 | | | | |
| +41.0 | +5 | −15.00 | +258.15 | +1832.0 | +1000 | +537.78 | +810.93 |
| +42.8 | +6 | −14.44 | +258.71 | +3632.0 | +2000 | +1093.33 | +1366.45 |
| +44.6 | +7 | −13.89 | +259.26 | +5432.0 | +3000 | +1648.89 | +1922.05 |

All systems of measuring temperature in degrees or units (kelvins) on a scale are based on the interval between the freezing and boiling points of water and differ only in the number of degrees or units into which this interval is divided.

**Fahrenheit:** interval is divided into 180 degrees (32° to 212°); 0° is at 32° below the freezing point of water.

**Rankine:** degree is the same as the Fahrenheit degree; 0° is at absolute zero (the theoretical point at which a thermodynamic system has the lowest energy, −459.67 °F). Once common in engineering applications in the US, the Rankine scale is now rarely used.

**Celsius:** interval is divided into 100 degrees; 0° is at the freezing point of water.

**Kelvin:** interval is the same as the Celsius degree; 0 K is at absolute zero (the theoretical point at which a thermodynamic system has the lowest energy, −273.15 °C).

**Réaumur:** interval is divided into 80 degrees; 0° is at the freezing point of water. One of the earliest (1730) temperature scales in widespread use, the Réaumur scale had been supplanted by other scales by the late 19th century.

*temperature conversion instructions:***
| °Fahrenheit | into | °Celsius | subtract 32, divide by 1.8** |
| °Celsius | into | °Fahrenheit | multiply by 1.8, add 32** |
| °Celsius | into | kelvin | add 273.15 |

*Because a kelvin is itself a unit of measurement, it is incorrect to use "degree" or the ° symbol with it, as is necessary with the units of the Rankine, Fahrenheit, Celsius, and Réaumur scales. One kelvin is equal to one degree Celsius.
**Instructions are for finding equivalent temperatures; to find the equivalent number of degrees in a temperature range (e.g., tomorrow's temperature will be 11.0 °F, or 6.1 °C, warmer than today's temperature), omit the step of adding or subtracting 32.

## Melting and Boiling Points of Selected Substances

Values are in °C at a pressure of 1 atmosphere (atm.; 101.325 kPa), except when a substance has a triple-point pressure greater than 1 atm.; in those cases the triple-point temperature and sublimation temperature are given and noted accordingly (see footnotes 1 and 2); figures are given only for those temperatures for which measurements or reliable estimates are available.

| SUBSTANCE | MELTING POINT (°C) | BOILING POINT (°C) | SUBSTANCE | MELTING POINT (°C) | BOILING POINT (°C) |
|---|---|---|---|---|---|
| **common compounds** | | | **selected elements (continued)** | | |
| ammonia ($H_3N$) | −77.74 | −33.34 | iodine (I) | 113.7 | 184.4 |
| carbon dioxide ($CO_2$) | −56.57[1] | −78.5[2] | iron (Fe) | 1,538 | 2,861 |
| ethyl alcohol ($C_2H_5OH$) | −114.1 | 78.5 | lead (Pb) | 327.46 | 1,749 |
| heavy water ($D_2O$) | 3.82 | 101.42 | lithium (Li) | 180.5 | 1,342 |
| hydrogen chloride (HCl) | −114 | −85 | magnesium (Mg) | 650 | 1,090 |
| hydrogen peroxide ($H_2O_2$) | −0.43 | 150.2 | manganese (Mn) | 1,246 | 2,061 |
| methane ($CH_4$) | −182.5 | −162 | mercury (Hg) | −38.83 | 356.73 |
| ozone ($O_3$) | −251.4 | −112 | molybdenum (Mo) | 2,623 | 4,639 |
| propane ($C_3H_8$) | −187.6 | −42.1 | neon (Ne) | −248.59 | −246.08 |
| sulfuric acid ($H_2SO_4$) | 10.37 | 338 | nickel (Ni) | 1,455 | 2,913 |
| water ($H_2O$) | 0.00 | 100.00 | nitrogen (N) | −210 | −195.79 |
| | | | oxygen (O) | −218.79 | −182.95 |
| **selected elements** | | | phosphorus (P) | 44.15 | 280.5 |
| aluminum (Al) | 660.32 | 2,519 | platinum (Pt) | 1,768.4 | 3,825 |
| argon (Ar) | −189.35 | −185.85 | plutonium (Pu) | 640 | 3,228 |
| arsenic (As) | 817[1] | 614[2] | potassium (K) | 63.38 | 759 |
| bromine (Br) | −7.2 | 58.8 | radon (Rn) | −71 | −61.7 |
| cadmium (Cd) | 321.07 | 767 | silicon (Si) | 1,414 | 3,265 |
| calcium (Ca) | 842 | 1,484 | silver (Ag) | 691.78 | 2,162 |
| carbon (C) | 4,492[1] | 3,642[2] | sodium (Na) | 97.80 | 883 |
| chlorine (Cl) | −101.5 | −34.04 | sulfur (S) | 115.21 | 444.6 |
| cobalt (Co) | 1,495 | 2,927 | tin (Sn) | 231.93 | 2,602 |
| copper (Cu) | 1,084.62 | 2,562 | titanium (Ti) | 1,668 | 3,287 |
| fluorine (F) | −219.62 | −188.12 | uranium (U) | 1,135 | 4,131 |
| gold (Au) | 1,064.18 | 2,856 | xenon (Xe) | −111.75 | −108.04 |
| helium (He) | | −268.93 | zinc (Zn) | 419.53 | 907 |
| hydrogen (H) | −259.34 | −252.87 | | | |

[1]Triple-point temperature (equilibrium between the solid, liquid, and gaseous phases).    [2]Sublimation temperature at 1 atm. (substance passes directly from solid to gaseous phase at a pressure of 1 atm.).

## Selected Physical Properties of Water

| | | | |
|---|---|---|---|
| molar mass | 18.0151 g/mol | heat of vaporization (100 °C) | 0.65 kJ/mol |
| melting point | 0.00 °C | heat of formation (25 °C) | −285.85 kJ/mol |
| boiling point | 100.00 °C | entropy of vaporization (25 °C) | 118.8 J/°C mol |
| vapor pressure (25 °C) | 23.75 torr | surface tension (25 °C) | 71.97 dynes/cm |
| heat of fusion (0 °C) | 6.010 kJ/mol | viscosity | 0.8903 centipoise |

**density**

freshwater

| | |
|---|---|
| ice | 0.92 g/cm³ |
| 0 °C | 0.99987 g/cm³ |
| 3.98 °C | 1.0000 g/cm³ (maximum density) |
| 20 °C | 0.99823 g/cm³ |
| 25 °C | 0.99701 g/cm³ |
| 100 °C | 0.95841 g/cm³ |

seawater (salinity 35 parts/thousand, at 0 °C)

| DEPTH (M) | PRESSURE (DECIBARS) | DENSITY (G/CM³) |
|---|---|---|
| 0 | 0 | 1.02813 |
| 1,000 | 1,000 | 1.03285 |
| 2,000 | 2,000 | 1.03747 |
| 4,000 | 4,000 | 1.04640 |
| 6,000 | 6,000 | 1.05495 |
| 8,000 | 8,000 | 1.06315 |
| 10,000 | 10,000 | 1.07104 |

# Playing Cards and Dice Chances

## Blackjack

Number of two-card combinations in a 52-card deck (where aces equal 11 and face cards equal 10) for each number between 13 and 21

Approximate chances of various hands reaching or exceeding 21

| TOTAL WITH TWO CARDS | POSSIBLE COMBINATIONS FROM 52 CARDS |
|---|---|
| 21 | 64 |
| 20 | 136 |
| 19 | 80 |
| 18 | 86 |
| 17 | 96 |
| 16 | 86 |
| 15 | 96 |
| 14 | 102 |
| 13 | 118 |

| TOTAL IN HAND BEFORE DEAL (TWO OR MORE CARDS) | CHANCE OF REACHING A COUNT OF 17 TO 21 (%) | CHANCE OF EXCEEDING 21 |  |
|---|---|---|---|
| | | ONE CARD (%) | ANY NUMBER OF CARDS (%) |
| 16 | 38 | 62 | 62 |
| 15 | 42 | 54 | 58 |
| 14 | 44 | 46 | 56 |
| 13 | 48 | 38 | 52 |

## Poker

Number of ways to reach and odds of reaching various five-card combinations on a single deal (52-card deck, no wild cards)

| HAND | NUMBER OF COMBINATIONS | ODDS OF RECEIVING ON A SINGLE DEAL |
|---|---|---|
| royal flush | 4 | 1 in 649,740 |
| straight flush | 36 | 1 in 72,193 |
| four of a kind | 624 | 1 in 4,165 |
| full house | 3,744 | 1 in 694 |
| flush | 5,108 | 1 in 509 |
| straight | 10,200 | 1 in 255 |
| three of a kind | 54,912 | 1 in 47 |
| two pairs | 123,552 | 1 in 21 |
| one pair | 1,098,240 | 1 in 2 |

## Dice

Probabilities of two-die totals

| TWO-DIE TOTAL | NUMBER OF COMBINATIONS | PROBABILITY (%) | TWO-DIE TOTAL | NUMBER OF COMBINATIONS | PROBABILITY (%) |
|---|---|---|---|---|---|
| 2 | 1 | 2.78 | 8 | 5 | 13.89 |
| 3 | 2 | 5.56 | 9 | 4 | 11.11 |
| 4 | 3 | 8.33 | 10 | 3 | 8.33 |
| 5 | 4 | 11.11 | 11 | 2 | 5.56 |
| 6 | 5 | 13.89 | 12 | 1 | 2.78 |
| 7 | 6 | 16.67 | total | 36 | 100[1] |

[1] Detail does not add to total because of rounding.

# Spirits Measure

*From smallest to largest. Many specific volumes have varied over time and from place to place, but the proportional relationships within the various families of measures have generally remained the same.*

| MEASURE | CONVENTIONAL EQUIVALENTS* | METRIC EQUIVALENT† |
|---|---|---|
| pony | 0.75 oz = ¾ shot= ½ jigger | 22.17 ml |
| shot/ounce/finger | 1 oz = 1⅓ ponies = ⅔ jigger | 29.57 ml |
| jigger | 1.5 oz = 2 ponies = 1½ shots | 44.36 ml |
| double | 2 oz = 2 shots | 59.15 ml |
| triple | 3 oz = 3 shots | 88.72 ml |
| noggin/imperial gill/drink (whiskey) | 4.8 oz | 142.1 ml |
| pint | 16 oz = ⅝ fifth = ½ quart | 473.2 ml |
| quarter yard | 20 oz = 1¼ pints | 591.5 ml |
| bottle (champagne or other wine) | about 25.5 oz or ⅙ imperial gallon | about 750 ml† |
| fifth | 25.6 oz = ⅘ quart = ⅕ gallon | 757.1 ml |
| quart | 32 oz = ½ magnum = ¼ gallon | 946.3 ml |
| half yard | 40 oz = 2½ pints | 1.182 l |
| magnum | 2 bottles (champagne or other wine) | 1.5 l |
| magnum | 64 oz = 2 quarts = ½ gallon | 1.893 l |
| yard | 80 oz = 5 pints | 2.365 l |
| jeroboam | 4 bottles (champagne or other wine) | 3 l |

## Spirits Measure (continued)

| MEASURE | CONVENTIONAL EQUIVALENTS* | METRIC EQUIVALENT† |
|---|---|---|
| gallon/double magnum | 128 oz = 4 quarts = 5 fifths = 2 magnums | 3.785 l |
| rehoboam | 6 bottles (champagne or other wine) | 4 l |
| imperial gallon | 1.20 gallons = ⅖ barn gallon = ¹⁄₁₀ anker | 4.546 l |
| ale/beer gallon | 1.22 gallons | 4.620 l |
| methuselah | 8 bottles (champagne or other wine) | 6 l |
| salmanazar | 12 bottles (champagne or other wine) | 9 l |
| barn gallon | 2½ imperial gallons = ¼ anker | 11.37 l |
| balthazar | 16 bottles (champagne or other wine) | 12 l |
| half keg | 5 gallons (type varies) | varies |
| nebuchadnezzar | 20 bottles (champagne or other wine) | 15 l |
| firkin | 9 gallons | 34.07 l |
| keg | 10 gallons (type varies) | varies |
| anker | 60 bottles = 10 imperial gallons = 4 barn gallons | 45.46 l |
| runlet/rundlet/rudlet | 144 pints = 72 quarts = 18 gallons = 2 firkins | 68.14 l |
| octave | 15.75 imperial gallons = ⅛ butt (wine) | 71.60 l |
| British bottle | 126 bottles = 21 imperial gallons | 95.47 l |
| aum | 120 quarts = 30 gallons | 113.6 l |
| barrel (wine) | 126 quarts = 31½ gallons = ¾ tierce | 119.2 l |
| barrel (ale/beer) | 144 quarts = 36 gallons = ½ puncheon (ale/beer) | 136.3 l |
| tierce | 168 quarts = 42 gallons = ½ puncheon (wine) | 159.0 l |
| British hogshead (ale/beer) | 54 imperial gallons = ½ butt (ale/beer) = ¼ tun (ale/beer) | 245.5 l |
| puncheon (ale/beer) | 72 gallons = 2 barrels (ale/beer) | 272.5 l |
| British hogshead (wine) | 63 imperial gallons = ½ butt (wine) = ¼ tun (wine) | 286.4 l |
| puncheon (wine) | 84 gallons = 2 tierces | 318.0 l |
| butt/pipe (ale/beer) | 108 imperial gallons = ½ tun (ale/beer) | 491.0 l |
| butt/pipe (wine) | 126 imperial gallons = ½ tun (wine) | 572.8 l |
| tun (ale/beer) | 216 imperial gallons = 4 British hogsheads (ale/beer) = 2 butts (ale/beer) | 982.0 l |
| tun (wine) | 252 imperial gallons = 12 British bottles = 2 butts (wine) | 1,146 l |

*All ounce measures are in US fluid ounces.   †Wine bottle sizes have varied from 700 to 800 ml in various countries; industry standard is 750 ml.

## Cooking Measurements

| MEASURE | CONVENTIONAL EQUIVALENTS* | METRIC EQUIVALENT |
|---|---|---|
| drop | ¹⁄₆₀ teaspoon | 0.08 ml |
| dash | ⅛ teaspoon | 0.62 ml |
| teaspoon | 8 dashes; ⅓ tablespoon; ⅙ fluid ounce | 4.93 ml |
| tablespoon | 3 teaspoons; ½ fluid ounce | 14.79 ml |
| ounce (weight) | ¹⁄₁₆ pound | 28.35 g |
| fluid ounce (volume) | 2 tablespoons | 29.57 ml |
| cup | 8 fluid ounces; 16 tablespoons; ½ pint | 236.59 ml |
| pound | 16 ounces | 453.6 g |
| pint | 16 fluid ounces; 2 cups; ½ quart | 473.18 ml |
| quart | 32 fluid ounces; 4 cups; 2 pints; ¼ gallon | 946.36 ml |
| gallon | 128 fluid ounces; 16 cups; 8 pints; 4 quarts | 3.785 l |
| peck | 2 gallons | 7.57 l |
| bushel | 8 gallons; 4 pecks | 30.28 l |

*All ounce measurements are in US ounces or fluid ounces.

### OVEN TEMPERATURE EQUIVALENTS

| °F | °C | AMERICAN OVEN TEMPERATURE TERMS | FRENCH OVEN TEMPERATURE TERMS AND THERMOSTAT SETTINGS | BRITISH "GAS MARK" OVEN THERMOSTAT SETTINGS |
|---|---|---|---|---|
| 160 | 71 | | #1 | |
| 170 | 77 | | | |
| 200 | 93 | | très doux; étuve | |
| 212 | 100 | | | |
| 221 | 105 | | #2 | |
| 225 | 107 | very slow | doux | |
| 230 | 110 | | #3 | #¼ (241 °F) |
| 250 | 121 | | | |

# Cooking Measurements (continued)

## OVEN TEMPERATURE EQUIVALENTS (CONTINUED)

| °F | °C | AMERICAN OVEN TEMPERATURE TERMS | FRENCH OVEN TEMPERATURE TERMS AND THERMOSTAT SETTINGS | BRITISH "GAS MARK" OVEN THERMOSTAT SETTINGS |
|---|---|---|---|---|
| 275 | 135 | | | #½ (266 °F) |
| 284 | 140 | slow | moyen; modéré | #1 (291 °F) |
| 300 | 149 | | | |
| 302 | 150 | | #4 | |
| 320 | 160 | | | #2 (313 °F) |
| 325 | 163 | | | |
| 350 | 177 | moderate | assez chaud; bon four | #3 (336 °F) |
| 356 | 180 | | | #4 (358 °F) |
| 375 | 190 | | #5 | |
| 390 | 200 | | | #5 (379 °F) |
| 400 | 205 | | | #6 (403 °F) |
| 410 | 210 | hot | chaud | |
| 425 | 218 | | #6 | #7 (424 °F) |
| 428 | 220 | | | |
| 437 | 225 | | | |
| 450 | 232 | | | #8 (446 °F) |
| 475 | 246 | very hot | très chaud; vif | #9 (469 °F) |
| 500 | 260 | | #7 | |
| 525 | 274 | | #8 | |
| 550 | 288 | | #9 | |

# Large Numbers

The American system of numeration for denominations above one million was modeled on the French system, but more recently the French system has been changed to correspond to the German and British systems. In the American system each of the denominations above 1,000 millions (the American *billion*) is 1,000 times the preceding one (one trillion = 1,000 billions; one quadrillion = 1,000 trillions). In the British system the first denomination above 1,000 millions (the British *milliard*) is 1,000 times the preceding one, but each of the denominations above 1,000 milliards (the British *billion*) is 1,000,000 times the preceding one (one trillion = 1,000,000 billions; one quadrillion = 1,000,000 trillions).

Source: *Merriam-Webster's Collegiate Dictionary*, Tenth Edition, Merriam-Webster, Inc., 1993.

| AMERICAN NAME | VALUE IN POWERS OF TEN | NUMBER OF ZEROS | BRITISH NAME | VALUE IN POWERS OF TEN | NUMBER OF ZEROS |
|---|---|---|---|---|---|
| billion | $10^9$ | 9 | milliard | $10^9$ | 9 |
| trillion | $10^{12}$ | 12 | billion | $10^{12}$ | 12 |
| quadrillion | $10^{15}$ | 15 | trillion | $10^{18}$ | 18 |
| quintillion | $10^{18}$ | 18 | quadrillion | $10^{24}$ | 24 |
| sextillion | $10^{21}$ | 21 | quintillion | $10^{30}$ | 30 |
| septillion | $10^{24}$ | 24 | sextillion | $10^{36}$ | 36 |
| octillion | $10^{27}$ | 27 | septillion | $10^{42}$ | 42 |
| nonillion | $10^{30}$ | 30 | octillion | $10^{48}$ | 48 |
| decillion | $10^{33}$ | 33 | nonillion | $10^{54}$ | 54 |
| undecillion | $10^{36}$ | 36 | decillion | $10^{60}$ | 60 |
| duodecillion | $10^{39}$ | 39 | undecillion | $10^{66}$ | 66 |
| tredecillion | $10^{42}$ | 42 | duodecillion | $10^{72}$ | 72 |
| quattuordecillion | $10^{45}$ | 45 | tredecillion | $10^{78}$ | 78 |
| quindecillion | $10^{48}$ | 48 | quattuordecillion | $10^{84}$ | 84 |
| sexdecillion | $10^{51}$ | 51 | quindecillion | $10^{90}$ | 90 |
| septendecillion | $10^{54}$ | 54 | sexdecillion | $10^{96}$ | 96 |
| octodecillion | $10^{57}$ | 57 | septendecillion | $10^{102}$ | 102 |
| novemdecillion | $10^{60}$ | 60 | octodecillion | $10^{108}$ | 108 |
| vigintillion | $10^{63}$ | 63 | novemdecillion | $10^{114}$ | 114 |
| centillion | $10^{303}$ | 303 | vigintillion | $10^{120}$ | 120 |
| | | | centillion | $10^{600}$ | 600 |

# Roman Numerals

Seven numeral-characters compose the Roman numeral system. When a numeral appears with a line above it, it represents the base value multiplied by 1,000. However, because Roman numerals are now seldom utilized for values beyond 4,999, this convention is no longer in use.

## Roman Numerals (continued)

| ARABIC | ROMAN | ARABIC | ROMAN | ARABIC | ROMAN | ARABIC | ROMAN |
|---|---|---|---|---|---|---|---|
| 1 | I | 15 | XV | 70 | LXX | 1,000 | M |
| 2 | II | 16 | XVI | 80 | LXXX | 1,001 | MI |
| 3 | III | 17 | XVII | 90 | XC | 1,002 | MII |
| 4 | IV | 18 | XVIII | 100 | C | 1,003 | MIII |
| 5 | V | 19 | XIX | 101 | CI | 1,900 | MCM |
| 6 | VI | 20 | XX | 102 | CII | 2,000 | MM |
| 7 | VII | 21 | XXI | 200 | CC | 2,001 | MMI |
| 8 | VIII | 22 | XXII | 300 | CCC | 2,002 | MMII |
| 9 | IX | 23 | XXIII | 400 | CD | 2,100 | MMC |
| 10 | X | 24 | XXIV | 500 | D | 3,000 | MMM |
| 11 | XI | 30 | XXX | 600 | DC | 4,000 | $\overline{\text{MMMM or MV}}$ |
| 12 | XII | 40 | XL | 700 | DCC | 5,000 | $\overline{V}$ |
| 13 | XIII | 50 | L | 800 | DCCC | | |
| 14 | XIV | 60 | LX | 900 | CM | | |

## Ancient Measures

*The standard unit of measure is listed first, with a rough modern equivalent in parentheses. Often, standard units varied over time, so a range is sometimes given. The subdivisions below relate to the standard unit of measure given first.*

| CULTURE | LENGTH | WEIGHT | LIQUID |
|---|---|---|---|
| Egyptian | cubit (524 mm; 20.62 in) | kite (4.5–29.9 g; 0.16–1.05 oz) | cubic cubit (0.14 cubic m; 37 gal)[1] |
| | digit (1/28 of a cubit) | deben (10 kites) | khar |
| | palm (4 digits) | sep (10 debens) | hekat |
| | hand (5 digits) | | hin |
| | small span (12 digits, or 3 palms) | | ro |
| | large span (14 digits, or 1/2 cubit) | | |
| | t'ser (16 digits, or 4 palms) | | |
| | small cubit (24 digits, or 6 palms) | | |
| Babylonian | kus[2] (530 mm; 20.9 in) | mina (640–978 g; 23–34 oz) | ka (99–102 cubic mm; 3.9–4.0 cubic in) |
| | foot (2/3 kus) | shekel | gur (300 ka) |
| | shusi (1/30 kus) | | |
| Hebrew[3] | | sacred mina (60 shekels) | bat[4] |
| | | sacred talent (3,000 shekels, or 50 sacred minas) | hin |
| | | Talmudic mina (25 shekels) | log |
| | | Talmudic talent (1,500 shekels, or 60 Talmudic minas) | |
| Greek | finger (19.3 mm; 0.76 in) | talent (25.8 kg; 56.9 lb) | metretes (39.4 l; 10.4 gal) |
| | foot (16 fingers) | | |
| | Olympic cubit (24 fingers) | | |
| Roman | foot (subdivided into the uncia [plural unciae; 1/12 ft]) | libra (327.45 g; 11.55 oz) | sextarius (0.53 l; 0.14 gal) |
| | pace, or double step (5 ft) | uncia (1/12 lb) | amphora (48 sextarii) |
| | mille passus (1,000 paces) | | |
| Chinese[5] | chih (25 cm; 9.8 in) | shih, or tan (60 kg; 132 lb) | |
| | chang (3 m; 9.8 ft) | | |

[1]Measures given below the cubic cubit run from small to large.    [2]Also called the Babylonian cubit.    [3]The Hittites, Assyrians, Phoenicians, and Hebrews derived their systems from the Babylonians and Egyptians. Hebrew standards were based on the relationship between the mina, the talent (the basic unit), and the shekel.    [4]Volumes are not definitely known but are listed from largest to smallest.    [5]The Chinese system of measurement exhibited all the principal characteristics of the Western. It was, however, fundamentally chaotic in that there was no relationship between different types of units, such as those of length and those of volume. It also fluctuated from region to region and according to use. The first emperor of China, Shi Huangdi (221–210/09 BC), fixed the basic units given here.

## Prime Numbers

A prime number is a positive integer greater than 1 that is divisible only by itself and 1. Every positive integer greater than 1 can be expressed as the product of only a single set of prime numbers. Primes have been recognized since at least 300 BC, when they were studied by the Greek mathematicians Euclid and Eratosthenes. They have always fascinated mathematicians, and even today there remain certain open questions regarding them. The first 100 prime numbers are: 2, 3, 5, 7, 11, 13,

17, 19, 23, 29, 31, 37, 41, 43, 47, 53, 59, 61, 67, 71, 73, 79, 83, 89, 97, 101, 103, 107, 109, 113, 127, 131, 137, 139, 149, 151, 157, 163, 167, 173, 179, 181, 191, 193, 197, 199, 211, 223, 227, 229, 233, 239, 241, 251, 257, 263, 269, 271, 277, 281, 283, 293, 307, 311, 313, 317, 331, 337, 347, 349, 353, 359, 367, 373, 379, 383, 389, 397, 401, 409, 419, 421, 431, 433, 439, 443, 449, 457, 461, 463, 467, 479, 487, 491, 499, 503, 509, 521, 523, and 541.
For more numbers, see <www.utm.edu/research/primes>

## Decimal Equivalents of Common Fractions

| 4THS | 8THS | 16THS | 32NDS | DECIMAL | | 3RDS | 6THS | 12THS | DECIMAL |
|---|---|---|---|---|---|---|---|---|---|
| | | | | 0.015625 | | | | 1 | 0.833334 |
| | | | 1 | 0.03125 | | | 1 | 2 | 0.166667 |
| | | 1 | 2 | 0.0625 | | | | 3 | 0.25 |
| | | | 3 | 0.09375 | | 1 | 2 | 4 | 0.333334 |
| | 1 | 2 | 4 | 0.125 | | | | 5 | 0.416667 |
| | | | 5 | 0.15625 | | | 3 | 6 | 0.5 |
| | | 3 | 6 | 0.1875 | | | | 7 | 0.583333 |
| | | | 7 | 0.21875 | | 2 | 4 | 8 | 0.666667 |
| 1 | 2 | 4 | 8 | 0.25 | | | | 9 | 0.75 |
| | | | 9 | 0.28125 | | | 5 | 10 | 0.833333 |
| | | 5 | 10 | 0.3125 | | | | 11 | 0.916667 |
| | | | 11 | 0.34375 | | | 6 | 12 | 1 |
| | 3 | 6 | 12 | 0.375 | | | | | |
| | | | 13 | 0.40625 | | | | | |
| | | 7 | 14 | 0.4375 | | | | 5THS | DECIMAL |
| | | | 15 | 0.46875 | | | | 1 | 0.2 |
| 2 | 4 | 8 | 16 | 0.5 | | | | 2 | 0.4 |
| | | | 17 | 0.53125 | | | | 3 | 0.6 |
| | | 9 | 18 | 0.5625 | | | | 4 | 0.8 |
| | | | 19 | 0.59375 | | | | 5 | 1 |
| | 5 | 10 | 20 | 0.625 | | | | | |
| | | | 21 | 0.65625 | | | | | |
| | | 11 | 22 | 0.6875 | | | | 7THS | DECIMAL |
| | | | 23 | 0.71875 | | | | 1 | 0.142857 |
| 3 | 6 | 12 | 24 | 0.75 | | | | 2 | 0.285714 |
| | | | 25 | 0.78125 | | | | 3 | 0.428571 |
| | | 13 | 26 | 0.8125 | | | | 4 | 0.571428 |
| | | | 27 | 0.84375 | | | | 5 | 0.714285 |
| | 7 | 14 | 28 | 0.875 | | | | 6 | 0.857142 |
| | | | 29 | 0.90625 | | | | 7 | 1 |
| | | 15 | 30 | 0.9375 | | | | | |
| | | | 31 | 0.96875 | | | | | |
| 4 | 8 | 16 | 32 | 1 | | | | | |

## Mathematical Formulas

*The ratio of the circumference of a circle to its diameter is π (3.14159265358979323846264338327..., generally rounded to 22/7 or 3.1416). It occurs in various mathematical problems involving the lengths of arcs or other curves, the areas of surfaces, and the volumes of many solids.*

| | ACTION | FORMULA |
|---|---|---|
| **circumference** | | |
| circle | multiply diameter by π | $\pi d$ |
| | | |
| **area** | | |
| circle | multiply radius squared by π | $\pi r^2$ |
| rectangle | multiply height by length | hl |
| sphere surface | multiply radius squared by π by 4 | $4\pi r^2$ |
| square | length of one side squared | $s^2$ |
| trapezoid | parallel side length A + parallel side length B multiplied by height and divided by 2 | (A+B)h/2 |
| triangle | multiply base by height and divide by 2 | hb/2 |
| | | |
| **volume** | | |
| cone | multiply base radius squared by π by height and divide by 3 | $br^2\pi h/3$ |
| cube | length of one edge cubed | a3 |
| cylinder | multiply base radius squared by π by height | $br^2\pi h$ |
| pyramid | multiply base area by height and divide by 3 | hb/3 |
| sphere | multiply radius cubed by π by 4 and divide by 3 | $4\pi r^3/3$ |

# Encyclopædia Britannica's Great Inventions

| INVENTION | YEAR | INVENTOR | COUNTRY |
|---|---|---|---|
| aerosol can | 1926 | Erik Rotheim | Norway |
| air conditioning | 1902 | Willis Haviland Carrier | US |
| airbag, automotive | 1952 | John Hetrick | US |
| airplane, engine-powered | 1903 | Wilbur & Orville Wright | US |
| airship | 1852 | Henri Giffard | France |
| alphabet | c. 1700–1500 BC | Semitic-speaking peoples | eastern coast of Mediterranean Sea |
| American Sign Language | 1817 | Thomas H. Gallaudet | US |
| animation, motion-picture | 1906 | J. Stuart Blackton | US |
| answering machine, telephone | 1898 | Valdemar Poulsen | Denmark |
| aspartame | 1965 | James Schlatter | US |
| aspirin | 1897 | Felix Hoffmann (Bayer) | Germany |
| assembly line | 1913 | Henry Ford | US |
| astrolabe | c. 2nd century | — | — |
| AstroTurf | 1965 | James M. Faria, Robert T. Wright | US |
| audiotape | 1928 | Fritz Pfleumer | Germany |
| automated teller machine (ATM) | 1968 | Don Wetzel | US |
| automobile | 1889 | Gottlieb Daimler | Germany |
| baby food, prepared | 1927 | Dorothy Gerber | US |
| bag, flat-bottomed paper | 1870 | Margaret Knight | US |
| Bakelite | 1907 | Leo Hendrik Baekeland | US |
| ball bearing | 1794 | Philip Vaughan | England |
| balloon, hot-air | 1783 | Joseph & Étienne Montgolfier | France |
| bandage, adhesive | 1921 | Earle Dickson | US |
| bar code | 1952 | Joseph Woodland | US |
| barbed wire | 1874 | Joseph Glidden | US |
| barometer | 1643 | Evangelista Torricelli | Italy |
| battery, electric storage | 1800 | Alessandro Volta | Italy |
| beer | before 6000 BC | Sumerians, Babylonians | Mesopotamia |
| bicycle | 1818 | Baron Karl de Drais de Sauerbrun | Germany |
| bifocal lens | 1784 | Benjamin Franklin | US |
| bikini | 1946 | Louis Réard | France |
| blood bank | late 1930s | Charles Richard Drew | US |
| blow-dryer | 1920 | Racine Universal Motor Co., Hamilton Beach Manufacturing Co. | US |
| bomb, atomic | 1945 | J. Robert Oppenheimer et al. | US |
| bomb, thermonuclear (hydrogen) | 1952 | Edward Teller et al. | US |
| boomerang | c. 15,000 years ago | Aboriginal peoples | Australia |
| Braille system | 1824 | Louis Braille | France |
| brassiere (bra) | 1913 | Mary Phelps Jacob | US |
| bread, sliced (bread-slicing machine) | 1928 | Otto Frederick Rohwedder | US |
| button | c. 700 BC | Greeks, Etruscans | Greece, Italy |
| buttonhole | 13th century | — | Europe |
| calculator, electronic hand-held | 1967 | Jack S. Kilby | US |
| calculus | 1680s | Sir Isaac Newton and Gottfried Wilhelm Leibniz (invented separately) | England and Germany (respectively) |
| calendar, modern (Gregorian) | 1582 | Pope Gregory XIII | Italy |
| camcorder | 1982 | Sony Corp. | Japan |
| camera, motion picture | 1891 | Thomas Alva Edison, William K.L. Dickson | US |
| camera, portable photographic | 1888 | George Eastman | US |
| can, metal beverage | 1933 | American Can Co. | US |
| can opener | 1858 | Ezra J. Warner | US |
| candle | c. 3000 BC | — | Egypt, Crete |
| canning, food | 1809 | Nicolas Appert | France |
| carbon-14 dating | 1946 | Willard F. Libby | US |
| cardboard, corrugated | 1871 | Albert Jones | US |
| cards, playing | c. 10th century | — | China |
| cash register | 1879 | James Ritty | US |
| cat litter | 1947 | Edward Lowe | US |
| catalog, mail-order | 1872 | Aaron Montgomery Ward | US |

## Encyclopædia Britannica's Great Inventions (continued)

| INVENTION | YEAR | INVENTOR | COUNTRY |
|---|---|---|---|
| cellophane | 1911 | Jacques E. Brandenberger | Switzerland |
| celluloid | 1869 | John Wesley Hyatt | US |
| cement, portland | 1824 | Joseph Aspdin | England |
| cereal flakes, breakfast | 1894 | John Harvey Kellogg | US |
| chewing gum (modern) | c. 1870 | Thomas Adams | US |
| chocolate | c. 3rd–10th century | Maya, Aztec | Central America, Mexico |
| chronometer | 1762 | John Harrison | England |
| clock, pendulum | 1656 | Christiaan Huygens | The Netherlands |
| clock, quartz | 1927 | Warren A. Marrison | Canada/US |
| cloning, animal | 1970 | John B. Gurdon | UK |
| coffee, drip | 1908 | Melitta Bentz | Germany |
| coffee, decaffeinated | 1905 | Ludwig Roselius | Germany |
| coins | c. 650 BC | Lydians | Turkey |
| compact disc (CD) | 1980 | Philips Electronics, Sony Corp. | The Netherlands, Japan |
| compass, magnetic | c. 12th century | — | China, Europe |
| computed tomography (CT scan, CAT scan) | 1972 | Godfrey Hounsfield, Allan Cormack | UK, US |
| computer, electronic digital | 1939 | John V. Atanasoff, Clifford E. Berry | US |
| computer, laptop | 1983 | Radio Shack Corp. | US |
| computer, personal | 1974 | MITS (Micro Instrumentation Telemetry Systems) | US |
| concrete, reinforced | 1867 | Joseph Monier | France |
| condom, latex | c. 1930 | — | — |
| contact lenses | 1887 | Adolf Fick | Germany |
| contraceptives, oral | early 1950s | Gregory Pincus, John Rock, Min Chueh Chang | US |
| corn, hybrid | 1917 | Donald F. Jones | US |
| correction fluid, white | 1951 | Bette Nesmith | US |
| cotton gin | 1793 | Eli Whitney | US |
| coupon, grocery | 1894 | Asa Candler | US |
| crayons, children's wax | 1903 | Edwin Binney, C. Harold Smith | US |
| cream separator (dairy processing) | 1878 | Carl Gustaf Patrik de Laval | Sweden |
| credit card | 1950 | Frank McNamara, Ralph Schneider (Diners' Club) | US |
| crossword puzzles | 1913 | Arthur Wynne | US |
| DDT | 1874 | Othmar Zeidler | Germany |
| defibrillator | 1952 | Paul M. Zoll | US |
| dentures | c. 700 BC | Etruscans | Italy |
| detector, metal | late 1920s | Gerhard Fisher | Germany/US |
| detector, home smoke | 1969 | Randolph Smith, Kenneth House | US |
| diamond, artificial | 1955 | General Electric Co. | US |
| diapers, disposable | 1950 | Marion Donovan | US |
| digital videodisc (DVD) | 1995 | consortium of international electronics companies | Japan, US, The Netherlands |
| dishwasher | 1886 | Josephine Cochrane | US |
| DNA fingerprinting | 1984 | Alec Jeffreys | UK |
| doughnut, ring-shaped | 1847 | Hanson Crockett Gregory | US |
| door, revolving | 1888 | Theophilus von Kannel | US |
| drinking fountain | c. 1905–1912 | Luther Haws, Halsey W. Taylor (invented separately) | US |
| dry cleaning | 1855 | Jean Baptiste Jolly | France |
| dynamite | 1867 | Alfred Nobel | Sweden |
| elastic, fabric | c. 1830 | Thomas Hancock | UK |
| electric chair | 1888 | Harold P. Brown, Arthur E. Kennelly | US |
| electrocardiogram (ECG, EKG) | 1903 | Willem Einthoven | The Netherlands |
| electroencephalogram (EEG) | 1929 | Hans Berger | Germany |
| electronic mail (e-mail) | 1971 | Ray Tomlinson | US |
| elevator, passenger | 1852 | Elisha Graves Otis | US |

## Encyclopædia Britannica's Great Inventions (continued)

| INVENTION | YEAR | INVENTOR | COUNTRY |
|---|---|---|---|
| encyclopedia | c. 4th century BC or 77 AD | Speusippus (compliation of Plato's teachings) or Pliny the Elder (comprehensive work) | Greece or Rome |
| engine, internal-combustion | 1859 | Étienne Lenoir | France |
| engine, jet | 1930 | Sir Frank Whittle | UK |
| engine, liquid-fueled rocket | 1926 | Robert H. Goddard | US |
| engine, steam | 1698 | Thomas Savery | England |
| escalator | 1891 | Jesse W. Reno | US |
| eyeglasses | 1280s | Salvino degli Armati or Alessandro di Spina | Italy |
| facsimile (fax) | 1842 | Alexander Bain | Scotland |
| fiber optics | 1955 | Narinder S. Kapany | India |
| fiberglass | 1938 | Owens Corning (corp.) | US |
| film, photographic | 1884 | George Eastman | US |
| flashlight, battery-operated portable | 1899 | Conrad Hubert | Russia/US |
| flask, vacuum (Thermos) | 1892 | Sir James Dewar | Scotland |
| food processor | 1971 | Pierre Verdon | France |
| foods, freeze-dried | 1946 | Earl W. Flosdorf | US |
| foods, frozen | c. 1924 | Clarence Birdseye | US |
| Fresnel lens | 1820 | Augustin-Jean Fresnel | France |
| fuel cell | 1839 | William R. Grove | UK |
| genetic engineering | 1973 | Stanley N. Cohen, Herbert W. Boyer | US |
| Geiger counter | 1908 | Hans Geiger | Germany |
| glass | c. 2500 BC | Egyptians or Phoenicians | Egypt or Lebanon |
| glass, safety | 1909 | Édouard Bénédictus | France |
| greeting card, Christmas | 1843 | John Callcott Horsley | England |
| guillotine | 1792 | Joseph-Ignace Guillotin | France |
| guitar, electric | 1941 | Les Paul | US |
| gunpowder | c. 10th century | — | China or Arabia |
| hanger, wire coat | 1903 | Albert J. Parkhouse | US |
| helicopter | 1939 | Igor Sikorsky | Russia/US |
| holography | 1948 | Dennis Gabor | Hungary |
| hypodermic syringe | 1853 | Charles Gabriel Pravaz | France |
| in vitro fertilization (IVF), human | 1978 | Patrick Steptoe, Robert Edwards | UK |
| ink | c. 2500 BC | — | Egypt, China |
| insulin, extraction and preparation of | 1921 | Sir Frederick Grant Banting, Charles H. Best | Canada |
| integrated circuit | 1958 | Jack S. Kilby | US |
| Internet | 1969 | Advanced Research Projects Agency (ARPA) at the Dept. of Defense | US |
| iron, electric | 1882 | Henry W. Seely | US |
| irradiation, food | 1905 | — | US/UK |
| jeans | 1873 | Levi Strauss, Jacob Davis | US |
| JELL-O (gelatin dessert) | 1897 | Pearle B. Wait | US |
| jukebox | 1889 | Louis Glass | US |
| Kevlar | 1965 | Stephanie Kwolek | US |
| Kool-Aid (fruit drink mix) | 1927 | Edwin E. Perkins | US |
| laser | 1958 | Gordon Gould and Charles Hard Townes, Arthur L. Schawlow (invented separately) | US |
| laundromat | 1934 | J.F. Cantrell | US |
| lawn mower, gasoline-powered | c. 1940 | Leonard Goodall | US |
| Lego | late 1940s | Ole Kirk Christiansen | Denmark |
| light bulb, incandescent | 1879 | Thomas Alva Edison | US |
| light bulb, fluorescent | 1934 | Arthur Compton | US |
| light-emitting diode (LED) | 1962 | Nick Holonyak, Jr. | US |
| linoleum | 1860 | Frederick Walton | UK |
| lipstick, tube | 1915 | Maurice Levy | US |
| liquid crystal display (LCD) | 1963 | George Heilmeier | US |
| lock and key | c. 2000 BC | Assyrians | Mesopotamia |

# Encyclopædia Britannica's Great Inventions (continued)

| INVENTION | YEAR | INVENTOR | COUNTRY |
|---|---|---|---|
| locomotive | 1829 | George Stephenson | England |
| longbow | c. 1000 | — | Wales |
| loudspeaker | 1924 | Chester W. Rice, Edward W. Kellogg | US |
| magnetic resonance imaging (MRI) | early 1970s | Raymond Damadian, Paul Lauterbur | US |
| margarine | 1869 | Hippolyte Mège-Mouriès | France |
| matches, friction | 1827 | John Walker | England |
| metric system of measurement | 1795 | French Academy of Sciences | France |
| microphone | 1878 | David E. Hughes | UK/US |
| microscope, compound optical | c. 1600 | Hans & Zacharias Jansen | The Netherlands |
| microscope, electron | 1933 | Ernst Ruska | Germany |
| microwave oven | 1945 | Percy L. Spencer | US |
| miniature golf | c. 1930 | Garnet Carter | US |
| mirror, glass | c. 1200 | Venetians | Italy |
| missile, guided | 1942 | Wernher von Braun | Germany |
| mobile home | 1919 | Glenn H. Curtiss | US |
| money, paper | late 900s | — | China |
| Monopoly (board game) | 1934 | Charles B. Darrow | US |
| Morse code | 1838 | Samuel F.B. Morse | US |
| motor, electric | 1834 | Thomas Davenport | US |
| motor, outboard | 1907 | Ole Evinrude | Norway/US |
| motorcycle | 1885 | Gottlieb Daimler, Wilhelm Maybach | Germany |
| mouse, computer | 1963–64 | Douglas Engelbart | US |
| Muzak | 1922 | George Owen Squier | US |
| nail, construction | c. 3300 BC | Sumerians | Mesopotamia |
| necktie | 17th century | — | Croatia |
| neon lighting | 1910 | Georges Claude | France |
| nuclear reactor | 1942 | Enrico Fermi | US |
| nylon | 1937 | Wallace H. Carothers | US |
| oil lamp | 1784 | Aimé Argand | Switzerland |
| oil well | 1859 | Edwin Laurentine Drake | US |
| pacemaker, cardiac | 1952 | Paul M. Zoll | US |
| paper | c. 105 | Ts'ai Lun | China |
| paper clip | 1899 | Johan Vaaler | Norway |
| paper towel | 1931 | Arthur Scott | US |
| parachute, modern | 1797 | André-Jacques Garnerin | France |
| parking meter | 1932 | Carl C. Magee | US |
| particle accelerator | 1929 | Sir John Douglas Cockcroft, Ernest Thomas Sinton Walton | Ireland/UK |
| pasteurization | 1864 | Louis Pasteur | France |
| pen, ballpoint | 1938 | Lazlo Biro | Hungary |
| pencil | 1565 | Conrad Gesner | Switzerland |
| periodic table | 1871 | Dmitry Ivanovich Mendeleyev | Russia |
| personal watercraft, motorized | 1968 | Bombardier, Inc. | Canada |
| petroleum jelly | 1870s | Robert Chesebrough | US |
| phonograph | 1877 | Thomas Alva Edison | US |
| photocopying (xerography) | 1937 | Chester F. Carlson | US |
| photography | 1837 | Louis-Jacques-Mandé Daguerre | France |
| photography, instant | 1947 | Edwin Herbert Land | US |
| Play-Doh | 1956 | Noah W. & Joseph S. McVicker | US |
| plow, steel | 1836 | John Deere | US |
| pocket watch | c. 1500 | Peter Henlein | Germany |
| polyethylene | 1935 | Eric Fawcett, Reginald Gibson | UK |
| polygraph (lie detector) | 1921 | John A. Larson | US |
| polyvinyl chloride (PVC) | 1872 | Eugen Baumann | Germany |
| Post-it Notes | mid-1970s | Arthur Fry (3M) | US |
| potato chips | 1853 | George Crum | US |
| printing press, movable type | c. 1450 | Johannes Gutenberg | Germany |
| Prozac | 1972 | Ray W. Fuller, Bryan B. Molloy, David T. Wong | US |

## Encyclopædia Britannica's Great Inventions (continued)

| INVENTION | YEAR | INVENTOR | COUNTRY |
|---|---|---|---|
| radar | c. 1904 | Christian Hülsmeyer | Germany |
| radio | 1896 | Guglielmo Marconi | Italy |
| radio, car | early 1920s | William P. Lear | US |
| rayon | 1884 | Louis-Marie-Hilaire Bernigaud, count of Chardonnet | France |
| razor, electric | 1928 | Jacob Schick | US |
| razor, safety | c. 1900 | King Camp Gillette | US |
| reaper, mechanical | 1831 | Cyrus Hall McCormick | US |
| record, long-playing (LP) | 1948 | Peter Carl Goldmark | US |
| refrigerator | 1842 | John Gorrie | US |
| remote control, television | 1950 | Robert Adler | US |
| respirator | c. 1955 | Forrest M. Bird | US |
| revolver | 1835–36 | Samuel Colt | US |
| Richter scale | 1935 | Charles Francis Richter, Beno Gutenberg | US |
| rifle, assault | 1944 | Hugo Schmeisser | Germany |
| roller coaster | 1884 | LeMarcus A. Thompson | US |
| rubber, vulcanized | 1839 | Charles Goodyear | US |
| rubber band | 1845 | Stephen Perry | UK |
| saccharin | 1879 | Ira Remsen, Constantin Fahlberg | US, Germany |
| saddle | c. 200 BC | — | China |
| safety pin | 1849 | Walter Hunt | US |
| satellite, successful artificial earth | 1957 | Sergey Korolyov, et al. | USSR |
| satellite, communications | 1960 | John Robinson Pierce | US |
| saxophone | 1846 | Antoine-Joseph Sax | Belgium |
| Scotch tape | 1930 | Richard Drew (3M) | US |
| scuba gear | 1943 | Jacques Cousteau, Émile Gagnan | France |
| seat belt, automotive shoulder | 1959 | Nils Bohlin (Volvo) | Sweden |
| sewing machine | 1841 | Barthélemy Thimonnier | France |
| shoelaces | 1790 | — | England |
| silicone | 1904 | Frederic Stanley Kipping | UK |
| skateboard | 1958 | Bill & Mark Richards | US |
| skates, ice | 1000 BC | — | Scandinavia |
| skates, roller | 1760s | Joseph Merlin | Belgium |
| ski, snow | c. 2000–3000 BC | — | Sweden, Finland, Norway |
| skyscraper, steel-frame | 1884 | William Le Baron Jenney | US |
| slot machine | 1890s | Charles Fey | US |
| snowmobile | 1922 | Joseph-Armand Bombardier | Canada |
| soap | 600 BC | Phoenicians | Lebanon |
| soft drinks, carbonated | 1772 | Joseph Priestley | UK |
| sonar | 1915 | Paul Langevin | France |
| stamps, postage | 1840 | Sir Rowland Hill | UK |
| stapler | 1866 | George W. McGill | US |
| steamboat, successful | 1807 | Robert Fulton | US |
| steel, mass-production | 1856 | Henry Bessemer | UK |
| steel, stainless | 1914 | Harry Brearley | UK |
| stereo, personal | 1979 | Sony Corp. | Japan |
| stereophonic sound recording | 1931 | Alan Dower Blumlein | UK |
| stethoscope | 1819 | René-Théophile-Hyacinthe Laënnec | France |
| stock ticker | 1867 | Edward A. Calahan | US |
| stove, electric | 1896 | William Hadaway | US |
| stove, gas | 1826 | James Sharp | UK |
| straw, drinking | 1888 | Marvin Stone | US |
| submarine | 1620 | Cornelis Drebbel | The Netherlands |
| sunglasses | 1752 | James Ayscough | UK |
| sunscreen | 1944 | Benjamin Green | US |
| supermarket | 1930 | Michael Cullen | US |
| synthesizer, music | 1955 | Harry Olson, Herbert Belar | US |
| synthetic skin | 1981 | Ioannis V. Yannas, John F. Burke | US |
| tampon, cotton | 1931 | Earle Cleveland Haas | US |

## Encyclopædia Britannica's Great Inventions (continued)

| INVENTION | YEAR | INVENTOR | COUNTRY |
|---|---|---|---|
| tank, military | 1915 | Admiralty Landships Committee | UK |
| tea bag | early 1900s | Thomas Sullivan | US |
| teddy bear | 1902 | Morris Michtom | US |
| Teflon | 1938 | Roy Plunkett | US |
| telegraph | 1832–35 | Samuel F.B. Morse | US |
| telephone, wired-line | 1876 | Alexander Graham Bell | Scotland/US |
| telephone, mobile | 1946 | Bell Laboratories | US |
| telescope, optical | 1608 | Hans Lippershey | The Netherlands |
| television | 1923, 1927 | Vladimir Kosma Zworykin, Philo Taylor Farnsworth | Russia/US, US |
| thermometer | 1592 | Galileo | Italy |
| thermostat | 1830 | Andrew Ure | UK |
| threshing machine | 1778 | Andrew Meikle | Scotland |
| tire, pneumatic | 1888 | John Boyd Dunlop | UK |
| tissue, disposable facial | 1924 | Kimberly-Clark Co. | US |
| tissue, toilet | 1857 | Joseph Gayetty | US |
| toaster, electric | 1893 | Crompton Co. | UK |
| toilet, flush | c. 1591 | Sir John Harington | England |
| toothbrush | 1498 | — | China |
| tractor | 1892 | John Froehlich | US |
| traffic lights, automatic | 1923 | Garrett A. Morgan | US |
| transistor | 1947 | John Bardeen, Walter H. Brattain, William B. Shockley | US |
| typewriter | 1868 | Christopher Latham Sholes | US |
| ultrasound imaging, obstetric | 1958 | Ian Donald | UK |
| vaccination | 1796 | Edward Jenner | England |
| vacuum cleaner, electric | 1901 | Herbert Cecil Booth | UK |
| Velcro | 1948 | George de Mestral | Switzerland |
| vending machine | c. 100–200 BC | — | Egypt |
| Viagra | 1997 | Pfizer Inc. | US |
| video games | 1972 | Nolan Bushnell | US |
| videocassette recorder | 1969 | Sony Corp. | Japan |
| videotape | 1950s | Charles Ginsburg | US |
| virtual reality | 1983 | Jaron Lanier | US |
| vision correction, laser | 1987 | Stephen Trokel | US |
| washing machine, electric | 1907 | Alva J. Fisher | US |
| wheel | about 3500 BC | proto-Aryan people or Sumerians | Russia/Kazakhstan or Mesopotamia |
| wheelbarrow | 1st century BC | — | China |
| wheelchair | 1590s | — | Spain |
| windmill | 644 | — | Persia |
| wine | before 4000 BC | — | Middle East |
| World Wide Web | 1989 | Tim Berners-Lee | UK |
| wristwatch, digital | 1970 | John M. Bergey | US |
| X-ray imaging | 1895 | Wilhelm Conrad Röntgen | Germany |
| Zamboni (ice resurfacing machine) | 1949 | Frank J. Zamboni | US |
| zipper | 1893 | Whitcomb L. Judson | US |

# Applied Science

## Chemistry

Chemistry is the science that deals with the properties, composition, and structure of substances (defined as elements and compounds), the transformations that they undergo, and the energy that is released or absorbed during these processes. Every substance, whether naturally occurring or artificially produced, consists of one or more of the hundred-odd species of atoms that have been identified as elements. Although these atoms, in turn, are composed of more elementary particles, they are the basic building blocks of chemical substances; there is no quantity of oxygen, mercury, or gold, for example, smaller than an atom of that substance. Chemistry, therefore, is concerned not with the subatomic domain but with the properties of atoms and the laws governing their combinations and with how the knowledge of these properties can be used to achieve specific purposes.

## Periodic Table of the Elements

The periodic table arranges the elements into groups (vertically) of elements sharing common physical and chemical characteristics, and into periods (horizontally) of sequentially increasing atomic number and electron-shell configuration. Elements 110, 111, 112, and 114 have been created experimentally and have temporary names.

| IA | | | | | | | | VIII | | | IB | IIB | IIIA | IVA | VA | VIA | VIIA | Zero |
|---|---|---|---|---|---|---|---|---|---|---|---|---|---|---|---|---|---|---|
| 1 H | IIA | | | | | | | | | | | | IIIA | IVA | VA | VIA | VIIA | 2 He |
| 3 Li | 4 Be | | | | | | | | | | | | 5 B | 6 C | 7 N | 8 O | 9 F | 10 Ne |
| 11 Na | 12 Mg | IIIB | IVB | VB | VIB | VIIB | | | | | IB | IIB | 13 Al | 14 Si | 15 P | 16 S | 17 Cl | 18 Ar |
| 19 K | 20 Ca | 21 Sc | 22 Ti | 23 V | 24 Cr | 25 Mn | 26 Fe | 27 Co | 28 Ni | 29 Cu | 30 Zn | 31 Ga | 32 Ge | 33 As | 34 Se | 35 Br | 36 Kr |
| 37 Rb | 38 Sr | 39 Y | 40 Zr | 41 Nb | 42 Mo | 43 Tc | 44 Ru | 45 Rh | 46 Pd | 47 Ag | 48 Cd | 49 In | 50 Sn | 51 Sb | 52 Te | 53 I | 54 Xe |
| 55 Cs | 56 Ba | 57 La | 72 Hf | 73 Ta | 74 W | 75 Re | 76 Os | 77 Ir | 78 Pt | 79 Au | 80 Hg | 81 Tl | 82 Pb | 83 Bi | 84 Po | 85 At | 86 Rn |
| 87 Fr | 88 Ra | 89 Ac | 104 Rf | 105 Db | 106 Sg | 107 Bh | 108 Hs | 109 Mt | 110 Uun | 111 Uuu | 112 Uub | | 114 Uuq | | | | | |

| Lanthanide Series | 58 Ce | 59 Pr | 60 Nd | 61 Pm | 62 Sm | 63 Eu | 64 Gd | 65 Tb | 66 Dy | 67 Ho | 68 Er | 69 Tm | 70 Yb | 71 Lu |
|---|---|---|---|---|---|---|---|---|---|---|---|---|---|---|
| Actinide Series | 90 Th | 91 Pa | 92 U | 93 Np | 94 Pu | 95 Am | 96 Cm | 97 Bk | 98 Cf | 99 Es | 100 Fm | 101 Md | 102 No | 103 Lr |

| Element | Symbol | Atomic no. | Atomic weight* | Element | Symbol | Atomic no. | Atomic weight* |
|---|---|---|---|---|---|---|---|
| Actinium | Ac | 89 | 227.028 | Molybdenum | Mo | 42 | 95.94 |
| Aluminum | Al | 13 | 26.9815 | Neodymium | Nd | 60 | 144.24 |
| Americium | Am | 95 | (243) | Neon | Ne | 10 | 20.180 |
| Antimony | Sb | 51 | 121.75 | Neptunium | Np | 93 | (237.0482) |
| Argon | Ar | 18 | 39.948 | Nickel | Ni | 28 | 58.69 |
| Arsenic | As | 33 | 74.9216 | Niobium | Nb | 41 | 92.9064 |
| Astatine | At | 85 | (210) | Nitrogen | N | 7 | 14.0067 |
| Barium | Ba | 56 | 137.33 | Nobelium | No | 102 | (259) |
| Berkelium | Bk | 97 | (247) | Osmium | Os | 76 | 190.2 |
| Beryllium | Be | 4 | 9.01218 | Oxygen | O | 8 | 15.9994 |
| Bismuth | Bi | 83 | 208.9804 | Palladium | Pd | 46 | 106.42 |
| Bohrium | Bh | 107 | (264) | Phosphorus | P | 15 | 30.97376 |
| Boron | B | 5 | 10.81 | Platinum | Pt | 78 | 195.08 |
| Bromine | Br | 35 | 79.904 | Plutonium | Pu | 94 | (244) |
| Cadmium | Cd | 48 | 112.41 | Polonium | Po | 84 | (209) |
| Calcium | Ca | 20 | 40.08 | Potassium | K | 19 | 39.0983 |
| Californium | Cf | 98 | (251) | Praseodymium | Pr | 59 | 140.9077 |
| Carbon | C | 6 | 12.011 | Promethium | Pm | 61 | (145) |
| Cerium | Ce | 58 | 140.12 | Protactinium | Pa | 91 | 231.0359 |
| Cesium | Cs | 55 | 132.9054 | Radium | Ra | 88 | (226.0254) |
| Chlorine | Cl | 17 | 35.453 | Radon | Rn | 86 | (222) |
| Chromium | Cr | 24 | 51.996 | Rhenium | Re | 75 | 186.207 |
| Cobalt | Co | 27 | 58.9332 | Rhodium | Rh | 45 | 102.9055 |
| Copper | Cu | 29 | 63.546 | Rubidium | Rb | 37 | 85.4678 |
| Curium | Cm | 96 | (247) | Ruthenium | Ru | 44 | 101.07 |
| Dubnium | Db | 105 | (262) | Rutherfordium | Rf | 104 | (261) |
| Dysprosium | Dy | 66 | 162.50 | Samarium | Sm | 62 | 150.36 |
| Einsteinium | Es | 99 | (252) | Scandium | Sc | 21 | 44.9559 |
| Erbium | Er | 68 | 167.26 | Seaborgium | Sg | 106 | (266) |
| Europium | Eu | 63 | 151.96 | Selenium | Se | 34 | 78.96 |
| Fermium | Fm | 100 | (257) | Silicon | Si | 14 | 28.0855 |
| Fluorine | F | 9 | 18.9984 | Silver | Ag | 47 | 107.868 |
| Francium | Fr | 87 | (223) | Sodium | Na | 11 | 22.98977 |
| Gadolinium | Gd | 64 | 157.25 | Strontium | Sr | 38 | 87.62 |
| Gallium | Ga | 31 | 69.72 | Sulfur | S | 16 | 32.07 |
| Germanium | Ge | 32 | 72.61 | Tantalum | Ta | 73 | 180.9479 |
| Gold | Au | 79 | 196.9665 | Technetium | Tc | 43 | (98) |
| Hafnium | Hf | 72 | 178.49 | Tellurium | Te | 52 | 127.60 |
| Hassium | Hs | 108 | (277) | Terbium | Tb | 65 | 158.9254 |
| Helium | He | 2 | 4.00260 | Thallium | Tl | 81 | 204.383 |
| Holmium | Ho | 67 | 164.930 | Thorium | Th | 90 | 232.0381 |
| Hydrogen | H | 1 | 1.0079 | Thulium | Tm | 69 | 168.9342 |
| Indium | In | 49 | 114.82 | Tin | Sn | 50 | 118.71 |
| Iodine | I | 53 | 126.9045 | Titanium | Ti | 22 | 47.867 |
| Iridium | Ir | 77 | 192.22 | Tungsten (wolfram) | W | 74 | 183.85 |
| Iron | Fe | 26 | 55.845 | Ununbium | Uub | 112 | (285) |
| Krypton | Kr | 36 | 83.80 | Ununnilium | Uun | 110 | (281) |
| Lanthanum | La | 57 | 138.9055 | Ununquadium | Uuq | 114 | (289) |
| Lawrencium | Lr | 103 | (262) | Unununium | Uuu | 111 | (272) |
| Lead | Pb | 82 | 207.2 | Uranium | U | 92 | 238.029 |
| Lithium | Li | 3 | 6.941 | Vanadium | V | 23 | 50.9415 |
| Lutetium | Lu | 71 | 174.967 | Xenon | Xe | 54 | 131.29 |
| Magnesium | Mg | 12 | 24.305 | Ytterbium | Yb | 70 | 173.04 |
| Manganese | Mn | 25 | 54.9380 | Yttrium | Y | 39 | 88.9059 |
| Meitnerium | Mt | 109 | (268) | Zinc | Zn | 30 | 65.39 |
| Mendelevium | Md | 101 | (258) | Zirconium | Zr | 40 | 91.224 |
| Mercury | Hg | 80 | 200.59 | | | | |

*Parentheses indicate the mass number of the most stable isotope of a radioactive element.

## Common Alloys

| ALLOY | COMPOSITION | ALLOY | COMPOSITION |
|-------|-------------|-------|-------------|
| brass | 55% copper, 45% zinc | pewter | tin, antimony, copper |
| bronze | copper, tin | solder | tin, lead |
| cast iron | iron, carbon, silicon, manganese, trace impurities | stainless steel | iron, carbon, chromium, nickel |
| | | steel | iron, carbon |
| cupronickel | copper, nickel | sterling silver | silver, copper |

## Physics

Physics is the science that deals with the structure of matter and the interactions between the fundamental constituents of the observable universe. The basic physical science, its aim is the discovery and formulation of the fundamental laws of nature. In the broadest sense, physics (from the Greek *physikos*) is concerned with all aspects of nature on both the macroscopic and submicroscopic levels. Its scope of study encompasses not only the behavior of objects under the action of given forces but also the nature and origin of gravitational, electromagnetic, and nuclear force fields. Its ultimate objective is the formulation of a few comprehensive principles that bring together and explain all such disparate phenomena. Physics can, at base, be defined as the science of matter, motion, and energy. Its laws are typically expressed with economy and precision in the language of mathematics.

**Did you know?** Ouroboros was the emblematic serpent of ancient Egypt and Greece, represented with its tail in its mouth as continually devouring itself and being reborn from itself. In the 19th century, a vision of Ouroboros gave the German chemist Friedrich August Kekule von Stradonitz the idea of linked carbon atoms forming the benzene ring.

## Weight, Mass, and Density

**Mass,** strictly defined, is the quantitative measure of inertia, the resistance a body offers to a change in its speed or position when force is applied to it. The greater the mass of a body, the smaller the change produced by an applied force. In more practical terms, it is the measure of the amount of material in an object, and in common usage is often expressed as weight. However, the mass of an object is constant regardless of its position, while weight varies according to gravitational pull.

In the International System of Units (SI, the metric system), the kilogram is the standard unit of mass, defined as equaling the mass of the international prototype of the kilogram, currently a platinum-iridium cylinder kept at Sèvres, near Paris, France; it is roughly equal to the mass of 1,000 cubic centimeters of pure water at the temperature of its maximum density. In the US customary system, the unit is the slug, defined as the mass which a one pound force can accelerate at a rate of one foot per second per second, which is the same as the mass of an object weighing 32.17 pounds on the earth's surface.

**Weight** is the gravitational force of attraction on an object, caused by the presence of a massive second object, such as the Earth or Moon. Weight is the product of an object's mass and the acceleration of gravity at the point where the object is located. A given object will have the same mass on the Earth's surface, on the Moon, or in the absence of gravity, while its weight on the Moon would be about one sixth of its weight on the Earth's surface, because of the Moon's smaller gravitational pull (due in turn to the Moon's smaller mass and radius), and in the absence of gravity the object would have no weight at all.

Weight is measured in units of force, not mass, though in practice units of mass (such as the kilogram) are often substituted because of mass's relatively constant relation to weight on the Earth's surface. The weight of a body can be obtained by multiplying the mass by the acceleration of gravity. In SI, weight is expressed in newtons, or the force required to impart an acceleration of one meter per second per second to a mass of one kilogram. In the US customary system, it is expressed in pounds.

**Density** is the mass per unit volume of a material substance. It offers a convenient means of obtaining the mass of a body from its volume, or vice versa; the mass is equal to the volume multiplied by the density, while the volume is equal to the mass divided by the density. In SI, density is expressed in kilograms per cubic meter.

# Communications

## Introduction to the Internet

The **Internet** is a dynamic collection of computer networks that has revolutionized communications and methods of commerce by enabling those networks around the world to interact with each other. Sometimes referred to as a "**network of networks,**" the Internet was developed in the United States in the 1970s but was not widely used by the general public until the early 1990s. By the beginning of the 21st century approximately 360 million people, or roughly 6% of the world's population, were estimated to have access to the Internet. It is widely assumed that at least half of the world's population will have some form of Internet access by 2010 and that wireless access will play a growing role.

The Internet is so powerful and general that it can be used for almost any purpose that depends on the processing of information, and it is accessible by every individual who connects to one of its constituent networks. It supports human communication via **electronic mail** (e-mail), as well as real-time "chat rooms," newsgroups, and audio and video transmission and allows people to work collaboratively at many different locations. It supports access to information by many applications, including the **World Wide Web**, which uses text and graphical presentations. Publish-

ing has been revolutionized, as whole novels and reference works are available on the Web, and periodicals, including data prepared daily for an individual subscriber (such as stock market reports or news summaries), are also common. The Internet has attracted a large and growing number of "e-businesses" (including subsidiaries of traditional "brick-and-mortar" companies) that carry out most of their sales and services over the Internet.

In 1996 researchers at universities began planning for Internet I, an even faster network to link university campuses.

## Estimated Number of Internet Users, 1992–2003

*Sources: International Telecommunications Union Yearbook of Statistics, CIA World Factbook.*

| YEAR | UNITED STATES | WORLD | YEAR | UNITED STATES | WORLD |
|---|---|---|---|---|---|
| 1992 | 4,500,000 | 12,300,000 | 1998 | 73,000,000 | 160,000,000 |
| 1993 | 5,500,000 | 15,000,000 | 1999 | 102,000,000 | 270,000,000 |
| 1994 | 8,500,000 | 17,500,000 | 2000 | 124,000,000 | 385,000,000 |
| 1995 | 20,000,000 | 23,700,000 | 2001 | 143,000,000 | 499,000,000 |
| 1996 | 30,000,000 | 55,000,000 | 2002 | 164,000,000 | 544,000,000 |
| 1997 | 45,000,000 | 101,000,000 | 2003 | 165,750,000 | 580,780,000 |

## Personal Computers (PCs)

Computers small and inexpensive enough to be purchased by individuals for home use first became feasible when large-scale integration made it possible to construct a sufficiently powerful microprocessor on a single semiconductor chip. The personal computer industry truly began in 1977, when Apple Computer introduced the **Apple II**, one of the first pre-assembled, mass-produced personal computers. Radio Shack and Commodore Business Machines also introduced personal computers that year. These machines all used 8-bit microprocessors and possessed limited memory.

The IBM Corporation entered the new market in 1981, when it introduced the **IBM PC**. The IBM PC was only slightly faster than rival machines, but it had about 10 times their memory capacity. It became the world's most popular personal computer, and both its microprocessor, the Intel 8088, and its operating system, which was adapted from the Microsoft Corporation's MS-DOS system, became industry standards. In 1983 Apple introduced **Lisa**, a personal computer with a **graphical user interface** (GUI), which allowed the user to perform routine operations using a mouse. The

Lisa's GUI became the basis of Apple's extremely successful **Macintosh** personal computer, which was introduced in 1984. In 1985 the Microsoft Corporation introduced **Microsoft Windows**, a GUI that gave MS-DOS–based computers many of the same capabilities of the Macintosh. Windows became the dominant operating environment for personal computers.

These advances in software and operating systems were matched by the development of microprocessors containing ever-greater numbers of circuits, with resulting increases in the processing speed and power of PCs, in part through the developments of chip manufacturers Intel and Motorola. The memory capacity of PCs had increased from 64 kilobytes (64,000 characters) in the late 1970s to 100 megabytes (100 million characters) by the early 1990s.

Laptop computers, notebook computers, and PDAs became increasingly common in the early 1990s, and by the middle of the decade the **Internet** had revolutionized computer use. By 1997 about 40% of all households in the US owned a personal computer; by 2001 there were 178,000,000 personal computers in the US and 495,366,000 worldwide.

## Worldwide Cellular Mobile Telephone Subscribers, 2002

*Source: International Telecommunication Union Yearbook of Statistics.*

| COUNTRY | SUBSCRIBERS | SUBSCRIBERS PER 1,000 RESIDENTS | COUNTRY | SUBSCRIBERS | SUBSCRIBERS PER 1,000 RESIDENTS |
|---|---|---|---|---|---|
| China | 206,620,000 | 161 | Taiwan | 23,905,400 | 1,065 |
| United States | 140,766,800 | 488 | Turkey | 23,374,400 | 348 |
| Japan | 79,083,300 | 621 | Russia | 17,668,100 | 121 |
| Germany | 59,200,000 | 717 | Thailand | 16,117,000 | 260 |
| Italy | 52,316,000 | 927 | Philippines | 14,216,200 | 178 |
| United Kingdom | 49,921,000 | 845 | Poland | 14,000,000 | 363 |
| France | 38,585,300 | 647 | India | 12,687,600 | 12 |
| Brazil | 34,881,000 | 201 | Australia | 12,579,000 | 640 |
| Spain | 33,475,000 | 823 | South Africa | 12,081,000 | 266 |
| South Korea | 32,342,000 | 680 | Canada | 11,849,000 | 377 |
| Mexico | 25,928,300 | 255 | The Netherlands | 11,700,000 | 722 |

# Growth of Cell Phone Use in the US

*Estimated number of cellular mobile telephone subscribers in the US, 1991–2002.*
*Source:* International Telecommunications Union Yearbook of Statistics.

| YEAR | SUBSCRIBERS | YEAR | SUBSCRIBERS | YEAR | SUBSCRIBERS | YEAR | SUBSCRIBERS |
|------|------------|------|------------|------|------------|------|------------|
| 1991 | 7,557,000 | 1994 | 24,134,000 | 1997 | 55,312,000 | 2000 | 109,478,000 |
| 1992 | 11,033,000 | 1995 | 33,786,000 | 1998 | 69,209,000 | 2001 | 128,375,000 |
| 1993 | 16,009,000 | 1996 | 44,043,000 | 1999 | 86,047,000 | 2002 | 140,767,000 |

# Encyclopædia Britannica's Favorite Web Sites

*Encyclopædia Britannica editors have chosen these dynamic Web sites for their excellence in providing useful and noteworthy content, design, function, and ease of navigation.*

| SITE | URL | SUBJECT |
|------|-----|---------|
| **art** | | |
| Aesthetics Online | <www.aesthetics-online.org> | art, aesthetics, *Journal of Aesthetics and Art Criticism* |
| Andy Deck–Art Context | <www.artcontext.org> | Net art |
| Smithsonian Archives | <www.archivesofamericanart.si.edu> | art, American art, archive of American art |
| Blinken Lights | <www.blinkenlights.de> | Net art |
| Children's Picture Book Database | <www.lib.muohio.edu/pictbks> | library database |
| Dictionary of Art Historians | <www.lib.duke.edu/lilly/dah.htm> | art, art historians, dictionary |
| The Fantastic in Art and Fiction | <http://fantastic.library.cornell.edu> | fantastic art, fantastic literature |
| Found Magazine | <www.foundmagazine.com> | found art, found objects, found photographs, art, Surrealism, Dadaism |
| The Grove Dictionary of Art | <www.groveart.com> | art |
| Laughing Squid: Underground Art and Culture from San Francisco and Beyond | <www.laughingsquid.org> | underground art, art |
| Listening Post | <www.earstudio.com/projects/listeningPost.html> | Net art |
| National Association of Comics Art Educators | <www.teachingcomics.org> | art, comics, education, organization |
| Panoramas: The North American Landscape in Art | <www.virtualmuseum.ca/Exhibitions/Landscapes> | North America, art, landscape art |
| PuppetTool | <www.lecielestbleu.com/puppettool> | Net art |
| Surveillance Camera Players | <www.notbored.org/the-scp.html> | Net art |
| **business** | | |
| Amazon.com | <www.amazon.com> | e-commerce |
| Art.com | <www.art.com> | e-commerce, art |
| The Cluetrain Manifesto | <www.cluetrain.com> | business |
| eBay | <www.ebay.com> | e-commerce |
| Ecommerce Dictionary | <www.ecommerce-dictionary.com> | e-commerce |
| Europages: The European Business Directory | <www.europages.com> | business news, Europe |
| Evite | <www.evite.com> | services |
| Flea Market Guide of US Flea Markets | <www.fleamarketguide.com> | flea markets |
| Fresh Direct | <www.freshdirect.com> | commerce |
| Hoover's | <www.hoovers.com> | business news |
| Kiplinger.com | <www.kiplinger.com> | business news |
| QVC | <www.qvc.com> | e-commerce |
| Reuters | <www.reuters.com> | business news |
| TaxGaga.com | <www.taxgaga.com/pages/c-taxhaha/dir-humor.html> | taxes, IRS, humor |
| The Tire Rack Online Performance Source | <www.tirerack.com> | commerce |
| World Cargo News | <www.worldcargonews.com> | news and features |
| XE.com | <www.xe.com> | currency converter |

## Encyclopædia Britannica's Favorite Web Sites (continued)

| SITE | URL | SUBJECT |
|---|---|---|
| **computers and Internet** | | |
| Annoyances.org | <www.annoyances.org> | computers, Microsoft Windows, "bugs" |
| The Apache Software Foundation | <www.apache.org> | technical |
| Art and the Zen of web sites | <www.tlc-systems.com/webtips.shtml> | Web site production, Web site design |
| Association for Computing Machinery | <www.acm.org> | computers |
| Blogger | <www.blogger.com> | Web log creation |
| Computer History Museum | <www.computerhistory.org> | computers |
| Computer Songs and Poems | <www.poppyfields.net/filks> | computers, songs, poems, humor |
| Fazzle | <www.fazzle.com> | Internet search |
| Geocaching | <www.geocaching.com> | community |
| Google | <www.google.com> | Internet search |
| Google (Klingon Version) | <www.google.com/intl/xx-klingon/> | Google, Klingon, *Star Trek* |
| I Hate Computers | <www.i-hate-computers.org> | computers |
| Internet Archive Wayback Machine | <http://web.archive.org/collections/web.html> | Internet search |
| Invisible-web | <www.invisible-web.net> | Web directory, "invisible information" |
| The Jargon File | <www.jargon.watson-net.com> | computers, hacking, computer jargon |
| Linux Online | <www.linux.org> | technical |
| Old-Computers.com | <www.old-computers.com/news/default.asp> | computers |
| Tom's Hardware Guide | <www.tomshardware.com> | computers |
| Toxic Lemon | <www.toxiclemon.co.uk> | Internet search |
| Web Style Guide, 2nd Edition | <www.webstyleguide.com/index.html?> | Web site production, Web site design |
| Web Wombat | <www.webwombat.com.au> | Internet search |
| Wise Nut | <www.wisenut.com> | Internet search |
| | | |
| **education** | | |
| Big Chalk | <www.bigchalk.com> | education for children |
| Encyclopædia Britannica Online: School Edition | <www.school.eb.com> | education for children |
| Idea Box | <www.theideabox.com> | education for children |
| Mothergoose.com | <www.mothergoose.com> | education for children, Mother Goose, nursery rhymes |
| The New York Times on the Web LearningNetwork | <www.nytimes.com/learning> | education |
| sodaplay | <www.sodaplay.com> | education |
| | | |
| **fashion** | | |
| Girl-on-the-street | <www.girlonthestreet.com> | lifestyle |
| The Hair Archives | <www.hairarchives.com> | hairstyles, hairdressing |
| Hint Fashion Magazine | <www.hintmag.com> | fashion |
| Japanese Streets | <www.japanesestreets.com> | fashion |
| Lucire | <www.lucire.com> | fashion |
| SHOWstudio | <www.showstudio.com> | fashion |
| Style.com | <www.style.com> | fashion |
| | | |
| **food** | | |
| Epicurious: Gourmet.com | <www.gourmet.com> | *Gourmet* magazine Web site |
| Food Network.com | <www.foodnetwork.com> | Food Network Web site |
| Food Reference Website | <www.foodreference.com> | food, cooking |
| Gernot Katzer's Spice Pages | <www-ang.kfunigraz.ac.at/~katzer/engl/> | facts about seasonings |
| Iowa State University's Tasty Insect Recipes | <www.ent.iastate.edu/misc/insectsasfood.html> | edible insects |
| Rolling Your Own Sushi | <www.rain.org/~hutch/sushi.html> | Japanese cuisine, sushi |
| Soup of the Evening | <www.soupsong.com> | recipes and trivia about soup |
| StarChefs | <www.starchefs.com> | cuisine |
| | | |
| **geography, maps, and travel** | | |
| Atlapedia Online | <www.atlapedia.com> | countries of the world |
| California Driving: A Survival Guide | <www.caldrive.com/index.html> | automobile driving, California |

# Encyclopædia Britannica's Favorite Web Sites (continued)

| SITE | URL | SUBJECT |
|---|---|---|
| **geography, maps, and travel (continued)** | | |
| Hostelling International-USA | <www.hiayh.org/homenew.shtml> | international travel organization |
| IgoUgo | <www.igougo.com> | travel |
| Joe Sent Me | <www.zyworld.com/brancatelli> | travel |
| Lonely Planet | <www.lonelyplanet.com> | travel destinations |
| The New York Times: Travel | <www.nytimes.com/pages/travel/index.html> | travel |
| RoadsideAmerica.com | <www.roadsideamerica.com> | curiosities, wonders, travel |
| SeatGuru.com | <www.seatguru.com> | travel |
| Tourism Offices Worldwide Directory | <www.towd.com> | tourism |
| Travel-Library.com | <www.travel-library.com> | personal travel |
| World City Photo Archive | <www.worldcityphotos.org> | distinguished global places |
| World Heritage Center: UNESCO | <http://whc.unesco.org/nwhc/pages/home/pages/homepage.htm> | distinguished global places |
| World Landmarks.com | <www.worldlandmarks.com> | distinguished global places |
| Zoom Into Maps | <http://lcweb2.loc.gov/ammem/ndlpedu/features/maps> | maps, cartography |
| **history, archaeology, and anthropology** | | |
| The Center for Archaeo-astronomy | <www.wam.umd.edu/~tlaloc/archastro/index.html> | astronomy, archaeology |
| Cyndi's List of Genealogy Sites on the Internet | <www.cyndislist.com> | 190,000+ genealogical links |
| Digital Pharoahs | <www.desk.nl/~pdenijs/faraos.html> | archaeology, Egyptology |
| Encyclopedia of Greek Mythology | <www.mythweb.com/encyc/index.html> | mythology |
| Fantastic Fish of the Middle Ages | <www.godecookery.com/ffissh/ffissh.htm> | fish, Middle Ages, folklore |
| Geometry Step-by-Step from the Land of the Incas | <www.agutie.homestead.com> | geometry, Incan culture |
| Great Archaeological Sites | <www.culture.fr/culture/arcnat/en> | archaeology, paleontology |
| HistoryWired: A Few of Our Favorite Things | <www.historywired.si.edu/index.html> | material culture, National Museum of American History |
| Internet Medieval Sourcebook | <www.fordham.edu/halsall/sbook.html> | medieval studies |
| Medieval Macabre | <www.godecookery.com/macabre/macabre.htm> | medieval studies, supernatural, fantasy |
| Medieval Names Archive | <www.panix.com/~mittle/names> | medieval studies |
| The Medieval Technology Pages | <http://scholar.chem.nyu.edu/tekpages/Technology.html> | medieval studies |
| Theban Mapping Project | <www.thebanmappingproject.com> | mapping Egyptian archaeological sites |
| The USGenWeb Project | <www.usgenweb.com> | network of genealogical groups |
| The Victorian Dictionary | <www.victorianlondon.org> | Victorian England, culture, lifestyle, society |
| **hobbies** | | |
| Do It Yourself Network | <www.diynet.com> | lifestyle |
| Early Office Museum | <www.officemuseum.com> | office equipment, collectibles |
| Halloween Online | <www.halloween-online.com> | Halloween, holidays |
| Kitchens.com | <www.kitchens.com> | lifestyle |
| KITEcast.com | <www.intellicast.com/KITEcast> | kites, kite flying |
| Pageant News Bureau | <www.pageant.com> | beauty pageant news and features |
| 3d&l | <www.3d-i.org> | design for youth |
| You Grow Girl | <www.yougrowgirl.com> | gardening |
| **humor** | | |
| Bad Girl Swirl | <www.badgirlswirl.com> | lifestyle |
| The Brains Trust | <www.thebrainstrust.co.uk> | wit, humor, Great Britain, satire |
| Cheese Racing | <www.apsmith.btinternet.co.uk/cheese> | cheese, sports |
| College Humor Magazines | <www.geocities.com/troyc22/collhumor.html> | humor magazine list |

## Encyclopædia Britannica's Favorite Web Sites (continued)

| SITE | URL | SUBJECT |
|---|---|---|
| **humor (continued)** | | |
| The Dead Grandmother/ Exam Syndrome and the Potential Downfall of American Society | <http://biology.ecsu.ctstateu.edu/ People/ConnRev> | humor |
| Dezmin's Archives | <www.dezmin.com> | humor magazine |
| Dress the Chief | <www.electricscotland.com/kids/ dress1.html> | toys, paper dolls, wit, humor, Scotland |
| Eric Conveys an Emotion | <www.emotioneric.com> | humor |
| HomestarRunner.com | <www.homestarrunner.com> | cartoons, games, wit, humor |
| The Ig Nobel Home Page | <www.improbable.com/ig/ig-top.html> | wit, humor |
| Joey Green's Wacky Uses.com | <www.wackyuses.com> | home economics, brand-name products |
| OddTodd.com | <www.oddtodd.com> | humor, wit |
| The Onion | <www.theonion.com> | humor magazine |
| Peep Research: A Study of Small Fluffy Creatures and Library Usage | <www.millikin.edu/staley/fluff/ peep_research.html> | Peeps, libraries, humor, food, candy |
| Peephenge | <www.lordofthepeeps.com/ peephenge/peephenge.html> | Peeps, Stonehenge, candy, humor, wit |
| rathergood.com | <www.rathergood.com> | weird |
| Recoil | <www.recoilmag.com> | humor magazine |
| SatireWire | <www.satirewire.com/index.shtml> | satire, wit |
| Sinkie | <www.sinkie.com> | special days, food habits, humor |
| | | |
| **language and literature** | | |
| Ancient Scripts.com | <www.ancientscripts.com> | linguistics |
| BIOSIS | <www.biosis.org/zrdocs/zoolinfo/ vernac.htm> | taxonomy |
| Book-a-Minute Classics | <www.rinkworks.com/bookaminute/ classics.shtml> | literature, humor |
| The Bulwer-Lytton Fiction Contest | <www.bulwer-lytton.com> | literature, wit, humor |
| A Collection of Word Oddities and Trivia | <www.members.aol.com/gulfhigh2/ words.html> | words, English language |
| The Devil's Dictionary | <www.alcyone.com/max/lit/devils> | Ambrose Bierce; humor |
| Dictionary of All-Consonant Words | <www.blueray.com/dictionary/ consonant/index.html> | dictionary |
| Dictionary of All-Vowel Words | <www.blueray.com/dictionary/vowel/ index.html> | dictionary |
| Ethnologue | <www.ethnologue.com> | languages of the world |
| Figures of Speech | <www.nipissingu.ca/faculty/williams/ figofspe.htm> | figures of speech, English language |
| The Foolish Dictionary Online Edition | <www.aaaugh.com/dictionary> | dictionary, humor |
| Grandiloquent Dictionary | <www.islandnet.com/~egbird/ dict/dict.htm> | dictionary |
| The Grapes of Wrath, 1998 | <http://home.att.net/~gkrist/ grapes.html> | satire, *The Grapes of Wrath*, John Steinbeck |
| I Love Languages | <www.ilovelanguages.com> | languages of the world |
| Jennifer's Language Page | <www.elite.net/~runner/jennifers> | languages of the world |
| Julia A. Moore Poetry Contest | <www.flint.lib.mi.us/about/programs/ jmoore> | Julia Moore; parody, wit, humor |
| Lexicon of Linguistics | <http://tristram.let.uu.nl/UIL-OTS/ Lexicon> | linguistics |
| Model Languages and the Art of Language Making | <www.langmaker.com> | linguistics |
| Nom de Guerre | <www.go.to/realnames> | pseudonyms |
| Pseudodictionary | <www.pseudodictionary.com> | dictionary, humor |
| Quoteland.com | <www.quoteland.com> | quotations |
| Rivertrout.com | <www.rivertrout.com/main.html> | letters, letter writing, literature |
| Social Security Administration's Popular Baby Names | <www.ssa.gov/OACT/babynames> | names, naming, babies |
| Symbols.com | <www.symbols.com> | symbols |
| Things People Said | <www.rinkworks.com/said> | language, humor |

## Encyclopædia Britannica's Favorite Web Sites (continued)

| SITE | URL | SUBJECT |
|---|---|---|
| **language and literature (continued)** | | |
| Twists, Slugs and Roscoes: A Glossary of Hardboiled Slang | <www.miskatonic.org/slang.html> | linguistics |
| Weird Tales: The Unique Magazine | <www.members.aol.com/weirdtales> | fantasy fiction, horror fiction, pulp fiction |
| The White Queen's Dictionary of One Letter Words | <www.blueray.com/dictionary/oneletter/index.html> | dictionary |
| Wordorigins.org | <www.wordorigins.org> | linguistics |
| Ye Olde English Sayings | <www.rootsweb.com/~genepool/sayings.htm> | linguistics |
| **media** | | |
| All Your Base Are Belong To Us | <www.planettribes.com/allyourbase> | comics, humor, popular cult interest |
| AlterNet | <www.alternet.org> | zines and magazines |
| The Astounding B Monster | <www.bmonster.com/index.html> | motion pictures |
| BBC Video Nation | <www.bbc.co.uk/videonation> | community |
| Bright Lights Film Journal | <www.brightlightsfilm.com> | motion pictures |
| The British Film Institute | <www.bfi.org.uk> | motion pictures |
| CartoonNetwork.com | <www.cartoonnetwork.com> | television |
| CBC Radio 3 | <www.cbcradio3.com> | broadband |
| Dermatology in the Cinema | <www.skinema.com> | motion pictures |
| Disney's Toontown Online | <www.toontown.com> | games |
| Don Markstein's Wired News | <www.wired.com> | film, video, technology, digital video |
| Epitonic Radio | <www.epitonic.com/radio.jsp> | radio |
| Filk Frequently Asked Questions | <www.home.earthlink.net/~kayshapero/filkfaq.htm> | folk music, science fiction, fantasy fiction |
| indieWIRE | <www.indiewire.com> | motion pictures |
| The Internet Movie Database | <www.imdb.com> | motion pictures |
| KEXP | <www.kexp.org> | radio |
| Love HK Film | <www.lovehkfilm.com> | motion pictures |
| Metacritic.com | <www.metacritic.com> | motion pictures |
| Metropolismag.com | <www.metropolismag.com> | zines and magazines |
| The Museum of Broadcast Communications: The Encyclopedia of Television | <www.museum.tv/archives/etv/index.html> | encyclopedia, television |
| Nick.com | <www.nick.com> | television |
| The Nitpickers Site | <www.nitpickers.com> | motion pictures |
| Oscar.com: Academy Awards | <www.oscar.com> | motion pictures |
| Planet Bollywood | <www.planetbollywood.com> | motion pictures |
| A Prairie Home Companion | <www.prairiehome.org> | wit, humor, public radio, radio programs |
| Rotten Tomatoes | <www.rottentomatoes.com> | motion pictures |
| Shift | <www.shift.com> | zines and magazines |
| Spongi | <www.spongi.com> | motion pictures |
| Toonopedia | <www.toonopedia.com> | encyclopedia, cartoons |
| **medicine and health** | | |
| American Association for Geriatric Psychiatry | <www.aagpgpa.org> | geriatrics, psychiatry |
| American Cancer Society | <www.cancer.org> | cancer |
| American College of Sports Medicine | <www.acsm.org/index.asp> | health and medicine |
| Antiqua Medicina | <www.med.virginia.edu/hs-library/historical/antiqua/anthome.html> | health and medicine |
| Cancer.gov | <www.cancer.gov> | health |
| eMedicine | <www.emedicine.com> | health and medicine |
| geriatricsandaging.ca | <www.geriatricsandaging.ca> | geriatrics |
| HIV Stops With Me | <www.hivstopswithme.org> | health |
| LifeClinic | <www.lifeclinic.com> | health |
| Medline Plus Health Information | <www.nlm.nih.gov/medlineplus> | health and medicine |
| National Alliance of Breast Cancer Organizations | <www.nabco.org> | cancer, breast cancer, women's issues |

## Encyclopædia Britannica's Favorite Web Sites (continued)

| SITE | URL | SUBJECT |
|---|---|---|
| **medicine and health (continued)** | | |
| National Institute on Aging | <www.nih.gov/nia> | geriatrics |
| The National Women's Health Information Center | <www.4woman.gov> | women's health, US |
| Planned Parenthood Golden Gate | <www.ppgg.org> | health |
| teenwire | <www.teenwire.com> | health |
| Third World Women's Health | <www.arches.uga.edu/~haneydaw/twwh/index.html> | women's health, women's issues, Third World issues |
| UNAIDS/WHO Global HIV/ AIDS and STD Surveillance | <www.who.int/emc-hiv> | STDs |
| UNAIDS/WHO Global Surveillance fact sheets | <www.unaids.org/hivaidsinfo/statistics/fact_sheets/all_countries_en.html> | STDs by country |
| | | |
| **nature, science, environment, and technology** | | |
| Airliners.net | <www.airliners.net> | aeronautics, airplanes, photographs |
| bioethics.net | <www.ajobonline.com> | genetics; ethics |
| Animal Planet: Future is Wild Interactive | <www.animal.discovery.com/convergence/futureiswild/animals/animals.html> | television |
| Anomalies | <www.anomalyinfo.com> | anomalies |
| The Asian Elephant Art and Conservation Project | <www.elephantart.com/catalog/splash.php> | elephants, elephant art, elephant artists, animal conservation, humor |
| The Astronomy Cafe: The Web Site for the Astonomically Disadvantaged | <www.astronomycafe.net> | astronomy |
| Astronomy Picture of the Day | <http://antwrp.gsfc.nasa.gov/apod/astropix.html> | astronomy, astronomical images |
| Astronomy Unbound: A Virtual Astronomy Text | <www.herts.ac.uk/astro_ub> | astronomy |
| Astronomy.com | <www.astronomy.com/home.asp> | astronomy |
| Awesome Amphibians, Remarkable Reptiles | <www.stlzoo.org/content.asp?page_name=herpfacts> | amphibians, reptiles |
| Bad Astronomy | <www.badastronomy.com> | astronomy, hoaxes |
| Bat Conservation International Inc. | <www.batcon.org> | mammals |
| Boxes and Arrows | <www.boxesandarrows.com> | zines and magazines, architecture, design |
| BrainPOP | <www.brainpop.com> | education, health, science, technology, math |
| Build a Solar System | <www.exploratorium.edu/ronh/solar_system> | solar system |
| California's Endangered Insects | <www.mip.berkeley.edu/essig/endins> | endangered species of the world, California |
| Carolina Raptor Center | <www.birdsofprey.org> | endangered species of the world, raptors |
| Chandra X-ray Center | <www.chandra.harvard.edu/pub.html> | astronomy, astronomical images |
| Comparative Mammalian Brain Collections | <www.brainmuseum.org> | mammals |
| The Council for Responsible Genetics | <www.gene-watch.org> | genetics, ethics |
| CuriousMath.com | <www.curiousmath.com> | mathematics |
| Dark Matter | <www.fmrib.ox.ac.uk/~dave/darkmatter> | outer space |
| Dateline Moon: The Media and the Space Race | <www.newseum.org/datelinemoon> | space exploration |
| DOEgenomes.org | <www.ornl.gov/hgmis> | genetics |
| The Dog Hause | <www.doghause.com> | pets, animals, quotations, humor |
| Ellijay Wildlife Rehab Sanctuary | <www.wildliferehabsanctuary.org> | global nature reserves |
| The EMBL Reptile Database | <www.embl-heidelberg.de/~uetz/LivingReptiles.html> | reptiles |
| Encyclopedia Astronautica | <www.astronautix.com> | outer space |
| Eric Weisstein's World of Mathematics | <www.mathworld.wolfram.com> | science |
| European Space Agency | <www.esa.int/export/esaCP/index.html> | outer space |

## Encyclopædia Britannica's Favorite Web Sites (continued)

| SITE | URL | SUBJECT |
|------|-----|---------|
| nature, science, environment, and technology (continued) | | |
| exploreMarsnow.org | <www.exploremarsnow.org> | science |
| Fish Reports.net | <www.fishreports.net> | fish |
| FishBase | <www.fishbase.org/home.htm> | fish |
| Fortean Times | <www.forteantimes.com> | weird |
| GardenWeb | <www.gardenweb.com> | gardening |
| Gene Tests | <www.genetests.org> | genetics |
| Gothic Gardening | <www.gothic.net/~malice> | gardening |
| Grand Illusions | <www.grand-illusions.com> | optical illusions |
| HowStuffWorks | <www.howstuffworks.com> | science |
| International Carnivorous Plant Society | <www.carnivorousplants.org> | plants |
| International Chindogu Society | <www.pitt.edu/~ctnst3/chindogu.html> | inventions, humor |
| The International Plant Names Index | <www.ipni.org/index.html> | plants |
| IUCN Red List of Threatened Species | <www.redlist.org> | endangered species of the world |
| The Japanese Garden Database | <www.jgarden.org> | gardening, Japan, Japanese gardens |
| The Knot Plot Site | <www.pims.math.ca/knotplot> | mathematics |
| Mammal Species of the World: Smithsonian | <www.nmnh.si.edu/msw> | mammals |
| Mythical Plants of the Middle Ages | <www.godecookery.com/mythical/mythical.htm> | mythology |
| NASA | <www.nasa.gov> | NASA, aeronautics, space flight, space travel |
| NASA Earth Observatory | <www.earthobservatory.nasa.gov> | education, NASA, Earth, astronomy, aeronautics |
| NASA Human Space Flight | <www.spaceflight.nasa.gov> | space exploration |
| NASA Jet Propulsion Laboratory | <www.jpl.nasa.gov/index.html> | astronomy |
| National Human Genome Research Institute | <www.genome.gov> | genetics |
| National Parks Worldwide | <http://hum.amu.edu.pl/~zbzw/ph/pnp/swiat.htm> | global nature reserves |
| National Weather Service | <www.weather.gov> | weather |
| NewCROP: The New Crop Resource Online Program | <www.hort.purdue.edu/newcrop> | plants, crops |
| The Nine Planets: A Multimedia Tour of the Solar System | <http://www.seds.org/billa/tnp | solar system |
| The Nobel Channel | <www.nobelchannel.com> | Nobel Prizes |
| Nobel e-Museum | <www.nobel.se> | Nobel Prizes |
| Origami Mathematics | <www.merrimack.edu/~thull/origamimath.html> | mathematics |
| Outer Space Tourist | <www.outerspacetourist.com> | outer space |
| Patently Absurd! | <www.patent.freeserve.co.uk> | patents, UK |
| PlaneCrashInfo.com | <www.planecrashinfo.com> | plane crashes |
| Plants Database: US Department of Agriculture | <http://plants.usda.gov> | plants |
| Plants-In-Motion | <www.sunflower.bio.indiana.edu/~rhangart/plantmotion> | plants |
| Plumb Design Visual Thesaurus | <www.visualthesaurus.com> | education, thesaurus, technology |
| Publius | <www.publius.org> | elections, voting |
| Science Hobbyist | <www.amasci.com> | science |
| Scirus | <www.scirus.com> | science |
| SkyandTelescope.com | <http://skyandtelescope.com/observing/skychart> | astronomy, constellations, stars |
| Skyscrapers.com | <www.skyscrapers.com/re/en/bu/sk/st/tp> | world's tallest buildings |
| Skywatching Center | <www.earthsky.com/Features/Skywatching> | astronomy |
| Snow Crystals | <www.its.caltech.edu/~atomic/snowcrystals> | snowflakes, ice crystals, physics |

# Encyclopædia Britannica's Favorite Web Sites (continued)

| SITE | URL | SUBJECT |
|------|-----|---------|
| nature, science, environment, and technology (continued) | | |
| Space Calendar | <www.jpl.nasa.gov/calendar> | space exploration |
| Space Science: NASA | <http://spacescience.nasa.gov> | outer space |
| Space.com | <www.space.com> | outer space |
| Spaceguard UK | <www.spaceguarduk.com> | solar system, asteroids, comets |
| StarChild: A Learning Center for Young Astronomers | <http://starchild.gsfc.nasa.gov/docs/ StarChild> | astronomy, children |
| StarDate Online: AstroGlossary | <www.stardate.org/resources/ astroglossary> | astronomy |
| Strange Science: The Rocky Road to Modern Paleontology and Biology | <www.strangescience.net> | paleontology, fossils, biology, geology |
| Totally Absurd Inventions | <www.totallyabsurd.com> | inventions, humor |
| 20th Century Castles | <www.missilebases.com> | weird real estate |
| ufoskeptic.org | <www.ufoskeptic.org> | outer space |
| University of St. Andrews School of Mathematics and Statistics | <www-groups.cs.st-and.ac.uk/ ~history/Indexes/HistoryTopics.html> | mathematics |
| VenomousReptiles.org | <www.venomousreptiles.org> | reptiles |
| What is the 'tallest structure in the world'? | <www.xs4all.nl/~hnetten/tallest.html> | world's tallest building |
| | | |
| news and features | | |
| BBC News | <www.bbcnews.com> | news and features |
| Google News | <www.news.google.com> | news and features |
| MSNBC News | <www.msnbc.com> | news and features |
| The New York Times on the Web | <www.nytimes.com> | news and features |
| Urban Legends Reference Pages | <www.snopes.com> | urban legends, folklore, rumor |
| Weird News Online | <www.weirdnewsonline.com> | news and features |
| Whyville | <www.whyville.net> | youth |
| | | |
| performing arts | | |
| Heavy | <www.heavy.com> | music |
| Instrument Jokes | <www.mit.edu/~jcb/other-instrument- jokes.html> | musical instruments, jokes, humor |
| Miserable Melodies | <www.miserablemelodies.com> | music, humor |
| Oddmusic.com: A Source for Unique and Experimental Music, Instruments, Players, and Listeners | <www.oddmusic.com> | music, musical instruments |
| Okayplayer.com | <www.okayplayer.com> | music |
| The Peter Schickele/ P.D.Q. Bach Web Site | <www.schickele.com> | Peter Schickele; P.D.Q. Bach; art music, humor |
| Pinknoises.com | <www.pinknoises.com> | women's music, electronic music, music |
| Rock's Backpages | <www.rocksbackpages.com> | rock and pop music |
| Tech.Nitions | <www.technitions.com/tech2.html> | music |
| | | |
| politics, government, world affairs, social issues | | |
| 2Camels.com | <www.2camels.com> | world festivals |
| Act For Change | <www.actforchange.com> | political activism |
| allAfrica.com | <www.allafrica.com> | news and features |
| Background Notes: US Department of State | <www.state.gov/r/pa/ei/bgn> | countries of the world |
| The Capitol Steps | <www.capsteps.com> | Congress, Capitol Hill, humor |
| CIA World Factbook | <www.cia.gov/cia/publications/ factbook> | country information |
| Citizens Against Government Waste | <www.cagw.org/site/PageServer> | governments |
| Clean Elections Institute Inc. | <www.azclean.org> | voting, "clean elections" |
| Commanding Heights: The Battle for the World Economy | <www.pbs.org/wgbh/ commandingheights/lo/> | economics |

## Encyclopædia Britannica's Favorite Web Sites (continued)

| SITE | URL | SUBJECT |
|------|-----|---------|
| politics, government, world affairs, social issues (continued) | | |
| Commission on Mental and Physical Disability Law | <www.abanet.org/disability> | US politics and legislation, American Bar Association |
| Congress.org | <www.congress.org> | politics |
| Country Reports.org | <www.countryreports.org> | countries of the world |
| Disinformation | <www.disinfo.com/site> | Web search engine, "invisible information" |
| Economist.com | <www.economist.com> | news and features |
| Edutopia Online | <www.glef.org> | George Lucas Educational Foundation; K–12 public education |
| Election Data Sites | <www.nd.edu/~kic/elecdata.htm> | world election data |
| Elections and Electoral Systems Around the World | <www.psr.keele.ac.uk/election.htm> | world politics |
| Electionworld.org | <www.electionworld.org> | world election data |
| Environmental Working Group | <www.ewg.org> | politics |
| The Evolutionary World Politics Homepage | <http://faculty.washington.edu/modelski> | world politics |
| Frontline/World | <www.pbs.org/frontlineworld> | television |
| Global IDP Project | <www.idpproject.org> | internally displaced persons |
| Global Security | <www.globalsecurity.org> | international organization |
| Governments on the WWW | <www.gksoft.com/govt/en> | governments |
| Great American Speeches | <www.pbs.org/greatspeeches> | US politics and legislation, speeches |
| Greenpeace | <www.greenpeace.org> | activism |
| Homeless | <www.abc.net.au/homeless> | homelessness, social issue |
| Images of American Political History | <http://teachpol.tcnj.edu/amer_pol_hist> | US politics and legislation, images, photographs |
| International Institute for Democracy and Electoral Assistance | <www.idea.int> | voter participation |
| International Rescue Committee | <www.theirc.org> | refugees |
| Inter-Parliamentary Union | <www.ipu.org> | world politics |
| The Jane Goodall Institute | <www.janegoodall.com> | activism |
| Legislation Related to the Attack of September 11, 2001 | <http://thomas.loc.gov/home/terrorleg.htm> | US politics and legislation |
| LiveJournal.com | <www.livejournal.com> | community |
| Meetup | <www.meetup.com> | community |
| MoveOn.org | <www.moveon.org> | politics |
| The Note: ABC News Political Unit | <www.abcnews.go.com/sections/politics/US/TheNote.html> | politics |
| Political Money Line | <www.fecinfo.com> | US political campaign donations |
| Political Resources on the Net | <www.politicalresources.net> | politics |
| The Punch Cartoon Library | <www.punch.co.uk/shop.asp?type=cartoon> | wit, humor, cartoons, Great Britain |
| PurePolitics.com | <www.purepolitics.com> | world politics, humor |
| Richard Kimber's Political Science Resources | <www.psr.keele.ac.uk> | politics |
| Romenesko | <www.poynter.org/medianews> | news and features, journalism |
| Rulers.org | <www.rulers.org> | country leaders |
| The Smoking Gun | <www.thesmokinggun.com> | news, humor, crime |
| Spinsanity | <www.spinsanity.org> | politics |
| Terrorism Law and Policy | <www.jurist.law.pitt.edu/terrorism.htm> | US politics and legislation, terrorism |
| This American Life | <www.thisamericanlife.org> | radio |
| Thomas–US Library of Congress | <http://thomas.loc.gov> | US politics and legislation |
| Transom.org | <www.transom.org> | radio |
| The UN Refugee Agency | <www.unhcr.ch/cgi-bin/texis/vtx/home> | refugees |
| United Nations | <www.un.org> | international organization |
| US Census Bureau | <www.census.gov> | US people |
| Virtual Presentation Assistant | <www.ukans.edu/cwis/units/coms2/vpa/vpa.htm> | public speaking, speeches |
| Visit a Refugee Camp | <www.refugeecamp.org> | refugees |

# Encyclopædia Britannica's Favorite Web Sites (continued)

| SITE | URL | SUBJECT |
|------|-----|---------|
| **politics, government, world affairs, social issues (continued)** | | |
| Voice Yourself | <www.voiceyourself.com> | activism |
| VolunteerMatch | <www.volunteermatch.org> | services |
| World Resources Institute | <www.wri.org> | activism |
| World Statesmen | <www.worldstatesmen.org> | country leaders |
| YourCongress.com | <www.yourcongress.com> | US Congress, humor |
| **reference** | | |
| Encyclopædia Britannica | <www.britannica.com> | encyclopedia |
| Merriam-Webster Online | <http://m-w.com> | dictionary |
| LibDex: The Library Index | <www.libdex.com> | library database |
| Lipstick Librarian | <www.lipsticklibrarian.com> | women's issues, libraries |
| OCLC FirstSearch | <http://newfirstsearch.oclc.org> | library database |
| Smithsonian Institution Research Information System | <www.siris.si.edu/#ari> | research, libraries, archives, Smithsonian Institution |
| **religion, philosophy, and mythology** | | |
| BBCi Religion & Ethics | <www.bbc.co.uk/religion> | spirituality |
| The Cat in Urban Mythology | <www.messybeast.com/urbancat.htm> | mythology |
| Dictionary of Philosophy of Mind | <www.artsci.wustl.edu/~philos/MindDict> | philosophy |
| An Exploration of Modern Monsters | <www.umich.edu/~umfandsf/symbolismproject/symbolism.html/Monstrosity/intropage/homepage.html> | monsters, folklore, symbolism |
| Film and Philosophy | <www.hanover.edu/philos/film> | philosophy |
| Guide to Philosophy on the Internet | <www.earlham.edu/~peters/gpi/index.htm> | philosophy |
| Philosophical Humor | <www.u.arizona.edu/~chalmers/phil-humor.html> | philosophy |
| Philosophy Comix | <www.members.aol.com/lshauser/phlcomix.html> | philosophy |
| The Pluralism Project | <www.pluralism.org> | spirituality |
| The Religious Movements Homepage at the University of Virginia | <http://religiousmovements.lib.virginia.edu/home.html> | new religious movements |
| The Ross Institute for the Study of Destructive Cults, Controversial Groups and Movements | <www.rickross.com> | new religious movements |
| Stanford Encyclopedia of Philosophy | <http://plato.stanford.edu> | philosophy |
| **sports and games** | | |
| Alternative Sports Magazine | <www.alternativesportsmag.com/index.html> | sports |
| Baseball Almanac | <www.baseball-almanac.com> | baseball, sports |
| Cool Quiz! | <www.coolquiz.com> | trivia, quizzes |
| ESPN | <www.espn.com> | sports |
| Guinness World Records | <www.guinnessworldrecords.com> | world records, curiosities, wonders |
| The Indie Game Jam | <www.indiegamejam.com> | games |
| Let's Play Scrabble | <www.thepixiepit.co.uk> | Scrabble, games |
| The Olympic Movement | <www.olympic.org> | Olympic sports |
| Orisinal | <www.orisinal.com> | games |
| PopCap Games | <www.popcap.com> | games |
| Strange Sports Stories | <www.members.aol.com/MG4273/sport.htm#Numbers> | sports |
| A Tale in the Desert | <www.atitd.com> | games |
| This Week in Chess | <www.chesscenter.com/twic/twic.html> | chess |
| Kidzworld: Useless Olympic Facts | <www.kidzworld.com/site/p1661.htm> | Olympic sports |

**Did you know?** In 1865 Jules Verne published *De la Terre à la Lune* (*From the Earth to the Moon*; 1873). Verne imagined a number of scientific devices and developments that eventually came to be, including the submarine, scuba gear, television, and space travel.

# Aerospace Technology

## Space Exploration

Three men were the first scientists to conceive pragmatically of spaceflight: the Russian **Konstantin Tsiolkovsky**, the American **Robert Goddard**, and the German **Hermann Oberth**. Technology in the early 20th century, however, was a long way from the level required for rocket-powered flight. Nonetheless, the theory and dynamics of such flights were rigorously studied. By the end of World War II, the German development of rocket propulsion for aircraft and guided missiles (notably the V-2) had reached a high level. With the German surrender in 1945, the US and its Allies fell heir to the technical knowledge of rocket power developed by the Germans. The technical director of the German missile effort, **Wernher von Braun**, and some 150 of his top aides surrendered to US troops. Most emigrated to the US, where they assembled and launched V-2 missiles that had been captured and shipped there. The USSR carried out an unpublicized but extensive program that must have been very similar; Britain and France conducted smaller programs.

In both the US and the USSR the development of **military missile technology** was essential to the achievement of satellite flight. Preparations for the International Geophysical Year (IGY, 1957–58) stimulated discussion of the possibility of launching **artificial Earth satellites** for scientific investigations. Both the US and the USSR became determined to prepare scientific satellites for launching during the IGY. While the US was still developing a space launch vehicle, the USSR startled the world by placing **Sputnik 1** in orbit on 4 Oct 1957. This was followed a month later by **Sputnik 2** carrying a live dog. The failure by the US to launch its small payload on 6 Dec 1957 heightened that nation's political discomfiture in view of its supposed advanced status in science. Following debates on the necessity of achieving parity, the US government established the **National Aeronautics and Space Administration (NASA)** in 1958. Since that time, NASA has conducted virtually all major aspects of the US space program.

The first successful US satellite, **Explorer 1**, was launched about four months after Sputnik 1. During the next decades the two nations participated in a space race, conducting thousands of successful launches of spacecraft of all varieties including scientific research, communications, meteorological, remote-sensing, military reconnaissance, early warning, and navigation satellites, lunar and planetary probes, and manned craft. The USSR launched the first human, **Yury Gagarin**, into orbit around Earth on 12 Apr 1961. On 20 July 1969, the US landed two men, **Neil Armstrong** and **Edwin ("Buzz") Aldrin**, on the surface of the Moon as part of the **Apollo 11** mission. On 12 Apr 1981, the 20th anniversary of manned space flight, the US launched the first reusable manned space transportation system, the space shuttle. From the 1960s the European nations, Japan, India, and other countries have formed their own agencies for space exploration and development. The **European Space Agency (ESA)**, consists of 15 member nations. Private corporations, too, offer space launches for communications and remote sensing satellites.

In the post-Apollo decades, while the US focused much of its manned space program on the **shuttle**, the USSR concentrated on launching a series of increasingly sophisticated Earth-orbiting **space stations**, beginning with the world's first in 1971. Station crews, who were carried up in two- and three-person spacecraft, carried out mostly scientific missions while gaining experience in living and working for long periods in the space environment. After the USSR was dissolved in 1991, its space program was continued by Russia on a much smaller scale owing to economic constraints. The US launched a space station in 1973 using surplus Apollo hardware and conducted shuttle missions to a Russian station, Mir, in the 1990s. In 1998, at the head of a 16-nation consortium and with Russia as a major partner, it began in-orbit assembly of the **International Space Station (ISS)**, using the shuttle and Russian expendable launch vehicles to ferry the facility's modular components and crews into space. In addition to manned and unmanned lunar exploration, space exploration programs have included deep-space robotic missions to the planets, their moons, and smaller bodies such as comets and asteroids. Also important has been the development of unmanned space-based astronomical observatories, which allow observation of near and distant cosmic objects above the filtering and distorting effects of Earth's atmosphere.

**Significant space programs and missions:**

**Sputnik** (Russian for "fellow traveler")
**Years launched:** 1957–58. **Country or space agency:** USSR. **Designation:** 1 through 3 (first series). **Not Manned. Events of note:** Sputnik 1 was the first satellite to be successfully launched into space; Sputnik 2 carried a small dog named Laika ("Barker"); Sputnik 3 became the first multipurpose space-science satellite.

**Vanguard**
**Years launched:** 1958–59. **Country or space agency:** US. **Designation:** 1 through 3. **Not Manned. Events of note:** The first attempted Vanguard launch, hastily mounted in December 1957 after the USSR's Sputnik successes, failed with the launch vehicle's explosion.

**Explorer**
**Years launched:** 1958–75. **Country or space agency:** US. **Designation:** 1 through 55. **Not Manned. Events**

of note: Explorer 1, the first successful US satellite, discovered Earth's inner radiation belt. Other Explorers in this long series conducted pioneering studies over a broad spectrum of Earth and space sciences.

### Pioneer
Years launched: 1958–78. Country or space agency: US. Designation: 1 through 13. Not Manned. Events of note: Pioneer 10 was the first spacecraft to travel through the asteroid belt, to fly by Jupiter, and to escape the solar system; Pioneer 11 was the first to visit Saturn. Complementary Pioneer 12 and 13 spacecraft (also called Pioneer Venus) explored Venus, one conducting radar mapping of the planet's cloud-shrouded surface from orbit while the other dropped atmospheric probes.

### Luna (Russian for "Moon")
Years launched: 1959–76. Country or space agency: USSR. Designation: 1 through 24. Not Manned. Events of note: Luna 2 was the first spacecaft to crash-land on the lunar surface; Luna 3 took the first photographs of the Moon's far side; three Lunas (16, 20, and 24) returned with samples of lunar soil.

### Mercury
Years launched: 1961–63 (manned missions). Country or space agency: US. Designation: Manned Mercury spacecraft had program designations, but they became better known by the individual names bestowed on them, such as "Freedom," followed by a "7" to honor the seven NASA astronauts chosen for the program. Manned. Events of note: Some 20 preliminary unmanned Mercury missions took place between 1959 and 1961. Of the six manned missions, Freedom 7 was launched in 1961 with Alan Shepard (the first American in space) aboard; Liberty Bell 7 in 1961 with Virgil "Gus" Grissom; Friendship 7 in 1962 with John Glenn (the first American to orbit Earth); Aurora 7 in 1962 with Scott Carpenter; Sigma 7 in 1962 with Walter Schirra; and Faith 7 in 1963 with Gordon Cooper.

### Vostok (Russian for "east")
Years launched: 1961–63. Country or space agency: USSR. Designation: 1 through 6. Manned. Events of note: The first man in space and to orbit Earth was Soviet cosmonaut Yury Gagarin in Vostok 1, launched on 12 April 1961. Vostok 2 was launched with Gherman Titov in 1961, Vostok 3 with Andriyan Nikolayev in 1962, Vostok 4 with Pavel Popovich in 1962, Vostok 5 with Valery Bykovsky in 1963, and Vostok 6 with Valentina Tereshkova, the first woman in space, in 1963.

### Venera (Russian for "Venus")
Years launched: 1961–83. Country or space agency: USSR. Designation: 1 through 16. Not Manned. Events of note: Venera 1 carried out the first Venus flyby. Venera 3 was the first spacecraft to impact on another planet, and Venera 7 was the first to soft-land on another planet. Venera 9 and 10 sent back the first closeup pictures of Venus's surface.

### Ranger
Years launched: 1961–65. Country or space agency: US. Designation: 1 through 9. Not Manned. Events of note: Ranger 4 was the first US spacecraft to crash-land on the Moon; the last three Rangers returned thousands of images of the lunar surface before impacting the lunar surface as planned.

### Mariner
Years launched: 1962–73. Country or space agency: US. Designation: 1 through 10. Not Manned. Events of note: Various Mariners in the program flew by Venus, Mercury, and Mars. Mariner 9 mapped Mars in detail from orbit, becoming the first spacecraft to orbit another planet. Mariner 10 is the only spacecraft to have visited the vicinity of Mercury.

### Voskhod (Russian for "sunrise" or "ascent")
Years launched: 1964–65. Country or space agency: USSR. Designation: 1 and 2. Manned. Events of note: Voskhod 1 was the first spacecraft to carry more than one person; Aleksey Leonov performed the first space walk, from the Voskhod 2 spacecraft, on 18 Mar 1965.

### Gemini
Years launched: 1965–66. Country or space agency: US. Designation: 1 through 12. Manned. Events of note: Ten two-person manned missions followed two unmanned test flights. Gemini 8 was the first spacecraft to dock with another craft, an unmanned launcher stage. The Gemini program showed that astronauts could carry out rendezvous and docking maneuvers and could live and work in space for the time needed for a round-trip to the Moon.

### Lunar Orbiter
Years launched: 1966–67. Country or space agency: US. Designation: 1 through 5. Not Manned. Events of note: Five consecutive spacecraft made detailed photographic surveys of most of the Moon's surface, providing the mapping essential for choosing landing sites for the manned Apollo missions.

### Soyuz (Russian for "union")
Years launched: 1967–present. Country or space agency: USSR. Designation: 1 through 40 (first series). Three subsequent series of upgraded spacecraft received the additional suffix letters T, TM, or TMA and were renumbered from 1. Manned. Events of note: On 24 Apr 1967 cosmonaut Vladimir Komarov conducted the inaugural test flight (Soyuz 1) of this multiperson transport craft but died returning to Earth after the parachute system failed, becoming the first fatality during a spaceflight. Soyuz 11 ferried the crew of the first space station, Salyut 1. Soyuz TM-2 made the inaugural manned flight of this TM upgrade while transporting the second crew of the Mir space station. Soyuz TM-31 carried up the International Space Station's first three-man crew. An automated unmanned cargo ferry, called Progress, was derived from the Soyuz design.

### Apollo
Years launched: 1968–72. Country or space agency: US. Designation: 7 through 17. Manned. Events of note: Several unmanned test flights preceded 11 manned Apollo missions, including two in Earth orbit (7 and 9), two in lunar orbit (8 and 10), one lunar swingby (13), and six lunar landings (11, 12, and 14–17) in which a total of 12 astronauts walked on the Moon. Apollo 11, crewed by Neil Armstrong, Michael Collins, and Buzz Aldrin, was the first mission to land humans on the Moon, on 20 Jul 1969. Apollo 13, planned as a lunar landing mission, experienced an onboard explosion en route to the Moon; after a swing around the Moon, the crippled spacecraft made a harrowing but safe return journey to Earth

with its crew, James Lovell, John Swigert, and Fred Haise. The six landing missions collectively returned almost 382 kg (842 pounds) of lunar rocks and soil for study on Earth.

## Salyut (Russian for "salute")

**Years launched: 1971–82. Country or space agency:** USSR. **Designation:** 1 through 7 (two designs). **Manned. Events of note:** Salyut 1, launched 19 Apr 1971, was the world's first space station; its crew, cosmonauts Georgy Dobrovolsky, Vladislav Volkov, and Viktor Patsayev, died returning to Earth when their Soyuz spacecraft depressurized. Salyut 6, the first of an improved design, operated as a highly successful scientific space platform, supporting a series of crews and international visitors over a 4-year period.

## Skylab

**Year launched: 1973. Country or space agency:** US. **Manned. Events of note:** Skylab, based on the outfit-ted and pressurized upper stage of a Saturn V Moon rocket, was the first US space station. Three succes-sive astronaut crews carried out solar astronomy studies, materials-sciences research, and biomedical experiments on the effects of weightlessness.

## Apollo-Soyuz

**Year launched: 1975. Countries or space agencies:** US and USSR. **Manned. Events of note:** As a sign of improved US-Soviet relations, an Apollo spacecraft carrying three astronauts docked in Earth orbit with a Soyuz vehicle carrying two cosmonauts. It was the first cooperative multinational space mission and the last use of an Apollo craft.

## Viking

**Year launched: 1975. Country or space agency:** US. **Designation:** 1 and 2. **Not Manned. Events of note:** Both space probes traveled to Mars, released land-ers, and took photographs of large expanses of Mars from orbit. The Viking 1 lander transmitted the first pictures from the Martian surface; both landers carried experiments designed to detect living organ-isms or life processes but found no convincing signs of life.

## Voyager

**Years launched: 1977. Country or space agency:** US. **Designation:** 1 and 2. **Not Manned. Events of note:** Both Voyager spacecraft flew past Jupiter and Sat-urn, transmitting measurements and photographs; Voyager 2 went on to Uranus in 1986 and then to Neptune. Both craft continued out of the solar sys-tem, with Voyager 1 overtaking Pioneer 10 in 1998 to become the most distant human-made object in space.

## space shuttle (Space Transportation System, or STS)

**Years launched: 1981–present. Country or space agency:** US. **Designation:** Individual missions were designated STS with a number (and sometimes let-ter) suffix, although the orbiter spacecraft them-selves were reused. **Manned. Events of note:** The first flight of a manned space shuttle, STS-1, was on 12 Apr 1981 with the orbiter Columbia. Other original op-erational orbiters included Challenger, Discovery, and Atlantis. During shuttle mission STS-51-L, Challenger exploded after liftoff on 28 Jan 1986, killing all seven astronauts aboard including a private citizen, Christa

McAuliffe; the orbiter Endeavour was built as a re-placement vehicle. Space shuttle missions were used to deploy satellites, space observatories, and plane-tary probes; to carry out in-space repairs of orbiting spacecraft; and to take US astronauts to the Russian space station Mir. Beginning in 1998 a series of shut-tle missions ferried components, supplies, and crews to the International Space Station during its assem-bly and operation. In 2003 the orbiter Columbia dis-integrated while returning from a space mission, claiming the lives of its seven-person crew including Ilan Ramon, the first Israeli astronaut to go into space.

## Giotto (named for the Italian artist)

**Year launched: 1985. Countries or space agency:** ESA. **Not Manned. Events of note:** This first deep-space probe launched by ESA made a close flyby of Halley's Comet, collecting data and transmitting im-ages of the icy nucleus. It was then redirected to a second comet, using a gravity-assist flyby of Earth, the first time that a spacecraft coming back from deep space had made such a maneuver.

## Mir (Russian for "peace" and "world")

**Years launched: 1986–96. Country or space agency:** USSR/Russia. **Manned. Events of note:** The core of this modular space station was launched on 20 Feb 1986; five additional modules were added over the next decade to create a large, versatile space labora-tory. Although intended for a 5-year life, it supported human habitation between 1986 and 2000, includ-ing an uninterrupted stretch of occupancy of almost 10 years, and it hosted a series of US astronauts as part of a Mir-space shuttle cooperative endeavor. In 1995, Mir cosmonaut Valery Polyakov set a space en-durance record of nearly 438 days.

## Magellan

**Year launched: 1989. Country or space agency:** US. **Not Manned. Events of note:** Magellan was the first deep-space probe deployed by the space shuttle. Dur-ing four years in orbit above Venus, it mapped some 98% of the surface of the cloud-covered planet with radar at high resolution. At the end of its mission, it was sent on a gradual dive into the Venusian atmo-sphere, where it measured various properties before burning up.

## Galileo

**Year launched: 1989. Country or space agency:** US. **Not Manned. Events of note:** En route to Jupiter, Galileo took the first detailed pictures of two aster-oids and returned unique images of a comet as it im-pacted Jupiter's atmosphere. Near the Jovian system, it released an atmospheric probe and then went into orbit around Jupiter for an extended study of the giant planet and its Galilean moons. Among many discov-eries, Galileo found evidence of a liquid water ocean below Europa's icy surface.

## Ulysses

**Year launched: 1990. Countries or space agency:** US and ESA. **Not Manned. Events of note:** Ulysses trav-eled first to Jupiter in order to use the giant planet's gravity to sling the probe out of the plane of the plan-ets. Ulysses successively passed over the Sun's south and north poles, studying properties of the corona, solar wind, and interplanetary space at high solar latitudes.

### Clementine
**Year launched:** 1994. **Country or space agency:** US. **Not Manned. Events of note:** This probe was designed to test new imaging sensors in space for defense applications. It mapped the Moon in various wavelengths from lunar orbit, determining mineral content of the surface and producing tantalizing hints of the existence of frozen water in permanently shadowed craters near the Moon's south pole.

### NEAR Shoemaker (Near Earth Asteroid Rendezvous Shoemaker)
**Year launched:** 1996. **Country or space agency:** US. **Not Manned. Events of note:** This spacecraft, targeted to the Earth-approaching asteroid Eros, was the first to orbit a small body and to touch down on its surface. It studied Eros for a year with cameras and instruments, then made a slow descent and a soft landing and transmitted gamma-ray data from the surface for more than two weeks.

### Mars Global Surveyor (MGS)
**Year launched:** 1996. **Country or space agency:** US. **Not Manned. Events of note:** MGS conducted long-term mapping from Martian orbit of the planet's entire surface and studies of its magnetic, atmospheric, and internal properties. Close-up images suggested, controversially, that liquid water may have flowed on or near the planet's surface in geologically recent times and still may exist in protected areas. They also showed that the "face on Mars" formation first photographed by Viking 1 was of natural origin and not a product of alien intelligence, as some had purported.

### Mars Pathfinder
**Year launched:** 1996. **Country or space agency:** US. **Not Manned. Events of note:** The first spacecraft to land on Mars since the 1976 Viking missions, Pathfinder descended to the Martian surface using a novel combination of parachutes, rockets, and air bags. The lander and its six-wheeled robotic surface rover, called Sojourner, which together successfully collected 17,000 images and other data, added to evidence that ancient Mars was much more Earth-like than it is today.

### Lunar Prospector
**Year launched:** 1998. **Country or space agency:** US. **Not Manned. Events of note:** Equipped with radiation- and particle-measuring equipment to assay geochemistry of the Moon's surface from orbit, the probe strengthened the evidence for water (first found by Clementine) in the south polar region. It later was deliberately crashed into a permanently shadowed crater at the south pole in an unsuccessful attempt to liberate water vapor, which could be detected from Earth.

### International Space Station (ISS)
**Years launched:** 1998–present. **Countries or space agencies:** US, Russia, ESA, Canada, Japan, and Brazil. **Manned. Events of note:** A large modular complex of habitat modules and laboratories powered by solar arrays, the ISS continued to be assembled in Earth orbit by means of space-shuttle and Proton and Soyuz rocket flights that ferried components, crews, and supplies between Earth and the station. The first component, a US-funded, Russian-built module called Zarya, was launched on 20 Nov 1998. The ISS received its first resident crew on 2 Nov 2000.

### 2001 Mars Odyssey
**Year launched:** 2001. **Country or space agency:** US. **Not Manned. Events of note:** This spacecraft was launched to study Mars from orbit and serve as a communications relay for future U.S. and multinational landers. Its instruments mapped the distribution of various elements on or near the surface; some of its data suggested the presence of huge subsurface reservoirs of frozen water in both polar regions.

 **Did you know?** The Baykonur Cosmodrome, the hub of the Russian space program and the place from which all Russian spaceflights are launched, is actually located in Kazakhstan, which leases the facility to Russia.

## Space Exploration Firsts

| EVENT | DETAILS | COUNTRY OR AGENCY | DATE ACCOMPLISHED |
|---|---|---|---|
| earliest known person to write about spaceflight | Lucian, in his satire *True History,* which includes a visit to the Moon | ancient Greece | 2nd century |
| earliest appearance of rocket-propulsion technology | recorded use of gunpowder-propelled arrows in battle | China | by 13th century |
| first publication of fictional works employing scientific principles to describe human space travel and encounters with alien life | examples: Jules Verne's *From the Earth to the Moon* (1865); H.G. Wells's *The War of the Worlds* (1898) and *The First Men in the Moon* (1901) | — | late 19th and early 20th centuries |
| first person to study in detail the use of rockets for spaceflight | Konstantin Tsiolkovsky | Russia | late 19th and early 20th centuries |
| first rigorous mathematical analysis of rocketry and its application to rocket design | Hermann Oberth, in "The Rocket into Interplanetary Space" (1923) and *Ways to Spaceflight* (1929) | Germany | 1920s |

## Space Exploration Firsts (continued)

| EVENT | DETAILS | COUNTRY OR AGENCY | DATE ACCOMPLISHED |
|---|---|---|---|
| first launch of a liquid-fueled rocket | Robert Goddard | US | 16 Mar 1926 |
| first launch of the V-2 ballistic missile, the forerunner of modern space rockets | Wernher von Braun | Germany | 3 Oct 1942 |
| first artificial Earth satellite | Sputnik 1 | USSR | 4 Oct 1957 |
| first animal launched into space | dog Laika aboard Sputnik 2 | USSR | 3 Nov 1957 |
| first spacecraft to hard-land on another celestial object (the Moon) | Luna 2 | USSR | 14 Sep 1959 |
| first pictures of the far side of the Moon | Luna 3 | USSR | 7 Oct 1959 |
| first applications satellite launched | Tiros 1 (weather observation) | US | 1 Apr 1960 |
| first recovery of a payload from Earth orbit | Discoverer 13 (part of Corona reconnaissance satellite program) | US | 11 Aug 1960 |
| first human to orbit Earth | Yury Gagarin on Vostok 1 | USSR | 12 Apr 1961 |
| first data transmitted to Earth from vicinity of another planet (Venus) | Mariner 2 | US | 14 Dec 1962 |
| first woman in space | Valentina Tereshkova on Vostok 6 | USSR | 16 Jun 1963 |
| first satellite to operate in geostationary orbit | Syncom 2 (telecommunications satellite) | US | 26 Jul 1963 |
| first space walk | Aleksey Leonov on Voskhod 2 | USSR | 18 Mar 1965 |
| first spacecraft pictures of Mars | Mariner 4 | US | 14 Jul 1965 |
| first spacecraft to soft-land on the Moon | Luna 9 | USSR | 3 Feb 1966 |
| first death during a space mission | Vladimir Komarov on Soyuz 1 | USSR | 24 Apr 1967 |
| first humans to orbit the Moon | Frank Borman, James Lovell, and William Anders on Apollo 8 | US | 24 Dec 1968 |
| first human to walk on the Moon | Neil Armstrong on Apollo 11 | US | 20 Jul 1969 |
| first unmanned spacecraft to carry lunar samples back to Earth | Luna 16 | USSR | 24 Sep 1970 |
| first soft landing on another planet (Venus) | Venera 7 | USSR | 15 Dec 1970 |
| first space station launched | Salyut 1 | USSR | 19 Apr 1971 |
| first spacecraft to orbit another planet (Mars) | Mariner 9 | US | 13 Nov 1971 |
| first spacecraft to soft-land on Mars | Mars 3 | USSR | 2 Dec 1971 |
| first spacecraft to fly by Jupiter | Pioneer 10 | US | 3 Dec 1973 |
| first international docking in space | Apollo and Soyuz spacecraft during Apollo-Soyuz Test Project | US/USSR | 17 Jul 1975 |
| first pictures transmitted from the surface of Mars | Viking 1 | US | 20 Jul 1976 |
| first spacecraft to fly by Saturn | Pioneer 11 | US | 1 Sep 1979 |
| first reusable spacecraft launched and returned from space | space shuttle Columbia | US | 12–14 Apr 1981 |
| first spacecraft to fly by Uranus | Voyager 2 | US | 24 Jan 1986 |
| first spacecraft to make a close flyby of a comet's nucleus | Giotto at Halley's Comet | European Space Agency | 13 Mar 1986 |
| first spacecraft to fly by Neptune | Voyager 2 | US | 24 Aug 1989 |
| first large optical space telescope launched | Hubble Space Telescope | US/European Space Agency | 25 Apr 1990 |
| first spacecraft to orbit Jupiter | Galileo | US | 7 Dec 1995 |
| first resident crew to occupy the International Space Station | William Shepherd, Yury Gidzenko, Sergey Krikalyov | US/Russia | 2 Nov 2000 |
| first spacecraft to orbit and land on an asteroid | NEAR at the asteroid Eros | US | 14 Feb 2000/ 12 Feb 2001 |

# Air Travel

## Flight History

Humanity has been fascinated with the possibility of flight for millennia; a myriad of myths and stories feature humans with the ability to fly. Indeed, an important characteristic of the history of flight is the pervasive human interest in the subject; inventors from many countries took up the challenge over the years, achieving varying degrees of success. The history of flight began at least as early as about AD 400 with historical references to a Chinese kite that used a rotary wing as a source of lift. Other toys using the principle of the helicopter—in this case a rotary blade turned by the pull of a string—were known during the Middle Ages. During the latter part of the 15th century, Leonardo da Vinci made drawings pertaining to flight. In the 1700s experiments were made with the ornithopter, a machine with flapping wings.

The history of successful flight begins with the hot-air balloon. In southwestern France, two brothers, Joseph and Étienne Montgolfier, papermakers, experimented with a large cell contrived of paper in which they could collect heated air. On 19 Sep 1783 the Montgolfiers sent aloft a balloon with a rooster, a duck, and a sheep, and on 21 November the first manned flight was made. Balloons gained importance as their flights increased into hundreds of miles, but they were essentially unsteerable.

During the American Civil War, a volunteer officer in the Union army, the former German cavalryman Count Ferdinand von Zeppelin, observed a free balloon ascent. He spent much of the remainder of his life working with balloons, particularly on the steering problem. As his experimentation on what would come to be known as dirigibles continued, hydrogen and illuminating gas were substituted for hot air, and a motor was mounted on a bag filled with gas that had been fitted with propellers and rudders. It was Zeppelin who first saw clearly that maintaining a steerable shape was essential, so he created a rigid but light frame. On 2 Jul 1900 Zeppelin undertook the first experimental flight of what he called an airship. All went well with the development of the dirigible until the docking procedure at Lakehurst NJ on 6 May 1937, when the *Hindenburg* burst into flames and exploded, with a loss of 36 lives. Public feeling about the craft made further development futile.

It should be remembered, however, that neither balloons or dirigibles had produced true flight: what they had done was harness the dynamics of the atmosphere to lift a craft off the ground, using what power (if any) they supplied primarily to steer. The first scientific exposition of the principles that ultimately led to the successful flight with a heavier-than-air device came in 1843 from Sir George Cayley, who is also regarded by many as the father of fixed-wing flight. It was Cayley who built the successful man-carrying glider that came closest to permitting real flight. Cayley's work was built upon in the experiments and writings on gliders from the late 1800s by aviation pioneers Otto Lilienthal of Germany and Octave Chanute of the United States. The works of Cayley, Lilienthal, and Chanute would eventually inspire and form the basis of the Wright brothers' work.

The Americans Wilbur and Orville Wright by 1902 had developed a fully practical biplane (double-winged) glider that could be controlled in every direc-

tion. Fitting a small engine and two propellers to another biplane, the Wrights on 17 Dec 1903 made the world's first successful flight of a man-carrying, engine-powered, heavier-than-air craft at a site near Kitty Hawk, on the coast of North Carolina.

The Wright brothers' success soon inspired successful aircraft designs and flights by others, and World War I (1914–18) further accelerated the expansion of aviation. Though initially used for aerial reconnaissance, aircraft were soon fitted with machine guns to shoot at other aircraft and with bombs to drop on ground targets; military aircraft with these types of missions and armaments became known, respectively, as fighters and bombers.

By the 1920s the first small commercial airlines had begun to carry mail, and the increased speed and range of aircraft made possible the first nonstop flights over the world's oceans, poles, and continents. In the 1930s more efficient monoplane (single-wing) aircraft with an all-metal fuselage (body) and a retractable undercarriage became standard. Aircraft played a vitally important role in World War II (1939–45), developing in size, weight, speed, power, range, and armament. The war marked the high point of piston-engined propeller craft while also introducing the first aircraft with jet engines, which could fly at higher speeds. Jet-engined craft became the norm for fighters in the late 1940s and proved their superiority as commercial transports beginning in the '50s. The high speeds and low operating costs of jet airliners led to a massive expansion of commercial air travel in the second half of the 20th century.

The next great aviation innovation after the jet engine was aircraft able to fly at supersonic speeds. The first was a Bell XS-1 rocket-powered research plane piloted by Maj. Charles E. Yeager of the US Air Force on 14 Oct 1947. The XS-1 broke the sound barrier at 1,066 km/hr (662 mph) and attained a top speed of 1,126 km/hr (700 mph). Thereafter many military aircraft capable of supersonic flight were built. The first supersonic, passenger-carrying, commercial airplane, the Concorde, was built jointly by aircraft manufacturers in Great Britain and France and was in regular commercial service between 1976 and 2003.

---

**Did you know?**

One of the most famous airplanes ever built was Howard Hughes's HK-1 Hercules Flying Boat. Crafted of laminated birch wood and popularly known as the "Spruce Goose," the plane was designed during World War II in an effort to build a troop-and-cargo transport plane that did not rely on precious wartime materials in its construction. After some five years and numerous design changes, the plane made its public debut on 2 Nov 1947, when Hughes piloted the aircraft for its first and only flight, which lasted for about a mile. At the time, the Spruce Goose (a nickname Hughes always hated) was three times larger than any plane ever built, and it still holds the record for the largest wingspan of any aircraft ever built.

---

## Airlines in the US: Best On-Time Arrival Performance
*September 1985–March 2003.*
*Source: US Department of Transportation.*

| | AIRLINE | % OF ALL FLIGHTS | | AIRLINE | % OF ALL FLIGHTS | | AIRLINE | % OF ALL FLIGHTS |
|---|---|---|---|---|---|---|---|---|
| 1 | Skywest | 86.1 | 6 | America West | 78.5 | 11 | JetBlue | 76.3 |
| 2 | Southwest | 82.4 | 7 | US Airways | 78.5 | 12 | Alaska | 76.0 |
| 3 | Northwest | 79.8 | 8 | Delta | 77.7 | 13 | United | 75.8 |
| 4 | American | 79.2 | 9 | ExpressJet | 77.4 | 14 | American Eagle | 75.1 |
| 5 | Continental | 78.8 | 10 | Airtran | 77.2 | 15 | ATA | 73.4 |

# US Aviation Safety, 1983–2002

*2002 data are preliminary.*
*Source: US National Transportation Safety Board.*

| | US AIRLINES* | | | | US GENERAL AVIATION | | | |
|---|---|---|---|---|---|---|---|---|
| YEAR | NO. OF ACCIDENTS | NO. OF ACCIDENTS WITH FATALITIES | TOTAL NO. OF DEATHS | HOURS FLOWN | ALL ACCIDENTS | FATAL ACCIDENTS | TOTAL FATALITIES | HOURS FLOWN |
| 1983 | 23 | 4 | 15 | 7,298,799 | 3,075 | 555 | 1,068 | 28,673,000 |
| 1984 | 16 | 1 | 4 | 8,165,124 | 3,017 | 545 | 1,042 | 29,099,000 |
| 1985 | 21 | 7 | 526 | 8,709,894 | 2,739 | 498 | 956 | 28,322,000 |
| 1986 | 24 | 3 | 8 | 9,976,104 | 2,581 | 474 | 967 | 27,073,000 |
| 1987 | 34 | 5 | 232 | 10,645,192 | 2,494 | 446 | 837 | 26,972,000 |
| 1988 | 30 | 3 | 285 | 11,140,548 | 2,388 | 460 | 797 | 27,446,000 |
| 1989 | 28 | 11 | 278 | 11,274,543 | 2,243 | 432 | 769 | 27,920,000 |
| 1990 | 24 | 6 | 39 | 12,150,116 | 2,241 | 443 | 767 | 28,510,000 |
| 1991 | 26 | 4 | 62 | 11,780,610 | 2,197 | 438 | 799 | 27,678,000 |
| 1992 | 18 | 4 | 33 | 12,359,715 | 2,111 | 451 | 867 | 24,780,000 |
| 1993 | 23 | 1 | 1 | 12,706,206 | 2,064 | 401 | 744 | 22,796,000 |
| 1994 | 23 | 4 | 239 | 13,124,315 | 2,022 | 404 | 730 | 22,235,000 |
| 1995 | 36 | 3 | 168 | 13,505,257 | 2,056 | 413 | 735 | 24,906,000 |
| 1996 | 37 | 5 | 380 | 13,746,112 | 1,908 | 361 | 636 | 24,881,000 |
| 1997 | 49 | 4 | 8 | 15,838,109 | 1,845 | 350 | 631 | 25,591,000 |
| 1998 | 50 | 1 | 1 | 16,816,555 | 1,904 | 364 | 624 | 25,518,000 |
| 1999 | 51 | 2 | 12 | 17,555,208 | 1,906 | 340 | 619 | 29,713,000 |
| 2000 | 56 | 3 | 92 | 18,299,257 | 1,837 | 344 | 595 | 29,057,000 |
| 2001 | 45 | 6 | 531 | 17,752,447 | 1,726 | 325 | 562 | 27,451,000 |
| 2002 | 41 | 0 | 0 | 18,011,700 | 1,714 | 343 | 576 | 26,078,000 |

*Scheduled and nonscheduled service.

# World's Busiest Airports

*Ranked by total aircraft movement (takeoffs and landings), 2002.*
*Source: Airports Council International (preliminary statistics). Web site: <www.airports.org>.*

| RANK | AIRPORT | LOCATION | AIRPORT CODE | TOTAL MOVEMENTS |
|---|---|---|---|---|
| 1 | O'Hare International Airport | Chicago IL | ORD | 923,555 |
| 2 | Hartsfield Atlanta International Airport | Atlanta GA | ATL | 889,974 |
| 3 | Dallas/Fort Worth International Airport | Dallas/Ft. Worth TX | DFW | 765,109 |
| 4 | Los Angeles International Airport | Los Angeles CA | LAX | 645,424 |
| 5 | Phoenix Sky Harbor International Airport | Phoenix AZ | PHX | 545,771 |
| 6 | Paris Charles de Gaulle International Airport | Paris, France | CDG | 510,098 |
| 7 | Minneapolis–St. Paul International Airport | Minneapolis/St. Paul MN | MSP | 506,656 |
| 8 | Van Nuys Airport | Los Angeles CA | VNY | 498,477 |
| 9 | McCarran International Airport | Las Vegas NV | LAS | 496,845 |
| 10 | Denver International Airport | Denver CO | DEN | 493,847 |
| 11 | Detroit Metropolitan Wayne County Airport | Detroit MI | DTW | 490,885 |
| 12 | Cincinnati/Northern Kentucky International Airport | Cincinnati OH | CVG | 486,657 |
| 13 | London Heathrow Airport | London, UK | LHR | 466,554 |
| 14 | Philadelphia International Airport | Philadelphia PA | PHL | 463,158 |
| 15 | Frankfurt Airport | Frankfurt, Germany | FRA | 458,359 |
| 16 | George Bush Intercontinental Airport | Houston TX | IAH | 456,849 |
| 17 | Charlotte/Douglas International Airport | Charlotte NC | CLT | 455,516 |
| 18 | Miami International Airport | Miami FL | MIA | 446,235 |
| 19 | Lambert St. Louis International Airport | St. Louis MO | STL | 437,117 |
| 20 | Pittsburgh International Airport | Pittsburgh PA | PIT | 424,974 |
| 21 | Amsterdam Airport Schiphol | Amsterdam, The Netherlands | AMS | 417,115 |
| 22 | Salt Lake City International Airport | Salt Lake City UT | SLC | 406,994 |
| 23 | Memphis International Airport | Memphis TN | MEM | 398,769 |
| 24 | Newark International Airport | Newark NJ | EWR | 394,079 |
| 25 | Logan International Airport | Boston MA | BOS | 392,079 |
| 26 | Phoenix Deer Valley Airport | Phoenix AZ | DVT | 389,570 |
| 27 | Lester B. Pearson International Airport | Toronto ON | YYZ | 383,189 |
| 28 | Washington Dulles International Airport | Washington DC | IAD | 372,624 |
| 29 | Oakland International Airport | Oakland CA | OAK | 371,986 |
| 30 | Orlando Sanford International Airport | Sanford FL | SFB | 368,831 |

# Meteorology

## Global Temperatures and Precipitation

*Listed in alphabetical order by city. For more information see <www.weatherbase.com>.*

| CITY | AVERAGE TEMPERATURE °F (°C) JAN | APR | JUL | OCT | AVERAGE ANNUAL RAIN LEVELS IN INCHES (MM) |
|---|---|---|---|---|---|
| Ankara, Turkey | 27 (−2) | 49 (9) | 69 (20) | 52 (11) | N/A |
| Beijing, China | 26 (−3) | 57 (13) | 79 (26) | 57 (13) | 25.1 (630) |
| Buenos Aires, Argentina | 75 (23) | 62 (16) | 50 (10) | 61 (16) | 38.5 (970) |
| Cairo, Egypt | 57 (13) | 71 (21) | 83 (28) | 75 (23) | 1 (25) |
| Casablanca, Morocco | 55 (12) | 60 (15) | 73 (22) | 66 (18) | 16.1 (400) |
| Christchurch, New Zealand | 63 (17) | 54 (12) | 44 (6) | 53 (11) | 25.5 (640) |
| Colombo, Sri Lanka | 81 (27) | 84 (28) | 83 (28) | 82 (27) | 87.8 (2,230) |
| Doha, Qatar | 63 (17) | 80 (26) | 96 (35) | 85 (29) | 3.2 (80) |
| Hanoi, Vietnam | 62 (16) | 76 (24) | 86 (30) | 78 (25) | N/A |
| Havana, Cuba | 71 (21) | 76 (24) | 82 (27) | 78 (25) | N/A |
| Jerusalem, Israel | 46 (7) | 59 (15) | 73 (22) | 66 (18) | 23 (580) |
| Johannesburg, South Africa | 69 (20) | 61 (16) | 52 (11) | 64 (17) | 28.7 (720) |
| Kandahar, Afghanistan | 44 (6) | 68 (20) | 89 (31) | 64 (17) | 7.4 (180) |
| Lima, Peru | 74 (23) | 71 (21) | 64 (17) | 65 (18) | 0.3 (7.5) |
| Lisbon, Portugal | 51 (10) | 58 (14) | 73 (22) | 64 (17) | N/A |
| London, UK | 39 (3) | 46 (7) | 62 (16) | 51 (10) | 29.7 (750) |
| Mbarara, Uganda | 69 (20) | 69 (20) | 68 (20) | 69 (20) | 35.3 (890) |
| Moscow, Russia | 16 (−8) | 42 (5) | 63 (17) | 39 (3) | 23.6 (590) |
| Nice, France | 48 (8) | 55 (12) | 74 (23) | 62 (16) | 32.4 (820) |
| Nuuk, Greenland | 17 (−8) | 25 (−3) | 45 (7) | 31 (0) | 23.9 (600) |
| Pala, Chad | 77 (25) | 87 (30) | 77 (25) | 78 (25) | 40.4 (1,027) |
| Reykjavík, Iceland | 31 (0) | 37 (2) | 52 (11) | 40 (4) | 32.2 (810) |
| Rotterdam, The Netherlands | 38 (3) | 47 (8) | 63 (17) | 52 (11) | N/A |
| Santiago, Chile | 70 (21) | 59 (15) | 47 (8) | 58 (14) | 13.4 (340) |
| São Paulo, Brazil | 74 (23) | 70 (21) | 63 (17) | 69 (20) | 53.2 (1,350) |
| South Pole, Antarctica | −16 (−26) | −69 (−56) | −74 (−58) | −58 (−50) | 0.1 (2.5) |
| Sydney, Australia | 72 (22) | 65 (18) | 53 (11) | 64 (17) | 44.5 (1,130) |
| Tokyo, Japan | 42 (5) | 57 (13) | 77 (25) | 64 (17) | 60.2 (1,520) |
| Toronto ON, Canada | 21 (−6) | 44 (6) | 70 (21) | 48 (8) | 30.1 (760) |
| Vilnius, Lithuania | 23 (−5) | 41 (5) | 62 (16) | 42 (5) | 26.3 (669) |

*N/A: not available*

## World Temperature Extremes

| REGION | highest recorded air temperature PLACE (ELEVATION) | °C | °F | lowest recorded air temperature PLACE (ELEVATION) | °C | °F |
|---|---|---|---|---|---|---|
| Africa | Al-'Aziziyah, Libya (112 m [367 ft]; 13 Sep 1922) | 57.7 | 136 | Ifrane, Morocco (1,635 m [5,364 ft]; 11 Feb 1935) | −23.9 | −11 |
| Antarctica | Vanda Station, Scott Coast (15 m [49 ft]; 5 Jan 1974) | 15 | 59 | Vostok, 78° 27″ S, 106° 52″ E (3,420 m [11,220 ft]; 21 Jul 1983) | −89.4 | −129 |
| Asia | Tirat Zevi, Israel (−220 m [−722 ft]; 21 Jun 1942) | 53.9 | 129 | Oymyakon, Russia (806 m [2,625 ft]; 6 Feb 1933) | −67.7 | −90 |
| Australia | Cloncurry, Queensland (190 m [622 ft]; 16 Jan 1889) | 53.3 | 128 | Charlotte Pass, New South Wales (1,755 m [5,758 ft]; 29 Jun 1994) | −23 | −9.4 |
| Europe | Seville, Spain (8 m [26 ft]; 4 Aug 1881) | 50 | 122 | Ust-Shchuger, Russia (85 m [279 ft]; exact date unknown) | −55 | −67 |
| North America | Greenland Ranch, Death Valley, California (−54 m [−178 ft]; 10 Jul 1913) | 56.6 | 134 | Snag, Yukon (646 m [2,120 ft]; 3 Feb 1947) | −63 | −81.4 |
| South America | Rivadavia, Argentina (206 m [676 ft]; 11 Dec 1905) | 48.9 | 120 | Colonia, Sarmiento, Argentina (268 m [879 ft]; 1 Jun 1907) | −33 | −27 |
| Tropical Pacific | Tuguegarao, Philippines (22 m [72 ft]; 29 Apr 1912) | 42.2 | 108 | Haleakala, Hawaii (2,972 m [9,750 ft]; 2 Jan 1961) | −10 | 14 |

## Normal Temperatures and Precipitation for Selected US Cities

*Statistics from city airports, 1971–2000. Alphabetical by state.*
*Source: National Oceanic and Atmospheric Administration, National Climatic Data Center, Asheville NC.*

| CITY | MEAN TEMPERATURE (°F) | | | | ANNUAL PRECIPITATION (IN) |
|------|------|------|------|------|------|
| | JAN | APR | JUL | OCT | |
| Montgomery AL | 46.6 | 64.3 | 81.8 | 65.4 | 54.77 |
| Anchorage AK | 15.8 | 36.3 | 58.4 | 34.1 | 16.08 |
| Phoenix AZ | 54.2 | 70.2 | 92.8 | 74.6 | 8.29 |
| Little Rock AR | 40.1 | 61.4 | 82.4 | 63.3 | 50.93 |
| Los Angeles CA | 57.1 | 60.8 | 69.3 | 66.9 | 13.15 |
| San Francisco CA | 49.4 | 56.2 | 62.8 | 61.0 | 20.11 |
| Denver CO | 29.2 | 47.6 | 73.4 | 51.0 | 15.81 |
| Hartford CT | 25.7 | 48.9 | 73.7 | 51.9 | 46.16 |
| Wilmington DE | 31.5 | 52.4 | 76.6 | 55.8 | 42.81 |
| Miami FL | 68.1 | 75.7 | 83.7 | 78.8 | 58.53 |
| Atlanta GA | 42.7 | 61.6 | 80.0 | 62.8 | 50.20 |
| Honolulu HI | 73.0 | 75.6 | 80.8 | 80.2 | 18.29 |
| Boise ID | 30.2 | 50.6 | 74.7 | 52.8 | 12.19 |
| Chicago IL[1] | 22.0 | 47.8 | 73.3 | 52.1 | 36.27 |
| Indianapolis IN | 26.5 | 52.0 | 75.4 | 54.6 | 40.95 |
| Des Moines IA | 20.4 | 50.6 | 76.1 | 52.8 | 34.72 |
| Topeka KS | 27.2 | 54.5 | 78.4 | 56.6 | 35.64 |
| Louisville KY | 33.0 | 56.4 | 78.4 | 58.5 | 44.54 |
| New Orleans LA | 52.6 | 68.2 | 82.7 | 70.0 | 64.16 |
| Portland ME | 21.7 | 43.7 | 68.7 | 47.7 | 45.83 |
| Baltimore MD | 32.3 | 53.2 | 76.5 | 55.4 | 41.94 |
| Boston MA | 29.3 | 48.3 | 73.9 | 54.1 | 42.53 |
| Detroit MI | 24.5 | 48.1 | 73.5 | 51.9 | 32.89 |
| Minneapolis MN | 13.1 | 46.6 | 73.2 | 48.7 | 29.41 |
| Jackson MS | 45.0 | 63.4 | 81.4 | 64.4 | 55.95 |
| St. Louis MO | 29.6 | 56.6 | 80.2 | 58.3 | 38.75 |
| Missoula MT | 23.5 | 45.2 | 66.9 | 44.4 | 13.82 |
| Lincoln NE | 22.4 | 51.2 | 77.8 | 53.5 | 28.37 |
| Las Vegas NV | 47.0 | 66.0 | 91.2 | 68.7 | 4.49 |
| Concord NH | 20.1 | 44.6 | 70.0 | 47.8 | 37.60 |
| Newark NJ | 31.3 | 52.3 | 77.2 | 56.4 | 46.25 |
| Albuquerque NM | 35.7 | 55.6 | 78.5 | 57.3 | 9.47 |
| New York NY[2] | 31.8 | 50.1 | 74.8 | 56.5 | 42.46 |
| Charlotte NC | 41.7 | 60.9 | 80.3 | 61.7 | 43.51 |
| Fargo ND | 6.8 | 43.5 | 70.6 | 45.3 | 21.19 |
| Cleveland OH | 25.7 | 47.6 | 71.9 | 52.2 | 38.71 |
| Tulsa OK | 36.4 | 60.8 | 83.5 | 62.6 | 42.42 |
| Portland OR | 39.9 | 51.2 | 68.1 | 54.3 | 37.07 |
| Philadelphia PA | 32.3 | 53.1 | 77.6 | 57.2 | 42.05 |
| Providence RI | 28.7 | 48.6 | 73.3 | 53.0 | 46.45 |
| Charleston SC | 47.9 | 64.2 | 81.7 | 66.2 | 51.53 |
| Rapid City SD | 22.4 | 44.7 | 71.7 | 48.2 | 16.64 |
| Memphis TN | 39.9 | 62.1 | 82.5 | 63.8 | 54.65 |
| Dallas TX[3] | 44.1 | 65.0 | 85.0 | 67.2 | 34.73 |
| Salt Lake City UT | 29.2 | 50.0 | 77.0 | 52.5 | 16.50 |
| Burlington VT | 18.0 | 43.5 | 70.6 | 47.7 | 36.05 |
| Richmond VA | 36.4 | 57.1 | 77.9 | 58.3 | 43.91 |
| Seattle WA | 40.9 | 50.2 | 65.3 | 52.7 | 37.07 |
| Charleston WV | 33.4 | 54.3 | 73.9 | 55.1 | 44.05 |
| Milwaukee WI | 20.7 | 45.2 | 72.0 | 51.4 | 34.81 |
| Casper WY | 22.3 | 42.7 | 70.0 | 45.7 | 13.03 |

[1]Data from O'Hare International Airport.    [2]Data from John F. Kennedy International Airport.    [3]Data from Dallas/Fort Worth International Airport.

## Hurricane and Tornado Classifications

The Saffir/Simpson Hurricane Scale* is used to rank tropical cyclones in the North Atlantic Ocean and the eastern North Pacific.

**Category 1.** *Barometric pressure:* 28.91 in or more; *wind speed:* 74–95 mph; *storm surge:* 4–5 ft; *damage:* minimal.

**Category 2.** *Barometric pressure:* 28.50–28.91 in; *wind speed:* 96–110 mph; *storm surge:* 6–8 ft; *damage:* moderate.

**Category 3.** *Barometric pressure:* 27.91–28.47 in; *wind speed:* 111–130 mph; *storm surge:* 9–12 ft; *damage:* extensive.

**Category 4.** *Barometric pressure:* 27.17–27.88 in; *wind speed:* 131–155 mph; *storm surge:* 13–18 ft; *damage:* extreme.

**Category 5.** *Barometric pressure:* less than 27.17 in; *wind speed:* 155 mph or more; *storm surge:* 18 ft or more; *damage:* catastrophic.

**Tornado classifications.**

Tornado intensity is commonly estimated after the fact by analyzing damaged structures and then correlating the damage with the wind speeds known to produce various degrees of damage. Tornadoes are assigned specific values on the Fujita Scale, or F-Scale, of tornado intensity established by meteorologist T. Theodore Fujita.

Categories:

**F0.** *Wind speed:* 40–72 mph; *damage:* light.

**F1.** *Wind speed:* 73–112 mph; *damage:* moderate.

**F2.** *Wind speed:* 113–157 mph; *damage:* considerable.

**F3.** *Wind speed:* 158–206 mph; *damage:* severe.

**F4.** *Wind speed:* 207–260 mph; *damage:* devastating.

**F5.** *Wind speed:* 261–318 mph; *damage:* incredible.

**Published by permission of Herbert Saffir, consulting engineer, and Robert Simpson, meteorologist.*

# Indexes

## Wind Chill Table

*The wind chill index is based upon a formula that determines how cold the atmosphere feels by combining the temperature and wind speed and applying other factors. For more information, see <www.nws.noaa.gov/om/windchill/index.shtml>.*

| | | TEMPERATURE (°F) | | | | | | | | | | | | | | |
|---|---|---|---|---|---|---|---|---|---|---|---|---|---|---|---|---|
| | **CALM** | **40** | **35** | **30** | **25** | **20** | **15** | **10** | **5** | **0** | **-5** | **-10** | **-15** | **-20** | **-25** | **-30** |
| **WIND SPEED (MPH)** | **5** | 36 | 31 | 25 | 19 | 13 | 7 | 1 | -5 | -11 | -16 | -22 | -28 | -34 | -40 | -46 |
| | **10** | 34 | 27 | 21 | 15 | 9 | 3 | -4 | -10 | -16 | -22 | -28 | -35 | -41 | -47 | -53 |
| | **15** | 32 | 25 | 19 | 13 | 6 | 0 | -7 | -13 | -19 | -26 | -32 | -39 | -45 | -51 | -58 |
| | **20** | 30 | 24 | 17 | 11 | 4 | -2 | -9 | -15 | -22 | -29 | -35 | -42 | -48 | -55 | -61 |
| | **25** | 29 | 23 | 16 | 9 | 3 | -4 | -11 | -17 | -24 | -31 | -37 | -44 | -51 | -58 | -64 |
| | **30** | 28 | 22 | 15 | 8 | 1 | -5 | -12 | -19 | -26 | -33 | -39 | -46 | -53 | -60 | -67 |
| | **35** | 28 | 21 | 14 | 7 | 0 | -7 | -14 | -21 | -27 | -34 | -41 | -48 | -55 | -62 | -69 |
| | **40** | 27 | 20 | 13 | 6 | -1 | -8 | -15 | -22 | -29 | -36 | -43 | -50 | -57 | -64 | -71 |
| | **45** | 26 | 19 | 12 | 5 | -2 | -9 | -16 | -23 | -30 | -37 | -44 | -51 | -58 | -65 | -72 |
| | **50** | 26 | 19 | 12 | 4 | -3 | -10 | -17 | -24 | -31 | -38 | -45 | -52 | -60 | -67 | -74 |
| | **55** | 25 | 18 | 11 | 4 | -3 | -11 | -18 | -25 | -32 | -39 | -46 | -54 | -61 | -69 | -75 |
| | **60** | 25 | 17 | 10 | 3 | -4 | -11 | -19 | -26 | -33 | -40 | -48 | -55 | -62 | -69 | -76 |

## Heat Index

*The Heat Index shows the effects of the combination of heat and humidity. Apparent temperature is the temperature as it feels to your body. For more information see <www.jeonet.com/heat.htm>.*

| | AIR TEMPERATURE (°F) | | | | | | | | | | |
|---|---|---|---|---|---|---|---|---|---|---|---|
| **relative humidity** | 70 | 75 | 80 | 85 | 90 | 95 | 100 | 105 | 110 | 115 | 120 |
| | **apparent temperature** | | | | | | | | | | |
| 0% | 64 | 69 | 73 | 78 | 83 | 87 | 91 | 95 | 99 | 103 | 107 |
| 10% | 65 | 70 | 75 | 80 | 85 | 90 | 95 | 100 | 105 | 111 | 116 |
| 20% | 66 | 72 | 77 | 82 | 87 | 93 | 99 | 105 | 112 | 120 | 130 |
| 30% | 67 | 73 | 78 | 84 | 90 | 96 | 104 | 113 | 123 | 135 | 148 |
| 40% | 68 | 74 | 79 | 86 | 93 | 101 | 110 | 123 | 137 | 151 | |
| 50% | 69 | 75 | 81 | 88 | 96 | 107 | 120 | 135 | 150 | | |
| 60% | 70 | 76 | 82 | 90 | 100 | 114 | 132 | 149 | | | |
| 70% | 70 | 77 | 85 | 93 | 106 | 124 | 144 | | | | |
| 80% | 71 | 78 | 86 | 97 | 113 | 136 | 157 | | | | |
| 90% | 71 | 79 | 88 | 102 | 122 | 150 | 170 | | | | |
| 100% | 72 | 80 | 91 | 108 | 133 | 166 | | | | | |

**HEAT INDEX/HEAT DISORDERS**

| Heat Index | Possible heat disorders for people in higher risk groups* |
|---|---|
| 130°F or higher | Heatstroke/sunstroke highly likely with continued exposure. |
| 105°-130°F | Sunstroke, heat cramps, or heat exhaustion likely, and heatstroke possible with prolonged exposure and/or physical activity. |
| 90°-105°F | Sunstroke, heat cramps, and heat exhaustion possible with prolonged exposure and/or physical activity. |
| 80°-90°F | Fatigue possible with prolonged exposure and/or physical activity. |

**Small children, the elderly, the chronically ill, those on certain medications or drugs (especially tranquilizers and anticholinergics), and persons with weight and alcohol problems are particularly susceptible to heat reactions, especially during heat waves in areas where moderate climate usually prevails.*

# Ultraviolet (UV) Index

The Ultraviolet (UV) Index predicts the intensity of the sun's ultraviolet rays. It was developed by the National Weather Service and the US Environmental Protection Agency to provide a daily forecast of the expected risk of overexposure to the sun. The Index is calculated on a next-day basis for dozens of cities across the US. Other local conditions, such as cloud cover, are taken into account in determining the UV Index number. UV Index numbers are: 0–2 (minimal exposure); 3–4 (low exposure); 5–6 (moderate exposure); 7–9 (high exposure); and 10 and over (very high exposure).

Some simple precautions can be taken to reduce the risk of sun-related illness: limit time in the sun between 10 AM and 4 PM, when rays are generally the strongest; seek shade whenever possible; use a broad spectrum sunscreen with an SPF of at least 15; wear a wide-brimmed hat and, if possible, tightly woven, full-length clothing; wear UV-protective sunglasses; avoid sunlamps and tanning salons; and watch for the UV Index daily. The UV Index should not be used by seriously sun-sensitive individuals, who should consult their doctors and take additional precautions regardless of the exposure level.

## National Weather Service Watches, Warnings, and Advisories

For more information, see *National Weather Service Web site: <www.crh.noaa.gov>*

**Blizzard warning.** Winter storms with sustained winds or frequent gusts of 35 mph (56 km/hr) or greater and considerable falling and/or blowing snow; visibility reduced to less than ¼ mile. Conditions expected to last at least three hours.

**Excessive heat warning.** Heat index is expected to equal or exceed 115 °F (46 °C) for three hours or more. In these cases, the heat becomes dangerous for a large portion of the population.

**Flash flood.** *Watch:* Flash flooding is possible in and close to the watch area. Those in the affected area are urged to be ready to take quick action if a flash flood warning is issued or flooding is observed. *Warning:* Rapid flooding of small rivers, streams, creeks, or urban areas is imminent or already occurring.

**Flood.** *Watch:* Widespread flooding is possible in and close to the watch area. Those in the affected area are urged to be ready to take quick action if a flood warning is issued or flooding is observed. Issued for general flooding that is expected to occur during or within 12 hours after heavy rain has ended. *Warning:* Issued for life- or property-threatening general flooding that occurs during or within 12 hours after heavy rainfall has ended. Can be issued for rural or urban areas as well as for areas along small streams and creeks. **Coastal flood.** *Watch:* Alerts coastal residents to the possibility of flooding. *Warning:* Flooding is imminent or occurring. Coastal waters extend out 100 nautical miles (100 mi; 185 km). **River flood.** *Warning:* Alerts residents of long-term flooding (more than 12 hours) along major streams and rivers that is a threat to life and/or property. Usually contains river stage forecast, crest information, and the history and impact of the flood.

**Gale warning.** Sustained winds of 34 to 47 knots (39 to 54 mph; 63 to 87 km/hr) are expected or occurring (not directly associated with tropical cyclones).

**Health warning.** Ground level ozone readings are expected to be in the unhealthful range. The elderly and persons with heart or respiratory problems should stay indoors near a fan or circulating air and reduce physical activity. Motorists are asked to reduce unnecessary driving by carpooling or using public transportation.

**Heavy snow warning.** Snowfall amounts of four inches or more in 12 hours or six inches or more in 24 hours are expected.

**Heavy surf advisory.** Describes all tropical cyclone watches and warnings in effect along with details concerning locations, intensity, movement, and precautions. Also issued to describe tropical cyclones and subtropical cyclones prior to the issuance of watches and warnings. High surf may pose a threat to life or property. May be issued alone or in conjunction with coastal flood watches or warnings.

**High wind warning.** Sustained winds of 40 mph (64 km/hr) or more are expected to last for at least one hour, or for nonthunderstorm winds of 58 mph (93 km/hr) or greater for any duration.

**Hurricane.** *Local statement:* A public release in or near the threatened area giving specific details on weather conditions, evacuation decisions made by local officials, and other necessary precautions to protect life and property. *Watch:* An announcement for specific locations that a hurricane poses a possible threat, generally within 36 hours. *Warning:* A warning that sustained surface winds of 64 knots (74 mph; 119 km/hr) or higher are expected in specified coastal areas within 24 hours or less. A hurricane warning can remain in effect when dangerously high water and/or exceptionally high waves continue even though winds may be less than hurricane force. **Inland hurricane force wind.** *Watch:* Issued for inland locations when hurricane force winds are anticipated beyond the coastal areas, though the actual occurrence, timing, and location are still uncertain.

**Ice storm warning.** Damaging ice accumulations are expected during freezing rain situations; walking and driving becomes extremely dangerous. Ice accumulations are usually ¼ inch or greater.

**Severe thunderstorm.** *Watch:* Conditions are favorable for the development of severe thunderstorms in and close to the watch area. Usually in effect for several hours. *Warning:* Issued when a thunderstorm produces hail ¾ of an inch or larger in diameter and/or winds of 58 mph (93 km/hr) or more.

**Sleet warning.** Accumulations of sleet covering the ground to a depth of ½ inch or more are expected.

**Special tropical disturbance statement.** Issued to furnish information on strong formative, nondepression systems. Focuses on major threats of the disturbance, such as the potential for torrential rains on island or inland areas.

**Storm warning (coastal, oceanic, or marine).** Sustained winds of 48 knots (55 mph; 89 km/hr) or greater are expected or occurring and are not directly associated with tropical cyclones.

**Strike probability forecast of tropical cyclone conditions.** The probability that the cyclone center will pass within 50 miles (80 km) to the right or 75 miles (121 km) to the left of the listed locations within the indicated time period when looking at the coast in the direction of the cyclone's movement.

**Tornado.** *Watch:* Conditions are favorable for the development of tornadoes in and close to the watch area. Usually in effect for several hours. *Warning:* A tornado is indicated by radar or sighted by storm spotters. The warning will include where the tornado is and what towns will be in its path.

**Tropical storm.** *Watch:* An announcement that a tropical storm or tropical storm conditions pose a threat to coastal areas, generally within 36 hours. A tropical storm watch is not usually issued if a tropical cyclone is expected to attain hurricane strength. *Warning:* Sustained winds of 34 to 63 knots (39 to 73 mph; 63 to 118 km/hr) inclusive are expected in specified coastal areas within 24 hours.

**Wind chill warning.** Wind chill temperatures are expected to reach −35 °F (−37 °C) or colder, with a minimum wind speed of about 10 mph (16 km/hr).

**Winter storm.** *Watch:* Conditions are favorable for the development of hazardous weather elements, such as heavy snow or sleet, blizzard conditions, significant accumulations of freezing rain or drizzle, or any combination thereof. Usually issued 12 to 48 hours in advance of an event. *Warning:* Hazardous winter weather conditions are imminent or very likely, including any occurrence or combination of heavy snow, wind-driven snow, sleet, or freezing rain or drizzle. Usually issued for up to 12 hours, but can be extended to 24 hours. The term "near-blizzard" may be incorporated into the winter storm warning for serious situations which fall just short of official blizzard conditions.

# Meteorological Phenomena

## Tides

"Tides" refer to any of the cyclic deformations of one astronomical body caused by the gravitational forces exerted by others. The most familiar are the **periodic variations in sea level** on the Earth that correspond to changes in the relative positions of the Moon and the Sun.

At the surface of the Earth the gravitational force of the Moon is about 2.2 times greater than that of the Sun. The tide-producing action of the Moon arises from the variations in its gravitational field over the surface of the Earth as compared with its strength at the Earth's center. The effect is that the water tends to accumulate on the parts of the Earth's surface directly toward and directly opposite the Moon and to be depleted elsewhere. The regions of accumulation move over the surface as the position of the Moon varies relative to the Earth, mainly because of the Earth's rotation but also because of the Moon's orbital motion around the Earth. There are approximately two high and two low tides per day at any given place, but they occur at times that change from day to day; the average interval between consecutive high tides is 12 hours 25 minutes. The effect of the Sun is similar and additive to that of the Moon. Consequently, the tides of largest range or amplitude (**spring tides**) occur at New Moon, when the Moon and the Sun are in the same direction, and at Full Moon, when they are in opposite directions; the tides of smallest range (**neap tides**) occur at intermediate phases of the Moon.

Although the observed tides possess the broad features discussed above, this pattern does not correspond to a pair of bulges that move around the Earth. The inertia of the water, the existence of continents, and effects associated with the water depth result in much more complicated behavior. For the main oceans, a combination of theory and observation indicates the existence of **amphidromic points**, at which the tidal rise and fall is zero: patterns of high and low tides rotate around these points (either clockwise or counterclockwise). Amplitudes are typically less than a meter.

Tides are most easily observed—and of greatest practical importance—along **seacoasts**, where the amplitudes are exaggerated. When tidal motions run into the shallow waters of the continental shelf, their rate of advance is reduced, energy accumulates in a smaller volume, and the rise and fall is amplified. The details of tidal motions in coastal waters, particularly in channels, gulfs, and estuaries, depend on the details of coastal geometry and water-depth variation. Tidal amplitudes, the contrast between spring and neap tides, and the variation of times of high and low tide all vary widely from place to place.

## Monsoons

A **monsoon** is a type of major wind system that seasonally reverses its direction—e.g., one that blows for approximately six months from the northeast and six months from the southwest. The most prominent examples of such seasonal winds occur in southern Asia and in Africa. Monsoonal tendencies also are apparent along the Gulf Coast of the United States and in central Europe, as well as in various other areas. The **primary cause** of monsoons lies in the difference of the annual temperature trends over land and sea. Seasonal changes in temperature are large over land but small over ocean waters. A monsoon blows from cold toward warm regions: from sea toward land in summer and from land toward sea in winter. Atmospheric pressure is high in cold regions and low in warm ones, permitting the movement of air to occur. Most **summer monsoons** have a dominant westerly component and a strong tendency to ascend and produce copious amounts of rain (because of the condensation of water vapor in the rising air). The intensity and duration, however, are not uniform from year to year. **Winter monsoons,** by contrast, have a dominant easterly component and a strong tendency to diverge, subside, and cause drought.

## El Niño

In oceanography and climatology, **El Niño** ("The Christ Child" in Spanish) is the anomalous appearance, every few years, of unusually warm ocean conditions along the tropical west coast of South America. This event is associated with adverse effects on fishing, agriculture, and local weather from Ecuador to Chile and with far-field climatic anomalies in the equatorial Pacific and occasionally in Asia and North America as well.

The **name El Niño** was originally used during the 19th century by the fishermen of northern Peru in reference to the annual flow of warm equatorial waters southward around Christmastime. Peruvian scientists later noted that more intense changes occurred at intervals of several years and were associated with catastrophic seasonal flooding along the normally arid coast, while the thermal anomalies lasted for a year or more. The more unusual episodes gained world attention during the 20th century, and the original annual connotation of the name was replaced by that of the anomalous occurrence.

The **timing and intensity** of El Niño events vary widely. The first recorded occurrence of unusual desert rainfall was in 1525, when the Spanish conquistador Francisco Pizarro landed in northern Peru.

Historians suggest that the desert rains and vegetation encountered by the Spaniards may have facilitated their conquest of the Inca empire. The intensity of El Niño episodes varies from weak thermal anomalies (2–3 °C [about 4–5 °F]) with only moderate local effects to very strong anomalies (8–10 °C [14–18 °F]) associated with worldwide climatic perturbations. El Niño events typically occur at **three- to four-year intervals**, with the strong events being less common. The intermittency varies widely, however, and the phenomenon is neither periodic nor predictable in the sense that ocean tides are.

The warm ocean conditions in the equatorial Pacific induce large-scale anomalies in the atmosphere. **Rainfall** increases manyfold in Ecuador and northern Peru, causing coastal flooding and erosion and consequent hardships in transportation and agriculture. Additionally, strong El Niño events are associated with **droughts** in Indonesia, Australia, and northeastern South America and with altered patterns of tropical storms in the tropical belt. During the stronger El Niño episodes, the atmospheric "teleconnections" are extensive enough to cause unusually severe winter weather at the higher latitudes of North and South America.

# Environmental Change

## Pollution

**Pollution** is the addition of any substance or form of energy to the environment at a rate faster than the environment can accommodate it by dispersion, breakdown, recycling, or storage in some harmless form. All living things exert some pressure on the natural environment, but modern efforts to improve the standard of living for humans—through the control of nature and the development of new consumer products—have partially contaminated much of the world's air, water, and land with chemical wastes. As a result, governments have passed laws to limit or reverse the threat of environmental pollution.

The branch of science that deals with how living things, including humans, are related to their surroundings is called **ecology**. The Earth supports some five million species of plants, animals, and microorganisms that form a vast network of interrelated environmental systems called **ecosystems**. The arctic tundra is an ecosystem and so is a Brazilian rain forest.

If left undisturbed, natural environmental systems tend to achieve **balance or stability** among the various species of plants and animals. Sudden changes in the relative population of a particular species can begin a kind of chain reaction among other elements of the ecosystem. For example, eliminating a species of insect through the use of a chemical pesticide also may eliminate a bird species that depends upon the

insect as a source of food. As another example, overhunting by humans caused the extinction of the passenger pigeon in 1914.

**Environmental pollution** has existed since people began to congregate in towns and cities; ancient Athenians and Romans stored garbage outside city walls, a practice that may have contributed to outbreaks of viral diseases. The adverse effects of pollution became more noticeable as cities grew during the Middle Ages, as the human population grew steadily after 1650, and with the advent of the Industrial Revolution in the 19th century. The reduction of the Earth's resources has been closely linked to the rise in human population.

In 1997 representatives from 160 nations signed the **Kyoto Protocol,** an international agreement that called for the gradual reduction of greenhouse-gas emissions. These are emissions that increase atmospheric carbon dioxide and contribute to the greenhouse effect, an overwarming of the Earth's surface and lower atmosphere. Originally a supporter of the Protocol, the US, shortly after George W. Bush became president, in 2001, opted not to participate.

The various **kinds of pollution** are most conveniently considered under three headings: air, ground, and water.

## Air Pollution

Air pollution is the release into the atmosphere of gases, finely divided solids, or finely dispersed liquid aerosols at rates that exceed the capacity of the atmosphere to dissipate them or to dispose of them through incorporation into the biosphere.

**Dust storms** in desert areas and **smoke** from forest

and grass fires contribute to particulate and chemical air pollution. **Volcanic activity** is the major natural source of air pollution, pouring huge amounts of ash and toxic fumes into the atmosphere.

Air pollution may affect humans directly, causing irritation of the eyes or coughing. More indirectly, its effects can be measured far from the source, as, for example, the fallout of tetraethyl lead from automobile exhausts, which has been observed in the oceans and on the Greenland ice sheet. Still less direct are possible effects on global climates.

Though not generally categorized as air pollution, **noise pollution**, or excessively loud noises, is another form of airborne contamination that has deleterious effects on the environment.

## Ground Pollution

Ground pollution occurs when the land is unable to accommodate in a natural manner the addition of substances to the soil, such as solid wastes that can't be broken down quickly, or, in some instances, at all. It can also refer to the unintended removal of needed components from the earth, such as topsoil. In many areas, the overuse of croplands in the quest to maximize yields results in the erosion of topsoil, which, in turn, causes the over-silting or sedimentation of rivers and streams.

One of the most hazardous forms of pollution comes from **agricultural pesticides**. These chemicals are designed to deter or kill insects, weeds, fungi, or rodents that pose a threat to crops. When airborne pesticides drift with the wind or become absorbed into the fruits and vegetables they are meant to protect, they can become a source of many illnesses, including cancer and birth defects. Pesticides are often designed to withstand rain, which means they are not always water-soluble, and therefore they may persist in the environment for long periods of time. In addition, some pests have developed a genetic resistance

to these chemicals, forcing farmers to increase the amounts or types of pesticide.

Some urban areas are experiencing serious problems regarding the disposal of **garbage and hazardous wastes**, such as solvents and industrial dyes and inks. In many areas landfill sites have reached full capacity, forcing municipalities to consider alternative disposal methods, including incineration. Giant high-temperature incinerators have become another source of air pollution, however, because incineration ashes sometimes contain very high concentrations of metals as well as dioxins, a dangerous family of chemical poisons.

One step toward solving the garbage problem is **recycling**. Some towns have passed ordinances that encourage or require residents to separate glass and aluminum cans and bottles from other refuse so that these substances can be melted down and reused. Although lightweight steel, cardboard, and paper are also economically recyclable, most industries and cities still burn or bury large amounts of scrap metal and paper products.

## Water Pollution

Water pollution occurs when substances are released into a body of water, where they become dissolved or suspended or deposited on the bottom, accumulating to the extent that they overwhelm the body of water's capacity to absorb, break down, or recycle them, and thus interfere with the functioning of aquatic ecosystems.

Contributions to water pollution include substances drawn from the air (such as **acid rain**), silt from **soil erosion**, chemical **fertilizers** and **pesticides**, runoff from **septic tanks**, outflow from **livestock feedlots**, **chemical wastes** from industries, and **sewage** and other urban wastes. A community far upstream in a watershed may thus receive relatively clean water,

whereas one farther downstream receives a partly diluted mixture of urban, industrial, and rural wastes.

When organic matter exceeds the capacity of microorganisms in the water to break it down and recycle it, the excess of nutrients in such matter encourages **algal water blooms**. When these algae die, their remains add further to the organic wastes already in the water, and eventually the water becomes deficient in oxygen. Organisms that do not require oxygen then attack the organic wastes, releasing gases such as methane and hydrogen sulfide, which are harmful to the oxygen-requiring forms of life. The result is a foul-smelling, waste-filled body of water.

# Natural Disasters

## Geologic Disasters

### Major Historical Earthquakes

*Magnitudes given for pre-20th-century events are generally estimations from intensity data. When no magnitude was available, the maximum intensity, written as a Roman numeral from I to XII, is given.*

| YEAR (AD) | AFFECTED AREA | MAGNITUDE OR INTENSITY | DEATHS | YEAR (AD) | AFFECTED AREA | MAGNITUDE OR INTENSITY | DEATHS |
|---|---|---|---|---|---|---|---|
| 365 | Knossos, Crete (Greece) | XI | 50,000 | 856 | Qumis, Damghan, Iran | unknown | 200,000 |
| 526 | Antioch, Syria | unknown | 250,000 | 893 | Caucasus | unknown | 82,000 |
| 844 | Damascus, Syria | VIII | 50,000 | 893 | Daipur, India | unknown | 180,000 |
| 847 | Mosul, Iraq | unknown | 50,000 | 893 | Ardabil, Iran | unknown | 150,000 |
| 847 | Damascus, Syria | X | 70,000 | 1042 | Palmyra, Baalbek, Syria | X | 50,000 |

## Major Historical Earthquakes (continued)

| YEAR (AD) | AFFECTED AREA | MAGNITUDE OR INTENSITY | DEATHS | YEAR (AD) | AFFECTED AREA | MAGNITUDE OR INTENSITY | DEATHS |
|---|---|---|---|---|---|---|---|
| 1138 | Ganzah, Aleppo, Syria | XI | 230,000 | 1963 | Skopje, Macedonia | 6.0 | 1,070 |
| 1201 | Upper Egypt or Syria | IX | 1,100,000 | 1964 | Prince William Sound AK | 8.3 | 131 |
| 1268 | Cilicia, Anatolia (Turkey) | unknown | 60,000 | 1970 | southern Yunnan province, China | 7.7 | 10,000 |
| 1290 | China | 6.7 | 100,000 | 1970 | northern Peru | 7.8 | 66,794 |
| 1556 | Shaanxi province, China | IX | 830,000 | 1972 | Managua, Nicaragua | 6.2 | 5,000 |
| | | | | 1976 | Guatemala City, Guatemala | 7.5 | 22,778 |
| 1667 | Shemakha, Azerbaijan | 6.9 | 80,000 | 1976 | northeastern Italy | 6.5 | 929 |
| 1668 | Shandong province, China | XII | 50,000 | 1976 | Tangshan, China | 7.8 | 240,000 |
| | | | | 1977 | Bucharest, Romania | 7.2 | 1,581 |
| 1693 | Sicily, Catania (Italy) | XI | 100,000 | 1978 | Khorasan, Iran | 7.4 | 25,000 |
| 1703 | Jeddo, Japan | unknown | 200,000 | 1979 | Colombia; Ecuador | 7.9 | 579 |
| 1727 | Tabriz, Iran | VIII | 77,000 | 1980 | El-Asnam (Ech-Cheliff), Algeria | 7.7 | 5,000 |
| 1730 | Hokkaido, Japan | unknown | 137,000 | | | | |
| 1731 | Beijing, China | unknown | 100,000 | 1980 | southern Italy | 6.9 | 3,114 |
| 1737 | Kolkata (Calcutta), India | unknown | 300,000 | 1983 | eastern Turkey | 6.9 | 1,400 |
| | | | | 1985 | Mexico City, Mexico | 8.1 | 9,500 |
| 1739 | China | X | 50,000 | 1986 | San Salvador, El Salvador | 5.4 | 1,000 |
| 1755 | Lisbon, Portugal; Spain; Morocco | XI | 62,000 | 1988 | Leninakan (Kumayri), Armenia | 6.8 | 25,000 |
| 1780 | Tabriz, Iran | unknown | 100,000 | 1989 | northern California | 7.1 | 62 |
| 1811 | New Madrid MO | 8.6 | unknown | 1990 | Rasht, Iran | 7.6 | 50,000 |
| 1835 | northern Japan | 7.6 | 28,300 | 1990 | Luzon, Philippines | 7.7 | 1,600 |
| 1857 | Tejon Pass (Palmdale) CA | 8.3 | unknown | 1991 | northern India | 7.1 | 2,000 |
| 1868 | Ecuador; Colombia | 7.7 | 70,000 | 1992 | Flores Island, Indonesia | 7.5 | 2,500 |
| 1883 | Java, Indonesia | unknown | 100,000 | 1993 | southern India | 6.4 | 30,000 |
| 1905 | Jammu and Kashmir, India | 8.6 | 19,000 | 1995 | Kobe, Japan | 7.2 | 5,000 |
| | | | | 1995 | Sakhalin Island, Russia | 7.1 | 2,000 |
| 1906 | San Francisco CA | 8.3 | 700 | 1997 | northwestern Iran | 5.5 | 1,000 |
| 1906 | Valparaíso, Chile | 8.6 | 1,500 | 1997 | eastern Iran | 7.1 | 1,560 |
| 1908 | Calabria, Messina, Italy | 7.5 | 58,000 | 1998 | Takhar province, Afghanistan | 6.1 | 4,000 |
| 1915 | Abruzzi, Italy | 7.5 | 32,600 | 1999 | Colombia | 6.2 | 1,185 |
| 1920 | Gansu province, China | 8.5 | 200,000 | 1999 | Turkey | 7.6 | 17,000 |
| | | | | 1999 | Taiwan | 7.7 | 2,400 |
| 1923 | Tokyo; Yokohama, Japan | 8.3 | 142,800 | 2000 | Sulawesi, Indonesia | 7.6 | 46 |
| | | | | 2000 | southern Sumatra, Indonesia | 7.9 | 103 |
| 1927 | Nan Ling, China | 8.0 | 40,900 | 2001 | El Salvador | 7.7 | 844 |
| 1932 | Gansu province, China | 7.6 | 70,000 | 2001 | India | 7.7 | 20,085 |
| 1935 | Quetta, India | 7.5 | 30,000 | 2001 | El Salvador | 6.6 | 315 |
| 1939 | Chillán, Chile | 8.3 | 28,000 | 2001 | southern Peru; northern Chile | 8.4 | 75 |
| 1939 | Erzincan, Turkey | 8.0 | 32,700 | | | | |
| 1948 | Ashkhabad, Turkmenistan | 7.3 | 19,800 | 2002 | Turkey | 6.5 | 44 |
| | | | | 2002 | Hindu Kush region, Afghanistan | 7.4 | 150 |
| 1950 | Assam, India | 8.7 | 574 | | | | |
| 1960 | Agadir, Morocco | 5.9 | 12,000 | 2002 | Hindu Kush region, Afghanistan | 6.1 | 1,000 |
| 1960 | Puerto Montt, Valdivia, Chile | 8.5 | 5,700 | 2003 | northern Algeria | 6.8 | 1,600 |

## Measuring Earthquakes

The seismologists Beno Gutenberg and Charles Francis Richter introduced measurement of the seismic energy released by earthquakes on a magnitude scale in 1935. Each increase of one unit on the scale represents a 10-fold increase in the magnitude of an earthquake. Seismographs are designed to measure different components of seismic waves, such as wave type, intensity, and duration. This table shows the typical effects of earthquakes in various magnitude ranges. For further information, see <www.seismo.unr.edu/ftp/pub/louie/class/100/magnitude.html>.

| MAGNITUDE | EARTHQUAKE EFFECTS |
|---|---|
| Less than 3.5 | Generally not felt, but recorded. |
| 3.5–5.4 | Often felt, but rarely causes damage. |

## Measuring Earthquakes (continued)

| MAGNITUDE | EARTHQUAKE EFFECTS |
|---|---|
| Less than 6.0 | At most, slight damage to well-designed buildings. Can cause major damage to poorly constructed buildings over small regions. |
| 6.1–6.9 | Can be destructive in areas up to about 100 km (61 mi) across where people live. |
| 7.0–7.9 | Major earthquake. Can cause serious damage over larger areas. |
| 8 or greater | Great earthquake. Can cause serious damage in areas several hundred km across. |

## Tsunamis

A tsunami is a **catastrophic ocean wave**, usually caused by a submarine earthquake occurring less than 30 mi (50 km) beneath the seafloor, with a magnitude greater than 6.5. Underwater or coastal landslides or volcanic eruptions also may cause a tsunami. The often-used term **tidal wave** is a misnomer: the wave has no connection with the tides. After the earthquake or other generating impulse, a train of simple, progressive oscillatory waves is propagated great distances at the ocean surface in ever-widening circles, much like the waves produced by a pebble falling into a shallow pool. In deep water, the wavelengths are enormous, about 60 to 125 mi (100 to 200 km), and the wave heights are very small, only 1 to 2 ft (0.3 to 0.6 m). The resulting wave steepness is extremely low; coupled with the waves' long periods that vary from five minutes to an hour, this enables normal wind waves and swell to completely obscure the waves in deep water. Thus, a ship in the open ocean experiences the passage of a tsunami as an insignificant rise and fall. As the waves approach continental coasts, friction with the increasingly shallow bottom reduces the velocity of the waves. The period must remain constant; consequently, as the velocity lessens, the wavelengths become shortened and the wave amplitudes increase, coastal waters rising as high as **100 feet (30 m)** in 10 to 15 minutes. By a poorly understood process, the continental shelf waters begin to oscillate after the rise in sea level. Between three and five major oscillations generate most of the damage; the oscillations cease, however, only several days after they begin. Occasionally, the first arrival of a tsunami at a coast may be a trough, the water receding and exposing the shallow seafloor.

## Avalanches

An **avalanche** is a large mass of rock debris or snow that moves rapidly down a mountain slope, sweeping and grinding everything in its path. An avalanche begins when a mass of material overcomes frictional resistance of the sloping surface, often after its foundation is loosened by spring rains or is rapidly melted by a warm, dry wind. Vibrations caused by loud noises, such as artillery fire, thunder, or blasting, can start the mass in motion. **Rock avalanches** (rockfalls) are commonly composed of bedrock fragments a few centimeters (an inch or so) in diameter and include much soil and dust; they are thought to ride on a cushion of compressed air that allows them to travel long distances. A **debris avalanche** usually occurs in unconsolidated earth materials when weakened by moisture. **Snow avalanches** may develop during heavy snowstorms and slide while the snow is still falling, but more often they occur after the snow has accumulated at a given site. One of the causes of snow avalanches is the slow formation of depth hoar (hexagonal cuplike ice crystals that begin to form at ground level) under the snowpack. Depth-hoar crystals develop in loose array from the evaporation of the original snow particles and the simultaneous vapor deposition of larger, denser ice crystals near the ground; thus a zone of weakness occurs within the snowpack near the ground, the particles of which act as a lubricant when the upper layers of the snow start sliding down the mountain. The **wet snow avalanche** is perhaps the most dangerous because of its great weight, heavy texture, and tendency to solidify as soon as it stops moving. The dry type is also dangerous because its entraining of great amounts of air makes it act like a fluid; this kind of avalanche may flow up the opposite side of a narrow valley. Avalanches can carry a considerable amount of rock debris with the snow.

## Deadly Volcano Eruptions
*Casualty figures are approximate.*

| VOLCANO (LOCATION) | YEAR | CASUALTIES | VOLCANO (LOCATION) | YEAR | CASUALTIES |
|---|---|---|---|---|---|
| Tambora (Indonesia) | 1815 | 92,000[1] | Raung (Indonesia) | 1730 | 3,000 |
| Krakatoa (Indonesia) | 1883 | 36,000[1] | Lamington (Papua New Guinea) | 1951 | 3,000 |
| Pelée (Martinique) | 1902 | 30,000 | Awu (Indonesia) | 1856 | 2,800 |
| Ruiz (Colombia) | 1985 | 25,000[2] | Taal, Luzon (Philippines) | 1906 | 1,500 |
| Etna (Italy) | 1669 | 20,000 | Taal, Luzon (Philippines) | 1911 | 1,300 |
| Unzen (Japan) | 1792 | 15,000 | Etna (Italy) | 1536 | 1,000 |
| Kelud (Indonesia) | 1586 | 10,000 | Paricutín (Mexico) | 1949 | 1,000 |
| Laki (Iceland) | 1783 | 9,000 | Purace (Colombia) | 1949 | 1,000 |
| Kelud (Indonesia) | 1919 | 5,000 | Pinatubo (Philippines) | 1991 | 350 |
| Vesuvius (Italy) | 79 | 3,360 | El Chichón (Mexico) | 1982 | 100 |
| Awu (Indonesia) | 1711 | 3,200 | St. Helens (Washington, US) | 1980 | 66[3] |
| Raung (Indonesia) | 1638 | 3,000 | | | |

[1]Includes tidal wave triggered by eruption.   [2]Includes mudflow triggered by eruption.   [3]Includes persons missing.

# Weather-Related Disasters

## Storms

A storm is simply a disturbed state of the atmosphere. The term strongly implies destructive or unpleasant weather conditions characterized by strong winds, heavy rain, snow, sleet, hail, lightning, or a combination of these occurrences. Each type of storm—thunderstorms, cyclonic storms and tornadoes, hurricanes and typhoons—follows a particular cycle and occurs in specific seasons when atmospheric conditions are right for its creation.

Thunderstorms arise when layers of warm, moist air rise in a large, swift updraft to cooler regions of the atmosphere. There the moisture contained in the updraft condenses to form towering cumulonimbus clouds and, eventually, precipitation. Columns of cooled air then sink earthward, striking the ground with strong downdrafts and horizontal winds. At the same time, electrical charges accumulate on cloud particles (water droplets and ice). Lightning discharges occur when the accumulated electric charge becomes sufficiently large. Lightning heats the air it passes through so intensely and quickly that shock waves are produced; these shock waves are heard as claps and rolls of thunder. On occasion, severe thunderstorms are accompanied by swirling vortices of air that become concentrated and powerful enough to form tornadoes. The temperate and tropical regions of the world are the most prone to thunderstorms.

A tornado is a small-diameter column of violently rotating air developed within a convective cloud and in contact with the ground. Tornadoes occur most often in association with thunderstorms during the spring and summer in the mid-latitudes of both the Northern and Southern Hemispheres. These whirling atmospheric vortices can generate the strongest winds known on Earth: wind speeds in the range of 500 km/h (300 mph) have been estimated. When winds of this magnitude strike a populated area, they can cause fantastic destruction and great loss of life, mainly through injuries from flying debris and collapsing structures. Most tornadoes, however, are comparatively weak events that occur in sparsely populated areas and cause minor damage.

A cyclone is any large system of winds that rotates about a center of low atmospheric pressure in a counterclockwise direction north of the Equator and in a clockwise direction to the south. Cyclonic winds move across nearly all regions of the Earth except the equatorial belt and are generally associated with rain or snow. In the Atlantic and Caribbean regions, tropical cyclones are commonly called hurricanes, while in the western Pacific and China Sea the term typhoon is applied.

Hurricanes are characterized by very strong winds and torrential rains; severe thunderstorms and waterspouts are embedded in the storm's cloud system. Storm surge, similar to a tidal wave, is sometimes created by the storm's high winds and by variations in air pressure. When a storm surge slams into a coastline, it usually inflicts severe damage.

Typhoons in the western Pacific are generally much stronger and more deadly than their Atlantic hurricane counterparts. This is because the Pacific Ocean is much larger than the Atlantic, and the typhoons have more time to develop before striking land.

A blizzard is a severe weather condition that is distinguished by low temperatures, strong winds, and large quantities of snow. The US Weather Service defines a blizzard as a storm with winds of more than 51 km/h (32 mph) and enough snow to limit visibility to 150 m (500 ft) or less. A severe blizzard has winds of over 72 km/h (about 45 mph), visibility near zero, and temperatures of −12 °C (10 °F) or lower. The name originated in the central US, where blizzards are brought by northwesterly winds following winter depressions, or low-pressure systems. In the US and in England, the term is commonly used for any strong, heavy snowstorm. In Antarctica, blizzards are associated with winds spilling over the edge of the ice plateau at an average velocity of 160 km/h (about 100 mph).

## Floods

A flood occurs when water overflows its natural or artificial banks onto normally dry land. The effects of floods on human well-being range from unqualified blessings to catastrophes. The regular seasonal spring floods of the Nile River prior to construction of the Aswan High Dam, for example, were depended upon to provide moisture and soil enrichment for the fertile floodplains of its delta. The uncontrolled floods of the Yangtze River and the Huang Ho (Yellow River) in China, however, have repeatedly wrought disaster when these rivers habitually rechart their courses. Uncontrollable floods likely to cause considerable damage commonly result from excessive rainfall over brief periods of time, as, for example, the floods of Paris (1658 and 1910), of Warsaw (1861 and 1964), and of Rome (1530 and 1557). Potentially disastrous floods may also result from ice jams during the spring rise, as with the Danube River (1342, 1402, 1501, and 1830); from storm tides such as those of 1099 and 1953 that flooded the coasts of England, Belgium, and The Netherlands; and from tsunamis, the mountainous sea waves caused by earthquakes, as in Lisbon (1755) and Hawaii (Hilo, 1946).

Floods can be measured for height, peak discharge, area inundated, and volume of flow. These factors are important to judicious land use, construction of bridges and dams, and prediction and control of floods. Common measures of flood control include the improvement of channels, the construction of protective levees and storage reservoirs, and, indirectly, the implementation of programs of soil and forest conservation to retard and absorb runoff from storms.

The discharge volume of an individual stream is often highly variable from month to month and year to year. A particularly striking example of this variability is the flash flood, a sudden, unexpected torrent of muddy and turbulent water rushing down a canyon or a gulch. It is uncommon, of relatively brief duration, and generally the result of summer thunderstorms in mountains. A flash flood can take place in a single tributary while the rest of the drainage basin remains dry. The suddenness of its occurrence makes a flash flood extremely dangerous.

## Wildfires

Fire danger in a wildland setting varies with weather conditions: drought, heat, and wind participate in drying out the timber or other fuel, making it easier to ignite. Once a fire is burning, these factors all increase its intensity. Topography also affects wildland fire, which spreads quickly uphill and slowly downhill.

In the past, a combination of high summer temperatures, strong winds, late summer drought, and accumulations of dead vegetation set the stage for many naturally caused **prairie fires**, which prevented trees from becoming abundant in prairie vegetation. Now the fertile prairie soils are cultivated or grazed.

**Peat bogs**, which cover vast areas in the tundra and boreal forest regions of Canada, northern Europe, Russia, and Britain, are also prone to potentially dangerous fires. Although usually moist, peat may dry out and then burns easily. Peat bog fires are especially hazardous, as they emit carbon monoxide and carbon dioxide and burn deep underground. They may smolder for years, nearly impossible to extinguish.

Dried grass, leaves, and light branches are considered **flash fuels**; they ignite readily and fire spreads quickly in them, often generating enough heat to ignite heavier fuels such as tree stumps, heavy limbs, and the matted duff of the forest floor. Such fuels, ordinarily slow to kindle, are difficult to extinguish. **Green fuels**—growing vegetation—are not considered flammable, but an intense fire can dry out leaves and needles quickly enough to allow ready ignition. Green fuels sometimes carry a special danger: evergreens, such as pine, cedar, fir, and spruce, contain flammable oils that burst into flames when heated sufficiently by the searing drafts of a forest fire.

Tools for fighting wildland fires range from the standard equipment of urban fire departments to portable pumps, tank trucks, and earth-moving equipment. **Firefighting forces** specially trained to deal with wildland fires are maintained by public and private owners of forestlands. Such a force may attack a fire directly by spraying water, beating out flames, and removing vegetation at the edge of the fire to contain it behind a **fire line**. When the edge is too hot to approach, a fire line is built at a safe distance, sometimes using **strip burning** or **backfire** to eliminate fuel in the path of the uncontrolled fire or to change the fire's direction or slow its progress. Backfiring is used only as a last resort.

**Aircraft** were first used in fighting wildland fires in California in 1919. Airplanes and helicopters are primarily used for dumping water, for observation, and occasionally for assisting in communication and transporting personnel, supplies, and equipment.

Humans cause most of the nation's wildfires, either intentionally or through negligence. In the summer of 2003 enormous wildfires burned in several western US states, including one in Arizona that consumed nearly 100,000 acres and destroyed hundreds of homes and buildings in the Santa Catalina Mountains before being contained.

**Did you know?** It is believed that Homo erectus used wood for fire at least 750,000 years ago. The oldest evidence of the use of wood for construction, found at the Kalambo Falls site in Tanzania, dates from some 60,000 years ago.

## Deadliest Hurricanes in the US

Listed below, in order of number of deaths, are the 30 deadliest hurricanes to hit the US mainland 1900–2001. Hurricane names are given in parentheses after the location, when applicable. The list includes Atlantic/Gulf Coast hurricanes only. Source: National Hurricane Center.

National Hurricane Center Web site: <www.nhc. noaa.gov/pastdead.html>

| | HURRICANE LOCATION | YEAR | CATEGORY | DEATHS | | | HURRICANE LOCATION | YEAR | CATEGORY | DEATHS |
|---|---|---|---|---|---|---|---|---|---|---|
| 1 | Galveston TX | 1900 | 4 | 8,000[1] | | 17 | SC; NC (Hazel) | 1954 | 4 | 95 |
| 2 | Lake Okeechobee FL | 1928 | 4 | 1,836 | | 18 | southeast FL; | | | |
| 3 | south TX; FL Keys | 1919 | 4 | 600[2] | | | southeast LA | 1965 | 3 | 75 |
| 4 | New England | 1938 | 3 | 600 | | | (Betsy) | | | |
| 5 | FL Keys | 1935 | 5 | 408 | | 19 | northeast US (Carol) | 1954 | 3 | 60 |
| 6 | southwest LA/ | 1957 | 4 | 390 | | 20 | eastern US (Floyd) | 1999 | 2 | 57 |
| | north TX (Audrey) | | | | | 21 | southeast FL; LA; | 1947 | 4 | 51 |
| 7 | northeast US | 1944 | 3 | 390[3] | | | MS | | | |
| 8 | Grand Isle LA | 1909 | 4 | 350 | | 22 | FL; eastern US | 1960 | 4 | 50 |
| 9 | New Orleans LA | 1915 | 4 | 275 | | | (Donna) | | | |
| 10 | Galveston TX | 1915 | 4 | 275 | | 23 | GA; SC; NC | 1940 | 2 | 50 |
| 11 | MS; LA (Camille) | 1969 | 5 | 256 | | 24 | TX (Carla) | 1961 | 4 | 46 |
| 12 | FL; LA; MS; AL | 1926 | 4 | 243 | | 25 | Velasco TX | 1909 | 3 | 41 |
| 13 | northeast US | 1955 | 1 | 184 | | 26 | Freeport TX | 1932 | 4 | 40 |
| | (Diane) | | | | | 27 | south TX | 1933 | 3 | 40 |
| 14 | southeast Florida | 1906 | 2 | 164 | | 28 | LA (Hilda) | 1964 | 3 | 38 |
| 15 | FL; MS; AL | 1906 | 3 | 134 | | 29 | southwest LA | 1918 | 3 | 34 |
| 16 | northeast US | 1972 | 1 | 122 | | 30 | southwest FL | 1910 | 3 | 30 |
| | (Agnes) | | | | | | | | | |

[1]*Death toll may actually have been as high as 12,000.*  [2]*More than 500 of these lost on ships at sea; 600–900 estimated deaths.*  [3]344 of these lost on ships at sea.

## Costliest Hurricanes in the US

*This table shows cyclones that caused the most damage on the US mainland. For more information see <www.nhc.noaa.gov/pastcost.html>. Note: ranking numbers 19 and 26 on the main list are repeated due to the equal damage amount in dollars of multiple separate hurricanes.*

| RANK | HURRICANE (LOCATION) | YEAR | CATEGORY | ESTIMATED DAMAGE ($), NOT ADJUSTED | DAMAGE IN CONSTANT 2000 DOLLARS |
|---|---|---|---|---|---|
| 1 | Andrew (southeastern FL/southeastern LA) | 1992 | 5 | 26,500,000,000 | 34,954,825,000 |
| 2 | Hugo (SC) | 1989 | 4 | 7,000,000,000 | 9,739,820,675 |
| 3 | Floyd (midatlantic and northeastern US) | 1999 | 2 | 4,500,000,000 | 4,666,817,360 |
| 4 | Fran (NC) | 1996 | 3 | 3,200,000,000 | 3,670,400,000 |
| 5 | Opal (northwestern FL/AL) | 1995 | 3 | 3,000,000,000 | 3,520,596,085 |
| 6 | Georges (Florida Keys, MS, AL) | 1998 | 2 | 2,310,000,000 | 2,494,800,000 |
| 7 | Frederic (AL/MS) | 1979 | 3 | 2,300,000,000 | 4,965,327,332 |
| 8 | Agnes (northeastern US) | 1972 | 1 | 2,100,000,000 | 8,602,500,000 |
| 9 | Alicia (northern TX) | 1983 | 3 | 2,000,000,000 | 3,421,660,182 |
| 10 | Bob (NC/northeastern US) | 1991 | 2 | 1,500,000,000 | 2,004,635,258 |
| 11 | Juan (LA) | 1985 | 1 | 1,500,000,000 | 2,418,795,844 |
| 12 | Camille (MS/AL) | 1969 | 5 | 1,420,700,000 | 6,992,441,549 |
| 13 | Betsy (FL/LA) | 1965 | 3 | 1,420,500,000 | 8,516,866,023 |
| 14 | Elena (MS/AL/ northwestern FL) | 1985 | 3 | 1,250,000,000 | 2,015,663,203 |
| 15 | Gloria (eastern US) | 1985 | 3[1] | 900,000,000 | 1,451,277,506 |
| 16 | Diane (northeastern US) | 1955 | 1 | 831,700,000 | 5,540,676,187 |
| 17 | Bonnie (NC/VA) | 1998 | 2 | 720,000,000 | N/A |
| 18 | Erin (central and northwestern FL/AL) | 1995 | 2 | 700,000,000 | N/A |
| 19 | Allison (northern TX) | 1989 | T.S.[2] | 500,000,000 | N/A |
| 19 | Alberto (northwestern FL/GA/AL) | 1994 | T.S.[2] | 500,000,000 | N/A |
| 19 | Frances (TX) | 1998 | T.S.[2] | 500,000,000 | N/A |
| 22 | Eloise (northwestern FL) | 1975 | 3 | 490,000,000 | 1,489,250,000 |
| 23 | Carol (northeastern US) | 1954 | 3[1] | 461,000,000 | 3,134,443,557 |
| 24 | Celia (southern TX) | 1970 | 3 | 453,000,000 | 2,015,663,203 |
| 25 | Carla (TX) | 1961 | 4 | 408,000,000 | 2,550,580,095 |
| 26 | Claudette (northern TX) | 1979 | T.S.[2] | 400,000,000 | N/A |
| 26 | Gordon (southern and central FL/NC) | 1994 | T.S.[2] | 400,000,000 | N/A |
| 28 | Donna (FL/eastern US) | 1960 | 4 | 387,000,000 | 2,407,888,443 |
| 29 | David (FL/eastern US) | 1979 | 2 | 320,000,000 | N/A |
| 30 | New England | 1938 | 3[1] | 306,000,000 | 4,748,580,000 |
| **non-Atlantic or non-Gulf coast systems** | | | | | |
| 4 | Georges (USVI/Puerto Rico) | 1998 | 3 | 3,600,000,000 | 3,888,000,000 |
| 10 | Iniki (Kauai, Hawaii) | 1992 | unknown[3] | 1,800,000,000 | 2,190,600,000 |
| 10 | Marilyn (USVI/eastern Puerto Rico) | 1995 | 2 | 1,500,000,000 | 1,624,110,320 |
| 15 | Hugo (USVI/Puerto Rico) | 1989 | 4 | 1,000,000,000 | 1,283,755,274 |
| 19 | Hortense (Puerto Rico) | 1996 | 4 | 500,000,000 | N/A |
| 29 | Lenny (USVI/Puerto Rico) | 1999 | 4 | 330,000,000 | N/A |
| 29 | Olivia (CA) | 1982 | T.D.[4] | 325,000,000 | N/A |
| 30 | Iwa (Kauai, Hawaii) | 1982 | unknown[3] | 312,000,000 | N/A |

[1] *Moving more than 30 mph.* [2] *Of tropical storm intensity but included because of high damage.* [3] *Intensity not sufficiently known to establish category.* [4] *Tropical depression.*

## Hurricane Names

*Source: National Hurricane Center.*

In 1953, the National Hurricane Center developed a list of given names for Atlantic tropical storms. This list is now maintained by the World Meteorological Organization (WMO). Until 1979, only women's names were used, but since then men's and women's names have alternated. There are six lists currently in rotation, so names are reused every six years. Any country affected by a hurricane, however, can request its name be retired for ten years. Also, if a storm has been particularly destructive, the WMO can remove it from the list and replace it with a different name.

# Civil Engineering

## History of Civil Engineering

Civil engineering describes the design and construction of public structures. The term first came into use in the 18th century, though the discipline has been in practice since antiquity. Civil engineering is generally distinguished from military engineering and often times from architecture. It is the oldest of the four traditional disciplines of engineering: civil, mechanical, electrical, and chemical.

The first engineer known by name and achievement is **Imhotep**, builder of the **Step Pyramid** at Saqqarah, Egypt, (c. 2550 BC). Imhotep's successors—Egyptian, Persian, Greek, and Roman—carried civil engineering to remarkable heights on the basis of empirical methods aided by arithmetic, geometry, and a smattering of physical science. The lighthouse **Pharos** of Alexandria, **Solomon's Temple** in Jerusalem, the **Colosseum** in Rome, the **Persian Royal Road** and **Roman road systems**, the **Pont du Gard** aqueduct in France, and many other large structures testify to their skill, imagination, and daring. Of many treatises written by them, one in particular survives to provide a picture of engineering education and practice in classical times: *De architectura* by Vitruvius of Rome, published in the 1st century AD.

In construction, medieval European engineers carried technique, in the form of the **Gothic arch** and the **flying buttress**, to a height unknown to the Romans. The sketchbook of the 13th-century French engineer **Villard de Honnecourt** reveals a wide knowledge of mathematics, geometry, natural and physical science, and draftsmanship.

In Asia, engineering had a separate but very similar development, with more and more sophisticated techniques of construction, hydraulics, and metallurgy helping to create advanced civilizations such as the **Mongol empire**, whose large, beautiful cities impressed Marco Polo in the 13th century.

The appearance of civil engineering as a distinct discipline began in France in 1747 with the establishment of the **École Nationale des Ponts et Chaussées** ("National School of Bridges and Highways"), whose faculty and students helped to define the emerging field. Soon, craftsmen, stonemasons, and toolmakers from France and England became civil engineers. In Britain, **James Brindley** began as a millwright and became the foremost canal builder of the century; **John Rennie** was a millwright's apprentice who eventually built the new London Bridge; **Thomas Telford**, a stonemason, became Britain's leading road builder; and **John Smeaton**, an instrument maker, built the Eddystone Lighthouse (1756–59), before founding the Society of Civil Engineers (1771; now known as the **Smeatonian Society**). Other institutions included the **École Polytechnique** in Paris (1794), the **Bauakademie** in Berlin (1799) and the **Institution of Civil Engineers** in London (1818).

Today civil engineering is taught in universities across the world and national organizations of civil engineers have been formed widely.

## The Seven Wonders of the Ancient World

The seven wonders of the ancient world were considered to be the preeminent architectural and sculptural achievements of the Mediterranean and Middle East. The best known are those of the 2nd-century-BC writer Antipater of Sidon. Some early lists included the Walls of Babylon or the Palace of King Cyrus of Persia, but the established list usually contained the following:

**Pyramids of Giza.** The oldest of the wonders and the only one substantially in existence today, the pyramids of Giza were erected c. 2575–c. 2465 BC on the west bank of the Nile River near Al-Jizah in northern Egypt. The designations of the pyramids—Khufu, Khafre, and Menkaure—correspond to the kings for whom they were built. Khufu (also called the Great Pyramid) is the largest of the three, the length of each side at the base averaging 230 m (755 ¾ ft). Its original height was 147 m (481.4 ft); none of the pyramids reach their original heights because they have been almost entirely stripped of their outer casings of smooth white limestone. According to Herodotus, the Great Pyramid took 20 years to construct and demanded the labor of 100,000 men.

**Hanging Gardens of Babylon.** A series of landscaped terraces ascribed to either Queen Sammuramat (810–783 BC) or King Nebuchadrezzar II (c. 605–c. 561 BC), the gardens were built within the walls of the royal palace at Babylon (in present-day southern Iraq). They did not actually "hang" but were instead "up in the air"—that is, they were roof gardens laid out on a series of ziggurat terraces that were irrigated by pumps from the Euphrates River. Although no traces of the Hanging Gardens have been found, classical authors related that the terraces were roofed with stone balconies on which were layered various materials, such as reeds, bitumen, and lead, so that the irrigation water would not seep through them.

**Statue of Zeus.** A large, ornate figure of Zeus on his throne, this wonder was made around 430 BC by Phidias of Athens. It was placed in the huge Temple of Zeus at Olympia in western Greece. The statue, almost 12 m (40 ft) high and plated with gold and ivory, represented the god sitting on an elaborate cedar-wood throne ornamented with ebony, ivory, gold, and precious stones. On his outstretched right hand was a statue of Nike (Victory), and in the god's left hand was a scepter on which an eagle was perched. The statue, which took eight years to construct, may have been destroyed along with the temple in AD 426, or in a fire at Constantinople (Istanbul) about 50 years later.

**Temple of Artemis.** The great temple was built by Croesus, king of Lydia, in about 550 BC and was rebuilt after being burned by a madman named Herostratus in 356 BC. The artemesium was famous not only for its great size (over 110 by 55 m [350 by 80 ft]) but also for the magnificent works of art that adorned it. It was destroyed by invading Goths in AD 262 and was never rebuilt. Little remains of the temple, but excavation has revealed traces of it, and copies survive of the famous statue of Artemis. A mummylike figure, this early representation of the goddess stands stiffly straight, with her hands extended outward. The original statue was made of gold, ebony, silver, and black stone, the legs and hips covered by a garment decorated with reliefs of animals and bees and the head adorned with a high-pillared headdress.

**Mausoleum of Halicarnassus.** Monumental tomb of Mausolus, the tyrant of Caria in southwestern Asia Minor, the mausoleum was built between about 353 and 351 BC by Mausolus' sister and widow, Artemisia. The architect was Pythius (Pytheos), and the sculptures that adorned the building were the work of four leading Greek artists. According to the description of Pliny the Elder, the monument was almost square, with a total periphery of 125 m (411 ft). It was bounded by 36 columns, and the top formed a 24-step pyramid surmounted by a four-horse marble chariot. Fragments of the mausoleum's sculpture are preserved in the British Museum. The mausoleum was probably destroyed by an earthquake between the 11th and 15th century AD, and the stones were reused in local buildings.

**Colossus of Rhodes.** This huge bronze statue was built at the harbor of Rhodes in ancient Greece in commemoration of the raising of the siege of Rhodes (305–304 BC). The sculptor was Chares of Lyndus, and the statue was made of bronze, reinforced with iron, and weighted with stones. The Colossus was said to be 70 cubits (32 m [105 ft]) high and stood beside Mandrákion harbor. It is technically impossible that the statue could have straddled the harbor entrance, and the popular belief that it did so dates only from the Middle Ages. The Colossus took 12 years to build (c. 294–282 BC) and was toppled by an earthquake about 225 BC. The fallen Colossus was left in place until AD 654, when Arabian forces raided Rhodes and had the statue broken up and the bronze sold for scrap.

**Pharos of Alexandria.** The most famous lighthouse of the ancient world, it was built by Sostratus of Cnidus, perhaps for Ptolemy I Soter, but was finished during the reign of his son, Ptolemy II of Egypt, about 280 BC. The lighthouse stood on the island of Pharos off Alexandria and is said to have been more than 100 m (350 ft) high; the only taller man-made structures at the time would have been the pyramids of Giza. It was a technological triumph and is the archetype of all lighthouses since. According to ancient sources, a broad spiral ramp led to the top, where a fire burned at night. The lighthouse was destroyed by an earthquake in the 1300s. In 1994 a large amount of masonry blocks and statuary was found in the waters off Pharos.

## 25 Tallest Buildings in the World

*Building height equals the distance from the sidewalk level of the main entrance to the structural top of the building, including spires. Source: Lehigh University Council on Tall Buildings and Urban Habitat.*

| RANK | BUILDING | CITY | YEAR COMPLETED | HEIGHT IN FT/M | STORIES |
|---|---|---|---|---|---|
| 1 | Petronas Tower 1 | Kuala Lumpur, Malaysia | 1996 | 1483/452 | 88 |
| 2 | Petronas Tower 2 | Kuala Lumpur, Malaysia | 1996 | 1483/452 | 88 |
| 3 | Sears Tower | Chicago IL | 1974 | 1450/442 | 110 |
| 4 | Jin Mao Building | Shanghai, China | 1998 | 1381/421 | 88 |
| 5 | Two International Finance Centre | Hong Kong, China | 2003 | 1352/412 | 88 |
| 6 | Sky Central Plaza | Guangzhou, China | 1996 | 1283/391 | 80 |
| 7 | Shun Hing Square | Shenzhen, China | 1996 | 1260/384 | 69 |
| 8 | Empire State Building | New York NY | 1931 | 1250/381 | 102 |
| 9 | Central Plaza | Hong Kong, China | 1992 | 1227/374 | 78 |
| 10 | Bank of China | Hong Kong, China | 1989 | 1209/369 | 70 |
| 11 | Emirates Tower One | Dubai, UAE | 1999 | 1165/355 | 55 |
| 12 | The Center | Hong Kong, China | 1998 | 1148/350 | 79 |
| 13 | T & C Tower | Kaohsiung, Taiwan | 1997 | 1140/348 | 85 |
| 14 | Aon Center | Chicago IL | 1973 | 1136/346 | 80 |
| 15 | John Hancock Center | Chicago IL | 1969 | 1127/344 | 100 |
| 16 | Burj al Arab | Dubai, UAE | 1999 | 1053/321 | 60 |
| 17 | Chrysler Building | New York NY | 1930 | 1046/319 | 77 |
| 18 | Bank of America Plaza | Atlanta GA | 1992 | 1023/312 | 55 |
| 19 | Library Tower | Los Angeles CA | 1990 | 1018/310 | 75 |
| 20 | Telekom Malaysia Headquarters | Kuala Lumpur, Malaysia | 1999 | 1017/310 | 55 |
| 21 | Emirates Tower Two | Dubai, UAE | 2000 | 1014/309 | 56 |
| 22 | AT&T Corporate Center | Chicago IL | 1989 | 1007/307 | 60 |
| 23 | JPMorgan Chase Tower | Houston TX | 1982 | 1000/305 | 75 |
| 24 | Baiyoke Tower II | Bangkok, Thailand | 1997 | 997/304 | 85 |
| 25 | Two Prudential Plaza | Chicago IL | 1990 | 995/303 | 64 |

## Notable Towers

A tower is any structure that is relatively tall in proportion to the dimensions of its base. It may be either freestanding or attached to a building or wall. Modifiers frequently denote a tower's function (e.g., watchtower, water tower, church tower, and so on).

Historically, there are several types of structures particularly implied by the name. **Defensive towers** served as platforms from which a defending force could rain missiles down upon an attacking force. The Romans, Byzantines, and medieval Europeans built such towers along their city walls and adjoining important gates. The Romans and other peoples also used offensive, or **siege,** towers as raised platforms for attacking troops to overrun high city walls. **Military towers** often gave their name to an entire fortress; the **Tower of London,** for example, includes the entire complex of buildings contiguous with the **White Tower** of William I the Conqueror.

Towers were an important feature of the **churches and cathedrals** built during the Romanesque and Gothic periods. Some Gothic church towers were designed to carry a spire, while others had flat roofs. Many church towers were used as belfries, though the most famous **campanile**, or bell tower, the **Leaning Tower of Pisa** (1174), is a freestanding structure. In civic architecture, towers were often used to hold clocks, as in town halls in France and Germany. The use of towers declined somewhat during the Renaissance but reappeared in the more flamboyant Baroque architecture of the 17th and 18th centuries.

The use of **steel frames** enabled buildings to reach unprecedented heights in the late 19th and 20th centuries; the **Eiffel Tower** (1889) in Paris was the first structure to reveal the true vertical potential of steel construction. The ubiquity of modern skyscrapers has robbed the word *tower* of most of its meaning, though the **Petronas Twin Towers** in Kuala Lumpur, Malaysia, the **Sears Tower** in Chicago, and other skyscrapers still bear the term in their official names.

The world's **tallest freestanding structure** is the CN Tower (1976), an observation and broadcasting tower in Toronto that rises to more than 553 m (1,815 ft). **The tallest supported structure** is a 629-m (2,063-ft) stayed television broadcasting tower, completed in 1963 and located between Fargo and Blanchard ND.

# Bridges

A bridge is a structure that spans horizontally between supports to allow pedestrians and vehicles to cross a void, such as a river or a valley. The bridge supports must be strong enough to hold the structure up, and the span between the supports must be strong enough to carry the vertical loads. Spans are generally made as short as possible; long spans are justified where good foundations are limited—for example, over estuaries with deep water.

The loads that bridges transfer to their vertical supports are of various kinds. Dead load is the weight of the bridge, live load is the weight of the traffic on it, and wind load is the pressure of the wind against the bridge. Major bridges are usually built with public money, and bridge-building can achieve a high level of prominence. Civil engineers often design a bridge to be elegant, as well as efficient and economical.

### Beam bridge
The simplest bridge is the beam (or girder) bridge, consisting of straight, rigid beams placed across a span (e.g., a tree trunk laid across a stream). A more complex example is a plate girder bridge over a highway; a plate girder is a built-up beam consisting of a steel plate to which angles are riveted or welded. Because a simple beam tends to bend down at its middle, particularly over a long chasm, the beam may rest on more than one support to form a continuous beam.

Another beam bridge is the **truss bridge**, made up of members forming rigid triangles. Trusses are popular because they use a relatively small amount of material to carry relatively large loads. A variation of the beam principle is used in the **cantilever bridge**. A cantilever is a beam that extends beyond its support. Sometimes two cantilever arms meet at mid-span or are connected by a light suspended span.

### Arch bridge
Based on a different principle than the beam is the arch bridge. In the beam bridge the load is transmitted vertically to the supports, whereas the arch bridge pushes outward against its supports, which must be heavy to resist the horizontal thrust of the arch. The arch may be fixed, with each end rigid; two-hinged, with a hinge at each support; or three-hinged, with a third hinge at its crown. The hinges permit movement because of loads or temperature changes.

### Suspension bridge
In the suspension bridge huge cables are hung over two high towers. The cable ends are fastened to heavy concrete or masonry anchorages. Suspender cables hanging from the main cables support the roadway. As in the arch, the thrust on the suspension bridge is horizontal. Instead of horizontal compression, or push, however, there is horizontal tension, or pull, upon the anchorages.

### Cable-stayed bridge
Cable-stayed bridges carry the vertical main-span loads by nearly straight diagonal cables in tension. The towers transfer the cable forces to the foundations through vertical compression. The tensile forces in the cables also put the deck into horizontal compression.

### Other bridges
A **drawbridge** over the moat of a medieval castle is an example of a movable bridge. The **bascule bridge**, in either single-leaf or double-leaf, is the modern-day version. Bascule in French means "a seesaw;" a counterweight balances the span in every open position.

The **swing span** bridge turns about a vertical axis to allow ships to pass. It is balanced on a pivot pier, usually in its center. Its span is measured by including the length of both arms. The vertical lift bridge has a tower at each end of its span. Cables attached to ends of the span pass over pulleys at the top of the towers and are fastened to counterweights that equal the weight of the span. The span moves up and down like an elevator.

In the **floating bridge**, boats or pontoons support the road. The bridge retracts or swings aside to allow ships to pass. The **transporter bridge** has two towers supporting a fixed span from which a moving platform or car is hung.

### Early history of bridgebuilding
The earliest bridges were made from materials at hand. The Swiss lake dwellers built their timber houses by driving piles into the lake bed. From this evolved the timber pile and trestle railroad bridge. In warmer parts of the world bridgebuilders erected suspension bridges. In one Chinese type the traveler sat in a basket or saddle suspended from a cable and slid to the opposite bank. Bridgemakers in the Himalayas threw ropes across a chasm and from these hung thinner ropes to carry the road. This was the origin of the modern suspension bridge. The cantilever bridge also originated in Asia, in India; wooden planks, weighted down by abutment stones, were projected from the two banks until they met in the center.

## Basic Types of Bridges

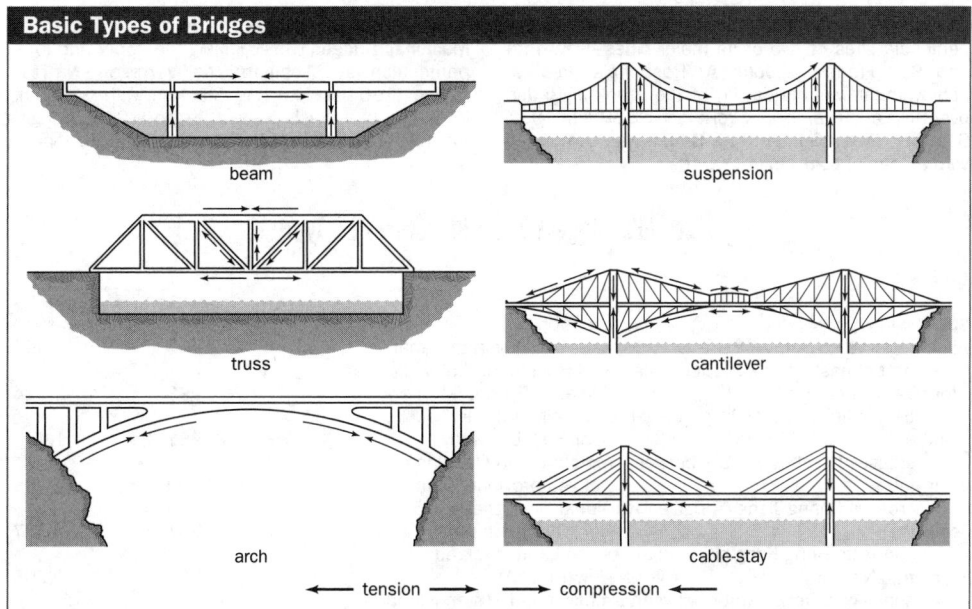

beam

suspension

truss

cantilever

arch

cable-stay

← tension → ← compression ←

The ancient **Romans** were notable bridgebuilders. Six of their masonry arch bridges over the Tiber River still stand in Rome. The most beautiful of the existing Roman bridges is the **Ponte di Augusto,** built at Rimini about 5 BC. The greatest Roman aqueduct is the **Pont du Gard** at Nîmes, France. It has three tiers of arches, which rise 47 m (155 ft) above the Gard River.

### Medieval bridges
During the Middle Ages the church became the chief builder of bridges. Churchmen formed the **Brotherhood of Bridgebuilders** in Italy and France at the end of the 12th century. St. Bénézet built a beautiful stone bridge over the Rhone at Avignon, in southern France. Four arches still remain.

Monks also built the old **London Bridge** (1209) over the River Thames, in London. By the 16th century more than a hundred shops and dwellings had been erected on it. Another covered bridge with shops along the sides was the **Ponte Vecchio** (1345), which still stands over the Arno River, at Florence, Italy.

A major contribution of the Renaissance was the theory of the truss. **Andrea Palladio** of Italy wrote about truss design in *The Four Books of Architecture* (1570). Typical of the bridgebuilding of this period is the stone arch **Rialto Bridge** over the Grand Canal, in Venice. Two Renaissance stone bridges remain over the Seine in Paris—the **Pont Notre Dame** (1505) and the **Pont Neuf** (1606).

### The 18th century
In the 18th century, bridge design came to be considered a science. **Hubert Gautier,** a French engineer, wrote a treatise on bridgebuilding. The first engineering school was founded in Paris. Its director, **Jean Perronet,** is called the father of modern bridgebuilding. He perfected the masonry arch, using a flat arch and slender piers. One of his finest bridges is the **Pont de la Concorde,** in Paris.

Also in the 1700s the **wooden truss bridge** was rediscovered, and the covered wooden bridge began to appear in Switzerland. The **Grubenmann brothers,** Swiss carpenters, built a 200-ft (60-m) span at Wettin-

gen. The picturesque covered bridge was highly developed in the American Colonies. **Col. Enoch Hale** built the first framed **timber bridge** in the United States, over the Connecticut River at Bellows Falls VT, in 1785.

The invention of the steam locomotive changed bridgebuilding, for stronger spans were needed. Iron was first used for chain cables of a suspension over the Tees River, in England, in 1741. Abraham Darby and John Wilkinson built the first **iron bridge** over the Severn River at Coalbrookdale, England, in 1779.

### Modern bridges
**Thomas Telford** built the first modern iron arch bridge in 1813—Craig Ellachie Bridge over the River Spey at Banffshire, Scotland. In the 1820s Telford built the forerunner of the modern suspension bridge—the 570-foot span over **Menai Strait,** in Wales. It had wrought-iron chains for cables. The first to design railroad bridges was George Stephenson, who with his son Robert invented the Rocket, the first practical locomotive. Many truss designs were patented in the 1850s for railroad bridges. After numerous failures of cast-iron bridges, wrought iron was used, then steel.

The first bridge to use steel extensively was the triple-arched **Eads Bridge** over the Mississippi at St. Louis MO, in 1874. The first major use of pneumatic caissons for large piers was made in this bridge. It was an important link in the transcontinental railroad and made St. Louis a crossroads.

At the turn of the 20th century, the construction of **masonry arch bridges** reached its peak. Then the more economical and easier to use concrete became common for arch bridges. Later, reinforced concrete and then prestressed concrete were used.

The first **modern cantilever bridge** was built in 1867 by **Heinrich Gerber** over the Main River at Hassfurt, Germany. The first major example of the cantilever, however, was the **Firth of Forth Bridge,** in Scotland. It was built in 1882–90 with two 1,700-ft (510-m) spans and steel truss members that are tubular in shape.

As the suspension bridge replaced the cantilever, the United States became the world leader in this type of long-span bridgebuilding. One reason was the peninsula sites of two of its major cities—New York and San Francisco. **John A. Roebling**'s greatest achievement was his design of the Brooklyn Bridge over the East River in New York City in 1883. In 1937 San Francisco's **Golden Gate Bridge** was completed with a span of 1280 m (4,200 ft).

After World War II, bridges of note included the **Mackinac Bridge** (1957), linking the upper and lower peninsulas of Michigan; the **Verrazano-Narrows Bridge** (1964) connecting Brooklyn with Staten Island; and the **Akashi Kaikyo Bridge** (1998), bringing together the islands of Honshu and Shikoku, Japan.

## World's Longest-Span Structures by Type

### Bridges

| SUSPENSION | LOCATION | YEAR OF COMPLETION | MAIN SPAN (M) |
|---|---|---|---|
| Akashi Kaikyo | Kobe–Awaji Island, Japan | 1998 | 1,991 |
| part of eastern link between islands of Honshu and Shikoku | | | |
| Store Bælt (Great Belt) | Zealand–Funen, Denmark | 1998 | 1,624 |
| part of link between Copenhagen and mainland Europe | | | |
| Humber | near Hull, England | 1981 | 1,410 |
| crosses Humber estuary between Yorkshire and Lincolnshire | | | |
| Jiangyin | Jiangsu province, China | 1999 | 1,385 |
| crosses Chang Jiang (Yangtze River) near Shanghai | | | |
| Tsing Ma | Hong Kong, China | 1997 | 1,377 |
| connects Hong Kong city with airport on Landao Island | | | |
| Verrazano-Narrows | New York NY | 1964 | 1,298 |
| spans New York Harbor between Brooklyn and Staten Island | | | |
| Golden Gate | San Francisco CA | 1937 | 1,280 |
| spans entrance to San Francisco Bay | | | |
| Höga Kusten (High Coast) | Kramfors, Sweden | 1997 | 1,210 |
| crosses Angerman River on scenic coastal route in northern Sweden | | | |
| Mackinac | Mackinaw City–St. Ignace MI | 1957 | 1,158 |
| spans Mackinac Straits between upper and lower peninsulas of Michigan | | | |
| Minami Bisan-Seto | Sakaide, Japan | 1988 | 1,100 |
| part of central link between islands of Honshu and Shikoku | | | |
| Bosporus II (Fatih Sultan Mehmet) | Istanbul, Turkey | 1988 | 1,090 |
| spans strait from Rumeli Fortress on European side to Anadolu Fortress on Asian side | | | |
| Bosporus I | Istanbul, Turkey | 1973 | 1,074 |
| provides highway link between European Turkey (Thrace) and Asian Turkey (Anatolia) | | | |
| George Washington | New York NY | 1931 | 1,067 |
| crosses Hudson River between New Jersey and Manhattan Island | | | |
| Kurushima-3 | Onomichi–Imabari, Japan | 1999 | 1,030 |
| part of western link between islands of Honshu and Shikoku | | | |
| Kurushima-2 | Onomichi–Imabari, Japan | 1999 | 1,020 |
| part of western link between islands of Honshu and Shikoku | | | |
| Ponte 25 de Abril (Salazar) | Lisbon, Portugal | 1966 | 1,013 |
| provides main crossing over Tagus River into Lisbon | | | |
| Forth Road | Queensferry, Scotland | 1964 | 1,006 |
| carries automobile traffic over Firth of Forth | | | |
| Kita Bisan-Seto | Kojima–Sakaide, Japan | 1988 | 990 |
| part of central link between islands of Honshu and Shikoku | | | |
| Severn | near Bristol, England | 1966 | 988 |
| crosses Severn estuary between England and Wales | | | |
| Yichang | Hubei province, China | 2001 | 960 |
| crosses Chang Jiang (Yangtze River) downstream of Three Gorges Dam | | | |
| | | | |
| **CABLE-STAYED (STEEL)** | | | |
| Tatara | Onomichi–Imabari, Japan | 1999 | 890 |
| part of western link between islands of Honshu and Shikoku | | | |
| Normandie | near Le Havre, France | 1995 | 856 |
| crosses Seine estuary between upper and lower Normandy | | | |
| Nancha | Nanjing, China | 2001 | 628 |
| southern span of Second Nanjing Yangtze Bridge | | | |
| Wuhan Baishazhou | Hubei province, China | 2000 | 618 |
| provides third crossing of Chang Jiang (Yangtze River) in city of Wuhan | | | |
| Qingzhou Minjiang | Fuzhou, China | 2001 | 605 |
| connects Fuzhou with airport across Minjiang (Min River) | | | |
| Yangpu | Shanghai, China | 1993 | 602 |
| crosses Huangpujiang (Huang-p'u River) between northeast Shanghai and Pudong New District | | | |
| Xupu | Shanghai, China | 1997 | 590 |
| crosses Huangpujiang (Huang-p'u River) between southwest Shanghai and Pudong New District | | | |

# World's Longest-Span Structures (continued)

| | LOCATION | YEAR OF COMPLETION | MAIN SPAN (M) |
|---|---|---|---|
| **CABLE-STAYED (STEEL)** | | | |
| Meikouchuou (Meiko Central) | Nagoya, Japan | 1998 | 590 |
| middle of three spans crossing Nagoya's port | | | |
| Skarnsundet | near Trondheim, Norway | 1991 | 530 |
| crosses scenic Trondheimsfjorden between northern and southern Norway | | | |
| Queshi | Shantou, China | 1998 | 518 |
| carries highway traffic across Shantou's harbor | | | |
| Tsurumi Tsubasa | Yokohama, Japan | 1994 | 510 |
| one of two spans crossing Yokohama's harbor | | | |
| Jingsha Yangtze River North | Jingzhou, China | 2002 | 500 |
| part of multispan crossing of Chang Jiang (Yangtze River) on north-south highway | | | |
| Ikuchi | Onomichi–Imabari, Japan | 1991 | 490 |
| part of western link between islands of Honshu and Shikoku | | | |
| Øresund (Öresund) | Copenhagen– Malmö | 2000 | 490 |
| part of link across The Sound between Denmark and Sweden | | | |
| | | | |
| **ARCH** | | | |
| **steel** | | | |
| Lupu | Shanghai, China | 2003 | 550 |
| crosses Huangpujiang (Huang-p'u River) between central Shanghai and Pudong New District | | | |
| New River Gorge | Fayetteville WV | 1977 | 518 |
| provides road link through scenic New River Gorge National River area | | | |
| Bayonne | Bayonne NJ–New York NY | 1931 | 504 |
| spans the Kill Van Kull between New Jersey and Staten Island | | | |
| Sydney Harbour | Sydney, Australia | 1932 | 503 |
| links the City of Sydney with North Sydney | | | |
| Fremont | Portland OR | 1973 | 383 |
| links interstate highways over Willamette River | | | |
| Port Mann | Vancouver, BC, Canada | 1964 | 366 |
| carries TransCanada Highway across Fraser River | | | |
| **concrete** | | | |
| Wanxian | Sichuan province, China | 1997 | 420 |
| crosses Chang Jiang (Yangtze River) in Three Gorges area | | | |
| Krk I | Krk Island, Croatia | 1980 | 390 |
| links scenic Krk Island with mainland Croatia | | | |
| Jiangjiehe | Guizhou province, China | 1995 | 330 |
| spans gorge of Wujiang (Wu River) | | | |
| Yongning | Guangxi province, China | 1996 | 312 |
| crosses Yongjiang (Yung River) near Nanning | | | |
| Gladesville | Sydney, Australia | 1964 | 305 |
| spans Parramatta River upstream from Sydney Harbour | | | |
| | | | |
| **CANTILEVER** | | | |
| **steel truss** | | | |
| Pont de Québec | Quebec City, QC, Canada | 1917 | 549 |
| provides rail crossing over St. Lawrence River | | | |
| Forth | Queensferry, Scotland | 1890 | 2 spans, each 521 |
| provides rail crossing over Firth of Forth | | | |
| Minato | Osaka–Amagasaki, Japan | 1974 | 510 |
| carries road traffic across Osaka's harbor | | | |
| Commodore John J. Barry | Bridgeport NJ–Chester PA | 1974 | 501 |
| provides road crossing over Delaware River | | | |
| Greater New Orleans-1 | New Orleans LA | 1958 | 480 |
| connects highway traffic across Mississippi River | | | |
| Greater New Orleans-2 | New Orleans LA | 1988 | 480 |
| provides parallel service to Greater New Orleans-1 Bridge | | | |
| Howrah | Calcutta | 1943 | 457 |
| provides automobile and pedestrian crossing of Hooghly River | | | |
| | | | |
| **PRESTRESSED CONCRETE** | | | |
| Stolmasundet | Austevoll, Norway | 1998 | 301 |
| links islands of Stolmen and Sjelbörn south of Bergen | | | |
| Raftsundet | Lofoten, Norway | 1998 | 298 |
| crosses Raft Sound in arctic Lofoten Islands | | | |
| Sundøy | Leirfjord, Norway | 2003 | 298 |
| links Alsten Island to mainland Norway | | | |
| Boca Tigris-2 | Humen, China | 1997 | 270 |
| part of multispan link across Tiger's Mouth (Boca Tigris) of Pearl River Delta | | | |

# World's Longest-Span Structures (continued)

| PRESTRESSED CONCRETE | LOCATION | YEAR OF COMPLETION | MAIN SPAN (M) |
|---|---|---|---|
| Gateway | Brisbane, Australia | 1986 | 260 |
| provides highway link between Queensland's Sunshine Coast and Gold Coast | | | |

**BEAM**
**steel truss**

| | | | |
|---|---|---|---|
| Ikitsuki Ohashi | Nagasaki prefecture, Japan | 1991 | 400 |
| connects islands of Iki and Hirado off of northwest Kyushu | | | |
| Astoria | Astoria OR | 1966 | 376 |
| carries Pacific Coast Highway across Columbia River between Oregon and Washington | | | |
| Francis Scott Key | Baltimore MD | 1977 | 366 |
| spans Patapsco River at Baltimore Harbor | | | |
| Oshima | Yamaguchi prefecture, Japan | 1976 | 325 |
| links Yanai City and Oshima Island | | | |
| Tenmon | Kumamoto prefecture, Japan | 1966 | 295 |
| part of Amakusa Gokyo (Five Bridges of Amakusa) linking islands in southwestern Kumamoto | | | |

**steel plate and box girder**

| | | | |
|---|---|---|---|
| Presidente Costa e Silva | Rio de Janeiro State, Brazil | 1974 | 300 |
| crosses Guanabara Bay between Rio de Janeiro and suburb of Niterói | | | |
| Neckartalbrücke-1 | Weitingen, Germany | 1978 | 263 |
| carries highway across Neckar River Valley | | | |
| Brankova | Belgrade, Serbia | 1956 | 261 |
| provides road crossing of Sava River between Old and New Belgrade | | | |
| Ponte de Vitória-3 | Espírito Santo State, Brazil | 1989 | 260 |
| provides road link to state capital on Vitória Island | | | |
| Zoobrücke (Zoo Bridge) | Cologne, Germany | 1966 | 259 |
| spans Rhine River between old city on left bank and convention centre on right bank | | | |

**MOVABLE**
**vertical lift**

| | | | |
|---|---|---|---|
| Arthur Kill | Elizabeth NJ–New York NY | 1959 | 170 |
| provides rail link between port of Elizabeth and Staten Island | | | |
| Cape Cod Canal | Cape Cod MA | 1935 | 166 |
| provides rail crossing over waterway near Buzzard's Bay | | | |
| Delair | Delair NJ–Philadelphia PA | 1960 | 165 |
| provides rail link across Delaware River between Philadelphia and South Jersey shore | | | |
| Marine Parkway-Gil Hodges Memorial | New York NY | 1937 | 165 |
| carries road traffic over mouth of Jamaica Bay between Brooklyn and the Rockaways, Queens | | | |

**swing span**

| | | | |
|---|---|---|---|
| Al-Firdan (El-Ferdan) | Suez Canal, Egypt | 2001 | 340 |
| provides road and rail link between Sinai Peninsula and eastern Nile Delta region | | | |
| Santa Fe | Fort Madison IA–Niota IL | 1927 | 160 |
| provides road and rail crossing of Mississippi River | | | |

**BASCULE**

| | | | |
|---|---|---|---|
| South Capitol Street/Frederick Douglass Memorial | Washington DC | 1949 | 118 |
| carries road traffic over Anacostia River | | | |
| Sault Sainte Marie | Sault Sainte Marie MI–Ontario | 1941 | 102 |
| connects rail systems of United States and Canada | | | |
| Charles Berry | Lorain OH | 1940 | 101 |
| carries road traffic over Black River | | | |
| Market Street/Chief John Ross | Chattanooga TN | 1917 | 94 |
| carries road traffic over Tennessee River | | | |

**Causeways**[1]

| | | | |
|---|---|---|---|
| Lake Pontchartrain-2 | Metairie–Mandeville LA | 1969 | 38,422 |
| carries northbound road traffic from suburbs of New Orleans to north lakeshore | | | |
| Lake Pontchartrain-1 | Mandeville–Metairie LA | 1956 | 38,352 |
| carries southbound road traffic from north lakeshore to suburbs of New Orleans | | | |
| King Fahd Causeway | Bahrain–Saudi Arabia | 1986 | 24,950 |
| carries road traffic across Gulf of Bahrain in Persian Gulf | | | |
| Confederation Bridge | Borden-Carleton, PE–Cape Jourimain, NB | 1997 | 12,900 |
| carries road traffic over Northumberland Strait | | | |

[1]Defined here as fixed link over water consisting almost entirely of multiple spans of identical beam or cantilever construction. Does not include links containing tunnels or bridges of suspension, cable-stayed, or arch construction.

# Roads

A road is the traveled way on which people, animals, or wheeled vehicles move. The term **street** implies an urban roadway, **boulevard** denotes a broad landscaped road, and **highway** suggests a high-speed or heavily traveled route, with controlled points of entrance and exit. **Thruway, expressway, motorway, tollway,** and **freeway** are variations of highway.

The earliest roads developed from paths and trails and appeared with the invention of wheeled vehicles, around 3000 BC. Road systems developed to facilitate trade in early civilizations. The **Persian Royal Road,** the first major road, extended 1,775 miles (2,857 km) from the Persian Gulf to the Aegean Sea and was used c. 3500–300 BC.

The **Romans** used roads to maintain control of their empire, with over 53,000 miles (85,000 km) of roadways extending across its lands. Their roads were often several feet thick, characteristically straight, and composed of layers of flintlike lava, gravel mixed with lime, flat stones, and sand or mortar—all stacked on a graded soil foundation. Roman construction techniques and design remained the most advanced until the late 1700s.

In the 19th century, invention of **macadam** road construction provided a quick and durable method for building roads, and **asphalt** and **concrete** also began to be used. The widespread use of bicycles created a demand for roads with smoother surfaces. New types of pavement were developed, in both flexible and rigid varieties.

Motorized traffic in the 20th century led to the **limited-access highway,** the first of which was the Bronx River Parkway in New York City (1925). In the 1930s superhighways also appeared in Italy, as the autostrada, and in Germany, as the autobahn. Military use was an important design feature of these highways, which could accommodate heavy traffic at high speeds. In the 1950s the **US interstate highway system** was inaugurated to link the country's major cities. It included toll roads, for which users pay in increments while traveling on them.

In industrialized nations, roadway planners must account for existing traffic congestion, future traffic needs, and the effects of urban sprawl, in addition to the measures of affordability, quality, and project duration. Engineers must consider material durability, local climatic conditions, drainage patterns, and safety improvements, such as reflective markings, rumble strips, guardrails, and crash cushions.

# Notable Tunnels

A tunnel is a horizontal underground or underwater passageway, generally produced by excavation. Tunnels are used for mining, as passageways for trains and motor vehicles, for diverting rivers around damsites, for housing underground installations such as power plants and military bases, and for conducting water.

When natural obstacles—such as mountains, hills, or rivers—block the path proposed for a railway, highway, or pipeline, engineers bore tunnels through or under the obstacles. Structures built as trenches and later covered are also often called tunnels. A tunnel that carries water from reservoirs to cities for drinking and irrigation is an aqueduct, while those transporting water-borne freight through hillsides are canals. Mass-transit railway tunnels constructed under cities to relieve crowded streets are known as subways.

Excavation of a drift, or horizontal shaft, can begin from a hill or mountain slope, in which case the entrance is called a portal. Work can also begin from a vertical shaft, in which workers and equipment are raised and lowered and out of which rubble or muck is removed. All tunnels need some form of ventilation to supply air to workers and, later, to traffic. Ventilation also draws out potentially dangerous fumes from blasting or from gas deposits and prevents temperatures from getting too high. Tunnels can be divided into four general categories, depending on the material through which they pass: soft ground, solid rock, soft rock, and under water.

### Tunneling in soft ground

Soft-ground tunnels are generally shallow and are often built for use as subways, water-supply systems, and sewers. Excavation in soft ground is much easier than it is in solid rock, but the stand-up time—that is, the time an excavated section will safely stand up without support—is very short. To prevent the tunnel from collapsing, a support structure is continuously built around the heading, or excavation face. A circular or arch-shaped design has been found to be the best at bearing the ground load from above. Brick and stone were used for support in early tunnels, but in modern tunneling steel is generally used to provide temporary support until a concrete lining can be installed.

Soft-soil excavation can be accomplished by a number of methods, from simple hand mining with shovel and pickax to full-face boring with sophisticated machinery. One such device, the tunneling mole, utilizes a rotating wheel set with teeth that continuously excavates material and loads it onto a conveyor belt. When the ground being excavated is extremely soft or a tunnel of large diameter is being constructed, it is sometimes necessary to use what is called the multiple-drift method: a number of small, parallel drifts are bored and connected to create the sides and crown, or top, of the tunnel; the core can then be safely excavated.

Soft-ground tunnels can be built under rivers or in water-bearing strata by using a tunneling shield. The problem of tunneling under a river had defied the engineering imagination for centuries because of the difficulty of preventing mud and water from seeping in and causing the tunnel to collapse. In 1818 Marc Isambard Brunel, a former French naval officer who had immigrated to England, observed the action of a tiny marine borer, the shipworm. The animal's shell plates permitted it to bore through timber and push the sawdust out behind it. Brunel built a giant iron casing, or shield, that could be pushed forward through soft ground by means of screw jacks, while miners dug through shutter openings in the face.

Brunel's rectangular shield was used successfully in driving the world's first underwater tunnel beneath the River Thames in London in 1825–42. Later improvements on Brunel's shield included that of Peter Barlow in 1865, perfected by James Henry Greathead to burrow under the Thames. In the 1880s Greathead used compressed air behind a shield in a

London subway tunnel to prevent flooding while the lining was being installed. Modern tunneling shields are essentially the same as the Greathead design—that is, strong steel cylinders shoved forward by hydraulic jacks.

### Tunneling through rock

Although tunnels through solid rock can be excavated at only about half the rate of tunnels through soft earth, rock bores have much longer stand-up times. If a tunnel is pushed through unfractured blocks, it may need little or no additional support. Tunnelers, however, must be able to change their method of tunneling quickly to suit the conditions. Jointed rock exists in much larger sections and may not settle or shift for several days. Rock bolts, which are rods driven into the joints and kept under tension with nuts, provide extra support.

The introduction of gunpowder blasting in the 17th century marked a great advance in solid-rock excavation. Railroad and, later, motor-vehicle transportation in the 19th–20th centuries led to a tremendous expansion in the number and length of tunnels. Brick and stone were used for support in early tunnels, but in modern tunneling steel is generally used until a concrete lining can be installed. A common method of lining involves spraying a cement mixture called shotcrete onto the tunnel crown immediately after excavation. A permanent shield can then be built by thickening the concrete lining; steel ribs can be used for additional support.

The problem of water inflow can occur in any type of tunneling operation; it is a constant danger during the construction of underwater tunnels. An early solution involved using a pressurized excavation chamber that held back incoming water. Alternative methods include the construction of drainage tunnels and the use of prefabricated sections that can be floated into position, sunk, and attached to other sections.

### History

Ancient civilizations used tunnels to divert water for consumption and farming, and cave dwellers cut short passageways through clay or soft rock to connect adjacent caves or burrow into the sides of hills. In about 2180–60 BC the Babylonians built a tunnel for pedestrian traffic under the Euphrates River. An early Greek tunnel was completed in 687 BC on the island of Samos as part of an aqueduct system.

Initial tunnel-building techniques varied. The Egyptians used copper saws that were capable of cutting soft rock, while the Babylonians constructed masonry tunnels. The Romans built aqueduct tunnels through mountains by heating the rock face with fire and rapidly cooling it with water, causing the rock to crack.

Their greatest feat was a 3.5-mile (5.6-kilometer) tunnel to drain Lake Fucino in Italy to create Fucino Basin.

The first tunnel that can rightly be called modern was built near Malpas, France, as part of the Canal du Midi, or Languedoc Canal. More than 500 feet (150 meters) long, the tunnel was completed in the late 1600s. The Union Canal Tunnel in Pennsylvania, several hundred miles long and completed in 1826, is the oldest existing transportation tunnel in the US. The Hoosac Tunnel, drilled for a railroad through the Berkshire Mountains in Massachusetts in 1851–75, contributed advances in tunneling, including the first use of nitroglycerin as a blasting agent, the first use of electric firing of explosives, and the introduction of power drills—initially steam and later air, from which there ultimately developed a compressed-air industry.

Simultaneously, more spectacular railroad tunnels were being started through the Alps, beginning with the Mont Cenis Tunnel (1857–71). Its engineer, Germain Sommeiller, introduced pioneering techniques such as rail-mounted drill carriages, hydraulic ram air compressors, and construction camps for workers. Subsequent Alpine railroad tunnels were the 9-mile St. Gotthard (1872–82), the 12-mile Simplon (1898–1906), and the 9-mile Lötschberg (1906–11). Nearly 7,000 feet below the mountain crest, Simplon encountered major problems from highly stressed rock bursting off the walls; from high pressure in weak schists and gypsum, requiring 10-foot-thick masonry lining to resist swelling; and from high-temperature water (130 °F [54 °C]), which was partly treated by spraying from cold springs. Driving Simplon as two parallel tunnels with frequent crosscut connections considerably aided ventilation and drainage. The Mont Blanc Tunnel, which links France and Italy through the Alps, was at its opening in 1965 the world's longest vehicular tunnel.

Other tunnels of note include the Cascade Tunnel (1925–29) in Washington, at 7.8 miles (12.5 km) in length, and the Kanmon Tunnel (1936–44), connecting the Japanese islands of Honshu and Kyushu—the first tunnel built under an ocean. The Seikan Tunnel (1964–88) links Honshu to Hokkaido and is the longest tunnel in the world, with a length of 33.5 miles (53.9 km). A series of passageways, extending the Italian high-speed railway system through the Apennine Range between Bologna and Florence, Italy, is projected to top Seikan as the world's longest, with 41 miles (66 km) of tunnel scheduled to be driven by 2006. One of the most famous tunnels, opened in 1994, is the Eurotunnel, or Channel Tunnel (or Chunnel), a 31-mile (50-kilometer) route beneath the English Channel, connecting Folkestone, England, with Sangatte (near Calais), France.

## The World's 25 Longest Tunnels

| TUNNEL | LOCATION | LENGTH IN KM (MI) | COMPLETED | USE |
|---|---|---|---|---|
| Seikan | Japan | 53.9 (33.5) | 1988 | railway |
| passes under the Tsugaru Strait between islands of Honshu and Hokkaido | | | | |
| Channel Tunnel (Eurotunnel) | UK–France | 50.5 (31.4) | 1994 | railway |
| passes under English Channel between Folkestone (UK) and Sangatte (France) | | | | |
| Iwate-Ichinohe | Japan | 25.8 (15.7) | 2002 | railway |
| carries Tohoku high-speed line through mountains between Tokyo and northern Honshu | | | | |
| Lærdal | Norway | 24.5 (15.3) | 2000 | highway |
| carries main cross-country highway through mountains in central Norway | | | | |
| Daishimizu | Japan | 22.2 (13.8) | 1982 | railway |
| on Joetsu Line across Honshu between Tokyo and Niigata | | | | |

## The World's 25 Longest Tunnels (continued)

| TUNNEL | LOCATION | LENGTH IN KM (MI) | COMPLETED | USE |
|---|---|---|---|---|
| Simplon II | Italy–Switzerland | 19.8 (12.3) | 1922 | railway |
| Simplon I | Italy–Switzerland | 19.8 (12.3) | 1906 | railway |
| rail links under Simplon Pass, traditional divide between northern and southern Europe | | | | |
| Vereina | Switzerland | 19.1 (11.9) | 1999 | railway |
| rail link under Flüela Pass between upper Rhine and lower Engadin valleys | | | | |
| Shin-Kanmon | Japan | 18.7 (11.6) | 1975 | railway |
| carries Sanyo high-speed line under Kanmon Strait between islands of Honshu and Kyushu | | | | |
| Great Apennine | Italy | 18.5 (11.5) | 1934 | railway |
| rail link through mountains between Bologna and Florence | | | | |
| Qinling | China | 18.5 (11.5) | 2001 | railway |
| traverses Qinling (Tsinling) Mountains, historic barrier between northern and southern China | | | | |
| Saint Gotthard | Switzerland | 16.9 (10.5) | 1980 | highway |
| links Uri and Ticino cantons under St. Gotthard Pass | | | | |
| Rokko | Japan | 16.3 (10.1) | 1972 | railway |
| carries Sanyo high-speed line through Rokko Mountains near Kobe | | | | |
| Furka | Switzerland | 15.4 (9.6) | 1982 | railway |
| carries scenic Glacier Express line under Furka Pass | | | | |
| Haruna | Japan | 15.4 (9.6) | 1982 | railway |
| on Joetsu Line across Honshu between Tokyo and Niigata | | | | |
| Saint Gotthard | Switzerland | 15 (9.3) | 1882 | railway |
| carries Luzern–Milan line under St. Gotthard Pass between Uri and Ticino cantons | | | | |
| Nakayama | Japan | 14.9 (9.2) | 1982 | railway |
| on Joetsu Line across Honshu between Tokyo and Niigata | | | | |
| Lötschberg | Switzerland | 14.6 (9.1) | 1913 | railway |
| rail link under Lötschen Pass between Bern and Valais cantons | | | | |
| Mount MacDonald | British Columbia | 14.6 (9.1) | 1988 | railway |
| carries Canadian Pacific Railway under Rogers Pass in Glacier National Park | | | | |
| Dayaoshan (Ta-yao Shan) | China | 14.3 (8.9) | 1988 | railway |
| carries dual-track line through Nan Mountains, northern Guangdong province | | | | |
| Arlberg | Austria | 14 (8.7) | 1978 | highway |
| provides road link under Arlberg Pass between Tirol and Vorarlberg provinces | | | | |
| Hokuriku | Japan | 13.9 (8.6) | 1962 | railway |
| on Hokuriku Line along Sea of Japan | | | | |
| Romeriks | Norway | 13.9 (8.6) | 1999 | railway |
| on high-speed rail line between Oslo and airport at Gardermoen | | | | |
| Mount Cenis | France–Italy | 13.7 (8.5) | 1871 | railway |
| carries main Paris–Turin line through Alps At Fréjus Pass | | | | |
| Shin-Shimizu | Japan | 13.5 (8.4) | 1967 | railway |
| on Joetsu Line across Honshu between Tokyo and Niigata | | | | |

## World's Largest Dams

*Source: International Water Power and Dam Construction Yearbook (1996).*

| NAME | TYPE* | DATE OF COMPLETION | RIVER | COUNTRY | |
|---|---|---|---|---|---|
| **by height** | | | | | height (m) |
| Nurek | E | 1980 | Vakhsh | Tajikistan | 300 |
| Grand Dixence | G | 1961 | Dixence | Switzerland | 285 |
| Inguri | A | 1980 | Inguri | Georgia | 272 |
| Vaiont[1] | A | 1961 | Vaiont | Italy | 262 |
| Chicoasen | ER | 1980 | Grijalva | Mexico | 261 |
| Tehri | ER | 2002[2] | Bhagirathi | India | 261 |
| Mauvoisin | A | 1957 | Drance de Bagnes | Switzerland | 250 |
| Guavio | ER | 1989 | Guavio | Colombia | 246 |
| Sayano-Shushensk | AG | 1989 | Yenisey | Russia | 245 |
| Mica | ER | 1973 | Columbia | Canada | 242 |
| Ertan | A | 1999 | Yalong (Ya-lung) | China | 240 |
| Chivor | ER | 1957 | Batá | Colombia | 237 |
| **by volume** | | | | | volume ('000 cubic m) |
| Syncrude Tailings | E | N/A | ...[3] | Canada | 540,000 |
| New Cornelia Tailings | E | 1973 | Ten Mile Wash | US | 209,500 |
| Tarbela | ER | 1976 | Indus | Pakistan | 106,000 |
| Fort Peck | E | 1937 | Missouri | US | 96,050 |
| Lower Usuma | E | 1990 | Usuma | Nigeria | 93,000 |

## World's Largest Dams (continued)

| NAME | TYPE* | DATE OF COMPLETION | RIVER | COUNTRY | volume ('000 cubic m) |
|---|---|---|---|---|---|
| **by volume (continued)** | | | | | |
| Tucurui | EGR | 1984 | Tocantins | Brazil | 85,200 |
| Ataturk | ER | 1990 | Euphrates | Turkey | 84,500 |
| Guri | EGR | 1986 | Caroni | Venezuela | 77,971 |
| Oahe | E | 1958 | Missouri | US | 66,517 |
| Gardiner | E | 1968 | Saskatchewan | Canada | 65,400 |
| Mangla | E | 1967 | Jhelum | Pakistan | 65,379 |
| Afsluitdijk | E | 1932 | IJsselmeer | The Netherlands | 63,430 |
| | | | | | **reservoir capacity ('000 cubic m)** |
| **by size of reservoir** | | | | | |
| Owen Falls | G | 1954 | Victoria Nile | Uganda | 2,700,000,000[4] |
| Kakhovsk | EG | 1955 | Dnieper | Ukraine | 182,000,000 |
| Kariba | A | 1959 | Zambezi | Zimbabwe–Zambia | 180,600,000 |
| Bratsk | EG | 1964 | Angara | Russia | 169,270,000 |
| Aswan High | ER | 1970 | Nile | Egypt | 168,900,000 |
| Akosombo | ER | 1965 | Volta | Ghana | 153,000,000 |
| Daniel Johnson | M | 1968 | Manicouagan | Canada | 141,852,000 |
| Guri (Raúl Leoni) | EGR | 1986 | Caroní | Venezuela | 138,000,000 |
| Krasnoyarsk | G | 1967 | Yenisey | Russia | 73,300,000 |
| W.A.C. Bennett | E | 1967 | Peace | Canada | 70,309,000 |
| Zeya | B | 1978 | Zeya | Russia | 68,400,000 |
| Cabora Bassa | A | 1974 | Zambezi | Mozambique | 63,000,000 |
| | | | | | **power capacity (megawatts)** |
| **by power capacity** | | | | | |
| Itaipú | EGR | 1983 | Paraná | Brazil–Paraguay | 12,600 |
| Guri (Raúl Leoni) | EGR | 1986 | Caroní | Venezuela | 10,300 |
| Grand Coulee | G | 1942 | Columbia | US | 6,809 |
| Sayano-Shushenskoye | GA | 1989 | Yenisey | Russia | 6,400 |
| Krasnoyarsk | G | 1968 | Yenisey | Russia | 6,000 |
| Churchill Falls | E | 1971 | Churchill | Canada | 5,428 |
| La Grande 2 | R | 1979 | LaGrande | Canada | 5,328 |
| Bratsk | EG | 1961 | Angara | Russia | 4,500 |
| Ust-Ilim | R | 1977 | Angara | Russia | 4,320 |
| Tucurui (Raúl G. Lhano) | EGR | 1984 | Tocantins | Brazil | 3,960 |
| Ilha Solteira | N/A | 1973 | Paraná | Brazil | 3,200 |
| Tarbela | ER | 1977 | Indus | Pakistan | 3,046 |

*Key: A, arch; B, buttress; E, earth fill; G, gravity; M, multi-arch; R, rock fill; RCC, roller-compacted-concrete. N/A indicates "not available." [1]Vaiont Dam was the scene of a massive landslide and flood in 1963 and no longer operates. [2]Diversion tunnels closed and reservoir filling begun December 2002. [3]Near Fort McMurray AB. [4]Most of this reservoir is a natural lake.

## Lighthouses

A lighthouse is a structure, usually with a tower, built onshore or on the seabed to signal danger or to help those on ships determine location. Lighthouses have been built for centuries in areas where naval or commercial vessels sail. They have guided marine navigators through busy and often tortuous coastal waters and harbor approaches. Lighthouses were initially manned by lighthouse keepers, who lived in or nearby the structure in order to keep the light shining. Most modern lighthouses, however, have automatic lights that need little tending.

### History
The first known lighthouse was built on the island of Pharos, near Alexandria, Egypt, about 280 BC. It was regarded as one of the seven wonders of the ancient world. The modern lighthouse dates only from the early 18th century. Initially made of **wood**, these towers were often washed away in severe storms.

The first lighthouse made of **interlocking masonry blocks** was built on the treacherous Eddystone Rocks reef, off Plymouth, England. Celebrated in ballad and folklore, it endured four successive constructions: in timber (1696–99), until it was swept out to sea in 1703; in oak and iron (1708), until it was destroyed by fire in 1755; in interlocking stone (1756–59), until its foundation deteriorated; and again in stone (1882). Interlocking masonry blocks remained the principal material of construction until they were replaced by **concrete** and **steel** in the 20th century.

### Lighthouse construction
Modern construction techniques have facilitated the building of lighthouses in the open sea. On soft ground, the **submerged caisson** method is used, a system applied first in the late 19th century in Germany and the United States. With this method a large steel caisson is sunk deep into the seabed, then

pumped dry and filled with concrete to form a solid base on which the lighthouse proper is built. Where the seabed is suitable, it is possible to build a **float-out lighthouse**, consisting of a cylindrical tower—constructed on shore, towed out to sea, and sunk into position—with a broad concrete base that is fillled with sand. This design was pioneered largely in Sweden.

Another design, which is more independent of seabed conditions, is the **conventional steel-piled structure** used for offshore oil and gas rigs. Piles may be driven as deep as 46 m (150 ft) into the seabed, depending on the underlying strata. Helicopters are widely employed in the servicing and maintenance of offshore towers, so that modern designs normally include a helipad.

### Lighthouse illumination

Historically illuminants included **wood** fires, discontinued c. 1800, and **coal**, begun c. 1550. In 1782 Swiss scientist Aimé Argand invented an **oil lamp** with a steady smokeless flame. It had a circular wick with a glass chimney that ensured an adequate current of air up the center and the outside of the wick for even combustion of the oil. These lamps originally burned **fish oil**, later **vegetable oil**, and by 1860 **mineral oil**. The Argand lamp became the principal lighthouse illuminant for more than 100 years. In 1901 the Briton Arthur Kitson invented the **vaporized oil burner**, which was subsequently improved by David Hood of Trinity House and others. This burner utilized **kerosene** vaporized under pressure, mixed with air, and burned to heat an incandescent mantle.

Early proposals to use **coal gas** at lighthouses did not meet with great success. However, **acetylene gas**, generated in situ from calcium carbide and water and safe to compress for storage, was pioneered by Gustaf Dalén of Sweden between 1900 and 1910. Its great advantage was that it could be readily controlled; thus, for the first time automatic unattended lights were possible. Its main use today is in buoys, which inherently have to operate unattended. **Floating lights** (i.e., lightships and buoys) have an important function in coastal waters, guiding both passing ships and those making for or leaving harbor.

**Liquefied petroleum gas**, such as propane, has also found use as an illuminant, although both oil and gas lamps have largely been superseded by **electricity**.

Electric illumination in the form of **carbon arc lamps** was first employed at Dungeness, England, in 1862, even while oil lamps were still in vogue. The **electric-filament lamp**, which came into general use in the 1920s, is now the standard illuminant. Most lamps are of the **tungsten-halogen** type for better efficiency and longer life.

### Optical equipment

With the advent of the **Argand lamp**, a reliable and steady illuminant, it became possible to develop effective optical apparatuses for increasing the intensity of the light. In the first equipment of this type, known as the **catoptric system**, paraboloidal reflectors concentrated the light into a beam. In 1777 William Hutchinson of Liverpool, England, produced the first practical mirrors for lighthouses. The first revolving-beam lighthouse was at Carlsten, near Marstrand, Sweden, in 1781.

In 1828 Augustin Fresnel of France produced the first apparatus using the refracting properties of glass, now known as the **dioptric system**. On a lens panel he surrounded a central bull's-eye lens with a series of concentric glass prismatic rings. The panel collected light emitted by the lamp over a wide horizontal angle and also the light that would otherwise escape to the sky or to the sea, concentrating it into a narrow, horizontal pencil beam, which he later expanded to several revolving beams and then a fixed all-around light. Thus emerged the full **Fresnel catadioptric system**, the basis of all lighthouse lens systems today, although many have been converted to electric lamps with electric-motor drives.

### Other innovations

The limitations of purely visual navigation very early led to the idea of supplementary audible warning in lighthouses. Early **sound signals** included cannonfire and bells, but at the beginning of the 20th century, **compressed-air** fog signals, which sounded a series of blasts, were developed. The most widely used were the siren and the diaphone. A later compressed-air signal was the tyfon, employing a metal diaphragm vibrated by differential air pressure. Modern fog signals are almost invariably electric.

**Radio** and **satellite-based** navigation systems have greatly reduced the need for large lighthouses in sighting land.

## Notable Civil Engineering Projects (in progress or completed as of December 2002)

| NAME | LOCATION | terminal area (sq m) | YEAR OF COMPLETION | NOTES |
|---|---|---|---|---|
| airports | | | | |
| Detroit Metro (new McNamara Terminal) | Romulus MI | 610,000 | 2002 | hub for Northwest Airlines; opened 24 Feb 2002 |
| Dallas/Fort Worth Int'l (new Terminal D) | Irving TX | 610,000 | 2005 | new international terminal |
| Suvarnabhumi ("Golden Land") | near Bangkok, Thailand | 563,000 | 2005 | to replace Don Muang Airport—Southeast Asia's busiest airport |
| Pearson International | Toronto ON | 332,000 | 2003 | new horseshoe-shaped terminal at Canada's busiest airport |
| Baiyun ("White Cloud") International (replacement) | near Guangzhou, China | 300,000 | 2003 | main hub airport of south China (excluding Hong Kong) |
| Munich Int'l (new Terminal 2) | northeast of Munich, Germany | 260,000 | 2003 | Germany's busiest domestic passenger airport as of 2001 |

## Notable Civil Engineering Projects (in progress or completed as of December 2002)
### (continued)

| NAME | LOCATION | length (main span; m) | YEAR OF COMPLETION | NOTES |
|---|---|---|---|---|
| **bridges** | | | | |
| I-95 (Woodrow Wilson #2) | Alexandria VA–MD suburbs of DC | 1,852[1] | 2007 | 2 bascule spans forming higher inverted v-shape for ships; begun 2000 |
| Nancha (1 bridge of 2-section Runyang) | Zhenjiang, China (across the Yangtze) | 1,490 | 2005 | to be world's third largest suspension bridge |
| Alfred Zampa Memorial (Carquinez #3) | Crockett CA–Vallejo CA | 728 | 2003 | begun 2000; first major US suspension bridge since 1973 |
| Rion–Antirion | near Patrai, Greece (across Gulf of Corinth) | 560 | 2004 | to be world's longest cable-stayed bridge (incl. all spans) |
| Lupu | Shanghai, China (across the Huangpu) | 550 | 2003 | world's longest steel-arch bridge; spans linked 7 Oct 2002 |
| new US 82 (Greenville #2) | Greenville MS–Lake Village AR | 420 | 2006 | to be longest cable-stayed bridge in US |
| San Francisco–Oakland Bay (East Span) | Yerba Buena Island CA–Oakland CA | 385 | 2006 | 2-km causeway and world's largest suspension bridge hung from single tower |
| William Natcher | Rockport IN–near Owensboro KY | 366 | 2002 | longest cable-stayed bridge over US inland waterway; opened 21 Oct 2002 |
| Rosario–Victoria | Rosario to Victoria, Argentina | 350 | 2003 | bridges/viaducts across 59-km-wide Paraná wetlands |
| Millau Viaduct | Tarn Gorge, west of Millau, France | 342 | 2005 | 7 cable-stayed spans; world's highest (270 m) road viaduct |
| Leonard P. Zakim Bunker Hill | Boston MA | 227 | 2002 | widest (56 m) cable-stayed bridge in world |
| **buildings** | | **height (m)** | | |
| Taipei 101 (Taipei Financial Center) | Taipei, Taiwan | 448 | 2004 | begun 1999; to be world's second tallest building |
| Two International Finance Centre | Hong Kong | 412 | 2003 | begun 2000; to be world's fourth tallest building |
| Kingdom Centre | Riyadh, Saudi Arabia | 296 | 2002 | tallest building in Saudi Arabia; no. 29 in the world |
| Mok-dong Hyperion Tower A | Seoul, South Korea | 256 | 2003 | will be tallest building in South Korea; no. 3 all-residential in the world |
| Torre Generali | Panama City, Panama | 250 | 2003 | begun mid-2000; will be Latin America's tallest building |
| Torre Mayor | Mexico City, Mexico | 225 | 2003 | will be tallest building in Mexico |
| Esplanade–Theatres on the Bay | Singapore | | 2002 | Has 2 unique spiked domes; opened 12 Oct 2002 |
| **dams and hydrological projects** | | **crest length (m)** | | |
| Three Gorges | west of Yichang, China | 1,983 | 2009 | world's largest hydroelectric project; third (final) phase from November 2002 |
| San Roque Multipurpose | Agno River, Luzon, Philippines | 1,100 | 2003 | irrigation and flood control; tallest earth-and-rock fill dam in Asia |
| Bakun Dam | Balui River, Sarawak, Borneo, Malaysia | 740 | 2007 | hydroelectricity to peninsular Malaysia via world's longest submarine cable |
| Mohale (Lesotho Highlands Water Project, Lesotho to South Africa water transfer | Senqunyane River, 100 km SE of Maseru, Lesotho | 700 | 2003 | filling of Mohale Reservoir began 29 Oct 2002 |
| Sardar Sarovar Project | Narmada River, Madhya Pradesh, India | ? | ? | largest dam of controversial 30-dam project; to benefit Gujarat state |
| Alqueva Dam | Guadiana River, 180 km SE of Lisbon | ? | 2002 | creates Europe's largest (250 sq km) reservoir; gates closed 8 Feb 2002 |
| Sheikh Zayed | into bedrock of Lake Nasser, Egypt (72 km) | NA[2] | 2002 | to feed irrigation systems for southern desert valleys |

## Notable Civil Engineering Projects (in progress or completed as of December 2002) (continued)

| NAME | LOCATION | | YEAR OF COMPLETION | NOTES |
|---|---|---|---|---|
| **dams and hydrological projects** (continued) | | **crest length (m)** | | |
| Davis (holding) Pond | near Mississippi River, New Orleans LA (36 sq km) | NA[2] | 2002 | world's largest freshwater diversion project; replenishes 31,000 sq km wetlands area with controlled seasonal flooding; opened 26 Mar 2002 |
| **highways** | | **length (km)** | | |
| Golden Quadrilateral superhighway | Mumbai– Chennai–Kolkata– Delhi, India | 5,846 | 2004 | Upgraded to 4 or 6 lanes; includes town by-passes and service roads |
| Indus Highway | Karachi–Peshawar, Pakistan | 1,265 | 2003 | main trunk road running the length of Pakistan |
| Highway 1 | Kabul–Kandahar– Herat, Afghanistan | 1,000 | 2005 | reconstruction paid for by US, Saudi Arabia, and Japan; |
| Egnatia Motorway | Igoumenitsa– Thessaloniki, Greece | 680 | 2006 | first Greek highway at modern int'l standards; 69 tunnels |
| Croatian Motorway (Section III) | Bosiljevo–Sveti Rok, Croatia | 145 | 2004 | built through mountainous terrain with unstable slopes, caverns, and unexploded ordnance |
| **railways (heavy)** | | **length (km)** | | |
| Alice Springs–Darwin ("ADrail") | Alice Springs– Darwin, Australia | 1,420 | 2004 | completes north-south rail link ("Darwin to Adelaide") |
| Qinghai–Tibet | Golmud, Qinghai, China–Lhasa, Tibet | 1,118 | 2007 | highest world railway (5,072 m at summit); half of the line travels across permafrost |
| Xi'an–Hefei | Xi'an–Hefei, China | 954 | 2005 | to promote economic growth in interior provinces |
| Ferronorte (extension to Cuiabá) | Alto Taquari–Cuiabá, Brazil | 525 | 2005 | to promote exports from Mato Grosso (Brazilian interior) |
| Alameda Corridor (incl. 16-km trench) | Long Beach/LA ports– downtown Los Angeles | 32 | 2002 | consolidated corridor for streamlined cargo handling; begun 1997 |
| **railways (high speed)** | | **length (km)** | | |
| Spanish High Speed (second line) | Madrid–Barcelona, Spain | 855 | 2005 | Madrid–Lleida corridor; extension to Figueras |
| Taiwan High Speed | Taipei–Kaohsiung, Taiwan | 326 | 2005 | links Taiwan's two largest cities along west coast |
| Kyongbu (phase 1) | Seoul–Taegu, South Korea | 323 | 2004 | connects largest and third largest cities |
| Italian High Speed (second line) | Rome–Naples, Italy | 222 | 2004 | begun 1994; part of planned 1,300-km high-speed network |
| German High Speed (third line) | Frankfurt–Cologne, Germany | 219 | 2002 | connects Cologne to Frank-furt International Airport; opened 1 Aug 2002 |
| Shanghai maglev ("magnetic levitation") | Pudong International Airport–financial district, Shanghai, China | 29.9 | 2003 | world's first maglev train for public use; 430 km/hr on metro line 2 |
| **subways/metros/light rails** | | **length (km)** | | |
| Oporto Light Rail | Oporto, Portugal | 70.0 | 2002–04 | Europe's largest total rail system project; service from 7 Dec 2002 |
| Hong Kong Railway (West Rail, phase 1) | Western New Territories to Kowloon, Hong Kong | 30.3 | 2003 | 11.5 km in tunnels and 13.4 km on viaducts |
| Guangzhou (Canton) Metro (line 2) | Guangzhou, China (north-south line) | 23.2 | 2003 | begun 1999; 34.7-km line 3 to be built 2003–07 |
| Los Angeles Metro (Gold Line) | LA Union Station to Pasadena CA | 22.0 | 2003 | |
| Copenhagen Metro | Copenhagen, Denmark | 21.0 | 2002–07 | Line 1 opened 19 Oct 2002; world's largest driverless system |

### Notable Civil Engineering Projects (in progress or completed as of December 2002)
### (continued)

| NAME | LOCATION | | YEAR OF COMPLETION | NOTES |
|---|---|---|---|---|
| subways/metros/light rails (continued) | | length (km) | | |
| Hiawatha Light Rail | Downtown Minneapolis– Bloomington MN | 18.7 | 2004 | difficult tunneling under M/SP airport in unstable limestone; begun 2001 |
| Tren Urbano (phase 1) | San Juan PR | 17.2 | 2003 | Service links Bayamón (western suburbs) to north San Juan; 60% elevated |
| New York Airtrain (light rail) | JFK Airport– subways + L.I. Railroad | 13.5 | 2003 | enables direct links between JFK terminals and Manhattan |
| tunnels | | length (m) | | |
| Apennine Range tunnels (9) | Bologna–Florence, Italy (high-speed railway) | 73,400 | 2007 | begun 1996; longest tunnel, 18.6 km; tunnels to cover 93% of railway |
| Lötschberg #2 | Frutigen–Raron, Switzerland | 34,800 | 2007 | to be world's 3rd longest rail tunnel; France–Italy link |
| Iwate Ichinohe | Morioka–Hachinohe, Japan | 25,810 | 2002 | world's 3rd longest rail tunnel; used by bullet train from 1 December |
| A86 Ring Road | around Paris, France | 17,700 | 2004–08 | two tunnels (to east [10,100 m], to west [7,600 m]) |
| Södra Länken ("Southern Link") | part of Stockholm, Sweden, ring road | 16,600 | 2004 | complex underground interchanges |
| Hsüeh–shan ("Snow Mountain") | near Taipei, Taiwan | 12,900 | 2004 | to be world's 4th longest road tunnel; Taipei–I-lan expressway link |
| Westerscheldetunnel ("Western Schelde") | Terneuzen to Ellewoutsdijk, Neth. | 6,600 | 2003 | longest world tunnel in "bored weak soil" |
| Vestmannasund Subsea Tunnel | Streym (Streymoy) and Vágar islands, Faroe Is. | 4,940 | 2002 | first subsea tunnel in the Faroe Islands |

[1]Length of each span.  [2]Not applicable.

**Did you know?** The platypus's sensitive snout has been shown by researchers to contain electroreceptors, which enable it to detect the electrical field produced by the moving muscles of its prey. The platypus finds its food chiefly in underwater mud, and each day it consumes nearly its own weight in crustaceans, fishes, frogs, mollusks, tadpoles, and earthworms.

# Life on Earth

## Taxonomy

Taxonomy is the classification of living and extinct organisms. The term is derived from the Greek *taxis* ("arrangement") and *nomos* ("law") and refers to the methodology and principles of systematic botany and zoology and sets up arrangements of the kinds of plants and animals in hierarchies of superior and subordinate groups.

Popularly, classifications of living organisms arise according to need and are often superficial; for example, although the term fish is common to the names shellfish, crayfish, and starfish, there are more anatomical differences between a shellfish and a starfish than there are between a bony fish and a human. Also, vernacular names vary widely. Biolo-

gists have attempted to view all living organisms with equal thoroughness and thus have devised a formal classification. A formal classification supports a relatively uniform and internationally understood nomenclature, thereby simplifying cross-referencing and retrieval of information.

Carolus Linnaeus, who is usually regarded as the founder of modern taxonomy and whose books are considered the beginning of modern botanical and zoological nomenclature, drew up rules for assigning names to plants and animals and was the first to use binomial nomenclature consistently, beginning in 1758. Classification since Linnaeus has incorporated newly discovered information and more closely approaches a natural system, and the process of clarifying relationships continues to this day. The table below shows the seven ranks that are accepted as obligatory by zoologists and botanists and sample listings for animals and plants.

|  | ANIMALS | PLANTS |
|---|---|---|
| Kingdom | Animalia | Plantae |
| Phylum/Division | Chordata | Tracheophyta |
| Class | Mammalia | Pteropsida |
| Order | Primates | Coniferales |
| Family | Hominidae | Pinaceae |
| Genus | *Homo* | *Pinus* |
| Species | *Homo sapiens* (human) | *Pinus strobus* (white pine) |

# Animals

## Notable Venomous Animals

*Instances where the exact chemical makeup of a toxin has not been established are indicated as "unknown."*

REPRESENTATIVE VENOMOUS ANIMALS THAT INFLICT A STING

### Marine animals

**cone shell** (*Conus* species; tropical Indo-Pacific region): quaternary ammonium compounds and others (blanching at site of injection, cyanosis of surrounding area, numbness, stinging or burning sensation, blurred vision, loss of speech, difficulty swallowing, nausea, extreme weakness, coma, death in some cases; no specific antidote)

**crown-of-thorns starfish** (*Acanthaster planci*; Indo-Pacific): unknown (penetration of spines produces a painful wound, redness, swelling, vomiting, numbness, and paralysis)

**long-spined sea urchin** (*Diadema setosum*; Indo-Pacific): unknown (penetration of spines produces an immediate and intense burning sensation, redness, swelling, numbness, muscular paralysis)

**Portuguese man-of-war** (*Physalia* species; tropical seas): tetramine, 5-hydroxytryptamine (immediate stinging, throbbing, or burning sensation; inflammatory rash; blistering; shock; collapse; death in very rare cases)

**scorpion fish** (*Scorpaena* species; temperate and tropical seas): unknown (fin spines can inflict painful stings and intense, immediate pain, followed by redness, swelling, loss of consciousness, ulceration of the wound, paralysis, cardiac failure, delirium, convulsions, nausea, prostration, and respiratory distress, but rarely death; no known antidote)

**sea anemone** (*Actinia equina*; Mediterranean, Black Sea, etc.): unknown (burning or stinging sensation, itching, swelling, redness, ulceration, nausea, vomiting, prostration; no specific antidote)

**sea urchin** (*Toxopneustes pileolus*; Indo-Pacific): unknown (bites from stinging jaws or small pincerlike organs produce an immediate, intense, radiating pain, faintness, numbness, muscular paralysis, respiratory distress, and occasionally death)

**sea wasp** (*Chironex fleckeri*; northern and northeast Australia): cardiotoxin (immediate and extremely painful stinging sensation, seared reddened lines wherever tentacles touched the skin, large indurated lesions, prostration, dizziness, circulatory failure, respiratory distress, rapid death in a high percentage of cases)

**spotted octopus** (*Octopus maculosus*; Indo-Pacific, Indian Ocean): cephalotoxin, a neuromuscular poison (sharp stinging pain, numbness of mouth and tongue, blurred vision, loss of tactile sensation, difficulty in speech and swallowing, paralysis of legs, nausea, prostration, coma, death in a high percentage of cases)

**stingray** (*Dasyatis* species; warm temperate and tropical seas): cardiotoxin (penetration of tail spines inflicts jagged wounds that produce sharp, shooting, throbbing pain, fall in blood pressure, nausea, vomiting, cardiac failure, muscular paralysis, and rarely death; no known antidote; stingrays are among the most common causes of envenomizations in the marine environment)

**stonefish** (*Synanceja* species; Indo-Pacific region): unknown (produces an extremely painful sting by means of the dorsal fin spines; symptoms similar to other scorpion fish stings but more serious)

**weever fish** (*Trachinus draco*; Mediterranean Sea): unknown (penetration of opercular and dorsal fin spines can produce instant pain, burning, stabbing, or crushing sensation; pain spreads and becomes progressively more intense, causing victim to lose consciousness; numbness around the wound, swelling, redness, nausea, delirium, difficulty breathing, convulsions, and death; no known antidote)

### Arthropods

**kissing bug** (*Triatoma* species; Latin America, US): unknown (bite usually painless; later itching, edema around the bite, nausea, palpitation, redness; the bite is of minor importance but spreads Chagas' disease caused by a trypanosome)

**puss caterpillar** (*Megalopyge* species; US, Latin America): unknown (contact with hairs produces an intense burning pain, itching, pustules, redness, nausea, fever, numbness, swelling, and paralysis; recovery usually within six days)

**honeybee** (*Apis* species; worldwide): neurotoxin, hemolytic, melittin, hyaluronidase, phospholipase A, histamine, and others (acute local pain or burning sensation, blanching at site of sting surrounded by redness, and itching; local symptoms usually disappear after 24 hours; severe cases may develop massive swelling, shock, prostration, vomiting, rapid heartbeat, respiratory distress, trembling, coma, and death; estimated that 500 stings in a short period of time can produce a lethal dose; bee stings kill more people in the US than do venomous reptiles)

**bumblebee** (*Bombus* species; temperate regions): similar to (*Apis*) honeybee venom (stings are similar to honeybee stings; bumblebees are not as vicious as honeybees)

**yellow jacket, hornet** (*Vespula* species; temperate regions): similar to bee venom; also acetylcholine (yellow jackets are quite aggressive and can both bite and sting; the sting is similar to a honeybee's but more painful and may be fatal)

**wasp** (*Polistes* and *Vespa* species; worldwide): similar to bee venom; also acetylcholine (wasps are less aggressive than hornets, and their stings are similar to the honeybee's but generally less painful than the hornet's; stings may be fatal)

**harvester ant** (*Pogonomyrmex* species; US): bradykinin, formic acid, hyaluronidase, hemolytic, phospholipase A, and others (immediate intense burning, pain, blanched area at site of sting surrounded by redness, ulceration, fever, blistering, itching, hemorrhaging into the skin, eczematoid dermatitis, pustules, respiratory distress, prostration, coma, and death in some instances)

**fire ant** (*Solenopsis* species; US, Latin America): similar to harvester ant venom

**millipede** (*Apheloria* species [and others]; temperate areas): hydrogen cyanide and benzaldehyde (toxic liquid or gas from lateral glands causes inflammation, swelling, and blindness in contact with eyes; brown stain, swelling, redness, and vesicle formation in contact with skin)

**centipede** (*Scolopendra* species; temperate and tropical regions): hemolytic phospholipase and serotonin (local pain, swelling, and redness at bite site)

**brown spider** (*Loxosceles* species; US, South America, Europe, Asia): cytotoxic, hyaluronidase, hemolytic, and others (bite causes stinging or burning, blanching at site of bite surrounded by redness, blistering, hemorrhaging into the skin and internal organs, ulceration, vomiting, fever, cardiovascular collapse, convulsions, and sometimes death)

**black widow** (*Latrodectus* species; tropical and temperate regions): neurotoxin (bite may be painful; two tiny red dots at site, localized swelling after a few minutes; intense cramping pain of abdomen, legs, chest, back; rigidity of muscles lasting 12–48 hours, nausea, sweating, respiratory distress, abnormal and painful erection of the penis, chills, skin rash, restlessness, fever, numbness, tingling; about 4% are fatal; antiserum is available)

**tarantula** (*Dugesiella* and *Lycosa* species; temperate and tropical regions): venom varies, usually mild (most of the large tarantulas found in the US, Mexico, and Central America are harmless to humans; some of the large tropical species may be more poisonous, but their effects are largely localized)

**scorpion** (species of *Centruroides*, *Tityus*, and *Leiurus*; warm temperate and tropical regions): neurotoxin, cardiotoxin, hemolytic, lecithinase, hyaluronidase, and others (symptoms vary depending upon species; sting from the tail causes a sharp burning sensation, swelling, sweating, restlessness, salivation, confusion, vomiting, abdominal pain, chest pain, numbness, muscular twitching, respiratory distress, convulsions, and often death; the mortality rate from certain species of scorpions is very high; antiserum is available)

## Reptiles

**Gila monster** (*Heloderma suspectum*; southwestern US): heloderma venom, primarily a neurotoxin (all of the teeth are venomous; bite causes local pain, swelling, weakness, ringing of the ears, nausea, respiratory distress, and cardiac failure; may cause death; no antiserum available)

## Sponges

**red moss** (*Microciona prolifera*; eastern US coastal waters): unknown (contact produces chemical irritation of the skin, redness, stiffness of finger joints, swelling, blisters, and pustules)

## Flatworms

**flatworm** (*Leptoplana tremellaris*; European coastal waters): unknown (poison is produced by epidermal skin glands; no human intoxications recorded, but extracts from the skin injected into laboratory animals produces cardiac arrest)

## Arthropods

**blister beetles** (*Cantharis vesicatorea*; US): cantharidin (toxic substance is found throughout the body of the beetle; no discomfort from initial contact; after about 8–10 hours large blisters on the skin accompanied by slight burning or tingling; swallowing of the beetles may cause kidney damage; cantharidin is used as an aphrodisiac known as Spanish Fly, a very dangerous substance; ingestion can cause severe gastroenteritis, kidney damage, blood in the urine, abnormal and painful erection of the penis, profound collapse, and death)

**millipedes** (species of *Orthoporus*, *Rhinocrichus*, *Julus*, and *Spirobolus*; temperate and tropical regions): unknown (a fluid distasteful to enemies may be exuded or forcefully squirted from body pores a distance of 76 cm [30 in] or more; contact with the skin induces mild to moderately intense burning pain, redness, and pigmentation of the skin; toxic fluid squirted in the eyes may cause temporary blindness, inflammation, and pain)

**venomous ticks** (species of *Ixodes* and *Ornithodoros*; temperate and tropical regions): unknown (bites result in swelling, redness, intense pain, headache, muscle cramps, loss of memory)

## Fishes

**sea lamprey** (*Petromyzon marinus*; Atlantic Ocean): unknown (slime is toxic; ingestion may cause diarrhea)

**soapfish** (*Rypticus saponaceus*; tropical and subtropical Atlantic): neurotoxin (slime is toxic; produces irritation of the mucous membrane)

## Amphibians

**European earth salamander** (*Salamandra maculosa*; Europe): skin glands are poisonous; contain the alkaloids samandarin, samandenone, samandine, samanine, samandarone, samandaridine, and others (effects on humans not known; affects the heart and nervous system; in animals causes convulsions, cardiac irregularity, paralysis, and death)

**toads** (*Bufo* species; temperate and tropical regions): bufotoxin, bufogenins, and 5-hydroxytryplanime; poison includes a complex of many substances (produces a poisonous secretion in parotid glands and skin; handling of some toads may cause skin irritation; ingestion causes nausea, vomiting, numbness of mouth and tongue, and tightness of chest; the poison has a digitalis-like action)

**frogs** (some species of *Dendrobates*, *Physalaemus*, and *Rana*; northern South America and Central

America): skin secretions are poisonous; histamine, bufotenine, physalaemin, serotonin, and other substances; composition varies with the species (secretions produce a burning sensation; used by indigenous peoples as an arrow poison)

**tree frogs** (some species of *Hyla* and *Phyllobates*; northern South America and Central America): skin secretions are poisonous; batrachotoxin, steroidal alkaloids, serotonin, histamine, and other substances; bufotenine varies with the species (burning sensation and skin rash; skin secretions in the eye may produce a severe inflammatory reaction; if ingested, poison causes vomiting and abdominal pain; batrachotoxin is extremely toxic if injected; used by indigenous peoples as an arrow poison)

**SELECTED HIGHLY VENOMOUS SNAKES**

**inland taipan** (*Oxyuranus microlepidotus*): Australia
**eastern brown snake** (*Pseudonaja textilis*): Australia
**Malayan krait** (*Bungarus candidus*): Southeast Asia and Indonesia
**coastal taipan** (*Oxyuranus scutellatus*): Australia
**tiger snake** (*Notechis scutatus*): Australia
**beaked sea snake** (*Enhydrina schistosa*): South Asian waters
**saw-scaled viper** (*Echis carinatus*): Middle East, Asia
**eastern coral snake** (*Micrurus fulvius*): North America
**boomslang** (*Dispholidus typus*): Africa
**death adder** (*Acanthophis antarcticus*): Australia and New Guinea

## Period of Gestation and Longevity of Selected Mammals

| ANIMAL | AVERAGE GESTATION (DAYS) | AVERAGE LONGEVITY (YEARS) | ANIMAL | AVERAGE GESTATION (DAYS) | AVERAGE LONGEVITY (YEARS) |
|---|---|---|---|---|---|
| bear (black) | 219 | 18 | horse | 330 | 20 |
| bear (grizzly) | 225 | 25 | human (worldwide) | 266–70 | Men: 64.7; Women: 68.9 |
| bear (polar) | 240 | 20 | | | |
| cat (domestic) | 63 | 12 | monkey (rhesus) | 164 | 15 |
| dog (domestic) | 61 | 12 | mouse (domestic white) | 19 | 3 |
| elephant (Asian) | 645 | 40 | pig (domestic) | 112 | 10 |
| fox (red) | 52 | 7 | rabbit (domestic) | 31 | 5 |
| guinea pig | 68 | 4 | sheep (domestic) | 154 | 12 |
| hippopotamus | 238 | 25–30 | squirrel (gray) | 44 | 9–10 |

## Names of the Male, Female, Young, and Group of Animals

| ANIMAL | MALE | FEMALE | YOUNG | GROUP |
|---|---|---|---|---|
| ape | male | female | baby | shrewdness |
| bear | boar | sow | cub | sleuth, sloth |
| camel | bull | cow | calf | flock |
| cattle | bull | cow | calf | drift, drove, herd, mob |
| chicken | rooster | hen | chick, pullet (hen), cockrell (rooster) | flock, brood (hens), clutch & peep (chicks) |
| deer | buck, stag | doe | fawn | herd |
| donkey | jack, jackass | jennet, jenny | colt, foal | drove, herd |
| elephant | bull | cow | calf | herd, parade |
| ferret | hob | jill | kit | business, fesynes |
| fox | reynard | vixen | kit, cub, pup | skulk, leash |
| giraffe | bull | doe | calf | herd, corps, tower, group |
| goat | buck, billy | doe, nanny | kid, billy | herd, tribe, trip |
| gorilla | male | female | infant | band |
| hamster | buck | doe | pup | horde |
| hippopotamus | bull | cow | calf | herd, bloat |
| horse | stallion, stud | mare, dam | foal, colt (male), filly (female) | stable, harras, herd, team (working) string or field (racing) |
| human | man | woman | baby, infant, toddler | clan (related), crowd, family (closely related), community, gang, mob, tribe, etc. |
| lion | lion | lioness | cub | pride |
| louse | male | female | nymph | lice, colony, infestation |
| mouse | buck | doe | pup, pinkie, kitten | horde, mischief |
| ostrich | cock | hen | chick | flock |
| pig | boar | sow | piglet, shoat, farrow | drove, herd, litter (of pups), sounder |
| quail | cock | hen | chick | bevy, covey, drift |
| rhinoceros | bull | cow | calf | crash |
| seal | bull | cow | pup | herd, pod, rookery, harem |
| sheep | buck, ram | ewe, dam | lamb, lambkin, cosset | drift, drove, flock, herd, mob, trip |
| turkey | tom | hen | poult | rafter |
| turtle | male | female | hatchling | bale |
| whale | bull | cow | calf | gam, grind, herd, pod, school |
| wolf | dog | bitch | pup, whelp | pack, rout |
| zebra | stallion | mare | colt, foal | herd, crossing |

# Plants

## Notable Medicinal Plants

*Sources: <http://world.std.com/~krahe/html1.html>; <www.hort.purdue.edu/newcrop/med-aro/toc.html>.*

| PLANT | NATIVE REGION | MAIN PROPERTIES (USES) |
|---|---|---|
| angelica | Europe | antispasmodic, promotes menstrual flow |
| basil (holy basil) | India | antispasmodic, analgesic, fungicidal, lowers blood pressure, lowers blood sugar, reduces fever, anti-inflammatory |
| chamomile | Europe, Western Asia, North America, Africa | anti-inflammatory, antispasmodic, relaxant, carminative, bitter, nervine |
| chicory | Europe | digestive, liver tonic, anti-rheumatic, mild laxative |
| cinnamon | Sri Lanka | warming stimulant, carminative, antispasmodic, antiseptic, anti-viral |
| coriander | Europe, Mediterranean | digestive, antispasmodic, anti-rheumatic |
| cymbopogon (lemon grass) | Sri Lanka, south India | digestive, antispasmodic, analgesic |
| dandelion | Asia | diuretic, digestive, antibiotic, bitter |
| eucalyptus | Australia | antiseptic, expectorant, stimulates local blood flow, anti-fungal |
| fennel | Mediterranean | digestive, antispasmodic, anti-inflammatory |
| garlic | Central Asia | antibiotic, expectorant, diaphoretic, hypotensive, antispasmodic, expels worms |
| ginger | Southeast Asia | diaphoretic, carminative, circulatory stimulant, anti-inflammatory, antiseptic, inhibits coughing |
| ginkgo | China | anti-asthmatic, antispasmodic, anti-allergenic, anti-inflammatory, circulatory stimulant and tonic |
| ginseng | northeastern China, eastern Russia, Korea | tonic, stimulant, physical and mental revitalizer |
| gumplant | Southwestern US, Mexico | antispasmodic, expectorant, hypotensive |
| hamamelis (witch hazel) | eastern North America | astringent, anti-inflammatory, stops external and internal bleeding |
| hyssop | Mediterranean | antispasmodic, expectorant, diaphoretic, anti-inflammatory, hepatic |
| jasmine | Iran | aromatic, antispasmodic, expectorant |
| lavender | Mediterranean | carminative, antidepressant, antiseptic, antibacterial, stimulates blood flow, relieves muscle spasms |
| marjoram (wild marjoram) | Asia | antiseptic, antispasmodic, digestive |
| melissa (lemon balm) | Mediterranean | relaxant, antispasmodic, carminative, anti-viral, nerve tonic, increases sweating |
| myrrh | northeast Africa | stimulant, antiseptic, anti-inflammatory, astringent, expectorant, antispasmodic, carminative |
| nettle | Eurasia | diuretic, tonic, astringent, anti-allergenic, prevents hemorrhaging, reduces prostate enlargement (root) |
| parsley | North & Central Europe, Western Asia | digestive, diuretic |
| passiflora (passion flower) | North America | anti-inflammatory, antispasmodic, hypotensive, sedative, tranquilizing |
| peppermint | unknown | carminative, antiseptic, relieves muscle spasms, increases sweating, stimulates secretion of bile |
| rosemary | Mediterranean | tonic, stimulant, astringent, nervine, anti-inflammatory, carminative |
| rue | southern Europe | antispasmodic, increases peripheral blood circulation, relieves eye tension |
| sesame | Africa | digestive, aromatic, antispasmodic |
| St. John's wort | Europe | antidepressant, antispasmodic, astringent, sedative, anti-viral, relieves pain |
| thyme | western Mediterranean, southwest Italy | antiseptic, expectorant, tonic, relieves muscle spasm |
| turmeric | India, southern Asia | anti-inflammatory, antioxidant, antibacterial, eases stomach pain, stimulates secretion of bile |
| valerian | Europe, Western Asia | sedative, relaxant, relieves muscle spasm, relieves anxiety, lowers blood pressure |
| verbena | Europe | nervine, tonic, mild sedative, stimulates bile secretion, mild bitter |
| wormwood | Europe | aromatic bitter, anti-inflammatory, mild antidepressant, stimulates bile secretion, eliminates worms, eases stomach pains |

## Notable Medicinal Plants (continued)

| PLANT | NATIVE REGION | MAIN PROPERTIES (USES) |
|---|---|---|
| yarrow | Europe | antispasmodic, astringent, bitter tonic, mild diuretic, urinary antiseptic, increases sweating, lowers blood pressure, reduces fever |

## World's Oldest Trees and Flowering Plants

| | MAXIMUM AGE IN YEARS | | |
|---|---|---|---|
| | ESTIMATED | VERIFIED | LOCATION |
| **trees** | | | |
| bristlecone pine | | 4,900 | Wheeler Peak, Humboldt National Forest, Nevada |
| Sierra redwood | 4,000 | 2,200–2,300 | northern California |
| Swiss stone pine | 1,200 | 750 | Riffel Alp, Switzerland |
| common juniper | 2,000 | 544 | Kola Peninsula, northeastern Russia |
| European larch | 700 | 417 | Riffel Alp, Switzerland |
| Norway spruce | 1,200 | 350–400 | Eichstätt, Bavaria, Germany |
| **flowering plants** | | | |
| bo tree | 2,000–3,000 | | Buddh Gaya, India; Anuradhapura, Ceylon |
| English oak | 2,000 | 1,500 | Hasbruch Forest, Lower Saxony, Germany |
| linden | | 815 | Lithuania |
| European beech | 900 | 250 | Montigny, Normandy, France |
| English ivy | 440 | | Ginac, near Montpellier, France |
| dragon tree | 200 | | Tenerife, Canary Islands |
| dwarf birch | | 80 | eastern Greenland |

# Endangerment

## Selected Endangered Species: Flora

*For a complete list of endangered and threatened flora, see*
*<http://endangered.fws.gov/wildlife.html#Species>.*

**Flowering plants**
Akoko, Ewa Plains
Alani (*Melicope reflexa*)
Arrowhead, bunched
Avens, spreading
Ayenia, Texas
Barberry, Truckee
Bird's-beak, salt marsh
Bittercress, small-anthered
Bladderpod, Missouri
Bluegrass, Hawaiian
Bluet, Roan Mountain
Boxwood, Vahl's
Buckwheat, steamboat
Bulrush, Northeastern
Cactus, Key tree
Cactus, Knowlton
Cactus, Pima pineapple
Cactus, Sneed pincushion
Cactus, star
Campion, fringed
Chaffseed, American
Checker-mallow, pedate
Clarkia, Pismo
Clover, running buffalo
Clover, showy Indian
Coneflower, smooth
Desert-parsley, Bradshaw's
Dropwort, Canby's
Flannelbush, Mexican
Frankenia, Johnston's
Geranium, Hawaiian red-flowered
Gerardia, sandplain
Grass, Tennessee yellow-eyed

**Flowering plants (continued)**
Ha'iwale (*Cyrtandra munroi*)
Haha (*Cyanea superba*)
Harperella
Hau kuahiwi (*Hibiscadelphus giffardianus*)
Iagu, Hayun
Ipomopsis, Holy Ghost
Jewelflower, California
Kamakahala (*Labordia lanaiensis*)
Koki'o, Cooke's
Larkspur, San Clemente Island
Lau'ehu
Lily, Western
Liveforever, Santa Barbara Island
Loosestrife, rough-leaved
Lo'ulu (*Pritchardia munroi*)
Lousewort, Furbish
Love grass, Fosberg's
Lupine, scrub
Manioc, Walker's
Mesa-mint, Otay
Milk-vetch, Jesup's
Milk-vetch, Mancos
Mint, longspurred red
Monardella, willowy
Na'ena'e (*Dubautia herbstobatae*)
Nehe (*Lipochaeta lobata*)
Niterwort, Amargosa
'Oha wai (*Clermontia mauiensis*)
Orcutt grass, California
Penstemon, blowout

**Flowering plants (continued)**
Phacelia, clay
Pinkroot, gentian
Pitcher-plant, green
Pitcher-plant, mountain sweet
Pondberry
Prairie-clover, leafy
Prickly-ash, St. Thomas
Rock-cress, Hoffmann's
Rock-cress, McDonald's
Rock-cress, shale barren
Rosemary, short-leaved
Sandwort, Cumberland
Sandwort, Marsh
Spineflower, slender-horned
Sumac, Michaux's
Sunflower, Schweinitz's
Thistle, Chorro Creek bog
Trillium, persistent
Trillium, relict
Wallflower, Contra Costa
Walnut, West Indian or nogal
Water-umbel, Huachuca

**Conifers and cycads**
Cypress, Santa Cruz
Torreya, Florida

**Ferns and allies**
Diellia, asplenium-leaved
Fern, Aleutian shield
Fern, Elfin tree
Fern, pendant kihi
Ihi'ihi

## Selected Endangered Species: Flora (continued)

**Ferns and allies (continued)**
Pauoa
Quillwort, black spored
Quillwort, Louisiana

**Ferns and allies (continued)**
Quillwort, mat-forming
Wawae'iole (*Huperzia mannii*)
Wawae'iole (*Lycopodium nutans*)

**Lichens**
Lichen, rock gnome

## The World's Forests

*This table shows the 50 countries that either lost or gained the most forest area between 1990 and 2000 as well as forest losses or gains by continent. Source: State of the World's Forests 2001. 1 hectare = x .01 sq km, .004 sq mi. Web site: <www.fao.org/forestry>.*

| COUNTRY/AREA | LAND AREA ('000 HA) | TOTAL FOREST, 1990 ('000 HA) | TOTAL FOREST IN 2000 ('000 HA) | PERCENTAGE OF LAND AREA IN 2000 (%) | % CHANGE 1990–2000 |
|---|---|---|---|---|---|
| Burundi | 2,568 | 241 | 94 | 3.7 | −61.00 |
| Haiti | 2,756 | 158 | 88 | 3.2 | −44.30 |
| Micronesia | 69 | 24 | 15 | 21.7 | −37.50 |
| El Salvador | 2,072 | 193 | 121 | 5.8 | −37.31 |
| Saint Lucia | 61 | 14 | 9 | 14.8 | −35.71 |
| Comoros | 186 | 12 | 8 | 4.3 | −33.33 |
| Rwanda | 2,466 | 457 | 307 | 12.4 | −32.82 |
| Niger | 126,670 | 1,945 | 1,328 | 1 | −31.72 |
| Togo | 5,439 | 719 | 510 | 9.4 | −29.07 |
| Côte d'Ivoire | 31,800 | 9,766 | 7,117 | 22.4 | −27.12 |
| Nicaragua | 12,140 | 4,450 | 3,278 | 27 | −26.34 |
| Sierra Leone | 7,162 | 1,416 | 1,055 | 14.7 | −25.49 |
| Mauritania | 102,522 | 415 | 317 | 0.3 | −23.61 |
| Nigeria | 91,077 | 17,501 | 13,517 | 14.8 | −22.76 |
| Malawi | 9,409 | 3,269 | 2,562 | 27.2 | −21.63 |
| Zambia | 74,339 | 39,755 | 31,246 | 42 | −21.40 |
| Belize | 2,280 | 1,704 | 1,348 | 59.1 | −20.89 |
| Benin | 11,063 | 3,349 | 2,650 | 24 | −20.87 |
| Samoa | 282 | 130 | 105 | 37.2 | −19.23 |
| Liberia | 11,137 | 4,241 | 3,481 | 31.3 | −17.92 |
| Uganda | 19,964 | 5,103 | 4,190 | 21 | −17.89 |
| Yemen | 52,797 | 541 | 449 | 0.9 | −17.01 |
| Nepal | 14,300 | 4,683 | 3,900 | 27.3 | −16.72 |
| Ghana | 22,754 | 7,535 | 6,335 | 27.8 | −15.93 |
| Guatemala | 10,843 | 3,387 | 2,850 | 26.3 | −15.85 |
| Greece | 12,890 | 3,299 | 3,599 | 27.9 | 9.09 |
| The Gambia | 1,000 | 436 | 481 | 48.1 | 10.32 |
| China | 932,743 | 145,417 | 163,480 | 17.5 | 12.42 |
| Swaziland | 1,721 | 464 | 522 | 30.3 | 12.50 |
| Cuba | 10,982 | 2,071 | 2,348 | 21.4 | 13.38 |
| Azerbaijan | 8,359 | 964 | 1,094 | 13.1 | 13.49 |
| Armenia | 2,820 | 309 | 351 | 12.4 | 13.59 |
| Bangladesh | 13,017 | 1,169 | 1,334 | 10.2 | 14.11 |
| Algeria | 238,174 | 1,879 | 2,145 | 0.9 | 14.16 |
| Libya | 175,954 | 311 | 358 | 0.2 | 15.11 |
| Liechtenstein | 15 | 6 | 7 | 46.7 | 16.67 |
| Portugal | 9,150 | 3,096 | 3,666 | 40.1 | 18.41 |
| Guadeloupe | 169 | 67 | 82 | 48.5 | 22.39 |
| Iceland | 10,025 | 25 | 31 | 0.3 | 24.00 |
| Kazakhstan | 267,074 | 9,758 | 12,148 | 4.5 | 24.49 |
| Kyrgyzstan | 19,180 | 775 | 1,003 | 5.2 | 29.42 |
| United Arab Emirates | 8,360 | 243 | 321 | 3.8 | 32.10 |
| Ireland | 6,889 | 489 | 659 | 9.6 | 34.76 |
| Belarus | 20,748 | 6,840 | 9,402 | 45.3 | 37.46 |
| Egypt | 99,545 | 52 | 72 | 0.1 | 38.46 |
| Cyprus | 925 | 119 | 172 | 18.6 | 44.54 |
| Israel | 2,062 | 82 | 132 | 6.4 | 60.98 |
| Uruguay | 17,481 | 791 | 1,292 | 7.4 | 63.34 |
| Kuwait | 1,782 | 3 | 5 | 0.3 | 66.67 |
| Cape Verde | 403 | 35 | 85 | 21.1 | 142.86 |
| Africa | 2,978,394 | 702,502 | 649,866 | 21.8 | −7.5 |
| Asia | 3,084,746 | 551,448 | 547,793 | 17.8 | −0.7 |

## The World's Forests (continued)

| COUNTRY/AREA | LAND AREA ('000 HA) | TOTAL FOREST, 1990 ('000 HA) | TOTAL FOREST IN 2000 ('000 HA) | PERCENTAGE OF LAND AREA IN 2000 (%) | % CHANGE 1990–2000 |
|---|---|---|---|---|---|
| Europe | 2,259,957 | 1,030,475 | 1,039,251 | 46 | 0.9 |
| North and Central America | 2,136,966 | 555,002 | 549,304 | 25.7 | −1.0 |
| Oceania | 849,096 | 201,271 | 197,623 | 23.3 | −1.8 |
| South America | 1,754,741 | 922,731 | 885,618 | 50.5 | −4.0 |
| World | 13,063,900 | 3,963,429 | 3,869,455 | 29.6 | −2.4 |

## Selected Endangered Species: Fauna

*For a complete list of endangered and threatened fauna, see*
*<http://endangered.fws.gov/wildlife.html#Species>.*

### Vertebrate animals
#### Mammals
Bat, gray
Bat, Indiana
Caribou, woodland
Deer, Columbian white-tailed
Deer, Key
Ferret, black-footed
Fox, San Joaquin kit
Jaguar
Manatee, West Indian
Mouse, Perdido Key beach
Ocelot
Panther, Florida
Pronghorn, Sonoran
Puma (cougar), eastern
Rabbit, Lower Keys marsh
Rabbit, pygmy
Rat, rice
Seal, Caribbean monk
Seal, Hawaiian monk
Sea-lion, Steller
Sheep, bighorn (two varieties)
Shrew, Buena Vista Lake ornate
Squirrel, Carolina northern flying
Squirrel, Delmarva Peninsula fox
Vole, Amargosa
Vole, Hualapai Mexican
Whale, blue
Whale, humpback
Whale, sperm
Wolf, gray
Wolf, red
Woodrat, Key Largo
Woodrat, riparian (San Joaquin Valley)

#### Birds
Albatross, short-tailed
Blackbird, yellow-shouldered
Bobwhite, masked (quail)
Broadbill, Guam
Condor, California
Coot, Hawaiian
Crane, whooping
Creeper, Molokai
Crow, Mariana
Crow, white-necked
Curlew, Eskimo
Duck, Hawaiian
Duck, Laysan
Elepaio, Oahu
Falcon, northern aplomado
Finch, Laysan

#### Birds (continued)
Finch, Nihoa
Flycatcher, southwestern willow
Goose, Hawaiian
Hawk, Hawaiian
Hawk, Puerto Rican broad-winged
Honeycreeper, crested
Kingfisher, Guam Micronesian
Kite, Everglade snail
Mallard, Mariana
Megapode, Micronesian
Millerbird, Nihoa (Old World warbler)
Parrot, Puerto Rican
Pelican, brown
Pigeon, Puerto Rican plain
Plover, piping
Pygmy-owl, cactus ferruginous
Rail, Yuma clapper
Sparrow, Cape Sable seaside
Stilt, Hawaiian
Stork, wood
Swiftlet, Mariana gray
Tern, least
Thrush, large Kauai
Thrush, small Kauai
Vireo, black-capped
Vireo, least Bell's
Warbler (wood), Bachman's
Warbler (wood), golden-cheeked
Warbler (wood), Kirtland's
White-eye, bridled
Woodpecker, ivory-billed
Woodpecker, red-cockaded

#### Reptiles
Anole, Culebra Island giant
Boa, Puerto Rican
Boa, Virgin Islands tree
Crocodile, American
Gecko, Monito
Lizard, blunt-nosed leopard
Lizard, St. Croix ground
Sea turtle, green
Sea turtle, hawksbill
Sea turtle, Kemp's ridley
Sea turtle, leatherback
Snake, San Francisco garter
Turtle, Alabama red-belly
Turtle, Plymouth redbelly

#### Amphibians
Frog, Mississippi gopher
Salamander, California tiger

#### Amphibians (continued)
Salamander, desert slender
Salamander, Santa Cruz long-toed
Salamander, Shenandoah
Salamander, Sonoran tiger
Salamander, Texas blind
Toad, arroyo (arroyo southwestern)
Toad, Houston
Toad, Wyoming

#### Fish
Chub, bonytail
Chub, humpback
Dace, Moapa
Darter, amber
Darter, boulder
Darter, Maryland
Gambusia, Pecos
Gambusia, San Marcos
Goby, tidewater
Logperch, Conasauga
Madtom, Scioto
Minnow, Rio Grande silvery
Pikeminnow (squawfish), Colorado
Pupfish, desert
Salmon, Atlantic
Salmon, sockeye
Shiner, palezone
Shiner, Topeka
Sturgeon, pallid
Sturgeon, shortnose
Sucker, Lost River
Sucker, razorback
Topminnow, Gila (incl. Yaqui)
Trout, Gila
Woundfin

### Invertebrate animals
#### Clams
Acornshell, southern
Bean, Cumberland (pearlymussel)
Bean, purple
Blossom, tubercled (pearlymussel)
Blossom, turgid (pearlymussel)
Catspaw (purple cat's paw pearlymussel)
Catspaw, white (pearlymussel)
Clubshell
Clubshell, southern
Combshell, Cumberlandian

## Selected Endangered Species: Fauna (continued)

**Invertebrate Animals** (continued)
**Clams** (continued)
Combshell, upland
Elktoe, Appalachian
Elktoe, Cumberland
Fanshell
Heelsplitter, Carolina
Higgins eye (pearlymussel)Kidneyshell, triangular
Lampmussel, Alabama
Lilliput, pale (pearlymussel)
Mapleleaf, winged (mussel)
Moccasinshell, Coosa
Moccasinshell, Gulf
Monkeyface, Appalachian (pearlymussel)
Monkeyface, Cumberland (pearlymussel)
Mussel, oyster
Mussel, scaleshell
Pearlymussel, cracking
Pearlymussel, littlewing
Pigtoe, finerayed
Pigtoe, rough
Pimpleback, orangefoot (pearlymussel)
Pocketbook, fat
Pocketbook, shinyrayed
Rabbitsfoot, rough
Riffleshell, northern
Riffleshell, tan
Ring pink (mussel)

**Clams** (continued)
Spinymussel, James
Stirrupshell
Three-ridge, fat (mussel)
Wartyback, white (pearlymussel)
Wedgemussel, dwarf

**Snails**
Ambersnail, Kanab
Riversnail, Anthony's
Snail, Iowa Pleistocene
Snail, Utah valvata
Springsnail, Idaho

**Insects**
Beetle, American burying
Beetle, Helotes mold
Beetle, Hungerford's crawling water
Butterfly, Karner blue
Butterfly, Mitchell's satyr
Dragonfly, Hine's emerald
Fly, Delhi Sands flower-loving
Grasshopper, Zayante bandwinged
Ground beetle (unnamed, *Rhadine exilis*)
Ground beetle (unnamed, *Rhadine infernalis*)
Moth, Blackburn's sphinx
Skipper, Carson wandering
Tiger beetle, Ohlone

**Arachnids**
Harvestman, Bee Creek Cave
Harvestman, Bone Cave
Meshweaver, Madla's cave
Meshweaver Robber Baron Cave
Pseudoscorpion, Tooth Cave
Spider, Government Canyon cave
Spider, Kauai cave wolf (pe'e pe'e maka 'ole)
Spider, spruce-fir moss
Spider, Tooth Cave

**Crustaceans**
Amphipod, Hay's Spring
Amphipod, Illinois cave
Amphipod, Kauai cave
Amphipod, Peck's cave
Crayfish, cave (*Cambarus aculabrum*)
Crayfish, cave (*Cambarus zophonastes*)
Crayfish, Nashville
Crayfish, Shasta
Fairy shrimp, Conservancy
Fairy shrimp, Riverside
Isopod, Lee County cave
Isopod, Socorro
Shrimp, Alabama cave
Shrimp, California freshwater
Shrimp, Kentucky cave
Tadpole shrimp, vernal pool

# Geology

## The Continents

*Figures given are approximate. Area and population as of 2001. Lowest points listed are all below sea level.*

| CONTINENT | POPULATION | AREA | % OF TOTAL LAND AREA[1] | HIGHEST/LOWEST POINT |
|---|---|---|---|---|
| Asia | 3,754,689,000 | 45,009,200 sq km<br>17,378,140 sq mi | 29.9 | Mount Everest (China, Nepal):<br>8,848 m (29,028 ft)<br>Dead Sea (Israel, Jordan):<br>−400 m (−1,312 ft) |
| Africa | 816,524,000 | 30,348,110 sq km<br>11,717,370 sq mi | 20.6 | Mt. Kilimanjaro (Tanzania):<br>5,895 m (19,340 ft)<br>Lake Assal (Djibouti):<br>−157 m (−515 ft) |
| North America | 490,780,000 | 24,221,490 sq km<br>9,351,970 sq mi | 14.8 | Mt. McKinley (Alaska):<br>6,194 m (20,320 ft)<br>Death Valley (California):<br>−86 m (−282 ft) |
| South America | 350,514,000 | 17,858,520 sq km<br>6,895,210 sq mi | 12.0 | Mt. Aconcagua (Argentina):<br>6,959 m (22,831 ft)<br>Valdés Peninsula (Argentina):<br>−40 m (−131 ft) |
| Antarctica | N/A | 14,000,000 sq km<br>5,400,000 sq mi | 10.5 | Vinson Massif: 4,897 m (16,066 ft)<br>Bentley Subglacial Trench:<br>−5,538 m (−8,327 ft) |
| Europe | 686,285,000 | 9,850,500 sq km<br>3,803,300 sq mi | 7.0 | Mt. Elbrus (Russia):<br>5,642 m (18,510 ft)<br>Caspian Sea (Russia): −27 m (−90 ft) |
| Oceania | 31,377,000 | 8,514,830 sq km<br>3,287,600 sq mi | 5.2 | Mt. Wilhelm (Papua New Guinea):<br>4,509 m (14,793 ft)<br>Lake Eyre: −15 m (−50 ft) |

[1]*Together, the continents make up about 29.2% of the Earth's surface.*

## Thermal structure of the atmosphere

## Electrical structure

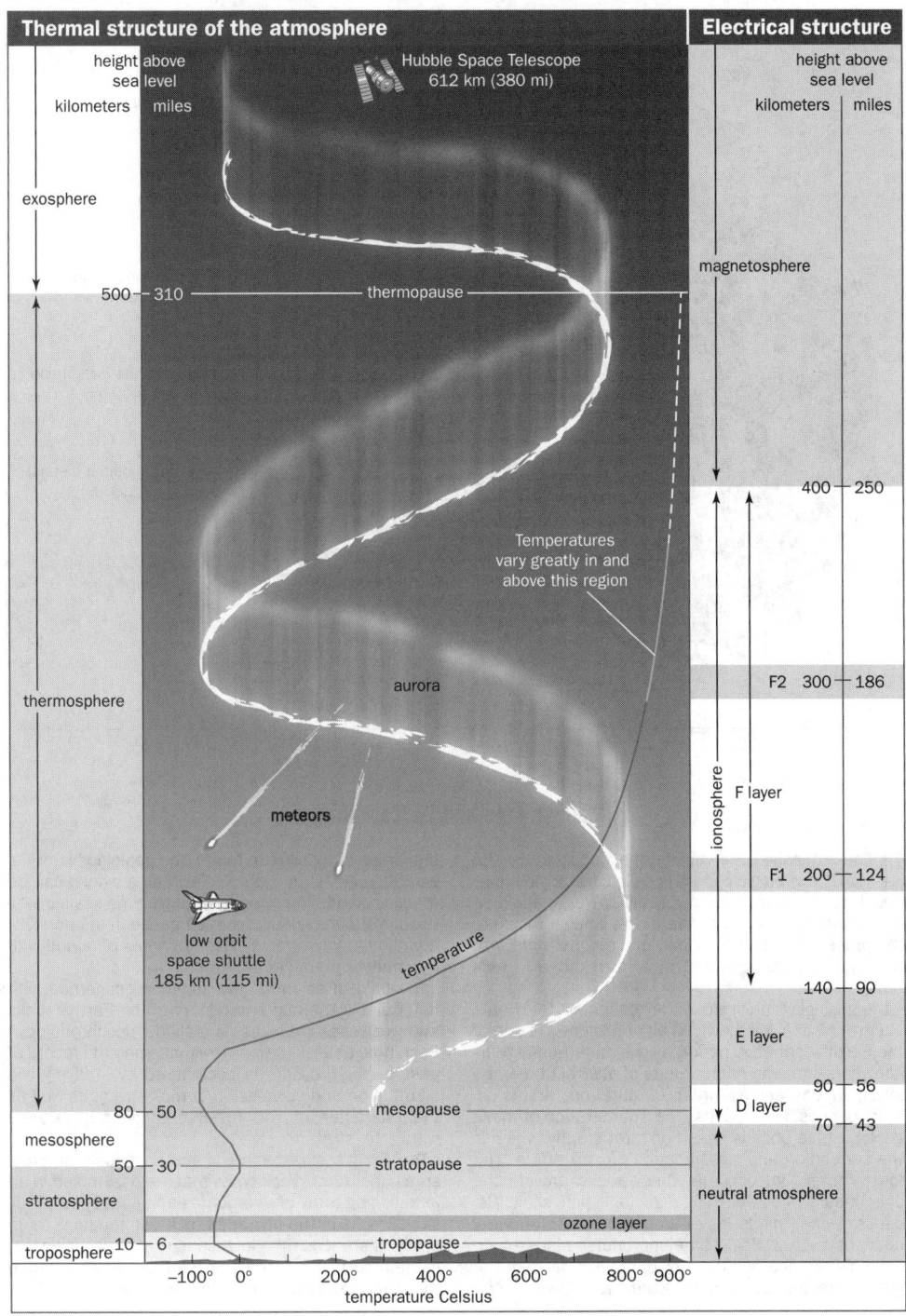

height above sea level
kilometers    miles

Hubble Space Telescope
612 km (380 mi)

exosphere

500 — 310 ———————————— thermopause ————————————

thermosphere

Temperatures vary greatly in and above this region

aurora

meteors

low orbit space shuttle
185 km (115 mi)

temperature

80 — 50 ————————————— mesopause —————————————

mesosphere

50 — 30 ————————————— stratopause —————————————

stratosphere

ozone layer

10 — 6 ————————————— tropopause —————————————

troposphere

−100°    0°    200°    400°    600°    800° 900°
temperature Celsius

height above sea level
kilometers    miles

magnetosphere

400 — 250

F2  300 — 186

F layer

F1  200 — 124

140 — 90

E layer

90 — 56
70 — 43

D layer

neutral atmosphere

ionosphere

**Earth's interior layers (depths below surface)**

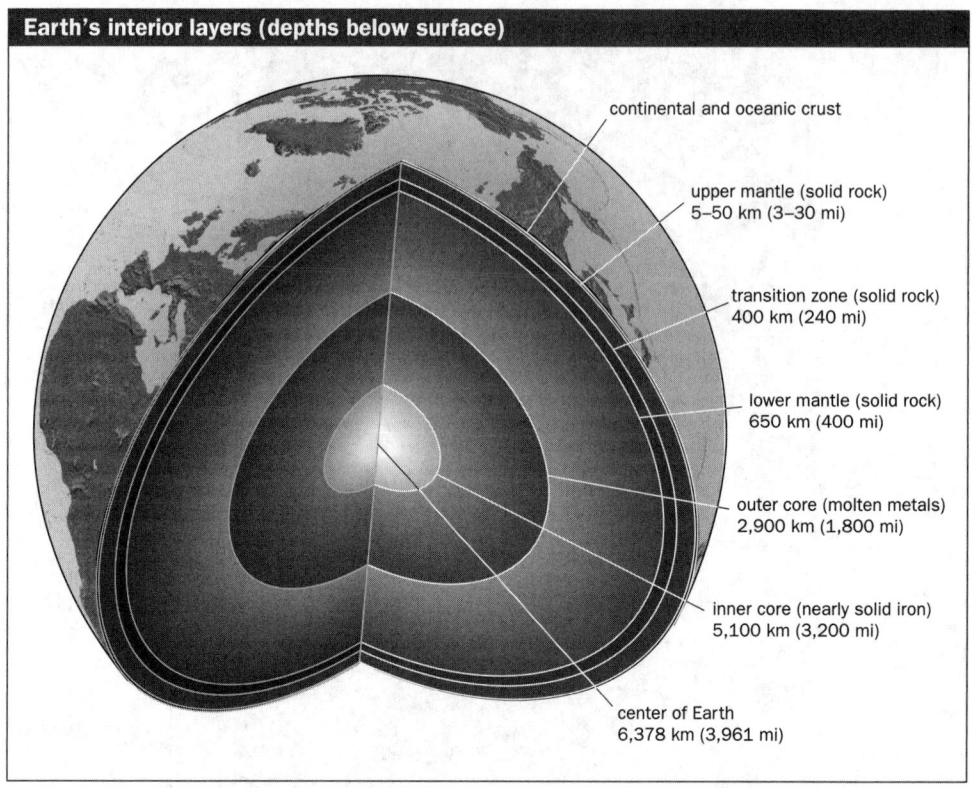

continental and oceanic crust

upper mantle (solid rock)
5–50 km (3–30 mi)

transition zone (solid rock)
400 km (240 mi)

lower mantle (solid rock)
650 km (400 mi)

outer core (molten metals)
2,900 km (1,800 mi)

inner core (nearly solid iron)
5,100 km (3,200 mi)

center of Earth
6,378 km (3,961 mi)

## Geologic Time and Geochronology

The extensive interval of time occupied by the Earth's geologic history is called "geologic time." It extends from about 3.9 billion years ago (corresponding to the age of the oldest known rocks) to the present day. It is, in effect, that segment of Earth history that is represented by and recorded in rock strata.

The geologic time scale is the "calendar" for events in Earth history. It subdivides all time since the end of the Earth's formative period as a planet (nearly 4 billion years ago) into named units of abstract time: the latter, in descending order of duration, are eons, eras, periods, and epochs. The enumeration of these geologic time units is based on stratigraphy, which is the correlation and classification of rock strata. The fossil forms that occur in these rocks provide the chief means of establishing a geologic time scale. Because living things have undergone evolutionary changes over geologic time, particular kinds of organisms are characteristic of particular parts of the geologic record. By correlating the strata in which cer-

tain types of fossils are found, the geologic history of various regions (and of the Earth as a whole) can be reconstructed. The relative geologic time scale developed from the fossil record has been numerically quantified by means of absolute dates obtained with radiometric dating methods.

The field of scientific investigation concerned with determining the age and history of the Earth's rocks and rock assemblages is called "geochronology." Such time determinations are made and the record of past geologic events is deciphered by studying the distribution and succession of rock strata, as well as the character of the fossil organisms preserved within the strata.

The Earth's surface is a complex mosaic of exposures of different rock types that are assembled in an astonishing array of geometries and sequences. Individual rocks in the myriad of rock outcroppings (or in some instances shallow subsurface occurrences) contain certain materials or mineralogic information that can provide insight as to their "age."

---

The oldest detected meteorite impact on Earth occurred 3.47 billion years ago. The meteor left geochemical evidence of its impact in southern Africa and Australia and is thought to have been about 20 km (12 mi) wide. It would have taken less than two seconds to pass through the atmosphere and slam into the surface of the planet, causing immense tsunamis and devastating erosion to the ocean floor and small continents.

# Geologic Time Scale

## Cenozoic Era

| mya* | period | | epoch | | age | boundaries* |
|---|---|---|---|---|---|---|
| | Quaternary | | Holocene | | | 0.01 |
| | | | Pleistocene | | Calabrian | 1.8 |
| | Tertiary | Neogene | Pliocene | L | Piacenzian | 3.6 |
| | | | | E | Zanclean | 5.3 |
| | | | Miocene | L | Messinian | 7.1 |
| | | | | | Tortonian | 11.2 |
| | | | | M | Serravallian | 14.8 |
| | | | | | Langhian | 16.4 |
| | | | | E | Burdigalian | 20.5 |
| | | | | | Aquitanian | 23.8 |
| | | Paleogene | Oligocene | L | Chattian | 28.5 |
| | | | | E | Rupelian | 33.7 |
| | | | Eocene | L | Priabonian | 37.0 |
| | | | | M | Bartonian | 41.3 |
| | | | | | Lutetian | 49.0 |
| | | | | E | Ypresian | 54.8 |
| | | | Paleocene | L | Thanetian | 57.9 |
| | | | | E | Selandian | 61.0 |
| | | | | | Danian | 65.0 |

## Mesozoic Era

| period | epoch | | age | boundaries* |
|---|---|---|---|---|
| Cretaceous | L | | Maastrichtian | 71.3 |
| | | | Campanian | 83.5 |
| | | | Santonian | 85.8 |
| | | | Coniacian | 89.0 |
| | | | Turonian | 93.5 |
| | | | Cenomanian | 99.0 |
| | E | | Albian | 112 |
| | | | Aptian | 121 |
| | | | Barremian | 127 |
| | | Neocomian | Hauterivian | 132 |
| | | | Valanginian | 137 |
| | | | Berriasian | 144 |
| Jurassic | L | | Tithonian | 151 |
| | | | Kimmeridgian | 154 |
| | | | Oxfordian | 159 |
| | M | | Callovian | 164 |
| | | | Bathonian | 169 |
| | | | Bajocian | 176 |
| | | | Aalenian | 180 |
| | E | | Toarcian | 190 |
| | | | Pliensbachian | 195 |
| | | | Sinemurian | 202 |
| | | | Hettangian | 206 |
| Triassic | L | | Rhaetian | 210 |
| | | | Norian | 221 |
| | | | Carnian | 227 |
| | M | | Ladinian | 234 |
| | | | Anisian | 242 |
| | E | | Olenekian | 245 |
| | | | Induan | 248 |

## Paleozoic Era

| period | epoch | age | boundaries* |
|---|---|---|---|
| Permian | L | Tatarian | 248 |
| | | Ufimian-Kazanian | 252 |
| | E | Kungurian | 256 |
| | | Artinskian | 260 |
| | | Sakmarian | 269 |
| | | Asselian | 282 |
| Carboniferous — Pennsylvanian | L | Gzelian (S.) | 290 |
| | | Kasimovian | 296 |
| | E | Moscovian (W.) | 303 |
| | | Bashkirian (N.) | 311 |
| Carboniferous — Mississippian | L | Serpukhovian | 323 |
| | | | 327 |
| | E | Visean | 342 |
| | | Tournaisian | 354 |
| Devonian | L | Famennian | 364 |
| | | Frasnian | 370 |
| | M | Givetian | 380 |
| | | Eifelian | 391 |
| | E | Emsian | 400 |
| | | Praghian | 412 |
| | | Lochkovian | 417 |
| Silurian | L | Pridolian | 419 |
| | | Ludlovian | 423 |
| | | Wenlockian | 428 |
| | E | Llandoverian | 443 |
| Ordovician | L | Ashgillian | 449 |
| | | Caradocian | 458 |
| | M | Llandeilian | 464 |
| | | Llanvirnian | 470 |
| | E | Arenigian | 485 |
| | | Tremadocian | 490 |
| Cambrian** | D | Sunwaptian** | 495 |
| | | Steptoean** | 500 |
| | C | Marjuman** | 506 |
| | B | Delamaran** | 512 |
| | | Dyeran** | 516 |
| | A | Montezuman** | 520 |
| | | | 543 |

## Precambrian time

| eon | era | boundaries* |
|---|---|---|
| Proterozoic | L | 543 |
| | | 900 |
| | M | |
| | | 1,600 |
| | E | |
| | | 2,500 |
| Archean | L | |
| | | 3,000 |
| | M | |
| | | 3,400 |
| | E | |
| | | 3,800? |

* Millions of years before the present.
** International ages have not been established. These are regional (Laurentian) only.

Published with permission of the Geological Society of America.

# Largest Islands of the World

| NAME AND LOCATION | CONTINENT | AREA* SQ MI | AREA* SQ KM |
|---|---|---|---|
| Greenland | North America | 822,700 | 2,130,800 |
| New Guinea, Papua New Guinea–Indonesia | Oceania | 309,000 | 800,000 |
| Borneo, Indonesia–Malaysia–Brunei | Asia | 283,400 | 734,000 |
| Madagascar | Africa | 226,658 | 587,041 |
| Baffin, Nunavut, Canada | North America | 195,928 | 507,451 |
| Sumatra, Indonesia | Asia | 167,600 | 434,000 |
| Honshu, Japan | Asia | 87,805 | 227,414 |
| Victoria, Northwest Territories–Nunavut, Canada | North America | 83,897 | 217,291 |
| Great Britain | Europe | 83,698 | 216,777 |
| Ellesmere, Nunavut, Canada | North America | 75,767 | 196,236 |
| Celebes, Indonesia | Asia | 69,100 | 179,000 |
| South Island, New Zealand | Oceania | 58,676 | 151,971 |
| Java, Indonesia | Asia | 49,000 | 126,900 |
| North Island, New Zealand | Oceania | 44,204 | 114,489 |
| Newfoundland, Canada | North America | 42,031 | 108,860 |
| Cuba | North America | 40,519 | 104,945 |
| Luzon, Philippines | Asia | 40,420 | 104,688 |
| Iceland | Europe | 39,699 | 102,819 |
| Mindanao, Philippines | Asia | 36,537 | 94,630 |
| Ireland, Ireland–UK | Europe | 32,589 | 84,406 |
| Hokkaido, Japan | Asia | 30,144 | 78,073 |
| Sakhalin, Russia | Asia | 29,500 | 76,400 |
| Hispaniola, Haiti–Dominican Republic | North America | 29,418 | 76,192 |
| Banks, Northwest Territories, Canada | North America | 27,038 | 70,028 |
| Sri Lanka, Ceylon | Asia | 25,332 | 65,610 |
| Tasmania, Australia | Oceania | 24,868 | 64,409 |
| Devon, Nunavut, Canada | North America | 21,331 | 55,247 |
| Severny, Novaya Zemlya, Russia | Europe | 18,882 | 48,904 |
| Tierra del Fuego, Argentina–Chile | South America | 18,530 | 47,992 |
| Alexander I | Antarctica | 16,700 | 43,200 |
| Axel Heiberg, Nunavut, Canada | North America | 16,671 | 43,178 |
| Melville, Northwest Territories–Nunavut, Canada | North America | 16,274 | 42,149 |
| Southampton, Nunavut, Canada | North America | 15,913 | 41,214 |
| Marajó, Pará, Brazil | South America | 15,500 | 40,100 |
| Spitsbergen, Svalbard, Norway | Europe | 15,075 | 39,044 |
| Kyushu, Japan | Asia | 14,114 | 36,554 |
| New Britain, Papua New Guinea | Oceania | 14,100 | 36,500 |
| Taiwan, Formosa | Asia | 13,851 | 35,873 |
| Hainan, China | Asia | 12,962 | 33,572 |
| Prince of Wales, Nunavut, Canada | North America | 12,872 | 33,339 |
| Yuzhny, Novaya Zemlya, Russia | Europe | 12,848 | 33,275 |
| Vancouver, British Columbia, Canada | North America | 12,079 | 31,285 |
| Timor, Indonesia–East Timor | Asia | 11,883 | 30,777 |
| Sicily, Italy | Europe | 9,830 | 25,460 |
| Somerset, Nunavut, Canada | North America | 9,570 | 24,786 |
| Sardinia, Italy | Europe | 9,194 | 23,813 |
| Bananal, Tocantins, Brazil | South America | 7,700 | 20,000 |
| Shikoku, Japan | Asia | 7,049 | 18,256 |
| Halmahera, Indonesia | Asia | 6,865 | 17,780 |
| Seram, Indonesia | Asia | 6,621 | 17,148 |

*Area given may include small adjoining islands. Conversions for rounded figures are rounded to nearest hundred.

# Highest Mountains of the World

"I" in the name of a peak refers to the highest in a group of numbered peaks of the same name.

| NAME AND LOCATION | HEIGHT IN M | HEIGHT IN FT | YEAR FIRST CLIMBED |
|---|---|---|---|
| **Africa** | | | |
| Kilimanjaro (Kibo peak), Tanzania | 5,895 | 19,340 | 1889 |
| Mt. Kenya (Batian peak), Kenya | 5,199 | 17,058 | 1899 |
| Margherita, Ruwenzori Range, Zaire–Uganda | 5,119 | 16,795 | 1906 |
| Ras Dashen, Simen Mtns., Ethiopia | 4,620 | 15,157 | 1841 |
| Meru, Tanzania | 4,565 | 14,978 | N/A |
| Lageda, Ethiopia | 4,532 | 14,869 | N/A |

# Highest Mountains of the World (continued)

| NAME AND LOCATION | HEIGHT IN M | HEIGHT IN FT | YEAR FIRST CLIMBED |
|---|---|---|---|
| **Africa (continued)** | | | |
| Karisimbi, Virunga Mtns., Zaire–Rwanda | 4,507 | 14,787 | 1903 |
| Analu, Ethiopia | 4,480 | 14,698 | N/A |
| Weynober, Ethiopia | 4,472 | 14,672 | N/A |
| Mikeno, Virunga Mtns., Zaire–Rwanda | 4,437 | 14,557 | 1927 |
| | | | |
| **Antarctica** | | | |
| Vinson Massif, Sentinel Range, Ellsworth Mtns. | 4,897 | 16,066 | 1966 |
| Tyree, Sentinel Range, Ellsworth Mtns. | 4,852 | 15,919 | 1967 |
| Shinn, Sentinel Range, Ellsworth Mtns. | 4,801 | 15,751 | 1966 |
| Kirkpatrick, Queen Alexandra Range | 4,528 | 14,856 | N/A |
| Markham, Queen Elizabeth Range | 4,350 | 14,272 | N/A |
| | | | |
| **Asia** | | | |
| Everest, Chomolungma), Himalayas, Nepal–Tibet, China | 8,848 | 29,028 | 1953 |
| K2 (Godwin Austen) (Chogori), Karakoram Range, Pakistan–Sinkiang, China | 8,611 | 28,251 | 1954 |
| Kanchenjunga I (Gangchhendzonga), Himalayas, Nepal–India | 8,586 | 28,169 | 1955 |
| Lhotse I, Himalayas, Nepal–Tibet, China | 8,516 | 27,940 | 1956 |
| Makalu I, Himalayas, Nepal–Tibet, China | 8,463 | 27,766 | 1955 |
| Cho Oyu, Himalayas, Nepal–Tibet, China | 8,201 | 26,906 | 1954 |
| Dhaulagiri I, Himalayas, Nepal | 8,167 | 26,795 | 1960 |
| Manaslu I, Himalayas, Nepal | 8,163 | 26,781 | 1956 |
| Nanga Parbat I, Himalayas, Pakistan | 8,126 | 26,660 | 1953 |
| Annapurna I, Himalayas, Nepal | 8,091 | 26,545 | 1950 |
| | | | |
| **Caucasus** | | | |
| Elbrus, Russia | 5,642 | 18,510 | 1874 |
| Dykh–Tau, Russia | 5,204 | 17,073 | 1888 |
| Koshtan–Tau, Russia | 5,151 | 16,900 | 1889 |
| Shkhara, Russia–Georgia | 5,068 | 16,627 | 1888 |
| Dzhangi–Tau, Russia–Georgia | 5,058 | 16,594 | 1903 |
| Kazbek, Georgia | 5,033 | 16,512 | 1868 |
| Shota Rustaveli, Russia–Georgia | 4,960 | 16,273 | N/A |
| Dzhimara, Georgia | 4,780 | 15,682 | N/A |
| Ushba, Georgia | 4,700 | 15,420 | 1888 |
| Uilpata, Russia | 4,649 | 15,253 | N/A |
| | | | |
| **Europe** | | | |
| Mont Blanc, Alps, France–Italy | 4,807 | 15,771 | 1786 |
| Dufourspitze (Monte Rosa), Alps, Switzerland–Italy | 4,634 | 15,203 | 1855 |
| Dom (Mischabel), Alps, Switzerland | 4,545 | 14,911 | 1858 |
| Weisshorn, Alps, Switzerland | 4,505 | 14,780 | 1861 |
| Matterhorn, Alps, Switzerland–Italy | 4,478 | 14,692 | 1865 |
| Mont Maudit, Alps, France–Italy | 4,471 | 14,669 | N/A |
| Dent Blanche, Alps, Switzerland | 4,357 | 14,295 | 1862 |
| Grand Combin, Alps, Switzerland | 4,314 | 14,154 | 1859 |
| Dôme du Goûter, Alps, France | 4,304 | 14,121 | 1784 |
| Finsteraarhorn, Alps, Switzerland | 4,274 | 14,022 | 1812 |
| | | | |
| **North America** | | | |
| McKinley, Alaska Range, Alaska | 6,194 | 20,320 | 1913 |
| Logan, St. Elias Mtns., Yukon, Canada | 5,951 | 19,524 | 1925 |
| Citlaltépetl (Orizaba), Cordillera Neo-Volcánica, Mexico | 5,610 | 18,406 | 1848 |
| St. Elias, St. Elias Mtns., Alaska–Canada | 5,489 | 18,009 | 1897 |
| Popocatépetl, Cordillera Neo-Volcánica, Mexico | 5,465 | 17,930 | 1519 |
| Foraker, Alaska Range, Alaska | 5,304 | 17,400 | 1934 |
| Iztaccíhuatl (Ixtacihuatl), Cordillera Neo-Volcánica, Mexico | 5,230 | 17,159 | 1889 |
| Lucania, St. Elias Mtns., Yukon, Canada | 5,226 | 17,146 | 1937 |
| King, St. Elias Mtns., Yukon, Canada | 5,173 | 16,972 | 1952 |
| Steele, St. Elias Mtns., Yukon, Canada | 5,073 | 16,644 | 1935 |

## Highest Mountains of the World (continued)

| NAME AND LOCATION | HEIGHT IN M | HEIGHT IN FT | YEAR FIRST CLIMBED |
|---|---|---|---|
| **Oceania** | | | |
| Jaya (Sukarno, Carstensz), Sudirman Range, Indonesia | 5,030 | 16,500[1] | 1962 |
| Pilimsit (Idenburg), Sudirman Range, Indonesia | 4,800 | 15,750[1] | 1962 |
| Trikora (Wilhelmina), Jayawijaya Mtns., Indonesia | 4,750 | 15,580[1] | 1912 |
| Mandala (Juliana), Jayawijaya Mtns., Indonesia | 4,700 | 15,420[1] | 1959 |
| Wisnumurti (Jan Pieterszoon Coen), Jayawijaya, Mtns., Indonesia | 4,595 | 15,080[1] | N/A |
| Wilhelm, Bismarck Range, Papua New Guinea | 4,509 | 14,793 | N/A |
| Giluwe, Hagen Range, Papua New Guinea | 4,368 | 14,331 | N/A |
| Kubor, Kubor Range, Papua New Guinea | 4,359 | 14,301 | N/A |
| Herbert, Bismarck Range, Papua New Guinea | 4,267 | 13,999 | N/A |
| Mauna Kea, Hawaii, US | 4,205 | 13,796 | N/A |
| | | | |
| **South America** | | | |
| Aconcagua, Andes, Argentina–Chile | 6,959 | 22,831 | 1897 |
| Ojos del Salado, Andes, Argentina–Chile | 6,893 | 22,615 | 1937 |
| Bonete, Andes, Argentina | 6,872 | 22,546 | 1913 |
| Tupungato, Andes, Argentina–Chile | 6,800 | 22,310 | 1897 |
| Pissis, Andes, Argentina | 6,779 | 22,241 | 1937 |
| Mercedario, Andes, Argentina | 6,770 | 22,211 | 1934 |
| Huascarán, Cordillera Blanca, Andes, Peru | 6,768 | 22,205 | 1908 |
| Tres Cruces, Andes, Argentina–Chile | 6,753 | 22,156 | 1937 |
| Llullaillaco, Cordillera Occidental, Andes, Argentina–Chile | 6,723 | 22,057 | 1952 |
| Cachi (El Libertador), Sierra de Pastos Grandes, Andes, Argentina | 6,720 | 22,047 | 1904 |

[1]Conversions rounded to the nearest 10 ft.

## Major Caves and Cave Systems of the World by Continent

| NAME AND LOCATION | DEPTH[1] FEET | DEPTH[1] M | LENGTH[2] MILES | LENGTH[2] KM |
|---|---|---|---|---|
| **Africa** | | | | |
| Achra Lemoun, Algeria | 1,060 | 323 | N/A | N/A |
| Ambatoanjahana, Madagascar | N/A | N/A | 6.7 | 10.8 |
| Ambatoharanana, Madagascar | N/A | N/A | 11.2 | 18.1 |
| Apocalypse Pothole, South Africa | 279 | 85 | 7.5 | 12.1 |
| Boussouil, Algeria | 2,641 | 805 | 2 | 3.2 |
| Ifflis, Algeria | 3,802 | 1,159 | 1 | 1.6 |
| Jabal As-Sarj, Tunisia | 876 | 267 | 1.1 | 1.7 |
| Leviathani, Kenya | 1,526 | 465 | 7 | 11.2 |
| Sof 'Umar, Ethiopia | N/A | N/A | 9.4 | 15.1 |
| Tafna (Bou Ma'za), Algeria | N/A | N/A | 11.4 | 18.4 |
| Toghobeït, Morocco | 2,339 | 713 | 2.3 | 3.7 |
| | | | | |
| **Antarctica: no significant caves** | | | | |
| | | | | |
| **Asia** | | | | |
| Air Jernih, Malaysia | 1,165 | 355 | 32.1 | 51.6 |
| Bilremos, South Korea | N/A | N/A | 7.3 | 11.7 |
| Byakuren, Japan | 1,476 | 450 | 0.7 | 1.1 |
| Faouar Dara, Lebanon | 2,041 | 622 | 1.5 | 2.5 |
| Kap-Kutan/Promezhutochnaya, Uzbekistan | N/A | N/A | 31.3 | 50.3 |
| Kiev, Uzbekistan | 3,248 | 990 | 1.1 | 1.8 |
| Manjung, South Korea | N/A | N/A | 8.3 | 13.3 |
| Omi-senri, Japan | 1,198 | 365 | N/A | N/A |
| Oreshnaya, Russia | 623 | 190 | 25.5 | 41 |
| Parau, Iran | 2,464 | 751 | 0.9 | 1.4 |
| Sallukan Kallang, Indonesia | 673 | 205 | 7.6 | 12.3 |
| Ural, Uzbekistan | 1,854 | 565 | 1.5 | 2.5 |
| Wu-chia, China | 1,430 | 436 | N/A | N/A |
| | | | | |
| **Europe** | | | | |
| Arañonera, Spain | 3,888 | 1,185 | 4 | 6.5 |
| Berger, France | 4,072 | 1,241 | 12.9 | 20.7 |

## Major Caves and Cave Systems of the World (continued)

| NAME AND LOCATION | DEPTH[1] FEET | M | LENGTH[2] MILES | KM |
|---|---|---|---|---|
| **Europe (continued)** | | | | |
| Coumo d'Hyouernèdo, France | 3,294 | 1,004 | 56.2 | 90.5 |
| Dachstein-Mammut, Austria | 3,871 | 1,180 | 23.9 | 38.5 |
| Dent de Crolles, France | 1,978 | 603 | 33.6 | 54.1 |
| Ease Gill, United Kingdom | N/A | N/A | 32.6 | 52.5 |
| Ffynnon Ddu, United Kingdom | 1,010 | 308 | 26.7 | 43 |
| Fighiera-Farolfi-Antro del Corchia, Italy | 3,986 | 1,215 | 28 | 45 |
| Hirlatz, Austria | 2,008 | 612 | 35.4 | 57 |
| Hölloch, Switzerland | 2,844 | 867 | 82.7 | 133.1 |
| Jean Bernard, France | 5,036 | 1,535 | 11.1 | 17.9 |
| L'Alpe, France | 2,014 | 614 | 28.7 | 46.2 |
| Laminako Ateak (Illamina), Spain | 4,619 | 1,408 | 7.4 | 11.9 |
| Ojo Guareña, Spain | N/A | N/A | 55.4 | 89.1 |
| Optimisticheskaya, Ukraine | N/A | N/A | 102.5 | 165 |
| Ozernaya, Ukraine | N/A | N/A | 66.5 | 107 |
| Pierre Saint-Martin, France-Spain | 4,403 | 1,342 | 32.3 | 52 |
| Raucherkar, Austria | 2,379 | 725 | 29.8 | 48 |
| Red del Río Silencio, Spain | 1,614 | 492 | 32.9 | 53 |
| Schwer, Austria | 3,999 | 1,219 | 3.8 | 6.1 |
| Siebenhengste-Hohgant-Höhlen, Switzerland | 3,346 | 1,020 | 68.4 | 110 |
| Snezhnoye-Mezhonnogo, Georgia | 4,495 | 1,370 | 11.8 | 19 |
| Trave, Spain | 4,528 | 1,380 | 1.8 | 2.9 |
| Vyacheslav Pantyukhina, Georgia | 4,948 | 1,508 | N/A | N/A |
| Xitu, Spain | 3,766 | 1,148 | 4.7 | 7.5 |
| Zolushka, Moldova | N/A | N/A | 51 | 82 |
| | | | | |
| **Oceania** | | | | |
| Atea, Papua New Guinea | 1,148 | 350 | 21.4 | 34.5 |
| Bulmer, New Zealand | 2,388 | 728 | 6.8 | 11 |
| Cora-Lynn, Australia | N/A | N/A | 8.3 | 13.3 |
| Gardners Gut, New Zealand | N/A | N/A | 7.4 | 11.9 |
| H.H. Hole, New Zealand | 2,044 | 623 | N/A | N/A |
| Honeycomb, New Zealand | N/A | N/A | 8.1 | 13.1 |
| Ipaku-Kukumbu, Papua New Guinea | 1,273 | 388 | 6.8 | 11 |
| Kavakuna II, Papua New Guinea | 1,499 | 457 | 2.2 | 3.5 |
| Mamo, Papua New Guinea | 1,732 | 528 | 34.1 | 54.8 |
| Mini-Martin-Exit, Australia | 722 | 220 | 9.9 | 16 |
| Muruk, Papua New Guinea | 2,090 | 637 | 2.9 | 4.6 |
| Nettlebed, New Zealand | 2,917 | 889 | 15.2 | 24.4 |
| Selminum, Papua New Guinea | N/A | N/A | 12.7 | 20.5 |
| | | | | |
| **North America** | | | | |
| Aztotempa, Mexico | 2,297 | 700 | 2.5 | 4 |
| Binkley's, Indiana | N/A | N/A | 19.1 | 30.7 |
| Butler-Sinking Creek, Virginia | 623 | 190 | 20 | 32.2 |
| Carlsbad Caverns, New Mexico | 1,027 | 313 | 20.8 | 33.5 |
| Crevice, Missouri | N/A | N/A | 28.2 | 45.4 |
| Cuicateca, Mexico | 4,035 | 1,230 | 5.8 | 9.3 |
| Cumberland Caverns, Tennessee | N/A | N/A | 27.6 | 44.4 |
| Fisher Ridge, Kentucky | N/A | N/A | 44.4 | 71.5 |
| Friars Hole, West Virginia | 617 | 188 | 42.8 | 68.8 |
| Guixani Ndia Guinjao, Mexico | 3,084 | 940 | 1.2 | 2 |
| The Hole, West Virginia | N/A | N/A | 22.9 | 36.8 |
| Huautla, Mexico | 4,439 | 1,353 | 32.4 | 52.1 |
| Jewel, South Dakota | 443 | 135 | 76.9 | 123.8 |
| Lechuguilla, New Mexico | 1,503 | 458 | 32.9 | 53 |
| Mammoth-Flint Ridge, Kentucky | 360 | 110 | 329.3 | 530 |
| Organ, West Virginia | N/A | N/A | 37.6 | 60.5 |
| Purificación, Mexico | 2,936 | 895 | 44.5 | 71.6 |
| Sloan's Valley, Kentucky | N/A | N/A | 24.6 | 39.6 |
| Sonyance, Mexico | 2,444 | 745 | 1.1 | 1.8 |
| Tilaco, Mexico | 2,129 | 649 | N/A | N/A |
| Trinidad, Mexico | 2,736 | 834 | N/A | N/A |
| Whigpistle, Kentucky | N/A | N/A | 22.5 | 36.2 |
| Xanadu, Tennessee | N/A | N/A | 24 | 38.6 |

## Major Caves and Cave Systems of the World (continued)

| NAME AND LOCATION | DEPTH[1] FEET | DEPTH[1] M | LENGTH[2] MILES | LENGTH[2] KM |
|---|---|---|---|---|
| **South America** | | | | |
| Angélica, Brazil | N/A | N/A | 4 | 6.4 |
| Aonda, Venezuela | 1,188 | 362 | N/A | N/A |
| Auyantepuy Norte, Venezuela | 1,050 | 320 | N/A | N/A |
| Brejões, Brazil | N/A | N/A | 4.8 | 7.8 |
| Guácharo, Venezuela | 164 | 50 | 6.3 | 10.2 |
| Guarataro, Venezuela | 1,001 | 305 | N/A | N/A |
| Kaukiran, Peru | 1,335 | 407 | 1.3 | 2.1 |
| Major de Sarisarinama, Venezuela | 1,030 | 314 | N/A | N/A |
| Ôlhos d'Água, Brazil | N/A | N/A | 3.9 | 6.3 |
| San Andrés, Peru | 1,096 | 334 | N/A | N/A |
| São Mateus-Imbira, Brazil | N/A | N/A | 12.7 | 20.5 |

[1]*Below highest entrance.*   [2]*Explored portion of cave.*
Source: Paul Courbon et al., *Atlas of the Great Caves of the World (1989).*

## Major Deserts of the World by Continent

| DESERT (LOCATION) | AREA SQ KM | AREA SQ MI | DESERT (LOCATION) | AREA SQ KM | AREA SQ MI |
|---|---|---|---|---|---|
| **Africa** | | | **Australia** | | |
| Sahara, northern Africa | 8,600,000 | 3,320,000 | Great Victoria, Western and | 647,000 | 250,000 |
| Libyan, Libya, Egypt, and | N/A | N/A | South Australia | | |
| Sudan | | | Great Sandy, northern | 400,000 | 150,000 |
| Kalahari, southwestern | 930,000 | 360,000 | Western Australia | | |
| Africa | | | Gibson, Western Australia | N/A | N/A |
| Namib, southwestern | 135,000 | 52,000 | Simpson, Northern Territory | 145,000 | 56,000 |
| Africa | | | | | |
| | | | **North America** | | |
| **Asia** | | | Great Basin, southwestern | 492,000 | 190,000 |
| Arabia, southwestern Asia | 2,330,000 | 900,000 | US | | |
| Rub'al-Khali, southern | 650,000 | 250,000 | Chihuahuan, northern | 450,000 | 175,000 |
| Arabian Peninsula | | | Mexico | | |
| Gobi, Mongolia and | 1,300,000 | 500,000 | Sonoran, southwestern US | 310,000 | 120,000 |
| northeastern China | | | and Baja California | | |
| Kyzylkum, Kazakhstan- | 300,000 | 115,000 | Colorado, California | N/A | N/A |
| Uzbekistan | | | and northern Mexico | | |
| Takla Makan, northern | 270,000 | 105,000 | Yuma, Arizona and | N/A | N/A |
| China | | | Sonora, Mexico | | |
| Karakum, Turkmenistan | 350,000 | 135,000 | Mojave, southwestern US | 65,000 | 25,000 |
| Kavir, central Iran | 260,000 | 100,000 | | | |
| Syrian, Saudi Arabia, | 260,000 | 100,000 | **South America** | | |
| Jordan, Syria, and Iraq | | | Patagonian, southern | 673,000 | 260,000 |
| Thar, India and Pakistan | 200,000 | 77,000 | Argentina | | |
| Lut, eastern Iran | 52,000 | 20,000 | Atacama, northern Chile | 140,000 | 54,000 |

## Major Volcanoes of the World by Continent

| VOLCANO, LOCATION | ELEVATION M | ELEVATION FT | FIRST RECORDED ERUPTION | MOST RECENT ERUPTION |
|---|---|---|---|---|
| **Africa** | | | | |
| Kilimanjaro, Tanzania[1] | 5,895 | 19,340 | N/A | N/A[2] |
| Cameroon, Cameroon | 4,100 | 13,451 | 1650 | 2000 |
| Teide (Tenerife), Canary Islands | 3,718 | 12,198 | N/A | 1909 |
| Nyiragongo, Dem. Rep. of the Congo | 3,475 | 11,400 | 1884 | 2002 |
| Nyamuragira, Dem. Rep. of the Congo | 3,055 | 10,023 | 1882 | 2001 |
| Fogo, Cape Verde | 2,829 | 9,281 | 1500 | 1995 |
| Karthala, Comoros | 2,361 | 7,745 | 1828 | 1991 |
| Fournaise, Reunion Islands | 1,823 | 5,981 | 1640 | 2001 |
| | | | | |
| **Antarctica** | | | | |
| Erebus, Ross Island | 3,743 | 12,280 | 1841 | 1991 |
| Darnley, Sandwich Islands | 1,100 | 3,608 | 1823 | N/A |

## Major Volcanoes of the World (continued)

| VOLCANO, LOCATION | ELEVATION M | ELEVATION FT | FIRST RECORDED ERUPTION | MOST RECENT ERUPTION |
|---|---|---|---|---|
| **Asia–Oceania–Pacific** | | | | |
| Klyuchevskaya, Kamchatka, Russia[3] | 4,750 | 15,584 | 1697 | 2002 |
| Mauna Kea, Hawaii[4] | 4,205 | 13,796 | N/A | *dormant* |
| Mauna Loa, Hawaii | 4,169 | 13,678 | 1750 | 1984 |
| Kerinci, Sumatra, Indonesia | 3,800 | 12,467 | 1838 | 1970 |
| Fuji, Honshu, Japan | 3,776 | 12,388 | 1050 BC | 1708 |
| Rinjani, Lombok, Indonesia | 3,726 | 12,224 | 1847 | 1994 |
| Tolbachik, Kamchatka, Russia | 3,682 | 12,080 | 1740 | 1976 |
| Semeru, Java, Indonesia | 3,676 | 12,060 | 1818 | 2002 |
| Ichinskaya, Kamchatka, Russia | 3,621 | 11,880 | N/A | N/A |
| Slamet, Java, Indonesia | 3,428 | 11,247 | 1772 | 1988 |
| Raung, Java, Indonesia | 3,332 | 10,932 | 1586 | 2000 |
| Shiveluch, Kamchatka, Russia | 3,283 | 10,771 | 1793 | 2002 |
| Dempo, Sumatra, Indonesia | 3,159 | 10,364 | 1817 | 1974 |
| Sundoro, Java, Indonesia | 3,151 | 10,338 | 1818 | 1971 |
| Ontake, Honshu, Japan | 3,063 | 10,049 | 1979 | 1979 |
| Papandayan, Java, Indonesia | 2,987 | 9,802 | 1772 | 1998 |
| Gede, Java, Indonesia | 2,958 | 9,705 | 1747 | 1957 |
| Zhupanovsky, Kamchatka, Russia | 2,958 | 9,705 | 1776 | 1959 |
| Merapi, Java, Indonesia | 2,911 | 9,551 | 1006 | 2002 |
| Bezymianny, Kamchatka, Russia | 2,900 | 9,514 | 1055 | 2001 |
| Marapi, Sumatra, Indonesia | 2,891 | 9,485 | 1770 | 1994 |
| Ruapehu, North Island, New Zealand | 2,797 | 9,177 | 1861 | 1999 |
| Peuet Sague, Sumatra, Indonesia | 2,780 | 9,121 | 1918 | 1998 |
| Avachinskaya, Kamchatka, Russia | 2,751 | 9,026 | 1737 | 1991 |
| Mayon, Luzon, Philippines | 2,421 | 7,943 | 1616 | 2001 |
| Alaid, Kuril Islands, Russia | 2,335 | 7,662 | 1790 | 1981 |
| Ulawun, New Britain, Papua New Guinea | 2,296 | 7,532 | 1700 | 2002 |
| Kelud, Java, Indonesia | 1,731 | 5,679 | 1000 | 2001 |
| Pinatubo, Luzon, Philippines | 1,460 | 4,800 | 1380 | 1991 |
| Lopevi, Vanuatu | 1,364 | 4,755 | 1864 | 2001 |
| Unzen, Kyushu, Japan | 1,360 | 4,462 | 860 | 1991 |
| Awu, Pulau Sangihe, Indonesia | 1,320 | 4,331 | 1640 | 1966 |
| Kilauea, Hawaii | 1,243 | 4,077 | 1750 | 2002 |
| Krakatoa, Krakatau, Indonesia | 813 | 2,667 | 1680 | 2001 |
| Suwanose-jima, Ryukyu Islands, Japan | 799 | 2,621 | 1813 | 1996 |
| Taal, Luzon, Philippines | 400 | 1,312 | 1572 | 1999 |
| | | | | |
| **Europe and the Atlantic** | | | | |
| Etna, Italy | 3,323 | 10,899 | N/A | 2002 |
| Beerenberg, Norway | 2,277 | 7,470 | 1558 | N/A |
| Tristan da Cunha, South Atlantic | 2,060 | 6,760 | 1700 | N/A |
| Askja, Iceland | 1,570 | 5,149 | 1875 | 1961 |
| Hekla, Iceland | 1,491 | 4,890 | 1104 | 2000 |
| Vesuvius, Italy | 1,280 | 4,198 | N/A | 1944 |
| Stromboli, Italy | 926 | 3,038 | N/A | 2002 |
| Krafla, Iceland | 818 | 2,683 | 1300 | 1984 |
| | | | | |
| **North America** | | | | |
| Citlaltépetl, Mexico | 5,610 | 18,406 | N/A | N/A |
| Popocatépetl, Mexico | 5,465 | 17,930 | 1347 | 2002 |
| Rainier, Washington | 4,392 | 14,410 | N/A | c. 200 BC |
| Shasta, California | 4,317 | 14,160 | N/A | 1786 (?) |
| Colima, Mexico | 4,240 | 13,911 | 1576 | 2002 |
| Tajumulco, Guatemala | 4,220 | 13,845 | 1821 | N/A |
| Acatenango, Guatemala | 3,976 | 13,041 | 1924 | 1972 |
| Fuego, Guatemala | 3,763 | 12,342 | 1524 | 2002 |
| Hood, Oregon | 3,424 | 11,235 | 1800 | c. 1800 |
| Spurr, Alaska | 3,374 | 11,067 | 1953 | 1992 |
| Baker, Washington | 3,285 | 10,775 | 1820 | 1880 |
| Lassen, California | 3,187 | 10,457 | 1650 | 1921 |
| Redoubt, Alaska | 3,108 | 10,194 | 1778 | 1990 |
| Iliamna, Alaska | 3,053 | 10,016 | 1768 | 1953 |
| Shishaldin, Alaska | 2,857 | 9,371 | 1775 | 2000 |
| Parícutin, Mexico | 2,807 | 9,210 | 1943 | 1952 |
| Pavlof, Alaska | 2,714 | 8,902 | 1790 | 1997 |

## Major Volcanoes of the World (continued)

| VOLCANO, LOCATION | ELEVATION M | FT | FIRST RECORDED ERUPTION | MOST RECENT ERUPTION |
|---|---|---|---|---|
| **North America (continued)** | | | | |
| Poas, Costa Rica | 2,704 | 8,869 | 1834 | N/A |
| Pacaya, Guatemala | 2,552 | 8,371 | 1565 | 2001 |
| St. Helens, Washington | 2,549 | 8,360 | 1500 | 1998 |
| Veniaminof, Alaska | 2,507 | 8,223 | c. 1750 | 1993 |
| San Miguel, El Salvador | 2,180 | 7,150 | 1586 | 1976 |
| Chiginagak, Alaska | 2,126 | 6,973 | 1852 | 1997 |
| Katmai, Alaska | 2,047 | 6,714 | 1912 | 1912 |
| Makushin, Alaska | 2,035 | 6,674 | 1786 | 1987 |
| Izalco, El Salvador | 1,965 | 6,445 | 1770 | 1966 |
| San Cristóbal, Nicaragua | 1,745 | 5,724 | 1522 | 2001 |
| Great Sitkin, Alaska | 1,737 | 5,697 | 1760 | 1974 |
| Arenal, Costa Rica | 1,633 | 5,356 | 1968 | 2001 |
| Pelée, Martinique | 1,397 | 4,582 | 1792 | 1932 |
| Momotombo, Nicaragua | 1,280 | 4,198 | 1550 | 1996 |
| Kiska, Alaska | 1,220 | 4,001 | 1907 | 1969 |
| Telica, Nicaragua | 1,060 | 3,477 | 1527 | 1999 |
| | | | | |
| **South America** | | | | |
| Guallatiri, Chile | 6,060 | 19,876 | 1825 | 1985 |
| Cotopaxi, Ecuador[5] | 5,897 | 19,347 | 1532 | 1904 |
| Tupungatito, Chile | 5,640 | 18,499 | 1829 | 1986 |
| Lascar, Chile | 5,592 | 18,342 | 1848 | 2000 |
| Ruiz, Colombia | 5,400 | 17,716 | 1595 | 1985 |
| Sangay, Ecuador | 5,230 | 17,154 | 1628 | 1983 |
| Tolima, Colombia | 5,215 | 17,105 | c. 1600 BC | 1822 |
| Tungurahua, Ecuador | 5,033 | 16,512 | 1534 | 2002 |
| Purace, Colombia | 4,800 | 15,744 | 1827 | 1977 |
| Guagua Pichincha, Ecuador | 4,794 | 15,724 | 1533 | 2000 |
| Lautaro, Chile | 3,380 | 11,115 | 1878 | N/A |
| Llaima, Chile | 3,125 | 10,250 | 1640 | 1995 |
| Villarrica, Chile | 2,840 | 9,318 | 1558 | 2000 |
| Hudson, Chile | 2,615 | 8,580 | 1971 | 1991 |

[1]Includes three dormant volcanoes (Kibo, Mawensi, and Shira) that have not erupted in historic times.    [2]Has not erupted in historic times.    [3]Highest active volcano on the Kamchatka Peninsula.    [4]Usually snowcapped dormant volcano.    [5]The world's highest continuously active volcano.

## Oceans & Seas

| | AREA SQ KM | SQ MI | VOLUME CU KM | CU MI |
|---|---|---|---|---|
| **Pacific Ocean** | | | | |
| without marginal seas | 165,250,000 | 63,800,000 | 707,600,000 | 169,900,000 |
| with marginal seas | 179,680,000 | 69,370,000 | 723,700,000 | 173,700,000 |
| **Atlantic Ocean** | | | | |
| without marginal seas | 82,440,000 | 31,830,000 | 324,600,000 | 77,900,000 |
| with marginal seas | 106,460,000 | 41,100,000 | 354,700,000 | 85,200,000 |
| **Indian Ocean** | | | | |
| without marginal seas | 73,440,000 | 28,360,000 | 291,000,000 | 69,900,000 |
| with marginal seas | 74,920,000 | 28,930,000 | 291,900,000 | 70,100,000 |
| **Arctic Ocean** | 14,090,000 | 5,440,000 | 17,000,000 | 4,100,000 |
| | | | | |
| Australasian Central Sea | 8,140,000 | 3,140,000 | 9,900,000 | 2,400,000 |
| Gulf of Mexico and Caribbean Sea | 4,320,000 | 1,670,000 | 9,600,000 | 2,300,000 |
| Mediterranean and Black Seas | 2,970,000 | 1,150,000 | 4,200,000 | 100,000 |
| Bering Sea | 2,304,000 | 890,000 | 3,330,000 | 80,000 |
| Sea of Okhotsk | 1,583,000 | 611,000 | 1,300,000 | 30,000 |
| Hudson Bay | 1,230,000 | 47,000 | 160,000 | 40,000 |
| North Sea | 570,000 | 22,000 | 50,000 | 10,000 |
| Baltic Sea | 420,000 | 16,000 | 20,000 | 5,000 |
| Irish Sea | 100,000 | 40,000 | 6,000 | 1,000 |
| English Channel | 75,000 | 2,900 | 4,000 | 1,000 |

# Oceans & Seas (continued)

| | AVERAGE DEPTH | | |
|---|---|---|---|
| | M | FT | DEEPEST POINT |
| **Pacific Ocean** | | | |
| without marginal seas | 4,280 | 14,040 | Mariana Trench |
| with marginal seas | 4,030 | 13,220 | (11,034 m; 36,201 ft) |
| **Atlantic Ocean** | | | |
| without marginal seas | 3,930 | 12,890 | Puerto Rico Trench |
| with marginal seas | 3,330 | 10,920 | (8,380 m; 27,493 ft) |
| **Indian Ocean** | | | |
| without marginal seas | 3,960 | 10,040 | Sunda Deep of the Java |
| with marginal seas | 3,900 | 12,790 | Trench (7,450 m; 24,442 ft) |
| **Arctic Ocean** | 1,205 | 3,950 | (5,502 m; 18,050 ft) |
| | | | |
| Australasian Central Sea | 1,210 | 3,970 | NA |
| Gulf of Mexico and | 2,220 | 7,280 | Cayman Trench |
| Caribbean Sea | | | (7,686 m; 25,216 ft) |
| Mediterranean and | 1,430 | 4,690 | Ionian Basin |
| Black Seas | | | (4,900 m; 16,000 ft) |
| Bering Sea | 1,440 | 4,720 | Bowers Basin (4,097 m; 13,442 ft) |
| Sea of Okhotsk | 838 | 2,750 | Kuril Basin (2,499 m; 8,200 ft) |
| Hudson Bay | 128 | 420 | (867 m; 2,846 ft) |
| North Sea | 94 | 310 | Skagerrak (700 m; 2,300 ft) |
| Baltic Sea | 55 | 180 | Landsort Deep (459 m; 1,506 ft) |
| Irish Sea | 60 | 200 | Mull of Galloway (175 m; 576 ft) |
| English Channel | 54 | 180 | Hurd Deep (172 m; 565 ft) |

# Major Natural Lakes of the World

*Conversions for figures have been rounded, thousands to the nearest hundred and hundreds to the nearest ten.*

| NAME | LOCATION | AREA SQ MI | AREA SQ KM | NAME | LOCATION | AREA SQ MI | AREA SQ KM |
|---|---|---|---|---|---|---|---|
| Caspian Sea | Central Asia | 149,200 | 386,400 | Nyasa (Malawi) | eastern Africa | 11,430 | 29,604 |
| Superior | Canada-US | 31,700 | 82,100 | Great Slave | Northwest | 11,031 | 28,570 |
| Victoria | eastern Africa | 26,828 | 69,485 | | Territories, | | |
| Huron | Canada-US | 23,000 | 59,600 | | Canada | | |
| Michigan | US | 22,300 | 57,800 | Erie | Canada-US | 9,910 | 25,667 |
| Aral Sea[1] | Central Asia | 13,000 | 33,800 | Winnipeg | Manitoba, | 9,417 | 24,390 |
| Tanganyika | eastern Africa | 12,700 | 32,900 | | Canada | | |
| Great Bear | Northwest | 12,028 | 31,153 | Ontario | Canada-US | 7,340 | 19,010 |
| | Territories, | | | | | | |
| | Canada | | | | | | |

[1]Salt lake.

# Longest Rivers of the World

*This list includes both rivers and river systems. Conversions of rounded figures are rounded to nearest 10 or 100 miles or kilometers.*

| NAME | OUTFLOW | LENGTH MI | LENGTH KM |
|---|---|---|---|
| **Africa** | | | |
| Nile | Mediterranean Sea | 4,132 | 6,650 |
| Congo | South Atlantic Ocean | 2,900 | 4,700 |
| Niger | Bight of Biafra | 2,600 | 4,200 |
| Zambezi | Mozambique Channel | 2,200 | 3,500 |
| Kasai | Congo River | 1,338 | 2,153 |
| Orange | South Atlantic Ocean | 1,300 | 2,100 |
| White Nile (al-Bahr al-Abyad) | Nile River | 1,295 | 2,084 |
| Lualaba | Congo River | 1,100 | 1,800 |
| Limpopo | Mozambique Channel | 1,100 | 1,800 |
| Jubba (Juba) | Indian Ocean | 1,030 | 1,658 |
| | | | |
| **Asia** | | | |
| Yangtze | East China Sea | 3,915 | 6,300 |
| Yenisey-Baikal-Selenga | Kara Sea | 3,442 | 5,540 |
| Huang Ho (Yellow) | Gulf of Chihli | 3,395 | 5,464 |

# Longest Rivers of the World (continued)

| NAME | OUTFLOW | LENGTH MI | LENGTH KM |
|---|---|---|---|
| **Asia (continued)** | | | |
| Ob–Irtysh | Gulf of Ob | 3,362 | 5,410 |
| Amur–Argun | Sea of Okhotsk | 2,761 | 4,444 |
| Lena | Laptev Sea | 2,734 | 4,400 |
| Mekong | South China Sea | 2,700 | 4,350 |
| Ob–Katun | Gulf of Ob | 2,696 | 4,338 |
| Irtysh–Chorny Irtysh | Ob River | 2,640 | 4,248 |
| Yenisey | Kara Sea | 2,549 | 4,102 |
| | | | |
| **Europe** | | | |
| Volga | Caspian Sea | 2,193 | 3,530 |
| Danube | Black Sea | 1,770 | 2,850 |
| Ural | Caspian Sea | 1,509 | 2,428 |
| Dnieper | Black Sea | 1,367 | 2,200 |
| Don | Sea of Azov | 1,162 | 1,870 |
| Pechora | Barents Sea | 1,124 | 1,809 |
| Kama | Volga River | 1,122 | 1,805 |
| Oka | Volga River | 932 | 1,500 |
| Belaya | Kama River | 889 | 1,430 |
| Dniester | Black Sea | 840 | 1,352 |
| | | | |
| **North America** | | | |
| Mississippi–Missouri–Red Rock | Gulf of Mexico | 3,710 | 5,971 |
| Mackenzie–Slave–Peace | Beaufort Sea | 2,635 | 4,241 |
| Missouri–Red Rock | Mississippi River | 2,540 | 4,090 |
| St. Lawrence–Great Lakes | Gulf of St. Lawrence | 2,500 | 4,000 |
| Mississippi | Gulf of Mexico | 2,340 | 3,770 |
| Missouri | Mississippi River | 2,315 | 3,726 |
| Yukon–McNeil | Bering Sea | 1,980 | 3,190 |
| Rio Grande | Gulf of Mexico | 1,900 | 3,060 |
| Yukon | Bering Sea | 1,875 | 3,018 |
| Nelson–Saskatchewan | Hudson Bay | 1,600 | 2,575 |
| | | | |
| **Oceania** | | | |
| Darling | Murray River | 1,702 | 2,739 |
| Murray | Great Australian Bight | 1,609 | 2,589 |
| Murrumbidgee | Murray River | 981 | 1,579 |
| Lachlan | Murrumbidgee River | 922 | 1,484 |
| Cooper Creek | Lake Eyre | 882 | 1,420 |
| | | | |
| **South America** | | | |
| Amazon–Ucayali–Apurimac | South Atlantic Ocean | 4,000 | 6,400 |
| Paraná | Río de la Plata | 3,032 | 4,880 |
| Madeira–Mamoré–Guaporé | Amazon River | 2,082 | 3,350 |
| Jurua | Amazon River | 2,040 | 3,283 |
| Purus | Amazon River | 1,995 | 3,211 |
| São Francisco | South Atlantic Ocean | 1,811 | 2,914 |
| Japurá (Caquetá) | Amazon River | 1,750 | 2,816 |
| Ucayali–Apurimac | Amazon River | 1,701 | 2,738 |
| Orinoco | South Atlantic Ocean | 1,700 | 2,736 |
| Tocantins | Pará River | 1,677 | 2,699 |

# Glaciers

A glacier is a large mass of perennial ice that originates on land by the recrystallization of snow or other forms of solid precipitation and that shows evidence of past or present flow. The term **ice sheet** is commonly applied to a glacier that occupies an extensive tract of relatively level land and that flows from the center outward. Exact limits for glaciers cannot be set. Except in size, a small snow patch that persists for more than one season is hydrologically indistinguishable from a true glacier.

Glaciers occur where snowfall in winter exceeds melting in summer, conditions that prevail only in high mountain areas and polar regions. Glaciers occupy about 11% of the earth's land surface but hold roughly three-fourths of its fresh water; 99% of glacier ice lies in Antarctica and Greenland. At the end of the 20th century, scientists became increasingly concerned with **glacial melting**, which is often linked to **global warming** trends and may lead to changes in sea level and weather patterns.

# Preserving Nature

## US National Parks

*Dates in parentheses indicate when the area was first designated a park, in most cases under a different name. Web site: <www.nps.gov/parks.html>.*

| PARK | LOCATION | DESIGNATION DATE | SQ MI | SQ KM |
|---|---|---|---|---|
| Acadia | Bar Harbor ME | 1929 (1916) | 74 | 192 |
| Arches | Moab UT | 1971 (1929) | 120 | 311 |
| Badlands | southwestern South Dakota | 1978 (1939) | 379 | 982 |
| Big Bend | curve of the Rio Grande river, Texas | 1944 | 1,252 | 3,243 |
| Biscayne | near Miami FL | 1980 (1968) | 270 | 699 |
| Black Canyon of the Gunnison | near Montrose CO | 1999 (1933) | 43 | 112 |
| Bryce Canyon | Bryce Canyon, Utah | 1928 (1923) | 56 | 145 |
| Canyonlands | near Moab UT | 1964 | 527 | 1,366 |
| Capitol Reef | near Torrey UT | 1971 (1937) | 379 | 982 |
| Carlsbad Caverns | near Carlsbad NM | 1930 (1923) | 73 | 189 |
| Channel Islands | Ventura CA | 1980 (1938) | 75 | 194 |
| Crater Lake | Crater Lake OR | 1902 | 286 | 741 |
| Cuyahoga Valley | near Cleveland and Akron OH | 2000 (1974) | 51 | 133 |
| Death Valley | Death Valley, California | 1994 (1933) | 5,219 | 13,518 |
| Denali | central Alaska | 1980 (1917) | 9,492 | 24,584 |
| Dry Tortugas | Key West FL | 1992 (1935) | 101 | 262 |
| Everglades | southern Florida | 1947 | 2,358 | 6,107 |
| Gates of the Arctic | Bettles AK | 1980 (1978) | 13,238 | 34,287 |
| Glacier | northwest Montana | 1910 | 1,584 | 4,102 |
| Glacier Bay | Gustavus AK | 1980 (1925) | 5,130 | 13,287 |
| Grand Canyon | Grand Canyon, Arizona | 1919 (1908) | 1,902 | 4,927 |
| Grand Teton | Moose WY | 1950 (1929) | 484 | 1,255 |
| Great Basin | near Baker NV | 1986 (1922) | 121 | 313 |
| Great Smoky Mountains | Tennessee and North Carolina | 1934 | 815 | 2,110 |
| Guadalupe Mountains | Salt Flat TX | 1972 | 135 | 350 |
| Haleakala | Kula, Maui HI | 1960 (1916) | 47 | 121 |
| Hawaii Volcanoes | near Hilo HI | 1961 (1916) | 328 | 849 |
| Hot Springs | Hot Springs AR | 1921 (1832) | 9 | 22 |
| Isle Royale | Houghton MI | 1940 (1931) | 893 | 2,314 |
| Joshua Tree | near Palm Springs CA | 1994 (1936) | 1,591 | 4,120 |
| Katmai | near King Salmon AK | 1980 (1918) | 7,385 | 19,128 |
| Kenai Fjords | Seward AK | 1980 (1978) | 1,047 | 2,711 |
| Kobuk Valley | Kotzebue AK | 1980 (1978) | 2,672 | 6,920 |
| Lake Clark | Port Alsworth AK | 1980 (1978) | 6,297 | 16,309 |
| Lassen Volcanic | Mineral CA | 1916 (1907) | 166 | 430 |
| Mammoth Cave | Mammoth Cave, Kentucky | 1941 | 83 | 214 |
| Mesa Verde | near Cortez and Mancos CO | 1906 | 81 | 211 |
| Mount Rainier | near Ashford WA | 1899 | 368 | 954 |
| North Cascades | near Marblemount WA | 1968 | 1,069 | 2,769 |
| Olympic | near Port Angeles WA | 1938 | 1,442 | 3,734 |
| Petrified Forest | Arizona | 1962 (1906) | 146 | 379 |
| Rocky Mountain | near Estes Park and Grand Lake CO | 1915 | 415 | 1,076 |
| Saguaro | Tucson AZ | 1994 (1933) | 143 | 370 |
| Sequoia & Kings Canyon | near Three Rivers CA | 1940 (1890) | 1,351 | 3,498 |
| Shenandoah | near Luray VA | 1935 | 311 | 805 |
| Theodore Roosevelt | Medora ND (south unit); near Watford City ND (north unit) | 1978 (1947) | 110 | 285 |
| Virgin Islands | St. John, US Virgin Islands | 1956 | 23 | 59 |
| Voyageurs | International Falls MN | 1975 | 341 | 883 |
| Wind Cave | near Hot Springs SD | 1903 | 44 | 115 |
| Wolf Trap | Vienna VA | 2002 (1966) | 130 acres | |
| Wrangell–St. Elias | near Copper Center AK | 1980 | 20,587 | 53,320 |
| Yellowstone | Idaho, Montana, and Wyoming | 1872 | 3,468 | 8,983 |
| Yosemite | in the Sierra Nevada, California | 1890 (1864) | 1,189 | 3,081 |
| Zion | Springdale UT | 1919 (1909) | 229 | 593 |

## Major World Zoos

*Numbers given for species and animals are approximate.*

| ZOO (LOCATION) | FOUNDED | NUMBER OF SPECIES | NUMBER OF ANIMALS | FEATURES OF INTEREST |
|---|---|---|---|---|
| Antwerp Zoo (Belgium) | 1843 | 1,160 | 6,000 | Père David's deer, white rhinoceroses, okapi, Congo peafowl |
| Bronx Zoo (New York) | 1899 | 700 | 6,000 | largest US metropolitan zoo, Wildlife Conservation Society headquarters, snow leopards, Congo Gorilla Forest |
| Cincinnati Zoo (Ohio) | 1875 | 750 | 17,000 | red pandas, Reptile House, Vanishing Giants exhibit |
| Columbus Zoo (Ohio) | 1927 | 700 | 6,000 | first lowland gorilla born in captivity, bonobos, koalas |
| Denver Zoo (Colorado) | 1896 | 700 | 4,000 | conservation center, Primate Panorama, Dragons of Komodo exhibit |
| Hagenbeck Zoo (Hamburg, Germany) | 1907 | 300 | 2,000 | first zoo with natural animal habitats |
| Indianapolis Zoo (Indiana) | 1964 | 320 | 3,800 | incorporates zoo, aquarium, and botanical garden; five biomes |
| Lincoln Park Zoo (Chicago IL) | 1868 | 210 | 1,330 | Great Ape House, wildlife conservation department |
| London Zoo (England) | 1828 | 650 | N/A | largest zoological library of any zoo, apes and monkeys, giant pandas |
| National Zoological Gardens of South Africa (Pretoria) | 1899 | 640 | 5,500 | antelope, cheetah-breeding area |
| Philadelphia Zoo (Pennsylvania) | 1874 | 400 | 1,800 | first white lions and blue-eyed lemurs exhibited in the US |
| Phoenix Zoo (Arizona) | 1962 | N/A | N/A | wildlife relief program, reptile exhibit |
| St. Petersburg Zoo (Russia) | 1865 | 410 | 2,000 | polar bears, ornithological exhibit, 130 threatened species |
| San Diego Zoo (California) | 1916 | 800 | 4,000 | international conservation program, koalas, white rhinoceroses |
| Scottish National Zoo (Edinburgh) | 1913 | 150 | 1,500 | largest penguin colony in Europe |
| National Zoological Park (Washington DC) | 1889 | 500 | 5,800 | giant pandas, Sumatran tigers |
| Sri Lanka Zoo (Dehiwala) | 1936 | 330 | 3,890 | elephant orphanage |
| Taronga Zoological Park (Sydney, Australia) | 1884 | 730 | 4,000 | native Australian wildlife, mountain pygmy possum, bird collection |
| Toronto Zoo (Ontario) | 1974 | 450 | 5,000 | gorillas, Siberian tigers, African bush elephants |
| Ueno Zoological Garden (Japan) | 1882 | 960 | 8,860 | insectarium, giant salamander, rare pheasants and wallabies, giant pandas |

## Major World Botanical Gardens

Most botanical gardens are concerned primarily with exhibiting ornamental plants, insofar as possible in a scheme that emphasizes natural relationships. A major contemporary objective of botanical gardens is to maintain extensive collections of plants, labeled with common and scientific names and regions of origin. Numbers given for species are approximate.

| GARDEN (LOCATION) | FOUNDED | NUMBER OF SPECIES | FEATURES OF INTEREST |
|---|---|---|---|
| Atlanta Botanical Garden (Georgia) | 1976 | N/A | plant conservation |
| Australian National Botanic Gardens (Canberra) | 1970 | 5,500 | Australian flora |
| The Botanical Garden of the University of Vienna (Austria) | 1754 | 9,000 | woody tropical plants, teaching and research |
| The Botanical Garden of Padova (Italy) | 1545 | N/A | oldest university garden, medicinal plants |
| Brooklyn Botanic Garden (New York) | 1911 | 12,000 | rose, cactus, and orchid collections; garden for the blind |
| Cheyenne Botanic Gardens (Wyoming) | 1977 | N/A | solar heated conservatory, solar energy research |
| Chicago Botanic Garden (Illinois) | 1890 | 8,819 taxa | 23 gardens, ornamentals, Midwest plant conservation |
| Denver Botanic Gardens (Colorado) | 1951 | 15,000 | Rocky Mountain region plants |
| Fort Worth Botanic Garden (Texas) | N/A | 2,500 | 21 specialty gardens |

## Major World Botanical Gardens (continued)

| GARDEN (LOCATION) | FOUNDED | NUMBER OF SPECIES | FEATURES OF INTEREST |
|---|---|---|---|
| National Botanic Gardens, Glasnevin (Dublin, Ireland) | 1795 | 20,000 | palms, native strawberry trees, Atlantic cedar |
| National Botanic Garden of Belgium (Meise) | 1829 | N/A | classical herbarium studies |
| The New York Botanical Garden (Bronx NY) | N/A | 18,000 | 48 gardens and plant collections, 50-acre forest, International Plant Science Center |
| Peradeniya Botanic Gardens (Sri Lanka) | 1821 | 4,000 | orchids, gymnosperms, flowering trees |
| Royal Botanic Garden Edinburgh (Scotland) | 1670 | 17,000 | botanical library, among largest collections of living plants |
| Royal Botanic Gardens, Kew (London, England) | 1759 | N/A | alpines, junipers, seed conservation |
| Santa Barbara Botanic Garden (California) | N/A | 1,000 taxa | native California vegetation |
| Singapore Botanic Gardens | 1859 | 2,700 | orchids, bromeliads, palms |
| Tower Hill Botanic Garden (Boylston MA) | 1986 | N/A | apples, flowering bulbs |
| University of Copenhagen Botanic Garden (Denmark) | 1872 | 13,000 | Palm House, research and education |
| United States Botanic Garden (Washington DC) | 1820 | N/A | conservatory, large greenhouse |

# Health

## Worldwide Health Indicators

Column data as follows: **Life expectancy** in 2000; **Doctors** = persons per doctor, latest data[1]. **Infant mortality** per 1,000 births in 2001; **Water** = percentage (%) of population with access to safe drinking water (1989–98); **Food** = percentage (%) of the FAO recommended minimum (1998)[2]. **N/A** = not available.

| REGION/BLOC | LIFE EXPECTANCY MALE | LIFE EXPECTANCY FEMALE | DOCTORS | INFANT MORTALITY | WATER | FOOD |
|---|---|---|---|---|---|---|
| **World** | **64.3** | **68.3** | **730** | **55.2** | **76** | **118** |
| | | | | | | |
| **Africa** | **51.1** | **53.1** | **2,560** | **86.7** | **57** | **104** |
| Central Africa | 47.3 | 50.4 | 12,890 | 107.3 | 44 | 83 |
| East Africa | 44.9 | 46.3 | 13,620 | 94.8 | 44 | 84 |
| North Africa | 63.2 | 66.7 | 890 | 59.0 | 82 | 125 |
| Southern Africa | 50.2 | 52.4 | 1,610 | 63.1 | 70 | 116 |
| West Africa | 50.3 | 51.5 | 6,260 | 85.6 | 52 | 113 |
| | | | | | | |
| **Americas** | **68.6** | **74.8** | **520** | **25.1** | **83** | **128** |
| Anglo-America[3] | 74.3 | 80.0 | 370 | 6.8 | 91 | 140 |
| Canada | 76.0 | 83.0 | 540 | 5.1 | 100 | 119 |
| United States | 74.1 | 79.7 | 360 | 6.9 | 90 | 142 |
| Latin America | 65.2 | 71.6 | 690 | 32.4 | 78 | 119 |
| Caribbean | 67.3 | 72.0 | 380 | 43.8 | 77 | 102 |
| Central America | 67.1 | 72.5 | 950 | 34.3 | 76 | 105 |
| Mexico | 68.5 | 74.7 | 810 | 26.2 | 85 | 135 |
| South America | 63.8 | 70.6 | 710 | 32.9 | 76 | 117 |
| Andean Group | 68.0 | 71.7 | 830 | 31.0 | 79 | 106 |
| Brazil | 58.5 | 67.6 | 770 | 38.0 | 76 | 122 |
| Other South America | 71.8 | 78.4 | 410 | 20.9 | 71 | 129 |
| | | | | | | |
| **Asia** | **65.9** | **68.9** | **970** | **53.5** | **75** | **117** |
| Eastern Asia | 69.9 | 74.3 | 610 | 34.2 | 71 | 125 |
| China | 69.0 | 73.0 | 620 | 37.0 | 67 | 126 |
| Japan | 77.5 | 84.0 | 530 | 3.4 | 97 | 123 |
| South Korea | 72.0 | 79.0 | 740 | 7.0 | 93 | 131 |
| Other Eastern Asia | 71.3 | 77.2 | 500 | 31.0 | 96 | 107 |
| South Asia | 61.4 | 62.3 | 2,100 | 70.4 | 80 | 108 |
| India | 61.9 | 63.1 | 1,920 | 64.9 | 81 | 112 |
| Pakistan | 61.0 | 60.0 | 1,840 | 85.0 | 79 | 106 |
| Other South Asia | 59.2 | 60.0 | 5,080 | 80.6 | 78 | 89 |

## Worldwide Health Indicators (continued)

| REGION/BLOC | LIFE EXPECTANCY MALE | LIFE EXPECTANCY FEMALE | DOCTORS | INFANT MORTALITY | WATER | FOOD |
|---|---|---|---|---|---|---|
| Asia (continued) | | | | | | |
| Southeast Asia | 65.9 | 69.8 | 3,120 | 40.0 | 70 | 120 |
| Southwest Asia | 66.4 | 71.0 | 610 | 45.2 | 79 | 116 |
| Central Asia | 63.1 | 71.0 | 330 | 45.4 | 85 | 98 |
| Gulf Cooperation Council | 67.8 | 71.3 | 620 | 45.7 | 95 | 122 |
| Iran | 68.3 | 71.5 | 1,200 | 30.0 | 95 | 117 |
| Other Southwest Asia | 66.4 | 70.6 | 690 | 49.3 | 65 | 122 |
| | | | | | | |
| **Europe** | **66.2** | **74.2** | **300** | **9.4** | **99** | **125** |
| Eastern Europe | 63.5 | 73.9 | 290 | 15.4 | 95 | 116 |
| Russia | 59.9 | 72.4 | 240 | 15.3 | N/A | 111 |
| Ukraine | 60.6 | 72.0 | 330 | 21.7 | 97 | 112 |
| Other Eastern Europe | 68.2 | 76.1 | 370 | 13.7 | 94 | 122 |
| Western Europe | 68.6 | 74.3 | 300 | 5.0 | 100 | 134 |
| European Union (EU) | 68.3 | 74.1 | 290 | 5.1 | 100 | 134 |
| France | 74.8 | 82.9 | 330 | 4.5 | 100 | 141 |
| Germany | 74.4 | 80.6 | 290 | 4.3 | 100 | 128 |
| Italy | 75.9 | 82.5 | 180 | 5.8 | 100 | 143 |
| Spain | 75.6 | 82.5 | 240 | 5.0 | 99 | 136 |
| United Kingdom | 75.4 | 80.2 | 720 | 5.8 | 100 | 129 |
| Other EU | 42.5 | 45.8 | 320 | 5.2 | 100 | 132 |
| Non-EU | 76.4 | 81.9 | 480 | 3.7 | 100 | 123 |
| | | | | | | |
| **Oceania** | **71.9** | **76.8** | **480** | **26.2** | **86** | **117** |
| Australia | 76.6 | 82.0 | 400 | 6.0 | 95 | 120 |
| Pacific Ocean Islands | 67.1 | 71.6 | 770 | 42.8 | 68 | 111 |

[1]Latest data available for individual countries.    [2]The Food and Agriculture Organization of the United Nations (FAO) calculates this percentage by dividing the caloric equivalent to the known average daily supply of food-stuffs for human consumption in a given country by its population, thus arriving at a minimum daily per capita caloric intake. The higher the percentage, the more calories consumed.    [3]Includes Canada, the US, Greenland, Bermuda, and St. Pierre and Miquelon.

## Causes of Death, Worldwide, by Sex

Global estimates for 2001 as published in the World Health Organization *World Health Report 2002.* Data are percentages of total deaths in each cate-gory. Gaps in the information below often reflect the difficulty of collecting accurate data.

| | LEADING CAUSES OF DEATH | ALL CATE-GORIES (%) | MALES (%) | FEMALES (%) |
|---|---|---|---|---|
| 1 | Ischemic heart disease | 12.7 | 12.7 | 12.7 |
| 2 | Cerebrovascular disease | 9.6 | 8.4 | 11.0 |
| 3 | Lower respiratory infections | 6.8 | 6.8 | 6.9 |
| 4 | HIV disease | 5.1 | 5.2 | 5.0 |
| 5 | Chronic obstructive pulmonary disease | 4.7 | 4.6 | 4.9 |
| 6 | Perinatal conditions | 4.4 | 4.7 | 4.1 |
| 7 | Diarrheal diseases | 3.5 | 3.5 | 3.6 |
| 8 | Tuberculosis | 2.9 | 3.6 | 2.1 |
| 9 | Road traffic accidents | 2.1 | 2.9 | 1.3 |
| 10 | Trachea, bronchus, lung cancers | 2.1 | 3.0 | 1.2 |
| 11 | Malaria | 2.0 | 1.8 | 2.2 |
| 12 | Diabetes mellitus | 1.6 | 1.4 | 1.8 |
| 13 | Hypertensive heart disease | 1.5 | 1.3 | 1.8 |
| 14 | Stomach cancer | 1.5 | 1.8 | 1.2 |
| 15 | Self-inflicted injuries | 1.5 | 1.8 | 1.2 |
| 16 | Cirrhosis of the liver | 1.4 | 1.7 | 1.1 |
| 17 | Measles | 1.3 | 1.3 | 1.4 |
| 18 | Nephritis and nephrosis | 1.1 | 1.1 | 1.1 |
| 19 | Liver cancer | 1.1 | 1.4 | 0.7 |
| 20 | Colon and rectum cancers | 1.1 | 1.1 | 1.1 |
| 21 | Congenital anomalies | 0.9 | 0.9 | 0.9 |
| 22 | Violence | 0.9 | 1.3 | 0.4 |
| 23 | Breast cancer | 0.8 | 0.0 | 1.8 |

## Causes of Death, Worldwide, by Sex (continued)

| | LEADING CAUSES OF DEATH | ALL CATE-GORIES (%) | MALES (%) | FEMALES (%) |
|---|---|---|---|---|
| 24 | Esophagus cancer | 0.8 | 0.9 | 0.6 |
| 25 | Drowning | 0.7 | 0.9 | 0.5 |
| 26 | Alzheimer's and other dementias | 0.7 | 0.4 | 0.9 |
| 27 | Poisoning | 0.6 | 0.7 | 0.5 |
| 28 | Mouth and oropharynx cancers | 0.6 | 0.8 | 0.4 |
| 29 | Whooping cough | 0.5 | 0.5 | 0.5 |
| 30 | Tetanus | 0.5 | 0.5 | 0.5 |
| 31 | Prostate cancer | 0.5 | 0.9 | — |
| 32 | Cervix uteri cancer | 0.5 | — | 1.0 |
| 33 | War | 0.4 | 0.7 | 0.1 |

## Causes of Death, Worldwide, by Region

*Global estimates for 2001 as published in the World Health Organization (WHO) World Health Report 2002. Regions are as defined by the WHO. Numbers are in thousands ('000).*

| | LEADING CAUSES OF DEATH | ALL CATE-GORIES (%) | ALL CATE-GORIES | REGION | | | | | |
|---|---|---|---|---|---|---|---|---|---|
| | | | | AFRI-CAN | AMER-ICAN | EASTERN MEDITER-RANEAN | EURO-PEAN | SOUTHEAST ASIAN | WESTERN PACIFIC |
| 1 | Ischemic heart disease | 12.7 | 7,181 | 333 | 967 | 523 | 2,423 | 1,972 | 963 |
| 2 | Cerebrovascular disease | 9.6 | 5,454 | 307 | 454 | 218 | 1,480 | 1,070 | 1,926 |
| 3 | Lower respiratory infections | 6.8 | 3,871 | 1,026 | 225 | 383 | 298 | 1,355 | 586 |
| 4 | HIV disease | 5.1 | 2,866 | 2,197 | 88 | 58 | 26 | 445 | 53 |
| 5 | Chronic obstructive pulmonary disease | 4.7 | 2,672 | 116 | 222 | 88 | 285 | 614 | 1,347 |
| 6 | Perinatal conditions | 4.4 | 2,504 | 577 | 167 | 313 | 70 | 1,023 | 353 |
| 7 | Diarrheal diseases | 3.5 | 2,001 | 703 | 76 | 326 | 21 | 802 | 74 |
| 8 | Tuberculosis | 2.9 | 1,644 | 336 | 46 | 133 | 77 | 701 | 351 |
| 9 | Road traffic accidents | 2.1 | 1,194 | 179 | 141 | 103 | 125 | 353 | 292 |
| 10 | Trachea, bronchus, lung cancers | 2.1 | 1,213 | 23 | 227 | 30 | 371 | 162 | 399 |
| 11 | Malaria | 2.0 | 1,124 | 963 | 1 | 55 | 0 | 95 | 10 |
| 12 | Diabetes mellitus | 1.6 | 895 | 55 | 230 | 52 | 141 | 238 | 179 |
| 13 | Hypertensive heart disease | 1.5 | 874 | 54 | 131 | 91 | 175 | 138 | 285 |
| 14 | Stomach cancer | 1.5 | 850 | 37 | 76 | 21 | 172 | 65 | 480 |
| 15 | Self-inflicted injuries | 1.5 | 849 | 28 | 65 | 35 | 168 | 234 | 318 |
| 16 | Cirrhosis of the liver | 1.4 | 796 | 70 | 104 | 60 | 166 | 214 | 183 |
| 17 | Measles | 1.3 | 745 | 426 | 0 | 85 | 6 | 193 | 32 |
| 18 | Nephritis and nephrosis | 1.1 | 625 | 80 | 95 | 61 | 77 | 155 | 157 |
| 19 | Liver cancer | 1.1 | 616 | 64 | 39 | 14 | 64 | 65 | 371 |
| 20 | Colon and rectum cancers | 1.1 | 615 | 27 | 108 | 15 | 235 | 58 | 174 |
| 21 | Congenital anomalies | 0.9 | 507 | 67 | 62 | 75 | 38 | 149 | 116 |
| 22 | Violence | 0.9 | 500 | 116 | 150 | 22 | 70 | 77 | 65 |
| 23 | Breast cancer | 0.8 | 479 | 38 | 90 | 28 | 154 | 90 | 79 |
| 24 | Esophagus cancer | 0.8 | 438 | 27 | 31 | 13 | 50 | 80 | 236 |
| 25 | Drowning | 0.7 | 403 | 92 | 24 | 27 | 37 | 91 | 132 |
| 26 | Alzheimer's and other dementias | 0.7 | 368 | 5 | 94 | 10 | 97 | 100 | 62 |
| 27 | Poisoning | 0.6 | 343 | 37 | 17 | 18 | 104 | 95 | 73 |
| 28 | Mouth and oropharynx cancers | 0.6 | 326 | 34 | 22 | 21 | 52 | 144 | 54 |
| 29 | Whooping cough | 0.5 | 285 | 157 | 7 | 59 | 0 | 60 | 2 |
| 30 | Tetanus | 0.5 | 282 | 110 | 0 | 53 | 0 | 101 | 18 |
| 31 | Prostate cancer | 0.5 | 269 | 45 | 77 | 8 | 95 | 26 | 19 |
| 32 | Cervix uteri cancer | 0.5 | 258 | 59 | 30 | 12 | 27 | 99 | 33 |
| 33 | War | 0.4 | 230 | 122 | 11 | 59 | 16 | 20 | 3 |

# Ten Leading Causes of Death in the US, by Age

*Data for 2000. Numbers in thousands. Rates per 100,000 population. Numbers are based on weighted data rounded to the nearest individual, so category percentages and rates may not add to totals.*
*Source:* National Vital Statistics Report, <www.cdc.gov/nchs>.

| CAUSE | NUMBER | % | RATE |
|---|---|---|---|
| **1–4 years** | | | |
| 1 Accidents | 1,826 | 36.7 | 12.1 |
| 2 Congenital malformations, deformations, and chromosomal abnormalities | 495 | 9.9 | 3.3 |
| 3 Malignant neoplasms | 420 | 8.4 | 2.8 |
| 4 Assault (homicide) | 356 | 7.2 | 2.3 |
| 5 Diseases of the heart | 181 | 3.6 | 1.2 |
| 6 Influenza and pneumonia | 103 | 2.1 | 0.7 |
| 7 Septicemia | 99 | 2.0 | 0.7 |
| 8 Conditions of perinatal origin | 79 | 1.6 | 0.5 |
| 9 Nonmalignant/unknown neoplasms | 53 | 1.1 | 0.3 |
| 10 Chronic lower respiratory diseases | 51 | 1.0 | 0.3 |
| All other causes | 1,316 | 26.4 | 8.7 |
| **All causes, 1–4 years** | **4,979** | **100.0** | **32.9** |
| **5–9 years** | | | |
| 1 Accidents | 1,391 | 42.8 | 7.0 |
| 2 Malignant neoplasms | 489 | 15.0 | 2.5 |
| 3 Congenital malformations, deformations, and chromosomal abnormalities | 198 | 6.1 | 1.0 |
| 4 Assault (homicide) | 140 | 4.3 | 0.7 |
| 5 Diseases of the heart | 106 | 3.3 | 0.5 |
| 6 Nonmalignant/unknown neoplasms | 62 | 1.9 | 0.3 |
| 7 Chronic lower respiratory diseases | 48 | 1.5 | 0.2 |
| 8 Influenza and pneumonia | 47 | 1.4 | 0.2 |
| 9 Septicemia | 38 | 1.2 | 0.2 |
| 10 Cerebrovascular diseases | 25 | 0.8 | 0.1 |
| 11 Conditions of perinatal origin | 25 | 0.8 | 0.1 |
| All other causes | 684 | 21.0 | 3.5 |
| **All causes, 5–9 years** | **3,253** | **100.0** | **16.4** |
| **10–14 years** | | | |
| 1 Accidents | 1,588 | 38.2 | 8.0 |
| 2 Malignant neoplasms | 525 | 12.6 | 2.6 |
| 3 Intentional self-harm (suicide) | 300 | 7.2 | 1.5 |
| 4 Assault (homicide) | 231 | 5.6 | 1.2 |
| 5 Congenital malformations, deformations, and chromosomal abnormalities | 201 | 4.8 | 1.0 |
| 6 Diseases of the heart | 165 | 4.0 | 0.8 |
| 7 Chronic lower respiratory diseases | 91 | 2.2 | 0.5 |
| 8 Cerebrovascular diseases | 51 | 1.2 | 0.3 |
| 9 Influenza and pneumonia | 40 | 1.0 | 0.2 |
| 10 Nonmalignant/unknown neoplasms | 37 | 0.9 | 0.2 |
| All other causes | 931 | 22.4 | 4.7 |
| **All causes, 10–14 years** | **4,160** | **100.0** | **20.9** |
| **15–19 years** | | | |
| 1 Accidents | 6,755 | 49.8 | 34.0 |
| 2 Assault (homicide) | 1,914 | 14.1 | 9.6 |
| 3 Intentional self-harm (suicide) | 1,621 | 12.0 | 8.2 |
| 4 Malignant neoplasms | 745 | 5.5 | 3.7 |
| 5 Diseases of the heart | 403 | 3.0 | 2.0 |

| CAUSE | NUMBER | % | RATE |
|---|---|---|---|
| **15–19 years (continued)** | | | |
| 6 Congenital malformations, deformations, and chromosomal abnormalities | 225 | 1.7 | 1.1 |
| 7 Chronic lower respiratory diseases | 86 | 0.6 | 0.4 |
| 8 Cerebrovascular diseases | 67 | 0.5 | 0.3 |
| 9 Influenza and pneumonia | 65 | 0.5 | 0.3 |
| 10 Diabetes mellitus | 48 | 0.4 | 0.2 |
| All other causes | 1,634 | 12.0 | 8.2 |
| **All causes, 15–19 years** | **13,563** | **100.0** | **68.2** |
| **20–24 years** | | | |
| 1 Accidents | 7,358 | 41.5 | 39.8 |
| 2 Assault (homicide) | 3,025 | 17.0 | 16.4 |
| 3 Intentional self-harm (suicide) | 2,373 | 13.4 | 12.8 |
| 4 Malignant neoplasms | 968 | 5.5 | 5.2 |
| 5 Diseases of the heart | 628 | 3.5 | 3.4 |
| 6 Congenital malformations, deformations, and chromosomal abnormalities | 216 | 1.2 | 1.2 |
| 7 HIV disease | 144 | 0.8 | 0.8 |
| 8 Cerebrovascular diseases | 132 | 0.7 | 0.7 |
| 9 Influenza and pneumonia | 124 | 0.7 | 0.7 |
| 10 Diabetes mellitus | 114 | 0.6 | 0.6 |
| All other causes | 2,662 | 15.0 | 14.4 |
| **All causes, 20–24 years** | **17,744** | **100.0** | **96.0** |
| **25–34 years** | | | |
| 1 Accidents | 11,769 | 29.1 | 31.4 |
| 2 Intentional self-harm (suicide) | 4,792 | 11.8 | 12.8 |
| 3 Assault (homicide) | 4,164 | 10.3 | 11.1 |
| 4 Malignant neoplasms | 3,916 | 9.7 | 10.5 |
| 5 Diseases of the heart | 2,958 | 7.3 | 7.9 |
| 6 HIV disease | 2,437 | 6.0 | 6.5 |
| 7 Diabetes mellitus | 623 | 1.5 | 1.7 |
| 8 Cerebrovascular diseases | 602 | 1.5 | 1.6 |
| 9 Congenital malformations, deformations, and chromosomal abnormalities | 477 | 1.2 | 1.3 |
| 10 Chronic liver disease and cirrhosis | 415 | 1.0 | 1.1 |
| All other causes | 8,298 | 20.5 | 22.2 |
| **All causes, 25–34 years** | **40,451** | **100.0** | **108.1** |
| **35–44 years** | | | |
| 1 Malignant neoplasms | 16,520 | 18.4 | 36.8 |
| 2 Accidents | 15,413 | 17.2 | 34.3 |
| 3 Diseases of the heart | 13,181 | 14.7 | 29.4 |
| 4 Intentional self-harm (suicide) | 6,562 | 7.3 | 14.6 |
| 5 HIV disease | 5,919 | 6.6 | 13.2 |
| 6 Chronic liver disease and cirrhosis | 3,371 | 3.8 | 7.5 |
| 7 Assault (homicide) | 3,219 | 3.6 | 7.2 |
| 8 Cerebrovascular diseases | 2,599 | 2.9 | 5.8 |
| 9 Diabetes mellitus | 1,929 | 2.1 | 4.3 |
| 10 Influenza and pneumonia | 1,068 | 1.2 | 2.4 |
| All other causes | 20,020 | 22.3 | 44.6 |
| **All causes, 35–44 years** | **89,798** | **100.0** | **200.0** |

# Ten Leading Causes of Death in the US, by Age (continued)

| CAUSE | NUMBER | % | RATE |
|---|---|---|---|
| **45–54 years** | | | |
| 1 Malignant neoplasms | 48,034 | 30.0 | 129.3 |
| 2 Diseases of the heart | 35,480 | 22.1 | 95.5 |
| 3 Accidents | 12,278 | 7.7 | 33.0 |
| 4 Chronic liver disease and cirrhosis | 6,654 | 4.1 | 17.9 |
| 5 Cerebrovascular diseases | 6,011 | 3.7 | 16.2 |
| 6 Intentional self-harm (suicide) | 5,437 | 3.4 | 14.6 |
| 7 Diabetes mellitus | 4,954 | 3.1 | 13.3 |
| 8 HIV disease | 4,142 | 2.6 | 11.1 |
| 9 Chronic lower respiratory diseases | 3,251 | 2.0 | 8.8 |
| 10 Viral hepatitis | 1,894 | 1.2 | 5.1 |
| All other causes | 32,206 | 20.1 | 86.7 |
| **All causes, 45–54 years** | **160,341** | **100.0** | **431.6** |

| CAUSE | NUMBER | % | RATE |
|---|---|---|---|
| **55–64 years** | | | |
| 1 Malignant neoplasms | 89,005 | 37.0 | 371.3 |
| 2 Diseases of the heart | 63,399 | 26.3 | 264.5 |
| 3 Chronic lower respiratory diseases | 10,739 | 4.5 | 44.8 |
| 4 Cerebrovascular diseases | 9,956 | 4.1 | 41.5 |
| 5 Diabetes mellitus | 9,186 | 3.8 | 38.3 |
| 6 Accidents | 7,505 | 3.1 | 31.3 |
| 7 Chronic liver disease and cirrhosis | 5,774 | 2.4 | 24.1 |
| 8 Nephritis, nephrotic syndrome, and nephrosis | 3,100 | 1.3 | 12.9 |
| 9 Intentional self-harm (suicide) | 2,945 | 1.2 | 12.3 |
| 10 Septicemia | 2,899 | 1.2 | 12.1 |
| All other causes | 36,338 | 15.1 | 151.6 |
| **All causes, 55–64 years** | **240,846** | **100.0** | **1,004.6** |

| CAUSE | NUMBER | % | RATE |
|---|---|---|---|
| **65–74 years** | | | |
| 1 Malignant neoplasms | 150,131 | 34.0 | 826.4 |
| 2 Diseases of the heart | 122,405 | 27.7 | 673.8 |
| 3 Chronic lower respiratory diseases | 31,157 | 7.1 | 171.5 |
| 4 Cerebrovascular diseases | 23,649 | 5.4 | 130.2 |
| 5 Diabetes mellitus | 16,674 | 3.8 | 91.8 |
| 6 Accidents | 7,698 | 1.7 | 42.4 |
| 7 Influenza and pneumonia | 7,189 | 1.6 | 39.6 |
| 8 Nephritis, nephrotic syndrome, and nephrosis | 6,990 | 1.6 | 38.5 |
| 9 Septicemia | 5,704 | 1.3 | 31.4 |
| 10 Chronic liver disease and cirrhosis | 5,482 | 1.2 | 30.2 |
| All other causes | 64,130 | 14.5 | 353.0 |
| **All causes, 65–74 years** | **441,209** | **100.0** | **2,428.6** |

| CAUSE | NUMBER | % | RATE |
|---|---|---|---|
| **75–84 years** | | | |
| 1 Diseases of the heart | 220,060 | 31.4 | 1,787.1 |
| 2 Malignant neoplasms | 165,099 | 23.6 | 1,340.8 |
| 3 Cerebrovascular diseases | 57,020 | 8.1 | 463.1 |
| 4 Chronic lower respiratory diseases | 47,722 | 6.8 | 387.6 |
| 5 Diabetes mellitus | 22,184 | 3.2 | 180.2 |
| 6 Influenza and pneumonia | 19,821 | 2.8 | 161.0 |
| 7 Alzheimer's disease | 17,253 | 2.5 | 140.1 |
| 8 Nephritis, nephrotic syndrome, and nephrosis | 12,458 | 1.8 | 101.2 |
| 9 Accidents | 11,758 | 1.7 | 95.5 |
| 10 Septicemia | 9,938 | 1.4 | 80.7 |
| All other causes | 117,132 | 16.7 | 951.25 |
| **All causes, 75–84 years** | **700,445** | **100.0** | **5,688.4** |

| CAUSE | NUMBER | % | RATE |
|---|---|---|---|
| **85 years and over** | | | |
| 1 Diseases of the heart | 251,242 | 38.2 | 5,848.7 |
| 2 Malignant neoplasms | 77,136 | 11.7 | 1,795.6 |
| 3 Cerebrovascular diseases | 67,376 | 10.2 | 1,568.4 |
| 4 Influenza and pneumonia | 31,547 | 4.8 | 734.4 |
| 5 Alzheimer's disease | 28,309 | 4.3 | 659.0 |
| 6 Chronic lower respiratory diseases | 27,496 | 4.2 | 640.1 |
| 7 Diabetes mellitus | 13,556 | 2.1 | 315.6 |
| 8 Nephritis, nephrotic syndrome, and nephrosis | 11,777 | 1.8 | 274.2 |
| 9 Accidents | 11,595 | 1.8 | 269.9 |
| 10 Septicemia | 9,144 | 1.4 | 212.9 |
| All other causes | 128,993 | 19.6 | 3,002.8 |
| **All causes, 85 years and over** | **658,171** | **100.0** | **15,321.5** |

| CAUSE | NUMBER | % | RATE |
|---|---|---|---|
| **All ages[1]** | | | |
| 1 Diseases of the heart | 710,760 | 29.6 | 258.2 |
| 2 Malignant neoplasms | 553,091 | 23.0 | 200.9 |
| 3 Cerebrovascular diseases | 167,661 | 7.0 | 60.9 |
| 4 Chronic lower respiratory diseases | 122,009 | 5.1 | 44.3 |
| 5 Accidents | 97,900 | 4.1 | 35.6 |
| 6 Diabetes mellitus | 69,301 | 2.9 | 25.2 |
| 7 Influenza and pneumonia | 65,313 | 2.7 | 23.7 |
| 8 Alzheimer's disease | 49,558 | 2.1 | 18.0 |
| 9 Nephritis, nephrotic syndrome, and nephrosis | 37,251 | 1.5 | 13.5 |
| 10 Septicemia | 31,224 | 1.3 | 11.3 |
| All other causes | 499,283 | 20.8 | 181.4 |
| **All causes, all ages** | **2,403,351** | **100.0** | **873.1** |

[1] Includes under 1 year.

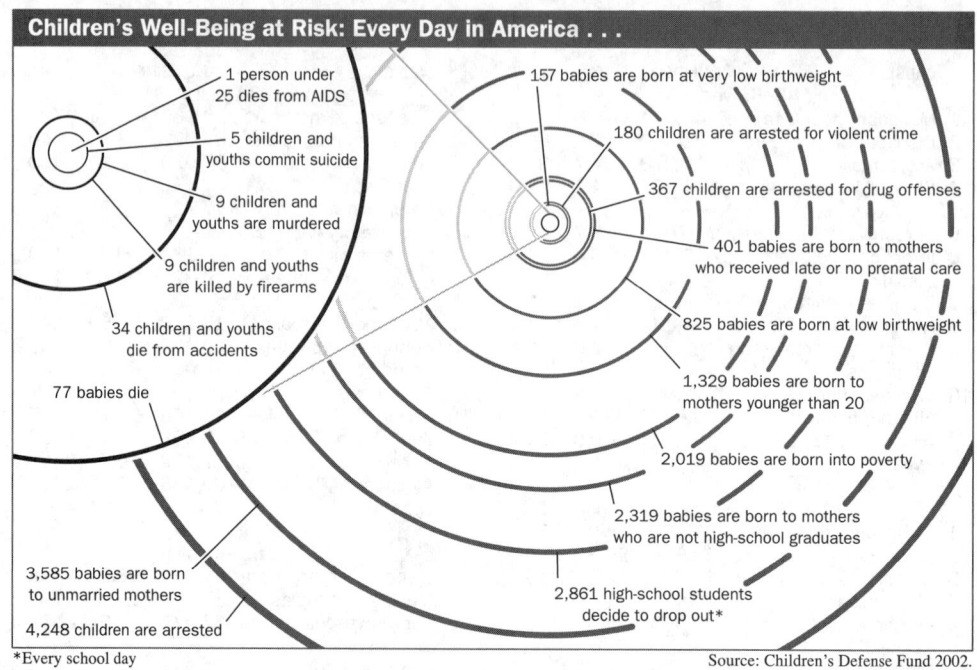

**Children's Well-Being at Risk: Every Day in America . . .**

- 1 person under 25 dies from AIDS
- 5 children and youths commit suicide
- 9 children and youths are murdered
- 9 children and youths are killed by firearms
- 34 children and youths die from accidents
- 77 babies die
- 3,585 babies are born to unmarried mothers
- 4,248 children are arrested
- 157 babies are born at very low birthweight
- 180 children are arrested for violent crime
- 367 children are arrested for drug offenses
- 401 babies are born to mothers who received late or no prenatal care
- 825 babies are born at low birthweight
- 1,329 babies are born to mothers younger than 20
- 2,019 babies are born into poverty
- 2,319 babies are born to mothers who are not high-school graduates
- 2,861 high-school students decide to drop out*

*Every school day

Source: Children's Defense Fund 2002.

## Infectious Diseases

Infectious diseases are caused by microscopic organisms, including viruses, bacteria, fungi, and animal parasites, that invade the body and multiply. Some infections, such as measles and malaria, affect the entire body; other infections affect only one body organ or system. **Infectious agents** may enter the body in a variety of ways, including inhalation of airborne microbes, skin-to-skin or sexual contact, ingestion of contaminated food or water, insect bites, and transmission from women to their unborn children. The outcome of any infection depends on the number and virulence of infectious agents, as well as on the response of the immune system.

Although progress has been made in the **eradication** of many infectious diseases, new diseases are emerging and many previously controlled diseases are making a resurgence. Unprecedented population growth, an increase in international travel, worldwide transport of animals and food products, and human encroachment on wilderness habitats all play a role in the spread of infectious diseases. In addition, microbial evolution has led to new strains of disease that are resistant to the antibiotics available to treat them. This has led to a call for a decrease in the use of antibiotics by health professionals, as the more often these drugs are administered, the more likely it is that antibiotic-resistant strains of microorganisms will emerge. **Immunization**, increased public health measures, and the development of new treatments are all crucial to controlling infectious diseases.

## Autoimmune Diseases

In autoimmune diseases, the immune system mistakenly attacks the cells, tissues, or organs of a person's own body. The cells that normally work to defend against infection effectively misrecognize parts of one's own body as alien. Autoimmune diseases are not contagious; genetic makeup increases one's chances of developing an autoimmune disease, but other environmental triggers may also play a role in disease onset. Many autoimmune diseases are rare, but as a group they afflict millions of Americans. For 2001 it was estimated that 50 million Americans (or one in five people) suffered from one of more than 80 autoimmune diseases. Women of childbearing age are most often afflicted.

Each autoimmune disease affects the body in a different way. Some of the most common diseases are listed by main target organs in the table below. All involve a collection of immune system cells and molecules at a target site, broadly referred to as **inflammation**. For example, in multiple sclerosis the autoimmune reaction is directed against the brain, and in inflammatory bowel diseases (Crohn's disease and ulcerative colitis) the immune system attacks the gut. In autoimmune diseases such as lupus, affected tissues and organs vary among individuals.

Autoimmune diseases are often difficult to **diagnose**, particularly in the early stages. Laboratory tests and close supervision are necessary for proper diagnosis and treatment. The majority of autoimmune diseases are **chronic**; health professionals seek to manage the inflammation caused by the disease rather than to cure it. Research into the intricate workings of the immune system and pathways of inflammation is being conducted in the hopes of future disease prevention.

# Autoimmune Diseases

*For information on specific autoimmune diseases, see <www.niaid.nih.gov>.*

**Blood**
Autoimmune hemolytic anemia
Autoimmune thrombocytopenia
Pernicious anemia

**Blood vessels**
Anti-phospholipid syndrome
Behcet's disease
Temporal artertis
Vasculitides (such as Wegener's granulomatosis)

**Endocrine glands**
Autoimmune disease of the adrenal gland
Autoimmune oophoritis and orchitis
Diabetes mellitus (type I or immune mediated)
Graves' disease
Hashimoto's thyroiditis

**Gastrointestinal system**
Autoimmune hepatitis
Crohn's disease
Primary biliary cirrhosis
Ulcerative colitis

**Multiple organs (including the musculoskeletal systems)**
Polymyositis, dermatomyositis
Rheumatoid arthritis
Scleroderma
Sjogren's syndrome
Spondyloarthropathies (such as ankylosing spondylitis)
Systemic lupus erythematosus

**Nervous systems**
Autoimmune neuropathies (such as Guillain-Barré)
Autoimmune ureitis
Multiple sclerosis
Myasthenia gravis

**Skin**
Dermatitis herpetiformis
Pemphigus vulgaris
Psoriasis
Vitiligo

# Cardiovascular Diseases

Cardiovascular diseases are the leading cause of death in the US, accounting for more than 40% of fatalities each year. There are many different diseases that can lead to congestive **heart failure**, a condition in which the heart muscle is less able to pump blood. Some of the common cardiovascular diseases are:

**Ischemic Heart Disease** (coronary heart disease)—the effect of an inadequate supply of oxygen-rich blood to the heart muscle because of narrowing or blocking of a coronary artery by fatty and fibrous tissue (arteriosclerosis). If the oxygen depletion is extreme, the effect may be the death of a section of heart muscle (myocardial infarction); if the deprivation is insufficient to cause infarction, the effect may be angina pectoris. Both conditions can be fatal because they can cause left ventricular failure or ventricular fibrillation—an uncontrolled and uncoordinated twitching of the ventricle muscle that induces sudden cardiac death. Coronary bypass surgery or balloon angioplasty are indicated if medication and diet do not control progressive coronary heart disease and if the myocardial damage is not too extensive.

**Pulmonary Heart Disease**—enlargement and eventual failure of the right ventricle of the heart because of disorders of the lungs, disorders of the blood vessels of the lungs, or abnormalities of the chest wall. The most common causes are chronic bronchitis and emphysema. The condition is such that the network of capillaries in the lungs is progressively destroyed, causing pressure in the pulmonary artery to be increased. The resultant back pressure on the right ventricle increases the work and the size of the chamber, leading to heart enlargement and eventually, if uncorrected, heart failure. The disease is characterized by a chronic cough, difficulty in breathing after exertion, wheezing, and weakness and fatigue. Treatment of the acute form of the disease is often by removal of the pulmonary blockage. Other treatment may include the use of antibiotics to combat respiratory infection; the use of a respirator to ease breathing; the restriction of sodium intake; and the administration of diuretics and digitalis.

**Heart Malformation** (congenital heart disease)—any deformity of the heart that develops within the first two months of fetal life. After birth, some of these deformities impair the supply of oxygen to the tissues and may cause disability or death. Approximately 40,000 children are born with a heart defect each year. These malformations can be repaired by modern surgical procedures with varying degrees of success.

Other cardiovascular-related conditions that may increase one's likelihood of heart disease include arrhythmias and blood pressure irregularities:

**Arrhythmias** are disorders of the rhythmic beating of the heart and are fairly common. Although often relatively harmless, they may indicate a more serious heart problem.

**Blood pressure** is the force originating in the pumping action of the heart, exerted by the blood against the walls of the blood vessels. It is usually measured indirectly over the brachial or femoral artery. The highest (systolic) pressure, normally about 120, occurs during contraction of the ventricles; the lowest (diastolic) pressure, normally about 80, occurs during ventricular relaxation. **Hypertension**, or high blood pressure, occurs when the blood vessels lose their flexibility or the muscles surrounding them force them to contract. As a result, the heart must pump more forcefully to move the same amount of blood through the narrowed vessels into the capillaries, thereby increasing blood pressure. The increased risk of death from congestive heart failure, kidney failure, or stroke is the chief danger of hypertension. **Hypotension**, or low blood pressure, is a condition in which the blood pressure is abnormally low, either because of reduced blood volume or because of increased blood-vessel capacity. Although not in itself an indication of ill health, it often accompanies disease conditions. Some causes are extensive bleeding or burns and exposure to cold.

To help prevent heart disease, the American Heart Association recommends maintaining a healthy diet, exercising, keeping cholesterol low, and managing stress.

**Internet resources:** <www.americanheart.org>

# Stroke

A stroke is a sudden impairment of brain function resulting either from a substantial reduction in blood flow to some part of the brain or from intracranial bleeding. The consequences may include transient or lasting paralysis on one or both sides of the body, difficulties in using words or in eating, and a loss in muscular coordination. A stroke may cause cerebral infarctions (dead sections of brain tissue).

Stroke occurs in conjunction with at least one of the following four events:

A blood clot forms within a blood vessel of the brain (thrombosis). This is the most common cause.

A blood clot lodges in an artery supplying brain tissue after originating in another portion of the body (embolism). A heart attack, damage to a valve, and an irregular heartbeat can cause blood clots that may reach the brain.

An intermittent insufficiency in the flow of blood results temporarily from a spasm of the arteries or the sludging of the blood as it passes through segments of vessels that have been narrowed by arteriosclerosis.

Hemorrhage occurs after an artery ruptures, usually as a result of a weakening of the arterial wall because of arteriosclerosis or because of a thinning of the wall along with bulging (an aneurysm), which may be congenital or develop later in life. The walls of arteries in the brain can become weakened by the assault of **high blood pressure**.

So-called "little strokes" result when long, thin arteries penetrating deep into the brain become blocked by arteriosclerosis, causing areas of surrounding tissue to lose their blood supply. Whereas the initial onset of stroke may be massive in its effects, producing widespread paralysis within several hours, the onset may also be manifested by a series of transient little strokes during which the patient may experience weakness and numbness of an arm, a leg, or a side of the face.

Precise history and physical examination are essential to differentiate stroke from a tumor and from brain injury resulting from other causes. Examination of spinal fluid for evidence of blood and diagnostic imaging may clarify the **diagnosis**. Surgery may be attempted to remove the obstruction or to insert a graft or synthetic bypass. Physical and speech therapy may also help prevent deformity. Many victims of stroke may live for a further 10 to 20 years or longer after the occurrence.

Smoking, high cholesterol, aging, diabetes, and heritable defects are among the major **risk factors** for stroke. Statistically, men and African Americans also have a higher stroke risk.

The National Stroke Association recommends maintaining a healthy diet that is low in sodium and fat, exercising, keeping cholestorol and alcohol consumption low, and not smoking.

**Internet resources:** <www.stroke.org>

# Diabetes

Diabetes mellitus is a disease in which the body does not produce or properly use insulin, a hormone that is needed to convert sugar, starches, and other food into energy. Two common problems thus caused by diabetes are hyperglycemia (high blood sugar) and hypoglycemia (low blood sugar). There are two types of diabetes: type I, insulin-dependent diabetes (formerly referred to as juvenile-onset diabetes as it usually arises in childhood); and type II, non-insulin-dependent diabetes (formerly referred to as adult-onset diabetes, as it usually occurs after 40 years of age). Despite their former classifications, either type of diabetes can occur at any age. Type II diabetes is by far the most common type of the disease, accounting for about 90% of all cases.

Type I diabetes is an **autoimmune disorder** in which the diabetic's immune system produces antibodies that destroy insulin-producing beta cells. People with type I diabetes require insulin injections to stay alive. Meal planning and exercise also help keep blood sugar levels regular.

Type II diabetes arises from either sluggish pancreatic secretion of insulin or reduced responsiveness in target cells of the body to secreted insulin, or both. It is linked to genetics and obesity. Some cases of type II diabetes can be controlled through diet and exercise, but often medication or insulin shots are needed as well.

It is estimated that 17 million Americans have diabetes, and one in three does not know it. Often diabetes goes undiagnosed because its symptoms seem harmless at first. Diabetes is also more common in African Americans, Latinos, Native Americans, Asian Americans, and Pacific Islanders. Some of the early **warning signs** of diabetes are: frequent urination, excessive thirst, extreme hunger, unusual weight loss, increased fatigue, irritability, and blurry vision.

Diabetes is the sixth leading cause of death by disease in the US. Each year, at least 190,000 people die as a result of complications associated with diabetes. Possible complications include:

**Blindness.** Each year, 12,000 to 24,000 people lose their sight due to diabetes. It is the leading cause of new blindness in people 20–74 years of age.

**Kidney disease.** Diabetic nephropathy, the most common cause of end-stage renal disease, requires dialysis or a kidney transplant to prevent death; 10–21% of all people with diabetes develop kidney disease.

**Heart disease and stroke.** People with diabetes are two to four times more likely to have heart disease, to die from heart disease, or to suffer a stroke.

**Nerve disease and amputations.** Approximately 70% of people with diabetes have mild to severe forms of diabetic nerve damage, which can lead to lower limb amputation. Diabetes is the most frequent cause of non-traumatic lower limb amputations in the US.

**Impotence.** Approximately 13% of men with Type I diabetes and 8% of men with Type II report problems with impotence.

Diabetes is a serious condition, but with proper treatment patients can lead productive lives. To avoid complications, people with diabetes should keep blood-sugar levels close to normal, control their weight, eat a healthy diet, exercise, see a doctor regularly, check their feet carefully for abnormalities, and refrain from smoking.

**Internet resources:** <www.diabetes.org>

## Cancer

Cancer is any of a group of related diseases characterized by uncontrolled multiplication and disorganized growth of the affected cells; it may arise in any of the body's tissues. If left untreated, cancer cells infiltrate and destroy adjacent tissues, eventually gain access to the circulatory system, are transported to distant parts of the body, and ultimately destroy the host. Not all abnormal growths are **malignant**, however; those that are not are referred to as **benign** tumors.

Cancer was known as far back as antiquity, and malignant tumors have been found in mummies 5,000 years old. It is estimated that nearly 1.3 million new cases will arise in the US in 2002. The disease can be caused by a variety of factors, including chemical substances, ionizing radiation, and viruses. Although much is known about how cancer is caused, the precise mechanism involved continues to elude researchers. Certain cancers have the ability to spread from their sites of origin, rendering their treatment and eradication difficult; this results either from direct extension from the primary site as a consequence of growth and tumor cell movement or from the cancer cells entering the vascular system by invading lymphatics or blood vessels (**metastasis**). The more the cancer spreads, the more difficult it is to treat, making early diagnosis of utmost importance.

Some of the major types of cancer are listed below, along with cancer-detection guidelines from the American Cancer Society.

**Breast cancer.** Breast cancer is the leading cause of death from cancer in women, afflicting approximately 192,200 US women in 2001. *Treatment:* Most patients will require some type of surgery to treat the tumor, possibly in combination with chemotherapy, hormone therapy, or radiation therapy. *Prevention:* Women age 20 and over should perform monthly breast self-exams. Women between the ages of 20 and 39 should have a clinical breast exam every 3 years; women over 40 should have one annually. Women 40 and over should also have a mammogram each year.

**Colorectal cancer.** Colorectal cancer is very common in the Western world, with an equal incidence in men and women. Generally, the tumors metastasize to the liver, lungs, and other distant sites. *Treatment:* Surgery is the most favored treatment, although chemotherapy and radiation may also be used. *Prevention:* There are five tests to detect colorectal cancer. Individuals 50 and over should choose one of the following options, even if they have no symptoms of the disease:

Fecal occult blood test (every year)
Flexible sigmoidoscopy (every 5 years)
Fecal occult blood test every year plus sigmoidoscopy every 5 years (preferred to either of the above treatments alone)
Double-contrast barium enema (every 5 years)
Colonoscopy (every 10 years)

**Leukemias.** Leukemias are a heterogeneous group of malignancies of the blood-forming tissues, which include the bone marrow, lymph nodes, and spleen. The acute form of the disease in adults is rapidly fatal, with infiltration of bone marrow and other blood-forming tissues by the malignant cells, while the acute form in children has yielded to treatment and a number of cures are documented. The best established cause involves chronic exposure to ionizing radiation. Other factors, including congenital disorders such as Down syndrome, viruses, and certain chemicals and drugs, have also been implicated. Patients afflicted with leukemia are rendered anemic and are susceptible to infection. *Treatment:* Treatment involves attempts to correct leukemia-related complications by transfusion of normal blood, as well as antibiotics to combat infection and chemotherapy to destroy malignant cells. *Prevention:* There are no special tests that can detect any form of leukemia and no known way to prevent most cases, as the disease is not linked to lifestyle risk factors.

**Lung cancer.** The most common forms of lung cancer are squamous-cell carcinomas, which arise in bronchial glandular epithelium that has been altered by long exposure to cigarette smoke. Cancers of the lung tend to metastasize widely; the average survival of persons with untreated lung cancer is about 9 months after diagnosis, and the spreading to regional or distant lymph nodes has already occurred in the majority of cases. *Treatment:* Removal of the tumor may prolong life for a number of months. *Prevention:* Do not smoke and avoid second-hand smoke as well as cancer-causing chemicals such as radon gas.

**Ovarian cancer.** Very common in the industrialized Western world, ovarian cancer may be linked to environmental factors. Many different types of ovarian cancer have been identified, arising either in the epithelium or in connective tissue components. *Treatment:* Tumors may be treated successfully through surgery if diagnosed early. Extension of the disease may require radiation or chemotheraphy. *Prevention:* Only 25% of ovarian cancers are found at an early stage, as they often manifest no symptoms early on. Therefore, women 18 and over should have a yearly pelvic exam. If symptoms do present, imaging studies or biopsy may be used to properly diagnose the disease.

**Prostate cancer.** A common form of cancer in men, prostate cancer commonly metastasizes to the bones and, together with involvement of nerves in the pelvis, creates considerable pain and discomfort. Fortunately, prostate cancer differs from other cancers in its slow rate of growth; if the cancer does not spread, the 5-year survival rate is nearly 100%, even if it remains untreated. *Treatment:* Surgery, radiation, and chemotherapy are the most-frequently used treatments. PSA blood tests and digital rectal exams can help diagnose the disease. *Prevention:* The exact cause of prostate cancer is not known, but a diet low in animal fat and high in vegetables, fruits, and grains is recommended for overall health.

**Skin cancer.** Approximately 82% of skin cancer arises from basal cells in the deepest layer of the skin, resulting in basal-cell carcinoma. This type of cancer grows slowly and rarely metastasizes, but does invade locally and can cause considerable destruction of adjacent tissues, which can result in disfigurement. Sqamous-cell carcinoma arises from the platelike flat cells that constitute the major cellular component of skin, and these cells may metastasize to regional lymph nodes. *Treatment*: Surgical excision or radiation therapy is often successful. *Prevention*:

The best way to lower one's risk of skin cancer is to avoid UV light. A sunscreen with an SPF of 15 or above is recommended, even on cloudy days. A self-exam each month should reveal any new or changing spots or blemishes on the skin; anything unusual should be reported to a health care provider.

**Internet resources:** <www.cancer.org>

## Alzheimer's Disease

Alzheimer's disease is the most common form of dementia—it is estimated that up to 4 million Americans are currently afflicted. An irreversible, progressive brain disorder that involves the death of brain cells and the breakdown of the connections between them, Alzheimer's usually begins gradually, with symptoms increasing as the disease progresses. On average, patients live for 8 to 10 years after diagnosis, but some have been known to survive for as long as 20.

Scientists are still trying to understand the underlying mechanisms of Alzheimer's; the disease develops differently among individuals, and this suggests that more than one pathological process may lead to the same outcome. One key element is the presence in the brain of two abnormalities—amyloid plaques and neurofibrillary tangles. Unfortunately, these growths can be detected only during an autopsy, and it is not known whether the plaques and tangles are a cause or a consequence of the disease. The majority of cases of Alzheimer's occur after age 60, but about 10% of those who develop the disease are younger. These cases, referred to as early-onset familial Alzheimer's disease, result from an inherited genetic mutation.

The Alzheimer's Association recognizes 10 **warning signs** of disease onset: memory loss; difficulty per-

forming familiar tasks; problems with language; disorientation to time and place; poor or decreased judgment; problems with abstract thinking; misplacing things; changes in mood or behavior; changes in personality; and loss of initiative. These symptoms become progressively more severe, and eventually people with Alzheimer's lose all memory, thinking, and reasoning abilities and become dependent on others for their daily needs.

No single diagnostic test can detect if a person has Alzheimer's. Standard clinical methods of **diagnosis** involve a complete medical history, various medical and neuropsychological tests, a mental status evaluation, a neurological examination, and a psychiatric evaulation. These procedures help rule out other diseases and enable physicians to make a positive clinical diagnosis of Alzheimer's with approximately 90% accuracy.

There is currently no **treatment** to prevent or reverse the effects of Alzheimer's disease; however, four FDA-approved drugs may help prevent worsening of some symptoms for a limited time. Other medications may help control the behavioral symptoms of the disease and make patients more comfortable and easier to care for.

**Internet resources:** <www.alz.org>

## Arthritis

There are more than 100 different medical conditions that fall under the category "arthritis," a blanket term for inflammation of the joints. Arthritis is the number one cause of disability in the US; nearly 43,000,00 (1 in 6) Americans are affected by it, including almost 300,000 children. Arthritis is generally a chronic condition that requires ongoing treatment. Many forms of arthritis are initially difficult to diagnose; health professionals will generally perform a physical exam, conduct various medical tests, and order X rays to confirm a **diagnosis.**

**Osteoarthritis,** the most common joint disease, is characterized by progressive deterioration of the articular cartilage and afflicts more than 80% of those who reach the age of 70. It often affects the hands and the weight-bearing joints, such as the knees, hips, feet, and back, resulting in stiffness, pain, and a limitation in movement as the disease progresses. The genesis of this disorder is not completely understood, but biomechanical forces that place stress on the joints are thought to interact with biochemical and genetic factors to contribute to the degenerative process. Obesity, joint injury owing to sports, and work-related activities may place individuals at increased risk for developing osteoarthritis. Corticosteroids and NSAIDS are commonly prescribed for **treatment**; glucocorticoids may be injected into the

affected joints; and surgery may be needed to relieve chronic pain and improve joint function. In addition, joint protection, weight control, and non-weight-bearing exercise are recommended.

**Rheumatoid arthritis** is an **autoimmune** disease that typically affects many different joints and may also affect other internal organs. Inflammation and thickening of the synovial membranes can result in irreversible damage to the joint as the inflamed joint lining invades and damages bone and cartilage. In addition to joint swelling, redness, warmth, stiffness, and pain, symptoms may include loss of appetite or energy, fever, anemia, and the development of rheumatoid nodules. Rheumatoid arthritis is about three times as common in women as in men and afflicts about 1% of the adult population in developed nations. Although the exact cause of the disease remains unknown, approximately 80% of individuals with rheumatoid arthritis have characteristic autoantibodies in their blood that are collectively called rheumatoid factor, and there is evidence that such individuals have a genetic susceptibility to some environmental agent related to disease onset. Rheumatoid arthritis is generally chronic, often with periods of disease flare-up and remission. There are a variety of drugs available for **treatment**. Symptomatic medications such as NSAIDS, analgesics, and glucocorticoids help reduce joint pain, stiffness, and swelling, while disease-modifying anti-rheumatic medications, including methotrexate, antimalarials, and biologic agents, may actually help stop disease progression.

**Fibromyalgia** is an arthritis-related syndrome that is characterized by widespread musculoskeletal pain, fatigue, and tenderness in precise areas of the body. It affects approximately 2% of Americans, primarily women of childbearing age. It was not until 1990 that fibromyalgia was officially recognized as a distinct syndrome. **Treatment** often includes a combination of exercise, medication (including antidepressants), physical therapy, and relaxation.

Other conditions related to arthritis include lupus, ankylosing spondylitis, gout, and psoriatic arthritis.

**Internet resources:** <www.arthritis.org>

# Allergies

An allergy is a hypersensitive reaction by the body to foreign substances that in similar amounts and circumstances are harmless within the bodies of other people.

Antigens that provoke allergic reactions are called **allergens**. Typical allergens include pollens, drugs, lints, bacteria, foods, and dyes or chemicals. Allergies tend to run in families and are common among children. Skin testing is often used to determine the source of the allergen.

Allergic reactions can be the result of inhaled allergens, such as weed, tree, and grass pollen, mold spores, animal dander, or house dust. These generally result in runny nose, sneezing, and watery and itchy eyes (allergic rhinitis). Eczema and contact dermatitis are common skin allergies that may result in a variety of problems, including rashes, hives, and itching. Certain foods, most frequently milk, fish, eggs, nuts, and wheat, tend to produce allergic reactions that result in intestinal disturbances.

**Anaphylactic shock** is the most severe allergic reaction and often occurs in individuals sensitive to stinging insects, penicillin, nuts, or shellfish. Anaphylaxis causes swelling of body tissues, vomiting, cramps, and a drop in blood pressure.

The most effective **treatment** is avoidance of the allergen. Additionally, allergy shots allow patients to build an immunity to the allergen. Antihistamines, decongestants, bronchodilators, and anti-inflammatory agents may also be used.

**Internet resources:** <www.aaaai.org>

# Asthma

Asthma is a chronic lung disorder affecting 12–17 million Americans, including approximately 5 million children. During an **asthmatic episode,** the airways become inflamed and may constrict, causing episodes of breathlessness, wheezing, coughing, and chest tightness that range in severity from mild to life-threatening. Although the mechanisms underlying an asthmatic episode are not fully understood, in general it is known that exposure to an inciting factor stimulates the release of chemicals from the immune system that cause spasmodic contraction of the smooth muscle surrounding the bronchi, swelling and inflammation of the bronchial tubes, and excessive secretion of mucus. The inflamed, mucus-clogged airways act as a one-way valve, preventing air from being expired.

Asthma is classified into four categories depending on severity and frequency: mild intermittent, mild persistent, moderate persistent, and severe persistent. Childhood asthma is often associated with an inherited susceptibility to **allergens,** substances such as pollen or dust mites. In adults, asthma also may develop in response to allergens, but viral infections, aspirin, exercise, and exposure to certain materials in the workplace may cause the disease as well.

Asthma sufferers are encouraged to minimize their exposure to substances that may trigger an attack. A number of **medications** are available to prevent and control the symptoms of asthma, including long-term and quick-relief prescriptions. A prolonged asthma attack that does not respond to medication may require hospitalization and administration of oxygen. Individuals can also monitor their level of airflow obstruction by using a pocket-size device called a **peak-flow meter.**

**Internet resources:** <www.aaaai.org>

# HIV/AIDS

Acquired Immunodeficiency Syndrome, or AIDS, is a fatal transmissable disorder of the immune system that is caused by the human immunodeficiency virus (HIV). HIV was first isolated in 1983. In most cases, HIV slowly attacks and destroys the **immune system,** leaving the infected individual vulnerable to malignancies and infections that eventually cause death. AIDS is the last stage of HIV infection, during which time these diseases arise. An average interval of 10 years exists between infection with HIV and development of the conditions typical of AIDS. **Pneumonia** and **Kaposi's sarcoma** are two of the most common diseases seen in AIDS patients.

HIV is contracted through semen, vaginal fluid, breast milk, blood, or other body fluids containing blood. Health care workers may come into contact with other body fluids that may transmit the HIV virus, including amniotic and synovial fluids. Although it is a transmissable virus, it is not contagious and it cannot be spread through coughing, sneezing, or casual physical contact. Other **STDs,** such as genital herpes, may increase the risk of contracting AIDS through sexual contact.

The main **cellular target** of HIV is a special class of white blood cells critical to the immune system known as T4 helper cells. Once HIV has entered a helper T cell, it can cause the cell to function poorly or it can destroy the cell. A hallmark of the onset of AIDS is a drastic reduction in the number of helper T cells in the body. Two predominant strains of the virus, designated HIV-1 and HIV-2, are known. World-wide the most common strain is HIV-1, with HIV-2 more common primarily in western Africa; the two strains act in a similar manner, but the latter causes a form of AIDS that progresses much more slowly.

**Diagnosis** is made on the basis of blood tests approved by the CDC that may be administered by a doctor or at a local health department. Alternately, a home collection kit may be purchased at many pharmacies. No vaccine or cure has yet been developed that can prevent HIV infection. Several **drugs** are now used to slow the development of AIDS, including azidothymidine (AZT). **Protease inhibitors**, such as ritonavir and indinavir, have been shown to block the development of AIDS, at least temporarily. Protease

inhibitors are most effective when used in conjunction with two different reverse transcriptase inhibitors—the so-called "triple-drug therapy."

HIV/AIDS is a major problem in developing countries, particularly sub-Saharan Africa. At the end of 2001, 40 million people were estimated to have contracted HIV, with 95% of those living in the developing world.

For information on **prevention**, see "Safer Sex Defined."

For confidential information on HIV/AIDS, call 1-800-342-AIDS.

**Internet resources:** <www.cdc.gov/hiv>

## Sexually Transmitted Diseases (STDs)

A sexually transmitted disease (STD) is usually passed from person to person by direct sexual contact. It may also be transmitted from a mother to her child before or at birth or, less frequently, may be passed from person to person in nonsexual contact. STDs usually initially affect the genitals, the reproductive tract, the urinary tract, the oral cavity, the anus, or the rectum but may mature in the body to attack various organs and systems. Following are some of the major STDs:

**Syphilis** was first widely reported by European writers in the 16th century, and a virtual epidemic swept Europe around the year 1500. Syphilis is spread through direct contact with a syphilis sore (chancre); development of this sore is the first stage of the disease. The second stage manifests itself as a rash on the palms and the bottoms of the feet. In the last stage, symptoms disappear, but the disease remains in the body and may damage internal organs and lead to paralysis, blindness, dementia, and even death. For individuals infected less than a year, a single dose of penicillin will cure the disease. Larger doses are needed for those who have had it for a longer period of time.

**Gonorrhea,** a form of urethritis (an infection and inflammation of the urethra), is one of the most common STDs. Although spread through sexual contact, the gonorrhea infection can also be spread to other parts of the body after touching the infected area. Men manifest symptoms, which include discharge and a burning sensation when urinating, more often than women. If gonorrhea is left untreated, women may develop pelvic inflammatory disease (PID) and men may become infertile. The disease can also spread to the blood or joints and is potentially life-threatening.

**Chlamydia,** another form of urethritis, can be transmitted during vaginal, anal, or oral sex. Since there are frequently no symptoms, most infected individuals do not know they have the disease until complications develop. Untreated chlamydia can cause urethral infection in men and PID in women. Antibiotics can successfully cure the disease.

**Genital herpes,** a disease that became especially widespread in the 1960s and 1970s, often presents minimal symptoms upon infection. The most common sign, however, is blistering in the genital area; outbreaks can occur over many years but generally decrease in severity and number. Genital herpes is caused by the herpes simplex viruses type 1 (HSV-1) and type 2 (HSV-2). The former causes infections on and around the mouth but may be spread through the saliva to the genitals; the latter is transmitted during sexual contact with someone who has a genital infection. The HSV-2 infection can cause problems for people with suppressed immune systems and for infants who contract the disease upon delivery. Herpes can also leave individuals more susceptible to HIV infection and make those carrying the disease more infectious. A variety of treatments, including antiviral medications, have been used to help manage genital herpes, but currently there is no cure for the disease.

Almost all STDs have reasonably effective drug cures. For information on STD **prevention**, see below, "Safer Sex Defined." For information on **HIV disease**, see individual entry.

**Internet resources:** <www.cdc.gov/nchstp/od/nch-stp.html>

## Safer Sex Defined

**Defining risky sexual behavior.** Any activity involving the exchange of body fluids—vaginal secretions, semen, or blood—could result in the transmission of HIV and other STDs. Unprotected vaginal and anal intercourse present the highest risks for contraction of STDs. Women are at greater risk than men of developing an infection as a result of heterosexual intercourse, and many STDs present fewer symptoms in women than in men. However, men and women of all sexual orientations should practice safer sex to reduce their risk of contracting an STD.

**HIV testing.** It can take years to develop symptoms

of HIV disease, so it is important to be tested for HIV after any behavior that might have resulted in infection. The CDC recommends undergoing two separate HIV-antibody tests, six months apart. If the second test is negative, there is a reasonable certainty that HIV is not present.

**STD testing.** It is important to get checked for other STDs at least once a year. Do not assume that STD testing is part of a routine checkup.

**Abstinence.** Refraining from any sexual activity that would allow the exchange of body fluids is by far the most effective method of birth control and disease prevention.

**Monogamous intercourse.** Sexual intercourse with only one partner can be as effective as abstinence in preventing disease transmission, if both partners have been properly tested for HIV and other STDs. Most health professionals, however, recommend continuing to practice safer sex, even in monogamous relationships, as there is no way to be sure a partner is being faithful.

**Condoms.** Using a latex or female condom correctly and consistently significantly reduces the chance of unplanned pregnancy. Condoms also reduce the risk of transmission of HIV, vaginitis, chlamydia, honeymoon cystitis, syphilis, pelvic inflammatory disease, chancroid, and gonorrhea. Condoms may be less ef-fective in preventing genital warts, herpes, cervical cancer, and hepatitis B. Male and female condoms should not be worn simultaneously.

**Birth control.** There are many methods of birth control for women that can help prevent unwanted pregnancy, including birth control pills, Norplant, Depo-Provera, condoms, diaphragms, and cervical caps. However, of these, only condoms protect against STDs. Emergency contraception, including the "morning-after" pill, should be used only when necessary and not relied upon as a regular method of birth control. Withdrawal and family planning are not recommended forms of birth control.

## Contraceptive Use by US Women

*Percent distribution by age. Totals may not add to 100% due to rounding. "..." indicates less than 0.05. Data are for 1995.*

| | AGE 15–44 | 15–19 | 20–24 | 25–29 | 30–34 | 35–39 | 40–44 |
|---|---|---|---|---|---|---|---|
| **Using contraception** | | | | | | | |
| Pill | 17.3 | 13.0 | 33.1 | 27.0 | 20.7 | 8.1 | 4.2 |
| Condom | 13.1 | 10.9 | 16.7 | 16.8 | 13.4 | 12.3 | 8.8 |
| Female sterilization | 17.8 | 0.1 | 2.5 | 11.8 | 21.4 | 29.8 | 35.6 |
| Male sterilization | 7.0 | 0.0 | 0.7 | 3.1 | 7.6 | 13.6 | 14.5 |
| Implant | 0.9 | 0.8 | 2.4 | 1.4 | 0.5 | 0.2 | 0.1 |
| Injectable | 1.9 | 2.9 | 3.9 | 2.9 | 1.3 | 0.8 | 0.2 |
| Intrauterine device (IUD) | 0.5 | 0.0 | 0.2 | 0.5 | 0.6 | 0.7 | 0.9 |
| Diaphragm | 1.2 | ... | 0.4 | 0.6 | 1.7 | 2.2 | 1.9 |
| Female condom | ... | 0.0 | 0.1 | 0.0 | 0.0 | 0.0 | 0.0 |
| Periodic abstinence | 1.5 | 0.4 | 0.6 | 1.2 | 2.3 | 2.1 | 1.8 |
| Natural family planning | 0.2 | 0.0 | 0.1 | 0.2 | 0.3 | 0.4 | 0.2 |
| Withdrawal | 2.0 | 1.2 | 2.1 | 2.6 | 2.1 | 2.3 | 1.4 |
| Other[1] | 1.0 | 0.3 | 0.9 | 1.2 | 1.3 | 0.9 | 1.8 |
| **Total using contraception** | **64.2** | **29.8** | **63.4** | **69.3** | **72.7** | **72.9** | **71.5** |
| | | | | | | | |
| **Not using contraception** | | | | | | | |
| Surgically sterile female | 3.0 | 0.1 | 0.1 | 0.6 | 1.7 | 5.1 | 9.6 |
| Nonsurgically sterile female | 1.3 | 0.7 | 0.5 | 0.7 | 1.2 | 2.3 | 1.9 |
| Pregnant or postpartum | 4.6 | 4.5 | 7.3 | 8.4 | 5.6 | 2.1 | 0.4 |
| Seeking pregnancy | 4.0 | 0.9 | 3.4 | 6.1 | 6.2 | 4.6 | 2.2 |
| Other | | | | | | | |
| Never had intercourse | 10.9 | 49.8 | 12.1 | 4.2 | 2.7 | 1.4 | 1.4 |
| No intercourse in last 3 months | 6.2 | 7.1 | 6.8 | 5.7 | 4.9 | 6.2 | 6.8 |
| Had intercourse in last 3 months | 5.2 | 7.1 | 6.0 | 4.7 | 4.4 | 4.3 | 5.1 |
| **Total not using contraception**[2] | **35.8** | **70.2** | **36.6** | **30.7** | **27.3** | **27.1** | **28.5** |

[1]Includes morning-after pill, cervical cap, Today™ sponge, suppository, and other methods.    [2]Includes other categories not listed.

## Complementary and Alternative Medicine and Treatment

In the past decade, the use of **alternative therapy** has doubled in North America and Europe, where conventional Western medicine generally had been the only accepted form of treatment. Alternative therapy encompasses both remedies and practices, including the use of herbs, homeopathy, therapeutic massage, acupuncture, hypnotism, and traditional Oriental medicine. Also called **complementary medicine** (as it may be used in conjunction with conventional practices), alternative medicine approaches are often **holistic**, or focused on the whole person, including physical, mental, emotional, and spiritual aspects. Related to alternative therapies in their treatment of the body as whole, **osteopathy** and **chiropractic** have also enjoyed greater acceptance in recent years, particularly in the US.

In 1998 Congress established the National Center for Complementary and Alternative Medicine as a division of the **NIH** to develop and support research on alternative medicine. In May 2002 WHO announced the development of a **global strategy** for researching and regulating alternative treatments; it is currently compiling reports on more than 100 medicinal plants. At issue is the safety and usefulness of alternative medicine, which remains largely unregulated. Often patients pursue treatment without the advice of a health care professional; as with conventional medicines, if used incorrectly alternative treatments can cause injury or even death. WHO is urging member states to adopt regulations to license providers and determine the authenticity and safety of alternative products. Only China, Vietnam, North Korea, and South Korea have integrated traditional medicines into their official health care systems.

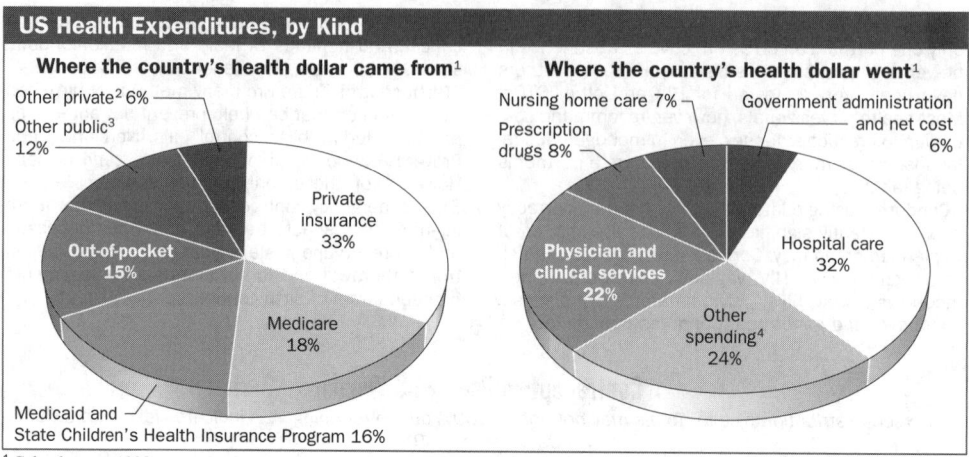

## US Health Expenditures, by Kind

**Where the country's health dollar came from**[1]

- Other private[2] 6%
- Other public[3] 12%
- Out-of-pocket 15%
- Private insurance 33%
- Medicare 18%
- Medicaid and State Children's Health Insurance Program 16%

**Where the country's health dollar went**[1]

- Nursing home care 7%
- Prescription drugs 8%
- Government administration and net cost 6%
- Physician and clinical services 22%
- Hospital care 32%
- Other spending[4] 24%

[1] Calendar year 1999.

[2] Other private includes industrial in-plant, privately funded construction, and non-patient revenues, including philanthropy.

[3] Other public includes programs such as workers' compensation, public health activity, US Department of Defense, US Department of Veterans Affairs, Indian Health Service, state and local hospital subsidies, and school health.

[4] Other spending includes dentist and other professional services, home health care, durable medical equipment, other nondurable medical products, government public health activities, and research and construction.

Source: Centers for Medicare & Medicaid Services, Office of the Actuary, National Health Statistics Group.

## The Centers for Disease Control and Prevention (CDC) and the National Institutes of Health (NIH)

*Both the CDC and the NIH are part of the US Department of Health and Human Services.*
*CDC Web site: <www.cdc.gov>*
*NIH Web site: <www.nih.gov>*

**C**enters for Disease Control. *Mission:* To promote health and quality of life by preventing and controlling disease, injury, and disability. *Location:* Atlanta, GA. *Acting Director:* Julie L. Gerberding. *Budget:* FY 2004 (requested) $6.5 billion. *Functions:* Monitors health problems and infectious diseases worldwide; conducts research to enhance disease prevention; develops public health policy; provides leadership and training; assists state and local health departments.

**National Institutes of Health.** *Mission:* To uncover new knowledge that will lead to better health for everyone. *Location:* Bethesda MD. *Director:* Elias A. Zerhouni. *Budget:* FY 2004 (requested) $27.9 billion. *Functions:* Supports and conducts biomedical research, both in its own laboratories and through research grants to universities, medical schools, hospitals, and research institutes. Future research will center on disease treatment and prevention in a variety of areas, including mental illness, cancer, AIDS, arthritis, and other unconquered diseases; improving the health of children, women, and minorities; and better understanding the aging process.

# Mental Health

## Diagnostic and Statistical Manual of Mental Disorders (DSM)

**T**he *Diagnostic and Statistical Manual of Mental Disorders* (*DSM*) is the standard reference for mental health professionals in the US (worldwide, the World Health Organization's *International Classification of Diseases* is used). Published by the American Psychiatric Association (APA), the *DSM* sets forth diagnostic criteria, descriptions, and other information to help classify and diagnose mental disorders.

There are three main components of the *DSM*. The **diagnostic classification** is a list of mental disorders that are officially recognized by the APA. These labels include diagnostic codes, which are used by institutions for data collection and billing. For each of these disorders, **diagnostic criteria** indicate what symptoms must be present and what others must not be present in order to make a particular diagnosis. A **descriptive text** also follows each disorder and includes information on subtypes, specific age and gender fea-

tures, prevalence, and familial patterns, among other categories.

The *DSM-I* was published in 1952, at a time when little empirical data existed for the evaluation of mental illness; its primary purpose was to standardize this data collection and establish a consensus among clinicians. Today the *DSM* is used mainly as a diagnostic, rather than a statistical, tool, but it is still an evolving entity, and changes are made with every new edition. One example of the way the *DSM* has evolved involves the classification of homosexuality as a mental disorder. Facing mounting empirical data, changing social norms, and pressure from the gay community, the board of trustees of the APA removed homosexuality from the *DSM* in 1973; it was subsequently replaced with a more refined diagnosis, ego-dystonic homosexuality, which was marked by a lack of heterosexual arousal despite the desire for such and by unwanted homosexual impulses. This disorder was in turn criticized, and homosexuality was entirely removed from the *DSM* in 1987.

The most recent edition, *DSM-IV*, was completed in 1994; a text revision, **DSM-IV-TR**, was made available in July 2000 (changes to the diagnostic criteria for Tourette's Disorder and Alzheimer's Disease were among the revisions). The *DSM-V* is slated for publication in 2010.

## Anxiety Disorders

Anxiety is defined as a feeling of fear, dread, or apprehension that arises without a clear or appropriate real-life justification. Generally, intense, persistent, or chronic anxiety that is not justified and that interferes with daily functioning is classified as a manifestation of a mental disorder. The most common anxiety disorders are:

**Panic disorder.** Panic disorder is characterized by recurrent panic attacks, with at least one of the attacks followed by persistent fear of having another attack, worry about the implications or consequences of the attack, or a change in behavior related to the attack; these feelings last for one month or more. A **panic attack** is the sudden onset of intense apprehension, fear, or terror and at least four of the following conditions: shortness of breath or a smothering sensation; palpitations or accelerated heart rate; chest pain or discomfort; choking; dizziness or faintness; trembling or shaking; sweating; nausea or abdominal distress; a feeling of unreality; numbness or tingling; hot flashes or chills; fear of dying; and fear of "going crazy" or losing control. A panic attack is unexpected and does not immediately precede or follow a stressful situation, although the person who experiences the attack usually is in a period of increased stress. It is easy to mistake the attack for other problems such as heart disease, as somatic symptoms play a prominent role. There is a close association between panic disorder and **depression**, and a large percentage of persons suffering from panic disorder go on to experience a major depression within the next few years. *Treatment:* Short-term individual psychotherapy is usually helpful, during which relaxation and imagery techniques may be taught. For more severe cases, benzodiazepines or selective serotonin reuptake inhibitor antidepressants may be prescribed.

**Generalized anxiety disorder.** Generalized anxiety disorder is characterized as the unrealistic or excessive worry about two or more life circumstances that is experienced more days than not for a period of six months or longer. Examples are excessive worry about finances or danger to one's child when there is no reason for this concern. The anxious behavior indicative of this disorder includes symptoms such as trembling, muscle soreness, restlessness, shortness of breath, palpitations, dizziness, difficulty concentrating, and an exaggerated startle response. *Treatment:* The first stage of treatment should be a full medical exam to rule out a biological or environmental cause. If the anxiety is found to be a psychological disorder, there are a number of treatment options, including cognitive-behavioral therapy, which often teaches relaxation techniques; hypnotherapy and self-help treatments can also be useful. Medication is often used in treatment as well. Traditionally, benzodiazepines were used, but they are often habit-forming and sedating; Buspar (buspirone) does not have these side effects and is now often prescribed. Some antidepressant medications may also relieve the symptoms of anxiety.

**Post-traumatic stress disorder.** The result of exposure to a very distressing event that elicits feelings of intense terror, fear, or helplessness, post-traumatic stress disorder often results in frequent flashbacks, nightmares, or an exaggerated startle response. Events that may cause this disorder include witnessing a murder, participating in a military battle, or being raped. *Treatment:* Three main psychotherapy treatments are used: stress inoculation, in which the patients learn coping skills to conquer their fears; prolonged exposure, in which the event is talked about repeatedly and thus rendered less threatening; and cognitive processing, in which memories of the event are written about and discussed with the therapist in order to reevaluate the emotions affected by the trauma. Medication is not generally used to treat this disorder except when specific symptoms, such as anxiety or depression, are also present. Self-help and a good support network are also valuable in the healing process.

**Phobias.** A phobic disorder involves the persistent and irrational fear of a specific object, activity, or situation that results in avoidance. Individuals with phobias recognize that their fear is excessive or unreasonable but cannot control the anxiety associated with it. **Specific phobias** usually develop in adolescence or adulthood and affect more than 1 in 10 people. Examples include fear of dogs, water, or flying; some of the most severe types are **agoraphobia** (characterized by a fear of being in open or public places) and **claustrophobia** (fear of confined spaces). The immediate response often resembles a panic attack. *Treatment:* Behavioral approaches are used, including desensitization, in which the patient is gradually exposed to a phobic object or situation, and emotive imagery, in which relaxation techniques help guide the patient through an imagined phobic encounter. **Social phobia** is the fear of social situations in which the individual dreads being criticized or humiliated. *Treatment:* Cognitive-behavioral therapy is widely used; tricyclic antidepressants can be useful in combatting panic attacks.

**Obsessive-compulsive disorder.** This disorder is marked by recurrent obsessions or compulsions that cause extreme distress and interfere with the normal activities of daily life. **Obsessions** are persistent ideas, thoughts, impulses, or images that are experienced as intrusive, senseless, and generally repugnant but which cannot be ignored or suppressed. Common obsessions include thoughts about committing violent acts, worries about contamination, and doubt (as in wondering whether one had turned off the stove before leaving the house). **Compulsions** are repetitive, intentional behaviors performed in a ritualized manner in an attempt to neutralize the obsession and control the anxiety associated with it. Persistent hand washing, counting, or touching are common compulsive behaviors. *Treatment:* Behavioral therapy, including systematic desensitization and flooding techniques, is common. The antidepressant drugs clomipramine (Anafranil), fluoxetine (Prozac), and fluvoxamine (Luvox) are helpful in relieving symptoms for the majority of sufferers.

**Internet resources:** <www.nimh.nih.gov/anxiety/anxietymenu.cfm>

# Autism

Autism is a neurobiological disorder that affects physical, social, and language skills. The term was first used by the psychiatrist Leo Kanner in the 1940s to describe children who appeared to be excessively withdrawn and self-preoccupied. The syndrome usually appears before 2½ years of age. According to the Autism Society of America, the following areas may be affected by autism:

**Social interaction.** Autistic infants generally appear indifferent or averse to affection and physical contact, though attachment to caregivers often develops later. Children are less responsive to eye contact or other social cues. Inappropriate attachment to objects may occur.

**Communication.** Speech develops slowly and abnormally or not at all. It may be characterized by meaningless repetition or strange mechanical sounds.

**Sensory impairment.** There may be underemphasized reaction to sound, no reaction to pain, or no recognition of genuine danger, as well as sensitivities in the areas of sight, touch, hearing, smell, and taste.

**Play.** Autistic children do not play spontaneously, imitate the play of others, or imagine their own games.

**Behaviors.** Usually the syndrome is accompanied by an obsessive desire to prevent environmental change, and frequently, rhythmic body movements such as rocking or hand-clapping. The behavior of children with autism varies greatly, from overactivity to passivity.

About 25% of autistic children develop **seizures** by late adolesence. Some individuals with autism also have other disorders of the brain, including epilepsy, Down syndrome, or mental retardation, or genetic disorders such as Tourette's syndrome, thus making the disease very difficult to diagnose. There are no medical tests for the **diagnosis** of autism, but tests may help rule out other diseases. Initial diagnosis may include a number of different health care professionals, including a psychologist, neurologist, developmental pediatrician, speech and language therapist, learning consultant, or other autism specialist.

The **cause** of autism remains unknown and the disease is incompletely understood. Recent research has revealed abnormalities in the brain structure of autistic individuals, abnormalities likely to have occurred during early brain development. Researchers also have noted a deficiency of large nerve cells called Purkinje cells and an excess of serotonin. There appears to be a complex genetic component as well. Since the early 1990s the global rate of autism has increased greatly; researchers speculate that over-vaccination has contributed to this disturbing rise.

**Treatment** of autism centers on helping the patient, as well as caregivers, to understand and cope with the disorder. Whereas most sufferers were previously institutionalized, children and adults with autism are now living more independently and becoming integrated into mainstream society. Some autistic individuals display remarkable talents, such as enhanced musical or mathematical prowess. Currently, there is no prescribed medical regime for autistic individuals.

# Depression

Clinical depression usually involves one or more of the following symptoms consistently for at least a two-week period: feelings of sadness, hopelessness, or pessimism; lowered self-esteem and heightened self-depreciation; a decrease or loss of ability to enjoy daily life; reduced energy and vitality; slowness of thought or action; loss of appetite; suicidal ideation; and disturbed sleep or insomnia. Depression differs from simple grief or mourning, which are appropriate emotional responses to the loss of loved persons or objects. Where there are clear grounds for a person's unhappiness, depression is considered to be present if the depressed mood is disproportionately long or severe.

Depression is probably the most common psychiatric complaint; the rate of incidence increases with age in men, while the peak for women is between the ages of 35 and 45 (women in general suffer from depression more often than men). Most professionals now agree that biological, social, and psychological factors all contribute to depression. The chief biochemical cause seems to be the defective regulation of the release of one or more naturally occurring monoamines in the brain, particularly norepinephrine and serotonin. Reduced quantities or reduced activity of these chemicals is linked to depression.

**Treatment** of depression has been a controversial topic in recent years as new drugs have been approved by the Food and Drug Administration. Many types of psychotherapy, both individual and group, are used to treat depressed patients; the medications most often prescribed are selective serotonin reuptake inhibitors (SSRIs), which regulate serotonin. A combination of psychotherapy and medication is generally the preferred choice for treatment. Hospitalization may be necessary if a patient is contemplating **suicide**. Although most depressed individuals are only mildly suicidal, poorly monitored administration of medications may actually increase the risk of suicide. The energizing effects of an anti-depressant can empower patients to act on suicidal thoughts, whereas they previously lacked the energy or will to do so; an inadequate or incomplete trial of a medication has also been correlated with increased suicide rates. An alternate or complementary approach to the treatment of depression involves the use of self-help techniques, including depression-oriented support groups.

**Internet resources:** <www.nimh.nih.gov/publicat/depressionmenu.cfm>

# Bipolar Disorder

Bipolar disorder, or **manic-depression**, is characterized by alternating periods of extreme moods, from excessive irritability or elation (manic state) to despondency or severe tension (depressed state), often with periods of normal mood in between. The frequency and duration of this cycling of moods varies between individuals but usually begins in adolescence or early adulthood. Bipolar disorder may also feature such psychotic symptoms as delusions and hallucinations. **Depression** is the more common symptom, and many patients never develop a genuine manic phase, although they may experience a brief period of overoptimism and mild euphoria while recovering from a depression. Patients in a manic state are highly sociable, gregarious, and optimistic and have grandiose notions and an inflated sense of self-esteem.

At any given time, at least two million Americans suffer from bipolar disorder. The first manic episode may be caused by some external stress the patient has experienced, but ensuing cycles are beyond control. Statistical studies have suggested a hereditary predisposition to the disorder, and this has now been linked to a defect on a dominant gene located on chromosome 11. In a physiological sense, it is believed that bipolar disorder is caused by the faulty regulation of one or more amines at sites in the brain where the transmission of nerve impulses takes place; a deficiency of the amines results in depression, and an excess of them causes mania. However, there is no single known cause for the disorder, and the best **treatment** involves individual or group therapy and medication. The two complement one another, as follow-up care can help ensure medical compliance, often an issue for manic-depressive patients: one of the main causes of a return of the disorder is the patient's discontinuance of medication. **Lithium** is the drug of choice and is generally prescribed long-term. However, if a patient first presents in a depressive state, appropriate antidepressants may be used initially. If left untreated, the disease worsens and the patient eventually experiences full-fledged mania and clinical depression. With proper treatment, people with bipolar disorder can lead productive, functional lives.

## Eating Disorders

Eating disorders are characterized by an unhealthy relationship with food in which normal eating habits are disrupted or polarized. They most often afflict women in adolescence or early adulthood and are linked to low self-esteem and poor body image rather than any biomedical cause. The main eating disorders are:

**Anorexia nervosa.** The most defining feature of anorexia is starvation, accompanied by the patients' misperception that they are actually overweight. Emotional manifestations may range from a neurotic overreaction to a weight-reduction diet to full-blown schizophrenic delusions resulting in the abhorrence of food. As with bulimia, **binging** (extreme overindulgence in food) may be part of this destructive eating cycle. These patterns are related to a preoccupation with self-control through starvation, and loss of that control leads to shame and self-loathing. Sufferers are often able to maintain their strength and daily activities at approximately normal levels; they appear characteristically unconcerned with their undernourished state. Associated symptoms include vomiting and, in women, failure to menstruate. *Treatment:* A complete medical examination is needed to assess any possible physical damage done during the course of the disease. In severe cases hospitalization may be necessary. Since people suffering from anorexia often rationalize their behavior, they may be unwilling to seek help. A trusting relationship with a therapist is key, though patients may relapse during the course of treatment. Group therapy may also prove useful. Often, specific childhood trauma triggers the patient's negative self-image; exploring these issues may help reach the goal of an improved self-evaluation. Medications, particularly anti-depressants, may be prescribed.

**Bulimia nervosa.** Bulimia is characterized by periods of **binging** followed by **purging** via one or more of the following: self-induced vomiting, unnecessary ingestion of laxatives, or exercising too much. Binging is often done in secret and is followed by a shame and self-loathing similar to that experienced by anorexic individuals, which results in the subsequent purging. Although sufferers are also obsessed with body image, unlike anorexic patients the majority are close to their proper weight. If left untreated, bulimia can result in serious medical complications, such as dental decay, stomach rupture, and dehydration, and can also be fatal. *Treatment:* Like anorexia, a prominent feature of bulimia is a negative self-image, and treatment options are the same. Since bulimic patients may purge medication, careful monitoring is necessary.

A new diagnostic category, **binge-eating disorder**, was recently classified as a medical condition. Patients with this disorder also overindulge in food but do not follow the cycle of purging.

## Personality Disorders

Personality disorders are marked by deeply ingrained and lasting patterns of inflexible, maladaptive, or antisocial behavior. A personality disorder is an accentuation of one or more personality traits. It need not disrupt a person's daily functioning, but in times of extreme stress symptoms increase and may interfere with psychological and emotional functioning. Individuals with personality disorders generally have difficulty with interpersonal relationships, range of emotion, self-perception, and impulse control. There are many different types of personality disorders, classified below according to the **DSM-IV**. All manifest themselves by early adulthood.

**Antisocial personality disorder.** Individuals follow a pattern of behavior that disregards and often violates the rights of others, including at least three of the following symptoms: failure to conform to social norms and the law (frequent arrests are common); deceitfulness, including lying, using aliases, and deceiving others for profit; impulsivity (failure to plan ahead); irritability and aggressiveness (physical fights); reckless disregard for individual's own safety or the safety of others; consistent irresponsibility, including failure to sustain work or be financially responsible; and a lack of remorse concerning mistreatment of others. *Treatment:* Psychotherapy is the usual treatment, with medication being used to help with mood swings or other specific problems. Many individuals will be mandated to therapy by the court, though not all people who commit crimes can be classified as having antisocial personality disorder, and thorough psychological testing is needed. Proper therapy may help individuals realize greater emotional depth. Group therapy centered around the disorder may also be useful in exploring these issues and establishing relationships.

**Avoidant personality disorder.** This disorder involves extreme social inhibition, hypersensitivity, and feelings of inadequacy. Four or more of the following symptoms must be present: avoidance of occupational activities involving significant interpersonal contact; unwillingness to become involved with people socially unless certain of being accepted; restraint within intimate relationships; preoccupation with social criticism or rejection; inhibition in new interpersonal situations; negative self-perception (views self as inferior and unappealing to others); and a reluctance to take risks or participate in new activities due to fear of embarrassment. *Treatment:* Short-term individual psychotherapy is the preferred treatment, though some patients may attend group therapy later in the process. Medication is not useful unless there is a concurrent disorder that requires it.

**Borderline personality disorder.** Individuals with this disorder experience unstable interpersonal relationships, self-image, and emotions and display impulsive behaviors. These problems are present in social, familial, and occupational settings. Five or more of the following are necessary for diagnosis: frantic efforts to avoid real or imagined abandonment; a pattern of unstable but intense interpersonal relationships characterized by alternating idealization and devaluation (a person is either "good" or "bad"); identity disturbance (unstable self-image); impulsivity in at least two areas that are potentially self-damaging (including spending, substance abuse, reckless driving, binge eating, and sexual activity); recurrent suicidal behavior or threats, or self-mutilation; emotional instability owing to a marked reactivity of mood (intense episodic irritability or anxiety usually lasting a few hours); long-term feelings of emptiness; inappropriate, intense anger and lack of control over this emotion; and transient, stress-related paranoia or severe dissociative symptoms. *Treatment:* People with this disorder are notoriously difficult to treat, as they place a considerable emotional burden on a therapist. Fairly long-term psychotherapy is the preferred treatment, and the use of medication is controversial. Suicidal feelings may require hospitalization and should always be evaulated by the therapist. A popular new treatment called dialectical behavior therapy teaches patients how to better control their emotions and lives through regulation and self-knowledge.

**Dependent personality disorder.** This disorder is characterized by a fear of separation or abandonment and manifests itself in submissive and clinging behavior. Five or more of the following symptoms are present: difficulty making everyday decisions; the need for others to assume responsibility over the patient's life; difficulty expressing disagreement; difficulty initiating projects or doing things alone; going to excessive lengths to garner other's support; discomfort or helplessness when left alone; need to seek a new relationship as soon as a close relationship ends; and fears of being left to care for oneself. *Treatment:* Psychotherapy is preferred, though the relationship between therapist and patient is often a delicate one given the latter's need for constant reassurance and support. Long-term therapy is generally not recommended, and ending therapy may be an indication of how well the patient has progressed. Assertiveness training and group therapy later in treatment may also be useful. Medication is generally avoided, as drug abuse and overdose are common in individuals with this disorder.

**Histrionic personality disorder.** Individuals exhibit excessive emotionality and seek attention. Five or more of the following symptoms are present: discomfort in situations in which the individual is not the center of attention; interaction with others that is often characterized by sexually seductive behavior; rapidly shifting emotions that appear shallow; use of physical appearance to draw attention; excessively impressionistic speech that lacks detail; self-dramatization, theatricality, and exaggerated emotional expression; suggestibility (easily influenced by criticism); and relationships that the individual deems more intimate than they actually are. *Treatment:* Individual psychotherapy is preferred, as group therapy may exacerbate the patients' needs to dramatize and draw attention to themselves. Boundary issues between therapist and client are key, and solution-focused treatment dedicated to helping the individual view social interactions objectively is usually helpful. Medication is generally prescribed with great caution, as suicidal behavior is common.

**Narcissistic personality disorder.** This disorder is characterized by a pattern of grandiosity, the need for admiration, and a lack of empathy; patients manifest five or more of the following symptoms: grandiose sense of self-importance; preoccupation with fantasies of unlimited success, power, brilliance, beauty, or ideal love; belief that they are unique and can only associate with or be understood by others who are equally special; need for excessive admiration; sense of entitlement (unreasonable expectations of favorable treatment or compliance with wishes); exploitation of interpersonal relationships; difficulty identifying with others' needs and a lack of empathy; envy of others or the belief that others envy them; and arrogance or haughtiness. *Treatment:* Frequently, patients with narcissistic personality disorder are hospitalized. Individual therapists will often be devalued by clients in an attempt to gain dominance and maintain their fragile sense of grandeur. In extreme cases, treatment may be symptom-oriented; less-resistant patients often are taught how to acknowledge the needs and ideas of others while maintaining a healthier sense of self (this goal may be aided by group therapy).

**Obsessive-compulsive personality disorder.** Defined as a pervasive preoccupation with orderliness, perfectionism, and mental and interpersonal control, individuals with this disorder engage in behaviors even when they impair flexibility, openness, and efficiency. Four or more of the following symptoms are present: preoccupation with details, rules, lists, order, organization, or schedules; perfectionism that interferes with task completion; excessive devotion to work and productivity (to the exclusion of leisure activities); inflexibility about morals, ethics, or values to the point of being overly scrupulous or conscientious; inability to discard worn-out objects; reluctance to delegate authority or to work with others; hoarding of money; and rigidity and stubbornness. *Treatment:* Psychotherapy is often focused on short-term symptom relief and coping mechanisms, as well as helping the patient identify and realize more complex emotions. Patients are usually resistent to long-term therapy with the goal of personality change. Group therapy and medication are not often used, though newer medications such as Prozac may provide some relief.

**Paranoid personality disorder.** Persons with this disorder are distrustful and suspicious of others and interpret others' motives as malevolent. Four or more of the following symptoms are present: suspicion that others are exploiting, harming, or deceiving them (without sufficient cause); preoccupation with the trustworthiness or loyalty of friends or associates; reluctance to confide in others (with the fear that this information will be used against them); misinterpretation of benign remarks or events; persistance in bearing a grudge; perception of character attacks that do not exist; and suspicions regarding the fidelity of a sexual partner. *Treatment:* Paranoid personality disorder is very difficult to treat, as individuals with this disorder rarely seek help and usually suffer from it their whole lives. There has been no substantive work done to determine a course of treatment, but a straightforward, trusting relationship with a therapist may prove promising. Clients often view medication with suspicion, and there is no specific drug used to treat this condition.

**Schizoid personality disorder.** A pervasive detachment from social relationships and a restricted range of emotions in interpersonal settings characterize this disorder, which may manifest itself in four or more of the following symptoms: lack of desire to form close relationships; limitation to solitary activities; little interest in sexual experiences; little plea-sure in most activities; no close friends other than immediate relatives; indifference to praise or criticism; and emotional coldness and detachment. *Treatment:* Psychotherapy is usually best kept short-term, with clear and simple goals in mind. Individuals may attempt group therapy following initial treatment. No medication has proven effective for this disorder.

**Schizotypal personality disorder.** Individuals with this disorder exhibit acute discomfort with close relationships as well as cognitive or perceptual distortions and eccentricities of behavior. Five or more of the following symptoms are present: ideas of reference; odd beliefs or magical thinking that influences behavior; unusual perceptual experiences, including bodily illusions; odd thinking and speech; suspiciousness or paranoid ideation; inappropriate or constricted emotions; behavior or appearance that is eccentric; lack of close friends other than immediate relatives; and excessive social anxiety that does not diminish with familiarity and tends to be associated with paranoia. *Treatment:* Psychotherapy usually focuses on developing a supportive, non-threatening relationship with the client as well as social skills training and other behavioral approaches. Group therapy may be appropriate after the initial treatment. Antipsychotic medications may be useful for treating the more acute phases of this disorder.

## Schizophrenia

Schizophrenia refers to any of a group of severe mental disorders that have in common such symptoms as hallucinations, delusions, blunted emotions, disordered thinking, and a withdrawal from reality. The most common psychotic disorder, schizophrenia affects approximately 1% of the world's population; it is estimated that between one third and one half of all homeless Americans have schizophrenia. There is no known cause, but scientists are currently researching possible genetic and hereditary factors (the disorder tends to run in families). There are four main types of this disorder:

**Paranoid type.** This type of schizophrenia usually arises later in life than others and is characterized primarily by delusions of persecution and grandeur combined with unrealistic, illogical thinking, often accompanied by hallucinations.

**Catatonic type.** Characterized by striking motor behavior, patients with this form may remain in a state of almost complete immobility, often assuming statuesque positions. Mutism (the inability to talk), extreme incompliance, and absence of almost all voluntary actions are also common. This state of inactivity is at times preceded or interrupted by episodes of excessive motor activity and excitement, generally of an impulsive, unpredictable nature.

**Disorganized (hebephrenic) type.** Patients display shallow and inappropriate emotional responses, fool-ish or bizarre behavior, disorganized speech, delusions, and hallucinations.

**Undifferentiated type.** The simplest form of schizophrenia, it manifests as an insidious and gradual reduction in external relations and interests. A lack of emotional depth, a simplicity of ideation, a relative absence of mental activity, a progressive lessening in the use of inner resources, and a retreat to simpler or sterotyped behavior is common.

These types are not mutually exclusive, and schizophrenic patients may display a combination of symptoms that defy convenient classification. There may also be a mixture of schizophrenic symptoms with those of other psychoses, notably those of **bipolar disorder**.

**Treatment** always focuses on medication. Unfortunately, patients often relapse after failing to take their medications; therapy, including family therapy, may aid in support and help prevent such a relapse. A combination of antipsychotic, antianxiety, and antidepressant medications are often combined. Newer antipsychotics, which block both serotonin and dopamine receptors, prove promising, as they effectively treat a fuller range of symptoms with fewer side effects.

**Internet resources:** <www.nimh.nih.gov/publicat/schizmenu.cfm>

## Alcohol and Substance Abuse

**Alcoholism.** Simply defined, alcoholism is the excessive and repeated use of alcoholic beverages that causes harm to the drinker; this harm may be physical, mental, social, or economic. It has recently been accepted that alcoholism is a disease, a compulsive behavior out of the user's control akin to other substance abuse problems. Unlike other ad-dictions, however, alcoholics do not need increased doses to produce the desired effect. Although consciousness of the disease is high, the nature and causes of alcoholism remain marginally understood.

Many theories of the **cause** of alcoholism rest on the limited perspectives of specialists in particular disciplines or professions, most of which have their own definitions of the disease. The most comprehensive conceptions recognize that alcoholism may have a genetic or constitutional underlying factor—not a fateful heredity but a predisposition that renders some people more disposed to alcoholism than others. Other factors, such as childhood trauma, may also make a person more vulnerable to addiction. Some evidence links alcoholism to other mental illness and hypothesizes that alcohol intake is a form of self-medicating behavior that masks a different condition, such as depression or anxiety.

Because of the lack of a precise definition, it is difficult to rely on statistics regarding alcoholism. However, in the US rates are generally higher in urban and industrialized areas and among men, and alcoholism is certainly in the front rank of public-health problems. Suicide rates are 2.5 times higher; accidental death rates are seven times higher; and there is an enormously higher rate of general morbidity among alcoholics.

**Treatment** may be physiological (with drugs that cause vomiting and a feeling of panic when alcohol is consumed); psychological (with therapy and rehabilitation); or social (group therapy). These may take place in or out of an institutional setting, though there is a growing trend in the US toward detoxification centers. Suddenly stopping heavy drinking can lead to **withdrawal** symptoms, including delirium tremens. Many professionals recommend a variety of treatments pursued simultaneously, and even clients in individual therapy are encouraged to attend Alcoholics Anonymous (AA) meetings. AA was founded in 1935 and is based on Twelve Steps, a nonsectarian spiritual program the central points of which are reliance on God or a higher power as each individual understands that concept and the value of help to other alcoholics. AA is thought by many to be the single most successful method yet devised for coping with alcoholism.

**Substance abuse.** Abused substances include anabolic steroids, which are used by some athletes to enhance performance, and psychotropic agents, substances that affect the user's mental state and are mood- and perception-altering. The latter category, which has a much longer history of abuse, includes opium (and the derivative heroin), hallucinogens, barbiturates, cocaine, amphetamines, tranquilizers, and cannabis (alcohol is also often included in this group). Dependence on prescribed drugs is increasingly common, particularly with tranquilizers and hypnotics. Ecstasy abuse and solvent abuse became increasingly popular among young people in the late 1990s.

Like alcoholics, individuals addicted to drugs are compelled to use them despite the deterioration in health, work, or social activities they may cause. This dependence varies from drug to drug in its extent and effect; it can be physical or psychological or both. Physical dependence becomes apparent only when the drug intake is decreased or stopped and **withdrawal** occurs. Psychological dependence is indicated when the user relies on a drug to produce a feeling of well-being. Another related phenomenon is **tolerance**, a gradual decrease in the effect of a certain dose as the drug is repeatedly taken, causing the user to consume larger doses to produce the desired effect (most marked with habitual opiate users). **Treatment** is similar to that for alcoholism and involves an initial process of detoxification, which should be medically supervised.

**Internet resources:**
<www.niaaa.nih.gov> (alcohol abuse)
<www.samhsa.gov> (substance abuse)

## Suicide

*Suicide prevention hotline: 1-800-SUICIDE; Suicide prevention online: <www.samaritans.org>;*
*Other Internet resources: <www.nimh.nih.gov/publicat/depsuicidemenu.cfm>*

Every year approximately 30,000 Americans commit suicide, making it the 11th leading cause of death in 1999. Suicide has historically been condoned by some groups, including the Brahmans of India and the samurai of Japan. In some countries suicide attempts are punishable by law, but in many there is now a greater readiness to sympathize with rather than condemn suicide, though a tendency to conceal suicidal acts still persists.

Although not classified as a distinct mental disorder, suicide is closely linked to **depression** and **bipolar disorder.** It is estimated that approximately 60% of people who commit suicide have had some form of mood disorder. In younger people, substance abuse often plays a role as well. Early recognition and treatment of mental disorders is thus an important deterrent.

Over half of all suicides occur in men aged 25–65; men are often more deliberate in their suicide intentions, are less likely to confide in someone about their plans, and often use more lethal measures.

Among the **warning signs** of suicide are: suicidal talk, including threats of self-harm; previous suicide attempts; preoccupation with death; signs of depression, including social withdrawal, agitation, and behavioral changes; a recent life crisis, such as divorce or the loss of a loved one; and disposal of possessions. Friends and relatives who suspect a person of suicidal ideation are encouraged to get help from agencies specializing in suicide prevention and to always take seriously the threat of suicide.

**Assisted suicide,** or euthanasia, is currently illegal in the US. The exception is Oregon, where physician-assisted suicide is permitted under tightly controlled conditions. Those in favor of assisted suicide argue that the terminally ill have a right to die with dignity and on their own terms. Many in the medical profession oppose physician-assisted suicide on ethical grounds, as health care workers are bound to prevent injury, even if it is self-induced. Others note that depression, and thus suicidal ideation, is a natural response to a debilitating disease.

## Incidence of Suicide in the US, 1900–2000

*Age-adjusted rates per 100,000 population. Figures based on death registration data.*
*Courtesy of National Center for Injury Prevention and Control.*

| YEAR | MALE | FEMALE | TOTAL | YEAR | MALE | FEMALE | TOTAL |
|------|------|--------|-------|------|------|--------|-------|
| 1900 | 17.7 | 5.0 | 11.3 | 1954 | 16.3 | 4.1 | 10.1 |
| 1906 | 22.0 | 6.2 | 14.3 | 1960 | 16.5 | 4.9 | 10.6 |
| 1912 | 26.0 | 7.9 | 17.3 | 1966 | 16.1 | 5.9 | 10.9 |
| 1918 | 20.0 | 6.9 | 13.6 | 1972 | 17.4 | 6.7 | 11.9 |
| 1924 | 20.2 | 6.2 | 13.4 | 1978 | 18.7 | 6.2 | 12.3 |
| 1930 | 26.2 | 7.4 | 17.0 | 1984 | 18.6 | 5.2 | 11.6 |
| 1936 | 22.4 | 7.0 | 14.8 | 1990 | 19.0 | 4.5 | 11.5 |
| 1942 | 18.0 | 5.8 | 11.8 | 1996 | 18.0 | 4.1 | 10.8 |
| 1948 | 16.7 | 5.1 | 10.8 | 2000 | 18.1 | 4.0 | 10.6 |

# Diet and Exercise

## The Food and Drug Administration (FDA)

*The FDA is a division of the US Department of Health and Human Services. FDA Web site: <www.fda.gov>.*

**Mission:** To promote and protect the public health by helping safe and effective products reach the market in a timely way and monitoring products for continued safety after they are in use. **Location:** Rockville, MD. **Commissioner of Food and Drugs:** Mark B. McClellan. **Budget:** FY 2004 (requested) $1.4 billion. **Functions:** The FDA is the agency of the US federal government authorized by Congress to inspect, test, approve, and set safety standards for foods and food additives, drugs, chemicals, cosmetics, and household and medical devices. Generally, the FDA is empowered to prevent untested products from being sold and to take legal action to halt sale of undoubtedly harmful products or of products which involve a health or safety risk. Through court procedure, the FDA can seize products and prosecute the persons or firms responsible for legal violation. FDA authority is limited to interstate commerce. The agency cannot control prices nor directly regulate advertising except of prescription drugs and medical devices.

## Vitamins, with Daily Recommendations

Vitamins are organic substances that are usually divided into two types: water-soluble and fat-soluble. Small quantities are necessary for normal health and growth in higher forms of animal life, as they work to regulate reactions that occur in metabolism (in contrast to macronutrients such as fats, carbohydrates, and proteins, which are the compounds utilized in the reactions regulated by vitamins). Absence of a vitamin blocks one or more specific metabolic reactions in a cell; thus, vitamin deficiency may result in specific diseases. As they generally cannot be synthesized by humans, vitamins must be obtained from the diet or from a synthetic source.

The name of each vitamin is followed by its alternative name and usual pharmaceutical preparation, respectively. Amounts shown indicate recommended daily consumption.

Abbreviations—mg: milligram; mcg: microgram; RE: retinol equivalent; IU: international unit

### Water-soluble vitamins

**Thiamin** (vitamin $B_1$; thiamine hydrochloride)
  **Purpose:** energy metabolism and initiation of nerve impulses. **Dietary sources:** pork, nuts, peas. **Men over 14:** 1.2 mg; **women over 18:** 1.1 mg; **pregnant women:** 1.4 mg; **lactating women:** 1.5 mg.

**Riboflavin** (vitamin $B_2$; riboflavin)
  **Purpose:** release of energy from carbohydrates, fats, and proteins; maintaining integrity of red blood cells. **Dietary sources:** milk, eggs, kidney, liver, peas, soybeans, leafy vegetables. **Men over 14:** 1.3 mg; **women over 18:** 1.0 mg; **pregnant women:** 1.4 mg; **lactating women:** 1.6 mg.

**Niacin** (nicotonic acid; nicotinamide; nicotinamide)
  **Purpose:** release of energy from carbohydrates and fats; red blood cell formation; metabolism of proteins. **Dietary sources:** cereal grains, nuts, green vegetables, liver, kidney. **Men over 14:** 16.0 mg; **women over 18:** 14.0 mg; **pregnant women:** 18.0 mg; **lactating women:** 17.0 mg.

**Vitamin $B_6$** (pyroxidine; pyroxidine hydrochloride)
  **Purpose:** amino acid, carbohydrate, and fat metabolism. **Dietary sources:** bananas, cereal grains, fish, nuts, spinach. **Men 14–50:** 1.3 mg; **men over 50:** 1.7 mg; **women 19–50:** 1.3 mg; **women over 50:** 1.5 mg; **pregnant women:** 1.9 mg; **lactating women:** 2.0 mg.

**Pantothenic acid** (vitamin $B_5$; calcium pantothenate)
  **Purpose:** metabolism of carbohydrates; synthesis and degradation of fats; synthesis of sterols and other compounds. **Dietary sources:** liver, kidney, eggs, avocados, bananas. **All adults:** 4.0–7.0 mg.

# Vitamins, with Daily Recommendations (continued)

## Water-soluble vitamins (continued)

**Biotin** (N/A; biotin)
    **Purpose:** carbohydrate and fat metabolism. **Dietary sources:** beef liver, yeast, oatmeal. **All adults:** 0.3 mg.

**Folate** (folacin; vitamin $B_9$; folic acid)
    **Purpose:** cellular metabolism, including synthesis of DNA components; normal red blood cell formation. **Dietary sources:** chicken, liver, green leafy vegetables, wheat bran and germ, citrus fruits, cereals, beans, asparagus. **Adults over 13:** 400 mcg; **pregnant women:** 600 mcg; **lactating women:** 500 mcg.

**Vitamin $B_{12}$** (cobalamin; cyanocobalamin; hydroxocobalamin)
    **Purpose:** proper functioning of many enzymes involved in carbohydrate, fat, and protein metabolism; synthesis of the insulating sheath around nerve cells; cell reproduction and normal growth; red blood cell formation. **Dietary sources:** eggs, meat, milk, nutritional yeast, fortified cereals. **Adults:** 2.4 mcg; **pregnant women:** 2.6 mcg; **lactating women:** 2.8 mcg.

**Vitamin C** (ascorbic acid; ascorbic acid)
    **Purpose:** prevention of oxidative damage to DNA, membrane lipids, and proteins; synthesis of collagen, hormones, transmitters of the nervous sytem, lipids, and proteins; proper immune function. **Dietary sources:** citrus fruits, green peppers, broccoli, cantaloupe, green leafy vegetables. **Adults over 14:** 60 mg; **pregnant women:** 70 mg; **lactating women** (first 6 months): 95 mg; (second 6 months): 90 mg.

## Fat-soluble vitamins

**Vitamin A** (retinol; retinol)
    **Purpose:** functioning of the retina; growth and maturation of epithelial cells; growth of bone; reproduction and embryonic development. **Dietary sources:** fish and fish-liver oils, liver, butter, orange vegetables and fruits, dark green leafy vegetables; tomatoes. **Men over 10:** 1000 RE; **women over 10:** 800 RE; **pregnant women:** 800 RE; **lactating women** (first 6 months): 1300 RE; (second 6 months): 1200 RE.

**Vitamin D** (vitamins $D_2$ and $D_3$; [ergo] calciferol)
    **Purpose:** promotes formation of bone by increasing the blood levels of calcium and phosphorus. **Dietary sources:** fish-liver oils, eggs, milk enriched with Vitamin D. **All adults:** 400 IU.

**Vitamin E** (N/A; tocopherol)
    **Purpose:** protection of cell membranes and prevention of damage to membrane-associated enzymes. **Dietary sources:** nuts, vegetable oils, margarine, cereal grains. **Men over 10:** 15 IU. **women over 10:** 12 IU; **pregnant women:** 15 IU; **lactating women** (first 6 months): 18 IU; (second 6 months): 16.5 IU.

**Vitamin K** (N/A; vitamin $K_1$)
    **Purpose:** formation of several blood clotting factors. **Dietary sources:** green leafy vegetables, vegetable oils. *No recommended daily allowance.*

## Food Guide Pyramid

The USDA recommends following the food guide pyramid as a way of maintaining a healthful diet. It is designed to help you get the proper nutrients while at the same time consuming the amount of calories necessary to maintain a healthy weight. It is important to choose a diet that is low in saturated fat and cholesterol and moderate in total fat. You should eat at least the lower number of servings from the five food groups and pick the lowest fat choices from each.

Serving amounts given are for a single day. Typical serving sizes are:

**Bread, Cereal, Rice, and Pasta Group:** 1 slice bread; 1 oz cereal; ½ cup rice or pasta.

**Vegetable Group:** 1 cup raw leafy vegetables; ½ cup other vegetables; ¾ cup vegetable juice.

**Fruit Group:** 1 medium apple, banana, or orange; ½ cup chopped, cooked, or canned fruit; ¾ cup fruit juice.

**Milk, Yogurt, and Cheese Group:** 1 cup milk or yogurt; 1 ½ oz natural cheese; 2 oz processed cheese.

**Fish, Meat, Poultry, Dry Beans, Eggs, and Nuts Group:** 2–3 oz cooked lean meat, poultry, or fish; ½ cup cooked dry beans; 1 egg; 2 tablespoons peanut butter.

No specific serving is recommended for the Fats, Oils, and Sweets Group, but you should use these only sparingly. Remember to count a larger portion as more than one serving—a typical restaurant serving of pasta, for example, would count as 2–3 servings on the pyramid.

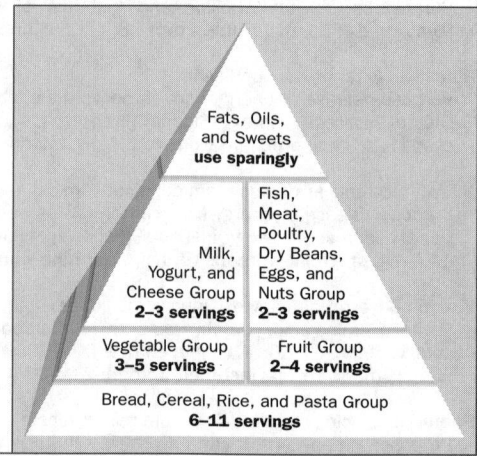

Fats, Oils, and Sweets
**use sparingly**

Fish, Meat, Poultry, Dry Beans, Eggs, and Nuts Group
**2–3 servings**

Milk, Yogurt, and Cheese Group
**2–3 servings**

Vegetable Group
**3–5 servings**

Fruit Group
**2–4 servings**

Bread, Cereal, Rice, and Pasta Group
**6–11 servings**

Source: USDA.

## Fat Intake in US Diet

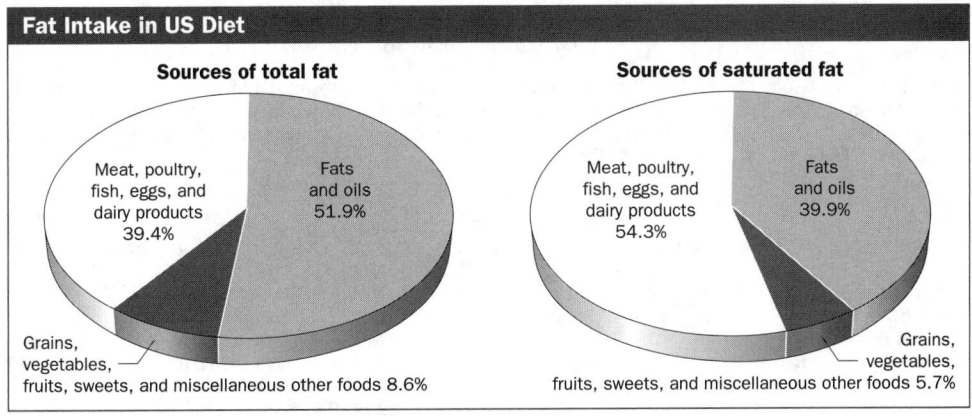

### Sources of total fat

Meat, poultry, fish, eggs, and dairy products 39.4%

Fats and oils 51.9%

Grains, vegetables, fruits, sweets, and miscellaneous other foods 8.6%

### Sources of saturated fat

Meat, poultry, fish, eggs, and dairy products 54.3%

Fats and oils 39.9%

Grains, vegetables, fruits, sweets, and miscellaneous other foods 5.7%

## US, Annual Per Capita Food Consumption (in pounds)

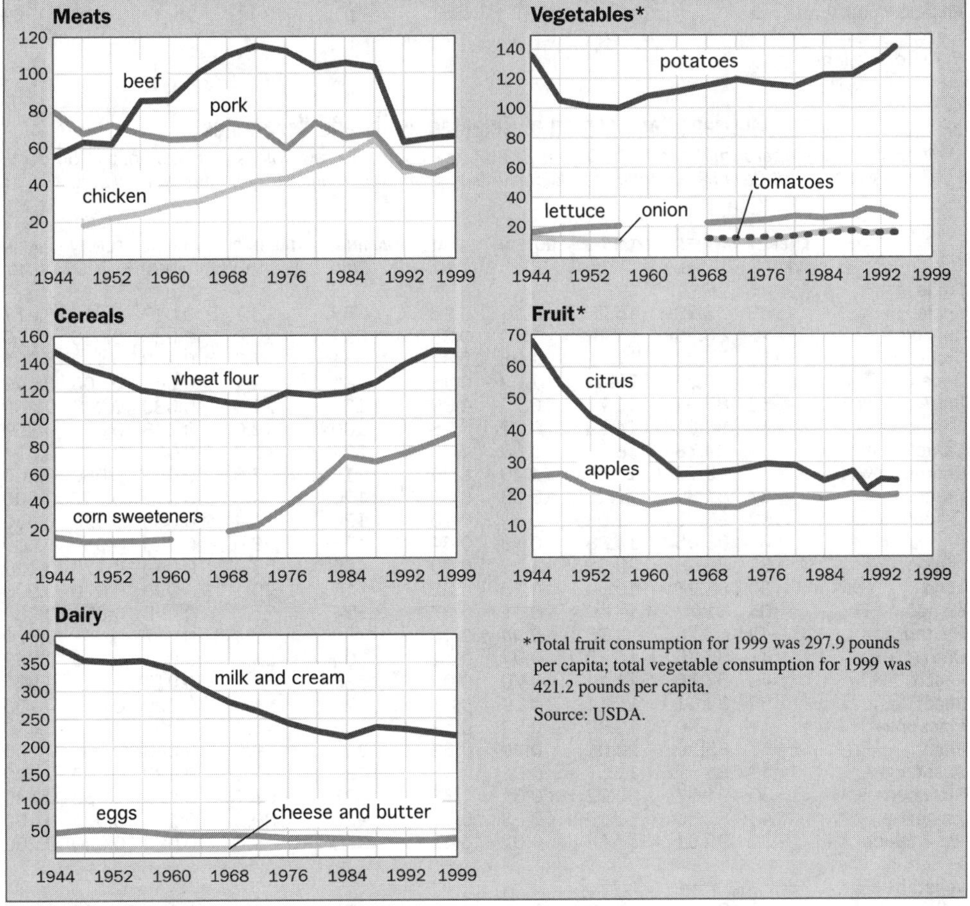

### Meats

beef
pork
chicken

(y-axis: 120, 100, 80, 60, 40, 20)
(x-axis: 1944, 1952, 1960, 1968, 1976, 1984, 1992, 1999)

### Vegetables*

potatoes
tomatoes
lettuce    onion

(y-axis: 140, 120, 100, 80, 60, 40, 20)
(x-axis: 1944, 1952, 1960, 1968, 1976, 1984, 1992, 1999)

### Cereals

wheat flour
corn sweeteners

(y-axis: 160, 140, 120, 100, 80, 60, 40, 20)
(x-axis: 1944, 1952, 1960, 1968, 1976, 1984, 1992, 1999)

### Fruit*

citrus
apples

(y-axis: 70, 60, 50, 40, 30, 20, 10)
(x-axis: 1944, 1952, 1960, 1968, 1976, 1984, 1992, 1999)

### Dairy

milk and cream
eggs    cheese and butter

(y-axis: 400, 350, 300, 250, 200, 150, 100, 50)
(x-axis: 1944, 1952, 1960, 1968, 1976, 1984, 1992, 1999)

*Total fruit consumption for 1999 was 297.9 pounds per capita; total vegetable consumption for 1999 was 421.2 pounds per capita.

Source: USDA.

## Individuals Meeting Dietary Guidelines
### 1977–78 and 1994–96.

Percentages of US population that meet or exceed the minimum dietary guidelines given in Nutrition and Your Health: Dietary Guidelines for Americans, 5th edition (2000), a joint publication of the departments of Health and Human Services and Agriculture. To view the complete publication or to order a print copy, visit <www.health.gov/dietaryguidelines>.

| AGE AND GENDER | CALORIES | TOTAL FAT | SATURA-TED FAT | CHOL-ESTEROL | SODIUM | FIBER | CALCIUM | IRON |
|---|---|---|---|---|---|---|---|---|
| | | | | **1977–78** | | | | |
| Children (2–17) | 33 | 14 | N/A | N/A | N/A | N/A | 37 | 39 |
| Adults (18 and over) | 23 | 13 | N/A | N/A | N/A | N/A | 15 | 43 |
| Males 60 and over | 29 | 12 | N/A | N/A | N/A | N/A | 11 | 66 |
| Females 60 and over | 18 | 17 | N/A | N/A | N/A | N/A | 4 | 40 |
| **All individuals 2 and over** | **26** | **13** | **N/A** | **N/A** | **N/A** | **N/A** | **22** | **42** |
| | | | | **1994–96** | | | | |
| AGE AND GENDER | | | | | | | | |
| Children (2–17) | 38 | 37 | 31 | 77 | 39 | 39 | 37 | 59 |
| Adults (18 and over) | 27 | 37 | 43 | 69 | 34 | 20 | 21 | 60 |
| Males 60 and over | 28 | 36 | 43 | 65 | 30 | 26 | 16 | 77 |
| Females 60 and over | 18 | 41 | 49 | 79 | 54 | 35 | 6 | 56 |
| **All individuals 2 and over** | **30** | **37** | **40** | **71** | **35** | **25** | **25** | **59** |

N/A: Not available

## Nutrient Composition of Selected Fruits and Vegetables

*Values shown are approximations for 100 grams (3.57 oz.). Foods are raw unless otherwise noted. Source: USDA Nutrient Data Laboratory. kcal: kilocalorie; g: gram; mg: milligram; IU: international unit.*

| | ENERGY (KCAL) | WATER (G) | CARBO-HYDRATE (G) | PROTEIN (G) | FAT (G) | VITAMIN A (IU) | VITAMIN C (MG) | THIAMINE (MG) | RIBO-FLAVIN (MG) | NIACIN (MG) |
|---|---|---|---|---|---|---|---|---|---|---|
| **Fruits** | | | | | | | | | | |
| Apple | 59 | 83.93 | 15.25 | 0.19 | 0.36 | 53 | 5.7 | 0.017 | 0.014 | 0.077 |
| Apricot | 48 | 86.35 | 11.12 | 1.40 | 0.39 | 2,612 | 10.0 | 0.030 | 0.040 | 0.600 |
| Avocado | 161 | 74.27 | 7.39 | 1.98 | 15.32 | 61 | 7.9 | 0.108 | 0.122 | 1.921 |
| Banana | 92 | 74.26 | 23.43 | 1.03 | 0.48 | 81 | 9.1 | 0.045 | 0.100 | 0.540 |
| Blackberries | 52 | 85.64 | 12.76 | 0.72 | 0.39 | 165 | 21.0 | 0.030 | 0.040 | 0.400 |
| Blueberries | 56 | 84.61 | 14.13 | 0.67 | 0.38 | 100 | 13.0 | 0.048 | 0.050 | 0.359 |
| Cantaloupe | 35 | 89.78 | 8.36 | 0.88 | 0.28 | 3,224 | 42.2 | 0.036 | 0.021 | 0.574 |
| Cherries (sweet) | 72 | 80.76 | 16.55 | 1.20 | 0.96 | 214 | 7.0 | 0.050 | 0.060 | 0.400 |
| Grapes | 67 | 81.30 | 17.15 | 0.63 | 0.35 | 100 | 4.0 | 0.092 | 0.057 | 0.300 |
| Grapefruit | 32 | 90.89 | 8.08 | 0.63 | 0.10 | 124 | 34.4 | 0.036 | 0.020 | 0.250 |
| Kiwi | 61 | 83.05 | 14.88 | 0.99 | 0.44 | 175 | 98.0 | 0.020 | 0.050 | 0.500 |
| Lemon | 29 | 88.98 | 9.32 | 1.10 | 0.30 | 29 | 53.0 | 0.040 | 0.020 | 0.100 |
| Lime | 30 | 88.26 | 10.54 | 0.70 | 0.20 | 10 | 29.1 | 0.030 | 0.020 | 0.200 |
| Mango | 65 | 81.71 | 17.00 | 0.51 | 0.27 | 3,894 | 27.7 | 0.058 | 0.057 | 0.584 |
| Nectarine | 49 | 86.28 | 11.78 | 0.94 | 0.46 | 736 | 5.4 | 0.017 | 0.041 | 0.990 |
| Orange | 47 | 86.75 | 11.75 | 0.94 | 0.12 | 205 | 53.2 | 0.087 | 0.040 | 0.282 |
| Peach | 43 | 87.66 | 11.10 | 0.70 | 0.09 | 535 | 6.6 | 0.017 | 0.041 | 0.990 |
| Pear | 59 | 83.81 | 15.11 | 0.39 | 0.40 | 20 | 4.0 | 0.020 | 0.040 | 0.100 |
| Pineapple | 49 | 86.50 | 12.39 | 0.39 | 0.43 | 23 | 15.4 | 0.092 | 0.036 | 0.420 |
| Plum | 55 | 85.20 | 13.01 | 0.79 | 0.62 | 323 | 9.5 | 0.043 | 0.096 | 0.500 |
| Raspberries | 49 | 86.57 | 11.57 | 0.91 | 0.55 | 130 | 25.0 | 0.030 | 0.090 | 0.900 |
| Strawberries | 30 | 91.57 | 7.02 | 0.61 | 0.37 | 27 | 56.7 | 0.020 | 0.066 | 0.230 |
| Tangerine | 44 | 87.60 | 11.19 | 0.63 | 0.19 | 920 | 30.8 | 0.105 | 0.022 | 0.160 |
| Watermelon | 32 | 91.51 | 7.18 | 0.62 | 0.43 | 366 | 9.6 | 0.080 | 0.020 | 0.200 |
| **Vegetables** | | | | | | | | | | |
| Artichoke[1] | 50 | 83.97 | 11.18 | 3.48 | 0.16 | 177 | 10.0 | 0.065 | 0.066 | 1.001 |
| Asparagus[1] | 24 | 92.20 | 4.23 | 2.59 | 0.31 | 539 | 10.8 | 0.123 | 0.126 | 1.082 |
| Beans (snap, green) | 31 | 90.27 | 7.14 | 1.82 | 0.12 | 668 | 16.3 | 0.084 | 0.105 | 0.752 |
| Beet | 43 | 87.58 | 9.56 | 1.61 | 0.17 | 38 | 4.9 | 0.031 | 0.040 | 0.334 |
| Broccoli | 28 | 90.69 | 5.24 | 2.98 | 0.35 | 1,542 | 93.2 | 0.065 | 0.119 | 0.638 |
| Brussels sprout | 43 | 86.00 | 8.96 | 3.38 | 0.30 | 883 | 85.0 | 0.139 | 0.090 | 0.745 |
| Cabbage | 25 | 92.15 | 5.43 | 1.44 | 0.27 | 133 | 32.2 | 0.050 | 0.040 | 0.300 |
| Carrot | 43 | 87.79 | 10.14 | 1.03 | 0.19 | 28,129 | 9.3 | 0.097 | 0.059 | 0.928 |
| Cauliflower | 25 | 91.91 | 5.20 | 1.98 | 0.21 | 19 | 46.4 | 0.057 | 0.063 | 0.526 |

## Nutrient Composition of Selected Fruits and Vegetables (continued)

| | ENERGY (KCAL) | WATER (G) | CARBO-HYDRATE (G) | PROTEIN (G) | FAT (G) | VITAMIN A (IU) | VITAMIN C (MG) | THIAMINE (MG) | RIBO-FLAVIN (MG) | NIACIN (MG) |
|---|---|---|---|---|---|---|---|---|---|---|
| **Vegetables (continued)** | | | | | | | | | | |
| Celery | 16 | 94.64 | 3.65 | 0.75 | 0.14 | 134 | 7.0 | 0.046 | 0.045 | 0.323 |
| Collards[1] | 26 | 91.86 | 4.90 | 2.11 | 0.36 | 3,129 | 18.2 | 0.040 | 0.106 | 0.575 |
| Corn (sweet, yellow)[1] | 108 | 69.57 | 25.11 | 3.32 | 1.28 | 217 | 6.2 | 0.215 | 0.072 | 1.614 |
| Cucumber | 13 | 96.01 | 2.76 | 0.69 | 0.13 | 215 | 5.3 | 0.024 | 0.022 | 0.221 |
| Eggplant[1] | 28 | 91.77 | 6.64 | 0.83 | 0.23 | 64 | 1.3 | 0.076 | 0.020 | 0.600 |
| Lettuce (iceberg) | 12 | 95.89 | 2.09 | 1.01 | 0.19 | 330 | 3.9 | 0.046 | 0.030 | 0.187 |
| Mushroom[1] | 27 | 91.08 | 5.14 | 2.17 | 0.47 | 0 | 4.0 | 0.073 | 0.300 | 4.460 |
| Okra[1] | 32 | 89.91 | 7.21 | 1.87 | 0.17 | 575 | 16.3 | 0.132 | 0.055 | 0.871 |
| Onion[1] | 44 | 87.86 | 10.15 | 1.36 | 0.19 | 0 | 5.2 | 0.042 | 0.023 | 0.165 |
| Pepper (sweet, green) | 27 | 92.19 | 6.43 | 0.89 | 0.19 | 632 | 89.3 | 0.066 | 0.030 | 0.509 |
| Pepper (sweet, red) | 27 | 92.19 | 6.43 | 0.89 | 0.19 | 5,700 | 190.0 | 0.066 | 0.030 | 0.509 |
| Potato[2] | 93 | 75.42 | 21.56 | 1.96 | 0.10 | 0 | 12.8 | 0.105 | 0.021 | 1.395 |
| Spinach | 22 | 91.58 | 3.50 | 2.86 | 0.35 | 6,715 | 28.1 | 0.078 | 0.189 | 0.724 |
| Sweet potato[2] | 103 | 72.85 | 24.27 | 1.72 | 0.11 | 21,822 | 24.6 | 0.073 | 0.127 | 0.604 |
| Tomato (red) | 21 | 93.76 | 4.64 | 0.85 | 0.33 | 623 | 19.1 | 0.059 | 0.048 | 0.628 |

[1]Boiled.  [2]Baked.

## Nutritional Value of Selected Foods

*Values shown are approximations.* Source: Home and Garden Bulletin No. 72, *USDA. kcal: kilocalorie; g: gram; mg: milligram; oz: ounce; fl oz: fluid ounce.*

| FOOD | AMOUNT | GRAMS | ENERGY (KCAL) | CARBO-HYDRATE (G) | PROTEIN (G) | TOTAL FAT (G) | SATU-RATED FAT (G) | CALCIUM (MG) | IRON (MG) | SODIUM (MG) |
|---|---|---|---|---|---|---|---|---|---|---|
| **Beverages** | | | | | | | | | | |
| Beer | 12 fl oz | 360 | 150 | 13 | 1 | 0 | 0 | 14 | 0.1 | 18 |
| Cola, regular | 12 fl oz | 369 | 160 | 41 | 0 | 0 | 0 | 11 | 0.2 | 18 |
| Cola, diet (w/aspartame and saccharine) | 12 fl oz | 355 | 0 | 0 | 0 | 0 | 0 | 14 | 0.2 | 32 |
| Coffee, brewed | 6 fl oz | 180 | 0 | 0 | 0 | 0 | 0 | 4 | 0 | 2 |
| Orange juice, canned | 8 fl oz | 249 | 105 | 25 | 1 | 0 | 0 | 20 | 1.1 | 5 |
| Tea, instant, prepared, un-sweetened | 8 fl oz | 241 | 0 | 1 | 0 | 0 | 0 | 1 | 0 | 1 |
| Wine, table, red | 3.5 fl oz | 102 | 75 | 3 | 0 | 0 | 0 | 8 | 0.4 | 5 |
| **Dairy** | | | | | | | | | | |
| Butter, salted | 4 oz | 113 | 810 | 0 | 1 | 92 | 57.1 | 27 | 0.2 | 933 |
| Cheese, American (pasteurized, processed) | 1 oz | 28.35 | 105 | 0 | 6 | 9 | 5.6 | 174 | 0.1 | 406 |
| Cheese, cheddar | 1 oz | 28.35 | 115 | 0 | 7 | 9 | 6 | 204 | 0.2 | 176 |
| Cheese, mozzarella (whole milk) | 1 oz | 28.35 | 80 | 1 | 6 | 6 | 3.7 | 147 | 0.1 | 106 |
| Cheese, swiss | 1 oz | 28.35 | 105 | 1 | 8 | 8 | 5 | 272 | 0 | 74 |
| Cottage cheese, small curd | 8 oz | 210 | 215 | 6 | 26 | 9 | 6 | 126 | 0.3 | 850 |
| Cream cheese | 1 oz | 28.35 | 100 | 1 | 2 | 10 | 6.2 | 23 | 0.3 | 84 |
| Cream, half and half | 0.5 oz | 15 | 20 | 1 | 0 | 2 | 1.1 | 16 | 0 | 6 |
| Cream, sour | 8 oz | 230 | 495 | 10 | 7 | 48 | 30 | 268 | 0.1 | 123 |
| Eggs, cooked, fried | 1 egg | 46 | 90 | 1 | 6 | 7 | 1.9 | 25 | 0.7 | 162 |
| Eggs, cooked, hard-cooked | 1 egg | 50 | 75 | 1 | 6 | 5 | 1.6 | 25 | 0.6 | 62 |
| Eggs, cooked, scrambled | 1 egg | 61 | 100 | 1 | 7 | 7 | 2.2 | 44 | 0.7 | 171 |
| Ice cream, vanilla, 11% fat | 8 oz | 133 | 270 | 32 | 5 | 14 | 8.9 | 176 | 0.1 | 116 |
| Milk, whole, 3.3% fat | 8 oz | 244 | 150 | 11 | 8 | 8 | 5.1 | 291 | 0.1 | 120 |
| Milk, low fat, 2% fat | 8 oz | 244 | 120 | 12 | 8 | 5 | 2.9 | 297 | 0.1 | 122 |
| Milk, skim | 8 oz | 245 | 85 | 12 | 8 | 0 | 0.3 | 302 | 0.1 | 126 |
| Milk, chocolate | 8 oz | 250 | 210 | 26 | 8 | 8 | 5.3 | 280 | 0.6 | 149 |
| Yogurt, plain, low fat | 8 oz | 227 | 145 | 16 | 12 | 4 | 2.3 | 415 | 0.2 | 159 |
| **Fats, oils** | | | | | | | | | | |
| Lard | 0.5 oz | 13 | 115 | 0 | 0 | 13 | 5.1 | 0 | 0 | 0 |
| Margarine, hard, 80% fat | 0.5 oz | 14 | 100 | 0 | 0 | 11 | 2.2 | 4 | 0 | 132 |

# Nutritional Value of Selected Foods (continued)

| FOOD | AMOUNT | GRAMS | ENERGY (KCAL) | CARBO-HYDRATE (G) | PROTEIN (G) | TOTAL FAT (G) | SATU-RATED FAT (G) | CALCIUM (MG) | IRON (MG) | SODIUM (MG) |
|---|---|---|---|---|---|---|---|---|---|---|
| **Fats, oils (continued)** | | | | | | | | | | |
| Olive oil | 0.5 oz | 14 | 125 | 0 | 0 | 14 | 1.9 | 0 | 0 | 0 |
| Vegetable shortening | 0.5 oz | 13 | 115 | 0 | 0 | 13 | 3.3 | 0 | 0 | 0 |
| | | | | | | | | | | |
| **Fish** | | | | | | | | | | |
| Crabmeat, canned | 8 oz | 135 | 135 | 1 | 23 | 3 | 0.5 | 61 | 1.1 | 1350 |
| Fish sticks, frozen | 1 piece | 28 | 70 | 4 | 6 | 3 | 0.8 | 11 | 0.3 | 53 |
| Ocean perch, breaded, fried | 1 piece | 85 | 185 | 7 | 16 | 11 | 2.6 | 31 | 1.2 | 138 |
| Oysters, raw | 8 oz | 240 | 160 | 8 | 20 | 4 | 1.4 | 226 | 15.6 | 175 |
| Salmon, baked, red | 3 oz | 85 | 140 | 0 | 21 | 5 | 1.2 | 26 | 0.5 | 55 |
| Shrimp, fried | 3 oz | 85 | 200 | 11 | 16 | 10 | 2.5 | 61 | 2 | 384 |
| Trout, broiled, w/butter and lemon juice | 3 oz | 85 | 175 | 0 | 21 | 9 | 4.1 | 26 | 1 | 122 |
| Tuna, canned, white, in water | 3 oz | 85 | 135 | 0 | 30 | 1 | 0.3 | 17 | 0.6 | 468 |
| | | | | | | | | | | |
| **Fruits, fruit products** | | | | | | | | | | |
| Apples, peeled, sliced | 8 oz | 110 | 65 | 16 | 0 | 0 | 0.1 | 4 | 0.1 | 0 |
| Applesauce, canned, sweetened | 8 oz | 255 | 195 | 51 | 0 | 0 | 0.1 | 10 | 0.9 | 8 |
| Apricots | 3 apricots | 106 | 50 | 12 | 1 | 0 | 0 | 15 | 0.6 | 1 |
| Bananas | 1 banana | 114 | 105 | 27 | 1 | 1 | 0.2 | 7 | 0.4 | 1 |
| Blackberries | 8 oz | 144 | 75 | 18 | 1 | 1 | 0.2 | 46 | 0.8 | 0 |
| Blueberries | 8 oz | 145 | 80 | 20 | 1 | 1 | 0 | 9 | 0.2 | 9 |
| Grapefruit, pink | ½ grapefruit | 120 | 40 | 10 | 1 | 0 | 0 | 14 | 0.1 | 0 |
| Grapes, European, Thompson | 10 grapes | 50 | 35 | 9 | 0 | 0 | 0.1 | 6 | 0.1 | 1 |
| Oranges | 1 orange | 131 | 60 | 15 | 1 | 0 | 0 | 52 | 0.1 | 0 |
| Peaches | 1 peach | 87 | 35 | 10 | 1 | 0 | 0 | 4 | 0.1 | 0 |
| Pears, Bartlett | 1 pear | 166 | 100 | 25 | 1 | 1 | 0 | 18 | 0.4 | 0 |
| Pineapple, canned, heavy syrup | 8 oz | 255 | 200 | 52 | 1 | 0 | 0 | 36 | 1 | 3 |
| Plums, 2⅛-in. diam. | 1 plum | 66 | 35 | 9 | 1 | 0 | 0 | 3 | 0.1 | 0 |
| Prunes, dried, large | 5 prunes | 49 | 115 | 31 | 1 | 0 | 0 | 25 | 1.2 | 2 |
| Raisins | 8 oz | 145 | 435 | 115 | 5 | 1 | 0.2 | 71 | 3 | 17 |
| Strawberries | 8 oz | 149 | 45 | 10 | 1 | 1 | 0 | 21 | 0.6 | 1 |
| Watermelon | 1 piece | 482 | 155 | 35 | 3 | 2 | 0.3 | 39 | 0.8 | 10 |
| | | | | | | | | | | |
| **Grains** | | | | | | | | | | |
| Bagels, plain | 1 bagel | 68 | 200 | 38 | 7 | 2 | 0.3 | 29 | 1.8 | 245 |
| Bread, rye, light | 1 slice | 25 | 65 | 12 | 2 | 1 | 0.2 | 20 | 0.7 | 175 |
| Bread, wheat | 1 slice | 25 | 65 | 12 | 2 | 1 | 0.2 | 32 | 0.9 | 138 |
| Bread, white | 1 slice | 25 | 65 | 12 | 2 | 1 | 0.3 | 32 | 0.7 | 129 |
| Bread, whole wheat | 1 slice | 28 | 70 | 13 | 3 | 1 | 0.4 | 20 | 1 | 180 |
| Cereal, Cheerios | 1 oz | 28.35 | 110 | 20 | 4 | 2 | 0.3 | 48 | 4.5 | 307 |
| Cereal, Kellogg's Corn Flakes | 1 oz | 28.35 | 110 | 24 | 2 | 0 | 0 | 1 | 1.8 | 351 |
| Cereal, Lucky Charms | 1 oz | 28.35 | 110 | 23 | 3 | 1 | 0.2 | 32 | 4.5 | 201 |
| Cereal, Post Raisin Bran | 1 oz | 28.35 | 85 | 21 | 3 | 1 | 0.1 | 13 | 4.5 | 185 |
| Cake, white, w/white frosting, commercial | 1 piece | 71 | 260 | 42 | 3 | 9 | 2.1 | 33 | 1 | 176 |
| Cheesecake | 1 piece | 92 | 280 | 26 | 5 | 18 | 9.9 | 52 | 0.4 | 204 |
| Chocolate chip cookies, commercial | 4 cookies | 42 | 180 | 28 | 2 | 9 | 2.9 | 13 | 0.8 | 140 |
| Cornmeal, whole-ground, dry | 8 oz | 122 | 435 | 90 | 11 | 5 | 0.5 | 24 | 2.2 | 1 |
| Doughnuts, cake, plain | 1 doughnut | 50 | 210 | 24 | 3 | 12 | 2.8 | 22 | 1 | 192 |
| English muffins, plain | 1 muffin | 57 | 140 | 27 | 5 | 1 | 0.3 | 96 | 1.7 | 378 |
| Oatmeal, instant, cooked, w/salt | 8 oz | 234 | 145 | 25 | 6 | 2 | 0.4 | 19 | 1.6 | 374 |
| Macaroni, cooked, firm | 8 oz | 130 | 190 | 39 | 7 | 1 | 0.1 | 14 | 2.1 | 1 |
| Muffins, blueberry, commercial mix | 1 muffin | 45 | 140 | 22 | 3 | 5 | 1.4 | 15 | 0.9 | 225 |
| Pancakes, plain, commercial mix | 1 pancake | 27 | 60 | 8 | 2 | 2 | 0.5 | 36 | 0.7 | 160 |
| Pie, apple | 1 piece | 158 | 405 | 60 | 3 | 18 | 4.6 | 13 | 1.6 | 476 |

## Nutritional Value of Selected Foods (continued)

| FOOD | AMOUNT | GRAMS | ENERGY (KCAL) | CARBO-HYDRATE (G) | PROTEIN (G) | TOTAL FAT (G) | SATU-RATED FAT (G) | CALCIUM (MG) | IRON (MG) | SODIUM (MG) |
|---|---|---|---|---|---|---|---|---|---|---|
| **Grains (continued)** | | | | | | | | | | |
| Popcorn, air-popped, unsalted | 8 oz | 8 | 30 | 6 | 1 | 0 | 0 | 1 | 0.2 | 0 |
| Pretzels, stick | 10 pieces | 3 | 10 | 2 | 0 | 0 | 0 | 1 | 0.1 | 48 |
| Rice, brown, cooked | 8 oz | 195 | 230 | 50 | 5 | 1 | 0.3 | 23 | 1 | 0 |
| Rice, white, instant, cooked | 8 oz | 165 | 180 | 40 | 4 | 0 | 0.1 | 5 | 1.3 | 0 |
| Saltines | 4 pieces | 12 | 50 | 9 | 1 | 1 | 0.5 | 3 | 0.5 | 165 |
| Spaghetti, cooked, tender | 8 oz | 140 | 155 | 32 | 5 | 1 | 0.1 | 11 | 1.7 | 1 |
| Waffles, from commercial mix | 1 waffle | 75 | 205 | 27 | 7 | 8 | 2.7 | 179 | 1.2 | 515 |
| | | | | | | | | | | |
| **Meat, poultry** | | | | | | | | | | |
| Bacon, regular, cooked | 3 slices | 19 | 110 | 0 | 6 | 9 | 3.3 | 2 | 0.3 | 303 |
| Beef, chuck, lean, cooked | 2.2 oz | 62 | 170 | 0 | 19 | 9 | 3.9 | 8 | 2.3 | 44 |
| Chicken, breast, roasted | 3 oz | 86 | 140 | 0 | 27 | 3 | 0.9 | 13 | 0.9 | 64 |
| Chicken, drumstick, floured, fried | 1.7 oz | 49 | 120 | 1 | 13 | 7 | 1.8 | 6 | 0.7 | 44 |
| Ground beef, broiled | 3 oz | 85 | 245 | 0 | 20 | 18 | 6.9 | 9 | 2.1 | 70 |
| Ham, roasted, lean and fat | 3 oz | 85 | 205 | 0 | 18 | 14 | 5.1 | 6 | 0.7 | 1009 |
| Hamburger | 4-oz patty | 174 | 445 | 38 | 25 | 21 | 7.1 | 75 | 4.8 | 763 |
| Lamb chops, braised, lean | 1.7 oz | 48 | 135 | 0 | 17 | 7 | 2.9 | 12 | 1.3 | 36 |
| Turkey, roasted, light and dark | 8 oz | 140 | 240 | 0 | 41 | 7 | 2.3 | 35 | 2.5 | 98 |
| Veal cutlet, med. fat, braised or broiled | 3 oz | 85 | 185 | 0 | 23 | 9 | 4.1 | 9 | 0.8 | 56 |
| | | | | | | | | | | |
| **Nuts, legumes, seeds** | | | | | | | | | | |
| Mixed nuts w/peanuts, dry, salted | 1 oz | 28.35 | 170 | 7 | 5 | 15 | 2 | 20 | 1 | 190 |
| Peanuts, oil-roasted, unsalted | 8 oz | 145 | 840 | 27 | 39 | 71 | 9.9 | 125 | 2.8 | 22 |
| Peanut butter | 0.5 oz | 16 | 95 | 3 | 5 | 8 | 1.4 | 5 | 0.3 | 75 |
| Pinto beans, dry, cooked | 8 oz | 180 | 265 | 49 | 15 | 1 | 0.1 | 86 | 5.4 | 3 |
| Sunflower seeds | 1 oz | 28.35 | 160 | 5 | 6 | 14 | 1.5 | 33 | 1.9 | 1 |
| Tofu | 1 piece | 120 | 85 | 3 | 9 | 5 | 0.7 | 108 | 2.3 | 8 |
| | | | | | | | | | | |
| **Sauces, dressings, condiments** | | | | | | | | | | |
| Catsup | 0.5 oz | 15 | 15 | 4 | 0 | 0 | 0 | 3 | 0.1 | 156 |
| Cheese sauce w/milk, from mix | 8 fl oz | 279 | 305 | 23 | 16 | 17 | 9.3 | 569 | 0.3 | 1565 |
| Honey | 0.5 oz | 21 | 65 | 17 | 0 | 0 | 0 | 1 | 0.1 | 1 |
| Jams/preserves | 0.5 oz | 20 | 55 | 14 | 0 | 0 | 0 | 4 | 0.2 | 2 |
| Mayonnaise | 0.5 oz | 14 | 100 | 0 | 0 | 11 | 1.7 | 3 | 0.1 | 80 |
| Mustard, yellow | 0.17 oz | 5 | 5 | 0 | 0 | 0 | 0 | 4 | 0.1 | 63 |
| Salad dressing, French | 0.5 oz | 16 | 85 | 1 | 0 | 9 | 1.4 | 2 | 0 | 188 |
| Salad dressing, Italian, low calorie | 0.5 oz | 15 | 5 | 2 | 0 | 0 | 0 | 1 | 0 | 136 |
| Syrup, table | 1 oz | 42 | 122 | 32 | 0 | 0 | 0 | 1 | 0 | 19 |
| | | | | | | | | | | |
| **Sugars, sweets, miscellaneous snacks** | | | | | | | | | | |
| Caramels, plain or chocolate | 1 oz | 28.35 | 115 | 22 | 1 | 3 | 2.2 | 42 | 0.4 | 64 |
| Chocolate, milk, candy, w/almonds | 1 oz | 28.35 | 150 | 15 | 3 | 10 | 4.8 | 65 | 0.5 | 23 |
| Chocolate, dark, sweet | 1 oz | 28.35 | 150 | 16 | 1 | 10 | 5.9 | 7 | 0.6 | 5 |
| Gelatin dessert, prepared | 4 oz | 120 | 70 | 17 | 2 | 0 | 0 | 2 | 0 | 55 |
| Hard candy | 1 oz | 28.35 | 110 | 28 | 0 | 0 | 0 | 0 | 0.1 | 7 |
| Popsicle | 1 popsicle | 95 | 70 | 18 | 0 | 0 | 0 | 0 | 0 | 11 |
| Potato chips | 10 chips | 20 | 105 | 10 | 1 | 7 | 1.8 | 5 | 0.2 | 94 |
| Pudding, chocolate, instant | 4 oz | 130 | 155 | 27 | 4 | 4 | 2.3 | 130 | 0.3 | 440 |
| Sugar, brown | 8 oz | 220 | 820 | 212 | 0 | 0 | 0 | 187 | 4.8 | 97 |
| Sugar, white, granulated | 8 oz | 200 | 770 | 199 | 0 | 0 | 0 | 3 | 0.1 | 5 |
| | | | | | | | | | | |
| **Vegetables** | | | | | | | | | | |
| Beans, snap, yellow, canned, no salt | 8 oz | 135 | 25 | 6 | 2 | 0 | 0 | 35 | 1.2 | 3 |
| Broccoli | 1 spear | 151 | 40 | 8 | 4 | 1 | 0.1 | 72 | 1.3 | 41 |

## Nutritional Value of Selected Foods (continued)

| FOOD | AMOUNT | GRAMS | ENERGY (KCAL) | CARBO-HYDRATE (G) | PROTEIN (G) | TOTAL FAT (G) | SATU-RATED FAT (G) | CALCIUM (MG) | IRON (MG) | SODIUM (MG) |
|---|---|---|---|---|---|---|---|---|---|---|
| **Vegetables (continued)** | | | | | | | | | | |
| Carrots, cooked from frozen | 8 oz | 146 | 55 | 12 | 2 | 0 | 0 | 41 | 0.7 | 86 |
| Cauliflower, cooked from raw | 8 oz | 125 | 30 | 6 | 2 | 0 | 0 | 34 | 0.5 | 8 |
| Celery, Pascal, raw | 1 stalk | 40 | 5 | 1 | 0 | 0 | 0 | 14 | 0.2 | 35 |
| Corn, yellow, cooked from frozen | 8 oz | 165 | 135 | 34 | 5 | 0 | 0 | 3 | 0.5 | 8 |
| Cucumber, w/peel | 6 slices | 28 | 5 | 1 | 0 | 0 | 0 | 4 | 0.1 | 1 |
| Lettuce, crisphead | 1 wedge | 135 | 20 | 3 | 1 | 0 | 0 | 26 | 0.7 | 12 |
| Mushrooms | 8 oz | 70 | 20 | 3 | 1 | 0 | 0 | 4 | 0.9 | 3 |
| Onions, sliced | 8 oz | 115 | 40 | 8 | 1 | 0 | 0.1 | 29 | 0.4 | 2 |
| Peas, green, cooked from frozen | 8 oz | 160 | 125 | 23 | 8 | 0 | 0.1 | 38 | 2.5 | 139 |
| Potatos, boiled, peeled after | 1 potato | 136 | 120 | 27 | 3 | 0 | 0 | 7 | 0.4 | 5 |
| Tomatoes, raw | 1 tomato | 123 | 25 | 5 | 1 | 0 | 0 | 9 | 0.6 | 10 |

## Reading Food Labels

The FDA requires most food manufacturers to provide standardized nutritional information about certain nutrients. Within strict guidelines the nutritional labels are designed to aid the consumer in making informed dietary decisions as well as to regulate claims made by manufacturers about their products.

The percent daily value is based on a 2,000-calorie-per-day diet. Some larger packages will have listings for both 2,000-calorie and 2,500-calorie diets. For products that require additional preparation before eating, such as dry cake mixes, manufacturers often provide two columns of nutritional information, one with the values of the food as purchased, the other with the values of the food as prepared.

The FDA selects mandatory label components (see sample label at right) based on current understanding of nutrition concerns, and component order on the label is consistent with the priority of dietary recommendations. Components that may appear in addition to the mandatory components are limited to the following: calories from saturated fat; polyunsaturated fat; monounsaturated fat; potassium; soluble fiber; insoluble fiber; sugar alcohol (for example, the sugar substitutes xylitol, mannitol, and sorbitol); other carbohydrate (the difference between total carbohydrate and the sum of dietary fiber, sugars, and sugar alcohol if declared); percent of vitamin A present as beta-carotene; and other essential vitamins and minerals. Any of these optional components that form the basis of product claims, fortification, or enrichment must appear in the nutrition facts. By 2006 labels must specify amounts of trans fatty acids.

Certain key descriptions are also regulated by the FDA. They include the following, in amounts per serving:

  Low fat: 3 g or less
  Low saturated fat: 1 g or less
  Low sodium: 140 mg or less
  Low cholesterol: 20 mg or less and 2 g or less of saturated fat
  Low calorie: 40 calories or less

US FDA Center for Food Safety & Applied Nutrition Web site: <www.cfsan.fda.gov>.

# Nutrition Facts

Serving Size 1/2 cup (114g)
Serving Per Container 4

**Amount Per Serving**

**Calories** 90    Calories from Fat 30

                                         **%Daily Value***

| | |
|---|---|
| **Total Fat** 3g | **5%** |
|   Saturated Fat 0g | **0%** |
| **Cholesterol** 0mg | **0%** |
| **Sodium** 300mg | **13%** |
| **Total Carbohydrate** 13g | **4%** |
|   Dietary Fiber 3g | **12%** |
|   Sugars 3g | |
| **Protein** 3g | |

Vitamin A 80%   •   Vitamin C 60%
Calcium 4%   •   Iron 4%

* Percent Daily Values are based on a 2,000 calorie diet. Your daily values may be higher or lower depending on your calorie needs:

| | | Calories | 2,000 | 2,500 |
|---|---|---|---|---|
| Total Fat | Less than | 65g | 80g |
|   Sat. Fat | Less than | 20g | 25g |
| Cholesterol | Less than | 300mg | 300mg |
| Sodium | Less than | 2,400mg | 2,400mg |
| Total Carbohydrate | | 300g | 375g |
|   Dietary Fiber | | 25g | 30g |

Calories per gram:
Fat 9   •   Carbohydrate 4   •   Protein 4

## Americans and Physical Activity

This table shows the percentage of participants who reported taking part in specific activities during the two weeks preceding the interview. Percentages do not total 100, as only the most popular activities are listed and participants may have taken part in more than one activity. Data from the National Health Interview Survey, 1991.

| males ACTIVITY | ALL AGES/ SEXES (%) | 18–29 (%) | 30–44 (%) | 45–64 (%) | 65–74 (%) | 75+ (%) | ALL (%) |
|---|---|---|---|---|---|---|---|
| 1 Walking | 44.1 | 32.8 | 37.6 | 43.3 | 50.1 | 47.1 | 39.4 |
| 2 Gardening/yard work | 29.4 | 22.2 | 36.0 | 39.8 | 42.6 | 38.4 | 34.2 |
| 3 Stretching | 25.5 | 32.1 | 27.2 | 20.0 | 15.5 | 15.7 | 25.0 |
| 4 Cycling[1] | 15.4 | 18.7 | 18.5 | 14.0 | 10.8 | 8.4 | 16.2 |
| 5 Weight lifting/ muscle strengthening | 14.1 | 33.6 | 21.2 | 12.2 | 6.4 | 4.7 | 20.0 |
| 6 Stair climbing | 10.8 | 10.5 | 11.4 | 9.6 | 6.0 | 4.0 | 9.9 |
| 7 Jogging/running | 9.1 | 22.6 | 14.1 | 7.7 | 1.4 | 0.5 | 12.8 |
| 8 Aerobics | 7.1 | 3.4 | 3.3 | 2.1 | 1.6 | 1.0 | 2.8 |
| 9 Swimming | 6.5 | 10.1 | 7.6 | 5.3 | 3.1 | 1.4 | 6.9 |
| 10 Basketball | 5.8 | 24.2 | 10.5 | 2.4 | 0.1 | 0.1 | 10.5 |
| 11 Golf | 4.9 | 7.9 | 8.6 | 7.9 | 9.7 | 4.9 | 8.2 |

| females ACTIVITY | ALL AGES/ SEXES (%) | 18–29 (%) | 30–44 (%) | 45–64 (%) | 65–74 (%) | 75+ (%) | ALL (%) |
|---|---|---|---|---|---|---|---|
| 1 Walking | 44.1 | 47.4 | 49.1 | 49.4 | 50.1 | 40.5 | 48.3 |
| 2 Gardening/yard work | 29.4 | 15.4 | 28.6 | 29.6 | 28.2 | 21.5 | 25.1 |
| 3 Stretching | 25.5 | 32.5 | 27.7 | 21.4 | 21.9 | 17.9 | 26.0 |
| 4 Cycling[1] | 15.4 | 17.4 | 16.9 | 12.6 | 11.4 | 6.0 | 14.6 |
| 5 Weight lifting/ muscle strengthening | 14.1 | 14.5 | 10.6 | 5.1 | 2.8 | 1.1 | 8.8 |
| 6 Stair climbing | 10.8 | 14.6 | 12.8 | 10.3 | 7.3 | 5.6 | 11.6 |
| 7 Jogging/running | 9.1 | 11.6 | 6.5 | 2.5 | 0.8 | 0.4 | 5.7 |
| 8 Aerobics | 7.1 | 19.3 | 12.3 | 6.6 | 4.2 | 1.6 | 11.1 |
| 9 Swimming | 6.5 | 8.0 | 7.5 | 4.6 | 4.2 | 1.5 | 6.2 |
| 10 Basketball | 5.8 | 3.1 | 1.7 | 0.4 | 0.0 | 0.2 | 1.5 |
| 11 Golf | 4.9 | 1.4 | 1.7 | 2.2 | 3.3 | 0.7 | 1.8 |

[1]Riding a bicycle or stationary bike.

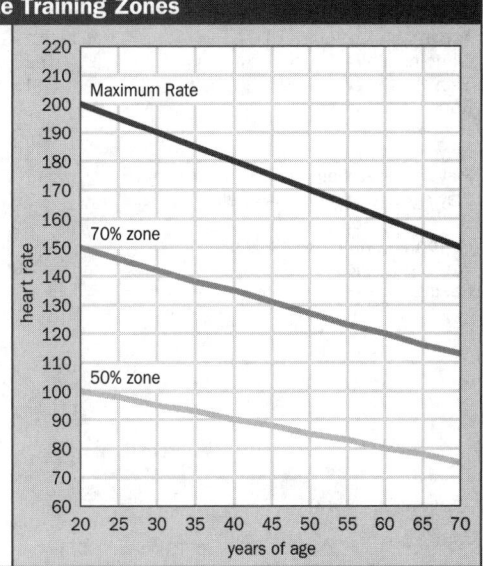

### Target Heart Rate Training Zones

Measuring **target heart rate** involves monitoring your pulse periodically as you exercise. To use the Target Heart Rate chart:

1. Calculate your maximum heart rate by subtracting your age from 220.
2. Determine your target heart rate zone (50–70% of your maximum heart rate).
3. While exercising, monitor your pulse regularly. Count the number of beats for 10 seconds, then multiply by 6 to determine in what zone you are working.

The American Heart Association recommends using the target heart rate scale when participating in more vigorous athletic activity, such as jogging or aerobics. If your activity is moderate or taking your pulse is too bothersome, a "talk test" can be used as a substitute. If you can converse with someone with minimal effort, you are not working too hard. Alternately, if you can sing without difficulty, you are not working hard enough.

Note: For optimal cardiovascular fitness, you should work toward the middle of your 50 and 70% zones. Always check with your physician before starting any fitness routine, especially if you have heart or respiratory concerns.

## Body Mass Index (BMI)

The BMI is a measure expressing the relationship of weight to height determined by dividing body weight in kilograms by the square of height in meters (for convenience, the information has been converted to standard US measurements in the table below). It is more highly correlated with body fat than any other indicator of height and weight. The National Institutes of Health recommend using the BMI scale to help assess the risk of diseases and disabilities associated with an unhealthy weight. Individuals with a BMI below 18.5 are considered underweight; those with a BMI from 18.5 to 24.9 are considered normal; those with a BMI between 25.0 and 29.9 are considered overweight; and those with a BMI of 30.0 or more are considered obese. The BMI may overestimate body fat in athletes and others who have a muscular build, and it may underestimate body fat in older persons and others who have lost muscle mass. Source: <www.nhlbi.nih.gov>.

| HEIGHT (INCHES) | | | | | | | BODY WEIGHT (POUNDS) | | | | | | | | | | | | | | |
|---|---|---|---|---|---|---|---|---|---|---|---|---|---|---|---|---|---|---|---|---|---|
| 58 | 91 | 96 | 100 | 105 | 110 | 115 | 119 | 124 | 129 | 134 | 138 | 143 | 148 | 153 | 158 | 162 | 167 | 172 | 177 | 181 | 186 |
| 59 | 94 | 99 | 104 | 109 | 114 | 119 | 124 | 128 | 133 | 138 | 143 | 148 | 153 | 158 | 163 | 168 | 173 | 178 | 183 | 188 | 193 |
| 60 | 97 | 102 | 107 | 112 | 118 | 123 | 128 | 133 | 138 | 143 | 148 | 153 | 158 | 163 | 168 | 174 | 179 | 184 | 189 | 194 | 199 |
| 61 | 100 | 106 | 111 | 116 | 122 | 127 | 132 | 137 | 143 | 148 | 153 | 158 | 164 | 169 | 174 | 180 | 185 | 190 | 195 | 201 | 206 |
| 62 | 104 | 109 | 115 | 120 | 126 | 131 | 136 | 142 | 147 | 153 | 158 | 164 | 169 | 175 | 180 | 186 | 191 | 196 | 202 | 207 | 213 |
| 63 | 107 | 113 | 118 | 124 | 130 | 135 | 141 | 146 | 152 | 158 | 163 | 169 | 175 | 180 | 186 | 191 | 197 | 203 | 208 | 214 | 220 |
| 64 | 110 | 116 | 122 | 128 | 134 | 140 | 145 | 151 | 157 | 163 | 169 | 174 | 180 | 186 | 192 | 197 | 204 | 209 | 215 | 221 | 227 |
| 65 | 114 | 120 | 126 | 132 | 138 | 144 | 150 | 156 | 162 | 168 | 174 | 180 | 186 | 192 | 198 | 204 | 210 | 216 | 222 | 228 | 234 |
| 66 | 118 | 124 | 130 | 136 | 142 | 148 | 155 | 161 | 167 | 173 | 179 | 186 | 192 | 198 | 204 | 210 | 216 | 223 | 229 | 235 | 241 |
| 67 | 121 | 127 | 134 | 140 | 146 | 153 | 159 | 166 | 172 | 178 | 185 | 191 | 198 | 204 | 211 | 217 | 223 | 230 | 236 | 242 | 249 |
| 68 | 125 | 131 | 138 | 144 | 151 | 158 | 164 | 171 | 177 | 184 | 190 | 197 | 203 | 210 | 216 | 223 | 230 | 236 | 243 | 249 | 256 |
| 69 | 128 | 135 | 142 | 149 | 155 | 162 | 169 | 176 | 182 | 189 | 196 | 203 | 209 | 216 | 223 | 230 | 236 | 243 | 250 | 257 | 263 |
| 70 | 132 | 139 | 146 | 153 | 160 | 167 | 174 | 181 | 188 | 195 | 202 | 209 | 216 | 222 | 229 | 236 | 243 | 250 | 257 | 264 | 271 |
| 71 | 136 | 143 | 150 | 157 | 165 | 172 | 179 | 186 | 193 | 200 | 208 | 215 | 222 | 229 | 236 | 243 | 250 | 257 | 265 | 272 | 279 |
| 72 | 140 | 147 | 154 | 162 | 169 | 177 | 184 | 191 | 199 | 206 | 213 | 221 | 228 | 235 | 242 | 250 | 258 | 265 | 272 | 279 | 287 |
| 73 | 144 | 151 | 159 | 166 | 174 | 182 | 189 | 197 | 204 | 212 | 219 | 227 | 235 | 242 | 250 | 257 | 265 | 272 | 280 | 288 | 295 |
| 74 | 148 | 155 | 163 | 171 | 179 | 186 | 194 | 202 | 210 | 218 | 225 | 233 | 241 | 249 | 256 | 264 | 272 | 280 | 287 | 295 | 303 |
| 75 | 152 | 160 | 168 | 176 | 184 | 192 | 200 | 208 | 216 | 224 | 232 | 240 | 248 | 256 | 264 | 272 | 279 | 287 | 295 | 303 | 311 |
| 76 | 156 | 164 | 172 | 180 | 189 | 197 | 205 | 213 | 221 | 230 | 238 | 246 | 254 | 263 | 271 | 279 | 287 | 295 | 304 | 312 | 320 |
| BMI | 19 | 20 | 21 | 22 | 23 | 24 | 25 | 26 | 27 | 28 | 29 | 30 | 31 | 32 | 33 | 34 | 35 | 36 | 37 | 38 | 39 |
| | | | NORMAL | | | | | OVERWEIGHT | | | | | | | | OBESE | | | | | |

## Ways to Burn 150 Calories

Values shown are approximations. Activities are listed from more to less vigorous—the more vigorous an activity, the less time it takes to burn a calorie. When specific distances are given, the activity must be performed in the time shown (for example, one must run 1.5 miles in 15 minutes to burn 150 calories).

| ACTIVITY | DURATION (MINUTES) | ACTIVITY | DURATION (MINUTES) |
|---|---|---|---|
| Climbing stairs | 15 | Pushing a stroller 1.5 miles | 30 |
| Shoveling snow | 15 | Dancing fast | 30 |
| Running 1.5 miles | 15 | Bicycling 5 miles | 30 |
| Jumping rope | 15 | Shooting baskets | 30 |
| Bicycling 4 miles | 15 | Walking 1.75 miles | 35 |
| Playing basketball | 15–20 | Wheeling oneself in a wheelchair | 30–40 |
| Playing wheelchair basketball | 20 | Gardening | 30–45 |
| Swimming laps | 20 | Playing touch football | 30–45 |
| Performing water aerobics | 30 | Playing volleyball | 45 |
| Walking 2 miles | 30 | Washing windows or floors | 45–60 |
| Raking leaves | 30 | Washing and waxing a car | 45–60 |

# The World

The information about the countries of the world that follows has been assembled and analyzed by Encyclopædia Britannica editors from hundreds of private, national, and international sources. Included are all the sovereign states of the world as well as the major dependent, or nonsovereign, areas. The historical background sketches have been adapted, augmented, and updated from *Britannica Concise Encyclopedia* (2002), the statistical sections from *Britannica World Data*, which is published annually as part of *Britannica Book of the Year*. The section called "Recent Developments" also has been adapted from material appearing in recent issues of the yearbook, as well as from other sources inside and outside Britannica. The locator maps have been prepared by Britannica's Cartography Department, and the recommended Web sites are from Britannica Online.

All information is the latest available to Britannica, although it must be understood that in many cases it takes several years for the various countries or agencies to gather and process data, such that the most current data available will normally be dated several years earlier.

A few definitions of terms used in the articles may be useful. **Gross domestic product** (GDP) is the total value of goods and services produced in a country during a given accounting period, usually a year. Unless otherwise noted, the value is given in current prices of the year indicated. **Gross national product** (GNP) is essentially GDP plus income from foreign transactions minus payments made outside the country. **Balance of payments** is a financial statement for a given period showing the balance among: (1) transactions in goods, services, and income between that country and the rest of the world, (2) changes in ownership or valuation of that country's monetary gold, special drawing rights (a unit of account utilized by the International Monetary Fund to denominate monetary reserves available under a quota system to IMF members to maintain the value of their national currency unit in international transactions), and claims on and liabilities to the rest of the world, and (3) unrequited transfers and counterpart entries needed (in an accounting sense) to balance transactions and changes among any of the foregoing types of exchange that are not mutually offsetting. There are slight differences in accounting methods among various countries so balance of payments figures may not be completely comparable from one country to another.

The symbol $ indicates US dollars unless otherwise indicated. A few helpful **conversions** for the statistical section are given at the foot of the left-hand pages.

## Afghanistan

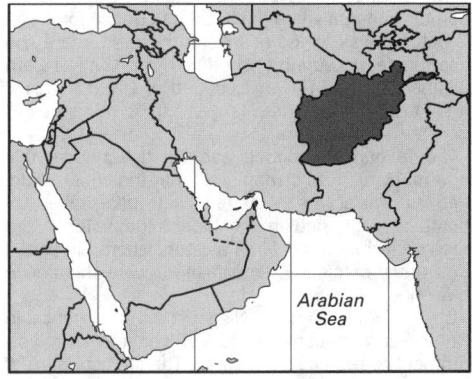

*Arabian Sea*

**Official name:** Islamic State of Afghanistan. **Form of government:** interim regime. **Head of state and government:** President Hamid Karzai (from 13 Jun 2002). **Capital:** Kabul. **Official languages:** Dari (Persian); Pashto. **Official religion:** Islam. **Monetary unit:** 1 afghani (Af) = 100 puls (puli); valuation (7 Jul 2003) $1 = Af 43.00 (black market rate in April 2000: $1 = Af 64,000; most currency transactions are conducted with the Pakistan rupee or US dollar).

### Demography

**Area:** 251,825 sq mi, 652,225 sq km. **Population** (2002): 27,756,000 (includes Afghan refugees [estimated to number about 1.1 million in Pakistan and about 1.4 million in Iran). **Density** (2002): persons per sq mi 110.2, persons per sq km 42.6. **Urban** (2001): 22.3%. **Sex distribution** (2000): male 51.31%; female 48.69%. **Age breakdown** (2000):

under 15, 43.8%; 15–29, 25.4%; 30–44, 16.8%; 45–59, 9.1%; 60–74, 4.2%; 75 and over, 0.7%. **Ethnolinguistic composition** (early 1990s): Pashtun 52.4%; Tajik 20.4%; Hazara 8.8%; Uzbek 8.8%; Chahar Aimak 2.8%; Turkmen 1.9%; other 4.9%. **Religious affiliation** (2000): Sunni Muslim 89.2%; Shi'i Muslim 8.9%; Zoroastrian 1.4%; Hindu 0.4%; other 0.1%. **Major cities** (1988): Kabul 2,602,000; Kandahar (Qandahar) 225,500; Herat 177,300; Mazar-e Sharif 130,600; Jalalabad 55,000. **Location:** southern Asia, bordering Uzbekistan, Tajikistan, China, Pakistan, Iran, and Turkmenistan.

### Vital statistics

**Birth rate** per 1,000 population (2000): 41.8 (world avg. 22.5). **Death rate** per 1,000 population (2000): 18.0 (world avg. 9.0). **Natural increase rate** per 1,000 population (2000): 23.8 (world avg. 13.5). **Total fertility rate** (avg. births per childbearing woman; 2000): 5.9. **Life expectancy** at birth (2000): male 46.6 years; female 45.1 years.

### National economy

**Budget** (1997–98). *Revenue:* primarily from narcotics trade. *Expenditures:* more than 90% of revenue used to finance war effort. **Gross national product** (1999): $21,000,000,000 ($840 per capita). **Public debt** (external, outstanding; 1993): $5,381,000,000. **Production** (metric tons except as noted). *Agriculture, forestry, fishing* (1999): wheat 2,834,000, rice 450,000, grapes 330,000, barley 300,000, corn (maize) 240,000, potatoes 235,000; livestock (number of live animals) 14,300,000 sheep, 2,200,000 goats, 1,500,000 cattle; roundwood (1998) 8,091,000 cu m; fish catch (1997) 1,250. *Mining and quarrying* (1997): salt 13,000;

copper (metal content) 5,000. *Manufacturing* (by production value in Af '000,000; 1988–89): food products 4,019; leather and fur products 2,678; textiles 1,760; printing and publishing 1,070; industrial chemicals (including fertilizers) 1,053. *Energy production (consumption)*: electricity (kW-hr; 1997) 513,000,000 (613,000,000); coal (metric tons; 1997) 2,000 (2,000); petroleum products (metric tons; 1997) none (237,000); natural gas (cu m; 1997) 147,355,000 (147,355,000). **Population economically active** (1994): total 5,557,000; activity rate of total population 29.4% (participation rates: female 9.0%; unemployed [1995] c. 8%). **Tourism:** receipts (1997) $1,000,000; expenditures (1997) $1,000,000. **Land use** (1994): forested 2.9%; meadows and pastures 46.0%; agricultural and under permanent cultivation 12.4%; other 38.7%.

## Foreign trade

**Imports** (1997-c.i.f.): $525,000,000 (1995; food 18.8%, machinery and transport equipment 15.2%, unspecified commodities 46.5%). *Major import sources* (1997): Singapore 19.2%; Japan 18.5%; China 6.9%; India 4.8%; Russia 4.0%. **Exports** (1997-f.o.b.): $149,000,000 (1995; carpets and rugs 54.3%, dried fruits and nuts 15.6%). *Major export destinations* (1997): Pakistan 20.1%; Belgium-Luxembourg 8.7%; France 7.4%; US 6.7%; Japan 6.0%.

## Transport and communications

**Transport.** *Railroads* (1997): length 16 mi (25 km). *Roads* (1996): total length 21,000 km (paved 13%). *Vehicles* (1996): passenger cars 31,000; trucks and buses 25,000. *Air transport* (Ariana Afghan Airlines only): passenger-km (1995) 276,000,000; metric ton-km cargo 38,000,000; airports (1996) 3. **Communications,** in total units (units per 1,000 persons). Daily newspaper circulation (1996): 113,000 (5.0); radio receivers (1997): 2,750,000 (116); television receivers (1997): 270,000 (11); telephone main lines (1999): 29,000 (1.2).

## Education and health

**Educational attainment** (1980). Percentage of population age 25 and over having: no formal schooling 88.5%; some primary education 6.8%; complete primary 0.3%; some secondary 1.2%; postsecondary 3.2%. **Literacy** (1995): population age 15 and over literate 31.5%; males 47.2%; females 15.1%. **Health:** physicians (1997) 2,555 (1 per 9,091 persons); hospital beds, n.a.; infant mortality rate per 1,000 live births (2000) 149.3. **Food** (1999): daily per capita caloric intake 1,755 (vegetable products 79%, animal products 21%); 72% of FAO recommended minimum.

## Military

**Total active duty personnel** (2002): first 600 troops of planned 68,000-member army completed basic training in April 2002 (foreign troops [June 2002]: 5,000-member, 19-nation International Security Assistance Force [ISAF] and 7,000-member, non-ISAF US troops searching for al-Qaeda and Taliban fighters).

## Background

The area was part of the Persian empire in the 6th century BC and was conquered by Alexander the Great in the 4th century BC. Hindu influence entered with the Hephthalites and Sasanians; Islam became entrenched during the rule of the Saffarids, c. AD 870. Afghanistan was divided between the Mughal empire of India and the Safavid empire of Persia until the 18th century, when other Persians under Nadir Shah took control. Great Britain and Russia fought several wars in the area in the 19th century. From the 1930s Afghanistan had a stable monarchy; it was overthrown in the 1970s. The rebels' intention was to institute Marxist reforms, but the reforms sparked rebellion, and troops from the USSR invaded to establish order. Afghan guerrillas prevailed, and the Soviet Union withdrew in 1988–89. In 1992 rebel factions overthrew the government and established an Islamic republic, but fighting among factions continued. In 1996 the government was taken over by the Taliban faction.

## Recent Developments

The terrorist attacks in the United States on 11 Sep 2001 set off a chain reaction that reversed fortunes and produced Afghanistan's first orderly change of government in decades. A year that saw the rigid control of the Taliban on the verge of total victory also witnessed its military defeat and political marginalization.

Blaming Saudi-born militant Osama Bin Laden for the 11 September attacks, the US turned its military wrath against the Taliban for protecting Bin Laden. A bombing campaign begun by US and British forces on 7 October was aimed at Taliban military targets and coordinated to support an offensive by the Northern Alliance, an anti-Taliban coalition of Uzbeks, Tajiks, and Hazaras—the three largest ethnic minorities of northern Afghanistan.

The Taliban abandoned Kabul and Kandahar fell, and many fighters disappeared into the countryside, fled to Pakistan, or shifted their allegiance. US bombing continued in the mountainous Tora Bora area near the border with Pakistan, where Bin Laden and many of his al-Qaeda fighters were thought to have fled.

On 27 Nov 2001, a UN-sponsored conference in Bonn, Germany, convened to settle on an interim government to replace the Taliban. The largest share of delegates represented the Northern Alliance, whose political leader, Burhanuddin Rabbani, had retained international recognition even after being driven from Kabul in 1996. Supporters of former king Zahir Shah also participated. The result was an agreement that Hamid Karzai, a Pashtun tribal leader and supporter of the former king, would lead an interim administration for six months, when a *loya jirga*, a traditional Afghan assembly of notables, would choose a new government. Karzai and a cabinet that included two women were installed in a peaceful ceremony joined by outgoing President Rabbani and most of the country's ethnic and political factions. On 13 Jun 2002 Karzai was elected president. The government continued to struggle against warlordism, ethnic rivalry, and terrorism into 2003, although the US declared in May that major combat was completed. Important progress was being

---

*1 metric ton = about 1.1 short tons;   1 kilometer = 0.6 mi (statute);   1 metric ton-km cargo = about 0.68 short ton-mi cargo;   c.i.f.: cost, insurance, and freight;   f.o.b.: free on board*

made toward building a stable, democratic social structure based on traditional Afghan values.

Internet resources: <www.afghan-web.com/politics>

# Albania

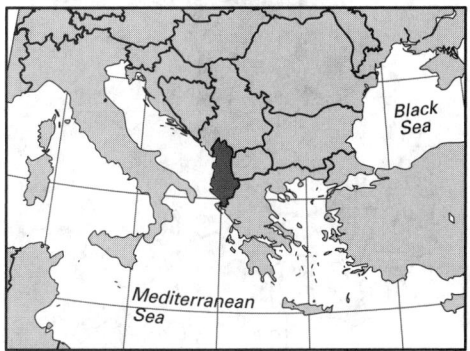

**Official name:** Republika e Shqipërisë (Republic of Albania). **Form of government:** unitary multiparty republic with one legislative house (Assembly [140]). **Chief of state:** President Alfred Moisiu (from 24 Jul 2002). **Head of government:** Prime Minister Fatos Nano (from 31 Jul 2002). **Capital:** Tirana (Tiranë). **Official language:** Albanian. **Official religion:** none. **Monetary unit:** 1 lek = 100 qindars; valuation (7 Jul 2003) $1 = 119.31 leks.

## Demography

**Area:** 11,082 sq mi, 28,703 sq km. **Population** (2002): 3,108,000. **Density** (2002): persons per sq mi 280.5, persons per sq km 108.3. **Urban** (2002): 43.0%. **Sex distribution** (2000): male 48.90%; female 51.10%. **Age breakdown** (2000): under 15, 30.2%; 15–29, 26.6%; 30–44, 19.8%; 45–59, 13.2%; 60–74, 7.9%; 75 and over, 2.3%. **Ethnic composition** (2000): Albanian 91.7%; Vlach (Aromanian) 3.6%; Greek 2.3%; other 2.4%. **Religious affiliation** (2000): Muslim 38.8%; Roman Catholic 16.7%; non-religious 16.6%; Albanian Orthodox 10.4%; other Orthodox 5.7%; other 11.8%. **Major cities** (1991): Tirana (Tiranë) (1999) 279,000; Durrës 86,900; Shkodër 83,700; Elbasan 83,200. **Location:** southeastern Europe, bordering Serbia and Montenegro, Macedonia, Greece, and the Mediterranean Sea.

## Vital statistics

**Birth rate** per 1,000 population (2001): 18.6 (world avg. 21.2). **Death rate** per 1,000 population (2001): 6.5 (world avg. 8.9). **Natural increase rate** per 1,000 population (2001): 12.1 (world avg. 13.2). **Total fertility rate** (avg. births per childbearing woman; 2001): 2.3. **Marriage rate** per 1,000 population (1998): 7.4. **Life expectancy** at birth (2001): male 69.3 years; female 75.1 years.

## National economy

**Budget** (2000). *Revenue*: 120,588,000,000 leks (taxes 86.3%, of which value-added tax 31.6%, import duties and export taxes 18.8%, income tax 11.9%, social security contributions 11.2%, other 12.8%; nontax revenue 13.7%). *Expenditures*:

169,423,000,000 leks (current expenditure 79.3%, of which social security 22.1%, interest on debt 17.5%, wages 15.2%, government operations 11.4%, other 13.1%; capital expenditure 20.7%). **Public debt** (2000): $644,200,000. **Production** (metric tons except as noted). *Agriculture, forestry, fishing* (2000): cereals 580,000, vegetables and melons 444,000 (mainly beans, peas, onions, tomatoes, cabbage, eggplants, and carrots), watermelons 240,000; livestock (number of live animals) 1,941,000 sheep, 1,120,000 goats, 720,000 cattle; roundwood (2000) 409,000 cu m; fish catch (1999) 3,055. *Mining and quarrying* (1999): chromium ore 79,000; copper ore 34,000. *Manufacturing* (1999): cement 106,000; bread 67,000; rolled steel 20,000; cheese 7,000; beer 91,000 hectolitres; wine 10,000 hectolitres. *Construction* (1990): 12,428 units. *Energy production (consumption)*: electricity (kW-hr; 1999) 5,396,000,000 (5,396,000,000); coal (metric tons; 1997) 80,000 (60,000); crude petroleum (barrels; 1999) 2,368,000 (2,413,000 [1997]); petroleum products (metric tons; 1997) 277,000 (382,000); natural gas (cu m; 1997) 17,939,000 (17,939,000). **Gross national product** (2000): $3,833,000,000 ($1,120 per capita). **Population economically active** (2000): total 1,940,000; activity rate of total population 57.0% (participation rates [1998]: ages 15–64, 69.9%; female 49.9%; unemployed 16.8%). **Household income and expenditure:** Average household size (1998) 3.9; annual income per rural household (1989) 80,835 leks ($ value, n.a.); sources of income: wages 53.0%, transfers from relatives abroad 21.5%, social insurance 11.4%; expenditure: n.a. **Tourism** (2000): receipts $389,000,000; expenditures $272,000,000.

## Foreign trade

**Imports** (2000): $1,070,000,000 (manufactured goods 23.8%; machinery and transport equipment 21.6%; food and beverages 19.8%; mineral fuels 9.0%; chemicals 7.0%; crude materials 1.4%). *Major import sources:* Italy 36.2%; Greece 28.0%; Germany 5.5%; Turkey 5.5%. **Exports** (2000): $256,000,000 (miscellaneous manufactured articles 68.0%; manufactured goods 12.1%; crude materials 8.7%; food and beverages 6.6%). *Major export destinations:* Italy 70.3%; Greece 12.9%; Germany 6.6%.

## Transport and communications

**Transport.** *Railroads* (1998): length 670 km; passenger-km 116,000,000; metric ton-km cargo 25,000. *Roads* (1998): total length 18,000 km (paved 30%). *Vehicles* (1998): passenger cars 90,766; trucks and buses 34,378. *Air transport* (1997): passenger-km 3,519,000; short ton-mi 223,000, metric ton-km 325,000; airports (1999) with scheduled flights 1. **Communications**, in total units (units per 1,000 persons). Daily newspaper circulation (1996): 116,000 (37); radio receivers (1997): 810,000 (259); television receivers (1998): 430,000 (137); telephone main lines (2001): 197,500 (50); cellular telephone subscribers (2001): 350,000 (88); Internet users (2001): 10,000 (3.2).

## Education and health

**Educational attainment** (1989). Percentage of population age 10 and over having: primary education 65.3%; secondary 29.1%; higher 5.6%. **Literacy**

(1989): population age 10 and over literate 91.8%; males 95.5%; females 88.0%. **Health** (1995): physicians 4,848 (1 per 657 persons); hospital beds (1994) 10,200 (1 per 333 persons); infant mortality rate per 1,000 live births (2000) 41.3. **Food** (1999): daily per capita caloric intake 2,717 (vegetable products 73%, animal products 27%); 113% of FAO recommended minimum requirement.

## Military

**Total active duty personnel** (2001): 27,000 (army 74.1%, navy 9.3%, air force 16.7%). **Military expenditure as percentage of GNP** (1999): 1.3% (world 2.4%); per capita expenditure $21.

Did you know? Albania is the poorest country in Europe, with an annual income in 1999 of only $930 per person.

## Background

The Albanians are descended from the Illyrians, an ancient Indo-European people who lived in central Europe and migrated south by the beginning of the Iron Age. Of the two major Illyrian migrating groups, the Ghegs settled in the north and the Tosks in the south, along with Greek colonizers. The area was under Roman rule by the 1st century BC; after AD 395 it was connected administratively to Constantinople. Turkish invasion began in the 14th century and continued into the 15th century; though the national hero, Skanderbeg, was able to resist them for a time, after his death (1468) the Turks consolidated their rule. The country achieved independence in 1912 and was admitted into the League of Nations in 1920. It was briefly a republic in 1925–28, then became a monarchy under Zog I, whose initial alliance with Benito Mussolini led to Italy's invasion of Albania in 1939. After the war a socialist government under Enver Hoxha was installed. Gradually Albania cut itself off from the nonsocialist international community and eventually from all nations, including China, its last political ally. By 1990 economic hardship had produced antigovernment demonstrations, and in 1992 a non-Communist government was elected and Albania's international isolation ended. In 1997 it plunged into chaos, brought on by the collapse of pyramid investment schemes. In 1999 it was overwhelmed by ethnic Albanians seeking refuge from Yugoslavia.

## Recent Developments

The fourth democratic general elections in Albania's history were held in June–July 2001. The Socialist Party (PS—the former Communists), with a reform-oriented program, gained an absolute majority in the parliament with 73 of the 140 seats. Political compromises were struck in 2002, both within the PS and between the Socialists and the opposition, that placed veteran party leader Fatos Nano in the prime minister's post and Alfred Moisiu, a retired general, in the presidency.

**Internet resources:** <www.albanian.com>

# Algeria

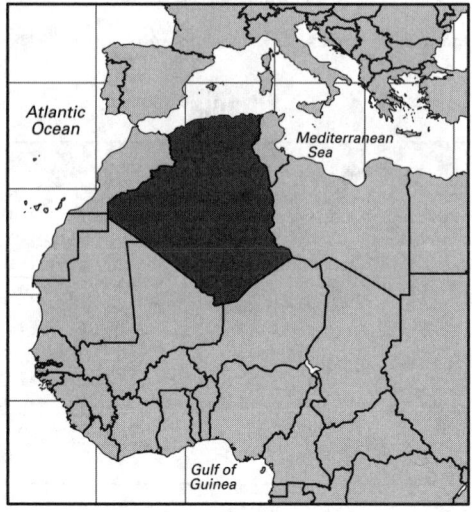

**Official name:** Al-Jumhuriyah al-Jaza'iriyah ad-Dimuqratiyah ash-Sha'biyah (Arabic) (People's Democratic Republic of Algeria). **Form of government:** multiparty republic with two legislative bodies (Council of the Nation [144] [includes 48 nonelected seats appointed by the president]; National People's Assembly [380]). **Chief of state:** President Abdelaziz Bouteflika (from 1999). **Head of government:** Prime Minister Ahmed Ouyahia (from 5 May 2003). **Capital:** Algiers. **Official language:** Arabic. **Official religion:** Islam. **Monetary unit:** 1 Algerian dinar (DA) = 100 centimes; valuation (7 Jul 2003) $1 = DA 77.82.

## Demography

**Area:** 919,595 sq mi, 2,381,741 sq km. **Population** (2002): 31,261,000. **Density** (2002): persons per sq mi 34.0, persons per sq km 13.0. **Urban** (1998): 80.8%. **Sex distribution** (1998): male 50.56%; female 49.44%. **Age breakdown** (1998): under 15, 36.2%; 15–29, 30.6%; 30–44, 17.7%; 45–59, 8.9%; 60–74, 5.1%; 75 and over, 1.5%. **Ethnic composition** (2000): Algerian Arab 59.1%; Berber 26.2%, of which Arabized Berber 3.0%; Bedouin Arab 14.5%; other 0.2%. **Religious affiliation** (2000): Muslim 99.7%, of which Sunni 99.1%, Ibadiyah 0.6%; Christian 0.3%. **Major cities** (1998): Algiers 1,519,570; Oran 692,516; Constantine 462,187; Annaba 348,554; Batna 242,514. **Location:** northern Africa, bordering the Mediterranean Sea, Tunisia, Libya, Niger, Mali, Mauritania, Western Sahara, and Morocco.

## Vital statistics

**Birth rate** per 1,000 population (2000): 19.8 (world avg. 22.5). **Death rate** per 1,000 population (2000): 5.5 (world avg. 9.0). **Natural increase rate** per 1,000 population (2000): 14.3 (world avg. 13.5). **Total fertility rate** (avg. births per childbearing woman; 2000): 2.8. **Marriage rate** per 1,000 population (2000): 5.8. **Life expectancy** at birth (2000): male 68.3 years; female 71.0 years.

*1 metric ton = about 1.1 short tons;   1 kilometer = 0.6 mi (statute);   1 metric ton-km cargo = about 0.68 short ton-mi cargo;   c.i.f.: cost, insurance, and freight;   f.o.b.: free on board*

## National economy

**Budget** (2000). *Revenue*: DA 1,578,100,000,000 (taxes on hydrocarbons 76.9%, value-added taxes 8.0%). *Expenditures*: DA 1,178,100,000,000 (current expenditure 72.7%, development expenditure 27.3%). **Land use** (1994): forested 1.6%; meadows and pastures 13.3%; agricultural and under permanent cultivation 3.4%; other (mostly desert) 81.7%. **Production** (metric tons except as noted). *Agriculture, forestry, fishing* (1999): wheat 1,503,000, potatoes 1,100,000, tomatoes 790,000; livestock (number of live animals) 18,000,000 sheep, 3,200,000 goats; roundwood (1997) 2,735,000 cu m; fish catch (1997) 99,332. *Mining and quarrying* (1999): iron ore (gross weight) 2,330,000; phosphate rock (gross weight) 1,300,000; mercury 12,000 flasks. *Manufacturing* (value added in $'000,000; 1997): food products 463; cement, bricks, and tiles 393; iron and steel 118. *Energy production (consumption)*: electricity (kW-hr; 1997) 21,489,000,000 (21,489,000,-000); coal (metric tons; 1997) 23,000 (1,193,000); crude petroleum (barrels; 2000) 307,091,000 ([1997] 165,974,000); petroleum products (metric tons; 1997) 41,601,000 (8,146,000); natural gas (cu m; 2000) 89,300,000,000 (25,981,000,000). **Household income and expenditure**. Average household size (1998) 7.1; sources of income (2000): wages and salaries 41.2%, self-employment 39.3%, transfers 19.5%; expenditure (1995): food and beverages 58.5%, transportation and communications 9.5%, clothing and footwear 13.9%, health 4.4%, other 13.7%. **Gross domestic product** (2000): $47,897,000,000 ($1,580 per capita). **Population economically active** (1994): total 6,814,000; activity rate of population 24.8% (participation rates [1987] ages 15–64, 44.3%; female 9.2%; unemployed [February 2000] 29.8%). **Public debt** (external, outstanding; 2000): $23,062,000,000. **Tourism**: receipts from visitors (1998) $24,000,000; expenditures by nationals abroad (1997) $64,000,000.

## Foreign trade

**Imports** (1999-c.i.f.): $9,162,000,000 (machinery and apparatus 25.0%, food 24.3%, transport equipment 7.6%). *Major import sources:* France 22.8%; Italy 9.9%; US 8.4%; Germany 7.4%; Spain 5.5%. **Exports** (1999-f.o.b.): $12,525,000,000 (natural and manufactured gas 41.7%, crude petroleum 39.7%, refined petroleum 15.0%). *Major export destinations:* Italy 23.5%; US 14.0%; France 13.7%; Spain 10.6%; The Netherlands 8.2%.

## Transport and communications

**Transport**. *Railroads* (1997): route length 3,945 km; (1996) passenger-km 1,826,000,000; metric ton-km cargo 2,139,000,000. *Roads* (1995): total length 102,424 km (paved 69%). *Vehicles* (1996): passenger cars 725,000; trucks and buses 780,000. *Air transport* (1998–Air Algérie): passenger-km 2,901,-000,000; metric ton-km cargo 18,285,000; airports (1996) 28. **Communications**, in total units (units per 1,000 persons). Daily newspaper circulation (1996): 1,080,000 (38); radio receivers (1997) 7,100,000 (253); television receivers (1999) 3,300,000 (110); telephone main lines (2001): 1,880,000 (60); cellular telephone subscribers (2001): 100,000 (3.2); personal computers (2001): 220,000 (7.1); Internet users (2001): 60,000 (1.9).

## Education and health

**Educational attainment** (1998). Percentage of economically active population age 6 and over having: no formal schooling 30.1%; primary education 29.9%; lower secondary 20.7%; upper secondary 13.4%; higher 4.3%; other 1.6%. **Literacy** (1998): total population age 10 and over literate 15,314,109 (68.1%); males literate 8,650,719 (76.3%); females literate 6,663,392 (59.7%). **Health** (1996): physicians 27,650 (1 per 1,015 persons); hospital beds 34,544 (1 per 812 persons); infant mortality rate per 1,000 live births (2000) 51.1. **Food** (1999): daily per capita caloric intake 2,965 (vegetable products 90%, animal products 10%); 124% of FAO recommended minimum.

## Military

**Total active duty personnel** (2001): 124,000 (army 86.3%, navy 5.6%, air force 8.1%). **Military expenditure as percentage of GNP** (1999): 4.0% (world 2.4%); per capita expenditure $60.

## Background

Phoenician traders settled the area early in the 1st millennium BC; several centuries later the Romans invaded, and by AD 40 they had control of the Mediterranean coast. The fall of Rome in the 5th century led to invasion by the Vandals and later by Byzantium. The Islamic invasion began in the 7th century; by 711 all of northern Africa was under the control of the Umayyad caliphate. Several Islamic Berber empires followed, most prominently the Almoravid (c. 1054–1130), which extended its domain to Spain, and the Almohad (c. 1130–1269). The Barbary Coast pirates, operating in the area, had menaced Mediterranean trade for centuries, and France seized this pretext to enter Algeria in 1830. By 1847 France had established control in the region, and by the late 19th century had instituted civil rule. Popular movements resulted in the bloody Algerian War (1954–62); independence was achieved following a referendum in 1962. In the 1990s Islamic fundamentalists opposing the military brought Algeria to a state of virtual civil war.

## Recent Developments

Algeria continued to suffer from the chronic and endemic violence that had taken thousands of lives over the past decade. Antar Zouabri, the head of the militant Armed Islamic Group, was killed in February 2002, but another radical organization, the Salafist Group for Call and Combat, widened its control over parts of the Skikda region and Kabylia. A measure of autonomy was granted by the government to Kabylia, the area where the Berber minority largely resides, and the Tamazight language was recognized as an official language in the Algerian constitution. A powerful earthquake and a major aftershock claimed hundreds of lives in May 2003.

**Internet resources:** <www.algeria.com>

# American Samoa

**Official name:** American Samoa (English); Amerika Samoa (Samoan). **Political status:** unincorporated and unorganized territory of the US with two legislative

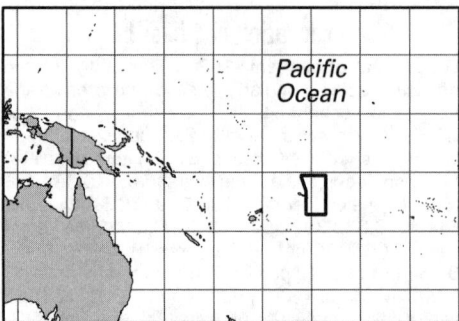

chickens; fish catch (1999) 1,000, of which tunas, bonitos, and billfish 950. *Manufacturing* (value of export in $; 1999): canned tuna 334,219,881; garments 4,598,766; other manufactures include pet food, handicrafts, soap, and alcoholic beverages. *Construction* (value of building permits in $; 1999) 15,209,000. *Energy production (consumption):* electricity (kW-hr; 1999) 158,576,000 (137,834,000); petroleum products (metric tons; 1997) none (94,000). **Population economically active** (2000): total 17,664, activity rate of total population 30.8% (participation rates: ages 16 and over 52.0%; female 41.5%; unemployed 5.3%). **Household income and expenditure.** Average household size (2000) 6.0; income per household (2000): $24,000; expenditure (1995): food and beverages 30.9%, housing and furnishings 25.8%, church donations 20.7%, transportation and communications 9.4%, clothing 2.9%, other 10.3%. **Tourism:** receipts from visitors (1997) $10,000,000; expenditures by nationals abroad (1996) $2,000,000. **Land use** (1994): forested 70%; agricultural and under permanent cultivation 15%; other 15%.

houses (Senate [18]; House of Representatives [20; excluding a nonvoting representative from Swains Island]). **Chief of state:** President of the US George W. Bush (from 2001). **Head of government:** Governor Tauese P.F. Sunia (from 1997). **Capital:** Fagatogo (legislative and judicial) and Utulei (executive), both within the Pago Pago urban agglomeration. **Official languages:** English; Samoan. **Official religion:** none. **Monetary unit:** US dollar ($) = 100 cents.

## Demography

**Area:** 84.4 sq mi, 218.6 sq km. **Population** (2002): 60,000. **Density** (2002): persons per sq mi 776.2, persons per sq km 299.7. **Urban** (1998): 51.5%. **Sex distribution** (2000): male 48.50%; female 51.50%. **Age breakdown** (2000): under 15, 38.7%; 15–29, 24.5%; 30–44, 20.5%; 45–59, 10.9%; 60–74, 4.4%; 75 and over, 1.0%. **Ethnic composition** (2000): Samoan 88.2%; Tongan 2.8%; Asian 2.8%; Caucasian 1.1%; other 5.1%. **Religious affiliation** (1995): 4 major Protestant groups 60.1%; Roman Catholic 19.4%; Mormon 12.5%; other 8.0%. **Major villages** (2000): Tafuna 8,406; Nu'uuli 5,154; Pago Pago 4,278 (urban agglomeration [2001] 15,000). **Location:** group of islands in the south Pacific Ocean.

## Vital statistics

**Birth rate** per 1,000 population (2001): 24.9 (world avg. 21.2). **Death rate** per 1,000 population (2001): 4.3 (world avg. 8.9). **Natural increase rate** per 1,000 population (2001): 20.6 (world avg. 12.3). **Total fertility rate** (avg. births per childbearing woman; 2000): 3.6. **Marriage rate** per 1,000 population (1999): 4.8. **Divorce rate** per 1,000 population (1993): 0.5. **Life expectancy** at birth (2001): male 70.9 years; female 80.0 years.

## National economy

**Budget** (1997). *Revenue*: $144,438,095 (US government grants 67.4%; taxes 23.6%; insurance claims 4.9%; other 4.1%). *Expenditures*: $152,912,308 (education and culture 28.5%; health and welfare 27.3%; general government 14.1%; public works and parks 12.8%; public safety 6.9%; economic development 6.1%; capital projects 3.4%; debt 0.9%). **Gross national product** (1997): $253,000,000 ($4,300 per capita). **Production** (metric tons except as noted). *Agriculture, forestry, fishing* (2001): coconuts 4,700, taros 1,500, fruits (excluding melons) 1,200; livestock (number of live animals; 2001) 10,700 pigs, 37,000

## Foreign trade

**Imports** (1999-c.i.f.): $452,600,000 (fish and cannery related products 57.4%, petroleum and petroleum products 10.8%, food 10.5%, manufactured goods 9.9%, transport equipment 4.3%, building materials 3.4%). *Major import sources* (1999): US 66.5%; New Zealand 9.2%; Australia 8.6%; Fiji 5.6%; Western Samoa 2.9%; Japan 1.9%; South Korea 1.4%; Taiwan 1.1%; China 0.7%. **Exports** (1999-f.o.b.): $345,100,000 (tuna in airtight containers 96.8%, finished garments 1.3%, pet food 1.2%, fish meal 0.6%). *Major export destinations:* US 100.0%.

## Transport and communications

**Transport.** *Roads* (1991): total length 350 km (paved, 43%). *Vehicles* (1999): passenger cars 5,984; trucks and buses 576. *Air transport* (1999): incoming flights 7,748; incoming passengers 92,368; incoming cargo 833 metric tons; airports (1999) with scheduled flights 3. **Communications,** in total units (units per 1,000 persons). Daily newspaper circulation (1996): 5,000 (85); radio receivers (1997): 57,000 (929); television receivers (1997): 14,000 (221); telephone main lines (1999): 11,919 (211); cellular telephone subscribers (1999): 2,643 (47).

## Education and health

**Educational attainment** (2000). Percentage of population age 25 and over having: no formal schooling to some secondary education 33.9%; completed secondary 39.3%; some college 19.4%; undergraduate degree 4.8%; graduate degree 2.6%. **Literacy** (2000): total population age 10 and over literate 33,993 (99.4%); males literate 17,704 (99.4%); females literate 16,589 (99.5%). **Health** (1991): physicians 26 (1 per 1,888 persons); hospital beds (1995) 140 (1 per 4.7 persons); infant mortality rate per 1,000 live births (2001) 10.4.

## Military

Military defense is the responsibility of the US.

*1 metric ton = about 1.1 short tons;   1 kilometer = 0.6 mi (statute);   1 metric ton-km cargo = about 0.68 short ton-mi cargo;   c.i.f.: cost, insurance, and freight;   f.o.b.: free on board*

## Background

The Samoan islands were probably inhabited by Polynesians 2,500 years ago. Dutch explorers first arrived in 1722. A haven for runaway sailors and escaped convicts, the islands were ruled by native chiefs until c. 1860. The US gained the right to establish a naval station at Pago Pago in 1878, and the US, Britain, and Germany administered a tripartite protectorate in 1889–99. The islands were ceded to the US in 1904 and 1925. The first constitution was approved in 1960, and in 1977 the territory's first elected governor took office.

## Recent Developments

The popular governor of American Samoa, Tauese Pita Fiti Sunia, died on 26 Mar 2003 aboard an airplane en route from Apia, Samoa, to Honolulu HI, where he was being flown for medical treatment. He was an educator and lawyer and had served as governor since 1996.

Internet resources: <http://amerikasamoa.info>

# Andorra

Official name: Principat d'Andorra (Principality of Andorra). Form of government: parliamentary coprincipality with one legislative house (General Council [28]). Chiefs of state: President of France Jacques Chirac (from 1995); Bishop of Urgell, Spain, Joan Martí Alanís (from 1971). Head of government: Head of Government Marc Forné Molné (from 1994). Capital: Andorra la Vella. Official language: Catalan. Official religion: none (Roman Catholicism enjoys special recognition in accordance with Andorran tradition). Monetary unit: 1 euro (€) = 100 cents; valuation (7 Jul 2003) $1 = €0.87 (at conversion on 1 Jan 2002; 1€ = 166.386 Spanish pesetas [Ptas]).

## Demography

Area: 181 sq mi, 468 sq km. Population (2002): 66,500. Density (2002): persons per sq mi 367.4, persons per sq km 142.1. Urban (1999): 93%. Sex distribution (2000): male 52.04%; female 47.96%. Age breakdown (2000): under 15, 15.3%; 15–29, 19.8%; 30–44, 29.1%; 45–59, 19.2%; 60–74, 10.9%; 75 and over, 5.7%. Ethnic composition (by nationality; 2000): Spanish 40.6%; Andorran 36.0%; Portuguese 10.2%; French 6.5%; British 1.4%; Moroccan 0.7%; German 0.5%; other 4.1%. Religious

affiliation (2000): Roman Catholic 89.1%; other Christian 4.3%; Muslim 0.6%; Hindu 0.5%; nonreligious 5.0%; other 0.5%. Major urban areas (2001): Andorra la Vella 20,845; Les Escaldes–Engordany 15,397; Encamp 10,576. Location: southwestern Europe, between France and Spain.

## Vital statistics

Birth rate per 1,000 population (2000): 11.3 (world avg. 21.2). Death rate per 1,000 population (2000): 3.9 (world avg. 8.9). Natural increase rate per 1,000 population (2000): 7.4 (world avg. 12.3). Total fertility rate (avg. births per childbearing woman; 2001): 1.2. Marriage rate per 1,000 population (2000): 3.4. Life expectancy at birth (2001): male 80.6 years; female 86.6 years.

## National economy

Budget (2001). *Revenue:* €234,705,780 (indirect taxes 75.2%, taxes from government enterprises 17.8%, revenue from capital 7.0%). *Expenditures:* €250,775,790 (current expenditures 51.5%, development expenditures 48.5%). Public debt (1995): about $500,000,000. *Production. Agriculture* (2000): tobacco 324 metric tons; other traditional crops include hay, potatoes, and grapes; livestock (number of live animals; 2000) 1,586 sheep, 1,181 cattle, 850 horses. Quarrying: small amounts of marble are quarried. *Manufacturing* (value of recorded exports in €'000; 2000): electrical machinery and apparatus 11,090; motor vehicles and parts 8,500; newspapers and periodicals 4,690. *Energy production (consumption):* electricity (kW-hr; 1997) 116,000,000 ([2000] 412,143,000); petroleum products, none ([2000] 201,677,000 litres). Household expenditure (1997): food, beverages, and tobacco 25.5%, housing and energy 19.4%, transportation 17.7%, clothing and footwear 9.2%. Land use (1994): forested 22.0%; meadows and pastures 56.0%; agricultural and under permanent cultivation 2.0%; other 20.0%. Population economically active (2000): total 39,895; activity rate of total population 52.4% (participation rates: ages 15–64, 72.6%; unemployed [2000] unofficially, none). Gross national product (at current market prices; 1998): $1,110,000,000 ($16,930 per capita). Tourism (2000): 10,991,284 visitors; number of hotels 271.

## Foreign trade

Imports (2000): €1,106,006,000 (food, beverages, and tobacco 20.0%; machinery and apparatus 16.2%; chemicals and chemical products 10.1%; transport equipment 9.1%; textiles and wearing apparel 9.1%; photographic and optical goods and watches and clocks 5.0%). *Major import sources:* Spain 48.5%; France 26.6%; Asia 6.2%; Germany 4.4%; Italy 4.1%; UK 2.5%. Exports (2000): €49,491,000 (electrical machinery and apparatus 17.2%; motor vehicles and parts 15.2%; newspapers, books, and periodicals 9.5%; chemicals 7.4%; optical and photo equipment 7.2%; tobacco 6.9%; clothing 4.4%). *Major export destinations:* Spain 60.9%; France 26.1%; Greece 1.7%; Germany 1.5%; The Netherlands 0.5%.

## Transport and communications

Transport. *Railroads:* none; however, both French and Spanish railways stop near the border. *Roads* (1999):

total length 269 km (paved 74%). *Vehicles* (2000): passenger cars 60,287; trucks and buses 4,400. Airports with scheduled flights: none. **Communications,** in total units (units per 1,000 persons). Daily newspaper circulation (1996): 4,000 (62); radio receivers (1997): 16,000 (247); television receivers (1998): 30,000 (457); telephone main lines (2001): 35,000 (438); cellular telephone subscribers (2001): 23,543 (302); Internet users (2001): 7,000 (88).

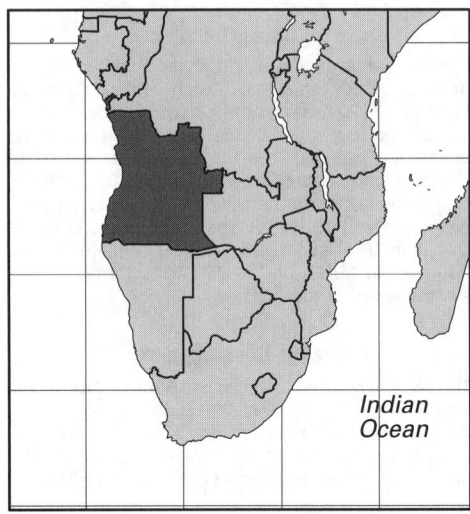

Indian Ocean

## Education and health

**Educational attainment** (mid-1980s). Percentage of population age 15 and over having: no formal schooling 5.5%; primary education 47.3%; secondary education 21.6%; postsecondary education 24.9%; unknown 0.7%. **Literacy:** resident population is virtually 100% literate. **Health** (1999): physicians 218 (1 per 303 persons); hospital beds 203 (1 per 323 persons); infant mortality rate per 1,000 live births (1999–2001 avg.) 4.1.

## Military

**Total active duty personnel:** none. France and Spain are responsible for Andorra's external security; the police force is assisted in alternate years by either French gendarmerie or Barcelona police.

## Background

Andorra's independence is traditionally ascribed to Charlemagne, who recovered the region from the Muslims in 803. It was placed under the joint suzerainty of the French counts of Foix and the Spanish bishops of the See of Urgell in 1278, and it was subsequently governed jointly by the Spanish bishop of Urgell and the French head of state. This feudal system of government, the last in Europe, lasted until 1993, when a constitution was adopted that transferred most of the coprinces' powers to the Andorran General Council, a body elected by universal suffrage. Andorra has long had a strong affinity with Catalonia; its institutions are based in Catalonian law, and it is part of the diocese of the See of Urgell (Spain). The traditional economy was based on sheep raising, but tourism has been very important since the 1950s.

## Recent Developments

Andorra's banking sector came under fire for its secrecy laws as the international search to uncover terrorist funds intensified in 2002. Along with six other countries, Andorra was named by the Organisation for Economic Co-operation and Development as an uncooperative tax haven and had action threatened against it.

**Internet resources:** <www.turisme.ad>

## Angola

**Official name:** República de Angola (Republic of Angola). **Form of government:** unitary multiparty republic with one legislative house (National Assembly [220]). **Head of state and government:** President José Eduardo dos Santos, assisted by Prime Minister Fernando da Piedade Dias dos Santos (from 6 Dec 2002). **Capital:** Luanda. **Official language:** Portuguese. **Official religion:** none. **Monetary unit:** 1 refloated kwanza (NKz) = 100 lwei; valuation (7 Jul 2003) $1 = refloated kwanza 78.55.

## Demography

**Area:** 481,354 sq mi, 1,246,700 sq km. **Population** (2002): 10,593,000. **Density** (2002): persons per sq mi 22.0, persons per sq km 8.5. **Urban** (2001): 34.9%. **Sex distribution** (2000): male 50.59%; female 49.41%. **Age breakdown** (2000): under 15, 43.2%; 15–29, 26.5%; 30–44, 16.9%; 45–59, 8.7%; 60 and over, 4.7%. **Ethnic composition** (2000): Ovimbundu 25.2%; Kimbundu 23.1%; Kongo 12.6%; Lwena (Luvale) 8.2%; Chokwe 5.0%; Kwanyama 4.1%; Nyaneka 3.9%; Luchazi 2.3%; Ambo (Ovambo) 2.0%; Mbwela 1.7%; Nyemba 1.7%; other 10.2%. **Religious affiliation** (2001): Christian 94.1%, of which Roman Catholic 62.1%, Protestant 15.0%; traditional beliefs 5.0%; other 0.9%. **Major cities** (1999): Luanda 2,555,000; Huambo 400,000 (1995); Benguela 155,000 (1983); Lobito 150,000 (1983); Lubango 105,000 (1984). **Location:** southern Africa, bordering Democratic Republic of the Congo, Zambia, Namibia, and the Atlantic Ocean.

## Vital statistics

**Birth rate** per 1,000 population (2000): 46.9 (world avg. 22.5). **Death rate** per 1,000 population (2000): 25.0 (world avg. 9.0). **Natural increase rate** per 1,000 population (2000): 21.9 (world avg. 13.5). **Total fertility rate** (avg. births per childbearing woman; 2000): 6.5. **Life expectancy** at birth (2000): male 37.1 years; female 39.6 years.

## National economy

**Budget** (1999). *Revenue:* NKz 7,540,000,000 (tax revenue 99.4%, of which petroleum corporate taxes 71.1%, tax on goods 20.5%, import duties 3.0%; nontax revenue 0.6%). *Expenditures:* NKz 8,940,000,-

---

*1 metric ton = about 1.1 short tons;    1 kilometer = 0.6 mi (statute);    1 metric ton-km cargo = about 0.68 short ton-mi cargo;    c.i.f.: cost, insurance, and freight;    f.o.b.: free on board*

000 (defense and internal security 41%; administration 16.1%; interest 10.7%; economic services 10.3%; education 4.8%; health 2.8%; other 14.3%). **Public debt** (external, outstanding; 2000): $8,758,000,000. **Production** (metric tons except as noted). *Agriculture, forestry, fishing* (2000): cassava 3,129,734, corn (maize) 428,045, sugarcane 330,000; livestock (number of live animals) 4,042,000 cattle, 2,150,000 goats, 800,000 pigs; roundwood (2000) 6,676,000 cu m; fish catch (1999) 177,497. *Mining and quarrying* (1999): diamonds 1,080,000 carats. *Manufacturing* (1999): bread 87,500; frozen fish 57,700; wheat flour 57,500. *Energy production (consumption):* electricity (kW-hr; 1998) 1,885,000,000 (1,885,000,000); coal, none (none); crude petroleum (barrels; 1999) 278,900,000 (14,100,000); petroleum products (metric tons; 1999) 1,956,000 (1,124,000); natural gas (cu m; 1997) 187,077,000 (187,077,000). **Tourism:** receipts (2000) $18,000,000; expenditures $11,000,000. **Population economically active** (1999): total 5,729,000; activity rate of total population 57.7% (participation rates over age 10 [1991] 60.1%; female 38.4%; unemployed [2002] 70%). Average household size (1998) 5.0. **Gross national product** (at current market prices; 2000): $3,847,000,000 ($290 per capita). **Land use** (1995): forested 18.5%; meadows and pastures 43.3%; agricultural and under permanent cultivation 2.8%; other 35.4%.

### Foreign trade

**Imports** (1999): $3,267,000,000 (1991; current consumption goods 50.2%, capital goods 20.2%, intermediate consumption goods 18.9%, transport equipment 6.8%). *Major import sources* (1999): Portugal 18.8%; US 14.6%; South Africa 11.9%; France 8.2%; UK 6.2%; Spain 5.9%; Brazil 5.1%. **Exports** (1999): $5,344,000,000 (mineral fuels 87.8%, diamonds 11.8%). *Major export destinations* (1999): US 59.5%; China 8.2%; Taiwan 7.7%; Germany 2.4%; France 2.1%.

### Transport and communications

**Transport.** *Railroads* (1998): route length 2,952 km; passenger-km 326,000,000 (1988); metric ton-km cargo 1,720,000,000 (1988). *Roads* (1998): total length 72,626 km (paved 25%). *Vehicles* (1997): passenger cars 207,000; trucks and buses 25,000. *Air transport* (1997): passenger-km 620,000,000; airports (1999) with scheduled flights 17. **Communications,** in total units (units per 1,000 persons). Daily newspaper circulation (1996): 128,000 (14); television receivers (1999): 190,000 (19); telephone main lines (2001): 80,000 (5.9); cellular telephone subscribers (2001): 86,500 (6.4); personal computers (2001): 17,000 (1.3); Internet users (2001): 60,000 (4.4).

### Education and health

**Literacy** (1998): population age 15 and over literate 41.7%; males literate 55.6%; females literate 28.5%. **Health** (1997): physicians 736 (1 per 12,985 persons); hospital beds (1990) 11,857 (1 per 845 persons); infant mortality rate per 1,000 live births (2000) 195.8. **Food** (2000): daily per capita caloric intake 1,903 (vegetable products 92%, animal products 8%); 81% of FAO recommended minimum.

### Military

**Total active duty personnel** (2001): 130,500 (army 92.0%, navy 1.9%, air force 6.1%). **Military expenditure as percentage of GNP** (1999): 21.2% (world 2.4%); per capita expenditure $248.

### Background

An influx of Bantu-speaking peoples in the 1st millennium AD led to their dominance in the area by c. 1500. The most important Bantu kingdom was the Kongo; south of the Kongo was the Ndongo kingdom of the Mbundu people. Portuguese explorers arrived in 1483 and over time gradually extended their rule. Angola's frontiers were largely determined with other European nations in the 19th century, but not without severe resistance by the indigenous peoples. Its status as a Portuguese colony was changed to that of an overseas province in 1951. Resistance to colonial rule led to the outbreak of fighting in 1961, which led ultimately to independence in 1975. Rival factions continued fighting after independence; although a peace accord was reached in 1994, forces led by Jonas M. Savimbi continued to resist government control. The killing of Savimbi in February 2002 changed the political balance and led to the signing of a cease-fire agreement in Luanda in April that effectively ended the civil war.

### Recent Developments

The legacy of decades of fighting was a country in tatters. In mid-2002 the UN World Food Programme estimated that half a million people in Angola were suffering from starvation and another million were entirely dependent upon food aid for their survival.

**Internet resources:** <www.angola.org>

# Antigua and Barbuda

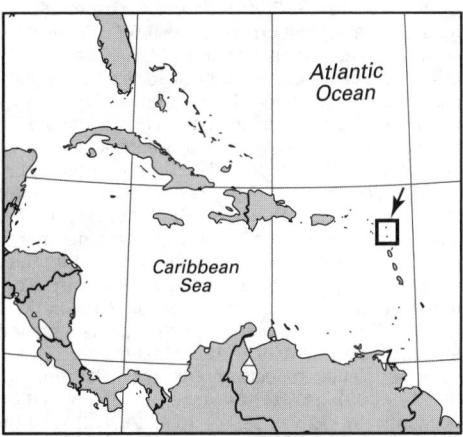

**Official name:** Antigua and Barbuda. **Form of government:** constitutional monarchy with two legislative houses (Senate [17]; House of Representatives [17] [directly elected seats only; attorney general and speaker may serve ex officio if they are not elected to House of Representatives]). **Chief of state:** British Monarch Queen Elizabeth II (from 1952) represented by Governor-General Sir James Carlisle (from 1993). **Head of government:** Prime Minister Lester Bird (from 1994). **Capital:** Saint John's. **Official language:** English. **Official religion:** none. **Monetary unit:** 1 Eastern Caribbean dollar (EC$) = 100 cents; valuation (7 Jul 2003) US$1 = EC$2.67.

## Demography

**Area:** 170.5 sq mi, 441.6 sq. km. **Population** (2002): 76,400. **Density** (2002): persons per sq mi 448.1, persons per sq km 173.0. **Urban** (2001): 36.9%. **Sex distribution** (2001): male 47.55%; female 52.45%. **Age breakdown** (1991): under 15, 30.4%; 15–29, 27.8%; 30–44, 20.5%; 45–59, 10.2%; 60–74, 7.7%; 75 and over, 3.4%. **Ethnic composition** (2000): black 82.4%; US white 12.0%; mulatto 3.5%; British 1.3%; other 0.8%. **Religious affiliation** (1991): Protestant 73.7%, of which Anglican 32.1%, Moravian 12.0%, Methodist 9.1%, Seventh-day Adventist 8.8%; Roman Catholic 10.8%; Jehovah's Witness 1.2%; Rastafarian 0.8%; other religion/no religion/not stated 13.5%. **Major city** (1991): Saint John's 22,342. **Location:** eastern Caribbean Sea.

## Vital statistics

**Birth rate** per 1,000 population (2000): 20.2 (world avg. 22.5); (1988) legitimate 23.4%; illegitimate 76.6%. **Death rate** per 1,000 population (2000): 6.0 (world avg. 9.0). **Natural increase rate** per 1,000 population (2000): 14.2 (world avg. 13.5). **Total fertility rate** (avg. births per childbearing woman; 2000): 2.3. **Marriage rate** per 1,000 population (1995): 22.1. **Divorce rate** per 1,000 population (1988): 0.2. **Life expectancy** at birth (2000): male 68.2 years; female 72.8 years.

## National economy

**Budget** (1998). *Revenue*: EC$362,300,000 (taxes on international transactions 35.6%, of which import duties 15.8%; consumption taxes 24.9%; nontax revenue 12.5%; corporate income taxes 7.1%). *Expenditures*: EC$427,300,000 (current expenditures 90.1%; development expenditures 9.9%). **Public debt** (external, outstanding; end of 1998): US$406,400,000. **Production** (metric tons except as noted). *Agriculture, forestry, fishing* (1999): tropical fruit (including papayas, guavas, soursops, and oranges) 6,500, mangoes 1,300, eggplants 250; livestock (number of live animals) 15,700 cattle, 12,200 sheep; fish catch (1997) 500. *Mining and quarrying*: crushed stone for local use. *Manufacturing* (1994): beer and malt 166,000 cases; T-shirts 179,000 units; other manufactures include cement, handicrafts, and furniture, as well as electronic components for export. *Construction* (1998): gross value of building applications EC$323,000,000. *Energy production (consumption)*: electricity (kW-hr; 1997) 153,700,000 (115,300,000); petroleum products (metric tons; 1997) negligible (110,000); natural gas, none (none). **Population economically active** (1991): total 26,753; activity rate of total population 45.1% (participation rates: ages 15–64, 69.7%; female 45.6%; unemployed [end of 1999] c. 5%). Average household size (2001) 3.1. **Gross national product** (2000): US$642,000,000 (US$9,440 per capita). **Land use** (1994): forested 11.0%; meadows and pastures 9.0%; agricultural and under permanent cultivation 18.0%;

other 62.0%. **Tourism:** receipts from visitors (2000) US$290,000,000; expenditures by nationals abroad (1997) US$26,000,000.

## Foreign trade

**Imports** (1998): US$357,500,000 (agricultural products 11.0%, other [including petroleum products for reexport] 89%). *Major import sources* (1997): US 26.3%; UK 10.0%; Caricom 7.8%. **Exports** (1998): US$36,200,000 (reexports [significantly, petroleum products reexported to neighboring islands] 59.1%, domestic exports 40.9%). *Major export destinations* (1994): US 40.0%; others include the UK, Canada, and Caricom.

## Transport and communications

**Transport.** *Roads* (1996): total length 250 km. *Vehicles* (1995): passenger cars 13,588; trucks and buses 1,342. *Air transport* (1995): passenger-km 252,000,000; (1991) metric ton-km cargo 200,000; airports (1996) with scheduled flights 2. **Communications,** in total units (units per 1,000 persons). Daily newspaper circulation (1996): 6,000 (87); radio receivers (1997): 36,000 (523); television receivers (1997): 31,000 (451); telephone main lines (2001): 37,300 (474); cellular telephone subscribers (2001): 25,000 (318); Internet users (2000): 5,000 (65).

## Education and health

**Educational attainment** (1991). Percentage of population age 25 and over having: no formal schooling 1.1%; primary education 50.5%; secondary 33.4%; higher (not university) 5.4%; university 6.2%; other/unknown 3.4%. **Literacy** (1995): total population age 15 and over literate, 90.0%. **Health** (1996): physicians 75 (1 per 915 persons); hospital beds 255 (1 per 269 persons); infant mortality rate per 1,000 live births (2000) 23.0. **Food** (1999): daily per capita caloric intake 2,396 (vegetable products 68%, animal products 32%); 102% of FAO recommended minimum.

## Military

**Total active duty personnel** (2000): a 170-member defense force (army 73.5%, navy 26.5%) is part of the Eastern Caribbean regional security system. **Military expenditure as percentage of GNP** (1998): 0.7% (world 2.5%); per capita expenditure US$57.

**Did you know?** Antigua, the "gateway to the Caribbean," is home to Nelson's Dockyard, constructed by British Adm. Horatio Nelson. The collection of buildings, most built between 1785–92, is considered an architectural treasure and is a major tourist attraction.

## Background

Christopher Columbus visited Antigua in 1493 and named it after a church in Seville, Spain. It was colonized in 1632 by English settlers, who imported

---

*1 metric ton = about 1.1 short tons; 1 kilometer = 0.6 mi (statute); 1 metric ton-km cargo = about 0.68 short ton-mi cargo; c.i.f.: cost, insurance, and freight; f.o.b.: free on board*

African slaves to grow tobacco and sugarcane. Barbuda was colonized by the English in 1678. In 1834 its slaves were emancipated. Antigua (with Barbuda) was part of the British colony of the Leeward Islands from 1871 until that colony was defederated in 1956. The islands achieved full independence in 1981.

## Recent Developments

Accusations of involvement in money-laundering activities continued to plague the country in 2002. The government yielded to demands for transparency and the "effective exchange of information in criminal tax matters" with countries of the Organisation for Economic Co-Operation and Development, thereby averting being blacklisted as an offshore tax haven.

Internet resources: <www.antigua-barbuda.org>

# Argentina

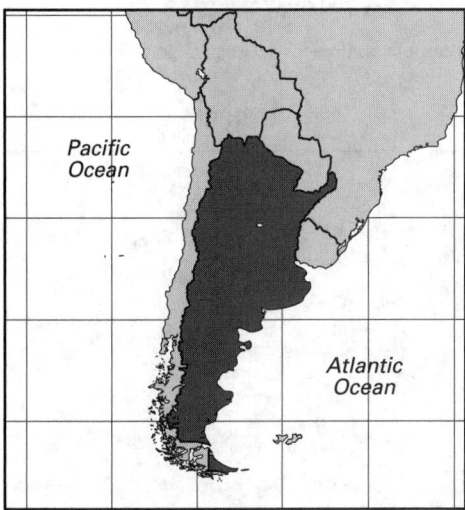

Pacific Ocean

Atlantic Ocean

**Official name:** República Argentina (Argentine Republic). **Form of government:** federal republic with two legislative houses (Senate [72]; Chamber of Deputies [257]). **Head of state and government:** President Néstor Kirchner (from 25 May 2003), assisted by Cabinet Chief Alberto Fernández (from 25 May 2003). **Capital:** Buenos Aires. **Official language:** Spanish. **Official religion:** Roman Catholicism. **Monetary unit:** 1 peso (pl. pesos) (Arg$) = 100 centavos; valuation (7 Jul 2003) $1 = Arg$2.79.

## Demography

**Area:** 1,073,400 sq mi, 2,780,092 sq km. **Population** (2002): 36,446,000. **Density** (2002): persons per sq mi 34.0, persons per sq km 13.1. **Urban** (2000): 89.6%. **Sex distribution** (2001): male 48.77%; female 51.23%. **Age breakdown** (2000): under 15, 27.7%; 15–29, 25.6%; 30–44, 18.8%; 45–59, 14.6%; 60–74, 9.6%; 75 and over, 3.7%. **Ethnic composition** (2000): European extraction 86.4%; mestizo 6.5%; Amerindian 3.4%; Arab 3.3%; other 0.4%. **Religious affiliation** (2000): Roman Catholic 79.8%; Protestant 5.4%; Muslim 1.9%; Jewish 1.3%; other 11.6%. **Major cities** (1999): Buenos

Aires 2,904,192 (12,423,000 [urban agglomeration]); Córdoba 1,275,585; Rosario 1,000,000; Mar del Plata 579,483; La Plata 556,308. **Location:** southern South America, bordering Bolivia, Paraguay, Brazil, Uruguay, the South Atlantic Ocean, and Chile.

## Vital statistics

**Birth rate** per 1,000 population (2001): 18.2 (world avg. 21.2). **Death rate** per 1,000 population (2001): 7.6 (world avg. 8.9). **Natural increase rate** per 1,000 population (2001): 10.6 (world avg. 12.3). **Total fertility rate** (avg. births per childbearing woman; 2001): 2.4. **Life expectancy** at birth (2001): male 72.1 years; female 79.0 years.

## National economy

**Budget** (1999). *Revenue*: Arg$56,621,300,000 (current revenue 98.2%, of which tax revenue 90.4%, nontax revenue 7.8%; capital revenue 1.8%). *Expenditure:* Arg$63,662,000,000 (social security 35.3%; debt service 13.6%; general public services 8.4%; education 5.0%; health 5.0%; economic services 3.9%; defense 3.3%). **Public debt** (external, outstanding; 2000): US$86,599,000,000. **Tourism** (2000): receipts US$2,874,000,000; expenditures US$4,338,-000,000. **Gross national product** (2002): US$276,-228,000,000 (US$7,460 per capita). **Production** (metric tons except as noted). *Agriculture, forestry, fishing* (1999): soybeans 19,500,000, sugarcane 16,700,000, wheat 14,200,000; livestock (number of live animals) 55,000,000 cattle, 14,000,000 sheep; roundwood (1998) 11,428,000 cu m; fish catch 1,012,804. *Mining and quarrying* (1999): silver 1,149,970 troy oz; gold 655,870 troy oz. *Manufacturing* (1999): cement 7,187,000; vegetable oil 5,658,000; wheat flour 3,563,000. *Energy production (consumption):* electricity (kW-hr; 2001) 84,540,000,000 ([1997] 78,190,000,000); coal (1999) 336,000 ([1997] 1,258,000); crude petroleum (barrels; 2001) 277,000,000 ([1997] 191,-000,000); petroleum products (metric tons; 1997) 21,923,000 (18,700,000); natural gas (cu m; 2001) 53,298,000,000 ([1997] 36,717,000,000). **Population economically active** (1995): total 14,345,171; activity rate of total population 41.5% (participation rates: ages 15–64, 64.5%; female 36.9%; unemployed [1996] 17.0%). **Household size and expenditure.** Average household size (1991) 3.8; expenditure (1985–86): food 38.2%, transportation 11.6%, housing 9.3%, energy 9.0%, clothing 8.0%, health 7.9%, recreation 7.5%, other 8.5%.

## Foreign trade

**Imports** (1999): US$25,508,000,000 (machinery and transport equipment 46.5%, chemical products 19.4%, manufactured products 15.0%, food products and live animals 4.4%). *Major import sources:* Brazil 21.9%; US 19.6%; France (includes Monaco) 5.9%; Germany 5.5%; Italy 5.3%; Japan 4.2%; Spain 3.9%. **Exports** (1999): US$23,333,000,000 (food products and live animals 35.1%, petroleum and petroleum products 12.1%, machinery and transport equipment 12.0%, manufactured products 10.8%, vegetable and animal oils 9.9%, crude materials 8.0%, chemical products 7.7%). *Major export destinations:* Brazil 24.4%; US 11.4%; Chile 8.0%; The Netherlands 4.3%; Spain 4.1%; Uruguay 3.5%; Italy 3.0%.

## Transport and communications

**Transport.** *Railroads* (1999): route length 33,958 km; passenger-km 9,102,000,000; metric ton-km cargo 9,101,852,000. *Roads* (1999): total length 215,471 km (paved 29%). *Vehicles* (1998): passenger cars 5,047,630; commercial vehicles and buses 1,496,567. *Air transport* (2001): passenger-km 4,575,000,000; metric ton-km cargo 105,342,000; airports (1997) 39. **Communications,** in total units (units per 1,000 persons). Daily newspaper circulation (1996): 4,320,000 (123); radio receivers (1998): 21,500,000 (595); television receivers (1998): 10,600,000 (293); telephone main lines (2001): 8,108,000 (216); cellular telephone subscribers (2001): 6,974,900 (186); personal computers (2001): 3,000,000 (80); Internet users (2001): 2,000,000 (53).

## Education and health

**Educational attainment** (1991). Percentage of population age 25 and over having: no formal schooling 5.7%; less than primary education 22.3%; primary 34.6%; incomplete secondary 12.5%; complete secondary 12.8%; higher 12.0%. **Literacy** (1995): total population age 15 and over literate 96.2%; males literate 96.2%; females literate 96.2%. **Health**: physicians (1992) 88,800 (1 per 376 persons); hospital beds (1996) 115,803 (1 per 304 persons); infant mortality rate per 1,000 live births (2000) 18.3. **Food** (2000): daily per capita caloric intake 3,181 (vegetable products 69%, animal products 31%); 135% of FAO recommended minimum.

## Military

**Total active duty personnel** (2001): 70,100 (army 59.1%, navy 23.1%, air force 17.8%). **Military expenditure as percentage of GNP** (1999): 1.6% (world 2.4%); per capita expenditure US$118.

## Background

Little is known of Argentina's indigenous population before the Europeans' arrival. The area was explored for Spain by Sebastian Cabot in 1526–30; by 1580, Asunción, Santa Fe, and Buenos Aires had been settled. At first attached to the viceroyalty of Peru (1620), it was later included with regions of modern Uruguay, Paraguay, and Bolivia in the viceroyalty of La Plata, or Buenos Aires (1776). With the establishment of the United Provinces of the Plate River in 1816, Argentina achieved its independence from Spain, but its boundaries were not set until the early 20th century. In 1943 the government was overthrown by the military; Col. Juan Perón took control in 1946. He in turn was overthrown in 1955. He returned in 1973 after two decades of turmoil. His second wife, Isabel, became president on his death in 1974 but lost power after a military coup in 1976. The military government tried to take the Falkland Islands (Islas Malvinas) in 1982 but was defeated by the British, with the result that the government returned to civilian rule in 1983. The government of Raúl Alfonsín worked to end the human-rights abuses that characterized the former regimes. Hyperinflation led to public riots and Alfonsín's electoral defeat in 1989; his Peronist successor,

Carlos Menem, instituted laissez-faire economic policies. In 1999 Fernando de la Rúa of the Alliance coalition was elected president, and his administration struggled with rising unemployment, foreign debt, and government corruption until the collapse of the government late in 2001.

## Recent Developments

On 1 Jan 2002 Eduardo Duhalde, a populist senator from Buenos Aires province, was elected president by the National Congress, but the economic collapse continued. The GDP had fallen by 21% since 1998 and unemployment reached 22% and one million Argentines found the value of their money had dropped by 60–70%. The government worked with the IMF and the World Bank to restructure its international debt, but Argentina defaulted on its $805 million World Bank loan in November. After former president Carlos Menem withdrew from the presidential race, it was clear sailing for Néstor Kirchner, governor of remote Santa Cruz province. He was inaugurated as president in May 2003.

**Internet resources:** <www.sectur.gov.ar>

# Armenia

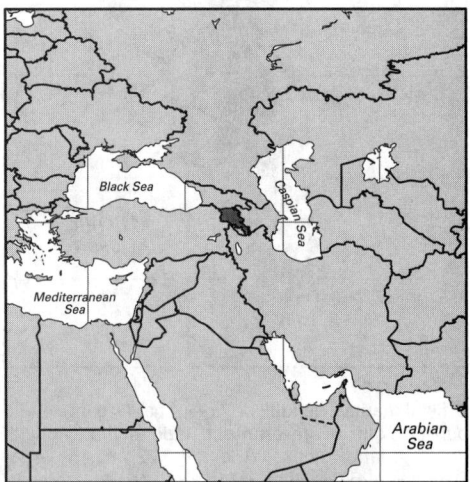

**Official name:** Hayastani Hanrape-tut'yun (Republic of Armenia). **Form of government:** unitary multiparty republic with a single legislative body (National Assembly [131]). **Head of state:** President Robert Kocharyan (from 1998). **Head of government:** Prime Minister Andranik Markaryan (from 2000). **Capital:** Yerevan. **Official language:** Armenian. **Official religion:** none (but a 1991 law establishes the Armenian Apostolic Church [the Armenian Orthodox Church] as having special status). **Monetary unit:** 1 dram = 100 lumas; valuation (7 Jul 2003), $1 = 558.14 drams.

## Demography

**Area:** 11,484 sq mi, 29,743 sq km; in addition, nearly 20% of neighboring Azerbaijan (including the 1,700-sq mi [4,400-sq km] geographic region of Nagorno-

*1 metric ton = about 1.1 short tons;   1 kilometer = 0.6 mi (statute);   1 metric ton-km cargo = about 0.68 short ton-mi cargo;   c.i.f.: cost, insurance, and freight;   f.o.b.: free on board*

Karabakh [Armenian: Artsakh]) has been occupied by Armenian forces since 1993. **Population** (2002): 3,800,000; actually present 3,008,000 (plus 14,000 in Nagorno-Karabakh). **Density** (2002): persons per sq mi 261.9, persons per sq km 101.1. **Urban** (2001): 66.6%. **Sex distribution** (2001): male 48.68%; female 51.32%. **Age breakdown** (2001): under 15, 23.2%; 15–29, 24.6%; 30–44, 23.3%; 45–59, 14.5%; 60–74, 11.6%; 75 and over, 2.8%. **Ethnic composition** (2000): Armenian 94.6%; Kurdish 1.7%; Russian 1.5%; Azerbaijani 0.5%; other 1.7%. **Religious affiliation** (1995): Armenian Apostolic 64.5%; other Christian 1.3%; other (mostly nonreligious) 34.2%. **Major cities** (2000): Yerevan 1,248,200; Gyumri 211,700 (1999); Kirovakan 172,700 (1999). **Location**: southwestern Asia, bordering Georgia, Azerbaijan, Iran, and Turkey.

## Vital statistics

**Birth rate** per 1,000 population (2001): 11.3 (world avg. 21.2); (1993) legitimate 86.0%; illegitimate 14.0%. **Death rate** per 1,000 population (2001): 7.9 (world avg. 8.9). **Natural increase rate** per 1,000 population (2001): 3.4 (world avg. 12.3). **Total fertility rate** (avg. births per childbearing woman; 2001): 1.5. **Marriage rate** per 1,000 population (2000): 2.9. **Divorce rate** per 1,000 population (2000): 0.4. **Life expectancy** at birth (2001): male 62.1 years; female 71.1 years.

## National economy

**Budget** (2000). *Revenue*: 202,005,000,000 drams (tax revenue 96.7%, of which value-added tax 33.4%, excise tax 12.5%, payroll tax 11.6%, enterprise profit tax 10.1%, income tax 7.3%, other taxes 21.8%; grants 3.3%). Expenditures: 267,411,000,000 drams (current expenditures 79.1%, of which pensions and social welfare 24.8%, wages 13.7%, interest 6.5%, health 5.5%, education 3.3%, other 25.3%; capital expenditure and net lending 20.9%). **Public debt** (external, outstanding; 2000): $677,700,000. **Tourism** (2000): receipts from visitors $45,000,000; expenditures by nationals abroad $37,000,000. **Land use** (1994): forest 13.4%; pasture 23.1%; agriculture 20.1%; other 43.4%. **Gross national product** (2000): $1,991,000,000 ($520 per capita). **Production** (metric tons except as noted). *Agriculture, forestry, fishing* (2001): potatoes 363,834, wheat 297,791, tomatoes 173,837; livestock (number of live animals) 497,306 cattle, 497,165 sheep, 68,912 pigs; roundwood (1998) 35,700 cu m; fish catch (1999) 1,730. *Mining and quarrying* (1999): copper 9,600,000; molybdenum 2,900; gold (metal content) 1,200 kg. *Manufacturing* (value in '000,000 drams; 1999): food products 109,016; jewelry 17,430; machinebuilding and metalworking equipment 15,286. *Construction* (1999): residential 190,400 sq m. *Energy production (consumption)*: electricity (kW-hr; 2000) 5,958,000,000 (5,958,000,000); coal (metric tons; 2000) none (5,000); crude petroleum (barrels; 1996) none (1,026,000); petroleum products (metric tons; 1997) none (139,000); natural gas (cu m; 1997) none (1,323,600). **Population economically active** (2000): total 1,436,900; activity rate of total population 37.8% (participation rates: ages 16–60, 77.4%; female 49.0%; unemployed 10.7%). **Household income and expenditure.** Average household size (1999) 4.5; income per household (1999) 664,700 drams ($1,200); sources of income (1999): agricul-

tural income 32.1%, wages and salaries 24.6%, transfers 19.3%, help from abroad 12.8%, self-employment 10.6%, other 0.6%; expenditure (1999): food 67.0%, beverages and tobacco 19.2%, services 12.4%, other 1.4%.

## Foreign trade

**Imports** (2000): $899,000,000 (minerals and chemicals 29.4%, food 16.6%, jewelry 12.6%, machinery and equipment 2.7%). *Major import sources:* EU countries 33.6%; former Soviet Union (FSU) 18.7%, of which Russia 14.7%; US 11.5%; Iran 9.3%. **Exports** (2000): $307,000,000 (jewelry 39.4%, machinery and equipment 14.3%, mineral products 12.4%, agricultural products 9.8%). *Major export destinations:* Belgium 24.5%; Russia 14.7%; US 12.4%; Iran 9.1%; Georgia 4.9%.

## Transport and communications

**Transport.** *Railroads* (1999): length 830 km; passenger-km 46,400,000; metric ton-km cargo 323,900,000. *Roads* (1997): 8,431 km (paved 100%). *Vehicles* (1996): passenger cars 1,300; trucks and buses 4,460. *Air transport* (2000): passenger-km 572,400,000; short ton-mi cargo 5,931,000, metric ton-km cargo 9,545,000; airports (2000) 1. **Communications**, in total units (units per 1,000 persons). Daily newspaper circulation (1995): 80,000 (23); television receivers (1998): 840,000 (221); telephone main lines (2001): 529,300 (140); cellular telephone subscribers (2001): 25,000 (6.6); personal computers (2001): 30,000 (7.9); Internet users (2001): 50,000 (14.2).

## Education and health

**Educational attainment** (1999). Percentage of population age 15 and over having: primary education or no formal schooling 5.9%; some secondary 15.2%; completed secondary and some postsecondary 60.2%; higher 15.0%. **Literacy** (1999): total population age 15 and over literate 99.3%. **Health** (2000): physicians 10,029 (1 per 301 persons); hospital beds 18,800 (1 per 166 persons); infant mortality rate per 1,000 live births (2000) 15.6. **Food** (2000): daily per capita caloric intake 1,944 (vegetable products 83%, animal products 17%); 77% of FAO recommended minimum.

## Military

**Total active duty personnel** (2001): 42,060 (army 92%, air force 8%). **Military expenditure as percentage of GNP** (1999): 5.8% (world 2.4%); per capita expenditure $170.

## Background

Armenia is a successor state to a historical region in southwestern Asia. Historical Armenia's boundaries have varied considerably, but the region extended over what is now northeastern Turkey and the Republic of Armenia. The area was later conquered by the Medes and Macedonia, and still later allied with the Roman empire. Armenia adopted Christianity as its national religion in AD 303. It came under the rule of the Ottoman Turks in 1514. Over the next centuries, as parts were ceded to other rulers, nationalism arose among the scattered Armenians; by the late 19th century it was causing widespread disruption. Fighting between Turks and Russians escalated when part of Armenia was ceded to Russia in 1878, and it continued through World War I, leading to Armenian deaths on a genocidal scale. With the Turkish defeat, the Russian-controlled part of Armenia was set up as a Soviet republic in 1921. Armenia became a constituent republic of the USSR in 1936. With the latter's dissolution in the late 1980s, Armenia declared its independence in 1990. It fought Azerbaijan for control over Nagorno-Karabakh until a cease-fire in 1994. About one-fifth of the population left the country beginning in 1993 because of an energy crisis. Political tension escalated, and in 1999 the prime minister and some legislators were killed in a terrorist attack on the legislature.

## Recent Developments

Armenia was accepted into full membership of the Council of Europe in January 2001. Robert Kocharyan in 2002 faced political pressure from increasingly united opposition groups seeking to unseat him as president.

**Internet resources:** <www.armeniaemb.org>

# Aruba

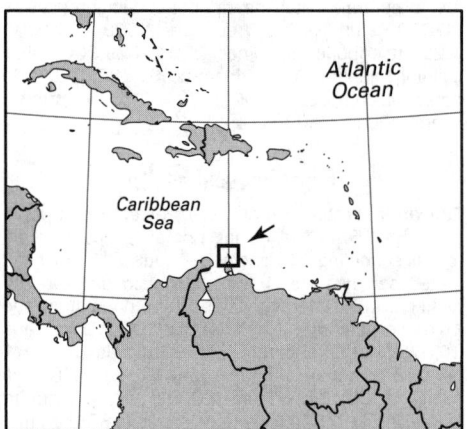

**Official name:** Aruba. **Political status:** nonmetropolitan territory of The Netherlands with one legislative house (States of Aruba [21]). **Chief of state:** Dutch Monarch Queen Beatrix (from 1980) represented by governor. **Head of government:** Prime Minister Nelson O. Oduber (from 2001). **Capital:** Oranjestad. **Official language:** Dutch. **Official religion:** none. **Monetary unit:** 1 Aruban florin; the Aruban florin (Af.) is pegged to the US dollar at a fixed rate of Af. 1.79 = $1).

## Demography

**Area:** 75 sq mi, 193 sq km. **Population** (2002): 91,600. **Density** (2002): persons per sq mi 1,221.3, persons per sq km 474.6. **Urban** (2000): 67.0%. **Sex distribution** (2000): male 47.99%; female 52.01%. **Age breakdown** (2000): under 15, 23.1%; 15–29, 19.3%; 30–44, 27.9%; 45–59, 18.1%; 60–74, 8.6%; 75 and over, 2.6%; unknown 0.4%. **Ethnolinguistic**

composition (2000): Papiamento 69.4%; Spanish 13.2%; English 8.1%; Dutch 6.1%; Portuguese 0.3%; other 2.0%; unknown 0.9%. **Religious affiliation** (2000): Christian 96.2%, of which Roman Catholic 81.9%, Protestant 7.3%, other Christian (Jehovah's Witness) 1.3%; Spiritist 1.0%; nonreligious 1.4%; other 1.4%. **Major urban areas** (2000): Oranjestad 26,355; San Nicolas 15,848. **Location:** southern Caribbean, north of Venezuela.

## Vital statistics

**Birth rate** per 1,000 population (2001): 13.9 (world avg. 21.2); legitimate 57.8%; illegitimate 42.2%. **Death rate** per 1,000 population (2001): 5.2 (world avg. 8.9). **Natural increase rate** per 1,000 population (2001): 8.7 (world avg. 12.3). **Total fertility rate** (avg. births per childbearing woman; 2000): 1.8. **Marriage rate** per 1,000 population (1998): 6.1. **Divorce rate** per 1,000 population (1998): 3.6. **Life expectancy** at birth (2000): male 70.0 years; female 76.0 years.

## National economy

**Budget** (1999). *Revenue:* Af. 712,900,000 (tax revenue 85.4%, of which taxes on wages and income 32.1%, import duties 13.7%, taxes on profits 11.2%, excise taxes on gasoline 8.4%; nontax revenue 14.4%). *Expenditures:* Af. 736,900,000. **Production** (metric tons except as noted). Agriculture, forestry, fishing: aloes are cultivated for export; small amounts of tomatoes, beans, cucumbers; (livestock; number of live animals) Aruba has very few livestock; fish catch (1997) 205. *Mining and quarrying:* excavation of sand for local use. *Manufacturing:* rum, cigarettes, aloe products. *Energy production (consumption):* electricity (kW-hr; 1999) 738,000,000 ([2000] 644,000,000); crude petroleum (barrels; 1997) none (2,353,000); petroleum products (metric tons; 1997) none (289,000). **Gross domestic product** (2000): $1,970,000,000 ($21,760 per capita). **Population economically active** (1997): total 44,840; activity rate of total population 48.9% (participation rates: ages 15–64, 68.3%; female 43.8%; unemployed 7.4%). **Public debt** (external, outstanding; December 2000): $209,800,000. **Household income and expenditure** (1999): average household size 3.6; average annual income per household: Af. 39,000 ($21,800); expenditure (1994): transportation and communications 20.7%, food and beverages 18.4%, clothing and footwear 11.3%, household furnishings 10.4%, housing 9.8%. **Tourism:** receipts from visitors (2000) $638,000,000; expenditures by nationals abroad (1999) $122,000,000. **Land use** (1998): forest, negligible; meadows and pastures, negligible; agricultural and under permanent cultivation 11.0%; other (dry savanna and built-up) 89.0%.

## Foreign trade

**Imports** (1999): $2,003,000,000 (petroleum [all forms] and free-zone imports 61.0%, electrical and nonelectrical machinery 8.0%, base and fabricated metals 4.3%). *Major import sources* (1999): US 63.3%; The Netherlands 11.1%; Venezuela 3.0%; Netherlands Antilles 2.8%. **Exports** (1999): $1,420,-000,000 (petroleum [all forms] and free-zone exports

---

*1 metric ton = about 1.1 short tons;   1 kilometer = 0.6 mi (statute);   1 metric ton-km cargo = about 0.68 short ton-mi cargo;   c.i.f.: cost, insurance, and freight;   f.o.b.: free on board*

97.9%). *Major export destinations*: US 41.4%; Colombia 20.3%; The Netherlands 12.1%; Netherlands Antilles 8.4%.

## Transport and communications

**Transport.** *Roads* (1995): total length 800 km (paved 64%). *Vehicles* (1999): passenger cars 38,834; trucks and buses 990. *Air transport* (2001–Air Aruba only): passenger-km 800,000,000; airports (1998) with scheduled flights 1. **Communications,** in total units (units per 1,000 persons). Daily newspaper circulation (1995): 80,000 (23); television receivers (1998): 840,000 (221); telephone main lines (2001): 529,300 (140); cellular telephone subscribers (2001): 25,000 (6.6); personal computers (2001): 30,000 (7.9); Internet users (2001): 50,000 (14.2).

## Education and health

**Educational attainment** (2000). Percentage of population age 25 and over having: no formal schooling or incomplete primary education 9.7%; primary education 33.9%; secondary/vocational 39.2%; advanced vocational/higher 16.2%; unknown status 1.0%. **Literacy** (2000): total population age 13 and over literate 96.3%. **Health** (1999): physicians (1997) 103 (1 per 870 persons); hospital beds 308 (1 per 306 persons); infant mortality rate per 1,000 live births (2000) 6.5.

## Military

**Total active duty personnel** (1999): a 45-member Dutch naval/air force contingent is stationed in Aruba and the Netherlands Antilles.

## Background

Aruba's earliest inhabitants were Arawak Indians, whose cave drawings can still be seen. Though the Dutch took possession of Aruba in 1636, they did not begin to develop it aggressively until 1816. In 1986 Aruba seceded from the Federation of the Netherlands Antilles in an initial step toward independence.

## Recent Developments

In 2001 Aruba was commended by the IMF for having improved surveillance and detection procedures relating to its growing offshore-banking sector. The opposition People's Electoral Movement emerged victorious in the September 2001 election.

**Internet resources:** <www.aruba.com>

# Australia

**Official name:** Commonwealth of Australia. **Form of government:** federal parliamentary state (formally a constitutional monarchy) with two legislative houses (Senate [76]; House of Representatives [150]). **Chief of state:** British Monarch Queen Elizabeth II (from 1952) represented by Governor-General Michael Jeffery (from 11 Aug 2003). **Head of government:** Prime Minister John Howard (from 1996). **Capital:** Canberra. **Official language:** English. **Official religion:** none. **Monetary unit:** 1 Australian dollar ($A) = 100 cents; valuation (7 Jul 2003) US$1 = $A1.47.

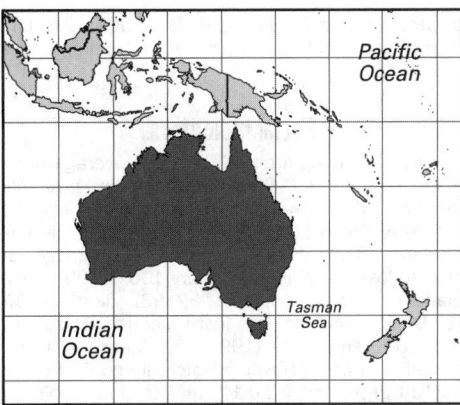

## Demography

**Area:** 2,969,910 sq mi, 7,692,030 sq km. **Population** (2002): 19,702,000. **Density** (2002): persons per sq mi 6.6, persons per sq km 2.6. **Urban** (2002): 85.0%. **Sex distribution** (2001): male 49.35%; female 50.65%. **Age breakdown** (2001): under 15, 20.8%; 15–24, 13.7%; 25–44, 29.8%; 45–64, 23.1%; 65 and over, 12.6%. **Ethnic composition** (1999): white 91.4%; Asian 6.4%; aboriginal 1.5%; other 0.7%. **Religious affiliation** (1996): Christian 70.9%, of which Roman Catholic 27.0%, Anglican Church of Australia 22.0%, other Protestant 21.9% (Uniting Church and Methodist 7.5%, Presbyterian 3.8%), Orthodox 2.8%, other Christian 2.4%; Muslim 1.1%; Buddhist 1.1%; Jewish 0.4%; Hindu 0.4%; no religion 16.6%; other 9.5%. **Metropolitan areas** (2001): Sydney 3,997,321; Melbourne 3,366,542; Brisbane 1,627,535; Perth 1,339,993; Adelaide 1,072,585; Newcastle 470,610; Gold Coast 444,077; Canberra 353,149; Wollongong 257,510; Caloundra 192,397; Hobart 191,169. **Location:** Oceania; continent between the Indian Ocean and the South Pacific Ocean. **Place of birth** (1999): 76.4% native-born; 23.6% foreign-born, of which Europe 10.8% (UK 6.5% [includes both Northern Ireland and Republic of Ireland], Italy 1.3%, Greece 0.7%, Germany 0.7%, The Netherlands 0.5%, other Europe 1.1%), Asia and Middle East 2.7%, New Zealand 1.9%, Africa, the Americas, and other 8.2%. **Mobility** (1995–96). Population age 15 and over living in the same residence as in 1994: 81.6%; different residence between states, regions, and neighborhoods 18.4%. **Households** (1996). Total number of households 7,100,000. Average household size 2.6; couples only 34.1%, couples with dependent children only 40.6%, couples with nondependent children 9.0%, single parent with children 9.9%, other 6.4%. **Immigration** (1996): permanent immigrants admitted 96,970, from UK and Ireland 12.8%, New Zealand 11.8%, China 7.6%, Vietnam 4.8%, Hong Kong 4.6%, India 4.4%, Philippines 3.9%, South Africa 3.2%, Bosnia and Herzegovina 3.2%, Yugoslavia 3.1%, Sri Lanka 2.2%. **Refugee arrivals** (1998–99): 8,790.

## Vital statistics

**Birth rate** per 1,000 population (2002): 12.8 (world avg. 21.2); (1997) legitimate 72.0%; illegitimate 28.0%. **Death rate** per 1,000 population (2002): 7.4 (world avg. 8.9). **Natural increase rate** per 1,000 population (2002): 5.4 (world avg. 12.3). **Total fertility rate** (avg. births per childbearing woman; 2000): 1.8. **Marriage rate** per 1,000 population (2001): 5.3.

Divorce rate per 1,000 population (2001): 2.8. **Life expectancy** at birth (2000): male 76.6 years; female 82.0 years.

## Social indicators

**Quality of working life** (1999–2000). Average workweek: 35.7 hours (16.8% (1994) overtime). Annual rate per 100,000 workers for: accidental injury and industrial disease, 3,200 (1992–93); death, n.a. Proportion of employed persons insured for damages or income loss resulting from: injury 100% (1994); permanent disability 100% (1992–93); death 100% (1992–93). Working days lost to industrial disputes per 1,000 employees (1999): 87. Means of transportation to work (1986): private automobile 69.4%; public transportation 10.1%; motorcycle and bicycle 3.2%; foot 6.6%; other 10.7%. Discouraged job seekers (considered by employers to be too young or too old, having language or training limitations, or no vacancies in line of work; 1999): 1.1% of labor force. **Access to services** (1976). Proportion of dwellings having access to: electricity 99.5%; bathroom 96.0%; flush toilet 92.2%; kitchen 97.9%; public sewer 73.4%. **Social participation.** Eligible voters participating in last national election (1996): 95.8%; voting is compulsory. Trade union membership in total workforce (1996): 31%. **Social deviance** (1999). Offense rate per 100,000 population for: murder 1.8; sexual assault 74.2; assault 704.5; auto theft 684.8; burglary and housebreaking 2,191.6; armed robbery 49.8. Incidence per 100,000 in general population of (1996): prisoners with drug offenses 539.5; suicide 13.1. **Material well-being** (1995). Households possessing: automobile 85%; telephone 95%; refrigerator 99.7%; personal computers 54.0% (1994); washing machine 90.0%

## National economy

**Gross national product** (2000): US$388,252,000,-000 (US$20,240 per capita). **Budget** (1998–99). *Revenue:* $A 146,444,000,000 (income tax 70.3%, of which individual 52.4%, corporate 14.2%; excise duties and sales tax 22.1%). *Expenditures:* $A 140,814,000,000 (social security and welfare 37.5%; health 16.6%; economic and public services 11.2%; defense 8.0%; education 6.9%; interest on public debt 5.3%). **Public debt** (2000–01): $A 69,226,000,000. **Tourism** (2000): receipts from visitors US$8,006,000,000; expenditures by nationals abroad US$5,740,000,000. **Production** (gross value in $A '000 except as noted). *Agriculture, forestry, fishing* (1998–99): livestock slaughtered 7,401,400 (cattle 4,476,600, sheep and lambs 1,045,500, poultry 1,174,300, pigs 689,700); wheat 3,860,000, wool 2,139,100, seed cotton 1,353,000, grapes 1,115,-600, sugarcane 1,044,000, barley 885,000, canola 638,000, potatoes 486,000, rice 332,000, apples 325,000, oranges 307,000, sorghum 285,000, bananas 264,000, lupins 244,000, tomatoes 222,000, carrots 162,000, oats 157,000, pears 114,000, sunflower seeds 74,000, peaches 65,000, corn (maize) 60,000, tobacco 40,000, pineapples 39,000; livestock (number of live animals; 1999) 115,456,000 sheep and lambs, 26,578,000 cattle, 2,626,000 pigs, 93,578,000 poultry; roundwood (1999) 22,938,000 cu m; fish catch (1998) 201,216 metric

tons. *Mining and quarrying* (metric tons [tons of contained metal]; 1997–98): iron ore 169,568,000; bauxite 50,418,000; zinc 2,029,000; copper 1,665,000; lead 943,000; uranium oxide 5,797; gold 330,095 kg; diamonds (1998–99) 36,000,000 carats. *Manufacturing* (value added in US$'000,000 except as noted; 1995): food products 12,239; transport equipment 5,745; printing and publishing 5,252; metal products 4,840; nonferrous metals 4,766; nonelectrical machinery 4,054. *Construction* (buildings completed, by value in $A '000; 1998–99): new dwellings 17,080,000; alterations and additions to dwellings 3,194,000; nonresidential 14,016,000. *Energy production (consumption):* electricity (kW-hr; 1997) 183,069,000,000 (183,069,000,000); coal (metric tons; 1997) 264,972,000 (115,424,000); crude petroleum (barrels; 1997) 153,000,000 (223,000,000); petroleum products (metric tons; 1997) 33,445,000 (31,038,000); natural gas (cu m; 1997) 31,909,000,000 (21,116,000,000). **Population economically active** (1999–2000): total 9,577,900; activity rate of total population 50.5% (participation rates: over age 15, 63.4%; female 43.6%; unemployed 6.9%). **Household income and expenditure** (1998–99). Average household size (1996) 2.6; average annual income per household $A 45,708 (US$24,200); sources of income: wages and salaries 39.9%, self-employment 32.1%, transfer payments 10.1%, other 17.9%; expenditure: food and nonbeverages 18.2%, transportation and communications 16.9%, housing 13.9%, recreation 12.7%, household durable goods 6.0%, household services and operation 5.9%, clothing and footwear 4.6%, health 4.6%, alcoholic beverages 2.9%, energy 2.6%, other 11.7%. **Land use** (1998): agricultural and under permanent cultivation 7.0%; other 93.0% (of which, meadows and pastures 54.0%).

## Foreign trade

**Imports** (1999–2000-f.o.b.): $A 110,083,000,000 (machinery and transport equipment 46.6%, of which road motor vehicles 11.6%, office machines and automatic data-processing equipment 6.9%, telecommunications equipment 6.2%; basic manufactures 12.4%, of which textile yarn and fabrics 2.4%, paper and paperboard products 2.1%; chemicals and related products 11.4%; mineral fuels and lubricants 7.0%; food and live animals 3.6%). *Major import sources:* US 20.9%; Japan 12.8%; China 6.8%; UK 5.8%; Germany 5.3%; New Zealand 4.0%; Singapore 4.0%. **Exports** (1999–2000-f.o.b.): $A 97,255,000,-000 (crude materials excluding fuels 18.9%, of which metalliferous ores and metal scrap 11.6%, textile fibers and their waste 4.4%; mineral fuels and lubricants 18.6%, of which coal, coke, and briquettes 8.6%, petroleum, petroleum products, and natural gas 7.3%; food and live animals 17.3%, of which cereals and cereal preparations 5.1%, meat and meat preparations 4.6%, dairy products 2.4%; basic manufactures 12.7%). *Major export destinations:* Japan 19.3%; US 9.8%; South Korea 7.8%; New Zealand 6.9%; China 5.1%; Singapore 5.0%; Taiwan 4.8%.

## Transport and communications

**Transport.** *Railroads* (1998–99; government railways only): route length 35,780 km; passengers carried

---

*1 metric ton = about 1.1 short tons;   1 kilometer = 0.6 mi (statute);   1 metric ton-km cargo = about 0.68 short ton-mi cargo;   c.i.f.: cost, insurance, and freight;   f.o.b.: free on board*

595,200,000; metric ton-km cargo 127,400,000,-000. *Roads* (2000): total length 808,465 km (paved 40%). *Vehicles* (1999): passenger cars 9,719,900; trucks and buses 2,214,900. *Air transport* (1999; includes Qantas and Ansett Australia [ceased operations 4 Mar 2002]): passenger-km 75,070,556,000; metric ton-km cargo 1,688,215,000; airports (1996) with scheduled flights 400. **Communications,** in total units (units per 1,000 persons). Daily newspaper circulation (1996): 5,370,000 (296); radio receivers (1997): 25,500,000 (1,391); television receivers (1999): 13,400,000 (706); telephone main lines (2001): 10,060,000 (520); cellular telephone subscribers (2001): 11,169,000 (578); personal computers (2001): 10,000,000 (517); Internet users (2001): 7,200,000 (372).

## Education and health

**Educational attainment** (1999). Percentage of population age 15 to 64 having: no formal schooling and incomplete secondary education 38.0%; completed secondary 18.3%; postsecondary, technical, or other certificate/diploma 28.3%; university 15.4%. **Literacy** (1996): total population literate, virtually 100%. **Health:** physicians (1999–2000) 55,200 (1 per 345 persons); hospital beds (1998–99) 77,631 (1 per 243 persons); infant mortality rate per 1,000 live births (2000) 6.0. **Food** (1999): daily per capita caloric intake 3,150 (vegetable products 69%, animal products 31%); (1997) 118% of FAO recommended minimum.

## Military

**Total active duty personnel** (2001): 50,700 (army 47.7%, navy 24.7%, air force 27.6%). **Military expenditure as percentage of GNP** (1999): 1.8% (world 2.4%); per capita expenditure US$372.

---

**Did you know?** Australia has more than 7,000 beaches, more than any other nation in the world.

---

## Background

Australia has long been inhabited by Aborigines, who arrived on the continent 40,000–60,000 years ago. Estimates of the population at the time of European settlement in 1788 range from 300,000 to more than 1,000,000. Widespread European knowledge of Australia began with 17th-century explorations. The Dutch landed in 1616 and the British in 1688, but the first large-scale expedition was that of James Cook in 1770, which established Britain's claim to Australia. The first English settlement, at Port Jackson (1788), consisted mainly of convicts and seamen; convicts were to make up a large proportion of the incoming settlers. By 1859 the colonial nuclei of all Australia's states had been formed, but with devastating effects on the Aborigines, whose population declined sharply with the introduction of European diseases and weaponry. Britain granted its colonies limited self-government in the mid 19th century, and Australia achieved federation in 1901. Australia fought alongside the British in World War I, notably at Gallipoli, and again in World War II, preventing the occupation of Australia by the Japanese. It joined the US in the Korean and Vietnam wars. Since the 1960s the government has sought to deal more fairly with the Aborigines, and

a loosening of immigration restrictions has led to a more heterogeneous population. Constitutional links allowing British interference in government were formally abolished in 1968, and Australia has assumed a leading role in Asian and Pacific affairs. During the 1990s, it experienced several debates about giving up its British ties and becoming a republic.

## Recent Developments

A terrorist bomb attack on 12 Oct 2002 killed nearly 100 Australians on holiday in the resort town of Kuta on the Indonesian island of Bali. Prime Minister John Howard declared that "our nation has been changed by this event" and wept when he visited the blackened bomb site where two popular night spots had once stood.

The Australian and Indonesian governments moved closer together in 2002, especially in the aftermath of the Bali bombing. Indonesian Pres. Megawati Sukarnoputri and Howard set up Operation Alliance to investigate the bomb blast. Many of the Indonesian victims were flown to Australia for medical treatment. In February 2002 Howard had visited Indonesia and signed a joint memorandum of understanding on sharing intelligence. Subsequently, Defense Minister Robert Hill visited Jakarta as part of Canberra's efforts to counter terrorism. Australia faced pressure from the new state of East Timor, however, when Prime Minister Mari Alkatiri made it clear that East Timor claimed an area that extended 200 nautical miles from its coastline. This area included the Greater Sunrise gas fields, 80% of which were in Australian waters.

The US and China were other focuses of Australian foreign policy in 2002–03. Howard said that he would commit troops to a US-led military strike against Saddam Hussein's regime in Iraq. Foreign Minister Alexander Downer, who held talks in Washington DC in July, offered strong backing to the Bush government. After the bombing on Bali Downer watered down his support for a war in Iraq, saying Australia "had an overwhelming focus on [its] own region and [its] own environment." President Bush telephoned Howard to express American sympathy, and a wattle tree was planted in the US embassy in Canberra as a mark of solidarity. In the event, Australia supplied 2,000 troops to the coalition forces. Australia signed a 25-year, $A 25-billion-liquid-gas supply contract to provide clean energy to China's Guangdong province.

Public opinion in Australia was quick to blame Howard for the bombing on Bali. Many people believed that Howard had made Australians a target for Muslim extremists by his overenthusiastic support for US foreign policy. The prime minister's high public standing on matters of immigration allowed him to remain firmly defiant regarding the treatment of asylum seekers in Australia. Throughout the year Immigration Minister Philip Ruddock defended Australia's Pacific Solution to the asylum problem against local and overseas condemnation. On 29 March 2002 a razor-wire fence at the Woomera Detention Centre was torn down, which allowed several detainees to escape and triggered violent local protests. Forty-two Iraqi asylum seekers, who were being held on Papua New Guinea's Manus Island, were eventually accepted as refugees in Australia, but almost all of the asylum seekers claiming to be Afghans were rejected. In order to provide a more humane form of detention, the government built the new Baxter detention center on the El Alamein Army Base near Port Augusta.

After having won a historic third term in office in the 2001 general elections, Howard and his Liberal Party of Australia (LPA) faced weak federal opposition parties. Governor-General Peter Hollingsworth resigned in May 2003 under the shadow of allegations that he had mishandled sex-abuse cases when he was archbishop of Brisbane (1990–2001).

Internet resources: <www.australia.com>

# Austria

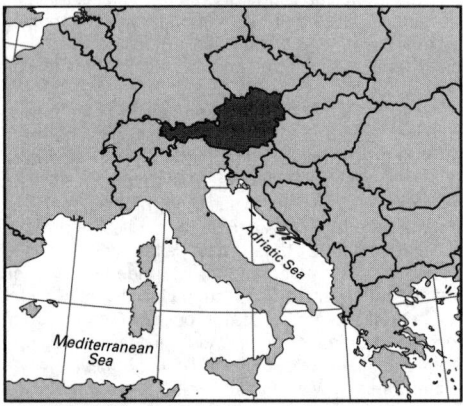

Official name: Republik Österreich (Republic of Austria). Form of government: federal state with two legislative houses (Federal Council [64]; National Council [183]). Chief of state: President Thomas Klestil (from 1992). Head of government: Chancellor Wolfgang Schüssel (from 2000). Capital: Vienna. Official language: German. Official religion: none. Monetary unit: 1 euro (€) = 100 cents; $1 = €0.87 (7 Jul 2003); at conversion on 1 Jan 2002, €1 = 13.76 Austrian schilling (S).

## Demography

Area: 32,378 sq mi, 83,858 sq km. Population (2002): 8,077,000. Density (2002): persons per sq mi 249.5, persons per sq km 96.3. Urban (2001): 67.4%. Sex distribution (2001): male 48.44%; female 51.56%. Age breakdown (2001): under 15, 16.8%; 15–29, 18.7%; 30–44, 24.9%; 45–59, 18.6%; 60–74, 13.8%; 75 and over, 7.2%. Ethnic composition (national origin; 1998): Austrian 91.2%; citizens of former Yugoslavia 4.0%; Turkish 1.6%; other 3.2%. Religious affiliation (1995): Roman Catholic 75.1%; nonreligious and atheist 8.6%; Protestant (mostly Lutheran) 5.4%; Muslim 2.1%; Eastern Orthodox 0.7%; Jewish 0.1%; other 1.9%; unknown 6.1%. Major cities (2001): Vienna 1,562,482; Graz 226,892; Linz 186,266; Salzburg 144,817; Innsbruck 113,826. Location: central Europe, bordering the Czech Republic, Slovakia, Hungary, Slovenia, Italy, Switzerland, Liechtenstein, and Germany.

## Vital statistics

Birth rate per 1,000 population (2001): 9.2 (world avg. 21.2); (2000) legitimate 68.7%; illegitimate 31.3%. Death rate per 1,000 population (2001): 9.2 (world avg. 8.9). Natural increase rate per 1,000 population (2001): 0.0 (world avg. 13.2). Total fertility rate (avg. births per childbearing woman; 2000): 1.3. Marriage rate per 1,000 population (1999): 4.9. Divorce rate per 1,000 population (1999): 2.3. Life expectancy at birth (2000): male 75.4 years; female 81.2 years.

## National economy

Budget (1997). Revenue: S 950,820,000,000 (tax revenue 92.0%, of which social security contributions 37.7%, individual income taxes 17.3%, value-added taxes 16.2%). Expenditures: S 1,017,870,000 (social security and welfare 42.0%; health 14.4%; education 9.2%; interest 9.2%; defense 2.0%). National debt (end of year 1998): $133,897,000,000. Production (metric tons except as noted). Agriculture, forestry, fishing (2000): sugar beets 2,600,000, corn (maize) 1,800,000, wheat 1,313,000; livestock (number of live animals) 3,790,000 pigs, 2,150,000 cattle, 13,540,000; roundwood (1999) 14,083,000 cu m; fish catch (1997) 3,486. Mining and quarrying (1999): iron ore 1,747,000; magnesite 748,600; talc 129,600. Manufacturing (value added in S '000,000,000; 1997): nonelectrical machinery and apparatus 46.1; food and beverages 44.1; electrical machinery and apparatus 42.9. Energy production (consumption): electricity (kW-hr; 1999) 60,348,000,-000 ([1997] 56,082,000,000); hard coal (metric tons; 1999) negligible ([1997] 4,087,000); lignite (metric tons; 1999) 1,137,000 ([1997] 1,287,000); crude petroleum (barrels; 1999) 7,054,000 ([1997] 66,323,000); petroleum products (metric tons; 1997) 8,792,000 (10,760,000); natural gas (cu m; 1999) 1,833,000,000 ([1997] 8,353,000,000). Tourism ($'000,000; 2000): receipts $10,031; expenditures $9,291. Population economically active (1999): total 3,909,000; activity rate of total population 48.3% (participation rates: ages 15–64 [1998] 70.7%; female 43.2%; unemployed [October 1999–September 2000] 6.0%). Gross national product (at current market prices; 2000): $204,525,000,000 ($25,220 per capita). Household income and expenditure. Average household size (2000) 2.5; sources of income (1995): wages and salaries 54.8%, transfer payments 25.9%; expenditure (1995): transportation and communications 15.4%, housing 15.4%, food and beverages 15.3%, café and hotel expenditures 12.6%. Land use (1994): forested 39.2%; meadows and pastures 24.3%; agricultural and under permanent cultivation 18.3%; other 18.2%.

## Foreign trade

Imports (1999-c.i.f.): €65,320,000,000 (machinery and transport equipment 41.3%, of which road vehicles 12.1%, electrical machinery and apparatus 7.5%; chemicals and related products 10.3%; food products 5.2%; clothing 4.4%). Major import sources: Germany 41.9%; Italy 7.6%; US 5.3%; France 5.0%; Switzerland 3.4%; Hungary 3.3%. Exports (1999): €60,270,000,000 (machinery and transport equipment 43.1%, of which road vehicles 10.0%, electrical machinery and apparatus 8.1%; chemical products 9.4%; fabricated metals 4.9%; paper and paper products 4.7%). Major export destinations: Germany 34.9%; Italy 8.4%; Switzerland 6.0%; Hungary 4.9%; US 4.6%; France 4.4%.

1 metric ton = about 1.1 short tons;   1 kilometer = 0.6 mi (statute);   1 metric ton-km cargo = about 0.68 short ton-mi cargo;   c.i.f.: cost, insurance, and freight;   f.o.b.: free on board

## Transport and communications

**Transport.** *Railroads* (1999; federal railways only): length 5,643 km; (1998) passenger-km 7,971,000,-000; (1998) metric ton-km cargo 15,348,000,000. *Roads* (1997): total length 200,000 km (paved 100%). *Vehicles* (1999): passenger cars 4,009,604; trucks and buses 328,591. *Air transport* (1999; Austrian Airlines and Lauda Air): passenger-km 12,460,-000,000; metric ton-km cargo 361,348,000; airports (1999) with scheduled flights 6. **Communications,** in total units (units per 1,000 persons). Daily newspaper circulation (1996): 2,382,000 (296); radio receivers (1996): 6,000,000 (744); television receivers (1998): 4,200,000 (520); telephone main lines (2001): 3,810,000 (468); cellular telephone subscribers (2001): 6,565,900 (807); personal computers (2000): 2,270,000 (279); Internet users (2001): 2,600,000 (319).

## Education and health

**Educational attainment** (1993). Percentage of population age 25 and over having: lower-secondary education 37.5%; vocational education ending at secondary level 44.6%; completed upper secondary 6.1%; higher vocational 5.5%; higher 6.3%. **Literacy:** virtually 100%. **Health:** physicians (2001) 25,001 (1 per 323 persons); hospital beds (2000) 67,964 (1 per 119 persons); infant mortality rate per 1,000 live births (2001) 4.9. **Food** (1998): daily per capita caloric intake 3,531 (vegetable products 65%, animal products 35%); 134% of FAO recommended minimum.

## Military

**Total active duty personnel** (2001): 41,100 (army 84.4%; air force 15.6%). **Military expenditure as percentage of GNP** (1999): 0.8% (world 2.4%); per capita expenditure $208.

## Background

Settlement in Austria goes back some 3,000 years, when Illyrians were probably the main inhabitants. The Celts invaded c. 400 BC and established Noricum. The Romans arrived after 200 BC and established the provinces of Raetia, Noricum, and Pannonia; prosperity followed and the population became romanized. With the fall of Rome in the 5th century AD, many tribes invaded, including the Slavs; they were eventually subdued by Charlemagne, and the area became ethnically Germanic. The distinct political entity that would become Austria emerged in 976 with Leopold I of Babenberg as margrave. In 1278 Rudolf I of the Holy Roman Empire (formerly Rudolf IV of Habsburg) conquered the area; Habsburg rule lasted until 1918. While in power, the Habsburgs created a kingdom centered on Austria, Bohemia, and Hungary. The Napoleonic Wars brought about the creation of the Austrian empire (1804) and the end of the Holy Roman Empire (1806). Count von Metternich tried to assure Austrian supremacy among Germanic states, but war with Prussia led Austria to divide the empire into the Dual Monarchy of Austria-Hungary. Nationalist sentiment plagued the kingdom, and the assassination of Francis Ferdinand by a Serbian nationalist in 1914 triggered World War I, which destroyed the Austrian empire. In the postwar carving up of Austria-Hungary, Austria became an independent republic. It was annexed by Nazi Germany in 1938 and joined the Axis powers in World War II. The republic was restored in 1955 after 10 years of Allied occupation. Austria became a member of the European Union in 1995.

## Recent Developments

In September 2002 the coalition of the conservative Austrian People's Party (ÖVP) and the populist right-wing Freedom Party of Austria (FPÖ) finally collapsed. Elections on 24 November saw support for the FPÖ plummet from 27% in 1999 to a mere 10%. The big winner was the senior coalition partner, the ÖVP, which took 42% of the vote and gave its leader, Chancellor Wolfgang Schüssel, the choice of making a coalition with any one of the other three parties represented in the Federal Assembly—the FPÖ, the SPÖ, or the environmentalist Greens. On 28 Feb 2003, to a chorus of international protests, he swore in a new ÖVP-FPÖ government. In May the National Federation of Austrian Unions declared a general strike to protest government plans to tighten state pension provisions.

**Internet resources:** <www.austria.org>

# Azerbaijan

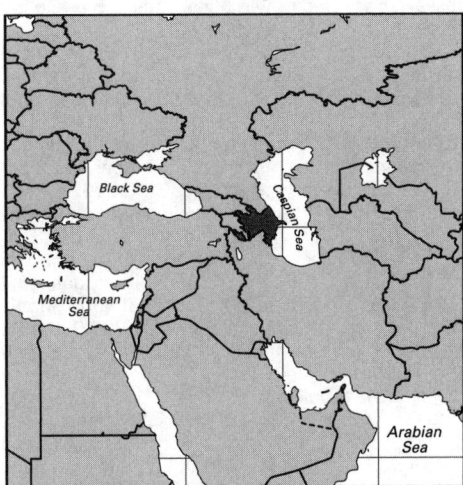

**Official name:** Azerbaycan Respublikasi (Azerbaijani Republic). **Form of government:** unitary multiparty republic with a single legislative body (National Assembly [124 seats, excluding one vacancy reserved for a Nagorno-Karabakh representative]). **Head of state and government:** President Heydar Aliyev (from 1993) assisted by Prime Minister Artur Rasizade (from 1996). **Capital:** Baku. **Official language:** Azerbaijani. **Official religion:** none. **Monetary unit:** 1 manat (A.M.) = 100 gopik; valuation (7 Jul 2003) free rate, $1 = A.M. 4,921.

## Demography

**Area:** 33,400 sq mi, 86,600 sq km. **Population** (2002): 8,176,000. **Density** (2002): persons per sq mi 244.8, persons per sq km 94.4. **Urban** (1998): 56.6%. **Sex distribution** (2000): male 48.94%; female 51.06%. **Age breakdown** (2000): under 15, 31.8%; 15–29, 25.6%; 30–44, 24.1%; 45–59, 9.5%; 60–69, 7.6%; 70 and over, 1.4%. **Ethnic composition** (1995): Azerbaijani 89.0%; Russian 3.0%; Lezgian

2.2%; Armenian 2.0%; other 3.8%. **Religious affiliation** (1995): Muslim 93.4%, of which Shi'i 65.4%, Sunni 28.0%; Russian Orthodox 1.1%; Armenian Apostolic (Orthodox) 1.1%; other 4.4%. **Major cities** (1997): Baku 1,727,200; Ganca (formerly Kirovabad) 291,900; Sumqayit (Sumgait) 248,500; Mingaevir (Mingechaur) 97,200. **Location:** eastern Transcaucasia, bordering Russia, the Caspian Sea, Iran, Turkey, Armenia, and Georgia.

## Vital statistics

**Birth rate** per 1,000 population (2001): 14.8 (world avg. 21.2); (1994) legitimate 94.8%; illegitimate 5.2%. **Death rate** per 1,000 population (2001): 5.9 (world avg. 8.9). **Natural increase rate** per 1,000 population (2001): 8.9 (world avg. 12.3). **Total fertility rate** (avg. births per childbearing woman; 2001): 1.6. **Life expectancy** at birth (2001): male 68.1 years; female 75.1 years.

## National economy

**Budget** (2000). *Revenue*: A.M. 4,004,000,000,000 (tax revenue 69.3%, of which value-added tax 22.8%, social security contributions 11.4%, enterprise profits tax 11.4%, personal income tax 8.3%, excise taxes 7.3%, tax on international trade 5.8%, other taxes 2.3%; nontax revenue 30.7%). *Expenditures*: A.M. 3,801,000,000,000 (education 23.8%; social security 18.3%; national economy 17.8%; defense 12.8%; health 5.4%; culture 2.8%; other 19.1%). **Public debt** (external, outstanding; 2000): $692,-100,000. **Production** (metric tons except as noted). *Agriculture, forestry, fishing* (2000): cereals 950,-000, vegetables (except potatoes) 780,800, fruit (except grapes) 477,000; livestock (number of live animals) 6,086,000 sheep and goats, 2,021,600 cattle, 63,700 horses; roundwood (2000) 13,500 cu m; fish catch (1999) 4,935. *Mining and quarrying* (1996): iron ore 1,000,000; alunite 600,000. *Manufacturing* (value of production in A.M. '000,000,000; 1998): oil refinery products 2,980; electricity and gas 2,005; food products 1,972. *Energy production (consumption)*: electricity (kW-hr; 1997) 16,800,-000,000 (16,800, 000,000); coal (metric tons; 1997) none (1,000); crude petroleum (barrels; 2000) 102,200,000 (47,200,000); petroleum products (metric tons; 2000) 7,520,000 ([1998] 6,200,-000); natural gas (cu m; 2000) 5,600,000,000 (5,600,000,000). **Household income and expenditure.** Average household size (1997) 5.2; sources of income (1993): wages and salaries 50.9%, agricultural income 24.0%, social benefits 10.2%; expenditure: food 61.2%, clothing 11.1%, services 3.0%. **Tourism** (2000): receipts $63,000,000; expenditures $132,000,000. **Gross national product** (2000): $4,960,000,000 ($610 per capita). **Population economically active** (2000): total 3,704,500, activity rate 45.8% (participation rates: ages 15–64, 73.1%; female 47.7%; unemployed 1.2%). **Land use** (2000): forest 11.5%; pasture 25.4%; agriculture 50.0%; other 12.6%.

## Foreign trade

**Imports** (2000): $1,172,069,000 (machinery and equipment 31.0%, food 19.0%, metals 10.5%,

minerals 9.8%, vehicles 8.5%, chemicals 7.2%). *Major import sources:* Russia 21.3%; Turkey 11.0%; US 8.9%; Germany 5.8%; Kazakhstan 4.9%; Iran 4.8%; Switzerland 4.8%; Ukraine 3.1%. **Exports** (2000): $1,744,900,000 (petroleum products 84.0%, food 3.3%, cotton 2.1%, chemicals 2.1%, machinery and equipment 1.9%, metals 1.8%). *Major export destinations:* Italy 43.7%; France 11.8%; Israel 7.7%; Turkey 6.0%; Russia 5.6%; Georgia 4.3%; Iceland 1.8%.

## Transport and communications

**Transport.** *Railroads* (2000): length 2,120 km; passenger-km 493,200,000; metric ton-km cargo 5,770,000. *Roads* (1999): total length 45,870 km (paved 94%). *Vehicles* (2000): passenger cars 332,100; trucks and buses 78,300. *Air transport* (1995): passenger-km 1,650,000,000; metric ton-km cargo 183,000,000; airports (2000) 3. **Communications,** in total units (units per 1,000 persons). Daily newspaper circulation (1995): 210,000 (28); radio receivers (1997): 175,000 (23); television receivers (1998): 1,950,000 (253); telephone main lines (2001): 865,500 (111); cellular telephone subscribers (2001): 620,000 (79); Internet users (2001): 25,000 (3.2).

## Education and health

**Educational attainment** (1995). Percentage of population age 15 and over having: primary education or no formal schooling 12.1%, some secondary 9.1%; completed secondary and some postsecondary 27.5%; higher 7.6%. **Literacy** (1989): total population 15 and over literate 97.3%; males literate 98.9%; females 95.9%. **Health** (2000): physicians 28,600 (1 per 283 persons); hospital beds (1998) 71,100 (1 per 110 persons); infant mortality rate per 1,000 live births (2001) 30.0. **Food** (2000): daily per capita caloric intake 2,468 (vegetable products 85%, animal products 15%); 96% of FAO recommended minimum.

## Military

**Total active duty personnel** (2001): 72,100 (army 86.0%, navy 3.0%, air force 11.0%). **Military expenditure as percentage of GNP** (1999): 6.6% (world 2.4%); per capita expenditure $120.

## Background

Azerbaijan adjoins the Iranian region of the same name, and the origin of their respective inhabitants is the same. By the 9th century AD it had come under Turkish influence, and in ensuing centuries it was fought over by Arabs, Mongols, Turks, and Iranians. Russia acquired the territory of what is now independent Azerbaijan in the early 19th century. After the Russian Revolution of 1917, Azerbaijan declared its independence; it was subdued by the Red Army in 1920 and became a Soviet Socialist Republic. It declared independence from the collapsing Soviet Union in 1991. Azerbaijan has two geographic peculiarities. The exclave Nakhichevan is separated from the rest of Azerbaijan by Armenian territory. Nagorno-Karabakh, which lies within

*1 metric ton = about 1.1 short tons;   1 kilometer = 0.6 mi (statute);   1 metric ton-km cargo = about 0.68 short ton-mi cargo;   c.i.f.: cost, insurance, and freight;   f.o.b.: free on board*

Azerbaijan and is administered by it, has a Christian Armenian majority. Azerbaijan and Armenia went to war over both territories in the 1990s, causing great economic disruption. Though a cease-fire was declared in 1994, the political situation remained unresolved.

## Recent Developments

Pres. Heydar Aliyev's four-week hospitalization in the US in February 2002 for prostate surgery and the fact that he collapsed, twice, during a televised speech on 21 Apr 2003 in Istanbul, Turkey, fueled speculation that failing health would ultimately compel him to abandon his stated intention of seeking a third presidential term in 2003. A nationwide referendum on sweeping constitutional changes that was held 24 Aug 2002 was apparently intended to facilitate the election of Aliyev's son Ilham to succeed him.

Internet resources: <www.president.az>

# The Bahamas

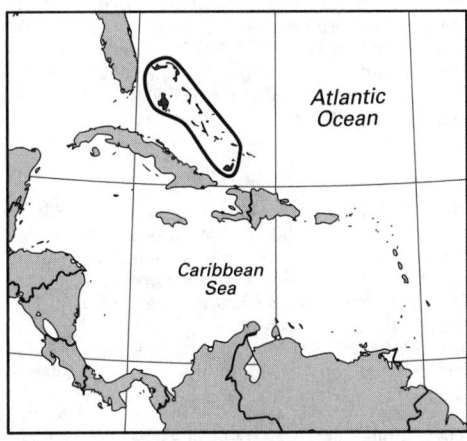

**Official name:** The Commonwealth of The Bahamas. **Form of government:** constitutional monarchy with two legislative houses (Senate [16]; House of Assembly [40]). **Chief of state:** Queen Elizabeth II represented by Governor-General Dame Ivy Dumont (from 13 Nov 2001). **Head of government:** Prime Minister Perry Christie (from 3 May 2002). **Capital:** Nassau. **Official language:** English. **Official religion:** none. **Monetary unit:** 1 Bahamian dollar (B$) = 100 cents; valuation (7 Jul 2003) US$1 = B$1.00.

## Demography

**Area:** 5,382 sq mi, 13,939 sq km. **Population** (2002): 309,000. **Density** (2002): persons per sq mi 79.4, persons per sq km 30.7. **Urban** (2000): 88.3%. **Sex distribution** (2000): male 49.34%; female 50.66%. **Age breakdown** (2000): under 15, 29.5%; 15–29, 27.2%; 30–44, 23.3%; 45–59, 12.1%; 60–74, 5.9%; 75 and over, 2.0%. **Ethnic composition** (2000): local black 67.5%; mulatto 14.2%; British 12.0%; Haitian black 3.0%; US white 2.4%; other 0.9%. **Religious affiliation** (1995): non-Anglican Protestant 45.4%, of which Baptist 17.5%; Roman Catholic 16.8%; Anglican 10.8%; nonreligious 5.3%; Spiritist 1.5%; other (mostly independent and

unaffiliated Christian) 20.2%. **Major cities** (2000): Nassau 210,832 (pop. of New Providence Island); Freeport/Lucaya 35,255. **Location:** chain of islands in the Caribbean Sea, southeast of Florida.

## Vital statistics

**Birth rate** per 1,000 population (2000): 19.5 (world avg. 22.5); (1995) legitimate 45.7%; illegitimate 54.3%. **Death rate** per 1,000 population (2000): 6.8 (world avg. 9.0). **Natural increase rate** per 1,000 population (2000): 12.7 (world avg. 13.5). **Total fertility rate** (avg. births per childbearing woman; 2000): 2.3. **Marriage rate** per 1,000 population (1996): 9.3. **Life expectancy** at birth (2000): male 68.3 years; female 73.9 years.

## National economy

**Budget** (1998–99). *Revenue*: B$730,102,000 (import taxes 45.1%, stamp taxes from imports 11.0%, business and professional licenses 7.4%, departure taxes 6.6%). *Expenditures*: B$748,150,000 (education 19.7%, health 15.5%, interest on public debt 13.2%, public order 11.1%, defense 3.7%). **National debt** (2001): US$1,483,800,000. **Production** (value of production in B$'000 except as noted). *Agriculture, forestry, fishing* (1998): crayfish 56,500 (2001), poultry products 28,300, citrus and other fruit 21,300; roundwood (1998) 117,000 cu m. *Mining and quarrying* (value of export production; 1996): salt 18,100, aragonite 4,900. *Manufacturing* (value of export production; 1996): pharmaceuticals and other chemical products (1995) 74,200; rum 5,200. *Energy production (consumption)*: electricity (kW-hr; 2000) 1,665,000,000 ([1997] 1,414,000,000); petroleum products (metric tons; 1997) none (566,000). **Tourism** (US$'000,000; 2000): receipts 1,814; expenditures 293. **Household income and expenditure**. Average household size (1996) 3.9; income per household (1996) B$27,252 (US$27,252); expenditure (1995): housing 32.8%, transportation and Communications. 14.8%, food and beverages 13.8%, household furnishings 8.9%. **Gross national product** (at current market prices; 2000): US$4,533,000,000 (US$14,960 per capita). **Population economically active** (1996): total 146,635; activity rate of total population 51.6% (participation rates: [1994] ages 15–64, 77.8%; female 47.5%; unemployed [1998] 9.5%). **Land use** (1994): forest 32.4%; pasture 0.2%; agriculture 1.0%; other 66.4%.

## Foreign trade

**Imports** (1999-c.i.f.): B$1,907,000,000 (machinery and transport equipment 30.8%; food products 13.7%; chemicals and chemical products 11.7%; petroleum for domestic use 8.7%). *Major import sources* (1998; excludes all petroleum): US 91.5%; EC 1.6%. **Exports** (1999-f.o.b.): B$486,300,000 (domestic exports 48.3%, of which crayfish 14.9%, rum 6.4%; reexports 44.2%; petroleum exports 7.5%). *Major export destinations* (1998; excludes all petroleum): US 56.5%; EC 31.4%; Canada 2.1%.

## Transport and communications

**Transport.** *Roads* (1999): total length 1,673 mi, 2,693 km (paved 57%). *Vehicles* (1996): passenger cars 89,263; trucks and buses 17,228. *Air transport*

(2001; Bahamasair only): passenger-mi 232,000,-000, passenger-km 374,000,000; short ton-mi cargo 1,208,000, metric ton-km cargo 1,764,000; airports (1997) with scheduled flights 22. **Communications**, in total units (units per 1,000 persons). Daily newspaper circulation (1996): 28,000 (99); radio receivers (1997): 215,000 (744); television receivers (1997): 67,000 (232); telephone main lines (2001): 123,300 (400); cellular telephone subscribers (2001): 60,600 (197); Internet users (2001): 16,900 (54).

## Education and health

**Educational attainment** (1990). Percentage of population age 25 and over having: no formal schooling 3.5%; incomplete primary education 25.4%; complete primary/incomplete secondary 57.6%; complete secondary/higher 13.5%. **Literacy** (1995): total population age 15 and over literate 98.2%. **Health**: physicians (1996) 419 (1 per 678 persons); hospital beds (1997) 1,119 (1 per 258 persons); infant mortality rate per 1,000 live births (2000) 17.0. **Food** (1999): daily per capita caloric intake 2,500 (vegetable products 71%, animal products 29%); 103% of FAO recommended minimum.

## Military

**Total active duty personnel** (2001): 860 (paramilitary coast guard 100%). **Military expenditure as percentage of GNP** (2000): 0.6% (world, n.a.); per capita expenditure US$85.

## Background

The islands were inhabited by Lucayan Indians when Christopher Columbus sighted them on 12 Oct 1492. He is thought to have landed on San Salvador (Watling) Island. The Spaniards made no attempt to settle but carried out slave raids that depopulated the islands; when English settlers arrived in 1648 from Bermuda, the islands were uninhabited. They became a haunt of pirates, and few of the ensuing settlements prospered. The islands enjoyed some prosperity following the American Revolution, when Loyalists fled the US and established cotton plantations there. The islands were a center for blockade runners during the American Civil War. Not until the development of tourism after World War II did permanent economic prosperity arrive. The Bahamas was granted internal self-government in 1964 and became independent in 1973.

## Recent Developments

In a referendum in February 2002, Bahamians voted against a package of proposals that included ending all discrimination against women in the country's constitution and creating an independent Electoral Boundaries Commission. The long-standing commitment to a tax-free environment in The Bahamas was reaffirmed even as the country bowed to pressure from the Organisation for Economic Co-operation and Development and agreed to improve the transparency of the tax system.

**Internet resources:** <www.bahamas.com>

# Bahrain

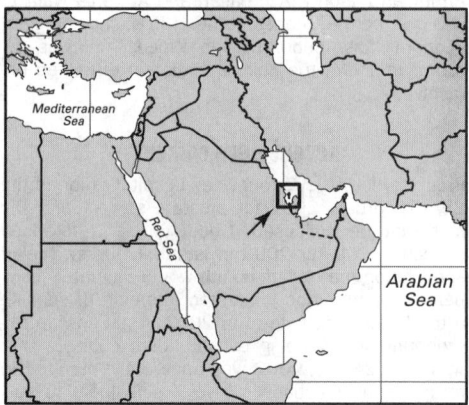

**Official name:** Mamlakat al-Bahrayn (Kingdom of Bahrain). **Form of government:** constitutional monarchy (declared 14 Feb 2002) with two legislative houses (Chamber of Deputies [40; elected] and Consultative Council [40; appointed by the king]). **Chief of state:** Sheikh Hamad ibn 'Isa al-Khalifah (from 1999). **Head of Government:** Prime Minister Khalifah ibn Sulman al-Khalifah (from 1970). **Capital:** Manama. **Official language:** Arabic. **Official religion:** Islam. **Monetary unit:** 1 Bahrain dinar (BD) = 1,000 fils; valuation (7 Jul 2003) $1 = BD 0.38.

## Demography

**Area:** 268.0 sq mi, 694.2 (rounded) sq km. **Population** (2002): 672,000. **Density** (2002): persons per sq mi 2,507.5, persons per sq km 968.0. **Urban** (1995): 90.3%. **Sex distribution** (2001): male 57.43%; female 42.57%. **Age breakdown** (2001): under 15, 27.9%; 15–29, 27.5%; 30–44, 29.7%; 45–59, 11.0%; 60–74, 3.2%; 75 and over, 0.7%. **Ethnic composition** (1991): Bahraini Arab 63.6%; Persian, Indian, Pakistani, and other Asians 30.3%; other Arab 3.5%; European 1.2%; other 1.4%. **Religious affiliation** (1991): Muslim 81.8%, of which Shi'i 61.3%, Sunni 20.5%; Christian 8.5%; other 9.7%. **Major cities** (2001): Manama 153,395; Ar-Rifa' 79,985; Hammad 52,718; Al-Muharraq (1991) 45,337; Madinat 'Isa 36,833. **Location:** Middle East, archipelago in the Persian Gulf, east of Saudi Arabia.

## Vital statistics

**Birth rate** per 1,000 population (2001): 20.1 (world avg. 21.2); legitimate 100%. **Death rate** per 1,000 population (2001): 3.9 (world avg. 8.9). **Natural increase rate** per 1,000 population (2001): 16.2 (world avg. 12.3). **Total fertility rate** (avg. births per childbearing woman; 2001): 2.8. **Marriage rate** per 1,000 population (1999): 5.5. **Divorce rate** per 1,000 population (1999): 1.3. **Life expectancy** at birth (2001): male 70.8 years; female 75.7 years.

## National economy

**Budget** (2000). *Revenue:* BD 572,000,000 ([1998] entrepreneurial and property income 53.7%, social security contribution 13.1%, import duties 12.3%,

---

*1 metric ton = about 1.1 short tons;   1 kilometer = 0.6 mi (statute);   1 metric ton-km cargo = about 0.68 short ton-mi cargo;   c.i.f.: cost, insurance, and freight;   f.o.b.: free on board*

foreign grants 7.3%). *Expenditures*: BD 732,000,000 ([1998] general administration and public order 29.9%, defense 17.3%, education 13.2%, fuel and energy 13.0%, health 9.0%, transportation, communications, and other services 8.6%). **Population economically active** (2001): total 308,341; activity rate of total population 47.4% (participation rates: ages 15 and over 63.3%; female 21.7%; unemployed 5.5%). **Production** (metric tons except as noted). *Agriculture, forestry, fishing* (2000): fruit (excluding melons) 21,500, dates 16,508, cow's milk 15,000; livestock (number of live animals) 18,000 sheep, 16,000 goats, 11,000 cattle; fish catch (1999) 10,295. *Manufacturing* (barrels; 1999): gas oil 32,958,000; fuel oil 22,067,000; kerosene and jet fuel 18,520,000. *Energy production (consumption)*: electricity (kW-hr; 1999) 5,041,000,000 (5,041,000,000); crude petroleum (barrels; 1999) 13,472,000 ([1997] 85,951,-000); petroleum products (metric tons; 1997) 10,990,000 (1,032,000); natural gas (cu m; 1999) 7,310,000,000 (7,310,000,000). **Gross national product** (1998): $4,909,000,000 ($7,640 per capita). **Public debt** (1999): BD 589,800,000 ($1,568,632,000). **Household income and expenditure.** Average household size (2001) 6.2; expenditure (1984): food and tobacco 33.3%, housing 21.2%, household durable goods 9.8%, transportation and communications 8.5%, recreation 6.4%, clothing and footwear 5.9%, education 2.7%, health 2.3%, energy and water 2.2%. **Land use** (1994): meadows and pastures 5.8%; agricultural and under permanent cultivation 2.9%; built-on and wasteland 91.3%. **Tourism** (2000): receipts from visitors $469,000,000; expenditures by nationals abroad $169,000,000.

## Foreign trade

**Imports** (2000-c.i.f.): BD 1,734,000,000 (petroleum products 44.4%, machinery and transport equipment 11.3%, food and live animals 9.5%, chemicals 8.1%). *Major import sources* (excludes trade in petroleum): Australia 10.1%; Saudi Arabia 8.8%; US 7.7%; UK 7.0%; Japan 6.8%; Germany 6.4%. **Exports** (2000): BD 2,154,000,000 (petroleum products 69.7%, metal and metal products 14.3%, textile 5.8%, mineral products 3.5%). *Major export destinations* (excludes trade in petroleum): US 22.9%; Saudi Arabia 14.1%; Taiwan 8.6%; Japan 5.7%; South Korea 4.1%; India 3.8%.

## Transport and communications

**Transport.** *Roads* (1999): total length 3,224 km (paved 77%). *Vehicles* (2000): passenger cars 170,161; trucks and buses 35,008. *Air transport* (1999; one-fourth apportionment of international flights of Gulf Air): passenger-km 2,835,900,000; metric ton-km cargo 118,681,000; airports (2000) with scheduled flights 1. **Communications,** in total units (units per 1,000 persons). Daily newspaper circulation (1996): 67,000 (117); radio receivers (1997): 338,000 (580); television receivers (1999): 270,000 (405); telephone main lines (2001): 173,900 (247); cellular telephone subscribers (2001): 299,600 (425); personal computers (2001): 100,000 (142); Internet users (2001): 140,200 (21,500).

## Education and health

**Educational attainment** (2001). Percentage of population age 15 and over having: no formal education 24.0%; primary education 37.1%; secondary 26.4%;

higher 12.5%. **Literacy** (2001): population age 15 and over literate 87.7%; males literate 92.5%; females literate 83.0%. **Health** (1998): physicians 709 (1 per 907 persons); hospital beds 1,832 (1 per 351 persons); infant mortality rate per 1,000 live births (2001) 19.8.

## Military

**Total active duty personnel** (2001): 11,000 (army 77.3%, navy 9.1%, air force 13.6%); . US troops in Bahrain (2002): 4,200. **Military expenditure as percentage of GNP** (1999): 8.1% (world 2.4%); per capita expenditure $666.

**Did you know?** The first petroleum well in the Middle East was drilled in Bahrain, beginning in 1931, near Jebel Dukhan ("Mountain of Smoke"), the highest point in the country. Oil was struck at a depth of 612 m (2,008 ft).

## Background

The area has long been an important trading center and is mentioned in Persian, Greek, and Roman references. It was ruled by Arabs from the 7th century AD but was then occupied by the Portuguese 1521–1602. Since 1783 it has been ruled by the Khalifah family, though through a series of treaties its defense remained a British responsibility from 1820 to 1971. After Britain withdrew its forces from the Persian Gulf (1968), Bahrain declared its independence in 1971. It served as a center for the allies in the Persian Gulf War (1990–1991). Since 1994 it has experienced bouts of political unrest, mainly by Shi'ites, who attempted to get the government to restore the parliament (abolished in 1975).

## Recent Developments

On 14 Feb 2002 Bahrain was officially transformed from an emirate into a kingdom as Emir Hamad ibn Isa al-Khalifah assumed the title of king. The new king immediately announced political reforms, calling for general elections for a municipal council and a new parliament and giving both men and women the right to vote.

**Internet resources:** <www.bahraintourism.com>

# Bangladesh

**Official name:** Gana Prajatantri Bangladesh (People's Republic of Bangladesh). **Form of government:** unitary multiparty republic with one legislative house (Parliament [330 seats, includes 30 reserved for women]). **Chief of state:** President Iajuddin Ahmed (from 6 Sep 2002). **Head of government:** Prime Minister Khaleda Zia (from 2001). **Capital:** Dhaka. **Official language:** Bengali. **Official religion:** Islam. **Monetary unit:** 1 Bangladesh taka (Tk) = 100 paisa; valuation (7 Jul 2003) $1 = Tk 58.40.

## Demography

**Area:** 56,977 sq mi, 147,570 sq km. **Population** (2002): 133,377,000. **Density** (2002): persons per

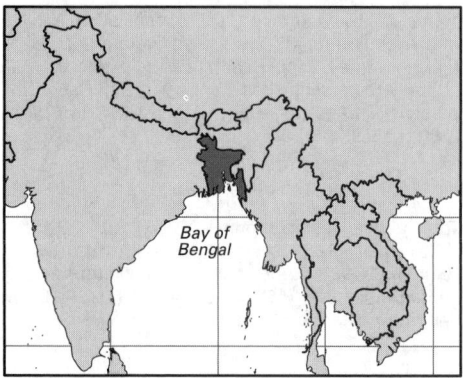

Bay of
Bengal

sq mi 2,479.3, persons per sq km 957.2. **Urban** (2002): 26.0%. **Sex distribution** (1999): male 51.44%; female 48.56%. **Age breakdown** (1996): under 15, 42.0%; 15–29, 26.4%; 30–44, 17.8%; 45–59, 8.9%; 60–74, 3.8%; 75 and over, 1.1%. **Ethnic composition** (1997): Bengali 97.7%; tribal 1.9%, of which Chakma 0.4%, Saontal 0.2%, Marma 0.1%; other 0.4%. **Religious affiliation** (2000): Muslim 85.8%; Hindu 12.4%; Christian 0.7%; Buddhist 0.6%; other 0.5%. **Major urban agglomerations** (2000): Dhaka (2001) 13,181,000; Chittagong 3,651,000; Khulna 1,442,000; Rajshahi 1,035,000. **Location:** South Asia, bordering India, Burma, and Bay of Bengal.

## Vital statistics

**Birth rate** per 1,000 population (2002): 30.1 (world avg. 21.2). **Death rate** per 1,000 population (2002): 8.8 (world avg. 8.9). **Natural increase rate** per 1,000 population (2002): 21.3 (world avg. 12.3). **Total fertility rate** (avg. births per childbearing woman; 2002): 3.6. **Marriage rate** per 1,000 population (1998): 9.2. **Divorce rate** per 1,000 population (1981): 3.6. **Life expectancy** at birth (2002): male 60.0 years; female 61.0 years.

## National economy

**Budget** (1998–99). *Revenue:* Tk 210,000,000,000 (value-added tax 37.4%; customs duties 24.0%; income taxes 11.7%; service charges 5.0%; public telephone enterprises 4.3%; interest receipts 2.8%). *Expenditures:* Tk 157,500,000,000 (goods and services 52.4%; transfer payments 28.4%; interest payments 16.3%). **Production** (metric tons except as noted). *Agriculture, forestry, fishing* (2000): paddy rice 35,821,000, sugarcane 6,951,000, wheat 1,900,000; livestock (number of live animals) 33,800,000 goats, 23,652,000 cattle, 1,121,000 sheep; roundwood 33,629,000 cu m; fish catch (1998) 839,141. *Mining and quarrying* (1997–98): marine salt 350,000; industrial limestone 26,000. *Manufacturing* (value added in $'000,000; 1995): textiles 651; industrial chemicals 441; food products 331. *Energy production (consumption):* electricity (kW-hr; 1997) 12,820,000,000 (12,820,000,000); coal (metric tons; 1997) none (646,000); crude petroleum (barrels; 1997) none (10,000,000); petroleum products (metric tons; 1997) 769,000 (2,337,000); natural gas (cu m; 1997) 8,135,000,-

000 (8,135,000,000). **Household income.** Average household size (1995–96) 5.3; average annual income per household Tk 52,389 ($1,277; sources of income: self-employment 56.9%, wages and salaries 28.1%, transfer payments 9.1%, other 5.9%; expenditure: food and drink 57.7%, housing and rent 11.1%, clothing and footwear 6.5%, energy 5.6%, other 19.1%. **Population economically active** (1995–96): total 56,014,000; activity rate of total population 46.0% (participation rates: over age 10, 64.8%; female 38.1%; unemployed 2.5%). **Public debt** (external, outstanding; 2000): $15,098,000,-000. **Gross national product** (2000): $47,864,000,-000 ($370 per capita). **Land use** (1998): pasture 4.6%; agriculture 68.6%; forest and other 26.8%. **Tourism** (2000): receipts $50,000,000; expenditures $301,000,000.

## Foreign trade

**Imports** (1997–98-f.o.b.): Tk 341,850,000,000 (textile yarn, fabrics, and made-up articles 24.6%; machinery and transport equipment 12.5%; petroleum and products 5.8%; iron and steel 5.2%; cereals and cereal preparations 3.9%). *Major import sources:* India 15.0%; Western Europe 13.0%; China 10.0%; Japan 9.0%; South Korea 7.0%; Hong Kong 6.0%; Singapore 5.0%; US 5.0%. **Exports** (1997–98): Tk 203,970,000,000 (ready-made garments 61.9%; fish and prawns 7.3%; jute manufactures 6.5%; hides, skins, and leather 4.0%; raw jute 2.4%; tea 1.0%). *Major export destinations:* Western Europe 49.0%; US 32.0%; Hong Kong 3.0%; Japan 2.7%; Canada 2.0%; Pakistan 1.2%.

## Transport and communications

**Transport.** *Railroads* (1998–99): route length 2,734 km; passenger-km 4,980,000,000; metric ton-km cargo 828,000,000. *Roads* (1996): total length 204,022 km (paved 12%). *Vehicles* (1998): passenger cars 54,784; trucks and buses 69,394. *Air transport* (1999; Bangladesh Biman only): 000, passenger-km 3,466,143,000; metric ton-km cargo 138,530,000; airports with scheduled flights (1997) 8. **Communications,** in total units (units per 1,000 persons). Daily newspaper circulation (1996): 1,117,000 (9.0); radio receivers (1998): 8,000,000 (64); television receivers (1999): 940,000 (7.4); telephone main lines (2001): 514,000 (3.9); cellular telephone subscribers (2001): 520,000 (4.0); personal computers (2001): 250,000 (1.9); Internet users (2001): 150,000 (1.1).

## Education and health

**Educational attainment** (1991). Percentage of population age 25 and over having: no formal schooling 65.4%; primary education 17.1%; secondary 13.8%; postsecondary 3.7%. **Literacy** (1995): total population age 15 and over literate 38.1%; males literate 49.4%; females literate 26.1%. **Health** (1997): physicians 26,608 (1 per 4,627 persons); hospital beds 39,900 (1 per 3,086 persons); infant mortality rate per 1,000 live births (2002) 68.0. **Food** (1999): daily per capita caloric intake 2,201 (vegetable products 97%, animal products 3%); (1997) 95% of FAO recommended minimum.

*1 metric ton = about 1.1 short tons;   1 kilometer = 0.6 mi (statute);   1 metric ton-km cargo = about 0.68 short ton-mi cargo;   c.i.f.: cost, insurance, and freight;   f.o.b.: free on board*

## Military

Total active duty personnel (2001): 137,000 (army 87.6%, navy 7.7%, air force 4.7%). Military expenditure as percentage of GNP (1999): 1.4% (world 2.4%); per capita expenditure $5.

## Background

In its early years Bangladesh was known as Bengal. When the British left the subcontinent in 1947, the area that was East Bengal became the part of Pakistan called East Pakistan. Bengali nationalist sentiment increased after the creation of an independent Pakistan. In 1971 violence erupted; some one million Bengalis were killed, and millions more fled to India, which finally entered the war on the side of the Bengalis, ensuring West Pakistan's defeat. East Pakistan became the independent nation of Bangladesh. Little of the devastation caused by the war has been repaired, and political instability, including the assassination of two presidents, has continued. In addition, the low-lying country has been repeatedly battered by natural disasters, notably tropical storms and flooding.

## Recent Developments

The most dramatic political event of 2002 was the forced resignation on 21 June of Pres. A.Q.M. Badruddoza Chowdhury, who was accused of having neglected to pay homage to ruling Bangladesh Nationalist Party (BNP) founder Ziaur Rahman on the anniversary of his death. In a move that some viewed as unconstitutional, the parliamentary wing of the BNP passed a resolution that removed him from office. The year was marked by the continued standoff between the ruling four-party alliance government, led by the BNP, and the opposition and long-time ruling party, the Awami League.

Internet resources: <www.bangladeshgov.org>

# Barbados

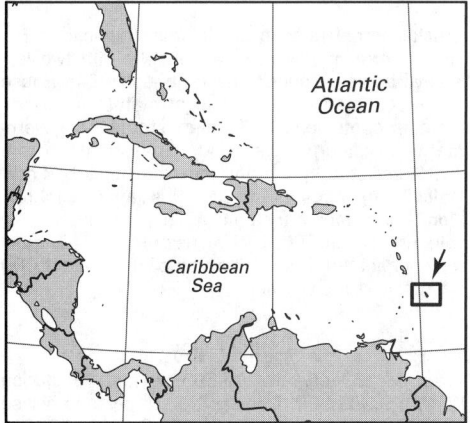

Atlantic
Ocean

Caribbean
Sea

Official name: Barbados. Form of government: constitutional monarchy with two legislative houses (Senate [21]; House of Assembly [28]). Chief of state: Queen Elizabeth II represented by Governor-General Sir Clifford Husbands (from 1996). Head of government: Prime Minister Owen Arthur (from 1994). Capital: Bridgetown. Official language: English. Official

religion: none. Monetary unit: 1 Barbados dollar (BDS$) = 100 cents; valuation (7 Jul 2003) US$1 = BDS$1.99.

## Demography

Area: 166 sq mi, 430 sq km. Population (2002): 270,000. Density (2002): persons per sq mi 1,627, persons per sq km 628. Urban (1998): 48.9%. Sex distribution (2000): male 48.07%; female 51.93%. Age breakdown (2000): under 15, 22.0%; 15–29, 24.2%; 30–44, 26.1%; 45–59, 15.7%; 60–74, 7.9%; 75 and over, 4.1%. Ethnic composition (2000): local black 87.1%; mulatto 6.0%; British expatriates 4.3%; US white 1.2%; Indo-Pakistani 1.1%; other 0.3%. Religious affiliation (1995): Protestant 63.0%, of which Anglican 26.3%, Pentecostal 10.6%, Methodist 5.7%; Roman Catholic 4.8%; other Christian 2.0%; nonreligious/other 30.2%. Major cities (1990): Bridgetown 6,070 (urban agglomeration [2001] 136,000); Speightstown, c. 3,500. Location: northeast of Venezuela at the eastern edge of the Caribbean Sea where it adjoins the North Atlantic Ocean.

## Vital statistics

Birth rate per 1,000 population (2000): 13.6 (world avg. 22.5); (1979) legitimate 26.9%; illegitimate 73.1%. Death rate per 1,000 population (2000): 8.7 (world avg. 9.0). Natural increase rate per 1,000 population (2000): 4.9 (world avg. 13.5). Total fertility rate (avg. births per childbearing woman; 2000): 1.6. Marriage rate per 1,000 population (1995): 13.5. Divorce rate per 1,000 population (1995): 1.5. Life expectancy at birth (2000): male 70.4 years; female 75.6 years.

## National economy

Budget (1997–98). Revenue: BDS$1,458,274,000 (tax revenue 94.7%, of which goods and services taxes 49.5%, personal income and company taxes 29.5%, import duties 8.8%; nontax revenue 5.3%). Expenditures: BDS$1,508,869,000 (current expenditure 83.2%, of which education 18.8%, economic services 11.5%, health 10.9%, social security and welfare 8.3%). Production (metric tons except as noted). Agriculture, forestry, fishing (1999): raw sugar 48,000, sweet potatoes 5,100, yams 1,350; livestock (number of live animals) 41,000 sheep, 33,000 pigs, 23,000 cattle; fish catch (1997) 2,764. Manufacturing (value added in BDS$'000; 1995): food, beverages, and tobacco (mostly sugar, molasses, rum, beer, and cigarettes) 108,000; paper products, printing, and publishing 33,400; metal products and assembly-type goods (mostly electronic components) 28,000. Energy production (consumption): electricity (kW-hr; 1997) 678,000,000 (678,000,000); crude petroleum (barrels; 1997) 328,000 (1,639,000); petroleum products (metric tons; 1997) 277,000 (307,000); natural gas (cu m; 1997) 23,372,000 (23,372,000). Household income and expenditure. Average household size (1990) 3.5; income per household (1988) BDS$13,455 (US$6,690); expenditure (1994): food 39.4%, housing 16.8%, transportation 10.5%, household operations 8.1%, alcohol and tobacco 6.4%, fuel and light 5.2%, clothing and footwear 5.0%, other 8.6%. Population economically active (1997): total 135,800; activity rate of total population 51.3% (participation rates: ages 15 and over, 67.5%; female 62.1%; unemployed 14.5%).

**Gross national product** (2000): US$2,469,000,000 (US$9,250 per capita). **Public debt** (external, outstanding; 1999): US$359,100,000. **Tourism**: receipts from visitors (2000) US$711,000,000; expenditures by nationals abroad (1999) US$87,000,000.

## Foreign trade

**Imports** (1997-c.i.f.): BDS$1,991,001,000 (retained imports 92.7%, of which capital goods 20.4%, food and beverages 15.0%, construction materials 8.2%, chemicals 5.6%, fuels 3.7%; reexported imports 7.3%). *Major import sources* (2000): US 41.6%[9]; Trinidad and Tobago 16.5%; UK 8.1%; Japan 5.2%. **Exports** (1997): BDS$565,887,000 (domestic exports 74.4%, of which sugar 12.7%, chemicals 10.0%, electrical components 9.2%, rum 4.9%, margarine and lard 2.0%, clothing 1.2%; reexports 25.6%). *Major export destinations* (2000): US 15.8%; Trinidad and Tobago 13.2%; UK 13.2%; Jamaica 7.0%; bunkers and ships' stores 16.3%.

## Transport and communications

**Transport.** *Roads* (1999): total length 1,600 km (paved 99%). *Vehicles* (1999): passenger cars 60,826; trucks and buses 9,578. *Air transport* (1995): passenger arrivals 699,000, passenger departures 707,400; cargo unloaded 8,382 metric tons, cargo loaded 4,717 metric tons; airports (1997) with scheduled flights 1. **Communications,** in total units (units per 1,000 persons). Daily newspaper circulation (1996): 53,000 (199); radio receivers (1997): 237,000 (888); television receivers (1999): 78,000 (292); telephone main lines (2001): 123,800 (460); cellular telephone subscribers (2000): 28,500 (106); personal computers (2001): 25,000 (93); Internet users (2000): 10,000 (37).

## Education and health

**Educational attainment** (1990). Percentage of population age 25 and over having: no formal schooling 0.4%; primary education 23.7%; secondary 60.3%; higher 11.2%; other 4.4%. **Literacy** (1995): total population age 15 and over literate 97.4%; males literate 98.0%; females literate 96.8%. **Health** (1992): physicians 312 (1 per 842 persons); hospital beds 1,966 (1 per 134 persons); infant mortality rate per 1,000 live births (2000) 12.4. **Food** (2000): daily per capita caloric intake 3,022 (vegetable products 77%, animal products 23%); 124% of FAO recommended minimum.

## Military

**Total active duty personnel** (2001): 610 (army 82.0%, navy 18.0%). **Military expenditure as percentage of GNP** (1999): 0.5% (world 2.4%); per capita expenditure US$44.

## Background

The island of Barbados was probably inhabited by Arawaks who originally came from South America. Spaniards may have landed by 1518, and by 1536 they had apparently wiped out the Indian population. Barbados was settled by the English in the 1620s. Slaves were brought in to work the sugar plantations,

which were especially prosperous in the 17th–18th century. The British empire abolished slavery in 1834, and all the Barbados slaves were freed by 1838. In 1958 Barbados joined the West Indies Federation. When the latter dissolved in 1962, Barbados sought independence from Britain; it achieved Commonwealth status in 1966.

## Recent Developments

The House of Assembly took an important step toward modernizing Barbados's constitution when in May 2000 it considered recommendations made by a Constitution Review Commission. The panel recommended that the country adopt a republican form of government—similar to the one in Trinidad and Tobago—with a nonexecutive president elected by the House of Assembly and the Senate.

**Internet resources:** <www.barbados.org>

# Belarus

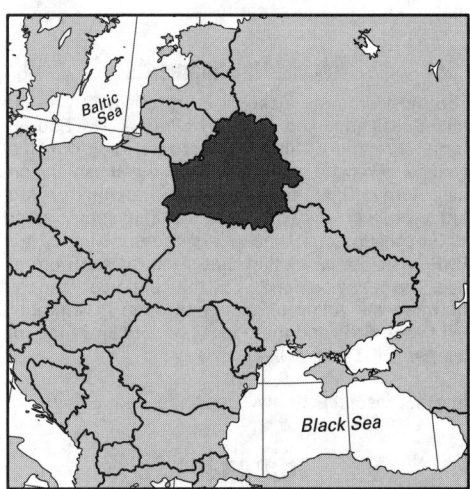

**Official name:** Respublika Belarus (Republic of Belarus). **Form of government:** republic with two legislative bodies (Council of the Republic [64]; House of Representatives [110]); legal status of government is controversial. **Head of state and government:** President Alyaksandr Lukashenka (from 1994) assisted by a prime minister. **Capital:** Minsk. **Official languages:** Belarusian; Russian. **Official religion:** none. **Monetary unit:** rubel (Rbl; plural rubli) valuation (7 Jul 2003) $1 = (new) Rbl 2,070; rubel re-denominated 1 Jan 2000; as of that date 1,000 old rubli = 1 (new) rubel.

## Demography

**Area:** 80,153 sq mi, 207,595 sq km. **Population** (2002): 9,933,000. **Density** (2002): persons per sq mi 123.9, persons per sq km 47.8. **Urban** (2001): 70.2%. **Sex distribution** (2001): male 46.92%; female 53.08%. **Age breakdown** (2001): under 15, 18.3%; 15–29, 22.5%; 30–44, 23.2%; 45–59, 16.9%; 60–69, 10.2%; 70 and over, 8.9%. **Ethnic**

---

*1 metric ton = about 1.1 short tons;    1 kilometer = 0.6 mi (statute);    1 metric ton-km cargo = about 0.68 short ton-mi cargo;    c.i.f.: cost, insurance, and freight;    f.o.b.: free on board*

composition (1999): Belarusian 81.2%; Russian 11.4%; Polish 3.9%; Ukrainian 2.4%; Jewish 0.3%; other 0.8%. **Religious affiliation** (1995): Belarusian Orthodox 31.6%; Roman Catholic 17.7%; other (mostly nonreligious) 50.7%. **Major cities** (2001): Minsk 1,699,000; Homel 490,000; Mahilyou 361,000; Vitebsk 349,000; Hrodno 307,000. **Location:** Eastern Europe, bordering Latvia, Russia, Ukraine, Poland, and Lithuania.

## Vital statistics

**Birth rate** per 1,000 population (2000): 9.4 (world avg. 22.5); legitimate 81.4%; illegitimate 18.6%. **Death rate** per 1,000 population (2000): 13.5 (world avg. 9.0). **Natural increase rate** per 1,000 population (2000): –4.1 (world avg. 13.5). **Total fertility rate** (avg. births per childbearing woman; 2000): 1.3. **Marriage rate** per 1,000 population (2000): 6.2. **Divorce rate** per 1,000 population (2000): 4.3. **Life expectancy** at birth (1999): male 63.4 years; female 74.7 years.

## National economy

**Budget** (2000). *Revenue:* Rbl 3,181,000,000,000 (tax revenue 76.5%, of which value-added tax 25.7%, taxes on profits 13.8%, taxes on income 8.7%, excise taxes 8.0%, taxes on international trade 4.5%, other 15.8%; nontax revenue 23.5%). *Expenditures:* Rbl 3,236,000,000,000 (target budgetary fund 17.6%, education 17.4%, health 14.1%, subsidies 7.7%, capital expenditure 6.9%, other 36.3%). **Public debt** (external, outstanding; 2000): US$692,000,000. **Production** (metric tons except as noted). *Agriculture, forestry, fishing* (2000): potatoes 8,718,000, cereal 4,856,000, sugar beets 1,474,000; livestock (number of live animals) 4,221,000 cattle, 3,431,000 pigs, 221,300 horses; roundwood (1998) 17,745,000 cu m; fish catch (1999) 450. *Mining and quarrying* (2000): potash 3,400,000; peat 2,211,000. *Manufacturing* (value of production in [old] Rbl '000,000; 1994): machine-building equipment 1,086,650; chemical products 659,438; food products 562,438; *Energy production (consumption):* electricity (kW-hr; 1997) 26,057,000,000 (33,677,000,000); coal (1994) none (1997; 810,000); crude petroleum (barrels; 1997) 13,355,000 (86,406,000); petroleum products (1997) 9,589,000 (10,473,000); natural gas (cu m; 2000) 257,000,000 (16,402,000,000). **Gross national product** (2000): US$28,735,000,000 (US$2,870 per capita). **Household income and expenditure.** Average household size (2000) 3.4; income per household (1995) (old) Rbl 2,400,000; sources of income (2000): wages and salaries 51.9%, business activities 28.3%, transfers 18.0%, property income 1.8%; expenditure (2000): food, beverages, and tobacco 64.9%; clothing 11.7%; transport 6.9%; household appliances 4.1%; rent 3.0%; health 2.2%; education 2.2%; other 5.0%. **Population economically active** (2000): 4,537,000; activity rate of total population 45.4% (participation rate: ages 16–59 [male], 16–54 [female] 97.9%; female 51.3%; unemployed 2.1%). **Tourism** (2000): receipts US$19,000,000; expenditures US$123,000,000. **Land use** (1994): forested 33.7%; meadows and pastures 14.1%; agricultural and under permanent cultivation 30.5%; other 21.7%; 25% of territory severely affected by radioactive fallout from Chernobyl.

## Foreign trade

**Imports** (2000-c.i.f.): US$8,492,000,000 (mineral products 31.2%, machinery and transport equipment 18.2%, chemical products 15.3%, food and beverages 12.5%, iron and steel 11.4%, light industry 3.3%, wood and paper products 3.2%). *Major import sources:* Russia 63.4%; Germany 6.9%; Ukraine 4.0%; Poland 2.5%; Italy 1.9%; US 1.6%; Czech Republic 1.6%; UK 1.3%. **Exports** (2000): US$7,331,000,000 (machinery and transport equipment 25.3%, mineral products 20.2%, chemicals and synthetic rubber 19.8%, ferrous metals 7.2%, food 6.9%, light industry 6.4%, wood and paper products 4.3%). *Major export destinations:* Russia 50.7%; Ukraine 7.6%; Latvia 6.4%; Lithuania 4.8%; Poland 3.8%; Germany 3.2%; China 2.0%.

## Transport and communications

**Transport.** *Railroads* (2000): length 5,533 km; (1997) passenger-km 17,722,000,000; metric ton-km cargo 31,425,000,000. *Roads* (2000): total length 74,400 km (paved 89.0%). *Vehicles* (2000): passenger cars 1,448,461; trucks and buses 85,791. *Air transport* (2000): passenger-km 513,000,000; metric ton-km cargo 18,000,000; airports 1. **Communications,** in total units (units per 1,000 persons). Daily newspaper circulation (1997): 1,437,000 (140); radio receivers (1998): 3,021,000 (296); television receivers (1999): 3,300,000 (327); telephone main lines (2001): 2,857,900 (279); cellular telephone subscribers (2001): 138,300 (8.6); Internet users (2001): 422,200 (41.2).

## Education and health

**Literacy** (1999): total population age 15 and over literate 99.5%; males literate 99.7%; females literate 99.4%. **Health** (2000): physicians 45,817 (1 per 218 persons); hospital beds 126,209 (1 per 79 persons); infant mortality rate per 1,000 live births (2000) 9.3. **Food** (2000): daily per capita caloric intake 2,902 (vegetable products 72%, animal products 28%); 113% of FAO recommended minimum.

## Military

**Total active duty personnel** (2001): 82,900 (army 52.3%, air force and air defense 27.1%, other 20.6%). **Military expenditure as percentage of GNP** (1999): 1.3% (world 2.4%); per capita expenditure US$89.

**Did you know?** The Pripet Marshes, a 270,000 sq km (104,000 sq mi) region in southern Belarus and northwestern Ukraine, is Europe's largest swamp and has been a major obstacle to invading armies for centuries.

## Background

While Belarusians share a distinct identity and language, they did not enjoy political sovereignty until the late 20th century. The territory that is now Belarus underwent partition and changed hands often; as a result its history is entwined with its neighbors'. In medieval times the region was ruled by Lithuanians and Poles. Following the Third Partition of Poland it was ruled by Russia. After World War I the western part was assigned to Poland and the eastern part became USSR territory. After World War II the Soviets expanded what had been the Belorussian SSR by annexing more of Poland. Much of the area suffered contamination from the Chernobyl accident in 1986, forcing many to evacuate. Belarus declared its independence in 1991 and later joined the Commonwealth of Independent States. Amid increasing political turmoil in the 1990s, it proposed a union with Russia in 1997 that was still being debated at the start of the 21st century.

## Recent Developments

In June 2002 Russian Pres. Vladimir Putin publicly condemned the "Soviet" (i.e., federal) model for the proposed union, pointing out that because the Belarusian economy was only 3% the size of Russia's, the two sides could hardly be regarded as equals. Putin proposed either a unified state or a union formed according to the principles of the European Union. Belarus Pres. Alyaksandr Lukashenka continued to press for a solution that would preserve full Belorussian sovereignty. Lukashenka's regime continued to come under close international scrutiny for its political and human rights policies.

**Internet resources:** <www.belarusembassy.org>

# Belgium

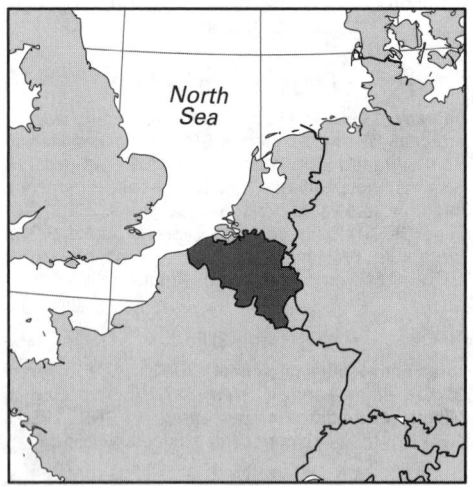

**Official name:** Koninkrijk België (Dutch); Royaume de Belgique (French) (Kingdom of Belgium). **Form of government:** federal constitutional monarchy with a Parliament composed of two legislative chambers (Senate [71, excluding children of the monarch serving ex officio from age 18]; House of Representatives [150]). **Chief of state:** King Albert II (from 1993). **Head of government:** Prime Minister Guy Verhofstadt (from 1999). **Capital:** Brussels. **Official languages:** Dutch; French; German. **Official religion:** none. **Monetary unit:** 1 euro (€) = 100 cents; $1 = €0.87 (7 Jul 2003); at conversion on 1 Jan 2002, €1 = BF40.3399.

## Demography

**Area:** 11,7874 sq mi, 30,528 sq km. **Population** (2002): 10,280,000. **Density** (2002): persons per sq mi 872.1, persons per sq km 336.7. **Urban** (2001): 97.4% (includes Luxembourg). **Sex distribution** (2000): male 48.89%; female 51.11%. **Age breakdown** (2000): under 15, 17.5%; 15–29, 18.8%; 30–44, 22.9%; 45–59, 18.8%; 60–74, 14.8%; 75 and over, 7.2%. **Ethnic composition** (2000): Flemish 53.7%; Walloon (French) 31.6%; Italian 2.6%; French 2.0%; Arab 1.8%; German 1.5%; Berber 0.9%; other 5.9%. **Religious affiliation** (1995): Roman Catholic 87.9%; Muslim 2.5%; other Christian 2.4%, of which Protestant 1.0%; Jewish 0.3%; other 6.9%. **Major cities** (2000): Brussels 959,318 (capital region); Antwerp 446,525; Ghent 224,180; Charleroi 200,827; Liège 185,639. **Location:** Western Europe, bordering The Netherlands, Germany, Luxembourg, France, and the North Sea.

## Vital statistics

**Birth rate** per 1,000 population (2001): 11.2 (world avg. 21.2). **Death rate** per 1,000 population (2001): 10.2 (world avg. 8.9). **Natural increase rate** per 1,000 population (2001): 1.0 (world avg. 12.3). **Total fertility rate** (avg. births per childbearing woman; 2000): 1.5. **Marriage rate** per 1,000 population (1999): 4.3. **Divorce rate** per 1,000 population (1994): 2.2. **Life expectancy** at birth (2000): male 74.5 years; female 81.3 years.

## National economy

**Budget** (1999). *Revenue:* €107,764,000,000 (social security contributions 29.6%, taxes on goods and services 26.9%, income tax 26.7%). *Expenditures:* €109,772,000,000 (transfer payments 49.4%, interest on debt 15.1%, other 35.5%). **Public debt** (1999): $250,459,000,000. **Production** (metric tons except as noted). *Agriculture, forestry, fishing* (2000; includes Luxembourg): sugar beets 6,200,000, potatoes 3,000,000, wheat 1,634,000; livestock (number of live animals) 7,671,000 pigs, 3,085,000 cattle, 152,000 sheep, 67,000 horses; roundwood (2000; includes Luxembourg) 4,400,000 cu m; fish catch (1999) 29,900. *Mining and quarrying* (1997): limestone 30,000,000; granite (Belgium bluestone) 2,115,000 cu m; marble 400 cu m. *Manufacturing* (value added in BF '000,000; 1996): metal products 468,894; food 263,382; chemicals 243,787. *Energy production (consumption):* electricity (kW-hr; 1998) 83,244,000,000 ([1997] 82,209,000,000); coal (metric tons; 1997) negligible (11,255,000); crude petroleum (barrels; 1997) none (239,860,000); petroleum products (metric tons; 1997) 28,995,000 (17,516,000); natural gas (cu m; 1997) 188,556 (16,468,000,000). **Gross national product** (2000): $251,583,000,000 ($24,540 per capita). **Household income and expenditure.** Avg. household size (1999) 2.5; sources of income (1992): wages 49.6%, transfer payments 20.7%, property income 18.8%, self-employment 10.9%; expenditure (1992): food 18.0%, housing 17.0%, transportation 13.3%, health 11.8%, durable goods 10.7%, clothing 7.7%. **Land use** (1994; includes Luxembourg): forest 21.3%; pasture 21.0%; agriculture 24.2%; other 33.5%. **Popula-**

tion economically active (1999): total 3,905,500; activity rate 38.2% (participation rates: ages 15–64, 58.0%; female 42.7%; unemployed 9.6%). **Tourism** (2000): receipts $7,422,000,000; expenditures $10,151,000,000.

## Foreign trade

**Imports** (1999; includes Luxembourg): BF 6,237,-963,000,000 (machinery and transport equipment 31.9%; basic manufactures 20.8%; chemicals 16.4%; food 7.8%; mineral fuels 5.7%, of which petroleum products 4.3%; diamonds 3.9%). Major import sources: Germany 17.4%; The Netherlands 16.7%; France 13.7%; UK 8.6%; US 7.5%. **Exports** (1999; includes Luxembourg): BF 6,780,785,-000,000 (machinery and transport equipment 30.0%; chemicals 20.3%, of which plastics 4.4%; food 8.7%; iron and steel 4.0%; textiles 3.7%; petroleum products 2.5%). Major export destinations: Germany 17.9%; France 17.7%; The Netherlands 12.8%; UK 10.0%; US 5.2%.

## Transport and communications

**Transport.** *Railroads* (1999): route length 3,380 km; passenger-km 7,354,000,000; metric ton-km cargo 7,392,000,000. *Roads* (1997): total length 143,800 km (paved 97%). *Vehicles* (1998): passenger cars 4,491,734; trucks and buses 453,122. *Air transport* (2000; Sabena Airlines [now Brussels Airlines] only): passenger-km 19,378,689,000; metric ton-km cargo 568,244,000; airports (1999) 2. **Communications,** in total units (units per 1,000 persons). Daily newspaper circulation (1996): 1,625,000 (161); radio receivers (1997): 8,075,000 (795); television receivers (1999): 5,300,000 (518); telephone main lines (2001): 5,074,000 (493); cellular telephone subscribers (2001): 7,690,000 (747); personal computers (2001): 3,500,000 (345); Internet users (2001): 2,881,000 (280).

## Education and health

**Educational attainment** (1981). Percentage of population age 15 and over having: less than secondary education 44.4%; lower secondary 26.5%; upper secondary 17.0%; vocational 2.9%; teacher's college 0.6%; university 3.5%. **Health:** physicians (1998) 40,300 (1 per 253 persons); hospital beds (1994) 77,181 (1 per 131 persons); infant mortality rate per 1,000 live births (2000) 4.8. **Food** (2000; includes Luxembourg): daily per capita caloric intake 3,701 (vegetable products 70%, animal products 30%); 140% of FAO recommended minimum.

## Military

**Total active duty personnel** (2001): 39,420 (army 67.0%, navy 6.5%, air force 21.8%, medical service 4.7%). **Military expenditure as percentage of GNP** (1999): 1.4% (world 2.4%); per capita expenditure $352.

## Background

Inhabited in ancient times by the Belgae, a Celtic people, the area was conquered by Caesar in 57 BC; under Augustus it became the Roman province of Belgica. Conquered by the Franks, it later broke up into semi-independent territories, including Brabant and Luxembourg. By the late 15th century the territories of the Netherlands, of which the future Belgium was a part, gradually united and passed to the Habsburgs. In the 16th century it was a center for European commerce. The basis of modern Belgium was laid in the southern Catholic provinces that split from the northern provinces after the Union of Utrecht in 1579. Overrun by the French and incorporated into France in 1801, it was reunited to Holland and with it became the independent Kingdom of The Netherlands in 1815. After the revolt of its citizens in 1830, it became the independent Kingdom of Belgium. Under Léopold II it acquired vast lands in Africa. Overrun by the Germans in World Wars I and II, Belgium was the scene of the Battle of the Bulge. Internal discord led to legislation in the 1970s and 1980s that created three nearly autonomous regions in accordance with language distribution: Flemish Flanders, French Wallonia, and bilingual Brussels. In 1993 it became a federation comprising the three regions. It is a member of the European Union.

## Recent Developments

The Belgian Parliament approved a further decentralization of power to the country's three regions during 2001, and responsibility for agricultural policy, foreign trade, development cooperation, and control over communal and provincial councils passed from the national to the regional level at the beginning of 2002. Belgium became the second country in the world, after The Netherlands, to legalize euthanasia, and the private use of cannabis has also been decriminalized. In June 2003, the Belgian government rescinded the unique global reach of its war crime law.

**Internet resources:** <www.visitbelgium.com>

# Belize

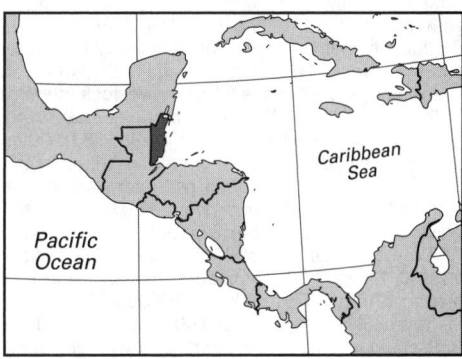

**Official name:** Belize. **Form of government:** constitutional monarchy with two legislative houses (Senate [8, excluding president of the Senate]; House of Representatives [29, excluding speaker of the House of Representatives]). **Chief of state:** Queen Elizabeth II represented by Governor-General Sir Colville Young (from 1993). **Head of government:** Prime Minister Said Musa (from 1998). **Capital:** Belmopan. **Official language:** English. **Official religion:** none. **Monetary unit:** 1 Belize dollar (BZ$) = 100 cents; valuation (7 Jul 2003) US$1 = BZ$1.97 (pegged to the US dollar).

## Demography

**Area:** 8,867 sq mi, 22,965 sq km (includes offshore cays totaling 266 sq mi (689 sq km). **Population** (2002): 251,000. **Density** (2002): persons per sq mi 28.3, persons per sq km 10.9. **Urban** (2000): 47.7%. **Sex distribution** (2000): male 50.49%; female 49.51%. **Age breakdown** (1998): under 15, 41.2%; 15–29, 26.5%; 30–44, 16.7%; 45–59, 8.8%; 60–74, 5.0%; 75 and over, 1.8%. **Ethnic composition** (2000): mestizo (Spanish-Indian) 48.7%; Creole (predominantly black) 24.9%; Mayan Indian 10.6%; Garifuna (black-Carib Indian) 6.1%; white 4.3%; East Indian 3.0%; other or not stated 2.4%. **Religious affiliation** (2000): Roman Catholic 49.6%; Protestant 31.8%, of which Pentecostal 7.4%, Anglican 5.3%, Seventh-day Adventist 5.2%, Mennonite 4.1%; other Christian 1.9%; nonreligious 9.4%; other 7.3%. **Major cities** (2000): Belize City 49,050; Orange Walk 13,483; San Ignacio/Santa Elena 13,260; Dangriga 8,814; Belmopan 8,130. **Location:** Central America, bordering Mexico, Caribbean Sea, and Guatemala.

## Vital statistics

**Birth rate** per 1,000 population (2000): 32.3 (world avg. 22.5); (1997) legitimate 40.3%; illegitimate 59.7%. **Death rate** per 1,000 population (2000): 4.8 (world avg. 9.0). **Natural increase rate** per 1,000 population (2000): 27.5 (world avg. 13.5). **Total fertility rate** (avg. births per childbearing woman; 2000): 4.1. **Marriage rate** per 1,000 population (1997): 6.6. **Divorce rate** per 1,000 population (1997): 0.2. **Life expectancy** at birth (2000): male 68.7 years; female 73.3 years.

## National economy

**Budget** (1997). *Revenue*: BZ$324,600,000 (tax revenue 77.4%, of which import duties 25.7%, general sales taxes 23.6%; grants 12.7%; nontax revenue 9.2%). *Expenditures*: BZ$362,300,000 (education 20.5%; transportation and communication 16.7%; general admin. 11.4%; health 8.2%; defense 5.4%). **Production** (metric tons except as noted). *Agriculture, forestry, fishing* (1998): sugarcane 1,208,000, oranges 170,000, bananas 81,000; livestock (number of live animals; 1999) 58,000 cattle, 23,000 pigs, 1,400,000 chickens; roundwood (1998) 187,600 cu m; fish catch (1998) 2,620, of which shrimp 1,682, conchs 253, lobsters 251, freshwater and marine fish 111. *Mining and quarrying* (1997): sand and gravel 350,000; limestone 310,000. *Manufacturing* (2000–01): sugar 105,500; molasses 35,000; flour 11,800. *Energy production (consumption)*: electricity (kW-hr; 1997) 167,000,000 (192,000,000); petroleum products (metric tons; 1997) none (127,000). **Household income and expenditure.** Average household size (2000) 4.5; average annual income of employed head of household (1993) BZ$6,450 (US$3,225); expenditure (1990): food, beverages, and tobacco 34.0%, transportation 13.7%, energy and water 9.1%, housing 9.0%, clothing and footwear 8.8%, household furnishings 8.0%. **Tourism** (2000): receipts from visitors US$121,000,000; expenditures by nationals abroad US$24,000,000. **Land use** (1994): forested 92.1%; meadows and pastures 2.2%; agricultural and under permanent cultivation

3.6%; other 2.1%. **Population economically active** (1998): total 85,595; activity rate of total population 36.2% (participation rates: ages 14–64, 64.1%; female 34.5%; unemployed [2001] 9.3%). **Gross national product** (2000): US$746,000,000 (US$3,110 per capita). **Public debt** (external, outstanding; 2000): US$449,000,000.

## Foreign trade

**Imports** (2001-c.i.f.): BZ$921,100,000 (machinery and transport equipment 27.7%; food 13.5%; mineral fuels and lubricants 18.2%; chemicals and chemical products 8.0%). *Major import sources*: US 47.2%; Mexico 11.2%; Caricom 5.0%; UK 2.7%; other EU 3.8%. **Exports** (2001-f.o.b.): BZ$538,200,000 (domestic exports 61.8%, of which citrus concentrate 16.5%; raw sugar 11.0%, shrimp 8.7%, bananas 8.0%, garments 5.6%; reexports [principally to Mexico] 38.2%). *Major export destinations* (domestic exports only): US 53.8%; UK 23.0%; other EU 6.7%; Caricom 6.4%.

## Transport and communications

**Transport.** *Roads* (1999): total length 2,872 km (paved 18%). *Vehicles* (1998): passenger cars 9,929; trucks and buses 11,755. *Air transport* (1998; Belize International Airport only): passenger arrivals 199,475, passenger departures 193,620; cargo loaded 166 metric tons, cargo unloaded 1,082 metric tons. Airports (1997) with scheduled flights 9. **Communications,** in total units (units per 1,000 persons). Radio receivers (1997): 133,000 (571); television receivers (1998): 42,000 (183); telephone main lines (2001): 35,200 (144); cellular telephone subscribers (2001): 28,200 (115); personal computers (2001): 33,000 (135); Internet users (2001): 18,000 (74).

## Education and health

**Educational attainment** (2000). Percentage of population age 25 and over having: no formal schooling 36.6%; primary education 40.9%; secondary 11.7%; postsecondary/advanced vocational 6.4%; university 3.8%; other/unknown 0.6%. **Literacy** (1991): total population age 14 and over literate 75,500 (70.3%). **Health** (1998): physicians 155 (1 per 1,558 persons); hospital beds 554 (1 per 435 persons); infant mortality rate per 1,000 live births (2000) 26.0. **Food** (1999): daily per capita caloric intake 2,889 (vegetable products 79%, animal products 21%); 128% of FAO recommended minimum.

## Military

**Total active duty personnel** (2001): 1,050 (army 100%); Foreign forces (2001): British army 180. **Military expenditure as percentage of GNP** (1999): 1.6% (world 2.4%); per capita expenditure US$47.

 **Did you know?** Belize's waters are home to the world's second-largest barrier reef, making the country a popular destination for underwater sports enthusiasts. Eco-tourists also come to visit the rainforests and view the abundant wildlife.

---

*1 metric ton = about 1.1 short tons;   1 kilometer = 0.6 mi (statute);   1 metric ton-km cargo = about 0.68 short ton-mi cargo;   c.i.f.: cost, insurance, and freight;   f.o.b.: free on board*

## Background

The area was inhabited by the Maya c. 300 BC–AD 900; the ruins of their ceremonial centers, including Caracol and Xunantunich, can still be seen. The Spanish claimed sovereignty from the 16th century but never tried to settle Belize, though they regarded as interlopers the British who did. British logwood cutters arrived in the mid-17th century; Spanish opposition was finally overcome in 1798. When settlers began to penetrate the interior they met with Indian resistance. In 1871 British Honduras became a crown colony, but an unfulfilled provision of a 1859 British-Guatemalan treaty led Guatemala to claim the territory. The situation had not been resolved when Belize was granted its independence in 1981. A British force, stationed there to ensure the new nation's security, was withdrawn after Guatemala officially recognized the territory's independence in 1991.

## Recent Developments

Under the auspices of the Organization of American States, great progress was registered during 2002 toward solving Belize's border dispute with Guatemala that had endured for more than a century. Six months after the event, Belize was still reeling from the tremendous devastation caused by Hurricane Iris, which struck the southern third of the country in October 2001.

Internet resources: <www.belize.gov.bz>

# Benin

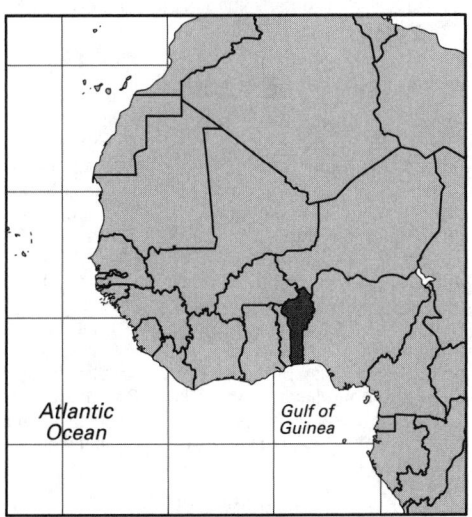

Atlantic Ocean

Gulf of Guinea

**Official name:** République du Bénin (Republic of Benin). **Form of government:** multiparty republic with one legislative house (National Assembly [83]). **Head of state and government:** President Matheiu Kérékou (from 1996). **Capital:** Porto-Novo (legislative capital; administrative capital in Cotonou). **Official language:** French. **Official religion:** none. **Monetary unit:** 1 CFA franc (CFAF) = 100 centimes; valuation (7 Jul 2003) $1 = CFAF 571.07 (formerly pegged to the French franc and since 1 Jan 2002 to the euro at €1 = CFAF 655.96).

## Demography

**Area:** 44,300 sq mi, 114,760 sq km. **Population** (2002): 6,788,000. **Density** (2002): persons per sq mi 156.1, persons per sq km 60.3. **Urban** (1999): 41.5%. **Sex distribution** (2001): male 49.26%; female 50.74%. **Age breakdown** (2001): under 15, 47.3%; 15–29, 27.8%; 30–44, 13.9%; 45–59, 7.1%; 60–74, 3.1%; 75 and over, 0.8%. **Ethnic composition** (1992): Fon 39.7%; Yoruba (Nago) 12.1%; Adjara 11.1%; Bariba 8.6%; Aizo 8.6%; Somba (Otomary) 6.6%; Fulani 5.6%; other 7.7%. **Religious affiliation** (1992): Christian 35.4%, of which Roman Catholic 25.9%, Protestant 9.5%; traditional beliefs, including voodoo 35.0%; Muslim 20.6%; other 9.0%. **Major cities** (1998): Cotonou 649,580; Porto-Novo 218,241; Djougou 132,000 (1994); Parakou 128,277; Abomey 80,000. **Location:** western Africa, bordering Burkina Faso, Niger, Nigeria, the Atlantic Ocean, and Togo.

## Vital statistics

**Birth rate** per 1,000 population (2001): 44.2 (world avg. 21.2). **Death rate** per 1,000 population (2001): 14.5 (world avg. 8.9). **Natural increase rate** per 1,000 population (2001): 24.7 (world avg. 12.3). **Total fertility rate** (avg. births per childbearing woman; 2001): 6.2. **Life expectancy** at birth (2001): male 49.0 years; female 50.9 years.

## National economy

**Budget** (2000). *Revenue:* CFAF 251,300,000,000 (1999; tax revenue 85.5%; nontax revenue 14.5%). *Expenditures:* CFAF 375,800,000,000 (1999; current expenditures 64.5%, of which salaries 26.8%, debt service 5.6%; development expenditure 35.5%). **Production** (metric tons except as noted). *Agriculture, forestry, fishing* (2001): cassava 2,800,000, yams 1,773,363, corn (maize) 662,958; livestock (number of live animals; 2001) 1,500,000 cattle, 1,182,527 goats, 644,997 sheep; roundwood (2000) 6,242,329 cu m; fish catch (1999) 38,542. *Manufacturing* (1998): cement 350,000; cotton fibre 175,000; meat 70,000. *Energy production (consumption):* electricity (kW-hr; 1997) 7,000,000 (272,000,000); crude petroleum (barrels; 1997) 426,000 (negligible); petroleum products (metric tons; 1997) none (151,000). **Public debt** (external, outstanding; 2000): $1,143,-000,000. **Gross national product** (2000): $2,345,-000,000 ($370 per capita). **Population economically active** (1997): total 2,608,000; activity rate of total population 44.2% (participation rates: ages 15–64, 84.3%; female 48.3%). **Household income.** Average household size (1992) 5.9; income per household (1983) $240; sources of income; self-employement 73.7%, wages and salaries 26.3%. **Land use** (1995): agricultural and under permanent cultivation 17.0%; other 83.0% (of which [1994] forested 30.7%, meadows and pastures 4.0%). **Tourism** (1998): receipts from visitors $33,000,000; expenditures by nationals abroad $7,000,000.

## Foreign trade

**Imports** (1999-c.i.f.): CFAF 346,400,000,000 (1997; cotton yarn and fabric 20.2%; machinery and transport equipment 16.2%; rice 7.4%; iron and steel 4.5%). *Major import sources* (1995): France 27.1%; UK 9.6%; China 9.3%; Thailand 9.1%; Hong Kong

8.8%; The Netherlands 5.6%; US 4.8%; Germany 4.3%. **Exports** (1999-f.o.b.): CFAF 237,200,000,000 (1997; cotton yarn 51.6%, reexport 38.5%, cotton seed 2.8%, crude petroleum 2.2%). *Major export destinations* (1997): Brazil 18.0%; Portugal 11.0%; Morocco 10.0%; India 6.5%; Libya 6.0%; Italy 4.5%; US 4.5%.

## Transport and communications

**Transport.** *Railroads* (1997): length 578 km; passenger-km 121,800,000; metric ton-km cargo 311,400,000. *Roads* (1999): total length 6,787 km (paved 20.0%). *Vehicles* (1996): passenger cars 37,772; trucks and buses 8,058. *Air transport* (1998; represents about 10% of the traffic of Air Afrique, which is operated by 11 West African states): passenger-km 258,263,000; metric ton-km cargo 13,524,000; airports (2000) with scheduled flights 1. **Communications,** in total units (units per 1,000 persons). Daily newspaper circulation (1996): 12,000 (2); radio receivers (1996): 620,000 (110); television receivers (1998): 65,000 (10.8); telephone main lines (2001): 59,300 (9.2); cellular telephone subscribers (2001): 125,000 (19.4); personal computers (2001): 11,000 (1.7); Internet users (2001): 25,000 (3.8).

## Education and health

**Educational attainment** (1992). Percentage of population age 25 and over having: no formal schooling 78.5%; primary education 10.8%; some secondary 8.2%; secondary 1.2%; postsecondary 1.3%. **Literacy** (1998): total population age 15 and over literate 37.7%; males literate 53.8%; females literate 22.6%. **Health:** physicians (1993) 363 (1 per 14,216 persons); hospital beds (1993) 1,235 (1 per 4,182 persons); infant mortality rate per 1,000 live births (2001) 89.7. **Food** (2000): daily per capita caloric intake 2,558 (vegetable products 96%, animal products 4%); 111% of FAO recommended minimum.

## Military

**Total active duty personnel** (2001): 4,750 (army 94.7%, navy 2.1%, air force 3.2%). **Military expenditure as percentage of GNP** (1999): 1.4% (world 2.4%); per capita expenditure $5.

## Background

In southern Benin, the Dahomey, or Fon, established the Abomey kingdom in 1625. In the 18th century the kingdom expanded to include Allada and Ouidah, where French forts had been established in the 17th century. In 1857 the French reestablished themselves in the area, and eventually fighting ensued. In 1894 Dahomey became a French protectorate; it was incorporated into the federation of French West Africa in 1904. It achieved independence in 1960. Dahomey was renamed Benin in 1975. At the end of the 20th century, its chronically weak economy produced tension between laborers and the government.

## Recent Developments

Amid widespread criticism of the handling of Benin's presidential elections in March 2001, incumbent

Pres. Mathieu Kérékou triumphed again at the polls. The victory ensured that Kérékou would maintain his grip upon a nation that he had ruled for all but five years since 1972.

**Internet resources:**
<www.siftthru.com/benintrav.htm>

# Bermuda

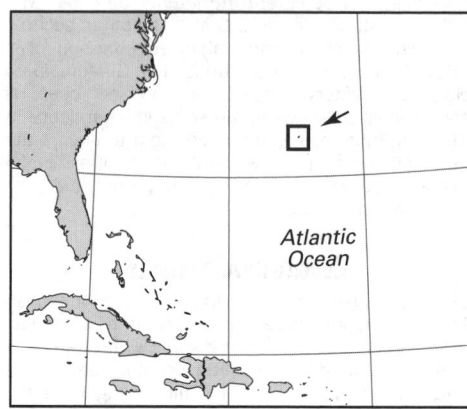

Atlantic Ocean

**Official name:** Bermuda. **Political status:** colony (UK) with two legislative houses (Senate [11]; House of Assembly [40]). **Chief of state:** Queen Elizabeth II, represented by Governor John Vereker (from 2002). **Head of government:** Premier Jennifer Smith (from 1998). **Capital:** Hamilton. **Official language:** English. **Official religion:** none. **Monetary unit:** 1 Bermuda dollar (Bd$) = 100 cents; valuation (28 Jun 2002) US$1 = Bd$1.00.

## Demography

**Area:** 20.5 sq mi, 53.1 sq km. **Population** (2001): 63,500. **Population** (2002): 63,600. **Density** (2002): persons per sq mi 3,102, persons per sq km 1,198. **Urban** (2000): 100.0%; rural, none. **Sex distribution** (1999): male 48.57%; female 51.43%. **Age breakdown** (1999): under 15, 19.8%; 15–29, 18.3%; 30–44, 27.5%; 45–59, 19.4%; 60–74, 11.2%; 75 and over, 3.8%. **Ethnic composition** (2000): black 50.4%; British expatriates 29.0%; mulatto 10.0%; US white 6.0%; Portuguese 4.5%; other 0.1%. **Religious affiliation** (2000): Protestant 67.2%, of which Anglican 37.2%; Roman Catholic 16.0%; unaffiliated Christian 7.0%; nonreligious 4.0%; other 5.8%. **Major cities** (1991): St. George 1,648; Hamilton 1,100. **Location:** North Atlantic Ocean, east of North Carolina (US).

## Vital statistics

**Birth rate** per 1,000 population (2000): 13.4 (world avg. 22.5); legitimate 64.3%; illegitimate 35.7%. **Death rate** per 1,000 population (2000): 7.5 (world avg. 9.0). **Natural increase rate** per 1,000 population (2000): 5.9 (world avg. 13.5). **Total fertility rate** (avg. births per childbearing woman; 2000): 1.8. **Marriage rate** per 1,000 population (2000): 16.3. **Divorce rate** per 1,000 population (1996): 3.7. **Life expectancy** at birth (2000): male 74.9 years; female 78.9 years.

---

*1 metric ton = about 1.1 short tons;    1 kilometer = 0.6 mi (statute);    1 metric ton-km cargo = about 0.68 short ton-mi cargo;    c.i.f.: cost, insurance, and freight;    f.o.b.: free on board*

## National economy

**Budget** (1999). *Revenue*: Bd$562,200,000 (customs duty 31.3%; payroll tax 27.0%; fees, sales, recoveries, and other miscellaneous receipts 15.0%; tax on international companies 6.3%). *Expenditures*: Bd$545,700,000 (current expenditure 91.4%, of which public debt 2.3%; development expenditure 8.6%). **Production** (value in Bd$'000 except as noted). *Agriculture, forestry, fishing* (1999): vegetables 3,000, milk 1,657, fruits 900; livestock (number of live animals; 1999) 900 horses, 600 cattle, 45,000 chickens; fish catch (metric tons; 1998) 457, of which crustaceans and mollusks 38. *Mining and quarrying*: crushed stone for local use. *Manufacturing*: industries include pharmaceuticals, cosmetics, electronics, fish processing, handicrafts, and small boat building; the economy of Bermuda is overwhelmingly based on service industries such as tourism, insurance companies, offshore financial centres, e-commerce companies, and ship repair facilities. *Energy production (consumption)*: electricity (kW-hr; 1997) 530,000,000 (530,000,000); petroleum products (metric tons; 1997) none (167,000). **Land use** (1988): forested 20.0%; meadows and pastures 0.9%; agricultural and under permanent cultivation 3.1%; built-on, wasteland, and other 76.0%. **Tourism**: receipts from visitors (2000) US$431,000,000; expenditures by nationals abroad (1997) US$148,000,000. **Population economically active** (1991): total 35,222; activity rate of total population 60.2% (participation rates: ages 15–64, 80.9%; female 47.1%[7]; unemployed [1995] 1.5%). **Gross domestic product** (1999–2000): US$2,624,000,000 (US$41,690 per capita). **Household income and expenditure**. Average household size (1993) 2.5; average annual income per household (2001) Bd$72,500 (US$72,500); sources of income (1993): wages and salaries 65.3%, imputed income from owner occupancy 10.6%, self-employment 9.0%, net rental income 4.8%, other 10.4%; expenditure (1993): housing 27.7%, household furnishings 16.6%, food and nonalcoholic beverages 14.6%, health care 7.6%, transportation 7.3%, foreign travel 6.0%, clothing and footwear 4.9%, recreation 4.8%.

## Foreign trade

**Imports** (1999): Bd$712,000,000 (machinery 21.7%; food, beverages, and tobacco 19.0%; chemicals and chemical products 10.6%; transport equipment 7.7%; clothing 5.7%). *Major import sources:* US 72.8%; Canada 5.7%; UK 4.9%. **Exports** (1999): Bd$51,000,000 (nearly all reexports; detail is unavailable). *Major export destinations* (1995): US 49.8%; UK 6.2%; nonspecified 44.0%.

## Transport and communications

**Transport.** *Roads* (1997): total length 225 km (paved 100%; [222 km of private roads are also paved]). *Vehicles* (1996): passenger cars 21,220; trucks and buses 4,007. *Air transport* (2000): passenger arrivals 913,000, passenger departures 913,000; cargo loaded and unloaded 5,600 metric tons; airports (1998) with scheduled flights 1. **Communications**, in total units (units per 1,000 persons). Daily newspaper circulation (1996): 17,000 (277); radio receivers (1997): 82,000 (1,328); television receivers (1997): 66,000 (1,069); telephone main lines (2001): 56,300 (872); cellular telephone subscribers (2001):

13,300 (206); personal computers (2001): 32,000 (495); Internet users (1999): 25,000 (390).

## Education and health

**Educational attainment** (1991). Percentage of total population age 25 and over having: no formal schooling 0.5%; incomplete or complete primary 18.2%; incomplete or complete secondary 62.9%; higher 18.4%. **Literacy** (1997): total population age 15 and over literate, 98%. **Health** (1996): physicians 96 (1 per 639 persons); hospital beds 251 (1 per 244 persons); infant mortality rate per 1,000 live births (1998–2000 avg.) 1.6. **Food** (1999): daily per capita caloric intake 2,883 (vegetable products 73%, animal products 27%); 114% of FAO recommended minimum.

## Military

**Total active duty personnel** (1997): 700; part-time defense force assists police and is drawn from Bermudian conscripts.

 **Did you know?** The "Bermuda Triangle," an area between Bermuda, the US, and the Greater Antilles, is notorious for the large number of airplanes and ships that have disappeared there without a trace, but scientific substantiation for the peril of the region does not exist.

## Background

The Bermuda archipelago was named for Juan de Bermúdez, who may have visited the islands in 1503. Colonized by the English in 1612, Bermuda became a crown colony in 1684. Its economy is based on tourism and international finance; its per capita gross national product is among the world's highest.

## Recent Developments

Attracted by favorable tax and corporate residency laws, some American companies have opted recently to establish their headquarters in Bermuda.

**Internet resources:** <www.bermudatourism.org>

# Bhutan

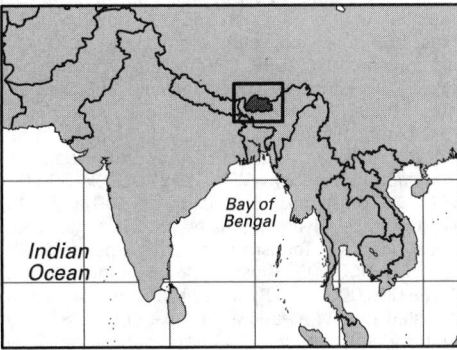

*Bay of Bengal*

*Indian Ocean*

**Official name:** Druk-Yul (Kingdom of Bhutan). **Form of government:** de facto constitutional monarchy with one legislative house (National Assembly [150 seats, including 45 nonelective seats representing the king and religious groups]). **Chief of state:** King Jigme Singye Wangchuk (from 1972). **Head of government:** Chairman of Council of Ministers Lyonpo Kinzang Dorji (from 14 Aug 2002). **Capital:** Thimphu. **Official language:** Dzongkha (a Tibetan dialect). **Official religion:** Mahayana Buddhism. **Monetary unit:** 1 ngultrum (Nu) = 100 chetrum; valuation (7 Jul 2003) $1 = Nu 46.33; Indian rupee also accepted legal tender.

## Demography

**Area:** 18,150 sq mi, 47,000 sq km. **Population** (2002): 721,000 (excluding more than 100,000 refugees in Nepal and India). **Density** (2002): persons per sq mi 39.7, persons per sq km 15.3. **Urban** (2002): 8.0%. **Sex distribution** (1988): male 50.97%; female 49.03%. **Age breakdown** (1988): under 15, 40.3%; 15–29, 26.4%; 30–44, 16.5%; 45–59, 10.5%; 60–74, 5.2%; 75 and over, 1.1%. **Ethnic composition** (1993): Bhutia (Ngalops) 50.0%; Nepalese (Gurung) 35.0%; Sharchops 15.0%. **Religious affiliation** (2000): Buddhist 74.0%; Hindu 20.5%; other 5.5%. **Major cities** (1997 est.): Thimphu 45,000; Phuntsholing 45,000. **Location:** southern Asia, bordering China and India.

## Vital statistics

**Birth rate** per 1,000 population (2002): 34.9 (world avg. 21.2). **Death rate** per 1,000 population (2002): 8.7 (world avg. 8.9). **Natural increase rate** per 1,000 population (2002): 26.2 (world avg. 12.3). **Total fertility rate** (avg. births per childbearing woman; 2002): 5.1. **Marital status** of population 15 years and over (1985): married 71.2%; single 19.7%; widowed 7.5%; divorced 1.6%. **Divorce rate** per 1,000 population: n.a. **Life expectancy** at birth (2002): male 62.0 years; female 64.0 years.

## National economy

**Budget** (1998–99). *Revenue*: Nu 6,844,000,000 (internal revenue 45.2%, grants from government of India 33.2%, grants from UN and other international agencies 21.6%). *Expenditures*: Nu 6,999,000,000 (capital expenditures 59.3%, current expenditures 40.7%). **Public debt** (external, outstanding; 2000): $197,300,000. **Production** (metric tons except as noted). *Agriculture, forestry, fishing* (1999): oranges 58,000, rice 50,000, corn (maize) 39,000; livestock (number of live animals) 435,000 cattle, 74,900 pigs, 58,500 sheep; roundwood (1998) 1,702,000 cu m; fish catch (1999) 330. *Mining and quarrying* (1997): limestone 270,000; dolomite 250,000; gypsum 50,000. *Manufacturing* (value in Nu '000,000; 1994): chemical products 419.0; cement 255.1; wood board products 230.6. *Energy production (consumption)*: electricity (kW-hr; 1997) 1,838,000,000 (415,000,000); coal (metric tons; 1997) 54,000 (71,000); petroleum products (metric tons; 1997) none (40,000). **Tourism** (2000): receipts from visitors $10,000,000. **Gross national product** (2000): $479,000,000 ($590 per capita). **Land use** (1994): forested 66.0%; meadows and pastures 5.8%; agricultural and under permanent cultivation 2.8%; other 25.4%.

## Foreign trade

**Imports** (1997-c.i.f.): Nu 4,978,000,000 (petroleum products 4.6%, rice 4.6%, vegetable fats and oils 3.0%, steel products 2.4%, wheat 2.0%, industrial machinery 1.7%). *Major import source* (1997–98): India 70.5%. **Exports** (1997): Nu 4,274,100,000 (electricity 21.0%, calcium carbide 15.0%, particle board 8.0%, cement 7.1%). *Major export destination* (1997–98): India 94.5%.

## Transport and communications

**Transport.** *Roads* (1999): total length 3,691 km (paved 60%). *Vehicles* (1999): passenger cars 6,468; trucks and buses 3,273. *Air transport* (1998): passenger-km 49,000,000; metric ton-km cargo 4,000,000; airports (1997) with scheduled flights 1. **Communications,** in total units (units per 1,000 persons). Radio receivers (1997): 37,000 (19); television receivers (1999): 13,000 (20); telephone main lines (2001): 14,000 (20); personal computers (2001): 4,000 (5.8); Internet users (2001): 2,500 (3.6).

## Education and health

**Literacy** (1995 est.): total population age 15 and over literate 42.2%; males literate 56.2%; females literate 28.1%. **Health:** physicians (1994) 100 (1 per 8,000 persons); hospital beds 970 (1 per 825 persons); infant mortality rate per 1,000 live births (2002) 55.0. **Food** (1975–77): daily per capita caloric intake 2,058 (vegetable products 98%, animal products 2%); 89% of FAO recommended minimum.

## Military

**Total active duty personnel** (2000): about 6,000 (army 100%).

## Background

Bhutan's mountains and forests long made it inaccessible to the outside world, and its feudal rulers banned foreigners until well into the 20th century. It nevertheless became the object of foreign invasions; in 1865 it came under British influence, and in 1910 it agreed to be guided by Britain in its foreign affairs. It later became oriented toward British-ruled India, though much of its trade was with Tibet. India took over Britain's role in 1949, and Communist China's 1950 occupation of neighboring Tibet further strengthened Bhutan's ties with India. The apparent Chinese threat made Bhutan's rulers aware of the need to modernize, and it embarked on a program to build roads and hospitals and to create a system of secular education.

## Recent Developments

A Civil and Criminal Procedure Code, under which the powers of the country's judiciary were expanded and the judicial process defined, was passed by the National Assembly in 2001. Bhutan's economy continued to flourish, and work proceeded on a new draft constitution.

**Internet resources:**
<lcweb2.loc.gov/frd/cs/bttoc.html>

*1 metric ton = about 1.1 short tons; 1 kilometer = 0.6 mi (statute); 1 metric ton-km cargo = about 0.68 short ton-mi cargo; c.i.f.: cost, insurance, and freight; f.o.b.: free on board*

# Bolivia

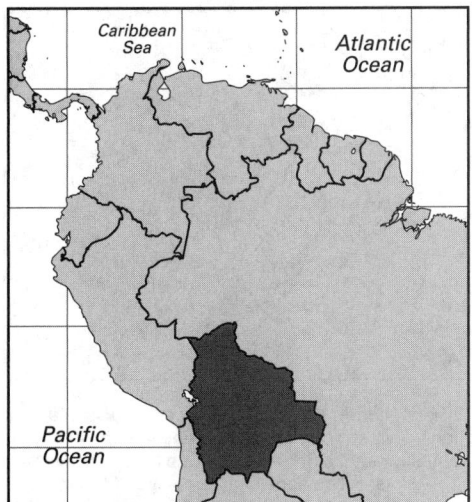

**Official name:** República de Bolivia (Republic of Bolivia). **Form of government:** unitary multiparty republic with two legislative houses (Chamber of Senators [27]; Chamber of Deputies [130]). **Head of state and government:** President Gonzalo Sánchez de Lozada (from 6 Aug 2002). **Capitals:** La Paz (administrative); Sucre (judicial). **Official languages:** Spanish, Aymara, Quechua. **Official religion:** Roman Catholicism. **Monetary unit:** 1 boliviano (Bs) = 100 centavos; valuation (7 Jul 2003) $1 = Bs 7.66.

## Demography

**Area:** 424,164 sq mi, 1,098,581 sq km. **Population** (2002): 8,401,000. **Density** (2002): persons per sq mi 19.8, persons per sq km 7.6. **Urban** (2001): 62.4%. **Sex distribution** (2001): male 49.84%; female 50.16%. **Age breakdown** (2000): under 15, 39.1%; 15–29, 28.1%; 30–44, 16.6%; 45–59, 9.9%; 60–74, 4.5%; 75 and over, 1.8%. **Ethnic composition** (1996): Indian 55.0%; mestizo 30.0%; white 15.0%. **Religious affiliation** (1995): Roman Catholic 88.5%; Protestant 9.0%; other 2.5%. **Major cities** (2001): Santa Cruz 1,116,059; La Paz 789,585 (urban agglomeration 1,499,000); El Alto 647,350 (within La Paz urban agglomeration); Cochabamba 516,683; Oruro 201,230. **Location:** central South America, bordering Brazil, Paraguay, Argentina, Chile, and Peru.

## Vital statistics

**Birth rate** per 1,000 population (2000): 31.9 (world avg. 22.5). **Death rate** per 1,000 population (2000): 8.6 (world avg. 9.0). **Natural increase rate** per 1,000 population (2000): 23.3 (world avg. 13.5). **Total fertility rate** (avg. births per childbearing woman; 2000): 3.7. **Marriage rate** per 1,000 population: n.a. **Life expectancy** at birth (2000): male 61.2 years; female 66.3 years.

## National economy

**Budget** (1998). *Revenue*: Bs 11,698,500,000 (tax revenue 78.9%, of which indirect taxes 49.0%, taxes on petroleum and petroleum products 18.8%; non-

tax revenue 8.9%). *Expenditures*: Bs 13,681,300,-000 (current expenditure 78.8%, of which wages and salaries 31.3%, transfers 21.9%; capital expenditure 21.2%). **Production** (metric tons except as noted). *Agriculture, forestry, fishing* (1999): sugarcane 4,160,000, soybeans 762,000, potatoes 783,000; livestock (number of live animals) 8,575,000 sheep, 6,556,000 cattle, 2,715,000 pigs; roundwood (1998) 1,989,000 cu m; fish catch (1998) 6,055. Mining and quarrying (metric tons of pure metal; 1998): zinc 150,709; lead 13,848; tin 10,542. *Manufacturing* (value added in $'000; 1994): petroleum products 375; food products 169; beverages 99. *Energy production (consumption)*: electricity (kW-hr; 1998) 3,771,000,000 (3,252,-000,000); crude petroleum (barrels; 1998) 12,628,000 (10,382,000); petroleum products (metric tons; 1997) 1,354,000 (1,514,000); natural gas (cu m; 1998) 3,106,000,000 (1,511,000,000). **Population economically active** (1997): total 3,645,165; activity rate of total population 46.6% (participation rates: ages 15–64, 72.1%; female 43.7%; unemployed 2.1%). **Tourism** (2000): receipts $160,000,000; expenditures $102,000,000. **Gross national product** (at current market prices; 2000): $8,206,000,000 ($990 per capita). **Public debt** (external, outstanding; 2000): $4,120,000,000. **Household income and expenditure.** Average household size (1997): 4.4; expenditure (1988): food 35.5%, transportation and communications 17.7%, housing 14.8%, household durable goods 7.3%, clothing and footwear 5.1%, beverages and tobacco 4.5%, recreation 2.7%, health 2.1%. **Land use** (1994): forested 53.5%; meadows and pastures 24.4%; agricultural and under permanent cultivation 2.2%; other 19.9%.

## Foreign trade

**Imports** (1998; f.o.b. in balance of trade and c.i.f. for commodities and trading partners): $1,983,000,-000 (raw materials 42.2%, of which raw materials for industry 32.8%; capital goods 40.0%, of which transportation equipment 23.1%, capital goods for industry 15.9%; consumer goods 18.2%, of which nondurable consumer goods 9.3%, durable consumer goods 8.9%; other 0.4%). *Major import sources*: US 26.3%; Japan 20.0%; Brazil 10.3%; Argentina 10.0%; Chile 6.0%; Peru 3.7%; France 1.1%. **Exports** (1998): $1,104,900,000 (zinc 14.1%; soybeans 13.6%; gold 10.1%; silver 6.6%; oils 5.8%; natural gas 5.1%; tin 5.1%; timber 4.6%). *Major export destinations*: US 18.4%; UK 17.8%; Peru 11.9%; Argentina 10.9%; Chile 2.9%; Brazil 2.4%; Germany 1.9%.

## Transport and communications

**Transport.** *Railroads* (1997): route length 3,519 km; passenger-km 136,700,000; metric ton-km cargo 524,200,000. *Roads* (1999): total length 52,216 km (paved 6%). *Vehicles* (1996): passenger cars 223,829; trucks and buses 138,536. *Air transport* (2000): passenger-km 1,914,566,000; metric ton-km cargo 192,838,000; airports (1997) with scheduled flights 14. **Communications**, in total units (units per 1,000 persons). Daily newspaper circulation (1996): 420,000 (55); radio receivers (1997): 5,250,-000 (675); television receivers (1999): 960,000 (118); telephone main lines (2001): 514,800 (62); cellular telephone subscribers (2001): 744,000 (90);

personal computers (2001): 170,000 (21); Internet users (2001): 120,000 (15).

## Education and health

**Educational attainment** (1992). Percentage of population age 25 and over having: no formal schooling 23.3%; some primary 20.3%; primary education 21.7%; some secondary 9.0%; secondary 6.5%; some higher 5.0%; higher 4.8%; not specified 9.4%. **Literacy** (1995): total population age 15 and over literate 82.3%; males literate 92.1%; females literate 79.4%. **Health** (1996): physicians 4,346 (1 per 1,747 persons); hospital beds (1998) 11,548 (1 per 689 persons); infant mortality rate per 1,000 live births (2000) 60.4. **Food** (2000): daily per capita caloric intake 2,218 (vegetable products 84%, animal products 16%); 93% of FAO recommended minimum.

## Military

**Total active duty personnel** (2001): 31,500 (army 79.4%, navy 11.1%, air force 9.5%). **Military expenditure as percentage of GNP** (1998): 1.8% (world 2.4%); per capita expenditure $18.

## Background

The Bolivian highlands were the location of the advanced Tiwanaku culture in the 7th–11th centuries and, with its passing, became the home of the Aymara, an Indian group conquered by the Incas in the 15th century. The Incas were overrun by the invading Spanish under Francisco Pizarro in the 1530s. By 1600 Spain had established the cities of Charcas (now Sucre), La Paz, Santa Cruz, and what would become Cochabamba, and had begun to exploit the silver wealth of Potosí. Bolivia flourished in the 17th century, and for a time Potosí was the largest city in the Americas. By the end of the century, the mineral wealth had dried up. Talk of independence began as early as 1809, but not until 1825 were Spanish forces finally defeated. Bolivia shrank in size when it lost Atacama province to Chile in 1884 at the end of the War of the Pacific, and again in 1939 when it lost most of Gran Chaco to Paraguay. One of South America's poorest countries, it was plagued by governmental instability for much of the 20th century. By the 1990s Bolivia had become one of the world's largest producers of coca, from which cocaine is derived. The government subsequently instituted a largely successful program to eradicate the crop, although such efforts were resisted by the many poor farmers who depended on coca.

## Recent Developments

Presidential balloting in August 2002 resulted in the election of the political centrist Gonzalo Sánchez de Lozada, a millionaire mining executive who grew up in the US and speaks Spanish with an accent, to the top post in the country. Controversy continued over the US-supported program to eradicate coca plantations. Clashes involving coca growers, police, and soldiers claimed dozens of lives between August 2001 and March 2002.

**Internet resources:** <www.boliviabiz.com>

# Bosnia and Herzegovina

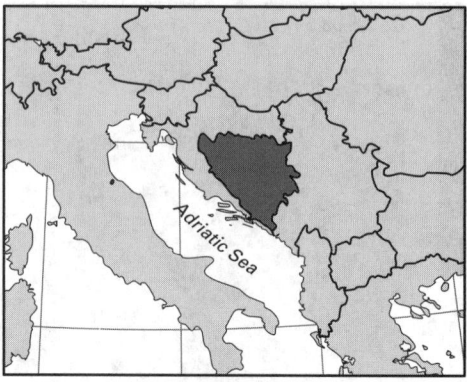

**Official name:** Bosna i Hercegovina (Bosnia and Herzegovina). **Form of government:** federal multiparty republic with bicameral legislature (House of Peoples [15—all seats are nonelective]; House of Representatives [42]). **Chiefs of state:** Tripartite presidency with 8-month-long rotating presidency. **Head of government:** Prime minister (chairman of Council of Ministers) with 8-month-long rotating chairmanship. **Capital:** Sarajevo. **Official language:** Bosnian (Serbo-Croatian). **Official religion:** none. **Monetary unit:** 1 marka (KM) = 100 fenning; valuation (7 Jul 2003) $1 = KM 1.70.

## Demography

**Area:** 19,741 sq mi, 51,129 sq km. **Population** (2002): 3,964,000 (excludes about 200,000 refugees in adjacent countries and Western Europe). **Density** (2002): persons per sq mi 200.8, persons per sq km 77.5. **Urban** (1999): 42.5%. **Sex distribution** (2001): male 50.46%; female 49.54%. **Age breakdown** (2001): under 15, 20.1%; 15–29, 22.2%; 30–44, 25.8%; 45–59, 17.4%; 60–74, 12.2%; 75 and over, 2.3%. **Ethnic composition** (1999): Bosniac 44.0%; Serb 31.0%; Croat 17.0%; other 8.0%. **Religious affiliation** (1999): Sunni Muslim 43.0%; Serbian Orthodox 30.0%; Roman Catholic 18.0%; other (mostly nonreligious) 9.0%. **Major cities** (1991): Sarajevo 360,000 (urban agglomeration [2001] 552,000); Banja Luka 160,000 (1997); Zenica 96,027; Tuzla 83,770; Mostar 75,865. **Location:** southeastern Europe, bordered by Croatia, Serbia and Montenegro, and the Adriatic Sea.

## Vital statistics

**Birth rate** per 1,000 population (2001): 12.9 (world avg. 21.2); (1993) legitimate 92.6%; illegitimate 7.4%. **Death rate** per 1,000 population (2001): 8.0 (world avg. 8.9). **Natural increase rate** per 1,000 population (2001): 4.9 (world avg. 12.3). **Total fertility rate** (avg. births per childbearing woman; 2001): 1.7. **Marriage rate** per 1,000 population (1991): 6.0. **Life expectancy** at birth (2001): male 69.0 years; female 74.7 years.

## National economy

**Budget** (2000). *Revenue:* KM 1,819,600,000 (tax revenue 75.9%, of which taxes on goods and services

*1 metric ton = about 1.1 short tons;   1 kilometer = 0.6 mi (statute);   1 metric ton-km cargo = about 0.68 short ton-mi cargo;   c.i.f.: cost, insurance, and freight;   f.o.b.: free on board*

58.1%, customs duties 9.2%; nontax revenue 24.1%). *Expenditures*: KM 2,042,900,000 (defense 21.0%; disability benefits 15.7%; wages 15.1%; social funds 14.3%; transfer to state government 12.0%). *Public debt* (external, outstanding; 2000): $2,575,000,000. **Gross national product** (2000): $4,899,000,000 ($1,230 per capita). **Production** (metric tons except as noted). *Agriculture, forestry, fishing* (2001): corn (maize) 640,329, potatoes 320,000, wheat 269,105; livestock (number of live animals) 640,000 sheep, 440,000 cattle; roundwood (1998) 40,000 cu m; fish catch (1999) 2,500. *Mining* (1996): iron ore (gross weight) 100,000; bauxite 75,000; kaolin 3,000. *Manufacturing* (1996): cement 150,000; crude steel 115,000; pig iron 100,000. *Energy production (consumption)*: electricity (kW-hr; 1999) 2,585,000,000 (2,684,000,000); coal (metric tons; 1997) 1,640,000 (1,640,000); petroleum products (metric tons; 1997) none (684,000); natural gas (cu m; 1997) none (115,600,-000). **Population economically active** (1991): total 992,000; activity rate of total population 22.7% (participation rates: ages 15–64, 35.6%; female [1990] 37.7%; unemployed [December 2000] c. 40%). **Household income and expenditure.** Average household size (1991) 3.4; sources of income (1990): wages 53.2%, transfers 18.2%, self-employment 12.0%, other 16.6%; expenditure (1988): food 41.3%, clothing 8.3%, fuel and lighting 7.8%, housing 7.8%, transportation 6.0%, beverages and tobacco 5.7%. **Tourism** (1999): receipts from visitors $21,000,000. **Land use** (1994): forested 53.1%; meadows and pastures 23.5%; agricultural and under permanent cultivation 15.7%; other 7.7%.

## Foreign trade

**Imports** (2000): $2,629,000,000. *Major import sources:* Croatia 20.6%; Italy 15.9%; Slovenia 14.2%; Germany 10.7%; Serbia and Montenegro 5.7%. **Exports** (2000): $968,000,000. *Major export destinations:* Italy 23.4%; Serbia and Montenegro 21.6%; Switzerland 11.9%; Germany 9.2%; Croatia 7.9%.

## Transport and communications

**Transport.** *Railroads* (2001; 1991–95 war destroyed much infrastructure; limited service resumed in 1998): length 1,031 km; passenger-km 38,740,000; metric ton-km cargo 239,138,000. *Roads* (2001): total length 21,846 km (paved 64%). *Vehicles* (1996): passenger cars 96,182; trucks and buses 10,919. *Air transport* (1998; Air Bosna only): passenger-km 40,390,000; metric ton-km 430,000. Airports (1997) with scheduled flights 1. **Communications,** in total units (units per 1,000 persons). Daily newspaper circulation (1995): 520,000 (155); radio receivers (1997): 940,000 (282); telephone main lines (2001): 450,100 (60); cellular telephone subscribers (2001): 233,300 (57); Internet users (2001): 45,000 (11).

## Education and health

**Literacy** (1991): total population age 10 and over literate 85.5%; males literate 96.5%; females literate 76.6%. **Health:** physicians (1998) 5,000 (1 per 700 persons); hospital beds (1996) 15,586 (1 per 208 persons); infant mortality rate per 1,000 live births (2001) 24.5. **Food** (2000): daily per capita caloric intake 2,661 (vegetable products 86%, animal products 14%); 115% of FAO recommended minimum.

## Military

**Total active duty personnel** (2001): 38,000 (army 100%); about 19,000 troops of the NATO-commanded Stabilization Force are stationed in Bosnia and Herzegovina to assure implementation of the Dayton accords. **Military expenditure as percentage of GNP** (1999): 4.5% (world 2.4%); per capita expenditure $75.

**Did you know?** A variety of fruits are commonly grown in Bosnia and Herzegovina, including apples, grapes, peaches, pears, nectarines, and especially plums. Slivovitz, distilled from plums, particularly those from the Posavina region in the far north of the country, is the liquor of choice for men in Bosnia and Herzegovina and in other Balkan countries.

## Background

Habitation long predates the era of Roman rule, when much of the country was included in the province of Dalmatia. Slav settlement began in the 6th century AD. For the next several centuries, parts of the region fell under the rule of Serbs, Croats, Hungarians, Venetians, and Byzantines. The Ottoman Turks invaded Bosnia in the 14th century, and after many battles it became a Turkish province in 1463. Herzegovina, then known as Hum, was taken in 1482. In the 16th–17th century the area was an important Turkish outpost, constantly at war with the Habsburgs and Venice. During this period much of the native population converted to Islam. At the Congress of Berlin after the Russo-Turkish War of 1877–78, Bosnia and Herzegovina was assigned to Austria-Hungary and annexed in 1908. Growing Serb nationalism resulted in the 1914 assassination of the Austrian Archduke Francis Ferdinand at Sarajevo by a Bosnian Serb, an event that precipitated World War I. After the war the area was annexed to Serbia. Following World War II the twin territory became a republic of communist Yugoslavia. With the collapse of communist regimes in Eastern Europe, Bosnia and Herzegovina declared its independence in 1992; its Serb population objected, and conflict ensued among Serbs, Croats, and Muslims. The 1995 peace accord established a loosely federated government roughly divided between a Muslim Croat federation and a Serb Republic (Republika Srpska). In 1996 a NATO peacekeeping force was installed there.

## Recent Developments

In October 2002 nationalist parties won in general elections organized without international supervision for the first time since war broke out in 1992. Electoral results suggested impatience with the pace of reforms by moderates over the previous two years rather than a victory for nationalists. In February 2003 Biljana Plavsic, a leader of the Bosnian Serbs during the 1992–95 civil war known as "the Ironlady," was sentenced to 11 years in prison by the International War Crimes Tribunal in The Hague. She had surrendered voluntarily and pleaded guilty to war crimes.

**Internet resources:** <www.bhembassy.org>

# Botswana

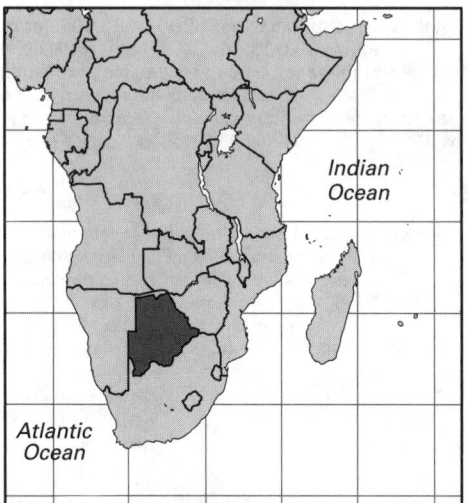

Indian Ocean

Atlantic Ocean

**Official name:** Republic of Botswana. **Form of government:** multiparty republic with one legislative body (National Assembly [47]) and House of Chiefs (15-member advisory board). **Head of state and government:** President Festus Mogae (from 1998). **Capital:** Gaborone. **Official language:** English (Tswana is the national language). **Official religion:** none. **Monetary unit:** 1 pula (P) = 100 thebe; valuation (7 Jul 2003) $1 = P 4.93.

## Demography

**Area:** 224,607 (rounded) sq mi, 581,730 sq km. **Population** (2002): 1,679,000. **Density** (2002): persons per sq mi 7.5, persons per sq km 2.9. **Urban** (1999): 29.4%. **Sex distribution** (2000): male 48.58%; female 51.42%. **Age breakdown** (2000): under 15, 40.6%; 15–29, 30.8%; 30–44, 15.0%; 45–59, 7.7%; 60–74, 4.3%; 75 and over, 1.6%. **Ethnic composition** (2000): Tswana 66.8%; Kalanga 14.8%; Ndebele 1.7%; Herero 1.4%; San (Bushman) 1.3%; Afrikaner 1.3%. **Religious affiliation** (2000): traditional beliefs 38.8%; African Christian 30.7%; Protestant 10.9%; Roman Catholic 3.7%. **Major cities** (2001): Gaborone 185,891; Francistown 84,406; Molepolole 54,124; Selebi-Pikwe 50,012; Maun 43,952.

## Vital statistics

**Birth rate** per 1,000 population (2002): 28.0 (world avg. 21.2). **Death rate** per 1,000 population (2002): 26.3 (world avg. 8.9). **Natural increase rate** per 1,000 population (2002): 1.7 (world avg. 12.3). **Total fertility rate** (avg. births per childbearing woman; 2002): 3.6. **Marriage rate** per 1,000 population (1987): 1.6. **Life expectancy** at birth (2001): male 36.8 years; female 37.5 years.

## National economy

**Budget** (1997–98). *Revenue*: P 8,468,900,000 (mineral royalties 57.7%, customs and excise taxes

14.0%, property income 13.2%, non-mineral income tax 6.4%). *Expenditures*: P 7,616,400,000 (education 24.2%, defense 8.4%, health 5.1%, interest 1.3%). **Population economically active** (1995): total 439,933; activity rate of total population 29.9% (participation rates: ages 15–64, 59.6%; female 35.5%, unemployed 21.5%). **Tourism:** receipts (2000) $313,000,000; expenditures (1999) $143,000,-000. **Production** (metric tons except as noted). *Agriculture, forestry, fishing* (1999): cereals 19,800 (of which sorghum 13,000, corn [maize] 5,000, millet 1,300), pulses 16,000, vegetables and melons 15,000; livestock (number of live animals) 2,380,000 cattle, 1,835,000 goats, 250,000 sheep; roundwood (1998) 1,066,000 cu m; fish catch (1998) 2,000. *Mining and quarrying* (1998): nickel 19,432; copper 15,593; diamonds 19,773,000 carats. *Manufacturing* (value added in P '000,000; 1994): food products 164.3; wearing apparel 78.9; paper and paper products 28.0. *Energy production (consumption)*: electricity (kW-hr; 1993) 970,000,-000 (970,000,000); coal (metric tons; 1992) 901,452 (n.a.); crude petroleum, none (n.a.). **Gross national product** (2000): $5,280,000,000 ($3,300 per capita). **Public debt** (external, outstanding; 2000): $397,600,000. **Household income and expenditure** (1991). Average household size 4.8; average annual income per household (1985–86) P 3,910 ($2,080); sources of income (1987): wages and salaries 73.3%, self-employment 15.9%, transfers 10.8%; expenditure: food 39.4%, household durable goods 14.0%, rent and services 13.3%, transportation 13.1%, clothing 5.6%, health 2.3%. **Land use** (1994): forest 46.8%; pasture 45.2%; agriculture 0.7%; other 7.3%.

## Foreign trade

**Imports** (1998): P 9,513,126,000 (machinery and transport equipment 37.5%, of which transport equipment 16.3%; food, beverages, and tobacco 13.1%; metal and metal products 10.1%; chemical and rubber products 8.9%). *Major import sources:* Customs Union of Southern Africa (CUSA) 74.9%; South Korea 4.8%; Zimbabwe 3.9%; UK 3.4%; US 1.4%. **Exports** (1998): P 8,696,922,000 (diamonds 69.4%; vehicles and parts 11.1%; copper-nickel matte 5.0%; textiles 3.5%; meat products 3.4%). *Major export destinations:* UK 55.5%; CUSA 17.2%; Zimbabwe 2.9%; US 1.0%.

## Transport and communications

**Transport.** *Railroads* (1996–97): length 1,135 km; passenger-km 96,000,000; metric ton-km cargo 795,000. *Roads* (1996): total length 18,327 km (paved 25%). *Vehicles* (1996): passenger cars 30,517; trucks and buses 59,710. *Air transport* (1998; Air Botswana only): passenger-km 56,835,-000; metric ton-km cargo 211,000; airports (1998) 7. **Communications**, in total units (units per 1,000 persons). Daily newspaper circulation (1996): 40,000 (27); radio receivers (1997): 237,000 (154); television receivers (1999): 33,000 (21); telephone main lines (2000): 150,300 (93); cellular telephone subscribers (2001): 278,000 (167); personal computers (2001): 65,000 (39); Internet users (2000): 25,000 (15).

*1 metric ton = about 1.1 short tons;    1 kilometer = 0.6 mi (statute);    1 metric ton-km cargo = about 0.68 short ton-mi cargo;    c.i.f.: cost, insurance, and freight;    f.o.b.: free on board*

## Education and health

**Educational attainment** (1993). Percentage of population age 25 and over having: no formal schooling 34.7%; primary education 44.1%; some secondary 19.8%; postsecondary 1.4%. **Literacy** (2000): total population over age 15 literate 934,200 (77.2%); males literate 449,200 (74.4%); females literate 485,000 (79.8%). **Health** (1994): physicians 339 (1 per 4,395 persons); hospital beds (1993) 3,299 (1 per 434 persons); infant mortality rate per 1,000 live births (2002) 64.7. **Food** (1998): daily per capita caloric intake 2,159 (vegetable products 82%, animal products 18%); 93% of FAO recommended minimum.

## Military

**Total active duty personnel** (2001): 9,000 (army 94.4%, navy, none [land locked], air force 5.6%). **Military expenditure as percentage of GNP** (1999): 4.7% (world 2.4%); per capita expenditure $142.

## Background

The region's earliest inhabitants were the Khoikhoi and San (Bushmen). Sites were settled as early as AD 190 during the southerly migration of Bantu-speaking farmers. Tswana dynasties, which developed in the western Transvaal in the 13th–14th century, moved into Botswana in the 18th century and established several powerful states. European missionaries arrived in the early 19th century, but it was the discovery of gold in 1867 that excited European interest. In 1885 the area became the British Bechuanaland Protectorate. The next year, the region south of the Molopo River became a crown colony, and it was annexed by the Cape Colony 10 years later. Bechuanaland itself continued as a British protectorate until the 1960s. In 1966 the Republic of Bechuanaland (later, Botswana) was proclaimed an independent member of the British Commonwealth. Independent Botswana tried to maintain a delicate balance between its economic dependence on South Africa and its relations with the surrounding black countries; the independence of Namibia in 1990 and South Africa's rejection of apartheid eased tensions.

## Recent Developments

Botswana enjoys a remarkably stable liberal democracy with solid growth, a by-product of the October 1999 elections that confirmed the mandate of the Botswana Democratic Party under Pres. Festus Mogae. In the Transparency International 2001 survey, Botswana was ranked the least corrupt state in Africa. On the health front, however, the country faces a growing crisis; nearly 36% of adults in Botswana are believed to have HIV, the virus that causes AIDS.

**Internet resources:** <www.gov.bw/tourism>

# Brazil

**Official name:** República Federativa do Brasil (Federative Republic of Brazil). **Form of government:** multiparty federal republic with 2 legislative houses (Federal Senate [81]; Chamber of Deputies [513]). **Chief of state and government:** President Luiz Inácio Lula

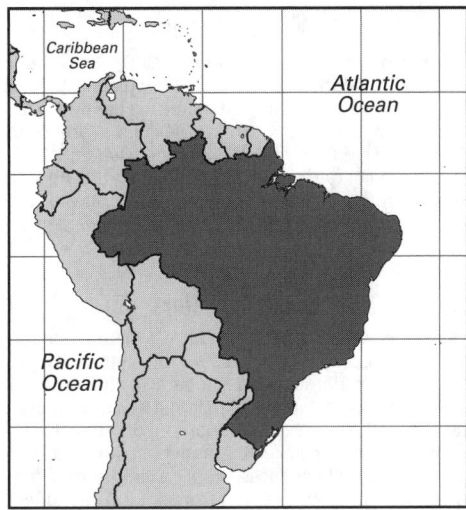

da Silva (from 1 Jan 2003). **Capital:** Brasília. **Official language:** Portuguese. **Official religion:** none. **Monetary unit:** real (R$) = 100 centavos; valuation (7 Jul 2003) US$1 = 2.83 reais.

## Demography

**Area:** 3,300,171 sq mi, 8,547,404 sq km (land area excluding inland water is 3,265,076 sq mi [8,456,508 sq km]). **Population** (2002): 174,619,-000. **Density** (2002): persons per sq mi 53.1, persons per sq km 20.5. **Urban** (1999): 79.7%. **Sex distribution** (2000): male 49.26%; female 50.74%. **Age breakdown** (2000): under 15, 29.0%; 15–29, 28.4%; 30–44, 22.2%; 45–59, 12.5%; 60–74, 6.3%; 75 and over, 1.6%. **Racial composition** (1999; excludes rural population of Acre, Amapá, Amazonas, Pará, Rondônia, and Roraima states): white 54.0%; mulatto and mestizo 39.9%; black and black/Amerindian 5.4%; Asian 0.5%; Amerindian 0.2%. **Religious affiliation** (1995; Christian data include nominal Christians): Catholic 74.3% (includes syncretic Afro-Catholic cults having Spiritist beliefs and rituals), of which Roman Catholic 72.3%; Protestant 23.2%, of which Pentecostal 19.1%; other Christian 0.9%; New-Religionist 0.3%; Buddhist 0.3%; Jewish 0.2%; Muslim 0.1%; other 0.7%. **Major cities and metropolitan areas** (2000; preliminary figures are for *municípios,* which may include adjacent urban or rural districts): São Paulo 9,785,640 (17,833,757); Rio de Janeiro 5,850,544 (10,871,960); Salvador 2,439,-881 (3,018,326); Belo Horizonte 2,229,697 (4,208,508); Fortaleza 2,138,234 (2,843,304); Brasília 2,043,169 (2,043,169); Curitiba 1,586,898 (2,697,924); Recife 1,421,947 (3,316,451); Manaus 1,394,724 (1,403,796); Porto Alegre 1,320,069 (3,507,624); Belém 1,271,615 (1,807,556); Goiânia 1,083,396 (1,616,370); Guarulhos 1,048,280 (within São Paulo metropolitan area); Campinas 951,824 (1,717,410). **Families** (1996). Average family size 3.9; 1–2 persons 25.2%, 3 persons 20.3%, 4 persons 22.2%, 5–6 persons 23.3%, 7 or more persons 9.0%. **Domestic migration.** Percent of population moving to different *município* between 1991 and 1996: 7.6%. **Number of emigrants/immigrants** (1986–96): 2,355,057/169,303. Emigrants' most popular destinations in order of preference are the US, Japan, and the UK.

## Vital statistics

**Birth rate** per 1,000 population (2000): 18.8 (world avg. 22.5). **Death rate** per 1,000 population (2000): 9.4 (world avg. 9.0). **Natural increase rate** per 1,000 population (2000): 9.4 (world avg. 13.5). **Total fertility rate** (avg. births per childbearing woman; 2000): 2.1. **Marriage rate** per 1,000 population (1995): 4.7. **Divorce rate** per 1,000 population (1995): 0.6. **Life expectancy** at birth (2000): male 58.5 years; female 67.6 years.

## Social indicators

**Quality of working life.** Annual estimated rate per 100,000 insured workers (1990) for: on-the-job injury 2,032; industrial illness 17; death 4. Proportion of labor force participating in national social insurance system (1990): 50.1%. Proportion of formally employed population receiving minimum wage (1993): 25.0%. **Access to services** (1999; excludes rural population of Acre, Amapá, Amazonas, Pará, Rondônia, and Roraima states). Proportion of households having access to: electricity 94.8%, of which urban households having access 99.2%, rural households having access 75.4%; safe public (piped) water supply 79.8%, of which urban households having access 92.3%, rural households having access 24.9%; public (piped) sewage system 43.6%, of which urban household having access 52.5%, rural households having access 4.5%; no sewage disposal 8.5%, of which urban households having no disposal 2.9%, rural households having no disposal 32.9%. **Social participation.** Voting is mandatory for national elections; abstention is punishable by a fine. Trade union membership in total workforce (1991): 16,748,155. **Social deviance.** Annual murder rate per 100,000 population (1996): Brazil 23, Rio de Janeiro alone 69, São Paulo alone 55. **Leisure.** Favorite leisure activities include: playing soccer, dancing, rehearsing all year in neighborhood samba groups for celebrations of Carnival, and competing in water sports, volleyball, and basketball. **Material well-being** (1999; excludes rural population of Acre, Amapá, Amazonas, Pará, Rondônia, and Roraima states). Households possessing: telephone lines (1997) 27.9%, of which urban 33.2%, rural 4.9%; television receiver 87.7%, of which urban 93.2%, rural 63.8%; refrigerator 82.8%, of which urban 89.7%, rural 52.5%; washing machine 32.8%, of which urban 38.0%, rural 10.0%.

## National economy

**Gross national product** (at current market prices; 2000): US$610,058,000,000 (US$3,580 per capita). **Budget** (1995). *Revenue* R$320,178,000,000 (development receipts 62.6%, of which credits 58.4%; current receipts 37.4%, of which social contributions 19.3% [including social security 9.2%], taxes 13.3%). *Expenditures:* R$320,178,000,000 (administration and planning 59.5%; social welfare 13.9%; regional development 6.0%; health and sanitation 4.9%; agriculture 3.1%; education 2.7%; defense and public order 2.6%). *Public debt* (external, outstanding; 2000): US$92,590,000,000. **Production** ('000 metric tons except as noted). *Agriculture, forestry, fishing* (2000): sugarcane 324,668, soybeans 32,687, corn (maize) 32,038, cassava 22,960, oranges 22,745, rice 11,168, bananas 6,339, tomatoes 3,043, dry beans 3,037, potatoes 2,582, seed cotton 1,915, wheat 1,895, coffee 1,824, coconuts 1,822, papayas 1,700, cashew apples 1,500, pineapples 1,353, apples 1,160, onions 1,078, grapes 978, sorghum 842, mangoes 605, tobacco 594, sweet potatoes 500, lemons and limes 480, oil palm fruit 387, maté 220, cacao beans 210, sisal 195, peanuts (groundnuts) 188, cashews 154, garlic 72, natural rubber 70, Brazil nuts 23; livestock (number of live animals) 167,471,000 cattle, 27,320,000 pigs, 18,300,000 sheep, 6,400,000 horses; roundwood (1999) 197,897,000 cu m, of which fuelwood 90,210,000 cu m, sawlogs and veneer logs 46,779,000 cu m, pulpwood 30,701,000 cu m; fish catch (1997) 820, of which freshwater fishes 267. *Mining and quarrying* (value of export production in US$'000,000; 1998): iron ore 3,066; ferroniobium 242; silicon 135; bauxite 122; kaolin (clay) 106; ferrosilicon 101; granite (1996) 97; copper 89; manganese 52; nickel 52; gold production for both domestic use and export 1,594,000 troy oz; Brazil is also a world-leading producer of high-quality grade quartz and tantalum. *Manufacturing* (value added in R$'000,000; 1995): industrial chemicals 21,937; transport equipment 20,434; food products 18,117; fabricated and base metals 13,813; electrical machinery 9,563; nonelectrical machinery 8,122; paper and paper products 5,667; cement, bricks, and tiles 5,125; pharmaceuticals 4,958; textiles 4,907; printing and publishing 4,807. **Land use** (1994): forested 57.7%; meadows and pastures 21.9%; agricultural and under permanent cultivation 6.0%; other 14.4%. **Population economically active** (1998; excludes rural population of Acre, Amapá, Amazonas, Pará, Rondônia, and Roraima states and members of armed forces in barracks): total 76,885,700; activity rate of total population 47.4% (participation rates: ages 15–59 [1997] 72.0%; female 40.7%; unemployed [May 1999] officially 8%). **Tourism** (2000): receipts from visitors US$4,228,000,000; expenditures by nationals abroad US$3,893,000,000. **Households.** Average household size (2000) 3.8. **Family income and expenditure.** Average family size (1997) 3.5; annual income per family (1993) US$2,178 (excludes rural population of Acre, Amapá, Amazonas, Pará, Rondônia, and Roraima states); sources of income (1987–88; based on 10,408,833 families in Brazil's nine largest metropolitan regions): wages and salaries 62.4%, self-employed 14.7%, transfers 10.9%, other 12.0%; expenditure (1995–96): housing, energy, and household furnishings 28.8%, food and beverages 23.4%, transportation and communications 13.8%, health care 9.2%, education and recreation 8.4%. *Energy production (consumption):* electricity (kW-hr; 1999) 332,304,000,000 ([1998] 287,864,000,000); coal (metric tons; 1999) 4,284,000 ([1997] 17,802,000); crude petroleum (barrels; 2001) 468,873,000 ([1997] 518,296,000); petroleum products (metric tons; 1997) 62,549,000 (71,404,000); natural gas (cu m; 2001) 13,999,000,-000 ([1997] 5,462,000,000); carburant alcohol (barrels; 1997) 76,650,000 (76,650,000).

## Foreign trade

**Imports** (2000; f.o.b. in balance of trade; c.i.f. in commodities and trading partners): US$55,783,-000,000 (electrical machinery and apparatus 32.5%;

*1 metric ton = about 1.1 short tons; 1 kilometer = 0.6 mi (statute); 1 metric ton-km cargo = about 0.68 short ton-mi cargo; c.i.f.: cost, insurance, and freight; f.o.b.: free on board*

chemicals and chemical products 16.7%; mineral fuels 13.7%; motor vehicles 8.8%; food products 3.4%). *Major import sources:* US 23.1%; Argentina 12.3%; Germany 7.9%; Japan 5.3%; Italy 3.9%; France 3.4%; Algeria 2.7%; South Korea 2.5%; Venezuela 2.4%; UK 2.2%. **Exports** (2000): US$55,086,000,000 (transportation equipment 16.6%; machinery and apparatus 11.2%; fabricated metal products 10.7%; soybeans 7.6%; chemicals and chemical products 7.4%; iron ore and other ores 5.9%; paper and cellulose 4.6%; meat 3.5%). *Major export destinations:* US 23.9%; Argentina 11.3%; Germany 5.1%; Germany 4.6%; Japan 4.5%; Italy 3.9%; Belgium 3.2%; Mexico 3.1%; France 3.1%; UK 2.7%.

## Transport and communications

**Transport.** *Railroads* (1998): route length (1997) 29,706 km; passenger-km 12,667,000,000; metric ton-km cargo 141,239,000,000. *Roads* (1999): total length 1,724,924 km (paved 9%). *Vehicles* (1998): passenger cars 21,313,351; trucks and buses 3,743,836. *Air transport* (1999; TAM Regional, TAM Meridional, VARIG, and VASP airlines only): passenger-km 35,028,000,000; metric ton-km cargo 1,301,000,000; airports (1995) with scheduled flights 139. **Communications,** in total units (units per 1,000 persons). Daily newspaper circulation (1996): 6,472,000 (41); radio receivers (1997): 71,000,000 (446); television receivers (1999): 56,000,000 (336); telephone main lines (2001): 37,430,800 (217); cellular telephone subscribers (2001): 28,745,800 (167); personal computers (2001): 10,800,000 (63); Internet users (2001): 8,000,000 (46).

## Education and health

**Educational attainment** (1996). Percentage of population age 25 and over having: no formal schooling or less than one year of primary education 17.7%; lower primary only 19.1%; upper primary 30.7%; complete primary to some secondary 11.6%; complete secondary to some higher 13.9%; complete higher 6.2%; unknown 0.8%. **Literacy** (2000): total population age 15 and over literate 103,500,000 (85.3%); males literate 50,300,000 (85.1%); females literate 53,200,000 (85.4%). **Health:** physicians (1997) 205,828 (1 per 774 persons); hospital beds (1999) 484,945 (1 per 343 persons); infant mortality rate per 1,000 live births (2000) 38.0. **Food** (1997): daily per capita caloric intake 2,974 (vegetable products 80%, animal products 20%); 124% of FAO recommended minimum.

## Military

**Total active duty personnel** (2001): 287,600 (army 65.7%, navy 16.9%, air force 17.4%). **Military expenditure as percentage of GNP** (1999): 1.9% (world 2.4%); per capita expenditure US$59.

## Background

Little is known about Brazil's early indigenous inhabitants. Though the area was theoretically allotted to Portugal by the 1494 Treaty of Tordesillas, it was not formally claimed by discovery until Pedro Alvares Cabral accidentally touched land in 1500. It was first settled by the Portuguese in the early 1530s on the southeastern coast and at São Vicente (near modern São Paulo); the French and Dutch created small settlements over the next century. A viceroyalty was established in 1640 and Rio de Janeiro became the capital in 1763. In 1808 Brazil became the refuge and seat of the government of John VI of Portugal when Napoleon invaded Portugal; ultimately the Kingdom of Portugal, Brazil, and the Algarves was proclaimed, and John ruled from Brazil in 1815–21. On John's return to Portugal, his son Pedro I proclaimed Brazilian independence. In 1889 his successor, Pedro II, was deposed, and a constitution mandating a federal republic was adopted. The 20th century saw increased immigration and growth in manufacturing along with frequent military coups and suspensions of civil liberties. Construction of a new capital at Brasília, intended to spur development of the country's interior, worsened the inflation rate. After 1979 the military government began a gradual return to democratic practices, and in 1989 the first popular presidential election in 29 years was held.

## Recent Developments

On 6 Oct 2002 more than 94 million Brazilians went to the polls in first-round elections. With no candidate receiving a majority of the valid votes cast for president, Luiz Inácio Lula da Silva, popularly called Lula, of the leftist Workers Party (PT) (46.4%) and José Serra of the Brazilian Social Democratic Party (PSDB) (23.2%) competed in a second-round runoff election on 27 October. The third- and fourth-place finishers threw their support behind Lula, who took an overwhelming 62% of the valid votes and was elected Brazil's first socialist president in 40 years. The PT platform stressed, among other provisions, an end to hunger, more job creation, economic growth of 5% per annum, and a reduction in the workweek from 44 to 40 hours. The PT also promised to continue to maintain a floating exchange rate with inflation targets and to honor the privatizations concluded and under way. The new president lacked a majority in the legislature, however.

Lula was inaugurated as president on 1 Jan 2003 and immediately put his socialist program into action by canceling a large order for new jet aircraft, suggesting that the money could be better used to alleviate hunger. In mid-March he announced a plan to eliminate slave labor, a practice that lingers on in logging concerns, mines, and ranches and is thought to involve as many as 25,000 poor and illiterate Brazilians. Lula also reached out to other socialist leaders in the hemisphere, notably Presidents Hugo Chávez of neighboring Venezuela and Fidel Castro of Cuba. Lula attracted worldwide attention in the week before the G8 Summit in Evian, France, in June when he offered to help eradicate world terrorism and drug trafficking—but only if the rich countries increased investment in developing countries.

Major demographic shifts continued to affect Brazil at the turn of the 21st century, including a growing population that was increasingly concentrated in cities. The nation's cities were, however, ill-prepared to serve the needs of their growing multitudes. At the same time, the frontiers of agricultural and mining operations persistently expanded, and Brazil remained embroiled in domestic and international controversies regarding threats to the Amazon rainforest and to Indian groups. At the end of May 2003, for the first time, a black was appointed to the Supreme Court.

**Internet resources:** <www.embratur.gov.br>

# Brunei

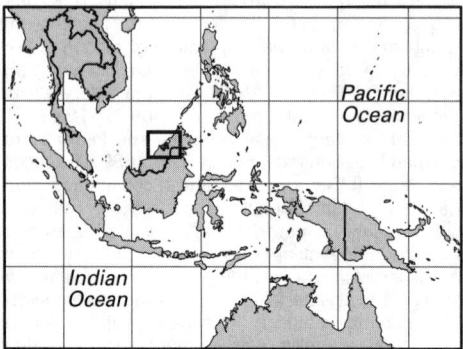

Pacific
Ocean

Indian
Ocean

**Official name:** Negara Brunei Darussalam (State of Brunei, Abode of Peace). **Form of government:** monarchy (advised on legislative matters by a 21-member appointed body). **Head of state and government:** Sultan Haji Hassanal Bolkiah Mu'izzadin Waddaulah (from 1967). **Capital:** Bandar Seri Begawan. **Official language:** Malay. **Official religion:** Islam. **Monetary unit:** 1 Brunei dollar (B$) = 100 cents; valuation (7 Jul 2003) US$1 = B$1.75.

## Demography

**Area:** 2,226 sq mi, 5,765 sq km. **Population** (2002): 351,000. **Density** (2002): persons per sq mi 157.7, persons per sq km 60.9. **Urban** (2002): 73.0%. **Sex distribution** (2002): male 52.35%; female 47.65%. **Age breakdown** (2002): under 15, 30.2%; 15–29, 27.0%; 30–44, 25.2%; 45–59, 13.2%; 60–74, 3.6%; 75 and over, 0.8%. **Ethnic composition** (1999): Malay 67.6%; Chinese 14.9%; other indigenous 5.9%; Indian and other 11.6%. **Religious affiliation** (2000): Muslim 64.4%; traditional beliefs 11.2%; Buddhist 9.1%; Christian 7.7%; other religions and nonreligious 7.6%. **Major cities** (1991): Bandar Seri Begawan (1999) 85,000 (urban agglomeration); Kuala Belait 21,163; Seria 21,082; Tutong 13,049. **Location:** southeastern Asia, bordering the South China Sea and Malaysia.

## Vital statistics

**Birth rate** per 1,000 population (2002): 20.1 (world avg. 21.2); (1982) legitimate 99.6%; illegitimate 0.4%. **Death rate** per 1,000 population (2002): 3.4 (world avg. 8.9). **Natural increase rate** per 1,000 population (2002): 16.7 (world avg. 12.3). **Total fertility rate** (avg. births per childbearing woman; 2002): 2.4. **Marriage rate** per 1,000 population (1995): 6.1. **Divorce rate** per 1,000 population (1992): 1.1. **Life expectancy** at birth (2002): male 71.7 years; female 76.6 years.

## National economy

**Budget** (1998). *Revenue*: B$2,775,000,000 (tax revenue 54.6%, of which corporate income tax 47.3%, import duty 7.2%; nontax revenue 45.4%, of which property income 33.8%, commercial receipts 10.9%). *Expenditures*: B$4,295,000,000 (current expenditure 65.5%; capital expenditure 34.5%). **Public debt** (external, outstanding): none. **Tourism** (1995):

receipts from visitors US$40,000,000; expenditures by nationals abroad US$1,000,000. **Production** (metric tons except as noted). *Agriculture, forestry, fishing* (1999): vegetables and melons 8,700, fruits (excluding melons) 5,225, cassava 1,500; livestock (number of live animals) 6,000 buffalo, 4,500 pigs, 3,302 goats; roundwood (1998) 296,000 cu m; fish catch (1997) 4,677. *Mining and quarrying*: other than petroleum and natural gas, none except sand and gravel for construction. *Manufacturing* (1998): gasoline 187,600; distillate fuel oils 147,800; kerosene 76,500. *Energy production (consumption)*: electricity (kW-hr; 1997) 1,705,000,000 (1,705,000,000); crude petroleum (barrels; 1997) 60,000,000 (1,400,000); petroleum products (metric tons; 1997) 861,000 (939,000); natural gas (cu m; 1997) 9,217,000,000 (1,318,000,000). **Population economically active** (1991): total 111,955; activity rate of total population 43.0% (participation rates: ages 15–64, 67.6%; female 32.9%; unemployed 4.7%). **Household income and expenditure.** Average household size (1991) 5.8; expenditure (1990): food 38.7%, transportation and communications 19.9%, housing 18.6%, clothing 6.4%, other 16.4%. **Gross national product** (at current market prices; 1998): US$7,209,000,000 (US$22,278 per capita). **Land use** (1994): forested 85.4%; meadows and pastures 1.1%; agricultural and under permanent cultivation 1.3%; other 12.2%.

## Foreign trade

**Imports** (1997-c.i.f.): B$3,154,000,000 (machinery and transport equipment 39.0%, manufactured goods 25.5%, miscellaneous manufactured articles 11.6%, food and live animals 11.1%, chemicals 6.4%, crude materials 3.4%, beverages and tobacco 1.9%). *Major import sources:* ASEAN 45.5%, of which Singapore 25.6%, Malaysia 13.6%; EEC 17.9%; Japan 11.2%; US 10.0%. **Exports** (1997): B$3,973,000,000 (natural gas 46.8%, crude petroleum 41.5%, petroleum products 2.8%). *Major export destinations:* Japan 53.1%; ASEAN 20.9%, of which Thailand 11.2%, Singapore 6.6%; South Korea 18.1%; Taiwan 2.7%.

## Transport and communications

**Transport.** *Railroads* (privately owned): length 19 km. *Roads* (1996): total length 1,712 km (paved 75%). *Vehicles* (1997): passenger cars 91,047; trucks and buses 15,918. *Air transport* (1998): passenger-km 2,803,000,000; metric ton-km cargo 109,527,000; airports (1996) with scheduled flights 1. **Communications**, in total units (units per 1,000 persons). Daily newspaper circulation (1996): 21,000 (69); radio receivers (1997): 93,000 (302); television receivers (1999): 205,000 (637); telephone main lines (2000): 80,500 (245); cellular telephone subscribers (2000): 95,000 (289); personal computers (2001): 25,000 (75); Internet users (2001): 35,000 (104).

## Education and health

**Educational attainment** (1991). Percentage of population age 25 and over having: no formal schooling 17.0%; primary education 43.3%; secondary 26.3%; postsecondary and higher 12.9%; not stated 0.5%.

---

*1 metric ton = about 1.1 short tons;   1 kilometer = 0.6 mi (statute);   1 metric ton-km cargo = about 0.68 short ton-mi cargo;   c.i.f.: cost, insurance, and freight;   f.o.b.: free on board*

**Literacy** (1995): total population age 15 and over literate 89.1%; males literate 93.2%; females literate 84.6%. **Health** (1996): physicians 281 (1 per 1,086 persons); hospital beds 961 (1 per 317 persons); infant mortality rate per 1,000 live births (2002) 14.0. **Food** (1999): daily per capita caloric intake 2,793 (vegetable products 82%, animal products 18%); (1997) 125% of FAO recommended minimum.

## Military

**Total active duty personnel** (2001): 5,900 (army 66.1%, navy 15.3%, air force 18.6%). British troops (a Gurkha batallion; 2000): 1,050. **Military expenditure as percentage of GNP** (1999): 4.0% (world 2.4%); per capita expenditure US$897.

## Background

Brunei traded with China in the 6th century AD. Through allegiance to the Javanese Majapahit kingdom (13th–15th century), it came under Hindu influence. In the early 15th century, with the decline of the Majapahit kingdom, many people converted to Islam, and Brunei became an independent sultanate. When Ferdinand Magellan's ships visited in 1521, the sultan of Brunei controlled almost all of Borneo and its neighboring islands. Beginning in the late 16th century, Brunei lost power because of the Portuguese, Dutch, and, later, British activities in the region. By the 19th century, the sultanate of Brunei included Sarawak (present-day Brunei) and part of North Borneo (now part of Sabah). In 1841 a revolt took place against the sultan, and a British soldier, James Brooke, helped put it down; he was later proclaimed governor. In 1847 the sultanate entered into a treaty with Great Britain and by 1906 had yielded all administration to a British Resident. Brunei rejected membership in the Federation of Malaysia in 1963, negotiated a new treaty with Britain in 1979, and achieved independence in 1984, with membership in the Commonwealth. Today Brunei is considering ways to diversify its economy and to encourage tourism.

## Recent Developments

In 2002 Brunei recovered somewhat from the adverse international publicity and the multibillion-dollar financial loss that had been brought about by the 1998 collapse of the Amedeo Development Corp. Prince Jeffri Bolkiah, the sultan's youngest brother, had been sued by the state in 2001 for squandering public funds on Amedeo projects. The cases were largely settled out of court, however, and the government was thus left room to focus on domestic development.

**Internet resources:** <www.brunet.bn>

## Bulgaria

**Official name:** Republika Balgariya (Republic of Bulgaria). **Form of government:** unitary multiparty republic with one legislative body (National Assembly [240]). **Chief of state:** President Georgi Parvanov (from 22 Jan 2002). **Head of government:** Prime Minister Simeon Saxecoburggotski (from 2001). **Capital:** Sofia. **Official language:** Bulgarian. **Official religion:** none. **Monetary unit:** 1 lev (Lw; leva) = 100 stotinki; valuation (7 Jul 2003) $1 = 1.69 (new) leva (re-denominated in 1999 to 1 new leva = 1,000 old leva).

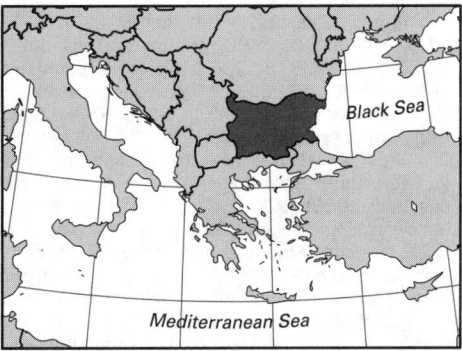

## Demography

**Area:** 110,971.4 sq mi, 8,190,876 sq km. **Population** (2002): 7,890,000. **Density** (2002): persons per sq mi 184.1, persons per sq km 71.1. **Urban** (2001) 67.4%. **Sex distribution** (2001): male 48.48%; female 51.52%. **Age breakdown** (2000): under 15, 15.6%; 15–29, 21.8%; 30–44, 20.0%; 45–59, 20.5%; 60–74, 16.3%; 75 and over, 5.8%. **Ethnic composition** (2000): Bulgarian 79.8%; Turkish 9.6%; Roma (Gypsy) 5.4%; Macedonian 2.5%; Pomak 0.9%; other 1.8%. **Religious affiliation** (1995): Bulgarian Orthodox 36.5%, Protestant 1.4%, Roman Catholic 0.8%; Sunni Muslim 13.1%; other/nonreligious 47.8%. **Major cities** (2001): Sofia 1,173,988; Plovdiv 338,302; Varna 320,668. **Location:** southeastern Europe, bordering Romania, the Black Sea, Turkey, Greece, Macedonia, and Serbia and Montenegro.

## Vital statistics

**Birth rate** per 1,000 population (2000): 9.0 (world avg. 21.2); legitimate 61.6%; illegitimate 38.4%. **Death rate** per 1,000 population (2000): 14.1 (world avg. 8.9). **Natural increase rate** per 1,000 population (2000): –5.1 (world avg. 12.3). **Total fertility rate** (avg. births per childbearing woman; 2000): 1.3. **Life expectancy** at birth (2000): male 68.2 years; female 75.3 years.

## National economy

**Budget** (2001). *Revenue*: 10,268,300,000 leva (tax revenue 74.8%, of which social insurance 24.3%, value-added tax 23.9%, income and profit tax 12.4%, excises 10.8%, customs and duties 1.9%, other 1.5%; nontax revenue 23.1%; grants 2.1%). *Expenditures*: 10,212,600,000 leva (social insurance 35.5%; administration and defense 13.4%; capital expenditure 10.7%; interest on debt 10.7%; health 9.6%; wages 7.6%; public safety 5.2%; education 4.5%). **Public debt** (external, outstanding; 2000): $7,513,000,000. **Gross national product** (2000): $12,391,000,000 ($1,520 per capita). **Production** (metric tons except as noted). *Agriculture, forestry, fishing* (2001): wheat 3,800,000, corn (maize) 1,739,969, sunflower seeds 605,832; livestock (number of live animals) 2,286,-000 sheep, 1,144,000 pigs, 970,000 goats; roundwood (2001) 3,991,890 cu m; fish catch (1999) 18,336. *Mining and quarrying* (2000): copper 23,297,000; iron ore 1,002,299; lead 351,449. *Manufacturing* (value of production in '000,000 [old] leva; 1997): food, beverages, and tobacco 2,834,413; chemical and oil processing 1,633,583; machine and metalworking 1,460,220. *Energy production* (consumption): electricity (kW-hr; 2000) 40,925,-011,000 (40,925,011,000); coal (metric tons; 2000) 26,583,426 (1998; 34,200,000); crude petroleum (barrels; 1998) 232,360 (50,979,000); petroleum products (metric tons; 1997) 4,966,000 (3,626,-000); natural gas (cu m; 1997) 37,210,000 (4,900,-029,000). **Household income and expenditure.** Average household size (2000) 3.0; income per household (2000) 4,610 leva ($2,154); sources of income: wages and salaries 36.8%, transfer payments 23.2%, self-employment in agriculture 15.8%, other 24.2%; expenditure (2000): food 42.1%, housing and energy 11.7%, transportation 4.9%, clothing 3.8%, health 3.5%, education and culture 3.1%, household durable goods 2.7%, other 28.2%. **Population economically active** (2001): total 3,264,700; activity rate of total population 48.1% (participation rates: age 16–59 [male], 16–54 [female] 54.2%; female 46.4%; unemployed 16.3%). **Tourism** (2000): receipts $1,074,000,000; expenditures $538,000,000.

## Foreign trade

**Imports** (2001-c.i.f.): $7,224,000,000 (petroleum and natural gas 22.5%; machine-building and metalworking equipment 14.0%; textile 10.9%; chemicals and plastics 6.4%; electrical and electronic equipment 4.4%; food, beverages, and tobacco 2.7%). *Major import sources:* Russia 19.9%; Germany 15.3%; Italy 9.6%; Turkey 3.8%; Ukraine 3.2%; US 2.6%. **Exports** (2001-f.o.b.): $5,096,000,000 (clothing and footwear 20.0%; mineral fuels 13.5%; metals 8.3%; iron and steel 6.9%; machine-building and metalworking equipment 6.0%; food, beverages, and tobacco 5.6%). *Major export destinations:* Italy 15.0%; Germany 9.6%; Greece 8.8%; Turkey 8.1%; France 5.6%; Belgium 5.6%; US 5.5%.

## Transport and communications

**Transport.** *Railroads* (2000): track length 6,518 km; passenger-km 3,472,000,000; metric ton-km cargo 5,538,000,000. *Roads* (2000): length 37,301 km (paved 92%). *Vehicles* (1999): cars 1,908,392; trucks and buses 272,102. Merchant marine (2000): vessels (100 gross tons and over) 94; deadweight tonnage 1,786,149. *Air transport* (2000): passenger-mi 1,402,000,000, passenger-km 2,257,000,000; short ton-mi cargo 29,000,000, metric ton-km cargo 46,000,000; airports (2000) with scheduled flights 3. **Communications,** in total units (units per 1,000 persons). Daily newspaper circulation (1998): 2,145,000 (254); television receivers (1998): 3,400,000 (418); telephone main lines (2001): 2,913,900 (359); cellular telephone subscribers (2001): 1,550,000 (191); personal computers (2001): 361,000 (44); Internet users (2001): 605,000 (74.6).

## Education and health

**Educational attainment** (1992). Percentage of population age 25 and over having: no formal schooling 4.7%; incomplete primary education 12.5%; primary 31.9%; secondary 35.7%; higher 15.0%. **Literacy** (1998): total population age 15 and over literate 98.2%; males 98.9%; females 97.6%. **Health** (2001): physicians 27,526 (1 per 288 persons); hospital beds 62,272 (1 per 127 persons); infant mortality rate per 1,000 live births (2000) 13.3. **Food** (2000): daily per capita caloric intake 2,467 (vegetable products 72%, animal products 28%); 99% of FAO recommended minimum.

## Military

**Total active duty personnel** (2001): 77,260 (army 54.9%, navy 6.8%, air force 23.7%, other 14.6%). **Military expenditure as percentage of GNP** (1999): 3.0% (world 2.4%); per capita expenditure $158.

The historical and cultural center of Bulgaria is the town of Veliko Tarnovo, which served as the medieval capital of Bulgaria. During its heyday in the 12th–14th centuries, European royal circles glorified it as "the third Rome and the second Constantinople."

## Background

Evidence of human habitation in Bulgaria dates from prehistoric times. Thracians were its first recorded inhabitants, dating from c. 3500 BC, and their first state dates from about the 5th century BC; the area was subdued by the Romans, who divided it into the provinces of Moesia and Thrace. In the 7th century AD the Bulgars took the region to the south of the Danube. The Byzantine Empire in 681 formally recognized Bulgar control over the area between the Balkans and the Danube. In the second half of the 14th century, Bulgaria fell to the Turks and ultimately lost its independence. At the end of the Russo-Turkish War (1877–78), Bulgaria rebelled. The ensuing Treaty of San Stefano was unacceptable to the Great Powers, and the Congress of Berlin (1878) resulted. In 1908 the Bulgarian ruler, Ferdinand, declared Bulgaria's independence. After its involvement in the Balkan Wars (1912–13), Bulgaria lost territory. It sided with the Central Powers in World War I and with Germany in World War II. A communist coalition seized power in 1944, and in 1946 a people's republic was declared. With other eastern European countries in the late 1980s, Bulgaria experienced political unrest; its communist leader resigned in 1989. A new constitution proclaiming a republic was implemented in 1991. The rest of the decade brought economic turmoil.

## Recent Developments

Bulgarian political life in 2002 was influenced by the need for national unity pending decisions on the country's applications to join NATO and the European Union. This meant that a number of confrontations were softened, though not eliminated. There were considerable differences between the prime minister (Bulgaria's former king, Simeon II) and the new, socialist president, Georgi Purvanov, who assumed office in January 2002, but both men played them down for the appearance of national unity. In November Bulgaria was invited to join NATO along with six other European nations.

**Internet resources:** <www.bulgaria2net.com>

*1 metric ton = about 1.1 short tons; 1 kilometer = 0.6 mi (statute); 1 metric ton-km cargo = about 0.68 short ton-mi cargo; c.i.f.: cost, insurance, and freight; f.o.b.: free on board*

# Burkina Faso

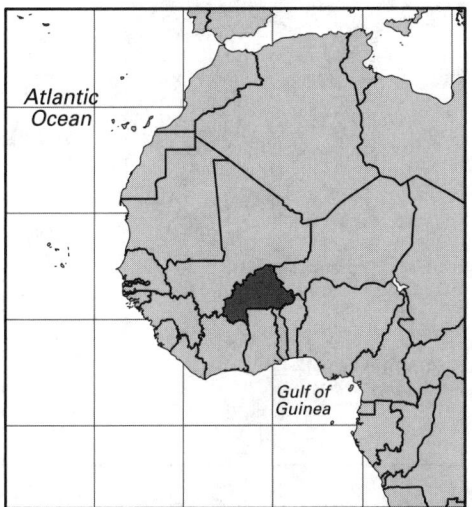

**Official name:** Burkina Faso. **Form of government:** multiparty republic with one advisory body (Chamber of Representatives [178 appointed or indirectly elected]) and one legislative body (National Assembly [111]). **Chief of state:** President Blaise Compaoré (from 1987). **Head of government:** Prime Minister Ernest Paramanga Yonli (from 2000). **Capital:** Ouagadougou. **Official language:** French. **Official religion:** none. **Monetary unit:** 1 CFA franc (CFAF) = 100 centimes; valuation (7 Jul 2003) $1 = CFAF 571.07 (formerly pegged to the French franc and since 1 Jan 2002 to the euro at €1 = CFAF 655.96).

## Demography

**Area:** 105,946 sq mi, 274,400 sq km. **Population** (2002): 12,603,000. **Density** (2002): persons per sq mi 119.0, persons per sq km 45.9. **Urban** (1999): 17.0%. **Sex distribution** (2000): male 48.76%; female 51.24%. **Age breakdown** (2000): under 15, 47.6%; 15–29, 27.5%; 30–44, 13.0%; 45–59, 7.3%; 60–74, 3.8%; 75 and over, 0.8%. **Ethnic composition** (1983): Mossi 47.9%; Mande 8.8%; Fulani 8.3%; Lobi 6.9%; Bobo 6.8%; Senufo 5.3%; Grosi 5.1%; Gurma 4.8%; Tuareg 3.3%. **Religious affiliation** (2000): Muslim 48.6%; traditional beliefs 34.1%; Christian 16.7%, of which Roman Catholic 9.5%. **Major cities** (1996): Ouagadougou 709,736; Bobo-Dioulasso 309,736; Koudougou 72,490; Banfora 62,548; Ouahigouya 52,193. **Location:** western Africa, bordering Mali, Niger, Benin, Togo, Ghana, and Côte d'Ivoire.

## Vital statistics

**Birth rate** per 1,000 population (2000): 45.3 (world avg. 22.5). **Death rate** per 1,000 population (2000): 17.0 (world avg. 9.0). **Natural increase rate** per 1,000 population (2000): 28.3 (world avg. 13.5). **Total fertility rate** (avg. births per childbearing woman; 2000): 6.4. **Life expectancy** at birth (2000): male 46.3 years; female 47.2 years.

## National economy

**Budget** (1999). *Revenue:* CFAF 238,100,000,000 (tax revenue 93.4%, of which sales tax 43.3%, import duties 25.3%, personal income taxes 22.6%, other 2.2%; nontax revenue 6.6%). *Expenditures:* CFAF 246,900,000,000 (wages and salaries 27.5%; investment 27.3%; health and education 22.4%; transfers 17.3%; debt service 5.5%). **Public debt** (external, outstanding; 2000): $1,135,000,000. **Household income and expenditure.** Average household size (1985) 6.2; average annual income per household CFAF 303,000 ($640); expenditure (1985): food 38.7%, transportation 18.6%, electricity and fuel 13.7%, beverages 9.0%, health 5.2%, housing 5.1%. **Tourism:** receipts (1998) $42,000,000; expenditures (1994) $23,000,000. **Production** (metric tons except as noted). *Agriculture, forestry, fishing* (1999): sorghum 1,178,400, millet 945,000, corn (maize) 468,900; livestock (number of live animals) 7,950,000 goats, 6,350,000 sheep, 4,550,000 cattle; roundwood (1998) 10,794,000 cu m; fish catch (1998) 8,335. *Mining and quarrying* (1999): gold 869 kg (officially marketed gold only; does not include substantial illegal production); silver 120 kg. *Manufacturing* (1999): sugar 29,905; flour 21,454; edible oils 11,850. *Energy production (consumption):* electricity (kW-hr; 1998) 267,000,000 (267,000,000); petroleum products (metric tons; 1997) none (317,000). **Gross national product** (2000): $2,422,000,000 ($210 per capita). **Population economically active** (1991): total 4,679,193; activity rate 50.9% (participation rates: over age [1988] 10, 78.1%; female 48.7%; unemployed 1.1%). **Land use** (1994): forest 50.5%; pasture 21.9%; agriculture 13.0%; other 14.6%.

## Foreign trade

**Imports** (2001): CFAF 373,300,000,000 (capital equipment 30.9%, petroleum products 18.2%, food products 14.4%, raw materials 9.8%). *Major import sources* (2000): Côte d'Ivoire 22.7%; France 22.4%; Japan 5.6%; China 4.1%; US 3.7%; Germany 3.6%; Italy 3.1%; Belgium-Luxembourg 2.8%. **Exports** (2001): CFAF 168,800,000,000 (raw cotton 56.9%, live animals 11.4%, hides and skins 6.4%, gold 2.1%). *Major export destinations* (2000): France 21.6%; Côte d'Ivoire 11.5%; Belgium-Luxembourg 8.4%; Italy 7.7%; Singapore 5.6%; Mali 5.0%.

## Transport and communications

**Transport.** *Railroads* (1995; passenger-km and metric ton-km cargo figures are based on traffic between Abidjan, Côte d'Ivoire, and Ouagadougou): route length 622 km; passenger-km 202,000,000; metric ton-km cargo 45,000,000. *Roads* (1996): total length 12,100 km (paved 16%). *Vehicles* (1996): passenger cars 38,220; trucks and buses 17,980. *Air transport* (1993): passenger-km 217,154,000; metric ton-km cargo 34,204,000; airports (1998) 2. **Communications,** in total units (units per 1,000 persons). Daily newspaper circulation (1996): 14,000 (1.3); radio receivers (1997): 370,000 (34.0); television receivers (1998): 120,000 (10.6); telephone main lines (2001): 57,600 (4.7); cellular telephone subscribers (2001): 75,000 (6.1); personal computers (2001): 17,000 (1.4); Internet users (2001): 21,000 (1.7).

## Education and health

**Educational attainment** (1985). Percentage of population age 10 and over having: no formal schooling 86.1%; some primary 7.3%; general secondary 2.2%; specialized secondary and postsecondary 3.8%; other

0.6%. **Literacy** (1995): total population age 15 and over literate 23.0%; males literate 31.2%; females literate 13.1%. **Health** (1991): physicians 341 (1 per 27,158 persons); hospital beds 5,041 (1 per 1,837 persons); infant mortality rate per 1,000 live births (2000) 108.5. **Food** (2000): daily per capita caloric intake 2,293 (vegetable products 95%, animal products 5%); 97% of FAO recommended minimum.

## Military

Total active duty personnel (2001): 5,800 (army 96.6%, air force 3.4%). **Military expenditure as percentage of GNP** (1999): 1.6% (world 2.4%); per capita expenditure $4.

## Background

Probably in the 14th century, the Mossi and Gurma peoples established themselves in eastern and central areas of what is now Burkina Faso. The Mossi kingdoms of Yatenga and Ouagadougou existed into the early 20th century. A French protectorate was established over the region (1895–97), and its southern boundary was demarcated through an Anglo-French agreement. It was part of the Upper Senegal–Niger colony, then became a separate colony in 1919. Named Upper Volta, it was constituted an overseas territory within the French Union in 1947, became an autonomous republic within the French Community in 1958, and achieved total independence in 1960. Since then, the country has been ruled primarily by the military and has experienced several coups; following one in 1983, the country received its present name. A new constitution, adopted in 1991, restored multiparty rule.

## Recent Developments

In the parliamentary elections held on 5 May 2002, Pres. Blaise Compaoré's Congress for Democracy and Progress barely maintained its majority, winning 57 of 111 seats—44 fewer than in the previous parliament. In 2002, despite a 36% increase in production, cotton growers faced a crisis as world prices continued to drop. International agencies granted Burkina Faso more than $1 billion in debt relief as well as substantial amounts of development aid.

Internet resources: <www.ouaganet.com>

## Burundi

**Official name:** Republika y'u Burundi (Rundi); République du Burundi (French) (Republic of Burundi). **Form of government:** transitional regime. **Head of state and government:** President Domitien Ndayizeye (from 30 Apr 2003) assisted by a vice president. **Capital:** Bujumbura. **Official languages:** Rundi; French. **Official religion:** none. **Monetary unit:** 1 Burundi franc (FBu) = 100 centimes; valuation (7 Jul 2003) $1 = FBu 1,075.

## Demography

**Area:** 10,740 sq mi, 27,816 sq km. **Population** (2002): 6,373,000. **Density** (2002): persons per sq

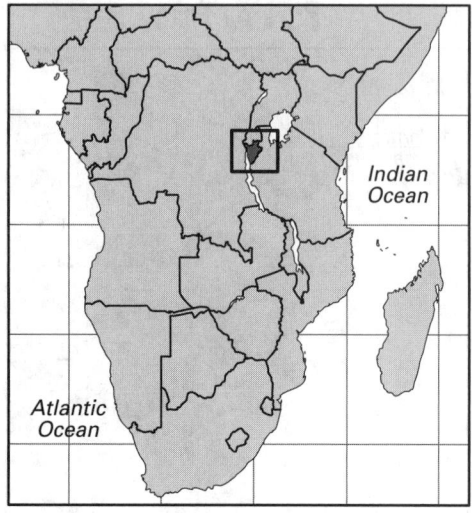

mi 636.1, persons per sq km 245.6. **Urban** (2001): 9.3%. **Sex distribution** (2001): male 49.58%; female 50.42%. **Age breakdown** (2001): under 15, 46.7%; 15–29, 27.2%; 30–44, 14.5%; 45–59, 7.3%; 60–74, 3.2%; 75 and over, 1.1%. **Ethnic composition** (1995): Rundi 98.0%, of which Hutu 82.5%, Tutsi 14.5%; Twa Pygmy 1.0%; other 2.0%. **Religious affiliation** (1990): Roman Catholic 65.1%; Protestant 13.8%; Muslim 1.6%; nonreligious 18.6%; traditional beliefs 0.3%; other 0.6%. **Major cities** (1990): Bujumbura (2001) 346,000; Gitega 101,827; Bururi 15,816; Ngozi 14,511; Cibitoke 8,280. **Location:** central Africa, bordering Rwanda, Tanzania, Lake Tanganyika, and the Dem. Rep. of the Congo.

## Vital statistics

**Birth rate** per 1,000 population (2001): 40.1 (world avg. 21.2). **Death rate** per 1,000 population (2001): 16.4 (world avg. 8.9). **Natural increase rate** per 1,000 population (2001): 23.7 (world avg. 12.3). **Total fertility rate** (avg. births per childbearing woman; 2001): 6.2. **Life expectancy** at birth (2001): male 45.2 years; female 47.0 years.

## National economy

**Budget** (1999). *Revenue:* FBu 70,400,000,000 (tax revenue 92.9%, of which taxes on goods and services 39.3%, taxes on international trade 23.3%, income tax 13.8%, corporate tax 13.1%, administrative receipts 3.4%; nontax revenue 7.1%). *Expenditures:* FBu 99,000,000,000 (wages and salaries 29.1%, goods and services 28.0%, subsidies and transfers 8.5%, public debt 6.1%). **Public debt** (external, outstanding; 2000): $1,028,000,000. **Production** (metric tons except as noted). *Agriculture, forestry, fishing* (2001): bananas 1,548,897, sweet potatoes 780,839, cassavas 712,713; livestock (number of live animals) 600,000 goats, 315,000 cattle, 230,000 sheep; roundwood (2001) 8,284,615 cu m; fish catch (1999) 9,254. *Mining and quarrying* (1995): peat 8,000; kaolin clay 5,000; gold 10 kg. *Manufacturing* (1998): beer 1,036,321 hectolitres; carbonated beverages 60,390 hectolitres; cotton-

---

*1 metric ton = about 1.1 short tons;   1 kilometer = 0.6 mi (statute);   1 metric ton-km cargo = about 0.68 short ton-mi cargo;   c.i.f.: cost, insurance, and freight;   f.o.b.: free on board*

seed oil 133,600 litres. *Energy production (consumption)*: electricity (kW-hr; 1999) 99,133,000 (128,450,000); petroleum products (metric tons; 1999) none (60,667); peat (metric tons; 1997) 12,000 (12,000). **Household income and expenditure**. Average household size (1998) 5.0; expenditure: (1990) food 59.6%, clothing and footwear 11.1%, furniture and household goods 6.0%, energy and water 5.8%, housing 4.4%, other 13.1%. **Land use** (1994): forested 12.7%; meadows and pastures 38.6%; agricultural and under permanent cultivation 45.9%; other 2.8%. **Gross national product** (at current market prices; 2000): $732,000,000 ($110 per capita). **Population economically active** (1997): total 3,475,000; activity rate of total population 63.1% (participation rates [1991]: ages 15–64, 91.4%; female 48.9%; unemployed, n.a.). **Tourism** (2000): receipts from visitors $800,000; expenditures by nationals abroad $14,000,000.

### Foreign trade

**Imports** (1999): FBu 55,300,000,000 (consumption goods 31.8%, of which food and food products 8.5%; capital goods 25.5%; petroleum products 17.2%). *Major import sources* (1998): Belgium-Luxembourg 19.3%; France 9.1%; Zambia 8.0%; Germany 6.1%; Kenya 5.6%; Japan 3.8%; US 1.5%. **Exports** (1999): FBu 32,200,000,000 (coffee 78.0%, tea 18.3%, animal hides and skins 0.2%). *Major export destinations* (1998): UK 28.4%; Germany 10.4%; Belgium-Luxembourg 9.2%; US 1.7%; The Netherlands 0.9%; Rwanda 0.8%.

### Transport and communications

**Transport**. *Roads* (1999): total length 14,480 km (paved 7%). *Vehicles* (1996): passenger cars 19,200; trucks and other vehicles 18,240. *Air transport* (1998; figures for Bujumbura airport only): passenger arrivals 12,113, departures 11,725; cargo loaded 1,490 metric tons, unloaded 9,329 metric tons; airports (2000) 1. **Communications**, in total units (units per 1,000 persons). Daily newspaper circulation (1996): 20,000 (3.2); radio receivers (1997): 440,000 (69); television receivers (1999): 100,000 (15.2); telephone main lines (2001): 20,000 (2.9); cellular telephone subscribers (2001): 20,000 (2.9); Internet users (2001): 6,000 (0.9).

### Education and health

**Literacy** (1995): total population age 15 and over literate 35.3%; males literate 49.7%; females literate 22.5%. **Health** (1996): physicians 329 (1 per 16,507 persons); hospital beds 3,560 (1 per 1,526 persons); infant mortality rate per 1,000 live births (2001) 70.7. **Food** (2000): daily per capita caloric intake 1,605 (vegetable products 98%, animal products 2%); 69% of FAO recommended minimum.

### Military

**Total active duty personnel** (2001): 40,000 (army 100%). **Military expenditure as percentage of GNP** (1999): 7.0% (world 2.4%); per capita expenditure $8.

### Background

Original settlement by the Twa people was followed by Hutu settlement, which occurred gradually and was completed by the 11th century. The Tutsi arrived 300–400 years later; though a minority, they established the kingdom of Burundi in the 16th century. In the 19th century the area came within the German sphere of influence, but the Tutsi remained in power. Following World War I the Belgians took control of the area, which became a UN trusteeship after World War II. Colonial-period conditions had intensified Hutu-Tutsi ethnic animosities, and as independence neared, hostilities flared. Independence was granted in 1962 in the form of a kingdom ruled by the Tutsi. In 1965 the Hutu rebelled but were brutally repressed. The rest of the 20th century saw violent clashes between the two groups, leading to charges of genocide in the 1990s. The very unstable government that existed in these surroundings was overthrown by the military in 1996.

### Recent Developments

In the ongoing effort to end Burundi's nine-year civil war, South African Deputy Pres. Jacob Zuma chaired cease-fire negotiations in Tanzania between the Bujumbura government and the main rebel groups in 2002. Government officials and Col. Jean-Bosco Ndayikengurukiye, the head of the Hutu rebel group Forces for Defense of Democracy, signed a draft peace accord in late August. At the end of April 2003 Domitien Ndayizeye, a Hutu, replaced Pierre Buyoya, a Tutsi, as president.

**Internet resources:** <www.burundi.gov.bi>

# Cambodia

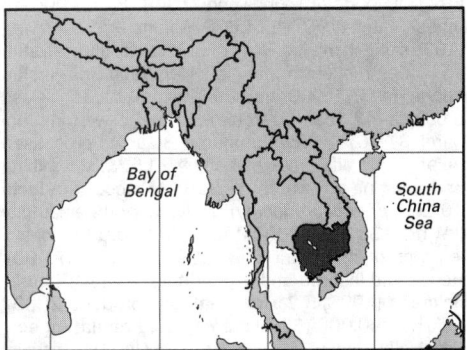

**Official name:** Preah Reach Ana Pak Kampuchea (Kingdom of Cambodia). **Form of government:** constitutional monarchy with two legislative houses (Senate [61; all seats appointed in 1999; all seats to be elected in future]; National Assembly [122]). **Chief of state:** King Norodom Sihanouk (from 1993). **Head of government:** Prime Minister Hun Sen (from 1998). **Capital:** Phnom Penh. **Official language:** Khmer. **Official religion:** Buddhism. **Monetary unit:** 1 riel = 100 sen; valuation (7 Jul 2003) $1 = 3,835 riels.

### Demography

**Area:** 69,898 sq mi, 181,035 sq km. **Population** (2002): 13,414,000. **Density** (2002): persons per sq mi 195.1, persons per sq km 75.3. **Urban** (2002): 17.0%. **Sex distribution** (1998): male 48.19%; female 51.81%. **Age breakdown** (1998): under 15, 42.8%; 15–29, 26.1%; 30–44, 17.3%; 45–59, 8.6%;

60–74, 4.2%; 75 and over, 1.0%. **Ethnic composition** (1994): Khmer 88.6%; Vietnamese 5.5%; Chinese 3.1%; Cham 2.3%; other (Thai, Lao, and Kola) 0.5%. **Religious affiliation** (2000): Buddhist 84.7%; Chinese folk religionist 4.7%; traditional beliefs 4.3%; Muslim 2.3%; Christian 1.1%; other 2.9%. **Major cities** (1998): Phnom Penh 999,804; Preah Sihanouk 155,690; Kaeb 28,660; Pailin 22,906. **Location**: southeastern Asia, bordering Thailand, Laos, Vietnam, and the Gulf of Thailand.

## Vital statistics

**Birth rate** per 1,000 population (2002): 35.2 (world avg. 21.2). **Death rate** per 1,000 population (2002): 10.6 (world avg. 8.9). **Natural increase rate** per 1,000 population (2002): 24.6 (world avg. 12.3). **Total fertility rate** (avg. births per childbearing woman; 2002): 4.9. **Life expectancy** at birth (2002): male 54.0 years; female 59.0 years.

## National economy

**Budget** (1999). *Revenue*: 1,224,000,000,000 riels (taxes on international trade 36.0%; indirect taxes 27.1%, of which value-added taxes 13.7%; nontax revenue 28.2%). *Expenditures*: 1,485,000,000,000 riels (current expenditure 74.4%, of which civil administration 36.1%, defense and security 30.7%; development expenditure 25.6%). **Public debt** (external, outstanding; 2000): $2,180,000,000. **Production** (metric tons except as noted). *Agriculture, forestry, fishing* (1999): rice 3,800,000, bananas 145,000, sugarcane 138,000; livestock (number of live animals; 1999) 2,821,000 cattle, 2,438,000 pigs, 694,000 buffalo; roundwood (1998) 8,008,000 cu m; fish catch (1997) 114,600. *Mining and quarrying* (1995): legal mining is confined to fertilizers, salt, and construction materials. *Manufacturing* (value added in '000,000 riels; 1995): glass and glass products 42,659; cigarettes 1,064.5; wearing apparel 37,567; rubber products 30,114; processed meat, fish, fruits, and vegetables 24,521; sawmilling and planing of wood 18,099; tobacco products 10,163. *Energy production (consumption)*: electricity (kW-hr; 1997) 208,000,000 (208,000,000); petroleum products (metric tons; 1997) none (167,000). **Household income and expenditure.** Average household size (1998) 5.2. **Gross national product** (2000): $3,150,000,000 ($260 per capita). **Population economically active** (1996): total 4,904,294; activity rate of total population 47.4% (participation rates: ages 15 and over, 78.9%; female 52.7%). **Tourism** (2000): receipts $228,000,000; expenditures $19,000,000. **Land use** (1994): forested 69.1%; meadows and pastures 8.5%; agricultural and under permanent cultivation 21.7%; other 0.7%.

## Foreign trade

**Imports** (1998-f.o.b.): $1,334,000,000 (cigarettes 11.2%; petroleum products 10.4%; motorcycles 2.8%; clothing 1.6%). *Major import sources* (1996): Singapore 34.2%; Thailand 23.9%; Vietnam 7.3%. **Exports** (1998): $999,000,000 (reexports 39.6%; garments 39.0%; sawn timber and logs 17.8%; rubber 2.5%). *Major export destinations* (1996): Thailand 13.0%; Singapore 13.0%; India 9.3%.

## Transport and communications

**Transport.** *Railroads* (1995): length (1999) 403 mi, 649 km; passenger-km 38,443,600; metric ton-km 7,797,600. *Roads* (1997): total length 22,226 mi, 35,769 km (paved 8%). *Vehicles* (1997): passenger cars 52,919; trucks and buses 13,574. Merchant marine (1992): vessels (100 gross tons and over) 3; total deadweight tonnage 3,839. *Air transport* (1977): passenger-mi 26,098,800, passenger-km 42,000,000; short ton-mi cargo 274,000, metric ton-km cargo 400,000; airports (1997) with scheduled flights 8. **Communications,** in total units (units per 1,000 persons). Daily newspaper circulation (1996): 17,000 (1.7); radio receivers (1997): 1,340,000 (128); television receivers (1999): 98,000 (9.0); telephone main lines (2001): 33,500 (2.5); cellular telephone subscribers (2001): 223,500 (17); Personal computers (2001): 20,000 (1.5); Internet users (2001): 10,000 (0.7).

## Education and health

**Educational attainment** (1998). Percentage of population age 25 and over having: no formal schooling 2.1%; some primary education 56.6%; primary 24.7%; some secondary 11.8%; secondary and above 4.8%. **Literacy** (1998): total population age 15 and over literate 67.3%; males literate 79.5%; females literate 57.0%. **Health:** physicians (1994) 1,200 (1 per 7,900 persons); hospital beds (1994) 12,098 (1 per 791 persons); infant mortality rate per 1,000 live births (2002) 74.0. **Food** (2000): daily per capita caloric intake 2,070 (vegetable products 91%, animal products 9%); 93% of FAO recommended minimum.

## Military

**Total active duty personnel** (2001): 140,000 (army 64.3%, navy 2.1%, air force 1.4%, provincial 32.2%). **Military expenditure as percentage of GNP** (1999): 4.0% (world 2.4%); per capita expenditure $28.

 **Did you know?** The Mekong River flows through Cambodia for about 500 km (300 mi) and is considered the country's most important waterway. The Kizuna bridge became the first bridge ever to span the Mekong when it opened to the public on 4 Dec 2001.

## Background

In the early Christian era, what is now Cambodia was under Hindu and, to a lesser extent, Buddhist influence. The Khmer state gradually spread in the early 7th century and reached its height under Jayavarman II and his successors in the 9th–12th centuries, when it ruled the Mekong Valley and the tributary Shan states and built Angkor. Widespread adoption of Buddhism occurred in the 13th century, resulting in a script change from Sanskrit to Pali. From the 13th century Cambodia was attacked by Annam and Siamese city-states and was alternately a province of one or the other. The area became a French protectorate in 1863. It was occupied by the Japanese in World War II and became independent in 1954.

*1 metric ton = about 1.1 short tons;   1 kilometer = 0.6 mi (statute);   1 metric ton-km cargo = about 0.68 short ton-mi cargo;   c.i.f.: cost, insurance, and freight;   f.o.b.: free on board*

Cambodia's borders were the scene of fighting in the Vietnam War from 1961, and in 1970 its northeastern and eastern areas were occupied by the North Vietnamese and penetrated by US and South Vietnamese forces. An indiscriminate US bombing campaign alienated much of the population, enabling the communist Khmer Rouge under Pol Pot to seize power in 1975. Their regime of terror resulted in the deaths of at least 1 million Cambodians. Vietnam invaded in 1979 and drove the Khmer Rouge into the western hinterlands, but it was unable to effect reconstruction of the country, and Cambodian infighting continued. A peace accord was reached by most Cambodian factions under UN auspices in 1991, and elections were held in 1993. Civil and military unrest continued. In 1997 King Norodom Sihanouk left the country, which was on the verge of civil war.

## Recent Developments

In February 2002, after five years of discussions about establishing an international tribunal to try perpetrators of Khmer Rouge atrocities in the 1970s, UN Secretary-General Kofi Annan abandoned the effort and blamed the intransigence of Prime Minister Hun Sen. The idea was revived in March 2003, however, and was approved by the UN General Assembly in May. As King Sihanouk approached his 80th birthday, questions arose about the succession. The constitution stipulated that a Throne Council, made up of legislative leaders, should nominate any suitable descendant of three related 19th-century kings.

Internet resources: <www.cambodia.org>

# Cameroon

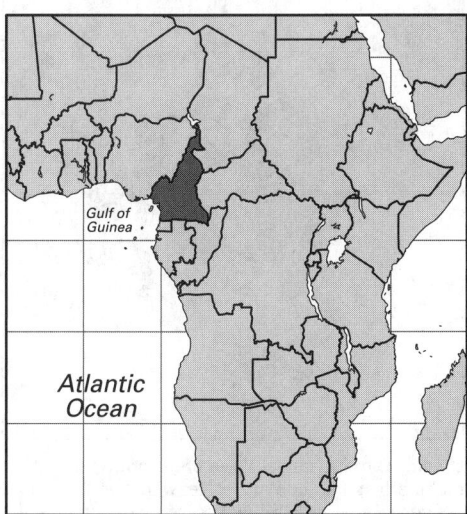

**Official name:** République du Cameroun (French); Republic of Cameroon (English). **Form of government:** unitary multiparty republic with one legislative house (National Assembly [180]). **Chief of state:** President Paul Biya (from 1982). **Head of government:** Prime Minister Peter Mafany Musonge (from 1996). **Capital:** Yaoundé. **Official languages:** French; English. **Official religion:** none. **Monetary unit:** 1 CFA franc (CFAF) = 100 centimes; valuation (7 Jul 2003) $1 = CFAF

571.07 (formerly pegged to the French franc and since 1 Jan 2002, to the euro at the rate of €1 = CFAF 655.96).

## Demography

**Area** (rounded): 183,569 sq mi, 475,442 sq km. **Population** (2002): 16,185,000. **Density** (2002): persons per sq mi 90.2, persons per sq km 34.8. **Urban** (2001): 49.7%. **Sex distribution** (2001): male 50.22%; female 49.78%. **Age breakdown** (2001): under 15, 42.4%; 15–29, 28.0%; 30–44, 15.6%; 45–59, 8.8%; 60–74, 4.2%; 75 and over, 1.0%. **Ethnic composition** (1983): Fang 19.6%; Bamileke and Bamum 18.5%; Duala, Luanda, and Basa 14.7%; Fulani 9.6%; Tikar 7.4%; Mandara 5.7%; Maka 4.9%; Chamba 2.4%; Mbum 1.3%; Hausa 1.2%; French 0.2%; other 14.5%. **Religious affiliation** (2000): Roman Catholic 26.4%; traditional beliefs 23.7%; Muslim 21.2%; Protestant 20.7%. **Major cities** (1992): Douala 1,200,000; Yaoundé 800,000; Garoua 160,000; Maroua 140,000; Bafoussam 120,000. **Location:** western Africa, bordering Chad, Central African Republic, Republic of the Congo, Equatorial Guinea, Gabon, the Bight of Biafra and Nigeria.

## Vital statistics

**Birth rate** per 1,000 population (2001): 36.1 (world avg. 21.2). **Death rate** per 1,000 population (2001): 12.0 (world avg. 8.9). **Natural increase rate** per 1,000 population (2001): 24.1 (world avg. 12.3). **Total fertility rate** (avg. births per childbearing woman; 2001): 4.8. **Life expectancy** at birth (2001): male 53.8 years; female 55.4 years.

## National economy

**Budget** (1998–99). *Revenue*: CFAF 838,000,000,-000 (taxes on goods and services 40.5%; income tax 20.8%; customs duties 16.5%; oil revenue 15.9%). *Expenditures*: CFAF 1,023,000,000,000 (current expenditure 80.9%, of which debt service 27.6%, wages and salaries 26.9%, goods and services 16.3%, transfers 9.8%; capital expenditure 19.1%). **Public debt** (external, outstanding; 2000): $7,357,-000,000. **Gross national product** (2000): $8,644,-000,000 ($580 per capita). **Household income and expenditure.** Average household size (1998) 5.7; average annual income per household (1983) $420; sources of income: n.a.; expenditure (1993): food 49.1%, housing 18.0%, transportation and communications 13.0%, health 8.6%, clothing 7.6%, recreation 2.4%. **Population economically active** (1991): total 4,740,000; activity rate of total population 40.0% (participation rates [1985]: ages 15–69, 66.3%; female 38.5%). **Production** (metric tons except as noted). *Agriculture, forestry, fishing* (2001): cassava 1,700,000, sugarcane 1,350,000, plantains 1,000,000; livestock (number of live animals) 5,900,-000 cattle, 4,400,000 goats, 3,880,000 sheep; roundwood (2001) 12,142,670 cu m; fish catch (1999) 95,067. *Mining and quarrying* (1996): pozzolana 100,000; aluminum 82,000; limestone 50,-000. *Manufacturing* (value added in CFAF '000,000; 1994): beverages 49,314; wood and wood products 42,756; rubber and plastic products 38,928. *Energy production (consumption)*: electricity (kW-hr; 1997) 2,758,000,000 (2,758,000,000); coal (metric tons; 1997) 1,000 (1,000); crude petroleum (barrels; 1997) 40,276,000 (4,928,000); petroleum products (metric tons; 1997) 1,045,000 (1,112,000). **Land use** (1994): forested 77.1%; meadows and pastures 4.3%; agricultural and under permanent cultivation 15.1%; other 3.5%. **Tourism** (1995): receipts $36,-000,000; expenditures $105,000,000.

## Foreign trade

**Imports** (1998–99): CFAF 881,500,000,000 (semi-finished goods 15.9%, industrial equipment 13.3%, food and beverages 11.3%, minerals 10.6%, transport equipment 10.3%, unrecorded trade 6.1%). *Major import sources:* France 25.6%; Germany 6.4%; US 5.7%; Japan 5.0%; Belgium-Luxembourg 4.8%; Italy 4.3%; The Netherlands 2.6%; UK 2.6%. **Exports** (1998–99): CFAF 993,900,000,000 (crude petroleum 31.6%, lumber 12.1%, coffee 7.5%, cocoa 7.4%, aluminum 5.0%, cotton 4.7%). *Major export destinations:* Italy 22.4%; France 12.6%; Spain 9.4%; The Netherlands 9.4%; Portugal 3.3%; Germany 1.9%.

## Transport and communications

**Transport.** *Railroads* (1997): route length 1,006 km; (1995) passenger-km 317,000,000; metric ton-km cargo 812,000,000. *Roads* (1997): total length 48,400 km (paved 8%). *Vehicles* (1997): passenger cars 98,000; trucks and buses 64,350. *Air transport* (1996): passenger-km 560,000,000; metric ton-km cargo 91,000,000; airports (1998) with scheduled flights 5. **Communications,** in total units (units per 1,000 persons). Daily newspaper circulation (1996): 91,000 (6.7); radio receivers (1997): 2,270,000 (163); television receivers (1998): 480,000 (33.5); telephone main lines (2001): 101,400 (6.7); cellular telephone subscribers (2001): 310,000 (20.4); Personal computers (2001): 60,000 (3.9); Internet users (2001): 45,000 (3.0).

## Education and health

**Educational attainment** (1976). Percentage of population age 15 and over having: no schooling 51.1%; primary education 41.7%; some postprimary 0.2%; secondary 5.7%; some postsecondary 0.3%; higher 0.2%; other 0.8%. **Literacy** (1995): total population age 15 and over literate 63.4%; males literate 75.0%; females literate 52.1%. **Health:** physicians (1996) 1,031 (1 per 13,510 persons); hospital beds (1988) 29,285 (1 per 371 persons); infant mortality rate per 1,000 live births (2001) 69.8. **Food** (2000): daily per capita caloric intake 2,255 (vegetable products 94%, animal products 6%); 97% of FAO recommended minimum.

## Military

**Total active duty personnel** (2001): 13,100 (army 87.8%, navy 9.9%, air force 2.3%). **Military expenditure as percentage of GNP** (1999): 1.8% (world 2.4%); per capita expenditure $10.

## Background

The Cameroon area had long been inhabited before European colonization. Bantu speakers from equatorial Africa settled in the south, followed by Muslim Fu-

lani from the Niger River basin, who settled in the north. Portuguese explorers visited in the late 15th century and established a foothold, but they lost control to the Dutch in the 17th century. In 1884 the Germans took control and extended their protectorate over Cameroon. In World War I joint French-British action forced the Germans to retreat, and after the war the region was divided into French and British administrative zones. After World War II the two areas became UN trusteeships. In 1960 the French trust territory became an independent republic. In 1961 the southern part of the British trust territory voted for union with the new republic of Cameroon, and the northern part for union with Nigeria. In recent decades economic problems have produced unrest in the country.

## Recent Developments

Pres. Paul Biya's Cameroon People's Democratic Movement crushed the opposition in the 30 June 2002 legislative elections, increasing its majority of the 180 seats from 116 to 133. The International Court of Justice resolved the long-standing dispute between Nigeria and Cameroon over ownership of the Bakassi peninsula and awarded the oil-rich peninsula to Cameroon in October. Oil company officials announced in April 2002 that construction of infrastructure for the Chad-Cameroon pipeline had begun. A stock exchange—the first in central Africa—opened in Douala in April 2003.

**Internet resources:**
<www.cameroon.net/index_cameroon.phtml>

# Canada

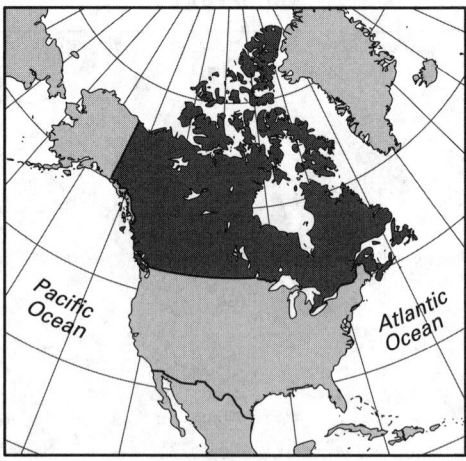

**Official name:** Canada. **Form of government:** federal multiparty parliamentary state with two legislative houses (Senate [105]; House of Commons [301]). **Chief of state:** Queen Elizabeth II. **Representative of chief of state:** Governor-General Adrienne Clarkson (from 1999). **Head of government:** Prime Minister Jean Chrétien (from 1993). **Capital:** Ottawa. **Official languages:** English; French. **Official religion:** none. **Monetary unit:** 1 Canadian dollar (Can$) = 100 cents; valuation (7 Jul 2003) US$1 = Can$1.34.

*1 metric ton = about 1.1 short tons;     1 kilometer = 0.6 mi (statute);     1 metric ton-km cargo = about 0.68 short ton-mi cargo;     c.i.f.: cost, insurance, and freight;     f.o.b.: free on board*

## Demography

**Area:** 3,849,674 sq mi, 9,970,610 sq km. **Population** (2002): 31,244,000. **Density** (2002): persons per sq mi 8.8, persons per sq km 3.4. **Urban** (2001): 78.9%. **Major metropolitan areas** (2001): Toronto 4,881,400; Montreal 3,511,800; Vancouver 2,078,800; Ottawa-Hull 1,106,900; Calgary 971,500; Edmonton 956,800; Quebec 693,100; Winnipeg 684,800; Hamilton 680,600; Kitchener 431,700. **Sex distribution** (2001): male 49.51%; female 50.49%. **Age breakdown** (2001): under 15, 18.8%; 15–29, 20.3%; 30–44, 24.4%; 45–59, 19.7%; 60–74, 11.1%; 75 and over, 5.7%. **Ethnic origin** (1996): British 11.5%; French 9.4%; other European 13.1%, of which Southern European 4.8%, Western European 3.9%, Eastern European 3.0%; Asian origin 7.0%; Amerindian and Inuit (Eskimo) 1.7%; Latin American origin 1.4%; Arab origin 0.6%; African origin 0.5%; multiple origin and other 54.8%. **Religious affiliation** (2000): Roman Catholic 41.8%; Protestant 39.7%; Eastern Orthodox 1.9%; Jewish 1.3%; Muslim 1.0%; Hindu 1.0%; Buddhist 0.8%; nonreligious 10.9%; other 1.6%. **Place of birth** (1996): 83.4% native-born; 16.6% foreign-born, of which UK 2.2%, other European 4.2%, Asian countries 5.2%, US 0.8%, other 4.2%. **Mobility** (1996). Population living in the same residence as in 1991: 56.7%; different residence, same municipality 23.0%; same province, different municipality 3.3%; different province 13.4%; different country 3.5%. **Households** (1999). Total number of households 11,553,000. Average household size 2.5; (1997) 1 person 25.2%, 2 persons 33.0%, 3 persons 16.7%, 4 persons 16.3%, 5 or more persons 8.8%. Family households (1999): 8,139,700 (70.6%), nonfamily 3,413,300 (29.4%, of which 1 person 83.6%). **Immigration** (1999–2000): permanent immigrants admitted 252,088; from Asia 62.1%, of which India 11.6%, Philippines 5.6%, Vietnam 0.7%, Hong Kong 0.3%; US 2.4%; UK 2.1%; refugee arrivals 22,899. **Location:** northern North America, bordering the Arctic Ocean, the North Atlantic Ocean, the US, and the North Pacific Ocean.

## Vital statistics

**Birth rate** per 1,000 population (2000): 10.8 (world avg. 22.5); (1997) legitimate 72.3%; illegitimate 27.7%. **Death rate** per 1,000 population (2000): 7.5 (world avg. 9.0). **Natural increase rate** per 1,000 population (2000): 3.3 (world avg. 13.5). **Total fertility rate** (avg. births per childbearing woman; 2000): 1.6. **Marriage rate** per 1,000 population (2000): 5.0. **Divorce rate** per 1,000 population (2000): 2.2. **Life expectancy** at birth (2000): male 76.0 years; female 83.0 years.

## Social indicators

**Quality of working life.** Average workweek (1997): 31.3 hours. Annual rate per 100,000 workers for (1997): injury, accident, or industrial illness 1,330; death 2.7. Average days lost to labor stoppages per 1,000 employee-workdays (1997): 0.9. Mode of transportation to work: automobile 80.6%, public transportation 10.1%, other 9.3%. Rate per 1,000 workers of discouraged (unemployed no longer seeking work; 1983): 10.5. **Access to services** (1999). Proportion of households having access to: electricity 100.0%; public water supply 99.8%; public sewage collection 99.3%. **Social participation.** Eligible voters participating in last national election (November

2000): 61.2%. Population over 18 years of age participating in voluntary work (2000): 26.7%. Union membership in total workforce (1999): 32.9%. Practicing religious population in total affiliated population (1996): 92.5%. **Social deviance** (2000). Offense rate per 100,000 population for: violent crime 981, of which assault 758.9, sexual assault 78.2, homicide 1.6; property crime 4,067, of which auto theft 521, burglary 954. **Leisure** (1998). Favorite leisure activities (hours weekly): television 15.4; social time 13.3; reading 2.8; sports and entertainment 1.4. **Material well-being** (1998). Households possessing: automobile 78.8%, of which two or more 34.5%; telephone 98.2%; color television 98.8%; refrigerator 99.8%; central air conditioner 33.1%; cable television 66.5%; video recorder 88.1%; microwave oven 88.7%; home computers 45.1%.

## National economy

**Gross national product** (2000): US$649,829,000,-000 (US$21,130 per capita). **Budget** (1999–2000). *Revenue:* Can$172,532,000,000 (individual income taxes 47.8%, value-added tax 20.3%, corporate income tax 13.0%, contributions to social security 10.8%, import duties 1.3%). *Expenditures:* Can$169,966,000,000 (social services 29.6%, public debt interest 24.5%, defense and social protection 10.8%, education 2.6%, health 1.0%). **National debt** (1997): Can$619,710,000,000. **Tourism** (2000): receipts US$10,704,000,000; expenditures US$12,140,000,000. **Production** (metric tons except as noted). *Agriculture, forestry, fishing* (2001): wheat 20,695,300, barley 11,103,300, rapeseed 7,778,-000, corn (maize) 7,550,000, potatoes 4,568,500, oats 2,838,300, dry peas 2,175,400, vegetables 2,135,000 (of which tomatoes 670,000, carrots 278,608, onions 189,334, cabbage 167,450), soybeans 2,040,100, sugar beets 821,000, linseed 703,700, apples 580,000; livestock (number of live animals) 12,860,000 cattle, 12,600,000 pigs, 694,800 sheep, 385,000 horses; roundwood (2000) 148,871,000 cu m; fish catch (1999) 1,135,516. *Mining and quarrying* (1999): iron ore 33,004,000; zinc 960,099; copper 580,036; nickel 177,029; lead 156,102; uranium 9,892; molybdenum 6,293; silver 1,173 kg; gold 157,790 kg. *Manufacturing* (value of shipments in Can$'000,000; 1999): transportation equipment 125,034.3; food 52,352.8; electrical machinery 36,760.6; paper products 33,150.3; wood industries 30,600.6; metal products 26,883.9; machinery 16,890.5; rubber and plastic products 16,885.0; printing and publishing 16,526.3; furniture 8,506.4; wearing apparel 6,996.3; textiles 3,683.3. *Energy production (consumption):* electricity (kW-hr; 1999) 541,900,-000,000 (545,460,300,000); coal (metric tons; 2000) 69,164,000 (60,761,000); crude petroleum (barrels; 1997) 719,729,000 (608,411,000); petroleum products (metric tons; 1997) 95,026,000 (81,240,000); natural gas (cu m; 1999) 163,384,-000,000 ([1998] 89,163,000,000). **Population economically active** (2000): total 15,999,200; activity rate of total population 52.0% (participation rates: ages 15 and over 65.9%; female 45.9%; unemployed [2001] 7.3%). **Household income and expenditure** (1999). Average household size 2.6; average annual income per family (1999) Can$63,818 (US$43,413); sources of income (1995): wages and salaries 57.0%, transfer payments 20.7%, property and entrepreneurial income 13.7%, profits 8.6%; expendi-

ture (1999): housing 27.2%, food, alcohol, and tobacco 19.3%, transportation and communications
18.2%, recreation 7.9%, utilities 6.4%, clothing 6.2%,
household durable goods 3.9%, health 3.3%, education 2.0%. **Land use** (1994): forested 53.6%; meadows and pastures 3.0%; agricultural and under permanent cultivation 4.9%; built-on, wasteland, and
other 38.5%.

## Foreign trade

**Imports** (2000): Can$363,281,300,000 (1999; ma-
chinery and transport equipment 56.3%, of which
motor vehicles 23.2%; chemical products 6.9%; food
5.4%; petroleum and energy products 3.3%; forestry
products 0.8%). *Major import sources* (1999): US
67.2%; Japan 4.7%; Mexico 3.0%; China 2.8%; UK
2.5%; Germany 2.2%; France 1.7%; Taiwan 1.4%;
Italy 1.1%; South Korea 1.1%. **Exports** (2000):
Can$422,558,700,000 (1999; machinery and trans-
port equipment 50.3%, of which motor vehicles
26.5%; mineral fuels 8.2%, of which crude petroleum
3.1%; food 7.1%; lumber 5.5%; newsprint and paper
products 3.5%; wood pulp 1.9%). *Major export destinations* (1999): US 86.8%; Japan 2.5%; UK 1.3%;
South Korea 0.6%.

## Transport and communications

**Transport.** *Railroads* (1998): length 65,403 km; passenger-km 1,458,000,000; metric ton-km cargo
299,508,000,000. *Roads* (1999): total length
901,903 km (paved 35%). *Vehicles* (1998): passenger cars 13,887,270; trucks and buses 3,694,125.
*Air transport* (2000): passenger-km 68,202,000,-
000; metric ton-km cargo 1,786,600,000; airports
(1997) with scheduled flights 269. **Communications,**
in total units (units per 1,000 persons). Daily newspaper circulation (1996): 4,718,000 (159); radio receivers (1997): 32,300,000 (1,077); television receivers (1998): 21,450,000 (715); telephone main
lines (2001): 20,319,000 (655); cellular telephone
subscribers (2001): 9,923,000 (320); personal computers (2001): 12,000,000 (390); Internet users
(2001): 13,500,000 (435).

## Education and health

**Educational attainment** (1996). Percentage of population age 15 and over having: no formal schooling or
not known 4.2%; at least primary education 12.3%;
some secondary 19.6%; completed secondary 19.8%;
postsecondary 30.5%; university graduates 13.6%.
**Literacy** (1996): total population age 15 and over literate virtually 100%. **Health:** physicians (2000) 60,559
(1 per 508 persons); hospital beds (1997) 161,867 (1
per 185 persons); infant mortality rate per 1,000 live
births (2000) 5.1. **Food** (1999): daily per capita caloric
intake 3,161 (vegetable products 71%, animal products 29%); 119% of FAO recommended minimum.

## Military

**Total active duty personnel** (2001): 56,800 (army
32.7%, navy 15.8%, air force 23.7%, not identified by
service 27.8%). **Military expenditure as percentage
of GNP** (1999): 1.4% (world 2.4%); per capita expenditure US$269.

## Background

Originally inhabited by American Indians and Inuit,
Canada was visited c. AD 1000 by Scandinavian explorers, whose discovery is confirmed by archaeolog-
ical evidence from Newfoundland. Fishing expedi-
tions off Newfoundland by the English, French,
Spanish, and Portuguese began as early as 1500.
The French claim to Canada was made in 1534
when Jacques Cartier entered the Gulf of St.
Lawrence. A small settlement was made in Nova
Scotia (Acadia) in 1605, and in 1608 Samuel de
Champlain founded Quebec. Fur trading was the im-
petus behind the early colonizing efforts. In response
to French activity, the English in 1670 formed the
Hudson's Bay Company.

The British-French rivalry for the interior of upper
North America lasted almost a century. The first
French loss occurred in 1713 at the conclusion of
Queen Anne's War (War of the Spanish Succession)
when Nova Scotia and Newfoundland were ceded to
the British. The Seven Years' War (French and Indian
War) resulted in France's expulsion from continental
North America in 1763. After the US War of Independence the population was augmented by Loyalists fleeing the US, and the increasing number arriving in Quebec led the British to divide the colony
into Upper and Lower Canada in 1791. The British
reunited the two provinces in 1841. Canadian ex-
pansionism resulted in the confederation movement
of the mid-19th century, and in 1867 the Dominion
of Canada, comprising Nova Scotia, New Brunswick,
Quebec, and Ontario, came into existence. After
confederation, Canada entered a period of westward expansion.

The prosperity that accompanied Canada into the
20th century was marred by continuing conflict between the English and French communities. Through
the Statute of Westminster (1931), Canada was recognized as an equal of Great Britain. With the Constitution Act of 1982, the British gave Canada total control over its constitution and severed the remaining
legal connections between the two countries. French
Canadian unrest continued to be a major concern,
with a movement growing for Quebec separatism in
the late 20th century. Referendums for more political
autonomy for Quebec were rejected in 1992 and
1995, but the issue remained unresolved. In 1999
Canada formed the new territory of Nunavut, and on
6 Dec 2001 Newfoundland was renamed Newfoundland and Labrador.

## Recent Developments

National politics in Canada in 2002 were dominated
by questions of party leadership, especially in the
governing Liberal Party. Prime Minister Jean Chrétien
faced a revolt against his continuation as party
chief. Many Liberals believed that it was time for
Chrétien to step down. At age 68, he had been a
member of Parliament, with a short break, since
1963, but he showed little vision for the country,
and his style of governance had become increasingly
authoritarian.

The Canadian economy moved forward steadily in
2002. The turmoil on the stock markets brought
down the value of many Canadian equities but did
not interrupt the economy's growth. Job creation was

---

*1 metric ton = about 1.1 short tons;    1 kilometer = 0.6 mi (statute);    1 metric ton-km cargo = about 0.68 short
ton-mi cargo;    c.i.f.: cost, insurance, and freight;    f.o.b.: free on board*

strong, with the unemployment rate hovering above 7%. The consumer price index stood at 3.2% in October, pushed upward by energy costs. For the economy on the whole, the increase in gross domestic product was expected to rise 3–4% to the end of 2003. A severe drought, reminiscent of the dust-bowl conditions of the 1930s, settled over the Western prairies in 2002. Overall wheat production was expected to decline 40% from 2001. To add to the farmers' misery, an infestation of grasshoppers consumed surviving crops.

Reverberations from the 2001 terrorist attacks in the US spurred the government of Canada to strengthen the country's security and join in the international coalition against global terrorism. In January 2002, 850 troops were prepared for service in Afghanistan to work under US Army command in the search for al-Qaeda fighters. This was the largest deployment of Canadian combat forces since the Korean War. A naval detachment of six vessels to patrol the Arabian Sea and a small group of transport and surveillance aircraft brought another 1,700 personnel to the troubled region. Satisfaction with the mission was marred by an unfortunate incident on 17 April, when four Canadian soldiers were killed by a 227-kg (500-lb) bomb dropped by a US Air National Guard F-16 pilot who apparently failed to observe his force's rules of engagement.

Canada did not adopt a firm position on a possible US strike on Iraq to topple Saddam Hussein and stop his alleged accumulation of weapons of mass destruction. At the United Nations, Canada had long criticized Iraq for its refusal, after 1998, to accept UN weapons inspectors. Foreign Minister Graham cautioned that the US should not intervene unilaterally but should seek UN approval for any action taken. Prime Minister Chrétien made it clear that Canada would not participate in military action against Iraq unless it were carried out under UN auspices. In the event, Canada did not send troops to join the US-led coalition forces against Iraq. As expected, American resentment of Canada's position affected relations between the two neighbors well into 2003.

Canada played host to the Group of Eight summit of leading industrialized nations in June 2002. The meeting, deep in the Rockies of Alberta, was undisturbed by the violent demonstrations that had taken place at past summits.

The mysterious epidemic of SARS affected Canada in the spring of 2003. Dozens of deaths were reported in the Toronto area, and the WHO at one point advised travelers to avoid the city. A brief scare over mad cow disease flared up in May after a cow in Alberta was found to be infected.

Internet resources: <www.travelcanada.ca>

# Cape Verde

**Official name:** República de Cabo Verde (Republic of Cape Verde). **Form of government:** multiparty republic with one legislative house (National Assembly [72]). **Chief of state:** President Pedro Pires (from 2001). **Head of government:** Prime Minister José Maria Neves (from 2001). **Capital:** Praia. **Official language:** Portuguese. **Official religion:** none. **Monetary unit:** 1 escudo (C.V.Esc.) = 100 centavos; valuation (7 Jul 2003) $1 = C.V.Esc. 108.95 (formerly pegged to

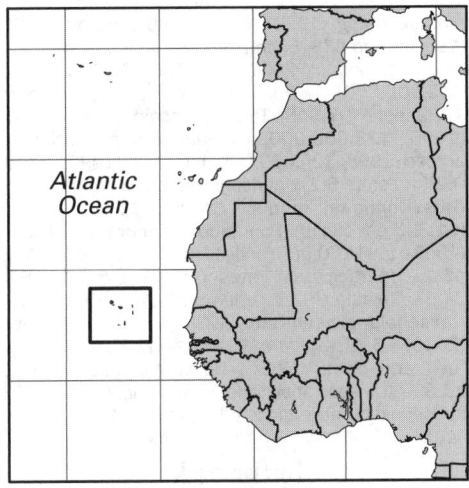

the Portuguese escudo and since 1 Jan 2002, to the euro at the rate of €1 = C.V.Esc. 110.27).

## Demography

**Area:** 1,557 sq mi, 4,033 sq km. **Population** (2002): 453,000. **Density** (2002): persons per sq mi 290.9, persons per sq km 112.3. **Urban** (2000): 53.3%. **Sex distribution** (2000): male 48.42%; female 51.58%. **Age breakdown** (2000): under 15, 43.6%; 15–29, 24.8%; 30–44, 17.1%; 45–59, 5.8%; 60–74, 6.3%; 75 and over, 2.4%. **Ethnic composition** (2000): Cape Verdean *mestico* (black-white admixture) 69.6%; Fulani 12.2%; Balanta 10.0%; Mandyako 4.6%; Portuguese white 2.0%; other 1.6%. **Religious affiliation** (2000): Roman Catholic 91.4%; Muslim 2.8%; other 5.8%. **Major cities** (2000): Praia 94,757; Mindelo 62,970; São Filipe 7,894. **Location:** off the coast of western Africa; consists of 10 islands in the North Atlantic Ocean.

## Vital statistics

**Birth rate** per 1,000 population (2001): 28.7 (world avg. 21.2); (1989) legitimate 28.9%; illegitimate 71.1%. **Death rate** per 1,000 population (2001): 7.2 (world avg. 8.9). **Natural increase rate** per 1,000 population (2001): 21.5 (world avg. 12.3). **Total fertility rate** (avg. births per childbearing woman; 2001): 4.0. **Marriage rate** per 1,000 population (1990): 4.5. **Life expectancy** at birth (2001): male 65.9 years; female 72.6 years.

## National economy

**Budget** (2000). *Revenue:* C.V.Esc. 13,228,000,000 (tax revenue 88.9%, of which taxes on international trade 52.9%, income taxes 29.8%, other taxes 6.2%; nontax revenue 11.1%). *Expenditures:* C.V.Esc. 29,114,000,000 (current expenditure 75.5%, of which transfers 23.5%, wages and salaries 22.1%, public debt 6.0%, goods and services 1.6%; capital expenditure 24.5%). **Public debt** (external, outstanding; 2000): $314,600,000. **Production** (metric tons except as noted). *Agriculture, forestry, fishing* (2001): corn (maize) 21,469, sugarcane 14,000, bananas 6,000; livestock (number of live animals) 636,000 pigs, 110,000 goats, 21,500 cattle; fish catch (1999) 10,371. *Mining and quarrying* (2000): salt 2,000.

*Manufacturing* (1999): flour 15,901; bread 5,628 (1995); soap 833. *Energy production (consumption)*: electricity (kW-hr; 2000) 148,783,000,000 (130,-792,000,000); petroleum products (metric tons; 1999) none (97,346). **Tourism**: receipts from visitors (2000) $23,000,000; expenditures by nationals abroad (1998) $24,000,000. **Land use** (1994): forest 0.2%; pasture 6.2%; agriculture 11.2%; other 82.4%. **Gross national product** (2000): $588,000,000 ($1,330 per capita). **Population economically active** (1997): total 160,000; activity rate of total population 41.2% (participation rates [1990]: ages 15–64, 64.3%; female 39.0%; unemployed [1990] 25.8%). **Household expenditure**. Average household size (2000) 4.6; expenditure (1988): food 51.1%, housing, fuel, and power 13.5%, beverages and tobacco 11.8%, transportation and communications. 8.8%, household durable goods 6.9%, other 7.9%.

## Foreign trade

**Imports** (2000): C.V.Esc. 25,212,000,000 (food 31.3%, machinery and apparatus 17.8%, nonmetallic mineral products 10.8%, transport equipment 10.4%, metal products 7.2%, chemicals 7.0%). *Major import sources* (2000): Portugal 52.4%; The Netherlands 13.0%; France 4.4%; US 3.6%; Spain 2.5%. **Exports** (2000): C.V.Esc. 2,774,000,000 (domestic export 45.9%, of which shoes 23.8%, clothing 16.1%, fish and fish preparations 3.4%, other 2.6%; reexports 54.1%). *Major export destinations* (2000): Portugal 80.1%; US 11.4%; Spain 3.5%.

## Transport and communications

**Transport**. *Roads* (1999): total length 1,100 km (paved [1996] 78%). *Vehicles* (2000): passenger cars 13,473; trucks and buses 3,085. *Air transport* (2001; TACV airline only): passenger-km 276,000,-000; metric ton-km cargo 26,000,000; airports (1997) with scheduled flights 9. **Communications**, in total units (units per 1,000 persons). Radio receivers (1997): 71,000 (179); television receivers (1999): 2,000 (4.7); telephone main lines (2001): 62,300 (143); cellular telephone subscribers (2001): 31,500 (72); Internet users (2001): 12,000 (27).

## Education and health

**Educational attainment** (1990). Percentage of population age 25 and over having: no formal schooling 47.9%; primary 40.9%; incomplete secondary 3.9%; complete secondary 1.4%; higher 1.5%; unknown 4.4%. **Literacy** (1999): total population age 15 and over literate 73.6%; males 84.5%; females 65.1%. **Health** (1998): physicians 165 (1 per 2,574 persons); hospital beds 792 (1 per 513 persons); infant mortality rate per 1,000 live births (2001) 53.2. **Food** (2000): daily per capita caloric intake 3,278 (vegetable products 86%, animal products 14%); 141% of FAO recommended minimum.

## Military

**Total active duty personnel** (2001): 1,200 (army 83.3%, air force 8.3%, coast guard 8.4%). **Military expenditure as percentage of GNP** (1999): 0.9% (world 2.4%); per capita expenditure $13.

## Background

When visited by the Portuguese in 1456–60, the islands were uninhabited. In 1460 Diogo Gomes sighted and named Maio and São Tiago, and in 1462 the first settlers landed on São Tiago, founding the city of Ribeira Grande. The city's importance grew with the development of the slave trade, and its wealth attracted pirates so often that it was abandoned after 1712. The prosperity of the Portuguese-controlled islands vanished with the decline of the slave trade in the 19th century, but later improved because of their position on the great trade routes between Europe, South America, and South Africa. In 1951 the colony became an overseas province of Portugal. Many islanders preferred outright independence, and it was finally granted in 1975. Once associated politically with Guinea-Bissau, Cape Verde split from it in 1981.

## Recent Developments

The year 2001 marked the end of 10 years of rule by the Movement for Democracy and the return to power of the African Party for the Independence of Cape Verde (PAICV). In legislative elections held in January, the PAICV won the majority of seats, and its leader, José Maria Neves, became the new prime minister.

**Internet resources:** <www.ine.cv>

# Central African Republic

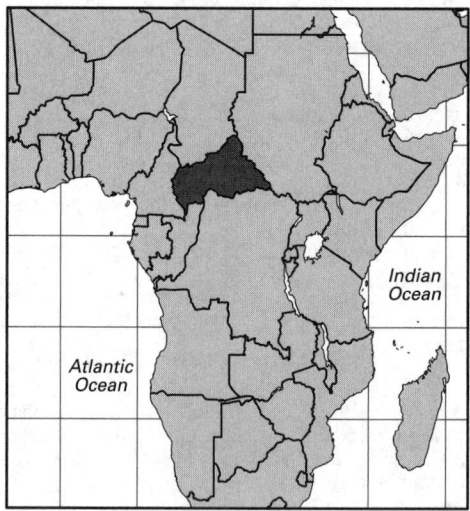

**Official name:** République Centrafricaine (Central African Republic). **Form of government:** multiparty republic with one legislative body (National Assembly [109]). **Chief of state:** President François Bozizé (from 15 Mar 2003). **Head of government:** Prime Minister Abel Goumba (from 23 Mar 2003). **Capital:** Bangui. **Official languages:** French; Sango. **Official religion:** none. **Monetary unit:** 1 CFA franc (CFAF) = 100 centimes; valuation (7 Jul 2003) $1 = CFAF 571.07 (formerly pegged to the French franc and

*1 metric ton = about 1.1 short tons; 1 kilometer = 0.6 mi (statute); 1 metric ton-km cargo = about 0.68 short ton-mi cargo; c.i.f.: cost, insurance, and freight; f.o.b.: free on board*

since 1 Jan 2002, to the euro at the rate of €1 = CFAF 655.96).

## Demography

**Area:** 240,324 sq mi, 622,436 sq km. **Population:** (2002): 3,643,000. **Density** (2002): persons per sq mi 15.2, persons per sq km 5.9. **Urban** (2001): 41.7%. **Sex distribution** (2001): male 49.43%; female 50.57%. **Age breakdown** (2001): under 15, 43.5%; 15–29, 28.0%; 30–44, 14.9%; 45–59, 8.1%; 60–74, 4.2%; 75 and over, 1.3%. **Ethnolinguistic composition** (1988): Gbaya (Baya) 23.7%; Banda 23.4%; Mandjia 14.7%; Ngbaka 7.6%; Sara 6.5%; Mbum 6.3%; Kare 2.4%; French 0.1%; other 15.3%. **Religious affiliation** (2000): Christian 67.8%, of which Roman Catholic 18.4%, Protestant 14.4%, African Christian 11.6%, other Christian 23.4%; Muslim 15.6%; traditional beliefs 15.4%; other 1.2%. **Major cities** (1994): Bangui 524,000; Berbérati 47,000; Bouar 43,000; Bambari 41,000; Carnot 41,000. **Location:** central Africa, bordering Chad, The Sudan, Democratic Republic of the Congo, Republic of the Congo, and Cameroon.

## Vital statistics

**Birth rate** per 1,000 population (2001): 37.1 (world avg. 21.2). **Death rate** per 1,000 population (2001): 18.5 (world avg. 8.9). **Natural increase rate** per 1,000 population (2001): 18.6 (world avg. 12.3). **Total fertility rate** (avg. births per childbearing woman; 2001): 4.9. **Life expectancy** at birth (2001): male 42.2 years; female 45.5 years.

## National economy

**Budget** (1999). *Revenue*: CFAF 59,700,000,000 (taxes 88.0%, of which international trade tax 38.0%, indirect domestic tax 30.1%, taxes on income and profits 19.9%; nontax receipts 12.0%). *Expenditures*: CFAF 116,100,000,000 (current expenditure 49.0%, of which wages 23.3%; public investment program 51.0%). **Production** (metric tons except as noted). *Agriculture, forestry, fishing* (2001): cassava 561,700, yams 360,000, bananas 118,000; livestock (number of live animals; 2002) 3,273,000 cattle, 2,921,000 goats, 738,000; roundwood (2000) 3,011,000 cu m; fish catch (1999) 15,117. *Mining and quarrying* (2000): gold 38.7 kg, diamonds 460,000 carats (legal trade only). *Manufacturing* (value added in $'000; 1994): food, beverages, and tobacco 19,000; chemical products 3,000; wood products 2,000. *Energy production (consumption)*: electricity (kW-hr; 1998) 114,700,000 (114,700,000); petroleum products (metric tons; 1997) none (79,000). **Household income and expenditure.** Average household size (1998) 5.9; average annual income per household (1988) CFAF 91,985 ($435); expenditure (1991): food 70.5%, clothing 8.5%, other manufactured products 7.6%, energy 7.3%, services (including transportation and communications, recreation, and health) 6.1%. **Gross national product** (2000): $1,031,000,000 ($280 per capita). **Public debt** (external, outstanding; 2000): $810,100,000. **Population economically active** (1988): total 1,186,972; activity rate of total population 48.2% (participation rates: ages 15–64, 78.3%; female 46.8%; unemployed 7.5%). **Land use** (1994): forest 75.0%; meadows 4.8%; agriculture 3.2%; other 17.0%. **Tourism** (1997): receipts $5,000,000; expenditures $39,000,000.

## Foreign trade

**Imports** (2000): CFAF 85,500,000,000 (1992; food products 22.2%, transportation equipment 16.6%, chemical products 13.7%, energy products 11.0%). Major import sources (1999): France 33.8%; Cameroon 12.2%; Belgium-Luxembourg 7.4%; UK 4.1%; Germany 2.7%; US 2.7%. **Exports** (2000): CFAF 114,200,000,000 (diamonds 45.9%, wood 18.2%, cotton 10.4%, coffee 10.2%). Major export destinations: Belgium-Luxembourg 64.7%; Spain 6.3%; France 3.2%; Taiwan 3.2%; Italy 1.4%; Germany 1.4%.

## Transport and communications

**Transport.** *Roads* (1998): total length 24,307 km (paved 3%). *Vehicles* (1996): passenger cars 8,900; trucks and buses 7,000. *Air transport* (1998; includes about 10% of the traffic of Air Afrique, which is operated by 11 West African states): passenger-km 258,000,000; metric ton-km cargo 38,000,000; airports (2001) 1. **Communications**, in total units (units per 1,000 persons). Daily newspaper circulation (1996): 6,000 (1.8); radio receivers (1997): 283,000 (83.0); television receivers (1999): 20,000 (5.6); telephone main lines (2001): 10,000 (2.6); cellular telephone subscribers (2001): 11,000 (2.9); personal computers (2001): 7,000 (1.9); Internet users (2001): 2,000 (0.5).

## Education and health

**Educational attainment** (1988). Percentage of population age 10 and over having: no formal schooling 59.3%; primary education 29.6%; lower secondary 7.5%; upper secondary 2.3%; higher 1.3%. **Literacy** (1999): total population age 15 and over literate 45.4%; males literate 58.6%; females literate 33.3%. **Health** (1992): physicians 157 (1 per 18,660 persons); hospital beds (1991) 4,258 (1 per 672 persons); infant mortality rate per 1,000 live births (2001) 105.3. **Food** (2000): daily per capita caloric intake 1,946 (vegetable products 90%, animal products 10%); 86% of FAO recommended minimum.

## Military

**Total active duty personnel** (2001): 3,150 (army 95.2%; navy, none; air force 4.8%; excludes 1,000 gendarmerie, who are part of the armed forces). **Military expenditure as percentage of GNP** (1999): 2.8% (world 2.4%); per capita expenditure $8.

---

**Did you know?** Although mining produces less than 4% of the gross domestic product in the Central African Republic, diamonds generate one-third of the value of exports, even though much of the production is smuggled out of the country.

---

## Background

For several centuries before the arrival of Europeans, the territory was subjected to slave traders. The French explored and claimed central Africa and in 1889 established a post at Bangui. In 1898 they partitioned the colony among commercial concessionaires. United with Chad in 1906 to form the French colony of Ubangi-Shari, it later became part of French Equatorial Africa. It was separated from Chad in 1920 and became an overseas territory in 1946. An autonomous republic within the French Community in 1958, the country achieved independence in 1960. In 1966 the military overthrew a civilian government and installed Jean-Bédel Bokassa, who in 1976 declared himself Emperor Bokassa I and renamed the country the Central African Empire. He was overthrown in 1979, but the military again seized power in the 1980s. Elections in 1993 led to the installation of a civilian government.

## Recent Developments

Continuing political turbulence in the country erupted in a coup on 15 March 2003 in which François Bozizé, the army chief who had been sacked by Pres. Ange-Félix Patassé, took advantage of the president's absence from the country and the disgruntlement of soldiers who had not been paid in many months. Bozizé declared himself president; Patassé, stranded in Cameroon, accused Chad of being behind the action; and the UN and the African Union initially condemned the coup.

Internet resources: <www.sas.upenn.edu/ African_Studies/Country_Specific/CAR.html>

# Chad

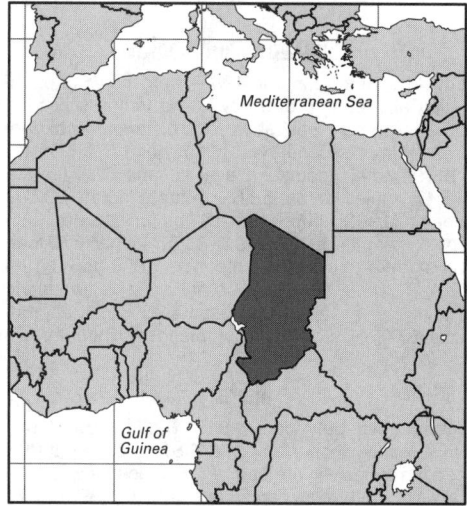

**Official name:** Jumhuriyah Tshad (Arabic); République du Tchad (French) (Republic of Chad). **Form of government:** unitary republic with one legislative body (National Assembly [125]). **Chief of state:** President Idriss Déby (from 1990). **Head of government:** Prime Minister Moussa Faki Mahamat (from 24 Jun 2003). **Capital:** N'Djamena. **Official languages:** Arabic; French. **Official religion:** none. **Monetary unit:** 1 CFA franc (CFAF) = 100 centimes; valuation (7 Jul 2003) $1 = CFAF 571.07 (formerly pegged to the French franc and since 1 Jan 2002, to the euro at the rate of €1 = CFAF 655.96).

## Demography

**Area:** 495,755 sq mi, 1,284,000 sq km. **Population** (2002): 8,997,000. **Density** (2002): persons per sq mi 18.1, persons per sq km 7.0. **Urban** (1999): 23.4%. **Sex distribution** (2001): male 48.56%; female 51.44%. **Age breakdown** (2001): under 15, 47.7%; 15–29, 26.1%; 30–44, 14.1%; 45–59, 7.6%; 60–74, 3.6%; 75 and over, 0.9%. **Ethnolinguistic composition** (1993): Sara 27.7%; Sudanic Arab 12.3%; Mayo-Kebbi peoples 11.5%; Kanem-Bornu peoples 9.0%; Ouaddaï peoples 8.7%; Hadjeray (Hadjaraï) 6.7%; Tangale (Tandjilé) peoples 6.5%; Gorane peoples 6.3%; Fitri-Batha peoples 4.7%; Fulani (Peul) 2.4%; other 4.2%. **Religious affiliation** (1993): Muslim 53.9%; Christian 34.7%, of which Roman Catholic 20.3%, Protestant 14.4%; traditional beliefs 7.4%; other 4.0%. **Major cities** (1993): N'Djamena 530,965; Moundou 282,103; Bongor 196,713; Sarh 193,753; Abéché 187,936. **Location:** central Africa, bordered by Libya, The Sudan, Central African Republic, Cameroon, Nigeria, and Niger.

## Vital statistics

**Birth rate** per 1,000 population (2001): 48.3 (world avg. 21.2). **Death rate** per 1,000 population (2001): 15.4 (world avg. 8.9). **Natural increase rate** per 1,000 population (2001): 32.9 (world avg. 12.3). **Total fertility rate** (avg. births per childbearing woman; 2001): 6.6. **Life expectancy** at birth (2001): male 48.9 years; female 53.0 years.

## National economy

**Budget** (2000). *Revenue:* CFAF 128,200,000,000 (tax revenue 53.3%, of which income tax 19.0%, taxes on international trade 17.0%, taxes on goods and services 14.7%, other taxes 2.6%; nontax revenue 9.3%; grants 37.4%). *Expenditures:* CFAF 203,200,000,000 (current expenditure 49.2%, of which government salaries 19.7%, materials and supply 10.2%, defense 7.5%, transfer payments 5.9%, debt service 5.1%, other 0.8%; capital expenditure 50.8%). **Public debt** (external, outstanding; 2000): $1,009,000,000. **Tourism** (1994): receipts from visitors $12,000,000; expenditures by nationals abroad $26,000,000. **Production** (metric tons except as noted). *Agriculture, forestry, fishing* (2001): sorghum 566,577, cassava 342,000, peanuts (groundnuts) 333,000; livestock (number of live animals) 5,900,000 cattle, 5,250,000 goats, 2,400,000 sheep; roundwood (1998) 1,919,000 cu m; fish catch (1999) 84,000. *Mining and quarrying* (1997): aggregate (gravel) 170,000; limited commercial production of natron (10,000) and salt; artisanal gold production. *Manufacturing* (2000): cotton fibre 86,260 (1998); refined sugar 27,000; gum arabic 3,420. *Energy production (consumption):* electricity (kW-hr; 2000) 86,400,000 (81,800,000); petroleum products (metric tons; 1998) none (47,057). **Household income and expenditure** (1993). Average household size 5.0; average annual income per household CFAF 96,806 ($458); sources of income (1995–96; urban) informal-sector employment and entrepreneurship 36.7%, transfers 24.8%, wages 23.6%, ownership of reals estate 8.6%; expenditure (1983): food 45.3%, health 11.9%, energy 5.8%, clothing 3.3%. **Population economically active** (1997): total 3,433,000; activity rate of total population 47.9% (participation rates: over age 15, 72.3%; female 44.5%; unemployed [1993] 0.6%). **Gross national**

---

*1 metric ton = about 1.1 short tons;  1 kilometer = 0.6 mi (statute);  1 metric ton-km cargo = about 0.68 short ton-mi cargo;  c.i.f.: cost, insurance, and freight;  f.o.b.: free on board*

product (2000): $1,541,000,000 ($200 per capita). **Land use** (1994): forested 25.7%; meadows and pastures 35.7%; agricultural and under permanent cultivation 2.6%; other 36.0%.

## Foreign trade

**Imports** (2000-c.i.f.): CFAF 234,300,000,000 (1995; petroleum products 17.9%; machinery 15.5%; transport equipment 8.3%; raw and refined sugar 7.9%; cereal products 7.4%; pharmaceutical and other chemical products 7.2%. *Major import sources* (1997): France 41.3%; Nigeria 10.1%; Cameroon 7.2%; India 5.8%; Belgium-Luxembourg 5.1%; Italy 4.3%; Portugal 2.9%. **Exports** (2000-f.o.b.): CFAF 130,200,000,000 (cotton fibre 55.9%; cattle, sheep, and goats 16.9%; other 27.2%). *Major export destinations* (1997): Portugal 29.9%; Germany 14.2%; Thailand 7.5%; Costa Rica 6.0%; Hong Kong 4.8%; Taiwan 4.8%; France 3.7%.

## Transport and communications

**Transport.** *Roads* (1999): total length 33,400 km (paved 1%). *Vehicles* (1996): passenger cars 10,560; trucks and buses 14,550. *Air transport* (1996; includes about 10% of the traffic of Air Afrique, which is operated by 11 West African states): passenger-km 233,000,000; metric ton-km cargo 37,000,000; airports (2000) with scheduled flights 1. **Communications,** in total units (units per 1,000 persons). Daily newspaper circulation (1997): 2,000 (0.2); radio receivers (1997): 1,310,000 (205.9); television receivers (1999): 10,300 (1.4); telephone main lines (2001): 11,000 (1.4); cellular telephone subscribers (2001): 22,000 (2.7); personal computers (2001): 12,000 (1.5); Internet users (2001): 4,000 (0.5).

## Education and health

**Educational attainment** (1993). Percentage of economically active population age 15 and over having: no formal schooling 81.1%; Quranic education 4.2%; primary education 11.2%; secondary education 2.7%; higher education 0.3%; professional education 0.5%. **Literacy** (1995): total population age 15 and over literate 48.1%; males literate 62.1%; females literate 34.7%. **Health** (2000): physicians 1,667 (1 per 4,471 persons); hospital beds (1993) 3,962 (1 per 1,521 persons); infant mortality rate per 1,000 live births (2001) 95.1. **Food** (2000): daily per capita caloric intake 2,046 (vegetable products 93%, animal products 7%); 86% of FAO recommended minimum.

## Military

**Total active duty personnel** (2001): 30,350 (army 82.4%; navy, none; air force 1.2%; paramilitary 16.4%; excludes 900 French troops). **Military expenditure as percentage of GNP** (1999): 2.4% (world 2.4%); per capita expenditure $5.

## Background

Around AD 800 the kingdom of Kanem was founded, and by the early 1200s its borders had expanded to form a new kingdom, Kanem-Bornu, in the northern regions of the area. Its power peaked in the 16th century with its command of the southern terminus of the trans-Sahara trade route to Tripoli. Around this time the rival kingdoms of Baguirmi and Wadai evolved in the south. In the years 1883–93 all three kingdoms fell to the Sudanese adventurer Rabih al-Zubayr, who was in turn pushed out by the French in 1891. Extending their power, the French in 1910 made Chad a part of French Equatorial Africa. Chad became a separate colony in 1920 and was made an overseas territory in 1946. The country achieved independence in 1960. This was followed by decades of civil war and frequent intervention by France and Libya.

## Recent Developments

The discovery in the Chadian desert of a fossil skull initially dated at some 6–7 million years (far older than any other hominid fossil found to date) and nicknamed "Toumai" excited scientists worldwide. In January 2002, after mediation by Libya, the government of Chad signed a peace agreement with the Movement for Democracy and Justice in Chad, which had been fighting since 1998 in the northern Tibesti region of the country, bordering Libya.

**Internet resources:** <www.chadembassy.org>

# Chile

**Official name:** República de Chile (Republic of Chile). **Form of government:** multiparty republic with two legislative houses (Senate [49, including 11 nonelective seats]; Chamber of Deputies [120]). **Head of state and government:** President Ricardo Lagos Escobar (from 2000). **Capital:** Santiago (legislative bodies meet in Valparaíso). **Official language:** Spanish. **Official religion:** none. **Monetary unit:** 1 peso (Ch$) = 100 centavos; valuation (7 Jul 2003) US$1 = Ch$698.15.

## Demography

**Area:** 292,135 sq mi, 756,626 sq km (includes 205 sq mi [530 sq km] of waters, known as Laguna del Desierto, lost in a border dispute with Argentina, resolved on 21 Oct 1994). **Population** (2002): 15,082,000. **Density** (2002): persons per sq mi 51.7, persons per sq km 19.9. **Urban** (2002): 86.7%. **Sex distribution** (2002): male 49.19%; female 50.81%. **Age breakdown** (2000): under 15, 28.5%;

15–29, 24.2%; 30–44, 22.9%; 45–59, 14.3%; 60–74, 7.5%; 75 and over, 2.6%. **Ethnic composition** (1992): European and mestizo 89.7%; Araucanian (Mapuche) 9.6%; Aymara 0.5%; Rapa Nui Polynesian 0.2%. **Religious affiliation** (1992): Roman Catholic 76.7%; Protestant 13.2%; atheist and nonreligious 5.8%; other 4.3%. **Major cities** (2002): Greater Santiago 4,647,444; Puente Alto 501,042; Concepción 376,043; Viña del Mar 298,828; Antofagasta 298,153. **Location:** southern South America, bordering Peru, Bolivia, Argentina, the South Atlantic Ocean, and the South Pacific Ocean.

## Vital statistics

**Birth rate** per 1,000 population (2000): 17.2 (world avg. 22.5). **Death rate** per 1,000 population (2000): 5.5 (world avg. 9.0). **Natural increase rate** per 1,000 population (2000): 11.7 (world avg. 13.5). **Total fertility rate** (avg. births per childbearing woman; 2000): 2.2. **Life expectancy** at birth (2000): male 72.4 years; female 79.2 years.

## National economy

**Budget** (2001). *Revenue:* Ch$9,537,200,000,000 (income from taxes 76.2%, nontax revenue 23.5%, capital 0.3%). *Expenditures:* Ch$9,932,200,000,000 (pensions 29.5%, wages 19.0%, capital expenditure 15.0%, interest 2.1%). **Population economically active** (1999): total 5,822,700; activity rate of total population 38.6% (participation rates [1995]: ages 15–64, 58.6%; female 32.4%; unemployed [1999] 9.7%). **Production** (metric tons except as noted). *Agriculture, forestry, fishing* (1999): sugar beets 3,100,000, grapes 1,575,000, tomatoes 1,243,000; livestock (number of live animals) 4,134,000 cattle, 4,116,000 sheep, 2,221,000 pigs; roundwood (1998) 31,670,000 cu m; fish catch (1998) 3,265,300. *Mining* (1998): iron 8,277,000; copper 3,843,000; zinc 26,000. *Manufacturing* (value added in Ch$'000,000; 1997): food products 3,810,200; metal and metal products 2,631,900; petroleum and petroleum products 1,100,200. *Energy production (consumption):* electricity (kW-hr; 1999) 38,389,000,000 (31,204,000,000); coal (metric tons; 1997) 1,080,000 (6,153,000); crude petroleum (barrels; 1997) 2,027,000 (63,163,000); petroleum products (metric tons; 1997) 8,151,000 (10,469,000); natural gas (cu m; 1997) 2,017,-000,000 (2,387,000,000). **Gross national product** (2000): US$69,850,000,000 (US$4,590 per capita). **Public debt** (external, outstanding; 2000): US$5,210,000,000. **Household income and expenditure.** Average household size (2002) 3.4; average annual income per household (1994) Ch$5,981,706 at November prices (US$12,552); sources of income (1990): wages and salaries 75.1%, transfer payments 12.0%, other 12.9%; expenditure (1989): food 27.9%, clothing 22.5%, housing 15.2%, transportation 6.4%. **Tourism** (2000): receipts US$827,000,-000; expenditures US$752,000,000.

## Foreign trade

**Imports** (1999): US$15,137,000,000 (intermediate goods 59.5%; capital goods 21.8%; consumer goods 18.7%). *Major import sources:* US 20.8%; Argentina 13.9%; Brazil 6.7%; Japan 4.4%; Germany 4.3%; France 2.9%. **Exports** (1999): US$15,616,000,000 (mining products 44.4%, of which copper 37.7%; industrial products 38.5%; foodstuffs 17.1%). *Major export destinations:* US 19.4%; Japan 14.3%; UK 6.8%; Argentina 4.6%; Brazil 4.3%; Germany 3.5%; Taiwan 3.2%.

## Transport and communications

**Transport.** *Railroads* (1999): route length 8,707 km; passenger-km 605,900,000; metric ton-km cargo 2,329,246,000. *Roads* (1996): total length 79,800 km (paved 14%). *Vehicles* (1999): passenger cars 1,323,800; trucks and buses 687,500. *Air transport* (1999): passenger-km 10,650,500,000; metric ton-km cargo 2,107,000,000; airports (1998) with scheduled flights 23. **Communications,** in total units (units per 1,000 persons). Daily newspaper circulation (1996): 1,410,000 (98); radio receivers (1997): 5,180,000 (354); television receivers (1999): 3,600,000 (240); telephone main lines (2001): 3,703,300 (249); cellular telephone subscribers (2001): 5,271,600 (353); personal computers (2001): 1,300,000 (87.2); Internet users (2001): 3,102,200 (208).

## Education and health

**Educational attainment** (1992). Percentage of population age 25 and over having: no formal schooling 5.7%; primary education 44.2%; secondary 42.2%; higher 7.9%. **Literacy** (1995): total population age 15 and over literate 95.2%; males 95.4%; females 95.0%. **Health** (1999): physicians 17,853 (1 per 841 persons); hospital beds (1998) 41,706 (1 per 355 persons); infant mortality rate per 1,000 live births (2000) 9.6. **Food** (2000): daily per capita caloric intake 2,882 (vegetable products 78%, animal products 22%); 118% of FAO recommended minimum.

## Military

**Total active duty personnel** (2002): 87,500 (army 58.3%, navy 27.4%, air force 14.3%). **Military expenditure as percentage of GNP** (1999): 3.0% (world 2.4%); per capita expenditure US$133.

## Background

Originally inhabited by native peoples, including the Mapuche, the Chilean coast was invaded by the Spanish in 1536. A settlement begun at Santiago in 1541 was governed under the viceroyalty of Peru but became a separate captaincy general in 1778. It revolted against Spanish rule in 1810; its independence was finally assured by the victory of José de San Martín in 1818, and the area was then governed by Bernardo O'Higgins to 1823. In the War of the Pacific against Peru and Bolivia, it won the rich nitrate fields on the coast of Bolivia, effectively forcing that country into a landlocked position. Chile remained neutral in World War I and in World War II but severed diplomatic ties with the Axis in 1943. In 1970 Salvador Allende was elected president, becoming the first avowed Marxist to be elected chief of state in Latin America. Following economic upheaval, he was ousted in 1973 in a coup led by Gen. Augusto

*1 metric ton = about 1.1 short tons; 1 kilometer = 0.6 mi (statute); 1 metric ton-km cargo = about 0.68 short ton-mi cargo; c.i.f.: cost, insurance, and freight; f.o.b.: free on board*

Pinochet, whose military junta for many years harshly suppressed all internal opposition. A national referendum in 1988 rejected Pinochet, and elections held in 1989 returned the country to civilian rule.

## Recent Developments

Ricardo Lagos Escobar won a five-year term as president of Chile after narrowly defeating Joaquín Lavín Infante in the 2000 elections. Lagos was the third consecutive Concertación coalition candidate elected to the post. In July 2002 the Supreme Court reaffirmed that Pinochet was not fit to stand trial for human rights abuses. The Supreme Court also refused to extradite five Chilean military men, as requested by an Argentine judge, to stand trial for the 1974 murder of Chilean Gen. Carlos Prats and his wife in a car bombing in Buenos Aires. Continuing controversy over a secret Air Force death squad forced Air Force head Patricia Rios to resign in October.

Internet resources: <www.visit-chile.org>

# China

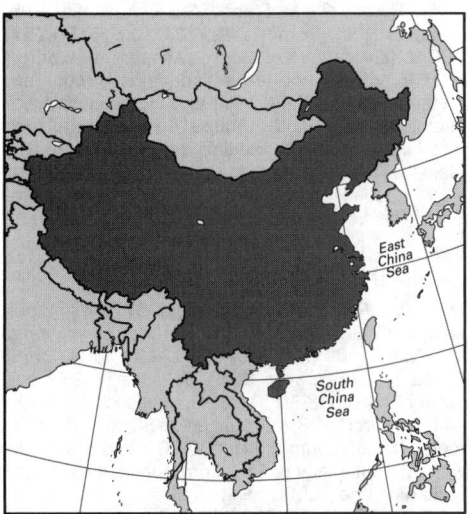

**Official name:** Zhonghua Renmin Gongheguo (People's Republic of China). **Form of government:** single-party people's republic with one legislative house (National People's Congress [2,989]). **Chief of state:** President Hu Jintao (from 15 Mar 2003). **Head of government:** Premier Wen Jiabao (from 16 Mar 2003). **Capital:** Beijing (Peking). **Official language:** Mandarin Chinese. **Official religion:** none. **Monetary unit:** 1 Renminbi (yuan) (Y) = 10 jiao = 100 fen; valuation (7 Jul 2003) $1 = Y 8.28.

## Demography

**Area** (includes 4,600 sq mi [11,900 sq km] not shown separately): 3,696,100 sq mi, 9,572,900 sq km. **Population** (2002): 1,284,211,000. **Density** (2002): persons per sq mi 347.5, persons per sq km 134.2. **Urban** (2002): 33.0%. **Sex distribution** (2000): male 51.63%; female 48.37%. **Age breakdown** (1998): under 15, 24.3%; 15–29, 24.6%; 30–44, 24.8%; 45–59, 15.2%; 60–74, 8.8%; 75 and over, 2.3%. **Ethnic composition** (1990): Han (Chinese)

91.96%; Chuang 1.37%; Manchu 0.87%; Hui 0.76%; Miao 0.65%; Uighur 0.64%; Yi 0.58%; Tuchia 0.50%; Mongolian 0.42%; Tibetan 0.41%; Puyi 0.23%; Tung 0.22%; Yao 0.18%; Korean 0.17%; Pai 0.14%; Hani 0.11%; Kazakh 0.10%; Tai 0.09%; Li 0.09%; other 0.51%. **Religious affiliation** (2000): nonreligious 42.1%; Chinese folk-religionist 28.5%; Buddhist 8.4%; atheist 8.1%; Christian 7.1%; traditional beliefs 4.3%; Muslim 1.5%. **Major cities** (1998): Shanghai 8,937,175; Peking 6,633,929; Tientsin 4,835,327; Wu-han 3,911,824; Shen-yang 3,876,289; Canton 3,306,277; Chungking 3,193,889; Harbin 2,586,978; Nanking 2,388,915; Sian 2,294,790; Ch'eng-tu 2,146,126; Ch'ang-ch'un 2,072,324; Talien (Dalian) 2,000,944; T'ai-yüan 1,768,530; Chi-nan 1,713,036; Ch'ing-tao (Qingdao) 1,702,108; Chengchou 1,465,069; Tzu-po (Zibo) 1,458,060; Lan-chou 1,429,673; K'un-ming 1,350,640; Hang-chou 1,346,148; Ch'ang-sha 1,334,036; Kuei-yang 1,320,566. **Location:** eastern Asia, bordering Mongolia, Russia, North Korea, the Yellow Sea, the East China Sea, the South China Sea, Vietnam, Laos, Myanmar (Burma), Bhutan, Nepal, India, Pakistan, Afghanistan, Tajikistan, Kyrgyzstan, and Kazakhstan. **Households.** Average rural household size (1996) 4.4; urban household size (1998) 3.2. Family households (1990): 277,390,000 (99.4%); collective 1,671,000 (0.6%).

## Vital statistics

**Birth rate** per 1,000 population (2001): 14.9 (world avg. 21.2). **Death rate** per 1,000 population (2001): 7.0 (world avg. 8.9). **Total fertility rate** (avg. births per childbearing woman; 2001): 1.8. **Marriage rate** per 1,000 population (1996): 7.6. **Divorce rate** per 1,000 population (1996): 0.9. **Life expectancy** at birth (2002): male 69.0 years; female 73.0 years.

## Social indicators

**Quality of working life** (1991). Average workweek: 48 hours. Funds for pensions and social welfare relief (1996): Y 181,780,000,000. **Access to services.** Proportion of communes having access to electricity (1979) 87.1%. Percentage of urban population with: safe public water supply (1996) 95.0%. **Social participation.** Trade union membership in total labor force (1996): 14.7%. **Social deviance.** Annual reported arrest rate per 100,000 population (1986) for: property violation 20.7; infringing personal rights 7.2; disruption of social administration 3.3; endangering public security 1.0 (excludes arrests for anti-Communist activities). **Material well-being.** Urban families possessing (number per family; 1996): bicycles 1.9; televisions 1.2; washing machines 0.9; refrigerators 0.7; sewing machines 0.6; cameras 0.3. Rural families possessing (number per family; 1998): bicycles 1.4; televisions 1.3; sewing machines 0.7; washing machines 0.2.

## National economy

**Gross national product** (at current market prices; 2000): $1,062,919,000,000 ($840 per capita). **Budget** (1997). *Revenue:* Y 492,650,000,000 (taxes on goods and services 66.6%; grants 12.3%; income taxes 8.2%; import duties 6.5%; nontax revenue 2.3%). *Expenditures:* Y 601,720,000,000 (defense 13.6%; general public services 7.5%; agriculture 6.0%; industry 2.9%; public order 2.6%; education 2.0%; utilities 1.8%; other economic affair expenditures 5.9%; nonfunctional expenditures 56.3%). **Public debt** (external, outstanding; 2000): $104,709,-000,000. **Tourism** (2000): receipts from visitors $16,224,000,000; expenditures by nationals abroad $13,114,000,000. **Production** (metric tons except as noted). *Agriculture, forestry, fishing* (2000): grains—rice 190,168,000, corn (maize) 105,231,000, wheat 99,370,000, sorghum 2,784,000, barley 3,940,000, millet 2,091,000; oilseeds—soybeans 15,400,000, peanuts (groundnuts) 15,067,000, rapeseed 11,350,000, sunflower seeds 2,100,000; fruits and nuts—watermelons 38,382,000, apples 22,888,000, pears 8,618,000, cantaloupes 6,418,000, oranges 3,508,000; other—sweet potatoes 121,024,000, sugarcane 70,205,000, potatoes 62,036,000, cabbage 20,209,000, tomatoes 19,309,000, sugar beets 7,700,000, cucumbers 17,176,000, seed cotton 13,050,000, onions 12,176,000, eggplants 11,915,-000, garlic 6,466,000, tobacco leaves 2,509,000, tea 721,000; livestock (number of live animals) 437,551,000 pigs, 148,401,000 goats, 131,095,-000 sheep, 104,582,000 cattle, 22,599,000 water buffalo, 9,348,000 asses, 8,916,000 horses, 3,625,000,000 chickens, 611,899,000 ducks; roundwood (1999) 291,330,000 cu m; fish catch (1998) 17,229,957. *Mining and quarrying* (1998): metal concentrates—zinc 1,540,000, copper 1,150,-000, lead 733,000, antimony 80,000, tin 79,000, tungsten 24,000; metal ores—iron ore 210,000,000, bauxite 8,500,000, manganese ore 6,100,000, silver 1,400, gold 178; nonmetals—salt 22,420,000, gypsum 7,900,000, soda ash 7,200,000, barite 3,200,000, fluorspar 2,550,000, magnesite 2,200,-000, talc 2,200,000, asbestos 250,000. *Manufacturing* (1998): cement 536,000,000; rolled steel 105,180,000; chemical fertilizer 30,100,000; sulfuric acid 21,710,000; paper and paperboard 21,260,-000; sugar 8,260,000; cotton yarn 5,420,000; cotton fabrics 24,100,000,000 m; color television sets 34,970,000 units; bicycles 23,125,000 units; household washing machines 12,073,000 units; household refrigerators 10,600,000 units; motor vehicles 1,630,000 units. *Distribution of industrial production* (percentage of total value of output by sector; 1978 [1996]): state-operated enterprises 80.6% (28.5%); collectives 19.2% (39.4%); privately operated enterprises 0.2% (32.1%). Retail sales (percentage of total sales by sector; 1978 [1996]): state-operated enterprises 90.5% (27.3%); collectives 7.4% (18.4%); privately operated enterprises 2.1% (54.3%). *Energy production (consumption):* electricity (kW-hr; 2001) 1,421,262,000,000 ([1997] 1,127,356,000,000); coal (metric tons; 2001) 960,476,000 ([1997] 1,331,589,000); crude petroleum (barrels; 2001) 1,207,000,000 ([1997] 1,281,000,000); petroleum products (metric tons; 1997) 125,698,000 (142,635,000); natural gas (cu m; 2001) 30,252,-000,000 ([1997] 22,449,000,000). **Household income and expenditure** (1996). Average household size (2000) 3.4; rural household 4.4, urban household (1998) 3.2. Average annual income per household Y 13,459; rural household Y 12,406, urban household (1998) Y 17,248. Sources of income: rural household—income from household businesses 79.6%, wages 16.1%, other 4.3%; urban household—wages 80.5%, business income 5.9%, other 13.6%. Expenditure: rural household—food 56.3%, housing 13.9%, cultural activities 8.4%, clothing 7.2%, household ma-

terials 5.4%, health 3.7%, transportation 3.0%; urban household (1998)—food 44.5%, clothing 11.1%, housing 9.4%, household materials 8.2%, education 6.3%, transportation and communications 5.9%, health 4.7%. **Population economically active** (1998): total 699,570,000; activity rate of total population 55.7% (participation rates: over age 15 [1996] 75.9%; female 49.7%; unemployed 3.1%). Urban workforce by sector 1978 (1998): state enterprises 74,500,000 (90,580,000); collectives 20,000,000 (19,630,000); self-employment or privately run enterprises 150,000 (96,570,000). **Land use** (1999): meadows and pastures 42.9%; agricultural and under permanent cultivation 14.5%; forested and other 42.6%.

## Foreign trade

**Imports** (1998-f.o.b.): $140,166,000,000 (machinery and transport equipment 40.5%; products of textile industries, rubber and metal products 22.2%; chemical and related products 14.4%; inedible raw materials 7.6%; mineral fuel and lubricants 4.8%; food and live animals 2.7%). *Major import sources:* Japan 20.1%; US 12.1%; Taiwan 11.9%; South Korea 10.7%; Germany 5.0%; Hong Kong 4.8%; Singapore 3.0%; Russia 2.6%; France 2.3%; Australia 1.9%; Malaysia 1.9%. **Exports** (1998-f.o.b.): $183,757,-000,000 (machinery and transport equipment 27.3%; products of textile industries, rubber and metal products 17.6%; food and live animals 5.8%; chemicals and allied products 5.6%; mineral fuels and lubricants 2.8%; inedible raw materials 1.9%). *Major export destinations:* Hong Kong 21.1%; US 20.7%; Japan 16.2%; Germany 4.0%; South Korea 3.4%; The Netherlands 2.8%; UK 2.5%.

## Transport and communications

**Transport.** *Railroads* (1998): length 57,584 km; passenger-km 369,598,000,000; metric ton-km cargo 1,231,200,000,000. *Roads* (1998): total length 1,278,474 km (paved 93%). *Vehicles* (1998): passenger cars 6,548,300; trucks and buses 6,278,900. *Air transport* (1998): passenger-km 80,024,000,000; metric ton-km cargo 3,345,000,000; airports (1996) with scheduled flights 113. **Communications**, in total units (units per 1,000 persons). Daily newspaper circulation (1994): 27,790,000 (23); radio receivers (1997): 417,000,000 (335); television receivers (1999): 370,000,000 (292); telephone main lines (2001): 179,034,000 (138); cellular telephone subscribers (2001): 144,812,000 (112); personal computers (2001): 25,000,000 (19); Internet users (2001): 33,700,000 (26).

## Education and health

**Educational attainment** (1997). Percentage of population age 15 and over having: no schooling and incomplete primary 20.7%; completed primary 37.6%; some secondary and complete secondary 39.2%; college and postsecondary education 2.5%. **Literacy** (1995): total population age 15 and over literate 81.5%; males literate 89.9%; females literate 72.7%. **Health** (1998): physicians 1,999,500 (1 per 629 persons); hospital beds 2,913,700 (1 per 431 persons); infant mortality rate per 1,000 live births (2002) 37.0. **Food** (1999): daily per capita caloric intake

---

*1 metric ton = about 1.1 short tons;   1 kilometer = 0.6 mi (statute);   1 metric ton-km cargo = about 0.68 short ton-mi cargo;   c.i.f.: cost, insurance, and freight;   f.o.b.: free on board*

3,042 (vegetable products 81%, animal products 19%); (1997) 129% of FAO recommended minimum.

## Military

**Total active duty personnel** (2001): 2,310,000 (army 69.3%, navy 12.5%, air force 18.2%). **Military expenditure as percentage of GNP** (1999): 2.3% (world 2.4%); per capita expenditure $71.

**Did you know?** Eugene Chen, Minister of Foreign Affairs for China in 1927 and secretary to the first president of China was born of African-Chinese parentage in Trinidad, British West Indies. He changed his family named from Akam to Chen when he left Trinidad for Peking, China, in 1912, and soon became a fighter against European imperialism in China.

## Background

The discovery of Peking man (*Homo erectus*) in 1927 dated the advent of early humans in what is now China to the Middle Pleistocene, about 900,000 to 130,000 years ago. Chinese civilization probably spread from the Huang He (Yellow River) valley, where it existed c. 3000 BC. The first dynasty for which there is definite historical material is the Shang (c. 16th century BC), which had a writing system and a calendar. The Zhou, a subject state of the Shang, overthrew its Shang rulers in the 11th century BC and ruled until the 3rd century BC. Taoism and Confucianism were founded in this era.

A time of conflict, called the Warring States Period, lasted from the 5th century BC until in 221 BC the Qin (Ch'in) dynasty (from whose name China is derived) was established after its rulers had conquered rival states and created a unified empire. The Han dynasty was established in 206 BC and ruled until AD 220. A time of turbulence followed, and Chinese reunification was not achieved until the Sui dynasty was established in 581.

After the founding of the Song dynasty in 960, the capital was moved to the south because of northern invasions. In 1279 this dynasty was overthrown and Mongol (Yuan) domination began. During this time, Marco Polo visited Kublai Khan. The Ming dynasty followed the period of Mongol rule and lasted from 1368 to 1644, cultivating antiforeign feelings to the point that China closed itself off from the rest of the world.

Peoples from Manchuria overran China in 1644 and established the Qing (Manchu) dynasty. Ever-increasing incursions by Western and Japanese interests led in the 19th century to the Opium Wars, the Taiping Rebellion, and the Sino-Japanese War, all of which weakened the Manchus.

The dynasty fell in 1911, and a republic was proclaimed in 1912 by Sun Yat-sen. The power struggles of warlords weakened the republic. Under Sun's successor, Chiang Kai-shek, some national unification was achieved in the 1920s, but Chiang soon broke with the Communists, who then formed their own armies. Japan invaded northern China in 1937; its occupation lasted until 1945. The Communists gained support after the Long March (1934–35), in which Mao Zedong emerged as their leader.

Upon Japan's surrender at the end of World War II, a fierce civil war began; in 1949 the Nationalists fled to Taiwan and the Communists proclaimed the People's Republic of China. The Communists undertook extensive reforms, but pragmatic policies alternated with periods of revolutionary upheaval, most notably in the Great Leap Forward and the Cultural Revolution. The chaos of the latter led, after Mao's death in 1976, to a turn to moderation under Deng Xiaoping, who undertook economic reforms and renewed China's ties to the West. The government established diplomatic ties with the US in 1979. It suppressed the Tiananmen Square student demonstration in 1989. The economy has been in transition since the late 1970s, moving from central planning and state-run industries to a mixture of state-owned and private enterprises in manufacturing and services. The death of Deng in 1997 marked the end of a political era, but power passed peacefully to Jiang Zemin. In 1997 Hong Kong reverted to Chinese rule, as did Macao in 1999.

## Recent Developments

The 16th Congress of the Communist Party of China (CPC) was convened in early November 2002. It affirmed the "Three Represents" doctrine, referring to the CPC's stated mission to represent three essential concerns: the development needs of the country, China's advanced culture, and the fundamental interests of the vast majority of the Chinese people. President Jiang ensured that the Congress's proceedings were carefully scripted to focus on his achievements in the 13 years since he became party chief. Vice President Hu Jintao was elected to succeed Jiang. The new Political Bureau consisted of only those younger than 70 years old and was dominated by technocrats—18 of 25 full and alternate members were engineers and 5 of them had received degrees from China's premier scientific and technological institution, Tsinghua University. Jiang maintained his position as the chairman of the CPC Central Military Affairs Commission. The pronouncements issued during the Congress suggested that the party indeed remained committed to a middle-class agenda: maintaining high growth and social stability, encouraging private enterprises, breaking up government monopolies, and respecting private rights. The party was expected to be ever more pro-private business.

In the first six months of 2002, according to one Chinese newspaper, 555 government officials were arrested on corruption charges, including one banking chief suspected of having laundered some $730 million. A new campaign to discredit the outlawed spiritual movement Falun Gong also got under way.

In February 2002, US Pres. George W. Bush traveled to Beijing—his second trip to China within four months. China reciprocated with two heavyweight visits to the US, first by Vice Pres. Hu and then by Jiang. The two countries seemed to find some common ground amid lingering mutual suspicion. Later in 2002 there were signs of a possible settlement between Beijing and the Dalai Lama regarding the latter's relationship with Tibet. Representatives of the exiled leader made a visit to Beijing in September. China was identified as the country of origin of the SARS (severe acute respiratory syndrome) virus in the spring of 2003. The deadly epidemic killed 225 people in China by early May and several more in other countries. The government came under criticism for covering up the seriousness of the problem. At the beginning of June, the sluice gates were closed, and the Three Gorges Dam began filling with water.

**Internet resources:** <www.chinaonline.com>

# Colombia

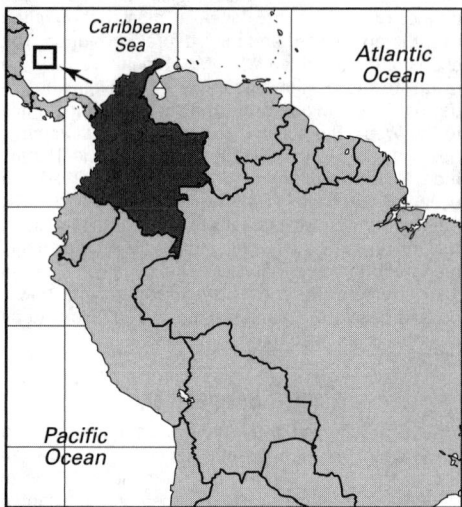

Caribbean Sea

Atlantic Ocean

Pacific Ocean

**Official name:** República de Colombia (Republic of Colombia). **Form of government:** unitary, multiparty republic with two legislative houses (Senate [102]; House of Representatives [163, including two representatives from indigenous communities]). **Head of state and government:** President Álvaro Uribe Vélez (from 7 Aug 2002). **Capital:** Bogotá. **Official language:** Spanish. **Official religion:** none. **Monetary unit:** 1 peso (Col$) = 100 centavos; valuation (7 Jul 2003) US$1 = Col$2,823.

## Demography

**Area:** 440,762 sq mi, 1,141,568 sq km. **Population** (2002): 41,008,000 (excludes at least 2,000,000 Colombians who left the country since 1997 because of violence and high unemployment). **Density** (2002): persons per sq mi 93.0, persons per sq km 35.9. **Urban** (1999): 73.5%. **Sex distribution** (2000): male 49.14%; female 50.86%. **Age breakdown** (2000): under 15, 32.2%; 15–29, 26.6%; 30–44, 22.6%; 45–59, 11.6%; 60–74, 5.6%; 75 and over, 1.4%. **Ethnic composition** (2000): mestizo 47.3%; mulatto 23.0%; white 20.0%; black 6.0%; black-Amerindian 1.0%; Amerindian/other 2.7%. **Religious affiliation** (1995): Roman Catholic 91.9%; other 8.1%. **Major cities** (1999): Bogotá, D.C., 6,276,428; Cali 2,110,571; Medellín 1,957,928; Barranquilla 1,226,292; Bucaramanga 520,874. **Location:** northern South America, bordering the Caribbean Sea, Venezuela, Brazil, Peru, Ecuador, the Pacific Ocean, and Panama.

## Vital statistics

**Birth rate** per 1,000 population (2000): 22.9 (world avg. 22.5). **Death rate** per 1,000 population (2000): 5.7 (world avg. 9.0). **Natural increase rate** per 1,000 population (2000): 17.2 (world avg. 13.5). **Total fertility rate** (avg. births per childbearing woman; 2000): 2.7. **Life expectancy** at birth (2000): male 66.4 years; female 74.3 years.

## National economy

**Budget** (1998). *Revenue:* Col$16,706,000,000,000 (tax revenue 70.8%, nontax revenue 25.6%, transfers 3.6%). *Expenditures:* Col$21,526,000,000,000 (current expenditure 77.0%, of which wages 23.9%; capital expenditure 23.0%). **Public debt** (external, outstanding; 2000): US$20,951,000,000. **Population economically active** (1998): total 6,550,679; activity rate 47.4% (participation rates: ages 15–69, 67.7%; female 45.1%; unemployed 19.7%). **Production** (metric tons except as noted). *Agriculture, forestry, fishing* (1999): sugarcane 36,900,000, plantains 2,789,-000, potatoes 2,705,413; livestock (number of live animals) 25,614,200 cattle, 2,195,600 sheep, 2,764,000 pigs; roundwood (1998) 18,618,000 cu m; fish catch (1998) 167,464. *Mining and quarrying* (1997): iron ore 631,500; salt 560,300; gold 521,800 troy oz. *Manufacturing* (value added in Col$'000,000; 1996): processed food 9,362,300; beverages 2,485,900; textiles 2,107,300. *Energy production (consumption):* electricity (kW-hr; 1997) 46,378,000,000 (46,577,000,000); coal (metric tons; 1997) 32,592,000 (5,069,000); crude petroleum (barrels; 2001) 243,208,000 ([1997] 111,247,-000); petroleum products (metric tons; 1997) 13,092,000 (11,141,000); natural gas (cu m; 1997) 5,681,838,000 (5,681,838,000). **Gross national product** (2000): US$85,279,000,000 (US$2,020 per capita). **Household income and expenditure.** Average household size (1998) 5.3; sources of income (1992): wages 45.1%, self-employment 35.4%, transfer payments 14.2%; expenditure (1992): food 34.2%, transportation 18.5%, housing 7.8%, health care 6.4%, household durable goods 5.7%, clothing 4.5%. **Tourism** (2000): receipts US$1,028,000,000; expenditures US$1,057,000,000.

## Foreign trade

**Imports** (2000-f.o.b.): US$11,538,500,000 (machinery and transport equipment 37.9%, chemicals 23.4%, food and tobacco 6.6%, textiles and leather products 6.5%, vegetable products 6.2%, metals 5.1%, paper and paper products 4.0%). Major import sources (2000): US 33.7%; Venezuela 8.2%; Japan 4.6%; Brazil 4.4%. **Exports** (2001): US$13,037,400,000 (petroleum products 35.0%, chemicals 13.0%, vegetable products 8.7%, coffee 8.2%, textiles and leather products 7.3%, food and tobacco 6.7%, coal 6.1%). Major export destinations (2000): US 50.0%; Venezuela 9.9%; Ecuador 3.5%; Germany 3.2%; Peru 2.8%.

## Transport and communications

**Transport.** *Railroads* (1997): route length 3,230 km; passenger-km 15,524,000 (1992); metric ton-km cargo 736,247,000. *Roads* (1999): total length 112,988 km (paved 14%). *Vehicles* (1999): cars 762,000; trucks 672,000. *Air transport* (2000): passenger-km 7,141,973,000; metric ton-km cargo 1,023,703,000; airports (1998) 43. **Communications,** in total units (units per 1,000 persons). Daily newspaper circulation (1996): 1,800,000 (46); radio receivers (1997): 21,000,000 (524); television receivers (1999): 8,273,000 (199); telephone main lines (2001): 7,300,000 (181); cellular telephone subscribers (2001): 3,160,000 (78); personal com-

---

*1 metric ton = about 1.1 short tons;   1 kilometer = 0.6 mi (statute);   1 metric ton-km cargo = about 0.68 short ton-mi cargo;   c.i.f.: cost, insurance, and freight;   f.o.b.: free on board*

puters (2001): 1,800,000 (45); Internet users (2001): 1,154,000 (29).

## Education and health

**Educational attainment** (1985). Percentage of population age 25 and over having: no schooling 15.3%; primary education 50.1%; secondary 25.4%; higher 6.8%; not stated 2.4%. **Literacy** (1995): population age 15 and over literate 91.3%; males literate 91.2%; females literate 91.4%. **Health**: physicians (1997) 40,355 (1 per 1,102 persons); hospital beds 40,043 (1 per 1,000 persons); infant mortality rate per 1,000 live births (1999) 25.6. **Food** (2000): daily per capita caloric intake 2,597 (vegetable products 84%, animal products 16%); 112% of FAO recommended minimum.

## Military

**Total active duty personnel** (2001): 158,000 (army 86.1%, navy 9.5%, air force 4.4%). **Military expenditure as percentage of GNP** (1999): 3.2% (world 2.4%); per capita expenditure US$68.

## Background

The Spanish arrived in what is now Colombia c. 1500 and by 1538 had defeated the area's Chibchan-speaking Indians and made the area subject to the viceroyalty of Peru. After 1740 authority was transferred to the newly created viceroyalty of New Granada. Parts of Colombia threw off Spanish jurisdiction in 1810, and full independence came after Spain's defeat by Simón Bolívar in 1819. Civil war in 1840 checked development. Conflict between the Liberal and Conservative parties led to the War of a Thousand Days (1899–1903). Years of relative peace followed, but hostility erupted again in 1948; the two parties agreed in 1958 to a scheme for alternating governments. A new constitution was adopted in 1991, but democratic power remained threatened by civil unrest. Many leftist rebels and right-wing paramilitary groups funded their activities through kidnappings and narcotics trafficking.

## Recent Developments

Economic uncertainties and the specter of political violence remained major issues in Colombia at the beginning of the 21st century. In February 2002 presidential candidate Ingrid Betancourt was abducted at a roadblock and held hostage by the Revolutionary Armed Forces of Colombia (FARC), one of the leading guerrilla groups that exercised de facto control over much of the country. The following month the outspoken Roman Catholic archbishop Isaias Duarte Cancino was gunned down outside his church in the city of Cali. In elections in May 2002, Álvaro Uribe Vélez, who campaigned on a strong anticrime platform and vowed to get tough on the guerrillas who have waged war with the government for almost four decades, was convincingly elected president. In May 2003, rebel forces killed Gov. Guillermo Gaviria, a former defense minister, and others whom they held hostage.

**Internet resources:** <www.dane.gov.co>

# Comoros

**Official name:** L'Union des Comores (Union of the Comoros). **Form of government:** transitional govern-

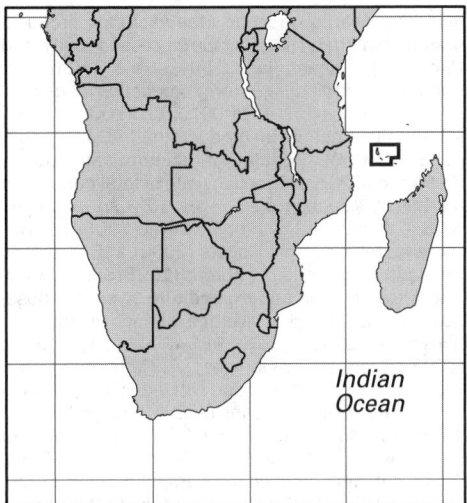

Indian Ocean

ment. **Head of state and government:** President Col. Azali Assoumani (from 26 May 2002). **Capital:** Moroni. **Official languages:** Comorian; Arabic; French. **Official religion:** Islam. **Monetary unit:** 1 Comorian franc (CF) = 100 centimes; valuation (7 Jul 2003) $1 = CF 454.33.

## Demography

**Area:** 719 sq mi, 1,862 sq km. **Population** (2002): 583,000 (includes 165,000 on Mayotte). **Density** (2002): persons per sq mi 810.8, persons per sq km 313.1. **Urban** (1995): 24.1%. **Sex distribution** (2000): male 49.62%; female 50.38%. **Age breakdown** (2000): under 15, 42.7%; 15–29, 28.6%; 30–44, 15.9%; 45–59, 8.1%; 60–74, 3.9%; 75 and over, 0.8%. **Ethnic composition** (2000): Comorian (a mixture of Bantu, Arab, Malay, and Malagasy peoples) 97.1%; Makua 1.6%; French 0.4%; Arab 0.1%; other 0.8%. **Religious affiliation** (2000): Sunni Muslim 98.0%; Christian 1.2%; other 0.8%. **Major cities** (1995): Moroni 34,168 (urban agglomeration [2001] 49,000); Mutsamudu (1991) 20,000; Domoni (1990) 8,000; Fomboni (1990) 5,600. **Location:** western Indian Ocean, lying between Madagascar and Mozambique.

## Vital statistics

**Birth rate** per 1,000 population (2000): 40.0 (world avg. 22.5). **Death rate** per 1,000 population (2000): 9.6 (world avg. 9.0). **Natural increase rate** per 1,000 population (2000) 30.4 (world avg. 13.5). **Total fertility rate** (avg. births per childbearing woman; 2000): 5.4. **Life expectancy** at birth (2000): male 57.8 years; female 62.2 years.

## National economy

**Budget** (1998). *Revenue:* CF 14,066,000,000 (tax revenue 64.0%, grants 29.4%, nontax revenue 6.6%). *Expenditures:* CF 16,307,000,000 (current expenditures 85.4%, development expenditures 14.6%). **Production** (metric tons except as noted). *Agriculture, forestry, fishing* (2000): coconuts 60,000 (includes Mayotte), bananas 60,000 (1998), cassava 45; livestock (number of live animals; 1998) 40,000 goats, 40,000 cattle; fish catch (2000) 13,200. *Mining and quarrying:* sand, gravel, and crushed stone from coral mining for local construction. *Manufacturing*: products of small-scale industries include processed vanilla and ylang-ylang, cement, handicrafts, soaps, soft drinks, woodwork, and clothing. *Energy production (consumption)*: electricity (kW-hr; 2000) 35,200,000 ([1999] 22,000,000); petroleum products (metric tons; 1997) none (22,000). **Population economically active** (1991): total 215,000; activity rate of total population 44.4% (participation rates: ages 10 years and over, 57.8%; female 40.0%; unemployed [2000] 20%). **Tourism:** receipts from visitors (2000) $15,000,000; expenditures by nationals abroad (1998) $3,000,000. **Household income and expenditure.** Average household size (1995) 6.3; average annual income per household (1995) CF 188,985 ($505); expenditure (1993): food and beverages 67.3%, clothing and footwear 11.6%, tobacco and cigarettes 4.1%, energy 3.8%. **Land use** (1994; includes Mayotte): forested 17.9%; meadows and pastures 6.7%; agricultural and under permanent cultivation 44.9%; other 30.5%. **Gross national product** (at current market prices; 2000): $212,000,000 ($380 per capita). **Public debt** (external, outstanding; 2000): $201,900,000.

## Foreign trade

**Imports** (20000-c.i.f.): CF 23,085,000,000 (petroleum products 20.0%, rice 12.3%, vehicles 10.8%, meat and fish 7.4%, cement 5.6%). *Major import sources:* France 36.6%; Pakistan 13.7%; Kenya 10.8%; South Africa 9.0%; Belgium-Luxembourg 3.8%. **Exports** (2000-f.o.b.): CF 6,259,000,000 (vanilla 49.5%, cloves 32.1%, ylang-ylang 14.2%). *Major export destinations:* France 38.6%; US 19.9%; Germany 6.6%.

## Transport and communications

**Transport.** *Roads* (1996): total length 900 km (paved [1995] 76%). *Vehicles* (1996): passenger cars 9,100; trucks and buses 4,950. *Air transport* (1996): passenger-km 3,000,000; airports (1997) with scheduled flights 2. **Communications,** in total units (units per 1,000 persons). Radio receivers (1997): 90,000 (170); television receivers (1997): 1,000 (1.8); telephone main lines (2001): 8,900 (12); personal computers (2001): 4,000 (5.5); Internet users (2001): 2,500 (3.4).

## Education and health

**Educational attainment** (1980). Percentage of population age 25 and over having: no formal schooling 56.7%; Quranic school education 8.3%; primary 3.6%; secondary 2.0%; higher 0.2%; not specified 29.2%. **Literacy** (1995): total population age 15 and over literate 192,000 (57.0%); males literate 108,000 (64.0%); females literate 84,000 (50.0%). **Health** (1995): physicians 64 (1 per 7,800 persons); hospital beds 1,450 (1 per 342 persons); infant mortality rate per 1,000 live births (2000) 86.3. **Food** (1997): daily per capita caloric intake 1,800 (vegetable products 94%, animal products 6%); 77% of FAO recommended minimum.

## Military

**Total active duty personnel** (1997): 1,500.

## Background

The Comoros islands were known to European navigators from the 16th century. In 1843 France officially took possession of Mayotte and in 1886 placed the other three islands under protection. Subordinated to Madagascar in 1912, the Comoros became an overseas territory of France in 1947. In 1961 they were granted autonomy. In 1974 majorities on three of the islands voted for independence, which was granted in 1975. The following decade saw several coup attempts, culminating in the assassination of the president in 1989. French intervention permitted multiparty elections in 1990, but the country remained in a state of chronic instability. Anjouan seceded from the Comoros federation in 1997. The army took control of the government in 1999. A referendum at the end of 2001 renamed the country the Union of the Comoros and granted the three main islands partially autonomous status.

## Recent Developments

Following the adoption of Comoros' new constitution, violence and protests attended the round of elections for union officials and the presidents and parliaments of the three islands. The new political structure was threatened in June 2002 when a struggle erupted between Union Pres. Azali Assoumani and Grande Comore Pres. Abdou Soule Elbak on how power should be shared. A coup attempt against Assoumani in February 2003 failed.

**Internet resources:**
<http://travel.state.gov/comoros>

# Democratic Republic of the Congo

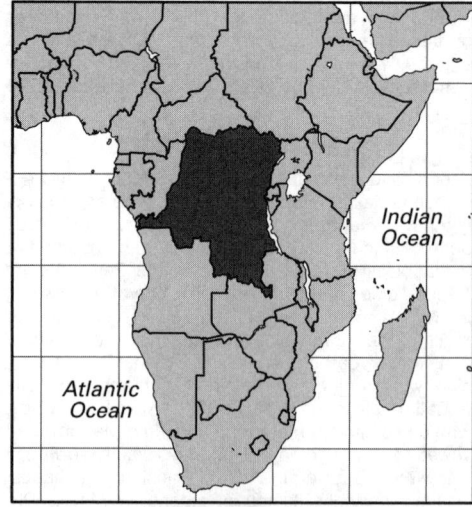

**Official name:** République Democratique du Congo (Democratic Republic of the Congo). **Form of government:** transitional military regime (civil war began in the Dem. Rep. of the Congo in 1998; peace talks were under way from Feb 2002). **Chief of state:** President Joseph Kabila (from 2001). **Capitals:** Kinshasa

*1 metric ton = about 1.1 short tons;    1 kilometer = 0.6 mi (statute);    1 metric ton-km cargo = about 0.68 short ton-mi cargo;    c.i.f.: cost, insurance, and freight;    f.o.b.: free on board*

(executive and judicial); Lubumbashi (legislative). **Official languages:** French; English. **Official religion:** none. **Monetary unit:** Congolese franc (FC); valuation (7 Jul 2003) $1 = FC 421.50.

## Demography

**Area:** 905,354 sq mi, 2,344,858 sq km. **Population** (2002): 52,557,000 (2002 population estimate adjusted for about 2.5 million war deaths between August 1998 and May 2001). **Density** (2002): persons per sq mi 58.1, persons per sq km 22.4. **Urban** (2001): 30.6%. **Sex distribution** (2000): male 49.40%; female 50.60%. **Age breakdown** (2000): under 15, 48.3%; 15–29, 26.9%; 30–44, 13.8%; 45–59, 7.0%; 60–74, 3.3%; 75 and over, 0.7%. **Ethnic composition** (1983): Luba 18.0%; Kongo 16.1%; Mongo 13.5%; Rwanda 10.3%; Azande 6.1%; Bangi and Ngale 5.8%; Rundi 3.8%; Teke 2.7%; Boa 2.3%; Chokwe 1.8%; Lugbara 1.6%; Banda 1.4%; other 16.6%. **Religious affiliation** (1995): Roman Catholic 41.0%; Protestant 32.0%; indigenous Christian 13.4%, of which Kimbanguist 13.0%; other Christian 0.8%; Muslim 1.4%; traditional beliefs and other 11.4%. **Major cities** (1994): Kinshasa 4,655,313; Lubumbashi 851,381; Mbuji-Mayi 806,475; Kolwezi 417,800; Kisangani 417,517. **Location:** central Africa, bordering the Central African Republic, The Sudan, Uganda, Rwanda, Burundi, Tanzania, Zambia, Angola, the South Atlantic Ocean, and the Republic of the Congo.

## Vital statistics

**Birth rate** per 1,000 population (2000): 46.4 (world avg. 22.5). **Death rate** per 1,000 population (2000): 15.4 (world avg. 9.0). **Natural increase rate** per 1,000 population (2000): 31.0 (world avg. 13.5). **Total fertility rate** (avg. births per childbearing woman; 2000): 6.9. **Life expectancy** at birth (2000): male 47.6 years; female 50.8 years.

## National economy

**Budget** (1999). *Revenue:* FC 2,328,600,000 (tax revenue 76.9%, of which taxes on international trade 18.5%, taxes on goods and services 13.8%, income tax 12.6%; nontax revenue 12.8%). *Expenditures:* FC 4,113,800,000; wages and salaries 50.5%; defense 14.6%; investment 13.5%; interest on debt 7.2%). **Public debt** (external, outstanding; 2000): $7,842,000,000. **Tourism** (1997): receipts $9,000,000; expenditures $7,000,000. **Production** (metric tons except as noted). *Agriculture, forestry, fishing* (2000): cassava 15,959,000, plantains 1,800,000, sugarcane 1,669,000; livestock (number of live animals) 4,131,321 goats, 1,048,710 pigs, 822,355 cattle; roundwood (2000) 50,754,000 cu m; fish catch (1999) 208,862. *Mining and quarrying* (1999): copper (metal content) 29,600; cobalt (metal content) 1,600; zinc (metal content) 1,300. *Manufacturing* (1999): iron and steel 965,000; cement 172,900; sugar 73,400. *Energy production (consumption):* electricity (kW-hr; 1999) 5,087,000,000 (5,087,000,000); coal (metric tons; 1997) 95,000 (141,000); crude petroleum (barrels; 1997) 8,425,000 (520,000); petroleum products (metric tons; 1997) 49,000 (469,000); natural gas, none (none). **Household expenditure.** Average household size (1998) 2.3; expenditure (1985): food 61.7%, housing and energy 11.5%,

clothing and footwear 9.7%, transportation 5.9%, furniture and utensils 4.9%. **Gross national product** (2000): $4,417,000,000 ($85 per capita). **Population economically active** (1997): total 19,618,000; activity rate 42.0% (participation rates [1987]: over age 10, 57.4%; female 43.5%). **Land use** (1994): forested 76.7%; meadows and pastures 6.6%; agricultural and under permanent cultivation 3.5%; other 13.2%.

## Foreign trade

**Imports** (1999): $1,108,000,000 (non-oil 95.0%; oil 5.0%). *Major import sources* (1999): South Africa 22.0%; Belgium 15.8%; Nigeria 10.0%; Zambia 5.3%; France 4.6%; US 3.2%; China 3.2%; Germany 2.7%; The Netherlands 2.5%. **Exports** (1999): $933,000,000 (diamonds 61.3%, crude petroleum 12.4%, coffee 9.8%, cobalt 8.6%, copper 5.1%). *Major export destinations* (1999): Belgium-Luxembourg 63.8%; US 19.0%; Finland 4.1%; Italy 3.0%.

## Transport and communications

**Transport.** *Railroads* (1996): length 5,138 km; passenger-km 29,000,000; metric ton-km cargo 176,000,000. *Roads* (1996): total length 154,027 km (paved 2%). *Vehicles* (1996): passenger cars 787,000; trucks and buses 60,000. *Air transport* (1996): passenger-km 279,000,000; metric ton-km cargo 42,000,000; airports (1997) with scheduled flights 22. **Communications,** in total units (units per 1,000 persons). Daily newspaper circulation (1996): 124,000 (2.7); radio receivers (1997): 18,030,000 (376.0); television receivers (1997): 6,478,000 (135.0); telephone main lines (2001): 20,000 (0.4); cellular telephone subscribers (2001): 150,000 (2.9); Internet users (2001): 6,000 (n.a.).

## Education and health

**Literacy** (1999): percentage of total population age 15 and over literate 60.3%; (1995) males literate 86.6%; females literate 67.7%. **Health:** physicians (1990) 2,469 (1 per 15,584 persons); hospital beds (1986) 68,508 (1 per 487 persons); infant mortality rate per 1,000 live births (2000) 101.6. **Food** (2000): daily per capita caloric intake 1,514 (vegetable products 97%, animal products 3%); 68% of FAO recommended minimum.

## Military

**Total active duty personnel** (2001): 81,400 (army 97.1%, navy 1.1%, air force 1.8%); national opposition forces (2001): 41,000; foreign forces were leaving DRC in September 2002. **Military expenditure as percentage of GNP** (1997): 14.4% (world 2.4%); per capita expenditure $102.

## Background

Prior to European colonization, several native kingdoms had emerged in the Congo region, including the 16th-century Luba kingdom and the Kuba federation, which reached its peak in the 18th century. European development began late in the 19th century when King Léopold II of Belgium financed Henry Morton Stanley's exploration of the Congo River. The 1884–85 Berlin West Africa Conference recognized the Congo Free State with Léopold as its sovereign.

The growing demand for rubber helped finance the exploitation of the Congo, but abuses against native peoples outraged Western nations and forced Léopold to grant the Free State a colonial charter as the Belgian Congo (1908). Independence was granted in 1960, and the country's name was changed to Zaire. The post-independence period was marked by unrest, culminating in a military coup that brought Gen. Mobutu Sese Seko to power in 1965. Mismanagement, corruption, and increasing violence devastated the infrastructure and economy. Mobutu was deposed in 1997 by Laurent Kabila, who restored the country's name to Congo. Regional instability and desire for Congo's mineral wealth led to military involvement by numerous African countries. Kabila was assassinated in 2001 and succeeded by his son.

## Recent Developments

A comprehensive peace settlement of the war that had raged in the Congo for three years seemed possible when agreement was reached in Sun City, South Africa, on 2 Apr 2003 to form a transitional government headed by Pres. Joseph Kabila, two vice presidents from the main rebel groups, one from the political opposition, and one from Kabila's government. Fighting continued nonetheless into the summer.

**Internet resources:** <www.un.int/drcongo>

# Republic of the Congo

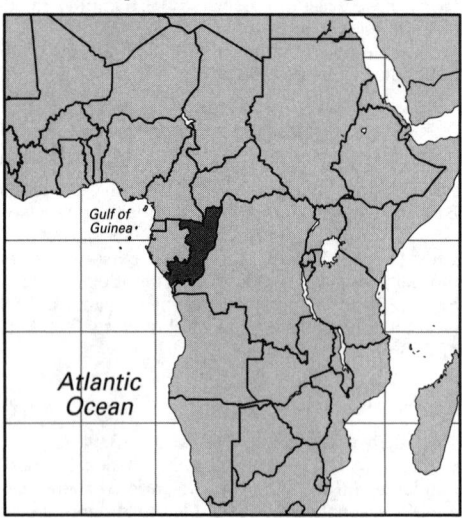

**Official name:** République du Congo (Republic of the Congo). **Form of government:** republic (new constitution effective from 10 Aug 2002) with two legislative houses (Senate [66]; National Assembly [137]). **Chief of state and government:** President Denis Sassou-Nguesso (from 1997). **Capital:** Brazzaville. **Official language:** French (Lingala and Monokutuba are national languages). **Official religion:** none. **Monetary unit:** 1 CFA franc (CFAF) = 100 centimes; valuation (7 Jul 2003) $1 = CFAF 571.07 (formerly pegged to the

French franc and since 1 Jan 2002, to the euro at the rate of €1 = CFAF 655.96).

## Demography

**Area:** 132,047 sq mi, 342,000 sq km. **Population** (2002): 2,899,000. **Density** (2002): persons per sq mi 22.0, persons per sq km 8.5. **Urban** (2001): 66.1%. **Sex distribution** (2000): male 49.17%; female 50.83%. **Age breakdown** (2000): under 15, 42.5%; 15–29, 28.7%; 30–44, 16.1%; 45–59, 7.7%; 60–74, 4.1%; 75 and over, 0.9%. **Ethnic composition** (1983): Kongo 51.5%; Teke 17.3%; Mboshi 11.5%; Mbete 4.9%; Punu 3.0%; Sango 2.7%; Maka 1.8%; Pygmy 1.5%; other 5.8%. **Religious affiliation** (2000): Roman Catholic 49.3%; Protestant 17.0%; African Christians 12.6%; unaffiliated Christians 11.9%; traditional beliefs 4.8%; other 4.4%. **Major cities** (1992): Brazzaville 937,579; Pointe-Noire 576,206; Loubomo 83,605; Nkayi 42,465; Mossendjo 16,405. **Location:** west-central Africa, bordering Cameroon, the Central African Republic, the Dem. Rep. of the Congo, Angola, the South Atlantic Ocean, and Gabon.

## Vital statistics

**Birth rate** per 1,000 population (2000): 38.6 (world avg. 22.5). **Death rate** per 1,000 population (2000): 16.4 (world avg. 9.0). **Natural increase rate** per 1,000 population (2000): 22.2 (world avg. 13.5). **Total fertility rate** (avg. births per childbearing woman; 2000): 5.1. **Life expectancy** at birth (2000): male 44.5 years; female 50.5 years.

## National economy

**Budget** (1999). *Revenue:* CFAF 390,600,000,000 (petroleum revenue 70.6%; nonpetroleum receipts 27.8%; grants 1.6%). *Expenditures:* CFAF 475,400,-000,000 (current expenditure 81.3%, of which debt service 35.4%, salaries 21.2%, transfers and subsidies 5.5%; capital expenditure 18.7%). **Public debt** (external, outstanding; 2001): $3,758,000,000. **Household income and expenditure.** Average household size (1984) 5.2. **Gross national product** (at current market prices; 2000): $1,735,000,000 ($570 per capita). **Production** (metric tons except as noted). *Agriculture, forestry, fishing* (2000): cassava 790,-000, sugarcane 450,000, oil palm fruit 90,000; livestock (number of live animals) 285,000 goats, 116,000 sheep, 77,000 cattle; roundwood (2000) 3,243,000 cu m; fish catch (1999) 43,886. *Mining and quarrying* (1998): gold 10 kg. *Manufacturing* (1998): residual fuel oil 240,000; cement 110,000; distillate fuel oils 85,000. *Energy production (consumption):* electricity (kW-hr; 1998) 408,000,000 (535,000,000); crude petroleum (barrels; 1996) 77,837,000 (11,882,000); petroleum products (metric tons; 1996) 534,000 (507,000); natural gas (cu m; 1996) 3,357,000 (3,357,000). **Population economically active** (1997): total 1,110,000; activity rate of total population 42.0% (participation rates [1984]: ages 15–64, 54.0%; female [1997] 43.4%; unemployed [1984] 2.3%). **Land use** (1994): forested 58.3%; meadows and pastures 29.3%; agricultural and under permanent cultivation 0.5%; other 11.9%. **Tourism** (1999): receipts $12,000,000; expenditures $60,000,000.

*1 metric ton = about 1.1 short tons;   1 kilometer = 0.6 mi (statute);   1 metric ton-km cargo = about 0.68 short ton-mi cargo;   c.i.f.: cost, insurance, and freight;   f.o.b.: free on board*

## Foreign trade

**Imports** (1999): CFAF 378,100,000,000 (machinery and transport equipment 20.8%, basic manufactures 20.1%, food and live animals 20.0%, chemicals and chemical products 14.2%, mineral fuels 12.1%). *Major import sources:* France 23.2%; US 7.8%; Italy 7.8%; Hong Kong 4.9%; Belgium 3.8%; UK 3.1%; The Netherlands 2.9%. **Exports** (1999): CFAF 1,022,200,-000,000 (petroleum and petroleum products 91.9%, wood and wood products 4.3%, other 3.8%). *Major export destinations:* Taiwan 31.5%; US 22.8%; South Korea 15.3%; Germany 6.7%; France 2.6%; Italy 2.3%.

## Transport and communications

**Transport.** *Railroads:* (1998) length 894 km; passenger-km 242,000,000; metric ton-km cargo 135,000,000. *Roads* (1997): total length 12,800 km (paved 10%). *Vehicles* (1997): passenger cars 37,240; trucks and buses 15,500. *Air transport* (1998; includes about 10% of the traffic of Air Afrique, which is operated by 11 West African states): passenger-km 258,272,000; metric ton-km cargo 13,524,000; airports (1998) with scheduled flights 10. **Communications**, in total units (units per 1,000 persons). Daily newspaper circulation (1995): 20,000 (7.8); radio receivers (1997): 341,000 (126); television receivers (1997): 33,000 (12); telephone main lines (2001): 22,000 (7.1); cellular telephone subscribers (2001): 150,000 (48); Internet users (1999): 500 (0.18).

## Education and health

**Educational attainment** (1984). Percentage of population age 25 and over having: no formal schooling 58.7%; primary education 21.4%; secondary education 16.9%; postsecondary 3.0%. **Literacy** (1995): total population age 15 and over literate 80.7%; males literate 87.5%; females literate 74.4%. **Health:** physicians (1995) 632 (1 per 4,083 persons); hospital beds (1989) 4,817 (1 per 446 persons); infant mortality rate per 1,000 live births (2000) 101.6. **Food** (1999): daily per capita caloric intake 2,212 (vegetable products 94%, animal products 6%); 100% of FAO recommended minimum.

## Military

**Total active duty personnel** (2001): 10,000 (army 80.0%, navy 8.0%, air force 12.0%). **Military expenditure as percentage of GNP** (1999): 3.5% (world 2.4%); per capita expenditure $21.

**Did you know?**  One of Africa's least-explored regions, the northern part of the Rep. of the Congo, an area of huge swamps and nearly impenetrable forests, was traversed by foot in 1999. Dr. Michael Fay, an ecologist with the Wildlife Conservation Society, and a team of 12 others undertook a 1,900-km (1,200-mi) survey of this area as well as similar areas in neighboring Gabon. The team concluded that this wilderness is seriously threatened.

## Background

In precolonial days the Congo area was home to several thriving kingdoms, including the Kongo, which had its beginnings in the 1st millennium AD. The slave trade began in the 15th century with the arrival of the Portuguese; it supported the local kingdoms and dominated the area until its suppression in the 19th century. The French arrived in the mid-19th century and established treaties with two of the kingdoms, placing them under French protection prior to their becoming part of the colony of French Congo. In 1910 the French possessions were renamed French Equatorial Africa, and Congo became known as Middle (Moyen) Congo. In 1946 Middle Congo became a French overseas territory and in 1958 voted to become an autonomous republic within the French Community. Full independence came two years later. The area has suffered from political instability since independence. Congo's first president was ousted in 1963. A Marxist party, the Congolese Labor Party, gained strength, and in 1968 another coup, led by Maj. Marien Ngouabi, created the People's Republic of the Congo. Ngouabi was assassinated in 1977. A series of military rulers followed, at first militantly socialist but later oriented toward social democracy. Fighting between local militias that began in 1997 badly disrupted the economy.

## Recent Developments

An outbreak of the disease caused by the Ebola virus had killed more than 100 persons in the Congo by March 2003 as well as two-thirds of the gorillas in the Lossi Park wildlife reserve. An agreement signed in March by the government and the "Ninja" rebel group promised to bring stability to the Pool region, which surrounds Brazzaville.

**Internet resources:** <www.cia.gov/cia/publications/factbook/geos/cf.html>

# Costa Rica

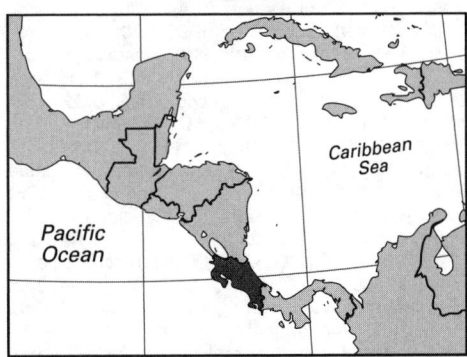

Caribbean Sea

Pacific Ocean

**Official name:** República de Costa Rica (Republic of Costa Rica). **Form of government:** unitary multiparty republic with one legislative house (Legislative Assembly [57]). **Head of state and government:** President Abel Pacheco de la Espriella (from 8 May 2002). **Capital:** San José. **Official language:** Spanish. **Official religion:** Roman Catholicism. **Monetary unit:** 1 Costa Rican colón (¢) = 100 céntimos; valuation (7 Jul 2003) $1 = ¢399.15.

## Demography

**Area:** 19,730 sq mi, 51,100 sq km. **Population** (2002): 3,960,000. **Density** (2002): persons per sq mi 200.7, persons per sq km 77.5. **Urban** (2000):

59.0%. **Sex distribution** (2000): male 49.94%; female 50.06%. **Age breakdown** (2000): under 15, 31.9%; 15–29, 27.1%; 30–44, 21.7%; 45–59, 11.4%; 60–74, 5.7%; 75 and over, 2.2%. **Ethnic composition** (2000): white 77.0%; mestizo 17.0%; black/mulatto 3.0%; East Asian (mostly Chinese) 2.0%; Amerindian 1.0%. **Religious affiliation** (1995): Roman Catholic 86.0%; Protestant 9.3%, of which Pentecostal 4.9%; other Christian 2.4%; other 2.3%. **Major cities** (2000): San José canton 309,672 (urban agglomeration 983,000); Limón district 60,298; Alajuela district 42,889; San Isidro de El General district 41,221; Cartago 39,958 (pop. of three districts). **Location:** Central America, bordering Nicaragua, the Caribbean Sea, Panama, and the North Pacific Ocean.

## Vital statistics

**Birth rate** per 1,000 population (2001): 19.7 (world avg. 21.2); (1999) legitimate 51.0%; illegitimate 49.0%. **Death rate** per 1,000 population (2001): 4.0 (world avg. 8.9). **Natural increase rate** per 1,000 population (2001): 15.7 (world avg. 12.3). **Total fertility rate** (avg. births per childbearing woman; 1999): 2.6. **Marriage rate** per 1,000 population (1999): 7.3. **Divorce rate** per 1,000 population (1995): 1.4. **Life expectancy** at birth (1999): male 74.2 years; female 79.9 years.

## National economy

**Budget** (1998). *Revenue:* ¢459,700,000,000 (general sales tax 38.3%, selective taxes on goods and services 21.6%, income and profit taxes 19.3%, import duties 11.0%). *Expenditures:* ¢562,300,000,000 (current expenditures 91.3%, development expenditures 8.7%). **Public debt** (external, outstanding; 2000): $3,274,000,000. **Gross national product** (2000): $14,510,000,000 ($3,810 per capita). **Production** (metric tons except as noted). *Agriculture, forestry, fishing* (1999): sugarcane 3,950,000, bananas 2,101,000, oil palm fruit 440,000; livestock (number of live animals) 1,617,000 cattle, 290,000 pigs, 17,000,000 chickens; roundwood (1998) 5,311,000 cu m; fish catch (1997) 33,613, of which shrimp 5,717. *Mining and quarrying* (1997): limestone 1,500,000; gold 17,700 troy oz. *Manufacturing* (value added in ¢'000,000; 1996): food products 90,498; beverages 43,101; fertilizers and pesticides 18,360. *Energy production (consumption):* electricity (kW-hr; 1997) 5,589,000,000 (5,714,000,000); crude petroleum (barrels; 1997) none (4,955,000); petroleum products (metric tons; 1997) 625,000 (1,462,000). **Population economically active** (1998): total 1,376,540; activity rate of total population 41.2% (participation rates: ages 12–59, 59.3%; female 32.6%; unemployed [1999] 6.0%). **Tourism** (2000): receipts $1,229,000,000; expenditures $482,000,000. **Household income and expenditure.** Average household size (2000) 4.1; average annual household income (1997) ¢1,468,597 ($6,314); sources of income (1987–88): wages and salaries 61.0%, self-employment 22.6%, transfers 9.6%; expenditure (1987–88): food and beverages 39.1%, housing and energy 12.1%, transportation 11.6%, household furnishings 10.9%. **Land use** (1994): forested 30.8%; meadows and pastures 45.8%; agricultural and under permanent cultivation 10.4%; other 13.0%.

## Foreign trade

**Imports** (2000-c.i.f.): $6,380,000,000 (general merchandise 68%; goods for reassembly 32%). *Major import sources:* US 33.5%; Mexico 8.4%; Venezuela 7.2%; Japan 4.5%; Guatemala 3.1%. **Exports** (2000-f.o.b.): $5,820,000,000 (reexports 57.1%; domestic exports 42.9%, of which bananas 9.4%, processed food and tobacco products 5.9%, coffee 4.7%, tropical fruit 3.4%). *Major export destinations:* US 33.9%; Nicaragua 6.9%; Guatemala 6.8%; Germany 5.3%; El Salvador 4.8%.

## Transport and communications

**Transport.** *Roads* (1999): total length 35,876 km (paved 17%). *Vehicles* (1999): passenger cars 326,524; trucks and buses 181,272. *Air transport* (1999; Lacsa (Costa Rican Airlines) only): passenger-km 2,112,000,000; metric ton-km cargo 84,697,000; airports (1996) 14. **Communications,** in total units (units per 1,000 persons). Daily newspaper circulation (1996): 320,000 (94); radio receivers (1997): 980,000 (283); television receivers (1999): 900,000 (242); telephone main lines (2001): 945,000 (230); cellular telephone subscribers (2001): 311,300 (78); personal computers (2001): 700,000 (170); Internet users (2001): 384,000 (93).

## Education and health

**Educational attainment** (1996). Percentage of population age 5 and over having: no formal schooling 11.7%; incomplete primary education 28.5%; complete primary 25.8%; incomplete secondary 16.0%; complete secondary 9.0%; higher 8.5%; other/unknown 0.5%. **Literacy** (1995): total population age 15 and over literate 2,118,000 (94.8%); males literate 1,054,000 (94.7%); females literate 1,064,000 (95.0%). **Health** (1997): physicians 5,500 (1 per 630 persons); hospital beds 5,953 (1 per 582 persons); infant mortality rate per 1,000 live births (2001) 10.8. **Food** (1999): daily per capita caloric intake 2,761 (vegetable products 82%, animal products 18%); 123% of FAO recommended minimum.

## Military

**Paramilitary expenditure as percentage of GNP** (1999): 0.5% (world 2.4%); per capita expenditure $19. The army was officially abolished in 1948. Paramilitary (police) forces had 8,400 members in 2001.

## Background

Christopher Columbus landed in Costa Rica in 1502 in an area inhabited by a number of small, independent Indian tribes. These peoples were not easily dominated, and it took almost 60 years for the Spanish to establish a permanent settlement. Ignored by the Spanish crown because of its lack of mineral wealth, the colony grew slowly. Coffee exports and the construction of a rail line improved its economy in the 19th century. It joined the short-lived Mexican empire in 1821, was a member of the United Provinces of Central America 1823–38, and adopted a constitution in 1871. In 1890 Costa Ricans held what is considered to be the first free and honest election in Cen-

---

*1 metric ton = about 1.1 short tons;   1 kilometer = 0.6 mi (statute);   1 metric ton-km cargo = about 0.68 short ton-mi cargo;   c.i.f.: cost, insurance, and freight;   f.o.b.: free on board*

tral America, beginning a tradition of democracy for which Costa Rica is renowned. In 1987 then president Oscar Arias Sánchez was awarded the Nobel Peace Prize. During the 1990s Costa Rica struggled with its economic policies. It suffered severe damage from a hurricane in 1996.

## Recent Developments

Abel Pacheco of Costa Rica's ruling Social Christian Unity Party continued his party's grip on the presidency by defeating Rolando Araya of the opposition National Liberation Party in a runoff election held in April 2002. Pacheco's victory broke a long tradition of alternation in power between the country's two leading parties. His administration was expected to focus on reversing a sharp decline in economic growth and taming a 10% inflation rate that ranked among the highest in Latin America.

Internet resources: <www.casapres.go.cr>

# Côte d'Ivoire

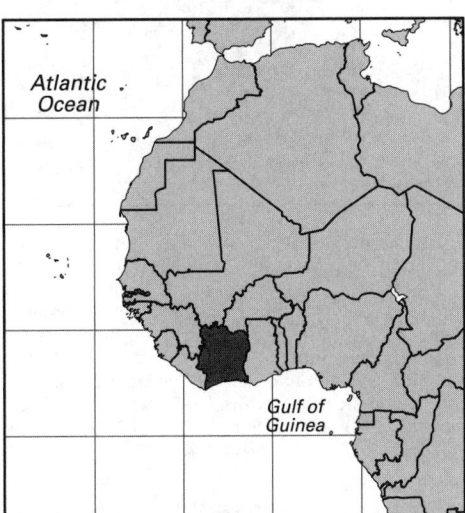

Atlantic Ocean

Gulf of Guinea

**Official name:** République de Côte d'Ivoire (Republic of Côte d'Ivoire). **Form of government:** republic with one legislative house (National Assembly [225, including unoccupied seats]); constitutional referendum approved Jul 2000, but status of new constitution unclear in 2003. **Chief of state and government:** President Laurent Gbagbo (from 2000) assisted by a prime minister. **Capital:** Abidjan (de facto; legislative). **Capital designate:** Yamoussoukro (de jure; administrative). **Official language:** French. **Official religion:** none. **Monetary unit:** 1 CFA franc (CFAF) = 100 centimes; valuation (7 Jul 2003) $1 = CFAF 571.07 (formerly pegged to the French franc and since 1 Jan 2002, to the euro at the rate of €1 = CFAF 655.96).

## Demography

**Area:** 124,504 sq mi, 322,463 sq km. **Population** (2002): 16,805,000 (local population only; foreigners constitute 26% of the population and 2/3 of all foreigners are from Burkina Faso). **Density** (2002): persons per sq mi 135.7, persons per sq km 52.4. **Urban** (2002): 44.0%. **Sex distribution** (2001): male 50.79%; female 49.21%. **Age breakdown** (2001): under 15, 46.2%; 15–29, 28.2%; 30–44, 14.2%; 45–59, 7.6%; 60–74, 3.0%; 75 and over, 0.8%. **Ethnolinguistic composition** (1998): Akan 42.1%; Mande 26.5%; other 31.4%. **Religious affiliation** (1998): Muslim 38.6%; Christian 30.4%; nonreligious 16.7%; animist 11.9%; other 2.4%. **Major cities** (1995): Abidjan (1999) 3,199,000; Bouaké 330,000; Daloa 123,000; Yamoussoukro 110,000. **Location:** western Africa, bordering Mali, Burkina Faso, Ghana, the Atlantic Ocean, Liberia, and Guinea.

## Vital statistics

**Birth rate** per 1,000 population (2001): 40.4 (world avg. 21.2). **Death rate** per 1,000 population (2001): 16.6 (world avg. 8.9). **Natural increase rate** per 1,000 population (2001): 23.8 (world avg. 12.3). **Total fertility rate** (avg. births per childbearing woman; 2001): 5.7. **Life expectancy** at birth (2001): male 43.6 years; female 46.3 years.

## National economy

**Budget** (2000). *Revenue:* CFAF 1,237,100,000,000 (tax revenue 87.1%, of which import taxes and duties 29.2%, export taxes 13.2%, taxes on profits 11.6%, income tax 10.2%; nontax revenue 12.9%). *Expenditures:* CFAF 1,358,200,000,000 (wages and salaries 33.0%, debt service 22.7%; capital expenditure 15.4%; transfers 13.1%; other 15.8%). **Production** (metric tons except as noted). *Agriculture, forestry, fishing* (2001): yams 3,000,000, cassava 1,900,000, plantains 1,500,000; livestock (number of live animals) 1,451,000 sheep, 1,409,000 cattle, 1,134,000 goats; roundwood (2001) 11,968,000 cu m; fish catch (1999) 77,000. *Mining and quarrying* (1999): gold 2,706 kg; diamonds (1994) 84,300 carats. *Manufacturing* (value added in CFAF '000,000,000; 1997): food 156.6, of which cocoa and chocolate 72.4, vegetable oils 62.7; chemicals 60.2; wood products 55.9. *Energy production (consumption):* electricity (kW-hr; 1997) 2,760,000,000 (2,760,000,000); crude petroleum (barrels; 1997) 9,267,000 (31,376,000); petroleum products (metric tons; 1997) 2,197,000 (2,165,000). **Household income and expenditure.** Average household size (1998) 8.0; expenditure (1992–93): food 48.0%, transportation 12.2%, clothing 10.1%, energy and water 8.5%, housing 7.8%, household equipment 3.4%. **Population economically active** (2000): total 6,531,000; activity rate of total population 40.9% (participation rates: [1994] over ages 10, 64.3%; female 33.0%; unemployed [1996] 38.8%). **Gross national product** (2000): $9,591,000,000 ($600 per capita). **Public debt** (external, outstanding; 2000): $9,063,000,000. **Tourism** (2000): receipts $57,000,000; expenditures $226,000,000.

## Foreign trade

**Imports** (1999): CFAF 1,739,500,000,000 (machinery and transport equipment 20.8%, food and food products 19.8%, crude and refined petroleum 18.9%, iron and steel products 4.5%, plastics 4.1%, pharmaceuticals 4.0%). *Major import sources* (1999): France 25.9%; Italy 5.6%; US 5.2%; Germany 4.3%; Japan 4.3%; Spain 3.5%. **Exports** (1999): CFAF 2,572,100,000,000 (cocoa beans and products 30.2%, crude petroleum and petroleum products 12.5%, fish products 6.2%, wood and wood products

6.1%, coffee beans 3.7%, cotton and cotton cloth 2.3%). *Major export destinations:* France 14.4%; The Netherlands 13.4%; US 8.5%; Brazil 7.7%; Mali 4.7%; Italy 4.3%; Burkina Faso 4.3%; Spain 3.7%; Germany 3.2%.

## Transport and communications

**Transport.** *Railroads* (1998): route length 655 km; passenger-km 118,800,000; metric ton-km cargo 529,800,000. *Roads* (1999): total length 50,400 km (paved 9.7%). *Vehicles* (1996): passenger cars 293,000; trucks and buses 163,000. *Air transport* (1998): passenger-km 318,000,000; metric ton-km cargo 44,000,000; airports (1999) 5. **Communications,** in total units (units per 1,000 persons). Daily newspaper circulation (1996): 231,000 (17); radio receivers (1998): 1,600,000 (97); television receivers (1998): 1,000,000 (65); telephone main lines (2001): 293,600 (18); cellular telephone subscribers (2001): 728,500 (45); personal computers (2001): 100,000 (6.1); Internet users (2001): 70,000 (4.3).

## Education and health

**Educational attainment** (1988). Percentage of population age 6 and over having: no formal schooling 60.0%; Qur'anic school 3.6%; primary education 24.8%; secondary 10.7%; higher 0.9%. **Literacy** (1999): total population age 15 and over literate 45.7%; males 53.8%; females 37.2%. **Health:** physicians (1996) 1,318 (1 per 11,111 persons); hospital beds (1993) 7,928 (1 per 1,698 persons); infant mortality rate per 1,000 live births (2001) 93.7. **Food** (2000): daily per capita caloric intake 2,590 (vegetable products 96%, animal products 4%); 112% of FAO recommended minimum.

## Military

**Total active duty personnel** (2001): 13,900 (army 81.0%, navy 10.7%, air force 8.3%; excludes 680 French troops.). **Military expenditure as percentage of GNP** (1999): 0.8% (world avg. 2.4%); per capita expenditure $5.

## Background

Europeans came to the area to trade in ivory and slaves beginning in the 15th century, and local kingdoms gave way to French influence in the 19th century. The French colony of Côte d'Ivoire was founded in 1893, and full occupation took place 1908–18. In 1946 it became a territory in the French Union. Côte d'Ivoire achieved independence in 1960, when Félix Houphouët-Boigny was elected president. The country's first multiparty presidential elections were held in 1990.

## Recent Developments

Former president Gen. Robert Gueï led a coup attempt in September 2002 but was killed by loyalist troops. The population was polarized, and fighting began. Rebel groups in the west of the country attacked French troops in early January 2003, after Pres. Laurent Gbagbo and leaders of northern rebel groups agreed to begin talks on 15 January. In Paris the parties agreed to form a government of national reconciliation that gave rebel leaders the key ministries of interior and defense. A former prime minister, Seydou Diarra, was tapped for this post again, and it was hoped that these measures would appease the opposition groups. Riots broke out immediately, however, against what was seen as a French-imposed giveaway of power. Negotiations on composition of the government continued. In July the rebels suddenly agreed to accept Gbagbo, and the war was declared finished.

**Internet resources:** <www.tourisme.ci>

# Croatia

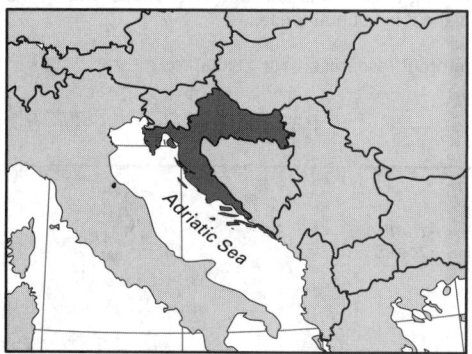

**Official name:** Republika Hrvatska (Republic of Croatia). **Form of government:** multiparty republic with one legislative house (House of Representatives [151—six seats represent Croatians living abroad]). **Head of state:** President Stipe Mesic (from 2000). **Head of government:** Prime Minister Ivica Racan (from 2000). **Capital:** Zagreb. **Official language:** Croatian (Serbo-Croatian). **Official religion:** none. **Monetary unit:** 1 kuna (HrK; plural kune) = 100 lipa; valuation (7 Jul 2003) $1 = HrK 6.54.

## Demography

**Area:** 56,542 sq km. **Population** (2002): 4,405,000. **Density** (2002): persons per sq mi 201.8, persons per sq km 77.9. **Urban** (2000): 57.7%. **Sex distribution** (2000): male 48.58%; female 51.42%. **Age breakdown** (2000): under 15, 18.0%; 15–29, 20.1%; 30–44, 21.6%; 45–59, 19.6%; 60–74, 15.4%; 75 and over, 5.3%. **Ethnic composition** (2000): Croat 82.0%; Serb 5.9%; other 12.1%. **Religious affiliation** (2000): Christian 95.2%, of which Roman Catholic 88.5%, Eastern Orthodox 5.6%, Protestant 0.6%; Sunni Muslim 2.3%; nonreligious/atheist 2.5%. **Major cities** (2001): Zagreb 682,598; Split 173,692; Rijeka 147,709; Osijek 91,046; Zadar 69,239. **Location:** southeastern Europe, bordering Slovenia, Hungary, Serbia and Montenegro, Bosnia and Herzegovina, and the Adriatic Sea.

## Vital statistics

**Birth rate** per 1,000 population (2001): 12.8 (world avg. 21.2); (1999) legitimate 91.8%; illegitimate

---

*1 metric ton = about 1.1 short tons;    1 kilometer = 0.6 mi (statute);    1 metric ton-km cargo = about 0.68 short ton-mi cargo;    c.i.f.: cost, insurance, and freight;    f.o.b.: free on board*

8.2%. **Death rate** per 1,000 population (2001): 11.4 (world avg. 8.9). **Natural increase rate** per 1,000 population (2001): 1.4 (world avg. 12.3). **Total fertility rate** (avg. births per childbearing woman; 2000): 1.4. **Marriage rate** per 1,000 population (1999): 5.2. **Divorce rate** per 1,000 population (1999): 0.8. **Life expectancy** at birth (2001): male 70.8 years; female 77.7 years.

## National economy

**Budget** (2000). *Revenue:* HrK 66,734,998,000 (sales tax 32.9%; extra budgetary social services 31.5%; excise taxes 11.3%; income tax 6.1%). *Expenditures:* HrK 74,432,276,000 (extra budgetary social services 50.7%, of which pensions 27.1%, health 18.7%; education 8.8%; defense 7.4%; public order 7.0%). **Population economically active** (2000): total 1,698,829; activity rate 38.8% (participation rates: ages 15–64, 51.1%; female 46.0%; unemployed (2000) 21.1%). **Production** (metric tons except as noted). *Agriculture, forestry, fishing* (2001): corn (maize) 2,005,900, sugar beets 1,040,000, potatoes 663,600; livestock (number of live animals) 1,234,000 pigs, 529,000 sheep, poultry 11,256,000; roundwood (1998) 3,398,000 cu m; fish catch (1999) 25,519. *Mining and quarrying* (2000): gypsum 100,000; ferrochromium 16,000. *Manufacturing* (value added in $'000,000; 1996): food products 895; transport equipment 425; electrical machinery 362. *Energy production (consumption)*: electricity (kW-hr; 2000) 10,293,000,000 ([1997] 13,633,-000,000,000); hard coal (metric tons; 1999) 50,839 ([1997] 286,000); lignite (metric tons; 1997) none (133,000); crude petroleum (barrels; 1999) 9,475,000 ([1997] 37,471,000); petroleum products (metric tons; 1997) 4,629,000 (3,540,000); natural gas (cu m; 2000) 1,768,000,000 ([1997] 2,679,000,000). **Gross national product** (2000): $20,240,000,000 ($4,620 per capita). **Public debt** (external, outstanding; 2000): $7,686,000,000. **Household income and expenditure.** Average household size (1999) 3.0; income per household HrK 53,534 ($8,200); sources: wages 47.7%, self-employment 19.6%, pension 19.6%, other 13.1%; expenditure (1999): food 37.9%, housing and energy 13.3%, transportation 11.0%, clothing 7.4%, household furnishings 5.9%, recreation and culture 5.7%, drink and tobacco 4.9%, health care 1.8%, education 0.7%, other 11.4%. **Tourism** (2000): receipts from visitors $2,758,000,000; expenditures by nationals abroad $1,257,000,000. **Land use** (1994): forest 37.1%; pasture 19.3%; agriculture 21.6%; other 22.0%.

## Foreign trade

**Imports** (2000-c.i.f.): $7,923,000,000 (machinery and transport equipment 32.9%; manufactured goods 29.4%; mineral fuels 14.4%; chemicals and chemical products 12.7%; food and live animals 7.0%; crude materials except fuels 2.4%). *Major import sources:* Italy 17.0%; Germany 16.3%; Russia 8.5%; Slovenia 7.9%; Austria 6.7%; France 4.3%. **Exports** (2000-f.o.b.): $4,432,000,000 (machinery and transport equipment 27.0%; manufactured goods 20.0%; chemical and chemical products 12.5%; mineral fuels and lubricants 11.0%; food 6.2%; crude materials except fuels 5.7%). *Major export destinations:* Italy 22.3%; Germany 14.3%; Bosnia and Herzegovina 11.2%; Slovenia 10.8%; Austria 6.6%.

## Transport and communications

**Transport.** *Railroads* (2000): length 2,726 km; passenger-km 996,000,000; metric ton-km cargo 1,928,000,000. *Roads* (2000): total length 28,123 km (paved 82%). *Vehicles* (2000): passenger cars 1,124,825; trucks and buses 113,134. *Merchant marine* (1999): cargo ships 260. *Air transport* (2000): passenger-km 763,000,000; metric ton-km cargo 3,219,000; airports (2000) 4. **Communications,** in total units (units per 1,000 persons). Daily newspaper circulation (1996): 515,000 (118); radio receivers (1999): 1,110,000 (261); television receivers (1999): 1,083,000 (254); telephone main lines (2001): 1,646,000 (365); cellular telephone subscribers (2001): 1,755,000 (377); personal computers (2001): 400,000 (86); Internet users (2001): 250,000 (56).

## Education and health

**Educational attainment** (1991). Percentage of population age 15 and over having: no schooling or unknown 10.1%; less than full primary education 21.2%; primary 23.4%; secondary 36.0%; postsecondary and higher 9.3%. **Literacy** (1995): total population age 15 and over literate 98.3%; males 99.4%; females 97.3%. **Health** (1999): physicians 8,046 (1 per 529 persons); hospital beds 27,000 (1 per 158 persons); infant mortality rate per 1,000 live births (2001) 7.2. **Food** (2000): daily per capita caloric intake 2,489 (vegetable products 79%, animal products 21%); 98% of FAO recommended minimum.

## Military

**Total active duty personnel** (2001): 58,300 (army 87.0%, navy 5.1%, air force and air defense 7.9%). **Military expenditure as percentage of GNP** (1999): 6.4% (world 2.4%); per capita expenditure $491.

**Did you know?** Split, a popular tourist destination on Croatia's Adriatic seacoast, is home to the ruins of the Roman city of Spalato ("little palace"), so-called because it was here that the Roman emperor Diocletian (AD 284-305) constructed his palace.

## Background

The Croats, a southern Slavic people, arrived in the area in the 7th century AD and in the 8th century came under Charlemagne. They converted to Christianity soon afterward and formed a kingdom in the 10th century. Most of Croatia was taken by the Turks in 1526; the rest voted to accept Austrian rule. In 1867 it became part of Austria-Hungary, with Dalmatia and Istria ruled by Vienna and Croatia-Slavonia a Hungarian crown land. In 1918, after the defeat of Austria-Hungary in World War I, it joined other south Slav territories to form the Kingdom of Serbs, Croats, and Slovenes, renamed Yugoslavia in 1929. In World War II, an independent state of Croatia was established by Germany and Italy, embracing Croatia-Slavonia, part of Dalmatia, and Bosnia and Herzegovina; after the war Croatia was rejoined to Yugoslavia as a people's republic. It declared its independence in 1991, sparking insurrections by Croatian Serbs, who carved out autonomous regions with

Serbian-led Yugoslav army help; Croatia had taken back most of these regions by 1995. With some stability returning, Croatia's economy began to revive in the late 1990s.

## Recent Developments

In 2002 Croatia continued to see its political landscape fragment and the broad-based ruling coalition split further amid slow economic recovery. Disagreements with its neighbors demonstrated that the country had not yet completely extricated itself from the aftermath of the breakup of Yugoslavia. Croatia squabbled with Slovenia over custodianship of the Krsko nuclear power plant as well as fishing rights and territorial boundaries in the Bay of Piran. Border disputes persisted with Bosnia and Herzegovina and Serbia and Montenegro. In February 2003 Croatia formally applied to join the European Union.

**Internet resources:** <www.mint.hr>

# Cuba

**Official name:** República de Cuba (Republic of Cuba). **Form of government:** unitary socialist republic with one legislative house (National Assembly of the People's Power [601]). **Head of state and government:** President Fidel Castro (from 1976). **Capital:** Havana. **Official language:** Spanish. **Official religion:** none. **Monetary unit:** 1 Cuban peso (CUP) = 100 centavos; valuation (7 Jul 2003) $1 = 21.00 CUP.

## Demography

**Area:** 42,804 sq mi, 110,861 sq km. **Population** (2002): 11,267,000. **Density** (2002): persons per sq mi 263.2, persons per sq km 101.6. **Urban** (2001): 75.5%. **Sex distribution** (2000): male 50.00%; female 50.00%. **Age breakdown** (2000): under 15, 21.4%; 15–29, 22.7%; 30–44, 26.2%; 45–59, 16.1%; 60–74, 9.2%; 75 and over, 4.4%. **Ethnic composition** (1994): mixed 51.0%; white 37.0%; black 11.0%; other 1.0%. **Religious affiliation** (1995): Roman Catholic 39.5%; Protestant 2.4%; other Christian 0.2%; other (mostly Santería) 57.9%. **Major cities** (1999): Havana 2,189,716; Santiago de Cuba 441,524; Camagüey 306,049; Holguín 259,300; Santa Clara 210,100. **Location:** island southeast of

Florida, US, between the North Atlantic Ocean and the Caribbean Sea.

## Vital statistics

**Birth rate** per 1,000 population (2000): 12.7 (world avg. 22.5). **Death rate** per 1,000 population (2000): 7.3 (world avg. 9.0). **Natural increase rate** per 1,000 population (2000): 5.4 (world avg. 13.5). **Total fertility rate** (avg. births per childbearing woman; 2000): 1.6. **Marriage rate** per 1,000 population (1999): 5.1. **Divorce rate** per 1,000 population (1993): 6.0. **Life expectancy** at birth (2000): male 73.8 years; female 78.3 years.

## National economy

**Budget** (1999). *Revenue*: CUP 13,575,000,000. *Expenditures*: CUP 14,270,000,000 (education and health 26.5%; investment 11.9%; other 61.6%). **Public debt** (external, outstanding; 1999): $11,078,-000,000. **Production** (metric tons except as noted). *Agriculture, forestry, fishing* (2000): sugarcane 36,000,000, oranges and tangerines 447,000, rice 368,770; livestock (number of live animals) 4,700,000 cattle, 2,800,000 pigs, 15,000,000 chickens; roundwood (2000) 1,593,000 cu m; fish catch (1999) 122,425. *Mining and quarrying* (2000): nickel (metal content) 68,305; cobalt (metal content) 3,096. *Manufacturing* (value added in $'000,000; 1990): tobacco products 2,629; food products 1,033; beverages 358. *Energy production (consumption)*: electricity (kW-hr; 1997) 14,087,000,000 (14,087,000,000); coal (metric tons; 1997) none (42,000); crude petroleum (barrels; 2000) 17,380,-000 ([1997] 20,772,000); petroleum products (metric tons; 1997) 2,284,000 (7,262,000); natural gas (cu m; 1997) 21,987,966 (21,987,966). **Household income and expenditure.** Average household size (1999) 3.6; average annual income per household (1982) CUP 3,680 ($4,330); sources of income (1982): wages and salaries 57.3%, bonuses and other payments 42.7%; personal consumption (1989): food 26.7%, other retail purchases 60.5%, transportation services 5.4%, energy 2.7%, value of self-produced and consumed food 1.5%, household repairs 1.3%, other 1.9%. **Population economically active** (1988): total 4,570,236; activity rate of total population 43.7% (participation rates: over age 15, 56.9%; female [1998] 37.0%; unemployed [2000–01] 4.1%). **Gross domestic product** (1999): $18,600,000,000 ($1,700 per capita). **Tourism:** receipts from visitors (2000) $1,756,000,000; expenditures by nationals abroad (1990) $48,000,000. **Land use** (1994): forested 23.7%; meadows and pastures 27.0%; agricultural and under permanent cultivation 30.7%; other 18.6%.

## Foreign trade

**Imports** (1999-c.i.f.): $3,200,000,000 (1996; mineral fuels and lubricants 27.9%, food and live animals 19.8%, machinery and transport equipment 16.1%, basic manufactures 14.9%, chemicals 8.7%, inedible crude materials 2.8%). *Major import sources* (1999): Spain 19.5%; France 8.2%; Canada 8.1%; China 7.7%; Italy 7.0%; Russia 3.8%. **Exports** (1999-f.o.b.): $1,400,000,000 (1996; sugar 52.8%, miner-

---

*1 metric ton = about 1.1 short tons;   1 kilometer = 0.6 mi (statute);   1 metric ton-km cargo = about 0.68 short ton-mi cargo;   c.i.f.: cost, insurance, and freight;   f.o.b.: free on board*

als and concentrates 23.7%, fish products 6.8%, raw tobacco and tobacco products 5.9%, citrus and other agricultural products 2.1%). *Major export destinations* (1999): Russia 23.3%; Canada 14.5%; The Netherlands 12.9%; Spain 8.0%; China 3.6%.

## Transport and communications

**Transport.** *Railroads* (1999): length 4,807 km; (1997) passenger-km 1,962,200; metric ton-km cargo 1,074,800,000. *Roads* (1997): total length 60,858 km (paved 49%). *Vehicles* (1998): passenger cars 172,574; trucks and buses 185,495. *Air transport* (1997): passenger-km 3,543,176,000; metric ton-km cargo 56,239,000; airports with scheduled flights (1999) 14. **Communications,** in total units (units per 1,000 persons). Daily newspaper circulation (1996): 1,300,000 (118); radio receivers (1997): 3,900,000 (352); television receivers (1999): 2,750,000 (246); telephone main lines (2001): 573,000 (51); cellular telephone subscribers (2001): 8,100 (0.7); personal computers (2001): 220,000 (20); Internet users (2001): 120,000 (11).

## Education and health

**Educational attainment** (1981). Percentage of population age 25 and over having: no formal schooling or some primary education 39.6%; completed primary 26.6%; secondary 29.6%; higher 4.2%. **Literacy** (1995): total population age 15 and over literate 95.7%; males 96.2%; females 95.3%. **Health** (1998): physicians 63,554 (1 per 175 persons); hospital beds 80,684 (1 per 123 persons); infant mortality rate per 1,000 live births (2000) 7.5. **Food** (2000): daily per capita caloric intake 2,564 (vegetable products 86%, animal products 14%); 111% of FAO recommended minimum.

## Military

**Total active duty personnel** (2001): 46,000 (army 76.1%, navy 6.5%, air force 17.4%). Military expenditure as percentage of GDP (1999): 1.9% (world 2.4%); per capita expenditure: $57.

## Background

Several Indian groups, including the Ciboney, the Taino, and the Arawak, inhabited Cuba at the time of the first Spanish contact. Christopher Columbus claimed the island for Spain in 1492, and the Spanish conquest began in 1511, when the settlement of Baracoa was founded. The native Indians were eradicated over the succeeding centuries, and African slaves, from the 18th century until slavery was abolished in 1886, were imported to work the sugar plantations. Cuba revolted unsuccessfully against Spain in the Ten Years' War (1868–78); a second war of independence began in 1895. In 1898 the US entered the war; Spain relinquished its claim to Cuba, which was occupied by the US for three years before gaining its independence in 1902. The US invested heavily in the Cuban sugar industry in the first half of the 20th century, and this, combined with tourism and gambling, caused the economy to prosper. Inequalities in the distribution of wealth persisted, however, as did political corruption. In 1958–59 the communist revolutionary Fidel Castro overthrew Cuba's longtime dictator, Fulgencio Batista, and established a socialist state aligned with the Soviet Union, abolishing capitalism and nationalizing foreign-owned enterprises. Relations with the US deteriorated, reaching a low point with the 1961 Bay of Pigs invasion and the 1962 Cuban missile crisis. In 1980 about 125,000 Cubans, including many that their government officially labeled "undesirables," were shipped to the US in the so-called Mariel Boat Lift. When communism collapsed in the USSR, Cuba lost important financial backing and its economy suffered greatly. The latter gradually improved in the 1990s with the encouragement of tourism, though diplomatic relations with the US were not resumed.

## Recent Developments

In 2002 Cuba's constitution was amended to declare the socialist revolution irreversible, despite increasing evidence of new and serious challenges to the Cuban system. In May the George W. Bush administration accused Cuba of having the capacity to develop an offensive bioweapons program; in September the State Department further implied that Cuba was intentionally trying to obstruct the American "war on terrorism." Meanwhile, quiet cooperation continued in areas such as counternarcotics operations, migration, and security regarding several hundred alleged al-Qaeda operatives captured in Afghanistan and transferred to the US naval base at Guantánamo Bay. Former US president Jimmy Carter led a delegation to Cuba in May for the purpose of fostering an exchange of ideas between the two countries. In a new clampdown in early 2003, veteran opposition leader Hector Palacios was sent to prison for 25 years. Countries of the European Union critical of Cuba's human rights record were targeted by protestors in Havana in June.

**Internet resources:** <www.cubatravel.cu>

# Cyprus

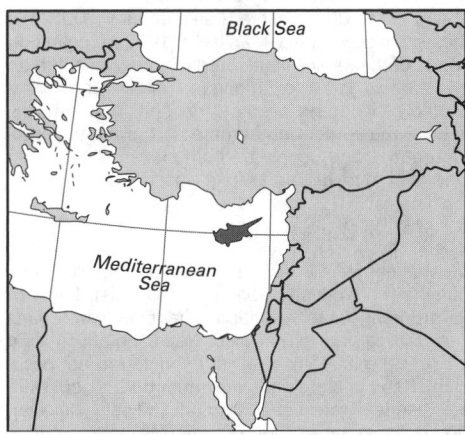

Two de facto states currently exist on the island of Cyprus: the Republic of Cyprus (ROC), predominantly Greek in character, occupying the southern two-thirds of the island, which is the original and still the internationally recognized de jure government of the whole island; and the Turkish Republic of Northern Cyprus (TRNC), proclaimed unilaterally 15 Nov 1983, on territory originally secured for the Turkish Cypriot population by the 20 Jul 1974 intervention of Turkey. Only Turkey recognizes the TRNC. The two ethnic communities have failed to reestablish a single state. Provision of separate data below does not imply recognition of either state's claims, but unified data is not collected for the whole island.

**Area:** 3,572 sq mi, 9,251 sq km. **Population** (2002): 907,000 (includes 75,000 "settlers" from Turkey and 31,000 Turkish military in the TRNC; excludes 3,200 British troops in the Sovereign Base Areas (SBA) in the ROC and 1,300 UN peacekeeping forces). **Location:** Middle East, island in the Mediterranean Sea, south of Turkey.

## Background

Cyprus was inhabited by the early Neolithic Age; by the late Bronze Age it had been visited and settled by Mycenaeans and Achaeans, who introduced Greek culture and language, and it became a trading center. By 800 BC Phoenicians had begun to settle there. Ruled over the centuries by the Assyrian, Persian, and Ptolemaic empires, it was annexed by Rome in 58 BC. It was part of the Byzantine empire in the 4th–12th centuries AD. Cyprus was conquered by Richard I in 1191. A part of the Venetian empire from 1489, it was taken by Ottoman Turks in 1571. In 1878 the British assumed control, and Cyprus became a British crown colony in 1925. It gained independence in 1960. Conflict between Greek and Turkish Cypriots led to the establishment of a UN peacekeeping mission in 1964. In 1974, fearing a movement to unite Cyprus with Greece, Turkish soldiers occupied the northern third of the country and Turkish Cypriots established a functioning government, which obtained recognition only from Turkey. Conflict has continued to the present, and the UN peacekeeping mission has remained in place. Reunification talks remained deadlocked.

## Recent Developments

A unification proposal by UN Secretary-General Kofi Annan led to UN-sponsored talks in early 2003, but these collapsed in mid-March. On 16 April, acting on behalf of the whole island, Greek Cyprus accepted an invitation to join the European Union. Then, unexpectedly, eight days later the Turkish Cypriot officials opened the border between the northern and southern entities and people on both sides of the Green Line flocked to visit areas long closed to them.

## Republic of Cyprus

**Official name:** Kipriakí Dhimokratía (Greek); Kibris Cumhuriyeti (Turkish) (Republic of Cyprus). **Form of government:** unitary multiparty republic with a unicameral legislature (House of Representatives [80]; 24 seats reserved for Turkish Cypriots are not occupied). **Head of state and government:** President Glafcos Clerides (from 1993). **Capital:** Lefkosía (Nicosia). **Official languages:** Greek; Turkish. **Monetary unit:** 1 Cyprus pound (£C) = 100 cents; valuation (7 Jul 2003) 1 £C = $0.51.

## Demography

**Area** (includes 99 sq mi [256 sq km] of British military SBA and c. 107 sq mi [c. 278 sq km] of the

UN Buffer Zone): 2,276 sq mi, 5,896 sq km. **Population** (2002): 692,000. **Urban** (2001): 68.7%. **Age breakdown** (1999): under 15, 23.8%; 15–29, 21.5%; 30–44, 22.3%; 45–59, 17.2%; 60–74, 10.6%; 75 and over, 4.6%. **Ethnic composition** (2000): Greek Cypriot 91.8%; Armenian 3.3%; Arab 2.9%, of which Lebanese 2.5%; British 1.4%; other 0.6%. **Religious affiliation** (1995): Greek Orthodox 93.4%; Armenian Apostolic 2.9%; Roman Catholic 1.5%; Muslim 1.0%; other 1.2%. **Urban areas** (2001): Lefkosía 198,697; Limassol 156,458; Larnaca 70,147.

## Vital statistics

**Birth rate** per 1,000 population (2000): 12.4 (world avg. 22.5). **Death rate** per 1,000 population (2000): 7.9 (world avg. 9.0). **Natural increase rate** per 1,000 population (2000): 4.5 (world avg. 13.5). **Life expectancy** at birth (1998–99): male 75.3 years; female 80.1 years.

## National economy

**Budget** (1998). *Revenue:* £C 1,473,900,000 (income taxes 19.7%, value-added taxes 15.3%, social security contributions 14.9%). *Expenditures:* £C 1,731,500,000 (current expenditures 89.7%, development expenditures 10.3%). **Tourism** (2000): receipts $1,894,000,000; expenditures $285,000,000. *Household expenditure* (1994): food and beverages 23.0%, transportation and communications 14.5%, expenditures in cafés and hotels 14.5%. **Gross national product** (at current market prices; 2000): $9,361,000,000 ($12,370 per capita). **Production.** *Agriculture* (in '000 metric tons; 2000): potatoes 117.0, grapes 108.0, cereals 48.0, oranges 42.7, grapefruit 28.1, olives 21.0. *Manufacturing* (value added in £C '000,000; 1999): food 102.7; cement, bricks, and tiles 47.1; tobacco products 46.3. *Energy production:* electricity (kW-hr; 2001) 3,552,000,000.

## Foreign trade

**Imports** (1998-c.i.f.): £C 1,904,700,000 (consumer goods 34.2%; transport equipment 12.9%; capital goods 11.2%; mineral fuels 6.6%). *Major import sources:* US 12.5%; UK 11.3%; Italy 9.4%; Germany 8.5%; Greece 8.2%. **Exports** (1998-f.o.b.): £C 551,134,000 (reexports 55.6%; domestic exports 38.7%, of which clothing 5.3%, chemicals 5.2%; ships' stores 5.7%). *Major export destinations:* UK 14.6%; Russia 10.3%; Greece 9.8%; Lebanon 5.5%; United Arab Emirates 4.9%.

## Transport and communications

**Transport.** *Roads* (1999): total length 11,009 km (paved 58%). *Vehicles* (1999): cars 256,989; trucks and buses 113,802. *Air transport* (2001; Cyprus Airways): passenger-km 3,017,000,000; metric ton-km cargo 39,981,000; airports (1996) 2. **Communications,** in total units (units per 1,000 persons). Daily newspaper circulation (1996): 84,000 (111); radio receivers (1997): 310,000 (406); television receivers (1999): 120,000 (180); telephone main lines (2001): 435,000 (642); cellular telephone sub-

---

*1 metric ton = about 1.1 short tons;    1 kilometer = 0.6 mi (statute);    1 metric ton-km cargo = about 0.68 short ton-mi cargo;    c.i.f.: cost, insurance, and freight;    f.o.b.: free on board*

scribers (2001): 314,400 (464); personal computers (2001): 170,000 (251); Internet users (2001): 150,000 (222).

## Education and health

**Educational attainment** (1997). Percentage of population age 20 and over having: no formal schooling 4%; higher education 17%. **Health** (2000): physicians 1,824 (1 per 372 persons); hospital beds 3,147 (1 per 216 persons); infant mortality rate per 1,000 live births (2000) 5.6.

## Turkish Republic of Northern Cyprus

**Official name:** Kuzey Kibris Türk Cumhuriyeti (Turkish) (Turkish Republic of Northern Cyprus). **Head of state:** Rauf Denktash (from 1975). **Capital:** Lefkosa (Nicosia). **Official language:** Turkish. **Monetary unit:** 1 Turkish lira (LT) = 100 kurush; valuation (7 Jul 2003) $1 = LT 1,393,500. **Population** (2002): 215,000 (includes 75,000 "settlers" from Turkey and 36,000 Turkish military in the TRNC); (1996 census) Lefkosa 36,834; Gazimagusa 23,295. **Ethnic composition** (1996): Turkish Cypriot/Turkish 96.4%; other 3.6%. **Budget** (1998). *Revenue:* $406,200,000 (aid from Turkey 33.3%, direct taxes 25.2%, indirect taxes 19.8%, loans 7.3%). *Expenditures:* $406,200,000 (investments 13.6%, defense 10.4%, other 76.0%). **Imports** (1998): $390,100,000 (transport equipment 18.6%, prepared foodstuffs 12.3%). *Major import sources:* Turkey 59.3%; UK 12.8%. **Exports** (1998): $53,400,000 (ready-made garments 40.2%, citrus fruits 24.0%). *Major export destinations:* Turkey 50.7%; UK 30.9%. **Health** (1998): physicians 451 (1 per 416 persons); hospital beds 1,002 (1 per 187 persons); infant mortality rate per 1,000 live births (1999) 3.7.

**Internet resources:** <www.pio.gov.cy> (Republic of Cyprus); <www.trncwashdc.org/> (Turkish Republic of Northern Cyprus)

# Czech Republic

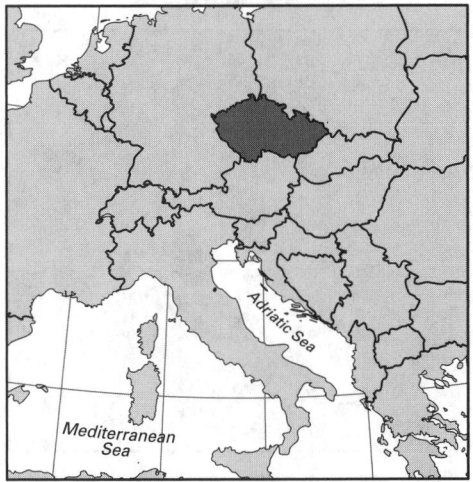

**Official name:** Ceska Republika (Czech Republic). **Form of government:** unitary multiparty republic with two legislative houses (Senate [81]; Chamber of Deputies [200]). **Chief of state:** President Vaclav

Klaus (from 7 Mar 2003). **Head of government:** Prime Minister Vladimir Spidla (from 12 Jul 2002). **Capital:** Prague. **Official language:** Czech. **Official religion:** none. **Monetary unit:** 1 koruna (Kc) = 100 halura; valuation (7 Jul 2003) $1 = 27.53 Kc.

## Demography

**Area:** 78,866 sq mi, 10,272,939 sq km. **Population** (2002): 10,210,060. **Density** (2002): persons per sq mi 335.3, persons per sq km 129.5. **Urban** (1999): 74.6%. **Sex distribution** (2001): male 48.76%; female 51.24%. **Age breakdown** (2001): under 15, 16.2%; 15–29, 23.5%; 30–44, 20.2%; 45–59, 21.6%; 60–74, 13.0%; 75 and over, 5.5%. **Ethnic composition** (2001): Czech 90.1%; Moravian 3.6%; Slovak 1.8%; Polish 0.5%; German 0.4%; Silesian 0.1%; Rom (Gypsy) 0.1%; other 3.5%. **Religious affiliation** (2000): Catholic 43.8%, of which Roman Catholic 40.4%, Hussite Church of the Czech Republic 2.2%; nonreligious 31.9%; atheist 5.0%; Protestant 3.1%; Orthodox Christian 0.6%; Jewish 0.1%; other (mostly unaffiliated Christian) 15.5%. **Major cities** (2001): Prague 1,178,576; Brno 379,185; Ostrava 319,293; Plzen 166,274; Olomouc 103,293. **Location:** central Europe, bordering Germany, Poland, Slovakia, and Austria.

## Vital statistics

**Birth rate** per 1,000 population (2000): 8.8 (world avg. 21.2); legitimate 78.2%; illegitimate 21.8%. **Death rate** per 1,000 population (2000): 10.6 (world avg. 9.0). **Natural increase rate** per 1,000 population (2000): –1.8 (world avg. 12.3). **Total fertility rate** (avg. births per childbearing woman; 2000): 1.0. **Marriage rate** per 1,000 population (2000): 5.4. **Divorce rate** per 1,000 population (2000): 2.9. **Life expectancy** at birth (2000): male 71.7 years; female 78.4 years.

## National economy

**Budget** (2000). *Revenue:* Kc 586,208,000,000 (tax revenue 93.6%, of which social security contributions 37.1%, value-added tax 18.8%, personal income tax 13.2%, excise tax 9.2%, corporate tax 9.2%; nontax revenue 6.4%). *Expenditures:* Kc 632,268,000,000 (1999; social security and welfare 37.1%; health 17.5%; education 9.9%; defense 5.0%; police 4.6%). **Production** (metric tons except as noted). *Agriculture, forestry, fishing* (2001): cereals 6,869,000 (of which wheat 4,545,729, barley 2,018,028, corn [maize] 349,951), sugar beets 3,517,570, potatoes 1,590,050; livestock (number of live animals) 3,593,717 pigs, 1,582,027 cattle, 90,241 sheep, 14,687,000 chickens; roundwood (2000) 14,441,000 cu m; fish catch (1999) 22,965. *Mining and quarrying* (1999): kaolin 3,600,000; feldspar 345,000. *Manufacturing* (value added in Kc '000,000,000; 1998): nonelectrical machinery and apparatus 47.0; food products 37.4; fabricated metals 35.2. *Energy production (consumption):* electricity (kW-hr; 2000) 73,466,000,000 (63,449,000,000); hard coal (metric tons; 2000) 14,855,000 (14,855,000); lignite (metric tons; 2000) 50,307,000 (50,307,000); crude petroleum (barrels; 2000) 1,176,500 (39,826,000); petroleum products (metric tons; 2000) 6,132,000 (7,998,000); natural gas (cu m; 2000) 219,000,000 (9,428,000,000). **Tourism** (2000): receipts from visitors $2,869,000,000;

expenditures by nationals abroad $1,257,000,000. **Household income and expenditure.** Average household size (2000) 2.5; disposable income per household Kc 286,920 ($8,900); sources of income (2000): wages and salaries 69.3%; transfer payments 24.2%, of which pensions 17.8%; other 6.5%; expenditure (2000): food and beverages 23.3%, housing and utilities 18.4%, transportation and communications. 14.1%, recreation 10.8%, clothing and footwear 6.7%. **Population economically active** (2001): total 4,663,885; activity rate of total population 45.0% (participation rates: ages 15–64, 70.1%; female 39.3%; unemployed 8.1%). **Public debt** (external, outstanding; 2000): $8,132,000,000. **Gross national product** (2000): $53,925,000,000 ($5,250 per capita). **Land use** (1994): forested 33.3%; meadows and pastures 11.3%; agricultural and under permanent cultivation 43.0%; other 12.4%.

## Foreign trade

**Imports** (2000): Kc 1,241,924,000,000 (machinery and apparatus 30.9%, chemicals and chemical products 12.0%, transport equipment 9.0%, mineral fuels 9.6%). *Major import sources* (2000): Germany 34.2%; Slovakia 6.1%; Austria 5.7%; Russia 5.7%; France 5.6%; Italy 5.3%. **Exports** (2000): Kc 1,121,099,000,000 (machinery and transport equipment 52.9%, basic manufactures 25.5%, chemicals and chemical products 9.3%, furniture 7.4%, iron and steel 7.1%, fabricated metals 5.2%). *Major export destinations* (2000): Germany 41.8%; Slovakia 8.5%; Austria 6.6%; Poland 5.5%; France 3.8%.

## Transport and communications

**Transport.** *Railroads* (2000): length 9,444 km; passenger-km 6,884,000,000; metric ton-km cargo 17,496,000,000. *Roads* (1999): total length 125,905 km. *Vehicles* (2000): passenger cars 3,720,316; trucks and buses 442,076. *Air transport* (2000): passenger-km 5,864,666,000; metric ton-km 37,788,000; airports (2000) with scheduled flights 2. **Communications,** in total units (units per 1,000 persons). Daily newspaper circulation (1996): 2,620,000 (254); television receivers (2000): 3,289,000 (341); telephone main lines (2001): 3,846,000 (374); cellular telephone subscribers (2001): 6,769,000 (659); personal computers (2001): 1,400,000 (136); Internet users (2001): 1,250,000 (121).

## Education and health

**Educational attainment** (1991). Percentage of adult population having: no schooling through complete primary education 31.7%; secondary 58.6%; higher 8.5%; unknown 1.2%. **Literacy** (1998): 99%. **Health** (2000): physicians 39,342 (1 per 261 persons); hospital beds 115,894 (1 per 89 persons); infant mortality rate per 1,000 live births (2000) 4.1. **Food** (2000): daily per capita caloric intake 3,104 (vegetable products 73%, animal products 27%); 126% of FAO recommended minimum.

## Military

**Total active duty personnel** (2001): 53,600 (army 44.4%, air force 21.6%, ministry of defense 34.0%).

**Military expenditure as percentage of GNP** (1999): 2.3% (world 2.4%); per capita expenditure: $292.

## Background

Until 1918, the history of what is now the Czech Republic was largely that of Bohemia. In that year the independent republic of Czechoslovakia was born through the union of Bohemia and Moravia with Slovakia. Czechoslovakia came under the domination of the Soviet Union after World War II, and from 1948 to 1989 it was ruled by a communist government. Its growing political liberalization was suppressed by a Soviet invasion in 1968. After communist rule collapsed in 1989–90, separatist sentiments emerged among the Slovaks, and in 1992 the Czechs and Slovaks agreed to break up their federated state. On 1 Jan 1993, the Czechoslovakian republic was peacefully dissolved and replaced by two new countries, the Czech Republic and Slovakia, with the region of Moravia remaining in the former. In the late 1990s the Czech Republic started membership talks with the European Union, and in 1999 it entered NATO.

## Recent Developments

General elections in the Czech Republic in mid-June 2002 resulted in a victory for the left-wing Czech Social Democratic Party (CSSD) over the center-right coalition that had been in power since 1998. CSSD leader Vladimir Spidla formed a government. The coalition cabinet, which included the participation of the centrist Twin-Coalition of the Christian Democrats and the Freedom Union, was announced on 15 July. Massive floods in August wreaked havoc on Prague and other important centers of tourism and industry and complicated the country's already strained fiscal situation. Vaclav Havel, the prominent playwright and former dissident who had been president since 1993, was replaced by former prime minister Vaclav Klaus in March 2003.

**Internet resources:** <www.visitczech.cz>

# Denmark

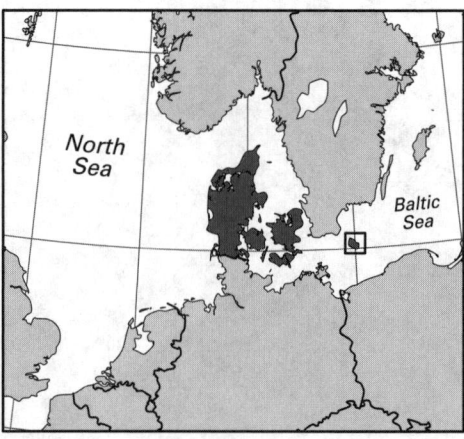

**Official name:** Kongeriget Danmark (Kingdom of Denmark). **Form of government:** parliamentary state and

---

*1 metric ton = about 1.1 short tons;   1 kilometer = 0.6 mi (statute);   1 metric ton-km cargo = about 0.68 short ton-mi cargo;   c.i.f.: cost, insurance, and freight;   f.o.b.: free on board*

constitutional monarchy with one legislative house (Folketing [179]). **Chief of state:** Queen Margrethe II (from 1972). **Head of government:** Prime Minister Anders Fogh Rasmussen (from 2001). **Capital:** Copenhagen. **Official language:** Danish. **Official religion:** Evangelical Lutheran. **Monetary unit:** 1 Danish krone (Dkr; plural kroner) = 100 øre; valuation (7 Jul 2003) $1 = Dkr 6.47.

## Demography

**Area:** 16,639 sq mi, 43,096 sq km (excludes the Faroe Islands and Greenland). **Population** (2002): 5,377,000. **Density** (2002): persons per sq mi 323.1, persons per sq km 124.8. **Urban** (2001): 85.1%. **Sex distribution** (2001): male 49.43%; female 50.57%. **Age breakdown** (2001): under 15, 18.6%; 15–29, 18.5%; 30–44, 22.3%; 45–59, 20.8%; 60–74, 12.7%; 75 and over, 7.1%. **Ethnic composition** (2001): Danish 95.2%; Asian 1.7%, of which Turkish 0.7%; residents of former Yugoslavia 0.7%; African 0.5%; German 0.2%; English 0.2%; other 1.5%. **Religious affiliation** (1998): Christian 87.5%, of which Evangelical Lutheran 85.8%; Muslim 2.2%; other/nonreligious 10.3%. **Major urban areas** (2001): Greater Copenhagen 1,081,673; Århus 218,380; Odense 144,849; Ålborg 119,996; Esbjerg 73,046. **Location:** northern Europe, bordering the North Sea, the Baltic Sea, and Germany. **Dependent territories:** Faroe Islands and Greenland.

## Vital statistics

**Birth rate** per 1,000 population (2000): 12.6 (world avg. 22.5); (1995) legitimate 53.5%; illegitimate 46.5%. **Death rate** per 1,000 population (2000): 10.9 (world avg. 9.0). **Natural increase rate** per 1,000 population (2000): 1.7 (world avg. 13.5). **Total fertility rate** (avg. births per childbearing woman; 2000): 1.7. **Marriage rate** per 1,000 population (2000): 7.2. **Divorce rate** per 1,000 population (2000): 2.7. **Life expectancy** at birth (2001): male 74.3 years; female 79.1 years.

## National economy

**Budget** (1997). *Revenue:* Dkr 612,077,000,000 (direct taxes 52.2%, indirect taxes 30.7%). *Expenditures:* Dkr 626,536,000,000 (social security assistance 31.8%, education 12.2%, welfare services 10.1%, health 8.4%, defense 2.8%). **National debt** (end of year; 1996): Dkr 664,128,000,000. **Tourism** (2000): receipts $4,025,000,000; expenditures $5,139,000,000. **Population economically active** (2000): total 2,877,000; activity rate of total population 54.0% (participation rates: ages 16–66 77.5%; female 46.5%; unemployed [May 2000–April 2001 avg.] 5.3%). **Household income and expenditure.** Average household size (2001) 2.2; income per household (1988) Dkr 199,354 ($29,613); expenditure (1993): housing 22.9%, food and beverages 17.9%, transportation and communications 15.5%, recreation 8.3%, household furnishings 6.1%, energy 6.1%. **Production** (in Dkr '000,000 except as noted). *Agriculture, forestry, fishing* (value added; 2000): meat 21,059 (of which pork 17,032, beef 2,654), milk 11,254, cereals 7,458 (of which wheat 3,732, barley 3,214); livestock (number of live animals) 11,921,573 pigs, 1,867,937 cattle; roundwood (2000) 3,086,000 cu m; fish catch (1999) 1,447,664 metric tons. *Mining and quarrying* (2000): sand and

gravel 23,000,000 cu m; chalk 400,000 metric tons. *Manufacturing* (value added in $'000; 1998): non-electrical machinery and apparatus 3,874; food products 3,848; fabricated metals 2,228. *Energy production (consumption):* electricity (kW-hr; 2000) 35,844,000,000 ([1996] 39,582,000,000); coal (metric tons; 1997) 23,000 (11,161,000); crude petroleum (barrels; 2000) 136,095,000 ([1997] 66,971,000); petroleum products (metric tons; 1997) 8,654,000 (7,274,000); natural gas (cu m; 2000) 8,168,000,000 ([1997] 3,787,000,000). **Gross national product** (2000): $172,238,000,000 ($32,280 per capita). **Land use** (1994): forested 10.5%; meadows and pastures 7.5%; agricultural and under permanent cultivation 55.9%; other 26.1%.

## Foreign trade

**Imports** (2000-c.i.f.): Dkr 360,790,000,000 (machinery and apparatus 14.2%, chemicals and chemical products 12.3%, food and live animals 8.2%, transport equipment and parts 7.8%, fuels 5.4%). *Major import sources:* Germany 21.0%; Sweden 12.2%; The Netherlands 8.6%; UK 7.6%; Norway 5.1%; France 5.1%. **Exports** (2000-f.o.b.): Dkr 403,285,000,000 (machinery and apparatus 23.5%, food and live animals 18.4%, pharmaceuticals 5.1%, mineral fuels and lubricants 4.8%, furniture 3.8%). *Major export destinations:* Germany 18.9%; Sweden 13.0%; UK 9.8%; Norway 5.5%; France 4.9%.

## Transport and communications

**Transport.** *Railroads* (2001): route length 2,743 km; passenger-km 5,318,000,000; metric ton-km cargo 2,025,000,000. *Roads* (2001): total length 71,663 km (paved 100%). *Vehicles* (2001): passenger cars 1,854,060; trucks and buses 335,690. *Air transport* (2001; Danish share of Scandinavian Airlines System [scheduled air service only] and Maersk Air): passenger-km 8,942,000,000; metric ton-km cargo 183,152,000; airports (1996) with scheduled flights 13. **Communications,** in total units (units per 1,000 persons). Daily newspaper circulation (1998): 1,613,000 (284); radio receivers (1997): 6,020,000 (1,145); television receivers (1999): 3,300,000 (621); telephone main lines (2001): 3,882,000 (723); cellular telephone subscribers (2001): 3,954,000 (737); personal computers (2001): 2,300,000 (432); Internet users (2001): 2,400,000 (447).

## Education and health

**Educational attainment** (2000). Percentage of population age 25–69 having: completed lower secondary or not stated 34.6%; completed upper secondary or vocational 42.3%; undergraduate 17.6%; graduate 5.5%. **Literacy:** 100%. **Health:** physicians (1994) 14,497 (1 per 358 persons); hospital beds (1999) 23,352 (1 per 228 persons); infant mortality rate per 1,000 live births (2001) 5.0. **Food** (2000): daily per capita caloric intake 3,396 (vegetable products 62%, animal products 38%); 126% of FAO recommended minimum.

## Military

**Total active duty personnel** (2001): 21,400 (army 60.3%, navy 18.7%, air force 21.0%). **Military expenditure as percentage of GNP** (1999): 1.6% (world 2.4%); per capita expenditure $524.

## Background

The Danes, a Scandinavian branch of the Teutons, settled the area in c. 6th century AD. During the Viking period the Danes expanded their territory, and by the 11th century the united Danish kingdom included parts of what are now Germany, Sweden, England, and Norway. Scandinavia was united under Danish rule from 1397 until 1523, when Sweden became independent; a series of debilitating wars with Sweden in the 17th century resulted in the Treaty of Copenhagen (1660), which established the modern Scandinavian frontiers. Denmark gained and lost various other territories, including Norway, in the 19th and 20th centuries; it went through three constitutions between 1849 and 1915 and was occupied by Nazi Germany in 1940–45. A founding member of NATO (1949), Denmark adopted its current constitution in 1953. It became a member of the European Community in 1973 and modified its membership during the 1990s. The island of Zealand, on which Copenhagen stands, was connected to the central island of Funen by a rail tunnel and bridge in 1997. This ended more than 100 years of ferry service and cut the crossing time from an hour to under 10 minutes.

## Recent Developments

In 2002, after storming to power in November 2001 following the biggest swing to the right in Danish politics since the 1920s, the Liberal-Conservative coalition government of Prime Minister Anders Fogh Rasmussen—with backing from the populist, nationalist Danish People's Party—introduced tighter immigration controls and sweeping expenditure cuts, denting Denmark's image abroad as a bastion of tolerance and humanitarianism. In 2001, 12,512 asylum seekers had entered the country, mainly from Iraq, Afghanistan, Bosnia and Herzegovina, and Yugoslavia; just over half were granted asylum. The influx fell sharply in 2002. Foreign citizens accounted for barely 5% of the population in homogeneous Denmark (only 1.7% were of non-European extraction).

Internet resources: <www.visitdenmark.com>

# Djibouti

**Official name:** Jumhuriyah Jibuti (Arabic); République de Djibouti (French) (Republic of Djibouti). **Form of government:** multiparty republic with one legislative house (National Assembly [65]). **Head of state and government:** President Ismail Omar Guelleh (from 1999) assisted by a prime minister. **Capital:** Djibouti. **Official languages:** Arabic; French. **Official religion:** none. **Monetary unit:** 1 Djibouti franc (DF) = 100 centimes; valuation (7 Jul 2003) $1 = DF 175.00.

## Demography

**Area:** 8,950 sq mi, 23,200 sq km. **Population** (2002): 473,000. **Density** (2002): persons per sq mi 52.8, persons per sq km 20.4. **Urban** (1999): 83.1%. **Sex distribution** (2001): male 51.59%; female 48.41%. **Age breakdown** (2001): under 15, 42.6%; 15–29, 26.4%; 30–44, 14.3%; 45–59, 11.5%; 60–74, 4.6%; 75 and over, 0.6%. **Ethnic composition**

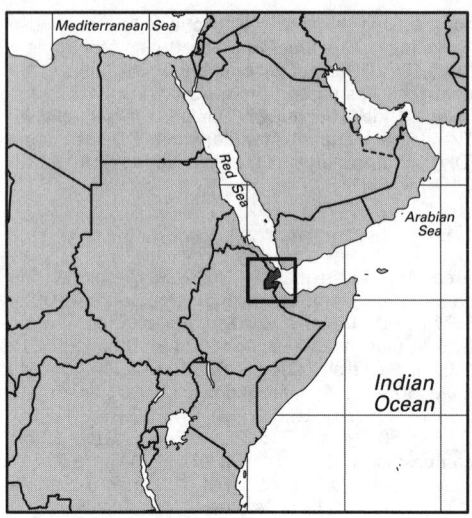

(2000): Somali 46.0%; Afar 35.4%; Arab 11.0%; mixed African and European 3.0%; French 1.6%; other/unspecified 3.0%. **Religious affiliation** (1995): Sunni Muslim 97.2%; Christian 2.8%, of which Roman Catholic 2.2%, Orthodox 0.5%, Protestant 0.1%. **Major city and towns** (1991): Djibouti 383,000 (1995); 'Ali Sabih 8,000; Tadjoura 7,500; Dikhil 6,500. **Location:** eastern Africa, bordering Eritrea, the Red Sea, the Gulf of Aden, Somalia, and Ethiopia.

## Vital statistics

**Birth rate** per 1,000 population (2001): 40.7 (world avg. 21.2). **Death rate** per 1,000 population (2001): 14.7 (world avg. 8.9). **Natural increase rate** per 1,000 population (2001): 26.0 (world avg. 12.3). **Total fertility rate** (avg. births per childbearing woman; 2001): 5.7. **Life expectancy** at birth (2001): male 49.4 years; female 53.1 years.

## National economy

**Budget** (1998). *Revenue:* DF 23,154,000,000 (tax revenue 87.5%, of which domestic consumption taxes 27.1%, wages and salary tax 13.7%, surcharge on khat 8.9%, income and profit tax 6.1%; nontax revenue 12.5%). *Expenditures:* DF 30,427,000,000 (current expenditures 80.0%, of which general administration 26.7%, defense and mobilization 20.0%, education 8.7%, health 5.4%; capital expenditures 20.0%). **Tourism** (1995): receipts from visitors $4,000,000; expenditures by nationals abroad $4,000,000. **Production** (metric tons except as noted). *Agriculture, forestry, fishing* (2001): vegetables and melons 23,060, of which tomatoes 1,100, onions 80, eggplant 33; lemons and limes 1,800; tropical fruit 1,700; livestock (number of live animals) 513,000 goats, 465,000 sheep, 269,000 cattle; fish catch (1999) 350. *Mining and quarrying:* mineral production limited to locally used construction materials and evaporated salt. *Manufacturing* (2000): main products include furniture, nonalcoholic beverages, meat and hides, light electromechanical goods, and mineral water. *Energy production (consumption):* electricity (kW-hr; 1999) 180,000,000 (167,400,-

---

*1 metric ton = about 1.1 short tons;     1 kilometer = 0.6 mi (statute);     1 metric ton-km cargo = about 0.68 short ton-mi cargo;     c.i.f.: cost, insurance, and freight;     f.o.b.: free on board*

000); petroleum products (metric tons; 1997) none (119,000); geothermal, wind, and solar resources are substantial but largely undeveloped. **Population economically active** (1991): total 282,000; activity rate of total population 61.5% (participation rates: over age 10, 70.4%; female 40.8%; unemployed [2000] c. 40–50%). **Household income and expenditure.** Average household size (1991) 3.6; expenditure (expatriate households; 1984): food 50.3%, energy 13.1%, recreation 10.4%, housing 6.4%, clothing 1.7%, personal effects 1.4%, health care 1.0%, household goods 0.3%, other 15.4%. **Public debt** (external, outstanding; 2000): $237,900,000. **Gross national product** (2000): $553,000,000 ($880 per capita). **Land use** (1994): forested 0.9%; meadows and pastures 56.1%; agricultural and under permanent cultivation; built-on, wasteland, and other 43.0%.

## Foreign trade

**Imports** (1998): $238,800,000 (food, beverages, khat, and tobacco 53.2%; petroleum products 12.4%; machinery and electric appliances 10.9%; base metals and base metal products 4.9%; chemical products 4.6%; transport equipment 4.3%; clothing and footwear 3.7%). *Major import sources:* France 12.5%; Ethiopia 12.0%; Italy 9.2%; UK 6.2%; Saudi Arabia 5.7%; Japan 4.2%. **Exports** (1998): $59,100,000 (1992; unspecified special transactions 60.0%; live animals [including camels] 21.3%; basic manufactures 5.2%; crude materials 4.5%). *Major export destinations:* Somalia 53.0%; Yemen 22.5%; Ethiopia 5.0%; Saudi Arabia 0.7%.

## Transport and communications

**Transport.** *Railroads* (1997): length (1989) 106 km; passenger-km 762,000,000; metric ton-km cargo 232,000,000. *Roads* (1999): total length 2,890 km (paved 13%). *Vehicles* (1996): passenger cars 9,200; trucks and buses 2,040. *Air transport* (1998): passengers handled 107,369; metric tons of freight handled 7,290; airports (2000) with scheduled flights 1. **Communications,** in total units (units per 1,000 persons). Daily newspaper circulation (1995): 500 (0.8); radio receivers (1997): 52,000 (84); television receivers (1999): 30,000 (67); telephone main lines (2001): 9,900 (15.4); cellular telephone subscribers (2001): 3,000 (4.7); personal computers (2001): 7,000 (10.9); Internet users (2001): 3,300 (5.1).

## Education and health

**Literacy** (1998): total population age 15 and over literate 62.7%; males literate 74.0%; females literate 51.4%. **Health** (1996): physicians 60 (1 per 7,100 persons); hospital beds (1989) 1,383 (1 per 369 persons); infant mortality rate per 1,000 live births (2001) 93.2. **Food** (2000): daily per capita caloric intake 2,050 (vegetable products 87%, animal products 13%); 88% of FAO recommended minimum.

## Military

**Total active duty personnel** (2001): 9,600 (army 83.3%, navy 2.1%, air force 2.1%, paramilitary 12.5%; excludes 3,200 French troops; other military forces from mid-2002 include 1,200 German naval personnel and 800 US troops). **Military expenditure as percentage of GNP** (1999): 4.3% (world 2.4%); per capita expenditure $51.

Djibouti, virtually a city-state, is a deepwater port city and railhead bordered on three sides by a sparsely populated, hot, arid landscape. In 1985 this small country won the first world cup men's team marathon.

## Background

Settled around the 3rd century BC by the Arab ancestors of the Afars, Djibouti was later populated by Somali Issas. In AD 825 Islam was brought to the area by missionaries. Arabs controlled the trade in this region until the 16th century; it became the French protectorate of French Somaliland in 1888. In 1946 it became a French overseas territory, and in 1977 gained its independence. In the late 20th century, the country received refugees from the Ethiopian-Somali war and from civil conflicts in Eritrea. In the 1990s it suffered from political unrest.

## Recent Developments

Djibouti's proximity to Yemen and Somalia, two countries cited by the US government as possible terrorist havens, became the dominant factor affecting the country's foreign relations in 2002. In late January German naval forces began to arrive in Djibouti to stage patrols of the regional maritime traffic, searching for terrorist suspects possibly fleeing Afghanistan. The US also assembled a military presence at a French base in the country. Pres. Ismael Omar Guelleh received the red-carpet treatment during a visit to Washington in January 2003.

**Internet resources:** <www.republique-djibouti.com>

# Dominica

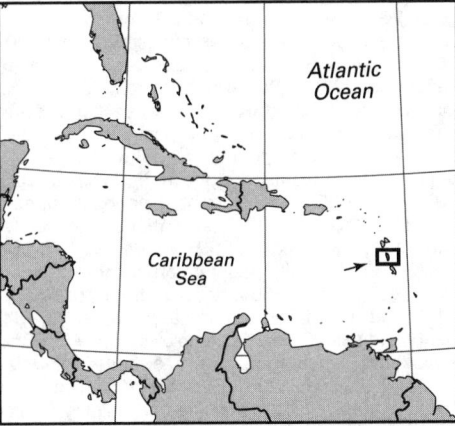

Atlantic Ocean

Caribbean Sea

**Official name:** Commonwealth of Dominica. **Form of government:** multiparty republic with one legislative house (House of Assembly [32; includes 22 seats that are elective [including speaker if elected from outside of the House of Assembly] and 10 seats that are nonelective [including 9 appointees of the president and the attorney general serving ex officio]). **Chief of state:** President Vernon Shaw (from 1998). **Head of government:** Prime Minister Pierre Charles (from 2000). **Capital:** Roseau. **Official language:** English. **Official religion:** none. **Monetary unit:** 1 East

Caribbean dollar (EC$) = 100 cents; valuation (7 Jul 2003) US$1 = EC$2.67.

## Demography

**Area:** 285.3 sq mi, 739.0 sq km (total area of Dominica per more recent survey is 290 sq mi [750 sq km]). **Population** (2002): 71,700. **Density** (2002): persons per sq mi 247.2, persons per sq km 95.6. **Urban** (2001): 70.4%. **Sex distribution** (2001): male 51%; female 49%. **Age breakdown** (2000): under 15, 29.1%; 15–29, 27.2%; 30–44, 23.7%; 45–59, 9.6%; 60–74, 7.0%; 75 and over, 3.4%. **Ethnic composition** (2000): black 88.3%; mulatto 7.3%; black-Amerindian 1.7%; British expatriates 1.0%; Indo-Pakistani 1.0%; other 0.7%. **Religious affiliation** (1991): Roman Catholic 70.1%; six largest Protestant groups 17.2%, of which Seventh-day Adventist 4.6%, Pentecostal 4.3%, Methodist 4.2%; other 8.9%; nonreligious 2.9%; unknown 0.9%. **Major towns** (1991): Roseau 15,853; Portsmouth 3,621; Marigot 2,919; Atkinson 2,518; Mahaut 2,372. **Location:** southern Caribbean Sea, south of Guadeloupe and north of Martinique.

## Vital statistics

**Birth rate** per 1,000 population (2000): 18.3 (world avg. 22.5); (1991) legitimate 24.1%; illegitimate 75.9%. **Death rate** per 1,000 population (2000): 7.3 (world avg. 9.0). **Natural increase rate** per 1,000 population (2000): 11.0 (world avg. 13.5). **Total fertility rate** (avg. births per childbearing woman; 2000): 2.0. **Marriage rate** per 1,000 population (1996): 3.1. **Divorce rate** per 1,000 population (1996): 0.7. **Life expectancy** at birth (2000): male 70.5 years; female 76.3 years.

## National economy

**Budget** (1998–99). *Revenue*: EC$232,700,000 (tax revenue 73.9%, of which consumption taxes on imports 26.9%, income taxes 20.9%; nontax revenue 14.7%; grants 9.2%). *Expenditures*: EC$260,300,000 (current expenditures 77.1%; development expenditures 22.9%). **Public debt** (external, outstanding; 2000): US$89,200,000. **Land use** (1994): forested 66.0%; meadows and pastures 3.0%; agricultural and under permanent cultivation 23.0%; other 8.0%. **Tourism:** receipts from visitors (2000) US$47,000,000; expenditures by nationals abroad (1998) US$8,000,000. **Gross national product** (at current market prices; 1999): US$238,000,000 (US$3,260 per capita). **Population economically active** (1991): total 26,364; activity rate of total population 38.0% (participation rates: ages 15–64, 62.4%; female 34.5%; unemployed [1994] 23%). **Household expenditure.** Average household size (1991) 3.6; expenditure (1984): food and nonalcoholic beverages 43.1%, housing and utilities 16.1%, transportation 11.6%, clothing and footwear 6.5%, household furnishings 6.0%. **Production** (metric tons except as noted). *Agriculture, forestry, fishing* (1998): bananas 28,640, root crops 23,168 (of which dasheens 11,903, yams 7,560, tanias 3,534), plantains 22,236; livestock (number of live animals; 1999) 13,400 cattle, 9,700 goats, 7,600 sheep; fish catch (1997) 855 metric tons. *Mining and quarrying*: pumice, limestone, and sand and gravel are quarried

primarily for local consumption. *Manufacturing* (value of production in EC$'000; 1998): toilet soap 21,816; laundry soap 16,467; crude coconut oil 1,848. *Energy production (consumption)*: electricity (kW-hr; 1996) 37,000,000 (37,000,000); petroleum products (metric tons; 1996) none (26,000).

## Foreign trade

**Imports** (1999-c.i.f.): EC$343,400,000 (food and beverages 20.8%; machinery 16.4%; transport equipment 9.3%; mineral fuels 6.4%). *Major import sources*: US 30.7%; Caricom 27.0%; UK 8.8%; Japan 7.8%; France 5.0%. **Exports** (1999-f.o.b.): EC$147,400,000 (manufactured exports 61.7%, of which coconut-based laundry and toilet soaps 26.7%; agricultural exports 38.3%, of which bananas 27.1%). *Major export destinations*: Caricom 55.3%; UK 27.5%; Guadeloupe 4.9%; US 4.0%.

## Transport and communications

**Transport.** *Roads* (1996): total length 780 km (paved 50%). *Vehicles* (1994): passenger cars 6,581; trucks and buses 2,825. *Air transport*: (1991) passenger arrivals 43,312; (1997) cargo unloaded 575 metric tons, cargo loaded 363 metric tons; airports (1996) with scheduled flights 2. **Communications,** in total units (units per 1,000 persons). Radio receivers (1997): 46,000 (608); television receivers (1997): 6,000 (79); telephone main lines (2001): 23,300 (291); cellular telephone subscribers (2001): 1,200 (16); personal computers (2001): 6,000 (77); Internet users (2000): 6,000 (77).

## Education and health

**Educational attainment** (1991). Percentage of population age 25 and over having: no formal schooling 4.2%; primary education 78.4%; secondary 11.0%; higher vocational 2.3%; university 2.8%; other/unknown 1.3%. **Literacy** (1994): total population age 15 and over literate, c. 44,000 (90.0%). **Health** (1998): physicians 38 (1 per 2,007 persons); hospital beds 262 (1 per 291 persons); infant mortality rate per 1,000 live births (2000) 17.1. **Food** (2000): daily per capita caloric intake 2,994 (vegetable products 77%, animal products 23%); 124% of FAO recommended minimum.

## Military

**Total active duty personnel** (1999): none (300-member police force includes a coast guard unit).

## Background

At the time of the arrival of Christopher Columbus in 1493, Dominica was inhabited by the Caribs. With its steep coastal cliffs and inaccessible mountains, it was one of the last islands to be explored by Europeans, and the Caribs remained in possession until the 18th century; it was then settled by the French and ultimately taken by Britain in 1783. Subsequent hostilities between the settlers and the native inhabitants resulted in the Caribs' near extinction. Incorporated with the Leeward Islands in 1883 and with the Windward Islands in 1940, it became a member of

---

*1 metric ton = about 1.1 short tons;    1 kilometer = 0.6 mi (statute);    1 metric ton-km cargo = about 0.68 short ton-mi cargo;    c.i.f.: cost, insurance, and freight;    f.o.b.: free on board*

the West Indies Federation in 1958. Dominica became independent in 1978.

## Recent Developments

In common with most other Caribbean states, Dominica agreed in March 2002 to improve the transparency of its tax-regulatory systems in order to secure its removal from the list of countries allegedly posing "harmful tax competition" to member states of the Organisation for Economic Co-operation and Development.

**Internet resources:** <www.ndcdominica.dm>

# Dominican Republic

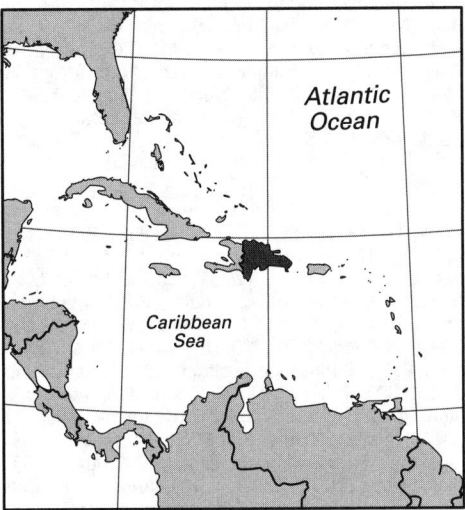

**Official name:** República Dominicana (Dominican Republic). **Form of government:** multiparty republic with two legislative houses (Senate [30]; Chamber of Deputies [149]). **Head of state and government:** President Hipólito Mejía Domínguez (from 2000). **Capital:** Santo Domingo. **Official language:** Spanish. **Official religion:** none (Roman Catholicism is the state religion per concordat with Vatican City). **Monetary unit:** 1 Dominican peso (RD$) = 100 centavos; valuation (7 Jul 2003) US$1 = RD$31.00.

## Demography

**Area:** 48,671 sq mi, 8,553,744 sq km. **Population** (2002): 8,833,000. **Density** (2002): persons per sq mi 470.0, persons per sq km 181.5. **Urban** (2000): 66.0%. **Sex distribution** (2000): male 50.80%; female 49.20%. **Age breakdown** (2000): under 15, 34.5%; 15–29, 27.3%; 30–44, 20.3%; 45–59, 10.8%; 60–74, 5.7%; 75 and over, 1.4%. **Ethnic composition** (2000): mulatto 69.5%; white 17.0%; local black 9.4%; Haitian black 2.4%; other/unknown 1.7%. **Religious affiliation** (1995): Roman Catholic 81.8%; Protestant 6.4%; other Christian 0.6%; other 11.2%. **Major urban centers** (1993): Santo Domingo (urban agglomeration; 2001) 2,629,000; Santiago 365,463; La Romana 140,204; San Pedro de Macorís 124,735; San Francisco de Macorís 108,485. **Location:** eastern two-thirds of the island of Hispaniola, bordered by the North Atlantic Ocean, the Caribbean Sea, and Haiti.

## Vital statistics

**Birth rate** per 1,000 population (2000): 25.2 (world avg. 22.5). **Death rate** per 1,000 population (2000): 4.7 (world avg. 9.0). **Natural increase rate** per 1,000 population (2000): 20.5 (world avg. 13.5). **Total fertility rate** (avg. births per childbearing woman; 2000): 3.0. **Marriage rate** per 1,000 population (1994): 2.0. **Life expectancy** at birth (2000): male 71.1 years; female 75.4 years.

## National economy

**Budget** (1998). *Revenue*: RD$38,566,000,000 (tax revenue 93.8%, of which taxes on goods and services 47.7%, import duties 27.0%, income taxes 17.9%; nontax revenue 5.3%). *Expenditures*: RD$41,179,000,000 (current expenditures 72.2%; development expenditures 27.8%). **Public debt** (external, outstanding; 2000): US$3,368,000,000. **Gross national product** (2000): US$17,847,000,000 (US$2,130 per capita). **Production** (metric tons except as noted). *Agriculture, forestry, fishing* (1998): sugarcane 5,097,000, rice 475,000, bananas 359,000; livestock (number of live animals) 2,528,000 cattle, 960,000 pigs, 38,000,000 chickens; roundwood (2000) 562,300 cu m; fish catch (2000) 11,029. *Mining* (2000): nickel (metal content) 68,300; gold 40,700 troy oz (the mining of gold was temporarily suspended from 1999 through late 2002). *Manufacturing* (1998; excludes free-zone sector for reexport [mostly ready-made garments] employing 195,000): cement 1,872,000; refined sugar 105,000; beer 2,990,000 hectolitres. *Energy production (consumption)*: electricity (kW-hr; 2000) 9,788,000,000 (5,777,000,000); coal (metric tons; 1996) none (128,000); crude petroleum (barrels; 1996) none (17,035,000); petroleum products (metric tons; 1996) 2,147,000 (3,671,000). **Tourism** (2000): receipts US$2,860,000,000; expenditures US$309,000,000. **Population economically active** (1993): total 2,556,225; activity rate of total population 35.0% (participation rates: ages 15–64, 54.3%; female 24.9%; unemployed [2000] 13.9%). **Household expenditure.** Average household size (1993) 3.9; expenditure (1980–85): food and beverages 46.0%, housing 10.0%, household goods 8.0%. **Land use** (1994): forested 12.4%; meadows and pastures 43.4%; agricultural and under permanent cultivation 30.6%; other 13.6%.

## Foreign trade

**Imports** (1998): US$4,897,000,000 (capital goods 22.1%, consumer durables 13.2%, crude petroleum and petroleum products 11.0%; excludes 1998 imports of free zones equaling US$2,701,000,000). *Major import sources* (1997): US 56%; Venezuela 23%; Mexico 9%; Japan 4%. **Exports** (1998): US$889,000,000 (ships' stores 15.8%, ferronickel 15.0%, cacao and cocoa 13.6%, raw sugar 13.2%, raw coffee 7.2%; excludes 1998 reexports of free zones equaling US$4,100,000,000). *Major export destinations* (1997): US 53.9%; Belgium 11.9%; Puerto Rico 7.0%.

## Transport and communications

**Transport.** *Railroads* (1997): route length 1,743 km. *Roads* (1996): total 12,600 km (paved 49%). *Vehicles* (1996): passenger cars 224,000; trucks and buses 151,550. *Air transport* (1997; Aerochago and Dominair airlines): passenger-km, 15,808,000; metric ton-km cargo 11,624,000; airports (2002) 6. **Communications,** in total units (units per 1,000 persons). Daily newspaper circulation (1996): 416,000 (53); radio receivers (1997): 1,440,000 (179); television receivers (1997): 770,000 (96); telephone main lines (2001): 939,500 (108); cellular telephone subscribers (2001): 1,073,000 (124); Internet users (2001): 186,000 (21).

## Education and health

**Literacy** (1995): total population age 15 and over literate, c. 4,164,000 (82.1%); males literate, c. 2,118,000 (82.0%); females literate, c. 2,046,000 (82.2%). **Health:** physicians (1997) 17,460 (1 per 460 persons); hospital beds (1996) 11,921 (1 per 662 persons); infant mortality rate per 1,000 live births (2000) 35.9. **Food** (2000): daily per capita caloric intake 2,325 (vegetable products 85%, animal products 15%); 103% of FAO recommended minimum.

## Military

**Total active duty personnel** (2001): 24,500 (army 61.2%, navy 16.3%, air force 22.4%). **Military expenditure as percentage of GNP** (1999): 0.7% (world 2.4%); per capita expenditure US$15.

## Background

The Dominican Republic was originally part of the Spanish colony of Hispaniola. In 1697 the western third of the island, which later became Haiti, was ceded to France; the remainder of the island passed to France in 1795. The eastern two-thirds of the island were returned to Spain in 1809, and the colony declared its independence in 1821. Within a matter of weeks it was overrun by Haitian troops and occupied until 1844. Since then the country has been under the rule of a succession of dictators, except for short interludes of democratic government, and the US has frequently been involved in its affairs. The termination of the dictatorship of Rafael Trujillo in 1961 led to civil war in 1965 and US military intervention. The country suffered from severe hurricanes in 1979 and 1998.

## Recent Developments

Legislative elections were held on 16 May 2002. The overwhelming victory of Pres. Hipólito Mejía's Dominican Revolutionary Party (PRD) was as much a surprise to PRD members as to local pundits. The party secured a majority in both legislative chambers. When the PRD pushed through a constitutional change permitting the reelection of a sitting president to a second term, it provoked widespread unease, but Mejía asserted that he would not stand for reelection.

**Internet resources:** <www.dominicana.com.do>

# East Timor

**Official name:** República Demokrátika Timor Lorosa'e (Tetum); República Democrática de Timor-Leste

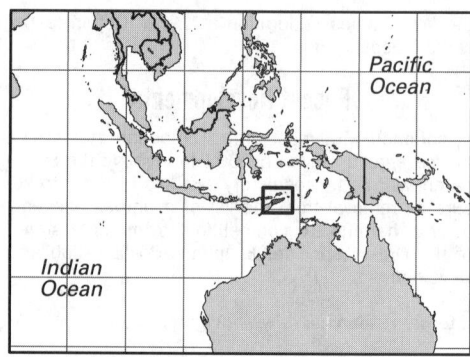

(Portuguese) (Democratic Republic of East Timor). **Form of government:** republic with one legislative body (National Parliament [88]). **Chief of State:** President Xanana Gusmão (from 20 May 2002). **Head of Government:** Prime Minister Mari Alkatiri (from 20 May 2002). **Capital:** Dili. **Official languages:** Tetum; Portuguese. **Official religion:** none. **Monetary unit:** 1 US dollar = 100 cents.

## Demography

**Area:** 5,639 sq mi, 14,604 sq km. **Population** (2002): 797,000. **Density:** persons per sq mi 141.3; per sq km 54.6. **Urban** (2001): 24.0%. **Sex distribution** (2000): male: 51.7%; female: 48.3%. **Age breakdown** (2000): under 15, 43%; 15–29, 23.9%; 30–44, 17.9%; 45–59, 10.5%; 60–74, 4.1%; 75 and over, 0.6%. **Ethnic composition** (1999): East Timorese c. 80%; other (nearly all Indonesian, and particularly West Timorese) c. 20%. **Religious affiliation** (2000): Roman Catholic c. 87%; Protestant c. 5%; Muslim c. 3%; traditional beliefs c. 3%; other c. 2%. **Major cities** (2000): Dili 48,200; Dare 17,100; Baucau 14,200; Maliana 12,300; Ermera 12,000. **Location:** southeast Asia, eastern end of the island of Timor plus an exclave on the western end, bordering the Timor Sea and Indonesia.

## Vital statistics

**Birth rate** per 1,000 population (2000–05): 21.0 (world avg. 21.2). **Death rate** per 1,000 population (2000–05): 11.0 (world avg. 8.9). **Natural increase rate** per 1,000 population (2000–05): 10.0 (world avg. 13.2). **Total fertility rate** (avg. births per childbearing woman; 2000–05): 3.8. **Marriage rate** per 1,000 population (1997–98): 0.4. **Divorce rate** per 1,000 population (1997–98): 0.1. **Life expectancy** at birth (2001): male 56.0 years; female 59.0 years.

## National economy

**Budget** (2000). *Revenue:* $107,000,000 (grants 86.0%; domestic sources 14.0%). *Expenditures:* $107,000,000 (reconstruction and development expenditure 72%; current expenditure 28.0%). **Gross domestic product** (2001) $375,000,000 ($490 per capita). **Production** (metric tons except as noted). *Agriculture, forestry, fishing* (1998): corn (maize) 58,900; rice 36,800; cassava 32,100; livestock (number of live animals) chickens 541,000, pigs (1996) 378,000, goats (1996) 187,000; fish catch

---

*1 metric ton = about 1.1 short tons;   1 kilometer = 0.6 mi (statute);   1 metric ton-km cargo = about 0.68 short ton-mi cargo;   c.i.f.: cost, insurance, and freight;   f.o.b.: free on board*

(1997) 2,804, of which marine 2,424. *Mining and quarrying* (2001): commercial quantities of marble are exported. *Manufacturing* (2001): principally the production of textiles, garments, and handicrafts, bottled water, and processed coffee. *Energy production (consumption)*: electricity (kW-hr; 1998) 40,000,000 (n.a.). **Tourism:** available beds for tourists (1998) 580. **Population economically active** (2001): total 232,000; activity rate of total population 28% (participation rates: ages 15–64 57%; unofficially unemployed [2000] 80%). **Land use** (2000): forested 34%; agricultural and under permanent cultivation 15%; meadows and pastures 10%; other 41%.

## Foreign trade

**Imports** (1998): $135,000,000 (foodstuffs 26%, of which rice 10%; construction materials 15%; petroleum products 10%; unspecified 49%). *Major import sources*: nearly 100% Indonesia. **Exports** (1998): $55,000,000 (agricultural products 93%, of which nonfood crops [nearly all coffee] 51%, livestock 22%, food crops 15%; garments, bottled water, handicrafts, and other manufactured goods 5%). *Major export destinations*: Indonesia 96%.

## Transport and communications

**Transport.** *Paved roads* (1999): total length 1,414 km. *Vehicles* (1998): passenger cars 3,156; trucks and buses 7,140. *Air transport*: airports (2001) with scheduled flights 1. **Communications,** in total units (units per 1,000 persons). Daily newspaper circulation (2002): 1,500 (1.9); telephone main lines (1996): 6,600 (8.0)

## Education and health

**Literacy** (2001): total population age 15 and over literate 203,000 (48%). **Health:** physicians (1996–97) 122 (1 per 6,667 persons); hospital beds (1999) 560 (1 per 1,329 persons); infant mortality rate per 1,000 live births (2001) 70–90.

## Military

**Total active duty personnel** (2002): 636 (army 94.3%, naval element 5.7%; to be expanded to 1,500 troops by the end of 2003).

## Background

The Portuguese first settled on the island of Timor in 1520 and were granted rule over Timor's eastern half in 1860. The Timor political party Fretilin declared East Timor independent in 1975 after Portugal withdrew its troops. It was invaded by Indonesian forces and was incorporated as a province of Indonesia in 1976. The takeover, which resulted in thousands of East Timorese deaths during the next two decades, was disputed by the UN. In 1999 an independence referendum won overwhelmingly; civilian militias, armed by the military and led by local supporters of integration, then rampaged through the province, killing 1,000–2,000 people. The Indonesian parliament rescinded Indonesia's annexation of the territory, and East Timor was returned to its preannexation status as a non-self-governing territory, though this time under UN supervision. Preparation for independence got under way in 2001, with East Timorese voting by universal suffrage in August for a Constituent Assembly

of 88 members; by the end of the year, the assembly had drafted a constitution for the new state.

## Recent Developments

On 14 Apr 2002 former guerrilla leader Xanana Gusmão easily won the country's first presidential election. East Timor officially declared its independence on 20 May, with UN Secretary-General Kofi Annan attending ceremonies in Taci Tolu, outside of the capital, Dili, where he formally ended the UN's authority over the territory. The declaration of independence was followed by the swearing in of Gusmão and the raising of the flag of the world's newest country.

**Internet resources:** <www.gov.east-timor.org>

# Ecuador

**Official name:** República del Ecuador (Republic of Ecuador). **Form of government:** unitary multiparty republic with one legislative house (National Congress [121]). **Head of state and government:** President Lucio Gutiérrez Borbúa (from 15 Jan 2003). **Capital:** Quito. **Official language:** Spanish (Quechua and Shuar are also official languages for the indigenous peoples). **Official religion:** none. **Monetary unit:** dollar ($) (7 Jul 2003; the US dollar became the principal national currency from March 2000 and was formally adopted as the national currency on 9 Sep 2000; the pegged value of the sucre [S/.], the former national currency from March 2000, was $1 = S/. 25,000).

## Demography

**Area:** 105,037 sq mi, 272,045 sq km (includes 884 sq mi [2,289 sq km] in nondelimited areas). **Population** (2002): 13,095,000. **Density** (2002): persons per sq mi 124.7, persons per sq km 48.1. **Urban** (2001): 61.0%. **Sex distribution** (2001): male 49.60%; female 50.40%. **Age breakdown** (2002): under 15, 35.3%; 15–29, 28.5%; 30–44, 19.2%; 45–59, 10.5%; 60–74, 4.8%; 75 and over, 1.7%. **Ethnic composition** (2000): mestizo 42.0%; Amerindian 40.8%; white 10.6%; black 5.0%; other 1.6%. **Religious affiliation** (2000): Roman Catholic 94.1%; Protestant 1.9%; other 4.0%. **Major cities**

(2001): Guayaquil 1,952,029; Quito 1,399,814; Cuenca 276,964; Santo Domingo de los Colorados 200,421; Machala 198,123. **Location:** northwestern South America, bordering Colombia, Peru, and the Pacific Ocean.

## Vital statistics

**Birth rate** per 1,000 population (2000; excluding nomadic Indian tribes): 26.5 (world avg. 22.5). **Death rate** per 1,000 population (2000; excluding nomadic Indian tribes): 5.5 (world avg. 9.0). **Total fertility rate** (avg. births per childbearing woman; 2000): 3.2. **Marriage rate** per 1,000 population (1997): 5.6. **Life expectancy** at birth (2000): male 68.3 years; female 74.0 years.

## National economy

**Budget** (1996). *Revenue:* S/. 10,233,300,000,000 (petroleum revenue 45.9%, indirect taxes 30.9%, direct taxes 11.1%). *Expenditures:* S/. 11,836,700,-000,000 (administration 40.8%, debt service 20.7%, subsidies 7.4%). **Public debt** (external, outstanding; 2000): $11,366,000,000. **Production** (metric tons except as noted). *Agriculture, forestry, fishing* (1999): sugarcane 6,800,000, bananas 4,563,000, rice 1,043,000; livestock (live animals) 5,534,000 cattle, 2,892,000 pigs, 2,182,000 sheep; roundwood (1998) 11,340,000 cu m; fish catch (2000) 592,547. *Mining and quarrying* (2000): limestone 3,147,000; gold 2,823 kg. *Manufacturing* (value added in S/. '000,000; 1996): chemical products 2,364,091; food products 1,779,894; nonmetallic mineral products 453,148. *Energy production (consumption):* electricity (kW-hr; 1997) 9,560,000,000 (9,560,000,000); crude petroleum (barrels; 2001) 146,200,000 (52,000,000 [1997]); petroleum products (metric tons; 1997) 7,602,000 (5,627,000); natural gas (cu m; 1997) 502,000,000 (502,000,000). **Household income and expenditure.** Average household size (1990) 4.1; average annual income per household (1995) S/. 9,825,610 ($3,830); sources of income (1995): self-employment 70.9%, wages 16.0%, transfer payments 6.7%, other 6.4%; expenditure (1995): food and tobacco 37.9%, transportation and communications 15.0%, clothing 9.2%, household furnishings 6.5%. **Population economically active** (1997): total 3,373,810; activity rate of total population 44.9% (participation rates: ages 15 and over, 64.2%; female 39.1%). **Gross national product** (2000): $15,256,000,000 ($1,210 per capita). **Tourism** (2000): receipts $402,000,000; expenditures $299,000,000.

## Foreign trade

**Imports** (1999; f.o.b. in balance of trade and c.i.f. for commodities and trading partners): $3,017,200,000 (machines and transport equipment 28.8%; chemicals and chemical products 22.0%; food and live animals 9.4%; mineral fuels 8.2%). *Major import sources:* US 30.4%; Colombia 12.0%; Venezuela 6.4%; Japan 4.7%; Germany 4.2%. **Exports** (1999): $4,451,100,000 (food 51.7%, of which bananas 21.4%, crustaceans 13.7%, fish 5.9%; crude petroleum 29.5%). *Major export destinations:* US 38.4%; Colombia 5.1%; Panama 4.9%; South Korea 4.8%.

## Transport and communications

**Transport.** *Railroads* (1999): route length 966 km; passenger-km (1998) 44,000,000; metric ton-km cargo (1996) 1,000,000. *Roads* (1997): total length 43,197 km (paved 19%). *Vehicles* (1996): passenger cars 464,902; trucks and buses 52,630. *Air transport* (2001; Ecuatoviana and TAME airlines): passenger-km 901,000,000; metric ton-km cargo 14,344,-000. **Communications,** in total units (units per 1,000 persons). Daily newspaper circulation (1996): 820,000 (70); radio receivers (1997): 4,150,000 (348); television receivers (1998): 2,500,000 (205); telephone main lines (2001): 1,335,800 (104); cellular telephone subscribers (2001): 859,200 (67); personal computers (2001): 300,000 (23); Internet users (2001): 327,700 (25).

## Education and health

**Educational attainment** (1990). Percentage of population age 25 and over having: no formal schooling 2.2%; incomplete primary 54.3%; primary 28.0%; postsecondary 15.5%. **Literacy** (1995): total population age 15 and over literate 90.1%; males 92.0%; females 88.2%. **Health** (1997): physicians 20,243 (1 per 590 persons); hospital beds 18,510 (1 per 645 persons); infant mortality rate per 1,000 live births (2002) 33.0. **Food** (2000): daily per capita caloric intake 2,693 (vegetable products 84%, animal products 16%); 118% of FAO recommended minimum.

## Military

**Total active duty personnel** (2001): 59,500 (army 84.0%, navy 9.3%, air force 6.7%). **Military expenditure as percentage of GNP** (1999): 3.7% (world 2.4%); per capita expenditure $38.

 **Did you know?**

Quito, the capital of Ecuador, came to be the northern capital of the Inca empire, the largest political unit of pre-Columbian America.

## Background

Ecuador was conquered by the Incas in AD 1450 and came under Spanish control in 1534. Under the Spaniards it was a part of the viceroyalty of Peru until 1740, when it became a part of the viceroyalty of New Granada. It gained its independence from Spain in 1822 as part of the republic of Gran Colombia, and in 1830 it became a sovereign state. A succession of authoritarian governments ruled into the mid-20th century, and economic hardship and social unrest prompted the military to take a strong role. Border disputes led to war between Peru and Ecuador in 1941; the two fought periodically until agreeing to a final demarcation in 1998. The economy, booming in the 1970s with petroleum profits, was depressed in the 1980s by reduced oil prices and earthquake damage. A new constitution was adopted in 1979. In the 1990s social unrest caused political instability and several changes of heads of state. In a controversial move to help stabilize the economy, the US dollar replaced the sucre as the national currency in 2000.

*1 metric ton = about 1.1 short tons;   1 kilometer = 0.6 mi (statute);   1 metric ton-km cargo = about 0.68 short ton-mi cargo;   c.i.f.: cost, insurance, and freight;   f.o.b.: free on board*

## Recent Developments

Lucio Gutiérrez Borbúa, a former army colonel who had participated in an antigovernment uprising in January 2000 and who was the richest man in Ecuador, took over as president on 15 Jan 2003. Despite widespread poverty, the Ecuadoran economy was one of the stronger performers in Latin America, with 3.5% growth forecast for 2002. Pressure from environmentalists dogged construction of a new $1.3 billion Ecuadoran pipeline to carry crude oil from the Amazon region to the Pacific coast, scheduled for completion in 2003. Activists said it would threaten the ecotourism industry and the habitat of endangered bird species.

Internet resources: <www.ecuador.com>

# Egypt

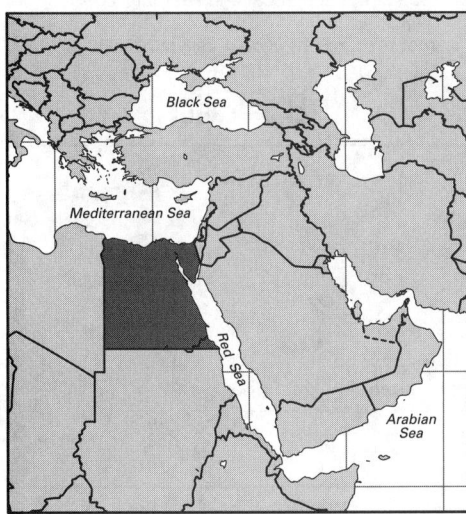

Official name: Jumhuriyah Misr al-'Arabiyah (Arab Republic of Egypt). Form of government: republic with one legislative house (People's Assembly [454, including 10 nonelective seats]). Chief of state: President Hosni Mubarak (from 1981). Head of government: Prime Minister Atef Ebeid (from 1999). Capital: Cairo. Official language: Arabic. Official religion: Islam. Monetary unit: 1 Egyptian pound (£E) = 100 piastres; valuation (7 Jul 2003) $1 = £E 6.10.

## Demography

Area: 385,210 sq mi, 997,690 sq km. Population (2002): 66,341,000. Density (2002): persons per sq mi 172.2; persons per sq km 66.5. Urban (2001): 42.7. Sex distribution (2000): male 50.50%; female 49.50%. Age breakdown (2000): under 15, 35.1%; 15–29, 28.5%; 30–44, 19.0%; 45–59, 11.3%; 60–74, 5.0%; 75 and over, 1.0%. Ethnic composition (2000): Egyptian Arab 84.1%; Sudanese Arab 5.5%; Arabized Berber 2.0%; Bedouin 2.0%; Rom (Gypsy) 1.6%; other 4.8%. Religious affiliation (1997): Sunni Muslim 89%; Christian 11%. Major cities (1996): Cairo 6,789,000 (1999 urban agglomeration: 10,345,000); Alexandria 3,328,000; Al-Jizah 2,222,000; Shubra al-Khaymah 871,000; Port Said 470,000. Location: northern Africa, bordering the Mediterranean Sea, the Gaza Strip, Israel, the Red Sea, The Sudan, and Libya.

## Vital statistics

Birth rate per 1,000 population (2000): 25.4 (world avg. 22.5). Death rate per 1,000 population (2000): 7.8 (world avg. 9.0). Natural increase rate per 1,000 population (2000): 17.6 (world avg. 13.5). Total fertility rate (avg. births per childbearing woman; 2000): 3.2. Life expectancy at birth (2000): male 61.3 years; female 65.5 years.

## National economy

Budget (1998–99). Revenue: £E 71,295,000,000 (income and profits taxes 21.9%, sales taxes 20.1%, customs duties 14.2%, Suez Canal fees 4.1%, oil revenue 3.1%). Expenditures: £E 75,285,000,000 (current expenditure 79.1%, of which wages and pensions 31.7%, public debt interest 20.8%, defense 11.0%; capital expenditure 20.9%). Public debt (external, outstanding; 2000): $24,279,000,000. Population economically active (1999–2000): total 18,818,000; activity rate 29.7% (participation rates [1995]: ages 15–64, 49.8%; female 22.0%; unemployed 7.4%). Production ('000; metric tons except as noted). Agriculture, forestry, fishing (2000): sugarcane 15,668, wheat 6,564, corn (maize) 6,395; livestock ('000; number of live animals) 4,450 sheep, 3,300 goats, 3,200 buffalo; roundwood 2,883,000 cu m; fish catch (1999) 606,780. Mining and quarrying (1998–99): iron ore 3,002; gypsum 2,666; salt 2,588. Manufacturing (1999–2000): cement 26,000; nitrate fertilizers 1,550; sugar 1,285. Energy production (consumption): electricity ('000,000 kW-hr; 1997) 54,924 (54,924); coal ('000 metric tons; 1997) none (1,880); crude petroleum ('000 barrels; 1999) 303,576 (210,243); petroleum products ('000 metric tons; 1999) 28,538 (23,761); natural gas ('000,000 cu m; 2000) 21,000 (14,897; 1997). Gross national product (2000): $95,380,000,000 ($1,490 per capita). Household income and expenditure. Average household size (1986) 4.9; expenditure (1986–87): food 55.7%, clothing 10.9%, housing 10.5%. Tourism (2000): receipts $4,345,000,000; expenditures $1,073,000,000.

## Foreign trade

Imports (1999): $15,165,000,000 (machinery and transport equipment 32.7%; foodstuffs 21.2%; iron and steel products 7.7%; wood and paper 6.2%; chemical products 5.1%). Major import sources (1999): US 14.3%; Germany 8.6%; Italy 6.6%; France 4.9%; Saudi Arabia 4.4%. Exports (1999): $5,327,000,000 (petroleum and petroleum products 22.9%; cotton yarn, textiles, and clothing 9.7%; basic metals and manufactures 9.4%). Major export destinations (1999): US 12.4%; Italy 10.1%; The Netherlands 7.1%; Israel 5.3%; bunkers and ships' stores 10.3%.

## Transport and communications

Transport. Railroads (1999): length 4,810 km; passenger-km (1998) 56,667,000,000; metric ton-km cargo (1996) 4,117,000,000. Roads (1998): length 64,000 km (paved 78%). Vehicles (1998): passenger cars 1,154,753; trucks and buses 510,766. Inland water (1999): Suez Canal, number of transits 13,490; metric ton cargo 384,994,000. Air transport

(1999): passenger-km 9,074,000,000; metric ton-km cargo 269,520,000; airports (1998) 11. **Communications**, in total units (units per 1,000 persons). Daily newspaper circulation (1996): 2,400,000 (38.0); radio receivers (1997): 20,500,000 (330); television receivers (1999): 11,400,000 (183); telephone main lines (2001): 6,650,000 (103); cellular telephone subscribers (2001): 2,793,800 (43); personal computers (2001): 1,000,000 (16); Internet users (2001): 600,000 (9.3).

## Education and health

**Literacy** (1995): total population age 15 and over literate 51.4%; males 63.6%; females 38.8%. **Health:** physicians (1996) 129,000 (1 per 472 persons); hospital beds (1994) 113,020 (1 per 515 persons); infant mortality rate per 1,000 live births (2000) 62.3. **Food** (2000): daily per capita caloric intake 3,346 (vegetable products 92%, animal products 8%); 133% of FAO recommended minimum.

## Military

**Total active duty personnel** (2001): 443,000 (army 72.2%, navy 4.3%, air force [including air defense] 23.5%). **Military expenditure as percentage of GNP** (1999): 2.7% (world 2.4%); per capita expenditure $36.

## Background

Egypt is home to one of the world's oldest continuous civilizations. Upper and Lower Egypt were united c. 3000 BC, beginning a period of cultural achievement and a line of native rulers that lasted nearly 3,000 years. Egypt's ancient history is divided into the Old, Middle, and New Kingdoms, spanning 31 dynasties and lasting to 332 BC. The pyramids date from the Old Kingdom; the cult of Osiris and the refinement of sculpture, from the Middle Kingdom; and the era of empire and the Exodus of the Jews, from the New Kingdom. An Assyrian invasion occurred in the 7th century BC, and the Persian Achaemenids established a dynasty in 525 BC. The invasion by Alexander the Great in 332 BC inaugurated the Macedonian Ptolemaic period and the ascendancy of Alexandria. The Romans held Egypt from 30 BC to AD 395; later it was placed under the control of Constantinople. Constantine's granting of tolerance in 313 to the Christians began the development of a formal Egyptian (Coptic) church. Egypt came under Arab control in 642 and ultimately was transformed into an Arabic-speaking state, with Islam as the dominant religion. Held by the Umayyad and Abbasid dynasties, in 969 it became the center of the Fatimid dynasty. In 1250 the Mamluks established a dynasty that lasted until 1517, when Egypt fell to the Ottoman Turks. An economic decline ensued, and with it a decline in Egyptian culture. Egypt became a British protectorate in 1914 and received nominal independence in 1922, when a constitutional monarchy was established. A coup overthrew the monarchy in 1952, with Gamal Abdel Nasser taking power. Following three wars with Israel, Egypt, under Nasser's successor, Anwar al-Sadat, ultimately played a leading role in Middle East peace talks. Sadat was succeeded by Hosni Mubarak, who followed Sadat's peace initiatives and in 1982 re-

gained Egyptian sovereignty (lost in 1967) over the Sinai peninsula. Although Egypt took part in the coalition against Iraq during the Persian Gulf War (1991), it later began peace overtures with countries in the region, including Iraq.

## Recent Developments

Egypt began the year 2002 with a devalued currency. On 13 Dec 2001 the government devalued the Egyptian pound 7.8%—to E£ 4.50 to the US dollar—in an effort to boost the economy and help the tourist industry, which had been hit hard in the aftermath of the 11 Sep 2001 attacks in the US. The case of Sa'd al-Din Ibrahim—a professor at the American University in Cairo who had been sentenced in May 2001 to seven years' hard labor for having accepted money from overseas without obtaining government approval—continued to capture the limelight. His third trial—following two convictions that were overturned on appeal—opened in Cairo in February 2003.

**Internet resources:** <www.touregypt.net>

# El Salvador

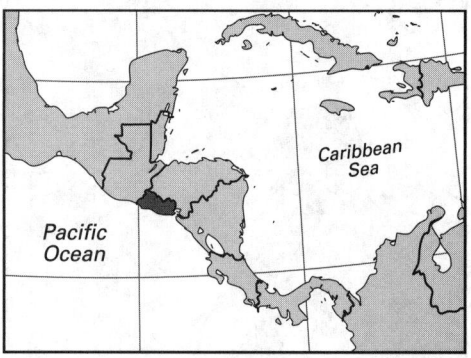

**Official name:** República de El Salvador (Republic of El Salvador). **Form of government:** republic with one legislative house (Legislative Assembly [84]). **Chief of state and government:** President Francisco Flores Pérez (from 1999). **Capital:** San Salvador. **Official language:** Spanish. **Official religion:** none (Roman Catholicism, although not official, enjoys special recognition in the constitution). **Monetary units:** 1 colón (¢) = 100 centavos; valuation (7 Jul 2003; pegged rate) $1 = ¢8.75 (the US dollar is also legal tender since 1 Jan 2001).

## Demography

**Area:** 8,124 sq mi, 21,041 sq km. **Population** (2002): 6,354,000. **Density** (2002): persons per sq mi 782.1, persons per sq km 302.0. **Urban** (2001): 61.5%. **Sex distribution** (2000): male 48.65%; female 51.35%. **Age breakdown** (2000): under 15, 38.0%; 15–29, 28.7%; 30–44, 16.6%; 45–59, 9.5%; 60–74, 5.3%; 75 and over 1.9%. **Ethnic composition** (2000): mestizo 88.3%; Amerindian 9.1%, of which Pipil 4.0%; white 1.6%; other/unknown 1.0%. **Religious affiliation** (1995): Roman Catholic 78.2%; Protestant 17.1%, of which Pentecostal 13.3%; other Christian 1.9%; other

2.8%. **Major urban areas** (1998): San Salvador 467,004 (urban agglomeration 1,856,788); Soyapango 282,066 (within San Salvador urban agglomeration); Santa Ana 241,266; San Miguel 227,414; Mejicanos 180,775 (within San Salvador urban agglomeration). **Location:** Central America, bordering Guatemala, Honduras, and the North Pacific Ocean.

## Vital statistics

**Birth rate** per 1,000 population (2000): 29.0 (world avg. 22.5); (1998) legitimate 27.2%; illegitimate 72.8%. **Death rate** per 1,000 population (2000): 6.3 (world avg. 9.0). **Natural increase rate** per 1,000 population (2000): 22.7 (world avg. 13.5). **Total fertility rate** (avg. births per childbearing woman; 2000): 3.4. **Marriage rate** per 1,000 population (1998): 4.4. **Life expectancy** at birth (2000): male 66.1 years; female 73.5 years.

## National economy

**Budget.** *Revenue* (1997): ¢11,345,000,000 (sales taxes 50.2%, corporate taxes 14.7%, individual income taxes 11.7%, import duties 11.2%). *Expenditures:* ¢12,027,000,000 (education 19.6%, police 16.3%, transportation and communications 12.4%, health 10.3%, defense 7.1%). **Public debt** (external, outstanding; 2000): $2,775,000,000. **Production** (metric tons except as noted). *Agriculture, forestry, fishing* (1999): sugarcane 5,500,000, corn (maize) 683,500, sorghum 181,500; livestock (number of live animals) 1,141,000 cattle, 335,000 pigs; roundwood (1998) 5,129,000 cu m; fish catch (1997) 10,987, of which crustaceans 3,920. *Mining and quarrying* (1997): limestone 3,000,000 metric tons. *Manufacturing* (value added in $'000,000; 1998): food products 306; wearing apparel 249; drugs and medicines 128. *Energy production (consumption):* electricity (kW-hr; 1998) 3,868,000,000 (3,906,000,000); crude petroleum (barrels; 1997) none (5,703,000); petroleum products (metric tons; 1997) 722,000 (1,592,000). **Household income and expenditure.** Average household size (1992–93) 4.8; average income per household (1992–93) ¢22,930 ($2,562); expenditure (1990–91): food and beverages 37.0%, housing 12.1%, transportation and communications 10.2%, clothing and footwear 6.7%. **Land use** (1994): forested 5.0%; meadows and pastures 29.5%; agricultural and under permanent cultivation 35.2%; other 30.3%. **Population economically active** (1995): total 2,136,400; activity rate of total population 39.1% (participation rates: ages 15–64, 62.9%; female 37.1%; unemployed [1998] 7.5%). **Gross national product** (at current market prices; 2000): $12,569,000,000 ($2,000 per capita). **Tourism** (2000): receipts $254,000,000; expenditures $171,000,000.

## Foreign trade

**Imports** (1999-c.i.f.): $3,128,100,000 (food 14.9%; chemicals and chemical products 14.2%; mineral fuels 11.5%; nonelectrical machinery and equipment 10.2%). Major import sources: US 37.5%; Guatemala 11.8%; Mexico 8.4%; Japan 4.1%; Costa Rica 3.7%. **Exports** (1999-f.o.b.): $1,164,200,000 (coffee 21.0%; yarn, fabrics, made-up articles 6.9%; paper and paper products 6.3%; wearing apparel 5.4%; refined petroleum products 4.6%). Major export destinations: Guatemala 23.4%; US 21.3%; Honduras 14.7%; Germany 9.0%; Costa Rica 7.9%.

## Transport and communications

**Transport.** *Railroads* (1997): operational route length 283 km; (1997) passenger-km 7,100,000; (1996) metric ton-km cargo 17,300,000. *Roads* (1999): total length 10,029 km (paved 20%). *Vehicles* (1997): passenger cars 177,488; trucks and buses 184,859. *Air transport* (1999; TACA International Airlines only): passenger-km 5,091,000,000; metric ton-km cargo 43,636,000; airports (1997) with scheduled flights 1. **Communications,** in total units (units per 1,000 persons). Daily newspaper circulation (1996): 278,000 (49); radio receivers (1997): 2,750,000 (475); television receivers (1999): 1,777,000 (196); telephone main lines (2001): 598,000 (93); cellular telephone subscribers (2001): 800,000 (125); personal computers (2001): 140,000 (22); Internet users (2000): 50,000 (8.0).

## Education and health

**Educational attainment** (1992). Percentage of population over age 25 having: no formal schooling 34.7%; incomplete primary education 37.6%; complete primary 10.8%; secondary 9.4%; higher technical 2.4%; incomplete undergraduate 1.1%; complete undergraduate 2.9%; other/unknown 1.1%. **Literacy** (1992): total population age 15 and over literate 2,326,800 (74.1%); males literate 1,141,007 (77.4%); females literate 1,185,793 (71.3%). **Health:** physicians (1997) 6,177 (1 per 936 persons); hospital beds (1996) 9,571 (1 per 593 persons); infant mortality rate per 1,000 live births (2000) 29.2. **Food** (1999): daily per capita caloric intake 2,503 (vegetable products 88%, animal products 12%); 109% of FAO recommended minimum.

## Military

**Total active duty personnel** (2001): 16,800 (army 89.3%, navy 4.2%, air force 6.5%). **Military expenditure as percentage of GNP** (1999): 0.9% (world 2.4%); per capita expenditure $18.

## Background

The Spanish arrived in the area in 1524 and subjugated the Pipil Indian kingdom of Cuzcatlán by 1539. The country was divided into two districts, San Salvador and Sonsonate, both attached to Guatemala. When independence came in 1821, San Salvador was incorporated into the Mexican empire; upon its collapse in 1823, Sonsonate and San Salvador combined to form the new state of El Salvador within the United Provinces of Central America. From its founding, El Salvador experienced a high degree of political turmoil and was under military rule from 1931 to 1979, when the government was ousted in a coup. Elections held in 1982 set up a new government, and in 1983 a new constitution was adopted, but civil war continued through the 1980s. An accord in 1992 brought an uneasy truce.

## Recent Developments

A UN Development Programme report for 2001 ranked El Salvador 95th among 162 countries for human development on the basis of its poverty, low rate of tax collection, and meager spending on social programs. Hopes on the left of a strengthened showing in the March 2003 local and legislative elections were only partly realized. The far-left Farabundo Martí Front for National Liberation took the capital from the rightist parties and showed well in the other most populous cities but failed to wrest control of the legislature from the National Republican Alliance and its conservative coalition partners.

Internet resources: <www.elsalvadorturismo.gob.sv>

# Equatorial Guinea

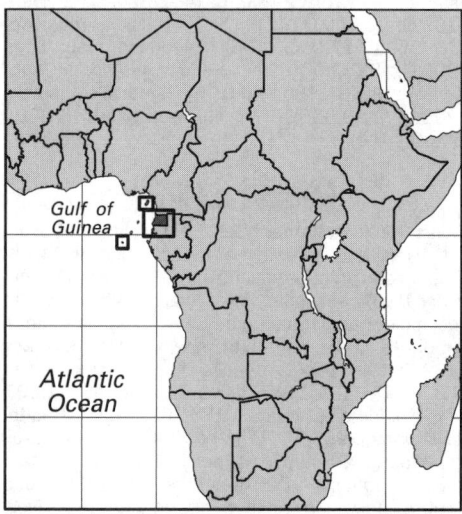

**Official name:** República de Guinea Ecuatorial (Spanish); République du Guinée Équatoriale (French) (Republic of Equatorial Guinea). **Form of government:** republic with one legislative house (House of Representatives of the People [80]). **Chief of state:** President Teodoro Obiang Nguema Mbasogo (from 1979). **Head of government:** Prime Minister Cándido Muatetema Rivas (from 2001). **Capital:** Malabo. **Official languages:** Spanish; French. **Official religion:** none. **Monetary unit:** 1 CFA franc (CFAF) = 100 centimes; valuation (7 Jul 2003) $1 = CFAF 571.07; the CFAF is pegged to the euro (€) at €1 = CFAF 655.96 from 1 Jan 2002.

## Demography

**Area:** 10,831 sq mi, 28,051 sq km. **Population** (2002): 498,000. **Density** (2002): persons per sq mi 46.0, persons per sq km 17.8. **Urban** (2001): 49.4%. **Sex distribution** (2000): male 48.71%; female 51.29%. **Age breakdown** (2000): under 15, 42.7%; 15–29, 26.8%; 30–44, 15.9%; 45–59, 8.6%; 60–74, 4.9%; 75 and over, 1.1%. **Ethnic composition** (1995): Fang 82.9%; Bubi 9.6%; other 7.5%. **Religious affiliation** (2000): Roman Catholic 80.1%; Muslim 4.0%; African Christian 3.7%; Protestant 3.1%; other 9.1%. **Major cities:** Malabo 47,500 (1995); Bata 37,000 (1995); Ela-Nguema 6,179 (1983); Campo Yaunde 5,199 (1983); Los Angeles 4,079 (1983). **Location:** western Africa, the mainland portion bordering Cameroon, Gabon, and the Bight of Biafra (inlet of the Atlantic Ocean).

## Vital statistics

**Birth rate** per 1,000 population (2000): 38.1 (world avg. 22.5). **Death rate** per 1,000 population (2000): 13.4 (world avg. 9.0). **Natural increase rate** per 1,000 population (2000): 24.7 (world avg. 13.5). **Total fertility rate** (avg. births per childbearing woman; 2000): 4.9. **Life expectancy** at birth (2000): male 51.5 years; female 55.7 years.

## National economy

**Budget** (1996). *Revenue:* CFAF 24,637,000,000 (domestic revenue 95.1%, of which oil revenue 46.9%, tax revenue 36.8%, nontax revenue 11.4%; foreign grants 4.9%). *Expenditures:* CFAF 32,955,000,000 (current expenditure 60.6%, of which goods and services 23.8%, salaries 17.3%, interest on debt 15.6%, transfers 3.9%; capital expenditure 9.7%). **Public debt** (external, outstanding; 2000): $198,000,000. **Gross national product** (at current market prices; 2000): $363,000,000 ($800 per capita). **Production** (metric tons except as noted). *Agriculture, forestry, fishing* (1999): roots and tubers 84,000 (of which cassava 49,000, sweet potatoes 35,000), bananas 15,000, coconuts 8,000; livestock (number of live animals) 36,000 sheep, 8,100 goats, 5,300 pigs; roundwood (1998) 811,000 cu m; fish catch (1997) 6,090. *Mining and quarrying:* construction materials. *Manufacturing* (1998): sawn timber 21,500 cu m; processed timber 3,900 cu m. *Energy production (consumption):* electricity (kW-hr; 1999) 21,000,000 ([1997] 20,000,000); coal, none (none); crude petroleum (barrels; 2001) 66,065,000 ([1996] 37,000); petroleum products (metric tons; 1996) none (42,000); natural gas, none (none). **Population economically active** (1997): total 177,000; activity rate of total population 40.0% (participation rates: ages 15–64, 74.7%; female 35.4%; unemployed [1983] 24.2%). **Household income and expenditure.** Average household size (1980) 4.5; sources of income (1988): wages and salaries 57.0%, business income 42.0%, other 1.0%; expenditure (1988): food and beverages 62.0%, clothing and footwear 10.0%; medical care 6.0%. **Tourism:** tourism is a government priority but remains undeveloped. **Land use** (1994): forested 65.2%; meadows and pastures 3.7%; agricultural and under permanent cultivation 8.2%; built-on, wasteland, and other 22.9%.

## Foreign trade

**Imports** (1998-c.i.f.): CFAF 256,200,000,000 (petroleum sector 83.1%; other 16.9%). *Major import sources:* US 35.4%; France 15.0%; Spain 9.9%; Cameroon 9.9%; UK 6.2%; The Netherlands 5.7%. **Exports** (1998-f.o.b.): CFAF 271,800,000,000 (petroleum 87.6%; wood 9.2%; cocoa 1.5%). *Major export destinations:* US 62.0%; Spain 17.3%; China 8.9%; Japan 3.4%; France 3.4%.

## Transport and communications

**Transport.** *Roads* (1996): total length 2,800 km (paved 13%). *Vehicles* (1994): passenger cars 6,500; trucks and buses 4,000. *Air transport* (1996): passenger-km 7,000,000; metric ton-km cargo 1,000,000; airports (1998) with scheduled flights 1.

---

*1 metric ton = about 1.1 short tons;    1 kilometer = 0.6 mi (statute);    1 metric ton-km cargo = about 0.68 short ton-mi cargo;    c.i.f.: cost, insurance, and freight;    f.o.b.: free on board*

**Communications,** in total units (units per 1,000 persons). Daily newspaper circulation (1996): 2,000 (4.9); radio receivers (1997): 180,000 (428); television receivers (1997): 4,000 (9.8); telephone main lines (2001): 6,900 (14.7); cellular telephone subscribers (2001): 15,000 (31.9); Internet users (2001): 6 (0.1).

## Education and health

**Educational attainment** (1983). Percentage of population age 15 and over having: no schooling 35.4%; some primary education 46.6%; primary 13.0%; secondary 2.3%; postsecondary 1.1%; not specified 1.6%. **Literacy** (1995): total population age 15 and over literate 77.8%; males literate 89.3%; females literate 67.4%. **Health:** physicians (1996) 106 (1 per 4,065 persons); hospital beds (1990) 992 (1 per 350 persons); infant mortality rate per 1,000 live births (2000) 94.8.

## Military

**Total active duty personnel** (2001): 1,320 (army 75.8%, navy 9.1%, air force 7.6%). **Military expenditure as percentage of GNP** (1999): 3.2% (world 2.4%); per capita expenditure $40.

## Background

The first inhabitants of the mainland region appear to have been Pygmies. The now-prominent Fang and Bubi reached the mainland region in the 17th-century Bantu migrations. Equatorial Guinea was ceded by the Portuguese to the Spanish in the late 18th century; it was frequented by slave traders, as well as by British, German, Dutch, and French merchants. Bioko was administered by British authorities (1827–58) before the official takeover by the Spanish. The mainland (Río Muni) was not effectively occupied by the Spanish until 1926. Independence was declared in 1968, followed by a reign of terror and economic chaos under the dictatorial president Macías Nguema, who was overthrown by a military coup in 1979 and later executed. A new constitution was adopted in 1982, but political unrest persisted.

## Recent Developments

The discovery in 2002 of new offshore oil fields made Equatorial Guinea one of the most exciting countries anywhere for new oil production. Western oil companies increased production to more than 200,000 bbl per day. While 70% of the population remained illiterate, the vast new wealth allowed the government to commit itself to providing basic education for all. The country remained notorious for its poor human rights record, however.

**Internet resources:** <www.cia.gov/cia/publications/factbook/geos/ek.html>

# Eritrea

**Official name:** State of Eritrea. **Form of government:** transitional regime with one interim legislative body (Transitional National Assembly [150]). **Head of state and government:** President Isaias Afwerki (from 1993). **Capital:** Asmara. **Official language:** none. Of-

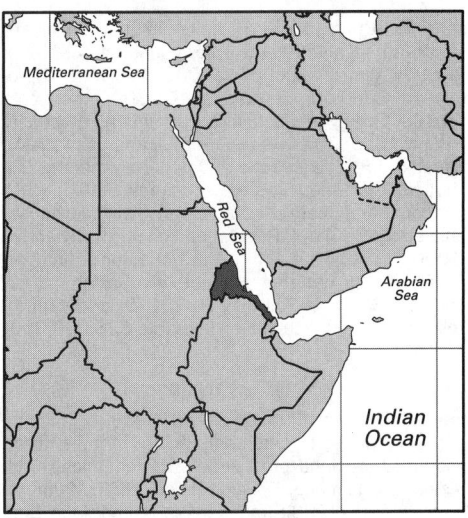

ficial religion: none. **Monetary unit:** nakfa (Nfa) = 100 cents; valuation (11 Jul 2003) $1 = Nfa 9.75.

## Demography

**Area:** 46,770 sq mi, 121,100 sq km. **Population** (2002 est.): 3,981,000. **Density** (2002): persons per sq mi 85.1, persons per sq km 32.9. **Urban** (1998): 18.0%. **Sex distribution** (2001): male 49.83%; female 50.17%. **Age breakdown** (2001): under 15, 42.8%; 15–29, 28.8%; 30–44, 14.3%; 45–59, 9.0%; 60–74, 4.1%; 75 and over, 1.0%. **Ethnolinguistic composition** (2000): Tigrinya (Tigray) 51.8%; Tigré 17.9%; Afar 8.1%; Saho 4.3%; Kunama 4.1%; other 13.8%. **Religious affiliation** (2000): Christian 50.5%, of which Eritrean Orthodox 46.1%; Muslim 44.7%; other 4.8%. **Major cities** (1992): Asmara 503,000 (2001); Asseb 50,000; Keren 40,000; Massawa 40,000. **Location:** the Horn of eastern Africa, bordering The Sudan, the Red Sea, Djibouti, and Ethiopia.

## Vital statistics

**Birth rate** per 1,000 population (2001): 42.5 (world avg. 21.2). **Death rate** per 1,000 population (2001): 12.1 (world avg. 8.9). **Natural increase rate** per 1,000 population (2001): 30.4 (world avg. 12.3). **Total fertility rate** (avg. births per childbearing woman; 2001): 5.9. **Marriage rate** per 1,000 population (1992): 6.8. **Life expectancy** at birth (2001): male 53.7 years; female 58.7 years.

## National economy

**Budget** (1999). *Revenue*: Nfa 1,822,900,000 (tax revenue 53.9%, of which direct taxes 26.1%, import duties 14.5%, indirect taxes 13.3%; nontax revenue 46.1%). *Expenditures*: Nfa 3,822,200,000 (current expenditure 61.1%, of which defense 38.2%, wages and salaries 14.5%; capital expenditure 38.9%). **Public debt** (external, outstanding; 2000): $298,000,-000. **Production** (metric tons except as noted). *Agriculture, forestry, fishing* (2001): sorghum 86,990, roots and tubers 85,000, barley 44,633; livestock (number of live animals) 1,570,000 sheep, 1,700,000 goats, 2,200,000 cattle; roundwood (2000) 2,246,265; fish catch (1999) 4,797, of which artisanal fisheries 941. *Mining and quarrying* (2000):

salt 200,000; marble and granite are quarried, as are sand and aggregate (gravel) for construction. *Manufacturing* (gross value in Nfa '000; 1998): food production 234,700; beverages 161,300; chemicals 59,800. *Energy production (consumption)*: electricity (kW-hr; 1999) 207,000,000 (n.a.). **Land use** (1994): forested 7.3%; agricultural and under permanent cultivation 5.1%; meadows and pastures 69.0%; other (predominantly barren land) 18.6%. **Average household size** (1998) 4.7. **Population economically active** (1996): 1,649,000; activity rate of total population 41.4%. **Gross national product** (at current market prices; 2000): $696,000,000 ($170 per capita). **Tourism** (2000): receipts from visitors $26,000,000.

## Foreign trade

**Imports** (1999-c.i.f.): $506,900,000 (1998; machinery and transport equipment 38.3%, manufactured goods 23.9%, food products 17.1%, chemical products 5.7%, animal and vegetable oil 2.6%). *Major import sources* (1998): Italy 17.4%; United Arab Emirates 16.2%; Germany 5.7%; UK 4.5%; US 4.2%; Japan 4.0%. **Exports** (1999): $26,300,000 (1998; raw materials 45.5%, food products 29.6%, manufactured goods 13.2%, machinery and transport equipment 2.4%, chemical products 2.1%). *Major export destinations* (1998): The Sudan 27.2%; Ethiopia 26.5%; Japan 13.2%; United Arab Emirates 7.3%; Italy 5.3%.

## Transport and communications

**Transport.** *Railroads* (2000): the 306-km rail line that formerly connected Massawa and Agordat is currently under reconstruction; a 82-km section between Massawa and Embatkala was reopened in stages by 2001. *Roads* (1999): total length 4,010 km (paved 22%). *Vehicles* (1996): automobiles 5,940. *Air transport* (1999; Asmara airport only): passenger arrivals and departures 93,007; metric ton cargo handled 3,279; airports (2000) with scheduled flights 2. **Communications,** in total units (units per 1,000 persons). Radio receivers (1995): 310,000 (89.6); television receivers (1999): 60,000 (15.1); telephone main lines (2001): 32,000 (8.4); personal computers (2001): 7,000 (1.8); Internet users (2001): 10,000 (2.6).

## Education and health

**Literacy** (1998): total population age 15 and over literate, 51.7%; males 65.7%; females 38.2%. **Health** (1993): physicians 69 (1 per 36,000 persons); hospital beds (1986–87): 2,449 (1 per 1,100 persons); infant mortality rate per 1,000 live births (2001) 75.1. **Food** (2000): daily per capita caloric intake 1,655 (vegetable 94%, animal products 6%); 71% of FAO recommended minimum.

## Military

**Total active duty personnel** (2000): estimated strength of Eritrean armed forces (predominantly former guerrillas) is between 200,000 and 250,000. UN peacekeeping force along Eritrean-Ethiopian border (May 2002): 4,200. **Military expenditure as percentage of GNP** (1999): 27.4% (world 2.4%); per capita expenditure $52.

**Did you know?** Tigrinya, spoken by about half of Eritrea's population, is a Semitic language based on Ge'ez, the ancient liturgical (and now extinct vernacular) language of the Ethiopian Orthodox Church. Written Tigrinya has its own script with more than 200 characters, each of which represents a particular syllable ("ba," "bo," etc.).

## Background

As the site of the main ports of the Aksumite empire, Eritrea was linked to the beginnings of the Ethiopian kingdom, but it retained much of its independence until it came under Ottoman rule in the 16th century. In the 17th and 19th centuries, control of the territory was disputed among Ethiopia, the Ottomans, the kingdom of Tigray, Egypt, and Italy; it became an Italian colony in 1890. Eritrea was used as the main base for the Italian invasions of Ethiopia (1896 and 1935–36) and in 1936 became part of Italian East Africa. It was captured by the British in 1941, federated to Ethiopia in 1952, and made a province of Ethiopia in 1962. Thirty years of guerrilla warfare by Eritrean secessionist groups ensued. A provisional Eritrean government was established in 1991 after the overthrow of the Ethiopian government, and independence came in 1993. A new constitution was ratified in 1997.

## Recent Developments

The years 2002–03 saw progress in postwar recovery and normalization of Eritrea's regional and international relations. Strained relations with the European Commission were patched up, allowing the disbursement during the year of some €25 million (about $25 million). In late March 2003 the UN Boundary Commission confirmed its decision that the village of Badme, disputed with Ethiopia, should go to Eritrea. The refugee repatriation program successfully oversaw the return of hundreds of Eritreans from The Sudan to their homeland.

**Internet resources:** <www.eriemb.se>

# Estonia

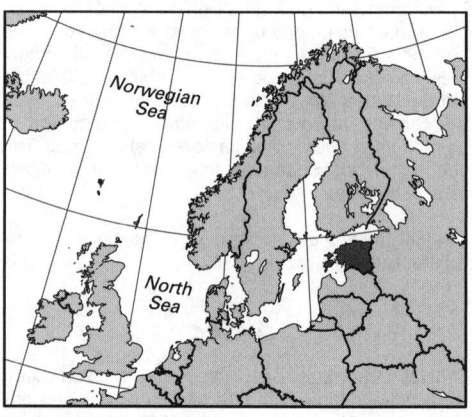

*1 metric ton = about 1.1 short tons;    1 kilometer = 0.6 mi (statute);    1 metric ton-km cargo = about 0.68 short ton-mi cargo;    c.i.f.: cost, insurance, and freight;    f.o.b.: free on board*

**Official name:** Eesti Vabariik (Republic of Estonia). **Form of government:** unitary multiparty republic with a single legislative body (Riigikogu [101]). **Chief of state:** President Arnold Ruutel (from 2001). **Head of government:** Prime Minister Juhan Parts (from 10 Apr 2003). **Capital:** Tallinn. **Official language:** Estonian. **Official religion:** none. **Monetary unit:** 1 kroon (EEK) = 100 sents; valuation (7 Jul 2003) $1 = EEK 13.63.

## Demography

**Area:** 16,769 sq mi, 43,431 sq km. **Population** (2002): 1,359,000. **Density** (2001): persons per sq mi 81.0, persons per sq km 31.3. **Urban** (2001): 69.4%. **Sex distribution** (2001): male 46.12%; female 53.88%. **Age breakdown** (2001): under 15, 18.0%; 15–29, 21.9%; 30–44, 21.5%; 45–59, 18.3%; 60–74, 15.0%; 75 and over, 5.3%. **Ethnic composition** (2000): Estonian 65.3%; Russian 28.1%; Ukrainian 2.5%; Belarusian 1.5%; Finnish 0.9%; other 1.7%. **Religious affiliation** (1995): Christian 38.1%, of which Orthodox 20.4%, Evangelical Lutheran 13.7%; other (mostly nonreligious) 61.9%. **Major cities** (2001): Tallinn 399,850; Tartu 101,240; Narva 68,538; Kohtla-Järve 47,484; Pärnu 44,978. **Location:** Eastern Europe, bordering the Gulf of Finland, Russia, Latvia, the Gulf of Riga, and the Baltic Sea.

## Vital statistics

**Birth rate** per 1,000 population (2001): 9.3 (world avg. 21.2); (2000) legitimate 45.5%; illegitimate 54.5%. **Death rate** per 1,000 population (2001): 13.6 (world avg. 8.9). **Natural increase rate** per 1,000 population (2001): –4.3 (world avg. 12.3). **Total fertility rate** (avg. births per childbearing woman; 1999): 1.2. **Marriage rate** per 1,000 population (2001): 4.1. **Divorce rate** per 1,000 population (2001): 3.2. **Life expectancy** at birth (1999): male 65.4 years; female 76.1 years.

## National economy

**Budget** (1998). *Revenue:* EEK 24,130,000,000 (social security contributions 32.9%, value-added taxes 26.6%, excise taxes 11.6%, personal income taxes 11.4%). *Expenditures:* EEK 24,103,000,000 (social security and welfare 30.6%, health 16.4%, education 8.6%, police 7.3%, defense 4.0%). **Public debt** (external, outstanding; 2000): $206,300,000. **Production** (metric tons except as noted). *Agriculture, forestry, fishing* (1999): potatoes 340,000, barley 198,000, wheat 135,000; livestock (number of live animals) 326,400 pigs, 307,500 cattle; roundwood (1998) 6,061,000 cu m; (1997) fish catch 123,873. *Mining and quarrying* (1998): oil shale 10,913,000; peat 333,500. *Manufacturing* (value of production in EEK '000,000; 1999): food products 6,770; wood products (excluding furniture) 4,703; furniture 2,546. *Energy production (consumption):* electricity (kW-hr; 2001) 8,484,000,000 ([2000] 5,422,000,-000); hard coal (metric tons; 1997) none (98,000); lignite (metric tons; 1997) 14,383,000 (15,951,-000); petroleum products (metric tons; 1997) 367,000 (1,231,000); natural gas (cu m; 1997) none (670,000,000). **Tourism** (2000): receipts $506,000,000; expenditures $204,000,000. **Population economically active** (1997): total 707,800; activity rate of total population 48.4% (participation

rates: ages 15–64, 71.3%; female 47.9%; unemployed [2001] 12.6%). **Household income and expenditure** (1998). Average household size 2.3; average disposable income per household EEK 53,049 ($3,769); sources of income: wages and salaries 63.8%, transfers 24.1%, self-employment 6.2%, other 5.9%; expenditure: food and beverages 35.5%, housing 14.6%, transportation 10.7%, clothing and footwear 9.0%. **Gross national product** (2000): $4,894,000,000 ($3,580 per capita). **Land use** (1994): forest 44.7%; pasture 7.2%; agriculture 32.2%; other 15.9%.

## Foreign trade

**Imports** (2000-c.i.f.): EEK 72,246,000,000 (electrical and nonelectrical machinery 38.5%, fabricated and base metals 8.1%, textiles and apparel 7.5%). *Major import sources:* Finland 27.4%; Sweden 9.8%; Germany 9.5%; Russia 8.5%; Japan 6.1%. **Exports** (2000-f.o.b.): EEK 53,877,000,000 (electrical and nonelectrical machinery 37.5%, wood and wood products 13.4%, textiles and clothing 11.3%). *Major export destinations:* Finland 32.3%; Sweden 20.5%; Germany 8.5%; Latvia 7.0%; UK 4.4%.

## Transport and communications

**Transport.** *Railroads* (2000): route length 968 km; passenger-km 263,000,000; metric ton-km cargo 8,102,000,000. *Roads* (2000): total length 16,430 km (paved 51%). *Vehicles* (1999): passenger cars 458,700; trucks and buses 87,226. *Air transport* (2001; Estonian Air): passenger-km 295,000,000; metric ton-km cargo 1,412,000; airports (1997) 1. **Communications,** in total units (units per 1,000 persons). Daily newspaper circulation (1996): 255,000 (174); radio receivers (1997): 1,010,000 (693); television receivers (1999): 800,000 (568); telephone main lines (2001): 503,600 (352); cellular telephone subscribers (2001): 651,200 (455); personal computers (2001): 250,000 (175); Internet users (2001): 429,700 (300).

## Education and health

**Educational attainment** (1989). Percentage of persons age 25 and over having: no formal schooling 2.2%; primary education 39.0%; secondary 45.1%; higher 13.7%. **Health** (1998): physicians 4,471 (1 per 324 persons); hospital beds 10,509 (1 per 138 persons); infant mortality rate per 1,000 live births (2000) 8.1. **Food** (1999): daily per capita caloric intake 3,154 (vegetable products 74%, animal products 26%); 123% of FAO recommended minimum.

## Military

**Total active duty personnel** (2001): 4,450 (army 90.8%, navy 6.7%, air force 2.5%). **Military expenditure as a percentage of GNP** (1999): 1.5% (world 2.4%); per capita expenditure $120.

## Background

The lands on the eastern shores of the Baltic Sea were invaded by Vikings in the 9th century AD and later by Danes, Swedes, and Russians, but the Estonians were able to withstand the assaults until the Danes took control in 1219. In 1346 the Danes sold their sovereignty to the Teutonic Order, which was then in possession of Livonia (southern Estonia and Latvia). In the mid-16th century Estonia was once again divided, with northern Estonia capitulating to Sweden and Poland gaining Livonia, which it surrendered to Sweden in 1629. Russia acquired Livonia and Estonia in 1721. Nearly a century later, serfdom was abolished, and from 1881 Estonia underwent intensive Russification. In 1918 Estonia obtained independence from Russia, which lasted until the Soviet Union occupied the country in 1940 and forcibly incorporated it into the USSR. Germany held the region (1941–44) during World War II, but the Soviet regime was restored in 1944, after which Estonia's economy was collectivized and integrated into that of the Soviet Union. In 1991, along with other parts of the former USSR, it proclaimed its independence and subsequently held elections. Estonia continued negotiations with Russia to settle their common border.

## Recent Developments

The closing months of 2002 brought to fruition two of Estonia's long-standing foreign policy goals: invitations for membership in NATO and in the European Union. Formal induction into both organizations was expected in 2004, following a ratification process in the case of NATO and a referendum, scheduled for September 2003, in the case of the EU.

**Internet resources:** <http://visitestonia.com>

# Ethiopia

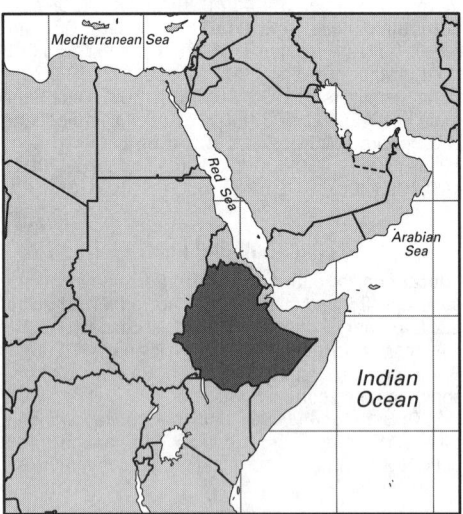

**Official name:** Federal Democratic Republic of Ethiopia. **Form of government:** federal republic with two legislative houses (Federal Council [108]; Council of People's Representatives [546]). **Chief of state:** President Wolde-Giorgis Girma (from 2001). **Head of government:** Prime Minister Meles Zenawi (from 1995). **Capital:** Addis Ababa. **Official language:** none (Amharic is the "working" language). **Official religion:** none. **Monetary unit:** 1 birr (Br) = 100 cents; valuation (7 Jul 2003) $1 = Br 8.58.

## Demography

**Area:** 437,794 sq mi, 1,133,882 sq km. **Population** (2002): 67,673,000. **Density** (2002): persons per sq mi 154.6, persons per sq km 59.7. **Urban** (2001): 15.9%. **Sex distribution** (2000): male 50.19%; female 49.81%. **Age breakdown** (2000): under 15, 47.0%; 15–29, 26.4%; 30–44, 14.2%; 45–59, 7.9%; 60–74, 3.7%; 75 and over, 0.8%. **Ethnolinguistic composition** (1994): Oromo 31.8%; Amharic 29.3%; Somali 6.2%; Tigrinya 5.9%; Walaita 4.6%; Gurage 4.2%; Sidamo 3.4%; Afar 1.9%; Hadya-Libide 1.7%; other 11.0%. **Religious affiliation** (1994): Ethiopian Orthodox 50.3%; Muslim 32.9%; Protestant 10.1%; traditional beliefs 4.8%; Roman Catholic 0.6%; other 1.3%. **Major cities** (1994): Addis Ababa 2,112,737; Dire Dawa 164,851; Harer 131,139; Nazret 127,842; Gonder 112,249. **Location:** the Horn of eastern Africa, bordering Eritrea, Djibouti, Somalia, Kenya, and The Sudan.

## Vital statistics

**Birth rate** per 1,000 population (2000): 45.1 (world avg. 22.5). **Death rate** per 1,000 population (2000): 17.6 (world avg. 9.0). **Natural increase rate** per 1,000 population (2000): 27.5 (world avg. 13.5). **Total fertility rate** (avg. births per childbearing woman; 2001): 7.1. **Life expectancy** at birth (2000): male 44.4 years; female 45.9 years.

## National economy

**Budget** (1997–98). *Revenue:* Br 9,686,000,000 (taxes 54.4%, of which import duties 21.0%, income and profit tax 17.1%, sales tax 12.2%, export duties 1.9%; nontax revenue 29.2%; grants 13.1%; privatization receipts 3.3%). *Expenditures:* Br 7,140,000,000 (general services 45.2%, of which defense 29.3%; social services 24.1%, of which education 15.8%, public health 5.6%; debt payment 12.3%). **Public debt** (external, outstanding; 2000): $5,325,000,000. **Tourism** (2000): receipts $68,000,000; expenditures $74,000,000. **Gross national product** (2000): $6,737,000,000 ($100 per capita). **Production** (metric tons except as noted). *Agriculture, forestry, fishing* (1999): corn (maize) 2,840,000, sugarcane 2,200,-000, sorghum 1,340,000; livestock (number of live animals) 35,095,230 cattle, 22,000,000 sheep, 16,950,000 goats; roundwood (1998) 50,148,000 cu m; fish catch (1998) 14,000. *Mining and quarrying* (1995): cement 400,000; limestone 200,000; salt 165,000; gold 4,500 kg; platinum 48 troy oz. *Manufacturing* (gross value in Br '000; 1997): food 1,351,200; beverages 876,408; textiles 593,341. *Energy production (consumption):* electricity (kW-hr; 1997) 1,662,000,000 (1,662,000,000); crude petroleum (barrels; 1997) n.a. (1,187,000); petroleum products (metric tons; 1996) 139,000 (389,000). **Land use** (1994): forest 13.3%; pasture 20.0%; agriculture 11.0%; other 55.7%. **Population economically active** (1997): total 26,408,000; activity rate of total population 44.8% (participation rates [1995]: ages 15–64, 72.2%; female [1997] 41.0%; unemployed [1994] 62.9%). **Household income and expenditure.** Average household size (1998) 5.0; income per household (1981–82; includes Eritrea) Br 1,728 ($835); sources of income (1981–82): self-employment 79.5%, wages and salaries 0.2%, other 20.3%;

*1 metric ton = about 1.1 short tons;    1 kilometer = 0.6 mi (statute);    1 metric ton-km cargo = about 0.68 short ton-mi cargo;    c.i.f.: cost, insurance, and freight;    f.o.b.: free on board*

expenditure (1988; includes Eritrea): food 66.7%, fuel and power 15.9%, clothing and footwear 6.8%, health care 3.1%, education 2.5%, household goods 2.1%.

## Foreign trade

**Imports** (1997–98): Br 7,615,100,000 (consumer goods 24.9%, semifinished goods 17.2%, petroleum products 16.2%, food and live animals 13.9%, transport equipment 13.2%, machinery 13.1%, raw materials 2.1%). *Major import sources:* Japan 10.5%; Germany 9.8%; Saudi Arabia 9.7%; Italy 9.5%; UK 6.0%; India 5.7%; US 4.7%. **Exports** (1997–98): Br 3,966,000,000 (coffee 69.8%, hides 8.4%, pulses 2.5%, petroleum products 0.2%). *Major export destinations:* Germany 24.8%; Japan 12.2%; Saudi Arabia 9.9%; Italy 6.8%; US 6.8%; Belgium 4.4%; France 3.6%.

## Transport and communications

**Transport.** *Railroads* (1996–97): length 682 km; passenger-km 157,000,000; metric ton-km cargo 106,000,000. *Roads* (1996): total length 19,500 km (paved 15%). *Vehicles* (1997): passenger cars 52,012; trucks and buses 39,936. *Air transport* (1997; Ethiopian Airlines only): passenger-km 1,915,000,000; metric ton-km cargo 328,000,000; airports (1997) 31. **Communications,** in total units (units per 1,000 persons). Daily newspaper circulation (1997): 86,000 (1.5); radio receivers (1997): 11,750,000 (202); television receivers (1999): 350,000 (6.1); telephone main lines (2001 (main lines (310,000) (4.8); cellular telephone subscribers (2001): 27,500 (0.4); personal computers (2001): 75,000 (1.2); Internet users (2001): 25,000 (0.3).

## Education and health

**Literacy** (1995): total population age 15 and over literate 35.5%; males 45.5%; females 25.3%. **Health:** physicians (1988; includes Eritrea) 1,466 (1 per 30,195 persons); hospital beds (1986–87; includes Eritrea) 11,745 (1 per 3,873 persons); infant mortality rate per 1,000 live births (2000) 101.3. **Food** (2000): daily per capita caloric intake 2,023 (vegetable products 95%, animal products 5%); 87% of FAO recommended minimum.

## Military

**Total active duty personnel** (2001): 252,500 (army 99.0%, air force 1.0%); UN peacekeeping personnel along Ethiopian-Eritrean border (May 2002): 4,200. **Military expenditure as percentage of GNP** (1999): 8.8% (world 2.4%); per capita expenditure $9.

## Background

Ethiopia, the Biblical land of Cush, was inhabited from earliest antiquity and was once under ancient Egyptian rule. Geez-speaking agriculturalists established the kingdom of Daamat in the 2nd millennium BC. After 300 BC they were superseded by the kingdom of Aksum, whose king Menilek I, according to legend, was the son of King Solomon and the Queen of Sheba. Christianity was introduced in the 4th century AD and became widespread. Ethiopia's prosperous Mediterranean trade was cut off by the Muslim Arabs in the 7th and 8th centuries and the area's interests were directed eastward. Contact with Europe resumed in the late 15th century with the arrival of the Portuguese. Modern Ethiopia

began with the reign of Tewodros II, who began the consolidation of the country. In the wake of European encroachment, the coastal region was made an Italian colony in 1890, but under Emperor Menilek II, the Italians were defeated and ousted in 1896. Ethiopia prospered under his rule, and his modernization programs were continued by Emperor Haile Selassie in the 1930s. In 1936 Italy again gained control of the country and held it as part of Italian Africa until 1941, when it was liberated by the British. Ethiopia incorporated Eritrea in 1952. In 1974 Haile Selassie was deposed and a Marxist government, plagued by civil wars and famine, controlled the country until 1991. In 1993 Eritrea gained its independence, but border conflicts with it and neighboring Somalia continued in the 1990s.

## Recent Developments

In April 2002 the border demarcation between Ethiopia and Eritrea was finalized. International coffee prices fell to a 40-year low in the first part of 2002. Coffee was Ethiopia's largest export, and this was bad news for an economy that had been growing at a rate of only about 2% for a few years. Drought affected the grain harvest in the highlands, and by year's end famine was looming in the northeastern Afar region, where rains failed for a second year. In June 2003 three crania were discovered in the Afar region that, at 160,000 years old, are believed to be the oldest fossils of *Homo sapiens* yet unearthed.

**Internet resources:** <www.ethiopians.com>

# Faroe Islands

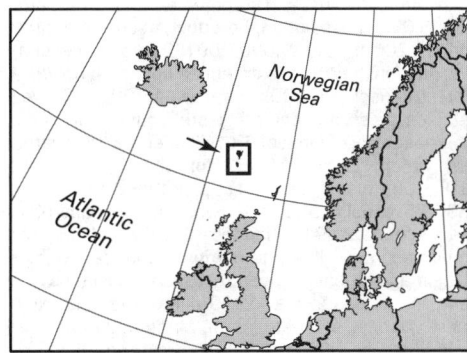

**Official name:** Føroyar (Faroese); Færøerne (Danish) (Faroe Islands; English-language alternative spelling is Faeroe Islands). **Political status:** self-governing region of the Danish realm with a single legislative body (Lagting [32]). **Chief of state:** Danish Queen Margrethe II (from 1972) represented by High Commissioner Birgit Kleis (from 2001). **Head of home government:** Prime Minister Anfinn Kallsberg (from 1998). **Capital:** Tórshavn (Thorshavn). **Official languages:** Faroese; Danish. **Official religion:** Evangelical Lutheran. **Monetary unit:** 1 Danish krone (Dkr) = 100 øre; valuation (7 Jul 2003) $1 = Dkr 6.47 (the local currency, the Faroese króna (Fkr), is equivalent to the Danish krone. Banknotes used are Faroese or Danish; coins are Danish).

## Demography

**Area:** 540 sq mi, 1,399 sq km. **Population** (2002): 47,400. **Density** (2002): persons per sq mi 87.8, persons per sq km 33.9. **Urban** (2000): urban 36.3%. **Sex distribution** (2001): male 51.88%; female 48.12%. **Age breakdown** (2000): under 15, 23.0%; 15–29, 21.1%; 30–44, 19.5%; 45–59, 18.4%; 60–74, 11.5%; 75 and over, 6.5%. **Ethnic composition** (2000): Faroese 97.0%; Danish 2.5%; other Scandinavian 0.4%; other 0.1%. **Religious affiliation** (1995): Evangelical Lutheran Church of Denmark 80.8%; Plymouth Brethren 10.1%; Roman Catholic 0.2%; other (mostly nonreligious) 8.9%. **Major towns** (2002): Tórshavn 18,070; Klaksvík 4,773; Runavík 2,516; Tvøroyri 1,837. **Location**: island group north of the British Isles between the Norwegian Sea and the North Atlantic Ocean.

## Vital statistics

**Birth rate** per 1,000 population (2001): 13.5 (world avg. 21.2); (1998) legitimate 62.0%; illegitimate 38.0%. **Death rate** per 1,000 population (2001): 7.7 (world avg. 8.9). **Natural increase rate** per 1,000 population (2001): 5.8 (world avg. 12.3). **Total fertility rate** (avg. births per childbearing woman; 2000): 2.3. **Marriage rate** per 1,000 population (2001): 5.9. **Divorce rate** per 1,000 population (2001): 0.8. **Life expectancy** at birth (2000): male 75.0 years; female 81.9 years.

## National economy

**Budget** (1999). *Revenue*: Dkr 3,104,530,000 (income taxes 33.8%; customs and excise duties 32.4%; transfers from the Danish government 30.4%). *Expenditures*: Dkr 3,105,530,000 (health and social welfare 43.3%; education 16.6%; debt service 7.7%; agriculture, fishing, and commerce 7.5%; administration 6.0%). **Gross national product** (at current market prices; 2000): $1,029,000,000 ($22,460 per capita). **Production** (metric tons except as noted). *Agriculture, forestry, fishing* (2000): potatoes 1,500, other vegetables, grass, hay, and silage are produced; livestock (number of live animals) 68,100 sheep, 2,000 cattle; fish catch (1999) 358,013 (of which blue whiting 105,106, mackerel 56,476, saithe 34,423, cod 33,725, capelin 24,275, prawns, shrimps, and other crustaceans 20,916, haddock 19,697). *Mining and quarrying*: negligible (the maritime boundary demarcation agreement between the Shetland Islands (UK) and the Faroes in May 1999 allowed for the exploration of deep-sea petroleum). *Manufacturing* (value added in Dkr '000,000; 1999): processed fish 393; all other manufacturing 351; important products include handicrafts and woolen textiles and clothing. *Energy production (consumption)*: electricity (kW-hr; 2001) 231,000,000 ([1997] 181,000,000); petroleum products (metric tons; 1997) none (207,000). **Population economically active** (1997): total 26,500; activity rate of total population c. 60% (participation rates: female c. 46%; unemployed c. 10%). **Public debt** (to Denmark; end of 1999): $653,000,000. **Household expenditure**. Expenditure (1998): food and beverages 25.1%, transportation and communications 17.7%, housing 12.5%, recreation 11.9%, energy 7.7%. **Tourism** (1987): receipts from visitors $10,000,000; expenditures by nationals abroad $42,600,000. **Land use** (1994): forested, none; meadows and pastures, none; agricultural and under permanent cultivation 2.1%; other 97.9%.

## Foreign trade

**Imports** (2000): Dkr 4,185,000,000 (machinery and transport equipment 31.0%; goods for household consumption 22.4%; petroleum products 12.1%). *Major import sources:* Norway 27.0%; Denmark 24.9%; Germany 6.6%; UK 5.3%; Sweden 4.8%. **Exports** (2000): Dkr 3,804,000,000 (fish for human consumption 92.1%, of which fresh chilled fish 28.5%, frozen fish 17.2%, dried, salted, and smoked fish 14.3%; ships 6.9%). *Major export destinations:* Denmark 31.2%; UK 19.0%; France 6.9%; Spain 6.7%; Germany 5.7%; US 5.3%.

## Transport and communications

**Transport**. *Roads* (1998): total length 458 km. *Vehicles* (2000): passenger cars 14,608; trucks and buses 3,455. *Air transport* (1998): airports with scheduled flights 1. **Communications**, in total units (units per 1,000 persons). Daily newspaper circulation (1996): 6,000 (136); radio receivers (1997): 26,000 (582); television receivers (1997): 15,000 (333); telephone main lines (2001): 25,471 (542); cellular telephone subscribers (1999): 11,000 (244); Internet users (1998): 5,000 (113).

## Education and health

**Health** (1998): physicians 83 (1 per 537 persons); hospital beds 277 (1 per 161 persons); infant mortality rate per 1,000 live births (2000) 6.9. **Food** (1979–81): daily per capita caloric intake 3,195 (vegetable products 68%, animal products 32%); 120% of FAO recommended minimum.

## Military

Defense responsibility lies with Denmark.

 **Did you know?** The Faroese Parliament (Lagting) has been in existence for more than 1,000 years. Evidence of the Lagting can be traced as far back as AD 800.

## Background

First settled by Irish monks (c. 700), the islands were colonized by the Vikings (c. 800) and were ruled by Norway from the 11th century until 1380, when they passed to Denmark. They unsuccessfully sought independence in 1946 but received self-government in 1948.

## Recent Developments

Relations between the Faroe Islands and Denmark remained strained following the postponement of a local referendum on the issue of independence that had been scheduled for May 2001. Danish Prime Minister Poul Nyrup Rasmussen had threatened to cut off Copenhagen's annual $120 million grant to the islands, about one-third of Faroese public expenditure. In April 2002 elections pro-independence parties captured 17 of 32 legislative seats and formed a coalition government, although the Union Party,

*1 metric ton = about 1.1 short tons;   1 kilometer = 0.6 mi (statute);   1 metric ton-km cargo = about 0.68 short ton-mi cargo;   c.i.f.: cost, insurance, and freight;   f.o.b.: free on board*

which opposed independence, received the largest number of votes (26%).

Internet resources: <www.tourist.fo>

# Fiji

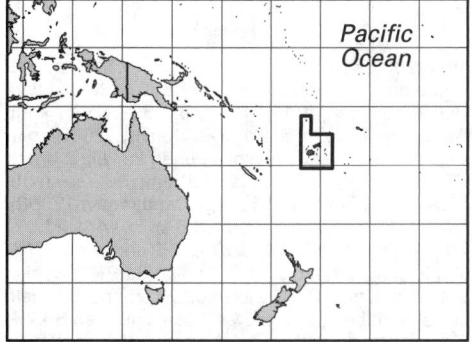

Pacific Ocean

**Official name:** Republic of the Fiji Islands. **Form of government:** multiparty republic with two legislative houses (Senate [32; all seats are nonelected]); House of Representatives [71]). **Chief of state:** President Ratu Josefa Iloilo (from 2000). **Head of government:** Prime Minister Laisenia Qarase (from 2001). **Capital:** Suva. **Official languages:** English, Fijian, and Hindustani have equal status per constitution. **Official religion:** none. **Monetary unit:** 1 Fiji dollar (F$) = 100 cents; valuation (7 Jul 2003) US$1 = F$1.85.

## Demography

**Area:** 7,055 sq mi, 18,272 sq km. **Population** (2002): 824,000. **Density** (2002): persons per sq mi 116.8, persons per sq km 45.1. **Urban** (1996): 46.4%. **Sex distribution** (2000): male 50.88%; female 49.12%. **Age breakdown** (2000): under 15, 32.8%; 15–29, 27.9%; 30–44, 20.9%; 45–59, 12.3%; 60–74, 5.0%; 75 and over, 1.1%. **Ethnic composition** (2000): Fijian 52.0%; Indian 41.5%[5]; other 6.5%. **Religious affiliation** (2000): Christian 56.8%, of which Protestant 37.1%, independent Christian 8.5%, Roman Catholic 8.4%; Hindu 33.3%; Muslim 6.9%; nonreligious 1.3%; Sikh 0.7%; other 1.0%. **Major cities** (1996; "urban centers"): Suva 167,421; Lautoka 42,917; Nadi 30,791; Labasa 24,187; Nausori 21,645. **Location:** archipelago in the South Pacific Ocean, between Hawaii (US) and New Zealand.

## Vital statistics

**Birth rate** per 1,000 population (2001): 23.3 (world avg. 21.2). **Death rate** per 1,000 population (2001): 5.8 (world avg. 8.9). **Natural increase rate** per 1,000 population (2000): 17.5 (world avg. 12.3). **Total fertility rate** (avg. births per childbearing woman; 2001): 2.9. **Life expectancy** at birth (2001): male 65.8 years; female 70.8 years.

## National economy

**Budget** (2000). *Revenue*: F$884,337,000 (income taxes, estate taxes, and gift duties 57.0%; customs duties and port dues 26.1%; fees, royalties, and sales 4.9%; other 12.0%). *Expenditures*: F$920,186,000 (departmental expenditure 72.9%; public-debt charges 23.2%; pensions and gratuities 3.9%). **Production** (metric tons except as noted). *Agriculture, forestry, fishing* (2001): sugarcane 3,500,000, coconuts 215,000, taro 37,000; livestock (number of live animals) 340,000 cattle, 245,749 goats, 137,000 pigs; roundwood (2000) 486,000 cu m; fish catch (1999) 25,100. *Mining and quarrying* (2000): cement 87,000; gold 3,794 kg; silver 1,462 kg. *Manufacturing* (2000): raw sugar 335,000; flour 54,931; soap 6,142. *Energy production (consumption):* electricity (kW-hr; 2000) 687,000,000 (687,000,000); coal (metric tons; 1997) none (22,000); petroleum products (metric tons; 1997) none (213,000). **Tourism** (2000): receipts from visitors US$195,000,-000; expenditures by nationals abroad US$66,000,-000. **Land use** (1994): forested 64.9%; agricultural and under permanent cultivation 14.2%; meadows and pastures 9.5%; other 11.4%. **Population economically active** (1997): total 297,800; activity rate of total population 33.8% (participation rates [1986]: ages 15–64, 56.0%; female 21.2%; unemployed [1990] 6.4%). **Gross national product** (2000): US$1,480,000,000 (US$1,820 per capita). **Public debt** (external, outstanding; 2000): US$101,200,-000. **Household expenditure.** Average household size (1999) 6.1; expenditure (1991): food, beverages, and tobacco 41.5%, housing and energy 21.4%, transportation and communications 12.9%, household durable goods 6.5%.

## Foreign trade

**Imports** (2000): F$1,758,338,000 (durable manufactures 27.3%; machinery and transport equipment 19.5%; petroleum products 16.8%; miscellaneous manufactured consumer articles 14.9%; food, beverages, and tobacco 12.5%; chemicals 6.6%). *Major import sources* (1999): Australia 41.1%; New Zealand 13.3%; US 12.4%; Japan 6.4%; China 4.6%. **Exports** (2000): F$1,057,285,000 (sugar 25.6%; clothing 25.3%; gold 7.4%; timber 5.7%; fish 5.2%; molasses 1.9%; coconut oil 0.8%). *Major export destinations*: Australia 40.6%; UK 19.6%; US 13.3%; New Zealand 4.8%; Japan 3.9%.

## Transport and communications

**Transport.** *Railroads* (1999): length 595 km. *Roads* (1999): total length 3,440 km (paved 49%). *Vehicles* (2000): passenger cars 50,005; trucks and buses 35,038. *Air transport* (1999; Air Pacific only): passenger-km 1,838,264,000; metric ton-km cargo 100,124,000; airports (1997) with scheduled flights 13. **Communications,** in total units (units per 1,000 persons). Daily newspaper circulation (1996): 40,000 (51); radio receivers (1997): 500,000 (636); television receivers (1999): 88,908 (111); telephone main lines (2001): 90,400 (84); cellular telephone subscribers (2001): 76,000 (92); personal computers (2001): 50,000 (61); Internet users (2001): 15,000 (18).

## Education and health

**Educational attainment** (1986). Percentage of population age 25 and over having: no formal schooling 28.3%; primary only 19.1%; some secondary 44.1%; secondary 4.1%; postsecondary 3.3%; other 1.1%. **Literacy** (1996): total population age 15 and over literate 92.9%; males 94.5%; females 91.4%. **Health** (1998): physicians 252 (1 per 3,147 persons); hospital beds 1,797 (1 per 441 persons); infant mortality rate per 1,000 live births (2001) 14.1. **Food** (2000): daily per capita caloric intake 2,861 (vegetable products 81%, animal products 19%); 125% of FAO recommended minimum.

## Military

**Total active duty personnel** (2001): 3,500 (army 91.4%, navy 8.6%, air force, none). **Military expenditure as percentage of GNP** (1999): 2.0% (world 2.4%); per capita expenditure US$42.

## Background

Archaeological evidence shows that the islands of Fiji were occupied in the late 2nd millennium BC and that the inhabitants had developed pottery by c. 1300 BC. The first European sighting was by the Dutch in the 17th century; in 1774 the islands were visited by Capt. James Cook, who found a mixed Melanesian-Polynesian population with a complex society. Traders and the first missionaries arrived in 1835. In 1857 a British consul was appointed, and in 1874 Fiji was proclaimed a crown colony. It became independent as a member of the Commonwealth in 1970 and was declared a republic in 1987 following a military coup. Elections in 1992 restored civilian rule. A new constitution was approved in 1997.

## Recent Developments

On 1 Oct 2001—after more than a year of political instability stemming from a coup in May 2000, when Fiji's Parliament was stormed by ethnic Fijian armed nationalists—newly elected lawmakers were sworn in amid tight security. Coup leader George Speight was imprisoned on treason and firearms charges. Aftershocks and recriminations from the coup continued to dominate Fijian politics into 2003.

**Internet resources:** <www.fiji.org.nz>

## Finland

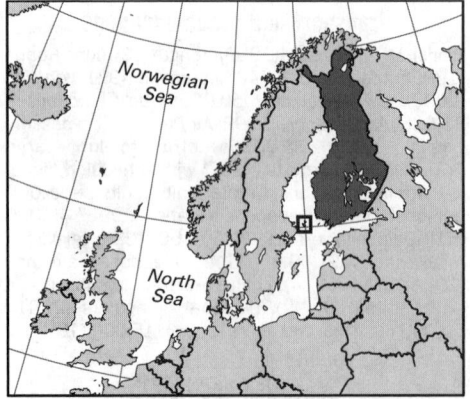

**Official names:** Suomen Tasavalta (Finnish); Republiken Finland (Swedish) (Republic of Finland). **Form of government:** multiparty republic with one legislative house (Parliament [200; includes one representative from Åland]). **Chief of state:** President Tarja Halonen

(from 2000). **Head of government:** Prime Minister Matti Vanhanen (from 24 Jun 2003). **Capital:** Helsinki. **Official languages:** none (Finnish and Swedish are national languages). **Official religion:** none. **Monetary unit:** 1 euro (€) = 100 cents; $1 = €0.87 (7 Jul 2003); at conversion on 1 Jan 2002, €1 = 5.95 Finnish markka (Fmk).

## Demography

**Area:** 130,559 sq mi, 338,145 sq km (total includes land area of 117,580 sq mi [304,530 sq km] and inland water area of 12,979 sq mi [33,615 sq km]). **Population** (2002): 5,201,000. **Density** (2002): persons per sq mi 44.2, persons per sq km 17.1. **Urban** (2002): 61.4%. **Sex distribution** (2002): male 48.85%; female 51.15%. **Age breakdown** (2002): under 15, 17.9%; 15–29, 18.6%; 30–44, 21.0%; 45–59, 22.1%; 60–74, 13.7%; 75 and over, 6.7%. **Ethnic composition** (2000): Finnish 91.9%; Swedish 5.9%; Karelian 0.8%; Russian 0.2%; other 1.2%. **Religious affiliation** (2000): Evangelical Lutheran 85.2%; Finnish (Greek) Orthodox 1.1%; nonreligious 12.6%; other 1.1%. **Major cities** (2002): Helsinki 559,718 (metro area 964,953); Tampere 197,774; Vantaa 179,856 (within Helsinki metro area); Turku 173,686; Oulu 123,274. **Location:** northern Europe, bordering Norway, Russia, the Gulf of Finland, the Baltic Sea, the Gulf of Bothnia, and Sweden.

## Vital statistics

**Birth rate** per 1,000 population (2001): 10.8 (world avg. 21.2); (2000) legitimate 60.8%; illegitimate 39.2%. **Death rate** per 1,000 population (2001): 9.4 (world avg. 8.9). **Natural increase rate** per 1,000 population (2001): 1.4 (world avg. 12.3). **Total fertility rate** (avg. births per childbearing woman; 2000): 1.7. **Marriage rate** per 1,000 population (2000): 5.1. **Divorce rate** per 1,000 population (2000): 2.7. **Life expectancy** at birth (2000): male 74.1 years; female 81.0 years.

## National economy

**Budget** (2000). *Revenue:* Fmk 199,579,000,000 (income and property taxes 33.7%, value-added taxes 27.7%, excise duties 13.8%). *Expenditures:* Fmk 199,575,000,000 (social security and health 21.8%, education 14.0%, interest on state debt 13.4%, agriculture and forestry 6.6%, defense 4.9%). **National debt** (2001): $86,666,000,000. **Production** (metric tons except as noted). *Agriculture, forestry, fishing* (1999): silage 6,799,000, barley 1,568,000, sugar beets 1,172,000; livestock (number of live animals; 2000) 1,541,000 pigs, 1,101,000 cattle, (1999) 195,000 reindeer; roundwood (1999) 53,851,000 cu m; fish catch (1999) 176,018. *Mining and quarrying* (1998): chromite (gross weight) 498,000; gold 5,000 kilograms. *Manufacturing* (value added in Fmk '000,000; 1998): wood pulp, paper, and paper products 24,304; radio, television, and communications equipment 21,271; nonelectrical machinery 17,398. *Energy production (consumption):* electricity (kW-hr; 2000) 67,278,000,000 (79,158,000,000); coal (metric tons; 1997) none (6,995,000); crude petroleum (barrels; 1997) none (70,904,000); petroleum products (metric tons; 1997) 10,721,000 (9,222,-

*1 metric ton = about 1.1 short tons;　1 kilometer = 0.6 mi (statute);　1 metric ton-km cargo = about 0.68 short ton-mi cargo;　c.i.f.: cost, insurance, and freight;　f.o.b.: free on board*

000); natural gas (cu m; 1997) none (3,509,000,-000). **Population economically active** (1999): total 2,557,000; activity rate of total population 49.5% (participation rates: ages 15–64, 73.6%; female 47.8%; unemployed [2001] 9.1%). **Household income and expenditure** (1998). Average household size 2.2; disposable income per household Fmk 146,400 ($27,395); sources of gross income: wages and salaries 55.4%, transfer payments 27.4%, other 17.2%; expenditure: housing and energy 27.3%, transportation and communications 18.9%, food, beverages, and tobacco 16.5%. **Gross national product** (2000): $130,106,000,000 ($25,130 per capita). **Tourism** (in $'000,000; 2000): receipts 1,397; expenditures 1,836. **Land use** (1994): forested 76.1%; meadows and pastures 0.4%; agricultural and under permanent cultivation 8.5%; other 15.0%.

## Foreign trade

**Imports** (1999-c.i.f.): €39,306,000,000 (electrical machinery and apparatus 16.7%; nonelectrical machinery and apparatus 15.4%; mineral fuels 8.5%; automobiles 8.4%). *Major import sources:* Germany 15.3%; Sweden 11.2%; US 7.9%; Russia 7.2%; UK 6.6%; Japan 6.2%; France 4.3%. **Exports** (1999-f.o.b.): €29,691,000,000 (electrical machinery and apparatus 23.7%; paper and paper products 20.5%; nonelectrical machinery and apparatus 11.8%; wood products and furniture 7.2%). *Major export destinations:* Germany 13.1%; Sweden 9.9%; UK 9.1%; US 7.9%; France 5.3%; The Netherlands 4.3%; Russia 4.1%.

## Transport and communications

**Transport.** *Railroads*: route length (1999) 5,836 km; passenger-km 3,415,000, 000; metric ton-km cargo 9,753,000,000. *Roads* (2000): total length 77,900 km (paved 65%). *Vehicles* (2000): passenger cars 2,069,055; trucks and buses 300,048. *Air transport* (1999): passenger-km 12,916,000,000; metric ton-km cargo 315,883,000; airports (1999) 27. **Communications,** in total units (units per 1,000 persons). Daily newspaper circulation (1996): 2,332,000 (455); radio receivers (1997): 7,700,000 (1,498); television receivers (1997): 3,200,000 (623); telephone main lines (2001): 2,845,000 (548); cellular telephone subscribers (2001): 4,044,000 (778); personal computers (2001): 2,200,000 (424); Internet users (2001): 2,235,300 (430).

## Education and health

**Educational attainment** (end of 1998). Percentage of population age 25 and over having: incomplete upper-secondary education 40.7%; complete upper secondary or vocational 33.6%; higher 25.7%. **Literacy:** virtually 100%. **Health** (1999): physicians 15,794 (1 per 327 persons); hospital beds (1998) 39,718 (1 per 130 persons); infant mortality rate per 1,000 live births 4.2. **Food** (1998): daily per capita caloric intake 3,180 (vegetable products 61%, animal products 39%); 117% of FAO recommended minimum.

## Military

**Total active duty personnel** (2001): 32,250 (army 76.1%, navy 15.5%, air force 8.4%). **Military expenditure as percentage of GNP** (1999): 1.4% (world 2.4%); per capita expenditure $344.

## Background

Recent archaeological discoveries have led some to suggest that human habitation in Finland dates back at least 100,000 years. Ancestors of the Sami apparently were present in Finland by about 7000 BC. The ancestors of the present-day Finns came from the southern shore of the Gulf of Finland in the 1st millennium BC. The area was gradually Christianized from the 11th century. From the 12th century Sweden and Russia contested for supremacy in Finland, until in 1323 Sweden ruled most of the country. Russia was ceded part of Finnish territory in 1721; in 1808 Alexander I of Russia invaded Finland, which in 1809 was formally ceded to Russia. The subsequent period saw the growth of Finnish nationalism. Russia's losses in World War I and the Russian Revolution of 1917 set the stage for Finland's independence in 1917. It was defeated by the Soviet Union in the Russo-Finnish War (1939–40) but then sided with Nazi Germany against the Soviets during World War II and regained the territory it had lost. Facing defeat again by the advancing Soviets in 1944, it reached a peace agreement with the USSR, ceding territory and paying reparations. Finland's economy recovered after World War II. It joined the European Union in 1995.

## Recent Developments

Finland's historically edgy relationship with Russia again dominated news in 2002. In July, Russian Defense Minister Sergey Ivanov indicated that Moscow would not be pleased if NATO bases were established near its borders. Finnish leaders said that they were not about to join NATO but that the option would be kept open. Elections in April 2003 were won by Anneli Jäätteenmäki's Center Party, and she became prime minister. Following a political scandal, however, she was replaced after only two months by Foreign Minister Matti Vanhanen.

**Internet resources:** <www.finland-tourism.com>

# France

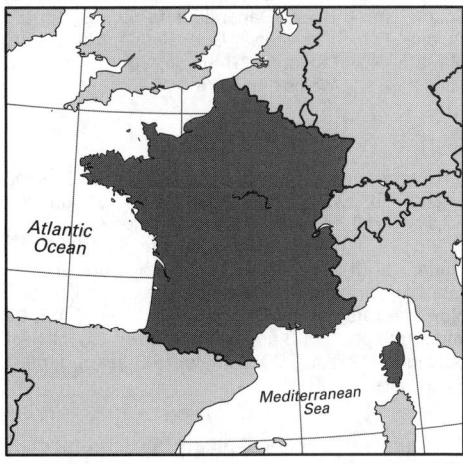

Atlantic Ocean

Mediterranean Sea

**Official name:** République Française (French Republic). **Form of government:** republic with two legislative houses (Parliament; Senate [321], National Assembly [577]). **Chief of state:** President Jacques Chirac (from

1995). **Head of government:** Prime Minister Jean-Pierre Raffarin (from 6 May 2002). **Capital:** Paris. **Official language:** French. **Official religion:** none. **Monetary unit:** 1 euro (€) = 100 cents; $1 = €0.87 (7 Jul 2003); at conversion on 1 Jan 2002, €1 = 6.56 French francs (F).

## Demography

**Area:** 210,026 sq mi, 543,965 sq km. **Population** (2002): 59,440,000. **Density** (2002): persons per sq mi 283.0, persons per sq km 109.3. **Urban** (1999): 75.5%. **Sex distribution** (1999): male 48.56%; female 51.44%. **Age breakdown** (1999): under 15, 17.9%; 15–29, 20.2%; 30–44, 21.9%; 45–59, 18.7%; 60–74, 13.6%; 75 and over, 7.7%. **Ethnic composition** (2000): French 76.9%; Algerian and Moroccan Berber 2.2%; Italian 1.9%; Portuguese 1.5%; Moroccan Arab 1.5%; Fleming 1.4%; Algerian Arab 1.3%; Basque 1.3%; Jewish 1.2%; German 1.2%; Vietnamese 1.0%; Catalan 0.5%; other 8.1%. **Religious affiliation** (2000): Roman Catholic 82.3%; Muslim 7.1%; atheist 4.4%; Protestant 3.7%; Orthodox 1.1%; Jewish 1.0%; other 0.4%. **Major cities** (1999): Paris 2,125,246 (metropolitan area 9,644,507); Marseille 798,430 (1,349,772); Lyon 445,452 (1,348,832); Toulouse 390,350 (761,090); Nice 342,738 (888,784); Nantes 270,251 (544,932); Strasbourg 264,115 (427,245); Montpellier 225,392 (287,981); Bordeaux 215,363 (753,931); Rennes 206,229 (272,263); Le Havre 190,905 (248,547); Reims 187,206 (215,581); Lille 184,493 (1,000,900); Saint-Étienne 180,210 (291,960); Toulon 160,639 (519,640). **Mobility** (1990). Population living in same residence as in 1982: 51.4%; same region 89.0%; different region 8.8%; different country 2.2%. **Households** (1993). Average household size 2.6; 1 person 27.7%, 2 persons 32.0%, 3 persons 17.4%, 4 persons 14.7%, 5 persons or more 8.2%. Family households (1990): 14,118,940 (72.1%); nonfamily 5,471,460 (27.9%, of which 1-person 24.6%). **Immigration** (1998): immigrants admitted 100,014 (Algeria 15.3%, Turkey 6.0%, Tunisia 4.9%, Sri Lanka 1.7%, Vietnam 1.0%). **Location:** western Europe, bordering the North Atlantic Ocean, Belgium, Luxembourg, Germany, Switzerland, Italy, the Mediterranean Sea, Spain, and Andorra. **Dependent territories:** French Guiana, French Polynesia, Guadeloupe, Martinique, Mayotte, New Caledonia, Réunion, Saint Pierre and Miquelon, and Wallis and Futuna.

## Vital statistics

**Birth rate** per 1,000 population (2000): 10.8 (world avg. 22.5); (1997) legitimate 59.9%; illegitimate 40.1%. **Death rate** per 1,000 population (2000): 9.1 (world avg. 9.0). **Natural increase rate** per 1,000 population (2000): 1.7 (world avg. 13.5). **Total fertility rate** (avg. births per childbearing woman; 2000): 1.7. **Marriage rate** per 1,000 population (1998): 4.6. **Divorce rate** per 1,000 population (1998): 2.0. **Life expectancy** at birth (2000): male 74.8 years; female 82.9 years.

## Social indicators

**Quality of working life.** Average workweek (1994): 38.9 hours. Annual rate per 100,000 workers for: in-

jury or accident 5,322 (deaths 0.8%); accidents in transit to work 708 (deaths 68.3). Average days lost to labor stoppages per 1,000 workers (1994): 21.0. Average length of journey to work (1990): 8.7 mi (14 km). **Access to services** (1992). Proportion of dwellings having: central heating 86.0%; piped water 97.0%; indoor plumbing 95.8%. **Social participation.** Eligible voters participating in last (June 2002) national election: 64.4%. Population over 15 years of age participating in voluntary associations (1997): 28.0%. **Social deviance.** Offense rate per 100,000 population (1998) for: murder 1.6, rape 13.4, other assault 583.8; theft (including burglary and housebreaking) 6,107.6. Incidence per 100,000 in general population of suicide (1993) 21.1. **Leisure** (1987–88). Participation rate for favorite leisure activities: watching television 82%; reading magazines 79%; listening to radio 75%; entertaining relatives 64%; visiting relatives 61%; attending fairs/expositions 56%. **Material well-being** (1994). Households possessing: automobile 79.5%; color television 92.4%; VCR 52.8%; refrigerator 99.0%; washing machine 89.4%.

## National economy

**Gross national product** (2000): $1,438,293,000,000 ($24,090 per capita). **Budget** (1998). *Revenue*: F 1,331,838,000,000 (value-added taxes 58.3%, personal income tax 22.2%, corporate income tax 16.5%). *Expenditures*: F 1,585,307,000,000 (education 21.1%, defense 15.0%, health and social services 4.6%, research and development 2.5%). **Production** (metric tons except as noted). *Agriculture, forestry, fishing* (2000): wheat 37,559,000, sugar beets 31,454,000, corn (maize) 16,469,000, barley 9,927,000, grapes 7,627,000, potatoes 6,652,000, rapeseed 3,569,000, apples 2,157,000, dry peas 1,918,000, sunflower seeds 1,813,000, triticale 1,213,000, tomatoes 898,000, carrots 633,000, green peas 550,000, lettuce 513,000, oats 503,000, peaches 476,000, onions 361,000; livestock (number of live animals) 20,527,000 cattle, 14,635,000 pigs, 10,004,000 sheep, 1,190,000 goats; roundwood 50,170,000 cu m; fish catch (1999) 845,649. *Mining and quarrying* (2000): gypsum 4,500,000; potash 360,000; kaolin 330,000; gold 84,600 troy oz. *Manufacturing* (value added in F '000,000,000; 1998): transport equipment 157.2, of which motor vehicles 75.7, aircraft 38.8; fabricated metals 83.0; nonelectrical machinery 80.5; electronics, radios, and televisions 58.9; pharmaceuticals 56.6; printing and publishing 55.0, of which publishing 33.9; other electrical machinery 48.6. *Energy production (consumption;* consumption data includes Monaco): electricity (kW-hr; 2000) 543,966,000,000 ([1997] 450,072,000,000); hard coal (metric tons; 2000) 3,168,000 ([1997] 21,527,000); lignite (metric tons; 2000) 300,000 ([1997] 852,000); crude petroleum (barrels; 2001) 11,027,000 ([1997] 651,981,000); petroleum products (metric tons; 1997) 79,634,000 (70,965,000); natural gas (cu m; 2000) 1,787,000,000 ([1997] 37,102,600,000). **Population economically active** (1998): total 25,459,200; activity rate of total population 43.4% (participation rates: ages 15–64, 67.6% [1994]; female 45.8%; unemployed 11.9%). **Household income and expenditure** (1995). Average household size 2.6; average annual income per household F 302,560

---

*1 metric ton = about 1.1 short tons;    1 kilometer = 0.6 mi (statute);    1 metric ton-km cargo = about 0.68 short ton-mi cargo;    c.i.f.: cost, insurance, and freight;    f.o.b.: free on board*

($60,610); sources of income: wages and salaries 70.0%, self-employment 24.4%, social security 5.6%; expenditure (1997): housing 22.5%, food 17.9%, transportation 16.3%, health 10.3%, recreation and education 7.4%, clothing 5.2%. **Tourism** (2000): receipts $29,900,000,000; expenditures $17,166,000,000. **Public debt** (1998): F 5,030,000,000,000 ($853,000,000,000). **Land use** (1994): forest 27.3%; pasture 19.3%; agriculture 35.4%; other 18.0%.

## Foreign trade

**Imports** (1998): F 1,687,500,000,000 (machinery and transport equipment 39.1%; chemicals 12.2%; agricultural products 7.9%; fuels 5.9%). *Major import sources*: Germany 17.2%; Italy 9.9%; UK 8.4%; US 8.2%; Belgium-Luxembourg 7.7%; Spain 7.1%. **Exports** (1998): F 1,773,200,000,000 (machinery and transport equipment 43.8%, of which transport equipment 17.7%; chemical products 12.7%; agricultural products 12.0%; plastics 3.3%). *Major export destinations*: Germany 16.1%; UK 10.0%; Italy 9.2%; Spain 8.7%; Belgium-Luxembourg 7.7%; US 7.4%.

## Transport and communications

**Transport.** *Railroads* (1999): route length 32,105 km; passenger-km 66,590,000,000; metric ton-km cargo 52,110,000,000. *Roads* (1999): total length 893,300 km (paved 100%). *Vehicles* (1999): passenger cars 27,480,000; trucks and buses 5,610,000. *Air transport* (2000): passenger-km 110,270,500,000; metric ton-km cargo 15,221,900,000; airports (1996) 61. **Communications**, in total units (units per 1,000 persons). Daily newspaper circulation (1996): 12,725,000 (218); radio receivers (1997): 55,300,000 (946); television receivers (1999): 36,500,000 (623); telephone main lines (2001): 34,033,000 (575); cellular telephone subscribers (2001): 35,922,000 (606); personal computers (2001): 20,000,000 (338); Internet users (2001): 15,653,000 (264).

## Education and health

**Educational attainment** (1990). Percentage of population age 25 and over having: primary 22.1%; lower secondary 7.8%; higher secondary and vocational 29.4%; postsecondary 11.6%; undeclared attainment 29.1%. **Health:** physicians (1996) 171,704 (1 per 346 persons); hospital beds (1998) 651,208 (1 per 91 persons); infant mortality rate per 1,000 live births (2000) 4.5. **Food** (2000): daily per capita caloric intake 3,591 (vegetable products 63%, animal products 37%); 143% of FAO recommended minimum.

## Military

**Total active duty personnel** (2002): 260,400 (army 52.6%, navy 17.5%, air force 24.6%, unallocated 5.3%). **Military expenditure as percentage of GNP** (1999): 2.7% (world 2.4%); per capita expenditure $658.

## Background

Archaeological excavations in France indicate continuous settlement from Paleolithic times. About 1200 BC the Gauls migrated into the area, and in 600 BC Ionian Greeks established several settlements, including one at Marseille. Julius Caesar completed the Roman conquest of Gaul in 50 BC. During the 6th century AD, the Salian Franks ruled; by the 8th century power had passed to the Carolingians, the greatest of whom was Charlemagne. The Hundred Years' War (1337–1453) resulted in the return to France of land that had been held by the British; by the end of the 15th century, France approximated its modern boundaries. The 16th century was marked by the Wars of Religion between Protestants (Huguenots) and Roman Catholics. Henry IV's Edict of Nantes (1598) granted substantial religious toleration, but this was revoked in 1685 by Louis XIV, who helped to raise monarchical absolutism to new heights. In 1789 the French Revolution proclaimed the rights of the individual and destroyed the ancient regime. Napoleon ruled from 1799 to 1814, after which a limited monarchy was restored until 1871, when the Third Republic was created. World War I (1914–18) ravaged the northern part of France. After Nazi Germany's invasion during World War II, the collaborationist Vichy regime governed. Liberated by Allied and Free French forces in 1944, France restored parliamentary democracy under the Fourth Republic. A costly war in Indochina and rising nationalism in French colonies during the 1950s overwhelmed the Fourth Republic. The Fifth Republic was established in 1958 under Charles de Gaulle, who presided over the dissolution of most of France's overseas colonies. In 1981 François Mitterrand became France's first elected Socialist president. During the 1990s the French government, balancing right- and left-wing forces, moved toward solidifying European unity.

## Recent Developments

On 5 May 2002 French Pres. Jacques Chirac won re-election over challenger Jean-Marie Le Pen of the far-right National Front. Le Pen had earned the right to challenge Chirac with a surprise second-place finish in the election's preliminary round. Prime Minister Lionel Jospin, who was among the candidates bested by Le Pen, resigned his post after the results of the first round were announced. Chirac's margin of victory over Le Pen in the final round, however, was the widest ever in a French presidential election.

Two elements of French statehood were recently phased out—the franc, which gave way to the euro in January 2002, and military conscription, which was abandoned in December 2001 in favor of a smaller volunteer army. Both changes could be seen in the context of a France far more willing to cooperate—at least with its European neighbors—than it had been under de Gaulle. France was active in the campaign to keep the United Nations involved in the international pressures being brought to bear on Saddam Hussein's Iraq and repeatedly endorsed UN-led arms inspections. Paris especially opposed the "go-it-alone" attitude of the United States and, together with Germany and Russia, led a majority of other European countries in their opposition to the US-UK military action in Iraq in the spring of 2003. France also favored international, rather than US-led, efforts to rebuild Iraq; relations between Washington and Paris were notably frosty.

In April 2003, Prime Minister Jean-Pierre Raffarin announced an effort to decentralize the government, which was especially welcome news to residents of Corsica. In July, in the first-ever referendum in France, however, Corsicans narrowly voted against greater autonomy.

**Internet resources:** <www.franceguide.com>

# French Guiana

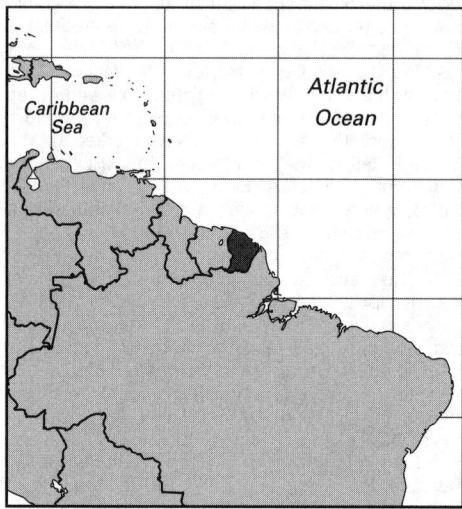

**Official name:** Département de la Guyane française (Department of French Guiana). **Political status:** overseas department of France with two legislative houses (General Council [19]; Regional Council [31]). **Chief of state:** President Jacques Chirac of France (from 1995). **Heads of government:** Prefect Ange Mancini (from 31 Jul 2002). **Capital:** Cayenne. **Official language:** French. **Official religion:** none. **Monetary unit:** 1 euro (€) = 100 cents; $1 = €0.87 (7 Jul 2003); at conversion on 1 Jan 2002, €1 = 6.56 French francs (F).

## Demography

**Area:** 33,399 sq mi, 86,504 sq km. **Population** (2002): 172,000. **Density** (2002): persons per sq mi 5.1, persons per sq km 2.0. **Urban** (2000): 78.2%. **Sex distribution** (1999): male 50.36%; female 49.64%. **Age breakdown** (1999): under 15, 34.0%; 15–29, 24.2%; 30–44, 23.3%; 45–59, 12.5%; 60–74, 4.3%; 75 and over, 1.7%. **Ethnic composition** (2000): Guianese Mulatto 37.9%; French 8.0%; Haitian 8.0%; Surinamese 6.0%; Antillean 5.0%; Chinese 5.0%; Brazilian 4.9%; East Indian 4.0%; other (other West Indian, Hmong, other South American) 21.2%. **Religious affiliation** (2000): Christian 84.6%, of which Roman Catholic 80.0%, Protestant 3.9%; Chinese folk-religionist 3.6%; Spiritist 3.5%; nonreligious/atheist 3.0%; traditional beliefs 1.9%; Hindu 1.6%; Muslim 0.9%; other 0.9%. **Major cities** (1999 [commune pop.]): Cayenne 50,594 (urban agglomeration 84,181); Saint-Laurent-du-Maroni 19,211; Kourou 19,107; Matoury 18,032 (within Cayenne urban agglomeration); Rémire-Montjoly 15,555 (within Cayenne urban agglomeration). **Location:** northern South America, bordering the Atlantic Ocean, Brazil, and Suriname.

## Vital statistics

**Birth rate** per 1,000 population (2000): 22.4 (world avg. 22.5); (1993) legitimate 20.0%; illegitimate 80.0%. **Death rate** per 1,000 population (2000): 4.7 (world avg. 9.0). **Natural increase rate** per 1,000 population (2000): 17.7 (world avg. 13.2). **Total fertility rate** (avg. births per childbearing woman; 2000): 3.2. **Marriage rate** per 1,000 population (1997): 4.5. **Divorce rate** per 1,000 population (1993): 0.4. **Life expectancy** at birth (2000): male 75.0 years; female 81.9 years.

## National economy

**Budget** (1995). *Revenue:* F 945,000,000 (current receipts 78.2%, of which taxes 50.8%, revenue from French central government 22.5%; development receipts 21.8%). *Expenditures:* F 945,000,000 (current expenditures 78.2%; capital expenditures 21.8%). **Production** (metric tons except as noted). *Agriculture, forestry, fishing* (2000): rice 31,000, cassava 10,400, sugarcane 5,300; livestock (number of live animals) 10,500 pigs, 9,000 cattle; roundwood (1998) 118,000 cu m; fish catch (1998) 7,709. *Mining and quarrying:* stone, sand, and gravel (1994) 1,034; gold (2000) 90,000 troy oz. *Manufacturing* (1998): pork 1,245; chicken meat 461; finished wood products 3,172 cu m (1996). Number of satellites launched from the Kourou Space Centre (1999): 10 (in 1991 the European Space Agency accounted for 28.7% of GDP, 28.2% of employed labor force, and 70.9% of imports). *Energy production (consumption):* electricity (kW-hr; 1998) 566,000,000 ([1997] 450,000,000); coal, none (none); crude petroleum, none (none); petroleum products (metric tons; 1997) none (284,000). **Household income and expenditure.** Average household size (1999) 3.3; income per household (1980) F 75,762 ($16,776); sources of income (1989): wages and salaries 64.4%, pensions and rents 18.0%, industrial and commercial profits 15.4%, other 2.2%; expenditure (1994): food and beverages 28.7%, housing 11.7%, energy 9.0%, clothing and footwear 6.4%, health 2.7%, other 41.5%. **Land use** (1994): forested 90.6%; meadows and pastures 0.1%; agricultural and under permanent cultivation 0.2%; other 9.1%. **Gross national product** (1997): $1,430,000,000 ($9,410 per capita). **Population economically active** (1998): total 61,100; activity rate of total population 39.0% (participation rates [1990]: ages 15–64, 67.3%; female 38.2%; unemployed [1998] 21.4%). **Tourism** (1999): receipts $50,000,000.

## Foreign trade

**Imports** (1998): F 3,449,000,000 (food products 21.3%; unspecified 78.7%). *Major import sources* (1997): France 51.6%; US 14.3%; Trinidad and Tobago 6.0%. **Exports** (1996): F 856,000,000 (gold 21.5%; shrimp 20.5%; parts for air and space vehicles 14.6%; rice 7.0%). *Major export destinations* (1997): France 61.5%; Switzerland 6.6%; US 2.2%.

## Transport and communications

**Transport.** *Roads* (1996): total length 1,245 km. *Vehicles* (1997): passenger cars 28,200; trucks and buses 9,400. *Air transport* (2000): passenger arrivals 215,745, passenger departures 219,676; cargo unloaded 4,117 metric tons, cargo loaded 1,935 metric tons; airports (1998) with scheduled flights 1. **Communications,** in total units (units per 1,000 persons): Daily newspaper circulation (1996): 2,000 (14); radio

---

*1 metric ton = about 1.1 short tons;    1 kilometer = 0.6 mi (statute);    1 metric ton-km cargo = about 0.68 short ton-mi cargo;    c.i.f.: cost, insurance, and freight;    f.o.b.: free on board*

receivers (1997): 104,000 (702); television receivers (1997): 30,000 (202); telephone main lines (1999): 49,000 (308); cellular telephone subscribers (1999): 18,000 (113); personal computers (1999): 23,000 (145); Internet users (1999): 2,000 (13).

## Education and health

**Educational attainment** (1990). Percentage of population age 25 and over having: incomplete primary education or no declaration 61.7%; completed primary 5.3%; some secondary 15.9%; completed secondary 8.2%; some higher 4.9%; completed higher 4.0%. **Literacy** (1982): total population age 16 and over literate 38,964 (82.0%); males literate 21,021 (82.5%); females literate 17,943 (81.3%). **Health:** physicians (1998) 223 (1 per 684 persons); hospital beds (1996) 730 (1 per 196 persons); infant mortality rate per 1,000 live births (2000) 14.0. **Food** (1992): daily per capita caloric intake 2,900 (vegetable products 70%, animal products 30%); 128% of FAO recommended minimum.

## Military

**Total active duty personnel** (2001): 3,250 (includes French Foreign Legion troops assigned to guard the Kourou Space Centre).

## Background

Originally settled by the Spanish, French, and Dutch, the territory of French Guiana was awarded to France in 1667, and the inhabitants were made French citizens after 1877. By 1852 the French began using the territory as a penal colony with one, on Devils Island, especially notorious. It became an overseas territory of France in 1946; the penal colonies were closed by 1939.

## Recent Developments

The European Space Agency has regularly launched communication satellites from French Guiana, and the space center near Kourou, completed in 1968, is a major factor in the local economy. With only 6 launches planned for 2003, compared with 12 the year before, however, the facility announced in March 2003 that it was cutting 400 jobs, or about one-quarter of its staff.

**Internet resources:**
<www.countryreports.org/french.htm>

# French Polynesia

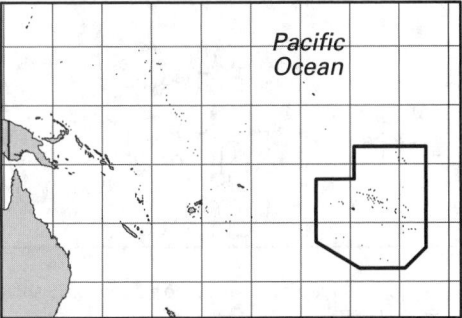

Pacific Ocean

**Official name:** Territoire de la Polynésie française (French); Polynesia Farani (Tahitian) (Territory of French Polynesia). **Political status:** overseas territory of France with one legislative house (Territorial Assembly [49]). **Chief of state:** President Jacques Chirac of France (from 1995). **Head of government:** President of the Government, Gaston Flosse (from 1991). **Capital:** Papeete. **Official languages:** French; Tahitian. **Official religion:** none. **Monetary unit:** 1 franc of the Comptoirs français du Pacifique (CFPF) = 100 centimes; valuation (7 Jul 2003) $1 = CFPF 100.29; the CFPF is pegged to the euro (€) at €1 = CFPF 119.25 from 1 Jan 2002.

## Demography

**Area:** 1,544 sq mi, 4,000 sq km (approximate total area including inland water). **Population** (2002): 242,000. **Density** (2002): persons per sq mi 178.1, persons per sq km 68.7. **Urban** (2002): 53.0%. **Sex distribution** (1996): male 51.92%; female 48.08%. **Age breakdown** (1996): under 15, 33.7%; 15–29, 27.3%; 30–44, 21.6%; 45–59, 11.4%; 60–74, 5.0%; 75 and over, 1.0%. **Ethnic composition** (1996): Polynesian and part-Polynesian 82.8%; European (mostly French) 11.9%; Asian (mostly Chinese) 4.7%; other 0.6%. **Religious affiliation** (1995): Protestant 50.2%, of which Evangelical Church of French Polynesia (Presbyterian) 46.1%; Roman Catholic 39.5%; other Christian 9.9%, of which Mormon 5.9%; other 0.4%. **Major cities** (1996 [commune pop.]): Faaa 25,888 (part of Papeete urban agglomeration); Papeete 25,553 (urban agglomeration [1999] 121,000); Punaauia 19,524 (part of Papeete urban agglomeration); Pirae 13,974 (part of Papeete urban agglomeration); Mahina 11,640 (part of Papeete urban agglomeration). **Location:** Oceania, an archipelago in the South Pacific Ocean, about halfway between South America and Australia.

## Vital statistics

**Birth rate** per 1,000 population (2002): 20.5 (world avg. 21.2); (1996) legitimate 35.4%; illegitimate 64.6%. **Death rate** per 1,000 population (2002): 4.8 (world avg. 8.9). **Natural increase rate** per 1,000 population (2002): 15.7 (world avg. 12.3). **Total fertility rate** (avg. births per childbearing woman; 2002): 2.5. **Marriage rate** per 1,000 population (1996): 5.7. **Life expectancy** at birth (2002): male 71.0 years; female 76.0 years.

## National economy

**Budget** (1998). *Revenue*: CFPF 85,671,000,000 (indirect taxes 60.3%, direct taxes and nontax revenue 39.7%). *Expenditures*: CFPF 114,143,000,000 (current expenditure 72.5%; capital expenses 27.5%). **Production** (metric tons except as noted). *Agriculture, forestry, fishing* (1999): coconuts 85,000, copra (1998) 11,000, cassava 5,500; livestock (number of live animals) 33,000 pigs, 6,500 cattle, 16,000 goats; fish catch (1998) 11,406; export production of black pearls (1998) 6,050 kg. *Mining and quarrying*: estimated annual production of phosphates ranges from 1,000,000 to 1,200,000 tons. *Manufacturing* (1999): coconut oil 6,386; other manufactures include *monoï* oil (primarily refined coconut and sandalwood oils), beer, printed cloth, and sandals. *Energy production (consumption)*: electricity (kW-hr; 1997) 360,000,000 (360,000,000); petroleum products (metric tons; 1997) none (183,000). **Tourism** (1999):

number of visitors 236,000; receipts from visitors $394,000,000; number of hotel rooms 3,396; occupancy 57.5%. **Household income and expenditure** (1986). Average household size (1996) 4.3; average annual income per household CFPF 2,153,112 ($17,831); sources of income (1993): salaries 61.9%, self-employment 21.5%, transfer payments 16.6%; expenditure: food and beverages 32.1%, household furnishings 12.3%, transportation 12.2%, energy 8.1%, recreation and education 6.9%, clothing 6.3%. **Land use** (1998): forested and other 81.4%; meadows and pastures 5.5%; agricultural and under permanent cultivation 13.1%. **Gross national product** (at current market prices; 2000): $4,064,000,000 ($17,290 per capita). **Population economically active** (1996): total 87,121; activity rate of total population 39.7% (participation rates: ages 14 and over, 68.3%; female 38.7%; unemployed 13.2%). **Public debt** (external, outstanding; 1999): $542,000,000.

## Foreign trade

**Imports** (1997-c.i.f.): CFPF 99,300,000,000 (machinery and appliances 16.3%, food products 6.8%, pharmaceutical products 3.1%, metal manufactures 2.6%). *Major import sources* (2000): France 35.9%; US 13.9%; Australia 9.3%; New Zealand 7.4%; Germany 4.8%. **Exports** (1997-f.o.b.): CFPF 16,481,000,-000 (black cultured pearls 61.6%, coconut oil 1.6%, mother-of-pearl 1.4%, vanilla 0.5%). *Major export destinations* (2000): Japan 36.9%; Hong Kong 20.9%; France 14.5%; US 12.1%; New Caledonia 5.0%.

## Transport and communications

**Transport.** *Roads* (1996): total length 884 km (paved 44%). Motor vehicles: passenger cars (1996) 47,300; trucks and buses (1993) 15,300. *Air transport* (1998): passengers carried 1,219,907; freight handled 9,542 metric tons; airports (1994) with scheduled flights 17. **Communications**, in total units (units per 1,000 persons). Daily newspaper circulation (1996): 24,000 (110); radio receivers (1997): 128,000 (574); television receivers (1999): 43,000 (186); telephone main lines (2001): 52,600 (222); cellular telephone subscribers (2001): 67,000 (283); personal computers (1995): 20,000 (1.2); Internet users (2001): 16,000 (68).

## Education and health

**Educational attainment** (1996). Percentage of population age 15 and over having: no formal schooling 4.9%; primary education 37.4%; secondary 49.0%; higher 8.7%. **Literacy** (1983): total population age 15 and over literate 98,314 (95.0%); males literate 51,910 (94.9%); females literate 46,404 (95.0%). **Health** (1996): physicians 384 (1 per 175 persons); hospital beds 981 (1 per 447 persons); infant mortality rate per 1,000 live births (2002) 9.0. **Food** (1999): daily per capita caloric intake 2,969 (vegetable products 72%, animal products 28%); (1997) 130% of FAO recommended minimum.

## Military

**Total active duty personnel** (2001): 3,100 French military personnel.

The cultured black pearl is found almost exclusively around the islands of French Polynesia. The harvest of these rare pearls comprises over 60% of the exports in the country.

## Background

European contact with the islands of French Polynesia was gradual. Portuguese navigator Ferdinand Magellan sighted Pukapuka in the Tuamotu group in 1521. The southern Marquesas Islands were discovered in 1595. Dutch explorer Jacob Roggeveen in 1722 discovered Makatea, Bora-Bora, and Maupiti. Captain Samuel Wallis in 1767 discovered Tahiti, Moorea, and Maiao Iti. The Society Islands were named after the Royal Society, which had sponsored the expedition under Captain James Cook that observed from Tahiti the 1769 transit of the planet Venus. Tubuai was discovered on Cook's last voyage, in 1777. The islands became French protectorates in the 1840s, and in the 1880s the French colony of Oceania was established. French Polynesia became an overseas territory of France after World War II and was granted partial autonomy in 1977.

## Recent Developments

Pres. Gaston Flosse has continued to pursue constitutional changes that would increase French Polynesia's autonomy while retaining its connection to France. In October 2002 agreement was reached on France's financial assistance to the territory, with the provision of €150 million (about $155.6 million) for 2003. The new Economic Restructuring Fund supplements grants made in 1996 as compensation for the loss of spending following the closure of France's nuclear testing facilities at Moruroa.

**Internet resources:** <www.polynesianislands.com/fp>

# Gabon

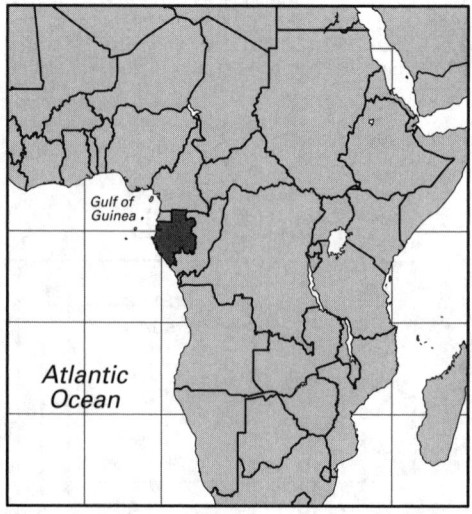

---

*1 metric ton = about 1.1 short tons;   1 kilometer = 0.6 mi (statute);   1 metric ton-km cargo = about 0.68 short ton-mi cargo;   c.i.f.: cost, insurance, and freight;   f.o.b.: free on board*

Official name: République Gabonaise (Gabonese Republic). Form of government: unitary multiparty republic with a Parliament comprising two legislative houses (Senate [91]; National Assembly [120]). Chief of state: President El Hadj Omar Bongo (from 1967). Head of government: Prime Minister Jean-François Ntoutoume-Emane (from 1999). Capital: Libreville. Official language: French. Official religion: none. Monetary unit: 1 CFA franc (CFAF) = 100 centimes; valuation (7 Jul 2003) $1 = CFAF 571.07; the CFAF is pegged to the euro (€) at €1 = 655.96 from 1 Jan 2002.

## Demography

Area: 103,347 sq mi, 267,667 sq km. Population (2002): 1,233,000. Density (2002): persons per sq mi 11.9, persons per sq km 4.6. Urban (1998): 46.9%. Sex distribution (2001): male 49.77%; female 50.23%. Age breakdown (1999): under 15, 33.3%; 15–29, 25.7%; 30–44, 15.3%; 45–59, 16.2%; 60–74, 8.0%; 75 and over, 1.4%. Ethnic composition (1983): Fang 35.5%; Punu, Sira, and Nzebi 16.9%; Mpongwe 15.1%; Mbete 14.2%; other 18.3%. Religious affiliation (2000): Christian 90.6%, of which Roman Catholic 56.6%, Protestant 17.7%; Muslim 3.1%; traditional beliefs 1.7%. Major cities (1993); Libreville 362,386; Port-Gentil 80,841; Franceville 30,246; Oyem 22,669; Moanda 21,921. Location: western Africa, bordering Cameroon, Rep. of the Congo, the South Atlantic Ocean, and Equatorial Guinea.

## Vital statistics

Birth rate per 1,000 population (2001): 27.4 (world avg. 21.2). Death rate per 1,000 population (2001): 17.2 (world avg. 8.9). Natural increase rate per 1,000 population (2001): 10.2 (world avg. 12.3). Total fertility rate (avg. births per childbearing woman; 2001): 3.7. Life expectancy at birth (2001): male 48.5 years; females 50.8 years.

## National economy

Budget (1997). Revenue: CFAF 914,700,000,000 (oil revenues 62.4%; taxes on international trade 18.8%; customs duties 10.7%; other revenues 8.1%). Expenditures: CFAF 756,100,000,000 (current expenditure 71.5%, of which wages and salaries 25.0%, service on public debt 23.5%; capital expenditure 28.5%). Public debt (external, outstanding; 2000): $3,512,000,000. Tourism (2000): receipts from visitors $7,000,000; expenditures by nationals abroad $174,000,000. Production (metric tons except as noted). Agriculture, forestry, fishing (1999): roots and tubers 436,300 (of which cassava 225,000, yams 150,000, taro 58,500), plantains 280,000, sugarcane 175,000; livestock (number of live animals) 212,000 pigs, 195,000 sheep, 90,000 goats, 3,100,000 chickens; roundwood (2000) 3,099,000 cu m; fish catch (2000) 47,470. Mining and quarrying (2000): manganese ore 1,700,000; gold 2,250 troy oz (excludes about 13,000 troy oz of illegally mined gold smuggled out of Gabon). Manufacturing (1995): fuel oil 295,000; diesel and gas oil 274,000; cement 130,000. Energy production (consumption): electricity (kW-hr; 1997) 1,257,000,000 (1,257,-000,000); crude petroleum (barrels; 2001) 110,-230,000 ([1997] 6,201,000); petroleum products (metric tons; 1997) 701,000 (520,000); natural gas (cu m; 1997) 1,020,000,000 (1,020,000,000). Pop-ulation economically active (1997): total 542,000; activity rate of total population 45.5% (participation rates [1985]: ages 15–64, 68.2%; female 44.5%; unemployed [1996] 20%). Gross national product (2000): $3,928,000,000 ($3,190 per capita). Household income. Average household size (1998) 6.1; sources of income (1983): private sector 73.4%, public sector 26.6%. Land use (1994): forested 77.2%; meadows and pastures 18.2%; agricultural and under permanent cultivation 1.8%; other 2.8%.

## Foreign trade

Imports (1997): CFAF 578,100,000,000 (machinery and mechanical equipment 26.4%, food and agricultural products 23.1%, consumer products 15.5%, transport equipment 11.5%, metals 6.2%). Major import sources: France 39.1%; Belgium 9.7%; US 8.1%; UK 4.3%; Japan 4.0%. Exports (1997): CFAF 1,776,300,000,000 (crude petroleum and petroleum products 77.1%, wood 14.5%, manganese ore and concentrate 5.0%, uranium ore and concentrate 0.7%). Major export destinations: US 68.2%; France 8.1%; other EU 4.4%; Japan 3.2%; Africa 1.6%.

## Transport and communications

Transport. Railroads (1998): route length 814 km; passenger-km 85,000,000 (1996); metric ton-km cargo carried 503,000,000 (1995). Roads (1996): total length 7,670 km (paved 8.2%). Vehicles (1997): passenger cars 24,750; trucks and buses 16,490. Air transport (1996): passenger-km 728,000,000; metric ton-km cargo 100,000,000; airports (1997) 17. Communications, in total units (units per 1,000 persons). Daily newspaper circulation (1997): 33,000 (30); radio receivers (1997): 195,000 (16); television receivers (1999): 300,000 (251); telephone main lines (2000): 39,000 (32); cellular telephone subscribers (2000): 120,000 (98); personal computers (2001): 15,000 (12); Internet users (2000): 15,000 (12).

## Education and health

Educational attainment of economically active population (1993): none, or incomplete primary 37.7%; complete primary 32.1%; complete secondary 16.4%; postsecondary certificate or degree 13.8%. Literacy (1995): total population age 15 and over literate 63.2%; males literate 73.7%; females literate 53.3%. Health: physicians (1989) 448 (1 per 2,377 persons); hospital beds (1988) 5,329 (1 per 199 persons); infant mortality rate per 1,000 live births (1998) 83.1. Food (2000): daily per capita caloric intake 2,564 (vegetable products 86%, animal products 14%); 109% of FAO recommended minimum.

## Military

Total active duty personnel (2001): 4,700 (army 68.1%, navy 10.6%, air force 21.3%), excluding 700 French troops. Military expenditure as percentage of GNP (1999): 2.4% (world 2.4%); per capita expenditure $78.

## Background

Artifacts dating from late Paleolithic and early Neolithic times have been found in Gabon, but it is not known when the Bantu speakers who established

Gabon's ethnic composition arrived. Pygmies were probably the original inhabitants. The Fang arrived in the late 18th century and were followed by the Portuguese and by French, Dutch, and English traders. The slave trade dominated commerce in the 18th and much of the 19th century. The French then took control, and Gabon was administered (1843–86) with French West Africa. In 1886 the colony of French Congo was established to include both Gabon and the Congo; in 1910 Gabon became a separate colony within French Equatorial Africa. An overseas territory of France from 1946, it became an autonomous republic within the French Community in 1958 and declared its independence in 1960. Rule by a sole political party was established in the 1960s, but discontent with it led to riots in Libreville in 1990. Legalization of opposition parties led to new elections in 1990. Peace negotiations with neighboring Chad rebels and with the Republic of the Congo were ongoing in the 1990s.

## Recent Developments

In January 2002, Pres. 'Omar Bongo's new government was the first in more than a decade to include members of the opposition. A constitutional amendment passed on 29 Jun 2003 would allow Bongo, already in power for 36 years, to rule indefinitely. A squabble broke out in March 2003 with Gabon's neighbor to the north, Equatorial Guinea, over the potentially oil-rich Isle of Mbagne in Corisco Bay.

Internet resources: <www.gabonnews.com>

# The Gambia

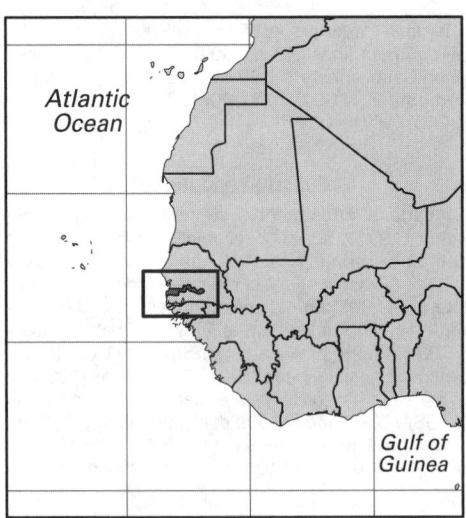

Atlantic
Ocean

Gulf of
Guinea

**Official name:** The Republic of the Gambia. **Form of government:** multiparty republic with one legislative house (National Assembly [53, including 5 non-elected seats]). **Head of state and government:** President Yahya A.J.J. Jammeh (from 1994). **Capital:** Banjul. **Official language:** English. **Official religion:** none. **Monetary unit:** 1 dalasi (D) = 100 butut; valuation (7 Jul 2003) $1 = D 26.75.

## Demography

**Area:** 4,127 sq mi, 10,689 sq km. **Population** (2002): 1,418,000. **Density** (2002): persons per sq mi 426.5, persons per sq km 164.7. **Urban** (1999): 36.8%. **Sex distribution** (2001): male 49.96%; female 50.04%. **Age breakdown** (2001): under 15, 45.2%; 15–29, 26.2%; 30–44, 15.6%; 45–59, 8.7%; 60–74, 3.5%; 75 and over, 0.8%. **Ethnic composition** (1993): Malinke 34.1%; Fulani 16.2%; Wolof 12.6%; Diola 9.2%; Soninke 7.7%; other 20.2%. **Religious affiliation** (1993): Muslim 95.0%; Christian 4.1%; traditional beliefs and other 0.9%. **Major cities/urban areas** (1993): Serekunda 151,450 (within Greater Banjul); Brikama 42,480; Banjul 42,326 (Greater Banjul 270,540); Bakau 38,062 (within Greater Banjul); Farafenni 21,142. **Location:** western Africa, bordering Senegal on three sides and the North Atlantic Ocean.

## Vital statistics

**Birth rate** per 1,000 population (2001): 41.8 (world avg. 21.2). **Death rate** per 1,000 population (2001): 12.9 (world avg. 8.9). **Natural increase rate** per 1,000 population (2001): 28.9 (world avg. 12.3). **Total fertility rate** (avg. births per childbearing woman; 2001): 5.7. **Life expectancy** at birth (2001): male 51.7 years; female 55.6 years.

## National economy

**Budget** (1999). *Revenue:* D 944,500,000 (tax revenue 81.9%, of which import duties and excises 29.0%, income taxes 19.4%, sales tax 6.9%; nontax revenue 11.1%; grants 7.0%). *Expenditures:* D 1,118,200,000 (wages and salaries 26.9%; interest payments 22.2%; goods and services 16.9%; education and culture 13.1%; health 7.9%; defense 3.6%). **Production** (metric tons except as noted). *Agriculture, forestry, fishing* (2001): peanuts (groundnuts) 153,000, millet 105,000, paddy rice 33,000; livestock (number of live animals) 365,000 cattle, 145,000 goats, 106,000 sheep; roundwood (1998) 661,000 cu m; fish catch (1998) 29,002, of which Atlantic Ocean 26,702, inland water 2,300. *Mining and quarrying:* sand and gravel are excavated for local use. *Manufacturing* (value of production in D '000; 1982): processed food, including peanut and palm-kernel oil 62,878; beverages 10,546; textiles 3,253. *Energy production (consumption):* electricity (kW-hr; 1998) 122,187,000 (122,187,000); petroleum products (metric tons; 1998) none (44,000). **Population economically active** (1998): total 575,140; activity rate of total population 47.3% (participation rates: [1983] ages 15–64, 78.2%; female 46.3%). **Tourism** (1998): receipts from visitors $33,000,000; expenditures by nationals abroad (1997) $16,000,000. **Household expenditure.** Average household size (1998) 9.4; expenditure (1991): food and beverages 58.0%, clothing and footwear 17.5%, energy and water 5.4%, housing 5.1%, education, health, transportation and communications, recreation, and other 14.0%. **Public debt** (external, outstanding; 2000): $425,200,000. **Gross national product** (at current market prices; 2000): $440,000,000 ($340 per capita). **Land use** (1994): forested 10.0%; meadows and pastures 19.0%; agricultural and under permanent cultivation 17.2%; built-on area, wasteland, and other 53.8%.

*1 metric ton = about 1.1 short tons;   1 kilometer = 0.6 mi (statute);   1 metric ton-km cargo = about 0.68 short ton-mi cargo;   c.i.f.: cost, insurance, and freight;   f.o.b.: free on board*

## Foreign trade

**Imports** (1999; c.i.f. in balance of trade and f.o.b. in commodities and trading partners): D 2,186,820,000 (food 32.9%; basic manufactures 23.9%; machinery and transport equipment 20.7%; chemicals and related products 7.3%; mineral fuels and lubricants 7.2%; vegetable oils 3.0%). *Major import sources:* China 17.2%; Hong Kong 10.6%; UK 8.7%; The Netherlands 7.3%; Senegal 5.2%; France 4.7%; Côte d'Ivoire 4.3%; Thailand 1.0%. **Exports** (1999): D 80,600,000 (domestic exports 13.3%, of which peanuts (groundnuts) 8.3%, fish products 2.2%; reexports 86.7%). *Major export destinations:* Belgium-Luxembourg 61.0%; Japan 19.4%; UK 6.8%; Spain 1.8%.

## Transport and communications

**Transport.** *Roads* (1999): total length 2,700 km (paved 35%). *Vehicles* (1997): passenger cars 7,267; trucks and buses (1996) 9,000. *Air transport* (1994): passenger-km 50,000,000; cargo metric ton-km 5,000,000; airports (2000) with scheduled flights 1. **Communications,** in total units (units per 1,000 persons). Daily newspaper circulation (1996): 2,000 (1.7); radio receivers (1997): 196,000 (165); television receivers (1999): 4,000 (3.1); telephone main lines (2001): 35,000 (26); cellular telephone subscribers (2001): 43,000 (32); personal computers (2001): 17,000 (13); Internet users (2001): 18,000 (14).

## Education and health

**Literacy** (1998): total population age 15 and over literate 34.6%; males literate 41.9%; females literate 27.5%. **Health:** physicians (2000) 105 (1 per 12,977 persons); hospital beds (2000) 1,140 (1 per 1,199 persons); infant mortality rate per 1,000 live births (2001) 77.8. **Food** (2000): daily per capita caloric intake 2,474 (vegetable products 95%, animal products 5%); 104% of FAO recommended minimum.

## Military

**Total active duty personnel** (2001): 800 (army 100%). **Military expenditure as percentage of GNP** (1999): 1.3% (world 2.4%); per capita expenditure $12.

## Background

Beginning about the 13th century AD, the Wolof, Malinke, and Fulani peoples settled in different parts of what is now Gambia and established villages and then kingdoms in the region. European exploration began when the Portuguese sighted the Gambia River in 1455. In the 17th century, when Britain and France both settled in the area, the British Fort James, on an island about 20 mi (32 km) from the river's mouth, was an important collection point for the slave trade. In 1783 the Treaty of Versailles reserved the Gambia River for Britain. After the British abolished slavery in 1807, they built a fort at the mouth of the river to block the continuing slave trade. In 1889 Gambia's boundaries were agreed upon by Britain and France; the British declared a protectorate over the area in 1894. Independence was proclaimed in 1965, and Gambia became a republic within the Commonwealth in 1970. It formed a limited confederation with Senegal in 1982 that was dissolved in 1989. During the 1990s, the government was in turmoil.

## Recent Developments

Internal controversy in 2002 focused on the enactment of the harsh Media Commission law that created a body to register all reporters, enforce the disclosure of sources, impose fines for the publication of "unauthorized stories," and close down papers for noncompliance with its orders. A controversial "alien tax" of $40 a year was imposed on non-Gambian residents in February 2003.

**Internet resources:** <www.gambiatourism.info>

# Georgia

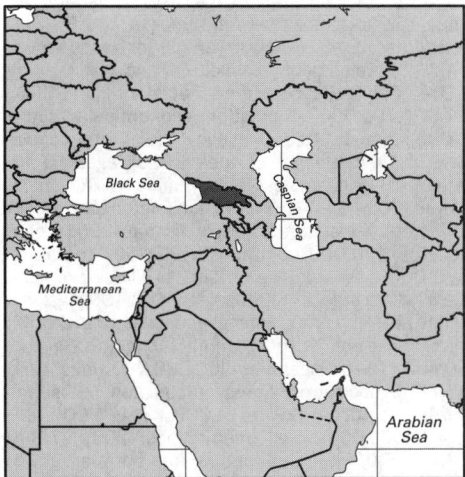

**Official name:** Sak'art'velo (Georgia). **Form of government:** unitary multiparty republic with a single legislative body (Parliament [235]). **Head of state and government:** President Eduard Shevardnadze (from 1992), assisted by Minister of State, Avtandil Jorbenadze. **Capital:** T'bilisi. **Official language:** Georgian. **Official religion:** none; but special recognition is given to the Georgian Orthodox Church. **Monetary unit:** 1 Georgian lari = 100 tetri; valuation (7 Jul 2003) $1 = 2.14 lari.

## Demography

**Area:** 26,911 sq mi, 69,700 sq km. **Population** (2002): 4,961,000. **Density** (2002): persons per sq mi 184.3, persons per sq km 71.2. **Urban** (2000): 60.7%. **Sex distribution** (2001): male 47.56%; female 52.44%. **Age breakdown** (2001): under 15, 19.6%; 15–29, 24.0%; 30–44, 22.4%; 45–59, 15.6%; 60–74, 14.4%; 75 and over, 4.0%. **Ethnic composition** (2000): Georgian 57.9%; Mingrelian 9.1%; Armenian 8.1%; Russian 6.3%; Azerbaijani 5.7%; Ossetian 3.0%; Greek 1.9%; Abkhazian 1.8%; other 6.2%. **Religious affiliation** (1995): Christian 46.2%, of which Georgian Orthodox 36.7%, Armenian Apostolic 5.6%, Russian Orthodox 2.7%, other Christian 1.2%; Sunni Muslim 11.0%; other (mostly nonreligious) 42.8%. **Major cities** (1997): T'bilisi (1998) 1,398,968; K'ut'aisi 240,000; Rust'avi 158,000; Bat'umi 137,100; Zugdidi 105,000 (includes internally displaced persons from Abkhazia). **Location:** Caucasus region of southwestern Asia, bordering Russia, Azerbaijan, Armenia, Turkey, and the Black Sea.

## Vital statistics

**Birth rate** per 1,000 population (2001): 11.2 (world avg. 21.2). **Death rate** per 1,000 population (2001): 14.6 (world avg. 8.9). **Natural increase rate** per 1,000 population (2001): –3.4 (world avg. 12.3). **Total fertility rate** (avg. births per childbearing woman; 2001): 1.4. **Marriage rate** per 1,000 population (1996): 3.7. **Life expectancy** at birth (2001): male 61.0 years; female 68.3 years.

## National economy

**Budget** (2000). *Revenue*: 913,300,000 lari (tax revenue 77.4%, of which valueadded tax 31.7%, excise tax 13.5%, income tax 11.8%; extrabudgetary revenue 15.9%; nontax revenue 4.9%; grants 1.8%). *Expenditures*: 1,155,900,000 lari (current expenditure 94.7%; development expenditure and net lending 5.3%). **Public debt** (external, outstanding; 2000): $1,609,700,000. **Population economically active** (2000): total 1,748,800; activity rate of total population 35.1% (participation rates [1993]: ages 16–65 [male], 16–60 [female] 55.6%; female 47.8%; unemployed [2000] 12.0%). **Production** (metric tons except as noted). *Agriculture, forestry, fishing* (2001): corn (maize) 420,000, potatoes 380,000, tomatoes 310,000; livestock (number of live animals) 1,177,400 cattle, 545,000 sheep, 443,400 pigs; fish catch (1999) 1,600. *Mining and quarrying* (2000): manganese ore 59,100. *Manufacturing* (2000): steel 56,400 (1998); cigarettes 300,000,000 units; wine 430,400 hectolitres. *Energy production (consumption)*: electricity (kW-hr; 2000) 7,400,000,000 (7,400,000,000); coal (metric tons; 2000) 7,300 (1997; 5,000); crude petroleum (barrels; 2000) 803,000 (803,000); petroleum products (metric tons; 2000) 10,600 (1997; 104,000); natural gas (cu m; 2000) 79,500,000 (1997; 914,935,000). **Gross national product** (2000): $3,183,000,000 ($630 per capita). **Household income and expenditure** (1993). Average household size 4.0; sources of income: wages and salaries 34.5%, benefits 21.9%, agricultural income 21.6%, other 22.0%; expenditure: taxes 42.5%, retail goods 32.3%, savings 16.4%, transportation 4.2%. **Tourism** ($'000,000; 2000): receipts 413; expenditures 110.

## Foreign trade

**Imports** (2000-c.i.f.): $700,200,000 (mineral fuels 18.5%; wheat and flour 6.5%; medicines 5.2%; tobacco products 4.5%; sugar 3.8%; unspecified 52.9%). *Major import sources:* Turkey 16.0%; Russia 14.1%; US 10.1%; Azerbaijan 8.5%; Germany 7.7%. **Exports** (2000-f.o.b.): $329,900,000 (scrap metals 11.5%; wine 8.6%; nuts 6.8%; fertilizers 4.9%; precious metallic ores 4.5%; ferroalloys 4.1%; crude oil 3.9%; aluminum waste 3.9%). *Major export destinations:* Turkey 22.7%; Russia 21.1%; Germany 10.4%; Azerbaijan 6.4%; Armenia 4.1%; Switzerland 4.1%.

## Transport and communications

**Transport.** *Railroads* (1997): 1,546 km; (1995) passenger-km 371,000,000; (1993) metric ton-km cargo 1,750,000,000. *Roads* (1999): 20,215 km (paved 93%). *Vehicles* (1999): passenger cars 247,872; trucks and buses 43,421. *Air transport* (1997): passenger-km 206,000,000; metric ton-km cargo 840,000 (Orbi Georgian Airways); airports (2000) with scheduled flights 1. **Communications**, in total units (units per 1,000 persons). Radio receivers (1997): 3,020,000 (586); television receivers (1998): 2,580,000 (506); telephone main lines (2001): 867,600 (159); cellular telephone subscribers (2001): 295,000 (54); Internet users (2001): 25,000 (4.6).

## Education and health

**Literacy** (1997): total population age 15 and over literate 99.5%; males literate 99.7%; females literate 99.4%. **Food** (2000): daily per capita caloric intake 2,412 (vegetable products 84%, animal products 16%); 92% of FAO recommended minimum. **Health** (1997): physicians 21,846 (1 per 236 persons); hospital beds 24,500 (1 per 210 persons); infant mortality rate per 1,000 live births (2001) 52.4.

## Military

**Total active duty personnel** (2001): 28,490 (army 50.5%, air force 4.7%, navy 3.7%, paramilitary 41.1%). About 4,000 Russian troops remained in Georgia in mid-2001. Withdrawal of Russian troops from Georgia began in June 2001 with the closure of the first of four Russian military bases. **Military expenditure as percentage of GNP** (1999): 1.2% (world 2.4%); per capita expenditure $33.

## Background

Ancient Georgia was the site of the kingdoms of Iberia and Colchis, whose fabled wealth was known to the ancient Greeks. The area was part of the Roman empire by 65 BC and became Christian in AD 337. For the next three centuries it was involved in the conflicts between the Byzantine and Persian empires; after 654 it was controlled by Arab caliphs, who established an emirate in Tbilisi. It was controlled by the Bagratids from the 8th to the 12th century, and the zenith of Georgia's power was reached in the reign of Queen Tamara, whose realm stretched from Azerbaijan to Circassia, forming a pan-Caucasian empire. Invasions by Mongols and Turks in the 13th and 14th centuries disintegrated the kingdom, and the fall of Constantinople (now Istanbul) to the Ottoman Turks in 1453 isolated it from western Christendom. The next three centuries saw repeated invasions by the Armenians, Turks, and Persians. Georgia sought Russian protection in 1783, and in 1801 it was annexed to Russia. After the Russian Revolution of 1917, the area was briefly independent; in 1921 a Soviet regime was installed, and in 1936 Georgia became the Georgian SSR, a full member of the Soviet Union. In 1990 a noncommunist coalition came to power in the first free elections ever held in Soviet Georgia, and in 1991 Georgia declared independence. In the 1990s, while Pres. Eduard Shevardnadze tried to steer a middle course, internal dissension resulted in conflicts with the northwestern republic of Abkhazia, and external distrust of Russian motives in the area grew. In 1992 Abkhazia reinstated its 1925 constitution and declared independence, which Georgia refused to recognize.

*1 metric ton = about 1.1 short tons; 1 kilometer = 0.6 mi (statute); 1 metric ton-km cargo = about 0.68 short ton-mi cargo; c.i.f.: cost, insurance, and freight; f.o.b.: free on board*

## Recent Developments

On 10 Oct 2002 the Georgian Parliament voted to amend the constitution to designate Abkhazia an autonomous republic. In May 2002 a contingent of US troops arrived in Georgia to help train Georgian forces in antiterrorism warfare. In November Georgia formally announced its intention to seek membership in NATO.

**Internet resources:**
<www.parliament.ge/gotoGeorgia.htm>

# Germany

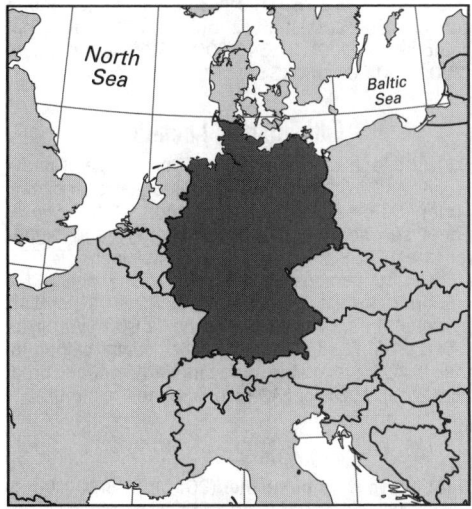

**Official name:** Bundesrepublik Deutschland (Federal Republic of Germany). **Form of government:** federal multiparty republic with two legislative houses (Federal Council [69]; Federal Diet [603]). **Chief of state:** President Johannes Rau (from 1999). **Head of government:** Chancellor Gerhard Schröder (from 1998). **Capital:** Berlin; some ministries remain in Bonn. **Official language:** German. **Official religion:** none. **Monetary unit:** 1 euro (€) = 100 cents; valuation (7 Jul 2003) $1 = €0.87; at conversion on 1 Jan 2002, €1= 1.96 Deutsche Mark (DM).

## Demography

**Area:** 137,846 sq mi, 357,021 sq km. **Population** (2002): 82,506,000. **Major cities** (1999): Berlin 3,392,900; Hamburg 1,701,800 (2,664,000); Munich 1,193,600 (2,291,000); Cologne 963,200; Frankfurt am Main 644,700 (3,681,000); Essen 600,700; Dortmund 590,300; Stuttgart 581,200; Düsseldorf 568,500; Bremen 542,300 (880,000); Duisburg 521,300; Hannover 515,200 (1,283,000); Leipzig 490,000; Nuremberg (Nürnberg) 486,400 (1,189,000). **Density** (2002): persons per sq mi 598.5, persons per sq km 231.1. **Urban** (1997): 82.4%. **Sex distribution** (2000): male 48.79%; female 51.21%. **Age breakdown** (2000): under 15, 15.7%; 15–29, 17.6%; 30–44, 24.7%; 45–59, 19.1%; 60–74, 15.9%; 75 and over, 7.0%. **Ethnic composition** (by nationality; 2000): German 88.2%; Turkish 3.4%, of which Kurdish 0.7%; Italian 1.0%; Greek 0.7%; Serb 0.6%; Russian 0.6%; Polish 0.4%;

other 5.1%. **Religious affiliation** (2000): Christian 75.8%, of which Protestant 35.6% (including Lutheran 33.9%), Roman Catholic 33.5%, Orthodox 0.9%, independent Christian 0.9%, other Christian 4.9%; Muslim 4.4%; Jewish 0.1%; nonreligious 17.2%; atheist 2.2%; other 0.3%. **Households** (2000). Number of households 38,124,000; average household size 2.2; 1 person 36.0%, 2 persons 33.4%, 3 persons 14.7%, 4 persons 11.5%, 5 or more persons 4.4%. **Location:** central Europe, bordering Denmark, the Baltic Sea, Poland, the Czech Republic, Austria, Switzerland, France, Luxembourg, Belgium, The Netherlands, and the North Sea.

## Vital statistics

**Birth rate** per 1,000 population (2001): 9.0 (world avg. 21.2); legitimate 75.0%; illegitimate 25.0%. **Death rate** per 1,000 population (2001): 10.0 (world avg. 8.9). **Natural increase rate** per 1,000 population (2001): −1.0 (world avg. 12.3). **Total fertility rate** (avg. births per childbearing woman; 2000): 1.3. **Marriage rate** per 1,000 population (2001): 4.7. **Divorce rate** per 1,000 population (2001): 2.4. **Life expectancy** at birth (1997–99): male 74.4 years; female 80.6 years.

## Social indicators

**Quality of working life.** Average workweek (1998): 39.8 hours. Annual rate per 100,000 workers (1993) for: injuries or accidents at work 4,808; deaths, including commuting accidents, 6.7. Proportion of labor force insured for damages of income loss resulting from: injury, virtually 100%; permanent disability, virtually 100%; death, virtually 100%. Average days lost to labor stoppages per 1,000 workers (2000): 0.3. **Access to services.** Proportion of dwellings (1996) having: electricity, virtually 100%; piped water supply, virtually 100%; flush sewage disposal (1993) 98.4%; public fire protection, virtually 100%. **Social participation.** Eligible voters participating in September 1998 national election c. 81%. Trade union membership in total workforce (1994): c. 27%. Practicing religious population (1994): 5% of Protestants and 25% of Roman Catholics "regularly" attend religious services. **Social deviance** (1996). Offense rate per 100,000 population for: murder and manslaughter 3.3; sexual abuse 46.0, of which rape and forcible sexual assault 13.4, child molestation 7.3; assault and battery 116.9; theft 688.9. **Material well-being** (2000; median income). Households possessing: automobile 75.4%; telephone 96.7%; color television receiver 95.5%; refrigerator 79.3%; washing machine 97.9%; home freezer 73.8%; personal computer 48.2%; video recorder 83.8%.

## National economy

**Budget** (2000). *Revenue:* DM 1,910,161,000,000 (taxes 84.7%, interest 7.7%). *Expenditures:* DM 1,873,837,000,000 (pensions and other social security payments 34.4%, purchase of current goods and services 21.9%, personnel costs 18.4%). **Total national debt** (May 2002): €715,800,000,000. **Production** (value of production in DM except as noted; 1999–2000). *Agriculture, forestry, fishing:* cereal grains 7,007,000,000, flowers and ornamental plants 3,010,000,000, sugar beets 2,541,000,000, grapes for wine 2,289,000,000, fruits 2,095,000,-000, potatoes 2,024,000,000, vegetables 1,960,-

000,000, tree nurseries 1,870,000,000, oilseed crops 1,601,000,000; livestock (number of live animals; 2000) 27,049,000 pigs, 14,658,000 cattle, 2,100,000 sheep, 110,000,000 chickens; roundwood (2000) 37,634,000 cu m; fish catch (metric tons; 1999) 312,492. *Mining and quarrying* (metric tons; 1998): potash 37,100,000. *Manufacturing* (value added at factor cost in DM '000,000; 1996): capital equipment 252,226, of which machinery 90,213, transport equipment 80,418; electrical equipment 57,269; chemicals (including pharmaceuticals) 60,842; food and beverages 39,184; plastics and other synthetic products 27,853; glass and ceramic products 22,730; furniture and other wood products 16,651; paper products 12,948; textiles 8,636; clothing 5,467. *Energy production (consumption)*: electricity (kW-hr; 2000) 557,004,000,000 ([1997] 544,063,000,000); hard coal (metric tons; 2001) 28,866,000 ([1997] 72,236,000); lignite (metric tons; 2001) 175,259,000 ([1997] 179,403,-000); crude petroleum (barrels; 2001) 21,502,000 ([1997] 745,355,000); petroleum products (metric tons; 1997) 93,230,000 (113,289,000); natural gas (cu m; 2000) 23,387,000,000 ([1997] 108,390,-000,000). **Gross national product** (at current market prices; 2000): $2,063,734,000,000 ($25,120 per capita). **Household income and expenditure.** Average annual income per household (1998) DM 75,144 ($42,702); sources of take-home income: wages 77.6%, self-employment 12.0%, transfer payments 10.4%; expenditure: rent 24.7%, food and beverages 13.9%, transportation 13.7%, entertainment, education, and leisure 11.8%, household operations, durables, and maintenance 7.0%, clothing and footwear 5.5%. **Tourism** (2000): receipts $17,879,-000,000; expenditures $47,785,000,000. **Population economically active** (2000): total 40,326,000; activity rate of total population 49.0% (participation rates [1998]: ages 15–64, 70.7%; female 43.1%; unemployed 10.7%). **Land use** (1994): forest 30.6%; pasture 15.1%; agriculture 19.9%; other 34.4%.

## Foreign trade

**Imports** (2000; f.o.b. in balance of trade and c.i.f. in commodities and trading partners): DM 1,064,308,-800,000 (machinery and transport equipment 37.0%, of which road transport equipment 8.3%, electrical machinery other than office equipment 7.9%; chemicals and chemical products 8.9%, of which organic chemical products 2.5%, unfabricated plastics 1.4%; mineral fuels 8.7%, of which crude petroleum and petroleum products 6.5%, natural gas 1.8%; food and beverages 6.1%, of which fruits and vegetables 1.8%, meat and meat products 0.7%, coffee, tea, and cocoa 0.6%; iron and steel 2.2%; furniture 1.3%). *Major import sources:* France 9.6%; The Netherlands 8.8%; US 8.5%; UK 7.0%; Italy 6.6%; Japan 4.9%; Belgium 4.8%; Austria 3.8%; Switzerland 3.4%. **Exports** (2000): DM 1,167,343,300,000 (machinery and transport equipment 51.2%, of which road transport equipment 17.4%, electrical machinery other than office equipment 8.4%; chemicals and chemical products 12.7%, of which organic chemical products 2.4%, unfabricated plastics 2.2%). *Major export destinations:* France 11.4%; US 10.2%; UK 8.3%; Italy 7.6%; The Netherlands 6.4%; Austria 5.3%; Belgium 5.1%; Spain 4.5%; Switzerland 4.3%; Poland 2.4%.

## Transport and communications

**Transport.** *Railroads* (1999): length 82,413 km (1998); passengers carried 1,943,000,000; passenger-km 73,587,000,000; metric ton-km cargo 71,356,000,000. *Roads* (1999): total length 230,735 km (paved 99%). *Vehicles* (2000): passenger cars 42,423,300; trucks and buses 2,576,000. *Air transport* (1999): passengers carried 41,118,000; passenger-km 88,867,173,000; metric ton-km cargo 6,598,776,000; airports (1997) 35. **Communications**, in total units (units per 1,000 persons). Daily newspaper circulation (1996): 25,500,000 (311); radio receivers (1997): 77,800,000 (948); television receivers (1999): 47,600,000 (580); telephone main lines (2001): 52,280,000 (635); cellular telephone subscribers (2001): 56,245,000 (683); personal computers (2000): 27,640,000 (336); Internet users (2001): 30,000,000 (364).

## Education and health

**Educational attainment** (2000). Percentage of population age 25 and over having: primary and lower secondary 50.6%; intermediate secondary 17.9%; vocational secondary 8.7%; post-secondary and higher (all levels) 22.8%. **Health** (2000): physicians 294,676 (1 per 279 persons); dentists 63,156 (1 per 1,302 persons); hospital beds (1999) 565,268 (1 per 145 persons); infant mortality rate per 1,000 live births (2001) 4.3. **Food** (1999): daily per capita caloric intake 3,411 (vegetable products 69%, animal products 31%); 128% of FAO recommended minimum.

## Military

**Total active duty personnel** (2001): 308,400 (army 68.7%, navy 8.4%, air force 22.9%); US troops in Germany (2001): 71,000. **Military expenditure as percentage of GNP** (1999): 1.6% (world 2.4%); per capita expenditure $395.

 **Did you know?**   Established in 1970, the Bavarian Forest National Park is Germany's oldest and best-developed national park. It occupies 50.5 sq mi (130.8 sq km) of the Bohemian Forest highlands along the border with the Czech Republic. A favorite of hikers, the park is Europe's largest closed-canopy forest.

## Background

Germanic tribes entered the region about the 2nd century BC, displacing the Celts. The Romans failed to conquer the region, which became a political entity only with the division of the Carolingian Empire in the 9th century AD. The monarchy's control was weak, and power increasingly devolved upon the nobility, organized in feudal states. The monarchy was restored under Saxon rule in the 10th century, and the Holy Roman Empire, centering on Germany and northern Italy, was revived. Continuing conflict between the Holy Roman emperors and the Roman Catholic popes undermined the empire, and its dissolution was accelerated by Martin Luther's revolt in 1517, which divided Germany, and ultimately Europe, into Protes-

---

*1 metric ton = about 1.1 short tons;    1 kilometer = 0.6 mi (statute);    1 metric ton-km cargo = about 0.68 short ton-mi cargo;   c.i.f.: cost, insurance, and freight;    f.o.b.: free on board*

tant and Roman Catholic camps, culminating in the Thirty Years' War (1618–48). Germany's population and borders were greatly reduced, and its numerous feudal princes gained virtually full sovereignty. In 1862 Otto von Bismarck came to power in Prussia and over the next decade reunited Germany in the German Empire. It was dissolved in 1918 after the German defeat in World War I. Germany was stripped of much of its territory and all of its colonies. In 1933 Adolf Hitler became chancellor and established a totalitarian state, the Third Reich, dominated by the Nazi Party. Hitler's invasion of Poland in 1939 plunged the world into World War II. Following its defeat in 1945, Germany was divided by the Allied Powers into four zones of occupation. Disagreement with the USSR over the reunification of the zones led to the creation in 1949 of the Federal Republic of Germany (West Germany) and the German Democratic Republic (East Germany). Berlin, the former capital, remained divided. West Germany became a prosperous parliamentary democracy, East Germany a one-party state under Soviet control. The East German Communist government was brought down peacefully in 1989, and Germany was reunited in 1990. After the initial euphoria over unity, the former West Germany sought to incorporate the former East Germany both politically and economically, resulting in heavy financial burdens for the wealthier western Germans. The country continued to move toward deeper political and economic integration with western Europe through its membership in the European Union.

## Recent Developments

Germany has witnessed a slowdown in the pace of economic growth and reform, though the country's involvement in world affairs is increasing. Unemployment hit 11.1% in early 2003. Despite diminished personal approval ratings, Chancellor Gerhard Schröder had gained in stature as a statesman as Germany embarked on a more active and assertive foreign policy course after more than half a century of restraint. Germany assumed a greater leadership role in European affairs and grew more active in other international trouble spots such as Macedonia and the Middle East. Germany adamantly opposed military action in Iraq, for example, and relations with the US suffered accordingly. Schröder was reelected in federal elections in September 2002, but his Social Democrats were stingingly upset in local elections in January 2003 in the states of Hesse and Lower Saxony, the chancellor's home territory.

Internet resources: <www.germany-tourism.de>

# Ghana

**Official name:** Republic of Ghana. **Form of government:** unitary multiparty republic with one legislative house (House of Parliament [200]). **Head of state and government:** President John Agyekum Kufuor (from 2001). **Capital:** Accra. **Official language:** English. **Official religion:** none. **Monetary unit:** 1 cedi ( ) = 100 pesewas; valuation (7 Jul 2003) $1 = 8,685.

## Demography

**Area:** 92,098 sq mi, 238,533 sq km. **Population** (2002): 20,244,000. **Density** (2002): persons per sq mi 219.8, persons per sq km 84.9. **Urban** (1999):

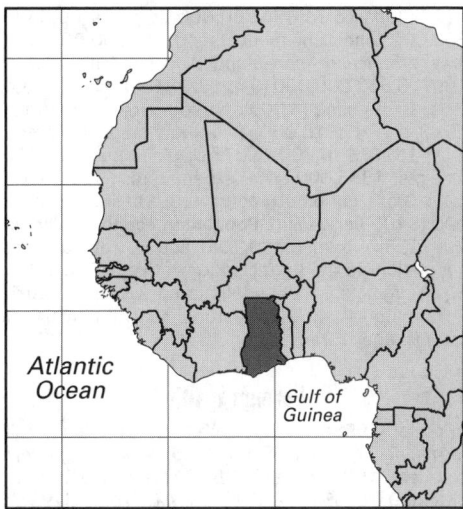

37.8%. **Sex distribution** (1999): male 49.77%; female 50.23%. **Age breakdown** (2000): under 15, 41.9%; 15–29, 27.7%; 30–44, 17.4%; 45–59, 7.8%; 60–74, 4.2%; 75 and over, 1.0%. **Ethnolinguistic composition** (1983): Akan 52.4%; Mossi 15.8%; Ewe 11.9%; Ga-Adangme 7.8%; Gurma 3.3%; Yoruba 1.3%; other 7.5%. **Religious affiliation** (2000): Christian 55.4%, of which Protestant 16.6%, African Christian 14.4%, Roman Catholic 9.5%; traditional beliefs 24.4%; Muslim 19.7%; other 0.5%. **Major cities** (2001): Accra 1,551,200; Kumasi 610,600; Tamale 259,200; Tema 225,900; Obuasi 118,000. **Location:** western Africa, bordering Burkina Faso, Togo, the Atlantic Ocean, and Côte d'Ivoire.

## Vital statistics

**Birth rate** per 1,000 population (2001): 29.0 (world avg. 21.2). **Death rate** per 1,000 population (2001): 10.3 (world avg. 8.9). **Natural increase rate** per 1,000 population (2001): 18.7 (world avg. 12.3). **Total fertility rate** (avg. births per childbearing woman; 2001): 3.8. **Life expectancy** at birth (2001): male 55.9 years; females 58.7 years.

## National economy

**Budget** (1996). *Revenue:* 1,997,600,000,000 cedi (excise and value-added taxes 36.7%, of which petroleum tax 14.5%; import-export duties 27.3%; income taxes 21.7%; nontax revenue 14.4%). *Expenditures* (1995): 1,697,893,000,000 cedi (1994: education 22.3%; debt service 20.1%; health 6.9%; transportation and communications 5.3%; social security and welfare 3.6%; defense 2.9%). **Public debt** (external, outstanding; 2000): $5,529,000,000. **Production** (metric tons except as noted). *Agriculture, forestry, fishing* (2000): roots and tubers 12,893,000 (of which cassava 7,845,000, yams 3,249,000, taro 1,707,000), cereals 1,686,000 (of which corn [maize] 1,014,000, sorghum 302,000, rice 210,000, millet 160,000), bananas and plantains 2,061,000; livestock (number of live animals) 2,739,000 goats, 2,516,000 sheep, 17,467,000 chickens; roundwood (2000) 21,765,000 cu m; fish catch (2000) 452,070. *Mining and quarrying* (2000): manganese (metal content) 287,000; bauxite 504,000; gold 2,317,000 troy oz. *Manufacturing* (value added in ;

1993): tobacco 71,474,700,000; footwear 60,350,-600,000; chemical products 40,347,600,000. *Energy production (consumption)*: electricity (kW-hr; 1997) 6,652,000,000 (6,426,000,000); coal (metric tons; 1998) none (3,000); crude petroleum (barrels; 1998) none (7,315,000); petroleum products (metric tons; 1998) 926,000 (1,077,000). **Tourism** (2000): receipts $335,000,000; expenditures $100,000,-000. **Gross national product** (1999): $7,451,000,-000 ($400 per capita). **Population economically active** (1984): total 5,580,104; activity rate of total population 45.4% (participation rates: over age 15, 82.5%; female 51.2%; unemployed 2.8%). **Land use** (1994): forest 42.2%; pasture 36.9%; agriculture 19.0%; other 1.9%.

## Foreign trade

**Imports** (1998): $2,896,900,000 (petroleum [all forms] 7.4%; unspecified 92.6%). *Major import sources* (1999): Nigeria 14.9%; UK 9.5%; Côte d'Ivoire 9.0%; US 8.1%; France 7.7%. **Exports** (1998): $2,091,400,000 (gold 32.9%; cacao 25.9%; wood products 8.2%; cocoa products 3.8%). *Major export destinations* (1999): Togo 12.6%; UK 11.6%; US 9.4%; Italy 8.9%; The Netherlands 7.5%.

## Transport and communications

**Transport.** *Railroads* (2000): route length 953 km; (1993) passenger-km 1,177,000,000; (1994) metric ton-km cargo 125,700,000. *Roads* (1996): total length 38,700 km (paved 40%). *Vehicles* (1996): passenger cars 90,000; trucks and buses 45,000. *Air transport* (2001; Ghana Airways only): passenger-km 1,259,000,000; metric ton-km cargo 32,970,000; airports (1996) with scheduled flights 1. **Communications**, in total units (units per 1,000 persons). Daily newspaper circulation (1996): 250,000 (14); radio receivers (1997): 4,400,000 (236); television receivers (1999): 2,266,000 (118); telephone main lines (2001): 242,100 (12); cellular telephone subscribers (2001): 193,800 (9.3); personal computers (2001): 70,000 (3.3); Internet users (2001): 40,500 (1.9).

## Education and health

**Educational attainment** (1984). Percentage of population age 25 and over having: no formal schooling 60.4%; primary education 7.1%; middle school 25.4%; secondary 3.5%; vocational and other postsecondary 2.9%; higher 0.6%. **Literacy** (2000): total population age 15 and over literate 8,070,000 (70.2%); males literate 4,520,000 (79.8%); females literate 3,550,000 (61.2%). **Health:** physicians (1994) 735 (1 per 22,970 persons); hospital beds (1994) 26,455 (1 per 638 persons); infant mortality rate per 1,000 live births (2001) 56.5. **Food** (2000): daily per capita caloric intake 2,699 (vegetable products 96%, animal products 4%); 118% of FAO recommended minimum.

## Military

**Total active duty personnel** (2001): 7,000 (army 71.4%, navy 14.3%, air force 14.3%). **Military expenditure as percentage of GNP** (1999): 0.8% (world 2.4%); per capita expenditure $3.

## Background

The modern state of Ghana is named after the ancient Ghana empire that flourished until the 13th century AD in the western Sudan, about 500 mi (800 km) northwest of the modern state. The Akan peoples then founded their first states in modern Ghana. Gold-seeking Mande traders arrived by the 14th century, and Hausa merchants arrived by the 16th century. During the 15th century the Mande founded the states of Dagomba and Mamprussi in the northern half of the region. The Ashanti, an Akan people, originated in the central forest region and formed a strongly centralized empire that was at its height in the 18th and 19th centuries. European exploration of the region began early in the 15th century, when the Portuguese landed on the Gold Coast; they later established a settlement at Elmina as headquarters for the slave trade. By the mid-18th century the Gold Coast was dominated by numerous forts controlled by Dutch, British, and Danish merchants. Britain made the Gold Coast a crown colony in 1874, and British protectorates over the Ashanti and the northern territories were established in 1901. In 1957 the Gold Coast became the independent state of Ghana. Since independence, numerous political coups have occurred, but that of 1981 produced a government that lasted into the 1990s.

## Recent Developments

Until recently Ghana had generally avoided the ethnic tensions that plagued other West African nations. In March 2002, however, fighting between rival clans and ethnic groups broke out in the northern region. Different clans claimed the right to certain chieftainships, and several ethnic groups—all minorities within Ghana itself—clashed over reportedly unfair treatment and discrimination in the region and the nation generally. Conflicts continued sporadically throughout the year, with more than 100 people killed.

**Internet resources:**
<www.africaonline.com.gh/Tourism>

# Greece

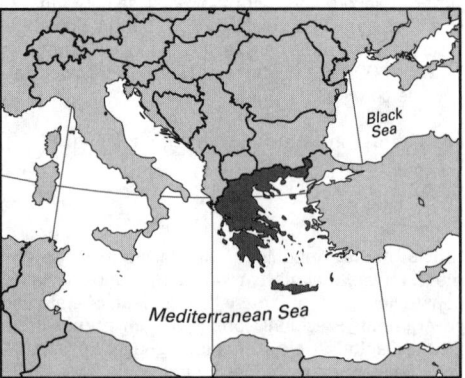

**Official name:** Elliniki Dhimokratia (Hellenic Republic). **Form of government:** unitary multiparty republic with one legislative house (Greek Chamber of

---

*1 metric ton = about 1.1 short tons; 1 kilometer = 0.6 mi (statute); 1 metric ton-km cargo = about 0.68 short ton-mi cargo; c.i.f.: cost, insurance, and freight; f.o.b.: free on board*

Deputies [300]). **Chief of state:** President Konstantinos (Kostis) Stephanopoulos (from 1995). **Head of government:** Prime Minister Konstantinos (Kostas) Simitis (from 1996). **Capital:** Athens. **Official language:** Greek. **Official religion:** Eastern Orthodox. **Monetary unit:** 1 euro (€) = 100 cents; valuation (7 Jul 2003) $1 = €0.87; at conversion on 1 Jan 2002, €1= 340.75 Greek drachma (Dr).

## Demography

**Area:** 50,949 sq mi, 131,957 sq km. **Population** (2002): 10,994,000. **Density** (2002): persons per sq mi 215.8, persons per sq km 83.3. **Urban** (2000): 60.1%. **Sex distribution** (1998): male 49.29%; female 50.71%. **Age breakdown** (1998): under 15, 15.6%; 15–29, 22.1%; 30–44, 21.5%; 45–59, 18.1%; 60–74, 16.3%; 75 and over, 6.5%. **Ethnic composition** (2000): Greek 90.4%; Macedonian 1.8%; Albanian 1.5%; Turkish 1.4%; Pomak 0.9%; Roma (Gypsy) 0.8%; other 3.2%. **Religious affiliation** (1995): Christian 95.2%, of which Eastern Orthodox 94.0%, Roman Catholic 0.5%; Muslim 1.3%; other 3.5%. **Major cities** (1991): Athens 772,072 (urban agglomeration [2001] 3,120,000); Thessaloniki 383,967 (urban agglomeration [2000] 789,000); Piraeus 182,671; Pátrai 152,570; Peristerion 137,288. **Location:** southern Europe, bordering Albania, Macedonia, Bulgaria, Turkey, and the Mediterranean Sea.

## Vital statistics

**Birth rate** per 1,000 population (2000): 11.7 (world avg. 22.5); (1998) legitimate 96.2%; illegitimate 3.8%. **Death rate** per 1,000 population (2000): 10.5 (world avg. 9.0). **Natural increase rate** per 1,000 population (2000): 1.2 (world avg. 13.5). **Total fertility rate** (avg. births per childbearing woman; 2000): 1.3. **Marriage rate** per 1,000 population (1998): 5.3. **Divorce rate** per 1,000 population (1997): 0.8. **Life expectancy** at birth (2000): male 75.9 years; female 81.2 years.

## National economy

**Budget** (1999). *Revenue:* Dr 12,409,000,000,000 (indirect taxes 47.2%, direct taxes 32.6%, nontax revenue 20.2%). *Expenditures:* Dr 17,737,000,000,000 (debt service 36.8%, health and social insurance 12.4%, education and culture 7.9%, agriculture 7.1%, defense 5.9%). **Public debt** (1997): $18,331,000,000. **Tourism** (2000): receipts $9,219,000,000; expenditures $4,558,000,000. **Production** (metric tons except as noted). *Agriculture, forestry, fishing* (2000): sugar beets 2,906,000, olives 2,000,000, tomatoes 1,960,000; livestock (number of live animals) 9,041,000 sheep, 5,293,000 goats, 906,000 pigs; roundwood (1999) 2,215,260 cu m; fish catch (1999) 215,964. *Mining and quarrying:* bauxite (1999) 1,813,000; nickel (1998) 18,000. *Manufacturing* (value added in Dr '000,000,000; 1999): food 573; paints, soaps, varnishes, drugs, and medicines 371; electrical machinery 287. *Energy production (consumption):* electricity (kW-hr; 1999) 44,724,000,000 ([1997] 36,528,000,000); hard coal (metric tons; 1997) none (1,153,000); lignite (metric tons; 1999) 61,464,000 ([1997] 58,678,000); crude petroleum (barrels; 1997) 3,145,000 (130,453,000); petroleum products (metric tons; 1997) 18,938,000 (15,669,000); natural gas (cu m; 1997) 52,177,000 (202,530,000). **Household income and expenditure.**

Average household size (1993–94) 2.9; income per household Dr 3,900,000 ($15,660); sources of income (1995): wages and salaries 36.6%, transfer payments 19.0%, other 44.4%; expenditure: food and beverages 32.7%, transportation and communications 13.5%, housing 11.5%, cafe/hotel expenditures 7.6%, household furnishings 7.4%. **Gross national product** (2000): $126,269,000,000 ($11,960 per capita). **Population economically active** (1998): total 4,445,700; activity rate of total population 42.3% (participation rates: ages 15 and over, 50.1%; female 39.4%; unemployed [2000] 11.1%). **Land use** (1994): forest 20.3%; pasture 40.7%; agriculture 27.2%; other 11.8%.

## Foreign trade

**Imports** (1998-c.i.f.): Dr 8,933,000,000,000 (machinery and transport equipment 34.7%, chemicals and chemical products 12.3%, food products 10.9%, mineral fuels 7.3%). *Major import sources:* Italy 15.9%; Germany 14.9%; France 8.6%; UK 6.4%; The Netherlands 6.2%; US 4.6%. **Exports** (1998-f.o.b.): Dr 3,203,000,000,000 (food 18.4%, of which fruits and nuts 7.7%; clothing and apparel 16.8%; petroleum 6.4%; aluminum 4.2%; tobacco products 4.1%). *Major export destinations:* Germany 18.3%; Italy 11.9%; UK 7.0%; US 4.7%; France 4.6%; Bulgaria 4.1%.

## Transport and communications

**Transport.** *Railroads* (1999): route length 2,299 km; passenger-km 1,434,000,000; metric ton-km cargo 347,000,000. *Roads* (1999): total length 117,000 km (paved 92%). *Vehicles* (1998): passenger cars 2,675,676; trucks and buses 1,013,677. *Air transport* (1999; Olympic Airways): passenger-km 8,305,451,000; metric ton-km cargo 103,243,000; airports (1997) 36. **Communications,** in total units (units per 1,000 persons). Daily newspaper circulation (1996): 1,600,000 (150); radio receivers (1997): 5,020,000 (470); television receivers (1999): 5,100,000 (471); telephone main lines (2001): 5,607,700 (529); cellular telephone subscribers (2001): 7,962,000 (751); personal computers (2001): 860,000 (81); Internet users (2001): 1,400,000 (132).

## Education and health

**Educational attainment** (1991). Percentage of population age 25 and over having: no formal schooling (illiterate) 6.8%; some primary education 10.6%; completed primary 39.7%; lower secondary 10.8%; higher secondary 20.6%; some postsecondary 4.9%; completed higher 6.6%. **Literacy** (2000): total population age 15 and over literate 9,080,000 (97.2%); males literate 4,570,000 (98.6%); females literate 4,510,000 (96.0%). **Health** (1997): physicians 43,030 (1 per 248 persons); hospital beds 52,474 (1 per 204 persons); infant mortality rate per 1,000 live births (1999) 6.7. **Food** (1999): daily per capita caloric intake 3,689 (vegetable products 78%, animal products 22%); 148% of FAO recommended minimum.

## Military

**Total active duty personnel** (2001): 159,170 (army 69.1%, navy 11.9%, air force 19.0%). **Military expenditure as percentage of GNP** (1999): 4.7% (world 2.4%); per capita expenditure $573.

## Background

The earliest urban society in Greece was the palace-centered Minoan civilization, which reached its height on Crete c. 2000 BC. It was succeeded by the mainland Mycenaean civilization, which arose c. 1600 BC following a wave of Indo-European invasions. In c. 1200 BC a second wave of invasions destroyed the Bronze Age cultures, and a dark age followed, known mostly through the epics of Homer. At the end of this time, classical Greece began to emerge (c. 750 BC) as a collection of independent city-states, including Sparta in the Peloponnese and Athens in Attica. The civilization reached its zenith after repelling the Persians at the beginning of the 5th century BC and began to decline after the civil strife of the Peloponnesian War at the century's end. In 338 BC the Greek city-states were taken over by Philip II of Macedon, and Greek culture was spread by Philip's son Alexander the Great throughout his empire. The Romans, themselves heavily influenced by Greek culture, conquered the Greek states in the 2nd century BC. After the fall of Rome, Greece remained part of the Byzantine empire until the mid-15th century, when it became part of the expanding Ottoman Empire; it gained its independence in 1832. It was occupied by Nazi Germany during World War II. Civil war followed and lasted until 1949, when communist forces were defeated. In 1952 Greece joined NATO. A military junta ruled the country from 1967 to 1974, when democracy was restored and a referendum declared an end to the Greek monarchy. In 1981 Greece joined the European Community, the first Eastern European country to do so. Upheavals in the Balkans in the 1990s strained Greece's relations with some neighboring states, notably the former Yugoslav entity that took the name Republic of Macedonia.

## Recent Developments

In 2002 Greek security forces managed to crack down on the elusive left-wing terrorist group called November 17. Until that time not a single suspected member of the group believed to have been responsible for 23 killings since 1975 had been arrested. Police arrested more than a dozen alleged members of the group. The trials of the accused terrorists began in March 2003 and were expected to last for months. Large infrastructure works continued in and around Athens in preparation for the 2004 Olympic Summer Games. The International Olympic Committee said that it was largely satisfied with preparations.

**Internet resources:** <www.gnto.gr>

# Greenland

**Official name:** Kalaallit Nunaat (Greenlandic); Grønland (Danish) (Greenland). **Political status:** integral part of the Danish realm with one legislative house (Parliament [31]). **Chief of state:** Danish monarch Queen Margrethe II (from 1972). **Heads of government:** High Commissioner (for Denmark) Gunnar Martens (from 1995); Prime Minister (for Greenland) Hans Enoksen (from 14 Dec 2002). **Capital:** Nuuk (Godthåb). **Official languages:** Greenlandic; Danish.

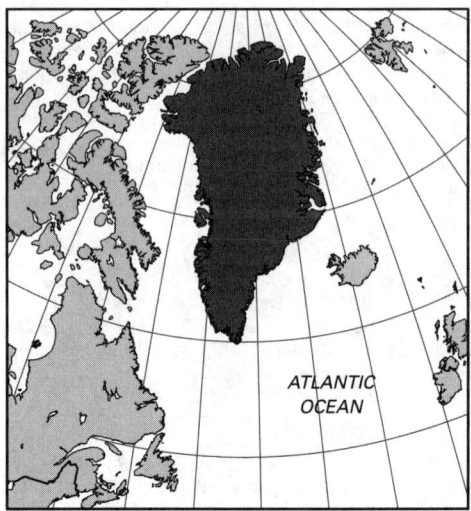

ATLANTIC OCEAN

**Official religion:** Evangelical Lutheran (Lutheran Church of Greenland). **Monetary unit:** 1 Danish krone (Dkr) = 100 øre; valuation (7 Jul 2003) $1 = Dkr 6.47.

## Demography

**Area:** 840,000 sq mi, 2,175,600 sq km. **Population** (2002): 56,600. **Density** (2002 [ice-free area only]): persons per sq mi 0.36, persons per sq km 0.14. **Town-dwelling** (2001): 84.3%. **Sex distribution** (2002): male 53.37%; female 46.63%. **Age breakdown** (2002): under 15, 26.4%; 15–29, 19.4%; 30–49, 35.4%; 50–64, 13.5%; 65 and over, 5.3%. **Ethnic composition** (2000): Greenland Eskimo 79.1%; Danish 13.6%; other 7.3%. **Religious affiliation** (2000): Protestant 69.2%, of which Evangelical Lutheran 64.2%, Pentecostal 2.8%; other Christian 27.4%; other/nonreligious 3.4%. **Major towns** (2001): Nuuk (Godthåb) 13,650; Sisimiut (Holsteinsborg) 5,165. **Location:** northern Atlantic Ocean, northeast of Canada.

## Vital statistics

**Birth rate** per 1,000 population (2000): 16.8 (world avg. 22.5); (1993) legitimate 29.2%; illegitimate 70.8%. **Death rate** per 1,000 population (2000): 7.6 (world avg. 9.0). **Natural increase rate** per 1,000 population (2000): 9.2 (world avg. 13.5). **Total fertility rate** (avg. births per childbearing woman; 2000): 2.3. **Marriage rate** per 1,000 population (1993): 7.1. **Divorce rate** per 1,000 population (1993): 2.7. **Life expectancy** at birth (2000): male 64.5 years; female 71.7 years.

## National economy

**Budget** (1998). *Revenue:* Dkr 4,304,000,000 (block grant from Danish government 59.8%; taxes and royalties for Greenland treasury 13.5%; import duties 11.3%; EEC fishery license fees 6.4%; other 6.6%). *Expenditures* (1997): Dkr 5,987,442,000 (current expenditure 93.3%, of which wages and salaries 35.9%, social welfare 22.3%, culture and education 15.3%, health 10.7%, defense 5.5%; capital [development]

*1 metric ton = about 1.1 short tons;   1 kilometer = 0.6 mi (statute);   1 metric ton-km cargo = about 0.68 short ton-mi cargo;   c.i.f.: cost, insurance, and freight;   f.o.b.: free on board*

expenditure 6.7%). **Public debt** (external, outstanding; 1995): $243,000,000. **Tourism** (1997): number of overnight visitors 181,043. **Production** (metric tons except as noted). *Fishing, animal products:* fish catch (1998) 372,974 (by local boats 128,630, of which shrimp 73,581, halibut 29,965, cod 11,776; by foreign boats 123,748); livestock (number of live animals; 1999) 22,000 sheep, 4,800 reindeer; animal products (value of external sales in Dkr '000; 1998) sealskins 31,044, polar bear skins 579. *Manufacturing:* principally handicrafts and fish processing. *Energy production (consumption):* electricity (kW-hr; 1999) 250,000,000 (232,000,000); crude petroleum (barrels; 1999) none (1,307,000); petroleum products (metric tons; 1991) none (214,000). **Gross national product** (1998): $1,021,000,000 ($18,205 per capita). **Population economically active** (2000): total 31,518; activity rate of total population 56.2% (participation rates: ages 15–60, 86.6%; female [1987] 43.4%; unemployed [1999] 10.0%). **Household income and expenditure.** Average household size (1998): 2.6; income per person (1997): Dkr 144,700 ($17,700); expenditure (1994): food, beverages, and tobacco 41.6%, housing and energy 22.4%, transportation and communications 10.2%, recreation 6.4%. **Land use** (1994): forested 0.03%; meadows and pastures 0.69%; agricultural and under permanent cultivation, none; other (principally ice cap) 99.28%.

## Foreign trade

**Imports** (2001): Dkr 2,466,000,000 (food, beverages, and tobacco products 17.3%; mineral fuels 16.6%; goods for construction industry 9.2%; machinery 7.0%; transport equipment 3.6%; unspecified 10.7%). *Major import sources* (2000): Denmark 72.8%; Norway 8.9%; Japan 2.6%; Germany 2.4%; Sweden 1.8%. **Exports** (2001): Dkr 2,251,000,000 (fish and fish products 87.2%, of which shrimp 54.8%, crab 11.4%). *Major export destinations* (2000): Denmark 86.0%; Japan 6.6%; US 4.7%; Thailand 1.4%.

## Transport and communications

**Transport.** *Roads* (1998): total length 150 km (paved 60%). *Vehicles* (1998): passenger cars 2,242; trucks and buses 1,474. *Air transport* (1998; Greenlandair only): passenger-km 167,000,000; metric ton-km cargo 339,000; airports (1998) with scheduled flights 18. **Communications,** in total units (units per 1,000 persons). Daily newspaper circulation (1996): 1,000 (18); radio receivers (1997): 27,000 (482); television receivers (1997): 22,000 (393); telephone main lines (1999): 26,000 (464); cellular telephone subscribers (1999): 14,000 (250).

## Education and health

**Literacy** (1999): total population age 15 and over literate virtually 100%. **Health** (1998): physicians 84 (1 per 668 persons); hospital beds (1993) 465 (1 per 125 persons); infant mortality rate per 1,000 live births (2000) 18.3.

## Military

**Total active duty personnel.** Denmark is responsible for Greenland's defense. Greenlanders are not liable for military service.

## Background

The Inuit probably crossed to northwestern Greenland from North America, along the islands of the Canadian Arctic, from 4000 BC to AD 1000. The Norwegian Erik the Red visited Greenland in 982; his son, Leif Eriksson, introduced Christianity in the 11th century. Greenland came under joint Danish-Norwegian rule in the late 14th century. The original Norse settlements became extinct in the 15th century, but Greenland was recolonized by Denmark in 1721. In 1776 Denmark closed the Greenland coast to foreign trade; it was not reopened until 1950. Greenland became part of the kingdom of Denmark in 1953. Home rule was established in 1979.

## Recent Developments

In December 2002 voters gave a majority of seats to parties advocating independence from Denmark. The ruling Siumut party, headed by Hans Enoksen, briefly formed a coalition government with the pro-independence Inuit Brotherhood, then joined its preelection coalition partner, the conservative Atassut party. Atassut advocates delaying independence until Greenland can manage it financially.

**Internet resources:** <www.greenland-guide.gl>

# Grenada

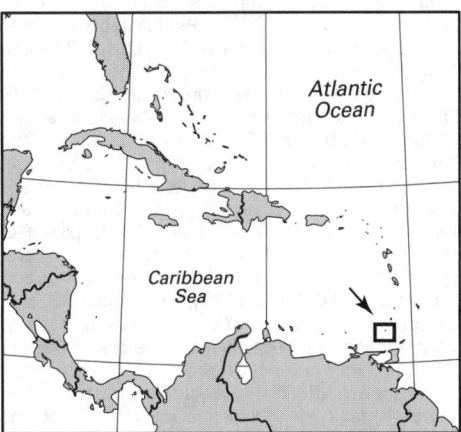

**Official name:** Grenada. **Form of government:** constitutional monarchy with two legislative houses (Senate [13]; House of Representatives [15, excluding the speaker]). **Chief of state:** Queen Elizabeth II (from 1952) represented by Governor-General Sir Daniel Williams (from 1996). **Head of government:** Prime Minister Keith Mitchell (from 1995). **Capital:** St. George's. **Official language:** English. **Official religion:** none. **Monetary unit:** 1 East Caribbean dollar (EC$) = 100 cents; valuation (7 Jul 2003) US$1 = EC$2.67.

## Demography

**Area:** 133 sq mi, 344 sq km. **Population** (2002): 101,000. **Density** (2002): persons per sq mi 759.4, persons per sq km 293.6. **Urban** (2000): 38.3%. **Sex distribution** (2000): male 51.70%; female 48.30%. **Age breakdown** (2000): under 15, 38.1%; 15–29, 33.3%; 30–44, 17.7%; 45–59, 4.9%; 60–74, 4.7%; 75 and over, 1.3%. **Ethnic composition** (2000): black

51.7%; mixed 40.0%; Indo-Pakistani 4.0%; white 0.9%; other 3.4%. **Religious affiliation** (1995): Roman Catholic 57.8%; Protestant 37.6%, of which Anglican 14.4%, Pentecostal 8.3%, Seventh-day Adventist 7.0%; other 4.6%, of which Rastafarian c. 3.0%. **Major localities** (2001): St. George's 3,908 (urban agglomeration 35,559); Gouyave 3,100 (1991); Grenville 2,300 (1991). **Location:** island between the Caribbean Sea and the Atlantic Ocean, north of Trinidad and Tobago.

## Vital statistics

**Birth rate** per 1,000 population (2001): 18.8 (world avg. 21.2); (1987) legitimate 18.1%; illegitimate 81.9%. **Death rate** per 1,000 population (2001): 7.2 (world avg. 8.9). **Natural increase rate** per 1,000 population (2001): 11.6 (world avg. 12.3). **Total fertility rate** (avg. births per childbearing woman; 2000): 2.6. **Marriage rate** per 1,000 population (1991): 4.3. **Divorce rate** per 1,000 population (1991): 0.8. **Life expectancy** at birth (2000): male 62.7 years; female 66.3 years.

## National economy

**Budget** (1998). *Revenue*: EC$229,000,000 (current revenue 90.0%, of which tax on international trade 52.3%, general sales taxes 17.8%, income taxes 9.6%; grants from abroad 10.0%). *Expenditures*: EC$281,700,000 (current expenditure 73.7%, of which wages 37.2%, transfers 16.1%, debt 11.6%; capital expenditure 26.3%). **Public debt** (external, outstanding; 2000): US$180,900,000. **Tourism** (2000): receipts from visitors US$67,000,000; expenditures by nationals abroad US$5,000,000. **Gross national product** (at current market prices; 2000): US$370,000,000 (US$3,770 per capita). **Production** (metric tons except as noted). *Agriculture, forestry, fishing* (1999): coconuts 6,800, sugarcane 6,600, bananas 4,400; livestock (number of live animals) 13,000 sheep, 7,000 goats, 5,300 pigs; fish catch (1998) 1,713. *Mining and quarrying*: excavation of gravel for local use. *Manufacturing* (value of production in EC$'000; 1997): wheat flour 13,390; soft drinks 9,798; beer 7,072. *Energy production (consumption)*: electricity (kW-hr; 1996) 95,000,000 (95,000,000); petroleum products (metric tons; 1996) none (55,000). **Household income and expenditure.** Average household size (1991) 3.7; income per household (1988) EC$7,097 (US$2,629); expenditure (1987): food, beverages, and tobacco 40.7%, household furnishings and operations 13.7%, housing 11.9%, transportation 9.1%, personal effects and medical care 8.6%. **Population economically active** (1988): total 38,920; activity rate of total population 39.9% (participation rate: ages 15–65, 72.7%; female 48.6%; unemployed [1997] 17.0%). **Land use** (1994): forested 9.0%; meadows and pastures 3.0%; agricultural and under permanent cultivation 35.0%; other 53.0%.

## Foreign trade

**Imports** (2000): US$242,700,000 (machinery and transport equipment 30.9%; basic manufactures 17.2%; food 16.2%; chemicals and chemical products 6.8%). *Major import sources*: US 37.9%; UK

8.4%; Japan 7.1%; Venezuela 5.0%; Canada 4.2%. **Exports** (2000): US$79,100,000 (domestic exports 95.0%, of which electronic components 54.7%, nutmeg 15.8%, fish 6.5%, cocoa beans 2.1%, paper products 2.1%; reexports 5.0%). *Major export destinations*: US 35.9%; UK 3.1%; Canada 1.9%.

## Transport and communications

**Transport.** *Roads* (1996): total length 1,040 km (paved 61%). *Vehicles* (1991): passenger cars 4,739; trucks and buses 3,068. *Air transport* (1997): passengers 322,000; cargo 2,300 metric tons; airports (1998) with scheduled flights 2. **Communications,** in total units (units per 1,000 persons). Radio receivers (1997): 57,000 (615); television receivers (1997): 33,000 (353); telephone main lines (2001): 73,700 (328); cellular telephone subscribers (2001): 61,400 (273); personal computers (2001): 13,000 (130); Internet users (2001): 5,200 (52).

## Education and health

**Educational attainment** (1991). Percentage of population age 25 and over having: no formal schooling 1.8%; primary education 74.9%; secondary 15.5%; higher 4.7%, of which university 2.8%; other/unknown 3.1%. **Literacy** (1995): total population age 15 and over literate 50,000 (85.0%). **Health** (1997): physicians 80 (1 per 1,236 persons); hospital beds 340 (1 per 290 persons); infant mortality rate per 1,000 live births (2001) 17.4. **Food** (2000): daily per capita caloric intake 2,764 (vegetable products 76%, animal products 24%); 114% of FAO recommended minimum.

## Military

**Total active duty personnel** (1997): the 730-member police force includes an 80-member paramilitary unit and a 30-member coast guard unit.

---

**Did you know?**  Grenada is widely known as "Spice Island" because of its extensive export of nutmeg and other spices.

---

## Background

The warlike Carib Indians dominated Grenada when Christopher Columbus sighted the island in 1498 and named it Concepción; they ruled it for the next 150 years. In 1674 it became subject to the French crown and remained so until 1762, when British forces captured it. In 1833 the island's black slaves were freed. Grenada was the headquarters of the government of the British Windward Islands 1885–1958 and a member of the West Indies Federation 1958–62. It became a self-governing state in association with Britain in 1967 and gained its independence in 1974. In 1979 a left-wing government took control in a bloodless coup. Relations with its US-oriented Latin American neighbors became strained as Grenada leaned toward Cuba and the Soviet bloc. In order to counteract this trend, the US invaded the island in 1983; democratic self-government was reestablished in 1984. Its relations with Cuba, once suspended, were restored in 1997.

---

*1 metric ton = about 1.1 short tons;    1 kilometer = 0.6 mi (statute);    1 metric ton-km cargo = about 0.68 short ton-mi cargo;    c.i.f.: cost, insurance, and freight;    f.o.b.: free on board*

## Recent Developments

In February 2002 Grenada was removed from the Organisation for Economic Co-operation and Development's list of "uncooperative" tax havens after it had made a commitment to transparency in the regulation of its offshore banking system and agreed to "effective exchange of information" on tax matters. Four questionable offshore banks were shut down in September as the government strove to improve the image of an industry that had been under attack in recent years.

Internet resources: <www.grenada.org>

# Guadeloupe

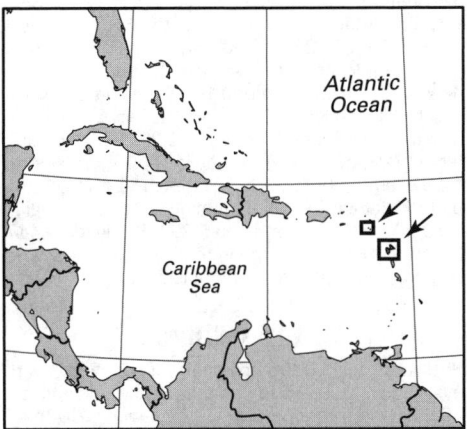

**Official name:** Département de la Guadeloupe (Department of Guadeloupe). **Political status:** overseas department (France) with two legislative houses (General Council [42]; Regional Council [43]). **Chief of state:** President Jacques Chirac of France (from 1995), represented by Prefect Dominique Vian (from 6 Aug 2002). **Heads of government:** President of the General Council Jacques Gillot (from 2001); President of the Regional Council Lucette Michaux-Chevry (from 1992). **Capital:** Basse-Terre. **Official language:** French. **Official religion:** none. **Monetary unit:** 1 euro (€) = 100 cents; $1 = €0.87 (7 Jul 2003); at conversion on 1 Jan 2002, €1 = 6.56 French francs (F).

## Demography

**Area:** 687 sq mi, 1,780 sq km. **Population** (2002): 432,000. **Density** (2002): persons per sq mi 656.5, persons per sq km 253.4. **Urban** (1999; communes larger than 2,000): 99.6%. **Sex distribution** (1999): male 48.11%; female 51.89%. **Age breakdown** (1999): under 15, 23.6%; 15–29, 22.4%; 30–44, 24.3%; 45–59, 15.7%; 60–74, 9.3%; 75 and over, 4.7%. **Ethnic composition** (2000): Creole (mulatto) 76.7%; black 10.0%; Guadeloupe mestizo (French-East Asian) 10.0%; white 2.0%; other 1.3%. **Religious affiliation** (1995): Roman Catholic 81.1%; Jehovah's Witness 4.8%; Protestant 4.7%; other 9.4%. **Major communes** (1999): Les Abymes 63,054; Saint-Martin 29,078; Le Gosier 25,360; Baie-Mahault 23,389; Pointe-à-Pitre 20,948. **Location:** islands in the eastern Caribbean Sea, southeast of Puerto Rico.

## Vital statistics

**Birth rate** per 1,000 population (2000): 17.2 (world avg. 22.5); (1997) legitimate 37.0%; illegitimate 63.0%. **Death rate** per 1,000 population (2000): 6.0 (world avg. 9.0). **Natural increase rate** per 1,000 population (2000): 11.2 (world avg. 13.5). **Total fertility rate** (avg. births per childbearing woman; 2000): 1.9. **Marriage rate** per 1,000 population (1997): 4.7. **Divorce rate** per 1,000 population (1997): 1.3. **Life expectancy** at birth (2000): male 73.8 years; female 80.3 years.

## National economy

**Budget** (1998). *Revenue:* F 4,227,000,000 (tax revenues 69.0%, of which direct taxes 42.5%, value-added taxes 25.1%; advances, loans, and transfers 26.8%). *Expenditures:* F 7,874,000,000 (current expenditures 70.6%, capital [development] expenditures 10.6%; advances and loans 18.8%). **Tourism** (2000): receipts from visitors $418,000,000; expenditures, n.a. **Production** (metric tons except as noted). *Agriculture, forestry, fishing* (1999): sugarcane 499,980, bananas 141,140, yams 9,030; livestock (number of live animals) 80,410 cattle, 63,000 goats, 15,000 pigs; roundwood (1998) 15,000 cu m; fish catch (1998) 9,084. *Mining and quarrying* (1993): pumice 210,000. *Manufacturing* (1996): cement 282,571; raw sugar 48,896; rum 66,483 hectolitres. *Energy production (consumption):* electricity (kW-hr; 1997) 1,211,000,000 (1,211,000,000); petroleum products (metric tons; 1997) none (462,000). **Population economically active** (1998): total 182,200; activity rate of total population 41.8% (participation rates: ages [1995] 15–64, 73.2%; female 46.8%; unemployed 30.7%). **Gross national product** (1995): $3,877,000,000 ($9,145 per capita). **Household income and expenditure.** Average household size (1990) 3.4; income per household (1988) F 105,400 ($17,700); sources of income (1988): wages and salaries 78.9%, self-employment 12.7%, transfer payments 8.4%; expenditure (1994–95): housing 26.2%, food and beverages 21.4%, transportation and communications 14.1%, household durables 6.0%, culture and leisure 4.2%. **Land use** (1994): forest 39.1%; pasture 14.2%; agriculture 16.0%; other 30.7%.

## Foreign trade

**Imports** (1998): F 10,663,000,000 (consumer goods 23.7%, food and agriculture products 21.1%, machinery and equipment 19.7%, transport vehicles and parts 12.3%). *Major import sources:* France 63.4%; Germany 4.4%; Italy 3.5%; Martinique 3.4%; US 2.9%; Japan 1.9%. **Exports** (1998): F 667,000,-000 (1995; bananas 25.4%, sugar 11.4%, rum 4.4%, melons 2.9%). *Major export destinations:* France 68.5%; Martinique 9.4%; Italy 4.8%; Belgium-Luxembourg 3.3%; French Guiana 3.0%.

## Transport and communications

**Transport.** *Roads* (1998): total length 3,415 km (paved [1986] 80%). *Vehicles* (1993): passenger cars 101,600; trucks and buses 37,500. *Air transport* (1998): passenger arrivals and departures 1,807,-100; cargo handled 16,496 metric tons, cargo unloaded 5,493 metric tons; airports (1997) with scheduled flights 7. **Communications,** in total units (units per 1,000 persons). Daily newspaper circulation (1995): 35,000 (81); radio receivers (1997):

113,000 (258); television receivers (1999): 118,000 (262); telephone main lines (2000): 204,900 (449); cellular telephone subscribers (2001): 292,500 (635); personal computers (2001): 100,000 (217); Internet users (2000): 8,000 (18).

## Education and health

**Educational attainment** (1990). Percentage of population age 25 and over having: incomplete primary, or no declaration 59.8%; primary education 14.5%; secondary 19.0%; higher 6.7%. **Literacy** (1982): total population age 15 and over literate 225,400 (90.1%); males literate 108,700 (89.7%); females literate 116,700 (90.5%). **Health** (1998): physicians 760 (1 per 550 persons); hospital beds 2,796 (1 per 149 persons); infant mortality rate per 1,000 live births (2000) 9.8. **Food** (1995): daily per capita caloric intake 2,732 (vegetable products 75%, animal products 25%); 129% of FAO recommended minimum.

## Military

**Total active duty personnel** (2002): French troops in Antilles (Guadeloupe and Martinique) 4,000.

## Background

The Carib Indians held off the Spanish and French for a number of years before the islands of Guadeloupe became part of France in 1674. The British occupied Guadeloupe for short periods in the 18th and 19th centuries; the islands became officially French in 1816. In 1946 Guadeloupe was made an overseas territory of France. Tourism has benefited the economy in recent decades.

## Recent Developments

French Pres. Jacques Chirac gave a clear hint in March 2000 that the hitherto highly centralized relationship between Paris and French overseas territories might be relaxed in favor of a looser arrangement. He said that the era of "uniform status" was over and that DOMs such as Guadeloupe might enjoy more local control in the future. The introduction of the euro as the currency in Guadeloupe in 2002 was expected to help attract more European tourists to the islands.

**Internet resources:** <www.guadeloupe-info.com>

# Guam

**Official name:** Teritorion Guam (Chamorro); Territory of Guam (English). **Political status:** self-governing, organized, unincorporated territory of the US with one legislative house (Guam Legislature [15]). **Chief of state:** President of the US George W. Bush (from 2001). **Head of government:** Governor Felix Camacho (from 6 Jan 2003). **Capital:** Agana. **Official languages:** Chamorro; English. **Official religion:** none. **Monetary unit:** 1 US dollar ($1) = 100 cents.

## Demography

**Area:** 209 sq mi, 541 sq km. **Population** (2002): 160,000. **Density** (2002): persons per sq mi 737.3,

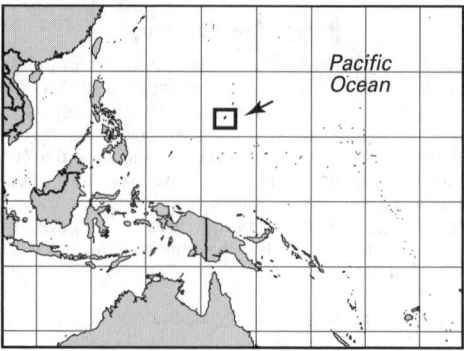

persons per sq km 285.2. **Urban** (2002): 40.0%. **Sex distribution** (2000): male 51.15%; female 48.85%. **Age breakdown** (2000): under 15, 30.5%; 15–34, 32.4%; 35–59, 28.9%; 60–74, 6.7%; 75 and over, 1.5%. **Ethnic composition** (2000): Pacific Islander 44.6%, of which Chamorro 37.0%; Asian 32.5%, of which Filipino 26.3%, Korean 2.5%; white 6.8%; mixed 13.9%; black 1.0%; other 1.2%. **Religious affiliation** (1995): Roman Catholic 74.7%; Protestant 12.8%; other Christian 2.4%; other 10.1%. **Major populated places** (2000): Tamuning 10,833; Mangilao 7,794; Yigo 6,391; Astumbo 5,207; Barrigada 4,417. **Location:** Oceania, island in the North Pacific Ocean, south of the Northern Mariana Islands.

## Vital statistics

**Birth rate** per 1,000 population (2002): 26.6 (world avg. 21.2); (1997) legitimate 50.1%; illegitimate 49.9%. **Death rate** per 1,000 population (2002): 4.9 (world avg. 8.9). **Natural increase rate** per 1,000 population (2002): 21.7 (world avg. 12.3). **Total fertility rate** (avg. births per childbearing woman; 2002): 4.0. **Marriage rate** per 1,000 population (1997): 9.5. **Divorce rate** per 1,000 population (1995): 4.3. **Life expectancy** at birth (2002): male 72.0 years; female 77.0 years.

## National economy

**Budget** (1997–98). *Revenue:* $738,100,000 (local taxes 68.7%, federal contributions 25.5%, interest 2.2%, licenses, fees, and permits 1.7%). *Expenditures:* $501,900,000 (current expenditures 80.2%, debt service 10.6%, capital expenditures 8.6%). **Production.** *Agriculture, forestry, fishing* (value of production in $'000; 1996): eggplant 625, long beans 592, bananas 418; livestock (number of live animals) 205,000 poultry, 4,000 pigs, 610 goats; fish catch (metric tons; 1998) 253, value of aquaculture production (1996) $1,442,000. *Mining and quarrying:* sand and gravel. *Manufacturing* (value of sales in $'000; 1997): printing and publishing 40,307; food processing 24,333; stone, clay, and glass products 16,914. *Energy production (consumption):* electricity (kW-hr; 1997) 825,000,000 (825,000,000); petroleum products (metric tons; 1997) none (1,329,000). **Household income and expenditure.** Average household size (1998; excludes US military and dependents) 3.9; average annual income per household (1998; excludes US military and dependents) $47,374; expenditure (1978): housing 28.6%, food 24.1%, transportation 18.0%, clothing 10.6%, entertainment 5.1%, medical

*1 metric ton = about 1.1 short tons;   1 kilometer = 0.6 mi (statute);   1 metric ton-km cargo = about 0.68 short ton-mi cargo;   c.i.f.: cost, insurance, and freight;   f.o.b.: free on board*

care 4.7%. **Gross domestic product** (1998): $3,302,-700,000 ($20,660 per capita). **Population economically active** (1997): total 71,400; activity rate of total population 45.7% (participation rates: over age 16 [1994] 69.3%; female [1994] 43.3%; unemployed [June 1999] 15.2%). **Tourism** (1999): receipts from visitors $1,908,000,000. **Land use** (1998): forested 14.6%; meadows and pastures 14.5%; agricultural and under permanent cultivation 21.8%; other 49.1%.

## Foreign trade

**Imports** (fiscal year November 1998–October 1999): $205,800,000 (food products 34.2%; leather products including footwear 15.8%; motor vehicles and parts 14.3%; construction materials 6.4%; clothing 5.0%). **Exports** (1999): $75,700,000 (food products 54.7%, of which fish 53.8%; petroleum and natural gas products 20.0%; tobacco products 6.7%). *Major export destinations:* Japan 53.9%; Federated States of Micronesia 18.6%; Palau 6.3%; Hong Kong 2.0%.

## Transport and communications

**Transport.** *Roads* (1999): total length 885 km (paved 76%). *Vehicles* (1995): passenger cars 79,800; trucks and buses 34,700. *Air transport* (1998): passenger arrivals 1,375,000; passenger departures 1,378,000; cargo loaded and unloaded (1997) 35,295 metric tons; airports (1999) with scheduled flights 1. **Communications,** in total units (units per 1,000 persons). Daily newspaper circulation (1996): 28,000 (178); radio receivers (1997): 221,000 (1,400); television receivers (1997): 106,000 (668); telephone main lines (2000): 80,300 (478); cellular telephone subscribers (2000): 27,200 (162); Internet users (1999): 5,000 (30).

## Education and health

**Educational attainment** (1995). Percentage of population age 25 and over having: no formal schooling to some secondary education 26.9%; completed secondary 55.4%; completed higher 17.7%. **Literacy** (1990): total population age 15 and over literate 99.0%; males literate 99.0%; females literate 99.0%. **Health** (1999): physicians 130 (1 per 1,169 persons); hospital beds 192 (1 per 792 persons); infant mortality rate per 1,000 live births (2002) 10.0.

## Military

**Total active duty US personnel** (2001): 3,490 (army 1.2%; navy 53.0%; air force 45.8%).

## Background

Possibly visited by Ferdinand Magellan in 1521, Guam was formally claimed by Spain in 1565. It remained Spanish until it was ceded to the US after the Spanish-American War in 1898. During World War II the Japanese occupied the island (1941–44). It subsequently became a major US air and naval base. In 1950 it was made a US territory.

## Recent Developments

In his state of the island speech on 13 May 2003 Gov. Felix Camacho spoke of the economic crisis on the island and its causes, notably the policies of previous administrations, the world economic downturn

(particularly in tourism) following the 11 Sep 2001 terrorist attacks, and Supertyphoon Pongsona, which struck Guam on 8 Dec 2002 and caused a quarter of a billion dollars in property damage.

**Internet resources:** <http://ns.gov.gu>

# Guatemala

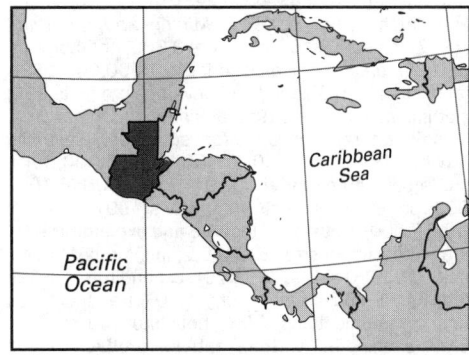

**Official name:** República de Guatemala (Republic of Guatemala). **Form of government:** republic with one legislative house (Congress of the Republic [113]). **Head of state and government:** President Alfonso Antonio Portillo Cabrera (from 2000). **Capital:** Guatemala City. **Official language:** Spanish. **Official religion:** none. **Monetary unit:** 1 quetzal (Q) = 100 centavos; valuation (7 Jul 2003) $1 = Q 7.94.

## Demography

**Area:** 42,042 (rounded) sq mi, 108,889 sq km. **Population** (2002): 11,987,000. **Density** (2002): persons per sq mi 284.5, persons per sq km 109.9. **Urban** (2000): 39.4%. **Sex distribution** (2002): male 50.31%; female 49.69%. **Age breakdown** (2002): under 15, 41.8%; 15–29, 28.1%; 30–44, 15.9%; 45–59, 8.8%; 60–74, 4.2%; 75 and over, 1.2%. **Ethnic composition** (1994): Amerindian 42.8%; non-Amerindian 57.2%. **Religious affiliation** (1995): Roman Catholic 75.9%, of which Catholic/traditional syncretist 25.0%; Protestant 21.8%; other Christian 1.3%; other 1.0%. **Major cities** (1995): Guatemala City 1,167,495; Mixco 436,668; Villa Nueva 165,567; Chinautla 61,335; Amatitlan 40,229. **Location:** Central America, bordering Mexico, Belize, the Caribbean Sea, Honduras, El Salvador, and the Pacific Ocean.

## Vital statistics

**Birth rate** per 1,000 population (2000): 35.1 (world avg. 22.5). **Death rate** per 1,000 population (2000): 6.9 (world avg. 9.0). **Natural increase rate** per 1,000 population (2000): 28.2 (world avg. 13.5). **Total fertility rate** (avg. births per childbearing woman; 2000): 4.7. **Marriage rate** per 1,000 population (1995): 4.6. **Divorce rate** per 1,000 population (1995): 0.05. **Life expectancy** at birth (2000): male 63.5 years; female 69.0 years.

## National economy

**Budget** (1998). *Revenue:* Q 11,997,000,000 (tax revenue 90.3%, nontax revenue 8.9%). *Expenditures:* Q 14,828,000,000 (current expenditures 61.7%, of which disbursements for wages and salaries 25.3%, transfer payments 18.0%; capital expenditures 38.3%). **Public debt** (external, outstanding; 2000): $3,146,000,000. **Tourism** (2000): receipts $518,-000,000; expenditures $182,000,000. **Production** (metric tons except as noted). *Agriculture, forestry, fishing* (1999): sugarcane 15,459,000, corn (maize) 1,109,000, bananas 733,000; livestock (number of live animals) 2,300,000 cattle, 825,000 pigs, 24,000,-000 chickens; roundwood (1998) 12,995,000 cu m; fish catch (1998) 10,847. *Mining and quarrying* (1997): gypsum 30,000; iron ore 3,300; antimony ore 880. *Manufacturing* (value added in Q '000,000; 1998 [at prices of 1958]): food and beverage products 298; clothing and textiles 119; machinery and metal products 55. *Energy production (consumption)*: electricity (kW-hr; 1997) 4,132,000,000 (4,044,000,000); crude petroleum (barrels; 1997) 7,000,000 (6,100,-000); petroleum products (metric tons; 1997) 713,000 (2,152,000). **Household income and expenditure.** Average household size (1994) 5.2; income per household (1989) Q 4,306 ($1,529); expenditure (1981): food 64.4%, housing and energy 16.0%, transportation and communications 7.0%, household furnishings 5.0%, clothing 3.1%. **Gross national product** (2000): $19,164,000,000 ($1,680 per capita). **Population economically active** (1996): total 3,183,173; activity rate of total population 29.1% (participation rates [1994] ages 15–64, 51.0%; female 19.5%; unemployed [1995] 1.4%). **Land use** (1998): forested and nonarable land 58.4%; meadows and pastures 24.0%; agricultural and under permanent cultivation 17.6%.

## Foreign trade

**Imports** (1998; f.o.b. in balance of trade and c.i.f. for commodities and trading partners): $4,650,900,000 (intermediate goods 34.9%, consumer goods 29.5%, capital goods 26.3%, lubricants and fuels 6.1%, construction materials 3.2%). *Major import sources:* US 41.5%; Mexico 10.4%; Japan 4.5%; Venezuela 3.3%; Germany 2.8%. **Exports** (1998): $2,846,700,000 (coffee 20.4%, sugar 11.0%, bananas 6.2%, petroleum 2.0%). *Major export destinations:* US 32.2%; Germany 4.3%; Mexico 4.1%; Japan 2.2%.

## Transport and communications

**Transport.** *Railroads* (1996): route length 884 km; passenger-km (1995) 16,580,000; metric ton-km cargo 85,615,000. *Roads* (1996): total length 13,100 km (paved 28%). *Vehicles* (1996): passenger cars 102,000; trucks and buses 97,000. *Air transport* (1995; Aviateca Airlines only): passenger-km 500,000,000; metric ton-km cargo 70,000,000; airports (1996) 2. **Communications**, in total units (units per 1,000 persons). Daily newspaper circulation (1996): 338,000 (33); radio receivers (1997): 835,000 (79); television receivers (1998): 660,000 (61); telephone main lines (2001): 756,000 (65); cellular telephone subscribers (2001): 1,134,000 (97); personal computers (2001): 150,000 (13); Internet users (2001): 200,000 (17).

## Education and health

**Educational attainment** (1994). Percentage of population age 25 and over having: no formal schooling

45.2%; incomplete primary education 20.8%; complete primary 18.0%; some secondary 4.8%; secondary 7.2%; higher 4.0%. **Literacy** (1995): total population age 15 and over literate 55.6%; males literate 62.5%; females literate 48.6%. **Health** (1988): physicians (1997) 9,812 (1 per 1,072 persons); hospital beds (1995) 10,974 (1 per 909 persons); infant mortality rate per 1,000 live births (2000) 47.0. **Food** (2000): daily per capita caloric intake 2,171 (vegetable products 90%, animal products 10%); 99% of FAO recommended minimum.

## Military

**Total active duty personnel** (2001): 31,400 (army 93.0%, navy 4.8%, air force 2.2%). **Military expenditure as percentage of GNP** (1999): 0.7% (world 2.4%); per capita expenditure $10.

**Did you know?** Antigua Guatemala, founded in the early 16th century, was the original capital city of Guatemala. The city was hit hard by earthquakes and constantly had to be rebuilt, and after a severe earthquake in 1773, the capital was moved to Guatemala City. Many of the structures from the old capital that survived have been restored and are preserved as national monuments.

## Background

From simple farming villages dating to 2500 BC, the Maya of Guatemala and the Yucatan developed an impressive civilization. The civilization of the Maya declined after AD 900, and the Spanish began the subjugation of their descendants in 1523. The Central American colonies declared independence from Spain in Guatemala City in 1821, and Guatemala was incorporated into the Mexican Empire until its collapse in 1823. In 1839 Guatemala became an independent republic under the first of a series of dictators who held power almost continuously for the next century. In 1945 a liberal-democratic coalition came to power and instituted sweeping reforms. Attempts to expropriate land belonging to US business interests prompted the US government in 1954 to sponsor an invasion. In the following years Guatemala's social revolution came to an end and most of the reforms were reversed. Chronic political instability and violence thenceforth marked Guatemalan politics; most of the 200,000 deaths that resulted were blamed on government forces. In 1991 it abandoned its long-standing claims of sovereignty over Belize, and the two countries established diplomatic relations. It continued to experience violence as guerrillas sought to seize power. A peace treaty was signed in 1996, and the country started slowly to recover from its civil war.

## Recent Developments

During 2002 Guatemala suffered from serious economic difficulties and widespread crime. Low coffee prices contributed to the country's declining export revenues, as did a serious drought on the Pacific coast. Declining investments and unemployment exacerbated widespread poverty and social injustice. Pres. Alfonso Portillo was implicated in multimillion-dollar corruption

---

*1 metric ton = about 1.1 short tons;   1 kilometer = 0.6 mi (statute);   1 metric ton-km cargo = about 0.68 short ton-mi cargo;   c.i.f.: cost, insurance, and freight;   f.o.b.: free on board*

schemes, but he resisted demands from civic organizations that he resign, citing improvements in health, education, road construction, and housing programs and a declining inflation rate during his tenure.

**Internet resources:** <www.guatemalatravel.com.gt>

# Guernsey

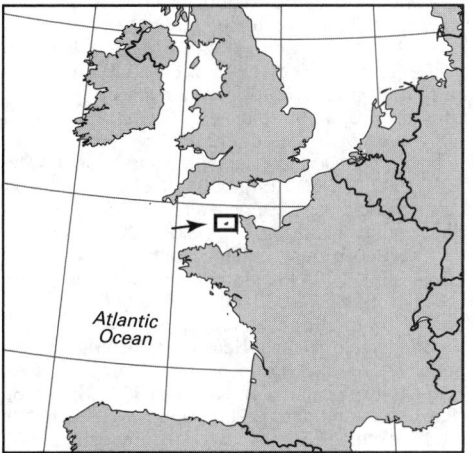

Atlantic
Ocean

Data exclude Guernsey dependencies (particularly Alderney and Sark) unless otherwise indicated. **Official name:** Bailiwick of Guernsey. **Political status:** crown dependency (UK) with one legislative house (States of Deliberation [57; elected seats only]); Alderney and Sark are dependencies of Guernsey having their own parliaments. **Chief of state:** Queen Elizabeth II represented by Lieutenant Governor Sir John Foley (from 2000). **Head of government:** The government of Guernsey is conducted by committees appointed by the States of Deliberation. **Capital:** St. Peter Port. **Official language:** English. **Official religion:** n.a. **Monetary unit:** 1 Guernsey pound (equivalent to pound sterling) = 100 pence; valuation (7 Jul 2003) 1 Guernsey pound = $1.67.

## Demography

**Area:** 30.2 sq mi, 78.1 sq km (including areas of Guernsey dependencies, of which Alderney 3.1 sq mi [7.9 sq km], Sark 1.6 sq mi [4.2 sq km], others 1.2 sq mi [3.0 sq km]. **Population** (2002): 63,000. **Density** (2002): persons per sq mi 2,085.1, persons per sq km 806.3. **Sex distribution** (2001): male 48.72%; female 51.28%. **Age breakdown** (1996): under 15, 17.6%; 15–29, 20.6%; 30–44, 22.3%; 45–59, 19.0%; 60–74, 13.2%; 75 and over, 7.3%. **Population by place of birth** (1996): Guernsey 65.5%; UK 27.2%; Portugal 1.9%; Jersey 0.7%; Ireland 0.7%; Alderney 0.3%; Sark 0.1%; other 3.6%. **Religious affiliation** (c. 1990): Anglican 65.2%; other 34.8%. **Major cities** (2001; pop. of parish): St. Peter Port 16,488; Vale 9,573; Castel 8,975; St. Sampson 8,592; St. Martin 6,267. **Location:** western Europe, island in the English Channel, northwest of France.

## Vital statistics

**Birth rate** per 1,000 population (2000): 10.5 (world avg. 22.5). **Death rate** per 1,000 population (2000): 9.3 (world avg. 9.0). **Natural increase rate** per 1,000 population (2000): 1.2 (world avg. 13.5). **Total

fertility rate** (avg. births per childbearing woman; 2000): 1.3. **Marriage rate** per 1,000 population (1995): 6.0. **Divorce rate** per 1,000 population (1993): 2.5. **Life expectancy** at birth (2000): male 76.7 years; female 82.8 years.

## National economy

**Budget** (1999). *Revenue:* £306,991,000 (income tax 79.7%, customs duties and excise taxes 5.7%, document duties 2.7%, corporation taxes 2.1%, automobile taxes 1.9%). *Expenditures:* £244,418,000 (welfare 31.1%, health 26.2%, education 15.9%, administrative services 6.7%, law and order 4.9%, community services 4.1%). **Gross national product** (at current market prices; 2000): $1,883,550,000 ($30,840 per capita). **Production** (metric tons except as noted). *Agriculture, forestry, fishing* (1999): tomatoes 2,449 (1998), flowers 1,153,857 boxes, of which roses 287,915 boxes, freesia 184,467 boxes, carnations 161,273 boxes; livestock (number of live animals) 3,262 cattle; fish catch (1997; includes Jersey): 4,368, of which crustaceans 2,934 (sea spiders and crabs 2,713), mollusks 743 (abalones, winkles, and conch 438), marine fish 691. *Manufacturing:* milk 98,830 hectolitres. *Energy production (consumption):* electricity (kW-hr; 1999–2000), n.a. (273,013,000). **Household income and expenditure** (1999). Average household size (2001) 2.5; expenditure (1996): housing 21.6%, food 12.7%, household goods and services 11.2%, recreation services 9.2%, transportation 8.5%, clothing and footwear 5.6%, personal goods 4.9%, energy 4.1%. **Population economically active** (1999): total 31,153; activity rate of total population 48.8%. **Tourism** (1996): receipts $275,000,000.

## Foreign trade

**Imports** (1997): principal imports, n.a. *Major import sources* (1997): mostly UK. **Exports** (1999): £525,718,000 (mostly flowers and tomatoes). *Major export destinations* (1999): mostly UK.

## Transport and communications

**Transport.** *Vehicles* (2000): passenger cars 37,598; trucks and buses 7,338. *Air transport:* (2000) passenger arrivals 884,284; (1996) freight loaded and unloaded 7,616 metric tons; airports (1999) with scheduled flights 2 (includes one airport on Alderney). **Communications,** in total units (units per 1,000 persons). Daily newspaper circulation (1998): 15,784 (260); telephone main lines (2001): 55,000 (877); cellular telephone subscribers (2001): 31,500 (502); Internet users (2000): 20,000 (320).

## Education and health

**Literacy** (1993): total population age 15 and over literate 100.0%; males literate 100.0%; females literate 100.0%. **Health** (1999): physicians 93 (1 per 654 persons); infant mortality rate per 1,000 live births (2000) 5.1. **Food** (2000; data for the UK): daily per capita caloric intake 3,334 (vegetable products 70%, animal products 30%); 132% of FAO recommended minimum.

## Military

The UK is responsible for defense.

**Internet resources:** <www.guernseymap.com>

# Guinea

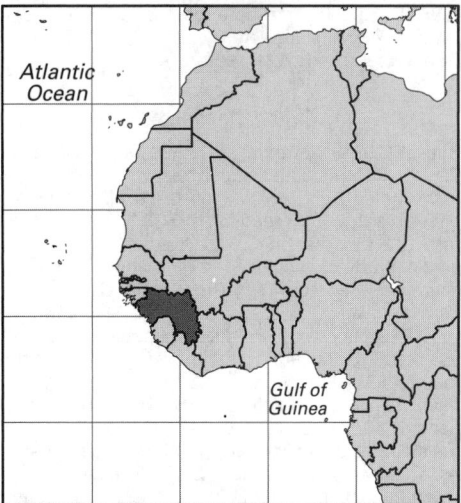

**Official name:** République de Guinée (Republic of Guinea). **Form of government:** unitary multiparty republic with one legislative house (National Assembly [114 seats]). **Head of state and government:** President Lansana Conté (from 1984) assisted by extraconstitutional Prime Minister Lamine Sidimé (from 1999). **Capital:** Conakry. **Official language:** French. **Official religion:** none. **Monetary unit:** 1 Guinean franc (GF) = 100 cauris; valuation (7 Jul 2003) $1 = GF 1,990.

## Demography

**Area:** 94,926 sq mi, 245,857 sq km. **Population** (2002): 7,775,000. **Density** (2002): persons per sq mi 81.9, persons per sq km 31.6. **Urban** (1998): 31.3%. **Sex distribution** (1998): male 50.28%; female 49.72%. **Age breakdown** (1999): under 15, 43.6%; 15–29, 26.9%; 30–44, 16.0%; 45–59, 9.0%; 60–74, 3.9%; 75 and over, 0.6%. **Ethnic composition** (1996): Fulani 38.6%; Malinke 23.2%; Susu 11.0%; Kissi 6.0%; Kpelle 4.6%; other 16.6%. **Religious affiliation** (1996): Muslim 85.0%; Christian 10.0%; other 5.0%. **Major cities** (2001): Conakry 1,565,200; Kankan 88,800; Labé 64,500; Kindia 56,000; Nzérékoré 55,000;. **Location:** western Africa, bordering Guinea-Bissau, Senegal, Mali, Côte d'Ivoire, Liberia, Sierra Leone, and the North Atlantic Ocean.

## Vital statistics

**Birth rate** per 1,000 population (2001): 39.8 (world avg. 21.2). **Death rate** per 1,000 population (2001): 17.5 (world avg. 8.9). **Natural increase rate** per 1,000 population (2001): 22.3 (world avg. 12.3). **Total fertility rate** (avg. births per childbearing woman; 2001): 5.4. **Life expectancy** at birth (2001): male 43.5 years; female 48.4 years.

## National economy

**Budget** (1998). *Revenue*: GF 624,500,000,000 (current revenues 79.5%, of which indirect taxes 34.8%,

mining sector 20.2%, tax on trade 11.5%, direct taxes 7.7%, nontax revenue 5.3%; foreign aid 20.5%). *Expenditures*: GF 655,600,000,000 (wages and salaries 27.6%, goods and services 13.6%, interest 9.8%, transfers 8.1%; capital spending 38.2%). **Production** (metric tons except as noted). *Agriculture, forestry, fishing* (1999): roots and tubers 1,064,888 (of which cassava 811,869, sweet potatoes 134,940, yams 88,635), fruits 996,078 (of which plantains 429,000, bananas 150,000, pineapples 71,858), paddy rice 750,000; livestock (number of live animals) 2,368,000 cattle, 864,000 goats, 8,900,000 chickens; roundwood (1998) 8,650,000 cu m; fish catch (1997) 102,589. *Mining and quarrying* (2000): bauxite 15,000,000; alumina 550,000; gold 427,600 troy oz. *Manufacturing* (2000): cement 250,000. *Energy production (consumption)*: electricity (kW-hr; 1997) 542,000,000 (542,000,000); petroleum products (metric tons; 1997) none (356,000). **Gross national product** (2000): $3,303,000,000 ($450 per capita). **Public debt** (external, outstanding; 2000): $2,940,000,000. **Population economically active** (1997): total 3,321,000; activity rate of total population 44.8% (participation rates [1983]: ages 15–64, 63.5%; female 47.3%). **Household income and expenditure.** Average household size (1997): 4.1; average annual income per capita (1984) GF 7,660 ($305); expenditure (1985): food 61.5%, health 11.2%, clothing 7.9%, housing 7.3%. **Tourism** (2000): receipts $7,000,000; expenditures $36,000,000. **Land use** (1994): forest 27.3%; pasture 43.5%; agriculture 3.3%; other 25.9%.

## Foreign trade

**Imports** (1997): $571,800,000 (capital goods 52.4%, consumer products 18.0%, food 17.1%, petroleum 12.5%). *Major import sources:* France 24.8%; US 9.8%; Belgium 7.9%; Côte d'Ivoire 6.6%; China 5.6%. **Exports** (1998): $709,200,000 (bauxite 45.7%, gold 17.7%, alumina 14.1%, diamonds 7.2%, fish 5.4%, coffee 3.3%). *Major export destinations:* US 16.4%; Hong Kong 14.7%; Belgium 13.7%; Spain 12.4%; Ireland 12.2%.

## Transport and communications

**Transport.** *Railroads* (2000): route length of operational lines for cargo (mostly bauxite) transport 274 km. *Roads* (1997): total length 30,500 km (paved 16.5%). *Vehicles* (1996): passenger cars 14,100; trucks and buses 21,000. *Air transport* (1998): passenger-km 50,000,000; metric ton-km cargo 5,000,000; airports (1998) 1. **Communications,** in total units (units per 1,000 persons). Daily newspaper circulation (1988): 13,000 (2.0); radio receivers (1998): 325,000 (43); television receivers (1999): 343,000 (44); telephone main lines (2001): 25,500 (3.2); cellular telephone subscribers (2001): 55,700 (6.9); personal computers (2001): 32,000 (4.0); Internet users (2001): 15,000 (1.9).

## Education and health

**Educational attainment** of those age 6 and over having attended school (1983): primary 55.2%; secondary 32.7%; vocational 3.4%; higher 8.7%. **Literacy** (1995): total population age 15 and over literate 35.9%; males

---

*1 metric ton = about 1.1 short tons;   1 kilometer = 0.6 mi (statute);   1 metric ton-km cargo = about 0.68 short ton-mi cargo;   c.i.f.: cost, insurance, and freight;   f.o.b.: free on board*

49.9%; females 21.9%. **Health:** physicians (1991) 920 (1 per 6,840 persons); hospital beds (1988) 3,382 (1 per 1,652 persons); infant mortality rate per 1,000 live births (2002) 127.1. **Food** (2000): daily per capita caloric intake 2,353 (vegetable products 97%, animal products 3%); 102% of FAO recommended minimum.

## Military

**Total active duty personnel** (2001): 9,700 (army 87.6%, navy 4.1%, air force 8.2%). **Military expenditure as percentage of GNP** (1999): 1.6% (world 2.4%); per capita expenditure $7.

## Background

About AD 900 successive migrations of the Susu swept down from the desert and pushed the original inhabitants of Guinea, the Baga, to the Atlantic coast. Small kingdoms of the Susu rose in importance in the 13th century and later extended their rule to the coast. In the mid-15th century the Portuguese visited the coast and developed a slave trade. In the 16th century the Fulani established domination over the Fouta Djallon region; they ruled into the 19th century. In the early 19th century the French arrived and in 1849 proclaimed the coastal region a French protectorate. In 1895 French Guinea became part of the federation of French West Africa. In 1946 it was made an overseas territory of France, and in 1958 it achieved independence. Following a military coup in 1984, Guinea began implementing Westernized government systems. A new constitution was adopted in 1991, and the first multiparty elections were held in 1993. During the 1990s Guinea accommodated several hundred thousand war refugees from neighboring Liberia and Sierra Leone.

## Recent Developments

Tensions along Guinea's borders with Liberia and Sierra Leone in 2002 prompted the three nations to seek a common solution to the general insecurity in the area. On 7 March cabinet ministers from the three governments agreed to revive the Mano River Union, a long-moribund economic group, and create a joint security commission under its umbrella. The body proposed that each country expel armed dissident groups from its territories and that joint border patrols be formed to prevent the smuggling of weapons.

**Internet resources:** <www.mirinet.net.gn/ont>

# Guinea-Bissau

**Official name:** República da Guiné-Bissau (Republic of Guinea-Bissau). **Form of government:** transitional regime with one legislative house (National People's Assembly [102]). **Chief of state:** President Kumba Ialá (from 2000). **Head of government:** Prime Minister Mário Pires (from 17 Nov 2002). **Capital:** Bissau. **Official language:** Portuguese. **Official religion:** none. **Monetary unit:** 1 CFA franc (CFAF) = 100 centimes; valuation (7 Jul 2003) $1 = CFAF 571.07 (formerly pegged to the French franc and since 1 Jan 2002 to the euro at €1 = CFAF 655.96).

## Demography

**Area:** 13,948 sq mi, 36,125 sq km; area figures include water area of about 3,089 sq mi (8,000 sq km).

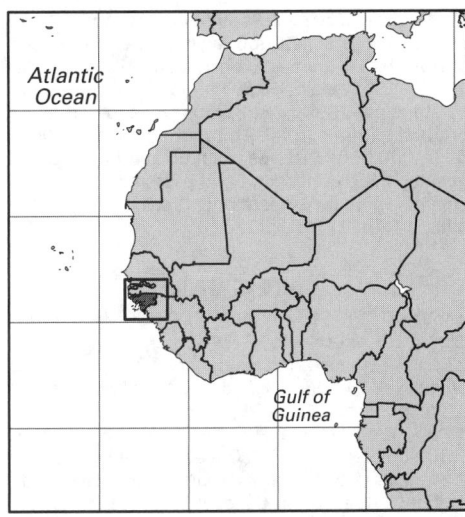

**Population** (2002): 1,345,000. **Density** (2002): persons per sq mi 123.9, persons per sq km 47.8. **Urban** (2001): 32.4%. **Sex distribution** (1997): male 48.52%; female 51.48%. **Age breakdown** (1997): under 15, 42.7%; 15–29, 28.1%; 30–44, 15.4%; 45–59, 9.2%; 60–74, 3.8%; 75 and over, 0.8%. **Ethnic composition** (1995): Balante 30%; Fulani 20%; Mandyako 14%; Malinke 13%; Pepel 7%; nonindigenous Cape Verdean mulatto 2%; other 14%. **Religious affiliation** (2000): traditional beliefs 45.2%; Muslim 39.9%; Christian 13.2%, of which Roman Catholic 9.9%; other 1.7%. **Major cities** (1997): Bissau 200,000 (urban agglomeration [2001] 292,000); Bafatá 15,000; Cacheu 14,000; Gabú 10,000. **Location:** western Africa, bordering Senegal, Guinea, and the North Atlantic Ocean.

## Vital statistics

**Birth rate** per 1,000 population (2000): 39.6 (world avg. 22.5). **Death rate** per 1,000 population (2000): 15.6 (world avg. 9.0). **Natural increase rate** per 1,000 population (2000): 24.0 (world avg. 13.5). **Total fertility rate** (avg. births per childbearing woman; 2000): 5.3. **Life expectancy** at birth (2000): male 46.8 years; female 51.4 years.

## National economy

**Budget** (1998). *Revenue:* CFAF 10,500,000,000 (foreign grants 37.1%; taxes on international trade 21.6%, of which import duties 12.9%; nontax revenues 19.8%, of which fishing licenses 7.3%; taxes on goods and services 10.7%; income taxes 8.2%). *Expenditures:* CFAF 30,200,000,000 (current expenditures 75.2%, of which scheduled external interest payments 27.0%; capital expenditures 24.8%). **Production** (metric tons except as noted). *Agriculture, forestry, fishing* (1999): rice 130,000, oil palm fruit 80,000, roots and tubers 77,500; livestock (number of live animals) 520,000 cattle, 340,000 pigs, 315,000 goats; roundwood (1998) 589,000 cu m; fish catch (2000) 3,993, of which marine fish 3,508, shrimp 415. *Mining and quarrying:* extraction of construction materials only. *Manufacturing* (2000): processed wood 11,200; wood products 4,400; dried and smoked fish 3,500. *Energy production (consumption):* electricity (kW-hr; 1999) 27,500,000 (10,200,000); petroleum products (metric tons;

1997) none (75,000). **Population economically active** (1992): total 471,000; activity rate of total population 46.9% (participation rates [1991]: over age 10, 67.1%; female 40.5%). **Public debt** (external, outstanding; 2000): $818,300,000. **Gross national product** (at current market prices; 2000): $217,000,000 ($180 per capita). **Land use** (1994): forested 38.1%; meadows and pastures 38.4%; agricultural and under permanent cultivation 12.1%; other 11.4%.

## Foreign trade

**Imports** (2001-c.i.f.): $96,700,000 (foodstuffs 18.7%, of which rice 6.6%; transport equipment 13.2%; equipment and machinery 7.7%; fuel and lubricants 6.2%; unspecified 39.3%). *Major import sources:* Portugal 30.9%; Senegal 28.3%; China 11.3%; The Netherlands 6.8%; Japan 5.8%. **Exports** (2001-f.o.b.): $47,200,000 (cashews 95.6%; cotton 2.3%; logs 1.5%). *Major export destinations:* India 85.6%; Portugal 3.8%; Senegal 2.5%; France 1.7%.

## Transport and communications

**Transport.** *Roads* (1999): total length 4,400 km (paved 10%). *Vehicles* (1996): passenger cars 7,120; trucks and buses 5,640. *Air transport* (1998): passenger-km 10,000,000; airports (1997) with scheduled flights 2. **Communications,** in total units (units per 1,000 persons). Daily newspaper circulation (1996): 6,000 (5.1); radio receivers (1997): 49,000 (41); telephone main lines (2001): 12,000 (9.8); Internet users (2001): 4,000 (3.3).

## Education and health

**Literacy** (1995): total population age 15 and over literate 54.9%; males literate 68.0%; females literate 42.5%. **Health:** physicians (1994) 184 (1 per 5,546 persons); hospital beds (1993) 1,300 (1 per 834 persons); infant mortality rate per 1,000 live births (2000) 112.3. **Food** (1999): daily per capita caloric intake 2,245 (vegetable products 93%, animal products 7%); 97% of FAO recommended minimum.

## Military

**Total active duty personnel** (2001): 7,250 (army 93.8%, navy 4.8%, air force 1.4%). **Military expenditure as percentage of GNP** (1999): 2.7% (world 2.4%); per capita expenditure $4.

---

**Did you know?** Historically, Guinea-Bissau was the center of the Portuguese West African slave trade. Military posts at Cacheu and Bissau served as collection points. Slaves were often transported from Guinea-Bissau to the slave trading center of Cape Verde.

---

## Background

More than 1,000 years ago the coast of Guinea-Bissau was occupied by iron-using agriculturists. They grew irrigated and dry rice and were also the major suppliers of marine salt to the western Sudan. At about the same time, it came under the influence of the Mali empire and became a tributary kingdom known as Gabú. After 1546 Gabú was virtually autonomous; vestiges of the kingdom lasted until 1867. The earliest overseas contacts came in the 15th century with the Portuguese, who imported slaves from the Guinea area to the offshore Cape Verde Islands. Portuguese control of Guinea-Bissau was marginal despite their claims to sovereignty there. The end of the slave trade forced the Portuguese inland in search of new profits. Their subjugation of the interior was slow and sometimes violent; it was not effectively achieved until 1915, though sporadic resistance continued until 1936. Guerrilla warfare in the 1960s led to the country's independence in 1974, but political turmoil continued and the government was overthrown by a military coup in 1980. A new constitution was adopted in 1984, and the first multiparty elections were held in 1994. A destructive civil war in 1998 was followed by a military coup in 1999.

## Recent Developments

Guinea-Bissau remained tense in 2002 after the failed coup attempt against Pres. Kumba Ialá in December 2001. In May the government claimed that there had been another coup attempt from within the military. Under pressure from the UN, President Ialá in June made a gesture of national reconciliation by proposing an amnesty for soldiers who had been involved in the coup attempts, but he also threatened to invade The Gambia, accusing it of supporting those plotting against him. Reports emerged in early 2003 that opposition politicians had been arrested for complicity in the coup attempts and were being tortured.

**Internet resources:** <www.bissau.com>

# Guyana

**Official name:** Co-operative Republic of Guyana. **Form of government:** unitary multiparty republic with one legislative house (National Assembly [65]). **Head of state and government:** President Bharrat Jagdeo

---

*1 metric ton = about 1.1 short tons;   1 kilometer = 0.6 mi (statute);   1 metric ton-km cargo = about 0.68 short ton-mi cargo;   c.i.f.: cost, insurance, and freight;   f.o.b.: free on board*

(from 1999) assisted by Prime Minister Samuel Hinds (from 1997). **Capital:** Georgetown. **Official language:** English. **Official religion:** none. **Monetary unit:** 1 Guyana dollar (G$) = 100 cents; valuation (7 Jul 2003) US$1 = G$179.00.

## Demography

**Area:** 83,044 sq mi, 215,083 sq km. **Population** (2002): 775,000. **Density** (2002): persons per sq mi 10.2, persons per sq km 3.9. **Urban** (2001): 36.7%. **Sex distribution** (2000): male 48.49%; female 51.51%. **Age breakdown** (2000): under 15, 30.6%; 15–29, 31.0%; 30–44, 21.0%; 45–59, 10.4%; 60–74, 5.1%; 75 and over, 1.9%. **Ethnic composition** (1992–93): East Indian 49.4%; black (African Negro and Bush Negro) 35.6%; mixed 7.1%; Amerindian 6.8%; Portuguese 0.7%; Chinese 0.4%. **Religious affiliation** (1995): Christian 40.9%, of which Protestant 27.5% (including Anglican 8.6%), Roman Catholic 11.5%, Ethiopian Orthodox 1.1%; Hindu 34.0%; Muslim 9.0%; other 16.1%. **Major cities** (1997): Georgetown 230,000 (urban agglomeration [2001] 280,000); Linden 35,000; New Amsterdam 25,000; Corriverton 24,000. **Location:** northern South America, bordering the North Atlantic Ocean, Suriname, Brazil, and Venezuela.

## Vital statistics

**Birth rate** per 1,000 population (2000): 17.9 (world avg. 22.5). **Death rate** per 1,000 population (2000): 8.4 (world avg. 9.0). **Natural increase rate** per 1,000 population (2000): 9.5 (world avg. 13.5). **Total fertility rate** (avg. births per childbearing woman; 2000): 2.1. **Life expectancy** at birth (2000): male 61.1 years; female 67.2 years.

## National economy

**Budget** (1999): *Revenue:* G$36,544,000,000 (tax revenue 91.6%, of which consumption taxes 32.0%, income taxes on companies 22.2%, personal income taxes 15.5%, import duties 11.4%; nontax revenue 8.2%). *Expenditures:* G$41,983,000,000 (current expenditure 71.2%, of which debt charges 13.8%; development expenditure 28.8%). **Production** (metric tons except as noted). *Agriculture, forestry, fishing* (1999): rice 365,469, raw sugar 321,438, coconuts 56,449; livestock (number of live animals) 220,000 cattle, 130,000 sheep, 11,600,000 chickens; roundwood 442,000 cu m; fish catch 54,450, of which shrimps and prawns 12,153. *Mining and quarrying* (2001): bauxite 2,011,901; gold 455,918 troy oz; diamonds 484,309 carats. *Manufacturing* (1999): flour 35,290; rum 137,800 hectolitres; beer and stout 129,200 hectolitres. *Energy production (consumption):* electricity (kW-hr; 2001) 505,000,000 ([1997] 404,000,000); petroleum products (metric tons; 1997) none (333,000). **Population economically active** (1992–93): total 278,000; activity rate of total population 38.8% (participation rates: ages 15–64, 61.8%; female 34.1%; unemployed [1998] c. 12%). **Gross national product** (at current market prices; 2000): US$652,000,000 (US$860 per capita). **Public debt** (external, outstanding; 2000): US$1,209,000,000. **Household income and expenditure.** Average household size (1997) 4.5. **Tourism:** receipts from visitors (1999) US$59,000,000; expenditures by nationals abroad (1997) US$22,000,000. **Land use** (1994): forested 83.8%; meadows and pastures 6.3%; agricultural and under permanent cultivation 2.5%; other 7.4%.

## Foreign trade

**Imports** (2001-c.i.f.): US$583,900,000 (consumer goods 28.3%, fuels and lubricants 22.5%, capital goods 19.7%). *Major import sources* (1999): US 29%; Trinidad and Tobago 18%; Netherlands Antilles 16%; UK 7%; Cuba 3%. **Exports** (2001-f.o.b.): US$490,-300,000 (gold 25.9%, sugar 22.3%, bauxite 12.4%, rice 10.2%, shrimp 10.1%, timber 6.7%). *Major export destinations* (1999): US 22%; Canada 22%; UK 18%; Netherlands Antilles 11%; Jamaica 5%.

## Transport and communications

**Transport.** *Roads* (1999): total length 7,970 km (paved 7%). *Vehicles* (1995): passenger cars 24,000; trucks and buses 9,000. *Air transport* (1998): passenger-km 231,000,000; (1996) metric ton-km cargo 3,300,000; airports (1996; international only) with scheduled flights 1. **Communications,** in total units (units per 1,000 persons) Daily newspaper circulation (1996): 42,000 (54); radio receivers (1997): 420,000 (539); television receivers (1999): 60,000 (77); telephone main lines (2001): 79,900 (92); cellular telephone subscribers (2001): 39,500 (45); personal computers (2001): 23,000 (26); Internet users (2001): 95,000 (109).

## Education and health

**Educational attainment** (1980). Percentage of population age 25 and over having: no formal schooling 8.1%; primary education 72.8%; secondary 17.3%; higher 1.8%. **Literacy** (1995): total population age 15 and over literate, c. 511,000 (98.1%); males literate, c. 254,000 (98.6%); females literate, c. 257,000 (97.5%). **Health:** physicians (1998) 334 (1 per 2,326 persons); hospital beds 3,293 (1 per 236 persons); infant mortality rate per 1,000 live births (2000) 39.1. **Food** (1999): daily per capita caloric intake 2,569 (vegetable products 84%, animal products 16%); 113% of FAO recommended minimum.

## Military

**Total active duty personnel** (2001): 1,600 (army 87.5%, navy 6.3%, air force 6.2%). **Military expenditure as percentage of GNP** (1998): 0.8% (world 2.4%); per capita expenditure US$7.

## Background

Guyana was colonized by the Dutch in the 17th century. During the Napoleonic Wars the British occupied the territory and afterward purchased the colonies of Demerara, Berbice, and Essequibo, united in 1831 as British Guiana. The slave trade was abolished in 1807, but emancipation of the 100,000 slaves in the colonies was not completed until 1838. From the 1840s East Indian and Chinese indentured servants were brought to work the plantations; by 1917 almost 240,000 East Indians had migrated to British Guiana. It was made a crown colony in 1928 and granted home rule in 1953. Political parties began to emerge, developing on racial lines as the People's Progressive Party (largely East Indian) and the People's National Congress (largely black). The PNC formed a coalition government and led the country into independence

as Guyana in 1966. In 1970 Guyana became a republic within the Commonwealth; in 1980 it adopted
a new constitution. Venezuela has long claimed land
west of the Essequibo River, and the UN has continued to arbitrate the issue.

## Recent Developments

For most of 2002 Guyana was in the grip of a crime
wave following the breakout from jail of five hardened criminals in February. The ruling People's Progressive Party/Civic alliance set up a new unit in
midyear to combat what the government described
as "domestic terrorism." Lawlessness in the country
took a new turn when in July antigovernment demonstrators stormed the presidential compound in
Georgetown to protest what they alleged to be racial
discrimination practiced by the government, which
had traditionally been supported by those of East Indian descent.

Internet resources: <www.guyana.org>

# Haiti

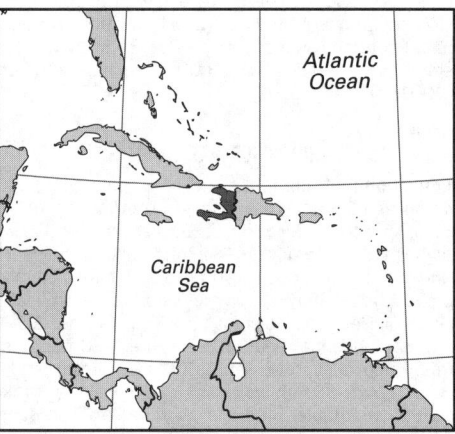

**Official name:** Repiblik Dayti (Haitian Creole);
République d'Haïti (French) (Republic of Haiti). **Form
of government:** multiparty republic with two legislative houses (Senate [27]; Chamber of Deputies [82]).
**Chief of state:** President Jean-Bertrand Aristide (from
2001). **Head of government:** Prime Minister Yvon
Neptune (from 15 Mar 2002). **Capital:** Port-au-Prince.
**Official languages:** Haitian Creole; French. **Official religion:** none. **Monetary unit:** 1 gourde (G) = 100 centimes; valuation (7 Jul 2003) $1 = G 39.15.

## Demography

**Area:** 10,695 sq mi, 27,700 sq km. **Population**
(2002): 7,064,000. **Density** (2002): persons per sq
mi 660.5, persons per sq km 255.0. **Urban** (2001):
36.3%. **Sex distribution** (2000): male 49.26%; female 50.74%. **Age breakdown** (2000): under 15,
41.1%; 15–29, 28.7%; 30–44, 15.2%; 45–59, 8.6%;
60–74, 5.0%; 75 and over, 1.4%. **Ethnic composition**
(2000): black 94.2%; mulatto 5.4%; other/unspeci-
fied 0.4%. **Religious affiliation** (1995): Roman
Catholic 68.5%; Protestant 24.1%, of which Baptist

5.9%, Pentecostal 5.3%, Seventh-day Adventist 4.6%;
other 7.4%. **Major cities** (1997): Port-au-Prince
917,112 (metropolitan area 1,556,588; including
Carrefour 306,074; Delmas 257,247; Pétion-Ville
76,155); Cap-Haïtien 107,026. **Location:** western
third of the island of Hispaniola, between the North
Atlantic Ocean and the Caribbean Sea.

## Vital statistics

**Birth rate** per 1,000 population (2000): 32.0 (world
avg. 22.5). **Death rate** per 1,000 population (2000):
15.1 (world avg. 9.0). **Natural increase rate** per
1,000 population (2000): 16.9 (world avg. 13.5).
**Total fertility rate** (avg. births per childbearing
woman; 2000): 4.5. **Life expectancy** at birth (2000):
male 47.5 years; female 51.1 years.

## National economy

**Budget** (2001). *Revenue*: G 6,509,000,000 (general
sales tax 31.3%; customs duties 27.2%; individual
taxes on income and profits 13.7%). *Expenditures*: G
8,728,000,000 (current expenditure 81.9%, of which
interest on public debt 8.8%; capital expenditure
18.1%). **Production** (metric tons except as noted).
*Agriculture, forestry, fishing* (1999): sugarcane
1,000,100, cassava (manioc) 325,000, plantains
290,000; livestock (number of live animals)
1,618,000 goats, 1,300,000 cattle, 800,000 pigs;
roundwood (1998) 6,397,000 cu m; fish catch
5,000. *Mining and quarrying*: small amounts of limestone, calcareous clay, salt, and marble. *Manufacturing* (1999–2000): soap 30,070; hectolitres; malt
liquor and beer 18,800,000 bottles; articles assembled for reexport (gross export value in $'000,000;
1999–2000) 270.3, of which garments 255.3,
leather manufactures from domestic sources 3.6;
sports equipment and toys 2.8. *Energy production
(consumption)*: electricity (kW-hr; 1997) 633,000,-
000 (633,000,000); petroleum products (metric
tons; 1997) none (453,000). **Land use** (1994):
forested 5.1%; meadows and pastures 18.0%; agricultural and under permanent cultivation 33.0%;
other 43.9%. **Population economically active** (1996):
total 3,209,000; activity rate of total population
49.3% (participation rates: ages 15–64 [1990]
64.8%; female 43.0%; unemployed unofficially about
60%). **Household income and expenditure.** Average
household size (1982) 4.4; average annual income
of urban wage earners (1984): G 1,545 ($309); ex-
penditure (1996): food, beverages, and tobacco
49.4%, housing and energy 9.1%, transportation
8.7%, clothing and footwear 8.5%. **Public debt** (external, outstanding; 2000): $1,040,000,000. **Gross na-
tional product** (2000): $4,059,000,000 ($510 per
capita). **Tourism** (2000): receipts from visitors
$54,000,000; expenditures by nationals abroad
(1998) $37,000,000.

## Foreign trade

**Imports** (2001; f.o.b. in balance of trade and c.i.f. in
commodities and trading partners): $1,061,500,000
(food and live animals 24.6%, basic manufactures
20.0%, machinery and transport equipment 16.5%,
petroleum and derivatives 15.4%). *Major import
sources* (1999): US 60%; Dominican Republic 4%;

*1 metric ton = about 1.1 short tons;     1 kilometer = 0.6 mi (statute);     1 metric ton-km cargo = about 0.68 short
ton-mi cargo;     c.i.f.: cost, insurance, and freight;     f.o.b.: free on board*

Japan 3%; France 3%; Canada 3%. **Exports** (2001): $293,300,000 (reexports 85.7%, of which clothing 83.9%; handicrafts and related products [including wood carvings, paintings, woven sisal products, and ceramics] 2.7%; cacao 2.4%). *Major export destinations* (1999): US 90%; Canada 3%; Belgium 2%, France 2%.

## Transport and communications

**Transport.** *Roads* (1999): total length 2,585 mi, 4,160 km (paved 24%). *Vehicles* (1996): passenger cars 32,000; trucks and buses 21,000. *Air transport* (2000; Port-au-Prince Airport only): passenger arrivals and departures 924,000; cargo unloaded and loaded 15,300 metric tons; airports (1997) with scheduled flights 2. **Communications,** in total units (units per 1,000 persons). Daily newspaper circulation (1996): 20,000 (3.1); radio receivers (1997): 415,000 (63); television receivers (1997): 38,000 (5.8); telephone main lines (2001): 80,000 (10); cellular telephone subscribers (2001): 91,500 (11); Internet users (2001): 30,000 (3.6).

## Education and health

**Educational attainment** (1986–87). Percentage of population age 25 and over having: no formal schooling 59.5%; primary education 30.5%; secondary 8.6%; vocational and teacher training 0.7%; higher 0.7%. **Literacy** (1995): total population age 15 and over literate 1,930,000 (45.0%); males literate 992,000 (48.0%); females literate 938,000 (42.2%). **Health**: physicians (1994–95) 641 (1 per 9,989 persons); hospital beds (1996) 5,241 (1 per 1,242 persons); infant mortality rate per 1,000 live births (2000) 97.1. **Food** (1999): daily per capita caloric intake 1,977 (vegetable products 94%, animal products 6%); 87% of FAO recommended minimum.

## Military

**Total active duty personnel:** The Haitian army was disbanded in 1995. The national police force had 5,300 personnel in 2001.

## Background

Haiti gained its independence when the former slaves of the island, initially led by Toussaint-Louverture, and later by Jean-Jacques Dessalines, rebelled against French rule in 1791–1804. The new republic encompassed the entire island of Hispaniola, but the eastern portion was restored to Spain in 1809. The island was reunited under Haitian Pres. Jean-Pierre Boyer (1818–43); after his overthrow the eastern portion revolted and formed the Dominican Republic. Haiti's government was marked by instability, with frequent coups and assassinations. It was occupied by the US in 1915–34. In 1957 the dictator François ("Papa Doc") Duvalier came to power. Despite an economic decline and civil unrest, Duvalier ruled until his death in 1971. He was succeeded by his son, Jean-Claude ("Baby Doc") Duvalier, who was forced into exile in 1986. Haiti's first free presidential elections, held in 1990, were won by Jean-Bertrand Aristide. He was deposed by a military coup in 1991, after which tens of thousands of Haitians attempted to flee to the US in small boats. The military government stepped down in 1994, and Aristide returned from exile and resumed the presidency.

## Recent Developments

The government's tenuous grasp on the economy and political institutions continued to weaken in 2002–03. It was unable to provide basic security, health care, education, or enough food and jobs for its citizens. The country lingered near the bottom of the UN's annual survey of living conditions. Life expectancy was less than 53 years. At least 23% of children aged 5 and under suffered from malnutrition, and roughly one out of every 12 Haitians had HIV/AIDS.

**Internet resources:** <www.haiti.org>

# Honduras

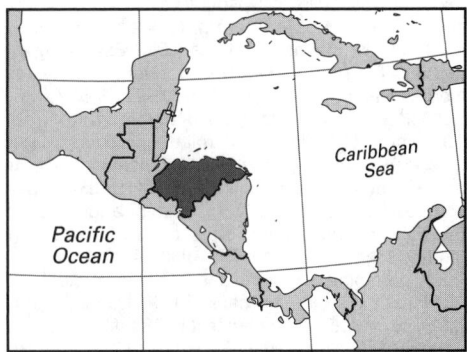

**Official name:** República de Honduras (Republic of Honduras). **Form of government:** multiparty republic with one legislative house (National Assembly [128]). **Head of state and government:** President Ricardo Maduro (from 27 Jan 2002). **Capital:** Tegucigalpa (jointly with the adjacent urban area of Comayagüela). **Official language:** Spanish. **Official religion:** none. **Monetary unit:** 1 Honduran lempira (L) = 100 centavos; valuation (7 Jul 2003) $1 = L 17.50.

## Demography

**Area:** 43,433 sq mi, 112,492 sq km. **Population** (2002): 6,561,000. **Density** (2002): persons per sq mi 151.1, persons per sq km 58.3. **Urban** (2001): 53.7%. **Sex distribution** (1999): male 48.94%; female 51.06%. **Age breakdown** (1998): under 15, 42.6%; 15–29, 28.4%; 30–44, 16.2%; 45–59, 7.8%; 60–74, 3.9%; 75 and over, 1.1%. **Ethnic composition** (2000): mestizo 86.6%; Amerindian 5.5%; black (including Black Carib) 4.3%; white 2.3%; other 1.3%. **Religious affiliation** (1995): Roman Catholic 86.7%; Protestant 10.4%, of which Pentecostal 5.7%; other 2.9%. **Major cities** (2000): Tegucigalpa 1,037,600; San Pedro Sula 471,000; El Progreso 109,400; La Ceiba 107,200; Choluteca 96,900. **Location:** Central America, bordering the Caribbean Sea, Nicaragua, the North Pacific Ocean, El Salvador, and Guatemala.

## Vital statistics

**Birth rate** per 1,000 population (2000): 32.7 (world avg. 22.5). **Death rate** per 1,000 population (2000): 5.3 (world avg. 9.0). **Natural increase rate** per 1,000 population (2000): 27.4 (world avg. 13.5). **Total fertility rate** (avg. births per childbearing woman; 2000):

4.3. **Life expectancy** at birth (2000): male 67.9 years; female 72.1 years.

## National economy

**Budget** (1998). *Revenue*: L 13,197,000,000 (current revenue 99.8%, of which indirect taxes 65.1%, direct taxes 25.6%, nontax revenue 6.9%, transfers 2.2%). *Expenditures*: L 11,367,000,000 (current expenditure 72.6%; capital expenditure 27.4%). **Public debt** (external, outstanding; 2000): $4,337,000,000. **Production** (metric tons except as noted). *Agriculture, forestry, fishing* (1999): sugarcane 4,286,000, bananas 861,000, oil palm fruit 522,000; livestock (number of live animals) 2,061,000 cattle, 700,000 pigs, 18,000,0000 chickens; roundwood (1998) 7,176,000 cu m; fish catch (1998) 14,881. *Mining and quarrying* (1997): gypsum 28,000; zinc 25,500; salt 25,000. *Manufacturing* (value added in L '000,000; 1996): food products 1,937.3; wearing apparel 1,266.4; beverages 699.6. *Energy production (consumption)*: electricity (kW-hr; 1997) 3,097,000,-000 (3,252,000,000); crude petroleum (barrels; 1992) none (3,064,000); petroleum products (metric tons; 1996) none (1,157,000). **Household income and expenditure**. Average household size (1988) 5.4; sources of income (1985): wages and salaries 58.8%, transfer payments 1.8%, other 39.4%; expenditure (1986): food 44.4%, utilities and housing 22.4%, clothing and footwear 9.0%, household furnishings 8.3%, health care 7.0%, transportation 3.0%, other 5.9%. **Land use** (1998): forested and other 67.9%; meadows and pastures 13.8%; agricultural and under permanent cultivation 18.3%. **Gross national product** (at current market prices; 2000): $5,517,000,000 ($860 per capita). **Population economically active** (1999): total 2,131,300; activity rate of total population 33.4% (participation rates: over age 15 [1998] 61.2%; female [1998] 34.6%; unemployed [1998] 4.3%). **Tourism** (2000): receipts $262,000,000; expenditures $99,000,000.

## Foreign trade

**Imports** (1999-c.i.f.): $2,727,800,000 (machinery and electrical equipment 20.8%, industrial chemicals 13.0%, transport equipment 12.1%, food products 10.3%, mineral fuels and lubricants 9.4%). *Major import sources*: US 47.1%; Guatemala 7.4%; Mexico 4.8%; Japan 4.7%; Costa Rica 2.5%. **Exports** (1999-f.o.b.): $1,303,900,000 (coffee 20.5%, shrimp and lobsters 15.5%, melons 3.7%, lead and zinc 3.4%). *Major export destinations*: US 35.4%; Germany 7.5%; El Salvador 6.4%; Guatemala 5.8%; Nicaragua 4.8%.

## Transport and communications

**Transport**. *Railroads* (2000): serviceable lines c. 205 km; most tracks are out of use but not dismantled. *Roads* (1999): total length 14,602 km (paved 18%). *Vehicles* (1995): passenger cars 81,439; trucks and buses 170,006. *Air transport* (1995): passenger-km 341,000,000; metric ton-km cargo 33,000,000; airports (1996) with scheduled flights 8. **Communications**, in total units (units per 1,000 persons). Daily newspaper circulation (1996): 320,000 (55); radio receivers (1997): 2,450,000 (410); television receivers (1999): 600,000 (95); telephone main lines

(2001): 309,700 (47); cellular telephone subscribers (2001): 237,600 (36); personal computers (2001): 80,000 (12); Internet users (2000): 40,000 (6.1).

## Education and health

**Educational attainment** (1988). Percentage of population age 10 and over having: no formal schooling 33.4%; primary education 50.1%; secondary education 13.4%; higher 3.1%. **Literacy** (1995): total population age 15 and over literate 72.7%; males literate 72.6%; females literate 72.7%. **Health**: physicians (1993) 3,803 (1 per 1,358 persons); hospital beds (1999) 5,720 (1 per 1,098 persons); infant mortality rate per 1,000 live births (2000) 31.3. **Food** (2000): daily per capita caloric intake 2,395 (vegetable products 86%, animal products 14%); (1997) 106% of FAO recommended minimum.

## Military

**Total active duty personnel** (2001): 8,300 (army 66.3%, navy 12.0%, air force 21.7%). **Military expenditure as percentage of GNP** (1999): 0.7% (world 2.4%); per capita expenditure $6.

**Did you know?** Honduras's history is richly displayed in the numerous Mayan archeological sites and vestiges of early Spanish colonization. In the town of Copán, the narrow, cobblestone streets pass between white adobe buildings with red-tiled roofs and a colonial church just a kilometer away from the famous Mayan ruins.

## Background

Early residents of Honduras were part of the Maya civilization that flourished in the 1st millennium AD. Christopher Columbus reached Honduras in 1502, and permanent settlement followed. A major war between the Spanish and the Indians broke out in 1537, culminating in the decimation of the Indian population through disease and enslavement. After 1570 Honduras was part of the captaincy general of Guatemala until Central American independence in 1821. Part of the United Provinces of Central America, Honduras withdrew in 1838 and declared its independence. In the 20th century, under military rule, there was constant civil war and some intervention by the US. A civilian government assumed office in 1982. The military remained in the background, however, as the activity of leftist guerrillas increased.

## Recent Developments

On 27 Jan 2002 Pres. Carlos Flores of the Liberal Party handed over power to Ricardo Maduro of the National Party. The new administration was the first to govern without a majority in the congress. The economy had largely rebounded from the widespread destruction caused by Hurricane Mitch in 1998, but economic performance was depressed owing to low world market prices for coffee, bananas, and sugar, Honduras's main exports.

**Internet resources:** <www.honduras.com>

---

*1 metric ton = about 1.1 short tons; 1 kilometer = 0.6 mi (statute); 1 metric ton-km cargo = about 0.68 short ton-mi cargo; c.i.f.: cost, insurance, and freight; f.o.b.: free on board*

# Hong Kong

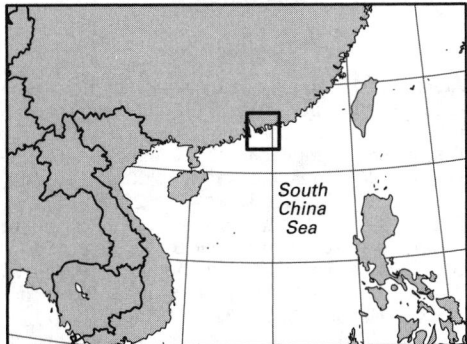

South
China
Sea

**Official name:** Xianggang Tebie Xingzhengqu (Chinese); Hong Kong Special Administrative Region (English). **Political status:** special administrative region (People's Republic of China) with one legislative house (Legislative Council [60]). **Chief of state:** President Hu Jintao of China (from 15 Nov 2002). **Head of government:** Chief Executive Tung Chee-hwa (from 1997). **Capital:** None. **Official languages:** Chinese; English. **Official religion:** none. **Monetary unit:** 1 Hong Kong dollar (HK$) = 100 cents; valuation (7 Jul 2003) US$1 = HK$7.80.

## Demography

**Area:** 421.6 sq mi, 1,091.9 sq km. **Population** (2002): 6,785,000. **Density** (2002): persons per sq mi 15,999, persons per sq km 6,177. **Urban** (2001): 100.0%. **Sex distribution** (2002): male 48.63%; female 51.37%. **Age breakdown** (2002): under 15, 16.1%; 15–29, 20.6%; 30–44, 28.9%; 45–59, 19.4%; 60–74, 10.4%; 75 and over, 4.6%. **Place of birth** (1996): Hong Kong 60.3%; China or Macau 33.7%; other 6.0%. **Religious affiliation** (1994): Buddhist and Taoist 73.8%; Christian 8.4%, of which Protestant 4.3%, Roman Catholic 4.1%; New Religionist 3.2%; Muslim 0.8%; Hindu 0.2%; nonreligious/atheist 13.5%; other 0.1%. **Location:** east Asia, bordering China and the South China Sea.

## Vital statistics

**Birth rate** per 1,000 population (2001): 7.2 (world avg. 21.2). **Death rate** per 1,000 population (2001): 5.0 (world avg. 8.9). **Natural increase rate** per 1,000 population (2001): 2.2 (world avg. 12.3). **Total fertility rate** (avg. births per childbearing woman; 2000): 1.3. **Marriage rate** per 1,000 population (2001): 4.8. **Life expectancy** at birth (2001): male 78.4 years; female 84.6 years.

## National economy

**Budget** (2000–01). *Revenue:* HK$222,855,000,000 (earning and profit taxes 32.0%; capital revenue 23.9%; indirect taxes 23.2%, of which entertainment and stamp duties 11.3%, duties 3.3%). *Expenditures:* HK$278,388,000,000 (housing 18.7%; education 18.6%; health 11.6%; social welfare 10.2%; law and order 9.7%; transportation and public works 8.2%; environment and food 4.1%). **Gross domestic product** (2000): US$162,397,000,000 (US$24,360 per capita). **Production** (metric tons except as noted). *Agriculture, forestry, fishing* (2000): vegetables 42,500, fruits and nuts 2,022, field crops 508; livestock (number of live animals) 446,000 pigs, 120 cattle; roundwood (1996) 206,000 cu m; fish catch (2000) 157,012. *Manufacturing* (value added in HK$; 1999): publishing and printed materials 10,748,000,000; electrical and electronic products 8,279,000,000; textiles 7,276,000,000. *Energy production (consumption):* electricity (kW-hr; 1997) 28,943,000,000 (36,260,000,000); coal (metric tons; 1997) none (5,711,000); petroleum products (metric tons; 1997) none (3,358,000). **Population economically active** (2000): total 3,382,700; activity rate of total population 49.3% (participation rates: over age 15, 60.7%; female 49.1%; unemployed 5.0%). **Household income and expenditure.** Average household size (2001) 3.2; monthly income per household (1996) HK$17,500 (US$2,300); expenditure (1994–95): food 29.5%, housing 28.8%, transportation and vehicles 7.8%, clothing and footwear 6.7%, durable goods 5.5%. **Tourism** (2000): receipts from visitors US$7,886,000,000. **Land use** (1995): forested 20.1%; agricultural and under permanent cultivation 5.8%; fishponds 1.5%; built-on, scrublands, and other 72.6%.

## Foreign trade

**Imports** (2001-c.i.f.): HK$1,568,194,000,000 (machinery and transport equipment 43.9%, manufactured goods 16.2%, chemicals and other related products 5.7%, food and beverages 4.1%, mineral fuels and lubricants 2.0%). Major import sources: China 43.5%; Japan 11.3%; Taiwan 6.9%; US 6.7%; Singapore 4.6%; South Korea 4.5%. **Exports** (2001-f.o.b.): HK$153,520,000,000 (clothing accessories and apparel 47.1%, electrical machinery 13.2%, textile fabrics 5.3%, office and automatic data-processing machines 3.1%, jewelry 3.1%, printed materials 2.6%, telecommunications equipment 2.3%, watches and clocks 1.5%, articles of artificial resins and plastics 0.7%; excludes re-exports). Major export destinations: China 32.3%; US 31.0%; UK 5.6%; Germany 3.8%; Taiwan 3.5%; The Netherlands 3.0%.

## Transport and communications

**Transport.** *Railroads* (1995): route length 34 km; passenger-km 3,591,000,000; metric ton-km cargo 99,000,000 (1994). *Roads* (2001): total length 1,911 km (paved 100%). *Vehicles* (2001): passenger cars 341,000; trucks and buses 132,000. *Air transport* (2001): passenger arrivals 11,533,000, passenger departures 11,488,000; airports (2000) with scheduled flights 1. **Communications,** in total units (units per 1,000 persons). Daily newspaper circulation (1996): 5,000,000 (792); radio receivers (1998): 3,700,000 (553); television receivers (1998): 1,749,000 (262); telephone main lines (2001): 3,926,000 (584); cellular telephone subscribers (2001): 5,701,700 (848); personal computers (2001): 2,600,000 (387); Internet users (2001): 3,100,000 (461).

## Education and health

**Educational attainment** (1996). Percentage of population age 15 and over having: no formal schooling 9.5%; primary education 22.6%; secondary 46.6%; matriculation 6.1%; nondegree higher 4.8%; higher degree 10.4%. **Literacy** (1995): total population age 15 and over literate 92.2%; males literate 96.0%;

females literate 88.2%. **Health** (2000): physicians 10,130 (1 per 658 persons); hospital beds 35,100 (1 per 190 persons); infant mortality rate per 1,000 live births (2001) 2.6. **Food** (1999): daily per capita caloric intake 3,231 (vegetable products 63%, animal products 37%); 141% of FAO recommended minimum.

## Military

Total active duty personnel (2001): 7,000 Chinese troops to intervene in local matters only at the request of the Hong Kong government.

## Background

The island of Hong Kong and adjacent islets were ceded by China to the British in 1842, and the Kowloon Peninsula and the New Territories were later leased by the British from China for 99 years (1898–1997). A joint Chinese-British declaration, signed on 19 Dec 1984, paved the way for the entire territory to be returned to China, which occurred on 1 Jul 1997.

## Recent Developments

Reactions were negative from human rights activists and international observers to a planned tightening of Hong Kong's security laws, which would permit local authorities to ban political organizations and otherwise limit expressions of unorthodox views. The final bill, submitted to the Legislative Council in February 2003, had been somewhat tempered. The territory was hit early and hard by the SARS (Severe Acute Respiratory Syndrome) virus, which originated in southern China in November 2002.

**Internet resources:** <www.info.gov.hk>

# Hungary

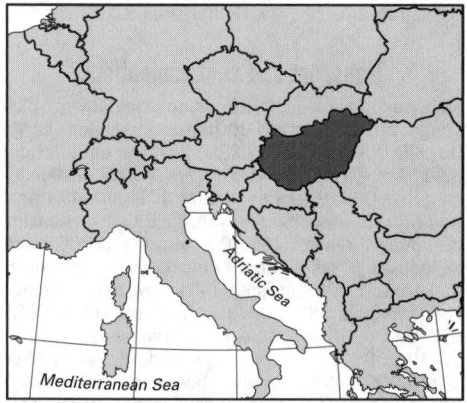

*Adriatic Sea*

*Mediterranean Sea*

**Official name:** Magyar Köztársaság (Republic of Hungary). **Form of government:** unitary multiparty republic with one legislative house (National Assembly [386, excluding 13 seats set aside for ethnic minorities]). **Chief of state:** President Ferenc Mádl (from 2000). **Head of government:** Prime Minister Péter Medgyessy (from 27 May 2002). **Capital:** Budapest. **Official language:** Hungarian. **Official religion:** none.

**Monetary unit:** 1 forint (Ft) = 100 filler; valuation (7 Jul 2003) $1 = Ft 229.53.

## Demography

**Area:** 35,919 sq mi, 93,030 sq km. **Population** (2002): 10,162,000. **Density** (2002): persons per sq mi 282.9, persons per sq km 109.2. **Urban** (2000): 63.6%. **Sex distribution** (2001): male 47.70%; female 52.30%. **Age breakdown** (2000): under 15, 17.1%; 15–29, 22.6%; 30–44, 20.2%; 45–59, 20.5%; 60–74, 14.0%; 75 and over, 5.6%. **Ethnic composition** (2000): Hungarian 84.4%; Roma (Gypsy) 5.3%; Ruthenian 2.9%; German 2.4%; Romanian 1.0%; Slovak 0.9%; Jewish 0.6%; other 2.5%. **Religious affiliation** (1998): Roman Catholic 57.8%; Reformed 17.7%; Lutheran 3.9%; Jewish 0.2%; nonreligious 18.5%; other/unknown 1.9%. **Major cities** (2001): Budapest 1,775,203; Debrecen 211,038; Miskolc 184,129; Szeged 168,276; Pécs 162,502. **Location:** central Europe, bordering Slovakia, Ukraine, Romania, Serbia and Montenegro, Croatia, Slovenia, and Austria.

## Vital statistics

**Birth rate** per 1,000 population (2001): 9.5 (world avg. 21.2); (2000) legitimate 71.0%; illegitimate 29.0%. **Death rate** per 1,000 population (2001): 13.0 (world avg. 8.9). **Natural increase rate** per 1,000 population (2001): –3.5 (world avg. 12.3). **Total fertility rate** (avg. births per childbearing woman; 2000): 1.3. **Marriage rate** per 1,000 population (2001): 4.3. **Life expectancy** at birth (2000): male 67.1 years; female 75.6 years.

## National economy

**Budget** (1999). *Revenue*: Ft 4,955,000,000,000 (social security contributions 29.6%, value-added taxes 19.0%, personal income taxes 15.5%, excise taxes 9.4%). *Expenditures*: Ft 5,396,000,000,000 (current expenditures 93.9%, development expenditures 6.1%). **Production** (metric tons except as noted). *Agriculture, forestry, fishing* (2000): corn (maize) 5,000,-000, wheat 3,709,000, sugar beets 2,300,000; livestock (number of live animals) 5,335,000 pigs, 857,000 cattle; roundwood (1999) 4,287,500 cu m; fish catch (1997) 21,916. *Mining and quarrying* (1999): bauxite 935,000. *Manufacturing* (value added in Ft '000,000; 1998): refined petroleum products 296,000; food and beverages 278,800; electrical machinery and apparatus 218,000. *Energy production (consumption)*: electricity (kW-hr; 2001) 33,986,000,000 ([1997] 33,348,000,000); hard coal (metric tons; 2001) 573,000 ([1999] 1,110,000); lignite (metric tons; 2001) 12,745,000 ([1999] 14,341,000); crude petroleum (barrels; 2001) 7,118,000 ([1999] 51,633,000); petroleum products (metric tons; 1997) 6,516,000 (6,393,-000); natural gas (cu m; 2001) 3,417,000,000 ([1999] 12,365,000,000). **Land use** (1994): forested 19.1%; meadows and pastures 12.4%; agricultural and under permanent cultivation 53.9%; other 14.6%. **Public debt** (external, outstanding; 2000): $14,251,000,000. **Population economically active** (1999): total 4,096,200; activity rate of total population 40.7% (participation rates: ages 15–64, 59.9%;

*1 metric ton = about 1.1 short tons;   1 kilometer = 0.6 mi (statute);   1 metric ton-km cargo = about 0.68 short ton-mi cargo;   c.i.f.: cost, insurance, and freight;   f.o.b.: free on board*

female 44.5%; unemployed [2001] 5.7%). **Tourism** ($'000,000; 2000): receipts 3,429; expenditures 1,094. **Gross national product** (2000): $47,249,-000,000 ($4,710 per capita). **Household income and expenditure.** Average household size (1998) 2.5; income per household (1998) Ft 1,828,441 ($8,528); sources of income (1998): wages 49.9%, transfers 17.9%, self-employment 17.2%, other 15.0%; expenditure (1999): food and beverages 33.6%; transportation and communications 14.9%; energy 14.6%; housing 8.0%.

## Foreign trade

**Imports** (2000): Ft 9,064,000,000,000 (electrical machinery 16.0%, nonelectrical machinery 14.4%, road vehicles 7.3%, computers and office machines 7.1%, telecommunications equipment 6.5%). *Major import sources:* Germany 25.5%; Russia 8.1%; Italy 7.5%; Austria 7.4%; Japan 5.3%. **Exports** (2000): Ft 7,942,800,000,000 (office machines and computers 13.9%, electrical machinery 11.9%, telecommunications equipment 10.8%, power generating machinery 10.0%, road vehicles 8.8%). *Major export destinations:* Germany 37.2%; Austria 8.7%; Italy 5.9%; The Netherlands 5.4%; US 5.3%.

## Transport and communications

**Transport.** *Railroads:* (2000) route length 7,768 km; (1999) passenger-km 9,514,000,000; (1999) metric ton-km cargo 7,733,000,000. *Roads* (1999): total length 188,203 km (paved 43%). *Vehicles* (1999): passenger cars 2,255,526; trucks and buses 321,634. *Air transport* (1999): passenger-km 3,513,000,000; metric ton-km cargo 55,500,000; airports (1997) with scheduled flights 1. **Communications,** in total units (units per 1,000 persons). Daily newspaper circulation (1996): 1,895,000 (186); radio receivers (1997): 7,000,000 (689); television receivers (1998): 4,500,000 (445); telephone main lines (2001): 3,730,000 (374); cellular telephone subscribers (2001): 4,968,000 (498); personal computers (2001): 1,000,000 (100); Internet users (2001): 1,480,000 (148).

## Education and health

**Educational attainment** (1990). Population age 25 and over having: no formal schooling 1.3%; primary education 57.9%; secondary 30.7%; higher 10.1%. **Health** (1999): physicians 32,240 (1 per 312 persons); hospital beds 83,992 (1 per 120 persons); infant mortality rate per 1,000 live births (2001) 8.1. **Food** (1998): daily per capita caloric intake 3,408 (vegetable products 69%, animal products 31%); 130% of FAO recommended minimum.

## Military

**Total active duty personnel** (2001): 33,810 (army 67.7%, air force 10.4%, headquarters staff 21.9%). **Military expenditure as percentage of GNP** (1999): 1.7% (world 2.4%); per capita expenditures $185.

## Background

The western part of Hungary was incorporated into the Roman Empire in 14 BC. The Magyars, a nomadic people, occupied the middle basin of the Danube River in the late 9th century AD. Stephen I, crowned in 1000, Christianized the country and organized it into a strong and independent state. Invasions by the Mongols in the 13th century and by the Ottoman Turks in the 14th century devastated the country, and by 1568 the territory of modern Hungary had been divided into three parts: Royal Hungary went to the Habsburgs; Transylvania gained autonomy in 1566 under the Turks; and the central plain remained under Turkish control until the late 17th century, when the Austrian Habsburgs took over. Hungary declared its independence from Austria in 1849, and in 1867 the dual monarchy of Austria-Hungary was established. Its defeat in World War I resulted in the dismemberment of Hungary, leaving it only those areas in which Magyars predominated. In an attempt to regain some of this lost territory, Hungary cooperated with the Germans against the Soviet Union during World War II. After the war, a pro-Soviet provisional government was established, and in 1949 the Hungarian People's Republic was formed. Opposition to this Stalinist regime broke out in 1956 but was suppressed. Nevertheless, from 1956 to 1988 communist Hungary grew to become the most tolerant of the Soviet-bloc nations of Eastern Europe. It gained its independence in 1989 and soon attracted the largest amount of direct foreign investment in east-central Europe. In 1999 it joined NATO.

## Recent Developments

In 2002 the ruling coalition of the Federation of Young Democrats (Fidesz)–Hungarian Civic Party and the Independent Smallholders' Party (FKGP) were ousted in Hungary's parliamentary elections. The Socialists, led by Peter Medgyessy, and its ally, the Alliance of Free Democrats, claimed 198 of parliament's 386 seats. Medgyessy took office as prime minister on 27 May. An economist and former banker, Medgyessy and his center-left coalition's first priority was to deliver on its main campaign promises—that is, raising pensions and public service salaries, especially in the health and education sectors.

**Internet resources:** <www.hungarytourism.hu>

# Iceland

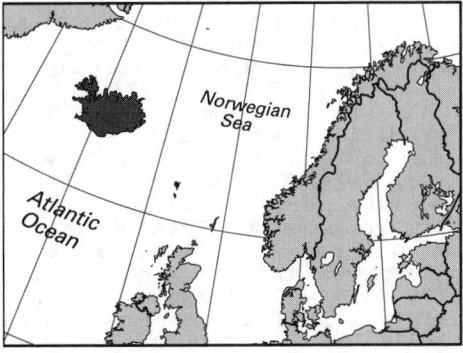

**Official name:** Lydhveldidh Ísland (Republic of Iceland). **Form of government:** unitary multiparty republic with one legislative house (Althing [63]). **Chief of state:** President Ólafur Ragnar Grímsson (from 1996). **Head of government:** Prime Minister Davíd Oddsson (from 1991). **Capital:** Reykjavík. **Official language:** Icelandic. **Official religion:** Evangelical Lutheran.

**Monetary unit:** 1 króna (ISK) = 100 aurar; valuation (7 Jul 2003) $1 = ISK 76.43.

## Demography

**Area:** 39,699 sq mi, 102,819 sq km. **Population** (2002): 288,000. **Density** (2002; calculated with reference to 9,191 sq mi (23,805 sq km) area free of glaciers, lava fields, wasteland or lakes): persons per sq mi 31.3, persons per sq km 12.1. **Urban** (1999) 93.5%. **Sex distribution** (2001): male 50.07%; female 49.93%. **Age breakdown** (2000): under 15, 23.2%; 15–29, 22.7%; 30–44, 22.2%; 45–59, 16.9%; 60–74, 9.9%; 75 and over, 5.1%. **Ethnic composition** (2000): Icelandic 96.9%; European 2.2%, of which Nordic 0.6%; Asian 0.5%; other 0.4%. **Religious affiliation** (2000): Protestant 92.3%, of which Evangelical Lutheran 87.8%, other Lutheran 3.9%; Roman Catholic 1.5%; other and not specified 6.2%. **Major cities** (2001): Reykjavík 112,268 (urban area 178,000, including Kópavogur 24,229; Hafnarfjördhur 20,223; Gardhabær 8,445); Akureyri 15,632. **Location:** northern Europe, an island between the Greenland Sea, the Norwegian Sea, and the North Atlantic Ocean.

## Vital statistics

**Birth rate** per 1,000 population (2000): 15.2 (world avg. 21.2); (1999) legitimate 37.4%; illegitimate 62.6%. **Death rate** per 1,000 population (2000): 6.4 (world avg. 8.9). **Natural increase rate** per 1,000 population (2000): 8.8 (world avg. 12.3). **Total fertility rate** (avg. births per childbearing woman; 2000): 2.1. **Marriage rate** per 1,000 population (2000): 6.3. **Divorce rate** per 1,000 population (2000): 1.9. **Life expectancy** at birth (1999–2000): male 77.6 years; female 81.4 years.

## National economy

**Budget** (1998). *Revenue*: ISK 220,840,000,000 (indirect taxes 49.5%, of which value-added taxes 26.0%; direct taxes 44.6%; nontax revenue 5.9%). *Expenditures*: ISK 198,216,000,000 (1997; health and welfare 39.6%; education 14.3%; general administration 8.7%; communications 7.5%; cultural affairs 6.2%; agriculture 4.0%). **Public debt** (2000): $2,242,600,000. **Production** (metric tons except as noted). *Agriculture, forestry, fishing* (2000): potatoes 9,843, cereals 3,041, tomatoes 931; livestock (number of live animals) 465,777 sheep, 73,995 horses, 72,135 cattle; fish catch (value in ISK '000,000; 2000) 57,858, of which cod 26,383, herring 5,728, redfish 4,570, shrimp 2,661, other 18,516. *Mining and quarrying* (2000): diatomite 28,300. *Manufacturing* (value added in ISK '000,000; 1996): preserved and processed fish 18,114; other food products 10,848; printing and publishing 6,914. *Energy production (consumption)*: electricity (kW-hr; 2000) 7,676,000,000 (7,676,000,000); coal (metric tons; 1997) none (58,000); petroleum products (metric tons; 1997) none (724,000). **Land use** (1994): forested 1.2%; meadows and pastures 22.7%; agricultural and under permanent cultivation 0.1%; other 76.0%. **Population economically active** (2000): total 160,100; activity rate of total population 55.6% (participation rates: ages 16–74, 83.5%; female 46.5%;

unemployed 2.3%). **Tourism** (2000): receipts $228,000,000; expenditures $467,000,000. **Gross national product** (2000): $8,540,000,000 ($30,390 per capita). **Household income and expenditure.** Average household size (1990) 3.6; annual income per household (1995) ISK 1,976,066 ($30,546); sources of income (1995): wages and salaries 74.1%, pension 10.5%, self-employment 2.7%, other 12.7%; expenditure (2000): transportation and communications 22.0%; food and beverages 20.1%, housing and energy 18.5%, recreation and education 12.4%.

## Foreign trade

**Imports** (2001-c.i.f.): ISK 220,874,000,000 (machinery and apparatus 15.1%; road vehicles 12.4%; food products 8.4%; chemicals 8.3%; crude petroleum and petroleum products 8.3%). *Major import sources* (2000): Germany 11.9%; US 11.0%; UK 9.0%; Norway 8.1%; Denmark 7.9%; The Netherlands 7.5%; Sweden 6.6%; Japan 4.9%. **Exports** (2001-f.o.b.): ISK 144,811,600,000 (marine products 62.5%, of which frozen fish 33.7%, salted fish 13.1%, lobster and shrimp 7.5%; manufactured products 31.3%). *Major export destinations* (2000): UK 19.3%; Germany 16.4%; US 12.2%; The Netherlands 7.7%; Portugal 5.7%; France 4.6%; Spain 4.5%.

## Transport and communications

**Transport.** *Roads* (2000): total length 12,682 km (paved 28%). *Vehicles* (2001): passenger cars 158,936; trucks and buses 21,105. *Air transport* (2000; Icelandair only): passenger-km 3,714,000,000; metric ton-km cargo 109,600,000; airports (1996) with scheduled flights 24. **Communications,** in total units (units per 1,000 persons). Daily newspaper circulation (1996): 145,000 (535); radio receivers (1997): 260,000 (950); television receivers (1999): 145,000 (523); telephone main lines (2001): 190,600 (664); cellular telephone subscribers (2001): 235,400 (820); personal computers (2001): 120,000 (418); Internet users (2001): 195,000 (679).

## Education and health

**Educational attainment** (2001): Percentage of population ages 25–64 having primary and some secondary education 36.6%; secondary 44.8%; higher 18.6%. **Literacy:** virtually 100%. *Health:* physicians (1999) 938 (1 per 296 persons); hospital beds (1993) 2,798 (1 per 95 persons); infant mortality rate per 1,000 live births (2000) 3.0. **Food** (2000): daily per capita caloric intake 3,313 (vegetable products 58%, animal products 42%); 126% of FAO recommended minimum.

## Military

**Total active duty personnel** (2001): 125 coast guard personnel; NATO-sponsored US-manned Iceland Defense Force: 1,640. **Military expenditure as percentage of GNP** (1999): none (world average 2.4%).

## Background

Iceland was settled by Norwegian seafarers in the 9th century and was Christianized by 1000. Its legisla-

---

*1 metric ton = about 1.1 short tons;   1 kilometer = 0.6 mi (statute);   1 metric ton-km cargo = about 0.68 short ton-mi cargo;   c.i.f.: cost, insurance, and freight;   f.o.b.: free on board*

ture, the Althing, was founded in 930, making it one of the oldest legislative assemblies in the world. Iceland united with Norway in 1262. It became an independent state of Denmark in 1918 but severed those ties to become an independent republic in 1944. Vigdís Finnbogadóttir became the world's first female elected president in 1980.

## Recent Developments

Planning was completed and deals were signed in early 2003 for the construction of a $3 billion complex including a hydroelectric dam at Kárahnjúkar and an aluminum plant at Reyðarfjörður. Despite vocal concerns by environmental groups concerned about potential damage to subarctic wilderness, the government ruled that construction could go ahead. The project to be realized together with the American aluminum giant Alcoa, Inc. would equal nearly one-third of Iceland's GDP. In April Iceland announced that after 13 years of inactivity it would resume whaling; like Japan, Iceland said it would take whales for scientific research.

Internet resources: <www.icetourist.is>

# India

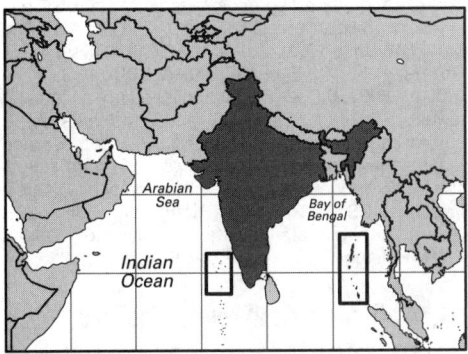

**Official name:** Bharat (Hindi); Republic of India (English). **Form of government:** multiparty federal republic with two legislative houses (Council of States [245], House of the People [545, including 2 non-elective seats]). **Chief of state:** President A.P.J. Abdul Kalam (from 25 Jul 2002). **Head of government:** Prime Minister Atal Bihari Vajpayee (from 1998). **Capital:** New Delhi. **Official languages:** Hindi; English. **Official religion:** none. **Monetary unit:** 1 Indian rupee (Re, plural Rs) = 100 paise; valuation (7 Jul 2003) $1 = Rs 46.33.

## Demography

**Area:** 1,222,559 sq mi, 3,166,414 sq km (excludes 46,660 sq mi [120,849 sq km] of territory claimed by India as part of Jammu and Kashmir but occupied by Pakistan or China). **Population** (2002): 1,047,671,-000. **Density** (2002; calculation excludes Pakistan- and China-controlled Jammu and Kashmir): persons per sq mi 856.9, persons per sq km 330.9. **Urban** (2001): 27.8%. **Sex distribution** (2001): male 51.73%; female 48.27%. **Age breakdown** (2000): under 15, 33.6%; 15–29, 27.7%; 30–44, 19.8%; 45–59, 11.9%; 60–74, 5.6%; 75 and over, 1.4%. **Major cities** (2001; urban agglomerations, 2001): Greater Mumbai

(Greater Bombay) 11,914,398 (16,368,084); Delhi 9,817,439 (12,791,458; includes New Delhi 294,783); Kolkata (Calcutta) 4,580,544 (13,216,-546); Bangalore 4,292,223 (5,686,844); Chennai (Madras) 4,216,268 (6,424,624); Ahmadabad 3,515,361 (4,519,278); Hyderabad 3,449,878 (5,533,640); Pune (Poona) 2,540,069 (3,755,525); Kanpur 2,532,138 (2,690,486); Surat 2,433,787 (2,811,466); Jaipur 2,324,319 (2,324,319). **Linguistic composition** (1991): Hindi 27.58% (including associated languages and dialects, 39.85%); Bengali 8.22%; Telugu 7.80%; Marathi 7.38%; Tamil 6.26%; Urdu 5.13%; Gujarati 4.81%; Kannada 3.87%; Malayalam 3.59%; Oriya 3.32%; Punjabi 2.76%; Assamese 1.55%; Bhili/Bhilodi 0.66%; Santhali 0.62%; Kashmiri 0.47%; Gondi 0.25%; Sindhi 0.25%; Nepali 0.25%; Konkani 0.21%; Tulu 0.18%; Kurukh 0.17%; Manipuri 0.15%; Bodo 0.14%; Khandeshi 0.12%; other 3.26%. Hindi (66.00%) and English (19.00%) are also spoken as lingua francas (second languages). **Religious affiliation** (2000): Hindu 73.72%; Muslim 11.96%, of which Sunni 8.97%, Shi'i 2.99%; Christian 6.08%, of which Independent 2.99%, Protestant 1.47%, Roman Catholic 1.35%, Orthodox 0.27%; traditional beliefs 3.39%; Sikh 2.16%; Buddhist 0.71%; Jain 0.40%; Baha'i 0.12%; Zoroastrian (Parsi) 0.02%; other 1.44%. **Households** (1991). Total households 151,032,898. Average household size 5.6; 1–2 persons 12.1%, 3–5 persons 44.4%, 6–8 persons 30.5%, 9 or more persons 13.0%. Average number of rooms per household 2.2; 1 room 40.5%, 2 rooms 30.6%, 3 rooms 13.8%, 4 rooms 7.1%, 5 rooms 3.2%, 6 or more rooms 3.9%, unspecified number of rooms 0.9%. Average number of persons per room 2.6. **Location:** southern Asia, bordering Pakistan, China, Nepal, Bhutan, Myanmar, Bangladesh, and the Indian Ocean.

## Vital statistics

**Birth rate** per 1,000 population (2000): 24.8 (world avg. 22.5). **Death rate** per 1,000 population (2000): 8.9 (world avg. 9.0). **Natural increase rate** per 1,000 population (2000): 15.9 (world avg. 13.5). **Total fertility rate** (avg. births per childbearing woman; 2000): 3.1. **Marital status** of male (female) population age 6 and over (1992–93): single 48.3% (37.1%); married 47.5% (55.2%); widowed 3.6% (7.2%); divorced or separated 0.6% (0.5%). **Life expectancy** at birth (2000): male 61.9 years; female 63.1 years.

## Social indicators

**Quality of working life** (data apply to the workers employed in the "organized sector" only [28.2 million in 1997–98, of which 19.4 million are employed in the public sector and 8.8 million are employed in the private sector]; few legal protections exist for the more than 350 million workers in the "unorganized sector"). Average workweek (1989): 42 hours. Rate of fatal (nonfatal) injuries per 100,000 industrial workers (1989) 17 (3,625). Agricultural workers in servitude to creditors (early 1990s) 10–20%. **Access to services** (1991). Percentage of total (urban, rural) households having access to: electricity for lighting purposes 42.4% (75.8%, 30.5%); attached toilet or nearby latrine 23.7% (63.9%, 9.5%). Source of drinking water: piped water 32.3%, well 32.2%, hand pump or tube well 30.0%, river or canal 2.0%, public tank 1.3%, other 2.2%. **Social participation.** Eligible voters participating in September/October 1999 national election: 59.6%. Trade union membership

(1998): c. 16,000,000 (primarily in the public sector). **Social deviance** (1990; crimes reported to National Crime Records Bureau). Offense rate per 100,000 population for: murder 4.1; dacoity (gang robbery) 1.3; theft and housebreaking 56.6; riots 12.0. Rate of suicide per 100,000 population (1991): 9.0. **Material well-being** (1994). Households possessing: black and white television receivers 18.8%, color television receivers 6.3%, videocassette recorders 1.3%, refrigerators 6.9%, washing machines 2.3%.

## National economy

**Gross national product** (2000): $454,800,000,000 ($450 per capita). **Budget** (1999–2000). *Revenue*: Rs 3,288,000,000,000 (tax revenue 48.6%, of which excise taxes 19.4%, customs duties 15.3%, corporation taxes 9.4%; nontax revenue 36.5%, of which economic services 20.7%, interest receipts 10.0%; other sources of revenue 14.9%). *Expenditures*: Rs 3,288,000,000,000 (interest payments and debt servicing 26.8%; transportation 11.0%; defense 10.5%; grants in aid to state governments 9.4%; communications 7.2%; agriculture 5.0%; social services 4.7%). **Public debt** (external, outstanding; 2000): $87,598,000,000. **Production** (in '000 metric tons except as noted). *Agriculture, forestry, fishing* (2000): sugarcane 315,100, cereals 239,814 (of which rice 134,150, wheat 74,251, corn [maize] 11,500, sorghum 9,500, millet 9,000), fruits 49,199 (of which mangoes 15,642, bananas 13,900, oranges 3,000, apples 1,580, pineapples 1,440, lemons and limes 1,000), oilseeds 31,015 (of which rapeseed 6,120, peanuts [groundnuts] 6,100, soybeans 5,400, sunflower seeds 1,200, castor beans 810, sesame 620 [1998]), pulses 14,237 (of which chickpeas 5,754, dry beans 3,600, pigeon peas 2,450 [1998]), coconuts 11,100, seed cotton 6,172, eggplants 6,100, jute 1,500, tea 749, tobacco 702, natural rubber 620, garlic 517, cashews 450, betel 315, coffee 282, ginger 235, pepper 58; livestock (number of live animals; 2000) 218,800,000 cattle, 123,000,000 goats, 93,772,000 water buffalo, 57,900,000 sheep, 16,500,000 pigs, 1,030,000 camels; roundwood (1999) 302,794,000 cu m, of which fuelwood 278,755,000 cu m, industrial roundwood 24,038,000; fish catch (metric tons; 1999) 5,352,000, of which freshwater fish 2,632,000, marine fish 2,248,000, crustaceans 377,000. *Mining and quarrying* (1999–2000): limestone 128,000; iron ore 48,100; bauxite 6,854; manganese 626; chromium 509; zinc 252; copper 37; gold 78,512 troy oz; gem diamonds 40,666 carats. *Manufacturing* (value added in Rs '000,000,000; 1999): iron and steel 188.1; industrial chemicals 167.7; paints, soaps, varnishes, drugs, and medicines 164.2; transport equipment 159.7; food products 139.0; textiles 136.8; electrical machinery 118.6; nonelectrical machinery 116.3; refined petroleum 79.2; cements, bricks, and tiles 67.2; fabricated metal products 39.5; nonferrous base metals 37.5. *Energy production (consumption)*: electricity (kW-hr; 2001) 509,209,000,000 ([1997] 465,867,000,000); hard coal (metric tons; 2001) 318,756,000 ([1997] 310,133,000); lignite (metric tons; 2001) 23,713,000 ([1997] 22,855,000); crude petroleum (barrels; 2001) 242,919,000 ([1997] 512,232,000); petroleum products (metric tons; 1997) 50,916,000

(69,390,000); natural gas (cu m; 2001) 29,016,000,000 ([1997] 19,430,000,000). **Land use** (1994): forested 23.0%; meadows and pastures 3.8%; agricultural and under permanent cultivation 57.1%; other 16.1%. **Population economically active** (1993–94): total 372,000,000; activity rate of total population c. 41% (female 32.5%). **Household income and expenditure.** Average household size (1991) 5.6; sources of income (1984–85): salaries and wages 42.2%, self-employed 39.7%, interest 8.6%, profits and dividends 6.0%, rent 3.5%; expenditure (1998–99): food, beverages, and tobacco 52.1%, transportation and communications 13.7%, housing and energy 10.2%, clothing and footwear 5.2%, health 4.4%. **Service enterprises** (net value added in Rs '000,000,000; 1998–99): wholesale and retail trade 1,562; finance, real estate, and insurance 1,310; transport and storage 804; community, social, and personal services 763; construction 545; electricity, gas, and steam 287. **Tourism** (2000): $3,168,000,000; expenditures $2,567,000,000.

## Foreign trade

**Imports** (1999–2000-c.i.f.): Rs 2,006,570,000,000 (crude petroleum and refined petroleum 22.3%; precious and semiprecious stones 11.6%; chemicals 6.0%; nonelectrical machinery 5.8%; electronic goods 5.6%). *Major import sources*: Belgium 7.7%; US 7.5%; UK 5.8%; Switzerland 5.5%; Japan 5.1%; Saudi Arabia 4.8%; United Arab Emirates 4.5%; Malaysia 4.3%; Germany 3.9%. **Exports** (1999–2000-f.o.b.): Rs 1,607,430,000,000 (cut and polished diamonds and jewelry 20.0%; cotton ready-made garments 9.2%; cotton yarn, fabrics, and thread 7.9%; leather and leather manufactures 4.2%; drugs and pharmaceuticals 4.2%; fabricated metals 3.2%). *Major export destinations*: US 22.2%; Hong Kong 6.7%; UK 5.6%; United Arab Emirates 5.6%; Germany 4.6%; Japan 4.5%; Belgium 3.6%; Italy 3.0%; Russia 2.5%.

## Transport and communications

**Transport.** *Railroads* (1998–99): route length 62,809 km; (1999–2000) passenger-km 420,449,000,000; (1999–2000) metric ton-km cargo 305,513,000,000. *Roads* (1999): total length 3,319,644 km (paved 46%). *Vehicles* (1997): passenger cars 4,662,000; trucks and buses 2,748,000. *Air transport* (2001; Air India and Indian Airlines): passenger-km 19,263,000,000; metric ton-km cargo 450,331,000; airports (1996) with scheduled flights 66. **Communications,** in total units (units per 1,000 persons). Daily newspaper circulation (1993): 18,800,000 (21); radio receivers (1997): 116,000,000 (120); television receivers (1999): 75,000,000 (75); telephone main lines (2001): 34,732,100 (34); cellular telephone subscribers (2001): 5,725,200 (5.6); personal computers (2001): 6,000,000 (5.8); Internet users (2001): 7,000,000 (6.8).

## Education and health

**Educational attainment** (1991). Percentage of population age 25 and over having: no formal schooling 57.5%; incomplete primary education 28.0%; complete primary or some secondary 7.2%; complete secondary or higher 7.3%. **Literacy** (2001): total population-

---

*1 metric ton = about 1.1 short tons; 1 kilometer = 0.6 mi (statute); 1 metric ton-km cargo = about 0.68 short ton-mi cargo; c.i.f.: cost, insurance, and freight; f.o.b.: free on board*

tion age 7 and over literate 566,715,000 (65.4%); males literate 339,969,000 (75.8%); females literate 226,746,000 (54.2%). **Health**: physicians (1992) 410,875 (1 per 2,173 persons); hospital beds (1993) 659,000 (1 per 1,364 persons); infant mortality rate per 1,000 live births (2000) 64.9. **Food** (1999): daily per capita caloric intake 2,417 (vegetable products 92%, animal products 8%); 109% of FAO recommended minimum.

## Military

**Total active duty personnel** (2001): 1,263,000 (army 87.1%, navy 4.2%, air force 8.7%); personnel in paramilitary forces 1,089,700. **Military expenditure as percentage of GNP** (1999): 2.5% (world 2.4%); per capita expenditure $11.

 **Did you know?** The Ganges (officially the Ganga), the great river of northern India, is sacred to Hindus. Its region (the Gangetic Plain or Hindustan) has been the cradle of many different civilizations from the 3rd century BC to the 16th century AD. About one-fourth of India's total population live in Uttar Pradesh and Bihar, the two states comprising nearly all of the plain.

## Background

India has been inhabited for thousands of years. Agriculture dates back to at least the 7th millennium BC, and an urban civilization, that of the Indus Valley, was established by 2600 BC. Buddhism and Jainism arose in the 6th century BC in reaction to the caste-based society created by the Vedic religion and its successor, Hinduism. Muslim invasions began c. AD 1000, establishing the long-lived Delhi sultanate in 1206 and the Mughal dynasty in 1526. Vasco da Gama's voyage to India in 1498 initiated several centuries of commercial rivalry among the Portuguese, Dutch, English, and French. British conquests in the 18th and 19th centuries led to the rule of the British East India Co., and direct administration by the British empire began in 1858. After Mohandas K. Gandhi helped end British rule in 1947, Jawaharlal Nehru became India's first prime minister and he, his daughter, Indira Gandhi, and his grandson Rajiv Gandhi guided the nation's destiny for all but a few years until 1989. The subcontinent was partitioned into two countries—India, with a Hindu majority, and Pakistan, with a Muslim majority—in 1947. A later clash with Pakistan resulted in the creation of Bangladesh in 1971. In the 1980s and '90s, Sikhs sought to establish an independent state in Punjab, and ethnic and religious conflicts took place in other parts of the country as well.

## Recent Developments

India's major preoccupations in 2002 were continuing infiltration of terrorists and an outbreak of violent Hindu-Muslim riots in the state of Gujarat. Muslim terrorists attacked Akshardham, a Hindu temple in Gandhinagar, in September and killed 28 worshipers. On the positive side was the fact that elections were held on 12 December for the state assembly of Jammu and Kashmir in spite of frantic efforts by militants to frighten voters and disrupt polling. The Bharatiya Janata Party (BJP), which campaigned on a plank of Hindu assertiveness and cultural nationalism, won a resounding victory, securing 126 seats in the 182-member house and 51% of the vote.

In order to de-escalate tension with Pakistan, India withdrew troops from the international border in October and also announced that it would be willing to hold talks with the new Pakistani government provided that infiltration of terrorists was ended.

During a visit to Beijing in June 2003, Prime Minister Atal Bihari Vajpayee signed an agreement to open a border pass between Tibet and Sifkim over which the two countries had gone to war in 1962.

There was a marked fall in India's economic growth rate in 2002 and a general belief that economic reform and liberalization had slowed because of increasing opposition within the BJP. A major decision to sell key petroleum companies was held over until the end of the year. There was some progress in disinvestment, however. Tatas, India's largest corporate conglomerate, acquired from the government the controlling stake in Videsh Sanchar Nigam Ltd., an international telecommunications carrier. Several state-owned hotels were also sold off.

The country mourned the death on 1 Feb 2003 aboard the space shuttle *Columbia* of Indian American astronaut Kalpana Chawla.

**Internet resources**: <www.tourismofindia.com>

# Indonesia

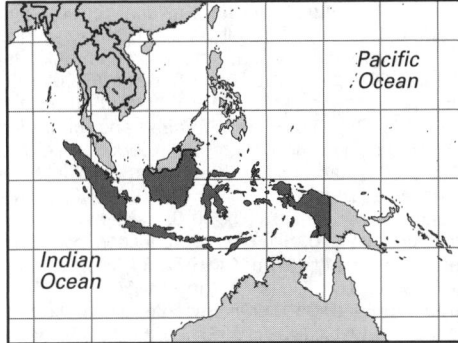

**Official name**: Republik Indonesia (Republic of Indonesia). **Form of government**: unitary multiparty republic with two legislative houses (People's Consultative Assembly [700, including members of the House of People's Representatives and 200 other appointees]; House of People's Representatives [500, including 38 nonelective seats reserved for the military]). **Head of state and government**: President Sukarnoputri Megawati (from 2001). **Capital**: Jakarta. **Official language**: Indonesian (Bahasa Indonesia). **Official religion**: monotheism. **Monetary unit**: 1 Indonesian rupiah (Rp) = 100 sen; valuation (7 Jul 2003) $1 = Rp 8,183.

## Demography

**Area**: 1,922,570 sq km. **Population** (2002): 211,023,000. **Density** (2002): persons per sq mi 284.3, persons per sq km 109.8. **Urban** (2002): 43.0%. **Sex distribution** (2000): male 50.14%; female 49.86%. **Age breakdown** (2000): under 15, 30.4%; 15–29, 29.3%; 30–44, 21.8%; 45–59, 11.3%; 60–74, 5.8%; 75 and over, 1.4%. **Ethnolinguistic**

composition (1990): Javanese 39.4%; Sundanese 15.8%; Indonesian (Malay) 12.1%; Madurese 4.3%; Minang 2.4%; other 26.0%. **Religious affiliation** (2000): Muslim 76.5%, of which syncretistic religions 21.8%; Christian 13.1%, of which Protestant 5.7%, independent Christian 4.0%, Roman Catholic 2.7%; Hindu 3.4%; traditional beliefs 2.5%; nonreligious 1.9%; other 2.6%. **Major cities** (1995): Jakarta (1996) 9,341,000; Surabaya (1996) 2,743,000; Bandung (1996) 2,429,000; Medan 1,909,700; Palembang 1,283,100. **Location:** archipelago in southeast Asia, bordering Malaysia, the Pacific Ocean, Papua New Guinea, and the Indian Ocean.

## Vital statistics

**Birth rate** per 1,000 population (2002): 20.3 (world avg. 21.2). **Death rate** per 1,000 population (2002): 7.1 (world avg. 8.9). **Total fertility rate** (avg. births per childbearing woman; 2002): 2.3. **Marriage rate** per 1,000 population (1997–98): 8.1. **Life expectancy** at birth (2002): male 65.0 years; female 69.0 years.

## National economy

**Budget** (1999–2000). *Revenue*: Rp 188,428,500,-000,000 (income tax 31.7%, oil and gas revenues 31.0%, value-added tax 17.6%, nontax revenue 9.1%, excise taxes 5.5%). *Expenditures*: Rp 204,-900,300,000,000 (development 23.9%, subsidies 22.9%, salaries 15.7%, debt repayment 10.1%, transfers 8.5%). **Production** (metric tons except as noted). *Agriculture, forestry, fishing* (2000): rice 51,000,000, palm fruit oil 34,000,000, sugarcane 21,400,000; livestock (number of live animals) 14,121,000 goats, 12,102,000 cattle, 7,502,000 sheep; roundwood (1999) 190,601,000 cu m; fish catch (1998) 3,699,000. *Mining and quarrying* (1998): copper concentrate 2,640,000; nickel ore 1,642,000; bauxite 513,000; gold 118,246 kg. *Manufacturing* (value added in Rp '000,000,000; 1997): transport equipment 10,038.6; textiles 9,629.7; food products 9,028.1. *Energy production (consumption)*: electricity (kW-hr; 1997) 84,096,000,000 (84,096,000,000); coal (metric tons; 2001) 90,648,-000 ([1997] 10,330,000); crude petroleum (barrels; 2001) 514,413,000 ([1997] 315,000,000); petroleum products (metric tons; 1997) 44,576,000 (42,492,000); natural gas (cu m; 2000) 82,326,-000,000 ([1997] 39,818,000,000). **Gross national product** (2000): $119,871,000,000 ($570 per capita). **Public debt** (external, outstanding; 2000): $69,161,000,000. **Population economically active** (1999): total 94,800,000; activity rate 46.0% (participation rates: over age 15, 70.7%; unemployed 6.3%). **Household.** Average household size (2000) 3.9. **Tourism** (2000): receipts $5,749,000,000; expenditures $3,197,000,000.

## Foreign trade

**Imports** (1998-f.o.b. in balance of trade): $27,336,-900,000 (machinery and transport equipment 36.3%, basic manufactures 16.6%, chemicals 15.1%, mineral fuels 9.8%, food and live animals 9.6%). *Major import sources:* Japan 15.7%; US 12.9%; Singapore 9.3%; Germany 8.7%; Australia 6.4%; South Korea 5.6%. **Exports** (1998–f.o.b. in balance of trade): $48,847,600,000 (crude petroleum 8.3%, natural gas 7.8%, garments 5.4%, plywood 4.3%, processed rubber 2.3%). *Major export destinations:* Japan 18.7%; US 14.4%; Singapore 10.6%; Australia 3.1%.

## Transport and communications

**Transport.** *Railroads* (1999): route length 6,458 km; passenger-km 18,585,000,000; metric ton-km cargo 5,035,000,000. *Roads* (1997): length 341,467 km (paved 56%). *Vehicles* (1998): passenger cars 2,734,769; trucks and buses 2,189,876. *Air transport* (1999): passenger-km 12,389,000,000; metric ton-km cargo 340,932,000; airports (1996) 81. **Communications,** in total units (units per 1,000 persons). Daily newspaper circulation (1996): 4,665,-000 (23); radio receivers (1998): 26,000,000 (128); television receivers (1999): 30,000,000 (143); telephone main lines (2001): 7,949,300 (37); cellular telephone subscribers (2001): 5,303,000 (25); personal computers (2001): 2,300,000 (11); Internet users (2001): 4,000,000 (19).

## Education and health

**Educational attainment** (1990). Percentage of population age 25 and over having: no schooling 34.6%; less than complete primary 28.2%; primary 23.3%; secondary 12.5%; higher 1.4%. **Literacy** (1995 est.): total population age 15 and over literate 83.8%; males literate 89.6%; females literate 78.0%. **Health:** physicians (1996) 31,435 (1 per 6,259 persons); hospital beds (1997) 121,996 (1 per 1,638 persons); infant mortality rate per 1,000 live births (2002) 40.0. **Food** (1999): daily per capita caloric intake 2,931 (vegetable products 95%, animal products 5%); (1997) 136% of FAO recommended minimum.

## Military

**Total active duty personnel** (2001): 297,000 (army 77.4%, navy 13.5%, air force 9.1%). **Military expenditure as percentage of GNP** (1999): 1.1% (world 2.4%); per capita expenditure $7.

## Background

Proto-Malay peoples migrated to Indonesia from mainland Asia before 1000 BC. Commercial relations were established with China in about the 5th century AD, and Hindu and Buddhist cultural influences from India began to take hold. Arab traders brought Islam to the islands in the 13th century; the religion took hold throughout the islands, except for Bali, which retained its Hindu religion and culture. European influence began in the 16th century, and the Dutch ruled Indonesia from the late 17th century until 1942, when the Japanese invaded. Independence leader Sukarno declared Indonesia's independence in 1945, which the Dutch granted, with nominal union to The Netherlands, in 1949; Indonesia dissolved this union in 1954. The suppression of an alleged coup attempt in 1965 resulted in the deaths of more than 300,000 people the government claimed to be communists, and by 1968 Gen. Suharto had taken power. His government forcibly incorporated East Timor into Indonesia in 1975–76, with much loss of life. In the

*1 metric ton = about 1.1 short tons;     1 kilometer = 0.6 mi (statute);     1 metric ton-km cargo = about 0.68 short ton-mi cargo;     c.i.f.: cost, insurance, and freight;     f.o.b.: free on board*

1990s the country was beset by political, economic, and environmental problems, and Suharto was deposed in 1998.

## Recent Developments

Megawati Sukarnoputri celebrated her first anniversary as president in July 2002 but received mixed assessments of her and her government's performance. Despite criticisms of her cautious and reticent presidential style and her resistance to making political reforms, opinion polls consistently showed her to be the clear favorite in the race for the presidency in 2004. Some progress was made on resolving the bloody religious conflicts in the eastern provinces of Central Sulawesi and Maluku when government ministers brokered peace agreements between warring Christian and Muslim groups, but sporadic violence returned to both areas. The situation in the restive provinces of Aceh and Papua was also little improved, despite the fact that both had been granted special autonomy. The aftermath of Indonesian rule in East Timor continued to make news, and in March 2003 Brig. Gen. Noer Muis was sentenced to five years in prison for failing to prevent militia attacks on Timorese civilians in 1999. On 12 Oct 2002 a massive bomb exploded at a nightclub on the resort island of Bali; the death toll was finally set at 202, the majority of whom were Westerners, mostly Australian tourists. This was the worst terrorist attack since 11 Sep 2001. By year's end authorities had taken more than 20 suspects into custody.

Internet resources: <www.bps.go.id>

# Iran

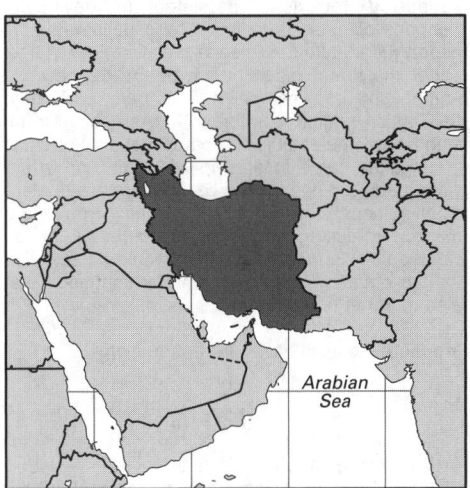

Arabian
Sea

**Official name:** Jomhuri-ye Eslami-ye Iran (Islamic Republic of Iran). **Form of government:** unitary Islamic republic with one legislative house (Islamic Consultative Assembly [290]). **Supreme political/religious authority:** Leader (not required to be a supreme theological authority) *Rahbar* (Spiritual Leader) Ayatollah Sayyed Ali Khamenei (from 1989). **Head of state and government:** President Mohammad Khatami (from 1997). **Capital:** Tehran. **Official language:** Farsi (Persian). **Official religion:** Islam. **Monetary unit:** 1 rial (Rls); valuation (7 Jul 2003) $1 = Rls 8,195 (official floating rate).

## Demography

**Area:** 629,315 sq mi, 1,629,918 sq km. **Population** (2002; excludes roughly 1.4 million Afghan refugees and about 220,000 Iraqi refugees): 65,457,000. **Density** (2002): persons per sq mi 104.0, persons per sq km 40.2. **Urban** (2001): 64.7%. **Sex distribution** (2000): male 50.73%; female 49.27%. **Age breakdown** (2000): under 15, 34.4%; 15–29, 32.0%; 30–44, 17.9%; 45–59, 9.2%; 60–74, 5.1%; 75 and over, 1.4%. **Ethnic composition** (1995): Persian 51%; Azerbaijani 24%; Gilaki/Mazandarani 8%; Kurd 7%; Arab 3%; Luri 2%; Balochi 2%; other 3%. **Religious affiliation** (2000): Muslim 95.6% (Shi'i 90.1%, Sunni 5.5%); Zoroastrian 2.8%; Christian 0.5%; other 1.1%. **Major cities** (1996): Tehran 6,758,845; Mashhad 1,887,405; Esfahan 1,266,072; Tabriz 1,191,043; Shiraz 1,053,025. **Location:** Middle East, bordering the Caspian Sea, Turkmenistan, Afghanistan, Pakistan, the Gulf of Oman, the Persian Gulf, Iraq, Turkey, Azerbaijan, and Armenia.

## Vital statistics

**Birth rate** per 1,000 population (2000): 18.3 (world avg. 22.5). **Death rate** per 1,000 population (2000): 5.5 (world avg. 9.0). **Natural increase rate** per 1,000 population (2000): 12.8 (world avg. 13.5). **Total fertility rate** (avg. births per childbearing woman; 2000): 2.2. **Life expectancy** at birth (2000): male 68.3 years; female 71.5 years.

## National economy

**Budget** (2000–01). *Revenue:* Rls 150,212,000,000,-000 (petroleum and natural gas revenue 55.2%; taxes 22.6%, of which corporate 8.9%; import duties 4.6%; other 17.6%). *Expenditures:* Rls 136,761,-000,000,000 (current expenditure 65.1%; development expenditures 22.0%; other 12.9%). **Public debt** (external, outstanding; 2000): $3,812,000,000. **Tourism** (1999): receipts $662,000,000; expenditures $918,000,000. **Gross national product** (2000): $106,707,000,000 ($1,680 per capita). **Production** (metric tons except as noted). *Agriculture, forestry, fishing* (1998): wheat 8,673,000, sugar beets 5,587,000, potatoes 3,433,000; livestock (number of live animals) 55,000,000 sheep, 8,100,000 cattle; roundwood (2000) 1,151,000 cu m; fish catch (1999) 419,000. *Mining and quarrying* (1998): copper ore 14,500,000; iron ore 12,300,000; gypsum 9,750,000. *Manufacturing* (value added in $'000,-000; 1995): iron and steel 1,393; food products 1,170; textiles 989. *Energy production (consumption):* electricity (kW-hr; 2000–01) 120,611,000,000 (120,611,000,000); coal (metric tons; 1997) 1,750,000 (1,320,000); crude petroleum (barrels; 1999–2000) 1,255,000,000 (496,000,000); petroleum products (metric tons; 1997) 50,135,000 (53,936,000); natural gas (cu m; 1999–2000) 80,000,000,000 (58,700,000,000). **Population economically active** (2000–01): total 18,700,000; activity rate 29.3% (participation rates: over age 15 [1996] 44.0%; female [1996] 12.7%; unemployed 13.9%). **Household income and expenditure.** Average household size (1999) 5.0; income per urban household (1988) Rls 1,339,970 ($19,536); sources of urban income (1988): wages 37.4%, self-employment 30.5%, other 32.1%; expenditure (1990–91): food, beverages, and tobacco 42.6%, housing and energy 24.9%, clothing 11.8%, household furnishings 6.4%. **Land use** (1994): forest 7.0%; pasture 26.9%; agriculture 11.1%; other 55.0%.

## Foreign trade

**Imports** (1998–99): $14,286,000,000 (nonelectrical machinery 24.4%, electrical machinery 10.6%, transportation equipment 9.3%, iron and steel 9.0%, grains and derivatives 6.1%). *Major import sources:* Germany 11.6%; Italy 8.3%; Japan 7.0%; Belgium 6.3%; UAE 5.3%; Argentina 4.4%. **Exports** (1998–99): $13,118,000,000 (petroleum and natural gas 75.7%, fruit 4.5%, carpets 4.3%, iron and steel 1.1%). *Major export destinations:* UK 16.8%; Japan 15.7%; Italy 8.6%; UAE 6.7%; South Korea 5.0%; Greece 5.0%; Turkey 3.8%.

## Transport and communications

**Transport.** *Railroads* (1999): route length 6,300 km; passenger-km 6,103,000,000 (1997); metric ton-km cargo 14,400,000,000 (1997). *Roads* (1997): length 165,724 km (paved 50%). *Vehicles* (1996): passenger cars 1,793,000; trucks and buses 692,000. *Air transport* (2000; Iran Air): passenger-km 6,228,670,000; metric ton-km cargo 72,150,-000; airports (1996) 19. **Communications,** in total units (units per 1,000 persons). Daily newspaper circulation (1996): 1,651,000 (28); radio receivers (1997): 17,000,000 (280); television receivers (1999): 10,500,000 (157); telephone main lines (2001): 10,005,000 (155); cellular telephone subscribers (2001): 1,485,000 (23); personal computers (2001): 4,500,000 (70); Internet users (2001): 402,000 (6.2).

## Education and health

**Educational attainment** (1986). Percentage of population age 25 and over having: no formal schooling 12.8%; secondary education 38.0%; higher 7.8%. **Literacy** (1997): total population age 15 and over literate 73.4%; males literate 79.7%; females literate 65.9%. **Health** (1998–99): physicians 60,000 (1 per 1,033 persons); hospital beds 98,669 (1 per 628 persons); infant mortality rate per 1,000 live births (2000) 30.0. **Food** (2000): daily per capita caloric intake 2,913 (vegetable products 91%, animal products 9%); 121% of FAO recommended minimum.

## Military

**Total active duty personnel** (2001): 513,000 (revolutionary guard corps 24.4%, army 63.4%, navy 3.5%, air force 8.7%). **Military expenditure as percentage of GNP** (1999): 2.9% (world 2.4%); per capita expenditure $106.

 **Did you know?** Iran is the only country in the Middle East that uses the Islamic solar calendar, which is based on the ancient Iranian calendar that came into use before the beginning of the Persian Empire (550 BC). The Arabic lunar calendar is used for religious observances.

## Background

Habitation in Iran dates to c. 100,000 BC, but recorded history began with the Elamites c. 3000 BC. The Medes flourished from c. 728 BC but were overthrown (550 BC) by the Persians, who were in turn conquered by Alexander the Great in the 4th century BC. The Parthians created a Greek-speaking empire that lasted from 247 BC to AD 226, when control passed to the Sasanians. Arab Muslims conquered them in 640 and ruled Iran for 850 years. In 1502 the Safavids established a dynasty that lasted until 1736. The Qajars ruled from 1779, but in the 19th century the country was economically controlled by the Russian and British empires. Reza Khan seized power in a coup (1921). His son Mohammad Reza Shah Pahlavi alienated religious leaders with a program of modernization and Westernization and was overthrown in 1979; Shi'ite cleric Ruhollah Khomeini then set up a fundamentalist Islamic republic, and Western influence was suppressed. The destructive Iran-Iraq War of the 1980s ended in a stalemate. During the 1990s the government gradually moved to a more liberal conduct of state affairs.

## Recent Developments

Iran was deeply affected by the state of the union address by Pres. George W. Bush on 29 Jan 2002, in which he denounced Iran's leading role in an "axis of evil." Senior officials in the Bush administration alleged that the Iranian government was sympathetic to the Taliban regime in Afghanistan and supportive of the al-Qaeda movement. For the rest of 2002, the president and other key US representatives continued to list Iran as a "rogue state" that supported terrorism, persisted in developing weapons of mass destruction, and deliberately impeded the Middle East peace process. Feeling itself under the threat of an attack by the US once the Afghan and Iraqi campaigns had been completed, the Iranian regime was forced into a change in foreign policy. The established pattern of anti-American propaganda came to a temporary halt, and efforts were made to appease the US. In response to alarm at allegations that Iran was developing weapons of mass destruction, it was announced that an advanced ballistic missile program would be curtailed, though other missile developments continued. Iran also rounded up al-Qaeda suspects.

**Internet resources:** <www.irantourism.org>

# Iraq

**Official name:** Al-Jumhuriyah al-'Iraqiyah (Republic of Iraq). **Form of government:** transitional regime. **Head of state and government:** President Saddam Hussein (1979—April 2003; Coalition military authority thereafter [Supreme Commander of occupational forces John Abizaid from 7 Jul 2003]). **Capital:** Baghdad. **Official language:** Arabic (Kurdish is official in the Kurdish Autonomous Region). **Official religion:** Islam. **Monetary unit:** 1 Iraqi dinar (ID) = 20 dirhams = 1,000 fils; valuation (7 Jul 2003) $1 = ID .311.

---

*1 metric ton = about 1.1 short tons;    1 kilometer = 0.6 mi (statute);    1 metric ton-km cargo = about 0.68 short ton-mi cargo;    c.i.f.: cost, insurance, and freight;    f.o.b.: free on board*

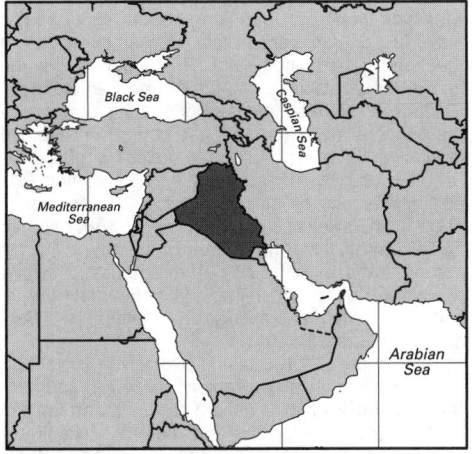

## Demography

**Area:** 167,975 sq mi, 435,052 sq km. **Population** (2002): 24,002,000. **Density** (2002): persons per sq mi 142.9, persons per sq km 55.2. **Urban** (1999): 76.4%. **Sex distribution** (2001): male 50.57%; female 49.43%. **Age breakdown** (2000): under 15, 42.1%; 15–29, 30.4%; 30–44, 15.6%; 45–59, 7.4%; 60–74, 3.5%; 75 and over, 1.0%. **Ethnic composition** (2000): Arab 64.7%; Kurd 23.0%; Azerbaijani 5.6%; Turkmen 1.2%; Persian 1.1%; other 4.4%. **Religious affiliation** (2000): Shi'i Muslim 62.0%; Sunni Muslim 34.0%; Christian (primarily Chaldean rite and Syrian rite Catholic and Nestorian) 3.2%; other (primarily Yazidi syncretist) 0.8%. **Major cities:** Baghdad (2001) 4,958,000; Irbil (2000) 2,369,000; Mosul (2000) 1,131,000; Karkuk (1987) 418,624; Al-Basrah (1987) 406,296. **Location:** Middle East, bordering Turkey, Iran, the Persian Gulf, Kuwait, Saudi Arabia, Jordan, and Syria.

## Vital statistics

**Birth rate** per 1,000 population (2001): 34.6 (world avg. 21.2). **Death rate** per 1,000 population (2001): 6.2 (world avg. 8.9). **Natural increase rate** per 1,000 population (2001): 28.4 (world avg. 12.3). **Total fertility rate** (avg. births per childbearing woman; 2001): 4.8. **Marriage rate** per 1,000 population (1997): 6.3. **Divorce rate** per 1,000 population (1997): 1.3. **Life expectancy** at birth (2001): male 65.9 years; female 68.0 years.

## National economy

**Budget** (1992). *Revenue*: ID 13,935,000,000. *Expenditures*: ID 13,935,000,000. Details of more recent budgets are not available. **Production** (metric tons except as noted). *Agriculture, forestry, fishing* (2001): wheat 550,000, tomatoes 500,000, barley 465,000; livestock (number of live animals) 6,780,-000 sheep, 1,350,000 cattle; roundwood (2000) 110,309 cu m; fish catch (1999) 26,789. *Mining and quarrying* (2000): phosphate rock 300,000, sulfur 250,000. *Manufacturing* (value added in $'000,000; 1994): refined petroleum 127; bricks, tiles, and cement 100; industrial chemicals 79. *Energy production (consumption)*: electricity (kW-hr; 1999) 26,000,000,000 (31,563,000,000); crude petroleum (barrels; 2001) 853,225,000 ([1997] 214,678,-000); petroleum products (metric tons; 1997)

23,730,000 (21,531,000); natural gas (cu m; 1999) 4,000,000,000 (4,000,000,000). **Household income and expenditure** (1988). Average household size 8.9; sources of income: self-employment 33.9%, wages and salaries 23.9%, transfers 23.0%, rent 18.6%; expenditure: food and beverages 50.2%, housing and energy 19.9%, clothing and footwear 10.6%. **Gross domestic product** (2000): $20,000,000,000 ($900 per capita). **Public debt** (external, outstanding; 1999): $23,000,000,000. **Population economically active** (1996): total 5,573,000; activity rate of total population 27.6% (participation rates: ages 15–64, 45.7%; female 25.0%). **Tourism** (1997): receipts $13,000,-000. **Land use** (1994): forest 0.4%; pasture 9.1%; agriculture 13.1%; other 77.4%.

## Foreign trade

UN-imposed trade sanctions were in place from August 1990 through September 2002. **Imports** (1999-c.i.f.): $4,400,000,000 (agricultural products 41.9%, of which cereals 17.5%; unspecified 58.1%). *Major import sources* (1996): Turkey 36.5%; Jordan 26.3%; Malaysia 3.7%; Australia 3.0%. **Exports** (1999-f.o.b.): $4,960,000,000 (mostly crude petroleum and petroleum products). *Major export destinations* (1996): Jordan 91.5%; Turkey 5.8%.

## Transport and communications

**Transport.** *Railroads* (1999): route length 2,603 km; passenger-km 499,600,000; metric ton-km cargo 830,200,000. *Roads* (1999): total length 45,550 km (paved 84%). *Vehicles* (1998): passenger cars 735,521; trucks and buses 349,202. **Communications**, in total units (units per 1,000 persons). Daily newspaper circulation (1996): 407,000 (20); radio receivers (1997): 4,850,000 (229); television receivers (1997): 1,750,000 (78); telephone main lines (1999): 675,000 (30).

## Education and health

**Educational attainment** (1987). Percentage of population age 10 and over having: no formal schooling 52.8%; primary education 21.5%; secondary 11.6%; higher 4.1%; unknown 10.0%. **Literacy** (1995): total population age 15 and over literate 58.0%; males 70.7%; females 45.0%. **Health** (1998): physicians 11,046 (1 per 1,937 persons); hospital beds 30,022 (1 per 713 persons); infant mortality rate per 1,000 live births (2001) 60.0. **Food** (2000): daily per capita caloric intake 2,197 (vegetable products 96%, animal products 4%); 91% of FAO recommended minimum.

## Military

**Total active duty personnel** (2001): 429,000 (army 91.3%, navy 0.5%, air force 8.2%). Military expenditure as percentage of GDP (1999): 5.5% (world 2.4%); per capita expenditure $57.

## Background

Called Mesopotamia in classical times, the region gave rise to the world's earliest civilizations, including those of Sumer, Akkad, and Babylon. Conquered by Alexander the Great in 330 BC, the area later became a battleground between Romans and Parthians, then between Sasanians and the Byzantines. Arab Muslims conquered it in the 7th century AD and ruled until the

Mongols took over in 1258. The Ottomans took control in the 16th century and ruled until 1917. The British occupied the country during World War I and created the kingdom of Iraq in 1921. The British occupied Iraq again during World War II. A king was restored following the war, but a revolution ended the monarchy in 1958. Following a series of military coups, the socialist Ba'th Party, led by Saddam Hussein, took control and established totalitarian rule in 1968. The Iran-Iraq War of the 1980s and the Persian Gulf War (precipitated by the Iraqi invasion of Kuwait in 1990) brought heavy casualties and disrupted the economy. The 1990s were dominated by economic turmoil.

## Recent Developments

In 2002 US Pres. George W. Bush accused Iraq—along with Iran and North Korea—of being part of an "axis of evil." Bush charged Iraq with being hostile toward the US and supporting terrorism. Bush adopted the notion of replacing Pres. Saddam Hussein with a democratic regime by any means, including the use of US military force. Iraqi officials vowed to fight this change, and the war of words continued throughout the year. In preparation for a possible invasion, the US increased its military presence at its bases in the Middle East and pressured Arab and European countries to join in an anti-Iraq political and military alliance. Among the countries approached by the US, the UK evinced the most support for military action against Iraq, while Germany was outspoken in its opposition. France and Russia objected to US unilateralism, claiming that punitive action could be taken only within the framework of the UN and only in the event that Iraq continued to defy UN resolutions.

After several months of discussion, on 14 May the Security Council adopted a new resolution easing the UN economic sanctions on Iraq imposed after Iraq's invasion of Kuwait in 1990. According to the new resolution, Iraq would be permitted, without seeking advance approval, to import all products needed for nonmilitary civilian use.

By the summer, international attention was focusing on the return of UN inspectors to Iraq to search for weapons of mass destruction and to destroy any that were found. Iraq objected to the return of inspectors, claiming that they had finished their work and that in any event Iraq no longer possessed chemical, biological, or nuclear weapons or proscribed long-range missiles. Faced with US threats and international pressure, Baghdad suddenly changed its policy and, on 16 September, announced that it would accept a new round of weapons inspections, thereby dividing the members of the UN Security Council over how to proceed. By the end of September, the Bush administration had proposed giving Iraq a seven-day deadline to accept a new UN resolution with stiff conditions for weapons inspections, which Iraqi leaders rejected. In October Congress gave the president the right to use force in Iraq. In late November the first UN weapons inspectors arrived, and in December Iraq submitted a 12,000-page declaration on the status of its weapons program, which indicated that in the past it had secretly attempted to get equipment from a number of countries for nuclear weapons.

Both sides hardened their positions during the first months of 2003. Weapons inspectors pressed ahead with their work, and Saddam Hussein continued to make just enough concessions to keep international reactions divided. The US and UK lost patience by the end of January and declared that Iraq was clearly in violation of UN resolutions—this despite a report by the weapons inspectors that Iraq had never resumed its nuclear weapons program, a major US allegation. On 5 February, working toward a UN resolution supporting the use of military force, US Secretary of State Colin Powell laid out the evidence that Iraq had not disarmed. Meanwhile, from mid-February, huge demonstrations were held throughout the world against military action in Iraq. In late February the US laid down an ultimatum for Iraq to disarm and Saddam to go into exile.

Forces of the US-UK coalition struck with Tomahawk cruise missiles at a government bunker in southern Baghdad on 20 March (local time) in an attempt to kill Saddam and his sons and thereby "decapitate" the Iraqi regime. Intense pinpoint bombing of Baghdad ensued. Coalition ground troops moved into Iraq from Kuwait. They quickly took the oil terminal at Umm Qasr and began moving up the great river valleys of central Iraq. A command in the northern, largely Kurdish part of the country was established on 24 March. Ground forces had taken Baghdad by 9 April. With the fall of the Saddam Hussein regime and the absence for several days of any civil authority by the coalition, widespread looting further damaged the country's infrastructure. An occupation administration was established, while the major powers again fell to squabbling over who would take the lead in the postwar rebuilding of Iraq.

**Internet resources:** <www.uruklink.net/iraqinfo>

# Ireland

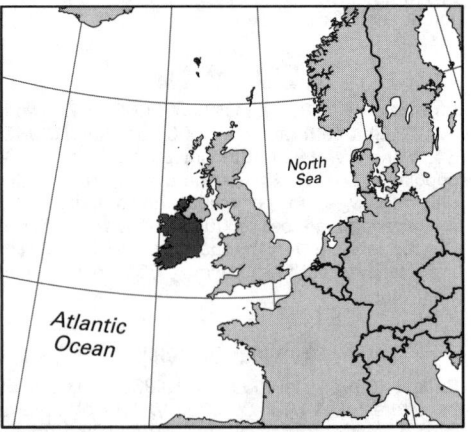

North Sea

Atlantic Ocean

**Official name:** Éire (Irish); Ireland (English). **Form of government:** unitary multiparty republic with two legislative houses (Senate [60, including 11 nonelective seats]; House of Representatives [166]). **Chief of state:** President Mary McAleese (from 1997). **Head of government:** Prime Minister Bertie Ahern (from 1997). **Capital:** Dublin. **Official languages:** Irish; English. **Official religion:** none. **Monetary unit:** 1 euro (€) = 100 cents; valuation (7 Jul 2003) $1 = €0.87; at conversion on 1 Jan 2002, €1= 0.79 Irish pound (£Ir).

1 metric ton = about 1.1 short tons;    1 kilometer = 0.6 mi (statute);    1 metric ton-km cargo = about 0.68 short ton-mi cargo;    c.i.f.: cost, insurance, and freight;    f.o.b.: free on board

## Demography

**Area:** 27,133 sq mi, 70,273 sq km. **Population** (2002): 3,926,000. **Density** (2002): persons per sq mi 147.6, persons per sq km 57.0. **Urban** (1996): 58.0%. **Sex distribution** (2002): male 49.66%; female 50.34%. **Age breakdown** (2000): under 15, 21.9%; 15–29, 24.9%; 30–44, 21.1%; 45–59, 16.9%; 60–74, 10.3%; 75 and over, 4.9%. **Ethnic composition** (2000): Irish 95.0%; British 1.7%, of which English 1.4%; Ulster Irish 1.0%; US white 0.8%; other 1.5%. **Religious affiliation** (1991): Roman Catholic 91.6%; Church of Ireland (Anglican) 2.5%; Presbyterian 0.4%; other 5.5%. **Major cities** (2002; for Ireland's five administrative county boroughs): Dublin 495,101 (urban agglomeration 1,122,600); Cork 123,338; Galway 65,774; Limerick 54,058; Waterford 44,564. **Location:** western Europe, bordering the UK (Northern Ireland), the Irish Sea, the Celtic Sea, and the North Atlantic Ocean.

## Vital statistics

**Birth rate** per 1,000 population (2000): 14.3 (world avg. 22.5). **Death rate** per 1,000 population (2000): 8.2 (world avg. 9.0). **Natural increase rate** per 1,000 population (2000): 6.1 (world avg. 13.5). **Marriage rate** per 1,000 population (2000): 5.1. **Total fertility rate** (avg. births per childbearing woman; 2000): 1.9. **Life expectancy** at birth (2000): male 74.1 years; female 79.7 years.

## National economy

**Budget** (2000). *Revenue*: £Ir 21,741,000,000 (income taxes 33.0%, value-added tax 27.0%, excise taxes 15.4%). *Expenditures*: £Ir 19,297,000,000 (social welfare 27.9%, health 20.9%, education 14.9%, debt service 10.5%). **Public debt** (1996): $47,876,-000,000. **Gross national product** (2000): $85,979,000,000 ($22,660 per capita). **Tourism** (2000): receipts $3,387,000,000; expenditures $2,957,000,000. **Production** (metric tons except as noted). *Agriculture, forestry, fishing* (2000): sugar beets 1,564,000, barley 1,129,000, wheat 706,000; livestock (number of live animals) 8,393,000 sheep, 6,607,500 cattle, 1,763,000 pigs; roundwood (2000) 2,673,000 cu m; fish catch (1999) 329,777. *Mining and quarrying* (1999): gypsum 480,000; zinc ore 199,300; lead ore 44,100. *Manufacturing* (value added in £Ir '000,000; 1995): office equipment and computers 2,163; basic chemicals 2,112; reproduction of recorded media 1,531. *Energy production (consumption)*: electricity (kW-hr; 1997) 19,856,-000,000 (19,856,000,000); coal (metric tons; 1997) none (3,070,000); crude petroleum (barrels; 1997) none (20,800,000); petroleum products (metric tons; 1997) 2,795,000 (5,616,000); natural gas (cu m; 1997) 1,012,000,000 (3,242,000,000). **Population economically active** (2000): total 1,745,600; activity rate 46.1% (participation rates: ages 15–64, c. 68%; female 40.3%; unemployed 4.3%). **Household income and expenditure.** Average household size (1997) 3.1; income per household (1994–95): £Ir 16,224 ($25,100); expenditure (1996): food and beverages 35.4%, transportation 13.9%, rent/household goods 11.6%.

## Foreign trade

**Imports** (1999-c.i.f.): £Ir 34,682,100,000 (machinery and transport equipment 51.5%, chemicals 11.2%, manufactured goods 11.0%, food 5.8%, petroleum and petroleum products 2.8%). *Major import sources:* UK 33.1%; US 16.7%; Germany 6.2%; Japan 5.8%; France 4.1%. **Exports** (1999-f.o.b.): £Ir 52,537,200,000 (machinery and transport equipment 38.8%, chemical products 31.6%, manufactured goods 11.1%, food 8.2%). *Major export destinations:* UK 22.0%; US 15.4%; Germany 11.9%; France 8.4%; The Netherlands 6.0%.

## Transport and communications

**Transport.** *Railroads* (1999): route length 1,945 km; passenger-km 1,295,000,000; metric ton-km cargo 570,000,000. *Roads* (1999): length 92,500 km (paved 94%). *Vehicles* (2000): passenger cars 1,269,245; trucks and buses 188,814. *Air transport* (2000; Aer Lingus only): passenger-km 9,385,039,-000; metric ton-km cargo 1,005,296,000; airports (1996) 9. **Communications,** in total units (units per 1,000 persons). Daily newspaper circulation (1996): 543,000 (150); radio receivers (1998): 2,150,000 (580); television receivers (1999): 2,144,000 (578); telephone main lines (2001): 1,860,000 (480); cellular telephone subscribers (2001): 2,800,000 (722); personal computers (2001): 1,500,000 (387); Internet users (2001): 895,000 (231).

## Education and health

**Educational attainment** (1991). Percentage of population age 15 and over having: primary education or no schooling 33.7%; secondary 42.7%; some postsecondary 12.6%; university or like institution 11.0%. **Health:** physicians (1998) 8,114 (1 per 457 persons); hospital beds (1995) 11,953 (1 per 301 persons); infant mortality rate per 1,000 live births (2000) 5.6. **Food** (2000): daily per capita caloric intake 3,613 (vegetable products 68%, animal products 32%); 144% of FAO recommended minimum.

## Military

**Total active duty personnel** (2001): 10,460 (army 81.3%, navy 10.5%, air force 8.2%). **Military expenditure as percentage of GNP** (1999): 1.0% (world 2.4%); per capita expenditure $208.

## Background

Human settlement in Ireland began c. 6000 BC, and Celtic migration dates from c. 300 BC. St. Patrick is credited with Christianizing the country in the 5th century AD. Norse domination began in 795 and ended in 1014, when the Norse were defeated by Brian Boru. Gaelic Ireland's independence ended in 1171 when English king Henry II proclaimed himself overlord of the island. Beginning in the 16th century, Irish Catholic landowners fled religious persecution by the English and were replaced by English and Scottish Protestant migrants. The United Kingdom of Great Britain and Ireland was established in 1801. The Great Famine of the 1840s led over 2 million people to emigrate and built momentum for Irish Home Rule. The Easter Rising (1916) was followed by civil war (1919–21) between the Catholic majority in southern Ireland, who favored complete independence, and the Protestant majority in the north, who preferred continued union with Britain. Southern Ireland was granted dominion status and became the Irish Free State in 1921, and in 1937 it adopted the name Éire and became a sovereign independent nation. It remained neutral during World War II. Britain recognized the status of Ireland in 1949 but declared that cession of the northern six counties could not occur without the consent of the Parliament of Northern Ireland. In 1973 Ireland joined the European Economic Community (later the European Community) and is now a member of the European Union. The late 20th century was dominated by sectarian hostilities between the island's Catholics and Protestants.

## Recent Developments

Double-digit growth, a healthy tax base, moderate inflation, and extremely low unemployment had earned Ireland the soubriquet "the Celtic Tiger," but the economic boom that peaked in 1999–2000 finally petered out in 2002. Budget surpluses became a memory, spending for health and education was cut back, and infrastructure developments were scaled down or deferred. On 19 October the Irish electorate said "yes" to a second referendum on the Treaty of Nice. The 63–37% vote cleared the way for reform of the EU and for the admission of 10 new member states. In an earlier referendum held in June 2001, the electorate had rejected the treaty by a small majority but with a low turnout.

Internet resources: <www.ireland.ie>

# Isle of Man

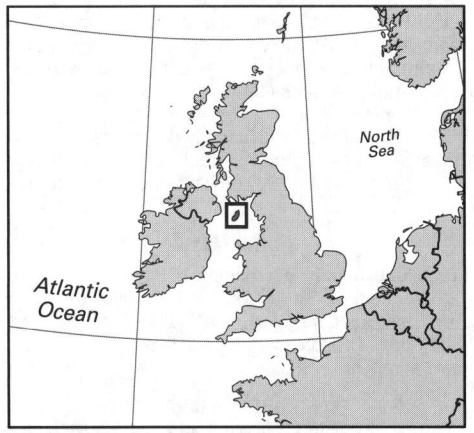

North Sea

Atlantic Ocean

**Official name:** Isle of Man (Manx Gaelic: Ellan Vannin). **Political status:** crown dependency (UK) with Tynwald comprising two legislative bodies (Legislative Council [11, including 3 nonelective seats]; House of Keys [24]). **Chief of state:** Queen Elizabeth II represented by Lieutenant Governor Ian David Macfadyen (from 2000). **Head of government:** Chief Minister Richard Corkill (from 2001). **Capital:** Douglas. **Official language:** English. **Official religion:** none. **Monetary unit:** 1 Manx pound (£M) = 100 new pence; valuation (7 Jul 2003) $1 = £M.60; the Manx pound is equivalent in value to the pound sterling.

## Demography

**Area:** 227 sq mi, 588.1 km. **Population** (2002): 76,900. **Density** (2002): persons per sq mi 338.6,

persons per sq km 130.8. **Urban** (1999): 76.3%. **Sex distribution** (2001): male 48.97%; female 51.03%. **Age breakdown** (2001): under 15, 17.9%; 15–29, 17.5%; 30–44, 22.6%; 45–59, 20.1%; 60–74, 13.6%; 75 and over, 8.3%. **Population by place of birth** (2001): Isle of Man 48.0%; UK 45.2%, of which England 38.2%, Scotland 3.5%, Northern Ireland 2.3%, Wales 1.2%; Ireland 2.3%; other Europe 1.0%; South Africa 0.5%. **Religious affiliation** (2000): Christian 63.7%, of which Anglican 40.5%, Methodist 9.9%, Roman Catholic 8.2%; other (mostly nonreligious) 36.3%. **Major towns** (2001): Douglas 25,347; Onchan 8,803; Ramsey 7,322; Peel 3,785; Port Erin 3,369. **Location:** Irish Sea, midway between Ireland and Great Britain.

## Vital statistics

**Birth rate** per 1,000 population (2000): 11.0 (world avg. 22.5); legitimate 66.2%; illegitimate 33.8%. **Death rate** per 1,000 population (2000): 11.9 (world avg. 9.0). **Natural increase rate** per 1,000 population (2000): –0.9 (world avg. 13.5). **Total fertility rate** (avg. births per childbearing woman; 1999): 1.6. **Marriage rate** per 1,000 population (2000): 5.5. **Divorce rate** per 1,000 population (1996): 4.0. **Life expectancy** at birth (1999): male 73.9 years; female 80.8 years.

## National economy

**Budget** (1999–2000). *Revenue:* £339,070,000 (customs duties and excise taxes 54.1%; income taxes 44.7%, of which resident 40.0%, nonresident 4.7%). *Expenditures:* £291,804,000 (health and social security 40.2%; education 18.8%; home affairs 6.8%; transportation 6.5%; tourism and recreation 5.5%). **Production.** *Agriculture, forestry, fishing* (1998): main crops include hay, oats, barley, wheat, and orchard crops; livestock (number of live animals) 173,900 sheep, 34,000 cattle, 6,600 pigs; fish catch (value of catch in £; 1997): scallops 1,666,000, whitefish 244,000, herring 138,000. *Mining and quarrying:* sand and gravel. *Manufacturing* (value added in $; 1996–97): electrical and nonelectrical machinery/apparatus, textiles, other 103,700,000; food and beverages 18,600,000. *Energy production (consumption):* electricity (kW-hr; 1999–2000), n.a. (307,400,000). **Household income and expenditure.** Average household size (2001) 2.4; income per household (1981–82) £7,479 ($13,721); sources of income (1981–82): wages and salaries 64.1%, transfer payments 16.9%, interest and dividends 11.2%, self-employment 6.6%; expenditure (1981–82): food and beverages 31.0%, transportation 14.9%, energy 11.0%, housing 7.9%, clothing and footwear 7.0%. **Gross national product** (at current market prices; 1998–99): $1,485,000,000 ($20,030 per capita). **Population economically active** (2001): total 39,685; activity rate of total population 52.0% (participation rates: ages 16 and over 64.2%; female 45.4%; unemployed 1.6%). **Tourism:** receipts from visitors (1999) $90,600,000.

## Foreign trade

**Imports** (1998): n.a. *Major import sources* (1998): mostly UK. **Exports** (1998): traditional exports include scallops, herring, beef, lambs, and tweeds. *Major export destinations* (1998): mostly UK.

*1 metric ton = about 1.1 short tons;   1 kilometer = 0.6 mi (statute);   1 metric ton-km cargo = about 0.68 short ton-mi cargo;   c.i.f.: cost, insurance, and freight;   f.o.b.: free on board*

## Transport and communications

**Transport.** *Railroads* (1998): route length 52 km. *Roads* (1998): total length, more than 805 km. *Vehicles* (1998): passenger cars 40,168. *Air transport* (1998; Manx Airlines): passenger-km 846,775,000; metric ton-km cargo 168,000; airports (1999) with scheduled flights 1. **Communications,** in total units (units per 1,000 persons). Daily newspaper circulation (1997): none (Isle of Man has 2 weekly and 1 biweekly newspapers); television receivers (1997): 27,000 (375); telephone main lines (1996): 46,000 (641).

## Health

**Health:** physicians (2000) 138 (1 per 547 persons); hospital beds (1998) 505 (1 per 143 persons); infant mortality rate per 1,000 live births (1998–2000 avg.) 4.5. **Food** (1998): daily per capita caloric intake 3,257 (vegetable products 68%, animal products 32%); 129% of FAO recommended minimum.

## Military

**Total active duty personnel:** the UK is responsible for defense.

## Israel

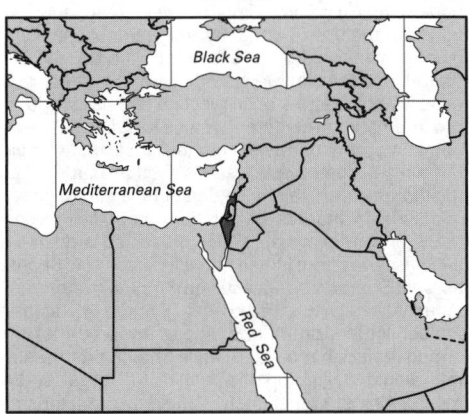

**Official name:** Medinat Yisra'el (Hebrew); Isra'il (Arabic) (State of Israel). **Form of government:** multiparty republic with one legislative house (Knesset [120]). **Chief of state:** President Moshe Katzav (from 2000). **Head of government:** Prime Minister Ariel Sharon (from 2001). **Capital:** Jerusalem is the proclaimed capital of Israel and the actual seat of government, but recognition of its status as capital by the international community has largely been withheld pending final settlement of territorial and other issues through peace talks between Israel and the Arab parties concerned. **Official languages:** Hebrew; Arabic. **Official religion:** none. **Monetary unit:** 1 New (Israeli) shekel (NIS) = 100 agorot; valuation (7 Jul 2003) $1 = NIS 4.30.

## Demography

**Area:** 7,886 sq mi, 20,425 sq km. **Population** (2002): 6,394,000. **Density** (2002; includes 2002 population of Golan Heights [35,000] and East Jerusalem and excludes 2002 Jewish population of

the West Bank and Gaza Strip [220,000]): persons per sq mi 810.8, persons per sq km 313.0. **Urban** (2000): 90.6%. **Sex distribution** (2000): male 49.33%; female 50.67%. **Age breakdown** (2000): under 15, 28.6%; 15–29, 25.1%; 30–44, 18.7%; 45–59, 14.5%; 60–74, 8.8%; 75 and over, 4.3%. **Ethnic composition** (2000): Jewish 78.1%; Arab and other 21.9%. **Religious affiliation** (2000): Jewish 78.1%; Muslim (mostly Sunni) 15.1%; Christian 2.1%; Druze 1.6%; other 3.1%. **Major cities** (2001): Jerusalem 657,500; Tel Aviv–Yafo 354,400; Haifa 270,500; Rishon LeZiyyon 202,200; Petah Tiqwa 167,500. **Location:** Middle East, bordering Lebanon, Syria, Jordan, West Bank, Egypt, and the Gaza Strip.

## Vital statistics

**Birth rate** per 1,000 population (2000): 21.7 (world avg. 22.5); (1994; Jewish only) legitimate 98.2%; illegitimate 1.8%. **Death rate** per 1,000 population (2000): 6.0 (world avg. 9.0). **Natural increase rate** per 1,000 population (2000): 15.7 (world avg. 13.5). **Total fertility rate** (avg. births per childbearing woman; 2000): 3.0. **Marriage rate** per 1,000 population (1999): 6.6. **Divorce rate** per 1,000 population (1999): 1.7. **Life expectancy** at birth (2000): male 76.6 years; female 80.4 years.

## National economy

**Budget** (2000). *Revenue:* NIS 178,037,000,000 (tax revenue 74.6%, of which income tax and property tax 34.7%, value-added tax 26.0%, sales tax and fuel tax 4.7%; nontax revenue 18.5%; grants 6.9%). *Expenditures:* NIS 188,927,000,000 (defense 20.7%; education 14.8%; interest on loans 13.9%; labor and welfare 12.1%; health 8.5%). **Public debt** (external, outstanding; 1999): $27,323,000,000. **Gross national product** (2000): $104,128,000,000 ($16,710 per capita). **Production** (metric tons except as noted). *Agriculture, forestry, fishing* (2000): tomatoes 550,200, grapefruit 370,000, potatoes 348,600; livestock (number of live animals) 388,000 cattle, 350,000 sheep; roundwood (2000) 113,000 cu m; fish catch (1999) 24,661. *Mining and quarrying* (1999): phosphate rock 4,100,000, potash 1,750,000. *Manufacturing* (1996): cement 6,723,000; paper 114,403; cardboard 113,278. *Energy production (consumption):* electricity (kW-hr; 2000) 42,916,000 (39,317,000); coal (metric tons; 1997) none (8,639,000); crude petroleum (barrels; 1997) 36,000 (80,340,000); petroleum products (metric tons; 1997) 9,637,000 (9,514,000); natural gas (cu m; 1997) 13,272,000 (13,272,000). **Population economically active** (2000): total 2,435,000; activity rate 39.9% (participation rates: over age 15, 54.3%; female 45.6%; unemployed 8.8%). **Household income and expenditure** (1999). Average household size 3.6; monthly income per household (1995) NIS 6,125 ($2,034); sources of income (1993): salaries and wages 63.4%, allowances and assistance 18.9%, self-employment 14.6%; expenditure (1998): housing 23.7%, food, beverages, and tobacco 21.1%, household durable goods 8.2%. **Tourism** (2000): receipts $3,819,000,000; expenditures $2,804,000,000.

## Foreign trade

**Imports** (2000): $35,749,500,000 (investment goods 21.3%; diamonds 17.0%; consumer goods 12.3%; fuel and lubricants 6.0%). *Major import* sources: US 20.7%; Belgium 11.1%; Germany 8.1%; UK 7.6%; Italy 5.3%. **Exports** (2000): $31,403,-700,000 (machinery and transport equipment 39.7%; diamonds 23.7%; chemicals 13.4%; apparel 4.9%; food, beverages, and tobacco 3.1%). Major export destinations: US 35.5%; UK 5.5%; Belgium 5.4%; Germany 4.5%; Hong Kong 3.4%; Japan 3.3%.

## Transport and communications

**Transport.** Railroads (1999): route length 610 km; passenger-km 529,000,000; metric ton-km cargo 1,128,000,000. Roads (1999): total length 15,464 km (paved 100%). Vehicles (2000): passenger cars 1,316,765; trucks and buses 319,581. Air transport (2000; El Al only): passenger-km 14,125,067,000; metric ton-km cargo 1,288,345,000; airports (1999) with scheduled flights 7. **Communications,** in total units (units per 1,000 persons). Daily newspaper circulation (1997): 1,650,000 (288); radio receivers (1997): 3,070,000 (524); television receivers (1999): 1,690,000 (288); telephone main lines (2001): 3,100,000 (476); cellular telephone subscribers (2001): 5,260,000 (808); personal computers (2001): 1,600,000 (246); Internet users (2001): 1,500,000 (231).

## Education and health

**Educational attainment** (2000). Percentage of population age 15 and over having: no formal schooling 3.3%; primary 1.9%; secondary 57.4%; postsecondary, vocational, and higher 37.4%. **Literacy** (2000): total population age 15 and over literate 96.7%. **Health** (2000): physicians 21,500 (1 per 284 persons); hospital beds 38,577 (1 per 158 persons); infant mortality rate per 1,000 live births (2000) 5.1. **Food** (2000): daily per capita caloric intake 3,562 (vegetable products 81%, animal products 19%); 139% of FAO recommended minimum.

## Military

**Total active duty personnel** (2001): 163,500 (army 73.4%, navy 4.0%, air force 22.6%). **Military expenditure as percentage of GNP** (1999): 8.8% (world 2.4%); per capita expenditure $1,510.

## Background

The record of human habitation in Israel is at least 100,000 years old. Efforts by Jews to establish a national state there began in the late 19th century. Britain supported Zionism and in 1922 assumed political responsibility for what was Palestine. Migration of Jews there during Nazi persecution led to deteriorating relations with Arabs. In 1947 the UN voted to partition the region into separate Jewish and Arab states, a decision opposed by neighboring Arab countries. The State of Israel was proclaimed in 1948, and Egypt, Transjordan, Syria, Lebanon, and Iraq immediately declared war on it. Israel won this war as well as the 1967 Six-Day War, in which it claimed the West Bank from Jordan and the Gaza Strip from Egypt. Another war with its Arab neighbors followed in 1973, but the Camp David Accords led to the signing of a peace treaty between Israel and Egypt in 1979. Israel invaded Lebanon to quell the Palestine Liberation Organization

(PLO) in 1982, and in the late 1980s a Palestinian resistance movement arose in the occupied territories. Peace negotiations between Israel and the Arab states and Palestinians began in 1991. Israel and the PLO agreed in 1993 upon a five-year extension of self-government to the Palestinians of the West Bank and the Gaza Strip. Israel signed a full peace treaty with Jordan in 1994. Israeli soldiers and Lebanon's Hezbollah forces clashed in 1997. Following numerous contentious talks between Israel and Lebanon, Israeli troops abruptly withdrew from Lebanon in 2000.

## Recent Developments

Renewed hopes for finding a solution to the intractable problems of Israel and Palestine were raised by a US-sponsored "road map for peace in the Middle East," a specific, graduated, and performance-based plan presented in the spring of 2003. In three planned phases projecting forward to 2005, the road map called for the renunciation of violence and terrorism, the establishment of Palestinian political institutions leading to multiparty elections, the establishment of a Palestinian state with provisional borders and the adoption of a constitution, and international recognition of the new state. Meanwhile Israel was to withdraw from Palestinian territories occupied since 28 Sep 2000, dismantle settlement outposts created since March 2001, and end further settlement activity. Israel was also called upon to cease actions that undermine trust and to improve the humanitarian situation in the area. For its part the international community, monitored by "the Quartet" (the US, the UN, the EU, and Russia), were gradually to normalize relations with both Israel and Palestine and participate in two international conferences, one to support the economic recovery of Palestine and the second to work out a resolution covering issues such as borders and the status of Jerusalem, settlements, and refugees.

Palestinian leaders quickly indicated their acceptance of the road map, which pressured a reluctant acquiescence from Israeli Prime Minister Ariel Sharon as well. Sharon and Palestinian Prime Minister Mahmoud Abbas met with US Pres. George W. Bush in Aqaba, Jordan, on 4 June. Abbas declared that the armed intifadah must end, while Sharon promised Israel would begin the dismantling of illegal settlements. Almost immediately, however, violence flared up as Israeli forces redoubled their attacks on the radical Islamic militant groups such as Hamas, the tempo of Palestinian suicide bombings increased, and Israeli settlers resisted the planned destruction of unofficial settlements. Israeli forces clamped down on the Gaza Strip and Bethlehem but relaxed these measures somewhat as Hamas, in June, declared a three-month cease-fire. At midyear 2003, the road to peace in the Middle East still seemed rocky indeed.

**Internet Resources:** <www.goisrael.com>

# Italy

**Official name:** Repubblica Italiana (Italian Republic). **Form of government:** republic with two legislative houses (Senate [321]; Chamber of Deputies [630]). **Chief of state:** President Carlo Azeglio Ciampi (from 1999). **Head of government:** Prime Minister Silvio

1 metric ton = about 1.1 short tons;   1 kilometer = 0.6 mi (statute);   1 metric ton-km cargo = about 0.68 short ton-mi cargo;   c.i.f.: cost, insurance, and freight;   f.o.b.: free on board

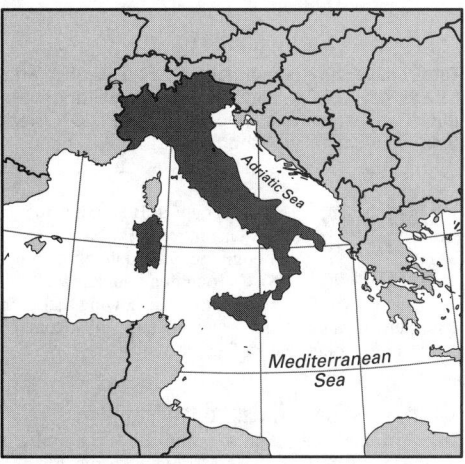

Berlusconi (from 2001). **Capital:** Rome. **Official language:** Italian. **Official religion:** none. **Monetary unit:** 1 euro (€) = 100 cents; valuation (7 Jul 2003) $1 = €0.87; at conversion on 1 Jan 2002, €1= 1,936.27 Italian lire (Lit).

## Demography

**Area:** 116,324 sq mi, 301,277 sq km. **Population** (2002): 57,988,000. **Density** (2002): persons per sq mi 498.4, persons per sq km 192.4. **Urban** (2000): 67.2%. **Sex distribution** (2000): male 48.55%; female 51.45%. **Age breakdown** (2000): under 15, 14.4%; 15–29, 19.5%; 30–44, 23.1%; 45–59, 19.1%; 60–74, 16.1%; 75 and over, 7.8%. **Ethnolinguistic composition** (2000): Italian 96.0%; North African Arab 0.9%; Italo-Albanian 0.8%; Albanian 0.5%; German 0.4%; Austrian 0.4%; other 1.0%. **Religious affiliation** (1996): Roman Catholic 81.7%; nonreligious 13.6%; Muslim 1.2%; other 3.5%. **Major cities** (2000): Rome 2,643,581; Milan 1,300,977; Naples 1,002,619; Turin 903,703; Palermo 683,794; Genoa 636,104; Bologna 381,161; Florence 376,682; Catania 337,862; Bari 331,848; Venice 277,305. **Location:** southern Europe, bordering Switzerland, Austria, Slovenia, the Mediterranean Sea, and France. **National origin** (1991): Italian 99.3%; foreign-born 0.7%, of which European 0.3%, African 0.2%, Asian 0.1%, other 0.1%. **Mobility** (1991). Population living in the same commune as in 1986: 93.3%; another commune, same province 3.4%; different province 2.5%; abroad 0.8%. **Households.** Average household size (1991) 2.7; composition of households: 1 person 19.5%, 2 persons 21.9%, 3 persons 25.2%, 4 persons 21.4%, 5 or more persons 12.0%. Family households (1991): 15,538,335 (73.8%); nonfamily 5,527,105 (26.2%), of which one-person 19.5%. **Immigration** (1997): immigrants 162,857, from Europe 41.1%, of which EU countries 14.2%; Africa 25.5%; Asia 19.0%; Western Hemisphere 14.0%.

## Vital statistics

**Birth rate** per 1,000 population (2000): 9.1 (world avg. 22.5); (1998) legitimate 91.0%; illegitimate 8.0%. **Death rate** per 1,000 population (2000): 10.1 (world avg. 9.0). **Natural increase rate** per 1,000 population (2000): –1.0 (world avg. 13.5). **Total fertility rate** (avg. births per childbearing woman; 2000): 1.2.

**Marriage rate** per 1,000 population (1998): 4.8. **Divorce rate** per 1,000 population (1994): 0.5. **Life expectancy** at birth (2001): male 75.9 years; female 82.5 years.

## Social indicators

**Quality of working life.** Average workweek (1995): 37.0 hours. Annual rate per 100,000 workers (1996) for: injury or accident 3,208; death 7.5. Percentage of labor force insured for damages or income loss (1992) resulting from: injury 100%; permanent disability 100%; death 100%. Number of working days lost to labour stoppages per 1,000 workers (1996): 97. Rate per 1,000 workers of discouraged (unemployed no longer seeking work; 1990): 1.1. **Material well-being.** Rate per 1,000 of population possessing (1995): telephone 434; automobile 550; television 436. **Social participation.** Eligible voters participating in last national election (May 13, 2001): 81.2%. Trade union membership in total workforce (1990): c. 28%. **Social deviance** (1999). Offense rate per 100,000 population for: murder 1.4; rape 68.3; assault 210.4 (1995); theft, including burglary and housebreaking 2,567; suicide 6.3 (1996). **Access to services** (1999). Nearly 100% of dwellings have access to electricity, a safe water supply, and toilet facilities. **Leisure** (1998). Favorite leisure activities (as percentage of household spending on culture): cinema 21.8%; sporting events 14.6%; theater 13.8%.

## National economy

**Gross national product** (2000): $1,163,211,000,000 ($20,160 per capita). **Budget** (1999). *Revenue*: Lit 620,534,000,000,000 (income taxes 46.9%, of which individual 37.5%, corporate 9.4%; value-added and excise taxes 30.6%). *Expenditures*: Lit 668,251,000,000,000 (1995; debt service 27.5%; social security 18.4%; education 9.1%; transportation 4.7%; defense 2.8%). **Public debt** (1999): $766,000,000,000. **Tourism** (2000): receipts $27,500,000,000; expenditures $15,693,000,000. **Production** (metric tons except as noted). *Agriculture, forestry, fishing* (2001): sugar beets 12,000,000, corn (maize) 11,300,000, grapes 9,770,000, tomatoes 6,990,000, wheat 6,500,000, olives 2,780,000, oranges 2,270,000, apples 2,160,000, potatoes 2,100,000, peaches and nectarines 1,730,000, rice 1,300,000, barley 1,250,000, soybeans 1,100,000; livestock (number of live animals) 10,970,000 sheep, 8,400,000 pigs, 7,180,000 cattle, 100,000,000 chickens; roundwood (2000) 9,329,000 cu m; fish catch (1999) 540,523. *Mining and quarrying* (1998): rock salt 3,413,522; feldspar 2,503,541; barite 31,792; lead 10,102; zinc 5,242. *Manufacturing* (1998): cement 33,714,914 (1995); crude steel 25,782,300; pig iron 10,792,700; glass 3,981,104 (1995); textiles 2,340,600 (1997); sulfuric acid 2,013,400; wine 56,896,000 hectolitres; beer 10,616,173 hectolitres (1995); olive oil (2000) 493,000 hectolitres; 6,995,818 washing machines (1995); 5,908,224 refrigerators (1995); 2,779,827 color televisions (1995); 2,723,541 motorized road vehicles, of which 1,378,517 automobiles, 1,062,570 motorcycles, 282,454 trucks and buses. *Energy production (consumption)*: electricity (kW-hr; 2001) 278,904,000,000 ([1997] 289,607,000,000); coal (metric tons; 1997) negligible (16,006,000); crude petroleum (barrels; 2001) 27,714,000 ([1997] 614,938,000); petroleum products (metric tons;

1997) 85,936,000 (90,037,000); natural gas (cu m; 2001) 15,298,000,000 ([1997] 58,001,000,000). **Population economically active** (1999): total 23,135,000; activity rate of total population 40.1% (participation rates: ages 15–64, 57.7% (1996); female 38.2%; unemployed 11.4%). **Household income and expenditure** (1995). Average household size 2.7; average annual income per household (1984) Lit 19,692,000 ($11,208); sources of income (1996): salaries and wages 38.8%, property income and self-employment 38.5%, transfer payments 22.0%; expenditure (1997): food and beverages 18.1%, housing 18.0%, transportation and communications 13.3%, recreation and education 8.4%. **Land use** (1994): forest 23.0%; pasture 15.4%; agriculture 37.9%; other 23.7%.

## Foreign trade

**Imports** (1999-c.i.f.): Lit 394,271,000,000,000 (machinery and transport equipment 38.4%, of which transport equipment 15.1%; chemicals 13.6%; metal 9.8%; food 7.5%; textiles 5.2%; plastics 2.3%). *Major import sources:* Germany 19.0%; France 12.6%; The Netherlands 6.3%; UK 6.1%; US 4.9%; Belgium-Luxembourg 4.6%; Spain 4.3%. **Exports** (1999-f.o.b.): Lit 419,124,000,000,000 (machinery and transport equipment 41.7%, of which transport equipment 11.5%, electrical machinery 9.8%; textiles and wearing apparel 10.7%; chemicals 8.9%; plastics 3.7%). *Major export destinations:* Germany 16.5%; France 13.0%; US 9.5%; UK 7.1%; Spain 6.3%.

## Transport and communications

**Transport.** *Railroads*: (1997) length 19,527 km; (1998) passenger-km 41,392,000,000; (1998) metric ton-km cargo 22,386,000,000. *Roads* (1997): total length 308,139 km (paved 100%). *Vehicles* (1998): passenger cars 31,370,000; trucks and buses 5,127,000. *Air transport* (2001; Alitalia only): passenger-km 36,524,000,000; metric ton-km cargo 1,530,000,000; airports (1997) 34. **Communications**, in total units (units per 1,000 persons). Daily newspaper circulation (1997): 5,970,000 (104); radio receivers (1997): 50,500,000 (880); television receivers (1998): 28,000,000 (488); telephone main lines (2001): 27,303,000 (471); cellular telephone subscribers (2001): 48,698,000 (839); personal computers (2001): 11,300,000 (195); Internet users (2001): 16,000,000 (278).

## Education and health

**Educational attainment** (1995). Percentage of labor force age 15 and over having: basic literacy or primary education 40.4%; secondary 30.5%; postsecondary technical training 5.1%; some college 19.2%; college degree 4.3%. **Literacy** (1995): total population age 15 and over literate 48,100,000 (98.1%); males literate 23,800,000 (98.6%); females literate 24,300,000 (97.6%). **Health** (1997): physicians (1993) 207,319 (1 per 193 persons); hospital beds 334,613 (1 per 172 persons); infant mortality rate per 1,000 live births (2001) 5.8. **Food** (1999): daily per capita caloric intake 3,629 (vegetable products 74%, animal products 26%); 144% of FAO recommended minimum.

## Military

**Total active duty personnel** (2001): 230,350 (army 59.5%, navy 16.5%, air force 24.0%). **Military expenditure as percentage of GNP** (1999): 2.0% (world 2.4%); per capita expenditure $412.

The University of Bologna is the oldest university in Europe. Although the exact date of the university's founding is unknown, there are artifacts showing that masters of rhetoric and logic began to study Roman law there around the 11th century.

## Background

The Etruscan civilization arose in the 9th century BC and was overthrown by the Romans in the 4th–3rd century BC. Barbarian invasions of the 4th–5th century AD destroyed the western Roman empire. Italy's political fragmentation lasted for centuries but did not diminish its impact on European culture, notably during the Renaissance. From the 15th to the 18th century, Italian lands were ruled by France, the Holy Roman Empire, Spain, and Austria. When Napoleonic rule ended in 1815, Italy was again a grouping of independent states. The Risorgimento successfully united most of Italy, including Sicily and Sardinia, by 1861, and the unification of peninsular Italy was completed by 1870. Italy joined the Allies during World War I, but social unrest in the 1920s brought to power the Fascist movement of Benito Mussolini, and Italy allied itself with Nazi Germany in World War II. Defeated by the Allies in 1943, Italy proclaimed itself a republic in 1946. It was a charter member of NATO (1949) and of the European Community. It completed the process of setting up regional legislatures with limited autonomy in the 1970s. Since World War II it has experienced rapid changes of government but has remained socially stable. It has worked with other European countries to establish the European Union.

## Recent Developments

Six and a half years of rule by center-left governments came to an end in 2001 when elections swept into power a center-right coalition led by media magnate Silvio Berlusconi. In January 2002 Foreign Minister Renato Ruggiero was forced to resign after he protested what he perceived as an increasingly anti-European stance taken by his fellow cabinet ministers and by Berlusconi himself. Very large-scale protests were mounted by organized labor. In April Italy's three main union federations staged the first daylong nationwide general strike in 20 years, paralyzing the country for the day. The government responded by quickly signing a compromise reform pact with two of the three main unions. In June 2003, at the time that Italy was taking over the rotating EU presidency, Berlusconi precipitated some European disunity with boorish remarks about Germans that caused German Chancellor Gerhard Schröder to cancel his planned Italian vacation.

Emblematic of a slowdown of the economy in 2002 was a decision in October by Italy's biggest automaker, Fiat, to lay off some 8,100 workers, nearly a fifth of the company's total employees. (The legendary

---

*1 metric ton = about 1.1 short tons;   1 kilometer = 0.6 mi (statute);   1 metric ton-km cargo = about 0.68 short ton-mi cargo;   c.i.f.: cost, insurance, and freight;   f.o.b.: free on board*

grandson of Fiat's founder, Gianni Agnelli, died in January 2003.) The flow of illegal immigrants into Italy continued to cause problems and spark controversy. By the end of September 2002, some 14,000 illegal immigrants had landed on Italy's coasts, and at least 85 had drowned while attempting to do so. Parliament approved some of the strictest immigration laws in Europe, including measures that would facilitate expulsions from the country and require immigrants to show proof of employment before being granted residence permits.

Internet resources: <www.italyemb.org>

# Jamaica

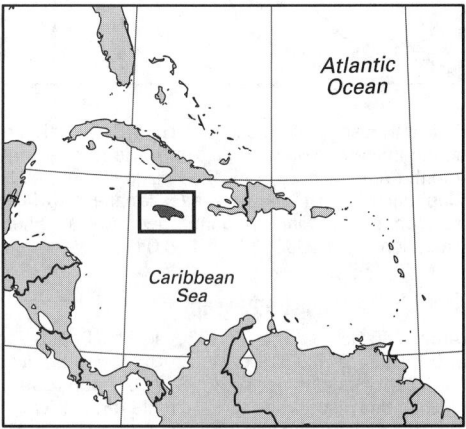

Atlantic Ocean

Caribbean Sea

Official name: Jamaica. Form of government: constitutional monarchy with two legislative houses (Senate [21]; House of Representatives [60]). Chief of state: Queen Elizabeth II (from 1952). Head of government: Prime Minister Percival James Patterson (from 1992). Capital: Kingston. Official language: English. Monetary unit: 1 Jamaica dollar (J$) = 100 cents; valuation (7 Jul 2003) US$1 = J$57.90.

## Demography

Area: 4,244 sq mi, 10,991 sq km. Population (2002): 2,630,000. Density (2002): persons per sq mi 619.7, persons per sq km 239.3. Urban (2001): 55.6%. Sex distribution (2001): male 48.96%; female 51.04%. Age breakdown (2001): under 15, 29.7%; 15–29, 28.3%; 30–44, 22.4%; 45–59, 10.5%; 60–74, 6.3%; 75 and over, 2.8%. Ethnic composition (2000): local black 77.0%; local mulatto 14.6%; Haitian 2.0%; East Indian 1.7%; black-East Indian 1.6%; other 3.1%. Religious affiliation (1995): Protestant 39.0%, of which Pentecostal 10.5%, Seventh-day Adventist 6.1%, Baptist 5.3%; Roman Catholic 10.4%; Anglican 3.7%; other (including nonreligious) 46.9% (includes c. 0.7% Rastafarian). Major cities (1991): Kingston 103,771 (metropolitan area 587,798); Spanish Town 92,383; Portmore 90,138; Montego Bay 83,446; May Pen 46,785. Location: island in the Caribbean Sea south of Cuba.

## Vital statistics

Birth rate per 1,000 population (2001): 21.2 (world avg. 21.2). Death rate per 1,000 population (2001): 6.6 (world avg. 8.9). Natural increase rate per 1,000

population (2001): 14.6 (world avg. 12.3). Total fertility rate (avg. births per childbearing woman; 2001): 2.1. Marriage rate per 1,000 population (1996): 7.4. Life expectancy at birth (2001): male 73.5 years; female 77.5 years.

## National economy

Budget (2000–01). Revenue J$101,018,000,000 (tax revenue 86.2%, of which income taxes 35.1%, consumption taxes 26.4%, custom duties 8.4%; nontax revenue 7.7%; bauxite levy 2.7%; capital revenue 1.7%; grants 1.7%). Expenditures: J$104,171,000,-000 (current expenditure 91.0%, of which debt interest 41.2%, wages 33.8%; capital expenditure 9.0%). Production (metric tons except as noted). Agriculture, forestry, fishing (2001): sugarcane 2,400,000, yams 145,000, vegetables and melons 144,500; livestock (number of live animals) 440,000 goats, 400,000 cattle, 180,000 pigs; roundwood (2001) 873,825 cu m; fish catch (1999) 12,658. Mining and quarrying (2001): bauxite 11,126,000; alumina 3,601,000; gypsum 331,000. Manufacturing (value added in constant 1991–95 prices, J$'000,000; 1995): machinery and equipment 593.6; food processing 580.3; petroleum products 351.3. Energy production (consumption): electricity (kW-hr; 1997) 6,255,000,-000 (6,255,000,000); crude petroleum (barrels; 1997) none (7,828,000); petroleum products (metric tons; 1997) 1,104,000 (3,294,000). Population economically active (April 2001): total 1,105,800; activity rate of total population 42.4% (participation rates: ages 14 and over 63.0%; female 43.9%; unemployed 14.8%). Gross national product (2000): US$6,883,-000,000 (US$2,610 per capita). Public debt (external, outstanding; 2000): US$3,373,000,000. Household income and expenditure. Average household size (1991) 4.2; average annual income per household (1988) J$8,356 (US$1,525); sources of income (1989): wages and salaries 66.1%, self-employment 19.3%, transfers 14.6%; expenditure (1988): food and beverages 55.6%, housing 7.9%, fuel and other household supplies 7.4%, health care 7.0%, transportation 6.4%. Tourism: receipts (2000) US$1,332,-600,000; expenditures US$209,000,000.

## Foreign trade

Imports (2000): US$2,921,000,000 (raw materials 53.4%, of which fuels 18.3%; consumer goods 30.6%, of which food 8.2%; capital goods 15.9%, of which machinery and apparatus 7.8%). Major import sources (2000): US 44.8%; Trinidad and Tobago 10.0%; Japan 6.0%; France 5.0%; Venezuela 3.9%; UK 3.1%; Canada 3.1%; Mexico 2.6%. Exports (2000): US$1,556,000,000 (crude materials 62.0%, of which alumina 44.4%; food 18.7%; manufactured articles 7.9%; chemicals 5.5%; beverages and tobacco 4.0%; machinery and transport equipment 0.1%). Major export destinations: US 39.1%; UK 11.5%; Canada 10.2%; Norway 9.1%; Japan 2.3%.

## Transport and communications

Transport. Railroads (2000): route length 339 km; passenger-km 19,516,000; metric ton-km cargo 2,442,000. Roads (1999): total length 18,700 km (paved 70%). Vehicles (1999–2000): passenger cars 160,948; trucks and buses 55,596. Air transport (1999; Air Jamaica only): passenger-km 4,412,000,-000; metric ton-km cargo 26,391,000; airports

(2000) with scheduled flights 4. **Communications**, in total units (units per 1,000 persons). Daily newspaper circulation (1996): 158,000 (63); radio receivers (1997): 1,215,000 (483); television receivers (1998): 480,000 (187); telephone main lines (2001): 512,-600 (197); cellular telephone subscribers (2001): 700,000 (269); personal computers (2001): 130,000 (50); Internet users (2001): 100,000 (38).

## Education and health

**Educational attainment** (1982). Percentage of population age 25 and over having: no formal schooling 3.2%; some primary education 79.8%; some secondary 15.0%; complete secondary and higher 2.0%. **Literacy** (2000): total population age 15 and over literate 88%; males 83%; females 91%. **Health** (2000): physicians 435 (1 per 5,988 persons); hospital beds 3,511 (1 per 742 persons); infant mortality rate per 1,000 live births (2001) 14.2. **Food** (2000): daily per capita caloric intake 2,693 (vegetable products 85%, animal products 15%); 120% of FAO recommended minimum.

## Military

**Total active duty personnel** (2001): 2,830 (army 88.3%; coast guard 6.7%; air force 5.0%). **Military expenditure as percentage of GNP** (1999): 0.8% (world 2.4%); per capita expenditure US$19.

## Background

The island of Jamaica was settled by Arawak Indians c. AD 600. It was sighted by Christopher Columbus in 1494; Spain colonized it in the early 16th century but neglected it because it lacked gold reserves. Britain gained control in 1655, and by the end of the 18th century Jamaica had become a prized colonial possession due to the volume of sugar produced by slave laborers. Slavery was abolished in the late 1830s, and the plantation system collapsed. Jamaica gained full internal self-government in 1959 and became an independent country within the British Commonwealth in 1962.

## Recent Developments

Tourism was dealt a severe blow in 2001 when four cruise lines dropped Jamaica from their itineraries following complaints about visitor harassment. Jamaica's police service was sharply criticized for its violations of human rights in an Amnesty International report that the government described as "one-sided, false, and misleading." In the general election held on 16 Oct 2002, the People's National Party won 35 seats in the 60-seat House of Representatives and clinched its fourth successive term in office. Prime Minister Percival J. Patterson would remain in office for a record third consecutive term.

**Internet Resources:** <www.discoverjamaica.com>

# Japan

**Official name:** Nihon (Japan). **Form of government:** constitutional monarchy with a national Diet consisting of two legislative houses (House of Councillors

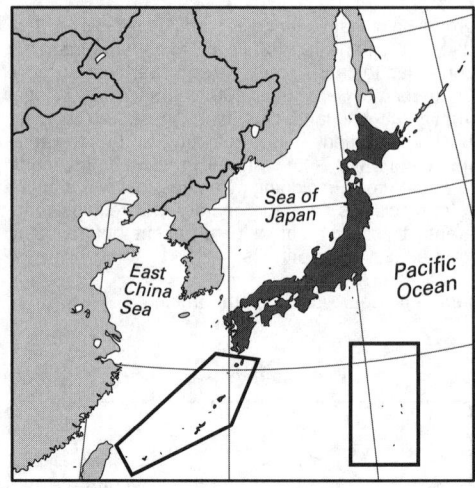

[247]; House of Representatives [480]). **Chief of state:** Emperor Akihito (from 1989). **Head of government:** Prime Minister Junichiro Koizumi (from 2001). **Capital:** Tokyo. **Official language:** Japanese. **Official religion:** none. **Monetary unit:** 1 yen (¥) = 100 sen; valuation (7 Jul 2003) $1 = ¥118.04.

## Demography

**Area:** 145,884 sq mi, 377,837 sq km. **Population** (2002): 127,347,000. **Density** (2002): persons per sq mi 872.8, persons per sq km 337.0. **Urban** (1999): 78.6%. **Sex distribution** (2001): male 48.9%; female 51.1%. **Age breakdown** (2001): under 15, 14.4%; 15–29, 19.8%; 30–44, 19.7%; 45–59, 21.9%; 60–74, 16.7%; 75 and over, 7.5%. **Composition** by nationality (1997): Japanese 99.1%; Korean 0.5%; Chinese 0.2%; other 0.2%. **Place of birth** (1995): 99.3% native-born; 0.7% foreign-born (mainly Korean). **Immigration** (2001): permanent immigrants/registered aliens admitted 1,686,444, from North and South Korea 37.7%, Taiwan, Hong Kong, and China 19.9%, Brazil 15.1%, Philippines 8.6%, Peru 2.7%, US 2.6%, Thailand 1.7%, Indonesia 1.1%, UK 1.0%, Vietnam 0.6%, Canada 0.6%, India 0.6%, Pakistan 0.4%, other 7.4%. **Major cities** (2000): Tokyo 8,134,408; Yokohama 3,426,506; Osaka 2,598,589; Nagoya 2,171,378; Sapporo 1,822,300; Kobe 1,493,595; Kyoto 1,467,705; Fukuoka 1,341,489; Kawasaki 1,249,851; Hiroshima 1,126,282; Kita-Kyushu 1,011,491; Sendai 1,008,024. **Religious affiliation** (1995): Shinto and related religions 93.1% (many Japanese practice both Shintoism and Buddhism); Buddhism 69.6%; Christian 1.2%; other 8.1%. **Households** (2000). Total households 46,376,000; average household size 2.7; composition of households 1 person 26.4%, 2 persons 25.5%, 3 persons 19.2%, 4 persons 17.3%, 5 persons 6.9%, 6 or more persons 4.7%. Family households 33,920,000 (73.2%); nonfamily 12,456,000 (26.8%), of which 1 person 12,268,000 (26.4%). **Mobility** (October 1990). Population living in same residence as in October 1985, 74.7%; different residence, same town 9.5%; same prefecture 7.9%; different prefecture 7.6%; different country 0.3%. **Location:** eastern Asia; island chain between the North Pacific Ocean and the Sea of Japan.

---

*1 metric ton = about 1.1 short tons;   1 kilometer = 0.6 mi (statute);   1 metric ton-km cargo = about 0.68 short ton-mi cargo;   c.i.f.: cost, insurance, and freight;   f.o.b.: free on board*

## Vital statistics

Birth rate per 1,000 population (1999): 9.4 (world avg. 22.5); (1985) legitimate 99.0%; illegitimate 1.0%. Death rate per 1,000 population (1999): 7.8 (world avg. 9.0). Natural increase rate per 1,000 population (1999): 1.6 (world avg. 13.5). Total fertility rate (avg. births per childbearing woman; 1999): 1.3. Marriage rate per 1,000 population (1999): 6.1; average age at first marriage (1996) men 28.5 years, women 26.4 years. Divorce rate per 1,000 population (1999): 2.0. Life expectancy at birth (2000): male 77.5 years; female 84.0 years.

## Social indicators

Quality of working life. Average hours worked per month (2000): 154.9. Annual rate of industrial deaths per 100,000 workers (1998): 1.7. Proportion of labor force insured for damages or income loss resulting from injury, permanent disability, and death (1991): 50.1%. Average man-days lost to labor stoppages per 1,000,000 workdays (1998): 6.8. Average duration of journey to work (1996): 19.0 minutes (1983; 26.7% private automobile, 67.4% public transportation, 5.5% taxi, 0.4% other). Rate per 1,000 workers of discouraged (unemployed no longer seeking work: 1997): 89.4. Access to services (1989). Proportion of households having access to: gas supply 64.6%; safe public water supply 94.0%; public sewage collection 89.4%. Social participation. Eligible voters participating in last national election (June 2000): 62.5%. Population 15 years and over participating in social-service activities on a voluntary basis (1991): 26.3%. Trade union membership in total workforce (2002): 21.5%. Social deviance (1999). Offense rate per 100,000 population for: homicide 1.0; rape 1.5; robbery 3.3; larceny and theft 1,505. Rate of suicide per 100,000 population: 24.8. Material well-being (1994). Households possessing: automobile 79.7%; telephone, virtually 100%; color television receiver 99.3%; refrigerator 98.9%; air conditioner 72.3%; washing machine 99.4%; vacuum cleaner 98.7%; videocassette recorder 82.8%; camera 86.8%; microwave oven 84.3%; compact disc player 53.8%.

## National economy

Gross national product (at current market prices; 2000): $4,519,067,000,000 ($35,620 per capita). Budget (2001–02). Revenue: ¥54,334,000,000,000 (income tax 34.2%; corporation tax 21.8%; value-added tax 18.6%; stamp and customs duties 2.8%). Expenditures: ¥66,731,000,000,000 (social security 26.3%; debt service 25.7%; public works 14.1%; national defense 7.4%). Public debt (1998): $2,412,200,000,000 (¥278,847,900,000,000). Population economically active (2000): total 67,660,000; activity rate of total population 52.7% (participation rates: age 15 and over, 63.7% [1997]; female 40.7%; unemployed 4.7%). Household income and expenditure (2000). Average annual income per household ¥6,601,000 ($61,120); sources of income (1994): wages and salaries 59.0%, transfer payments 20.5%, self-employment 12.8%, other 7.3%; expenditure (1999): food 23.7%, transportation and communications 10.6%, recreation 10.3%, fuel, light, and water charges 6.7%, housing 6.5%, clothing and footwear 5.4%, education 4.2%, furniture and household utensils 3.6%, medical care 3.5%. Tourism (2000): receipts from visitors

$3,373,000,000; expenditures by nationals abroad $31,886,000,000. Land use (1994): forested 66.4%; meadows and pastures 1.8%; agricultural and under permanent cultivation 11.7%; other 20.1%. Energy production (consumption): electricity (kW-hr; 1998) 1,046,294,000,000 (1,046,294,000,000); coal (metric tons; 1998) 3,681,000 (132,849,000); crude petroleum (barrels; 1998) 3,298,000 (1,569,000); petroleum products (metric tons; 1998) 187,410,000, of which (by volume) diesel 32.8%, heavy fuel oil 21.7%, gasoline 21.7%, kerosene and jet fuel 12.0% (192,747,000); natural gas (cu m; 1998) 2,320,400,000 (68,211,000,000). Composition of energy supply by source (1998): crude oil and petroleum products 50.9%, coal 17.0%, nuclear power 14.2%, natural gas 12.8%, hydroelectric power 4.1%, other 1.0%. Domestic energy demand by end use (1998): mining and manufacturing 46.3%, residential and commercial 26.3%, transportation 25.2%, other 2.2%. Production (metric tons except as noted). Agriculture, forestry, fishing (2001): rice 11,320,000, sugar beets 4,000,000, potatoes 2,900,000, cabbages 2,600,000, sugarcane 1,600,000, sweet potatoes 1,073,000, onions 1,000,000, apples 894,000, tomatoes 800,000, cucumbers 766,700, wheat 700,000, carrots 680,000, watermelons 580,600, lettuce 540,000, eggplant 476,900, pears 411,800, spinach 330,000, cantaloupes 315,000, persimmons 278,800, pumpkins 253,600, soybeans 240,000, grapes 234,200, taro 231,000, barley 220,000, yams 200,000, strawberries 200,000, peaches 174,600, peppers 170,900, plums 121,000, cauliflower 116,000; livestock (number of live animals) 9,785,000 pigs, 4,530,000 cattle, 297,000,000 chickens; roundwood (1999) 17,987,000 cu m; fish catch (2000) 5,752,178, of which squid 671,100, scallops 515,000, cod 398,900, crabs 42,000. Mining and quarrying (1999): limestone 180,193,000; silica stone 18,312,000; dolomite 3,648,000; pyrophyllite 694,000; zinc 64,263; lead 6,074; copper 1,038; silver 94,004 kg; gold 9,405 kg. Manufacturing (1999): crude steel 94,192,000; steel products 86,335,000 (1998); cement 80,120,000; pig iron 74,520,000; sulfuric acid 6,493,000; plastic products 6,035,000 (1998); fertilizers 4,156, (1998); spun yarn 507,475 (1998); newsprint 3,192,300; cotton fabrics 814,000,000 sq m (1998); synthetic fabrics 2,087,000 sq m (1998); finished products (in number of units) 552,269,000 watches and clocks, 30,350,000 (1996) air conditioners, 12,051,000 (1998) videocassette recorders, 10,326,000 cameras, 9,684,000 (1998) video cameras, 9,639,000 (1998) computers, 8,100,000 passenger cars, 6,056,000 (1998) facsimile machines, 5,975,000 (1997) bicycles, 4,851,000 (1998) electric refrigerators, 4,468,000 (1998) automatic washing machines, 3,444,000 color television receivers, 2,959,000 (1998) microwave ovens, 2,252,000 motorcycles, 1,903,000 (1997) photocopy machines.

## Foreign trade

Imports (1999): ¥35,268,000,000,000 (machinery and transport equipment 31.3%, food products 14.3%, petroleum and petroleum products 10.5%, chemicals and chemical products 7.4%, textiles 5.4%). Major import sources: US 21.7%; China 13.8%; South Korea 5.2%; Australia 4.1%; Taiwan 4.1%; Indonesia 4.0%; Germany 3.7%; Malaysia 3.5%; Thailand 2.9%; United Arab Emirates 2.8%.

**Exports** (1999): ¥47,548,000,000 (electrical machinery 24.3%, transport equipment 22.7%, chemicals 7.4%, scientific and optical equipment 5.0%, iron and steel products 3.2%, textiles and allied products 1.9%). *Major export destinations:* US 30.7%; Taiwan 6.9%; China 5.6%; Hong Kong 5.3%; South Korea 5.2%; Germany 4.5%; Singapore 3.8%; UK 3.4%; The Netherlands 2.9%; Thailand 2.7%.

## Transport and communications

**Transport.** *Railroads* (1999): length 27,454 km; rolling stock—locomotives 1,787 (1995), passenger cars 25,973 (1995), freight cars 12,688 (1995); passengers carried 21,750,000,000; passenger-km 385,101,000,000; metric ton-km cargo 22,541,000,-000. *Roads* (1999): total length 1,155,439 km (paved 73%). *Vehicles* (1999): passenger cars 51,164,000; trucks and buses 18,630,000. *Air transport* (1998): passengers carried 102,749,000; passenger-km 157,305,000,000; metric ton-km cargo 7,183,-000,000; airports (1996) with scheduled flights 73. **Communications,** in total units (units per 1,000 persons). Daily newspaper circulation (1999): 72,218,-000 (567); radio receivers (1997): 120,500,000 (955); television receivers (1997): 86,500,000 (686); telephone main lines (2001): 76,000,000 (597); cellular telephone subscribers (2001): 72,796,000 (572); personal computers (2001): 44,400,000 (349); Internet users (2001): 57,900,000 (455). Radio and television broadcasting (1994): total radio stations 1,340, of which commercial 481; total television stations 14,625, of which commercial 7,736. Commercial broadcasting hours (by percentage of programs; 1994): reports—radio 13.0%, television 21.0%; education—radio 3.4%, television 12.0%; culture—radio 14.9%, television 24.7%; entertainment—radio 67.6%, television 40.0%. Advertisements (daily average; 1994): radio 148, television 295.

## Education and health

**Educational attainment** (1990). Percentage of population age 25 years and over having: primary education 34.3%; secondary 44.5%; postsecondary 21.2%. **Literacy:** total population age 15 and over literate, virtually 100%. **Health** (1999): physicians 248,611 (1 per 508 persons); dentists 88,061 (1 per 1,436 persons); nurses 985,821 (1 per 128 persons); pharmacists 205,953 (1 per 614 persons); midwives 24,202 (1 per 5,223 persons); hospital beds 1,648,217 (1 per 77 persons), of which general 76.5%, mental 21.7%, other 1.8%; infant mortality rate per 1,000 live births (1999) 3.4. **Food** (2000): daily per capita caloric intake 2,762 (vegetable products 79%, animal products 21%); 118% of FAO recommended minimum.

## Military

**Total active duty personnel** (2001): 239,800 (army 62.0%, navy 18.4%, air force 18.9%). **Military expenditure as percentage of GNP** (1999): 1.0% (world 2.4%); per capita expenditure $342.

## Background

Japan's history began with the accession of the legendary first emperor, Jimmu, in 660 BC. The Yamato court established the first unified Japanese state in the 4th–5th century AD; during this period, Buddhism arrived in Japan by way of Korea. For centuries Japan borrowed heavily from Chinese culture, but it began to sever its links with the mainland by the 9th century. In 1192 Minamoto Yoritomo established Japan's first *bakufu*, or shogunate. Unification was achieved in the late 1500s under the leadership of Oda Nobunaga, Toyotomi Hideyoshi, and Tokugawa Ieyasu. During the Tokugawa shogunate, beginning in 1603, the government imposed a policy of isolation. Under the leadership of Emperor Meiji (1868–1912), it adopted a constitution (1889) and began a program of modernization and Westernization. Japanese imperialism led to war with China (1894–95) and Russia (1904–05) as well as to the annexation of Korea (1910) and Manchuria (1931). During World War II Japan attacked US forces in Hawaii and the Philippines (December 1941) and occupied European colonial possessions in South Asia. In 1945 the US dropped atomic bombs on Hiroshima and Nagasaki, and Japan surrendered to the Allied powers. US postwar occupation of Japan led to a new democratic constitution in 1947. In rebuilding Japan's ruined industrial plant, new technology was used in every major industry. A tremendous economic recovery followed, and it was able to maintain a favorable balance of trade into the 1990s.

## Recent Developments

Even in his first year in office Prime Minister Junichiro Koizumi encountered opposition by conservative factions within his Liberal Democratic Party. They were led by party bosses entrenched in the postal service, construction and retail trades, and rice farming. Japan's economy, the second largest in the world, remained enmeshed in its fourth recession in a decade. A government report noted that property values had declined 5.9% in 2001, the sharpest fall in nine years. In October 2002 the Nikkei 225 stock index fell to 8,439, its lowest level since June 1983. Meanwhile, the prime minister had felt the force of opposition within his cabinet. On 29 Jan 2002 he dismissed Makiko Tanaka, the first woman to have served as Japan's foreign minister. Koizumi appointed Yoriko Kawaguchi, who had previously served as environment minister. Agriculture Minister Tadamori Oshima resigned amid a scandal in late March 2003.

In late January 2002 Tokyo hosted a gathering of delegates from more than 50 nations to discuss the rebuilding of Afghanistan. The prime minister pledged $250 million for the first year and a like amount to be paid later. On 17 February US Pres. George W. Bush began a delayed trip to Japan and South Korea. In March a US sergeant stationed on the Japanese island of Okinawa was found guilty of rape by a Japanese court. The incident evoked loud protests, and some officials called for a renegotiation of the status of forces agreement governing the US military presence in Japan. (Some 47,000 military personnel were based on Okinawa.) Also in February Japan notified the International Whaling Commission that it planned to double its catch for the purpose of "scientific research." American officials charged that Japan was actually engaging in commercial whaling.

The possibility of a breakthrough in generally sour relations with North Korea came on 17 September

---

*1 metric ton = about 1.1 short tons;    1 kilometer = 0.6 mi (statute);    1 metric ton-km cargo = about 0.68 short ton-mi cargo;    c.i.f.: cost, insurance, and freight;    f.o.b.: free on board*

when Koizumi became the first Japanese prime minister to visit Pyongyang. The following month, however, the North Koreans confessed that they were involved in work on nuclear weapons, and the Japanese placed normalization on hold. The year 2002 witnessed an unusual cooperation between Japan and South Korea; the two countries served as the first cohosts of the World Cup association football (soccer) tournament—the world's biggest sporting event. On 10 Jan 2003, during a visit to Russia, Koizumi and Russian Pres. Vladimir Putin signed an "action plan" that called for the two sides to find a solution to the "Northern Territories" issue, the ownership of several islets between Japan's Hokkaido and Russia's Kuril Islands.

Internet Resources: <www.jnto.go.jp>

# Jersey

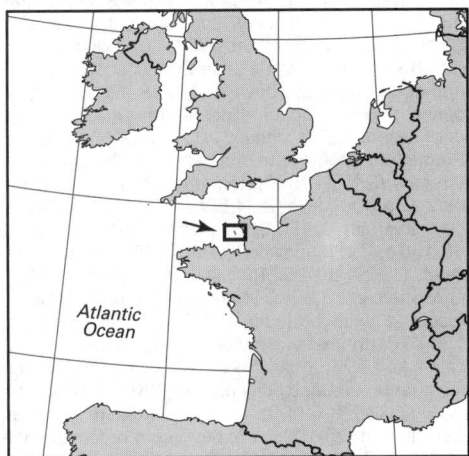

Atlantic
Ocean

**Official name:** Bailiwick of Jersey. **Political status:** Crown dependency (UK) with one legislative house (States of Jersey [57; 53 elected members include 12 senators popularly elected for 6-year terms, 12 constables popularly elected triennially, and 29 deputies also popularly elected triennially; 4 non-elected members include the bailiff, the dean of Jersey, the attorney general, and the solicitor general]). **Chief of state:** British Monarch Queen Elizabeth II (from 1952) represented by Lieutenant Governor Sir John Cheshire (from 2001). **Head of government:** Executive committees appointed by the States of Jersey (alternately called States Assembly). **Capital:** Saint Helier. **Official language:** English (until the 1960s French was an official language of Jersey and is still used by the court and legal professions; Jèrriais, a Norman-French dialect, is spoken by a small number of residents). **Official religion:** none. **Monetary unit:** 1 Jersey pound (£J) = 100 pence; valuation (7 Jul 2003) $1 = £J.60.

## Demography

**Area:** 44.9 sq mi, 116.2 sq km. **Population** (2002): 87,400. **Density** (2002): persons per sq mi 1,946.5, persons per sq km 752.2. **Sex distribution** (2001): male 48.73%; female 51.27%. **Age breakdown** (2001): under 15, 16.9%; 15–29, 18.4%; 30–44, 25.9%; 45–59, 19.7%; 60–74, 12.6%; 75 and over,

6.5%. **Population by place of birth** (2001): Jersey 52.6%; UK, Guernsey, or Isle of Man 35.8%; Portugal 5.9%; France 1.2%; other 4.5%. **Religious affiliation** (2000; includes Guernsey): Christian 86.0%, of which Anglican 44.1%, Roman Catholic 14.6%, other Protestant 6.9%, unaffiliated Christian 20.1%; nonreligious/atheist 13.4%; other 0.6%. **Major cities** (2001; pop. of parishes): St. Helier 28,310; St. Saviour 12,491; St. Brelade 10,134. **Location:** western Europe, island in the English Channel.

## Vital statistics

**Birth rate** per 1,000 population (2000): 11.6 (world avg. 22.5). **Death rate** per 1,000 population (2000): 9.3 (world avg. 9.0). **Natural increase rate** per 1,000 population (2000): 2.3 (world avg. 13.5). **Total fertility rate** (avg. births per childbearing woman; 2000): 1.6. **Life expectancy** at birth (2000): male 76.1 years; female 81.1 years.

## National economy

**Budget** (2000). *Revenue*: £388,389,000 (corporate income tax 43.0%, individual income tax 26.9%, self-employment tax 11.6%, spirits and tobacco tax 6.0%, international business 5.4%, tax on fuel 3.0%). *Expenditures*: £300,030,000 (current expenditure 79.2%, of which health 27.8%, education 21.3%, social security 20.5%; capital expenditure 20.8%). **Production.** *Agriculture, forestry, fishing*: fruits and vegetables, mostly potatoes and greenhouse tomatoes; greenhouse flowers are important export crops; livestock (number of live animals; 1999) 7,315 cattle, of which about 4,500 dairy cattle; fish catch (metric tons; 1997; includes Guernsey): 4,368, of which crustaceans 2,934 (including sea spiders and crabs 2,713), mollusks 743 (including abalones, winkles, and conch 438), marine fish 691. *Manufacturing*: light industry, mainly electrical goods, textiles and clothing; dairy products (including 179 hectolitres of milk in 1999). *Energy production (consumption)*: electricity (kW-hr; 1995) 266,000,000 (467,000,000). **Gross national product** (at current market prices; 1995): $2,670,000,000 ($30,940 per capita). **Household expenditure.** Average household size (1996) 2.4; expenditure (1998–99): housing 20.1%, recreation 16.5%, transportation 12.8%, household furnishings 11.6%, food 11.5%, alcoholic beverages 6.0%, clothing and footwear 5.5%. **Population economically active** (2001): total 46,602; activity rate of total population 53.4% (participation rates: ages 15–64, 81.7%; female 45.5%; unemployed 2.1%). **Public debt:** none. **Tourism** (1996): receipts $429,000,000; number of visitors for at least one night 670,000. **Land use** (1997): land under cultivation 56.8%; other 43.2%.

## Foreign trade

**Imports:** n.a. *Major import sources* (1999): mostly UK. **Exports:** agricultural exports (1996): £45,400,000 (potatoes 61.2%, greenhouse tomatoes 17.2%, zucchini 6.4%, greenhouse carnations and narcissus 6.0%). *Major export destinations:* mostly UK.

## Transport and communications

**Transport.** *Roads* (1995): total length 557 km (paved 100%). *Vehicles* (1995): passenger cars 58,491; trucks and buses 9,109. *Air transport* (1999; Jersey

European Airways): passenger-km 890,438,000; metric ton-km cargo 923,000; airports (1999) with scheduled flights 1. **Communications,** in total units (units per 1,000 persons). Daily newspaper circulation (1997): 25,542 (299); telephone main lines (2001): 73,900 (848); cellular telephone subscribers (2001): 61,400 (704); Internet users (2000): 8,000 (92).

## Education and health

**Literacy** (1996): total population age 15 and over literate 71,033 (100.0%). **Health** (1995): physicians 95 (1 per 895 persons); hospital beds 651 (1 per 130 persons); infant mortality rate per 1,000 live births (2000) 5.7.

## Military

**Total active duty personnel** (2000): defense is the responsibility of the UK.

# Jordan

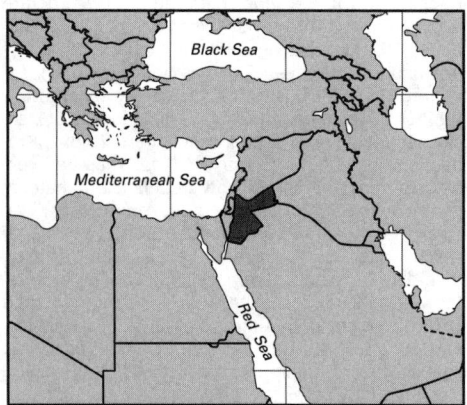

*Official name:* Al-Mamlakah al-Urdunniyah al-Hashimiyah (Al-Urdun) (Hashemite Kingdom of Jordan). **Form of government:** constitutional monarchy with two legislative houses (Senate [40; all members are appointed by the king]; House of Representatives [80]). **Head of state and government:** King Abdullah II (from 1999) assisted by Prime Minister 'Ali Abu al-Raghib (from 2000). **Capital:** Amman. **Official language:** Arabic. **Official religion:** Islam. **Monetary unit:** 1 Jordan dinar (JD) = 1,000 fils; valuation (7 Jul 2003) JD 1.00 = $0.71.

## Demography

**Area:** 34,495 sq mi, 89,342 sq km. **Population** (2002): 5,260,000. **Density** (2002): persons per sq mi 152.5, persons per sq km 58.9. **Urban** (2000): 74.2%. **Sex distribution** (2001): male 52.35%; female 47.65%. **Age breakdown** (2000): under 15, 37.9%; 15–29, 30.9%; 30–44, 18.3%; 45–59, 7.8%; 60–74, 4.2%; 75 and over, 0.9%. **Ethnic composition** (2000): Arab 97.8%, of which Jordanian 32.4%, Palestinian 32.2%, Iraqi 14.0%, Bedouin 12.8%; Circassian 1.2%; other 1.0%. **Religious affiliation** (2000): Sunni Muslim 93.5%; Christian 4.1%; other 2.4%. **Major cities** (1994): Amman 969,598;

Az-Zarqa' 350,849; Irbid 208,329; Ar-Rusayfah 137,247; Wadi Essier 89,104. **Location:** the Middle East, bordering Syria, Iraq, Saudi Arabia, the Gulf of Aqaba, Israel, and parts of the Emerging Palestinian Autonomous Areas.

## Vital statistics

**Birth rate** per 1,000 population (2001): 25.4 (world avg. 21.2). **Death rate** per 1,000 population (2001): 2.6 (world avg. 8.9). **Natural increase rate** per 1,000 population (2001): 22.8 (world avg. 12.3). **Total fertility rate** (avg. births per childbearing woman; 2001): 3.3. **Life expectancy** at birth (2001): male 75.1 years; female 80.0 years.

## National economy

**Budget** (2000 est.). *Revenue:* JD 1,804,700,000 (taxes 53.3%, of which sales tax 28.8%, custom duties 14.7%, income and profits taxes 8.9%; nontax 33.5%, of which licenses and fees 13.2%; foreign grants 13.2%). *Expenditures:* JD 2,004,600,000 (current 85.7%, of which defense 26.5%, social security and other transfers 20.4%, wages 18.3%, interest expense 14.6%; capital expenditure 14.3%). **Public debt** (external, outstanding; 2000): $7,055,000,000. **Production** (metric tons except as noted). *Agriculture, forestry, fishing* (2000): tomatoes 354,300, cucumbers 135,600, olives 134,300; livestock (number of live animals) 1,850,000 sheep, 640,000 goats, 65,400 cattle; roundwood (2000) 226,143 cu m; fish catch (1999) 1,025. *Mining and quarrying* (2001): phosphate ore 5,878,100; potash 1,962,600. *Manufacturing* (value added in JD '000; 1997): chemicals 130,276; nonmetallic mineral products, pottery, and china 114,897; tobacco 96,380. *Energy production (consumption):* electricity (kW-hr; 2001) 7,365,700,000 (7,365,700,000); crude petroleum (barrels; 1997) none (25,100,000); petroleum products (metric tons; 2001) 3,596,800 (3,596,800); natural gas (cu m; 2000) 283,000,000 (283,000,000). **Land use** (1994): forest 0.8%; pasture 8.9%; agriculture 4.6%; other 85.7%. **Tourism** (2000): receipts $722,000,000; expenditures $387,000,000. **Population economically active** (1993): total 859,300; activity rate of total population 22.2% (participation rates: over age 15, 43.6%; female 14.0%; unemployed [1999] 14.4%). **Gross national product** (2000): $8,360,000,000 ($1,710 per capita). **Household income and expenditure.** Average household size (1997) 6.1; income per household (1997) JD 5,464 ($7,700); sources of income (1997): wages and salaries 52.4%, rent and property income 24.5%, transfer payments 12.8%, self-employment 10.3%; expenditure (1997): food and beverages 44.3%, housing and energy 23.5%, transportation 8.2%, clothing and footwear 6.2%, education 4.5%, health care 2.5%.

## Foreign trade

**Imports** (2000): JD 3,218,100,000 (machinery and transport equipment 28.6%; food and live animals 16.1%; mineral fuels 15.8%; chemicals and chemical products 10.6%; iron and steel 3.0%). *Major import sources:* Iraq 15.1%; Germany 11.5%; US 10.0%; UK 4.6%; Japan 4.0%; Italy 3.6%. **Exports** (2000): JD 1,345,300,000 (domestic goods 80.3%, of which

---

*1 metric ton = about 1.1 short tons;    1 kilometer = 0.6 mi (statute);    1 metric ton-km cargo = about 0.68 short ton-mi cargo;    c.i.f.: cost, insurance, and freight;    f.o.b.: free on board*

chemicals and chemical products 25.8%, potash 10.3%, manufactured goods 8.4%, phosphate fertilizers 6.8%, fruits, vegetables, and nuts 5.3%, machinery and transport equipment 5.1%; reexports 19.7%). *Major export destinations*: India 15.9%; Iraq 9.3%; Saudi Arabia 8.5%; US 4.2%; China 3.0%; Kuwait 1.8%; Syria 1.5%.

## Transport and communications

**Transport.** *Railroads* (1998): route length 677 km; passenger-km 2,000,000; metric ton-km cargo 596,000,000. *Roads* (1998): total length 7,133 km (paved 100%). *Vehicles* (1996): passenger cars 213,874; trucks and buses 79,153. *Air transport* (2001; Royal Jordanian Airlines only): passenger-km 3,848,000,000; metric ton-km cargo 181,408,000; airports (1999) 3. **Communications,** in total units (units per 1,000 persons). Daily newspaper circulation (1996): 250,000 (57); radio receivers (1997): 1,660,000 (395); television receivers (1999): 540,000 (83); telephone main lines (2001): 660,000 (127); cellular telephone subscribers (2001): 745,500 (144); personal computers (2001): 170,000 (33); Internet users (2001): 212,000 (41).

## Education and health

**Educational attainment** (2000). Percentage of population age 25 and over having: no formal schooling 16.7%; primary education 49.2%; secondary 16.7%; postsecondary and vocational 9.5%; higher 8.2%. **Literacy** (2000): total population age 15 and over literate 88.8%; males literate 94.9%; females literate 84.4%. **Health** (1998): physicians 7,480 (1 per 625 persons); hospital beds 8,565 (1 per 546 persons); infant mortality rate per 1,000 live births (2001) 20.4. **Food** (2000): daily per capita caloric intake 2,749 (vegetable products 88%, animal products 12%); 112% of FAO recommended minimum.

## Military

**Total active duty personnel** (2001): 100,240 (army 84.5%, navy 0.5%, air force 15.0%). **Military expenditure as percentage of GDP** (1999): 9.2% (world 2.4%); per capita expenditure $150.

---

**Did you know?** Since 1986 Jordan's only seaport, Aqaba, has been the site of an on-going archaeological excavation that is revealing the plan of an Islamic city in existence from the mid-7th century to the early 12th century.

---

## Background

Jordan shares much of its history with Israel, since both occupied the area known historically as Palestine. Much of present-day eastern Jordan was incorporated into Israel under kings David and Solomon c. 1000 BC. It fell to the Seleucids in 330 BC and to Muslim Arabs in the 7th century AD. The Crusaders extended the kingdom of Jerusalem east of the Jordan River in 1099. Jordan submitted to Ottoman Turkish rule during the 16th century. In 1920 the area comprising Jordan (then known as the Transjordan) was established within the British mandate of Palestine. Transjordan became an independent state in 1927, although the British mandate did not end

until 1948. After hostilities with the new state of Israel ceased in 1949, Jordan annexed the West Bank of the Jordan River, administering the territory until Israel gained control of it in the Six-Day War of 1967. In 1970–71 Jordan was wracked by fighting between the government and guerrillas of the Palestine Liberation Organization (PLO), a struggle that ended in the expulsion of the PLO from Jordan. In 1988 King Hussein renounced all Jordanian claims to the West Bank in favor of the PLO. In 1994 Jordan and Israel signed a full peace agreement. Upon the death of King Hussein in 1999, his son Abdullah took over the throne.

## Recent Developments

King Abdullah II pursued an active foreign policy to consolidate Jordan's relationships with other Middle Eastern nations and to advance the Israeli-Palestinian peace process. He also voiced continued support of the US-declared war on terrorism. The king stood behind Palestinian leader Yasir Arafat, but he fully supported the Saudi peace initiative that was publicly announced by Saudi Crown Prince Abdullah and was subsequently endorsed by the Arab League. There remained strong opposition among Islamists and leftists in Jordan to normalization with Israel, especially in the wake of the second Palestinian *intifadah*. While there was popular opposition in Jordan to the US-UK invasion of neighboring Iraq, King Abdullah took a more pragmatic position toward the coalition.

**Internet resources:** <www.seejordan.org>

# Kazakhstan

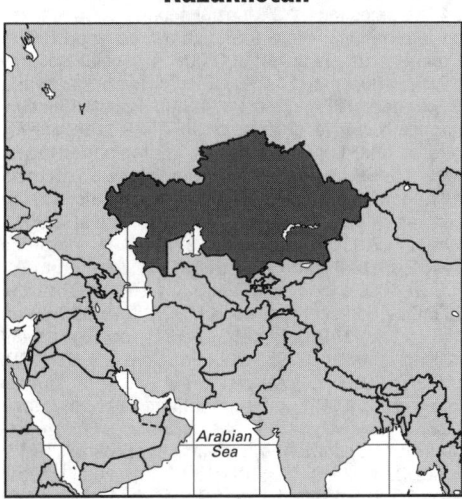

Arabian Sea

**Official name:** Qazaqstan Respublikasy (Republic of Kazakhstan). **Form of government:** unitary republic with a Parliament consisting of two chambers (Senate [39, including 7 nonelective seats] and Assembly [77]). **Head of state and government:** President Nursultan Nazarbayev (from 1991) assisted by Prime Minister Daniyal Akhmetov (from 13 Jun 2003). **Capital:** Astana. **Official language:** Kazakh (Russian commands equal status at state-owned organizations and local government bodies). **Official religion:** none. **Monetary unit:** 1 tenge (T) = 100 tiyn; valuation (7 Jul 2003) free rate, $1 = 147.69 tenge.

## Demography

**Area:** 1,052,100 sq mi, 2,724,900 sq km. **Population** (2002): 14,884,000. **Density** (2002): persons per sq mi 14.1, persons per sq km 5.5. **Urban** (2001): 56.3%. **Sex distribution** (2001): male 48.07%; female 51.93%. **Age breakdown** (2001): under 15, 26.7%; 15–29, 27.1%; 30–44, 21.5%; 45–59, 13.2%; 60–74, 9.2%; 75 and over, 2.3%. **Ethnic composition** (1999): Kazakh 53.4%; Russian 30.0%; Ukrainian 3.7%; Uzbek 2.5%; German 2.4%; Tatar 1.7%; other 6.3%. **Religious affiliation** (1995): Muslim (mostly Sunni) 47.0%; Russian Orthodox 8.2%; Protestant 2.1%; other (mostly nonreligious) 42.7%. **Major cities** (1999): Almaty (Alma-Ata) 1,130,068; Qaraghandy (Karaganda) 436,900; Shymkent (Chimkent) 360,100; Taraz 330,100; Astana 319,318. **Location:** central Asia, bordering Russia, China, Kyrgyzstan, Uzbekistan, the Aral Sea, Turkmenistan, and the Caspian Sea.

## Vital statistics

**Birth rate** per 1,000 population (2001): 14.9 (world avg. 21.2); (1996) legitimate 82.4%, illegitimate 17.6%. **Death rate** per 1,000 population (2001): 10.0 (world avg. 8.9). **Natural increase rate** per 1,000 population (2001): 4.9 (world avg. 12.3). **Total fertility rate** (avg. births per childbearing woman; 2001): 2.0. **Life expectancy** at birth (2002): male 58.3 years; female 71.1 years.

## National economy

**Budget** (2001). *Revenue*: 743,550,000,000 T (tax revenue 91.1%, of which income, profits, and taxes 34.8%, sales tax 29.3%, social security 17.5%, taxes on international trade 3.6%; nontax revenue 8.9%). *Expenditures*: 749,092,000,000 T (social security 24.9%, education 14.0%, public order 8.5%, health 8.3%, debt 6.7%, defense 4.3%). **Population economically active** (2001): total 7,479,100; activity rate of total population 50.4% (participation rates: ages 16–59 [male], 16–54 [female] 73.6%; female 46%; unemployed 4.4%). **Production** (metric tons except as noted). *Agriculture, forestry, fishing* (2001): wheat 12,910,000, barley 2,330,000, potatoes 1,600,000; livestock (number of live animals) 8,939,400 sheep and goats, 4,106,600 cattle, 976,000 horses; roundwood (1998) 315,000 cu m; fish catch (1999) 26,951. *Mining and quarrying* (2000): copper 32,751,200; iron ore 16,157,000; nickel 7,000,000. *Manufacturing* (value of production in T '000,000; 2001): metallurgy 215,862; food 128,934; oil and nuclear energy 58,270. *Energy production (consumption)*: electricity (kW-hr; 1997) 52,000,000,000 (58,700,000,000); coal (metric tons; 2000) 74,872,400 ([1997] 46,274,000); crude petroleum (barrels; 2000) 258,872,000 ([1997] 66,828,000); petroleum products (metric tons; 1997) 8,249,000 (7,381,000); natural gas (cu m; 2000) 11,541,900,000 ([1997] 7,394,800,000). **Gross national product** (2000): $18,773,000,000 ($1,260 per capita). **Public debt** (external, outstanding; 2000): $3,602,000,000. **Household income and expenditure.** Average household size (1999) 3.6; sources of income (2001): salaries and wages 72.1%, social benefits 9.2%, agricultural income 8.1%, other 10.6%; expenditure (2001): food and beverages 56.0%, housing 11.7%, clothing 7.9%, transportation 5.1%, health 2.6%, education 2.4%, other 14.3%. **Tourism** (2000): receipts $356,000,000; expenditures $408,000,000.

## Foreign trade

**Imports** (2001; f.o.b. in balance of trade): $6,363,000,000 (2000; electrical equipment and mechanical tools 20.3%, vehicles 6.6%, nonfood consumer goods 6.4%, foodstuffs 3.4%, petroleum products 3.4%). *Major import sources:* Russia 50.1%; Germany 6.2%; US 5.3%; UK 3.7%; Ukraine 1.9%; Uzbekistan 1.5%. **Exports** (2001; f.o.b. in balance of trade): $8,646,900,000 (2000; oil and gas condensate 46.9%, refined copper 6.7%, grain 5.3%, ferrous metals 3.1%). *Major export destinations:* Russia 21.8%; Italy 10.8%; Germany 7.3%; China 6.8%.

## Transport and communications

**Transport.** *Railroads*: (2001) route length 13,500 km; passenger-km 10,384,000,000; metric ton-km cargo 135,653,000,000. *Roads* (1999): total length 109,445 km (paved 90%). *Vehicles* (1997): passenger cars 987,724; trucks and buses 291,114. *Air transport* (2001): passenger-km 1,901,100,000; metric ton-km cargo 44,000,000; airports (1999) with scheduled flights 20. **Communications**, in total units (units per 1,000 persons). Radio receivers (1997): 6,470,000 (395); television receivers (1998): (3,890,000) (238); telephone main lines (2001): 1,834,200 (113); cellular telephone subscribers (2001): 582,000 (36); Internet users (2001): 100,000 (6.2).

## Education and health

**Educational attainment** (1989). Population age 25 and over having: primary education or no formal schooling 16.2%; some secondary 19.8%; completed secondary and some postsecondary 54.1%; higher 9.9%. **Literacy** (1989): population age 15 and over literate 97.5%; males 99.1%; females 96.1%. **Health** (2001): physicians 51,300 (1 per 289 persons); hospital beds 110,200 (1 per 134 persons); infant mortality rate per 1,000 live births (2001) 19.4. **Food** (2000): daily per capita caloric intake 2,991 (vegetable products 78%, animal products 22%); 117% of FAO minimum requirement.

## Military

**Total active duty personnel** (2001): 64,000 (army 70.3%, air force 29.7%). **Military expenditure as percentage of GNP** (1999): 0.9% (world avg. 2.4%); per capita expenditure $40.

## Background

Named for its earliest inhabitants, the Kazakhs, the area came under Mongol rule in the 13th century. The Kazakhs consolidated a nomadic empire in the 15th–16th century. Under Russian rule by the mid-19th century, it became part of the Kirgiz Autonomous Republic formed by the Soviets in 1920, and in 1925 its name was changed to the Kazakh

---

*1 metric ton = about 1.1 short tons;   1 kilometer = 0.6 mi (statute);   1 metric ton-km cargo = about 0.68 short ton-mi cargo;   c.i.f.: cost, insurance, and freight;   f.o.b.: free on board*

Autonomous Soviet Socialist Republic. Kazakhstan obtained its independence from the Soviet Union in 1991, and during the 1990s it attempted to stabilize its economy.

## Recent Developments

Kazakhstan's economy continued to perform relatively well in 2002, particularly in the petroleum sector. It was reported that the Kashagan field in the Caspian Sea was proving to be as oil-rich as the Persian Gulf. A deal for an international consortium led by ChevronTexaco to finance a $3 billion expansion of the Tengiz oil field was finally signed in January 2003. In June the parliament passed a law that for the first time would allow private ownership of land.

Internet resources:
<www.kazstat.asdc.kz/indexe.htm>

# Kenya

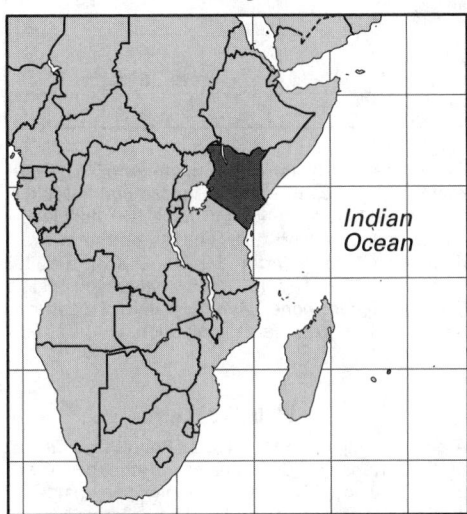

Indian Ocean

**Official name:** Jamhuri ya Kenya (Swahili); Republic of Kenya (English). **Form of government:** unitary multiparty republic with one legislative house (National Assembly [224; including 14 nonelective seats]). **Head of state and government:** President Mwai Kibaki (from 30 Dec 2002). **Capital:** Nairobi. **Official languages:** Swahili; English. **Official religion:** none. **Monetary unit:** 1 Kenya shilling (K Sh) = 100 cents; valuation (7 Jul 2003) $1 = K Sh 74.40.

## Demography

**Area:** 224,961 sq mi, 582,646 sq km. **Population** (2002): 31,139,000. **Density** (2002): persons per sq mi 138.4, persons per sq km 53.4. **Urban** (2002): 34.4%. **Sex distribution** (2001): male 50.16%; female 49.84%. **Age breakdown** (2001): under 15, 41.9%; 15–29, 32.1%; 30–44, 14.6%; 45–59, 7.0%; 60–74, 3.4%; 75 and over, 1.0%. **Ethnic composition** (1989): Kikuyu 17.7%; Luhya 12.4%; Luo 10.6%; Kalenjin 9.8%; Kamba 9.8%; other 39.7%. **Religious affiliation** (2000): Christian 79.3%, of which Roman Catholic 22.0%, African Christian 20.8%, Protestant 20.1%; Muslim 7.3%; other 13.4%. **Major cities** (1999): Nairobi 2,143,254; Mombasa 461,753

(1989); Nakuru 231,262; Kisumu 192,733 (1989); Meru 126,427. **Location:** eastern Africa, bordering Ethiopia, Somalia, the Indian Ocean, Tanzania, Uganda, and The Sudan.

## Vital statistics

**Birth rate** per 1,000 population (2001): 28.5 (world avg. 21.2). **Death rate** per 1,000 population (2001): 14.4 (world avg. 8.9). **Natural increase rate** per 1,000 population (2001): 14.1 (world avg. 12.3). **Total fertility rate** (avg. births per childbearing woman; 2000): 3.7. **Life expectancy** at birth (2001): male 46.6 years; female 48.4 years.

## National economy

**Budget** (2001–02). *Revenue:* K Sh 206,665,600,-000 (tax revenue 86.6%, of which income and profit taxes 29.0%, value-added tax 27.2%, import duties 15.3%, excise tax 15.1%; nontax revenue 13.4%). *Expenditures:* K Sh 235,832,000,000 (recurrent expenditure 80.4%, of which administration 29.7%, education 22.2%, defense 6.1%, health 6.0%; development expenditure 19.6%). **Production** (metric tons except as noted). *Agriculture, forestry, fishing* (2001): sugarcane 5,150,000, corn (maize) 2,700,-000, cassava 950,000; livestock (number of live animals) 12,500,000 cattle, 9,000,000 goats, 6,500,-000 sheep; roundwood (2001) 21,803,900 cu m; fish catch (1999) 205,587, of which freshwater fish 95.0%. *Mining and quarrying* (2000): soda ash 238,200; fluorite 100,100; salt 16,400. *Manufacturing* (value added in K£'000 [Kenya pound (K£) as a unit of account equals 20 K Sh]; 1995): food products 847,000; beverages and tobacco 249,000; machinery and transport equipment 226,000. *Energy production (consumption):* electricity (kW-hr; 2001) 4,338,400,000 (3,654,800,000); coal (metric tons; 1997) none (114,000); crude petroleum (barrels; 1997) none (13,194,000); petroleum products (metric tons; 2001) 1,695,600 (2,385,200). **Household expenditure.** Average household size (1998) 3.4; expenditure (1993–94): food 42.4%, housing and energy 24.1%, clothing and footwear 9.1%, transportation 6.4%, other 18.0%. **Tourism** (2000): receipts from visitors $257,000,000; expenditures by nationals abroad $132,000,000. **Population economically active** (1997): total 14,592,000; activity rate of total population 50.0% (participation rates [1985]: ages 15–64, 76.2%; female [1997] 46.1%). **Public debt** (external, outstanding; 2000): $5,180,000,000. **Gross national product** (2000): $10,610,000,000 ($350 per capita). **Land use** (1994): forest 29.5%; pasture 37.4%; agriculture 8.0%; other 25.1%.

## Foreign trade

**Imports** (2000-c.i.f.): K Sh 247,803,900,000 (machinery and transport equipment 29.1%, mineral fuels 26.1%, chemical products 13.2%, basic manufactures 11.1%, food and beverages 8.6%). *Major import sources:* U.A.E. 19.5%; UK 10.1%; South Africa 6.7%; Saudi Arabia 6.1%; Japan 5.1%; US 4.1%; India 4.1%; Germany 3.5%. **Exports** (2000): K Sh 134,527,100,000 (tea 29.3%, coffee 9.8%, petroleum products 7.9%, horticulture 7.8%, fruits and vegetables 6.5%, chemicals 5.6%, iron and steel 2.2%). *Major export destinations:* Uganda 17.9%; UK 13.9%; Tanzania 8.2%; Pakistan 7.4%; The Netherlands 5.4%; Egypt 5.3%; Germany 4.2%.

## Transport and communications

**Transport.** *Railroads* (2000): route length 2,700 km; passenger-km 302,000,000; metric ton-km cargo 1,557,000,000. *Roads* (1999): total length 63,800 km (paved 14%). *Vehicles* (2000): passenger cars 244,836; trucks and buses 96,726. *Air transport* (1998): passenger-km 2,091,000,000; metric ton-km cargo 243,000,000; airports (1997) with scheduled flights 11. **Communications,** in total units (units per 1,000 persons). Daily newspaper circulation (1996): 263,000 (9.4); radio receivers (1997): 3,070,000 (107); television receivers (1999): 660,000 (23); telephone main lines (2001): 313,100 (10); cellular telephone subscribers (2001): 500,0009 (16); personal computers (2001): 175,0009 (5.6); Internet users (2001): 500,0009 (16).

## Education and health

**Literacy** (1999): total population over age 15 literate 81.5%; males literate 88.3%; females literate 74.8%. **Health** (2001): physicians 4,630 (1 per 6,645 persons); hospital beds 57,540 (1 per 535 persons); infant mortality rate per 1,000 live births (2001): 68.0. **Food** (2000): daily per capita caloric intake 1,965 (vegetable products 88%, animal products 12%); 85% of FAO recommended minimum.

## Military

**Total active duty personnel** (2001): 24,400 (army 82.0%, navy 5.7%, air force 12.3%). **Military expenditure as percentage of GNP** (1999): 1.9% (world 2.4%); per capita expenditure $7.

## Background

The coastal region of East Africa was dominated by Arabs until it was seized by the Portuguese in the 16th century. The Masai people held sway in the north and moved into central Kenya in the 18th century, while the Kikuyu expanded from their home region in south-central Kenya. The interior was explored by European missionaries in the 19th century. After the British took control, Kenya was established as a British protectorate (1890) and a crown colony (1920). The Mau Mau rebellion of the 1950s was directed against European colonialism. In 1963 the country became fully independent, and a year later a republican government under Jomo Kenyatta was elected. In 1992 Kenyan president Daniel arap Moi allowed the country's first multiparty elections in three decades, though the balloting was marred by violence and fraud. Political turmoil occurred over the next years.

## Recent Developments

The December 2002 presidential election was a pivotal event in Kenya's modern history because longtime authoritarian president Daniel arap Moi could not seek reelection. Moi did try to retain a grip on power by backing Uhuru Kenyatta, the son of Kenya's founder Jomo Kenyatta, as the KANU party's candidate. Meanwhile, 12 opposition parties formed the National Rainbow Coalition (NARC) and put forward one candidate, Mwai Kibaki. Kibaki won in a landslide, with 62.3% of the vote, and was sworn in on 30 December. The early days of Kibaki's tenure were marked by concern for his health (he had been injured in a car accident during the campaign), the death and severe injuries of several top government officials in a plane crash in January 2003, and the resignation a month later, under pressure for condoning corruption, of the chief justice.

**Internet resources:** <www.magicalkenya.com>

# Kiribati

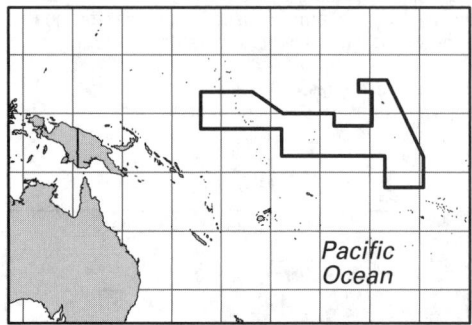

*Pacific Ocean*

**Official name:** Republic of Kiribati. **Form of government:** unitary republic with a unicameral legislature (House of Assembly [42, including two nonelective members]). **Head of state and government:** President Anote Tong (from 10 Jul 2003). **Capital:** Bairiki, on Tarawa Atoll. **Official language:** English. **Official religion:** none. **Monetary unit:** 1 Australian dollar ($A) = 100 cents; valuation (7 Jul 2003) US$1 = $A 1.47.

## Demography

**Area:** 313 sq mi, 811 sq km. **Population** (2002): 90,600. **Density** (2002; based on inhabited island areas (280 sq mi [726 sq km] only): persons per sq mi 323.6, persons per sq km 124.8. **Urban** (2002): 40.0%. **Sex distribution** (2000): male 49.40%; female 50.60%. **Age breakdown** (1995): under 15, 41.2%; 15–29, 25.8%; 30–44, 18.3%; 45–59, 9.3%; 60–74, 4.4%; 75 and over, 1.0%. **Ethnic composition** (1995): I-Kiribati 97.7%; mixed (part I-Kiribati and other) 1.5%; Tuvaluan 0.3%; European 0.2%; other 0.3%. **Religious affiliation** (1995): Roman Catholic 54.3%; Kiribati Protestant (Congregational) 37.9%; Baha'i 2.6%; other Protestant 2.5%; other Christian (Mormon) 1.7%; other/nonreligious 1.0%. **Major cities** (1999): Tarawa (urban area) 32,000. **Location:** western Pacific Ocean, south of the Hawaiian Islands (US).

## Vital statistics

**Birth rate** per 1,000 population (2002): 31.6 (world avg. 21.2). **Death rate** per 1,000 population (2002): 8.8 (world avg. 8.9). **Total fertility rate** (avg. births per childbearing woman; 2002): 4.3. **Marriage rate** per 1,000 population (1988): 5.2. **Life expectancy** at birth (2002): male 57.6 years; female 63.6 years.

*1 metric ton = about 1.1 short tons;   1 kilometer = 0.6 mi (statute);   1 metric ton-km cargo = about 0.68 short ton-mi cargo;   c.i.f.: cost, insurance, and freight;   f.o.b.: free on board*

## National economy

**Budget** (1997). *Revenue*: $A 79,100,000 (nontax revenue 46.6%, tax revenue 20.4%, grants 33.0%). *Expenditures*: $A 79,100,000 (current expenditures 66.3%, of which wages 25.4%; capital expenditures 33.7%). **Public debt** (external, outstanding; 1999): US$9,500,000. **Tourism**: receipts from visitors (2000) US$2,100,000; expenditures by nationals abroad (1999) US$2,000,000. **Land use** (1994): forest 2.7%; agricultural and under permanent cultivation 50.7%; other 46.6%. **Production** (metric tons except as noted). *Agriculture, forestry, fishing* (1999): coconuts 85,000, roots and tubers 6,500 (of which taro 1,600), vegetables and melons 5,000; livestock (number of live animals) 9,500 pigs, 300,000 chickens; fish catch (1997) 23,000. *Mining and quarrying*: none. *Manufacturing* (1996): processed copra 9,321; other important products are processed fish, baked goods, clothing, and handicrafts. *Energy production (consumption)*: electricity (kW-hr; 1997) 7,000,000 (7,000,000); petroleum products (metric tons; 1997) none (7,000). **Gross national product** (2000): US$86,000,000 (US$950 per capita). **Population economically active** (1995): total 38,407; activity rate of total population 49.5% (participation rates: over age 15, 84.0%; female 47.8%; unemployed 0.2%). **Household income and expenditure**. Average household size (1995) 6.5; sources of income (1978): wages 69.7%, self-employment 21.4%, transfer payments 6.0%, other 2.9%; expenditure (1982): food 50.0%, tobacco and alcohol 14.0%, clothing 8.0%, transportation 8.0%, housing, energy, and household operation 7.5%.

## Foreign trade

**Imports** (1996): $A 47,829,000 (food and live animals 33.4%; machinery and transport equipment 18.1%; basic manufactures 14.6%; mineral fuels 10.3%; beverages and tobacco 6.7%; chemicals 6.6%; crude materials 2.1%). *Major import sources*: Australia 46.1%; Fiji 18.7%; Japan 8.6%; New Zealand 8.4%; China 5.9%; US 3.3%. **Exports** (1996): $A 7,447,000 (domestic exports 91.7%, of which copra 62.8%, pet fish 11.6%, fish and fish preparations 4.0%, seaweed 3.6%; reexports 8.3%). *Major export destinations* (1994): Japan 32.9%; US 17.1%; Hong Kong 12.9%; Bangladesh 8.6%; Germany 8.6%; Malaysia 7.1%.

## Transport and communications

**Transport.** *Roads* (1996): total length 670 km (paved 5%). *Vehicles* (1988): passenger cars 222; trucks and buses 115. *Air transport* (1996): passenger-km 7,000,000; metric ton-km cargo 1,000,000; airports 9. **Communications,** in total units (units per 1,000 persons). radio receivers (1997): 17,000 (212); television receivers (1997): 1,000 (15); telephone main lines (2000): 3,400 (40); cellular telephone subscribers (2000): 400 (4.8); personal computers (2001): 2,000 (25); Internet users (2001): 2,000 (25).

## Education and health

**Educational attainment** (1995). Percentage of population age 25 and over having: no schooling 7.8%; primary education 68.5%; secondary or higher 23.7%. **Literacy** (1995): population age 15 and over literate 90%. **Health:** physicians (1998) 26 (1 per 3,378 persons); hospital beds (1990) 283 (1 per 253 persons);

infant mortality rate per 1,000 live births (2002) 52.6. **Food** (1999): daily per capita caloric intake 2,982 (vegetable products 89%, animal products 11%); (1997) 131% of FAO recommended minimum.

## Background

The islands were settled by Austronesian-speaking peoples before the 1st century AD. In 1765 the British discovered the island of Nikunau; the first permanent European settlers arrived in 1837. In 1916 the Gilbert and Ellice islands and Banaba became a crown colony of Britain; they were later joined by the Phoenix and Line islands. In 1979 the colony became the nation of Kiribati.

## Recent Developments

In his address in September 2002 at the World Summit on Sustainable Development in Johannesburg, South Africa, Pres. Teburoro Tito suggested that international development plans focus on social and environmental issues as well as economic concerns. Kiribati, comprised of low-lying coral islands and atolls, is threatened by rising sea levels and increased cyclonic storms as a result of global warming.

**Internet Resources:** <www.tskl.net.ki/Kiribati>

# North Korea

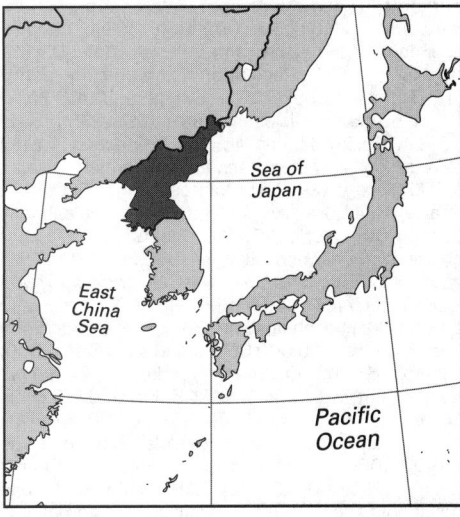

**Official name:** Choson Minjujuui In'min Konghwaguk (Democratic People's Republic of Korea). **Form of government:** unitary single-party republic with one legislative house (Supreme People's Assembly [687]). **Chief of state:** Chairman of the National Defense Commission Kim Jong Il (from 1998) (enhanced military post with revised constitutional powers). **Head of state and government:** Premier Hong Sang Nam (from 1998). **Capital:** Pyongyang. **Official language:** Korean. **Official religion:** none. **Monetary unit:** 1 won = 100 chon; valuation (7 Jul 2003) $1 = 2.20 won.

## Demography

**Area:** 47,399 sq mi, 122,762 sq km. **Population** (2002): 22,224,000. **Density** (2002): persons per sq mi 468.9, persons per sq km 181.0. **Urban** (1998): 62.2%. **Sex distribution** (2000): male 48.48%; female 51.52%. **Age breakdown** (2000): under 15, 25.6%; 15–29, 24.5%; 30–44, 24.7%; 45–59, 14.4%; 60–74, 9.0%; 75 and over, 1.8%. **Ethnic composition** (1999): Korean 99.8%; Chinese 0.2%. **Religious affiliation** (1980): atheist or nonreligious 68.3%; traditional beliefs 15.6%; Ch'ondogyo 13.9%; Buddhist 1.7%; Christian 0.5%. **Major cities** (1993): Pyongyang 2,500,000 (1996 estimate; urban agglomeration for 1999 3,136,000); Namp'o 731,448; Hamhung 709,000; Ch'ongjin 582,480; Kaesong 334,433. **Location:** eastern Asia, bordering China, Russia, the Sea of Japan (East Sea), South Korea, and the Yellow Sea.

## Vital statistics

**Birth rate** per 1,000 population (2000): 20.4 (world avg. 22.5). **Death rate** per 1,000 population (2000): 6.9 (world avg. 9.0). **Natural increase rate** per 1,000 population (2000): 13.5 (world avg. 13.5). **Total fertility rate** (avg. births per childbearing woman; 2000): 2.3. **Marriage rate** per 1,000 population (1987): 9.3. **Divorce rate** per 1,000 population (1987): 0.2. **Life expectancy** at birth (2000): male 67.8 years; female 73.9 years.

## National economy

**Budget** (1999). *Revenue*: 19,801,000,000 won (turnover tax and profits from state enterprises). *Expenditures*: 20,018,200,000 won (1994; national economy 67.8%, social and cultural affairs 19.0%, defense 11.6%). **Population economically active** (1997): total 11,898,000; activity rate of total population 55.8% (participation rates [1988–93]: ages 15–64, 49.5%; female 46.0%). **Production** (metric tons except as noted). *Agriculture, forestry, fishing* (2000): rice 1,690,000, potatoes 1,402,000, corn (maize) 1,041,000; livestock (number of live animals) 2,970,000 pigs, 2,100,000 goats, 10,371,000 chickens; roundwood (2000) 4,900,000 cu m; fish catch (1999): 278,500. *Mining and quarrying* (2000): iron ore (metal content) 300,000; magnesite 1,000,000; phosphate rock 350,000. *Manufacturing* (1999): cement 16,000,000; crude steel 8,100,000; pig iron 6,600,000. *Energy production (consumption)*: electricity (kW-hr; 1999) 28,600,000 (28,600,-000); coal (metric tons; 1999) 85,500,000 (87,600,-000); crude petroleum (barrels; 1999) none (26,000,000); petroleum products (metric tons; 1997) 2,785,000 (4,258,000). **Households.** Average household size (1999) 4.6. **Public debt** (external, outstanding; 1999): $12,000,000,000. **Gross national product** (1999): $9,912,000,000 ($457 per capita). **Land use** (1994): forested 61.2%; meadows and pastures 0.4%; agricultural and under permanent cultivation 16.6%; other 21.8%.

## Foreign trade

**Imports** (1999-f.o.b.): $965,000,000 (crude petroleum, coal and coke, industrial machinery and transport equipment [including trucks], industrial chemicals, textile yarn and fabrics, and grain are among the major imports). *Major import sources* (1995): China 30.0%; Japan 15.8%; Austria 9.3%; Ukraine 5.9%. Ex-

ports (1999): $515,000,000 (minerals [including lead, magnesite, zinc], metallurgical products [iron and steel, nonferrous metals], cement, agricultural products [including fish, grain, fruit and vegetables, tobacco], and manufactured goods [textile fabrics, clothing] are among the major exports). *Major export destinations* (1995): Japan 31.4%; Austria 17.3%; India 6.9%.

## Transport and communications

**Transport.** *Railroads* (1999): length 8,533 km. *Roads* (1998): total length 14,544 mi, 23,407 km (paved 8%). *Vehicles* (1990): passenger cars 248,000. *Air transport* (1997): passenger-km 286,000,000; metric ton-km cargo 30,000,000; airports (2001) with scheduled flights 1. **Communications,** in total units (units per 1,000 persons). Daily newspaper circulation (1996): 4,500,000 (199); radio receivers (1997): 3,360,000 (146); television receivers (1997): 1,200,-000 (52); telephone main lines (1999): 1,100,000 (46).

## Education and health

**Educational attainment** (1987–88). Percentage of population age 16 and over having attended or graduated from postsecondary-level school: 13.7%. **Literacy** (1997): 95%. **Health** (1993): physicians 61,200 (1 per 370 persons); hospital beds (1989) 290,590 (1 per 74 persons); infant mortality rate (2001) 22.5. **Food** (2000): daily per capita caloric intake 2,185 (vegetable products 94%, animal products 6%); 93% of FAO recommended minimum.

## Military

**Total active duty personnel** (2001): 1,082,000 (army 87.8%, navy 4.2%, air force 8.0%). **Military expenditure as percentage of GNP** (1997): 27.5% (world 2.4%); per capita expenditure $282.

---

 **Did you know?** Many association football (soccer) aficionados consider North Korea's 1966 1–0 first round victory over Italy to be the greatest upset in the history of World Cup competition.

---

## Background

According to tradition, the ancient kingdom of Choson was established in the northern part of the Korean Peninsula, probably by peoples from northern China, in the 3rd millennium BC and was conquered by China in 108 BC. The kingdom was ruled by the Yi dynasty from 1392 to 1910. That year Korea was formally annexed by Japan. It was freed from Japanese control in 1945, at which time the USSR occupied the area north of latitude 38° N and the US occupied the area south of it. The Democratic People's Republic of Korea was established as a communist state in 1948. North Korea launched an invasion of South Korea in 1950, initiating the Korean War, which ended with an armistice in 1953. Under Kim Il-sung, North Korea became one of the most harshly regimented societies in the world, with a state-owned

---

*1 metric ton = about 1.1 short tons;   1 kilometer = 0.6 mi (statute);   1 metric ton-km cargo = about 0.68 short ton-mi cargo;   c.i.f.: cost, insurance, and freight;   f.o.b.: free on board*

economy that failed to produce adequate food. In the late 1990s, under Kim Il-sung's successor, Kim Jong Il, the country endured a serious famine; as many as a million Koreans may have died.

## Recent Developments

North Korea's relations with other states, notably the US, continued to seesaw wildly in 2002–03. Pyongyang vigorously protested Pres. George W. Bush's characterization of the regime as part of an "axis of evil" and announced that planned talks with the US would be called off until the criticism was withdrawn. This was followed later in 2002 by a threat to deal the US "merciless blows" should armed forces ever land in North Korea. An American delegation visited Pyongyang in October, but any hopes of improved relations between the two countries were dashed when North Korea admitted that it was still attempting to develop nuclear weapons. In January 2003, under pressure from its regional allies and mindful of its growing problems in Iraq, the US signaled its willingness to talk with North Korea about the nuclear weapons problem. Pyongyang, however, abruptly announced its decision to withdraw from the Nuclear Non-proliferation Treaty. The US countered with offers of aid if the North Koreans would abandon their pursuit of nuclear weapons. The Koreans test-fired a missile on 24 February. The next day the US announced it would resume food aid, and the day after that North Korea restarted a nuclear reactor at its main nuclear complex.

**Internet resources:** <www.kcna.co.jp/index-e.htm>

# South Korea

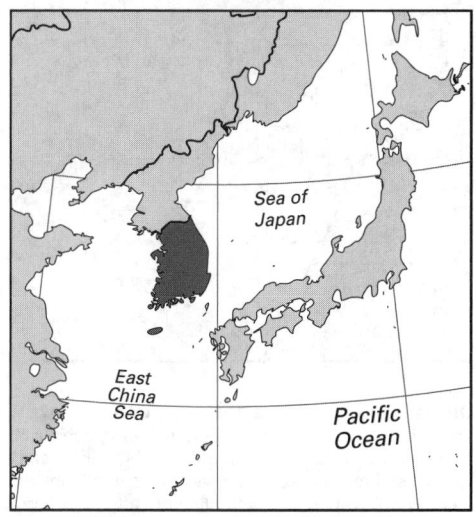

Sea of Japan

East China Sea

Pacific Ocean

**Official name:** Taehan Min'guk (Republic of Korea). **Form of government:** unitary multiparty republic with one legislative house (National Assembly [273]). **Head of state and government:** President Roh Moo Hyun (from 25 Feb 2003), assisted by Prime Minister Goh Kun (from 26 Feb 2003). **Capital:** Seoul. **Official language:** Korean. **Official religion:** none. **Monetary unit:** 1 won (W) = 100 chon; valuation (7 Jul 2003) $1 = W 1,180.50.

## Demography

**Area:** 38,402 sq mi, 99,461 sq km. **Population** (2002): 47,640,000. **Density** (2002): persons per sq mi 1,240.6, persons per sq km 479.0. **Urban** (2002): 83.0%. **Sex distribution** (2002): male 50.34%; female 49.66%. **Age breakdown** (2002): under 15, 20.6%; 15–29, 24.1%; 30–44, 26.9%; 45–59, 16.5%; 60–74, 9.4%; 75 and over, 2.5%. **Ethnic composition** (2000): Korean 97.7%; Japanese 2.0%; US white 0.1%; Han Chinese 0.1%; other 0.1%. **Religious affiliation** (1995): religious 50.7%, of which Buddhist 23.2%, Protestant 19.7%, Roman Catholic 6.6%, Confucian 0.5%, Wonbulgyo 0.2%, Ch'ondogyo 0.1%, other 0.4%; nonreligious 49.3%. **Major cities** (2000): Seoul 9,853,972; Pusan 3,655,437; Taegu 2,473,990; Inch'on 2,466,338; Taejon 1,365,961. **Location:** northeast Asia, bordering North Korea, the Sea of Japan (East Sea), and the Yellow Sea.

## Vital statistics

**Birth rate** per 1,000 population (2001): 11.6 (world avg. 21.2). **Death rate** per 1,000 population (2001): 5.1 (world avg. 8.9). **Natural increase rate** per 1,000 population (2001): 6.5 (world avg. 12.3). **Total fertility rate** (avg. births per childbearing woman; 1999): 1.7. **Marriage rate** per 1,000 population (2000): 7.0. **Divorce rate** per 1,000 population (2000): 2.5. **Life expectancy** at birth (2002): male 72.0 years; female 79.0 years.

## National economy

**Budget** (1998). *Revenue*: W 96,673,000,000,000 (taxes on income and profits 28.9%, taxes on goods and services 28.1%, nontax revenue 18.1%, social security contributions 10.9%, education tax 5.4%). *Expenditures*: W 115,689,000,000,000 (economic services 24.6%, education 15.4%, defense 11.8%, social security and welfare 10.6%, general public services 9.4%, housing and community amenities 6.3%). **Public debt** (external, outstanding; 2000): $46,941,000,000. **Production** (metric tons except as noted). *Agriculture, forestry, fishing* (2000): rice 7,067,000, cabbages 2,755,000, dry onions 936,000; livestock (number of live animals) 7,864,000 pigs, 2,486,000 cattle, 97,000,000 chickens; roundwood 1,722,000 cu m; fish catch (1998) 2,026,934. *Mining and quarrying* (1998): copper ore 226,000; iron ore 133,000; zinc concentrate 10,488. *Manufacturing* (2000): cement 51,424,000; computer peripherals $12,060,000,000; motor vehicles 3,115,000 units. *Energy production (consumption)*: electricity (kW-hr; 1999) 239,328,000,000 ([1997] 248,653,000,000); coal (metric tons; 1999) 4,140,000 ([1997] 53,942,000); crude petroleum (barrels; 1997) none (873,000,000); petroleum products (metric tons; 1997) 97,118,000 (76,056,000); natural gas (cu m; 1997) none (15,620,000,000). **Household income and expenditure** (2000). Average household size (1998) 3.6; income per household W 54,025,000 ($47,769); sources of income: wages 53.0%, other 47.0%; expenditure: food and beverages 27.5%, transportation and communications 16.4%, education and recreation 16.2%, clothing and footwear 5.7%, utilities 5.1%, health care 4.1%, household durable goods 3.7%, housing 3.3%, other 18.0%. **Gross national product** (2000): $421,069,000,000 ($8,910 per capita). **Population economically active** (2000): total 21,950,000; activity rate

46.4% (participation rates: ages 15 and over, 60.7%; female [1998] 38.8%; unemployed 4.1%). **Tourism** (2000): receipts $6,811,000,000; expenditures $6,174,000,000.

## Foreign trade

**Imports** (2000-c.i.f.): $160,481,000,000 (electric and electronic products 27.0%, crude petroleum 15.7%, machinery and transport equipment 13.2%, manufactured consumer goods 10.0%, chemicals 7.4%, iron and steel products 3.7%). *Major import sources:* Japan 19.8%; US 18.2%; China 8.0%; Saudi Arabia 6.0%; Australia 3.7%; Malaysia 3.0%. **Exports** (2000-f.o.b.): $172,267,500,000 (electric and electronic products 36.0%, machinery and transport equipment 18.2%, chemicals 7.0%, crude materials and fuels 6.7%). *Major export destinations:* US 21.8%; Japan 11.9%; China 10.7%; Hong Kong 6.2%; Taiwan 4.7%; Singapore 3.3%; UK 3.1%.

## Transport and communications

**Transport.** *Railroads* (1998): length (2000) 6,706 km; passenger-km 30,072,-000,000; metric ton-km cargo 12,708,000,000. *Roads* (2000): total length 88,775 km (paved 76%). *Vehicles* (2000): passenger cars 8,084,000; trucks and buses 3,938,000. *Air transport* (1998): passenger-km 47,712,000,000; metric ton-km cargo 7,280,640,000; airports (1996) with scheduled flights 14. **Communications,** in total units (units per 1,000 persons). Daily newspaper circulation (1995): 17,700,000 (394); radio receivers (1997): 47,500,000 (1,033); television receivers (1999): 16,896,000 (361); telephone main lines (2001): 22,724,700 (476); cellular telephone subscribers (2001): 29,045,600 (608); personal computers (2001): 12,000,000 (251); Internet users (2001): 24,380,000 (511).

## Education and health

**Educational attainment** (1995). Percentage of population age 25 and over having: no formal schooling 8.5%; primary education or less 17.7%; some secondary and secondary 53.1%; postsecondary 20.6%. **Literacy** (1995): total population age 15 and over literate 98.0%; males 99.3%; females 96.7%. **Health** (1999): physicians 69,724 (1 per 672 persons); hospital beds (1997) 220,427 (1 per 209 persons); infant mortality rate per 1,000 live births (2002): 7.0. **Food** (2000): daily per capita caloric intake 3,073 (vegetable products 86%, animal products 14%); (1997) 131% of FAO recommended minimum.

## Military

**Total active duty personnel** (2001): 683,000 (army 82.0%, navy 8.8%, air force 9.2%); US military forces (2001): 36,000. **Military expenditure as percentage of GNP** (1999): 2.9% (world 2.4%); per capita expenditure $246.

## Background

Civilization in the Korean Peninsula dates to the 3rd millennium BC (see background of Democratic People's Republic of Korea, above). The Republic of

Korea was established in 1948 in the southern portion of the Korean peninsula. In 1950 North Korean troops invaded South Korea, precipitating the Korean War. UN forces intervened on the side of South Korea, while Chinese troops backed North Korea in the war, which ended with an armistice in 1953. The devastated country was rebuilt with US aid, and South Korea prospered in the postwar era, developing a strong export-oriented economy. It experienced an economic downturn in the mid-1990s that affected many economies in the area.

## Recent Developments

As South Korea prepared for a presidential election on 19 Dec 2002, three candidates emerged. The president, Kim Dae Jung, could not run for reelection so he threw his support behind Roh Moo Hyun, a lawyer and former maritime affairs and fisheries minister. Roh, of the ruling Millennium Democratic Party, narrowly defeated Lee Hoi Chang, a contender in previous elections. Roh took office on 25 Feb 2003. Aside from the election, the biggest stories in South Korea for 2002 were in sports. In June the country cohosted, with Japan, the World Cup association football championships, a remarkable, even historic, event. In September and October it played host to the Asian Games in Pusan, also a huge success.

**Internet resources:** <www.nso.go.kr/eng>

# Kuwait

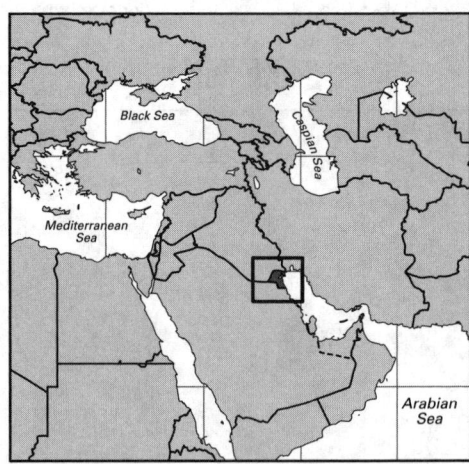

**Official name:** Dawlat al-Kuwayt (State of Kuwait). **Form of government:** constitutional monarchy with one legislative body (National Assembly [65; including 50 elected members plus cabinet ministers not elected to National Assembly serving ex offico]). **Head of state and government:** Emir Sheikh Jabir al-Ahmad al-Jabir Al Sabah (from 1977) assisted by Prime Minister Sheikh Sabah al-Ahmad al-Jabir Al Sabah (from 13 Jul 2003). **Capital:** Kuwait City. **Official language:** Arabic. **Official religion:** Islam. **Monetary unit:** 1 Kuwaiti dinar (KD) = 1,000 fils; valuation (7 Jul 2003) $1 = KD 0.30.

---

*1 metric ton = about 1.1 short tons;   1 kilometer = 0.6 mi (statute);   1 metric ton-km cargo = about 0.68 short ton-mi cargo;   c.i.f.: cost, insurance, and freight;   f.o.b.: free on board*

## Demography

**Area:** 6,880 sq mi, 17,818 sq km. **Population** (2002): 2,253,000. **Density** (2002): persons per sq mi 327.5, persons per sq km 126.4. **Urban** (2001): 96.1%. **Sex distribution** (2000): male 60.04%; female 39.96%. **Age breakdown** (2000): under 15, 29.4%; 15–29, 28.2%; 30–44, 25.8%; 45–59, 12.6%; 60–74, 3.5%; 75 and over, 0.5%. **Ethnic composition** (2000): Arab 74%, of which Kuwaiti 30%, Palestinian 17%, Jordanian 10%, Bedouin 9%; Kurd 10%; Indo-Pakistani 8%; Persian 4%; other 4%. **Religious affiliation** (1995): Muslim 85%, of which Sunni 45%, Shi'i 30%; other Muslim 10%; other (mostly Christian and Hindu) 15.0%. **Major cities** (1995): As-Salimiyah 130,215; Qalib ash-Shuyukh 102,178; Hawalli 82,238; Kuwait City 28,859 (urban agglomeration [2001] 888,000). **Location:** the Middle East, bordering Iraq, the Persian Gulf, and Saudi Arabia.

## Vital statistics

**Birth rate** per 1,000 population (2000): 22.0 (world avg. 22.5). **Death rate** per 1,000 population (2000): 2.4 (world avg. 9.0). **Natural increase rate** per 1,000 population (2000): 19.6 (world avg. 13.5). **Total fertility rate** (avg. births per childbearing woman; 2000): 3.3. **Marriage rate** per 1,000 population (1999): 7.0. **Divorce rate** per 1,000 population (1999): 3.9. **Life expectancy** at birth (2000): male 75.3 years; female 76.9 years.

## National economy

**Budget** (2001–02). *Revenue:* KD 2,224,000,000 (oil revenue 79.2%). *Expenditures:* KD 4,295,000,-000 (transfers 21.2%, defense 20.9%, education 9.1%, economic development 8.0%, health 6.3%). **Tourism** (2000): receipts from visitors $98,000,000; expenditures by na-tionals abroad $2,451,000,000. **Gross national product** (2000): $35,771,000,000 ($18,030 per capita). **Production** (metric tons except as noted). *Agriculture, forestry, fishing* (2000): cucumbers and gherkins 33,004, tomatoes 31,788, eggplants 12,002; livestock (number of live animals) 450,000 sheep, 150,000 goats, 20,400 cattle; fish catch (1999) 6,535. *Mining and quarrying* (1997): sulfur 600,000; lime 40,000. *Manufacturing* (value added in KD '000,000; 1997): refined petroleum products 3,632; industrial chemicals 962; fabricated metal products 68. *Energy production (consumption):* electricity (kW-hr; 1998) 29,988,000,-000 ([1997] 27,224,000,000); crude petroleum (barrels; 2000) 867,000,000 ([1998] 315,000,-000); petroleum products (metric tons; 1997) 41,109,000 (7,722,000); natural gas (cu m; 1998) 11,081,000,000 (11,081,000,000). **Population economically active** (1999): total 1,226,134; activity rate of total population 53.9% (participation rates [1995]: ages 15–59, 70.7%; female 26.1%; unemployed 0.7%). **Household income and expenditure.** Average household size (1995) 3.9; sources of income (1986): wages and salaries 53.8%, self-employment 20.8%, other 25.4; expenditure (1992): food, beverages, and tobacco 37.0%, housing and energy 18.7%, transportation 15.3%, household appliances and services 11.1%, clothing and footwear 10.0%, education and health 2.5%. **Land use** (1994): forest 0.1%; pasture 7.7%; agriculture 0.3%; other 91.9%.

## Foreign trade

**Imports** (1999-f.o.b.): KD 2,318,305,000 (machinery and transport equipment 39.7%, manufactured goods 16.3%, food and live animals 14.9%, miscellaneous manufactured articles 14.5%, chemical products 8.7%). *Major import sources:* Japan 12.8%; US 12.3%; Germany 7.7%; Saudi Arabia 6.2%; UK 5.8%; Italy 5.8%; France 3.7%; India 3.7%. **Exports** (1999-f.o.b.): KD 3,696,000,000 (crude petroleum and petroleum products 96.5%, chemicals 2.9%). *Major export destinations:* Japan 27%; US 14%; South Korea 13%; Singapore 10%; The Netherlands 8%; Pakistan 8%.

## Transport and communications

**Transport.** *Roads* (1997): total length 4,450 km (paved 81%). *Vehicles* (1998): passenger cars 747,042; trucks and buses 140,480. *Air transport* (2000): passenger-km 6,137,195,000; metric ton-km cargo 243,204,000; airports (1999) with scheduled flights 1. **Communications,** in total units (units per 1,000 persons). Daily newspaper circulation (1996): 635,000 (377); radio receivers (1997): 1,175,000 (678); television receivers (1999): 910,000 (520); telephone main lines (2001): 472,000 (240); cellular telephone subscribers (2001): 489,000 (248); personal computers (2001): 260,000 (132); Internet users (2001): 200,000 (101).

## Education and health

**Educational attainment** (1988). Percentage of population age 25 and over having: no formal schooling 44.8%; primary education 8.6%; some secondary 15.1%; complete secondary 15.1%; higher 16.4%. **Literacy** (1995): total population age 15 and over literate 79.3%; males literate 82.3%; females literate 76.0%. **Health** (1998): physicians 3,447 (1 per 541 persons); hospital beds 4,389 (1 per 425 persons); infant mortality rate per 1,000 live births (2000) 11.5. **Food** (2000): daily per capita caloric intake 3,132 (vegetable products 77%, animal products 23%); 129% of FAO recommended minimum.

## Military

**Total active duty personnel** (2001): 15,500 (army [including central staff] 71.0%, navy 12.9%, air force 16.1%); US troops (2002) 10,000. **Military expenditure as percentage of GNP** (1999): 7.7% (world 2.4%); per capita expenditure $1,410.

## Background

Faylakah Island, in Kuwait Bay, had a civilization dating back to the 3rd millennium BC that flourished until 1200 BC. Greek colonists again settled the island in the 4th century BC. Abd Rahim of the Sabah dynasty became sheikh in 1756, the first of a family that continues to rule Kuwait. In 1899, to thwart German and Ottoman influences, Kuwait gave Britain control of its foreign affairs. Following the outbreak of war in 1914, Britain established a protectorate there. In 1961, after Kuwait became independent, Iraq laid claim to it. British troops defended Kuwait, the Arab League recognized its independence, and Iraq dropped its claim. Iraqi forces invaded and occupied Kuwait in 1990, and a US-led military coalition drove them out in 1991. The destruction of many of Kuwait's oil wells complicated reconstruction efforts.

## Recent Developments

The political situation in Kuwait was clouded in 2002 by the comeback of "movement Islamists" (those associated with organizations such as the Islamic Constitution Movement, which in turn was linked to the Muslim Brotherhood). Following revelations after 11 Sep 2001 about Kuwaiti involvement in Osama bin Laden's operations, the Islamists were subjected to rare public criticism, and there were even calls for government supervision of Islamist-run "charities" that solicited money from the population. By the spring of 2002, however, reports of civilian casualties from US bombing in Afghanistan and the staunchly pro-Israel stance of US Pres. George W. Bush had helped restore Islamist credibility and popularity. October saw two attacks by Kuwaitis on American servicemen who were training in the country for a possible attack on Iraq, and two other Americans were shot, one fatally, in an attack in January 2003. US and UK military bases in Kuwait housed the bulk of ground troops for the invasion of Iraq in the spring of 2003, and their presence sent the local stock market soaring.

**Internet resources:** <www.kuwait-info.org>

# Kyrgyzstan

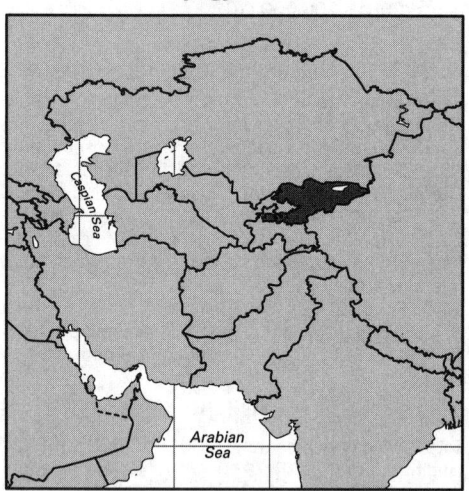

**Official name:** Kyrgyz Respublikasy (Kyrgyz); Respublika Kirgizstan (Russian) (Kyrgyz Republic). **Form of government:** unitary multiparty republic with two legislative houses (Assembly of People's Representatives [45]; Legislative Assembly [60]). **Head of state and government:** President Askar Akayev (from 1990) assisted by Prime Minister Nikolay Tanayev (from 22 May 2002). **Capital:** Bishkek. **Official languages:** Kyrgyz; Russian. **Official religion:** none. **Monetary unit:** 1 som (K.S.) = 100 tyiyn; valuation (7 Jul 2003) $1 = K.S. 41.61.

## Demography

**Area:** 77,200 sq mi, 199,900 sq km. **Population** (2002): 5,002,000. **Density** (2002): persons per sq mi 64.8, persons per sq km 25.0. **Urban** (1999): 34.3%. **Sex distribution** (2001): male 48.84%; female 51.16%. **Age breakdown** (2001): under 15, 35.0%; 15–29, 28.1%; 30–44, 18.6%; 45–59, 9.2%; 60–74, 7.0%; 75 and over, 2.1%. **Ethnic composition** (1999): Kyrgyz 64.9%; Uzbek 13.8%; Russian 12.5%; Hui 1.1%; Ukrainian 1.0%; Uighur 1.0%; other 5.7%. **Religious affiliation** (1997): Muslim (mostly Sunni) 75.0%; Christian 6.7%, of which Russian Orthodox 5.6%; other (mostly nonreligious) 18.3%. **Major cities** (1999): Bishkek (Frunze) 762,308; Osh 220,500; Jalal-Abad 74,200 (1991); Tokmok 71,200 (1991); Kara-Kol 64,300 (1991). **Location:** central Asia, bordering Kazakhstan, China, Tajikistan, and Uzbekistan.

## Vital statistics

**Birth rate** per 1,000 population (2001): 20.6 (world avg. 21.2); (1994) legitimate 83.2%; illegitimate 16.8%. **Death rate** per 1,000 population (2001): 7.3 (world avg. 8.9). **Natural increase rate** per 1,000 population (2001): 13.3 (world avg. 12.3). **Total fertility rate** (avg. births per childbearing woman; 2001): 2.5. **Marriage rate** per 1,000 population (1999): 5.6. **Divorce rate** per 1,000 population (1999): 4.6. **Life expectancy** at birth (2001): male 64.0 years; female 72.0 years.

## National economy

**Budget** (2000). *Revenue:* K.S. 9,896,000,000 (tax revenue 93.9%, of which taxes on goods and services 60.8%, taxes on income and profits 13.9%, taxes on international trade 2.8%; nontax revenue 6.1%). *Expenditures:* K.S. 11,850,000,000 (education 19.4%; health 11.0%; economic development 10.0%; defense 9.9%; social security 9.4%). **Public debt** (external, outstanding; 2000): $1,223,600,000. **Land use** (1994): forest 3.7%; pasture 45.4%; agriculture 7.2%; other 43.7%. **Population economically active** (2000): total 1,905,400; activity rate of total population 39.0% (participation rates: ages 16–59 [male], 16–54 [female] 62.0%; female (1999) 44.9%; unemployed 7.6%). **Production** (metric tons except as noted). *Agriculture, forestry, fishing* (2000): grain 1,569,000, potatoes 1,046,000, vegetables and melons 747,000; livestock (number of live animals) 3,570,000 sheep and goats, 825,000 cattle, 320,000 horses; roundwood (2000) 45,000 cu m; fish catch (1999) 198. *Mining and quarrying* (2000): antimony 1,500; mercury 700; gold 22,000 kg. *Manufacturing* (value of production in '000,000 som; 1994): textiles 1,112; processed foods 729; ferrous and nonferrous metals 678. *Energy production (consumption):* electricity (kW-hr; 2000) 14,886,000,000 (12,054,000,000); coal (metric tons; 2000) 419,400 (1,141,600); crude petroleum (barrels; 2000) 564,000 (564,000); petroleum products (metric tons; 2000) 141,000 (420,000); natural gas (cu m; 2000) 31,900,000 (681,800,000). **Household income and expenditure.** Average household size (1999) 4.3; income per household (1994) 4,359 som ($325); sources of income (1999): wages and salaries 55.2%, pensions and stipends 14.3%, income from agricultural products 4.1%, other 26.4%; expenditure (1990): food and clothing 48.0%, health care 13.1%, housing 5.9%, cultural affairs 5.2%, appliances 4.4%. **Gross national product** (2000): $1,345,000,000 ($270 per capita). **Tourism** (2000): receipts from visitors, $14,000,000; expenditures by nationals abroad, $11,000,000.

*1 metric ton = about 1.1 short tons;    1 kilometer = 0.6 mi (statute);    1 metric ton-km cargo = about 0.68 short ton-mi cargo;    c.i.f.: cost, insurance, and freight;    f.o.b.: free on board*

## Foreign trade

**Imports** (2000-f.o.b. in balance of trade): $502,100,000 (oil and gas 24.5%, machine-building equipment 22.1%, food products 11.4%, chemical products 9.0%, light industrial products 6.4%). *Major import sources:* Russia 26.4%; Uzbekistan 15.0%; Kazakhstan 11.4%; US 10.7%; China 7.3%; Turkey 5.3%. **Exports** (2000-f.o.b. in balance of trade): $510,900,000 (nonferrous metals 45.8%, electricity 15.6%, machinery 9.9%, light industrial products 9.2%, agricultural products 9.2%, food 3.3%). *Major export destinations:* Germany 28.3%; Uzbekistan 17.5%; Russia 13.4%; China 8.6%; Kazakhstan 7.1%; Switzerland 6.7%.

## Transport and communications

**Transport.** *Railroads* (1999): length 424 km; (1998) passenger-km 59,000,000; metric ton-km cargo 471,000,000. *Roads* (1999): total length 18,500 km (paved 91%). *Vehicles* (1999): passenger cars 187,734. *Air transport* (1997): passenger-km 5,301,000,000; metric ton-km cargo 52,000,000; airports with scheduled flights 2. **Communications,** in total units (units per 1,000 persons). Daily newspaper circulation (1996): 67,000 (15); radio receivers (1997): 520,000 (113); television receivers (1998): 220,000 (47); telephone main lines (2001): 376,100 (79); cellular phones (2001): 27,000 (5.4); Internet users (2001): 51,600 (10.5).

## Education and health

**Educational attainment** (1999). Percentage of population age 15 and over having: primary education 6.3%; some secondary 18.3%; completed secondary 50.0%; some postsecondary 14.9%; higher 10.5%. **Literacy** (1999): total population age 15 and over literate 97.5%; males literate 98.5%; females literate 96.5%. **Health** (1997): physicians 15,100 (1 per 307 persons); hospital beds 40,700 (1 per 114 persons); infant mortality rate per 1,000 live births (2001) 39.0. **Food** (2000): daily per capita caloric intake 2,871 (vegetable products 81%, animal products 19%); 111% of FAO recommended minimum.

## Military

**Total active duty personnel** (2001): 9,000 (army 73.3%, air force 26.7%); US troops (June 2002) 1,000. **Military expenditure as percentage of GNP** (1999): 2.4% (world 2.4%); per capita expenditure $62.

---

**Did you know?** Kyrgyzstan boasts a landscape highlighted by soaring mountains that cover more than 95% of the country. The massive Tien Shan system in the southeast dominates the terrain and includes the country's highest point, Victory (Pobeda) Peak (7,439 meters [24,406 feet]). The nearby Mt. Khan-Tengri contains Lake Ysyk-Kol (Issyk-Kul), one of the largest mountain lakes in the world.

---

## Background

The Kyrgyz, a nomadic people of Central Asia, settled in the Tian Shan region in ancient times. They were conquered by Genghis Khan's son Jochi in 1207. The area became part of the Qing empire of China in the mid-18th century. The region came under Russian control in the 19th century, and its rebellion against Russia in 1916 resulted in a long period of brutal repression. Kirgiziya became an autonomous province of the USSR in 1924 and was made the Kirgiz Soviet Socialist Republic in 1936. Kyrgyzstan gained independence in 1991. In the 1990s it struggled with its democratization process and with establishing a thriving economy.

## Recent Developments

Kyrgyzstan in 2002–03 continued to host a large international military presence, mostly American and French, at Bishkek's Manas International Airport in support of the antiterrorist coalition. Opposition parliamentarians questioned the presence of a foreign air base on Kyrgyz soil, but government leaders asserted that it was to the country's benefit to help crush international terrorism. On 17 March 2002 five people were killed and many were wounded in a clash between police and protesters in the southern district of Aksy. Recriminations between the government and the opposition over the punishment of those responsible dominated political life for the rest of the year. On 12 May 2003 Kyrgyzstan closed its border with China to prevent the spread of SARS.

**Internet resources:** <www.kyrgyzstan.org>

# Laos

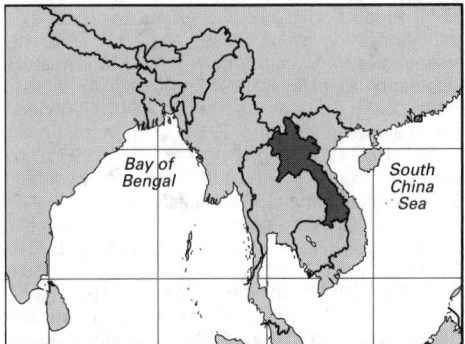

**Official name:** Sathalanalat Paxathipatai Paxaxon Lao (Lao People's Democratic Republic). **Form of government:** unitary single-party people's republic with one legislative house (National Assembly [109]). **Chief of state:** President Khamtai Siphandon (from 1998). **Head of government:** Prime Minister Boungnang Vorachith (from 2001). **Capital:** Vientiane (Viangchan). **Official language:** Lao. **Official religion:** none. **Monetary unit:** 1 kip (KN) = 100 at; valuation (7 Jul 2003) managed floating rate, $1 = KN 7,600.

## Demography

**Area:** 91,429 sq mi, 236,800 sq km. **Population** (2002): 5,777,000. **Density** (2002): persons per sq mi 63.2, persons per sq km 24.4. **Urban** (2002): 25.0%. **Sex distribution** (1996): male 49.42%; female 50.58%. **Age breakdown** (1996): under 15, 44.2%; 15–29, 25.4%; 30–44, 16.0%; 45–59, 8.7%; 60–74, 4.5%; 75 and over, 1.2%. **Ethnic composition** (2000): Lao-Lum (Lao) 53.0%; Lao-Theung (Mon-

Khmer) 23.0%; Lao-Tai (Tai) 13.0%; Lao-Soung (Miao [Hmong] and Man [Yao]) 10.0%; other (ethnic Chinese or Vietnamese) 1.0%. **Religious affiliation** (2000): Buddhist 48.8%; traditional beliefs 41.7%; nonreligious 4.3%; Christian 2.1%; other 3.1%. **Major cities** (1995): Vientiane 528,100; Louangphrabang 55,300; Savannakhet 47,500; Salavan 42,500; Pakxe 32,500. **Location:** southeastern Asia, bordering China, Vietnam, Cambodia, Thailand, and Myanmar (Burma).

## Vital statistics

**Birth rate** per 1,000 population (2002): 36.0 (world avg. 21.2). **Death rate** per 1,000 population (2002): 12.8 (world avg. 8.9). **Natural increase rate** per 1,000 population (2002): 23.2 (world avg. 12.3). **Total fertility rate** (avg. births per childbearing woman; 2001): 5.0. **Life expectancy** at birth (2002): male 52.0 years; female 55.9 years.

## National economy

**Budget** (2000–01). *Revenue:* KN 2,614,000,000,-000 (taxes 66.6%, nontax revenue 17.3%, foreign grants 16.1%). *Expenditures:* KN 3,382,000,000,-000 (capital expenditure 58.1%, current expenditure 41.9%). **Public debt** (external, outstanding; 2000): $2,449,000,000. **Tourism** (2000): receipts from visitors $114,000,000; expenditures by nationals abroad $17,000,000. **Population economically active** (1989): total 1,888,000; activity rate of total population 49.0% (participation rates [1985]: ages 15–64, 84.2%; female 45.3%; unemployed [1994] 2.6%). **Production** (metric tons except as noted). *Agriculture, forestry, fishing* (1999): rice 2,103,000, sugarcane 174,000, corn (maize) 96,000; livestock (number of live animals) 1,937,000 pigs, 1,497,000 cattle, 1,286,000 water buffalo, 13,882,000 chickens; roundwood (1998) 4,591,000 cu m; fish catch (1997) 40,000. *Mining and quarrying* (1997): gypsum 145,000; rock salt 18,000; tin (metal content) 618. *Manufacturing* (1998): plastic products 3,225; tobacco 1,000; detergent 912. *Energy production (consumption):* electricity (kW-hr; 1997) 1,219,-000,000 (495,000,000); coal (metric tons; 1997) 1,000 (1,000); petroleum products (metric tons; 1997) none (112,000). **Gross national product** (2000): $1,519,000,000 ($290 per capita). **Household income.** Average household size (1995) 6.1%; average annual income per household KN 3,710 ($371). **Land use** (1994): forested 54.4%; meadows and pastures 3.5%; agricultural and under permanent cultivation 3.9%; other 38.2%.

## Foreign trade

**Imports** (1998-c.i.f. in balance of trade and commodities): $552,800,000 (consumption goods 42.3%; investment goods 41.0%, of which construction and electrical equipment 14.7%, motor vehicles 7.1%; materials for garment assembly 12.1%). *Major import sources* (1997): Thailand 52.0%; Vietnam 3.9%; Japan 1.6%; Hong Kong 1.5%; China 0.8%. **Exports** (1998): $369,500,000 (wood products 34.3%; garments 20.8%; electricity 18.0%; coffee 14.3%). *Major export destinations* (1997): Vietnam 42.7%; Thailand 22.1%; France 6.3%; Belgium 5.6%; Germany 5.1%.

## Transport and communications

**Transport.** *Roads* (1996): total length 22,321 km (paved [1995] 14%). *Vehicles* (1996): passenger cars 16,320; trucks and buses 4,200. *Air transport* (1997): passenger-km 48,000,000; metric ton-km cargo 5,000,000; airports (1996) with scheduled flights 11. **Communications,** in total units (units per 1,000 persons). Daily newspaper circulation (1996): 18,000 (3.7); radio receivers (1997): 730,000 (145); television receivers (1999): 51,000 (9.6); telephone main lines (2001): 52,600 (9.3); cellular telephone subscribers (2001): 29,500 (5.2); personal computers (2001): 16,000 (2.8); Internet users (2001): 10,000 (1.8).

## Education and health

**Educational attainment** (1985). Percentage of population age 6 and over having: no schooling 49.3%; primary 41.2%; secondary 9.1%; higher 0.4%. **Literacy** (1995): total population age 15 and over literate 56.6%; males literate 69.4%; females literate 44.4%. **Health:** physicians (1995) 3,100 (1 per 1,563 persons); hospital beds (1990) 10,364 (1 per 402 persons); infant mortality rate per 1,000 live births (2002) 91.0. **Food** (1999): daily per capita caloric intake 2,152 (vegetable products 93%, animal products 7%); (1997) 97% of FAO recommended minimum.

## Military

**Total active duty personnel** (2001): 29,100 (army 85.9%, navy 2.1%, air force 12.0%). **Military expenditure as percentage of GNP** (1999): 2.0% (world 2.4%); per capita expenditure $5.

## Background

The Lao people migrated into Laos from southern China after the 8th century AD, displacing indigenous tribes. In the 14th century Fa Ngum founded the first Laotian state, Lan Xang. Except for a period of rule by Burma (1574–1637), the Lan Xang kingdom ruled Laos until 1713, when it split into three kingdoms. France gained control of the region in 1893. In 1945 Japan seized it and declared Laos independent. The area reverted to French rule after World War II. The Geneva Conference of 1954 unified and granted independence to Laos. Communist forces took control in 1975, establishing the Lao People's Democratic Republic. Laos held its first election in 1989 and promulgated a new constitution in 1991. Although its economy was adversely affected by the mid-1990s Asian monetary crises, it realized a longtime goal in 1997 when it joined the Association of Southeast Asian Nations.

## Recent Developments

The elections on 24 Feb 2002 for the 109-seat National Assembly returned many members of the ruling Central Committee of the Lao People's Revolutionary Party. Prime Minister Boungnang Vorachith, promoted from finance minister in 2001, was reappointed. In June the government claimed that in four years opium poppy cultivation in the country had been reduced by 50%.

**Internet resources:** <http://visit-laos.com>

*1 metric ton = about 1.1 short tons;   1 kilometer = 0.6 mi (statute);   1 metric ton-km cargo = about 0.68 short ton-mi cargo;   c.i.f.: cost, insurance, and freight;   f.o.b.: free on board*

# Latvia

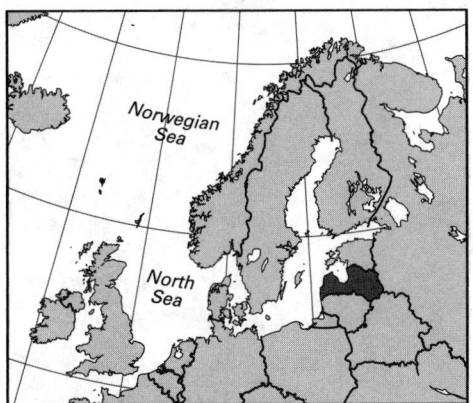

**Official name:** Latvijas Republika (Republic of Latvia). **Form of government:** unitary multiparty republic with a single legislative body (Parliament, or Saeima [100]). **Chief of state:** President Vaira Vike-Freiberga (from 1999). **Head of government:** Prime Minister Einars Repse (from 7 Nov 2002). **Capital:** Riga. **Official language:** Latvian. **Official religion:** none. **Monetary unit:** 1 lats (Ls; plural lati) = 100 santimi; valuation (7 Jul 2003) $1 = 0.56 lats.

## Demography

**Area:** 24,938 sq mi, 64,589 sq km. **Population** (2002): 2,331,000. **Density** (2002): persons per sq mi 93.9, persons per sq km 36.2. **Urban** (2000): 68.1%. **Sex distribution** (2000): male 46.06%; female 53.94%. **Age breakdown** (2000): under 15, 18.1%; 15–29, 21.2%; 30–44, 21.4%; 45–59, 18.3%; 60–74, 15.7%; 75 and over, 5.3%. **Ethnic composition** (2000): Latvian 57.7%; Russian 29.6%; Belarusian 4.1%; Ukrainian 2.7%; Polish 2.5%; Lithuanian 1.4%; other 2.0%. **Religious affiliation** (1995): Christian 39.6%, of which Protestant 16.7% (of which Lutheran 14.6%), Roman Catholic 14.9%, Orthodox 8.0%; Jewish 0.6%; other (mostly nonreligious) 59.8%. **Major cities** (2000): Riga (2001) 755,600; Daugavpils 115,265; Liepaja 89,448; Jelgava 63,652; Jurmala 55,718. **Location:** eastern Europe, bordering Estonia, Russia, Belarus, Lithuania, and the Baltic Sea.

## Vital statistics

**Birth rate** per 1,000 population (2001): 8.3 (world avg. 21.2); (1998) legitimate 62.9%; illegitimate 37.1%. **Death rate** per 1,000 population (2001): 13.9 (world avg. 8.9). **Natural increase rate** per 1,000 population (2001): –5.6 (world avg. 12.3). **Total fertility rate** (avg. births per childbearing woman; 2000): 1.1. **Marriage rate** per 1,000 population (2001): 3.9. **Divorce rate** per 1,000 population (2001): 2.4. **Life expectancy** at birth (1999): male 64.9 years; female 76.2 years.

## National economy

**Budget** (1998). *Revenue:* Ls 1,577,400,000 (social security contributions 27.1%, value-added taxes 20.1%, personal income taxes 13.9%, excises 10.7%, nontax revenue 10.1%). *Expenditures:* Ls 1,572,300,-000 (social security and welfare 34.4%, education

15.7%, health 9.4%, police 5.8%, defense 2.4%). **Production** (metric tons except as noted). *Agriculture, forestry, fishing* (1999): grasses for forage and silage 13,800,000, hay 1,355,000, potatoes 795,500; livestock (number of live animals) 403,400 pigs, 375,700 cattle; roundwood (2001) 14,037,000 cu m; fish catch (1999) 125,827. *Mining and quarrying* (1998): peat 171,700; gypsum 119,100. *Manufacturing* (value added in Ls '000,000; 1998): alcoholic beverages 79.4; sawn wood 64.4; veneer/plywood 37.6. *Energy production (consumption):* electricity (kW-hr; 2001) 4,236,000,000 ([1998] 5,133,000,-000); coal (1997) none (196,000); petroleum products (1997) none (1,690,000); natural gas (cu m; 1997) none (1,143,000,000). **Household income and expenditure.** Average household size (2000) 2.7; annual disposable income per household (1996) Ls 1,659 ($3,011); sources of income (1998): wages and salaries 55.8%, pensions and transfers 25.7%, self-employment 9.5%; expenditure (1998): food, beverages, and tobacco 46.4%, housing and energy 16.6%, transportation and communications 9.8%. **Public debt** (external, outstanding; 2000): $827,100,-000. **Gross national product** (2000): $6,925,000,-000 ($2,920 per capita). **Population economically active** (2000): total 1,131,900; activity rate of total population 46.7% (participation rates: ages 15–64, 67.5%; female 48.5%; unemployed 14.6%). **Tourism** (in $'000,000; 2000): receipts 131; expenditures 248. **Land use** (1994): forested 44.4%; meadows and pastures 12.4; agricultural and under permanent cultivation 27.0%; other 16.2%.

## Foreign trade

**Imports** (1999-c.i.f.): Ls 1,724,000,000 (machinery and equipment 22.0%; chemicals and chemical products 12.0%; mineral fuels 11.4%; transport vehicles 8.3%; textiles and clothing 7.7%). *Major import sources:* Germany 15.2%; Russia 10.5%; Finland 9.1%; Lithuania 7.3%; Sweden 7.2%. **Exports** (1999-f.o.b.): Ls 1,008,000,000 (wood and paper products 37.3%, of which sawn wood 22.0%; textiles and clothing 15.4%; base and fabricated metals 11.5%). *Major export destinations:* Germany 16.9%; UK 16.4%; Sweden 10.7%; Lithuania 7.5%; Russia 6.6%.

## Transport and communications

**Transport.** *Railroads* (2000): length 2,413 km; passenger-km (1999) 984,000,000; metric-km cargo (1999) 12,210,000,000. *Roads* (1999): total length 73,227 km (paved 39%). *Vehicles* (1999): passenger cars 525,572; trucks and buses 101,776. *Air transport* (1999): passenger-km 238,000,000; metric ton-km cargo 10,000,000; airports with scheduled flights (2001) 2. **Communications,** in total units (units per 1,000 persons). Daily newspaper circulation (1996): 616,000 (247); radio receivers (1997): 1,760,000 (713); television receivers (1999): 1,808,000 (755); telephone main lines (2001): 724,800 (308); cellular telephone subscribers (2001): 656,800 (279); personal computers (2001): 360,000 (153); Internet users (2001): 170,000 (72).

## Education and health

**Educational attainment** (2000). Percentage of population age 15 and over having: incomplete primary education 2.4%; complete primary 6.1%; lower secondary 26.5%; upper secondary 51.1%; higher 13.9%.

Literacy (1995): percentage of total population age 15 and over literate 99.6%. **Health** (1998): physicians 6,900 (1 per 355 persons); hospital beds 23,165 (1 per 106 persons); infant mortality rate per 1,000 live births (2001) 10.9. **Food** (1999): daily per capita caloric intake 2,904 (vegetable products 75%, animal products 25%); 113% of FAO recommended minimum.

## Military

Total active duty personnel (2001): 6,500 (army 47.7%, navy 12.9%, air force 3.2%, national guard 36.2%; excludes 3,500 border guards classified as paramilitary). **Military expenditure as percentage of GNP** (1999): 0.9% (world 2.4%); per capita expenditure $59.

## Background

Latvia was settled by the Balts in ancient times. It was conquered by the Vikings in the 9th century and later dominated by its German-speaking neighbors, who Christianized the people in the 12th–13th centuries. By 1230 German rule was established. From the mid-16th to the early 18th century, the region was split between Poland and Sweden, but by the end of the 18th century all of Latvia had been annexed by Russia. Latvia declared its independence after the Russian Revolution of 1917, but in 1940 the Soviet Red Army invaded. Held by Nazi Germany in 1941–44, the country was recaptured by the Soviets and incorporated into the Soviet Union. Latvia gained its independence in 1991 with the breakup of the Soviet Union; throughout the 1990s it sought to privatize the economy and build ties with western Europe.

## Recent Developments

Latvians celebrated the 800th anniversary of the capital, Riga, in 2001. The parliamentary elections in October 2002 altered the composition of the Saeima and led to the formation of a four-party center-right coalition government. In November Latvia received the long-awaited invitation to begin membership negotiations with NATO, and in December came a bid to join the European Union.

Internet resources: <www.eunet.lv/VT>

## Lebanon

**Official name:** Al-Jumhuriyah al-Lubnaniyah (Lebanese Republic). **Form of government:** unitary multiparty republic with one legislative house (National Assembly [128]). **Chief of state:** President Émile Lahoud (from 1998). **Head of government:** Prime Minister Rafiq al-Hariri (from 2000). **Capital:** Beirut. **Official language:** Arabic. **Official religion:** none. **Monetary unit:** 1 Lebanese pound (£L) = 100 piastres; valuation (7 Jul 2003) $1 = £L 1,514.

## Demography

**Area:** 4,016 sq mi, 10,400 sq km. **Population** (2002; excludes about 375,000 Palestinian refugees): 3,678,000. **Density** (2002): persons per sq mi 915.8, persons per sq km 353.7. **Urban** (2001):

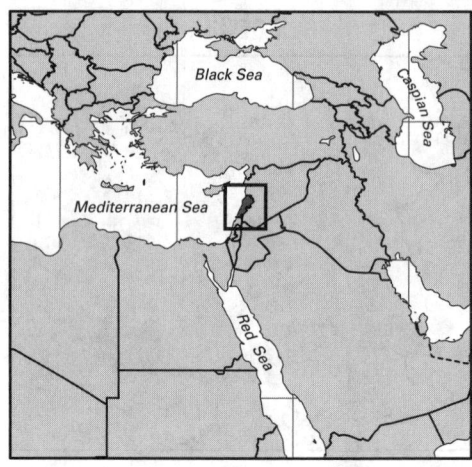

90.1%. **Sex distribution** (2000): male 48.44%; female 51.56%. **Age breakdown** (2000): under 15, 27.9%; 15–29, 33.5%; 30–44, 19.0%; 45–59, 10.1%; 60–74, 7.2%; 75 and over, 2.3%. **Ethnic composition** (2000): Arab 84.5%, of which Lebanese 71.2%, Palestinian 12.1%; Armenian 6.8%; Kurd 6.1%; other 2.6%. **Religious affiliation** (1995): Muslim 55.3%, of which Shi'i 34.0%, Sunni 21.3%; Christian 37.6%, of which Catholic 25.1% (Maronite 19.0%, Greek Catholic or Melchite 4.6%), Orthodox 11.7% (Greek Orthodox 6.0%, Armenian Apostolic 5.2%), Protestant 0.5%; Druze 7.1%. **Major cities** (1998): Beirut 1,100,000 (urban agglomeration; 2,115,000 [2001]); Tripoli 200,000; Sidon (Sayda) 140,000; Tyre (Sur) 110,000; An-Nabatiyah 84,000. **Location:** the Middle East, bordering Syria, Israel, and the Mediterranean Sea.

## Vital statistics

**Birth rate** per 1,000 population (2000): 20.3 (world avg. 22.5). **Death rate** per 1,000 population (2000): 6.4 (world avg. 9.0). **Natural increase rate** per 1,000 population (2000): 13.9 (world avg. 13.5). **Total fertility rate** (avg. births per childbearing woman; 2000): 2.1. **Life expectancy** at birth (1999): male 68.9 years; female 73.7 years.

## National economy

**Budget** (2000). *Revenue:* £L 4,091,435,000,000 (1998; tax revenue 74.6%, of which customs revenues 44.1%, income tax 9.0%, taxes on goods and services 8.4%, property tax 8.4%, miscellaneous taxes and fees 2.1%; nontax revenue 25.4%). *Expenditures:* £L 8,190,034,000,000 (current expenditures 81.1%, of which debt service 40.0%, public services 13.3%, defense 9.7%, education 8.3%, social security 6.4%, health 2.6%; capital expenditures 18.9%). **Production** (metric tons except as noted). *Agriculture, forestry, fishing* (2000): tomatoes 335,000, sugar beets 330,000, potatoes 270,000; livestock (number of live animals) 445,000 goats, 380,000 sheep, 32,000,000 chickens; roundwood (2000) 412,150 cu m; fish catch (1999) 3,860. *Mining and quarrying* (1996): lime 16,000; salt 4,000; gypsum 2,000. *Manufacturing* (1999): cement

*1 metric ton = about 1.1 short tons;   1 kilometer = 0.6 mi (statute);   1 metric ton-km cargo = about 0.68 short ton-mi cargo;   c.i.f.: cost, insurance, and freight;   f.o.b.: free on board*

2,715,000; flour 411,300; olive oil 6,000. *Energy production (consumption)*: electricity (kW-hr; 2000) 9,236,000,000 ([1998] 9,010,000,000); coal, n.a. (none); crude petroleum (barrels; 1998) none (1,358,000); petroleum products (metric tons; 1998) none (3,204,000). **Gross national product** (2000): $17,355,000,000 ($4,010 per capita). **Population economically active** (1995): total 1,028,000; activity rate of total population 25.4% (participation rates: over age 15 [1988] 44%; female c. 30%.). **Public debt** (external, outstanding; 2000): $7,034,000,000. **Household income and expenditure.** Average household size (1998) 4.4; average annual income per household (1994) £L 2,400,000 ($1,430); sources of income (1974): wages 27.9%, transfers 3.0%, other 69.1%; expenditure (1966): food 42.8%, housing 16.8%, clothing 8.6%, health care 7.2%. **Tourism** (2000): receipts from visitors $742,000,000. **Land use** (1994): forested 7.8%; meadows and pastures 1.0%; agricultural and under permanent cultivation 29.9%; wasteland and other areas 61.3%.

## Foreign trade

**Imports** (1999-c.i.f.): $6,177,000,000 (food and live animals 15.2%; machinery and apparatus 14.6%; road vehicles 9.7%; refined petroleum 7.9%; nonmonetary gold 6.3%). *Major import sources:* Italy 10.9%; France 9.6%; Germany 8.9%; US 8.1%; Switzerland 7.1%. **Exports** (1999): $674,000,000 (food 13.7%, of which fruits and vegetables 8.8%; machinery and transport equipment 12.0%; precious metal jewelry 7.7%; apparel 5.7%; aluminum 4.9%). *Major export destinations:* Saudi Arabia 10.5%; UAE 8.0%; France 7.7%; Switzerland 6.6%; US 6.2%.

## Transport and communications

**Transport.** *Roads* (1996): total length 6,350 km (paved 95%). *Vehicles* (1997): passenger cars 1,299,398; trucks and buses 85,242. *Air transport* (2001; Middle East Airlines and Trans-Mediterranean Airways): passenger-km 1,661,000,000; metric ton-km cargo 216,700,000; airports (1999) 1. **Communications,** in total units (units per 1,000 persons). Daily newspaper circulation (1996): 435,000 (141); radio receivers (1997): 2,850,000 (907); television receivers (1998): 1,120,000 (351); telephone main lines (2000): 681,000 (195); cellular telephone subscribers (2000): 743,000 (213); personal computers (2001): 200,000 (56); Internet users (2000): 300,000 (86).

## Education and health

**Literacy** (1995): total population age 15 and over literate 1,829,000 (92.4%); males literate 94.7%; females literate 90.3%. **Health** (1997): physicians 7,203 (1 per 476 persons); hospital beds (1995) 11,596 (1 per 319 persons); infant mortality rate per 1,000 live births (2000) 29.3. **Food** (2000): daily per capita caloric intake 3,155 (vegetable products 87%, animal products 13%); 127% of FAO recommended minimum.

## Military

**Total active duty personnel** (2001): Lebanese national armed forces 71,830 (army 97.5%, navy 1.1%, air force 1.4%). External regular military forces include: UN peacekeeping force in Lebanon (July 2002) 3,400; Syrian army 18,000. **Military expenditure as**

percentage of GNP (1999): 4.0% (world 2.4%); per capita expenditure: $185.

**Did you know?** The Phoenicians, inventors of the alphabet, originally occupied the area of what is now Lebanon. Many scholars believe that the first alphabet was created in the city of Byblos around 1300 BC.

## Background

Much of present-day Lebanon corresponds to ancient Phoenicia, which was settled c. 3000 BC. In the 6th century AD, Christians fleeing Syrian persecution settled in what is now northern Lebanon and founded the Maronite Church. Arab tribesmen settled in southern Lebanon and by the 11th century had founded the Druze faith. Lebanon was later ruled by the Mamluks. In 1516 the Ottoman Turks seized control. the Turks ended the local rule of the Druze Shihab princes in 1842. After the massacre of Maronites by Druze in 1860, France forced the Ottomans to form an autonomous province for the Christian area, known as Mount Lebanon. Following World War I, it was administered by the French military, but by late 1946 it was fully independent. After the Arab–Israeli War of 1948–49, Palestinian refugees settled in southern Lebanon. In 1970 the Palestine Liberation Organization (PLO) moved its headquarters there and began raids into northern Israel. The Christian-dominated Lebanese government tried to curb them, and in response the PLO sided with Lebanon's Muslims in their conflict with Christians, sparking a civil war by 1975. In 1982 Israeli forces invaded in an effort to drive Palestinian forces out of southern Lebanon. Israeli troops withdrew from most of Lebanon in 1985, leaving the conflict unresolved, but later returned. A cease-fire, agreed to in 1996, was broken in 1997 when Israeli soldiers and Lebanon's Hezbollah forces clashed.

## Recent Developments

Two major world meetings took place in Lebanon in 2002—the Arab summit on 27–28 March and the 9th Francophone Summit (which had been postponed a year because of the events of 11 Sep 2001) on 18–20 October. The Arab summit adopted a Saudi Arabian peace plan and transformed it into an Arab peace initiative that called upon Israel to withdraw from the Palestinian and Syrian lands occupied since 1967 and promised an Arab normalization of relations with Israel in return. Prime Minister Rafiq al-Hariri resigned but was immediately reappointed to office in early 2003; he named a new 30-member cabinet on 17 April.

**Internet resources:** <www.presidency.gov.lb>

# Lesotho

**Official name:** Lesotho (Sotho); Kingdom of Lesotho (English). **Form of government:** transitional regime with 2 legislative houses (Senate [33]; National Assembly [120]); traditionally a hereditary monarchy; an interim political authority was mandated in 1998 to make Lesotho more democratic. **Chief of state:** King Letsie III (from 1996). **Head of government:** Prime Minister Pakalitha Mosisili (from 1998). **Capital:**

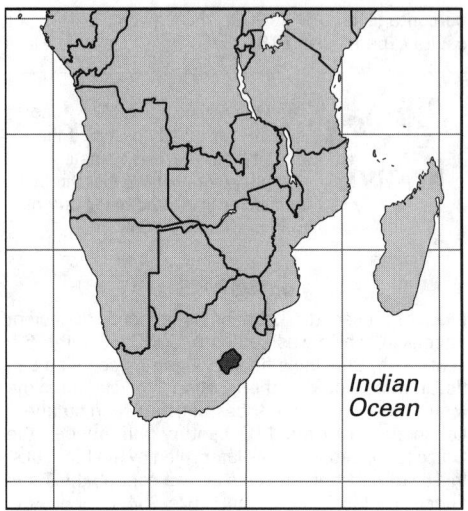

*Indian Ocean*

Maseru. **Official languages:** Sotho; English. **Official religion:** Christianity. **Monetary unit:** 1 loti (plural maloti [M]) = 100 lisente; valuation (7 Jul 2003) $1 = M 7.51.

## Demography

**Area:** 11,720 sq mi, 30,355 sq km. **Population** (2002): 2,208,000. **Density** (2002): persons per sq mi 188.4, persons per sq km 72.7. **Urban** (1996): 16.9%. **Sex distribution** (1996): male 49.20%; female 50.80%. **Age breakdown** (1996): under 15, 43.1%; 15–29, 27.6%; 30–44, 15.0%; 45–59, 8.6%; 60–74, 4.8%; 75 and over, 0.9%. **Ethnic composition** (2000): Sotho 80.3%; Zulu 14.4%; other 5.3%. **Religious affiliation** (2000): Christian 91.0%, of which Roman Catholic 37.5%, Protestant (mostly Presbyterian) 13.0%, African Christian 11.8%; other (mostly traditional beliefs) 9.0%. **Major urban centers** (1996): Maseru 137,837; Teyateyaneng 48,869; Maputsoe 27,951; Hlotse 23,122; Mafeteng 20,804. **Location:** southern Africa, surrounded by South Africa.

## Vital statistics

**Birth rate** per 1,000 population (2002): 30.7 (world avg. 21.2). **Death rate** per 1,000 population (2002): 16.8 (world avg. 8.9). **Natural increase rate** per 1,000 population (2002): 13.9 (world avg. 12.3). **Total fertility rate** (avg. births per childbearing woman; 2002): 4.0. **Life expectancy** at birth (2002): male 46.3 years; female 47.8 years.

## National economy

**Budget** (2000–01). *Revenue*: M 2,752,200,000 (customs receipts 40.9%, grants and nontax revenue 29.4%, income tax 11.4%, sales tax 10.2%). *Expenditures*: M 2,897,900,000 (personal emoluments 31.8%, capital expenditure 17.8%, subsidies and transfers 9.6%, interest payments 9.0%). **Production** (metric tons except as noted). *Agriculture, forestry, fishing* (1999): corn (maize) 125,000, roots and tubers 85,000, sorghum 33,000; livestock (number of live animals) 720,000 sheep, 560,000 goats, 1,700,-000 chickens; roundwood (1998) 1,594,000 cu m;

fish catch (1998) 30. *Mining and quarrying* (1998): diamonds 2,398 carats. *Manufacturing* (value added in $'000,000; 1995): food products 58; beverages 38; textiles 14. **Tourism** (2000): receipts from visitors $24,000,000; expenditures by nationals abroad $9,000,000. **Population economically active** (1993): total 617,871; activity rate of total population 45.1% (participation rates: ages 15–64 [1986] 79.8%; female 23.7%; unemployed [1992] 35.0%). **Household income and expenditure.** Average household size (1996) 5.0; average annual income per household (1986–87) M 2,832 ($1,297); sources of income (1986–87): transfer payments 44.7%, self-employment 27.8%, wages and salaries 22.4%, other 5.1%; expenditure (1989): food 48.0%, clothing 16.4%, household durable goods 11.9%, housing and energy 10.1%, transportation 4.7%. **Gross national product** (2000): $1,181,000,000 ($580 per capita). **Public debt** (external, outstanding; 2000): $697,800,000. **Land use** (1998): meadows and pastures 65.9%; agricultural and under permanent cultivation 10.7%; other 23.4%.

## Foreign trade

**Imports** (1998- f.o.b. in balance of trade and c.i.f. in commodities and trading partners): M 5,199,800,-000 (1990; manufactured goods [excluding chemicals, machinery, and transport equipment] 42.5%; food and live animals 19.1%; machinery and transport equipment 15.3%; petroleum products 8.6%). *Major import sources:* Customs Union of Southern Africa 88.7%; Asia 7.2%; Europe 2.3%, of which European Economic Community 2.0%; the Americas 1.3%. **Exports** (1998): M 1,109,600,000 (manufactured goods 71.6%; machinery and transport equipment 15.1%; food and live animals 4.0%; beverages and tobacco 3.5%; crude materials 1.8%). *Major export destinations:* Customs Union of Southern Africa 65.5%; the Americas 33.6%; Europe 0.5%.

## Transport and communications

**Transport.** *Railroads* (1999): length 2.6 km. *Roads* (1996): total length 4,955 km (paved 18%). *Vehicles* (1996): passenger cars 12,610; trucks and buses 25,000. *Air transport* (1996): passenger-km 6,200,-000; metric ton-km cargo 577,000; airports (1997) with scheduled flights 1. **Communications,** in total units (units per 1,000 persons). Daily newspaper circulation (1996): 15,000 (7.6); radio receivers (1997): 104,000 (52); television receivers (1999): 33,000 (16); telephone main lines (2000): 22,200 (10); cellular telephone subscribers (2001): 33,000 (15); Internet users (2001): 5,000 (2.3).

## Education and health

**Educational attainment** (1986–87). Percentage of population age 10 and over having: no formal education 22.9%; primary 52.8%; secondary 23.2%; higher 0.6%. **Literacy** (1995): total population age 15 and over literate 849,700 (71.3%); males literate 468,000 (81.1%); females literate 381,700 (62.3%). **Health:** physicians (1995) 105 (1 per 18,527 persons); hospital beds (1992) 2,400 (1 per 765 persons); infant mortality rate per 1,000 live births (2002) 82.6. **Food** (1999): daily per capita

*1 metric ton = about 1.1 short tons;    1 kilometer = 0.6 mi (statute);    1 metric ton-km cargo = about 0.68 short ton-mi cargo;    c.i.f.: cost, insurance, and freight;    f.o.b.: free on board*

caloric intake 2,300 (vegetable products 95%, animal products 5%); (1997) 101% of FAO recommended minimum.

## Military

Total active duty personnel (2001): 2,000. Military expenditure as percentage of GNP (1999): 2.6% (world 2.4%); per capita expenditure $14.

## Background

Bantu-speaking farmers began to settle the area in the 16th century, and a number of chiefdoms arose. The most powerful organized the Basotho in 1824 and obtained British protection in 1843, as tension between the Basotho and the South African Boers increased. The area became a British territory in 1868 and was annexed to the Cape Colony in 1871. The colony's effort to disarm the Basotho resulted in revolt in 1880, and four years later it separated from the colony and became a British High Commission Territory. In 1966 it declared its independence. A new constitution (1993) ended seven years of military rule. In the late 20th century, Lesotho suffered from internal political problems and a deteriorating economy.

## Recent Developments

After years of delay, general elections were held in Lesotho on 25 May 2002. Many feared a repetition of problems that had plagued the 1998 elections, which were marred by claims of voting fraud, but South Africa and the Southern African Development Community worked with the Lesotho government, the Interim Political Authority, and the Independent Electoral Commission to try to prevent this. The many observer missions found the elections free and fair.

Internet resources: <www.lesotho.gov.ls>

# Liberia

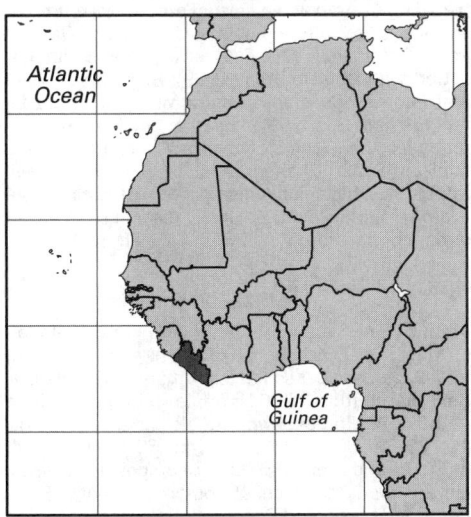

Atlantic
Ocean

Gulf of
Guinea

**Official name:** Republic of Liberia. **Form of government:** multiparty republic with two legislative houses

(Senate [26]; House of Representatives [64]). **Head of state and government:** President Charles Taylor (from 1997 to 12 Aug 2003). **Capital:** Monrovia. **Official language:** English. **Official religion:** none. **Monetary unit:** 1 Liberian dollar (L$) = 100 cents; valuation (7 Jul 2003) US$1 = L$1.00 (par value rate to US$ ineffective from January 1998; the independent free market exchange rate was roughly US$1 = L$60 in August 2001).

## Demography

**Area:** 37,743 sq mi, 97,754 sq km. **Population** (2002): 3,288,000. **Density** (2001): persons per sq mi 87.1, persons per sq km 33.6. **Urban** (2001): 45.5%. **Sex distribution** (2001): male 49.42%; female 50.58%. **Age breakdown** (2001): under 15, 43.2%; 15–29, 27.0%; 30–44, 15.1%; 45–59, 9.4%; 60–74, 4.2%; 75 and over, 1.1%. **Ethnic composition** (1984): Kpelle 19.4%; Bassa 13.9%; Grebo 9.0%; Gio 7.8%; Kru 7.3%; Mano 7.1%; other 35.5%. **Religious affiliation** (1995): traditional beliefs 63.0%; Christian 21.0%, of which Protestant 13.5%, African Christian 5.1%, Roman Catholic 2.4%; Muslim 16.0%. **Major cities** (2002): Monrovia 543,000; Zwedru 33,800; Buchanan 27,000; Yekepa 22,500; Harper 19,600. **Location:** western Africa, bordering Guinea, Côte d'Ivoire, the Atlantic Ocean, and Sierra Leone.

## Vital statistics

**Birth rate** per 1,000 population (2001): 46.6 (world avg. 21.2). **Death rate** per 1,000 population (2001): 16.4 (world avg. 8.9). **Natural increase rate** per 1,000 population (2001): 30.2 (world avg. 12.3). **Total fertility rate** (avg. births per childbearing woman; 2001): 6.4. **Life expectancy** at birth (2001): male 50.0 years; female 52.9 years.

## National economy

**Budget** (2001). *Revenue:* US$80,700,000 (tax revenue 85.1%, of which import duties 22.4%, maritime revenue 19.8%, stamps and land rental 15.9%, income and profit taxes 13.8%; grants 8.3%; nontax revenue 6.6%). *Expenditures:* US$73,100,-000 (current expenditures 76.2%, of which goods and services 42.1%, wages 27.9%, interest on debt 4.5%; development expenditures 23.8%). **Population economically active** (1997): total 1,183,000; activity rate 51.4% (participation rates: ages 10–64 [1994] 64.0%; female 39.5%; unemployed [1996] 95%). **Production** (metric tons except as noted). *Agriculture, forestry, fishing* (2001): cassava 440,-500, sugarcane 250,000, rice 183,400; livestock (number of live animals) 220,000 goats, 210,000 sheep, 4,000,000 chickens; roundwood (2001) 5,261,930 cu m; fish catch (1999) 15,472. *Mining and quarrying* (1998): diamonds 150,000 carats; gold 500 kg. *Manufacturing* (1999): palm oil 42,000; cement 8,300 (1993); cigarettes 22,000,-000 units (1992). *Energy production (consumption):* electricity (kW-hr; 1997) 493,000,000 (493,000,-000); petroleum products (metric tons; 1997) none (107,000). **Public debt** (external, outstanding; 2000): US$1,040,000,000. **Households.** Average household size (1983) 4.3. **Gross national product** (1996): US$1,174,000,000 (US$490 per capita). **Land use** (1994): forested 47.8%; meadows and pastures 20.8%; agricultural and under permanent cultivation 3.8%; other 27.6%.

## Foreign trade

**Imports** (2001): US$180,900,000 (food and live animals 31.1%, petroleum and petroleum products 19.5%, machinery and transport equipment 17.6%, basic manufactures 10.7%, chemicals 4.6%, beverages and tobacco 3.2%). *Major import sources* (1999): South Korea 27.4%; Japan 24.8%; Germany 14.1%; Singapore 7.1%; Croatia 5.2%. **Exports** (2001): US$127,400,000 (rubber 52.9%, logs and timber 46.2%, cocoa 0.4%, other 0.5%). *Major export destinations* (2001): Norway 23.8%; Germany 10.5%; France 7.5%; Singapore 6.5%; Belgium 4.8%; Italy 3.8%; Spain 3.4%; Turkey 3.1%; South Korea 2.0%.

## Transport and communications

**Transport.** *Railroads* (1998): route length 490 km; metric ton-km cargo 860,000,000. *Roads* (1999): total length 10,600 km (paved 6%). *Vehicles* (1996): passenger cars 9,400; trucks and buses 25,000. *Air transport* (1992): passenger-km 7,000,000; metric ton-km cargo 1,000,000; airports (2000) with scheduled flights 2. **Communications,** in total units (units per 1,000 persons). Daily newspaper circulation (1996): 35,000 (16); radio receivers (1997): 790,-000 (329); television receivers (1997): 70,000 (29); telephone main lines (1999): 6,600 (2.2).

## Education and health

**Literacy** (1995): total population age 15 and over literate 705,000 (38.3%); males literate 523,000 (53.9%); females literate 182,000 (22.4%). **Health:** physicians (1992) 257 (1 per 8,333 persons); infant mortality rate per 1,000 live births (2001) 132.4. **Food** (2000): daily per capita caloric intake 2,076 (vegetable products 97%, animal products 3%); 90% of FAO recommended minimum.

## Military

**Total active duty personnel:** About 11,000–15,000 in all armed forces as of 2001. West African (ECOMOG) peacekeepers withdrew in January 1999 and the civil war resumed in April 1999. The fighting continued into 2003. **Military expenditure as percentage of GNP** (1999): 1.2% (world 2.4%); per capita expenditure US$2.

## Background

Africa's oldest republic, Liberia was established as a home for freed US slaves under the American Colonization Society, which founded a colony at Cape Mesurado in 1821. In 1822 Jehudi Ashmun, a Methodist minister, became the director of the settlement and Liberia's real founder. Joseph Jenkins Roberts, Liberia's first nonwhite governor, proclaimed Liberian independence in 1847 and expanded its boundaries, which were officially established in 1892. In 1980 a coup led by Samuel K. Doe marked the end of the Americo-Liberians' long political dominance over the indigenous Africans. A rebellion in 1989 escalated into a destructive civil war in the 1990s. A peace agreement was reached in 1996, and elections were held in 1997.

## Recent Developments

Violence and instability continued into 2003, despite the official end of the civil war. The Liberian government accused neighboring Guinea of supporting antigovernment rebels in northern Liberia. Fighting centered on Monrovia, the capital, as rebel forces advanced and were pushed back. The world waited for the US, at the time of President George W. Bush's trip to Africa in July, to send in peacekeeping forces, but only two dozen troops were provided. Pres. Charles Taylor stepped down on 12 August and went into voluntary exile.

**Internet resources:** <http://www.cia.gov/cia/publications/factbook/geos/li.html>

# Libya

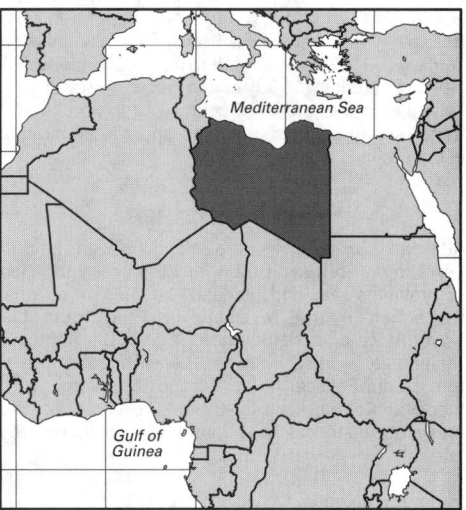

**Official name:** Al-Jamahiriyah al-'Arabiyah al-Libiyah al-Sha'biyah al-Ishtirakiyah al-Uzma (Socialist People's Libyan Arab Jamahiriya). **Form of government:** socialist state with one policy-making body (General People's Congress [760]). **Chief of state:** Muammar al-Qaddafi (de facto; from 1969); Secretary of General People's Congress Zentani Muhammad al-Zentani (de jure; from 1992). **Head of government:** Secretary of the General People's Committee (prime minister) Shokri Ghanem (from 14 Jun 2003). **Capital:** Tripoli. **Official language:** Arabic. **Official religion:** Islam. **Monetary unit:** 1 Libyan dinar (LD) = 1,000 dirhams; valuation (7 Jul 2003) $1 = LD 1.21.

## Demography

**Area:** 678,400 sq mi, 1,757,000 sq km. **Population** (2002): 5,369,000. **Density** (2002): persons per sq mi 7.9, persons per sq km 3.1. **Urban:** (2000) 87.6%. **Sex distribution** (2001): male 51.41%; female 48.59%. **Age breakdown** (2001): under 15, 35.4%; 15–29, 31.7%; 30–44, 19.1%; 45–59, 8.0%; 60–74, 4.5%; 75 and over, 1.3%. **Ethnic composition** (1995): Libyan Arab 78%; Berber 1%; other 21% (mostly Egyptians, Sudanese, and Chadians). **Religious affiliation**

---

*1 metric ton = about 1.1 short tons;    1 kilometer = 0.6 mi (statute);    1 metric ton-km cargo = about 0.68 short ton-mi cargo;    c.i.f.: cost, insurance, and freight;    f.o.b.: free on board*

(1995): Sunni Muslim 97.0%; other 3.0%. **Major cities** (1995): Tripoli 1,140,000; Banghazi 650,000; Misratah 280,000; Surt 150,000. **Location:** northern Africa, bordering the Mediterrranean Sea, Egypt, The Sudan, Chad, Niger, Algeria, and Tunisia.

## Vital statistics

**Birth rate** per 1,000 population (2001): 27.6 (world avg. 21.2). **Death rate** per 1,000 population (2001): 3.5 (world avg. 8.9). **Natural increase rate** per 1,000 population (2001): 24.1 (world avg. 12.3). **Total fertility rate** (avg. births per childbearing woman; 2001): 3.6. **Life expectancy** at birth (2001): male 73.5 years; female 77.9 years.

## National economy

**Budget** (2000). *Revenue:* LD 6,850,000,000 (oil revenues 69.1%, other 30.9%). *Expenditures:* LD 4,400,000,000 (1990–91; current expenditures 55.7%, of which municipalities 39.4%, education and scientific research 4.3%, health 2.7%; capital expenditures 44.3%, of which agriculture and land reclamation 13.6%, industry 5.3%). **Production** (metric tons except as noted). *Agriculture, forestry, fishing* (2001): tomatoes 250,000, watermelons 215,000, potatoes 210,000; livestock (number of live animals; 2001) 5,100,000 sheep, 1,950,000 goats, 25,000,000 chickens; roundwood (2000) 652,000 cu m; fish catch (1999) 32,550. *Mining and quarrying* (2000): lime 290,000; gypsum 175,000; salt 40,000. *Manufacturing* (value of production in '000,000 LD; 1996): base metals 212, electrical equipment 208, petrochemicals 175. *Energy production (consumption):* electricity (kW-hr; 1999) 18,900,000,000 (17,577,000,000); coal (metric tons; 1997) none (5,000); crude petroleum (barrels; 2001) 490,294,000 ([1997] 114,348,-000); petroleum products (metric tons; 1997) 14,266,000 (7,695,000); natural gas (cu m; 1997) 6,542,000,000 (5,442,000,000). **Land use** (1994): forested 0.5%; meadows and pastures 7.6%; agricultural and under permanent cultivation 1.2%; desert and built-up areas 90.7%. **Population economically active** (1996): total 1,224,000; activity rate of total population 26.1% (participation rates [1993]: ages 10 and over, 35.2%; female 9.8%; unemployed [2000] 30.0%). **Public debt** (2000): none. **Gross domestic product** (2000): $38,000,000,000 ($6,200 per capita). **Household.** Average household size (1980) 5.1. **Tourism** (2000): receipts $114,000,000; expenditures $17,000,000.

## Foreign trade

**Imports** (2000-f.o.b. in balance of trade and c.i.f. in commodities and trading partners): $7,600,000,000 (1997; machinery 25.9%; food products 20.0%; road vehicles 10.1%; chemical products 7.5%). *Major import sources:* Italy 24.0%; Germany 12.0%; Tunisia 9.0%; UK 7.0%; France 6.0%. **Exports** (2000): $13,900,000,000 (1997; crude petroleum 76.4%; refined petroleum 16.5%; iron and steel 1.5%). *Major export destinations:* Italy 33.0%; Germany 24.0%; Spain 10.0%; France 5.0%; Turkey 4.0%.

## Transport and communications

**Transport.** *Roads* (1999): total length 83,200 km (paved 57%). *Vehicles* (1996): passenger cars 809,54; trucks and buses 357,528. *Air transport* (2001):

passenger-km 410,000,000; metric ton-km cargo 259,000. **Communications,** in total units (units per 1,000 persons). Daily newspaper circulation (1996): 71,000 (14); radio receivers (1997): 1,350,000 (259); television receivers (1999): 730,000 (133); telephone main lines (2001): 610,000 (115); cellular telephone subscribers (2001): 50,000 (9.0); Internet users (2001): 20,000 (3.6).

## Education and health

**Educational attainment** (1984). Percentage of population age 25 and over having: no formal schooling (illiterate) 59.7%; incomplete primary education 15.4%; complete primary 8.5%; some secondary 5.2%; secondary 8.5%; higher 2.7%. **Literacy** (1998): percentage of total population age 15 and over literate 78.1%; males literate 89.6%; females literate 65.4%. **Health:** physicians (1997) 6,092 (1 per 781 persons); hospital beds (1998) 18,100 (1 per 312 persons); infant mortality rate per 1,000 live births (2001) 29.0. **Food** (2000): daily per capita caloric intake 3,305 (vegetable products 89%, animal products 11%); 140% of FAO recommended minimum.

## Military

**Total active duty personnel** (2001): 76,000 (army 59.2%, navy 10.5%, air force 30.3%). **Military expenditure as percentage of GNP** (1995): 6.1% (world 2.4%); per capita expenditure $342.

---

 The world's largest civil engineering scheme, called the "Great Man-Made River Project," will tap Libya's vast underground reserves of water beneath the southern deserts and deliver it via a series of 4-m (14-ft) pipes to cities and agricultural areas as far as 1500 km (900 mi) away.

---

## Background

Greeks and Phoenicians settled the area in the 7th century BC. It was conquered by Rome in the 1st century BC and by Arabs in the 7th century AD. In the 16th century the Ottoman Turks combined Libya's three regions under one regency in Tripoli. In 1911 Italy claimed control of Libya, and by the outbreak of World War II 150,000 Italians had immigrated there. The scene of much fighting in the war, it became an independent state in 1951. The discovery of oil in 1959 brought wealth to Libya. A decade later a group of army officers led by Muammar al-Qaddafi deposed the king and made the country an Islamic republic. Under Qaddafi's rule it supported the Palestinian Liberation Organization and terrorist groups, bringing protests from many countries, particularly the US. Intermittent warfare with Chad during the 1970s and '80s ended with Chad's defeat of Libya in 1987. International relations in the 1990s were dominated by the consequences of the 1988 bombing of a US airliner over Lockerbie, Scotland; the US accused Libyan nationalists of the deed and imposed a trade embargo on Libya, endorsed by the UN in 1992.

## Recent Developments

The Libyan leadership continued to seek improved international relations with the US and European Union countries. Diplomatic relations had been restored with all except the US by the beginning of 2002. Muammar al-Qaddafi adopted a low profile regarding the major Middle East flash points of Palestine-Israel, the aftermath of Afghanistan, and Iraq. The outcome of the Lockerbie trial in January 2001 was unconvincing internationally, unsatisfactory from the point of view of the families of the American victims, and unhelpful in advancing the Libyan campaign.

Internet resources: <www.arab.net/libya>

# Liechtenstein

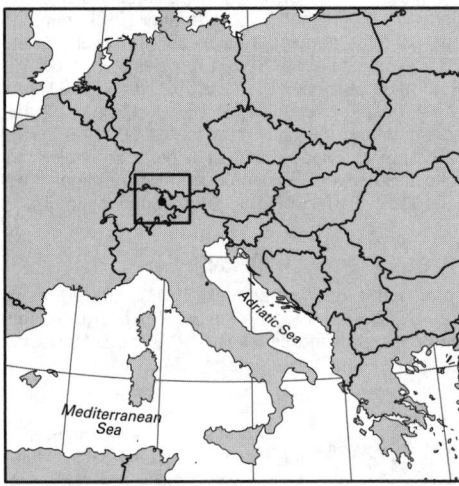

Official name: Fürstentum Liechtenstein (Principality of Liechtenstein). Form of government: constitutional monarchy with one legislative house (Diet [25]). Chief of state: Prince Hans Adam II (from 1989). Head of government: Prime Minister Otmar Hasler (from 2001). Capital: Vaduz. Official language: German. Official religion: none. Monetary unit: 1 Swiss franc (Sw F) = 100 centimes; valuation (7 Jul 2003) $1 = Sw F 1.35.

## Demography

Area: 61.8 sq mi, 160.0 sq km. Population (2002): 33,300. Density (2002): persons per sq mi 538.8, persons per sq km 208.1. Urban (2001): 21.2%. Sex distribution (2000): male 48.70%; female 51.30%. Age breakdown (2000): under 15, 18.7%; 15–29, 22.3%; 30–44, 25.4%; 45–59, 19.4%; 60–74, 9.7%; 75 and over, 4.5%. Ethnic composition (2000): Liechtensteiner 65.5%; Swiss 11.9%; Austrian 6.2%; German 3.4%; Italian 2.8%; other 10.2%. Religious affiliation (1998): Roman Catholic 80.0%; Protestant 7.5%; Muslim 3.3%; Eastern Orthodox 0.7%; atheist 0.6%; other 7.9%. Major cities (1999): Schaan 5,262; Vaduz 5,106. Location: central Europe, between Austria and Switzerland.

## Vital statistics

Birth rate per 1,000 population (2000): 11.8 (world avg. 22.5); (1997) legitimate 86.0%; illegitimate 14.0%. Death rate per 1,000 population (2000): 6.7

(world avg. 9.0). Natural increase rate per 1,000 population (2000): 5.1 (world avg. 13.5). Total fertility rate (avg. births per childbearing woman; 2000): 1.5. Marriage rate per 1,000 population (1998): 13.2. Divorce rate per 1,000 population (1994): 1.4. Life expectancy at birth (2000): male 75.2 years; female 82.5 years.

## National economy

Budget (1999). Revenue: Sw F 690,200,000 (taxes and duties 78.2%, investment income 11.3%, charges and fees 8.5%, real estate capital-gains taxes and death and estate taxes 2.0%). Expenditures: Sw F 537,200,000 (financial affairs 35.8%, social welfare 17.0%, education 15.1%, transportation 9.1%, general administration 9.4%, public safety 4.9%, health 4.7%). Public debt: none. Tourism (2001): 123,273 tourist overnight stays. Population economically active (2000): total 16,368; activity rate of total population 50.1% (participation rates: ages 15–64, 71.2%; female 40.3%; unemployed 1.8%). Household income and expenditure. Average household size (1990) 2.7; sources of earned income (1987): wages and salaries 92.9%, self-employment 7.1%; expenditure (1990): rent 20.9%, food 17.7%, transportation 11.0%, education and self-improvement 9.7%, clothing 7.0%, health 4.7%. Production (metric tons except as noted). Agriculture, forestry, fishing (2000): significantly market gardening, other crops include cereals and apples; livestock (number of live animals; 2000) 6,000 cattle, 3,000 pigs, 2,900 sheep; commercial timber (1998) 19,527 cu m. Manufacturing (1997): processed milk 13,304; milk for whipped cream 262; yogurt 82; cheese 3; wine (1993) 635.2 hectolitres. Energy production (consumption): electricity (kW-hr; 1997) 75,842,000 (302,018,000 [2000]); coal (metric tons; 1996) none (24); petroleum products (metric tons; 1995) none (49,291); natural gas (cu m; 1994) none (19,350,000). Gross national product (1998): $1,164,000,000 ($36,760 per capita). Land use (latest): forested 34.8%; meadows and pastures 15.7%; agricultural and under permanent cultivation 24.3%; other 25.2%.

## Foreign trade

Imports (1997): Sw F 1,179,000,000 (machinery and transport equipment 35.2%; other finished goods 23.6%; metal products 12.5%; limestone, cement, and other building materials 12.4%; unrefined and semifabricated metal 5.7%; chemical products 5.2%). Major import sources: EU and Switzerland. Exports (1997): Sw F 2,694,000,000 (machinery and transport equipment 49.2%; metal products 15.1%; other finished goods 12.7%; limestone, cement, and other building materials 9.8%; chemical products 7.7%; food and beverages 4.2%). Major export destinations (1998): EU 49.5%; Switzerland 12.7%; other 37.8%.

## Transport and communications

Transport. Railroads (1998): length 18.5 km. Roads (1999): total length 323 km. Vehicles (1999): passenger cars 21,150; trucks and buses (1998) 2,684. Air transport: the nearest scheduled airport service is through Zürich, Switzerland. Communications, in total units (units per 1,000 persons). Daily newspaper circulation (1998): 17,900 (565); radio receivers (1997):

1 metric ton = about 1.1 short tons;     1 kilometer = 0.6 mi (statute);     1 metric ton-km cargo = about 0.68 short ton-mi cargo;     c.i.f.: cost, insurance, and freight;     f.o.b.: free on board

21,000 (658); television receivers (1997): 12,000 (364); telephone main lines (1999): 19,763 (597).

## Education and health

**Educational attainment** (1990). Percentage of population not of preschool age or in compulsory education having: no formal schooling 0.3%; primary and lower secondary education 39.3%; higher secondary and vocational 47.6%; some postsecondary 7.4%; university 4.2%; other and unknown 1.1%. **Literacy:** virtually 100%. **Health:** physicians (1997) 41 (1 per 764 persons); hospital beds 108 (1 per 288 persons); infant mortality rate per 1,000 live births (2000) 5.7. **Food** (1999): daily per capita caloric intake 3,600 (vegetable products 65%, animal products 35%); 134% of FAO recommended minimum.

## Military

**Total active duty personnel:** none; Liechtenstein has had no standing army since 1868. **Military expenditure as percentage of GNP:** none.

## Background

The Rhine plain was occupied for centuries by two independent lordships of the Holy Roman Empire, Vaduz and Schellenberg. The principality of Liechtenstein, consisting of these two lordships, was founded in 1719 and remained part of the Holy Roman Empire. It was included in the German Confederation (1815–66). In 1866 it became independent, recognizing Vaduz and Schellenberg as unique regions forming separate electoral districts. An almost 60-year ruling coalition dissolved in 1997, and the prince urged adoption of constitutional reforms.

## Recent Developments

Prince Hans Adam II won a referendum in mid-March 2003 that made him the most powerful monarch in Europe. He was given the power to kill any bill in the legislature, dissolve the elected government, approve judicial nominees, and ignore rulings of the constitutional court. Some 64% of the residents of Liechtenstein voted to give up their rights to the prince, who had threatened to move out of the country if the vote went against him.

Internet resources: <www.news.li>

# Lithuania

**Official name:** Lietuvos Respublika (Republic of Lithuania). **Form of government:** unitary multiparty republic with a single legislative body, the Seimas (141). **Head of state:** President Rolandas Paksas (from 26 Feb 2003). **Head of government:** Premier Algirdas Brazauskas (from 2001). **Capital:** Vilnius. **Official language:** Lithuanian. **Official religion:** none. **Monetary unit:** 1 litas (LTL) = 100 centai; valuation (7 Jul 2003) $1 = LTL 3.01.

## Demography

**Area:** 25,212 sq mi, 65,300 sq km. **Population** (2002): 3,473,000. **Density** (2002): persons per sq mi 137.8, persons per sq km 53.2. **Urban** (2001): 66.9%. **Sex distribution** (2001): male 46.76%; female 53.24%. **Age

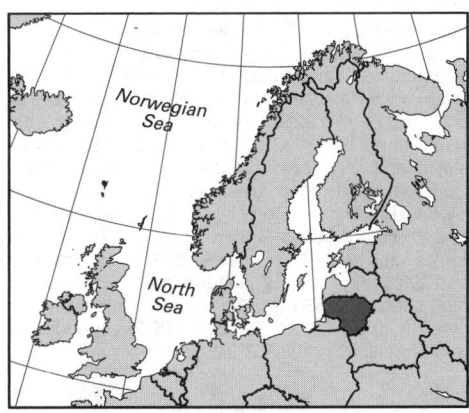

breakdown** (2001): under 15, 19.5%; 15–29, 21.2%; 30–44, 22.8%; 45–59, 17.2%; 60–74, 14.2%; 75 and over, 5.1%. **Ethnic composition** (2001): Lithuanian 83.5%; Polish 6.7%; Russian 6.3%; Belarusian 1.2%; Ukrainian 0.7%; other 1.6%. **Religious affiliation** (1995): Roman Catholic 72.2%; Orthodox 3.3%; Protestant 1.3%; other (mostly nonreligious) 23.2%. **Major cities** (2001): Vilnius 542,287; Kaunas 378,943; Klaipeda 192,954; Siauliai 133,883; Panevezys 119,749. **Location:** eastern Europe, bordering Latvia, Belarus, Poland, Russia, and the Baltic Sea.

## Vital statistics

**Birth rate** per 1,000 population (2001): 9.0 (world avg. 21.2); (2000) legitimate 77.4%; illegitimate 22.6%. **Death rate** per 1,000 population (2001): 11.6 (world avg. 8.9). **Natural increase rate** per 1,000 population (2001): –2.6 (world avg. 12.3). **Total fertility rate** (avg. births per childbearing woman; 2000): 1.3. **Marriage rate** per 1,000 population (2000): 4.6. **Divorce rate** per 1,000 population (2000): 2.9. **Life expectancy** at birth (2000): male 67.6 years; female 77.9 years.

## National economy

**Budget** (1998). *Revenue:* LTL 9,378,000,000 (value-added tax 38.5%, individual income tax 25.8%, excise taxes 14.3%, nontax revenue 7.5%). *Expenditures:* LTL 9,916,000,000 (education 27.7%, police 12.3%, social security and welfare 10.0%, health 6.6%, defense 4.5%). **Gross national product** (2000): $10,809,000,000 ($2,930 per capita). **Production** (metric tons except as noted). *Agriculture, forestry, fishing* (1999): hay 2,621,000, potatoes 1,699,000, sugar beets 890,000, wheat 837,300; livestock (number of live animals) 1,168,000 pigs, 928,000 cattle; roundwood (2000) 5,500,000 cu m; fish catch (1999) 35,244. *Mining and quarrying* (1998): limestone 250,000; peat 195,300. *Manufacturing* (value of production in LTL '000,000; 1997): food and beverages 5,785; refined petroleum products 3,488; wearing apparel 1,378. *Energy production (consumption):* electricity (kW-hr; 2000) 11,388,000,000 ([1997] 12,105,000,000); coal (metric tons; 1997) none (256,000); crude petroleum (barrels; 1997) 1,554,000 (36,782,000); petroleum products (metric tons; 1997) 5,151,000 (3,326,000); natural gas (cu m; 1997) none (2,148,000,000). **Public debt** (external outstanding; 2000): $2,188,300,000. **Population economically active** (1997): total 1,819,800; activity rate of total population 49.1% (participation rates: ages 14–64, 71.1%; female 47.3%; registered unemployed [2000] 11.5%). **Household income and expenditure**. Average household size (1997) 2.9; average annual household disposable income (1997): LTL 12,914 ($3,228); sources of income (1998): wages and salaries 52.7%, transfers 21.3%, self-employment 14.8%, other 11.2%; expenditure (1998): food, beverages, and expenditures in cafés/hotels 54.6%, housing and energy 12.4%, transportation and communications 8.6%, clothing and footwear 8.0%. **Land use** (1994): forested 30.4%; meadows and pastures 7.6%; agricultural and under permanent cultivation 53.9%; other 8.1%. **Tourism** (2000): receipts from visitors $391,000,000; expenditures by nationals abroad $253,000,000.

## Foreign trade

**Imports** (2000-c.i.f.): LTL 21,826,000,000 (mineral fuels 23.3%, machinery/apparatus 15.7%, textiles and clothing 9.3%, chemicals and chemical products 9.1%, food products 8.3%). *Major import sources:* Russia 27.4%; Germany 15.1%; Poland 4.9%; UK 4.5%; France 4.2%. **Exports** (2000-f.o.b.): LTL 15,238,000,000 (mineral fuels 21.2%, textiles and clothing 18.6%, machinery/apparatus 10.6%, food products 9.4%, chemicals and chemical products 7.9%). *Major export destinations:* Latvia 15.0%; Germany 14.3%; UK 7.8%; Russia 7.1%; Poland 5.5%.

## Transport and communications

**Transport.** *Railroads* (1998): route length 1,997 km; passenger-km 715,000,000; metric ton-km cargo 8,265,000,000. *Roads* (1999): total length 73,650 km (paved 91%). *Vehicles* (1999): passenger cars 1,089,334; trucks and buses 102,414. *Air transport* (2001; Lithuanian Airlines): passenger-km 438,000,-000; metric ton-km cargo 1,531,000; airports with scheduled flights (1996) 3. **Communications,** in total units (units per 1,000 persons). Daily newspaper circulation (1996): 344,000 (93); radio receivers (1997): 1,900,000 (513); television receivers (1999): 1,555,000 (420); telephone main lines (2001): 1,151,700 (313); cellular telephone subscribers (2001) 932,000 (253); personal computers (2001): 260,000 (71); Internet users (2001): 250,000 (68).

## Education and health

**Educational attainment** (1989). Percentage of population age 25 and over having: no schooling 9.1%; incomplete and complete primary education 21.3%; incomplete and complete secondary 57.0%; postsecondary 12.6%. **Literacy** (1995): total population age 15 and over literate 99.2%. **Health** (1998): physicians 14,622 (1 per 253 persons); hospital beds 35,612 (1 per 104 persons); infant mortality rate per 1,000 live births (2001) 7.9. **Food** (1999): daily per capita caloric intake 2,959 (vegetable products 77%, animal products 23%); 116% of FAO recommended minimum.

## Military

**Total active duty personnel** (2001): 12,190 (army 61.5%, navy 4.8%, air force 6.6%, volunteer national defense force 27.1%; excludes 4,400 paramilitary in border police or coast guard). **Military expenditure as percentage of GNP** (1999): 1.3% (world 2.4%); per capita expenditure $87.

## Background

Lithuanian tribes united in the mid-13th century to oppose the Teutonic knights. Gediminas, one of the grand dukes, expanded Lithuania into an empire that dominated much of Eastern Europe in the 14th through 16th centuries. In 1386 the Lithuanian grand duke became the king of Poland, and the two countries remained closely associated until Lithuania was acquired by Russia in the Third Partition of Poland in 1795. Occupied by Germany during World War I, it declared its independence in 1918. In 1940 the Red Army gained control of Lithuania. Germany occupied it again in 1941–44, but the USSR regained control in 1944. With the breakup of the USSR, Lithuania became independent in 1991. During the 1990s it sought economic stability and hoped to join the European Union and NATO. It signed a border treaty with Russia in 1997.

## Recent Developments

The year 2003 brought a shock from polls as underdog Rolandas Paksas unseated the popular incumbent, Pres. Valdas Adamkus, a former US citizen. Paksas, a right-wing former prime minister, was considered something of an eccentric: a trained pilot, he performed a dangerous aerial stunt during the campaign and later raised eyebrows when he admitted to links with a faith healer. Lithuania remained on track to join NATO and the EU.

**Internet resources:** <www.tourism.lt>

# Luxembourg

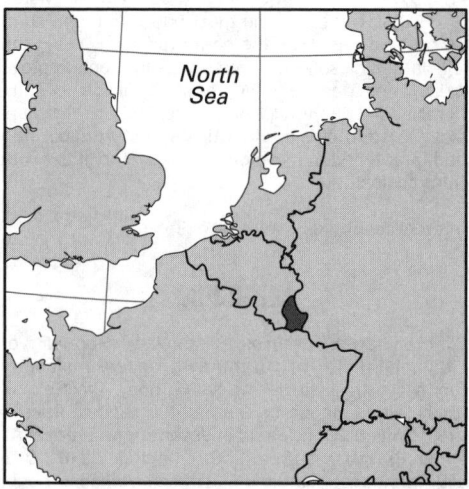

**Official name:** Groussherzogtum Lëtzebuerg (Luxemburgian); Grand-Duché de Luxembourg (French); Grossherzogtum Luxemburg (German) (Grand Duchy of Luxembourg). **Form of government:** constitutional monarchy with two legislative houses (Council of

*1 metric ton = about 1.1 short tons;   1 kilometer = 0.6 mi (statute);   1 metric ton-km cargo = about 0.68 short ton-mi cargo;   c.i.f.: cost, insurance, and freight;   f.o.b.: free on board*

State [21]; Chamber of Deputies [60]). **Chief of state:** Grand Duke Henri (from 2000). **Head of government:** Prime Minister Jean-Claude Juncker (from 1995). **Capital:** Luxembourg. **Official language:** none; Luxemburgian (national); French (used for most official purposes); German (lingua franca). **Official religion:** none. **Monetary unit:** 1 euro (€) = 100 cents; valuation (7 Jul 2003) $1 = €0.87; at conversion on 1 Jan 2002, €1= 40.3 Luxembourg franc (Lux F).

## Demography

**Area:** 999 sq mi, 2,586 sq km. **Population** (2002): 447,000. **Density** (2002): persons per sq mi 447.4, persons per sq km 172.9. **Urban** (2002): 91.9%. **Sex distribution** (2001): male 49.26%; female 50.74%. **Age breakdown** (2001): under 15, 18.9%; 15–29, 18.2%; 30–44, 25.4%; 45–59, 18.7%; 60–74, 13.1%; 75 and over, 5.7%. **Ethnic composition** (nationality; 2001): Luxemburger 63.1%; Portuguese 13.4%; French 4.6%; Italian 4.3%; Belgian 3.4%; German 2.3%; English 1.0%; other 7.9%. **Religious affiliation** (1996): Roman Catholic 95.1%; other 4.9%. **Major cities** (2001): Luxembourg 76,687; Esch-sur-Alzette 27,186; Dudelange 17,348; Schifflange 7,854; Bettembourg 7,162. **Location:** western Europe, bordering Belgium, Germany, and France.

## Vital statistics

**Birth rate** per 1,000 population (2001): 12.4 (world avg. 21.2); (1998) legitimate 82.5%; illegitimate 17.5%. **Death rate** per 1,000 population (2001): 8.8 (world avg. 8.9). **Natural increase rate** per 1,000 population (2001): 3.6 (world avg. 12.3). **Total fertility rate** (avg. births per childbearing woman; 2001): 1.7. **Marriage rate** per 1,000 population (2001): 4.5. **Divorce rate** per 1,000 population (2001): 2.3. **Life expectancy** at birth (2001): male 74.2 years; female 81.0 years.

## National economy

**Budget** (2002). *Revenue:* €5,977,200,000 (1998; income and excise taxes 58.2%, customs taxes 13.4%). *Expenditures:* €5,976,100,000 (1998; social security 21.3%, education 11.7%, transportation 8.2%, administration 6.5%, defense 2.7%, debt service 0.9%). **Public debt** (1997): $668,420,000. **Production** (metric tons except as noted). *Agriculture, forestry, fishing* (2000): barley 64,787, wheat 53,500, potatoes 23,430; livestock (number of live animals) 205,072 cattle, 80,141 pigs; roundwood (2000) 355,000 cu m. *Mining and quarrying* (1999): gypsum and anhydrite 400,000. *Manufacturing* (2001): rolled steel 4,519,000; crude steel 2,725,000; cement 748,600. *Energy production (consumption):* electricity (kW-hr; 2000) 1,124,000,000 (6,445,000,000); coal (metric tons; 1997) none (194,000); petroleum products (metric tons; 1997) none (1,615,000); natural gas (cu m; 1997) none (730,700,000). **Land use** (1992): forested 34.2%; meadows and pastures 25.6%; agricultural and under permanent cultivation 23.2%; other 17.0%. **Tourism** (1997): receipts from visitors $297,000,000. **Gross national product** (2000): $18,439,000,000 ($42,060 per capita). **Population economically active** (2001): total 277,000; activity rate of total population 63.0% (participation rates: ages 15–64 [1997] 51.4%; female [1997] 38.2%; unemployed [2001] 2.6%). **Household income and expenditure.** Average household size (1991) 2.6; income

per household (1992) Lux F 1,438,000 ($44,700); sources of income (1992): wages and salaries 67.1%, transfer payments 28.1%, self-employment 4.8%; expenditure (1994): food, beverages, and tobacco 19.7%, housing 17.3%, transportation and communications 16.2%, household goods and furniture 9.9%, clothing and footwear 8.2%, health 7.9%.

## Foreign trade

**Imports** (2000-c.i.f.): €11,126,400,000 (machinery and other equipment 22.0%; fabricated metals 12.7%; transport equipment 12.1%; chemicals and chemical products 9.9%; food, beverages, and tobacco 5.2%). *Major import sources:* Belgium 37.1%; Germany 25.2%; France 12.9%; The Netherlands 4.8%; US 3.5%; UK 2.9%. **Exports** (2000-f.o.b.): €8,483,400,000 (fabricated metals 30.0%; machinery and equipment 24.4%; basic manufactures 16.0%; chemicals and chemical products 6.7%; transport equipment 4.0%; food products 3.7%). *Major export destinations:* Germany 23.9%; France 21.0%; Belgium 12.6%; UK 7.6%; Italy 5.5%; The Netherlands 5.3%; US 4.1%.

## Transport and communications

**Transport.** *Railroads* (2001): route length 274 km; passenger-km 346,000,000; metric ton-km cargo 634,000,000. *Roads* (1999): total length 5,166 km (paved 100%). *Vehicles* (2001): passenger cars 273,088; trucks and buses 21,490. *Air transport* (2001): passengers carried 1,625,000; cargo 510,965 metric tons; airports (2001) with scheduled flights 1. **Communications,** in total units (units per 1,000 persons). Daily newspaper circulation (1996): 135,000 (325); radio receivers (1997): 285,000 (677); television receivers (1998): 165,000 (389); telephone main lines (2001): 350,000 (783); cellular telephone subscribers (2001): 432,400 (967); personal computers (2001): 230,000 (515); Internet users (2001): 100,000 (227).

## Education and health

**Literacy** (2001): virtually 100% literate. **Health** (2001): physicians 1,123 (1 per 392 persons); hospital beds 3,035 (1 per 145 persons); infant mortality rate per 1,000 live births (2001) 4.7. **Food** (1995): daily per capita caloric intake 3,530 (vegetable products 68%, animal products 32%); 134% of FAO recommended minimum.

## Military

**Total active duty personnel** (2000): 899 (army 100.0%). **Military expenditure as percentage of GNP** (1999): 0.8% (world 2.4%); per capita expenditure $326.

## Background

At the time of Roman conquest (57–50 BC), Luxembourg was inhabited by a Belgic tribe. After AD 400, Germanic tribes invaded the region. Made a duchy in 1354, it was ceded to the house of Burgundy in 1443 and to the Habsburgs in 1477. In the mid-16th century it became part of the Spanish Netherlands. It was made a grand duchy in 1815. After an uprising in 1830, its western portion became part of Belgium, while the remainder was held by The Netherlands. In

1867 the European powers guaranteed the neutrality and independence of Luxembourg. In the late 19th century it exploited its extensive iron-ore deposits. It was invaded and occupied by Germany in both world wars. It abandoned its neutrality by joining NATO in 1949; it had joined the Benelux Economic Union in 1944. A member of the European Union, its economy has continued to expand. On 7 Oct 2000, Grand Duke Jean abdicated power in favor of his son, Crown Prince Henri, after 36 years on the throne.

## Recent Developments

A peace march of about 1,000 demonstrators—large for Luxembourg—was held on 19 Oct 2002 to protest the threatened war with Iraq.

**Internet resources:** <www.luxembourg.co.uk>

# Macau

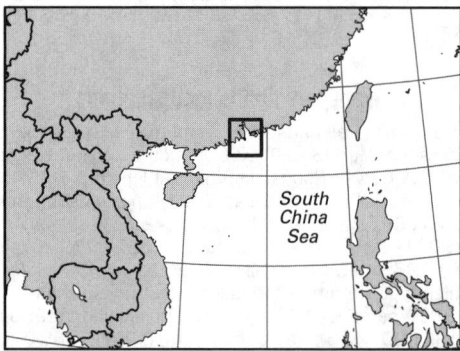

South China Sea

**Official name:** Aomen Tebie Xingzhengqu (Chinese); Região Administrativa Especial de Macau (Portuguese) (Macau Special Administrative Region). **Political status:** special administrative region (China) with one legislative house (Legislative Council [27, including 10 directly elected seats, 7 seats appointed by the chief executive, and 10 seats appointed by special-interest groups]). **Chief of state:** President Hu Jintao of China (from 15 Nov 2002). **Head of government:** Chief Executive Edmund Ho Hau-wah (from 1999). **Capital:** Macau. **Official languages:** Chinese; Portuguese. **Official religion:** none. **Monetary unit:** 1 pataca (MOP) = 100 avos; valuation (7 Jul 2003) $1 = MOP 8.03.

## Demography

**Area:** 9.1 sq mi, 23.6 sq km. **Population** (2002): 438,000. **Density** (2002): persons per sq mi 43,800, persons per sq km 16,977. **Urban** (2002): urban, virtually 100% (about 1% of Macau's population live on sampans and other vessels). **Sex distribution** (2001): male 47.55%; female 52.45%. **Age breakdown** (1999): under 15, 23.2%; 15–29, 22.9%; 30–44, 29.0%; 45–59, 15.0%; 60–74, 6.6%; 75 and over, 3.3%. **Nationality** (1991): Chinese 68.2%; Portuguese 27.9%; English 1.8%; other 2.1%. **Religious affiliation** (1998): nonreligious 60.8%; Buddhist 16.7%; other 22.5%. **Major city** (2000 est.): Macau 437,900. **Location:** eastern Asia, bordering China and the South China Sea.

## Vital statistics

**Birth rate** per 1,000 population (2002): 9.0 (world avg. 21.2). **Death rate** per 1,000 population (2002): 4.6 (world avg. 8.9). **Natural increase rate** per 1,000 population (2002): 4.4 (world avg. 12.3). **Total fertility rate** (avg. births per childbearing woman; 2002): 1.1. **Marriage rate** per 1,000 population (2001): 2.8. **Divorce rate** per 1,000 population (2001): 0.8. **Life expectancy at birth** (2002): male 77.0 years; female 82.0 years.

## National economy

**Budget** (1998). *Revenue*: MOP 14,831,099,000 (recurrent receipts 69.1%, autonomous agency receipts 21.4%, capital receipts 2.2%). *Expenditures*: 14,831,099,000 MOP (recurrent payments 61.1%, autonomous agency expenditures 21.4%, capital payments 17.5%). **Tourism**: receipts from visitors (2000) $2,999,000,000; expenditures by nationals abroad (1999) $131,000,000. **Land use** (1992): built-on area, wasteland, and other 100.0%. **Gross domestic product** (at current market prices; 2000): $6,385,000,000 ($14,580 per capita). **Production** (metric tons except as noted). *Agriculture, forestry, fishing* (1999): eggs 650; livestock (number of live animals) 500,000 chickens; fish catch (1997) 1,500. *Quarrying* (value added in '000,000 MOP; 1997): 13. *Manufacturing* (value added in MOP '000,000; 1997): wearing apparel 2,161; textiles 607; electrical appliances 131. *Energy production (consumption)*: electricity (kW-hr; 1997) 1,409,000,000 (1,584,000,000); petroleum products (metric tons; 1997) none (480,000). **Public debt** (long-term, external; 1999): $706,000,000. **Population economically active** (1998): total 210,700; activity rate of total population 48.9% (participation rates: age 15–64, 70.2%; female 44.8%; unemployed [1999] 6.6%). **Household expenditure.** Average household size (1991) 3.5; expenditure (1987–88): food 38.3%, housing 19.7%, education, health, and other services 12.1%, transportation 7.4%, clothing and footwear 6.8%, energy 4.0%, household durable goods 3.7%, other goods 8.0%.

## Foreign trade

**Imports** (1998-c.i.f.): MOP 15,596,446,000 (raw materials 54.1%, capital goods 14.2%, foodstuffs 9.3%, fuels and lubricants 6.3%). *Major import sources*: China 32.7%; Hong Kong 23.7%; European Community 10.5%; Taiwan 9.9%; Japan 7.8%; US 4.7%. **Exports** (1998): MOP 17,083,616,000 (garments 76.4%, textiles 4.5%, machinery and mechanical appliances 3.5%, textile yarn and thread 3.1%, footwear 2.2%). *Major export destinations*: US 47.7%; European Community 30.5%; Hong Kong 7.6%; China 6.8%; Taiwan 1.5%; Japan 0.7%.

## Transport and communications

**Transport.** *Roads* (1996): total length 50 km (paved 100%). *Vehicles* (1998): passenger cars 45,184; trucks and buses 6,578. **Communications**, in total units (units per 1,000 persons). Daily newspaper circulation (1996): 200,000 (455); radio receivers (1997): 160,000 (356); television receivers (1999): 125,492 (287); telephone main lines (2001): 176,400 (394); cellular telephone subscribers

---

*1 metric ton = about 1.1 short tons;     1 kilometer = 0.6 mi (statute);     1 metric ton-km cargo = about 0.68 short ton-mi cargo;     c.i.f.: cost, insurance, and freight;     f.o.b.: free on board*

(2001): 194,500 (434); personal computers (2001): 80,000 (179); Internet users (2001): 101,000 (225).

## Education and health

**Educational attainment** (1991). Population age 25 and over having: no formal schooling 13.1%; incomplete primary education 16.0%; completed primary 19.9%; some secondary 45.1%; postsecondary 5.9%. **Literacy** (1995): percentage of population age 15 and over literate 91.7%; males literate 95.6%; females literate 88.2%. **Health** (1998): physicians 369 (1 per 1,167 persons); hospital beds 1,086 (1 per 396 persons); infant mortality rate per 1,000 live births (2002) 8.0. **Food** (1998): daily per capita caloric intake 2,471 (vegetable products 76%, animal products 24%); 108% of FAO recommended minimum.

## Military

**Total active duty personnel:** Chinese troops (2001) 500.

---

**Did you know?** Macau's name is derived from the Chinese A-mangao, or "Bay of A-ma," named for A-ma, the Chinese goddess popular among sailors.

---

## Background

Portuguese traders first arrived in Macau in 1513, and it soon became the chief market center for the trade between China and Japan. It was declared a Portuguese colony in 1849 and an overseas territory in 1951. In December 1999 Portugal returned it to Chinese rule.

## Recent Developments

In 2002 Macau broke the long-standing monopoly on its important casino industry by awarding three new gaming licenses. Two of the licenses went to Las Vegas–connected enterprises. Plans were under way to boost the struggling economy by bringing flashy Las Vegas glamour to the industry.

**Internet resources:** <www.macautourism.gov.mo>

# Macedonia

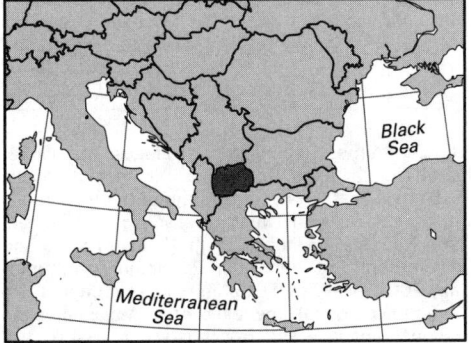

**Official name:** Republika Makedonija (Republic of Macedonia [member of the UN under the name The Former Yugoslav Republic of Macedonia]). **Form of**

**government:** unitary multiparty republic with a unicameral legislative (Assembly [120]). **Head of state:** President Boris Trajkovski (from 1999). **Head of government:** Prime Minister Branko Crvenkovski (from 1 Nov 2002). **Capital:** Skopje. **Official language:** Macedonian (pending approval of Albanian as second official language at the local level). **Official religion:** none. **Monetary unit:** denar; valuation (7 Jul 2003) $1 = 53.47 denar.

## Demography

**Area:** 25,713 sq km. **Population** (2002): 2,031,000. **Density** (2002): persons per sq mi 204.6, persons per sq km 79.0. **Urban** (2000): 62.0%. **Sex distribution** (2001): male 50.06%; female 49.94%. **Age breakdown** (2001): under 15, 22.9%; 15–29, 24.4%; 30–44, 21.5%; 45–59, 16.8%; 60–64, 11.2%; 65 and over, 3.2%. **Ethnic composition** (2000): Macedonian 53.9%; Albanian 18.0%; Turkish 7.7%; Roma (Gypsy) 5.3%; Aromanian 5.0%; Serbian 2.1%; Croat 2.0%; other 6.0%. **Religious affiliation** (1995): Serbian (Macedonian) Orthodox 54.2%; Sunni Muslim 30.0%; other 15.8%. **Major cities** (1994): Skopje 440,577; Bitola 75,386; Prilep 67,371; Kumanovo 66,237; Tetovo 50,376. **Location:** southeastern Europe, bordering Serbia and Montenegro, Bulgaria, Greece, and Albania.

## Vital statistics

**Birth rate** per 1,000 population (2001): 13.5 (world avg. 21.2); (1998) legitimate 90.5%; illegitimate 9.5%. **Death rate** per 1,000 population (2001): 7.7 (world avg. 8.9). **Natural increase rate** per 1,000 population (2001): 5.8 (world avg. 12.3). **Total fertility rate** (avg. births per childbearing woman; 2001): 1.6. **Marriage rate** per 1,000 population (1999): 7.0. **Life expectancy** at birth (2001): male 71.8 years; female 76.4 years.

## National economy

**Budget** (2002). *Revenue:* 53,089,000,000 denar (tax revenue 94.2%, of which value-added tax 33.7%, excise taxes 20.6%, income and profit tax 19.6%; import duties 10.0%; nontax revenue 5.8%). *Expenditure:* 59,979,000,000 denar (wages and salaries 29.5%, pensions 26.1%, goods and services 20.0%, interest 6.1%). **External debt** (2000): $1,165,000,-000. **Production** (metric tons except as noted). *Agriculture, forestry, fishing* (2001): wheat 246,000, grapes 229,800, potatoes 176,000; livestock (number of live animals) 1,251,000 sheep, 265,000 cattle, 3,350,000 chickens; roundwood (2000) 1,052,-000 cu m; fish catch (1999) 1,804 (all freshwater). *Mining and quarrying* (1999): copper 38,200; lead 12,300; zinc 10,200. *Manufacturing* (1998): cement 461,195; steel sheets 276,464; detergents 21,990. *Energy production (consumption):* electricity (kW-hr; 1997) 6,719,000,000 (6,719,000,000); coal (metric tons; 1997) 6,700,000 (6,800,000); crude petroleum (barrels; 1997) none (2,932,000); petroleum products (metric tons; 1997) 385,000 (976,000). **Household income and expenditure** (1994). Average household size 3.8; income per household Din 49,635 ($1,223); sources of income: wages and salaries 59.9%, transfer payments 17.0%, transfers from abroad 13.4%, other 9.7%; expenditure: food 42.2%, fuel and lighting 7.5%, clothing and footwear 7.4%, transportation and communications 7.2%, drink and tobacco 7.0%, health care 4.7%, education and entertainment 3.2%. **Gross national product** (2000): $3,902,000,000 ($1,920 per capita). **Population economically active** (2000): total 811,000; activity rate 39.9% (participation rates: ages 15–64, 52.9%; female 38.5%; unemployed 28.4%). **Tourism** (2000): receipts from visitors $37,000,000; expenditures by nationals abroad $34,000,000.

## Foreign trade

**Imports** (2000): $1,875,000,000 (machinery and transport equipment 19.6%, manufactured products 12.9%, mineral fuels 13.9%, food products and beverages 11.2%, chemical products 9.0%). *Major import sources:* Germany 12.1%; Ukraine 9.8%; Greece 9.6%; Russia 9.2%; Serbia and Montenegro 9.2%; Slovenia 6.9%; Italy 5.3%; US 4.0%. **Exports** (2000): $1,319,000,000 (manufactured products 36.8%, machinery and transport equipment 6.3%, food products 5.0%, chemical products 4.5%, raw materials 3.7%). *Major export destinations:* Serbia and Montenegro 25.2%; Germany 19.4%; US 12.6%; Italy 6.6%; Greece 6.4%; Croatia 3.6%.

## Transport and communications

**Transport.** *Railroads* (1999): length 925 km; passenger-km 150,000,000; metric ton-km cargo 380,000,000. *Roads* (1998): length 11,513 km (paved 63%). *Vehicles* (1998): passenger cars 288,678; trucks and buses 24,745. *Air transport* (2001; Macedonian Airlines): passenger-km 168,000,000; metric tons cargo transported 130,000,000; airports (2001) with scheduled flights 2. **Communications,** in total units (units per 1,000 persons). Daily newspaper circulation (1996): 41,000 (20); radio receivers (1997): 410,000 (204); television receivers (1999): 500,000 (248); telephone main lines (2001): 538,000 (264); cellular telephone subscribers (2001): 223,300 (109); Internet users (2001): 70,000 (34).

## Education and health

**Educational attainment** (1981). Percentage of population age 15 and over having: less than full primary education 45.3%; primary 28.1%; secondary 21.2%; postsecondary and higher 5.1%; unknown 0.3%. **Literacy** (1998): 94.6%. **Health** (1998): physicians 4,508 (1 per 445 persons); hospital beds 10,333 (1 per 194 persons); infant mortality rate per 1,000 live births (2001) 13.0. **Food** (2000): daily per capita caloric intake 3,006 (vegetable products 83%, animal products 17%); 118% of FAO recommended minimum.

## Military

**Total active duty personnel** (2001): 16,000 (army 95.6%, air force 4.4%). **Military expenditure as percentage of GNP** (1999): 2.5% (world 2.4%); per capita expenditure $112.

## Background

Macedonia has been inhabited since before 7000 BC. Part of it was incorporated into a Roman province in AD 29. It was settled by Slavic tribes by the mid-6th century AD. Seized by the Bulgarians in 1185, it was ruled by the Ottoman Empire from 1371 to 1912. The north and center of the region were annexed by Serbia in 1913 and in 1918 became part of what was later known as Yugoslavia. When Yugoslavia was partitioned by the Axis powers in 1941, Yugoslav Macedonia was occupied principally by Bulgaria. Macedonia again became part of Yugoslavia in 1946. After Croatia and Slovenia seceded from Yugoslavia, fear of Serbian dominance drove Macedonia to declare its independence in 1991. Because of Greek objections to the new state using the name of an ancient Greek province, it entered the UN as "the Former Yugoslav Republic of Macedonia."

## Recent Developments

In 2002 Macedonia tried to overcome the consequences of the previous year's armed conflict between the ethnic Albanian National Liberation Army (UCK) and state security forces. Implementing the August 2001 Ohrid agreement, the parliament passed several key pieces of legislation aimed at improving relations between Macedonia's two largest ethnic communities. These included a new law in January on local self-government that transferred some powers from the central government to the municipal level, an amnesty law in March, and a package of language laws in June that established Albanian as the second official language. Macedonia joined the World Trade Organization in April 2003.

**Internet resources:** <www.sinf.gov.mk>

# Madagascar

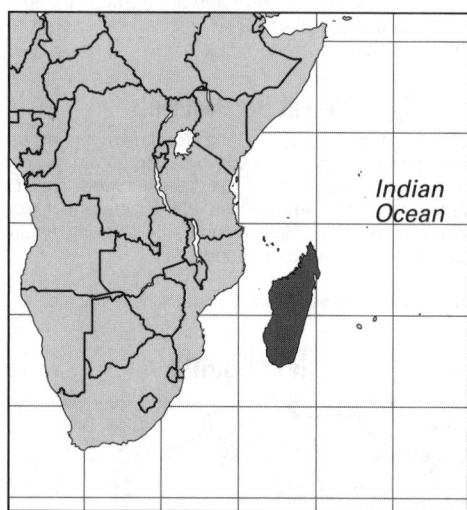

*Indian Ocean*

**Official name:** Repoblikan'i Madagasikara (Malagasy); République de Madagascar (French) (Republic of Madagascar). **Form of government:** federal multiparty republic with two legislative houses (Senate [90]; National Assembly [150]). **Heads of state and government:** President Marc Ravalomanana (from 6 May 2002) assisted by a prime minister. **Capital:** Antananarivo. **Official languages:** none; Malagasy is the national language and French is widely spoken; two versions of the constitution are in Malagasy and

*1 metric ton = about 1.1 short tons;    1 kilometer = 0.6 mi (statute);    1 metric ton-km cargo = about 0.68 short ton-mi cargo;    c.i.f.: cost, insurance, and freight;    f.o.b.: free on board*

French. **Official religion:** none. **Monetary unit:** 1 Malagasy franc (FMG) = 100 centimes; valuation (7 Jul 2003) $1 = FMG 5,920.

## Demography

**Area:** 226,658 sq mi, 587,041 sq km. **Population** (2002): 16,473,000. **Density** (2002): persons per sq mi 72.7, persons per sq km 28.1. **Urban** (2001): 30.1%. **Sex distribution** (2000): male 49.70%; female 50.30%. **Age breakdown** (2000): under 15, 45.0%; 15–29, 26.5%; 30–44, 15.8%; 45–59, 7.9%; 60–74, 3.8%; 75 and over, 1.0%. **Ethnic composition** (2000): Malagasy 95.9%, of which Merina 24.0%, Betsimisaraka 13.4%, Betsileo 11.3%, Tsimihety 7.0%, Sakalava 5.9%; Makua 1.1%; French 0.6%; Comorian 0.5%; Reunionese 0.4%; other 1.5%. **Religious affiliation** (2000): Christian 49.5%, of which Protestant 22.7%, Roman Catholic 20.3%; traditional beliefs 48.0; Muslim 1.9%; other 0.6%. **Major cities** (1993): Antananarivo 1,103,304; Toamasina 137,782; Antsirabe 126,062; Fianarantsoa 109,248; Mahajanga 106,780. **Location:** island in the Indian Ocean, east of the mainland of southern Africa.

## Vital statistics

**Birth rate** per 1,000 population (2000): 42.9 (world avg. 22.5). **Death rate** per 1,000 population (2000): 12.7 (world avg. 9.0). **Natural increase rate** per 1,000 population (2000): 30.2 (world avg. 13.5). **Total fertility rate** (avg. births per childbearing woman; 2000): 5.8. **Life expectancy** at birth (2000): male 52.7 years; female 57.3 years.

## National economy

**Budget** (1999). *Revenue:* FMG 2,667,000,000,000 (taxes 96.7%, of which duties on trade 55.5%, value-added tax 15.0%, income tax 14.9%; nontax receipts 3.3%). *Expenditures:* FMG 3,791,000,000,000 (current expenditure 57.4%, of which debt service 13.0%, general administration 10.8%, education 10.3%, defense 7.5%, health 4.0%, agriculture 1.5%; capital expenditure 42.6%). **Public debt** (external, outstanding; 2000): $4,295,000,000. **Production** (metric tons except as noted). *Agriculture, forestry, fishing* (2000): paddy rice 2,300,000, cassava 2,228,000, sugarcane 2,200,000; livestock (number of live animals) 10,364,000 cattle, 1,370,000 goats, 20,000,000 chickens; roundwood (2000) 10,359,000 cu m; fish catch (1999) 141,057. *Mining and quarrying* (2000): chromite ore 97,200; graphite 15,200; mica 800. *Manufacturing* (1998): refined sugar 79,775; cement 44,327; soap 14,513. *Energy production (consumption):* electricity (kW-hr; 1998) 642,000,000 (642,000,000); coal (metric tons; 1997) none (14,000); crude petroleum (barrels; 1997) none (1,539,000); petroleum products (metric tons; 1997) 193,000 (361,000). **Population economically active** (1993): total 5,914,000; activity rate of total population 48.9% (participation rates [1995]: over age 10, 59.4%; female 38.4%). **Gross national product** (2000): $3,869,000,000 ($250 per capita). **Household expenditure.** Average household size (1993) 4.6; expenditure (1983) food 60.4%, fuel and light 9.1%, clothing and footwear 8.6%, household goods and utensils 2.4%. **Land use** (1994): forest 39.9%; pasture 41.3%; agriculture 5.3%; other 13.5%. **Tourism** (2000): receipts from visitors $119,000,000; expenditures by nationals abroad $114,000,000.

## Foreign trade

**Imports** (1998): FMG 2,748,989,000,000 (chemical products 14.9%; food 14.1%; minerals 11.2%, of which crude petroleum 7.1%; machinery and equipment 9.3%). *Major import sources* (1999): France 24.1%; Iran 7.1%; Japan 6.2%; South Africa 6.0%; US 4.0%. **Exports** (1998): FMG 1,273,787,000,000 (coffee 17.2%, cotton fabrics 14.1%, minerals 11.3%, shrimp 6.0%, cloves and clove oil 3.9%, vanilla 3.0%). *Major export destinations* (1998): France 39.4%; Mauritius 6.8%; US 5.5%; Germany 4.5%; Italy 3.7%.

## Transport and communications

**Transport.** *Railroads:* route length (1998) 1,095 km; passenger-km 35,000,000; metric ton-km cargo 71,000,000. *Roads* (1996): total length 49,837 km (paved 17%). *Vehicles* (1996): passenger cars 62,000; trucks and buses 16,460. *Air transport* (1998): passenger-km 836,000,000; metric ton-km cargo 29,533,000; airports (1994) with scheduled flights 44. **Communications,** in total units (units per 1,000 persons). Daily newspaper circulation (1996): 66,000 (4.6); radio receivers (1997): 3,050,000 (209); television receivers (1998): 340,000 (22); telephone main lines (2001): 54,100 (4.7); cellular telephone subscribers (2001): 147,500 (9.0); personal computers (2001): 40,000 (2.4); Internet users (2001): 35,000 (2.1).

## Education and health

**Literacy** (1995): percentage of total population age 15 and over literate 45.7%; males literate 59.8%; females literate 32.0%. **Health:** physicians (1996) 1,470 (1 per 9,351 persons); hospital beds (1989) 10,900 (1 per 1,029 persons); infant mortality rate per 1,000 live births (2000) 87.0. **Food** (2000): daily per capita caloric intake 2,007 (vegetable products 90%, animal products 10%); 88% of FAO recommended minimum.

## Military

**Total active duty personnel** (2001): 13,500 (army 92.6%, navy 3.7%, air force 3.7%). **Military expenditure as percentage of GNP** (1999): 1.2% (world 2.4%); per capita expenditure $3.

## Background

Indonesians migrated to Madagascar about AD 700. The first European to visit the island was Portuguese navigator Diogo Dias in 1500. Trade in arms and slaves allowed the development of Malagasy kingdoms at the beginning of the 17th century. In the 18th century the Merina kingdom became dominant and in 1868 signed a treaty granting France control over the northwestern coast. In 1895 French troops took the island, and Madagascar became a French overseas territory in 1946. As the Malagasy Republic, it gained independence in 1960. It severed ties with France in the 1970s, taking its present name in 1975. A new constitution was adopted in 1992. The country has since been both politically and economically unstable.

## Recent Developments

Disputed presidential elections resulted in violent demonstrations in early 2002. Challenger Marc Ravalomanana, the wealthy mayor of Antananarivo, declared himself president in February and was named the winner by a court in April, a decision the incumbent, Pres. Didier Ratsiraka, refused to accept. In April the Constitutional Court found that Ravalomanana had indeed won more than half of the vote. The OAU refused to accept Ravalomanana as the legitimate president, but he was officially sworn in as president on 6 May. Although he received US recognition, Ravalomanana continued to be cold-shouldered by most other African states and was not invited to the African Union summit in Durban, South Africa, in July.

Internet resources: <www.embassy.org/madagascar>

# Malawi

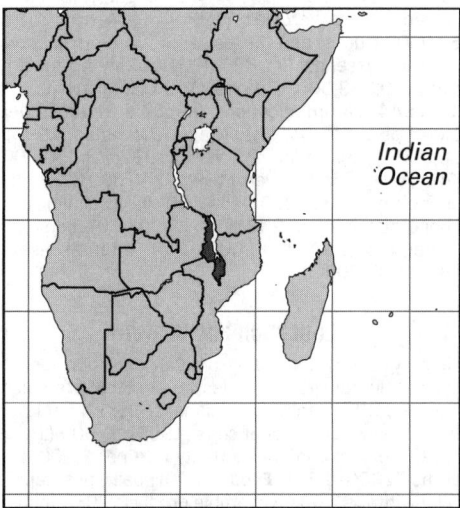

Indian Ocean

**Official name:** Republic of Malawi. **Form of government:** multiparty republic with one legislative house (National Assembly [192]). **Head of state and government:** President Bakili Muluzi (from 1994). **Capital:** Lilongwe (ministerial, financial, and legislative government operations) and Blantyre (executive and judicial government operations). **Official language:** none. **Official religion:** none. **Monetary unit:** 1 Malawi kwacha (MK) = 100 tambala; valuation (7 Jul 2003) $1 = MK 89.70.

## Demography

**Area:** 45,747 sq mi, 118,484 sq km. **Population** (2002): 10,520,000. **Density** (2002): persons per sq mi 289.0, persons per sq km 111.6. **Urban** (2002): 15.1%. **Sex distribution** (2001): male 49.39%; female 50.61%. **Age breakdown** (2001): under 15, 44.4%; 15–29, 30.4%; 30–44, 13.5%; 45–59, 7.2%; 60–74, 3.7%; 75 and over, 0.8%. **Ethnic composition** (2000): Chewa 34.7%; Maravi 12.2%; Ngoni 9.0%; Yao 7.9%; Tumbuka 7.9%; Lomwe 7.7%; Ngonde 3.5%; other 17.1%. **Religious affiliation** (1995): Christian 50.3%, of which Protestant 20.5%, Roman Catholic 18.0%; Muslim 20.0%; traditional beliefs 10.0%; other 19.7%. **Major cities** (1998): Blantyre 478,155; Lilongwe 435,964; Mzuzu 87,030. **Loca-**

**tion:** southeastern Africa, bordering Tanzania, Mozambique, and Zambia.

## Vital statistics

**Birth rate** per 1,000 population (2001): 37.8 (world avg. 21.2). **Death rate** per 1,000 population (2001): 22.8 (world avg. 8.9). **Natural increase rate** per 1,000 population (2001): 15.0 (world avg. 12.3). **Total fertility rate** (avg. births per childbearing woman; 2001): 5.2. **Life expectancy** at birth (2001): male 36.6 years; female 37.6 years.

## National economy

**Budget** (2000–01). *Revenue:* MK 31,233,000,000 (tax revenue 61.7%, of which income and profit tax 28.0%, sales tax 26.2%, import tax 7.6%; grants 33.1%; nontax revenue 5.2%). *Expenditures:* MK 37,303,000,000 (administration 33.4%; education 11.6%; social security 9.1%; health 6.1%). **Public debt** (external, outstanding; 2000): $2,555,000,000. **Production** (metric tons except as noted). *Agriculture, forestry, fishing* (2001): corn (maize) 2,500,000, potatoes 2,000,000, sugarcane 1,900,000; livestock (number of live animals) 1,450,000 goats, 750,000 cattle, 250,000 pigs; roundwood (2000) 9,964,000 cu m; fish catch (1999) 45,982. *Mining and quarrying* (1999): gemstones account for 95% of all mineral exports. *Manufacturing* (value added in MK '000,000; 1998): beverages 793; food products 571; chemicals 505, of which industrial 245. *Energy production (consumption):* electricity (kW-hr; 1997) 878,000,000 (878,000,000); coal (metric tons; 1999) 43,800 (43,800); petroleum products (metric tons; 1997) none (199,000). **Land use** (1994): forested 39.3%; meadows and pastures 19.6%; agricultural and under permanent cultivation 18.1%; other 23.0%. **Population economically active** (1998): total 4,509,290; activity rate 45.4% (participation rates: age 10 and over 66.9%; female 50.2%; unemployed 1.1%). **Gross national product** (2000): $1,744,000,000 ($170 per capita). **Household expenditure.** Average household size (1998) 4.3; expenditure (1990): food 55.5%, clothing and footwear 11.7%, housing 9.6%, household goods 8.4%. **Tourism:** receipts (2000) $27,000,-000; expenditures (1994) $15,000,000.

## Foreign trade

**Imports** (2001): $582,200,000 (1995; machinery 14.6%, transport equipment 13.0%, petroleum products 10.6%, food 10.6%, pharmaceutical products 7.9%, fertilizers 7.5%, textiles 5.1%). *Major import sources:* South Africa 39.7%; Zimbabwe 16.0%; Zambia 10.9%; US 2.6%. **Exports** (2001): $406,800,000 (tobacco 58.0%, sugar 11.3%, tea 11.2%, cotton 1.3%). *Major export destinations:* South Africa 19.1%; US 15.4%; Germany 11.2%; Japan 7.6%; The Netherlands 5.4%; UK 3.9%; France 2.3%.

## Transport and communications

**Transport.** *Railroads* (1995–96): route length 797 km; passenger-km 18,048,000; metric ton-km cargo 43,431,000. *Roads* (1998): total length 16,451 km (paved 19%). *Vehicles* (1996): passenger cars 27,000; trucks and buses 29,700. *Air transport*

*1 metric ton = about 1.1 short tons;     1 kilometer = 0.6 mi (statute);     1 metric ton-km cargo = about 0.68 short ton-mi cargo;     c.i.f.: cost, insurance, and freight;     f.o.b.: free on board*

(2001; Air Malawi only): passenger-km 241,000,000; metric ton-km cargo 798,000; airports (1998) 5. **Communications,** in total units (units per 1,000 persons). Daily newspaper circulation (1996): 22,000 (2.3); radio receivers (1997): 2,600,000 (258); television receivers (1999): 27,000 (2.5); telephone main lines (2001): 54,100 (4.7); cellular telephone subscribers (2001): 55,700 (4.8); personal computers (2001): 13,000 (1.1); Internet users (2001): 20,000 (1.7).

### Education and health

**Educational attainment** (1987). Percentage of population age 25 and over having: no formal education 55.0%; primary education 39.8%; secondary and higher 5.2%. **Literacy** (1998): total population age 15 and over literate 58.2%; males literate 73.2%; females literate 44.1%. **Health:** physicians (1989) 186 (1 per 47,634 persons); hospital beds (1987) 12,617 (1 per 627 persons); infant mortality rate per 1,000 live births (2001) 121.0. **Food** (2000): daily per capita caloric intake 2,181 (vegetable products 98%, animal products 2%); 94% of FAO recommended minimum.

### Military

**Total active duty personnel** (2001): 5,000 (army 100%; navy, none; air force, none). **Military expenditure as percentage of GNP** (1999): 0.6% (world 2.4%); per capita expenditure $1.

**Did you know?** Cape Maclear Beach, located at the southern tip of Lake Malawi (in Lake Malawi National Park), is a favorite vacation spot in Africa because of its 5 km (3 mi) of beaches and its fine restaurants.

### Background

Inhabited since 8000 BC, the region was settled by Bantu-speaking peoples between the 1st and the 4th century AD. About 1480 they founded the Maravi Confederacy, which encompassed most of central and southern Malawi. In northern Malawi the Ngonde people established a kingdom about 1600. The slave trade flourished during the 18th–19th century. Britain established colonial authority in 1891, and the area became known as Nyasaland in 1907. The colonies of Northern and Southern Rhodesia and Nyasaland formed a federation (1951–53), which was dissolved in 1963. The next year Malawi achieved independence. In 1966 it became a republic, with Hastings Banda as president. In 1971 he was designated president for life, and he ruled until he was defeated in multiparty elections in 1994. A new constitution was adopted in 1995.

### Recent Developments

Floods followed by a season of drought made for a food crisis affecting as many as 3 million people in Malawi by early 2002, and the government made an international appeal for food aid. Charged with mismanagement and corruption, the government claimed that it had sold off reserves of corn (maize) on the advice of the World Bank and the IMF, though there was no trace of the proceeds of the sale. Apparently

bowing to external and internal pressures, the government issued a budget statement aimed at living within its means. In April 2003 Pres. Bakili Muluzi sacked his entire cabinet and formed what he called a government of national unity.

**Internet resources:**
<http://members.tripod.com/~malawi>

# Malaysia

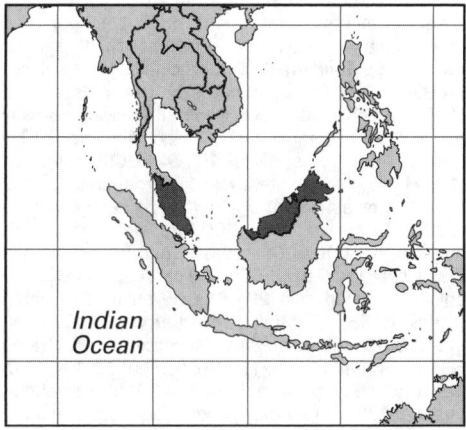

*Indian Ocean*

**Official name:** Malaysia. **Form of government:** federal constitutional monarchy with two legislative houses (Senate [70]; House of Representatives [193]). **Chief of state:** Yang di-Pertuan Agong (Paramount Ruler) Tuanku Syed Sirajuddin ibni al-Marhum Tuanku Syed Putra Jamalullail (from 13 Dec 2001). **Head of government:** Prime Minister Datuk Seri Mahathir bin Mohamad (from 1981). **Capital:** transferring from Kuala Lumpur to Putrajaya between 1999 and 2012. **Official language:** Malay. **Official religion:** Islam. **Monetary unit:** 1 ringgit, or Malaysian dollar (RM) = 100 cents; pegged since 6 Oct 2000 to the US dollar at the rate of $1 = RM 3.80.

### Demography

**Area:** 127,354 sq mi, 329,845 sq km. **Population** (2002): 24,370,000. **Density** (2002): persons per sq mi 191.4, persons per sq km 73.9. **Urban** (2002): 59.0%. **Sex distribution** (2000): male 50.45%; female 49.55%. **Age breakdown** (1999): under 15, 33.5%; 15–29, 28.2%; 30–44, 21.0%; 45–59, 11.3%; 60–74, 4.9%; 75 and over, 1.1%. **Ethnic composition** (2000): Malay and other indigenous 61.3%; Chinese 24.5%; Indian 7.2%; other nonindigenous 1.1%; noncitizen 5.9%. **Religious affiliation** (2000): Muslim 60.4%; Buddhist 19.2%; Christian 9.1%; Hindu 6.3%; Chinese folk religionist 2.6%; other 2.4%. **Major cities** (2000): Kuala Lumpur 1,297,526; Ipoh 566,211; Kelang 563,173; Petaling Jaya 438,084; Johor Baharu 384,613. **Location:** southeastern Asia, on the Malay Peninsula and the northern third of the island of Borneo, bordering Thailand, the South China Sea, Brunei, and Indonesia.

### Vital statistics

**Birth rate** per 1,000 population (2002): 23.2 (world avg. 21.2). **Death rate** per 1,000 population (2002): 4.4 (world avg. 8.9). **Natural increase rate** per 1,000 population (2002): 18.8 (world avg. 12.3). **Total fertility rate** (avg. births per childbearing woman; 2000): 3.1. **Life expectancy** at birth (2002): male 70.4 years; female 75.3 years.

## National economy

**Budget** (1999). *Revenue*: RM 59,157,000,000 (income tax 42.5%, taxes on goods and services 24.6%, nontax revenue 19.0%, taxes on international trade 9.1%). *Expenditures*: RM 71,429,000,000 (education 21.5%, defense and internal security 12.9%, interest payments 11.1%, health 6.2%, transport and communications 6.1%, social security 5.7%, agriculture 3.2%). **Tourism** (2000): receipts from visitors $4,936,000,000; expenditures by nationals abroad (1999) $1,973,000,000. **Population economically active** (1999): total 9,010,000; activity rate 39.7% (participation rates: ages 15–64, 60.6%; female [1997] 34.0%; unemployed 3.0%). **Production** (metric tons except as noted). *Agriculture, forestry, fishing* (2000): palm fruit oil 56,600,000, rice 2,037,000, sugarcane 1,600,000; livestock (number of live animals) 1,829,000 pigs, 723,000 cattle, 120,000,000 chickens; roundwood 29,461,000 cu m; fish catch (1998) 1,153,719. *Mining and quarrying* (1998): iron ore 316,808; bauxite 134,077; copper concentrates 53,001. *Manufacturing* (1999): cement 10,104,000; iron and steel bars and rods 2,261,000; refined sugar 1,226,000. *Energy production (consumption)*: electricity (kW-hr; 1997) 58,675,000,000 (58,638,-000,000); coal (metric tons; 2001) 540,000 ([1997] 2,636,000); crude petroleum (barrels; 2001) 247,000,000 ([1997] 140,000,000; Sabah and Sarawak only); petroleum products (metric tons; 1997) 15,395,000 (19,655,000); natural gas (cu m; 2001) 46,378,000,000 ([1997] 21,110,000,000). **Gross national product** (2000): $78,727,000,000 ($3,380 per capita). **Public debt** (external, outstanding; 2000): $19,090,000,000. **Household income and expenditure.** Average household size (2000) 4.5; annual income per household (1997) RM 31,280 ($11,120); expenditure (1983): food 28.7%, transportation 20.9%, recreation and education 11.0%, housing 10.2%, household durable goods 7.7%.

## Foreign trade

**Imports** (1998-f.o.b. in balance of trade): RM 228,309,000,000 (machinery and transport equipment 63.0%, basic manufactures 11.1%, chemicals 7.1%, food 4.6%, mineral fuels 3.1%). *Major import sources*: Japan 20.8%; US 17.4%; Singapore 14.0%; Taiwan 5.3%; South Korea 5.2%; Thailand 3.8%. **Exports** (1998): RM 286,756,000,000 (machinery and transport equipment 59.2%, basic manufactures 8.3%, animal and vegetable oils 7.5%, mineral fuels 6.2%, chemicals 3.5%, inedible crude materials 3.3%). *Major export destinations*: US 21.9%; Singapore 16.5%; Japan 11.6%; The Netherlands 5.1%; Taiwan 4.5%; Hong Kong 4.2%; UK 3.8%.

## Transport and communications

**Transport.** *Railroads* (1999): route length 2,227 km; passenger-km 1,332,000,000; metric ton-km cargo 912,000,000. *Roads* (1998): total length 66,437 km (paved 76%). *Vehicles* (1998): passenger cars 3,517,484; trucks and buses 644,792. *Air transport* (1999): passenger-km 33,708,000,000; metric ton-km cargo 1,424,556,000; airports (1997) 39. **Communications,** in total units (units per 1,000 persons). Daily newspaper circulation (1996): 3,345,000 (163); radio receivers (1997): 9,100,000 (434); television receivers (1999): 3,800,000 (174); telephone main lines (2001): 4,738,000 (199); cellular telephone subscribers (2001): 7,128,000 (300); personal computers (2001): 3,000,000 (126); Internet users (2001): 5,700,000 (239).

## Education and health

**Educational attainment** (1996). Percentage of population age 25 and over having: no formal schooling 16.7%; primary education 33.7%; secondary 42.8%; higher 6.8%. **Literacy** (1995): total population age 15 and over literate 83.5%; males literate 89.1%; females literate 78.1%. **Health** (1998): physicians 15,016 (1 per 1,402 persons); hospital beds 42,398 (1 per 497 persons); infant mortality rate per 1,000 live births (2002) 7.9. **Food** (2000): daily per capita caloric intake 2,919 (vegetable products 81%, animal products 19%); 131% of FAO recommended minimum.

## Military

**Total active duty personnel** (2001): 100,500 (army 79.6%, navy 12.4%, air force 8.0%). **Military expenditure as percentage of GDP** (1999): 2.3% (world 2.4%); per capita expenditure $78.

## Background

Malaya has been inhabited for 6,000–8,000 years, and small kingdoms existed in the 2nd–3rd century AD, when adventurers from India first arrived. Sumatran exiles founded the city-state of Malacca about 1400, and it flourished as a trading and Islamic religious center until its capture by the Portuguese in 1511. Malacca passed to the Dutch in 1641. The British founded a settlement on Singapore Island in 1819, and by 1867 they had established the Straits Settlements, including Malacca, Singapore, and Penang. During the late 19th century the Chinese began to migrate to Malaya. Japan invaded in 1941. Opposition to British rule led to the creation of the United Malays National Organization (UNMO) in 1946, and in 1948 the peninsula was federated with Penang. Malaya gained independence in 1957, and the federation of Malaysia was established in 1963. Its economy expanded greatly from the late 1970s, but it suffered from the economic slump that struck the area in the mid-1990s.

## Recent Developments

Malaysia's long-awaited political transition was under way in 2002. Prime Minister Datuk Seri Mahathir bin Mohamad, in his closing address to the United Malays National Organization (UMNO) General Assembly in June, announced his intention to retire. Soon after, he outlined a 16-month transition scenario. Leadership of the politically dominant UMNO and the governing National Front coalition would pass to his deputy prime minister, Datuk Seri Abdullah Ahmad Badawi. Some questioned whether Badawi would have the

*1 metric ton = about 1.1 short tons;   1 kilometer = 0.6 mi (statute);   1 metric ton-km cargo = about 0.68 short ton-mi cargo;   c.i.f.: cost, insurance, and freight;   f.o.b.: free on board*

guile and will to dominate the unruly UMNO organization, but he had been centrally involved in Malaysian politics for 30 years; he had survived a falling-out with Mahathir in the mid-1980s; and he enjoyed a reputation for Islamic piety and knowledge that could make him a more credible opponent of the fundamentalist Islamic Party of Malaysia (PAS) than Mahathir had ever managed to be.

Internet resources: <www.geographia.com/malaysia>

# Maldives

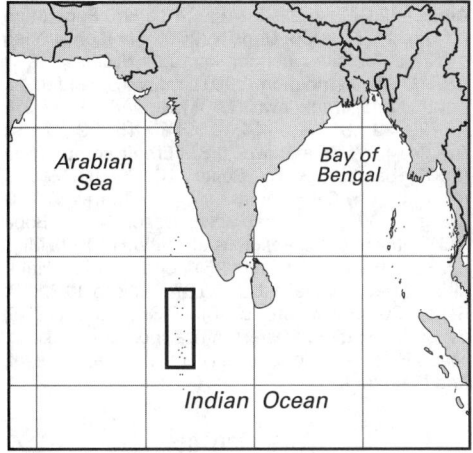

**Official name:** Divehi Jumhuriyya (Republic of Maldives). **Form of government:** republic with one legislative house (Majlis [42]). **Head of state and government:** President Maumoon Abdul Gayoom (since 1978). **Capital:** Male. **Official language:** Divehi. **Official religion:** Islam. **Monetary unit:** 1 Maldivian rufiyaa (Rf) = 100 laari; valuation (7 Jul 2003) $1 = Rf 12.80.

## Demography

**Area:** 115 sq mi, 298 sq km. **Population** (2002): 281,000. **Density** (2002): persons per sq mi 2,443, persons per sq km 943.0. **Urban** (2002): 27.0%. **Sex distribution** (2002): male 50.74%; female 49.26%. **Age breakdown** (2002): under 15, 37.7%; 15–29, 30.6%; 30–44, 17.8%; 45–59, 7.6%; 60–74, 5.2%; 75 and over, 1.1%. **Ethnic composition:** the majority is principally of Sinhalese and Dravidian extraction; Arab, African, and Negrito influences are also present. **Religious affiliation:** virtually 100% Sunni Muslim. **Major city** (2000): Male 74,069. **Location:** islands in the Indian Ocean, south of India.

## Vital statistics

**Birth rate** per 1,000 population (2002): 36.1 (world avg. 21.2). **Death rate** per 1,000 population (2002): 6.1 (world avg. 8.9). **Natural increase rate** per 1,000 population (2002): 30.0 (world avg. 12.3). **Total fertility rate** (avg. births per childbearing woman; 2002): 5.4. **Marriage rate** per 1,000 population (2001): 11.6. **Divorce rate** per 1,000 population (2001): 5.5. **Life expectancy** at birth (2002): male 68.0 years; female 67.0 years.

## National economy

**Budget** (2000). *Revenue*: Rf 2,548,800,000 (nontax revenue 51.1%, taxation 40.8%, foreign aid 7.9%). *Expenditures*: Rf 2,819,900,000 (general public services 23.6%, education 17.8%, defense 16.8%, health 10.2%, housing 9.1%, transportation and communications. 9.1%). **Public debt** (external, outstanding; 2000): $185,300,000. **Production** (metric tons except as noted). *Agriculture, forestry, fishing* (1999): vegetables and melons 25,300, coconuts 13,000, fruits (excluding melons) 8,850; fish catch (2000) 132,427. *Mining and quarrying*: coral for construction materials. *Manufacturing*: details, n.a.; however, major industries include boat building and repairing, coir yarn and mat weaving, coconut and fish processing, lacquerwork, garment manufacturing, and handicrafts. *Energy production (consumption)*: electricity (kW-hr; 1997) 66,000,000 (66,000,000); petroleum products (metric tons; 1997) none (99,000). **Tourism** (2000): receipts from visitors $344,000,000; expenditures by nationals abroad $46,000,000. **Population economically active** (1995): total 67,476; activity rate of total population 27.6% (participation rates: ages 15–64, 62.6%; female 27.1%; unemployed [1995] 0.9%). **Household income and expenditure** (1990). Average household size 7.2; annual income per household Rf 2,616 ($274), expenditure (1981): food and beverages 61.8%, housing equipment 17.0%, clothing 8.0%, recreation and education 5.9%, transportation 2.6%, health 2.5%, rent 1.6%. **Gross national product** (2000): $541,000,000 ($1,960 per capita). **Land use** (1994): forested 3.3%; meadows and pastures 3.3%; agricultural and under permanent cultivation 10.0%; built-on, wasteland, and other 83.4%.

## Foreign trade

**Imports** (1996-f.o.b. in balance of trade and c.i.f. for commodities and trading partners): Rf 3,551,289,-000 (machinery and transport equipment 27.9%, basic manufactures 23.7%, food and live animals 21.4%, petroleum products 9.1%). *Major import sources:* Singapore 32.0%; India 12.0%; Malaysia 8.5%; Sri Lanka 7.6%; UK 3.6%; Japan 3.5%. **Exports** (1996): Rf 699,190,000 (canned fish 28.0%, yellowfin tuna 20.5%, apparel and clothing 17.4%, dried skipjack tuna 11.0%). *Major export destinations:* UK 21.7%; Sri Lanka 18.3%; US 10.2%; Germany 10.8%; Japan 10.6%; Thailand 9.5%.

## Transport and communications

**Transport.** *Vehicles* (1999): passenger cars 3,037; trucks and buses 1,003. *Air transport* (1997): passengers carried 189,000; passenger-km 292,000,-000; airports (1997) with scheduled flights 5. **Communications,** in total units (units per 1,000 persons). Daily newspaper circulation (1996): 5,000 (19); radio receivers (1997): 34,000 (129); television receivers (1999): 10,650 (38); telephone main lines (2001): 27,200 (101); cellular telephone subscribers (2001): 18,400 (68); personal computers (2001): 6,000 (22); Internet users (2001): 10,000 (37).

## Education and health

**Educational attainment** (1990). Percentage of population age 15 and over having: no standard passed 25.6%; primary standard 37.2%; middle standard

25.9%; secondary standard 6.3%; preuniversity 3.4%; higher 0.4%; not stated 1.2%. **Literacy** (1995): total population age 15 and over literate 93.2%; males literate 93.0%; females literate 93.3%. **Health** (1996): physicians 99 (1 per 1,995 persons); hospital beds 318 (1 per 806 persons); infant mortality rate per 1,000 live births (2002) 38.0. **Food** (1999): daily per capita caloric intake 2,298 (vegetable products 81%, animal products 19%); (1997) 104% of FAO recommended minimum.

## Military

**Total active duty personnel:** Maldives maintains a single security force numbering about 700–1,000; it performs both army and police functions.

## Background

The archipelago was settled in the 5th century BC by Buddhists from Sri Lanka and southern India, and Islam was adopted in 1153. The Portuguese held sway in Male in 1558–73. The islands were a sultanate under the Dutch rulers of Ceylon (now Sri Lanka) during the 17th century. After the British gained control of Ceylon in 1796, the area became a British protectorate, a status formalized in 1887. The islands won full independence from Britain in 1965, and in 1968 a republic was founded. During the 1990s its economy gradually developed.

## Recent Developments

The development policy outlined by Pres. Maumoon Abdul Gayoom on 19 Feb 2002 placed emphasis on diversification and revitalization of the country's economy, which had grown only slowly in 2001 owing to a slump in the tourism industry. Development of human resources, improvement of child welfare, and preservation of the environment were also given priority.

**Internet resources:** <www.visitmaldives.com>

# Mali

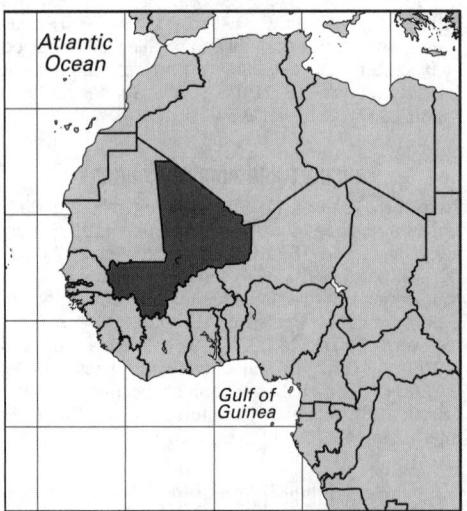

Official name: République du Mali (Republic of Mali). **Form of government:** multiparty republic with one legislative house (National Assembly [147]). **Chief of state:** President Amadou Toumani Touré (from 8 Jun 2002). **Head of government:** Prime Minister Ahmed Mohamed Ag Hamani (from 9 Jun 2002). **Capital:** Bamako. **Official language:** French. **Official religion:** none. **Monetary unit:** 1 CFA franc (CFAF) = 100 centimes; valuation (7 Jul 2003) $1 = CFAF 571.07; the CFAF is pegged to the euro (€) at €1 = 655.96 from 1 Jan 2002.

## Demography

**Area:** 482,077 sq mi, 1,248,574 sq km. **Population** (2002): 11,340,000. **Density** (2002): persons per sq mi 23.5, persons per sq km 9.1. **Urban** (1998): 28.7%. **Sex distribution** (2001): male 48.9%; female 51.1%. **Age breakdown** (2001): under 15, 47.2%; 15–29, 26.8%; 30–44, 13.3%; 45–59, 7.9%; 60–74, 4.0%; 75 and over, 0.8%. **Ethnic composition** (2000): Bambara 30.6%; Senufo 10.5%; Fula Macina (Niafunke) 9.6%; Soninke 7.4%; Tuareg 7.0%; Maninka 6.6%; Songhai 6.3%; Dogon 4.3%; Bobo 3.5%; other 14.2%. **Religious affiliation** (2000): Muslim 82%; traditional beliefs 16%; Christian 2%. **Major cities** (1998): Bamako 1,016,167; Sikasso 113,803; Ségou 90,898; Mopti (1996) 86,355; Gao (1996) 62,667. **Location:** western Africa, bordering Algeria, Niger, Burkina Faso, Côte d'Ivoire, Guinea, Senegal, and Mauritania.

## Vital statistics

**Birth rate** per 1,000 population (2001): 48.8 (world avg. 21.2). **Death rate** per 1,000 population (2001): 18.7 (world avg. 8.9). **Natural increase rate** per 1,000 population (2001): 30.1 (world avg. 12.3). **Total fertility rate** (avg. births per childbearing woman; 2001): 6.8. **Life expectancy** at birth (2001): male 45.8 years; female 48.2 years.

## National economy

**Budget** (1999). *Revenue*: CFAF 356,000,000,000 (tax revenue 66.1%, grants 23.4%, nontax revenue 10.5%). *Expenditures*: CFAF 417,400,000,000 (current expenditure 46.3%, of which wages and salaries 15.6%, education 10.3%, defense 8.3%, interest on public debt 3.6%, health 2.8%; capital expenditure 53.7%). **Public debt** (external, outstanding; 2000): $2,645,000,000. **Tourism** (2000): receipts from visitors $71,000,000; expenditures by nationals abroad $41,000,000. **Population economically active** (1997): total 5,042,000; activity rate of total population 51.5% (participation rates [1987] ages 15–64, 67.4%; female 46.3%; unemployed 0.8%). **Production** (metric tons except as noted). *Agriculture, forestry, fishing* (2001): millet 802,500, rice 745,100, sorghum 591,700; livestock (number of live animals) 14,550,000 goats and sheep, 6,200,-000 cattle, 652,000 asses; roundwood (2000) 6,596,900 cu m; fish catch (1999) 98,776. *Mining and quarrying* (1999): limestone 20,000 (1997); phosphate 3,000 (1997); iron oxide 708 (1997). *Manufacturing* (1999): sugar 27,000; cement 20,000; soap 10,097 (1995). *Energy production (consumption)*: electricity (kW-hr; 1997) 391,000,-

1 metric ton = about 1.1 short tons;    1 kilometer = 0.6 mi (statute);    1 metric ton-km cargo = about 0.68 short ton-mi cargo;    c.i.f.: cost, insurance, and freight;    f.o.b.: free on board

000 (391,000,000); petroleum products (metric tons; 1997) none (154,000). **Gross national product** (2000): $2,548,000,000 ($240 per capita). **Household expenditure**. Average household size (1997) 5.0; expenditure (1986–87): food 54.6%, clothing 14.2%, transportation and communications 11.9%, housing and energy 8.7%, household durable goods 4.2%. **Land use** (1994): forested 5.7%; meadows and pastures 24.6%; forest 9.7%; agricultural and under permanent cultivation 2.1%; other 63.6%.

## Foreign trade

**Imports** (1999-c.i.f.): CFAF 490,600,000,000 (machinery, appliances, and transport equipment 31.1%; petroleum products 14.3%; food products 13.9%; construction products 10.5%; chemicals 10.2%). *Major import sources:* African countries 49.9%, of which Côte d'Ivoire 18.9%; France 18.7%; China 4.4%; Germany 2.7%; Belgium-Luxembourg 2.4%. **Exports** (1999): CFAF 348,600,000,000 (raw cotton and cotton products 43.9%; gold 40.8%; live animals 9.4%). *Major export destinations:* Western Europe, US, and other non-Asian industrial countries 52.7%; Asian countries 33.9%; African countries 8.4%.

## Transport and communications

**Transport.** *Railroads* (1996): route length 729 km; passenger-km 189,000,000; metric ton-km cargo 256,000,000. *Roads* (1996): total length 15,100 km (paved 12%). *Vehicles* (1996): passenger cars 26,190; trucks and buses 18,240. *Air transport* (1997; represents about 10% of the traffic of Air Afrique, which is operated by 11 West African states): passenger-km 242,000,000; metric ton-km cargo 38,000,000; airports (1999) 9. **Communications,** in total units (units per 1,000 persons). Daily newspaper circulation (1997): 45,000 (4.6); radio receivers (1997): 1,600,000 (163); television receivers (1999): 130,000 (12); telephone main lines (2001): 49,900 (4.3).Cellular phones (2001): 45,300 (3.9); personal computers (2001): 14,000 (1.2); Internet users (2001): 30,000 (2.6).

## Education and health

**Educational attainment** (1987). Percentage of population age 6 and over having: no formal schooling 86.0%; primary education 12.5%; secondary 1.2%; postsecondary and higher 0.3%. **Literacy** (1995): Percentage of total population age 15 and over literate 1,760,000 (31.0%); males literate 1,084,000 (39.4%); females literate 676,000 (23.1%). **Health:** physicians (1993) 483 (1 per 18,376 persons); hospital beds (1987) 3,430 (1 per 2,253 persons); infant mortality rate per 1,000 live births (2001) 121.4. **Food** (1999): daily per capita caloric intake 2,314 (vegetable products 91%, animal products 9%); 90% of FAO recommended minimum.

## Military

**Total active duty personnel** (2000): 7,350 (army 100.0%). **Military expenditure as percentage of GNP** (1999): 2.3% (world 2.4%); per capita expenditure $6.

## Background

Inhabited since prehistoric times, the region was situated on a caravan route across the Sahara. In the 12th century the Malinke empire of Mali was founded on the Upper and Middle Niger. In the 15th century the Songhai empire in the Timbuktu-Gao region gained control. In 1591 Morocco invaded the area, and Timbuktu remained under the Moors for two centuries. In the mid-19th century the French conquered the area, which became a part of French West Africa known as the French Sudan. In 1946 it became an overseas territory of the French Union. It was proclaimed the Sudanese Republic in 1958, briefly joined with Senegal (1959–60) to form the Mali Federation, and formed the Republic of Mali in 1960. The government was overthrown by military coups in 1968 and 1991. Elections were held in 1992 and 1997, but political instability continued.

## Recent Developments

Presidential elections in May 2002 resulted in a win for Amadou Toumani Touré, an army general who had led the 1991 coup and who had led the state for 14 months in 1991–92. Bamako was the site of the African Nations Cup soccer championship in February 2002.

**Internet resources:** <www.oxfam.org.uk/coolplanet/ontheline/explore/journey/mali/malindex.htm>

# Malta

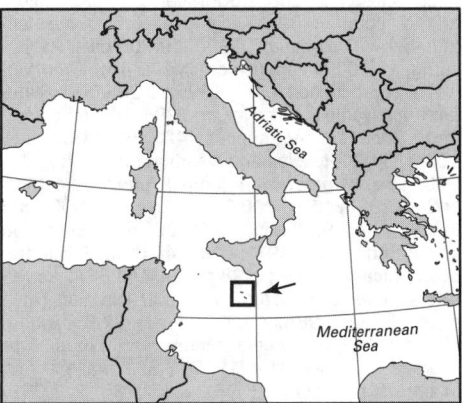

**Official name:** Repubblikka ta' Malta (Maltese); Republic of Malta (English). **Form of government:** unitary multiparty republic with one legislative house (House of Representatives [65]). **Chief of state:** President Guido de Marco (from 1999). **Head of government:** Prime Minister Eddie Fenech Adami (from 1998). **Capital:** Valletta. **Official languages:** Maltese; English. **Official religion:** Roman Catholicism. **Monetary unit:** 1 Maltese lira (Lm) = 100 cents = 1,000 mils; valuation (7 Jul 2003) $1 = Lm 0.37.

## Demography

**Area:** 122 sq mi, 316 sq km (rounded). **Population** (2002): 386,000. **Density** (2002): persons per sq mi 3,164, persons per sq km 1,222. **Urban** (2000): 90.5%%. **Sex distribution** (2000): male 49.49%; female 50.51%. **Age breakdown** (2000): under 15, 20.3%; 15–29, 21.6%; 30–44, 20.8%; 45–59, 20.4%; 60–74, 12.0%; 75 and over, 4.9%. **Ethnic composition** (by nationality; 2000): Maltese 93.8%; British 2.1%; Arab 2.0%; other 2.1%. **Religious affiliation**

(1996): Roman Catholic 93.4%; other 6.6%. **Major cities** (1999): Birkirkara 21,350; Qormi 17,881; Sliema 12,308; Hamrun 11,014; Valletta 7,100. **Location:** islands in the Mediterranean Sea, south of Sicily (Italy).

## Vital statistics

**Birth rate** per 1,000 population (2001): 10.0 (world avg. 21.2); (2000) legitimate 89.4%; illegitimate 10.6%. **Death rate** per 1,000 population (2001): 7.6 (world avg. 8.9). **Natural increase rate** per 1,000 population (2001): 2.4 (world avg. 12.3). **Total fertility rate** (avg. births per childbearing woman; 2000): 1.9. **Marriage rate** per 1,000 population (1998): 6.3. **Life expectancy** at birth (2002): male 75.8 years; female 81.0 years.

## National economy

**Budget** (1999). *Revenue:* Lm 637,852,000 (direct taxes 42.7%; indirect taxes 32.6%; nontax revenue 23.1%; foreign grants 1.5%). *Expenditures:* Lm 690,965,000 (recurrent expenditures 84.6%, of which social security 27.2%, education 10.4%, health 10.0%, debt service 4.9%, defense 4.2%; capital expenditure 15.4% [1997]). **Public debt** (2001): $2,150,800,000. **Production** (metric tons except where noted). *Agriculture, forestry, fishing* (1999): vegetables 58,850 (of which tomatoes 32,800, cabbage 3,500, melons 2,600, garlic 2,000, onions 1,200), potatoes 32,000, grapes 10,000; livestock (number of live animals; 1999) 69,000 pigs, 21,000 cattle, 16,000 sheep; fish catch 979,432. *Quarrying* (value of production in Lm; 1996): 6,898,000. *Manufacturing* (value of sales in Lm; 1994–95): machinery and transport equipment 402,993,000; food 103,733,000; textiles and wearing apparel 80,813,-000. *Energy production (consumption):* electricity (kW-hr; 1997) 1,515,000,000 (1,515,000,000); coal (metric tons; 1997) none (310,000); petroleum products (metric tons; 1997) none (344,000). **Population economically active** (1998): total 144,824; activity rate of total population 38.4% (participation rates: ages 15–64 [1985] 45.9%; female 27.6%; unemployed 5.1%). **Household income and expenditure.** Average household size (1985) 3.3; average annual income per household (1982) Lm 4,736 ($11,399); sources of income (1993): wages and salaries 63.8%, professional and unincorporated enterprises 19.3%, rents, dividends, and interest 16.9%; expenditure (1993): food and beverages 27.9%, transportation and communications 15.7%, household furnishings and operations 9.5%, recreation, entertainment, and education 7.2%, clothing and footwear 6.9%, housing 5.5%, health 3.3%, tobacco 2.6%. **Tourism** (2000): receipts from visitors $614,000,000; expenditures by nationals abroad $201,000,000. **Gross domestic product** (2000): $3,559,000,000 ($9,120 per capita). **Land use** (1994): agricultural and under permanent cultivation 40.6%; other (infertile clay soil with underlying limestone) 59.4%.

## Foreign trade

**Imports** (1999-c.i.f. in balance of trade and f.o.b. for commodities and trading partners): Lm 1,135,796,-000 (machinery and transport equipment 52.3%, manufactured and semimanufactured goods 22.8%, food 8.8%, chemicals 7.3%, mineral fuels 5.2%). *Major import sources:* France 19.1%; Italy 16.7%; UK 10.9%; Germany 10.0%; Singapore 9.5%. **Exports** (1999): Lm 712,481,000 (machinery and transport equipment 59.8%, other finished manufactured goods 30.5%, food and live animals 0.8%). *Major export destinations:* US 22.0%; Singapore 17.5%; France 16.5%; Germany 13.1%; UK 8.9%; Italy 4.4%.

## Transport and communications

**Transport.** *Roads* (1997): total length 1,961 km (paved 94%). *Vehicles* (1998): passenger cars 185,247; trucks and buses 49,520. *Air transport* (1998): passenger-km 1,887,736,000; metric ton-km cargo 11,227,000; airports (1999) with scheduled flights 1. **Communications,** in total units (units per 1,000 persons). Daily newspaper circulation (1996): 54,000 (145); radio receivers (1997): 255,000 (680); television receivers (1999): 212,000 (549); telephone main lines (2001): 207,700 (530); cellular telephone subscribers (2001): 138,800 (354); personal computers (2001): 90,000 (230); Internet users (2001): 99,000 (253).

## Education and health

**Educational attainment** (1967). Percentage of economically active population having: no formal schooling 10.8%; primary education 60.4%; lower secondary 3.4%; upper secondary 17.6%; technical secondary 3.9%; postsecondary and higher 3.9%. **Literacy** (2000): total population age 15 and over literate 279,000 (92.1%); males literate 138,000 (91.4%); females literate 141,000 (92.8%). **Health** (1996): physicians 925 (1 per 403 persons); hospital beds 2,140 (1 per 174 persons); infant mortality rate per 1,000 live births (2001) 4.3. **Food** (1999): daily per capita caloric intake 3,482 (vegetable products 72%, animal products 28%); 139% of FAO recommended minimum.

## Military

**Total active duty personnel** (2001): 2,140 (army 100%). **Military expenditure as percentage of GNP** (1999): 0.8% (world 2.4%); per capita expenditure $73.

---

**Did you know?** Founded in 1592, the University of Malta is one of the oldest universities in the world. Originally called Collegium Melitense, the Jesuit-run institution granted mostly degrees in religion and philosophy.

---

## Background

Inhabited as early as 3800 BC, Malta was ruled by the Carthaginians from the 6th century BC until it came under Roman control in 218 BC. In AD 60 the apostle Paul converted the inhabitants to Christianity. It was under Byzantine rule until the Arabs seized control in 870. In 1091 the Normans defeated the Arabs, and it was ruled by feudal lords until it came under the Knights of Malta in 1530. Napoleon seized control in

*1 metric ton = about 1.1 short tons; 1 kilometer = 0.6 mi (statute); 1 metric ton-km cargo = about 0.68 short ton-mi cargo; c.i.f.: cost, insurance, and freight; f.o.b.: free on board*

1798, the British took it in 1800, and it was returned to the Knights in 1802. The Maltese protested and acknowledged the British as sovereign, an arrangement ratified in 1814. It became self-governing in 1921 but reverted to a colonial regime in 1936. Malta was severely bombed by Germany and Italy during World War II, and in 1942 it received the George Cross, Britain's highest civilian decoration. In 1964 it gained independence within the Commonwealth, and in 1974 became a republic. When its alliance with Britain ended in 1979, Malta proclaimed its neutral status.

## Recent Developments

A yea vote of 54% in a referendum in March 2003 and a win by the incumbent Nationalist Party in the April elections seemed to have settled once and for all the question of whether Malta's accession to the European Union was the will of the people. Prime Minister Eddie Fenech Adami signed the accession documents on 16 April.

**Internet resources:** <www.mol.net.mt>

# Marshall Islands

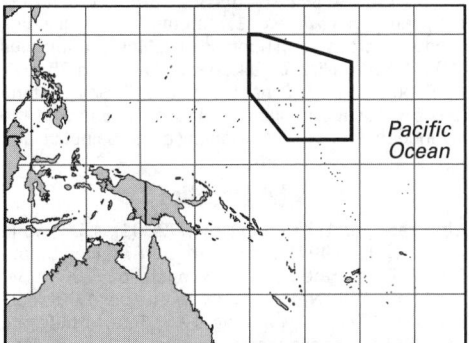

Pacific Ocean

**Official name:** Majol (Marshallese); Republic of the Marshall Islands (English). **Form of government:** unitary republic with two legislative houses (Council of Iroij [12]; Nitijela [33]). **Head of state and government:** President Kessai Note (from 2000). **Capital:** Majuro. **Official languages:** Marshallese (Kajin-Majol); English. **Official religion:** none. **Monetary unit:** 1 US dollar ($) = 100 cents.

## Demography

**Area:** 70.07 sq mi, 181.48 sq km. **Population** (2002): 56,600. **Density** (2002): persons per sq mi 807.8, persons per sq km 311.9. **Urban** (2001): 65.4%. **Sex distribution** (1999): male 51.20%; female 48.80%. **Age breakdown** (1999): under 15, 42.9%; 15–29, 28.7%; 30–44, 16.7%; 45–59, 8.2%; 60–74, 2.6%; 75 and over, 0.9%. **Ethnic composition** (nationality; 2000): Marshallese 88.5%; US white 6.5%; other Pacific islanders and East Asians 5.0%. **Religious affiliation** (1995): Protestant 62.8%; Roman Catholic 7.1%; Mormon 3.1%; Jehovah's Witness 1.0%; other (mostly nonreligious) 26.0%. **Major cities:** Majuro (1999) 23,676; Ebeye (1988) 8,324. **Location:** Oceania, group of atolls and reefs in the North Pacific Ocean, halfway between Hawaii and Papua New Guinea.

## Vital statistics

**Birth rate** per 1,000 population (2000): 41.8 (world avg. 22.5). **Death rate** per 1,000 population (2000): 4.9 (world avg. 9.0). **Natural increase rate** per 1,000 population (2000): 36.9 (world avg. 13.5). **Total fertility rate** (avg. births per childbearing woman; 2000): 6.6. **Life expectancy** at birth (2000): male 63.7 years; female 67.4 years.

## National economy

**Budget** (1997–98). *Revenue:* $61,400,000 (US government grants 59.7%, income tax 12.7%, import tax 10.7%, value-added and excise taxes 4.4%, fishing rights 2.9%, fees and charges 2.1%). *Expenditures:* $50,900,000 (wages and salaries 33.4%, goods and services 32.4%, capital expenditures 14.3%, interest payments 10.8%, subsidies 7.1%). **Production** (metric tons except as noted). *Agriculture, forestry, fishing* (value of production for household consumption in $'000; 1999): fish 3,920; pork 1,496; breadfruit 646; foreign fish catch (1999) 12,993, of which Japanese 6,762. *Mining and quarrying:* for local construction only. *Manufacturing* (1999): copra 3,348; coconut oil and processed (chilled or frozen) fish are important products; the manufacture of handicrafts and personal items (clothing, mats, boats, etc.) by individuals is also significant. *Energy production (consumption):* electricity (kW-hr; 1994) 57,891,000 (57,891,000); gasoline, oil, and lubricants (barrels; 1988; imports only) n.a. (84,588). **Public debt** (external, outstanding; 1996–97): $124,900,000. **Gross national product** (at current market prices; 1999): $99,000,000 ($1,950 per capita). **Land use** (1989; data are for the former Trust Territory of the Pacific Islands): forested 22.5%; meadows and pastures 13.5%; agricultural and under permanent cultivation 33.1%; other 30.9%. **Household income and expenditure.** Average household size (1999) 7.8; annual median income per household (1999) $6,840; expenditure (1982): food 57.7%, housing 15.6%, clothing 12.0%, personal effects and other 14.7%. **Population economically active** (1999): total 14,677; activity rate of total population 28.9% (participation rates: over age 15, 53.1%; female [1988] 30.1%; unemployed 9.5%). **Tourism** (2000): receipts $4,000,000.

## Foreign trade

**Imports** (1997-c.i.f. in balance of trade): $60,995,000 (mineral fuels and lubricants 23.4%, food, beverages, and tobacco 22.8%, machinery and transport equipment 9.5%, manufactured goods 7.4%, chemical products 6.6%). *Major import sources:* US 47.2%; Guam 4.8%; Australia 4.0%; Singapore 3.4%; Japan 3.3%. **Exports** (1997): $12,665,000 (chilled fish 78.2%, frozen fish 10.7%, crude coconut oil 9.6%). *Major export destinations:* US c. 80.0%; other c. 20.0%.

## Transport and communications

**Transport.** *Roads:* only Majuro and Kwajalein atolls have paved roads. *Vehicles* (1995): passenger cars 1,374; trucks and buses 262. *Air transport* (2001; Air Marshall Islands only): passenger-km 24,972,000; metric ton-km cargo 183,000; airports (1997) 25. **Communications,** in total units (units per 1,000 persons). Telephones (2001): 4,200 (60); cellular telephone subscribers (2001): 500 (7.0); Internet users (2001): 900 (13); personal computers (2001): 4,000 (50).

## Education and health

**Educational attainment** (1999). Percentage of population age 25 and over having: no formal schooling 3.1%; elementary education 35.5%; secondary 46.5%; some higher 12.3%; undergraduate degree 1.7%; advanced degree 0.9%. **Literacy**: total population age 15 and over literate 19,377 (91.2%); males literate 9,993 (92.4%); females literate 9,384 (90.0%). **Health** (1997): physicians 34 (1 per 1,785 persons); hospital beds 129 (1 per 470 persons); infant mortality rate per 1,000 live births (2000) 41.0.

## Military

Under the 1984 Compact of Free Association, the US provides for the defense of the Republic of the Marshall Islands.

## Background

The islands were sighted in 1529 by the Spanish navigator Álvaro Saavedra. Germany purchased them from Spain in 1899, and Japan seized them in 1914. During World War II the US took Kwajalein and Enewetak, and the Marshall Islands were made part of a UN trust territory under US jurisdiction in 1947. Bikini and Enewetak atolls served as testing grounds for US nuclear weapons from 1946 to 1958. The country became an internally self-governing republic in 1979. In 1986 it entered into a Compact of Free Association with the US, some provisions of which were set to expire in 2001, and became fully self-governing.

## Recent Developments

Negotiations on an amended compact continued into 2003, and a new agreement was signed on 30 April that will bring $3 billion to the Marshall Islands over 20 years. Especially sensitive was the issue of funding for ongoing compensation to the peoples of four islands affected by nuclear testing—Bikini, Enewetak, Utirik, and Rongelap.

**Internet resources:** <http://marshall.csu.edu.au>

# Martinique

**Official name:** Département de la Martinique (Department of Martinique). **Political status:** overseas department (France) with two legislative houses (General Council [45]; Regional Council [41]). **Chief of state:** President Jacques Chirac of France (from 1995). **Head of government:** Prefect (for France) Michel Cadot (from 2000). **Capital:** Fort-de-France. **Official language:** French. **Official religion:** none. **Monetary unit:** 1 euro (€) = 100 cents; $1 = €0.87 (7 Jul 2003); at conversion on 1 Jan 2002, €1 = 6.56 French francs (F).

## Demography

**Area:** 436 sq mi, 1,128 sq km. **Population** (2002): 386,000. **Density** (2002): persons per sq mi 885.3,

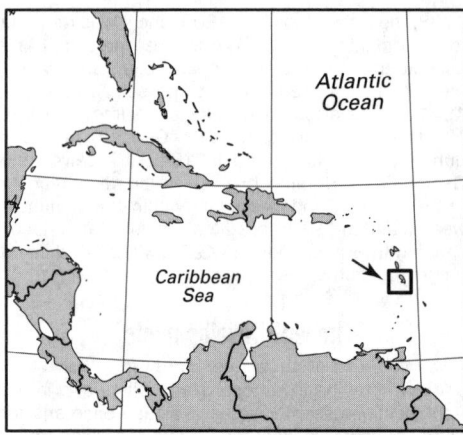

persons per sq km 342.2. **Urban** (2001): 95.2%. **Sex distribution** (2001): male 49.47%; female 50.53%. **Age breakdown** (2001): under 15, 23.1%; 15–29, 23.3%; 30–44, 26.3%; 45–59, 13.8%; 60–74, 9.1%; 75 and over, 4.4%. **Ethnic composition** (2000): mixed race (black/white/Asian) 93.4%; French (metropolitan and Martinique white) 3.0%; East Indian 1.9%; other 1.7%. **Religious affiliation** (1995): Roman Catholic 86.5%; Protestant 8.0% (mostly Seventh-day Adventist); Jehovah's Witness 1.6%; other 3.9%, including Hindu, syncretist, and nonreligious. **Major communes** (1999): Fort-de-France 94,049; Le Lamentin 35,460; Le Robert 21,201; Schoelcher 20,845; Sainte-Marie 20,058. **Location:** island in Atlantic Ocean and the Caribbean Sea, between Dominica and Saint Lucia.

## Vital statistics

**Birth rate** per 1,000 population (2001): 15.8 (world avg. 21.2); (1997) legitimate 31.8%; illegitimate 68.2%. **Death rate** per 1,000 population (2001): 6.4 (world avg. 8.9). **Natural increase rate** per 1,000 population (2001): 9.4 (world avg. 12.3). **Total fertility rate** (avg. births per childbearing woman; 2001): 1.4. **Marriage rate** per 1,000 population (1997): 4.1. **Divorce rate** per 1,000 population (1997): 1.1. **Life expectancy** at birth (2001): male 79.1 years; female 77.7 years.

## National economy

**Budget** (1999). *Revenue*: F 1,298,000,000 (general receipts from French central government and local administrative bodies 45.0%; tax receipts 34.0%, of which indirect taxes 19.5%, direct taxes 14.5%). *Expenditures*: F 1,298,000,000 (health and social assistance 42.0%; wages and salaries 16.7%; other administrative services 7.2%; debt amortization 5.0%). **Public debt** (1994): $186,700,000. **Production** (metric tons except as noted). *Agriculture, forestry, fishing* (2001): bananas 310,000, sugarcane 207,000, pineapples 20,800; livestock (number of live animals) 35,000 pigs, 34,000 sheep, 25,000 cattle; roundwood (2000) 12,000 cu m; fish catch (1999) 5,040. *Mining and quarrying* (1996): pumice 130,000; sand and gravel for local construction. *Manufacturing* (1998): cement 232,300; processed pineapples 20,210; sugar 6,543. *Energy production (consumption)*: electricity (kW-hr; 1998) 988,000,000 (988,-000,000); crude petroleum (barrels; 1997) none

---

*1 metric ton = about 1.1 short tons;   1 kilometer = 0.6 mi (statute);   1 metric ton-km cargo = about 0.68 short ton-mi cargo;   c.i.f.: cost, insurance, and freight;   f.o.b.: free on board*

(5,900,000); petroleum products (metric tons; 1997) 740,000 (565,000). **Household income and expenditure.** Average household size (1999) 3.0; income per household (1996) F 194,387 ($38,900); sources of income (1989): wages and salaries 80%, other 20%; expenditure (1993): food and beverages 32.1%, transportation and communications 20.7%, housing and energy 10.6%, household durable goods 9.4%, clothing and footwear 8.0%, education and recreation 5.4%, health care 5.2%, other 8.6%. **Tourism** (2000): receipts from visitors $302,000,000; number of visitors 816,000. **Gross national product** (1998): $4,888,000,000 ($12,875 per capita). **Population economically active** (1998): total 165,900; activity rate of total population 43.7% (participation rates: ages 15–64, 70.7%; female 45.9%; unemployed [2000] 27.9%). **Land use** (1998): forested 43.2%; meadows and pastures 12.5%; agricultural and under permanent cultivation 18.1%; other 26.2%.

## Foreign trade

**Imports** (1999-c.i.f.): F 10,605,600,000 (1996; consumer goods 23.9%, goods for intermediate consumption [inputs to the manufacturing process changed or destroyed in the final product] 15.9%, automobiles 15.0%, professional equipment 15.2%, energy products 8.3%). *Major import sources* (1998): France 64.2%; Germany 3.8%; Italy 3.6%; Venezuela 3.2%; US 2.7%; UK 2.6%; Japan 1.8%. **Exports** (1999-f.o.b.): F 1,715,100,000 (1998; bananas 39.3%, refined petroleum 12.2%, rum 7.5%, yachts and boats 4.4%). *Major export destinations* (1998): France 51.8%; Guadeloupe 22.4%; UK 10.2%; Belgium 5.0%; French Guiana 3.2%.

## Transport and communications

**Transport.** *Roads* (1994): total length 2,077 km (paved [1988] 75%). *Vehicles* (1998): passenger cars 147,589; trucks and buses 35,615. *Air transport* (1998): passenger arrivals and departures 1,570,700; cargo handled 15,655 metric tons; airports (2000) 1. **Communications,** in total units (units per 1,000 persons). Daily newspaper circulation (1996): 32,000 (83); radio receivers (1997): 82,000 (213); television receivers (1999): 66,000 (168); telephone main lines (2001): 172,192 (417); cellular telephone subscribers (2001): 286,100 (715); personal computers (2001): 52,000 (130); Internet users (1999): 5,000 (12.7).

## Education and health

**Educational attainment** (1990). Percentage of population age 25 and over having: incomplete primary, or no declaration 54.3%; primary education 18.0%; secondary 20.0%; higher 7.7%. **Literacy** (1982): total population age 15 and over literate 206,807 (92.5%); males literate 97,538 (91.8%); females literate 109,269 (93.2%). **Health** (1998): physicians 780 (1 per 487 persons); hospital beds 2,585 (1 per 128 persons); infant mortality rate per 1,000 live births (2001) 7.8. **Food** (1998): daily per capita caloric intake 2,865 (vegetable products 75%, animal products 25%); 118% of FAO recommended minimum.

## Military

Total active duty personnel (2001): 3,800 French troops.

## Background

Carib Indians, who had ousted earlier Arawak inhabitants, resided on the island when Christopher Columbus visited it in 1502. In 1635 the French established a colony there. The British captured and held the island in 1762–63 and again during the Napoleonic Wars, but each time it was returned to France. Made a department of France in 1946, Martinique remains under French rule despite a 1970s independence movement.

## Recent Developments

French Pres. Jacques Chirac gave a clear hint in 2000 that the hitherto highly centralized relationship between Paris and French overseas departments might be relaxed and that Martinique might enjoy more local control in the future. As a part of France, Martinique joined in the adoption of the euro in 2002.

**Internet resources:** <www.martinique.org>

# Mauritania

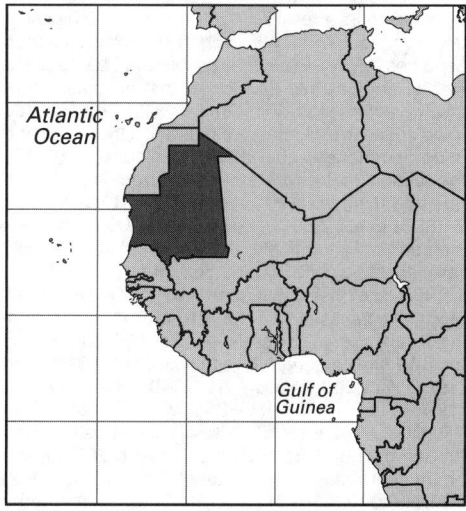

**Official name:** Al-Jumhuriyah al-Islamiyah al-Muritaniyah (Arabic) (Islamic Republic of Mauritania). **Form of government:** unitary multiparty republic with two legislative houses (Senate [56]; National Assembly [81]). **Head of state and government:** President Maaouya Ould Sidi Ahmad Taya (from 1984), assisted by Prime Minister Sghair Ould M'Bareck (from 6 Jul 2003). **Capital:** Nouakchott. **Official language:** Arabic (Arabic, Fulani, Soninke, and Wolof are national languages). **Official religion:** Islam. **Monetary unit:** 1 ouguiya (UM) = 5 khoums; valuation (7 Jul 2003) $1 = UM 266.75.

## Demography

**Area:** 398,000 sq mi, 1,030,700 sq km. **Population** (2002): 2,656,000. **Density** (2002): persons per sq mi 6.7, persons per sq km 2.6. **Urban** (1999): 56.5%. **Sex distribution** (2000): male 48.68%; female 51.32%. **Age breakdown** (2000): under 15, 46.2%; 15–29, 26.6%; 30–44, 15.6%; 45–59, 7.8%; 60–74, 3.3%; 75 and over, 0.5%. **Ethnic composition**

(1993): Moor 70% (of which about 40% "black" Moor [Haratin, or African Sudanic] and about 30% "white" Moor [Bidan, or Arab-Berber]); other black African 30% (mostly Wolof, Tukulor, Soninke, and Fulani). **Religious affiliation** (2000): Sunni Muslim 99.1%; traditional beliefs 0.5%; Christian 0.3%; other 0.1%. **Major cities** (1998): Nouakchott 611,883 (2000); Nouadhibou 97,600; Kiffa 48,300; Kaédi 43,000; Rosso 35,000. **Location:** northern Africa, bordering Western Sahara (annexed by Morocco), Algeria, Mali, Senegal, and the North Atlantic Ocean.

## Vital statistics

**Birth rate** per 1,000 population (2001): 42.5 (world avg. 21.2). **Death rate** per 1,000 population (2001): 13.3 (world avg. 8.9). **Natural increase rate** per 1,000 population (2001): 29.2 (world avg. 12.3). **Total fertility rate** (avg. births per childbearing woman; 2001): 6.1. **Life expectancy** at birth (2001): male 49.2 years; female 53.7 years.

## National economy

**Budget** (1997). *Revenue:* UM 44,800,000,000 (tax revenue 58.3%, of which taxes on goods and services 26.5%, import taxes 12.1%, income taxes 9.6%; nontax revenue 39.9%, of which fishing royalties and penalties 32.3%). *Expenditures:* UM 32,110,000,000 (wages and salaries 24.9%; interest on public debt 15.3%; defense 11.4%). **Land use** (1994): forested 4.3%; meadows and pastures 38.3%; agricultural and under permanent cultivation 0.2%; desert 57.2%. **Production** (metric tons except as noted). *Agriculture, forestry, fishing* (1999): rice 101,900, sorghum 74,800, dates 22,000, cow peas 22,000; livestock (number of live animals) 6,200,000 sheep, 4,133,000 goats, 1,395,000 cattle; roundwood (1998) 15,000 cu m; fish catch (metric tons; 1997) 82,000, of which octopuses 23,500; fish catch (1996) including foreign fishing vessels equals 564,200 metric tons. *Mining and quarrying* (gross weight; 1998): iron ore 11,411,000; gypsum 100,000. *Manufacturing* (1996): cow's milk 91,000 (1994); goat's milk 77,000 (1994); meat 58,200, of which fresh mutton and lamb 24,600, fresh beef and veal 10,200. *Energy production (consumption):* electricity (kW-hr; 1999) 226,700,000 ([1997] 153,000,000); coal (metric tons; 1997) none (6,000); crude petroleum (barrels; 1997) none (6,927,000); petroleum products (metric tons; 1997) 845,000 (932,000). **Population economically active** (1994): total 687,000; activity rate of total population 31.3% (participation rates: over age 10 [1991] 45.5%; female 22.9%). **Household income and expenditure.** Average household size (1996): 5.3; expenditure (1990): food and beverages 73.1%, clothing and footwear 8.1%, energy and water 7.7%, transportation and communications 2.0%. **Gross national product** (2000): $978,000,000 ($370 per capita). **Public debt** (external, outstanding; 2000): $2,150,000,000. **Tourism** (1999): receipts $28,000,000; expenditures $55,000,000.

## Foreign trade

**Imports** (1997): $403,400,000 (imports for National Industrial and Mining Company 20.2%; petroleum products 13.6%; investment including food aid

10.0%; equipment and machinery 6.5%). *Major import sources:* France 25.5%; Spain 7.5%; Germany 6.7%; Belgium-Luxembourg 6.4%; Thailand 5.1%. **Exports** (1997): $405,000,000 (iron ore 52.4%; fish 47.6%, of which cephalopods 28.3%). *Major export destinations:* Japan 23.3%; Italy 16.7%; France 13.9%; Spain 8.3%; Belgium-Luxembourg 7.1%.

## Transport and communications

**Transport.** *Railroads* (1998): route length 704 km; passenger-km, negligible; (1997) metric ton-km cargo 2,340,000,000. *Roads* (1996): total length 7,660 km (paved 11%). *Vehicles* (1996): passenger cars 18,810; trucks and buses 10,450. *Air transport* (1998; data represent about 10% of the total scheduled traffic of Air Afrique): passenger-km 258,263,000; metric ton-km cargo 13,524,000; airports (1997) with scheduled flights 9. **Communications,** in total units (units per 1,000 persons). Daily newspaper circulation (1996): 1,000 (0.4); radio receivers (1997): 360,000 (147); television receivers (1999): 247,000 (100); telephone main lines (2000): 19,000 (7.2); cellular telephone subscribers (2000): 7,000 (2.7); personal computers (2001): 27,000 (9.8); Internet users (2001): 7,000 (2.7).

## Education and health

**Educational attainment** (1988). Percentage of population age 25 and over having: no formal schooling 60.8%; primary and incomplete secondary 34.1%; secondary 3.8%; higher 1.3%. **Literacy** (1995): percentage of total population age 15 and over literate 37.7%; males literate 49.6%; females literate 26.3%. **Health:** physicians (1994) c. 200 (1 per 11,085 persons); hospital beds (1988) 1,556 (1 per 1,217 persons); infant mortality rate per 1,000 live births (2001) 75.2. **Food** (1999): daily per capita caloric intake 2,702 (vegetable products 85%, animal products 15%); 117% of FAO recommended minimum.

## Military

**Total active duty personnel** (2001): 15,650 (army 95.8%, navy 3.2%, air force 1.0%). **Military expenditure as percentage of GNP** (1999): 4.0% (world 2.4%); per capita expenditure $14.

**Did you know?** The Atlantic Ocean off Mauritania has historically been among the richest fisheries in the world for both pelagic (open sea) and demersal (seafloor) species. Since gaining its independence in 1960, Mauritania has derived a significant proportion of national revenue from regulating the fishing fleets of Japan, China, the EU, and others. A lack of enforcement of these regulations by 2002 had led to a dramatic fall in overall species catch because of overfishing (particularly for octopus), as well as a damaged marine environment.

## Background

Inhabited in ancient times by Sanhadja Berbers, in the 11th and 12th centuries Mauritania was the center of the Berber Almoravid movement, which

*1 metric ton = about 1.1 short tons;    1 kilometer = 0.6 mi (statute);    1 metric ton-km cargo = about 0.68 short ton-mi cargo;    c.i.f.: cost, insurance, and freight;    f.o.b.: free on board*

imposed Islam. Arab tribes arrived in the 15th century and formed powerful confederations; the Portuguese also arrived then. France gained control of the coast in 1817 and in 1903 made the territory a protectorate. In 1904 it was added to French West Africa, and later it became a colony. In 1960 Mauritania achieved independence. Its first president was ousted in a 1978 military coup. After a series of military rulers, in 1991 a new constitution was adopted, and multiparty elections were held in 1992. During the 1990s, relations between the government and opposition groups deteriorated, even as there was some success in liberalizing the economy.

## Recent Developments

On 3 Jan 2002 the government banned the opposition Action for Change (AC) party, claiming that it advocated racism and violence. The AC, which promoted the rights of black Mauritanians and descendents of slaves, would, however, be permitted to retain the four seats in the National Assembly that it had won in the October 2001 elections.

Internet resources: <www.mauritania.mr/ami>

# Mauritius

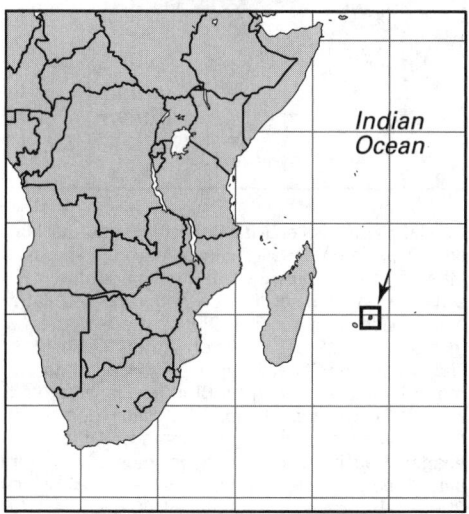

Indian Ocean

**Official name:** Republic of Mauritius. **Form of government:** republic with one legislative house (National Assembly [70—includes 8 "bonus" seats allocated to minor parties). **Chief of state:** President Karl Offman (from 25 Feb 2002). **Head of government:** Prime Minister Sir Anerood Jugnaugth (from 2000). **Capital:** Port Louis. **Official language:** English. **Official religion:** none. **Monetary unit:** 1 Mauritian rupee (Mau Re; plural Mau Rs) = 100 cents; valuation (7 Jul 2003) $1 = Mau Rs 29.15.

## Demography

**Area:** 788 sq mi, 2,040 sq km. **Population** (2002): 1,211,000. **Density** (2002): persons per sq mi 1,536.8, persons per sq km 593.6. **Urban** (2000): 42.7%. **Sex distribution** (2000): male 49.47%; female 50.53%. **Age breakdown** (2000): under 15, 25.7%; 15–29, 25.6%; 30–44, 24.7%; 45–59,

15.1%; 60–74, 6.8%; 75 and over, 2.1%. **Ethnic composition** (2000): Indo-Pakistani 67.0%; Creole (mixed Caucasian, Indo-Pakistani, and African) 27.4%; Chinese 3.0%; other 2.6%. **Religious affiliation** (2000): Hindu 49.6%; Christian 32.2%, of which Roman Catholic 23.6%; Muslim 16.6%; Buddhist 0.4%; other 1.2%. **Major urban areas** (2000): Port Louis 144,303; Beau Bassin-Rose Hill 103,872; Vacoas-Phoenix 100,066; Curepipe 78,920; Quatre Bornes 75,884. **Location:** island in the Indian Ocean, east of Madagascar.

## Vital statistics

**Birth rate** per 1,000 population (2001): 16.3 (world avg. 21.2). **Death rate** per 1,000 population (2001): 6.6 (world avg. 8.9). **Natural increase rate** per 1,000 population (2001): 9.7 (world avg. 12.3). **Total fertility rate** (avg. births per childbearing woman; 2001): 2.0. **Marriage rate** per 1,000 population (1998): 9.4. **Divorce rate** per 1,000 population (1997): 0.8. **Life expectancy** at birth (2001): male 67.3 years; female 75.3 years.

## National economy

**Budget** (1997–98). *Revenue*: Mau Rs 18,501,000,-000 (tax revenue 84.8%, of which import duties 33.3%, taxes on goods and services 32.5%, income tax 13.0%; nontax revenue 14.0%; grants 1.2%). *Expenditures*: Mau Rs 21,872,000,000 (social security 19.4%, government services 18.8%, education 16.0%, interest on debt 16.0%, economic services 11.4%, health 8.1%). **Tourism** (2000): receipts from visitors $542,000,000; expenditures by nationals abroad $182,000,000. **Public debt** (external, outstanding; 2000): $889,000,000. **Gross national product** (2000): $4,449,000,000 ($3,750 per capita). **Production** (metric tons except as noted). *Agriculture, forestry, fishing* (1999): sugarcane 3,500,000, vegetables 23,000, potatoes 15,000; livestock (number of live animals) 93,000 goats, 27,000 cattle, 20,000 pigs; roundwood (1998) 14,760 cu m; fish catch (1998) 13,734. *Manufacturing* (value added in Mau Rs '000; 1994): apparel 5,065,000; beverages and tobacco 1,995,800; food products 1,580,400. *Energy production (consumption)*: electricity (kW-hr; 1998) 1,364,800 (1,364,-800); coal (metric tons; 1998) none (86,300); petroleum products (metric tons; 1998) none (576,000). **Population economically active** (1998): total 507,000; activity rate of total population 43.8% (participation rates: ages 12 and over, 55.6%; female 37.1%; unemployed 5.7%). **Household income and expenditure.** Average household size (2000) 4.2; annual income per household (1996–97) Mau Rs 122,148 ($6,263); sources of income (1990): salaries and wages 48.4%, entrepreneurial income 41.2%, transfer payments 10.4%; expenditure (1996–97): food, beverages, and tobacco 45.2%, transportation and communications 14.2%, housing and household furnishings 13.2%, clothing and footwear 7.9%, recreation and education 6.0%, energy 4.4%, health 3.8%. **Land use** (1994): forested 21.7%; meadows and pastures 3.4%; agricultural and under permanent cultivation 52.2%; other 22.7%.

## Foreign trade

**Imports** (1998): Mau Rs 49,811,000,000 (manufactured goods classified chiefly by material 34.6%, machinery and transport equipment 22.8%, food 13.8%, chemicals 7.8%, mineral fuels and lubricants 6.3%, inedible crude materials excluding fuels 3.9%, animal and vegetable oils and fats 1.3%). *Major import sources:* France 11.1%; South Africa 10.5%; India 9.3%; Taiwan 5.2%; UK 5.2%; Japan 5.1%; Hong Kong 5.0%; Germany 4.1%. **Exports** (1998): Mau Rs 39,634,000,000 (clothing 55.9%, sugar 21.3%, yarn 3.7%, chemicals 0.5%, other 18.6%). *Major export destinations:* UK 32.3%; France 17.1%; US 16.3%; Germany 5.3%; Italy 3.5%.

## Transport and communications

**Transport.** *Roads* (1998): total length 1,905 km (paved 93%). *Vehicles* (1998): passenger cars 46,300; trucks and buses 12,100. *Air transport* (1998; Air Mauritius only): passenger-km 3,858,695; metric ton-km cargo 819,432,000; airports (1998) with scheduled flights 1. **Communications,** in total units (units per 1,000 persons). Daily newspaper circulation (1996): 85,000 (76); radio receivers (1997): 420,000 (371); television receivers (1999): 265,000 (230); telephone main lines (2001): 306,800 (256); cellular telephone subscribers (2001): 300,000 (250); personal computers (2001): 130,000 (108); Internet users (2001): 158,000 (132).

## Education and health

**Educational attainment** (1990). Percentage of population age 25 and over having: no formal education 18.3%; incomplete primary 42.6%; primary 6.1%; incomplete secondary 18.0%; secondary 13.1%; higher 1.9%. **Literacy** (1995): percentage of total population age 15 and over literate 82.9%; males literate 87.1%; females literate 78.8%. **Health** (1998): physicians 1,033 (1 per 1,123 persons); hospital beds 3,826 (1 per 303 persons); infant mortality rate per 1,000 live births (2001) 13.8. **Food** (1999): daily per capita caloric intake 2,972 (vegetable products 86%, animal products 14%); 131% of FAO recommended minimum.

## Military

**Total active duty personnel**: none; however, a special 1,500-person paramilitary force ensures internal security. **Military expenditure as percentage of GNP** (1999): 0.2% (world 2.4%); per capita expenditure $7.

## Background

The island was visited by the Portuguese in the early 16th century. The Dutch took possession in 1598 and attempted to settle it (1638–58, 1664–1710) before abandoning it to pirates. The French East India Company occupied Mauritius in 1721 and administered it until the French government took over in 1767. Sugar production allowed the colony to prosper. The British captured the island in 1810 and were granted formal control in 1814. In the late 19th century competition from beet sugar and the opening of the Suez Canal caused an economic decline. After World War II, Mauritius adopted political and economic reforms, and in 1968 it became an independent state within the Commonwealth. In 1992 it became a republic. It experienced political unrest during the 1990s.

## Recent Developments

In February 2002 Mauritius's presidency changed hands three times. Pres. Cassam Uteem decided to resign rather than approve a controversial antiterrorism bill that would limit the rights of persons accused of terror-related crimes. After the bill was passed into law, Karl Offmann of the Militant Socialist Movement was elected as the new president.

**Internet resources:** <http://ncb.intnet.mu/cso.htm>

# Mayotte

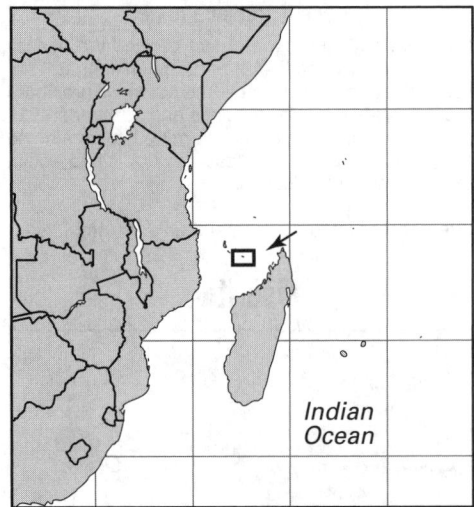

*Indian Ocean*

**Official name:** Collectivité Départementale de Mayotte (Departmental Collectivity of Mayotte); known as Mahoré in Comorian Swahili. **Political status:** overseas dependency of France with one legislative house (General Council [19]); claimed by the Comoros since 1975. **Chief of state:** President of France Jacques Chirac (from 1995). **Head of government:** Prefect Jean-Jacques Brot (for France; from 3 Jul 2002). **Capitals:** Dzaoudzi (French administrative); Mamoudzou (local administrative). **Official language:** French. **Official religion:** none. **Monetary unit:** 1 euro (€) = 100 cents; $1 = €0.87 (7 Jul 2003); at conversion on 1 Jan 2002, €1 = 6.56 French francs (F).

## Demography

**Area:** 144.1 sq mi, 373.2 sq km. **Population** (2002): 165,000. **Density** (2002): persons per sq mi 1,145, persons per sq km 442.1. **Urban** (1985): 59.7%. **Sex distribution** (2001): male 52.44%; female 47.56%. **Age breakdown** (2001): under 15, 46.6%; 15–29, 24.9%; 30–44, 18.3%; 45–59, 7.4%; 60–74, 2.4%; 75 and over, 0.4%. **Place of birth** (1997): Mayotte 73.6%; nearby islands of the Comoros 19.9%; metropolitan France 2.8%; other 3.7%. **Ethnic composition** (2000): Comorian (Mauri, Mahorais) 92.3%; Swahili 3.2%; white (French) 1.8%; Makua 1.0%; other 1.7%. **Religious affiliation** (2000): Sunni Muslim 96.5%; Christian, principally

---

*1 metric ton = about 1.1 short tons;   1 kilometer = 0.6 mi (statute);   1 metric ton-km cargo = about 0.68 short ton-mi cargo;   c.i.f.: cost, insurance, and freight;   f.o.b.: free on board*

Roman Catholic, 2.2%; other 1.3%. **Major towns** (1997): Mamoudzou 32,733; Dzaoudzi 10,792; Koungou 10,165. **Location:** island in the Indian Ocean, between the northern tip of Madagascar and the African mainland.

## Vital statistics

**Birth rate** per 1,000 population (2001): 44.4 (world avg. 21.2). **Death rate** per 1,000 population (2001): 8.8 (world avg. 8.9). **Natural increase rate** per 1,000 population (2001): 35.6 (world avg. 12.3). **Total fertility rate** (avg. births per childbearing woman; 2001): 6.2. **Marital status of adult population** (1997): monogamous marriage 48.5%, polygamous marriage 6.9%, other 44.6%. **Divorce rate** per 1,000 population (1997): 16.2. **Life expectancy** at birth (2000): male 57.8; female 62.0.

## National economy

**Budget** (1997). *Revenue*: F 1,022,400,000 (1993; current revenue 68.8%, of which subsidies 40.0%, indirect taxes 16.8%, direct taxes 4.9%; development revenue 31.2%, of which loans 11.6%, subsidies 7.9%). *Expenditures*: F 964,200,000 (current expenditure 75.2%, development expenditure 24.8%). **Production** (metric tons except as noted). *Agriculture, forestry, fishing* (1997): bananas 30,200, cassava 10,000, cinnamon 27,533 kg; livestock (number of live animals; 1997) 25,000 goats, 17,000 cattle, 2,000 sheep; fish catch (1999) 1,502. *Mining and quarrying*: negligible. *Manufacturing*: mostly processing of agricultural products and materials used in housing construction (including siding and roofing materials, joinery, and latticework). *Energy production (consumption)*: electricity (kW-hr; 1999) 68,387,000 (68,387,000). **Tourism** (number of visitors; 1999): 21,000; receipts $10,000,000. **Gross national product** (1998): $486,409,000 ($3,704 per capita). **Household income and expenditure**. Average household size (1997) 4.6; expenditure (1991): food 42.2%, clothing and footwear 31.5%, household furnishings 8.8%, energy and water 6.8%, transportation 5.1%. **Population economically active** (1997): total 42,896; activity rate of total population 32.7% (participation rates: ages 15–64, 58.6%; female 43.4%; unemployed 41.5%). **Land use** (1987): meadows 35.0%; agricultural 29.0%; other 36.0%.

## Foreign trade

**Imports** (1999): F 628,266,000 (1997; food products 23.8%; machinery 20.4%; transport equipment 10.4%; metals and metal products 10.3%; chemical products 7.7%). *Major import sources* (1997): France 66.0%; South Africa 14.0%; Asia 11.0%. **Exports** (1999): F 12,540,000 (1997; domestic exports 37.2%, of which ylang-ylang 27.9%, vanilla 3.5%; re-exports 62.8%). *Major export destinations* (1997): France 80.0%; Comoros 15.0%.

## Transport and communications

**Transport.** *Roads* (1998): total length 233 km (paved 77%). *Vehicles* (1998): 8,213. *Air transport* (1998): passenger arrivals and departures 88,034; cargo unloaded and loaded 1,012 metric tons; airports (2000) with scheduled flights 1. **Communications,** in total units (units per 1,000 persons). Daily

newspapers (1998): none (one weekly newspaper has a total circulation of 15,000); radio receivers (1996): 50,000 (427); television receivers (1999): 3,500 (30); telephone main lines (2001): 10,000 (70).

## Education and health

**Educational attainment** (1991). Percentage of population age 25 and over having: no formal education 72.8%; primary 14.2%; lower secondary 7.5%; higher secondary 3.2%; higher 2.3%. **Literacy** (1997): total population age 15 and over literate 63,053 (86.1%). **Health:** physicians (1997) 57 (1 per 2,304 persons); hospital beds 186 (1 per 706 persons); infant mortality rate per 1,000 live births (2001) 69.5.

## Military

**Total active duty personnel** (2001): 4,200 French troops are assigned to Mayotte and Réunion.

## Background

Originally inhabited by descendants of Bantu and Malayo-Indonesian peoples, Mayotte was converted to Islam by Arab invaders in the 15th century. Taken by a Malagasy tribe from Madagascar at the end of the 18th century, it came under French control in 1843. Together with the other Comoros islands and Madagascar, it became part of a single French overseas territory in the early 20th century. It has been administered separately since 1975, when the three northernmost islands of the Comoros declared independence.

## Recent Developments

Mayotte's geographic (and geopolitical) location halfway between the Comoros Islands and Madagascar once more exposed the island in 2002–03 to the social and political instabilities of its surroundings—the island of Anjouan in the Comoros continued its secessionist tendencies, and Antsiranana remained one of the six traditional provinces of Madagascar that expressed a desire for greater autonomy, even independence.

**Internet resources:** < www.ac-mayotte.fr>

# Mexico

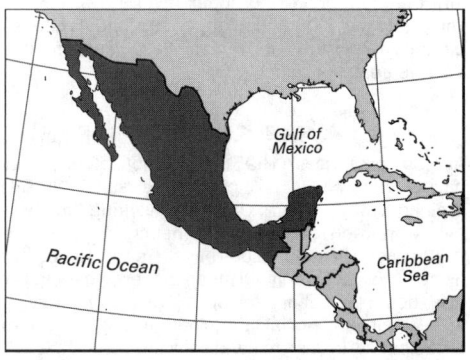

**Official name:** Estados Unidos Mexicanos (United Mexican States). **Form of government:** federal republic with two legislative houses (Senate [128]; Chamber of Deputies [500]). **Head of state and government:** President Vicente Fox Quesada (from 2000). **Capital:** Mexico City. **Official language:** Spanish. **Official religion:** none. **Monetary unit:** 1 Mexican peso (Mex$) = 100 centavos; valuation (7 Jul 2003) US$1 = Mex$10.39.

## Demography

**Area:** 758,449 sq mi, 1,964,375 sq km. **Population** (2002): 100,977,000. **Density** (2002): persons per sq mi 133.1, persons per sq km 51.4. **Urban** (1990): 71.3%. **Sex distribution** (2000): male 49.28%; female 50.72%. **Age breakdown** (2000): under 15, 33.8%; 15–29, 29.8%; 30–44, 19.1%; 45–59, 10.7%; 60–74, 5.2%; 75 and over, 1.4%. **Ethnic composition** (2000): mestizo 64.3%; Amerindian 18.0%, of which detribalized 10.5%; Mexican white 15.0%; Arab 1.0%; Mexican black 0.5%; Spaniard 0.3%; US white 0.2%; other 0.7%. **Religious affiliation** (1995): Roman Catholic 90.4%; Protestant (including Evangelical) 3.8%; other 5.8%. **Major cities** (2000): Mexico City 8,591,309; Guadalajara 1,647,000; Puebla 1,270,989; Ciudad Netzahualcóyotl 1,224,500; Juárez 1,190,000; Tijuana 1,150,000; Monterrey 1,108,400; León 1,019,510; Mérida 660,848; Chihuahua 650,000. **Location:** middle America, bordering the US, the Gulf of Mexico, the Caribbean Sea, Belize, Guatemala, and the North Pacific Ocean. **Place of birth** (1990): 93.1% native-born; 6.9% foreign-born and unknown. **Mobility** (1990). Population 5 years and older living in the same place as in 1985: 94.3%; different state 4.9%; unspecified 0.8%. **Households.** Total households (2000) 21,948,000; distribution by size (1995): 1 person 5.7%, 2 persons 10.9%, 3 persons 15.8%, 4 persons 20.1%, 5 persons 17.7%, 6 persons 11.6%, 7 or more persons 18.2%. Family households (1990): 17,064,507 (98.4%); nonfamily 1,039,738 (1.3%); unspecified 256,554 (0.3%). **Emigration** (1998): legal immigrants into the US 131,600.

## Vital statistics

**Birth rate** per 1,000 population (2000): 23.2 (world avg. 22.5); (1983) legitimate 72.5%; illegitimate 27.5%. **Death rate** per 1,000 population (2000): 5.0 (world avg. 9.0). **Natural increase rate** per 1,000 population (2000): 18.2 (world avg. 13.5). **Total fertility rate** (avg. births per childbearing woman; 2000): 2.7. **Marriage rate** per 1,000 population (1997): 7.5. **Divorce rate** per 1,000 population (1995): 0.4. **Life expectancy** at birth (2000): male 68.5 years; female 74.7 years.

## Social indicators

**Access to services** (1995). Proportion of dwellings having: electricity 93.2%; piped water supply 85.6%; drained sewage 74.7%. **Quality of working life.** Average workweek (1999): 44.4 hours. Annual rate (1992) per 100,000 insured workers for: temporary disability 6,426; indemnification for permanent injury 239; death 18. Labor stoppages (1997): 39, involving 9,375 workers. **Social participation.** Eligible voters participating in last national election (2000): 64%.

Practicing religious population in total affiliated population: national average of weekly attendance (1993) 11%; (1970) weekly attendance 10% of urban dwellers, 25% of rural dwellers; yearly attendance 55% of urban dwellers, 73% of rural dwellers. **Social deviance** (1991). Criminal cases tried by local authorities per 100,000 population for: murder 60.3; rape 22.4; other assault 301.0; theft 703.8. Incidence per 100,000 in general population of: suicide (1994) 2.47.

## National economy

**Gross national product** (2000): US$497,025,000,-000 (US$5,070 per capita). **Budget** (2000). *Revenue*: Mex$866,231,000,000 (1997; income tax 30.9%, VAT 20.9%, social security contributions 12.3%, excise tax 9.9%, import duties 3.9%). *Expenditures*: Mex$936,738,000,000 (1997; education 22.1%, social security and welfare 18.0%, interest on public debt 13.7%). **Public debt** (external, outstanding; 2000): US$81,550,000,000. **Tourism** (2000): receipts from visitors US$8,295,000,000; expenditures by nationals abroad US$5,499,000,-000. **Production** (metric tons except as noted). *Agriculture, forestry, fishing* (2000): sugarcane 49,274,780, corn (maize) 17,988,060, sorghum 5,981,835, oranges 4,059,769, wheat 3,404,576, tomatoes 2,176,557, bananas 1,978,032, peppers 1,826,140, mangoes 1,499,382, lemons and limes 1,639,196, coconuts 1,213,000, watermelons 1,069,000, avocados 933,337, dry beans 914,379, pineapples 881,000, papayas 748,000, barley 732,706, grapes 446,470, rice 410,210, carrots 372,869, coffee (green) 353,999, cauliflower 205,000; livestock (number of live animals) 30,540,000 cattle, 14,900,000 pigs, 9,600,000 goats, 8,000,000 ducks, 6,250,000 horses, 5,950,000 sheep, 3,000,000 turkeys, 3,280,000 mules, 3,250,000 asses, 476,000,000 chickens; roundwood (2000) 24,122,000 cu m; fish catch (1999) 1,250,592. *Mining and quarrying* (1999): salt 8,900,000, iron 6,855,219, gypsum 4,100,-000, silica 1,700,000, phosphate 950,649, sulfur 855,482, dolomite 415,284, fluorite 557,106, zinc 339,758, copper 340,148, barite 157,952, manganese 169,107, lead 131,402, silver 2,456,000 kg, gold 23,476 kg. *Manufacturing* (gross value of production in Mex$'000; 1998): machinery and equipment 423,579,725; food, beverages, and tobacco products 279,104,375; chemical products 212,479,904; metal products 108,951,844; mineral products 55,612,499; paper and paper products 56,522,215; textiles 54,458,821. *Energy production (consumption)*: electricity (kW-hr; 1997) 170,751,000,000 (172,212,000,000); coal (metric tons; 1997) 10,337,000 (11,538,000); crude petroleum (barrels; 1997) 1,099,400,000 (470,400,-000); petroleum products (metric tons; 1997) 72,362,000 (83,281,000); natural gas (cu m; 1997) 29,708,000,000 (30,314,000,000). **Population economically active** (1999): total 39,751,000; activity rate of total population 41.2% (participation rates: ages 15–64, 63.4%; female 33.5%; unemployed [2000] 4.0%). **Household income and expenditure.** Average household size (1999) 4.4; income per household (1989) Mex$3,461 (US$1,384); sources of income (1992): wages and salaries

61.5%, property and entrepreneurship 29.1%, transfer payments 7.8%, other 1.6%; expenditure (1992): food, beverages, and tobacco 36.9%, housing (includes household furnishings) 25.2%, transportation and communications 10.1%, clothing and footwear 8.5%, recreation and entertainment 5.5%, health and medical services 3.5%. **Land use** (1994): forest 25.5%; pasture 39.0%; agriculture 13.0%; other 22.5%.

## Foreign trade

**Imports** (2000): US$174,458,000,000 (intermediate goods 76.6%; capital goods 13.8%; consumer goods 9.6%). *Major import sources:* US 73.1%; Japan 3.7%; Germany 3.6%; Canada 2.3%; Italy 1.2%; China 1.1%. **Exports** (2000): US$166,455,-000,000 (machinery and transport equipment 33.3%; electrical equipment 10.7%; crude petroleum 8.9%; agricultural goods 3.3%). *Major export destinations:* US 88.7%; Europe 3.9%; Canada 2.0%; Japan 0.6%.

## Transport and communications

**Transport.** *Railroads* (1998): route length 26,623 km; passenger-km 1,089,000,000; metric ton-km cargo 31,747,000,000. *Roads* (1999): total length 365,119 km (paved 29%). *Vehicles* (1999): passenger cars 9,842,006; trucks and buses 4,749,789. *Air transport* (2000): passenger-km 32,005,000,-000; metric ton-km cargo 3,050,000,000; airports (1997) 83. **Communications,** in total units (units per 1,000 persons). Daily newspaper circulation (1996): 9,030,000 (97); radio receivers (1997): 31,000,000 (329); television receivers (1999): 26,000,000 (267); telephone main lines (2001): 13,533,000 (136); cellular telephone subscribers (2001): 20,136,000 (202); personal computers (2001): 6,900,000 (69); Internet users (2001): 3,500,000 (35).

## Education and health

**Educational attainment** (1995). Population age 15 and over having: no primary education 13.4%; some primary 22.8%; completed primary 19.3%; incomplete secondary 19.9%; complete secondary 16.3%; higher 8.3%. **Literacy** (1995): total population age 15 and over literate 89.6%; males literate 91.8%; females literate 87.4%. **Health:** physicians (1994) 146,021 (1 per 613 persons); hospital beds 107,288 (1 per 864 persons); infant mortality rate per 1,000 live births (2000) 26.2. **Food** (2000): daily per capita caloric intake 3,165 (vegetable products 82%, animal products 18%); 136% of FAO recommended minimum.

## Military

**Total active duty personnel** (2001): 192,770 (army 74.7%, navy 19.2%, air force 6.1%). **Military expenditure as percentage of GNP** (1999): 0.6% (world 2.4%); per capita expenditure US$27.

## Background

Inhabited for more than 20,000 years, Mexico produced great civilizations in AD 100–900, including the Olmec, Toltec, Mayan, and Aztec. The Aztec were conquered in 1521 by Spanish explorer Hernán Cortés, who established Mexico City on the site of the Aztec capital, Tenochtitlán. Francisco de Montejo conquered the remnants of Maya civilization in the mid-16th century, and Mexico became part of the viceroyalty of New Spain. In 1821 rebels negotiated a status quo independence from Spain, and in 1823 a new congress declared Mexico a republic. In 1845 the US voted to annex Texas, initiating the Mexican War. Under the Treaty of Guadalupe Hidalgo in 1848, Mexico ceded a vast territory in what is now the western and southwestern US. The Mexican government endured several rebellions and civil wars in the late 19th and early 20th centuries. During World War II it declared war on the Axis powers (1942), and in the postwar era it was a founding member of the UN (1945) and the Organization of American States (1948). In 1993 it ratified the North American Free Trade Agreement. The election of Vicente Fox to the presidency in 2000 ended 71 years of rule by the Institutional Revolutionary Party.

## Recent Developments

Although Pres. Vicente Fox's personal popularity remained high, divisions within the government and its lack of a legislative majority in the Congress severely hindered major legislative initiatives. Midterm elections in 2003 saw his party lose some 40 additional seats. Analysts expected the economy to grow by 1.6% in real terms during 2002, and the official target for inflation was a low 4.5%. The future of the important *maquiladora* industry (manufacturing plants that import and assemble duty-free components for export) remained especially uncertain.

In 2002 Mexico assumed one of the 10 rotating seats on the UN Security Council, and in March in Monterrey the government hosted the UN International Conference on Financing for Development. In early September the Mexican government formally withdrew from the 1947 Inter-American Treaty of Reciprocal Assistance (known as the Rio Treaty). Although the Fox administration continued to seek US legislative changes that would safeguard the rights of undocumented Mexican workers already resident in the US, as well as increase the availability of visas for Mexican citizens seeking temporary employment there, American concerns remained focused on the "war on terrorism" and heightened border controls. Foreign Minister Jorge G. Castañeda finally threw in the towel in January 2003, admitting that he could not cope with American foreign policy objectives. In March 2002 the Tijuana drug cartel, the largest drug-trafficking organization in Mexico, was brought down as one of its leaders was arrested and the other killed. Later that month Fox and Bush signed a border security agreement to make legal crossings easier while also improving security. The head of the Gulf drug cartel, Osiel Cárdenas, wanted by police in both Mexico and the US, was arrested in March 2003.

An uproar ensued when the Ministry of Foreign Relations signaled that Mexico would vote in favor of the UN Human Rights Commission's critical statement on the Cuban government's human rights record. The Mexican political opposition strongly denounced the Fox government's alignment with the US and its "betrayal" of Mexico's historic ties with the Cuban Revolution.

**Internet resources:** <www.mexonline.com>

# Micronesia

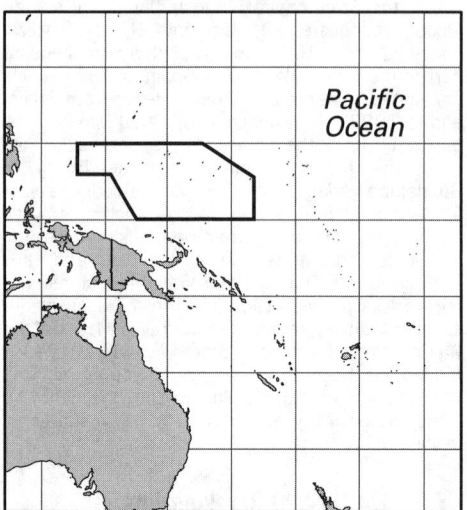

Pacific
Ocean

**Official name:** Federated States of Micronesia. **Form of government:** federal nonparty republic in free association with the US with one legislative house (Congress [14]). **Head of state and government:** President Joseph J. Urusemal (from 11 May 2003). **Capital:** Palikir, on Pohnpei. **Official language:** none. **Official religion:** none. **Monetary unit:** 1 US dollar ($) = 100 cents.

## Demography

**Area** (rounded): 270.8 sq mi, 701.4 sq km. **Population** (2002): 109,000. **Density** (2002): persons per sq mi 402.5, persons per sq km 155.4. **Urban** (2000): 28.5%. **Sex distribution** (2000): male 50.64%; female 49.36%. **Age breakdown** (2000): under 15, 40.3%; 15–29, 28.4%; 30–44, 16.9%; 45–59, 9.1%; 60–74, 3.9%; 75 and over, 1.4%. **Ethnic composition** (2000): Chuukese/Mortlockese 48.8%; Pohnpeian 24.2%; Yapese 9.2%; Kosraean 6.7%; Polynesian 1.4%; Asian 1.2%; other 8.5%. **Religious affiliation** (2000): Christianity is the predominant religious tradition; Roman Catholic 52.7%, Protestant 40.1%; the Kosraeans, Pohnpeians, and Chuukese are mostly Protestant and the Yapese mostly Roman Catholic. **Major towns** (2000): Weno, in Chuuk state 22,000; Tol, in Chuuk state 9,500; Palikir, on Pohnpei 8,600; Kolonia, on Pohnpei 5,600; Colonia, on Yap 4,800. **Location:** Oceania, island group in the North Pacific Ocean, northeast of New Guinea.

## Vital statistics

**Birth rate** per 1,000 population (2000): 26.7 (world avg. 22.5). **Death rate** per 1,000 population (2000): 3.9 (world avg. 9.0). **Natural increase rate** per 1,000 population (2000): 22.8 (world avg. 13.5). **Total fertility rate** (avg. births per childbearing woman; 2000): 3.8. **Life expectancy** at birth (2000): male 66.5 years; female 67.6 years.

## National economy

**Budget** (1997–98). *Revenue:* $152,300,000 (external grants 60.0%; tax revenue 15.1%; fishing rights fees 13.4%). *Expenditures:* $154,700,000 (current expenditures 79.6%, of which government services 71.4%, transfer payments 4.7%, debt services 3.4%; capital expenditure 20.4%). **Public debt** (external, outstanding; 2000): $85,700,000. **Population economically active** (2000): total 37,414; activity rate of total population 35.0% (participation rates: ages 15–64, 61.7%; female 42.9%; unemployed 22.0%). **Production** (metric tons except as noted). *Agriculture, forestry, fishing:* Micronesia's major crops include coconuts (which provide annually more than 4,000 tons of copra), breadfruit, cassava, sweet potatoes, peppers, and a variety of tropical fruits (including bananas); livestock comprises mostly pigs and poultry; fish catch (1998) 20,000, of which skipjack tuna 15,000, yellowfin tuna 5,000. *Mining and quarrying:* quarrying of sand and aggregate for local construction only. *Manufacturing:* copra and coconut oil, traditionally important products, are being displaced by garment production; the manufacture of handicrafts and personal items (clothing, mats, boats, etc.) by individuals is also important. *Energy production (consumption):* electricity (kW-hr; 1997) 100,333,000 (100,333,000); petroleum products (metric tons; 1992) none (77,000). **Household income and expenditure.** Average household size (2000) 6.7; annual income per household $8,944 (median income; $4,618); sources of income (1994): wages and salaries 51.8%, operating surplus 23.0%, social security 2.1%; expenditure (1985): food and beverages 73.5%. **Land use** (1984; includes all areas formerly constituting the US Trust Territory of the Pacific Islands): forested 22.5%; meadows and pastures 13.5%; agricultural and under permanent cultivation 33.5%; other 30.5%. **Gross national product** (2000): $250,000,000 ($2,110 per capita). **Tourism** (1998): expenditures $4,383,000; number of visitors 16,283.

## Foreign trade

**Imports** (1998): $82,486,915 (1997; food, beverages, and tobacco 41.9%; manufactured goods 32.0%; machinery and transport equipment 28.4%; petroleum products 11.2%; chemicals 4.4%). *Major import sources* (1997): US (including Guam) 72.5%; Japan 13.5%; Australia 6.6%. **Exports** (1998): $8,037,207 (1997; marine products 89.2%; agricultural products 4.4%, of which bananas 3.2%, copra 1.2%). *Major export destinations* (1992): Japan 80.0%; US 9.3%; Guam 8.3%; South Pacific Region 2.4%.

## Transport and communications

**Transport.** *Roads* (1990): total length 226 km (paved 17%). *Vehicles* (1998): passenger cars 2,044; trucks and buses 354. *Air transport:* airports (1997) with scheduled flights 4. **Communications,** in total units (units per 1,000 persons). Radio receivers (1996): 70,000 (667); television receivers (1999): 2,400 (21); telephone main lines (2001): 10,000 (93); cellular telephone subscribers (2001): 49,900 (466); Internet users (2000): 4,000 (37).

## Education and health

**Educational attainment** (2000). Percentage of population age 25 and over having: no formal schooling

---

*1 metric ton = about 1.1 short tons;    1 kilometer = 0.6 mi (statute);    1 metric ton-km cargo = about 0.68 short ton-mi cargo;    c.i.f.: cost, insurance, and freight;    f.o.b.: free on board*

12.3%; primary education 37.0%; some secondary 18.3%; secondary 12.9%; some college 18.4%. **Literacy** (2000): total population age 10 and over literate 72,140 (92.4%); males literate 36,528 (92.9%); females literate 35,612 (91.9%). **Health** (1998): physicians 68 (1 per 1,677 persons); hospital beds (1997) 260 (1 per 447 persons); infant mortality rate per 1,000 live births (2000) 38.0.

## Military

External security is provided by the US.

**Did you know?** Pohnpei, the largest island in Micronesia, has over 767 varieties of plant species, 111 of which are not found anywhere else in the world. Many of these unique plants grow in the upland forest regions, where rainfall can average over 400 in (10,000 mm) annually.

## Background

The islands of Micronesia were probably settled by people from eastern Melanesia some 3,500 years ago. Europeans first landed on the islands in the 16th century. Spain took control of the islands in 1886, then sold them to Germany in 1899. The islands came under Japanese rule after World War I. They were captured by US forces during World War II, and in 1947 they were included as a UN trust territory administered by the US. The islands became an internally self-governing federation in 1979. In 1986 Micronesia entered into a Compact of Free Association with the US, some provisions of which were set to expire in 2001. In the late 1990s, the republic was struggling to solve its economic difficulties.

## Recent Developments

A two-year negotiation period (2001–03) included in the compact of free association allowed US financial assistance to continue while discussions were ongoing. In 2002 the US proposed a new funding plan for Micronesia, which was to be voted on by Congress by October 2003.

Internet resources: <www.fm>

# Moldova

**Official name:** Republica Moldova (Republic of Moldova). **Form of government:** unitary parliamentary republic with a single legislative body (Parliament [101]). **Head of state:** President Vladimir Voronin (from 2001). **Head of government:** Prime Minister Vasile Tarlev (from 2001). **Capital:** Chisinau. **Official language:** Romanian (constitutionally designated as Moldovan). **Official religion:** none. **Monetary unit:** 1 Moldovan leu (plural lei) = 100 bani; valuation (7 Jul 2003) free rate, $1 = 14.05 Moldovan lei.

## Demography

**Area:** 13,000 sq mi, 33,700 sq km. **Population** (2002): 3,621,000. **Density** (2002): persons per sq mi 277.1, persons per sq km 107.0. **Urban** (2001): 41.4%. **Sex distribution** (2001): male 47.66%; female 52.34%. **Age breakdown** (2001): under 15,

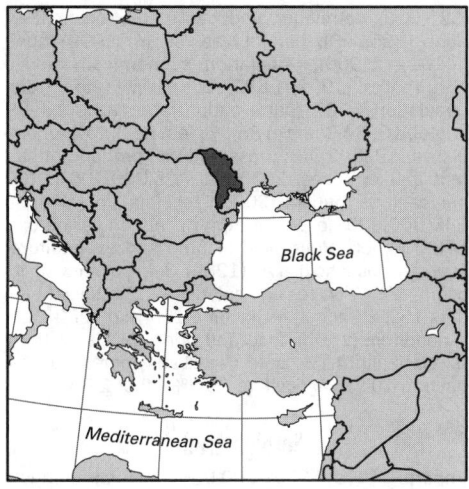

Black Sea

Mediterranean Sea

22.4%; 15–29, 25.5%; 30–44, 21.1%; 45–59, 16.6%; 60–74, 11.0%; 75 and over, 3.4%. **Ethnic composition** (2000): Moldovan 48.2%; Ukrainian 13.8%; Russian 12.9%; Bulgarian 8.2%; Rom (Gypsy) 6.2%; Gagauz 4.2%; other 6.5%. **Religious affiliation** (1995): Orthodox 46.0%, of which Romanian Orthodox 35.0%, Russian Orthodox 9.5%; Muslim 5.5%; Catholic 1.8%, of which Roman Catholic 0.6%; Protestant 1.7%; Jewish 0.9%; other (mostly nonreligious) 44.1%. **Major cities** (1999): Chisinau 655,000; Tiraspol 200,700; Balti 156,600. **Location:** eastern Europe, bordering Ukraine and Romania.

## Vital statistics

**Birth rate** per 1,000 population (2001): 13.3 (world avg. 21.2); (1995) legitimate 87.7%; illegitimate 12.3%. **Death rate** per 1,000 population (2001): 12.6 (world avg. 8.9). **Natural increase rate** per 1,000 population (2001): 0.7 (world avg. 12.3). **Total fertility rate** (avg. births per childbearing woman; 2001): 1.7. **Marriage rate** per 1,000 population (1998): 6.0. **Life expectancy** at birth (2001): male 60.2 years; female 69.3 years.

## National economy

**Budget** (1999). *Revenue:* 3,745,000,000 lei (value-added tax 25.1%, social fund contributions 20.9%, excise taxes 11.9%, profits tax 6.2%, duties and customs taxes 6.2%, personal income tax 5.9%). *Expenditures:* 4,535,000,000 lei (current expenditures 97.7%, of which interest payments 20.0%, social fund expenditures 19.6%, education 12.7%, health care 7.4%, national economy 6.3%; capital expenditure 2.3%). **Public debt** (external, outstanding; 2000): $854,000,000. **Production** (metric tons except as noted). *Agriculture, forestry, fishing* (2001): sugar beets 1,138,000, wheat 980,000, corn (maize) 825,400; livestock (number of live animals) 866,000 sheep, 543,000 pigs, 402,000 cattle; roundwood (2000) 58,300 cu m; fish catch (1999) 1,630. *Mining and quarrying* (1995): sand and gravel 376,000; gypsum 13,600. *Manufacturing* ('000,000 lei; 1995): food 1,446,824; machinery 383,153; construction materials 164,198. *Energy production (consumption):* electricity (kW-hr; 1999) 3,819,000,000 (4,997,000,000); coal (metric tons; 1999) none

(620,000); petroleum products (metric tons; 1999) none (835,000); natural gas (cu m; 1999) none (2,100,000,000). **Population economically active** (1994): total (1999) 1,682,000; activity rate of total population 44.8% (participation rates: ages 16–59 [male], 16–54 [female] 85.2%; female 53.0%; unemployed [1998] 2.0%). **Gross national product** (at current market prices; 2000): $1,428,000,000 ($400 per capita). **Tourism** (2000): receipts from visitors $46,000,000; expenditures by nationals abroad $78,000,000. **Household income and expenditure.** Average household size (1989) 3.4; sources of income (1994): wages and salaries 41.2%, social benefits 15.3%, agricultural income 10.4%, other 33.1%; expenditure (1995): food and drink 49.1%, clothing 9.7%, health 4.1%. **Land use** (1994): forest 10.6%; pasture 10.9%; agriculture 75.9%; other 2.6%.

## Foreign trade

**Imports** (1999): $597,000,000 (mineral products 38.2%, machinery 12.1%, textiles 11.6%, chemical products 8.0%, agricultural goods 6.6%). *Major import sources* (1997): Russia 28.4%; Ukraine 18.0%; Romania 8.6%; Germany 8.1%. **Exports** (1999): $469,000,000 (food and agricultural goods 42.5%, textile products 13.9%, machinery 5.9%, metals and metal products 3.5%). *Major export destinations* (1997): Russia 58.2%; Romania 6.7%; US 6.7%; Ukraine 5.6%.

## Transport and communications

**Transport.** *Railroads* (1998): length 2,710 km; passenger-km 656,000,000; metric ton-km cargo 2,575,000,000. *Roads* (1999): total length 12,657 km (paved 87%). *Vehicles* (1999): passenger cars 232,278; trucks and buses 66,012. *Air transport* (1997): passenger-km 61,000,000; metric ton-km cargo 6,000,000; airports (2000) 1. **Communications,** in total units (units per 1,000 persons). Daily newspaper circulation (1996): 261,000 (59); radio receivers (1997): 3,220,000 (736); television receivers (1998): 1,300,000 (297); telephone main lines (2001): 676,100 (154); cellular telephone subscribers (2001): 210,000 (48); personal computers (2001): 70,000 (16); Internet users (2001): 60,000 (14).

## Education and health

**Educational attainment** (1989). Percentage of population age 15 and over having: no formal schooling or some primary education 24.5%; some secondary 20.4%; secondary 46.4%; higher 8.7%. **Literacy** (2000): total population age 15 and over literate 98.9%; males 99.6%; females 98.3%. **Health** (1995): physicians 17,200 (1 per 250 persons); hospital beds 53,000 (1 per 82 persons); infant mortality rate per 1,000 live births (2001) 42.7. **Food** (2000): daily per capita caloric intake 2,764 (vegetable products 86%, animal products 14%); 108% of FAO recommended minimum.

## Military

**Total active duty personnel** (2001): 8,220 (army 86.6%, air force 13.4%). **Military expenditure as per-**

centage of **GNP** (1999): 1.6% (world 2.4%); per capita expenditure $10.

## Background

Moldova, once part of the principality of Moldavia, was founded by the Vlachs in the 14th century. In the mid-16th century it was under the Ottoman Empire. In 1774 it came under Russian control and lost portions of its territory. In 1859 it joined with the principality of Walachia to form the state of Romania, and in 1918 some of the territory it had ceded earlier also joined Romania. Romania was compelled to cede some of the Moldavian area to Russia in 1940, and that area combined with what Russia already controlled to become the Moldavian SSR. In 1991 Moldavia declared independence from the Soviet Union. It adopted the Romanian spelling of Moldova after having legitimized (1989) the use of the Roman rather than the Cyrillic alphabet. During the 1990s the country struggled to find economic equilibrium.

## Recent Developments

In the February 2001 elections Moldova became the first former Soviet republic to return unreformed Communists to power. They proposed a number of highly controversial Russification policies: the planned introduction of compulsory Russian courses in primary schools, the proclamation of Russian as an official language, and the replacement of courses in the history of the Romanian people with the Soviet-style version of the history of Moldova.

**Internet resources:** <www.ournet.md>

# Monaco

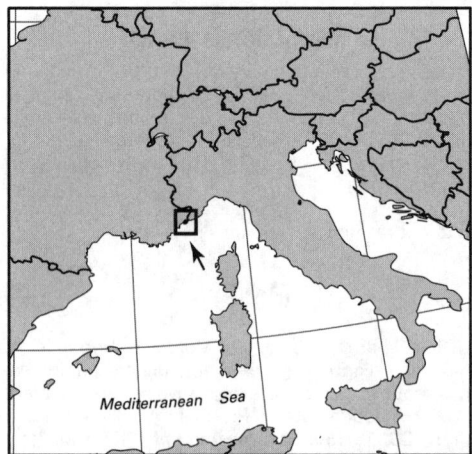

*Mediterranean Sea*

**Official name:** Principauté de Monaco (Principality of Monaco). **Form of government:** constitutional monarchy with one legislative body (National Council [18]). **Chief of state:** Prince Rainier III (from 1949). **Head of government:** Minister of State Patrick Leclercq (from 2000). **Capital:** (no separate area is distinguished as such). **Official language:** French. **Official religion:** Roman Catholicism. **Monetary unit:** 1 euro (€) = 100

*1 metric ton = about 1.1 short tons;    1 kilometer = 0.6 mi (statute);    1 metric ton-km cargo = about 0.68 short ton-mi cargo;    c.i.f.: cost, insurance, and freight;    f.o.b.: free on board*

cents; (7 Jul 2003) $1 = €0.87; at conversion on 1 Jan 2002, €1 = 6.56 French francs (F).

## Demography

**Area:** 0.75 sq mi, 1.95 sq km. **Population** (2002): 32,000. **Density** (2002): persons per sq mi 42,105, persons per sq km 16,326. **Urban** (2000): 100%. **Sex distribution** (2000): male 47.58%; female 52.42%. **Age breakdown** (2000): under 15, 15.1%; 15–29, 14.0%; 30–44, 21.2%; 45–59, 21.3%; 60–74, 17.2%; 75 and over, 11.2%. **Ethnic composition** (2000): French 45.8%; Ligurian (Genoan) 17.2%; Monegasque 16.9%; British 4.5%; Jewish 1.7%; other 13.9%. **Religious affiliation** (2000): Christian 93.2%, of which Roman Catholic 89.3%; Jewish 1.7%; nonreligious and other 5.1%. **Location:** western Europe, bordering the Mediterranean Sea and France.

## Vital statistics

**Birth rate** per 1,000 population (2000): 22.8 (world avg. 22.5). **Death rate** per 1,000 population (2000): 16.4 (world avg. 9.0). **Natural increase rate** per 1,000 population (2000): 6.4 (world avg. 13.5). **Total fertility rate** (avg. births per childbearing woman; 2000): 1.8. **Marriage rate** per 1,000 population (1997): 6.0. **Divorce rate** per 1,000 population (1997): 2.5. **Life expectancy** at birth (2000): male 74.9 years; female 83.0 years.

## National economy

**Budget** (1997). *Revenue:* F 3,225,658,000 (value-added taxes 50.0%). *Expenditures:* F 3,139,854,000. **Production.** *Agriculture, forestry, fishing:* some horticulture and greenhouse cultivation; no agriculture as such. *Manufacturing:* in the 1990s, principal manufactures included chemicals, cosmetics, perfumery, and pharmaceuticals; light electronics and precision instruments; paper and card manufactures; fabricated plastics; and clothing. *Energy production (consumption):* electricity (kW-hr; 1997), n.a. (403,000,-000 [imported from France]). **Gross domestic product** (1994): $765,000,000 ($24,460 per capita). **Population economically active** (1990): total 12,574 (42.0%); female participation in labor force 5,002 (39.8%); ages 17–64, 63.6%; unemployed (1996) 3.0%. **Household.** Average household size (1998) 2.2. **Tourism** (1999): 2,219 hotel rooms; 278,000 overnight stays. **Land use** (2000): forested 0%; meadows and pastures 0%; agricultural and under permanent cultivation 0%; built-up and other 100%.

## Foreign trade

Monaco participates in a customs union (since 1963) with France; separate figures are not available.

## Transport and communications

**Transport.** *Railroads* (1997): length 1.7 km; passengers 2,171,100; cargo 3,357 tons. *Roads* (1997): total length 50 km (paved 100%). *Vehicles* (1997): passenger cars 21,120; trucks and buses 2,770. **Communications,** in total units (units per 1,000 persons). Daily newspaper circulation (1999): 10,000 (300); radio receivers (1997): 34,000 (1,030); television receivers (1997): 25,000 (758); telephone main lines (1999): 33,000 (990); cellular telephone subscribers (1999): 12,000 (360).

## Education and health

**Literacy:** virtually 100%. **Health** (1997): physicians 188 (1 per 170 persons); hospital beds 555 (1 per 58 persons); infant mortality rate per 1,000 live births (2000) 5.9. **Food:** daily per capita caloric intake, n.a.; assuming consumption patterns similar to France (2000) 3,591 (vegetable products 62%, animal products 38%); 143% of FAO recommended minimum.

## Military

Defense responsibility lies with France according to the terms of the Versailles Treaty of 1919.

**Did you know?** Monaco is the second smallest country in the world and the smallest country in the United Nations. Its area covers only two square kilometers.

## Background

Inhabited since prehistoric times, Monaco was known to the Phoenicians, Greeks, Carthaginians, and Romans. In 1191 the Genoese took possession of it; in 1297 the reign of the Grimaldi family began. The Grimaldis allied themselves with France except for the period 1524–1641, when they were under the protection of Spain. France annexed Monaco in 1793, and it remained under French control until the fall of Napoleon, when the Grimaldis returned. In 1815 it was put under the protection of Sardinia. A treaty in 1861 called for the sale of the towns of Menton and Roquebrune to France and the establishment of Monaco's independence. Monaco is one of Europe's most luxurious resorts. In 1997 the 700-year rule of the Grimaldis, now under Prince Rainier III, was celebrated.

## Recent Developments

On 24 Oct 2002 Monaco and France signed a revision of the 1918 treaty that governed their interstate relations. Monaco gained in its ability to conduct its own foreign policy, and it is now likely that the principality will eventually join the EU.

**Internet Resources:** <www.monaco.mc>

# Mongolia

**Official name:** Mongol Uls (Mongolia). **Form of government:** unitary multiparty republic with one legislative house (State Great Hural [76]). **Chief of state:** President Natsagiyn Bagabandi (from 1997). **Head of government:** Prime Minister Nambaryn Enkhbayar (from 2000). **Capital:** Ulaanbaatar (Ulan Bator). **Official language:** Khalkha Mongolian. **Official religion:** none. **Monetary unit:** 1 tugrik (Tug) = 100 mongo; valuation (7 Jul 2003) $1 = Tug 1,126.

## Demography

**Area:** 603,930 sq mi, 1,564,160 sq km. **Population** (2002): 2,457,000. **Density** (2002): persons per sq mi 4.1, persons per sq km 1.6. **Urban** (2000): 56.6%. **Sex distribution** (2000): male

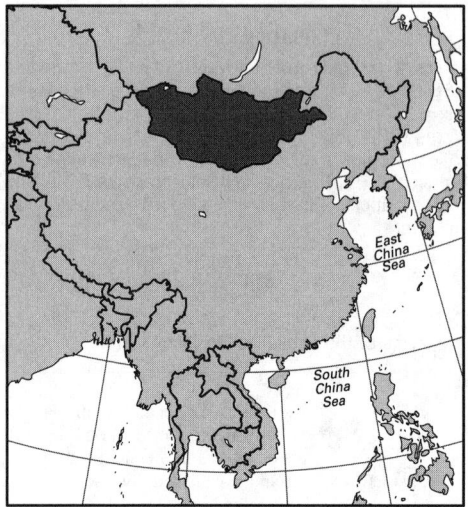

(number of live animals) 13,876,400 sheep, 10,077,500 goats, 2,660,700 horses; roundwood (2000) 631,000 cu m; fish catch (1999) 524. *Mining and quarrying* (2000): fluorspar 733,500; copper 357,800; molybdenum 2,843. *Manufacturing* (value added by manufacturing in Tug '000,000; 1996): food products 10,261.3; textiles 6,522.8; beverages 3,316.6. *Energy production (consumption)*: electricity (kW-hr; 2000) 2,946,000,000 (3,042,000,000); coal (metric tons; 2000) 5,185,-000 (4,986,000); petroleum products (metric tons; 1998) none (278,300). **Gross national product** (2000): $947,000,000 ($390 per capita). **Household income and expenditure** (2000): Average household size 4.4; monthly income per household (1999) Tug 67,426 ($66); sources of income (1999): wages 36.4%, transfer payments 11.7%, self-employment 41.2%, other 10.7%; expenditure (1999): food 41.1%, housing 11.4%, clothing 9.7%, education 7.5%, transportation and communications 7.1%, health care 3.6%. **Land use** (1998): forest and other 24.4%; pasture 74.8%; agriculture 0.8%.

49.63%; female 50.37%. **Age breakdown** (2000): under 15, 35.8%; 15–29, 30.2%; 30–44, 20.5%; 45–59, 8.3%; 60–69, 3.3%; 70 and over, 1.9%. **Ethnic composition** (2000): Khalkha Mongol 81.5%; Kazakh 4.3%; Dörbed Mongol 2.8%; Bayad 2.1%; Buryat Mongol 1.7%; Dariganga Mongol 1.3%; Zakhchin 1.3%; Tuvan (Uriankhai) 1.1%; other 3.9%. **Religious affiliation** (1995): Tantric Buddhist (Lamaism) 96.0%; Muslim 4.0%. **Major cities** (2000): Ulaanbaatar (Ulan Bator) 760,077; Erdenet 68,310; Darhan 65,791; Choybalsan 41,714; Ulaangom 26,319. **Location**: north-central Asia, bordering Russia and China.

## Vital statistics

**Birth rate** per 1,000 population (2001): 21.8 (world avg. 21.2). **Death rate** per 1,000 population (2001): 7.1 (world avg. 8.9). **Natural increase rate** per 1,000 population (2001): 14.7 (world avg. 12.3). **Total fertility rate** (avg. births per childbearing woman; 2001): 2.4. **Marriage rate** per 1,000 population (2000): 5.0. **Divorce rate** per 1,000 population (2000): 1.5. **Life expectancy** at birth (2001): male 62.1 years; female 66.5 years.

## National economy

**Budget** (2001). *Revenue*: Tug 333,491,400,000 (taxes 75.0%, of which sales tax 26.8%, social security contributions 13.3%, special taxes 12.1%, income taxes 11.3%, custom duties 8.8%; nontax revenue 25.0%). *Expenditures*: Tug 423,985,500 (education, health, social services 58.4%; transfers to provincial governments 14.0%; capital investment 6.9%; wages 7.9%; defense 6.0%). **Public debt** (external; 2000): $794,800,000. **Tourism** (1999): receipts $36,000,000; expenditures $41,000,000. **Population economically active** (2000): total 944,083; activity rate of total population 39.8% (participation rates: ages 15 and over 61.9%; female 50.8%; unemployed [2002] 11.5%). **Production** (metric tons except as noted). *Agriculture, forestry, fishing* (2000): wheat 142,100, potatoes 58,900, vegetables and melons 44,000; livestock

## Foreign trade

**Imports** (2000): $574,200,000 (1998; capital equipment 33.5%, energy 15.7%, food 13.9%, consumer goods 12.6%, raw materials and spare parts 10.8%). *Major import sources*: Russia 33.6%; China 20.5%; Japan 11.9%; South Korea 9.1%; US 4.6%; Germany 4.6%. **Exports** (2000): $432,300,000 (mineral products 59.3%, of which copper 33.1%; textiles 23.2%; cashmere 11.3%; wool, hides, and leather goods 6.2%). *Major export destinations*: China 58.9%; US 19.9%; Russia 9.7%; Italy 3.1%; UK 2.4%.

## Transport and communications

**Transport.** *Railroads* (2000): length 1,815 km; passenger-km (1999): 559,800,000; metric ton-km cargo 4,282,500. *Roads* (1999): total length 49,250 km (paved 4%). *Vehicles* (2000): passenger cars 44,100; trucks and buses 37,600. *Air transport* (1996): passenger-km 525,000,000; metric ton-km cargo 48,000,000; airports (2000) with scheduled flights 1. **Communications**, in total units (units per 1,000 persons). Daily newspaper circulation (1996): 68,000 (27); radio receivers (1997): 360,000 (142); television receivers (2000): 169,100 (58); telephone main lines (2001): 123,000 (48); cellular telephone subscribers (2001): 195,000 (76); personal computers (2001): 35,000 (14); Internet users (2001): 40,000 (16).

## Education and health

**Educational attainment** (2000). Percentage of population age 10 and over having: no formal education 11.6%; primary education 23.5%; secondary 46.1%; vocational secondary 11.2%; higher 7.6%. **Literacy** (2000): total population age 15 and over literate 97.8%; males 98.0%; females 97.5%. **Health** (1999): physicians 6,162 (1 per 384 persons); hospital beds 17,877 (1 per 132 persons); infant mortality rate per 1,000 live births (2001) 53.5. **Food** (2000): daily per capita caloric intake 1,981 (vegetable products 52%, animal products 48%); 82% of FAO recommended minimum.

---

*1 metric ton = about 1.1 short tons;    1 kilometer = 0.6 mi (statute);    1 metric ton-km cargo = about 0.68 short ton-mi cargo;    c.i.f.: cost, insurance, and freight;    f.o.b.: free on board*

## Military

Total active duty personnel (2001): 9,100 (army 82.4%, air force 17.6%). **Military expenditure as percentage of GNP** (1999): 2.1% (world 2.4%); per capita expenditure $5.

## Background

In Neolithic times Mongolia was inhabited by small groups of nomads. During the 3rd century BC it became the center of the Xiongnu empire. Turkic-speaking peoples held sway in the 4th–10th century AD. In the early 13th century Genghis Khan united the Mongol tribes and conquered central Asia. His successor, Ogodei, conquered the Chin dynasty of China in 1234. Kublai Khan established the Yuan, or Mongol, dynasty in China in 1279. After the 14th century, the Ming dynasty of China confined the Mongols to their homeland in the steppes; later they became part of the Chinese Ch'ing dynasty. Inner Mongolia was incorporated into China in 1644. After the fall of the Ch'ing dynasty in 1911, Mongol princes declared Mongolia's independence from China, and in 1921 Russian forces helped drive off the Chinese. The Mongolian People's Republic was established in 1924 and recognized by China in 1946. The nation adopted a new constitution in 1992 and shortened its name to Mongolia.

## Recent Developments

In June 2002 the Great Hural adopted the Law on Land and the Law on Land Privatization, due to come into force in 2003. The area to be privatized was limited, however, to 1% of Mongolia's total territory. As a result of two years of autumn drought and severe winters, 2.7 million livestock perished in early 2002.

**Internet resources:** <www.travelmongolia.com>

# Morocco

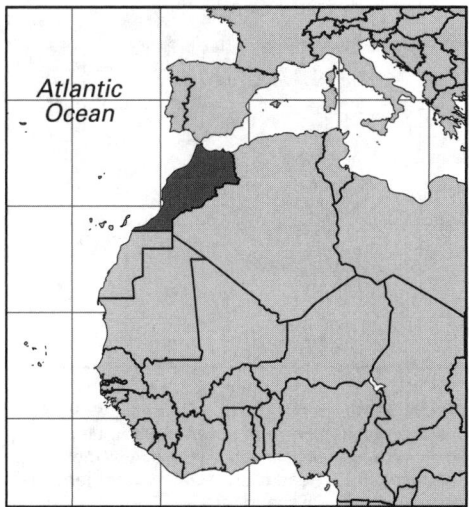

Atlantic Ocean

**Official name:** Al-Mamlakah al-Maghribiyah (Kingdom of Morocco). **Form of government:** constitutional monarchy with two legislative houses (House of Councillors [270 {indirectly elected seats}]; House of Representatives [325]). **Chief of state and head of government:** King Muhammad VI (from 1999) assisted by Prime Minister Driss Jettou (from 9 Oct 2002). **Capital:** Rabat. **Official language:** Arabic. **Official religion:** Islam. **Monetary unit:** 1 Moroccan dirham (DH) = 100 Moroccan francs; valuation (7 Jul 2003) $1 = DH 9.45.

## Demography

**Area** (includes Western Sahara): 274,461 sq mi, 710,850 sq km. **Population** (2002; includes annexed territory of Western Sahara [area: 97,344 sq mi, 252,120 sq km; pop. {2002} 256,000]): 29,632,000. **Density** (2002): persons per sq mi 108.0, persons per sq km 41.7. **Urban** (1999): 52.7%. **Sex distribution** (1999): male 49.89%; female 50.11%. **Age breakdown** (1999): under 15, 35.7%; 15–29, 28.9%; 30–44, 18.9%; 45–59, 9.2%; 60–74, 5.3%; 75 and over, 2.0%. **Ethnolinguistic composition** (1995): Arab 65%; Berber 33%; other 2%. **Religious affiliation** (2000): Muslim (mostly Sunni) 98.3%; Christian 0.6%; other 1.1%. **Major urban areas** (1994): Casablanca 2,940,623; Rabat-Salé 1,385,872; Fès 774,574; Marrakech 745,541; Oujda 678,778. **Location:** northern Africa, bordering the Mediterranean Sea, Algeria, and the North Atlantic Ocean.

## Vital statistics

**Birth rate** per 1,000 population (2002): 23.6 (world avg. 21.2). **Death rate** per 1,000 population (2002): 5.9 (world avg. 8.9). **Natural increase rate** per 1,000 population (2002): 17.7 (world avg. 12.3). **Total fertility rate** (avg. birth per childbearing woman; 2002): 3.0. **Life expectancy** at birth (2002): male 67.5 years; female 72.1 years.

## National economy

**Budget.** *Revenue* (1997): DH 79,747,000,000 (taxes on income and profits 25.2%; value-added tax 22.7%; excise taxes 17.9%; international trade 15.0%; stamp tax 4.4%). *Expenditures* (1997): DH 86,058,000,000 (current expenditure 78.7%, of which wages 39.7%, debt payment 20.1%; capital expenditure 21.3%). **Public debt** (external, outstanding; 2000): $15,793,000,000. **Tourism** (2000): receipts $2,040,000; expenditures $430,000,000. **Production** (metric tons except as noted). *Agriculture, forestry, fishing* (1999): sugar beets 3,223,400, wheat 2,153,540, barley 1,473,980; livestock (number of live animals) 16,576,400 sheep, 5,114,400 goats, 2,559,800 cattle; roundwood (1998) 1,746,000 cu m; fish catch (1997) 625,000. *Mining and quarrying* (1996): phosphate rock 20,792,000; barite 283,000; zinc 152,000. *Manufacturing* (value added in DH '000,000; 1996): food 39,280; chemical products 13,508; textiles 12,392. *Energy production (consumption):* electricity (kW-hr; 2001) 13,339,000,000 ([1997] 14,192,000,000); coal (metric tons; 2001) 135,000 ([1997] 3,009,000); crude petroleum (barrels; 1997) 88,000 (43,460,000); petroleum products (metric tons; 1997) 5,056,000 (6,146,000); natural gas (cu m; 1997) 30,625,000 (30,625,000). **Population economically active** (1998): total 5,137,539; activity rate 34.4% (participation rates: over age 15, 48.1%; female 23.8%; unemployed 19.0%). **Gross national product** (2000): $33,940,000,000 ($1,180 per capita). **Household income and expenditure.** Average household size

(1998) 5.7; expenditure (1994): food 45.2%, housing 12.5%, transportation 7.6%.

## Foreign trade

**Imports** (2000-c.i.f.): DH 121,983,000,000 (finished consumer products 23.5%, of which textiles and apparel 8.8%; finished industrial products 20.2%; mineral fuels 17.8%, of which crude petroleum 12.1%; food 11.7%, of which wheat 4.5%). *Major import sources:* France 24.3%; Spain 9.8%; UK 6.0%; US 5.6%; Germany 4.9%. **Exports** (2000-f.o.b.): DH 78,673,000,000 (finished consumer products 37.5%, of which hosiery 11.2%; food 20.8%, of which crustaceans and mollusks 8.1%; phosphoric acid 6.8%; phosphates 5.8%; electronic components 5.3%). *Major export destinations:* France 33.6%; Spain 12.7%; UK 9.3%; Italy 7.6%; Germany 4.4%.

## Transport and communications

**Transport.** *Railroads* (1996): route length 1,768 km; passenger-km 1,776,000,000; metric ton-km cargo 4,757,000,000. *Roads* (1996): total length 57,810 km (paved 52%). *Vehicles* (1996): passenger cars 1,018,146; trucks and buses 278,075. *Air transport* (2001; Royal Air Maroc only): passenger-km 7,362,000,000; metric ton-km cargo 76,005,000; airports (1998) 11. **Communications,** in total units (units per 1,000 persons). Daily newspaper circulation (1996): 704,000 (27); radio receivers (1997): 6,640,000 (247); television receivers (1997): 3,100,000 (115); telephone main lines (2001): 1,191,000 (39); cellular telephone subscribers (2001): 4,772,000 (157); personal computers (2001): 400,000 (13); Internet users (2001): 400,000 (13).

## Education and health

**Educational attainment** (1982). Percentage of population age 25 and over having: no formal education 47.8%; some primary education 47.8%; some secondary 3.8%; higher 0.6%. **Literacy** (1995): total population over age 15 literate 43.7%; males literate 56.6%; females literate 31.0%. **Health** (1994): physicians 8,838 (1 per 2,923 persons); hospital beds 26,407 (1 per 978 persons); infant mortality rate per 1,000 live births (2001) 48.1. **Food** (1999): daily per capita caloric intake 3,010 (vegetable products 94%, animal products 6%); 124% of FAO recommended minimum.

## Military

**Total active duty personnel** (2001): 198,500 (army 88.2%, navy 5.0%, air force 6.8%). **Military expenditure as percentage of GDP** (1999): 4.3% (world 2.4%); per capita expenditure $49.

## Background

The Berbers entered Morocco near the end of the 2nd millennium BC. Phoenicians established trading posts along the Mediterranean during the 12th century BC, and Carthage had settlements along the Atlantic in the 5th century BC. After the fall of Carthage, Morocco became a loyal ally of Rome, and in AD 42 it was annexed by Rome as part of the province of Mauretania. It was invaded by Muslims in the 7th century. Beginning in the mid-11th century, the Almoravids, Almohads, and Marinids ruled successively. After the fall of the Marinids in the mid-15th century, the Sa'dis ruled for a century after 1550. The French fought Morocco over the Algerian boundary in the 1840s, and the Spanish seized part of Moroccan territory in 1859. It was a French protectorate from 1912 until its independence in 1956. In the mid-1970s it reasserted claim to the Western Sahara, and in 1976 Spanish troops left. Conflicts with Mauritania and Algeria over the region continued into the 1990s. As the decade wore on, the UN tried to solve the dispute. King Hassan II died in July 1999 after 38 years on the throne and was succeeded by his eldest son, Sidi Muhammad, who took the name Muhammad VI.

## Recent Developments

Morocco's poor relations with Spain were further strained in July 2002. After Morocco sent soldiers to the disputed though unoccupied islet of Leila/Perejil, Spain invaded the islet (near Ceuta in the Strait of Gibraltar) and expelled the six gendarmes. Though the US brokered an agreement to leave the islet unoccupied, relations between the two countries remained at a low level for the remainder of the year. The Polisario Front, which seeks independence for Western Sahara and has been occupied by Morocco for 25 years, in January 2003 rejected another UN plan to resolve the problem.

**Internet resources:** <www.mincom.gov.ma>

# Mozambique

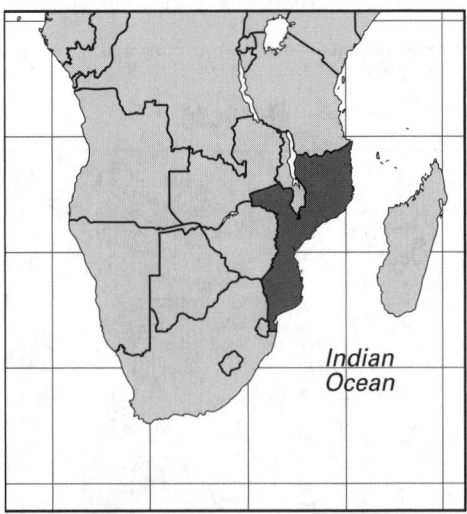

*Indian Ocean*

**Official name:** República de Moçambique (Republic of Mozambique). **Form of government:** multiparty republic with a single legislative house (Assembly of the Republic [250]). **Head of state and government:** President Joaquim Chissano (from 1986) assisted by Prime Minister Pascoal Mocumbi (from 1994). **Capital:** Maputo. **Official language:** Portuguese. **Official**

religion: none. **Monetary unit:** 1 metical (Mt; plural meticais) = 100 centavos; valuation (7 Jul 2003) $1 = Mt 23,338.

## Demography

**Area:** 313,661 sq mi, 812,379 sq km. **Population** (2002): 18,083,000. **Density** (2002): persons per sq mi 57.7, persons per sq km 22.3. **Urban** (2000): 40.2%. **Sex distribution** (2002): male 48.12%; female 51.88%. **Age breakdown** (2001): under 15, 42.7%; 15–29, 29.2%; 30–44, 15.2%; 45–59, 8.4%; 60–74, 3.8%; 75 and over, 0.7%. **Ethnic composition** (2000): Makuana 15.3%; Makua 14.5%; Tsonga 8.6%; Sena 8.0%; Lomwe 7.1%; Tswa 5.7%; Chwabo 5.5%; other 35.3%. **Linguistic composition** (1997): Makua 26.3%; Tsonga 11.4%; Lomwe 7.6%; Sena 7.0%; Portuguese 6.5%; Chuaba 6.3%; other Bantu languages 33.0%; other 1.9%. **Religious affiliation** (2000): traditional beliefs 50.4%; Christian 38.4%, of which Roman Catholic 15.8%, Protestant 8.9%; Muslim 10.5%. **Major cities** (1997): Maputo 989,386; Matola 440,927; Beira 412,588; Nampula 314,965; Chimoio 177,608. **Location:** southern Africa, bordering Tanzania, the Indian Ocean, South Africa, Swaziland, Zimbabwe, Zambia, and Malawi.

## Vital statistics

**Birth rate** per 1,000 population (2001): 37.2 (world avg. 21.2). **Death rate** per 1,000 population (2001): 24.2 (world avg. 8.9). **Natural increase rate** per 1,000 population (2001): 13.0 (world avg. 12.3). **Total fertility rate** (avg. births per childbearing woman; 2001): 4.8. **Life expectancy** at birth (2001): male 37.3 years; female 35.6 years.

## National economy

**Budget** (2001). *Revenue*: Mt 19,253,000,000 (grants 50.1%; tax revenue 44.6%, of which sales tax 27.9%, customs taxes 7.7%, individual income tax 7.7%; nontax revenue 5.3%). *Expenditures*: Mt 23,221,000,000 (current expenditures 45.2%, of which administrative salaries 21.1%, goods and services 10.3%, transfers 9.6%; capital expenditures 44.9%; net lending 9.9%). **Public debt** (external, outstanding; 2000): $4,599,000,000. **Production** (metric tons except as noted). *Agriculture, forestry, fishing* (2001): cassava 5,361,974, corn (maize) 1,143,263, sugarcane 397,276; livestock (number of live animals) 1,320,000 cattle, 392,000 goats, 28,000,000 chickens; roundwood (2001) 18,043,000 cu m; fish catch (1999) 35,560. *Mining and quarrying* (2000): gold 23 kg; semiprecious gemstones 3,400 carats. *Manufacturing* (gross production value in Mt '000,000; 1998): beverages and tobacco 1,753,706; food 1,238,569; chemicals 497,406. *Energy production (consumption)*: electricity (kW-hr; 1997) 570,-000,000 (1,174,000,000); coal (metric tons; 2000) 16,100 ([1997] 60,000); petroleum products (metric tons; 1997) none (277,000); natural gas (cu m; 2000) 55,000,000 (n.a.). **Household income and expenditure.** Average family size (1997) 4.1; source of income (1992–93): wages and salaries 51.6%, self-employment 12.5%, barter 11.5%, private farming 7.7%; expenditure (1992–93): food, beverages, and tobacco 74.6%; housing and energy 11.7%; transportation and communications 4.7%; clothing and footwear 3.7%; education and recreation 1.4%; health 0.8%. **Population economically active** (1999):

total 9,985,000; activity rate 59.3% (participation rates [1980]: over age 15, 87.3%; female [1980] 52.4%; unemployed [1980] 1.7%). **Gross national product** (2000): $3,746,000,000 ($270 per capita). **Land use** (1994): forested 22.1%; meadows and pastures 56.1%; agricultural and under permanent cultivation 4.0%; other 17.8%.

## Foreign trade

**Imports** (2000-c.i.f.): $1,162,300,000 (1996; machinery and transport equipment 32.3%, food and beverages 18.3%, basic manufactures 17.4%, petroleum products 9.6%). *Major import sources:* South Africa 49.8%; European Union 28.6%, of which Portugal 7.6%; Japan 4.6%; US 3.5%. **Exports** (2000): $364,000,000 (prawns 25.1%, electricity 18.4%, aluminum 16.5%, cotton 7.0%, cashews 5.6%). *Major export destinations:* Zimbabwe 17.7%; South Africa 14.6%; Portugal 11.6%; Spain 10.7%; US 4.7%; Japan 4.2%.

## Transport and communications

**Transport.** *Railroads* (1999): route length 3,123 km; passenger-km 144,700,000; metric ton-km cargo 721,300,000. *Roads* (1996): total length 30,400 km (paved 19%). *Vehicles* (1995): passenger cars 84,000; trucks and buses 26,800. *Air transport* (1999): passenger-km 311,700,000; metric ton-km cargo 6,100,000; airports (1997) with scheduled flights 7. **Communications,** in total units (units per 1,000 persons). Daily newspaper circulation (1996): 49,000 (2.7); radio receivers (1997): 730,000 (40); television receivers (1999): 95,000 (5.0); telephone main lines (2001): 89,400 (4.4); cellular telephone subscribers (2001): 169,900 (8.4); personal computers (2001): 70,000 (3.5); Internet users (2001): 15,000 (0.7).

## Education and health

**Literacy** (2000): total population age 15 and over literate 43.8%; males literate 59.9%; females literate 28.4%. **Health:** physicians (1996) 120 (1 per 124,697 persons); hospital beds (1997) 12,630 (1 per 1,210 persons); infant mortality rate per 1,000 live births (2001) 139.2. **Food** (2000): daily per capita caloric intake 1,927 (vegetable products 97%, animal products 3%); 83% of FAO recommended minimum.

## Military

**Total active duty personnel** (2001): c. 11,100 (army 86%, navy 5%, air force 9%). **Military expenditure as percentage of GNP** (1999): 2.5% (world 2.4%); per capita expenditure $5.

## Background

Inhabited in prehistoric times, Mozambique was settled by Bantu peoples about the 3rd century AD. Arab traders occupied the coastal region from the 14th century, and the Portuguese controlled the area from the early 16th century. The slave trade later became an important part of the economy. In the late 19th century private trading companies began to administer parts of the inland areas. It became an overseas province of Portugal in 1951. After years of war beginning in the 1960s, the country was granted independence in 1975. It was wracked by civil war in the

1970s and '80s. In 1990 a new constitution was promulgated, and a peace treaty was signed with the
rebels in 1992.

## Recent Developments

In December 2002 Pres. Joaquim Chissano welcomed his counterparts Robert Mugabe of Zimbabwe
and Thabo Mbeki of South Africa to Maputo to sign
the treaty officially launching the Great Limpopo
Transfrontier Park, which linked game reserves in all
three countries. In March 2003 plans were completed to privatize the port of Maputo, making it likely
that it would develop into a major southern African
commercial center.

Internet resources: <www.mozambique.mz>

# Myanmar (Burma)

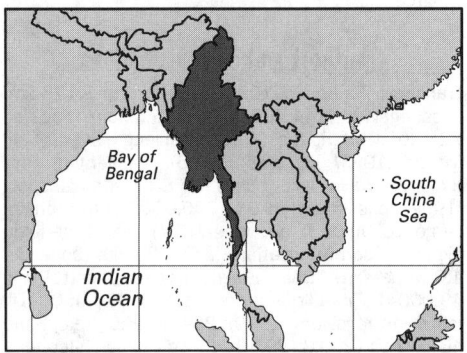

Official name: Pyidaungzu Myanma Naingngandaw
(Union of Myanmar). Form of government: military
regime. Head of state and government: Chairman of
the State Peace and Development Council and Prime
Minister Gen. Than Shwe (from 1992). Capital: Yangon (Rangoon). Official language: Burmese. Official
religion: none. Monetary unit: 1 Myanmar kyat (K) =
100 pyas; valuation (7 Jul 2003) $1 = K 6.20 (pegged
rate to the Special Drawing Right of the International
Monetary Fund).

## Demography

Area: 261,228 sq mi, 676,577 sq km. Population
(2002): 42,238,000. Density (2002): persons per sq
mi 161.7, persons per sq km 62.4. Urban (2002):
29.0%. Sex distribution (1997): male 49.65%; female 50.35%. Age breakdown (1997): under 15,
33.3%; 15–29, 27.7%; 30–44, 19.8%; 45–59,
11.5%; 60 and over, 7.7%. Ethnic composition
(2000): Burman 55.9%; Karen 9.5%; Shan 6.5%;
Han Chinese 2.5%; Mon 2.3%; Yangbye 2.2%;
Kachin 1.5%; other 19.6%. Religious affiliation
(1983): Buddhist 89.4%; Christian 4.9%; Muslim
3.8%; traditional beliefs 1.2%; other 0.7%. Major
cities (1993 est.): Yangon (Rangoon) 3,361,700;
Mandalay 885,300; Moulmein (Mawlamyine)
307,600; Pegu (Bago) 190,900; Bassein (Pathein)
183,900. Location: southeastern Asia, bordering
China, Laos, Thailand, the Andaman Sea, the Bay of
Bengal, and India.

## Vital statistics

Birth rate per 1,000 population (2002): 23.5 (world
avg. 21.2). Death rate per 1,000 population (2002):
11.6 (world avg. 8.9). Natural increase rate per
1,000 population (2002): 11.9 (world avg. 12.3).
Total fertility rate (avg. births per childbearing
woman; 2002): 2.9. Life expectancy at birth (2002):
male 54.0 years; female 59.0 years.

## National economy

Budget (1999–2000). Revenue: K 90,900,000,000
(nontax revenue 55.7%; revenue from taxes 43.8%,
of which taxes on goods and services 19.0%, taxes
on income 15.8%; foreign grants 0.5%). Expenditures: K 92,500,000,000 (defense 34.3%; interest
payments 13.4%; agriculture and forestry 12.4%; education 10.7%; public works and housing 10.5%;
general services 6.2%). Public debt (external, outstanding; 2000): $5,360,000,000. Tourism (2000):
receipts from visitors $42,000,000; expenditures by
nationals abroad $25,000,000. Production (metric
tons except as noted). Agriculture, forestry, fishing
(1999): rice 17,075,000, sugarcane 5,429,000,
pulses 1,895,000; livestock (number of live animals)
10,740,000 cattle, 6,100,000 ducks, 3,715,000
pigs; roundwood (1998) 22,430,000 cu m; fish
catch (1997) 917,666. Mining and quarrying
(1997–98): gypsum 40,642; copper concentrates
14,634; refined lead 1,585. Manufacturing (1996):
cement 513,000; fresh meat 116,000; fertilizers
66,000. Energy production (consumption): electricity
(kW-hr; 1997) 4,211,000,000 (4,211,000,000); coal
(metric tons; 1997) 59,000 (125,000); crude petroleum (barrels; 1997) 2,800,000 (7,300,000); petroleum products (metric tons; 1997) 890,000
(1,452,000); natural gas (cu m; 1997) 1,703,000,-
000 (1,703,000,000). Household expenditure. Average household size (1994) 5.6; expenditure (1994):
food and beverages 67.1%, fuel and lighting 6.6%,
transportation 4.0%, charitable contributions 3.1%,
medical care 3.1%. Gross national product (1996):
$119,334,000,000 ($2,610 per capita). Population
economically active (1997–98): total 19,743,000;
activity rate of total population 42.5% (participation
rates: ages 15–64 [1983] 64.2%; female [1987–88]
35.3%; unemployed 6.2%). Land use (1994):
forested 49.3%; meadows and pastures 0.5%; agricultural and under permanent cultivation 15.3%;
other 34.9%.

## Foreign trade

Imports (1997–98-c.i.f. in balance of trade and in
commodities and trading partners): K 12,735,900,-
000 (machinery and transport equipment 28.6%, intermediate raw materials 19.9%, basic manufactures
15.8%, capital construction materials 12.3%, consumer durable goods 4.3%). Major import sources:
Singapore 31.1%; Japan 15.3%; Thailand 9.8%;
China 9.4%; Malaysia 7.0%; South Korea 5.5%; Indonesia 4.8%. Exports (1997–98): K 5,415,800,000
(pulses and beans 22.3%, teak 11.1%, fish and fish
products 4.6%, hardwood 2.5%, rubber 2.1%). Major
export destinations: India 22.6%; Singapore 13.2%;
Thailand 11.9%; China 10.6%; Hong Kong 5.8%;
Japan 3.8%; US 3.5%.

1 metric ton = about 1.1 short tons;   1 kilometer = 0.6 mi (statute);   1 metric ton-km cargo = about 0.68 short
ton-mi cargo;   c.i.f.: cost, insurance, and freight;   f.o.b.: free on board

## Transport and communications

**Transport.** *Railroads* (1999): route length (1999–2000) 3,955 km; passenger-km 4,112,000,000; metric ton-km cargo 1,043,000,000. *Roads* (1996): total length 28,200 km (paved 12%). *Vehicles* (1996): passenger cars 27,000; trucks and buses 42,000. *Air transport* (1998): passenger-km 345,000,000; metric ton-km cargo 40,000,000; airports (1996) 19. **Communications,** in total units (units per 1,000 persons). Daily newspaper circulation (1996): 449,000 (10); radio receivers (1997): 4,200,000 (96); television receivers (1999): 323,000 (7.2); telephone main lines (2001): 281,200 (5.8); cellular telephone subscribers (2001): 13,800 (0.3); personal computers (2001): 55,000 (1.1); Internet users (2001): 10,000 (0.2).

## Education and health

**Educational attainment** (1983). Percentage of population age 25 and over having: no formal schooling 55.8%; primary education 39.4%; secondary 4.6%; religious 0.1%; postsecondary 0.1%. **Literacy** (1995): total population age 15 and over literate 83.1%; males literate 88.7%; females literate 77.7%. **Health** (1995–96): physicians 12,950 (1 per 3,114 persons); hospital beds 28,732 (1 per 1,404 persons); infant mortality rate per 1,000 live births (2002) 88.0. **Food** (2000): daily per capita caloric intake 2,843 (vegetable products 96%, animal products 4%); 132% of FAO recommended minimum.

## Military

**Total active duty personnel** (2001): 444,000 (army 95.7%, navy 2.3%, air force 2.0%). **Military expenditure as percentage of GNP** (1999): 7.8% (world 2.4%); per capita expenditure $112.

---

**Did you know?**

Myanmar was one of the first areas in Southeast Asia to receive Buddhism, and by the 11th century it had become the center of the Theravada branch. Almost 90% of the population practices Buddhism.

---

## Background

Myanmar, until 1989 known as Burma, has long been inhabited, with the Mon and Pyu states dominant between the 1st century BC and the 9th century AD. It was united in the 11th century under a Burmese dynasty that was overthrown by the Mongols in the 13th century. The Portuguese, Dutch, and English traded there in the 16th–17th centuries. The modern Burmese state was founded in the 18th century. It fell to the British in 1885 and became a province of India. It was occupied by Japan in World War II and became independent in 1948. A military coup took power in 1962 and nationalized major economic sectors. Civilian unrest in the 1980s led to antigovernment rioting. In 1990 opposition parties won in national elections, but the army remained in control. Trying to negotiate for a freer government amid the unrest, Aung San Suu Kyi, the National League for Democracy (NLD) leader, was awarded the Nobel Peace Prize in 1991.

## Recent Developments

International pressure on the Myanmar government's human rights policy increased sharply following the taking into custody on 30 May 2003 of Suu Kyi and the closing of local offices of her party, the NLD. The EU imposed a travel ban and froze the assets of the regime, Japan announced it was suspending aid, and even Myanmar's neighbors in ASEAN dropped their reticence to criticize the junta's conduct. On 28 June US Pres. George W. Bush signed a bill imposing trade sanctions.

**Internet resources:** <www.myanmar-tourism.com>

# Namibia

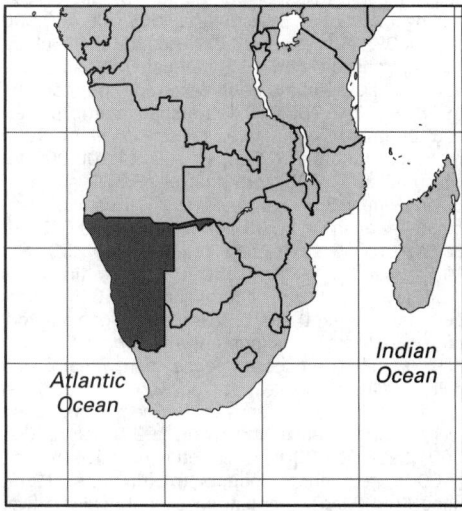

Atlantic Ocean

Indian Ocean

**Official name:** Republic of Namibia. **Form of government:** republic with two legislative houses (National Council [mostly an advisory body; 26]; National Assembly [72]). **Head of state and government:** President Sam Nujoma (from 1990) assisted by Prime Minister Theo-Ben Gurirab (from 28 Aug 2002). **Capital:** Windhoek. **Official language:** English. **Official religion:** none. **Monetary unit:** 1 Namibian dollar (N$) = 100 cents; valuation (7 Jul 2003) US$1 = N$7.51.

## Demography

**Area:** 318,580 sq mi, 825,118 sq km. **Population** (2002): 1,837,000. **Density** (2002): persons per sq mi 5.8, persons per sq km 2.2. **Urban** (1999): 39.8%. **Sex distribution** (2001): male 48.73%; female 51.27%. **Age breakdown** (1999): under 15, 43.2%; 15–29, 28.6%; 30–44, 15.1%; 45–59, 7.7%; 60–74, 4.0%; 75 and over, 1.4%. **Ethnic composition** (2000): Ovambo 34.4%; mixed race (black/white) 14.5%; Kavango 9.1%; Afrikaner 8.1%; San (Bushmen) and Bergdama 7.0%; Herero 5.5%; Nama 4.4%; Kwambi 3.7%; German 2.8%; other 10.5%. **Religious affiliation** (2000): Protestant (mostly Lutheran) 47.5%; Roman Catholic 17.7%; African Christian 10.8%; traditional beliefs 6.0%; other 18.0%. **Major cities** (2001): Windhoek urban agglomeration 216,000; Walvis Bay 40,849; Rehoboth 21,782; Oshakati (1991) 21,603; Rundu 19,597. **Location:**

southwestern Africa, bordering Angola, Zambia, Botswana, South Africa, and the Atlantic Ocean.

## Vital statistics

**Birth rate** per 1,000 population (2002): 34.2 (world avg. 21.2). **Death rate** per 1,000 population (2002): 22.3 (world avg. 8.9). **Natural increase rate** per 1,000 population (2002): 11.9 (world avg. 12.3). **Total fertility rate** (avg. births per childbearing woman; 2002): 4.8. **Life expectancy** at birth (2002): male 40.8 years; female 37.1 years.

## National economy

**Budget** (1999–2000). *Revenue*: N$7,128,400,000 (customs taxes 31.4%, general sales tax 28.2%, individual income taxes 17.9%, nontax revenues 8.9%, mining taxes 3.1%). *Expenditures*: N$8,009,400,000 (1996–97; education 23.2%, health and welfare 10.3%, transportation 6.1%, defense 5.8%, social security 5.4%). **Public debt** (external, outstanding 1998): US$747,700,000. **Production** (metric tons except as noted). *Agriculture, forestry, fishing* (1999): roots and tubers 260,000, cereals 71,100,000 (of which millet 46,300, corn [maize] 18,300, sorghum 3,300, wheat 3,000), fruits 10,000; livestock (number of live animals) 2,100,000 sheep, 2,000,000 cattle, 1,700,000 goats; fish catch (1998) 352,188. *Mining and quarrying* (2000): gem diamonds 1,542,000 carats; zinc (metal content) 40,266; copper (metal content) 5,070. *Manufacturing*: n.a.; products include cut gems (primarily diamonds), fur products (karakul), processed foods (fish, meats, and dairy products), textiles, carved wood products, refined metals (copper and lead). *Energy production (consumption)*: electricity (kW-hr; 1999) 1,948,000,000 (2,838,000,000); coal (metric tons; 1999) none (7,000); petroleum products (metric tons; 1999) none (7,000,000). **Population economically active**: total (1991) 493,580; activity rate of total population, 34.9% (participation rates: ages 15–64, 61.3%; female 43.5%; unemployed 20.1%). **Gross national product** (2000): US$3,569,000,000 (US$2,030 per capita). **Household income.** Average household size (2001) 5.1; average annual income per household (1980) US$4,143; sources of income (1992): wages and salaries 69.0%, income from property 25.6%, transfer payments 5.4%. **Tourism** (1998): receipts US$288,000,000; expenditures US$88,000,000. **Land use** (1994): forested 15.2%; meadows and pastures 46.2%; agricultural and under permanent cultivation 0.8%; other 37.8%.

## Foreign trade

**Imports** (1998): N$8,021,000,000 (1994; machinery and transport equipment 27.1%, of which transport equipment 16.2%; food and live animals 22.3%; minerals and fuels 11.4%; chemical products 8.1%). *Major import sources* (1993): South Africa 87.0%; Germany 3.0%; France 2.0%; Japan 2.0%. **Exports** (1998): N$7,076,000,000 (manufactured products 46.7%, of which fish processing 28.4%; minerals 45.1%, of which diamonds 30.4%; food and live animals 8.0%, of which cattle 3.7%; karakul pelts 0.3%). *Major export destinations* (1993): UK 34.0%; South Africa 27.0%; Japan 10.0%; Spain 6.0%.

## Transport and communications

**Transport.** *Railroads*: route length (1999) 2,382 km; (1995–96) passenger-km 48,300,000; (1995–96) metric ton-km 1,082,000,000. *Roads* (1996): total length 65,220 km (paved 7.7%). *Vehicles* (1996): passenger cars 74,875; trucks and buses 66,500 (1995). *Air transport* (2001; Air Namibia only): passenger-km 624,000,000; metric ton-km cargo 72,575,000; airports (1997) 11. **Communications,** in total units (units per 1,000 persons). Daily newspaper circulation (1996): 30,000 (19); radio receivers (1997): 232,000 (143); television receivers (1999): 65,000 (38); telephone main lines (2001): 117,400 (66); cellular telephone subscribers (2001): 100,000 (56); personal computers (2001): 65,000 (36); Internet users (2001): 45,000 (25).

## Education and health

**Educational attainment** (1991). Percentage of population age 25 and over having: no formal schooling 35.1%; primary education 31.9%; secondary 28.5%; higher 4.5%. **Literacy** (2000): total population age 15 and over literate 830,200 (82.1%); males literate 416,000 (82.9%); females literate 414,200 (81.2%). **Health**: physicians (1997) 458 (1 per 3,390 persons); hospital beds (1989) 6,997 (1 per 216 persons); infant mortality rate per 1,000 live births (2001) 71.7. **Food** (1999): daily per capita caloric intake 2,096 (vegetable products 89%, animal products 11%); 92% of FAO recommended minimum.

## Military

**Total active duty personnel** (2001): 9,200 (army 97.8%, navy 2.2%). **Military expenditure as percentage of GNP** (1999): 2.9% (world 2.4%); per capita expenditure US$53.

## Background

Long inhabited by indigenous peoples, Namibia was explored by the Portuguese in the late 15th century. In 1884 it was annexed by Germany as German South West Africa. It was captured in World War I by South Africa, which received it as a mandate from the League of Nations in 1920 and refused to give it up after World War II. A UN resolution in 1966 ending the mandate was challenged by South Africa in the 1970s and '80s. Through long negotiations involving many factions and interests, Namibia achieved independence in 1990.

## Recent Developments

The November 2001 announcement that Sam Nujoma would not seek another term as president heightened speculation regarding the identity of his successor after his term ended in March 2005. In August 2002, after denouncing "factions" within SWAPO, the ruling party, Nujoma unexpectedly reshuffled his cabinet, presumably with his succession in mind. He himself took charge of the Ministry of Information and Broadcasting and soon insisted that the Namibian Broadcasting Corp. replace foreign television programs with ones containing local content.

**Internet resources:** <www.met.gov.na>

---

*1 metric ton = about 1.1 short tons;    1 kilometer = 0.6 mi (statute);    1 metric ton-km cargo = about 0.68 short ton-mi cargo;    c.i.f.: cost, insurance, and freight;    f.o.b.: free on board*

# Nauru

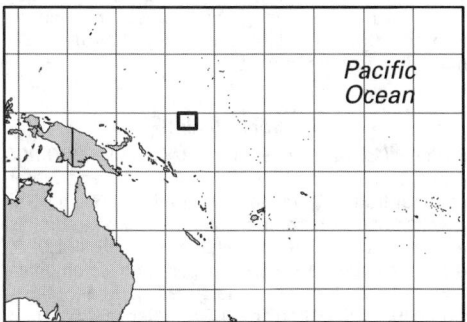

Pacific
Ocean

**Official name:** Naoero (Republic of Nauru). **Form of government:** republic with one legislative house (Parliament [18]). **Head of state and government:** President René Harris (from 8 Aug 2003). **Capital:** government offices are located in Yaren district. **Official language:** none. **Official religion:** none. **Monetary unit:** 1 Australian dollar ($A) = 100 cents; valuation (7 Jul 2003) US$1 = $A 1.47.

## Demography

**Area:** 8.2 sq mi, 21.2 sq km. **Population** (2002): 12,300. **Density** (2002): persons per sq mi 1,500, persons per sq km 580.2. **Urban** (2001): 100%. **Sex distribution** (2001): male 50.50%; female 49.50%. **Age breakdown** (2001): under 15, 40.3%; 15–29, 26.8%; 30–44, 19.0%; 45–59, 10.7%; 60–74, 3.0%; 75 and over, 0.2%. **Ethnic composition** (1992): Nauruan 68.9%; other Pacific Islander 23.7%, of which Kiribati 12.8%, Tuvaluan 8.7%; Asian 5.9%, of which Filipino 2.5%, Chinese 2.3%; other 1.5%. **Religious affiliation** (1995): Protestant 53.5%, of which Congregational 35.3%, Pentecostal 4.8%; Roman Catholic 27.5%; other 19.0%. **Major cities:** none; population of Yaren district (1996) 700. **Location:** western Pacific Ocean, near the equator east of Papua New Guinea.

## Vital statistics

**Birth rate** per 1,000 population (2001): 27.2 (world avg. 21.2). **Death rate** per 1,000 population (2001): 7.2 (world avg. 8.9). **Natural increase rate** per 1,000 population (2001): 20.0 (world avg. 12.3). **Total fertility rate** (avg. births per childbearing woman; 2001): 3.6. **Marriage rate** per 1,000 population (1995): 5.3. **Divorce rate** per 1,000 population: n.a. **Life expectancy** at birth (2001): male 57.7 years; female 64.9 years.

## National economy

**Budget** (1999). *Revenue:* $A 38,700,000. *Expenditures:* $A 37,200,000. **Public debt** (external, outstanding; beginning of 1996): c. US$150,000,000. **Tourism:** receipts from visitors, virtually none; expenditures by nationals abroad, n.a. **Gross national product** (at current market prices; 1997): US$128,000,000 (US$11,538 per capita). **Production** (metric tons except as noted). *Agriculture, forestry, fishing* (2001): coconuts 1,600, vegetables 450, tropical fruit (including mangoes) 275; livestock (number of live animals) 2,800 pigs; roundwood, none; fish catch (1999) 250. *Mining and quarrying* (2001): phosphate rock (gross weight) 400,000. *Manufacturing:* none;

virtually all consumer manufactures are imported. *Energy production (consumption):* electricity (kW-hr; 1999) 30,000,000 (27,900,000); petroleum products (metric tons; 1997) none (45,000). **Population economically active** (1992): 2,453; activity rate of total population 35.9% (participation rates: unemployed, 18.2%). **Household.** Average household size (1992) 10.0. **Land use** (1995): agricultural and under permanent cultivation c. 10%; other c. 90%.

## Foreign trade

**Imports** (1999): US$20,000,000 (agricultural products 65.0%, of which food 45.0%; remainder 35.0%). Major import sources (1995): Australia more than 50%; UK c. 10%; New Zealand c. 10%. **Exports** (1999): US$40,000,000 (phosphate, virtually 100%). Major export destinations (1995): New Zealand c. 50%; Australia c. 25%.

## Transport and communications

**Transport.** *Railroads* (2001): length 35 km. *Roads* (2001): total length 30 km (paved 79%). *Vehicles* (1989): passenger cars, trucks, and buses 1,448. *Air transport* (1996): passenger-km 243,000,000; metric ton-km cargo 24,000,000; airports (2001) with scheduled flights 1. **Communications,** in total units (units per 1,000 persons). Radio receivers (1997): 7,000 (609); television receivers (1997): 500 (48); telephone main lines (1998): 1,700 (149); cellular telephone subscribers (1998): 850 (75).

## Education and health

**Educational attainment** (1992). Percentage of population age 5 and over having primary education or less 77.4%; secondary education 12.9%; higher 4.1%; not stated 5.6%. **Literacy** (1999): total population age 15 and over literate 99%. **Health:** physicians (1995) 17 (1 per 637 persons); hospital beds (1990) 207 (1 per 46 persons); infant mortality rate per 1,000 live births (2001) 10.7. **Food** (2000; data for Oceania): daily per capita caloric intake 2,991 (vegetable products 70%, animal products 30%); 131% of FAO recommended minimum.

## Military

**Total active duty personnel** (2001): Nauru does not have any military establishment. The defense is assured by Australia, but no formal agreement exists.

## Background

Nauru was inhabited by Pacific islanders when British explorers arrived in 1798 and named it Pleasant Island for the friendly welcome they received. Annexed by Germany in 1888, it was occupied by Australia at the start of World War I, and in 1919 it was placed under a joint mandate of Britain, Australia, and New Zealand. During World War II it was occupied by the Japanese. Made a UN trust territory under Australian administration in 1947, it gained independence in 1968. During the mid-1990s Nauru suffered political unrest.

## Recent Developments

In January 2003 the telephone network collapsed in Nauru, and the tiny equatorial Pacific country was out of touch with the rest of the world for weeks. It was known that the presidential mansion had burned down in January, but it was not known who was in charge. Longtime Pres. René Harris was unseated in a vote of no confidence led by Bernard Dowiyogo, who then became president but died in a US hospital in early March. The country was also tottering on the edge of bankruptcy.

**Internet resources:** <www.travelershub.com/ destination_guide/pacific/nauru.html>

# Nepal

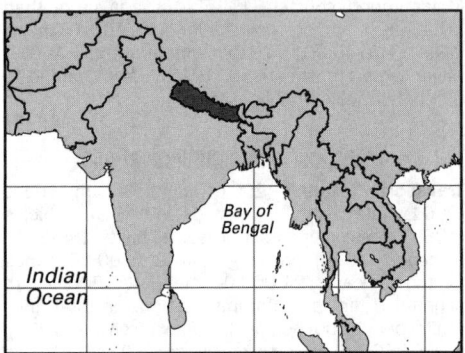

**Official name:** Nepal Adhirajya (Kingdom of Nepal). **Form of government:** constitutional monarchy with a bicameral parliament consisting of two legislative houses (National Council [60, including 10 members appointed by king]; House of Representatives [205]). **Chief of state:** King Gyanendra Bir Bikram Shah Deva (from 2001). **Head of government:** Prime Minister Surya Bahadur Thapa (from 5 Jun 2003). **Capital:** Kathmandu. **Official language:** Nepali. **Official religion:** Hinduism. **Monetary unit:** 1 Nepalese rupee (NRs) = 100 paisa (pice); valuation (7 Jul 2003) $1 = NRs 75.65.

## Demography

**Area:** 56,827 sq mi, 147,181 sq km. **Population** (2002): 23,692,000. **Density** (2002): persons per sq mi 416.9, persons per sq km 161.0. **Urban** (2002): 13.0%. **Sex distribution** (2001): male 49.96%; female 50.04%. **Age breakdown** (2001): under 15, 39.3%; 15–29, 27.0%; 30–44, 17.1%; 45–59, 10.1%; 60–74, 5.2%; 75 and over, 1.3%. **Ethnic composition** (1991): Nepalese 53.2%; Bihari (including Maithili and Bhojpuri) 18.4%; Tharu 4.8%; Tamang 4.7%; Newar 3.4%; Magar 2.2%; Abadhi 1.7%; other 11.6%. **Religious affiliation** (2001): Hindu 80.6%; Buddhist 10.7%; Muslim 4.2%; Kirat 3.6%; Christian 0.5%; other 0.4%. **Major cities** (2001): Kathmandu 696,852; Biratnagar 166,902; Lalitpur 161,617; Pokhara 159,104; Birganj 112,031. **Location:** south-central Asia, bordering China and India.

## Vital statistics

**Birth rate** per 1,000 population (2002): 34.2 (world avg. 21.2). **Death rate** per 1,000 population (2002):

10.0 (world avg. 8.9). **Natural increase rate** per 1,000 population (2002): 24.2 (world avg. 12.3). **Total fertility rate** (avg. births per childbearing woman; 2002): 4.5. **Life expectancy** at birth (2002): male 60.0 years; female 59.0 years.

## National economy

**Budget** (1999). *Revenue*: NRs 40,698,000,000 (taxes on goods and services 29.2%, taxes on international trade 23.9%, foreign grants 14.5%, income taxes 14.2%, state property revenues 8.4%, administrative fees 5.5%). *Expenditures*: NRs 58,391,000,-000 (education 13.6%, transport and communications 11.4%, fuel and energy 9.0%, health 6.5%, agriculture 5.5%, housing 4.7%, defense 4.5%, public order 4.3%, general public services 3.7%). **Public debt** (external, outstanding; 2000): $2,784,000,-000. **Land use** (1994): forested 42.0%; meadows and pastures 14.6%; agricultural and under permanent cultivation 17.2%; other 26.2%. **Tourism** (2000): receipts from visitors $167,000,000; expenditures by nationals abroad $73,000,000. **Production** (metric tons except as noted). *Agriculture, forestry, fishing* (1999): rice 3,710,000, sugarcane 1,972,000, corn (maize) 1,346,000; livestock (number of live animals) 7,030,698 cattle, 6,204,616 goats, 3,470,600 buffalo; roundwood (1998) 21,474,000 cu m; fish catch (1997) 23,206. *Mining and quarrying* (1997): limestone 369,000; salt 7,000; talc 6,800. *Manufacturing* (value added in $'000,000; 1995): textiles 78; food products 74; wearing apparel 54. *Energy production (consumption)*: electricity (kW-hr; 1997) 1,232,000,000 (1,262,000,000); coal (metric tons; 1997) none (119,000); petroleum products (metric tons; 1997) none (509,000). **Population economically active** (1991): total 7,339,586; activity rate of total population 39.7% (participation rates: ages 10 years and over, 57.0%; female 45.5%; unemployed [1996] 4.9%). **Gross national product** (at current market prices; 2000): $5,584,000,000 ($240 per capita). **Household income and expenditure** (1984–85). Average household size (2001) 5.4; income per household NRs 14,796 ($853); sources of income: self-employment 63.4%, wages and salaries 25.1%, rent 7.5%, other 4.0%; expenditure: food and beverages 61.2%, housing 17.3%, clothing 11.7%, health care 3.7%, education and recreation 2.9%, transportation and communications 1.2%, other 2.0%.

## Foreign trade

**Imports** (1996–97-f.o.b. in balance of trade and c.i.f. for commodities and trading partners): NRs 96,006,000,000 (basic manufactured goods 47.6%; machinery and transport equipment 14.7%; chemicals 8.8%; mineral fuels and lubricants 7.5%; food and live animals, chiefly for food 6.6%; crude materials except fuels 5.5%). *Major import sources:* India 23.3%; Hong Kong 14.3%; Singapore 13.0%; Japan 11.2%; China 6.4%; New Zealand 5.1%. **Exports** (1996–97): NRs 22,481,000,000 (basic manufactures 48.7%; miscellaneous manufactures 29.2%; food and live animals, chiefly for food 12.6%; chemicals and drugs 5.9%; crude materials except fuels 2.6%). *Major export destinations:* US 34.4%; India 9.5%; Bangladesh 1.4%; China 0.9%.

*1 metric ton = about 1.1 short tons;    1 kilometer = 0.6 mi (statute);    1 metric ton-km cargo = about 0.68 short ton-mi cargo;    c.i.f.: cost, insurance, and freight;    f.o.b.: free on board*

## Transport and communications

**Transport.** *Railroads* (1995–96): route length (1999) 59 km; passengers carried 1,379,000; freight handled 5,320 metric tons. *Roads* (1997): total length 7,700 km (paved 42%). *Vehicles* (1998–99): passenger cars 49,426; trucks and buses 30,620. *Air transport* (1997): passenger-km 908,000,000; metric ton-km cargo 99,000,000; airports (1996) with scheduled flights 24. **Communications,** in total units (units per 1,000 persons). Daily newspaper circulation (1996): 250,000 (11); radio receivers (1997): 840,000 (38); television receivers (1999): 150,000 (6.7); telephone main lines (2001): 298,100 (13); cellular telephone subscribers (2001): 17,300 (0.7); personal computers (2001): 80,000 (3.4); Internet users (2001): 60,000 (2.5).

## Education and health

**Educational attainment** (1981). Percentage of population age 25 and over having: no formal schooling 41.2%; primary education 29.4%; secondary 22.7%; higher 6.8%. **Literacy** (1995): total population age 15 and over literate 27.5%; males literate 40.9%; females literate 14.0%. **Health** (1996): physicians 872 (1 per 25,745 persons); hospital beds 3,604 (1 per 6,229 persons); infant mortality rate per 1,000 live births (2002) 72.0. **Food** (2000): daily per capita caloric intake 2,435 (vegetable products 93%, animal products 7%); 111% of FAO recommended minimum.

## Military

**Total active duty personnel** (2001): 46,000 (army 99.5%, air force 0.5%). **Military expenditure as percentage of GNP** (1999): 0.8% (world 2.4%); per capita expenditure $2.

**Did you know?** Mt. Everest, the tallest mountain on Earth at 8,850 m (29,035 feet), is located between Nepal and China on Nepal's northern border.

## Background

Nepal developed under early Buddhist influence, and dynastic rule dates from about the 4th century AD. It was formed into a single kingdom in 1769 and fought border wars with China, Tibet, and British India in the 18th–19th century. Its independence was recognized by Britain in 1923. A new constitution in 1990 restricted royal authority and accepted a democratically elected parliamentary government. Nepal signed trade agreements with India in 1997. On 1 Jun 2001, King Birendra, the queen, and seven other members of the royal family were fatally shot by Crown Prince Dipendra, who then turned the gun on himself.

## Recent Developments

Hopes ran high that the government's seven-year violent struggle against Maoist rebels, which had cost some 7,000 lives, was winding down after the rebels declared a truce on 29 Jan 2003. The leadership struggled against allegations of corruption and caste privilege, while a large pro-rebel demonstration greeted the arrival in Kathmandu of Maoist negotiators in April. The talks continued into May. World attention turned upward to Nepal in 2003 as the 50th anniversary of the first ascent of Mt. Everest, by New Zealander Edmund Hillary and Nepalese Sherpa Tenzing Norgay (29 May 1953), was commemorated.

**Internet resources:** <www.welcomenepal.com>

# The Netherlands

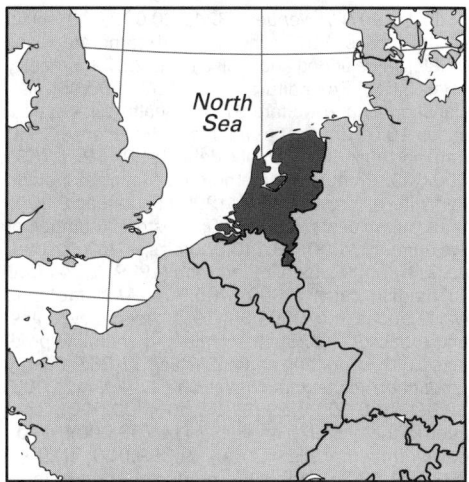

**Official name:** Koninkrijk der Nederlanden (Kingdom of The Netherlands). **Form of government:** constitutional monarchy with a parliament (States General) comprising two legislative houses (First Chamber [75]; Second Chamber [150]). **Chief of state:** Queen Beatrix (from 1980). **Head of government:** Prime Minister Jan Peter Balkenende (from 22 Jul 2002). **Seat of government:** The Hague. **Capital:** Amsterdam. **Official language:** Dutch. **Official religion:** none. **Monetary unit:** 1 euro (€) = 100 cents; $1 = €0.87 (7 Jul 2003); at conversion on 1 Jan 2002, €1 = 2.20 Netherlands guilders (f.).

## Demography

**Area:** 16,033 sq mi, 41,526 sq km (including inland water area totaling 2,955 sq mi [7,653 sq km]). **Population** (2002): 16,142,000. **Density** (2002): persons per sq mi 1,234.2, persons per sq km 476.5. **Urban** (2001): 89.6%. **Sex distribution** (2002): male 49.50%; female 50.50%. **Age breakdown** (2000): under 15, 18.6%; 15–29, 19.3%; 30–44, 24.2%; 45–59, 19.8%; 60–74, 12.1%; 75 and over, 6.0%. **Ethnic composition** (by place of origin [including 2nd generation]; 2000): Netherlander 82.5%; Indonesian 2.6%; Turkish 1.9%; Surinamese 1.9%; Moroccan 1.7%; Netherlands Antillean/Aruban 0.7%; other 8.7%. **Religious affiliation** (1999): Roman Catholic 31.0%; Reformed (NHK) 14.0%; other Reformed 7.0%; Muslim 4.5%; Hindu 0.5%; nonreligious 41.0%; other 2.0%. **Major urban agglomerations** (2000): Amsterdam 1,002,868; Rotterdam 989,956; The Hague 610,245; Utrecht 366,186; Eindhoven 302,274. **Location:** northwestern Europe, bordering the North Sea, Germany, and Belgium.

## Vital statistics

**Birth rate** per 1,000 population (2001): 12.6 (world avg. 21.2); legitimate 72.8%; illegitimate 27.2%.

**Death rate** per 1,000 population (2001): 8.8 (world avg. 8.9). **Natural increase rate** per 1,000 population (2001): 3.8 (world avg. 12.3). **Total fertility rate** (avg. births per childbearing woman; 2001): 1.7. **Marriage rate** per 1,000 population (2000): 5.3. **Life expectancy at birth** (2001): male 75.8 years; female 80.7 years.

## National economy

**Budget** (1997). *Revenue:* f. 324,360,000,000 (social security taxes 41.1%; income and corporate taxes 24.8%; value-added and excise taxes 22.7%; property taxes 3.0%). Expenditures: f. 337,620,000,000 (social security and welfare 37.4%; health 14.8%; education 10.0%; interest payments 9.1%; defense 3.9%; transportation 3.5%). **Public debt** (1999): $251,763,-000,000. **Production** (metric tons except as noted). *Agriculture, forestry, fishing* (2000): potatoes 8,200,-000, sugar beets 5,504,000; livestock (number of live animals; 2000) 13,140,000 pigs, 4,200,000 cattle, 1,401,000 sheep; roundwood (1999) 1,044,000 cu m; fish catch (2000) 495,804. *Manufacturing* (value added in f. '000,000; 1998): food, beverages, and tobacco 24,323; chemicals and chemical products 15,009; printing and publishing 11,267. *Energy production (consumption):* electricity (kW-hr; 2000) 89,580,000,000 ([1999] 93,505,000,000); coal (metric tons; 1997) negligible (14,793,000); crude petroleum (barrels; 2000) 9,389,000 ([1997] 392,581,000); petroleum products (metric tons; 1997) 63,072,000 (31,863,000); natural gas (cu m; 2000) 67,864,000,000 ([1997] 51,783,000,000). **Household income and expenditure**. Average household size (2000) 2.3; disposable income per household (1999) f. 51,600 ($26,444); sources of income (1996): wages 48.4%, transfers 28.5%, self-employment 11.3%; expenditure (1999): housing and energy 20.8%; transportation and communications 15.6%; food and beverages 14.8%; recreation and culture 11.1%. **Gross national product** (2000): $397,544,-000,000 ($24,970 per capita). **Population economically active** (1998): total 7,735,000; activity rate of total population 49.3% (participation rates: ages 15–64, 72.9%; female 42.5%; unemployed [February 2001–January 2002] 2.0%). **Tourism** (2000): receipts $7,206,000,000; expenditures $12,198,000,-000. **Land use** (1994): forested 10.3%; meadows and pastures 31.0%; agricultural and under permanent cultivation 28.0%; other 30.7%.

## Foreign trade

**Imports** (2001-c.i.f.): €217,151,000,000 (computers and related equipment 11.9%, chemicals and chemical products 11.4%, mineral fuels 10.1%, food 8.2%, road vehicles 7.0%). *Major import sources:* Germany 18.5%; US 9.8%; Belgium-Luxembourg 9.3%; UK 8.9%; France 5.7%. **Exports** (2001-f.o.b.): €240,833,000,000 (chemicals and chemical products 15.4%, food 12.3%, computers and related equipment 11.7%, mineral fuels 9.2%). *Major export destinations:* Germany 25.6%; Belgium-Luxembourg 11.9%; UK 11.2%; France 10.3%; Italy 6.2%.

## Transport and communications

**Transport**. *Railroads* (1999): length 2,808 km; passenger-km 14,330,000,000; metric ton-km cargo 3,521,000,000. *Roads* (1999): total length 116,500 km (paved 90%). *Vehicles* (2000): passenger cars 6,343,000; trucks and buses 826,000. *Air transport* (2001; KLM only): passenger-km 57,848,000,000; metric ton-km cargo 4,464,000,000; airports (1996) 6. **Communications**, in total units (units per 1,000 persons). Daily newspaper circulation (1996): 4,753,000 (306); radio receivers (1998): 12,000,000 (764); television receivers (1999): 9,500,000 (601); telephone main lines (2001): 10,000,000 (621); cellular telephone subscribers (2001): 11,900,000 (739); personal computers (2001): 6,900,000 (429); Internet users (2001): 5,300,000 (329).

## Education and health

**Educational attainment** (1999). Percentage of population ages 15–64 having: primary education 13.4%; lower secondary 10.4%; upper secondary/vocational 53.9%; tertiary vocational 15.5%; university 6.8%. **Health** (1999): physicians 27,090 (1 per 582 persons); hospital beds 81,328 (1 per 194 persons); infant mortality rate per 1,000 live births (2001) 5.4. **Food** (1999): daily per capita caloric intake 3,243 (vegetable products 64%, animal products 36%); 121% of FAO recommended minimum.

## Military

**Total active duty personnel** (2001): 50,430 (army 45.8%, navy 24.0%, air force 19.8%, paramilitary 10.4%). **Military expenditure as percentage of GNP** (1999): 1.8% (world 2.4%); per capita expenditure $445.

## Background

Celtic and Germanic tribes inhabited The Netherlands at the time of the Roman conquest. Under the Romans, trade and industry flourished, but by the mid-3rd century AD Roman power had waned, eroded by resurgent German tribes and the encroachment of the sea. A Germanic invasion (406–07) ended Roman control. The Merovingian dynasty followed the Romans but was supplanted in the 7th century by the Carolingian dynasty, which converted the area to Christianity. After Charlemagne's death in 814, the area was increasingly the target of Viking attacks. It became part of the kingdom of Lotharingia, which established an Imperial Church. In the 12th–14th centuries dike building occurred on a large scale. The dukes of Burgundy gained control in the late 14th century. By the early 16th century the Low Countries were ruled by the Spanish Habsburgs. In 1581 the seven northern provinces, led by Calvinists, declared their independence from Spain, and in 1648, following the Thirty Years' War, Spain recognized Dutch independence. The 17th century was the golden age of Dutch civilization. The Dutch East India Company secured Asian colonies, and the country's standard of living soared. In the 18th century the region was conquered by the French and became the kingdom of Holland under Napoleon (1806). It remained neutral in World War I and declared neutrality in World War II but was occupied by Germany. It joined NATO in 1949, was a founding member of what is now the European Community, and is part of the European Union.

---

*1 metric ton = about 1.1 short tons;   1 kilometer = 0.6 mi (statute);   1 metric ton-km cargo = about 0.68 short ton-mi cargo;   c.i.f.: cost, insurance, and freight;   f.o.b.: free on board*

## Recent Developments

A variety of political shakeups occurred in 2002, beginning with the resignation of the government in April. A report blaming the Dutch military and government for their failure to prevent the 1995 Srebrenica massacre in Bosnia led to the resignation of the prime minister and his cabinet. In May flamboyant nationalist politician Pim Fortuyn was murdered, and later that month the ruling Labor Party was defeated in national elections by the conservative Christian Democrats. The Dutch royals enlivened the social scene: on 2 Feb 2002 Crown Prince Willem-Alexander married Argentine Máxima Zorreguieta in a civil ceremony in Amsterdam, followed by a church blessing. Queen Beatrix's niece Princess Margarita, who had married a commoner, Edwin de Roy van Zuydewijn, in 2001, spiced gossip columns in 2003 with her revelations of behind-the-scenes life in the royal family.

Internet resources: <www.holland.com>

# Netherlands Antilles

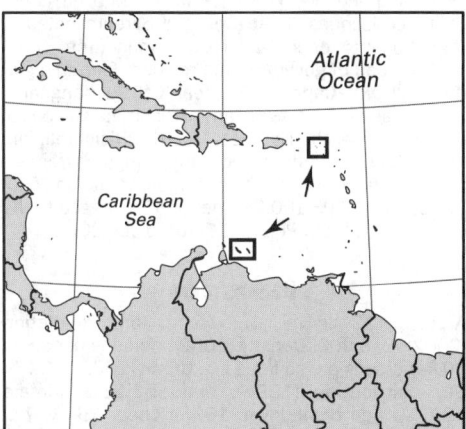

**Official name:** Nederlandse Antillen (Netherlands Antilles). **Political status:** nonmetropolitan territory of The Netherlands with one legislative house (States of the Netherlands Antilles [22]). **Chief of state:** Queen Beatrix (from 1980), represented by Governor-General Frits Goedgedrag (from 1 Jul 2002). **Head of government:** Prime Minister Ben Komproe (from 22 Jul 2003). **Capital:** Willemstad. **Official language:** Dutch. **Official religion:** none. **Monetary unit:** 1 Netherlands Antillean guilder (NA f.) = 100 cents; valuation (7 Jul 2003) $1 = NA f. 1.78.

## Demography

**Area:** 308 sq mi, 800 sq km. **Population** (2002): 175,000. **Density** (2002): persons per sq mi 568.2, persons per sq km 218.8. **Urban** (2001): 69.6%. **Sex distribution** (2001): male 46.98%; female 53.02%. **Age breakdown** (2001): under 15, 24.2%; 15–29, 18.2%; 30–44, 25.5%; 45–59, 19.0%; 60–74, 9.4%; 75 and over, 3.7%. **Ethnic composition** (2000): local black-other (Antillean Creole) 81.1%; Dutch 5.3%; Surinamese 2.9%; other (significantly West Indian black) 10.7%. **Religious affiliation** (2001): Roman Catholic 72.0%; Protestant 16.0%; Spiritist 0.9%; Buddhist 0.5%; Jewish 0.4%; Baha'i 0.3%; Hindu

0.2%; Muslim 0.2%; other/unknown 4.3%. **Major cities:** Willemstad (urban area; 1999) 123,000; Kralendijk (2001) 7,900; Philipsburg (2001) 6,300. **Location:** two separate island groups in the Caribbean Sea, one just north of Venezuela, the other east of Puerto Rico.

## Vital statistics

**Birth rate** per 1,000 population (2001): 13.6 (world avg. 21.2); (1988) legitimate 51.6%; illegitimate 48.4%. **Death rate** per 1,000 population (2001): 6.4 (world avg. 8.9). **Natural increase rate** per 1,000 population (2001): 7.2 (world avg. 12.3). **Total fertility rate** (avg. births per childbearing woman; 2001): 2.1. **Marriage rate** per 1,000 population (1999): 4.7. **Divorce rate** per 1,000 population (1999): 2.6. **Life expectancy** at birth (2001): male 72.8 years; female 77.2 years.

## National economy

**Budget** (2000). *Revenue*: NA f. 621,300,000 (tax revenue 83.5%, of which sales tax 37.3%, import duties 20.6%, excise on gasoline 12.8%; nontax revenue 14.9%; grants 1.6%). *Expenditures*: NA f. 743,700,-000 (current expenditures 92.6%, of which wages 35.3%, transfers 32.4%, goods and services 12.9%, interest payments 10.4%; development expenditures 7.4%). **Production** (metric tons except as noted). Agriculture, forestry, fishing: mostly tomatoes, beans, cucumbers, gherkins, melons, and lettuce grown on hydroponic farms; aloes grown for export, divi-divi pods, and sour orange fruit are nonhydroponic crops; livestock (number of live animals; 2001) 13,000 goats, 7,300 sheep, 135,000 chickens; fish catch (1999) 905. *Mining and quarrying* (1997): salt 432,225, sulfur by-product 27,600. *Manufacturing* (1996): residual fuel oil 5,013,000; gas-diesel oils 2,218,000; other manufactures include electronic parts, cigarettes, textiles, rum, and Curaçao liqueur. *Energy production (consumption)*: electricity (kW-hr; 1999) 1,112,500,000 (1,112,500,000); crude petroleum (barrels; 1997) none (100,289,000); petroleum products (metric tons; 1997) 9,966,000 (863,000). **Land use** (1998): forested, negligible; meadows and pastures, negligible; agricultural and under permanent cultivation 10.0%; other (dry savanna) 90.0%. **Tourism** (2000): receipts from visitors $765,000,-000; expenditures by nationals abroad $339,000,-000. **Household expenditure.** Average household size (2001) 2.9; expenditure (1996): housing 26.5%, transportation and communications 19.9%, food 14.7%, household furnishings 8.8%, recreation and education 8.2%, clothing and footwear 7.5%. **Gross national product** (at current market prices; 1997): $2,609,000,000 ($12,490 per capita). **Population economically active** (2001): total 81,558; activity rate of total population 46.4% (participation rates: ages 15–64, 68.7%; female 49.0%; unemployed 14.6%). **Public debt** (external, outstanding; 1999): $294,600,000.

## Foreign trade

**Imports** (1999): NA f. 2,375,000,000 (nonpetroleum domestic imports 71.3%, crude petroleum and petroleum products 14.8%, imports of Curaçao free zone 13.9%). *Major import sources* (1998): Venezuela 35.3%; US 21.0%; Mexico 9.8%; Italy 5.4%; The Netherlands 4.8%; Brazil 3.1%. **Exports** (1999): NA f.

470,000,000 (reexports of Curaçao free zone 59.1%, nonpetroleum domestic exports 37.5%, petroleum products 3.4%). *Major export destinations* (1998): US 17.5%; Guatemala 8.0%; Costa Rica 6.5%; The Bahamas 4.6%; Jamaica 4.1%; Chile 3.4%.

## Transport and communications

**Transport.** *Roads* (1992): total length 590 km (paved 51%). *Vehicles* (1999): passenger cars 74,840; trucks and buses 17,415. *Air transport* (2000; Curaçao airport only): passenger arrivals and departures 911,000; freight loaded and unloaded 14,500 metric tons; airports (2000) with scheduled flights 5. **Communications,** in total units (units per 1,000 persons). Daily newspaper circulation (1996): 70,000 (341); radio receivers (1997): 217,000 (1,039); television receivers (1997): 69,000 (330); telephone main lines (1999): 79,000 (386); cellular telephone subscribers (1998): 16,000 (77).

## Education and health

**Educational attainment** (2001). Percentage of population 25 and over having: no formal schooling 0.8%; primary education 24.2%; lower secondary 42.8%; upper secondary 16.8%; higher 11.4%; unknown 4.0%. **Literacy** (1995): total population age 15 and over literate 194,900 (96.6%); males literate 93,300 (96.6%); females literate 101,600 (96.6%). **Health** (1999): physicians 341 (1 per 616 persons); hospital beds 1,466 (1 per 142 persons); infant mortality rate per 1,000 live births (2001) 11.4. **Food** (2000): daily per capita caloric intake 2,573 (vegetable products 68%, animal products 32%); 107% of FAO recommended minimum.

## Military

**Total active duty personnel** (2001): a 45-member Dutch naval/air force contingent is stationed in the Netherlands Antilles and Aruba.

## Background

The Netherlands Antilles were sighted by Christopher Columbus in 1493 and claimed for Spain. In the 17th century the Dutch gained control, and in 1845 the islands became the Netherlands Antilles. In 1954 they became an integral part of The Netherlands, with full autonomy in domestic affairs. Aruba seceded from the group in 1986.

## Recent Developments

The Netherlands Antilles signaled its willingness to cooperate in criminal tax investigations by signing a Tax Information Exchange Agreement with the US in April 2002. The Netherlands Antilles government indicated in October that tougher visa restrictions on nationals of Colombia, Haiti, and the Dominican Republic were being implemented following 26 execution-style murders that had taken place in Curaçao since January. The killings were blamed on professional assassins from the countries concerned, particularly Colombia.

**Internet resources:** <http://netherlandsantilles.com>

# New Caledonia

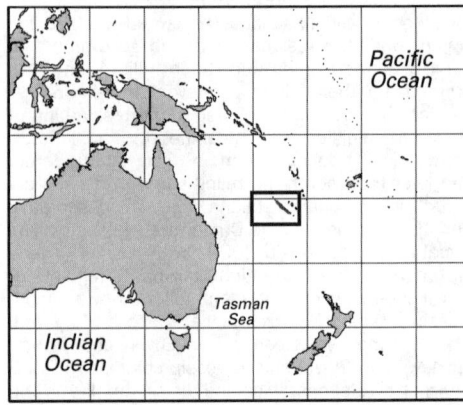

**Official name:** Nouvelle-Calédonie (New Caledonia). **Political status:** overseas territory (France) with one legislative house (Congress [54]; operates in association with 3 provincial assemblies). The Nouméa Accord of 1999 granted New Caledonia limited autonomy with likely independence by 2013. **Chief of state:** President of France Jacques Chirac (from 1995) represented by High Commissioner Daniel Constantin (from 3 Jul 2002). **Head of government:** President Pierre Frogier (from 2001). **Capital:** Nouméa. **Official language:** none; Kanak languages and French have special recognition per the Nouméa Accord. **Official religion:** none. **Monetary unit:** 1 franc of the Comptoirs français du Pacifique (CFPF) = 100 centimes; valuation (7 Jul 2003) $1 = CFPF 100.29; the CFPF is pegged to the euro (€) at €1 = CFPF 119.25 from 1 Jan 2002.

## Demography

**Area:** 7,172 sq mi, 18,575 sq km. **Population** (2002): 218,000. **Density** (2002): persons per sq mi 30.4, persons per sq km 11.7. **Urban** (2002): 79.0%. **Sex distribution** (1996): male 51.23%; female 48.77%. **Age breakdown** (1996): under 15, 30.7%; 15–29, 27.2%; 30–44, 21.3%; 45–59, 13.3%; 60–74, 5.9%; 75 and over, 1.6%. **Ethnic composition** (1996): Melanesian 45.3%, of which local (Kanak) 44.1%, Vanuatuan 1.2%; European 34.1%; Wallisian or Futunan 9.0%; Indonesian 2.6%; Tahitian 2.6%; Vietnamese 1.4%; other 5.0%. **Religious affiliation** (1995): Roman Catholic 61.3%; Protestant 14.5%, of which Presbyterian 12.3%; Muslim 2.7%; other Christian 2.3%; other 19.2%. **Major cities** (1996): Nouméa 76,293 (urban agglomeration 118,823; includes Mont-Dore 20,780 and Dumbéa 13,888). **Location:** south Pacific Ocean, about 1,100 mi (1,800 km) east of Queensland, Australia.

## Vital statistics

**Birth rate** per 1,000 population (2002): 19.7 (world avg. 21.2); (1996) legitimate 36.4%; illegitimate 63.6%. **Death rate** per 1,000 population (2002): 4.9 (world avg. 8.9). **Natural increase rate** per 1,000 population (2002): 14.8 (world avg. 12.3). **Total fertility rate** (avg. births per childbearing woman; 2002): 2.5. **Marriage rate** per 1,000 population (2001): 4.3. **Divorce rate** per 1,000 population (1999): 0.8. **Life**

---

*1 metric ton = about 1.1 short tons;    1 kilometer = 0.6 mi (statute);    1 metric ton-km cargo = about 0.68 short ton-mi cargo;    c.i.f.: cost, insurance, and freight;    f.o.b.: free on board*

expectancy at birth (2002): male 72.0 years; female 78.0 years.

## National economy

**Budget** (1999). *Revenue*: CFPF 77,477,000,000 (indirect taxes 49.7%, direct taxes 30.9%, French government subsidies 8.6%, tobacco excises 6.3%). *Expenditures*: CFPF 74,218,000,000 (current expenditure 93.4%, development expenditure 6.6%). **Production** (metric tons except as noted). *Agriculture, forestry, fishing* (1999): roots and tubers 21,100, of which yams 11,000, sweet potatoes 3,000; coconuts 16,000; vegetables 3,785; livestock (number of live animals) 120,000 cattle, 38,000 pigs, 390,000 chickens; roundwood (1998) 4,800 cu m; fish catch (1997) 3,421, of which shrimp 1,107, sea urchins and echinoderms 505. *Mining and quarrying* (metric tons; 1999): nickel ore 6,562,000, of which nickel content (1997) 110,000; cobalt (1997) 800. *Manufacturing* (metric tons; 1999): cement 92,714; ferronickel (metal content) 45,289; nickel matte (metal content) 11,353. *Energy production (consumption)*: electricity (kW-hr; 1997) 1,567,000,000 (1,567,-000,000); coal (metric tons; 1997) none (168,000); petroleum products (metric tons; 1997) none (409,000). **Tourism**: receipts from visitors (2000) $110,000,000. **Population economically active** (1996): total 80,589; activity rate of total population 40.9% (participation rates: over age 14, 57.3%; female 39.7%; unemployed 18.6%). **Public debt** (external, outstanding; 1999): $746,000,000. **Gross national product** (2000): $3,203,000,000 ($15,060 per capita). **Household income and expenditure** (1991). Average household size (1996) 3.8; average annual income per household CFPF 3,361,233 ($32,879); sources of income: wages and salaries 68.2%, transfer payments 13.7%, other 18.1%; expenditure: food and beverages 25.9%, housing 20.4%, transportation and communications 16.1%, recreation 4.8%. **Land use** (1994): forested 38.7%; meadows and pastures 11.8%; agricultural and under permanent cultivation 0.7%; other 48.8%.

## Foreign trade

**Imports** (1999-c.i.f.): CFPF 112,888,000,000 (machinery and apparatus 20.0%, food 16.2%, transportation equipment 15.6%, mineral fuels 9.4%, chemicals and chemical products 7.8%). *Major import sources* (1998): France 52.2%; Australia 13.9%; New Zealand 5.3%; Singapore 4.2%; Japan 3.4%. **Exports** (1999-f.o.b.): CFPF 44,763,000,000 (ferronickel 54.8%, nickel ore 18.8%, nickel matte 13.9%, shrimp 4.2%). *Major export destinations*: Japan 32.2%; France 22.1%; Taiwan 8.4%; South Korea 7.6%; Australia 7.1%.

## Transport and communications

**Transport.** *Roads* (1996): total length 5,764 km (paved [1993] 52%). *Vehicles*: passenger cars (1996) 56,700; trucks and buses (1993) 21,200. *Air transport* (1999; La Tontouta international airport only): passenger arrivals 171,887, passenger departures 170,815; freight unloaded 3,914 metric tons, freight loaded 1,163 metric tons; airports (1999) with scheduled flights 11. **Communications**, in total units (units per 1,000 persons). Daily newspaper circulation (1996): 24,000 (121); radio receivers (1997): 107,000 (533); television receivers (1999):

101,000 (480); telephone main lines (2000): 51,000 (237); cellular telephone subscribers (2000): 49,900 (232); Internet users (2000): 24,-000 (111).

## Education and health

**Educational attainment** (1996). Percentage of population age 14 and over having: no formal schooling 5.7%; primary education 28.9%; lower secondary 30.2%; upper secondary 24.6%; higher 10.5%. **Health** (1999): physicians 418 (1 per 497 persons); hospital beds 838 (1 per 248 persons); infant mortality rate per 1,000 live births (2002) 7.0. **Food** (1999): daily per capita caloric intake 2,772 (vegetable products 73%, animal products 27%); (1997) 122% of FAO recommended minimum.

## Military

**Total active duty personnel** (2001): 3,100 French troops.

## Background

Excavations indicate an Austronesian presence in New Caledonia about 2000–1000 BC. The islands were visited by James Cook in 1774 and by various navigators and traders in the 18th–19th centuries. They were occupied by France in 1853 and were a penal colony from 1864 to 1897. During World War II the islands were the site of Allied bases. They became a French overseas territory in 1946. In 1987 residents voted by referendum to remain part of France.

## Recent Developments

With a quarter of the world's nickel reserves, there were several proposals for new nickel ventures under consideration in New Caledonia. A major venture at Goro in the south was deferred because of cost escalations. Indigenous Kanak groups opposed this proposed development and another at nearby Prony because of environmental concerns and the low financial returns to New Caledonia.

Internet resources:
<www.newcaledoniatourism-south.com>

# New Zealand

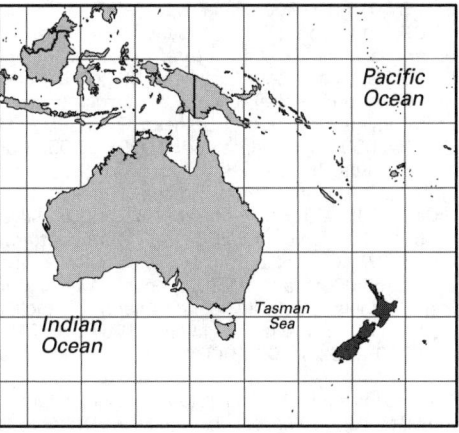

**Official name:** New Zealand (English); Aotearoa (Maori). **Form of government:** constitutional monarchy with one legislative house (House of Representatives [120, including six elected seats allocated to Maoris]). **Chief of state:** Queen Elizabeth II (from 1952), represented by Governor-General Dame Silvia Cartwright (from 2001). **Head of government:** Prime Minister Helen Clark (from 1999). **Capital:** Wellington. **Official languages:** English; Maori. **Official religion:** none. **Monetary unit:** 1 New Zealand dollar ($NZ) = 100 cents; valuation (7 Jul 2003) US$1 = $NZ1.68.

## Demography

**Area:** 104,454 sq mi, 270,534 sq km. **Population** (2002): 3,893,000. **Density** (2002): persons per sq mi 37.3, persons per sq km 14.4. **Urban** (2002): 86.0%. **Sex distribution** (2001): male 48.73%; female 51.27%. **Age breakdown** (2001): under 15, 22.9%; 15–29, 20.1%; 30–44, 23.0%; 45–59, 17.9%; 60–74, 10.7%; 75 and over, 5.4%. **Ethnic composition** (2001): European 73.8%; Maori (local Polynesian) 13.5%; Asian 6.1%; other Pacific Peoples (mostly other Polynesian) 6.0%; other 0.6%. **Religious affiliation** (2001): Christian 55.2%, of which Anglican 15.3%, Roman Catholic 12.7%, Presbyterian 11.3%; nonreligious 26.9%; Buddhist 1.1%; Hindu 1.0%; other religions/not specified 15.8%. **Major cities** (2001): Auckland 371,313 (urban agglomeration 1,087,152); Christchurch 342,285; Wellington 166,362; Hamilton 140,088; Dunedin 110,757. **Dependent territories:** Cook Islands, Niue, and Tokelau. **Location:** between the South Pacific Ocean and the Tasman Sea, southeast of Australia.

## Vital statistics

**Birth rate** per 1,000 population (2002): 14.2 (world avg. 21.2); (1996) legitimate 58.0%; illegitimate 42.0%. **Death rate** per 1,000 population (2002): 7.6 (world avg. 8.9). **Natural increase rate** per 1,000 population (2002): 6.6 (world avg. 12.3). **Total fertility rate** (avg. births per childbearing woman; 2002): 1.8. **Life expectancy** at birth (2002): male 75.0 years; female 81.0 years.

## National economy

**Budget** (2000–2001). *Revenue:* $NZ 37,156,000,000 (income taxes 59.4%, taxes on goods and services 34.4%, nontax revenue 6.2%). *Expenditures:* $NZ 37,019,000,000 (social welfare 37.0%, health 19.0%, education 17.6%). **Production** (metric tons except as noted). *Agriculture, forestry, fishing* (2000): apples 482,000, wheat 360,000, barley 281,000, corn (maize) 174,000; livestock (number of live animals) 45,800,000 sheep, 9,457,000 cattle, 344,000 pigs; roundwood (1999) 17,953,000 cu m; fish catch (1998) 635,711. *Mining and quarrying* (1998): iron ore and sand concentrate 2,000,000; aluminum metal 315,600; silver 31,500 kg; gold 11,250 kg. *Manufacturing* (1996–97): wood pulp 1,405,300; chemical fertilizers 1,365,000; yarn 21,302; beer 343,457,000 liters; carpets 9,980,000 sq m. *Energy production (consumption):* electricity (kW-hr; 1997) 36,219,000,000 (36,219,000,000); coal (metric tons;

1997) 3,370,000 (2,651,000); crude petroleum (barrels; 1997) 21,000,000 (38,000,000); petroleum products (metric tons; 1997) 4,911,000 (5,039,000); natural gas (cu m; 1997) 5,059,000,000 (5,060,000,000). **Household income and expenditure.** Average household size (1996) 2.8; annual income per household (1996–97) $NZ 59,444 (US$40,143); sources of income (1998): wages and salaries 65.8%, transfer payments 15.2%, self-employment 9.8%, other 9.2%; expenditure (1996–97): housing 20.2%, transportation 18.2%, food 16.4%, household goods 13.7%, clothing 3.8%. **Tourism** (2000): receipts US$2,100,000,000; expenditures US$1,786,000,000. **Gross national product** (2000): US$49,750,000,000 (US$12,990 per capita). **Population economically active** (2000): total 1,923,700; activity rate 50.1% (participation rates: over age 15, 66.2%; female 45.3%; unemployed 5.7%). **Land use** (1999): pasture 49.6%; agriculture 12.2%; forest and other 38.2%.

## Foreign trade

**Imports** (1999-f.o.b. in balance of trade and c.i.f. in commodities and trading partners): $NZ 24,248,000,000 (machinery 24.6%; transport equipment 17.2%; mineral fuels 5.7%; textiles and textile products 4.7%; plastics 4.1%). *Major import sources:* Australia 22.1%; US 17.7%; Japan 12.6%; China 5.1%; Germany 4.5%; UK 4.4%. **Exports** (1998–99): $NZ 22,600,000,000 (food 47.2%; wood and wood products 10.6%; machinery 7.7%; metals and metal products 7.2%; wool 3.8%). *Major export destinations:* Australia 21.4%; US 13.3%; Japan 12.7%; UK 6.2%; South Korea 3.9%; Germany 2.8%; China 2.7%.

## Transport and communications

**Transport.** *Railroads* (1999): route length 3,912 km; passengers carried (1998) 11,751,000; metric ton-km cargo 3,960,000,000. *Roads* (1999): total length 92,075 km (paved 62%). *Vehicles* (1998–99): passenger cars 1,831,118; trucks and buses (1998) 368,723. *Air transport* (1999; Air New Zealand only): passenger-km 19,879,000,000; metric ton-km cargo 851,744,000; airports (1997) 36. **Communications,** in total units (units per 1,000 persons). Daily newspaper circulation (1999): 850,000 (223); radio receivers (1997): 3,750,000 (997); television receivers (1999): 1,975,000 (518); telephone main lines (2001): 1,833,600 (471); cellular telephone subscribers (2001): 2,417,000 (621); personal computers (2001): 1,500,000 (386); Internet users (2001): 1,091,900 (281).

## Education and health

**Educational attainment** (1991). Percentage of population age 25 and over having: primary and some secondary education 54.9%; secondary 31.1%; higher 6.9%; not specified 7.1%. **Literacy:** virtually 100.0%. **Health:** physicians (1999) 13,360 (1 per 285 persons); hospital beds (2000) 31,425 (1 per 122 persons); infant mortality rate per 1,000 live births (2002) 6.0. **Food** (1999): daily per capita caloric intake 3,152 (vegetable products 68%, animal products 32%); 119% of FAO recommended minimum.

---

*1 metric ton = about 1.1 short tons;    1 kilometer = 0.6 mi (statute);    1 metric ton-km cargo = about 0.68 short ton-mi cargo;    c.i.f.: cost, insurance, and freight;    f.o.b.: free on board*

## Military

Total active duty personnel (2001): 9,230 (army 48.2%, air force 30.3%, navy 21.5%). **Military expenditure as percentage of GNP** (1999): 1.2% (world 2.4%); per capita expenditure US$156.

The kiwi is the national bird and symbol of New Zealand. It is the best-known of four flightless birds that are native to New Zealand. The kiwi as a symbol first appeared in military badges of New Zealand soldiers sent overseas in the late 19th century. It became a household term internationally after Kiwi shoe polish was launched in the early 20th century.

## Background

Polynesian occupation of New Zealand dates to about AD 1000. First sighted by Dutch explorer Abel Janszoon Tasman in 1642, the main islands were charted by Captain James Cook in 1769. Named a British crown colony in 1840, the area was the scene of warfare between colonists and native Maori through the 1860s. In 1907 the colony became the Dominion of New Zealand. It administered Western Samoa during 1919–62 and participated in both world wars. When Britain joined what is now the European Union in the early 1970s, its influence led New Zealand to expand its export markets and diversify its economy.

## Recent Developments

Prime Minister Helen Clark spent the last parliamentary term cementing her grip on power. As leader of the Labour Party, she had seen her team come from behind in the general election in July 2002. Neither Labour, which won 41.3% of the votes and a total of 52 seats in the 120-seat House, nor the once-mighty National Party (NP), with 20.9% and 27 seats, won a clear majority. The real victor was mixed member proportional (MMP) voting, which distributed some seats on the basis of proportional representation. Some strain was evident between Australia and New Zealand when Canberra moved to limit the access of New Zealanders to Australian government benefits. New Zealanders, too, were critical of visitors to the larger country living like residents there without joining in any payment for resettlement. New Zealanders were not far behind Australians, however, in deploying Special Air Service forces alongside American troops in Afghanistan. In June 2003 Parliament voted to decriminalize prostitution and to license brothels.

**Internet resources:** <www.stats.govt.nz>

# Nicaragua

**Official name:** República de Nicaragua (Republic of Nicaragua). **Form of government:** unitary multiparty republic with one legislative house (National Assembly [93, including three unsuccessful presidential candidates in 2001 elections]). **Head of state and government:** President Enrique Bolaños Geyer (from 10 Jan 2002). **Capital:** Managua. **Official language:** Spanish. **Official religion:** none. **Monetary unit:** 1 córdoba oro (C$) = 100 centavos; valuation (7 Jul 2003) US$1 = C$15.01.

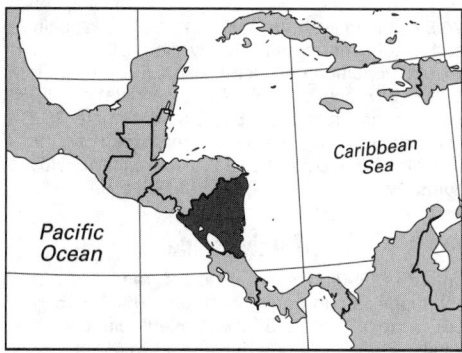

## Demography

**Area:** 50,337 sq mi, 130,373 sq km; land area only equals 46,464 sq mi, 120,340 sq km. **Population** (2002): 5,024,000. **Density** (2002): persons per sq mi 108.1, persons per sq km 41.7. **Urban** (2001): 56.5%. **Sex distribution** (2000): male 49.96%; female 50.04%. **Age breakdown** (2000): under 15, 39.7%; 15–29, 30.6%; 30–44, 17.0%; 45–59, 8.2%; 60–74, 3.7%; 75 and over, 0.8%. **Ethnic composition** (1997): mestizo (Spanish/Indian) 69.0%; white 17.0%; black 9.0%; Amerindian 5.0%. **Religious affiliation** (1995): Roman Catholic 72.9%; Protestant 16.7%, of which Evangelical 15.1%, Moravian 1.5%; nonreligious 8.5%; other 1.9%. **Major cities** (1995): Managua (2001) 1,039,000; León 123,865; Chinandega 97,387; Masaya 88,971; Granada 71,783; Estelí 71,550. **Location:** Central America, bordering Honduras, the Caribbean Sea, Costa Rica, and the North Pacific Ocean.

## Vital statistics

**Birth rate** per 1,000 population (2000): 28.3 (world avg. 22.5). **Death rate** per 1,000 population (2000): 4.9 (world avg. 9.0). **Natural increase rate** per 1,000 population (2000): 23.4 (world avg. 13.5). **Total fertility rate** (avg. births per childbearing woman; 2000): 3.3. **Life expectancy** at birth (2000): male 66.8 years; female 70.8 years.

## National economy

**Budget** (1998). *Revenue:* C$6,581,000,000 (tax revenue 85.7%, of which import duties 23.0%, excise taxes on petroleum products 16.7%, general sales taxes 14.2%, income taxes 12.3%; grants 10.3%). *Expenditures:* C$7,037,000,000 (current expenditure 67.2%; development expenditure 31.6%). **Public debt** (external, outstanding; 2000): US$5,602,000,000. **Production** (metric tons except as noted). *Agriculture, forestry, fishing* (1999): sugarcane 3,748,000, corn (maize) 302,000, rice 137,000; livestock (number of live animals) 1,693,000 cattle, 400,000 pigs; roundwood (2000) 5,984,000 cu m; fish catch (2000) 28,008, of which crustaceans 11,379. *Mining and quarrying* (2000): gold 90,000 troy oz. *Manufacturing* (value added in C$'000,000; 2000 at 1980 prices): food 1,936; beverages 1,261; cement, bricks, tiles 538. *Energy production (consumption):* electricity (kW-hr; 1998) 2,084,000,000 (1,392,-000,000); crude petroleum (barrels; 1997) none (5,468,000); petroleum products (metric tons; 1997) 735,000 (947,000). **Tourism** (2000): receipts from visitors US$111,000,000; expenditures by nationals abroad US$79,000,000. **Land use** (1994): forested

26.3%; meadows and pastures 45.3%; agricultural and under permanent cultivation 10.5%; other 17.9%. **Population economically active** (2000): total 1,815,300; activity rate of total population 35.8% (participation rates: 15–64, 64.1%; female 29.5%; unemployed 9.8%). **Gross national product** (2000): US$2,053,000,000 (US$410 per capita). **Households.** Average household size (1995) 5.8.

## Foreign trade

**Imports** (1999-f.o.b. in balance of trade and c.i.f. in commodities and trading partners): US$1,845,700,-000 (capital goods 32.2%, nondurable consumer goods 23.9%, mineral fuels 8.7%). *Major import sources:* US 34.5%; Costa Rica 11.4%; Guatemala 7.3%; Panama 6.9%. **Exports** (1999): US$543,800,-000 (coffee 24.9%, manufactured products 19.9%, crustaceans 15.4%, beef 7.7%, raw sugar 5.6%, gold 5.6%). *Major export destinations:* US 37.7%; El Salvador 12.5%; Germany 9.8%; Honduras 6.5%; Costa Rica 5.1%.

## Transport and communications

**Transport.** *Roads* (1999): total length 16,382 km (paved 11%). *Vehicles* (1998): passenger cars 52,220; trucks and buses 73,402. *Air transport* (1998): passenger-km 93,000,000; metric ton-km cargo 10,000,000; airports (1997) with scheduled flights 10. **Communications,** in total units (units per 1,000 persons). Daily newspaper circulation (1996): 135,000 (30); radio receivers (1997): 1,240,000 (265); television receivers (1999): 340,000 (72); telephone main lines (2001): 158,000 (31); cellular telephone subscribers (2001): 156,000 (30); personal computers (2000): 50,000 (9.9); Internet users (2000): 50,000 (9.9).

## Education and health

**Educational attainment** (1995). Percentage of population age 25 and over having: no formal schooling 30.6%, no formal schooling (literate) 3.9%, primary education 39.2%, secondary 17.0%, technical 3.1%, incomplete undergraduate 2.2%; complete undergraduate 4.0%. **Literacy** (1995): total population age 15 and over literate 1,769,000 (74.0%); males literate 853,000 (74.4%); females literate 916,000 (73.6%). **Health:** physicians (1997) 3,725 (1 per 1,255 persons); hospital beds (1996) 6,666 (1 per 674 persons); infant mortality rate per 1,000 live births (2000) 34.8. **Food** (1999): daily per capita caloric intake 2,314 (vegetable products 93%, animal products 7%); 103% of FAO recommended minimum.

## Military

**Total active duty personnel** (2001): 16,000 (army 87.5%, navy 5.0%, air force 7.5%). **Military expenditure as percentage of GNP** (1999): 1.2% (world 2.4%); per capita expenditure US$5.

## Background

Nicaragua has been inhabited for thousands of years, most notably by the Maya. Christopher Columbus arrived in 1502, and Spanish explorers discovered

Lake Nicaragua soon thereafter. Nicaragua was governed by Spain until 1821, when it declared its independence. It was part of Mexico and then the United Provinces of Central America until 1938, when full independence was achieved. The US intervened in political affairs by maintaining troops there in 1912–33. Ruled by the dictatorial Somoza dynasty from 1936 to 1979, it was taken over by the Sandinistas after a popular revolt. They were opposed by armed insurgents, the US-backed contras, from 1981. The Sandinista government nationalized several sectors of the economy but lost the national elections in 1990. The new government returned many economic activities to private control, but unrest continued through the 1990s.

## Recent Developments

Per capita income, second lowest in the hemisphere, fell for the second consecutive year, ending the modest recovery (1994–2000) that followed the end of the contra insurgency against the Sandinista government. Pres. Enrique Bolaños Geyer, inaugurated in January 2002 after promising a "new era," asked the legislature to strip former president Arnoldo Alemán Lacayo's immunity to prosecute him for having allegedly stolen $100 million from the public treasury and laundered it through domestic and foreign accounts.

**Internet resources:** <www.intur.gob.ni>

# Niger

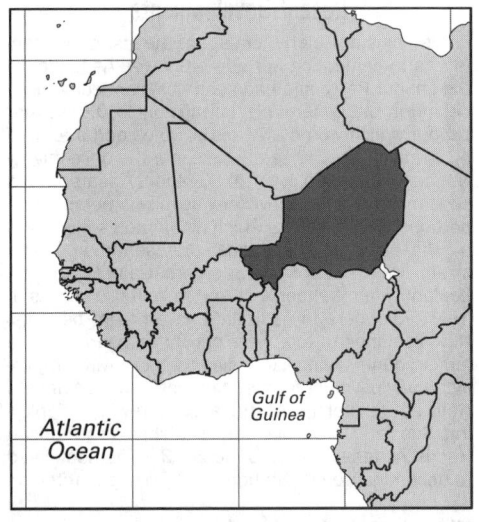

**Official name:** République du Niger (Republic of Niger). **Form of government:** multiparty republic with one legislative house (National Assembly [83]). **Head of state and government:** President Tandja Mamadou (from 1999), assisted by Prime Minister Hama Amadou (from 2000). **Capital:** Niamey. **Official language:** French. **Official religion:** none. **Monetary unit:** 1 CFA franc (CFAF) = 100 centimes; valuation (7 Jul 2003) $1 = CFAF 571.07 (earlier pegged to the French franc, after 1 Jan 2002 the CFAF was pegged at 655.96 to the euro).

*1 metric ton = about 1.1 short tons;   1 kilometer = 0.6 mi (statute);   1 metric ton-km cargo = about 0.68 short ton-mi cargo;   c.i.f.: cost, insurance, and freight;   f.o.b.: free on board*

## Demography

**Area:** 458,075 sq mi, 1,186,408 sq km. **Population** (2002): 10,640,000. **Density** (2002): persons per sq mi 21.8, persons per sq km 8.4. **Urban** (2000): 20.1%. **Sex distribution** (2001): male 49.93%; female 50.07%. **Age breakdown** (2001): under 15, 48.0%; 15–29, 26.3%; 30–44, 14.1%; 45–59, 7.8%; 60–74, 3.2%; 75 and over, 0.6%. **Ethnic composition** (1988): Hausa 53.0%; Zerma- (Djerma-) Songhai 21.2%; Tuareg 10.4%; Fulani (Peul) 9.8%; Kanuri-Nanga 4.4%; Teda 0.4%; Arab 0.3%; Gurma 0.3%; other 0.2%. **Religious affiliation** (2000): Sunni Muslim 90.7%; traditional beliefs 8.7%; Christian 0.5%; other 0.1%. **Major cities** (1988): Niamey 391,876 (urban agglomeration [2001] 821,000); Zinder 119,827; Maradi 110,005; Tahoua 49,948; Agadez 32,272. **Location:** western Africa, bordering Algeria, Libya, Chad, Nigeria, Benin, Burkina Faso, and Mali.

## Vital statistics

**Birth rate** per 1,000 population (2001): 50.7 (world avg. 21.2). **Death rate** per 1,000 population (2001): 22.7 (world avg. 8.9). **Natural increase rate** per 1,000 population (2001): 28.0 (world avg. 12.3). **Total fertility rate** (avg. births per childbearing woman; 2001): 7.1. **Life expectancy** at birth (2001): male 41.7 years; female 41.4 years.

## National economy

**Budget** (2000). *Revenue:* CFAF 162,166,000,000 (taxes 63.4%, external aid and gifts 32.1%, nontax revenue 4.5%). *Expenditures:* CFAF 204,800,000,000 (current expenditures 67.6%, of which education 13.7%, defense 6.8%, economic services 4.5%, health 3.9%; development expenditures 32.4%). **Public debt** (external, outstanding; 2000): $1,413,000,000. **Tourism** (2000): receipts from visitors $24,000,000; expenditures by nationals abroad $28,000,000. **Gross national product** (2000): $1,939,000,000 ($180 per capita). **Production** (metric tons except as noted). *Agriculture, forestry, fishing* (2001): millet 2,414,394, sorghum 655,729, cowpeas 300,000; livestock (number of live animals) 6,900,000 goats, 4,500,000 sheep, 2,260,000 cattle; roundwood (2001) 8,406,463 cu m; fish catch (1999) 11,014. *Mining and quarrying:* salt (1997) 3,000; uranium (2000) 2,898. *Manufacturing* (value added in CFAF '000,000; 1998): paper and products 3,171; food 1,697; soaps and other chemical products 1,547. *Energy production (consumption):* electricity (kW-hr; 2000) 199,200,000 (326,600,000); coal (metric tons; 1997) 174,000 (174,000); crude petroleum, none (none); petroleum products (metric tons; 2000) none (165,700). **Population economically active** (1988; excludes nomadic population): total 2,315,694; activity rate of total population 31.9% (participation rates: ages 15–64, 55.2%; female 20.4%). **Household income and expenditure.** Average household size (1998) 6.3; income per household: n.a.; expenditure (1987): food and beverages 43.1%, housing 22.8%, clothing 10.0%. **Land use** (1994): forested 2.0%; meadows and pastures 8.2%; agricultural and under permanent cultivation 2.9%; other (largely desert) 86.9%.

## Foreign trade

**Imports** (2000): CFAF 230,400,000,000 (food products 27.5%, petroleum products 20.7%; capital goods 19.4%; intermediate goods 7.5%). *Major import sources:* France 20.1%; Côte d'Ivoire 13.2%; Nigeria 10.3%; Japan 6.2%; Germany 2.2%; Italy 1.5%. **Exports** (2000): CFAF 201,200,000,000 (uranium 31.8%; livestock [mostly live cattle, sheep, and goats] 18.4%; cowpeas 6.7%). *Major export destinations:* France 48.1%; Nigeria 40.6%; Côte d'Ivoire 1.6%; Japan 0.5%.

## Transport and communications

**Transport.** *Roads* (1999): total length 10,100 km (paved 8%). *Vehicles* (1996): passenger cars 38,220, trucks and buses 15,200. *Air transport* (1998; represents about 10% of the traffic of Air Afrique, which is operated by 11 West African states): passenger-km 258,263,000; metric ton-km cargo 13,524,000; airports (1999) with scheduled flights 6. **Communications,** in total units (units per 1,000 persons). Daily newspaper circulation (1996): 2,000 (0.2); radio receivers (1997): 680,000 (73); television receivers (1999): 285,000 (29); telephone main lines (2001): 21,700 (1.9); cellular telephone subscribers (2001): 1,800 (0.1); personal computers (2001): 6,000 (0.5); Internet users (2001): 12,000 (1.1).

## Education and health

**Educational attainment** (1988). Percentage of population age 25 and over having: no formal schooling 85.0%; Qur'anic education 11.2%; primary education 2.5%; secondary 1.1%; higher 0.2%. **Literacy** (1995): total population age 15 and over literate 641,000 (13.6%); males literate 482,000 (20.9%); females literate 159,000 (6.6%). **Health:** physicians (1997) 324 (1 per 28,171 persons); infant mortality rate per 1,000 live births (2001) 123.6. **Food** (2000): daily per capita caloric intake 2,089 (vegetable products 95%, animal products 5%); 88% of FAO recommended minimum.

## Military

**Total active duty personnel** (2001): 5,300 (army 98%, air force 2%). **Military expenditure as percentage of GNP** (1999): 1.2% (world 2.4%); per capita expenditure $2.

## Background

On the territory of Niger, there is evidence of Neolithic culture, and several kingdoms existed there before the colonialists arrived. First explored by Europeans in the late 18th century, it became a French colony in 1922. It became an overseas territory of France in 1946 and gained independence in 1960. The first multiparty elections were held in 1993.

## Recent Developments

The severe drought in Niger continued, with 70% of villages reporting insufficient water supplies. On 31 Jul 2002 soldiers demanding higher pay and better conditions of service mutinied in Diffa, N'Guigmi, and N'Gourti in southeastern Niger. Several army officers and government officials, including Diffa's prefect, were taken hostage. The former sultan of Zinder, Aboubacar Sanda, deposed by the government in 2001 on fraud charges, was sentenced to two years in prison on 11 Sep 2002.

**Internet resources:**
<www.nigerembassyusa.org/travel.html>

# Nigeria

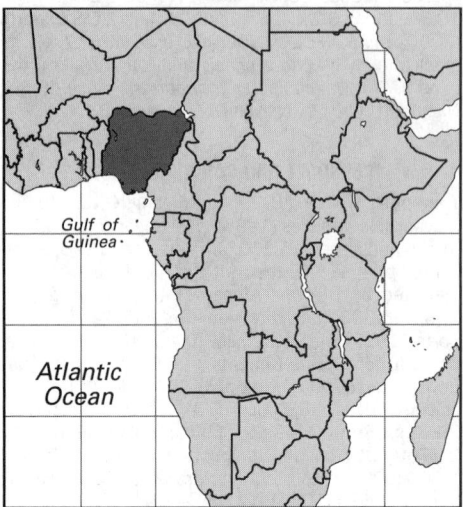

Gulf of
Guinea·

Atlantic
Ocean

**Official name:** Federal Republic of Nigeria. **Form of government:** federal republic with two legislative bodies (Senate [109]; House of Representatives [360]). **Head of state and government:** President Olusegun Obasanjo (from 1999). **Capital:** Abuja (statutory transfer from Lagos occurred in 1991; judiciary and some ministries remain in Lagos). **Official language:** English. **Official religion:** none. **Monetary unit:** 1 Nigerian naira (N) = 100 kobo; valuation (7 Jul 2003) $1 = N 130.10.

## Demography

**Area:** 356,669 sq mi, 923,768 sq km. **Population** (2002): 129,935,000. **Density** (2002): persons per sq mi 364.4, persons per sq km 140.7. **Urban** (2002): 44.9%. **Sex distribution** (2001): male 50.60%; female 49.40%. **Age breakdown** (2001): under 15, 43.7%; 15–29, 27.8%; 30–44, 15.3%; 45–59, 8.6%; 60–74, 3.9%; 75 and over, 0.7%. **Ethnic composition** (2000): Yoruba 17.5%; Hausa 17.2%; Igbo (Ibo) 13.3%; Fulani 10.7%; Ibibio 4.1%; Kanuri 3.6%; Egba 2.9%; Tiv 2.6%; Bura 1.1%; Nupe 1.0%; Edo 1.0%; other 25.0%. **Religious affiliation** (2000): Christian 45.9%, of which independent Christian 15.0%, Anglican 13.0%, other Protestant 9.0%, Roman Catholic 8.0%; Muslim 43.9%; African indigenous 9.8%; other 0.4%. **Major cities** (1991): Lagos 5,197,247 (urban agglomeration [2000] 13,427,-000); Kano 2,166,554; Ibadan (2000) 1,731,000; Kaduna 993,642; Benin City 762,719. **Location:** western Africa, bordering Niger, Chad, Cameroon, the Gulf of Guinea, and Benin.

## Vital statistics

**Birth rate** per 1,000 population (2001): 39.7 (world avg. 21.2). **Death rate** per 1,000 population (2001): 13.9 (world avg. 8.9). **Natural increase rate** per 1,000 population (2001): 25.8 (world avg. 12.3). **Total fertility rate** (avg. births per childbearing woman; 2001): 5.6. **Life expectancy** at birth (2001): male 51.1 years; female 51.7 years.

## National economy

**Budget** (2000). *Revenue:* N 1,927,087,000,000 (tax revenue 33.1%, of which petroleum profit tax 17.3%; import duties, excise taxes, and fees 6.0%; nontax revenue 66.9%, of which oil export proceeds 49.1%). *Expenditures:* N 1,834,305,000,000 (1999; recurrent expenditure 75.6%, of which debt service 18.8%, education 5.2%, defense 4.6%; capital expenditure 24.4%). **Production** (metric tons except as noted). *Agriculture, forestry, fishing* (2001): cassava 33,854,000, yams 26,201,000, sorghum 7,711,-000; livestock 24,300,000 goats, 20,500,000 sheep, 19,830,000 cattle; roundwood (2001) 69,115,550 cu m; fish catch (1999) 477,365. *Mining and quarrying* (2000): limestone 2,000,000; marble 30,000. *Manufacturing* (value added in N'000,000; 1995): food and beverages 25,415; textiles 16,193; chemical products 11,181. *Energy production (consumption):* electricity (kW-hr; 1999) 18,700,000,000 ([1997] 14,830,000,000); coal (metric tons; 1999) 63,500 (72,500); crude petroleum (barrels; 2001) 757,498,000 (106,580,000); petroleum products (metric tons; 1997) 5,550,000 (6,175,000); natural gas (cu m; 2001) 757,498,000 (106,580,000). **Tourism** (2000): receipts $200,000,000; expenditures $730,000,000. **Household income and expenditure.** Avg. household size (1995) 4.7; annual income per household (1992–93) N 15,000 ($760): sources of income (1979): self-employment 49.4%, wages 30.2%, interest 5.4%, rent 4.7%, transfer payments 4.3%; expenditures (1979): food 53.0%, fuel and light 11.4%, clothing 6.0%, transportation 4.7%, household goods 3.8%, other 21.1%. **Gross national product** (2000): $32,705,000,000 ($260 per capita). **Public debt** (external, outstanding; 2000): $32,735,000,000. **Population economically active** (1993–94): total 29,000,000; activity rate 31.0% (participation rates: ages 15–59, 64.4%; female 44.0%). **Land use** (1994): forest 15.7%; pasture 43.9%; agriculture 35.9%; other 4.5%.

## Foreign trade

**Imports** (2000): $12,372,000,000 (1995; machinery and transport equipment 42.0%; manufactured goods [mostly iron and steel products, textiles, and paper products] 24.0%; chemicals 17.0%; food 8.4%). *Major import sources* (2000): UK 10.9%; US 9.2%; France 8.9%; Germany 7.4%; China 6.3%; Italy 5.3%; The Netherlands 5.2%. **Exports** (2000): $20,441,000,000 (crude petroleum 98.9%; ships and boats 0.3%; food products 0.3%). *Major export destinations* (2000): US 46.1%; Spain 10.7%; India 6.1%; France 5.2%; Portugal 3.6%.

## Transport and communications

**Transport.** *Railroads* (2000): length 3,505 km; passenger-km 179,000,000 (1997); metric ton-km cargo 120,000,000 (1997). *Roads* (1999): total length 62,598 km (paved 19%). *Vehicles* (1996): passenger cars 773,000; trucks and buses 68,300 (1995). *Air transport* (2000; Nigeria Airways only): passenger-km 111,566,000; metric ton-km cargo 2,068,000; airports (1998) 12. **Communications,** in total units (units per 1,000 persons). Daily newspaper circulation (1996): 2,500,000 (24); radio receivers (1996):

---

*1 metric ton = about 1.1 short tons;   1 kilometer = 0.6 mi (statute);   1 metric ton-km cargo = about 0.68 short ton-mi cargo;   c.i.f.: cost, insurance, and freight;   f.o.b.: free on board*

20,500,000 (197); television receivers (1998): 7,200,000 (66); telephone main lines (2001): 500,000 (4.3); cellular telephone subscribers (2001): 330,000 (2.8); personal computers (2001): 800,000 (6.8); Internet users (2000): 200,000 (1.8).

## Education and health

**Literacy** (2000): total population age 15 and over literate 40,700,000 (64.1%); males literate 22,600,000 (62.3%); females literate 18,100,000 (56.2%). **Health** (1995): physicians 27,230 (1 per 3,707 persons); hospital beds 68,350 (1 per 1,477 persons); infant mortality rate per 1,000 live births (2001) 73.3. **Food** (2000): daily per capita caloric intake 2,850 (vegetable products 97%, animal products 3%); 121% of FAO recommended minimum.

## Military

**Total active duty personnel** (2001): 78,500 (army 79.0%, navy 8.9%, air force 12.1%). **Military expenditure as percentage of GNP** (1999): 1.7% (world 2.4%); per capita expenditure $13.

Nigeria is Africa's most populous country and a land of extreme diversity, with at least 250 different ethnic groups and more than 500 spoken languages.

## Background

Inhabited for thousands of years, Nigeria was the center of the Nok culture from 500 BC to AD 200 and of several precolonial empires, including the state of Kanem-Bornu and the Songhai, Hausa, and Fulani kingdoms. Visited in the 15th century by Europeans, it became a center for the slave trade. The area began to come under British control in 1861; by 1903 British rule was total. Nigeria gained independence in 1960 and became a republic in 1963. Ethnic strife soon led to military coups, and military groups ruled the country from 1966–79 and from 1983–99. Civil war between the central government and the former Eastern Region, which seceded and called itself Biafra, in 1967–70 ended in Biafra's surrender after widespread starvation and civilian deaths. In 1991 the capital was moved from Lagos to Abuja. The government's execution of environmental activist Ken Saro-Wiwa in 1995 led to international sanctions, and civilian rule was finally reestablished in 1999. By far the most populous nation in Africa, Nigeria suffers from rapid population increase, political instability, foreign debt, slow economic growth, a high rate of violent crime, and rampant government corruption.

## Recent Developments

Throughout 2002 Nigeria suffered from violence of many kinds, including communal clashes and religious, ethnic, or land disputes. Ethnic conflicts in Lagos in early February killed more than 100 people. In mid-March, disputes over land in southeastern Nigeria resulted in more than 40 deaths. Ethnic and religious clashes broke out periodically in northern states. Clashes between rival university cult groups at the University of Nigeria in southeastern Enugu state in mid-June left at least 12 students dead. Ethnic, political, and economic rioting broke out again in the south-

eastern Rivers state in March 2003 in protest mainly against the central government's policies, which were seen to favor some ethnic groups over others.

The incumbent president, Olusegun Obasanjo, won an easy victory in the elections in April, although the run-up to the balloting was marked by violence that included the assassination of a leading opposition politician, Marshall Harry. The case of Amina Lawal, a woman who was sentenced by a Nigerian Shariah (Islamic law) court in March 2002 to death by stoning for adultery, made headlines worldwide as her appeals continued into mid-2003. The Miss World beauty pageant, scheduled for 7 Dec 2002 in the Nigerian capital, Abuja, was moved to London after a newspaper in the Islamic north of Nigeria suggested that the Prophet Muhammad would have approved of the beauty contest, inciting riots in which more than 100 people were killed.

Internet resources:
<www.nigeriahighcommottawa.com>

# Northern Mariana Islands

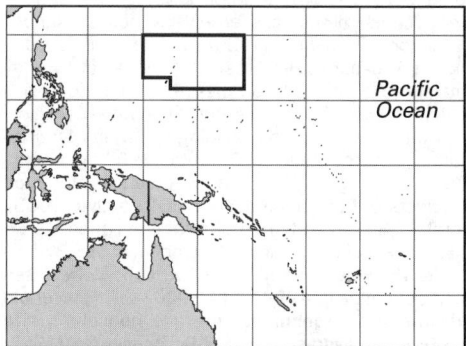

Pacific Ocean

**Official name:** Commonwealth of the Northern Mariana Islands. **Political status:** self-governing commonwealth in association with the US, having two legislative houses (Senate [9]; House of Representatives [18]; residents elect a nonvoting representative to the US Congress). **Chief of state:** President George W. Bush (from 20 Jan 2001). **Head of government:** Governor Juan N. Babauta (from 14 Jan 2002). **Capital:** Capital Hill, Saipan. **Official languages:** Chamorro, Carolinian, and English. **Official religion:** none. **Monetary unit:** 1 US dollar ($) = 100 cents.

## Demography

**Area:** 176.5 sq mi, 457.1 sq km. **Population** (2002): 70,000. **Density** (2002): persons per sq mi 396.6, persons per sq km 153.1. **Urban** (2002; all of Saipan was designated an urban area in 2002): 90.0%. **Sex distribution** (2000): male 46.21%; female 53.79%. **Age breakdown** (2000): under 15, 22.5%; 15–34, 45.8%; 35–59, 29.0%; 60–74, 2.3%; 75 and over, 0.4%. **Ethnic composition** (2000): Filipino 26.2%; Chinese 22.1%; Chamorro 21.3%; Carolinian 3.8%; other Asian 7.5%; other Pacific Islander 6.6%; white 1.8%; multiethnic and other 10.7%. **Religious affiliation** (1995): Roman Catholic 59.6%; Protestant 18.7%; other Christian 1.4%; other 20.3%. **Major villages** (2000): San Antonio 4,741; Garapan 3,588; Capital Hill 1,498. **Location:** Oceania, islands in the North Pacific Ocean, between Hawaii (US) and the Philippines.

## Vital statistics

**Birth rate** per 1,000 population (2002): 20.3 (world avg. 21.2); legitimate, 32.4%; illegitimate, 67.6%. **Death rate** per 1,000 population (2002): 2.4 (world avg. 8.9). **Natural increase rate** per 1,000 population (2002): 17.9 (world avg. 12.3). **Total fertility rate** (avg. births per childbearing woman; 2002): 1.8. **Marriage rate** per 1,000 population (1989): 28.5. **Divorce rate** per 1,000 population (1986): 2.9. **Life expectancy** at birth (2002): male 72.9 years; female 79.2 years.

## National economy

**Budget** (1999–2000). *Revenue*: $297,200,000 (local revenue 83.3%, grants from US Office of Insular Affairs for capital improvements 16.7%). *Expenditures*: $225,500,000 (education 22.0%, health and social welfare 19.3%, general government 16.0%, public safety 9.6%). **Tourism** (1998): receipts from visitors, $394,000,000. **Land use** (1990): meadows and pastures 3.7%; agricultural and under permanent cultivation 4.0%; other 92.3%. **Gross national product** (1999): $664,600,000 ($9,600 per capita). **Production** (metric tons except as noted). *Agriculture, forestry, fishing* (1989): melons 165, cucumbers 83, bananas 46; livestock (number of live animals) 4,513 cattle, 1,260 pigs, 9,580 chickens; fish catch (1998) 235. *Mining and quarrying*: negligible amount of quarrying for building material. *Manufacturing* (value of sales in $'000,000; 1997): garments 700; stone, glass, or ceramic products 21; food products 6. **Population economically active** (1995): total 37,393; activity rate of total population 63.5% (participation rates: ages 16 and over, 85.3%; female 48.1%; unemployed 7.1%). **Public debt** (external, outstanding; 1999): $146,000,000. **Household income and expenditure.** Average household size (1995) 4.0; average income per household (1995) $30,296; sources of income (1994): wages 83.9%, interest and rental 7.2%, self-employment 7.2%, transfer payments 1.7%.

## Foreign trade

**Imports** (1997): $836,200,000 (clothing and accessories 37.0%, foodstuffs 9.6%, petroleum and petroleum products 8.2%, transport equipment and parts 5.0%, construction materials 4.2%). *Major import sources:* Guam 35.6%, Hong Kong 24.0%, Japan 14.1%, South Korea 9.6%, US 7.6%. **Exports** (1999): $1,049,000,000 (clothing and accessories 99.9%). *Major export destinations:* nearly all to the US.

## Transport and communications

**Transport.** *Roads* (1998): total length c. 360 km (paved, nearly 100%). *Vehicles* (1993): passenger cars 12,000; trucks and buses 6,300. *Air transport* (1999; Saipan International Airport only): aircraft landings 23,853; boarding passengers 562,364; airports (1999) with scheduled flights 2. **Communications**, in total units (units per 1,000 persons). Radio receivers (1999): 10,500 (152); television receivers (1999): 4,100 (59); telephone main lines (2000): 26,800 (506); cellular telephone subscribers (2000): 3,000 (57).

## Education and health

**Educational attainment** (1995). Percentage of population age 25 and over having: no formal schooling 0.7%; primary education, 5.5%; some secondary 13.5%; completed secondary 38.8%; some postsecondary 23.3%; completed undergraduate 18.2%. **Literacy** (1990): total population age 10 and over literate 35,490 (98.8%); males literate 18,790 (99.0%); females literate 16,700 (98.6%). **Health**: physicians (1986): 23 (1 per 1,326 persons); hospital beds (1998): 74 (1 per 899 persons); infant mortality rate per 1,000 live births (2002): 5.6.

## Military

The US is responsible for military defense; headquarters of the US Pacific Command are in Hawaii.

## Background

The Northern Mariana Islands were discovered by Ferdinand Magellan in 1521 and colonized by Spain in 1668. Sold to Germany in 1899, they were occupied by Japan in 1914 and became a Japanese mandate from the League of Nations after 1919. They were the scene of fierce fighting in World War II; Tinian was the base for US planes that dropped atomic bombs on Hiroshima and Nagasaki. They were granted to the US in 1947 as a UN trust territory, became self-governing in 1978, and became a commonwealth under US sovereignty in 1986, when its residents became US citizens. The UN trusteeship ended in 1986.

## Recent Developments

Garment manufacturers reached a major legal settlement and agreed to compensation payments for as many as 30,000 Asian workers who allegedly had been made to work under sweatshop conditions in Saipan. Nearly half of Saipan's population of some 64,000 were migrants, mostly Filipinos and Chinese working in the garment industry. During October the government reached agreement with the US on a $120 million financial assistance package over 11 years to be introduced when the current agreement expired in 2003.

**Internet resources:** <www.mariana-islands.gov.mp>

# Norway

**Official name:** Kongeriket Norge (Kingdom of Norway). **Form of government:** constitutional monarchy with one legislative house (Parliament [165]). **Chief of state:** King Harald V (from 1991). **Head of government:** Prime Minister Kjell Magne Bondevik (from 2001). **Capital:** Oslo. **Official language:** Norwegian. **Official religion:** Evangelical Lutheran. **Monetary unit:** 1 Norwegian krone (NKr) = 100 øre; valuation (7 Jul 2003) $1 = NKr 7.22.

## Demography

**Area:** 125,004 sq mi, 323,758 sq km. **Population** (2002): 4,537,000. **Density** (2002): persons per sq

*1 metric ton = about 1.1 short tons;    1 kilometer = 0.6 mi (statute);    1 metric ton-km cargo = about 0.68 short ton-mi cargo;    c.i.f.: cost, insurance, and freight;    f.o.b.: free on board*

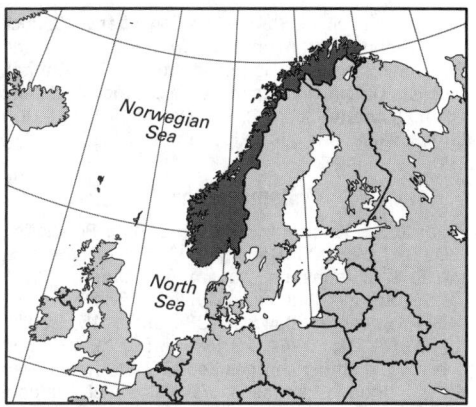

mi 36.3, persons per sq km 14.0. **Urban** (1990): 75.0%. **Sex distribution** (2002): male 49.56%; female 50.44%. **Age breakdown** (2000): under 15, 20.0%; 15–29, 19.6%; 30–44, 22.3%; 45–59, 18.8%; 60–74, 11.5%; 75 and over, 7.8%. **Ethnic composition** (by country of citizenship; 2002): Norway 95.9%; Sweden 0.6%; Denmark 0.4%; UK 0.2%; Iraq 0.2%; Bosnia and Herzegovina 0.2%; US 0.2%; Germany 0.2%; Pakistan 0.2%; Somalia 0.1%; Yugoslavia 0.1%; Finland 0.1%; Iran 0.1%; other 1.5%. **Major cities** (2002): Oslo 512,589; Bergen 233,291; Trondheim 151,408. **Location:** northern Europe, bordering the Barents Sea, Russia, Sweden, the North Sea, and the Norwegian Sea.

## Vital statistics

**Birth rate** per 1,000 population (2000): 13.2 (world avg. 22.5); (1999) legitimate 49.1%; illegitimate 50.9%. **Death rate** per 1,000 population (2000): 9.8 (world avg. 9.0). **Natural increase rate** per 1,000 population (2000): 3.4 (world avg. 13.5). **Total fertility rate** (avg. births per childbearing woman; 1999): 1.9. **Marriage rate** per 1,000 population (1998): 5.3. **Divorce rate** per 1,000 population (2000): 2.2. **Life expectancy** at birth (2000): male 76.0 years; female 81.4 years.

## National economy

**Budget** (2001). *Revenue*: NKr 829,345,000,000 (value-added taxes 30.7%, tax on income 28.6%, social security taxes 20.2%). *Expenditures*: NKr 617,372,000,000 (social security and welfare 37.8%, health 15.9%, education 13.6%, debt service 4.6%). **Land use** (1994): forested 27.2%; meadows and pastures 0.4%; agricultural and under permanent cultivation 2.9%; built-up and other 69.5%. **Production** (metric tons except as noted). *Agriculture, forestry, fishing* (2000): barley 649,400, potatoes 446,000, oats 372,400; livestock (number of live animals) 2,400,000 sheep, 1,042,000 cattle, 690,000 pigs; roundwood (1999) 8,424,000 cu m; fish catch (1999) 2,598,733, of which herring 807,635, cod 256,621, saithe 197,857, capelin 86,767. *Mining and quarrying* (1998): iron ore 621,000, ilmenite-titanium 589,500, copper 11,400. *Manufacturing* (value added in NKr '000,000; 1997): machinery and transport equipment 27,779; food products 25,646; paper and paper products 18,139. *Energy production (consumption)*: electricity (kW-hr; 1997) 111,551,000,000 (115,369,000,000); coal (metric tons; 1997) 386,000 (996,000); crude petroleum

(barrels; 1997) 1,191,000,000 (109,000,000); petroleum products (metric tons; 1997) 15,425,000 (8,648,000); natural gas (cu m; 1997) 47,485,-000,000 (4,652,000,000). **Household income and expenditure**. Average household size (2001) 2.3; consumption expenditure per household (1998) NKr 357,458 ($47,376); expenditure (1996–98): transportation 24.1%, housing 16.6%, food 12.9%, recreation and education 11.3%, household furniture and equipment 8.7%, clothing and footwear 6.1%. **Gross national product** (2000): $155,064,000,000 ($34,530 per capita). **Population economically active** (1999): total 2,333,000; activity rate of total population 52.4% (participation rates: ages 16–64 [1996] 79.1%; female 46.0%; unemployed 4.9%). **Public debt** (1998): $29,289,000,000. **Tourism** (2000): receipts from visitors $1,937,000,000.

## Foreign trade

**Imports** (2001-c.i.f. in balance of trade): NKr 296,161,000,000 (machinery and transport equipment 42.1%, of which road vehicles 8.7%; ships 3.4%; metals and metal products 7.7%, of which iron and steel 2.6%; food products 6.7%, of which fruits and vegetables 1.4%; petroleum products 3.0%). *Major import sources:* Sweden 15.2%; Germany 12.6%; UK 7.9%; Denmark 7.1%. **Exports** (2001): NKr 529,966,000,000 (petroleum products 48.5%; machinery and transport equipment 11.4%; metals and metal products 7.9%; food products 6.1%, of which fish 5.6%). *Major export destinations:* UK 19.6%; Germany 12.2%; The Netherlands 10.4%; Sweden 8.0%.

## Transport and communications

**Transport**. *Railroads* (2001): route length 4,178 km; passenger-km 2,536,000,000; metric ton-km cargo 2,451,000,000. *Roads* (2002): total length 91,545 km (paved 74% [1998]). *Vehicles* (2001): passenger cars 1,872,862; trucks and buses 444,626. *Air transport* (2000): passenger-km 10,754,711,000; metric ton-km cargo 1,254,364,000; airports (1996) 50. **Communications**, in total units (units per 1,000 persons). Daily newspaper circulation (1999): 2,294,000 (514); radio receivers (1996): 4,000,000 (913); television receivers (1999): 2,900,000 (650); telephone main lines (2001): 3,262,000 (723); cellular telephone subscribers (2001): 3,737,000 (828); personal computers (2001): 2,300,000 (510); Internet users (2001): 2,700,000 (598).

## Education and health

**Educational attainment** (1998). Percentage of population age 16 and over having: primary and lower secondary education 30.0%; higher secondary 45.9%; higher 20.8%; unknown 3.3%. **Literacy** (1998): virtually 100%. **Health:** physicians (1996) 15,368 (1 per 285 persons); hospital beds (2000) 22,486 (1 per 199 persons); infant mortality rate per 1,000 live births (1999) 3.9. **Food** (2000): daily per capita caloric intake 3,414 (vegetable products 66%, animal products 34%); 127% of FAO recommended minimum.

## Military

**Total active duty personnel** (2001): 25,800 (army 57.0%, navy 23.6%, air force 19.4%). **Military expenditure as percentage of GNP** (1999): 2.2% (world avg. 2.4%); per capita expenditure $742.

## Background

Several principalities were united into the kingdom of Norway in the 11th century. From 1380 it had the same king as Denmark until it was ceded to Sweden in 1814. The union with Sweden was dissolved in 1905, and Norway's economy grew rapidly. The country remained neutral during World War I, although its shipping industry played a vital role in the conflict. It declared its neutrality in World War II but was invaded and occupied by German troops. Norway is a member of NATO but turned down membership in the European Union in 1994. Its economy grew consistently during the 1990s.

## Recent Developments

In 2002 the coalition government of Prime Minister Kjell Magne Bondevik met with considerable resistance in its attempt to persuade Norwegians to accept tighter economic policies despite the fact that, as a major oil and gas producer, Norway ranked among the most prosperous countries of the world. In its call to limit spending the government cited the risk of economic overheating in the near future and the long-term need to secure pensions for the country's growing elder population. The Storting (parliament) had decided in 2001 that Norway should join the war against terrorism in Afghanistan, sending soldiers trained in mine clearing and high-mountain winter warfare. As one of the rotating members of the UN Security Council for 2001–02, Norway insisted that the UN have a say in any decision regarding Iraq. In September 2002 Norwegian Foreign Minister Jan Petersen called a British intelligence report on Iraq's weapons program "disturbing" and voiced support for a new UN resolution outlining demands on Saddam Hussein's regime. Mullah Krekar, the leader of Ansar al-Islam, a militant northern Iraqi group suspected of links to international terrorists, was arrested in March 2003 in Oslo. In May 2002 Princess Märtha Louise, older sister to the crown prince and the second heiress to the throne, married writer Ari Behn in Trondheim.

**Internet resources:** <www.norway.org>

## Oman

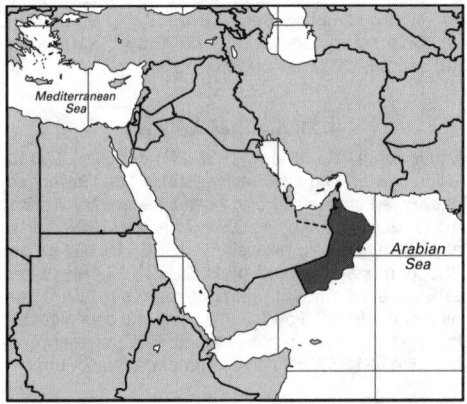

**Official name:** Saltanat 'Uman (Sultanate of Oman). **Form of government:** monarchy with two advisory

bodies (Council of State [41]; Consultative Council [83]). **Head of state and government:** Sultan and Prime Minister Qabus ibn Sa'id (from 1970). **Capital:** Muscat. **Official language:** Arabic. **Official religion:** Islam. **Monetary unit:** 1 rial Omani (RO) = 1,000 baizas; valuation (7 Jul 2003) $1 = RO 0.39.

## Demography

**Area:** 119,500 sq mi, 309,500 sq km. **Population** (2002): 2,522,000. **Density** (2002): persons per sq mi 21.1, persons per sq km 8.1. **Urban** (2001): 76.5%. **Sex distribution** (2000): male 56.8%; female 43.2%. **Age breakdown** (1998): under 15, 36.8%; 15–29, 29.7%; 30–44, 22.1%; 45–59, 7.9%; 60 and over, 3.5%. **Ethnic composition** (2000): Omani Arab 48.1%; Indo-Pakistani 31.7%, of which Balochi 15.0%, Bengali 4.4%, Tamil 2.5%; other Arab 7.2%; Persian 2.8%; Zanzibari (blacks originally from Zanzibar) 2.5%; other 7.7%. **Religious affiliation** (1993): Muslim 87.7%, of which Ibadiyah Muslim c. 75% (principal minorities are Sunni Muslim and Shi'i Muslim); Hindu 7.4%; Christian 3.9%; Buddhist 0.5%; other 0.5%. **Major cities** (1993): Salalah 116,000; Suhar 84,300; 'Ibri 76,000; Muscat 40,900 (urban agglomeration [2001] 540,000; includes Al-Sib; Bawshar 107,500). **Location:** Middle East, bordering the Gulf of Oman, the Arabian Sea, Yemen, Saudi Arabia, and the United Arab Emirates.

## Vital statistics

**Birth rate** per 1,000 population (2000): 38.1 (world avg. 22.5). **Death rate** per 1,000 population (2000): 4.2 (world avg. 9.0). **Natural increase rate** per 1,000 population (2000): 33.9 (world avg. 13.5). **Total fertility rate** (avg. births per childbearing woman; 2000): 6.1. **Life expectancy** at birth (1999): male 69.7 years; female 74.0 years.

## National economy

**Budget** (2000). *Revenue:* RO 2,284,300,000 (oil revenue 75.3%; other 24.7%). *Expenditures:* RO 2,608,-200,000 (current expenditure 78.8%, of which civil ministries 41.0%, defense 30.6%, interest paid on loans 4.1%; capital development projects and subsidies 21.2%). **Public debt** (external, outstanding; 2000): $2,673,000,000. **Gross national product** (1998): $13,135,000,000 ($5,950 per capita). **Tourism** (2000): receipts $120,000,000; expenditures $341,000,000. **Household expenditure.** Average household size (1999) 6.9; expenditure (1990): housing and utilities 27.8%, food, beverage, and tobacco 26.4%, transportation 19.8%, clothing and shoes 7.8%, household goods and furniture 6.1%, education, health services, entertainment, and other 12.1%. **Production** (metric tons except as noted). *Agriculture, forestry, fishing* (2000): vegetables and melons 165,000 (of which watermelons 32,000), dates 135,000, bananas 28,000; *livestock* (number of live animals) 729,000 goats, 180,000 sheep, 3,400,000 chickens; fish catch (1999) 108,819. *Mining and quarrying* (2000): copper 26,000; chromite 15,000; silver 4,692 kg. *Manufacturing* (value of production in RO '000,000; 1993): textiles and apparel 78,200; food and beverages 72,930; chemical products 40,950. *Energy production (con-*

---

*1 metric ton = about 1.1 short tons;    1 kilometer = 0.6 mi (statute);    1 metric ton-km cargo = about 0.68 short ton-mi cargo;    c.i.f.: cost, insurance, and freight;    f.o.b.: free on board*

*sumption)*: electricity (kW-hr; 1999) 8,600,000,000 (8,600,000,000); crude petroleum (barrels; 2001) 350,300,000 (20,100,000); petroleum products (metric tons; 1997) 3,540,000 (1,889,000); natural gas (cu m; 2001) 9,100,000,000 (6,300,000,000). **Population economically active** (1993; non-Omani workers constitute 61.3% of the labor force): total 704,798; activity rate of total population 34.9% (participation rates: over age 15, 60.9%; female 9.7%; unemployed [1996] c. 20%). **Land use** (1994): meadows and pastures 4.7%; agricultural and under permanent cultivation 0.3%; other (mostly desert and developed area) 95.0%.

## Foreign trade

**Imports** (2000-c.i.f.): RO 1,937,700,000 (machinery and transport equipment 43.1%; basic manufactured goods 16.0%; food and live animals 12.2%; beverages and tobacco 8.7%; miscellaneous manufactured articles 6.6%). *Major import sources:* UAE 29.5%; Japan 18.1%; UK 5.8%; US 5.4%; Germany 3.7%; South Korea 3.4%; India 3.3%; Saudi Arabia 2.7%. **Exports** (2000-f.o.b.): RO 4,352,000,000 (domestic exports 88.5%, of which petroleum 82.8%, manufactured goods 2.4% [of which copper and copper products 0.5%], food and live animals 1.9%, mineral fuels 0.7%; reexports 11.5%, of which machinery and transport equipment 7.8%). *Major export destinations:* UAE 40.1%; Saudi Arabia 8.4%; Iran 7.8%; Yemen 7.8%; US 5.5%; UK 3.8%; Tanzania 2.9%.

## Transport and communications

**Transport.** *Roads* (1999): total length 33,020 km (paved 24%). *Vehicles* (1999): passenger cars 229,029; trucks and buses 110,717. *Air transport* (2000; Oman Air only): passenger-km 968,000,000; metric ton-km cargo 18,106,000; airports (1999) with scheduled flights 6. **Communications,** in total units (units per 1,000 persons). Daily newspaper circulation (1996) 63,000 (28); radio receivers (1997): 1,400,000 (607); television receivers (1999): 1,415,000 (608); telephone main lines (2001): 235,300 (90); cellular telephone subscribers (2001): 324,500 (124); personal computers (1999): 85,000 (32); Internet users (2001): 120,000 (46).

## Education and health

**Educational attainment** (1993). Percentage of population age 15 and over having: no formal schooling (illiterate) 41.2%; no formal schooling (literate) 14.9%; primary 18.9%; secondary 21.1%; higher technical 2.0%; higher undergraduate 1.5%; higher graduate 0.1%; other 0.3%. **Literacy** (1995): percentage of total population age 15 and over literate 64.0%; males literate 74.6%; females literate 50.7%. **Health** (1998): physicians 3,061 (1 per 747 persons); hospital beds 5,075 (1 per 444 persons); infant mortality rate per 1,000 live births (2000) 23.3.

## Military

**Total active duty personnel** (2001): 43,400 (army 57.6%, navy 9.7%, air force 9.4%, royal household 23.3%); US troops in Oman (2002) 2,400. **Military expenditure as percentage of GNP** (1999): 15.3% (world 2.4%); per capita expenditure $726.

## Background

Oman has been inhabited for at least 10,000 years. The Arab migration began in the 9th century BC. Tribal warfare continued until the conversion to Islam in the 7th century AD. It was ruled by Ibadi imams until 1154, when a royal dynasty was established. The Portuguese controlled the coastal areas from about 1507 to 1650, when they were expelled. The Al Bu Sa'id dynasty, founded in the mid-18th century, still rules Oman. Oil was discovered in 1964. In 1970 the sultan was deposed by his son, who began a policy of modernization and joined the Arab League and the UN. In the Persian Gulf War, Oman cooperated with the allied forces against Iraq. In the 1990s it continued to expand its foreign relations.

## Recent Developments

Throughout 2002 Oman—as chair of the Supreme Council of the six-member Gulf Cooperation Council—carried an international burden greater than most of its neighboring states. As the US government increasingly favored an invasion of Iraq, Oman remained at the forefront of Arab and Islamic countries cautioning that any and all international action relating to Iraq should take place solely within the framework of the United Nations. Domestic priorities were the further streamlining and regulation of the country's securities exchange as well as its banking and financial sectors and the ongoing promotion of Oman's extraordinarily favorable geographic location as a regional hub for corporate headquarters and the transshipment of goods.

**Internet resources:** <www.exploreoman.com>

# Pakistan

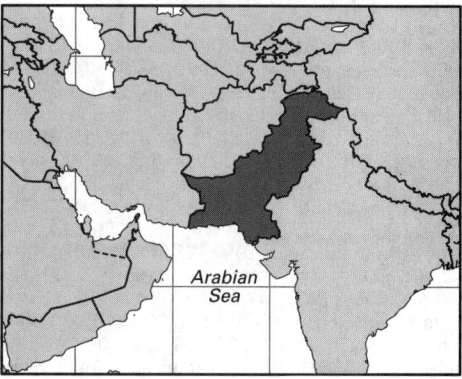

*Arabian Sea*

**Official name:** Islam-i Jamhuriya-e Pakistan (Islamic Republic of Pakistan). **Form of government:** interim military regime. **Chief of state and government:** President Pervez Musharraf (from 2001). **Capital:** Islamabad. **Official language:** Urdu. **Official religion:** Islam. **Monetary unit:** 1 Pakistan rupee (PRs) = 100 paisa, valuation (7 Jul 2003) $1 = PRs 57.75.

## Demography

**Area:** 307,374 sq mi, 796,095 sq km. **Population** (2002; excludes c. 1,100,000 Afghan refugees and the population of Pakistan-administered Jammu and Kashmir [c. 4,300,000]): 145,960,000. **Density** (2002): persons per sq mi 474.9, persons per sq km

183.3. **Urban** (2002; excludes Federally Administered Tribal Areas): 38.0%. **Sex distribution** (2002): male 51.92%; female 48.08%. **Age breakdown** (1998): under 15, 43.2%; 15–29, 26.9%; 30–44, 15.6%; 45–59, 8.8%; 60–74, 4.3%; 75 and over, 1.2%. **Ethnic composition** (2000): Punjabi 52.6%; Pashtun 13.2%; Sindhi 11.7%; Urdu-speaking muhajirs 7.5%; Balochi 4.3%; other 10.7%. **Religious affiliation** (2000): Muslim 96.1% (mostly Sunni, with Shi'i comprising about 17% of total population); Christian 2.5%; Hindu 1.2%; others (including Ahmadiyah) 0.2%. **Major cities** (1998): Karachi 9,269,000; Lahore 5,063,000; Faisalabad 1,977,000; Rawalpindi 1,406,000; Multan 1,182,000; Islamabad 525,000. **Location:** southern Asia, bordering China, India, the Arabian Sea, Iran, and Afghanistan.

## Vital statistics

**Birth rate** per 1,000 population (2002): 36.5 (world avg. 21.2). **Death rate** per 1,000 population (2002): 9.8 (world avg. 8.9). **Natural increase rate** per 1,000 population (2002): 26.7 (world avg. 12.3). **Total fertility rate** (avg. births per childbearing woman; 2002): 4.1. **Life expectancy** at birth (2002): male 61.0 years; female 61.0 years.

## National economy

**Budget** (1999–2000). *Revenue:* PRs 505,921,000,000 (nontax receipts 23.5%, sales tax 23.1%, income taxes 21.3%, customs duties 12.2%, excise taxes 11.0%). *Expenditures:* PRs 573,788,000,000 (public-debt service 42.7%, defense 26.2%, development 11.8%, general administration 8.3%, grants and subsidies 5.9%). **Public debt** (external, outstanding; 2000): $27,140,000,000. **Production** (metric tons except as noted). *Agriculture, forestry, fishing* (2000): sugarcane 46,333,000, wheat 21,079,000, rice 7,000,000; livestock (number of live animals) 47,400,000 goats, 24,100,000 sheep, 148,000,000 chickens; roundwood (1999) 33,075,000 cu m; fish catch (1998) 596,980. *Mining and quarrying* (1998–99): limestone 9,467,000; rock salt 1,190,000; gypsum 242,000. *Manufacturing* (1998–99): cement 9,635,000; refined sugar 3,568,000; chemical fertilizers 3,543,000, of which urea 3,522,000. *Energy production (consumption):* electricity (kW-hr; 1997–98) 59,088,000,000 ([1997] 59,119,000,000); coal (metric tons; 1997–98) 3,144,000 ([1997] 4,393,000); crude petroleum (barrels; 1997–98) 20,520,000 ([1997] 47,000,000); petroleum products (metric tons; 1997) 5,528,000 (15,712,000); natural gas (cu m; 1997–98) 19,809,000,000 ([1997] 18,466,000). **Population economically active** (1999): total 38,590,000; activity rate of total population 28.7% (participation rates: ages 15–64, 43.1%; female [1996–97] 14.4%; unemployed 6.1%). **Gross national product** (2000): $61,022,000,000 ($440 per capita). **Household income and expenditure** (1988). Average household size 6.3; income per household PRs 25,572 ($1,420); sources of income: self-employment 56.0%, wages and salaries 22.0%, other 22.0%; expenditure: food 47.0%, housing 12.0%, clothing and footwear 8.0%, other 33.0%. **Tourism** (2000): receipts $84,000,000; expenditures $252,000,000. **Land use** (1999): pasture 6.5%; agriculture 28.4%; forest and other 65.1%.

## Foreign trade

**Imports** (1999–2000-f.o.b.): $10,361,000,000 (1998–99; petroleum products 14.7%, fixed vegetable oil and fats 8.9%, specialized machinery 6.9%, organic chemicals 5.6%, wheat 4.1%, general industrial machinery 3.7%, road vehicles and parts 3.4%, iron and steel manufactures 3.2%). *Major import sources* (1998–99): Japan 8.3%; US 7.7%; Saudi Arabia 6.8%; UAE 6.7%; Malaysia 6.7%; Kuwait 5.9%; UK 4.4%; China 4.2%; Germany 4.2%. **Exports** (1999–2000): $8,569,000,000 (textile fabrics 18.1%, ready-made apparel and made-up articles 14.2%, cotton yarn 12.5%, rice 6.3%, leather goods 6.0%). *Major export destinations* (1998–99): US 21.8%; Hong Kong 7.1%; Germany 6.6%; UK 6.6%; UAE 5.4%; Japan 3.5%; France 3.2%; The Netherlands 3.1%; Italy 2.7%.

## Transport and communications

**Transport.** *Railroads* (1998–99): route length 8,774 km; passenger-km 19,164,000,000; metric ton-km cargo 4,020,000,000. *Roads* (1997–98): total length 149,679 mi, 240,885 km (paved 55%). *Vehicles* (1998): passenger cars 1,167,635; trucks and buses 251,407. *Air transport* (1999): passenger-km 10,466,000,000; metric ton-km cargo 329,832,000; airports (1997) 35. **Communications,** in total units (units per 1,000 persons). Daily newspaper circulation (1995): 2,800,000 (21); radio receivers (1997): 13,500,000 (102); television receivers (1999): 16,000,000 (119); telephone main lines (2001): 3,400,000 (24); cellular telephone subscribers (2001): 800,000 (5.5); personal computers (2001): 600,000 (4.1); Internet users (2001): 500,000 (3.4).

## Education and health

**Educational attainment** (1990). Percentage of population age 25 and over having: no formal schooling 73.8%; some primary education 9.7%; secondary 14.0%; postsecondary 2.5%. **Literacy** (1995): total population age 15 and over literate 37.8%; males literate 50.0%; females literate 24.4%. **Health** (1998): physicians 82,682 (1 per 1,638 persons); hospital beds 90,659 (1 per 1,494 persons); infant mortality rate per 1,000 live births (2002) 85.0. **Food** (1999): daily per capita caloric intake 2,462 (vegetable products 83%, animal products 17%); 107% of FAO recommended minimum.

## Military

**Total active duty personnel** (2001): 620,000 (army 88.7%, navy 4.0%, air force 7.3%). **Military expenditure as percentage of GNP** (1999): 5.9% (world 2.4%); per capita expenditure $25.

**Did you know?** The mountainous northern region of Pakistan is home to the world's highest road, the Karakoram Highway, which extends for about 800 km (500 mi) from Kashgar, China, to Islamabad, Pakistan.

*1 metric ton = about 1.1 short tons;    1 kilometer = 0.6 mi (statute);    1 metric ton-km cargo = about 0.68 short ton-mi cargo;    c.i.f.: cost, insurance, and freight;    f.o.b.: free on board*

## Background

Pakistan has been inhabited since about 3500 BC. From the 3rd century BC to the 2nd century AD, it was part of the Mauryan and Kushan kingdoms. The first Muslim conquests were in the 8th century AD. The British East India Company subdued the reigning Mughal dynasty in 1757. During the period of British colonial rule, what is now Pakistan was part of India. The new state of Pakistan came into existence in 1947 by act of the British Parliament. Kashmir remained a disputed territory between Pakistan and India, resulting in military clashes and full-scale war in 1965. Civil war between East Pakistan (now Bangladesh) and West Pakistan in 1971 resulted in independence for Bangladesh that same year. Many Afghan refugees migrated to Pakistan during the Soviet-Afghan War in the 1980s. Pakistan elected Benazir Bhutto, the first woman to head a modern Islamic state, in 1988. She was ousted in 1990 on charges of corruption and incompetence. During the 1990s conditions were volatile. Border flare-ups with India continued, and Pakistan conducted nuclear tests.

## Recent Developments

Relations between Pakistan and India deteriorated severely after India blamed two Pakistan-based organizations for a terrorist attack on Parliament on 13 Dec 2001 that was prompted by the standoff over the Kashmir region. As 2002 began both nations massed troops along their common border and continued to conduct attacks; international fear of war between the two countries was heightened, especially since both possessed nuclear weapons. The sides exchanged fire along the border in May, where as many as a million soldiers were stationed; Pakistan also began testing missiles, and India threatened to take more serious action. Early in 2002, *Wall Street Journal* reporter Daniel Pearl was kidnapped and eventually murdered by a militant group; four suspects went on trial in April. A top al-Qaeda official was captured in Pakistan in March.

For a brief period in April, terrorism took a backseat to politics. Insisting on holding to his multiple roles and already having given himself an extended term as chief of the army staff, Pres. and Chief Executive Gen. Pervez Musharraf called for a confirmation of his status as the country's principal leader. He announced that a national referendum would be held to determine whether he should be given an additional five-year term as president and chief executive. Challenged by criticism from every quarter, the general deflected all opposition to his plan, arguing that the country needed his brand of leadership. Despite protests and petitions calling for the rescinding of the referendum it was held on schedule on April 30, and those casting ballots gave Musharraf the expected resounding victory. Musharraf's new term began in October. That month also saw the first national election held during Musharraf's tenure, a vital step, the president said, in Pakistan's return to civilian rule. Musharraf's party, the Pakistan Muslim League (Q), won the most seats, 118 in the 342-seat Parliament; in February 2003 the PML (Q) won elections to the Senate.

**Internet resources:** <www.pak.gov.pk>

# Palau

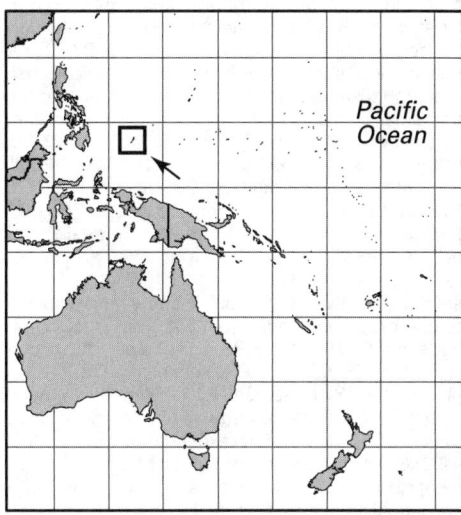

Pacific Ocean

**Official name:** Belu'u er a Belau (Palauan); Republic of Palau (English). **Form of government:** unitary republic with a national congress composed of two legislative houses (Senate [14]; House of Delegates [16]). **Head of state and government:** President Tommy Remengesau (from 2001). **Capital:** Koror; Melekeok on Babelthuap (the main island of Palau) is to be the eventual permanent capital. **Official languages:** Palauan; English. **Official religion:** none. **Monetary unit:** 1 US dollar ($) = 100 cents.

## Demography

**Area:** 188 sq mi, 488 sq km. **Population** (2002): 19,900. **Density** (2002): persons per sq mi 105.9, persons per sq km 40.8. **Urban** (2002): 73.0%. **Sex distribution** (2000): male 54.63%; female 45.37%. **Age breakdown** (2000): under 15, 23.9%; 15–29, 24.2%; 30–44, 29.9%; 45–59, 14.2%; 60–74, 5.5%; 75 and over 2.3%. **Ethnic composition** (1997): Palauan 74.5%; Filipino 16.0%; Chinese 3.2%; other Micronesian and other 6.3%. **Religious affiliation** (1995): Roman Catholic 38.4%; Protestant 24.7%; Modekngei (marginal Christian sect) 26.5%; other 10.4%. **Major city** (2000): Koror 13,303. **Location:** island group in the North Pacific Ocean, east of the Philippines.

## Vital statistics

**Birth rate** per 1,000 population (2002): 19.3 (world avg. 21.2). **Death rate** per 1,000 population (2002): 7.1 (world avg. 8.9). **Natural increase rate** per 1,000 population (2002): 12.2 (world avg. 12.3). **Total fertility rate** (avg. births per childbearing woman; 2002): 2.5. **Life expectancy** at birth (2002): male 66.1 years; female 72.5 years.

## National economy

**Budget** (2002). *Revenue:* $70,058,000 (grants from the US 49.4%, tax revenue 36.0%, nontax revenue 14.6%). *Expenditures:* $79,691,000 (current expenditure 74.6%, of which wages and salaries 38.1%; capital expenditure 25.4%). **Gross national product** (at current market prices; 2000): $118,206,000 ($6,179 per capita). **Production.** *Agriculture, forestry,* *fishing* (value of sales in $; 1993): eggs 262,701, fruit and vegetables 126,325, betel nuts 60,376; livestock (number of live animals; 1984) 1,343 pigs, 82 cows, 9,500 poultry; fish catch (1997) 1,500 (major species are parrot fish, snapper, unicorn fish, and rabbitfish). *Manufacturing*: includes handicrafts and small items. *Energy production (consumption)*: electricity (kW-hr; 1997) 208,000,000 (208,000,-000); petroleum products, none (78,000). **Public debt** (external, outstanding; 2000): $20,000,000. **Tourism** (2000): receipts from visitors $53,750,000. **Population economically active** (2000): total 9,845; activity rate of total population 51.5% (participation rates: over age 15, 67.6%; female [1995] 39.6%; unemployed 2.3%). **Household income and expenditure.** Average household size (2000) 5.7; income per household (1989) $8,882; sources of income (1989): wages 63.7%, social security 12.0%, self-employment 7.4%, retirement 5.5%, interest, dividend, or net rental 4.3%, remittance 4.1%, public assistance 1.0%, other 2.0%; expenditure (1997): food 42.2%, beverages and tobacco 14.8%, entertainment 13.1%, transportation 6.4%, clothing 5.7%, household goods 2.7%, other 15.1%.

### Foreign trade

**Imports** (1997–98): $63,222,000 (1997; machinery and transport equipment 27.8%; food, beverages, and tobacco 27.1%; manufactured articles 27.1%; mineral fuels 13.2%; chemicals and related products 4.5%). *Major import sources* (1997): US 44.1%; Guam 19.3%; Japan 14.8%; Singapore 14.3%; Taiwan 5.4%; China 2.6%; Hong Kong 1.9%. **Exports** (1997–98): $11,095,000 (mostly high-grade tuna; also garments and handicrafts). *Major export destinations*: mostly Japan.

### Transport and communications

**Transport.** *Roads* (1993): total length 64 km (paved 59%). *Vehicles* (1994): passenger cars and trucks 4,271. *Air transport* (1993): passenger arrivals 50,366, passenger departures 49,376; airports (1997) with scheduled flights 1. **Communications,** in total units (units per 1,000 persons). Radio receivers (1997): 12,000 (663.0); television receivers (1997): 11,000 (606.0); telephone main lines (1994): 2,615 (160.0).

### Education and health

**Educational attainment** (1997). Percentage of population age 25 and over having: no formal schooling 0.1%; some primary education 4.4%; completed primary 5.7%; some secondary 16.3%; completed secondary 41.0%; some postsecondary 13.0%; higher 19.5%. **Literacy** (1997): total population age 15 and over literate 99.9%. **Health** (1990): physicians (1998) 20 (1 per 906 persons); hospital beds (1990) 70 (1 per 200 persons); infant mortality rate per 1,000 live births (1999) 17.7.

### Military

The US is responsible for the external security of Palau, as specified in the Compact of Free Association of 1 Oct 1994.

### Background

Palau's inhabitants began arriving 3,000 years ago in successive waves from the Indonesian and Philippine archipelagos and from Polynesia. The islands had been under nominal Spanish ownership for more than three centuries when they were sold to Germany in 1899. They were seized by Japan in 1914 and taken by Allied forces in 1944 during World War II. Palau became part of the UN Trust Territory of the Pacific Islands in 1947 and became a sovereign state in 1994; the US provides economic assistance and maintains a military presence in the islands.

### Recent Developments

Palau improved its relationships with both the US and Taiwan in 2002. A nine-member delegation made a five-day visit to Taiwan to support its mission to join the UN. Palau was sympathetic to the major US diplomatic drive to exempt its troops from prosecution by the International Criminal Court, and it became one of a group of signatories to an agreement not to extradite US soldiers for prosecution to the Hague-based court.

**Internet resources:** <www.visit-palau.com>

# Panama

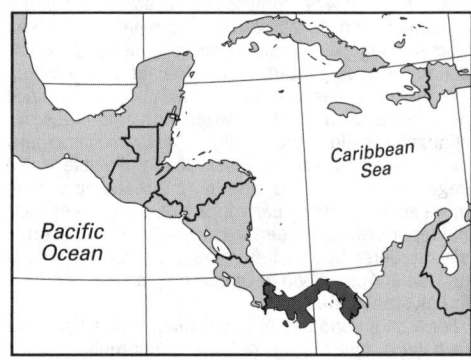

*Caribbean Sea*

*Pacific Ocean*

**Official name:** República de Panamá (Republic of Panama). **Form of government:** multiparty republic with one legislative house (Legislative Assembly [71]). **Head of state and government:** President Mireya Elisa Moscoso Rodríguez (from 1999). **Capital:** Panama City. **Official language:** Spanish. **Official religion:** none. **Monetary unit:** 1 balboa (B) = 100 cents; valuation (7 Jul 2003) $1 = B 1.00.

### Demography

**Area:** 28,950 sq mi, 74,979 sq km. **Population** (2002): 2,915,000. **Density** (2002): persons per sq mi 100.7, persons per sq km 38.9. **Urban** (1999): 56.0%. **Sex distribution** (2000): male 50.46%; female 49.54%. **Age breakdown** (1999): under 15, 31.7%; 15–29, 27.4%; 30–44, 20.9%; 45–59, 12.0%; 60–74, 5.9%; 75 and over, 2.1%. **Ethnic composition** (2000): mestizo 58.1%; black and mulatto 14.0%; white 8.6%; Amerindian 6.7%; Asian 5.5%; other 7.1%. **Religious affiliation** (1995): Roman

---

*1 metric ton = about 1.1 short tons;  1 kilometer = 0.6 mi (statute);  1 metric ton-km cargo = about 0.68 short ton-mi cargo;  c.i.f.: cost, insurance, and freight;  f.o.b.: free on board*

Catholic 80.2%; Protestant 15.0%, of which Pentecostal 8.4%; other Christian 1.6%; other 3.2%. **Major cities** (2000): Panama City 415,964 (urban agglomeration [1999] 1,141,000; includes San Miguelito 293,745); David 77,734; Arraiján 63,753; La Chorrera 55,871; Colón 42,133. **Location:** Central America, bordering the Caribbean Sea, Colombia, the North Pacific Ocean, and Costa Rica.

## Vital statistics

**Birth rate** per 1,000 population (2000): 19.5 (world avg. 22.5). **Death rate** per 1,000 population (2000): 5.0 (world avg. 9.0). **Natural increase rate** per 1,000 population (2000): 14.5 (world avg. 13.5). **Total fertility rate** (avg. births per childbearing woman; 2000): 2.3. **Marriage rate** per 1,000 population (1997; excludes indigenous population): 4.1. **Divorce rate** per 1,000 population (1997; excludes indigenous population): 0.7. **Life expectancy** at birth (2002): male 73.1 years; female 78.7 years.

## National economy

**Budget** (1997). *Revenue:* B 2,266,300,000 (tax revenue 70.3%, of which income taxes 20.2%, social security contributions 19.1%; nontax revenue 26.8%, of which entrepreneurial and property income 15.4%). *Expenditures:* B 2,341,300,000 (social security and welfare 20.5%; health 18.7%; education 18.3%; economic affairs 8.0%; defense 5.0%). **Production** (metric tons except as noted). *Agriculture, forestry, fishing* (1999): sugarcane 2,050,000, bananas 650,000, rice 232,000; livestock (number of live animals; 1999) 1,400,000 cattle, 252,000 pigs, 165,000 horses; roundwood (1998) 1,098,300 cu m; fish catch (value of production in B '000,000; 1998): fish 63, shrimps 40. *Mining and quarrying* (2001): limestone 270,000; gold 48,600 troy oz. *Manufacturing* (value of production in B '000,000; 1998): food products 1,203, of which meat 341, dairy products 144; refined petroleum 299; beverages 176. *Energy production (consumption):* electricity (kW-hr; 2001) 4,858,000,000 ([1998] 3,416,000,000); coal (metric tons; 1997) none (57,000); crude petroleum (barrels; 1997) none (17,277,000); petroleum products (metric tons; 1997) 1,479,000 (1,440,000); natural gas (cu m; 1997) none (60,992,000). **Tourism** (2000): receipts from visitors $576,000,000; expenditures by nationals abroad $187,000,000. **Household income and expenditure.** Average household size (2000) 4.2; average annual income per household (1990) B 5,450 ($5,450); expenditure (1983–84): food and beverages 34.9%, transportation and communications 15.1%, housing and energy 12.6%, education and recreation 11.7%. **Population economically active** (1998; excludes indigenous population): total 1,083,580; activity rate of total population 42.2% (participation rates: ages 15–69 [1997] 64.3%, female [1997] 35.6%, unemployed 13.6%). **Public debt** (external, outstanding; 2000): $5,723,000,000. **Gross national product** (2000): $9,308,000,000 ($3,260 per capita). **Land use** (1994): forested 43.8%; meadows and pastures 19.8%; agricultural and under permanent cultivation 8.9%; other 27.5%.

## Foreign trade

**Imports** (1998-c.i.f.): B 3,398,000,000 (machinery and apparatus 22.9%, transport equipment 15.1%, mineral fuels 10.3%, chemicals and chemical products 9.6%). *Major import sources:* US 39.7%; Colón Free Zone 12.8%; Japan 9.0%; Mexico 4.8%; Ecuador 3.2%. **Exports** (1998-f.o.b.): B 705,000,000 (bananas 19.7%, shrimps 19.4%, fish 7.9%, sugar 3.6%, clothing 3.6%). *Major export destinations:* US 40.0%; Sweden 7.2%; Costa Rica 6.6%; Spain 5.4%; Belgium 4.3%. Excludes Colón Free Zone (1998 imports f.o.b. B 5,319,000,000; 1998 reexports f.o.b. B 5,969,000,000, of which machinery and apparatus 28.4%, textiles and clothing 21.3%).

## Transport and communications

**Transport.** *Railroads* (2000): route length 354 km. *Roads* (1997): total length 11,301 km (paved 33%). *Vehicles:* passenger cars (1996) 203,760; trucks and buses 74,637. Panama Canal traffic (2000–01): oceangoing transits 12,197; cargo 196,242,000 metric tons. *Air transport* (2001; COPA only): passenger-km 3,004,000,000; metric ton-km cargo 25,235,000; airports (1996) 10. **Communications,** in total units (units per 1,000 persons). Daily newspaper circulation (1996): 166,000 (63); radio receivers (1997): 815,000 (306); television receivers (1998): 530,000 (195); telephone main lines (2001): 430,000 (148); cellular telephone subscribers (2001): 600,000 (207); personal computers (2001): 110,000 (38); Internet users (2000): 90,000 (32).

## Education and health

**Educational attainment** (1990). Percentage of population age 25 and over having: no formal schooling 11.6%; primary 41.6%; secondary 28.7%; undergraduate 12.4%; graduate 0.7%; other/unknown 5.0%. **Literacy** (1995): total population age 15 and over literate 1,590,000 (90.8%). **Health** (1998): physicians 3,518 (1 per 772 persons); hospital beds 7,287 (1 per 373 persons); infant mortality rate per 1,000 live births (2002) 19.6. **Food** (2000): daily per capita caloric intake 2,488 (vegetable products 77%, animal products 23%); 108% of FAO recommended minimum.

## Military

**Total active duty personnel** (2001): none; Panama has an 11,800-member national police force. **Military expenditure as percentage of GNP** (1999): 1.4% (world avg. 2.4%); per capita expenditure $45.

## Background

Panama was inhabited by Native Americans when the Spanish arrived in 1501. The first successful Spanish settlement was founded by Vasco Núñez de Balboa in 1510. Panama was part of the viceroyalty of New Granada until it declared its independence from Spain in 1821 to join the Gran Colombia union. In 1903 it revolted against Colombia and was recognized by the US, to which it ceded the Canal Zone. The completed Panama Canal was opened in 1914; its jurisdiction reverted from the US to Panama in 1999. An invasion by US troops in 1989 overthrew the de facto ruler, Gen. Manuel Noriega.

## Recent Developments

During 2002 Pres. Mireya Moscoso was repeatedly accused of nepotism for appointing to government offices relatives and members of various prominent families who supported her political party. The legislative assembly, protected by delegates' immunity from legal prosecution, was embroiled in a major scandal involving accusations of vote buying in the approval of Supreme Court justices and of a transportation and industrial development project. Measures were taken to enable US military forces and law-enforcement agencies to pursue and arrest drug traffickers in Panamanian territory.

Internet resources: <www.ipat.gob.pa>

# Papua New Guinea

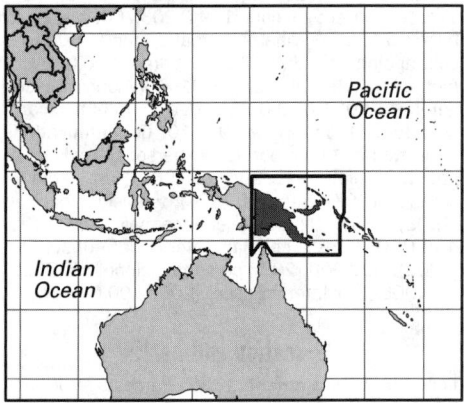

**Official name:** Independent State of Papua New Guinea. **Form of government:** constitutional monarchy with one legislative house (National Parliament [109]). **Chief of state:** Queen Elizabeth II represented by Governor-General Sir Silas Atopare (from 1997). **Head of government:** Prime Minister Sir Michael Somare (from 5 Aug 2002). **Capital:** Port Moresby. **Official language:** English; English, Motu, and Tok Pisin (English Creole) are national languages. **Official religion:** none. **Monetary unit:** 1 Papua New Guinea kina (K) = 100 toea; valuation (7 Jul 2003) $1 = K 3.46.

## Demography

**Area:** 178,704 sq mi, 462,840 sq km. **Population** (2002): 5,426,000. **Density** (2002): persons per sq mi 30.4, persons per sq km 11.7. **Urban** (2001): 17.6%. **Sex distribution** (2000): male 51.30%; female 48.70%. **Age breakdown** (2000): under 15, 38.8%; 15–29, 28.7%; 30–44, 17.1%; 45–59, 9.7%; 60–74, 4.7%; 75 and over, 1.0%. **Ethnic composition** (1983): New Guinea Papuan 84.0%; New Guinea Melanesian 15.0%; other 1.0%. **Religious affiliation** (1990): non-Anglican Protestant 64.3%, of which Evangelical Lutheran 23.2%, Uniting Church 12.7%, Seventh-day Adventist 8.1%, Pentecostal 7.1%, Roman Catholic 28.3%; Anglican 3.9%; other (mostly animists) 3.5%. **Major cities** (1997): Port Moresby 271,813; Lae 113,118; Madang 32,117; Wewak 25,143; Goroka 17,269. **Location:** group of islands, including the eastern half of the island of New Guinea, in the South Pacific Ocean near the Equator, bordering Indonesia and to the north of Australia.

## Vital statistics

**Birth rate** per 1,000 population (2000): 32.7 (world avg. 22.5). **Death rate** per 1,000 population (2000): 8.0 (world avg. 9.0). **Natural increase rate** per 1,000 population (2000): 24.7 (world avg. 13.5). **Total fertility rate** (avg. births per childbearing woman; 2000): 4.4. **Life expectancy** at birth (2000): male 61.1 years; female 65.3 years.

## National economy

**Budget** (2000). *Revenue*: K 2,866,700,000 (tax revenue 72.5%, of which income tax 19.5%, corporate tax 18.3%, VAT 11.8%; foreign grants 18.9%, nontax revenue 8.6%). *Expenditures*: K 3,081,800,000 (current expenditure 70.8%, of which transfer to provincial governments 16.8%, interest payments 12.4%; development expenditure 29.2%). **Public debt** (external, outstanding; 2000): $1,502,000,000. **Production** (metric tons except as noted). *Agriculture, forestry, fishing* (2000): coconuts 826,000, bananas 700,000, sweet potatoes 480,000; livestock (number of live animals) 1,500,000 pigs, 87,000 cattle, 3,600,000 chickens; roundwood (2000) 8,597,000 cu m; fish catch (1999) 53,763. *Mining and quarrying* (1999): copper (metal content) 187,900; silver 66,500 kg; gold 65,700 kg. *Manufacturing* (1998): palm oil 241,485; copra 124,349; coffee 80,700. *Energy production (consumption)*: electricity (kW-hr; 1997) 1,161,900,000 (1,790,-000,000; 1996); coal (metric tons; 1997) none (1,000); crude petroleum (barrels; 1997) 29,000,-000 (440,000); natural gas (cu m; 1997) 83,416,-000 (83,416,000); petroleum products (metric tons; 1997) 52,000 (738,000). **Land use** (1997): forested 92.3%; agricultural and under permanent cultivation 1.5%; meadows and pastures 0.2%; other 6.0%. **Gross national product** (2000): $3,607,000,000 ($700 per capita). **Population economically active** (1990): total 1,715,330; activity rate 36.9% (participation rates: over age 10, 35.2%; female 41.5%; unemployed 7.7%). **Tourism** (1999): receipts $76,-000,000; expenditures $53,000,000.

## Foreign trade

**Imports** (2000): K 2,758,100,000 (1998; nonelectrical machinery 18.3%; food and live animals 16.2%; transport equipment 14.8%; chemicals and chemical products 9.6%; fabricated metals 8.6%). *Major import sources* (1999): Australia 53.5%; Singapore 12.9%; Japan 5.6%; New Zealand 4.1%; US 3.6%; China 2.6%. **Exports** (2000): K 4,695,000,000 (gold 35.3%; crude petroleum 19.8%; copper 14.7%; coffee 7.0%; palm oil 5.2%; cocoa beans 2.8%). *Major export destinations* (1999): Australia 38.1%; Japan 16.9%; Germany 9.6%; US 6.6%; South Korea 5.8%; China 4.0%; UK 2.7%.

## Transport and communications

**Transport.** *Roads* (1986): total length 19,736 km (paved 6%). *Vehicles* (1994): passenger cars 13,000; trucks and buses 32,000. *Air transport* (1997): passenger-km 735,000,000; metric ton-km cargo 86,000,000; airports (1999) with scheduled flights 42. **Communications,** in total units (units per

*1 metric ton = about 1.1 short tons;   1 kilometer = 0.6 mi (statute);   1 metric ton-km cargo = about 0.68 short ton-mi cargo;   c.i.f.: cost, insurance, and freight;   f.o.b.: free on board*

1,000 persons). Daily newspapers (1996): 65,000 (15); radio receivers (1997): 410,000 (91); television receivers (1999): 60,000 (13); telephone main lines (2000): 64,800 (14); cellular telephone subscribers (2000): 8,600 (1.8); Internet users (2001): 300,000 (61).

## Education and health

**Educational attainment** (1990). Percentage of population age 25 and over having: no formal schooling 82.6%; some primary education 8.2%; completed primary 5.0%; some secondary 4.2%. **Literacy** (1995 est.): total population age 15 and over literate 72.2%; males literate 81.0%; females literate 62.7%. **Health:** physicians (1998) 342 (1 per 13,708 persons); hospital beds (1989) 15,335 (1 per 234 persons); infant mortality rate per 1,000 live births (2000) 59.9. **Food** (1999): daily per capita caloric intake 2,175 (vegetable products 90%, animal products 10%); 95% of FAO recommended minimum.

## Military

**Total active duty personnel** (2001): 4,400 (army 86.4%, navy 9.1%, air force 4.5%). **Military expenditure as percentage of GNP** (1999): 1.1% (world 2.4%); per capita expenditure $7.

---

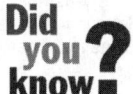

**Did you know?** Papua New Guinea's 96-km (60-mi) Kokoda Trail across the Owen Stanley Range to the northeast of Port Moresby was the site of an epic World War II struggle (in 1942) between invading Japanese forces and Australian troops.

---

## Background

Papua New Guinea has been inhabited since prehistoric times. The Portuguese sighted the coast in 1512, and in 1545 the Spanish claimed the island. The first colony was founded in 1793 by the British. In 1828 the Dutch claimed the western half as part of the Dutch East Indies. In 1884 Britain annexed the southeastern part and Germany took over the northeastern sector. The British part became the Territory of Papua in 1906 and passed to Australia, which also governed the German sector after World War I. After World War II, Australia governed both sectors as the Territory of Papua and New Guinea. Dutch New Guinea was annexed to Indonesia in 1969. Papua New Guinea achieved independence in 1975 and joined the British Commonwealth. It moved to resolve its war with Bougainville independence fighters in 1997. The decade-long war on the island of Bougainville ended when final terms for peace were negotiated on 1 Jun 2001.

## Recent Developments

Sir Michael Somare was elected—88 votes to 0—prime minister of Papua New Guinea on 5 Aug 2002. It was his third term as prime minister, and he had also served as chief minister (1972–75) prior to independence. Upon taking office, Somare was urged to act quickly to deal with the sharply declining economy.

**Internet resources:** <www.pngembassy.org>

# Paraguay

**Official name:** República del Paraguay (Spanish); Tetä Paraguáype (Guaraní) (Republic of Paraguay). **Form of government:** multiparty republic with two legislative houses (Senate [46, including 1 nonelective seat]; Chamber of Deputies [80]). **Head of state and government:** President Nicanor Duarte Frutos (from 15 Aug 2003). **Capital:** Asunción. **Official languages:** Spanish; Guaraní. **Official religion:** none, although Roman Catholicism enjoys special recognition in the 1992 constitution. **Monetary unit:** 1 Paraguayan Guaraní (G) = 100 céntimos; valuation (7 Jul 2003) $1 = G 6,200.

## Demography

**Area:** 157,048 sq mi, 406,752 sq km. **Population** (2002): 5,774,000. **Density** (2002): persons per sq mi 36.8, persons per sq km 14.2. **Urban** (2000): 54.5%. **Sex distribution** (2000): male 50.43%; female 49.57%. **Age breakdown** (1999): under 15, 39.3%; 15–29, 26.2%; 30–44, 17.9%; 45–59, 9.9%; 60–74, 5.1%; 75 and over, 1.6%. **Ethnic composition** (2000): mixed (white/Amerindian) 85.6%; white 9.3%, of which German 4.4%, Latin American 3.4%; Amerindian 1.8%; black 1.0%; other 2.3%. **Religious affiliation** (1995): Roman Catholic 88.5%; Protestant 5.0%; other 6.5%. **Major cities** (1992): Asunción 500,938 (urban agglomeration [2001] 1,302,000; includes San Lorenzo 133,395; Lambaré 99,572; Fernando de la Mora 95,072). **Location:** central South America, bordering Brazil, Argentina, and Bolivia.

## Vital statistics

**Birth rate** per 1,000 population (2000): 31.3 (world avg. 22.5). **Death rate** per 1,000 population (2000): 4.8 (world avg. 9.0). **Natural increase rate** per 1,000 population (2000): 26.5 (world avg. 13.5). **Total fertility rate** (avg. births per childbearing woman; 2000): 4.2. **Marriage rate** per 1,000 population (1999): 3.6. **Life expectancy** at birth (2000): male 71.2 years; female 76.3 years.

## National economy

**Budget** (1999). *Revenue:* G4,011,200,000,000 (tax revenue 69.4%, of which taxes on goods and services

39.0%, income tax 13.4%, customs duties 10.3%, social security 6.7%; nontax revenue including grants 30.6%). *Expenditures:* G4,605,800,000,000 (current expenditure 75.6%; capital expenditure 24.4%). **Public debt** (external, outstanding; 2000): $2,061,000,-000. **Population economically active** (1996): total 1,747,488; activity rate 35.3% (participation rates [1992]: ages 12 and over, 51.0%; female 23.8%; unemployed [1998] 7.2%). **Production** (metric tons except as noted). *Agriculture, forestry, fishing* (1999): cassava 3,500,000, soybeans 3,303,500, sugarcane 2,872,270; livestock (number of live animals) 9,863,000 cattle, 2,500,000 pigs, 15,000,000 chickens; roundwood (1998) 8,097,000 cu m; fish catch (1998) 26,000. *Mining and quarrying* (1997): limestone 600,000; kaolin 66,700; gypsum 4,500. *Manufacturing* (value added in constant prices of 1982, G'000,000; 1998): food products 59,100; wood products and furniture 23,500; handicrafts 10,300. *Energy production (consumption):* electricity (kW-hr; 2000) 51,500,000,000 (2,000,000,000); crude petroleum (barrels; 1997) none (1,158,000); petroleum products (metric tons; 1997) 149,000 (1,147,000). **Gross national product** (2000): $7,933,000,000 ($1,440 per capita). **Household income and expenditure.** Average household size (2000) 4.4; sources of income (1989): wages and salaries 33.9%, transfer payments 2.5%. **Tourism** (2000): receipts $101,-000,000; expenditures $97,000,000.

## Foreign trade

**Imports** (1998-f.o.b.): $2,470,800,000 (machinery and transport equipment 30.6%, of which transport equipment 8.1%; food, beverages, and tobacco 23.7%; fuels and lubricants 7.6%; chemicals and pharmaceuticals 5.4%). *Major import sources:* Brazil 32.2%; US 20.2%; Argentina 15.6%; Hong Kong 6.9%; Japan 2.7%. **Exports** (1998): $1,014,100,000 (soybean flour 43.4%; cotton fibers 9.1%; vegetable oil 7.5%, of which soybean oil 6.0%; timber 6.9%; processed meats 6.7%; hides and skins 3.8%). *Major export destinations:* Brazil 28.1%; Argentina 25.7%; The Netherlands 15.3%; Japan 4.8%; Chile 4.7%.

## Transport and communications

**Transport.** *Railroads* (1998): route length 441 km; passenger-km 3,000,000; metric ton-km cargo 5,500,000. *Roads* (1999): total length 29,500 km (paved 51%). *Vehicles* (2002): passenger cars 274,186; trucks 189,115. *Air transport* (2000): passenger-km 270,503,000; metric ton-km cargo 24,346,000; airports (1998) 5. **Communications,** in total units (units per 1,000 persons). Daily newspaper circulation (1996): 213,000 (43); radio receivers (1997): 925,000 (182); television receivers (1999): 1,100,000 (205); telephone main lines (2001): 288,800 (51); cellular telephone subscribers (2001): 1,150,000 (204); personal computers (2001): 60,000 (11); Internet users (2001): 80,000 (14.2).

## Education and health

**Educational attainment** (1999). Percentage of population age 15 and over having: no formal schooling 5.5%; primary education 52.8%; secondary 34.0%; higher 7.6%; not stated 0.1%. **Literacy** (1999): total

population age 15 and over literate 92.3%; males literate 94.1%; female literate 90.6%. **Health** (1995): physicians 3,730 (1 per 1,294 persons); hospital beds 6,759 (1 per 714 persons); infant mortality rate per 1,000 live births (2000) 30.8. **Food** (2000): daily per capita caloric intake 2,533 (vegetable products 77%, animal products 23%); 110% of FAO recommended minimum.

## Military

**Total active duty personnel** (2001): 18,600 (army 80.1%, navy 10.8%, air force 9.1%). **Military expenditure as percentage of GNP** (1999): 1.1% (world 2.4%); per capita expenditure $15.

## Background

Seminomadic tribes speaking Guaraní were in Paraguay long before it was settled by Spain in the 16th and 17th centuries. Paraguay was part of the viceroyalty of Río de la Plata until it became independent in 1811. It suffered from dictatorial governments in the 19th century and from the 1865 war with Brazil, Argentina, and Uruguay. The Chaco War with Bolivia over disputed territory was settled primarily in Paraguay's favor by the peace treaty of 1938. Military governments, including that of Alfredo Stroessner, predominated in the mid-20th century until the election of a civilian president, Juan Carlos Wasmosy, in 1993. Paraguay suffered a financial crisis in the late 1990s, and democratic government was in jeopardy.

## Recent Developments

The year 2002 in Paraguay ended much where it had begun, mired in a cycle of economic recession, social protest, corruption, and political paralysis. Transparency International, a global organization that monitors corruption, rated Paraguay as the nation perceived to be the most corrupt in Latin America and the third worst in the world. Nearly bankrupt, the government began the year hoping to raise $400 million from the privatization of state enterprises, specifically the state water and sanitation company and COPACO, the public telecommunications firm. In March the government fell behind on debt repayments and found itself unable to pay public-sector wages. Lino Oviedo, a former general living in asylum in Brazil who was suspected of having masterminded an attempted coup in 1996 and of having arranged the murder of Vice Pres. Luis María Argaña in 1999, formed an alliance with Vice Pres. Julio César Franco known as the National Patriotic Front that sought to impeach the president. In July Pres. Luis González decreed a state of emergency after nationwide protests against his economic policies led to riots and violent confrontations with police. Elections in April 2003 returned the ruling Colorado Party to power; Nicanor Duarte Frutos became president in August.

**Internet resources:** <www.onparaguay.com>

# Peru

**Official name:** República del Perú (Spanish) (Republic of Peru). **Form of government:** unitary multiparty re-

*1 metric ton = about 1.1 short tons;    1 kilometer = 0.6 mi (statute);    1 metric ton-km cargo = about 0.68 short ton-mi cargo;    c.i.f.: cost, insurance, and freight;    f.o.b.: free on board*

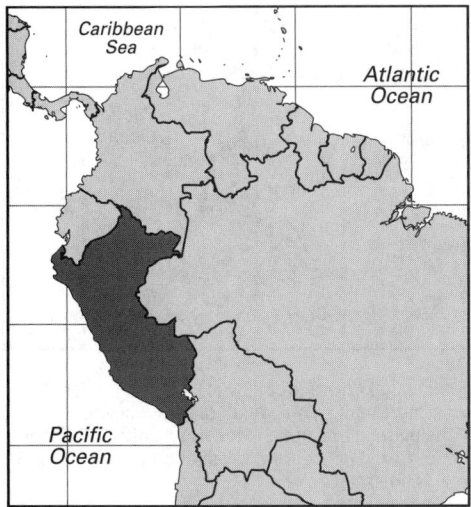

public with one legislative house (Congress [120]). **Head of state and government:** President Alejandro Toledo (from 2001). **Capital:** Lima. **Official languages:** Spanish; Quechua; Aymara. **Official religion:** Roman Catholicism. **Monetary unit:** 1 nuevo sol (S/.) = 100 céntimos; valuation (7 Jul 2003) $1 = S/. 3.47.

## Demography

**Area:** 496,225 sq mi, 1,285,216 sq km. **Population** (2002): 26,749,000. **Density** (2002): persons per sq mi 53.9, persons per sq km 20.8. **Urban** (2000): 72.3%. **Sex distribution** (2000): male 49.59%; female 50.41%. **Age breakdown** (2000): under 15, 33.4%; 15–29, 29.1%; 30–44, 19.3%; 45–59, 10.9%; 60–74, 5.7%; 75 and over, 1.6%. **Ethnic composition** (2000): Quechua 47.0%; mestizo 31.9%; white 12.0%; Aymara 5.4%; Japanese 0.5%; other 3.2%. **Religious affiliation** (1995): Roman Catholic 88.8%; Protestant 6.7%; other Christian 1.5%; other 3.0%. **Major cities** (1998 est.): metropolitan Lima 7,060,600; Arequipa 710,103; Trujillo 603,657; Chiclayo 469,200; Iquitos 334,013. **Location:** western South America, bordering Ecuador, Colombia, Brazil, Bolivia, Chile, and the South Pacific Ocean.

## Vital statistics

**Birth rate** per 1,000 population (2002): 23.4 (world avg. 21.2). **Death rate** per 1,000 population (2002): 5.7 (world avg. 8.9). **Natural increase rate** per 1,000 population (2002): 17.7 (world avg. 12.3). **Total fertility rate** (avg. births per childbearing woman; 2002): 2.9. **Life expectancy** at birth (2002): male 68.2 years; female 73.1 years.

## National economy

**Budget** (2000). *Revenue*: S/. 27,978,000,000 (taxes on goods and services 44.7%, income taxes 18.3%, nontax revenue 16.5%, import duties 10.3%, payroll tax 3.7%). *Expenditures*: S/. 32,900,000,000 (current expenditure 71.9%, capital expenditure 15.5%, interest payments 12.6%). **Public debt** (external, outstanding; 2000): $19,205,000,000. **Tourism** (2000): receipts $911,000,000; expenditures $531,000,000. **Production** (metric tons except as noted). *Agriculture, forestry, fishing* (1999): sugarcane 6,900,-

000, potatoes 3,050,000, rice 1,947,000; livestock (number of live animals) 13,700,000 sheep, 4,898,000 cattle, 79,917,000 chickens; roundwood (1998) 9,157,000 cu m; fish catch (1998) 4,338,437. *Mining and quarrying* (2001): iron ore 3,892,000; zinc (metal) 201,498; copper (metal) 471,875. *Manufacturing* (value in S/. '000,000; 1996): processed foods 275.1; base metal products 188.6; textiles and leather products 129.5. *Energy production (consumption)*: electricity (kW-hr; 1997) 17,951,000,000 (17,953000,000); coal (metric tons; 1997) 22,000 (310,000); crude petroleum (barrels; 1997) 44,000,000 (57,000,000); petroleum products (metric tons; 1997) 6,896,000 (7,866,-000); natural gas (cu m; 1997) 142,000,000 (142,000,000). **Population economically active** (1998): total 7,407,280; activity rate of total population 45.7% (participation rates: over age 15, 66.9%; female 43.8%; unemployed 7.7%). **Gross national product** (at current market prices; 2000): $53,392,-000,000 ($2,080 per capita). **Household income and expenditure.** Average household size (1993) 5.1; income per household (1988) $2,173; sources of income (1991): business income 67.1%, wages 23.3%, transfers 7.6%, other 2.0%; expenditure (1990): food 29.4%, recreation and education 13.2%, household durables 10.1%, clothing and footwear 8.5%, transportation 7.5%, health 7.0%. **Land use** (1998): forest and other 75.7%; pasture 21.1%; agricultural 3.2%.

## Foreign trade

**Imports** (1998-f.o.b. in balance of trade): $8,200,000,000 (raw and intermediate materials 41.3%, machinery 24.9%, consumer goods 23.0%, transport equipment 6.7%). Major import sources: US 32.5%; Colombia 7.4%; Germany 5.6%; Venezuela 4.3%. **Exports** (1998—f.o.b. in balance of trade): $5,722,900,000 (gold 16.2%, copper and copper products 13.6%, zinc products 7.8%, fish meal fodder 6.8%, coffee 5.0%, petroleum and derivatives 3.9%, lead products 3.7%, silver 2.3%, tin 2.1%). Major export destinations: US 32.3%; Japan 8.7%; UK 4.8%; Switzerland 4.2%; Spain 4.1%; Venezuela 3.9%; South Korea 3.4%.

## Transport and communications

**Transport.** *Railroads* (2000): route length 1,608 km; (1996) passenger-km 171,091,000; (1996) metric ton-km cargo 850,329,000. *Roads* (1999): total length 78,128 km (paved 13%). *Vehicles* (1999): passenger cars 684,533; trucks and buses 403,652. *Air transport* (1998): passenger-km 3,014,000,000; metric ton-km cargo 286,000,000; airports (1996) 27. **Communications,** in total units (units per 1,000 persons). Daily newspaper circulation (1996): 2,000,000 (84); radio receivers (1997): 6,650,000 (273); television receivers (1999): 3,700,000 (147); telephone main lines (2001): 2,022,300 (78); cellular telephone subscribers (2001): 1,545,000 (59); personal computers (2001): 1,250,000 (48); Internet users (2001): 3,000,000 (115).

## Education and health

**Educational attainment** (1993). Percentage of population age 15 and over having: no formal schooling 12.3%; less than primary education 0.3%; primary 31.5%; secondary 35.5%; higher 20.4%. **Literacy** (1995): total population age 15 and over literate

88.0%; males 93.5%; females 82.7%. **Health**: physicians (1996) 24,708 (1 per 969 persons); hospital beds (1994) 42,979 (1 per 538 persons); infant mortality rate per 1,000 live births (2002) 38.2. **Food** (2000): daily per capita caloric intake 2,624 (vegetable products 87%, animal products 13%); 112% of FAO recommended minimum.

## Military

**Total active duty personnel** (2001): 100,000 (army 60.0%, navy 25.0%, air force 15.0%). **Military expenditure as percentage of GNP** (1999): 2.4% (world 2.4%); per capita expenditure $45.

## Background

Peru was the center of the Inca empire, which was established about 1230 with its capital at Cuzco. In 1533 it was conquered by Francisco Pizarro, and it was dominated by Spain for almost 300 years as the viceroyalty of Peru. It declared its independence in 1821, and freedom was achieved in 1824. Peru was defeated in the War of the Pacific with Chile (1879–83). A boundary dispute with Ecuador erupted into war in 1941 and gave Peru control over a larger part of the Amazon basin; further disputes ensued until the border was demarcated again in 1998. The government was overthrown by a military junta in 1968, and civilian rule was restored in 1980. The government of Alberto Fujimori dissolved the legislature in 1992 and promulgated a new constitution the following year. It later successfully combated the Shining Path and Tupac Amarú rebel movements. Fujimori won a second term in 1995.

## Recent Developments

Peru went through 2002 with its rather fragile democracy intact under Pres. Alejandro Toledo, but the year had more than its share of disruptions and worries. Toledo's election promise that he would create a million new jobs had not been kept, and his public approval ratings fell steadily after he took office, hovering around an abysmal 20% for much of 2002. Nationwide regional and municipal elections were held on 17 November. The opposition American Popular Revolutionary Alliance won 12 regional elections and finished far ahead of Toledo's party and all others. In addition, Toledo had been pursued by a scandal that he was the father of an illegitimate 14-year-old girl; after denying the allegation for years he admitted in October that he was indeed the girl's father and reportedly agreed to a financial settlement in the case. Toledo also was accused of leading a lavish personal lifestyle, and a series of intemperate remarks by his Belgian-born wife added fuel to the fire.

**Internet resources:** <www.peru.org.pe>

# Philippines

**Official name:** Republika ng Pilipinas (Pilipino); Republic of the Philippines (English). **Form of government:** unitary republic with two legislative houses (Senate [24]; House of Representatives [260]). **Chief of state and head of government:** President Gloria

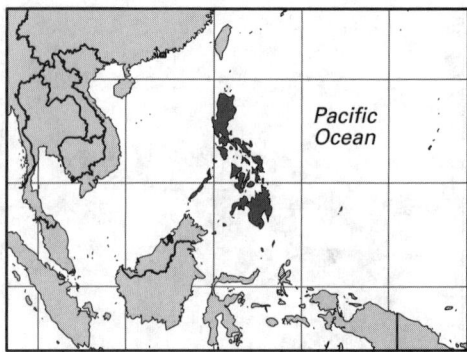

Macapagal Arroyo (from 2001). **Capital** (region): Quezon City/Manila. **Official languages:** Pilipino; English. **Official religion:** none. **Monetary unit:** 1 Philippine peso (P) = 100 centavos; valuation (7 Jul 2003) $1 = P 53.41.

## Demography

**Area:** 115,860 sq mi, 300,076 sq km. **Population** (2002): 79,882,000. **Density** (2002): persons per sq mi 689.5, persons per sq km 266.2. **Urban** (2002): 60.0%. **Sex distribution** (2000): male 50.37%; female 49.63%. **Age breakdown** (2000): under 15, 36.2%; 15–29, 28.1%; 30–44, 19.0%; 45–59, 10.7%; 60–74, 4.8%; 75 and over, 1.2%. **Ethnolinguistic composition** (by mother tongue of households; 1995): Pilipino (Tagalog) 29.3%; Cebuano 23.3%; Ilocano 9.3%; Hiligaynon Ilongo 9.1%; Bicol 5.7%; Waray 3.8%; Pampango 3.0%; Pangasinan 1.8%; other 14.7%. **Religious affiliation** (1996): Roman Catholic 82.9%; Protestant 5.4%; Muslim 4.6%; Aglipayan (Philippine Independent Church) 2.6%; other 4.5%. **Major cities** (2000): Quezon City 2,173,831; Manila 1,581,082; Caloocan 1,177,604; Davao 1,147,116; Cebu 718,821. **Location:** southeastern Asia, archipelago between the Philippine Sea and the South China Sea, east of Vietnam.

## Vital statistics

**Birth rate** per 1,000 population (2002): 26.2 (world avg. 21.2); (1982) legitimate 93.9%; illegitimate 6.1%. **Death rate** per 1,000 population (2002): 5.2 (world avg. 8.9). **Natural increase rate** per 1,000 population (2002): 21.0 (world avg. 12.3). **Total fertility rate** (avg. births per childbearing woman; 2002): 3.2. **Life expectancy** at birth (2002): male 68.0 years; female 72.0 years.

## National economy

**Budget** (2000). *Revenue*: P 514,762,000,000 (income taxes 39.6%, taxes on goods and services 27.1%, international duties 18.5%, nontax revenues 10.6%). *Expenditures*: P 649,484,000,000 (debt service 20.0%, education 18.7%, transportation and communications 9.5%, public order and safety 7.0%, general administration 5.4%, defense 5.0%). **Production** (metric tons except as noted). *Agriculture, forestry, fishing* (2000): sugarcane 33,732,000, rice 12,415,000, coconuts 5,761,000; livestock (number of live animals) 10,398,000 pigs, 6,780,000 goats,

*1 metric ton = about 1.1 short tons;     1 kilometer = 0.6 mi (statute);     1 metric ton-km cargo = about 0.68 short ton-mi cargo;     c.i.f.: cost, insurance, and freight;     f.o.b.: free on board*

142,000,000 chickens; roundwood (1999) 43,399,-000 cu m; fish catch (1998) 1,827,971. *Mining and quarrying* (1999): nickel ore 436,970; copper concentrate 98,857; chrome concentrate 17,562. *Manufacturing* (gross value added in ₱ '000,000; 1998): food products 246,300; electrical machinery 53,000; chemicals 49,100. *Energy production (consumption)*: electricity (kW-hr; 2001) 46,340,000,000 ([1997] 39,816,000,000); hard coal (metric tons; 2001) 1,235,000 ([1997] 5,182,000); crude petroleum (barrels; 1997) 300,000 (127,000,000); petroleum products (metric tons; 1997) 16,281,000 (17,234,-000). **Household income and expenditure** (2000). Average household size 5.0; income per family P144,506 ($3,150); sources of income (1997): wages 45.6%, entrepreneurial income 26.2%, rent 10.3%, transfers 6.8%, other 11.1%; expenditure: food, beverage, and tobacco 45.0%, housing 15.1%, transportation 6.8%, fuel and power 6.2%, education 4.2%, personal care 3.6%. **Gross national product** (at current market prices; 2000): $78,778,000,000 ($1,040 per capita). **Public debt** (external, outstanding; 2000): $33,429,000,000. **Population economically active** (2000): total 31,848,000; activity rate 41.5% (participation rates: ages 15–64, 65.0%; female [1995] 37.4%; unemployed [July 2002] 11.2%). **Tourism** (2000): receipts $2,134,000,000; expenditures $1,005,000,000.

## Foreign trade

**Imports** (1999-f.o.b. in balance of trade and c.i.f. for commodities and trading partners): $30,723,340,-000 (chemicals 8.1%, mineral fuels and lubricants 7.9%, power generating and specialized machinery 7.8%, telecommunications equipment and electrical machinery 7.6%, base metals 4.3%). *Major import sources:* US 20.7%; Japan 19.9%; South Korea 8.9%; Singapore 5.7%; Taiwan 5.3%; Hong Kong 4.0%. **Exports** (1999): $35,036,560,000 (electronics 56.2%, garments 6.5%, ignition wiring sets 1.5%, woodcraft and furniture 1.4%, coconut oil 1.0%, bananas 0.7%). *Major export destinations:* US 29.6%; Japan 13.3%; Taiwan 8.5%; The Netherlands 8.2%; Singapore 7.0%; Hong Kong 5.6%.

## Transport and communications

**Transport.** *Railroads* (2000): route length 897 km; passenger-km 12,000,000; metric ton-km cargo 660,000,000. *Roads* (1998): total length 199,950 km (paved 39%). *Vehicles* (2000): passenger cars 763,834; trucks and buses 282,231. *Air transport* (1999; Philippines Airlines only): passenger-km 10,292,338,000; metric ton-km cargo 240,918,000; airports (1996) with scheduled flights 21. **Communications**, in total units (units per 1,000 persons). Daily newspaper circulation (1996): 5,700,000 (82); radio receivers (1997): 11,500,000 (161); television receivers (1999): 8,200,000 (110); telephone main lines (2001): 3,100,000 (40); cellular telephone subscribers (2001): 10,568,000 (137); personal computers (2001): 1,700,000 (22); Internet users (2001): 2,000,000 (26).

## Education and health

**Education attainment** (1995). Percentage of population age 15 and over having: no schooling 3.7%; elementary education 35.8%; secondary 38.4%; post-secondary 21.9%; not stated 0.2%. **Literacy** (1995):

total population age 15 and over literate 94.6%; males literate 95.0%; females literate 94.3%. **Health:** physicians (1993) 78,445 (1 per 849 persons); hospital beds (2000) 81,016 (1 per 948 persons); infant mortality rate per 1,000 live births (2002) 30.0. **Food** (2000): daily per capita caloric intake 2,379 (vegetable products 85%, animal products 15%); 105% of FAO recommended minimum.

## Military

**Total active duty personnel** (2001): 107,000 (army 62.6%, navy 22.4%, air force 15.0%). **Military expenditure as percentage of GNP** (1999): 1.4% (world 2.4%); per capita expenditure $14.

## Background

In ancient times, the inhabitants of the Philippines were a diverse agglomeration of peoples who arrived in various waves of immigrants from the Asian mainland. Ferdinand Magellan arrived in 1521. The islands were colonized by the Spanish, who retained control until the islands were ceded to the US in 1898 following the Spanish-American War. The Commonwealth of the Philippines was established in 1935 to prepare the country for political and economic independence, which was delayed by World War II and the Japanese invasion. The islands were liberated by US forces during 1944–45, and the Republic of the Philippines was proclaimed in 1946, with a government patterned on that of the US. In 1965 Ferdinand Marcos was elected president. He declared martial law in 1972, which lasted until 1981. After 20 years of dictatorial rule, he was driven from power in 1986. Corazon Aquino became president and instituted a period of democratic rule that continued with the 1992 election of Fidel Ramos. Through the 1990s the government tried to come to terms with independence fighters in the southern islands.

## Recent Developments

Kidnappings and bombings plagued the Philippines during much of 2002. Pres. Gloria Macapagal Arroyo appealed for "grassroots vigilance" and improved police and military work. Most trouble occurred in the southern islands, where the Abu Sayyaf group claimed to be fighting for a separate Muslim state. Intelligence reports linked the guerrilla organization to the al-Qaeda terrorist network. Abu Sayyaf had kidnapped three Americans in May 2001 and beheaded one of them. After its army failed to catch the kidnappers, the Philippines requested American military advice, training, and equipment; some 4,000 personnel began arriving in January 2002 with orders to fight only if attacked. Most American military advisers left in July, but the US offered a $5 million reward for the capture of five other Abu Sayyaf leaders. Bombings occurred in several cities of predominately Christian inhabitants in mostly Muslim southern islands. Two bombings on 21 April killed 15 and wounded 45 in General Santos City. Five bombings within a few weeks in September–October killed 12 people, including an American soldier in Zamboanga. A bomb exploded at the airport in the southern city of Davao in March 2003, killing 21 people.

The trial on corruption charges of former president Joseph Estrada dragged inconclusively throughout

2002. The government's budget deficit ballooned as projects such as new irrigation systems were hurried in expectation of drought. The economy expanded, however, partly because of increased exports of electronics and greater demand for domestic vehicles.

**Internet resources:** <www.gov.ph>

# Poland

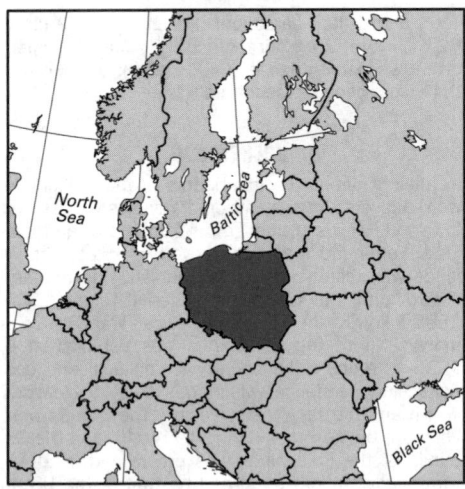

**Official name:** Rzeczpospolita Polska (Republic of Poland). **Form of government:** unitary multiparty republic with two legislative houses (Senate [100]; Diet [460]). **Chief of state:** President Aleksander Kwasniewski (from 1995). **Head of government:** Prime Minister Leszek Miller (from 2001). **Capital:** Warsaw. **Official language:** Polish. **Official religion:** none (Roman Catholicism has special recognition per 1997 concordat with the Holy See). **Monetary unit:** 1 zloty (Zl; redenominated at a rate of 10,000 old zloty to 1 new zloty in 1995) = 100 groszy; valuation (7 Jul 2003) $1 = Zl 3.87.

## Demography

**Area:** 120,728 sq mi, 312,685 sq km. **Population** (2002): 38,644,000. **Density** (2002): persons per sq mi 319.9, persons per sq km 123.6. **Urban** (2000): 61.8%. **Sex distribution** (2000): male 48.60%; female 51.40%. **Age breakdown** (2000): under 15, 19.1%; 15–29, 24.3%; 30–44, 21.3%; 45–59, 18.7%; 60–74, 12.2%; 75 and over, 4.4%. **Ethnolinguistic composition** (1997): Polish 94.2%; Ukrainian 3.9%; German 1.3%; Belarusian 0.6%. **Religious affiliation** (1995): Roman Catholic 90.7%; Ukrainian Catholic 1.4%; Polish Orthodox 1.4%; Protestant 0.5%; Jehovah's Witness 0.5%; other (mostly nonreligious) 5.5%. **Major cities** (2001): Warsaw 1,610,471; Lodz 793,217; Krakow 741,510; Wroclaw 633,857; Poznan 574,896. **Location:** central Europe, bordering the Baltic Sea, Russia (exclave of Kaliningrad), Lithuania, Belarus, Ukraine, Slovakia, Czech Republic, and Germany.

## Vital statistics

**Birth rate** per 1,000 population (2001): 9.5 (world avg. 21.2); (2000) legitimate 87.9%; illegitimate 12.1%. **Death rate** per 1,000 population (2001): 9.4 (world avg. 8.9). **Natural increase rate** per 1,000 population (2001): 0.1 (world avg. 12.3). **Total fertility rate** (avg. births per childbearing woman; 2000): 1.3. **Marriage rate** per 1,000 population (2000): 5.5. **Divorce rate** per 1,000 population (2000): 1.1. **Life expectancy** at birth (2000): male 69.7 years; female 78.0 years.

## National economy

**Budget** (1998). *Revenue:* Zl 126,560,000,000 (income tax 39.1%, value-added tax 33.9%, excise tax 16.6%). *Expenditures:* Zl 139,752,000,000 (social security 18.0%, health 15.0%, education 8.1%, welfare 6.6%, defense 6.0%). **Gross national product** (2000): $161,832,000,000 ($4,190 per capita). **Production** (metric tons except as noted). *Agriculture, forestry, fishing* (1999): (gross value of production in Zl '000,000) potatoes 4,066, wheat 3,747, fruit 3,578; livestock (number of live animals) 18,538,000 pigs, 6,555,000 cattle; roundwood (1999) 24,300,000 cu m; fish catch (2000) 218,354. *Mining and quarrying* (1998): sulfur 1,672,000; copper ore (metal content) 432,243; silver (recoverable metal content) 1,108. *Manufacturing* (value added in Zl '000,000; 1999): food products 13,764; beverages 13,582; transport equipment 10,596. *Energy production (consumption):* electricity ('000,000 kW-hr; 2001) 142,584 ([1997] 140,576); hard coal ('000 metric tons; 2001) 103,896 ([1997] 104,337); lignite ('000 metric tons; 2001) 59,544 ([1997] 63,143); crude petroleum (barrels; 1997) 2,144,000 (110,424,000); petroleum products (metric tons; 1997) 14,153,000 (17,565,000); natural gas (cu m; 2001) 5,178,000,000 ([1997] 11,227,000,000). **Public debt** (external, outstanding; 2000): $30,785,000,000. **Population economically active** (1998): total 17,162,000; activity rate of total population 44.4% (participation rates: 15–64, 66.1%; female 45.7%; unemployed [May 2001–April 2002] 16.7%). **Household income and expenditure.** Average household size (2000) 2.9; average annual income (1995) Zl 8,431 ($2,990); sources of income (1996): wages 43.9%, transfers 25.2%, self-employment 21.9%; expenditure (1999): food, beverages, and tobacco 32.3%, housing and energy 23.4%, transportation and communications 14.3%, recreation 6.6%. **Tourism** (2000): receipts $6,100,000,000; expenditures $3,600,000,000. **Land use** (1994): forest 28.8%; meadow 13.3%; agricultural and under permanent cultivation 47.0%; other 10.9%.

## Foreign trade

**Imports** (1999-c.i.f.): Zl 182,362,000,000 (machinery and transport equipment 38.2%, chemicals and chemical products 14.3%, mineral fuels and lubricants 7.2%, food 5.5%). *Major import sources:* Germany 25.2%; Italy 9.4%; France 6.8%; Russia 5.9%; UK 4.6%. **Exports** (1999-f.o.b.): Zl 108,706,000,000 (machinery and transport equipment 30.3%, food 8.5%, chemicals and chemical products 6.2%, mineral fuels and lubricants 5.0%). *Major export destina-*

*tions:* Germany 36.1%; Italy 6.5%; The Netherlands 5.3%; France 4.8%; UK 4.0%.

## Transport and communications

**Transport.** *Railroads* (2000): length 22,981 km; (1999) passenger-km 26,198,000,000; (1999) metric ton-km cargo 55,471,000,000. *Roads* (1997): total length 381,046 km (paved 66%). *Vehicles* (2000): passenger cars 9,283,000; trucks and buses 1,762,000. *Air transport* (2001; LOT only): passenger-km 6,052,000,000; metric ton-km cargo 69,039,000; airports (1997) 8. **Communications,** in total units (units per 1,000 persons). Daily newspaper circulation (1996): 4,351,000 (113); radio receivers (1997): 20,200,000 (523); television receivers (1999): 15,000,000 (388); telephone main lines (2001): 11,400,000 (295); cellular telephone subscribers (2001): 10,050,000 (260); personal computers (2001): 3,300,000 (85); Internet users (2001): 3,800,000 (98).

## Education and health

**Educational attainment** (1995). Percentage of population age 15 and over having: no formal schooling/incomplete primary education 6.3%; primary 33.7%; secondary/vocational 53.2%; higher 6.8%. **Literacy** (2000): 99.8%. **Health** (1999): physicians 90,086 (1 per 429 persons); hospital beds (2000) 239,341 (1 per 161 persons); infant mortality rate per 1,000 live births (2001) 7.7. **Food** (1999): daily per capita caloric intake 3,368 (vegetable products 73%, animal products 27%); 129% of FAO recommended minimum.

## Military

**Total active duty personnel** (2001): 206,045 (army 58.3%, navy 8.1%, air force 21.2%, paramilitary 12.4%). **Military expenditure as percentage of GNP** (1999): 2.1% (world 2.4%); per capita expenditure $173.

---

**Did you know?**
Jan Heweliusz (1611–1687) was a Polish astronomer who charted the first accurate maps of the lunar surface. A crater on the moon was named after him.

---

## Background

Established as a kingdom in 922 under Mieszko I, Poland was united with Lithuania in 1386 under the Jagiellon Dynasty (1386–1572) to become the dominant power in east-central Europe. In 1466 it wrested western and eastern Prussia from the Teutonic Order, and its lands eventually stretched to the Black Sea. Wars with Sweden and Russia in the late 17th century led to the loss of considerable territory. In 1697 the electors of Saxony became kings of Poland, virtually ending Polish independence. In the late 18th century Poland was divided among Prussia, Russia, and Austria and ceased to exist. After 1815 the former Polish lands came under Russian domination, and from 1863 Poland was a Russian province. After World War I an independent Poland was established by the Allies. The invasion of Poland in 1939 by the USSR and Germany precipitated World War II, during which the Nazis sought to purge its culture and its

large Jewish population. Reoccupied by Soviet forces in 1945, it was controlled by a Soviet-dominated government from 1947. In the 1980s the Solidarity labor movement achieved major political reforms, and free elections were held in 1989. An economic austerity program instituted in 1990 sped the transition to a market economy.

## Recent Developments

Despite Prime Minister Leszek Miller's pledge of continuity with the policies of the previous Polish government, the first months of 2002 saw a series of dismissals followed by often controversial appointments to midlevel public service and administrative positions. The turnover was described as necessary to bring in more competent staff. Opinion surveys showed that the level of public frustration was growing. Perhaps this was not surprising, considering that the unemployment rate—which topped 17%—was the highest in more than a decade.

In mid-August 2002 Pope John Paul II made what seemed likely to be his farewell visit to his homeland. The pontiff's homecoming was also important to the government, which, determined to lead the country into the EU, recognized the influence of the Roman Catholic Church and its potential for impact upon the results of a referendum held on 8 Jun 2003. Poland, struggling to find an advantageous stance between its close relations with the US and its desire to join the EU, opted to support the policies of the Bush administration on Iraq. Poland provided some 2,200 officers and troops and assumed command of one of the three peacekeeping forces in Iraq.

**Internet resources:** <www.stat.gov.pl/english>

# Portugal

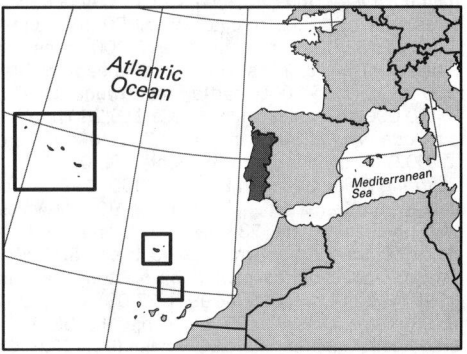

**Official name:** República Portuguesa (Portuguese Republic). **Form of government:** republic with one legislative house (Assembly of the Republic [230]). **Chief of state:** President Jorge Sampaio (from 1996). **Head of government:** Prime Minister José Manuel Durão Barroso (from 6 Apr 2002). **Capital:** Lisbon. **Official language:** Portuguese. **Official religion:** none. **Monetary unit:** 1 euro (€) = 100 cents; valuation (7 Jul 2003) $1 = €0.87; at conversion on 1 Jan 2002, € 1= 200.482 Portuguese escudos (Esc).

## Demography

**Area:** 35,662 sq mi, 92,365 sq km (includes the 169 sq mi [439 sq km] of water areas comprising the

Tagus and Sado estuaries and the Aveiro lagoon). **Population** (2002): 10,384,000. **Density** (2002): persons per sq mi 291.1, persons per sq km 112.4. **Urban** (2001): 65.8%. **Sex distribution** (2001): male 48.34%; female 51.66%. **Age breakdown** (2000): under 15, 17.1%; 15–29, 23.0%; 30–44, 21.5%; 45–59, 17.8%; 60–74, 14.5%; 75 and over, 6.1%. **Ethnic composition** (2000): Portuguese 91.9%; mixed race 1.6%; Brazilian 1.4%; Marrano 1.2%; other European 1.2%; Han Chinese 0.9%; other 1.8%. **Religious affiliation** (1995): Christian 94.8%, of which Roman Catholic 92.2%, Protestant 1.5%, other Christian (Jehovah's Witness 0.7%; Mormon 0.4%) 1.1%; Muslim 0.1%; other and nonreligious 5.1%. **Major cities** (2001): Lisbon 564,657 (urban agglomeration 3,447,173); Porto 263,131; Amadora 175,872; Braga 164,193; Coimbra 148,474. **Location:** southwestern Europe, bordering Spain and the North Atlantic Ocean.

## Vital statistics

**Birth rate** per 1,000 population (2001): 11.5 (world avg. 21.2). **Death rate** per 1,000 population (2001): 10.2 (world avg. 8.9). **Natural increase rate** per 1,000 population (2001): 1.3 (world avg. 12.3). **Total fertility rate** (avg. births per childbearing woman; 2001): 1.5. **Life expectancy** at birth (2001): male 72.4 years; females 79.7 years.

## National economy

**Budget** (1998). *Revenue:* Esc 7,633,800,000,000 (1997; social security contributions 22.5%, general sales tax 19.3%, individual income tax 14.9%, excise tax 11.6%, grants 9.2%, nontax revenue 9.1%). *Expenditures:* Esc 7,881,500,000,000 (1997; current expenditure 87.3%, development expenditure 12.7%). **Public debt** (1996): $40,504,000,000. **Production** (metric tons except as noted). *Agriculture, forestry, fishing* (2000): potatoes 1,250,000, tomatoes 1,075,000, corn (maize) 975,000; livestock (number of live animals) 5,900,000 sheep, 2,350,000 pigs, 1,250,000 cattle; roundwood (2000) 9,450,000 cu m; fish catch (1999) 215,230. *Mining and quarrying* (2000): marble 1,324,700; tin ore 1,200,000; copper (metal content) 76,200. *Manufacturing* (value added in Esc '000,000; 1998): machinery and transport equipment 605,966, of which transport equipment 231,893; petroleum refining 517,170; wearing apparel and footwear 307,275. *Energy production (consumption):* electricity (kW-hr; 1998) 33,144,000,000 ([1997] 37,086,000,000); coal (metric tons; 1997) negligible (5,758,000); crude petroleum (barrels; 1997) none (90,452,000); petroleum products (metric tons; 1997) 11,333,000 (11,100,000); natural gas (cu m; 1997) none (103,328,000). **Tourism** (2000): receipts $5,257,000,000; expenditures $2,230,000,000. **Land use** (1994): forest 35.9%; pasture 10.9%; agriculture 31.5%; other 21.7%. **Population economically active** (2001): total 5,200,600; activity rate of total population 50.1% (participation rates: ages 15–64 [1997], 68.5%; female 45.7%; unemployed 4.1%). **Gross national product** (at current market prices; 1999): $111,291,000,000 ($11,120 per capita). **Household income and expenditure.** Average household size (1999) 3.1; sources of income (1994–95): wages

and salaries 45.8%, property and entrepreneurial income 32.4%, transfer payments 21.5%; expenditure (1994–95): food 23.9%, housing 20.6%, transportation and communications 18.9%, clothing and footwear 6.3%, health 4.6%, other 25.7%.

## Foreign trade

**Imports** (1999-c.i.f.): Esc 7,519,000,000,000 (machinery and transport equipment 37.8%, of which road vehicles and parts 14.5%; basic manufactures 20.1%, of which textiles 5.8%; food products 10.4%; chemicals and chemical products 9.4%; mineral fuels 5.6%). *Major import sources* (1999): Spain 25.3%; Germany 14.7%; France 11.4%; Italy 7.7%; UK 7.7%; The Netherlands 4.8%. **Exports** (1999-f.o.b.): Esc 4,616,000,000,000 (machinery and transport equipment 34.1%, of which transport equipment 14.7%; textiles and wearing apparel 20.5%; footwear 6.5%; chemicals and chemical products 4.8%; food 3.8%; cork and wood products 3.8%). *Major export destinations* (1999): Germany 19.8%; Spain 18.1%; France 13.9%; UK 12.0%; US 5.0%; Belgium 4.7%.

## Transport and communications

**Transport.** *Railroads* (1998): route length 3,259 km; passenger-km 4,602,185; metric ton-km cargo 2,339,895,000. *Roads* (1996): total length 68,732 km (paved 88%). *Vehicles* (1998): passenger cars 3,200,000; trucks and buses 1,097,000. *Air transport* (2001): passenger-km 10,457,000,000; metric ton-km cargo 53,865,000; airports (2000) 16. **Communications,** in total units (units per 1,000 persons). Daily newspaper circulation (1996): 744,000 (74); radio receivers (1997): 3,020,000 (298); television receivers (1999): 5,600,000 (547); telephone main lines (2001): 4,369,700 (424); cellular telephone subscribers (2001): 7,977,500 (774); personal computers (2001): 1,210,000 (117); Internet users (2001): 3,600,000 (349).

## Education and health

**Educational attainment** (1991). Percentage of population age 25 and over having: no formal schooling 16.1%; some primary education 61.5%; some secondary 10.6%; postsecondary 3.5%. **Literacy** (2000): total population age 15 and over literate 92.2%; males 94.8%; females 90.0%. **Health** (1998): physicians 31,087 (1 per 321 persons); hospital beds 39,870 (1 per 250 persons); infant mortality rate per 1,000 live births (2000) 6.1. **Food** (2000): daily per capita caloric intake 3,716 (vegetable products 72%, animal products 28%); 146% of FAO recommended minimum.

## Military

**Total active duty personnel** (2001): 43,600 (army 58.3%, navy 24.8%, air force 16.9%). **Military expenditure as percentage of GNP** (1999): 2.1% (world 2.4%); per capita expenditure $240.

## Background

Celtic peoples settled the Iberian peninsula in the 1st millennium BC. They were conquered about 140 BC by the Romans, who ruled until the 5th century AD, when

---

*1 metric ton = about 1.1 short tons;    1 kilometer = 0.6 mi (statute);    1 metric ton-km cargo = about 0.68 short ton-mi cargo;    c.i.f.: cost, insurance, and freight;    f.o.b.: free on board*

the area was invaded by Germanic tribes. A Muslim invasion in 711 left only the northern part of Portugal in Christian hands. In 1139 it became the kingdom of Portugal and expanded as it reconquered the Muslim-held sectors. The boundaries of modern continental Portugal were completed in 1270 under King Afonso III. In the 15th and 16th centuries the monarchy encouraged exploration that took Portuguese navigators to Africa, India, Indonesia, China, the Middle East, and South America, where colonies were established. António de Oliveira Salazar ruled Portugal as a dictator in the mid-20th century; he died in office in 1970, and his successor was ousted in a coup in 1974. A new constitution was adopted in 1976 (revised 1982), and civilian rule resumed. Portugal was a charter member of NATO and is a member of the European Union.

## Recent Developments

Economic stagnation, political turmoil, an embarrassing reprimand from the European Union, and a feeble showing at the association football (soccer) World Cup all brought clouds of pessimism to Portugal and a sense that after more than a decade of robust growth and modernization, the country had lost its way. In December 2001 the Socialist-led government, headed by Prime Minister António Guterres, ran into trouble after losing ground in key municipal elections. Two major cities—Lisbon and Oporto—saw Socialist mayors ousted in favor of candidates from the Social Democratic Party (PSD). The political shift to the right, as well as slow economic growth, forced Guterres to call early elections. In the March 2002 vote the Socialists lost to the right-leaning PSD, led by José Manuel Durão Barroso, who fell short of an absolute majority in the parliament but was able to form a coalition government with the more conservative Partido Popular. A midyear audit of the public finances revealed that the combination of a sharp downturn and spending overruns by the previous government reversed seven straight years of deficit reduction and left the gap at a whopping 4.1% of GDP in 2001. That figure breached the EU's limit of 3%, which forced the EU to reprimand Portugal and initiate its excessive-deficit procedure, which could eventually lead to a fine.

Internet resources: <www.portugal.org>

# Puerto Rico

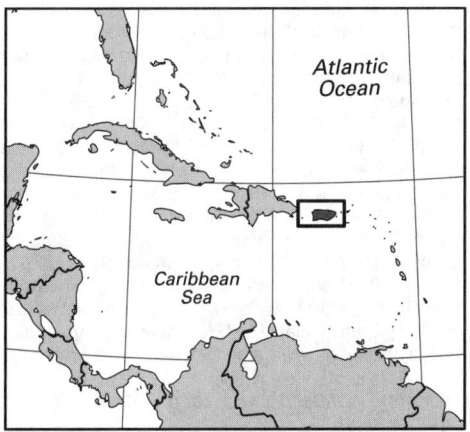

Official name: Estado Libre Asociado de Puerto Rico; Commonwealth of Puerto Rico. Political status: self-governing commonwealth in association with the US, having two legislative houses (Senate [27]; House of Representatives [51]). Chief of state: President of the US George W. Bush (from 2001). Head of government: Governor Sila Maria Calderón (from 2001). Capital: San Juan. Official languages: Spanish; English. Monetary unit: 1 US dollar ($) = 100 cents.

## Demography

Area: 3,515 sq mi, 9,104 sq km. Population (2002): 3,856,000. Density (2002): persons per sq mi 1,097.0, persons per sq km 423.5. Urban (2001): 75.6%. Sex distribution (2000): male 48.14%; female 51.86%. Age breakdown (2000): under 15, 23.8%; 15–34, 30.1%; 35–54, 25.7%; 55–64, 9.2%; 65 and over, 11.2%. Ethnic composition (2000): local white 72.1%; black 15.0%; mulatto 10.0%; US white 2.2%; other 0.7%. Religious affiliation (1995): Roman Catholic 64.8%; Protestant 28.7%; other 6.5%. Major urban agglomerations (1998): San Juan 2,004,054; Ponce 366,273; Caguas 315,921; Mayagüez 258,283; Arecibo 176,814. Location: island in the Caribbean Sea, east of Cuba.

## Vital statistics

Birth rate per 1,000 population (2001): 15.4 (world avg. 21.2). Death rate per 1,000 population (2001): 7.6 (world avg. 8.9). Natural increase rate per 1,000 population (2001): 7.8 (world avg. 12.3). Total fertility rate (avg. births per childbearing woman; 2000): 2.0. Marriage rate per 1,000 population (1996): 8.7. Life expectancy at birth (2001): male 72.9 years; female 81.1 years.

## National economy

Budget. Revenue (1997–98): $8,784,000,000 (tax revenue 68.3%, of which income taxes 45.5%, excise taxes 15.5%, intergovernment transfers 31.7%). Expenditures (1997–98): $6,263,000,000 (welfare 25.6%; education 20.3%; debt service 9.0%; public safety and protection 8.7%; health 3.5%). Public debt (outstanding; 1999): $22,678,200,000. Tourism (2000): receipts $2,388,000,000; expenditures $931,000,000. Production (in metric tons except as noted). Agriculture, forestry, fishing (1999): sugarcane 307,358, plantains 76,140, bananas 38,215; livestock (number of live animals) 388,307 cattle, 174,748 pigs; fish catch (1997) 2,744. Mining (value of production in $'000; 1999): crushed stone 57. Manufacturing (value added in $'000,000; 1997): chemicals, pharmaceuticals, and allied products 21,393; food 3,532; machinery and metal products 2,940. Energy production (consumption): electricity (kW-hr; 1996) 19,029,000,000 ([2001] 20,500,-000,000); coal (metric tons; 2001) none (172,000); crude petroleum (barrels; 2001) none (58,400,000); petroleum products (metric tons; 1996) 5,877,000 (6,743,000). Gross national product (2001): $45,-300,000,000 ($11,783 per capita). Population economically active (1997): total 1,298,000; activity rate 34.1% (participation rates: ages 16 and over, 48.0%; female 39.5%; unemployed 13.1%). Household income and expenditure (1999). Average family size (2000) 3.0; income per family $32,892; sources of income: wages and salaries 60.6%, transfers 31.3%, rent 6.5%, self-employment 6.1%; expenditure: food and beverages 18.8%, health care 17.8%, transportation 12.8%, housing 12.1%, household furnishings 11.6%, clothing 7.9%, recreation 7.7%.

## Foreign trade

**Imports** (1997–98): $27,308,700,000 (chemicals [all forms] 26.8%, electrical machinery 11.8%, food 10.2%, transport equipment 9.6%, petroleum and petroleum products 7.2%, nonelectrical machinery 6.8%, professional and scientific instruments 4.2%, clothing and textiles 4.2%). *Major import sources* (1995–96): US 62.5%; Japan 6.4%; Dominican Republic 4.0%; UK 2.9%. **Exports** (1997–98): $33,416,-400,000 (chemicals and chemical products 43.6%, nonelectrical machinery 13.2%, food 12.1%, electrical machinery 7.7%). *Major export destinations:* US 88.5%; other 11.5%.

## Transport and communications

**Transport.** *Railroads* (1988): length 96 km. *Roads* (1996): total length 14,400 km (paved 100%). *Vehicles* (1996): passenger cars 878,000; trucks and buses 190,000. *Air transport* (1998): passenger arrivals and departures 9,285,000; cargo loaded and unloaded 275,500 metric tons; airports (1998) with scheduled flights 7. **Communications,** in total units (units per 1,000 persons). Daily newspaper circulation (1996): 475,000 (128); radio receivers (1997): 2,700,000 (724); television receivers (1998): 1,250,000 (333); telephone main lines (2001): 1,330,000 (336); cellular telephone subscribers (2001): 1,211,000 (307); Internet users (2001): 600,000 (152).

## Education and health

**Educational attainment** (2000). Percentage of population age 25 and over having: no formal schooling to secondary education 25.4%; some upper secondary to some higher 60.0%; undergraduate or graduate degree 18.3%. **Literacy** (1995): total population age 15 and over literate 92.8%; males literate 92.7%; females literate 92.8%. **Health:** physicians (1992) 6,269 (1 per 575 persons); hospital beds (1993–94) 9,598 (1 per 381 persons); infant mortality rate per 1,000 live births (2001) 9.8.

## Military

**Total active duty personnel** (2001): 2,840 US personnel.

## Background

Puerto Rico was inhabited by Arawak Indians when it was settled by the Spanish in the early 16th century. It remained largely undeveloped economically until the late 18th century. After 1830 it gradually developed a plantation economy based on the export crops of sugarcane, coffee, and tobacco. The independence movement began in the late 19th century, and Spain ceded the island to the US in 1898, after the Spanish-American War. In 1917 Puerto Ricans were granted US citizenship, and in 1952 the island became a commonwealth with autonomy in internal affairs. The question of Puerto Rican statehood has been a political issue, with commonwealth status approved by voters in 1967, 1993, and 1998.

## Recent Developments

The US Navy resumed target practice off the coast of Puerto Rico on Vieques Island in April 2002, and the inevitable protests followed. Puerto Rican authorities reiterated their conviction that US Pres. George W. Bush would stick to his pledge to halt the bombing and close the Vieques naval base by May 2003. A poll of Puerto Rican opinions in April 2003, however, found that as many as 43.8% of those surveyed wanted the navy to retain a presence in Puerto Rico.

**Internet resources:** <www.prtourism.com>

# Qatar

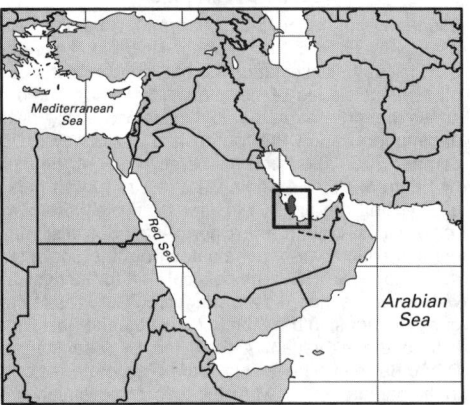

**Official name:** Dawlat Qatar (State of Qatar). **Form of government:** monarchy (emirate); Islamic law is the basis of legislation in the state. **Heads of state and government:** Emir Sheikh Hamad ibn Khalifah Al Thani (from 1995) assisted by Prime Minister Sheikh Abdullah ibn Khalifah Al Thani. **Capital:** Doha. **Official language:** Arabic. **Official religion:** Islam. **Monetary unit:** 1 riyal (QR) = 100 dirhams; valuation (7 Jul 2003) $1 = QR 3.64.

## Demography

**Area:** 4,412 sq mi, 11,427 sq km (includes area of Hawar Island and adjacent islets, most of which were awarded to Bahrain in 2001). **Population** (2002): 606,000. **Density** (2001): persons per sq mi 137.4, persons per sq km 53.0. **Urban** (2001): 92.9%. **Sex distribution** (2000): male 65.9%; female 34.1%. **Age breakdown** (2000): under 15, 26.3%; 15–29, 22.6%; 30–44, 27.1%; 45–59, 19.4%; 60–74, 4.1%; 75 and over, 0.5%. **Ethnic composition** (2000): Arab 52.5%, of which Palestinian 13.4%, Qatari 13.3%, Lebanese 10.4%, Syrian 9.4%; Persian 16.5%; Indo-Pakistani 15.2%; black African 9.5%; other 6.3%. **Religious affiliation** (2000): Muslim (mostly Sunni) 82.7%; Christian 10.4%; Hindu 2.5%; other 4.4%. **Major cities** (1997): Ad-Dawhah (Doha) 264,009 (urban agglomeration [1999] 391,000); Ar-Rayyan 161,453; Al-Wakrah 20,205; Umm Salal 15,935. **Location:** the Middle East, bordering the Persian Gulf and Saudi Arabia.

*1 metric ton = about 1.1 short tons;   1 kilometer = 0.6 mi (statute);   1 metric ton-km cargo = about 0.68 short ton-mi cargo;   c.i.f.: cost, insurance, and freight;   f.o.b.: free on board*

## Vital statistics

**Birth rate** per 1,000 population (2000): 16.1 (world avg. 22.5). **Death rate** per 1,000 population (2000): 4.2 (world avg. 9.0). **Natural increase rate** per 1,000 population (2000): 11.9 (world avg. 13.5). **Total fertility rate** (avg. births per childbearing woman; 2000): 3.3. **Marriage rate** per 1,000 population (1994): 2.8. **Divorce rate** per 1,000 population (1994): 1.0. **Life expectancy** at birth (2000): male 69.9 years; female 74.9 years.

## National economy

**Budget** (1999–2000). *Revenue*: QR 14,098,000,-000 (crude oil about 90%). *Expenditures*: QR 14,353,000,000 (current expenditure 91.7%, of which wages and salaries 37.5%; capital expenditure 8.3%). **Production** (metric tons except as noted). *Agriculture, forestry, fishing* (2000): dates 16,500, tomatoes 11,000, pumpkin and squash 8,500; livestock (number of live animals; 2000) 215,000 sheep, 179,000 goats, 50,000 camels; fish catch (1999) 4,207. *Mining and quarrying* (1996): limestone 900,000; sulfur 61,000; gypsum, sand and gravel, and clay are also produced. *Manufacturing* (value added in QR '000,000; 1998): industrial chemicals 516; fertilizers and pesticides 474; iron and steel 459. *Energy production (consumption)*: electricity (kW-hr; 1997) 6,868,000,000 (6,868,000,000); crude petroleum (barrels; 2001) 243,788,000 ([1997] 22,500,000); petroleum products (metric tons; 1997) 5,367,000 (873,000); natural gas (cu m; 1997) 17,900,000,000 (17,900,000,000). **Tourism** (1997): total number of tourists staying in hotels 435,000. **Population economically active** (1997): total 280,122; activity rate of total population 53.7% (participation rates: ages 15–64, 59.7%; female 21.0%). **Gross national product** (1998): $6,473,000,-000 ($11,600 per capita). **Household income and expenditure.** Average household size (1998) 7.0; sources of income (1988): wages and salaries 80.8%, rents and royalties 10.6%, self-employment 5.6%, other 3.0%; expenditure (1993): food 28.7%, transportation 19.3%, housing 12.4%, clothing 10.6%, education 7.6%, health 1.2%. **Land use** (1994): meadows and pastures 4.5%; agricultural and under permanent cultivation 0.7%; built-up, desert, and other 94.7%.

## Foreign trade

**Imports** (1999): QR 9,098,400,000 (machinery and transport equipment 34.6%, manufactured goods 19.0%, food and live animals 13.2%, chemicals and chemical products 8.2%, raw materials 3.1%). *Major import sources* (1999): UK 11.5%; US 11.4%; Japan 10.3%; UAE 8.0%; Saudi Arabia 7.1%; Germany 6.1%; France 4.9%; Italy 4.9%. **Exports** (1999): QR 26,258,000,000 (1994; mineral fuels and lubricants 81.2%, chemicals and chemical products 10.4%, manufactured goods 5.9%). *Major export destinations* (1999): Japan 51.0%; South Korea 12.9%; Singapore 9.1%; US 4.3%; Thailand 3.4%; UAE 2.3%; India 1.1%.

## Transport and communications

**Transport.** *Roads* (1996): total length 1,230 km (paved 90%). *Vehicles* (1996): passenger cars 126,000; trucks and buses 64,000. *Air transport*

(1999; Qatar Airways): passenger-km 2,857,529,-000; metric ton-km cargo 104,947,000; airports (1999) with scheduled flights 1. **Communications,** in total units (units per 1,000 persons). Daily newspaper circulation (1995): 90,000 (161); radio receivers (1997): 250,000 (432); television receivers (1998): 490,000 (846); telephone main lines (2001): 167,400 (275); cellular telephone subscribers (2001): 178,800 (293); personal computers (2001): 100,000 (163.9); Internet users (2001): 40,000 (65).

## Education and health

**Educational attainment** (1986). Percentage of population age 25 and over having: no formal education 53.3%, of which illiterate 24.3%; primary 9.8%; preparatory (lower secondary) 10.1%; secondary 13.3%; postsecondary 13.3%; other 0.2%. **Literacy** (1995): total population age 15 and over literate 460,000 (79.4%); males literate 298,000 (79.2%); females literate 122,000 (79.9%). **Health:** physicians (1996) 703 (1 per 793 persons); hospital beds (1995) 892 (1 per 555 persons); infant mortality rate per 1,000 live births (2000) 22.1.

## Military

**Total active duty personnel** (2001): 12,330 (army 68.9%, navy 14.0%, air force 17.1%); US troops (2002) 3,300. **Military expenditure as percentage of GNP** (1999): 10.0% (world 2.4%); per capita expenditure $1,470.

## Background

Qatar was partly controlled by Bahrain in the 18th and 19th centuries and was nominally part of the Ottoman Empire until World War I. In 1916 it became a British protectorate. Oil was discovered in 1939, and the country rapidly modernized. Qatar declared independence in 1971, when the British protectorate ended. In 1991 it served as a base for air strikes against Iraq in the Persian Gulf War.

## Recent Developments

Qatar continued to figure prominently in regional and international news, largely as a result of its ongoing chairmanship of the Organization of the Islamic Conference. Qatar was a prominent interlocutor with international and regional organizations and, in particular, with the UN, the US, and other allied governments engaged in the global campaign against terrorism. The image of the tiny Persian Gulf state grew even larger when the Al-Udeid Air Base served as command center for Coalition forces invading Iraq in the spring of 2003. The Qatari capital, Doha, is also the home base for the major source of news and TV footage in the Middle East, Al-Jazeera.

In April 2003 a referendum overwhelmingly approved a constitution for the country that would temper the power of the royal family and establish a legislature. In August 2003 Prince Jassim bin Hamad was abruptly replaced as crown prince by his younger brother, Prince Tamim.

**Internet resources:** <www.mofa.gov.qa>

# Réunion

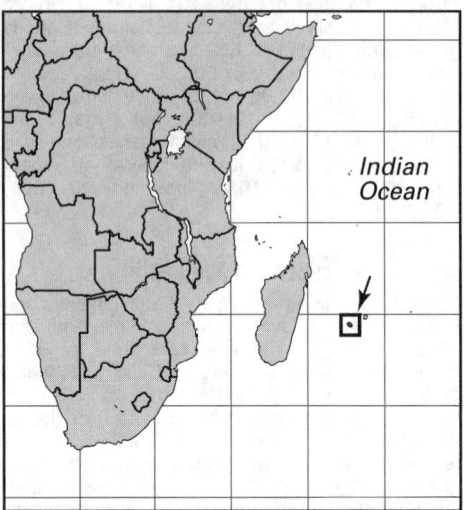

*Indian Ocean*

**Official name:** Département de la Réunion (Department of Réunion). **Political status:** overseas department (France) with two legislative houses (General Council [47]; Regional Council [45]). **Chief of state:** President of France Jacques Chirac (from 1995). **Head of government:** Prefect Gonthier Friederici (from 2001). **Capital:** Saint-Denis. **Official language:** French. **Official religion:** none. **Monetary unit:** 1 euro (€) = 100 cents; valuation (7 Jul 2003) $1 = €0.87 (1 French franc [F] = 100 centimes; at conversion on 1 Jan 2002, €1 = 6.56 French francs [F]).

## Demography

**Area:** 968 sq mi, 2,507 sq km. **Population** (2002): 743,000. **Density** (2002): persons per sq mi 767.6, persons per sq km 296.4. **Urban** (1999): 71.6%. **Sex distribution** (1999): male 49.15%; female 50.85%. **Age breakdown** (1999): under 15, 27.0%; 15–29, 24.8%; 30–44, 24.4%; 45–59, 13.8%; 60–74, 7.2%; 75 and over, 2.8%. **Ethnic composition** (2000): mixed race (black-white-South Asian) 42.6%; local white 25.6%; South Asian 23.0%, of which Tamil 20.0%; Chinese 3.4%; East African 3.4%; Malagasy 1.4%; other 0.6%. **Religious affiliation** (1995): Roman Catholic 89.4%; Pentecostal 2.7%; other Christian 1.8%; other (mostly Muslim) 6.1%. **Major cities** (1999): Saint-Denis 131,557 (pop. of commune; agglomeration 158,139); Saint-Paul 87,712 (pop. of commune); Saint-Pierre 68,915 (pop. of commune; agglomeration 129,238); Le Tampon 60,323 (pop. of commune; within Saint-Pierre agglomeration); Saint-Louis 43,519 (pop. of commune). **Location:** island in the western Indian Ocean, east of Madagascar and near Mauritius.

## Vital statistics

**Birth rate** per 1,000 population (1999): 19.9 (world avg. 22.5); (1997) legitimate 41.5%; illegitimate 58.5%. **Death rate** per 1,000 population (1999): 5.4 (world avg. 9.0). **Natural increase rate** per 1,000 population (1999): 14.5 (world avg. 13.5). **Total fertility rate** (avg. births per childbearing woman; 1997): 2.2. **Marriage rate** per 1,000 population (1998): 4.8. **Divorce rate** per 1,000 population (1997): 1.3. **Life expectancy** at birth (2000): male 70.6 years; female 78.7 years.

## National economy

**Budget** (1998). *Revenue:* F 4,624,000,000 (receipts from the French central government and local administrative bodies 52.7%, tax receipts 20.2%, loans 8.9%). *Expenditures:* F 4,300,000,000 (current expenditures 68.7%, development expenditures 31.3%). **Tourism** (2000): receipts $254,000,000. **Gross national product** (at current market prices; 1998): $5,070,000,000 ($7,270 per capita). **Production** (metric tons except as noted). *Agriculture, forestry, fishing* (1999): sugarcane 1,800,000, corn (maize) 17,000, cabbages 14,000; livestock (number of live animals) 89,000 pigs, 38,000 goats, 27,000 cattle; roundwood (2000) 36,100 cu m; fish catch (2000) 5,091. *Mining and quarrying:* gravel and sand for local use. *Manufacturing* (value added in F '000,000; 1997): food and beverages 1,019, of which meat and milk products 268; construction materials (mostly cement) 394; fabricated metals 258. *Energy production (consumption):* electricity (kW-hr; 2000) 1,757,000,000 ([1997] 1,133,000,000); petroleum products (metric tons; 1997) none (511,000). **Population economically active** (1998): total 288,760; activity rate of total population 41.2% (participation rates: ages 15–64, 57.5%; female 44.3%; unemployed [2000] 36.5%). **Household income and expenditure.** Average household size (1999) 3.3; average annual income per household (1997) F 136,800 ($23,438); sources of income (1997): wages and salaries and self-employment 41.8%, transfer payments 41.3%, other 16.9%; expenditure (1994–95): food and beverages 22.0%, transportation and communications 19.0%, housing and energy 10.0%, household furnishings 8.0%, recreation 6.0%. **Land use** (1994): forested 35.2%; meadows and pastures 4.8%; agricultural and under permanent cultivation 19.6%; other 40.4%.

## Foreign trade

**Imports** (1998): F 15,310,000,000 (food and agricultural products 17.1%, transport equipment 14.7%, machinery and apparatus 13.4%, clothing and footwear 6.8%). *Major import sources:* France 66.0%; EC 14.0%. **Exports** (1998): F 1,215,000,000 (sugar 58.9%, machinery, apparatus, and transport equipment 17.5%, rum 2.5%, lobster 1.7%). *Major export destinations:* France 70.0%; EC 9.0%; Madagascar 4.5%; Mauritius 2.3%.

## Transport and communications

**Transport.** *Roads* (1994): total length 2,754 km (paved [1991] 79%). *Vehicles* (1999): passenger cars 190,300; trucks and buses 44,300. *Air transport* (2000; Saint-Denis airport only): passenger arrivals 736,499, passenger departures 730,980; cargo unloaded 17,206 metric tons, cargo loaded 8,934 metric tons; airports (1999) with scheduled flights 2. **Communications,** in total units (units per 1,000 persons). Daily newspaper circulation (1996): 83,000

---

*1 metric ton = about 1.1 short tons;    1 kilometer = 0.6 mi (statute);    1 metric ton-km cargo = about 0.68 short ton-mi cargo;    c.i.f.: cost, insurance, and freight;    f.o.b.: free on board*

(123); radio receivers (1997): 173,000 (252); television receivers (1997): 127,000 (185); telephone main lines (1999): 268,496 (378); cellular telephone subscribers (1998): 50,300 (72).

## Education and health

**Educational attainment** (1986–87). Percentage of population age 25 and over having: no formal schooling 18.8%; primary education 44.3%; lower secondary 21.6%; upper secondary 11.0%; higher 4.3%. **Literacy** (1996): total population age 16–66 literate 373,487 (91.3%); males literate 179,154 (89.9%); females literate 194,333 (92.7%). **Health** (2000): physicians 1,595 (1 per 449 persons); hospital beds (2000) 2,124 (1 per 337 persons); infant mortality rate per 1,000 live births (1999) 6.0.

## Military

**Total active duty personnel** (2001): 4,200 French troops (includes troops stationed on Mayotte).

**Did you know?** Piton de la Fournaise, an active 500,000-year-old volcano lying in the southeastern part of Réunion Island, erupts almost annually, putting on a spectacular show.

## Background

The island of Réunion was settled in the 17th century by the French, who brought slaves from eastern Africa to work on coffee and sugar plantations there. It was a French colony until 1946, when it became an overseas territory of France. Its economy is based almost entirely on the export of sugar.

## Recent Developments

A proposal to split the island into two separate dependencies was rejected by the voters, as reflected in the victory in March 2001 elections of rightist parties opposed to the split. Social unrest was traced to inequities between the various ethnic groups, a very high rate of unemployment (40%), exploding population, and dependence on welfare and foreign aid.

**Internet resources:**
<www.runweb.com/uk_main.asp>

# Romania

**Official name:** Romania. **Form of government:** unitary republic with two legislative houses (Senate [143]; Assembly of Deputies [346, including 19 non-elective seats]). **Chief of state:** President Ion Iliescu (from 2000). **Head of government:** Prime Minister Adrian Nastase (from 2000). **Capital:** Bucharest. **Official language:** Romanian. **Official religion:** none. **Monetary unit:** 1 Romanian leu (plural lei) = 100 bani; valuation (7 Jul 2003) $1 = 32,742 lei.

## Demography

**Area:** 91,699 sq mi, 237,500 sq km. **Population** (2002): 21,667,000. **Density** (2002): persons per sq mi 236.3, persons per sq km 91.2. **Urban** (2002): 52.7%. **Sex distribution** (2002): male 48.77%; fe-

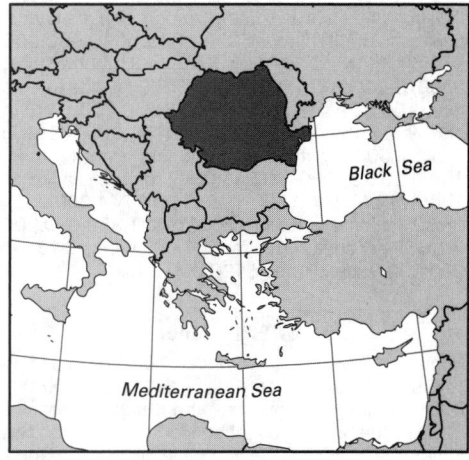

male 51.23%. **Age breakdown** (2000): under 15, 18.4%; 15–29, 24.1%; 30–44, 21.0%; 45–59, 17.7%; 60–74, 14.3%; 75 and over, 4.5%. **Ethnic composition** (2002): Romanian 89.5%; Hungarian 6.6%; Roma (Gypsy) 2.5%; other 1.4%. **Religious affiliation** (2002): Romanian Orthodox 86.7%; Protestant 6.4%; Roman Catholic 4.7%; Greek Orthodox 0.9%; Muslim 0.3%; other 1.0%. **Major cities** (1997): Bucharest 2,027,512; Iasi 348,399; Constanta 344,876; Timisoara 334,098; Cluj-Napoca 332,792. **Location:** southeastern Europe, bordering Ukraine, Moldova, the Black Sea, Bulgaria, Serbia and Montenegro, and Hungary.

## Vital statistics

**Birth rate** per 1,000 population (2000): 10.8 (world avg. 22.5). **Death rate** per 1,000 population (2000): 12.3 (world avg. 9.0). **Natural increase rate** per 1,000 population (2000): −1.7 (world avg. 13.5). **Total fertility rate** (avg. births per childbearing woman; 2000): 1.4. **Marriage rate** per 1,000 population (1995): 6.8. **Life expectancy** at birth (2000): male 66.1 years; female 74.0 years.

## National economy

**Budget** ('000,000,000,000 lei; 1996). *Revenue:* 76.7 (social security 23.0%, personal income tax 18.2%, value-added tax 15.2%). *Expenditures:* 85.6 (social security 28.2%, debt service 10.0%, education 9.6%, health 7.5%). **Public debt** (external, outstanding; 2000): $6,430,000,000. **Population economically active** (1998): total 11,577,300; activity rate 51.4% (participation rates: ages 15–64, 67.2%; female 42.8%; unemployed 6.3%). **Household income and expenditure.** Average household size (1992) 3.1; income per household (1989) 73,500 lei ($4,940); sources of income (1982): wages 62.6%; expenditure (1989): food 51.1%, housing 16.4%. **Production** (metric tons except as noted). *Agriculture, forestry, fishing* (2000): wheat 4,320,000, corn (maize) 4,200,000, potatoes 3,650,000; livestock (number of live animals) 7,972,000 sheep, 5,951,000 pigs, 3,154,000 cattle; roundwood (1998) 11,515,000 cu m; fish catch (1998) 9,020. *Mining* (2000): iron (metal content) 55,000; bauxite 135,000; zinc (metal content of concentrate) 27,455. *Manufacturing* (value-added in '000,000,000,000 lei; 1996): food products 5.8; beverages

3.0; iron and steel 1.6. *Energy production (consumption)*: electricity (kW-hr; 2001) 53,640,000,000 ([1997] 57,369,000,000); hard coal (metric tons; 2000) 3,240,000 ([1997] 6,637,000); lignite (metric tons; 2001) 29,431,000 ([1997] 31,504,000); crude petroleum (barrels; 2001) 45,164,000 ([1997] 91,427,000); petroleum products (metric tons; 1997) 10,520,000 (10,941,000); natural gas (cu m; 2001) 12,172,000,000 ([1997] 16,744,000,000). **Gross national product** (2000): $37,380,000,000 ($1,670 per capita). **Tourism** (2000): receipts $359,-000,000; expenditures $420,000,000.

## Foreign trade

**Imports** (1999-f.o.b. in balance of trade and c.i.f. in commodities and trading partners): $10,395,300,-000 (textile yarn, fabrics, and made-up articles 30.7%; chemicals and chemical products 10.6%; mineral fuels 10.1%; electrical machinery and apparatus 6.9%; food 5.8%). *Major import sources:* Italy 19.7%; Germany 17.1%; Russia 6.8%; France 6.7%; UK 4.2%. **Exports** (1999): $8,503,000,000 (clothing and apparel 24.0%; iron and steel 8.6%; footwear 5.0%; chemicals and chemical products 4.9%; sawn wood 3.8%; refined petroleum 3.8%). *Major export destinations:* Italy 23.4%; Germany 17.8%; France 6.2%; Turkey 5.5%; UK 4.9%.

## Transport and communications

**Transport.** *Railroads* (1997): length 11,365 km (1994); passenger-km 15,794,000,000; metric ton-km cargo 24,789,000,000. *Roads* (1996): length 153,358 km (paved 51%). *Vehicles* (1997): cars 2,605,565; trucks and buses 427,579. *Air transport* (1998): passenger-km 1,712,300,000; metric ton-km cargo 12,110,000; airports (1997) 8. **Communications,** in total units (units per 1,000 persons). Daily newspaper circulation (1996): 6,800,000 (297); radio receivers (1997): 7,200,000 (319); television receivers (1999): 7,000,000 (312); telephone main lines (2001): 4,094,000 (183); cellular telephone subscribers (2001): 3,860,000 (172); personal computers (2001): 800,000 (36); Internet users (2001): 1,000,000 (45).

## Education and health

**Educational attainment** (1992). Percentage of population age 25 and over having: no schooling 5.4%; some primary education 24.4%; some secondary 63.2%; postsecondary 6.9%. **Literacy** (2000): total population age 15 and over literate 98.2%; males 99.1%; females 97.3%. **Health:** physicians (1998) 40,658 (1 per 543 persons); hospital beds (1992) 174,900 (1 per 130 persons); infant mortality rate per 1,000 live births (2002) 18.9. **Food** (2000): daily per capita caloric intake 3,274 (vegetable products 79%, animal products 21%); 124% of FAO recommended minimum.

## Military

**Total active duty personnel** (2001): 103,000 (army 51.4%, navy 9.9%, air force 18.3%, other 20.4%). **Military expenditure as percentage of GNP** (2001): 1.6% (world 2.4%); per capita expenditure $97.

## Background

Romania was formed in 1862 by the unification of the principalities Moldavia and Walachia, which had once been part of the ancient country of Dacia. During World War I, Romania sided with the Allies and doubled its territory in 1918 with the addition of Transylvania, Bukovina, and Bessarabia. Allied with Germany in World War II, it was occupied by Soviet troops in 1944 and became a satellite country of the USSR in 1948. During the 1960s Romania's foreign policy was frequently independent of the Soviet Union's. The communist regime of Nicolae Ceausescu was overthrown in 1989, and free elections were held in 1990. Throughout the 1990s Romania struggled with rampant corruption and organized crime as it tried to stabilize its economy.

## Recent Developments

The 11 Sep 2001 terrorist attacks transformed Romania's strategic importance in Washington's eyes. Romania's willingness to act as a bridgehead in the event of US military operations in the Middle East meant that the daunting economic and political handicaps that had seemed to make early NATO membership a remote possibility no longer counted against it. In fact, Romania was invited to open negotiations to join NATO at the Atlantic Alliance's summit in Prague on 22 Nov 2002. The next day, US Pres. George W. Bush paid an official visit to Bucharest to show his approval for the active backing provided by the government not only in the war against terrorism but in the mounting confrontation with Iraq.

**Internet resources:** <www.rotravel.com>

# Russia

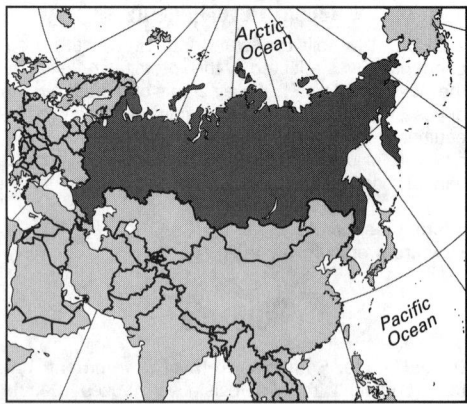

**Official name:** Rossiyskaya Federatsiya (Russian Federation). **Form of government:** federal multiparty republic with a bicameral legislative body (Federal Assembly comprising a Federation Council [178] and a State Duma [450]). **Head of state:** President Vladimir Putin (from 2000). **Head of government:** Prime Minister Mikhail Kasyanov (from 2000). **Capital:** Moscow. **Official language:** Russian. **Official religion:** none. **Monetary unit:** 1 ruble (Rub) = 100 kopecks; valuation (7 Jul 2003) market rate, $1 = Rub 30.31.

*1 metric ton = about 1.1 short tons; 1 kilometer = 0.6 mi (statute); 1 metric ton-km cargo = about 0.68 short ton-mi cargo; c.i.f.: cost, insurance, and freight; f.o.b.: free on board*

## Demography

**Area:** 6,592,800 sq mi, 17,075,400 sq km. **Population** (2002): 143,673,000. **Density** (2002): persons per sq mi 21.7, persons per sq km 8.4. **Urban** (2001): 73.1%. **Sex distribution** (2001): male 46.68%; female 53.32%. **Age breakdown** (2001): under 15, 13.3%; 15–29, 22.9%; 30–44, 23.0%; 45–59, 17.8%; 60 and over, 23.0%. **Ethnic composition** (1997): Russian 86.6%; Tatar 3.2%; Ukrainian 1.3%; Chuvash 0.9%; Bashkir 0.7%; Chechen 0.6%; Mordovian 0.5%; Belorussian 0.3%; other 5.9%. **Religious affiliation** (1997): Russian Orthodox 16.3%; Muslim 7.6%; other Orthodox 1.6%; Protestant 0.9%; Jewish 0.4%; Roman Catholic 0.3%; other Catholic 0.3%; other (mostly nonreligious) 72.6%. **Major cities** (2001): Moscow 8,546,000; St. Petersburg 4,628,000; Novosibirsk 1,393,200; Nizhny Novgorod 1,343,300; Yekaterinburg 1,256,900; Samara 1,146,400; Omsk 1,138,400; Kazan 1,090,200; Ufa 1,088,800; Chelyabinsk 1,081,100; Perm 1,004,800; Rostov-na-Donu 997,800. **Migration** (2000): immigrants 350,876; emigrants 161,046. *Refugees* (2001): 808,280, of which from Kazakhstan 291,445, Uzbekistan 102,125, Tajikistan 85,101, Georgia 60,067. **Households** (1999). Total family households 52,116,000; average household size 2.8; distribution by size (1995): 1 person 19.2%; 2 persons 26.2%; 3 persons 22.6%; 4 persons 20.5%; 5 persons or more 11.5%. Population in family households (1989): 87.0%, nonfamily population 13.0%. **Location:** eastern Europe and northern Asia, bordering the Arctic Ocean, the Pacific Ocean, North Korea, China, Mongolia, Kazakhstan, the Caspian Sea, Azerbaijan, Georgia, the Black Sea, Ukraine, Belarus, Latvia, Estonia, Finland, and Norway; the exclave of Kaliningrad on the Baltic Sea borders Lithuania and Poland.

## Vital statistics

**Birth rate** per 1,000 population (2001): 8.7 (world avg. 21.2); legitimate 70.5%; illegitimate 29.5%. **Death rate** per 1,000 population (2001): 15.4 (world avg. 8.9). **Natural increase rate** per 1,000 population (2000): -6.7 (world avg. 12.3). **Total fertility rate** (avg. births per childbearing woman; 2001): 1.3. **Life expectancy** at birth (2001): male 59.0 years; female 72.2 years.

## Social indicators

**Quality of working life** (2000). Average workweek: 40 hours. Annual rate per 100,000 workers of: injury or accident 510; industrial illness 18.1; death 14.9. Proportion of labor force insured for damages or income loss resulting from: injury 100%; permanent disability 100%; death 100%. Average days lost to labor strikes per 1,000 employees (1999): 35.7. **Access to services** (1990). Proportion of dwellings having access to: electricity, virtually 100%; safe public water supply 94%; public sewage collection 92%; central heating 92%; bathroom 87%; gas 72%; hot water 79%. **Social participation.** Eligible voters participating in last national election (2000): 64.2%. Trade union membership in total workforce (2000; state enterprises only): 100%. Practicing religious population in total affiliated population (1991): 32%. **Social deviance.** Offense rate per 100,000 population (2000) for: murder 21.9; rape 5.4; serious injury 34.3; larceny-theft 1,023.2. Incidence per 100,000 population (2000) of: alcoholism (1992) 1,727.5; substance abuse 25.6; suicide 39.2. **Material well-being** (1999). Durable goods possessed per 100 family households: automobile 37; radio receiver 100; television receiver 112; refrigerator or freezer 93; washing machine 80; camera 35; motorcycle 22; bicycle 51.

## National economy

**Public debt** (external, outstanding: 2000): $111,419,-000,000. **Budget** (2000). *Revenue*: Rub 1,132,100,-000,000 (tax revenue 85.2%, of which value-added tax 32.8%, profit tax 15.7%, individual income tax 11.6%, excise tax 6.0%; nontax revenue 14.8%). *Expenditures*: Rub 1,029,200,000 (interest on foreign debt 25.0%; defense 18.6%; social and cultural 13.0%; law enforcement 10.2%; administrative 2.4%). **Gross national product** (2000): $241,027,000,000 ($1,660 per capita). **Production** (metric tons except as noted). *Agriculture, forestry, fishing* (2001): wheat 46,871,000, potatoes 34,500,000, barley 19,500,-000, sugar beets 14,539,000, vegetables (other than potatoes) 12,533,800, oats 8,010,000, rye 6,000,-000, sunflower seeds 2,700,000, apples 1,800,000, millet 1,315,000, corn (maize) 831,000, peas 800,-000, buckwheat 570,000, rice 497,000; livestock (number of live animals) 27,300,000 cattle, 15,700,-000 pigs, 14,800,000 sheep; roundwood (2000) 158,100,000 cu m; fish catch (1999) 4,209,772. *Mining and quarrying* (2000): nickel 275,600,000; chrome ore 169,000,000; iron ore 86,800,000; tin 5,000,000; molybdenum 4,600,000; antimony 4,500,000; gold 4,113,000 troy oz; silver 270. *Manufacturing* (2000): crude steel 59,200,000; rolled steel 46,700,000; pig iron 44,600,000; cement 32,400,000; mineral fertilizers 12,213,000; sulfuric acid 8,300,000; cellulose 4,960,000; synthetic resins and plastics 2,576,000; cardboard 1,985,000; caustic soda 1,241,000; detergents 436,000; synthetic fibers 164,000; cotton fabrics 1,822,000,000 sq m; silk fabrics 178,000,000 sq m; linen fabrics 113,000,000 sq m; wool fabrics 54,600,000 sq m; cigarettes 290,000,000,000 units; watches 6,500,-000 units; refrigerators 1,327,000 units; television receivers 1,116,000 units; passenger cars 959,000 units; washing machines 954,000 units; vacuum cleaners 745,000 units; bicycles 639,000 units; cameras 183,600 units; sewing machines 31,800 units; motorcycles 28,700 units; leather footwear 22,500,-000 pairs; vodka and liquors 12,300,000 hectoliters; champagne 6,800,000 hectoliters; grape wine 2,401,000 hectoliters; beer 516,000 hectoliters; brandy 174,900 hectoliters. *Energy production (consumption)*: electricity (kW-hr; 2000) 877,800,-000,000 (863,700,000,000); hard coal (metric tons; 2000) 172,000,000 ([1997] 153,100,000); lignite (metric tons; 2000) 86,300,000 ([1997] 80,080,-000); crude petroleum (barrels; 2000) 2,323,730,-000 ([1997] 1,312,200,000); petroleum products (metric tons; 1997) 156,920,000 (102,980,000); natural gas (cu m; 2000) 584,000,000,000 ([1997] 308,646,800,000); peat (metric tons; 1997) 3,224,-000 (3,224,000). **Population economically active** (2000): total 72,900,000; activity rate of total population 49.9% (participation rates: ages over 15, 78.0%; female 47.6%; unemployed 12.3%). **Household income and expenditure.** Average household size (2000) 2.8; income per household: Rub 38,300 ($1,320); sources of income (2000): wages 61.4%, pensions and stipends 14.4%, income from entrepreneurial activities 15.9%, property income 7.1%, other 1.2%; expenditure (2000): food 47.6%, clothing

15.5%, furniture and household appliances 7.7%, housing 4.6%, transportation 2.6%. **Tourism** (1999): receipts $7,510,000,000; expenditures $7,434,000,000.

## Foreign trade

**Imports** (2000-c.i.f.): $30,142,000,000 (machinery and transport equipment 30.6%, food 23.1%, chemicals 18.6%, ferrous and nonferrous metals 8.3%, textiles and clothing 4.8%, fuels and lubricants 4.6%, wood and wood products 3.8%). *Major import sources* (2000): Germany 11.5%; Belarus 11.1%; Ukraine 10.8%; US 8.0%; Kazakhstan 6.5%; Italy 3.6%; France 3.3%; Finland 2.8%; Poland 2.1%. **Exports** (2000): $97,467,000,000 (fuels and lubricants 53.5%, of which oil and oil products 24.3%, gas 16.0%; ferrous and nonferrous metals 17.1%; machinery and transport equipment 8.6%; chemicals 7.0%; precious metals 5.0%; forestry products 4.4%). *Major export destinations:* Germany 9.0%; US 7.7%; Italy 7.0%; Belarus 5.4%; China 5.1%; Ukraine 4.9%; Poland 4.3%; The Netherlands 4.2%; Switzerland 3.9%; Finland 3.0%.

## Transport and communications

**Transport.** *Railroads* (2000): length 139,000 km; passenger-km 167,000,000,000; metric ton-km cargo 1,373,000,000. *Roads* (2000): total length 584,000 km (paved 91%). *Vehicles* (2000): passenger cars 20,247,800; trucks and buses (1999) 5,021,000. *Air transport* (2000): passenger-km 53,400,000,000; metric ton-km cargo 2,500,000,000; airports (1998) 75. **Communications**, in total units (units per 1,000 persons). Daily newspaper circulation (1996): 15,517,000 (105); radio receivers (1997): 61,500,000 (417); television receivers (1999): 62,000,000 (425); telephone main lines (2001): 35,700,000 (243); cellular telephone subscribers (2001): 5,560,000 (38); personal computers (2001): 7,300,000 (49.7); Internet users (2001): 4,300,000 (29.3).

## Education and health

**Educational attainment** (1998). Percentage of population age 16 and over having: primary or no formal education 11.2%; some secondary 25.3%; secondary and some postsecondary 40.9%; higher and postgraduate 22.6%. **Health** (2001): physicians 680,200 (1 per 213 persons); hospital beds 1,671,600 (1 per 87 persons); infant mortality rate per 1,000 live births (2000) 15.3. **Food** (2000): daily per capita caloric intake 2,917 (vegetable products 78%; animal products 22%); 114% of FAO recommended minimum.

## Military

**Total active duty personnel** (2001): 1,026,100 (army 31.3%, navy 16.7%, air force 18.0%, strategic deterrent forces 14.5%, other 19.5% [represents 200,000 military personnel not included elsewhere {including Ministry of Defense staff and centrally controlled units for electronic warfare}]). **Military expenditure as percentage of GNP** (1999): 5.6% (world 2.4%); per capita expenditure $239.

## Background

The region between the Dniester and Volga rivers was inhabited from ancient times by various peoples, including the Slavs. The area was overrun from the 8th century BC to the 6th century AD by successive nomadic peoples, including the Sythians, Sarmatians, Goths, Huns, and Avars. Kievan Rus, a confederation of principalities ruled from Kiev, emerged c. 10th century. It lost supremacy in the 11th and 12th centuries to independent principalities, including Novgorod and Vladimir. Novgorod ascended in the north and was the only Russian principality to escape the domination of the Mongol Golden Horde in the 13th century. In the 14th–15th centuries the princes of Moscow gradually overthrew the Mongols. Under Ivan IV, Russia began to expand. The Romanov dynasty arose in 1613. Expansion continued under Peter I (the Great) and Catherine II (the Great). The area was invaded by Napoleon in 1812; after his defeat, Russia received most of the grand duchy of Warsaw (1815). Russia annexed Georgia, Armenia, and Caucasus territories in the 19th century. The Russian southward advance against the Ottoman empire was of key importance to Europe. Russia was defeated in the Crimean War. It sold Alaska to the US in 1867. Russia's defeat in the Russo-Japanese War led to an unsuccessful uprising in 1905. In World War I it fought against the Central Powers.

The Russian Revolution that overthrew the czarist regime in 1917 marked the beginning of a government of soviets ("councils"). The Bolsheviks brought the main part of the former empire under communist control and organized it as the Russian Soviet Federated Socialist Republic (RSFSR; coextensive with present-day Russia). The Russian SFSR joined other soviet republics in 1922 to form the USSR. Although it fought with the Allies in World War II, after the war tensions with the West led to the decades-long Cold War.

Upon the dissolution of the USSR in 1991, the Russian SFSR was renamed Russia and became the leading member of the Commonwealth of Independent States. It adopted a new constitution in 1993. During the 1990s it struggled on several fronts, beset with economic difficulties, political corruption, and independence movements. Vladimir Putin was elected president in 2000, with economic reform, governmental reorganization, cutbacks in the military, and rooting out corruption and favoritism as his chief goals.

## Recent Developments

Pres. Vladimir Putin's popularity remained high in 2002 and his political position continued to be strong. Russia's regions remained compliant, many of them repudiating the idiosyncratic power-sharing treaties they had signed during Boris Yeltsin's presidency. The economy saw its fourth consecutive year of growth since the prolonged output collapse of 1989–98. GDP growth slowed in 2002 to around 4% from the annual average rate of 6% recorded in 1999–2001. Growth was expected to continue at this relatively healthy pace into 2003.

The year 2002 saw the continuation of the trend toward warmer relations with the West that began with Putin's election to office and that received a further boost when Russia joined the US-led antiterror coalition after 11 Sep 2001. Russian officials sought to

*1 metric ton = about 1.1 short tons;    1 kilometer = 0.6 mi (statute);    1 metric ton-km cargo = about 0.68 short ton-mi cargo;    c.i.f.: cost, insurance, and freight;    f.o.b.: free on board*

link their protracted war in the Chechen Republic with other manifestations of international terrorism. Moscow reacted calmly not only when the US abandoned the 1972 Anti-Ballistic Missile Treaty but also when it established temporary military bases in several of the former Soviet states in Central Asia and dispatched special forces on a training mission to Georgia. Moscow continued to express unhappiness at the prospect that the three Baltic States would be invited to join NATO but was not prepared to oppose the move. Russian relations with the US and the UK cooled appreciably in early 2003 when Moscow aligned with France and Germany in opposing a coalition invasion of Iraq.

Internet resources: <www.russia-travel.com>

# Rwanda

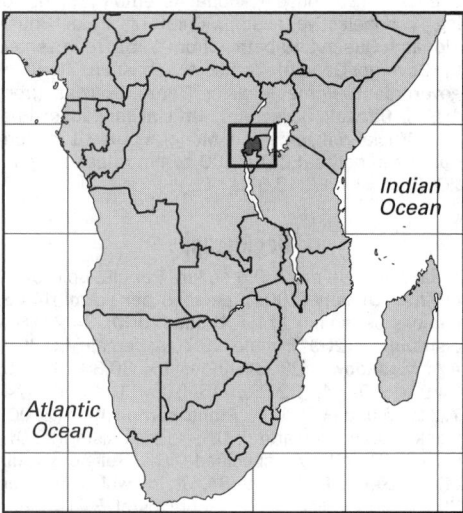

Official name: Repubulika y'u Rwanda (Rwanda); République Rwandaise (French); Republic of Rwanda (English). Form of government: transitional regime (until July 2003) with one legislative body (Transitional National Assembly [74]). Head of state and government: President Paul Kagame (from 2000) assisted by a prime minister. Capital: Kigali. Official languages: Rwanda; French; English. Official religion: none. Monetary unit: 1 Rwanda franc (RF); valuation (7 Jul 2003) $1 = RF 525.05.

## Demography

Area: 10,169 sq mi, 26,338 sq km. Population (2002): 7,398,000. Density (2002): persons per sq mi 758.2, persons per sq km 292.7. Urban (2001): 6.3%. Sex distribution (2001): male 49.60%; female 50.40%. Age breakdown (2001): under 15, 43.0%; 15–29, 30.4%; 30–44, 15.0%; 45–59, 7.3%; 60–74, 3.5%; 75 and over, 0.8%. Ethnic composition (1996): Hutu 80.0%; Tutsi 19.0%; Twa 1.0%. Religious affiliation (2000): Roman Catholic 51.0%; Protestant 28.8%; traditional beliefs 9.0%; Muslim 7.9%; independent Christian 2.1%; other 1.2%. Major cities (1991): Kigali (1999) 369,000; Ruhengeri 29,578; Butare 28,645; Gisenyi 21,918. Location: east-central Africa, bordering Uganda, Tanzania, Burundi, and the Dem. Rep. of the Congo.

## Vital statistics

Birth rate per 1,000 population (2001): 34.0 (world avg. 21.2). Death rate per 1,000 population (2001): 21.1 (world avg. 8.9). Natural increase rate per 1,000 population (2001): 12.9 (world avg. 12.3). Total fertility rate (avg. births per childbearing woman; 2001): 4.9. Marriage rate per 1,000 population (1984): 2.5. Life expectancy at birth (2001): male 38.4 years; female 39.7 years.

## National economy

Budget (2000). Revenue: RF 132,400,000,000 (grants 47.8%, taxes on goods and services 26.6%, income tax 13.5%, import and export duties 10.6%). Expenditures: RF 131,700,000,000 (current expenditures 67.7%, of which wages 27.8%, goods and services 18.1%, transfers 8.4%, defense 5.9%, debt payment 4.9%; capital expenditure 32.3%). Production (metric tons except as noted). Agriculture, forestry, fishing (2001): plantains 2,103,100, sweet potatoes 1,136,600, potatoes 988,900; livestock (number of live animals) 756,522 goats, 732,123 cattle, 248,345 sheep; roundwood (2001) 7,836,000 cu m; fish catch (1999) 6,773. Mining and quarrying (2001): cassiterite (tin ore) 555; wolframite (tungsten ore) 161; gold (1999) 10 kg. Manufacturing (value added in RF '000,000; 2000): food and nonalcoholic beverages 37,981; nonmetallic products 3,109; metal products 1,087. Energy production (consumption): electricity (kW-hr; 2000) 110,800,000 (210,770,000); petroleum products (metric tons; 1998) none (95,500); natural gas (cu m; 2000) 1,373,000,000 ([1996] 300,000). Population economically active (1996): total 3,021,000; activity rate of total population 50.8% (participation rates: ages 14–74 [1989] 46.3%; female 49.0%). Land use (1994): forested 10.1%; meadows and pastures 28.4%; agricultural and under permanent cultivation 47.4%; other 14.1%. Gross national product (2000): $1,998,000,000 ($230 per capita). Public debt (external, outstanding; 2000): $1,306,000,000. Household income. Average household size (1991) 4.7; average annual income per household (1983) RF 122,870 ($1,300). Tourism: receipts (1993) $2,000,-000; expenditures (1992) $17,000,000.

## Foreign trade

Imports (2000): $239,800,000 (capital goods 22.1%, food 19.4%, energy products 18.7%, intermediate goods 18.1%). Major import sources (1999): Japan 13.1%; Belgium 12.8%; Kenya 12.5%; Saudi Arabia 8.0%; Germany 5.1%. Exports (2000): $89,800,000 (tea 27.1%, coffee 25.1%, cassiterite and tin 1.1%). Major export destinations (1999): Kenya 62.4%; Tanzania 13.9%; Germany 7.9%; Belgium 6.5%.

## Transport and communications

Transport. Roads (1999): total length 7,460 mi, 12,000 km (paved 8%). Vehicles (1996): passenger cars 13,000; trucks 17,100. Air transport (2000; Kigali airport only): passengers embarked and disembarked 101,000; cargo loaded and unloaded 4,300 metric tons; airports (1998) with scheduled flights 2. Communications, in total units (units per 1,000 persons). Daily newspaper circulation (1995): 500 (0.1); radio receivers (1997): 601,000 (101); telephone main lines (2001): 21,500 (2.7); cellular telephone subscribers (2001): 65,000 (8.2); Internet users (2001): 20,000 (2.5).

## Education and health

**Literacy** (1995): percentage of total population age 15 and over literate 67.0%; males literate 73.7%; females literate 60.6%. **Health:** physicians (1992) 150 (1 per 50,000 persons); hospital beds (1990) 12,152 (1 per 588 persons); infant mortality rate per 1,000 live births (2001) 107.0. **Food** (2000): daily per capita caloric intake 2,077 (vegetable products 98%, animal products 2%); 90% of FAO recommended minimum.

## Military

**Total active duty personnel** (2001): 49,000–64,000 (army 100%). **Military expenditure as percentage of GNP** (1999): 4.5% (world 2.4%); per capita expenditure $12.

## Background

Originally inhabited by the Twa, a Pygmy people, Rwanda became home to the Hutu, who were well established there when the Tutsi appeared in the 14th century. The Tutsi conquered the Hutu and in the 15th century founded a kingdom near Kigali. The Belgians occupied Rwanda in 1916, and the League of Nations created Ruanda-Urundi as a Belgian mandate in 1923. The Tutsi retained their dominance until shortly before Rwanda reached independence in 1962, when the Hutu took control of the government and stripped the Tutsi of much of their land. Many Tutsi fled Rwanda, and the Hutu dominated the country's political system, waging sporadic civil wars until mid-1994, when the death of the country's leader in a plane crash—apparently shot down—led to massive violence. The Tutsi-led Rwandan Patriotic Front (RPF) took over the country by force after the massacre of almost 500,000 Tutsi by Hutu. Two million refugees, mostly Hutu, fled to neighboring countries after the RPF's victory.

## Recent Developments

In January 2002, the Rwandan government convened *gacacas* ("traditional courts") to help alleviate the backlog of cases involving the 1994 genocide. Owing to the size of the caseload—there were 115,000 suspects awaiting trial in Rwandan prisons—it would take the International Criminal Tribunal for Rwanda 200 years to complete all the hearings. A peace accord between Rwanda and the Democratic Republic of the Congo was signed in July, four years after Rwandan troops had entered the country to track down militias accused of genocide. Rwanda was withdrawing its troops from South Kivu province when fighting erupted anew on 18 October between a Congolese militia and rebels supported by Rwanda.

**Internet resources:**
<www.rwandemb.org/tourism.html>

# Saint Kitts and Nevis

**Official name:** Federation of Saint Kitts and Nevis. **Form of government:** constitutional monarchy with

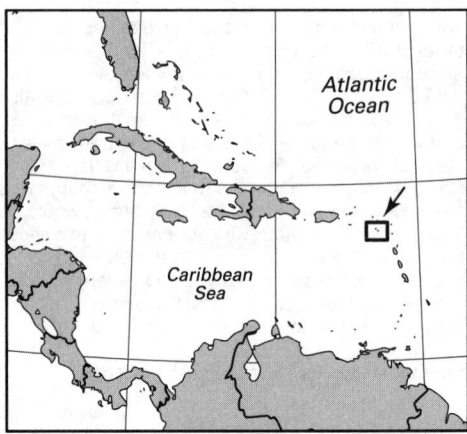

one legislative house (National Assembly [15, including 4 nonelective seats]). **Chief of state:** British Monarch Queen Elizabeth II (from 1952) represented by Governor-General Cuthbert Sebastian. **Head of government:** Prime Minister Denzil Douglas (from 1995). **Capital:** Basseterre. **Official language:** English. **Official religion:** none. **Monetary unit:** 1 Eastern Caribbean dollar (EC$) = 100 cents; valuation (7 Jul 2003) US$1 = EC $2.67.

## Demography

**Area:** 104.0 sq mi, 269.4 sq km. **Population** (2002): 46,200. **Density** (2002): persons per sq mi 444.2, persons per sq km 171.7. **Urban** (2000): 34.2%. **Sex distribution** (2001): male 49.70%; female 50.30%. **Age breakdown** (2000): under 15, 30.3%; 15–29, 24.9%; 30–44, 22.2%; 45–59, 11.2%; 60–74, 7.1%; 75 and over, 4.3%. **Ethnic composition** (2000): black 90.4%; mulatto 5.0%; Indo-Pakistani 3.0%; white 1.0%; other/unspecified 0.6%. **Religious affiliation** (1995): Protestant 84.6%, of which Anglican 25.2%, Methodist 25.2%, Pentecostal 8.4%, Moravian 7.6%; Roman Catholic 6.7%; Hindu 1.5%; other 7.2%. **Major towns** (2001): Basseterre 13,033; Charlestown (1994) 1,411. **Location:** island in the Caribbean Sea, between Puerto Rico and Trinidad and Tobago.

## Vital statistics

**Birth rate** per 1,000 population (2000): 19.1 (world avg. 22.5); (1983) legitimate 19.2%; illegitimate 80.8%. **Death rate** per 1,000 population (2000): 9.4 (world avg. 9.0). **Natural increase rate** per 1,000 population (2000): 9.7 (world avg. 13.5). **Total fertility rate** (avg. births per childbearing woman; 2000): 2.4. **Life expectancy** at birth (2000): male 67.9 years; female 73.7 years.

## National economy

**Budget** (1999). *Revenue:* EC$252,400,000 (tax revenue 72.8% of which taxes on income and profits 19.6%, consumption taxes 16.3%, import duties 15.4%, taxes on domestic goods and services 14.9%; nontax revenue 26.1%). *Expenditures:* EC$298,300,000 (current expenditure 88.4%; development expenditure 11.6%). **Production** (metric tons except as

*1 metric ton = about 1.1 short tons;   1 kilometer = 0.6 mi (statute);   1 metric ton-km cargo = about 0.68 short ton-mi cargo;   c.i.f.: cost, insurance, and freight;   f.o.b.: free on board*

noted). *Agriculture, forestry, fishing* (1999): sugar-cane 196,784, tropical fruit 1,300, coconuts 1,000; livestock (number of live animals) 14,500 goats, 8,000 sheep, 3,600 cattle; fish catch (2000) 257. *Mining and quarrying*: excavation of sand for local use. *Manufacturing* (2001): raw sugar 20,193; carbonated beverages 45,000 hectoliters (1995); beer 20,000 hectoliters (1995). *Energy production (consumption)*: electricity (kW-hr; 1997) 90,000,000 (90,000,000); petroleum products (metric tons; 1997) none (33,000). **Gross national product** (2000): US$269,000,000 (US$6,570 per capita). **Household income and expenditure**. Average household size (2001) 2.9; average annual income per wage earner (1994) EC$9,940 (US$3,681); expenditure (1978): food, beverages, and tobacco 55.6%, household furnishings 9.4%, housing 7.6%, clothing and footwear 7.5%, fuel and light 6.6%, transportation 4.3%, other 9.0%. **Public debt** (external, outstanding; 2000): US$135,800,000. **Population economically active** (1980): total 17,125; activity rate of total population 39.5% (participation rates: ages 15–64, 69.5%; female 41.0%; unemployed [1997] 4.5%). **Land use** (1994): forested 17%; meadows and pastures 3%; agricultural and under permanent cultivation 39%; other 41%. **Tourism**: receipts from visitors (2000) US$56,000,000; expenditures by nationals abroad (1998) US$6,000,000.

### Foreign trade

**Imports** (1997): EC$401,100,000 (machinery and transport equipment 30.3%, basic and miscellaneous manufactures 20.6%, food 16.1%, chemicals and chemical products 8.2%). *Major import sources*: US 45.5%; Caricom countries 13.4%, of which Trinidad and Tobago 9.8%; UK 9.7%. **Exports** (1997): EC$109,900,000 (food 56.0%, machinery and transport equipment [mostly electronic goods] 31.7%). *Major export destinations* (1997): US 55.0%; UK 32.6%; Caricom countries 2.9%.

### Transport and communications

**Transport**. *Railroads* (2000): length 58 km. *Roads* (1999): total length 250 km (paved 50%). *Vehicles* (1999): passenger cars 5,326; trucks and buses 3,742. *Air transport*: passenger arrivals (1992; Saint Kitts airport only) 123,195; airports (1998) with scheduled flights 2. **Communications**, in total units (units per 1,000 persons). Radio receivers (1997): 28,000 (701); television receivers (1997): 10,000 (264); telephone main lines (2000): 21,900 (568); cellular telephone subscribers (2000): 1,200 (31); personal computers (1999): 8,000 (190); Internet users (1999): 2,000 (52).

### Education and health

**Educational attainment** (1980). Percentage of population age 25 and over having: no formal schooling 1.1%; primary education 29.6%; secondary 67.2%; higher 2.1%. **Literacy** (1990): total population age 15 and over literate 25,500 (90.0%); males literate 13,100 (90.0%); females literate 12,400 (90.0%). **Health** (1998): physicians 50 (1 per 815 persons); hospital beds 244 (1 per 167 persons); infant mortality rate per 1,000 live births (2000): 16.7. **Food** (2000): daily per capita caloric intake 2,685 (vegetable products 72%, animal products 28%); 111% of FAO recommended minimum.

### Military

**Total active duty personnel**: in July 1997 the National Assembly approved a bill creating a 50-member army. **Military expenditure as percentage of GNP** (1998; includes expenditure for police): 3.5%; per capita expenditure US$226.

 Charlestown, the capital of the island of Nevis, is the birthplace of American statesman Alexander Hamilton. Hamilton was born in 1757, the illegitimate son of a Scotsman and a woman from Nevis. He was sent to King's College (which later became Columbia University) and was a member of the Continental Congress and the first secretary of the Treasury. Hamilton's portrait appears on the $10 bill. A replica of the Hamilton house stands in Charlestown.

### Background

Saint Kitts became the first British colony in the West Indies in 1623. Anglo-French rivalry grew in the 17th century and lasted more than a century. In 1783, by the Treaty of Versailles, the islands became wholly British possessions. They were united with Anguilla from 1882 to 1980 but became an independent federation within the British Commonwealth in 1983. In 1997 Nevis considered becoming independent.

### Recent Developments

Prime Minister Denzil Douglas pledged in April 2002 to readjust the focus of Saint Kitts and Nevis's offshore financial services policy away from an emphasis on tax exemption to other attractions that a "reputable" offshore location could offer. That same month the country was removed from the OECD's blacklist of centers posing "harmful tax competition."

**Internet resources**: <www.stkittsnevis.net>

# Saint Lucia

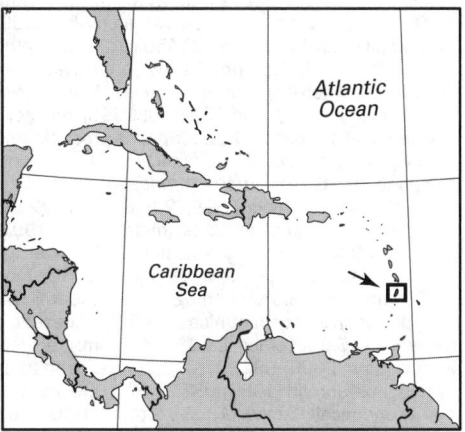

**Official name**: Saint Lucia. **Form of government**: constitutional monarchy with a Parliament consisting of two legislative chambers (Senate [11]; House of Assembly [17]). **Chief of state**: Queen Elizabeth II (from 1952) represented by Governor General Perlette

Louisy (from 1997). **Head of government:** Prime Minister Kenneth Anthony (from 1997). **Capital:** Castries. **Official language:** English. **Official religion:** none. **Monetary unit:** 1 Eastern Caribbean dollar (EC$) = 100 cents; valuation (7 Jul 2003) US$1 = EC$2.67.

## Demography

**Area:** 238 sq mi, 617 sq km. **Population** (2002): 160,000. **Density** (2002): persons per sq mi 672.3, persons per sq km 259.3. **Urban** (1998): 37.3%. **Sex distribution** (2000): male 49.04%; female 50.96%. **Age breakdown** (2000): under 15, 31.8%; 15–29, 29.6%; 30–44, 20.5%; 45–59, 10.2%; 60–74, 5.3%; 75 and over, 2.6%. **Ethnic composition** (2000): black 50%; mulatto 44%; East Indian 3%; white 1%; other 2%. **Religious affiliation** (2001): Roman Catholic 67.5%; Protestant 22.0%, of which Seventh-day Adventist 8.4%, Pentecostal 5.6%; Rastafarian 2.1%; nonreligious 4.5%; other/unknown 3.9%. **Major urban area** (2001): Castries 35,070. **Location:** island between the Caribbean Sea and North Atlantic Ocean, north of Trinidad and Tobago.

## Vital statistics

**Birth rate** per 1,000 population (2000): 18.2 (world avg. 22.5); legitimate 14.3%; illegitimate 85.7%. **Death rate** per 1,000 population (2000): 6.0 (world avg. 9.0). **Natural increase rate** per 1,000 population (2000): 12.2 (world avg. 13.5). **Total fertility rate** (avg. births per childbearing woman; 2000): 2.0. **Marriage rate** per 1,000 population (2000): 4.1. **Divorce rate** per 1,000 population (2000): 0.3. **Life expectancy** at birth (2000): male 68.7 years; female 73.6 years.

## National economy

**Budget** (1998–99). *Revenue:* EC$469,900,000 (current revenue 86.9%, of which consumption duties on imported goods 24.4%; taxes on income and profits 21.9%; import duties 14.7%; nontax revenue 9.2%; grants 3.9%). *Expenditures:* EC$496,600,000 (current expenditures 69.4%; development expenditures and net lending 30.6%). **Production** (metric tons except as noted). *Agriculture, forestry, fishing* (1999): bananas 80,000, mangoes 27,000, coconuts 12,000; livestock (number of live animals; 1999) 14,750 pigs, 12,500 sheep, 12,450 cattle; fish catch (2000) 1,759. *Mining and quarrying:* excavation of sand for local construction and pumice. *Manufacturing* (value of production in EC$'000; 1998): alcoholic beverages and tobacco 31,120; paper products and cardboard boxes 28,747; electrical and electronic components 16,245. *Energy production (consumption):* electricity (kW-hr; 1998) 235,881,000 (213,-000,000); petroleum products (metric tons; 1997) none (65,000). **Household expenditure.** Average household size (2001) 3.3; expenditure (1982): food 46.8%, housing 13.5%, clothing and footwear 6.5%, transportation and communications 6.3%, household furnishings 5.8%, other 21.1%. **Tourism:** receipts from visitors (2000) US$277,000,000; expenditures by nationals abroad (1997) US$29,000,000. **Population economically active** (1998): total 73,660; activity rate of total population 49.2% (participation rates: ages 15–64, 79.1%; female 44.4%; unemployed [2001] 18.9%). **Public debt** (external, outstanding;

2000): US$169,200,000. **Gross national product** (at current market prices; 2000): US$642,000,000 (US$4,120 per capita). **Land use** (1994): forested 13%; meadows and pastures 5%; agricultural and under permanent cultivation 30%; other 52%.

## Foreign trade

**Imports** (2000): US$355,100,000 (machinery and transportation equipment 24.6%; food products 20.0%; crude petroleum and petroleum products 9.3%; chemicals and chemical products 8.2%). *Major import sources:* US 37.5%; Caricom countries 21.7%, of which Trinidad and Tobago 14.4%; UK 8.5%; Japan 4.5%; Canada 3.8%. **Exports** (2000): US$43,400,-000 (1999; bananas 58.4%; beer and ale 11.7%; clothing 6.0%; cardboard boxes 4.1%). *Major export destinations:* UK 55.9%; Caricom countries 26.6%, of which Barbados 10.3%, Antigua and Barbuda 4.8%; US 14.8%.

## Transport and communications

**Transport.** *Roads* (1999): total length 1,210 km (paved 5%). *Vehicles* (1997): passenger cars 14,783; trucks and buses 1,020. *Air transport* (2000): passenger arrivals and departures 726,000; cargo unloaded and loaded 4,200 metric tons; airports (2000) with scheduled flights 2. **Communications,** in total units (units per 1,000 persons). Radio receivers (1997): 100,000 (668); television receivers (1997): 40,000 (267); telephone main lines (1999): 44,465 (289); cellular telephone subscribers (1998): 1,900 (12.5).

## Education and health

**Educational attainment** (2000). Percentage of population age 15 and over having: no formal schooling 6.5%; primary education 56.2%; secondary 27.5%; higher vocational 4.5%; university 2.7%; other/unknown 2.6%. **Literacy** (1995): about 82%. **Health** (1998): physicians 60 (1 per 2,533 persons); hospital beds 521 (1 per 292 persons); infant mortality rate per 1,000 live births (2000) 13.4. **Food** (1999): daily per capita caloric intake 2,812 (vegetable products 77%, animal products 23%); 116% of FAO recommended minimum.

## Military

**Total active duty personnel** (2000): The 300-member police force includes a specially trained paramilitary unit and a coast guard unit.

## Background

Caribs replaced early Arawak inhabitants on the island c. AD 800–1300. Settled by the French in 1650, it was ceded to Great Britain in 1814 and became one of the Windward Islands in 1871. It became fully independent in 1979. The economy is based on agriculture and tourism.

## Recent Developments

Saint Lucia, normally among the most buoyant of the smaller Caribbean economies, has been facing severe economic problems. Banana exports were stag-

---

*1 metric ton = about 1.1 short tons;   1 kilometer = 0.6 mi (statute);   1 metric ton-km cargo = about 0.68 short ton-mi cargo;   c.i.f.: cost, insurance, and freight;   f.o.b.: free on board*

nant, and tourism declined by about 8%, primarily because of the effects of the 11 Sep 2001 attacks in the US. In addition, in September Tropical Storm Lili destroyed almost 50% of the banana crop. Real growth in 2002 was considered unlikely.

Internet resources: <www.slucia.com>

# Saint Vincent and the Grenadines

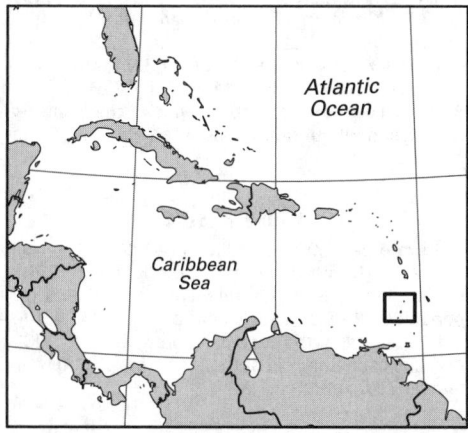

**Official name:** Saint Vincent and the Grenadines. **Form of government:** constitutional monarchy with one legislative house (House of Assembly [21, including 6 nonelective seats]). **Chief of state:** British Monarch Queen Elizabeth II (from 1952) represented by Governor-General Frederick Ballantyne (from 2 Sep 2002). **Head of government:** Prime Minister Ralph Gonsalves (from 2001). **Capital:** Kingstown. **Official language:** English. **Official religion:** none. **Monetary unit:** 1 Eastern Caribbean dollar (EC$) = 100 cents; valuation (7 Jul 2003) US$1 = EC$2.67.

## Demography

**Area:** 150.3 sq mi, 389.3 sq km. **Population** (2002): 113,000. **Density** (2002): persons per sq mi 751.8, persons per sq km 290.3. **Urban** (2000): 54.4%. **Sex distribution** (1999): male 50.50%; female 49.50%. **Age breakdown** (1999): under 15, 31.3%; 15–29, 31.2%; 30–44, 19.6%; 45–59, 9.4%; 60–74, 5.9%; 75 and over, 2.6%. **Ethnic composition** (1999): black 65.5%; mulatto 23.5%; Indo-Pakistani 5.5%; white 3.5%; black-Amerindian 2.0%. **Religious affiliation** (1995): Protestant 57.6%; unaffiliated Christian 20.6%; Roman Catholic 10.7%; Hindu 3.3%; Muslim 1.5%; other/nonreligious 6.3%. **Major city** (2000): Kingstown 16,209. **Location:** islands in the Caribbean Sea, north of Trinidad and Tobago.

## Vital statistics

**Birth rate** per 1,000 population (2001): 18.0 (world avg. 21.2); (1999) legitimate 17.9%; illegitimate 82.1%. **Death rate** per 1,000 population (2001): 6.6 (world avg. 8.9). **Natural increase rate** per 1,000 population (2001): 11.4 (world avg. 12.3). **Total fertility rate** (avg. births per childbearing woman; 2000): 2.1. **Marriage rate** per 1,000 population (1999): 5.7. **Divorce rate** per 1,000 population (1999): 0.6. **Life expectancy** at birth (2000): male 70.6 years; female 74.1 years.

## National economy

**Budget** (1998). *Revenue:* EC$285,200,000 (current revenue 73.8%, of which income tax 25.1%, consumption duties on imports 23.3%, taxes on goods and services 9.3%, import duties 7.9%; grants 14.5%; nontax revenue 9.5%; capital revenue 2.2%). *Expenditures:* EC$303,100,000 (current expenditure 65.9%; development expenditure 34.1%). **Public debt** (external, outstanding; 2000): US$161,000,000. **Production** (metric tons except as noted). *Agriculture, forestry, fishing* (1999): bananas 43,000, coconuts 23,600, eddoes and dasheens 4,118; livestock (number of live animals) 13,000 sheep, 9,400 pigs, 6,200 cattle; fish catch (2000) 7,294. *Mining and quarrying:* sand and gravel for local use. *Manufacturing* (export value of manufactures in US$'000,000; 1995): packaged flour 8.7; packaged rice 6.4; other goods (mostly garments, sporting goods, and electronic goods) 8.1. *Energy production (consumption):* electricity (kW-hr; 1999) 95,900,000 (84,800,000); petroleum products (metric tons; 1997) none (43,000). **Tourism:** receipts from visitors (2000) US$74,000,000; expenditures by nationals abroad (1998) US$8,000,000. **Land use** (1994): forested 36%; meadows and pastures 5%; agricultural and under permanent cultivation 28%; other 31%. **Gross national product** (2000): US$313,000,000 (US$2,720 per capita). **Population economically active** (1991): total 41,682; activity rate of total population 39.1% (participation rates: ages 15–64, 67.5%; female 35.9%; unemployed [1996] more than 30%). **Household income.** Average household size (1991) 3.9; income per household (1988) EC$4,579 (US$1,696).

## Foreign trade

**Imports** (1999-c.i.f.): US$202,300,000 (basic manufactures 33.9%; machinery and transport equipment 24.1%; food products 21.2%; chemicals and chemical products 9.9%; fuels 5.5%). Major import sources: US 37.5%; Caricom countries 23.2%, of which Trinidad and Tobago 15.7%; UK 12.0%; Japan 4.5%. **Exports** (1998-f.o.b.): US$49,600,000 (domestic exports 90.7%, of which bananas 38.5%, packaged flour 13.6%, packaged rice 10.1%, eddoes and dasheens 3.8%; reexports 9.3%). Major export destinations: Caricom countries 51.6%, of which Trinidad and Tobago 10.3%, St. Lucia 8.7%, Barbados 8.7%; UK 40.3%.

## Transport and communications

**Transport.** *Roads* (1999): total length 1,040 km (paved 31%). *Vehicles* (1999): passenger cars 7,989; trucks and buses 3,920. *Air transport* (1999): passenger arrivals 122,815; passenger departures 126,924; airports (1998) with scheduled flights 5. **Communications,** in total units (units per 1,000 persons). Radio receivers (1995): 65,000 (591); television receivers (1995): 17,700 (161); telephone main lines (2001): 24,900 (220); cellular telephone subscribers (2001): 2,400 (21); Internet users (2001): 3,500 (31); personal computers (2001): 13,000 (116).

## Education and health

**Educational attainment** (1980). Percentage of population age 25 and over having: no formal schooling 2.4%; primary education 88.0%; secondary 8.2%;

higher 1.4%. **Literacy** (1991): total population age 15 and over literate 64,000 (96.0%). **Health** (1998): physicians 59 (1 per 1,883 persons); hospital beds 209 (1 per 531 persons); infant mortality rate per 1,000 live births (1999) 17.7. **Food** (1999): daily per capita caloric intake 2,540 (vegetable products 83%, animal products 17%); 105% of FAO recommended minimum.

## Military

**Total active duty personnel** (1992): 634-member police force includes a coast guard and paramilitary unit.

## Background

The French and the British contested for control of St. Vincent and the Grenadines until 1763, when it was ceded to England by the Treaty of Paris. The original inhabitants, the Caribs, recognized British sovereignty but revolted in 1795. Most of the Caribs were deported; many who remained were killed in volcanic eruptions in 1812 and 1902. In 1969 Saint Vincent and the Grenadines became a self-governing state in association with the United Kingdom, and in 1979 it achieved full independence.

## Recent Developments

The country received a boost to its flagging tourism industry in 2002 when American real-estate tycoon Donald Trump took over management of the $300 million Carenage Beach Resort on the Vincentian island of Canouan. The government expected that the Trump name would be a magnet for other investors.

**Internet resources:** <www.svgtourism.com>

# Samoa

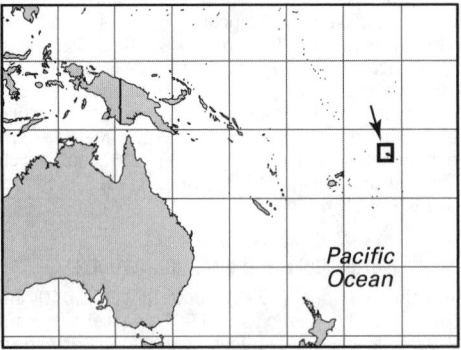

*Pacific Ocean*

**Official name:** Malo Sa'oloto Tuto'atasi o Samoa (Samoan); Independent State of Samoa (English). **Form of government:** constitutional monarchy with one legislative house (Legislative Assembly [49]). **Chief of state:** Chief Malietoa Tanumafili II (from 1962). **Head of government:** Prime Minister Tuila'epa Sailele Malielegaoi (from 1998). **Capital:** Apia. **Official languages:** Samoan; English. **Official religion:** none. **Monetary unit:** 1 tala (SA$ [WS$ prior to July 1997], plural tala) = 100 sene; valuation (7 Jul 2003) US$1 = SA$2.95.

## Demography

**Area:** 1,093 sq mi, 2,831 sq km. **Population** (2002): 178,000. **Density** (2002): persons per sq mi 162.9, persons per sq km 62.9. **Urban** (2002): 22.0%. **Sex distribution** (2001): male 52.0%; female 48.0%. **Age breakdown** (1991): under 15, 40.6%; 15–29, 29.9%; 30–44, 14.6%; 45–59, 8.8%; 60–74, 5.0%; 75 and over, 1.1%. **Ethnic composition** (1997): Samoan (Polynesian) 92.6%; Euronesian (European and Polynesian) 7.0%; European 0.4%. **Religious affiliation** (1995): Mormon 25.8%; Congregational 24.6%; Roman Catholic 21.3%; Methodist 12.2%; Pentecostal 8.0%; Seventh-day Adventist 3.9%; other Christian 1.7%; other 2.5%. **Major city** (2001): Apia 38,836. **Location:** group of islands in the South Pacific Ocean, about halfway between Hawaii (US) and New Zealand.

## Vital statistics

**Birth rate** per 1,000 population (2002): 28.0 (world avg. 21.2). **Death rate** per 1,000 population (2002): 5.6 (world avg. 8.9). **Natural increase rate** per 1,000 population (2002): 22.4 (world avg. 12.3). **Total fertility rate** (avg. births per childbearing woman; 2002): 4.2. **Life expectancy** at birth (2002): male 67.0 years; female 73.0 years.

## National economy

**Budget** (2000–01). *Revenue*: SA$262,400,000 (tax revenue 66.6%; grants 24.8%; nontax revenue 8.6%). *Expenditures*: SA$281,700,000 (current expenditure 58.4%; development expenditure 36.6%; net lending 5.0%). **Production** (metric tons except as noted). *Agriculture, forestry, fishing* (1999): coconuts 130,000, taro 36,900, bananas 10,000; livestock (number of live animals) 178,800 pigs, 26,000 cattle, 350,000 chickens; roundwood (1998) 131,000 cu m; fish catch (2000) 13,004. *Manufacturing* (in WS$'000; 1990): beer 8,708; cigarettes 6,551; coconut cream 5,576; sawn wood 3,662. *Energy production (consumption)*: electricity (kW-hr; 1997) 65,000,000 (65,000,000); petroleum products (metric tons; 1997) none (43,000). **Household expenditure.** Average household size (1999) 5.4; expenditure (1987): food 58.8%, transportation 9.0%, housing and furnishings 5.1%, fuel and lighting 5.0%, clothing 4.2%, other goods and services 1.9%, other 16.0%. **Tourism:** receipts from visitors (2000) US$40,000,000; expenditures by nationals abroad (1999) US$4,000,000. **Land use** (1994): forested 47.3%; meadows and pastures 0.4%; agricultural and under permanent cultivation 43.1%; other 9.2%. **Gross national product** (at current market prices; 2000): US$246,000,000 (US$1,450 per capita). **Population economically active** (1994): total 47,207; activity rate of total population 28.7% (participation rates: ages 15–64 [1981] 48.6%; female [1991] 32.0%). **Public debt** (external, outstanding; 2000): US$147,000.

## Foreign trade

**Imports** (1997-c.i.f.): WS$247,377,000 ([1996] food 33.9%, industrial supplies 26.4%, machinery 16.9%, petroleum products 11.8%, consumer goods 11.0%).

*1 metric ton = about 1.1 short tons; 1 kilometer = 0.6 mi (statute); 1 metric ton-km cargo = about 0.68 short ton-mi cargo; c.i.f.: cost, insurance, and freight; f.o.b.: free on board*

*Major import sources:* New Zealand 37.9%; Australia 20.7%; US 15.6%; Fiji 15.0%; Japan 4.5%; Hong Kong 0.9%; Singapore 0.5%. **Exports** (1997-f.o.b.): WS$38,531,000 (fresh fish 33.0%, copra 21.1%, coconut oil 18.1%, coconut cream 12.8%, beer 4.3%, kava 4.0%, copra meal 1.5%). *Major export destinations:* New Zealand 48.1%; American Samoa 15.3%; Australia 9.2%; US 3.3%; Germany 2.9%.

## Transport and communications

**Transport.** *Roads* (1996): total length 790 km (paved 42%). *Vehicles* (1995): passenger cars 1,068; trucks and buses 1,169. *Air transport* (1998): passenger-km 250,000,000; metric ton-km cargo 24,000,000; airports (1997) with scheduled flights 3. **Communications,** in total units (units per 1,000 persons). Radio receivers (1997): 178,000 (1,035); television receivers (1998): 9,000 (52); telephone main lines (2001): 10,000 (56); cellular telephone subscribers (2001): 3,000 (17); personal computers (2001): 1,000 (6.7); Internet users (2001): 3,000 (17).

## Education and health

**Educational attainment** (1981). Percentage of population age 25 and over having: some primary education 16.5%; complete primary 24.5%; some secondary 52.1%; complete secondary 3.1%; higher 2.0%; unknown 1.8%. **Literacy:** virtually 100%. **Health:** physicians (1996) 62 (1 per 2,919 persons); hospital beds (1991) 863 (1 per 255 persons); infant mortality rate per 1,000 live births (2002) 26.0. **Food** (1992): daily per capita caloric intake 2,828 (vegetable products 74%, animal products 26%); 124% of FAO recommended minimum.

## Military

No military forces are maintained; New Zealand is responsible for defense.

## Background

Polynesians inhabited the islands of the Samoan archipelago for thousands of years before they were visited by Europeans in the 18th century. Control of the islands was contested by the US, Britain, and Germany until 1899, when they were divided between the US and Germany. In 1914, Western Samoa was occupied by New Zealand, which received it as a League of Nations mandate in 1920. After World War II, it became a UN trust territory administered by New Zealand, and it achieved independence in 1962. In 1997, the word Western was dropped from the country's name.

## Recent Developments

In June 2002 Samoa celebrated 40 years of independence. Among the leaders in the region who traveled there to mark the anniversary were New Zealand Prime Minister Helen Clark, who made a formal apology for acts committed by the New Zealand government against a nationalist movement in the 1920s and '30s. In May, Samoa declared its 124,000-sq-km (48,000-sq-mi) exclusive economic zone to be a whale, turtle, and shark sanctuary.

**Internet resources:** <www.samoaobserver.ws>

# San Marino

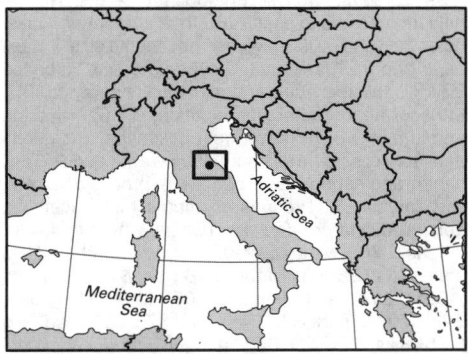

**Official name:** Serenissima Repubblica di San Marino (Most Serene Republic of San Marino). **Form of government:** unitary multiparty republic with one legislative house (Great and General Council [60]). **Heads of state and government:** two Captains-Regent who serve six-month terms beginning in April and October. **Capital:** San Marino. **Official language:** Italian. **Official religion:** none. **Monetary unit:** 1 euro (€) = 100 cents; valuation (7 Jul 2003) $1 = €0.87; at conversion on 1 Jan 2002, €1= 1,936.27 Italian lire (Lit).

## Demography

**Area:** 23.63 sq mi, 61.19 sq km. **Population** (2002): 27,700. **Density** (2002): persons per sq mi 1,172.2, persons per sq km 452.7. **Urban** (1999): 96.2%. **Sex distribution** (2000): male 48.34%; female 51.66%. **Age breakdown** (2000): under 15, 15.7%; 15–29, 18.8%; 30–44, 25.5%; 45–59, 18.8%; 60–74, 14.0%; 75 and over, 7.2%. **Ethnic composition** (1997): Sammarinesi 83.1%; Italian 12.0%; other 4.8%. **Religious affiliation** (2000): Roman Catholic 88.7%; Pentecostal 1.8%; other 9.5%. **Major cities** (1997): Serravalle/Dogano 4,802; Borgo Maggiore 2,394; San Marino 2,294. **Location:** southern Europe, completely surrounded by Italy.

## Vital statistics

**Birth rate** per 1,000 population (2000): 10.8 (world avg. 22.5); (1985) legitimate 95.2%; illegitimate 4.8%. **Death rate** per 1,000 population (2000): 7.0 (world avg. 9.0). **Natural increase rate** per 1,000 population (2000): 3.8 (world avg. 13.5). **Total fertility rate** (avg. births per childbearing woman; 2000): 1.3. **Marriage rate** per 1,000 population (1992–96): 8.1. **Divorce rate** per 1,000 population (1991–95): 1.0. **Life expectancy** at birth (2000): male 77.6 years; female 85.0 years.

## National economy

**Budget** (1997). *Revenue:* Lit 411,000,000,000 (taxes on goods and services 37.2%; taxes on income and profits 31.6%; social security 19.7%). *Expenditures:* Lit 448,000,000,000 (current expenditures 90.4%, of which social security and subsidies 48.2%, wages and salaries 31.2%; capital expenditures 6.9%; other 2.7%). **Public debt** (external outstanding; 2000): $3,873,000. **Tourism:** number of tourist arrivals (1999) 3,148,000; receipts from visitors (1994) $252,500,000. **Population economically active** (2000): total 19,072; activity rate of total population 73.1% (participation rates: ages 15–64, 88.4% [1999]; female 40.8%; unemployed 2.2%). **House-hold income and expenditure**. Total number of house-holds (1997) 10,093; average household size 2.5; expenditure (1991): food, beverages, and tobacco 22.1%, housing, fuel, and electrical energy 20.9%, transportation and communications 17.6%, clothing and footwear 8.0%, furniture, appliances, and goods and services for the home 7.2%, education 7.1%, health and sanitary services 2.6%, other goods and services 14.5%. **Production** (metric tons except as noted). *Agriculture, forestry, fishing:* wheat c. 4,400, grapes c. 700, barley c. 500; livestock (number of live animals; 1998) 831 cattle, 748 pigs. *Manufacturing* (1998): processed meats 324,073 kg, of which beef 226,570 kg, pork 87,764 kg, veal 7,803 kg; cheese 61,563 kg; butter 12,658 kg. *Energy production (consumption):* all electrical power is imported via electrical grid from Italy. **Gross national product** (at current market prices; 1999): $715,300,000 ($26,600 per capita). **Land use** (1985): agricultural and under permanent cultivation 74%; meadows and pastures 22%; forested, built-on, wasteland, and other 4%.

## Foreign trade

**Imports** (1996): $1,719,300,000 (manufactured goods of all kinds, oil, and gold). *Major import source:* Italy. **Exports** (1996): $1,741,900,000 (manufactured goods, traditionally wine, wheat, woolen goods, furniture, wood, ceramics, building stone, dairy products, meat, and postage stamps). *Major export destination:* Italy.

## Transport and communications

**Transport**. *Roads* (1999): total length 252 km. *Vehicles* (1999): passenger cars 26,320; trucks and buses 2,763. *Air transport:* airports with scheduled flights, none. **Communications**, in total units (units per 1,000 persons). Daily newspaper circulation (1996): 2,000 (72); radio receivers (1998): 16,000 (610); television receivers (1998): 9,055 (358); telephone main lines (1999): 19,970 (769); cellular telephone subscribers (1999): 10,000 (369).

## Education and health

**Educational attainment** (1997). Percentage of population age 14 and over having: basic literacy or primary education 35.6%; secondary 30.7%; some postsecondary 27.9%; higher degree 5.8%. **Literacy** (1997): total population age 15 and over literate 21,885 (99.1%); males literate 10,546 (99.4%); females literate 11,339 (98.8%). **Health** (2000): physicians 117 (1 per 230 persons); hospital beds 141 (1 per 191 persons); infant mortality rate per 1,000 live births (2000) 6.3. **Food** (2000): daily per capita caloric intake 3,661 (vegetable products 74%, animal products 26%); 146% of FAO recommended minimum.

## Military

**Total active duty personnel** (2000): none; defense is provided by a public security force of about 50; all fit males ages 16–55 constitute a militia. **Military expenditure as percentage of national budget** (1992): 1.0% (world 3.6%); per capita expenditure (1987) $155.

## Background

According to tradition, San Marino was founded in the early 4th century AD by St. Marinus. By the 12th century it had developed into a commune and remained independent despite challenges from neighboring rulers, including the Malatesta family in nearby Rimini, Italy. San Marino survived the Renaissance as a relic of the self-governing Italian city-state and remained an independent republic after the unification of Italy in 1861. It is one of the smallest republics in the world, and it may be the oldest one in Europe.

## Recent Developments

International pressure has been brought on San Marino, which had come under close scrutiny as a suspected fiscal haven, to bring its banking practices into alignment with those of major industrialized nations. The small republic has also attempted to ensure its future security by taking steps to explore eventual membership in the European Union.

Internet resources:
<http://emulateme.com/sanmarino.htm>

# São Tomé and Príncipe

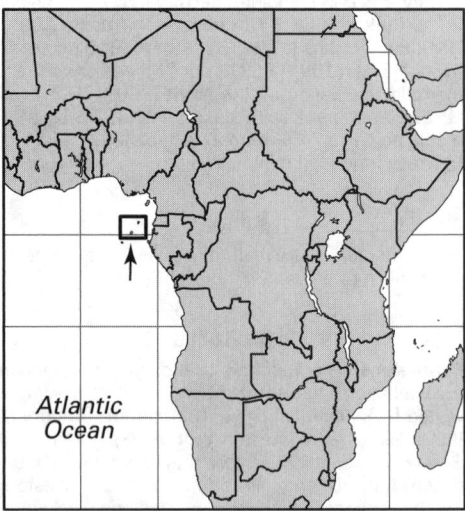

**Official name:** República democrática de São Tomé e Príncipe (Democratic Republic of São Tomé and Príncipe). **Form of government:** Multiparty republic with one legislative house (National Assembly [55]). **Chief of state:** President Fradique de Menezes (from 2001). **Head of government:** Prime Minister Maria das Neves (from 7 Oct 2002). **Capital:** São Tomé. **Official language:** Portuguese. **Official religion:** none. **Monetary unit:** 1 dobra (Db) = 100 cêntimos; valuation (7 Jul 2003) $1 = Db 8,700.

## Demography

**Area:** 386 sq mi, 1,001 sq km. **Population** (2002): 147,000. **Density** (2002): persons per sq mi 379.9,

---

*1 metric ton = about 1.1 short tons;     1 kilometer = 0.6 mi (statute);     1 metric ton-km cargo = about 0.68 short ton-mi cargo;     c.i.f.: cost, insurance, and freight;     f.o.b.: free on board*

persons per sq km 146.5. **Urban** (1999): 46.0%. **Sex distribution** (2001): male 49.28%, female 50.72%. **Age breakdown** (2001): under 15, 47.7%; 15–29, 27.5%; 30–44, 12.6%; 45–59, 6.3%; 60–74, 4.5%; 75 and over, 1.4%. **Ethnic composition** (2000): black-white admixture 79.5%; Fang 10.0%; angolares (descendants of former Angolan slaves) 7.6%; Portuguese 1.9%; other 1.0%. **Religious affiliation** (1995): Roman Catholic, about 89.5%; remainder mostly Protestant, predominantly Seventh-day Adventist and an indigenous Evangelical Church. **Major cities** (1981): São Tomé 49,541 (1997); Trindade 11,388; Santana 6,190; Neves 5,919; Santo Amaro 5,878. **Location:** islands in the Gulf of Guinea, straddling the Equator west of Gabon.

## Vital statistics

**Birth rate** per 1,000 population (2001): 42.7 (world avg. 21.2). **Death rate** per 1,000 population (2001): 7.5 (world avg. 8.9). **Natural increase rate** per 1,000 population (2001): 35.2 (world avg. 12.3). **Total fertility rate** (avg. births per childbearing woman; 2001): 6.0. **Life expectancy** at birth (2001): male 64.2 years; female 67.1 years.

## National economy

**Budget** (2000). *Revenue*: Db 183,400,000,000 (grants 56.4%; taxes 32.4%, of which sales taxes 10.9%, import taxes 9.8%, income and profit taxes 9.1%; nontax revenue 11.2%). *Expenditures*: Db 244,400,000,000 (capital expenditure 63.3%; recurrent expenditure 36.7%, of which personnel costs 11.8%, debt service 10.0%, goods and services 6.2%, transfers 3.0%, defense 0.5%). **Public debt** (external, outstanding; 2000): $294,400,000. **Production** (metric tons except as noted). *Agriculture, forestry, fishing* (2001): coconuts 25,500, taro 23,160, bananas 20,000; livestock (number of live animals) 4,800 goats, 4,100 cattle, 2,600 sheep; roundwood (2001) 9,000 cu m; fish catch (1999) 3,756, principally marine fish and shellfish. *Mining and quarrying*: some quarrying to support local construction industry. *Manufacturing* (value in Db; 1995): beer 880,000; clothing 679,000; lumber 369,000. *Energy production (consumption)*: electricity (kW-hr; 2000) 26,050,000 (16,574,000); petroleum products (metric tons; 1997) none (25,000). **Household expenditure.** Average household size (1981): 4.0; expenditure (1995): food 71.9%, housing and energy 10.2%, transportation and communications 6.4%, clothing and other items 5.3%, household durable goods 2.8%, education and health 1.7%. **Population economically active** (1994): total 51,789; activity rate of total population 40.8% (participation rates [1981] ages 15–64, 61.1%; female [1991] 32.4%; unemployed [1994] 29.0%). **Gross national product** (2000): $43,000,-000 ($290 per capita). **Tourism** (1997): receipts from visitors $2,000,000; expenditures by nationals abroad $1,000,000. **Land use** (1994): meadows and pastures 1.3%; agricultural and under permanent cultivation 54.0%; forest, built-on, wasteland, and other 44.7%.

## Foreign trade

**Imports** (2000): $22,300,000 (investment goods 52.9%, food and other agricultural products 20.2%,

petroleum products 17.9%). *Major import sources:* Portugal 41.7%; Angola 13.0%; Japan 10.8%; Belgium 8.5%; France 7.6%; Gabon 3.1%; Germany 0.4%. **Exports** (2000): $3,200,000 (cocoa 90.6%). *Major export destinations:* The Netherlands 57.7%; Portugal 10.9%.

## Transport and communications

**Transport.** *Roads* (1999): total length 320 km (paved 68%). *Vehicles* (1996): passenger cars 4,040; trucks and buses 1,540. *Air transport* (1997): passenger-km 9,000,000; short ton-km cargo 1,000,000; airports (2000) 2. **Communications,** in total units (units per 1,000 persons). Radio receivers (1997): 38,000 (272); television receivers (1997): 23,000 (163); telephone main lines (2001): 5,400 (36); Internet users (2001): 9,000 (60).

## Education and health

**Literacy** (1991): total population age 15 and over literate 73.0%; males literate 85.0%; females literate 62.0%. **Health:** physicians (1996) 61 (1 per 2,147 persons); hospital beds (1983) 640 (1 per 158 persons); infant mortality rate per 1,000 live births (2001) 49.0. **Food** (2000): daily per capita caloric intake 2,390 (vegetable products 96%, animal products 4%); 102% of FAO recommended minimum.

## Military

**Total active duty personnel** (2001): 18,043. **Military expenditure as percentage of GNP** (1999): 1.0% (world 2.4%); per capita expenditure $3.

Cocoa has been the chief export of São Tomé and Príncipe since the late 19th century. Prior to independence in 1975, the cocoa plantations (*roças*) were worked by indentured laborers (slavery was offically abolished in 1875) recruited by Portuguese plantation managers. Some of the distinctive colonial buildings on the *roças* are now tourist attractions.

## Background

First visited by European navigators in the 1470s, the islands of São Tomé and Príncipe were colonized by the Portuguese in the 16th century and were used in the trade and transshipment of slaves. Sugarcane and cacao were the main cash crops. The islands became an overseas province of Portugal in 1951 and achieved independence in 1975. During recent decades its economy was heavily dependent on international assistance.

## Recent Developments

A coup in São Tomé and Príncipe in July 2003 overthrew Pres. Fradique de Menezes and sent a scare through the multinational oil companies that view the country as likely to be rich in petroleum. The coup leaders agreed to the president's reinstatement, however, although his powers would be somewhat reduced.

**Internet resources:** <www.sao-tome.com>

# Saudi Arabia

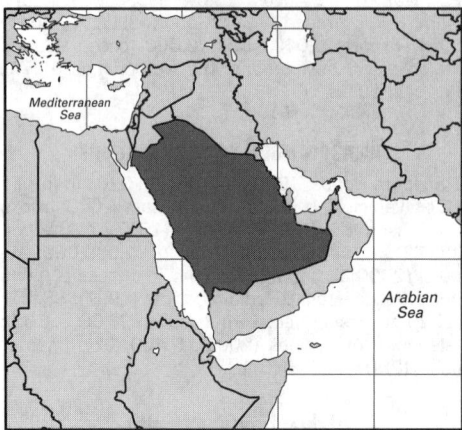

**Official name:** Al-Mamlakah al-'Arabiyah al-Sa'udiyah (Kingdom of Saudi Arabia). **Form of government:** monarchy (assisted by the Consultative Council consisting of 90 appointed members). **Head of state and government:** King Fahd (Crown Prince Abdullah has been de facto ruler since 1996). **Capital:** Riyadh. **Official language:** Arabic. **Official religion:** Islam. **Monetary unit:** 1 Saudi riyal (SRls) = 100 halalah; valuation (7 Jul 2003) $1 = SRls 3.75.

## Demography

**Area:** 868,000 sq mi, 2,248,000 sq km. **Population** (2002): 23,370,000. **Density** (2002): persons per sq mi 28.2, persons per sq km 10.9. **Urban** (2001): 86.7%. **Sex distribution** (2000): male 55.33%; female 44.67%. **Age breakdown** (2000): under 15, 42.6%; 15–29, 22.8%; 30–44, 17.9%; 45–59, 12.1%; 60–74, 3.9%; 75 and over, 0.7%. **Ethnic composition** (2000): Arab 88.1%, of which Saudi Arab 74.2%, Bedouin 3.9%, Gulf Arab 3.0%; Indo-Pakistani 5.5%; African black 1.5%; Filipino 1.0%; other 3.9%. **Religious affiliation** (1992): Sunni Muslim 93.3%; Shi'i Muslim 3.3%; Christian 3.0%; other 0.4%. **Major urban agglomerations** (2000): Riyadh 4,549,000; Jiddah 3,192,000; Mecca 1,335,000; Medina 891,000; Ad-Dammam 764,000. **Location:** the Middle East, bordering Iraq, Kuwait, the Persian Gulf, Qatar, United Arab Emirates, Oman, Yemen, the Red Sea, the Gulf of Aqaba, and Jordan.

## Vital statistics

**Birth rate** per 1,000 population (2000): 37.5 (world avg. 22.5). **Death rate** per 1,000 population (2000): 6.0 (world avg. 9.0). **Natural increase rate** per 1,000 population (2000): 31.5 (world avg. 13.5). **Total fertility rate** (avg. births per childbearing woman; 2000): 6.3. **Life expectancy** at birth (2000): male 66.1 years; female 69.5 years.

## National economy

**Budget** (2000). *Revenue:* SRls 157,000,000,000 (oil revenues 75.1%). Expenditures: SRls 185,000,000,000 (defense and security 40.5%, human resource

development 26.6%, public administration, municipal transfers, and subsidies 16.5%, health and social development 8.9%). **Production** (metric tons except as noted). *Agriculture, forestry, fishing* (2000): wheat 2,046,000, alfalfa 1,400,000, dates 712,000; livestock (number of live animals) 7,576,000 sheep, 4,305,000 goats, 400,000 camels; fish catch (1999) 51,949. *Mining and quarrying* (1999): gypsum 330,000; silver 20,000 kg; gold 9,000 kg. *Manufacturing* (value added in $'000,000; 1995): industrial chemicals 3,014; cement, glass, and other nonmetal mineral products 943; refined petroleum 830. *Energy production (consumption):* electricity (kW-hr; 1996) 106,979,000,000 (106,979,000,-000); crude petroleum (barrels; 2001) 2,862,000,-000 ([1997] 603,789,000); petroleum products (metric tons; 1997) 94,298,000 (44,873,000); natural gas (cu m; 1999) 46,200,000,000 ([1997] 43,400,000,000). **Population economically active** (1994): total 5,614,000; activity rate of total population 32.2% (participation rates [1988] ages 15–64, 59.1%, female 3.5%; unemployed [1997] c. 25%). **Gross national product** (2000): $149,932,000,000 ($7,230 per capita). **Household expenditure.** Average household size (1992) 6.1; expenditure (1994): food and tobacco 38.5%, transportation and communications 16.4%, housing 15.2%, clothing 8.8%, household furnishings 9.7%, education and entertainment 2.3%, other 9.1%. **Tourism** (in $'000,000): receipts (1997) 1,420. **Land use** (1994): forested 0.8%; meadows and pastures 55.8%; agricultural and under permanent cultivation 1.8%; built-on, waste, and other 41.6%.

## Foreign trade

**Imports** (1999-c.i.f.): SRls 104,980,000,000 (machinery and appliances 24.0%, transport equipment 14.5%, chemicals and chemical products 9.0%, base metals and articles 8.4%, vegetables 7.3%, textiles and clothing 6.2%). *Major import sources:* US 18.9%; Japan 9.2%; UK 8.1%; Germany 7.3%; Italy 4.2%. **Exports** (1999-f.o.b.): SRls 190,100,000,-000 (crude petroleum 72.8%; refined petroleum 15.8%; chemical products 4.8%; plastic products 1.9%). *Major export destinations* (1998): US 16.3%; Japan 14.9%; S. Korea 9.6%; Singapore 6.0%; The Netherlands 4.2%.

## Transport and communications

**Transport.** *Railroads* (1997–98): route length 1,390 km; passenger-km 222,000,000 metric ton-km cargo 856,000,000. *Roads* (1996): total length 162,000 km (paved 42.7%). *Vehicles* (1996): passenger cars 1,744,000; trucks and buses 1,192,000. *Air transport* (2001; Saudi Arabian Airlines only): passenger-km 20,216,000,000; metric ton-km cargo 798,968,000; airports (1998) with scheduled flights 28. **Communications,** in total units (units per 1,000 persons). Daily newspaper circulation (1996): 1,105,000 (59); radio receivers (1997): 6,250,000 (313); television receivers (1999): 5,500,000 (256); telephone main lines (2001): 3,233,000 (145); cellular telephone subscribers (2001): 2,529,000 (133); personal computers (2001): 1,400,000 (63); Internet users (2001): 300,000 (14).

*1 metric ton = about 1.1 short tons;    1 kilometer = 0.6 mi (statute);    1 metric ton-km cargo = about 0.68 short ton-mi cargo;   c.i.f.: cost, insurance, and freight;    f.o.b.: free on board*

## Education and health

Educational attainment (1986). Percentage of population age 25 and over having: no formal schooling 31.8%; primary, secondary, or higher education 68.2%. Literacy (1995): population age 15 and over literate 62.8%; males literate 71.5%; females literate 50.2%. Health (1995): physicians 30,306 (1 per 590 persons); hospital beds 41,916 (1 per 427 persons); infant mortality rate per 1,000 live births (2000) 52.9. Food (2000): daily per capita caloric intake 2,875 (vegetable products 84%, animal products 16%); 119% of FAO recommended minimum.

## Military

Total active duty personnel (2001): 126,500 (army 59.3%, navy 12.3%, air force 28.4%); US military (2001) 5,200. Military expenditure as percentage of GNP (1999): 14.9% (world 2.4%); per capita expenditure $996.

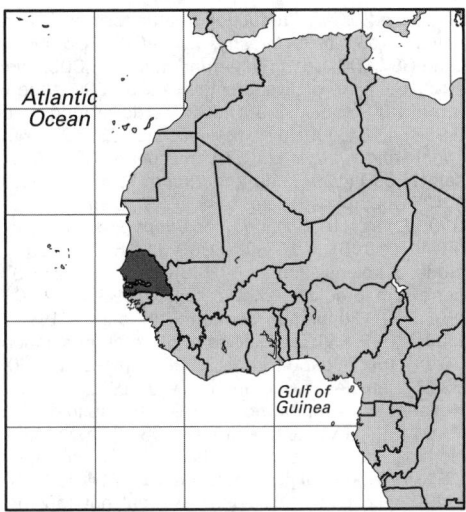

## Background

Saudi Arabia is the historical home of Islam, founded by Muhammad in Medina in 622. During medieval times, local and foreign rulers fought for control of the Arabian Peninsula; in 1517 the Ottomans prevailed. In the 18th–19th century Islamic leaders supporting religious reform struggled to regain Saudi territory, all of which was restored by 1904. The British held Saudi lands as a protectorate from 1915 to 1927; then they acknowledged the sovereignty of the Kingdom of the Hejaz and Najd. The two kingdoms were unified as the Kingdom of Saudi Arabia in 1932. Since World War II, it has supported the Palestinian cause in the Middle East and maintained close ties with the US.

## Recent Developments

As part of a diplomatic effort aimed at improving Saudi-US relations, early in 2002 Crown Prince Abdullah launched a comprehensive peace initiative toward Israel, which called for an Israeli withdrawal from Palestinian territories in exchange for full Arab normalization of relations with the Jewish state. The crown prince traveled to the US to meet with Pres. George W. Bush in April, and, while there were points of disagreement, the White House described Abdullah's proposal as "constructive." Relations became strained again, however, after Saudi Arabia made clear its unwillingness to support any attack on Iraq. An especially tense time ensued after the publication of a study by the RAND Corporation, a California-based think tank, that described Saudi Arabia as "an enemy disguised as a friend" and "active in every level of terrorism." Further strains were visible in early 2003, when the *New York Times* reported that the Saudis were preparing to ask the US to remove its military presence from the country. A string of terrorist bombings of US-occupied facilities in Riyadh in May killed 34 people and wounded 200 others; the attacks were tied to al-Qaeda.

Internet resources: <www.saudinf.com>

# Senegal

Official name: République du Sénégal (Republic of Senegal). Form of government: multiparty republic with one legislative house (National Assembly [120]).

Head of state and government: President Abdoulaye Wade (from 2000) assisted by a prime minister. Capital: Dakar. Official language: French. Official religion: none. Monetary unit: 1 CFA franc (CFAF) = 100 centimes; valuation (7 Jul 2003) $1 = CFAF 571.07; the CFAF is pegged to the euro (€) at €1 = CFAF 655.96 from 1 Jan 2002.

## Demography

Area: 75,951 sq mi, 196,712 sq km. Population (2002): 9,905,000. Density (2002): persons per sq mi 130.4, persons per sq km 50.4. Urban (2000): 47.4%. Sex distribution (2000): male 48.98%; female 50.02%. Age breakdown (2000): under 15, 44.6%; 15–29, 27.5%; 30–44, 15.6%; 45–59, 7.7%; 60–74, 3.7%; 75 and over, 0.9%. Ethnic composition (1988): Wolof 48.1%; Serer 12.6%; Peul (Fulani) and Tukulor 21.7%; Diola 5.0%; Malinke (Mandingo) 3.7%; other 8.9%. Religious affiliation (1988): Sunni Muslim 92.0%; traditional beliefs and other 6.0%; Christian (predominantly Roman Catholic) 2.0%. Major cities (1994): Dakar 785,071 (urban agglomeration [1998] 1,905,000; includes Pikine [1994 population estimate 855,287] and Rufisque [138,837]); Thiès 216,381; Kaolack 193,115; Ziguinchor 161,680; Saint-Louis 132,444. Location: western Africa, bordering Mauritania, Mali, Guinea, Guinea-Bissau, the North Atlantic Ocean, and The Gambia.

## Vital statistics

Birth rate per 1,000 population (2000): 37.9 (world avg. 22.5). Death rate per 1,000 population (2000): 8.6 (world avg. 9.0). Natural increase rate per 1,000 population (2000): 29.3 (world avg. 13.5). Total fertility rate (avg. births per childbearing woman; 2000): 5.2. Life expectancy at birth (2000): male 60.6 years; female 63.8 years.

## National economy

Budget (1997). *Revenue:* CFAF 432,200,000,000 (value-added taxes 30.3%, individual income tax 12.4%, taxes on petroleum products 9.1%, corporate income tax 6.7%). *Expenditures:* CFAF 432,200,000,-000 (current expenditures 73.5%, of which education 19.0%, defense 9.3%, health 3.7%; development expenditure 26.5%). **Production** (metric tons except as noted). *Agriculture, forestry, fishing* (2000): sugarcane 887,000, peanuts (groundnuts) 828,000; livestock (number of live animals) 4,300,000 sheep, 3,595,000 goats, 2,960,000 cattle; roundwood (1998) 4,934,000 cu m; fish catch (1998) 425,766. *Mining and quarrying* (1996): phosphate 1,376,000; salt 87,600 (1994). *Manufacturing* (1996): tobacco 1,425,000; phosphates 1,384,000; cement 811,-000. *Energy production (consumption)*: electricity (kW-hr; 1998) 1,160,000,000 (1,160,000,000); crude petroleum (barrels; 1998) none (6,392,000); petroleum products (metric tons; 1998) 852,000 (895,000). **Population economically active** (1991): total 2,739,476; activity rate of total population 36.1% (participation rates [1988]: ages 15–60, 53.1%; female 25.6%; unemployed [1992] 24.4%). **Household expenditure**. Average household size (1991) 8.7; expenditure (early 1980s): food 49%, clothing and footwear 11%, housing 7%, education 6%. **Gross national product** (2000): $4,714,000,000 ($490 per capita). **Public debt** (external, outstanding; 2000): $2,958,000,000. **Tourism** (2000): receipts $140,000,000; expenditures (1999) $54,000,000. **Land use** (1994): forested 39.5%; meadows and pastures 29.6%; agricultural and under permanent cultivation 12.2%; other 18.7%.

## Foreign trade

**Imports** (1998-c.i.f.): CFAF 793,000,000,000 (1995; agricultural products 34.5%, of which rice 7.1%, fixed vegetable oils 5.2%; capital goods 15.0%; refined petroleum 11.0%). *Major import sources:* France 35.8%; US 5.9%; Germany 5.2%; Spain 4.6%; Nigeria 4.4%. **Exports** (1998-f.o.b.): CFAF 575,700,000,000 (1995; fish and crustaceans 28.0%; chemical products 12.0%; peanut [groundnut] oil 11.0%; phosphates 3.0%). *Major export destinations:* France 9.8%; Mali 8.5%; Mauritania 3.9%; Cameroon 1.6%.

## Transport and communications

**Transport.** *Railroads*: (1995) route length 1,225 km; (1993) passenger-km 206,000,000; metric ton-km cargo 695,000,000. *Roads* (1996): total length 14,700 km (paved 29%). *Vehicles* (1996): passenger cars 85,488, trucks and buses 36,962. *Air transport* (1996; represents about 10% of total international scheduled traffic of Air Afrique (government-supported airline of 11 West African countries): passenger-km 224,736,000; metric ton-km cargo 16,420,-000; airports (1996) with scheduled flights 7. **Communications**, in total units (units per 1,000 persons). Daily newspaper circulation (1996): 45,000 (5.3); radio receivers (1997): 1,240,000 (141); television receivers (1998): 370,000 (41); telephone main lines (2001): 237,200 (24); cellular telephone subscribers (2001): 390,800 (40); personal computers (2001): 180,000 (19); Internet users (2001): 100,000 (10).

## Education and health

**Educational attainment** (1988). Percentage of population age 6–34 having: no formal schooling 62.6%; primary education 25.7%; secondary 8.4%; higher 0.8%; other 2.5%. **Literacy** (1995): total population

age 15 and over literate 1,960,000 (37.3%); males literate 1,220,000 (47.2%); females literate 740,000 (27.6%). **Health** (1992): physicians 520 (1 per 14,825 persons); hospital beds 7,408 (1 per 1,041 persons); infant mortality rate per 1,000 live births (2000): 58.1. **Food** (2000): daily per capita caloric intake 2,257 (vegetable products 91%, animal products 9%); 95% of FAO recommended minimum.

## Military

**Total active duty personnel** (2001): 9,400 (army 85.1%, navy 6.4%, air force 8.5%; excludes 1,170 French troops). **Military expenditure as percentage of GNP** (1999): 1.7% (world 2.4%); per capita expenditure $8.

 Africa's largest slave trading center from the 15th to the 19th century was Gorée Island, off the coast of Senegal at the entrance to the Dakar roadstead. The preserved slave quarters and elegant residences of slave merchants, some of which have been turned into museums, are a popular destination for tourists in Gorée.

## Background

Links between the peoples of Senegal and North Africa were established in the 10th century AD. Islam was introduced in the 11th century, although animism retained a hold on the country into the 19th century. The Portuguese explored the coast in 1445, and in 1638 the French established a trading post at the mouth of the Senegal River. Throughout the 17th and 18th centuries, Europeans exported slaves, ivory, and gold from Senegal. The French gained control over the coast in the early 19th century and moved inland, checking the expansion of the Tukulor empire; in 1895 Senegal became part of French West Africa. Its inhabitants were made French citizens in 1946, and it became an overseas territory of France. It became an autonomous republic in 1958 and was federated with Mali 1959–60. It became an independent state in 1960. In 1982 it entered a confederation with The Gambia, called Senegambia, which was dissolved in 1989.

## Recent Developments

Despite a series of peace meetings between representatives of the government and leaders of the secessionist Movement of Democratic Forces of the Casamance, a solution to the rebellion remained elusive. A succession of armed clashes added to the death toll on both sides. Thousands had been killed in the 20-year-long conflict. An estimated 1,863 people drowned when the ferry *Le Joola* capsized in a violent storm off the coast of The Gambia on 26 Sep 2002.

**Internet resources:** <www.senegal-tourism.com>

# Serbia and Montenegro

**Official name:** Srbija i Crna Gora (Serbia and Montenegro). **Form of government:** state union (*drzavna*

*1 metric ton = about 1.1 short tons;   1 kilometer = 0.6 mi (statute);   1 metric ton-km cargo = about 0.68 short ton-mi cargo;   c.i.f.: cost, insurance, and freight;   f.o.b.: free on board*

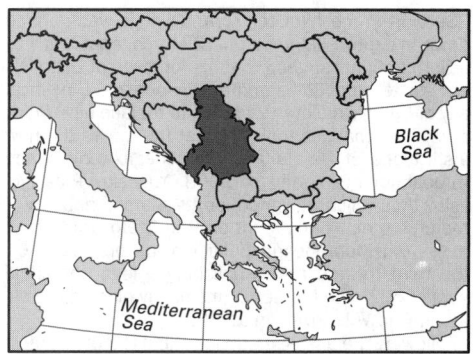

*zajednica*) of two republics; one legislative house (Skupstina) with 126 deputies (91 from Serbia and 35 from Montenegro). **Chief of state and head of government:** President Svetozar Marovic (from 7 Mar 2003). **Capital:** Belgrade. **Official language:** none; Serbian (Serbo-Croatian) is the national language. **Official religion:** none. **Monetary unit:** in Serbia, 1 Yugoslav dinar = 100 paras; valuation (7 Jul 2003) $1 = 56.67 Yugoslav dinars; the euro (valuation [7 Jul 2003] $1 = €0.87) also circulates widely in Serbia and, since 2002, is the official currency in Montenegro.

## Demography

**Area:** 39,449 sq mi, 102,173 sq km. **Population** (2002): 10,664,000. **Density** (2002): persons per sq mi 270.3, persons per sq km 104.4. **Urban** (2002): 51.7%. **Sex distribution** (1999): male 49.53%; female 50.47%. **Age breakdown** (1991): under 15, 22.8%; 15–29, 21.6%; 30–44, 21.7%; 45–59, 17.1%; 60–74, 12.2%; 75 and over, 3.5%; unknown, 1.1%. **Ethnic composition** (2000): Serb 62.1%; Albanian 17.1%; Montenegrin 4.3%; Hungarian 4.3%; Croat 3.1%; Bosniak Muslim 1.8%; Roma (Gypsy) 1.4%; Slovak 0.9%; Romanian 0.8%; other 4.2%. **Religious affiliation** (1995): Serbian Orthodox 62.6%; Muslim 19.0%; Roman Catholic 5.8%; other, mostly nonreligious 12.6%. **Major cities** (2000): Belgrade 1,168,454; Novi Sad 179,626; Nis 175,391; Kragujevac 147,305; Podgorica 117,875. **Location:** southeastern Europe, bordering Romania, Bulgaria, Macedonia, Albania, the Adriatic Sea, Bosnia and Herzegovina, Croatia, and Hungary.

## Vital statistics

**Birth rate** per 1,000 population (2000): 11.8 (world avg. 22.5). **Death rate** per 1,000 population (2000): 11.1 (world avg. 9.0). **Natural increase rate** per 1,000 population (2000): 0.7 (world avg. 13.5). **Total fertility rate** (avg. births per childbearing woman; 2000): 2.0. **Life expectancy** at birth (2000): male 69.8 years; female 74.9 years.

## National economy

**Budget** (2001). *Revenue:* 421,000,000,000 Yugoslav new dinars (tax revenue 91.5%, of which social security tax 26.8%, VAT 26.2%, income tax 12.5%, excise tax 11.9%; nontax revenue 8.5%). Expenditure: 477,000,000,000 Yugoslav new dinars (transfers 50.1%, wages 20.7%, other 29.2%). **Public debt** (external, outstanding; 2000): US$6,074,000,-000. **Production** (metric tons except as noted). *Agriculture, forestry, fishing* (2001): corn (maize) 3,828,-

000, wheat 2,949,000, sugar beets 2,500,000; livestock (number of live animals) 4,372,000 pigs, 1,917,000 sheep, 21,118,000 poultry; roundwood (2000) 1,140,000 cu m; fish catch (2000) 9,940. *Mining and quarrying* (1998): copper ore 19,939,000; lead-zinc ore 1,249,000; aluminum and ingots 100,000. *Manufacturing* (1998): cement 2,418,000; crude steel 949,000; wheat flour 830,000. *Energy production (consumption):* electricity (kW-hr; 2001) 34,594,000,000 (34,594,000,-000); coal (metric tons; 2001) 32,225,000 (32,225,000); crude petroleum (barrels; 2001) 5,534,000,000 (5,534,000,000); petroleum products (metric tons; 1998) 763,000 ([1997] 1,285,-000); natural gas (cu m; 1998) 731,000,000 ([1997] 2,944,000,000). **Tourism** (2000): receipts from visitors $26,000,000; **Population economically active** (2001; excludes Kosovo): total 3,092,000; activity rate 37.1% (1998; participation rates: over age 15, 58.3%; female [1995] 43.7%; [2001] unemployed 27.5%). **Gross domestic product** (2000): $10,028,-000,000 ($940 per capita). **Household income and expenditure** (excludes Kosovo). Average household size (2000) 4.2; income per household (2000) 93,185 Yugoslav new dinars ($7,280); sources of income (2000): wages and salaries 50.6%, pensions 21.2%, self-employment 9.5%, other 18.7%; expenditure (2000): food 47.0%, fuel and light 9.9%, beverages and tobacco 7.3%, clothing and footwear 6.6%, transportation and communications 6.2%, health 5.6%, education 2.1%, housing 1.3%, other 14.0%.

## Foreign trade

**Imports** (2001): $4,837,000,000 (machinery and transport equipment 21.3%, mineral fuels 20.7%, chemicals 14.4%, food and live animals 9.1%). *Major import sources:* Russia 14.2%; Germany 12.2%; Italy 10.3%; Greece 4.5%; Hungary 4.0%. **Exports** (2001): $1,903,000,000 (manufactured goods 19.1%, food 14.5%, machinery and transport equipment 12.8%, chemicals 7.0%). *Major export destinations:* Italy 16.4%; Bosnia 13.1%; Germany 12.1%; Macedonia 9.2%; Switzerland 8.4%; Russia 4.2%; Greece 3.3%; Hungary 3.3%; UK 2.9%.

## Transport and communications

**Transport.** *Railroads* (2000): length 4,058 km; passenger-km 1,436,000,000; metric ton-km cargo 1,969,000,000. *Roads* (2000): total length 44,777 km (paved 63%). *Vehicles* (1998): passenger cars 1,863,315; trucks and buses 158,667. *Air transport* (2000): passenger-km 979,000,000; metric ton-km cargo 7,629,000,000; airports (2000) 5. **Communications,** in total units (units per 1,000 persons). Daily newspaper circulation (1995): 1,363,000 (256); radio receivers (1997): 1,384,000 (131); television receivers (1999): 2,900,000 (272); telephone main lines (2001): 2,443,900 (229); cellular telephone subscribers (2001): 1,997,800 (187); personal computers (2001): 250,000 (23); Internet users (2001): 600,000 (56).

## Education and health

**Educational attainment** (1991). Percentage of population age 15 and over having: less than full primary education 33.5%; primary 25.0%; secondary 32.2%; postsecondary and higher 9.3%. **Literacy** (1991): total population age 10 and over literate 93.0%;

males literate 97.2%; females literate 88.9%. **Health** (2000): physicians 27,010 (1 per 394 persons); hospital beds 56,928 (1 per 187 persons); infant mortality rate per 1,000 live births (2000) 13.0. **Food** (2000): daily per capita caloric intake 2,570 (vegetable products 61%, animal products 39%); 101% of FAO recommended minimum.

## Military

**Total active duty personnel** (2001; 38,600 troops from over 30 NATO and non-NATO countries were deployed in Kosovo in 2002): 105,500 (army 74.9%, air force 18.5%, navy 6.6%). **Military expenditure as percentage of government expenditure** (1991): 3.9% (world 4.0%); per capita expenditure $176.

## Background

The Kingdom of the Serbs, Croats, and Slovenes was created after the collapse of Austria-Hungary at the end of World War I. The country signed treaties with Czechoslovakia and Romania in 1920–21, marking the beginning of the Little Entente. In 1929 an absolute monarchy was established, the country's name was changed to Yugoslavia, and it was divided without regard to ethnic boundaries. Axis powers invaded Yugoslavia in 1941, and German, Italian, Hungarian, and Bulgarian troops occupied it for the rest of World War II. In 1945 the Socialist Federal Republic of Yugoslavia was established; it included the republics of Bosnia and Herzegovina, Croatia, Macedonia, Montenegro, Serbia, and Slovenia. Its independent form of communism under Josip Broz Tito's leadership provoked the USSR. Internal ethnic tensions flared up in the 1980s, causing the country to collapse. In 1991–92 independence was declared by Croatia, Slovenia, Macedonia, and Bosnia and Herzegovina; the new Federal Republic of Yugoslavia (containing roughly 45% of the population and 40% of the area of its predecessor) was proclaimed by Serbia and Montenegro. Still fueled by long-standing ethnic tensions, hostilities continued into the 1990s. Despite the approval of the Dayton peace accord (1995), sporadic fighting continued and was followed in 1998–99 by Serbian repression and expulsion of ethnic populations in Kosovo. In September and October 2000, the battered nation of Yugoslavia ended the autocratic rule of Pres. Slobodan Milosevic. In April 2001 he was arrested and in June extradited to The Hague to stand trial for war crimes, genocide, and crimes against humanity committed during the fighting in Kosovo.

## Recent Developments

On 4 Feb 2003 both houses of the Yugoslav federal legislature voted to accept a new state charter and change the name of the country from Yugoslavia to Serbia and Montenegro. Henceforth, defense, international political and economic relations, and human rights matters would be handled centrally, while all other functions would be run from the republican capitals, Belgrade and Podgorica, respectively. The move was seen as an acknowledgment that Serbia and Montenegro had little in common, and a provision was included for both states to vote on independence after three years.

Serbian Prime Minister Zoran Djindjic was gunned down in central Belgrade on 12 March, apparently by a Serb nationalist gang that disapproved of Djindjic's pro-Western politics. Parliament approved a political ally of Djindjic's, Zoran Zivkovic, to replace him. Many personnel changes took place at the top as the new institutions of Serbia and Montenegro took shape throughout the spring of 2003. Yugoslav Pres. Vojislav Kostunica resigned on 3 March, and on 7 March the new parliament elected Svetozar Marovic, a veteran Montenegrin politician, as president. On the third try and after abolishing a legal threshold vote of 50%, the Montenegrins finally elected a president, Filip Vujanovic, on 11 May.

Following the assassination of Djindjic, police crackdowns on criminal gangs and quasi-governmental paramilitary units such as the shadowy "Red Berets" implicated family and cronies of the deposed Serbian leader, Slobodan Milosevic, and a warrant was issued for the arrest of his wife, Mirjana Markovic, who was believed to be in Russia, for complicity on the disappearance of a prominent politician, Ivan Stambolic, in 2000. Stambolic's remains were found in late March. Earlier Vojislav Seselj, a fiery Serb nationalist leader who had come in second in the December 2002 Serbian presidential election, was indicted by the UN war crimes tribunal. He flew voluntarily to The Hague on 24 February and gave himself up to officials, vowing to defend himself "with a greater vigor" than had Milosevic.

No solution was found to the problem of the final status of Kosovo. In November 2002, Kosovo's Albanian-dominated assembly approved a resolution denouncing the preamble of the draft constitution for the new union between Serbia and Montenegro as proof of Belgrade's intention to annex Kosovo.

**Internet resources:** <www.gov.yu>

# Seychelles

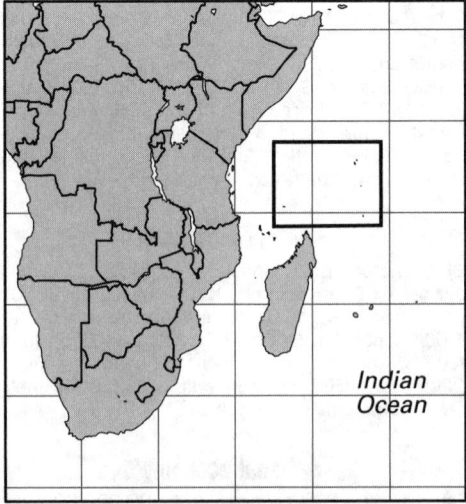

Indian Ocean

**Official name:** Repiblik Sesel (Creole); Republic of Seychelles (English); République des Seychelles (French). **Form of government:** multiparty republic with one legislative house (National Assembly [34]).

*1 metric ton = about 1.1 short tons;     1 kilometer = 0.6 mi (statute);     1 metric ton-km cargo = about 0.68 short ton-mi cargo;     c.i.f.: cost, insurance, and freight;     f.o.b.: free on board*

**Head of state and government:** President France-Albert René (from 1977). **Capital:** Victoria. **Official languages:** none. **Official religion:** none. **Monetary unit:** 1 Seychelles rupee (SR) = 100 cents; valuation (7 Jul 2003) $1 = SR 5.62.

## Demography

**Area:** 176 sq mi, 455 sq km. **Population** (2002): 83,400. **Density** (2002): persons per sq mi 473.9, persons per sq km 183.3. **Urban** (2002): 64.6%. **Sex distribution** (2000): male 49.57%; female 50.43%. **Age breakdown** (2000): under 15, 28.8%; 15–29, 29.6%; 30–44, 24.6%; 45–59, 8.6%; 60–74, 5.8%; 75 and over, 2.6%. **Ethnic composition** (2000): Seychellois Creole (mixture of Asian, African, and European) 93.2%; British 3.0%; French 1.8%; Chinese 0.5%; Indian 0.3%; other unspecified 1.2%. **Religious affiliation** (1996): Roman Catholic 86.6%; other Christian (mostly Anglican) 9.3%; Hindu 1.3%; other 2.8%. **Major city** (1999): Victoria 28,000. **Location:** group of islands in the Indian Ocean, northeast of Madagascar.

## Vital statistics

**Birth rate** per 1,000 population (2000): 18.6 (world avg. 22.5); (1998) legitimate 24.7%; illegitimate 75.3%. **Death rate** per 1,000 population (2000): 6.8 (world avg. 9.0). **Natural increase rate** per 1,000 population (2000): 11.8 (world avg. 13.5). **Total fertility rate** (avg. births per childbearing woman; 2000): 2.1. **Marriage rate** per 1,000 population (2000): 6.0. **Divorce rate** per 1,000 population (2000): 1.1. **Life expectancy** at birth (2000): male 67.9 years; female 77.9 years.

## National economy

**Budget** (2000). *Revenue:* SR 1,332,700,000 (tax revenue 71.0%, of which customs taxes and duties 23.7%, sales tax 19.7%, tax on income and profit 18.3%; nontax revenue 25.3%; grants 3.7%). *Expenditures:* SR 1,674,800,000 (current expenditure 76.1%, of which debt service 15.7%, wages and salaries 13.0%, education 8.1%, health 7.9%; capital expenditure 23.9%). **Tourism** (2000): receipts from visitors $112,000,000; expenditures by nationals abroad $21,000,000. **Land use** (1994): forested 11.1%; agricultural and under permanent cultivation 15.6%; built-on, wasteland, and other 73.3%. **Gross national product** (1999): $573,000,000 ($7,050 per capita). **Production** (metric tons except as noted). *Agriculture, forestry, fishing* (2001): coconuts 3,200, bananas 1,970, cinnamon 400; livestock (number of live animals) 18,400 pigs, 5,250 goats, 560,000 chickens; fish catch (2000) 4,768, of which (1998) jack 30.2%, snapper 18.3%, capitaine 8.3%, mackerel 4.8%. *Mining and quarrying* (1998): guano 5,000. *Manufacturing* (2000): canned tuna 28,781; copra 377; tea 246. *Energy production (consumption):* electricity (kW-hr; 2000) 189,100,000,000 (166,500,000,000); petroleum products (metric tons; 2000) none (291,000). **Population economically active** (2000): total 31,935; activity rate of total population 39.4% (participation rates: ages 15–64, 81.5%; female 43.0%; unemployed [1999] 11.5%). **Public debt** (external, outstanding; 2000): $134,-400,000. **Household income and expenditure.** Average household size (1997) 4.2; average annual income per household (1978) SR 18,480 ($2,658);

sources of income: wages and salaries 77.2%, self-employment 3.8%, transfer payments 3.2%; expenditure (1991–92): food and beverages 47.6%, housing 15.1%, clothing and footwear 8.6%, transportation 8.0%, energy and water 7.4%, recreation 6.7%, household and personal goods 6.6%.

## Foreign trade

**Imports** (2000): SR 1,591,400,000 (food, beverages, and tobacco 29.0%, manufactured goods 21.7%, machinery and transport equipment 20.3%, mineral fuels [including petroleum], lubricants, and related materials 17.0%, chemicals 7.2%). *Major import sources* (2000): South Africa 13.6%; France 11.5%; UK 10.6%; Italy 10.6%; Singapore 9.7%; UAE 2.1%; Thailand 1.4%. **Exports** (2000): SR 1,114,900,000 (canned tuna 54.4%, petroleum products 32.0%, other fish, including dried shark fins 4.5%, frozen prawns 1.6%, cinnamon bark 0.1%). *Major export destinations* (2000): UK 44.4%; France 21.6%; Germany 12.1%; Italy 9.1%.

## Transport and communications

**Transport.** *Roads* (2000): total length 275 mi, 443 km (paved 88%). *Vehicles* (2000): passenger cars 6,970; trucks and buses 2,483. *Merchant marine* (1992): vessels (100 gross tons and over) 9; total deadweight tonnage 3,337. *Air transport* (2000): passenger arrivals 157,000, passenger departures 158,000; metric ton cargo unloaded 4,592; metric ton cargo loaded 1,801; airports (2000) with scheduled flights 2. **Communications,** in total units (units per 1,000 persons). Daily newspaper circulation (1996): 3,000 (46); radio receivers (1997): 42,000 (560); television receivers (1998): 12,000 (149); telephone main lines (2001): 21,400 (267); cellular telephone subscribers (2001): 44,100 (552); personal computers (2001): 12,000 (150); Internet users (2001): 9,000 (112).

## Education and health

**Educational attainment** (1994). Percentage of population age 12 and over having: primary education 37.0%; some secondary 16.8%; complete secondary 19.0%; vocational 15.2%; postsecondary 3.0%; not stated 9.0%. **Literacy** (2000): total population age 12 and over literate 91.0%; males literate 92.0%; females literate 91.0%. **Health** (2000): physicians 105 (1 per 854 persons); hospital beds 420 (1 per 193 persons); infant mortality rate per 1,000 live births (2000) 9.9. **Food** (2000): daily per capita caloric intake 2,432 (vegetable products 80%, animal products 20%); 104% of FAO recommended minimum.

## Military

**Total active duty personnel** (2001): 450. **Military expenditure as percentage of GNP** (1997): 3.8% (world 2.6%); per capita expenditure $194.

## Background

The first recorded landing on the uninhabited Seychelles was made in 1609 by an expedition of the British East India Co. The archipelago was claimed by the French in 1756 and surrendered to the British in 1810. Seychelles became a British crown colony in 1903 and a republic within the Commonwealth in

1976. A one-party socialist state since 1979, Seychelles began moving toward democracy in the 1990s; it adopted a new constitution in 1993.

## Recent Developments

The slump in the global economy adversely affected Seychelles, which relied heavily on tourism. In March 2002 Pres. France-Albert René refused to implement economic reforms recommended by the IMF. René also denied allegations that members of the al-Qaeda terrorist network had fled Afghanistan and found refuge in Seychelles.

Internet resources: <www.seychelles-online.com.sc>

# Sierra Leone

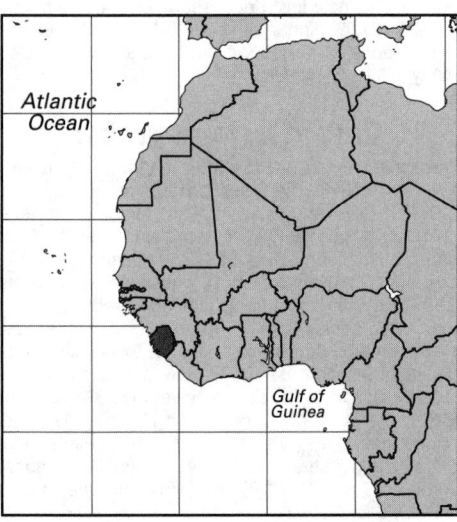

Atlantic Ocean

Gulf of Guinea

Official name: Republic of Sierra Leone. Form of government: republic with one legislative body (Parliament [80, including 12 paramount chiefs]). Head of state and government: President Ahmad Tejan Kabbah (from 1998). Capital: Freetown. Official language: English. Official religion: none. Monetary unit: 1 leone (Le) = 100 cents; valuation (7 Jul 2003) $1 = Le 2,370.

## Demography

Area: 27,699 sq mi, 71,740 sq km. Population (2002): 4,823,000. Density (2002): persons per sq mi 174.1, persons per sq km 67.2. Urban (2000): 36.6%. Sex distribution (2000): male 48.44%; female 51.56%. Age breakdown (2000): under 15, 44.7%; 15–29, 26.1%; 30–44, 14.9%; 45–59, 9.2%; 60–74, 4.3%; 75 and over, 0.8%. Ethnic composition (2000): Mende 26.0%; Temne 24.6%; Limba 7.1%; Kuranko 5.5%; Kono 4.2%; Fulani 3.8%; Bullom-Sherbro 3.5%; other 25.3%. Religious affiliation (2000): Sunni Muslim 45.9%; traditional beliefs 40.4%; Christian 11.4%; other 2.3%. Major cities (1985): Freetown 469,776 (urban agglomeration [2001] 837,000); Koidu–New Sembehun 80,000; Bo 26,000; Kenema 13,000; Makeni 12,000. Location:

western Africa, bordering Guinea, Liberia, and the North Atlantic Ocean.

## Vital statistics

Birth rate per 1,000 population (2000): 45.6 (world avg. 22.5). Death rate per 1,000 population (2000): 19.6 (world avg. 9.0). Natural increase rate per 1,000 population (2000): 26.0 (world avg. 13.5). Total fertility rate (avg. births per childbearing woman; 2000): 6.1. Life expectancy at birth (2000): male 42.4 years; female 48.2 years.

## National economy

Budget (1996–97). Revenue: Le 85,708,000,000 (customs duties 47.4%; excise taxes 25.4%; corporate income tax 9.5%; personal income tax 7.3%). Expenditures: Le 143,293,000,000 (recurrent expenditures 75.6%, of which transfers 24.4%, wages and salaries 19.8%, goods and services 18.9%, debt service 12.5%; capital expenditures 24.4%). Gross national product (2000): $647,000,000 ($130 per capita). Production (metric tons except as noted). Agriculture, forestry, fishing (1999): rice 247,235, cassava 239,597, oil palm fruit 163,000; livestock (number of live animals) 400,000 cattle, 350,000 sheep, 190,000 goats; roundwood (1998) 3,315,000 cu m; fish catch (1998) 52,700. Mining and quarrying (2000): rutile and ilmenite (titanium ores) (1994; production was suspended after 1994 because of civil war) 184,000; diamonds 350,000 carats; gold 965 troy oz. Manufacturing (value added in Le '000,000; 1993): food 36,117; chemicals 10,560; earthenware 1,844. Energy production (consumption): electricity (kW-hr; 1997) 242,000,000 (242,000,000); crude petroleum (barrels; 1997) none (1,700,000); petroleum products (metric tons; 1997) 177,000 (130,000). Household income and expenditure. Average household size (1998) 6.3; average annual income per household (1984): $320; sources of income (1984): self-employment 61.6%, wages and salaries 27.9%, other 10.5%; expenditure (1989): food 66.2%, clothing 9.9%, housing 5.8%, transportation 4.4%, household goods 4.0%, recreation and education 3.8%, health 3.5%. Public debt (external, outstanding; 2000): $969,000,000. Population economically active (1996): total 1,610,000; activity rate of total population 34.8% (participation rates [1991]: ages 10–64, 53.3%; female 32.4%; unemployed [registered; 1992] 10.6%). Tourism (1999): receipts $8,000,000; expenditures $4,000,000. Land use (1994): forest 28.5%; pasture 30.7%; agriculture 7.5%; other 33.3%.

## Foreign trade

Imports (1999-c.i.f.): Le 153,856,000,000 (1995–96; food and live animals 51.6%; fuels 11.6%; chemicals 10.2%; machinery and transport equipment 8.9%; beverages and tobacco 2.7%; crude minerals 2.5%). Major import sources (1998): UK 20.0%; US 13.0%; Belgium 7.5%; Italy 6.5%; Nigeria 5.5%. Exports (1999-f.o.b.): Le 11,347,000,000 (1995–96; mineral exports 56.4%, of which diamonds 50.6%, rutile [titanium ore] 5.7%; cocoa 5.0%; coffee 3.7%; re-exports 4.8%). Major export destinations (1999): Belgium 40.8%; US 7.5%; Spain 6.1%; UK 4.1%.

1 metric ton = about 1.1 short tons;    1 kilometer = 0.6 mi (statute);    1 metric ton-km cargo = about 0.68 short ton-mi cargo;    c.i.f.: cost, insurance, and freight;    f.o.b.: free on board

## Transport and communications

**Transport.** *Railroads* (1995): length 84 km. *Roads* (1996): total length 11,700 km (paved 11%). *Vehicles* (1996): passenger cars 17,640; trucks and buses 10,890. *Air transport* (1996): passenger-km 24,000,000; metric ton-km cargo 2,000,000; airports (1998) with scheduled flights 1. **Communications**, in total units (units per 1,000 persons). Daily newspaper circulation (1996): 20,000 (4.7); radio receivers (1997): 1,121,000 (253); television receivers (1998): 60,000 (13); telephone main lines (2001): 22,700 (4.7); cellular telephone subscribers (2001): 26,900 (5.5); personal computers (1999): 100 (—); Internet users (2001): 7,000 (1.4).

## Education and health

**Educational attainment** (1985). Percentage of population age 5 and over having: no formal schooling 64.1%; primary education 18.7%; secondary 9.7%; higher 1.5%. **Literacy** (1995): total population age 15 and over literate 791,000 (31.4%); males literate 555,000 (45.4%); females 236,000 (18.2%). **Health:** physicians (1996) 339 (1 per 13,696 persons); hospital beds (1988) 4,025 (1 per 980 persons); infant mortality rate per 1,000 live births (2000) 148.7. **Food** (2000): daily per capita caloric intake 1,863 (vegetable products 97%, animal products 3%); 81% of FAO recommended minimum.

## Military

**Total active duty personnel** (2001): 6,000 (army 96.7%, navy 3.3%, air force, none; UN troops authorized from October 1999 numbered 17,100 in September 2002). **Military expenditure as percentage of GNP** (1999): 3.0% (world 2.4%); per capita expenditure $4.

Freetown, the capital of Sierra Leone, was founded in 1792 as a home for freed slaves from various origins (including slaves from Nova Scotia who had fought for the British during the American Revolution, runaway slaves from Jamaica ["Maroons"], and slaves from captured slave ships). With the British abolition of slave trade in 1807, Freetown served as the base of operations against slave ships along the west coast of Africa.

## Background

The earliest inhabitants of Sierra Leone were probably the Buloms; the Mende and Temne peoples arrived in the 15th century. The coastal region was visited by the Portuguese in the 15th century, and by 1495 there was a Portuguese fort on the site of modern Freetown. European ships visited the coast regularly to trade for slaves and ivory, and the English built trading posts on offshore islands in the 17th century. British abolitionists and philanthropists founded Freetown in 1787 as a private venture for freed and runaway slaves. In 1808 the coastal settlement became a British colony. The region became a British protectorate in 1896. It achieved independence in 1961 and became a republic in 1971. It was marked by political and economic turmoil in the late 20th century as successive military regimes tried

to assume power. UN peacekeeping forces were stationed there but were ineffectual in preventing bloodletting and atrocities.

## Recent Developments

An official end to the civil war that had plagued the country since 1991 was declared on 5 Jan 2002 with a symbolic weapons-burning ceremony in Freetown. More than 45,000 rebels belonging to the Revolutionary United Front turned in their weapons. In early July riots broke out in Freetown between youth gangs and Nigerian businessmen, but calm was quickly restored by the armed forces. Areas near the Liberian border remained unstable as a result of numerous border incursions by Liberian armed forces and rebels of the Liberians United for Reconciliation and Democracy. Sierra Leone also had to cope with tens of thousands of refugees fleeing into the country from Liberia. In August the UN sent 17,000 peacekeepers to Sierra Leone.

**Internet resources:** <www.Sierra-Leone.org>

# Singapore

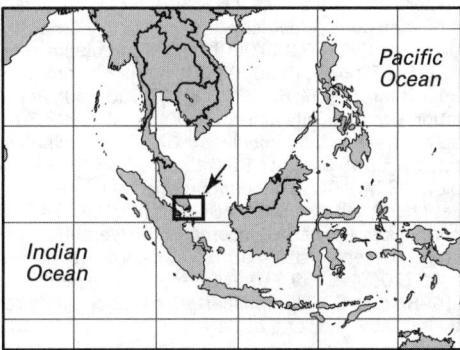

**Official name:** Hsin-chia-p'o Kung-ho-kuo (Mandarin Chinese); Republik Singapura (Malay); Singapore Kudiyarasu (Tamil); Republic of Singapore (English). **Form of government:** unitary multiparty republic with one legislative house (Parliament [93]). **Chief of state:** President Sellapan Rama (S.R.) Nathan (from 1999). **Head of state government:** Prime Minister Goh Chok Tong (from 1990). **Capital:** Singapore. **Official languages:** Chinese; Malay; Tamil; English. **Official religion:** none. **Monetary unit:** 1 Singapore dollar (S$) = 100 cents; valuation (7 Jul 2003) US$1 = S$1.75.

## Demography

**Area:** 263.6 sq mi, 682.7 sq km. **Population** (2002): 4,204,000. **Density** (2002): persons per sq mi 15,948, persons per sq km 6,158. **Urban** 100.0%. **Sex distribution** (2000): male 49.96%; female 50.04%. **Age breakdown** (2000): under 15, 21.5%; 15–34, 30.1%; 35–54, 33.9%; 55–74, 12.1%; 75 and over, 2.4%. **Ethnic composition** (2000): Chinese 76.8%; Malay 13.9%; Indian 7.9%. **Religious affiliation** (2000): Buddhist 42.5%; Muslim 14.9%; Christian 14.6%; Taoist 8.5%; Hindu 4.0%; traditional beliefs 0.6%; nonreligious 14.9%. **Location:** southeastern Asia, islands between Malaysia and Indonesia.

## Vital statistics

**Birth rate** per 1,000 population (2001): 11.9 (world avg. 21.2). **Death rate** per 1,000 population (2001): 4.4 (world avg. 8.9). **Natural increase rate** per 1,000 population (2001): 7.5 (world avg. 12.3). **Total fertility rate** (avg. births per childbearing woman; 2000): 1.4. **Marriage rate** per 1,000 population (2000): 6.9. **Life expectancy** at birth (2000): male 76.0 years; female 80.0 years.

## National economy

**Budget** (2000). *Revenue*: S$33,526,600,000 (income tax 40.0%, nontax revenue 24.6%, goods and services tax 6.7%, motor vehicle taxes 6.5%, customs and excise duties 5.3%). *Expenditures*: S$18,896,-900,000 (security 47.0%, education 20.6%, communications 12.8%, health 5.2%, trade and industry 2.1%). **Production**. *Agriculture, forestry, fishing* (metric tons; 2000): vegetables and fruits 4,811; livestock (number of live animals) 2,000,000 chickens; fish catch (1999) 6,489. *Mining and quarrying* (value of output in S$; 1994): granite 75,800,000. *Manufacturing* (value added in S$'000,000; 1996): electronic products 16,982.1; chemical products 3,326.5; machinery and equipment 2,623.3. *Energy production (consumption)*: electricity (kW-hr; 1997) 26,188,-000,000 (26,188,000,000); crude petroleum (barrels; 1997) none (453,000,000); petroleum products (metric tons; 1997) 53,592,000 (24,636,000). **Population economically active** (2000): total 2,192,300; activity rate of total population 67.2% (participation rates: ages 15 and over, 85.6%; female 55.5%; unemployed 3.5%). **Gross national product** (at current market prices; 2000): US$99,404,000,000 (US$24,740 per capita). **Household income and expenditure**. Average household size (2000) 3.7; income per household (2000) S$59,316 (US$34,406); expenditure (1998): food 23.7%, transportation and communications 22.8%, housing costs and furnishings 21.6%, education 6.9%, clothing and footwear 4.1%, health 3.3%, other 17.6%. **Tourism** (2000): receipts from visitors US$6,018,000,000; expenditures by nationals abroad US$4,970,000,000.

## Foreign trade

**Imports** (2000-c.i.f.): S$232,175,000,000 (office machines 12.4%, crude petroleum 6.5%, petroleum products 5.6%, telecommunications apparatus 4.7%, electric power machinery 4.7%, scientific instruments 3.7%, industrial machinery 2.1%). *Major import sources* (1999): US 17.0%; Japan 16.6%; Malaysia 15.6%; China 5.1%; Thailand 4.7%; Taiwan 4.0%; South Korea 3.8%. **Exports** (2000-c.i.f.): S$237,826,-000,000 (office machines 22.6%, petroleum products 7.2%, telecommunications apparatus 5.5%, electrical generators 3.4%, optical instruments 2.6%, industrial machinery 1.4%, clothing 1.3%). *Major export destinations* (1999): US 19.2%; Malaysia 16.6%; Hong Kong 7.7%; Japan 7.4%; Taiwan 4.9%; Thailand 4.4%; UK 3.7%.

## Transport and communications

**Transport**. *Railroads* (2000): length 117 km. *Roads* (1997): total length 3,017 km (paved 97%). *Vehicles* (2000): passenger cars 413,545; trucks and buses 147,325. *Air transport* (1999): passenger-km 64,528,800,000; metric ton-km cargo 5,481,708,-000; airports (2000) 1. **Communications**, in total units (units per 1,000 persons). Daily newspaper circulation (2000): 1,197,301 (367); radio receivers (1997): 2,550,000 (821); television receivers (1999): 1,200,000 (373); telephone main lines (2001): 1,948,500 (472); cellular telephone subscribers (2001): 2,858,800 (692); personal computers (2001): 2,100,000 (508); Internet users (2001): 1,500,000 (363).

## Education and health

**Educational attainment** (2000). Percentage of population age 15 and over having: no schooling 19.6%; primary education 23.1%; secondary 39.5%; postsecondary 17.8%. **Literacy** (1995): total population age 15 and over literate 90.8%; males literate 95.6%; females literate 86.1%. **Health** (2000): physicians 5,577 (1 per 585 persons); hospital beds 11,798 (1 per 277 persons); infant mortality rate per 1,000 live births (2001) 2.2. **Food** (1988–90): daily per capita caloric intake 3,121 (vegetable products 76%, animal products 24%); 136% of FAO recommended minimum.

## Military

**Total active duty personnel** (2001): 60,500 (army 82.7%, navy 7.4%, air force 9.9%). **Military expenditure as percentage of GNP** (1999): 4.8% (world 2.4%); per capita expenditure US$1,100.

## Background

Long inhabited by fishermen and pirates, Singapore was an outpost of the Sumatran empire of Srivijaya until the 14th century, when it passed to Java and then Siam. It became part of the Malacca empire in the 15th century. In the 16th century the Portuguese controlled the area; they were followed by the Dutch in the 17th century. In 1819 Singapore was ceded to the British East India Co., becoming part of the Straits Settlements and the center of British colonial activity in southeast Asia. The Japanese occupied the islands in 1942–45. In 1946 it became a crown colony. It achieved full internal self-government in 1959, became a part of Malaysia in 1963, and became independent in 1965. It is influential in the affairs of the Association of Southeast Asian Nations. The country's dominant voice in politics for 30 years after independence was Lee Kuan Yew.

## Recent Developments

A year after suffering its worst-ever recession, Singapore experienced a modest economic comeback in 2002. The economy had witnessed double-digit percentage falls throughout the last half of 2001, but 3.9% growth was achieved in the second quarter of 2002—the first expansion in five quarters. The boost was attributed in part to an increase in electronics exports, which had been in a steep slump. While most forecasters were predicting an overall growth rate of between 2% and 4% for Singapore for the year, the government warned that the jobless rate could rise as high as 6% before the economy made a full recov-

*1 metric ton = about 1.1 short tons;   1 kilometer = 0.6 mi (statute);   1 metric ton-km cargo = about 0.68 short ton-mi cargo;   c.i.f.: cost, insurance, and freight;   f.o.b.: free on board*

ery. The weakened demand for imports in American and Asian markets posed serious problems for a country whose manufacturing sector was heavily geared toward exports. Singapore was also worried about losing foreign investment to such regional competitors as China and Malaysia.

Internet resources: <www.sg>

# Slovakia

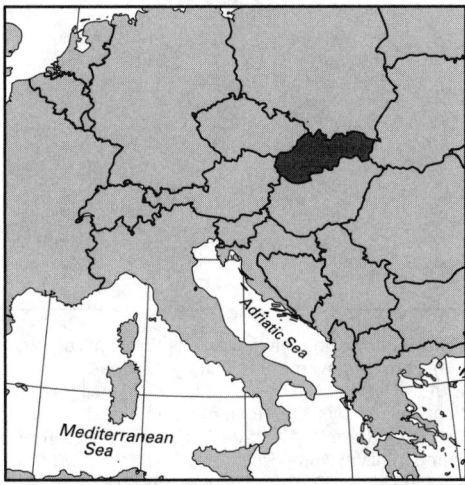

**Official name:** Slovenska Republika (Slovak Republic). **Form of government:** unitary multiparty republic with one legislative house (National Council [150]). **Chief of state:** President Rudolf Schuster (from 1999). **Head of government:** Prime Minister Mikulas Dzurinda (from 1998). **Capital:** Bratislava. **Official language:** Slovak. **Official religion:** none. **Monetary unit:** 1 Slovak koruna (Sk) = 100 halura; valuation (7 Jul 2003) $1 = Sk 36.17.

## Demography

**Area:** 18,933 sq mi, 49,035 sq km (de jure). **Population** (2002): 5,383,000. **Density** (2002): persons per sq mi 284.3, persons per sq km 109.8. **Urban** (2002): 57.6%. **Sex distribution** (2001): male 48.56%; female 51.44%. **Age breakdown** (2001): under 15, 18.9%; 15–29, 25.1%; 30–44, 21.5%; 45–59, 18.9%; 60–74, 11.0%; 75 and over, 4.6%. **Ethnic composition** (2001): Slovak 85.8%; Hungarian 9.7%; Rom (Gypsy) 1.7%; Czech 0.8%; Ruthenian and Ukrainian 0.7%; other 1.3%. **Religious affiliation** (2001): Roman Catholic 68.9%; Protestant 9.2%, of which Slovak Evangelical 6.9%, Reformed Christian 2.0%; Greek Catholic 4.1%; Eastern Orthodox 0.9%; nonreligious and other 16.9%. **Major cities** (2001): Bratislava 428,672; Kosice 236,093; Presov 92,786; Nitra 87,285; Zilina 85,400. **Location:** central Europe, bordering Poland, Ukraine, Hungary, Austria, and the Czech Republic.

## Vital statistics

**Birth rate** per 1,000 population (2001): 10.5 (world avg. 21.2); (1999) legitimate 83.1%; illegitimate 16.9%. **Death rate** per 1,000 population (2001): 9.3 (world avg. 8.9). **Natural increase rate** per 1,000 population (2001): 1.2 (world avg. 12.3). **Total fertility rate** (avg. births per childbearing woman; 2001): 1.3. **Marriage rate** per 1,000 population (2002): 4.4. **Divorce rate** per 1,000 population (2002): 1.8. **Life expectancy** at birth (2001): male 70.0 years; female 78.2 years.

## National economy

**Budget** (2000). *Revenue*: Sk 347,600,000,000 (tax revenue 87.4%, of which social security contribution 33.3%, value-added tax 20.3%, income tax 11.9%; nontax revenue 12.6%). *Expenditures*: Sk 378,800,-000,000 (current expenditures 89.4%, of which social welfare 32.5%, wages 15.8%, health 12.8%, debt service 6.3%; investment 10.6%). **Production** (metric tons except as noted). *Agriculture, forestry, fishing* (2001): wheat 1,894,000, sugar beets 1,293,140, corn [maize] 721,000; livestock (number of live animals) 1,488,400 pigs, 646,100 cattle, 347,983 sheep; roundwood (2000) 5,213,000 cu m; fish catch (2000) 2,115. *Mining and quarrying* (2000): iron ore 750,000; gold (1998) 10,900 troy oz. *Manufacturing* (value added in Sk '000,000; 1998): food 10,203; nonelectrical machinery 10,116; transport equipment 9,422. *Energy production (consumption)*: electricity (kW-hr; 2000) 30,685,000,000 (22,957,000,-000); coal (metric tons; 1997) 5,236,000 (4,875,000); crude petroleum (barrels; 1997) 462,800 (38,497,000); petroleum products (metric tons; 1997) 3,973,000 (1,998,000); natural gas (cu m; 2000) 358,800,000 ([1997] 5,743,400,000). **Population economically active** (2001): total 2,665,837; activity rate of total population 49.6% (participation rates: ages 15–64, 79.6%; female 47.7%; unemployed 18.0%). **Household income and expenditure.** Average household size (1999) 3.3; income per household (1999) Sk 74,010 ($2,100); sources of income: wages and salaries 68.0%, transfer payments 21.8%, other 10.2%; expenditure: food, beverages, and tobacco 26.3%, housing and energy 12.4%, transportation and communications 8.9%, clothing and footwear 7.3%. **Public debt** (external, outstanding; 2000): $4,883,000,000. **Gross national product** (2000): $19,969,000,000 ($3,700 per capita). **Tourism:** receipts from visitors (2000) $432,000,000; expenditure by nationals abroad $295,000,000. **Land use** (1994): forested 40.6%; meadows and pastures 17.0%; agricultural and under permanent cultivation 32.9%; other 9.5%.

## Foreign trade

**Imports** (2000): $12,812,000,000 (machinery and transport equipment 35.6%; semimanufactured products 17.7%; mineral fuels 17.5%; chemicals and chemical products 10.9%). *Major import sources* (2000): Germany 25.0%; Czech Republic 18.7%; Russia 17.0%; Italy 6.2%; Austria 3.9%. **Exports** (2000): $11,914,000,000 (machinery and transport equipment 39.4%; manufactured goods 26.6%; chemicals and chemical products 7.9%; mineral fuels 7.0%). *Major export destinations* (2000): Germany 26.7%; Czech Republic 20.0%; Italy 9.1%; Austria 8.3%; Poland 5.8%; Hungary 4.8%.

## Transport and communications

**Transport.** *Railroads* (1998): length 3,673 km; passenger-km 3,092,000,000; metric ton-km cargo 11,754,000,000. *Roads* (1999): total length 17,710 km. *Vehicles* (2000): passenger cars 1,274,244; trucks and buses 121,634. *Air transport* (2000): passenger-km 250,900,000; metric ton-km cargo 220,000; airports (2000) with scheduled flights 2. **Communications**, in total units (units per 1,000 persons). Daily newspaper circulation (1996): 989,000 (184); television receivers (1999): 2,250,000 (417); telephone main lines (2001): 1,556,300 (288); cellular telephone subscribers (2001): 2,147,300 (397); personal computers (2001): 80,000 (148); Internet users (2000): 650,000 (120).

### Education and health

**Educational attainment** (1991). Percentage of adult population having: incomplete primary education 0.7%; primary and incomplete secondary 37.9%; complete secondary 50.9%; higher 9.5%; unknown 1.0%. **Literacy** (2001): total population age 15 and over literate virtually 100%. **Health** (1999): physicians 19,171 (1 per 281 persons); hospital beds 60,169 (1 per 90 persons); infant mortality rate per 1,000 live births (2001) 9.0. **Food** (2000): daily per capita caloric intake 3,133 (vegetable products 75%, animal products 25%); 127% of FAO recommended minimum.

### Military

**Total active duty personnel** (2001): 33,000 (army 60.0%, air force 30.9%, headquarters staff 9.1%). **Military expenditure as percentage of GNP** (1999): 1.8% (world 2.4%); per capita expenditure $187.

### Background

Slovakia was inhabited in the first centuries AD by Illyrian, Celtic, and Germanic tribes. Slovaks settled there around the 6th century. It became part of Great Moravia in the 9th century but was conquered by the Magyars c. 907. It remained in the kingdom of Hungary until the end of World War I, when the Slovaks joined the Czechs to form the new state of Czechoslovakia in 1918. In 1938 Slovakia was declared an autonomous unit within Czechoslovakia; it was nominally independent under German protection in 1939–45. After the expulsion of the Germans, Slovakia joined a reconstituted Czechoslovakia, which came under Soviet domination in 1948. In 1969 a partnership between the Czechs and Slovaks established the Slovak Socialist Republic. The fall of the Communist regime in 1989 led to a revival of interest in autonomy, and Slovakia became an independent nation in 1993.

### Recent Developments

Parliamentary elections held on 20–21 September were the major event of 2002. The outcome was considered crucial for the future direction of Slovakia, particularly in light of the upcoming decisions on the enlargement of NATO and the European Union. Many feared that Slovaks would turn away from the reformist, pro-Western government that had held office since 1998 and would instead support the return of populist and nationalist forces that could lead the country to international isolation. In fact, four center-right parties managed to win a majority

in the elections, with 78 of 150 parliamentary seats. Mikulas Dzurinda was reappointed prime minister on 15 October.

**Internet resources:** <www.slovakiatourism.sk>

# Slovenia

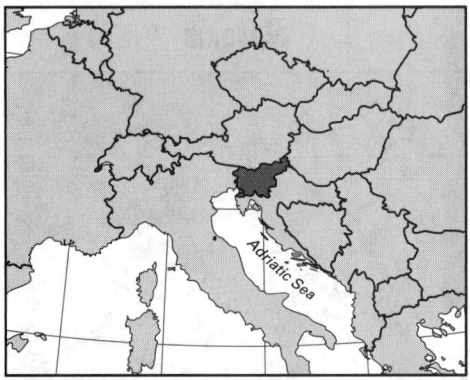

**Official name:** Republika Slovenija (Republic of Slovenia). **Form of government:** unitary multiparty republic with two legislative houses (National Council [40]; National Assembly [90]). **Head of state:** President Janez Drnovsek (from 23 Dec 2002). **Head of government:** Prime Minister Anton Rop (from 11 Dec 2002). **Capital:** Ljubljana. **Official language:** Slovene (Hungarian and Italian are official where indigenous). **Official religion:** none. **Monetary unit:** 1 Slovene tolar (SIT; plural tolarji) = 100 stotin; valuation (7 Jul 2003) $1 = 203.90 tolarji.

### Demography

**Area:** 7,827 sq mi, 20,273 sq km. **Population** (2002): 1,948,000. **Density** (2001): persons per sq mi 248.9, persons per sq km 96.1. **Urban** (2001): 49.1%. **Sex distribution** (2000): male 48.84%; female 51.16%. **Age breakdown** (2000): under 15, 16.1%; 15–29, 21.9%; 30–44, 23.4%; 45–59, 19.6%; 60–74, 14.0%; 75 and over, 5.0%. **Ethnic composition** (2000): Slovene 89.8%; Croat 4.9%; Austrian 1.3%; German 1.0%; Serb 0.6%; other 2.4%. **Religious affiliation** (1995): Christian 86.2%, of which Roman Catholic 82.7%, Orthodox 2.0%, Protestant 1.3%; Muslim 1.0%; other 12.8%. **Major cities** (2000): Ljubljana 270,986; Maribor 115,532; Kranj 51,923; Celje 49,572; Koper 47,905. **Location:** southeastern Europe, bordering Austria, Hungary, Croatia, the Adriatic Sea, and Italy.

### Vital statistics

**Birth rate** per 1,000 population (2001): 9.3 (world avg. 21.2); legitimate 64.4%; illegitimate 35.6%. **Death rate** per 1,000 population (2001): 10.0 (world avg. 8.9). **Natural increase rate** per 1,000 population (2001): –0.7 (world avg. 12.3). **Total fertility rate** (avg. births per childbearing woman; 2001): 1.3. **Marriage rate** per 1,000 population (2000): 3.6. **Divorce rate** per 1,000 population (2000): 1.1. **Life expectancy** at birth (2001): male 71.2 years; female 79.2 years.

---

*1 metric ton = about 1.1 short tons;   1 kilometer = 0.6 mi (statute);   1 metric ton-km cargo = about 0.68 short ton-mi cargo;   c.i.f.: cost, insurance, and freight;   f.o.b.: free on board*

## National economy

**Budget** (2000). *Revenue*: SIT 1,725,791,000,000 (taxes on goods and services 34.9%, social security contributions 32.0%, personal income tax 15.0%, nontax revenue 7.3%). *Expenditures*: SIT 1,781,311,-000,000 (current expenditures 90.4%, development expenditures 9.6%). **Public debt** (external, outstanding; 2000): $2,665,000,000. **Production** (metric tons except as noted). *Agriculture, forestry, fishing* (2000): silage 1,900,000, sugar beets 467,000, corn (maize) 308,000; livestock (number of live animals) 552,000 pigs, 471,000 cattle; roundwood (1999) 2,133,000 cu m; fish catch (1997) 3,262. *Mining and quarrying* (1998): ferrosilicon 10,000; kaolin 10,000. *Manufacturing* (value added in SIT '000,000; 1997): base and fabricated metals 89,189; food, beverages, and tobacco products 81,998; chemicals and chemical products 81,408. *Energy production (consumption)*: electricity (kW-hr; 1999) 12,456,000,000 (10,432,-000,000); coal (metric tons; 1998) 5,200,000 ([1997] 5,456,000); crude petroleum (barrels; 1999) 6,000 ([1997] 3,914,000); petroleum products (metric tons; 1997) 463,000 ([1998] 2,328,000); natural gas (cu m; 1999) 5,700,000 (996,000,000). **Land use** (1994): forest 53.2%; pasture 24.8%; agricultural 11.6%; other 10.4%. **Household income and expenditure** (1999). Average household size 2.8; income per household SIT 2,557,500 ($14,070); sources of income: wages 58.8%, transfers 29.7%, self-employment 7.0%, other 4.5%; expenditure: transportation and communications 18.9%, food and beverages 18.6%, housing 11.3%, recreation 8.2%, clothing and footwear 8.1%. **Gross national product** (at current market prices; 2000): $19,979,000,000 ($10,050 per capita). **Population economically active** (1998): total 967,000; activity rate 49.6% (participation rates: ages 15–64, 69.1%; female 46.3%; unemployed [2000] 12.2%). **Tourism** (2000): receipts $961,000,-000; expenditures $461,000,000.

## Foreign trade

**Imports** (2000-c.i.f.): $10,115,000,000 (machinery and transport equipment 34.2%, other manufactured goods 21.9%, chemicals and chemical products 12.4%, mineral fuels 9.1%, food products 5.1%). *Major import sources*: Germany 19.0%; Italy 17.4%; France 10.3%; Austria 8.2%; Croatia 4.4%. **Exports** (2000-f.o.b.): $8,731,000,000 (machinery and transport equipment 36.0%, other manufactured goods 27.3%, chemicals and chemical products 11.2%, food products 2.3%). *Major export destinations:* Germany 27.2%; Italy 13.6%; Croatia 7.9%; Austria 7.5%; France 7.1%.

## Transport and communications

**Transport.** *Railroads* (1999): length 1,201 km; passenger-km 625,000,000; metric ton-km cargo 2,784,000,000. *Roads* (1999): total length 20,128 km (paved 81%). *Vehicles* (1999): passenger cars 829,674; trucks and buses 67,111. *Air transport* (1999): passenger-km 832,000,000; metric ton-km cargo 4,160,000; airports (1999) with scheduled flights 3. **Communications**, in total units (units per 1,000 persons). Daily newspaper circulation (1996): 397,000 (199); radio receivers (1997): 630,000 (317); television receivers (1998): 710,000 (358); telephone main lines (2001): 799,700 (401); cellular telephone subscribers (2001): 1,515,700 (760); In-

ternet users (2001): 600,000 (301); personal computers (2001): 550,000 (276).

## Education and health

**Educational attainment** (1991). Percentage of population age 25 and over having: no formal schooling 0.7%; incomplete and complete primary education 45.1%; incomplete and complete secondary 42.4%; higher 10.4%; unknown 1.4%. **Literacy** (2000): 99.7%. **Health** (1999): physicians 4,486 (1 per 440 persons); hospital beds 10,959 (1 per 180 persons); infant mortality rate per 1,000 live births 4.5.

## Military

**Total active duty personnel** (2001): 7,600 (army 100%). **Military expenditure as percentage of GNP** (1999): 1.4% (world 2.4%); per capita expenditure $227.

## Background

The Slovenes settled the region in the 6th century AD. In the 8th century it was incorporated into the Frankish empire of Charlemagne, and in the 10th century it came under Germany as part of the Holy Roman Empire. Except for 1809–14, when Napoleon ruled the area, most of the lands belonged to Austria until the formation of the Kingdom of Serbs, Croats, and Slovenes in 1918. It became a constituent republic of Yugoslavia in 1946 and received a section of the former Italian Adriatic coastline in 1947. In 1990 Slovenia held the first contested multiparty elections in Yugoslavia since before World War II. In 1991 it seceded from Yugoslavia; its independence was internationally recognized in 1992.

## Recent Developments

Janez Drnovsek, Slovenia's prime minister for most of its 11 years of independence, was elected the country's president on 1 Dec 2002. The four parties constituting the country's left-of-center coalition government chose Anton Rop, a Liberal Democrat like Drnovsek, to form a new government. Slovenia achieved two long-sought foreign policy objectives: first, on 21 November, when it was invited to become a member of NATO in 2004, and a few weeks later, on 13 December, when it got a bid to join the European Union. Slovenia's membership would mean that its southern border would also become the EU's border. This would impose special financial and security obligations on the small country, and it remained a concern for Slovenia and for the EU.

**Internet resources:** <www.slovenia-tourism.si>

# Solomon Islands

**Official name:** Solomon Islands. **Form of government:** constitutional monarchy with one legislative house (National Parliament [50]). **Chief of state:** Queen Elizabeth II (from 1952), represented by Governor-General John Lapli (from 1999). **Head of government:** Prime Minister Allan Kemakeza (from 2001). **Capital:** Honiara. **Official language:** English. **Official religion:** none. **Monetary unit:** 1 Solomon Islands dollar (SI$) = 100 cents; valuation (7 Jul 2003) US$1 = SI$7.52.

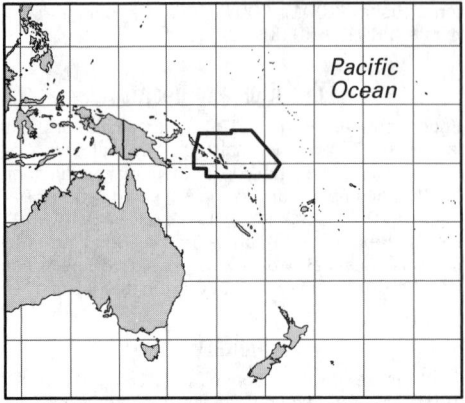

Pacific
Ocean

ing 11.0%, household operations 10.9%, transportation 9.9%, recreation and health 7.9%, clothing 5.7%, drinks and tobacco 5.0%. **Population economically active** (1993): total 29,577; activity rate of total population 8.3% (participation rates: ages 15–60 [1986] 98.6%; female 22.6%; unemployed [1999] 11%). **Production** (metric tons except as noted). *Agriculture, forestry, fishing* (1999): coconuts 240,000, palm oil fruit 140,000, sweet potatoes 73,000; livestock (number of live animals) 58,000 pigs, 10,000 cattle, 185,000 chickens; roundwood (1998) 872,000 cu m; fish catch (2000) 23,443. *Mining and quarrying* (1998): gold 33,300 troy oz. *Manufacturing* (1997): palm oil 30,100, copra 23,500, coconut oil 3,900. *Energy production (consumption)*: electricity (kW-hr; 1997) 32,000,000 (32,000,000); petroleum products (metric tons; 1997) none (52,000). **Public debt** (external, outstanding; 2000): US$120,700,000.

## Demography

**Area:** 10,954 sq mi, 28,370 sq km. **Population** (2002): 439,000. **Density** (2002): persons per sq mi 40.1, persons per sq km 15.5. **Urban** (2002): 21.0. **Sex distribution** (1999): male 51.68%; female 48.32%. **Age breakdown** (1996): under 15, 43.7%; 15–29, 28.7%; 30–44, 15.2%; 45–59, 8.1%; 60–74, 3.6%; 75 and over, 0.7%. **Ethnic composition** (1986): Melanesian 94.2%; Polynesian 3.7%; other Pacific Islander 1.4%; European 0.4%; Asian 0.2%; other 0.1%. **Religious affiliation** (1995): Christian 85.6%, of which Protestant 67.1% (including Church of Melanesia [Anglican] 31.0%), Roman Catholic 17.4%; traditional beliefs 3.1%; other 11.3%. **Major cities** (1999): Honiara 49,107 (urban agglomeration [2001] 78,000; Noro 3,482; Gizo 2,960; Auki 1,606; Tulagi 1,333. **Location:** southwestern Pacific Ocean, east of Papua New Guinea.

## Vital statistics

**Birth rate** per 1,000 population (2002): 37.9 (world avg. 21.2). **Death rate** per 1,000 population (2002): 4.7 (world avg. 8.9). **Natural increase rate** per 1,000 population (2002): 33.2 (world avg. 12.3). **Total fertility rate** (avg. births per childbearing woman; 2002): 5.3. **Life expectancy** at birth (2002): male 68.0 years; female 71.0 years.

## National economy

**Budget** (1998). *Revenue:* SI$557,800,000 (foreign grants 33.0%, taxes on foreign trade 25.8%, income taxes 19.5%, taxes on goods and services 13.1%, nontax revenue 8.6%). *Expenditures:* SI$558,700,000 (capital expenditure 35.9%, administrative 28.6%, wages and salaries 27.2%, interest payments 8.3%). **Tourism:** receipts from visitors (1999) US$6,000,000; expenditures by nationals abroad US$7,000,000. **Land use** (1994): forested 87.5%; meadows and pastures 1.4%; agricultural and under permanent cultivation 2.0%; other 9.1%. **Gross national product** (at current market prices; 2000): US$278,000,000 (US$620 per capita). **Household income and expenditure.** Average household size (1999) 6.3; average annual income per household (1991) US$2,387; sources of income (1983): wages and salaries 74.1%, self-employment, remittances, gifts, and other assistance 25.9%; expenditure (1992): food 46.8%, hous-

## Foreign trade

**Imports** (1996-f.o.b.): SI$536,870,000 (machinery and transport equipment 30.3%, basic manufactured goods 22.2%, food and live animals 15.1%, mineral fuels and lubricants 11.3%). *Major import sources:* Australia 44.1%; Japan 12.5%; Singapore 7.0%; US 2.1%; Thailand 1.8%; UK 1.6%. **Exports** (1996): SI$656,300,000 (timber products 60.6%, fish products 18.3%, palm oil products 10.9%, copra 4.1%, cacao beans 2.2%). *Major export destinations:* Japan 40.1%; South Korea 19.4%; UK 18.4%; Thailand 3.8%; Australia 2.3%; Singapore 2.2%.

## Transport and communications

**Transport.** *Roads* (1996): total length 1,360 km (paved 2.5%). *Vehicles* (1993): passenger cars 2,052; trucks and buses 2,574. *Air transport* (1999): passenger-km 47,278,000; metric ton-km cargo 1,250,000; airports (1997) with scheduled flights 21. **Communications,** in total units (units per 1,000 persons). Radio receivers (1997): 57,000 (141); television receivers (1998): 6,000 (14); telephone main lines (2001): 7,400 (16); cellular telephone subscribers (2001): 1,000 (2.1); personal computers (2001): 22,000 (48); Internet users (2001): 2,000 (4.3).

## Education and health

**Educational attainment** (1986). Percentage of population age 25 and over having: no schooling 44.4%; primary education 46.2%; secondary 6.8%; higher 2.6%. **Literacy** (1999): total population age 15 and over literate 181,000 (76%); males 102,500 (83%); females 78,500 (68%). **Health:** physicians (1999) 53 (1 per 7,692 persons); hospital beds (1997) 210 (1 per 1,957 persons); infant mortality rate per 1,000 live births (1999) 66.0. **Food** (1999): daily per capita caloric intake 2,222 (vegetable products 92%, animal products 8%); (1997) 97% of FAO recommended minimum.

## Military

**Total active duty personnel:** no military forces are maintained, but the Solomon Islands Peace Plan of 2000 permits the establishment of a defense force.

*1 metric ton = about 1.1 short tons;   1 kilometer = 0.6 mi (statute);   1 metric ton-km cargo = about 0.68 short ton-mi cargo;   c.i.f.: cost, insurance, and freight;   f.o.b.: free on board*

## Background

The Solomon Islands were probably settled c. 2000 BC by Austronesian people. Visited by the Spanish in 1568, they were subsequently explored and charted by the Dutch, French, and British. They came under British protection in 1893 and became the British Solomon Islands. During World War II, the Japanese invasion of 1942 ignited three years of the most bitter fighting in the Pacific, particularly on Guadalcanal. The protectorate became self-governing in 1975 and fully independent in 1978. (Another island group named Solomon Islands, which includes Bougainville, is part of Papua New Guinea.)

## Recent Developments

Solomon Islands remained in a state of crisis in 2002 in regard to both public order and the economy. Two years after the Townsville Peace Agreement nominally ended ethic conflict, many had still not surrendered their weapons. An international intervention force led by Australia sent in 2,500 troops in August 2003 to quell the violence. Cyclone Zoe, with winds of over 300 km/hr (186 mph) and 10-m (33-ft) waves, struck the Solomon Islands on 29 Dec 2002, and, because of the remoteness of some islands, it was weeks before the extent of the massive damage was known.

**Internet resources:** <www.solomons.com>

## Somalia

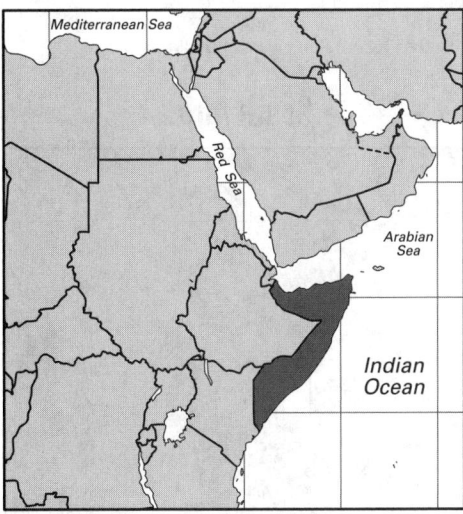

**Official name:** Soomaaliya (Somali); As-Sumal (Arabic) (Somalia). **Form of government:** Since 1991 there has been no sovereign Somalia, only chaos as numerous warlords vie for whatever resources they can secure from the remnants of what was Somalia. In recent years a number of attempts have been made to establish a legitimate national government; to date none has been recognized by the international community. At present Somalia is divided into three autonomous regions: Somaliland in the northwest, Puntland in the northeast, and Somalia in the south. **Chief of state:** Pres. Abdiqasim Salad Hassan (from 2000). **Head of government:** Hassan Abshir Farah (from 2001). **Capital:** Mogadishu. **Official lan-**

guages: Somali; Arabic. **Official religion:** Islam. **Monetary unit:** 1 Somali shilling (So.Sh.) = 100 cents; valuation (7 Jul 2003) $1 = So.Sh. 2,620.00 (in the spring of 2001 the "black market" value was about 17,000 So.Sh = $1).

## Demography

**Area:** 246,000 sq mi, 637,000 sq km. **Population** (2002): 7,753,000. **Density** (2002): persons per sq mi 31.5, persons per sq km 12.2. **Urban** (2001): 27.9. **Sex distribution** (2000): male 50.18%; female 49.82%. **Age breakdown** (2000): under 15, 44.4%; 15–29, 26.8%; 30–44, 17.9%; 45–59, 6.6%; 60–74, 3.5%; 75 and over, 0.8%. **Ethnic composition** (2000): Somali 92.4% (the Somali are divided into six major clans, of which four are predominantly pastoral (representing c. 70% of the population) and two are predominantly agricultural (representing c. 20% of the population); the remainder are urban dwellers with less clan identification); Arab 2.2%; Afar 1.3%; other 4.1%. **Religious affiliation** (1995): Sunni Muslim 99.9%; other 0.1%. **Major cities** (1990): Mogadishu 1,212,000 (2001); Hargeysa 90,000; Kismaayo 90,000; Berbera 70,000; Marka 62,000. **Location:** eastern Africa, bordering Djibouti, the Gulf of Aden, the Indian Ocean, Kenya, and Ethiopia.

## Vital statistics

**Birth rate** per 1,000 population (2001): 47.2 (world avg. 21.2). **Death rate** per 1,000 population (2001): 18.4 (world avg. 8.9). **Natural increase rate** per 1,000 population (2001): 28.8 (world avg. 12.3). **Total fertility rate** (avg. births per childbearing woman; 2000): 7.1. **Life expectancy** at birth (2001): male 45.0 years; female 48.3 years.

## National economy

**Budget** (1991). *Revenue:* So.Sh. 151,453,000,000 (domestic revenue sources, principally indirect taxes and import duties 60.4%; external grants and transfers 39.6%). *Expenditures:* So.Sh. 141,141,000,000 (general services 46.9%; economic and social services 31.2%; debt service 7.0%). **Public debt** (external, outstanding; 2000): $1,825,000,000. **Production** (metric tons except as noted). *Agriculture, forestry, fishing* (1999): fruits (excluding melons) 210,000, sugarcane 210,000, corn (maize) 150,000; livestock (number of live animals) 13,000,000 sheep, 12,000,000 goats, 6,000,000 camels; roundwood (2000) 9,338,000 cu m; fish catch (2000) 20,200. *Mining and quarrying* (2001): gypsum 1,500; salt 1,000. *Manufacturing* (value added in So.Sh. '000,000; 1988): food 794; cigarettes and matches 562; hides and skins 420. *Energy production (consumption):* electricity (kW-hr; 1998) 265,000,000 (246,000,000); crude petroleum (barrels; 1991) none (806,000); petroleum products (metric tons; 1991) none (59,000). **Household expenditure.** Average household size (1980) 4.9; expenditure (1983): food and tobacco 62.3%, housing 15.3%, clothing 5.6%, energy 4.3%, other 12.5%. **Population economically active** (1991): total 3,215,000; activity rate of total population 40.9% (participation rates [1987] over age 10, 63.1%; female 48.7%; unemployed n.a.). **Gross national product** (1996): $706,000,000 ($110 per capita). **Land use** (1994): forest 25.5%; pasture 68.6%; agriculture 1.6%; other 4.3%.

## Foreign trade

**Imports** (1999-c.i.f.): $180,000,000 (agricultural products 49.2%, of which refined sugar 23.9%, wheat 14.3%, rice 9.4%; unspecified 50.8%). *Major import sources:* Djibouti 27%; Kenya 12%; India 9%; Thailand 5%; UAE 4%. **Exports** (1999-f.o.b.): $150,000,000 (agricultural products 47.6%, of which live sheep and goats 38.7%, bananas 5.3%; other [including bagged charcoal] 52.4%). *Major export destinations:* Yemen 29%; Saudi Arabia 28%; UAE 28%; Oman 6%.

## Transport and communications

**Transport.** *Roads* (1996): total length 22,100 km (paved 12%). *Vehicles* (1996): passenger cars 1,020; trucks and buses 6,440. *Air transport* (1991): passenger-km 131,000,000; metric ton-km cargo 5,000,-000; airports (1998) with scheduled flights 1. **Communications,** in total units (units per 1,000 persons). Daily newspaper circulation (1996): 10,000 (1.2); radio receivers (1997): 470,000 (53); television receivers (1997): 135,000 (15); telephone main lines (1999): 15,000 (2.1).

## Education and health

**Literacy** (1995): percentage of total population age 15 and over literate 24%; males literate 36%; females literate 14%. **Health:** physicians (1997) 265 (1 per 25,034 persons); hospital beds (1985) 5,536 (1 per 1,130 persons); infant mortality rate per 1,000 live births (2001) 124.0. **Food** (2000): daily per capita caloric intake 1,628 (vegetable products 62%, animal products 38%); 70% of FAO recommended minimum.

## Military

**Total active duty personnel:** clan warfare between 1991 and mid-2003. **Military expenditure as percentage of GNP** (1990): 0.9% (world 4.3%); per capita expenditure $1.

---

 **Did you know?** Somalia has been a lively trading center for millennia. The area was known to ancient Egyptians as a land of aromatics and incense, and later was the source of exotic products as varied as ostrich feathers, clarified butter, and precious vegetable gums.

---

## Background

Muslim Arabs and Persians first established trading posts along the coasts of Somalia in the 7th–10th centuries. By the 10th century Somali nomads occupied the area inland from the Gulf of Aden, and the south and west were inhabited by various groups of pastoral Oromo peoples. Intensive European exploration began after the British occupation of Aden in 1839, and in the late 19th century Britain and Italy set up protectorates in the region. During World War II the Italians invaded British Somaliland (1940); a year later British troops retook the area, and Britain administered the region until 1950, when Italian So-

maliland became a UN trust territory. In 1960 it was united with the former British Somaliland, and the two became the independent Republic of Somalia. Since then it has suffered political and civil strife, including military dictatorship, civil war, drought, and famine. In the 1990s no effective central government existed. In 1991 a proclamation of a Republic of Somaliland, on territory corresponding to the former British Somaliland, was issued by a breakaway group, but it did not receive international recognition. A multinational force intervened from 1992 to 1994 in an unsuccessful attempt to stabilize the region. The country remained in turmoil.

## Recent Developments

By 2002 the Transitional National Government (TNG) set up in 2000 had failed to bring unity to the country and had little effective power. In effect it represented one alliance of clans, which was opposed by a counteralliance. Even in the former capital of Mogadishu, the TNG struggled for control with other factions. Acts of banditry and kidnapping continued there in spite of the attempts by the TNG to form a police force and enforce a weapons ban, and in May and again in July there was bloody factional fighting. Violence continued to break out from time to time over local disputes in different parts of the country. By contrast, the self-declared Republic of Somaliland in the north remained stable, even after Pres. Muhammad Ibrahim Egal died in May and was succeeded by the vice president, Dahir Riyale Kahin. Kahin won presidential elections in April 2003 by the barest of margins.

**Internet resources:** <www.somalirepublic.org>

# South Africa

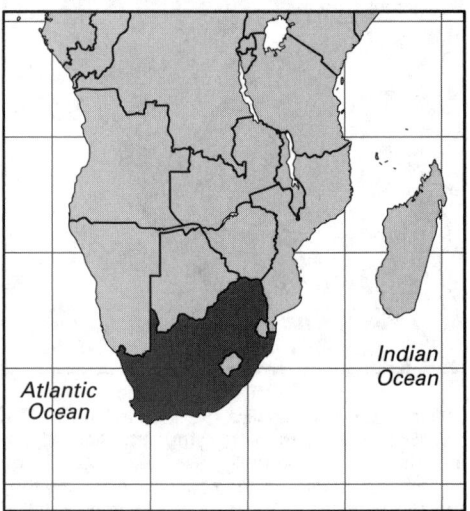

**Official name:** Republiek van Suid-Afrika (Afrikaans); Republic of South Africa (English). **Form of government:** multiparty republic with two legislative houses (National Council of Provinces [90]; National Assembly [400]). **Head of state and government:** President

---

Thabo Mbeki (from 1999). **Capitals** (de facto): Pretoria/Tshwane (executive); Bloemfontein/Mangaung (judicial); Cape Town (legislative). **Official languages:** Afrikaans; English; Ndebele; Pedi; Sotho; Swazi; Tsonga; Tswana; Venda; Xhosa; Zulu. **Official religion:** none. **Monetary unit:** 1 rand (R) = 100 cents; valuation (7 Jul 2003) $1 = R 7.51.

## Demography

**Area:** 470,693 sq mi, 1,219,090 sq km. **Population** (2002): 45,172,000. **Density** (2002): persons per sq mi 96.0, persons per sq km 37.1. **Urban** (2002): 57.7%. **Sex distribution** (2002): male 48.15%; female 51.85%. **Age breakdown** (1996): under 15, 33.9%; 15–29, 28.6%; 30–44, 19.4%; 45–59, 9.9%; 60–74, 5.3%; 75 and over, 1.7%; unknown, 1.2%. **Ethnic composition** (2000): black 77.6%, of which Zulu c. 22.0%, Xhosa c. 18.0%, Pedi c. 9.0%, Sotho c. 7.0%, Tswana c. 7.0%, Tsonga c. 3.5%, Swazi c. 3.0%; white 10.4%; Coloured 8.7%; Asian 2.5%; other 0.8%. **Religious affiliation** (2000): Christian 83.1%, of which black independent churches 39.1%, Protestant 31.8%, Roman Catholic 7.1%; traditional beliefs 8.4%; Hindu 2.4%; Muslim 2.4%; nonreligious 2.4%; Baha'i 0.6%; Jewish 0.4%; other 0.3%. **Major urban agglomerations** (2000): Johannesburg 2,950,000; Cape Town 2,930,000; Durban 2,391,000; Pretoria 1,590,000; Port Elizabeth 1,060,000. **Location:** southern Africa, bordering Namibia, Botswana, Zimbabwe, Mozambique, Swaziland, and the southern Atlantic and western Indian Oceans; wholly contained within South Africa is the country of Lesotho.

## Vital statistics

**Birth rate** per 1,000 population (2001): 19.8 (world avg. 21.2). **Death rate** per 1,000 population (2001): 15.0 (world avg. 8.9). **Natural increase rate** per 1,000 population (2001): 4.8 (world avg. 12.3). **Marriage rate** per 1,000 population (1998): 3.4. **Total fertility rate** (avg. births per childbearing woman; 2001): 2.4. **Life expectancy** at birth (2001): male 50.7 years; female 51.4 years.

## National economy

**Budget** (2000–01). *Revenue*: R 213,385,700,000 (personal income taxes 42.8%, value-added taxes 24.3%, company income taxes 11.6%, other 21.3%). *Expenditures*: R 235,048,400,000 (transfer to provinces 46.3%, interest on public debt 19.6%, police and prisons 9.1%, defense 5.9%). **Public debt** (external, outstanding; 2000): $9,088,000,000. **Production** (in R '000,000 except as noted). *Agriculture, forestry, fishing* (in value of production; 2000): poultry 8,270, corn (maize) 5,654, beef 3,904, temperate fruits 2,975, sugarcane 2,530; roundwood (2000) 30,616,000 cu m; fish catch (1999) 592,144 metric tons. *Mining and quarrying* (in value of sales; 2000): platinum-group metals 27,111; gold 25,272; rough diamonds 10,015,000 carats. *Manufacturing* (in R '000,000 value added; 1996): food products 11,437; iron and steel 7,515; transport equipment 7,445. *Energy production (consumption)* (includes Botswana, Lesotho, Namibia, and Swaziland, except electricity): electricity (kW-hr; 1999) 203,532,-000,000 ([1998] 187,517,000,000); coal (metric tons; 1999) 223,357,000 ([1997] 149,076,000); crude petroleum (barrels; 1999) 5,493,000 ([1997] 159,061,000); petroleum products (metric tons;

1997) 19,193,000 (17,252,000); natural gas (cu m; 1999): 1,616,500,000 (1,616,500,000). **Tourism** (2000): receipts $2,707,000,000; expenditures $2,004,000,000. **Household income and expenditure.** Average household size (1996) 4.5; average annual disposable income per household (1996) R 47,600 ($11,070); expenditure (1998): food, beverages, and tobacco 31.3%; transportation 14.3%; housing 9.3%; household furnishings and operation 8.9%. **Population economically active** (2000): total 13,527,000; activity rate of total population 31.2% (participation rates [1995]: over age 15, c. 53%; female 43.6%; unemployed [2000] 23.3%). **Gross national product** (2000): $129,171,000,000 ($3,020 per capita). **Land use** (1994): forest 6.7%; pasture 66.7%; agriculture 10.8%; other 15.8%.

## Foreign trade

**Imports** (2000): $27,202,000,000 (1997; machinery and apparatus 33.7%, petroleum and products 11.1%, basic manufactures 10.5%, chemicals and chemical products 10.5%, food 3.9%). *Major import sources* (1999): Germany 14.5%; US 13.3%; UK 9.4%; Japan 7.5%; France 4.3%. **Exports** (2000): $31,434,000,000 (1997; machinery and transport equipment 14.8%; pearls, precious and semiprecious stones 14.7%; gem diamonds 14.7%; chemicals 9.1%; food 8.9%; iron and steel 6.8%). *Major export destinations* (1999): UK 8.3%; US 8.2%; Germany 7.0%; Japan 5.2%; Italy 4.2%; unspecified 21.8%.

## Transport and communications

**Transport.** *Railroads*: route length (1998) 20,319 km; passenger-km (1997–98) 1,775,000,000; metric ton-km cargo (1997–98) 103,866,000,000. *Roads* (1999): length 331,265 km (paved 41%). *Vehicles* (1999): passenger cars 3,966,252; trucks and buses 1,904,871. *Air transport* (2000; SAA only): passenger-km 19,320,000,000; metric ton-km cargo 677,048,000; airport (1996) 24. **Communications**, in total units (units per 1,000 persons). Daily newspaper circulation (1996): 1,288,000 (31); radio receivers (1997): 13,750,000 (324); television receivers (1999): 5,450,000 (124); telephone main lines (2001): 4,969,000 (101); cellular telephone subscribers (2001): 9,197,000 (210); personal computers (2001): 3,000,000 (69); Internet users (2001): 3,068,000 (70).

## Education and health

**Educational attainment** (1994). Percentage of population age 25 and over having: no formal schooling 14.5%; primary/incomplete secondary 61.6%; secondary/incomplete higher 20.4%; complete higher 3.1%; other/unknown 0.4%. **Literacy** (1995): total population age 15 and over literate: 81.8%. **Health:** physicians (2000) 29,788 (1 per 1,453 persons); hospital beds (1998) 144,363 (1 per 290 persons); infant mortality rate per 1,000 live births (2001) 58.1. **Food** (2000): daily per capita caloric intake 2,886 (vegetable products 87%, animal products 13%); 114% of FAO recommended minimum.

## Military

**Total active duty personnel** (2001): 61,500 (army 67.9%, navy 8.1%, air force 15.0%, intraservice medical service 9.0%). **Military expenditure as percent-**

age of GNP (1999): 1.5% (world 2.4%); per capita expenditure $45.

## Background

San and Khoikhoi peoples roamed southern Africa as hunters and gatherers in the Stone Age, and the latter had developed a pastoralist culture by the time of European contact. By the 14th century, Bantu-speaking peoples had settled in the area and developed gold and copper mining and an active east African trade. In 1652 the Dutch established a colony at the Cape of Good Hope; the Dutch settlers became known as Boers and later as Afrikaners, after their Afrikaans language. In 1795 British forces captured the Cape, and in the 1830s, to escape British rule, Dutch settlers began the Great Trek northward and established the independent Boer republics of Orange Free State and the South African Republic (later the Transvaal region), which the British annexed as colonies by 1902. In 1910 the British colonies of Cape Colony, Transvaal, Natal, and Orange River were unified into the new Union of South Africa. It became independent and withdrew from the Commonwealth in 1961. Throughout the 20th century South African politics were dominated by the issue of maintaining white supremacy over the country's black majority, and in 1948 South Africa formally instituted apartheid. Faced by increasing worldwide condemnation, it began dismantling the policy in the 1980s and ended it in 1990. In free elections in 1994, Nelson Mandela became the country's first black president. South Africa also rejoined the Commonwealth in 1994.

## Recent Developments

In his 2002 annual address to Parliament, South African Pres. Thabo Mbeki of the African National Congress (ANC) detailed the progress made in land reform and in the provision of water, electricity, and housing; he defined as national goals black economic empowerment, poverty eradication, and nation building driven by volunteerism. During the year a mining charter was enacted, requiring that 15% of the industry be black owned within 5 years and 26% within 10 years; similar goals were set for the oil industry. The government's policy on HIV/AIDS continued to be controversial. In March an ANC document portrayed AIDS as the result of a conspiracy with the aim of dehumanizing Africans. The prominent social activist and politician Winnie Madikizela-Mandela was found guilty of fraud in April 2003 and sentenced to five years in prison, a judgment she appealed.

President Mbeki continued as a resolute advocate of the New Partnership for Africa's Development, a plan for the economic development of Africa that was adopted by the World Economic Forum held in Durban, South Africa, in June; by the African Union, launched in Durban in July; and by the UN General Assembly in September. The UN World Summit on Sustainable Development was also held in South Africa—in Johannesburg—in August. The South African government brokered eight weeks of peace talks on the civil war in the Democratic Republic of the Congo in March and April and was involved in other efforts to secure peace in Central Africa.

Internet resources: <http://tourism.org.za>

# Spain

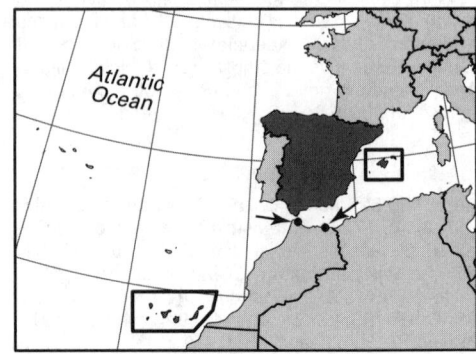

**Official name:** Reino de España (Kingdom of Spain). **Form of government:** constitutional monarchy with two legislative houses (Senate [259; 208 directly elected, 51 indirectly elected]; Congress of Deputies [350]). **Chief of state:** King Juan Carlos I (from 1975). **Head of government:** Prime Minister José María Aznar López (from 1996). **Capital:** Madrid. **Official language:** Castilian Spanish. **Official religion:** none. **Monetary unit:** 1 euro (€) = 100 cents; valuation (7 Jul 2003) $1 = €0.87 (at conversion on 1 Jan 2002; €1 = 166.386 pesetas [Ptas]).

## Demography

**Area:** 195,364 sq mi, 505,990 sq km. **Population** (2002): 40,998,000. **Density** (2002): persons per sq mi 209.8, persons per sq km 81.0. **Urban** (2002): 77.8%. **Sex distribution** (2002): male 48.95%; female 51.05%. **Age breakdown** (2002): under 15, 14.6%; 15–29, 21.7%; 30–44, 24.0%; 45–59, 18.0%; 60–74, 14.2%; 75 and over, 7.5%. **Ethnolinguistic composition** (1991): Spanish 74.4%; Catalan 16.9%; other 8.7%. **Religious affiliation** (2000): Roman Catholic 92.0%; Muslim 0.5%; Protestant 0.3%; other 7.2%. **Major cities** (2001): Madrid 2,938,723; Barcelona 1,503,884; Valencia 738,441; Seville 684,633; Zaragoza 614,905. **Location:** southwestern Europe, bordering France, Andorra, the Mediterranean Sea, Gibraltar, the Atlantic Ocean, and Portugal.

## Vital statistics

**Birth rate** per 1,000 population (2001): 10.0 (world avg. 21.2). **Death rate** per 1,000 population (2001): 9.3 (world avg. 8.9). **Natural increase rate** per 1,000 population (2001): 0.7 (world avg. 12.3). **Total fertility rate** (avg. births per childbearing woman; 2001): 1.2. **Life expectancy** at birth (2001): male 75.6 years; female 82.5 years.

## National economy

**Budget** (2002). *Revenue:* €108,824,300,000 (direct taxes 46.6%, of which income tax 27.2%; indirect taxes 41.8%, of which value-added tax on products 27.8%; other taxes 11.6%). *Expenditures:* €112,586,900,000 (public debt 15.7%; health 9.8%; pensions 5.7%; defense 5.6%; public works 4.4%). **Tourism** (2000): receipts $31,454,000,000; expen-

*1 metric ton = about 1.1 short tons;   1 kilometer = 0.6 mi (statute);   1 metric ton-km cargo = about 0.68 short ton-mi cargo;   c.i.f.: cost, insurance, and freight;   f.o.b.: free on board*

ditures $5,572,000,000. **Gross national product** (2000): $595,255,000,000 ($15,080 per capita). **Production** (metric tons except as noted). *Agriculture, forestry, fishing* (2000): barley 11,283,100, sugar beets 8,343,800, wheat 7,333,100; livestock (number of live animals) 23,700,000 sheep, 23,682,000 pigs, 6,203,000 cattle; roundwood (2000) 14,810,000 cu m; fish catch (1999) 1,485,000. *Mining and quarrying* (metal content in metric tons; 1999): zinc 109,400; lead 28,000; copper 3,500. *Manufacturing* (value added in Ptas '000,000,000; 1999): machinery 2,475; transport equipment 1,687; food products 1,585;. *Energy production (consumption)*: electricity (kW-hr; 2000) 212,244,000,000 ([1997] 187,128,000,000); hard coal (metric tons; 2000) 11,916,000 ([1997] 27,940,000); lignite (metric tons; 1997) 12,587,000 (12,805,000); crude petroleum (barrels; 2000) 1,711,000 ([1997] 331,765,000); petroleum products (metric tons; 1997) 48,528,000 (44,200,000); natural gas (cu m; 2000) 183,336,000 ([1997] 12,999,000,000). **Public debt** (2001): €307,434,000,000. **Population economically active** (2000): total 16,844,200; activity rate of total population 41.6% (participation rates: ages [1995] 16–64, 60.7%, female 38.3%; unemployed 22.9%). **Household income and expenditure.** Average household size (1999) 3.3; income per household (2000) Ptas 3,205,693 ($18,470); expenditure (1995): housing 26.0%, food 24.0%, transportation 12.8%, clothing and footwear 7.4%, household goods and services 6.1%.

## Foreign trade

**Imports** (2000-f.o.b. in balance of trade): Ptas 27,643,097,000,000 (machinery 12.5%; energy products 12.0%; transportation equipment 10.9%; agricultural products 8.1%). *Major import sources:* France 17.1%; Germany 14.9%; Italy 14.3%; UK 7.0%. **Exports** (2000): Ptas 20,482,039,900,000 (transport equipment 19.5%; agricultural products 12.9%; machinery 7.9%). *Major export destinations:* France 19.4%; Germany 12.4%; Portugal 9.4%; Italy 8.8%; UK 8.3%.

## Transport and communications

**Transport.** *Railroads* (2000): route length 13,832 km; passenger-km 19,927,000,000; metric ton-km cargo 12,071,000,000. *Roads* (1999): length 346,548 km (paved 99%). *Vehicles* (2000): cars 17,449,000; trucks and buses 3,835,000. *Air transport* (1999): passenger-km 60,696,083,000; metric ton-km cargo 6,406,562,000; airports (1997) with scheduled flights 25. **Communications,** in total units (units per 1,000 persons). Daily newspaper circulation (1996): 3,931,000 (99); radio receivers (1998): 12,000,000 (332); television receivers (1998): 22,000,000 (553); telephone main lines (2001): 17,427,000 (431); cellular telephone subscribers (2001): 26,494,200 (655); personal computers (2001): 6,800,000 (168); Internet users (2001): 7,388,000 (183).

## Education and health

**Educational attainment** (1997). Percentage of economically active population age 16 and over having: no formal schooling 6.4%; primary 26.6%; secondary 58.9%; higher 8.1%. **Literacy** (1999): total population age 15 and over literate 97.6%; males 98.5%; females 96.7%. **Health** (1997): physicians 168,630 (1

per 236 persons); hospital beds (1999) 164,097 (1 per 244 persons); infant mortality rate per 1,000 live births (2001) 4.7. **Food** (2000): daily per capita caloric intake 3,352 (vegetable products 73%, animal products 27%); 136% of FAO recommended minimum.

## Military

**Total active duty personnel** (2001): 143,450 (army 64.1%, navy 18.8%, air force 17.1%). **Military expenditure as percentage of GNP** (1999): 1.3% (world 2.4%); per capita expenditure $192.

## Background

Remains of Stone Age populations dating back some 35,000 years have been found throughout Spain. Celtic peoples arrived in the 9th century BC, followed by the Romans, who dominated Spain from c. 200 BC until the Visigoth invasion in the early 5th century. In the early 8th century most of the peninsula fell to Muslims (Moors) from North Africa and remained under their control until it was gradually reconquered by the Christian kingdoms of Castile, Aragon, and Portugal. Spain was reunited in 1479 following the marriage of Ferdinand II (of Aragon) and Isabella I (of Castile). The last Muslim kingdom, Granada, was reconquered in 1492, and around this time Spain also established a colonial empire in the Americas. In 1516 the throne passed to the Habsburgs, whose rule ended in 1700 when Philip V became the first Bourbon king of Spain. His ascendancy caused the War of the Spanish Succession, which resulted in the loss of numerous European possessions and sparked revolution within most of Spain's American colonies. Spain lost its remaining overseas possessions to the US in the Spanish-American War (1898). It became a republic in 1931. The Spanish Civil War (1936–39) ended in victory for the Nationalists under General Francisco Franco, who ruled as dictator until his death in 1975. His successor as head of state, King Juan Carlos I, restored the monarchy upon his accession to the throne; a new constitution in 1978 established a parliamentary monarchy. Spain joined NATO in 1982 and the European Community in 1986.

## Recent Developments

Movements for Basque and Catalan autonomy dominated headlines in 2002–03. With the support of the Socialist opposition, the ruling Popular Party government intensified its fight against terrorism, combining successful police operations against the armed Basque separatists in Euskadi Ta Askatasuna (ETA) with legal action against the organization's political wing, Batasuna. Batasuna was officially outlawed in March 2003. A week later, with an eye on October elections, the ruling nationalist coalition in Catalonia published a plan for the region to acquire sovereignty and increased national rights and representation.

Tensions with Morocco flared up in July 2002 when a small detachment of Moroccan armed police landed on Leila/Perejil, a barren rock a few hundred meters off the North African mainland over which both countries claimed sovereignty. After a weeklong standoff, Spanish troops seized the islet, but they withdrew three days later after the two countries reached an agreement to return to the status quo and initiate talks on the various issues souring relations. Prime Minister José María Aznar López put his political career on the line by strongly supporting, against the will of his people, US Pres. George W. Bush's aggressive policy on Iraq. Aznar's position also signaled a new foreign policy independence by Spain in relation to, especially, France and Germany. A meeting of more than 100 Iraqi opposition leaders was convened in Madrid in late April to help the Iraqi people "build their own future."

Internet resources: <www.tourspain.es>

# Sri Lanka

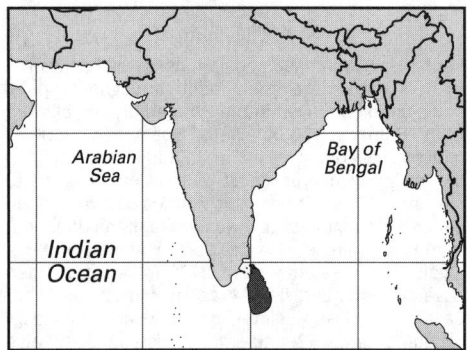

**Official name:** Sri Lanka Prajatantrika Samajavadi Janarajaya (Sinhala); Ilangai Jananayaka Socialisa Kudiarasu (Tamil) (Democratic Socialist Republic of Sri Lanka). **Form of government:** unitary multiparty republic with one legislative house (Parliament [225]). **Head of state and government:** President Chandrika Kumaratunga (from 1994) assisted by Prime Minister Ranil Wickremesinghe (from 2001). **Capitals:** Colombo (executive); Sri Jayewardenepura Kotte (Colombo suburb; legislative and judicial). **Official languages:** Sinhala; Tamil. **Official religion:** none. **Monetary unit:** 1 Sri Lanka rupee (SL Rs) = 100 cents; valuation (7 Jul 2003) $1 = SL Rs 97.18.

## Demography

**Area:** 25,332 sq mi, 65,610 sq km. **Population** (2002): 18,870,000. **Density** (2002): persons per sq mi 744.9, persons per sq km 287.6. **Urban** (2002): 25.0%. **Sex distribution** (1999): male 50.97%; female 49.03%. **Age breakdown** (1996): under 15, 28.0%; 15–29, 26.9%; 30–44, 22.5%; 45–59, 13.6%; 60–74, 7.0%; 75 and over, 2.0%. **Ethnic composition** (2000): Sinhalese 72.4%; Tamil 17.8%; Sri Lankan Moor 7.4%; other 2.4%. **Religious affiliation** (2000): Buddhist 68.4%; Hindu 11.3%; Christian 9.4%; Muslim 9.0%; other 1.9%. **Major cities** (2001): Colombo 642,020; Dehiwala–Mount Lavinia 201,787; Moratuwa 177,190; Negombo 121,933; Kandy 110,049. **Location:** island in the northern Indian Ocean, lying southeast of India.

## Vital statistics

**Birth rate** per 1,000 population (2002): 17.3 (world avg. 21.2); (1986) legitimate 96.3%; illegitimate 3.7%. **Death rate** per 1,000 population (2002): 6.3 (world avg. 8.9). **Natural increase rate** per 1,000 population (2002): 11.0 (world avg. 12.3). **Total fertility**

rate (avg. births per childbearing woman; 2002): 2.1. **Marriage rate** per 1,000 population (1997): 8.9. **Life expectancy** at birth (2002): male 70.0 years; female 76.0 years.

## National economy

**Budget** (2000). *Revenue*: SL Rs 233,974,000,000 (sales and turnover tax 22.8%, excise taxes 19.9%, nontax revenue 13.8%, income taxes 12.5%, import duties 11.5%). *Expenditures*: SL Rs 329,012,000,-000 (interest payments 21.1%, defense 11.7%, transport and communications 11.7%, social welfare 10.5%, education 9.5%, administration 8.5%). **Public debt** (external, outstanding; 2000): $8,035,000,000. **Production** (metric tons except as noted). *Agriculture, forestry, fishing* (2000): rice 2,767,000, coconuts 1,950,000, sugarcane 1,114,000; livestock (number of live animals) 1,616,700 cattle, 727,700 buffalo, 514,400 goats; roundwood (1999) 10,344,000 cu m; fish catch (1998) 266,100. *Mining and quarrying* (1998); limestone 950,000; titanium concentrate 23,000; graphite 5,000. *Manufacturing* (value added, in $'000,000; 1995): food, beverages, and tobacco 601; textiles and apparel 391; petrochemicals 116. *Energy production (consumption)*: electricity (kW-hr; 1997) 5,145,000,000 (5,145,000,000); coal (metric tons; 1997) none (negligible); crude petroleum (barrels; 1997) none (13,000,000); petroleum products (metric tons; 1997) 1,675,000 (2,399,000). **Gross national product** (2000): $16,408,000,000 ($850 per capita). **Population economically active:** total (1997) 6,213,086; activity rate 40.2% (participation rates: ages 15 and over, 55.2%; female 32.4%; unemployed [2000] 8.0%). **Household income and expenditure** (1992). Average household size (1994) 4.6; income per household SL Rs 116,100 ($2,600); sources of income: wages 48.5%, property income and self-employment 41.8%, transfers 9.7%; expenditure: food 58.6%, transportation 16.0%, clothing 8.4%. **Tourism** (2000): receipts $253,000,000; expenditures $244,000,000.

## Foreign trade

**Imports** (1999): $5,981,000,000 (textile products 22.1%, machinery and equipment 11.3%, transport equipment 8.7%, petroleum 8.4%, processed foods 6.7%). *Major import sources:* Japan 10.4%; India 9.5%; Singapore 8.4%; UK 4.7%; US 4.0%. **Exports** (1999): $4,600,000,000 (clothing and accessories 52.7%, tea 13.5%, gems 4.7%, coconuts 1.8%). *Major export destinations:* US 39.6%; UK 13.3%; Germany 4.8%; Japan 3.5%; The Netherlands 2.4%.

## Transport and communications

**Transport.** *Railroads* (1998): route length 1,447 km; passenger-km 3,264,000,000; metric ton-km cargo 132,000,000. *Roads* (1996): total length 99,200 km (paved 40%). *Vehicles* (1996): passenger cars 107,000; trucks and buses 150,160. *Air transport* (1999): passenger-km 5,156,000,000; metric ton-km cargo 669,700,000; airports (1996) 1. **Communications,** in total units (units per 1,000 persons). Daily newspaper circulation (1996): 530,000 (29); radio receivers (1997): 3,850,000 (211); television receivers (1999): 1,900,000 (102); telephone main

*1 metric ton = about 1.1 short tons;    1 kilometer = 0.6 mi (statute);    1 metric ton-km cargo = about 0.68 short ton-mi cargo;    c.i.f.: cost, insurance, and freight;    f.o.b.: free on board*

lines (2001): 828,000 (43); cellular telephone sub-scribers (2001): 720,000 (38); personal computers (2001): 150,000 (7.9); Internet users (2001): 150,000 (7.9).

## Education and health

**Literacy** (1995): percentage of population age 15 and over literate 90.2%; males literate 93.4%; females literate 87.2%. **Health** (1999): physicians 6,938 (1 per 2,740 persons); hospital beds (1997) 52,298 (1 per 355 persons); infant mortality rate per 1,000 live births (2002) 20.0. **Food** (2000): daily per capita caloric intake 2,405 (vegetable products 94%, animal products 6%); 108% of FAO recommended minimum.

## Military

**Total active duty personnel** (2001): 120,500 (army 76.8%, navy 14.9%, air force 8.3%). **Military expenditure as percentage of GNP** (1999): 4.7% (world 2.4%); per capita expenditure $38.

---

Adam's Peak (Sri Pada), a modest-sized mountain in southern Sri Lanka, has a long history as a sacred monument. Early inhabitants of the island (the Veddas) were the first known to worship it as a religious place. Present day Buddhists, Christians, Hindus, and Muslims in Sri Lanka, for various reasons, have Adam's Peak as a centerpiece in their religious histories.

---

## Background

The Sinhalese people of Sri Lanka (Ceylon) probably originated with the blending of aboriginal inhabitants and migrating Indo-Aryans from India c. 5th century BC. The Tamils were later immigrants from Dravidian India, migrating over a period from the early centuries AD to c. 1200. Buddhism was introduced during the 3rd century BC. As Buddhism spread, the Sinhalese kingdom extended its political control over Ceylon but lost it to invaders from southern India in the 10th century AD. Between 1200 and 1505 Sinhalese power gravitated to southwestern Ceylon, while a southern Indian dynasty seized power in the north and established the Tamil kingdom in the 14th century. Foreign invasions from India, China, and Malaya occurred in the 13th–15th centuries. In 1505 the Portuguese arrived, and by 1619 they controlled most of the island. The Sinhalese enlisted the Dutch to help oust the Portuguese and eventually came under the control of the Dutch East India Co., which relinquished power in 1796 to the British. In 1802 Ceylon became a crown colony, gaining independence in 1948. It became the Republic of Sri Lanka in 1972 and was renamed the Democratic Socialist Republic of Sri Lanka in 1978. Civil strife between Tamil and Sinhalese groups has beset the country in recent years, with the Tamils demanding a separate autonomous state in northern Sri Lanka.

## Recent Developments

In 2002 hope of ending Sri Lanka's long-standing civil war at last emerged, but negotiations between the government and the secessionist Liberation Tigers of Tamil Eelam (LTTE) dragged on into 2003. Norwegian mediators had negotiated an indefinite cease-fire in February 2002. Internal political opposition delayed the start of peace talks, but in September the talks began at a naval base in Thailand. Following the initial round, the LTTE unexpectedly dropped its claim for independence, saying it would accept "genuine autonomy and self-determination" in place of a separate state. The two sides agreed to cooperate on such matters as clearing land mines and resettling displaced persons. Encouraging progress was suspended in April 2003, however, when the LTTE delegates refused a call to give up their arms and suspended the talks, purportedly to give the government a chance to improve its treatment of the Tamil minority.

**Internet resources:** <www.infolanka.com>

# The Sudan

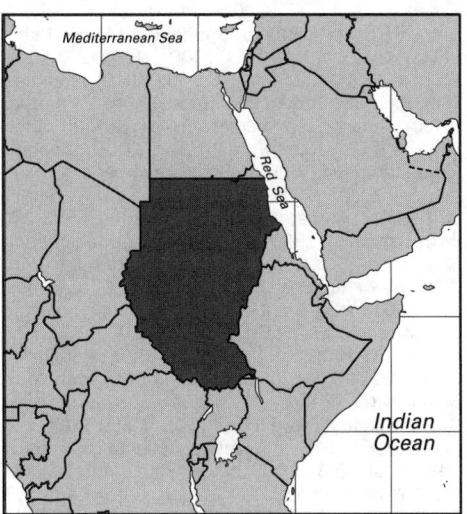

**Official name:** Jumhuriyat al-Sudan (Republic of the Sudan). **Form of government:** federal republic with one legislative body (National Assembly [360; includes 90 seats not elected directly]). **Head of state and government:** President Omar Hassan Ahmad al-Bashir (from 1989). **Capitals:** Khartoum (executive); Omdurman (legislative). **Official language:** Arabic. **Official religion:** Islam. **Monetary unit:** 1 Sudanese dinar (Sd); valuation (7 Jul 2003) $1 = Sd 258.70.

## Demography

**Area:** 2,503,890 sq km (includes about 130,000 sq km of inland water). **Population** (2002): 37,090,000. **Density** (2002): persons per sq mi 38.3, persons per sq km 14.8. **Urban** (2002) 37.1%%. **Sex distribution** (2001): male 50.64%; female 49.36%. **Age breakdown** (2001): under 15, 44.6%; 15–29, 27.6%; 30–44, 15.6%; 45–59, 8.4%; 60–74, 3.3%; 75 and over, 0.5%. **Ethnic composition** (1983): Sudanese Arab 49.1%; Dinka 11.5%; Nuba 8.1%; Beja 6.4%, Nuer 4.9%; Zande 2.7%; Bari 2.5%; Fur 2.1%; other 12.7%. **Religious affiliation** (2000): Sunni Muslim 70.3%; Christian 16.7%, of which Roman Catholic c. 8%, Anglican c. 6%; traditional beliefs 11.9%; other 1.1%. **Major cities** (1993): Omdurman 1,267,077; Khartoum 924,505; Khartoum North 879,105; Port Sudan 305,385; Kassala 234,270. **Location:** northeastern Africa, bordering Egypt, the Red Sea, Eritrea,

Ethiopia, Kenya, Uganda, Democratic Republic of the Congo, Central African Republic, Chad, and Libya.

## Vital statistics

**Birth rate** per 1,000 population (2001): 37.9 (world avg. 21.2). **Death rate** per 1,000 population (2001): 10.0 (world avg. 8.9). **Natural increase rate** per 1,000 population (2001): 27.9 (world avg. 12.3). **Total fertility rate** (avg. births per childbearing woman; 2001): 5.3. **Life expectancy** at birth (2001): male 55.9 years; female 58.1 years.

## National economy

**Budget** (1999–2000). *Revenue:* Sd 206,700,000,-000 (import duties 26.0%, nontax revenue 25.8%, excise duties 11.9%, taxes on business profits 11.1%). *Expenditures:* Sd 227,200,000,000 (current expenditure 85.8%, development expenditure 14.2%). **Public debt** (external, outstanding; 2000): $8,647,000,000. **Tourism** (2000): receipts $5,000,000; expenditures $55,000,000. **Production** (metric tons except as noted). *Agriculture, forestry, fishing* (2000): sugarcane 4,982,000, sorghum 2,488,000, peanuts (groundnuts) 947,000; livestock (number of live animals) 46,095,000 sheep, 38,548,000 goats, 37,093,000 cattle; roundwood (2000) 18,853,000 cu m; fish catch (1999) 50,500. *Mining and quarrying* (2000): salt 50,000; gold 6,000 kg. *Manufacturing* (2000): raw sugar 662,000; flour 600,000; cement 161,000. *Energy production (consumption):* electricity (kW-hr; 2000) 2,569,200,000 (1,337,000,000); crude petroleum (barrels; August 1999 through July 2000) 60,700,000 ([1997] 6,441,000); petroleum products (metric tons; 2000) 1,913,600 (1,753,000). **Gross national product** (2000): $9,599,000,000 ($310 per capita). **Population economically active** (1993): total 8,866,000; activity rate of total population 32.3% (participation rates: ages 15–64 [1983] 57.4%; female 22.3%; unemployed c. 30.0%). **Household expenditure** (1983): food and beverages 63.6%, housing 11.5%, household goods 5.5%, clothing and footwear 5.3%. **Land use** (1994): forested 18.1%; meadows and pastures 46.3%; agricultural and under permanent cultivation 5.5%; desert and other 30.1%.

## Foreign trade

**Imports** (2000-c.i.f.): $1,552,700,000 (1999; machinery and equipment 25.4%; foodstuffs 19.5%, of which wheat and wheat flour 8.7%; petroleum products 13.0%; transport equipment 9.3%). *Major import sources:* Saudi Arabia 11.8%; France 8.6%; Italy 6.3%; UAE 5.5%; Germany 5.4%; UK 5.1%. **Exports** (2000-f.o.b.): $1,806,700,000 (1999; crude petroleum 35.4%; sesame seeds 16.3%; sheep and lambs 13.0%; gold 7.1%; cotton 5.8%). *Major export destinations:* Saudi Arabia 18.1%; Japan 15.7%; UK 9.2%; South Korea 7.9%; Italy 7.1%.

## Transport and communications

**Transport.** *Railroads:* route length (2000) 5,901 km; (1995–96) passenger-km 161,000,000; (1995–96) metric ton-km cargo 1,965,000,000. *Roads* (1999): total length 11,900 km (paved 36%). *Vehicles* (1996): passenger cars 285,000; trucks and buses 53,000.

*Air transport* (2001): passenger-km 803,000,000; metric ton-km cargo 54,542,000; airports (1997) with scheduled flights 3. **Communications,** in total units (units per 1,000 persons). Daily newspaper circulation (1996): 737,000 (24); radio receivers (1997): 7,550,000 (235); television receivers (1999): 5,000,000 (147); telephone main lines (2001): 453,000 (14); cellular telephone subscribers (2001): 105,000 (3.3); personal computers (2001): 115,000 (3.6); Internet users (2001): 56,000 (1.8).

## Education and health

**Educational attainment** (1983). Percentage of population age 25 and over having: no formal schooling 76.7%; complete secondary 2.0%; higher 0.8%. **Literacy** (1998): total population age 15 and over literate 55.7%; males 68.0%; females 43.4%. **Health:** physicians (1997) 3,423 (1 per 9,395 persons); hospital beds (1997) 22,656 (1 per 1,420 persons); infant mortality rate per 1,000 live births (2001) 68.7. **Food** (2000): daily per capita caloric intake 2,444 (vegetable products 81%, animal products 19%); 100% of FAO recommended minimum.

## Military

**Total active duty personnel** (2001): 117,000 (army 96.2%, navy 1.2%, air force 2.6%). **Military expenditure as percentage of GNP** (1999): 4.8% (world 2.4%); per capita expenditure $33.

## Background

From the end of the 4th millennium BC Nubia (now northern Sudan) periodically came under Egyptian rule, and it was part of the kingdom of Cush from the 11th century BC to the 4th century AD. Christian missionaries converted The Sudan's three principal kingdoms during the 6th century AD; these black Christian kingdoms coexisted with their Muslim Arab neighbors in Egypt for centuries, until the influx of Arab immigrants brought about their collapse in the 13th–15th centuries. Egypt had conquered all of The Sudan by 1874 and encouraged British interference in the region; this aroused Muslim opposition and led to the revolt of al-Mahdi, who captured Khartoum in 1885 and established a Muslim theocracy in The Sudan that lasted until 1898, when his forces were defeated by the British. The British ruled the country, generally in partnership with Egypt, until The Sudan achieved independence in 1956. Since then the country has fluctuated between ineffective parliamentary government and unstable military rule. The non-Muslim population of the south has engaged in ongoing rebellion against the Muslim-controlled government of the north, leading to famines and the displacement of some four million people.

## Recent Developments

On 19 Jan 2002 the US special envoy to The Sudan, John Danforth, brokered a six-month cease-fire between the government and the rebel Sudanese People's Liberation Army (SPLA). The agreement covered only a limited area but proved sufficiently successful for it to be renewed for a further six months in July. On 20 July, after five weeks of peace talks under the aegis

*1 metric ton = about 1.1 short tons;   1 kilometer = 0.6 mi (statute);   1 metric ton-km cargo = about 0.68 short ton-mi cargo;   c.i.f.: cost, insurance, and freight;   f.o.b.: free on board*

of Kenyan Pres. Daniel arap Moi, the two sides signed the Machakos Protocol. After a six-year "interim" period, there would be an internationally monitored referendum to allow the southerners to vote either for a continuation of the interim arrangement or for secession. No provision was made in the agreement for a cease-fire, and on 31 July the government launched a large-scale attack on SPLA positions. Ten weeks later the rival combatants agreed to a total cessation of hostilities with effect from 17 October to allow for discussions aimed at achieving a political settlement. Talks in Kenya continued into the spring of 2003.

Internet resources: <www.sudan.net>

# Suriname

**Official name:** Republiek Suriname (Republic of Suriname). **Form of government:** multiparty republic with one legislative house (National Assembly [51]). **Head of state and government:** President Ronald Venetiaan (from 2000), assisted by Prime Minister Jules Rattankoemar Ajodhia (from 2000). **Capital:** Paramaribo. **Official language:** Dutch. **Official religion:** none. **Monetary unit:** 1 Suriname guilder (Sf) = 100 cents; valuation (7 Jul 2003) $1 = Sf 2,515.

## Demography

**Area:** 63,251 sq mi, 163,820 sq km. **Population** (2002): 436,000. **Density** (2002): persons per sq mi 6.9, persons per sq km 2.7. **Urban** (1998): 51.0. **Sex distribution** (2000): male 50.77%; female 49.23%. **Age breakdown** (2000): under 15, 32.1%; 15–29, 27.2%; 30–44, 22.7%; 45–59, 9.9%; 60–74, 6.4%; 75 and over, 1.7%. **Ethnic composition** (1999): Indo-Pakistani 37.0%; Suriname Creole 31.0%; Javanese 15.0%; Bush Negro 10.0%; Amerindian 2.5%; Chinese 2.0%; white 1.0%; other 1.5%. **Religious affiliation** (1995): Hindu 27.4%; Roman Catholic 21.0%; Muslim 19.6%; Protestant (mostly Moravian) 16.4%; other 15.6%. **Major cities** (1996/1997): Paramaribo 222,800 (urban agglomeration 289,000); Lelydorp 15,600; Nieuw Nickerie 11,100; Mungo (Moengo) 6,800; Meerzorg 6,600. **Location:** northern South America, bordering the North Atlantic Ocean, French Guiana, Brazil, and Guyana.

## Vital statistics

**Birth rate** per 1,000 population (2000): 21.1 (world avg. 22.5). **Death rate** per 1,000 population (2000): 5.7 (world avg. 9.0). **Natural increase rate** per 1,000 population (2000): 15.4 (world avg. 13.5). **Total fertility rate** (avg. births per childbearing woman; 2000): 2.5. **Marriage rate** per 1,000 population (1991): 4.9. **Divorce rate** per 1,000 population (1991): 2.5. **Life expectancy** at birth (2000): male 68.7 years; female 74.1 years.

## National economy

**Budget** (1996). *Revenue:* Sf 90,874,600,000 (direct taxes 42.2%; indirect taxes 32.2%; bauxite levy 25.0%; other 0.6%). *Expenditures:* Sf 96,957,700,-000 (current expenditures 99.6%, of which wages and salaries 28.5%, transfers 13.7%, debt service 1.7%; capital expenditures 0.4%). **Production** (metric tons except as noted). *Agriculture, forestry, fishing* (1999): rice 180,400, sugarcane 90,000, bananas 55,000; livestock (number of live animals) 102,000 cattle, 25,000 pigs, 2,200,000 chickens; roundwood (2000) 226,700 cu m; fish catch (2000) 16,200. *Mining and quarrying* (2000): bauxite 3,600,000; gold 9,600 troy oz (unrecorded production may be as high as 950,000 troy oz). *Manufacturing* (value of production at factor cost in Sf; 1993): food products 992,000,000; beverages 558,000,000; tobacco 369,000,000. *Energy production (consumption):* electricity (kW-hr; 1997) 1,626,000,000 (1,626,-000,000); crude petroleum (barrels; 2000) 4,400,-000 ([1997] 1,451,000); petroleum products (metric tons; 1997) none (482,000). **Households.** Average household size (1998) 4.8. **Population economically active** (1994): total 98,240; activity rate of total population 24.3% (participation rates (1992): ages 15–64, 56.0%; female 37.5%; unemployed [1996] 10.7%). **Gross national product** (at current market prices; 2000): $788,000,000 ($1,890 per capita). **Public debt** (external, outstanding; 1996): $216,-500,000. **Tourism** (2000): receipts from visitors $16,000,000; expenditures by nationals abroad $23,000,000. **Land use** (1994): forested 96.2%; meadows and pastures 0.1%; agricultural and under permanent cultivation 0.4%; other 3.3%.

## Foreign trade

**Imports** (1998-c.i.f.): Sf 216,860,000,000 (machinery and transport equipment 31.9%, food and live animals 10.8%, road vehicles 10.2%, inorganic chemicals 8.5%, refined petroleum 8.1%). *Major import sources:* US 41.2%; The Netherlands 25.0%; Trinidad and Tobago 9.6%; Netherlands Antilles 5.8%; Japan 5.5%. **Exports** (1998-f.o.b.): Sf 192,680,000,000 (metalliferous ores [mostly alumina and bauxite] 61.5%, rolled silver 11.6%, processed nickel 7.6%, fish 5.8%, rice 3.8%). *Major export destinations:* The Netherlands 21.3%; Norway 21.2%; US 19.1%; Canada 11.0%; France 8.6%.

## Transport and communications

**Transport.** *Railroads* (1997): length 187 mi, 301 km. *Roads* (1996): total length 2,815 mi, 4,530 km (paved 26%). *Vehicles* (1996): passenger cars 46,408; trucks and buses 19,255. *Air transport* (1996): passenger-km 883,347,000; metric ton-km cargo 106,000,000; airports (1998) with scheduled flights 1. **Communications,** in total units (units per 1,000 persons). Daily newspaper circulation (1996): 50,000 (122); radio receivers (1997): 300,000 (728); television receivers (1999): 98,000 (236); telephone main lines (2001): 77,400 (176); cellular telephone subscribers (2001): 84,100 (191); Internet users (2001): 14,500 (33).

## Education and health

**Literacy** (1995): total population age 15 and over literate 271,000 (93.0%); males literate 137,000 (95.1%); females literate 134,000 (91.0%). **Health:** physicians (1998) 166 (1 per 2,518 persons); hospital beds (1998) 1,449 (1 per 288 persons); infant mortality rate per 1,000 live births (2000) 25.1. **Food** (2000): daily per capita caloric intake 2,652 (vegetable products 86%, animal products 14%); 118% of FAO recommended minimum.

## Military

**Total active duty personnel** (2001): 2,040 (army 78.4%, navy 11.8%, air force 9.8%). **Military expenditure as percentage of GNP** (1999): 1.8% (world 2.4%); per capita expenditure $33.

## Background

Suriname was inhabited by various native peoples prior to European settlement. Spanish explorers claimed it in 1593, but the Dutch began to settle there in 1602, followed by the English in 1651. It was ceded to the Dutch in 1667, and in 1682 the Dutch West India Co. introduced coffee and sugarcane plantations and African slaves to cultivate them. Slavery was abolished in 1863, and indentured servants were brought from China, Java, and India to work the plantations, adding to the population mix. Except for brief interludes of British rule (1799–1802, 1804–15), it remained a Dutch colony. It gained internal autonomy in 1954 and independence in 1975. A military coup in 1980 ended civilian control until the electorate approved a new constitution in 1987. Military control resumed after a coup in 1990. Elections were held in 1991, followed by a resumption of democratic government.

## Recent Developments

The modest successes that had characterized Pres. Ronald Venetiaan's first two years in office became mostly wistful memories in 2002. Key to a disquieting range of political and economic difficulties was the government's failure to curb a sharply rising fiscal deficit. Substantial pay increases fueled inflation, increased depreciation of the Surinam guilder, and apparently provoked the IMF into seeking the preparation of a revised government budget. Agriculture suffered owing to the closure of the commercial banana industry and the loss of the key Jamaican market for rice. The vast informal economy of narcotics smuggling, ecologically corrosive mining, fish poaching, and timber cutting continued to resist government control measures while creating hazards for potentially productive new industrial-scale bauxite and gold projects.

**Internet resources:** <www.surinam.net>

# Swaziland

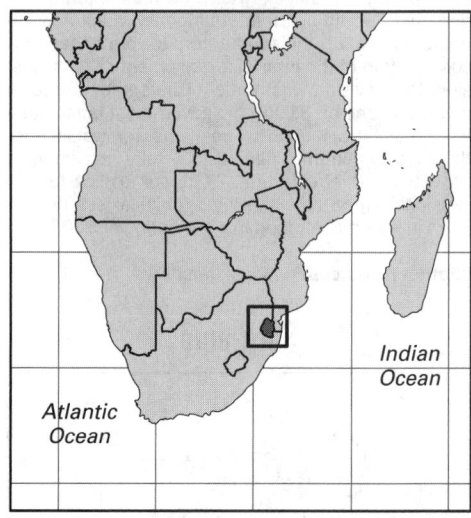

*Indian Ocean*

*Atlantic Ocean*

**Official name:** Umbuso weSwatini (Swazi); Kingdom of Swaziland (English). **Form of government:** monarchy with two legislative houses (Senate [30]; House of Assembly [65]). **Head of state:** King Mswati III (from 1986). **Head of government:** Prime Minister Sibusiso Barnabas Dlamini (from 1996). **Capitals:** Mbabane (administrative and judicial); Lozitha and Ludzidzini (royal); Lobamba (legislative). **Official languages:** Swazi; English. **Official religion:** none. **Monetary unit:** 1 lilangeni (plural emalangeni [E]) = 100 cents; valuation (7 Jul 2003) 1 $ = E 7.51.

## Demography

**Area:** 6,704 sq mi, 17,364 sq km. **Population** (2002): 1,124,000. **Density** (2002): persons per sq mi 167.7; persons per sq km 64.7. **Urban** (2001): 26.7%. **Sex distribution** (1997): male 48.28%; female 51.72%. **Age breakdown** (1997): under 15, 42.5%; 15–29, 29.2%; 30–44, 15.5%; 45–59, 7.8%; 60–74, 3.3%; 75 and over, 1.2%; unknown 0.5%. **Ethnic composition** (2000): Swazi 82.3%; Zulu 9.6%; Tsonga 2.3%; Afrikaner 1.4%; mixed (black-white) 1.0%; other 3.4%. **Religious affiliation** (1995): Christian 66.7%, of which African indigenous 44.7%, Protestant 14.8%, Roman Catholic 5.3%; other (mostly traditional beliefs) 33.3%. **Major cities** (1986): Manzini (2000) 80,000; Mbabane (2000) 60,000; Big Bend 9,676; Simunye/Ngomane 9,060; Mhlume 6,509. **Location:** southern Africa, bordering South Africa and Mozambique.

## Vital statistics

**Birth rate** per 1,000 population (2001): 31.0 (world avg. 21.2). **Death rate** per 1,000 population (2001): 17.8 (world avg. 8.9). **Natural increase rate** per 1,000 population (2001): 13.2 (world avg. 12.3). **Total fertility rate** (avg. births per childbearing woman; 2001): 4.1. **Life expectancy** at birth (2001): male 44.8 years; female 41.8 years.

---

*1 metric ton = about 1.1 short tons;     1 kilometer = 0.6 mi (statute);     1 metric ton-km cargo = about 0.68 short ton-mi cargo;     c.i.f.: cost, insurance, and freight;     f.o.b.: free on board*

## National economy

**Budget** (1999–2000). *Revenue*: E 2,436,400,000 (receipts from Customs Union of Southern Africa 50.1%; tax on income and profits 25.8%; sales tax 12.0%; foreign-aid grants 3.5%; property income 2.1%; fees, services, and fines 1.1%). *Expenditures*: E 2,630,700,000 (recurrent expenditure 78.2%, of which general administration 28.0%, education 17.3%, economic services 11.2%, justice and police 8.0%, health 6.5%, defense 4.8%). **Gross national product** (2000): $1,451,000,000 ($1,390 per capita). **Population economically active** (1986): total 160,355; activity rate of total population 23.5% (participation rates: ages 15 and over, 44.1%; female 34.2%; unemployed 27.0%). **Public debt** (external, outstanding; 2000): $198,200,000. **Production** (metric tons except as noted). *Agriculture, forestry, fishing* (1999): sugarcane 3,700,000, corn (maize) 113,000, oranges 31,200; livestock (number of live animals) 652,000 cattle, 438,000 goats, 980,000 chickens; roundwood (1998) 1,494,000 cu m; fish catch (1998) 60. *Mining and quarrying* (2000): asbestos 12,690; diamonds 64,000 carats (1994). *Manufacturing* (value added in $'000; 1994): food and beverages 244,000, of which beverage processing 153,000; paper and paper products 35,000; textiles 19,000. *Energy production (consumption)*: electricity (kW-hr; 2000) 265,000,000 (702,000,000); coal (metric tons; 2000) 378,000 (n.a.). **Household income and expenditure**. Average household size (1986) 5.7; annual income per household (1985) E 332 ($151); sources of income (1985): wages and salaries 44.4%, self-employment 22.2%, transfers 12.2%, other 21.2%; expenditure (1985): food and beverages 33.5%, rent and fuel 13.4%, household durable goods 12.8%, transportation and communications 8.8%, clothing and footwear 6.0%, recreation 3.3%. **Tourism** (2000): receipts $34,000,000; expenditures $36,000,000.

## Foreign trade

**Imports** (1998): $1,068,000,000 (machinery and transport equipment 26.2%; manufactured items 17.0%; foodstuffs 15.8%; chemicals 13.9%; minerals, fuels, and lubricants 11.8%). *Major import sources* (1997–98): South Africa 82.9%; UK 1.7%; US 0.9%; Zimbabwe 0.2%; Spain 0.2%. **Exports** (1998): $921,000,000 (sugar 11.0%; wood and wood products 8.1%; refrigerators 7.5%; cotton yarn 2.3%; paper and paper products 2.0%; canned fruits 1.4%; citrus fruits 1.3%; asbestos 1.0%). *Major export destinations* (1997): South Africa 74.0%; Italy 8.7%; Mozambique 5.2%; US 2.4%; UK 2.1%; Zimbabwe 1.7%.

## Transport and communications

**Transport.** *Roads* (1996): total length 3,810 km (paved 29%). *Vehicles* (1997): passenger cars 31,882; trucks and buses 32,772. *Air transport* (1995; Royal Swazi National Airways only; international flights only): passenger-km 49,423,000; metric ton-km cargo 127,000; airports (1997) with scheduled flights 1. **Communications**, in total units (units per 1,000 persons). Daily newspaper circulation (1996): 24,000 (24.3); radio receivers (1997): 155,000 (153); television receivers (1999): 110,000 (104); telephone main lines (2001): 32,000 (32); cellular telephone subscribers (2001): 66,000 (65); personal computers (1998): 278 (0.3); Internet users (2001): 14,000 (14).

## Education and health

**Educational attainment** (1986). Percentage of population age 25 and over having: no formal schooling 42.1%; some primary education 23.9%; complete primary 10.5%; some secondary 19.2%; complete secondary and higher 4.3%. **Literacy** (1995): total population age 15 and over literate 76.7%; males literate 78.0%; females literate 75.6%. **Health:** physicians (1996) 148 (1 per 6,663 persons); hospital beds (1984) 1,608 (1 per 396 persons); infant mortality rate per 1,000 live births (2001) 65.7. **Food** (2000): daily per capita caloric intake 2,620 (vegetable products 85%, animal products 15%); 113% of FAO recommended minimum.

## Military

**Military expenditure as percentage of GNP** (1999): 1.5% (world 2.4%); per capita expenditure $20.

## Background

Stone tools and rock paintings indicate prehistoric habitation in the region, but it was not settled until the Bantu-speaking Swazi people migrated there in the 18th century and established the nucleus of the Swazi nation. The British gained control in the 19th century after the Swazi king sought their aid against the Zulus. Following the South African War, the British governor of Transvaal administered Swaziland; his powers were transferred to the British high commissioner in 1906. In 1949 the British rejected the Union of South Africa's request to control Swaziland. The country gained limited self-government in 1963 and achieved independence in 1968. In the 1970s new constitutions were framed based on the supreme authority of the king and traditional tribal government. During the 1990s forces demanding democracy arose, but the kingdom remained in place.

## Recent Developments

King Mswati III, the world's last remaining absolute monarch, found himself at odds with pro-democracy forces in 2002–03. In September 2002 the parliament rejected financing for an expensive jet for the king; critics argued that the money could be better spent fighting rampant poverty and the HIV/AIDS epidemic. Protests intensified when Mswati chose three high-school-age women as his intended brides despite his 2001 decree that young women should not engage in sexual activity for the next five years. In March 2003 the Commonwealth threatened to exclude Swaziland if the king did not yield his powers to rule the country by decree, but on Easter Sunday Mswati told his people, "Democracy is not good for us, because God gave us our own way of doing things."

**Internet resources:** <www.swazi.com>

# Sweden

**Official name:** Konungariket Sverige (Kingdom of Sweden). **Form of government:** constitutional monarchy and parliamentary state with one legislative house (Parliament [349]). **Chief of state:** King Carl Gustaf XVI (from 1973). **Head of government:** Prime Minister Göran Persson (from 1996). **Capital:** Stockholm. **Official language:** Swedish. **Official religion:**

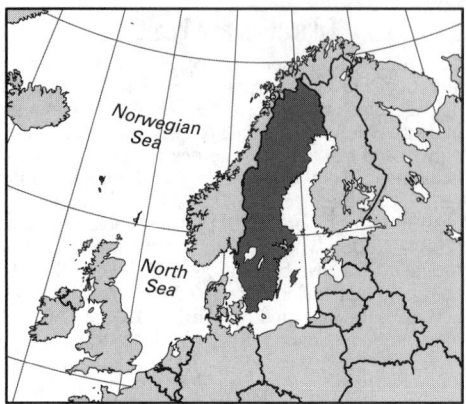

none. **Monetary unit:** 1 Swedish krona (SKr) = 100 ore; valuation (7 Jul 2003) $1 = SKr 8.01.

## Demography

**Area:** 173,732 sq mi, 449,964 sq km. **Population** (2002): 8,925,000. **Density** (2002): persons per sq mi 56.2, persons per sq km 21.7. **Urban** (1999): 83.3%. **Sex distribution** (2000): male 49.42%; female 50.58%. **Age breakdown** (2000): under 15, 18.5%; 15–29, 18.3%; 30–44, 20.8%; 45–59, 20.3%; 60–74, 13.3%; 75 and over, 8.8%. **Ethnic composition** (1997): Swedish 89.3%; Finnish 2.3%; Yugoslavian 0.8%; Iranian 0.6%; Bosnian 0.5%; other 6.5%. **Religious affiliation** (1999): Church of Sweden (Lutheran Church) 86.5% (nominally; about 30% non-practicing); Muslim 2.3%; Roman Catholic 1.8%; Pentecostal 1.1%; other 8.3%. **Major cities** (2001): Stockholm 754,948; Göteborg 471,267; Malmö 262,397; Uppsala 191,110; Linköping 134,039. **Location:** northern Europe, bordering Finland, the Gulf of Bothnia, the Baltic Sea, and Norway.

## Vital statistics

**Birth rate** per 1,000 population (2001): 10.3 (world avg. 21.2); (1999) legitimate 48.2%; illegitimate 51.8%. **Death rate** per 1,000 population (2001): 10.5 (world avg. 8.9). **Natural increase rate** per 1,000 population (2001): −0.2 (world avg. 12.3). **Total fertility rate** (avg. births per childbearing woman; 2001): 1.5. **Marriage rate** per 1,000 population (2001): 4.0. **Divorce rate** per 1,000 population (2001): 2.4. **Life expectancy** at birth (2001): male 77.6 years; female 82.1 years.

## National economy

**Budget** (2000). *Revenue:* SKr 800,000,000,000 (value-added and excise taxes 33.2%, social security 28.2%, income and capital gains taxes 15.9%, property taxes 4.7%). *Expenditures:* SKr 698,068,000,000 (health and social affairs 29.3%, debt service 14.0%, defense 7.2%, education 4.9%). **Production** (metric tons except as noted). *Agriculture, forestry, fishing* (2001): sugar beets 2,752,600, wheat 2,390,000, barley 1,600,000; livestock (number of live animals) 1,891,456 pigs, 1,713,000 cattle, 451,594 sheep; roundwood (2000) 55,250,000 cu m; fish catch (1999) 357,317. *Mining and quarrying*

(1998): iron ore 20,930,000; zinc 297,000; copper 270,000. *Manufacturing* (value added, in SKr '000,000; 1999): transport equipment 76,274; machinery, except electrical 76,133; paper products 46,363. *Energy production (consumption):* electricity (kW-hr; 2000) 144,966,000,000 (160,203,000,-000); coal (metric tons; 1997) none (3,113,000); crude petroleum (barrels; 1997) none (146,382,000); petroleum products (metric tons; 1997) 18,840,000 (12,757,000); natural gas (cu m; 1997) none (856,941,000). **Household income and expenditure.** Average household size (1999) 2.2; median income per household (1994) SKr 396,100 ($51,330); sources of income (1992): wages and salaries 58.9%, transfer payments 25.8%, self-employment 15.3%; expenditure (1995): housing and energy 29.6%, food 20.9%, transportation 16.1%, education and recreation 9.2%. **Gross national product** (2000): $240,707,000,000 ($27,140 per capita). **Public debt** (2000): $61,046,000,000. **Population economically active** (2000): total 4,362,000; activity rate of total population 49.1% (participation rates: ages 16–64, 77.9%; female 47.7%; unemployed 4.7%). **Tourism** (2000): receipts $4,034,000,000; expenditures $8,015,000,000. **Land use** (1994): forest 68.0%; pasture 1.4%; agriculture 6.8%; other 23.8%.

## Foreign trade

**Imports** (2000): SKr 666,864,000,000 (machinery and transport equipment 44.9%; manufactured goods 13.9%; chemicals 9.6%; food 5.3%). *Major import sources* (1999): Germany 17.6%; UK 9.5%; Norway 8.2%; Denmark 7.6%; US 6.7%. **Exports** (2000): SKr 796,549,000,000 (machinery and transport equipment 50.2%, of which electrical machinery 23.0%, road vehicles 11.4%; chemicals 9.4%; paper products 7.8%; iron and steel products 4.7%). *Major export destinations* (2000): Germany 11.0%; US 9.5%; UK 9.4%; Norway 7.5%; Finland 6.2%; Denmark 5.9%.

## Transport and communications

**Transport.** *Railroads* (2000): length 6,811 mi, 10,961 km; (1999) passenger-km 7,638,000,000; metric ton-km cargo 19,088,000,000. *Roads* (2000): total length 130,500 mi, 210,000 km (paved 74%). *Vehicles* (2000): passenger cars 3,890,159; trucks and buses 352,897. *Merchant marine* (2000): vessels (100 gross tons and over) 412; total deadweight tonnage 2,861,000. *Air transport* (2000; one-third of SAS): passenger-km 11,261,000; metric ton-km cargo 286,404,000; airports (1996) 48. **Communications,** in total units (units per 1,000 persons). Daily newspaper circulation (1996): 3,933,000 (446); radio receivers (1997): 8,250,000 (932); television receivers (1999): 4,900,000 (553); telephone main lines (2001): 6,585,000 (740); cellular telephone subscribers (2001): 6,867,000 (771); personal computers (2001): 4,600,000 (517); Internet users (2001): 5,000,000 (562).

## Education and health

**Educational attainment** (2000). Percentage of population age 16–64 having: primary education 32.0%; lower secondary education 28.0%; higher secondary

---

*1 metric ton = about 1.1 short tons;     1 kilometer = 0.6 mi (statute);     1 metric ton-km cargo = about 0.68 short ton-mi cargo;     c.i.f.: cost, insurance, and freight;     f.o.b.: free on board*

16.0%; some postsecondary 24.0%. **Literacy** (2000): virtually 100%. **Health** (2000): physicians 24,500 (1 per 362 persons); hospital beds 31,765 (1 per 279 persons); infant mortality rate per 1,000 live births (2000) 3.5. **Food** (2000): daily per capita caloric intake 3,109 (vegetable 67%, animal 33%); 116% of FAO recommended minimum.

## Military

**Total active duty personnel** (2001): 33,900 (army 56.3%, navy 20.9%, air force 22.7%). **Military expenditure as percentage of GNP** (1999): 2.3% (world 2.4%); per capita expenditure $601.

## Background

The first inhabitants of Sweden were apparently hunters who crossed the land bridge from Europe c. 9000 BC. During the Viking era (9th–10th centuries), the Swedes controlled river trade in eastern Europe between the Baltic Sea and the Black Sea and also raided western European lands. Sweden was loosely united and Christianized in the 11th–12th centuries. It conquered the Finns in the 12th century and in the 14th united with Norway and Denmark under a single monarchy. It broke away in 1523 under Gustav I Vasa. In the 17th century it emerged as a great European power in the Baltic region, but its dominance declined after its defeat in the Second Northern War (1700–21). Sweden became a constitutional monarchy in 1809 and united with Norway 1814–1905; it acknowledged Norwegian independence in 1905. It maintained its neutrality during both world wars. It was a charter member of the UN but abstained from membership in the European Union (EU) until the 1990s and in NATO altogether. A new constitution drafted in 1975 reduced the monarch's powers to ceremonial head of state. In 1997 it decided to begin the controversial shutdown of its nuclear power industry.

## Recent Developments

The center-left Social Democratic Party (SDP), under the leadership of Prime Minister Göran Persson, was returned to power in the 2002 general election but faced the challenge of convincing Swedes that they should abandon the krona and adopt the single European currency, the euro. Against a backdrop of low unemployment and with tax cuts and reduced fees for key public services boosting household consumption, the SDP was able to portray itself as the party of economic competence. Persson's unequivocal support of the US and its "war on terrorism" in the aftermath of the attacks of 11 Sep 2001 also hit a chord with voters. In the weeks before the vote, however, opinion polls indicated that the contest was much closer than had been predicted. Instead of focusing on the upbeat economic news, voters turned their attention to the problems of integrating the country's immigrant community, by far the largest in the Nordic region, with about 22% of the population born outside the country or with a parent born abroad. The excesses of the Internet and telecommunications investment bubbles continued to batter the economy. The most high-profile victim, Ericsson, the world's largest producer of wireless telecom systems, was forced to fire thousands of staff and raise about $3 billion from its shareholders.

**Internet resources:** <www.sverigeturism.se>

# Switzerland

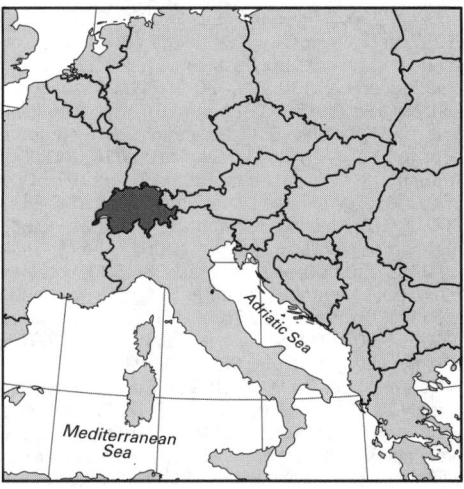

**Official name:** Confédération Suisse (French); Schweizerische Eidgenossenschaft (German); Confederazione Svizzera (Italian); Confederaziun Svizra (Romansh) (Swiss Confederation). **Form of government:** federal state with two legislative houses (Council of States [46]; National Council [200]). **Head of state and government:** President of the Federal Council Pascal Couchepin (from 1 Jan 2003). **Capitals:** Bern (administrative); Lausanne (judicial). **Official languages:** French; German; Italian; Romansh (locally). **Official religion:** none. **Monetary unit:** 1 Swiss Franc (Sw F) = 100 centimes; valuation (7 Jul 2003) $1 = Sw F 1.35.

## Demography

**Area:** 15,940 sq mi, 41,284 sq km. **Population** (2002): 7,282,000. **Density** (2002): persons per sq mi 456.8, persons per sq km 176.4. **Urban** (2001): 67.3%. **Sex distribution** (2001): male 48.86%; female 51.14%. **Age breakdown** (2001): under 15, 17.4%; 15–29, 18.3%; 30–44, 24.4%; 45–59, 19.8%; 60–74, 13.0%; 75 and over, 7.1%. **National composition** (2001; includes 1,424,370 resident aliens; excludes 71,957 refugees): Swiss 80.2%; Yugoslav 4.8%; Italian 4.5%; Portuguese 1.9%; German 1.5%; Spanish 1.2%; other 5.9%. **Religious affiliation** (1990): Roman Catholic 46.2%; Protestant 40.0%; Muslim 2.2%; Orthodox Christian 1.0%; Jewish 0.3%; other 10.3%. **Major urban agglomerations** (2001): Zürich 953,800; Geneva 464,000; Basel 401,500; Bern 319,600; Lausanne 289,600; Luzern 182,500. **Location:** central Europe, bordering Germany, Austria, Liechtenstein, Italy, and France.

## Vital statistics

**Birth rate** per 1,000 population (2000): 11.0 (world avg. 22.5); legitimate 90.0%; illegitimate 10.0%. **Death rate** per 1,000 population (2000): 8.7 (world avg. 9.0). **Natural increase rate** per 1,000 population (2000): 2.3 (world avg. 13.5). **Total fertility rate** (avg. births per childbearing woman; 2000): 1.5. **Marriage rate** per 1,000 population (2001): 4.9. **Divorce rate** per 1,000 population (2001): 2.1. **Life expectancy** at birth (2000): male 76.9 years; female 82.6 years.

## National economy

**Budget** (2002). *Revenue*: Sw F 130,595,000,000 (1997; social security contributions 46.7%, taxes on goods and services 20.2%, income taxes 11.6%). *Expenditures:* Sw F 132,989,000,000 (1997; social security and welfare 50.5%, health 19.7%, economic affairs 10.4%, defense 5.2%, education 2.3%). **National debt** (end of year; 2001): Sw F 106,810,000,000. **Tourism** (2000): receipts from visitors $7,500,000,000; expenditures by nationals abroad $6,238,000,000. **Production** (metric tons except as noted). *Agriculture, forestry, fishing* (2001): cow's milk (2000) 3,910,000, sugar beets 1,065,600, potatoes 526,000; livestock (number of live animals) 1,611,000 cattle, 1,556,000 pigs; roundwood (2001) 5,000,000 cu m; fish catch (1999) 2,975. *Mining* (1999): salt 300,000. *Manufacturing* (value added in Sw F '000,000; 1998): nonelectrical machinery and transport equipment 20,757; chemicals and chemical products 13,026; fabricated metal products 8,143; food 5,667. *Energy production (consumption)*: electricity (kW-hr; 2000) 63,374,000,000 (56,304,000,000); coal (metric tons; 1997) none (133,000); crude petroleum (barrels; 1997) none (35,726,000); petroleum products (metric tons; 2000) 4,861,000 ([1997] 10,907,000); natural gas (cu m; 1997) negligible (2,801,700,000). **Gross national product** (2000): $273,829,000,000 ($38,140 per capita). **Population economically active** (2000): total 3,985,000; activity rate of total population 55.6% (participation rates: ages 15 and over, 67.4%; female 44.2%; unemployed [2001] 1.9%). **Household income and expenditure** (2000). Average household size 2.4; average gross income per household Sw F 104,352 ($64,400); sources of income (2000): work 72.4%, transfers 22.3%; expenditure (2000): housing 17.6%, taxes 13.6%, recreation, entertainment, restaurants 13.2%, social security contribution 9.5%, health 8.8%, food 8.3%, transportation 7.5%.

## Foreign trade

**Imports** (2001-c.i.f.): Sw F 130,052,000,000 (machinery 22.7%, chemical products 20.2%, vehicles 10.9%, food products 7.6%). *Major import sources:* Germany 32.2%; France 11.0%; Italy 10.2%; The Netherlands 5.9%; US 5.3%. **Exports** (2001-f.o.b.): Sw F 131,717,100,000 (chemical products 31.8%; machinery 27.3%; precision instruments, watches, jewelry 16.4%; fabricated metals 7.9%). *Major export destinations:* Germany 22.2%; US 10.6%; France 9.0%; Italy 8.0%; UK 5.3%; Japan 3.9%; Hong Kong 3.2%.

## Transport and communications

**Transport.** *Railroads*: length (1999) 5,035 km; passenger-km 14,104,000,000; metric ton-km cargo 8,688,000,000. *Roads* (1998): total length 71,211 km. *Vehicles* (2001): passenger cars 3,629,713; trucks and buses 289,897. *Air transport* (2001; Swissair only [Swissair ceased operations on 31 Mar 2002]): passenger-km 32,981,000,000; metric ton-km cargo 1,793,704,000; airports (1996) with scheduled flights 5. **Communications,** in total units (units per 1,000 persons). Daily newspaper circulation (1996): 2,383,000 (337); radio receivers (1997): 7,100,000 (1,002); television receivers

(1999): 3,700,000 (518); telephone main lines (2001): 5,183,000 (718); cellular telephone subscribers (2001): 5,226,000 (724); personal computers (2001): 3,600,000 (500); Internet users (2001): 2,917,000 (404).

## Education and health

**Educational attainment** (2000). Percentage of resident Swiss and resident alien population age 25–64 having: compulsory education 19.0%; secondary 56.8%; higher 24.2%. **Health** (1999): physicians 27,863 (1 per 256 persons); hospital beds (1998) 45,959 (1 per 155 persons); infant mortality rate per 1,000 live births (2000) 3.3. **Food** (2000): daily per capita caloric intake 3,293 (vegetable products 67%, animal products 33%); 122% of FAO recommended minimum.

## Military

**Total active duty personnel** (2001): 3,600 (excludes 351,200 reservists). **Military expenditure as percentage of GNP** (1999): 1.2% (world 2.4%); per capita expenditure $469.

Bellinzona, a small city south of the central Alps, has long been of strategic importance because of its location at the juncture of roads extending northward to the mountain passes of St. Gotthard, Lukmanier, and San Bernardino. Fortifications last rebuilt in the 15th century to control the juncture at Bellinzona include three castles and a series of walls. Together they are an outstanding example of a medieval defensive ensemble. In 2000 all were declared a UNESCO World Heritage site.

## Background

The original inhabitants of Switzerland were the Helvetians, who were conquered by the Romans in the 1st century BC. Germanic tribes penetrated the region from the 3rd to the 6th century AD, and Muslim and Magyar raiders ventured in during the 10th century. It came under the Holy Roman Empire in the 11th century. In 1291 three cantons formed an anti-Habsburg league that became the nucleus of the Swiss Confederation. It was a center of the Reformation, which divided the confederation and led to a period of political and religious conflict. The French organized Switzerland as the Helvetic Republic in 1798. In 1815 the Congress of Vienna recognized Swiss independence and guaranteed its neutrality. A new federal state was formed in 1848 with Bern as the capital. It remained neutral in both world wars and continued to guard this stance. With the formation of the European Union (EU), it took steps toward provisional association with the European economic area.

## Recent Developments

Long known for its conservatism and carefully protected neutrality, Switzerland took a major step into the international arena in March 2002 when its voters narrowly approved a referendum in favor of join-

---

*1 metric ton = about 1.1 short tons;    1 kilometer = 0.6 mi (statute);    1 metric ton-km cargo = about 0.68 short ton-mi cargo;    c.i.f.: cost, insurance, and freight;    f.o.b.: free on board*

ing the UN; it would become the 190th member. Geneva had long been home to UN agencies, and the country had participated in many UN activities. Switzerland remained outside the EU, in part because of the potential for disruption of the banking industry, which would have to adhere to EU requirements. In 2000 several banks were fined for having accepted $600 million in deposits on behalf of Nigerian dictator Sani Abacha. The assets held in Swiss banks since before World War II, mainly those of Jews, had come under scrutiny in 1999.

Although the economy was generally strong, the national airline Swissair collapsed, the worldwide drop in passengers after 11 Sep 2001 providing the final blow after several years of financial difficulties. Crossair took over 52 of Swissair's planes, bolstered by bankruptcy protection and an influx of capital. A new national airline, called "swiss," began operations on 31 March 2002. Domestic issues included the scaling back of army personnel by more than 40% and restrictions on immigration.

**Internet resources:** <www.myswitzerland.com>

# Syria

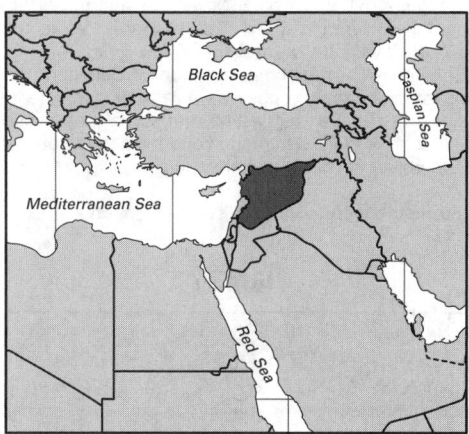

**Official name:** Al-Jumhuriyah al-'Arabiyah al-Suriyah (Syrian Arab Republic). **Form of government:** unitary multiparty (parties ideologically compatible with the ruling Ba'th Party) republic with one legislative house (People's Council [250]). **Head of state and government:** President Bashar al-Assad, assisted by Prime Minister Muhammad Mustafa Mero (from 2000). **Capital:** Damascus. **Official language:** Arabic. **Official religion:** none, although Islam is the required religion of the head of state and is the basis of the legal system. **Monetary unit:** 1 Syrian pound (LS) = 100 piastres; valuation (7 Jul 2003) $1 = LS 46.00.

## Demography

**Area** (includes territory in the Golan Heights recognized internationally as part of Syria): 71,498 sq mi, 185,180 sq km. **Population** (2002): 17,156,000. **Density** (2002): persons per sq mi 240.0, persons per sq km 92.6. **Urban** (2001): 51.8%. **Sex distribution** (2000): male 51.23%; female 48.77%. **Age breakdown** (2000): under 15, 40.1%; 15–29, 30.6%; 30–44, 16.6%; 45–59, 7.4%; 60–74, 3.8%; 75 and over, 1.5%. **Ethnic composition** (2000): Syrian Arab 74.9%; Bedouin Arab 7.4%; Kurd 7.3%; Palestinian

Arab 3.9%; Armenian 2.7%; other 3.8%. **Religious affiliation** (1992): Muslim 86.0%, of which Sunni 74.0%, 'Alawite (Shi'i) 12.0%; Christian 5.5%; Druze 3.0%; other 5.5%. **Major cities** (1994): Aleppo 1,591,400; Damascus 1,549,932; Homs 644,204; Latakia 306,535; Hamah 229,000. **Location:** the Middle East, bordering Turkey, Iraq, Jordan, Israel, Lebanon, and the Mediterranean Sea.

## Vital statistics

**Birth rate** per 1,000 population (2001): 30.6 (world avg. 21.2). **Death rate** per 1,000 population (2001): 5.2 (world avg. 8.9). **Natural increase rate** per 1,000 population (2001): 25.4 (world avg. 12.3). **Total fertility rate** (avg. births per childbearing woman; 2001): 3.9. **Marriage rate** per 1,000 population (1995): 8.4. **Life expectancy** at birth (2001): male 67.6 years; female 70.0 years.

## National economy

**Budget** (1999). *Revenue*: LS 255,300,000,000 (current revenues 85.4%, capital [development] revenues 14.6%). *Expenditures*: LS 255,300,000,000 (current expenditures 56.4%, capital [development] expenditures 43.6%). **Public debt** (external, outstanding; 2000): $15,930,000,000. **Gross national product** (2000): $15,146,000,000 ($940 per capita). **Production** (metric tons except as noted). *Agriculture, forestry, fishing* (2000): wheat 3,104,969, sugar beets 1,300,000, seed cotton 930,000; livestock (number of live animals) 15,000,000 sheep, 1,200,000 goats, 905,000 cattle; roundwood (2000) 50,400 cu m; fish catch (1999) 14,024. *Mining and quarrying* (1999): phosphate rock 2,127,000; gypsum 232,000; salt 104,000. *Manufacturing* (1998): cement 5,016,000; refined sugar 89,000; cottonseed cake 226,000. *Energy production (consumption)*: electricity (kW-hr; 2000) 23,952,000,000 (21,568,000,000); crude petroleum (barrels; 1997) 192,433,000 (86,817,000); petroleum products (metric tons; 1997) 11,573,000 (10,473,000); natural gas (cu m; 1997) 3,588,000,000 (3,588,000,000). **Population economically active** (1999): total 4,527,258; activity rate of total population 28.8% (participation rates: ages 10 and over, 32.9%; female 11.3%; unemployed 9.5%). **Household expenditure.** Average household size (1999): 5.0; expenditure (1987): food 58.8%, rent, fuel, and light 16.0%, clothing 7.5%, household goods 5.8%, transportation 2.4%. **Tourism** (2000): receipts $1,082,000,000; expenditures $640,000,000. **Land use** (1994): steppe and pasture 45.2%; agricultural and under permanent cultivation 30.1%; forested 2.6%; other 22.1%.

## Foreign trade

**Imports** (1999-c.i.f.): LS 43,010,000,000 (basic metals and manufactures 16.9%, food and beverages 13.8%, machinery and transport equipment 13.0%, textiles 9.9%, chemicals and chemical products 8.9%, resins 5.8%). *Major import sources*: Germany 7.0%; France 5.7%; Italy 5.6%; Turkey 4.7%; US 4.6%; Japan 4.1%; China 3.3%; Belgium 2.9%. **Exports** (1999): LS 38,880,000,000 (crude petroleum and petroleum products 62.9%, fresh vegetables and fruits 12.4%, textiles and fabrics 7.2%, raw cotton 4.5%, live animals and meat 1.3%). *Major export destinations*: Italy 26.6%; France 20.6%; Turkey 9.2%; Saudi Arabia 8.3%; Spain 6.9%; Lebanon 4.0%.

## Transport and communications

**Transport.** *Railroads* (2000): route length 2,676 km (excludes length of Syrian part of railway opened in August 2000 linking Aleppo, Syria, and Mosul, Iraq); (1998) passenger-km 181,575,000; (1998) metric ton-km cargo 1,440,000,000. *Roads* (1998): total length 41,451 km (paved 23%). *Vehicles* (1998): passenger cars 138,900; trucks and buses 282,664. *Air transport* (2000): passenger-km 1,421,537,000; metric ton-km cargo 20,813,000; airports (1999) with scheduled flights 5. **Communications,** in total units (units per 1,000 persons). Daily newspaper circulation (1996): 287,000 (20); radio receivers (1997): 4,150,000 (278); television receivers (1999): 1,070,000 (66.4); telephone main lines (2001): 1,807,600 (109); cellular telephone subscribers (2001): 200,000 (12); personal computers (2001): 270,000 (16.3); Internet users (2001): 60,000 (3.6).

## Education and health

**Educational attainment** (1984). Percentage of population age 10 and over having: no schooling 20.1%; knowledge of reading and writing 26.3%; primary education 29.3%; secondary 18.4%; certificate 3.3%; higher 2.7%. **Literacy** (1995): percentage of population age 15 and over literate 74.4%; males literate 88.3%; females literate 60.4%. **Health** (1998): physicians 22,293 (1 per 694 persons); hospital beds (1995) 17,623 (1 per 832 persons); infant mortality rate per 1,000 live births (2001) 33.8. **Food** (1999): daily per capita caloric intake 3,038 (vegetable products 86.5%, animal products 13.5%); 123% of FAO recommended minimum.

## Military

**Total active duty personnel** (2001): 321,000 (army 67.0%, navy 1.9%, air force 12.5%). **Military expenditure as percentage of GNP** (1999): 7.0% (world 2.4%); per capita expenditure $280.

## Background

Syria has been inhabited for several thousand years. From the 3rd millennium BC, it was under the control variously of Sumerians, Akkadians, Amorites, Egyptians, Hittites, Assyrians, and Babylonians. In the 6th century BC it became part of the Persian Achaemenian dynasty, which fell to Alexander the Great in 330 BC. Seleucid rulers governed it from 301 BC to c. 164 BC; then Parthians and Nabataean Arabs divided the region. It flourished as a Roman province (64 BC–AD 300) and as part of the Byzantine Empire (300–634) until Muslims invaded and established control. It came under the Ottoman Empire in 1516, which held it, except for brief rules by Egypt, until the British invaded in World War I. After the war it became a French mandate; it achieved independence in 1945. It united with Egypt in the United Arab Republic (1958–61). During the Six-Day War (1967), it lost the Golan Heights to Israel. Syrian troops frequently clashed with Israeli troops in Lebanon during the 1980s and '90s. Hafez al-Assad's long and harsh regime was marked also by antagonism toward Syria's neighbors Turkey and Iraq.

## Recent Developments

The problems of its neighbors to the west and east, Israel/Palestine and Iraq respectively, occupied Syria's attention in 2002–03. Spontaneous popular demonstrations in defense of Palestinian rights became a regular occurrence in Damascus in the spring of 2002. Meanwhile, allies of Pres. Bashar al-Assad continued to purge the top levels of the armed forces and security services. Dozens of midlevel government bureaucrats were also dismissed on charges of mismanagement and misconduct throughout the spring and summer.

Syria served on the UN Security Council but abstained from voting on a March 2002 resolution that for the first time referred explicitly to a Palestinian state and walked out before the vote on an April resolution that demanded the withdrawal of Israeli troops from Palestinian-administered towns in the West Bank. Syrian troops undertook the delicate task of restraining, but tolerating, Hezbollah operations against Israel's continued occupation of the disputed border between Lebanon and the Golan Heights. Despite Damascus's long-standing opposition to US military intervention in the region, Syria voted in favor of the US-sponsored resolution on Iraq passed by the UN Security Council on 8 November and closed its border with Iraq in March 2003, shortly before the US-UK invasion, to prevent Iraqis from leaving. Nonetheless, after the occupation of Baghdad, the US intimated that Damascus was assisting Iraqi leaders to flee and suggested that Syria possessed weapons of mass destruction and might itself be the next object of US military attention.

**Internet resources:** <http://syriatourism.org>

# Taiwan

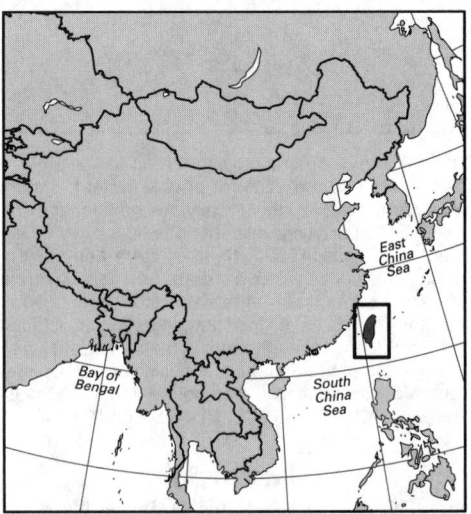

**Official name:** Chung-hua Min-kuo (Republic of China). **Form of government:** multiparty republic with a Legislature (Legislative Yuan [225]). **Chief of state:** President Chen Shui-bian (from 2000). **Head of government:** Premier Yu Shyi-kun (from 1 Feb 2002).

---

*1 metric ton = about 1.1 short tons;     1 kilometer = 0.6 mi (statute);     1 metric ton-km cargo = about 0.68 short ton-mi cargo;     c.i.f.: cost, insurance, and freight;     f.o.b.: free on board*

Capital: Taipei. **Official language:** Mandarin Chinese. **Official religion:** none. **Monetary unit:** 1 New Taiwan dollar (NT$) = 100 cents; valuation (7 Jul 2003) US$1 = NT$34.37.

## Demography

**Area:** 13,972 sq m, 36,188 sq km. **Population** (2002): 22,457,000. **Density** (2002): persons per sq mi 1,607.7, persons per sq km 620.7. **Urban** (1991): 74.7%. **Sex distribution** (2002): male 51.03%; female 48.97%. **Age breakdown** (2002): under 15, 20.8%; 15–29, 24.9%; 30–44, 25.3%; 45–59, 16.7%; 60–74, 9.1%; 75 and over, 3.2%. **Ethnic composition** (1997): Han Chinese, Chinese mainland minorities, and others 98.2%; indigenous tribal peoples 1.8%, of which Ami 0.6%. **Religious affiliation** (1997): Buddhism 22.4%; Taoism 20.7%; I-kuan Tao 4.3%; Protestant 1.6%; Roman Catholic 1.4%; other Christian 0.3%; Muslim 0.2%; Baha'i 0.1%; other (mostly Christian folk-religionists) 49.0%. **Major cities** (2002): Taipei 2,635,678; Kao-hsiung 1,504,061; T'ai-chung 990,041; T'ai-nan 742,574; Chung-ho (1998) 388,174. **Location:** between the East China Sea, the Philippine Sea, and the South China Sea north of the Philippines and southeast of mainland China.

## Vital statistics

**Birth rate** per 1,000 population (2001): 11.7 (world avg. 21.2). **Death rate** per 1,000 population (2001): 5.7 (world avg. 8.9). **Natural increase rate** per 1,000 population (2001): 6.0 (world avg. 12.3). **Total fertility rate** (avg. births per childbearing woman; 2000): 1.8. **Life expectancy** at birth (2000): male 73.6 years; female 79.3 years.

## National economy

**Budget** (1999). *Revenue:* NT$3,391,948,000,000 (income taxes 18.0%, business tax 9.1%, commodity tax 6.5%, land tax 6.4%, customs duties 4.6%). *Expenditures:* NT$3,371,702,000,000 (administration and defense 24.5%, education 19.4%). **Population economically active** (1990): total 10,236,324; activity rate 50.5% (participation rates: ages 15–64, 72.5%; female 38.5%; unemployed [2000] 3.0%). **Production** (metric tons except as noted). *Agriculture, forestry, fishing* (2000): sugarcane 2,894,000, rice 1,559,000, citrus fruits 440,382; livestock (number of live animals) 7,494,954 pigs, 202,491 goats, 161,700 cattle; timber 21,134 cu m; fish catch 1,356,275. *Mining and quarrying* (2000): marble 17,800,000. *Manufacturing* (2000): cement 17,572,303; steel ingots 17,302,396; paperboard 3,233,864. *Energy production (consumption):* electricity (kW-hr; 2001) 178,358,000,000 ([1996] 111,140,000,000); coal (metric tons; 2000) 83,400 ([1999] 40,700,000); crude petroleum (barrels; 2000) 234,000 (285,400,-000); natural gas (cu m; 2000) 670,000,000 ([1999] 6,230,000,000). **Tourism** (2000): receipts from visitors US$3,738,000,000; expenditures by nationals abroad US$6,376,000,000. **Gross national product** (2001): US$288,267,000,000 (US$12,941 per capita). **Household income and expenditure** (1999). Average household size (2002) 3.3; income per household NT$1,181,082 (US$37,153); expenditure: food, beverage, and tobacco 25.1%, rent, fuel, and power 24.9%, education and recreation 13.0%, transportation 11.1%, health care 11.0%, clothing 4.1%, furniture 2.9%.

## Foreign trade

**Imports** (2001-c.i.f.): US$107,237,400,000 (electronic machinery 25.4%, nonelectrical machinery 15.9%, minerals 13.1%, chemicals 12.2%, metals and metal products 10.3%, precision instruments, clocks, watches, and musical instruments 8.5%). *Major import sources:* Japan 36.0%; US 17.0%; South Korea 6.3%; Germany 4.0%; Malaysia 3.9%; Singapore 3.1%. **Exports** (2001): US$122,866,300,000 (nonelectrical machinery, electrical machinery, and electronics 67.2%, textile products 12.4%, plastic articles 7.4%, transportation equipment 4.7%). *Major export destinations:* US 22.5%; Hong Kong 21.9%; Japan 10.4%; Germany 3.6%; Singapore 3.3%.

## Transport and communications

**Transport.** *Railroads* (2001): track length 3,733 km; passenger-km 12,269,000,000; metric ton-km cargo 1,010,000,000. *Roads* (2001): total length 36,624 km (paved 88% [1999]). *Vehicles* (2001): passenger cars 4,825,581; trucks and buses 854,726. *Air transport* (1998): passenger-km 39,218,000,000; metric ton-km cargo 4,129,300,000; airports (1996) 13. **Communications,** in total units (units per 1,000 persons). Radio receivers (1996): 8,620,000 (402); television receivers (1999): 9,200,000 (418); telephone main lines (2001): 12,846,906 (575); cellular telephone subscribers (2001): 21,632,978 (968); personal computers (2001): 5,000,000 (223); Internet users (2001): 6,231,917 (279).

## Education and health

**Educational attainment** (1999). Percentage of population age 25 and over having: no formal schooling 7.0%; less than complete primary education 6.3%; primary 21.3%; incomplete secondary 25.7%; secondary 21.8%; some college 10.4%; higher 7.5%. **Literacy** (1999): population age 15 and over literate 16,414,896 (94.6%); males 8,641,549 (97.6%); females 7,773,347 (91.4%). **Health** (2001): physicians 30,562 (1 per 731 persons); hospital beds 127,676 (1 per 175 persons); infant mortality rate per 1,000 live births (2000) 7.1.

## Military

**Total active duty personnel** (2001): 370,000 (army 64.9%, navy 16.8%, air force 18.4%). **Military expenditure as percentage of GNP** (1999): 5.2% (world 2.4%); per capita expenditure US$690.

## Background

Known to the Chinese as early as the 7th century, Taiwan was widely settled by them early in the 17th century. In 1646 the Dutch seized control of the island, only to be ousted in 1661 by a large influx of Chinese Ming-dynasty refugees. Taiwan fell to the Manchus in 1683 and was not open to Europeans again until 1858. In 1895 it was ceded to Japan following the Sino-Japanese War. A Japanese military center in World War II, it was frequently bombed by US planes. After Japan's defeat, it was returned to China, which was then governed by the Nationalists. When the Communists took over mainland China in 1949, the Nationalist government fled to Taiwan and made it their seat of government, with Gen. Chiang Kai-shek as president. In 1954 he and the US signed a mutual defense treaty, and Taiwan received US support for almost three decades, developing its economy in spectacular fashion. It was recognized by many noncommunist countries as the representative of all China until 1971, when it was replaced in the UN by the People's Republic of China. Martial law was lifted in Taiwan in 1987 and travel restrictions with mainland China in 1988. In 1989 opposition parties were legalized. The relationship with the mainland became increasingly close in the 1990s.

## Recent Developments

The year 2002 began with a major cabinet reshuffle that was widely perceived to be part of an effort by Pres. Chen Shui-bian to lay the groundwork for re-election in 2004. Meanwhile, leaders of two opposition parties agreed in April 2003 to join forces and run together in the 2004 elections.

Early in 2002 China extended an invitation to members of Taiwan's governing Democratic Progressive Party (DPP) to visit the mainland. In the past, Chinese leaders had made general invitations to party officials from Taiwan, but this was the first offer expressly issued to the officially pro-independence DPP. Chinese Vice-Premier Qian Qichen made another diplomatic overture later in the year when he called for negotiations with Taiwan on the establishment of direct cross-strait transportation operations. A milestone was reached in January 2003 when almost-direct flights between Taipei and Shanghai were permitted.

Taiwan's economy grew only 0.9% in the first months of 2002, which was even lower than experts had forecast. In November President Chen announced a five-year plan to address economic woes, vowing to bring the jobless rate down by one percentage point to 4.5% in 2003. Four days after the announcement, some 120,000 demonstrators took to the streets of Taipei to protest the proposed financial reforms, which included abolishing agricultural cooperatives that provided funding to poor farmers and fishermen.

Internet resources: <www.tbroc.gov.tw>

# Tajikistan

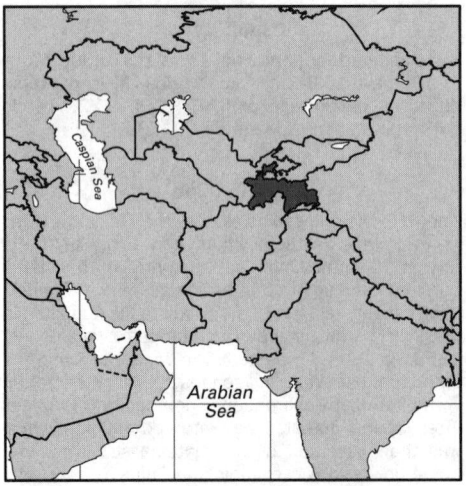

**Official name:** Jumhurii Tojikiston (Republic of Tajikistan). **Form of government:** parliamentary republic with two legislative houses (National Assembly [33]; Assembly of Representatives [63]). **Chief of state:** President Imomali Rakhmonov (from 1994). **Head of government:** Prime Minister Akil Akilov (from 1999). **Capital:** Dushanbe. **Official language:** Tajik. **Official religion:** none. **Monetary unit:** 1 somoni = 100 dinar; valuation (7 Jul 2003) $1 = 2.79 somoni.

## Demography

**Area:** 55,300 sq mi, 143,100 sq km. **Population** (2002): 6,327,000. **Density** (2002): persons per sq mi 114.4, persons per sq km 44.2. **Urban** (2000): 26.5%. **Sex distribution** (2000): male 50.30%; female 49.70%. **Age breakdown** (2000): under 15, 39.4%; 15–29, 27.7%; 30–44, 18.4%; 45–59, 7.6%; 60–74, 5.4%; 75 and over, 1.5%. **Ethnic composition** (2000): Tajik 64.9%; Uzbek 25.9%; Russian 3.5%; Tatar 1.4%; Kyrgyz 1.3%; other 3.0%. **Religious affiliation** (1995): Sunni Muslim 80.0%; Shi'i Muslim 5.0%; Russian Orthodox 1.5%; Jewish 0.1%; other (mostly nonreligious) 13.4%. **Major cities** (2000): Dushanbe 562,000; Khujand 149,000; Kulyab 78,000; Kurgan-Tyube 60,000; Ura-Tyube 51,000. **Location:** central Asia, bordering Kyrgzstan, China, Afghanistan, and Uzbekistan.

## Vital statistics

**Birth rate** per 1,000 population (2001): 24.7 (world avg. 21.2); (1994) legitimate 90.8%; illegitimate 9.2%. **Death rate** per 1,000 population (2001): 6.4 (world avg. 8.9). **Natural increase rate** per 1,000 population (2001): 18.3 (world avg. 12.3). **Total fertility rate** (avg. births per childbearing woman; 2001): 4.4. **Marriage rate** per 1,000 population (1994): 6.8. **Divorce rate** per 1,000 population (1994): 0.8. **Life expectancy** at birth (2001): male 65.0 years; female 71.0 years.

## National economy

**Budget** (2000). *Revenue*: 218,803,000 somoni (tax revenue 93.9%, of which taxes on aluminum and cotton 26.9%, value-added tax 20.3%, income and profit taxes 15.2%, customs duties 12.5%, excise taxes 4.1%; nontax revenue 5.4%; grants 0.7%). *Expenditures*: 225,410,000 somoni (current expenditures 78.2%, of which state authorities 19.7%, education 18.3%, state bodies and administration 12.0%, defense 9.7%, law enforcement 9.7%, health 7.4%; capital expenditures 21.8%). **Production** (metric tons except as noted). *Agriculture, forestry, fishing* (2000): grain 550,000, vegetables and fruit 523,000, raw cotton 335,000; livestock (number of live animals) 2,222,000 sheep and goats, 1,062,000 cattle, 72,000 horses; fish catch (1999) 80. *Mining and quarrying* (2000): aluminum 520,000; lead (metal content of concentrate) 800; gold 2,700 kg. *Manufacturing* (value of production in '000,000 Tajik rubles; 1996 [the somoni {equal to 1,000 Tajik rubles} was introduced on 30 Oct 2000]): ferrous and nonferrous metals 80,333; textiles 35,023; grain mill products 23,526. *Energy production (consumption)*: electricity (kW-hr; 2000) 14,200,000,000 (12,500,-000,000); coal (metric tons; 2001) 24,900 (122,-

1 metric ton = about 1.1 short tons;   1 kilometer = 0.6 mi (statute);   1 metric ton-km cargo = about 0.68 short ton-mi cargo;   c.i.f.: cost, insurance, and freight;   f.o.b.: free on board

000); crude petroleum (barrels; 1997) 183,000 (183,000); petroleum products (metric tons; 1997) none (1,116,000); natural gas (cu m; 1997) 41,000,000 (1,015,000,000). **Public debt** (external, outstanding; 2000): $625,600,000. **Population economically active** (2000): total 1,754,000; activity rate of total population 28.6% (participation rates: ages 15–59 [male], 15–54 [female] 55.0%; female [1996] 46.5%; unemployed 3.1%). **Gross national product** (2000): $1,109,000,000 ($180 per capita). **Land use** (1994): forest 3.8%; pasture 24.8%; agriculture 6.0%; other 65.4%. **Household income and expenditure.** Average household size (1989) 6.1; (1995) income per household 18,744 Tajik rubles ($114); sources of income (1995): wages and salaries 34.5%, self-employment 34.0%, borrowing 2.4%, pension 2.0%, other 27.1%; expenditure: food 81.5%, clothing 10.2%, transport 2.5%, fuel 2.1%, other 3.7%.

## Foreign trade

**Imports** (2000): $864,000,000 (electricity 24.3%, alumina 21.3%, petroleum products and natural gas 14.2%, grain and flour 5.1%). *Major import sources* (1996): Uzbekistan 29.8%; Switzerland 14.9%; UK 11.7%; Russia 11.1%; Kazakhstan 7.8%; Turkmenistan 3.9%; Ukraine 2.9%. **Exports** (2000): $792,000,000 (aluminum 49.6%, electricity 23.2%, cotton fibre 11.6%). *Major export destinations* (1996): The Netherlands 28.3%; Uzbekistan 24.8%; Switzerland 10.8%; Russia 10.2%; Kazakhstan 3.2%.

## Transport and communications

**Transport.** *Railroads* (1999): length 482 km; passenger-km 61,200,000; metric ton-km cargo 1,300,000,-000. *Roads* (1996): total length 13,700 km (paved 83%). *Vehicles* (1996): passenger cars 680,000; trucks and buses 8,190. *Air transport* (2001; Tajikistan Airlines only): passenger-km 605,000,000; metric ton-km cargo 4,841,000; airports (1997) 1. **Communications,** in total units (units per 1,000 persons). Daily newspaper circulation (1996): 120,000 (21); radio receivers (1997): 850,000 (143); television receivers (1999): 2,000,000 (328); telephone main lines (2001): 223,000 (36); cellular phones (2001): 1,600 (0.3); Internet users (2001): 3,200 (0.5).

## Education and health

**Educational attainment** (1989). Percentage of population age 25 and over having: primary education or no formal schooling 16.3%; some secondary 21.1%; completed secondary and some postsecondary 55.1%; higher 7.5%. **Literacy** (1998): percentage of total population age 15 and over literate 99.0%; males literate 99.5%; females literate 98.6%. **Health** (1998): physicians 14,292 (1 per 416 persons); hospital beds 36,920 (1 per 161 persons); infant mortality rate per 1,000 live births (2001) 54.0. **Food** (2000): daily per capita caloric intake 1,720 (vegetable products 91%, animal products 9%); 67% of FAO recommended minimum.

## Military

**Total active duty personnel** (2001): 6,000 (army 100%); Russian troops (2002) 25,000. **Military expenditure as percentage of GNP** (1999): 1.3% (world 2.4%); per capita expenditure $13.

## Background

Settled by the Persians c. 6th century BC, Tajikistan was part of the empires of the Persians and of Alexander the Great and his successors. In the 7th–8th centuries AD, it was conquered by the Arabs, who introduced Islam. The Uzbeks controlled the region in the 15th–18th centuries. In the 1860s Russia took over much of Tajikistan. In 1924 it became an autonomous republic under the administration of the Uzbek Soviet Socialist Republic, and it gained republic status in 1929. It achieved independence with the collapse of the Soviet Union in 1991. Civil war raged through much of the 1990s between government forces and an opposition of mostly Islamic forces. Peace was reached in 1997.

## Recent Developments

Tajikistan was able to benefit from its participation in the international antiterrorism coalition to forge closer ties with a number of countries, including the US, France, the UK, China, and Iran. These states, as well as international financial institutions, promised their assistance in overcoming the legacy of widespread poverty and lagging economic development that was left by Tajikistan's civil war in the first years of independence. Despite its own difficult economic situation, Tajikistan promised such assistance as it was able to provide for the reconstruction of Afghanistan. Although in 2002 there was little evidence that Islamic extremists were entering Tajikistan from outside, the government asserted that there were plenty of the homegrown variety operating in the northern part of the country. The international movement Hizb-ut Tahrir, which sought to create a medieval-style caliphate in the Fergana Valley, had already gained a foothold in the northern, Tajik portion of the valley.

**Internet resources:** <www.traveltajikistan.com>

# Tanzania

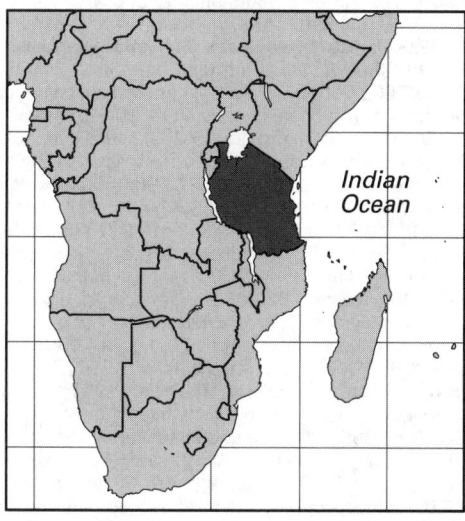

Indian Ocean

**Official name:** Jamhuri ya Muungano wa Tanzania (Swahili); United Republic of Tanzania (English). **Form of government:** unitary multiparty republic with one legislative house (National Assembly [275]). **Head of**

**state and government:** President Benjamin William Mkapa (from 1995), assisted by Prime Minister Frederick Tulway Sumaye (from 1995). **Seat of government:** Dar es Salaam (capital designate, Dodoma). **Official languages:** Swahili; English. **Official religion:** none. **Monetary unit:** 1 Tanzania shilling (T Sh) = 100 cents; valuation (7 Jul 2003) $1 = T Sh 1,042.

## Demography

**Area:** 942,799 sq km. **Population** (2002): 34,902,000. **Density** (2002): persons per sq mi 102.3, persons per sq km 39.5. **Urban** (2002) 33.3%. **Sex distribution** (2001): male 49.72%; female 50.28%. **Age breakdown** (2001): under 15, 44.8%; 15–29, 28.9%; 30–44, 14.2%; 45–59, 7.6%; 60–74, 3.6%; 75 and over, 0.9%. **Ethnolinguistic composition** (1987): Nyamwezi and Sukuma 21.1%; Swahili 8.8%; Hehet and Bena 6.9%; Haya 5.9%; Makonde 5.9%; Nyakyusa 5.4%; Chagga 4.9%; other 41.1%. **Religious affiliation** (1997): Christian c. 44%; Muslim c. 37%; animist c. 19%. **Location:** eastern Africa, bordering Kenya, the Indian Ocean, Mozambique, Malawi, Zambia, the Dem. Rep. of the Congo, Burundi, Rwanda, and Uganda.

## Vital statistics

**Birth rate** per 1,000 population (2001): 39.7 (world avg. 21.2). **Death rate** per 1,000 population (2001): 13.0 (world avg. 8.9). **Natural increase rate** per 1,000 population (2001): 26.7 (world avg. 12.3). **Total fertility rate** (avg. births per childbearing woman; 2001): 5.4. **Life expectancy** at birth (2001): male 51.0 years; female 53.0 years.

## National economy

**Budget** (1999–2000). *Revenue*: T Sh 777,644,700,-000 (sales and excise tax 28.7%, income tax 26.9%, import duties 22.9%). *Expenditures*: T Sh 1,168,-778,800,000 (current payments 58.2%, interest payments on debt 11.0%; capital expenditure 30.8%). **Public debt** (external, outstanding; 2000): $6,325,-000,000. **Tourism** (2000): receipts from visitors $739,000,000; expenditures by nationals abroad $337,000,000. **Gross national product** (2000): $9,013,000,000 ($270 per capita). **Production** (metric tons except as noted). *Agriculture* (2000): cassava 5,758,000, corn (maize) 2,009,000, sweet potatoes 798,000; livestock (number of live animals) 14,380,-000 cattle, 9,950,000 goats, 27,798,000 chickens; roundwood (2000) 23,100,000 cu m; fish catch (1999) 310,300. *Mining and quarrying* (2000): gemstones (excluding diamonds) 150,800 kg; gold 15,060 kg; diamonds 354,400 carats. *Manufacturing* (2000): cement 833,000; sugar 135,300; petroleum products 117,000. *Energy production (consumption)*: electricity (kW-hr; 1997) 1,744,000,000 (1,744,000,000); coal (metric tons; 1997) 5,000 (5,000); crude petroleum (barrels; 1997) none (4,354,000); petroleum products (metric tons; 1997) 589,000 (665,000). **Population economically active** (2000): total 18,088,000; activity rate 51.2% (participation rates [1991]: over age 10, 87.8%; female 40.0%). **Household expenditure.** Average household size (1998) 5.4; expenditure (1994): food 64.2%, clothing 9.9%, housing 8.3%, energy 7.6%, trans-portation 4.1%. **Land use** (1995): forested 37.0%; meadows and pastures 39.6%; agricultural and under permanent cultivation 4.2%; other 19.2%.

## Foreign trade

**Imports** (1999): $1,630,600,000 (consumer goods 33.9%, machinery 20.9%, transport equipment 18.2%, food 10.8%). *Major import sources:* Japan 10.9%; UK 7.8%; US 6.0%; Kenya 5.8%; India 5.6%. **Exports** (1999): $541,000,000 (cashew nuts 18.3%, coffee 14.2%, minerals 13.2%, tobacco 8.0%, cotton 5.2%, tea 4.5%). *Major export destinations:* India 19.5%; UK 17.0%; Japan 8.0%; The Netherlands 5.7%; Singapore 4.5%; Germany 4.0%; Kenya 3.8%; US 3.3%.

## Transport and communications

**Transport.** *Railroads* (1997): length 3,569 km; passenger-journeys 694,000,000 (1995); metric ton-km cargo 1,354,000,000 (1995). *Roads* (1999): length 88,200 km (paved 4.2%). *Vehicles* (1996): passenger cars 23,760; trucks and buses 115,700. *Air transport* (2001; Air Tanzania only): passenger-km 155,-000,000; metric ton-km 2,772,000; airports (1999) with scheduled flights 11. **Communications,** in total units (units per 1,000 persons). Daily newspaper circulation (1996): 120,000 (3.9); radio receivers (1997): 8,800,000 (280); television receivers (1999): 690,000 (20); telephone main lines (2001): 148,500 (4.1); cellular telephone subscribers (2001): 427,-000 (12); personal computers (2001): 120,000 (3.3); Internet users (2001): 300,000 (8.3).

## Education and health

**Literacy** (1999): percentage of population age 15 and over literate 74.7%; males 84.0%; females 65.7%. **Health** (1993): physicians 1,365 (1 per 20,511 persons); hospital beds 26,820 (1 per 1,000 persons); infant mortality rate per 1,000 live births (2001) 79.4. **Food** (2000): daily per capita caloric intake 1,906 (vegetable products 94%, animal products 6%); 82% of FAO recommended minimum.

## Military

**Total active duty personnel** (2001): 27,000 (army 85.2%, navy 3.7%, air force 11.1%). **Military expenditure as percentage of GNP** (1999): 1.4% (world 2.4%); per capita expenditure $4.

## Background

Inhabited from the 1st millennium BC, Tanzania was occupied by Arab and Indian traders and Bantu-speaking peoples by the 10th century AD. The Portuguese gained control of the coastline in the late 15th century, but they were driven out by the Arabs of Oman and Zanzibar in the late 18th century. German colonists entered the area in the 1880s, and in 1891 the Germans declared the region a protectorate as German East Africa. In World War I Britain captured the German holdings, which became a British mandate (1920) under the name Tanganyika. Britain retained control of the region after World War II when it became a UN trust territory (1947). Tanganyika gained independence in 1961

---

*1 metric ton = about 1.1 short tons;     1 kilometer = 0.6 mi (statute);     1 metric ton-km cargo = about 0.68 short ton-mi cargo;     c.i.f.: cost, insurance, and freight;     f.o.b.: free on board*

and became a republic in 1962. In 1964 it united with Zanzibar under the name Tanzania. It experienced both political and economic struggles in recent years.

## Recent Developments

In January 2002 a new deal was made between the ruling Chama Cha Mapinduzi party and the leading opposition party, the Civic United Front. The arrangement restored working relations that had been disrupted in 2001 and called for the implementation of the peace accord signed in October of that year. The corporate privatization program encouraged by the World Bank and the IMF continued to make steady progress in 2002. On 3 March Pres. Benjamin William Mkapa announced that he would defy the World Bank and implement an air traffic control system supplied by the British aerospace company BAE Systems. British Prime Minister Tony Blair had authorized the transaction against the advice of Chancellor of the Exchequer Gordon Brown. Brown argued that Tanzania, one of the world's poorest countries, should not invest in such an unnecessarily expensive system. The task of creating a customs union with Kenya and Uganda within the East African Community was proving difficult. Government officials and businessmen feared that freeing the regional market would benefit only the stronger economy of Kenya.

Internet resources: <www.tanzanianews.com>

# Thailand

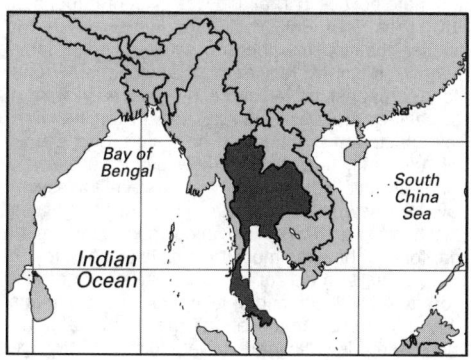

Bay of Bengal

South China Sea

Indian Ocean

**Official name:** Muang Thai, or Prathet Thai (Kingdom of Thailand). **Form of government:** constitutional monarchy with two legislative houses (Senate [200]; House of Representatives [500]). **Chief of state:** King Bhumibol Adulyadej (from 1946). **Head of government:** Prime Minister Thaksin Shinawatra (from 9 Feb 2001). **Capital:** Bangkok. **Official language:** Thai. **Official religion:** Buddhism. **Monetary unit:** 1 Thai baht (B) = 100 stangs; valuation (7 Jul 2003) $1 = B 41.67.

## Demography

**Area:** 198,115 sq mi, 513,115 sq km. **Population** (2002): 63,430,000. **Density** (2002): persons per sq mi 320.2, persons per sq km 123.6. **Urban** (2002): 31.0%. **Sex distribution** (2000): male 49.24%; female 50.76%. **Age breakdown** (1999): under 15, 26.0%; 15–29, 27.7%; 30–44, 23.3%; 45–59, 14.1%; 60–74, 7.2%; 75 and over, 1.7%. **Ethnic composition** (2000): Tai peoples 81.4%, of which Thai (Siamese) 34.9%, Lao 26.5%; Han Chinese 10.6%; Malay 3.7%;

Khmer 1.9%; other 2.4%. **Religious affiliation** (2000): Buddhist 94.2%; Muslim 4.6%; Christian and other 1.2%. **Major cities** (2000): Bangkok 5,680,380; Nonthaburi 522,669; Songkhla 273,113; Samut Prakan 268,583; Chon Buri 256,300. **Location:** southeastern Asia, bordering Laos, Cambodia, the Gulf of Thailand, Malaysia, and Myanmar (Burma).

## Vital statistics

**Birth rate** per 1,000 population (2002): 14.0 (world avg. 21.2). **Death rate** per 1,000 population (2002): 6.0 (world avg. 8.9). **Natural increase rate** per 1,000 population (2002): 8.0 (world avg. 12.3). **Total fertility rate** (avg. births per childbearing woman; 2002): 1.8. **Marriage rate** per 1,000 population (1999): 5.7. **Divorce rate** per 1,000 population (1999): 1.1. **Life expectancy** at birth (2002): male 70.0 years; female 75.0 years.

## National economy

**Budget** (2000). *Revenue:* B 794,700,000,000 (taxes on goods and services 40.5%; income taxes 29.6%; taxes on international trade 11.0%). *Expenditures:* B 949,500,000,000 (education 20.7%; transportation and communications 11.1%; defense 7.6%; agriculture 7.4%; health 7.3%; public order and safety 5.8%; social security 5.8%). **Production** (metric tons except as noted). *Agriculture, forestry, fishing* (2000): sugarcane 51,210,472, rice 23,402,900, cassava 18,508,568; livestock (number of live animals) 7,682,000 pigs, 6,100,000 cattle, 172,000,000 chickens; roundwood (1999) 36,631,000 cu m; fish catch (1998) 2,900,320. *Mining and quarrying* (1998): limestone 37,251,000; gypsum 4,334,000; kaolin clay 266,000. *Manufacturing* (1996): cement 38,739,000; refined sugar 6,323,000; crude steel 2,143,000. *Energy production (consumption):* electricity (kW-hr; 2000) 67,104,000,000 ([1997] 98,194,000,000); hard coal (metric tons; 1997) negligible (3,204); lignite (metric tons; 2001) 19,619,000 ([1997] 22,614,000); 23,393,000 (25,818,000); crude petroleum (barrels; 2001) 21,900,000 ([1997] 278,000, 000); petroleum products (metric tons; 1997) 36,727,000 (33,927,000); natural gas (cu m; 2001) 20,633,000,000 ([1997] 15,046,000,000). **Tourism** (2000): receipts from visitors $7,112,000,000; expenditures by nationals abroad $2,068,000,000. **Land use** (1998): meadows and pastures 1.6%; agricultural and under permanent cultivation 39.8%; forested and other 58.6%. **Population economically active** (2000): total 33,973,000; activity rate of total population 54.4% (participation rates: over age 13, 69.7%; female 45.0%; unemployed 2.4%). **Gross national product** (2000): $121,602,000,000 ($2,000 per capita). **Public debt** (external, outstanding; 2000): $29,418,000,000. **Household income and expenditure** (1998). Average household size (2000) 3.9; average annual income per household B 149,904 ($3,624); sources of income: wages and salaries 40.1%, self-employment 29.8%, transfer payments 7.9%, other 22.2%; expenditure: food, tobacco, and beverages 37.7%, housing 21.4%, transportation and communications 13.3%, medical and personal care 5.1%, clothing 3.5%, education 2.3%.

## Foreign trade

**Imports** (1998-f.o.b. in balance of trade and c.i.f. for commodities and trading partners): B 1,778,564,-

000,000 (electrical machinery 26.2%, power generating equipment 14.6%, mineral fuels and lubricants 8.0%, iron and steel products 8.0%, plastics
4.2%, organic chemicals 3.3%, aircraft and parts
2.7%). *Major import sources:* Japan 23.6%; US
14.0%; Singapore 5.6%; Taiwan 5.2%; Malaysia
5.1%; Germany 4.3%; China 4.2%; South Korea
3.5%. **Exports** (1998): B 2,242,579,000,000 (electrical machinery 18.9%, power generating equipment 18.6%, garments 6.1%, rubber products 4.1%,
live fish 4.0%, meat and fish preparations 3.9%, cereals 3.9%). *Major export destinations:* US 22.3%;
Japan 13.7%; Singapore 8.6%; Hong Kong 5.1%;
The Netherlands 4.0%; UK 3.9%; Malaysia 3.3%;
China 3.2%.

## Transport and communications

**Transport.** *Railroads* (1998): route length 4,623 km;
passenger-km 10,680,000,000; metric ton-km
cargo 2,832,000,000. *Roads* (1996): total length
64,600 km (paved 98%). *Vehicles* (1999): passenger cars 1,661,000; trucks and buses 2,855,000.
*Air transport* (1999): passenger-km 38,345,195,-
000; metric ton-km cargo 1,670,717,000; airports
(1996) 25. **Communications,** in total units (units
per 1,000 persons). Daily newspaper circulation
(1996): 3,800,000 (64); radio receivers (1997):
13,959,000 (234); television receivers (1999):
17,600,000 (289); telephone main lines (2001):
5,973,500 (94); cellular telephone subscribers
(2001): 7,550,000 (119); personal computers
(2001): 1,700,000 (27); Internet users (2001):
3,536,000 (56).

## Education and health

**Educational attainment** (1990). Percentage of population age 25 and over having: no formal schooling
11.8%; primary education 71.3%; secondary 9.5%;
postsecondary 6.6%; unknown 0.8%. **Literacy**
(1995): total population age 15 and over literate
93.8%; males literate 96.0%; females literate 91.6%.
**Health** (1997): physicians 16,569 (1 per 3,553 persons); hospital beds 132,405 (1 per 445 persons); infant mortality rate per 1,000 live births (2002) 21.0.
**Food** (2000): daily per capita caloric intake 2,506
(vegetable products 89%, animal products 11%);
113% of FAO recommended minimum.

## Military

**Total active duty personnel** (2001): 306,000 (army
62.1%, navy 22.2%, air force 15.7%). **Military expenditure as percentage of GNP** (1999): 1.7% (world
2.4%); per capita expenditure $34.

---

**Did you know** ■  Residents of Bangkok, one of the
most congested cities in the world,
hoped that the SkyTrain, a commuter train inaugurated in 2002
that travels 40 ft (12 m) over the
city streets along a 14-mi (23-km) route, would alleviate the crush. By early 2002, however, ridership
was only about half of what was needed for the private owner to break even.

## Background

The region of Thailand has been continuously occupied for 20,000 years. It was part of the Mon and
Khmer kingdoms from the 9th century AD. Thai-speak-
ing peoples emigrated from China c. the 10th century.
During the 13th century two Thai states emerged: the
Sukhothai kingdom, founded c. 1220 after a successful revolt against the Khmer, and Chiang Mai,
founded in 1296 after the defeat of the Mon. In 1350
the Thai kingdom of Ayutthaya succeeded Sukhothai.
The Burmese were its most powerful rivals, occupying
it briefly in the 16th century and destroying the kingdom in 1767. The Chakri dynasty came to power in
1782, moving the capital to Bangkok and extending
the empire along the Malay Peninsula and into Laos
and Cambodia. The country was named Siam in
1856. Though Western influence increased during
the 19th century, Siam's rulers avoided colonization
by granting concessions to European countries; it was
the only southeast Asian nation able to do so. In
1917 it entered World War I on the side of the Allies.
It became a constitutional monarchy following a military coup in 1932 and was officially renamed Thailand in 1939. It was occupied by Japan in World War
II. It participated in the Korean War as a UN forces
member. It was allied with South Vietnam in the Vietnam War. Along with other southeast Asian nations, it
suffered from the 1990s regional financial crisis.

## Recent Developments

Prime Minister Thaksin Shinawatra's ambition to
dominate politics in Thailand was evident throughout
2002. His Thai Rak Thai Party merged with two
smaller coalition members to secure a huge parliamentary majority, leaving the Democrats virtually
alone in opposition. A far-reaching reorganization of
the cabinet, state bureaucracy, and military hierarchy
was enacted in October, but not before King Bhumibol Adulyadej had unexpectedly used his constitutional prerogative to delay royal assent for several
days. Six new ministries were created, bringing the
total number to 20. Thaksin faced criticism during the
year for spending too much time on overseas trips, including one to India for reasons critics claimed had
more to do with protecting his family's vast personal
fortune in telecommunications than with statecraft.
There were also allegations that old-style patronage,
nepotism, and cronyism were very much alive. Nevertheless, anticorruption reforms implemented under
the 1997 constitution snared several of the country's
leading figures in 2002. Relations with neighboring
Myanmar (Burma) deteriorated steadily, as Yangon
(Rangoon) accused Bangkok of siding with the Shan
States Army, an ethnic Thai rebel group active in
Myanmar. Thailand in turn accused Myanmar of border encroachments.

**Internet resources:** <www.ithailand.com>

## Togo

**Official name:** République Togolaise (Togolese Republic). **Form of government:** multiparty republic with
one legislative body (National Assembly [81]). **Chief
of state:** President Gen. Gnassingbé Eyadéma (from

---

*1 metric ton = about 1.1 short tons; 1 kilometer = 0.6 mi (statute); 1 metric ton-km cargo = about 0.68 short
ton-mi cargo; c.i.f.: cost, insurance, and freight; f.o.b.: free on board*

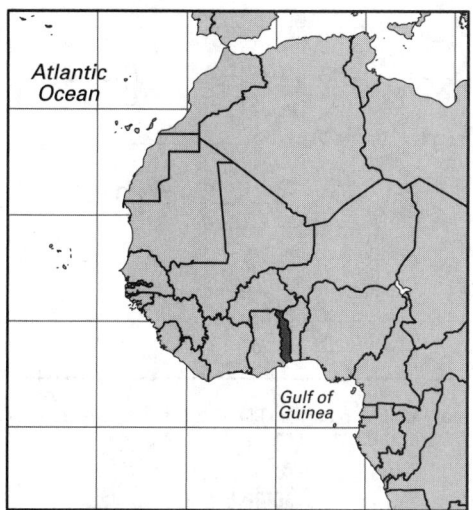

Atlantic Ocean

Gulf of Guinea

1967; personal military-supported rule from 1967 continues under constitution approved by referendum in September 1992). **Head of government:** Prime Minister Koffi Sama (from 29 Jun 2002). **Capital:** Lomé. **Official language:** French. **Official religion:** none. **Monetary unit:** 1 CFA franc (CFAF) = 100 centimes; valuation (7 Jul 2003) $1 = CFAF 571.07; the CFAF is pegged to the euro (€) at 1€ = CFAF 655.96 from 1 Jan 2002.

## Demography

**Area:** 21,925 sq mi, 56,785 sq km. **Population** (2002): 5,286,000. **Density** (2002): persons per sq mi 241.1, persons per sq km 93.1. **Urban** (2002) 33.9%%. **Sex distribution** (2001): male 49.22%; female 50.78%. **Age breakdown** (2001): under 15, 45.6%; 15–29, 28.1%; 30–44, 14.8%; 45–59, 7.5%; 60–74, 3.3%; 75 and over, 0.7%. **Ethnic composition** (2000): Ewe 22.2%; Kabre 13.4%; Wachi 10.0%; Mina 5.6%; Kotokoli 5.6%; Bimoba 5.2%; Losso 4.0%; Gurma 3.4%; Lamba 3.2%; Adja 3.0%; other 24.4%. **Religious affiliation** (1993): traditional beliefs 50%; Christian 35%, of which Roman Catholic 23%; Muslim 15%. **Major cities** (1997): Lomé 375,000 (urban agglomeration [2001] 732,000); Sokodé 51,000; Kara 30,000; Kpalimé 30,000; Atakpamé 30,000. **Location:** western Africa, bordering Burkina Faso, Benin, the Bight of Benin, and Ghana.

## Vital statistics

**Birth rate** per 1,000 population (2001): 37.0 (world avg. 21.2). **Death rate** per 1,000 population (2001): 11.2 (world avg. 8.9). **Natural increase rate** per 1,000 population (2001): 25.8 (world avg. 12.3). **Total fertility rate** (avg. births per childbearing woman; 2001): 5.3. **Life expectancy** at birth (2001): male 52.4 years; female 56.4 years.

## National economy

**Budget** (1999). *Revenue:* CFAF 140,400,000,000 (tax revenue 80.1%; grants 10.5%; nontax revenue 9.4%). *Expenditures:* CFAF 173,700,000,000 (current expenditure 83.3%, of which wages 33.9%, materials and supplies 20.0%, transfers 13.8%, debt service 10.8%, other 4.8%; capital expenditure 16.7%). **Public**

**debt** (external, outstanding; 2000): $1,232,000,000. **Production** (metric tons except as noted). *Agriculture, forestry, fishing* (2000): cassava 700,700, yams 563,300, corn (maize) 495,500; livestock (number of live animals) 1,110,000 goats, 850,000 pigs, 7,500,000 chickens; roundwood (2000) 5,805,000 cu m; fish catch (1999) 23,100. *Mining and quarrying* (2000): phosphate rock 1,400,000; limestone is quarried for cement manufacture. *Manufacturing* (value added in CFAF '000,000; 1998): food products, beverages, and tobacco manufactures 41,400; metallic goods 12,000; nonmetallic manufactures 8,500. *Energy production (consumption)*: electricity (kW-hr; 1998) 48,320,000 ([1997] 282,200,000); petroleum products (metric tons; 1998) none (231,000). **Household income and expenditure.** Average household size (1999) 6.0; average annual income per household (1980) CFAF 102,000 ($452); expenditure (1987): food and beverages 45.9%, services 20.5%, household durable goods 13.9%, clothing 11.4%, housing 5.9%. **Gross national product** (2000): $1,318,000,000 ($290 per capita). **Population economically active** (2000): total 1,913,000; activity rate of total population 38.1% (participation rates over age 15, 70.7%; female 39.9%; unemployed ([1994]) 16–18%). **Tourism** (2000): receipts $5,000,000; expenditures $3,000,000.

## Foreign trade

**Imports** (2001-c.i.f.): CFAF 260,016,000,000 (1999; fuels 39.7%, manufactured goods 17.2%, machinery and transport equipment 11.1%, food 8.4%, chemicals 7.3%). *Major import sources* (1999): France 17.5%; Côte d'Ivoire 11.6%; Benin 6.0%; Italy 4.1%; The Netherlands 4.1%; Japan 3.7%. **Exports** (2001): CFAF 165,922,000,000 (1999; cotton 24.2%, phosphates 18.0%, coffee 7.1%, cocoa 4.2%, tea 2.5%). *Major export destinations* (1999): Benin 16.6%; Ghana 10.9%; Canada 5.1%; Brazil 4.8%; Nigeria 4.1%; France 2.5%.

## Transport and communications

**Transport.** *Railroads* (1999): route length 395 km; (1998) passenger-km 35,200,000; metric ton-km cargo 758,700,000. *Roads* (1999): total length 7,520 km (paved 32%). *Vehicles* (1996): passenger cars 79,200; trucks and buses 34,240. *Air transport* (1997; includes about 10% of the traffic of Air Afrique, which is operated by 11 West African states): passenger-km 242,000,000; metric ton-km cargo 38,000,000; airports (1998) 2. **Communications,** in total units (units per 1,000 persons). Daily newspaper circulation (1996): 15,000 (3.6); radio receivers (1998): 720,000 (167); television receivers (1999): 100,000 (21); telephone main lines (2001): 48,100 (11); cellular telephone subscribers (2001): 95,000 (20); personal computers (2001): 100,000 (22); Internet users (2001): 50,000 (11).

## Education and health

**Educational attainment** (1981). Percentage of population age 25 and over having: no formal schooling 76.5%; primary education 13.5%; secondary 8.7%; higher 1.3%. **Literacy** (1995): total population age 15 and over literate 51.7%; males 67.0%; females 37.0%. **Health:** physicians (1995) 320 (1 per 13,158 persons); hospital beds (1990) 5,307 (1 per 694 persons); infant mortality rate per 1,000 live births

(2001) 70.4. **Food** (1999): daily per capita caloric intake 2,527 (vegetable products 96%, animal products 4%); 110% of FAO recommended minimum.

## Military

**Total active duty personnel** (2001): 6,950 (army 93.5%, navy 2.9%, air force 3.6%). **Military expenditure as percentage of GNP** (1999): 1.8% (world 2.4%); per capita expenditure $5.

## Background

Until 1884 what is now Togo was an intermediate zone between the black African military states of Ashanti and Dahomey, and its various ethnic groups lived in general isolation from each other. In 1884 it became part of the Togoland German protectorate, which was occupied by British and French forces in 1914. In 1922 the League of Nations assigned eastern Togoland to France and the western portion to Britain. In 1946 the British and French governments placed the territories under UN trusteeship. Ten years later British Togoland was incorporated into the Gold Coast, and French Togoland became an autonomous republic within the French Union. Togo gained independence in 1960. It suspended its constitution 1967–80. A multiparty constitution was approved in 1992, but the political situation remained unstable.

## Recent Developments

Modifications to Togo's electoral code were introduced early in 2002. These included new residency requirements and exclusive Togolese nationality for all political candidates, measures clearly designed to prevent participation in the political process of certain high-profile opponents of the regime, most notably the exile Gilchrist Olympio. National and international protests over these changes to the code led to the cancellation of the March legislative elections. On 27 June Pres. Gnassingbé Eyadéma fired Prime Minister Agbéyomé Kodjo, who fled the country. On 17 September the government issued an international warrant for his arrest. The government issued a statement in August strongly protesting allegations brought by Amnesty International that it engaged in systematic repression of political opponents. In October Togolese officials testified before the UN Human Rights Committee, denying such abuses as torture, extrajudicial executions, and illegal detention of prisoners.

Internet resources:
<www.republicoftogo.com/en/home.asp>

# Tonga

**Official name:** Pule'anga Fakatu'i 'o Tonga (Tongan); Kingdom of Tonga (English). **Form of government:** constitutional monarchy with one legislative house (Legislative Assembly [30; includes 12 nonelective seats and 9 nobles elected by the 33 hereditary nobles of Tonga]). **Head of state and government:** King Taufa'ahau Tupou IV (from 1965), assisted by Prime Minister of the Privy Council Prince 'Ulukalala Lavaka Ata (from 2000). **Capital:** Nuku'alofa. **Official languages:** Tongan; English. **Official religion:** none. **Mon-**

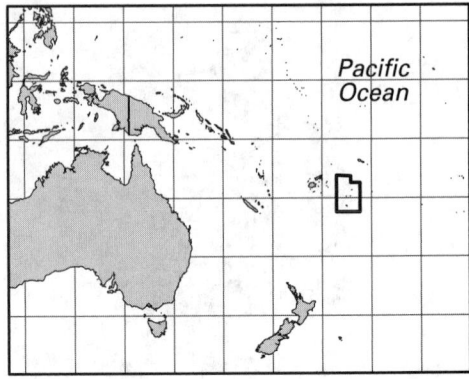

etary unit: 1 pa'anga (T$) = 100 seniti; valuation (7 Jul 2003) US$1 = T$1.47.

## Demography

**Area:** 289.5 sq mi, 749.9 sq km, of which land area equals 278.1 sq mi, 720.3 sq km. **Population** (2002): 101,000. **Density** (2002): persons per sq mi 363.2, persons per sq km 140.2. **Urban** (2002) 39.0%. **Sex distribution** (2000): male 50.87%; female 49.13%. **Age breakdown** (1996): under 15, 39.1%; 15–29, 28.0%; 30–44, 15.1%; 45–59, 10.0%; 60–74, 6.0%; 75 and over, 1.8%. **Ethnic composition** (1996): Tongan and part Tongan 98.2%; other 1.8%. **Religious affiliation** (1998): Free Wesleyan 41.2%; Roman Catholic 15.8%; Mormon 13.6%; other (mostly other Protestant) 29.4%. **Major cities** (1986): Nuku'alofa (1996) 22,400 (urban agglomeration [2001] 33,000); Neiafu 3,879; Haveluloto 3,070. **Major city** (1996): Nuku'alofa 22,400. **Location:** archipelago in the South Pacific Ocean between Hawaii and New Zealand.

## Vital statistics

**Birth rate** per 1,000 population (2002): 24.1 (world avg. 21.2). **Death rate** per 1,000 population (2002): 5.6 (world avg. 8.9). **Natural increase rate** per 1,000 population (2002): 18.5 (world avg. 12.3). **Total fertility rate** (avg. births per childbearing woman; 2000): 4.2. **Marriage rate** per 1,000 population (1992): 8.2. **Divorce rate** per 1,000 population (1992): 1.1. **Life expectancy** at birth (2000): male 71.0 years; female 73.0 years.

## National economy

**Budget** (2000–01). *Revenue:* T$77,500,000 (foreign-trade taxes 45.7%, government services revenue 15.4%, direct taxes 13.2%, indirect taxes 10.2%, interest and rent 5.8%). *expenditures:* T$84,700,000 (general administration 20.9%, education 14.0%, health 10.2%, social security 6.7%, agriculture 6.5%, law and order 5.7%, defense 4.6%). **Public debt** (external, outstanding; 2000): US$58,000,000. **Production** (metric tons except as noted). *Agriculture, forestry, fishing* (1999): yams 31,000, cassava 28,000, taro 27,200; livestock (number of live animals) 80,853 pigs, 13,939 goats, 11,400 horses; roundwood (1998) 4,600 cu m; fish catch (2000) 3,531. *Mining and quarrying:* coral and sand for local

*1 metric ton = about 1.1 short tons;   1 kilometer = 0.6 mi (statute);   1 metric ton-km cargo = about 0.68 short ton-mi cargo;   c.i.f.: cost, insurance, and freight;   f.o.b.: free on board*

use. *Manufacturing* (output in T$'000,000; 1996): food products and beverages 8,203; paper products 1,055; chemical products 964. *Energy production (consumption)*: electricity (kW-hr; 1997) 34,000,000 (34,000,000); petroleum products (metric tons; 1997) n.a. (39,000). **Tourism**: receipts (2000) US$7,000,000; expenditures (1997) US$3,000,000. **Gross national product** (2000): US$166,000,000 (US$1,660 per capita). **Population economically active** (1996): total 33,908; activity rate 34.7% (participation rates: ages 15 and over 57.0%; female 36.0%; unemployed 13.3%). **Household expenditure.** Average household size (1996) 6.0; expenditure (1991–92): food 43.2%, transportation 15.5%, household 14.2%, housing 6.4%, tobacco and beverages 5.4%, clothing and footwear 4.2%. **Land use** (1994): forest 11.1%; pasture 5.6%; agriculture 66.7%; other 16.6%.

## Foreign trade

**Imports** (1999–2000): US$54,300,000 (food and live animals 32.0%, basic manufactures 17.3%, machinery and transport equipment 15.7%, mineral fuels 14.7%, chemicals and chemical products 7.2%). *Major import sources:* US 35.2%; Australia 23.0%; New Zealand 12.3%; Fiji 10.3%; Japan 6.1%. **Exports** (1999–2000): US$11,300,000 (squash 48.7%, fish 36.3%, manufactured goods 7.1%, vanilla beans 4.4%). *Major export destinations:* Japan 57.5%; US 18.5%; New Zealand 7.6%; Australia 2.6%; Fiji 1.4%.

## Transport and communications

**Transport.** *Roads* (1996): total length 680 km (paved 27%). *Vehicles* (1998): passenger cars 6,419, commercial vehicles 9,189. *Air transport* (1998): passenger-km 10,000,000; metric ton-km cargo 1,000,000; airports (1996) with scheduled flights 6. **Communications**, in total units (units per 1,000 persons). Daily newspaper circulation (1996): 7,000 (72); radio receivers (1997): 61,000 (619); television receivers (1997): 2,000 (21); telephone main lines (2000): 9,700 (99); cellular telephone subscribers (1999): 140 (1.4); Internet users (1999): 1,000 (10).

## Education and health

**Educational attainment** (1996). Percentage of population age 25 and over having: primary education 26%; lower secondary 58%; upper secondary 8%; higher 6%; not stated 2%. **Health**: physicians (1997) 43 (1 per 2,279 persons); hospital beds (1992) 307 (1 per 320 persons); infant mortality rate per 1,000 live births (2002) 13.7. **Food** (1992): daily per capita caloric intake 2,946 (vegetable products 82%, animal products 18%); 129% of FAO recommended minimum.

## Military

**Total active duty personnel** (1999): 125-member naval force; an air force was created in 1996. **Military expenditure as percentage of GNP** (1989): 4.9% (world 4.7%); per capita expenditure US$21.

## Background

Tonga was inhabited at least 3,000 years ago by people of the Lapita culture. The Tongans developed a stratified social system headed by a paramount ruler whose dominion by the 13th century extended as far as the Hawaiian Islands. The Dutch visited the islands

in the 17th century; in 1773 Capt. James Cook arrived and named the archipelago the Friendly Islands. The modern kingdom was established during the reign (1845–93) of King George Tupou I. It became a British protectorate in 1900. This was dissolved in 1970, when Tonga, the only ancient kingdom surviving from the pre-European period in Polynesia, achieved complete independence within the Commonwealth.

## Recent Developments

Parliamentary elections in March 2002 attracted 52 candidates competing for the nine seats available to commoners; seven of the nine seats were won by the Tonga Human Rights and Democracy Movement (THRDM) and the other two went to independents. Later in the year, the THRDM unsuccessfully proposed a constitutional change that would have removed the king's legislative and executive powers, established a bicameral legislature, and shifted the balance of power to elected members. In June, American J.D. Bogdonoff, onetime financial adviser and court jester to King Taufa'ahau Tupou IV, was sued in a US district court for having defrauded the Tonga Trust Fund of $25 million.

**Internet resources:** <www.vacations.tvb.gov.to>

# Trinidad and Tobago

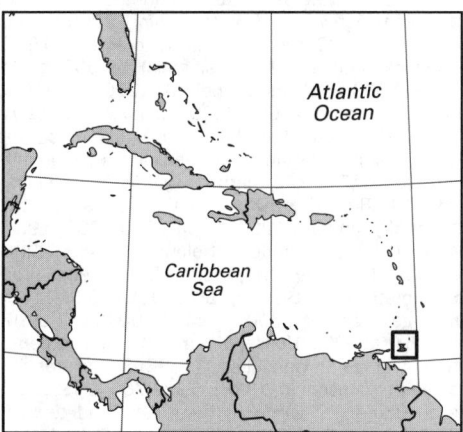

**Official name:** Republic of Trinidad and Tobago. **Form of government:** multiparty republic with two legislative houses (Senate [31]; House of Representatives [36; excludes speaker]). **Chief of state:** President George Maxwell Richards (from 17 Mar 2003). **Head of government:** Prime Minister Patrick Manning (from 2001). **Capital:** Port of Spain. **Official language:** English. **Official religion:** none. **Monetary unit:** 1 Trinidad and Tobago dollar (TT$) = 100 cents; valuation (7 Jul 2003) US$1 = TT$6.14.

## Demography

**Area:** 5,128 sq km. **Population** (2002): 1,304,000. **Density** (2002): persons per sq mi 658.4, persons per sq km 254.2. **Urban** (2002) 74.5%. **Sex distribution** (2001): male 51.22%; female 48.78%. **Age breakdown** (2001): under 15, 24.3%; 15–29, 27.1%; 30–44, 22.5%; 45–59, 15.5%; 60–74, 7.7%; 75 and over, 2.9%. **Ethnic composition** (2000): black 39.2%; East Indian 38.6%; mixed 16.3%; Chinese 1.6%; white

1.0%; other/not stated 3.3%. **Religious affiliation** (1990): six largest Protestant bodies 29.7%; Roman Catholic 29.4%; Hindu 23.7%; Muslim 5.9%; other 11.3%. **Major cities** (1990): Chaguanas 56,601; Port of Spain 43,396 (1996); San Fernando 30,115 (1991); Arima 29,483 (1991); Point Fortin 20,025. **Location:** islands northeast of Venezuela between the North Atlantic Ocean and the Caribbean Sea.

## Vital statistics

**Birth rate** per 1,000 population (2001): 12.8 (world avg. 21.2). **Death rate** per 1,000 population (2001): 8.2 (world avg. 8.9). **Natural increase rate** per 1,000 population (2001): 4.6 (world avg. 12.3). **Total fertility rate** (avg. births per childbearing woman; 2001): 1.8. **Marriage rate** per 1,000 population (1996): 5.6. **Divorce rate** per 1,000 population (1996): 1.2. **Life expectancy** at birth (2001): male 67.4 years; female 72.8 years.

## National economy

**Budget** (2000). *Revenue:* TT$12,144,000,000 (income taxes 29.7%; petroleum sector 26.4%; sales tax 25.8%; taxes on international trade 6.4%; other taxes 1.6%; nontax revenues 10.1%). *Expenditures:* TT$12,068,000,000 (current expenditures 90.0%, of which transfers and subsidies 36.6%, wages 28.9%, interest payment 23.6%, other 0.9%; development expenditures 10.0%). **Production** (metric tons except as noted). *Agriculture, forestry, fishing* (2000): sugarcane 1,500,000, coconuts 23,000, oranges 19,500; livestock (number of live animals) 59,000 goats, 10,000,000 chickens; roundwood (2000) 116,500 cu m; fish catch (2000) 15,000. *Mining and quarrying* (2000): natural asphalt 9,900. *Manufacturing* (2000): anhydrous ammonia and urea (nitrogenous fertilizers) 3,718,700; methanol 2,480,200; steel billets 743,800. *Energy production (consumption):* electricity (kW-hr; 1997) 4,848,000,000 ([1997] 4,848,000,000); crude petroleum (barrels; 2000) 39,337,000 ([1997] 37,963,000); petroleum products (metric tons; 1997) 5,259,000 (1,310,000); natural gas (cu m; 2000) 15,483,000,000 ([1997] 8,136,000,000). **Household income and expenditure.** Average household size (1998) 3.8; average income per household (1988) TT$21,760 (US$5,661); expenditure (1993): food, beverages, and tobacco 25.5%, housing 21.6%, transportation 15.2%, household furnishings 14.3%, clothing and footwear 10.4%. **Tourism** (1999): receipts from visitors US$210,000,000; expenditures by nationals abroad (1998) US$67,000,000. **Land use** (1994): forested 45.8%; meadows and pastures 2.1%; agricultural and under permanent cultivation 23.8%; other 28.3%. **Gross national product** (at current market prices; 2000): US$6,415,000,000 (US$4,930 per capita). **Population economically active** (2000): total 572,300; activity rate of total population 44.2% (participation rates: ages 15 and over 61.4%; female 39.3%; unemployed 12.3%). **Public debt** (external, outstanding; 2000): US$1,496,000,000.

## Foreign trade

**Imports** (1999-c.i.f.): TT$17,263,000,000 (machinery and apparatus 26.6%, fuels 20.1%, food 7.0%, transport equipment 5.6%). *Major import sources* (2000): US 32.0%; Venezuela 18.4%; UK 4.3%; Japan 3.8%; Canada 3.3%. **Exports** (1999-f.o.b.): TT$17,661,200,000 (refined petroleum 32.7%, crude petroleum 13.0%, anhydrous ammonia 10.4%, iron and steel 5.8%, reexports 4.4%, methanol 1.7%). *Major export destinations* (2000): US 42.6%; Caricom 23.8%, of which Jamaica 8.9%, Barbados 5.0%; EC (excluding UK) 5.7%.

## Transport and communications

**Transport.** *Roads* (1999): total length 7,900 km (paved 51%). *Vehicles* (1996): passenger cars 122,000; trucks and buses 24,000. *Air transport* (2001; BWIA only): passenger-km 2,496,000,000; metric ton-km cargo 56,236,000; airports (2000) with scheduled flights 2. **Communications,** in total units (units per 1,000 persons). Daily newspaper circulation (1996): 156,000 (123); radio receivers (1997): 680,000 (535); television receivers (1999): 435,000 (338); telephone main lines (2001): 311,800 (239); cellular telephone subscribers (2001): 225,400 (173); personal computers (2001): 90,000 (69); Internet users (2001): 120,000 (92).

## Education and health

**Educational attainment** (1990). Percentage of population age 25 and over having: no formal schooling 4.5%; primary education 56.4%; secondary 32.1%; higher 3.4%; other/not stated 3.6%. **Literacy** (1999): total population age 15 and over literate 93.5%; males 95.4%, females 91.7%. **Health:** physicians (1997) 1,074 (1 per 1,183 persons); hospital beds (1996) 6,622 (1 per 191 persons); infant mortality rate per 1,000 live births (2001) 25.6. **Food** (2000): daily per capita caloric intake 2,760 (vegetable products 85%, animal products 15%); 114% of FAO recommended minimum.

## Military

**Total active duty personnel** (2001): 2,700 (army 74.1%, coast guard 25.9%). **Military expenditure as percentage of GNP** (1999): 1.4% (world 2.4%); per capita expenditure US$78.

---

Trinidad's Carnival is the biggest, most famous, and liveliest festival in the Caribbean. It is celebrated two days before Ash Wednesday. Integral to the festivities are the uniquely Trinidadian steel drum music and the singing of calypso.

---

## Background

When Christopher Columbus visited Trinidad in 1498, it was inhabited by the Arawak Indians; Caribs inhabited Tobago. The islands were settled by the Spanish in the 16th century. In the 17th and 18th centuries African slaves were imported for plantation labor to replace the original Indian population, which had been worked to death by the Spanish. Trinidad was surrendered to the British in 1797. The British attempted to settle Tobago in 1721, but the French captured the is-

---

*1 metric ton = about 1.1 short tons;   1 kilometer = 0.6 mi (statute);   1 metric ton-km cargo = about 0.68 short ton-mi cargo;   c.i.f.: cost, insurance, and freight;   f.o.b.: free on board*

land in 1781 and transformed it into a sugar-producing colony; the British acquired it in 1802. After slavery ended in the islands in 1834–38, immigrants from India were brought in to work the plantations. Trinidad and Tobago were administratively combined in 1889. Granted limited self-government in 1925, the islands became an independent state within the Commonwealth in 1962 and a republic in 1976. Political unrest was followed in 1990 by an attempted Muslim-fundamentalist coup against the government.

## Recent Developments

Parliament failed to elect a speaker at its first meeting of 2002 in April. The opposition United National Congress party declined to cooperate in the process, even voting against its own nominees. A second attempt was made at another sitting in August and produced the same result, which left Prime Minister Patrick Manning with no option but to advise the president to dissolve Parliament and call a fresh election. This was duly held on 7 October, and Manning's People's National Movement emerged clearly victorious. Prior to the election, the authorities had charged former prime minister Basdeo Panday with having failed to declare money held in a London bank account.

Internet resources: <www.tidco.co.tt>

# Tunisia

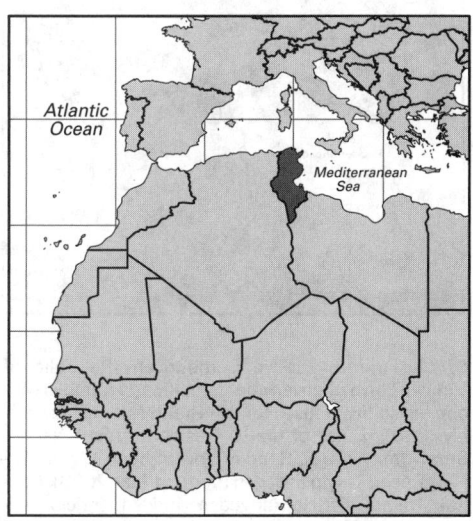

Official name: Al-Jumhuriyah al-Tunisiyah (Republic of Tunisia). Form of government: multiparty republic with one legislative house (Chamber of Deputies [182]). Chief of state: President Zine El Abidine Ben Ali (from 1987). Head of government: Prime Minister Mohamed Ghannouchi (from 1999). Capital: Tunis. Official language: Arabic. Official religion: Islam. Monetary unit: 1 dinar (D) = 1,000 millimes; valuation (7 Jul 2003) $1= D 1.27.

## Demography

Area: 63,378 sq mi, 164,150 sq km. Population (2002): 9,764,000. Density (2002): persons per sq mi 154.1, persons per sq km 59.5. Urban (2001): 66.2%. Sex distribution (2000): male 50.40%; female 49.60%. Age breakdown (2000): under 15, 29.7%; 15–29, 30.4%; 30–44, 21.2%; 45–59, 10.6%; 60–74, 6.8%; 75 and over, 1.3%. Ethnic composition (2000): Tunisian Arab 67.2%; Bedouin Arab 26.6%; Algerian Arab 2.4%; Berber 1.4%; other 2.4%. Religious affiliation (2000): Sunni Muslim 98.9%; Christian 0.5%; other 0.6%. Major cities (commune; 1994): Tunis 674,100 (urban agglomeration [2001] 1,927,000); Safaqis 230,900; Al-Arianah 152,700; Ettadhamen 149,200; Susah 125,000. Location: northern Africa, bordering the Mediterranean Sea, Libya, and Algeria.

## Vital statistics

Birth rate per 1,000 population (2001): 17.1 (world avg. 21.2). Death rate per 1,000 population (2001): 5.0 (world avg. 8.9). Total fertility rate (avg. births per childbearing woman; 2001): 2.1. Marriage rate per 1,000 population (1995): 6.0. Life expectancy at birth (2001): male 72.4 years; female 75.6 years.

## National economy

Budget (2000). Revenue: D 7,625,000,000 (tax revenue 91.1%, of which goods and services 39.1%, income tax 20.0%, social security 17.8%, import duties 9.8%; nontax revenue 8.9%). Expenditures: D 8,454,-000,000 (current expenditure 77.2%, of which interest on public debt 10.3%; development expenditure 22.8%). Public debt (external, outstanding; 2000): $8,869,000,000. Production (metric tons except as noted). Agriculture, forestry, fishing (2000): wheat 1,144,000, olives 1,000,000, tomatoes 905,000; livestock (live animals) 6,600,000 sheep, 1,400,000 goats, 790,000 cattle; roundwood (2000) 2,841,800 cu m; fish catch (2000) 90,100. Mining and quarrying (2000): phosphate rock 8,339,000; iron ore 182,000; zinc (metal content) 41,200. Manufacturing (2000): cement 5,398,900; phosphoric acid 845,000; flour 745,500. Energy production (consumption): electricity (kW-hr; 2001) 9,787,000,000 ([2000] 8,150,400,-000); coal (metric tons; 1997) none (2,000); crude petroleum (barrels; 2001) 25,712,000 ([1996] 7,097,000); petroleum products (metric tons; 1997) 1,855,000 (3,230,000); natural gas (cu m; 2001) 2,143,100,000 ([1997] 2,107,300,000). Household income and expenditure. Average household size (2000) 4.8; expenditure (1995): food and beverages 37.7%, housing and energy 22.2%, health and personal care 9.6%, transportation 8.9%, recreation 8.7%, other 12.9%. Tourism (2000): receipts $1,496,-000,000; expenditures $263,000,000. Gross national product (2000): $20,057,000,000 ($2,100 per capita). Population economically active (1997): total 3,502,000; activity rate of total population 37.9% (participation rates [1989]: ages 15–64, 42.2%; female [1997] 30.9%; unemployed [2000] 15.9%). Land use (1994): forested 4.3%; meadows and pastures 20.0%; agricultural and under permanent cultivation 31.9%; other 43.8%.

## Foreign trade

Imports (2000-c.i.f.): D 11,728,000,000 (textiles, clothing, and leather 22.9%, nonelectrical equipment 20.3%, electrical equipment 10.2%, transport equipment 10.2%). Major import sources: France 26.3%; Italy 19.1%; Germany 10.0%; US 4.6%; Libya 3.7%. Exports (2000): D 8,005,000,000 (textiles, clothing, and leather products 46.6%, mineral fuels and lubricants 12.1%, electrical equipment 10.1%, phosphates and phosphate derivatives 9.0%). *Major export destinations:* France 26.8%; Italy 23.0%; Germany 12.5%; Belgium 5.1%; Libya 3.6%.

## Transport and communications

**Transport.** *Railroads* (2000): route length 2,169 km; passenger-km 1,196,000,000; metric ton-km cargo 2,365,000,000. *Roads* (1997): total length 23,100 km (paved 79%). *Vehicles* (1996): passenger cars 269,000; trucks and buses 312,000. *Air transport* (2000; Tunis Air only): passenger-km 2,694,167,000; metric ton-km cargo 20,821,000; airports (1998) 5. **Communications,** in total units (units per 1,000 persons). Daily newspaper circulation (1996): 280,000 (31); radio receivers (1997): 2,060,000 (224); television receivers (1999): 1,800,000 (190); telephone main lines (2001): 1,056,000 (109); cellular telephone subscribers (2001): 389,200 (40); personal computers (2001): 230,000 (24); Internet users (2001): 400,000 (41).

## Education and health

**Educational attainment** (1989). Percentage of population age 25 and over having: no formal schooling 54.9%; primary 26.9%; secondary 14.3%; higher 3.4%; unspecified 0.5%. **Literacy** (2000): total population age 10 and over literate 74.4%; males literate 83.5%; females literate 65.3%. **Health** (2000): physicians 7,444 (1 per 1,284 persons); hospital beds (1999) 16,256 (1 per 581 persons); infant mortality rate per 1,000 live births (2001) 29.0. **Food** (2000): daily per capita caloric intake 3,299 (vegetable products 89%, animal products 11%); 138% of FAO recommended minimum.

## Military

**Total active duty personnel** (2002): 35,000 (army 77.1%, navy 12.9%, air force 10.0%). **Military expenditure as percentage of GNP** (1999): 1.8% (world 2.4%); per capita expenditure $38.

## Background

From the 12th century BC the Phoenicians had a series of trading posts on the north African coast. By the 6th century BC the Carthaginian kingdom encompassed most of present-day Tunisia. The Romans ruled from 146 BC until the Muslim Arab invasions in the mid-7th century AD. The area was fought over, won, and lost by many, including the Abbasids, the Almohads, the Spanish, and the Ottoman Turks, who finally conquered it in 1574 and held it until the late 19th century. For a time it maintained autonomy as the French, British, and Italians contended for the region. In 1881 it became a French protectorate. In World War II US and British forces captured it (1943) to end a brief German occupation. In 1956 France granted it full independence; Habib Bourguiba assumed power and remained in office until 1987.

## Recent Developments

In Tunisia the year 2002 was dominated by the explosion of a bomb placed outside the El-Ghriba syna-

gogue in Jarbah (Djerba) on 11 April. A group of tourists was visiting the synagogue when an oil tanker parked next to the building exploded, killing 19 people, including 14 Germans from a tourist party. The incident was believed to be the first successful al-Qaeda assault since the 11 Sep 2001 attacks in the US. The perpetrator, Nizar Nawar, a local man who had been trained in Afghanistan, died in the explosion. In November several arrests were made in connection with the bombing. Pres. Zine al-Abidine Ben Ali's government continued its harsh treatment of internal dissidents after the bombing. Amnesty International visited Tunisia in late September and subsequently called for the immediate liberation of prisoners of conscience and the review of all trials of political prisoners. Despite a significant decline in tourism, the Tunisian economy continued to grow at a rate of approximately 5% annually, earning praise from the IMF. Controversy continued to rage over the president's plan to seek a fourth term in 2004, a move prohibited by Tunisia's constitution.

**Internet resources:** <www.tourismtunisia.com>

# Turkey

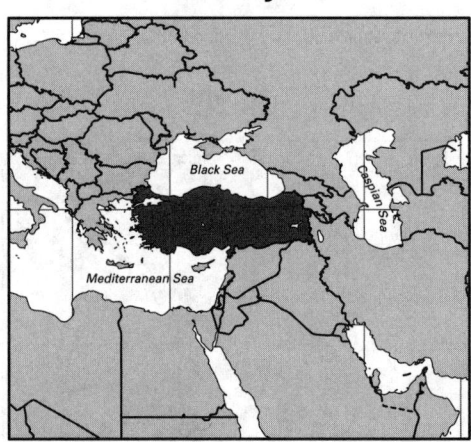

**Official name:** Turkiye Cumhuriyeti (Republic of Turkey). **Form of government:** multiparty republic with one legislative house (Turkish Grand National Assembly [550]). **Chief of state:** President Ahmet Necdet Sezer (from 2000). **Head of government:** Prime Minister Recep Tayyip Erdogan (from 14 Mar 2003). **Capital:** Ankara. **Official language:** Turkish. **Official religion:** none. **Monetary unit:** 1 Turkish lira (LT) = 100 kurush; valuation (7 Jul 2003) $1 = LT 1,393,500.

## Demography

**Area:** 300,948 sq mi, 779,452 sq km. **Population** (2002): 69,359,000. **Density** (2002): persons per sq mi 230.5, persons per sq km 89.0. **Urban** (2001): 66.2%. **Sex distribution** (2000): male 50.57%; female 49.43%. **Age breakdown** (2000): under 15, 29.1%; 15–29, 28.8%; 30–44, 21.5%; 45–59, 11.8%; 60–74, 6.8%; 75 and over, 2.0%. **Ethnic composition** (2000): Turk 65.1%; Kurd 18.9%; Crimean Tatar 7.2%; Arab 1.8%; Azerbaijani 1.0%; Yoruk 1.0%; other

*1 metric ton = about 1.1 short tons; 1 kilometer = 0.6 mi (statute); 1 metric ton-km cargo = about 0.68 short ton-mi cargo; c.i.f.: cost, insurance, and freight; f.o.b.: free on board*

5.0%. **Religious affiliation** (2000): Muslim 97.2%, of which Sunni c. 67%, Shi'i c. 30% (including nonorthodox Alevi c. 26%); Christian (mostly Eastern Orthodox) 0.6%; other 2.2%. **Major urban agglomerations** (2001): Istanbul 10,243,000; Ankara 4,611,000; Izmir 3,437,000; Bursa (2000) 1,166,000; Adana (2000) 1,091,000. **Location:** southwestern Asia and a small part in southeastern Europe, bordering the Black Sea, Georgia, Armenia, Azerbaijan, Iran, Iraq, Syria, the Mediterranean Sea, Greece, and Bulgaria.

## Vital statistics

**Birth rate** per 1,000 population (2000): 18.7 (world avg. 22.5). **Death rate** per 1,000 population (2000): 6.0 (world avg. 9.0). **Natural increase rate** per 1,000 population (2000): 12.7 (world avg. 13.5). **Total fertility rate** (avg. births per childbearing woman; 2000): 2.2. **Marriage rate** per 1,000 population (1997): 7.8. **Divorce rate** per 1,000 population (1997): 0.5. **Life expectancy** at birth (2000): male 68.6 years; female 73.4 years.

## National economy

**Budget** (2000). *Revenue:* LT 33,756,347,000,-000,000 (tax revenue 78.5%, nontax revenue 10.3%, special funds 9.7%, other 1.5%). *Expenditures:* LT 46,602,627,000,000,000 (interest payments 38.3%, personnel 24.7%, investments 5.5%). **Public debt** (external, outstanding; 2000): $55,293,-000,000. **Production** (in '000 metric tons except as noted). *Agriculture, forestry, fishing* (2000): wheat 21,000, sugar beets 18,000, barley 8,000; livestock (number of live animals) 29,435,000 sheep, 11,031,000 cattle, 615,000 (1997) angora goats; roundwood (2000) 17,767,000 cu m; fish catch (1999) 638,097. *Mining* (1999): boron minerals 2,600; chromite 770; copper ore (metal content) 45. *Manufacturing* (1995; value added in $'000,000): refined petroleum 4,583; food products 3,944; textiles 3,907; transport equipment 3,048; iron and steel 2,453; paints, soaps, and pharmaceuticals 2,301. Energy production (consumption): electricity (kW-hr; 2001) 123,096,000,000 ([1997] 80,862,000,000); hard coal (metric tons; 2001) 3,719,000 ([1997] 12,537,000); lignite (metric tons; 2001) 57,157,000 ([1997] 59,503,000); crude petroleum (barrels; 2001) 18,218,000 ([1997] 192,771,000); petroleum products (metric tons; 1997) 22,914,000 (25,336,000); natural gas (cu m; 2000) 611,800,000 ([1997] 10,420,000,-000). **Tourism** (2000): receipts $7,636,000,000; expenditures $1,711,000,000. **Household income and expenditure** (1994). Average household size (1999) 4.6; income per household LT 165,089,000 ($5,576); expenditure: food, tobacco, and café expenditures 38.5%, housing 22.8%, clothing 9.0%. **Population economically active** (1997): total 22,359,000; activity rate of total population 35.8% (participation rates: ages 15–64, 53.1%; female 26.8%; unemployed [2000] 6.6%). **Gross national product** (2000): $202,131,000,000 ($3,100 per capita). **Land use** (1994): forested 26.2%; meadows and pastures 16.1%; agricultural and under permanent cultivation 36.1%; other 21.6%.

## Foreign trade

**Imports** (2000-c.i.f.): $53,983,000,000 (mineral fuels 17.6%; nonelectrical machinery 14.3%; electrical machinery 11.2%; transport equipment 10.1%; iron and steel 5.1%; chemicals 3.7%). *Major import sources:* Germany 13.2%; Italy 8.0%; US 7.2%; France 6.5%; UK 5.0%. **Exports** (2000-f.o.b.): $27,324,000,000 (textiles and clothing 22.6%; electrical and electronic machinery 7.1%; vehicles 5.7%; iron and steel 5.7%). *Major export destinations:* Germany 18.8%; US 11.2%; Russia and Eastern Europe 10.8%; UK 7.4%; Italy 6.3%; France 6.0%.

## Transport and communications

**Transport.** *Railroads* (2000): length 8,671 km; passenger-km 6,122,000,000; metric ton-km cargo 10,032,000,000. *Roads* (2000): total length 383,-636 km (paved [1997] 25%). *Vehicles* (2000): passenger cars 4,283,080; trucks and buses 1,488,016. *Air transport* (2000): passenger-km 16,492,416; metric ton-km cargo 379,630,000; airports (1996) 26. **Communications,** in total units (units per 1,000 persons). Daily newspaper circulation (1996): 6,845,000 (111); radio receivers (1997): 11,300,000 (181); television receivers (1999): 21,500,000 (331); telephone main lines (2001): 18,900,000 (285); cellular telephone subscribers (2001): 20,000,000 (302); personal computers (2001): 2,700,000 (41); Internet users (2001): 2,500,000 (38).

## Education and health

**Educational attainment** (1993). Percentage of population age 25 and over having: no formal schooling 30.5%; incomplete primary education 6.6%; complete primary 40.4%; incomplete secondary 3.1%; complete secondary or higher 19.1%; unknown 0.3%. **Literacy** (1995): total population age 15 and over literate 33,605,000 (82.3%); males literate 19,191,000 (91.7%); females literate 14,414,000 (72.4%). **Health:** physicians (1997) 73,659 (1 per 853 persons); hospital beds (1997) 144,984 (1 per 431 persons); infant mortality rate per 1,000 live births (2000) 48.9. **Food** (2000): daily per capita caloric intake 3,416 (vegetable products 89%, animal products 11%); 136% of FAO recommended minimum.

## Military

**Total active duty personnel** (2002): 515,100 (army 78.0%, navy 10.3%, air force 11.7%). **Military expenditure as percentage of GNP** (1999): 5.3% (world 2.4%); per capita expenditure $154.

## Background

Turkey's early history corresponds to that of Asia Minor, the Byzantine Empire, and the Ottoman Empire. Byzantine rule emerged when Constantine the Great made Constantinople (now Istanbul) his capital. The Ottoman Empire, begun in the 12th century, dominated for more than 600 years; it ended in 1918 after the Young Turk revolt precipitated its demise. Under the leadership of Mustafa Kemal Ataturk, a republic was proclaimed in 1923, and the caliphate was abolished in 1924. Turkey remained neutral throughout most of World War II, siding with the Allies in 1945. Since the war it has alternated between civil and military governments and has had several conflicts with Greece over Cyprus. The 1990s saw political and civic turmoil between Islamists and secularists.

## Recent Developments

In 2003 Turkey found itself in the vanguard of the political and strategic battles that preceded the US-UK invasion of Iraq. Not only was Turkey a Muslim state that bordered Iraq, but a large and fractious Kurdish nation lived on both sides of the border. Further, Turkey was a member of NATO and host of US military facilities, including key air bases, as well as an aspirant to membership in the EU. In November 2002, after his party's election victory, the country's most powerful politician, Recep Tayyip Erdogan, asked for UN authorization of any military action against Saddam Hussein in Iraq.

Early in 2003 Turkey led regional diplomatic efforts to avert the gathering war on Iraq. When these fizzled out, the government indicated its willingness to grant permission to the US to use bases in Turkey to launch attacks on Iraq. Immediately coming under intense popular pressures, Ankara upped the ante and demanded a $32 billion aid package in exchange for Turkish participation. For its part, the US-UK coalition was not eager to encourage the presence of Turkish ground troops in northern Iraq, fully aware that Turkey's key objective was to prevent any possibility of an autonomous Kurdish state taking hold there—which, of course, was exactly what the Kurds were seeking. In March Parliament astonished everyone and denied permission for deployment of US troops in its territory. Later, Turkey agreed to allow Coalition overflights of its territory but insisted on its right to send troops into northern Iraq if it saw the need to do so.

Erdogan was named prime minister in March. Shortly thereafter, Turks were enraged by a decision from the European Court of Human Rights that the 1999 trial of Kurdish rebel leader Abdullah Ocalan had not been fair. The same week, a Turkish court banned the largest pro-Kurdish party in Turkey, alleging it had links with international terrorists.

**Internet resources:** <www.turizm.gov.tr>

# Turkmenistan

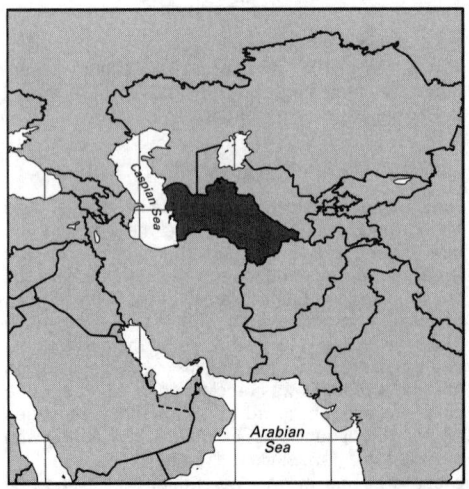

**Official name:** Turkmenistan. **Form of government:** unitary republic with one legislative body (Majlis [Parliament; 50]). **Head of state and government:** President Saparmurad Niyazov (from 1990). **Capital:** Ashgabat. **Official language:** Turkmen. **Official religion:** none. **Monetary unit:** manat; valuation (11 Jul 2003) $1 = 5,195.10 manat.

## Demography

**Area:** 188,500 sq mi, 488,100 sq km. **Population** (2002): 4,946,000. **Density** (2002): persons, per sq mi 26.2, persons per sq km 10.1. **Urban** (2002): 44.9%. **Sex distribution** (2001): male 49.44%; female 50.56%. **Age breakdown** (2001): under 15, 37.9%; 15–29, 27.9%; 30–44, 23.7%; 45–59, 6.5%; 60–74, 3.5%; 75 and over, 0.5%. **Ethnic composition** (1997): Turkmen 77.0%; Uzbek 9.2%; Russian 6.7%; Kazakh 2.0%; Tatar 0.8%; other 4.3%. **Religious affiliation** (1995): Muslim (mostly Sunnī) 87.0%; Russian Orthodox 2.4%; other (mostly nonreligious) 10.6%. **Major cities** (1999 est.): Ashgabat 605,000; Turkmenabad 203,000; Dashhowuz 165,000; Mary 123,000; Nebitdag 119,000. **Location:** central Asia, bordering Kazakhstan, Uzbekistan, Afghanistan, Iran, and the Caspian Sea.

## Vital statistics

**Birth rate** per 1,000 population (2001): 28.6 (world avg. 21.2); (1998) legitimate 96.2%; illegitimate 3.8%. **Death rate** per 1,000 population (2001): 8.0 (world avg. 8.9). **Natural increase rate** per 1,000 population (2001): 20.6 (world avg. 12.3). **Total fertility rate** (avg. births per childbearing woman; 2001): 3.5. **Marriage rate** per 1,000 population (1998): 5.4. **Divorce rate** per 1,000 population (1994): 1.5. **Life expectancy** at birth (2001): male 57.5 years; female 64.8 years.

## National economy

**Budget** (1999). *Revenue:* 3,693,100,000,000 manat (value-added tax 25.6%, pension and social security fund 22.5%, repayments of scheduled gas 13.0%, excise tax 10.2%, personal income tax 6.1%). *Expenditures:* 3,894,300,000,000 manat (education 26.9%, pension and social security 15.6%, defense and security 14.9%, health 14.1%, agriculture 5.7%). **Public debt** (external, outstanding; 2000): $1,731,000,000. **Production** (metric tons except as noted). *Agriculture, forestry, fishing* (2001): seed cotton 1,800,000, wheat 1,200,000, vegetables and melons 347,000; livestock (number of live animals) 6,375,000 sheep and goats, 860,000 cattle, 5,000,000 poultry; roundwood (2000) 2,000,000 cu m; fish catch (1999) 9,292. *Mining and quarrying* (2000): gypsum 100,000, sodium sulfate 60,000, sulfur 9,000. *Manufacturing* (value of production in '000,000 manat; 1994): ferrous and nonferrous metals 278; machinery and metalworks 223; food products 129. *Energy production (consumption):* electricity (kW-hr; 1997) 9,400,000,000 (6,750,000,000); crude petroleum (barrels; 2001) 58,000,000 (19,000,000); petroleum products (metric tons; 1997) 3,886,000 (2,332,000); natural gas (cu m; 2001) 46,439,-000,000 (7,362,000,000). **Household income and expenditure.** Average household size (1998) 5.0;

*1 metric ton = about 1.1 short tons;	1 kilometer = 0.6 mi (statute);	1 metric ton-km cargo = about 0.68 short ton-mi cargo;	c.i.f.: cost, insurance, and freight;	f.o.b.: free on board*

sources of income (1996): wages and salaries 70.6%, pensions and grants 20.9%, self-employment (mainly agricultural income) 2.3%, nonwage income of workers 1.1%; expenditure (1996): goods 26.8%, services 13.5%, taxes and other payments 9.4%. **Land use** (1994): forested 8.2%; meadows and pastures 61.6%; agricultural and under permanent cultivation 3.0%; other 27.2%. **Population economically active** (1999): total 1,838,700; activity rate of total population 38.8% (participation rates [1995]: ages 16–59 [male], 16–54 [female] 81.0%; female 41.0%; unemployed 3.0%). **Gross national product** (2000): $3,886,000,000 ($750 per capita). **Tourism:** receipts from visitors (1998) $192,000,000; expenditures (1997) $125,000,000.

## Foreign trade

**Imports** (1998-c.i.f. in balance of trade): $1,137,-100,000 (machinery and equipment 39.1%, food products 8.0%, chemicals 5.1%, medicines 1.8%). *Major import sources:* Ukraine 16.1%; Turkey 13.1%; Russia 11.6%; Germany 6.9%; US 6.4%; Uzbekistan 5.2%; Armenia 3.0%. **Exports** (1998): $614,100,000 (natural gas and oil products 54.6%, cotton 22.0%, electricity 5.2%). *Major export destinations:* Iran 24.1%; Turkey 18.3%; Azerbaijan 6.9%; UK 4.9%; Russia 4.7%; Tajikistan 4.5%.

## Transport and communications

**Transport.** *Railroads* (1998): length 2,313 km; passenger-km (1996) 2,104,000,000, metric ton-km cargo (1996) 6,779,000,000. *Roads* (1999): total length 24,000 km (paved 81%). *Vehicles* (1995): passenger cars 220,000; trucks and buses 58,200. *Air transport* (2001; Turkmenavia only): passenger-km 1,631,000,000; metric ton-km cargo 35,000,000; airports (2000) with scheduled flights 1. **Communications,** in total units (units per 1,000 persons). Radio receivers (1997): 1,225,000 (289); television receivers (1998): 865,000 (201); telephone main lines (2001): 387,600 (80); cellular telephone subscribers (2001): 9,500 (2.1); Internet users (2001): 8,000 (1.6).

## Education and health

**Educational attainment** (1989). Percentage of population age 25 and over having: primary education or no formal schooling 13.6%; some secondary 21.3%; completed secondary and some postsecondary 56.8%; higher 8.3%. **Literacy** (1999): total population age 15 and over literate 98.0%. **Health** (1995): physicians 13,500 (1 per 330 persons); hospital beds 46,000 (1 per 97 persons); infant mortality rate per 1,000 live births (2001) 73.2. **Food** (2000): daily per capita caloric intake 2,675 (vegetable products 83%, animal products 17%); 104% of FAO recommended minimum.

## Military

**Total active duty personnel** (2001): 17,500 (army 82.9%; air force 17.1%). **Military expenditure as percentage of GNP** (1999): 3.4% (world 2.4%); per capita expenditure $122.

## Background

The earliest traces of human settlement in Central Asia, dating back to Paleolithic times, have been

 Present proven natural gas reserves of more than one trillion cubic feet place Turkmenistan among the world's critical suppliers of energy well into the 21st century. Its claims on some of the huge Caspian Sea reserves of petroleum, as well as natural gas, promise to make its position even more important.

found in Turkmenistan. The nomadic, tribal Turkmen probably entered the area in the 11th century AD. They were conquered by the Russians in the early 1880s, and the region became part of Russian Turkistan. It was organized as the Turkmen Soviet Socialist Republic in 1924 and became a constituent republic of the USSR in 1925. The country gained full independence from the USSR in 1991 under the name Turkmenistan. From 1990 the country was ruled by the ever more autocratic and mercurial strongman Saparmurad Niyazov.

## Recent Developments

Throughout 2002 Niyazov continued to destabilize his own government through an increasingly rapid turnover of top officials and the concentration of progressively more tasks in the hands of fewer and fewer ministries. In early August 2002 the Turkmen National Council voted to change the names of the months and days. Henceforth, for example, January would be known as Turkmenbashi, the official name by which President Niyazov is known. A summit of leaders of the Caspian littoral states held in Ashgabat in April failed to agree on the division of the sea. Niyazov actively sought to revive a project to build a pipeline from Turkmenistan across Afghanistan to Pakistan. While the other two countries were enthusiastic about the project, potential investors were cautious. In April 2003 the Royal Dutch/Shell oil company announced that it was closing its offices in Turkmenistan because it could see no prospects for realistic projects in the country.

**Internet resources:** <www.turkmenistanembassy.org>

# Tuvalu

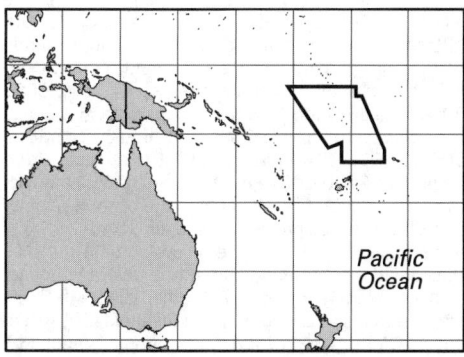

Pacific Ocean

**Official name:** Tuvalu. **Form of government:** constitutional monarchy with one legislative house (Parliament [12]). **Chief of state:** British Queen Elizabeth II (from 1952), represented by Governor-General Tomasi Puapua (from 1998). **Head of government:**

Prime Minister Saufatu Sopoanga (from 2 Aug 2002). **Capital:** government offices are at Vaiaku, Fongafale islet, on Funafuti Atoll. **Official language:** none. **Official religion:** none. **Monetary units:** 1 Tuvalu dollar = 1 Australian dollar ($T = $A) = 100 Tuvalu and Australian cents; valuation (7 Jul 2003) US$1 = $A 1.47.

## Demography

**Area:** 9.90 sq mi, 25.63 sq km. **Population** (2002): 10,900. **Density** (2002): persons per sq mi 1,101, persons per sq km 425. **Urban** (2002): 54.0%. **Sex distribution** (2000): male 48.65%; female 51.35%. **Age breakdown** (2000): under 15, 33.7%; 15–29, 22.1%; 30–44, 21.9%; 45–59, 12.8%; 60–74, 7.3%; 75 and over, 2.2%. **Ethnic composition** (2000): Tuvaluan (Polynesian) 96.3%; mixed (Pacific Islander/European/Asian) 1.0%; Micronesian 1.0%; European 0.5%; other 1.2%. **Religious affiliation** (1995): Church of Tuvalu (Congregational) 85.4%; Seventh-day Adventist 3.6%; Roman Catholic 1.4%; Jehovah's Witness 1.1%; Baha'i 1.0%; other 7.5%. *Major locality* (1995): Fongafale, on Funafuti atoll, 4,000. **Location:** western Pacific Ocean, lying east of Papua New Guinea near the equator.

## Vital statistics

**Birth rate** per 1,000 population (2002): 21.4 (world avg. 21.2); (1989) legitimate 82.2%; illegitimate 17.8%. **Death rate** per 1,000 population (2002): 7.5 (world avg. 8.9). **Natural increase rate** per 1,000 population (2002): 13.9 (world avg. 12.3). **Total fertility rate** (avg. births per childbearing woman; 2002): 3.1. **Life expectancy** at birth (2002): male 64.8 years; female 69.2 years.

## National economy

**Budget** (1996). *Revenue:* $A 7,905,000 (nontax revenues 67.2%; taxes 32.8%). *Expenditures:* $A 8,203,000 (1987; capital [development] expenditures 68.9%, of which marine transport 20.7%, education 13.0%, fisheries 5.6%, health 3.1%; current expenditures 31.1%). **Public debt** (external; 1993): US$6,000,000. **Gross national product** (1998): US$14,700,000 (US$1,400 per capita). **Production** (metric tons except as noted). *Agriculture, forestry, fishing* (1999): coconuts 1,800, bananas 180, eggs 12; livestock (number of live animals) 27,000 chickens, 12,600 pigs, 7,000 ducks; fish catch (1998) 400. *Manufacturing:* tiny amounts of copra, handicrafts, and garments. Overseas employment (2000) of Tuvaluan seafarers contributes about US$5,000,000 annually to the Tuvalu economy. *Energy production (consumption):* electricity (kW-hr; 1992) 1,300,000 (1,300,000). **Tourism** (1998): receipts from visitors US$200,000. **Population economically active** (1991): total 5,910; activity rate of total population 65.3% (participation rates: ages 15–64, 85.5%; female [1979] 51.3%; unemployed [1979] 4.0%). **Household income and expenditure.** Average household size (1994): Funafuti 7.0, other islands 5.8; average annual gross income per household (1994): Funafuti $A 12,012 (US$8,789), other islands $A 3,536 (US$2,587); sources of income (1987): agriculture and other 45.0%, cash economy only 38.0%, overseas remittances 17.0%; expenditure (1992):

food 45.5%, housing and household operations 11.5%, transportation 10.5%, alcohol and tobacco 10.5%, clothing 7.5%, other 14.5%. **Land use** (1987): agricultural and under permanent cultivation 73.6%; scrub 16.1%; other 10.3%.

## Foreign trade

**Imports** (1999): $A 16,461,000 (food 26%, machinery and transport equipment 25%, refined petroleum 9%, chemicals and chemical products 5%, beverages and tobacco 5%). *Major import sources:* Australia 38%; Fiji 32%; New Zealand 11%; Japan 6%; China 2%. **Exports** (1999): $A 2,108,000 (primarily copra, stamps, and handicrafts). *Major export destinations* (1995): South Africa 64%; Colombia 9%; Belgium-Luxembourg 9%.

## Transport and communications

**Transport.** *Roads* (2000): total length 28 km (paved, none). *Air transport:* airports (1997) 1. **Communications,** in total units (units per 1,000 persons). Radio receivers (1997): 4,000 (384); television receivers (1996): 100 (13); telephone main lines (1999): 630 (55).

## Education and health

**Educational attainment** (mid-1990s). Percentage of population age 15 and over (on Funafuti) having: no formal schooling through completed primary education 31.9%; some secondary 46.6%; completed secondary to some higher 18.6%; completed higher 2.9%. **Literacy** (1990): total population literate in Tuvaluan 8,593 (95.0%); **Literacy** in English estimated at 45.0%. **Health** (1999): physicians 8 (1 per 1,375 persons); hospital beds (1990) 30 (1 per 302 persons); infant mortality rate per 1,000 live births (2002): 22.0.

## Military

**Total active duty personnel:** none; Tuvalu relies on Australian-trained volunteers from Fiji and Papua New Guinea.

## Background

The original Polynesian settlers of Tuvalu probably came mainly from Samoa or Tonga. The islands were sighted by the Spanish in the 16th century. Europeans settled there in the 19th century and intermarried with Tuvaluans. During this period Peruvian slave traders, known as "blackbirders," decimated the population. In 1856 the US claimed the four southern islands for guano mining. Missionaries from Europe arrived in 1865 and rapidly converted the islanders to Christianity. In 1892 Tuvalu joined the British Gilbert Islands, a protectorate that became the Gilbert and Ellice Islands Colony in 1916. Tuvaluans voted in 1974 for separation from the Gilberts (now Kiribati), whose people are Micronesian. Tuvalu gained independence in 1978, and in 1979 the US relinquished its claims. Elections were held in 1981, and a revised constitution was adopted in 1986. In recent decades, the government has tried to find overseas job opportunities for its citizens.

---

*1 metric ton = about 1.1 short tons;    1 kilometer = 0.6 mi (statute);    1 metric ton-km cargo = about 0.68 short ton-mi cargo;    c.i.f.: cost, insurance, and freight;    f.o.b.: free on board*

## Recent Developments

In the July 2002 elections, 39 candidates, including 2 women, vied for seats in the 15-member Parliament; 6 sitting members, including Prime Minister Koloa Talake, lost their seats. The new prime minister was Saufatu Sopoaga, the former minister of finance. At the World Summit on Sustainable Development in Johannesburg, South Africa, in August, Tuvalu highlighted the environmental vulnerability of its coral islands to global warming, rising sea levels, and cyclonic storms. It particularly attacked the position of the US (the world's largest producer of greenhouse gases) and Australia (which produced the highest levels of greenhouse gases on a per capita basis). Tuvalu threatened to take legal action in international courts. Australia rejected the claims and announced an aid package for improved meteorological services and projects that would allow Pacific island countries to adapt to changing climatic conditions.

Internet resources:
<www.tcsp.com/destinations/tuvalu/index.shtml>

# Uganda

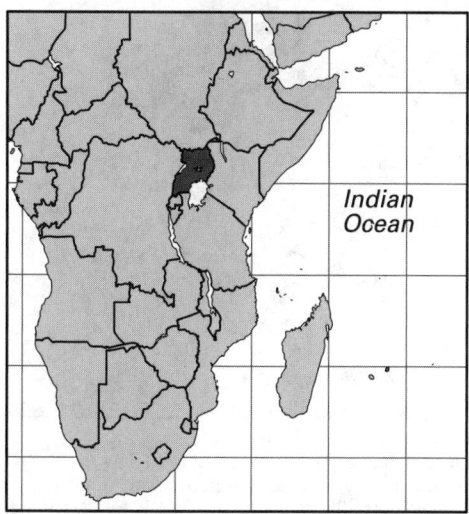

Indian Ocean

**Official name:** Republic of Uganda. **Form of government:** nonparty republic with one legislative house (Parliament [305, including 10 unelected members]). **Head of state and government:** President Yoweri Museveni (from 1986) assisted by Prime Minister Apolo Nsibambi (from 1999). **Capital:** Kampala. **Official language:** English. **Official religion:** none. **Monetary unit:** 1 Uganda shilling (U Sh) = 100 cents; valuation (7 Jul 2003) $1 = U Sh 1,991.

## Demography

**Area:** 93,065 sq mi, 241,038 sq km (includes 16,984 sq mi [43,989 sq km] water area). **Population (2002):** 24,378,000. **Density (2002):** persons per sq mi 320.4, persons per sq km 123.7. **Urban (1999–2000):** 13.0%. **Sex distribution (2002):** male 49.11%; female 50.89%. **Age breakdown (2000):** under 15, 51.1%; 15–29, 26.2%; 30–44, 13.6%; 45–59, 5.7%; 60–74, 2.9%; 75 and over, 0.5%. **Ethnolinguistic composition (1991):** Ganda 18.1%;

Nkole 10.7%; Kiga 8.4%; Soga 8.2%; Lango 5.9%; Lugbara 4.7%; Gisu 4.5%; Acholi 4.4%. **Religious affiliation (1995):** Christian 66%, of which Roman Catholic 33%, Protestant 33% (of which mostly Anglican); traditional beliefs 18%; Muslim 16%. **Major cities (1991):** Kampala urban agglomeration 1,274,000 (2001); Jinja 61,000; Mbale 53,600; Masaka 49,100; Gulu 42,800. **Location:** eastern Africa, bordering The Sudan, Kenya, Lake Victoria, Tanzania, Rwanda, and the Dem. Rep. of the Congo.

## Vital statistics

**Birth rate** per 1,000 population (2000): 48.0 (world avg. 22.5). **Death rate** per 1,000 population (2000): 22.4 (world avg. 9.0). **Natural increase rate** per 1,000 population (2000): 25.6 (world avg. 13.5). **Total fertility rate** (avg. births per childbearing woman; 2000): 7.0. **Life expectancy** at birth (2000): male 42.2 years; female 43.7 years.

## National economy

**Budget (1997–98).** *Revenue:* U Sh 1,193,100,000,-000 (taxes 62.7%, of which customs duties 25.5%, sales taxes 20.2%, income taxes 10.5%; grants 33.3%). *Expenditures:* U Sh 1,239,900,000,000 (current expenditures 58.7%, of which wages and salaries 20.6%, education 16.6%, security 11.0%, health 4.3%; capital expenditures 41.3%). **Public debt** (external, outstanding; 2000): $2,997,000,000. **Production** (metric tons except as noted). *Agriculture, forestry, fishing* (1999): plantains 9,400,000, cassava 3,400,000, sweet potatoes 2,520,000; livestock (number of live animals) 5,700,000 cattle, 3,650,000 goats, 23,000,000 chickens; roundwood (1998) 15,649,000 cu m; fish catch (2000) 355,831. *Mining and quarrying* (2000): gold (officially reported export figure) 7,303 kg. *Manufacturing* (1998): cement 278,800; sugar 93,000; soap 36,100. *Energy production (consumption):* electricity (kW-hr; 1998) 1,282,800,000 (872,000,000); petroleum products (metric tons; 1997) none (330,000). **Tourism (1999):** receipts from visitors $149,000,000; expenditures by nationals abroad $141,000,000. **Gross national product (2000):** $6,699,000,000 ($300 per capita). **Population economically active (1991):** total 8,365,000; activity rate of total population 49.6% (participation rates: ages 15–64, 78.9%; female 35.2%). **Household income and expenditure (1999–2000).** Average household size 5.2; income per household U Sh 141,000 ($91); sources of income: wages and self-employment 78.0%, transfers 13.0%, rent 9.0%; expenditure: food and beverages 51.0%, rent, energy, and services 17.0%, education 7.0%, household durable goods 6.0%, transportation 5.0%, health 4.0%. **Land use (1994):** forest 31.5%; pasture 9.1%; agriculture 34.0%; other 25.4%.

## Foreign trade

**Imports (1999–c.i.f.):** $1,015,200,000 (1998; machinery and apparatus 18.5%, food and live animals 11.4%, road vehicles 11.0%, refined petroleum 10.1%, pharmaceuticals 4.8%). *Major import sources:* Kenya 23.8%; UK 10.2%; Japan 8.1%; India 6.4%; US 5.6%; UAE 5.5%. **Exports (1999–f.o.b.):** $505,700,000 (unroasted coffee 52.8%, fish waste 8.0%, nonmonetary gold [excl. gold ores and concentrates] 6.6%, cotton 5.8%, fresh fish 4.7%). *Major export destinations:* UK 18.0%; Southern African Customs Union 6.5%; Kenya 6.3%; Singapore 4.9%; Switzerland 4.8%.

## Transport and communications

**Transport.** *Railroads* (1998): route length 1,241 km; passenger-km (1996) 27,000,000; metric ton-km cargo (1996) 236,000,000. *Roads* (1996): total length 26,800 km (paved 7.7%). *Vehicles* (1996): passenger cars 35,361; trucks and buses 48,430. *Air transport* (1997): passenger-km 52,117,000; metric ton-km cargo 5,000,000; airports (1998) 1. **Communications,** in total units (units per 1,000 persons). Daily newspaper circulation (1997): 40,000 (2.1); radio receivers (1997): 2,600,000 (130); television receivers (1998): 580,000 (28.0); telephone main lines (2001): 63,700 (2.8); cellular telephone subscribers (2001): 322,700 (14); personal computers (2001): 70,000 (3.1); Internet users (2001): 60,000 (2.7).

## Education and health

**Educational attainment** (1991). Percentage of population age 25 and over having: no formal schooling or less than one full year 46.9%; primary education 42.1%; secondary 10.5%; higher 0.5%. **Literacy** (1999–2000): population age 10 and over literate 65.0%; males literate 74.0%; females literate 57.0%. **Health** (1993): physicians 840 (1 per 22,399 persons); hospital beds (1989) 20,136 (1 per 817 persons); infant mortality rate per 1,000 live births (2000) 93.3. **Food** (2000): daily per capita caloric intake 2,359 (vegetable products 94%, animal products 6%); 101% of FAO recommended minimum.

## Military

**Total active duty personnel** (2001): 50,000–60,000. **Military expenditure as percentage of GNP** (1999): 2.3% (world 2.4%); per capita expenditure $6.

## Background

By the 19th century the region around Uganda comprised several separate kingdoms inhabited by various peoples, including Bantu- and Nilotic-speaking tribes. Arab traders reached the area in the 1840s. The native kingdom of Buganda was visited by the first European explorers in 1862. Protestant and Roman Catholic missionaries arrived in the 1870s, and the development of religious factions led to persecution and civil strife. In 1894 Buganda was formally proclaimed a British protectorate. As Uganda, it gained its independence in 1962, and in 1967 it adopted a republican constitution. The civilian government was overthrown in 1971 and replaced by a military regime under Idi Amin. His invasion of Tanzania in late 1978 resulted in the collapse of his regime. In 1985 the civilian government was again deposed by the military, which in turn was overthrown in 1986. A constituent assembly enacted a new constitution in 1995.

## Recent Developments

In August 2002 Pres. Yoweri Museveni accused international donor agencies of undue interference in the affairs of African states, and, at the Earth Summit

meeting in Johannesburg, South Africa, in September, he charged the IMF and nongovernmental organizations with inhibiting environmental improvements to Uganda. These attempts to assert his country's sovereignty came at a time of difficulty for Uganda. The world price for coffee, the country's chief export commodity, had fallen from about $400 million in 1994–95 to $90 million in 2001–02. Many farmers abandoned coffee in favor of the more profitable cocoa or vanilla. Operations by the rebel Lord's Resistance Army in the north caused grave concern. In March the government launched Operation Iron Fist, aimed at putting an end to the rebellion. Uganda's military operations against the Democratic Republic of the Congo, already considerably reduced, came nearer to a conclusion. In September Uganda withdrew more than 2,000 of its troops, with the rest—1,000 in all—remaining until its western border was secure.

**Internet resources:** <www.visituganda.com>

# Ukraine

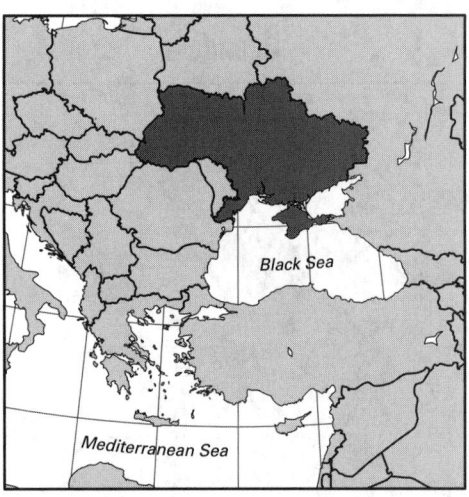

**Official name:** Ukrayina (Ukraine). **Form of government:** unitary multiparty republic with a single legislative body (Supreme Council [450]). **Head of state:** President Leonid Kuchma (from 1994). **Head of government:** Prime Minister Viktor Yanukovich (from 21 Nov 2002). **Capital:** Kiev (Kyyiv). **Official language:** Ukrainian. **Official religion:** none. **Monetary unit:** hryvnya (pl. hryvnyas); valuation (7 Jul 2003) $1 = 5.34 hryvnyas.

## Demography

**Area:** 603,700 sq km. **Population** (2002): 48,120,000. **Density** (2002): persons per sq mi 206.4, persons per sq km 79.7. **Urban** (2002): 68.0%. **Sex distribution** (2001): male 46.25%; female 53.75%. **Age breakdown** (2001): under 15, 17.3%; 15–29, 22.3%; 30–44, 21.7%; 45–59, 17.8%; 60–74, 15.7%; 75 and over, 5.2%. **Ethnic composition** (2000): Ukrainian 70.4%; Russian 20.0%; Polish 2.3%; Rom (Gypsy) 1.3%; Ruthenian 1.1%; other/unspecified 4.9%. **Religious affiliation** (1995): Ukrainian Orthodox (Russian

*1 metric ton = about 1.1 short tons;   1 kilometer = 0.6 mi (statute);   1 metric ton-km cargo = about 0.68 short ton-mi cargo;   c.i.f.: cost, insurance, and freight;   f.o.b.: free on board*

patriarchy) 19.5%; Ukrainian Orthodox (Kiev patriarchy) 9.7%; Ukrainian Catholic (Uniate) 7.0%; Protestant 3.6%; other Orthodox 1.6%; Roman Catholic 1.2%; Jewish 0.9%; other (mostly nonreligious) 56.5%. **Major cities** (2001): Kiev 2,602,000; Kharkiv 1,470,000; Dnipropetrovsk 1,064,000; Odessa 1,029,000; Donetsk 1,016,000. **Location:** eastern Europe bordering Belarus, Russia, the Black Sea, Romania, Moldova, Hungary, Slovakia, and Poland.

## Vital statistics

**Birth rate** per 1,000 population (2001): 9.3 (world avg. 21.2); (1993) legitimate 87.0%; illegitimate 13.0%. **Death rate** per 1,000 population (2001): 16.4 (world avg. 8.9). **Natural increase rate** per 1,000 population (2001): –7.1 (world avg. 12.3). **Total fertility rate** (avg. births per childbearing woman; 2001): 1.3. **Life expectancy** at birth (2001): male 60.6 years; female 72.0 years.

## National economy

**Budget** (2000). *Revenue:* 24,792,000,000 hryvnyas (tax revenue 87.0%, of which taxes on goods and services 29.1%, payroll tax 26.9%, income tax 24.8%, excise tax 2.6%, property tax 2.2%, other 1.4%; nontax revenue and grants 13.0%). *Expenditures:* 25,100,000,000 hryvnyas (social security 37.5%; education 11.6%; debt payment 8.7%; health 8.3%; defense 3.5%). **Production** (metric tons except as noted). *Agriculture, forestry, fishing* (2001): wheat 21,333,000, sugar beets 15,489,000, potatoes 13,500,000; livestock (number of live animals) 9,914,000 cattle, 9,078,000 pigs, 1,770,000 sheep and goats; roundwood (2000) 5,920,000 cu m; fish catch (1999) 441,700. *Mining and quarrying* (1999): iron ore 47,709,000; manganese (metal content) 675,000; uranium 500,000. *Manufacturing* (value of production in '000,000 hryvnyas; 1998): iron and steel 14,525; food and beverages 12,974; nonelectrical machinery 3,838. *Energy production (consumption):* electricity (kW-hr; 2000) 171,000,000,000 ([1999] 168,600,000,000); hard coal (2001) 82,896,000,000 ([1997] 81,509,000,000); lignite (2001) 1,035,000 ([1997] 1,915,000); crude petroleum (barrels; 2001) 27,150,000 ([2000] 126,290,000); petroleum products (barrels; 1997) 11,867,000 (15,468,000); natural gas (cu m; 2001) 15,954,000,000 ([1999] 78,013,000,000). **Population economically active** (1999): total 21,824,000; activity rate of total population 43.6% (participation rates: ages 16–59 [male] 15–64 [female] 56.6%; female [1994] 51.0%; unemployed [2000] 6.4%). **Gross national product** (2000): $34,565,000,000 ($700 per capita). **Public debt** (external; 2000): $8,139,000,000. **Tourism** (1999): receipts $2,124,000,000; expenditures $1,774,000,000. **Household income and expenditure** (1996). Average household size (1998) 3.0; income per household (1996) 4,968 hryvnyas ($2,715); sources of income (1995): wages and salaries 66.4%, sales of agricultural products 9.3%, subsidies 6.9%, pensions 6.5%, remuneration from abroad 5.3%; expenditures (1995): food and beverages 43.1%, consumer goods 27.5%, services 7.2%, housing 6.7%, taxes 6.2%.

## Foreign trade

**Imports** (1999): $12,945,000,000 (fuel and energy products 39.9%; machinery 17.4%; chemicals and

chemical products 11.3%; food and raw materials 7.0%). *Major import sources:* Russia 47.9%; Germany 7.3%; Turkmenistan 3.7%; US 3.1%; Belarus 2.6%. **Exports** (1999): $12,463,000,000 (ferrous and nonferrous metals 39.1%; food and raw materials 11.4%; machinery 11.1%; chemicals and chemical products 11.1%). *Major export destinations:* Russia 19.2%; China 5.9%; Turkey 5.4%; Germany 4.5%; Italy 3.7%; US 3.5%.

## Transport and communications

**Transport.** *Railroads* (1999): length 22,302 km; passenger-km 47,600, 000,000; metric ton-km cargo 156,336,000,000. *Roads* (2000): total length 168,674 km (paved 97%). *Vehicles* (1997): passenger cars 5,210,774. *Air transport* (1998): passenger-km 1,720,000,000; metric ton-km cargo 188,000,000; airports (1998) with scheduled flights 12. **Communications,** in total units (units per 1,000 persons). Daily newspaper circulation (1996): 2,780,000 (54); radio receivers (1997): 45,050,000 (889); television receivers (1998): 21,000,000 (418); telephone main lines (2001): 10,669,600 (212); cellular telephone subscribers (2001): 2,224,600 (44); personal computers (2001): 920,000 (18); Internet users (2001): 600,000 (12).

## Education and health

**Educational attainment** (1989). Percentage of population age 15 and over having: some primary education 6.8%; completed primary 13.8%; some secondary 18.4%; completed secondary 31.1%; some postsecondary 19.5%; higher 10.4%. **Literacy** (1999): total population age 15 and over literate 99.6%; males literate 99.7%; females literate 99.5%. **Health** (1998): physicians 150,382 (1 per 334 persons); hospital beds 508,030 (1 per 99 persons); infant mortality rate per 1,000 live births (2001) 21.4. **Food** (2000): daily per capita caloric intake 2,871 (vegetable products 80%, animal products 20%); 112% of FAO recommended minimum.

## Military

**Total active duty personnel** (2001): 303,800 (army 49.8%, air force 31.6%, navy 4.3%, headquarters 14.3%). **Military expenditure as percentage of GNP** (1999): 3.0% (world 2.4%); per capita expenditure $103.

 **Did you know?** Lviv, the largest city of western Ukraine and a principal center of Ukrainian culture, has long been an economic and cultural crossroads. In 1998 the historic center was declared a UNESCO World Heritage Site because of its urban landscape displaying Eastern European, German, and Italian architectural traditions of different eras.

## Background

The area around Ukraine was invaded and occupied in the first millennium BC by the Cimmerians, Scythians, and Sarmatians, and in the first millennium AD by the Goths, Huns, Bulgars, Avars, Khazars, and Magyars. Slavic tribes settled there after the 4th century. Kiev was its chief town. The Mongol conquest in the mid-13th century decisively ended Kievan power. Ruled by Lithuania in the 14th century and Poland in the 16th century, it fell to Russian rule in the 18th century. The Ukrainian National Republic, established in 1917, declared its independence from Soviet Russia in 1918 but was reconquered in 1919; it was made the Ukrainian Soviet Socialist Republic of the USSR in 1922. The northwestern region was held by Poland from 1919 to 1939. Ukraine suffered a severe famine in 1932–33 under Soviet leader Joseph Stalin; over five million Ukrainians died of starvation in an unprecedented peacetime catastrophe. Overrun by Axis armies in 1941 in World War II, it was further devastated before being retaken by the Soviets in 1944. It was the site of the 1986 accident in Chernobyl, at a Soviet-built nuclear power plant. Ukraine declared independence in 1991. In recent years it has struggled both politically and economically.

## Recent Developments

Parliamentary balloting was held on 31 March 2002 in two stages: the election of 225 deputies based on party lists by proportional representation and the election of a further 225 in one-seat constituencies. In the former, Our Ukraine won 70 seats, the Communists 59, and For a United Ukraine, the party endorsed by Pres. Leonid Kuchma, 36 seats. In single-mandate constituencies, however, For a United Ukraine won 66 seats, and 18 independent deputies were persuaded to join its ranks. Our Ukraine won 42 seats, the Communists 7, and the Social Democratic Party 5. A government report of August 2002 indicated that some 13 million people (about 27%) were living below an official poverty line of $33 per month. The year was marked by industrial and military accidents, especially in the Donets Basin coal mines, perhaps the most dangerous workplace in the world. World attention also focused on Ukraine following a disaster at the Lviv air show on 27 July, when a fighter jet crashed shortly after takeoff, killing 76 people and injuring more than 100.

Internet resources: <www.ukremb.com>

## United Arab Emirates

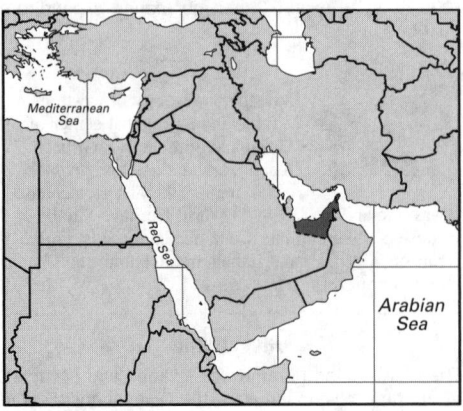

**Official name:** Al-Imarat al-'Arabiyah al-Muttahidah (United Arab Emirates). **Form of government:** federation of seven emirates with one advisory body (Federal National Council [40; all appointed seats]). **Chief of state:** President Sheikh Zaid ibn Sultan Al Nahayan (from 1971). **Head of government:** Prime Minister Sheikh Maktum ibn Rashid Al Maktum (from 1990). **Capital:** Abu Dhabi. **Official language:** Arabic. **Official religion:** Islam. **Monetary unit:** 1 UAE dirham (Dh) = 100 fils; valuation (7 Jul 2003) $1 = Dh 3.67.

## Demography

**Area:** 32,280 sq mi, 83,600 sq km. **Population** (2002): 3,550,000. **Density** (2002): persons per sq mi 110.0, persons per sq km 42.5. **Urban** (2001): 87.2%. **Sex distribution** (2001): male 67.54%; female 32.46%. **Age breakdown** (2001): under 15, 26.2%; 15–29, 29.2%; 30–44, 33.4%; 45–59, 9.6%; 60–74, 1.4%; 75 and over, 0.2%. **Ethnic composition** (2000): Arab 48.1%, of which U.A.E. Arab 12.2%, U.A.E Bedouin 9.4%, Egyptian Arab 6.2%, Omani Arab 4.1%, Saudi Arab 4.0%; South Asian 35.7%, of which Pashtun 7.1%, Balochi 7.1%, Malayali 7.1%; Persian 5.0%; Filipino 3.4%; white 2.4%; other 5.4%. **Religious affiliation** (1995): Muslim 96.0% (Sunni 80.0%, Shi'i 16.0%); other (mostly Christian and Hindu) 4.0%. **Major cities** (1995): Dubai 669,181; Abu Dhabi 398,695; Sharjah 320,095; Al-Ayn 225,970; Ajman 114,395. **Location:** the Middle East, bordering the Persian Gulf, the Gulf of Oman, Oman, Saudi Arabia, and Qatar.

## Vital statistics

**Birth rate** per 1,000 population (2001): 18.1 (world avg. 21.2). **Death rate** per 1,000 population (2001): 3.8 (world avg. 8.9). **Natural increase rate** per 1,000 population (2001): 14.3 (world avg. 12.3). **Total fertility rate** (avg. births per childbearing woman; 2001): 1.6. **Marriage rate** per 1,000 population (1999): 3.5. **Divorce rate** per 1,000 population (1999): 0.9. **Life expectancy** at birth (2001): male 71.8 years; female 76.9 years.

## National economy

**Budget** (1999). *Revenue:* Dh 52,003,000,000 (oil revenue 54.2%, non-oil revenue 45.8%). *Expenditures:* Dh 77,089,000,000 (current expenditures 66.2%, capital [development] expenditure 33.8%). **Gross national product** (1999): $52,098,000,000 ($17,730 per capita). **Tourism** (2000): total number of tourist arrivals 3,907,000. **Production** (metric tons except as noted). *Agriculture, forestry, fishing* (2000): tomatoes 780,000, dates 318,000, cantaloupes and watermelons 64,000; livestock (number of live animals) 1,200,000 goats, 467,281 sheep, 14,650,000 chickens; fish catch (1999) 117,607. *Mining and quarrying* (1998): sulfur 268,000; gypsum 110,000; chromite 54,000. *Manufacturing* (value of production in Dh '000,000; 1998): chemical products (including refined petroleum) 10,096; textiles and wearing apparel 2,397; fabricated metal products 1,999. *Energy production (consumption):* electricity (kW-hr; 1997) 20,571,-000,000 (20,571,000,000); crude petroleum (barrels; 2001) 740,000,000 ([1997] 86,000,000); pe-

*1 metric ton = about 1.1 short tons;    1 kilometer = 0.6 mi (statute);    1 metric ton-km cargo = about 0.68 short ton-mi cargo;    c.i.f.: cost, insurance, and freight;    f.o.b.: free on board*

troleum products (metric tons; 1997) 18,995,000 (7,190,000); natural gas (cu m; 2000) 39,000,-000,000 ([1997] 28,839,000,000). **Population economically active** (2001): total 1,947,000; activity rate of total population 59.2% (participation rates [1995]: over age 15, 55.4%; female 13.2%; unemployment [2000] 2.3%). **Household expenditure.** Average household size (1999) 6.1; expenditure (1991): rent, fuel, and light 23.9%, food 22.7%, transportation and communications 14.1%, durable household goods 11.6%, education, recreation, and entertainment 8.6%. **Land use** (1994): forested, virtually none; meadows and pastures 2.4%; agricultural and under permanent cultivation 0.5%; built-on, wasteland, and other 97.1%.

## Foreign trade

**Imports** (1997): Dh 109,100,000,000 (machinery and transport equipment 38.4%, basic manufactures 24.8%, food and live animals 9.7%, chemicals 6.1%, crude minerals 1.6%, mineral fuels 1.4%). *Major import sources:* Japan 10.2%; US 9.4%; UK 8.7%; China 8.0%; Germany 6.9%; India 5.8%; Italy 5.2%; South Korea 5.1%. **Exports** (1997): Dh 139,500,000,000 (domestic exports 76.0%, of which crude petroleum 37.6%, nonmonetary gold 11.8%, natural gas 7.1%, refined petroleum products 4.8%; reexports 24.0%). *Major export destinations:* Japan 36.2%; India 6.6%; Singapore 6.4%; South Korea 6.1%; Iran 3.7%; Oman 3.7%.

## Transport and communications

**Transport.** *Roads* (1999): total length 3,791 km (paved 100%). *Vehicles* (1996): passenger cars 201,000; trucks and buses 56,950. *Air transport* (2000; Emirates Air and one-fourth apportionment of Gulf Air): passenger-km 19,552,500,000; metric ton-km cargo 1,427,500,000; airports (1999) with scheduled flights 6. **Communications,** in total units (units per 1,000 persons). Daily newspaper circulation (1996): 384,000 (170); radio receivers (1997): 820,000 (355); television receivers (1999): 740,000 (252); telephone main lines (2001): 1,053,000 (397); cellular telephone subscribers (2001): 1,909,300 (720); personal computers (2001): 420,000 (158); Internet users (2001): 900,000 (339).

## Education and health

**Educational attainment** (1995). Percentage of population age 10 and over having: no formal schooling 47.6%; primary education 27.8%; secondary 16.0%, higher 8.6%. **Literacy** (1995): total population age 15 and over literate 79.2%; males literate 78.9%; females literate 79.8%. **Health** (1999): physicians 6,059 (1 per 485 persons); hospital beds 7,448 (1 per 394 persons); infant mortality rate per 1,000 live births (2001) 16.7. **Food** (2000): daily per capita caloric intake 3,192 (vegetable products 75%, animal products 25%); 132% of FAO recommended minimum.

## Military

**Total active duty personnel** (2001): 65,000 (army 90.8%, navy 3.1%, air force 6.2%). Military expenditure as percentage of GDP (1999): 4.1% (world 2.4%); per capita expenditure $935.

## Background

The Persian Gulf was the location of important trading centers as early as Sumerian times. Its people converted to Islam in Muhammad's lifetime. The Portuguese entered the region in the early 16th century, and the British East India Company arrived about 100 years later. In 1820 the British exacted a peace treaty with local rulers along the coast of the eastern Arabian Peninsula. The area formerly called the Pirate Coast became known as the Trucial Coast. In 1892 the rulers agreed to restrict foreign relations to Britain. Though the British administered the region from 1853, they never assumed sovereignty; each state maintained full internal control. The states formed the Trucial States Council in 1960. In 1971 the sheiks terminated defense treaties with Britain and established the six-member federation. Ra's al-Khaymah joined it in 1972. The UAE aided coalition forces against Iraq in the Persian Gulf War (1991).

## Recent Developments

Sheikh Hamdan ibn Zayid Al Nahayan, the minister of state for foreign affairs and son of the president, made an official visit to Tehran in May 2002, seeking to ameliorate the tension that existed between his country and Iran. The UAE government worked closely with the US to combat terrorism by taking steps in banking and law enforcement designed to help close channels that might be used by al-Qaeda and other international terrorists. The UAE president, however, expressed opposition to US use of force against Iraq, saying in an October 2002 interview that "war never solves a problem." In March 2001 a major deal was struck with Qatar to develop Qatar's North Field natural gas and to import it by an undersea pipeline to Abu Dhabi and Dubai. In May 2002 the UAE selected Occidental Petroleum and a French company as new partners in the huge Dolphin gas project, which would involve the international pipeline.

**Internet resources:** <www.emirates.org>; <www.uae.org.ae>

# United Kingdom

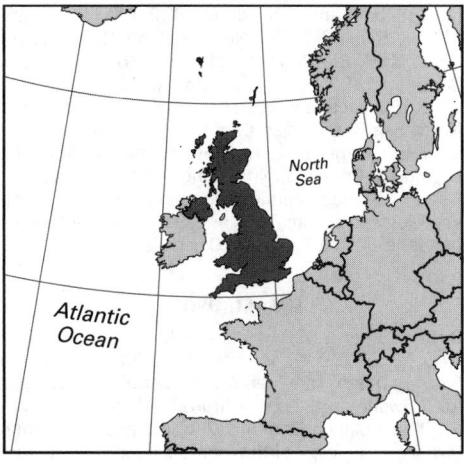

**Official name:** United Kingdom of Great Britain and Northern Ireland. **Form of government:** constitutional monarchy with two legislative houses (House of Lords [695]; House of Commons [659]). **Chief of state:** Queen Elizabeth II (from 1952). **Head of government:** Prime Minister Anthony C.L. (Tony) Blair (from 1997). **Capital:** London. **Official language:** English. **Official religion:** Churches of England and Scotland "established" (protected by the state, but not official) in their respective countries; no established church in Northern Ireland or Wales. **Monetary unit:** 1 pound sterling (£) = 100 new pence; valuation (7 Jul 2003) £1 = $1.67; $1 = £0.60.

## Demography

**Population** (2002): 60,178,000. **Area:** 94,248 sq mi, 244,101 sq km, of which England 50,351 sq mi, 130,410 sq km; Wales 8,015 sq mi, 20,758 sq km; Scotland 30,421 sq mi, 78,789 sq km; Northern Ireland (figures represent remainder) 5,461 sq mi, 14,144 sq km. **Density** (2002): persons per sq mi 638.5, persons per sq km 246.5. **Urban** (1999): 88.2%. **Age breakdown** (2001): under 15, 18.9%; 15–29, 18.8%; 30–44, 22.5%; 45–59, 18.9%; 60–74, 13.3%; 75 and over, 7.6%. **Ethnic composition** (1998): white 93.2%; black 1.8%, of which Caribbean origin 0.9%, African origin 0.7%; Asian Indian 1.7%; Pakistani 1.2%; Bangladeshi 0.5%; Chinese 0.2%; other and not stated 1.4%. **Sex distribution** (2001): male 48.62%; female 51.38%. **Religious affiliation** (2000): Christian 66.4%, of which Protestant 53.3% (Anglican 45.0%), Roman Catholic 9.6%, Orthodox 0.9%; Muslim 2.0%; Hindu 0.7%; Sikh 0.5%; Jewish 0.4%; other/nonreligious 30.0%. **Major cities** (2000): Greater London 7,375,100; Birmingham 1,010,400; Leeds 726,100; Glasgow 609,400; Sheffield 530,100; Bradford 486,100; Liverpool 457,300; Edinburgh 453,400; Manchester 439,500; Bristol 406,200; Kirklees 395,100; Fife 350,400. **Mobility** (1991; Great Britain only). Population living in the same residence as 1990: 90.1%; different residence, same country (of Great Britain) 8.1%; different residence, different country of Great Britain 1.2%; from outside Great Britain 0.6%. **Households** (1994; Great Britain only). Average household size 2.4; 1 person 27%, 2 persons 34%, 3 persons 16%, 4 persons 15%, 5 persons 6%, 6 or more persons 2%. Family household: 16,900,000 (72.0%), nonfamily 6,600,000 (28.0%, of which 1-person 12.0%). **Immigration** (1998): permanent residents 332,000, from Australia 7.5%, US 5.7%, New Zealand 4.2%, South Africa 3.6%, Bangladesh, India, and Sri Lanka 3.0%, Canada 1.5%, Pakistan 1.2%, other 73.3%, of which EU 8.7%. **Location:** western Europe, bordering the North Sea, the English Channel, the Celtic Sea, the Irish Sea, and Ireland. **Dependencies:** Anguilla, Bermuda, British Virgin Islands, Cayman Islands, Falkland Islands, Gibraltar, Guernsey, Isle of Man, Jersey, Montserrat, Pitcairn Island, Saint Helena and Dependencies, and Turks and Caicos Islands.

## Vital statistics

**Birth rate** per 1,000 population (2000): 11.4 (world avg. 22.5); (1999) legitimate 61.2%; illegitimate 38.8%. **Death rate** per 1,000 population (2000): 10.2 (world avg. 9.0). **Natural increase rate** per 1,000 population (2000): 1.2 (world avg. 13.5). **Total fertility rate** (avg. births per childbearing woman;

1999): 1.7. **Marriage rate** per 1,000 population (1999): 5.1. **Divorce rate** per 1,000 population (1999): 2.7. **Life expectancy** at birth (1998–2000): male 75.4 years; female 80.2 years.

## Social indicators

**Quality of working life** (2000). Average workweek (hours): male 41.2, female 37.4. Annual rate per 100,000 workers for (1996): injury or accident 553.6; death 1.0. Proportion of labor force (employed persons) insured for damages or income loss resulting from: injury 100%; permanent disability 100%; death 100%. Average days lost to labor stoppages per 1,000 employee workdays: 20. Principal means of transport to work (1991; London only): public transportation 81%, private automobile 15%, motor or pedal cycle 2%, other 2%. **Access to services** (1991; Great Britain only). Proportion of households having access to: bath or shower 98.7%; toilet 99.8%. **Social participation.** Eligible voters participating in last national election (May 1997): 71.4%. Population age 16 and over participating in voluntary work (1987; Great Britain only): 22%. Trade union membership in total workforce (1999) 27.0%. **Social deviance** (1998–99). Offense rate per 100,000 population for: theft and handling stolen goods 3,574.2; burglary 1,599.8; violence against the person 387.9; fraud and forgery 291.9; robbery 111.3; sexual offense 58.6. **Leisure** (1994). Favorite leisure activities (hours weekly): watching television 17.1; listening to radio 10.3; reading 8.8, of which books 3.8, newspapers 3.3; gardening 2.1. **Material well-being** (2000). Households possessing: automobile 72.0%, telephone 93.0%, television receiver 98.3% (color 95%; 1992), refrigerator 98.5%, washing machine 92.0%, central heating 91.0%, video recorder 87.0%.

## National economy

**Budget** (2000–01). *Revenue*: £372,561,000,000 (income tax 37.7%, customs and excise taxes 35.3%, social security contributions 15.8%). *Expenditures*: £354,867,000,000 (social protection 40.6%, health 15.5%, debt interest 7.6%, defense 7.5%). **Total national debt** (March 31, 2000): £426,239,200,000 ($679,894,200,000). **Gross national product** (at current market prices; 2000): $1,459,500,000,000 ($24,430 per capita). **Land use** (1994): forested 10.4%; meadows and pastures 45.9%; agricultural and under permanent cultivation 24.8%; other 18.9%. **Tourism** (2000): receipts from visitors $19,544,000,000; expenditures by nationals abroad $36,267,000,000. **Production** (metric tons except as noted). *Agriculture, forestry, fishing* (2001): wheat 12,060,000, sugar beets 10,000,000, barley 6,690,000, potatoes 6,647,000, rapeseed 1,129,000, oats 680,000, carrots 674,000, green peas 436,000; livestock (number of live animals) 42,000,000 sheep, 11,000,000 cattle, 6,500,000 pigs; roundwood (1999) 7,451,000 cu m; fish catch (1999) 992,552. *Mining and quarrying* (1999): china clay (kaolin) 2,304,000; ball clay and pottery clay 985,000. *Manufacturing* (value added in £'000,000; 1998): electrical and optical equipment 19,478; food and beverages 19,337; paper, printing, and publishing 17,717; iron and ferro-alloys 17,375; transport equipment 16,968; chemicals and chemical prod-

*1 metric ton = about 1.1 short tons;    1 kilometer = 0.6 mi (statute);    1 metric ton-km cargo = about 0.68 short ton-mi cargo;    c.i.f.: cost, insurance, and freight;    f.o.b.: free on board*

ucts 14,582; machinery and equipment 13,295; textiles and leather products 6,704. *Energy production (consumption)*: electricity (kW-hr; 2000) 341,808,-000,000 ([1997] 361,529,000,000); hard coal (metric tons; 2000) 31,200,000 ([1999] 58,800,000); crude petroleum (barrels; 2000) 884,273,000 (620,500,000); petroleum products (metric tons; 1997) 89,779,000 (72,673,000); natural gas (cu m; 2000) 128,425,000,000 ([1997] 102,506,000,-000). **Population economically active** (2000): total 29,412,000, activity rate of total population 49.2% (participation rates: ages 16–64, 74.3%; female 44.5%; unemployed 5.5%). **Household income and expenditure** (1999–2000). Average household size 2.3; average annual disposable income per household £17,170 ($27,750); sources of income: wages and salaries 67.0%, social security benefits 12.0%, income from self-employment 8.8%, dividends and interest 4.0%; expenditure: food and beverages 19.9%, transport and vehicles 16.7%, housing 16.6%, household goods 8.4%, clothing 5.7%, energy 3.1%.

## Foreign trade

**Imports** (2000): £218,036,000,000 (machinery and transport equipment 45.5%, of which electrical equipment 23.2%, road vehicles 10.6%; chemicals 9.4%, of which organic chemicals 2.4%, plastics 1.9%; clothing and footwear 4.8%; petroleum and petroleum products 4.1%; food 3.4%; textiles 2.0%; paper and paperboard 2.0%). *Major import sources:* US 13.1%; Germany 12.7%; France 8.4%; The Netherlands 6.9%; Belgium-Luxembourg 5.3%; Japan 4.7%; Ireland 4.4%; Italy 4.3%; Spain 2.7%; Hong Kong 2.7%. **Exports** (2002): £187,656,000,000 (machinery and transport equipment 46.7%, of which electrical equipment 22.6%, road vehicles 8.3%; chemicals 13.3%, of which medicinal products 3.8%, organic chemicals 3.0%; petroleum and petroleum products 8.3%; professional and scientific products 3.9%; iron and steel products 1.5%; food 0.9%). *Major export destinations:* US 15.7%; Germany 12.1%; France 9.9%; The Netherlands 8.0%; Ireland 6.6%; Belgium-Luxembourg 5.5%; Italy 4.5%; Spain 4.4%; Sweden 2.2%; Japan 2.0%; Switzerland 1.6%.

## Transport and communications

**Transport.** *Railroads* (1999–2000; Great Britain only): length 37,849 km (1990); passenger-km 39,218,000,000 (2000–01); metric ton-km cargo 18,400,000,000. *Roads* (1999): total length 371,914 km (paved 100%). *Vehicles* (2000): passenger cars 22,758,000, trucks and buses 2,511,000. *Air transport* (2000): passenger-km 170,469,000,-000; metric ton-km cargo 5,159,900,000; airports (1997) 57. **Communications,** in total units (units per 1,000 persons). Daily newspaper circulation (1996): 19,332,000 (332); radio receivers (1997): 84,500,000 (1,443); television receivers (1999): 38,800,000 (652); telephone main lines (2001): 34,710,000 (578); cellular telephone subscribers (2001): 47,026,000 (783); personal computers (2001): 22,000,000 (366); Internet users (1999): 24,000,000 (400).

## Education and health

**Educational attainment** (1999). Percentage of population age 25–64 having: up to lower secondary education only 38%; completed secondary 37%; higher

25%, of which at least some university 17%. **Literacy** (1990): total population literate, virtually 100%. **Health:** physicians (1993) 164,000 (1 per 355 persons); hospital beds (2000) 242,671 (1 per 246 persons); infant mortality rate per 1,000 live births (1999) 5.8. **Food** (2000): daily per capita caloric intake 3,334 (vegetable products 70%, animal products 30%); 133% of FAO recommended minimum.

## Military

**Total active duty personnel** (2001): 211,430 (army 53.9%, navy 20.6%, air force 25.5%); US troops (2001) 11,300. **Military expenditure as percentage of GNP** (1999): 2.5% (world 2.4%); per capita expenditure $615.

## Background

The early pre-Roman inhabitants of Britain were Celtic-speaking peoples, including the Brythonic people of Wales, the Picts of Scotland, and the Britons of Britain. Celts also settled in Ireland c. 500 BC. Julius Caesar invaded and took control of the area in 55–54 BC. The Roman province of Britannia endured until the 5th century and included present-day England and Wales. In the 5th century Nordic tribes of Angles, Saxons, and Jutes invaded Britain. The invasions had little effect on the Celtic peoples of Wales and Scotland.

Christianity began to flourish in the 6th century. During the 8th–9th centuries, Vikings, particularly Danes, raided the coasts of Britain. In the late 9th century Alfred the Great repelled a Danish invasion, which helped bring about the unification of England under Athelstan. The Scots attained dominance in Scotland, which was finally unified under Malcolm II (1005–34).

William of Normandy took England in 1066. The Norman kings established a strong central government and feudal state. The French language of the Norman rulers eventually merged with the Anglo-Saxon of the common people to form the English language. From the 11th century, Scotland came under the influence of the English throne. Henry II conquered Ireland in the late 12th century. His sons Richard I and John had conflicts with the clergy and nobles, and eventually John was forced to grant the nobles concessions in Magna Carta (1215). The concept of community of the realm developed during the 13th century, providing the foundation for parliamentary government. During the reign of Edward I, statute law developed to supplement English common law, and the first Parliament was convened. In 1314 Robert Bruce won independence for Scotland.

The Tudors became the ruling family of England following the Wars of the Roses (1455–85). Henry VIII established the Church of England and made Wales part of his realm. The reign of Elizabeth I began a period of colonial expansion; 1588 brought the defeat of the Spanish Armada. In 1603 James VI of Scotland ascended to the English throne, becoming James I, and established a personal union of the two kingdoms.

The English Civil Wars erupted in 1642 between Royalists and Parliamentarians, ending in the execution of Charles I (1649). After eleven years of Puritan rule under Oliver Cromwell and his son (1649–60), the monarchy was restored with Charles II. In 1707 England and Scotland assented to the Act of Union, forming the kingdom of Great Britain. The Hanoverians ascended to the English throne in 1714, when

George Louis, elector of Hanover, became George I of Great Britain. During the reign of George III, Great Britain's American colonies won independence (1783). This was followed by a period of war with revolutionary France and later with the empire of Napoleon (1789–1815).

In 1801 legislation united Great Britain with Ireland to create the United Kingdom of Great Britain and Ireland. Britain was the birthplace of the Industrial Revolution in the late 18th century, and it remained the world's foremost economic power until the late 19th century. During the reign of Queen Victoria, Britain's colonial expansion reached its zenith, though the older dominions, including Canada and Australia, were granted independence (1867 and 1901, respectively).

The United Kingdom entered World War I allied with France and Russia in 1914. Following the war, revolutionary disorder erupted in Ireland, and in 1921 the Irish Free State was granted dominion status. The six counties of Ulster, however, remained in the United Kingdom as Northern Ireland. The United Kingdom entered World War II in 1939. Following the war the Irish Free State became the Irish Republic and left the Commonwealth. India gained independence from the United Kingdom in 1947.

Throughout the postwar period and into the 1970s, the United Kingdom continued to grant independence to its overseas colonies and dependencies. With UN forces, it participated in the Korean War (1950–53). In 1956 it intervened militarily in Egypt during the Suez Crisis. In 1982 it defeated Argentina in the Falkland Islands War. As a result of continuing social strife in Northern Ireland, it joined with Ireland in several peace initiatives, which eventually resulted in an agreement to establish an assembly in Northern Ireland. In 1997 referenda approved in Scotland and Wales devolved power to both countries, though both remained part of the United Kingdom.

## Recent Developments

The year 2002 was noteworthy as the Golden Jubilee of Queen Elizabeth II, but the two months of official celebrations were preceded by the deaths of her sister, Princess Margaret, and their mother, Queen Elizabeth, the Queen Mother. Further, in a controversial court case in November the queen faced criticism for having held back evidence in the trial of Paul Burrell, a former butler to Diana, princess of Wales. Prime Minister Tony Blair remained the commanding figure in British politics, but he faced economic difficulties, troubles inside his own government, tensions with the trade unions, a widespread popular perception that public services had not improved since he took office in 1997, and a storm of criticism over his unflagging dedication to American policy on Iraq. In June 2003 Blair reshuffled his cabinet and proposed sweeping changes in the British constitutional system including abolishing the ancient post of lord chancellor and instituting a US-style supreme court.

Blair worked closely with US Pres. George W. Bush on strategy regarding Iraq. The prime minister expressed his willingness to commit British troops to fight alongside American troops, but preferred that any such action be authorized by the UN Security Council. In September 2002 Blair published a 50-page dossier setting out evidence of Iraq's accumulation of weapons of mass destruction. The report argued that Iraq had "military plans" for the use of chemical and biological weapons, even against its own population. It also said that Iraqi leader Saddam Hussein could have a nuclear weapon within two years if he could obtain weapons-grade material from abroad.

When push came to shove, Blair proved to be Bush's only ally among leaders of the major powers. British troops partnered with the Americans in the invasion in March 2003 and were responsible for taking and occupying key Iraqi cities. In May and June, like Bush, Blair felt the consequences: the prime minister suffered a severe crisis of confidence as a prominent cabinet minister resigned in protest over his policies. Especially vexing was the question of whether or not there had been indisputable knowledge in the government that the Iraqi regime possessed or was constructing weapons of mass destruction. A public opinion survey in July revealed that nearly two-thirds of those polled did not trust the prime minister.

Turbulence continued to characterize the situation in Northern Ireland, and on 14 Oct 2002 the government and Assembly there were suspended for the fourth time since their establishment in 1998. In 2002, for the second successive year, growth in the British economy slowed, declining to less than 2%, but fears of a recession, prompted by weaknesses in the global economy, did not materialize. Unemployment remained broadly stable throughout 2002, at just over 5%, while inflation remained subdued at around 2%.

**Internet resources:** <www.uktravel.com>

# United States

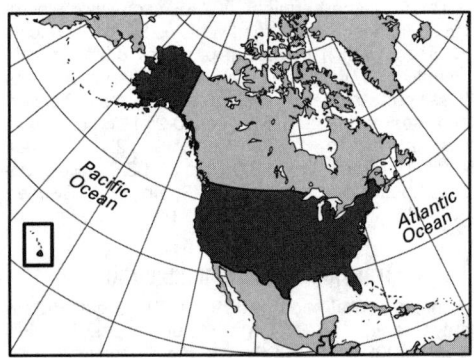

**Official name:** United States of America. **Form of government:** federal republic with two legislative houses (Senate [100]; House of Representatives [435; excludes 5 delegates having only committee voting rights]). **Head of state and government:** President George W. Bush (from 2001). **Capital:** Washington DC. **Official language:** none. **Official religion:** none. **Monetary unit:** 1 dollar ($) = 100 cents.

## Demography

**Area:** 3,675,031 sq mi, 9,518,323 sq km (total area per most recent official survey equals 3,675,267 sq mi [9,518,898 sq km], of which land area equals 3,536,278 sq mi [9,158,918 sq km], inland water area equals 78,937 sq mi [204,446 sq km], and

---

*1 metric ton = about 1.1 short tons;   1 kilometer = 0.6 mi (statute);   1 metric ton-km cargo = about 0.68 short ton-mi cargo;  c.i.f.: cost, insurance, and freight;  f.o.b.: free on board*

Great Lakes water area equals 60,052 sq mi [155,534 sq km]). **Population** (2002): 287,602,000. **Density** (2002): persons per sq mi 78.3, persons per sq km 30.2. **Urban** (2000): 77.2%. **Sex distribution** (2000): male 49.06%; female 50.94%. **Age breakdown** (2000): under 15, 21.4%; 15–29, 20.8%; 30–44, 23.3%; 45–59, 18.2%; 60–74, 10.4%; 75 and over, 5.9%. **Population by race and Hispanic origin** (2000): non-Hispanic white 70.5%; Hispanic 12.5%; non-Hispanic black 12.3%; Asian and Pacific Islander 3.8%; American Indian and Eskimo 0.9%. **Religious affiliation** (1995): Christian 85.3%, of which Protestant 57.9%, Roman Catholic 21.0%, other Christian 6.4%; Jewish 2.1%; Muslim 1.9%; nonreligious 8.7%; other 2.0%. **Mobility** (2000). Population living in the same residence as in 1999: 84.0%; different residence, same county 9.0%; different county, same state 3.0%; different state 3.0%; moved from abroad 1.0%. **Households** (2000). Total households 105,480,000 (married-couple families 54,493,000 [51.7%]). Average household size (2000) 2.7; 1 person 25.9%, 2 persons 32.1%, 3 persons 16.9%, 4 persons 14.9%, 5 or more persons 10.2%. Family households: 71,787,000 (68.1%); nonfamily 33,693,000 (31.9%), of which 1-person 80.8%. *Immigration* (2000): permanent immigrants admitted 849,807, from Mexico 20.2%, former USSR 5.2%, China 4.9%, the Philippines 4.8%, Africa 4.8%, India 4.6%, Vietnam 3.0%, Haiti 2.6%, El Salvador 2.6%, Canada 2.5%, Cuba 2.3%, Dominican Republic 2.1%, Jamaica 1.8%, South Korea 1.8%, other 36.8%. Refugees (end of 2000) 508,222. Asylum seekers (end of 2000): 386,330. **Major cities** (2000): New York 8,008,278; Los Angeles 3,694,820; Chicago 2,896,016; Houston 1,953,631; Philadelphia 1,517,550; Phoenix 1,321,045; San Diego 1,223,400; Dallas 1,188,580; San Antonio 1,144,646; Detroit 951,270. **Place of birth** (2000): native-born 245,708,000 (89.6%); foreign-born 28,379,000 (10.4%), of which Mexico 7,841,000, the Philippines 1,222,000, China and Hong Kong 1,067,000, India 1,007,000, Cuba 952,000, Vietnam 863,000, El Salvador 765,000, South Korea 701,000. **Location:** North America, bordering Canada, the Atlantic Ocean, the Gulf of Mexico, Mexico, and the Pacific Ocean. Outlying state of Alaska nearly touches eastern Russia and borders the Arctic Ocean and the Atlantic Ocean; Hawaii is an island group in the Pacific Ocean. **Dependencies:** American Samoa, Guam, Northern Mariana Islands, Puerto Rico, and Virgin Islands (of the US).

## Vital statistics

**Birth rate** per 1,000 population (2000): 14.7 (world avg. 22.5); (1999) legitimate 67.0%; illegitimate 33.0%. **Death rate** per 1,000 population (2000): 8.7 (world avg. 9.0). **Natural increase rate** per 1,000 population (2000): 6.0 (world avg. 13.5). **Total fertility rate** (avg. births per childbearing woman; 2000): 2.0. **Marriage rate** per 1,000 population (1999): 8.6; median age at first marriage (1991): men 26.3 years, women 24.1 years. **Divorce rate** per 1,000 population (1998): 4.2. **Life expectancy** at birth (2000): white male 74.8 years, black and other male (1996) 68.9 years; white female 80.4 years, black and other female 76.1 (1996) years.

## Social indicators

**Quality of working life** (1999). Average workweek: 39.5 hours. Annual death rate per 100,000 workers

(1999): 4.5; leading causes of occupational deaths: transportation incidents 43.4%, contact with objects/equipment 17.1%, assaults/violent acts 14.8%. Average days per 1,000 workdays lost to labor stoppages (2000): 1.8. Average duration of journey to work (1990): 22.4 minutes (private automobile 94.7%, of which drive alone 80.0%, carpool 14.7%; take public transportation 5.3%). Rate per 1,000 employed workers of discouraged workers (unemployed no longer seeking work; 2000): 1.8. **Access to services** (1995). Proportion of occupied dwellings having access to: electricity, virtually 100.0%; safe public water supply 99.4% (12.6% from wells); public sewage collection 77.0%, septic tanks 22.8%. **Social participation.** Eligible voters participating in last presidential election (2000): 51.2%. Population age 18 and over participating in voluntary work (1999): 66.0%. Trade-union membership in total workforce (2000): 14.9%. **Social deviance** (1999). Offense rate per 100,000 population for: murder 5.7; rape 32.7; robbery 150.0; aggravated assault 336.0; motor-vehicle theft 421.0; burglary and housebreaking 770.0; larceny-theft 2,551.0; drug-abuse violation 583.7; drunkenness 200.2 (1995). Estimated drug and substance users (population age 12 and over; 1999): cigarettes 57,296,000; binge alcohol 44,486,000; marijuana 11,476,000; other illicit drugs 6,645,000. Rate per 100,000 population of suicide (1999): 10.7. **Leisure** (1997). Favorite leisure activities (percentage of total population age 18 and over that undertook activity at least once in the previous year): movie 66.0%, amusement park 57.0%, sports event 41.0%, exercise program 76.0%, home improvement 66.0%; charity work 43.0%, playing sports 45.0%. **Material well-being** (1995). Occupied dwellings with householder possessing: automobile 95.6%; telephone 93.9%; radio receiver 99.0%; television receiver 98.3%; videocassette recorder 81.0%; washing machine 78.3%; air conditioner 69.7%; cable television 63.4%. **Recreational expenditures** (1999): $534,-900,000,000 (television and radio receivers, computers, and video equipment 18.5%; sports supplies 11.8%; golfing, bowling, and other participatory activities 11.4%; nondurable toys and sports equipment 6.9%; magazines and newspapers 6.9%; books and maps 5.6%; spectator amusements 4.8%, of which theatre and opera 1.9%, movies 1.4%, spectator sports 1.5%; flowers, seeds, and potted plants 3.3%; other 29.3%).

## National economy

**Budget** (2001). *Revenue:* $2,136,900,000,000 (individual income tax 48.8%, social-insurance taxes and contributions 36.4%, corporation income tax 10.4%, excise taxes 3.4%, customs duties 1.0%). *Expenditures:* $1,856200,000,000 (social security and medicare 37.5%, defense 16.1%, interest on debt 11.1%, other 35.3%). **Total national debt** (2000): $5,686,338,000,000. **Gross national product** (2000): $9,860,800,000,000 ($35,040 per capita). **Business activity** (1997): number of businesses 23,645,000 (sole proprietorships 72.6%, active corporations 19.9%, active partnerships 7.5%), of which services 10,114,000, wholesaling and retailing 4,455,000; business receipts $18,057,000,000,-000 (active corporations 88.0%, sole proprietorships 4.8%, active partnerships 7.2%), of which wholesaling and retailing $5,136,000,000,000, services $2,130,000,000,000; net profit $1,270,000,000,-000 (active corporations 72.0%, sole proprietorships

14.7%, partnerships 13.3%), of which services $203,000,000,000, wholesaling and retailing $10,000,000,000. New business starts and business failures (1995): total number of new business starts 168,158; total failures 71,194, of which commercial service 21,850, retail trade 12,952; failure rate per 10,000 concerns 90.0; current liabilities of failed concerns $37,507,000,000; average liability $526,830. Business expenditures for new plant and equipment (1995): total $594,465,000,000, of which trade, services, and communications $244,829,000,000, manufacturing businesses $172,308,000,000 (durable goods 53.0%, nondurable goods 47.0%), public utilities $42,816,000,000, transportation $37,021,000,000, mining and construction $35,985,000. **Production.** *Agriculture, forestry, fishing* (value of production/catch in $'000,000 except as noted; 2000): corn (maize) 18,621, soybeans 13,073, wheat 5,970, cotton lint 4,781, grapes 3,063, potatoes 2,539, tobacco 2,056, oranges 1,752, apples 1,554, head lettuce 1,259, tomatoes 1,160, rice 1,073, strawberries 1,013, almonds 852, peanuts (groundnuts) 844, sorghum 822, onions 732, cottonseed 677, barley 632, bell peppers 614, broccoli 597, peaches 495, sweet corn 474, carrots 436, dry beans 423, grapefruit 423, cantaloupes 359, cabbage 332, lemons 318, avocados 318, sweet cherries 286, cauliflower 259, pears 255, sunflower seeds 241, watermelons 236, pecans 234; livestock (number of live animals; 2000) 98,048,000 cattle, 59,337,000 pigs, 7,215,000 sheep, 5,320,000 horses, 1,720,000,000 chickens; roundwood (2000) 500,434,000 cu m; fish and shellfish catch (1999) 3,095, of which fish 1,395 (including salmon 308, Alaska pollack 187), shellfish 1,700 (including shrimp 519, crabs 480). *Mining* (metal content in metric tons except as noted; 2001): iron 37,800,000; copper 1,340,000; zinc 830,000; lead 420,000; molybdenum 38,300; vanadium 2,700; mercury 550; silver 1,800,000 kg; gold 350,000 kg; helium 101,000,000 cu m. *Quarrying* (metric tons; 2000): crushed stone 1,300,000,000; sand and gravel 1,139,000,000; cement 75,000,000; clay 40,700,000; phosphate rock 34,200,000; common salt 45,000,000; gypsum 18,800,000; lime 20,000,000. *Manufacturing* (value added in $'000,000; 1999): transportation equipment 268,511, of which motor vehicle parts 86,310, motor vehicles 80,134, aerospace products and parts 73,897; computers and electronic products 265,442, of which semiconductors and related components 102,003; chemicals and chemical products 229,284, of which pharmaceuticals and medicine 74,108; food 177,659; fabricated metal products 142,451; nonelectrical machinery 138,798; paper and paper products 74,602; plastics 72,183; base metals 66,733; printing 62,428; electrical machinery 60,458. *Construction* (completed; 2000): private $640,654,000,000, of which residential $374,274,000,000, nonresidential $210,140,000,000; public $174,860,000,000. *Energy production (consumption):* electricity (kW-hr; 2001) 3,778,500,000,000 ([1998] 3,399,600,000,000); coal (metric tons; 1998) 934,790,000 (846,813,000); lignite (metric tons; 1998) 78,593,000 (79,821,000); crude petroleum (barrels; 2001) 2,163,000,000 ([1998] 5,608,000,000); petroleum products (metric tons; 1998) 747,623,000 (757,728,000); natural gas (cu m;

2001) 549,557,000,000 ([1998] 601,880,000,000). Domestic production of energy by source (1998): coal 32.5%, natural gas 26.3%, crude petroleum 18.0%, nuclear power 9.8%, renewable energy 9.1%, other 0.9%. Energy consumption by source (1999): petroleum and petroleum products 39.7%, natural gas 23.3%, coal 21.4%, nuclear electric power 8.1%, hydroelectric and thermal 7.5%; by end use: industrial 37.8%, residential and commercial 35.4%, transportation 26.8%. **Household income and expenditure.** Average household size (2000) 2.7; median annual income per household (2001) $42,228, of which median Asian and Pacific Islander household $53,635, median non-Hispanic household $46,305, median Hispanic household $33,565, median black (including Hispanic) household $29,470; sources of personal income (2000): wages and salaries 57.6%, self-employment 8.6%, transfer payments 8.5%, other 25.3%; expenditure (1999): transportation 18.9%, housing 18.9%, food at home 7.9%, household furnishings 7.2%, fuel and utilities 6.4%, food away from home 5.7%, recreation 5.5%, health 5.3%, wearing apparel 4.7%, education 1.7%, other 17.8%. Average annual expenditure of "consumer units" (households, plus individuals sharing households or budgets; 1999): total $37,027, of which housing $12,057, transportation $7,011, food $5,031, pensions and social security $3,436, health care $1,959, clothing $1,743, other $5,790. Selected household characteristics (2000). Total number of households 104,705,000, of which (family households by race) white 84.8%, black 12.2%, other 3.0%; in central cities 31.4% (1994), in suburbs 46.3% (1994), outside metropolitan areas 22.3% (1994); (by tenure; 1994) owned 64,045,000 (64.7%), rented 34,946,000 (35.3%); family households 72,025,000, of which married couple 76.8%, female head with children under age 18, 10.5%, female head without children under 18, 7.1%; nonfamily households 32,680,000, of which female living alone 47.6%, male living alone 34.2%, other 18.2%. **Population economically active** (2000): total 140,863,000; activity rate of total population 50.1% (participation rates: age 16 and over 67.2%; female 46.6%; unemployed [November 2002] 6.0%). **Tourism** (1999): receipts from visitors $94,657,000,000; expenditures by nationals abroad $80,756,000,000; number of foreign visitors 48,491,000,000 (14,110,000 from Canada, 9,915,000 from Mexico, 11,243,000 from Europe); number of nationals traveling abroad 58,358,000 (17,743,000 to Mexico, 16,036,000 to Canada). **Land use** (1997): forested 20.9%; meadows and pastures 27.1%; agricultural and under permanent cultivation 21.1%; other 30.9%.

## Foreign trade

**Imports** (2000): $1,216,743,000,000 (manufactured goods 84.8%, of which motor vehicles and parts 13.3%, electrical machinery 8.9%, computers and office equipment 7.5%, petroleum and petroleum products 7.4%, chemicals and chemical products 6.0%, wearing apparel 5.3%; food and live animals 3.1%). *Major import sources:* Canada 19.0%; Japan 12.0%; Mexico 11.2%; China 8.2%; Germany 4.8%; UK 3.6%; Taiwan 3.3%; South Korea 3.3%; France 2.4%; Italy 2.1%; Malaysia 2.1%; Singapore 1.6%; Thailand 1.3%; Philippines 1.1%; Brazil 1.1%.

*1 metric ton = about 1.1 short tons;    1 kilometer = 0.6 mi (statute);    1 metric ton-km cargo = about 0.68 short ton-mi cargo;    c.i.f.: cost, insurance, and freight;    f.o.b.: free on board*

Exports (2000): $782,429,000,000 (manufactured goods 79.7%, of which electrical machinery 11.4%, chemicals and related products 10.2%, motor vehicles 7.3%, scientific and precision equipment 3.9%; food and live animals 6.4%). *Major export destinations:* Canada 22.9%; Mexico 14.2%; Japan 8.3%; UK 5.3%; Germany 3.7%; South Korea 3.6%; Taiwan 3.1%; The Netherlands 2.8%; France 2.6%; Singapore 2.3%; Brazil 2.0%.

## Transport and communications

**Transport.** *Railroads* (1998): length 212,433 km; (1999) passenger-km 21,568,000,000; metric ton-km cargo (1997) 2,075,000,000. *Roads* (1999): total length 6,348,227 km (paved 91%). *Vehicles* (2000): passenger cars 133,621,000; trucks and buses 87,107,000. *Air transport* (2000): passenger-km 1,139,000,000,000; metric ton-km cargo 48,636,000,000; localities (1996) with scheduled flights 834. Certified route passenger/cargo air carriers (1992) 77; operating revenue ($'000,000; 1991) 74,942, of which domestic 56,119, international 18,823; operating expenses 76,669, of which domestic 56,596, international 20,073. **Communications,** in total units (units per 1,000 persons). Daily newspaper circulation (2000): 55,773,000 (198); radio receivers (1997): 575,000,000 (2,116); television receivers (1999): 233,000,000 (843); telephone main lines (2001): 190,000,000 (665); cellular telephone subscribers (2001): 127,000,000 (444); personal computers (2001): 178,000,000 (623); Internet users (2001): 142,823,000 (500).

## Education and health

**Educational attainment** (2000). Percentage of population age 25 and over having: primary and incomplete secondary 15.9%; secondary 33.1%; some postsecondary 25.4%; 4-year higher degree 17.0%; advanced degree 8.6%. Number of earned degrees (1998): bachelor's degree 1,183,033; master's degree 429,296; doctor's degree 45,925; first-professional degrees (in fields such as medicine, theology, and law) 78,353. **Food** (2000): daily per capita caloric intake 3,772 (vegetable products 72%, animal products 28%); 143% of FAO recommended minimum. Per capita consumption of major food groups (kilograms annually; 2000): milk 259.5; fresh vegetables 125.8; fresh fruits 124.8; cereal products 113.6; red meat 74.2; potatoes 65.3; poultry products 47.6; sweeteners 37.2; fats and oils 31.2; fish and shellfish 21.4. **Health** (1999): doctors of medicine 797,600 (1 per 341 persons), of which office-based practice 473,200 (including specialties in internal medicine 17.9%, general and family practice 14.0%, pediatrics 8.5%, obstetrics and gynecology 6.5%, general surgery 6.6%, psychiatry 5.2%, anesthesiology 5.6%, orthopedics 3.6%, ophthalmology 3.2%); doctors of osteopathy 43,500; nurses 2,271,000 (1 per 120 persons); dentists 196,000 (1 per 1,390 persons; 1996); hospital beds 994,000 (1 per 274 persons), of which nonfederal 94.5% (community hospitals 88.4%, psychiatric 9.3%, long-term general and special 2.1%), federal 5.5%; infant mortality rate per 1,000 live births (2000) 7.1.

## Military

**Total active duty personnel** (2002): 1,414,000 (army 34.3%, navy 27.3%, air force 26.1%, marines 12.3%).

**Military expenditure as percentage of GNP** (1999): 3.0% (world 2.4%); per capita expenditure $1,030. Security assistance to the world (2002): $7,209,000,000, for underwriting the purchase of US weapons 50.6%, of which Israel 28.3%, Egypt 18.0%, Jordan 1.0%; for economic support 30.5%, of which Israel 10.0%, Egypt 9.1%, Jordan 2.1%; for the Andean Counterdrug Initiative 9.2%; for nonproliferation, antiterrorism, and de-mining 4.3%; for international narcotics and law enforcement 3.0%; for peacekeeping operations 1.9%.

**Did you know?** America was the first of the European colonies to separate successfully from its motherland, and it was the first state in the world to be established on the premise that sovereignty rests with its citizens and not with the government.

## Background

The territory that is now the US was originally inhabited for several thousand years by numerous American Indian peoples who had probably emigrated from Asia. European exploration and settlement from the 16th century began displacement of the Indians. The first permanent European settlement, by the Spanish, was at St. Augustine FL, in 1565; the British settled Jamestown VA (1607); Plymouth MA (1620); Maryland (1632); and Pennsylvania (1681). They took New York, New Jersey, and Delaware from the Dutch in 1664, a year after the Carolinas had been granted to British noblemen. The British defeat of the French in 1763 assured British political control over the 13 colonies.

Political unrest caused by British colonial policy culminated in the American Revolution (1775–83) and the Declaration of Independence (1776). The US was first organized under the Articles of Confederation (1781), then finally under the Constitution (1787) as a federal republic. Boundaries extended west to the Mississippi River, excluding Spanish Florida. Land acquired from France by the Louisiana Purchase (1803) nearly doubled the country's territory. The US fought the War of 1812 with the British and acquired Florida from Spain in 1819. In 1830 it legalized removal of American Indians to lands west of the Mississippi River. Settlement expanded to the west coast in the mid-19th century, especially after the discovery of gold in California in 1848. Victory in the Mexican War (1846–48) brought the territory of seven more future states (including California and Texas) into US hands. The northwestern boundary was established by treaty with Great Britain in 1846. The US acquired southern Arizona by the Gadsden Purchase (1853). It suffered disunity during the conflict between the slavery-based plantation economy in the South and the free industrial and agricultural economy in the North, culminating in the American Civil War, and the abolition of slavery under the 13th Amendment.

After Reconstruction (1865–77), the US experienced rapid growth, urbanization, industrial development, and European immigration. In 1877 it authorized allotment of Indian reservation land to individual tribesmen, resulting in widespread loss of land to whites. By the beginning of the 20th century, it had acquired outlying territories, including Alaska, the Midway Islands, the Hawaiian Islands, the

Philippines, Puerto Rico, Guam, Wake Island, American Samoa, the Panama Canal Zone, and the Virgin Islands.

The US participated in World War I during 1917–18. It granted suffrage to women in 1920 and citizenship to American Indians in 1924. The stock market crash of 1929 led to the Great Depression. The US entered World War II after the Japanese bombing of Pearl Harbor (7 Dec 1941). The explosion of the first atomic bomb on Hiroshima, Japan (6 Aug 1945), brought about the end of the war and set the US apart as a military power. After the war the US was involved in the reconstruction of Europe and Japan and embroiled in a rivalry with the Soviet Union that became known as the Cold War. It participated in the Korean War. In 1952 it granted autonomous commonwealth status to Puerto Rico.

Racial segregation in schools was declared unconstitutional in 1954. Alaska and Hawaii were made states in 1959, bringing the total to 50. In 1964 Congress passed the Civil Rights Act and authorized full-scale intervention in the Vietnam War. The mid- to late 1960s were marked by widespread civil disorders, including race riots and antiwar demonstrations. The US accomplished the first manned lunar landing in 1969. All US troops were withdrawn from Vietnam by 1973. The US led a coalition of forces against Iraq in the Persian Gulf War (1991), sent troops to Somalia (1992) to aid starving populations, and participated in NATO air strikes against Serb forces in the former Yugoslavia in 1995 and 1999. Administration of the Panama Canal was turned over to Panama in 1999.

## Recent Developments

In the decade following the collapse of the Soviet Union, the reign of the United States as the world's sole superpower was widely acknowledged, if not universally accepted. US military might was virtually unchallenged, complementing a dependable US economic engine that seemed to pull the global economy through good times and bad. In 2002, however, Americans came to understand that dominance was costly and often involved disquieting risk. The year started with the US determinedly addressing fallout from the 11 Sep 2001 terrorist attacks and apparently emerging from a mild economic recession. By year-end, however, both external and internal problems appeared far more complicated. Confrontation with the al-Qaeda terrorist network produced modest progress, but the overall terrorism conflict actually expanded; the US was preparing for a potential military assault on Iraq and attempting to defuse a nuclear crisis with North Korea.

The national economy, plagued by war jitters and corporate accounting irregularities, stalled in mid-recovery, with stock prices plunging and unemployment edging upward, which threw the federal budget back into long-term deficit. Contributing to the national malaise were a series of crises suffered by major American institutions. Virtually unprecedented revelations of dishonesty in corporate executive suites, accompanied by a wave of major business bankruptcies, shook confidence in the foundations of US economic prosperity. A sexual-abuse scandal rocked the Roman Catholic Church. In addition, the competency of the CIA and the FBI was questioned during inquiries into intelligence lapses before 11 September. Nevertheless, Pres. George W. Bush managed to solidify his position with the American people, in large part owing to his purposeful handling of the "war on terrorism." He announced a new policy favoring preemptive strikes against increased terrorist threats, asserting the national right of self-defense, and his allies steered several measures through Congress that increased US military spending. Bush took the issue into the midterm election in November, and his party regained total control of Congress.

In his January 2002 state of the union address, President Bush effectively broadened the antiterrorist struggle by declaring that nations attempting to produce "weapons of mass destruction" were part of the world terrorist threat. He specifically named Iraq, Iran, and North Korea as "an axis of evil" developing nuclear, chemical, or biological weaponry, and he challenged other governments to confront these states as well. The speech set the tone for a period in which the new terrorist threat dominated foreign relations as well as US domestic politics. US forces led a coalition military effort in Afghanistan that claimed an estimated 500 Taliban and al-Qaeda dead but left the top al-Qaeda and Taliban leaders, Osama bin Laden and Mullah Mohammad Omar, apparently still at large. The president strove to increase domestic precautions against terrorist attacks—to beef up the military and to lead the world response to the threat. Bush proposed a 14% increase for defense spending, the largest increase in two decades, and he sought a doubling of expenditures for homeland security. The government generally accepted Bush's expanded definition of the war on terrorism, including his call for a "regime change" in Iraq. In October, only days before national elections, Congress overwhelmingly approved a resolution authorizing the use of force against Saddam Hussein and Iraq. After an extended delay led by Russia, France, and other countries, the United Nations also agreed to demand Iraqi compliance with inspections to ensure that weapons prohibited in the 1991 peace agreement were not being developed. By year's end a US-dominated coalition had more than 100,000 troops deployed or en route to the region.

Finally, after several months of brinksmanship between Bush and British Prime Minister Tony Blair on the one side and Saddam Hussein on the other—with most world powers looking on disapprovingly and the United Nations declining to sponsor military action—in March 2003 the US–British-led coalition forces attacked Iraq. Within a few weeks Baghdad and other major cities had fallen. An occupation regime was set up, but not before a wave of looting swept the country. Again, as in Afghanistan, the fate of Iraq's top leaders, including Saddam Hussein, was unclear months after the military victory. The failure of coalition forces to unearth evidence of Iraqi weapons of mass destruction, a principal reason given for the attack mentioned by Bush in his 2003 state of the union message, led to a period of intense questioning of the integrity of US intelligence reporting in early summer.

**Internet resources:** <www.tourstates.com>

---

*1 metric ton = about 1.1 short tons;   1 kilometer = 0.6 mi (statute);   1 metric ton-km cargo = about 0.68 short ton-mi cargo;   c.i.f.: cost, insurance, and freight;   f.o.b.: free on board*

# Uruguay

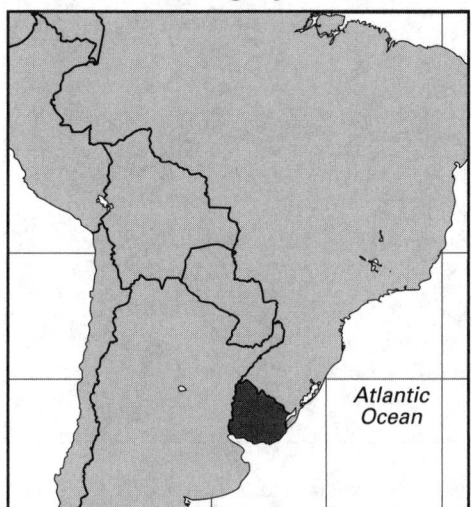

Atlantic
Ocean

**Official name:** República Oriental del Uruguay (Oriental Republic of Uruguay). **Form of government:** republic with two legislative houses (Senate [31, includes the vice president who serves as ex-officio presiding officer]; Chamber of Representatives [99]). **Head of state and government:** President Jorge Batlle (from 2000). **Capital:** Montevideo. **Official language:** Spanish. **Official religion:** none. **Monetary unit:** 1 peso uruguayo ($U; replaced the Uruguayan peso [Nur$] in 1993) = 100 centesimos; valuation (7 Jul 2003) US$1 = $U 26.77.

## Demography

**Area:** 68,037 sq mi, 176,215 sq km. **Population** (2002): 3,383,000. **Density** (2002): persons per sq mi 49.7, persons per sq km 19.2. **Urban** (1996): 88.7%. **Sex distribution** (2001): male 48.43%; female 51.57%. **Age breakdown** (2001): under 15, 24.6%; 15–29, 22.8%; 30–44, 19.7%; 45–59, 15.5%; 60–74, 11.8%; 75 and over, 5.6%. **Ethnic composition** (2000): white (mostly Spanish, Italian, or mixed Spanish-Italian) 94.5%; mestizo 3.1%; mulatto 2.0%; other 0.4%. **Religious affiliation** (1997): Roman Catholic 78.5%; Protestant 4.5%; other Christian 3.5%; Jewish 0.9%; other 12.6%. **Major cities** (1996): Montevideo 1,378,707; Salto 93,113; Paysandú 74,568; Las Piedras 66,584; Rivera 62,859. **Location:** southern South America, bordering Brazil, the South Atlantic Ocean, and Argentina.

## Vital statistics

**Birth rate** per 1,000 population (2001): 16.1 (world avg. 21.2). **Death rate** per 1,000 population (2001): 9.5 (world avg. 8.9). **Total fertility rate** (avg. births per childbearing woman; 2001): 2.2. **Marriage rate** per 1,000 population (2001): 4.2. **Divorce rate** per 1,000 population (2001): 2.0. **Life expectancy** at birth (2001): male 70.9 years; female 78.8 years.

## National economy

**Budget** (1998). *Revenue:* $U 70,664,000,000 (taxes on goods and services 39.4%, social security contributions 28.6%, income taxes 12.6%, nontax revenue 7.1%, receipts from foreign trade 3.7%). *Expenditures:* $U 72,673,000,000 (social security and welfare 61.4%, general public services 7.4%, education 7.0%, health 5.8%, interest payments 4.7%). **Public debt** (external, outstanding; 2000): US$5,597,000,000. **Production** (metric tons except as noted). *Agriculture, forestry, fishing* (1999): rice 1,328,000, wheat 377,000, corn (maize) 243,000; livestock (number of live animals) 15,500,000 sheep, 10,700,000 cattle; roundwood (1998) 6,163,000 cu m. *Mining and quarrying* (2001): limestone 1,300,000; gold 67,000 troy oz; gypsum 183,000. *Manufacturing* (value added in $U '000,000; 1998): food products 6,955; refined petroleum 4,966; beverages 3,175. *Energy production (consumption):* electricity (kW-hr; 1997) 7,147,000,000 (7,003,000,000); crude petroleum (barrels; 1997) none (10,000,000); petroleum products (metric tons; 1997) 1,317,000 (1,665,000). **Land use** (1998): forested and other 15.2%; meadows and pastures 77.3%; agricultural and under permanent cultivation 7.5%. **Household income and expenditure.** Avg. household size (1999) 3.3; avg. annual income per household (1985) NUr$266,261 (US$2,625); sources of income: wages 53.5%, self-employment 17.0%, transfer payments and other 29.5%; expenditure (1982–83): food 39.9%, housing 17.6%, transportation and communications 10.4%, health care 9.3%, clothing 7.0%. **Gross national product** (2000): US$20,010,000,000 (US$6,000 per capita). **Population economically active** (1998): total 1,239,400; activity rate 47.0% (participation rates: ages 14 and over, 60.4%; female 44.0%). **Tourism** (2000): receipts US$652,000,000; expenditures US$281,000,000.

## Foreign trade

**Imports** (1999-f.o.b. in balance of trade): US$3,356,770,000 (machinery and appliances 22.2%; chemical products 14.6%; mineral products 11.6%; transport equipment 9.1%; processed foods 7.1%; synthetic plastics, resins, and rubber 7.0%; metal products 4.8%). *Major import sources* (1998): Argentina 22.0%; Brazil 20.8%; US 12.1%; France 4.7%; Italy 4.6%; Spain 3.7%. **Exports** (1999): US$2,236,848,000 (live animals and live-animal products 30.1%; vegetable products 15.8%; textiles and textile products 11.8%; hides and skins 9.8%; processed foods 5.4%). *Major export destinations* (1998): Brazil 33.8%; Argentina 18.5%; US 5.7%; Germany 4.0%.

## Transport and communications

**Transport.** *Railroads* (1998): track length 3,002 km; passenger-km 14,000,000; metric ton-km cargo 244,000,000. *Roads* (1997): length 8,683 km (paved 30%). *Vehicles* (1997): passenger cars 516,889; trucks and buses 50,264. *Air transport* (1998): passenger-km 642,000,000; metric ton-km cargo 70,000,000; airports (1997) 1. **Communications,** in total units (units per 1,000 persons). Daily newspaper circulation (1996): 950,000 (293); radio receivers (1997): 1,970,000 (603); television receivers (1999): 1,760,000 (531); telephone main lines (2001): 950,900 (283); cellular telephone subscribers (2001): 520,000 (155); personal computers (2001): 370,000 (110); Internet users (2001): 400,000 (119).

## Education and health

**Educational attainment** (1996). Percentage of population age 25 and over having: no formal schooling

3.4%; primary education 53.6%; secondary 31.7%; higher 10.1%; unknown 1.2%. **Literacy** (2000 est.): population age 15 and over literate 97.7%; males 97.3%; females 98.1%. **Health** (1999): physicians 12,357 (1 per 263 persons); hospital beds 6,651 (1 per 488 persons); infant mortality rate per 1,000 live births (2002) 14.3. **Food** (2000): daily per capita caloric intake 2,879 (vegetable products 66%, animal products 34%); 108% of FAO recommended minimum.

## Military

**Total active duty personnel** (2001): 23,900 (army 63.6%, navy 23.8%, air force 12.6%). **Military expenditure as percentage of GNP** (1999): 1.3% (world 2.4%); per capita expenditure US$83.

## Background

The Spanish navigator Juan Díaz de Solís sailed into the Río de la Plata in 1516. The Portuguese established Colonia in 1680. Subsequently, the Spanish established Montevideo in 1726, driving the Portuguese from their settlement; 50 years later Uruguay became part of the viceroyalty of Río de la Plata. It gained independence from Spain in 1811. The Portuguese regained it in 1821, incorporating it into Brazil as a province. A revolt against Brazil in 1825 led to its being recognized as an independent state in 1828. It battled Paraguay 1865–70. For much of World War II it remained neutral. The presidential office was abolished in 1951 and replaced with a nine-member council. The country adopted a new constitution and restored the presidential system in 1966. A military coup occurred in 1973, but the country returned to civilian rule in 1985. The 1990s brought a general upturn in the economy.

## Recent Developments

The year 2002 was a time of worsening economic crisis for Uruguay. The most negative effect on the economy was produced by a freeze on deposits in Argentina following the collapse of the Argentine peso when that government abandoned its convertibility plan, which pegged its currency one-to-one with the US dollar. This forced many Argentines to withdraw dollars from their bank accounts in the traditionally safe haven of Montevideo. The subsequent collapse of two banks in Uruguay had many Uruguayans fearing for the safety of their banking system. The result was that in the first seven months of the year Uruguay lost about 80% of its foreign reserves. GDP fell 7.8% in the first half of the year and was expected to contract 11% for the year as a whole. Unemployment climbed to a record 19%. Inflation, which had been a mere 3.59% in 2001, hit 24% by September and was expected by the IMF to increase to almost 30% by the end of the year.

**Internet resources:** <www.uruguay.com>

# Uzbekistan

**Official name:** Uzbekiston Respublikasi (Republic of Uzbekistan). **Form of government:** multiparty republic with a single legislative body (Supreme Assembly [250]). **Heads of state and government:** President

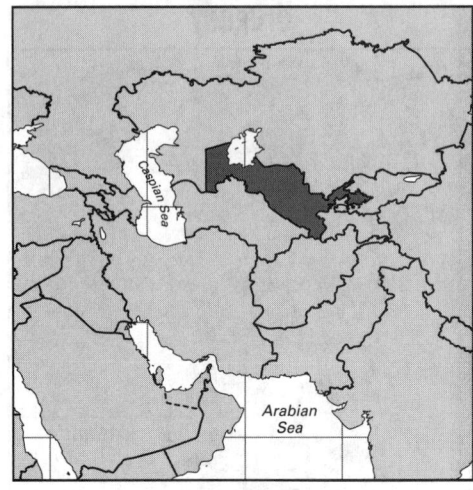

Islam Karimov (from 1990) assisted by Prime Minister Otkir Sultonov (from 1995). **Capital:** Tashkent (Toshkent). **Official language:** Uzbek. **Official religion:** none. **Monetary unit:** sum (plural sumy); valuation (7 Jul 2003) $1 = 974.07 sumy.

## Demography

**Area:** 172,700 sq mi, 447,400 sq km. **Population** (2002): 25,484,000. **Density** (2002): persons per sq mi 147.6, persons per sq km 57.0. **Urban** (2002): 36.6%. **Sex distribution** (2001): male 49.55%; female 50.45%. **Age breakdown** (2001): under 15, 36.4%; 15–29, 28.6%; 30–44, 19.6%; 45–59, 8.5%; 60–74, 5.4%; 75 and over, 1.5%. **Ethnic composition** (1998): Uzbek 75.8%; Russian 6.0%; Tajik 4.8%; Kazakh 4.1%; Tatar 1.6%; other 7.7%. **Religious affiliation** (2000): Muslim (mostly Sunni) 76.2%; nonreligious 18.1%; Russian Orthodox 0.8%; Jewish 0.2%; other 4.7%. **Major cities** (1999): Tashkent 2,142,700; Namangan 376,600; Samarkand 362,300; Andijon 323,900; Bukhara 237,900. **Location:** Central Asia, bordering Kazakhstan, Kyrgyzstan, Tajikistan, Afghanistan, and Turkmenistan.

## Vital statistics

**Birth rate** per 1,000 population (2001): 21.7 (world avg. 21.2); (1994) legitimate 96.5%; illegitimate 3.5%. **Death rate** per 1,000 population (2001): 5.9 (world avg. 8.9). **Natural increase rate** per 1,000 population (2001): 15.8 (world avg. 12.3). **Total fertility rate** (avg. births per childbearing woman; 2001): 3.1. **Marriage rate** per 1,000 population (1997): 7.7. **Divorce rate** per 1,000 population (1994): 1.1. **Life expectancy** at birth (2001): male 66.0 years; female 72.0 years.

## National economy

**Budget** (1999). *Revenue:* 611,897,000,000 sumy (taxes on income and profits 30.5%, value-added tax 27.3%, excise taxes 22.8%, property and land taxes 12.1%, other 7.3%). *Expenditures:* 654,259,000,000 sumy (social and cultural affairs 36.7%, investments 18.7%, national economy 10.4%, transfers 10.4%, administration 2.2%, interest on debt 1.9%, other

*1 metric ton = about 1.1 short tons;   1 kilometer = 0.6 mi (statute);   1 metric ton-km cargo = about 0.68 short ton-mi cargo;   c.i.f.: cost, insurance, and freight;   f.o.b.: free on board*

19.2%). **Household income and expenditure** (1995). Average household size (1998) 5.5; income per household 35,165 sumy ($1,040); sources of income: wages and salaries 63.0%, subsidies, grants, and nonwage income 34.9%, other 2.1%; expenditure: food and beverages 71%, clothing and footwear 14%, recreation 6%, household durables 4%, housing 3%. **Public debt** (external, outstanding; 2000): $3,578,000,000. **Production** (metric tons except as noted). *Agriculture, forestry, fishing* (2001): seed cotton 3,300,000, wheat 3,127,000, vegetables 2,700,000; livestock (number of live animals) 8,100,000 sheep, 5,344,000 cattle, 14,420,000 chickens; roundwood (2001) 24,980 cu m; fish catch (1999) 8,536. *Mining and quarrying* (2000): copper (metal content) 91,800; gold 62,276 kg. *Manufacturing* (metric tons except as noted; 1998): cement 3,358,000; cotton fiber 1,138,000; mineral fertilizer 897,000. *Energy production (consumption):* electricity (kW-hr; 1999) 45,108,000,000 ([1998] 46,100,000,000); hard coal (metric tons; 1997) 59,000 (75,000); lignite (metric tons; 1999) 2,904,000 ([1998] 2,792,000); crude petroleum (barrels; 1998) 59,400,000 (57,870,000); petroleum products (metric tons; 1998) 8,104,000 (6,934,000); natural gas (cu m; 2000) 56,350,000,000 (42,758,-000,000). **Gross national product** (2000): $8,843,-000,000 ($360 per capita). **Population economically active** (1999): total 8,831,000; activity rate of total population 36.4% (participation rates: ages 16–59 [male], 16–54 [female] 70.4%; female [1994] 43.0%; unemployed 0.6%). **Tourism** (1997): receipts $19,-000,000. **Land use** (1994): forested 2.9%; meadows and pastures 46.5%; agricultural and under permanent cultivation 10.1%; other 40.5%.

## Foreign trade

**Imports** (1998): $2,717,000,000 (machinery and metalworking products 49.6%, food products 20.9%, other 29.5%). *Major import sources:* western Europe 30.6%; Russia 20.5%; Asia 14.2%; Kazakhstan 5.2%; Ukraine 3.2%. **Exports** (1998): $2,888,000,-000 (cotton fiber 41.5%, energy 22.7%, gold 6.0%, other 29.8%). *Major export destinations:* western Europe 33.7%; Russia 22.6%; Asia 11.6%; Ukraine 5.4%; Kazakhstan 5.4%; Tajikistan 2.9%; Turkmenistan 2.5%.

## Transport and communications

**Transport.** *Railroads* (2000): length 3,950 km; (1999) passenger-km 1,900,000,000; (1999) metric ton-km cargo 13,900,000,000. *Roads* (1997): total length 84,400 km (paved 87%). *Vehicles* (1994): passenger cars 865,300; buses 14,500. *Air transport* (2000; Uzbekistan Airways): passenger-km 3,732,000,000; metric ton-km cargo 76,600,000; airports (1998) with scheduled flights 9. **Communications,** in total units (units per 1,000 persons). Daily newspaper circulation (1996): 75,000 (3.3); television receivers (1999): 6,700,000 (276); telephone main lines (2001): 1,663,000 (66); cellular telephone subscribers (2001): 62,800 (2.5); Internet users (2001): 150,000 (5.9).

## Education and health

**Educational attainment** (1989). Percentage of population age 25 and over having: primary education or no formal schooling 13.3%; some secondary 19.8%; completed secondary and some postsecondary

57.7%; higher 9.2%. **Literacy** (1998): total population age 15 and over literate 88.0% (male 92.7%, female 83.4%). **Health** (1995): physicians 76,200 (1 per 302 persons); hospital beds 192,000 (1 per 120 persons); infant mortality rate per 1,000 live births (2001) 38.0. **Food** (2000): daily per capita caloric intake 2,371 (vegetable products 82%, animal products 18%); 93% of FAO recommended minimum.

## Military

**Total active duty personnel** (2001): 78,100 (army 64.0%, air force 11.7%, other 24.3%). **Military expenditure as percentage of GNP** (1999): 1.7% (world 2.4%); per capita expenditure $38.

**Did you know?** The name Uzbek probably originated in the 14th century from Öz Beg Khan, under whom the Golden Horde of the Mongols reached its apogee.

## Background

Genghis Khan's grandson Shibaqan received the territory of Uzbekistan as his inheritance in the 13th century AD. His Mongols ruled over nearly 100 mainly Turkic tribes, who would eventually intermarry with the Mongols to form the Uzbeks and other Turkic peoples of Central Asia. In the early 16th century, a federation of Mongol-Uzbeks invaded and occupied settled regions, including an area called Transoxania that would become the Uzbeks' permanent homeland. By the early 19th century, the region was dominated by the khanates of Khiva, Bukhara, and Quqon, all of which eventually succumbed to Russian domination. The Uzbek Soviet Socialist Republic was created in 1924. In June 1990 Uzbekistan became the first Central Asian republic to declare sovereignty. It achieved full independence from the USSR in 1991. During the 1990s its economy was considered the strongest in Central Asia, though its political system was deemed harsh.

## Recent Developments

During 2002 Uzbekistan sought to strengthen and solidify the relationship it had established with the US as one of the main partners in the international antiterrorist coalition. Although some questions were raised on the US side about the depth of Uzbek Pres. Islam Karimov's commitment to economic reform and improving his country's human rights record, Uzbekistan appeared to be doing well out of the relationship. For 2002 the US provided $193 million to promote democracy, market reform, and security projects, with the largest amount going for humanitarian aid. In March Karimov visited Washington, where he was promised that economic and military relations would continue to be close even after the departure of the US military presence in Uzbekistan when operations ceased in Afghanistan. In April 2003 the parliament adopted a number of constitutional changes including a provision to divide civil and criminal courts systems and another to separate the posts of president and head of government, the responsibilities of the latter going to the prime minister. Henceforth the country was to be ruled by a government answerable to the parliament.

**Internet resources:**
<www.tashkent.org/uzland/index.html>

# Vanuatu

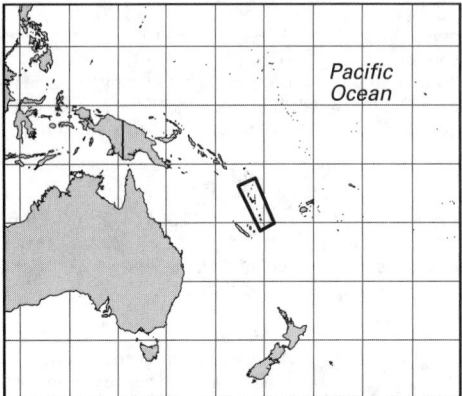

Pacific Ocean

**Official name:** Ripablik blong Vanuatu (Bislama); République de Vanuatu (French); Republic of Vanuatu (English). **Form of government:** republic with a single legislative house (Parliament [52]). **Chief of state:** President John Bani (from 1999). **Head of government:** Prime Minister Edward Natapei (from 2001). **Capital:** Vila. **Official languages:** Bislama; French; English. **Official religion:** none. **Monetary unit:** vatu (VT); valuation (7 Jul 2003) $1 = VT 118.85.

## Demography

**Area:** 4,707 sq mi, 12,190 sq km. **Population** (2002): 207,000. **Density** (2002): persons per sq mi 44.0, persons per sq km 17.0. **Urban** (2002): 21.0%. **Sex distribution** (1999): male 51.46%; female 48.54%. **Age breakdown** (1999): under 15, 37.8%; 15–29, 29.4%; 30–44, 18.2%; 45–59, 9.7%; 60–74, 4.0%; 75 and over, 0.9%. **Ethnic composition** (1999): Ni-Vanuatu 98.7%; European and other Pacific Islanders 1.3%. **Religious affiliation** (1989): Christian 89.7%, of which Presbyterian 35.8%, Roman Catholic 14.5%, Anglican 14.0%, Seventh-day Adventist 8.2%; Custom (traditional beliefs) 4.6%; unknown 4.0%; nonreligious 1.7%. **Major towns** (1999): Vila (Port-Vila) 30,139; Luganville 11,360. **Location:** island group in Oceania, between the South Pacific Ocean and the Coral Sea.

## Vital statistics

**Birth rate** per 1,000 population (2002): 31.6 (world avg. 21.2). **Death rate** per 1,000 population (2002): 5.5 (world avg. 8.9). **Natural increase rate** per 1,000 population (2002): 26.1 (world avg. 12.3). **Total fertility rate** (avg. births per childbearing woman; 2002): 4.3. **Marriage rate** per 1,000 population (1985): c. 7.4. **Divorce rate** per 1,000 population (1985): less than 0.7. **Life expectancy** at birth (2002): male 67.0 years; female 70.0 years.

## National economy

**Budget** (1998). *Revenue*: VT 8,536,000,000 (taxes on international trade 33.0%; taxes on goods and services 32.0%; foreign grants 20.9%; nontax revenue 10.2%). *Expenditures*: VT 12,611,000,000 (current expenditure 58.0%, of which general public services 17.2%, education 13.2%, public order and safety

8.4%, health 6.6%, economic affairs and services 5.8%; capital expenditure 42.0%). **Public debt** (external, outstanding; 2000): $67,200,000. **Household income and expenditure** (1985). Average household size (1989) 5.1; income per household $11,299; sources of income: wages and salaries 59.0%, self-employment 33.7%; expenditure (1990): food and nonalcoholic beverages 30.5%, housing 20.7%, transportation 13.2%, health and recreation 12.3%, tobacco and alcohol 10.4%. **Production** (metric tons except as noted). *Agriculture, forestry, fishing* (1999): coconuts 339,000, roots and tubers 65,000, bananas 12,500; livestock (number of live animals) 151,000 cattle, 62,000 pigs, 320,000 chickens; roundwood (1998) 63,200 cu m; fish catch (2000) 73,490, of which tuna 71,120. *Mining and quarrying*: small quantities of coral-reef limestone, crushed stone, sand, and gravel. *Manufacturing* (value added in VT '000,000; 1995): food, beverages, and tobacco 645; wood products 423; fabricated metal products 377; paper products 125; chemical, rubber, plastic, and nonmetallic products 84; textiles, clothing, and leather 54. *Energy production (consumption)*: electricity (kW-hr; 1997) 30,000,000 (30,000,000); petroleum products (metric tons; 1997) none (20,000). **Land use** (1994): forested 75.0%; meadows and pastures 2.0%; agricultural 11.8%; other 11.2%. **Population economically active** (1999): total 76,370; activity rate of total population 40.9% (participation rates: ages 15–64, 78.2%; female 49.6%). **Gross national product** (2000): $226,000,000 ($1,150 per capita). **Tourism** (2000): receipts from visitors $58,000,000; expenditures by nationals abroad $9,000,000.

## Foreign trade

**Imports** (1997-c.i.f.): VT 10,888,000,000 (machinery and transport equipment 25.7%, food and live animals 19.7%, basic manufactures 15.2%, mineral fuels 10.6%, chemical products 6.2%, beverages and tobacco 3.6%). *Major import sources:* Australia 42.1%; France 13.5%; New Zealand 12.2%; Japan 7.3%; Fiji 6.0%. **Exports** (1997-f.o.b.): VT 4,087,000,000 (copra 49.0%, timber 12.3%, beef 10.2%, cacao beans 5.9%). *Major export destinations:* EU 45.9%; Bangladesh 12.6%; Japan 10.4%; New Caledonia 4.5%; Australia 2.3%.

## Transport and communications

**Transport.** *Roads* (1996): total length 1,070 km (paved 24%). *Vehicles* (1996): passenger cars 4,000; trucks and buses 2,600. *Air transport* (2001; Air Vanuatu only): passenger-km 212,039,000; metric ton-km 1,899,000; airports (1996) with scheduled flights 29. **Communications**, in total units (units per 1,000 persons). Radio receivers (1997): 62,000 (350); television receivers (1997): 2,000 (14); telephone main lines (2001): 6,800 (34); cellular telephone subscribers (2001): 300 (1.7); Internet users (2001): 5,500 (27).

## Education and health

**Educational attainment** (1999). Percentage of population age 15 and over having: no formal schooling 18.0%; incomplete primary education 20.6%; completed primary 35.5%; some secondary 12.2%; com-

---

*1 metric ton = about 1.1 short tons;    1 kilometer = 0.6 mi (statute);    1 metric ton-km cargo = about 0.68 short ton-mi cargo;    c.i.f.: cost, insurance, and freight;    f.o.b.: free on board*

pleted secondary 8.5%; higher 5.2%, of which university 1.3%. **Literacy** (1998): total population age 15 and over literate 64%. **Health** (1997): physicians 21 (1 per 8,524 persons); hospital beds 573 (1 per 312 persons); infant mortality rate per 1,000 live births (2002) 29.0. **Food** (1999): daily per capita caloric intake 2,766 (vegetable products 86%, animal products 14%); (1997) 121% of FAO recommended minimum.

## Military

**Total active duty personnel:** Vanuatu has a paramilitary force of about 300.

## Background

The islands of Vanuatu were inhabited for at least 3,000 years by Melanesian peoples before being discovered in 1606 by the Portuguese. They were rediscovered by French navigator Louis-Antoine de Bougainville in 1768, then explored by English mariner Capt. James Cook in 1774 and named New Hebrides. Sandalwood merchants and European missionaries arrived in the mid-19th century; they were followed by British and French cotton planters. Control of the islands was sought by both the French and British, who agreed in 1906 to form a condominium government. During World War II a major Allied naval base was on Espíritu Santo; the island group escaped Japanese invasion. New Hebrides became the independent Republic of Vanuatu in 1980. Much of the nation's housing was ravaged by a hurricane in 1987.

## Recent Developments

In the May 2002 elections, Prime Minister Edward Natapei's Vanua'aku Party and its coalition partner, the Union of Moderate Parties, won 14 and 15 seats, respectively, in the 52-member Parliament. With additional support from independent members, Natapei was returned as prime minister. The election was monitored by Transparency International observers, who found fundamental flaws with the electoral roll and noted delays, discrepancies, and errors in counting and reporting of results. In July former prime minister Barak Sopé was jailed for fraud in connection with his signing of unauthorized government guarantees worth millions of dollars, but Pres. John Bernard Bani later pardoned and released him on medical grounds.

**Internet resources:** <www.vanuatutourism.com>

# Vatican City State

**In full:** State of the Vatican City (Holy See). **Form of government:** ecclesiastical. **Chief of state:** Pope John Paul II. **Head of government:** Secretary of State Cardinal Angelo Sodano. **Capital:** Vatican City. **Languages:** Italian, Latin. **Religion:** Roman Catholic. **Monetary unit:** 1 euro (€) = 100 cents; $1 = €0.87 (7 Jul 2003); at conversion on 1 Jan 2002, €1 = 1,936.3 lira (Lit).

## Demography

**Area:** 0.44 sq km, 0.17 sq mi. **Population:** (2002 est.): 900. **Density:** (2001): persons per sq mi 5,298,

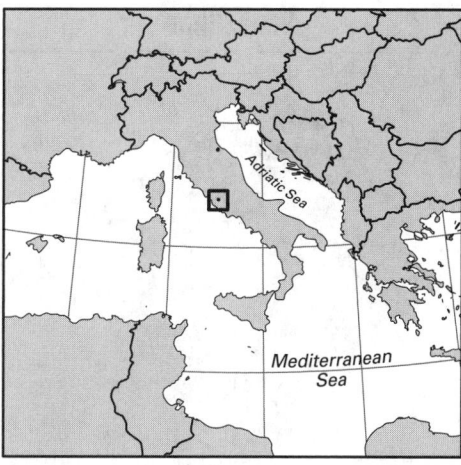

persons per sq km 2,045. **Location:** southern Europe, within the commune of Rome, Italy. **Annual budget:** $209 million. **Industries:** banking and finance; printing; production of a small amount of mosaics and uniforms; tourism.

## Background

Vatican City, the independent papal state, is the smallest independent state in the world. Its medieval and Renaissance walls form its boundaries except on the southeast, at St. Peter's Square. Within the walls is a miniature nation, with its own diplomatic missions, newspaper, post office, radio station, banking system, army of more than 100 Swiss Guards, and publishing house. Extraterritoriality of the state extends to Castel Gandolfo, summer home of the Pope, and to several churches and palaces in Rome proper. Its independent sovereignty was recognized in the Lateran Treaty of 1929. The pope has absolute executive, legislative, and judicial powers within the city. He appoints the members of the Vatican's government organs, which are separate from those of the Holy See. Its many imposing buildings include St. Peter's Basilica, the Vatican Palace, and the Vatican Museums. Frescoes by Michelangelo and Pinturicchio in the Sistine Chapel and Raphael's Stanze are also there. The Vatican Library contains a priceless collection of manuscripts from the pre-Christian and Christian eras.

## Recent Developments

On 24 Jan 2002 Pope John Paul II, joined by more than 200 religious leaders representing established and folk religions, gathered in Assisi, Italy, for a day of prayer denouncing violence and terror perpetrated under any auspices, especially in the name of religion. The value of modern telecommunications technology in facilitating the Vatican's apostolic mission was witnessed when the aging pontiff made his first "virtual visit" to Moscow to pray the rosary with the Roman Catholic faithful. The restructuring of the Roman Church in Russia and its restoration to the status it occupied in the precommunist era occupied a prominent position in the year's activities. On 14 November Pope John Paul II addressed the Italian Parliament, the first time a pontiff had done so, and urged a continuing important role for Christianity in the EU.

**Internet resources:**

# Venezuela

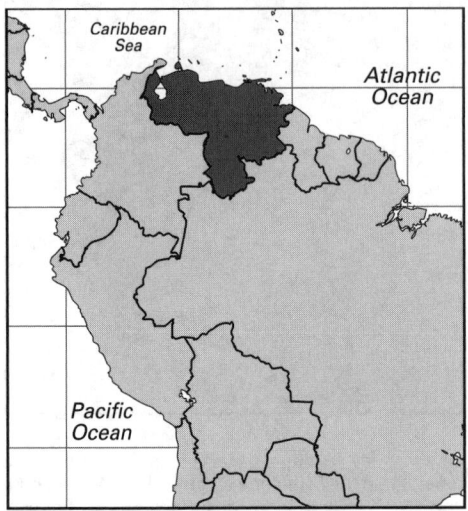

**Official name:** República Bolivariana de Venezuela (Bolivarian Republic of Venezuela). **Form of government:** federal multiparty republic with a unicameral legislature (National Assembly [165]). **Head of state and government:** President Hugo Chávez Frias (from 14 Apr 2002). **Capital:** Caracas. **Official language:** Spanish; 31 indigenous Indian languages were made official in May 2002. **Official religion:** none. **Monetary unit:** 1 bolívar (B, plural Bs) = 100 céntimos; valuation (7 Jul 2003) $1 = Bs 1,598.

## Demography

**Area:** 353,841 sq mi, 916,445 sq km. **Population** (2002): 25,093,000. **Density** (2002): persons per sq mi 70.9, persons per sq km 27.4. **Urban** (2000): 87.1%. **Sex distribution** (2000): male 50.31%; female 49.69%. **Age breakdown** (2000): under 15, 34.0%; 15–29, 27.5%; 30–44, 20.2%; 45–59, 11.7%; 60–74, 5.2%; 75 and over, 1.4%. **Ethnic composition** (1993): mestizo 67%; white 21%; black 10%; Indian 2%. **Religious affiliation** (2000): Roman Catholic 89.5%; Protestant 2.0%; other Christian 1.4%; Spiritist 1.1%; nonreligious/atheist 2.2%; other 3.8%. **Major cities** (2000): Caracas 1,975,787 (urban agglomeration [2001] 3,177,000); Maracaibo 1,764,038; Valencia 1,338,833; Barquisimeto 875,790; Ciudad Guayana 704,168. **Location:** northern South America, bordering the Caribbean Sea, the North Atlantic Ocean, Guyana, Brazil, and Colombia.

## Vital statistics

**Birth rate** per 1,000 population (2002): 20.2 (world avg. 21.2). **Death rate** per 1,000 population (2002): 4.9 (world avg. 8.9). **Total fertility rate** (avg. births per childbearing woman; 2002): 2.4. **Marriage rate** per 1,000 population (2000): 3.8. **Divorce rate** per 1,000 population (2000): 0.8. **Life expectancy** at birth (2002): male 70.5 years; female 76.8 years.

## National economy

**Budget** (1998). *Revenue*: Bs 9,017,475,000,000 (tax revenues 73.6%; nontax revenues 26.4%, of which oil revenues 24.9%). *Expenditures*: Bs 10,460,235,000,000 (subsidies 43.7%; goods and services 23.9%; capital expenditure 18.9%; debt service 11.8%). **Public debt** (external, outstanding; 2000): $27,628,000,000. **Production** (metric tons except as noted). *Agriculture, forestry, fishing* (1999): sugarcane 6,850,000, corn (maize) 1,024,-000, bananas 1,000,394; livestock (number of live animals) 15,992,400 cattle, 4,500,000 pigs, 110,000,000 chickens; roundwood (1998) 2,038,-000 cu m; fish catch (1998) 506,177. *Mining and quarrying* (1998): iron ore 19,305,000; bauxite 4,633,000; gold 14,046 kg. *Manufacturing* (value added in 1984 Bs '000,000; 1997): ferrous and nonferrous metals 16,355; food products 13,277; chemicals 10,004. *Energy production (consumption)*: electricity (kW-hr; 1997) 75,300,000,000 (75,145,000,000); coal (metric tons; 1999) 6,588,-000 (419,000); crude petroleum (barrels; 2001) 972,000,000 ([1997] 374,000,000); petroleum products (metric tons; 1997) 59,974,000 (25,090,-000); natural gas (cu m; 1997) 43,690,000,000 (43,690,000,000). **Gross national product** (2000): $104,065,000,000 ($4,310 per capita). **Population economically active** (1997): total 9,507,125; activity rate 41.7% (participation rates: over age 15, 64.6%; female 35.9%; unemployed 10.6%). **Household income and expenditure.** Average household size (1990) 5.1; average annual income per household (1981) Bs 42,492 ($9,899); expenditure (1995): food 40.6%, housing 13.8%, transportation and communications 8.6%, clothing 5.3%, health 3.1%, education and recreation 2.9%. **Tourism** (2000): receipts $563,000,000; expenditures $1,824,000,000. **Land use** (1998): forest and other 75.3%; pasture 20.7%; agriculture 4.0%.

## Foreign trade

**Imports** (2000-f.o.b. in balance of trade): $9,907,500,000 (nonelectrical machinery 18.8%, chemicals and chemical products 13.8%, transport equipment 11.6%, electrical machinery 11.1%). *Major import sources:* US 37.8%; Colombia 7.4%; Brazil 5.0%; Italy 4.4%; Mexico 4.3%. **Exports** (2000-f.o.b. in balance of trade): $21,602,200,000 (crude petroleum 58.9%, refined petroleum 26.6%, iron and steel 2.7%, aluminum 2.5%). *Major export destinations:* US 59.6%; Netherlands Antilles 5.6%; Brazil 3.6%; Colombia 2.8%.

## Transport and communications

**Transport.** *Railroads* (1996): length (1994) 627 km; passenger-km 149,905; metric ton-km cargo 54,474,000. *Roads* (1999): total length 96,155 km (paved 34%). *Vehicles* (1997): passenger cars 1,505,000; trucks and buses 542,000. *Air transport* (1998): passenger-km 3,133,000,000; metric ton-km cargo 332,000,000; airports (1997) with scheduled flights 20. **Communications,** in total units (units per 1,000 persons). Daily newspaper circulation (1996): 4,600,000 (206); radio receivers (1997): 10,750,000 (472); television receivers (1998):

---

*1 metric ton = about 1.1 short tons; 1 kilometer = 0.6 mi (statute); 1 metric ton-km cargo = about 0.68 short ton-mi cargo; c.i.f.: cost, insurance, and freight; f.o.b.: free on board*

4,300,000 (185); telephone main lines (2001): 2,758,300 (112); cellular telephone subscribers (2001): 6,489,900 (264); personal computers (2001): 1,300,000 (53); Internet users (2001): 1,300,000 (53).

## Education and health

**Educational attainment** (1993). Percentage of population age 25 and over having: no formal schooling 8.0%; primary education or less 43.7%; some secondary and secondary 38.3%; postsecondary 10.0%. **Literacy** (1995 est.): total population age 15 and over literate 91.1%; males 91.8%; females 90.3%. **Health** (1997): physicians 28,341 (1 per 804 persons); hospital beds 38,924 (1 per 585 persons); infant mortality rate per 1,000 live births (2002) 24.6. **Food** (1999): daily per capita caloric intake 2,229 (vegetable products 84%, animal products 16%); (1997) 90% of FAO recommended minimum.

## Military

**Total active duty personnel** (2001): 82,300 (army 69.3%, navy 22.2%, air force 8.5%). **Military expenditure as percentage of GNP** (1999): 1.4% (world 2.4%); per capita expenditure $61.

## Background

In 1498 Christopher Columbus sighted Venezuela; in 1499 the navigators Alonso de Ojeda, Amerigo Vespucci, and Juan de la Cosa traced the coast. A Spanish missionary established the first European settlement at Cumaná c. 1520. In 1718 it was included in the viceroyalty of New Granada and was made a captaincy general in 1731. Venezuelan Creoles led by Francisco de Miranda and Simón Bolívar spearheaded the South American independence movement, and though Venezuela declared independence from Spain in 1811, it was not assured until 1821. Military dictators generally ruled the country from 1830 until the overthrow of Marcos Pérez Jiménez in 1958. A new constitution adopted in 1961 marked the beginning of democracy. As a founding member of OPEC, it enjoyed relative economic prosperity from oil production during the 1970s, and its economy has remained dependent on the world petroleum market. The leftist president Hugo Chávez Frías promulgated a new constitution in 1999, and he was reelected in 2002; a period of great political and economic tumult ensued.

## Recent Developments

Loyalist military officers restored Venezuelan Pres. Hugo Chávez Frías to the presidency on the morning of 14 Apr 2002, just 48 hours after he had been removed from office. The overthrow had followed a massive protest march by Chávez's opponents that ended in the death of at least 17 demonstrators. The demonstrators had hoped to convince Chávez that his high-handed efforts to implement leftist policies had destroyed his government's legitimacy and that he should resign. Divisions between and among the three groups encouraged supporters of the ousted president, and the coup collapsed. A general strike paralyzed much of the country on 21 October, and several days later disgruntled military officers called for the overthrow of the government. On 4 November the opposition delivered two million signatures demanding a referendum (deemed unconstitutional by the government) on whether President Chávez should remain in office. A defiant Chávez took control of the Caracas Metropolitan Police Force, and protests against the action were met with riot troops and tear gas. The crisis deepened on 2 December when opposition forces (labor unions, business federations, and a coordinating committee of democratic political parties) declared a general strike for the purpose of forcing Chávez to resign or call early elections. When the strike spread to the petroleum sector, oil production was drastically curtailed, and Chávez threatened to impose a state of emergency. In late January 2003, deep in the second month of the crippling strike, former US president Jimmy Carter traveled to Caracas and proposed a constitutional solution. In early February Chávez's opponents petitioned for early elections and an easing of the strike. The key labor and business leaders left the country, while Chávez agreed to hold the referendum on his presidency, probably in August 2003.

**Internet resources:** <www.venezuelatuya.com>

# Vietnam

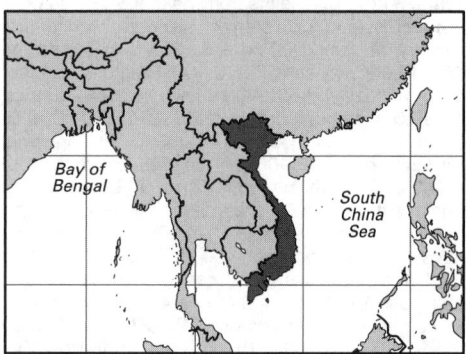

**Official name:** Cong Hoa Xa Hoi Chu Nghia Viet Nam (Socialist Republic of Vietnam). **Form of government:** socialist republic with one legislative house (National Assembly [450]). **Head of state:** President Tran Duc Luong (from 1997). **Head of government:** Prime Minister Phan Van Khai (from 1997). **Capital:** Hanoi. **Official language:** Vietnamese. **Official religion:** none. **Monetary unit:** 1 dong (D) = 10 hao = 100 xu; valuation (7 Jul 2003) $1 = D 15,503.

## Demography

**Area:** 127,816 sq mi, 331,041 sq km. **Population** (2002): 80,200,000. **Density** (2002): persons per sq mi 624.7, persons per sq km 241.2. **Urban** (1999): 23.5%. **Sex distribution** (1999): male 49.15%; female 50.85%. **Age breakdown** (2001): under 15, 32.1%; 15–29, 29.4%; 30–44, 21.1%; 45–59, 9.7%; 60–74, 5.8%; 75 and over, 1.9%. **Ethnic composition** (2000): Vietnamese 85.0%; Han Chinese 3.5%; Montagnards 1.9%; Tho (Tay) 1.6%; Tai 1.5%; Muong 1.4%; Khmer 1.2%; Nung 1.0%; other 2.9%. **Religious affiliation** (1995): Buddhist 66.7%; Christian 8.7%, of which Roman Catholic 7.7%, Protestant 1.0%; Cao Dai (a New-Religionist group) 3.5%; Hoa Hao (a New-Religionist group) 2.1%; other 19.0%. **Major cities** (1992): Ho Chi Minh City 4,549,000 (1999); Hanoi

2,154,900 (1993); Haiphong 783,133; Da Nang 382,674; Buon Ma Thuot 282,095. **Location:** southeastern Asia, bordering China, the Gulf of Tonkin, the South China Sea, the Gulf of Thailand, Cambodia, and Laos.

## Vital statistics

**Birth rate** per 1,000 population (2000): 21.6 (world avg. 22.5). **Death rate** per 1,000 population (2000): 6.3 (world avg. 9.0). **Natural increase rate** per 1,000 population (2000): 15.3 (world avg. 13.5). **Total fertility rate** (avg. births per childbearing woman; 2000): 2.5. **Life expectancy** at birth (2000): male 66.8 years; female 71.9 years.

## National economy

**Budget** (1998). *Revenue*: D 73,000,000,000,000 (tax revenue 80.8%, of which taxes on trade 20.4%, corporate income taxes 17.9%, turnover taxes 16.2%; nontax revenues 16.3%; grants 2.9%). *Expenditures*: D 80,200,000,000,000 (current expenditures 67.6%, of which social services 30.4%; capital expenditures 25.6%; other 6.8%). **Public debt** (external, outstanding; 2000): $11,546,000,000. **Gross national product** (2000): $30,439,000,000 ($390 per capita). **Tourism** (1997): receipts from visitors $88,000,000. **Production** (metric tons except as noted). *Agriculture, forestry, fishing* (2000): rice 32,554,000, sugarcane 15,145,000, cassava 2,036,000; livestock (number of live animals) 54,500,000 ducks, 20,194,000 pigs, 4,137,000 cattle; roundwood (1999) 36,730,000 cu m, of which fuelwood 32,174,000 cu m, industrial roundwood 4,556,000 cu m; fish catch (2000) 1,442,000, of which marine fish 1,008,000. *Mining and quarrying* (1998): phosphate rock (gross weight) 860,000; tin (metal content) 5,000. *Manufacturing* (gross value of production in D '000,000,000; 1998): food and beverages 36.5; cement, bricks, pottery, and glass 13.7; textiles 8.4. *Energy production (consumption)*: electricity (kW-hr; 1998) 21,847,000,000 ([1997] 19,253,000,000); coal (metric tons; 1998) 10,800,000 ([1997] 6,984,000); crude petroleum (barrels; 1998) 83,000,000 ([1997] 293,200); petroleum products (metric tons; 1997) 38,000 (5,691,-000); natural gas (cu m; 1997) 11,550,000 (11,550,-000). **Population economically active** (1989): total 30,521,019; activity rate 47.4% (participation rates: ages 15–64, 79.9%; female 51.7%; unemployed [1997] 10.3%). **Household income and expenditure.** Average household size (1989) 4.8; income per household (1990) D 577,008 ($93); expenditure (1990): food 62.4%, clothing 5.0%, household goods 4.6%, education 2.9%, housing 2.5%. **Land use** (1994): forested 29.6%; meadows and pastures 1.0%; agricultural and under permanent cultivation 21.5%; other 47.9%.

## Foreign trade

**Imports** (1998-f.o.b. in balance of trade and c.i.f. in commodities and trading partners): $11,527,000,-000 (machinery equipment [including aircraft] 17.8%; petroleum products 7.2%; textiles, clothing, and leather 7.1%; iron and steel 4.5%; unspecified 50.1%). *Major import sources:* Singapore 13.4%; South Korea 12.1%; Japan 11.8%; Taiwan 10.8%;

China 9.1%. **Exports** (1998): $9,365,000,000 (garments 14.4%; crude petroleum 13.2%; rice 10.9%; footwear 10.7%; fish, crustaceans, and mollusks 8.7%; coffee 6.3%). *Major export destinations:* Japan 18.0%; Germany 9.2%; US 6.2%; France 5.8%; Australia 5.4%.

## Transport and communications

**Transport.** *Railroads* (1999): route length 3,142 km; passenger-km 2,727,000,000; metric ton-km cargo 1,398,000,000. *Roads* (1996): total length 93,300 km (paved 25%). *Vehicles* (1994): passenger cars, trucks, and buses 200,000. *Air transport* (1999; Vietnam Airlines only): passenger-km 3,831,000,-000; metric ton-km cargo 98,455,000; airports (1997) with scheduled flights 12. **Communications,** in total units (units per 1,000 persons). Daily newspaper circulation (1996): 300,000 (4.1); radio receivers (1997): 8,200,000 (109); television receivers (1999): 14,500,000 (187); telephone main lines (2001): 3,049,900 (38); cellular telephone subscribers (2001): 1,251,200 (15); personal computers (2001): 800,000 (10); Internet users (2001): 400,000 (4.9).

## Education and health

**Educational attainment** (1989). Percentage of population age 25 and over having: no formal education (illiterate) 16.6%; incomplete and complete primary 69.8%; incomplete and complete secondary 10.6%; higher 2.6%; unknown 0.4%. **Literacy** (2000): population age 15 and over literate 93.3%; males 95.7%; females 91.0%. **Health** (1999): physicians 37,100 (1 per 2,092 persons); hospital beds (1997) 197,900 (1 per 380 persons); infant mortality rate per 1,000 live births (2000) 31.1. **Food** (2000): daily per capita caloric intake 2,583 (vegetable products 89%, animal products 11%); 120% of FAO recommended minimum.

## Military

**Total active duty personnel** (2002): 484,000 (army 85.1%, navy 8.7%, air force 6.2%). **Military expenditure as percentage of GNP** (1997): 2.4% (world 2.5%); per capita expenditure $44.

Did you know? Vietnam is perhaps best known for its wars of rebellion and unification in the latter half of the 20th century, yet perhaps even more important to the national psyche are the 2,000 years of struggle against recurrent invasions from the north.

## Background

A distinct Vietnamese group began to emerge c. 200 BC in the independent kingdom of Nam Viet, which was annexed to China in the 1st century BC. The Vietnamese were under continuous Chinese control until the 10th century AD. The southern region was gradually overrun by Vietnamese from the north in the late 15th century. The area was divided into two parts in the early 17th century, with the northern part known

*1 metric ton = about 1.1 short tons;     1 kilometer = 0.6 mi (statute);     1 metric ton-km cargo = about 0.68 short ton-mi cargo;     c.i.f.: cost, insurance, and freight;     f.o.b.: free on board*

as Tonkin, and the southern part as Cochin China. In 1802 the northern and southern parts of Vietnam were unified under a single dynasty.

Following several years of attempted French colonial expansion in the region, the French captured Saigon in 1859 and later the rest of the area, controlling it until World War II. The Japanese occupied Vietnam 1940–45 and declared it independent at the end of World War II, a move the French opposed. The French and Vietnamese fought the First Indochina War until French forces with US financial backing were defeated at Dien Bien Phu in 1954; evacuation of French troops ensued.

Following an international conference at Geneva, Vietnam was partitioned along the 17th parallel, with the northern part under Ho Chi Minh, and the southern part under Bao Dai; the partition was to be temporary, but the reunification elections scheduled for 1956 were never held. Bao Dai declared the independence of South Vietnam (Republic of Vietnam), while the Communists established North Vietnam (Democratic Republic of Vietnam). The activities of North Vietnamese guerrillas and pro-communist rebels in South Vietnam led to US intervention and the Vietnam War. A cease-fire agreement was signed in 1973, and US troops were withdrawn. The civil war soon resumed, and in 1975 North Vietnam invaded South Vietnam and the South Vietnamese government collapsed. In 1976 the two Vietnams were united as the Socialist Republic of Vietnam. From the mid-1980s, the government enacted a series of economic reforms and began to open up to Asian and western nations. During the 1990s the US moved to normalize relations with it.

## Recent Developments

At the first meeting of the Central Committee, the Vietnam Communist Party's top decision-making body, in February–March 2002, the plenum adopted policies to boost the role of the private sector and to permit party members to engage in private business for the first time. On 19 May Vietnamese voters went to the polls to elect deputies to the 11th legislature of the National Assembly, but election proceedings were marred when three candidates were disqualified for corruption. The National Assembly reelected Tran Duc Luong and Phan Van Khai for another five-year term as president and prime minister, respectively. In November the Central Committee adopted an economic development plan for 2003 that included two controversial projects, the Son La hydroelectric power plant and the Cau Mau fertilizer complex. In May 2002 Russia completed its withdrawal from Cam Ranh Bay and turned over its naval facilities to Vietnam. Relations with the US underwent strains as American lobby groups charged Vietnam with dumping catfish and shrimp on the American market. Vietnam's human rights and religious practices also attracted official criticism.

Internet resources: <www.vietnamtourism.com>

# Virgin Islands (US)

**Official name:** Virgin Islands of the US. **Political status:** organized unincorporated territory of the US with one legislative house (Senate [15]). **Chief of state:** President of the US George W. Bush (from 2001). **Head of government:** Governor Charles Turnbull (from 1999). **Capital:** Charlotte Amalie. **Official lan-**

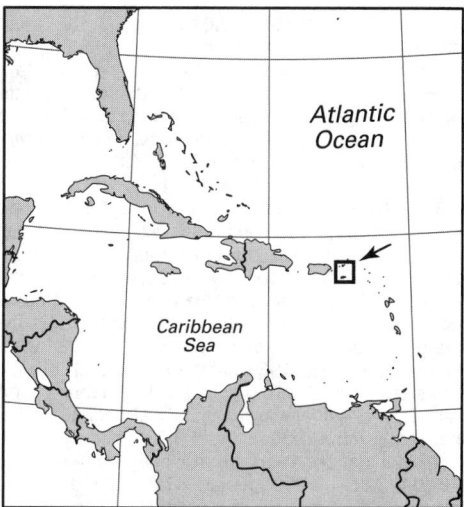

guage: English. **Official religion:** none. **Monetary unit:** 1 US dollar ($) = 100 cents.

## Demography

**Area:** 136 sq mi, 353 sq km. **Population** (2002): 110,000. **Density** (2002): persons per sq mi 808.8, persons per sq km 311.6. **Urban** (1998): 45.7%. **Sex distribution** (2000): male 46.91%; female 53.09%. **Age breakdown** (2000): under 15, 27.8%; 15–29, 22.4%; 30–44, 17.9%; 45–59, 19.1%; 60–74, 9.7%; 75 and over, 3.1%. **Ethnic composition** (1995): black 76.7%, of which Hispanic 6.7%; white 10.4%, of which Hispanic 1.5%; other 12.9%, of which Hispanic 9.1%. **Religious affiliation** (2000): Christian 96.3%, of which Protestant 51.0% (including Anglican 13.0%), Roman Catholic 27.5%, independent Christian 12.2%; nonreligious 2.2%; other 1.5%. **Major towns** (2000): Charlotte Amalie 11,004 (urban agglomeration 18,914); Christiansted 2,637; Frederiksted 732. **Location:** northeastern Caribbean, islands between the Caribbean Sea and the North Atlantic Ocean.

## Vital statistics

**Birth rate** per 1,000 population (2001): 15.9 (world avg. 21.2); (1998) legitimate 30.2%; illegitimate 69.8%. **Death rate** per 1,000 population (2001): 5.5 (world avg. 8.9). **Natural increase rate** per 1,000 population (2001): 10.4 (world avg. 12.3). **Total fertility rate** (avg. births per childbearing woman; 2001): 2.3. **Marriage rate** per 1,000 population (1993): 35.1. **Divorce rate** per 1,000 population (1993): 4.5. **Life expectancy** at birth (2001): male 74.4 years; female 82.4 years.

## National economy

**Budget.** *Revenue* (1998): $459,485,000 (personal income tax 45.7%, gross receipts tax 18.5%, property tax 9.9%, corporate income tax 5.4%, excise tax 3.7%). *Expenditures* (1998): $398,394,000 (education 30.4%, health 17.8%, executive branch 7.8%, public safety 7.6%, public works 6.3%, College of the Virgin Islands 5.7%). **Production.** *Agriculture, forestry, fishing* (value of sales in $'000; 1998): milk 1,263, livestock and livestock products 655 (of which cattle and calves 439, hogs and pigs 46), ornamental plants and other nursery products 364; livestock (number of live animals) 3,636 cattle, 3,074 sheep, 3,538 chickens; fish catch (1998) 910 metric tons. *Mining and quarrying*: sand and crushed stone for local use. *Manufacturing* ($'000; 1997): food and food products 31,949; stone, clay, and glass products 21,897; print and publishing 21,127. *Energy production (consumption)*: electricity (kW-hr; 1997) 1,079,000,000 (1,079,000,000); coal (metric tons; 1997) none (252,000); crude petroleum (barrels; 1997) none (120,212,000); petroleum products (metric tons; 1997) 15,142,000 (2,290,000). **Tourism** (2001): receipts from visitors $1,196,000,000; number of hotel rooms 5,049; occupancy percentage 56.6%. **Household income**. Average household size (2000) 2.6; average annual income per household (2000) $34,991; sources of income (1984): wages and salaries 65.7%, transfer payments 13.0%, interest, dividends, and rent 12.7%, self-employment 2.6%. **Population economically active** (2000): total 50,933; activity rate of total population 46.9% (participation rates: ages 16–64, 72.5% [1990]; female 47.8% [1990]; unemployed 8.6%). **Gross national product** (at current market prices; 1997): $2,666,000,000 ($18,287 per capita). **Public debt** (1999): $1,200,000,000. **Land use** (1994): forested 5.9%; meadows and pastures 26.5%; agricultural and under permanent cultivation 20.6%; other 47.0%.

### Foreign trade

**Imports** (2001-c.i.f.): $4,608,700,000. *Major import sources*: US 15.8%; other countries 84.2%. **Exports** (2001): $4,234,200,000. *Major export destinations* (1995): US 92.7%; other countries 7.3%.

### Transport and communications

**Transport**. *Roads* (1996): total length 856 km. *Vehicles* (1993): passenger cars 51,000; trucks and buses 13,300. *Shipping* (1988): cruise ship arrivals 1,228; passenger arrivals 1,062,010. *Air transport* (1989): passenger arrivals and departures 1,897,000; cargo loaded and unloaded 4,600 metric tons; airports (1999) with scheduled flights 2. **Communications**, in total units (units per 1,000 persons). Daily newspaper circulation (1996): 42,000 (364); radio receivers (1996): 107,000 (927); television receivers (1996): 67,000 (580); telephone main lines (2000): 69,000 (570); cellular telephone subscribers (2000): 35,000 (289); Internet users (1999): 12,000 (100).

### Education and health

**Educational attainment** (1997). Percentage of population age 25 and over having: incomplete primary education 4.4%; completed lower secondary 18.5%; incomplete upper secondary 27.3%; completed upper secondary 24.0%; incomplete undergraduate 14.0%; completed undergraduate 11.8%. **Health** (1989); physicians 130 (1 per 780 persons); hospital beds 252 (1 per 402 persons); infant mortality rate per 1,000 live births (2001) 9.4.

### Military

**Total active duty personnel**: no domestic military force is maintained; the US is responsible for defense and external security.

### Background

The Virgin Islands of the US probably were originally settled by Arawak Indians, but they were inhabited by the Caribs when Christopher Columbus landed on St. Croix in 1493. St. Croix was occupied by the Dutch, English, French, and Spanish and was at one time owned by the Knights of Malta. Denmark occupied St. Thomas, St. John, and St. Croix and established them as a Danish colony in 1754. The US purchased the Danish West Indies in 1917 for $25 million and changed the name to the Virgin Islands. They were administered by the US Department of the Interior from 1931. In 1954 the Organic Act of the Virgin Islands created the current governmental structure, and in 1970 the first popularly elected governor took office. The area suffered extensive damage by hurricanes in 1995.

### Recent Developments

A sharp rise in crime in the US Virgin Islands and the effect this could have on tourism prompted Gov. Charles Turnbull to announce the introduction in May 2002 of a string of unprecedented measures, including a reduction in the age at which a minor could be prosecuted as an adult for murder (from 14 to 13 years) and the enforcement of curfews obliging minors to be off the streets by 10 PM. Funds were also made available for additional police personnel and vehicles. In June Carnival Cruise Lines blamed crime for its decision to cancel calls to the islands by its ships during the 2002–03 winter season.

**Internet resources**: <www.usvitourism.vi>

# Yemen

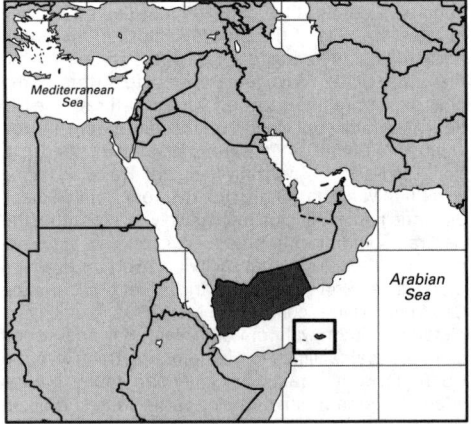

**Official name**: Al-Jumhuriyah al-Yamaniyah (Republic of Yemen). **Form of government**: multiparty republic with two legislative houses (Consultative Council [111]; House of Representatives [301]). **Head of state**: President Field Marshall 'Ali 'Abdallah Salih (from 1990). **Head of government**: Prime Minister 'Abd al-Qadir al-Ba Jamal (from 2001). **Capital**: Sanaa. **Official language**: Arabic. **Official religion**: Islam. **Monetary unit**: 1 Yemeni Rial (YRls) = 100 fils; valuation (7 Jul 2003): $1 = YRls 178.01.

---

*1 metric ton = about 1.1 short tons; 1 kilometer = 0.6 mi (statute); 1 metric ton-km cargo = about 0.68 short ton-mi cargo; c.i.f.: cost, insurance, and freight; f.o.b.: free on board*

## Demography

**Area:** 182,278 sq mi, 472,099 sq km. **Population** (2002): 19,495,000. **Density** (2002): persons per sq mi 91.0, persons per sq km 35.1. **Urban** (2001): 25.0%. **Sex distribution** (2000): male 50.98%; female 49.02%. **Age breakdown** (2000): under 15, 47.5%; 15–29, 27.8%; 30–44, 13.2%; 45–59, 7.1%; 60–74, 3.3%; 75 and over, 1.1%. **Ethnic composition** (2000): Arab 92.8%; Somali 3.7%; black 1.1%; Indo-Pakistani 1.0%; other 1.4%. **Religious affiliation** (1995): Muslim 99.9%, of which Sunni c. 60%, Shi'i c. 40%; other 0.1%. **Major cities** (1994): Sanaa 954,400 (urban agglomeration [2001] 1,410,000); Aden 398,300; Ta'izz 317,600; Al-Hudaydah 298,500; Al-Mukalla 122,400. **Location:** the Middle East, bordering Oman, the Arabian Sea, the Gulf of Aden, the Red Sea, and Saudi Arabia.

## Vital statistics

**Birth rate** per 1,000 population (2001): 43.4 (world avg. 21.2). **Death rate** per 1,000 population (2001): 9.6 (world avg. 8.9). **Natural increase rate** per 1,000 population (2001): 33.8 (world avg. 12.3). **Total fertility rate** (avg. births per childbearing woman; 2001): 3.4. **Life expectancy** at birth (2001): male 58.5 years; female 62.1 years.

## National economy

**Budget** (2000). *Revenue:* YRls 388,950,000,000 (1999; tax revenue 90.1%, of which oil revenue 64.1%, taxes on income and profits 9.4%, customs duties 7.8%; nontax revenue 9.9%). *Expenditures:* YRls 422,250,000,000 (1999; wages and salaries 23.0%; defense 18.1%; economic development 17.5%; interest on debt 13.8%; subsidies 7.7%). **Population economically active** (1999): total 4,118,000; activity rate of total population 24.3% (participation rates [1994]: age 15 and over, 45.8%; female 18.2%; unemployed [1995] 30%). **Production** (metric tons except as noted). *Agriculture, forestry, fishing* (2000): sorghum 401,212, tomatoes 244,720, potatoes 213,445; livestock (number of live animals) 4,760,389 sheep, 4,214,170 goats, 28,000,000 chickens; roundwood (1998) 324,000 cu m; fish catch (1999) 123,252. *Mining and quarrying* (1999): salt 149,000; gypsum 103,000. *Manufacturing* (value of production in YRls '000,000; 1996): food, beverages, and tobacco 43,927; chemicals and chemical products 42,369; nonmetallic mineral products 8,571. *Energy production (consumption):* electricity (kW-hr; 1999) 2,633,000,000 ([1997] 2,482,000,000); crude petroleum (barrels; 2001) 165,200,000 ([1997] 42,700,000); petroleum products (metric tons; 1997) 5,692,000 (4,937,000). **Gross national product** (2000): $6,554,000,000 ($370 per capita). **Household income and expenditure.** Average household size (1998) 7.1; income per household YRls 29,035 ($217). **Tourism** (2000): receipts $64,000,000; expenditures $83,000,000. **Public debt** (external, outstanding; 2000): $4,525,-000,000. **Land use** (1994): forest 3.8%; pasture 30.4%; agriculture 2.9%; other 62.9%.

## Foreign trade

**Imports** (1999-c.i.f. in balance of trade and f.o.b. in commodities and trading partners): $1,535,900,000 (food and live animals 36.2%, of which cereals and re-lated products 17.1%; machinery 15.3%; chemicals and chemical products 8.5%; mineral fuels 7.4%). *Major import sources:* UAE 11.7%; Saudi Arabia 10.2%; US 5.5%; Australia 4.8%; UK 4.7%; Kuwait 4.6%. **Exports** (1999): $2,435,800,000 (crude petroleum 87.5%; petroleum products 8.0%; coffee 0.5%; fish 0.5%). *Major export destinations:* China 28.8%; Thailand 25.5%; South Korea 14.5%; Singapore 8.6%.

## Transport and communications

**Transport.** *Roads* (1996): total length 64,725 km (paved 8.1%). *Vehicles* (1996): passenger cars 240,567; trucks and buses 291,149. *Air transport* (2000): passenger-km 1,574,000,000; metric ton-km cargo 32,000,000; airports (1998) with scheduled flights 12. **Communications,** in total units (units per 1,000 persons). Daily newspaper circulation (1996): 230,000 (15); radio receivers (1997): 1,050,000 (64); television receivers (1999): 5,000,000 (286); telephone main lines (2001): 423,200 (22); cellular telephone subscribers (2001): 152,000 (8.0); Internet users (2001): 17,000 (0.9); personal computers (2001): 37,000 (1.9).

## Education and health

**Educational attainment** (1998). Percentage of population age 10 and over having: no formal schooling 49.5%; reading and writing ability 32.2%; primary education 11.0%; secondary education 4.6%; higher 2.7%. **Literacy** (1998): total population age 10 and over literate 50.5%; males literate 71.8%; females literate 29.1%. **Health** (1998): physicians 3,883 (1 per 4,211 persons); hospital beds 9,143 (1 per 1,788 persons); infant mortality rate per 1,000 live births (2001) 68.5. **Food** (2000): daily per capita caloric intake 2,002 (vegetable products 93%, animal products 7%); 84% of FAO recommended minimum.

## Military

**Total active duty personnel** (2001): 54,000 (army 90.7%, navy 2.8%, air force 6.5%). **Military expenditure as percentage of GNP** (1999): 6.1% (world 2.4%); per capita expenditure $22.

## Background

Yemen was the home of ancient Minaean, Sabaean, and Himyarite kingdoms. The Romans invaded the region in the 1st century AD. In the 6th century it was conquered by Ethiopians and Persians. Following conversion to Islam in the 7th century, it was ruled nominally under a caliphate. The Egyptian Ayyubid dynasty ruled there from 1173 to 1229, after which the region passed to the Rasulids. From 1517 through 1918, the Ottoman Empire maintained varying degrees of control, especially in the northwestern section. A boundary agreement was reached in 1934 between the northwestern imam-controlled territory, which subsequently became the Yemen Arab Republic (North Yemen), and the southeastern British-controlled territory, which subsequently became the People's Democratic Republic of Yemen (South Yemen). Relations between the two Yemens remained tense and were marked by conflict throughout the 1970s and 1980s. Reaching an accord, the two officially united as the Republic of Yemen in 1990. Its 1993 elections were the first free, multiparty general elections held in the Arabian

Peninsula, and they were the first in which women participated. In 1994, after a two-month civil war, a new constitution was approved.

## Recent Developments

Following the 11 Sep 2001 terrorist attacks in the US, the Yemeni and US governments substantially increased their cooperation in combating terrorism, quietly exchanging information and working together to identify possible supporters of Osama bin Laden's al-Qaeda network. Yemen also closed a number of Koranic schools and instructed mosque preachers to use moderation in their sermons. In early October 2002, however, a terrorist-related explosion and fire erupted on the large French-flagged oil tanker *Limburg,* near the Yemeni port of Al-Mukalla. On 3 November the CIA and Yemen coordinated a missile attack that claimed the lives of six alleged al-Qaeda operatives in Yemen. On 30 December three Baptist missionaries were gunned down in a hospital in Jibla by a man believed to have links to an Islamist cell. Yemen's third general election since the country was reunited in 1990 was held in late April 2003; international observers found it peaceful but flawed in a number of respects.

**Internet resources:** <www.y.net.ye>

# Zambia

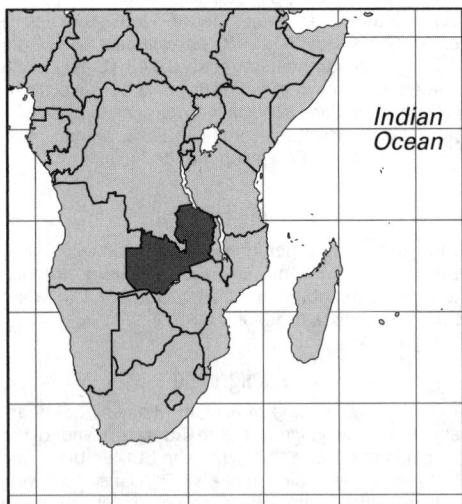

**Official name:** Republic of Zambia. **Form of government:** multiparty republic with one legislative house (National Assembly [156, including 5 nonelective seats]). **Head of state and government:** President Levy Mwanawasa (from 2 Jan 2002). **Capital:** Lusaka. **Official language:** English. **Official religion:** none. **Monetary unit:** 1 Zambian kwacha (K) = 100 ngwee; valuation (7 Jul 2003) $1 = K 4,768.

## Demography

**Area:** 290,586 sq mi, 752,614 sq km. **Population** (2002): 9,959,000. **Density** (2002): persons per sq mi 34.3, persons per sq km 13.2. **Urban** (2001): 43.9%. **Sex distribution** (2000): male 49.30%; female 50.70%. **Age breakdown** (2000): under 15, 47.6%; 15–29, 30.6%; 30–44, 12.4%; 45–59, 5.5%; 60–74, 3.1%; 75 and over, 0.8%. **Ethnolinguistic composition** (1990): Bemba peoples 39.7%; Maravi (Nyanja) peoples 20.1%; Tonga peoples 14.8%; North-Western peoples 8.8%; Barotze peoples 7.5%; Tumbuka peoples 3.7%; Mambwe peoples 3.4%; other 2.0%. **Religious affiliation** (1995): Christian 47.8%, of which Protestant 22.9%, Roman Catholic 16.9%, African Christian 5.6%; traditional beliefs 27.0%; Muslim 1.0%; other 24.2%. **Major cities** (1990): Lusaka 982,362 (urban agglomeration [1999] 1,577,000); Ndola 370,000; Kitwe 290,000; Chingola 167,954; Kabwe 159,000. **Location:** southern Africa, bordering Tanzania, Malawi, Mozambique, Zimbabwe, Botswana, Namibia, Angola, and the Dem. Rep. of the Congo.

## Vital statistics

**Birth rate** per 1,000 population (2000): 41.9 (world avg. 22.5). **Death rate** per 1,000 population (2000): 22.1 (world avg. 9.0). **Natural increase rate** per 1,000 population (2000): 19.8 (world avg. 13.5). **Total fertility rate** (avg. births per childbearing woman; 2000): 5.6. **Life expectancy** at birth (2000): male 37.1 years; female 37.4 years.

## National economy

**Budget** (1999). *Revenue*: K 1,430,400,000 (1998; tax revenue 71.5%, of which income tax 24.9%, excise taxes 13.8%, value-added tax 13.1%, company income tax 5.9%; grants 26.0%; nontax revenue 2.5%). *Expenditures*: K 1,874,300,000 (1998; current expenditures 65.0%, of which debt service 21.7%, education 7.7%, transfers 7.7%, health 5.7%, defense 1.4%; capital expenditures 35.0%). **Public debt** (external, outstanding; 2000): $4,448,000,000. **Production** (metric tons except as noted). *Agriculture, forestry, fishing* (2001): sugarcane 1,800,000, corn (maize) 980,000, cassava 950,000; livestock (number of live animals) 2,400,000 cattle, 1,270,000 goats, 30,000,000 chickens; roundwood (2000) 8,053,000 cu m; fish catch (1999) 71,507. *Mining and quarrying* (1999): copper (metal content) 260,000; cobalt (metal content) 4,700; silver 8,000 kg (in 1999 legal and illegal exports of emeralds were estimated to equal $20,000,000 [about 20% of world total]). *Manufacturing* (value added in K '000,000; 1994): food products 39,765.1; beverages 36,596.5; chemicals and pharmaceuticals 32,141.5. *Energy production (consumption)*: electricity (kW-hr; 1997) 7,795,000,000 (6,315,000,000); coal (metric tons; 1997) 360,000 (355,000); crude petroleum (barrels; 1997) none (4,215,000); petroleum products (metric tons; 1997) 517,000 (455,000). **Households.** Average household size (1997) 5.0. **Tourism** (1999): receipts $85,000,000. **Population economically active** (1996): total 3,454,000; activity rate of total population 38.2% (participation rates [1991]: over age 10, 52.6%; female 29.6%). **Gross national product** (2000): $3,026,000,000 ($300 per capita). **Land use** (1994): forest 43.0%; pasture 40.4%; agriculture 7.1%; other 9.5%.

*1 metric ton = about 1.1 short tons;   1 kilometer = 0.6 mi (statute);   1 metric ton-km cargo = about 0.68 short ton-mi cargo;   c.i.f.: cost, insurance, and freight;   f.o.b.: free on board*

## Foreign trade

**Imports** (1998): $1,022,000,000 (1995; machinery 24.5%, transport equipment 13.4%, chemicals and chemical products 13.3%, crude petroleum 11.3%, cereals and related products 6.5%). *Major import sources* (1999): South Africa 50.3%; Zimbabwe 9.3%; UK 5.9%; Saudi Arabia 5.7%. **Exports** (1998): $873,600,000 (copper 49.3%, cobalt 17.7%, non-metal exports 33.0%). *Major export destinations* (1999): Japan 11.3%; UK 8.5%; India 6.6%; Thailand 5.7%; Saudi Arabia 4.8%; US 4.5%; Germany 4.1%.

## Transport and communications

**Transport.** *Railroads* (1997; excludes Tanzania-Zambia Railway Authority [TAZARA] data): length 1,266 km; passenger-km 267,000,000; metric ton-km cargo 462,000,000. *Roads* (1999): total length 38,898 km (paved 18%). *Vehicles* (1996): passenger cars 157,000; trucks and buses 81,000. *Air transport* (1994): passenger-km 428,000,000; metric ton-km cargo 54,000,000; airports (1998) 4. **Communications**, in total units (units per 1,000 persons). Daily newspaper circulation (1996): 114,000 (14); radio receivers (1997): 1,030,000 (120); television receivers (1999): 1,300,000 (156); telephone main lines (2001): 85,400 (8.0); cellular telephone subscribers (2001): 98,300 (9.0); Internet users (2001): 25,000 (2.4); personal computers (2001): 75,000 (7.0).

## Education and health

**Educational attainment** (1993). Percentage of population age 14 and over having: no formal schooling 18.6%; some primary education 54.8%; some secondary 25.1%; higher 1.5%. **Literacy** (1995): population age 15 and over literate 3,890,000 (78.2%); males literate 2,060,000 (85.6%); females literate 1,830,000 (71.3%). **Health:** physicians (1993) 786 (1 per 10,917 persons); hospital beds (1989) 22,461 (1 per 349 persons); infant mortality rate per 1,000 live births (2000) 92.4. **Food** (2000): daily per capita caloric intake 1,912 (vegetable products 95%, animal products 5%); 83% of FAO recommended minimum.

## Military

**Total active duty personnel** (2001): 21,600 (army 92.6%; navy, none; air force 7.4%). **Military expenditure as percentage of GNP** (1999): 1.0% (world 2.4%); per capita expenditure $3.

---

**Did you know?** Zambia is home to 19 national parks and 33 game management areas that contribute to the protection of its biodiversity. Cookson's wildebeest, the red lechwa, and Thornicroft's giraffe are among the rare and endangered species enjoying protection in Zambia.

---

## Background

Archaeological evidence suggests that early humans roamed present-day Zambia one–two million years ago. Ancestors of the modern Tonga tribe reached the region early in the 2nd millennium BC, but other modern peoples from Congo and Angola reached the country only in the 17th and 18th centuries. Portuguese trading missions were established early in the 18th century. Emissaries of Cecil Rhodes and the British South Africa Co. concluded treaties with most of the Zambian chiefs during the 1890s. The company administered the region known as Northern Rhodesia until 1924, when it became a British protectorate. It was part of the Central African Federation of Rhodesia and Nyasaland in 1953–63. In 1964 Northern Rhodesia became the independent republic of Zambia. A constitutional amendment was passed in 1990 allowing opposition parties; the following years were filled with political tension.

## Recent Developments

The results of the presidential and legislative elections in late December 2001 had been so close that the defeated parties took to the streets in early January 2002 to protest the outcome. Levy Mwanawasa, the successful Movement for Multiparty Democracy (MMD) candidate who polled only 28.69% of the votes cast, was sworn in as president on 2 January 2002. Although his party could not command an overall majority in the National Assembly, Mwanawasa demonstrated that he would not countenance the corruption and mismanagement that had tarnished the reputation of the MMD under former president Frederick Chiluba. He dismissed a number of senior military personnel, became his own minister of defense, and sacked one of his ministers, Vernon Mwaanga, for disloyalty. On 11 July Foreign Minister Katele Kalumba resigned amid allegations of corruption. Five days later Chiluba, who had already been stripped of his retirement benefits because of his continued involvement in politics, had his immunity from prosecution lifted by the National Assembly in response to an appeal from Mwanawasa. Chiluba was arrested in February 2003 and charged with corruption and looting the state treasury. In May 2002 Mwanawasa was forced to declare a national disaster and appeal for international aid when food shortages threatened more than 2.5 million Zambians with starvation. The US offered to make up 50% of the deficit, but the government refused to accept food containing genetically modified organisms.

**Internet resources:** <www.zambia.co.zm>

# Zimbabwe

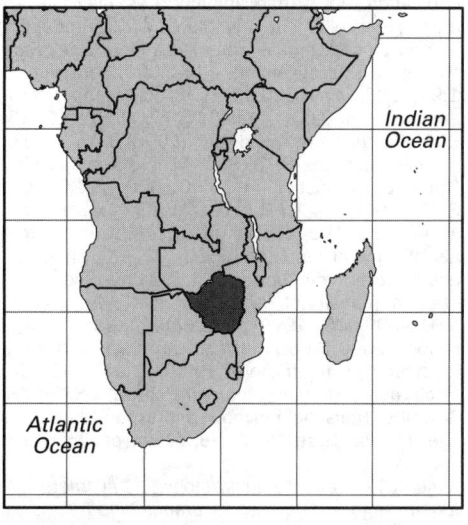

Indian Ocean

Atlantic Ocean

**Official name:** Republic of Zimbabwe. **Form of government:** multiparty republic with one legislative house (House of Assembly [150, including 30 non-elective seats]). **Head of state and government:** President Robert Mugabe (from 1987). **Capital:** Harare. **Official language:** English. **Official religion:** none. **Monetary unit:** 1 Zimbabwe dollar (Z$) = 100 cents; valuation (7 Jul 2003) US$1 = Z$824.00.

## Demography

**Area:** 150,872 sq mi, 390,757 sq km. **Population** (2002): 11,377,000. **Density** (2002): persons per sq mi 75.4, persons per sq km 29.1. **Urban** (2001): 36.0%. **Sex distribution** (2001): male 50.52%; female 49.48%. **Age breakdown** (2000): under 15, 39.6%; 15–29, 33.1%; 30–44, 14.8%; 45–59, 7.2%; 60–74, 4.1%; 75 and over, 1.2%. **Ethnic composition** (2000): Shona 67.1%; Ndebele 13.0%; Chewa 4.9%; British 3.5%; other 11.5%. **Religious affiliation** (1995): Christian 45.4%, of which Protestant (including Anglican) 23.5%, African indigenous 13.5%, Roman Catholic 7.0%; animist 40.5%; other 14.1%. **Major cities** (1992): Harare 1,184,169; Bulawayo 620,936; Chitungwiza 274,035; Mutare 131,808; Gweru 124,735. **Location:** southern Africa, bordering Mozambique, South Africa, Botswana, Namibia, and Zambia.

## Vital statistics

**Birth rate** per 1,000 population (2001): 31.0 (world avg. 21.2). **Death rate** per 1,000 population (2001): 19.7 (world avg. 8.9). **Natural increase rate** per 1,000 population (2001): 11.3 (world avg. 12.2). **Total fertility rate** (avg. births per childbearing woman; 2001): 1.9. **Life expectancy** at birth (2001): male 43.1 years; female 39.7 years.

## National economy

**Budget** (1997–98). *Revenue:* Z$57,596,000,000 (tax revenue 93.0%, of which income tax 48.0%, sales tax 20.4%, customs duties 17.3%, excise tax 4.2%; nontax revenue 7.0%). *Expenditures:* Z$70,332,-000,000 (recurrent expenditures 92.1%, of which goods and services 48.5%, interest payments 25.0%, transfer payments 18.4%). **Population economically active** (1992): total 3,600,000; activity rate of total population 34.6% (participation rates: over age 15, 63.4%; female 39.8%; unemployed 7.2%). **Production** (metric tons except as noted). *Agriculture, forestry, fishing* (1999): sugarcane 4,657,000, corn (maize) 1,520,000, wheat 320,000; livestock (number of live animals) 5,500,000 cattle, 2,770,000 goats, 15,-000,000 chickens; roundwood (1998) 8,378,000 cu m; fish catch (1998) 16,386. *Mining and quarrying* (value of production in Z$'000,000; 2000): gold 8,521; asbestos 2,776; coal 2,690. *Manufacturing* (value in Z$; 1994): foodstuffs 6,746,300,000; metals and metal products 5,662,700,000; chemicals and petroleum products 3,314,800,000. *Energy production (consumption):* electricity (kW-hr; 2000) 7,016,000,000 ([1999] 10,926,000,000); coal (metric tons; 2000) 3,986,000 ([1997] 5,095,000); petroleum products (metric tons; 1997) none (1,395,000). **Public debt** (external, outstanding; 2000): US$2,948,-000,000. **Household income and expenditure.** Average household size (1992) 4.8; income per household

Z$1,689 (US$2,628); expenditure (1990): food, beverages, and tobacco 39.1%, housing 18.7%, clothing and footwear 9.8%, transportation 8.4%, education 7.6%, household durable goods 7.2%, health 2.8%, recreation 2.0%, other 4.4%. **Gross national product** (2000): US$5,851,000,000 (US$460 per capita). **Tourism:** receipts (2000) US$125,000,000; expenditures (1998) US$131,000,000.

## Foreign trade

**Imports** (1999-f.o.b. in balance of trade and c.i.f. in commodities and trading partners): US$2,208,-000,000 (machinery and transport equipment 34.1%, chemicals and chemical products 16.4%, petroleum products 9.7%, food 4.7%, electricity 3.9%). *Major import sources* (2000): South Africa 38.4%; US 6.0%; UK 4.8%; Botswana 4.3%; Japan 4.1%. **Exports** (1999): US$1,924,000,000 (tobacco 31.8%, gold sales 11.9%, ferroalloys 8.7%, cotton lint 5.8%, horticultural products [including cut flowers] 4.3%). *Major export destinations* (2000): South Africa 15.0%; UK 8.7%; Germany 7.8%; Japan 7.3%; US 5.7%; China 5.2%.

## Transport and communications

**Transport.** *Railroads* (1998): route length 2,759 km; passenger-km 408,223,000; metric ton-km cargo 4,603,000. *Roads* (1996): total length 18,338 km (paved 47%). *Vehicles* (1996): passenger cars 323,000; trucks and buses 32,000. *Air transport* (2001; Air Zimbabwe only): passenger-km 723,000,-000; metric ton-km cargo 28,829,000; airports (1997) with scheduled flights 7. **Communications,** in total units (units per 1,000 persons). Daily newspaper circulation (1996): 209,000 (19); radio receivers (1997): 1,140,000 (102); television receivers (1999): 2,074,000 (183); telephone main lines (2001): 253,700 (19); cellular telephone subscribers (2001): 329,000 (24); personal computers (2001): 165,000 (12); Internet users (2001): 100,000 (7.3).

## Education and health

**Educational attainment** (1992). Percentage of population age 25 and over having: no formal schooling 22.3%; primary 54.3%; secondary 13.1%; higher 3.4%. **Literacy** (1995): total population age 15 and over literate 85.1%; males literate 90.4%; females literate 79.9%. **Health:** physicians (1996) 1,603 (1 per 6,904 persons); hospital beds (1996) 22,975 (1 per 501 persons); infant mortality rate per 1,000 live births (2001) 65.3. **Food** (2000): daily per capita caloric intake 2,117 (vegetable products 93%, animal products 7%); 89% of FAO recommended minimum.

## Military

**Total active duty personnel** (2001): 39,000 (army 89.7%, air force 10.3%). **Military expenditure as percentage of GNP** (1999): 5.0% (world 2.4%); per capita expenditure US$23.

## Background

Remains of Stone Age cultures dating back 500,000 years have been found in the Zimbabwe

---

*1 metric ton = about 1.1 short tons; 1 kilometer = 0.6 mi (statute); 1 metric ton-km cargo = about 0.68 short ton-mi cargo; c.i.f.: cost, insurance, and freight; f.o.b.: free on board*

area. The first Bantu-speaking peoples reached it during the 5th–10th centuries AD, driving the San (Bushmen) inhabitants into the desert. A second migration of Bantu-speakers began c. 1830. During this period the British and Afrikaners moved up from the south, and the area came under the administration of the British South Africa Co. 1889–1923. Called Southern Rhodesia (1911–64), it became a self-governing British colony in 1923. The colony united in 1953 with Nyasaland (Malawi) and Northern Rhodesia (Zambia) to form the Central African Federation of Rhodesia and Nyasaland. The federation dissolved in 1963, and Southern Rhodesia reverted to its former colonial status. In 1965 it issued a unilateral declaration of independence considered illegal by the British government, which led to economic sanctions against it. The country proclaimed itself a republic in 1970 and called itself Rhodesia 1964–79. In 1979 it instituted limited majority rule and changed its name to Zimbabwe Rhodesia. It was granted independence by Britain in 1980 and became Zimbabwe. Robert Mugabe, Zimbabwe's first prime minister, became president in 1987. Although a multiparty system was established in 1990, Mugabe's rule became more and more autocratic.

## Recent Developments

Mugabe again held center stage in 2002–03. The early months of 2002 were dominated by preparations for the March presidential elections. In the run-up to the election, the president took measures to control the press and hobble the opposition, but on 13 March it was announced that Mugabe had gained 54% of the vote to his opponent's 40%. Western nations were highly skeptical about the conduct of the elections, and the UK, already angered by the forcible eviction of white farmers as a result of Mugabe's land-reform program, took the lead in urging Commonwealth and EU countries to take action against him. In late March Zimbabwe was suspended from membership in the Commonwealth. Mugabe, in turn, depicted the West as attempting to reintroduce colonialism. He claimed that he was defending his country's sovereignty and argued that the political opposition was wholly financed by Western capital. In so saying, he won the sympathy of other African leaders and diverted attention from the violent attacks by his party's activists on black Zimbabwean opponents. The land-reform program was relaunched in June; 2,900 white farmers were told to leave their land by 8 August. Attacks on black opponents of the government grew steadily more violent as well.

These political struggles occurred against a background of acute food shortages, which Mugabe attributed to the West's failure to give appropriate assistance, while the West claimed that the shortages were the result of the president's land-reform program. The opposition called a general strike in March 2003 that was widely honored throughout the country, and the US imposed economic sanctions against Zimbabwe. In response, taking advantage of a time when world attention was focused on the Middle East, Mugabe imposed a new reign of terror in which some 1,000 opposition politicians were imprisoned and worse.

**Internet resources:** <www.rbz.co.zw>

# Antarctica

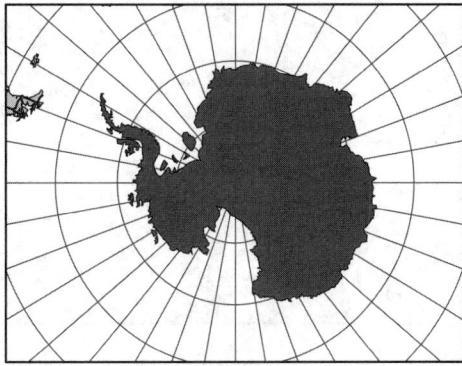

## Background

The Russian F.G. von Bellingshausen (1778–1852), the Englishman Edward Bransfield (1795?–1852), and the American Nathaniel Palmer (1799–1877) all claimed first sightings of the continent in 1820. The period from the 1760s to c. 1900 was dominated by the exploration of Antarctic and subantarctic seas. In the early 20th century, the "heroic era" of Antarctic exploration, Robert Scott and later Ernest Shackleton made expeditions deep into the interior. Roald Amundsen reached the South Pole in December 1911, and Scott followed in 1912. The first half of the 20th century was also Antarctica's colonial period. Seven nations claimed sectors of the continent, while many other nations carried out explorations. In 1957–58, 12 nations established over 50 stations on the continent for cooperative study. In 1961 the Antarctic Treaty, which reserved Antarctica for free and nonpolitical scientific study, was enacted. A 1991 agreement imposed a permanent ban on mineral exploitation.

## Recent Developments

The Antarctic Treaty had 45 signatories by 2003. Of the 45 nations, 27 were pursuing programs of Antarctic scientific research. Some 8,000 scientists and supporting personnel in these programs were in Antarctica and aboard ships in the adjacent Southern Ocean. The National Ice Center reported in March 2002 that a new iceberg—some 85 km (53 mi) long and 65 km (40 mi) wide—was adrift in the waters off Antarctica. The iceberg, designated B-22, had broken off from the Thwaites Ice Tongue, a peninsula of ice extending from the continent's mainland into the Amundsen Sea. The large number of icebergs that had calved from Antarctica in recent years, as well as the collapse of the Larsen B Ice Shelf in February 2002, caused some experts to question whether there was a connection to global warming.

**Internet resources:**
<www.antarctica.org/Hp_Uk/homepage_UK.htm>

# Arctic Regions

The Arctic regions may be defined in physical terms (astronomical [north of the Arctic Circle, latitude 66° 30' N], climatic [above the 10 °C (50 °F) July isotherm], or vegetational [above the northern limit of

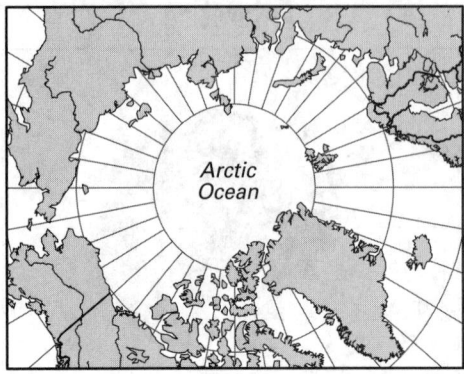

Arctic
Ocean

Aleut in North America and Russia, Sami [Lapp] in northern Scandinavia and Russia, and 29 other peoples of the Russian North, Siberia, and East Asia). No single national sovereignty or treaty regime governs the region, which includes portions of eight countries: Canada, the United States, Russia, Finland, Sweden, Norway, Iceland, and Greenland (part of Denmark). The Arctic Ocean, 14.09 million sq km (5.44 million sq mi) in area, constitutes about two-thirds of the region. The land area consists of permanent ice cap, tundra, or taiga. The population (2002 est.) of peoples belonging to the circumpolar cultures is about 375,000. International organizations concerned with the Arctic include the Arctic Council, institutions of the Barents Region, the Inuit Circumpolar Conference, and the Indigenous Peoples' Secretariat. International scientific cooperation of the Arctic is the focus of the International Arctic Research Center of the University of Alaska at Fairbanks.

the tree line]) or in human terms (the territory inhabited by the circumpolar cultures—Inuit [Eskimo] and

# Membership in International Organizations

**African Union (AU; formerly [until 2002] Organization for African Unity)**
Founded: 1963. Members: 52 countries of Africa, excluding Guinea-Bissau and Morocco
Web site: <www.africa-union.org>

**Andean Community**
Founded: 1969. Members: Bolivia, Colombia, Ecuador, Peru, Venezuela
Web site: <www.comunidadandina.org>

**Asia-Pacific Economic Cooperation (APEC)**
Founded: 1989. Members: Australia, Brunei, Canada, Chile, China, Hong Kong, Indonesia, Japan, Malaysia, Mexico, New Zealand, Papua New Guinea, Peru, the Philippines, Russia, Singapore, South Korea, Taiwan, Thailand, US, Vietnam
Web site: <www.apec.org>

**Association of Southeast Asian Nations (ASEAN)**
Founded: 1967. Members: Brunei, Cambodia, Indonesia, Laos, Malaysia, Myanmar (Burma), the Philippines, Singapore, Thailand, Vietnam
Web site: <www.aseansec.org>

**Caribbean Community and Common Market (CARICOM)**
Founded: 1973. Members: Antigua and Barbuda, the Bahamas (Community member only), Barbados, Belize, Dominica, Grenada, Guyana, Haiti, Jamaica, Montserrat, St. Kitts and Nevis, St. Lucia, St. Vincent and the Grenadines, Suriname, Trinidad and Tobago; also 8 observers and 4 associate members
Web site: <www.caricom.org>

**Central American Common Market (CACM)**
Founded: 1960. Members: Costa Rica, El Salvador, Guatemala, Honduras, Nicaragua

**Common Market for Eastern and Southern Africa (COMESA)**
Founded: 1994. Members: Angola, Burundi, Comoros, Democratic Republic of the Congo, Djibouti, Egypt, Eritrea, Ethiopia, Kenya, Madagascar, Malawi, Mauritius, Namibia, Rwanda, Seychelles, the Sudan, Swaziland, Uganda, Zambia, Zimbabwe
Web site: <www.comesa.int>

**Commonwealth (also known as the Commonwealth of Nations)**
Founded: 1931. Members: United Kingdom and 53 other countries, all of which (except Mozambique) were once under British rule or administratively connected to another member country
Web site: <www.thecommonwealth.org>

**Commonwealth of Independent States (CIS)**
Founded: 1991. Members: Armenia, Azerbaijan, Belarus, Georgia, Kazakhstan, Kyrgyzstan, Moldova, Russia, Tajikistan, Turkmenistan, Uzbekistan, Ukraine
Web site: <www.cis.minsk.by>

**Council of Europe**
Founded: 1949. Members: 45 European and former Soviet countries; 8 observer states
Web site: <www.coe.int>

**Economic Community of West African States (ECOWAS)**
Founded: 1975. Members: Benin, Burkina Faso, Cape Verde, Cote d'Ivoire, the Gambia, Ghana, Guinea, Guinea-Bissau, Liberia, Mali, Niger, Nigeria, Senegal, Sierra Leone, Togo
Web site: <www.ecowas.int>

**European Free Trade Association (EFTA)**
Founded: 1960. Members: Iceland, Liechtenstein, Norway, Switzerland
Web site: <www.efta.int>

**European Union (EU)**
Founded: 1950. Members: Austria, Belgium, Denmark, Finland, France, Germany, Greece, Ireland, Italy, Luxembourg, The Netherlands, Portugal, Spain, Sweden, UK; in mid-2003, 13 additional countries in Eastern and southern Europe were undergoing membership preparations
Web site: <www.europa.eu.int>

**Group of Eight (G-8)**
Founded: 1975. Members: Canada, France, Germany, Italy, Japan, Russia, UK, US
Web site: <www.g8.utoronto.ca>

**Gulf Cooperation Council (GCC)**
Founded: 1981. Members: Bahrain, Kuwait, Oman,

Qatar, Saudi Arabia, United Arab Emirates
Web site: <www.gcc-sg.org/home_e.html>

**Latin American Integration Association (ALADI)**
Founded: 1980. Members: Argentina, Bolivia, Brazil, Chile, Colombia, Cuba, Ecuador, Mexico, Paraguay, Peru, Uruguay, Venezuela
Web site: <www.aladi.org>

**League of Arab States (Arab League)**
Founded: 1945. Members: Algeria, Bahrain, Comoros, Djibouti, Egypt, Iraq, Jordan, Kuwait, Lebanon, Libya, Mauritania, Morocco, Oman, Palestine Liberation Organization, Qatar, Saudi Arabia, Somalia, the Sudan, Syria, Tunisia, United Arab Emirates, Yemen
Web site: <www.arableagueonline.org>

**Nordic Council of Ministers**
Founded: 1971. Members: Denmark, Finland, Iceland, Norway, Sweden; autonomous regions of Greenland, Faroe Islands, Åland Islands
Web site: <www.norden.org>

**North Atlantic Treaty Organization (NATO)**
Founded: 1949. Members: Belgium, Canada, Czech Republic, Denmark, France, Germany, Greece, Hungary, Iceland, Italy, Luxembourg, The Netherlands, Norway, Poland, Portugal, Spain, Turkey, UK, US
Web site: <www.nato.int>

**Organisation for Economic Co-operation and Development (OECD)**
Founded: 1961. Members: Australia, Austria, Belgium, Canada, Czech Republic, Denmark, Finland, France, Germany, Greece, Hungary, Iceland, Ireland, Italy, Japan, Luxembourg, Mexico, The Netherlands, New Zealand, Norway, Poland, Portugal, Slovak Republic, South Korea, Spain, Sweden, Switzerland, Turkey, UK, US
Web site: <www.oecd.org>

**Organization for Security and Co-operation in Europe (OSCE)**
Founded: 1973. Members: 53 countries of Europe and Central Asia, plus Canada and the US
Web site: <www.osce.org>

**Organization of American States (OAS)**
Founded: 1948. Members: 35 countries of North, Central, and South America and the Caribbean
Web site: <www.oas.org>

**Organization of Petroleum Exporting Countries (OPEC)**
Founded: 1960. Members: Algeria, Indonesia, Iran,
Iraq, Kuwait, Libya, Nigeria, Qatar, Saudi Arabia, United Arab Emirates, Venezuela
Web site: <www.opec.org>

**Organization of the Islamic Conference (OIC)**
Founded: 1969. Members: 57 Islamic countries, mainly in Africa and Asia; 3 observer countries
Web site: <www.oic-oci.org>

**Pacific Islands Forum (formerly [until 2000] South Pacific Forum)**
Founded: 1971. Members: Australia, Cook Islands, Fiji, Kiribati, Marshall Islands, Micronesia, Nauru, New Zealand, Niue, Palau, Papua New Guinea, Samoa, Solomon Islands, Tonga, Tuvalu, Vanuatu
Web site: <www.forumsec.org.fj>

**Secretariat of the Pacific Community (SPC; formerly South Pacific Commission)**
Founded: 1947. Members: American Samoa, Australia, Cook Islands, Fiji, France, French Polynesia, Guam, Kiribati, Marshall Islands, Micronesia, Nauru, New Caledonia, New Zealand, Niue, Northern Mariana Islands, Palau, Papua New Guinea, Pitcairn Island, Samoa, Solomon Islands, Tokelau, Tonga, Tuvalu, UK, US, Vanuatu, Wallis and Futuna
Web site: <www.spc.org.nc>

**South Asian Association for Regional Cooperation (SAARC)**
Founded: 1985. Members: Bangladesh, Bhutan, India, Maldives, Nepal, Pakistan, Sri Lanka
Web site: <www.saarc-sec.org>

**Southern African Development Community (SADC)**
Founded: 1980. Members: Angola, Botswana, Democratic Republic of the Congo, Lesotho, Malawi, Mauritius, Mozambique, Namibia, Seychelles, South Africa, Swaziland, Tanzania, Zambia, Zimbabwe
Web site: <www.sadcreview.com>

**Southern Common Market (MERCOSUR)**
Founded: 1991. Members: Argentina, Brazil, Paraguay, Uruguay; associate members Chile, Bolivia
Web site: <www.mercosur.org.uy>

**United Nations (UN)**
Founded: 1945. Members: 191 countries (nearly all world countries)
Web site: <www.un.org>

**World Trade Organization (WTO)**
Founded: 1995. Members: 146 member countries worldwide; 30 observer states
Web site: <www.wto.org>

# Rulers and Regimes
## Europe

### Roman Emperors

Overlapping reigns denote co-rulers. Diocletian (284–305) laid the foundation for the Byzantine Empire in the East when he appointed Maximian (286–305) to rule over the Western portion of the empire. Rome thus remained a unified state but was divided administratively. Theodosius I (379–395) was the last emperor to rule over a unified Roman Empire. When he died, Rome split into Eastern and Western empires. For a complete list of the Eastern emperors after the fall of Rome, see "Byzantine Empire."

## Roman Emperors (continued)

| REIGN | BYNAME | FULL NAME |
|---|---|---|
| 27 BC–AD 14 | Augustus | Caesar Augustus |
| 14–37 | Tiberius | Tiberius Caesar Augustus |
| 37–41 | Caligula | Gaius Caesar Augustus Germanicus |
| 41–54 | Claudius | Tiberius Claudius Caesar Augustus Germanicus |
| 54–68 | Nero | Nero Claudius Caesar Augustus Germanicus |
| 68–69 | Galba | Servius Galba Caesar Augustus |
| 69 | Otho | Marcus Otho Caesar Augustus |
| 69 | Vitellius | Aulus Vitellius Germanicus |
| 69–79 | Vespasian | Caesar Vespasianus Augustus |
| 79–81 | Titus | Titus Vespasianus Augustus |
| 81–96 | Domitian | Caesar Domitianus Augustus |
| 96–98 | Nerva | Nerva Caesar Augustus |
| 98–117 | Trajan | Caesar Nerva Traianus Augustus |
| 117–138 | Hadrian | Caesar Traianus Hadrianus Augustus |
| 138–161 | Antoninus Pius | Caesar Titus Aelius Hadrianus Antoninus Augustus Pius |
| 161–180 | Marcus Aurelius | Marcus Aurelius Antoninus |
| 161–169 | Lucius Verus | Lucius Aurelius Verus |
| 177–192 | Commodus | Lucius Aelius Aurelius Commodus |
| 193 | Pertinax | Publius Helvius Pertinax |
| 193 | Didius Julianus | Marcus Didius Severus Julianus |
| 193–211 | Septimius Severus | Lucius Septimius Severus Pertinax |
| 198–217 | Caracalla | Marcus Aurelius Severus Antoninus |
| 209–212 | Geta | Publius Septimius Geta |
| 217–218 | Macrinus | Marcus Opellius Severus Macrinus |
| 218–222 | Elagabalus | Sacerdos dei invicti solis Elagabali Marcus Aurelius Antoninus |
| 222–235 | Alexander Severus | Marcus Aurelius Severus Alexander |
| 235–238 | Maximin | Gaius Julius Verus Maximinus |
| 238 | Gordian I | Marcus Antonius Gordianus Sempronianus Romanus Africanus |
| 238 | Gordian II | Marcus Antonius Gordianus Sempronianus Romanus Africanus |
| 238 | Maximus | Marcus Clodius Pupienus Maximus |
| 238 | Balbinus | Decius Caelius Calvinus Balbinus |
| 238–244 | Gordian III | Marcus Antonius Gordianus |
| 244–249 | Philip | |
| 249–251 | Decius | Galus Messius Quintus Trianus Decius |
| 251 | Hostilian | Gaius Valens Hostilianus Messius Quintus |
| 251–253 | Gallus | Gaius Vibius Trebonianus Gallus |
| 253 | Aemilian | Marcus Aemilius Aemilianus |
| 253–260 | Valerian | Publius Licinius Valerianus |
| 253–268 | Gallienus | Publius Licinius Egnatius Gallienus |
| 268–270 | Claudius II Gothicus | Marcus Aurelius Valerius Claudius |
| 269–270 | Quintillus | Marcus Aurelius Claudius Quintillus |
| 270–275 | Aurelian | Lucius Domitius Aurelianus |
| 275–276 | Tacitus | Marcus Claudius Tacitus |
| 276 | Florian | Marcus Annius Florianus |
| 276–282 | Probus | Marcus Aurelius Probus |
| 282–283 | Carus | Marcus Aurelius Carus |
| 283–285 | Carinus | Marcus Aurelius Carinus |
| 283–284 | Numerian | Marcus Aurelius Numerius Numerianus |
| 284–305[1] | Diocletian | Gaius Aurelius Valerius Diocletianus |
| 286–305[2] | Maximian | Marcus Aurelius Valerius Maximianus Heraclius |
| 305–311[1] | Galerius | Gaius Galerius Valerius Maximianus |
| 305–306[2] | Constantius I Chlorus | Flavius Valerius Constantius |
| 306–307[2] | Severus | Flavius Valerius Severus |
| 306–312[2] | Maxentius | Marcus Aurelius Valerius Maxentius |
| 308–324[1] | Licinius | Valerius Licinianus Licinius |
| 312–337[2] | Constantine I | Flavius Valerius Constantinus |
| 337–340[2] | Constantine II | Flavius Claudius [or Julius] Constantinus |
| 337–350[2] | Constans I | Flavius Julius Constans |
| 337–361[2] | Constantius II | Flavius Julius [or Valerius] Constantius |
| 350–353[2] | Magnentius | Flavius Magnus Magnentius |
| 361–363[2] | Julian | Flavius Claudius Julianus |
| 363–364[2] | Jovian | Flavius Jovianus |
| 364–375[2] | Valentinian I | Flavius Valentinianus |
| 364–378[1] | Valens | Flavius Valens |
| 365–366[1] | Procopius | |
| 375–383[2] | Gratian | Flavius Gratianus Augustus |
| 375–392[2] | Valentinian II | Flavius Valentinianus |

## Roman Emperors (continued)

| REIGN | BYNAME | FULL NAME |
|---|---|---|
| 379–395[2] | Theodosius I | Flavius Theodosius |
| 395–408[1] | Arcadius | Flavius Arcadius |
| 395–423[2] | Honorius | Flavius Honorius |
| 408–450[1] | Theodosius II | |
| 421[2] | Constantius III | |
| 425–455[2] | Valentinian III | Flavius Placidius Valentinianus |
| 450–457[1] | Marcian | Marcianus |
| 455[2] | Petronius Maximus | Flavius Ancius Petronius Maximus |
| 455–456[2] | Avitus | Flavius Maccilius Eparchus Avitus |
| 457–474[1] | Leo I | Leo Thrax Magnus |
| 457–461[2] | Majorian | Julius Valerius Majorianus |
| 461–467[2] | Libius Severus | Libius Severianus Severus |
| 467–472[2] | Anthemius | Procopius Anthemius |
| 472[2] | Olybrius | Anicius Olybrius |
| 473–474[2] | Glycerius | |
| 474–475[2] | Julius Nepos | |
| 474[1] | Leo II | |
| 474–491[1] | Zeno | |
| 475–476[2] | Romulus Augustulus | Flavius Momyllus Romulus Augustulus |

[1]Ruled in the East only.    [2]Ruled in the West only.

## Sovereigns of Britain

| SOVEREIGN | DYNASTY OR HOUSE | REIGN | SOVEREIGN | DYNASTY OR HOUSE | REIGN |
|---|---|---|---|---|---|
| **Kings of Wessex (West Saxons)** | | | **Sovereigns of England (continued)** | | |
| Egbert | Saxon | 802–839 | Henry V | Plantagenet: Lancaster | 1413–22 |
| Aethelwulf (Ethelwulf) | Saxon | 839–856/858 | | | |
| Aethelbald (Ethelbald) | Saxon | 855/856–860 | Henry VI | Plantagenet: Lancaster | 1422–61 |
| Aethelberht (Ethelbert) | Saxon | 860–865/866 | | | |
| Aethelred I (Ethelred) | Saxon | 865/866–871 | Edward IV | Plantagenet: York | 1461–70 |
| Alfred the Great | Saxon | 871–899 | | | |
| Edward the Elder | Saxon | 899–924 | Henry VI (restored) | Plantagenet: Lancaster | 1470–71 |
| | | | Edward IV (restored) | Plantagenet: York | 1471–83 |
| **Sovereigns of England** | | | | | |
| Athelstan[1] | Saxon | 925–939 | | | |
| Edmund I | Saxon | 939–946 | Edward V | Plantagenet: York | 1483 |
| Eadred (Edred) | Saxon | 946–955 | | | |
| Eadwig (Edwy) | Saxon | 955–959 | Richard III | Plantagenet: York | 1483–85 |
| Edgar | Saxon | 959–975 | | | |
| Edward the Martyr | Saxon | 975–978 | Henry VII | Tudor | 1483–1509 |
| Ethelred II the Unready (Aethelred) | Saxon | 978–1013 | Henry VIII | Tudor | 1509–47 |
| | | | Edward VI | Tudor | 1547–53 |
| Sweyn Forkbeard | Danish | 1013–14 | Mary I | Tudor | 1553–58 |
| Ethelred II the Unready (restored) | Saxon | 1014–16 | Elizabeth I | Tudor | 1558–1603 |
| Edmund II Ironside | Saxon | 1016 | **Sovereigns of Great Britain and the United Kingdom[2, 3]** | | |
| Canute | Danish | 1016–35 | James I (VI of Scotland)[2] | Stuart | 1603–25 |
| Harold I Harefoot | Danish | 1035–40 | Charles I | Stuart | 1625–49 |
| Hardecanute | Danish | 1040–42 | | | |
| Edward the Confessor | Saxon | 1042–66 | **Commonwealth** | | |
| Harold II | Saxon | 1066 | Oliver Cromwell, Lord Protector | | 1653–58 |
| William I the Conqueror | Norman | 1066–87 | | | |
| William II | Norman | 1087–1100 | Richard Cromwell, Lord Protector | | 1658–59 |
| Henry I | Norman | 1100–35 | | | |
| Stephen | Blois | 1135–54 | | | |
| Henry II | Plantagenet | 1154–89 | **Sovereigns of Great Britain and the United Kingdom (restored)** | | |
| Richard I | Plantagenet | 1189–99 | | | |
| John | Plantagenet | 1199–1216 | Charles II | Stuart | 1660–85 |
| Henry III | Plantagenet | 1216–72 | James II | Stuart | 1685–88 |
| Edward I | Plantagenet | 1272–1307 | William III and Mary II[4] | Orange/ Stuart | 1689–1702 |
| Edward II | Plantagenet | 1307–27 | | | |
| Edward III | Plantagenet | 1327–77 | Anne | Stuart | 1702–14 |
| Richard II | Plantagenet | 1377–99 | George I | Hanover | 1714–27 |
| Henry IV | Plantagenet: Lancaster | 1399–1413 | George II | Hanover | 1727–60 |

## Sovereigns of Britain (continued)

| SOVEREIGN | DYNASTY OR HOUSE | REIGN | SOVEREIGN | DYNASTY OR HOUSE | REIGN |
|---|---|---|---|---|---|
| Sovereigns of Great Britain and the United Kingdom (restored) | | | Sovereigns of Great Britain and the United Kingdom (restored) continued | | |
| George III[3] | Hanover | 1760–1820 | George V[6] | Windsor | 1910–36 |
| George IV[5] | Hanover | 1820–30 | Edward VIII[7] | Windsor | 1936 |
| William IV | Hanover | 1830–37 | George VI | Windsor | 1936–52 |
| Victoria | Hanover | 1837–1901 | Elizabeth II | Windsor | 1952– |
| Edward VII | Saxe-Coburg-Gotha | 1901–10 | | | |

[1]Athelstan was king of Wessex and the first king of all England.    [2]James VI of Scotland became also James I of England in 1603. Upon accession to the English throne he styled himself "King of Great Britain" and was so proclaimed. Legally, however, he and his successors held separate English and Scottish kingships until the Act of Union of 1707, when the two kingdoms were united as the Kingdom of Great Britain.    [3]The United Kingdom was formed on 1 Jan 1801, with the union of Great Britain and Ireland. After 1801 George III was styled "King of the United Kingdom of Great Britain and Ireland."    [4]William and Mary, as husband and wife, reigned jointly until Mary's death in 1694. William then reigned alone until his own death in 1702.    [5]George IV was regent from 5 Feb 1811.    [6]In 1917, during World War I, George V changed the name of his house from Saxe-Coburg-Gotha to Windsor.    [7]Edward VIII succeeded upon the death of his father, George V, on 20 Jan 1936, but abdicated on 11 Dec 1936, before coronation.

## Rulers of Scotland

*Knowledge about the early Scottish kings (until Malcolm II) is slim and is partly based on traditional lists. The dating of reigns is thus inexact.*

| RULER | REIGN | RULER | REIGN |
|---|---|---|---|
| Kenneth I MacAlpin | 843–858 | Malcolm IV | 1153–65 |
| Donald I | 858–862 | William I the Lion | 1165–1214 |
| Constantine I | 862–877 | Alexander II | 1214–49 |
| Aed (Aodh) | 877–878 | Alexander III | 1249–86 |
| Eochaid (Eocha) and Giric (Ciric)[1] | 878–889 | Margaret, Maid of Norway | 1286–90 |
| Donald II | 889–900 | | |
| Constantine II | 900–943 | **Interregnum** | 1290–92 |
| Malcolm I | 943–954 | | |
| Indulf | 954–962 | John de Balliol | 1292–96 |
| Dub | 962–966 | | |
| Culen | 966–971 | **Interregnum** | 1296–1306 |
| Kenneth II | 971–995 | | |
| Constantine III | 995–997 | Robert I the Bruce | 1306–29 |
| Kenneth III | 997–1005 | David II | 1329–71 |
| Malcolm II | 1005–34 | | |
| Duncan I | 1034–40 | **House of Stewart (Stuart)[2]** | |
| Macbeth | 1040–57 | Robert II | 1371–90 |
| Lulach | 1057–58 | Robert III | 1390–1406 |
| Malcolm III Canmore | 1058–93 | James I | 1406–37 |
| Donald Bane (Donalbane) | 1093–94 | James II | 1437–60 |
| Duncan II | 1093–94 | James III | 1460–88 |
| Donald Bane (restored) | 1094–97 | James IV | 1488–1513 |
| Edgar | 1097–1107 | James V | 1513–42 |
| Alexander I | 1107–24 | Mary, Queen of Scots | 1542–67 |
| David I | 1124–53 | James VI[3] | 1567–1625 |

[1]Eochaid may have been a minor and Giric his guardian, or Giric may have been a usurper. Both appear in the lists of kings for the period.    [2]"Stewart" was the original spelling for the Scottish family, but during the 16th century French influence led to the adoption of the spelling Stuart (or Steuart), owing to the absence of the letter "w" in the French alphabet.    [3]James VI of Scotland became also James I of England in 1603. Upon accession to the English throne he styled himself "King of Great Britain" and was so proclaimed. Legally, however, he and his successors held separate English and Scottish kingships until the Act of Union of 1707, when the two kingdoms were united as the Kingdom of Great Britain.

**Did you know?** There occasionally arise weather conditions that allow the accumulation of pollutants over an urban area for several days. Such conditions, termed inversions (increasing air temperature with increasing altitude), strongly inhibit atmospheric mixing. Atmospheric inversion caused an air-pollution disaster in London in 1952, when about 3,500 people died from respiratory diseases.

# British Prime Ministers

The origin of the term prime minister and the question to whom it should originally be applied have long been issues of scholarly and political debate. Although the term was used as early as the reign of Queen Anne (1702–14), it acquired wider currency during the reign of George II (1727–60), when it began to be used as a term of reproach toward Robert Walpole. The title prime minister did not become official until 1905, to refer to the leader of a government.

Before the development of the Conservative and Liberal parties in the mid-19th century, parties in Britain were largely simply alliances of prominent groups or aristocratic families. The designations Whig and Tory tend often to be approximate. In all cases, the party designation is that of the prime minister; he might lead a coalition government, as did David Lloyd George and Winston Churchill (in his first term).

| PRIME MINISTER | PARTY | TERM | PRIME MINISTER | PARTY | TERM |
|---|---|---|---|---|---|
| Robert Walpole | Whig | 1721–42 | Edward Geoffrey Stanley | Conservative | 1858–59 |
| Spencer Compton | Whig | 1742–43 | Henry John Temple | Liberal | 1859–65 |
| Henry Pelham | Whig | 1743–54 | John Russell | Liberal | 1865–66 |
| Thomas Pelham-Holles | Whig | 1754–56 | Edward Geoffrey Stanley | Conservative | 1866–68 |
| William Cavendish | Whig | 1756–57 | Benjamin Disraeli | Conservative | 1868 |
| Thomas Pelham-Holles | Whig | 1757–62 | William Ewart Gladstone | Liberal | 1868–74 |
| John Stuart | | 1762–63 | Benjamin Disraeli | Conservative | 1874–80 |
| George Grenville | | 1763–65 | William Ewart Gladstone | Liberal | 1880–85 |
| Charles Watson Wentworth | Whig | 1765–66 | Robert Cecil | Conservative | 1885–86 |
| | | | William Ewart Gladstone | Liberal | 1886 |
| William Pitt | | 1766–68 | Robert Cecil | Conservative | 1886–92 |
| Augustus Henry Fitzroy | | 1768–70 | William Ewart Gladstone | Liberal | 1892–94 |
| Frederick North | | 1770–82 | Archibald Philip Primrose | Liberal | 1894–95 |
| Charles Watson Wentworth | Whig | 1782 | Robert Cecil | Conservative | 1895–1902 |
| | | | Arthur James Balfour | Conservative | 1902–05 |
| William Petty-Fitzmaurice | | 1782–83 | Henry Campbell-Bannerman | Liberal | 1905–08 |
| William Henry Cavendish-Bentinck | Whig | 1783 | | | |
| | | | H.H. Asquith | Liberal | 1908–16 |
| William Pitt | Tory | 1783–1801 | David Lloyd George | Liberal | 1916–22 |
| Henry Addington | Tory | 1801–04 | Bonar Law | Conservative | 1922–23 |
| William Pitt | Tory | 1804–06 | Stanley Baldwin | Conservative | 1923–24 |
| William Wyndham Grenville | | 1806–07 | Ramsay Macdonald | Labour | 1924 |
| | | | Stanley Baldwin | Conservative | 1924–29 |
| William Henry Cavendish-Bentinck | Whig | 1807–09 | Ramsay Macdonald | Labour | 1929–35 |
| | | | Stanley Baldwin | Conservative | 1935–37 |
| Spencer Perceval | Tory | 1809–12 | Neville Chamberlain | Conservative | 1937–40 |
| Robert Banks Jenkinson | Tory | 1812–27 | Winston Churchill | Conservative | 1940–45 |
| George Canning | Tory | 1827 | Clement Attlee | Labour | 1945–51 |
| Frederick John Robinson | Tory | 1827–28 | Winston Churchill | Conservative | 1951–55 |
| Arthur Wellesley | Tory | 1828–30 | Anthony Eden | Conservative | 1955–57 |
| Charles Grey | Whig | 1830–34 | Harold Macmillan | Conservative | 1957–63 |
| William Lamb | Whig | 1834 | Alec Douglas-Home | Conservative | 1963–64 |
| Arthur Wellesley | Tory | 1834 | Harold Wilson | Labour | 1964–70 |
| Robert Peel | Tory | 1834–35 | Edward Heath | Conservative | 1970–74 |
| William Lamb | Whig | 1835–41 | Harold Wilson | Labour | 1974–76 |
| Robert Peel | Conservative | 1841–46 | James Callaghan | Labour | 1976–79 |
| John Russell | Whig-Liberal | 1846–52 | Margaret Thatcher | Conservative | 1979–90 |
| Edward Geoffrey Stanley | Conservative | 1852 | John Major | Conservative | 1990–97 |
| George Hamilton-Gordon | | 1852–55 | Tony Blair | Labour | 1997– |
| Henry John Temple | Liberal | 1855–58 | | | |

# Rulers of France

| RULER | REIGN | RULER | REIGN |
|---|---|---|---|
| **Carolingian dynasty** | | **Robertian (Capetian) dynasty** | |
| Pippin III the Short | 751–768 | Eudes | 888–898 |
| Charles I (Charlemagne, Kingdom of the Franks) | 768–814 | | |
| | | **Carolingian dynasty** | |
| Louis I (Kingdom of the Franks) | 840–843 | Charles III | 893/898–923 |
| *Civil War* | | | |
| Charles II (Kingdom of the West Franks) | 843–877 | **Robertian (Capetian) dynasty** | |
| Louis II (Kingdom of the West Franks) | 877–879 | Robert I | 922–923 |
| Louis III (Kingdom of the West Franks) | 879–882 | Rudolf (Raoul, or Rodolphe) | 923–936 |
| Carloman (Kingdom of the West Franks) | 879–884 | | |
| Charles (III) (Charles III, Holy Roman Empire) | 884–887 | **Carolingian dynasty** | |
| | | Louis IV | 936–954 |

# Rulers of France (continued)

| RULER | REIGN |
|---|---|
| **Carolingian dynasty (continued)** | |
| Lothair (Lothaire) | 954–986 |
| Louis V | 986–987 |
| | |
| **Capetian dynasty** | |
| Hugh Capet (Hugues Capet) | 987–996 |
| Robert II | 996–1031 |
| Henry I (Henri) | 1031–60 |
| Philip I (Philippe) | 1060–1108 |
| Louis VI | 1108–37 |
| Louis VII | 1137–80 |
| Philip II (Philippe) | 1180–1223 |
| Louis VIII | 1223–26 |
| Louis IX (Saint Louis) | 1226–70 |
| Philip III (Philippe) | 1270–85 |
| Philip IV (Philippe) | 1285–1314 |
| Louis X | 1314–16 |
| John I (Jean) | 1316 |
| Philip V (Philippe) | 1316–22 |
| Charles IV | 1322–28 |
| | |
| **Valois dynasty** | |
| Philip VI (Philippe) | 1328–50 |
| John II (Jean) | 1350–64 |
| Charles V | 1364–80 |
| Charles VI | 1380–1422 |
| Charles VII | 1422–61 |
| Louis XI | 1461–83 |
| Charles VIII | 1483–98 |
| | |
| **Valois dynasty (Orléans branch)** | |
| Louis XII | 1498–1515 |
| | |
| **Valois dynasty (Angoulême branch)** | |
| Francis I (François) | 1515–47 |
| Henry II (Henri) | 1547–59 |
| Francis II (François) | 1559–60 |
| Charles IX | 1560–74 |
| Henry III (Henri) | 1574–89 |
| | |
| **House of Bourbon** | |
| Henry IV (Henri) | 1589–1610 |
| Louis XIII | 1610–43 |
| Louis XIV | 1643–1715 |
| Louis XV | 1715–74 |
| Louis XVI | 1774–92 |
| Louis (XVII) | 1793–95 |
| | |
| **First Republic** | |
| National Convention | 1792–95 |
| Directorate | 1795–99 |
| Consulate (Napoléon Bonaparte) | 1799–1804 |

| RULER | REIGN |
|---|---|
| **First Empire (emperors)** | |
| Napoleon I (Napoléon Bonaparte) | 1804–14, 1815 |
| Napoleon (II) | 1815 |
| | |
| **House of Bourbon** | |
| Louis XVIII | 1814–24 |
| Charles X | 1824–30 |
| | |
| **House of Orléans** | |
| Louis-Philippe | 1830–48 |
| | |
| **Second Republic (president)** | |
| Louis-Napoléon Bonaparte | 1848–52 |
| | |
| **Second Empire (emperor)** | |
| Napoleon III (Louis-Napoléon Bonaparte) | 1852–70 |
| | |
| **Third Republic (presidents)** | |
| Adolphe Thiers | 1871–73 |
| Marie-Edmé-Patrice-Maurice, comte de Mac-Mahon, duc de Magenta | 1873–79 |
| Jules Grévy | 1879–87 |
| Sadi Carnot | 1887–94 |
| Jean Casimir-Périer | 1894–95 |
| Félix Faure | 1895–99 |
| Émile Loubet | 1899–1906 |
| Armand Fallières | 1906–13 |
| Raymond Poincaré | 1913–20 |
| Paul Deschanel | 1920 |
| Alexandre Millerand | 1920–24 |
| Gaston Doumergue | 1924–31 |
| Paul Doumer | 1931–32 |
| Albert Lebrun | 1932–40 |
| | |
| **French State (État Français, or Vichy France)** | |
| Philippe Pétain | 1940–44 |
| | |
| **Provisional government** | 1944–47 |
| | |
| **Fourth Republic (presidents)** | |
| Vincent Auriol | 1947–54 |
| René Coty | 1954–58 |
| | |
| **Fifth Republic (presidents)** | |
| Charles de Gaulle | 1959–69 |
| Georges Pompidou | 1969–74 |
| Valéry Giscard d'Estaing | 1974–81 |
| François Mitterrand | 1981–95 |
| Jacques Chirac | 1995– |

# Rulers of Spain

| RULER | REIGN |
|---|---|
| **House of Habsburg** | |
| Charles I (Carlos) | 1516–56 |
| Philip II (Felipe) | 1556–98 |
| Philip III (Felipe) | 1598–1621 |
| Philip IV (Felipe) | 1621–65 |
| Charles II (Carlos) | 1665–1700 |
| | |
| **House of Bourbon (Borbón)** | |
| Philip V (Felipe) | 1700–24 |
| Louis (Luis) | 1724 |
| Philip V (2nd time) | 1724–46 |

| RULER | REIGN |
|---|---|
| **House of Bourbon (Borbón) continued** | |
| Ferdinand VI (Fernando) | 1746–59 |
| Charles III (Carlos) | 1759–88 |
| Charles IV (Carlos) | 1788–1808 |
| Ferdinand VII (Fernando) | 1808 |
| | |
| **House of Bonaparte** | |
| Joseph (José) | 1808–13 |
| | |
| **House of Bourbon (Borbón)** | |
| Ferdinand VII (2nd time) | 1814–33 |

## Rulers of Spain (continued)

| RULER | REIGN | RULER | REIGN |
|---|---|---|---|
| **House of Bourbon (Borbón) continued** | | **Republic** | 1931–39 |
| Isabella II (Isabel) | 1833–68 | | |
| | | **Nationalist Regime** | |
| **Interregnum** | 1868–70 | Francisco Franco | 1939–75 |
| **House of Savoy** | | **House of Bourbon (Borbón)** | |
| Amadeus I (Amadeo) | 1870–73 | Juan Carlos | 1975– |
| **Republic** | 1873–74 | | |
| **House of Bourbon (Borbón)** | | | |
| Alfonso XII | 1874–85 | | |
| Alfonso XIII | 1886–1931 | | |

**Did you know?** Gazpacho is a cold soup of Spanish cuisine, especially that of Andalusia. It is an ancient dish mentioned in Greek and Roman literature, although two of the main ingredients of the modern version, tomatoes and green peppers, were taken to Spain from the New World only in the 16th century. Spanish cookbooks classify gazpacho as a salad.

## Rulers of Germany

On 25 Jul 1806 the Confederation of the Rhine was founded, with Carl Theodor Reichsfreiherr von Dalberg as Prince-Primate (1806–13). After the dissolution of the Rhine Confederation, there was no true central power until 1815, when the German Confederation was founded. In 1867 the governing structure became the North German Confederation, and in 1871 the German Reich. For rulers of Germany before the Confederation of the Rhine, see "Holy Roman Emperors."

| RULER | REIGN OR TERM | RULER | REIGN OR TERM |
|---|---|---|---|
| **Emperors** | | **Chancellors (continued)** | |
| **Hohenzollern dynasty** | | Wilhelm Cuno | 1922–23 |
| Wilhelm I | 1871–88 | Gustav Stresemann | 1923 |
| Friedrich III | 1888 | Wilhelm Marx | 1923–24 |
| Wilhelm II | 1888–1918 | Hans Luther | 1925–26 |
| | | Wilhelm Marx | 1926–28 |
| **Presidents** | | Hermann Müller | 1928–30 |
| Richard Müller | 1918 | Heinrich Brüning | 1930–32 |
| Robert Leinert | 1918–19 | Franz von Papen | 1932 |
| Wilhelm Pfannkuch | 1919 | Kurt von Schleicher | 1932–33 |
| Eduard David | 1919 | Adolf Hitler | 1933–45 |
| Friedrich Ebert | 1919–25 | Joseph Goebbels | 1945 |
| Hans Luther (acting) | 1925 | Lutz Graf Schwerin von Krosigk | 1945 |
| Walter Simons (acting) | 1925 | (chairman of interim government) | |
| Paul von Hindenburg | 1925–34 | | |
| Adolf Hitler (Führer) | 1934–45 | **Allied occupation** | 1945–49 |
| Karl Dönitz | 1945 | | |
| | | **German Democratic Republic (East Germany)[1]** | |
| **Chancellors** | | **Presidents** | |
| Otto Fürst von Bismarck | 1871–90 | Johannes Dieckmann (acting) | 1949 |
| Leo Graf von Caprivi | 1890–94 | Wilhelm Pieck | 1949–60 |
| Chlodwig Fürst zu Hohenlohe-Schillingsfürst | 1894–1900 | Johannes Dieckmann (acting) | 1960 |
| Bernhard Graf Fürst von Bülow | 1900–09 | **Chairmen of the Council of State** | |
| Theobald von Bethmann Hollweg | 1909–17 | Walter Ulbricht | 1960–73 |
| Georg Michaelis | 1917 | Friedrich Ebert (acting) | 1973 |
| Georg Graf von Hertling | 1917–18 | Willi Stoph | 1973–76 |
| Maximilian Prinz von Baden | 1918 | Erich Honecker | 1976–89 |
| Friedrich Ebert | 1918 | Egon Krenz | 1989 |
| Philipp Scheidemann | 1919 | Manfred Gerlach (acting) | 1989–90 |
| Gustav Bauer | 1919–20 | Sabine Bergmann-Pohl[2] | 1990 |
| Wolfgang Kapp (in rebellion) | 1920 | | |
| Hermann Müller | 1920 | **Federal Republic of Germany (West Germany)[1]** | |
| Konstantin Fehrenbach | 1920–21 | **Presidents** | |
| Joseph Wirth | 1921–22 | Karl Arnold (acting) | 1949 |

## Rulers of Germany (continued)

| RULER | REIGN OR TERM | RULER | REIGN OR TERM |
|---|---|---|---|
| **Federal Republic of Germany (West Germany)**[1] | | **Chancellors** | |
| **Presidents (continued)** | | Konrad Adenauer | 1949–63 |
| Theodor Heuss | 1949–59 | Ludwig Erhard | 1963–66 |
| Heinrich Lübke | 1959–69 | Kurt Georg Kiesinger | 1966–69 |
| Gustav Heinemann | 1969–74 | Willy Brandt | 1969–74 |
| Walter Scheel | 1974–79 | Walter Scheel (acting) | 1974 |
| Karl Carstens | 1979–84 | Helmut Schmidt | 1974–82 |
| Richard von Weizsäcker | 1984–94 | Helmut Kohl | 1982–98 |
| Roman Herzog | 1994–99 | Gerhard Schröder | 1998– |
| Johannes Rau | 1999– | | |

[1]After WWII, Germany was split into four occupational zones, governed by the French, British, American, and Soviet powers. The Western zones were merged and, on 23 May 1949, became the independent Federal Republic of Germany. On 7 October of the same year, the Soviet zone was proclaimed the German Democratic Republic. On 3 Oct 1990, the latter was incorporated into the Federal Republic of Germany.
[2]Bergmann–Pohl was president of the People's Chamber.

## Holy Roman Emperors

*The Holy Roman Empire encompassed a varying complex of lands in Western and Central Europe. Ruled over by Frankish and then German kings, the empire officially dissolved on 6 Aug 1806, when Francis II resigned his title.*

| EMPEROR | REIGN | EMPEROR | REIGN |
|---|---|---|---|
| **Carolingian dynasty** | | **House of Hohenstaufen** | |
| Charlemagne (Charles I) | 800–814 | Conrad III | 1138–52 |
| Louis I | 814–840 | Frederick I (Barbarossa) | 1152–90 |
| *Civil War* | 840–843 | Henry VI | 1190–97 |
| Lothair I | 843–855 | Philip | 1198–1208 |
| Louis II | 855–875 | | |
| Charles II | 875–877 | **Welf dynasty** | |
| *Interregnum* | 877–881 | Otto IV | 1198–1214 |
| Charles III | 881–887 | | |
| *Interregnum* | 887–891 | **House of Hohenstaufen** | |
| | | Frederick II | 1215–50 |
| **House of Spoleto** | |   Rival claimants: | |
| Guy | 891–894 |    Henry (VII) | 1220–35 |
| Lambert | 894–898 |    Henry Raspe | 1246–47 |
| | |    William of Holland | 1247–56 |
| **Carolingian dynasty** | | Conrad IV | 1250–54 |
| Arnulf | 896–899 | *Great Interregnum* | 1254–73 |
| Louis III | 901–905 |   Richard | 1257–72 |
| | |   Alfonso (Alfonso X of Castile) | 1257–75 |
| **House of Franconia** | | | |
| Conrad I | 911–918 | **House of Habsburg** | |
| | | Rudolf I | 1273–91 |
| **Carolingian dynasty** | | | |
| Berengar | 915–924 | **House of Nassau** | |
| | | Adolf | 1292–98 |
| **House of Saxony (Liudolfings)** | | | |
| Henry I | 919–936 | **House of Habsburg** | |
| Otto I | 936–973 | Albert I | 1298–1308 |
| Otto II | 973–983 | | |
| Otto III | 983–1002 | **House of Luxembourg** | |
| Henry II | 1002–24 | Henry VII | 1308–13 |
| | | | |
| **Salian dynasty** | | **House of Habsburg** | |
| Conrad II | 1024–39 | Frederick (III) | 1314–26 |
| Henry III | 1039–56 | | |
| Henry IV | 1056–1106 | **House of Wittelsbach** | |
|   Rival claimants: | | Louis IV | 1314–46 |
|    Rudolf | 1077–80 | | |
|    Hermann | 1081–93 | **House of Luxembourg** | |
|    Conrad | 1093–1101 | Charles IV | 1346–78 |
| Henry V | 1105/06–25 | Wenceslas | 1378–1400 |
| | | | |
| **House of Supplinburg** | | **House of Wittelsbach** | |
| Lothair II | 1125–37 | Rupert | 1400–10 |

# Holy Roman Emperors (continued)

| EMPEROR | REIGN | EMPEROR | REIGN |
|---|---|---|---|
| **House of Luxembourg** | | **House of Habsburg (continued)** | |
| Jobst | 1410–11 | Ferdinand III | 1637–57 |
| Sigismund | 1410–37 | Leopold I | 1658–1705 |
| | | Joseph I | 1705–11 |
| **House of Habsburg** | | Charles VI | 1711–40 |
| Albert II | 1438–39 | | |
| Frederick III | 1440–93 | **House of Wittelsbach** | |
| Maximilian I | 1493–1519 | Charles VII | 1742–45 |
| Charles V | 1519–56 | | |
| Ferdinand I | 1556–64 | **House of Habsburg** | |
| Maximilian II | 1564–76 | Francis I | 1745–65 |
| Rudolf II | 1576–1612 | Joseph II | 1765–90 |
| Matthias | 1612–19 | Leopold II | 1790–92 |
| Ferdinand II | 1619–37 | Francis II | 1792–1806 |

# Rulers of Russia[1]

| RULER | REIGN | RULER | REIGN |
|---|---|---|---|
| **Princes and Grand Princes of Moscow** | | **Tsars and Empresses of Russia and the** | |
| **(Muscovy): Danilovich dynasty[2]** | | **Russian Empire: Romanov dynasty[3] (continued)** | |
| Daniel (son of Alexander Nevsky) | c. 1276–1303 | Catherine I | 1725–27 |
| Yury | 1303–25 | Peter II | 1727–30 |
| Ivan I | 1325–40 | Anna | 1730–40 |
| Semyon (Simeon) | 1340–53 | Ivan VI | 1740–41 |
| Ivan II | 1353–59 | Elizabeth | 1741–61 (O.S.) |
| Dmitry Donskoy | 1359–89 | Peter III[4] | 1761–62 (O.S.) |
| Vasily I | 1389–1425 | Catherine II | 1762–96 |
| Vasily II | 1425–62 | Paul | 1796–1801 |
| Ivan III | 1462–1505 | Alexander I | 1801–25 |
| Vasily III | 1505–33 | Nicholas I | 1825–55 |
| Ivan IV | 1533–47 | Alexander II | 1855–81 |
| | | Alexander III | 1881–94 |
| **Tsars of Russia: Danilovich dynasty** | | Nicholas II | 1894–1917 |
| Ivan IV | 1547–84 | | |
| Fyodor I | 1584–98 | **Provisional government** | 1917 |
| | | | |
| **Tsars of Russia: Time of Troubles** | | **Chairmen (or First Secretaries) of the** | |
| Boris Godunov | 1598–1605 | **Communist Party of the Soviet Union** | |
| Fyodor II | 1605 | Vladimir Lenin | 1917–24 |
| False Dmitry | 1605–06 | Joseph Stalin | 1924–53 |
| Vasily (IV) | 1606–10 | Georgy Malenkov | 1953 |
| | | Nikita Khrushchev | 1953–64 |
| **Interregnum** | 1610–12 | Leonid Brezhnev | 1964–82 |
| | | Yury Andropov | 1982–84 |
| | | Konstantin Chernenko | 1984–85 |
| **Tsars and Empresses of Russia and the** | | Mikhail Gorbachev | 1985–91 |
| **Russian Empire: Romanov dynasty[3]** | | | |
| Michael III | 1613–45 | **Presidents of Russia** | |
| Alexis | 1645–76 | Boris Yeltsin | 1990–99 |
| Fyodor III | 1676–82 | Vladimir Putin | 2000– |
| Peter I (Ivan V coruler 1682–96) | 1682–1725 | | |

[1]This table includes leaders of Muscovy, Russia, the Russian Empire, and the Soviet Union.    [2]The Danilovich dynasty is a late branch of the Rurik dynasty, named after its progenitor, Daniel.    [3]On 22 (O.S.) Oct 1721, Peter I the Great took the title of "emperor." However, despite the official titling, conventional usage took an odd turn. Every male sovereign continued usually to be called tsar, but every female sovereign was conventionally called empress.    [4]The direct line of the Romanov dynasty came to an end in 1761 with the death of Elizabeth, daughter of Peter I, but subsequent rulers of the "Holstein-Gottorp dynasty" (the first, Peter III, was son of Charles Frederick, duke of Holstein-Gottorp, and Anna, daughter of Peter I) took the family name of Romanov.

**Did you know?** The deepest continental body of water on Earth is Lake Baikal in southern Siberia. It reaches a maximum depth of 5,314 feet. Plant and animal life in the lake is rich and varied, and about three-quarters of the species are peculiar to Baikal. Approximately 600 plant species live on or near the surface. There are more than 1,200 animal species at different depths, including one mammal, the Baikal seal.

# Middle East

## Byzantine Emperors

The Byzantine Empire comprised what was previously the eastern half of the Roman Empire. It survived for nearly 1,000 years after the western half had crumbled into various feudal kingdoms; it finally fell to Ottoman Turkish onslaughts in 1453. For emperors of the Eastern Roman Empire (at Constantinople) before the fall of Rome, see "Roman Emperors."

| EMPEROR | REIGN | EMPEROR | REIGN |
|---|---|---|---|
| Zeno | 474–491 | Theodora (empress) | 1055–56 |
| Anastasius I | 491–518 | Michael VI Stratioticus | 1056–57 |
| Justin I | 518–527 | Isaac I Comnenus | 1057–59 |
| Justinian I | 527–565 | Constantine X Ducas | 1059–67 |
| Justin II | 565–578 | Romanus IV Diogenes | 1067–71 |
| Tiberius II Constantine | 578–582 | Michael VII Ducas | 1071–78 |
| Maurice Tiberius | 582–602 | Nicephorus III Botaniates | 1078–81 |
| Phocas | 602–610 | Alexius I Comnenus | 1081–1118 |
| Heraclius | 610–641 | John II Comnenus | 1118–43 |
| Heraclius Constantine | 641 | Manuel I Comnenus | 1143–80 |
| Heraclonas (or Heraclius) | 641 | Alexius II Comnenus | 1180–83 |
| Constans II (Constantine Pogonatus) | 641–668 | Andronicus I Comnenus | 1183–85 |
| Constantine IV | 668–685 | Isaac II Angelus | 1185–95 |
| Justinian II Rhinotmetus | 685–695 | Alexius III Angelus | 1195–1203 |
| Leontius | 695–698 | Isaac II Angelus (restored) | 1203–04 |
| Tiberius III | 698–705 | and Alexius IV Angelus (joint ruler) | |
| Justinian II Rhinotmetus (restored) | 705–711 | Alexius V Ducas Murtzuphlus | 1204 |
| Philippicus | 711–713 | | |
| Anastasius II | 713–715 | **Latin emperors** | |
| Theodosius III | 715–717 | Baldwin I | 1204–06 |
| Leo III | 717–741 | Henry | 1206–16 |
| Constantine V Copronymus | 741–775 | Peter | 1217 |
| Leo IV | 775–780 | Yolande (empress) | 1217–19 |
| Constantine VI | 780–797 | Robert | 1221–28 |
| Irene (empress) | 797–802 | Baldwin II | 1228–61 |
| Nicephorus I | 802–811 | John | 1231–37 |
| Stauracius | 811 | | |
| Michael I Rhangabe | 811–813 | **Nicaean emperors** | |
| Leo V | 813–820 | Constantine (XI) Lascaris | 1204–05? |
| Michael II Balbus | 820–829 | Theodore I Lascaris | 1205?–22 |
| Theophilus | 829–842 | John III Ducas Vatatzes | 1222–54 |
| Michael III | 842–867 | Theodore II Lascaris | 1254–58 |
| Basil I | 867–886 | John IV Lascaris | 1258–61 |
| Leo VI | 886–912 | | |
| Alexander | 912–913 | **Greek emperors restored** | |
| Constantine VII Porphyrogenitus | 913–959 | Michael VIII Palaeologus | 1261–82 |
| Romanus I Lecapenus | 920–944 | Andronicus II Palaeologus | 1282–1328 |
| Romanus II | 959–963 | Andronicus III Palaeologus | 1328–41 |
| Nicephorus II Phocas | 963–969 | John V Palaeologus | 1341–76 |
| John I Tzimisces | 969–976 | John VI Cantacuzenus | 1347–54 |
| Basil II Bulgaroctonus | 976–1025 | Andronicus IV Palaeologus | 1376–79 |
| Constantine VIII | 1025–28 | John V Palaeologus (restored) | 1379–90 |
| Romanus III Argyrus | 1028–34 | John VII Palaeologus | 1390 |
| Michael IV | 1034–41 | John V Palaeologus (restored) | 1390–91 |
| Michael V Calaphates | 1041–42 | Manuel II Palaeologus | 1391–1425 |
| Zoe (empress) | 1042–56 | John VIII Palaeologus | 1421–48 |
| Constantine IX Monomachus | 1042–55 | Constantine XI Palaeologus | 1449–53 |

## Caliphs

When Muhammad died on 8 Jun 632, Abu Bakr, his father-in-law, succeeded to his political and administrative functions. He and his three immediate successors are known as the "perfect" or "rightly guided" caliphs. After them, the title was borne by the 14 Umayyad caliphs of Damascus (from 661–750) and subsequently by the 38 'Abbasid caliphs of Baghdad (both are named after their clans of origin). The empire of the caliphate grew rapidly through conquest during its first two centuries to include most of southwestern Asia, North Africa, and Spain. 'Abbasid power ended in 945, when the Buyids took Baghdad under their rule. They retained the 'Abbasid caliphs as figureheads; other dynasties in Central Asia and the Ganges River basin acknowledged the 'Abbasid caliphs as spiritual leaders. The Fatimids, however, proclaimed a new caliphate in

## Caliphs (continued)

920 in their capital of al-Mahdiyah in Tunisia; it lasted until 1171, by which time opposition within the sect caused it to disintegrate. 'Abbasid authority was partially restored in the 12th century, but the caliphate ceased to exist with the Mongol destruction of Baghdad in 1258. Some principal caliphs are listed below.

| CALIPH | REIGN | CALIPH | REIGN |
|---|---|---|---|
| **"Perfect" caliphs** | | **Fatimid caliphs (al-Mahdiyah)** | |
| Abu Bakr | 632–634 | al-Mahdi | 909–934 |
| 'Umar I | 634–644 | al-Qa'im | 934–946 |
| 'Uthman ibn 'Affan | 644–656 | al-Mansur | 946–953 |
| 'Ali | 656–661 | al-Mu'izz | 953–975 |
| | | al-Hakim | 996–1021 |
| **Umayyad caliphs (Damascus)** | | al-Mustansir | 1036–94 |
| Mu'awiyah I | 661–680 | al-Musta'li | 1094–1101 |
| Abd al-Malik | 685–705 | | |
| al-Walid | 705–715 | **'Abbasid caliph (Baghdad)** | |
| Hisham | 724–743 | al-Nasir | 1180–1225 |
| Marwan II | 744–750 | | |
| | | | |
| **'Abbasid caliphs (Baghdad)** | | | |
| as-Saffah | 749–754 | | |
| Harun | 786–809 | | |
| al-Ma'mun | 813–833 | | |

## Sultans of the Ottoman Empire

One of the most powerful states in the world during the 15th and 16th centuries, the Ottoman empire was created by Turkish tribes in Anatolia and spanned more than 600 years. It came to an end in 1922, when it was replaced by the Turkish Republic and various successor states in southeastern Europe and the Middle East. At its height the empire included most of southeastern Europe, the Middle East as far east as Iraq, North Africa as far west as Algeria, and most of the Arabian Peninsula. The term Ottoman is a dynastic appellation derived from Osman (Arabic: 'Uthman), the nomadic Turkmen chief who founded both the dynasty and the empire.

| SULTAN | REIGN | SULTAN | REIGN |
|---|---|---|---|
| Osman I | c. 1300–1324 | Ibrahim | 1640–1648 |
| Orhan | 1324–1360 | Mehmed IV | 1648–1687 |
| Murad I | 1360–1389 | Suleyman II | 1687–1691 |
| Bayezid I | 1389–1402 | Ahmed II | 1691–1695 |
| Mehmed I | 1413–1421 | Mustafa II | 1695–1703 |
| Murad II | 1421–1444 | Ahmed III | 1703–1730 |
| Mehmed II | 1444–1446 | Mahmud I | 1730–1754 |
| Murad II (second reign) | 1446–1451 | Osman III | 1754–1757 |
| Mehmed II (second reign) | 1451–1481 | Mustafa III | 1757–1774 |
| Bayezid II | 1481–1512 | Abdulhamid I | 1774–1789 |
| Selim I | 1512–1520 | Selim III | 1789–1807 |
| Suleyman I | 1520–1566 | Mustafa IV | 1807–1808 |
| Selim II | 1566–1574 | Mahmud II | 1808–1839 |
| Murad III | 1574–1595 | Abdulmecid I | 1839–1861 |
| Mehmed III | 1595–1603 | Abdulaziz | 1861–1876 |
| Ahmed I | 1603–1617 | Murad V | 1876 |
| Mustafa I | 1617–1618 | Abdulhamid II | 1876–1909 |
| Osman II | 1618–1622 | Mehmed V | 1909–1918 |
| Mustafa I (second reign) | 1622–1623 | Mehmed VI | 1918–1922 |
| Murad IV | 1623–1640 | | |

## Persian Dynasties
*Dates given are approximate and may overlap.*

| DYNASTY/KINGDOM | PERIOD | DYNASTY/KINGDOM | PERIOD |
|---|---|---|---|
| Median | 728–550 BC | Arab invasion and the advent of | |
| Achaemenian | 559–330 BC | Islam | 640–829 |
| Hellenistic period of Alexander and the Seleucids[1] | 330 BC–247 BC | Iranian intermezzo[3] | 821–1055 |
| | | Seljuqs | 1038–1157 |
| Parthian period (Arsacid dynasty)[2] | 247 BC–AD 224 | Mongols[4] | 1220–1335 |
| Sasanian | 224–651 | Timurids and Ottoman Turks | 1380–1501 |

## Persian Dynasties (continued)

*Dates given are approximate and may overlap.*

| DYNASTY/KINGDOM | PERIOD | DYNASTY/KINGDOM | PERIOD |
|---|---|---|---|
| Safavid | 1502–1736 | Zand | 1750–79 |
| Afghan interlude | 1723–36 | Qajars | 1794–1925 |
| Nader Shah | 1736–47 | Pahlavi | 1925–79 |

[1]Dates from the death of Darius III, the last Achaemenian king, and the invasion of Alexander the Great. [2]Dates from the year in which the Parnian chief Arsaces first battled the Seleucids. [3]Includes the Tahirid, Samanid, Ghaznavids, and Buyid dynasties. [4]Mainly the Il-Khanid dynasty (1256–1353).

# Asia

## Indian Dynasties

*Dates given are approximations.*

| DYNASTY | LOCATION | DATES | DYNASTY | LOCATION | DATES |
|---|---|---|---|---|---|
| Nanda | Ganges Valley | 400 BC | Pala | Bengal | 800–1100 |
| Maurya | India, barring the area south of Mysore (Karnataka) | 400–200 BC | Pratihara | western India and upper Ganges Valley | 900–1100 |
| Indo-Greeks | northern India | 200–100 BC | Rastrakuta | western and central Deccan | 800–1100 |
| Sunga | Ganges Valley and parts of central India | 200–100 BC | Cola | Tamil Nadu | 900–1300 |
|  |  |  | Candella | Bundelkhand | 1000–1200 |
|  |  |  | Cauhan | Rajasthan | 1000–1200 |
| Satavahana | northern Deccan | 100 BC–AD 300 | Caulukya | Gujarat | 1000–1300 |
| Saka | western India | 100 BC–AD 400 | Paramara | western and central India | 1000–1100 |
| Kusana | northern India and Central Asia | AD 100–300 | Later Calukya | western and central Deccan | 1000–1200 |
| Gupta | northern India | 400–600 | Hoysala | central and southern Deccan | 1200–1400 |
| Harsa | northern India | 700 |  |  |  |
| Pallava | Tamil Nadu | 400–900 | Yadava | northern Deccan | 1200–1300 |
| Calukya | western and central Deccan | 600–800 | Pandya | Tamil Nadu | 1300–1400 |

## Japanese Historical Periods and Rulers

| PERIOD | DATES | PERIOD | DATES |
|---|---|---|---|
| Asuka | 552–710 | Muromachi (or Ashikaga) | 1338–1573 |
| Nara | 710–784 | Azuchi-Momoyama | 1574–1600 |
| Heian | 794–1185 | Edo (or Tokugawa) | 1603–1867 |
| Kamakura | 1192–1333 | Meiji | 1868–1912 |

Reign dates for the first 28 sovereigns (Jimmu through Senka) are taken from the *Nihon shoki* ("Chronicles of Japan"). The first 14 sovereigns are considered legendary, and while the next 14 are known to have existed, their exact reign dates have not been verified historically. When the year of actual accession and year of formal coronation are different, the latter is placed in parenthesis after the former. If the two events took place in the same year, no special notation is used. If only the coronation year is known, it is placed in parenthesis.

| EMPEROR | REIGN | EMPEROR | REIGN |
|---|---|---|---|
| Jimmu | (660)–585 BC | Nintoku | (313)–399 |
| Suizei | (581)–549 BC | Richu | (400)–405 |
| Annei | 549–511 BC | Hanzei | (406)–410 |
| Itoku | (510)–477 BC | Ingyo | (412)–453 |
| Kosho | (475)–393 BC | Anko | 453–456 |
| Koan | (392)–291 BC | Yuryaku | 456–479 |
| Korei | (290)–215 BC | Seinei | (480)–484 |
| Kogen | (214)–158 BC | Kenzo | (485)–487 |
| Kaika | 158–98 BC | Ninken | (488)–498 |
| Sujin | (97)–30 BC | Buretsu | 498–506 |
| Suinin | (29 BC)–AD 70 | Keitai | (507)–531 |
| Keiko | (71)–130 | Ankan | 531 (534)–535 |
| Seimu | (131)–190 | Senka | 535–539 |
| Chuai | (192)–200 | Kimmei | 539–571 |
| Jingu Kogo (regent) | 201–269 | Bidatsu | (572)–585 |
| Ojin | (270)–310 | Yomei | 585–587 |

## Japanese Historical Periods and Rulers (continued)

| EMPEROR | REIGN | EMPEROR | REIGN |
|---|---|---|---|
| Sushun | 587–592 | Juntoku | 1210 (1211)–21 |
| Suiko (empress regnant) | 593–628 | Chukyo | 1221 |
| Jomei | (629)–641 | Goshirakawa | 1221 (1222)–32 |
| Kogyoku (empress regnant) | (642)–645 | Shijo | 1232 (1233)–42 |
| Kotoku | 645–654 | Go–Saga | 1242–46 |
| Saimei (empress regnant: | (655)–661 | Go–Fukakusa | 1246–59/60 |
| Kogyoku rethroned) | | Kameyama | 1259/60–74 |
| Tenji | 661 (668)–672 | Gouda | 1274–87 |
| Kobun | 672 | Fushimi | 1287 (1288)–98 |
| Temmu | 672 (673)–686 | Go–Fushimi | 1298–1301 |
| Jito (empress regnant) | 686 (690)–697 | Go–Nijo | 1301–08 |
| Mommu | 697–707 | Hanazono | 1308–18 |
| Gemmei (empress regnant) | 707–715 | Go–Daigo | 1318–39 |
| Gensho (empress regnant) | 715–724 | Go–Murakami | 1339–68 |
| Shomu | 724–749 | Chokei | 1368–83 |
| Koken (empress regnant) | 749–758 | Go–Kameyama | 1383–92 |
| Junnin | 758–764 | | |
| Shotoku (empress regnant: | 764 (765)–770 | **The Northern court[2]** | |
| Koken rethroned) | | Kogon | 1331 (1332)–33 |
| Konin | 770–781 | Komyo | 1336 (1337/38)–48 |
| Kammu | 781–806 | Suko | 1348 (1349/50)–51 |
| Heizei | 806–809 | Go–Kogon | 1351 (1353/54)–71 |
| Saga | 809–823 | Go–Enyu | 1371 (1374/75)–82 |
| Junna | 823–833 | Go–Komatsu | 1382–92 |
| Nimmyo | 833–850 | Go–Komatsu | 1392–1412 |
| Montoku | 850–858 | Shoko | 1412 (1414)–28 |
| Seiwa | 858–876 | Go–Hanazono | 1428 (1429/30)–64 |
| Yozei | 876 (877)–884 | Go–Tsuchimikado | 1464 (1465/66)–1500 |
| Koko | 884–887 | Go–Kashiwabara | 1500 (1521)–26 |
| Uda | 887–897 | Go–Nara | 1526 (1536)–57 |
| Daigo | 897–930 | Ogimachi | 1557 (1560)–86 |
| Suzaku | 930–946 | Go–Yozei | 1586 (1587)–1611 |
| Murakami | 946–967 | Go–Mizunoo | 1611–29 |
| Reizei | 967–969 | Meisho (empress regnant) | 1629 (1630)–43 |
| En'yu | 969–984 | Go–Komyo | 1643–54 |
| Kazan | 984–986 | Go–Sai | 1654/55 (1656)–63 |
| Ichijo | 986–1011 | Reigen | 1663–87 |
| Sanjo | 1011–16 | Higashiyama | 1687–1709 |
| Go–Ichijo | 1016–36 | Nakamikado | 1709 (1710)–35 |
| Go–Suzaku | 1036–45 | Sakuramachi | 1735–47 |
| Go–Reizei | 1045–68 | Momozono | 1747–62 |
| Go–Sanjo | 1068–72 | Go–Sakuramachi | 1762 (1763)–71 |
| Shirakawa | 1072–86 | (empress regnant) | |
| Horikawa | 1086–1107 | Go–Momozono | 1771–79 |
| Toba | 1107–23 | Kokaku | 1780–1817 |
| Sutoku | 1123–41 | Ninko | 1817–46 |
| Konoe | 1141–55 | Komei | 1846 (1847)–66 |
| Go–Shirakawa | 1155–58 | Meiji (personal name: | 1867 (1868)–1912 |
| Nijo | 1158–65 | Mutsuhito; era name: Meiji) | |
| Rokujo | 1165–68 | Taisho (personal name: | 1912 (1915)–26 |
| Takakura | 1168–80 | Yoshihito; era name: Taisho) | |
| Antoku | 1180–85[1] | Hirohito (era name: Showa) | 1926 (1928)–1989 |
| Go–Toba | 1183 (1184)–98 | Akihito (era name: Heisei) | 1989 (1990)– |
| Tsuchimikado | 1198–1210 | | |

[1]Antoku's reign overlaps that of Go-Toba. Go-Toba was placed on the throne by the Minamoto clan after the rival Taira clan had fled Kyoto with Antoku.    [2]From 1336 until 1392 Japan witnessed the spectacle of two contending Imperial courts—the Southern court of Go-Daigo and his descendants, whose sphere of influence was restricted to the immediate vicinity of the Yoshino Mountains, and the Northern court of Kogon and his descendants, which was under the domination of the Ashikaga family.

## Chinese Dynasties

*Dates given for early dynasties are approximate and may overlap.*

| DYNASTY | ALTERNATE NAME | DATES | DYNASTY | ALTERNATE NAME | DATES |
|---|---|---|---|---|---|
| Hsia[1] | Xia | c. 2205–1766 BC | Western Zhou | Chou | c. 1050–771 BC |
| Shang | | c. 1760–1030 BC | Eastern Zhou | Chou | c. 771–255 BC |

## Chinese Dynasties (continued)

*Dates given for early dynasties are approximate and may overlap.*

| DYNASTY | ALTERNATE NAME | DATES | DYNASTY | ALTERNATE NAME | DATES |
|---|---|---|---|---|---|
| Qin | Ch'in | 221–206 BC | Sui | | 581–618 |
| Han | | 206 BC–AD 220 | T'ang | Tang | 618–907 |
| Western Jin | Chin | 265–317 | Five Dynasties[3] | Ten Kingdoms[3] | 907–960 |
| Eastern Jin[2] | Chin | 317–420 | Sung | Song | 960–1279 |
| Six Dynasties[2] | | 220–589 | Yüan | Yuan, Mongol | 1206–1368 |
| Wu | | 222–80 | Ming | | 1368–1644 |
| Eastern Jin[2] | | 317–420 | Ch'ing | Qing, Manchu | 1644–1911/12 |
| Liusong | | 420–79 | | | |
| Southern Qi | | 479–502 | | | |
| Southern Liang | | 502–57 | | | |
| Southern Chen | | 557–89 | | | |

[1]The Hsia Dynasty is mentioned in legends but is of undetermined historicity.    [2]Between the fall of the Han and the establishment of the Sui, China was divided into two societies, northern and southern. The Six Dynasties had their capital at Nanjing in the south. The Eastern Jin is considered one of these six dynasties and so is listed twice.    [3]Period of time between the fall of the T'ang dynasty and the founding of the Sung dynasty, when five would-be dynasties followed one another in quick succession in North China. The era is also known as the period of the Ten Kingdoms because 10 regimes dominated separate regions of South China during the same period.

## Leaders of the People's Republic of China Since 1949

**Chinese Communist Party leaders**

| NAME | TITLE | DATES |
|---|---|---|
| Mao Zedong | CCP chairman | 1949–1976 |
| Hua Guofeng | CCP chairman | 1976–1981 |
| Hu Yaobang | CCP chairman; after September 1982, general secretary of the CCP | 1981–1987 |
| Zhao Ziyang | CCP general secretary | 1987–1989 |
| Jiang Zemin | CCP general secretary | 1989–2002 |
| Hu Jintao | CCP general secretary | 2002– |

**premiers**

| NAME | DATES |
|---|---|
| Zhou Enlai | 1949–1976 |
| Hua Guofeng | 1976–1980 |
| Zhao Ziyang | 1980–1987 |
| Li Peng | 1987–1998 |
| Zhu Rongji | 1998–2003 |
| Wen Jiabao | 2003– |

*Note: although he held no top party or state position, Deng Xiaoping was de facto leader of China from 1977 to 1997.*

## Dalai Lamas

The Dalai Lama is the head of the dominant Dge-lugs-pa (Yellow Hat) order of Tibetan Buddhists and, until 1959, was both spiritual and temporal ruler of Tibet. In accordance with the belief in reincarnate lamas, which began to develop in the 14th century, the successors of the first Dalai Lama were considered his rebirths and came to be regarded as physical manifestations of the compassionate bodhisattva ("buddha-to-be"), Avalokitesvara.

| DALAI LAMA | NAME | LIVED | DALAI LAMA | NAME | LIVED |
|---|---|---|---|---|---|
| first | Dge-'dun-grub-pa | 1391–1475 | eighth | 'Jam-dpal-rgya-mtsho | 1758–1804 |
| second | Dge-'dun-rgya-mtsho | 1475–1542 | ninth | Lung-rtogs-rgya-mtsho | 1806–1815[1] |
| third | Bsod-nams-rgya-mtsho | 1543–1588 | tenth | Tshul-khrims-rgya-mtsho | 1816–1837[1] |
| fourth | Yon-tan-rgya-mtsho | 1589–1617 | eleventh | Mkhas-grub-rgya-mtsho | 1838–1856[1] |
| fifth | Ngag-dbang-rgya-mtsho | 1617–1682 | twelfth | 'Phrin-las-rgya-mtsho | 1856–1875[1] |
| sixth | Tshangs-dbyangs-rgya-mtsho | 1683–1706 | thirteenth | Thub-bstan-rgya-mtsho | 1875–1933[2] |
| seventh | Bskal-bzang-rgya-mtsho | 1708–1757 | fourteenth | Bstan-'dzin-rgya-mtsho | 1935–[3] |

[1]Dalai Lamas 9–12 all died young, and the country was ruled by regencies.    [2]Reigned as head of a sovereign state from 1912.    [3]Ruled from exile in Dharmsala, India, from 1960.

---

**Did you know?** The amount of water in river systems at any time is but a tiny fraction of the Earth's total water. The oceans contain 97% of all water. About three-quarters of fresh water is stored as land ice; nearly all the remainder occurs as groundwater. Lakes account for less than 0.5% of all fresh water, soil moisture 0.05%, and water in river channels only 0.025%, or about one four-thousandth of the Earth's total fresh water.

# The Americas

## Pre-Columbian Civilizations

Various aboriginal American Indian cultures evolved in Meso-America (part of Mexico and Central America) and the Andean region (western South America) prior to Spanish exploration and conquest in the 16th century. These pre-Columbian civilizations were extraordinary developments in human society and culture, characterized by kingdoms and empires, great monuments and cities, and refinements in the arts, metallurgy, and writing. Dates given below are approximations.

| CULTURE | LOCATION | DATES |
|---|---|---|
| **Meso-American civilizations** | | |
| Olmec | Gulf coast of southern Mexico | 1150 BC–800 BC |
| Zapotec | Oaxaca, particularly Monte Albán | 500 BC–AD 900 |
| Totonac | east-central Mexico | 500 BC–AD 900 |
| Teotihuacán | Teotihuacán, in the Valley of Mexico | AD 400–600 |
| Maya | southern Mexico and Guatemala | 250–900 |
| Toltec | central Mexico | 900–1200 |
| Aztec | central and southern Mexico | 1400–early 1500s |
| | | |
| **Andean civilizations** | | |
| Nazca | southern coast of Peru | 200 BC–AD 600 |
| Recuay | northern highlands of Peru | 200 BC–AD 600 |
| Tiwanaku | Lake Titicaca, Bolivia | 200 BC–AD 1000 |
| Moche (Mochica) | northern coast of Peru | AD 1–700 |
| Inca | Pacific coast of South America | 1100–1532 |

**Did you know?** The sweet potato originated in South America (where native Americans called it *batata*) and was introduced from there to Europe. It is the swollen root of a vine that trails along the ground. Some American varieties are erroneously known as yams. The term yam actually refers to tubers of the genus *Dioscorea;* they are native to the warmer regions of both hemispheres.

# Africa

## Historic Sub-Saharan African States

| STATE | LOCATION IN PRESENT-DAY COUNTRIES | FLOURISHED |
|---|---|---|
| Aksumite kingdom | Ethiopia, Sudan | 1st–10th centuries |
| Asante empire | Ghana | 18th–19th centuries |
| Basuto kingdom | Lesotho | 19th century |
| Benin kingdom | Nigeria | 12th–19th centuries |
| kingdom of Buganda | Uganda | 14th–20th centuries |
| kingdom of Bunyoro | Uganda | 15th–19th centuries |
| kingdom of Burundi | Burundi | 17th–20th centuries |
| kingdom of Dahomey | Benin | 17th–19th centuries |
| Darfur | Sudan | 17th–19th centuries |
| kingdom of Dongola | Sudan | 7th–14th centuries |
| Fulani empire | Cameroon, Niger, Nigeria | 19th–20th centuries |
| Ghana empire | Mali, Mauritania | 4th–13th centuries |
| Hausa states | Nigeria | 14th–19th centuries |
| Kanem-Bornu | Nigeria, Chad, Cameroon, Niger, Libya | 9th–19th centuries |
| Kongo kingdom | Angola, Dem. Rep. of Congo | 14th–17th centuries |
| Kuba kingdom | Dem. Rep. of Congo | 17th–19th centuries |
| kingdom of Kush | Egypt, Sudan | c. 850 BC–c. AD 325 |
| Luba empire | Dem. Rep. of Congo | 16th–19th centuries |
| Lunda empire | Dem. Rep. of Congo, Angola, Zambia | 17th–19th centuries |
| Mali empire | Mali, Mauritania, Senegal, Gambia, Guinea-Bissau | 13th–16th centuries |
| Ndongo kingdom | Angola | 14th–17th centuries |
| kingdom of Nubia | Egypt, Sudan | 4th–7th centuries |
| Oyo empire | Nigeria | 16th–19th centuries |
| Rozwi empire | Zimbabwe, Botswana | 17th–19th centuries |
| Shewa empire | Ethiopia | 15th–19th centuries |
| Songhai empire | Nigeria, Niger | 6th–17th centuries |
| Tukulor empire | Mali | 19th century |

## Historic Sub-Saharan African States (continued)

| STATE | LOCATION IN PRESENT-DAY COUNTRIES | FLOURISHED |
|---|---|---|
| Wolof empire | Senegal | 14th–19th centuries |
| Zeng empire | Somalia, Kenya, Tanzania, Mozambique | 10th–16th centuries |
| Zulu kingdom | South Africa | 19th century |

Baghdad was the world's first city to reach a population of more than one million. It was the world's largest city during the years 775–935.

# Populations

## Largest Urban Agglomerations

*Agglomerations include a central city and associated neighboring communities.*
*Source: United Nations, World Urbanization Prospects, the 2001 Revision.*

| RANK | AGGLOMERATION | COUNTRY | POPULATION (2000) | RANK | AGGLOMERATION | COUNTRY | POPULATION (2000) |
|---|---|---|---|---|---|---|---|
| 1 | Tokyo | Japan | 26,444,000 | 16 | Karachi | Pakistan | 10,032,000 |
| 2 | Mexico City | Mexico | 18,066,000 | 17 | Manila | Philippines | 9,950,000 |
| 3 | São Paulo | Brazil | 17,962,000 | 18 | Seoul | Korea | 9,888,000 |
| 4 | New York City | US | 16,732,000 | 19 | Paris | France | 9,630,000 |
| 5 | Bombay | India | 16,086,000 | 20 | Cairo | Egypt | 9,462,000 |
| 6 | Los Angeles | US | 13,213,000 | 21 | Tianjin | China | 9,156,000 |
| 7 | Calcutta | India | 13,058,000 | 22 | Istanbul | Turkey | 8,953,000 |
| 8 | Shanghai | China | 12,887,000 | 23 | Lagos | Nigeria | 8,665,000 |
| 9 | Dhaka | Bangladesh | 12,519,000 | 24 | Moscow | Russia | 8,367,000 |
| 10 | Delhi | India | 12,441,000 | 25 | London | UK | 7,640,000 |
| 11 | Buenos Aires | Argentina | 12,024,000 | 26 | Lima | Peru | 7,443,000 |
| 12 | Jakarta | Indonesia | 11,018,000 | 27 | Bangkok | Thailand | 7,372,000 |
| 13 | Osaka | Japan | 11,013,000 | 28 | Chicago | US | 6,989,000 |
| 14 | Beijing | China | 10,839,000 | 29 | Tehran | Iran | 6,979,000 |
| 15 | Rio de Janeiro | Brazil | 10,652,000 | 30 | Hong Kong | China | 6,860,000 |

## Migration of Foreigners Into and Out of Selected Countries

*Inflows and outflows of foreign population into selected OECD countries, estimates for 2000. N/A indicates not available. Source: Organisation for Economic Co-operation and Development,*
*Trends in International Migration (2002).*

| COUNTRY | FOREIGN INFLOW | FOREIGN OUTFLOW | COUNTRY | FOREIGN INFLOW | FOREIGN OUTFLOW |
|---|---|---|---|---|---|
| Australia | 92,300 | 50,800 | Luxembourg | 10,800 | 7,100 |
| Belgium | 68,600 | 35,600 | The Netherlands | 91,400 | 20,700 |
| Canada | 227,200 | N/A | New Zealand | 38,800 | 15,600 |
| Finland | 9,100 | 4,100 | Norway | 27,800 | 14,900 |
| France | 119,300 | N/A | Portugal | 15,900 | N/A |
| Germany | 648,800 | 562,400 | Sweden | 33,800 | 12,100 |
| Ireland | 24,100 | N/A | Switzerland | 87,400 | 55,800 |
| Italy | 271,500 | N/A | United Kingdom | 288,800 | 137,000 |
| Japan | 345,800 | 210,900 | United States | 849,800 | N/A |

## Principal Sources of Refugees Worldwide

*Estimates as of 31 Dec 2002. Source: US Committee for Refugees: World Refugee Survey 2003.*

| AREA | REFUGEES | AREA | REFUGEES | AREA | REFUGEES |
|---|---|---|---|---|---|
| Afghanistan | 3,500,000 | Vietnam | 302,000 | China (including Tibet) | 178,000 |
| Palestine | 3,000,000 | Somalia | 300,000 | Bosnia and Herzegovina | 160,000 |
| Myanmar (Burma) | 510,000 | Iraq | 294,000 | Sri Lanka | 155,000 |
| Sudan | 475,000 | Eritrea | 290,000 | Sierra Leone | 130,000 |
| Angola | 410,000 | Liberia | 280,000 | Guatemala | 129,000 |
| Dem. Rep. of the Congo | 410,000 | Croatia | 251,000 | Bhutan | 127,000 |
| Burundi | 400,000 | El Salvador | 203,000 | Western Sahara | 110,000 |

## Internally Displaced Persons (IDPS)

*Estimates of major populations of internally displaced persons (individuals forced to move within their own countries as the result of armed conflict or natural disasters) as of 31 Dec 2002. Estimates vary widely for some countries. Source: US Committee for Refugees, World Refugee Survey 2003.*

| COUNTRY | IDPS | COUNTRY | IDPS |
|---|---|---|---|
| Sudan | 4,000,000 | Indonesia | 600,000–1,000,000 |
| Colombia | 2,500,000 | Turkey | 380,000–1,000,000 |
| Angola | 2,000,000–3,500,000 | Jordan | 800,000 |
| Dem. Rep. of the Congo | 2,000,000 | Afghanistan | 700,000 |
| Iraq | 1,100,000 | Uganda | 600,000–700,000 |
| Burma | 600,000–1,000,000 | Côte d'Ivoire | 500,000–700,000 |

## Areas with High Ratios of Refugee Populations

*Ratio of refugees to host-country populations, selected estimates as of 31 Dec 2002. Source: US Committee for Refugees, World Refugee Survey 2003.*

| HOST AREA | RATIO OF REFUGEE POPULATION TO TOTAL POPULATION | NUMBER OF REFUGEES | HOST AREA | RATIO OF REFUGEE POPULATION TO TOTAL POPULATION | NUMBER OF REFUGEES |
|---|---|---|---|---|---|
| Gaza Strip | 1:2 | 879,000 | Saudi Arabia | 1:98 | 245,000 |
| West Bank | 1:3 | 627,000 | Uganda | 1:112 | 221,000 |
| Lebanon | 1:11 | 409,000 | Sudan | 1:114 | 287,000 |
| Djibouti | 1:27 | 23,000 | Switzerland | 1:165 | 44,200 |
| Rep. of Congo | 1:29 | 118,000 | Nepal | 1:181 | 132,000 |
| Iran | 1:30 | 2,209,000 | Dem. Rep. | 1:201 | 274,000 |
| Serbia and Montenegro | 1:30 | 353,000 | of Congo | | |
| | | | Thailand | 1:228 | 336,000 |
| Zambia | 1:40 | 247,000 | Canada | 1:399 | 78,400 |
| Guinea | 1:46 | 182,000 | Malaysia | 1:414 | 59,000 |
| Liberia | 1:51 | 65,000 | United States | 1:450 | 638,000 |
| Tanzania | 1:72 | 516,000 | United Kingdom | 1:760 | 79,200 |
| Pakistan | 1:95 | 1,518,000 | Germany | 1:788 | 104,000 |

 **Did you know?** The Khoisan languages of southern Africa have highly complex systems of clicks (which are considered consonants), influenced by a number of articulations such as nasality. Combined with non-click consonants, these systems have resulted in some uniquely large and complicated consonant systems, especially the !Xóõ language, which has 126 consonants.

# Languages of the World

## Most Widely Spoken Languages

*Listing the languages spoken by more than 1% of humankind, this table enumerates speakers of each tongue as a primary or secondary language. Figures based on data from Linguasphere 2000. For more information visit <www.linguasphere.org>.*

| LANGUAGE | NUMBER OF SPEAKERS (MILLIONS) | % OF WORLD POPULATION (APPROXIMATE) | LANGUAGE FAMILY |
|---|---|---|---|
| English | 1,000 | 16 | Indo-European (Germanic) |
| Mandarin | 1,000 | 16 | Sino-Tibetan (Chinese) |
| Hindi/Urdu[1] | 900 | 15 | Indo-European (Indo-Aryan) |
| Spanish | 450 | 7 | Indo-European (Romance) |
| Russian/Belarusian | 320 | 5 | Indo-European (Slavic) |
| Arabic | 250 | 4 | Afro-Asiatic (Semitic) |
| Bengali/Sylhetti | 250 | 4 | Indo-European (Indo-Aryan) |
| Malay/Indonesian | 200 | 3 | Austronesian (Malayo-Polynesian) |
| Portuguese | 200 | 3 | Indo-European (Romance) |
| Japanese | 130 | 2 | isolated language |
| French | 125 | 2 | Indo-European (Romance) |
| German | 125 | 2 | Indo-European (Germanic) |
| Thai/Lao | 90 | 1 | Tai |
| Punjabi | 85 | 1 | Indo-European (Indo-Aryan) |
| Wu | 85 | 1 | Sino-Tibetan (Chinese) |

## Most Widely Spoken Languages (continued)

| LANGUAGE | NUMBER OF SPEAKERS (MILLIONS) | % OF WORLD POPULATION (APPROXIMATE) | LANGUAGE FAMILY |
|---|---|---|---|
| Javanese | 80 | 1 | Austronesian (Malayo-Polynesian) |
| Marathi | 80 | 1 | Indo-European (Indo-Aryan) |
| Turkish/Azeri/Turkmen | 80 | 1 | Altaic (Turkic) |
| Korean | 75 | 1 | isolated language |
| Vietnamese | 75 | 1 | Mon-Khmer (Vietic) |
| Cantonese | 70 | 1 | Sino-Tibetan (Chinese) |
| Italian | 70 | 1 | Indo-European (Romance) |
| Tamil | 70 | 1 | Dravidian |
| Telugu | 70 | 1 | Dravidian |
| Ukrainian | 65 | 1 | Indo-European (Slavic) |
| Bhojpuri/Maithili | 60 | 1 | Indo-European (Indo-Aryan) |
| Persian/Tajik | 60 | 1 | Indo-European (Iranian) |
| Swahili | 60 | 1 | Afro-Asiatic (Niger-Congo) |
| Tagalog | 60 | 1 | Austronesian (Malayo-Polynesian) |

[1]Although Hindi and Urdu use different writing systems, these languages are branches of Hindustani and are orally mutually intelligible.

## Foreign Words and Phrases

**à droite** [F] : to or on the right hand

**à gauche** [F] : to or on the left hand

**aloha oe** [Hawaiian] : love to you : greetings : farewell

**amor patriae** [L] : love of one's country

**amor vincit omnia** [L] : love conquers all things

**aqua et igni interdictus** [L] : forbidden to be furnished with water and fire : outlawed

**ars longa, vita brevis** [L] : art is long, life is short

**à votre santé** [F] : to your health—used as a toast

**bella figura** [It] : fine appearance or impression

**bien entendu** [F] : well understood : of course

**bon appétit** [F] : good appetite : enjoy your meal

**bonjour** [F] : good day : good morning

**bonne foi** [F] : good faith

**bonsoir** [F] : good evening

**carte d'identité** [F] : identity card

**c'est la guerre** [F] : that's war : it cannot be helped

**c'est la vie** [F] : that's life : that's how things happen

**chacun à son goût** [F] : everyone to his taste

**cherchez la femme** [F] : look for the woman

**che sarà, sarà** [It] : what will be, will be

**cogito, ergo sum** [L] : I think, therefore I exist

**comédie humaine** [F] : human comedy : the whole variety of human life

**comme ci, comme ça** [F] : so-so

**compte rendu** [F] : report (as of proceedings in an investigation)

**cum grano salis** [L] : with a grain of salt

**d'accord** [F] : in accord : agreed

**de gustibus non est disputandum** [L] : there is no disputing about tastes

**Dei gratia** [L] : by the grace of God

**de integro** [L] : anew : afresh

**Deo gratias** [L] : thanks (be) to God

**de profundis** [L] : out of the depths

**dies irae** [L] : day of wrath—used of the Judgment Day

**Dieu et mon droit** [F] : God and my right—motto on the British royal arms

**Dominus vobiscum** [L] : the Lord be with you

**d'un certain âge** [F] : of a certain age : no longer young

**en famille** [F] : in or with one's family : at home : informally

**en garde** [F] : on guard

**en plein air** [F] : in the open air

**e pluribus unum** [L] : one out of many—used on the Great Seal of the US and on several US coins

**Erin go bragh** [Ir *go brách* or *go bráth*, lit., till doomsday] : Ireland forever

**errare humanum est** [L] : to err is human

**et tu Brute** [L] : thou too, Brutus—exclamation attributed to Julius Caesar on seeing his friend Brutus among his assassins

**eureka** [Gk] : I have found it—motto of California

**excelsior** [L] : still higher—motto of New York

**ex libris** [L] : from the books of—used on bookplates

**façon de parler** [F] : manner of speaking : figurative or conventional expression

**faire suivre** [F] : have forwarded : please forward

**fils** [F] : son—used orig. after French and now also after other family names to distinguish a son from his father

**force de frappe** [F] : military striking force esp. with nuclear weapons

**gardez la foi** [F] : keep faith

**guten Tag** [G] : good day

**hasta la vista** [Sp] : good-bye

**homme d'affaires** [F] : man of business : business agent

**hors commerce** [F] : outside the trade : not offered through regular commercial channels

**id est** [L] : that is (*i.e.*)

**ignorantia juris neminem excusat** [L] : ignorance of the law excuses no one

**in aeternum** [L] : forever

**inshallah** [Ar] : if Allah wills : God willing

**in vino veritas** [L] : there is truth in wine

**j'accuse** [F] : I accuse : bitter denunciation

**januis clausis** [L] : behind closed doors

**le roi est mort, vive le roi** [F] : the king is dead, long live the king

**l'état, c'est moi** [F] : the state, it is I

**mal vu** [F] : badly regarded : disapproved of

**mano a mano** [Sp] : hand to hand : in direct competition or confrontation

**mens sana in corpore sano** [L] : a sound mind in a sound body

**nolens volens** [L] : unwilling (or) willing : willy-nilly

**nuit blanche** [F] : white night : a sleepless night

## Foreign Words and Phrases (continued)

**nyet** [Russ] : no

**omertà** [It] : submission : code chiefly among members of the criminal underworld that enjoins private vengeance and the refusal to give information to outsiders (as the police)

**ora pro nobis** [L] : pray for us

**outre-mer** [F] : overseas : distant lands

**par avion** [F] : by airplane—used on airmail

**pax vobiscum** [L] : peace (be) with you

**père** [F] : father—used orig. after French and now also after other family names to distinguish a father from his son

**pour rire** [F] : for laughing : not to be taken seriously

**pro bono publico** [L] : for the public good

**pro hac vice** [L] : for this occasion

**pro patria** [L] : for one's country

**quis custodiet ipsos custodes?** [L] : who will keep the keepers themselves?

**qui s'excuse s'accuse** [F] : he who excuses himself accuses himself

**quod vide** [L] : which see (*q.v.*)

**raison d'état** [F] : reason of state

**répondez s'il vous plaît** [F] : reply, if you please (*RSVP*)

**requiescat in pace** [L] : may he or she rest in peace—used on tombstones (*RIP*)

**sans souci** [F] : without worry

**sayonara** [Jp] : good-bye

**semper fidelis** [L] : always faithful—motto of the US Marine Corps

**s'il vous plaît** [F] : if you please

**tout à fait** [F] : altogether : quite

**tout de suite** [F] : immediately *also* : all at once : consecutively

**tout le monde** [F] : all the world : everybody

**tristesse** [F] : melancholy

**über alles** [G] : above everything else

**uebermensch** [G] : superman

**und so weiter** [G] : and so on

**urbi et orbi** [L] : to the city (Rome) and the world : to everyone

**veni, vidi, vici** [L] : I came, I saw, I conquered

**voilà tout** [F] : that's all

**wie geht's?** [G] : how goes it?

## English Neologisms

*New entries from* Merriam-Webster's Collegiate® Dictionary, *Eleventh Edition (© 2003)*

**agita** (1982): a feeling of agitation or anxiety

**barista** (1982): a person who makes and serves coffee (as espresso) to the public

**brewski** (1978): beer

**bubkes** also **bupkes** or **bupkus** (1942): the least amount; beans

**buckytube** (1991): a nanotube composed of pure carbon with a molecular arrangement similar to that of fullerene

**burka** or **burqa** (1836): a loose enveloping garment that covers the face and body and is worn in public by certain Muslim women

**cack-handed** (1854) left-handed; clumsy, awkward

**chappie** (1821) fellow

**cheesed off** (1942) angry, irritated

**collateral damage** (1972): injury inflicted on something other than the intended target; specifically, civilian casualties of a military operation

**comb-over** (1980): an arrangement of hair on a balding man in which hair from the side of the head is combed over the bald spot

**compadre** (1834): a close friend; buddy

**dead-cat bounce** (1985): a brief and insignificant recovery (as of stock prices) after a steep decline

**dead presidents** (1944) slang: US money in the form of bills; specifically, dollars

**def** (1979): cool

**dog's breakfast** (c. 1934): a confused mess or mixture

**dot-commer** (1997): a person who owns or works for a dot-com

**exfoliant** (1983): a mechanical or chemical agent (as an abrasive skin wash or salicylic acid) that is applied to the skin to remove dead cells from the surface

**fen-phen** [fenfluramine + phentermine] (1994): a former drug combination of phentermine with either fenfluramine or dexfenfluramine—called also phen-fen

**Frankenfood** (1992): genetically engineered food

**funplex** (1986): an entertainment complex that includes facilities for various sports and games and often restaurants

**gimme cap** (1978): an adjustable visored cap that often features a corporate logo or slogan

**golden handcuffs** (1976): special benefits offered to an employee as an inducement to continue service

**headbanger** (1979): a musician who performs hard rock; a fan of hard rock

**headhunt** (1969): to recruit (personnel and especially executives) for top-level jobs

**heart-healthy** (1980): conducive to a healthy heart and circulatory system

**identity theft** (1991): the illegal use of someone else's personal information (as a Social Security number) in order to obtain money or credit

**junk DNA** (1972): a region of DNA that usually consists of a repeating DNA sequence, does not code for protein, and has no known function

**killer app** (1988): a computer application of such great value or popularity that it assures the success of the technology with which it is associated; broadly, a feature or component that in itself makes something worth having

**longneck** (1978): beer served in a bottle that has a long neck

**lookism** also **looksism** (1978): prejudice or discrimination based on physical appearance and especially physical appearance believed to fall short of societal notions of beauty

**McJob** (1986): a low-paying job that requires little skill and provides little opportunity for advancement

**mosh pit** (1988): an area in front of a stage where very physical and rough dancing takes place at a rock concert

**nanoscale** (1986): having dimensions measured in nanometers

**NIMBY** [not in my backyard] (1980): opposition to the locating of something considered undesirable (as a prison or incinerator) in one's neighborhood—**NIMBYism**

**peloton** (1951): the main body of riders in a bicycle race

**phat** (1963): highly attractive or gratifying; excellent

## English Neologisms (continued)

**psyops** [psychological operations] (1966): military operations usually aimed at influencing the enemy state of mind through noncombative means (as distribution of leaflets)

**punditocracy** (1987): a group of powerful and influential political commentators

**shootaround** (1978): a usually informal basketball practice session

**tweener** (1978): a player who has some but not all of the necessary characteristics for each of two or more positions (as in football or basketball)

**vermiculture** (1976): the cultivation of annelid worms (as earthworms or bloodworms) especially for use as bait or in composting

# Scholarship

## National and Public Libraries of the World

The national and public libraries listed below are generally open to the public. National libraries are usually the primary repository for a nation's printed works. Sources: "National Libraries of the World: an Address List," IFLA Publications. *International Dictionary of Library Histories*, 2001, Fitzroy Dearborn Publishers. *The Bowker Annual Library and Book Trade Almanac 2002*, R.R. Bowker.

| LIBRARY | LOCATION | YEAR FOUNDED | NUMBER OF VOLUMES (MILLIONS) | SPECIAL COLLECTIONS, ARCHIVES, PAPERS |
|---|---|---|---|---|
| **national libraries** | | | | |
| Biblioteca Nacional Venezuela | Caracas | 1833 | 5.8 | politics and diplomacy, Simón Bolívar |
| Biblioteca Nazionale Centrale | Florence | 1861 | 5.4 | Reformation, Galileo Galilei |
| Biblioteca Nazionale Centrale Vittorio Emanuele II | Rome | 1876 | 6.0 | Jesuit collections, Gabriele D'Annunzio |
| Bibliothèque nationale de France | Paris | 1461 | 14.0 | Denis Diderot, Jean-Paul Sartre |
| Bibliothèque nationale du Québec | Montreal | 1967 | 0.594 | artist's books, musical scores |
| British Library[1] | London | 1973 | 16.0 | Charles Dickens, George B. Shaw |
| Deutsche Bibliothek | Frankfurt[2] | 1947 | 6.3 | bibliographies, exile literature (1933–45) |
| Deutsche Bücherei | Leipzig | 1990 | 9.2 | socialism, Anne-Frank-Shoah-Bibliothek |
| Jewish National and University Library[3] | Jerusalem | 1892 | 3.0 | world Jewish history, Albert Einstein |
| Library of Congress | Washington DC | 1800 | 27.8 | Americana, Irving Berlin, Walt Whitman |
| National Diet Library[4] | Tokyo | 1948 | 7.3 | Japanese culture, Allied occupation |
| National Library of China[5] | Beijing | 1909 | 20 | art, early communism |
| National Library of India | Calcutta | 1903 | 3.0 | rare journals of vernacular languages |
| National Library of Mexico | Mexico City | 1867 | 3.0 | Jesuit works, Mexican printing |
| National Library of Russia | St. Petersburg | 1795 | 2.0 | rare books, Russian history |
| | | | | |
| **public libraries** | | | | |
| Biblioteca Luis Angel Arango | Bogotá | 1932 | 0.95 | Spanish New World chroniclers |
| Bibliothèque Mazarine Institut de France | Paris | 1643 | 0.5 | French theology, Jansenist materials |
| Bibliothèque municipale de Lyon | Lyon | 1765 | 2.0 | history of the book, occult studies |
| Bibliothèque publique et universitaire de Genéve | Switzerland | 1562 | 1.9 | Reformation, Jean Calvin, Voltaire |
| Birmingham Central Library | England | 1865 | 1.2 | Industrial Revolution, Shakespeare |
| Boston Public Library | Massachusetts | 1848 | 6.9 | music, fine arts, Emily Dickinson |
| Chetham's Library | Manchester, UK | 1653 | 0.1 | religious history, Robert Southey |
| Chicago Public Library | Illinois | 1873 | 5.8 | African American studies, blues music |
| Enoch Pratt Free Library | Baltimore MD | 1886 | 2.4 | Henry L. Mencken, Edgar Allan Poe |
| Free Library of Philadelphia | Pennsylvania | 1891 | 3.0 | Oliver Goldsmith, Edgar Allan Poe |
| Los Angeles Public Library | California | 1872 | 2.2 | Calif. cookbooks, fairy tales, Mexicana |
| Manchester Central Library | UK | 1852 | 2.1 | music, commerce, Samuel T. Coleridge |
| Mitchell Library | Glasgow | 1877 | 1.2 | angling, architecture, Robert Burns |
| New York Public Library | New York | 1895 | 8.0 | gay and lesbian works, theater and music |
| Öffentliche Bibliothek der Universität Basel | Switzerland | 1470 | 3.1 | Swiss Medical Academy, F. Nietzsche[6] |

## National and Public Libraries of the World (continued)

| LIBRARY | LOCATION | YEAR FOUNDED | NUMBER OF VOLUMES (MILLIONS) | SPECIAL COLLECTIONS, ARCHIVES, PAPERS |
|---|---|---|---|---|
| public libraries (continued) | | | | |
| Shanghai Tushu Guang | China | 1952 | 10.0 | chronicles, genealogies |
| Toronto Public Library[7] | Ontario | 1884 | 1.9 | science fiction, Arthur Conan Doyle |

[1]Originally founded in 1753 as the British Museum Library.   [2]Frankfurt am Main, Germany.   [3]Bet Ha-Sefarim Ha-Leummi Weha-Universitai Giv'at Ram.   [4]Kokuritsu Kokkai Toshokam.   [5]Zhongguo Guojia Tushuguan.   [6]Friedrich Nietzsche.   [7]Metropolitan Toronto Library Board Reference Library.

## World Education Profile

This table provides comparative data about the education systems in 30 selected countries. Definitions as well as information gathering and reporting methods vary widely from country to country, so the statistics presented here are not always comparable.

**Compulsory education** = the number of years of education and ages of pupils required by the system; **Net enrollment ratio** = the actual number of children attending primary school or secondary school as a percentage of all children in the primary school or secondary school age group as defined by the country (number may exceed 100%); **Gross enrollment ratio** for higher education = total enrollment in higher education, regardless of age, as a percentage of all persons of school-leaving age to five years therafter; **Student/teacher ratio** = number of pupils or students per teacher at each level; **Expenditure** = total public expenditure on education as a percentage of GNP.

Sources: *Britannica World Data*, 2003; *UNESCO Statistical Yearbook*, 1999.

| YEAR | COUNTRY | LITERACY RATE TOTAL | M | F | COMPULSORY EDUCATION # YEARS | AGES | ENROLLMENT RATIO NET PRI. | NET SEC. | GROSS HIGHER | STUDENT/TEACHER RATIO PRI. | SEC. | HIGHER | EXPEN-DITURE |
|---|---|---|---|---|---|---|---|---|---|---|---|---|---|
| | **Africa** | | | | | | | | | | | | |
| 1997 | Egypt | 55.3 | 66.6 | 43.7 | 8 | 6-14 | 93 | 64 | 20.0 | 24.2 | 18.6 | — | 4.8 |
| 1995 | Kenya | 82.5 | 89.0 | 76.0 | 8 | 6-14 | 91 | 11 | 2.0 | 30.5 | 15.2 | — | 6.5 |
| 1997 | Senegal | 37.3 | 47.2 | 27.6 | 6 | 7-13 | 60 | 16 | 3.0 | 57.6 | 33.3 | 25.0[1] | 3.7 |
| 1996 | South Africa | 85.1 | 85.8 | 84.5 | 9 | 6-14 | 103 | 58 | 19.0 | 36.3 | 29.2 | 22.8[2] | 8.0 |
| | **Asia** | | | | | | | | | | | | |
| 1997 | China | 85.0 | 92.3 | 77.4 | 9 | 7-15 | 101 | — | 6.0 | 24.2 | 16.8 | 7.8 | 2.3 |
| 1997 | India | 55.8 | 68.6 | 42.1 | 8 | 6-14 | — | — | 7.0 | 61.7 | 23.9 | 17.5 | 3.2 |
| 1997 | Indonesia | 87.0 | 91.9 | 82.1 | 9 | 7-15 | 95 | 45 | 11.0 | 21.3 | 14.4 | 15.0 | 1.4 |
| 1997 | Iran | 76.9 | 83.7 | 70.0 | 5 | 6-11 | 90 | 71 | 18.0 | 31.2 | 31.3 | 14.3 | 4.0 |
| 1998 | Israel | 96.1 | 97.9 | 94.3 | 11 | 5-15 | — | — | 41.0 | 9.2 | — | 19.0 | 7.6 |
| 1997 | Japan | 100.0 | 100.0 | 100.0 | 9 | 6-15 | 103 | 99 | 41.0 | 18.7 | 16.2 | 18.9 | 3.6 |
| 1997 | Philippines | 95.4 | 95.5 | 95.2 | 6 | 6-12 | 101 | 59 | 29.0 | 34.9 | 31.6 | — | 3.4 |
| 1997 | Saudi Arabia | 77.0 | 84.1 | 67.2 | — | — | 61 | 42 | 16.0 | 12.9 | 13 | 18.4 | 7.5 |
| 1997 | Thailand | 95.6 | 97.2 | 94.0 | 6 | 7-15 | — | — | 22.0 | — | — | 19.1 | 4.6 |
| 1997 | Turkey | 85.2 | 93.6 | 76.7 | 8 | 6-14 | 99 | 51 | 21.0 | 29.4 | 23.9 | 22.7 | 2.2 |
| | **Europe** | | | | | | | | | | | | |
| 1995 | France | 98.8 | 98.9 | 98.7 | 10 | 6-16 | 100 | 95 | 51.0 | 18.8 | 12.7 | 39.6 | 6.0 |
| 1998 | Germany | 100.0 | 100.0 | 100.0 | 12 | 6-18 | 86 | 88 | 47.0 | 18.7 | 13.8 | 11.2 | 4.8 |
| 1997 | Greece | 97.2 | 98.6 | 96.0 | 9 | 6-15 | 90 | 87 | 47.0 | 13.9 | 12 | 22.6 | 3.1 |
| 1997 | Italy | 98.5 | 98.9 | 98.1 | 8 | 6-14 | 100 | 67 | 47.0 | 9.7 | 8.4 | 32.0 | 4.9 |
| 1998 | Poland | 99.8 | 99.8 | 99.8 | 8 | 7-15 | 95 | 85 | 25.0 | 15.2 | 19.3 | 14.9 | 7.5 |
| 1999 | Russia | 99.4 | 99.8 | 99.2 | 9 | 6-15 | 93 | — | 43.0 | 12.1 | — | 12.7 | 3.5 |
| 1997 | Sweden | 100.0 | 100.0 | 100.0 | 9 | 7-15 | 102 | 99 | 50.0 | 11.7 | 10.9 | 8.2 | 8.3 |
| 1997 | United Kingdom | 100.0 | 100.0 | 100.0 | 11 | 5-16 | 99 | 91 | 52.0 | 18.5 | 13.2 | 20.4 | 5.3 |
| | **Latin America** | | | | | | | | | | | | |
| 1997 | Argentina | 96.9 | 96.9 | 96.9 | 10 | 5-14 | 96 | 42 | 38.0 | 16.7 | 10.3 | — | 3.5 |
| 1998 | Brazil | 85.3 | 85.5 | 85.4 | 8 | 7-14 | 90 | 19 | 15.0 | 24.5 | 18.3 | 11.2 | 5.1 |
| 1997 | Cuba | 96.4 | 96.5 | 96.4 | 6 | 6-16 | 101 | 59[3] | 12.0 | 13 | 11 | 5.3[3] | 6.7 |
| 1996 | Mexico | 91.0 | 93.1 | 89.1 | 6 | 6-14 | 101 | 51 | 16.0 | 28.3 | 16.2 | 9.4 | 4.9 |
| 1997 | Peru | 89.9 | 94.7 | 85.4 | 6 | 6-12 | 91 | 55 | 26.0 | 27 | 18.5 | 14.2 | 2.9 |
| | **North America** | | | | | | | | | | | | |
| 1996 | Canada | 96.6 | — | — | 10 | 6-16 | 95 | 91 | 88.0 | 16.5 | 18.8 | 14.4 | 6.9 |
| 1998 | United States | 95.5 | 95.7 | 95.3 | 10 | 6-16 | 95 | 90 | 81.0 | 18.5 | 14.4 | 15.3 | 5.4 |
| | **Oceania** | | | | | | | | | | | | |
| 1998 | Australia | 99.5 | — | — | 10 | 6-15 | 95 | 89 | 80.0 | 17.9 | 12.7 | 20.6 | 5.5 |

[1]Universities only.   [2]1994 data.   [3]1996 data.

## Selected World Universities and Colleges

Universities and colleges are selected based on enrollment, age of the institution, and prominence. Enrollment represents the latest available figures for all affiliated campuses and colleges and for all students, including correspondence and part-time students. Locations are included when the place is not mentioned in the name of the institution. Source: *The World of Learning* (2003). Web site: <http://geowww.uibk.ac.at/univ/>

| COUNTRY | INSTITUTION (LOCATION) | FOUNDING YEAR | ENROLLMENT |
|---|---|---|---|
| Afghanistan | Kabul University | 1932 | 9,334 |
| Albania | University of Tiranë | 1957 | 8,755 |
| Algeria | University of Algiers | 1879 | 32,000 |
|  | Mentouri University (Constantine) | 1969 | 27,995 |
| Angola | University Agostinho Neto (Luanda) | 1963 | 6,290 |
| Argentina | University of Buenos Aires | 1821 | 183,397 |
|  | National University of Córdoba | 1613 | 114,918 |
|  | National Technical University (Buenos Aires) | 1959 | 70,087 |
|  | National University of Rosario | 1968 | 54,319 |
|  | National University of La Plata | 1905 | 50,000 |
|  | National University of Tucumán (San Miguel de Tucumán) | 1914 | 42,946 |
|  | National University of the Northeast (Corrientes) | 1957 | 28,459 |
| Armenia | Yerevan State University | 1919 | 9,000 |
| Aruba | University of Aruba (Oranjestad) | 1988 | 300 |
| Australia | Royal Melbourne Institute of Technology | 1887 | 55,515 |
|  | Monash University (Clayon, Victoria) | 1958 | 43,934 |
|  | University of Sydney | 1850 | 39,982 |
|  | Swinburne University of Technology (Hawthorn, Victoria) | 1908 | 38,000 |
|  | Queensland University of Technology (Brisbane) | 1965 | 34,000 |
|  | University of Melbourne (Parkville [Melbourne], Victoria) | 1853 | 33,716 |
|  | Charles Sturt University (Bathurst, NSW) | 1989 | 32,618 |
|  | University of Western Sydney (Sydney) | 1989 | 32,000 |
|  | University of Queensland (Brisbane) | 1910 | 31,764 |
|  | University of South Australia (Adelaide) | 1991 | 27,263 |
| Austria | Vienna University | 1365 | 84,459 |
|  | Innsbruck University | 1669 | 27,000 |
|  | Graz University | 1585 | 24,059 |
| Azerbaijan | Baku State University | 1919 | 13,000 |
| The Bahamas | College of the Bahamas (Nassau) | 1974 | 3,463 |
| Bahrain | University of Bahrain (Madinah 'Isa) | 1986 | 6,760 |
| Bangladesh | University of Dhaka | 1921 | 25,797 |
|  | University of Rajshahi | 1953 | 24,032 |
|  | University of Chittagong | 1966 | 10,273 |
| Barbados | University of the West Indies (Bridgetown) | 1963 | 3,995 |
| Belarus | Belarus State University (Minsk) | 1921 | 13,000 |
|  | Yanka Kupala State University of Grodno | 1940 | 10,600 |
| Belgium | Catholic University of Leuven (Louvain [Leuven]) | 1425 | 27,189 |
|  | Catholic University of Louvain (Louvain-la-Neuve) | 1425 | 20,517 |
|  | Ghent University | 1817 | 24,021 |
| Belize | University of Belize (Belize City) | 1986 | 5,000 |
| Benin | National University of Benin (Cotonou) | 1970 | 18,533 |
| Bermuda | Bermuda College (Paget PG-BX) | 1974 | 1,200 |
| Bolivia | Major University of San Simón (Cochabamba) | 1832 | 40,641 |
|  | Major University of San Andrés (La Paz) | 1930 | 37,109 |
| Bosnia and Herzegovina | University of Sarajevo | 1949 | 34,800 |
| Botswana | University of Botswana (Gaborone) | 1976 | 12,286 |
| Brazil | University of São Paulo | 1934 | 62,100 |
|  | University of Brazil (Rio de Janeiro) | 1920 | 40,000 |
|  | Federal University of Rio Grande do Sul (Pôrto Alegre) | 1934 | 29,117 |
| Brunei | University of Brunei Darussalam (Gadong) | 1985 | 2,879 |
| Bulgaria | St. Kliment Ohridsky University of Sofia | 1888 | 25,454 |
| Burkina Faso | University of Ouagadougou | 1969 | 10,000 |
| Burundi | University of Burundi (Bujumbura) | 1960 | 2,749 |
| Cambodia | Royal University of Phnom Penh | 1960 | 3,686 |
| Cameroon | University of Yaoundé I | 1962 | 20,343 |
| Central African Republic | University of Bangui | 1969 | 6,474 |
| Chad | University of N'Djamena | 1971 | 4,047 |
| Chile | University of Chile (Santiago) | 1738 | 24,822 |
|  | University of Santiago | 1947 | 20,000 |
|  | Catholic University of Chile (Santiago) | 1888 | 18,000 |
| China | Zhejiang University | 1897 | 80,178 |

## Selected World Universities and Colleges (continued)

| COUNTRY | INSTITUTION (LOCATION) | FOUNDING YEAR | ENROLLMENT |
|---|---|---|---|
| China (continued) | Peking University (Beijing) | 1898 | 55,000 |
| | Wuhan University | 1893 | 40,000 |
| | Hong Kong Polytechnic University (Hung Hom) | 1937 | 23,218 |
| | Hunan University (Yule, Changsha) | 976 | 34,000 |
| | China University of Mining and Technology (Xuzhou City, Jiangsu) | 1909 | 30,942 |
| | Xian Jiaotong University (Sian [Xian], Shensi) | 1896 | 26,410 |
| | Harbin Engineering University | 1953 | 23,000 |
| | Nankai University (Tientsin) | 1919 | 23,000 |
| | Dalian University of Technology | 1949 | 22,344 |
| | Northeastern University (Shenyang, Liaoning) | 1923 | 20,621 |
| | University of Macao | 1981 | 4,274 |
| Colombia | National University of Colombia (Bogotá) | 1867 | 28,000 |
| | Javeriana Pontifical University (Bogotá) | 1622 | 26,749 |
| Democratic Republic of the Congo | University of Lubumbashi | 1955 | 13,158 |
| Republic of the Congo | Marien-Ngouabi University (Brazzaville) | 1961 | 16,000 |
| Costa Rica | University of Costa Rica (San Pedro de Montes de Oca) | 1843 | 28,986 |
| Côte d'Ivoire | University of Cocody (Abidjan) | 1958 | 45,000 |
| Croatia | University of Zagreb | 1669 | 53,000 |
| Cuba | University of Havana | 1728 | 15,980 |
| Cyprus | Eastern Mediterranean University (Gazi Magusa, Turkish Republic of Northern Cyprus) | 1979 | 10,300 |
| | University of Cyprus (Nicosia, Republic of Cyprus) | 1989 | 2,234 |
| Czech Republic | Charles (Karlova) University (Prague) | 1348 | 37,569 |
| | Czech Technical University in Prague | 1707 | 20,079 |
| | Masaryk University in Brno | 1919 | 19,462 |
| Denmark | University of Copenhagen | 1479 | 35,000 |
| | Aarhus University (Århus) | 1928 | 20,800 |
| | University of Southern Denmark (Odense) | 1964 | 15,000 |
| Dominican Republic | Autonomous University of Santo Domingo | 1538 | 26,040 |
| Ecuador | University of Guayaquil | 1867 | 60,000 |
| | Central University of Ecuador (Quito) | 1586 | 31,663 |
| Egypt | Al-Azhar University (Cairo) | 970 | 185,000 |
| | Alexandria University | 1942 | 130,500 |
| | Ain Shams University (Cairo) | 1950 | 126,835 |
| | Zagazig University | 1974 | 110,952 |
| | Cairo University | 1908 | 101,427 |
| | Helwan University | 1975 | 96,206 |
| El Salvador | University of El Salvador (San Salvador) | 1841 | 28,306 |
| Eritrea | University of Asmara | 1958 | 4,086 |
| Estonia | University of Tartu | 1632 | 15,350 |
| Ethiopia | Addis Ababa University | 1950 | 19,258 |
| Faroe Islands | University of the Faroe Islands (Tórshavn) | 1965 | 150 |
| Fiji | University of the South Pacific (Suva) | 1968 | 10,000 |
| Finland | University of Helsinki | 1640 | 37,244 |
| | University of Turku | 1920 | 17,025 |
| France | University of Paris | | |
| | I Panthéon-Sorbonne | 1971 | 43,256 |
| | IV Paris-Sorbonne | 1970 | 30,898 |
| | V René Descartes | 1970 | 30,400 |
| | VI Pierre and Marie Curie | 1971 | c. 30,000 |
| | VII Denis Diderot | 1970 | 30,000 |
| | X Paris-Nanterre | 1964 | 34,000 |
| | XI Paris-Sud | 1970 | 28,000 |
| | University of Toulouse I, II, and III | 1229 | 73,531 |
| | University of Lille I, II, and III | 1560 | 67,573 |
| | University of Nancy I and II | 1572 | 38,718 |
| | University of Strasbourg I, II, and III | 1538 | 38,443 |
| | University of Nantes | 1962 | 33,278 |
| | University of Rouen (Mont-Saint-Aignan) | 1966 | 30,000 |
| | University of Bourgogne (Dijon) | 1722 | 29,098 |
| | University of Caen | 1432 | 26,667 |
| | University of Grenoble I | 1339 | 17,273 |
| French Polynesia | University of French Polynesia (Tahiti) | 1999 | 1,600 |
| Gabon | Omar Bongo University (Libreville) | 1970 | 2,400 |
| The Gambia | University of The Gambia (Serrekunda) | 1999 | N/A |

## Selected World Universities and Colleges (continued)

| COUNTRY | INSTITUTION (LOCATION) | FOUNDING YEAR | ENROLLMENT |
|---|---|---|---|
| Georgia | Georgian Technical University (Tbilisi) | 1922 | 16,000 |
| | Javakhishvili State University (Tbilisi) | 1918 | 16,000 |
| Germany | University of Cologne | 1388 | 64,000 |
| | Westphalian Wilhelm University of Münster | 1780 | 44,688 |
| | Free University of Berlin | 1948 | 43,000 |
| | Ludwig Maximilian University of Munich | 1472 | 43,000 |
| | University of Hamburg | 1919 | 40,996 |
| | University of the Ruhr (Bochum) | 1961 | 37,600 |
| | Rhenish Friedrich Wilhelm University of Bonn | 1786 | 37,000 |
| | Johann Wolfgang Goethe University of Frankfurt (Frankfurt am Main) | 1914 | 36,679 |
| | Humboldt University of Berlin | 1810 | 33,740 |
| | University of Hannover | 1831 | 31,880 |
| | Technical University of Berlin | 1799 | 31,700 |
| | Johannes Gutenberg University of Mainz | 1477 | 30,000 |
| | Rhenish-Westphalian Technical University (Aachen) | 1870 | 30,000 |
| | University of Leipzig | 1409 | 26,553 |
| | Ruprecht Karl University of Heidelberg | 1386 | 24,290 |
| | Georg August University of Göttingen | 1737 | 23,000 |
| | Friedrich Alexander University of Erlangen-Nuremberg (Erlangen) | 1743 | 19,623 |
| | Eberhard-Karls University of Tübingen | 1477 | 18,780 |
| Ghana | Kwame Nkrumah University of Science and Technology (Kumasi) | 1951 | 11,633 |
| | University of Ghana (Accra) | 1948 | 8,822 |
| Greece | Aristotle University of Thessaloniki | 1925 | 75,000 |
| | National and Capodistrian University of Athens | 1837 | 45,000 |
| Greenland | University of Greenland (Nuuk) | 1984 | 100 |
| Grenada | St. George's University | 1977 | 2,000 |
| Guatemala | San Carlos University of Guatemala (Guatemala City) | 1676 | 71,199 |
| Guinea | Gamal Abdel Nasser University of Conakry | 1962 | 5,000 |
| Guyana | University of Guyana (Georgetown) | 1963 | 4,607 |
| Haiti | State University of Haiti (Port-au-Prince) | 1920 | 10,446 |
| Honduras | National Autonomous University of Honduras (Tegucigalpa) | 1847 | 33,000 |
| Hungary | University of Pécs | 1367 | 27,013 |
| | Loránd Eötvös University (Budapest) | 1635 | 24,427 |
| | University of Debrecen | 1538 | 23,062 |
| Iceland | University of Iceland (Reykjavík) | 1911 | 6,700 |
| India | University of Calcutta | 1857 | 300,000 |
| | University of Mumbai (Bombay [Mumbai]) | 1857 | 262,350 |
| | Chhatrapati Shahuji Maharaj University (Kanpur) | 1966 | 220,000 |
| | Utkal University (Bhubaneswar) | 1943 | 200,000 |
| | University of Rajasthan (Gandhi Nagar) | 1947 | 175,000 |
| | Magadh University (Bodh Gaya) | 1962 | 170,500 |
| | Gujarat University (Ahmedabad) | 1949 | 153,379 |
| | Shivaji University (Kolhapur) | 1962 | 149,427 |
| | Bangalore University | 1964 | 142,697 |
| | Madurai-Kamaraj University (Madurai) | 1966 | 133,100 |
| | Meerut University | 1966 | 125,365 |
| | Mahatma Gandhi University (Kottayam) | 1983 | 125,000 |
| | University of Kerala (Thiruvananthapuram) | 1937 | 123,310 |
| | Deen Dayal Upadhyay Gorakhpur University | 1957 | 115,000 |
| | Lalit Narayan Mithila University (Darbhanga) | 1972 | 110,355 |
| | University of Madras | 1857 | 107,518 |
| | University of Delhi | 1922 | 101,493 |
| | Karnataka University (Dharwad) | 1949 | 100,562 |
| | Hemvati Nandan Bahuguna Garhwal University (Srinagar) | 1973 | 100,000 |
| Indonesia | Padjadjaran University (Bandung) | 1957 | 40,482 |
| | Gadjah Mada University (Yogyakarta) | 1949 | 40,404 |
| | Indonesia University (Jakarta) | 1950 | 32,222 |
| Iran | Islamic Azad University (Tehran) | 1982 | 850,000 |
| | University of Tehran | 1932 | 32,000 |
| Iraq | University of Baghdad | 1957 | 50,000 |
| | Al-Mustansiriya University (Baghdad) | 1963 | 23,748 |
| Ireland | University College Dublin | 1908 | 18,357 |
| | University of Dublin (Trinity College) | 1592 | 14,750 |

## Selected World Universities and Colleges (continued)

| COUNTRY | INSTITUTION (LOCATION) | FOUNDING YEAR | ENROLLMENT |
|---|---|---|---|
| Israel | Tel Aviv University (Tel Aviv–Yafo) | 1953 | 26,000 |
| | Hebrew University of Jerusalem | 1918 | 23,077 |
| | Bar-Ilan University (Ramat-Gan) | 1953 | 20,000 |
| Italy | University of Rome | 1303 | 189,000 |
| | University of Bologna | 1088 | 101,000 |
| | University of Naples | 1224 | 83,975 |
| | University of Padua | 1222 | 65,579 |
| | University of Turin | 1404 | 65,000 |
| | University of Milan | 1923 | 60,158 |
| | University of Florence | 1321 | 59,847 |
| | University of Catania | 1434 | 53,674 |
| | University of Pisa | 1343 | 47,000 |
| | University of Bari | 1924 | 42,439 |
| | University of Messina | 1548 | 42,300 |
| | University of Genoa | c.1307 | 40,125 |
| | Catholic University of the Sacred Heart (Milan) | 1920 | 40,586 |
| | Polytechnic Institute of Milan | 1863 | 42,402 |
| Jamaica | University of the West Indies (Kingston) | 1948 | 9,073 |
| Japan | Nihon University (Tokyo) | 1889 | 82,158 |
| | Waseda University (Tokyo) | 1882 | 53,441 |
| | Keio University (Tokyo) | 1858 | 46,737 |
| | Meiji University (Tokyo) | 1881 | 35,504 |
| | Ritsumeikan University (Kyoto) | 1900 | 33,420 |
| | Kinki University (Osaka) | 1925 | 32,237 |
| | Tokai University (Tokyo) | 1946 | 31,481 |
| | Chuo University (Tokyo) | 1885 | 29,573 |
| | Hosei University (Tokyo) | 1880 | 29,339 |
| | University of Tokyo | 1877 | 28,103 |
| Jordan | University of Jordan (Amman) | 1962 | 23,623 |
| Kazakhstan | Karaganda State University | 1972 | 15,294 |
| | Kazakh al-Farabi State National University (Almaty) | 1934 | 12,089 |
| Kenya | University of Nairobi | 1956 | 12,359 |
| North Korea | Kim Il-Sung University (P'yongyang) | 1946 | 12,000 |
| South Korea | Hanyang University (Seoul) | 1939 | c. 27,000 |
| | Yonsei University (Seoul) | 1885 | 42,669 |
| | Seoul National University | 1946 | 32,115 |
| | Chosun University (Kwangju) | 1946 | 26,164 |
| | Pusan National University | 1946 | 25,942 |
| Kuwait | Kuwait University (Safat) | 1962 | 18,168 |
| Kyrgyzstan | Osh State University | 1951 | 25,000 |
| | Kyrgyz State National University (Frunze) | 1932 | 22,000 |
| Laos | National University of Laos (Vientiane) | 1995 | 15,791 |
| Latvia | University of Latvia (Riga) | 1919 | 30,242 |
| Lebanon | Lebanese University (Beirut) | 1951 | 69,627 |
| Lesotho | National University of Lesotho (Roma) | 1945 | 1,800 |
| Liberia | University of Liberia (Monrovia) | 1862 | 5,056 |
| Libya | Al-Fateh University (Tripoli) | 1957 | 35,988 |
| Lithuania | Vilnius University | 1579 | 19,120 |
| Luxembourg | Central University of Luxembourg | 1969 | 1,100 |
| Macedonia | University of Skopje | 1949 | 25,967 |
| Madagascar | University of Antananarivo | 1961 | 14,069 |
| Malawi | University of Malawi (Zomba) | 1964 | 4,000 |
| Malaysia | Putra University (Serdang) | 1971 | 33,566 |
| | Malaysia University of Technology (Skudai) | 1904 | 31,529 |
| | University of Malaya (Kuala Lumpur) | 1962 | 24,345 |
| Malta | University of Malta (Msida) | 1592 | 8,118 |
| Mauritania | University of Nouakchott | 1981 | 9,839 |
| Mauritius | University of Mauritius (Réduit) | 1965 | 5,590 |
| Mexico | National Autonomous University of Mexico (Mexico City) | 1551 | 269,000 |
| | University of Guadalajara | 1792 | 180,776 |
| | National Polytechnic Institute (Mexico City) | 1936 | 107,200 |
| | Autonomous University of Nuevo León (San Nicolás de los Garza) | 1933 | 104,300 |
| | Autonomous University of Guerrero (Chilpancingo) | 1869 | 49,000 |
| | University of Veracruz (Jalapa) | 1944 | 47,067 |
| | Autonomous Metropolitan University (Mexico City) | 1973 | 45,000 |
| | Autonomous University of Puebla | 1937 | 42,055 |

## Selected World Universities and Colleges (continued)

| COUNTRY | INSTITUTION (LOCATION) | FOUNDING YEAR | ENROLLMENT |
|---|---|---|---|
| Moldova | Moldova State University (Chisinau) | 1946 | 10,000 |
| Mongolia | Mongolian University of Science and Technology (Ulaanbaatar) | 1969 | 10,000 |
| | National University of Mongolia (Ulaanbaatar) | 1942 | 6,500 |
| Morocco | Cadi Ayyad University (Marrakech) | 1978 | 36,522 |
| | Hassan II University (Casablanca) | 1975 | 33,213 |
| | Mohammed V University (Rabat) | 1957 | 25,387 |
| Mozambique | Eduardo Mondlane University (Maputo) | 1962 | 7,000 |
| Myanmar (Burma) | University of Yangon | 1920 | 47,131 |
| | University of Mandalay | 1925 | 21,045 |
| Namibia | University of Namibia (Windhoek) | 1992 | 8,532 |
| Nepal | Tribhuvan University (Kathmandu) | 1959 | 146,749 |
| The Netherlands | Utrecht University | 1636 | 25,125 |
| | University of Amsterdam | 1632 | 24,000 |
| | University of Groningen | 1614 | 19,000 |
| | Leiden University | 1575 | 15,262 |
| Netherlands Antilles | University of The Netherlands Antilles (Willemstad Curaçao) | 1970 | 600 |
| New Caledonia | University of New Caledonia (Nouméa) | 1999 | 1,800 |
| New Zealand | Massey University (Palmerston North) | 1926 | 31,000 |
| | University of Auckland | 1882 | 30,000 |
| | Auckland University of Technology | 1895 | 23,288 |
| Nicaragua | National Autonomous University of Nicaragua (Managua) | 1812 | 22,000 |
| Niger | Abdou Moumouni University (Niamey) | 1971 | 5,850 |
| Nigeria | Lagos State University (Apapa) | 1983 | 36,683 |
| | University of Lagos | 1962 | 35,083 |
| | Ahmadu Bello University (Zaria) | 1962 | 29,832 |
| Norway | University of Oslo | 1811 | 34,000 |
| Oman | Sultan Qaboos University (Al-Khod) | 1985 | 7,500 |
| Pakistan | University of Peshawar | 1950 | 17,000 |
| | University of Sindh (Jamshoro) | 1947 | 13,349 |
| | University of Karachi | 1951 | 12,500 |
| Panama | University of Panamá (Panama City) | 1935 | 65,225 |
| Papua New Guinea | University of Papua New Guinea (Port Moresby) | 1965 | 4,416 |
| Paraguay | National University of Asunción | 1889 | 19,898 |
| Peru | National University of San Marcos (Lima) | 1551 | 34,223 |
| | Federico Villarreal National University  (Lima) | 1960 | 25,000 |
| Philippines | University of the Philippines (Quezon City) | 1908 | 48,090 |
| | Polytechnic University of the Philippines (Manila) | 1904 | 42,988 |
| | University of Santo Tomás (Manila) | 1611 | 32,061 |
| Poland | University of Warsaw | 1816 | 55,790 |
| | Adam Mickiewicz University in Poznan | 1919 | 43,000 |
| | University of Lodz | 1945 | 41,215 |
| | University of Silesia (Bankowa) | 1968 | 39,452 |
| | University of Wroclaw | 1702 | 33,222 |
| | Jagiellonian University (Krakow) | 1364 | 29,000 |
| Portugal | University of Coimbra | 1290 | 21,165 |
| | University of Lisbon | 1288 | 19,917 |
| | University of Porto | 1911 | 19,906 |
| Qatar | University of Qatar (Doha) | 1973 | 7,794 |
| Réunion | French University of the Indian Ocean (Saint-Denis) | 1970 | 9,103 |
| Romania | University of Oradea | 1990 | 30,000 |
| | Alexandru Ioan Cuza University (Iasi) | 1860 | 27,736 |
| | University of Bucharest | 1864 | 24,650 |
| | Polytechnic University of Bucharest | 1818 | 22,921 |
| Russia | Moscow M.V. Lomonosov State University | 1755 | 28,000 |
| | St. Petersburg State University | 1724 | 25,423 |
| | Udmurt State University (Izhevsk) | 1972 | 21,628 |
| | Kuban State University (Krasnodar) | 1920 | 20,000 |
| | Nizhny Novgorod N.I. Lobachevsky State University | 1916 | 20,000 |
| | Mordovian N.P. Ogarev State University (Saransk) | 1931 | 18,500 |
| | Novgorod State University | 1993 | 17,000 |
| | Far Eastern State University (Vladivostok) | 1899 | 16,000 |
| | Russian Peoples' Friendship University (Moscow) | 1960 | 16,000 |
| | St. Petersburg State Technical University | 1899 | 16,000 |
| | Voronezh State University | 1918 | 16,000 |
| Rwanda | National University of Rwanda (Butare) | 1963 | 4,840 |
| Samoa | National University of Samoa (Apia) | 1984 | 1,400 |

## Selected World Universities and Colleges (continued)

| COUNTRY | INSTITUTION (LOCATION) | FOUNDING YEAR | ENROLLMENT |
|---|---|---|---|
| Saudi Arabia | Islamic University of Imam Muhammad ibn Saud (Riyadh) | 1953 | 39,938 |
| | King Saud University (Riyadh) | 1957 | 37,324 |
| Senegal | Cheikh Anta Diop University of Dakar | 1949 | 20,000 |
| Serbia and Montenegro | University of Belgrade | 1863 | 67,985 |
| | University of Novi Sad | 1960 | 30,000 |
| Sierra Leone | University of Sierra Leone (Freetown) | 1967 | 4,310 |
| Singapore | National University of Singapore | 1980 | 30,698 |
| Slovakia | Comenius University in Bratislava | 1465 | 25,596 |
| Slovenia | University of Ljubljana | 1595 | 40,000 |
| Solomon Islands | Solomon Islands College of Higher Education (Honiara) | 1984 | 1,200 |
| Somalia | Somali National University (Mogadishu) | 1954 | 4,640 |
| South Africa | University of South Africa (Pretoria) | 1873 | 117,046 |
| | Rand Afrikaans University (Johannesburg) | 1966 | 28,200 |
| | University of Pretoria | 1908 | 26,684 |
| Spain | University of Madrid | 1293 | 135,000 |
| | University of Seville | 1502 | 75,000 |
| | University of the Basque Country (Bilbao) | 1968 | 70,000 |
| | University of Valencia | 1502 | 63,293 |
| | University of Barcelona | 1450 | 59,666 |
| | University of Granada | 1526 | 58,960 |
| | University of Valladolid | 1293 | 47,000 |
| | University of Zaragoza | 1542 | 43,331 |
| | University of Oviedo | 1608 | 41,070 |
| | University of Santiago de Compostela | 1495 | 35,000 |
| Sri Lanka | University of Peradeniya | 1942 | 9,500 |
| | University of Sri Jayewardenepura (Gangodawila) | 1959 | 8,200 |
| | University of Colombo | 1921 | 7,057 |
| The Sudan | University of Khartoum | 1956 | 14,000 |
| Suriname | Anton de Kom University of Suriname (Paramaribo) | 1968 | 3,081 |
| Swaziland | University of Swaziland (Kwaluseni) | 1964 | 4,198 |
| Sweden | Göteborg University | 1891 | 39,000 |
| | Uppsala University | 1477 | 36,000 |
| | Lund University | 1666 | 35,000 |
| | Stockholm University | 1877 | 32,000 |
| Switzerland | University of Zürich | 1833 | 20,600 |
| | University of Geneva | 1559 | 13,361 |
| | University of Lausanne | 1537 | 9,000 |
| | University of Basel | 1460 | 7,612 |
| Syria | University of Damascus | 1903 | 85,512 |
| | University of Aleppo | 1960 | 53,465 |
| Taiwan | Tamkang University (Taipei) | 1950 | 26,600 |
| | National Taiwan University (Taipei) | 1928 | 26,212 |
| Tajikistan | Tajik State University (Dushanbe) | 1948 | 11,578 |
| Tanzania | University of Dar es Salaam | 1961 | 8,653 |
| Thailand | Ramkhamhaeng University (Bangkok) | 1971 | 340,231 |
| | Kasetsart University (Bangkok) | 1943 | 27,366 |
| | Chiang Mai University | 1964 | 23,904 |
| Togo | University of Benin (Lomé) | 1965 | 14,293 |
| Trinidad and Tobago | University of the West Indies (St. Augustine) | 1948 | 6,641 |
| Tunisia | University of Tunis I and II | 1988 | 55,291 |
| Turkey | Istanbul University | 1453 | 73,061 |
| | Gazi University (Ankara) | 1982 | 61,447 |
| | Selcuk University (Konya) | 1975 | 60,000 |
| | Ankara University | 1946 | 42,438 |
| | Hacettepe University (Ankara) | 1206 | 28,000 |
| Turkmenistan | Turkmen State University (Ashkhabad) | 1950 | 11,000 |
| Uganda | Makerere University (Kampala) | 1922 | 27,976 |
| Ukraine | Ivan Franko National University of Lviv | 1661 | 22,000 |
| | Odessa I.I. Mechnikov National University | 1865 | 18,200 |
| | Taras Shevchenko University of Kiev | 1834 | 18,000 |
| United Arab Emirates | United Arab Emirates University (Al-'Ayn) | 1976 | 16,000 |
| United Kingdom | University of London (England) | 1836 | 116,288 |
| | University of Wales (Cardiff, Wales) | 1893 | 47,934 |
| | Manchester Metropolitan University (England) | 1970 | 31,080 |
| | University of Leeds (England) | 1874 | 27,682 |
| | De Montfort University (Leicester, England) | 1969 | 27,500 |
| | University of Nottingham (England) | 1881 | 26,500 |

## Selected World Universities and Colleges (continued)

| COUNTRY | INSTITUTION (LOCATION) | FOUNDING YEAR | ENROLLMENT |
|---|---|---|---|
| United Kingdom | Thames Valley University (London, England) | 1991 | 25,741 |
| (continued) | Sheffield Hallam University (England) | 1969 | 24,396 |
| | Nottingham Trent University (England) | 1970 | 24,000 |
| | University of Plymouth (England) | 1970 | 24,000 |
| | University of Sheffield (England) | 1897 | 23,186 |
| | Middlesex University (London, England) | 1973 | 22,412 |
| | University of Westminster (London, England) | 1838 | 21,504 |
| | University of Central England in Birmingham (England) | 1971 | 20,650 |
| | University of Edinburgh (Scotland) | 1583 | 20,483 |
| | University of Ulster (Coleraine, Co. Londonderry N.Ire.) | 1984 | 20,132 |
| | University of Manchester (England) | 1851 | 19,508 |
| | Queen's University of Belfast (N.Ire.) | 1845 | 19,783 |
| | University of Glasgow (Scotland) | 1451 | 19,306 |
| | University of Oxford (England) | c. 1096 | 16,411 |
| | University of Cambridge (England) | c. 1226 | 15,821 |
| Uruguay | University of the Republic (Montevideo) | 1849 | 59,436 |
| Uzbekistan | Tashkent State University | 1920 | 19,300 |
| Vatican City | Pontifical Lateran University (Rome) | 1773 | 4,000 |
| | Pontifical Gregorian University (Rome) | 1553 | 3,569 |
| Venezuela | University of Zulia (Maracaibo) | 1891 | 47,590 |
| | Central University of Venezuela (Caracas) | 1721 | 45,000 |
| | University of Carabobo (Valencia) | 1852 | 44,654 |
| | University of the Andes (Mérida) | 1785 | 34,294 |
| | University of the East (Cumaná) | 1958 | 23,084 |
| Vietnam | University of Hue | 1957 | 48,000 |
| | Hanoi University of Technology | 1956 | 31,000 |
| | Vietnam National University (Hanoi) | 1993 | 22,761 |
| West Bank | Birzeit University | 1924 | 5,320 |
| Yemen | University of Aden | 1975 | 22,538 |
| Zambia | University of Zambia (Lusaka) | 1965 | 3,464 |
| Zimbabwe | University of Zimbabwe (Harare) | 1955 | 8,784 |

 **Did you know?** In 1928, the replacement of the Arabic script by the Latin alphabet was a reform of truly revolutionary proportions in Turkey. This action set Turkey on the path to achieving one of the highest literacy rates in the Middle East.

## Selected North American Universities and Colleges

Universities and colleges are selected based on enrollment, age of the institution, and prominence. Enrollment represents the latest available figures for all students, including correspondence and part-time students. Locations are included when the place is not mentioned in the name of the institution. Source: *The World of Learning* (2003). Web site: <http://geowww.uibk.ac.at/univ/>.

| COUNTRY | STATE/PROVINCE | INSTITUTION (LOCATION) | FOUNDING YEAR | ENROLLMENT |
|---|---|---|---|---|
| United States | Alabama | University of Alabama | | |
| | | Tuscaloosa | 1831 | 19,046 |
| | | Birmingham | 1969 | 16,252 |
| | | Huntsville | 1950 | 6,464 |
| | | Auburn University | 1856 | 21,860 |
| | | Jacksonville State University | 1883 | 7,619 |
| | | Alabama State University (Montgomery) | 1867 | 5,608 |
| | | Troy State University | 1887 | 5,200 |
| | | Tuskegee University | 1881 | 3,000 |
| | Alaska | University of Alaska | | |
| | | Anchorage | 1954 | 17,800 |
| | | Fairbanks | 1917 | 9,400 |
| | | Southeast (Juneau) | 1987 | 4,600 |
| | Arizona | University of Phoenix (Tempe) | 1976 | 107,842[1] |
| | | Arizona State University (Tempe) | 1885 | 43,000 |
| | | University of Arizona (Tucson) | 1885 | 31,158 |
| | | Northern Arizona University (Flagstaff) | 1899 | 19,728 |

## Selected North American Universities and Colleges (continued)

| COUNTRY | STATE/PROVINCE | INSTITUTION (LOCATION) | FOUNDING YEAR | ENROLLMENT |
|---|---|---|---|---|
| United States (continued) | Arkansas | University of Arkansas | | |
| | | Fayetteville | 1871 | 15,795 |
| | | Little Rock | 1927 | 10,959 |
| | | Pine Bluff | 1873 | 3,710 |
| | | Arkansas State University (State University) | 1909 | 9,828 |
| | | Arkansas Tech University (Russellville) | 1909 | 4,500 |
| | | Henderson State University (Arkadelphia) | 1890 | 3,636 |
| | | Harding University (Searcy) | 1924 | 3,566 |
| | California | California State University | | |
| | | Long Beach | 1949 | 32,875 |
| | | Northridge | 1958 | 30,000 |
| | | Sacramento | 1947 | 26,556 |
| | | Fullerton | 1957 | 24,000 |
| | | Fresno | 1911 | 20,013 |
| | | Los Angeles | 1947 | 18,000 |
| | | Chico | 1887 | 14,000 |
| | | Hayward | 1957 | 12,825 |
| | | San Bernardino | 1960 | 12,153 |
| | | Dominguez Hills | 1960 | 10,400 |
| | | Bakersfield | 1965 | 6,210 |
| | | Stanislaus (Turlock) | 1957 | 5,900 |
| | | University of California | | |
| | | Los Angeles | 1919 | 34,713 |
| | | Berkeley | 1868 | 31,123 |
| | | Davis | 1905 | 26,426 |
| | | Santa Barbara | 1909 | 18,940 |
| | | San Diego (La Jolla) | 1912 | 18,324 |
| | | Irvine | 1965 | 17,888 |
| | | Santa Cruz | 1965 | 11,302 |
| | | Riverside | 1954 | 8,865 |
| | | San Francisco | 1873 | 3,443 |
| | | San Diego State University | 1897 | 34,186 |
| | | University of Southern California (Los Angeles) | 1880 | 29,194 |
| | | San Francisco State University | 1899 | 27,420 |
| | | San Jose State University | 1857 | 27,000 |
| | | California Polytechnic State University (San Luis Obispo) | 1901 | 18,079 |
| | | California State Polytechnic University (Pomona) | 1938 | 16,605 |
| | | Stanford University | 1885 | 14,173 |
| | | University of San Francisco | 1855 | 7,662 |
| | | Sonoma State University (Rohnert Park) | 1960 | 7,537 |
| | | Loyola Marymount University (Los Angeles) | 1911 | 7,515 |
| | | Pepperdine University (Malibu) | 1937 | 7,466 |
| | | Humboldt State University (Arcata) | 1913 | 7,433 |
| | | Santa Clara University | 1851 | 7,368 |
| | | University of San Diego | 1949 | 6,880 |
| | | Alliant International University (San Diego) | 2001 | 6,400 |
| | | University of the Pacific (Stockton) | 1851 | 5,428 |
| | | Azusa Pacific University | 1899 | 4,547 |
| | | St. Mary's College of California (Moraga) | 1863 | 4,204 |
| | | University of La Verne | 1891 | 4,088 |
| | | Biola University (La Mirada) | 1908 | 3,447 |
| | Colorado | University of Colorado | | |
| | | Boulder | 1861 | 25,571 |
| | | Denver | 1912 | 10,932 |
| | | Colorado Springs | 1965 | 6,066 |
| | | Colorado State University | | |
| | | Fort Collins | 1870 | 22,523 |
| | | Pueblo | 1933 | 4,343 |
| | | University of Northern Colorado (Greeley) | 1889 | 12,234 |
| | | University of Denver | 1864 | 8,667 |
| | | US Air Force Academy (Colorado Springs) | 1954 | 4,100 |
| | | Colorado School of Mines (Golden) | 1874 | 3,200 |
| | Connecticut | University of Connecticut (Storrs) | 1881 | 24,051 |
| | | Southern Connecticut State University (New Haven) | 1893 | 13,000 |
| | | Central Connecticut State University (New Britain) | 1849 | 12,252 |

## Selected North American Universities and Colleges (continued)

| COUNTRY | STATE/PROVINCE | INSTITUTION (LOCATION) | FOUNDING YEAR | ENROLLMENT |
|---|---|---|---|---|
| United States | Connecticut | Yale University (New Haven) | 1701 | 10,975 |
| (continued) | (continued) | University of Hartford (West Hartford) | 1877 | 6,844 |
| | | Western Connecticut State University (Danbury) | 1903 | 5,607 |
| | | Quinnipiac University (Hamden) | 1929 | 5,434 |
| | | Eastern Connecticut State University (Willimantic) | 1889 | 5,337 |
| | | Fairfield University | 1942 | 5,188 |
| | | University of New Haven (West Haven) | 1920 | 5,113 |
| | | Wesleyan University (Middletown) | 1831 | 3,210 |
| | Delaware | University of Delaware (Newark) | 1743 | 20,868 |
| | | Delaware State University (Dover) | 1891 | 3,381 |
| | District of Columbia | George Washington University | 1821 | 18,986 |
| | | Georgetown University | 1789 | 12,629 |
| | | American University | 1893 | 11,093 |
| | | Howard University | 1867 | 10,987 |
| | | University of the District of Columbia | 1851 | 9,660 |
| | | Catholic University of America | 1887 | 5,510 |
| | Florida | University of Florida (Gainesville) | 1853 | 35,753 |
| | | Florida International University (Miami) | 1965 | 34,000 |
| | | University of South Florida (Tampa) | 1956 | 32,360 |
| | | Florida State University (Tallahassee) | 1851 | 29,630 |
| | | University of Central Florida (Orlando) | 1963 | 29,000 |
| | | Florida Atlantic University (Boca Raton) | 1961 | 19,699 |
| | | Nova Southeastern University (Fort Lauderdale) | 1964 | 19,067 |
| | | University of Miami (Coral Gables) | 1925 | 14,436 |
| | | University of North Florida (South Jacksonville) | 1972 | 10,500 |
| | | Florida Agricultural and Mechanical University (Tallahassee) | 1887 | 9,933 |
| | | Saint Leo University | 1889 | 8,720 |
| | | Barry University (Miami Shores) | 1940 | 8,650 |
| | | Florida Institute of Technology (Melbourne) | 1958 | 4,409 |
| | | Stetson University (DeLand) | 1883 | 3,053 |
| | Georgia | University of Georgia (Athens) | 1785 | 31,288 |
| | | Georgia State University (Atlanta) | 1913 | 22,712 |
| | | Georgia Southern University (Statesboro) | 1906 | 14,371 |
| | | Georgia Institute of Technology (Atlanta) | 1885 | 12,901 |
| | | Emory University (Atlanta) | 1836 | 10,762 |
| | | Valdosta State University | 1906 | 8,755 |
| | | State University of West Georgia (Carrollton) | 1933 | 8,665 |
| | | Mercer University (Macon) | 1833 | 6,800 |
| | | Clark Atlanta University | 1988 | 5,912 |
| | | Georgia College and State University (Milledgeville) | 1889 | 5,800 |
| | | North Georgia College and State University (Dahlonega) | 1873 | 3,863 |
| | Hawaii | University of Hawaii (Honolulu) | 1907 | 44,579 |
| | | Hawaii Pacific University (Honolulu) | 1965 | 9,000 |
| | Idaho | Boise State University | 1932 | 14,969 |
| | | Idaho State University (Pocatello) | 1901 | 12,739 |
| | | University of Idaho (Moscow) | 1889 | 11,027 |
| | Illinois | University of Illinois | | |
| | |   Urbana-Champaign | 1867 | 38,291 |
| | |   Chicago | 1894 | 24,583 |
| | | Southern Illinois University | | |
| | |   Carbondale | 1869 | 21,598 |
| | |   Edwardsville | 1957 | 12,200 |
| | | Northern Illinois University (DeKalb) | 1895 | 23,149 |
| | | Illinois State University (Normal) | 1857 | 21,129 |
| | | DePaul University (Chicago) | 1898 | 16,499 |
| | | Loyola University Chicago | 1870 | 13,759 |
| | | Northwestern University (Evanston) | 1851 | 13,585 |
| | | Western Illinois University (Macomb) | 1899 | 13,206 |
| | | University of Chicago | 1890 | 13,000 |
| | | Eastern Illinois University (Charleston) | 1895 | 10,637 |
| | | Chicago State University | 1867 | 9,500 |
| | | Columbia College (Chicago) | 1890 | 8,076 |
| | | National-Louis University (Chicago) | 1886 | 7,700 |
| | | Roosevelt University (Chicago) | 1945 | 6,300 |
| | | Illinois Institute of Technology (Chicago) | 1893 | 6,287 |

## Selected North American Universities and Colleges (continued)

| COUNTRY | STATE/PROVINCE | INSTITUTION (LOCATION) | FOUNDING YEAR | ENROLLMENT |
|---|---|---|---|---|
| United States | Illinois | Bradley University (Peoria) | 1897 | 6,200 |
| (continued) | (continued) | Saint Xavier University (Chicago) | 1846 | 4,951 |
| | | Lewis University (Romeoville) | 1932 | 4,400 |
| | | School of the Art Institute of Chicago | 1866 | 3,000 |
| | Indiana | Indiana University | | |
| | | Bloomington | 1820 | 34,700 |
| | | South Bend | 1940 | 7,088 |
| | | Southeast (New Albany) | 1968 | 5,396 |
| | | Northwest (Gary) | 1963 | 5,149 |
| | | Purdue University | | |
| | | West Lafayette | 1869 | 36,878 |
| | | Calumet (Hammond) | 1943 | 9,400 |
| | | North Central (Westville) | 1949 | 3,657 |
| | | Indiana University–Purdue University at Indianapolis | 1969 | 23,468 |
| | | Ball State University (Muncie) | 1918 | 17,459 |
| | | Indiana State University (Terre Haute) | 1865 | 11,321 |
| | | University of Notre Dame | 1842 | 10,275 |
| | | Indiana University–Purdue University at Fort Wayne | 1964 | 10,186 |
| | | Butler University (Indianapolis) | 1855 | 4,800 |
| | | Valparaiso University | 1859 | 3,603 |
| | | University of Indianapolis | 1902 | 3,408 |
| | | University of Evansville | 1854 | 3,264 |
| | Iowa | University of Iowa (Iowa City) | 1847 | 28,705 |
| | | Iowa State University (Ames) | 1858 | 24,899 |
| | | University of Northern Iowa (Cedar Falls) | 1876 | 13,553 |
| | | Upper Iowa University (Fayette) | 1857 | 4,859 |
| | | Drake University (Des Moines) | 1881 | 4,826 |
| | Kansas | University of Kansas (Lawrence) | 1864 | 28,329 |
| | | Kansas State University (Manhattan) | 1863 | 20,885 |
| | | Wichita State University | 1894 | 14,568 |
| | | Washburn University of Topeka | 1865 | 6,626 |
| | | Pittsburg State University | 1903 | 6,589 |
| | | Emporia State University | 1863 | 6,006 |
| | | Fort Hays State University (Hays) | 1902 | 5,620 |
| | | Friends University (Wichita) | 1898 | 3,190 |
| | Kentucky | University of Kentucky (Lexington) | 1865 | 23,114 |
| | | University of Louisville | 1798 | 21,218 |
| | | Western Kentucky University (Bowling Green) | 1906 | 15,767 |
| | | Eastern Kentucky University (Richmond) | 1906 | 15,161 |
| | | Murray State University | 1922 | 8,914 |
| | | Morehead State University | 1922 | 8,171 |
| | Louisiana | Louisiana State University | | |
| | | Baton Rouge | 1860 | 29,000 |
| | | Shreveport | 1965 | 4,400 |
| | | Eunice | 1964 | 3,000 |
| | | University of Louisiana | | |
| | | Lafayette | 1898 | 15,489 |
| | | Monroe | 1931 | 11,553 |
| | | University of New Orleans | 1956 | 16,000 |
| | | Southeastern Louisiana University (Hammond) | 1925 | 14,522 |
| | | Tulane University (New Orleans) | 1834 | 11,158 |
| | | Louisiana Tech University (Ruston) | 1894 | c. 10,000 |
| | | Southern University and Agricultural and Mechanical College (Baton Rouge) | 1880 | 9,172 |
| | | Northwestern State University of Louisiana (Natchitoches) | 1884 | 8,600 |
| | | McNeese State University (Lake Charles) | 1939 | 7,780 |
| | | Nicholls State University (Thibodaux) | 1948 | 7,184 |
| | | Grambling State University | 1901 | 4,716 |
| | | Loyola University (New Orleans) | 1905 | 4,665 |
| | | Xavier University of Louisiana (New Orleans) | 1915 | 3,506 |
| | Maine | University of Maine | | |
| | | Orono | 1865 | 9,213 |
| | | Augusta | 1965 | 5,722 |
| | | University of Southern Maine (Portland) | 1878 | 10,820 |

## Selected North American Universities and Colleges (continued)

| COUNTRY | STATE/PROVINCE | INSTITUTION (LOCATION) | FOUNDING YEAR | ENROLLMENT |
|---|---|---|---|---|
| United States (continued) | Maryland | University of Maryland System | | |
| | | University College (Adelphi) | 1947 | 71,303 |
| | | College Park | 1859 | 33,889 |
| | | Baltimore County campus | 1963 | 10,265 |
| | | Baltimore City campus | 1807 | 5,975 |
| | | Eastern Shore (Princess Anne) | 1886 | 3,166 |
| | | Johns Hopkins University (Baltimore) | 1876 | 17,967 |
| | | Towson University | 1866 | 15,105 |
| | | Salisbury University | 1925 | 6,682 |
| | | Frostburg State University | 1898 | 5,295 |
| | | Bowie State University | 1865 | 5,181 |
| | | Morgan State University (Baltimore) | 1867 | 5,034 |
| | | University of Baltimore | 1925 | 5,000 |
| | | US Naval Academy (Annapolis) | 1845 | 4,265 |
| | | Coppin State College (Baltimore) | 1900 | 4,003 |
| | | McDaniel College (Westminster) | 1867 | 3,124 |
| | Massachusetts | University of Massachusetts | | |
| | | Amherst | 1863 | 24,884 |
| | | Boston | 1964 | 12,142 |
| | | Lowell | 1894 | 8,863 |
| | | Dartmouth (North Dartmouth) | 1895 | 7,460 |
| | | Boston University | 1839 | 29,544 |
| | | Northeastern University (Boston) | 1898 | 24,009 |
| | | Harvard University (Cambridge) | 1636 | 18,847 |
| | | Boston College (Chestnut Hill) | 1863 | 14,307 |
| | | Massachusetts Institute of Technology (Cambridge) | 1861 | 10,204 |
| | | Tufts University (Medford) | 1852 | 8,883 |
| | | Bridgewater State College | 1840 | 8,400 |
| | | Fitchburg State College | 1894 | 7,000 |
| | | Suffolk University (Boston) | 1906 | 6,203 |
| | | Bentley College (Waltham) | 1917 | 6,169 |
| | | Framingham State College | 1839 | 6,093 |
| | | Salem State College | 1854 | 5,400 |
| | | Worcester State College | 1874 | 5,369 |
| | | Springfield College | 1885 | 5,007 |
| | | Brandeis University (Waltham) | 1948 | 4,882 |
| | | Western New England College (Springfield) | 1919 | 4,732 |
| | | Worcester Polytechnic Institute | 1865 | 4,000 |
| | | Simmons College (Boston) | 1899 | 3,334 |
| | | Babson College (Wellesley) | 1919 | 3,328 |
| | | Westfield State College | 1838 | 3,200 |
| | | Smith College (Northampton) | 1871 | 2,758 |
| | | Wellesley College | 1870 | 2,340 |
| | | Amherst College | 1821 | 1,668 |
| | Michigan | University of Michigan | | |
| | | Ann Arbor | 1817 | 37,197 |
| | | Dearborn | 1959 | 8,215 |
| | | Flint | 1956 | 6,488 |
| | | Michigan State University (East Lansing) | 1855 | 43,038 |
| | | Wayne State University (Detroit) | 1868 | 32,149 |
| | | Western Michigan University (Kalamazoo) | 1903 | 28,931 |
| | | Central Michigan University (Mount Pleasant) | 1892 | 28,015 |
| | | Eastern Michigan University (Ypsilanti) | 1849 | 25,000 |
| | | Oakland University (Rochester) | 1957 | 14,379 |
| | | Ferris State University (Big Rapids) | 1884 | 10,930 |
| | | Northern Michigan University (Marquette) | 1899 | 8,577 |
| | | University of Detroit Mercy | 1877 | 7,000 |
| | | Michigan Technological University (Houghton) | 1885 | 6,620 |
| | | Marygrove College (Detroit) | 1905 | 6,097 |
| | | Calvin College (Grand Rapids) | 1876 | 4,162 |
| | | Madonna University (Livonia) | 1947 | 4,000 |
| | Minnesota | Minnesota State University System | | |
| | | St. Cloud State University | 1869 | 16,000 |
| | | Minnesota State University (Mankato) | 1868 | 12,316 |
| | | Metropolitan State University (St. Paul) | 1971 | 8,600 |
| | | Minnesota State University (Moorhead) | 1887 | 7,400 |

## Selected North American Universities and Colleges (continued)

| COUNTRY | STATE/PROVINCE | INSTITUTION (LOCATION) | FOUNDING YEAR | ENROLLMENT |
|---|---|---|---|---|
| United States | Minnesota | Winona State University | 1858 | 7,356 |
| (continued) | (continued) | Bemidji State University | 1919 | 4,991 |
| | | Southwest State University (Marshall) | 1963 | 3,000 |
| | | University of Minnesota | | |
| | | Twin Cities (Minneapolis) | 1851 | 46,597 |
| | | Duluth | 1895 | 9,380 |
| | | University of St. Thomas (St. Paul) | 1885 | 11,473 |
| | | St. Mary's University (Winona) | 1912 | 8,000 |
| | | Augsburg College (Minneapolis) | 1869 | 3,023 |
| | | St. Olaf College (Northfield) | 1874 | 3,011 |
| | Mississippi | Mississippi State University | 1878 | 14,831 |
| | | University of Southern Mississippi (Hattiesburg) | 1910 | 11,570 |
| | | University of Mississippi (University) | 1844 | 11,000 |
| | | Jackson State University | 1877 | 6,224 |
| | | Delta State University (Cleveland) | 1924 | 4,000 |
| | | Mississippi College (Clinton) | 1826 | 3,400 |
| | | Mississippi University for Women (Columbus) | 1884 | 3,314 |
| | | Alcorn State University | 1871 | 3,096 |
| | Missouri | University of Missouri | | |
| | | Columbia | 1839 | 23,667 |
| | | St. Louis | 1963 | 14,993 |
| | | Kansas City | 1929 | 12,000 |
| | | Rolla | 1870 | 4,715 |
| | | Southwest Missouri State University (Springfield) | 1905 | 16,439 |
| | | Webster University (St. Louis) | 1915 | 15,402 |
| | | Washington University in Saint Louis | 1853 | 12,118 |
| | | Central Missouri State University (Warrensburg) | 1871 | 11,300 |
| | | Saint Louis University | 1818 | 11,112 |
| | | Southeast Missouri State University (Cape Girardeau) | 1873 | 8,234 |
| | | Northwest Missouri State University (Maryville) | 1905 | 6,280 |
| | | Truman State University (Kirksville) | 1867 | 5,919 |
| | | Lindenwood University (St. Charles) | 1827 | 5,000 |
| | | Lincoln University (Jefferson City) | 1866 | 3,347 |
| | | Maryville University of Saint Louis | 1872 | 3,055 |
| | Montana | Montana State University | | |
| | | Bozeman | 1893 | 10,700 |
| | | Billings | 1927 | 4,300 |
| | | University of Montana (Missoula) | 1893 | 10,953 |
| | Nebraska | University of Nebraska | | |
| | | Lincoln | 1869 | 24,491 |
| | | Omaha | 1908 | 15,899 |
| | | Kearney | 1903 | 8,045 |
| | | Creighton University (Omaha) | 1878 | 6,297 |
| | | Wayne State College | 1910 | 4,000 |
| | | Chadron State College | 1911 | 3,206 |
| | Nevada | University of Nevada | | |
| | | Las Vegas | 1957 | 21,820 |
| | | Reno | 1874 | 14,316 |
| | New Hampshire | University of New Hampshire (Durham) | 1866 | 13,650 |
| | | Dartmouth College (Hanover) | 1769 | 5,495 |
| | | Keene State College | 1909 | 4,839 |
| | | Plymouth State College | 1871 | 3,990 |
| | New Jersey | Rutgers University | | |
| | | New Brunswick | 1766 | 35,650 |
| | | Newark | 1935 | 10,346 |
| | | Camden | 1926 | 5,248 |
| | | Montclair State University (Upper Montclair) | 1908 | 13,502 |
| | | Kean University (Union) | 1855 | 11,838 |
| | | Fairleigh Dickinson University (Teaneck) | 1942 | 11,000 |
| | | William Paterson University (Wayne) | 1855 | 9,945 |
| | | Seton Hall University (South Orange) | 1856 | 9,920 |
| | | Rowan University (Glassboro) | 1923 | 9,368 |
| | | New Jersey Institute of Technology (Newark) | 1881 | 7,837 |
| | | Jersey City State College | 1927 | 7,000 |
| | | College of New Jersey (Ewing) | 1855 | 6,706 |
| | | Princeton University | 1746 | 6,350 |

# Selected North American Universities and Colleges (continued)

| COUNTRY | STATE/PROVINCE | INSTITUTION (LOCATION) | FOUNDING YEAR | ENROLLMENT |
|---|---|---|---|---|
| United States | New Jersey | Rider University (Lawrenceville) | 1865 | 5,519 |
| (continued) | (continued) | Monmouth University (West Long Branch) | 1933 | 5,311 |
| | | Saint Peter's College (Jersey City) | 1872 | 4,698 |
| | New Mexico | University of New Mexico (Albuquerque) | 1889 | 25,009 |
| | | New Mexico State University (Las Cruces) | 1888 | 15,409 |
| | | Eastern New Mexico University (Portales) | 1934 | 3,632 |
| | New York | City University of New York | | |
| | |  Hunter College (New York) | 1870 | 19,689 |
| | |  Queens College (Flushing) | 1937 | 16,381 |
| | |  Baruch College (New York) | 1919 | 15,071 |
| | |  Brooklyn College | 1930 | 14,964 |
| | |  City College (New York) | 1847 | 12,083 |
| | |  College of Staten Island | 1976 | 12,023 |
| | |  New York City Technical College (Brooklyn) | 1881 | 11,124 |
| | |  John Jay College of Criminal Justice (New York) | 1964 | 10,834 |
| | |  Lehman College (Bronx) | 1931 | 9,283 |
| | |  York College (Jamaica) | 1966 | 6,030 |
| | |  Medgar Evers College (Brooklyn) | 1969 | 5,063 |
| | |  Graduate School and University Center (New York) | 1961 | 3,813 |
| | | Colleges of the State University of New York | | |
| | |  Empire State College (Saratoga Springs) | 1971 | 15,657 |
| | |  Buffalo | 1871 | 11,743 |
| | |  Brockport | 1841 | 8,500 |
| | |  Oswego | 1861 | 8,407 |
| | |  New Paltz | 1828 | 7,838 |
| | |  Cortland | 1868 | 7,500 |
| | |  Plattsburgh | 1889 | 6,100 |
| | |  College of Technology (Farmingdale) | 1912 | 5,700 |
| | |  Oneonta | 1889 | 5,700 |
| | |  Fredonia | 1826 | 5,301 |
| | |  Geneseo | 1867 | 5,000 |
| | |  Potsdam | 1816 | 4,001 |
| | |  Purchase | 1967 | 4,000 |
| | |  Old Westbury | 1968 | 3,000 |
| | | State University of New York | | |
| | |  Buffalo | 1846 | 24,830 |
| | |  Stony Brook | 1957 | 19,924 |
| | |  Albany | 1844 | 16,751 |
| | |  Binghamton | 1946 | 12,473 |
| | | New York University | 1831 | 37,134 |
| | | Long Island University | 1926 | 23,540 |
| | | Columbia University (New York) | 1754 | 20,504 |
| | | Cornell University (Ithaca) | 1865 | 19,000 |
| | | Syracuse University | 1870 | 18,600 |
| | | St. John's University (Jamaica) | 1870 | 18,478 |
| | | Pace University (New York) | 1906 | 15,000 |
| | | Rochester Institute of Technology | 1829 | 15,000 |
| | | Fordham University (Bronx) | 1841 | 14,000 |
| | | Hofstra University (Hempstead) | 1935 | 12,439 |
| | | University of Rochester | 1850 | 7,885 |
| | | Iona College (New Rochelle) | 1940 | 7,466 |
| | | Rensselaer Polytechnic Institute (Troy) | 1824 | 6,509 |
| | | College of New Rochelle | 1904 | 6,475 |
| | | Adelphi University (Garden City) | 1896 | 6,349 |
| | | Yeshiva University (New York) | 1886 | 6,335 |
| | | Dowling College (Oakdale) | 1968 | 6,000 |
| | | Ithaca College | 1892 | 5,897 |
| | | Canisius College (Buffalo) | 1870 | 4,944 |
| | | College of Saint Rose (Albany) | 1920 | 4,167 |
| | | US Military Academy (West Point) | 1802 | 4,112 |
| | | Marist College (Poughkeepsie) | 1929 | 4,025 |
| | | Siena College (Loudonville) | 1937 | 3,436 |
| | | Pratt Institute (Brooklyn) | 1887 | 3,384 |
| | | Polytechnic University (Brooklyn) | 1854 | 3,282 |
| | | Niagara University | 1856 | 3,146 |
| | | Le Moyne College (Syracuse) | 1946 | 3,130 |
| | | Manhattan College (Riverdale) | 1853 | 3,070 |

## Selected North American Universities and Colleges (continued)

| COUNTRY | STATE/PROVINCE | INSTITUTION (LOCATION) | FOUNDING YEAR | ENROLLMENT |
|---|---|---|---|---|
| United States | New York | Colgate University (Hamilton) | 1819 | 2,675 |
| (continued) | (continued) | Vassar College (Poughkeepsie) | 1861 | 2,400 |
| | | Sarah Lawrence College (Bronxville) | 1926 | 1,111 |
| | North Carolina | University of North Carolina | | |
| | | Chapel Hill | 1789 | 24,189 |
| | | Charlotte | 1946 | 18,308 |
| | | Greensboro | 1891 | 12,731 |
| | | Wilmington | 1947 | 10,599 |
| | | Asheville | 1927 | 3,179 |
| | | Pembroke | 1887 | 3,034 |
| | | North Carolina State University (Raleigh) | 1887 | 27,169 |
| | | East Carolina University (Greenville) | 1907 | 19,412 |
| | | Duke University (Durham) | 1838 | 12,192 |
| | | Appalachian State University (Boone) | 1899 | 11,641 |
| | | Campbell University (Buie's Creek) | 1887 | 9,220 |
| | | North Carolina Agricultural and Technical State University (Greensboro) | 1891 | 7,533 |
| | | Western Carolina University (Cullowhee) | 1889 | 6,619 |
| | | Wake Forest University (Winston-Salem) | 1834 | 5,841 |
| | | North Carolina Central University (Durham) | 1910 | 5,643 |
| | | Elon University | 1889 | 4,138 |
| | North Dakota | University of North Dakota (Grand Forks) | 1883 | 11,031 |
| | | North Dakota State University (Fargo) | 1890 | 10,000 |
| | Ohio | Ohio State University (Columbus) | 1870 | 54,781 |
| | | University of Cincinnati | 1819 | 33,342 |
| | | Kent State University | 1910 | 30,000 |
| | | Ohio University (Athens) | 1804 | 27,386 |
| | | University of Akron | 1870 | 24,000 |
| | | Miami University (Oxford) | 1809 | 20,517 |
| | | University of Toledo | 1872 | 20,307 |
| | | Bowling Green State University | 1910 | 18,200 |
| | | Cleveland State University | 1964 | 17,137 |
| | | Youngstown State University | 1908 | 12,222 |
| | | Wright State University (Dayton) | 1967 | 11,878 |
| | | University of Dayton | 1850 | 9,906 |
| | | Case Western Reserve University (Cleveland) | 1826 | 9,530 |
| | | Xavier University (Cincinnati) | 1831 | 6,523 |
| | | Ashland University | 1878 | 6,105 |
| | | John Carroll University (University Heights) | 1886 | 4,500 |
| | | Capital University (Columbus) | 1850 | 4,047 |
| | | University of Findlay | 1882 | 4,018 |
| | | Antioch University (Yellow Springs) | 1852 | 3,250 |
| | | Oberlin College | 1833 | 2,900 |
| | Oklahoma | University of Oklahoma (Norman) | 1890 | 24,887 |
| | | Oklahoma State University (Stillwater) | 1890 | 21,087 |
| | | University of Central Oklahoma (Edmond) | 1890 | 15,400 |
| | | Northeastern State University (Tahlequah) | 1851 | 8,750 |
| | | Southwestern Oklahoma State University (Weatherford) | 1901 | 5,226 |
| | | Oral Roberts University (Tulsa) | 1965 | 5,000 |
| | | Oklahoma City University | 1904 | 4,400 |
| | | East Central University (Ada) | 1909 | 4,378 |
| | | University of Tulsa | 1894 | 4,119 |
| | | Southeastern Oklahoma State University (Durant) | 1909 | 4,000 |
| | | Langston University | 1897 | 3,482 |
| | Oregon | Portland State University | 1946 | 21,046 |
| | | University of Oregon (Eugene) | 1872 | 17,207 |
| | | Oregon State University (Corvallis) | 1858 | 16,061 |
| | | Southern Oregon University (Ashland) | 1926 | 4,800 |
| | | Lewis and Clark College (Portland) | 1867 | 3,388 |
| | Pennsylvania | Pennsylvania State University | | |
| | | Pennsylvania State University (University Park) | 1855 | 75,489 |
| | | Erie, The Behrend College | 1948 | 3,700 |
| | | Harrisburg, The Capital College (Middletown) | 1966 | 3,200 |
| | | Temple University (Philadelphia) | 1884 | 31,001 |
| | | University of Pittsburgh | 1787 | 26,710 |

## Selected North American Universities and Colleges (continued)

| COUNTRY | STATE/PROVINCE | INSTITUTION (LOCATION) | FOUNDING YEAR | ENROLLMENT |
|---|---|---|---|---|
| United States | Pennsylvania | University of Pennsylvania (Philadelphia) | 1740 | 22,326 |
| (continued) | (continued) | Indiana University of Pennsylvania | 1875 | 13,410 |
| | | Drexel University (Philadelphia) | 1891 | 13,128 |
| | | West Chester University | 1871 | 11,344 |
| | | Villanova University | 1842 | 9,833 |
| | | Duquesne University (Pittsburgh) | 1878 | 9,451 |
| | | Carnegie Mellon University (Pittsburgh) | 1900 | 8,514 |
| | | Kutztown University | 1866 | 7,920 |
| | | Millersville University | 1855 | 7,556 |
| | | Bloomsburg University | 1839 | 7,500 |
| | | Edinboro University of Pennsylvania | 1857 | 7,498 |
| | | Widener University (Chester) | 1821 | 7,355 |
| | | Slippery Rock University of Pennsylvania | 1889 | 7,197 |
| | | Shippensburg University of Pennsylvania | 1871 | 7,193 |
| | | Saint Joseph's University (Philadelphia) | 1851 | 7,027 |
| | | Lehigh University (Bethlehem) | 1865 | 6,479 |
| | | Clarion University of Pennsylvania | 1867 | 6,300 |
| | | California University of Pennsylvania | 1852 | 5,850 |
| | | La Salle University (Philadelphia) | 1863 | 5,500 |
| | | University of Scranton | 1888 | 4,615 |
| | | Gannon University (Erie) | 1925 | 4,491 |
| | | Lock Haven University of Pennsylvania | 1870 | 3,945 |
| | | Philadelphia University | 1884 | 3,600 |
| | | Bucknell University (Lewisburg) | 1846 | 3,491 |
| | | Mansfield University | 1857 | 3,223 |
| | | Bryn Mawr College | 1885 | 1,701 |
| | Rhode Island | University of Rhode Island (Kingston) | 1892 | 13,698 |
| | | Rhode Island College (Providence) | 1854 | 9,066 |
| | | Brown University (Providence) | 1764 | 7,333 |
| | | Providence College | 1917 | 3,597 |
| | | Bryant College (Smithfield) | 1863 | 3,332 |
| | | Rhode Island School of Design (Providence) | 1877 | 1,912 |
| | South Carolina | University of South Carolina | | |
| | | Columbia | 1801 | 25,140 |
| | | Spartanburg | 1967 | 4,283 |
| | | Aiken | 1961 | 3,100 |
| | | Clemson University | 1889 | 16,980 |
| | | College of Charleston | 1770 | 10,600 |
| | | The Citadel (Charleston) | 1842 | 7,500 |
| | | Winthrop University (Rock Hill) | 1886 | 5,107 |
| | | South Carolina State University (Orangeburg) | 1896 | 4,500 |
| | South Dakota | South Dakota State University (Brookings) | 1881 | 9,350 |
| | | University of South Dakota (Vermillion) | 1862 | 7,317 |
| | | Black Hills State University (Spearfish) | 1883 | 4,068 |
| | | Northern State University (Aberdeen) | 1901 | 3,315 |
| | Tennessee | University of Tennessee System | | |
| | | Knoxville | 1794 | 27,971 |
| | | Chattanooga | 1886 | 8,200 |
| | | Martin | 1900 | 5,800 |
| | | University of Memphis | 1912 | 20,100 |
| | | Middle Tennessee State University (Murfreesboro) | 1911 | 17,000 |
| | | East Tennessee State University (Johnson City) | 1911 | 12,000 |
| | | Vanderbilt University (Nashville) | 1873 | 10,496 |
| | | Tennessee State University (Nashville) | 1912 | 8,625 |
| | | Tennessee Technological University (Cookeville) | 1915 | 8,500 |
| | | Austin Peay State University (Clarksville) | 1927 | 7,033 |
| | Texas | University of Texas System | | |
| | | Austin | 1883 | 50,616 |
| | | San Antonio | 1969 | 22,000 |
| | | Arlington | 1895 | 21,200 |
| | | El Paso | 1913 | 16,220 |
| | | Pan American (Edinburg) | 1927 | 13,700 |
| | | Dallas (Richardson) | 1969 | 10,945 |
| | | Tyler | 1971 | 4,250 |
| | | Texas A & M University System | | |
| | | College Station | 1876 | 41,461 |
| | | Tarleton State University (Stephenville) | 1899 | 7,545 |

## Selected North American Universities and Colleges (continued)

| COUNTRY | STATE/PROVINCE | INSTITUTION (LOCATION) | FOUNDING YEAR | ENROLLMENT |
|---|---|---|---|---|
| United States | Texas | Commerce | 1889 | 7,260 |
| (continued) | (continued) | West Texas A & M (Canyon) | 1910 | 6,775 |
| | | Corpus Christi | 1947 | 6,300 |
| | | Kingsville | 1917 | 5,876 |
| | | Prairie View A & M | 1876 | 5,600 |
| | | University of Houston | | |
| | | University of Houston | 1927 | 32,651 |
| | | University of Houston–Downtown | 1974 | 8,194 |
| | | University of Houston–Clear Lake | 1974 | 7,738 |
| | | University of North Texas (Denton) | 1890 | 25,605 |
| | | Texas Tech University (Lubbock) | 1923 | 24,007 |
| | | Southwest Texas State University (San Marcos) | 1899 | 21,765 |
| | | Stephen F. Austin State University (Nacogdoches) | 1923 | 12,500 |
| | | Sam Houston State University (Huntsville) | 1879 | 12,358 |
| | | Baylor University (Waco) | 1845 | 12,000 |
| | | Southern Methodist University (Dallas) | 1911 | 10,266 |
| | | Texas Woman's University (Denton) | 1901 | 8,690 |
| | | Lamar University (Beaumont) | 1923 | 8,235 |
| | | Texas Southern University (Houston) | 1947 | 8,219 |
| | | Texas Christian University (Fort Worth) | 1873 | 8,054 |
| | | Angelo State University (San Angelo) | 1928 | 6,234 |
| | | Midwestern State University (Wichita Falls) | 1922 | 5,832 |
| | | Abilene Christian University | 1906 | 4,673 |
| | | Rice University (Houston) | 1891 | 4,274 |
| | | St. Edwards University (Austin) | 1885 | 4,151 |
| | | University of Dallas (Irivng) | 1956 | 3,008 |
| | Utah | Brigham Young University (Provo) | 1875 | 30,465 |
| | | University of Utah (Salt Lake City) | 1850 | 26,359 |
| | | Utah State University (Logan) | 1888 | 21,234 |
| | | Weber State University (Ogden) | 1889 | 14,000 |
| | Vermont | University of Vermont (Burlington) | 1791 | 10,081 |
| | | Bennington College | 1925 | 400 |
| | Virginia | Virginia Polytechnic Institute and State University (Blacksburg) | 1872 | 25,912 |
| | | Virginia Commonwealth University (Richmond) | 1838 | 25,001 |
| | | George Mason University (Fairfax) | 1957 | 24,897 |
| | | University of Virginia (Charlottesville) | 1819 | 22,739 |
| | | Old Dominion University (Norfolk) | 1930 | 17,077 |
| | | James Madison University (Harrisonburg) | 1908 | 15,000 |
| | | Radford University | 1910 | 9,142 |
| | | College of William and Mary (Williamsburg) | 1693 | 7,530 |
| | | Hampton University | 1868 | 5,305 |
| | | University of Richmond | 1830 | 4,705 |
| | | Virginia State University (Petersburg) | 1882 | 4,007 |
| | | Longwood College (Farmville) | 1839 | 3,558 |
| | | Virginia Military Institute (Lexington) | 1839 | 1,300 |
| | Washington | University of Washington (Seattle) | 1861 | 30,227 |
| | | Washington State University (Pullman) | 1890 | 21,073 |
| | | Western Washington University (Bellingham) | 1893 | 11,708 |
| | | Eastern Washington University (Cheney) | 1882 | 8,000 |
| | | Central Washington University (Ellensburg) | 1891 | 7,471 |
| | | Seattle University | 1891 | 5,981 |
| | | Gonzaga University (Spokane) | 1887 | 5,572 |
| | | Evergreen State College (Olympia) | 1971 | 4,367 |
| | | Seattle Pacific University | 1891 | 3,615 |
| | West Virginia | West Virginia University (Morgantown) | 1867 | 22,774 |
| | | Marshall University (Huntington) | 1837 | 16,038 |
| | | Fairmont State College | 1867 | 6,500 |
| | | West Virginia State College (Institute) | 1891 | 4,545 |
| | | Shepherd College (Shepherdstown) | 1871 | 4,000 |
| | Wisconsin | University of Wisconsin System | | |
| | | Madison | 1849 | 41,219 |
| | | Milwaukee | 1885 | 23,000 |
| | | Oshkosh | 1871 | 10,619 |
| | | Eau Claire | 1916 | 10,500 |
| | | Whitewater | 1868 | 9,946 |
| | | La Crosse | 1909 | 8,500 |

## Selected North American Universities and Colleges (continued)

| COUNTRY | STATE/PROVINCE | INSTITUTION (LOCATION) | FOUNDING YEAR | ENROLLMENT |
|---|---|---|---|---|
| United States | Wisconsin | Stevens Point | 1894 | 8,500 |
| (continued) | (continued) | Stout (Menomonie) | 1891 | 7,702 |
| | | River Falls | 1874 | 5,849 |
| | | Green Bay | 1965 | 5,500 |
| | | Platteville | 1866 | 5,100 |
| | | Parkside (Kenosha) | 1968 | 5,000 |
| | | Marquette University (Milwaukee) | 1881 | 10,892 |
| | | Cardinal Stritch University (Milwaukee) | 1937 | 5,600 |
| | Wyoming | University of Wyoming (Laramie) | 1886 | 12,402 |
| | Guam | University of Guam (Mangilao) | 1952 | 3,200 |
| | Puerto Rico | University of Puerto Rico (San Juan) | 1903 | 69,567 |
| | | Inter-America University of Puerto Rico (San Juan) | 1912 | 39,000 |
| | US Virgin Islands | University of the Virgin Islands (St. Thomas) | 1962 | 2,610 |
| Canada | Alberta | University of Alberta (Edmonton) | 1906 | 32,253 |
| | | University of Calgary | 1945 | 27,448 |
| | | University of Lethbridge | 1967 | 5,361 |
| | British Columbia | University of British Columbia (Vancouver) | 1908 | 31,331 |
| | | Simon Fraser University (Burnaby) | 1963 | 19,347 |
| | | University of Victoria | 1963 | 18,195 |
| | Manitoba | University of Manitoba (Winnipeg) | 1877 | 23,618 |
| | | University of Winnipeg | 1871 | 6,152 |
| | New Brunswick | University of New Brunswick (Fredericton) | 1785 | 12,315 |
| | | University of Moncton | 1864 | 5,608 |
| | Newfoundland and Labrador | Memorial University of Newfoundland (St. John's) | 1925 | 16,000 |
| | Nova Scotia | Dalhousie University (Halifax) | 1818 | 13,642 |
| | | Saint Mary's University (Halifax) | 1802 | 7,109 |
| | | St. Francis Xavier University (Antigonish) | 1853 | 4,200 |
| | | Acadia University (Wolfville) | 1838 | 3,700 |
| | | University College of Cape Breton (Sydney) | 1974 | 3,243 |
| | Ontario | University of Toronto | 1827 | 55,024 |
| | | York University (Toronto) | 1959 | 33,749 |
| | | University of Western Ontario (London) | 1878 | 30,080 |
| | | University of Ottawa | 1848 | 24,477 |
| | | University of Waterloo | 1957 | 22,677 |
| | | Carleton University (Ottawa) | 1942 | 18,444 |
| | | McMaster University (Hamilton) | 1887 | 17,775 |
| | | Queens University at Kingston | 1841 | 17,510 |
| | | University of Guelph | 1964 | 14,000 |
| | | Ryerson University (Toronto) | 1948 | 13,864 |
| | | University of Windsor | 1857 | 12,632 |
| | | Brock University (St. Catharines) | 1964 | 10,500 |
| | | Wilfrid Laurier University (Waterloo) | 1911 | 10,287 |
| | | Lakehead University (Thunder Bay) | 1965 | 6,585 |
| | | Laurentian University of Sudbury | 1960 | 5,873 |
| | | Trent University (Peterborough) | 1963 | 5,564 |
| | | Nipissing University (North Bay) | 1967 | 4,746 |
| | Prince Edward Island | University of Prince Edward Island (Charlottetown) | 1969 | 2,800 |
| | Quebec | University of Quebec | | |
| | | Montreal | 1969 | 37,395 |
| | | Trois-Rivières | 1969 | 9,647 |
| | | Chicoutimi | 1969 | 6,500 |
| | | Hull | 1970 | 4,766 |
| | | Rimouski | 1969 | 4,400 |
| | | University of Montreal | 1878 | 49,997 |
| | | Laval University (Quebec City) | 1852 | 35,412 |
| | | McGill University (Montreal) | 1821 | 28,552 |
| | | Concordia University (Montreal) | 1974 | 26,450 |
| | | University of Sherbrooke | 1954 | 22,272 |
| | Saskatchewan | University of Saskatchewan (Saskatoon) | 1907 | 17,424 |
| | | University of Regina | 1974 | 11,593 |

[1]Classes are offered over the Internet and at learning centers around the country.

# Religion

## World Religions

At the beginning of the 21st century, one-third of the world's population is Christian, another one-fifth is Muslim, about one-eighth is Hindu, and one-eighth is nonreligious. Most people living in Europe and the Americas are Christian, while the vast majority of Muslims and Hindus are found in Asia. The plurality of Christians are Roman Catholics, of Muslims are Sunni, and of Hindus are Vaishnavites. Africa hosts slightly more Christians than Muslims, with much of the rest of the population listed as ethnic religionists, which describes followers of local, tribal, animistic, or shamanistic religions.

In addition to the predominant world religions (Christianity, Islam, Hinduism), there are small but noticeable percentages of Chinese folk religionists, Buddhists, other ethnic religionists, atheists, and new-religionists. Among the remaining distinct religions, Sikhs, Spiritists, Jews, Baha'is, Confucianists, Jains, Shintoists, Taoists, and Zoroastrians each make up less than one-half of one percent of religious adherents.

### Christianity

Christianity traces its origins to the 1st century AD and to Jesus of Nazareth, whom it affirms to be the chosen one (Christ) of God. Geographically the most widely diffused of all faiths, it has a constituency of more than two billion people. Its largest groups are the Roman Catholic Church, the Eastern Orthodox churches, and the Protestant churches; in addition, there are several independent churches of Eastern Christianity as well as numerous sects throughout the world.

Christianity's sacred scripture is the Bible, particularly the New Testament. Its principal tenets are that Jesus is the son of God (the second person of the Holy Trinity), that God's love for the world is the essential component of his being, and that Jesus died to redeem humankind.

Christianity was originally a movement of Jews who accepted Jesus as the messiah, but the movement quickly became predominantly Gentile. Nearly all Christian churches have an ordained clergy, which lead group worship services and are viewed as intermediaries between the laity and the divine in some churches. Most Christian churches administer at least two sacraments: baptism and the Lord's Supper.

### Islam

Islam is a religion that originated in the Middle East and was promulgated by the Prophet Muhammad in Arabia in the 7th century AD. The Arabic term *islam*, literally "surrender," illuminates the fundamental religious idea of Islam—that the believer (called a Muslim, from the active particle of *islam*) accepts "surrender to the will of Allah (Arabic: God)." Allah's will is made known through the sacred scriptures, the Qur'an (Koran), which Allah revealed to his messenger, Muhammad. In Islam, Muhammad is considered the last of a series of prophets (including Adam, Noah, Jesus, and others), and his message simultaneously consummates and abrogates the "revelations" attributed to earlier prophets.

The religious obligations of all Muslims are summed up in the Five Pillars of Islam. The fundamental concept in Islam is the Shari'ah, or Law, which embraces the total way of life commanded by God. Observant Muslims pray five times a day and join in community worship on Fridays at the mosque, where worship is led by an imam. Every believer is required to make a pilgrimage to Mecca, the holiest city, at least once in a lifetime, barring poverty or physical incapacity. The month of Ramadan is set aside for fasting. Jihad, considered a sixth pillar by some sects, is not accepted by most of the Islamic community as a call to wage physical war against unbelievers.

Divisions occurred early in Islam, brought about by disputes over the succession to the caliphate, resulting in various sects (Sunni, Shi'ite, Ismaili, Sufi). From the 19th century, the concept of the Islamic community inspired Muslim peoples to cast off Western colonial rule, and in the late 20th century fundamentalist movements toppled a number of secular Middle Eastern governments. A movement of African American Muslims emerged in the 20th century in the US.

### Hinduism

Hinduism is the oldest of the world's major religions, dating back more than 3,000 years, though its present forms are of more recent origin. It evolved from Vedism, the religion of the Indo-European peoples who settled in India at the end of the 2nd millennium BC. The vast majority of the world's Hindus live in India, though significant minorities may be found in Pakistan and Sri Lanka, and smaller numbers live in Myanmar, South Africa, Trinidad, Europe, and the US.

Though the various Hindu sects each rely on their own set of scriptures, they all revere the ancient Vedas, which were brought to India by Aryan invaders after 1200 BC. The philosophical Vedic texts called the Upanishads explored the search for knowledge that would allow mankind to escape the cycle of reincarnation. Fundamental to Hinduism is the belief in a cosmic principle of ultimate reality called brahman, and its identity with the individual soul, or atman. All creatures go through a cycle of rebirth, or samsara, which can be broken only by spiritual self-realization, after which liberation, or moksha, is attained. The principle of karma determines a being's status within the cycle of rebirth.

The greatest Hindu deities are Brahma, Vishnu, and Shiva. The major sources of classical mythology are the Mahabharata (which includes the Bhagavadgita, the most important religious text of Hinduism), the Ramayana, and the Puranas. The hierarchical social structure of the caste system is important in Hinduism; it is supported by the principle of dharma. During the 20th century Hinduism was blended with Indian nationalism to become a potent political force.

### Other major religions

**Buddhism**, a religion concentrated in Asia with some representation in North America, was founded by the Buddha (Siddhartha Gautama, or Gotama) in northeast India in the 5th century BC. By adhering to the Buddha's teachings, the believer can alleviate suffering through an understanding of the transitory nature of existence, in the hopes of achieving enlightenment. Distinct from Buddhism, **Shinto** is the indige-

# World Religions (continued)

nous religion of Japan and has no founder, sacred scriptures, or fixed dogmas. Also based in Asia, **Chinese folk religionists** are followers of local deities and engage in ancestor worship and divination. They also adhere to Confucian ethics, though statistically

**Confucianists** are categorized as non-Chinese (mostly Korean) followers of Confucius, a Chinese philosopher of the 6th century BC. Confucianism is not an organized religion as much as it is a political and social ideology. Also in the Confucian tradition, a **Taoist**

## Worldwide Adherents of All Religions, mid-2003

*This table and the US table that follows were prepared by David B. Barrett and Todd M. Johnson, coauthors of the* World Christian Encyclopedia, *and will appear in* Britannica Book of the Year 2004.

| | AFRICA | ASIA | EUROPE | LATIN AMERICA |
|---|---|---|---|---|
| Christians | 394,640,000 | 325,034,000 | 554,234,000 | 501,319,000 |
| Affiliated Christians | 373,110,000 | 319,090,000 | 530,451,000 | 495,550,000 |
| Roman Catholics | 138,970,000 | 117,710,000 | 276,490,000 | 473,000,000 |
| Protestants | 105,710,000 | 54,684,000 | 74,015,000 | 51,306,000 |
| Orthodox | 36,953,000 | 13,985,000 | 158,450,000 | 477,000 |
| Anglicans | 43,809,000 | 726,000 | 26,053,000 | 950,000 |
| Independents | 86,395,000 | 169,070,000 | 24,675,000 | 41,776,000 |
| Marginal Christians | 3,108,000 | 2,776,000 | 4,071,000 | 9,201,000 |
| *Multiple affiliation* | *−41,835,000* | *−39,861,000* | *−33,303,000* | *−81,160,000* |
| Unaffiliated Christians | 21,530,000 | 5,944,000 | 23,783,000 | 5,769,000 |
| Muslims | 344,920,000 | 869,880,000 | 32,117,000 | 1,752,000 |
| Hindus | 2,547,000 | 830,530,000 | 1,504,000 | 801,000 |
| Chinese Universists | 34,900 | 396,720,000 | 271,000 | 200,400 |
| Buddhists | 152,000 | 366,790,000 | 1,594,000 | 698,000 |
| Ethnoreligionists | 100,420,000 | 132,590,000 | 1,247,000 | 2,531,000 |
| New-Religionists | 37,000 | 103,230,000 | 191,000 | 660,000 |
| Sikhs | 58,700 | 23,410,000 | 243,000 | 0 |
| Jews | 220,000 | 4,465,000 | 2,427,000 | 1,152,000 |
| Spiritists | 3,100 | 2,000 | 137,000 | 12,426,000 |
| Baha'is | 1,937,000 | 3,632,000 | 146,000 | 822,000 |
| Confucianists | 300 | 6,330,000 | 17,000 | 500 |
| Jains | 73,000 | 4,332,000 | 0 | 0 |
| Zoroastrians | 1,000 | 2,553,000 | 91,000 | 0 |
| Taoists | 0 | 2,684,000 | 0 | 0 |
| Shintoists | 0 | 2,615,000 | 0 | 7,100 |
| Other religionists | 70,000 | 65,000 | 250,000 | 103,000 |
| Nonreligious | 5,863,000 | 620,290,000 | 107,210,000 | 16,693,000 |
| Atheists | 579,000 | 120,950,000 | 22,111,000 | 2,707,000 |
| **Total population** | **851,556,000** | **3,816,102,000** | **723,790,000** | **541,872,000** |

**Continents.** *These follow current UN demographic terminology, which now divides the world into the six major areas shown above. See United Nations,* World Population Prospects: The 2000 Revision *(New York: UN, 2001), with populations of all continents, regions, and countries covering the period 1950–2050, with 100 variables for every country each year. Note that "Asia" includes the former Soviet Central Asian states and "Europe" includes all of Russia eastward to the Pacific.*

**Countries.** *The last column enumerates sovereign and nonsovereign countries in which each religion or religious grouping has a numerically significant and organized following.*

**Adherents.** *As defined in the 1948 Universal Declaration of Human Rights, a person's religion is what he or she professes, confesses, or states that it is. Totals are enumerated for each of the world's 238 countries following the methodology of the* World Christian Encyclopedia, *2nd ed. (2001), and* World Christian Trends *(2001), using recent censuses, polls, surveys, yearbooks, reports, Web sites, literature, and other data. Religions are ranked in order of size in mid-2003.*

**Christians.** *Followers of Jesus Christ, enumerated here under* **Affiliated Christians,** *those affiliated with churches (church members, with names written on church rolls, usually total baptized persons including children baptized, dedicated, or undedicated): total in 2003 being 1,960,715,000, shown above divided among the six standardized ecclesiastical blocs and with (negative and italicized) figures for those with* **Multiple affiliation** *persons (members of more than one denomination); and* **Unaffiliated Christians,** *who are persons professing or confessing in censuses or polls to be Christians though not so affiliated.*

**Independents.** *This term here denotes members of Christian churches and networks that regard themselves as postdenominationalist and neo-apostolic and thus independent of historic, mainstream, organized, institutionalized, confessional, denominationalist Christianity.*

**Marginal Christians.** *Members of denominations who define themselves as Christians but who are on the margins of organized mainstream Christianity (e.g. Unitarians, Mormons, Jehovah's Witnesses, Christian Science, and Religious Science).*

# World Religions (continued)

seeks the correct path of human conduct and an understanding of the Absolute Tao.

**Zoroastrianism** is an ancient pre-Islamic religion of Iran that survives there and in India. It was founded by the Iranian prophet Zoroaster in the 6th century BC and has both monotheistic and dualistic features. Also founded in Iran is the **Baha'i** faith, created as a universal religion in the mid-19th century AD for the worship of Baha' Ullah and his forerunner, the Bab; it

| NORTHERN AMERICA | OCEANIA | WORLD | % | NUMBER OF COUNTRIES |
|---|---|---|---|---|
| 269,399,000 | 25,257,000 | 2,069,883,000 | 32.9 | 238 |
| 221,060,000 | 21,454,000 | 1,960,715,000 | 31.2 | 238 |
| 78,310,000 | 8,373,000 | 1,092,853,000 | 17.4 | 235 |
| 70,795,000 | 8,020,000 | 364,530,000 | 5.8 | 232 |
| 6,426,000 | 739,000 | 217,030,000 | 3.5 | 134 |
| 3,121,000 | 5,329,000 | 79,988,000 | 1.3 | 163 |
| 82,533,000 | 1,625,000 | 406,074,000 | 6.5 | 221 |
| 11,344,000 | 619,000 | 31,119,000 | 0.5 | 215 |
| −31,469,000 | −3,251,000 | −230,879,000 | −3.67 | 100 |
| 48,339,000 | 3,803,000 | 109,168,000 | 1.7 | 232 |
| 4,828,000 | 725,000 | 1,254,222,000 | 19.9 | 206 |
| 1,410,000 | 470,000 | 837,262,000 | 13.3 | 114 |
| 695,000 | 185,000 | 398,106,300 | 6.3 | 91 |
| 3,086,000 | 654,000 | 372,974,000 | 5.9 | 129 |
| 1,010,000 | 298,000 | 238,096,000 | 3.8 | 144 |
| 900,000 | 88,100 | 105,106,100 | 1.7 | 107 |
| 551,000 | 32,500 | 24,295,200 | 0.4 | 34 |
| 6,182,000 | 105,000 | 14,551,000 | 0.2 | 134 |
| 157,000 | 7,500 | 12,732,600 | 0.2 | 56 |
| 844,000 | 122,000 | 7,503,000 | 0.1 | 218 |
| 0 | 77,500 | 6,425,300 | 0.1 | 16 |
| 7,500 | 1,200 | 4,413,700 | 0.1 | 11 |
| 82,700 | 6,200 | 2,733,900 | 0.0 | 23 |
| 11,600 | 0 | 2,695,600 | 0.0 | 5 |
| 58,200 | 0 | 2,680,300 | 0.0 | 8 |
| 620,000 | 10,000 | 1,118,000 | 0.0 | 78 |
| 30,923,000 | 3,290,000 | 784,269,000 | 12.5 | 236 |
| 1,944,000 | 369,000 | 148,660,000 | 2.4 | 217 |
| **322,709,000** | **31,698,000** | **6,287,732,000** | **100.0** | **238** |

**Muslims.** *83% Sunnites, 16% Shi'ites, 1% other schools.*
**Hindus.** *70% Vaishnavites, 25% Shaivites, 2% neo-Hindus and reform Hindus.*
**Nonreligious.** *Persons professing no religion, nonbelievers, agnostics, freethinkers, uninterested, or derelegionized secularists indifferent to all religion but not militantly so.*
**Chinese Universists.** *Followers of a unique complex of beliefs and practices that may include: universism (yin/yang cosmology with dualities earth/heaven, evil/good, darkness/light), ancestor cult, Confucian ethics, divination, festivals, folk religion, goddess worship, household gods, local deities, mediums, metaphysics, monasteries, neo-Confucianism, popular religion, sacrifices, shamans, spirit writing, and Taoist and Buddhist elements.*
**Buddhists.** *56% Mahayana, 38% Theravada (Hinayana), 6% Tantrayana (Lamaism).*
**Ethnoreligionists.** *Followers of local, tribal, animistic, or shamanistic religions, with members restricted to one ethnic group.*
**Atheists.** *Persons professing atheism, skepticism, disbelief, or irreligion, including the militantly antireligious (opposed to all religion).*
**New-Religionists.** *Followers of Asian 20th-century New Religions, New Religious movements, radical new crisis religions, and non-Christian syncretistic mass religions, all founded since 1800 and most since 1945.*
**Jews.** *Adherents of Judaism. For detailed data on "core" Jewish population, see the annual "World Jewish Populations" article in the American Jewish Committee's American Jewish Year Book.*
**Confucianists.** *Non-Chinese followers of Confucius and Confucianism, mostly Koreans in Korea.*
**Other religionists.** *Including a handful of religions, quasi-religions, pseudoreligions, pararaligions, religious or mystic systems, and religious and semireligious brotherhoods of numerous varieties.*
**Total population.** *UN medium variant figures for mid-2003, as given in* World Population Prospects: The 2000 Revision.

# World Religions (continued)

has no priesthood or formal sacraments and is chiefly concerned with social ethics.

**Jainism** was founded in India in the 6th century BC by Vardhamana, or Mahavira, a monastic reformer in the Vedic, or early Hindu, tradition. Jainism emphasizes a path to spiritual purity and enlightenment through a disciplined mode of life founded upon the tradition of ahimsa, nonviolence to all living creatures.

**Sikhism** is a monotheistic religion founded in the late 15th century AD in India, historically associated with the Punjab region, though it includes representation in Europe and North America.

**Judaism**, like Christianity and Islam, is monotheistic and maintains the manifestation of God in human events, particularly through Moses in the Torah at Mount Sinai in the 13th century BCE. Jews, who

## Religious Adherents in the US, 1900–2005

*For categories not described below, see notes to "Worldwide Adherents of All Religions," pp. 682–683.*

| | 1900 | % | MID–1970 | % | MID–1990 | % |
|---|---|---|---|---|---|---|
| **Christians** | **73,260,000** | **96.4** | **191,182,000** | **91.0** | **217,623,000** | **85.4** |
| Affiliated Christians | 54,425,000 | 71.6 | 153,300,000 | 73.0 | 176,030,000 | 69.1 |
| Roman Catholics | 10,775,000 | 14.2 | 48,305,000 | 23.0 | 56,500,000 | 22.2 |
| Protestants | 35,000,000 | 46.1 | 58,568,000 | 27.9 | 60,216,000 | 23.6 |
| Orthodox | 400,000 | 0.5 | 4,139,000 | 2.0 | 5,150,000 | 2.0 |
| Anglicans | 1,600,000 | 2.1 | 3,196,000 | 1.5 | 2,450,000 | 1.0 |
| Multiple affiliation | 0 | 0.0 | –2,726,000 | –1.3 | –24,126,000 | –9.5 |
| Independents | 5,850,000 | 7.7 | 35,691,000 | 17.0 | 66,900,000 | 26.3 |
| Marginal Christians | 800,000 | 1.1 | 6,126,000 | 2.9 | 8,940,000 | 3.5 |
| *Evangelicals* | *32,068,000* | *42.2* | *33,752,000* | *16.1* | *37,349,000* | *14.7* |
| *evangelicals* | *11,000,000* | *14.5* | *45,500,000* | *21.7* | *87,656,000* | *34.4* |
| Unaffiliated Christians | 18,835,000 | 24.8 | 37,882,000 | 18.0 | 41,593,000 | 16.3 |
| **Jews** | 1,500,000 | 2.0 | 6,700,000 | 3.2 | 5,535,000 | 2.2 |
| **Muslims** | 10,000 | 0.0 | 800,000 | 0.4 | 3,500,000 | 1.4 |
| Black Muslims | 0 | 0.0 | 200,000 | 0.1 | 1,250,000 | 0.5 |
| **Buddhists** | 30,000 | 0.0 | 200,000 | 0.1 | 1,880,000 | 0.7 |
| **Hindus** | 1,000 | 0.0 | 100,000 | 0.1 | 750,000 | 0.3 |
| **Ethnoreligionists** | 100,000 | 0.1 | 70,000 | 0.0 | 780,000 | 0.3 |
| **New-Religionists** | 10,000 | 0.0 | 110,000 | 0.3 | 700,000 | 0.3 |
| **Baha'is** | 3,000 | 0.0 | 138,000 | 0.1 | 600,000 | 0.2 |
| **Sikhs** | 0 | 0.0 | 1,000 | 0.0 | 160,000 | 0.1 |
| **Spiritists** | 0 | 0.0 | 0 | 0.0 | 120,000 | 0.0 |
| **Chinese Universists** | 70,000 | 0.1 | 90,000 | 0.0 | 76,000 | 0.0 |
| **Shintoists** | 0 | 0.0 | 0 | 0.0 | 50,000 | 0.0 |
| **Zoroastrians** | 0 | 0.0 | 0 | 0.0 | 43,000 | 0.0 |
| **Taoists** | 0 | 0.0 | 0 | 0.0 | 10,000 | 0.0 |
| **Jains** | 0 | 0.0 | 0 | 0.0 | 5,000 | 0.0 |
| **Other religionists** | 10,000 | 0.0 | 450,000 | 0.2 | 530,000 | 0.2 |
| **Nonreligious** | 1,000,000 | 1.3 | 10,070,000 | 4.8 | 21,414,000 | 8.4 |
| **Atheists** | 1,000 | 0.0 | 200,000 | 0.1 | 1,000,000 | 0.4 |
| **Total population** | **75,995,000** | **100.0** | **210,111,000** | **100.0** | **254,776,000** | **100.0** |

*Methodology.* This table extracts and analyzes a microcosm of the world religion table. It depicts the United States, the country with the largest number of adherents to Christianity, the world's largest religion. Statistics at five points in time from 1900–2005 are presented. Each religion's Annual Change for 1990–2000 is also analyzed by Natural increase (births minus deaths, plus immigrants minus emigrants) per year and Conversion increase (new converts minus new defectors) per year, which together constitute the Total increase per year. Rate increase is then computed as percentage per year.

*Structure.* Vertically the table lists 30 major religious categories. The major categories (including nonreligious) in the US are listed with largest (Christians) first. Indented names of groups in the "Adherents" column are subcategories of the groups above them and are also counted in these unindented totals, so they should not be added twice into the column total. Figures in italics draw adherents from all categories of Christians above and so cannot be added together with them. Figures for Christians are built upon detailed head counts by churches, often to the last digit. Totals are then rounded to the nearest 1,000. Because of rounding, the corresponding percentage figures may sometimes not total exactly to 100%.

*Christians.* All persons who profess publicly to follow Jesus Christ as God and Savior. This category is subdivided into **Affiliated Christians** (church members) and **Unaffiliated** (nominal) **Christians** (professing Christians not affiliated with any church). See also the note on Christians at the world religion table.

# World Religions (continued)

come together in both religious and ethnic communities, have worldwide representation, with the greatest concentration in North America and the Middle East.

**New-Religionists** are followers of New Religious movements and non-Christian syncretistic mass religions.

**Did you know?** The colorful onion domes of Saint Basil the Blessed above Red Square are perhaps the most common vision Westerners conjure up of Moscow. The church was commissioned by Ivan the Terrible in honor of the Russian victory over the Tatars in Kazan and Astrakhan.

| MID-2000 | % | MID-2005 | % | ANNUAL CHANGE, 1990-2000 | | | |
|---|---|---|---|---|---|---|---|
| | | | | NATURAL | CONVERSION | TOTAL | RATE (%) |
| 238,893,000 | 84.3 | 248,722,000 | 84.0 | 2,429,510 | −291,013 | 2,138,497 | 0.94 |
| 195,470,000 | 69.0 | 203,800,000 | 68.8 | 1,977,068 | −21,063 | 1,956,004 | 1.05 |
| 62,970,000 | 22.2 | 65,655,000 | 22.2 | 635,802 | 15,356 | 651,157 | 1.09 |
| 61,003,000 | 21.5 | 62,524,000 | 21.1 | 645,109 | −566,357 | 78,752 | 0.13 |
| 5,638,000 | 2.0 | 5,914,000 | 2.0 | 57,412 | −8,357 | 49,055 | 0.91 |
| 2,325,000 | 0.8 | 2,299,000 | 0.8 | 25,412 | −37,882 | −12,470 | −0.52 |
| −24,607,000 | −8.7 | −26,336,000 | −8.9 | −259,350 | 211,201 | −48,149 | 0.20 |
| 77,957,000 | 27.5 | 82,423,000 | 27.8 | 770,907 | 345,464 | 1,116,371 | 1.54 |
| 10,108,000 | 3.6 | 11,286,000 | 3.8 | 101,796 | 24,001 | 125,798 | 1.32 |
| 40,735,000 | 14.4 | 41,950,000 | 14.2 | 415,551 | −75,265 | 340,287 | 0.87 |
| 97,750,000 | 34.5 | 102,200,000 | 34.5 | 986,703 | 29,222 | 1,015,925 | 1.10 |
| 43,423,000 | 15.3 | 44,922,000 | 15.2 | 452,442 | −269,020 | 183,423 | 0.43 |
| 5,620,000 | 2.0 | 5,700,000 | 1.9 | 59,365 | −50,859 | 8,507 | 0.15 |
| 4,200,000 | 1.5 | 4,641,000 | 1.6 | 40,978 | 29,859 | 70,838 | 1.84 |
| 1,650,000 | 0.6 | 1,850,000 | 0.6 | 12,700 | 17,300 | 30,000 | 2.29 |
| 2,500,000 | 0.9 | 2,872,000 | 1.0 | 23,310 | 40,007 | 63,317 | 2.89 |
| 1,050,000 | 0.4 | 1,127,000 | 0.4 | 9,579 | 21,218 | 30,798 | 3.42 |
| 1,010,000 | 0.4 | 1,100,000 | 0.4 | 9,526 | 13,903 | 23,429 | 2.62 |
| 850,000 | 0.3 | 950,000 | 0.3 | 8,249 | 6,945 | 15,194 | 1.96 |
| 767,000 | 0.3 | 845,000 | 0.3 | 7,275 | 9,717 | 16,992 | 2.49 |
| 238,000 | 0.1 | 251,000 | 0.1 | 2,118 | 5,943 | 8,061 | 4.05 |
| 141,000 | 0.0 | 147,000 | 0.0 | 1,389 | 733 | 2,122 | 1.63 |
| 79,900 | 0.0 | 81,000 | 0.0 | 830 | −439 | 391 | 0.50 |
| 57,200 | 0.0 | 59,600 | 0.0 | 571 | 155 | 726 | 1.35 |
| 53,600 | 0.0 | 58,700 | 0.0 | 514 | 562 | 1,076 | 2.23 |
| 11,300 | 0.0 | 11,700 | 0.0 | 113 | 18 | 131 | 1.23 |
| 7,000 | 0.0 | 8,000 | 0.0 | 64 | 141 | 205 | 3.42 |
| 577,000 | 0.2 | 602,000 | 0.2 | 5,100 | −390 | 4,700 | 0.85 |
| 25,853,000 | 9.1 | 27,500,000 | 9.3 | 251,548 | 197,884 | 449,432 | 1.90 |
| 1,319,000 | 0.5 | 1,388,000 | 0.5 | 12,341 | 20,211 | 32,552 | 2.81 |
| 283,230,000 | 100.0 | 296,064,000 | 100.0 | 2,845,000 | 0 | 2,845,000 | 1.06 |

*Evangelicals/evangelicals. These two designations—italicized and enumerated separately here—cut across all of the six Christian traditions or ecclesiastical blocs listed above and should be considered separately from them. The **Evangelicals** are mainly Protestant churches, agencies, and individuals that call themselves by this term (for example, members of the National Association of Evangelicals); they usually emphasize 5 or more of 7, 9, or 21 fundamental doctrines (salvation by faith, personal acceptance, verbal inspiration of Scripture, depravity of man, Virgin Birth, miracles of Christ, atonement, evangelism, Second Advent, et al.). The **evangelicals** are Christians of evangelical conviction from all traditions who are committed to the evangel (gospel) and involved in personal witness and mission in the world but who do not belong to specifically Evangelical churches or agencies or give their primary identity as "Evangelical." Alternatively these are all termed Great Commission Christians.*
*Jews. Core Jewish population relating to Judaism, excluding Jewish persons professing a different religion.*
*Other categories. Definitions are as given under the world religion table.*

## Chronological List of Popes

According to Roman Catholic doctrine, the pope is the successor of **St. Peter**, who was head of the Apostles. The pope thus is seen to have full and supreme power of jurisdiction over the universal church in matters of faith and morals, as well as in church discipline and government. Until the 4th century, the popes were usually known only as bishops of Rome. From 1309–77, the popes' seat was at Avignon, France. In the table, **antipopes**, who opposed the legitimately elected bishop of Rome and endeavored to secure the papal throne, are listed in italics. The elections of several antipopes are greatly obscured by incomplete or biased records, and at times even their contemporaries could not decide who was the true pope. It is impossible, therefore, to establish an absolutely definitive list of antipopes.

| POPE | REIGN | POPE | REIGN | POPE | REIGN |
|---|---|---|---|---|---|
| Peter | ?–c. 64 | Anastasius II | 496–498 | Valentine | 827 |
| Linus | c. 67–76/79 | Symmachus | 498–514 | Gregory IV | 827–844 |
| Anacletus | 76–88 or 79–91 | *Laurentius* | 498, 501–c. 505/507 | *John* | 844 |
| Clement I | 88–97 or 92–101 | Hormisdas | 514–523 | Sergius II | 844–847 |
| Evaristus | c. 97–c. 107 | John I | 523–526 | Leo IV | 847–855 |
| Alexander I | 105–115 or 109–119 | Felix IV (or III)[1] | 526–530 | Benedict III | 855–858 |
| Sixtus I | c. 115–c. 125 | *Dioscorus* | 530 | *Anastasius* | 855 |
| Telesphorus | c. 125–c. 136 | Boniface II | 530–532 | *(Anastasius the Librarian)* | |
| Hyginus | c. 136–c. 140 | John II | 533–535 | Nicholas I | 858–867 |
| Pius I | c. 140–155 | Agapetus I | 535–536 | Adrian II | 867–872 |
| Anicetus | c. 155–c. 166 | Silverius | 536–537 | John VIII | 872–882 |
| Soter | c. 166–c. 175 | Vigilius | 537–555 | Marinus I | 882–884 |
| Eleutherius | c. 175–189 | Pelagius I | 556–561 | Adrian III | 884–885 |
| Victor I | c. 189–199 | John III | 561–574 | Stephen V (or VI)[2] | 885–891 |
| Zephyrinus | c. 199–217 | Benedict I | 575–579 | Formosus | 891–896 |
| Calixtus I (Callistus) | 217?–222 | Pelagius II | 579–590 | Boniface VI | 896 |
| *Hippolytus* | 217, 218–235 | Gregory I | 590–604 | Stephen VI (or VII)[2] | 896 |
| Urban I | 222–230 | Sabinian | 604–606 | Romanus | 897 |
| Pontian | 230–235 | Boniface III | 604 | Theodore II | 897 |
| Anterus | 235–236 | Boniface IV | 608–615 | John IX | 898–900 |
| Fabian | 236–250 | Deusdedit (Adeodatus I) | 615–618 | Benedict IV | 900 |
| Cornelius | 251–253 | Boniface V | 619–625 | Leo V | 903 |
| *Novatian* | 251 | Honorius I | 625–638 | *Christopher* | 903–904 |
| Lucius I | 253–254 | Severinus | 640 | Sergius III | 904–911 |
| Stephen I | 254–257 | John IV | 640–642 | Anastasius III | 911–913 |
| Sixtus II | 257–258 | Theodore I | 642–649 | Lando | 913–914 |
| Dionysius | 259–268 | Martin I | 649–655 | John X | 914–928 |
| Felix I | 269–274 | Eugenius I | 654–657 | Leo VI | 928 |
| Eutychian | 275–283 | Vitalian | 657–672 | Stephen VII (or VIII)[2] | 929–931 |
| Gaius | 283–296 | Adeodatus II | 672–676 | John XI | 931–935 |
| Marcellinus | 291/296–304 | Donus | 676–678 | Leo VII | 936–939 |
| Marcellus I | 308–309 | Agatho | 678–681 | Stephen VIII (or IX)[2] | 939–942 |
| Eusebius | 309/310 | Leo II | 682–683 | Marinus II | 942–946 |
| Miltiades (Melchiades) | 311–314 | Benedict II | 684–685 | Agapetus II | 946–955 |
| Sylvester I | 314–335 | John V | 685–686 | John XII | 955–964 |
| Mark | 336 | Conon | 686–687 | Leo VIII[3] | 963–965 |
| Julius I | 337–352 | Sergius I | 687–701 | Benedict V[3] | 964–966? |
| Liberius | 352–366 | *Theodore* | 687 | John XIII | 965–972 |
| *Felix (II)* | 355–358 | *Paschal* | 687 | Benedict VI | 973–974 |
| Damasus I | 366–384 | John VI | 701–705 | *Boniface VII (1st time)* | 974 |
| *Ursinus* | 366–367 | John VII | 705–707 | Benedict VII | 974–983 |
| Siricius | 384–399 | Sisinnius | 708 | John XIV | 983–984 |
| Anastasius I | 399–401 | Constantine | 708–715 | *Boniface VII (2nd time)* | 984–985 |
| Innocent I | 401–417 | Gregory II | 715–731 | John XV (or XVI)[4] | 985–996 |
| Zosimus | 417–418 | Gregory III | 731–741 | Gregory V | 996–999 |
| Boniface I | 418–422 | Zacharias (Zachary) | 741–752 | *John XVI (or XVII)[4]* | 997–998 |
| *Eulalius* | 418–419 | Stephen (II)[2] | 752 | Sylvester II | 999–1003 |
| Celestine I | 422–432 | Stephen II (or III)[2] | 752–757 | John XVII (or XVIII)[4] | 1003 |
| Sixtus III | 432–440 | Paul I | 757–767 | John XVIII (or XIX)[4] | 1004–09 |
| Leo I | 440–461 | *Constantine (II)* | 767–768 | Sergius IV | 1009–12 |
| Hilary | 461–468 | *Philip* | 768 | *Gregory (VI)* | 1012 |
| Simplicius | 468–483 | Stephen III (or IV)[2] | 768–772 | Benedict VIII | 1012–24 |
| Felix III (or II)[1] | 483–492 | Adrian I | 772–795 | John XIX (or XX)[4] | 1024–32 |
| Gelasius I | 492–496 | Leo III | 795–816 | Benedict IX (1st time) | 1032–44 |
| | | Stephen IV (or V)[2] | 816–817 | Sylvester III | 1045 |
| | | Paschal I | 817–824 | | |
| | | Eugenius II | 824–827 | | |

## Chronological List of Popes (continued)

| POPE | REIGN | POPE | REIGN | POPE | REIGN |
|---|---|---|---|---|---|
| Benedict IX | 1045 | Clement IV | 1265–68 | Innocent VIII | 1484–92 |
| (2nd time) | | Gregory X | 1271–76 | Alexander VI | 1492–1503 |
| Gregory VI | 1045–46 | Innocent V | 1276 | Pius III | 1503 |
| Clement II | 1046–47 | Adrian V | 1276 | Julius II | 1503–13 |
| Benedict IX | 1047–48 | John XXI[4] | 1276–77 | Leo X | 1513–21 |
| (3rd time) | | Nicholas III | 1277–80 | Adrian VI | 1522–23 |
| Damasus II | 1048 | Martin IV[5] | 1281–85 | Clement VII | 1523–34 |
| Leo IX | 1049–54 | Honorius IV | 1285–87 | Paul III | 1534–49 |
| Victor II | 1055–57 | Nicholas IV | 1288–92 | Julius III | 1550–55 |
| Stephen IX (or X)[2] | 1057–58 | Celestine V | 1294 | Marcellus II | 1555 |
| *Benedict X* | 1058–59 | Boniface VIII | 1294–1303 | Paul IV | 1555–59 |
| Nicholas II | 1059–61 | Benedict XI | 1303–04 | Pius IV | 1559–65 |
| Alexander II | 1061–73 | Clement V (at | 1305–14 | Pius V | 1566–72 |
| *Honorius (II)* | 1061–72 | Avignon from | | Gregory XIII | 1572–85 |
| Gregory VII | 1073–85 | 1309) | | Sixtus V | 1585–90 |
| *Clement (III)* | 1080–1100 | John XXII[4] | 1316–34 | Urban VII | 1590 |
| Victor III | 1086–87 | (at Avignon) | | Gregory XIV | 1590–91 |
| Urban II | 1088–99 | *Nicholas (V)* | 1328–30 | Innocent IX | 1591 |
| Paschal II | 1099–1118 | *(at Rome)* | | Clement VIII | 1592–1605 |
| *Theodoric* | 1100–02 | Benedict XII | 1334–42 | Leo XI | 1605 |
| *Albert (Aleric)* | 1102 | (at Avignon) | | Paul V | 1605–21 |
| *Sylvester (IV)* | 1105–11 | Clement VI | 1342–52 | Gregory XV | 1621–23 |
| Gelasius II | 1118–19 | (at Avignon) | | Urban VIII | 1623–44 |
| *Gregory (VIII)* | 1118–21 | Innocent VI | 1352–62 | Innocent X | 1644–55 |
| Calixtus II | 1119–24 | (at Avignon) | | Alexander VII | 1655–67 |
| (Callistus) | | Urban V | 1362–70 | Clement IX | 1667–69 |
| Honorius II | 1124–30 | (at Avignon) | | Clement X | 1670–76 |
| *Celestine (II)* | 1124 | Gregory XI | 1370–78 | Innocent XI | 1676–89 |
| Innocent II | 1130–43 | (at Avignon, then | | Alexander VIII | 1689–91 |
| *Anacletus (II)* | 1130–38 | Rome from 1377) | | Innocent XII | 1691–1700 |
| *Victor (IV)* | 1138 | Urban VI | 1378–89 | Clement XI | 1700–21 |
| Celestine II | 1143–44 | *Clement (VII)* | 1378–94 | Innocent XIII | 1721–24 |
| Lucius II | 1144–45 | *(at Avignon)* | | Benedict XIII | 1724–30 |
| Eugenius III | 1145–53 | Boniface IX | 1389–1404 | Clement XII | 1730–40 |
| Anastasius IV | 1153–54 | *Benedict (XIII)* | 1394–1423 | Benedict XIV | 1740–58 |
| Adrian IV | 1154–59 | *(at Avignon)* | | Clement XIII | 1758–69 |
| Alexander III | 1159–81 | Innocent VII | 1404–06 | Clement XIV | 1769–74 |
| *Victor (IV)* | 1159–64 | Gregory XII | 1406–15 | Pius VI | 1775–99 |
| *Paschal (III)* | 1164–68 | *Alexander (V)* | 1409–10 | Pius VII | 1800–23 |
| *Calixtus (III)* | 1168–78 | *(at Bologna)* | | Leo XII | 1823–29 |
| *Innocent (III)* | 1179–80 | *John (XXIII)* | 1410–15 | Pius VIII | 1829–30 |
| Lucius III | 1181–85 | *(at Bologna)* | | Gregory XVI | 1831–46 |
| Urban III | 1185–87 | Martin V[5] | 1417–31 | Pius IX | 1846–78 |
| Gregory VIII | 1187 | Clement (VIII) | 1423–29 | Leo XIII | 1878–1903 |
| Clement III | 1187–91 | Eugenius IV | 1431–47 | Pius X | 1903–14 |
| Celestine III | 1191–98 | *Felix (V) (Amadeus* | 1439–49 | Benedict XV | 1914–22 |
| Innocent III | 1198–1216 | *VIII of Savoy)* | | Pius XI | 1922–39 |
| Honorius III | 1216–27 | Nicholas V | 1447–55 | Pius XII | 1939–58 |
| Gregory IX | 1227–41 | Calixtus III | 1455–58 | John XXIII | 1958–63 |
| Celestine IV | 1241 | (Callistus) | | Paul VI | 1963–78 |
| Innocent IV | 1243–54 | Pius II | 1458–64 | John Paul I | 1978 |
| Alexander IV | 1254–61 | Paul II | 1464–71 | John Paul II | 1978– |
| Urban IV | 1261–64 | Sixtus IV | 1471–84 | | |

[1]*The higher number is used if Felix (II), who reigned from 355 to 358 and is ordinarily classed as an antipope, is counted as a pope.* [2]*Though elected on 23 Mar 752, Stephen (II) died two days later before he could be consecrated and thus is ordinarily not counted. The issue has made the numbering of subsequent Stephens somewhat irregular.* [3]*Either Leo VIII or Benedict V may be considered an antipope.* [4]*A confusion in the numbering of popes named John after John XIV (reigned 983–984) resulted because some 11th-century historians mistakenly believed that there had been a pope named John between antipope Boniface VII and the true John XV (reigned 985–996). Therefore they mistakenly numbered the real popes John XV to XIX as John XVI to XX. These popes have since customarily been renumbered XV to XIX, but John XXI and John XXII continue to bear numbers that they themselves formally adopted on the assumption that there had indeed been 20 Johns before them. In current numbering there thus exists no pope by the name of John XX.* [5]*In the 13th century the papal chancery misread the names of the two popes Marinus as Martin, and as a result of this error Simon de Brie in 1281 assumed the name of Pope Martin IV instead of Martin II. The enumeration has not been corrected, and thus there exist no Martin II and Martin III.*

# Roman Catholic Cardinals

Members of the **Sacred College of Cardinals** elect the pope, act as his principal counselors, and aid in the government of the Roman Catholic church throughout the world. Cardinals serve as chief officials of the **Roman Curia** (the papal administration), as bishops of major dioceses, and often as papal envoys. New cardinals are appointed only by the pope. He calls a secret **consistory** (meeting) of the cardinals and announces to them the names of the new cardinals. The newly named cardinals then receive the red biretta and the ring symbolic of the office in a public consistory. There are three orders of cardinals: bishops, priests, and deacons. These ranks correspond not to a cardinal's rank of ordination but to his position within the College of Cardinals. These distinctions are not made in the table below. The total **number of cardinals** was fixed at 70 by Sixtus V in 1586. John XXIII eliminated the restriction of 70 in 1959, although the number of papal electors was later set at 120. Those aged over 80 no longer serve as papal electors.

The following cardinals hold specific offices within the college. **Dean:** Joseph Ratzinger; **Sub-Dean:** Angelo Sodano; **Protodeacon:** Luigi Poggi; **Camerlengo of the Holy Roman Church:** Eduardo Martínez Somalo; **Dean Emeritus:** Bernardin Gantin.

| NAME | COUNTRY (BIRTH YEAR) | DATE APPOINTED CARDINAL |
|---|---|---|
| Franz König | Austria (1905) | 15 Dec 1958 |
| Corrado Ursi | Italy (1908) | 26 Jun 1967 |
| Eugênio de Araújo Sales | Brazil (1920) | 28 Apr 1969 |
| Stephen Sou Hwan Kim | Korea (1922) | 28 Apr 1969 |
| Johannes Willebrands | The Netherlands (1909) | 28 Apr 1969 |
| Luis Aponte Martínez | Puerto Rico (1922) | 5 Mar 1973 |
| Paulo Evaristo Arns | Brazil (1921) | 5 Mar 1973 |
| Marcelo González Martín | Spain (1918) | 5 Mar 1973 |
| Maurice Michael Otunga | Kenya (1923) | 5 Mar 1973 |
| Salvatore Pappalardo | Italy (1918) | 5 Mar 1973 |
| Raúl Francisco Primatesta | Argentina (1919) | 5 Mar 1973 |
| Pio Taofinu'u | Samoa (1923) | 5 Mar 1973 |
| Juan Carlos Aramburu | Argentina (1912) | 24 May 1976 |
| Corrado Bafile | Italy (1903) | 24 May 1976 |
| William Wakefield Baum | US (1926) | 24 May 1976 |
| Aloísio Lorscheider | Brazil (1924) | 24 May 1976 |
| Opilio Rossi | US (1910) | 24 May 1976 |
| Jaime L. Sin | Philippines (1928) | 24 May 1976 |
| Hyacinthe Thiandoum | Senegal (1921) | 24 May 1976 |
| Bernardin Gantin | Benin (1922) | 27 Jun 1977 |
| Joseph Ratzinger | Germany (1927) | 27 Jun 1977 |
| Giuseppe Caprio | Italy (1914) | 30 Jun 1979 |
| Marco Cé | Italy (1925) | 30 Jun 1979 |
| Ernesto Corripio Ahumada | Mexico (1919) | 30 Jun 1979 |
| Roger Etchegaray | France (1922) | 30 Jun 1979 |
| Franciszek Macharski | Poland (1927) | 30 Jun 1979 |
| Godfried Danneels | Belgium (1933) | 2 Feb 1983 |
| Alexandre do Nascimento | Angola (1925) | 2 Feb 1983 |
| Józef Glemp | Poland (1929) | 2 Feb 1983 |
| Michael Michai Kitbunchu | Thailand (1929) | 2 Feb 1983 |
| Alfonso López Trujillo | Colombia (1935) | 2 Feb 1983 |
| Jean-Marie Lustiger | France (1926) | 2 Feb 1983 |
| Carlo Maria Martini | Italy (1927) | 2 Feb 1983 |
| Joachim Meisner | Poland (1933) | 2 Feb 1983 |
| Thomas Stafford Williams | New Zealand (1930) | 2 Feb 1983 |
| Francis Arinze | Nigeria (1932) | 25 May 1985 |
| Giacomo Biffi | Italy (1928) | 25 May 1985 |
| Rosalio José Castillo Lara | Venezuela (1922) | 25 May 1985 |
| Andrzej Maria Deskur | Poland (1924) | 25 May 1985 |
| Juan Francisco Fresno Larraín | Chile (1914) | 25 May 1985 |
| Edouard Gagnon | Canada (1918) | 25 May 1985 |
| Henryk Roman Gulbinowicz | Poland (1928) | 25 May 1985 |
| Antonio Innocenti | Italy (1915) | 25 May 1985 |
| Bernard Francis Law | US (1931) | 25 May 1985 |
| D. Simon Lourdusamy | India (1924) | 25 May 1985 |
| Paul Augustin Mayer | Germany (1911) | 25 May 1985 |
| Miguel Obando Bravo | Nicaragua (1926) | 25 May 1985 |
| Silvano Piovanelli | Italy (1924) | 25 May 1985 |
| Paul Poupard | France (1930) | 25 May 1985 |
| Adrianus Johannes Simonis | The Netherlands (1931) | 25 May 1985 |
| Alfons Maria Stickler | Austria (1910) | 25 May 1985 |

## Roman Catholic Cardinals (continued)

| NAME | COUNTRY (BIRTH YEAR) | DATE APPOINTED CARDINAL |
|---|---|---|
| Angel Suquía Goicoechea | Spain (1916) | 25 May 1985 |
| Jozef Tomko | Slovakia (1924) | 25 May 1985 |
| Paulos Tzadua | Ethiopia (1921) | 25 May 1985 |
| Louis-Albert Vachon | Canada (1912) | 25 May 1985 |
| Ricardo Vidal | Philippines (1931) | 25 May 1985 |
| Friedrich Wetter | Germany (1928) | 25 May 1985 |
| Giovanni Canestri | Italy (1918) | 28 Jun 1988 |
| Edward Bede Clancy | Australia (1923) | 28 Jun 1988 |
| José Freire Falcão | Brazil (1925) | 28 Jun 1988 |
| Angelo Felici | Italy (1919) | 28 Jun 1988 |
| Michele Giordano | Italy (1930) | 28 Jun 1988 |
| James Aloysius Hickey | US (1920) | 28 Jun 1988 |
| Antonio María Javierre Ortas | Spain (1921) | 28 Jun 1988 |
| Jean Margéot | Mauritius (1916) | 28 Jun 1988 |
| Eduardo Martínez Somalo | Spain (1927) | 28 Jun 1988 |
| László Paskai | Hungary (1927) | 28 Jun 1988 |
| Simon Ignatius Pimenta | India (1920) | 28 Jun 1988 |
| Alexandre José Maria dos Santos | Mozambique (1924) | 28 Jun 1988 |
| Achille Silvestrini | Italy (1923) | 28 Jun 1988 |
| Edmund Casimir Szoka | US (1927) | 28 Jun 1988 |
| Christian Wiyghan Tumi | Cameroon (1930) | 28 Jun 1988 |
| John Baptist Wu Cheng-Chung | China (1925) | 28 Jun 1988 |
| Fiorenzo Angelini | Italy (1916) | 28 Jun 1991 |
| Anthony Joseph Bevilacqua | US (1923) | 28 Jun 1991 |
| Edward Idris Cassidy | Australia (1924) | 28 Jun 1991 |
| Cahal Brendan Daly | Ireland (1917) | 28 Jun 1991 |
| Frédéric Etsou-Nzabi-Bamungwabi | Dem. Rep. of the Congo (1930) | 28 Jun 1991 |
| Ján Chryzostom Korec | Slovakia (1924) | 28 Jun 1991 |
| Pio Laghi | Italy (1922) | 28 Jun 1991 |
| Nicolás de Jesús López Rodríguez | Dominican Rep. (1936) | 28 Jun 1991 |
| Roger Michael Mahony | US (1936) | 28 Jun 1991 |
| Virgilio Noè | Italy (1922) | 28 Jun 1991 |
| Camillo Ruini | Italy (1931) | 28 Jun 1991 |
| Giovanni Saldarini | Italy (1924) | 28 Jun 1991 |
| José T. Sánchez | Philippines (1920) | 28 Jun 1991 |
| Henri Schwery | Switzerland (1932) | 28 Jun 1991 |
| Angelo Sodano | Italy (1927) | 28 Jun 1991 |
| Georg Maximilian Sterzinsky | Germany (1936) | 28 Jun 1991 |
| Gilberto Agustoni | Switzerland (1922) | 26 Nov 1994 |
| Ricardo María Carles Gordó | Spain (1926) | 26 Nov 1994 |
| Julius Riyadi Darmaatmadja | Indonesia (1934) | 26 Nov 1994 |
| Carlo Furno | Italy (1921) | 26 Nov 1994 |
| William Henry Keeler | US (1931) | 26 Nov 1994 |
| Adam Joseph Maida | US (1930) | 26 Nov 1994 |
| Jaime Lucas Ortega y Alamino | Cuba (1936) | 26 Nov 1994 |
| Paul Joseph Pham Dình Tung | Vietnam (1919) | 26 Nov 1994 |
| Luigi Poggi | Italy (1917) | 26 Nov 1994 |
| Vinko Puljic | Bosnia-Herzegovina (1945) | 26 Nov 1994 |
| Armand Gaétan Razafindratandra | Madagascar (1925) | 26 Nov 1994 |
| Juan Sandoval Iñiguez | Mexico (1933) | 26 Nov 1994 |
| Jan Pieter Schotte | Belgium (1928) | 26 Nov 1994 |
| Nasrallah Pierre Sfeir | Lebanon (1920) | 26 Nov 1994 |
| Peter Seiichi Shirayanagi | Japan (1928) | 26 Nov 1994 |
| Adolfo Antonio Suárez Rivera | Mexico (1927) | 26 Nov 1994 |
| Kazimierz Swiatek | Estonia (1914) | 26 Nov 1994 |
| Ersilio Tonini | Italy (1914) | 26 Nov 1994 |
| Jean-Claude Turcotte | Canada (1936) | 26 Nov 1994 |
| Miloslav Vlk | Czech Rep. (1932) | 26 Nov 1994 |
| Emmanuel Wamala | Uganda (1926) | 26 Nov 1994 |
| Aloysius Matthew Ambrozic | Slovenia (1930) | 21 Feb 1998 |
| Lorenzo Antonetti | Italy (1922) | 21 Feb 1998 |
| Serafim Fernandes de Araújo | Brazil (1924) | 21 Feb 1998 |
| Darío Castrillón Hoyos | Colombia (1929) | 21 Feb 1998 |
| Giovanni Cheli | Italy (1918) | 21 Feb 1998 |
| Francesco Colasuonno | Italy (1925) | 21 Feb 1998 |

## Roman Catholic Cardinals (continued)

| NAME | COUNTRY (BIRTH YEAR) | DATE APPOINTED CARDINAL |
|------|---------------------|------------------------|
| Salvatore de Giorgi | Italy (1930) | 21 Feb 1998 |
| Francis Eugene George | US (1937) | 21 Feb 1998 |
| Adam Kozlowiecki | Poland (1911) | 21 Feb 1998 |
| Jorge Arturo Medina Estévez | Chile (1926) | 21 Feb 1998 |
| Dino Monduzzi | Italy (1922) | 21 Feb 1998 |
| Polycarp Pengo | Tanzania (1944) | 21 Feb 1998 |
| Norberto Rivera Carrera | Mexico (1942) | 21 Feb 1998 |
| Antonio María Rouco Varela | Spain (1936) | 21 Feb 1998 |
| Christoph Schönborn | Bohemia (present-day Czech Rep.) (1945) | 21 Feb 1998 |
| Paul Shan Kuo-Hsi | China (1923) | 21 Feb 1998 |
| James Francis Stafford | US (1932) | 21 Feb 1998 |
| Dionigi Tettamanzi | Italy (1934) | 21 Feb 1998 |
| Marian Jaworski[1] | Ukraine (1926) | 28 Jan 2001 |
| Karl Lehmann | Germany (1936) | 28 Jan 2001 |
| Wilfrid Fox Napier | South Africa (1941) | 28 Jan 2001 |
| Janis Pujats[1] | Latvia (1930) | 28 Jan 2001 |
| Julio Terrazas Sandoval | Bolivia (1936) | 28 Jan 2001 |
| Geraldo Majella Agnelo | Brazil (1933) | 21 Feb 2001 |
| Bernard Agré | Côte d'Ivoire (1926) | 21 Feb 2001 |
| Francisco Álvarez Martínez | Spain (1925) | 21 Feb 2001 |
| Audrys Juozas Backis | Lithuania (1937) | 21 Feb 2001 |
| Jorge Mario Bergoglio | Argentina (1936) | 21 Feb 2001 |
| Agostino Cacciavillan | Italy (1926) | 21 Feb 2001 |
| Juan Luis Cipriani Thorne | Peru (1943) | 21 Feb 2001 |
| Desmond Connell | Ireland (1926) | 21 Feb 2001 |
| José da Cruz Policarpo | Portugal (1936) | 21 Feb 2001 |
| Ignace Moussa I Daoud | Syria (1930) | 21 Feb 2001 |
| Ivan Dias | India (1936) | 21 Feb 2001 |
| Avery Dulles | US (1918) | 21 Feb 2001 |
| Edward Michael Egan | US (1932) | 21 Feb 2001 |
| Francisco Javier Errázuriz Ossa | Chile (1933) | 21 Feb 2001 |
| Stéphanos II Ghattas | Egypt (1920) | 21 Feb 2001 |
| Antonio José González Zumárraga | Ecuador (1925) | 21 Feb 2001 |
| Zenon Grocholewski | Poland (1939) | 21 Feb 2001 |
| Jean Honoré | France (1920) | 21 Feb 2001 |
| Cláudio Hummes | Brazil (1934) | 21 Feb 2001 |
| Lubomyr Husar | Ukraine (1933) | 21 Feb 2001 |
| Walter Kasper | Germany (1933) | 21 Feb 2001 |
| Theodore Edgar McCarrick | US (1930) | 21 Feb 2001 |
| Jorge María Mejía | Argentina (1923) | 21 Feb 2001 |
| Cormac Murphy-O'Connor | UK (1932) | 21 Feb 2001 |
| Severino Poletto | Italy (1933) | 21 Feb 2001 |
| Mario Francesco Pompedda | Italy (1929) | 21 Feb 2001 |
| Giovanni Battista Re | Italy (1934) | 21 Feb 2001 |
| Oscar Andrés Rodríguez Maradiaga | Honduras (1942) | 21 Feb 2001 |
| Pedro Rubiano Sáenz | Colombia (1932) | 21 Feb 2001 |
| José Saraiva Martins | Portugal (1932) | 21 Feb 2001 |
| Leo Scheffczyk | Germany (1920) | 21 Feb 2001 |
| Sergio Sebastiani | Italy (1931) | 21 Feb 2001 |
| Crescenzio Sepe | Italy (1943) | 21 Feb 2001 |
| Roberto Tucci | Italy (1921) | 21 Feb 2001 |
| Ignacio Antonio Velasco García | Venezuela (1929) | 21 Feb 2001 |
| Varkey Vithayathil | India (1927) | 21 Feb 2001 |

[1]*Held* in pectore *(in secret) from the consistory of 21 Feb 1998; officially announced 28 Jan 2001.*

**Did you know?** The first recorded use of cryptography for correspondence was by the Spartans, who as early as 400 BC employed the scytale for secret communication between military commanders. The scytale consisted of a tapered baton, around which was spirally wrapped a strip of parchment or leather on which the message was written. When unwrapped, the letters were scrambled, but when the strip was wrapped around another baton of identical proportions to the original, the plain text appeared.

## Archbishops of Canterbury

The Archbishop of Canterbury has served as the diocesan Bishop of Canterbury since AD 597, when Augustine (Austin) founded the Christian church in England. The archbishop also serves as the Metropolitan for the Southern Province of the Church of England and as the Primate of All England, which recognizes the seat's lead ecclesiastical role in England. Until the middle of the 16th century, the English church was part of the Roman Catholic Church. In the early 1530s King Henry VIII established the Church of England as a separate faith, subject not to the authority of Rome but to that of the English monarch.

| ARCHBISHOP | TERM | ARCHBISHOP | TERM | ARCHBISHOP | TERM |
|---|---|---|---|---|---|
| Augustine (Austin) | 597–604 | Thomas Becket | 1162–1170 | William Sancroft | 1677–1690 |
| Laurentius (Lawrence) | 604–619 | Richard of Dover | 1174–1184 | John Tillotson | 1691–1694 |
| Mellitus | 619–624 | Baldwin | 1184–1190 | Thomas Tenison | 1694–1715 |
| Justus | 624–627 | Hubert Walter | 1193–1205 | William Wake | 1715–1737 |
| Honorius | 627–653 | Stephen Langton | 1206–1228 | John Potter | 1737–1747 |
| Deusdedit | 655–664 | Richard le Grant | 1229–1231 | Thomas Herring | 1747–1757 |
| Theodore (Theodorus) | 668–690 | Edmund Rich | 1233–1240 | Matthew Hutton | 1757–1758 |
| Berhtwald (Beorht-weald) | 693–731 | Boniface of Savoy | 1241–1270 | Thomas Secker | 1758–1768 |
| | | Robert Kilwardby | 1272–1278 | Frederick Cornwallis | 1768–1783 |
| Tatwine | 731–734 | John Pecham | 1279–1292 | | |
| Nothelm | 735–739 | Robert Winchelsey | 1293–1313 | John Moore | 1783–1805 |
| Cuthbert (Cuthbeorht) | 740–760 | Walter Reynolds | 1313–1327 | Charles Manners Sutton | 1805–1828 |
| Bregowine (Bregu-wine) | 761–764 | Simon Mepham | 1327–1333 | | |
| | | John Stratford | 1333–1348 | William Howley | 1828–1848 |
| Jaenberht (Jaen-beorht) | 765–792 | Thomas Bradwardine | 1348–1349 | John Bird Sumner | 1848–1862 |
| | | | | Charles Thomas Longley | 1862–1868 |
| Aethelheard | 793–805 | Simon Islip | 1349–1366 | | |
| Wulfred | 805–832 | Simon Langham | 1366–1368 | Archibald Campbell Tait | 1868–1882 |
| Feologild | 832 | William Whittlesey | 1368–1374 | | |
| Ceolnoth | 833–870 | Simon Sudbury | 1375–1381 | Edward White Benson | 1883–1896 |
| Aethelred | 870–889 | William Courtenay | 1381–1396 | | |
| Plegmund | 890–914 | Thomas Arundel | 1396–1397 | Frederick Temple | 1896–1902 |
| Aethelhelm | 914–923 | Roger Walden | 1397–1399 | Randall Thomas Davidson | 1903–1928 |
| Wulfhelm | 923–942 | Thomas Arundel (restored) | 1399–1414 | | |
| Oda | 942–958 | | | Cosmo Gordon Lang (from 1942, Baron Lang of Lambeth) | 1928–1942 |
| Aelfsige | 959 | Henry Chichele | 1414–1443 | | |
| Beorhthelm | 959 | John Stafford | 1443–1452 | | |
| Dunstan | 960–988 | John Kempe | 1452–1454 | | |
| Aethelgar | 988–990 | Thomas Bourgchier | 1454–1486 | William Temple | 1942–1944 |
| Sigeric Serio | 990–994 | John Morton | 1486–1500 | Geoffrey Francis Fisher (from 1961, Baron Fisher of Lambeth) | 1945–1961 |
| Aelfric | 995–1005 | Henry Deane | 1501–1503 | | |
| Aelfheah | 1005–1012 | William Warham | 1504–1532 | | |
| Lyfing | 1013–1020 | Thomas Cranmer | 1533–1556 | | |
| Aethelnoth | 1020–1038 | Reginald Pole | 1556–1558 | Arthur Michael Ramsey | 1961–1974 |
| Eadsige | 1038–1050 | Matthew Parker | 1559–1575 | | |
| Robert of Jumièges | 1051–1052 | Edmund Grindal | 1575–1583 | Frederick Donald Coggan | 1974–1980 |
| Stigand | 1052–1070 | John Whitgift | 1583–1604 | | |
| Lanfranc | 1070–1089 | Richard Bancroft | 1604–1610 | Robert A.K. Runcie | 1980–1991 |
| Anselm | 1093–1109 | George Abbot | 1611–1633 | George Carey | 1991–2002 |
| Ralph d'Escures | 1114–1122 | William Laud | 1633–1645 | Rowan Williams | 2002– |
| William of Corbeil | 1123–1136 | William Juxon | 1660–1663 | | |
| Theobald | 1138–1161 | Gilbert Sheldon | 1663–1677 | | |

# Law & Crime

## International Terrorist Organizations

*"Terrorism" is a subjective term. The list of organizations included here is that of the US Department of State, issued on 23 Oct 2002. The list is updated every year.*

**Abu Nidal Organization (ANO)** (Fatah Revolutionary Council, Arab Revolutionary Brigades, Black September, Revolutionary Organization of Socialist Muslims)
Founded in 1974 as splinter group from PLO; led by Sabri al-Banna.
**country or region of operation:** Middle East, primarily Iraq and Lebanon; has also operated in Asia and Europe

**primary goals:** elimination of Israel, establishment of Palestinian state

**Abu Sayyaf Group (ASG)**
Founded in early 1990s as splinter group from Moro National Liberation Front by Abdurajak Abubakar Janjalani; nominally led by Khadaffy Janjalani, but mainly made up of semiautonomous factions.

**country or region of operation:** the Philippines, Malaysia
**primary goals:** establishment of independent Islamic state in southern Philippines

**Armed Islamic Group (GIA)**
Founded in 1992; leadership uncertain, but may be led by Rachid Abou Tourab.
**country or region of operation:** Algeria
**primary goals:** replacement of secular Algerian government with an Islamic state

**Aum Shinrikyo** (Aum Supreme Truth, Aleph)
Founded in 1987 by Shoko Asahara; led by Fumihiro Joyu.
**country or region of operation:** Japan
**primary goals:** takeover of Japan and the world

**Basque Fatherland and Liberty (ETA)** (Euzkadi Ta Askatasuna)
Founded in 1959; leadership uncertain.
**country or region of operation:** Basque autonomous regions of northern Spain and southwestern France
**primary goals:** establishment of independent Basque state based on Marxism

**Al-Gama'a al-Islamiyya (Islamic Group, IG)**
Founded late 1970s; loosely organized in two factions led by Mustafa Hamza and Rifa'i Taha Musa; spiritual leader Sheikh Umar Abd al-Rahman.
**country or region of operation:** Egypt; also operates in several countries worldwide
**primary goals:** replacement of Egyptian government with an Islamic state

**Hamas (Islamic Resistance Movement)**
Founded in 1987 by Sheikh Ahmed Yasin as offshoot of Muslim Brotherhood; political leaders include Yasin, Abdel Aziz al-Rantisi, and Khalid Meshal.
**country or region of operation:** Gaza Strip, West Bank, Israel; also present throughout Middle East
**primary goals:** elimination of Israel, establishment of Islamic Palestinian state

**Harakat ul-Mujahidin (HUM)** (Movement of Holy Warriors)
Founded in mid-1980s or early 1990s; led by Farooq Kashmiri.
**country or region of operation:** the Kashmir region of Pakistan and India
**primary goals:** to make Kashmir part of an Islamic state

**Hezbollah (Party of God)** (Islamic Jihad, Revolutionary Justice Organization, Organization of the Oppressed on Earth, Islamic Jihad for the Liberation of Palestine)
Founded in 1982; governed by the Majlis al-Shura (Consultative Council) headed by Hassan Nasrallah; spiritual leader Sheikh Muhammad Hussein Fadlallah.
**country or region of operation:** Lebanon; also has cells worldwide
**primary goals:** establishment of Islamic rule in Lebanon, elimination of Israel, liberation of occupied Arab lands

**Islamic Movement of Uzbekistan (IMU)**
Founded in 1996; led by Tohir Yoldashev.

**country or region of operation:** Central and South Asia, primarily Uzbekistan, Tajikistan, Kyrgyzstan, Afghanistan, Iran, and Pakistan
**primary goals:** replacement of secular Uzbekistan government with an Islamic state

**al-Jihad** (Egyptian Islamic Jihad, Jihad Group, Islamic Jihad)
Founded late 1970s by Ayman al-Zawahiri; merged with al-Qaeda in 2001.
**country or region of operation:** Egypt and other countries, including Yemen, Afghanistan, Pakistan, Lebanon, and Great Britain; activities now centered mainly outside Egypt
**primary goals:** replacement of Egyptian government with an Islamic state, attacks on US and Israeli interests

**Kahane Chai (Kach)**
Kach founded in 1971 by Meir Kahane; Kahane Chai founded as follow-up group by Binyamin Kahane after Meir's assassination in 1990; Binyamin assassinated in 2000.
**country or region of operation:** Israel, West Bank
**primary goals:** expansion of Israel, removal of Palestinians

**Kurdistan Workers' Party (PKK)**
Founded in 1974; led by Abdullah Ocalan (imprisoned since 1999).
**country or region of operation:** Turkey; also operates in Europe and the Middle East
**primary goals:** establishment of independent Kurdish state

**Liberation Tigers of Tamil Eelam (LTTE)**
Founded in 1976; led by Velupillai Prabhakaran.
**country or region of operation:** Sri Lanka
**primary goals:** establishment of independent Tamil state

**Mujahedin-e Khalq Organization (MEK)** (National Liberation Army of Iran [NLA, the militant wing], People's Mujahidin of Iran [PMOI], National Council of Resistance [NCR], Muslim Iranian Student's Society [front organization to garner financial support])
Founded 1960s; led by Maryam and Masud Rajavi.
**country or region of operation:** Iran, Iraq
**primary goals:** establishment of secular government in Iran

**National Liberation Army (ELN)**
Founded in 1965; led by Nicolas Rodríguez Bautista.
**country or region of operation:** Colombia
**primary goals:** replacement of ruling government with Marxist state

**Palestine Islamic Jihad (PIJ)**
Founded in 1970s; most active faction led by Ramadan Shallah.
**country or region of operation:** Israel, West Bank, Gaza Strip; also elsewhere in Middle East, primarily Lebanon and Syria
**primary goals:** elimination of Israel, establishment of Islamic Palestinian state

**Palestine Liberation Front (PLF)**
Founded in mid-1970s as splinter group from PFLP–GC; pro-PLO faction led by Muhammad Abbas (Abu Abbas).

country or region of operation: Israel, Iraq
primary goals: elimination of Israel, establishment of Palestinian state

**Popular Front for the Liberation of Palestine (PFLP)**
Founded as part of PLO in 1967 by George Habash (discontinued PLO participation in 1993); led by Ahmed Sadat.
country or region of operation: Syria, Lebanon, Israel, West Bank, Gaza Strip
primary goals: promotion of national unity and revitalization of PLO, opposition to peace negotiations with Israel

**Popular Front for the Liberation of Palestine–General Command (PFLP–GC)**
Founded in 1968 as splinter group from PFLP; led by Ahmad Jabril.
country or region of operation: Syria, Lebanon, Israel, West Bank, Gaza Strip
primary goals: opposition to PLO and to peace negotiations with Israel

**al-Qaeda**
Founded in late 1980s; established and led by Osama bin Laden.
country or region of operation: worldwide
primary goals: establishment of worldwide Islamic rule, overthrow of non-Islamic governments, expulsion of Western influences from Muslim states, killing of US citizens

**Real IRA** (True IRA)
Founded in 1998 as splinter group of Irish Republican Army (IRA); led by Michael "Mickey" McKevitt (imprisoned since 2001).
country or region of operation: Northern Ireland; also elsewhere in Great Britain and in Ireland
primary goals: removal of British forces from Northern Ireland, unification of Ireland

**Revolutionary Armed Forces of Colombia (FARC)**
Founded in 1964 as military branch of Colombian Communist Party; governed by group led by Manuel Marulanda and including Jorge Briceno and five others.
country or region of operation: Colombia; also some operations in Venezuela, Ecuador, and Panama

primary goals: replacement of ruling government with Marxist state

**Revolutionary Nuclei** (Revolutionary Cells)
Founded in 1995 as offshoot of or successor to Revolutionary People's Struggle (ELA).
country or region of operation: Greece, primarily Athens
primary goals: elimination of US military bases in Greece, opposition to capitalism and NATO/EU membership

**Revolutionary Organization 17 November**
Founded in 1975; relatively small group operating secretly.
country or region of operation: Greece, primarily Athens
primary goals: elimination of US military bases in Greece, removal of Turkish forces from Cyprus, opposition to capitalism and NATO/EU membership

**Revolutionary People's Liberation Party/Front (DHKP/C)** (Devrimci Sol, Revolutionary Left, Dev Sol)
Founded in 1978 as splinter group from Turkish People's Liberation Party/Front; led by Dursun Karatas.
country or region of operation: Turkey, primarily Istanbul
primary goals: promotion of Marxism, opposition to US and NATO

**Shining Path (Sendero Luminoso, SL)**
Founded late 1960s by Abimael Guzman; led by Macario Ala.
country or region of operation: Peru, primarily rural areas
primary goals: replacement of Peruvian government with communist state, opposition to influence by foreign governments

**United Self-Defense Forces of Colombia (Autodefensas Unidas de Colombia, AUC)**
Founded in 1997 as umbrella organization of paramilitary groups; led by Carlos Castaño.
country or region of operation: Colombia
primary goals: opposition to and defense against leftist guerrilla groups

# Universal Declaration of Human Rights

*Completed by the UN Commission on Human Rights in June 1948, the Declaration was adopted by the General Assembly on 10 Dec 1948 by unanimous vote (with the six members of the Soviet bloc, Saudi Arabia, and the Union of South Africa abstaining). The declaration contained general definitions not only of those principal civil and political rights recognized in democratic constitutions but also of several so-called economic, social, and cultural rights.*

**Preamble**
*Whereas* recognition of the inherent dignity and of the equal and inalienable rights of all members of the human family is the foundation of freedom, justice and peace in the world,

*Whereas* disregard and contempt for human rights have resulted in barbarous acts which have outraged the conscience of mankind, and the advent of a world in which human beings shall enjoy freedom of speech and belief and freedom from fear and want has been proclaimed as the highest aspiration

of the common people,

*Whereas* it is essential, if man is not to be compelled to have recourse, as a last resort, to rebellion against tyranny and oppression, that human rights should be protected by the rule of law,

*Whereas* it is essential to promote the development of friendly relations between nations,

*Whereas* the peoples of the United Nations have in the Charter reaffirmed their faith in fundamental human rights, in the dignity and worth of the human person and in the equal rights of men and women and have determined to promote social progress and better standards of life in larger freedom,

*Whereas* Member States have pledged themselves to achieve, in co-operation with the United Nations, the promotion of universal respect for and observance of human rights and fundamental freedoms,

*Whereas* a common understanding of these rights and freedoms is of the greatest importance for the full realization of this pledge,

*Now, therefore,*

*The General Assembly*

Proclaims this Universal Declaration of Human Rights as a common standard of achievement for all peoples and all nations, to the end that every individual and every organ of society, keeping this Declaration constantly in mind, shall strive by teaching and education to promote respect for these rights and freedoms and by progressive measures, national and international, to secure their universal and effective recognition and observance, both among the peoples of Member States themselves and among the peoples of territories under their jurisdiction.

### Article 1
All human beings are born free and equal in dignity and rights. They are endowed with reason and conscience and should act towards one another in a spirit of brotherhood.

### Article 2
Everyone is entitled to all the rights and freedoms set forth in this Declaration, without distinction of any kind, such as race, colour, sex, language, religion, political or other opinion, national or social origin, property, birth or other status.

Furthermore, no distinction shall be made on the basis of the political, jurisdictional or international status of the country or territory to which a person belongs, whether it be independent, trust, non-self-governing or under any other limitation of sovereignty.

### Article 3
Everyone has the right to life, liberty and the security of person.

### Article 4
No one shall be held in slavery or servitude; slavery and the slave trade shall be prohibited in all their forms.

### Article 5
No one shall be subjected to torture or to cruel, inhuman or degrading treatment or punishment.

### Article 6
Everyone has the right to recognition everywhere as a person before the law.

### Article 7
All are equal before the law and are entitled without any discrimination to equal protection of the law. All are entitled to equal protection against any discrimination in violation of this Declaration and against any incitement to such discrimination.

### Article 8
Everyone has the right to an effective remedy by the competent national tribunals for acts violating the fundamental rights granted him by the constitution or by law.

### Article 9
No one shall be subjected to arbitrary arrest, detention or exile.

### Article 10
Everyone is entitled in full equality to a fair and public hearing by an independent and impartial tribunal, in the determination of his rights and obligations and of any criminal charge against him.

### Article 11
1. Everyone charged with a penal offence has the right to be presumed innocent until proved guilty according to law in a public trial at which he has had all the guarantees necessary for his defence.

2. No one shall be held guilty of any penal offence on account of any act or omission which did not constitute a penal offence, under national or international law, at the time when it was committed. Nor shall a heavier penalty be imposed than the one that was applicable at the time the penal offence was committed.

### Article 12
No one shall be subjected to arbitrary interference with his privacy, family, home or correspondence, nor to attacks upon his honour and reputation. Everyone has the right to the protection of the law against such interference or attacks.

### Article 13
1. Everyone has the right to freedom of movement and residence within the borders of each state.

2. Everyone has the right to leave any country, including his own, and to return to his country.

### Article 14
1. Everyone has the right to seek and to enjoy in other countries asylum from persecution.

2. This right may not be invoked in the case of prosecutions genuinely arising from non-political crimes or from acts contrary to the purposes and principles of the United Nations.

### Article 15
1. Everyone has the right to a nationality.

2. No one shall be arbitrarily deprived of his nationality nor denied the right to change his nationality.

### Article 16
1. Men and women of full age, without any limitation due to race, nationality or religion, have the right to marry and to found a family. They are entitled to equal rights as to marriage, during marriage and at its dissolution.

2. Marriage shall be entered into only with the free and full consent of the intending spouses.

3. The family is the natural and fundamental group unit of society and is entitled to protection by society and the State.

### Article 17

1. Everyone has the right to own property alone as well as in association with others.

2. No one shall be arbitrarily deprived of his property.

### Article 18

Everyone has the right to freedom of thought, conscience and religion; this right includes freedom to change his religion or belief, and freedom, either alone or in community with others and in public or private, to manifest his religion or belief in teaching, practice, worship and observance.

### Article 19

Everyone has the right to freedom of opinion and expression; this right includes freedom to hold opinions without interference and to seek, receive and impart information and ideas through any media and regardless of frontiers.

### Article 20

1. Everyone has the right to freedom of peaceful assembly and association.

2. No one may be compelled to belong to an association.

### Article 21

1. Everyone has the right to take part in the government of his country, directly or through freely chosen representatives.

2. Everyone has the right of equal access to public service in his country.

3. The will of the people shall be the basis of the authority of government; this will shall be expressed in periodic and genuine elections which shall be by universal and equal suffrage and shall be held by secret vote or by equivalent free voting procedures.

### Article 22

Everyone, as a member of society, has the right to social security and is entitled to realization, through national effort and international co-operation and in accordance with the organization and resources of each State, of the economic, social and cultural rights indispensable for his dignity and the free development of his personality.

### Article 23

1. Everyone has the right to work, to free choice of employment, to just and favourable conditions of work and to protection against unemployment.

2. Everyone, without any discrimination, has the right to equal pay for equal work.

3. Everyone who works has the right to just and favourable remuneration ensuring for himself and his family an existence worthy of human dignity, and supplemented, if necessary, by other means of social protection.

4. Everyone has the right to form and to join trade unions for the protection of his interests.

### Article 24

Everyone has the right to rest and leisure, including reasonable limitation of working hours and periodic holidays with pay.

### Article 25

1. Everyone has the right to a standard of living adequate for the health and well-being of himself and of his family, including food, clothing, housing and medical care and necessary social services, and the right to security in the event of unemployment, sickness, disability, widowhood, old age or other lack of livelihood in circumstances beyond his control.

2. Motherhood and childhood are entitled to special care and assistance. All children, whether born in or out of wedlock, shall enjoy the same social protection.

### Article 26

1. Everyone has the right to education. Education shall be free, at least in the elementary and fundamental stages. Elementary education shall be compulsory. Technical and professional education shall be made generally available and higher education shall be equally accessible to all on the basis of merit.

2. Education shall be directed to the full development of the human personality and to the strengthening of respect for human rights and fundamental freedoms. It shall promote understanding, tolerance and friendship among all nations, racial or religious groups, and shall further the activities of the United Nations for the maintenance of peace.

3. Parents have a prior right to choose the kind of education that shall be given to their children.

### Article 27

1. Everyone has the right freely to participate in the cultural life of the community, to enjoy the arts and to share in scientific advancement and its benefits.

2. Everyone has the right to the protection of the moral and material interests resulting from any scientific, literary or artistic production of which he is the author.

### Article 28

Everyone is entitled to a social and international order in which the rights and freedoms set forth in this Declaration can be fully realized.

### Article 29

1. Everyone has duties to the community in which alone the free and full development of his personality is possible.

2. In the exercise of his rights and freedoms, everyone shall be subject only to such limitations as are determined by law solely for the purpose of securing due recognition and respect for the rights and freedoms of others and of meeting the just requirements of morality, public order and the general welfare in a democratic society.

3. These rights and freedoms may in no case be exercised contrary to the purposes and principles of the United Nations.

### Article 30

Nothing in this Declaration may be interpreted as implying for any State, group or person any right to engage in any activity or to perform any act aimed at the destruction of any of the rights and freedoms set forth herein.

 In 2000 The Netherlands became the first country in the world to legalize same-sex marriages.

# The International Court of Justice

*The International Court of Justice is the principal judicial organ of the United Nations. Its seat is at the Peace Palace in The Hague (The Netherlands). It began work in 1946, when it replaced the Permanent Court of International Justice which had functioned in the Peace Palace since 1922. It operates under a Statute largely similar to that of its predecessor, which is an integral part of the Charter of the United Nations.*

## Functions of the Court

The Court has a dual role: to settle in accordance with international law the legal disputes submitted to it by States, and to give advisory opinions on legal questions referred to it by duly authorized international organs and agencies.

## Composition

The Court is composed of 15 judges elected to nine-year terms of office by the United Nations General Assembly and Security Council sitting independently of each other. It may not include more than one judge of any nationality. Elections are held every three years for one-third of the seats, and retiring judges may be re-elected. The Members of the Court do not represent their governments but are independent magistrates.

The judges must possess the qualifications required in their respective countries for appointment to the highest judicial offices, or be jurists of recognized competence in international law. The composition of the Court has also to reflect the main forms of civilization and the principal legal systems of the world.

When the Court does not include a judge possessing the nationality of a State party to a case, that State may appoint a person to sit as a judge ad hoc for the purpose of the case.

The present composition of the Court is as follows: President Gilbert Guillaume (France), Vice-President Shi Jiuyong (China), Judges Shigeru Oda (Japan), Raymond Ranjeva (Madagascar), Géza Herczegh (Hungary), Carl-August Fleischhauer (Germany), Abdul G. Koroma (Sierra Leone), Vladlen S. Vereshchetin (Russian Federation), Rosalyn Higgins (United Kingdom), Gonzalo Parra-Aranguren (Venezuela), Pieter H. Kooijmans (Netherlands), Francisco Rezek (Brazil), Awn Shawkat Al-Khasawneh (Jordan), Thomas Buergenthal (United States of America) and Nabil Elaraby (Egypt).

The Registrar of the Court is Mr. Philippe Couvreur (Belgium) and Deputy-Registrar of the Court is Mr. Jean-Jacques Arnaldez (France).

## Cases between States

**The Parties:** Only States may apply to and appear before the Court. The States Members of the United Nations (at present numbering 189), and one State which is not a Member of the United Nations but which has become party to the Court's Statute (Switzerland), are so entitled.

**Jurisdiction:** The Court is competent to entertain a dispute only if the States concerned have accepted its jurisdiction in one or more of the following ways:
1. by the conclusion between them of a special agreement to submit the dispute to the Court;

2. by virtue of a jurisdictional clause, i.e., typically, when they are parties to a treaty containing a provision whereby, in the event of a disagreement over its interpretation or application, one of them may refer the dispute to the Court. Several hundred treaties or conventions contain a clause to such effect;
3. through the reciprocal effect of declarations made by them under the Statute whereby each has accepted the jurisdiction of the Court as compulsory in the event of a dispute with another State having made a similar declaration. The declarations of 64 States are at present in force, a number of them having been made subject to the exclusion of certain categories of dispute.

In cases of doubt as to whether the Court has jurisdiction, it is the Court itself which decides.

**Procedure:** The procedure followed by the Court in contentious cases is defined in its Statute, and in the Rules of Court adopted by it under the Statute. The latest version of the Rules dates from 5 December 2000. The proceedings include a written phase, in which the parties file and exchange pleadings, and an oral phase consisting of public hearings at which agents and counsel address the Court. As the Court has two official languages (English and French) everything written or said in one is translated into the other.

After the oral proceedings the Court deliberates in camera and then delivers its judgment at a public sitting. The judgment is final and without appeal. Should one of the States involved fail to comply with it, the other party may have recourse to the Security Council of the United Nations.

The Court discharges its duties as a full court but, at the request of the parties, it may also establish a special chamber. The Court constituted such a chamber in 1982 for the first time, formed a second one in 1985 and constituted two more in 1987. A Chamber of Summary Procedure is elected every year by the Court in accordance with its Statute. In July 1993 the Court has also established a seven-member Chamber to deal with any environmental cases falling within its jurisdiction.

Since 1946 the Court has delivered 74 Judgments on disputes concerning inter alia land frontiers and maritime boundaries, territorial sovereignty, the non-use of force, non-interference in the internal affairs of States, diplomatic relations, hostage-taking, the right of asylum, nationality, guardianship, rights of passage and economic rights.

**Sources of applicable law:** The Court decides in accordance with international treaties and conventions in force, international custom, the general principles of law and, as subsidiary means, judicial decisions and the teachings of the most highly qualified publicists.

### Advisory Opinions

The advisory procedure of the Court is open solely to international organizations. The only bodies at present authorized to request advisory opinions of the Court are five organs of the United Nations and 16 specialized agencies of the United Nations family.

On receiving a request, the Court decides which States and organizations might provide useful information and gives them an opportunity of presenting written or oral statements. The Court's advisory procedure is otherwise modelled on that for contentious proceedings, and the sources of applicable law are the same.

In principle the Court's advisory opinions are consultative in character and are therefore not binding as such on the requesting bodies. Certain instruments or regulations can, however, provide in advance that the advisory opinion shall be binding.

Since 1946 the Court has given 24 Advisory Opinions, concerning inter alia admission to United Nations membership, reparation for injuries suffered in the service of the United Nations, territorial status of South-West Africa (Namibia) and Western Sahara, judgments rendered by international administrative tribunals, expenses of certain United Nations operations, applicability of the United Nations Headquarters Agreement, the status of human rights rapporteurs, and the legality of the threat or use of nuclear weapons.

Internet resources: <www.icj-cij.org>.

---

Sweden has been at peace since 1814, following the doctrine of "nonalignment in peace aiming at neutrality in war." Disavowing the military aggressiveness that once involved its armies deeply in Europe's centuries of dynastic warfare, Sweden has chosen instead to play a balancing role among the world's conflicting ideological and political systems. It is for this reason that Swedish statesmen have often been sought out to fill major positions in the United Nations.

---

# Military Affairs

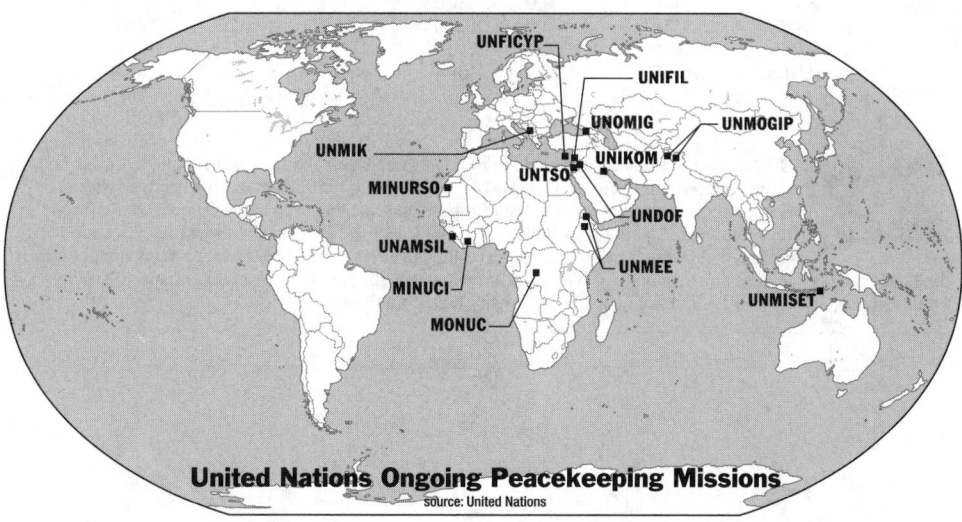

United Nations Ongoing Peacekeeping Missions
source: United Nations

**MINUCI** – United Nations Mission in Côte d'Ivoire – since May 2003

**MINURSO** – United Nations Mission for the Referendum in Western Sahara – since April 1991

**MONUC** – United Nations Organization Mission in the Democratic Republic of the Congo – since December 1999

**UNAMSIL** – United Nations Mission in Sierra Leone – since October 1999

**UNDOF** – United Nations Disengagement Observer Force – since June 1974

**UNFICYP** – United Nations Peacekeeping Force in Cyprus – since March 1964

**UNIFIL** – United Nations Interim Force in Lebanon – since March 1978

**UNIKOM** – United Nations Iraq-Kuwait Observation Mission – since April 1991

**UNMEE** – United Nations Mission in Ethiopia and Eritrea – since July 2000

**UNMIK** – United Nations Interim Administration Mission in Kosovo – since June 1999

**UNMISET** – United Nations Mission of Support in East Timor – since May 2002

**UNMOGIP** – United Nations Military Observer Group in India and Pakistan – since January 1949

**UNOMIG** – United Nations Observer Mission in Georgia – since August 1993

**UNTSO** – United Nations Truce Supervision Organization – since June 1948

## Nations with Largest Armed Forces

*Countries with a military strength of at least 200,000 active personnel. Personnel numbers are in thousands ('000), except for Chinese and Vietnamese reserves. Dollars refer to US currency.*
*Source: The Military Balance, 2002–03, The International Institute of Strategic Studies.*

| COUNTRY | MILITARY PERSONNEL ACTIVE | MILITARY PERSONNEL RESERVES | DEFENSE SPENDING ($ BILLIONS) | ARMY MAIN BATTLE TANKS | NAVY MAJOR WARSHIPS/ CARRIERS | NAVY SUB-MARINES | AIR FORCE COMBAT AIRCRAFT | STRATEGIC NUCLEAR WEAPONS |
|---|---|---|---|---|---|---|---|---|
| China | 2,270.0 | >500 | 47.0 | 7,010 | 63/0 | 69 | >1,900 | yes |
| US | 1,414.0 | 1,259.3 | 347.9 | 7,620 | 129/12 | 72 | 3,136 | yes |
| India | 1,298.0 | 535.0 | 14.3 | 3,898 | 27/1 | 16 | 701 | yes |
| N. Korea | 1,082.0 | 4,700.0 | 2.1 | 3,500 | 3/0 | 26 | 621 | yes |
| Russia | 988.1 | 2,400.0 | 65.0 | 21,870 | 32/1 | 53 | 1,736 | yes |
| S. Korea | 686.0 | 4,500.0 | 11.4 | 2,330 | 39/0 | 20 | 538 | |
| Pakistan | 620.0 | 513.0 | 2.4 | >2,300 | 8/0 | 10 | 366 | yes |
| Iran | 520.0 | 350.0 | 4.8 | 1,565 | 3/0 | 6 | 306 | |
| Turkey | 514.9 | 378.7 | 7.4 | 4,205 | 19/0 | 13 | 485 | |
| Vietnam | 484.0 | >3,000 | 2.4 | 1,315 | 6/0 | 2 | 189 | |
| Myanmar | 444.0 | 0.0 | 1.1 | 100 | 0/0 | 0 | 113 | |
| Egypt | 443.0 | 254.0 | 4.4 | 3,860 | 11/0 | 4 | 608 | |
| Iraq | 389.0 | 650.0 | 1.4 | 2,600 | 0/0 | 0 | 316 | |
| Taiwan | 370.0 | 1,657.0 | 10.7 | >926 | 32/0 | 4 | 479 | |
| Syria | 319.0 | 354.0 | 1.9 | 4,700 | 2/0 | 0 | 611 | |
| Thailand | 306.0 | 200.0 | 1.9 | 333 | 13/1 | 0 | 194 | |
| Ukraine | 302.3 | 1,000.0 | 5.0 | 3,905 | 3/0 | 1 | 499 | |
| Indonesia | 297.0 | 400.0 | 0.9 | 0 | 17/0 | 2 | 90 | |
| Germany | 296.0 | 390.3 | 27.5 | 2,490 | 14/0 | 14 | 446 | |
| Brazil | 287.6 | 1,115.0 | 10.7 | 87 | 19/1 | 4 | 264 | |
| France | 260.4 | 100.0 | 33.6 | 786 | 35/1 | 10 | 449 | yes |
| Ethiopia | 252.5 | 0.0 | 0.6 | >300 | 0/0 | 0 | 55 | |
| Japan | 239.9 | 47.4 | 40.3 | 1,040 | 54/0 | 16 | 280 | |
| Italy | 216.8 | 65.2 | 21.4 | 1,018 | 20/1 | 6 | 261 | |
| UK | 210.5 | 256.8 | 35.4 | 594 | 35/3 | 16 | 332 | yes |

**Did you know?** In 17th-century Holland a speculative frenzy erupted over the sale of tulip bulbs. Tulips had been introduced into Europe from Turkey shortly after 1550. Demand for new varieties soon exceeded the supply, and prices rose to astonishing heights. The craze, known as the Tulip Mania, reached its peak in Holland in 1633–37. Homes, estates, and industries were mortgaged so that bulbs could be purchased; bulbs of rare varieties sold for the equivalent of hundreds of dollars each. The crash came in 1637, when almost overnight the price structure collapsed, sweeping away fortunes and leaving behind financial ruin for many Dutch families.

# United States

## United States History

### United States Chronology

**1492** Christopher Columbus, sailing under the Spanish flag, discovers America, 12 October.

**1497** John Cabot, representing England, explores Atlantic coast of what is now Canada.

**1513** Ponce de León of Spain lands in Florida and gives that region its name.

**1519–22** Magellan's Spanish ship—the *Vittoria*—is the first to sail around the world.

**1534** France sends out Jacques Cartier to find a route to the Far East; he explores along the St. Lawrence River, and France then lays claim to part of North America.

**1541** Hernando de Soto of Spain discovers Mississippi River near site of Memphis.

**1565** St. Augustine, oldest permanent settlement in the US, founded by Spaniards.

**1587** A party under John White lands at Roanoke Island (now North Carolina); when White returns three years later, entire settlement has disappeared.

**1607** English make first permanent settlement in New World at Jamestown; Virginia becomes first of 13 English colonies.

**1619** First representative assembly in America, the House of Burgesses, meets in Virginia; first blacks land in Virginia.

**1620** Pilgrims from ship *Mayflower* found settlement at Plymouth.

**1649** Act Concerning Religion passed by Maryland legislature is first law of religious toleration in English colonies.

**1682** La Salle explores lower Mississippi Valley and claims entire region for France.

**1733** Georgia, 13th and last of English colonies in America, is founded.

**1754** Both England and the colonies reject Albany Plan of Union to unite colonies. Decisive French and Indian War between France and England begins in America.

**1763** Treaty of Paris ends French and Indian War; Britain wins control of New World; Louisiana ceded to Spain; Florida, to Britain.

**1765** Quartering Act and Stamp Act anger Americans; nine colonies represented at Stamp Act Congress.

**1770** British troops fire on a crowd, killing five people in the so-called Boston Massacre.

**1772** Committees of Correspondence organized in almost all colonies.

**1773** Boston Tea Party is first action in chain leading to war with Britain.

**1774** First Continental Congress meets at Philadelphia; protests Five Intolerable Acts.

**1775** Battles of Lexington and Concord, Bunker Hill; Second Continental Congress meets.

**1776** Declaration of Independence is adopted. Washington crosses the Delaware to fight at Trenton.

**1777** Americans capture General Burgoyne and large British force at Saratoga, New York.

**1778–79** Gen. George Rogers Clark leads victorious expedition into Northwest Territory.

**1781** Washington accepts surrender of Cornwallis at Yorktown, Virginia. Articles of Confederation become government of the US.

**1783** Treaty of peace with Great Britain signed at Paris, formally ending Revolutionary War.

**1786–87** Shays's Rebellion in Massachusetts shows weaknesses of Confederation government.

**1787** Northwest Territory organized by Congress. Convention meets to draft new constitution.

**1788** US Constitution is ratified by necessary nine states to ensure adoption.

**1789** New US government goes into effect; Washington inaugurated president; first Congress meets in New York City.

**1791** Bill of Rights added to Constitution. Vermont is first new state admitted to Union.

**1793** Eli Whitney invents cotton gin, which leads to large-scale cotton growing in the South.

**1800** National capital moved from Philadelphia PA to Washington DC.

**1803** Louisiana purchased from France. Supreme Court makes *Marbury* v. *Madison* decision; Congress halts the importation of slaves into the US after 1807.

**1804–06** Lewis and Clark blaze overland trail to the Pacific and return.

**1807** Robert Fulton's steamboat makes successful journey from New York City to Albany NY.

**1812–14** US maintains its independence in conflict with Britain, War of 1812.

**1818** US and Canada settle boundary dispute, agree on open border between countries.

**1820** Missouri Compromise settles problem of slavery in new states for next 30 years.

**1823** Monroe Doctrine warns European nations that US will protect the Americas.

**1825** Erie Canal, from Hudson River to Great Lakes, becomes great water highway to Middle West.

**1829** Inauguration of Pres. Andrew Jackson introduces era of Jacksonian Democracy.

**1836** Texas wins its independence from Mexico.

**1843** First great migration begins on Oregon Trail.

**1845** Texas annexed and admitted as a state.

**1846** Oregon boundary dispute settled with Britain. Mexican War begins.

**1847** Brigham Young leads party of Mormons into Salt Lake Valley UT.

**1848** Mexican War ends; US gains possession of California and New Mexico regions.

**1849** Gold rush to California begins.

**1850** Compromise of 1850 admits California as free state; postpones war between North and South.

**1853** Gadsden Purchase adds 117,935 sq km (45,535 sq mi) to what is now southern Arizona and New Mexico.

**1854** Kansas-Nebraska Act reopens slavery issue, leads to organization of Republican party.

**1857** Dred Scott Decision of Supreme Court declares Missouri Compromise illegal.

**1860** Lincoln elected president; South Carolina secedes from the Union.

**1861** Confederate States of America formed; Civil War begins; Union forces routed at Bull Run VA. Telegraph links New York City with San Francisco CA.

**1862** Grant launches Union attack in the West; Confederate invasion of Maryland halted at Antietam. Homestead Act grants 160 acres to each settler.

**1863** Federal forces win decisive battles at Gettysburg, Vicksburg, and Chattanooga. Emancipation Proclamation takes effect.

**1864** Sherman captures Atlanta and marches across Georgia. Grant closes in on Richmond VA.

**1865** Lee surrenders to Grant at Appomattox Court House VA, ending Civil War. Lincoln is assassinated.

**1867** Reconstruction acts impose military rule on South. Alaska purchased from Russia.

**1869** First transcontinental railroad completed as two lines meet at Promontory UT.

**1876** Telephone is invented. Centennial Exposition in Philadelphia PA celebrates 100th birthday of the US.

**1877** Withdrawal of last federal troops from South ends Reconstruction period. Railroad workers begin first nationwide strike.

**1879** First practical electric light is invented by Thomas A. Edison.

**1883** Pendleton Civil Service Act provides for examinations as basis of appointment to some government positions.

**1884–85** First skyscraper, the Home Insurance Building, is erected in Chicago.

**1886** American Federation of Labor is organized; first president is Samuel Gompers.

**1887** Interstate Commerce Act adopted to control railroads that cross state lines.

**1889–90** First Pan American Conference is held in Washington DC.

**1890** Sherman Anti-Trust Act is passed in effort to curb growth of monopolies.

**1896** Henry Ford's first car is driven on streets of Detroit MI.

**1898** US wins Spanish-American War; gains Philippines, Puerto Rico, and Guam.

**1903** Air age begins with successful airplane flight by Wright brothers.

**1906** Federal Food and Drug Act passed to protect public from impure food and drugs.

**1912** New Mexico and Arizona, 47th and 48th states, admitted to the Union.

**1913** Federal income tax authorized by 16th Amendment; 17th Amendment provides for popular election of US senators.

**1914** Panama Canal opened. World War I breaks out in Europe; Pres. Woodrow Wilson appeals for neutrality in the US.

**1915** German submarine sinks *Lusitania* with loss of 124 American lives. Telephone line established coast to coast.

**1917** Germany begins open submarine warfare; US declares war against Germany.

**1918** Pres. Wilson proposes "Fourteen Points" as basis for peace. Americans fight at Chateau-Thierry, Belleau Wood, St-Mihiel, Argonne Forest. Armistice ends war.

**1918–19** Pres. Wilson attends Paris Peace Conference of victorious nations.

**1919** US Senate rejects League of Nations. Navy pilots make first flight across Atlantic. Prohibition established by 18th Amendment.

**1920** Right to vote given women by 19th Amendment. Pittsburgh PA radio station, KDKA, begins broadcasting.

**1921** Immigration restricted according to national quotas.

**1921–22** Washington Conference restricts warship construction among chief naval powers.

**1924** Army plane *Chicago* makes first flight around the world.

**1927** Charles A. Lindbergh makes first nonstop solo flight across Atlantic.

**1928** US signs Kellogg-Briand Pact to outlaw war.

**1929** Stock market reaches new high, then crashes. Panic marks beginning of Great Depression; millions of workers are unemployed.

**1932** Franklin Delano Roosevelt elected president.

**1933** New Deal launched; gold standard suspended; National Recovery Act passed; bank deposits insured; Tennessee Valley Authority organized. 21st Amendment repeals prohibition.

**1934** Congress tightens control over securities; passes first Reciprocal Trade Agreement Act; launches federal housing program.

**1935** National Labor Relations (Wagner) Act guarantees collective bargaining to labor. Social Security Act passed. CIO founded.

**1936** Hoover Dam (Boulder Dam) completed across Colorado River.

**1938** Fair Labor Standards Act provides federal yardstick for wages and hours of workers.

**1939** Germany invades Poland to start World War II. US declares neutrality.

**1940** US begins huge rearmament program; first peacetime draft takes effect. Roosevelt defies tradition and accepts presidential nomination for a third term.

**1941** Lend-Lease Act passed. Atlantic Charter signed. Japanese attack on Pearl Harbor brings US into World War II.

**1942** Americans launch counteroffensive in Pacific. Allies invade North Africa.

**1943** Allied invasion of Italy is first landing on European continent.

**1944** Allies launch greatest sea-to-land assault in history in invasion of France. Allies invade Philippines. "GI Bill of Rights" passed.

**1945** Germany surrenders, 8 May; atomic bomb dropped on Hiroshima, 6 August; Japan surrenders, 2 September. Cold War begins between US and Soviet Union. United Nations (UN) formally launched on 24 October.

**1946** Philippines granted independence by US. Atomic Energy Commission created.

**1947** Senate passes Truman Doctrine. Taft-Hartley labor law enacted. Department of Defense consolidates Army, Navy, and Air Force.

**1948** European Recovery Program enacted. Truman elected president.

**1949** Fair Deal program announced. US and its allies force Soviet Union to lift Berlin blockade. North Atlantic Treaty Organization (NATO) founded.

**1950** US and several other members of UN send military forces to aid of Republic of Korea; bitter war develops.

**1951** Two-term limit put on presidency by ratification of 22nd Amendment to Constitution.

**1952** US and allies end occupation of West Germany. Election of Eisenhower ends 20 years of Democratic governance.

**1953** Korean War ends. Department of Health, Education, and Welfare becomes 10th Cabinet post.

**1954** Racial segregation of public schools declared illegal by Supreme Court. Southeast Asia Treaty Organization (SEATO) founded.

**1955** Two largest labor organizations merge into one group—the AFL-CIO. Salk poliomyelitis vaccine is proved successful.

**1956** Eisenhower reelected president. Democrats win control of Congress.

**1957** Eisenhower Doctrine to strengthen US position in Middle East adopted.

**1958** First US artificial Earth satellite launched. US joins the International Atomic Energy Agency.

**1959** Alaska becomes 49th state, Hawaii the 50th.

**1960** US reconnaissance plane shot down over Soviet Union.

**1961** CIA is involved in unsuccessful invasion of Cuba at Bay of Pigs. 23rd Amendment to Constitution gives Washington DC residents right to vote in presidential elections. First American makes spaceflight. American troops sent to defend West Berlin.

**1962** Cuban missile crisis erupts; Soviets remove missiles from Cuba on US urging.

**1963** March on Washington for Jobs and Freedom takes place. Pres. John F. Kennedy assassinated in Dallas TX. Nuclear test-ban treaty signed.

**1964** 24th Amendment to Constitution bans poll taxes in federal elections. Civil rights bill passed. Supreme Court makes possible reapportionment.

**1965** US combat forces fight in Vietnam. Voting-rights bill and Medicare act signed. Department of Housing and Urban Development becomes 11th Cabinet post.

**1966** Department of Transportation becomes 12th Cabinet post.

**1967** 25th Amendment to Constitution provides for presidential succession.

**1968** Assassinations of Martin Luther King, Jr., and Robert F. Kennedy provoke race riots.

**1969** US astronauts become the first men to land on the moon.

**1970** Four students at Kent State University in Ohio killed by National Guard during anti-Vietnam War protest.

**1971** 26th Amendment to Constitution gives 18-year-olds right to vote in all elections.

**1972** Pres. Richard M. Nixon visits China and Soviet Union.

**1973** US withdraws troops from Vietnam. Vice-Pres. Spiro T. Agnew resigns. OPEC raises price of petroleum 400%.

**1974** Watergate scandal and threat of impeachment force Nixon to resign.

**1977** Department of Energy becomes new Cabinet post. Treaty altered to return Panama Canal to Panama by year 2000.

**1978** Pres. Jimmy Carter hosts Camp David talks between Israel's Menachem Begin and Egypt's Anwar el-Sadat.

**1979** Strategic Arms Limitation Talks (SALT II) signed by US and Soviet Union. Militants seize 66 American hostages in takeover of US embassy in Iran.

**1980** Department of Health, Education, and Welfare is separated into Department of Health and Human Services and Department of Education.

**1981** Pres. Ronald Reagan wounded in assassination attempt. Major tax cut and increased defense spending pass Congress. Sandra Day O'Connor appointed first woman Supreme Court justice.

**1983** Reagan announces Star Wars missile-defense program. US invades Grenada.

**1985** Summit conference between Reagan and Soviet leader Mikhail Gorbachev held in Geneva, Switzerland.

**1986** Space shuttle *Challenger* explodes shortly after liftoff. US bombs targets in Libya. Summit conference in Iceland fails. Iran-contra affair revealed.

**1987** Iran-contra hearings held. Stock market collapses. Reagan and Gorbachev sign Intermediate-Range Nuclear Forces (INF) treaty.

**1988** Fourth Reagan-Gorbachev summit held in Moscow. Department of Veterans Affairs approved as Cabinet post.

**1989** *Exxon Valdez* supertanker spills 10 million gallons of crude oil off Alaskan coast. US invades Panama. Berlin Wall ceases to divide the two Germanys, signaling the end of the Cold War.

**1990** Troops sent to Saudi Arabia in response to Iraq's invasion of Kuwait.

**1991** Air and ground war leads to Iraqi surrender and withdrawal from Kuwait. Soviet Union comes apart.

**1992** 27th Amendment to Constitution bars Congress from giving itself a midterm pay raise. Riots erupt in Los Angeles CA after jury fails to convict white policemen accused of beating African American Rodney King. North American Free Trade Agreement (NAFTA) signed by US, Canada, and Mexico.

**1993** Janet Reno becomes the first woman attorney general. World Trade Center in New York City bombed.

**1995** Timothy McVeigh detonates a bomb in a terrorist attack on the Alfred P. Murrah Federal Building in Oklahoma City OK, killing 168 people.

**1998** Pres. Clinton impeached for perjury and obstruction of justice; he is acquitted by the Senate the following year.

**2000** The results of the presidential election are challenged by Vice Pres. Al Gore; US Supreme Court overrules Florida Supreme Court's order for a statewide manual recount of ballots; George W. Bush wins the presidency.

**2001** On 11 September, two hijacked airplanes hit the World Trade Center in New York City; another crashes into the Pentagon outside Washington DC; and a fourth crashes in the southern Pennsylvania countryside. Pres. Bush calls for a global war on terrorism and sends US troops into Afghanistan, eventually helping to displace the Taliban regime.

**2002** Republicans take control of both houses of Congress, holding both the legislative and the executive branches of government for the first time since 1952.

**2003** The US launches a war to depose the Saddam Hussein regime in Iraq and takes control of the country after just weeks of fighting. Congress passes a $350 billion tax cut. Tens of millions in the Northeast lose electricity when a massive failure on the nation's eastern power grid occurs.

# Important Documents in US History

## Mayflower Compact

*On 21 Nov 1620 (11 November, Old Style), 41 male passengers on the Mayflower signed the following compact prior to their landing at Plymouth (now Massachusetts). The compact resulted from the fear that some members of the company might leave the group and settle on their own. The Mayflower Compact bound the signers into a body politic for the purpose of forming a government and pledged them to abide by any laws and regulations that would later by established. The document was not a constitution but rather an adaptation of the usual church covenant to a civil situation. It became the foundation of Plymouth's government.*

In the name of God, Amen.

We whose names are underwritten, the loyal subjects of our dread sovereign Lord, King James, by the grace of God, of Great Britain, France and Ireland king, defender of the faith, etc., having undertaken, for the glory of God, and advancement of the Christian faith, and honor of our king and country, a voyage to plant the first colony in the Northern parts of Virginia, do by these presents solemnly and mutually in the presence of God, and one of another, covenant and combine ourselves together into a civil body politic, for our better ordering and preservation and furtherance of the ends aforesaid; and by virtue hereof to enact, constitute, and frame such just and equal laws, ordinances, acts, constitutions, and offices, from time to time, as shall be thought most meet and convenient for the general good of the colony, unto which we promise all due submission and obedience.

In witness whereof we have hereunder subscribed our names at Cape-Cod the 11 of November, in the year of the reign of our sovereign lord, King James, of England, France, and Ireland the eighteenth, and of Scotland the fifty-fourth. Anno Domine 1620.

## Declaration of Independence

*On 4 Jul 1776 the Continental Congress officially adopted the Declaration of Independence. Two days before, the Congress had "unanimously" voted (with New York abstaining) to be free and independent from Britain. The Declaration of Independence was written largely by Thomas Jefferson. After modifications by the Congress, the document was prepared and voted upon. New York delegates voted to accept it on 15 July, and on 19 July the Congress ordered the document to be engrossed as "The Unanimous Declaration of the Thirteen United States of America." It was accordingly put on parchment, and members of the Congress present on 2 August affixed their signatures to this parchment copy on that day, and others later. The last signer was Thomas McKean of Delaware, whose name was not placed on the document before 1777.*

The Unanimous Declaration of the Thirteen United States of America

When in the Course of human events, it becomes necessary for one people to dissolve the political bands which have connected them with another, and to assume among the powers of the earth, the separate and equal station to which the Laws of Nature and of Nature's God entitle them, a decent respect to the opinions of mankind requires that they should declare the causes which impel them to the separation.—We hold these truths to be self-evident, that all men are created equal, that they are endowed by their Creator with certain unalienable Rights, that among these are Life, Liberty and the pursuit of Happiness.—That to secure these rights, Governments are instituted among Men, deriving their just powers from the consent of the governed,—That whenever any Form of Government becomes destructive of these ends, it is the Right of the People to alter or to abolish it, and to institute new Government, laying its foundation on such principles and organizing its powers in such form, as to them shall seem most likely to effect their Safety and Happiness. Prudence, indeed, will dictate that Governments long established should not be changed for light and transient causes; and accordingly all experience hath shown, that mankind are more disposed to suffer, while evils are sufferable, than to right themselves by abolishing the forms to which they are accustomed. But when a long train of abuses and usurpations, pursuing invariably the same Object evinces a design to reduce them under absolute Despotism, it is their right, it is their duty, to throw off such Government, and to provide new Guards for their future security.—Such has been the patient sufferance of these Colonies; and such is now the necessity which constrains them to alter their former Systems of Government. The history of the present King of Great Britain is a history of repeated injuries and usurpations, all having in direct object the establishment of an absolute Tyranny over these States.

To prove this, let Facts be submitted to a candid world.—He has refused his Assent to Laws, the most wholesome and necessary for the public good.—He has forbidden his Governors to pass Laws of immediate and pressing importance, unless suspended in their operation till his Assent should be obtained; and when so suspended, he has utterly neglected to attend to them.—He has refused to pass other Laws for the accommodation of large districts of people, unless those people would relinquish the right of Representation in the Legislature, a right inestimable to them and formidable to tyrants only.—He has called together legislative bodies at places unusual, uncomfortable, and distant from the depository of their public Records, for the sole purpose of fatiguing them into compliance with his measures.—He has dissolved Representative Houses repeatedly, for opposing with manly firmness his invasions on the rights of the people.—He has refused for a long time, after such dissolutions, to cause others to be elected; whereby the Legislative powers, incapable of Annihilation, have returned to the People at large for their exercise; the State remaining in the mean time exposed to all the dangers of invasion from without, and convulsions within.—He has endeavoured to prevent the population of these States; for that purpose obstructing the Laws for Naturalization of Foreigners; refusing to pass others to encourage their migration hither, and raising the conditions of new Appropriations of Lands.—He has obstructed the Administration of Justice, by refusing his Assent to Laws for establishing Judiciary powers.—He has made judges dependent on his Will alone, for the tenure of their offices, and the amount and payment of their salaries.—He has erected a multitude of New Offices, and sent hither swarms of Officers to harrass our people, and eat out their substance.—He has kept among us, in times of peace, Standing Armies, without the Consent of our legislatures.—He has affected to render the Military independent of and superior to the Civil power.—He has combined with others to subject us to a jurisdiction foreign to our constitution, and unacknowledged by our laws; giving his Assent to their Acts of pretended Legislation:—For quartering large bodies of armed troops among us:—For protecting them, by a mock Trial, from punishment for any Murders which they should commit on the Inhabitants of these States:—For cutting off our Trade with all parts of the world:—For imposing Taxes on us without our Consent:—For depriving us in many cases, of the benefits of Trial by Jury:—For transporting us beyond Seas to be tried for pretended offences:—For abolishing the free System of English Laws in a neighbouring Province, establishing therein an Arbitrary government, and enlarging its Boundaries so as to render it at once an example and fit instrument for introducing the same absolute rule into these Colonies:—For taking away our Charters, abolishing our most valuable Laws, and altering fundamentally the Forms of our Governments:—For suspending our own Legislatures, and declaring themselves invested with power to legislate for us in all cases whatsoever.—He has abdicated Government here, by declaring us out of his Protection and waging War against us.—He has plundered our seas, ravaged our Coasts, burnt our towns, and destroyed the lives of our people.—He is at this time transporting large Armies of foreign Mercenaries to compleat the works of death, desolation and tyranny, already begun with circumstances of Cruelty & perfidy scarcely paralleled in the most barbarous ages, and totally unworthy the Head of a civilized nation.—He has constrained our fellow Citizens taken Captive on the high Seas to bear Arms against their Country, to become the executioners of their friends and Brethren, or to fall themselves by their Hands.—He has excited domestic insurrections amongst us, and has endeavoured to bring on the inhabitants of our frontiers, the merciless Indian Savages, whose known rule of warfare, is an undistinguished destruction of all ages, sexes and conditions. In every stage of these Oppressions We have Petitioned for Redress in the most humble terms: Our repeated Petitions have been answered only by repeated injury. A Prince, whose character is thus marked by every act which may define a Tyrant, is unfit to be the ruler of a free people. Nor have We been wanting in attentions to our Brittish brethren. We have warned them from time to time of attempts by their legislature to extend an unwarrantable jurisdiction over us. We have reminded them of the circumstances of our emigration and settlement here. We have appealed to their native justice and magnanimity, and we have conjured them by the ties of our common kindred to disavow these usurpations, which, would inevitably interrupt our connections and correspondence. They too have been deaf to the voice of justice and of consanguinity. We must, therefore, acquiesce in the necessity, which denounces our Separation, and hold them, as we hold the rest of mankind. Enemies in War, in Peace Friends.—

We, therefore, the Representatives of the United States of America, in General Congress, Assembled, appealing to the Supreme Judge of the world for the rectitude of our intentions, do, in the Name, and by Authority of the good People of these Colonies, solemnly publish and declare, That these United Colonies are, and of Right ought to be Free and Independent States; that they are Absolved from all Allegiance to the British Crown, and that all political connection between them and the State of Great Britain, is and ought to be totally dissolved; and that as Free and Independent States, they have full Power to levy War, conclude Peace, contract Alliances, establish Commerce, and to do all other Acts and Things which Independent States may of right do.—And for the support of this Declaration, with a firm reliance on the protection of Divine Providence, we mutually pledge to each other our Lives, our Fortunes and our sacred Honor.

## Signers of the Declaration of Independence

| | BIRTHPLACE | OCCUPATION |
|---|---|---|
| **Connecticut** | | |
| Samuel Huntington (1731–1796) | Windham CT | lawyer, judge |
| Roger Sherman (1721–1793) | Newton MA | cobbler, surveyor, lawyer, judge |
| William Williams (1731–1811) | Lebanon CT | merchant, judge |
| Oliver Wolcott (1726–1797) | Windsor CT | soldier, sheriff, judge |
| | | |
| **Delaware** | | |
| Thomas McKean (1734–1817) | New London PA | lawyer, judge |
| George Read (1733–1798) | North East MD | lawyer, judge |
| Caesar Rodney (1728–1784) | Dover DE | judge |
| | | |
| **Georgia** | | |
| Button Gwinnett (c. 1735–1777) | bapt. Gloucester, England | merchant |
| Lyman Hall (1724–1790) | Wallingford CT | physician |
| George Walton (c. 1741–1804) | Farmville VA | lawyer, judge |

# Signers of the Declaration of Independence (continued)

| | BIRTHPLACE | OCCUPATION |
|---|---|---|
| **Maryland** | | |
| Charles Carroll of Carrollton (1737–1832) | Annapolis MD | lawyer |
| Samuel Chase (1741–1811) | Somerset county MD | lawyer, judge |
| William Paca (1740–1799) | Abingdon MD | lawyer, judge |
| Thomas Stone (1743–1787) | Charles county MD | lawyer |
| | | |
| **Massachusetts** | | |
| John Adams (1735–1826) | Braintree (Quincy) MA | lawyer |
| Samuel Adams (1722–1803) | Boston MA | politician |
| Elbridge Gerry (1744–1814) | Marblehead MA | merchant |
| John Hancock (1737–1793) | Braintree (Quincy) MA | merchant |
| Robert Treat Paine (1731–1814) | Boston MA | lawyer, judge |
| | | |
| **New Hampshire** | | |
| Josiah Bartlett (1729–1795) | Amesbury MA | physician, judge |
| Matthew Thornton (c. 1714–1803) | Ireland | physician |
| William Whipple (1730–1785) | Kittery ME | merchant, soldier, judge |
| | | |
| **New Jersey** | | |
| Abraham Clark (1726–1794) | Elizabethtown NJ | surveyor, lawyer, sheriff |
| John Hart (c. 1711–1779) | Stonington CT | farmer, judge |
| Francis Hopkinson (1737–1791) | Philadelphia PA | lawyer, judge, author |
| Richard Stockton (1730–1781) | near Princeton NJ | lawyer |
| John Witherspoon (1723–1794) | Gifford, Scotland | clergyman, author, educator |
| | | |
| **New York** | | |
| William Floyd (1734–1821) | Brookhaven NY | soldier |
| Francis Lewis (1713–1802) | Llandaff, Wales | merchant |
| Philip Livingston (1716–1778) | Albany NY | merchant |
| Lewis Morris (1726–1798) | Morrisania (Bronx county) NY | farmer, soldier, judge |
| | | |
| **North Carolina** | | |
| Joseph Hewes (1730–1779) | Kingston NJ | merchant |
| William Hooper (1742–1790) | Boston MA | lawyer, judge |
| John Penn (1741–1788) | near Port Royal VA | lawyer |
| | | |
| **Pennsylvania** | | |
| George Clymer (1739–1813) | Philadelphia PA | merchant |
| Benjamin Franklin (1706–1790) | Boston MA | printer, publisher, author, scientist |
| Robert Morris (1734–1806) | Lancashire, England | merchant |
| John Morton (1724–1777) | Ridley PA | judge |
| George Ross (1730–1779) | New Castle DE | lawyer, judge |
| Benjamin Rush (1746–1813) | Byberry PA | physician |
| James Smith (c. 1719–1806) | Dublin, Ireland | lawyer |
| George Taylor (1716–1781) | Ireland | ironmaster |
| James Wilson (1742–1798) | Fife, Scotland | lawyer, judge |
| | | |
| **Rhode Island** | | |
| William Ellery (1727–1820) | Newport RI | lawyer, judge |
| Stephen Hopkins (1707–1785) | Providence RI | judge, educator |
| | | |
| **South Carolina** | | |
| Thomas Heyward, Jr. (1746–1809) | St. Helena's (now St. Luke's) parish SC | lawyer, judge |
| Thomas Lynch, Jr. (1749–1779) | Winyah SC | lawyer |
| Arthur Middleton (1742–1787) | near Charleston SC | planter, legislator |
| Edward Rutledge (1749–1800) | Charleston SC | lawyer |
| | | |
| **Virginia** | | |
| Carter Braxton (1736–1797) | Newington Plantation VA | planter |
| Thomas Jefferson (1743–1826) | Shadwell VA | lawyer, author, educator |
| Benjamin Harrison (c. 1726–1791) | Berkeley VA | planter, politician |
| Francis Lightfoot Lee (1734–1797) | Westmoreland county VA | farmer |
| Richard Henry Lee (1732–1794) | Westmoreland county VA | planter, judge |
| Thomas Nelson, Jr. (1738–1789) | Yorktown VA | planter |
| George Wythe (1726–1806) | Elizabeth City county (Hampton) VA | lawyer, educator |

# The Constitution of the United States

*The Constitution was written during the summer of 1787 in Philadelphia by 55 delegates to a Constitutional Convention that was called ostensibly to amend the Articles of Confederation. It was submitted for ratification to the 13 states on 28 Sep 1787. In June 1788, after the Constitution had been ratified by nine states (as required by Article VII), Congress set 4 Mar 1789 as the date for the new government to commence proceedings.*

## Preamble

We the People of the United States, in Order to form a more perfect Union, establish Justice, insure domestic Tranquility, provide for common defence, promote the general Welfare, and secure the Blessings of Liberty to ourselves and our Posterity, do ordain and establish this Constitution for the United States of America.

## Article I

**Section 1—**

All legislative Powers herein granted shall be vested in a Congress of the United States, which shall consist of a Senate and House of Representatives.

**Section 2—**

The House of Representatives shall be composed of Members chosen every second Year by the People of the several States, and the Electors in each State shall have the Qualifications requisite for Electors of the most numerous Branch of the State Legislature.

No Person shall be a Representative who shall not have attained to the Age of twenty five Years, and been seven Years a Citizen of the United States, and who shall not, when elected, be an Inhabitant of that State in which he shall be chosen.

Representatives and direct Taxes shall be apportioned among the several States which may be included within this Union, according to their respective Numbers, which shall be determined by adding to the whole Number of free Persons, including those bound to Service for a Term of Years, and excluding Indians not taxed, three fifths of all other Persons. The actual Enumeration shall be made within three Years after the first Meeting of the Congress of the United States, and within every subsequent Term of ten Years, in such Manner as they shall by Law direct. The Number of Representatives shall not exceed one for every thirty Thousand, but each State shall have at Least one Representative; and until such enumeration shall be made, the State of New Hampshire shall be entitled to chuse three, Massachusetts eight, Rhode-Island and Providence Plantations one, Connecticut five, New-York six, New Jersey four, Pennsylvania eight, Delaware one, Maryland six, Virginia ten, North Carolina five, South Carolina five, and Georgia three.

When vacancies happen in the Representation from any State, the Executive Authority thereof shall issue Writs of Election to fill such Vacancies.

The House of Representatives shall chuse their speaker and other Officers; and shall have the sole Power of Impeachment.

**Section 3—**

The Senate of the United States shall be composed of two Senators from each State, chosen by the Legislature thereof for six Years; and each Senator shall have one Vote.

Immediately after they shall be assembled in Consequence of the first Election, they shall be divided as equally as may be into three Classes. The Seats of the Senators of the first Class shall be vacated at the Expiration of the second Year, of the second Class at the Expiration of the fourth Year, and of the third Class at the Expiration of the sixth Year, so that one third may be chosen every second Year; and if Vacancies happen by Resignation, or otherwise, during the Recess of the Legislature of any State, the Executive thereof may make temporary Appointments until the next Meeting of the Legislature, which shall then fill such Vacancies.

No Person shall be a Senator who shall not have attained to the Age of thirty Years, and been nine Years a Citizen of the United States, and who shall not, when elected, be an Inhabitant of that State for which he shall be chosen.

The Vice President of the United States shall be President of the Senate, but shall have no Vote, unless they be equally divided.

The Senate shall chuse their other Officers, and also a President pro tempore, in the Absence of the Vice President, or when he shall exercise the Office of President of the United States.

The Senate shall have the sole Power to try all Impeachments. When sitting for that Purpose, they shall be on Oath or Affirmation. When the President of the United States is tried, the Chief Justice shall preside: And no Person shall be convicted without the concurrence of two thirds of the Members present. Judgment in Cases of Impeachment shall not extend further than to removal from Office, and disqualification to hold and enjoy any Office of honor, Trust or Profit under the United States: but the Party convicted shall nevertheless be liable and subject to Indictment, Trial, Judgment and Punishment, according to law.

**Section 4—**

The Times, Places and Manner of holding Elections for Senators and Representatives, shall be prescribed in each State by the Legislature thereof; but the Congress may at any time by Law make or alter such Regulations, except as to the Places of chusing Senators.

The Congress shall assemble at least once in every Year, and such Meeting shall be on the first Monday in December, unless they shall by Law appoint a different Day.

**Section 5—**

Each House shall be the Judge of the Elections, Returns and Qualifications of its own Members, and a Majority of each shall constitute a Quorum to do business; but a smaller Number may adjourn from day to day, and may be authorized to compel the Attendance of absent Members, in such Manner, and under such Penalties as each House may provide.

Each House may determine the Rules of its Proceedings, punish its Members for disorderly Behaviour, and, with the Concurrence of two thirds, expel a Member.

Each House shall keep a journal of its Proceedings, and from time to time publish the same, excepting such Parts as may in their Judgment require Secrecy; and the yeas and Nays of the Members of either House on any question shall, at the Desire of one fifth of those Present, be entered on the journal.

Neither House, during the Session of Congress, shall, without the Consent of the other, adjourn for more than three days, nor to any other place than that in which the two Houses shall be sitting.

## Section 6—

The Senators and Representatives shall receive a Compensation for their Services, to be ascertained by Law, and paid out of the Treasury of the United States. They shall in all Cases, except Treason, Felony and Breach of the Peace, be privileged from Arrest during their Attendance at the Session of their respective Houses, and in going to and returning from the same; and for any Speech or Debate in either House, they shall not be questioned in any other Place.

No Senator or Representative shall, during the Time for which he was elected, be appointed to any civil Office under the Authority of the United States, which shall have been created, or the Emoluments whereof shall have been encreased during such time; and no Person holding any Office under the United States, shall be a Member of either House during his Continuance in Office.

## Section 7—

All Bills for raising Revenue shall originate in the House of Representatives; but the Senate may propose or concur with Amendments as on other Bills.

Every Bill which shall have passed the House of Representatives and the Senate, shall, before it become a Law, be presented to the President of the United States; If he approve he shall sign it, but if not he shall return it, with his Objections to that House in which it shall have originated, who shall enter the Objections at large on their Journal, and proceed to reconsider it. If after such Reconsideration two thirds of that House shall agree to pass the Bill, it shall be sent, together with the Objections, to the other House, by which it shall likewise be reconsidered, and if approved by two thirds of that House, it shall become a Law. But in all such Cases the Votes of both Houses shall be determined by yeas and Nays, and the Names of the Persons voting for and against the Bill shall be entered on the Journal of each House respectively. If any Bill shall not be returned by the President within ten Days (Sundays excepted) after it shall have been presented to him, the Same shall be a Law, in like Manner as if he had signed it, unless the Congress by their Adjournment prevent its Return, in which Case it shall not be a Law.

Every Order, Resolution, or Vote to which the Concurrence of the Senate and House of Representatives may be necessary (except on a question of Adjournment) shall be presented to the President of the United States; and before the Same shall take Effect, shall be approved by him, or being disapproved by him, shall be repassed by two thirds of the Senate and House of Representatives, according to the Rules and Limitations prescribed in the Case of a Bill.

## Section 8—

The Congress shall have Power To lay and collect Taxes, Duties, Imposts and Excises, to pay the Debts and provide for the common Defence and general Welfare of the United States; but all Duties, Imposts and Excises shall be uniform throughout the United States;

To borrow Money on the credit of the United States;

To regulate Commerce with foreign Nations, and among the several States, and with the Indian Tribes;

To establish an uniform Rule of Naturalization, and uniform Laws on the subject of Bankruptcies throughout the United States;

To coin Money, regulate the Value thereof, and of foreign Coin, and fix the Standard of Weights and Measures;

To provide for the Punishment of counterfeiting the Securities and current Coin of the United States;

To establish Post Offices and post Roads;

To promote the Progress of Science and useful Arts, by securing for limited Times to Authors and Inventors the exclusive Right to their respective Writings and Discoveries;

To constitute Tribunals inferior to the supreme Court;

To define and punish Piracies and Felonies committed on the high Seas, and Offences against the Law of Nations;

To declare War, grant Letters of Marque and Reprisal, and make rules concerning Captures on Land and Water;

To raise and support Armies, but no Appropriation of Money to that Use shall be for a longer Term than two Years;

To provide and maintain a Navy;

To make Rules for the Government and Regulation of the land and naval Forces;

To provide for calling forth the Militia to execute the Laws of the Union, suppress Insurrections and repel Invasions;

To provide for organizing, arming, and disciplining, the Militia, and for governing such Part of them as may be employed in the Service of the United States, reserving to the States respectively, the Appointment of the Officers, and the Authority of training the Militia according to the discipline prescribed by Congress;

To exercise exclusive Legislation in all Cases whatsoever, over such District (not exceeding ten Miles square), as may, by Cession of particular States, and the Acceptance of Congress, become the Seat of the Government of the United States, and to exercise like Authority over all Places purchased by the Consent of the Legislature of the State in which the Same shall be for the Erection of Forts, Magazines, Arsenals, dock-Yards, and other needful Buildings; — And

To make all Laws which shall be necessary and proper for carying into Execution the foregoing Powers, and all other Powers vested by this Constitution in the Government of the United States, or in any Department or Officer thereof.

## Section 9—

The Migration or Importation of such Persons as any of the States now existing shall think proper to admit, shall not be prohibited by the Congress prior to the Year one thousand eight hundred and eight, but a Tax or duty may be imposed on such Importation, not exceeding ten dollars for each Person.

The Privilege of the Writ of Habeas Corpus shall not be suspended, unless when in Cases of Rebellion or Invasion the public Safety may require it.

No Bill of Attainder or ex post facto Law shall be passed.

No Capitation, or other direct, Tax shall be laid, unless in Proportion to the Census or Enumeration herein before directed to be taken.

No Tax or Duty shall be laid on Articles exported from any State.

No Preference shall be given by any Regulation of Commerce or Revenue to the Ports of one State over those of another; nor shall Vessels bound to, or from, one State, be obliged to enter, clear or pay Duties in another.

No money shall be drawn from the Treasury, but in Consequence of Appropriations made by Law; and a regular Statement and Account of the Receipts and Expenditures of all public Money shall be published from time to time.

No Title of Nobility shall be granted by the United States: And no Person holding any Office of Profit or Trust under them, shall, without the Consent of the Congress, accept of any present, Emolument, Office, or Title, of any kind whatever, from any King, Prince, or foreign State.

## Section 10—

No State shall enter into any Treaty, Alliance, or Confederation; grant Letters of Marque and Reprisal; coin Money; emit Bills of Credit; make any Thing but gold and silver Coin a Tender in Payment of Debts; pass any Bill of Attainder, ex post facto Law, or Law impairing the Obligation of Contracts, or grant any Title of Nobility.

No State shall, without the Consent of the Congress, lay any Imposts or Duties on Imports or Exports, except what may be absolutely necessary for executing it's inspection Laws: and the net Produce of all Duties and Imposts, laid by any State on Imports or Exports, shall be for the Use of the Treasury of the United States; and all such Laws shall be subject to the Revision and Controul of the Congress.

No State shall, without the Consent of Congress, lay any Duty of Tonnage, keep Troops, or Ships of War in time of Peace, enter into any Agreement or Compact with another State, or with a foreign Power, or engage in War, unless actually invaded, or in such imminent Danger as will not admit of delay.

## Article II

### Section 1—

The executive Power shall be vested in a President of the United States of America. He shall hold his Office during the Term of four Years, and, together with the Vice President, chosen for the same Term, be elected, as follows

Each State shall appoint, in such Manner as the Legislature thereof may direct, a Number of Electors, equal to the whole Number of Senators and Representatives to which the State may be entitled in the Congress: but no Senator or Representative, or Person holding an Office of Trust or Profit under the United States, shall be appointed an Elector.

The Electors shall meet in their respective States, and vote by Ballot for two Persons, of whom one at least shall not be an Inhabitant of the same State with themselves. And they shall make a List of all the Persons voted for, and of the Number of Votes for each; which List they shall sign and certify, and transmit sealed to the Seat of the Government of the United States, directed to the President of the Senate. The President of the Senate shall, in the Presence of the Senate and House of Representatives, open all the Certificates, and the Votes shall then be counted. The Person having the greatest Number of Votes shall be the President, if such Number be a Majority of the whole Number of Electors appointed; and if there be more than one who have such Majority, and have an equal Number of Votes, then the House of Representatives shall immediately chuse by Ballot one of them for President: and if no Person have a Majority, then from the five highest on the List the said House shall in like Manner chuse the President. But in chusing the President, the Votes shall be taken by States, the Representation from each State having one Vote; A quorum for this Purpose shall consist of a Member or Members from two thirds of the States, and a Majority of all the States shall be necessary to a Choice. In every Case, after the Choice of the President, the Person having the greatest Number of Votes of the Electors shall be the Vice President. But if there should remain two or more who have equal Votes, the Senate shall chuse from them by Ballot the Vice President.

The Congress may determine the Time of chusing the Electors, and the Day on which they shall give their Votes; which Day shall be the same throughout the United States.

No Person except a natural born Citizen, or a Citizen of the United States, at the time of the Adoption of this Constitution, shall be eligible to the Office of President; neither shall any Person be eligible to that Office who shall not have attained to the Age of thirty five Years, and been fourteen Years a Resident within the United States.

In Case of the Removal of the President from Office, or of his Death, Resignation, or Inability to discharge the Powers and Duties of the said Office, the Same shall devolve on the Vice President, and the Congress may by Law provide for the Case of Removal, Death, Resignation or Inability, both of the President and Vice President, declaring what Officer shall then act as President, and such Officer shall act accordingly, until the Disability be removed, or a President shall be elected.

The President shall, at stated Times, receive for his Services, a Compensation, which shall neither be encreased nor diminished during the Period for which he shall have been elected, and he shall not receive within that Period any other Emolument from the United States, or any of them.

Before he enter on the Execution of his Office, he shall take the following Oath or Affirmation: "I do solemnly swear (or affirm) that I will faithfully execute the Office of President of the United States, and will to the best of my Ability, preserve, protect and defend the Constitution of the United States."

### Section 2—

The President shall be Commander in Chief of the Army and Navy of the United States, and of the Militia of the several States, when called into the actual Service of the United States; he may require the Opinion, in writing, of the principal Officer in each of the executive Departments, upon any Subject relating to the Duties of their respective Offices, and he shall have Power to grant Reprieves and Pardons for Offences against the United States, except in Cases of Impeachment.

He shall have Power, by and with the Advice and Consent of the Senate, to make Treaties, provided two thirds of the Senators present concur; and he shall nominate, and by and with the Advice and Consent of the Senate, shall appoint Ambassadors, other public Ministers and Consuls, Judges of the supreme Court, and all other Officers of the United States, whose Appointments are not herein otherwise provided for, and which shall be established by Law: but the Congress may by Law vest the Appointment of such inferior Officers, as they think proper, in the President alone, in the Courts of Law, or in the Heads of Departments.

The President shall have Power to fill up all Vacancies that may happen during the Recess of the Senate, by granting Commissions which shall expire at the End of their next Session.

## Section 3—

He shall from time to time give to the Congress Information of the State of the Union, and recommend to their Consideration such Measures as he shall judge necessary and expedient; he may, on extraordinary Occasions, convene both Houses, or either of them, and in Case of Disagreement between them, with Respect to the Time of Adjournment, he may adjourn them to such Time as he shall think proper; he shall receive Ambassadors and other public Ministers; he shall take Care that the Laws be faithfully executed, and shall Commission all the Officers of the United States.

## Section 4—

The President, Vice President and all civil Officers of the United States, shall be removed from Office on Impeachment for, and Conviction of, Treason, Bribery, or other High Crimes and Misdemeanors.

## Article III

## Section 1—

The judicial Power of the United States, shall be vested in one supreme Court, and in such inferior Courts as the Congress may from time to time ordain and establish. The Judges, both of the supreme and inferior Courts, shall hold their Offices during good Behaviour, and shall, at stated Times, receive for their Services, a Compensation, which shall not be diminished during their Continuance in Office.

## Section 2—

The judicial Power shall extend to all Cases, in Law and Equity, arising under this Constitution, the Laws of the United States, and Treaties made, or which shall be made, under their Authority; — to all Cases affecting Ambassadors, other public Ministers and Consuls; — to all Cases of admiralty and maritime jurisdiction; — to Controversies to which the United States shall be a Party; — to Controversies between two or more States;-between a State and Citizens of another State; — between Citizens of different States; — between Citizens of the same State claiming Lands under Grants of different States, and between a State, or the Citizens thereof, and foreign States, Citizens or Subjects.

In all Cases affecting Ambassadors, other public Ministers and Consuls, and those in which a State shall be Party, the supreme Court shall have original Jurisdiction. In all the other Cases before mentioned, the supreme Court shall have appellate Jurisdiction, both as to Law and Fact, with such Exceptions, and under such Regulations as the Congress shall make.

The Trial of all Crimes, except in Cases of Impeachment, shall be by Jury; and such Trial shall be held in the State where the said Crimes shall have been committed; but when not committed within any State, the Trial shall be at such Place or Places as the Congress may by Law have directed.

## Section 3—

Treason against the United States, shall consist only in levying War against them, or in adhering to their Enemies, giving them Aid and Comfort. No Person shall be convicted of Treason unless on the Testimony of two Witnesses to the same overt Act, or on Confession in open Court.

The Congress shall have Power to declare the Punishment of Treason, but no Attainder of Treason shall work Corruption of Blood, or Forfeiture except during the Life of the Person attainted.

## Article IV

## Section 1—

Full Faith and Credit shall be given in each State to the public Acts, Records, and judicial Proceedings of every other State. And the Congress may by general Laws prescribe the Manner in which such Acts, Records and Proceedings shall be proved, and the Effect thereof.

## Section 2—

The Citizens of each State shall be entitled to all Privileges and Immunities of Citizens in the several States.

A person charged in any State with Treason, Felony, or other Crime, who shall flee from justice, and be found in another State, shall on Demand of the executive Authority of the State from which he fled, be delivered up, to be removed to the State having Jurisdiction of the Crime.

No Person held to Service or Labour in one State, under the Laws thereof, escaping into another, shall in Consequence of any Law or Regulation therein, be discharged from such Service or Labour, but shall be delivered upon on Claim of the Party to whom such Service or Labour may be due.

## Section 3—

New States may be admitted by the Congress into this Union; but no new State shall be formed or erected within the Jurisdiction of any other State; nor any State be formed by the Junction of two or more States, or Parts of States, without the Consent of the Legislatures of the States concerned as well as of the Congress.

The Congress shall have Power to dispose of and make all needful Rules and Regulations respecting the Territory or other Property belonging to the United States; and nothing in this Constitution shall be so construed as to Prejudice any Claims of the United States, or of any particular State.

## Section 4—

The United States shall guarantee to every State in this Union a Republican Form of Government, and shall protect each of them against Invasion; and on Application of the Legislature, or of the Executive (when the Legislature cannot be convened) against domestic Violence.

## Article V

The Congress, whenever two thirds of both Houses shall deem it necessary, shall propose Amendments to this Constitution, or, on the Application of the Legislatures of two thirds of the several States, shall call a Convention for proposing Amendments, which, in either Case, shall be valid to all Intents and Purposes, as Part of this Constitution, when ratified by the Legislatures of three fourths of the several States, or by Conventions in three fourths thereof, as the one or the other Mode of Ratification may be proposed by the Congress; Provided that no Amendment which may be made prior to the Year One thousand eight hundred and eight shall in any Manner affect the first and fourth Clauses in the Ninth Section of the first Article; and that no State, without its Consent, shall be deprived of its equal Suffrage in the Senate.

## Article VI

All Debts contracted and Engagements entered into, before the Adoption of this Constitution, shall be as valid against the United States under this Constitution, as under the Confederation.

This Constitution, and the Laws of the United States which shall be made in Pursuance thereof; and all Treaties made, or which shall be made, under the Authority of the United States, shall be the supreme Law of the Land; and the Judges in every State shall be bound thereby, any Thing in the Constitution or Laws of any State to the Contrary notwithstanding.

The Senators and Representatives before mentioned, and the Members of the several State Legislatures, and all executive and judicial Officers, both of the United States and of the several States, shall be bound by Oath or Affirmation, to support this Constitution; but no religious Test shall ever be required as a Qualification to any Office or public Trust under the United States.

## Article VII

The Ratification of the Conventions of nine States, shall be sufficient for the Establishment of this Constitution between the States so ratifying the Same.

Done in Convention by the Unanimous Consent of the States present the Seventeenth Day of September in the Year of our Lord one thousand seven hundred and Eighty seven and of the Independence of the United States of America the Twelfth      IN WITNESS whereof We have hereunto subscribed our Names,

G⁰ Washington—
*Presidᵗ. and deputy from Virginia*

*New Hampshire*
John Langdon
Nicholas Gilman

*Massachusetts*
Nathaniel Gorham
Rufus King

*Connecticut*
Wm. Saml. Johnson
Roger Sherman

*New York*
Alexander Hamilton

*New Jersey*
Wil: Livingston
David Brearley
Wm. Paterson
Jona: Dayton

*Pennsylvania*
B. Franklin
Thomas Mifflin
Robᵗ Morris
Geo. Clymer
Thos. FitzSimons
Jared Ingersoll
James Wilson
Gouv Morris

*Delaware*
Geo: Read
Gunning Bedford jun
John Dickinson
Richard Bassett
Jaco: Broom

*Maryland*
James McHenry
Dan of Sᵗ Thos. Jenifer
Danˡ Carroll

*Virginia*
John Blair—
James Madison Jr.

*North Carolina*
Wm. Blount
Rich'd Dobbs Spaight
Hu Williamson

*South Carolina*
J. Rutledge
Charles Cotesworth Pinckney
Charles Pinckney
Pierce Butler

*Georgia*
William Few
Abr Baldwin

Attest:
William Jackson, *Secretary*

[*Rhode Island and the Providence Plantations*
Rhode Island did not send delegates to the Constitutional Convention.]

# Bill of Rights

*The first 10 amendments to the Constitution were adopted as a single unit on 15 Dec 1791. Together, they constitute a collection of mutually reinforcing guarantees of individual rights and of limitations on federal and state governments.*

## Amendment I

Congress shall make no law respecting an establishment of religion, or prohibiting the free exercise thereof; or abridging the freedom of speech, or of the press; or the right of the people peaceably to assemble, and to petition the Government for a redress of grievances.

## Amendment II

A well regulated Militia, being necessary to the security of a free State, the right of the people to keep and bear Arms, shall not be infringed.

## Amendment III

No Soldier shall, in time of peace be quartered in any house, without the consent of the Owner, nor in time of war, but in a manner to be prescribed by law.

## Amendment IV

The right of the People to be secure in their persons,

houses, papers, and effects, against unreasonable searches and seizures, shall not be violated, and no Warrants shall issue, but upon probable cause, supported by Oath or affirmation, and particularity describing the place to be searched, and the persons or things to be seized.

### Amendment V

No person shall be held to answer for a capital, or otherwise infamous crime, unless on a presentment or indictment of a Grand Jury, except in cases arising in the land or naval forces, or in the Militia, when in actual service in time of War or public danger; nor shall any person be subject for the same offence to be twice put in jeopardy of life or limb; nor shall be compelled in any criminal case to be a witness against himself, nor be deprived of life, liberty, or property, without due process of law; nor shall private property be taken for public use, without just compensation.

### Amendment VI

In all criminal prosecutions, the accused shall enjoy the right to a speedy and public trial, by an impartial jury of the State and district wherein the crime shall have been committed, which district shall have been previously ascertained by law, and to be informed of the nature and cause of the accusation; to be confronted with the witnesses against him; to have compulsory process for obtaining witnesses in his favor, and to have Assistance of Counsel for his defence.

### Amendment VII

In Suits at common law, where the value in controversy shall exceed twenty dollars, the right of trial by jury shall be preserved, and no fact tried by a jury, shall be otherwise re-examined in any Court of the United States, than according to the rules of the common law.

### Amendment VIII

Excessive bail shall not be required, nor excessive fines imposed, nor cruel and unusual punishments inflicted.

### Amendment IX

The enumeration in the Constitution, of certain rights, shall not be construed to deny or disparage others retained by the people.

### Amendment X

The powers not delegated to the United States by the Constitution, nor prohibited by it to the States, are reserved to the States respectively, or to the people.

## Further Amendments

### Amendment XI
#### (ratified 7 Feb 1795)

The Judicial power of the United States shall not be construed to extend to any suit in law or equity, commenced or prosecuted against one of the United States by Citizens of another State, or by Citizens or Subjects of any Foreign State.

### Amendment XII
#### (ratified 15 Jun 1804)

The Electors shall meet in their respective states and vote by ballot for President and Vice-President, one of whom, at least, shall not be an inhabitant of the same state with themselves; they shall name in their ballots the person voted for as President, and in distinct ballots the person voted for as Vice-President, and they shall make distinct lists of all persons voted for as President, and of all persons voted for as Vice-President, and of the number of votes for each, which lists they shall sign and certify, and transmit sealed to the seat of the government of the United States, directed to the President of the Senate; — The President of the Senate shall, in the presence of the Senate and House of Representatives, open all the certificates and the votes shall then be counted; — The person having the greatest number of votes for President, shall be the President, if such number be a majority of the whole number of Electors appointed; and if no person have such majority, then from the persons having the highest numbers not exceeding three on the list of those voted for as President, the House of Representatives shall choose immediately, by ballot, the President. But in choosing the President, the votes shall be taken by states, the representation from each state having one vote; a quorum for this purpose shall consist of a member or members from two-thirds of the states, and a majority of all the states shall be necessary to a choice. And if the House of Representatives shall not choose a President whenever the right of choice shall devolve upon then, before the fourth day of March next following, then the Vice-President shall act as President, as in the case of the death or other constitutional disability of the President. — The person having the greatest number of votes as Vice-President, shall be the Vice-President, if such number be a majority of the whole number of Electors appointed, and if no person have a majority, then from the two highest numbers on the list, the Senate shall choose the Vice-President; a quorum for the purpose shall consist of two-thirds of the whole number of Senators, and a majority of the whole number shall be necessary to a choice. But no person constitutionally ineligible to the office of President shall be eligible to that of Vice-President of the United States.

### Amendment XIII
#### (ratified 6 Dec 1865)

**Section 1—**
Neither slavery nor involuntary servitude, except as a punishment for crime whereof the party shall have been duly convicted, shall exist within the United States, or any place subject to their jurisdiction.

**Section 2—**
Congress shall have power to enforce this article by appropriate legislation.

### Amendment XIV
#### (ratified 9 Jul 1868)

**Section 1—**
All persons born or naturalized in the United States, and subject to the jurisdiction thereof, are citizens of the United States and of the State wherein they reside. No State shall make or enforce any law which shall abridge the privileges or immunities of citizens of the United States; nor shall any State deprive any person of life, liberty, or property, without due process of law; nor deny to any person within its jurisdiction the equal protection of the laws.

**Section 2—**

Representatives shall be apportioned among the several States according to their respective numbers, counting the whole number of persons in each State, excluding Indians not taxed. But when the right to vote at any election for the choice of electors for President and Vice President of the United States, Representatives in Congress, the Executive and Judicial officers of a State, or the members of the Legislature thereof, is denied to any of the male inhabitants of such State, being twenty-one years of age, and citizens of the United States, or in any way abridged, except for participation in rebellion, or other crime, the basis of representation therein shall be reduced in the proportion which the number of such male citizens shall bear to the whole number of male citizens twenty-one years of age in such State.

**Section 3—**

No person shall be a Senator or Representative in Congress, or elector of President and Vice President, or hold any office, civil or military, under the United States, or under any State, who, having previously taken an oath, as a member of Congress, or as an officer of the United States, or as a member of any State legislature, or as an executive or judicial officer of any State, to support the Constitution of the United States, shall have engaged in insurrection or rebellion against the same, or given aid or comfort to the enemies thereof. But Congress may by a vote of two-thirds of each House, remove such disability.

**Section 4—**

The validity of the public debt of the United States, authorized by law, including debts incurred for payment of pensions and bounties for services in suppressing insurrection or rebellion, shall not be questioned. But neither the United States nor any State shall assume or pay any debt or obligation incurred in aid of insurrection or rebellion against the United States, or any claim for the loss or emancipation of any slave; but all such debts, obligations and claims shall be held illegal and void.

**Section 5—**

The Congress shall have power to enforce, by appropriate legislation, the provisions of this article.

### Amendment XV
#### (ratified 8 Feb 1870)

**Section 1—**

The right of citizens of the United States to vote shall not be denied or abridged by the United States or by any State on account of race, color, or previous condition of servitude.

**Section 2—**

The Congress shall have power to enforce this article by appropriate legislation.

### Amendment XVI
#### (ratified 3 Feb 1913)

The Congress shall have power to lay and collect taxes on incomes, from whatever source derived, without apportionment among the several States, and without regard to any census or enumeration.

### Amendment XVII
#### (ratified 13 Feb 1913)

The Senate of the United States shall be composed of two Senators from each State, elected by the people thereof for six years; and each Senator shall have one vote. The electors in each State shall have the qualifications requisite for electors of the most numerous branch of the State legislatures.

When vacancies happen in the representation of any State in the Senate, the executive authority of such State shall issue writs of election to fill such vacancies: Provided, That the legislature of any State may empower the executive thereof to make temporary appointments until the people fill the vacancies by election as the legislature may direct.

This amendment shall not be so construed as to affect the election or term of any Senator chosen before it becomes valid as part of the Constitution.

### Amendment XVIII
#### (ratified 16 Jan 1919; repealed 5 Dec 1933 by Amendment XXI)

**Section 1—**

After one year from the ratification of this article the manufacture, sale, or transportation of intoxicating liquors within, the importation thereof into, or the exportation thereof from the United States and all territory subject to the jurisdiction thereof for beverage purposes is hereby prohibited.

**Section 2—**

The Congress and the several States shall have concurrent power to enforce this article by appropriate legislation.

**Section 3—**

This article shall be inoperative unless it shall have been ratified as an amendment to the Constitution by the legislatures of the several States as provided in the Constitution, within seven years from the date of the submission hereof to the States by the Congress.

### Amendment XIX
#### (ratified 18 Aug 1920)

The right of citizens of the United States to vote shall not be denied or abridged by the United States or by any State on account of sex.

Congress shall have power to enforce this article by appropriate legislation.

### Amendment XX
#### (ratified 23 Jan 1933)

**Section 1—**

The terms of the President and Vice President shall end at noon on the 20th day of January, and the terms of Senators and Representatives at noon on the 3d day of January, of the years in which such terms would have ended if this article had not been ratified; and the terms of their successors shall then begin.

**Section 2—**

The Congress shall assemble at least once in every year, and such meeting shall begin at noon on the 3d day of January, unless they shall by law appoint a different day.

**Section 3—**

If, at the time fixed for the beginning of the term of the President, the President elect shall have died, the Vice President elect shall become President. If a President shall not have been chosen before the time fixed for the beginning of his term, or if the President elect shall have failed to qualify, then the Vice President elect shall act as President until a President shall have qualified; and the Congress may by law provide for the case wherein neither a President elect nor a Vice President elect shall have qualified, declaring who shall then act as President, or the manner in which one who is to act shall be selected, and such person shall act accordingly until a President or Vice President shall have qualified.

## Section 4—

The Congress may by law provide for the case of the death of any of the persons from whom the House of Representatives may choose a President whenever the right of choice shall have devolved upon them, and for the case of the death of any of the persons from whom the Senate may choose a Vice President whenever the right of choice shall have devolved upon them.

## Section 5—

Sections 1 and 2 shall take effect on the 15th day of October following the ratification of this article.

## Section 6—

This article shall be inoperative unless it shall have been ratified as an amendment to the Constitution by the legislatures of three-fourths of the several States within seven years from the date of its submission.

### Amendment XXI
### (ratified 5 Dec 1933)

## Section 1—

The eighteenth article of amendment to the Constitution of the United States is hereby repealed.

## Section 2—

The transportation or importation into any State, Territory, or possession of the United States for delivery or use therein of intoxicating liquors, in violation of the laws thereof, is hereby prohibited.

## Section 3—

This article shall be inoperative unless it shall have been ratified as an amendment to the Constitution by conventions in the several States, as provided in the Constitution, within seven years from the date of the submission hereof to the States by the Congress.

### Amendment XXII
### (ratified 27 Feb 1951)

## Section 1—

No person shall be elected to the office of the President more than twice, and no person who has held the office of President, or acted as President, for more than two years of a term to which some other person was elected President shall be elected to the office of the President more than once. But this Article shall not apply to any person holding the office of President when this Article was proposed by the Congress, and shall not prevent any person who may be holding the office of President, or acting as President, during the term within which this Article becomes operative from holding the office of President or acting as President during the remainder of such term.

## Section 2—

This Article shall be inoperative unless it shall have been ratified as an amendment to the Constitution by the legislatures of three-fourths of the several States within seven years from the date of its submission to the States by the Congress.

### Amendment XXIII
### (ratified 29 Mar 1961)

## Section 1—

The District constituting the seat of Government of the United States shall appoint in such manner as the Congress may direct:

A number of electors of President and Vice President equal to the whole number of Senators and Representatives in Congress to which the District would be entitled if it were a State, but in no event more than the least populous State; they shall be in addition to those appointed by the States, but they shall be considered, for the purposes of the election of President and Vice President, to be electors appointed by a State; and they shall meet in the District and perform such duties as provided by the twelfth article of amendment.

## Section 2—

The Congress shall have power to enforce this article by appropriate legislation.

### Amendment XXIV
### (ratified 23 Jan 1964)

## Section 1—

The right of citizens of the United States to vote in any primary or other election for President or Vice President, for electors for President or Vice President, or for Senator or Representative in Congress, shall not be denied or abridged by the United States or any State by reason of failure to pay any poll tax or other tax.

## Section 2—

The Congress shall have power to enforce this article by appropriate legislation.

### Amendment XXV
### (ratified 23 Jan 1967)

## Section 1—

In case of the removal of the President from office or of his death or resignation, the Vice President shall become President.

## Section 2—

Whenever there is a vacancy in the office of the Vice President, the President shall nominate a Vice President who shall take office upon confirmation by a majority vote of both Houses of Congress.

## Section 3—

Whenever the President transmits to the President pro tempore of the Senate and the Speaker of the House of Representatives his written declaration that he is unable to discharge the powers and duties of his office, and until he transmits to them a written declaration to the contrary, such powers and duties shall be discharged by the Vice President as Acting President.

## Section 4—

Whenever the Vice president and a majority of either the principal officers of the executive departments or of such other body as Congress may by law provide, transmit to the President pro tempore of the Senate and the Speaker of the House of Representatives their written declaration that the President is unable to discharge the powers and duties of his office, the Vice President shall immediately assume the powers and duties of the office as Acting President.

Thereafter, when the President transmits to the President pro tempore of the Senate and the Speaker of the House of Representatives his written declaration that no inability exists, he shall resume the powers and duties of his office unless the Vice President and a majority of either the principal officers of the executive department or of such other body as Congress may by law provide, transmit within four days to the President pro tempore of the Senate and the Speaker of the House of Representatives their written declaration that the President is unable to discharge the powers and duties of his office. Thereupon Congress shall decide the issue, assembling within forty-eight hours for that purpose if not in session. If the Congress, within twenty-one days after receipt of the latter written declaration, or, if Congress is not in session, within twenty-one days after Congress is required to assemble, determines by two-thirds vote of both Houses that the President is unable to discharge the powers and duties of his office, the Vice President shall continue to discharge the same as Acting President; otherwise, the President shall resume the powers and duties of his office.

## Amendment XXVI
(ratified 1 Jul 1971)

Section 1—
The right of citizens of the United States, who are eighteen years of age or older, to vote shall not be denied or abridged by the United States or by any State on account of age.

Section 2—
The Congress shall have power to enforce this article by appropriate legislation.

## Amendment XXVII
(ratified 7 May 1992)

No law, varying the compensation for the services of the Senators and Representatives, shall take effect, until an election of representatives shall have intervened.

---

## Confederate States and Secession Dates

In the months following Abraham Lincoln's election as president in 1860, seven states of the Deep South held conventions and approved secession, thus precipitating the Civil War. After the attack on Fort Sumter SC on 12 Apr 1861, Virginia, Arkansas, North Carolina, and Tennessee also seceded (Tennessee was the only state to hold a popular referendum without a convention on secession). The Confederacy operated as a separate government, with Jefferson Davis as president and Alexander H. Stephens as vice president. Its principal goals were the preservation of states' rights and the institution of slavery. Although it enjoyed a series of military victories in the first two years of fighting, the surrender at Appomattox VA by Gen. Robert E. Lee on 9 Apr 1865 signaled its dissolution.

| STATE | DATE | STATE | DATE | STATE | DATE |
|---|---|---|---|---|---|
| South Carolina | 20 Dec 1860 | Georgia | 19 Jan 1861 | Arkansas | 6 May 1861 |
| Mississippi | 9 Jan 1861 | Louisiana | 26 Jan 1861 | North Carolina | 20 May 1861 |
| Florida | 10 Jan 1861 | Texas | 1 Feb 1861 | Tennessee | 8 Jun 1861 |
| Alabama | 11 Jan 1861 | Virginia | 17 Apr 1861 | | |

---

## Emancipation Proclamation

*The Emancipation Proclamation was issued by Pres. Abraham Lincoln and freed the slaves of the Confederate states in rebellion against the Union. After the Battle of Antietam (17 Sep 1862), Lincoln issued his proclamation calling on the revolted states to return to their allegiance before the next year, otherwise their slaves would be declared free men. No state returned, and the threatened declaration was issued on 1 Jan 1863.*

By the President of the United States of America:

A Proclamation.

Whereas, on the twenty-second day of September, in the year of our Lord one thousand eight hundred and sixty-two, a proclamation was issued by the President of the United States, containing, among other things, the following, to wit:

"That on the first day of January, in the year of our Lord one thousand eight hundred and sixty-three, all persons held as slaves within any State or designated part of a State, the people whereof shall then be in rebellion against the United States, shall be then, thenceforward, and forever free; and the Executive Government of the United States, including the military and naval authority thereof, will recognize and maintain the freedom of such persons, and will do no act or acts to repress such persons, or any of them, in any efforts they may make for their actual freedom.

"That the Executive will, on the first day of January aforesaid, by proclamation, designate the States and parts of States, if any, in which the people thereof, respectively, shall then be in rebellion against the United States; and the fact that any State, or the people thereof, shall on that day be, in good faith, represented in the Congress of the United States by members chosen thereto at elections wherein a majority of the qualified voters of such State shall have participated, shall, in the absence of strong countervailing testimony, be deemed conclusive evidence that such State, and the people thereof, are not then in rebellion against the United States."

Now, therefore I, Abraham Lincoln, President of the United States, by virtue of the power in me vested as Commander-in-Chief, of the Army and Navy of the United States in time of actual armed rebellion against the authority and government of the United States, and as a fit and necessary war measure for suppressing said rebellion, do, on this first day of January, in the year of our Lord one thousand eight hundred and sixty-three, and in accordance with my purpose so to do publicly proclaimed for the full period of one hundred days, from the day first above mentioned, order and designate as the States and parts of States wherein the people thereof respectively, are this day in rebellion against the United States, the following, to wit:

Arkansas, Texas, Louisiana, (except the Parishes of St. Bernard, Plaquemines, Jefferson, St. John, St. Charles, St. James Ascension, Assumption, Terrebonne, Lafourche, St. Mary, St. Martin, and Orleans, including the City of New Orleans) Mississippi, Alabama, Florida, Georgia, South Carolina, North Carolina, and Virginia, (except the forty-eight counties designated as West Virginia, and also the counties of Berkley, Accomac, Northampton, Elizabeth City, York, Princess Ann, and Norfolk, including the cities of Norfolk and Portsmouth[]), and which excepted parts, are for the present, left precisely as if this proclamation were not issued.

And by virtue of the power, and for the purpose aforesaid, I do order and declare that all persons held as slaves within said designated States, and parts of States, are, and henceforward shall be free; and that the Executive government of the United States, including the military and naval authorities thereof, will recognize and maintain the freedom of said persons.

And I hereby enjoin upon the people so declared to be free to abstain from all violence, unless in necessary self-defence; and I recommend to them that, in all cases when allowed, they labor faithfully for reasonable wages.

And I further declare and make known, that such persons of suitable condition, will be received into the armed service of the United States to garrison forts, positions, stations, and other places, and to man vessels of all sorts in said service.

And upon this act, sincerely believed to be an act of justice, warranted by the Constitution, upon military necessity, I invoke the considerate judgment of mankind, and the gracious favor of Almighty God.

In witness whereof, I have hereunto set my hand and caused the seal of the United States to be affixed.

Done at the City of Washington, this first day of January, in the year of our Lord one thousand eight hundred and sixty three, and of the Independence of the United States of America the eighty-seventh.

By the President: Abraham Lincoln.
William H. Seward, Secretary of State.

## Gettysburg Address

*On 19 Nov 1863 Pres. Abraham Lincoln delivered this speech at the consecration of the National Cemetery at Gettysburg PA, the site of one of the most decisive battles of the American Civil War. The main address at the dedication ceremony was one of two hours, delivered by Edward Everett, the best-known orator of the time. It is Lincoln's short speech, however, which is remembered, not only as a memorial to those who gave their lives on the battlefield, but as a statement of the ideals on which the nation was founded.*

Four score and seven years ago our fathers brought forth on this continent a new nation, conceived in Liberty, and dedicated to the proposition that all men are created equal. Now we are engaged in a great civil war, testing whether that nation or any nation so conceived and so dedicated, can long endure. We are met on a great battle-field of that war. We have come to dedicate a portion of that field, as a final resting place for those who here gave their lives that that nation might live. It is altogether fitting and proper that we should do this. But, in a larger sense, we can not dedicate—we can not consecrate—we can not hallow—this ground. The brave men, living and dead, who struggled here, have consecrated it, far above our poor power to add or detract. The world will little note, nor long remember what we say here, but it can never forget what they did here. It is for us the living, rather, to be dedicated here to the unfinished work which they who fought here have thus far so nobly advanced. It is rather for us to be here dedicated to the great task remaining before us—that from these honored dead we take increased devotion to that cause for which they gave the last full measure of devotion—that we here highly resolve that these dead shall not have died in vain—that this nation, under God, shall have a new birth of freedom—and that government of the people, by the people, for the people, shall not perish from the earth.

# United States Government

## The Presidency at a Glance

| | PRESIDENCY | POLITICAL PARTY | TIME IN OFFICE | VICE PRESIDENT |
|---|---|---|---|---|
| 1 | George Washington | Federalist | 1789–1797 | John Adams |
| 2 | John Adams | Federalist | 1797–1801 | Thomas Jefferson |
| 3 | Thomas Jefferson | Jeffersonian Republican | 1801–1809 | Aaron Burr George Clinton |
| 4 | James Madison | Jeffersonian Republican | 1809–1817 | George Clinton Elbridge Gerry |
| 5 | James Monroe | Jeffersonian Republican | 1817–1825 | Daniel D. Tompkins |

## The Presidency at a Glance (continued)

| | PRESIDENCY | POLITICAL PARTY | TIME IN OFFICE | VICE PRESIDENT |
|---|---|---|---|---|
| 6 | John Quincy Adams | National Republican | 1825–1829 | John C. Calhoun |
| 7 | Andrew Jackson | Democratic | 1829–1837 | John C. Calhoun |
| | | | | Martin Van Buren |
| 8 | Martin Van Buren | Democratic | 1837–1841 | Richard M. Johnson |
| 9 | William Henry Harrison* | Whig | 4 Mar–4 Apr 1841 | John Tyler |
| 10 | John Tyler | Whig | 1841–1845 | none |
| 11 | James K. Polk | Democratic | 1845–1849 | George Mifflin Dallas |
| 12 | Zachary Taylor* | Whig | 1849–1850 | Millard Fillmore |
| 13 | Millard Fillmore | Whig | 1850–1853 | none |
| 14 | Franklin Pierce | Democratic | 1853–1857 | William Rufus de Vane King |
| 15 | James Buchanan | Democratic | 1857–1861 | John C. Breckinridge |
| 16 | Abraham Lincoln*† | Republican | 1861–1865 | Hannibal Hamlin |
| | | | | Andrew Johnson |
| 17 | Andrew Johnson | Democratic (Union) | 1865–1869 | none |
| 18 | Ulysses S. Grant | Republican | 1869–1877 | Schuyler Colfax |
| | | | | Henry Wilson |
| 19 | Rutherford B. Hayes | Republican | 1877–1881 | William A. Wheeler |
| 20 | James A. Garfield*† | Republican | 4 Mar–19 Sep 1881 | Chester A. Arthur |
| 21 | Chester A. Arthur | Republican | 1881–1885 | none |
| 22 | Grover Cleveland | Democratic | 1885–1889 | Thomas A. Hendricks |
| 23 | Benjamin Harrison | Republican | 1889–1893 | Levi Parons Morton |
| 24 | Grover Cleveland | Democratic | 1893–1897 | Adlai E. Stevenson |
| 25 | William McKinley*† | Republican | 1897–1901 | Garret A. Hobart |
| | | | | Theodore Roosevelt |
| 26 | Theodore Roosevelt | Republican | 1901–1909 | Charles Warren Fairbanks |
| 27 | William Howard Taft | Republican | 1909–1913 | James Schoolcraft Sherman |
| 28 | Woodrow Wilson | Democratic | 1913–1921 | Thomas R. Marshall |
| 29 | Warren G. Harding* | Republican | 1921–1923 | Calvin Coolidge |
| 30 | Calvin Coolidge | Republican | 1923–1929 | Charles G. Dawes |
| 31 | Herbert Hoover | Republican | 1929–1933 | Charles Curtis |
| 32 | Franklin D. Roosevelt* | Democratic | 1933–1945 | John Nance Garner |
| | | | | Henry A. Wallace |
| | | | | Harry S. Truman |
| 33 | Harry S. Truman | Democratic | 1945–1953 | Alben W. Barkley |
| 34 | Dwight D. Eisenhower | Republican | 1953–1961 | Richard M. Nixon |
| 35 | John F. Kennedy*† | Democratic | 1961–1963 | Lyndon B. Johnson |
| 36 | Lyndon B. Johnson | Democratic | 1963–1969 | Hubert H. Humphrey |
| 37 | Richard M. Nixon** | Republican | 1969–1974 | Spiro T. Agnew |
| | | | | Gerald R. Ford |
| 38 | Gerald R. Ford | Republican | 1974–1977 | Nelson A. Rockefeller |
| 39 | Jimmy Carter | Democratic | 1977–1981 | Walter F. Mondale |
| 40 | Ronald Reagan | Republican | 1981–1989 | George H.W. Bush |
| 41 | George H.W. Bush | Republican | 1989–1993 | Dan Quayle |
| 42 | William J. Clinton | Democratic | 1993–2001 | Albert Gore |
| 43 | George W. Bush | Republican | 2001– | Richard B. Cheney |

*Died in office.    **Resigned from office.    †Assassinated.

# Presidential Biographies

**George Washington** (22 Feb [11 Feb, Old Style] 1732, Westmoreland county VA–14 Dec 1799, Mt. Vernon, in Fairfax county VA), American Revolutionary commander-in-chief (1775–83) and first president of the US (1789–97). Born into a wealthy family, he was educated privately and worked as a surveyor from age 14. In 1752 he inherited his brother's estate at Mount Vernon, including 18 slaves whose ranks grew to 49 by 1760, though he disapproved of slavery. In the French and Indian War he was commissioned a colonel and sent to the Ohio Territory. After Edward Braddock was killed, Washington became commander of all Virginia forces, entrusted with defending the western frontier (1755–58). He resigned to manage his estate and in 1759 married Martha Dandridge Custis (1731–1802), a widow. He served in the House of Burgesses 1759–74, where he supported the colonists' cause, and in the Continental Congress 1774–75. In 1775 he was elected to command the Continental Army. In the ensuing American Revolution, he proved a brilliant commander and stalwart leader despite several defeats. With the war effectively ended by the capture of Yorktown (1781), he resigned his commission and returned to Mount Vernon (1783). He was a delegate to and presiding officer of the Constitutional Convention (1787) and helped secure ratification of the Constitution in Virginia. When the state electors met to select the first president (1789), Washington was the unanimous choice. He formed a cabinet to balance sectional and political differences but was committed to a strong central government. Elected to a second term, he followed a middle course between the political factions that became the Federalist Party and Democratic Party. He proclaimed a policy of neutrality in the war between Britain and France (1793) and sent troops to suppress the Whiskey Rebellion (1794). He declined to serve a third term, setting a 144-year precedent, and retired in 1797 after delivering his "Farewell Address." Known as the "father of his country," he is regarded as one of the greatest figures in US history.

**John Adams** (30 Oct [19 Oct, Old Style] 1735, Braintree [now in Quincy] MA—4 Jul 1826, Quincy MA), first vice president (1789–97) and second president (1797–1801) of the US. He practiced law in Boston and in 1764 married Abigail Smith. Active in the American independence movement, he was elected to the Massachusetts legislature and served as a delegate to the Continental Congress (1774–78), where he was appointed to several committees, including one with Thomas Jefferson and others to draft the Declaration of Independence. He served as a diplomat in France, The Netherlands, and England (1778–88). In the first US presidential election, he received the second-largest number of votes and became vice president under George Washington. Adams's term as president was marked by controversy over his signing the Alien and Sedition Acts in 1798 and by his alliance with the conservative Federalist Party. In 1800 he was defeated for reelection by Jefferson and retired to live a secluded life in Massachusetts. In 1812 he was reconciled with Jefferson, with whom he began an illuminating correspondence. Both men died on 4 Jul 1826, the Declaration's 50th anniversary. Pres. John Quincy Adams was his son.

**Thomas Jefferson** (13 Apr [2 Apr, Old Style] 1743, Shadwell VA—4 Jul 1826, Monticello VA), third president of the US (1801–9). He was a planter and lawyer from 1767, as well as a slaveholder who opposed slavery. While a member of the House of Burgesses (1769–75), he initiated the Committee of Correspondence (1773) with Richard Henry Lee and Patrick Henry. In 1774 he wrote the influential *Summary View of the Rights of British America*, stating that the British Parliament had no authority to legislate for the colonies. A delegate to the second Continental Congress, he was appointed to the committee to draft the Declaration of Independence and became its primary author. He was elected governor of Virginia (1779–81) but was unable to organize effective opposition when British forces invaded the colony (1780–81). Criticized for his conduct, he retired, vowing to remain a private citizen. Again a member of the Continental Congress (1783–85), he proposed territorial provisions later incorporated in the Northwest Ordinances. He traveled in Europe on diplomatic missions and became minister to France (1785–89). George Washington made him secretary of state (1790–93). He soon became embroiled in conflict with Alexander Hamilton over their opposing interpretations of the Constitution. This led to the rise of factions and political parties, with Jefferson representing the Democratic-Republicans. He served as vice president (1797–1801) but opposed the Alien and Sedition Acts enacted under Pres. John Adams. As part of this opposition, Jefferson drafted one of the Virginia and Kentucky Resolutions. In 1801 he be-

came president after an electoral-vote tie with Aaron Burr was settled by the House of Representatives. Jefferson initiated frugal fiscal policies and simplicity in the ceremonial role of the president. He oversaw the Louisiana Purchase and authorized the Lewis and Clark Expedition. He sought to avoid involvement in the Napoleonic Wars by signing the Embargo Act. He retired to his plantation, Monticello, where he pursued his many interests in science, philosophy, and architecture. He served as president of the American Philosophical Society 1797–1815, and in 1819 founded and designed the University of Virginia. In January 2000, the Thomas Jefferson Memorial Foundation accepted the conclusion, supported by DNA evidence, that Jefferson had fathered at least one, and perhaps as many as six, children with Sally Hemings, one of his house slaves. After a long estrangement, he and Adams became reconciled in 1813 and exchanged views on national issues. They both died on July 4, 1826, the 50th anniversary of the signing of the Declaration of Independence.

**James Madison** (16 Mar [5 Mar, Old Style] 1751, Port Conway VA—28 Jun 1836, Montpelier VA), fourth president of the US (1809–17). He served in the state legislature (1776–80, 1784–86). At the Constitutional Convention (1787), his active participation and his careful notes on the debates earned him the title "father of the Constitution." To promote ratification, he collaborated with Alexander Hamilton and John Jay on *The Federalist*. In the House of Representatives (1789–97), he sponsored the Bill of Rights, was a leading Jeffersonian Republican, and split with Hamilton over funding state war debts. In reaction to the Alien and Sedition Acts, he drafted one of the Virginia and Kentucky Resolutions (1798). He was appointed secretary of state (1801–9) by Thomas Jefferson, with whom he developed US foreign policy. Elected president in 1808, he was occupied by the trade and shipping embargo problems caused by France and Britain that led to the War of 1812. He was reelected in 1812; his second term was marked principally by the war, during which he reinvigorated the Army, and also saw approval of the charter of the Second Bank of the US and the first US protective tariff. He retired to his Virginia estate, Montpelier, with his wife, Dolley (1768–1849), whose political acumen he had long prized. He continued to write articles and letters and served as rector of the University of Virginia (1826–36).

**James Monroe** (28 Apr 1758, Westmoreland county VA—4 Jul 1831, New York NY), fifth president of the US (1817–25). He fought in the American Revolution and studied law under Thomas Jefferson. He served in the Congress (1783–86) and Senate (1790–94), where he opposed George Washington's administration. He nevertheless became minister to France (1794–96), where he misled the French about US politics and was recalled. He served as governor of Virginia 1799–1802. Pres. Jefferson sent him to France, where he helped negotiate the Louisiana Purchase (1803), then named him minister to Britain (1803–7). He returned to Virginia and became governor (1811), but resigned to become US secretary of state (1811–17) and secretary of war (1814–15). He served two terms as president, presiding in a period that became known as the Era of Good Feelings. He oversaw the Seminole War (1817–18) and the acquisition of the Floridas (1819–21), and signed the Missouri Compromise (1820). With secretary of state John Quincy Adams, he developed the principles of US foreign policy later called the Monroe Doctrine.

**John Quincy Adams** (11 Jul 1767, Braintree [now in Quincy] MA—23 Feb 1848, Washington DC), sixth president of the US (1825–29). He was the eldest son of Pres. John Adams and Abigail. He accompanied his father to Europe on diplomatic missions (1778–80) and was later appointed minister to The Netherlands (1794) and Prussia (1797). In 1801 he returned to Massachusetts and served in the Senate (1803–8). Resuming his diplomatic service, he became minister to Russia (1809–11) and Britain (1815–17). Appointed secretary of state (1817–24), he was instrumental in acquiring Florida from Spain and in drafting the Monroe Doctrine. He was one of three candidates in the 1824 presidential election, in which none received a majority of the electoral votes, though Andrew Jackson received a plurality. The decision went to the House of Representatives, where Adams received crucial support from Henry Clay and the electoral votes necessary to elect him president. He appointed Clay secretary of state, which further angered Jackson. Adams's presidency was unsuccessful; when he ran for reelection, Jackson defeated him. In 1830 he was elected to the House of Representatives, where he served until his death. He was outspoken in his opposition to slavery and in 1839 proposed a constitutional amendment forbidding slavery in any new state admitted to the Union. Southern congressmen prevented discussion of antislavery petitions by passing gag rules (repealed in 1844 as a result of Adams's persistence). In 1841 he successfully defended the slaves in the Amistad Mutiny case.

**Andrew Jackson** (15 Mar 1767, Waxhaws region SC—8 Jun 1845, the Hermitage, near Nashville TN), seventh president of the US (1829–37). He fought briefly in the American Revolution near his frontier home, where his family was killed. He studied law and in 1788 was appointed prosecuting attorney for western North Carolina. When the region became the state of Tennessee, he was elected to the House of Representatives (1796–97) and Senate (1797–98). He served on the state supreme court (1798–1804) and in 1802 was elected major general of the Tennessee militia. When the War of 1812 began, he offered the US the services of his 50,000-volunteer militia. He was sent to fight the Creek Indians allied with the British in Mississippi Territory. After a lengthy battle (1813–14), he defeated them at the Battle of Horseshoe Bend. After capturing Pensacola FL from the British-allied Spanish, he marched overland to engage the British in Louisiana. A decisive victory at the Battle of New Orleans made him a national hero, dubbed "Old Hickory" by the press. After US acquisition of Florida, he was named governor of the territory (1821). One of four candidates in the 1824 presidential election, he won an electoral-votes plurality but the House gave the election to John Quincy Adams. In 1828 Jackson defeated Adams after a fierce campaign and became the first president elected from west of the Appalachian Mountains. His election was considered a triumph of political democracy. He replaced many federal officeholders with his supporters, a process that became known as the spoils system. He pursued a policy of moving

Native Americans westward with the Indian Removal Acts. He split with his vice president, John C. Calhoun, over the nullification movement. His reelection in 1832 was due in part to support for his anticapitalistic fiscal policies and a controversial veto that affected the Bank of the US. His popularity continued to build throughout his presidency. During his tenure a strong Democratic Party developed that led to a vigorous two-party system.

**Martin Van Buren** (5 Dec 1782, Kinderhook NY—24 Jul 1862, Kinderhook NY), eighth president of the US (1837–41). He practiced law and served in the NY state senate (1812–20) and as state attorney general (1816–19). He became the leader of an informal group of political supporters, called the Albany Regency because they dominated state politics even while Van Buren was in Washington. He was elected to the US Senate (1821–28), where he supported states' rights and opposed a strong central government. After John Quincy Adams became president, he joined with Andrew Jackson and others to form a group that later became the Democratic Party. He was elected governor of New York (1828) but resigned to become US secretary of state (1829–31). He was nominated for vice president at the first Democratic Party convention (1832) and served under Jackson (1833–37). As Jackson's chosen successor, he defeated William H. Harrison to win the 1836 election. His presidency was marked by an economic depression, the Maine–Canada border dispute, the Seminole War in Florida, and debate over the annexation of Texas. He was defeated in his bid for reelection and failed to win the Democratic nomination in 1844 because of his antislavery views. In 1848 he was nominated for president by the Free Soil Party but failed to win the election and retired.

**William Henry Harrison** (9 Feb 1773, Charles City county VA—4 Apr 1841, Washington DC), ninth president of the US (1841). Born into a political family, he enlisted in the army at 18 and served under Anthony Wayne at the Battle of Fallen Timbers. In 1798 he became secretary of the Northwest Territories, and in 1800 governor of the new Indiana Territory. In response to pressure from white settlers, he negotiated treaties with the Native Americans that ceded millions of acres of additional land to the US When Tecumseh organized an uprising in 1811, Harrison led a US force to defeat the Indians at the Battle of Tippecanoe, a victory that largely established his reputation in the public mind. In the War of 1812 he was made a brigadier general and defeated the British and their Indian allies at the Battle of the Thames in Ontario. After the war he moved to Ohio, where he became prominent in the Whig Party. He served in the House of Representatives (1816–19) and Senate (1825–28). As the Whig candidate in the 1836 presidential election, he lost narrowly. In 1840 he and his running mate, John Tyler, won election with a slogan emphasizing Harrison's frontier triumph: "Tippecanoe and Tyler too." The 68-year-old Harrison delivered his inaugural speech without a hat or overcoat in a cold drizzle, contracted pneumonia, and died one month later, the first president to die in office.

**John Tyler** (29 Mar 1790, Charles City county VA—18 Jan 1862, Richmond VA), 10th president of the US (1841–45). He practiced law before serving in the state legislature (1811–16, 1823–25, 1839) and as governor of Virginia (1825–27). In the House of

Representatives (1817–21) and Senate (1827–36), he was a states-rights supporter. Though a slaveholder, he sought to prohibit the slave trade in the District of Columbia, provided Maryland and Virginia concurred. He resigned from the Senate rather than acquiesce to state instructions to change his vote on a censure of Pres. Andrew Jackson. After breaking with the Democratic Party, he was nominated by the Whig Party for vice president under William H. Harrison. They won the 1840 election, carefully avoiding the issues and stressing party loyalty and the slogan "Tippecanoe and Tyler too!" Harrison died a month after taking office, and Tyler became the first to attain the presidency "by accident." He vetoed a national bank bill supported by the Whigs, and all but one member of the cabinet resigned, leaving him without party support. Nonetheless, he reorganized the navy, settled the second of the Seminole Wars in Florida, and oversaw the annexation of Texas. He was nominated for reelection but withdrew in favor of James Polk and retired to his Virginia plantation. Committed to states' rights but opposed to secession, he organized the Washington Peace Conference (1861) to resolve sectional differences. When the Senate rejected a proposed compromise, Tyler urged Virginia to secede.

**James Knox Polk** (2 Nov 1795, Mecklenburg county NC—15 Jun 1849, Nashville TN), 11th president of the US (1845–49). He became a lawyer in Tennessee and a friend and supporter of Andrew Jackson, who helped Polk win election to the House of Representatives (1825–39). He left the House to become governor of Tennessee (1839–41). At the deadlocked 1844 Democratic convention Polk was nominated as the compromise candidate; he is considered the first dark-horse presidential candidate. A proponent of western expansion, he campaigned with the slogan "Fifty-four Forty or Fight," to bring a solution to the Oregon Question. Elected at 49, the youngest president to that time, he successfully concluded the Oregon border dispute with Britain (1846) and secured passage of the Walker Tariff Act (1846), which lowered import duties and helped foreign trade. He led the prosecution of the Mexican War, which resulted in large territorial gains but reopened the debate over the extension of slavery. His administration also established the Department of the Interior, the US Naval Academy, and the Smithsonian Institution, oversaw revision of the treasury system, and proclaimed the validity of the Monroe Doctrine. Though an efficient and competent president, deft in his handling of Congress, he was exhausted by his efforts and did not seek reelection; he died three months after leaving office.

**Zachary Taylor** (24 Nov 1784, Montebello VA—9 Jul 1850, Washington DC), 12th president of the US (1849–50). Born in Virginia, he grew up on the Kentucky frontier. He fought in the War of 1812, the Black Hawk War (1832), and the Seminole War in Florida (1835–42), earning the nickname "Old Rough-and-Ready" for his indifference to hardship. Sent to Texas in anticipation of war with Mexico, he defeated the Mexican invaders at the battles of Palo Alto and Resaca de la Palma (1846). After the Mexican War formally began, he captured Monterrey and granted the Mexican army an eight-week armistice. Displeased, Pres. James Polk moved Taylor's best troops to serve under Winfield Scott in the invasion of Veracruz. Taylor ignored orders to remain in Monterrey and marched south to defeat a large Mexican force at the Battle of Buena Vista (1847). He became a national hero and was nominated as the Whig candidate for president (1848). He defeated Lewis Cass to win the election. His brief term was marked by a controversy over the new territories that produced the Compromise of 1850 and by a scandal involving members of his cabinet. He died, probably of cholera, after only 16 months in office and was succeeded by Millard Fillmore.

**Millard Fillmore** (7 Jan 1800, Locke Township, NY—8 Mar 1874, Buffalo NY), 13th president of the US (1850–53). Born into poverty, he became an indentured apprentice at 15. He studied law with a local judge and began to practice in Buffalo in 1823. Initially identified with the Anti-Masonic Party (1828–34), he followed his political mentor, Thurlow Weed, to the Whigs and was soon a leader of the party's northern wing. He served in the House of Representatives (1833–35, 1837–43), where he became a follower of Henry Clay. In 1848 the Whigs nominated Fillmore as vice president, and he was elected with Zachary Taylor. He became president on Taylor's death in 1850. Though he abhorred slavery, he supported the Compromise of 1850 and insisted on federal enforcement of the Fugitive Slave Act. His stand, which alienated the North, led to his defeat by Winfield Scott at the Whigs' nominating convention in 1852 and effectively led to the death of the party. Throughout his career he advocated US internal development and was an early champion of expansion in the Pacific. In 1853 he sent Matthew Perry with a US fleet to Japan, forcing its isolationist government to enter into trade and diplomatic relations. He returned to Buffalo and was nominated for president by the third-party Know-Nothing Party in 1856, won by Democrat James Buchanan.

**Franklin Pierce** (23 Nov 1804, Hillsboro NH—8 Oct 1869, Concord NH), 14th president of the US (1853–57). He practiced law and served in the House of Representatives (1833–37) and Senate (1837–42). He returned to his law practice, serving briefly in the Mexican War. At the deadlocked Democratic convention of 1852, he was nominated as the compromise candidate; though largely unknown nationally, he unexpectedly trounced Winfield Scott in the general election. For the sake of harmony and business prosperity, he was inclined to oppose antislavery agitation so as to placate Southern opinion. He promoted US territorial expansion, resulting in the diplomatic controversy of the Ostend Manifesto. He reorganized the diplomatic and consular service and created the Court of Claims. He encouraged plans for a transcontinental railroad and approved the Gadsden Purchase. To promote northwestern migration and conciliate sectional demands, he approved the Kansas-Nebraska Act but was unable to settle the resultant problems. Defeated for renomination by James Buchanan in 1856, he retired from politics.

**James Buchanan** (23 Apr 1791, near Mercersburg PA—1 Jun 1868, near Lancaster PA), 15th president of the US (1857–61). He became a lawyer and member of the Pennsylvania legislature before serving in the House of Representatives (1821–31), as minister to Russia (1832–34), and in the Senate (1834–45). He was secretary of state in James Polk's cabinet (1845–49). As minister to Britain (1853–56), he helped draft the Ostend Manifesto. In 1856 he secured the Democratic nomination and election as president, defeating John C. Fremont. Though experienced in government and law, he lacked the moral courage to deal effectively with the slavery crisis and equivocated on the question of Kansas's status as a slaveholding state. The ensuing split within his party allowed Abraham Lincoln to win the election of 1860. He denounced the secession of South Carolina following the election and sent reinforcements to Fort Sumter, but failed to respond further to the mounting crisis.

**Abraham Lincoln** (12 Feb 1809, near Hodgenville KY—15 Apr 1865, Washington DC), 16th president of the US (1861–65). Born in a Kentucky log cabin, he moved to Indiana in 1816 and to Illinois in 1830. He worked as a storekeeper, rail-splitter, postmaster, and surveyor, then enlisted as a volunteer in the Black Hawk War and became a captain. Though largely self-taught, he practiced law in Springfield IL and served in the state legislature (1834–40). He was elected as a Whig to the House of Representatives (1847–49). As a circuit-riding lawyer from 1849, he became one of the state's most successful lawyers, noted for his shrewdness, common sense, and honesty (earning the nickname "Honest Abe"). In 1856 he joined the Republican Party, which nominated him as its candidate in the 1858 Senate election. In a series of seven debates with Stephen A. Douglas (the Lincoln-Douglas Debates), he argued against the extension of slavery into the territories, though not against slavery itself. Although morally opposed to slavery, he was not an abolitionist. During the campaign, he attempted to rebut Douglas' charge that he was a dangerous radical by reassuring audiences that he did not favor political equality for blacks. Despite his loss in the election, the debates brought him national attention. He again ran against Douglas in the 1860 presidential election, which he won by a large margin. But the South opposed his position on slavery in the territories, and before his inauguration seven Southern states had seceded from the Union. The ensuing American Civil War completely consumed Lincoln's administration. He excelled as a wartime leader, creating a high command for directing all the country's energies and resources toward the war effort and combining statecraft and overall command of the armies with what some have called military genius. However, his abrogation of some civil liberties, especially the writ of habeas corpus, and the closing of several newspapers by his generals disturbed both Democrats and Republicans, including some members of his own cabinet. To unite the North and influence foreign opinion, he issued the Emancipation Proclamation (1863); his Gettysburg Address (1863) further ennobled the war's purpose. The continuing war affected some Northerners' resolve and his reelection was not assured, but strategic battle victories turned the tide and he easily defeated George B. McClellan in 1864. His platform included passage of the 13th Amendment outlawing slavery (ratified 1865). At his second inaugural, with victory in sight, he spoke of moderation in reconstructing the South and building a harmonious Union. On 14 Apr, five days after the war ended, he was shot by John Wilkes Booth and soon after died.

**Andrew Johnson** (29 Dec 1808, Raleigh NC—31 Jul 1875, near Carter Station TN), 17th president of the US (1865–69). Born in North Carolina and reared in Tennessee, he was self-educated and initially worked as a tailor. He organized a workingman's party and was elected to the state legislature (1835–43), where he became a spokesman for small farmers. He served in the House of Representatives (1843–53) and as governor of Tennessee (1853–57). Elected to the Senate (1857–62), he opposed antislavery agitation, but in 1860 he opposed Southern secession, even after Tennessee seceded in 1861, and during the Civil War he was the only Southern senator who refused to join the Confederacy. In 1862 he was appointed military governor of Tennessee, then under Union control. In 1864 he was selected to run for vice president with Pres. Abraham Lincoln; he assumed the presidency after Lincoln's assassination. During Reconstruction he favored a moderate policy that readmitted former Confederate states to the Union with few provisions for reform or civil rights for freedmen. In 1867 the Radical Republicans in Congress passed civil rights legislation and established the Freedmen's Bureau. His veto angered Congress, which passed the Tenure of Office Act. In 1868 in defiance of the act, Johnson dismissed secretary of war Edwin M. Stanton, an ally of the Radicals. The House responded by impeaching the president for the first time in US history. In the subsequent Senate trial, the charges proved weak and the necessary two-thirds vote needed for conviction failed by one vote. Johnson remained in office until 1869, but his effectiveness had ended. He returned to Tennessee, where he won reelection to the Senate shortly before he died.

**Ulysses S. Grant (Hiram Ulysses Grant)** (27 Apr 1822, Point Pleasant OH—23 Jul 1885, Mount McGregor NY), 18th president of the US (1869–77). He served in the Mexican War under Zachary Taylor; he resigned his commission in 1854 when he could not afford to bring his family west. Allegations that he became a drunkard in the lonely years in the West and in later life, though never proved, would affect his reputation. He worked unsuccessfully at farming in Missouri and at his family's leather business in Illinois. When the Civil War began (1861), he was appointed brigadier general; his 1862 attack on Fort Donelson TN, produced the first major Union victory. He drove off a Confederate attack at Shiloh but was criticized for heavy Union losses. He devised the campaign to take the stronghold of Vicksburg MS, in 1863, cutting the Confederacy in half from east to west. Following his victory at the Battle of Chattanooga in 1864, he was appointed commander of the Union army. While William T. Sherman made his famous march across Georgia, Grant attacked Robert E. Lee's forces in Virginia, bringing the war to an end in 1865. Grant's administrative ability and innovative strategies were largely responsible for the Union victory. His successful Republican presidential campaign made him, at 46, the youngest man yet elected president. His two terms were marred by administrative inaction and political scandal involving members of his cabinet, including the Crédit Mobilier scandal and the Whiskey Ring operation. He was more successful in foreign affairs, in which he was aided by his secretary of state, Hamilton Fish. He supported amnesty for Confederate leaders and protection for black civil rights. His veto of a bill to increase the amount of legal tender (1874) diminished the currency crisis in the next 25 years. In 1881 he moved to New York; when a partner defrauded an investment firm co-owned by his son, the family was impoverished. His memoirs were published by his friend Mark Twain.

**Rutherford Birchard Hayes** (4 Oct 1822, Delaware OH–17 Jan 1893, Fremont OH), 19th president of the US (1877–81). He practiced law in Cincinnati, representing defendants in several fugitive-slave cases and becoming associated with the new Republican Party. After fighting in the Union army, he served in the House of Representatives (1865–67). As governor of Ohio (1868–72, 1875–76), he advocated a sound currency backed by gold. In 1876 he won the Republican nomination for president. His opponent, Samuel Tilden, won a larger popular vote, but Hayes's managers contested the electoral-vote returns in four states, and a special Electoral Commission awarded the election to Hayes. As part of a secret compromise reached with Southerners, he withdrew the remaining federal troops from the South, ending Reconstruction, and promised not to interfere with elections there, ensuring the return of white Democratic supremacy. He introduced civil-service reform based on merit, incurring a dispute with Roscoe Conkling and the conservative "stalwart" Republicans. At the request of state governors, he used federal troops against strikers in the railroad strikes of 1877. Declining to run for a second term, he retired to work for humanitarian causes.

**James Abram Garfield** (19 Nov 1831, near Orange [in Cuyahoga county] OH–19 Sep 1881, Elberon [now in Long Branch] NJ), 20th president of the US (1881). He graduated from Williams College, then returned to Ohio to teach and head an academy that became Hiram College. In the Civil War he led the 42nd Ohio Volunteers and fought at Shiloh and Chickamauga. He resigned as a major general to serve in the House of Representatives (1863–80). A Radical Republican during Reconstruction, he served on the Electoral Commission in the 1876 election, and was the House Republican leader from 1876 to 1880, when he was elected to the Senate. At the 1880 Republican nominating convention, the delegates supporting Ulysses S. Grant and James Blaine became deadlocked. On the 36th ballot Garfield was nominated as a compromise presidential candidate, with Chester Arthur as vice president, and won by a narrow margin. His brief term, less than 150 days, was marked by a dispute with Sen. Roscoe Conkling over patronage. On July 2 he was shot at Washington's railroad station by Charles J. Guiteau, an Arthur supporter. He died on September 19 after 11 weeks of public debate over the ambiguous constitutional conditions for presidential succession (later clarified by the 20th and 25th Amendments).

**Chester Alan Arthur** (5 Oct 1829, North Fairfield VT–18 Nov 1886, New York NY), 21st president of the US (1881–85). He practiced law in New York City from 1854. He became active in local Republican politics and a close associate of party leader Roscoe Conkling, and was appointed customs collector for the port of New York (1871–78), an office long known for its employment of the spoils system. He conducted the business of the office with integrity but continued to pad its payroll with Conkling loyalists. At the Republican national convention in 1880, Arthur became the compromise choice for vice president on the ticket with James Garfield, and became president on Garfield's assassination. As president, Arthur displayed unexpected independence by vetoing measures that rewarded polit-

ical patronage. He also signed the Pendleton Act, which created a civil-service system based on merit. He recommended the appropriations that initiated the rebuilding of the Navy toward the strength it later achieved in the Spanish–American War (1898). He failed to win his party's nomination for a second term.

**(Stephen) Grover Cleveland** (18 Mar 1837, Caldwell NJ–24 Jun 1908, Princeton NJ), 22nd and 24th president of the US (1885–89, 1893–97). He practiced law in Buffalo NY from 1859, where he entered Democratic Party politics. As mayor of Buffalo (1881–82), he was known as a foe of corruption. As governor of New York (1883–85), he earned the hostility of Tammany Hall with his independence, but in 1884 he won the Democratic nomination for president. The first Democratic president since 1856, he supported civil–service reform and opposed high protective tariffs, which became an issue in the 1888 election, when he was narrowly defeated by Benjamin Harrison. In 1892 he was reelected by a huge popular plurality. In 1893 he attributed the US's severe economic depression to the Sherman Silver Purchase Act of 1890 and strongly urged Congress to repeal the act. The economic unrest resulted in the Pullman Strike in 1894. An isolationist, he opposed territorial expansion. In 1895 he invoked the Monroe Doctrine in the border dispute between Britain and Venezuela. By 1896 supporters of the Free Silver Movement controlled the Democratic Party, which nominated William Jennings Bryan instead of Cleveland for president. He retired to New Jersey, where he lectured at Princeton University.

**Benjamin Harrison** (20 Aug 1833, North Bend OH–13 Mar 1901, Indianapolis IN), 23rd president of the US (1889–93). The grandson of Pres. William H. Harrison, he practiced law in Indianapolis from the mid-1850s. He served in the Union army in the Civil War, rising to brigadier general. He served a term in the Senate (1881–87) and, even though he lost reelection, was nominated for president by the Republicans. He went on to defeat the incumbent, Grover Cleveland, who lost despite winning more of the popular vote. As president, his domestic policy was marked by passage of the Sherman Antitrust Act. His foreign policy expanded US influence abroad. His secretary of state, James Blaine, presided at the conference that led to the establishment of the Pan-American Union, resisted pressure to abandon US interests in the Samoan Islands (1889), and negotiated a treaty with Britain in the Bering Sea Dispute (1891). Defeated for reelection by Cleveland in 1892, he returned to Indianapolis to practice law. In 1898–99 he was the leading counsel for Venezuela in its boundary dispute with Britain.

**William McKinley** (29 Jan 1843, Niles OH–14 Sep 1901, Buffalo NY), 25th president of the US (1897–1901). He served in the Civil War as an aide to Col. Rutherford B. Hayes, who later encouraged his political career. He was elected to the House of Representatives (1877–91), where he favored protective tariffs and sponsored the McKinley Tariff of 1890. With the support of Mark Hanna, he was elected governor (1892–96). In 1896 he won the Republican presidential nomination and the general election, defeating William Jennings Bryan. He called a special session of Congress to increase customs duties, but was soon embroiled in events in Cuba and responses to the sinking of the USS

*Maine*, which led to the Spanish-American War. At the war's end, he advocated US dependency status for the Philippines, Puerto Rico, and other former Spanish territories. He again defeated Bryan by a large majority in 1900, and began a tour to urge control of trusts and commercial reciprocity to boost foreign trade, issues neglected during the war. In Buffalo NY on 6 Sep 1901, he was fatally shot by an anarchist, Leon Czolgosz. He was succeeded by Theodore Roosevelt.

**Theodore Roosevelt** (27 Oct 1858, New York NY—6 Jan 1919, Oyster Bay NY), 26th president of the US (1901–9). He was elected to the New York legislature in 1882, where he became a Republican leader opposed to the Democratic political machine. After political defeats and the death of his wife, he went to the Dakota Territory to ranch. He returned to New York to serve on the US Civil Service Commission (1889–95) and as head of the city's board of police commissioners (1895–97). A supporter of William McKinley, he served as assistant secretary of the navy (1897–98). When the Spanish–American War was declared, he resigned to organize a cavalry unit, the Rough Riders. He returned to New York a hero and was elected governor in 1899. As the Republican vice-presidential nominee, he took office when McKinley was reelected, and he became president on McKinley's assassination in 1901. One of his early initiatives was to urge enforcement of the Sherman Antitrust Act against business monopolies. He won election in his own right in 1904, defeating Alton Parker. At his urging, Congress regulated railroad rates and passed the Pure Food and Drug Act and Meat Inspection Act (1906) to provide new consumer protections. He set aside national forests, parks, and mineral, oil, and coal lands for conservation. He and secretary of state Elihu Root announced the Roosevelt corollary to the Monroe Doctrine, which reinforced the US position as defender of the Western Hemisphere. For mediating an end to the Russo–Japanese War, he received the 1906 Nobel Peace Prize. He secured a treaty with Panama for construction of a trans-isthmus canal. Declining to seek reelection, he secured the nomination for William H. Taft. After traveling in Africa and Europe, he tried to win the Republican presidential nomination in 1912; when he was rejected, he organized the Bull Moose Party and ran on a policy of New Nationalism, but failed to win the election. Throughout his life he continued to write, publishing extensively on history, politics, travel, and nature.

**William Howard Taft** (15 Sep 1857, Cincinnati OH—8 Mar 1930, Washington DC), 27th president of the US (1909–13). He served on the state superior court (1887–90), as US solicitor general (1890–92), and as US appellate judge (1892–1900). He was appointed head of the Philippine Commission to set up a civilian government in the islands and was its first civilian governor (1901–4). He served as US secretary of war (1904–8) under Pres. Theodore Roosevelt, who supported Taft's nomination for president in 1908. He won the election but became allied with the conservative Republicans, causing a rift with party progressives. He was again the nominee in 1912, but the split with Roosevelt and the Bull Moose Party resulted in the electoral victory of Woodrow Wilson. Taft later taught law at Yale University (1913–21), served on the National War Labor Board (1918), and was a supporter of the League of Nations. As chief justice of the Supreme Court (1921–30), he introduced reforms that made it more efficient. He secured passage of the Judges Act of 1925, which gave the Court wider discretion in accepting cases. His important opinion in *Myers* v *US* (1926) upheld the president's authority to remove federal officials. In poor health, he resigned in 1930.

**(Thomas) Woodrow Wilson** (28 Dec 1856, Staunton VA—3 Feb 1924, Washington DC), 28th president of the US (1913–21). He earned a law degree and later received his doctorate from Johns Hopkins University. He taught political science at Princeton University (1890–1902), and as its president (1902–10), he introduced various reforms. With the support of progressives, he was elected governor of New Jersey. His reform measures attracted national attention, and he became the Democratic presidential nominee in 1912. His campaign emphasized the progressive measures of his New Freedom policy, and he defeated Theodore Roosevelt and William H. Taft to win the presidency. As president, he approved legislation that lowered tariffs, created the Federal Reserve System, established the Federal Trade Commission, and strengthened labor unions. In foreign affairs he promoted self-government for the Philippines and sought to contain the Mexican civil war. From 1914 he maintained US neutrality in World War I, offering to mediate a settlement and initiate peace negotiations. After the sinking of the *Lusitania* (1915) and other unarmed ships, he obtained a pledge from Germany to stop its submarine campaign. Campaigning on the theme that he had "kept us out of war," he was narrowly reelected in 1916, defeating Charles Evans Hughes. Germany's renewed submarine attacks on unarmed passenger ships caused Wilson to ask for a declaration of war in April 1917. In a continuing effort to negotiate a peace agreement, he presented the Fourteen Points (1918). He led the US delegation to the Paris Peace Conference, where he attempted to stand on his original principles but was forced to compromise by the demands of various countries. The Treaty of Versailles faced opposition in the Senate from the Republican majority led by Henry C. Lodge. In search of popular support for the treaty and its League of Nations, Wilson began a cross-country speaking tour, but he collapsed and returned to Washington DC (Sep 1919), where a stroke left him partially paralyzed. He rejected any attempts to compromise his version of the League of Nations and urged his Senate followers to vote against ratification of the treaty, which was defeated in 1920. He was awarded the 1919 Nobel Peace Prize for his work on the League of Nations.

**Warren Gamaliel Harding** (2 Nov 1865, Caledonia (now Blooming Grove) OH—2 Aug 1923, San Francisco CA), 29th president of the US (1921–23). He became a newspaper publisher in Marion OH, where he was allied with the Republican Party's political machine. He served successively as state senator (1899–1902), lieutenant governor (1903–4), and US senator (1915–21), supporting conservative policies. At the deadlocked 1920 Republican presidential convention, he was chosen as the compromise candidate. Pledging a "return to normalcy" after World War I, he defeated James Cox with over 60% of the popular vote, the largest margin to that time. On his recommendation, Congress established a budget system for the federal government, passed a high protective tariff, revised wartime taxes, and restricted immigration. His administration convened the Washington Conference (1921–22). His ill-advised cabinet and patronage appointments, including Albert Fall, led to the Teapot Dome scandal and characterized his administration as corrupt. While in Alaska, he received word of the corruption about to be exposed and headed back. He arrived in San Francisco exhausted, reportedly suffering from food poisoning and other ills, and died there under unclear circumstances. He was succeeded by his vice president, Calvin Coolidge.

**(John) Calvin Coolidge** (4 Jul 1872, Plymouth VT–5 Jan 1933, Northampton MA), 30th president of the US (1923–29). He practiced law in Massachusetts from 1897 and served as lieutenant governor before being elected governor in 1918. He gained national attention by calling out the state guard during the Boston police strike in 1919. At the 1920 Republican convention, "Silent Cal" was nominated for vice president on Warren G. Harding's winning ticket. When Harding died in office in 1923, Coolidge became president. He restored confidence in an administration discredited by scandals and won the presidential election in 1924, defeating Robert La Follette. He vetoed measures to provide farm relief and bonuses to World War I veterans. His presidency was marked by apparent prosperity. Congress maintained a high protective tariff and instituted tax reductions that favored capital. Coolidge declined to run for a second term. His conservative policies of domestic and international inaction have come to symbolize the era between World War I and the Great Depression.

**Herbert Clark Hoover** (10 Aug 1874, West Branch IA–20 Oct 1964, New York NY), 31st president of the US (1929–33). As a mining engineer, he administered engineering projects on four continents (1895–1913). He then headed Allied relief operations in England and Belgium prior to World War I, at which time he was appointed national food administrator (1917–19) and instituted programs that furnished food to the Allies and famine-stricken areas of Europe. Appointed secretary of commerce (1921–27), he reorganized the department, creating divisions to regulate broadcasting and aviation. He oversaw commissions to build Boulder (later Hoover) Dam and the St. Lawrence Seaway. In 1928, as the Republican presidential candidate, he soundly defeated Alfred E. Smith. His hopes for a "New Day" program were quickly overwhelmed by the Great Depression. As a believer in individual freedom, he vetoed bills to create a federal unemployment agency and to fund public-works projects, instead favoring private charity. In 1932 he finally allowed relief to farmers through the Reconstruction Finance Corp. He was overwhelmingly defeated in 1932 by Franklin Roosevelt. He continued to speak out against relief measures and criticized New Deal programs. After World War II he participated in famine-relief work in Europe and was appointed head of the Hoover Commission.

**Franklin Delano Roosevelt** (30 Jan 1882, Hyde Park NY–12 Apr 1945, Warm Springs GA), 32nd president of the US (1933–45). He was attracted to politics as an admirer of his cousin Pres. Theodore Roosevelt and became active in the Democratic Party. In 1905 he married distant cousin Eleanor Roosevelt, who would become a valued adviser in future years. He served in the state senate (1910–13) and as assistant secretary of the navy (1913–20). In 1920 he was nominated for vice president. The next year he was stricken with polio; though unable to walk, he remained active in politics. As governor of New York (1929–33), he set up the first state relief agency in the US In 1932 he won the Democratic presidential nomination with the help of James Farley and easily defeated Pres. Herbert Hoover. In his inaugural address to a nation of more than 13 million unemployed, he pronounced that "the only thing we have to fear is fear itself." Congress passed most of the changes he sought in his New Deal program in the first hundred days of his term. He was overwhelmingly reelected in 1936 over Alf Landon. To solve legal challenges to the New Deal, he proposed enlarging the Supreme Court, but his "court-packing" plan aroused strong opposition and had to be abandoned. By the late 1930s economic recovery had slowed, but Roosevelt was more concerned with the growing threat of war. In 1940 he was reelected to an unprecedented third term, defeating Wendell Willkie. He maintained US neutrality toward the war in Europe, but approved the principle of lend-lease and in 1941 met with Winston Churchill to draft the Atlantic Charter. With US entry into World War II, he mobilized industry for military production and formed an alliance with Britain and the Soviet Union; he met with Churchill and Joseph Stalin to form war policy at Tehran (1943) and Yalta (1945). Despite declining health, he won reelection for a fourth term against Thomas Dewey (1944) but served only briefly before his death. His presidency is well regarded in US history.

**Harry S. Truman** (8 May 1884, Lamar MO–26 Dec 1972, Kansas City MO), 33rd president of the US (1945–53). He worked at various jobs before serving with distinction in World War I. He became a partner in a Kansas City haberdashery; when the business failed, he entered Democratic Party politics with the help of Thomas Pendergast. He was elected county judge (1922–24), and later became presiding judge of the county court (1926–34). His reputation for honesty and good management gained him bipartisan support. In the Senate (1935–45), he led a committee that exposed fraud in defense production. In 1944 he was chosen to replace the incumbent Henry Wallace as vice-presidential nominee and was elected with Pres. Franklin Roosevelt. After only 82 days as vice president, he became president on Roosevelt's death (April 1945). He quickly made final arrangements for the San Francisco charter-writing meeting of the UN, helped arrange Germany's unconditional surrender on 8 May, which ended World War II in Europe, and in July attended the Potsdam Conference. The Pacific war ended officially on 2 Sep, after he ordered atomic bombs dropped on Hiroshima and Nagasaki; his justification was a report that 500,000 US troops would be lost in a conventional invasion of Japan. He announced the Truman Doctrine to aid Greece and Turkey (1947), established the Central Intelligence Agency, and pressed for passage of the Marshall Plan to aid European countries. In 1948 he defeated Thomas Dewey despite widespread expectation of his own defeat. He initiated a foreign policy of containment to restrict the Soviet Union's sphere of influence, pursued his Point Four Program, and initiated the Berlin airlift and the NATO pact of 1949. In the Korean War he sent troops under Gen. Douglas MacArthur to head the UN forces. Problems of pursuing the war occupied his administration until he retired. Though he was often criticized during his presidency, Truman's reputation grew steadily in later years.

**Dwight David Eisenhower** (14 Oct 1890, Denison TX — 28 Mar 1969, Washington DC), 34th president of the US (1953–61). He graduated from West Point (1915), then served in the Panama Canal Zone (1922–24) and in the Philippines under Douglas MacArthur (1935–39). In World War II Gen. George Marshall appointed him to the army's war-plans division (1941), then chose him to command US forces in Europe (1942). After planning the invasions of North Africa, Sicily, and Italy, he was appointed supreme commander of Allied forces (1943). He planned the Normandy Campaign (1944) and the conduct of the war in Europe until the German surrender (1945). He was promoted to five-star general (1944) and was named army chief of staff in 1945. He served as president of Columbia University from 1948 until being appointed supreme commander of NATO in 1951. Both Democrats and Republicans courted Eisenhower as a presidential candidate; in 1952, as the Republican candidate, he defeated Adlai Stevenson with the largest popular vote up to that time. He defeated Stevenson again in 1956 in an even larger landslide. His achievements included efforts to contain Communism with the Eisenhower Doctrine. He sent federal troops to Little Rock AR to enforce integration of a city high school (1957). When the Soviet Union launched Sputnik I (1957), he was criticized for failing to develop the US space program and responded by creating NASA (1958). In his last weeks in office the US broke diplomatic relations with Cuba.

**John Fitzgerald Kennedy** (29 May 1917, Brookline MA—22 Nov 1963, Dallas TX), 35th president of the US (1961–63). The son of Joseph P. Kennedy, he graduated from Harvard University and joined the Navy in World War II, where he earned medals for heroism. Elected to the House of Representatives (1947–53) and the Senate (1953–60), he supported social legislation and became increasingly committed to civil rights legislation. He supported the policies of Harry Truman but accused the State Department of trying to force Chiang Kai-shek into a coalition with Mao Zedong. In 1960 he won the Democratic nomination for president; after a vigorous campaign, managed by his brother Robert F. Kennedy and aided financially by his father, he narrowly defeated Richard Nixon. He was the youngest person and the first Roman Catholic elected president. In his inaugural address he called on Americans to "ask not what your country can do for you, ask what you can do for your country." He proposed tax-reform and civil rights legislation but received little congressional support. He established the Peace Corps and the Alliance for Progress. His foreign policy began with the abortive Bay of Pigs invasion (1961), which emboldened the Soviet Union to move missiles to Cuba, sparking the Cuban missile crisis. In 1963 he successfully concluded the Nuclear Test-Ban Treaty. In November 1963 he was assassinated while riding in a motorcade in Dallas by a sniper, allegedly Lee Harvey Oswald. The killing is considered the most notorious political murder of the 20th century. Kennedy's youth, energy, and charming family brought him world adulation and sparked the idealism of a generation, for whom the Kennedy White House became known as

"Camelot." Details about his powerful family and personal life, especially concerning his extramarital affairs, tainted his image in later years.

**Lyndon Baines Johnson** (27 Aug 1908, Gillespie county TX—22 Jan 1973, San Antonio TX), 36th president of the US (1963–69). He taught school in Houston before going to Washington DC in 1932 as a congressional aide. There he was befriended by Sam Rayburn and his political career blossomed. He won a seat in the House of Representatives (1937–49) as the New Deal was under conservative attack. His loyalty impressed Pres. Franklin Roosevelt, who made Johnson a protégé. He won election to the Senate in 1949 in a vicious campaign that saw fraud on both sides. As Democratic whip (1951–55) and majority leader (1955–61), he developed a talent for consensus building among dissident factions with methods both tactful and ruthless. He was largely responsible for passage of the civil rights bills of 1957 and 1960, the first in the 20th century. In 1960 he was elected vice president; he became president after the assassination of John F. Kennedy. In his first few months in office he won from Congress passage of a huge quantity of important civil rights, tax-reduction, antipoverty, and conservation legislation. He defeated Barry Goldwater in the 1964 election by the largest popular majority to that time and announced his Great Society program. He was diverted from overseeing its enactment by the escalation of US involvement in the Vietnam War, beginning with the Gulf of Tonkin Resolution. His approval ratings diminished markedly and led to his decision not to seek reelection in 1968. He retired to his Texas ranch.

**Richard Milhous Nixon** (9 Jan 1913, Yorba Linda CA— 22 Apr 1994, New York NY), 37th president of the US (1969–74). He studied law at Duke University and practiced in California 1937–42. After serving in World War II, he was elected to the House of Representatives in 1947, employing harsh campaign tactics. He came to national attention with the Alger Hiss case, and was elected to the Senate in 1951, again following a bitter campaign. He won the vice presidency in 1952 on a ticket with Dwight D. Eisenhower; they were reelected easily in 1956. As presidential candidate in 1960, he lost narrowly to John F. Kennedy. After failing to win the 1962 California gubernatorial race, he retired from politics and moved to New York to practice law. He reentered politics by running for president in 1968, and he defeated Hubert H. Humphrey with his "southern strategy" of seeking votes from southern and western conservatives in both parties. As president, he began to gradually withdraw US military forces in an effort to end the Vietnam War while ordering the secret bombing of North Vietnamese military centers in Laos and Cambodia. Attacks on North Vietnamese sanctuaries in Cambodia drew widespread protest. Economic problems caused by inflation made the US budget deficit the largest to date, and in 1971 Nixon established unprecedented peacetime controls on wages and prices. He won reelection in 1972 with a landslide victory over George McGovern. Assisted by Henry A. Kissinger, he concluded the Vietnam War. He reopened communications with Communist China and made a state visit there. On his visit to the Soviet Union, the first by a US president, he signed the bilateral SALT agreements. The Watergate scandal overshadowed his second term; his complicity in efforts to cover up his involvement and the likelihood of impeachment led to his becoming, in August 1974, the first president to resign from office. Though never convicted of wrongdoing, he was pardoned by his successor, Gerald Ford. He retired to write his memoirs and books on foreign policy.

**Gerald Rudolph Ford, Jr.** (Leslie Lynch King, Jr.; 14 Jul 1913, Omaha NE), 38th president of the US (1974–77). He was an infant when his parents divorced, and his mother later married Gerald R. Ford. He attended the University of Michigan and Yale Law School, and practiced law in Michigan after World War II. He served in the House of Representative 1948–73, becoming minority leader in 1965. After Spiro Agnew resigned as vice president in 1973, Richard Nixon nominated Ford to fill the vacant post. When the Watergate scandal forced Nixon's departure, Ford became the first president who had not been elected to either the vice presidency or the presidency. A month later he pardoned Nixon; to counter widespread outrage, he voluntarily appeared before a House subcommittee to explain his action. His administration gradually lowered the high inflation rate it inherited. Ford's relations with the Democratic-controlled Congress were typified by his more than 50 vetoes, of which more than 40 were sustained. In the final days of the Vietnam War in 1975, he ordered an airlift of 237,000 anti-Communist Vietnamese refugees, most of whom came to the US. Reaction against Watergate contributed to his defeat by James Earl Carter, Jr., in 1976.

**James Earl Carter, Jr.** (1 Oct 1924, Plains GA), 39th president of the US (1977–81). He graduated from the US Naval Academy and served in the navy until 1953, when he left to manage the family peanut business. He served in the state senate 1962–66. Elected governor (1971–75), he opened Georgia's government offices to blacks and women and introduced stricter budgeting procedures for state agencies. In 1976, though lacking a national political base or major backing, he won the Democratic nomination and the presidency, defeating the sitting president, Gerald Ford. As president, Carter helped negotiate a peace treaty between Egypt and Israel, signed a treaty with Panama to make the Panama Canal a neutral zone after 1999, and established full diplomatic relations with China. In 1979–80 the Iran hostage crisis became a major political liability. He responded more forcefully to the USSR's invasion of Afghanistan in 1979, embargoing the shipment of US grain to that country and leading a boycott of the 1980 Summer Olympics in Moscow. Hampered by high inflation and a recession engineered to tame it, he lost his bid for reelection to Ronald Reagan. He subsequently became involved in international diplomatic negotiations and helped oversee elections in countries with insecure democratic traditions. Carter was awarded the Nobel Peace Prize in 2002.

**Ronald Wilson Reagan** (6 Feb 1911, Tampico IL), 40th president of the US (1981–89). He attended Eureka College and worked as a radio sports announcer before going to Hollywood in 1937. In his career as a movie actor, he had roles in 50 films and was twice president of the Screen Actors Guild (1947–52, 1959–60). Reagan became a spokesman for the General Electric Co. and hosted its television theater program 1954–62. Having gradually changed his political affiliation from liberal Democrat to conservative Republican, he was elected governor of California and served 1967–74.

In 1980 he defeated incumbent Pres. James Earl Carter, Jr., to become president. Shortly after taking office, he was wounded in an assassination attempt. Reagan adopted supply-side economics to promote rapid economic growth and reduce the federal deficit. Congress approved most of his proposals (1981), which succeeded in lowering inflation but doubled the national debt by 1986. He began the largest peacetime military buildup in US history and in 1983 proposed construction of the Strategic Defense Initiative. His foreign policy included the INF Treaty to restrict intermediate-range nuclear weapons and the invasion of Grenada. In 1984 Reagan defeated Walter Mondale in a landslide for reelection. Details of his administration's involvement in the Iran-Contra Affair emerged in 1986 and significantly weakened his popularity and authority. Though his intellectual capacity for governing was often disparaged, his artful communication skills enabled him to pursue numerous conservative policies with conspicuous success. In 1994 he revealed that he had Alzheimer disease.

**George Herbert Walker Bush** (12 Jun 1924, Milton MA), 41st president of the US (1989–93). The son of Prescott Bush, later a Connecticut senator, he served in World War II, graduated from Yale University, and started an oil business in Texas. He served in the House of Representatives 1966–70 as a Republican. He then served as ambassador to the UN (1971–72), chief of liaison to China (1974–76), and head of the CIA (1976–77). In 1980 he ran for president but lost the nomination to Ronald Reagan. Bush served as vice president with Reagan (1981–88), whom he succeeded as president, defeating Michael Dukakis. He made no dramatic departures from Reagan's policies. In 1989 he ordered a brief military invasion of Panama, which toppled that country's leader, Gen. Manuel Noriega. He helped impose a UN-approved embargo against Iraq in 1990 to force its withdrawal from Kuwait. When Iraq refused, he authorized a US-led air offensive that began the Persian Gulf War. Despite general approval of his foreign policy, an economic recession led to his defeat by William Jefferson Clinton in 1992. His son George W. Bush was elected president in 2000.

**William Jefferson Clinton** (William Jefferson Blythe III; 19 Aug 1946, Hope, AR), 42nd president of the US (1993–2001). He was adopted, after his father's death in a car crash, by his mother's second husband, Roger Clinton. He attended Georgetown University, Oxford University (as a Rhodes Scholar), and Yale law school, then taught at the University of Arkansas School of Law. He served as state attorney general (1977–79) and served several terms as governor (1979–81, 1983–92), during which he reformed Arkansas's educational system and encouraged the growth of industry through favorable tax policies. He won the Democratic presidential nomination in 1992 after withstanding charges of personal impropriety, and defeated the incumbent, George H.W. Bush. As president, he obtained approval of the North American Free Trade Agreement in 1993. He and his wife, Hillary Rodham Clinton, strongly advocated their plan to overhaul the US health care system, but Congress rejected it. He committed US forces to a peacekeeping initiative in Bosnia and Herzegovina. In 1994 the Democrats lost control of Congress for the first time since 1954. Clinton defeated Robert Dole to win reelection in 1996. He faced renewed charges of personal impropriety, this time involving Monica Lewinsky, and as a result, in 1998 he became the second president in history to be impeached. Charged with perjury and obstruction of justice, he was acquitted at his Senate trial in 1999. His two terms saw sustained economic growth and successive budget surpluses, the first in three decades.

**George Walker Bush** (6 Jul 1946, New Haven CT), 43rd president of the US (from 2001). The eldest child of Pres. George H.W. Bush, he attended Yale University and Harvard Business School. After spending a decade in the oil business with mixed success, he served as managing general partner of the Texas Rangers baseball franchise. In 1994 he was elected governor of Texas (1995–2000). Despite losing the national popular vote to Vice President Al Gore by more than 500,000 votes, he gained the presidency when a Supreme Court ruling effectively ended a recount of ballots in Florida, whose 25 electoral votes were needed by both candidates to secure a narrow majority in the electoral college. His response to the terrorist attacks on 11 Sep 2001, which included military retaliation in Afghanistan and the invasion of Iraq by American and other forces in March 2003, gave shape to his administration, as did his commitment to lower taxes.

## Presidents' Wives and Children

*Maiden names of the presidents' wives appear in small capital letters.*

DATE OF MARRIAGE    PRESIDENTS, WIVES, AND CHILDREN

**George Washington**
6 Jan 1759    **Martha** DANDRIDGE **Custis** (2 Jun 1731–22 May 1802)
no children

**John Adams**
25 Oct 1764    **Abigail** SMITH (22 Nov 1744–28 Oct 1818)
▸ Abigail Amelia Adams (1765–1813), ▸ John Quincy Adams (1767–1848), ▸ Susanna Adams (1768–1770), ▸ Charles Adams (1770–1800), ▸ Thomas Boylston Adams (1772–1832)

**Thomas Jefferson**
1 Jan 1772    **Martha** WAYLES **Skelton** (30 Oct 1748–6 Sep 1782)
▸ Martha Washington Jefferson (1772–1836), ▸ Jane Randolph Jefferson (1774–1775), ▸ infant son (1777–1777), ▸ Mary Jefferson (1778–1804), ▸ Lucy Elizabeth Jefferson (1780–1781), ▸ Lucy Elizabeth Jefferson (1782–1785)

**James Madison**
15 Sep 1794    **Dolley Dandridge** PAYNE **Todd** (20 May 1768–12 Jul 1849)
no children

**James Monroe**
16 Feb 1786    **Elizabeth** KORTRIGHT (30 Jun 1768–23 Sep 1830)
▸ Eliza Kortright Monroe (1786–1835?), ▸ James Spence Monroe (1799–1800), ▸ Maria Hester Monroe (1803–1850)

**John Quincy Adams**
26 Jul 1797    **Louisa Catherine** JOHNSON (12 Feb 1775–15 May 1852)
▸ George Washington Adams (1801–1829), ▸ John Adams (1803–1834), ▸ Charles Francis Adams (1807–1886), ▸ Louisa Catherine Adams (1811–1812)

**Andrew Jackson**
Aug 1791    **Rachel** DONELSON **Robards** (15? Jun 1767–22 Dec 1828)
no children

**Martin Van Buren**
21 Feb 1807    **Hannah** HOES (8 Mar 1783–5 Feb 1819)
▸ Abraham Van Buren (1807–1873), ▸ John Van Buren (1810–1866), ▸ Martin Van Buren (1812–1855), ▸ Smith Thompson Van Buren (1817–1876)

**William Henry Harrison**
25 Nov 1795    **Anna Tuthill** SYMMES (25 Jul 1775–25 Feb 1864)
▸ Elizabeth Bassett Harrison (1796–1846), ▸ John Cleves Symmes Harrison (1798–1830), ▸ Lucy Singleton Harrison (1800–1826), ▸ William Henry Harrison (1802–1838), ▸ John Scott Harrison (1804–1878), ▸ Benjamin Harrison (1806–1840), ▸ Mary Symmes Harrison (1809–1842), ▸ Carter Bassett Harrison (1811–1839), ▸ Anna Tuthill Harrison (1813–1865), ▸ James Findlay Harrison (1814–1817)

# Presidents' Wives and Children (continued)

| DATE OF MARRIAGE | PRESIDENTS, WIVES, AND CHILDREN |
|---|---|

**John Tyler**

29 Mar 1813  **Letitia** CHRISTIAN (12 Nov 1790–10 Sep 1842)
▸ Mary Tyler (1815–1848), ▸ Robert Tyler (1816–1877), ▸ John Tyler (1819–1896), ▸ Letitia Tyler (1821–1907), ▸ Anne Contesse Tyler (1825–1825), ▸ Alice Tyler (1827–1854), ▸ Tazewell Tyler (1830–1874)

26 Jun 1844  **Julia** GARDINER (4 May 1820–10 Jul 1889)
▸ David Gardiner Tyler (1846–1927), ▸ John Alexander Tyler (1848–1883), ▸ Julia Gardiner Tyler (1849?–1871), ▸ Lachlan Tyler (1851–1902), ▸ Lyon Gardiner Tyler (1853–1935), ▸ Robert Fitzwalter Tyler (1856–1927), ▸ Pearl Tyler (1860–1947)

**James K. Polk**

1 Jan 1824  **Sarah** CHILDRESS (4 Sep 1803–14 Aug 1891)
no children

**Zachary Taylor**

21 Jun 1810  **Margaret Mackall** SMITH (21 Sep 1788–14 Aug 1852)
▸ Anne Margaret Mackall Taylor (1811–1875), ▸ Sarah Knox Taylor (1814–1835), ▸ Octavia Pannel Taylor (1816–1820), ▸ Margaret Smith Taylor (1819–1820), ▸ Mary Elizabeth Taylor (1824–1909), ▸ Richard Taylor (1826–1879)

**Millard Fillmore**

5 Feb 1826  **Abigail** POWERS (13 Mar 1798–30 Mar 1853)
▸ Millard Powers Fillmore (1828–1889), ▸ Mary Abigail Fillmore (1832–1854)

10 Feb 1858  **Caroline** CARMICHAEL **McIntosh** (21 Oct 1813–11 Aug 1881)
no children

**Franklin Pierce**

10 Nov 1834  **Jane Means** APPLETON (12 Mar 1806–2 Dec 1863)
▸ Franklin Pierce (1836–1836), ▸ Frank Robert Pierce (1839–1843), ▸ Benjamin Pierce (1841–1853)

**James Buchanan**
never married

**Abraham Lincoln**

4 Nov 1842  **Mary Ann** TODD (13 Dec 1818–16 Jul 1882)
▸ Robert Todd Lincoln (1843–1926), ▸ Edward Baker Lincoln (1846–1850), ▸ William Wallace Lincoln (1850–1862), ▸ Thomas Lincoln (1853–1871)

**Andrew Johnson**

17 May 1827  **Eliza** McCARDLE (4 Oct 1810–15 Jan 1876)
▸ Martha Johnson (1828–1901), ▸ Charles Johnson (1830–1863), ▸ Mary Johnson (1832–1883), ▸ Robert Johnson (1834–1869), ▸ Andrew Johnson (1852–1879)

**Ulysses S. Grant**

22 Aug 1848  **Julia Boggs** DENT (26 Jan 1826–14 Dec 1902)
▸ Frederick Dent Grant (1850–1912), ▸ Ulysses Simpson Grant (1852–1929), ▸ Ellen Wrenshall Grant (1855–1922), ▸ Jesse Root Grant (1858–1934)

**Rutherford B. Hayes**

30 Dec 1852  **Lucy Ware** WEBB (28 Aug 1831–25 Jun 1889)
▸ Birchard Austin Hayes (1853–1926), ▸ James Webb Cook Hayes (1856–1934), ▸ Rutherford Platt Hayes (1858–1927), ▸ Joseph Thompson Hayes (1861–1863), ▸ George Crook Hayes (1864–1866), ▸ Fanny Hayes (1867–1950), ▸ Scott Russell Hayes (1871–1923), ▸ Manning Force Hayes (1873–1874)

**James A. Garfield**

11 Nov 1858  **Lucretia** RUDOLPH (19 Apr 1832–13 Mar 1918)
▸ Eliza Arabella Garfield (1860–1863), ▸ Harry Augustus Garfield (1863–1942), ▸ James Rudolph Garfield (1865–1950), ▸ Mary Garfield (1867–1947), ▸ Irvin McDowell Garfield (1870–1951), ▸ Abram Garfield (1872–1958), ▸ Edward Garfield (1874–1876)

**Chester A. Arthur**

25 Oct 1859  **Ellen Lewis** HERNDON (30 Aug 1837–12 Jan 1880)
▸ William Lewis Herndon Arthur (1860–1863), ▸ Chester Alan Arthur (1864–1937), ▸ Ellen Herndon Arthur (1871–1915)

# Presidents' Wives and Children (continued)

| DATE OF MARRIAGE | PRESIDENTS, WIVES, AND CHILDREN |
|---|---|

**Grover Cleveland**

2 Jun 1886 — **Frances FOLSOM** (21 Jul 1864–29 Oct 1947)
▸ Ruth Cleveland (1891–1904), ▸ Esther Cleveland (1893–1980), ▸ Marion Cleveland (1895–1977), ▸ Richard Folsom Cleveland (1897–1974), ▸ Francis Grover Cleveland (1903–1995)

**Benjamin Harrison**

20 Oct 1853 — **Caroline Lavinia SCOTT** (1 Oct 1832–25 Oct 1892)
▸ Russell Benjamin Harrison (1854–1936), ▸ Mary Scott Harrison (1858–1930)

6 Apr 1896 — **Mary Scott LORD Dimmick** (30 Apr 1858–5 Jan 1948)
▸ Elizabeth Harrison (1897–1955)

**William McKinley**

25 Jan 1871 — **Ida SAXTON** (8 Jun 1847–26 May 1907)
▸ Katherine McKinley (1871–1875), ▸ Ida McKinley (1873–1873)

**Theodore Roosevelt**

27 Oct 1880 — **Alice Hathaway LEE** (29 Jul 1861–14 Feb 1884)
▸ Alice Lee Roosevelt (1884–1980)

2 Dec 1886 — **Edith Kermit CAROW** (6 Aug 1861–30 Sep 1948)
▸ Theodore Roosevelt (1887–1944), ▸ Kermit Roosevelt (1889–1943), ▸ Ethel Carow Roosevelt (1891–1977), ▸ Archibald Bulloch Roosevelt (1894–1979), ▸ Quentin Roosevelt (1897–1918)

**William Howard Taft**

19 Jun 1886 — **Helen HERRON** (2 Jun 1861–22 May 1943)
▸ Robert Alphonso Taft (1889–1953), ▸ Helen Herron Taft (1891–1987), ▸ Charles Phelps Taft (1897–1983)

**Woodrow Wilson**

24 Jun 1885 — **Ellen Louise AXSON** (15 May 1860–6 Aug 1914)
▸ Margaret Woodrow Wilson (1886–1944), ▸ Jessie Woodrow Wilson (1887–1933), ▸ Eleanor Randolph Wilson (1889–1967)

18 Dec 1915 — **Edith BOLLING Galt** (15 Oct 1872–28 Dec 1961)
no children

**Warren G. Harding**

8 Jul 1891 — **Florence Mabel KLING De Wolf** (15 Aug 1860–21 Nov 1924)
no children

**Calvin Coolidge**

4 Oct 1905 — **Grace Anna GOODHUE** (3 Jan 1879–8 Jul 1957)
▸ John Coolidge (1906–2000), ▸ Calvin Coolidge (1908–1924)

**Herbert Hoover**

10 Feb 1899 — **Lou HENRY** (29 Mar 1874–7 Jan 1944)
▸ Herbert Clark Hoover (1903–1969), ▸ Allan Henry Hoover (1907–1993)

**Franklin D. Roosevelt**

17 Mar 1905 — **(Anna) Eleanor ROOSEVELT** (11 Oct 1884–7 Nov 1962)
▸ Anna Eleanor Roosevelt (1906–1975), ▸ James Roosevelt (1907–1991), ▸ Franklin Roosevelt (1909–1909), ▸ Elliott Roosevelt (1910–1990), ▸ Franklin Delano Roosevelt (1914–1988), ▸ John Aspinwall Roosevelt (1916–1981)

**Harry S. Truman**

28 Jun 1919 — **Elizabeth Virginia (Bess) WALLACE** (13 Feb 1885–18 Oct 1982)
▸ Margaret (Mary) Truman (1924–   )

**Dwight D. Eisenhower**

1 Jul 1916 — **Marie (Mamie) Geneva DOUD** (14 Nov 1896–1 Nov 1979)
▸ Doud Dwight Eisenhower (1917–1921), ▸ John Sheldon Doud Eisenhower (1922–   )

**John F. Kennedy**

12 Sep 1953 — **Jacqueline Lee BOUVIER** (28 Jul 1929–19 May 1994)
▸ Caroline Bouvier Kennedy (1957–   ), ▸ John Fitzgerald Kennedy (1960–1999), Patrick Bouvier Kennedy (1963–1963)

## Presidents' Wives and Children (continued)

| DATE OF MARRIAGE | PRESIDENTS, WIVES, AND CHILDREN |
|---|---|
| | **Lyndon B. Johnson** |
| 17 Nov 1934 | **Claudia Alta (Lady Bird) TAYLOR** (22 Dec 1912– ) |
| | ▸ Lynda Bird Johnson (1944– ), ▸ Luci Baines Johnson (1947– ) |
| | |
| | **Richard M. Nixon** |
| 21 Jun 1940 | **Thelma Catherine (Patricia) RYAN** (16 Mar 1912–22 Jun 1993) |
| | ▸ Patricia Nixon (1946– ), ▸ Julie Nixon (1948– ) |
| | |
| | **Gerald R. Ford** |
| 15 Oct 1948 | **Elizabeth Ann (Betty) BLOOMER Warren** (8 Apr 1918– ) |
| | ▸ Michael Gerald Ford (1950– ), ▸ John Gardner Ford (1952– ), ▸ Steven Meigs Ford (1956– ), ▸ Susan Elizabeth Ford (1957– ) |
| | |
| | **Jimmy Carter** |
| 7 Jul 1946 | **(Eleanor) Rosalynn SMITH** (18 Aug 1927– ) |
| | ▸ John William Carter (1947– ), ▸ James Earl Carter (1950– ), ▸ Donnel Jeffrey Carter (1952– ), ▸ Amy Lynn Carter (1967– ) |
| | |
| | **Ronald Reagan** |
| 24 Jan 1940 | **Jane Wyman (née Sarah Jane FULKS)** (4 Jan 1914– ) |
| | ▸ Maureen Elizabeth Reagan (1941–2001), ▸ Michael Edward Reagan (1945– ) |
| 4 Mar 1952 | **Nancy Davis (née Anne Frances ROBBINS)** (6 Jul 1921– ) |
| | ▸ Patricia Ann Reagan (1952– ), ▸ Ronald Prescott Reagan (1958– ) |
| | |
| | **George H.W. Bush** |
| 6 Jan 1945 | **Barbara PIERCE** (8 Jun 1925– ) |
| | ▸ George Walker Bush (1946– ), ▸ Robin Bush (1949–1953), ▸ John Ellis (Jeb) Bush (1953– ), ▸ Neil Mallon Bush (1955– ), ▸ Marvin Pierce Bush (1956– ), ▸ Dorothy Walker Bush (1959– ) |
| | |
| | **William J. Clinton** |
| 11 Oct 1975 | **Hillary Diane RODHAM** (26 Oct 1947– ) |
| | ▸ Chelsea Clinton (1980– ) |
| | |
| | **George W. Bush** |
| 5 Nov 1977 | **Laura Lane WELCH** (4 Nov 1946– ) |
| | ▸ Barbara Bush (1981– ), ▸ Jenna Bush (1981– ) |

Thomas Jefferson was the first governor of a US state—Virginia—to go on to serve as president. Sixteen governors since have been elected president, including four of the last five executives. Andrew Jackson and William Henry Harrison served as territorial governors of Florida and Indiana prior to their elections to the presidency.

# Presidential Succession

The president is the chief executive of the US. In contrast to the parliamentary form of government, under which the head of state is mainly ceremonial, the presidential system, such as that in the US, vests the president with great authority. The role of the president—including the process of presidential succession—is outlined in Article II of the Constitution of 1787, the fundamental law of the US federal system of government. Presidential nomination procedures are often recognized as constitutional elements, though they are outside the letter of the Constitution.

The Presidential Succession Act of 1792 established the stages of succession: from the president to the vice president, then to the Senate president pro tempore and next to the speaker of the House of Representatives. In 1886 new legislation removed the latter two from succession, replacing them with cabinet officers. The pattern of presidential succession was again changed in 1947, when the the speaker of the House was placed next in line after the vice president, followed by the Senate president pro tempore, the secretary of state, and finally, the remaining cabinet officers in the order that their departments were first formed.

## History

The administration of the first president, George Washington, set the customary precedent of serving only two terms, a tradition maintained until Pres. Franklin D. Roosevelt was elected to a third and fourth term in the 1940s. Congress adopted the 22nd Amendment in 1951, which limits presidents to two terms in office.

In 1841 William Henry Harrison became the first president to die in office and was succeeded by his vice president, John Tyler. In 1850, when Zachary Taylor died after only 16 months in office, he was succeeded by Millard Fillmore. In the same manner, vice president Andrew Johnson assumed the presidency after Pres. Abraham Lincoln's assassination.

When Pres. James Garfield was shot on 2 Jul 1881, he became incapacitated, raising serious constitutional questions over who should perform the functions of the presidency. For 80 days the president lay ill, and it was generally agreed that, in such cases, the vice president (Chester Arthur) was empowered by the Constitution to assume the powers and duties of the office of president. But should Arthur serve merely as acting president until Garfield recovered, or would he receive the office itself and thus displace his predecessor? Because of an ambiguity in the Constitution, opinion was divided, and, because Congress was not in session, the problem could not be debated there. No further action was taken before the death of the president, the result of slow blood poisoning, on 19 Sep. This ambiguity over succession was later clarified by the 20th (1933) and 25th (1967) Amendments. Other vice presidents who succeeded upon the death of presidents included Theodore Roosevelt in 1901; Calvin Coolidge in 1923; Harry S. Truman in 1945; and Lyndon B. Johnson in 1963.

In the 2000 presidential election, Republican George W. Bush lost the popular vote but narrowly defeated Democratic Vice President Al Gore after a divided Supreme Court intervened to halt the manual recounting of disputed ballots in Florida, thereby giving Bush enough electoral votes to capture the presidency.

## Vice Presidents

| | NAME | DATES OF BIRTH/DEATH | BIRTHPLACE | TIME IN OFFICE | PRESIDENT |
|---|---|---|---|---|---|
| 1 | John Adams | 30 Oct 1735–4 Jul 1826 | Braintree (now Quincy) MA | 1789–97 | George Washington |
| 2 | Thomas Jefferson | 13 Apr 1743–4 Jul 1826 | Shadwell VA | 1797–1801 | John Adams |
| 3 | Aaron Burr | 6 Feb 1756–14 Sep 1836 | Newark NJ | 1801–05 | Thomas Jefferson |
| 4 | George Clinton[1] | 26 Jul 1739–20 Apr 1812 | Little Britain NY | 1805–09 1809–12 | Thomas Jefferson James Madison |
| 5 | Elbridge Gerry | 17 Jul 1744–23 Nov 1814 | Marblehead MA | 1813–14 | James Madison |
| 6 | Daniel D. Tompkins | 21 Jun 1774–11 Jun 1825 | Scarsdale NY | 1817–25 | James Monroe |
| 7 | John C. Calhoun[2] | 18 Mar 1782–31 Mar 1850 | Abbeville district SC | 1825–29 1829–32 | John Quincy Adams Andrew Jackson |
| 8 | Martin Van Buren | 5 Dec 1782–24 Jul 1862 | Kinderhook NY | 1833–37 | Andrew Jackson |
| 9 | Richard M. Johnson | 17 Oct 1781–19 Nov 1850 | Beargrass VA (now Louisville KY) | 1837–41 | Martin Van Buren |
| 10 | John Tyler | 29 Mar 1790–18 Jan 1862 | Charles City county VA | 1841 | William Henry Harrison[1] |
| 11 | George Mifflin Dallas | 10 Jul 1792–31 Dec 1864 | Philadelphia PA | 1845–49 | James K. Polk |
| 12 | Millard Fillmore | 7 Jan 1800–8 Mar 1874 | Locke township NY | 1849–50 | Zachary Taylor[1] |
| 13 | William Rufus de Vane King[1] | 7 Apr 1786–18 Apr 1853 | Sampson county NC | 4 Mar– 18 Apr 1853 | Franklin Pierce |
| 14 | John C. Breckinridge | 21 Jan 1821–17 May 1875 | near Lexington KY | 1857–61 | James Buchanan |
| 15 | Hannibal Hamlin | 27 Aug 1809–4 Jul 1891 | Paris Hill ME | 1861–65 | Abraham Lincoln[1] |
| 16 | Andrew Johnson | 29 Dec 1808–31 Jul 1875 | Raleigh NC | 1865 | |
| 17 | Schuyler Colfax | 23 Mar 1823–13 Jan 1885 | New York NY | 1869–73 | Ulysses S. Grant |
| 18 | Henry Wilson[1] | 16 Feb 1812–22 Nov 1875 | Farmington NH | 1873–75 | Ulysses S. Grant |
| 19 | William A. Wheeler | 30 Jun 1819–4 Jun 1887 | Malone NY | 1877–81 | Rutherford B. Hayes |
| 20 | Chester A. Arthur | 5 Oct 1829–18 Nov 1886 | North Fairfield VT | 1881 | James A. Garfield[1] |
| 21 | Thomas A. Hendricks[1] | 7 Sep 1819–25 Nov 1885 | Zanesville OH | 4 Mar– 25 Nov 1885 | Grover Cleveland |
| 22 | Levi Parsons Morton | 16 May 1824–16 May 1920 | Shoreham VT | 1889–93 | Benjamin Harrison |
| 23 | Adlai E. Stevenson | 23 Oct 1835–14 Jun 1914 | Christian county KY | 1893–97 | Grover Cleveland |
| 24 | Garret A. Hobart[1] | 3 Jun 1844–21 Nov 1899 | Long Branch NJ | 1897–99 | William McKinley |
| 25 | Theodore Roosevelt | 27 Oct 1858–6 Jan 1919 | New York NY | 1901 | William McKinley[1] |
| 26 | Charles Warren Fairbanks | 11 May 1852–4 Jun 1918 | Union county OH | 1905–09 | Theodore Roosevelt |
| 27 | James Schoolcraft Sherman[1] | 24 Oct 1855–30 Oct 1912 | Utica NY | 1909–12 | William Howard Taft |
| 28 | Thomas R. Marshall | 14 Mar 1854–1 Jun 1925 | North Manchester IN | 1913–21 | Woodrow Wilson |
| 29 | Calvin Coolidge | 4 Jul 1872–5 Jan 1933 | Plymouth VT | 1921–23 | Warren G. Harding[1] |
| 30 | Charles G. Dawes | 27 Aug 1865–23 Apr 1851 | Marietta OH | 1925–29 | Calvin Coolidge |
| 31 | Charles Curtis | 25 Jan 1860–8 Feb 1936 | Kansas Territory | 1929–33 | Herbert Hoover |

## Vice Presidents (continued)

| | NAME | DATES OF BIRTH/DEATH | BIRTHPLACE | TIME IN OFFICE | PRESIDENT |
|---|---|---|---|---|---|
| 32 | John Nance Garner | 22 Nov 1868–7 Nov 1967 | Red River county TX | 1933–41 | Franklin D. Roosevelt |
| 33 | Henry A. Wallace | 7 Oct 1888–18 Nov 1965 | Adair county IA | 1941–45 | Franklin D. Roosevelt |
| 34 | Harry S. Truman | 8 May 1884–26 Dec 1972 | Lamar MO | 1945 | Franklin D. Roosevelt[1] |
| 35 | Alben W. Barkley | 24 Nov 1877–30 Apr 1956 | Graves county KY | 1949–53 | Harry S. Truman |
| 36 | Richard M. Nixon | 9 Jan 1913–22 Apr 1994 | Yorba Linda CA | 1953–61 | Dwight D. Eisenhower |
| 37 | Lyndon B. Johnson | 27 Aug 1908–22 Jan 1973 | Gillespie county TX | 1961–63 | John F. Kennedy[1] |
| 38 | Hubert H. Humphrey | 27 May 1911–13 Jan 1978 | Wallace SD | 1965–69 | Lyndon B. Johnson |
| 39 | Spiro T. Agnew[2] | 9 Nov 1918–17 Sep 1996 | Baltimore MD | 1969–73 | Richard M. Nixon |
| 40 | Gerald R. Ford | 14 Jul 1913 | Omaha NE | 1973–74 | Richard M. Nixon[2] |
| 41 | Nelson A. Rockefeller | 8 Jul 1908–26 Jan 1979 | Bar Harbor ME | 1974–77 | Gerald R. Ford |
| 42 | Walter F. Mondale | 5 Jan 1928 | Ceylon MN | 1977–81 | Jimmy Carter |
| 43 | George H.W. Bush | 12 Jun 1924 | Milton MA | 1981–89 | Ronald Reagan |
| 44 | Dan Quayle | 4 Feb 1947 | Indianapolis IN | 1989–93 | George H.W. Bush |
| 45 | Albert Gore | 31 Mar 1948 | Washington DC | 1993–2001 | William J. Clinton |
| 46 | Richard B. Cheney | 30 Jan 1941 | Lincoln NE | 2001– | George W. Bush |

[1]*Died in office.*
[2]*Resigned from office.*

## US Presidential Cabinets

The cabinet is composed of the heads of executive departments chosen by the president with the consent of the Senate. Cabinet officials do not hold seats in Congress and are not regulated by the US Constitution, which makes no mention of such a body. The existence of the cabinet is a matter of custom dating back to George Washington, who consulted regularly with his department heads as a group. Original dates of service are given for officials appointed midterm and for newly created posts. Ad interim officials are not listed. Presidencies and new positions are indicated in bold.

### George Washington

**4 MAR 1789–3 MARCH 1793 (TERM 1)**

| | |
|---|---|
| State | Thomas Jefferson |
| Treasury | Alexander Hamilton |
| War | Henry Knox |
| Attorney General | Edmund Randolph |

**4 MAR 1793–3 MAR 1797 (TERM 2)**

| | |
|---|---|
| State | Thomas Jefferson; Edmund Randolph (2 Jan 1794); Timothy Pickering (20 Aug 1795) |
| Treasury | Alexander Hamilton; Oliver Wolcott, Jr. (2 Feb 1795) |
| War | Henry Knox; Timothy Pickering (2 Jan 1795); James McHenry (6 Feb 1796) |
| Attorney General | Edmund Randolph; William Bradford (29 Jan 1794); Charles Lee (10 Dec 1795) |

### John Adams

**4 MAR 1797–3 MAR 1801**

| | |
|---|---|
| State | Timothy Pickering; John Marshall (6 Jun 1800) |
| Treasury | Oliver Wolcott, Jr.; Samuel Dexter (1 Jan 1801) |
| War | James McHenry; Samuel Dexter (12 Jun 1800) |
| **Navy** | Benjamin Stoddert (18 Jun 1798) |
| Attorney General | Charles Lee |

### Thomas Jefferson

**4 MAR 1801–3 MAR 1805 (TERM 1)**

| | |
|---|---|
| State | James Madison |
| Treasury | Samuel Dexter; Albert Gallatin (14 May 1801) |
| War | Henry Dearborn |
| Navy | Benjamin Stoddert; Robert Smith (27 Jul 1801) |
| Attorney General | Levi Lincoln |

# US Presidential Cabinets (continued)

### Thomas Jefferson (continued)

**4 MAR 1805–3 MAR 1809 (TERM 2)**

| | |
|---|---|
| State | James Madison |
| Treasury | Albert Gallatin |
| War | Henry Dearborn |
| Navy | Robert Smith |
| Attorney General | John Breckenridge; Caesar Augustus Rodney (20 Jan 1807) |

### James Madison

**4 MAR 1809–3 MAR 1813 (TERM 1)**

| | |
|---|---|
| State | Robert Smith |
| Treasury | Albert Gallatin |
| War | John Smith; William Eustis (8 Apr 1809); John Armstrong (5 Feb 1813) |
| Navy | Robert Smith; Paul Hamilton (15 May 1809); William Jones (19 Jan 1813) |
| Attorney General | Caesar Augustus Rodney; William Pinkney (6 Jan 1812) |

**4 MAR 1813–3 MAR 1817 (TERM 2)**

| | |
|---|---|
| State | James Monroe |
| Treasury | Albert Gallatin; George Washington Campbell (9 Feb 1814); Alexander James Dallas (14 Oct 1814); William Harris Crawford (22 Oct 1816) |
| War | John Armstrong; James Monroe (1 Oct 1814); William Harris Crawford (8 Aug 1815) |
| Navy | William Jones; Benjamin Williams Crowninshield (16 Jan 1815) |
| Attorney General | William Pinkney; Richard Rush (11 Feb 1814) |

### James Monroe

**4 MAR 1817–3 MAR 1821 (TERM 1)**

| | |
|---|---|
| State | John Quincy Adams |
| Treasury | William Harris Crawford |
| War | John C. Calhoun |
| Navy | Benjamin Willliams Crowninshield; Smith Thompson (1 Jan 1819) |
| Attorney General | Richard Rush; William Wirt (15 Nov 1817) |

**4 MAR 1821–3 MAR 1825 (TERM 2)**

| | |
|---|---|
| State | John Quincy Adams |
| Treasury | William Harris Crawford |
| War | John C. Calhoun |
| Navy | Smith Thompson; Samuel Lewis Southard (16 Sep 1823) |
| Attorney General | William Wirt |

### John Quincy Adams

**4 MAR 1825–3 MAR 1829**

| | |
|---|---|
| State | Henry Clay |
| Treasury | Richard Rush |
| War | James Barbour; Peter Buell Porter (21 Jun 1828) |
| Navy | Samuel Lewis Southard |
| Attorney General | William Wirt |

### Andrew Jackson

**4 MAR 1829–3 MAR 1833 (TERM 1)**

| | |
|---|---|
| State | Martin Van Buren; Edward Livingston (24 May 1831) |
| Treasury | Samuel Delucenna Ingham; Louis McLane (8 Aug 1831) |
| War | John Henry Eaton; Lewis Cass (8 Aug 1831) |
| Navy | John Branch; Levi Woodbury (23 May 1831) |
| Attorney General | John Macpherson Berrien; Roger Brooke Taney (20 Jul 1831) |

**4 MAR 1833–3 MAR 1837 (TERM 2)**

| | |
|---|---|
| State | Edward Livingston; Louis McLane (29 May 1833); John Forsyth (1 Jul 1834) |
| Treasury | Louis McLane; William John Duane (1 Jun 1833); Roger Brooke Taney (23 Sep 1833); Levi Woodbury (1 Jul 1834) |
| War | Lewis Cass |
| Navy | Levi Woodbury; Mahlon Dickerson (30 Jun 1834) |
| Attorney General | Roger Brooke Taney; Benjamin Franklin Butler (18 Nov 1833) |

# US Presidential Cabinets (continued)

### Martin Van Buren

**4 MAR 1837–3 MAR 1841**

| | |
|---|---|
| State | John Forsyth |
| Treasury | Levi Woodbury |
| War | Joel Roberts Poinsett |
| Navy | Mahlon Dickerson; James Kirke Paulding (1 Jul 1838) |
| Attorney General | Benjamin Franklin Butler; Felix Grundy (1 Sep 1838); Henry Dilworth Gilpin (11 Jan 1840) |

### William Henry Harrison

**4 MAR 1841–4 APR 1841**

| | |
|---|---|
| State | Daniel Webster |
| Treasury | Thomas Ewing |
| War | John Bell |
| Navy | George Edmund Badger |
| Attorney General | John Jordan Crittenden |

### John Tyler

**6 APR 1841–3 MAR 1845**

| | |
|---|---|
| State | Daniel Webster; Abel Parker Upshur (24 Jul 1843); John C. Calhoun (1 Apr 1844) |
| Treasury | Thomas Ewing; Walter Forward (13 Sep 1841); John Canfield Spencer (8 Mar 1843); George Mortimer Bibb (4 Jul 1844) |
| War | John Bell; John Canfield Spencer (12 Oct 1841); James Madison Porter (8 Mar 1843); William Wilkins (20 Feb 1844) |
| Navy | George Edmund Badger; Abel Parker Upshur (11 Oct 1841); David Henshaw (24 Jul 1843); Thomas Walker Gilmer (19 Feb 1844); John Young Mason (26 Mar 1844) |
| Attorney General | John Jordan Crittenden; Hugh Swinton Legaré (20 Sep 1841); John Nelson (1 Jul 1843) |

### James K. Polk

**4 MAR 1845–3 MAR 1849**

| | |
|---|---|
| State | James Buchanan |
| Treasury | Robert James Walker |
| War | William Learned Marcy |
| Navy | George Bancroft; John Young Mason (9 Sep 1846) |
| Attorney General | John Young Mason; Nathan Clifford (17 Oct 1846); Isaac Toucey (29 Jun 1848) |

### Zachary Taylor

**4 MAR 1849–9 JUL 1850**

| | |
|---|---|
| State | John Middleton Clayton |
| Treasury | William Morris Meredith |
| War | George Washington Crawford |
| Navy | William Ballard Preston |
| Attorney General | Reverdy Johnson |
| **Interior** | Thomas Ewing (8 Mar 1849) |

### Millard Fillmore

**10 JUL 1850–3 MAR 1853**

| | |
|---|---|
| State | Daniel Webster; Edward Everett (6 Nov 1852) |
| Treasury | Thomas Corwin |
| War | George Washington Crawford; Charles Magill Conrad (15 Aug 1850) |
| Navy | William Alexander Graham; John Pendleton Kennedy (26 Jul 1852) |
| Attorney General | Reverdy Johnson; John Jordan Crittenden (14 Aug 1850) |
| Interior | Thomas Ewing; Thomas McKean Thompson McKennan (15 Aug 1850); Alexander Hugh Holmes Stuart (16 Sep 1850) |

### Franklin Pierce

**4 MAR 1853–3 MAR 1857**

| | |
|---|---|
| State | William Learned Marcy |
| Treasury | James Guthrie |
| War | Jefferson Davis |
| Navy | James Cochran Dobbin |
| Attorney General | Caleb Cushing |
| Interior | Robert McClelland |

# US Presidential Cabinets (continued)

### James Buchanan

**4 MAR 1857–3 MAR 1861**

| | |
|---|---|
| State | Lewis Cass; Jeremiah Sullivan Black (17 Dec 1860) |
| Treasury | Howell Cobb; Philip Francis Thomas (12 Dec 1860); John Adams Dix (15 Jan 1861) |
| War | John Buchanan Floyd |
| Navy | Isaac Toucey |
| Attorney General | Jeremiah Sullivan Black; Edwin McMasters Stanton (22 Dec 1860) |
| Interior | Jacob Thompson |

### Abraham Lincoln

**4 MAR 1861–3 MAR 1865 (TERM 1)**

| | |
|---|---|
| State | William Henry Seward |
| Treasury | Salmon Portland Chase; William Pitt Fessenden (5 Jul 1864) |
| War | Simon Cameron; Edwin McMasters Stanton (20 Jun 1862) |
| Navy | Gideon Welles |
| Attorney General | Edward Bates; James Speed (5 Dec 1864) |
| Interior | Caleb Blood Smith; John Palmer Usher (8 Jan 1863) |

**4 MAR 1865–15 APR 1865 (TERM 2)**

| | |
|---|---|
| State | William Henry Seward |
| Treasury | Hugh McCulloch |
| War | Edwin McMasters Stanton |
| Navy | Gideon Welles |
| Attorney General | James Speed |
| Interior | John Palmer Usher |

### Andrew Johnson

**15 APR 1865–3 MAR 1869**

| | |
|---|---|
| State | William Henry Seward |
| Treasury | Hugh McCulloch |
| War | Edwin McMasters Stanton; John McAllister Schofield (1 Jun 1868) |
| Navy | Gideon Welles |
| Attorney General | James Speed; Henry Stanbery (23 Jul 1866); William Maxwell Evarts (20 Jul 1868) |
| Interior | John Palmer Usher; James Harlan (15 May 1865); Orville Hickman Browning (1 Sep 1866) |

### Ulysses S. Grant

**4 MAR 1869–3 MAR 1873 (TERM 1)**

| | |
|---|---|
| State | Elihu Benjamin Washburne; Hamilton Fish (17 Mar 1869) |
| Treasury | George Sewall Boutwell |
| War | John Aaron Rawlins; William Tecumseh Sherman (11 Sep 1869); William Worth Belknap (1 Nov 1869) |
| Navy | Adolph Edward Borie; George Maxwell Robeson (25 Jun 1869) |
| Attorney General | Ebenezer Rockwood Hoar; Amos Tappan Akerman (8 Jul 1870); George Henry Williams (10 Jan 1872) |
| Interior | Jacob Dolson Cox; Columbus Delano (1 Nov 1870) |

**4 MAR 1873–3 MAR 1877 (TERM 2)**

| | |
|---|---|
| State | Hamilton Fish |
| Treasury | William Adams Richardson; Benjamin Helm Bristow (4 Jun 1874); Lot Myrick Morrill (7 Jul 1876) |
| War | William Worth Belknap; Alphonso Taft (11 Mar 1876); James Donald Cameron (1 Jun 1876) |
| Navy | George Maxwell Robeson |
| Attorney General | George Henry Williams; Edward Pierrepont (15 May 1875); Alphonso Taft (1 Jun 1876) |
| Interior | Columbus Delano; Zachariah Chandler (19 Oct 1875) |

### Rutherford B. Hayes

**4 MAR 1877–3 MAR 1881**

| | |
|---|---|
| State | William Maxwell Evarts |
| Treasury | John Sherman |
| War | George Washington McCrary; Alexander Ramsey (12 Dec 1879) |
| Navy | Richard Wigginton Thompson; Nathan Goff, Jr. (6 Jan 1881) |
| Attorney General | Charles Devens |
| Interior | Carl Schurz |

# US Presidential Cabinets (continued)

### James A. Garfield

**4 MAR 1881–19 SEP 1881**

| | |
|---|---|
| State | James Gillespie Blaine |
| Treasury | William Windom |
| War | Robert Todd Lincoln |
| Attorney General | Wayne McVeagh |
| Navy | William Henry Hunt |
| Interior | Samuel Jordan Kirkwood |

### Chester A. Arthur

**20 SEP 1881–3 MAR 1885**

| | |
|---|---|
| State | James Gillespie Blaine; Frederick Theodore Frelinghuysen (19 Dec 1881) |
| Treasury | William Windom; Charles James Folger (14 Nov 1881); Walter Quintin Gresham (24 Sep 1884); Hugh McCulloch (31 Oct 1884) |
| War | Robert Todd Lincoln |
| Navy | William Henry Hunt; William Eaton Chandler (17 Apr 1882) |
| Attorney General | Wayne MacVeagh; Benjamin Harris Brewster (3 Jan 1882) |
| Interior | Samuel Jordan Kirkwood; Henry Moore Teller (17 Apr 1882) |

### Grover Cleveland

**4 MAR 1885–3 MAR 1889**

| | |
|---|---|
| State | Thomas Francis Bayard |
| Treasury | Daniel Manning; Charles Stebbins Fairchild (1 Apr 1887) |
| War | William Crowninshield Endicott |
| Navy | William Collins Whitney |
| Attorney General | Augustus Hill Garland |
| Interior | Lucius Quintus Cincinnatus Lamar; William Freeman Vilas (16 Jan 1888) |
| **Agriculture** | Norman Jay Colman (13 Feb 1889) |

### Benjamin Harrison

**4 MAR 1889–3 MAR 1893**

| | |
|---|---|
| State | James Gillespie Blaine; John Watson Foster (29 Jun 1892) |
| Treasury | William Windom; Charles Foster (24 Feb 1891) |
| War | Redfield Proctor; Stephen Benton Elkins (24 Dec 1891) |
| Navy | Benjamin Franklin Tracy |
| Attorney General | William Henry Harrison Miller |
| Interior | John Willock Noble |
| Agriculture | Jeremiah McLain Rusk |

### Grover Cleveland

**4 MAR 1893–3 MAR 1897**

| | |
|---|---|
| State | Walter Quintin Gresham; Richard Olney (10 Jun 1895) |
| Treasury | John Griffin Carlisle |
| War | Daniel Scott Lamont |
| Navy | Hilary Abner Herbert |
| Attorney General | Richard Olney; Judson Harmon (11 Jun 1895) |
| Interior | Hoke Smith; David Rowland Francis (4 Sep 1896) |
| Agriculture | Julius Sterling Morton |

### William McKinley

**4 MAR 1897–3 MAR 1901 (TERM 1)**

| | |
|---|---|
| State | John Sherman; William Rufus Day (28 Apr 1898); John Hay (30 Sep 1898) |
| Treasury | Lyman Judson |
| War | Russell Alexander Alger; Elihu Root (1 Aug 1899) |
| Navy | John Davis Long |
| Attorney General | Joseph McKenna; John William Griggs (1 Feb 1898) |
| Interior | Cornelius Newton Bliss; Ethan Allen Hitchcock (20 Feb 1899) |
| Agriculture | James Wilson |

**4 MAR 1901–14 SEP 1901 (TERM 2)**

| | |
|---|---|
| State | John Hay |
| Treasury | Lyman Judson Gage |
| War | Elihu Root |
| Navy | John Davis Long |
| Attorney General | John William Griggs; Philander Chase Knox (10 Apr 1901) |
| Interior | Ethan Allen Hitchcock |
| Agriculture | James Wilson |

# US Presidential Cabinets (continued)

### Theodore Roosevelt

**14 SEP 1901–3 MAR 1905 (TERM 1)**

| | |
|---|---|
| State | John Hay |
| Treasury | Lyman Judson Gage; Leslie Mortier Shaw (1 Feb 1902) |
| War | Elihu Root; William Howard Taft (1 Feb 1904) |
| Navy | John Davis Long; William Henry Moody (1 May 1902); Paul Morton (1 Jul 1904) |
| Attorney General | Philander Chase Knox; William Henry Moody (1 Jul 1904) |
| Interior | Ethan Allen Hitchcock |
| Agriculture | James Wilson |
| **Commerce and Labor** | George Bruce Cortelyou (16 Feb 1903); Victor Howard Metcalf (1 Jul 1904) |

**4 MAR 1905–3 MAR 1909 (TERM 2)**

| | |
|---|---|
| State | John Hay; Elihu Root (19 Jul 1905); Robert Bacon (27 Jan 1909) |
| Treasury | Leslie Mortier Shaw; George Bruce Cortelyou (4 Mar 1907) |
| War | William Howard Taft; Luke Edward Wright (1 Jul 1908) |
| Navy | Paul Morton; Charles Joseph Bonaparte (1 Jul 1905); Victor Howard Metcalf (17 Dec 1906); Truman Handy Newberry (1 Dec 1908) |
| Attorney General | William Henry Moody; Charles Joseph Bonaparte (17 Dec 1906) |
| Interior | Ethan Allen Hitchcock; James Rudolph Garfield (4 Mar 1907) |
| Agriculture | James Wilson |
| Commerce and Labor | Victor Howard Metcalf; Oscar Solomon Straus (17 Dec 1906) |

### William Howard Taft

**4 MAR 1909–3 MAR 1913**

| | |
|---|---|
| State | Philander Chase Knox |
| Treasury | Franklin MacVeagh |
| War | Jacob McGavock Dickinson; Henry Lewis Stimson (22 May 1911) |
| Navy | George von Lengerke Meyer |
| Attorney General | George Woodward Wickersham |
| Interior | Richard Achilles Ballinger; Walter Lowrie Fisher (7 Mar 1911) |
| Agriculture | James Wilson |
| Commerce and Labor | Charles Nagel |

### Woodrow Wilson

**4 MAR 1913–3 MAR 1917 (TERM 1)**

| | |
|---|---|
| State | William Jennings Bryan; Robert Lansing (23 Jun 1915) |
| Treasury | William Gibbs McAdoo |
| War | Lindley Miller Garrison; Newton Diehl Baker (9 Mar 1916) |
| Navy | Josephus Daniels |
| Attorney General | James Clark McReynolds; Thomas Watt Gregory (3 Sep 1914) |
| Interior | Franklin Knight Lane |
| Agriculture | David Franklin Houston |
| **Commerce** | William Cox Redfield (5 Mar 1913) |
| **Labor** | William Bauchop Wilson (5 Mar 1913) |

**4 MAR 1917–3 MAR 1921 (TERM 2)**

| | |
|---|---|
| State | Robert Lansing; Bainbridge Colby (23 Mar 1920) |
| Treasury | William Gibbs McAdoo; Carter Glass (16 Dec 1918); David Franklin Houston (2 Feb 1920) |
| War | Newton Diehl Baker |
| Navy | Josephus Daniels |
| Attorney General | Thomas Watt Gregory; Alexander Mitchell Palmer (5 Mar 1919) |
| Interior | Franklin Knight Lane; John Barton Payne (13 Mar 1920) |
| Agriculture | David Franklin Houston; Edwin Thomas Meredith (2 Feb 1920) |
| Commerce | William Cox Redfield; Joshua Willis Alexander (16 Dec 1919) |
| Labor | William Bauchop Wilson |

### Warren G. Harding

**4 MAR 1921–2 AUG 1923**

| | |
|---|---|
| State | Charles Evans Hughes |
| Treasury | Andrew William Mellon |
| War | John Wingate Weeks |
| Navy | Edwin Denby |
| Attorney General | Harry Micajah Daugherty |

## US Presidential Cabinets (continued)

### Warren G. Harding (continued)

**4 MAR 1921–2 AUG 1923 (CONTINUED)**

| | |
|---|---|
| Interior | Albert Bacon Fall; Hubert Work (5 Mar 1923) |
| Agriculture | Henry Cantwell Wallace |
| Commerce | Herbert Hoover |
| Labor | James John Davis |

### Calvin Coolidge

**3 AUG 1923–3 MAR 1925 (TERM 1)**

| | |
|---|---|
| State | Charles Evans Hughes |
| Treasury | Andrew William Mellon |
| War | John Wingate Weeks |
| Navy | Edwin Denby; Curtis Dwight Wilbur (18 Mar 1924) |
| Attorney General | Harry Micajah Daugherty; Harlan Fiske Stone (9 Apr 1924) |
| Interior | Hubert Work |
| Agriculture | Henry Cantwell Wallace; Howard Mason Gore (21 Nov 1924) |
| Commerce | Herbert Hoover |
| Labor | James John Davis |

**4 MAR 1925–3 MAR 1929 (TERM 2)**

| | |
|---|---|
| State | Frank Billings Kellogg |
| Treasury | Andrew William Mellon |
| War | John Wingate Weeks; Dwight Filley Davis (14 Oct 1925) |
| Navy | Curtis Dwight Wilbur |
| Attorney General | John Garibaldi Sargent |
| Interior | Hubert Work; Roy Owen West (21 Jan 1929) |
| Agriculture | William Marion Jardine |
| Commerce | Herbert Hoover; William Fairfield Whiting (11 Dec 1928) |
| Labor | James John Davis |

### Herbert Hoover

**4 MAR 1929–3 MAR 1933**

| | |
|---|---|
| State | Henry Lewis Stimson |
| Treasury | Andrew William Mellon; Ogden Livingston Mills (13 Feb 1932) |
| War | James William Good; Patrick Jay Hurley (9 Dec 1929) |
| Navy | Charles Francis Adams |
| Attorney General | William De Witt Mitchell |
| Interior | Ray Lyman Wilbur |
| Agriculture | Arthur Mastick Hyde |
| Commerce | Robert Patterson Lamont; Roy Dikeman Chapin (14 Dec 1932) |
| Labor | James John Davis; William Nuckles Doak (9 Dec 1930) |

### Franklin D. Roosevelt

**4 MAR 1933–20 JAN 1937 (TERM 1)**

| | |
|---|---|
| State | Cordell Hull |
| Treasury | William Hartman Woodin; Henry Morgenthau, Jr. (8 Jan 1934) |
| War | George Henry Dern |
| Navy | Claude Augustus Swanson |
| Attorney General | Homer Stille Cummings |
| Interior | Harold Le Claire Ickes |
| Agriculture | Henry Agard Wallace |
| Commerce | Daniel Calhoun Roper |
| Labor | Frances Perkins |

**20 JAN 1937–20 JAN 1941 (TERM 2)**

| | |
|---|---|
| State | Cordell Hull |
| Treasury | Henry Morgenthau, Jr. |
| War | Harry Hines Woodring; Henry Lewis Stimson (10 Jul 1940) |
| Attorney General | Homer Stille Cummings; Frank Murphy (17 Jan 1939); Robert Houghwout Jackson (18 Jan 1940) |
| Navy | Claude Augustus Swanson; Charles Edison (11 Jan 1940); Frank Knox (10 Jul 1940) |
| Interior | Harold Le Claire Ickes |
| Agriculture | Henry Agard Wallace; Claude Raymond Wickard (5 Sep 1940) |
| Commerce | Daniel Calhoun Roper; Harry Lloyd Hopkins (23 Jan 1939); Jesse Holman Jones (19 Sep 1940) |
| Labor | Frances Perkins |

# US Presidential Cabinets (continued)

### Franklin D. Roosevelt (continued)

**20 JAN 1941–20 JAN 1945 (TERM 3)**

| | |
|---|---|
| State | Cordell Hull; Edward Reilly Stettinius (1 Dec 1944) |
| Treasury | Henry Morgenthau, Jr. |
| War | Henry Lewis Stimson |
| Navy | Frank Knox; James Vincent Forrestal (18 May 1944) |
| Attorney General | Robert Houghwout Jackson; Francis Biddle (5 Sep 1941) |
| Interior | Harold Le Claire Ickes |
| Agriculture | Claude Raymond Wickard |
| Commerce | Jesse Holman Jones |
| Labor | Frances Perkins |

**20 JAN 1945–12 APR 1945 (TERM 4)**

| | |
|---|---|
| State | Edward Reilly Stettinius |
| Treasury | Henry Morgenthau, Jr. |
| War | Henry Lewis Stimson |
| Navy | James Vincent Forrestal |
| Attorney General | Francis Biddle |
| Interior | Harold Le Claire Ickes |
| Agriculture | Claude Raymond Wickard |
| Commerce | Jesse Holman Jones; Henry Agard Wallace (2 Mar 1945) |
| Labor | Frances Perkins |

### Harry S. Truman

**12 APR 1945–20 JAN 1949 (TERM 1)**

| | |
|---|---|
| State | Edward Reilly Stettinius; James Francis Byrnes (3 Jul 1945); George Catlett Marshall (21 Jan 1947) |
| Treasury | Henry Morgenthau, Jr.; Frederick Moore (23 Jul 1945); John Wesley Snyder (25 Jun 1946) |
| War | Henry Lewis Stimson; Robert Porter Patterson (27 Sep 1945); Kenneth Clairborne Royall (25 Jul 1947) |
| **Defense** | James Vincent Forrestal (17 Sep 1947) |
| Navy | James Vincent Forrestal |
| Attorney General | Francis Biddle; Thomas Campbell Clark (1 Jul 1945) |
| Interior | Harold Le Claire Ickes; Julius Albert Krug (18 Mar 1946) |
| Agriculture | Claude Raymond Wickard; Clinton Presba Anderson (30 Jun 1945); Charles Franklin Brannan (2 Jun 1948) |
| Commerce | Henry Agard Wallace; William Averell Harriman (28 Jan 1947); Charles Sawyer (6 May 1948) |
| Labor | Frances Perkins; Lewis Baxter Schwellenbach (1 Jul 1945) |

**20 JAN 1949–20 JAN 1953 (TERM 2)**

| | |
|---|---|
| State | Dean Gooderham Acheson |
| Treasury | John Wesley Snyder |
| Defense | James Vincent Forrestal; Louis Arthur Johnson (28 Mar 1949); George Catlett Marshall (21 Sep 1950); Robert Abercrombie Lovett (17 Sep 1951) |
| Attorney General | Thomas Campbell Clark; James Howard McGrath (24 Aug 1949) |
| Interior | Julius Albert Krug; Oscar Littleton Chapman (19 Jan 1950) |
| Agriculture | Charles Franklin Brannan |
| Commerce | Charles Sawyer |
| Labor | Maurice Joseph Tobin |

### Dwight D. Eisenhower

**20 JAN 1953–20 JAN 1957 (TERM 1)**

| | |
|---|---|
| State | John Foster Dulles |
| Treasury | George Magoffin Humphrey |
| Defense | Charles Erwin Wilson |
| Attorney General | Herbert Brownell |
| Interior | Douglas McKay; Frederick Andrew Seaton (8 Jun 1956) |
| Agriculture | Ezra Taft Benson |
| Commerce | Sinclair Weeks |
| Labor | Martin Patrick Durkin; James Paul Mitchell (9 Oct 1953) |
| **Health, Education, and Welfare** | Oveta Culp Hobby (11 Apr 1953); Marion Bayard Folson (1 Aug 1955) |

**20 JAN 1957–20 JAN 1961 (TERM 2)**

| | |
|---|---|
| State | John Foster Dulles; Christian Archibald Herter (22 Apr 1959) |
| Treasury | George Magoffin Humphrey; Robert Bernerd Anderson (29 Jul 1957) |

## US Presidential Cabinets (continued)

### Dwight D. Eisenhower (continued)

**20 JAN 1957–20 JAN 1961 (TERM 2) (CONTINUED)**

| | |
|---|---|
| Defense | Charles Erwin Wilson; Neil Hosler McElroy (9 Oct 1957); Thomas Sovereign Gates, Jr. (2 Dec 1959) |
| Attorney General | Herbert Brownell, Jr.; William Pierce Rogers (27 Jan 1958) |
| Interior | Frederick Andrew Seaton |
| Agriculture | Ezra Taft Benson |
| Commerce | Sinclair Weeks; Frederick Henry Mueller (10 Aug 1959) |
| Labor | James Paul Mitchell |
| Health, Education, and Welfare | Marion Bayard Folsom; Arthur Sherwood Flemming (1 Aug 1958) |

### John F. Kennedy

**20 JAN 1961–22 NOV 1963**

| | |
|---|---|
| State | (David) Dean Rusk |
| Treasury | C. (Clarence) Douglas Dillon |
| Defense | Robert Strange McNamara |
| Attorney General | Robert F. Kennedy |
| Interior | Stewart Lee Udall |
| Agriculture | Orville Lothrop Freeman |
| Commerce | Luther Hartwell Hodges |
| Labor | Arthur Joseph Goldberg; W. (William) Willard Wirtz (25 Sep 1962) |
| Health, Education, and Welfare | Abraham Alexander Ribicoff; Anthony Joseph Celebrezze (31 Jul 1962) |

### Lyndon B. Johnson

**22 NOV 1963–20 JAN 1965 (TERM 1)**

| | |
|---|---|
| State | (David) Dean Rusk |
| Treasury | C. (Clarence) Douglas Dillon |
| Defense | Robert Strange McNamara |
| Attorney General | Robert F. Kennedy |
| Interior | Stewart Lee Udall |
| Agriculture | Orville Lothrop Freeman |
| Commerce | Luther Hartwell Hodges |
| Labor | W. (William) Willard Wirtz |
| Health, Education, and Welfare | Anthony Joseph Celebrezze |

**20 JAN 1965–20 JAN 1969 (TERM 2)**

| | |
|---|---|
| State | (David) Dean Rusk |
| Treasury | C. (Clarence) Douglas Dillon; Henry Hamill Fowler (1 Apr 1965); Joseph Walker Barr (23 Dec 1968) |
| Defense | Robert Strange McNamara; Clark McAdams Clifford (1 Mar 1968) |
| Attorney General | Nicholas deBelleville Katzenbach; William Ramsey Clark (10 Mar 1967) |
| Interior | Stewart Lee Udall |
| Agriculture | Orville Lothrop Freeman |
| Commerce | John Thomas Connor; Alexander Buel Trowbridge (14 Jun 1967); Cyrus Rowlett Smith (6 Mar 1968) |
| Labor | W. William Willard Wirtz |
| Health, Education, and Welfare | Anthony Joseph Celebrezze; John William Gardner (18 Aug 1965); Wilbur Joseph Cohen (9 May 1968) |
| **Housing and Urban Development** | Robert Clifton Weaver (18 Jan 1966); Robert Coldwell Wood (7 Jan 1969) |
| **Transportation** | Alan Stephenson Boyd (16 Jan 1967) |

### Richard Nixon

**20 JAN 1969–20 JAN 1973 (TERM 1)**

| | |
|---|---|
| State | William Pierce Rogers |
| Treasury | David Matthew Kennedy; John Bowden Connally, Jr. (11 Feb 1971); George Pratt Shultz (12 Jun 1972) |
| Defense | Melvin Robert Laird |
| Attorney General | John Newton Mitchell; Richard Gordon Kleindienst (12 Jun 1972) |
| Interior | Walter Joseph Hickel; Rogers Clark Ballard Morton (29 Jan 1971) |
| Agriculture | Clifford Morris Hardin; Earl Lauer Butz (2 Dec 1971) |
| Commerce | Maurice Hubert Stans; Peter George Peterson (21 Feb 1972) |
| Labor | George Pratt Shultz; James Day Hodgson (2 Jul 1970) |
| Health, Education, and Welfare | Robert Hutchinson Finch; Elliot Lee Richardson (24 Jun 1970) |
| Housing and Urban Development | George Wilcken Romney |
| Transportation | John Anthony Volpe |

**20 JAN 1973–9 AUG 1974 (TERM 2)**

| | |
|---|---|
| State | William Pierce Rogers; Henry Alfred Kissinger (22 Sep 1973) |
| Treasury | George Pratt Shultz; William Edward Simon (8 May 1974) |

# US Presidential Cabinets (continued)

### Richard Nixon (continued)

**20 JAN 1973–9 AUG 1974 (TERM 2) (CONTINUED)**

| | |
|---|---|
| Defense | Elliot Lee Richardson; James Rodney Schlesinger (2 Jul 1973) |
| Attorney General | Richard Gordon Kleindienst; Elliot Lee Richardson (25 May 1973); William Bart Saxbe (4 Jan 1974) |
| Interior | Rogers Clark Ballard Morton |
| Agriculture | Earl Lauer Butz |
| Commerce | Frederick Baily Dent |
| Labor | Peter Joseph Brennan |
| Health, Education, and Welfare | Caspar Willard Weinberger |
| Housing and Urban Development | James Thomas Lynn |
| Transportation | Claude Stout Brinegar |

### Gerald Ford

**9 AUG 1974–20 JAN 1977**

| | |
|---|---|
| State | Henry Alfred Kissinger |
| Treasury | William Edward Simon |
| Defense | James Rodney Schlesinger; Donald Henry Rumsfeld (20 Nov 1975) |
| Attorney General | William Bart Saxbe; Edward Hirsch Levi (7 Feb 1975) |
| Interior | Rogers Clark Ballard Morton, Jr.; Stanley Knapp Hathaway (13 Jun 1975); Thomas Savig Kleppe (17 Oct 1975) |
| Agriculture | Earl Lauer Butz; John Albert Knebel (4 Nov 1976) |
| Commerce | Frederick Baily Dent; Rogers Clark Ballard Morton, Jr. (1 May 1975); Elliot Lee Richardson (2 Feb 1976) |
| Labor | Peter Joseph Brennan; John Thomas Dunlop (18 Mar 1975); Willie Julian Usery, Jr. (10 Feb 1976) |
| Health, Education, and Welfare | Caspar Willard Weinberger; Forrest David Matthews (8 Aug 1975) |
| Housing and Urban Development | James Thomas Lynn; Carla Anderson Hills (10 Mar 1975) |
| Transportation | Claude Stout Brinegar; William Thaddeus Coleman, Jr. (7 Mar 1975) |

### Jimmy Carter

**20 JAN 1977–20 JAN 1981**

| | |
|---|---|
| State | Cyrus Vance; Edmund Sixtus Muskie (8 May 1980) |
| Treasury | Werner Michael Blumenthal; George William Miller (6 Aug 1979) |
| Defense | Harold Brown |
| Attorney General | Griffin Boyette Bell; Benjamin Richard Civiletti (16 Aug 1979) |
| Interior | Cecil Dale Andrus |
| Agriculture | Robert Selmer Bergland |
| Commerce | Juanita Morris Kreps; Philip Morris Klutznick (9 Jan 1980) |
| Labor | Fred Ray Marshall |
| Health, Education, and Welfare | Joseph Anthony Califano, Jr.; Patricia Roberts Harris (3 Aug 1979) |
| **Health and Human Services** | Patricia Roberts Harris (27 Sep 1979) |
| Housing and Urban Development | Patricia Roberts Harris; Moon Landrieu (24 Sep 1979) |
| Transportation | Brockman Adams; Neil Edward Goldschmidt (24 Sep 1979) |
| **Energy** | James Rodney Schlesinger (1 Oct 1977); Charles William Duncan, Jr. (24 Aug 1979) |
| **Education** | Shirley Mount Hufstedler (6 Dec 1979) |

### Ronald Reagan

**20 JAN 1981–20 JAN 1985 (TERM 1)**

| | |
|---|---|
| State | Alexander Meigs Haig, Jr.; George Pratt Shultz (16 Jul 1982) |
| Treasury | Donald Thomas Regan |
| Defense | Caspar Willard Weinberger |
| Attorney General | William French Smith |
| Interior | James Gaius Watt; William Patrick Clark (21 Nov 1983) |
| Agriculture | John Rusling Block |
| Commerce | Malcolm Baldrige |
| Labor | Raymond Joseph Donovan |
| Health and Human Services | Richard Schultz Schweiker; Margaret Mary O'Shaughnessy Heckler (9 Mar 1983) |
| Housing and Urban Development | Samuel Riley Pierce, Jr. |
| Transportation | Drew (Andrew) Lindsay Lewis, Jr.; Elizabeth Hanford Dole (7 Feb 1983) |
| Energy | James Burrows Edwards; Donald Paul Hodel (8 Dec 1982) |
| Education | Terrel Howard Bell |

**20 JAN 1985–20 JAN 1989 (TERM 2)**

| | |
|---|---|
| State | George Pratt Shultz |
| Treasury | Donald Thomas Regan; James Addison Baker III (25 Feb 1985); Nicholas Frederick Brady (18 Aug 1988) |

## US Presidential Cabinets (continued)

### Ronald Reagan (continued)

**20 JAN 1985–20 JAN 1989 (TERM 2) (CONTINUED)**

| | |
|---|---|
| Defense | Caspar Willard Weinberger; Frank Charles Carlucci III (21 Nov 1987) |
| Attorney General | William French Smith; Edwin Meese III (25 Feb 1985); Richard Lewis (Dick) Thornburgh (11 Aug 1988) |
| Interior | Donald Paul Hodel |
| Agriculture | John Rusling Block; Richard Edmund Lyng (7 Mar 1986) |
| Commerce | Malcolm Baldrige; Calvin William Verity, Jr. (19 Oct 1987) |
| Labor | Raymond James Donovan; William Emerson (Bill) Brock III (29 Apr 1985); Ann Dore McLaughlin (17 Dec 1987) |
| Health and Human Services | Margaret Mary O'Shaughnessy Heckler; Otis Ray Bowen (13 Dec 1985) |
| Housing and Urban Development | Samuel Riley Pierce, Jr. |
| Transportation | Elizabeth Hanford Dole; James Horace Burnley IV (3 Dec 1987) |
| Energy | John Stewart Herrington |
| Education | Terrel Howard Bell; William John Bennett (7 Feb 1985); Lauro Fred Cavazos, Jr. (20 Sep 1988) |

### George H.W. Bush

**20 JAN 1989–20 JAN 1993**

| | |
|---|---|
| State | James Addison Baker III |
| Treasury | Nicholas Frederick Brady |
| Attorney General | Richard Lewis (Dick) Thornburgh; William P. Barr (20 Nov 1991) |
| Interior | Manuel Lujan, Jr. |
| Agriculture | Clayton Keith Yeutter; Edward Madigan (7 Mar 1991) |
| Commerce | Robert Adam Mosbacher |
| Labor | Elizabeth Hanford Dole |
| Defense | Richard (Dick) Cheney |
| Health and Human Services | Louis Wade Sullivan |
| Housing and Urban Development | Jack F. Kemp |
| Transportation | Samuel K. Skinner; Andrew H. Card (22 Jan 1992) |
| Energy | James David Watkins |
| Education | Lauro Fred Cavazos, Jr.; Lamar Alexander (14 Mar 1991) |
| **Veterans Affairs** | Edward Joseph Derwinski (15 Mar 1989) |

### William J. Clinton

**20 JAN 1993–20 JAN 1997 (TERM 1)**

| | |
|---|---|
| State | Warren M. Christopher |
| Treasury | Lloyd Bentsen, Jr.; Robert E. Rubin (10 Jan 1995) |
| Attorney General | Janet Reno |
| Interior | Bruce Babbitt |
| Agriculture | Mike Espy; Dan Glickman (30 Mar 1995) |
| Commerce | Ronald H. Brown; Mickey Kantor (12 Apr 1996) |
| Labor | Robert B. Reich |
| Defense | Les Aspin; William J. Perry (3 Feb 1994) |
| Health and Human Services | Donna E. Shalala |
| Housing and Urban Development | Henry G. Cisneros |
| Transportation | Federico Peña |
| Energy | Hazel R. O'Leary |
| Education | Richard W. Riley |
| Veterans Affairs | Jesse Brown |

**20 JAN 1997–20 JAN 2001 (TERM 2)**

| | |
|---|---|
| State | Madeleine Albright |
| Treasury | Robert E. Rubin; Lawrence H. Summers (2 Jul 1999) |
| Attorney General | Janet Reno |
| Interior | Bruce Babbitt |
| Agriculture | Dan Glickman |
| Commerce | William M. Daley; Norman Mineta (21 Jul 2000) |
| Labor | Alexis M. Herman |
| Defense | William Cohen |
| Health and Human Services | Donna E. Shalala |
| Housing and Urban Development | Andrew M. Cuomo |
| Transportation | Rodney Slater |
| Energy | Federico Peña; Bill Richardson (18 Aug 1998) |
| Education | Richard W. Riley |
| Veterans Affairs | Togo D. West, Jr.; Hershel W. Gober (25 Jul 2000) |

# US Presidential Cabinets (continued)

### George W. Bush

(20 JAN 2001– )

| | |
|---|---|
| State | Colin Powell |
| Treasury | Paul O'Neill; John Snow (7 Feb 2003) |
| Attorney General | John Ashcroft |
| Interior | Gale Norton |
| Agriculture | Ann M. Veneman |
| Commerce | Don Evans |
| Labor | Elaine Chao |
| Defense | Donald Rumsfeld |
| Health and Human Services | Tommy Thompson |
| Housing and Urban Development | Mel Martinez |
| Transportation | Norman Mineta |
| Energy | Spencer Abraham |
| Education | Rod Paige |
| Veterans Affairs | Anthony Principi |
| **Homeland Security** | Tom Ridge |

Additionally, the White House lists the following as cabinet-rank members: Vice President Richard (Dick) Cheney, Chief of Staff Andrew H. Card, Jr., Environmental Protection Agency Administrator Marianne L. Horinko (acting), US Trade Representative Robert B. Zoellick, Office of Management and Budget Director Mitchell E. Daniels, Jr., and Office of National Drug Control Policy Director John Walters.

# Presidential Libraries

The presidential libraries serve as repositories for the papers, records, and materials of the US presidents since Herbert Hoover. Each of the 10 libraries contains a museum and conducts public programs. The network is administered by the the Office of Presidential Libraries, which is itself a division of the US National Archives and Records Administration (NARA). The system also includes the Nixon Presidential Materials Staff and the William J. Clinton Presidential Materials Project.

**NAME, ADDRESS, & CONTACT INFORMATION**

Herbert Hoover Library
210 Parkside Drive
P.O. Box 488
West Branch IA 52358-0488
Web site: <hoover.nara.gov>

Franklin D. Roosevelt Library
4079 Albany Post Road
Hyde Park NY 12538-1999
Web site: <www.fdrlibrary.marist.edu>

Harry S. Truman Library
500 West US Highway 24
Independence MO 64050-1798
Web site: <www.trumanlibrary.org>

Dwight D. Eisenhower Library
200 SE 4th Street
Abilene KS 67410-2900
Web site: <www.eisenhower.utexas.edu>

John F. Kennedy Library
Columbia Point
Boston MA 02125-3398
Web site: <www.jfklibrary.org>

Lyndon B. Johnson Library
2313 Red River Street
Austin TX 78705-5702
Web site: <www.lbjlib.utexas.edu>

Richard Nixon Library and Birthplace
18001 Yorba Linda Boulevard
Yorba Linda CA 92886-3949
Web site: <www.nixonlibrary.org>

**NAME, ADDRESS, & CONTACT INFORMATION**

Nixon Presidential Materials Staff
National Archives at College Park
8601 Adelphi Road
College Park MD 20740-6001
Web site: <www.nara.gov/nixon>

Gerald R. Ford Library
1000 Beal Avenue
Ann Arbor MI 48109-2114
Web site: <www.ford.utexas.edu>

Jimmy Carter Library
441 Freedom Parkway
Atlanta GA 30307-1498
Web site: <www.jimmycarterlibrary.org>

Ronald Reagan Library
40 Presidential Drive
Simi Valley CA 93065-0600
Web site: <www.reagan.utexas.edu>

George Bush Library
1000 George Bush Drive West
College Station TX 77845
Web site: <bushlibrary.tamu.edu>

William J. Clinton Presidential Materials Project
1000 LaHarpe Boulevard
Little Rock AR 72201
Web site: <www.clinton.nara.gov>

Office of Presidential Libraries
National Archives at College Park
8601 Adelphi Road
College Park MD 20740-6001
Web site: <www.nara.gov>

# Impeachment

The American federal impeachment process is rooted in Article II, Section 4, of the US Constitution. Impeachment has rarely been employed, largely because it is such a cumbersome process. It can occupy Congress for a lengthy period of time, fill thousands of pages of testimony, and involve conflicting and troublesome political pressures. Repeated attempts in the US Congress to amend the procedure, however, have been unsuccessful, partly because impeachment is regarded as an integral part of the system of checks and balances in the US government.

Andrew Johnson was the first US president ever impeached. In 1868 he was charged with attempting to remove, contrary to statute, the secretary of war, Edwin M. Stanton, with inducing a general of the army to violate an act of Congress, and with contempt of Congress. Johnson was acquitted by a margin of a single vote. In 1974 the Judiciary Committee of the House of Representatives voted three articles of impeachment against Pres. Richard M. Nixon, but he resigned before impeachment proceedings in the full House could begin. In December 1998 the House of Representatives voted to impeach Pres. William J. Clinton, charging him with perjury and obstruction of justice in investigations of his relationship with a White House intern, Monica Lewinsky. In the trial, the Senate voted not guilty on the perjury charge (55–45) and not guilty on the obstruction of justice charge (50–50); since 67 guilty votes are needed for a conviction, President Clinton was acquitted.

Every US state except Oregon provides for the removal of executive and judicial officers by impeachment. Exact procedures vary somewhat from state to state, but they are all similar to federal impeachment.

# Executive Departments

**Department of Agriculture**
**Secretary:** Ann M. Veneman
**Deputy secretary:** Jim Moseley
**Web site:** <www.usda.gov>
**Mission:** To enhance the quality of life for the American people by supporting production of agriculture.
**Selected divisions and agencies:**
  Farm and Foreign Agricultural Service
  Farm Service Agency
  Foreign Agricultural Service
  Risk Management Agency
  Food Safety
  Food Safety and Inspection Service
  Natural Resources and Environment
  Forest Service
  Natural Resources Conservation Service
  Rural Development
  Rural Business—Cooperative Service
  Office of Community Development
  Rural Housing Service
  Rural Utilities Service
  Food, Nutrition, and Consumer Services
  Food and Nutrition Service
  Center for Nutrition Policy and Promotion
  Marketing and Regulatory Programs
  Agricultural Marketing Service
  Animal and Plant Health Inspection Service
  Grain Inspection, Packers and Stockyards
    Administration
  Research, Education, and Economics
  Agricultural Research Service
  Cooperative State Research, Education, and
    Extension Service
  Economic Research Service
  National Agricultural Statistics Service

**Department of Commerce**
**Secretary:** Donald L. Evans
**Deputy secretary:** Samuel W. Bodman
**Web site:** <www.commerce.gov>
**Mission:** To promote job creation, economic growth, sustainable development, and improved living standards for all Americans by working in partnership with business, universities, communities, and workers.
**Selected divisions and agencies:**
  Economics and Statistics Administration
  Bureau of Economic Analysis

  Bureau of the Census
  National Oceanic and Atmospheric Administration
    National Weather Service
  Technology Administration
    National Institute of Standards and Technology
    National Technical Information Service
    Office of Technology Policy
  Economic Development Administration
  Bureau of Industry and Security
  International Trade Administration
  Minority Business Development Agency
  National Telecommunications and Information
    Administration
  Patent and Trademark Office

**Department of Defense**
**Secretary:** Donald H. Rumsfeld
**Deputy secretary:** Paul Wolfowitz
**Web site:** <www.defenselink.mil>
**Mission:** To provide the military forces needed to deter war and to protect the security of the US.
**Selected divisions and agencies:**
  Army Department
  Navy Department
    Marine Corps
  Air Force Department
  Defense Advanced Research Projects Agency
  Defense Commissary Agency
  Defense Contract Audit Agency
  Defense Contract Management Agency
  Defense Finance and Accounting Service
  Defense Information Systems Agency
  Defense Intelligence Agency
  Defense Legal Services Agency
  Defense Logistics Agency
  Defense Security Cooperation Agency
  Defense Security Service
  Defense Threat Reduction Agency
  Missile Defense Agency
  National Imagery and Mapping Agency
  National Security Agency
  Pentagon Force Protection Agency

**Department of Education**
**Secretary:** Rod Paige
**Deputy secretary:** William D. Hansen
**Web site:** <www.ed.gov>

## Department of Education (continued)

**Mission:** To establish policies relating to federal financial aid for education, administer distribution of these funds, and monitor their use; to collect data and oversee research on US schools and disseminate this information; to identify the major issues and problems in education and focus national attention on them; and to enforce federal statutes prohibiting discrimination in programs and activities receiving federal funds and ensure equal access to education for every individual.

**Selected divisions and agencies:**
White House Initiatives
  Center for Faith-Based and Community Initiatives
  Historically Black Colleges and Universities
  Educational Excellence for Hispanic Americans
  Tribal Colleges and Universities
Institute of Education Sciences
Office of Elementary and Secondary Education
Office of Postsecondary Education
Office of Innovation and Improvement
Office of Safe and Drug-Free Schools
Office of Special Education and Rehabilitative Services
Office of Federal Student Aid
Office of Vocational and Adult Education
Office for Civil Rights
Office of English Language Acquisition
Office of Educational Technology

## Department of Energy

**Secretary:** Spencer Abraham
**Deputy secretary:** Kyle McSlarrow
**Web site:** <www.energy.gov>
**Mission:** To ensure the integrity and safety of US nuclear weapons; to promote international nuclear safety; to advance nonproliferation; to provide safe, efficient, and effective nuclear power plants for the US Navy; to increase domestic energy production; to revolutionize the approach to energy conservation and efficiency; to promote the development of renewable and alternative energy sources; to ensure that safety legacies of the cold war are addressed and resolved; to dispose of the nation's radioactive wastes safely and permanently; and to sponsor cutting-edge science and technology research and development that revolutionizes the nation's approach to energy.

**Selected divisions and agencies:**
National Nuclear Security Administration
  Defense Programs
  Defense Nuclear Nonproliferation
  Naval Reactors
  Office of Emergency Operations
  Infrastructure and Security
  Management and Administration
Energy, Science and Environment
  Office of Science
  Office of Civilian Radioactive Waste Management
  Office of Nuclear Energy, Science, and Technology
  Office of Worker and Community Transition
Office of Counterintelligence
Office of Intelligence
Office of Security
Office of the Inspector General
Office of Independent Oversight and Performance Assurance
Office of Hearings and Appeals
Office of Energy Assurance
Office of Management, Budget and Evaluation/CFO
Energy Information Administration

## Department of Energy (continued)

Office of Economic Impact and Diversity
Office of Public Affairs

## Department of Health and Human Services

**Secretary:** Tommy G. Thompson
**Deputy secretary:** Claude A. Allen
**Web site:** <www.hhs.gov>
**Mission:** To protect the health of all Americans and provide essential human services, especially for those who are least able to help themselves.

**Selected divisions and agencies:**
Administration for Children and Families
Administration on Aging
Centers for Medicare and Medicaid Services
Agency for Healthcare Research and Quality
Centers for Disease Control and Prevention
Agency for Toxic Substances and Disease Registry
Food and Drug Administration
Health Resources and Services Administration
Indian Health Service
National Institutes of Health
Substance Abuse and Mental Health Services Administration
Program Support Center
Office of Public Health Emergency Preparedness
Faith-Based and Community Initiatives
Office for Civil Rights
Departmental Appeals Board

## Department of Homeland Security

**Secretary:** Tom Ridge
**Deputy Secretary:** Gordon England
**Web site:** <www.dhs.gov>
**Mission:** To prevent terrorist attacks within the United States, reduce America's vulnerablity to terrorism, and minimize the damage from potential attacks and natural disasters.

**Selected divisions and agencies, as planned (with former departments):**
Directorate of Border and Transportation Security
  US Customs Service (Treasury)
  Immigration and Naturalization Service (part) (Justice)
  Federal Protective Service (General Services Administration)
  Transportation Security Administration (Transportation)
  Federal Law Enforcement Training Center (Treasury)
  Animal and Plant Health Inspection Service (part) (Agriculture)
  Office for Domestic Preparedness (Justice)
Directorate of Emergency Preparedness and Response
  Federal Emergency Management Agency (independent)
  Strategic National Stockpile and the National Disaster Medical System (HHS)
  Nuclear Incident Response Team (Energy)
  Domestic Emergency Support Teams (Justice)
  National Domestic Preparedness Office (Justice—FBI)
Directorate of Science and Technology
  CBRN Countermeasures Programs (Energy)
  Environmental Measurements Laboratory (Energy)
  National BW Defense Analysis Center (Defense)
  Plum Island Animal Disease Center (Agriculture)
Directorate of Information Analysis and Infrastructure Protection

## Department of Homeland Security (continued)
Critical Infrastructure Assurance Office (Commerce)
Federal Computer Incident Response Center (General Services Administration)
National Communications System (Defense)
National Infrastructure Protection Center (Justice—FBI)
Energy Security and Assurance Program (Energy)
US Coast Guard (Defense)
US Secret Service (Treasury)

## Department of Housing and Urban Development
**Secretary:** Mel R. Martinez
**Deputy secretary:** Alphonso R. Jackson
**Web site:** <www.hud.gov>
**Mission:** To create a safe and sanitary living environment for every American by creating opportunities for homeownership; by providing housing assistance for low-income persons; by working to create, rehabilitate, and maintain the nation's affordable housing; by enforcing the nation's fair housing laws; by helping the homeless; by spurring economic growth in distressed neighborhoods; and by helping local communities meet their development needs.
**Selected divisions and agencies:**
Office of Housing
Office of Community Planning and Development
Office of Fair Housing and Equal Opportunity
Government National Mortgage Association (Ginnie Mae)
Office of Multifamily Housing Assistance Restructuring
Office of Public and Indian Housing

## Department of the Interior
**Secretary:** Gale A. Norton
**Deputy secretary:** James Steven Griles
**Web site:** <www.doi.gov>
**Mission:** To protect and provide access to the nation's natural and cultural heritage, and to honor responsibilities to Indian tribes and commitments to island communities.
**Selected divisions and agencies:**
National Park Service
US Fish and Wildlife Service
Bureau of Indian Affairs
Bureau of Land Management
Minerals Management Service
Office of Surface Mining Reclamation and Enforcement
US Geological Survey
Bureau of Reclamation

## Department of Justice
**Attorney General:** John Ashcroft
**Deputy Attorney General:** Larry D. Thompson
**Web site:** <www.usdoj.gov>
**Mission:** To enforce the law and defend the interests of the US according to the law; to provide federal leadership in preventing and controlling crime; to seek just punishment for those guilty of unlawful behavior; to administer and enforce the nation's immigration laws fairly and effectively; and to ensure fair and impartial administration of justice for all Americans.
**Selected divisions and agencies:**
Office of Legal Policy
Office of Legislative Affairs
Office of Intergovernmental and Public Liaison
Office of Public Affairs

## Department of Justice (continued)
Office of Legal Counsel
Office of the Solicitor General
Office of Justice Programs
Community Oriented Policing Office
Executive Office for United States Trustees
Office of Dispute Resolution
Office of Information and Privacy
Foreign Claims Settlement Commission
Civil Rights Division
Civil Division
Antitrust Division
Environment and Natural Resources Division
Tax Division
Community Relations Service
Federal Bureau of Investigation
Drug Enforcement Administration
Executive Office for United States Attorneys
Criminal Division
Bureau of Prisons
United States Marshals Service
US National Central Bureau—Interpol
Office of the Detention Trustee
Office of the Inspector General
Office of Intelligence Policy and Review
Justice Management Division
Executive Office for Immigration Review
Office of Professional Responsibility
Office of the Pardon Attorney
United States Parole Commission
National Drug Intelligence Center
Professional Responsibility Advisory Office

## Department of Labor
**Secretary:** Elaine L. Chao
**Deputy secretary:** D. Cameron Findlay
**Web site:** <www.dol.gov>
**Mission:** To foster and promote the welfare of the job seekers, wage earners, and retirees of the US by improving their working conditions, advancing their opportunities for profitable employment, protecting their retirement and health care benefits, helping employers find workers, strengthening free collective bargaining, and tracking changes in employment, prices, and other national economic measurements.
**Selected divisions and agencies:**
Office of Disability Employment Policy
Occupational Safety and Health Administration
Mine Safety and Health Administration
Employee Benefits Security Administration
Bureau of Labor Statistics
Pension Benefit Guaranty Corporation
Employment and Training Administration
Women's Bureau
Veterans' Employment and Training Service
Bureau of International Labor Affairs
Office of the Assistant Secretary for Policy
Employment Standards Administration
Office of Small Business Programs

## Department of State
**Secretary:** Colin L. Powell
**Deputy secretary:** Richard L. Armitage
**Web site:** <www.state.gov>
**Mission:** To promote peace and stability in regions of vital interest; to create jobs in the US by opening markets abroad; to help developing nations establish stable economic environments that provide investment and export opportunities; and to bring nations together to address global problems.

## Department of State (continued)

**Selected divisions, agencies, and bureaus:**

Political affairs
  African Affairs
  East Asian and Pacific Affairs
  European and Eurasian Affairs
  Near Eastern Affairs
  South Asian Affairs
  Western Hemisphere Affairs
  International Organization Affairs
Economic, Business and Agricultural Affairs
  Economic and Business Affairs
  Arms Control
  Nonproliferation
  Political-Military Affairs
  Verification and Compliance
Public Diplomacy and Public Affairs
  Educational and Cultural Affairs
  Public Affairs
  International Information Programs
Management
  Consular Affairs
  Diplomatic Security and Foreign Missions
  Foreign Service Institute
  Information Resource Management
  Office of White House Liaison
  Overseas Buildings Operations
Global Affairs
  Democracy, Human Rights, and Labor
  International Narcotics and Law Enforcement Affairs
  Oceans and International Environmental and Scientific Affairs
  Population, Refugees, and Migration
Policy Planning Staff
Office of Civil Rights
Intelligence and Research
Office of Protocol
Counterterrorism Office
Office of War Crimes Issues

## Department of Transportation

**Secretary:** Norman Y. Mineta
**Deputy secretary:** Michael P. Jackson
**Web site:** <www.dot.gov>
**Mission:** To serve the US by ensuring a fast, safe, efficient, accessible, and convenient transportation system that meets vital national interests and enhances the quality of life of the American people.
**Selected divisions and agencies:**
Federal Aviation Administration
Federal Highway Administration
Federal Railroad Administration

## Department of Transportation (continued)

National Highway Traffic Safety Administration
Federal Transit Administration
Saint Lawrence Seaway Development Corporation
Maritime Administration
Research and Special Programs Administration
Bureau of Transportation Statistics
Federal Motor Carrier Safety Administration

## Department of the Treasury

**Secretary:** John W. Snow
**Deputy secretary:** Susan C. Schwab
**Web site:** <www.ustreas.gov>
**Mission:** To promote prosperous and stable US and world economies; to manage the government's finances; to safeguard US financial systems; to protect US leaders; and to secure a safe and drug-free America.
**Selected divisions and agencies:**
Treasurer of the United States
Alcohol and Tobacco Tax and Trade Bureau
Bureau of Engraving and Printing
Bureau of the Public Debt
Financial Crimes Enforcement Network
Financial Management Service
Internal Revenue Service
Office of the Comptroller of the Currency
Office of Thrift Supervision
US Mint

## Department of Veterans Affairs

**Secretary:** Anthony J. Principi
**Deputy secretary:** Leo S. Mackay, Jr.
**Web site:** <www.va.gov>
**Mission:** To serve US veterans and their families with dignity and compassion and be their principal advocate in ensuring that they receive medical care, benefits, social support, and lasting memorials promoting the health, welfare, and dignity of all veterans in recognition of their service.
**Selected divisions and agencies:**
Veterans Health Administration
Veterans Benefits Administration
National Cemetery Administration
Board of Contract Appeals
Board of Veterans' Appeals
Center for Minority Veterans
Center for Women Veterans

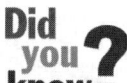

**Did you know?** The Constitution requires that US presidents be native-born citizens and residents of the US for at least 14 years. The last "foreign-born" president, therefore, was William Henry Harrison, who was born in Virginia in 1773, before the US was formed. Herbert Hoover was the first US president born (in 1874) west of the Mississippi River.

# United States Congress

## The Senate, 108th Congress

According to Article I, Section 3, of the US Constitution, a US senator must be at least 30 years old, must reside in the state he or she represents at the time of the election, and must have been a citizen of the United States for 9 years. Voters elect two senators from each state; terms are for 6 years and begin on 3 January. Senators originally made $6.00 per day; each current senator's salary is $154,700 per year. The majority and minority leaders and the president pro tempore receive $171,900 per year.

US Senate Web site: <www.senate.gov>

**Senate leadership**

| | |
|---|---|
| president: | Richard Cheney |
| president pro tempore: | Ted Stevens |
| majority leader: | Bill Frist |
| minority leader: | Tom Daschle |
| asst. majority leader (majority whip): | Mitch McConnell |
| asst. minority leader (minority whip): | Harry Reid |

| STATE | NAME AND PARTY | SERVICE BEGAN | TERM ENDS |
|---|---|---|---|
| Alabama | Richard Shelby (R) | 1987 | 2005 |
| | Jeff Sessions (R) | 1997 | 2003 |
| Alaska | Ted Stevens (R) | 1968[1] | 2003 |
| | Lisa Murkowski (R) | 2002 | 2005 |
| Arizona | John McCain (R) | 1987 | 2005 |
| | Jon Kyl (R) | 1995 | 2007 |
| Arkansas | Blanche Lambert Lincoln (D) | 1999 | 2005 |
| | Mark Pryor (D) | 2003 | 2009 |
| California | Dianne Feinstein (D) | 1992[2] | 2007 |
| | Barbara Boxer (D) | 1993 | 2005 |
| Colorado | Ben Nighthorse Campbell (R) | 1993 | 2005 |
| | Wayne Allard (R) | 1997 | 2003 |
| Connecticut | Chris Dodd (D) | 1981 | 2005 |
| | Joe Lieberman (D) | 1989 | 2007 |
| Delaware | Joseph R. Biden, Jr. (D) | 1973 | 2003 |
| | Tom Carper (D) | 2001 | 2007 |
| Florida | Bob Graham (D) | 1987 | 2005 |
| | Bill Nelson (D) | 2001 | 2007 |
| Georgia | Zell Miller (D) | 2000[3] | 2005 |
| | Saxby Chambliss (R) | 2003 | 2009 |
| Hawaii | Daniel K. Inouye (D) | 1963 | 2005 |
| | Daniel Kahikina Akaka (D) | 1990[4] | 2007 |
| Idaho | Larry Craig (R) | 1991 | 2003 |
| | Mike Crapo (R) | 1999 | 2005 |
| Illinois | Dick Durbin (D) | 1997 | 2003 |
| | Peter G. Fitzgerald (R) | 1999 | 2005 |
| Indiana | Richard G. Lugar (R) | 1977 | 2007 |
| | Evan Bayh (D) | 1999 | 2005 |
| Iowa | Chuck Grassley (R) | 1981 | 2005 |
| | Tom Harkin (D) | 1985 | 2003 |
| Kansas | Sam Brownback (R) | 1996[5] | 2005 |
| | Pat Roberts (R) | 1997 | 2003 |
| Kentucky | Mitch McConnell (R) | 1985 | 2003 |
| | Jim Bunning (R) | 1999 | 2005 |
| Louisiana | John Breaux (D) | 1987 | 2005 |
| | Mary L. Landrieu (D) | 1997 | 2003 |
| Maine | Olympia J. Snowe (R) | 1995 | 2007 |
| | Susan Collins (R) | 1997 | 2003 |
| Maryland | Paul S. Sarbanes (D) | 1977 | 2007 |
| | Barbara A. Mikulski (D) | 1987 | 2005 |
| Massachusetts | Edward M. Kennedy (D) | 1963 | 2007 |
| | John Kerry (D) | 1985 | 2003 |
| Michigan | Carl Levin (D) | 1979 | 2003 |
| | Debbie Stabenow (D) | 2001 | 2007 |
| Minnesota | Mark Dayton (D) | 2001 | 2007 |
| | Norm Coleman (R) | 2003 | 2009 |
| Mississippi | Thad Cochran (R) | 1979 | 2003 |
| | Trent Lott (R) | 1989 | 2007 |
| Missouri | Kit Bond (R) | 1987 | 2005 |
| | James Talent (R) | 2002 | 2007 |

## The Senate, 108th Congress (continued)

| STATE | NAME AND PARTY | SERVICE BEGAN | TERM ENDS |
|---|---|---|---|
| Montana | Max Baucus (D) | 1979 | 2003 |
| | Conrad Burns (R) | 1989 | 2007 |
| Nebraska | Chuck Hagel (R) | 1997 | 2003 |
| | Ben Nelson (D) | 2001 | 2007 |
| Nevada | Harry Reid (D) | 1987 | 2005 |
| | John Ensign (R) | 2001 | 2007 |
| New Hampshire | Judd Gregg (R) | 1993 | 2005 |
| | John Sununu (R) | 2003 | 2009 |
| New Jersey | Jon S. Corzine (D) | 2001 | 2007 |
| | Frank Lautenberg (D) | 2003 | 2009 |
| New Mexico | Pete V. Domenici (R) | 1973 | 2003 |
| | Jeff Bingaman (D) | 1983 | 2007 |
| New York | Charles E. Schumer (D) | 1999 | 2005 |
| | Hillary Rodham Clinton (D) | 2001 | 2007 |
| North Carolina | John Edwards (D) | 1999 | 2005 |
| | Elizabeth Dole (R) | 2003 | 2009 |
| North Dakota | Kent Conrad (D) | 1987 | 2007 |
| | Byron Dorgan (D) | 1993 | 2005 |
| Ohio | Mike DeWine (R) | 1995 | 2007 |
| | George V. Voinovich (R) | 1999 | 2005 |
| Oklahoma | Don Nickles (R) | 1981 | 2005 |
| | James M. Inhofe (R) | 1995[6] | 2003 |
| Oregon | Ron Wyden (D) | 1996[7] | 2005 |
| | Gordon H. Smith (R) | 1997 | 2003 |
| Pennsylvania | Arlen Specter (R) | 1981 | 2005 |
| | Rick Santorum (R) | 1995 | 2007 |
| Rhode Island | Jack Reed (D) | 1997 | 2003 |
| | Lincoln D. Chafee (R) | 1999[8] | 2007 |
| South Carolina | Ernest Hollings (D) | 1967 | 2005 |
| | Lindsey Graham (R) | 2003 | 2009 |
| South Dakota | Tom Daschle (D) | 1987 | 2005 |
| | Tim Johnson (D) | 1997 | 2003 |
| Tennessee | Bill Frist (R) | 1995 | 2007 |
| | Lamar Alexander (R) | 2003 | 2009 |
| Texas | Kay Bailey Hutchison (R) | 1993[9] | 2007 |
| | John Cornyn (R) | 2002 | 2009 |
| Utah | Orrin G. Hatch (R) | 1977 | 2007 |
| | Bob Bennett (R) | 1993 | 2005 |
| Vermont | Patrick Leahy (D) | 1975 | 2005 |
| | Jim Jeffords (I) | 1989 | 2007 |
| Virginia | John Warner (R) | 1979 | 2003 |
| | George Allen (R) | 2001 | 2007 |
| Washington | Patty Murray (D) | 1993 | 2005 |
| | Maria Cantwell (D) | 2001 | 2007 |
| West Virginia | Robert C. Byrd (D) | 1959 | 2007 |
| | Jay Rockefeller (D) | 1985 | 2003 |
| Wisconsin | Herb Kohl (D) | 1989 | 2007 |
| | Russ Feingold (D) | 1993 | 2005 |
| Wyoming | Craig Thomas (R) | 1995 | 2007 |
| | Mike Enzi (R) | 1997 | 2003 |

Republicans: 51; Democrats: 48; Independents: 1

[1]Ted Stevens was appointed in December 1968 to fill the vacancy caused by the death of Edward Lewis (Bob) Bartlett. [2]Dianne Feinstein was elected in November 1992 to complete the term of Pete Wilson, who resigned in 1991 to become California's governor. [3]Zell Miller was appointed in July 2000 to fill the vacancy caused by the death of Paul Coverdell. [4]Daniel Kahikina Akaka was appointed in April 1990 after winning a special election to fill the vacancy caused by the death of Spark M. Matsunaga. [5]Sam Brownback was elected in November 1996 to complete the term of Bob Dole, who resigned to campaign for the presidency. [6]James M. Inhofe was elected in November 1994 to complete the term of David Boren, who resigned to become president of the University of Oklahoma. [7]Ron Wyden was elected in January 1996 to complete the term of Bob Packwood, who resigned in 1995. [8]Lincoln D. Chafee was appointed in November 1999 to fill the vacancy caused by the death of his father, John H. Chafee. [9]Kay Bailey Hutchison was elected in June 1993 to fill the vacancy left by the retirement of Lloyd Bentsen, Jr.

## Senate Standing Committees

| COMMITTEE | CHAIRMAN (PARTY–STATE) | RANKING MINORITY MEMBER (PARTY–STATE) | NUMBER OF MEMBERS: MAJORITY | NUMBER OF MEMBERS: MINORITY | NUMBER OF SUBCOM-MITTEES |
|---|---|---|---|---|---|
| Agriculture, Nutrition, and Forestry | Thad Cochran (R-MS) | Tom Harkin (D-IA) | 11 | 10 | 4 |
| Appropriations | Ted Stevens (R-AK) | Robert C. Byrd (D-WV) | 15 | 14 | 13 |
| Armed Services | John Warner (R-VA) | Carl Levin (D-MI) | 13 | 12 | 6 |
| Banking, Housing, and Urban Affairs | Richard C. Shelby (R-AL) | Paul S. Sarbanes (D-MD) | 11 | 10 | 5 |
| Budget | Don Nickles (R-OK) | Kent Conrad (D-ND) | 12 | 11 | none |
| Commerce, Science, and Transportation | John McCain (R-AZ) | Ernest Hollings (D-SC) | 12 | 11 | 7 |
| Energy and Natural Resources | Pete V. Domenici (R-NM) | Jeff Bingaman (D-NM) | 12 | 11 | 4 |
| Environment and Public Works | James M. Inhofe (R-OK) | James M. Jeffords (I-VT) | 10 | 9 | 4 |
| Finance | Chuck Grassley (R-IA) | Mac Baucus (D-MT) | 11 | 10 | 5 |
| Foreign Relations | Richard G. Lugar (R-IN) | Joseph R. Biden, Jr. (D-DE) | 10 | 9 | 7 |
| Governmental Affairs | Susan Collins (R-ME) | Joseph Lieberman (D-CT) | 9 | 8 | 3 |
| Health, Education, Labor, and Pensions | Judd Gregg (R-NH) | Edward M. Kennedy (D-MA) | 11 | 10 | 4 |
| Judiciary | Orrin G. Hatch (R-UT) | Patrick Leahy (D-VT) | 10 | 9 | 6 |
| Rules and Administration | Trent Lott (R-MS) | Christopher Dodd (D-CT) | 10 | 9 | none |
| Small Business and Entrepreneurship | Olympia J. Snowe (R-ME) | John F. Kerry (D-MA) | 10 | 9 | none |
| Veterans' Affairs | Arlen Specter (R-PA) | Bob Graham (D-FL) | 8 | 7 | none |

## Senate Special, Select, and Other Committees

| COMMITTEE | CHAIRMAN (PARTY–STATE) | RANKING MINORITY MEMBER (PARTY–STATE) | NUMBER OF MEMBERS: MAJORITY | NUMBER OF MEMBERS: MINORITY |
|---|---|---|---|---|
| Special Committee on Aging | Larry Craig (R-ID) | John Breaux (D-LA) | 11 | 10 |
| Select Committee on Ethics | George V. Voinovich (R-OH) | Harry Reid (D-NV) | 3 | 3 |
| Committee on Indian Affairs | Ben Nighthorse Campbell (R-CO) | Daniel K. Inouye (D-HI) | 8 | 7 |
| Select Committee on Intelligence | Pat Roberts (R-KS) | John D. Rockefeller IV (D-WV) | 9 | 8 |

## Joint Committees of Congress

The joint committees of Congress include members from both the Senate and the House of Representatives. They function as overseeing entities but do not have the power to approve appropriations or legislation. Chairmanship of the Joint Economic Committee is determined by seniority and alternates between the Senate and the House every Congress. The Joint Committee on the Library of Congress is evenly made up of members from the House Administration Committee and the Senate Rules and Administration Committees. Chairmanship and vice chairmanship of the Joint Committee on Printing alternates between the House and the Senate every Congress. The Joint Committee on Taxation is composed of five members from the Senate Committee on Finance and five members from the House Committee on Ways and Means (three majority and two minority members from each).

| COMMITTEE | CHAIRMAN (PARTY-STATE) | VICE CHAIRMAN (PARTY-STATE) | NUMBER OF MEMBERS: REPUBLICANS | NUMBER OF MEMBERS: DEMOCRATS |
|---|---|---|---|---|
| Economic | Sen. Robert F. Bennett (R-UT) | Rep. Jim Saxton (R-NJ) | 12 | 8 |
| Library | vacant | Sen. Christopher J. Dodd (D-CT) | 2 | 3 |
| Printing | Rep. Robert W. Ney (R-OH) | Sen. Saxby Chambliss (R-GA) | 5 | 5 |
| Taxation | Rep. William M. Thomas (R-CA) | Sen. Charles E. Grassley (R-IA) | 6 | 4 |

**Did you know?** Out of the 45 vice presidents of the United States, 14 have gone on to serve as president. Only Richard Nixon served two terms as vice president and was elected to two terms as president.

# The House of Representatives, 108th Congress

*Parties: Democrat (D); Republican (R); Independent (I).*
*Party totals: **Republicans** 229; **Democrats** 205; **Independents** 1.*

According to Article I, Section 2, of the US Constitution, a US representative must be at least 25 years old, must reside in the state he or she represents at the time of the election, and must have been a citizen of the United States for 7 years. Each state is entitled to at least one representative, with additional seats apportioned based on population. Each congressperson originally represented 30,000 people; the current range is from 495,304 (Wyoming) to 905,316 (Montana) persons per representative. Terms are for 2 years and begin on 3 January (unless otherwise noted). The current representative's salary is $154,700 per year. The majority and minority leaders receive $171,900 per year; the speaker of the house receives $198,600 per year.

American Samoa, the District of Columbia, Guam, and the Virgin Islands elect delegates; Puerto Rico elects a resident commissioner. Their formal duties are the same, but the resident commissioner serves a 4-year term. They may participate in debate and serve on committees but are not permitted to vote. US House Web site: <www.house.gov>.

Numbers preceding the names refer to districts. Certain states gained (+) or lost (–) districts by reapportionment since the 107th Congress.

**House leadership**

| | |
|---|---|
| Speaker of the house: | J. Dennis Hastert (R-IL) |
| Majority leader: | Tom DeLay (R-TX) |
| Minority leader: | Nancy Pelosi (D-CA) |
| Republican whip: | Roy Blunt (MO) |
| Democratic whip: | Steny H. Hoyer (MD) |

| STATE | REPRESENTATIVES | SERVICE BEGAN |
|---|---|---|
| Alabama | 1. Jo Bonner (R) | Jan 2003 |
| | 2. Terry Everett (R) | Jan 1993 |
| | 3. Mike Rogers (R) | Jan 2003 |
| | 4. Robert B. Aderholt (R) | Jan 1997 |
| | 5. Robert E. (Bud) Cramer, Jr. (D) | Jan 1991 |
| | 6. Spencer Bachus (R) | Jan 1993 |
| | 7. Artur Davis (D) | Jan 2003 |
| Alaska | Don Young (R) | Mar 1973 |
| Arizona (+2) | 1. Rick Renzi (R) | Jan 2001 |
| | 2. Trent Franks (R) | Jan 2003 |
| | 3. John B. Shadegg (R) | Jan 1995 |
| | 4. Ed Pastor (D) | Jun 1991 |
| | 5. J.D. Hayworth (R) | Jan 1995 |
| | 6. Jeff Flake (R) | Jan 2001 |
| | 7. Raúl M. Grijalva (D) | Jan 2003 |
| | 8. Jim Kolbe (R) | Jan 1985 |
| Arkansas | 1. Marion Berry (D) | Jan 1997 |
| | 2. Vic Snyder (D) | Jan 1997 |
| | 3. John Boozman (R)[1] | Nov 2001 |
| | 4. Mike Ross (D) | Jan 2001 |
| California (+1) | 1. Mike Thompson (D) | Jan 1999 |
| | 2. Wally Herger (R) | Jan 1987 |
| | 3. Doug Ose (R) | Jan 1999 |
| | 4. John T. Doolittle (R) | Jan 1991 |
| | 5. Robert T. Matsui (D) | Jan 1979 |
| | 6. Lynn C. Woolsey (D) | Jan 1993 |
| | 7. George Miller (D) | Jan 1975 |
| | 8. Nancy Pelosi (D) | Jun 1987 |
| | 9. Barbara Lee (D) | Jan 1999 |
| | 10. Ellen O. Tauscher (D) | Jan 1997 |
| | 11. Richard W. Pombo (R) | Jan 1993 |
| | 12. Tom Lantos (D) | Jan 1981 |
| | 13. Fortney Pete Stark (D) | Jan 1973 |
| | 14. Anna G. Eshoo (D) | Jan 1993 |
| | 15. Michael M. Honda (D) | Jan 2001 |
| | 16. Zoe Lofgren (D) | Jan 1995 |
| | 17. Sam Farr (D) | Jun 1993 |
| | 18. Dennis A. Cardoza (D) | Jan 2003 |
| | 19. George Radanovich (R) | Jan 1995 |
| | 20. Calvin M. Dooley (D) | Jan 1991 |
| | 21. Devin Nunes (R) | Jan 2003 |
| | 22. William M. Thomas (R) | Jan 1979 |
| California (continued) | 23. Lois Capps (D) | Mar 1998 |
| | 24. Elton Gallegly (R) | Jan 1987 |
| | 25. Howard P. "Buck" McKeon (R) | Jan 1993 |
| | 26. David Dreier (R) | Jan 1981 |
| | 27. Brad Sherman (D) | Jan 1997 |
| | 28. Howard L. Berman (D) | Jan 1983 |
| | 29. Adam B. Schiff (D) | Jan 2001 |
| | 30. Henry A. Waxman (D) | Jan 1975 |
| | 31. Xavier Becerra (D) | Jan 1993 |
| | 32. Hilda L. Solis (D) | Jan 2001 |
| | 33. Diane E. Watson (D)[2] | Jun 2001 |
| | 34. Lucille Roybal-Allard (D) | Jan 1993 |
| | 35. Maxine Waters (D) | Jan 1991 |
| | 36. Jane F. Harman (D)[3] | Jan 1993 |
| | 37. Juanita Millender-McDonald (D) | Mar 1996 |
| | 38. Grace F. Napolitano (D) | Jan 1999 |
| | 39. Linda T. Sánchez (D) | Jan 2003 |
| | 40. Edward R. Royce (R) | Jan 1993 |
| | 41. Jerry Lewis (R) | Jan 1979 |
| | 42. Gary G. Miller (R) | Jan 1999 |
| | 43. Joe Baca (D) | Nov 1999 |
| | 44. Ken Calvert (R) | Jan 1993 |
| | 45. Mary Bono (R) | Apr 1998 |
| | 46. Dana Rohrabacher (R) | Jan 1989 |
| | 47. Loretta Sanchez (D) | Jan 1997 |
| | 48. Christopher Cox (R) | Jan 1989 |
| | 49. Darrell E. Issa (R) | Jan 2001 |
| | 50. Randy "Duke" Cunningham (R) | Jan 1991 |
| | 51. Bob Filner (D) | Jan 1993 |
| | 52. Duncan Hunter (R) | Jan 1981 |
| | 53. Susan A. Davis (D) | Jan 2001 |
| Colorado (+1) | 1. Diana DeGette (D) | Jan 1997 |
| | 2. Mark Udall (D) | Jan 1999 |
| | 3. Scott McInnis (R) | Jan 1993 |
| | 4. Marilyn N. Musgrave (R) | Jan 2003 |
| | 5. Joel Hefley (R) | Jan 1987 |
| | 6. Thomas G. Tancredo (R) | Jan 1999 |
| | 7. Bob Beauprez (R) | Jan 2003 |
| Connecticut (–1) | 1. John B. Larson (D) | Jan 1999 |
| | 2. Rob Simmons (R) | Jan 2001 |
| | 3. Rosa L. DeLauro (D) | Jan 1991 |
| | 4. Christopher Shays (R) | Aug 1987 |

## The House of Representatives, 108th Congress (continued)

| STATE | REPRESENTATIVES | SERVICE BEGAN |
|---|---|---|
| Connecticut (continued) | 5. Nancy L. Johnson (R) | Jan 1983 |
| Delaware | Michael N. Castle (R) | Jan 1993 |
| Florida (+2) | 1. Jeff Miller (R)[4] | Oct 2001 |
| | 2. Allen Boyd (D) | Jan 1997 |
| | 3. Corrine Brown (D) | Jan 1993 |
| | 4. Ander Crenshaw (R) | Jan 2001 |
| | 5. Ginny Brown-Waite (R) | Jan 2003 |
| | 6. Cliff Stearns (R) | Jan 1989 |
| | 7. John L. Mica (R) | Jan 1993 |
| | 8. Ric Keller (R) | Jan 2001 |
| | 9. Michael Bilirakis (R) | Jan 1983 |
| | 10. C.W. Bill Young (R) | Jan 1971 |
| | 11. Jim Davis (D) | Jan 1997 |
| | 12. Adam H. Putnam (R) | Jan 2001 |
| | 13. Katherine Harris (R) | Jan 2003 |
| | 14. Porter J. Goss (R) | Jan 1989 |
| | 15. Dave Weldon (R) | Jan 1995 |
| | 16. Mark Foley (R) | Jan 1995 |
| | 17. Kendrick B. Meek (D) | Jan 2003 |
| | 18. Ileana Ros-Lehtinen (R) | Jan 1991 |
| | 19. Robert Wexler (D) | Jan 1997 |
| | 20. Peter Deutsch (D) | Jan 1993 |
| | 21. Lincoln Diaz-Balart (R) | Jan 1993 |
| | 22. E. Clay Shaw, Jr. (R) | Jan 1981 |
| | 23. Alcee L. Hastings (D) | Jan 1993 |
| | 24. Tom Feeney (R) | Jan 2003 |
| | 25. Mario Diaz-Balart (R) | Jan 2003 |
| Georgia (+2) | 1. Jack Kingston (R) | Jan 1993 |
| | 2. Sanford D. Bishop, Jr. (D) | Jan 1993 |
| | 3. Jim Marshall (D) | Jan 2003 |
| | 4. Denise L. Majette (D) | Jan 2003 |
| | 5. John Lewis (D) | Jan 1987 |
| | 6. Johnny Isakson (R) | Jan 2001 |
| | 7. John Linder (R) | Jan 1993 |
| | 8. Mac Collins (R) | Jan 1993 |
| | 9. Charlie Norwood (R) | Jan 1995 |
| | 10. Nathan Deal (R) | Jan 1997 |
| | 11. Phil Gingrey (R) | Jan 2003 |
| | 12. Max Burns (R) | Jan 2003 |
| | 13. David Scott (D) | Jan 2003 |
| Hawaii | 1. Neil Abercrombie (D)[5] | Sep 1986 |
| | 2. Ed Case (D)[6] | Jan 2003 |
| Idaho | 1. C.L. "Butch" Otter (R) | Jan 2001 |
| | 2. Michael K. Simpson (R) | Jan 1999 |
| Illinois (−1) | 1. Bobby L. Rush (D) | Jan 1993 |
| | 2. Jesse L. Jackson, Jr. (D) | Jan 1997 |
| | 3. William O. Lipinski (D) | Jan 1983 |
| | 4. Luis V. Gutierrez (D) | Jan 1993 |
| | 5. Rahm Emanuel (D) | Jan 2003 |
| | 6. Henry J. Hyde (R) | Jan 1975 |
| | 7. Danny K. Davis (D) | Jan 1997 |
| | 8. Philip M. Crane (R) | Jan 1971 |
| | 9. Janice D. Schakowsky (D) | Jan 1999 |
| | 10. Mark Steven Kirk (R) | Jan 2001 |
| | 11. Jerry Weller (R) | Jan 1995 |
| | 12. Jerry F. Costello (D) | Jan 1989 |
| | 13. Judy Biggert (R) | Jan 1999 |
| | 14. J. Dennis Hastert (R) | Jan 1987 |
| | 15. Timothy V. Johnson (R) | Jan 2001 |
| | 16. Donald A. Manzullo (R) | Jan 1993 |
| | 17. Lane Evans (D) | Jan 1983 |

| STATE | REPRESENTATIVES | SERVICE BEGAN |
|---|---|---|
| Illinois (continued) | 18. Ray LaHood (R) | Jan 1995 |
| | 19. John Shimkus (R) | Jan 1997 |
| Indiana (−1) | 1. Peter J. Visclosky (D) | Jan 1985 |
| | 2. Chris Chocola (R) | Jan 2003 |
| | 3. Mark E. Souder (R) | Jan 1995 |
| | 4. Steve Buyer (R) | Jan 1993 |
| | 5. Dan Burton (R) | Jan 1983 |
| | 6. Mike Pence (R) | Jan 2001 |
| | 7. Julia Carson (D) | Jan 1997 |
| | 8. John N. Hostettler (R) | Jan 1995 |
| | 9. Baron P. Hill (D) | Jan 1999 |
| Iowa | 1. Jim Nussle (R) | Jan 1991 |
| | 2. James A. Leach (R) | Jan 1977 |
| | 3. Leonard L. Boswell (D) | Jan 1997 |
| | 4. Tom Latham (R) | Jan 1995 |
| | 5. Steve King (R) | Jan 2003 |
| Kansas | 1. Jerry Moran (R) | Jan 1997 |
| | 2. Jim Ryun (R) | Nov 1996 |
| | 3. Dennis Moore (D) | Jan 1999 |
| | 4. Todd Tiahrt (R) | Jan 1995 |
| Kentucky | 1. Ed Whitfield (R) | Jan 1995 |
| | 2. Ron Lewis (R) | May 1994 |
| | 3. Anne M. Northup (R) | Jan 1997 |
| | 4. Ken Lucas (D) | Jan 1999 |
| | 5. Harold Rogers (R) | Jan 1981 |
| | 6. Ernie Fletcher (R) | Jan 1999 |
| Louisiana | 1. David Vitter (R) | May 1999 |
| | 2. William J. Jefferson (D) | Jan 1991 |
| | 3. W.J. (Billy) Tauzin (R) | May 1980 |
| | 4. Jim McCrery (R) | Apr 1988 |
| | 5. Rodney Alexander (D) | Jan 2003 |
| | 6. Richard H. Baker (R) | Jan 1987 |
| | 7. Christopher John (D) | Jan 1997 |
| Maine | 1. Thomas H. Allen (D) | Jan 1997 |
| | 2. Michael H. Michaud (D) | Jan 2003 |
| Maryland | 1. Wayne T. Gilchrest (R) | Jan 1991 |
| | 2. C.A. Dutch Ruppersberger (D) | Jan 2003 |
| | 3. Benjamin L. Cardin (D) | Jan 1987 |
| | 4. Albert Russell Wynn (D) | Jan 1993 |
| | 5. Steny H. Hoyer (D) | May 1981 |
| | 6. Roscoe G. Bartlett (R) | Jan 1993 |
| | 7. Elijah E. Cummings (D) | Apr 1996 |
| | 8. Chris Van Hollen (D) | Jan 2003 |
| Massa-chusetts | 1. John W. Olver (D) | Jun 1991 |
| | 2. Richard E. Neal (D) | Jan 1989 |
| | 3. James P. McGovern (D) | Jan 1997 |
| | 4. Barney Frank (D) | Jan 1981 |
| | 5. Martin T. Meehan (D) | Jan 1993 |
| | 6. John F. Tierney (D) | Jan 1997 |
| | 7. Edward J. Markey (D) | Nov 1976 |
| | 8. Michael E. Capuano (D) | Jan 1999 |
| | 9. Stephen F. Lynch (D)[7] | Oct 2001 |
| | 10. William D. Delahunt (D) | Jan 1997 |
| Michigan (−1) | 1. Bart Stupak (D) | Jan 1993 |
| | 2. Peter Hoekstra (R) | Jan 1993 |
| | 3. Vernon J. Ehlers (R) | Dec 1993 |
| | 4. Dave Camp (R) | Jan 1991 |
| | 5. Dale E. Kildee (D) | Jan 1977 |

## The House of Representatives, 108th Congress (continued)

| STATE | REPRESENTATIVES | SERVICE BEGAN | STATE | REPRESENTATIVES | SERVICE BEGAN |
|---|---|---|---|---|---|
| Michigan | 6. Fred Upton (R) | Jan 1987 | New Mexico | 3. Tom Udall (D) | Jan 1999 |
| (continued) | 7. Nick Smith (R) | Jan 1993 | (continued) | | |
| | 8. Mike Rogers (R) | Jan 2001 | | | |
| | 9. Joe Knollenberg (R) | Jan 1993 | New York | 1. Timothy H. Bishop (D) | Jan 2003 |
| | 10. Candice S. Miller (R) | Jan 2003 | (−2) | 2. Steve Israel (D) | Jan 2001 |
| | 11. Thaddeus G. McCotter (R) | Jan 2003 | | 3. Peter T. King (R) | Jan 1993 |
| | | | | 4. Carolyn McCarthy (D) | Jan 1997 |
| | 12. Sander M. Levin (D) | Jan 1983 | | 5. Gary L. Ackerman (D) | Mar 1983 |
| | 13. Carolyn C. Kilpatrick (D) | Jan 1997 | | 6. Gregory W. Meeks (D) | Feb 1998 |
| | 14. John Conyers, Jr. (D) | Jan 1965 | | 7. Joseph Crowley (D) | Jan 1999 |
| | 15. John D. Dingell (D) | Dec 1955 | | 8. Jerrold Nadler (D) | Nov 1992 |
| | | | | 9. Anthony D. Weiner (D) | Jan 1999 |
| Minnesota | 1. Gil Gutknecht (R) | Jan 1995 | | 10. Edolphus Towns (D) | Jan 1983 |
| | 2. John Kline (R) | Jan 2003 | | 11. Major R. Owens (D) | Jan 1983 |
| | 3. Jim Ramstad (R) | Jan 1991 | | 12. Nydia M. Velázquez (D) | Jan 1993 |
| | 4. Betty McCollum (D) | Jan 2001 | | 13. Vito Fossella (R) | Nov 1997 |
| | 5. Martin Olav Sabo (D) | Jan 1979 | | 14. Carolyn B. Maloney (D) | Jan 1993 |
| | 6. Mark R. Kennedy (R) | Jan 2001 | | 15. Charles B. Rangel (D) | Jan 1971 |
| | 7. Collin C. Peterson (D) | Jan 1991 | | 16. José E. Serrano (D) | Mar 1990 |
| | 8. James L. Oberstar (D) | Jan 1975 | | 17. Eliot L. Engel (D) | Jan 1989 |
| | | | | 18. Nita M. Lowey (D) | Jan 1989 |
| Mississippi | 1. Roger F. Wicker (R) | Jan 1995 | | 19. Sue W. Kelly (R) | Jan 1995 |
| (−1) | 2. Bennie G. Thompson (D) | Apr 1993 | | 20. John E. Sweeney (R) | Jan 1999 |
| | | | | 21. Michael R. McNulty (D) | Jan 1989 |
| | 3. Charles W. "Chip" Pickering (R) | Jan 1997 | | 22. Maurice D. Hinchey (D) | Jan 1993 |
| | | | | 23. John M. McHugh (R) | Jan 1993 |
| | 4. Gene Taylor (D) | Oct 1989 | | 24. Sherwood L. Boehlert (R) | Jan 1983 |
| Missouri | 1. William Lacy Clay (D) | Jan 2001 | | 25. James T. Walsh (R) | Jan 1989 |
| | 2. W. Todd Akin (R) | Jan 2001 | | 26. Thomas M. Reynolds (R) | Jan 1999 |
| | 3. Richard A. Gephardt (D) | Jan 1977 | | | |
| | 4. Ike Skelton (D) | Jan 1977 | | 27. Jack Quinn (R) | Jan 1993 |
| | 5. Karen McCarthy (D) | Jan 1995 | | 28. Louise McIntosh Slaughter (D) | Jan 1987 |
| | 6. Sam Graves (R) | Jan 2001 | | | |
| | 7. Roy Blunt (R) | Jan 1997 | | 29. Amo Houghton (R) | Jan 1987 |
| | 8. Jo Ann Emerson (R) | Jan 1997 | | | |
| | 9. Kenny C. Hulshof (R) | Jan 1997 | North Carolina | 1. Frank W. Ballance, Jr. (D) | Jan 2003 |
| | | | (+1) | | |
| Montana | Dennis R. Rehberg (R) | Jan 2001 | | 2. Bob Etheridge (D) | Jan 1997 |
| | | | | 3. Walter B. Jones (R) | Jan 1995 |
| Nebraska | 1. Doug Bereuter (R) | Jan 1979 | | 4. David E. Price (D) | Jan 1997 |
| | 2. Lee Terry (R) | Jan 1999 | | 5. Richard Burr (R) | Jan 1995 |
| | 3. Tom Osborne (R) | Jan 2001 | | 6. Howard Coble (R) | Jan 1985 |
| | | | | 7. Mike McIntyre (D) | Jan 1997 |
| Nevada | 1. Shelley Berkley (D) | Jan 1999 | | 8. Robin Hayes (R) | Jan 1999 |
| (+1) | 2. Jim Gibbons (R) | Jan 1997 | | 9. Sue Wilkins Myrick (R) | Jan 1995 |
| | 3. Jon C. Porter (R) | Jan 2003 | | 10. Cass Ballenger (R) | Nov 1986 |
| | | | | 11. Charles H. Taylor (R) | Jan 1991 |
| New Hampshire | 1. Jeb Bradley (R) | Jan 2003 | | 12. Melvin L. Watt (D) | Jan 1993 |
| | 2. Charles F. Bass (R) | Jan 1995 | | 13. Brad Miller (D) | Jan 2003 |
| New Jersey | 1. Robert E. Andrews (D) | Nov 1990 | North Dakota | Earl Pomeroy (D) | Jan 1993 |
| | 2. Frank A. LoBiondo (R) | Jan 1995 | | | |
| | 3. Jim Saxton (R) | Nov 1984 | Ohio | 1. Steve Chabot (R) | Jan 1995 |
| | 4. Christopher H. Smith (R) | Jan 1981 | (−1) | 2. Rob Portman (R) | May 1993 |
| | 5. Scott Garrett (R) | Jan 2003 | | 3. Michael R. Turner (R) | Jan 2003 |
| | 6. Frank Pallone, Jr. (D) | Nov 1988 | | 4. Michael G. Oxley (R) | Jun 1981 |
| | 7. Mike Ferguson (R) | Jan 2001 | | 5. Paul E. Gillmor (R) | Jan 1989 |
| | 8. Bill Pascrell, Jr. (D) | Jan 1997 | | 6. Ted Strickland (D) | Jan 1997 |
| | 9. Steven R. Rothman (D) | Jan 1997 | | 7. David L. Hobson (R) | Jan 1991 |
| | 10. Donald M. Payne (D) | Jan 1989 | | 8. John A. Boehner (R) | Jan 1991 |
| | 11. Rodney P. Frelinghuysen (R) | Jan 1995 | | 9. Marcy Kaptur (D) | Jan 1983 |
| | | | | 10. Dennis J. Kucinich (D) | Jan 1997 |
| | 12. Rush D. Holt (D) | Jan 1999 | | 11. Stephanie Tubbs Jones (D) | Jan 1999 |
| | 13. Robert Menendez (D) | Jan 1993 | | | |
| | | | | 12. Patrick J. Tiberi (R) | Jan 2001 |
| New Mexico | 1. Heather Wilson (R) | Jun 1998 | | 13. Sherrod Brown (D) | Jan 1993 |
| | 2. Steven Pearce (R) | Jan 2003 | | | |

## The House of Representatives, 108th Congress (continued)

| STATE | REPRESENTATIVES | SERVICE BEGAN |
|---|---|---|
| Ohio (continued) | 14. Steven C. LaTourette (R) | Jan 1995 |
| | 15. Deborah Pryce (R) | Jan 1993 |
| | 16. Ralph Regula (R) | Jan 1973 |
| | 17. Timothy J. Ryan (D) | Jan 2003 |
| | 18. Robert W. Ney (R) | Jan 1995 |
| Oklahoma (–1) | 1. John Sullivan (R)[8] | Feb 2002 |
| | 2. Brad Carson (D) | Jan 2001 |
| | 3. Frank D. Lucas (R) | May 1994 |
| | 4. Tom Cole (R) | Jan 2003 |
| | 5. Ernest J. Istook, Jr. (R) | Jan 1993 |
| Oregon | 1. David Wu (D) | Jan 1999 |
| | 2. Greg Walden (R) | Jan 1999 |
| | 3. Earl Blumenauer (D) | May 1996 |
| | 4. Peter A. DeFazio (D) | Jan 1987 |
| | 5. Darlene Hooley (D) | Jan 1997 |
| Pennsylvania (–2) | 1. Robert A. Brady (D) | May 1998 |
| | 2. Chaka Fattah (D) | Jan 1995 |
| | 3. Phil English (R) | Jan 1995 |
| | 4. Melissa A. Hart (R) | Jan 2001 |
| | 5. John E. Peterson (R) | Jan 1997 |
| | 6. Jim Gerlach (R) | Jan 2003 |
| | 7. Curt Weldon (R) | Jan 1987 |
| | 8. James C. Greenwood (R) | Jan 1993 |
| | 9. Bill Shuster (R) | May 2001 |
| | 10. Don Sherwood (R) | Jan 1999 |
| | 11. Paul E. Kanjorski (D) | Jan 1985 |
| | 12. John P. Murtha (D) | Feb 1974 |
| | 13. Joseph M. Hoeffel (D) | Jan 1999 |
| | 14. Michael F. Doyle (D) | Jan 1995 |
| | 15. Patrick J. Toomey (R) | Jan 1999 |
| | 16. Joseph R. Pitts (R) | Jan 1997 |
| | 17. Tim Holden (D) | Jan 1993 |
| | 18. Tim Murphy (R) | Jan 2003 |
| | 19. Todd Russell Platts (R) | Jan 2001 |
| Rhode Island | 1. Patrick J. Kennedy (D) | Jan 1995 |
| | 2. James R. Langevin (D) | Jan 2001 |
| South Carolina | 1. Henry E. Brown, Jr. (R) | Jan 2001 |
| | 2. Joe Wilson (R)[9] | Dec 2001 |
| | 3. J. Gresham Barrett (R) | Jan 2003 |
| | 4. Jim DeMint (R) | Jan 1999 |
| | 5. John M. Spratt, Jr. (D) | Jan 1983 |
| | 6. James E. Clyburn (D) | Jan 1993 |
| South Dakota | William J. Janklow (R) | Jan 2003 |
| Tennessee | 1. William L. Jenkins (R) | Jan 1997 |
| | 2. John J. Duncan, Jr. (R) | Nov 1988 |
| | 3. Zach Wamp (R) | Jan 1995 |
| | 4. Lincoln Davis (D) | Jan 2003 |
| | 5. Jim Cooper (D)[10] | Jan 1983 |
| | 6. Bart Gordon (D) | Jan 1985 |
| | 7. Marsha Blackburn (R) | Jan 2003 |
| | 8. John S. Tanner (D) | Jan 1989 |
| | 9. Harold E. Ford, Jr. (D) | Jan 1997 |
| Texas (+2) | 1. Max Sandlin (D) | Jan 1997 |
| | 2. Jim Turner (D) | Jan 1997 |
| | 3. Sam Johnson (R) | May 1991 |
| | 4. Ralph M. Hall (D) | Jan 1981 |
| | 5. Jeb Hensarling (R) | Jan 2003 |

| STATE | REPRESENTATIVES | SERVICE BEGAN |
|---|---|---|
| Texas (continued) | 6. Joe Barton (R) | Jan 1985 |
| | 7. John Abney Culberson (R) | Jan 2001 |
| | 8. Kevin Brady (R) | Jan 1997 |
| | 9. Nick Lampson (D) | Jan 1997 |
| | 10. Lloyd Doggett (D) | Jan 1995 |
| | 11. Chet Edwards (D) | Jan 1991 |
| | 12. Kay Granger (R) | Jan 1997 |
| | 13. Mac Thornberry (R) | Jan 1995 |
| | 14. Ron Paul (R) | Jan 1997 |
| | 15. Rubén Hinojosa (D) | Jan 1997 |
| | 16. Silvestre Reyes (D) | Jan 1997 |
| | 17. Charles W. Stenholm (D) | Jan 1979 |
| | 18. Sheila Jackson-Lee (D) | Jan 1995 |
| | 19. Randy Neugebauer (R)[11] | June 2003 |
| | 20. Charles A. Gonzalez (D) | Jan 1999 |
| | 21. Lamar S. Smith (R) | Jan 1987 |
| | 22. Tom DeLay (R) | Jan 1985 |
| | 23. Henry Bonilla (R) | Jan 1993 |
| | 24. Martin Frost (D) | Jan 1979 |
| | 25. Chris Bell (D) | Jan 2003 |
| | 26. Michael C. Burgess (R) | Jan 2003 |
| | 27. Solomon P. Ortiz (D) | Jan 1983 |
| | 28. Ciro D. Rodriguez (D) | Apr 1997 |
| | 29. Gene Green (D) | Jan 1993 |
| | 30. Eddie Bernice Johnson (D) | Jan 1993 |
| | 31. John R. Carter (R) | Jan 2003 |
| | 32. Pete Sessions (R) | Jan 1997 |
| Utah | 1. Rob Bishop (R) | Jan 2003 |
| | 2. Jim Matheson (D) | Jan 2001 |
| | 3. Chris Cannon (R) | Jan 1997 |
| Vermont | Bernard Sanders (I) | Jan 1991 |
| Virginia | 1. Jo Ann Davis (R) | Jan 2001 |
| | 2. Edward L. Schrock (R) | Jan 2001 |
| | 3. Robert C. Scott (D) | Jan 1993 |
| | 4. J. Randy Forbes (R)[12] | Jun 2001 |
| | 5. Virgil H. Goode, Jr. (R) | Jan 1997 |
| | 6. Bob Goodlatte (R) | Jan 1993 |
| | 7. Eric Cantor (R) | Jan 2001 |
| | 8. James P. Moran (D) | Jan 1991 |
| | 9. Rick Boucher (D) | Jan 1983 |
| | 10. Frank R. Wolf (R) | Jan 1981 |
| | 11. Tom Davis (R) | Jan 1995 |
| Washington | 1. Jay Inslee (D)[13] | Jan 1993 |
| | 2. Rick Larsen (D) | Jan 2001 |
| | 3. Brian Baird (D) | Jan 1999 |
| | 4. Doc Hastings (R) | Jan 1995 |
| | 5. George R. Nethercutt, Jr. (R) | Jan 1995 |
| | 6. Norman D. Dicks (D) | Jan 1977 |
| | 7. Jim McDermott (D) | Jan 1989 |
| | 8. Jennifer Dunn (R) | Jan 1993 |
| | 9. Adam Smith (D) | Jan 1997 |
| West Virginia | 1. Alan B. Mollohan (D) | Jan 1983 |
| | 2. Shelley Moore Capito (R) | Jan 2001 |
| | 3. Nick J. Rahall II (D) | Jan 1977 |

## The House of Representatives, 108th Congress (continued)

| STATE | REPRESENTATIVES | SERVICE BEGAN | | | |
|---|---|---|---|---|---|
| Wisconsin | 1. Paul Ryan (R) | Jan 1999 | Wisconsin | 6. Thomas E. Petri (R) | Apr 1979 |
| (–1) | 2. Tammy Baldwin (D) | Jan 1999 | (continued) | 7. David R. Obey (D) | Apr 1969 |
| | 3. Ron Kind (D) | Jan 1997 | | 8. Mark Green (R) | Jan 1999 |
| | 4. Gerald D. Kleczka (D) | Apr 1984 | | | |
| | 5. F. James Sensen- | Jan 1979 | Wyoming | Barbara Cubin (R) | Jan 1995 |
| | brenner, Jr. (R) | | | | |

| JURISDICTION | REPRESENTATIVES | SERVICE BEGAN |
|---|---|---|
| American Samoa | (Delegate) Eni F.H. Faleomavaega (D) | Jan 1989 |
| District of Columbia | (Delegate) Eleanor Holmes Norton (D) | Jan 1991 |
| Guam | (Delegate) Madeleine Bordallo (D) | Jan 2003 |
| Puerto Rico | (Res. Comm.) Aníbal Acevedo-Vilá (D) | Jan 2001 |
| Virgin Islands | (Delegate) Donna M. Christensen (D) | Jan 1997 |

[1]*John Boozman was elected 20 Nov 2001 following the resignation of Asa Hutchinson.* [2]*Diane E. Watson was elected 5 Jun 2001 to complete the term of the late Julian C. Dixon.* [3]*Jane Harman did not serve 3 Jan 1999–3 Jan 2001.* [4]*Jeff Miller was elected 16 Oct 2001 following the resignation of Joe Scarborough.* [5]*Neil Abercrombie did not serve 3 Jan 1987–3 Jan 1991.* [6]*Ed Case was elected 4 Jan 2003 following the death of Patsy Mink.* [7]*Stephen F. Lynch was elected 16 Oct 2001 to complete the term of the late John Joseph Moakley.* [8]*John Sullivan was elected 8 Jan 2002 following the resignation of Steve Largent.* [9]*Joe Wilson was elected 18 Dec 2001 to complete the term of the late Floyd Spence.* [10]*Jim Cooper did not serve 3 Jan 1995–3 Jan 2003.* [11]*Randy Neugebauer was elected 3 June 2003 following the resignation of Larry Combest.* [12]*J. Randy Forbes was elected 19 Jun 2001 to complete the term of the late Norman Sisisky.* [13]*Jay Inslee did not serve 3 Jan 1995–3 Jan 1999.*

---

 **Did you know?** California sends the most representatives to Congress of any state: 53 to the House (more than 12% of House members), plus 2 to the Senate. By contrast, Alaska, Delaware, Montana, North Dakota, South Dakota, Vermont, and Wyoming send only one representative each to the House, plus 2 each to the Senate.

---

## House of Representatives Standing Committees

| COMMITTEE | CHAIRMAN (STATE) | RANKING DEMOCRAT (STATE) | NUMBER OF MEMBERS: MAJORITY | MINORITY | NUMBER OF SUBCOM- MITTEES |
|---|---|---|---|---|---|
| Agriculture | Bob Goodlatte (R-VA) | Charlie Stenholm (D-TX) | 27 | 24 | 5 |
| Appropriations | C.W. Bill Young (R-FL) | David Obey (D-WI) | 36 | 29 | 13 |
| Armed Services | Duncan Hunter (R-CA) | Ike Skelton (D-MO) | 33 | 28 | 6 |
| Budget | Jim Nussle (R-IA) | John Spratt (D-SC) | 24 | 19 | none |
| Education and the Workforce | John A. Boehner (R-OH) | George Miller (D-CA) | 27 | 22 | 5 |
| Energy and Commerce | W.J. "Billy" Tauzin (R-LA) | John D. Dingell (D-MI) | 31 | 26 | 6 |
| Financial Services | Michael G. Oxley (R-OH) | Barney Frank (D-MA) | 37 | 33[1] | 5 |
| Government Reform | Tom Davis (R-VA) | Henry A. Waxman (D-CA) | 24 | 20[1] | 7 |
| House Administration | Robert W. Ney (R-OH) | John B. Larson (D-CT) | 6 | 3 | none |
| International Relations | Henry J. Hyde (R-IL) | Tom Lantos (D-CA) | 26 | 23 | 6 |
| Judiciary | F. James Sensenbrenner, Jr. (R-WI) | John Conyers, Jr. (D-MI) | 21 | 16 | 5 |
| Resources | Richard W. Pombo (R-CA) | Nick J. Rahall II (D-WV) | 28 | 24 | 5 |
| Rules | David Dreier (R-CA) | Martin Frost (D-TX) | 9 | 4 | 2 |
| Science | Sherwood L. Boehlert (R-NY) | Ralph M. Hall (D-TX) | 25 | 22 | 4 |
| Small Business | Donald Manzullo (R-IL) | Nydia M. Velazquez (D-NY) | 19 | 17 | 4 |
| Standards of Official Conduct | Joel Hefley (R-CO) | Alan B. Mollohan (D-WV) | 5 | 5 | none |
| Transportation and Infrastructure | Don Young (R-AK) | James L. Oberstar (D-MN) | 41 | 34 | 6 |
| Veterans' Affairs | Christopher H. Smith (R-NJ) | Lane Evans (D-IL) | 17 | 14 | 3 |
| Ways and Means | Bill Thomas (R-CA) | Charles B. Rangel (D-NY) | 24 | 17 | 6 |
| Permanent Select Committee on Intelligence | Porter J. Goss (R-FL) | Jan Harman (D-CA) | 12 | 10 | 4 |
| Select Committee on Homeland Security | Christopher Cox (R-CA) | Jim Turner (D-TX) | 27 | 23 | 5 |

[1]*Bernard Sanders (VT) is an independent but caucuses with the Democratic Party.*

## Congressional Apportionment

The US Constitution requires a decennial census to determine the apportionment of representatives for each state in the House of Representatives. There was no reapportionment based on 1920 census figures.

| STATE | representatives | | | | | | | | | | |
|---|---|---|---|---|---|---|---|---|---|---|---|
| | 1790 | 1800 | 1810 | 1820 | 1830 | 1840 | 1850 | 1860 | 1870 | 1880 | 1890 |
| Alabama | NA | NA | 1[1] | 3 | 5 | 7 | 7 | 6 | 8 | 8 | 9 |
| Alaska | NA | NA | NA | NA | NA | NA | NA | NA | NA | NA | NA |
| Arizona | NA | NA | NA | NA | NA | NA | NA | NA | NA | NA | NA |
| Arkansas | NA | NA | NA | NA | 1[1] | 1 | 2 | 3 | 4 | 5 | 6 |
| California | NA | NA | NA | NA | NA | 2[1] | 2 | 3 | 4 | 6 | 7 |
| Colorado | NA | NA | NA | NA | NA | NA | NA | NA | 1[1] | 1 | 2 |
| Connecticut | 7 | 7 | 7 | 6 | 6 | 4 | 4 | 4 | 4 | 4 | 4 |
| Delaware | 1 | 1 | 2 | 1 | 1 | 1 | 1 | 1 | 1 | 1 | 1 |
| Florida | NA | NA | NA | NA | NA | 1[1] | 1 | 1 | 2 | 2 | 2 |
| Georgia | 2 | 4 | 6 | 7 | 9 | 8 | 8 | 7 | 9 | 10 | 11 |
| Hawaii | NA | NA | NA | NA | NA | NA | NA | NA | NA | NA | NA |
| Idaho | NA | NA | NA | NA | NA | NA | NA | NA | NA | 1[1] | 1 |
| Illinois | NA | NA | 1[1] | 1 | 3 | 7 | 9 | 14 | 19 | 20 | 22 |
| Indiana | NA | NA | 1[1] | 3 | 7 | 10 | 11 | 11 | 13 | 13 | 13 |
| Iowa | NA | NA | NA | NA | NA | 2[1] | 2 | 6 | 9 | 11 | 11 |
| Kansas | NA | NA | NA | NA | NA | NA | NA | 1 | 3 | 7 | 8 |
| Kentucky | 2 | 6 | 10 | 12 | 13 | 10 | 10 | 9 | 10 | 11 | 11 |
| Louisiana | NA | NA | 1[1] | 3 | 3 | 4 | 4 | 5 | 6 | 6 | 6 |
| Maine | NA | NA | NA | 7 | 8 | 7 | 6 | 5 | 5 | 4 | 4 |
| Maryland | 8 | 9 | 9 | 9 | 8 | 6 | 6 | 5 | 6 | 6 | 6 |
| Massachusetts | 14 | 17 | 20 | 13 | 12 | 10 | 11 | 10 | 11 | 12 | 13 |
| Michigan | NA | NA | NA | NA | 1[1] | 3 | 4 | 6 | 9 | 11 | 12 |
| Minnesota | NA | NA | NA | NA | NA | NA | 2[1] | 2 | 3 | 5 | 7 |
| Mississippi | NA | NA | 1[1] | 1 | 2 | 4 | 5 | 5 | 6 | 7 | 7 |
| Missouri | NA | NA | NA | 1 | 2 | 5 | 7 | 9 | 13 | 14 | 15 |
| Montana | NA | NA | NA | NA | NA | NA | NA | NA | NA | 1[1] | 1 |
| Nebraska | NA | NA | NA | NA | NA | NA | NA | 1[1] | 1 | 3 | 6 |
| Nevada | NA | NA | NA | NA | NA | NA | NA | 1[1] | 1 | 1 | 1 |
| New Hampshire | 4 | 5 | 6 | 6 | 5 | 4 | 3 | 3 | 3 | 2 | 2 |
| New Jersey | 5 | 6 | 6 | 6 | 6 | 5 | 5 | 5 | 7 | 7 | 8 |
| New Mexico | NA | NA | NA | NA | NA | NA | NA | NA | NA | NA | NA |
| New York | 10 | 17 | 27 | 34 | 40 | 34 | 33 | 31 | 33 | 34 | 34 |
| North Carolina | 10 | 12 | 13 | 13 | 13 | 9 | 8 | 7 | 8 | 9 | 9 |
| North Dakota | NA | NA | NA | NA | NA | NA | NA | NA | NA | 1[1] | 1 |
| Ohio | NA | 1[1] | 6 | 14 | 19 | 21 | 21 | 19 | 20 | 21 | 21 |
| Oklahoma | NA | NA | NA | NA | NA | NA | NA | NA | NA | NA | NA |
| Oregon | NA | NA | NA | NA | NA | NA | 1[1] | 1 | 1 | 1 | 2 |
| Pennsylvania | 13 | 18 | 23 | 26 | 28 | 24 | 25 | 24 | 27 | 28 | 30 |
| Rhode Island | 2 | 2 | 2 | 2 | 2 | 2 | 2 | 2 | 2 | 2 | 2 |
| South Carolina | 6 | 8 | 9 | 9 | 9 | 7 | 6 | 4 | 5 | 7 | 7 |
| South Dakota | NA | NA | NA | NA | NA | NA | NA | NA | NA | 2[1] | 2 |
| Tennessee | 1[1] | 3 | 6 | 9 | 13 | 11 | 10 | 8 | 10 | 10 | 10 |
| Texas | NA | NA | NA | NA | NA | 2[1] | 2 | 4 | 6 | 11 | 13 |
| Utah | NA | NA | NA | NA | NA | NA | NA | NA | NA | NA | 1[1] |
| Vermont | 2 | 4 | 6 | 5 | 5 | 4 | 3 | 3 | 3 | 2 | 2 |
| Virginia | 19 | 22 | 23 | 22 | 21 | 15 | 13 | 11 | 9 | 10 | 10 |
| Washington | NA | NA | NA | NA | NA | NA | NA | NA | NA | 1[1] | 2 |
| West Virginia | NA | NA | NA | NA | NA | NA | NA | NA | 3 | 4 | 4 |
| Wisconsin | NA | NA | NA | NA | NA | 2[1] | 3 | 6 | 8 | 9 | 10 |
| Wyoming | NA | NA | NA | NA | NA | NA | NA | NA | NA | 1[1] | 1 |
| Total | 106 | 142 | 186 | 213 | 242 | 232 | 237 | 243 | 293 | 332 | 357 |

# Congressional Apportionment (continued)

| STATE | representatives | | | | | | | | | |
|---|---|---|---|---|---|---|---|---|---|---|
| | 1900 | 1910 | 1930 | 1940 | 1950 | 1960 | 1970 | 1980 | 1990 | 2000 |
| Alabama | 9 | 10 | 9 | 9 | 9 | 8 | 7 | 7 | 7 | 7 |
| Alaska | NA | NA | NA | NA | 1[1] | 1 | 1 | 1 | 1 | 1 |
| Arizona | NA | 1[2] | 1 | 2 | 2 | 3 | 4 | 5 | 6 | 8 |
| Arkansas | 7 | 7 | 7 | 7 | 6 | 4 | 4 | 4 | 4 | 4 |
| California | 8 | 11 | 20 | 23 | 30 | 38 | 43 | 45 | 52 | 53 |
| Colorado | 3 | 4 | 4 | 4 | 4 | 4 | 5 | 6 | 6 | 7 |
| Connecticut | 5 | 5 | 6 | 6 | 6 | 6 | 6 | 6 | 6 | 5 |
| Delaware | 1 | 1 | 1 | 1 | 1 | 1 | 1 | 1 | 1 | 1 |
| Florida | 3 | 4 | 5 | 6 | 8 | 12 | 15 | 19 | 23 | 25 |
| Georgia | 11 | 12 | 10 | 10 | 10 | 10 | 10 | 10 | 11 | 13 |
| Hawaii | NA | NA | NA | NA | 1[1] | 2 | 2 | 2 | 2 | 2 |
| Idaho | 1 | 2 | 2 | 2 | 2 | 2 | 2 | 2 | 2 | 2 |
| Illinois | 25 | 27 | 27 | 26 | 25 | 24 | 24 | 22 | 20 | 19 |
| Indiana | 13 | 13 | 12 | 11 | 11 | 11 | 11 | 10 | 10 | 9 |
| Iowa | 11 | 11 | 9 | 8 | 8 | 7 | 6 | 6 | 5 | 5 |
| Kansas | 8 | 8 | 7 | 6 | 6 | 5 | 5 | 5 | 4 | 4 |
| Kentucky | 11 | 11 | 9 | 9 | 8 | 7 | 7 | 7 | 6 | 6 |
| Louisiana | 7 | 8 | 8 | 8 | 8 | 8 | 8 | 8 | 7 | 7 |
| Maine | 4 | 4 | 3 | 3 | 3 | 2 | 2 | 2 | 2 | 2 |
| Maryland | 6 | 6 | 6 | 6 | 7 | 8 | 8 | 8 | 8 | 8 |
| Massachusetts | 14 | 16 | 15 | 14 | 14 | 12 | 12 | 11 | 10 | 10 |
| Michigan | 12 | 13 | 17 | 17 | 18 | 19 | 19 | 18 | 16 | 15 |
| Minnesota | 9 | 10 | 9 | 9 | 9 | 8 | 8 | 8 | 8 | 8 |
| Mississippi | 8 | 8 | 7 | 7 | 6 | 5 | 5 | 5 | 5 | 4 |
| Missouri | 16 | 16 | 13 | 13 | 11 | 10 | 10 | 9 | 9 | 9 |
| Montana | 1 | 2 | 2 | 2 | 2 | 2 | 2 | 2 | 1 | 1 |
| Nebraska | 6 | 6 | 5 | 4 | 4 | 3 | 3 | 3 | 3 | 3 |
| Nevada | 1 | 1 | 1 | 1 | 1 | 1 | 1 | 2 | 2 | 3 |
| New Hampshire | 2 | 2 | 2 | 2 | 2 | 2 | 2 | 2 | 2 | 2 |
| New Jersey | 10 | 12 | 14 | 14 | 14 | 15 | 15 | 14 | 13 | 13 |
| New Mexico | NA | 1[2] | 1 | 2 | 2 | 2 | 2 | 3 | 3 | 3 |
| New York | 37 | 43 | 45 | 45 | 43 | 41 | 39 | 34 | 31 | 29 |
| North Carolina | 10 | 10 | 11 | 12 | 12 | 11 | 11 | 11 | 12 | 13 |
| North Dakota | 2 | 3 | 2 | 2 | 2 | 2 | 1 | 1 | 1 | 1 |
| Ohio | 21 | 22 | 24 | 23 | 23 | 24 | 23 | 21 | 19 | 18 |
| Oklahoma | 5[1] | 8 | 9 | 8 | 6 | 6 | 6 | 6 | 6 | 5 |
| Oregon | 2 | 3 | 3 | 4 | 4 | 4 | 4 | 5 | 5 | 5 |
| Pennsylvania | 32 | 36 | 34 | 33 | 30 | 27 | 25 | 23 | 21 | 19 |
| Rhode Island | 2 | 3 | 2 | 2 | 2 | 2 | 2 | 2 | 2 | 2 |
| South Carolina | 7 | 7 | 6 | 6 | 6 | 6 | 6 | 6 | 6 | 6 |
| South Dakota | 2 | 3 | 2 | 2 | 2 | 2 | 2 | 1 | 1 | 1 |
| Tennessee | 10 | 10 | 9 | 10 | 9 | 9 | 8 | 9 | 9 | 9 |
| Texas | 16 | 18 | 21 | 21 | 22 | 23 | 24 | 27 | 30 | 32 |
| Utah | 1 | 2 | 2 | 2 | 2 | 2 | 2 | 3 | 3 | 3 |
| Vermont | 2 | 2 | 1 | 1 | 1 | 1 | 1 | 1 | 1 | 1 |
| Virginia | 10 | 10 | 9 | 9 | 10 | 10 | 10 | 10 | 11 | 11 |
| Washington | 3 | 5 | 6 | 6 | 7 | 7 | 7 | 8 | 9 | 9 |
| West Virginia | 5 | 6 | 6 | 6 | 6 | 5 | 4 | 4 | 3 | 3 |
| Wisconsin | 11 | 11 | 10 | 10 | 10 | 10 | 9 | 9 | 9 | 8 |
| Wyoming | 1 | 1 | 1 | 1 | 1 | 1 | 1 | 1 | 1 | 1 |
| Total | 391 | 435 | 435 | 435 | 437 | 435 | 435 | 435 | 435 | 435 |

NA: Not applicable.   [1]Number assigned after apportionment.   [2]Included in anticipation of statehood.

## Electoral Votes by State

Each state receives one electoral vote for each of its representatives and one for each of its two senators, ensuring at least three votes for each state, as the Constitution guarantees at least one representative regardless of population. Allocations are based on the 2000 census and applicable for the 2004 presidential election.

*Total: 538; Majority needed to elect president and vice president: 270*

| STATE | NUMBER OF VOTES | STATE | NUMBER OF VOTES | STATE | NUMBER OF VOTES |
|---|---|---|---|---|---|
| Alabama | 9 | Kentucky | 8 | North Dakota | 3 |
| Alaska | 3 | Louisiana | 9 | Ohio | 20 |
| Arizona | 10 | Maine | 4 | Oklahoma | 7 |
| Arkansas | 6 | Maryland | 10 | Oregon | 7 |
| California | 55 | Massachusetts | 12 | Pennsylvania | 21 |
| Colorado | 9 | Michigan | 17 | Rhode Island | 4 |
| Connecticut | 7 | Minnesota | 10 | South Carolina | 8 |
| Delaware | 3 | Mississippi | 6 | South Dakota | 3 |
| District of Columbia | 3 | Missouri | 11 | Tennessee | 11 |
| Florida | 27 | Montana | 3 | Texas | 34 |
| Georgia | 15 | Nebraska | 5 | Utah | 5 |
| Hawaii | 4 | Nevada | 5 | Vermont | 3 |
| Idaho | 4 | New Hampshire | 4 | Virginia | 13 |
| Illinois | 21 | New Jersey | 15 | Washington | 11 |
| Indiana | 11 | New Mexico | 5 | West Virginia | 5 |
| Iowa | 7 | New York | 31 | Wisconsin | 10 |
| Kansas | 6 | North Carolina | 15 | Wyoming | 3 |

# Supreme Court

## Justices of the Supreme Court of the United States

*Listed under presidents who made appointments (bold). Chief justices' names appear in italics.*

| NAME | TERM OF SERVICE[1] | NAME | TERM OF SERVICE[1] | NAME | TERM OF SERVICE[1] |
|---|---|---|---|---|---|
| **George Washington** | | **Martin Van Buren** | | **James Garfield** | |
| *John Jay* | 1789–95 | John Catron | 1837–65 | Stanley Matthews | 1881–89 |
| James Wilson | 1789–98 | John McKinley | 1838–52 | **Chester A. Arthur** | |
| John Rutledge | 1790–91 | Peter V. Daniel | 1842–60 | Horace Gray | 1882–1902 |
| William Cushing | 1790–1810 | **John Tyler** | | Samuel Blatchford | 1882–93 |
| John Blair | 1790–96 | Samuel Nelson | 1845–72 | **Grover Cleveland** | |
| James Iredell | 1790–99 | **James Polk** | | Lucius Q.C. Lamar | 1888–93 |
| Thomas Johnson | 1792–93 | Levi Woodbury | 1845–51 | *Melville Weston Fuller* | 1888–1910 |
| William Paterson | 1793–1806 | Robert C. Grier | 1846–70 | **Benjamin Harrison** | |
| *John Rutledge*[2] | 1795 | **Millard Fillmore** | | David J. Brewer | 1890–1910 |
| Samuel Chase | 1796–1811 | Benjamin R. Curtis | 1851–57 | Henry B. Brown | 1891–1906 |
| *Oliver Ellsworth* | 1796–1800 | **Franklin Pierce** | | George Shiras, Jr. | 1892–1903 |
| **John Adams** | | John Archibald Campbell | 1853–61 | Howell E. Jackson | 1893–95 |
| Bushrod Washington | 1799–1829 | **James Buchanan** | | **Grover Cleveland** | |
| Alfred Moore | 1800–04 | Nathan Clifford | 1858–81 | Edward Douglass White | 1894–1910 |
| *John Marshall* | 1801–35 | **Abraham Lincoln** | | Rufus Wheeler Peckham | 1896–1909 |
| **Thomas Jefferson** | | Noah H. Swayne | 1862–81 | **William McKinley** | |
| William Johnson | 1804–34 | Samuel Freeman Miller | 1862–90 | Joseph McKenna | 1898–1925 |
| Brockholst Livingston | 1807–23 | David Davis | 1862–77 | **Theodore Roosevelt** | |
| Thomas Todd | 1807–26 | Stephen Johnson Field | 1863–97 | Oliver Wendell Holmes | 1902–32 |
| **James Madison** | | *Salmon P. Chase* | 1864–73 | William R. Day | 1903–22 |
| Gabriel Duvall | 1811–35 | **Ulysses S. Grant** | | William H. Moody | 1906–10 |
| Joseph Story | 1812–45 | William Strong | 1870–80 | **William H. Taft** | |
| **James Monroe** | | Joseph P. Bradley | 1870–92 | Horace H. Lurton | 1910–14 |
| Smith Thompson | 1823–43 | Ward Hunt | 1873–82 | Charles Evans Hughes | 1910–16 |
| **John Quincy Adams** | | *Morrison Remick Waite* | 1874–88 | Willis Van Devanter | 1911–37 |
| Robert Trimble | 1826–28 | **Rutherford B. Hayes** | | Joseph R. Lamar | 1911–16 |
| **Andrew Jackson** | | John Marshall Harlan | 1877–1911 | *Edward Douglass White* | 1910–21 |
| John McLean | 1830–61 | William B. Woods | 1881–87 | Mahlon Pitney | 1912–22 |
| Henry Baldwin | 1830–44 | | | | |
| James M. Wayne | 1835–67 | | | | |
| *Roger Brooke Taney* | 1836–64 | | | | |
| Philip P. Barbour | 1836–41 | | | | |

## Justices of the Supreme Court of the United States (continued)

| NAME | TERM OF SERVICE[1] | NAME | TERM OF SERVICE[1] | NAME | TERM OF SERVICE[1] |
|---|---|---|---|---|---|
| **Woodrow Wilson** | | William O. Douglas | 1939–75 | **Lyndon B. Johnson** | |
| James C. McReyn- | 1914–41 | Frank Murphy | 1940–49 | Abe Fortas | 1965–69 |
| olds | | *Harlan Fiske Stone* | 1941–46 | Thurgood Marshall | 1967–91 |
| Louis Brandeis | 1916–39 | James F. Byrnes | 1941–42 | **Richard M. Nixon** | |
| John H. Clarke | 1916–22 | Robert H. Jackson | 1941–54 | *Warren E. Burger* | 1969–86 |
| **Warren G. Harding** | | Wiley B. Rutledge | 1943–49 | Harry A. Blackmun | 1970–94 |
| *William Howard Taft* | 1921–30 | **Harry S. Truman** | | Lewis F. Powell, Jr. | 1972–87 |
| George Sutherland | 1922–38 | Harold H. Burton | 1945–58 | William H. Rehnquist | 1972–86 |
| Pierce Butler | 1923–39 | *Fred M. Vinson* | 1946–53 | **Gerald Ford** | |
| Edward T. Sanford | 1923–30 | Tom C. Clark | 1949–67 | John Paul Stevens | 1975– |
| **Calvin Coolidge** | | Sherman Minton | 1949–56 | **Ronald Reagan** | |
| Harlan Fiske Stone | 1925–41 | **Dwight D. Eisenhower** | | Sandra Day O'Connor | 1981– |
| **Herbert Hoover** | | *Earl Warren* | 1953–69 | *William H. Rehnquist* | 1986– |
| *Charles Evans Hughes* | 1930–41 | John Marshall Harlan | 1955–71 | Antonin Scalia | 1986– |
| Owen Roberts | 1930–45 | William J. Brennan, | 1956–90 | Anthony M. Kennedy | 1988– |
| Benjamin Nathan | 1932–38 | Jr. | | **George H.W. Bush** | |
| Cardozo | | Charles E. Whittaker | 1957–62 | David H. Souter | 1990– |
| **Franklin D. Roosevelt** | | Potter Stewart | 1958–81 | Clarence Thomas | 1991– |
| Hugo L. Black | 1937–71 | **John F. Kennedy** | | **Bill Clinton** | |
| Stanley F. Reed | 1938–57 | Byron R. White | 1962–93 | Ruth Bader Ginsburg | 1993– |
| Felix Frankfurter | 1939–62 | Arthur J. Goldberg | 1962–65 | Stephen G. Breyer | 1994– |

[1]*The year the justice took the judicial oath is here used as the beginning date of service, for until that oath is taken the justice is not vested with the prerogatives of the office. Justices, however, receive their commissions ("letters patent") before taking their oaths—in some instances, in the preceding year.* [2]*John Rutledge was acting chief justice; the U.S. Senate refused to confirm him.*

## Milestones of US Supreme Court Jurisprudence

*Information includes cases' short names, year of release, citation, and a short description of the Supreme Court's findings and importance for US law.*

**Marbury v. Madison, 5 U.S. 137 (1803):** the first instance in which the high court declared an act of Congress (the Judiciary Act of 1789, which in part authorized the court to compel action by the executive branch) to be unconstitutional, thus establishing the doctrine of judicial review.

**Martin v. Hunter's Lessee, 14 U.S. 304 (1816):** asserted the US Supreme Court's power of appellate review of state supreme court decisions.

**McCulloch v. Maryland, 17 U.S. 316 (1819):** affirmed the constitutional doctrine of the "implied powers" of Congress, determining that Congress had not only the powers expressly conferred upon it by the Constitution but also all authority "appropriate" to carry out such powers.

**Dred Scott v. Sandford, 60 U.S. 393 (1857):** ruled that blacks, free or enslaved, were not citizens under the Constitution, and further determined that only states, and not Congress or territorial governments, had the power to prohibit slavery, thus overturning the Missouri Compromise of 1820 and legalizing slavery in all US territories. The citizenship of all races was affirmed with the ratification of the Fourteenth Amendment in 1868.

**Santa Clara County v. Southern Pacific Railroad Co., 118 U.S. 394 (1886):** established that corporations are "persons" within the meaning of the Fourteenth Amendment, extending to them the rights of due process and equal protection.

**Plessy v. Ferguson, 163 U.S. 537 (1896):** permitted racial segregation in "separate but equal" public facilities.

**Lochner v. New York, 198 U.S. 45 (1905):** found that a state labor law limiting the number of hours in the work week violated due process because the "right of contract between the employer and employees" is protected under the Fourteenth Amendment.

**Standard Oil Co. of New Jersey et al. v. United States, 221 U.S. 1 (1911):** ruled that the activities of the Standard Oil Company of New Jersey, a holding company that through its subsidiaries controlled most of the US petroleum industry, constituted an undue restraint of trade, and ordered the company's dissolution under the Sherman Antitrust Act.

**Schenck v. United States, 249 U.S. 47 (1919):** found, in the case of an American socialist convicted of espionage for distributing antidraft leaflets during wartime, that First Amendment freedom of expression is limited when there exists a "clear and present danger that [the speech] will bring about the substantive evils that Congress has a right to prevent."

**Brown v. Board of Education of Topeka, 349 U.S. 294 (1954):** ruled that racial segregation in public schools violated the Fourteenth Amendment, overturning the doctrine of "separate but equal" facilities reached in *Plessy v. Ferguson*.

**Mapp v. Ohio, 367 U.S. 643 (1961):** found that the Fourth Amendment prohibition of unreasonable search and seizure, and the inadmissibility of evidence obtained in violation of it, applied to state as well as to federal government.

**Baker v. Carr, 369 U.S. 186 (1962):** ruled that, under the equal protection clause of the Fourteenth Amendment, issues relating to the apportionment of congressional districts could be resolved in federal courts.

**Gideon v. Wainwright, 372 U.S. 335 (1963):** declared that the Sixth Amendment right to counsel applies to defendants in state as well as federal courts.

*New York Times* Co. v. *Sullivan,* 376 U.S. 254 (1964): protected the press from the prospects of large damage awards in libel cases by requiring that "actual malice" be demonstrated; public officials who sue for damages must prove that a falsehood had been issued with knowledge that it was false or in reckless disregard of whether it was false or not.

*Heart of Atlanta Motel* v. *United States,* 379 U.S. 241; *Katzenbach* v. *McClung,* 379 U.S. 294 (1964): upheld Title II of the Civil Rights Act of 1964 (which prohibits segregation or discrimination in places of public accommodation involved in interstate commerce) in the cases of an Atlanta motel and a Birmingham AL restaurant, both of which discriminated against blacks. The court ruled that both engaged in transactions affecting interstate commerce and thus were within the purview of congressional regulation, and that the Civil Rights Act itself was constitutional.

*Griswold* v. *Connecticut,* 381 U.S. 479 (1965): ruled that a state law prohibiting the use of contraceptives (including providing information, advice, or prescriptions for them) violated "the right of marital privacy" implied within the Bill of Rights.

*Miranda* v. *Arizona,* 384 U.S. 436 (1966): ruled that the prosecution may not use statements made by a person in police custody unless minimum procedural safeguards were followed and established guidelines to guarantee arrested persons' Fifth Amendment right not to be compelled to incriminate themselves. These guidelines included informing arrestees prior to questioning that they have the right to remain silent, that anything they say may be used against them as evidence, and that they have the right to the counsel of an attorney.

*Loving* v. *Virginia,* 388 U.S. 1 (1967): declared that antimiscegenation laws (prohibitions of interracial marriage) have no legitimate purpose outside of racial discrimination, and thus violate the Fourteenth Amendment.

*New York Times Co.* v. *United States,* 403 U.S. 713 (1971): in what was known as the "Pentagon Papers" case, the court vacated a US Justice Department injunction that restrained the *New York Times* and *Washington Post* from publishing excerpts of a top-secret report on the Vietnam War, ruling that such prior restraint of the press was subject to a "heavy burden of . . . justification" which the government failed to meet.

*Wisconsin* v. *Yoder,* 406 U.S. 205 (1972): in the case of members of an Old Order Amish community who refused on religious grounds to keep their children in school past the eighth grade, found that the right to free exercise of religion outweighed the state's interest in universal education.

*Roe* v. *Wade,* 410 U.S. 113 (1973): held that overly restrictive state regulation of abortion is unconstitutional. In balancing the "compelling state interest[s]" in protecting the health of pregnant women and the potential life of fetuses, the court ruled that regulation of abortion could begin no sooner than about the end of the first trimester, with increasing regulation permissible in the second and third trimesters; the state's interest in protecting the fetus was found to increase with the fetus's "capability for meaningful life outside the mother's womb."

*Gregg* v. *Georgia,* 428 U.S. 153; *Proffitt* v. *Florida,* 428 U.S. 242; *Jurek* v. *Texas,* 428 U.S. 262 (1976): ruled that the death penalty, in and of itself, does not violate the Eighth Amendment if applied under certain guidelines in first-degree murder cases.

*Regents of the University of California* v. *Bakke,* 438 U.S. 265 (1978): in a test of the constitutionality of "affirmative action" programs to redress racial iniquities, the court ruled that the admissions policy of the Medical School of the University of California at Davis, which set aside a certain number of places for members of racial minorities, violated the Fourteenth Amendment and the Civil Rights Act of 1964 because it discriminated on the basis of race. The court did, however, permit "consideration of race in admissions decisions under some circumstances" in pursuit of diversity, a "compelling interest" in itself.

*Cruzan by Cruzan* v. *Director, Missouri Department of Health,* 497 U.S. 261 (1990): found that, in the absence of "clear and convincing evidence" of a person's desire to refuse medical treatment or not to live on life support, a state could require that such treatment continue. When such evidence exists, however, a patient's wishes must be respected.

*Rust* v. *Sullivan,* 500 U.S. 173 (1991): ruled that Congress could prohibit recipients of family-planning funds from providing or discussing abortion as a family planning option. The court held that this did not violate the First Amendment because clinics were still free to provide such counseling as a "financially and physically" separate activity.

*Planned Parenthood of Southeastern Pennsylvania* v. *Casey,* 505 U.S. 833 (1992): softened the ruling in *Roe* v. *Wade* by finding that some state regulation of abortion prior to fetal viability, including a 24-hour waiting period, mandatory counseling, and a parental-consent requirement for minors, is permissible as long as the regulations do not place an "undue burden" on the woman.

*Romer* v. *Evans,* 517 U.S. 620 (1996): invalidated a Colorado referendum passed by popular vote that prohibited conferral of protected status on the basis of sexual orientation; the court ruled that the referendum was overbroad, bore little relationship to legimate state interests, and violated the Fourteenth Amendment of the US Constitution.

*Faragher* v. *City of Boca Raton,* 524 U.S. 775; *Burlington Industries, Inc.* v. *Ellerth* 524 U.S. 742 (1998): held that, under by Title VII of the Civil Rights Act of 1964, an employer is responsible for workplace sexual harassment by supervisory employees if the employer does not act to prevent such harassment and to correct it should it occur.

*Oncale* v. *Sundowner Offshore Services, Inc., et al.,* 523 U.S. 75 (1998): found that Title VII's prohibition of workplace sexual discrimination applied equally in cases when the harasser and victim are of the same sex.

*Boy Scouts of America* v. *Dale,* 530 U.S. 640 (2000): ruled that the Boy Scouts, because it is a private organization, was within its rights when it dismissed a scoutmaster expressly because of his avowed homosexuality. The court reasoned that a state statute banning discrimination on the basis of sexual orientation in places of public accommodation was outweighed by the Scouts' First Amendment right to freedom of association.

*Stenberg* v. *Carhart,* 530 U.S. 914 (2000): ruled that a state law criminalizing the performance of dilation and extraction—or late-term—abortions violated the Constitution (following the same reasoning as in *Roe* v. *Wade*) because it allowed no consideration of the health of the woman in choosing the procedure.

*Bush* v. *Gore*, **531 U.S. 98 (2000):** stopped the manual recounts, then underway in certain Florida counties at the demand of Al Gore, of disputed ballots from the November 2000 presidential election on the grounds that inconsistent vote-counting standards among the several counties involved amounted to a violation of the Fourteenth Amendment's equal protection clause. Because George W. Bush at the time led Al Gore in the number of officially recognized Florida votes, the decision meant that he would win the state and thus the general election, despite having lost the popular vote.

*Republican Party of Minnesota* v. *White*, **536 U.S. 765 (2002):** held that candidates for judicial office may state their views on disputed legal or political issues within the purview of the court for which they are running.

*Atkins* v. *Virginia*, **536 U.S. 304 (2002):** ruled that the death penalty, when applied to mentally retarded individuals, constitutes a "cruel and unusual punishment" prohibited by the Eighth Amendment.

*Ring* v. *Arizona*, **536 U.S. 584 (2002):** ruled that under the Sixth Amendment, a jury, rather than a judge, must indicate those aggravating factors that would subject a convicted criminal to death rather than a lesser sentence.

*Eldred* v. *Ashcroft*, **123 S.Ct. 769 (2003):** upheld a 1998 federal statute that granted a 20-year extension to all existing copyrights.

*Lockyer* v. *Andrade*, **123 S.Ct. 1166;** *Ewing* v. *California*, **123 S.Ct. 1179 (2003):** upheld a "three-strikes" law that imposes long prison sentences for a third offense, even nonviolent crimes.

*State Farm Mutual Auto Insurance Co.* v. *Campbell*, **123 S.Ct. 1513 (2003):** placed limits on "irrational and arbitrary" punitive damages and established new guidelines that generally bar consideration of a defendant's wealth or conduct outside the state's borders and lower the ratio of punitive to compensatory damages.

*Brown* v. *Legal Foundation of Washington*, **123 S.Ct. 1406 (2003):** held that channeling interest on short-term deposits by lawyers on accounts held in trust for their clients to legal assistance programs for the poor is not an unconstitutional taking of property.

*Nevada Department of Human Resources* v. *Hibbs*, **123 S.Ct. 714 (2003):** held that state governments may be sued by their employees for failing to honor the federally guaranteed right to take time off from work for family emergencies.

*United States* v. *American Library Association*, **123 S.Ct. 22 (2003):** upheld the Children's Internet Protection Act, which conditions access to federal grants and subsidies upon the installation of antipornography filters on all Internet-connected computers.

*Grutter* v. *Bollinger*, cite; *Gratz* v. *Bollinger*, cite **(2003):** in a pair of decisions addressing affirmative action in admissions at the University of Michigan, the Court endorsed *Bakke*'s articulation of diversity as a compelling interest (*see above*), so long as the admissions program's operation is "holistic" and "individualized," and upheld Michigan's law school admissions program. In *Gratz*, the Court struck down Michigan's undergraduate admissions program because reserving spaces for underrepresented minorities was the "functional equivalent of a quota."

*Georgia* v. *Ashcroft*, cite **(2003):** ruled that race-sensitive redistricting could consider more general minority influence in the political process when drawing particular district lines rather than addressing only the actual number of minority voters present.

*Wiggins* v. *Smith*, cite **(2003):** found that trial lawyers' failure to perform "reasonably" under "prevailing professional norms" may support a writ for habeas corpus in a death penalty case.

*Lawrence* v. *Texas*, cite **(2003):** explicitly overruling *Bowers* v. *Hardwick*, 478 U.S. 186 (1986), the Court declared that gay men and lesbians are "entitled to respect for their private lives" under the Due Process Clause of the Fourteenth Amendment and rendered unconstitutional state statutes outlawing sex between adults of the same gender.

*Stogner* v. *California*, cite **(2003):** ruled that states cannot enact new statutes of limitations that retroactively extend the period of liability on crimes for which the statute of limitation had already expired, such as had been done to enable prosecutions in instances of long-ago child molestation.

# Military Affairs

## US Military Leadership

| | |
|---|---|
| President, Commander in Chief: | George W. Bush |
| Secretary of Defense: | Donald Rumsfeld |
| Chairman, Joint Chiefs of Staff: | Richard B. Myers |
| Vice Chairman, Joint Chiefs of Staff: | Peter Pace |

*The Joint Chiefs of Staff include the Chairman, Joint Chiefs of Staff; the Vice Chairman, Joint Chiefs of Staff; the Chief of Staff, US Army; the Chief of Naval Operations; the Commandant, US Marine Corps; and the Chief of Staff, US Air Force.*

| RANK/POSITION | NAME/DATE ASSUMED POST | RANK/POSITION | NAME/DATE ASSUMED POST |
|---|---|---|---|
| **Army** | | **Army (continued)** | |
| Chief of Staff | Gen. Peter J. Schoomaker (1 Aug 2003) | Sec. of the Army | vacant |
| | | Under Sec. of the Army | Les Brownlee (14 Nov 2001) |
| Vice Chief of Staff | John M. Keane (22 Jun 1999) | | |
| Sergeant Major | Jack L. Tilley (23 Jun 2000) | | |

# US Military Leadership (continued)

| RANK/POSITION | NAME/DATE ASSUMED POST |
|---|---|
| **Navy** | |
| Chief of Naval Operations | Vern Clark (21 Jul 2000) |
| Vice Chief of Naval Operations | William J. Fallon (11 Oct 2000) |
| Master Chief Petty Officer | Terry D. Scott (22 Apr 2002) |
| Sec. of the Navy | Hansford T. Johnson (7 Aug 2001) |
| Under Sec. of the Navy | vacant |
| **Air Force** | |
| Chief of Staff | John P. Jumper (6 Sep 2001) |
| Vice Chief of Staff | Robert H. Foglesong (5 Nov 2001) |
| Asst. Vice Chief of Staff | Joseph H. Wehrle, Jr. (25 Mar 2002) |
| Chief Master Sergeant | Frederick J. Finch (2 Aug 1999) |

| RANK/POSITION | NAME/DATE ASSUMED POST |
|---|---|
| **Air Force (continued)** | |
| Sec. of the Air Force | James G. Roche (1 Jun 2001) |
| Under Sec. of the Air Force | Peter B. Teets (13 Dec 2001) |
| **Marine Corps** | |
| Commandant | Michael W. Hagee (13 Jan 2003) |
| Asst. Commandant | Michael J. Williams (9 Sep 2000) |
| Sergeant Major | Alford L. McMichael (1 Jul 1999) |
| **Coast Guard** | |
| Commandant | Thomas H. Collins (30 May 2002) |
| Vice Commandant | Thomas Barrett (30 May 2002) |
| Chief of Staff | Timothy W. Josiah (31 May 1998) |
| Master Chief Petty Officer | Vincent Patton III (22 May 1998) |

# Unified Combatant Commands

The Unified Combatant Commands provide operational control of US combat forces and are organized geographically. Unified Commanders receive orders through the chairman of the Joint Chiefs of Staff. Although the number of commands may vary, each command must be composed of forces from at least two of the armed services. Information is current as of June 2003.

| COMMAND | HEADQUARTERS | COMMANDER IN CHIEF |
|---|---|---|
| US European Command | Stuttgart-Vaihingen, Germany | Gen. James L. Jones, USMC |
| US Pacific Command | Honolulu HI | Adm. Thomas B. Fargo, USN |
| US Joint Forces Command | Norfolk VA | Adm. E.P. Giambastiani, USN |
| US Southern Command | Miami FL | Gen. James T. Hill, USA |
| US Central Command | MacDill Air Force Base, Florida | Gen. Tommy R. Franks, USA |
| US Northern Command | Peterson Air Force Base, Colorado | Gen. Ralph E. Eberhart, USAF |
| US Special Operations Command | MacDill Air Force Base, Florida | Gen. Charles R. Holland, USAF |
| US Transportation Command | Scott Air Force Base, Illinois | Gen. John W. Handy, USAF |
| US Strategic Command | Offutt Air Force Base, Nebraska | Adm. James O. Ellis, Jr., USN |

# North Atlantic Treaty Organization (NATO) International Commands

*The NATO military command structure comprises two main strategic commands, Allied Command Europe and Allied Command Atlantic. Their subordinate regional commands are also listed.*

**ALLIED COMMAND FOR OPERATIONS (ACO)**
Mons, Belgium
Supreme Allied Commander, Operations:
  Gen. James L. Jones (USMC) (17 Jan 2003– )

**SUBORDINATE REGIONAL COMMANDS**
Allied Forces South Europe (AFSOUTH)
Naples, Italy
Commander-in-Chief: Adm. Gregory G. Johnson (USN)
  (24 Oct 2001– )

Allied Forces North Europe (AFNORTH)
Brunssum, The Netherlands
Commander-in-Chief: Gen. Sir Jack Deverell
  (Royal Army, UK) (23 Mar 2001– )

**ALLIED COMMAND TRANSFORMATION (ACT)**
Norfolk VA
Supreme Allied Commander, Transformation: Adm.
  Edmund P. Giambastiani, Jr. (USN) (19 Jun 2003– )

**SUBORDINATE REGIONAL COMMANDS**
Allied Forces East Atlantic (EASTLANT)
Northwood, United Kingdom
Commander-in-Chief: Adm. Sir Jonathon Band KCB
  (Royal Navy, UK) (2 Aug 2002– )

Allied Forces West Atlantic (WESTLANT)
Norfolk VA
  Commander-in-Chief: Adm. Robert J. Natter (USN)
  (23 Jun 2000– )

Allied Forces South Atlantic (SOUTHLANT)
Oeiras, Portugal
Commander-in-Chief: Vice Adm. Américo da Silva
  Santos (Portuguese Navy) (10 Nov 2000– )

# Chairmen of the Joint Chiefs of Staff, 1949–2003

The 1949 Amendments to the National Security Act of 1947 created the position of chairman of the Joint Chiefs of Staff. The president appoints the chairman with the advice and consent of the Senate. Terms are for two years. On 1 Oct 1986 the chairman's eligibility for service increased from two to three reappointments. (During wartime, there is no limit on reappointment.) The chairman's term begins on 1 October of odd-numbered years.

| NAME | MILITARY BRANCH | DATES OF SERVICE |
|---|---|---|
| Gen. of the Army Omar N. Bradley | US Army | 16 Aug 1949–15 Aug 1953 |
| Adm. Arthur W. Radford | US Navy | 15 Aug 1953–15 Aug 1957 |
| Gen. Nathan F. Twining | US Air Force | 15 Aug 1957–30 Sep 1960 |
| Gen. Lyman L. Lemnitzer | US Army | 1 Oct 1960–30 Sep 1962 |
| Gen. Maxwell D. Taylor | US Army | 1 Oct 1962–1 Jul 1964 |
| Gen. Earle G. Wheeler | US Army | 3 Jul 1964–2 Jul 1970 |
| Adm. Thomas H. Moorer | US Navy | 2 Jul 1970–1 Jul 1974 |
| Gen. George S. Brown | US Air Force | 1 Jul 1974–20 Jun 1978 |
| Gen. David C. Jones | US Air Force | 21 Jun 1978–18 Jun 1982 |
| Gen. John W. Vessey, Jr. | US Army | 18 Jun 1982–30 Sep 1985 |
| Adm. William J. Crowe, Jr. | US Navy | 1 Oct 1985–30 Sep 1989 |
| Gen. Colin L. Powell | US Army | 1 Oct 1989–30 Sep 1993 |
| Adm. David E. Jeremiah (acting) | US Navy | 1 Oct 1993–24 Oct 1993 |
| Gen. John M. Shalikashvili | US Army | 25 Oct 1993–30 Sep 1997 |
| Gen. Harry Shelton | US Army | 1 Oct 1997–1 Oct 2001 |
| Gen. Richard B. Myers | US Air Force | 1 Oct 2001– |

# Worldwide Deployment of the US Military

*Deployments of 1,000 or more active duty military personnel as of 30 Sept 2002. Regional totals include countries and areas not shown in the table. N/A means not available. Source: US Department of Defense.*

| COUNTRY/REGIONAL AREA | TOTAL | ARMY | NAVY | MARINE CORPS | AIR FORCE |
|---|---|---|---|---|---|
| US and territories | | | | | |
| continental US | 969,215 | 354,831 | 190,074 | 133,164 | 291,146 |
| Alaska | 15,906 | 6,630 | 99 | 41 | 9,136 |
| Hawaii | 34,608 | 15,985 | 8,654 | 5,680 | 4,289 |
| Guam | 3,149 | 34 | 1,591 | 91 | 1,433 |
| Puerto Rico | 2,592 | 818 | 1,688 | 22 | 64 |
| transients | 27,863 | 4,080 | 12,742 | 2,222 | 8,819 |
| afloat | 127,767 | 0 | 127,767 | 0 | 0 |
| **total ashore and afloat** | **1,181,150** | **382,402** | **342,617** | **141,220** | **314,911** |
| | | | | | |
| Europe | | | | | |
| Belgium | 1,458 | 898 | 102 | 29 | 429 |
| Bosnia and Herzegovina | 3,082 | 3,047 | 0 | 34 | 1 |
| Germany | 68,701 | 54,154 | 310 | 246 | 13,991 |
| Iceland | 1,665 | 3 | 1,054 | 57 | 551 |
| Italy | 12,466 | 2,940 | 5,475 | 65 | 3,986 |
| Serbia (including Kosovo) | 2,804 | 2,793 | 0 | 6 | 5 |
| Spain | 2,621 | 46 | 1,432 | 896 | 247 |
| Turkey | 1,587 | 122 | 24 | 23 | 1,418 |
| United Kingdom | 10,258 | 450 | 1,213 | 87 | 8,508 |
| afloat | 5,003 | 0 | 2,664 | 2,339 | 0 |
| **total ashore and afloat** | **112,548** | **65,146** | **12,820** | **4,030** | **30,552** |
| | | | | | |
| East Asia and Pacific | | | | | |
| Japan | 41,848 | 1,856 | 7,676 | 19,217 | 13,099 |
| South Korea | 37,743 | 28,527 | 342 | 155 | 8,719 |
| afloat | 16,090 | 0 | 13,802 | 2,288 | 0 |
| **total ashore and afloat** | **96,385** | **30,500** | **22,023** | **21,873** | **21,989** |
| | | | | | |
| North Africa, Near East, and South Asia | | | | | |
| Afghanistan | N/A[1] | | | | |
| Bahrain | 1,560 | 19 | 1,166 | 353 | 22 |
| Iraq | N/A[2] | | | | |
| **total ashore and afloat** | **4,820** | **1,175** | **2,338** | **914** | **393** |
| | | | | | |
| Western Hemisphere | | | | | |
| **total ashore and afloat** | **1,913** | **326** | **612** | **622** | **353** |

## Worldwide Deployment of the US Military (continued)

| | | | | | |
|---|---|---|---|---|---|
| all foreign countries | | | | | |
| ashore | 208,479 | 104,140 | 23,421 | 27,578 | 53,340 |
| afloat | 22,005 | 0 | 17,070 | 4,935 | 0 |
| **total ashore and afloat** | **230,484** | **104,140** | **40,491** | **32,513** | **53,340** |
| | | | | | |
| worldwide | | | | | |
| ashore | 1,261,862 | 486,542 | 238,271 | 168,798 | 368,251 |
| afloat | 149,772 | 0 | 144,837 | 4,935 | 0 |
| **total ashore and afloat** | **1,411,634** | **486,542** | **383,108** | **173,733** | **368,251** |

[1]*Estimated total as of April 2003: 8,500. Source: Associated Press.*
[2]*Estimated total as of May 2003: 130,000. Source: Jane's Defence Weekly.*

## Military Ranks and Monthly Pay

*Pay given in dollars as of 1 Jan 2003.*

### Enlisted personnel

| | E-1 | E-2 | E-3 | E-4 | E-5 |
|---|---|---|---|---|---|
| Army | private | private | private first class | corporal | sergeant |
| Navy | seaman recruit | seaman apprentice | seaman | petty officer third class | petty officer second class |
| Air Force | airman basic | airman | airman first class | senior airman | staff sergeant |
| Marine Corps | private | private first class | lance corporal | corporal | sergeant |
| | | | | | |
| 0–6 years | 1,065–1,151 | 1,290 | 1,357–1,529 | 1,503–1,749 | 1,625–1,903 |
| 6–12 years | | | | 1,824 | 2,037–2,237 |
| 12–18 years | | | | | 2,283 |
| 18–24 years | | | | | |
| over 24 years | | | | | |

| | E-6 | E-7 | E-8 | E-9 |
|---|---|---|---|---|
| Army | staff sergeant | sergeant first class | first sergeant | sergeant major |
| Navy | petty officer first class | chief petty officer | senior chief petty officer | master chief petty officer |
| Air Force | technical sergeant | master sergeant | senior master sergeant | chief master sergeant |
| Marine Corps | staff sergeant | gunnery sergeant | master sergeant, first sergeant | master gunnery sergeant, sergeant major, command sergeant major |
| | | | | |
| 0–6 years | 1,771–2,117 | 2,068–2,428 | | |
| 6–12 years | 2,204–2,477 | 2,516–2,753 | 2,975–3,061 | 3,564 |
| 12–18 years | 2,562–2,663 | 2,838–3,066 | 3,141–3,342 | 3,645–3,867 |
| 18–24 years | 2,710 | 3,139–3,331 | 3,530–3,787 | 3,987–4,344 |
| over 24 years | | 3,428–3,671 | 3,877–4,099 | 4,506–4,757 |

### Warrant officers

| | W-1 | W-2 | W-3 | W-4 | W-5 |
|---|---|---|---|---|---|
| Army | warrant officer | chief warrant officer | chief warrant officer | chief warrant officer | chief warrant officer |
| Navy | " | " | " | " | " |
| Air Force | " | " | " | " | " |
| Marine Corps | " | " | " | " | " |
| | | | | | |
| 0–6 years | 2,134–2,501 | 2,416–2,763 | 2,747–3,018 | 3,008–3,421 | |
| 6–12 years | 2,662–2,888 | 2,838–3,148 | 3,141–3,467 | 3,578–3,891 | |
| 12–18 years | 3,007–3,203 | 3,264–3,454 | 3,580–3,916 | 4,045–4,356 | |
| 18–24 years | 3,321–3,409 | 3,580–3,831 | 4,058–4,266 | 4,512–4,822 | 5,169–5,347 |
| over 24 years | | 3,957 | 4,407–4,548 | 4,978–5,137 | 5,524–5,703 |

### Officers (with more than 4 years served as an enlisted or warrant member of the armed services)

| | O-1E | O-2E | O-3E |
|---|---|---|---|
| Army | second lieutenant | first lieutenant | captain |
| Navy | ensign | lieutenant, jr. grade | lieutenant |
| Air Force | second lieutenant | first lieutenant | captain |
| Marine Corps | second lieutenant | first lieutenant | captain |
| | | | |
| 0–6 years | 2,747 | 3,411 | 3,883 |
| 6–12 years | 2,934–3,153 | 3,481–3,779 | 4,069–4,406 |

## Military Ranks and Monthly Pay (continued)

**Officers (with more than 4 years served as an enlisted or warrant member of the armed services) (continued)**

|  | O-1E | O-2E | O-3E |
|---|---|---|---|
| Army | second lieutenant | first lieutenant | captain |
| Navy | ensign | lieutenant, jr. grade | lieutenant |
| Air Force | second lieutenant | first lieutenant | captain |
| Marine Corps | second lieutenant | first lieutenant | captain |
|  |  |  |  |
| 12–18 years | 3,262–3,411 | 3,923–4,031 | 4,623–4,911 |
| 18–24 years |  |  | 5,054 |
| over 24 years |  |  |  |

**Officers**

|  | O-1 | O-2 | O-3 | O-4 | O-5 |
|---|---|---|---|---|---|
| Army | second lieutenant | first lieutenant | captain | major | lieutenant colonel |
| Navy | ensign | lieutenant, jr. grade | lieutenant | lieutenant commander | commander |
| Air Force | second lieutenant | first lieutenant | captain | major | lieutenant colonel |
| Marine Corps | second lieutenant | first lieutenant | captain | major | lieutenant colonel |
|  |  |  |  |  |  |
| 0–6 years | 2,184–2,747 | 2,515–3,411 | 2,911–3,883 | 3,311–4,146 | 3,838–4,678 |
| 6–12 years |  | 3,481 | 4,069–4,406 | 4,383–4,854 | 4,865–5,223 |
| 12–18 years |  |  | 4,623–4,736 | 5,201–5,471 | 5,403–5,992 |
| 18–24 years |  |  |  | 5,528 | 6,162–6,520 |
| over 24 years |  |  |  |  |  |

|  | O-6 | O-7 | O-8 | O-9 | O-10 |
|---|---|---|---|---|---|
| Army | colonel | brigadier general | major general | lieutenant general | general |
| Navy | captain | rear admiral (lower half) | rear admiral (upper half) | vice admiral | admiral |
| Air Force | colonel | brigadier general | major general | lieutenant general | general |
| Marine Corps | colonel | brigadier general | major general | lieutenant general | general |
|  |  |  |  |  |  |
| 0–6 years | 4,603–5,389 | 6,211–6,739 | 7,474–7,927 |  |  |
| 6–12 years | 5,410–5,672 | 6,931–7,340 | 8,129–8,547 |  |  |
| 12–18 years | 5,672–6,564 | 7,559–8,469 | 8,869–9,238 |  |  |
| 18–24 years | 6,899–7423 | 9,051 | 9,639–10,256 | 10,564–10,716 | 12,078–12,137 |
| over 24 years | 7,616–7,990 | 9,097 |  | 10,936–11,320 | 12,389–12,829 |

# Women in the Armed Forces

Few early American women were soldiers. With the rise of the women's movement in the late 19th century, women gradually made inroads into the US military, most often in auxiliary roles. It was not until the late 20th century that they achieved regular combat status in the armed forces. By the 21st century, women continued to fight for full equality across all branches of the military, especially in terms of combat duty.

During World War I many women had enlisted as volunteers in the military services; they usually served in clerical roles. When the war ended, they were released from their duties. The same was true during World War II, when an even greater number of women volunteers served in the armed forces. The war did open other employment opportunities for women—as factory workers ("Rosie the Riveter" became an American icon), nurses, and journalists—but these doors of opportunity were largely closed after the war, when women routinely lost their jobs to men discharged from military service.

During World War II several gender-specific military organizations were formed. Never before had women, with the exception of nurses, served within the ranks of the US Army until the advent of the **Women's Army Corps** (WAC), which placed more than 150,000 women in noncombat positions. In anticipation of the expiration of the WAC law in 1948, the leaders of the Army in 1946 requested that the WACs be made a permanent part of its personnel. Following two years of legislative debate, the bill was passed by Congress and signed into law by Pres. Harry S. Truman on 12 Jun 1948, as the **Women's Armed Services Integration Act**. It enabled women to serve as permanent, regular members of not only the Army but also the Navy, the Marine Corps, and the recently formed Air Force. The law limited the number of women who could serve in the military to 2% of the total forces in each branch. The WAC remained a separate unit of the Army until 1978, when male and female forces were integrated.

Another group formed during World War II was the **Coast Guard Women's Reserve**, founded in 1942 for the purpose of making more men available to serve at sea by assigning women to onshore duties. Also established in 1942, the military unit **Women Accepted for Volunteer Emergency Service** (WAVES) was the Navy's corps of female members. During the war some 100,000 WAVES served in a wide variety of capacities, ranging from performing essential clerical duties to serving as instructors for male pilots-in-training. Several thousand WAVES later participated in the Korean War. Unlike the WAC, the WAVES was not an auxiliary and its members were accorded a status comparable to that of male members of the reserve. The Navy, however, did come under fire for excluding African American women from the ranks until the final months of the war, when Pres. Franklin D. Roosevelt ordered racial integration. The corps continued its separate existence until 1978.

At the advent of the 21st century, about 200,000 women were listed as active members of the US armed forces, comprising about 15% of the total military balance. The largest representation of women was in the Air Force, where nearly one-fifth were female, though a larger gross number of women were active in the Army. The smallest number and smallest female-to-male proportion were found in the Marine Corps. Women served in a number of combat and combat-support roles in Operation **Iraqi Freedom** in 2003.

**Military education**
In the late 20th century women made advances in military education. In 1976 they were first admitted to the **US Military Academy**, **US Naval Academy**, and **US Air Force Academy**; the previous year they had been admitted to the **US Coast Guard Academy**. In 1990 the Justice Department ruled that the **Virginia Military Institute's** male-only admissions policy was unconstitutional. In response, the institute established an associated military program for women at **Mary Baldwin College** in Staunton VA in 1995.

Nonetheless, the Supreme Court ruled in 1996 that the admissions policy was unconstitutional, and the school admitted its first women cadets in 1997.

**Military figures**
**Deborah Sampson** of Massachusetts assumed a male identity to serve for the Continental Army in the American Revolutionary War in 1782 until her true identity was discovered and she was discharged; her heirs received a full military pension in 1838. **Sarah Emma Evelyn Edmonds** enlisted as a man in the American Civil War and saw military action as a Union soldier and a spy until she deserted in April 1863; she later received a veteran's pension. According to legend, **Lucy Brewer** was the first woman marine, who, perhaps inspired by the story of Deborah Sampson, disguised herself as a man to serve on the USS *Constitution* during the War of 1812. Officially, however, **Opha Mae Johnson** is credited as the first female in the Marine Corps, enrolling in 1918.

Among the female leaders of military outfits during and after World War II were **Florence A. Blanchfield** (Army Nurse Corps), **Sue Sophia Dauser** (Navy Nurse Corps), **Joy Bright Hancock** (WAVES), **Oveta Culp Hobby** and **Mary Agnes Hallaren** (WAC), **Dorothy Constance Stratton** (Coast Guard Women's Reserve), and **Katherine Amelia Towle**, who was director of the women's reserve of the Marine Corps from 1948 to 1953.

---

**Did you ? know■** Although he is remembered as the "Rebel General," Robert E. Lee was a disbeliever in slavery and was devoutly attached to the republic that his father and kinsmen had helped bring into being. Moreover, he rejected war as a means of resolving political conflict. In late 1860 he wrote, "[If] strife and civil war are to take the place of brotherly love and kindness, I shall mourn for my country and for the welfare and progress of mankind."

---

# African American Service in US Wars

During the American Civil War the Union Army enlisted some 179,000 soldiers in 166 all-black regiments, but the first official group of African American professional soldiers was not recognized until the war had ended and the US was reunified. A 1866 law authorized the creation of African American cavalry regiments in the Army; though it required their officers to be white. The resulting units were the 9th and 10th cavalries and the 38th through 41st infantries. These **buffalo soldiers**, as they came to be known, patrolled the Western frontier in the late 19th century, helping to pacify Native Americans.

The 9th and 10th cavalries later distinguished themselves by their fighting in the Spanish-American War and in the 1916 Mexican campaign. One of the 10th Cavalry's officers was **John J. Pershing**, afterwards a World War I general, whose nickname "Black Jack" reflected his advocacy of black troops.

The Medal of Honor, which became a permanent military decoration in 1863, was bestowed upon African Americans in the Civil War, Indian campaigns, Spanish-American War, both World Wars, the Korean

conflict, and the Vietnam War. The seven Medals of Honor awarded to black soldiers in World War II were not granted until 1997, after a study revealed there was racial disparity in the awarding process.

More than 1.2 million African Americans served during World War II. Mostly restricted to segregated units, black soldiers not only fought for the Army but first saw combat duty in the Navy, Marines, and Army Air Corps (later Air Force). The **Tuskegee Airmen** of the all-black 99th Pursuit Squadron of the Air Corps were commanded by Lt. Col. **Benjamin Oliver Davis, Jr.**, whose father, **Benjamin O. Davis, Sr.**, was the first African American to become a US general (Army).

In 1948 President Truman integrated all branches of the military, and all-black units were phased out by 1954. In the decades following, the **Civil Rights Movement** continued to erode public racial segregation, and African Americans continued to figure prominently in the military. **Colin Powell** became the the first black officer to hold the highest military post in the US when Pres. George Bush nominated him chairman of the Joint Chiefs of Staff in 1989.

# Number of Living Veterans[1]

| AGE IN YEARS | KOREAN CONFLICT | VIETNAM ERA | GULF WAR | TOTAL WARTIME | TOTAL VETERANS[2] |
|---|---|---|---|---|---|
| Under 35 | — | — | 1,833,000 | 1,833,000 | 2,105,000 |
| 35-39 | — | — | 432,000 | 432,000 | 1,444,000 |
| 40-44 | — | 35,000 | 295,000 | 331,000 | 1,808,000 |
| 45-49 | — | 1,249,000 | 128,000 | 1,487,000 | 2,028,000 |
| 50-54 | — | 2,810,000 | 26,000 | 2,962,000 | 3,049,000 |
| 55-59 | — | 2,667,000 | 6,000 | 2,722,000 | 3,098,000 |
| 60-64 | 69,000 | 789,000 | 2,000 | 882,000 | 2,263,000 |
| 65 and over | 2,994,000 | 169,000 | 1,000 | 8,470,000[3] | 9,553,000 |
| Total[4] | 3,064,000 | 7,718,000 | 2,723,000 | 19,120,000 | 25,349,000 |

[1]As of 1 Jul 2001. Includes Puerto Rico. Estimated. [2]Includes those serving during periods of armed conflict not listed. [3]Includes an estimate of fewer than 1,000 veterans of World War I and 5,039,000 veterans of World War II, all 65 or over. [4]Veterans who served in more than one wartime period are counted only once.

# Disabled Veterans Receiving Compensation

*Numbers of veterans receiving compensation for service-related disabilities.*

| TIME OF SERVICE | 1980 | 1990 | 1996 | 1997 | 1998 | 1999 | 2000 | 2001 |
|---|---|---|---|---|---|---|---|---|
| World War I[1] | 30,000 | 3,000 | —[2] | — | — | — | — | — |
| World War II | 1,193,000 | 876,000 | 655,000 | 616,000 | 578,000 | 541,000 | 505,000 | 470,000 |
| Korean Conflict | 236,000 | 209,000 | 187,000 | 182,000 | 179,000 | 175,000 | 171,000 | 166,000 |
| Vietnam Era | 553,000 | 652,000 | 714,000 | 724,000 | 729,000 | 736,000 | 741,000 | 750,000 |
| Gulf War | N/A[3] | N/A | 168,000 | 202,000 | 241,000 | 282,000 | 325,000 | 366,000 |
| Peacetime | 262,000 | 444,000 | 529,000 | 539,000 | 550,000 | 561,000 | 567,000 | 569,000 |
| Total[1] | 2,274,000 | 2,184,000 | 2,253,000 | 2,263,000 | 2,277,000 | 2,294,000 | 2,308,000 | 2,321,000 |

[1]Includes Spanish-American War and Mexican Border service. [2]Fewer than 500. [3]Not applicable.

# US Casualties of War

*Data prior to World War I are based on incomplete records. Casualty data exclude personnel captured or missing in action. N/A means not available or unknown. Sources: US Department of Defense and US Coast Guard.*

| WAR | SERVICE BRANCH | NUMBER OF COMBATANTS | WOUNDED[1] | CASUALTIES BATTLE DEATHS | OTHER DEATHS | TOTAL DEATHS |
|---|---|---|---|---|---|---|
| Revolutionary War | Army | N/A | 6,004 | 4,044 | N/A | 4,044 |
| (1775–1783) | Navy | N/A | 114 | 342 | N/A | 342 |
| | Marines | N/A | 70 | 49 | N/A | 49 |
| | total | 184,000–250,000[2] | 6,188 | 4,435 | N/A | 4,435 |
| War of 1812 | Army | N/A | 4,000 | 1,950 | N/A | 1,950 |
| (1812–1815) | Navy | N/A | 439 | 265 | N/A | 265 |
| | Marines | N/A | 66 | 45 | N/A | 45 |
| | Coast Guard | 100 | N/A | 0 | N/A | 0 |
| | total | 286,830 | 4,505 | 2,260 | N/A | 2,260 |
| Mexican War | Army | N/A | 4,102 | 1,721 | 11,550 | 13,271 |
| (1846–1848) | Navy | N/A | 3 | 1 | N/A | 1 |
| | Marines | N/A | 47 | 11 | N/A | 11 |
| | Coast Guard | 71 | N/A | N/A | N/A | N/A |
| | total | 78,789 | 4,152 | 1,733 | 11,550 | 13,283 |
| Civil War (1861–1865) | | | | | | |
| Union | Army | 2,128,948 | 280,040 | 138,154 | 221,374 | 359,528 |
| | Navy | N/A | 1,710 | 2,112 | 2,411 | 4,523 |
| | Marines | 84,415 | 131 | 148 | 312 | 460 |
| | Coast Guard | 219 | N/A | 1 | N/A | 1 |
| | total | 2,213,582 | 281,881 | 140,415 | 224,097 | 364,512 |
| Confederate[3] | total | 600,000–1,500,000 | N/A | 74,524 | 59,297 | 133,821 |
| Spanish-American War | Army | 280,564 | 1,594 | 369 | 2,061 | 2,430 |
| (1898) | Navy | 22,875 | 47 | 10 | N/A | 10 |
| | Marines | 3,321 | 21 | 6 | N/A | 6 |
| | Coast Guard | 660 | N/A | 0 | N/A | 0 |
| | total | 307,420 | 1,662 | 385 | 2,061 | 2,446 |

## US Casualties of War (continued)

| WAR | SERVICE BRANCH | NUMBER OF COMBATANTS | WOUNDED[1] | CASUALTIES BATTLE DEATHS | OTHER DEATHS | TOTAL DEATHS |
|---|---|---|---|---|---|---|
| World War I | Army[4] | 4,057,101 | 193,663 | 50,510 | 55,868 | 106,378 |
| (1917–1918) | Navy | 599,051 | 819 | 431 | 6,856 | 7,287 |
| | Marines | 78,839 | 9,520 | 2,461 | 390 | 2,851 |
| | Coast Guard | 8,835 | N/A | 111 | 81 | 192 |
| | total | 4,743,826 | 204,002 | 53,513 | 63,195 | 116,708 |
| World War II | Army[4] | 11,260,000 | 565,861 | 234,874 | 83,400 | 318,274 |
| (1941–1946) | Navy | 4,183,466 | 37,778 | 36,950 | 25,664 | 62,614 |
| | Marines | 669,100 | 68,207 | 19,733 | 4,778 | 24,511 |
| | Coast Guard | 241,093 | N/A | 574 | 1,343 | 1,917 |
| | total | 16,353,659 | 671,846 | 292,131 | 115,185 | 407,316 |
| Korean War[5] | Army | 2,834,000 | 77,596 | 27,731 | 2,125 | 29,856 |
| (1950–1953) | Navy | 1,177,000 | 1,576 | 506 | 154 | 660 |
| | Marines | 424,000 | 23,744 | 4,266 | 242 | 4,508 |
| | Air Force | 1,285,000 | 368 | 1,238 | 314 | 1,552 |
| | Coast Guard | 44,143 | 0 | 0 | N/A | 0 |
| | total | 5,764,143 | 103,284 | 33,741 | 2,835 | 36,576 |
| Vietnam War[5] | Army | 4,368,000 | 96,802 | 30,950 | 7,261 | 38,211 |
| (1964–1973) | Navy | 1,842,000 | 4,178 | 1,628 | 934 | 2,562 |
| | Marines | 794,000 | 51,392 | 13,091 | 1,749 | 14,840 |
| | Air Force | 1,740,000 | 931 | 1,744 | 841 | 2,585 |
| | Coast Guard | 8,000 | 60 | 7 | N/A | 7 |
| | total | 8,752,000 | 153,363[6] | 47,420 | 10,785 | 58,205 |
| Persian Gulf War[7] | Army | 338,636 | 354 | 98 | 126 | 224 |
| (1990–1991) | Navy | 152,419 | 12 | 5 | 50 | 55 |
| | Marines | 97,878 | 92 | 24 | 44 | 68 |
| | Air Force | 76,543 | 9 | 20 | 15 | 35 |
| | Coast Guard | 400 | 0 | 0 | 0 | 0 |
| | total | 665,876 | 467 | 147 | 235 | 382 |
| War on Terrorism[8] | Army | N/A | N/A | 16 | 24 | 40 |
| (2001– ) | Navy | N/A | N/A | 1 | 5 | 6 |
| | Marines | N/A | N/A | 1 | 10 | 11 |
| | Air Force | N/A | N/A | 2 | 5 | 7 |
| | Coast Guard | N/A | N/A | N/A | N/A | N/A |
| | total | N/A | N/A | 20 | 44 | 64 |
| Operation Iraqi Freedom[9] | Army | N/A | N/A | 53 | 14 | 67 |
| (2003) | Navy | N/A | N/A | 3 | 0 | 3 |
| | Marines | N/A | N/A | 56 | 9 | 65 |
| | Air Force | N/A | N/A | 3 | 1[10] | 4 |
| | Coast Guard | N/A | N/A | N/A | N/A | N/A |
| | total | N/A | N/A | 115 | 24 | 139 |

[1]Data in this column account for the total number of wounds. Marine Corps data for World War II, the Spanish-American War, and earlier wars represent the number of combatants wounded. [2]Estimate. [3]Authoritative statistics are not available. In addition to combat deaths, an estimated 26,000–31,000 Confederates died in Union prisons. [4]Includes air service. [5]As of 15 Mar 2003. Korean War casualty figures are under review. [6]Excludes 150,332 wounded that did not require hospital care. [7]Data for military personnel serving in the theater of operation. [8]Data as of 15 Mar 2003. First casualty was on 10 Oct 2001. Includes service deaths in and around Afghanistan, the Philippines, and the Persian Gulf. [9]Through the end of major combat actions as of 13 May 2003, though data is subject to change. On 26 Mar 2003 a Pentagon news release mentioned that more than 250,000 US personnel were involved in Operation Iraqi Freedom. [10]Pending.

# Treaties Regarding Weapons of Mass Destruction

Following the explosion of the first atomic bombs in 1945 during World War II, critics were less concerned about the economic and military inefficacies of an arms buildup than about the danger that nuclear weapons threatened the continued existence of civilization itself. During the Cold War the world's two superpowers, the US and the Soviet Union, each developed large arsenals of nuclear weapons. The possibility of both nations' mutual destruction in an intercontinental exchange of nuclear-armed missiles prompted them to undertake increasingly serious efforts to limit first the testing, then the deployment, and finally the possession of these weapons. Often their negotiations were facilitated by the UN. The US and the Soviet Union sponsored several international agreements of a limited-risk character. The first agreement was the Nuclear Test-Ban Treaty (1963), which banned tests of nuclear weapons in the atmosphere, in outer space, and underwater, thus effectively confining nuclear explosions to underground sites. With the Treaty on the Non-proliferation of Nuclear Weapons (1968), the two superpowers agreed not to promote the spread of nuclear weapons to countries that did not already possess them. Per other treaties, nuclear weapons could not be orbited around the Earth (the Outer Space Treaty of 1967) or placed on the seabed (the Seabed Treaty of 1971).

Substantial advances in limiting the nuclear arms race in the 1970s came out of the Strategic Arms Limitation Talks (SALT), which were intended to restrain the continuing buildup in nuclear-armed intercontinental (long-range or strategic) ballistic missiles (ICBMs). Part of SALT, the Anti-Ballistic Missile Treaty (1972), severely limited each nation's future deployment of antiballistic missiles, which could be used to destroy incoming ICBMs; the agreement thus kept both sides subject to the deterrent effect of the other's strategic offensive forces. The SALT II agreement of 1979 set limits on each side's store of multiple independent reentry vehicles (MIRVs), which are strategic missiles equipped with multiple nuclear warheads capable of hitting different targets on the ground.

Arms-control efforts between the two superpowers were facilitated in 1985 by the more liberal Soviet regime under Mikhail Gorbachev and bore their first fruits in the Intermediate-Range Nuclear Forces Treaty (1987), in which the US and the Soviet Union agreed to eliminate their stocks of intermediate- and medium-range land-based missiles. Also in the 1980s, the nations decided to reduce rather than merely limit their arsenals of nuclear warheads and launch platforms (missiles and bombers), during the Strategic Arms Reduction Treaty (START), signed in 1991.

Following the breakup of the Soviet Union in late 1991, a followup agreement, START II (1993), further reduced each nation's strategic nuclear forces. Both START II and the Comprehensive Test Ban Treaty (1996) were ratified by Russia in 2000. The following year, however, the US announced its intention to withdraw from the 1972 Anti-Ballistic Missile Treaty because it presented an obstacle to its proposed National Missile Defense.

There have also been attempts to eliminate other weapons of mass destruction. In 1971 the UN General Assembly approved a convention (in effect in 1975) prohibiting the manufacture, stockpiling, and use of biological weapons, although many states have never acceded to it. In 1993 the Chemical Weapons Convention, prohibiting the development, production, stockpiling, and use of chemical weapons and providing for their destruction, was opened for signature.

## Leading Department of Defense Contractors

*Top 100 Department of Defense contractors listed according to net value of prime contract awards, fiscal year 2002. Source: <www.defenselink.mil.pubs>.*

| RANK | CONTRACTOR | AMOUNT, IN '000 (US$) | RANK | CONTRACTOR | AMOUNT, IN '000 (US$) |
|---|---|---|---|---|---|
| 1 | Lockheed Martin | 16,997,272 | 32 | Veritas Capital Management | 521,866 |
| 2 | Boeing | 16,551,756 | 33 | Washington Group International | 505,916 |
| 3 | Northrop Grumman | 8,732,668 | 34 | Dell Computer | 504,969 |
| 4 | Raytheon | 6,995,085 | 35 | Titan | 501,630 |
| 5 | General Dynamics | 6,962,131 | 36 | Jacobs Engineering Group | 486,024 |
| 6 | United Technologies | 3,607,184 | 37 | Halliburton | 483,670 |
| 7 | Science Applications International | 2,074,920 | 38 | Mitre | 474,294 |
|  |  |  | 39 | Aerospace | 473,061 |
| 8 | TRW | 2,026,546 | 40 | Electronic Data Systems | 468,395 |
| 9 | Health Net | 1,691,430 | 41 | Stewart & Stevenson Services | 439,939 |
| 10 | L-3 Communications Holding | 1,660,048 | 42 | Johnson Controls | 434,210 |
| 11 | General Electric | 1,559,979 | 43 | Longbow | 411,099 |
| 12 | United Defense Industries | 1,514,163 | 44 | WorldCom | 403,530 |
| 13 | Dyncorp | 1,359,408 | 45 | Javelin Joint Venture | 401,438 |
| 14 | Humana | 1,304,691 | 46 | Government of Canada | 394,578 |
| 15 | Honeywell International | 1,278,371 | 47 | FedEx | 385,781 |
| 16 | B A E Systems | 1,115,608 | 48 | Harris | 381,477 |
| 17 | Bechtel Group | 1,029,712 | 49 | IBM | 379,892 |
| 18 | I T T Industries | 994,167 | 50 | Johns Hopkins University | 370,571 |
| 19 | Textron | 908,785 | 51 | Rockwell Collins | 362,797 |
| 20 | Triwest Healthcare Alliance | 823,741 | 52 | Massachusetts Institute of Technology | 357,378 |
| 21 | Computer Sciences | 807,671 |  |  |  |
| 22 | URS | 800,825 | 53 | Goodrich | 355,278 |
| 23 | Booz Allen & Hamilton | 687,553 | 54 | Veridian | 354,593 |
| 24 | GM GDLS Defense Group | 678,307 | 55 | Sierra Health Services | 353,891 |
| 25 | Alliant Techsystems | 674,013 | 56 | The Renco Group | 337,913 |
| 26 | Boeing Sikorsky Comanche Team | 661,832 | 57 | Anteon International | 335,534 |
| 27 | Cardinal Health | 649,582 | 58 | Amerisourcebergen | 333,506 |
| 28 | North American Airlines | 622,199 | 59 | A T & T | 328,223 |
| 29 | Oshkosh Truck | 601,664 | 60 | Engineered Support Systems | 322,616 |
| 30 | Exxon Mobil | 570,877 |  |  |  |
| 31 | N.V. Koninklijke Nederlandsche | 539,104 | 61 | GTSI | 317,392 |
|  |  |  | 62 | Battelle Memorial Institute | 311,679 |

## Leading Department of Defense Contractors (continued)

| RANK | CONTRACTOR | AMOUNT, IN '000 (US$) | RANK | CONTRACTOR | AMOUNT, IN '000 (US$) |
|---|---|---|---|---|---|
| 63 | CACI International | 310,689 | 82 | Mantech International | 210,179 |
| 64 | US Department of Energy | 298,995 | 83 | Wallenius Holdings | 204,319 |
| 65 | Chugach Alaska | 293,965 | 84 | United Industrial Corp. | 199,946 |
| 66 | Arinc | 285,739 | 85 | Cubic Corp. | 197,481 |
| 67 | Motorola | 283,827 | 86 | Caltex Tradign and | 196,499 |
| 68 | British Petroleum | 269,898 | | Transport | |
| 69 | Rolls-Royce | 265,413 | 87 | Leo Burnett USA | 194,654 |
| 70 | Hensel Phelps Construction | 262,919 | 88 | Philipp Holzmann AG | 189,983 |
| 71 | AMEC | 259,795 | 89 | A P Moller Gruppen | 188,079 |
| 72 | Federal Prison Industries | 255,757 | 90 | The Shaw Group | 177,867 |
| 73 | Valero Energy | 255,166 | 91 | National Oil Distribution | 177,457 |
| 74 | CH2M Hill Companies | 242,719 | 92 | Parker Hannifin | 175,083 |
| 75 | The Parsons Corporation | 235,388 | 93 | NCED | 171,495 |
| 76 | General Atomic Technologies | 229,774 | 94 | Charles Stark Draper Laboratories | 162,183 |
| 77 | Sumitomo Heavy Industries | 227,096 | 95 | Pepco Holdings | 160,432 |
| | | | 96 | Great Lakes Dredge and Dock | 159,770 |
| 78 | TYCO International | 221,201 | 97 | Bahrain Petroleum | 158,259 |
| 79 | Proctor & Gamble | 219,349 | 98 | Day & Zimmermann Group | 157,490 |
| 80 | Kuwait Petroleum | 218,840 | 99 | Bearingpoint | 156,024 |
| 81 | Foster Wheeler | 216,244 | 100 | LG-Caltex Oil | 155,889 |

# The Central Intelligence Agency (CIA)

The CIA is the principal intelligence and counterintelligence agency of the US government. Formally created in 1947, the agency grew out of the World War II Office of Strategic Services (OSS). Previous US intelligence and counterintelligence efforts had been conducted by the Army and Navy and by the Federal Bureau of Investigation (FBI) and suffered from duplication, competition, and lack of coordination. US allies had criticized the lack of any central intelligence function.

In June 1942 Pres. Franklin D. Roosevelt created the OSS so that the fragmented and uncoordinated strands of US intelligence-gathering would be brought together under a single organization. William J. ("Wild Bill") Donovan became head of the OSS upon its founding and was largely responsible for building that organization. During World War II the OSS was responsible for collecting and analyzing foreign intelligence concerning areas where US military forces operated. The OSS obtained intelligence through secret agents in enemy territory, it carried out counterpropaganda and disinformation activities, and it staged special operations behind enemy lines involving sabotage, demolition, and the supplying and direction of resistance fighters. Under Donovan's direction, the OSS was remarkably effective despite the initial inexperience of most of its personnel.

The OSS was dismantled in October 1945, but the administration of Pres. Harry S. Truman recognized the need for a coordinated postwar intelligence establishment. In 1946 the president established by executive order a Central Intelligence Group and a National Intelligence Authority. These bodies selected key personnel from the group assembled under wartime pressures by the OSS and tried to impose some central direction on postwar intelligence operations, although the armed forces maintained their own independent intelligence services.

In 1947 Congress created the National Security Council (NSC) and, under its direction, the Central Intelligence Agency, which was to advise the NSC on intelligence matters bearing on national security, make recommendations on coordinating intelligence activities of government agencies generally, correlate and evaluate intelligence and see to its proper communication within government, and carry out such other national-security intelligence functions as the NSC might direct.

The CIA is organized into four major groups. The Directorate of Intelligence analyzes intelligence that is gathered overtly from available sources and that which is obtained covertly through espionage, aerial and satellite photography, and interception of radio, telephone, and other forms of communication. Its analyses are distributed variously as bulletins, reports, and exhaustive surveys. It also monitors foreign radio broadcasts. The Directorate of Operations is responsible for covert operations, including clandestine collection of intelligence (i.e., espionage) and special covert activities. The Directorate of Science and Technology is charged with keeping the agency abreast of scientific and technological advances, and it develops technical devices useful to the agency and supplies technical and scientific support to agency operations. The Mission Support Offices not only administers but also contains the Office of Security, which is responsible for the security of personnel, facilities, information, and information sources such as defectors from other governments.

Clandestine activities are carried on under various guises—including the diplomatic cloak used by virtually every intelligence service, as well as fronts such as corporations that the CIA creates or acquires. The agency also "debriefs" business travelers, journalists willing to be so interviewed, and others returning to the US from a sensitive or professionally interesting place.

Among the CIA's major covert operations were the expulsion of Mohammad Mosaddeq as premier and the restoration of the shah of Iran in 1953, and the following year the toppling of an unfriendly leftist government in Guatemala. The attempted Bay of Pigs invasion of Cuba (1961) by CIA-supported Cuban dissidents was a fiasco. In 1973 and 1974 the agency was damaged by the revelation that former CIA operatives had repeatedly played illegal roles in the Watergate affair.

The CIA has come under intense scrutiny in the wake of the the attacks of 11 Sep 2001, and efforts to improve the coordination and sharing of intelligence, particularly with the FBI, have been undertaken.

## CIA Directors

The National Security Act of 26 Jul 1947 established the CIA on 18 Sep 1947. By authority of a presidential directive of 22 Jan 1946, the director of central intelligence serves as a member of the National Intelligence Authority and as head of the Central Intelligence Group. The director coordinates the nation's intelligence activities and informs the president on issues of national security.

| NAME | DATES OF SERVICE | NAME | DATES OF SERVICE |
|---|---|---|---|
| Rear Adm. Sidney W. Souers, USNR | 23 Jan 1946–10 Jun 1946 | Richard M. Helms | 30 Jun 1966–2 Feb 1973 |
| Lt. Gen. Hoyt S. Vandenberg, USA | 10 Jun 1946–1 May 1947 | James R. Schlesinger | 2 Feb 1973–2 Jul 1973 |
| | | William E. Colby | 4 Sep 1973–30 Jan 1976 |
| Rear Adm. Roscoe H. Hillenkoetter, USN | 1 May 1947–7 Oct 1950 | George H.W. Bush | 30 Jan 1976–20 Jan 1977 |
| Gen. Walter Bedell Smith, USA | 7 Oct 1950–9 Feb 1953 | Adm. Stansfield Turner, USN (Ret) | 9 Mar 1977–20 Jan 1981 |
| Allen W. Dulles | 26 Feb 1953–29 Nov 1961 | William J. Casey | 28 Jan 1981–29 Jan 1987 |
| John A. McCone | 29 Nov 1961–28 Apr 1965 | William H. Webster | 26 May 1987–31 Aug 1991 |
| Vice Adm. William F. Raborn, Jr., USN (Ret) | 28 Apr 1965–30 Jun 1966 | Robert M. Gates | 6 Nov 1991–20 Jan 1993 |
| | | R. James Woolsey | 5 Feb 1993–10 Jan 1995 |
| | | John M. Deutch | 10 May 1995–15 Dec 1996 |
| | | George J. Tenet | 11 Jul 1997– |

## The National Security Council (NSC)

The National Security Act of 1947 established the NSC to advise the president on policies relating to national security. In addition to regular attendees, the chief of staff to the president, counsel to the president, and assistant to the president for economic policy are invited to attend all meetings. The attorney general and the director of the office of management and budget are also invited to attend when needed.

| | |
|---|---|
| **chair** | George W. Bush (president) |
| **regular attendees** | Richard B. Cheney (vice president) |
| | Colin L. Powell (secretary of state) |
| | John Snow (secretary of the treasury) |
| | Donald H. Rumsfeld (secretary of defense) |
| | Condoleezza Rice (assistant to the president for national security affairs) |
| **military advisor** | Richard B. Myers (chairman of the joint chiefs of staff) |
| **intelligence advisor** | George J. Tenet (director of the CIA) |
| **additional participants** | Andrew H. Card, Jr. (chief of staff) |
| | John B. Bellinger, III (counsel to the president) |
| | Stephen E. Friedman (assistant to the president for economic policy) |
| | John Ashcroft (attorney general) |
| | Joshua B. Bolten (director of the Office of Management and Budget) |

On 23 Mar 1953 Pres. Dwight D. Eisenhower established the office of assistant to the president for national security affairs (commonly referred to as the national security advisor). Holders of this office are listed below.

| NAME | DATES OF SERVICE | NAME | DATES OF SERVICE |
|---|---|---|---|
| Robert Cutler | 23 Mar 1953–2 Apr 1955 | William P. Clark | 4 Jan 1982–17 Oct 1983 |
| Dillon Anderson | 2 Apr 1955–1 Sep 1956 | Robert C. McFarlane | 17 Oct 1983–4 Dec 1985 |
| Robert Cutler | 7 Jan 1957–24 Jun 1958 | John M. Poindexter | 4 Dec 1985– 25 Nov 1986 |
| Gordon Gray | 24 Jun 1958–13 Jan 1961 | Frank C. Carlucci | 2 Dec 1986–23 Nov 1987 |
| McGeorge Bundy | 20 Jan 1961–28 Feb 1966 | Colin L. Powell | 23 Nov 1987–20 Jan 1989 |
| Walt W. Rostow | 1 Apr 1966–2 Dec 1968 | Brent Scowcroft | 20 Jan 1989–20 Jan 1993 |
| Henry A. Kissinger | 2 Dec 1968–3 Nov 1975[1] | W. Anthony Lake | 20 Jan 1993–14 Mar 1997 |
| Brent Scowcroft | 3 Nov 1975–20 Jan 1977 | Samuel R. Berger | 14 Mar 1997–20 Jan 2001 |
| Zbigniew Brzezinski | 20 Jan 1977–21 Jan 1981 | Condoleezza Rice | 20 Jan 2001– |
| Richard V. Allen | 21 Jan 1981–4 Jan 1982 | | |

[1]Henry A. Kissinger served concurrently as secretary of state from 21 Sep 1973.

# United States Population

## The Census, History and Gathering

A census enumerates people, houses, firms, or other important items in a country or region at a particular time. Used alone, the term usually refers to a population census and considers population size and density, distribution, and vital statistics. National population censuses, being expensive, are taken only at infrequent intervals: every 10 years in many countries, every 5 years or at irregular intervals in other countries. Specialists such as demographers interpret the statistical results, which are useful to policymakers and businessmen.

Census, a Latin word, was first used by the ancient Romans to describe the counting of the citizenry in order to value their estates for the purpose of taxation. The Domesday Book was an inquest of England in 1086 that was made to acquaint William the Conqueror with the landholders and holdings of his new domain. In 1449, under the threat of siege, the German city of Nürnberg made an almost complete count of its people.

Strictly speaking, though, the modern population census as a complete enumeration of all the people and their characteristics began to evolve only in the 17th century. The United States was the first modern nation to adopt a legal provision for taking a census at regular intervals, which it began in 1790 to establish a basis for representation in Congress. Censuses were taken in England, France, and Canada in 1801, 1836, and 1871, respectively. China was the last major country to report a census, in 1953.

Over time, improvements were made in the administration of census taking and in the compilation of its data. Census information is obtained by using a fixed questionnaire covering such topics as place of residence, sex, age, marital status, occupation, citizenship, language, ethnicity, religious affiliation, and education. From the responses demographers derive data on population distribution, household and family composition, internal migration, labor–force participation, and other topics.

A "de jure" census tallies people according to their regular or legal residence, whereas a "de facto" census allocates them to the place where enumerated—normally where they spend the night of the day enumerated. By either method, the reported territorial distribution is according to where people sleep (nighttime population) rather than where they work (daytime population).

## Census 2000—Interpreting the Numbers

The undertaking of a national census every 10 years was mandated in the Constitution of 1787. Since the first census in 1790, each census counts the population of the states, and that population total determines each state's congressional representation. In general, the results of Census 2000 showed states in the Northeast and Midwest losing representatives to states in the West and South.

Twelve seats in the 435-member House of Representatives shifted with the changes in population. Arizona, Florida, Georgia, and Texas each gained two representatives, while California, Colorado, Nevada, and North Carolina each gained one. New York and Pennsylvania each lost two representatives. Connecticut, Illinois, Indiana, Michigan, Mississippi, Ohio, Oklahoma, and Wisconsin all lost one congressional seat.

## The Changing Face of America

The population of the United States increased by 32.7 million people between the censuses of 1990 and 2000. That increase represented the largest population growth in census history. Census 2000 revealed a nation with more ethnic and racial diversity. During the 1990s the Hispanic population (Hispanics may be of any race) increased by 58%, the Asian population by 48%. The immigration of these and other groups accounted for about 13.3 million of the country's total population—a number not equaled in United States history. The second largest number of immigrants recorded—10.1 million people—occurred between 1905 and 1914. Of the 281.4 million people residing in the United States on census day, non-Hispanic whites accounted for 69.1% of the population; Hispanics, 12.5%; blacks, 12.3%; and Asians, 3.6%.

The changing face of the United States was reflected in cities, suburbs, and rural areas. For the first time, nearly half of the nation's 100 largest cities were home to more African Americans, Hispanics, Asians, and other minorities than to non-Hispanic whites. While the population of the country's fastest-growing cities, such as Las Vegas and Phoenix, increased in all racial and ethnic categories, the vast majority of cities—71 of the top 100—lost non-Hispanic white residents to the suburbs and beyond. The nation's largest cities gained 3.8 million Hispanic residents, a 43% increase from a decade ago. Many cities, including Boston, Los Angeles, and Dallas, would have lost population in the 1990s were it not for large gains in the number of Hispanics.

Even with the arrival of a record number of immigrants (who tend to be relatively young), the United States continued to age as a nation. The median age of the country's population in 2000 was 35.3—five years older than the median age in 1950. (The median age splits the population in half, 50% are over the median age, 50% under it.) This increase in median age was tied to the graying of the post-World War II "Baby Boom" generation. Born from 1946 through 1964, Baby Boomers between 36 and 54 years of age represented 28% of the country's total population. The median age for non-Hispanic whites was 38.6, for Asians 32.7, blacks 30.2, and Hispanics 25.8. Census 2000 revealed that the country's population was 50.9% female and 49.1% male. There were 37.1 million males under the age of 18 as compared to 35.2 million females. By the age of 36, however, there were more females than males. Female senior citizens 65 years and older outnumbered males 20.6 million to 14.4 million.

Although they were not totally comprised of Baby Boomers and their parents, the Northeast and Midwest regions had the country's oldest populations. Median ages for those regions were 36.8 and 35.6, respectively. Interestingly, the Northeast was the only region in the country where all of its states had median ages above the national level. In contrast, the West had the population with the youngest median age, 33.8.

## Total US Population and Area, 1790–2000

*The total land/water area numbers from 1790 to 1970 were recalculated for the 1980 census. Information for Alaska and Hawaii is included in all censuses after 1940. The entry N/A means not applicable. Source: US Census Bureau.*

| CENSUS | POPULATION | POPULATION GROWTH (%) | TOTAL LAND/WATER AREA (SQ MI) | LAND AREA (SQ MI) | PEOPLE/ SQ MI OF LAND AREA |
|---|---|---|---|---|---|
| 1790 | 3,929,214 | N/A | 891,364 | 864,746 | 4.5 |
| 1800 | 5,308,483 | 35.1 | 891,364 | 864,746 | 6.1 |
| 1810 | 7,239,881 | 36.4 | 1,722,685 | 1,681,828 | 4.3 |
| 1820 | 9,638,453 | 33.1 | 1,792,552 | 1,749,462 | 5.5 |
| 1830 | 12,866,020 | 33.5 | 1,792,552 | 1,749,462 | 7.4 |
| 1840 | 17,069,453 | 32.7 | 1,792,552 | 1,749,462 | 9.8 |
| 1850 | 23,191,876 | 35.9 | 2,991,655 | 2,940,042 | 7.9 |
| 1860 | 31,443,321 | 35.6 | 3,021,295 | 2,969,640 | 10.6 |
| 1870 | 39,818,449 | 26.6 | 3,021,295 | 2,969,640 | 13.4 |
| 1880 | 50,155,783 | 26.0 | 3,021,295 | 2,969,640 | 16.9 |
| 1890 | 62,947,714 | 25.5 | 3,021,295 | 2,969,640 | 21.2 |
| 1900 | 75,994,575 | 20.7 | 3,021,295 | 2,969,834 | 25.6 |
| 1910 | 91,972,266 | 21.0 | 3,021,295 | 2,969,565 | 31.0 |
| 1920 | 105,710,620 | 14.9 | 3,021,295 | 2,969,451 | 35.6 |
| 1930 | 122,775,046 | 16.1 | 3,021,295 | 2,977,128 | 41.2 |
| 1940 | 131,669,275 | 7.2 | 3,021,295 | 2,977,128 | 44.2 |
| 1950 | 151,325,798 | 14.5 | 3,618,770 | 3,552,206 | 42.6 |
| 1960 | 179,323,175 | 18.5 | 3,618,770 | 3,540,911 | 50.6 |
| 1970 | 203,302,031 | 13.4 | 3,618,770 | 3,540,023 | 57.4 |
| 1980 | 226,542,199 | 11.4 | 3,618,770 | 3,539,289 | 64.0 |
| 1990 | 248,718,302 | 9.8 | 3,717,796 | 3,536,278 | 70.3 |
| 2000 | 281,422,426 | 13.1 | 3,794,083 | 3,537,438 | 79.6 |

## US Population by Race, Sex, Median Age, and Residence

*Numbers are in thousands ('000) except for the median age figures and the residency percentages. N/A means not available. Source: US Census Bureau.*

| YEAR | WHITE | RACE[1] BLACK | OTHER | MALE | SEX FEMALE | MEDIAN AGE | RESIDENCE[2] URBAN (%) | RURAL (%) |
|---|---|---|---|---|---|---|---|---|
| 1790 | 3,172 | 757 | N/A | N/A | N/A | N/A | 5.1 | 94.9 |
| 1800 | 4,306 | 1,002 | N/A | N/A | N/A | N/A | 6.1 | 93.9 |
| 1810 | 5,862 | 1,378 | N/A | N/A | N/A | N/A | 7.3 | 92.7 |
| 1820 | 7,867 | 1,772 | N/A | 4,897 | 4,742 | 16.7 | 7.2 | 92.8 |
| 1830 | 10,537 | 2,329 | N/A | 6,532 | 6,334 | 17.2 | 8.8 | 91.2 |
| 1840 | 14,196 | 2,874 | N/A | 8,689 | 8,381 | 17.8 | 10.8 | 89.2 |
| 1850 | 19,553 | 3,639 | N/A | 11,838 | 11,354 | 18.9 | 15.4 | 84.6 |
| 1860 | 26,923 | 4,442 | 79 | 16,085 | 15,358 | 19.4 | 19.8 | 80.2 |
| 1870 | 34,337 | 5,392 | 89 | 19,494 | 19,065 | 20.2 | 25.7 | 74.3 |
| 1880 | 43,403 | 6,581 | 172 | 25,519 | 24,637 | 20.9 | 28.2 | 71.8 |
| 1890 | 55,101 | 7,489 | 358 | 32,237 | 30,711 | 22.0 | 35.1 | 64.9 |
| 1900 | 66,809 | 8,834 | 351 | 38,816 | 37,178 | 22.9 | 39.6 | 60.4 |
| 1910 | 81,732 | 9,828 | 413 | 47,332 | 44,640 | 24.1 | 45.6 | 54.4 |
| 1920 | 94,821 | 10,463 | 427 | 53,900 | 51,810 | 25.3 | 51.2 | 48.8 |
| 1930 | 110,287 | 11,891 | 597 | 62,137 | 60,638 | 26.4 | 56.1 | 43.9 |
| 1940 | 118,215 | 12,866 | 589 | 66,062 | 65,608 | 29.0 | 56.5 | 43.5 |
| 1950 | 134,942 | 15,042 | 713 | 74,833 | 75,864 | 30.2 | 64.0 | 36.0 |
| 1960 | 158,832 | 18,872 | 1,620 | 88,331 | 90,992 | 29.5 | 69.9 | 30.1 |
| 1970 | 178,098 | 22,581 | 2,557 | 98,926 | 104,309 | 28.0 | 73.6 | 26.3 |
| 1980 | 194,713 | 26,683 | 5,150 | 110,053 | 116,493 | 30.0 | 73.7 | 26.3 |
| 1990 | 199,686 | 29,986 | 9,233 | 121,271 | 127,494 | 32.8 | 75.2 | 24.8 |
| 2000 | 211,461 | 34,658 | 13,118 | 138,054 | 143,368 | 35.3 | N/A | N/A |

[1]The population in the column heading "other" consists of Asians, Pacific Islanders, American Indians, and Alaska Natives. Alaska and Hawaii are excluded from the population numbers until 1960, the first census after they became states in 1959.  [2]The census definitions for urban and rural areas have changed through the decades.

# State Populations, 1790–2000

*Resident population of the states and the District of Columbia. Numbers are in thousands ('000).*
*Source: US Census Bureau.*

| STATE | 1790 | 1800 | 1810 | 1820 | 1830 | 1840 | 1850 | 1860 | 1870 | 1880 | 1890 |
|---|---|---|---|---|---|---|---|---|---|---|---|
| Alabama | | 1 | 9 | 128 | 310 | 591 | 772 | 964 | 997 | 1,263 | 1,513 |
| Alaska | | | | | | | | | | 33 | 32 |
| Arizona | | | | | | | | | 10 | 40 | 88 |
| Arkansas | | | 1 | 14 | 30 | 98 | 210 | 435 | 484 | 803 | 1,128 |
| California | | | | | | | 93 | 380 | 560 | 865 | 1,213 |
| Colorado | | | | | | | | 34 | 40 | 194 | 413 |
| Connecticut | 238 | 251 | 262 | 275 | 298 | 310 | 371 | 460 | 537 | 623 | 746 |
| Delaware | 59 | 64 | 73 | 73 | 77 | 78 | 92 | 112 | 125 | 147 | 168 |
| Dist. of Columbia | | 8 | 15 | 23 | 30 | 34 | 52 | 75 | 132 | 178 | 230 |
| Florida | | | | | 35 | 54 | 87 | 140 | 188 | 269 | 391 |
| Georgia | 83 | 163 | 252 | 341 | 517 | 691 | 906 | 1,057 | 1,184 | 1,542 | 1,837 |
| Hawaii | | | | | | | | | | | |
| Idaho | | | | | | | | | 15 | 33 | 89 |
| Illinois | | | 12 | 55 | 157 | 476 | 851 | 1,712 | 2,540 | 3,078 | 3,826 |
| Indiana | | 6 | 25 | 147 | 343 | 686 | 988 | 1,350 | 1,681 | 1,978 | 2,192 |
| Iowa | | | | | | 43 | 192 | 675 | 1,194 | 1,625 | 1,912 |
| Kansas | | | | | | | | 107 | 364 | 996 | 1,428 |
| Kentucky | 74 | 221 | 407 | 564 | 688 | 780 | 982 | 1,156 | 1,321 | 1,649 | 1,859 |
| Louisiana | | | 77 | 153 | 216 | 352 | 518 | 708 | 727 | 940 | 1,119 |
| Maine | 97 | 152 | 229 | 298 | 399 | 502 | 583 | 628 | 627 | 649 | 661 |
| Maryland | 320 | 342 | 381 | 407 | 447 | 470 | 583 | 687 | 781 | 935 | 1,042 |
| Massachusetts | 379 | 423 | 472 | 523 | 610 | 738 | 995 | 1,231 | 1,457 | 1,783 | 2,239 |
| Michigan | | | 5 | 9 | 32 | 212 | 398 | 749 | 1,184 | 1,637 | 2,094 |
| Minnesota | | | | | | | 6 | 172 | 440 | 781 | 1,310 |
| Mississippi | | 8 | 31 | 75 | 137 | 376 | 607 | 791 | 828 | 1,132 | 1,290 |
| Missouri | | | 20 | 67 | 140 | 384 | 682 | 1,182 | 1,721 | 2,168 | 2,679 |
| Montana | | | | | | | | | 21 | 39 | 143 |
| Nebraska | | | | | | | | 29 | 123 | 452 | 1,063 |
| Nevada | | | | | | | | 7 | 42 | 62 | 47 |
| New Hampshire | 142 | 184 | 214 | 244 | 269 | 285 | 318 | 326 | 318 | 347 | 377 |
| New Jersey | 184 | 211 | 246 | 278 | 321 | 373 | 490 | 672 | 906 | 1,131 | 1,445 |
| New Mexico | | | | | | | 62 | 94 | 92 | 120 | 160 |
| New York | 340 | 589 | 959 | 1,373 | 1,919 | 2,429 | 3,097 | 3,881 | 4,383 | 5,083 | 6,003 |
| North Carolina | 394 | 478 | 556 | 639 | 738 | 753 | 869 | 993 | 1,071 | 1,400 | 1,618 |
| North Dakota | | | | | | | | | 5 | 2 | 37 | 191 |
| Ohio | | 45 | 231 | 581 | 938 | 1,519 | 1,980 | 2,340 | 2,665 | 3,198 | 3,672 |
| Oklahoma | | | | | | | | | | | 259 |
| Oregon | | | | | | | 12 | 52 | 91 | 175 | 318 |
| Pennsylvania | 434 | 602 | 810 | 1,049 | 1,348 | 1,724 | 2,312 | 2,906 | 3,522 | 4,283 | 5,258 |
| Rhode Island | 69 | 69 | 77 | 83 | 97 | 109 | 148 | 175 | 217 | 277 | 346 |
| South Carolina | 249 | 346 | 415 | 503 | 581 | 594 | 669 | 704 | 706 | 996 | 1,151 |
| South Dakota | | | | | | | | | 12 | 98 | 349 |
| Tennessee | 36 | 106 | 262 | 423 | 682 | 829 | 1,003 | 1,110 | 1,259 | 1,542 | 1,768 |
| Texas | | | | | | | 213 | 604 | 819 | 1,592 | 2,236 |
| Utah | | | | | | | 11 | 40 | 87 | 144 | 211 |
| Vermont | 85 | 154 | 218 | 236 | 281 | 292 | 314 | 315 | 331 | 332 | 332 |
| Virginia | 692 | 808 | 878 | 938 | 1,044 | 1,025 | 1,119 | 1,220 | 1,225 | 1,513 | 1,656 |
| Washington | | | | | | | 1 | 12 | 24 | 75 | 357 |
| West Virginia | 56 | 79 | 105 | 137 | 177 | 225 | 302 | 377 | 442 | 618 | 763 |
| Wisconsin | | | | | | 31 | 305 | 776 | 1,055 | 1,315 | 1,693 |
| Wyoming | | | | | | | | | 9 | 21 | 63 |
| US total[1] | 3,929 | 5,308 | 7,240 | 9,638 | 12,866 | 17,069 | 23,192 | 31,443 | 39,818[2] | 50,156 | 62,948 |

[1]*Alaska and Hawaii are not included in the US total until 1960, the year after both achieved statehood.*

## State Populations, 1790–2000 (continued)

| 1900 | 1910 | 1920 | 1930 | 1940 | 1950 | 1960 | 1970 | 1980 | 1990 | 2000 |
|---|---|---|---|---|---|---|---|---|---|---|
| 1,829 | 2,138 | 2,348 | 2,646 | 2,833 | 3,062 | 3,267 | 3,444 | 3,894 | 4,040 | 4,447 |
| 64 | 64 | 55 | 59 | 73 | 129 | 226 | 300 | 402 | 550 | 627 |
| 123 | 204 | 334 | 436 | 499 | 750 | 1,302 | 1,771 | 2,718 | 3,665 | 5,131 |
| 1,312 | 1,574 | 1,752 | 1,854 | 1,949 | 1,910 | 1,786 | 1,923 | 2,286 | 2,351 | 2,673 |
| 1,485 | 2,378 | 3,427 | 5,677 | 6,907 | 10,586 | 15,717 | 19,953 | 23,668 | 29,811 | 33,872 |
| 540 | 799 | 940 | 1,036 | 1,123 | 1,325 | 1,754 | 2,207 | 2,890 | 3,294 | 4,301 |
| 908 | 1,115 | 1,381 | 1,607 | 1,709 | 2,007 | 2,535 | 3,032 | 3,108 | 3,287 | 3,406 |
| 185 | 202 | 223 | 238 | 267 | 318 | 446 | 548 | 594 | 666 | 784 |
| 279 | 331 | 438 | 487 | 663 | 802 | 764 | 757 | 638 | 607 | 572 |
| 529 | 753 | 968 | 1,468 | 1,897 | 2,771 | 4,952 | 6,789 | 9,746 | 12,938 | 15,982 |
| 2,216 | 2,609 | 2,896 | 2,909 | 3,124 | 3,445 | 3,943 | 4,590 | 5,463 | 6,478 | 8,186 |
| 154 | 192 | 256 | 368 | 423 | 500 | 633 | 769 | 965 | 1,108 | 1,212 |
| 162 | 326 | 432 | 445 | 525 | 589 | 667 | 713 | 944 | 1,007 | 1,294 |
| 4,822 | 5,639 | 6,485 | 7,631 | 7,897 | 8,712 | 10,081 | 11,114 | 11,427 | 11,431 | 12,419 |
| 2,516 | 2,701 | 2,930 | 3,239 | 3,428 | 3,934 | 4,662 | 5,194 | 5,490 | 5,544 | 6,080 |
| 2,232 | 2,225 | 2,404 | 2,471 | 2,538 | 2,621 | 2,758 | 2,824 | 2,914 | 2,777 | 2,926 |
| 1,470 | 1,691 | 1,769 | 1,881 | 1,801 | 1,905 | 2,179 | 2,247 | 2,364 | 2,478 | 2,688 |
| 2,147 | 2,290 | 2,417 | 2,615 | 2,846 | 2,945 | 3,038 | 3,219 | 3,661 | 3,687 | 4,042 |
| 1,382 | 1,656 | 1,799 | 2,102 | 2,364 | 2,684 | 3,257 | 3,641 | 4,206 | 4,222 | 4,469 |
| 694 | 742 | 768 | 797 | 847 | 914 | 969 | 992 | 1,125 | 1,228 | 1,275 |
| 1,188 | 1,295 | 1,450 | 1,632 | 1,821 | 2,343 | 3,101 | 3,922 | 4,217 | 4,781 | 5,296 |
| 2,805 | 3,366 | 3,852 | 4,250 | 4,317 | 4,691 | 5,149 | 5,689 | 5,737 | 6,016 | 6,349 |
| 2,421 | 2,810 | 3,668 | 4,842 | 5,256 | 6,372 | 7,823 | 8,875 | 9,262 | 9,295 | 9,938 |
| 1,751 | 2,076 | 2,387 | 2,564 | 2,792 | 2,982 | 3,414 | 3,805 | 4,076 | 4,376 | 4,919 |
| 1,551 | 1,797 | 1,791 | 2,010 | 2,184 | 2,179 | 2,178 | 2,217 | 2,521 | 2,575 | 2,845 |
| 3,107 | 3,293 | 3,404 | 3,629 | 3,785 | 3,955 | 4,320 | 4,677 | 4,917 | 5,117 | 5,595 |
| 243 | 376 | 549 | 538 | 559 | 591 | 675 | 694 | 787 | 799 | 902 |
| 1,066 | 1,192 | 1,296 | 1,378 | 1,316 | 1,326 | 1,411 | 1,483 | 1,570 | 1,578 | 1,711 |
| 42 | 82 | 77 | 91 | 110 | 160 | 285 | 489 | 800 | 1,202 | 1,998 |
| 412 | 431 | 443 | 465 | 492 | 533 | 607 | 738 | 921 | 1,109 | 1,236 |
| 1,884 | 2,537 | 3,156 | 4,041 | 4,160 | 4,835 | 6,067 | 7,168 | 7,365 | 7,748 | 8,414 |
| 195 | 327 | 360 | 423 | 532 | 681 | 951 | 1,016 | 1,303 | 1,515 | 1,819 |
| 7,269 | 9,114 | 10,385 | 12,588 | 13,479 | 14,830 | 16,782 | 18,237 | 17,558 | 17,991 | 18,976 |
| 1,894 | 2,206 | 2,559 | 3,170 | 3,572 | 4,062 | 4,556 | 5,082 | 5,882 | 6,632 | 8,049 |
| 319 | 577 | 647 | 681 | 642 | 620 | 632 | 618 | 653 | 639 | 642 |
| 4,158 | 4,767 | 5,759 | 6,647 | 6,908 | 7,947 | 9,706 | 10,652 | 10,798 | 10,847 | 11,353 |
| 790 | 1,657 | 2,028 | 2,396 | 2,336 | 2,233 | 2,328 | 2,559 | 3,025 | 3,146 | 3,451 |
| 414 | 673 | 783 | 954 | 1,090 | 1,521 | 1,769 | 2,091 | 2,633 | 2,842 | 3,421 |
| 6,302 | 7,665 | 8,720 | 9,631 | 9,900 | 10,498 | 11,319 | 11,794 | 11,864 | 11,883 | 12,281 |
| 429 | 543 | 604 | 687 | 713 | 792 | 859 | 947 | 947 | 1,003 | 1,048 |
| 1,340 | 1,515 | 1,684 | 1,739 | 1,900 | 2,117 | 2,383 | 2,591 | 3,122 | 3,486 | 4,012 |
| 402 | 584 | 637 | 693 | 643 | 653 | 681 | 666 | 691 | 696 | 755 |
| 2,021 | 2,185 | 2,338 | 2,617 | 2,916 | 3,292 | 3,567 | 3,924 | 4,591 | 4,877 | 5,689 |
| 3,049 | 3,897 | 4,663 | 5,825 | 6,415 | 7,711 | 9,580 | 11,197 | 14,229 | 16,986 | 20,852 |
| 277 | 373 | 449 | 508 | 550 | 689 | 891 | 1,059 | 1,461 | 1,723 | 2,233 |
| 344 | 356 | 352 | 360 | 359 | 378 | 390 | 444 | 511 | 563 | 609 |
| 1,854 | 2,062 | 2,309 | 2,422 | 2,678 | 3,319 | 3,967 | 4,648 | 5,347 | 6,189 | 7,079 |
| 518 | 1,142 | 1,357 | 1,563 | 1,736 | 2,379 | 2,853 | 3,409 | 4,132 | 4,867 | 5,894 |
| 959 | 1,221 | 1,464 | 1,729 | 1,902 | 2,006 | 1,860 | 1,744 | 1,950 | 1,793 | 1,808 |
| 2,069 | 2,334 | 2,632 | 2,939 | 3,138 | 3,435 | 3,952 | 4,418 | 4,706 | 4,892 | 5,364 |
| 93 | 146 | 194 | 226 | 251 | 291 | 330 | 332 | 470 | 454 | 494 |
| **75,995** | **91,972** | **105,711** | **122,775** | **131,669** | **150,697** | **179,323** | **203,302**[2] | **226,546**[2] | **248,791**[2] | **281,422** |

[2]Numbers were revised after the census.

## US Population by Race and Hispanic Origin

Census 2000 was the first US census in which individuals could report themselves as being of more than one race. For the comparison with the 1990 census results, this table uses the 2000 census information for the population indicating one race. Hispanic or Latino people may be of any race.

Source: US Census Bureau.

| RACE | 1990 CENSUS NUMBER | % | 2000 CENSUS NUMBER | % | % DIFFERENCE 1990/2000 |
|---|---|---|---|---|---|
| White | 199,686,070 | 80.3 | 211,460,626 | 75.1 | +5.9 |
| Black or African American | 29,986,060 | 12.1 | 34,658,190 | 12.3 | +15.6 |
| American Indian or Alaska Native | 1,959,234 | 0.8 | 2,475,956 | 0.9 | +26.4 |
| Asian | 6,908,638 | 2.8 | 10,242,998 | 3.6 | +48.3 |
| Native Hawaiian/other Pacific Islander | 365,024 | 0.1 | 398,835 | 0.1 | +9.3 |
| Some other race | 9,804,847 | 3.9 | 15,359,073 | 5.5 | +56.6 |
| Two or more races | N/A[1] | N/A | 6,826,228 | 2.4 | N/A |
| **Total population** | **248,709,873** | **100.0** | **281,421,906** | **100.0[2]** | **+13.2** |

| HISPANIC OR LATINO POPULATION | 1990 CENSUS NUMBER | % | 2000 CENSUS NUMBER | % | % DIFFERENCE 1990/2000 |
|---|---|---|---|---|---|
| Hispanic or Latino (of any race) | 22,354,059 | 9.0 | 35,305,818 | 12.5 | +57.9 |
| Not Hispanic or Latino | 226,355,814 | 91.0 | 246,116,088 | 87.5 | +8.7 |
| **Total population** | **248,709,873** | **100.0** | **281,421,906** | **100.0** | **+13.2** |

[1]N/A: not available.   [2]Totals may not equal 100% due to rounding.

## Foreign-Born Population in the US, 1850–2000

The foreign-born population consists of persons born outside the United States to parents who were not US citizens. Information from 1950 to 1990 was taken from sample data. Year 2000 information was an estimate derived before the decennial census was conducted. Populations of Alaska and Hawaii were included starting in 1960. In 1850 and 1860, information on nativity was not collected for slaves. The data in the table includes the slave population as part of the native-born population.

Source: US Census Bureau.

| YEAR | POPULATION TOTAL | FOREIGN-BORN | % OF TOTAL | YEAR | POPULATION TOTAL | FOREIGN-BORN | % OF TOTAL |
|---|---|---|---|---|---|---|---|
| 1850 | 23,191,876 | 2,244,602 | 9.7 | 1930 | 122,775,046 | 14,204,149 | 11.6 |
| 1860 | 31,443,321 | 4,138,697 | 13.2 | 1940 | 131,669,275 | 11,594,896 | 8.8 |
| 1870 | 38,558,371 | 5,567,229 | 14.4 | 1950 | 150,216,110 | 10,347,395 | 6.9 |
| 1880 | 50,155,783 | 6,679,943 | 13.3 | 1960 | 179,325,671 | 9,738,091 | 5.4 |
| 1890 | 62,622,250 | 9,249,547 | 14.8 | 1970 | 203,210,158 | 9,619,302 | 4.7 |
| 1900 | 75,994,575 | 10,341,276 | 13.6 | 1980 | 226,545,805 | 14,079,906 | 6.2 |
| 1910 | 91,972,266 | 13,515,886 | 14.7 | 1990 | 248,709,873 | 19,767,316 | 7.9 |
| 1920 | 105,710,620 | 13,920,692 | 13.2 | 2000 | 274,087,000 | 28,379,000 | 10.4 |

## Total Immigrants Admitted to the US, 1901–2000

*Numbers shown include only immigrant aliens admitted for permanent residence and are for fiscal years. Currently the fiscal year begins 1 October and ends 30 September. Prior to 1976, the fiscal year began 1 July and ended 30 June.*

| YEAR | NUMBER | YEAR | NUMBER | YEAR | NUMBER | YEAR | NUMBER |
|---|---|---|---|---|---|---|---|
| 1901 | 487,918 | 1911 | 878,587 | 1921 | 805,228 | 1931 | 97,139 |
| 1902 | 648,743 | 1912 | 838,172 | 1922 | 309,556 | 1932 | 35,576 |
| 1903 | 857,046 | 1913 | 1,197,892 | 1923 | 522,919 | 1933 | 23,068 |
| 1904 | 812,870 | 1914 | 1,218,480 | 1924 | 706,896 | 1934 | 29,470 |
| 1905 | 1,026,499 | 1915 | 326,700 | 1925 | 294,314 | 1935 | 34,956 |
| 1906 | 1,100,735 | 1916 | 298,826 | 1926 | 304,488 | 1936 | 36,329 |
| 1907 | 1,285,349 | 1917 | 295,403 | 1927 | 335,175 | 1937 | 50,244 |
| 1908 | 782,870 | 1918 | 110,618 | 1928 | 307,255 | 1938 | 67,895 |
| 1909 | 751,786 | 1919 | 141,132 | 1929 | 279,678 | 1939 | 82,998 |
| 1910 | 1,041,570 | 1920 | 430,001 | 1930 | 241,700 | 1940 | 70,756 |
| Totals 1901–10 | 8,795,386 | 1911–20 | 5,735,811 | 1921–30 | 4,107,209 | 1931–40 | 528,431 |

## Total Immigrants Admitted to the US, 1901–2000 (continued)

| YEAR | NUMBER | YEAR | NUMBER | YEAR | NUMBER | YEAR | NUMBER |
|---|---|---|---|---|---|---|---|
| 1941 | 51,776 | 1951 | 205,717 | 1961 | 271,344 | 1971 | 370,478 |
| 1942 | 28,781 | 1952 | 265,520 | 1962 | 283,763 | 1972 | 384,685 |
| 1943 | 23,725 | 1953 | 170,434 | 1963 | 306,260 | 1973 | 400,063 |
| 1944 | 28,551 | 1954 | 208,177 | 1964 | 292,248 | 1974 | 394,861 |
| 1945 | 38,119 | 1955 | 237,790 | 1965 | 296,697 | 1975 | 386,194 |
| 1946 | 108,721 | 1956 | 321,625 | 1966 | 323,040 | 1976 | 398,613 |
| 1947 | 147,292 | 1957 | 326,867 | 1967 | 361,972 | 1976 (TQ)[1] | 103,676 |
| 1948 | 170,570 | 1958 | 253,265 | 1968 | 454,448 | 1977 | 462,315 |
| 1949 | 188,317 | 1959 | 260,686 | 1969 | 358,579 | 1978 | 601,442 |
| 1950 | 249,187 | 1960 | 265,398 | 1970 | 373,326 | 1979 | 460,348 |
| Totals 1941–50 | 1,035,039 | 1951–60 | 2,515,479 | 1961–70 | 3,321,677 | 1980 | 530,639 |
| | | | | | | 1971–80 | 4,493,314 |

| YEAR | NUMBER | YEAR | NUMBER |
|---|---|---|---|
| 1981 | 596,600 | 1991 | 1,827,167 |
| 1982 | 594,131 | 1992 | 973,977 |
| 1983 | 559,763 | 1993 | 904,292 |
| 1984 | 543,903 | 1994 | 804,416 |
| 1985 | 570,009 | 1995 | 720,461 |
| 1986 | 601,708 | 1996 | 915,900 |
| 1987 | 601,516 | 1997 | 798,378 |
| 1988 | 643,025 | 1998 | 654,451 |
| 1989 | 1,090,924 | 1999 | 646,568 |
| 1990 | 1,536,483 | 2000 | 849,807 |
| Totals 1981–90 | 7,338,062 | 1991–2000 | 9,095,417 |

Totals 1901–2000: 46,965,825

[1]Transition quarter (TQ) to new fiscal year, 1 July through 30 September 1976.

## Immigrants Admitted to the US by Selected Country of Birth and State of Intended Residence

Fiscal Year 2001. Source: <www.bcis.gov>.

| STATE OF INTENDED RESIDENCE | TOTAL IMMIGRANTS | TOP FIVE COUNTRIES OF BIRTH (NUMBER OF IMMIGRANTS) |
|---|---|---|
| Alabama | 2,257 | Mexico (313), India (215), China (182), Vietnam (106), Canada (96) |
| Alaska | 1,401 | Philippines (366), Mexico (126), Canada (94), Russia (89), Korea (79) |
| Arizona | 16,362 | Mexico (7,932), Bosnia and Herzegovina (1,139), Canada (597), India (584), Vietnam (490) |
| Arkansas | 2,572 | Mexico (1,148), India (136), Vietnam (115), Philippines (113), China (101) |
| California | 282,957 | Mexico (97,293), Philippines (23,177), China (17,312), India (16,512), Vietnam (13,025) |
| Colorado | 12,494 | Mexico (4,107), India (786), China (648), Vietnam (612), Canada (458) |
| Connecticut | 12,148 | India (1,001), Jamaica (721), China (654), Poland (652), Bosnia and Herzegovina (502) |
| Delaware | 1,850 | India (270), China (182), Mexico (166), Korea (137), Philippines (118) |
| District of Columbia | 3,043 | El Salvador (752), China (136), Philippines (88), Guatemala (70), Nicaragua (69), Vietnam (69) |
| Florida | 104,715 | Cuba (21,729), Haiti (17,136), Nicaragua (10,712), Colombia (5,302), Jamaica (4,560) |
| Georgia | 19,431 | Mexico (2,531), India (1,743), Vietnam (1,242), Bosnia and Herzegovina (1,030), China (836) |
| Hawaii | 6,313 | Philippines (3,341), Japan (585), China (530), Korea (286), Vietnam (228) |
| Idaho | 2,296 | Mexico (942), Bosnia and Herzegovina (296), China (108), Germany (74), Canada (72) |
| Illinois | 48,296 | Mexico (11,821), India (4,961), Poland (4,158), Philippines (2,967), China (2,323) |
| Indiana | 6,010 | Mexico (944), India (575), China (485), Bosnia and Herzegovina (324), Philippines (306) |
| Iowa | 5,029 | Bosnia and Herzegovina (1,477), Mexico (1,053), Vietnam (291), India (268), China (190) |
| Kansas | 4,030 | Mexico (1,195), India (414), Vietnam (354), China (230), Philippines (138) |
| Kentucky | 4,548 | Bosnia and Herzegovina (864), Cuba (389), India (289), Mexico (260), China (240) |
| Louisiana | 3,778 | Vietnam (519), Mexico (247), China (210), India (200), Canada (139) |
| Maine | 1,186 | Canada (168), Bosnia and Herzegovina (95), China (71), Russia (65), Philippines (52) |

# Immigrants Admitted to the US by Selected Country of Birth and State of Intended Residence (continued)

| STATE OF INTENDED RESIDENCE | TOTAL IMMIGRANTS | TOP FIVE COUNTRIES OF BIRTH (NUMBER OF IMMIGRANTS) |
|---|---|---|
| Maryland | 22,060 | El Salvador (2,014), India (1,831), China (1,648), Philippines (993), Korea (958) |
| Massachusetts | 28,965 | China (2,450), India (2,332), Haiti (1,822), Dominican Rep. (1,538), Vietnam (1,405) |
| Michigan | 21,528 | India (2,978), Bosnia and Herzegovina (1,435), China (1,433), Canada (1,119), Mexico (1,003) |
| Minnesota | 11,166 | India (795), Mexico (772), China (643), Vietnam (637), Russia (474) |
| Mississippi | 1,340 | Mexico (160), India (130), Philippines (110), China (109), Vietnam (89) |
| Missouri | 7,616 | Bosnia and Herzegovina (1,494), China (575), India (543), Vietnam (474), Mexico (419) |
| Montana | 488 | Canada (116), China (36), Russia (36), Mexico (30), Philippines (20) |
| Nebraska | 3,850 | Mexico (1,370), Vietnam (246), India (216), Bosnia and Herzegovina (184), China (121) |
| Nevada | 9,618 | Mexico (3,308), Philippines (1,218), Cuba (540), El Salvador (339), China (324) |
| New Hampshire | 2,595 | India (305), Bosnia and Herzegovina (270), Canada (191), Philippines (172), China (157) |
| New Jersey | 59,920 | India (9,154), Dominican Rep. (3,427), China (3,262), Philippines (2,905), Colombia (2,245) |
| New Mexico | 5,207 | Mexico (3,575), China (129), Cuba (117), Vietnam (116), Canada (110) |
| New York | 114,116 | Dominican Rep. (10,394), China (8,071), Jamaica (5,727), India (4,942), Haiti (4,531) |
| North Carolina | 13,918 | Mexico (2,103), India (1,021), Canada (807), China (710), Vietnam (652) |
| North Dakota | 558 | Bosnia and Herzegovina (147), Canada (70), India (23), China (19), Philippines (19), Russia (19) |
| Ohio | 14,725 | India (1,651), China (1,126), Ukraine (682), Bosnia and Herzegovina (646), Mexico (633) |
| Oklahoma | 3,492 | Mexico (877), Vietnam (330), India (284), China (149), Pakistan (111) |
| Oregon | 9,638 | Mexico (1,985), Ukraine (872), Vietnam (704), India (611), China (557) |
| Pennsylvania | 21,411 | India (2,904), China (1,858), Vietnam (1,159), Ukraine (1,047), Mexico (1,031) |
| Rhode Island | 2,820 | Dominican Rep. (423), Guatemala (303), Colombia (136), China (129), El Salvador (81) |
| South Carolina | 2,882 | India (288), Canada (239), Mexico (231), Philippines (178), China (165) |
| South Dakota | 671 | Bosnia and Herzegovina (130), Ukraine (55), China (53), Russia (29), Philippines (28) |
| Tennessee | 6,257 | Mexico (703), India (444), Philippines (388), Vietnam (343), Bosnia and Herzegovina (309) |
| Texas | 86,315 | Mexico (43,524), India (4,313), Vietnam (3,772), El Salvador (3,644), China (2,623) |
| Utah | 5,247 | Mexico (1,103), Bosnia and Herzegovina (548), China (249), Canada (229), Vietnam (205) |
| Vermont | 954 | Bosnia and Herzegovina (240), Canada (111), China (71), UK (50), Vietnam (50) |
| Virginia | 26,876 | India (2,970), El Salvador (2,565), China (1,400), Pakistan (1,282), Philippines (1,214) |
| Washington | 23,085 | Ukraine (3,333), Mexico (2,518), Vietnam (1,533), Russia (1,435), Philippines (1,406) |
| West Virginia | 737 | India (106), China (80), Canada (43), Philippines (41), UK (41) |
| Wisconsin | 8,477 | Mexico (2,007), India (645), China (494), Russia (328), Canada (282) |
| Wyoming | 308 | Mexico (70), India (23), Canada (22), Philippines (22), Pakistan (21) |

## Americans 65 and Older, 1900–2000

Data for Hawaii and Alaska are included after 1950. Source: US Census Bureau.

| CENSUS YEAR | NUMBER OF PEOPLE 65 AND OLDER | % OF TOTAL POPULATION | CENSUS YEAR | NUMBER OF PEOPLE 65 AND OLDER | % OF TOTAL POPULATION |
|---|---|---|---|---|---|
| 1900 | 3,080,498 | 4.1 | 1960 | 16,559,580 | 9.2 |
| 1910 | 3,949,524 | 4.3 | 1970 | 20,065,502 | 9.8 |
| 1920 | 4,933,215 | 4.7 | 1980 | 25,549,427 | 11.3 |
| 1930 | 6,633,805 | 5.4 | 1990 | 31,241,831 | 12.6 |
| 1940 | 9,019,314 | 6.8 | 2000 | 34,991,753 | 12.4 |
| 1950 | 12,269,537 | 8.1 | | | |

## Poverty Level by State

Source: US Census Bureau. Totals may differ due to rounding. For the definition of poverty, see <www.census.gov/hhes/poverty/povdef.html>.

| STATE | % OF PEOPLE IN POVERTY | | | NUMBER OF PEOPLE IN POVERTY ('000) | | |
|---|---|---|---|---|---|---|
| | 1980 | 1990 | 2000 | 1980 | 1990 | 2000 |
| Alabama | 21.2 | 19.2 | 14.4 | 810 | 779 | 642 |
| Alaska | 9.6 | 11.4 | 8.2 | 36 | 57 | 53 |
| Arizona | 12.8 | 13.7 | 12.0 | 354 | 484 | 590 |
| Arkansas | 21.5 | 19.6 | 17.8 | 484 | 472 | 467 |
| California | 11.0 | 13.9 | 12.8 | 2,619 | 4,128 | 4,441 |
| Colorado | 8.6 | 13.7 | 8.1 | 247 | 461 | 343 |
| Connecticut | 8.3 | 6.0 | 6.6 | 255 | 196 | 219 |
| Delaware | 11.8 | 6.9 | 9.1 | 68 | 48 | 72 |
| District of Columbia | 20.9 | 21.1 | 14.9 | 131 | 120 | 75 |
| Florida | 16.7 | 14.4 | 10.6 | 1,692 | 1,896 | 1,604 |
| Georgia | 13.9 | 15.8 | 11.2 | 727 | 1,001 | 869 |
| Hawaii | 8.5 | 11.0 | 9.9 | 81 | 121 | 115 |
| Idaho | 14.7 | 14.9 | 12.9 | 138 | 157 | 161 |
| Illinois | 12.3 | 13.7 | 11.5 | 1,386 | 1,606 | 1,406 |
| Indiana | 11.8 | 13.0 | 8.7 | 645 | 714 | 504 |
| Iowa | 10.8 | 10.4 | 7.2 | 311 | 289 | 206 |
| Kansas | 9.4 | 10.3 | 9.6 | 215 | 259 | 251 |
| Kentucky | 19.3 | 17.3 | 11.9 | 701 | 628 | 471 |
| Louisiana | 20.3 | 23.6 | 17.3 | 868 | 952 | 730 |
| Maine | 14.6 | 13.1 | 8.4 | 158 | 162 | 106 |
| Maryland | 9.5 | 9.9 | 7.6 | 389 | 468 | 387 |
| Massachusetts | 9.5 | 10.7 | 10.1 | 542 | 626 | 629 |
| Michigan | 12.9 | 14.3 | 10.0 | 1,194 | 1,315 | 993 |
| Minnesota | 8.7 | 12.0 | 6.0 | 342 | 524 | 285 |
| Mississippi | 24.3 | 25.7 | 12.9 | 591 | 684 | 358 |
| Missouri | 13.0 | 13.4 | 8.0 | 625 | 700 | 440 |
| Montana | 13.2 | 16.3 | 15.7 | 102 | 134 | 136 |
| Nebraska | 13.0 | 10.3 | 9.0 | 199 | 167 | 148 |
| Nevada | 8.3 | 9.8 | 8.5 | 70 | 119 | 170 |
| New Hampshire | 7.0 | 6.3 | 5.2 | 63 | 68 | 64 |
| New Jersey | 9.0 | 9.2 | 8.0 | 659 | 711 | 666 |
| New Mexico | 20.6 | 20.9 | 16.8 | 268 | 319 | 299 |
| New York | 13.8 | 14.3 | 13.4 | 2,391 | 2,571 | 2,460 |
| North Carolina | 15.0 | 13.0 | 12.1 | 877 | 829 | 911 |
| North Dakota | 15.5 | 13.7 | 10.1 | 99 | 87 | 61 |
| Ohio | 9.8 | 11.5 | 10.0 | 1,046 | 1,256 | 1,157 |
| Oklahoma | 13.9 | 15.6 | 15.4 | 406 | 481 | 504 |
| Oregon | 11.5 | 9.2 | 11.2 | 309 | 267 | 382 |
| Pennsylvania | 9.8 | 11.0 | 8.9 | 1,142 | 1,328 | 1,062 |
| Rhode Island | 10.7 | 7.5 | 9.1 | 97 | 71 | 85 |
| South Carolina | 16.8 | 16.2 | 10.6 | 534 | 548 | 400 |
| South Dakota | 18.8 | 13.3 | 9.6 | 127 | 93 | 67 |
| Tennessee | 19.6 | 16.9 | 14.7 | 884 | 833 | 820 |
| Texas | 15.7 | 15.9 | 14.7 | 2,247 | 2,684 | 3,013 |
| Utah | 10.0 | 8.2 | 9.6 | 148 | 143 | 212 |
| Vermont | 12.0 | 10.9 | 11.3 | 62 | 61 | 71 |
| Virginia | 12.4 | 11.1 | 7.7 | 647 | 705 | 534 |
| Washington | 12.7 | 8.9 | 10.1 | 538 | 434 | 593 |
| West Virginia | 15.2 | 18.1 | 14.0 | 297 | 328 | 248 |
| Wisconsin | 8.5 | 9.3 | 9.6 | 403 | 448 | 518 |
| Wyoming | 10.4 | 11.0 | 11.0 | 49 | 51 | 54 |
| **All US** | **13.0** | **13.5** | **11.3** | **29,272** | **33,585** | **31,139** |

## Population of US Territories

Total midyear population. Source: US Census Bureau.

| YEAR | PUERTO RICO | GUAM | VIRGIN ISLANDS | AMERICAN SAMOA | NORTHERN MARIANA ISLANDS |
|---|---|---|---|---|---|
| 1970 | 2,721,754 | 86,470 | 63,476 | 27,267 | 12,359 |
| 1975 | 2,935,124 | 102,110 | 94,484 | 29,640 | 14,938 |
| 1980 | 3,209,648 | 106,869 | 99,636 | 32,418 | 16,890 |
| 1985 | 3,382,106 | 120,615 | 100,760 | 38,633 | 21,386 |
| 1990 | 3,536,910 | 134,110 | 104,235 | 47,199 | 44,037 |
| 1995 | 3,731,006 | 143,856 | 113,896 | 56,911 | 58,128 |
| 2000 | 3,915,798 | 154,623 | 120,917 | 65,446 | 71,912 |
| 2001 | 3,937,316 | 157,557 | 122,211 | 67,084 | 74,612 |
| 2002 | 3,957,988 | 160,796 | 123,498 | 68,688 | 77,311 |

# States and Other Areas of the United States

## Alabama

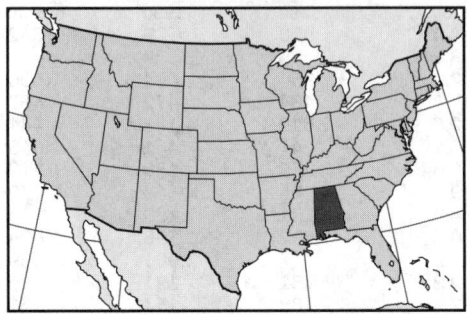

**Name:** Alabama, from the Choctaw language, meaning "thicket clearers." **Nickname:** Heart of Dixie. **Capital:** Montgomery. **Rank:** population: 23rd; area: 28th. **Motto:** *Audemus Jura Nostra Defendere* (We Dare Defend Our Rights). **Song:** "Alabama," words by Julia S. Tutwiler and music by Edna Gockel Gussen. **Amphibian:** Red Hills salamander. **Bird:** yellowhammer. **Fish:** largemouth bass (freshwater); tarpon (saltwater). **Flower:** camellia. **Fossil:** *Basilosaurus cetoides*. **Gemstone:** star blue quartz. **Insect:** monarch butterfly. **Mineral:** hematite. **Reptile:** Alabama red-bellied turtle. **Rock:** marble. **Tree:** southern longleaf pine.

## Natural features

**Area:** 52,237 sq mi, 135,293 sq km. **Mountain ranges:** Appalachians, Raccoon, Lookout. **Highest point:** Cheaha Mountain, 2,407 ft (734 m). **Largest lake:** Lake Guntersville. **Major rivers:** Mobile, Alabama, Tombigbee, Tennessee, Chattahoochee, Conecuh, Pea, Tensaw, Tallapoosa. **Natural regions:** the Appalachian Plateaus, extending across the north central region; interior low plateaus, far north; valley and ridge province and small portion of the Piedmont Province, covering the east; coastal plain, covering the southern half of the state. **Location:** South, bordering Tennessee, Georgia, Florida, Mississippi. **Climate:** temperate, with mild winters and hot, humid summers; temperatures mellowed by altitude in the northern counties and relatively higher in the southern counties; summer heat is often alleviated by winds blowing in from the Gulf of Mexico. **Land use:** forested, 67.5%; agricultural, 13.8%; pasture, 5.7%; other, 13.0%.

## People (2000 census)

**Population:** 4,447,100; 87.6 persons per sq mi (33.8 persons per sq km) (land area only). **Vital statistics** (1998; per 1,000 population): birth rate, 14.2 (1999); death rate, 10.1; marriage rate, 11.5; divorce rate, 6.0. **Major cities:** Birmingham, 242,820; Montgomery, 201,568; Mobile, 198,915; Huntsville, 158,216.

## Government

**Statehood:** entered the Union on 14 Dec 1819 as the 22nd state. **State constitution:** adopted 1901. **Representation in US Congress:** 2 senators; 7 represen-

tatives. **Electoral college:** 9 votes (in the 2004 general elections based on the 2000 census). **Political divisions:** 67 counties.

## Economy

**Employment:** services, 25.2%; trade, 21.6%; manufacturing, 16.9%; government, 16.4%; construction, 6.2%; finance, insurance, real estate, 4.9%; transportation, public utilities, 4.6%; agriculture, forestry, fishing, 3.5%; mining, 0.5%. **Production:** manufacturing, 19.0%; services, 16.9%; trade, 16.9%; government, 15.8%; finance, insurance, real estate, 14.7%; transportation, utilities, 8.7%; construction, 4.7%; agriculture, forestry, fisheries, 2.0%; mining, 1.3%. **Chief agricultural products:** *Crops:* cotton, corn, soybeans, peanuts (groundnuts), potatoes, sweet potatoes, peaches, pecans, fruits and vegetables, winter wheat, hay, honey. *Livestock:* cattle, poultry, hogs. *Fish catch:* marine fish, including red snapper; freshwater fish, including catfish; marine crustaceans, including shrimp, crab; marine mollusks, including mussels, oysters. **Chief manufactured products:** food products, meat products, poultry processing, textiles, apparel, wood products, mobile homes, paper and paperboard, petroleum products, plastics and rubber products, iron and steel, aluminum products, semiconductors, electronic components, motor vehicle parts.

**Internet resources:** <www.touralabama.org>; <www.alabama.gov>.

## Alaska

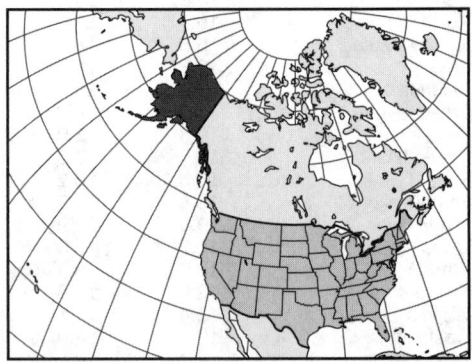

**Name:** Alaska, from the Aleut word *Alyeska,* meaning "great land." **Nickname:** The Last Frontier. **Capital:** Juneau. **Rank:** population: 48th; area: 1st. **Motto:** North to the Future. **Song:** "Alaska's Flag," words by Marie Drake and music by Elinor Dusenbury. **Bird:** willow ptarmigan. **Fish:** giant king salmon. **Flower:** forget-me-not. **Fossil:** *Mammuthus primigenius* (woolly mammoth). **Gemstone:** jade. **Insect:** four spot skimmer dragonfly. **Mammal:** moose. **Marine mammal:** bowhead whale. **Mineral:** gold. **Tree:** sitka spruce.

## Natural features

**Area:** 615,230 sq mi, 1,593,444 sq km. **Mountain ranges:** Wrangell, Chugach, Alaska, Brooks, Aleutian,

---

*For details about state governments, see pages 812–817; for energy data, see pages 840–842.*

Boundary. **Highest point:** Mount McKinley (Denali), 20,320 ft (6,194 m). **Largest lake:** Iliamna. **Major rivers:** Yukon, Porcupine, Tanana, Koyukuk, Noatak, Kuskokwim, Susitna, Copper. **Natural regions:** panhandle, a narrow strip of land that includes portions of the Coast Mountains; coastal archipelago and the Gulf of Alaska islands; the Alaska Peninsula and Aleutian island chain that separates the North Pacific from the Bering Sea; the Alaska Range, extending across the south-central region; the Interior Plateau, including the basin of the Yukon River, and the central plains and tablelands of the interior, the Seward Peninsula to the west, and the Brooks Range, sometimes called the North Slope, to the north; the Arctic Coastal Plain, a treeless region of tundra lying at the northernmost edge of the state; tundra-covered islands of the Bering Sea. **Location:** bordered by Canada. **Climate:** temperate with much regional variation in temperature and precipitation; *southern coastal and southeastern region, Gulf of Alaska and Aleutian islands:* cool summers and moderate winters, with high precipitation; *interior basin:* moderate summers and very cold winters, with low to moderate precipitation; *islands and coast of the Bering Sea:* cool summers and very cold winters; *central plains and uplands:* moderate summers and frigid winters; *North Slope:* moderate summers and frigid winters, though not as severe as interior regions. **Land use:** forested, 24.1 (24)%; pasture, 0.0%; other, 75.6 (76)%.

## People (2000 census)

Population: 626,932; 1.1 persons per sq mi (0.4 person per sq km) (land area only). **Vital statistics** (1998; per 1,000 population): birth rate, 16.1 (1999); death rate, 4.2; marriage rate, 9.7; divorce rate, 5.2. **Major cities:** Anchorage (metropolitan area), 260,283; Juneau (metropolitan area), 30,711; College, 11,402; Sitka, 8,835.

## Government

**Statehood:** entered the Union on 3 Jan 1959 as the 49th state. **State constitution:** adopted 1956. **Representation in US Congress:** 2 senators; 1 representative. **Electoral college:** 3 votes. **Political divisions:** 16 boroughs.

## Economy

**Employment:** services, 26.9%; government, 24.4%; trade, 18.7%; transportation, public utilities, 7.7%; finance, insurance, real estate, 5.3%; construction, 5.1%; manufacturing, 4.8%; agriculture, forestry, fishing, 4.1%; mining, 3.0%. **Production:** mining, 20.1%; government, 19.4%; transportation, utilities, 16.7%; services, 13.0%; trade, 10.1%; finance, insurance, real estate, 10.1%; construction, 4.6%; manufacturing, 4.2%; agriculture, forestry, fishing, 1.7%. **Chief agricultural products:** *Crops:* hay, milk, potatoes, timber. *Livestock:* cattle, pigs. *Fish catch:* marine fish, salmon, herring, groundfish, shellfish, crab, shrimp. **Chief manufactured products:** processed fish and seafood (fresh, frozen, canned, and cured), lumber and wood products, paper products, transportation products.

**Internet resources:** <www.travelalaska.com>; <www.alaska.gov>.

# Arizona

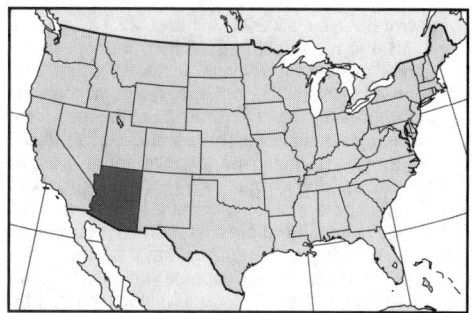

**Name:** Arizona, from *arizonac,* derived from two Papago Indian words meaning "place of the young spring." **Nickname:** Grand Canyon State. **Capital:** Phoenix. **Rank:** population: 20th; area: 6th. **Motto:** *Ditat Deus* (God Enriches). **Song:** "Arizona March Song," words by Margaret Rowe Clifford and music by Maurice Blumenthal. **Amphibian:** Arizona treefrog. **Bird:** cactus wren. **Fish:** Arizona trout. **Flower:** saguaro blossom. **Fossil:** petrified wood. **Gemstone:** turquoise. **Mammal:** ringtail. **Reptile:** Arizona ridgenose rattlesnake. **Tree:** palo verde.

## Natural features

**Area:** 114,006 sq mi, 295,276 sq km. **Mountain ranges:** Black, Gila Bend, Chuska, Hualapai, San Francisco, White. **Highest point:** Humphreys Peak, 12,633 ft (3,851 m). **Largest lake:** Lake Roosevelt. **Major rivers:** Colorado, Little Colorado, Verde, Salt, Gila. **Natural regions:** the Colorado Plateaus, northeast third of the state, include Grand Canyon and Painted Desert; the basin and range province, south, east, central, and northwest, includes Sonoran Desert in the southwest corner and part of the Great Basin Desert to the northwest. **Location:** Southwest, bordering Utah, Colorado, New Mexico, California, and Nevada; international border with Mexico. **Climate:** varies with location; half of Arizona is semiarid, one-third is arid, and the remainder is humid; *basin and range region:* arid and semiarid to subtropical climate; *Colorado Plateaus:* cool to cold winters and a semiarid climate; *Transition Zone:* climate ranges widely, from arid to humid. **Land use:** pasture, 55.7%; forested, 22.4%; agricultural, 1.7%; other, 20.2%.

## People (2000 census)

Population: 5,130,632; 45.1 persons per sq mi (17.4 persons per sq km) (land area only). **Vital statistics** (1998; per 1,000 population): birth rate, 17.0 (1999); death rate, 8.2; marriage rate, 8.1; divorce rate, 5.5. **Major cities:** Phoenix, 1,321,045; Tucson, 486,699; Mesa, 396,375; Glendale, 218,812; Scottsdale, 202,705; Chandler, 176,581; Tempe, 158,625.

## Government

**Statehood:** entered the Union on 14 Feb 1912 as the 48th state. **State constitution:** adopted 1911. **Representation in US Congress:** 2 senators; 6 representatives. **Electoral college:** 10 votes (in the 2004 general elections based on the 2000 census). **Political divisions:** 15 counties.

## Economy

**Employment:** services, 32.5%; trade, 22.7%; government, 13.4%; manufacturing, 8.8%; finance, insurance, real estate, 8.3%; construction, 6.6%; transportation, public utilities, 4.5%; agriculture, forestry, fishing, 2.6%; mining, 0.6%. **Production:** services, 22.0%; finance, insurance, real estate, 18.7%; trade, 17.4%; manufacturing, 14.4%; government, 12.1%; transportation, public utilities, 7.3%; construction, 5.8%; agriculture, forestry, fishing, 1.5%; mining, 0.8%. **Chief agricultural products:** *Crops:* cotton and cottonseed, wheat, sorghum, hay, barley, corn (maize), potatoes, grapes, apples, vegetables and melons, dairy products, lettuce. *Livestock:* cattle and calves, hogs and pigs, sheep and lambs, angora goats. **Chief manufactured products:** semiconductors, communications equipment, electric and electronic equipment, transportation equipment, soap products, nonferrous metal products.

**Internet resources:** <www.arizonaguide.com>; <www.az.gov>.

# Arkansas

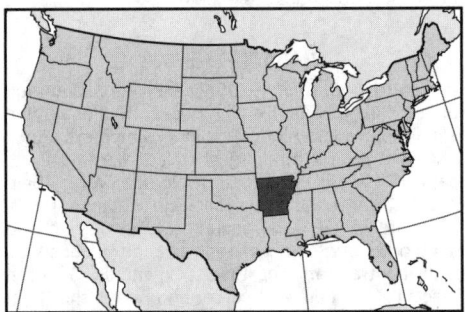

**Name:** Arkansas, from an unknown Native American word describing the Quapaw tribe (also known as the Arkansaw), meaning "people who live downstream." **Nickname:** The Natural State. **Capital:** Little Rock. **Rank:** population: 33rd; area: 27th. **Motto:** *Regnat Populus* (The People Rule). **Song:** "Arkansas," words and music by Eva Ware Barnett. **Bird:** mockingbird. **Flower:** apple blossom. **Gemstone:** diamond. **Insect:** honeybee. **Mammal:** whitetail deer. **Mineral:** quartz crystal. **Rock:** bauxite. **Tree:** pine tree.

## Natural features

**Area:** 53,182 sq mi, 137,742 sq km. **Mountain ranges:** Ozark, Ouachita. **Highest point:** Mount Magazine, 2,753 ft (839 m). **Largest lake:** Lake Chicot. **Major rivers:** Arkansas, Red, Quachita, White. **Natural regions:** the Ozark Plateaus, including the Boston Mountains, north and northwest regions; the Ouachita Province, including the Arkansas valley and the Ouachita Mountains, central region; Coastal Plain, extends from southwest to northeast. **Location:** South, bordering Missouri, Tennessee, Mississippi, Louisiana, Texas, and Oklahoma. **Climate:** temperate, with mild winters and hot summers. **Land use:** forested, 55.2%; agricultural, 30.3%; pasture, 6.0%; other, 8.5%.

## People (2000 census)

**Population:** 2,673,400; 51.3 persons per sq mi (19.8 persons per sq km) (land area only). **Vital statistics** (1998; per 1,000 population): birth rate, 14.4 (1999); death rate, 6.1; marriage rate, 15.1; divorce rate, 10.8. **Major cities:** Little Rock, 183,133; Fort Smith, 80,268; North Little Rock, 60,433; Fayetteville, 58,047; Jonesboro, 55,515.

## Government

**Statehood:** entered the Union on 15 Jun 1836 as the 25th state. **State constitution:** adopted 1874. **Representation in US Congress:** 2 senators; 4 representatives. **Electoral college:** 6 votes (in the 2004 general elections based on the 2000 census). **Political divisions:** 75 counties.

## Economy

**Employment:** services, 24.4%; trade, 21.3%; manufacturing, 18.3%; government, 13.9%; agriculture, forestry, fishing, 6.6%; construction, 5.8%; transportation, public utilities, 5.5%; finance, insurance, real estate, 4.8%; mining, 0.4%. **Production:** manufacturing, 22.5%; trade, 18.4%; services, 15.6%; government, 12.3%; finance, insurance, real estate, 11.6%; transportation, public utilities, 10.5%; construction, 4.6%; agriculture, forestry, fisheries, 3.7%; mining, 0.8%. **Chief agricultural products:** *Crops:* corn (maize), cotton, hay, rice, sorghum, soybeans, wheat, apples, blueberries, grapes, peaches, pecans, strawberries, tomatoes, watermelon. *Livestock:* cattle and calves, hogs and pigs, poultry. *Aquaculture:* catfish. **Chief manufactured products:** food products, meatpacking, poultry processing, lumber, paper and paper products, refined petroleum, chemical products, plastic and rubber products, iron and steel manufacturing, fabricated metal products, machinery, transportation products.

**Internet resources:** <www.arkansas.com>; <www.arkansas.gov>.

# California

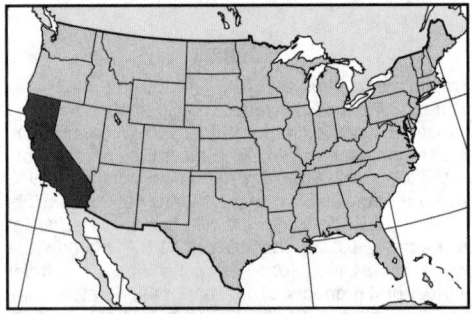

**Nickname:** Golden State. **Capital:** Sacramento. **Rank:** population: 1st; area: 3rd. **Motto:** *Eureka* (I Have Found It). **Song:** "I Love You, California," words by F.B. Silverwood and music by A.F. Frankenstein. **Bird:** California quail. **Fish:** golden trout (freshwater); garibaldi (saltwater). **Flower:** California poppy. **Fossil:** sabertooth cat. **Gemstone:** benitoite. **Insect:** California

*For details about state governments, see pages 812–817; for energy data, see pages 840–842.*

dogface butterfly. **Mammal:** California grizzly bear. **Marine mammal:** California gray whale. **Mineral:** gold. **Reptile:** desert tortoise. **Rock:** serpentine. **Tree:** California redwood.

## Natural features

**Area:** 158,869 sq mi, 411,470 sq km. **Mountain ranges:** Coast Range, Sierra Nevada, Santa Lucia, Cascade Range, Klamath Mountains, Tehachapi Mountains, San Gabriel Mountains, San Bernadino Mountains. **Highest point:** Mount Whitney, 14,494 ft (4,417 m). **Largest lake:** Lake Tahoe. **Major rivers:** Colorado, Sacramento, Pit, San Joaquin. **Natural regions:** Basin and Range Province, northeast corner, also eastern border with Arizona and southern Nevada; Cascade-Sierra Mountains, running from north to south along the east-central region; Pacific Border Province, west, including the Coast Ranges to the west, the Klamath Mountains to the north, the Los Angeles Ranges to the south, and the California Trough (commonly referred to as the Central Valley) to the east; Lower Californian Province, southwest tip. **Location:** West, bordering Oregon, Nevada, and Arizona; international border with Mexico. **Climate:** Mediterranean climate, with moderate temperatures, warm, dry summers, and cool, rainy winters. **Land use:** forested, 32.6%; pasture, 22.4%; agricultural, 10.6%; other, 34.4%.

## People (2000 census)

**Population:** 33,871,648; 217.2 persons per sq mi (83.8 persons per sq km) (land area only). **Vital statistics** (1998; per 1,000 population): birth rate, 15.6 (1999); death rate, 6.9; marriage rate, 5.9; divorce rate, N/A. **Major cities:** Los Angeles, 3,694,820; San Diego, 1,223,400; San Jose, 894,943; San Francisco, 776,733; Long Beach, 461,522; Fresno, 427,652; Sacramento, 407,018; Oakland, 399,484.

## Government

**Statehood:** entered the Union on 9 Sep 1850 as the 31st state. **State constitution:** adopted 1879. **Representation in US Congress:** 2 senators; 52 representatives. **Electoral college:** 55 votes (in the 2004 general elections based on the 2000 census). **Political divisions:** 58 counties.

## Economy

**Employment:** services, 33.8%; trade, 20.7%; government, 13.3%; manufacturing, 11.2%; finance, insurance, real estate, 8.0%; construction, 4.6%; transportation, public utilities, 4.5%; agriculture, forestry, fishing, 3.7%; mining, 0.2%. **Production:** services, 23.4%; finance, insurance, real estate, 21.7%; trade, 15.9%; manufacturing, 14.6%; government, 10.7%; transportation, utilities, 7.3%; construction, 3.8%; agriculture, forestry, fishing, 1.9%; mining, 0.6%. **Chief agricultural products:** *Crops:* wheat, oats, rice, grains, apples, apricots, cherries, grapes, olives, peaches, pears, citrus fruits, strawberries, onions, lima beans, artichokes, broccoli, snap beans, vegetables, dairy products, eggs. *Livestock:* cattle and calves, sheep and lambs. *Fish catch:* bonito, halibut, mackerel, groundfish, rockfish (commonly called Pacific red snapper), sablefish (also called black cod), soles and sanddabs, sardines, white seabass, shark, swordfish, tuna, crab, California spiny lobster, Pacific Ocean

(pink) shrimp, prawns, squid. *Extractive products:* timber. **Chief manufactured products:** food products, meat and poultry processing, soft drink products, beer and wine, textiles, apparel, lumber and wood products, paper and paper products, printing, refined petroleum, asphalt, chemical products, pharmaceuticals, plastic and rubber products, glass and glass products, construction materials, steel products, metal products, machinery, communications equipment, semiconductors and computers, electronics, transportation equipment, furniture, medical equipment, sporting goods.

**Internet resources:** <www.gocalif.com>; <www.ca.gov>.

# Colorado

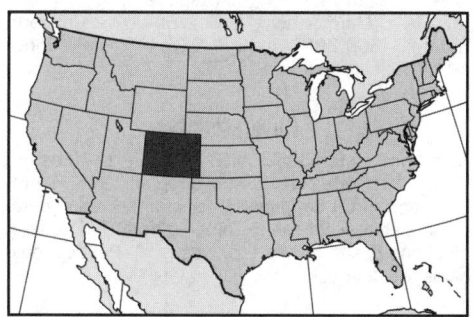

**Name:** Colorado, from a Spanish word meaning red colored earth. **Nickname:** Centennial State. **Capital:** Denver. **Rank:** population: 24th; area: 8th. **Motto:** *Nil Sine Numine* (Nothing Without Providence). **Song:** "Where the Columbines Grow," words and music by A.J. Flynn. **Bird:** lark bunting. **Fish:** greenback cutthroat trout. **Flower:** white and lavender columbine. **Fossil:** stegosaurus. **Gemstone:** aquamarine. **Insect:** Colorado hairstreak butterfly. **Mammal:** Rocky Mountain bighorn sheep. **Tree:** Colorado blue spruce.

 **Did you know?** There are 54 peaks higher than 14,000 ft (4,200 m) in the Colorado Rockies.

## Natural features

**Area:** 104,100 sq mi, 269,618 sq km. **Mountain ranges:** Rocky Mountains, Front, Medicine Bow, Park, Rabbit Ears, San Juan Mountains, Sangre de Cristo Range, Sawatch. **Highest point:** Mount Elbert, 14,433 ft (4,399 m). **Largest lakes:** Blue Mesa Reservoir (man-made); Grand Lake (natural). **Major rivers:** Colorado, Arkansas, South Platte, Rio Grande. **Natural regions:** the Great Plains Province, eastern half of state, includes the High Plains to the east, Colorado Piedmont to the west, and Raton Section to the south; Southern Rocky Mountains, running down the middle of the state; Middle Rocky Mountains and Wyoming Basin, northwest corner; Colorado Plateaus, western and southwestern border, include the Uinta Basin to the north, the Canyon Lands in the middle, and the Navajo Section to the south. **Location:** West, bordering Wyoming, Nebraska, Kansas, Oklahoma, New Mexico, and Utah. **Climate:** *Eastern* *plains:* with hot summers and dry, cold, windy, and generally harsh winters; *piedmont:* similar to eastern plains, also experiences the Chinook wind, a dry, descending winter airstream from the high mountains that is warmed by compression as it descends; *mountains and high plateaus:* cool summers, cold winters and much increased precipitation; snow may fall during any month of the year, with amounts ranging from about 20 to 50 inches. **Land use:** pasture, 42.0%; forest, 28.3%; agricultural, 17.2%; other, 12.5%.

## People (2000 census)

**Population:** 4,301,261; 41.5 persons per sq mi (16.0 persons per sq km) (land area only). **Vital statistics** (1998; per 1,000 population): birth rate, 15.3 (1999); death rate, 6.7; marriage rate, 7.9; divorce rate, N/A. **Major cities:** Denver, 554,636; Colorado Springs, 360,890; Aurora, 276,393; Lakewood, 144,126; Fort Collins, 118,652.

## Government

**Statehood:** entered the Union on 1 Aug 1876 as the 38th state. **State constitution:** adopted 1876. **Representation in US Congress:** 2 senators; 6 representatives. **Electoral college:** 9 votes (in the 2004 general elections based on the 2000 census). **Political divisions:** 63 counties.

## Economy

**Employment:** services, 32.3%; trade, 22.0%; government, 13.5%; finance, insurance, real estate, 8.4%; manufacturing, 8.2%; construction, 6.5%; transportation, public utilities, 5.4%; agriculture, forestry, fishing, 2.8%; mining, 0.9%. **Production:** services, 23.1%; finance, insurance, real estate, 17.5%; trade, 16.1%; transportation, utilities, 12.2%; government, 11.9%; manufacturing, 10.2%; construction, 6.0%; mining, 1.6%; agriculture, 1.5%. **Chief agricultural products:** *Crops:* millet, corn (maize), hay, potatoes, onions, sugar beets, sunflowers, wheat, dairy products, eggs, greenhouse products. *Livestock:* cattle and calves, hogs and pigs, sheep and lambs. **Chief manufactured products:** meat products, beverages, printing, semiconductors, computer and electronic products.

**Internet resources:** <www.colorado.com>; <www.colorado.gov>.

# Connecticut

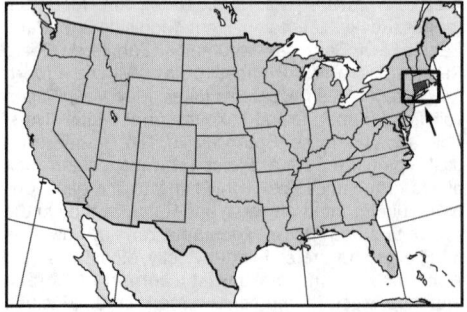

**Name:** Connecticut, from the Mohegan word *Quinnehtukqut,* meaning "Long River Place" or "Beside the Long Tidal River." **Nickname:** Constitution State. **Capital:** Hartford. **Rank:** population: 29th; area: 48th. **Motto:** *Qui Transtulit Sustinet* (He Who Transplanted Still Sustains). **Song:** "Yankee Doodle," words from folk tradition, melody from an English tune, "The World Turned Upside Down." **Bird:** robin. **Flower:** mountain laurel. **Fossil:** *Eubrontes giganteus.* **Insect:** praying mantis. **Mammal:** sperm whale. **Mineral:** garnet. **Shellfish:** eastern oyster. **Tree:** white oak.

## Natural features

**Area:** 5,544 sq mi, 14,358 sq km. **Mountain range:** Berkshire Hills. **Highest point:** Mount Frissell, 2,380 ft (725 m). **Largest lake:** Candlewood Lake. **Major rivers:** Connecticut, Housatonic, Thames. **Natural regions:** the New England Province covers the state, divided into the Western Upland, Central Lowland (Connecticut Valley), and Eastern Upland. **Location:** New England, bordering Massachusetts, Rhode Island, and New York. **Climate:** moderate temperate climate; coastal portions have somewhat warmer winters and cooler summers than does the interior; northwestern uplands have cooler and longer winters with heavier falls of snow; occasional hurricanes cause flooding and damage, particularly along the coastline. **Land use:** forest, 54.2%; agricultural, 5.4%; pasture, 1.0%; other, 39.4%.

## People (2000 census)

**Population:** 3,405,565; 702.9 persons per sq mi (271.4 persons per sq km) (land area only). **Vital statistics** (1998; per 1,000 population): birth rate, 13.2 (1999); death rate, 9.1; marriage rate, 6.1; divorce rate, 2.9. **Major cities:** Bridgeport, 139,529; New Haven, 123,626; Hartford, 121,578; Stamford, 117,083.

## Government

**Statehood:** entered the Union on 9 Jan 1788 as the 5th state. **State constitution:** adopted 1965. **Representation in US Congress:** 2 senators; 6 representatives. **Electoral college:** 7 votes (in the 2004 general elections based on the 2000 census). **Political divisions:** 8 counties.

## Economy

**Employment:** services, 34.3%; trade, 20.2%; manufacturing, 14.0%; government, 11.2%; finance, insurance, real estate, 9.5%; construction, 4.8%; transportation, public utilities, 4.2%; agriculture, forestry, fishing, 1.5%; mining, 0.1%. **Production:** finance, insurance, real estate, 28.7%; services, 22.0%; manufacturing, 16.5%; trade, 14.5%; government, 8.3%; transportation, utilities, 5.9%; construction, 3.3%; agriculture, 0.7%; mining, 0.1%. **Chief agricultural products:** *Crops:* corn (maize), silage, hay, tobacco, apples, pears, dairy products, eggs. *Livestock:* poultry, cattle, sheep, horses. *Fish catch:* lobster, clams, oysters, shad, marine fish. **Chief manufactured products:** printing, pharmaceutical products, soap and cleaning products, plastics, metal products, machinery, communications equipment, electronics, aerospace products, aircraft engines.

**Internet resources:** <www.ctbound.org>; <www.ct.gov>.

*For details about state governments, see pages 812–817; for energy data, see pages 840–842.*

# Delaware

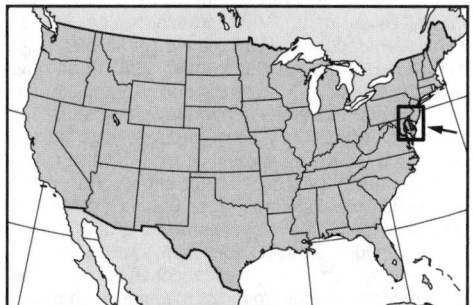

**Name:** Delaware, from Delaware River and Bay; named in turn for Sir Thomas West, Baron De La Warr. **Nickname:** First State. **Capital:** Dover. **Rank:** population: 45th; area: 49th. **Motto:** Liberty and Independence. **Song:** "Our Delaware," words by George B. Hynson and music by Will M.S. Brown. **Bird:** Blue Hen Chicken. **Fish:** weakfish. **Flower:** peach blossom. **Insect:** ladybug. **Mineral:** sillimanite. **Tree:** American holly.

## Natural features

**Area:** 2,396 sq mi, 6,206 sq km. **Highest point:** Ebright Road, New Castle County, 442 ft (135 m). **Largest lake:** Red Mill Pond. **Major rivers:** Delaware, Nanticoke, Pocomoke. **Natural regions:** the Piedmont Province, including the Piedmont Upland, covers the northernmost tip of the state; the remainder consists of the Coastal Plain. **Location:** East Coast, bordering Pennsylvania, New Jersey, and Maryland. **Climate:** temperate, with high humidity, hot summers and cold winters. **Land use:** agricultural, 36.1%; forest, 30.1%; pasture, 0.6%; other, 33.3%.

## People (2000 census)

**Population:** 783,600; 383.2 persons per sq mi (148.0 persons per sq km) (land area only). **Vital statistics:** (1998; per 1,000 population): birth rate, 14.2 (1999); death rate, 8.8; marriage rate, 6.8; divorce rate, 4.5. **Major cities:** Wilmington, 72,664; Dover, 32,135; Newark, 28,547.

## Government

**Statehood:** entered the Union on 7 Dec 1787 as the 1st state. **State constitution:** adopted 1897. **Representation in US Congress:** 2 senators; 1 representative. **Electoral college:** 3 votes. **Political divisions:** 3 counties.

## Economy

**Employment:** services, 28.6%; trade, 20.6%; government, 13.5%; finance, insurance, real estate, 12.8%; manufacturing, 12.6%; construction, 6.1%; transportation, public utilities, 3.8%; agriculture, forestry, fishing, 1.9%. **Production:** finance, insurance, real estate, 39.8%; services, 15.5%; manufacturing, 14.2%; trade, 11.1%; government, 9.2%; transportation, utilities, 5.1%; construction, 4.3%; agriculture, 0.8%. **Chief agricultural products:** *Crops:* corn, soybeans, wheat, barley, peas, vegetables, dairy products. *Livestock:* poultry, cattle, hogs. *Fish catch:* crustaceans, crab, clams. **Chief manufactured products:** chemi-cals, food products, paper products, rubber and plastics products, metal products, printed materials.

**Internet resources:** <www.visitdelaware.net>; <www.delaware.gov>.

# District of Columbia

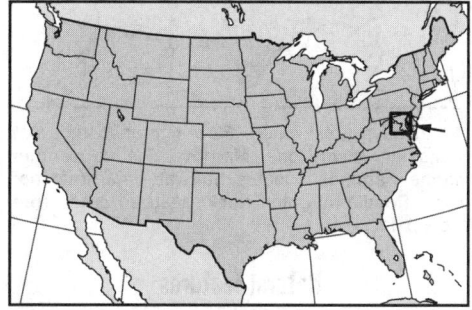

**Motto:** *Justitia Omnibus* (Justice for All). **Bird:** woodthrush. **Flower:** American Beauty rose. **Tree:** scarlet oak.

## Natural features

**Area:** 68 sq mi, 177 sq km. **Major river:** Potomac. **Location:** Atlantic seaboard, bordered by Maryland and Virginia. **Climate:** humid, subtropical climate.

## People (2000 census)

**Population:** 572,059; 9,378 persons per sq mi (3,620 persons per sq km) (land area only). **Vital statistics:** (1998; per 1,000 population): birth rate, 14.5 (1999); death rate, 11.6; marriage rate, 4.6; divorce rate, 3.6.

## Government

**Representation in US Congress:** 1 congressional delegate. **Political divisions:** 8 wards.

## Economy

**Employment** (1997): services, 43.5%; government, 36.0%; trade, 7.3%; finance, insurance, real estate, 5.2%; transportation, public utilities, 3.0%; manufacturing, 1.9%; construction, 1.5%; agricultural service, forestry, fishing, 1.4%. **Production** (2000): services, 38.3%; government, 36.6%; finance, insurance, real estate, 13.5%; transportation, utilities, 5.0%; trade, 4.0%; manufacturing, 1.4%; construction, 1.0%; others, 0.2%. **Chief manufactured products:** printing and publishing products.

**Internet resources:** <www.dc.gov>.

# Florida

**Name:** Florida, in honor of *Pascua florida* ("feast of the flowers"), Spain's Easter celebration. **Nickname:** Sunshine State. **Capital:** Tallahassee. **Rank:** population: 4th; area: 26th. **Motto:** In God We Trust. **Song:** "Old Folks at Home" ("Swanee River"), words and music by Stephen Foster. **Bird:** mockingbird. **Butterfly:** zebra longwing. **Fish:** sailfish (saltwater); large-

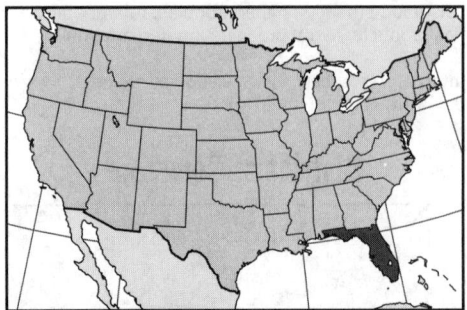

mouth bass (freshwater). **Flower:** orange blossom. **Gemstone:** moonstone. **Mammal:** Florida panther. **Marine mammal:** manatee. **Saltwater mammal:** porpoise. **Reptile:** alligator. **Rock:** agatized coral. **Tree:** sabal palm.

## Natural features

**Area:** 59,928 sq mi, 155,214 sq km. **Highest point:** 345 ft (105 m), in Walton County. **Largest lake:** Lake Okeechobee. **Major rivers:** Kissimmee, Suwannee, St. Johns, Caloosahatchee, Indian, Withlacoochee, Apalachicola, Perdido, St. Marys. **Natural regions:** Western Highlands, a region at the westernmost end of the panhandle; Marianna Lowlands, east of the Western Highlands; Tallahassee Hills, covering the northern border with Georgia; Central Highlands, extending down the middle two-thirds of the peninsula; Coastal Lowlands, curving along the east, south, and west coasts of the peninsula; the Everglades, far southern quarter of the peninsula. **Location:** Southeast, bordering Georgia and Alabama. **Climate:** tropical south of a west–east line drawn from Bradenton along the south shore of Lake Okeechobee to Vero Beach, and subtropical north of this line; hot, humid summers and mild, pleasant winters; hurricane season from June to November. **Land use:** forest, 42.3%; pasture, 15.8%; agricultural, 10.6%; other, 31.4%.

## People (2000 census)

**Population:** 15,982,378; 296.0 persons per sq mi (114.3 persons per sq km) (land area only). **Vital statistics** (1998; per 1,000 population): birth rate, 13.0 (1999); death rate, 10.6; marriage rate, 9.4; divorce rate, 5.4. **Major cities:** Jacksonville, 735,617; Miami, 362,470; Tampa, 303,447; St. Petersburg, 248,232; Hialeah, 226,419; Orlando, 185,951; Fort Lauderdale, 152,397; Tallahassee, 150,624.

## Government

**Statehood:** entered the Union on 3 Mar 1845 as the 27th state. **State constitution:** adopted 1968. **Representation in US Congress:** 2 senators; 23 representatives. **Electoral college:** 27 votes (in the 2004 general elections based on the 2000 census). **Political divisions:** 67 counties.

## Economy

**Employment:** services, 35.3%; trade, 23.2%; government, 13.1%; finance, insurance, real estate, 8.2%; manufacturing, 6.4%; construction, 5.7%; transportation, public utilities, 4.8%; agriculture, forestry,

fishing, 3.0%; mining, 0.1%. **Production:** services, 24.4%; finance, insurance, real estate, 21.5%; trade, 19.1%; government, 12.2%; transportation, utilities, 8.6%; manufacturing, 7.2%; construction, 5.1%; agriculture, 1.8%; mining, 0.2%. **Chief agricultural products:** *Crops:* citrus fruit, fruits and vegetables, corn (maize), cotton, peanuts (groundnuts), soybeans, sugarcane, tobacco, honey, dairy products, eggs, nursery plants and flowers. *Livestock:* cattle and calves, poultry, hogs and pigs. *Aquaculture:* catfish. *Fish catch:* marine fish, crab, shrimp, oyster. **Chief manufactured products:** food products, meatpacking, soft drinks, apparel, paper products, pesticides and fertilizers, agricultural chemicals, plastics, construction materials, fabricated metal products, machinery, communications equipment, semiconductors, electronics, aerospace products, airplane engines, ships and boats, medical and surgical equipment.

**Internet resources:** <www.flausa.com>; <www.state.fl.us>.

# Georgia

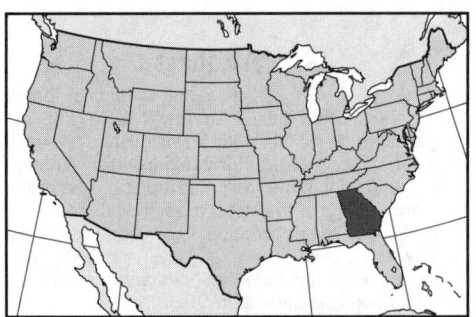

**Name:** Georgia, named for George II, king of England at the time the colony of Georgia was founded. **Nickname:** Empire State of the South; Peach State. **Capital:** Atlanta. **Rank:** population: 10th; area: 21st. **Mottos:** Wisdom, Justice, and Moderation; Agriculture and Commerce, 1776. **Song:** "Georgia on My Mind," words by Stuart Gorrell and music by Hoagy Carmichael. **Bird:** brown thrasher. **Fish:** largemouth bass. **Flower:** cherokee rose. **Fossil:** shark tooth. **Gemstone:** quartz. **Insect:** honeybee. **Marine mammal:** right whale. **Mineral:** staurolite. **Reptile:** gopher tortoise. **Tree:** live oak.

## Natural features

**Area:** 58,977 sq mi, 152,750 sq km. **Mountain range:** Blue Ridge Mountains. **Highest point:** Brasstown Bald, 4,784 ft (1,458 m). **Largest lake:** Lanier. **Major rivers:** Chattahoochee, Flint, Apalachicola, Ocmulgee, Oconee, Altamaha, Savannah. **Natural regions:** Blue Ridge Province, north-central edge; Valley and Ridge Province, northwest corner; Piedmont Province, northern half of state; Coastal Plain, southern half of state, divided into the Sea Island Section (southeast) and the East Gulf Coastal Plain (southwest). **Location:** South, bordering North Carolina, South Carolina, Florida, Alabama, and Tennessee. **Climate:** temperate, though maritime tropical air masses dominate the climate in summer; generally hot summers and cool winters; precipitation

*For details about state governments, see pages 812–817; for energy data, see pages 840–842.*

somewhat evenly distributed throughout the seasons in the north, whereas the southern and coastal areas have more summer rains; snow seldom occurs outside the mountainous northern counties. **Land use:** forest, 62.1%; agricultural, 19.8%; pasture, 3.6%; other, 14.6%.

## People (2000 census)

**Population:** 8,186,453; 139.0 persons per sq mi (53.7 persons per sq km) (land area only). **Vital statistics** (1998; per 1,000 population): birth rate, 16.0; death rate, 7.9; marriage rate, 7.8; divorce rate, 4.7. **Major cities:** Atlanta, 416,474; Columbus, 186,291; Savannah, 131,510; Macon, 97,255.

## Government

**Statehood:** entered the Union on 2 Jan 1788 as the 4th state. **State constitution:** adopted 1982. **Representation in US Congress:** 2 senators; 11 representatives. **Electoral college:** 15 votes (in the 2004 general elections based on the 2000 census). **Political divisions:** 159 counties.

## Economy

**Employment:** services, 27.7%; trade, 23.1%; government, 14.9%; manufacturing, 13.5%; finance, insurance, real estate, 6.7%; transportation, public utilities, 5.8%; construction, 5.7%; agriculture, forestry, fishing, 2.5%; mining, 0.2%. **Production:** services, 19.2%; trade, 18.4%; manufacturing, 17.0%; finance, insurance, real estate, 15.3%; government, 11.9%; transportation, utilities, 11.4%; construction, 5.0%; agriculture, 1.3%; mining, 0.5%. **Chief agricultural products:** *Crops:* peanuts (groundnuts), pecans, rye, corn (maize), cotton, cottonseed, hay, oats, sorghum, soybeans, tobacco, wheat, peaches, apples, onions, watermelon, snap beans, cabbage, cucumbers, blueberries, grapes, honey, dairy products. *Livestock:* poultry, pigs, cattle. *Aquaculture:* catfish, trout. *Extractive products:* timber. **Chief manufactured products:** food products, soft drinks, textiles, wood products, paper products, chemical products, transportation equipment.

**Internet resources:** <www.georgia.org>; <www.georgia.gov>.

## Hawaii

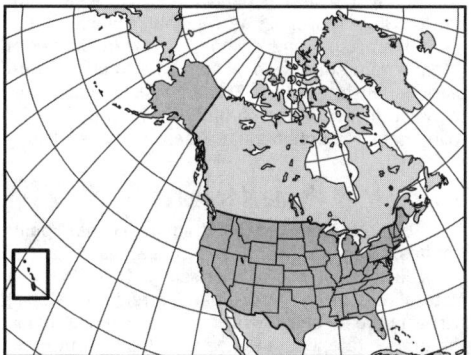

**Nickname:** Aloha State. **Capital:** Honolulu. **Rank:** population: 42nd; area: 47th. **Motto:** *Ua Mau ke Ea o*

*ka Aina i ka Pono* (The Life of the Land Is Perpetuated in Righteousness). **Song:** *"Hawaii Ponoi"* ("Our Hawaii"). **Bird:** nene, or Hawaiian goose. **Fish:** rectangular triggerfish (in Hawaiian, *humuhumunukunuku apua'a*). **Flower:** yellow hibiscus (in Hawaiian, *pua ma'o hau hele*). **Gemstone:** black coral. **Marine mammal:** humpback whale. **Tree:** kukui, or candlenut.

## Natural features

**Area:** Total area, 6,459 sq mi, 16,729 sq km; the eight largest islands are: *Hawaii:* 4,028 sq mi, 10,433 sq km; *Maui:* 728 sq mi, 1,886 sq km; *Oahu:* 607 sq mi, 1,574 sq km; *Kauai:* 552 sq mi, 1,430 sq km; *Molokai:* 280 sq mi, 725 sq km; *Lanai:* 140 sq mi, 363 sq km; *Niihau:* 72 sq mi, 186 sq km; *Kahoolawe:* 45 sq mi, 117 sq km. **Highest point:** Mauna Kea, Hawaii, 13,796 ft (4,205 m). **Major rivers:** *Hawaii:* Wailuku; *Kauai:* Waimea, Hanalei. **Natural regions:** The eight major islands at the eastern end of the 1,500-mile-long chain of islands are, from west to east, Niihau, Kauai, Oahu, Molokai, Lanai, Kahoolawe, Maui, and Hawaii; each island contains regions of mountains, deeps, ridges, and wide beaches; active volcanoes are found on the island of Hawaii. **Location:** islands surrounded by the Pacific Ocean. **Climate:** tropical; rainfall variations throughout the state are dramatic, ranging from 8.7 inches (220 mm) a year at Kawaihae on the island of Hawaii, to roughly 444 inches (11,280 mm) at Mount Waialeale on the island of Kauai. **Land use:** forest, 28.9%; pasture, 23.4%; agricultural, 7.1%; other, 40.6%.

## People (2000 census)

**Population:** Total, 1,211,537; 188.6 persons per sq mi (72.8 persons per sq km) (land area only). Populations of the eight largest islands: *Niihau:* 230 (1990 estimate); *Kauai:* 50,947 (1990 estimate); *Maui:* 105,336 (1995 estimate); *Molokai:* 6,838 (1995 estimate); *Lanai:* 2,989 (1995 estimate); *Oahu:* 872,478 (1998 estimate); *Hawaii:* 143,135 (1998 estimate); *Kahoolawe:* uninhabited. **Vital statistics** (1998; per 1,000 population): birth rate, 14.4 (1999); death rate, 6.8; marriage rate, 17.5; divorce rate, 4.0. **Major cities:** Honolulu, 371,657; Hilo, 40,759; Kailua, 36,513; Kaneohe, 34,970; Waipahu, 33,108.

## Government

**Statehood:** entered the Union on 21 Aug 1959 as the 50th state. **State constitution:** adopted 1950. **Representation in US Congress:** 2 senators; 2 representatives. **Electoral college:** 4 votes. **Political divisions:** 5 counties.

## Economy

**Employment:** services, 31.3%; government, 22.3%; trade, 22.0%; finance, insurance, real estate, 8.4%; transportation, public utilities, 6.3%; construction, 4.2%; agriculture, forestry, fishing, 2.8%; manufacturing, 2.7%; mining, 0.1%. **Production:** finance, insurance, real estate, 23.2%; services, 22.1%; government, 21.8%; trade, 14.7%; transportation, utilities, 10.4%; construction, 4.0%; manufacturing, 2.5%; agriculture, 1.2%; mining, 0.1%. **Chief agricultural products:** *Crops:* pineapples, sugarcane, flowers, macadamia nuts, coffee, milk, eggs. *Livestock:*

cattle. *Aquaculture:* fish, shellfish. **Chief manufactured products:** food products, processed sugar, canned pineapple, preserved fruits and vegetables, apparel and textile products, printing and publishing.

**Internet resources:** <www.gohawaii.com>; <www. hawaii.gov>.

# Idaho

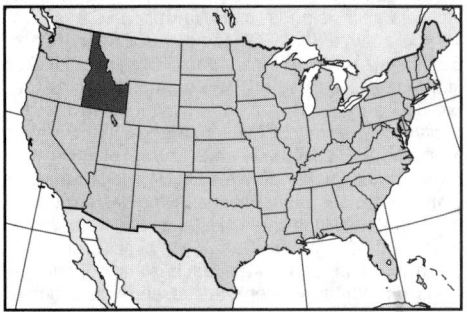

**Nickname:** Gem State. **Capital:** Boise. **Rank:** population: 39th; area: 11th. **Motto:** *Esto Perpetua* (It Is Forever). **Song:** "Here We Have Idaho," words by McKinley Helm and Albert J. Tompkins, music by Sallie Hume Douglas. **Bird:** mountain bluebird. **Fish:** cutthroat trout. **Flower:** syringa. **Fossil:** Hagerman horse fossil (*Equus simplicidens*). **Gemstone:** star garnet. **Horse:** Appaloosa. **Insect:** monarch butterfly. **Tree:** western white pine.

## Natural features

**Area:** 83,574 sq mi, 216,456 sq km. **Mountain ranges:** Northern Rocky Mountains, Middle Rocky Mountains, Sawtooth, Pioneer, Continental Divide, Beaverhead, Clearwater, Bitterroot, Salmon River, Lost River Range, Lemhi Range. **Highest point:** Borah Peak, 12,662 ft (3,859 m). **Largest lake:** Lake Pend Oreille. **Major rivers:** Snake, Salmon. **Natural regions:** Northern Rocky Mountains, covering most of the northern half of the state; Columbia Plateaus, extending across the south-central and southwestern regions; Great Basin region of the Basin and Range Province, southeast; Middle Rocky Mountains, extreme southeast tip. **Location:** Northwest, bordering Montana, Wyoming, Utah, Nevada, Oregon, and Washington; international border with Canada. **Climate:** continental, with warm wet summers and cold dry winters, but regionally diverse: in general, precipitation increases and mean temperatures drop with increases in altitude. **Land use:** pasture, 40.0%; forest, 32.3%; agricultural, 10.9%; other, 16.8%.

## People (2000 census)

**Population:** 1,293,953; 15.6 persons per sq mi (6.0 persons per sq km) (land area only). **Vital statistics** (1998; per 1,000 population): birth rate, 15.9 (1999); death rate, 7.5; marriage rate, 12.6; divorce rate, 5.7. **Major cities:** Boise, 185,787; Nampa, 51,867; Pocatello, 51,466; Idaho Falls, 50,730; Meridian, 34,919.

## Government

**Statehood:** entered the Union on 3 Jul 1890 as the 43rd state. **State constitution:** adopted 1889. **Representation in US Congress:** 2 senators; 2 representatives. **Electoral college:** 4 votes. **Political divisions:** 44 counties.

## Economy

**Employment:** services, 26.1%; trade, 22.7%; government, 15.0%; manufacturing, 11.4%; agriculture, forestry, fishing, 7.5%; construction, 7.1%; finance, insurance, real estate, 5.4%; transportation, public utilities, 4.4%; mining, 0.5%. **Production:** manufacturing, 21.6%; trade, 16.6%; services, 16.3%; government, 13.4%; finance, insurance, real estate, 11.8%; transportation, utilities, 7.8%; construction, 6.6%; agriculture, 5.2%; mining, 0.6%. **Chief agricultural products:** *Crops:* potatoes, wheat, hay, sugar beets, barley, alfalfa seed, Kentucky Blue Grass seed, hops, beans, onions, lentils, peas, honey, dairy products. *Livestock:* cattle, calves, sheep, lambs. *Extractive products:* timber, trout. **Chief manufactured products:** food processing, lumber and wood products, paper, printing, chemicals, plastics and rubber products, nonmetallic mineral products, fabricated metal products, machinery, computers and electronic products, transportation equipment, furniture.

**Internet resources:** <www.visitid.org>; <www. idaho.gov>.

# Illinois

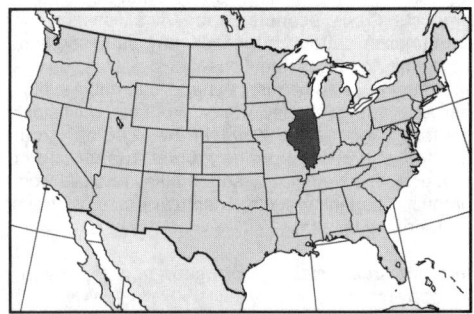

**Name:** Illinois, from a Native American word meaning "tribe of superior men." **Nickname:** Prairie State. **Capital:** Springfield. **Rank:** population: 5th; area: 24th. **Motto:** State Sovereignty, National Union. **Slogan:** Land of Lincoln. **Song:** "Illinois," words by Charles H. Chamberlain and music by Archibald Johnston. **Bird:** cardinal. **Fish:** bluegill. **Flower:** violet. **Fossil:** tully monster. **Insect:** monarch butterfly. **Mammal:** white-tailed deer. **Mineral:** fluorite. **Tree:** white oak.

## Natural features

**Area:** 57,918 sq mi, 150,007 sq km. **Highest point:** Charles Mound, 1,235 ft (376 m). **Largest lake:** Carlyle Lake. **Major rivers:** Mississippi, Ohio, Wabash. **Natural regions:** central Lowland, a region of sloping hills and broad, shallow river valleys covering almost the entire state; Ozark Plateaus, extreme southwest; Interior Low Plateaus and Coastal Plain, extreme

*For details about state governments, see pages 812–817; for energy data, see pages 840–842.*

southeastern tip. **Location:** Midwest, bordering Wisconsin, Indiana, Kentucky, Missouri, and Iowa. **Climate:** continental, with hot summers and cold, snowy winters; wide seasonal and regional variations. **Land use:** agricultural, 70.1%; forest, 11.4%; pasture, 4.4%; other, 14.2%.

## People (2000 census)

**Population:** 12,419,293; 223.4 persons per sq mi (85.1 persons per sq km) (land area only). **Vital statistics** (1998; per 1,000 population): birth rate, 15.0 (1999); death rate, 8.7; marriage rate, 7.0; divorce rate, 3.4. **Major cities:** Chicago, 2,896,016; Rockford, 150,115; Aurora, 142,990; Naperville, 128,358; Peoria, 112,936; Springfield, 111,454; Joliet, 106,221.

## Government

**Statehood:** entered the Union on 3 Dec 1818 as the 21st state. **State constitution:** adopted 1970. **Representation in US Congress:** 2 senators; 20 representatives. **Electoral college:** 21 votes (in the 2004 general elections based on the 2000 census). **Political divisions:** 102 counties.

## Economy

**Employment:** services, 30.9%; trade, 21.2%; manufacturing, 14.0%; government, 12.2%; finance, insurance, real estate, 9.0%; transportation, public utilities, 5.5%; construction, 4.7%; agriculture, forestry, fishing, 2.3%; mining, 0.3%. **Production:** services, 22.6%; finance, insurance, real estate, 20.4%; manufacturing, 16.3%; trade, 16.2%; government, 9.9%; transportation, utilities, 9.2%; construction, 4.5%; agriculture, 0.8%; mining, 0.3%. **Chief agricultural products:** *Crops:* corn (maize), soybeans, wheat, hay, oats, sorghum, apples, peaches, snap beans, sweet corn, potatoes, cabbage, dairy products, eggs. *Livestock:* pigs, cattle, calves, horses, poultry. **Chief manufactured products:** food products, beverages, textiles, leather goods, apparel, wood products, paper products, printing, petroleum and coal products, asphalt paving, chemicals, pharmaceuticals, plastics and rubber products, nonmetallic mineral products, iron and steel products, fabricated metals, machinery, computers and electronics, appliances, and transportation equipment.

**Internet resources:** <www.enjoyillinois.com>; <www.illinois.gov>.

# Indiana

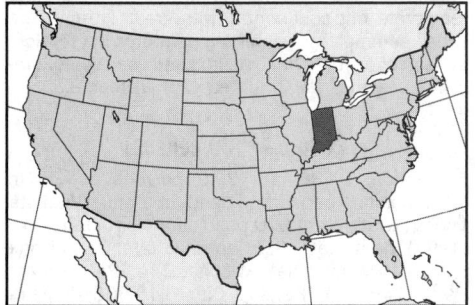

**Name:** Indiana, generally thought to mean "Land of the Indians." **Nickname:** Hoosier State. **Capital:**

Indianapolis. **Rank:** population: 14th; area: 38th. **Motto:** The Crossroads of America. **Song:** "On the Banks of the Wabash, Far Away," words and music by Paul Dresser. **Bird:** cardinal. **Flower:** peony. **Rock:** limestone. **Tree:** tulip tree (yellow poplar).

## Natural features

**Area:** 36,420 sq mi, 94,328 sq km. **Highest point:** 1,257 ft (383 m), near Fountain City. **Largest lake:** Lake Monroe. **Major rivers:** Wabash, Ohio. **Natural regions:** Central Lowland comprises most of the state and includes the Eastern Lake section to the north, and the Till Plains in the center; Interior Low Plateaus, including the Highland Rim section, cover the southern quarter of the state. **Location:** Midwest, bordering Michigan, Ohio, Kentucky, and Illinois. **Climate:** continental, with four distinct seasons; hot summers, cold winters, mild spring and fall, with increased risk of tornadoes in spring. **Land use:** agricultural, 59.6%; forest, 18.9%; pasture, 5.0%; other, 16.4%.

## People (2000 census)

**Population:** 6,080,485; 169.5 persons per sq mi (65.4 persons per sq km) (land area only). **Vital statistics** (1998; per 1,000 population): birth rate, 14.5 (1999); death rate, 9.1; marriage rate, 5.9; divorce rate, N/A. **Major cities:** Indianapolis, 791,926; Fort Wayne, 205,727; Evansville, 121,582; South Bend, 107,789; Gary, 102,746; Hammond, 83,048.

**Did you know?** Eating peanuts at the Indy 500 has been considered bad luck since the 1940s, when peanut shells were found in the seat of a crashed car.

## Government

**Statehood:** entered the Union on 11 Dec 1816 as the 19th state. **State constitution:** adopted 1851. **Representation in US Congress:** 2 senators; 10 representatives. **Electoral college:** 11 votes (in the 2004 general elections based on the 2000 census). **Political divisions:** 92 counties.

## Economy

**Employment:** services, 26.2%; trade, 22.7%; manufacturing, 19.7%; government, 11.7%; finance, insurance, real estate, 6.0%; construction, 5.8%; transportation, public utilities, 4.8%; agriculture, forestry, fishing, 3.0%; mining, 0.3%. **Production:** manufacturing, 30.9%; services, 16.6%; trade, 15.4%; finance, insurance, real estate, 13.0%; government, 10.0%; transportation, utilities, 7.6%; construction, 5.1%; agriculture, 1.0%; mining, 0.4%. **Chief agricultural products:** *Crops:* corn (maize), soybeans, wheat, hay, popcorn, tobacco, tomatoes, peppermint, spearmint, watermelon, blueberries, snap beans, cucumbers, apples, milk, eggs. *Livestock:* pigs, cattle, calves, poultry. **Chief manufactured products:** iron and steel, metal products, motor vehicle parts, machinery, food products, dairy products, soft drinks, wood products, paper products, mobile homes, asphalt.

**Internet resources:** <www.enjoyindiana.com>; <www.state.in.us>.

# Iowa

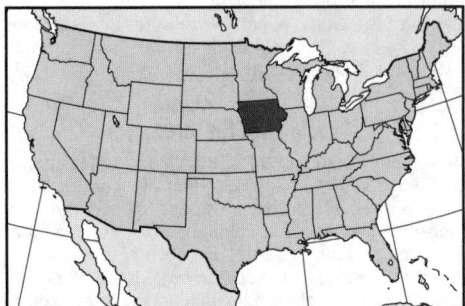

**Name:** Iowa, named for the Iowa (or Ioway) Indians who once inhabited the area. **Nickname:** Hawkeye State. **Capital:** Des Moines. **Rank:** population: 30th; area: 23rd. **Motto:** Our Liberties We Prize and Our Rights We Will Maintain. **Song:** "The Song of Iowa," words by S.H.M. Byers, to the tune of "O Tannenbaum." **Bird:** eastern goldfinch. **Flower:** wild rose. **Rock:** geode. **Tree:** oak.

## Natural features

**Area:** 56,276 sq mi, 145,754 sq km. **Highest point:** near Sibley, 1,670 ft (509 m). **Largest lake:** Spirit Lake. **Major rivers:** Des Moines, Mississippi, Missouri, Big Sioux. **Natural regions:** overall, Central Lowland, including the Western Lake section, north and central regions; Dissected Till Plains, south; Wisconsin Driftless Section, northeast corner. **Location:** Midwest, bordering Minnesota, Wisconsin, Illinois, Missouri, Nebraska, and South Dakota. **Climate:** continental, with hot summers and cold, snowy winters. **Land use:** agricultural, 78.1%; forest, 5.4%; pasture, 4.1%; other, 12.4%.

## People (2000 census)

**Population:** 2,926,324; 52.4 persons per sq mi (20.2 persons per sq km) (land area only). **Vital statistics** (1998; per 1,000 population): birth rate, 13.1 (1999); death rate, 9.9; marriage rate, 8.2; divorce rate, 3.3. **Major cities:** Des Moines, 198,682; Cedar Rapids, 120,758; Davenport, 98,359; Sioux City, 85,013; Waterloo, 68,747.

## Government

**Statehood:** entered the Union on 28 Dec 1846 as the 29th state. **State constitution:** adopted 1857. **Representation in US Congress:** 2 senators, 5 representatives. **Electoral college:** 7 votes. **Political divisions:** 99 counties.

## Economy

**Employment:** services, 26.8%; trade, 22.4%; manufacturing, 14.0%; government, 13.2%; agriculture, forestry, fishing, 7.7%; finance, insurance, real estate, 6.2%; construction, 5.1%; transportation, public utilities, 4.4%; mining, 0.1%. **Production:** manufacturing, 22.4%; services, 17.0%; trade, 16.9%; finance, insurance, real estate, 15.1%; government, 12.0%; transportation, utilities, 8.5%; construction, 4.4%; agriculture, 3.5%; mining, 0.3%. **Chief agricul-**tural products: *Crops:* corn (maize), soybeans, hay, oats, grain, milk, eggs, butter, honey, popcorn, sorghum. *Livestock:* poultry, hogs and pigs, beef cattle, sheep. **Chief manufactured products:** food products, dairy products, meatpacking, pesticide, fertilizer, and other agricultural chemicals, farm machinery, construction machinery, household appliances, motor vehicle parts.

**Internet resources:** <www.traveliowa.com>; <www.iowa.gov>.

# Kansas

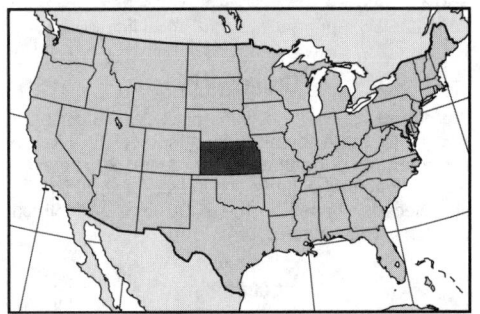

**Name:** Kansas, from the Sioux word *Kansa* ("people of the south wind") for the Native Americans who lived in the region. **Nickname:** Sunflower State. **Capital:** Topeka. **Rank:** population: 32nd; area: 13th. **Motto:** *Ad Astra Per Aspera* (To the Stars Through Difficulties). **Song:** "Home on the Range," words by Brewster Higley and music by Dan Kelly. **Amphibian:** barred tiger salamander. **Bird:** western meadowlark. **Flower:** wild native sunflower. **Insect:** honeybee. **Mammal:** American buffalo. **Reptile:** ornate box turtle. **Tree:** cottonwood.

## Natural features

**Area:** 82,282 sq mi, 213,110 sq km. **Highest point:** Mount Sunflower, 4,039 ft (1,231 m). **Largest lake:** Milford Lake. **Major rivers:** Kansas, Arkansas, Big Blue, Republican, Solomon, Saline, Smoky Hill, Cimarron, Verdigris, Neosho (Grand). **Natural regions:** the Great Plains Province, covering the western half of the state, consists of the High Plains to the west and the Plains Border to the east; the Central Lowland covers the eastern half of the state and consists of the Dissected Till Plains to the north and the Osage Plains to the south. **Location:** Midwest, bordering Nebraska, Missouri, Oklahoma, and Colorado. **Climate:** temperate but continental, with great extremes between summer and winter temperatures but few long periods of extreme hot or cold. **Land use:** agricultural, 64.4%; pasture, 24.0%; forest, 2.8%; other, 8.8%.

## People (2000 census)

**Population:** 2,688,418; 32.9 persons per sq mi (12.7 persons per sq km) (land area only). **Vital statistics** (1998; per 1,000 population): birth rate, 14.6 (1999); death rate, 9.2; marriage rate, 7.9; divorce rate, 4.1. **Major cities:** Wichita, 344,284; Overland Park, 149,080; Kansas City, 146,866; Topeka, 122,377; Olathe, 92,962.

*For details about state governments, see pages 812–817; for energy data, see pages 840–842.*

## Government

**Statehood:** entered the Union on 29 Jan 1861 as the 34th state. **State constitution:** adopted 1859. **Representation in US Congress:** 2 senators; 4 representatives. **Electoral college:** 6 votes. **Political divisions:** 105 counties.

## Economy

**Employment:** services, 26.5%; trade, 22.2%; government, 16.0%; manufacturing, 12.6%; agriculture, forestry, fishing, 5.9%; finance, insurance, real estate, 5.7%; construction, 5.2%; transportation, public utilities, 4.9%; mining, 1.2%. **Production:** trade, 18.2%; services, 17.4%; manufacturing, 16.8%; government, 13.5%; finance, insurance, real estate, 12.9%; transportation, utilities, 12.5%; construction, 4.6%; agriculture, 2.9%; mining, 1.3%. **Chief agricultural products:** *Crops:* wheat, corn (maize), sorghum, hay, soybeans, sunflower seed and oil, apples, peaches, pecans. *Livestock:* beef cattle and calves, hogs, lambs, sheep, dairy cows, horses and other equines. **Chief manufactured products:** food products, grain and oilseed milling, meat products, printing, refined petroleum, soap and cleaning products, plastic products, aerospace products and parts, aircraft.

**Internet resources:** <www.kansas-travel.com>; <www.kansas.gov>.

# Kentucky

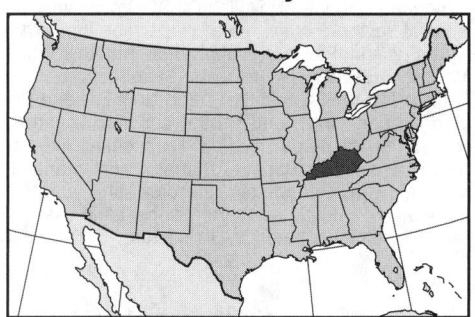

**Name:** Kentucky, possibly from the Iroquois word for "prairie." **Nickname:** Bluegrass State. **Capital:** Frankfort. **Rank:** population: 25th; area: 36th. **Motto:** United We Stand, Divided We Fall. **Song:** "My Old Kentucky Home," words and music by Stephen Foster. **Bird:** cardinal. **Butterfly:** viceroy butterfly. **Fish:** Kentucky bass. **Flower:** goldenrod. **Horse:** thoroughbred. **Tree:** tulip popular. **Wild animal:** gray squirrel.

## Natural features

**Area:** 40,411 sq mi, 104,665 sq km. **Mountain ranges:** Cumberland, Pine. **Highest point:** Black Mountain, 4,145 ft (1,263 m). **Largest lake:** Kentucky Lake. **Major rivers:** Mississippi, Ohio, Big Sandy, Licking, Kentucky, Salt, Green, Tradewater, Cumberland, Tennessee. **Natural regions:** Appalachian Plateaus, eastern third of the state; Interior Low Plateaus, including the Highland Rim section and the Lexington Plain, cover the remainder, with the exception of the Coastal Plain, which covers the extreme southwest tip. **Location:** Midwest, bordering Indiana,

Ohio, West Virginia, Virginia, Tennessee, Missouri, and Illinois. **Climate:** temperate continental climate, with hot, humid summers and cold winters. **Land use:** forest, 48.6%; agricultural, 34.8%; pasture, 5.9%; other, 10.7%.

## People (2000 census)

**Population:** 4,041,769; 101.7 persons per sq mi (39.3 persons per sq km) (land area only). **Vital statistics** (1998; per 1,000 population): birth rate, 13.7 (1999); death rate, 9.6; marriage rate, 11.3; divorce rate, 5.7. **Major cities:** Lexington-Fayette, 260,512; Louisville, 256,231; Owensboro, 54,067; Bowling Green, 49,296; Covington, 43,370.

## Government

**Statehood:** entered the Union on 1 Jun 1792 as the 15th state. **State constitution:** adopted 1891. **Representation in US Congress:** 2 senators; 6 representatives. **Electoral college:** 8 votes. **Political divisions:** 120 counties.

## Economy

**Employment:** services, 25.4%; trade, 21.7%; government, 14.9%; manufacturing, 14.9%; agriculture, forestry, fishing, 6.4%; construction, 5.8%; transportation, public utilities, 5.2%; finance, insurance, real estate, 4.5%; mining, 1.2%. **Production:** manufacturing, 27.5%; services, 16.0%; trade, 15.7%; government, 13.5%; finance, insurance, real estate, 10.9%; transportation, utilities, 8.0%; construction, 4.5%; mining, 2.1%; agriculture, 1.8%. **Chief agricultural products:** *Crops:* tobacco, soybeans, corn (maize), wheat, hay, sorghum, eggs, dairy products. *Livestock:* racing and show horses, beef and dairy cattle, hogs, poultry, sheep. **Chief manufactured products:** food products, meat packing, beverages, tobacco, apparel, paper products, printing, chemical products, paint, resin and synthetic rubber products, plastic products, iron and steel, aluminum, fabricated metal products, machinery, appliances, motor vehicles.

**Internet resources:** <www.kentuckytourism.com>; <www.kentucky.gov>.

# Louisiana

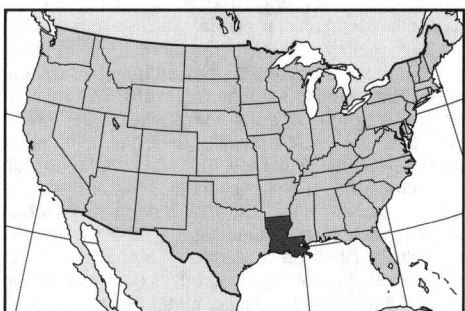

**Name:** Louisiana, named for Louis XIV, king of France. **Nickname:** Pelican State. **Capital:** Baton Rouge. **Rank:** population: 22nd; area: 33rd. **Motto:** Union, Justice and Confidence. **Songs:** "Give Me Louisiana," words and music by Doralice Fontane, arranged by John W. Schaum; "You Are My Sunshine,"

words and music by Jimmy H. Davis and Charles Mitchell. **Amphibian:** green tree frog. **Bird:** brown pelican. **Crustacean:** crawfish. **Freshwater fish:** white perch. **Flower:** magnolia. **Fossil:** petrified palmwood. **Gemstone:** agate. **Insect:** honeybee. **Mammal:** black bear. **Reptile:** alligator. **Tree:** bald cypress.

## Natural features

**Area:** 49,651 sq mi, 128,595 sq km. **Highest point:** Driskill Mountain, 535 ft (163 m). **Largest lake:** Lake Ponchartrain. **Major rivers:** Mississippi, Red, Sabine. **Natural regions:** the entire state consists of the Coastal Plain and is divided into the West Gulf Coastal Plain to the west, the Mississippi Alluvial Plain to the northeast, and the East Gulf Coastal Plain in the southeast. **Location:** South, bordering Arkansas, Mississippi, and Texas. **Climate:** subtropical, with hot, humid summers, tempered by frequent afternoon thunder showers, alternating with mild winters; subject to tropical storms: the hurricane season extends for six months, from June through November. **Land use:** forest, 49.1%; agricultural, 19.7%; pasture, 5.7%; other, 25.6%.

## People (2000 census)

**Population:** 4,468,976; 102.6 persons per sq mi (39.6 persons per sq km) (land area only). **Vital statistics** (1998; per 1,000 population): birth rate, 15.4 (1999); death rate, 9.2; marriage rate, 9.7; divorce rate, N/A. **Major cities:** New Orleans, 484,674; Baton Rouge, 227,818; Shreveport, 200,145; Lafayette, 110,257; Lake Charles, 71,757.

## Government

**Statehood:** entered the Union on 30 Apr 1812 as the 18th state. **State constitution:** adopted 1974. **Representation in US Congress:** 2 senators; 7 representatives. **Electoral college:** 9 votes. **Political divisions:** 64 parishes.

## Economy

**Employment:** services, 29.2%; trade, 21.6%; government, 17.4%; manufacturing, 8.7%; construction, 6.8%; transportation, public utilities, 5.6%; finance, insurance, real estate, 5.3%; agriculture, forestry, fishing, 2.8%; mining, 2.7%. **Production:** services, 17.6%; manufacturing, 15.2%; trade, 15.1%; finance, insurance, real estate, 13.0%; government, 12.3%; mining, 11.7%; transportation, utilities, 9.2%; construction, 4.9%; agriculture, 1.0%. **Chief agricultural products:** *Crops:* soybeans, cotton, corn (maize), sorghum, hay, sugarcane, rice, wheat, sweet potatoes, pecans, strawberries, peaches, milk, eggs. *Livestock:* cattle, chickens, hogs. *Aquaculture:* catfish, crawfish. *Fish catch:* shrimp, oysters, marine fish, freshwater fish. *Extractive products:* timber. **Chief manufactured products:** industrial chemicals, agricultural chemicals, plastics materials and resins, petroleum refining, cane sugar products, beverages, food products, paper, metal products, wood products, communications equipment, ships and boats.

**Internet resources:** <www.louisianatravel.com>; <www.louisiana.gov>.

# Maine

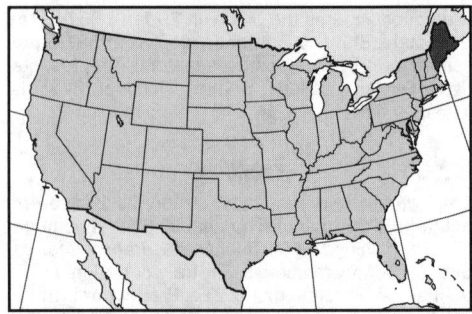

**Name:** Maine, possibly named for the former French province of Maine, or used to distinguish the mainland portion of the territory from offshore islands. **Nickname:** Pine Tree State. **Capital:** Augusta. **Rank:** population: 40th; area: 39th. **Motto:** *Dirigo* (I Direct). **Song:** "State of Maine Song," words and music by Roger Vinton Snow. **Bird:** chickadee. **Fish:** landlocked salmon. **Flower:** white pine cone and tassel. **Fossil:** *Pertica quadrifaria.* **Gemstone:** tourmaline. **Insect:** honeybee. **Mammal:** moose. **Tree:** white pine.

## Natural features

**Area:** 33,741 sq mi, 87,388 sq km. **Mountain ranges:** Appalachians, Longfellow. **Highest point:** Mount Katahdin, 5,268 ft (1,606 m). **Largest lake:** Moosehead Lake. **Major rivers:** Saco, Androscoggin, Kennebec, Penobscot, St. John's, St. Croix, Allagash. **Natural regions:** entire state is part of the larger New England Province, subdivided into the White Mountain section (southwest), Seaboard Lowland Section (southeast coastline), and New England Upland Section (north and central regions). **Location:** New England, bordering New Hampshire; international border with Canada. **Climate:** cool maritime climate, with coldest temperatures and greatest snowfall occurring in northern regions. **Land use:** forest, 85.8%; agricultural, 2.4%; pasture, 0.2%; other, 11.6%.

## People (2000 census)

**Population:** 1,274,923; 41.3 persons per sq mi (15.9 persons per sq km) (land area only). **Vital statistics** (1998; per 1,000 population): birth rate, 10.9 (1999); death rate, 9.8; marriage rate, 8.4; divorce rate, 4.1. **Major cities:** Portland, 64,249; Lewiston, 35,690; Bangor, 31,473; South Portland, 23,324; Auburn, 23,203.

## Government

**Statehood:** entered the Union on 15 Mar 1820 as the 23rd state. **State constitution:** adopted 1819. **Representation in US Congress:** 2 senators; 2 representatives. **Electoral college:** 4 votes. **Political divisions:** 16 counties.

## Economy

**Employment:** services, 30.2%; trade, 23.0%; government, 13.7%; manufacturing, 13.1%; construction,

*For details about state governments, see pages 812–817; for energy data, see pages 840–842.*

6.3%; finance, insurance, real estate, 5.9%; transportation, public utilities, 4.1%; agriculture, forestry, fishing, 3.7%. **Production:** services, 20.1%; finance, insurance, real estate, 18.8%; trade, 18.0%; manufacturing, 15.4%; government, 14.0%; transportation, utilities, 7.0%; construction, 4.6%; agriculture, forestry, fishing 2.0%. **Chief agricultural products:** *Crops:* potatoes, blueberries, hay, apples, cranberries, oats, honey, corn (maize), dairy products, eggs. *Livestock:* poultry, cattle, sheep. *Aquaculture:* salmon, rainbow trout. *Fish catch:* marine fish, lobster, shrimp, crab, clams, haddock, cod, mackerel. *Extractive industries:* timber. **Chief manufactured products:** paper, leather, lumber and wood products, food products, semiconductors, apparel, printing and publishing, plastic products, ships and boats.

**Internet resources:** <www.visitmaine.com>; <www.maine.gov>.

# Maryland

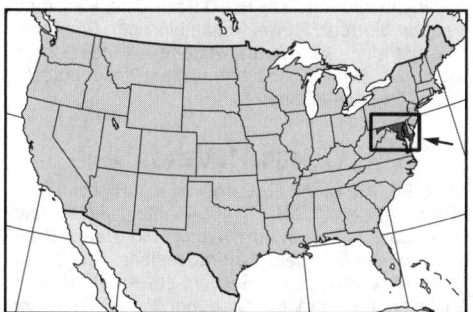

**Name:** Maryland, in honor of Henrietta Maria (queen of Charles I of England). **Nickname:** Old Line State. **Capital:** Annapolis. **Rank:** population: 19th; area: 42nd. **Motto:** *Fatti Maschii, Parole Femine* (Manly Deeds, Womanly Words). **Song:** "Maryland, My Maryland," words by James Ryder Randall, to the tune of "Lauriger Horatius." **Bird:** Baltimore oriole. **Crustacean:** Maryland blue crab. **Dinosaur:** *Astrodon johnstoni.* **Fish:** rockfish (striped bass). **Flower:** black-eyed Susan. **Insect:** Baltimore checkerspot. **Reptile:** diamondback terrapin. **Tree:** white oak.

## Natural features

**Area:** 12,297 sq mi, 31,849 sq km. **Mountain ranges:** Allegheny Mountains, Appalachians. **Highest point:** Backbone Mountain, 3,360 ft (1,024 m). **Largest lake:** Deep Creek Lake. **Major rivers:** Potomac, Patuxent, Susquehanna. **Natural regions:** Coastal Plain, eastern half of the state, includes the Embayed Section near the southwest corner of the peninsula; Piedmont Province, central, and including the Piedmont Upland to the north and the Piedmont Lowlands to the west; Blue Ridge Province, northwest; Valley and Ridge Province, part of western neck; Appalachian Plateau, extreme western neck. **Location:** East coast, bordering Pennsylvania, Delaware, District of Columbia, Virginia, and West Virginia. **Climate:** continental in the west, but a humid, subtropical climate prevails in the east; hurricanes often bring much rain to eastern regions. **Land use:** forest, 38.7%; agricultural, 24.9%; pasture, 3.3%; other, 33.1%.

## People (2000 census)

**Population:** 5,296,486; 541.8 persons per sq mi (209.2 persons per sq km) (land area only). **Vital statistics** (1998; per 1,000 population): birth rate, 13.9 (1999); death rate, 8.2; marriage rate, 7.3; divorce rate, 3.2. **Major cities:** Baltimore, 651,154; Frederick, 52,767; Gaithersburg, 52,613; Bowie, 50,269; Rockville, 47,388.

## Government

**Statehood:** entered the Union on 28 Apr 1788 as the 7th state. **State constitution:** adopted 1867. **Representation in US Congress:** 2 senators; 8 representatives. **Electoral college:** 10 votes. **Political divisions:** 23 counties.

## Economy

**Employment:** services, 34.4%; trade, 21.1%; government, 17.3%; finance, insurance, real estate, 8.3%; manufacturing, 6.4%; construction, 6.3%; transportation, public utilities, 4.4%; agriculture, forestry, fishing, 1.8%; mining, 0.1%. **Production:** services, 24.2%; finance, insurance, real estate, 21.3%; government, 17.5%; trade, 15.2%; manufacturing, 8.1%; transportation, utilities, 7.5%; construction, 5.4%; agriculture, 0.8%; mining, 0.1%. **Chief agricultural products:** *Crops:* corn (maize), soybeans, wheat, vegetables, potatoes, tobacco, dairy products, eggs. *Livestock:* cattle, pigs, poultry. *Aquaculture:* hybrid striped bass, catfish, tilapia, trout, oysters. *Fish catch:* blue crab, other crustaceans, oysters, mollusks, marine fish. **Chief manufactured products:** primary metals, ships and boats, food products, motor vehicles, chemical products, paper and printing, plastics and rubber, fabricated metal products, machinery, computers and electronics, transportation equipment.

**Internet resources:** <www.mdisfun.org>; <www.maryland.gov>.

# Massachusetts

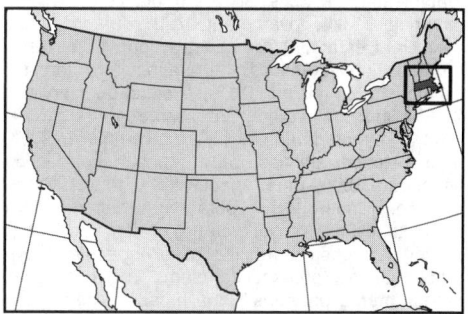

**Name:** Massachusetts, named for the Massachusett tribe of Native Americans who lived in the Great Blue Hill region south of Boston; the word *Massachusett* means "at or about the great hill." **Nickname:** Bay State. **Capital:** Boston. **Rank:** population: 13th; area: 45th. **Motto:** *Ense Petit Placidam Sub Libertate Quietem* (By the Sword We Seek Peace, but Peace Only Under Liberty). **Song:** "All Hail to Massachusetts," words and music by Arthur J. Marsh. **Bird:** black-capped chickadee. **Fish:** cod. **Flower:** mayflower. **Fossil:** theropod dinosaur tracks. **Gemstone:** rhodonite.

Insect: ladybug. Marine mammal: right whale. Mineral: babingtonite. Rock: Roxbury puddingstone. Tree: American elm.

## Natural features

Area: 9,241 sq mi, 23,934 sq km. Mountain ranges: Berkshire Mountains, Hoosac Range, Taconic Range. Highest point: Mount Greylock, 3,491 ft (1,064 m). Largest lake: Webster Lake. Major rivers: Connecticut, Charles, Merrimack, Housatonic, Taunton. Natural regions: the New England Province, comprising most of the state, subdivided into the Taconic Section along the west, the New England Upland Section in the central region, and the Seaboard Lowland Section covering the eastern third of the state; Coastal Plain, comprising the peninsula region. Location: New England, bordering New Hampshire, Rhode Island, Connecticut, New York, and Vermont. Climate: temperate continental climate, with cold snowy winters and warm, humid summers; climate is colder but drier in western Massachusetts, although its winter snowfalls may be more severe. Land use: forest, 53.3%; agricultural, 4.2%; pasture, 0.7%; other, 41.8%.

## People (2000 census)

Population: 6,349,097; 810.0 persons per sq mi (312.8 persons per sq km) (land area only). Vital statistics (1998; per 1,000 population): birth rate, 13.1 (1999); death rate, 9.0; marriage rate, 6.4; divorce rate, 2.7. Major cities: Boston, 589,141; Worcester, 172,648; Springfield, 152,082; Lowell, 105,167; Cambridge, 101,355.

## Government

Statehood: entered the Union on 6 Feb 1788 as the 6th state. State constitution: adopted 1780. Representation in US Congress: 2 senators; 10 representatives. Electoral college: 12 votes. Political divisions: 14 counties.

## Economy

Employment: services, 38.2%; trade, 20.6%; manufacturing, 11.9%; government, 11.2%; finance, insurance, real estate, 8.2%; construction, 4.6%; transportation, public utilities, 4.1%; agriculture, forestry, fishing, 1.3%; mining, 0.1%. Production: services, 26.8%; finance, insurance, real estate, 24.5%; trade, 15.3%; manufacturing, 13.9%; government, 9.1%; transportation, utilities, 5.6%; construction, 4.1%; agriculture, 0.5%. Chief agricultural products: Crops: tobacco, cranberries, hay, potatoes, sweet corn, dairy products, eggs. Livestock: cattle, poultry. Fish catch: marine fish, lobster, crab, mollusks. Aquaculture: oysters, quahogs, soft-shelled clams, scallops. Chief manufactured products: Food products, dairy products, soft drinks, textiles, paper products, printing, pharmaceuticals, plastic products, nonferrous metal products, fabricated metal products, machinery, communications equipment, semiconductors and electronics, electrical equipment, software, aerospace equipment, aircraft engines, surgical and medical equipment.

Internet resources: <www.mass-vacation.com>; <www.state.ma.us>.

# Michigan

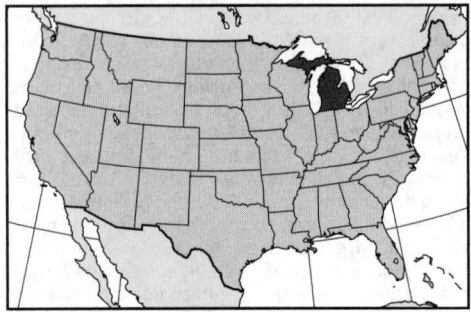

Name: Michigan, from Native American word Michigana meaning "great, or, large lake." Nicknames: Wolverine State and Great Lake State. Capital: Lansing. Rank: population: 8th; area: 22nd. Motto: Si Quaeris Peninsulam Amoenam, Circumspice (If You Seek a Pleasant Peninsula, Look Around You). Song: "Michigan, My Michigan," words by Giles Kavanagh and music by H.J. O'Reilly Clint. Bird: robin. Fish: brook trout. Flower: apple blossom. Gemstone: chlorastrolite. Mammal: white-tailed deer (game mammal). Reptile: painted turtle. Rock: petoskey stone. Tree: white pine.

## Natural features

Area: 96,705 sq mi, 250,465 sq km. Highest point: Mount Arvon, 1,980 ft (604 m). Largest lake: Houghton Lake. Major rivers: Montreal, Brule, Menominee, St. Clair. Natural regions: the Central Lowland, Eastern Lake Section, covers all of Lower Michigan and part of the Upper Peninsula region; the western half of the Upper Peninsula consists of Superior Upland, as do two small areas at the eastern end. Location: Midwest, bordering Ohio, Indiana, and Wisconsin; international border with Canada. Climate: continental; the Great Lakes cool the hot winds of summer and warm the cold winds of winter, giving Michigan a milder climate than some other north-central states, although the Upper Peninsula is relatively cooler; very high snowfall along the coast of Lake Michigan. Land use: forest, 51.3%; agricultural, 22.8%; pasture, 4.4%; other, 21.4%.

## People (2000 census)

Population: 9,938,444; 174.9 persons per sq mi (67.5 persons per sq km) (land area only). Vital statistics (1998; per 1,000 population): birth rate, 13.5 (1999); death rate, 8.7; marriage rate, 6.7; divorce rate, 4.0. Major cities: Detroit, 951,270; Grand Rapids, 197,800; Warren, 138,247; Flint, 124,943; Sterling Heights, 124,471; Lansing, 119,128; Ann Arbor, 114,024; Livonia, 100,545.

## Government

Statehood: entered the Union on 26 Jan 1837 as the 26th state. State constitution: adopted 1963. Representation in US Congress: 2 senators; 16 representatives. Electoral college: 17 votes (in the 2004 general elections based on the 2000 census). Political divisions: 83 counties.

For details about state governments, see pages 812–817; for energy data, see pages 840–842.

## Economy

**Employment:** services, 29.2%; trade, 22.2%; manufacturing, 18.4%; government, 12.1%; finance, insurance, real estate, 6.9%; construction, 4.9%; transportation, public utilities, 3.8%; agriculture, forestry, fishing, 2.3%; mining, 0.2%. **Production:** manufacturing, 26.2%; services, 19.6%; trade, 17.1%; finance, insurance, real estate, 14.1%; government, 10.3%; transportation, utilities, 6.6%; construction, 4.8%; agriculture, 0.9%; mining, 0.3%. **Chief agricultural products:** *Crops:* apples, asparagus, beans, blueberries, carrots, celery, cherries, corn (maize), flowers, grapes and wine, honey, wool, maple syrup, mint, onions, peaches, plums, potatoes, dairy products, eggs, strawberries, sugar, soybeans. *Livestock:* beef and dairy cattle and calves, pigs, poultry, sheep and lambs. *Aquaculture:* Rainbow, brook and brown trout, yellow perch, catfish. *Extractive industries:* Christmas trees. **Chief manufactured products:** Motor vehicles, salt, plastics, pharmaceuticals, soaps and cleansers, milled grain, dry cereals, agricultural machinery, office furniture, dairy products, preserved fruits and vegetables, printed matter, electrical equipment, construction materials, measuring and control devices.

**Internet resources:** <www.michigan.org>; <www.michigan.gov>.

# Minnesota

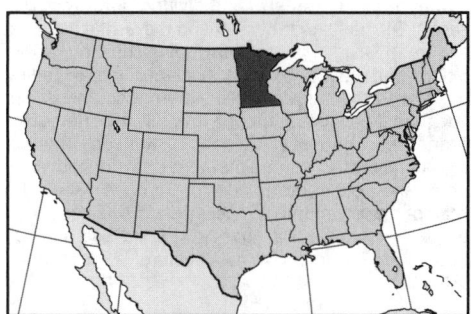

**Name:** Minnesota, from a Dakota word meaning "sky-tinted water." **Nickname:** North Star State. **Capital:** St. Paul. **Rank:** population: 21st; area: 14th. **Motto:** *L'Etoile du Nord* (The Star of the North). **Song:** "Hail! Minnesota," first verse and music by Truman E. Rickard, second verse by Arthur E. Upson. **Bird:** common loon. **Fish:** walleye pike. **Flower:** pink and white lady slipper. **Gemstone:** Lake Superior agate. **Insect:** monarch butterfly. **Tree:** Norway pine.

## Natural features

**Area:** 86,943 sq mi, 225,182 sq km. **Mountain ranges:** Mesabi, Vermillion, Cuyuna. **Highest point:** Eagle Mountain, 2,301 ft (701 m). **Largest lake:** Red Lake. **Major rivers:** Minnesota, St. Croix, Mississippi. **Natural regions:** Superior Upland, northeast corner; Central Lowland, covering most of the state; Western Lake Section, center; Dissected Till Plains, extreme southwest corner and south-central edge; Wisconsin Driftless Section, extreme southeast. **Location:** North central, bordering Wisconsin, Iowa, South Dakota, and North Dakota; international border with Canada. **Climate:** continental, with very cold winters and warm

summers. **Land use:** agricultural, 44.8 (45)%; forest, 29.1 (29)%; pasture, 3.0%; other, 23.1 (23)%.

## People (2000 census)

**Population:** 4,919,479; 61.8 persons per sq mi (23.9 persons per sq km) (land area only). **Vital statistics** (1998; per 1,000 population): birth rate, 13.8 (1999); death rate, 7.9; marriage rate, 6.8; divorce rate, 3.2. **Major cities:** Minneapolis, 382,618; St. Paul, 287,151; Duluth, 86,918; Rochester, 85,806; Bloomington, 85,172.

## Government

**Statehood:** entered the Union on 11 May 1858 as the 32nd state. **State constitution:** adopted 1857. **Representation in US Congress:** 2 senators; 8 representatives. **Electoral college:** 10 votes. **Political divisions:** 87 counties.

## Economy

**Employment:** services, 30.3%; trade, 22.0%; manufacturing, 14.3%; government, 12.0%; finance, insurance, real estate, 7.6%; transportation, public utilities, 4.7%; construction, 4.6%; agriculture, forestry, fishing, 4.2%; mining, 0.3%. **Production:** services, 20.8%; finance, insurance, real estate, 18.5%; manufacturing, 18.1%; trade, 17.6%; government, 10.2%; transportation, utilities, 7.6%; construction, 5.0%; agriculture, 1.7%; mining, 0.5%. **Chief agricultural products:** *Crops:* corn (maize), green peas, dry beans, onions, carrots, apples, oats, hay, spring wheat, barley, soybeans, potatoes, sugar beets, flaxseed, dairy products, eggs. *Livestock:* pigs, cattle and calves, poultry, sheep and lambs. **Chief manufactured products:** food processing, beer and malt beverages, dairy products, meatpacking, industrial machinery, computers and office machines, electronics and electric equipment, precision instruments, printing and publishing, call centers and communications, information technology, forest products, medical manufacturing, plastics manufacturing.

**Internet resources:** <www.exploreminnesota.com>; <www.state.mn.us>.

# Mississippi

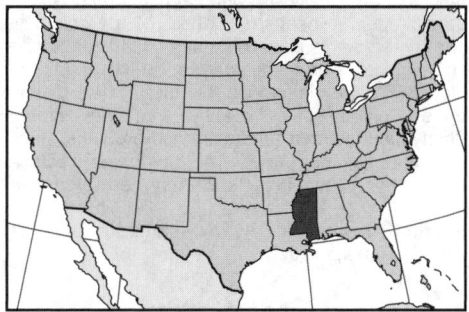

**Name:** Mississippi, from a Native American word meaning "great waters" or "father of waters." **Nickname:** Magnolia State. **Capital:** Jackson. **Rank:** population: 31st; area: 31st. **Motto:** *Virtute et Armis* (By Valor and Arms). **Song:** "Go, Mississippi," words and music by Houston Davis. **Bird:** mockingbird. **Fish:**

largemouth bass. **Flower:** magnolia. **Fossil:** prehistoric whale. **Insect:** honeybee. **Mammal:** white-tailed deer. **Marine mammal:** bottle-nosed dolphin (porpoise). **Rock:** petrified wood. **Tree:** magnolia tree.

## Natural features

**Area:** 48,286 sq mi, 125,060 sq km. **Highest point:** Woodall Mountain, 806 ft (246 m). **Major rivers:** Mississippi, Pearl, Big Black, Yazoo, Tombigbee, Pascagoula, Tennessee. **Natural regions:** the entire state consists of the Coastal Plain, subdivided into the Mississippi Alluvial Plain in the west, and the East Gulf Coastal Plain comprising the central and eastern regions. **Location:** South, bordering Tennessee, Alabama, Louisiana, and Arkansas. **Climate:** mild, with hot, humid summers and mild winters; coastal area is subject to hurricanes from June to October. **Land use:** forest, 61.9%; agricultural, 21.5%; pasture, 6.5%; other, 10.1%.

## People (2000 census)

**Population:** 2,844,658; 60.6 persons per sq mi (23.4 persons per sq km) (land area only). **Vital statistics** (1998; per 1,000 population): birth rate, 15.4 (1999); death rate, 10.1; marriage rate, 7.5; divorce rate, 4.7. **Major cities:** Jackson, 184,256; Gulfport, 71,127; Biloxi, 50,644; Hattiesburg, 44,779; Greenville, 41,633.

## Government

**Statehood:** entered the Union on 10 Dec 1817 as the 20th state. **State constitution:** adopted 1890. **Representation in US Congress:** 2 senators; 5 representatives. **Electoral college:** 6 votes (in the 2004 general elections based on the 2000 census). **Political divisions:** 82 counties.

## Economy

**Employment:** services, 24.5%; trade, 19.7%; government, 17.8%; manufacturing, 17.5%; construction, 5.5%; agriculture, forestry, fishing, 5.2%; finance, insurance, real estate, 4.7%; transportation, public utilities, 4.5%; mining, 0.6%. **Production:** manufacturing, 20.6%; services, 17.4%; trade, 16.8%; government, 16.0%; finance, insurance, real estate, 11.4%; transportation, utilities, 9.5%; construction, 4.7%; agriculture, 2.6%; mining, 1.0%. **Chief agricultural products:** *Crops:* cotton, soybeans, rice, wheat, corn, greenhouse and nursery plants, sweet potatoes, pecans, eggs. *Livestock:* poultry, cattle. *Aquaculture:* catfish, pearl farming. *Fish catch:* marine fish, freshwater fish, shrimp, oysters, crustaceans. *Extractive industries:* timber. **Chief manufactured products:** food products, transportation equipment, apparel, textiles, paper, electrical equipment, rubber products, primary metal products.

**Internet resources:** <www.visitmississippi.org>; <www.mississippi.gov>.

# Missouri

**Name:** Missouri, named for Native American tribe that lived in the region; the name means "town of the large canoes." **Nickname:** Show Me State. **Capital:**

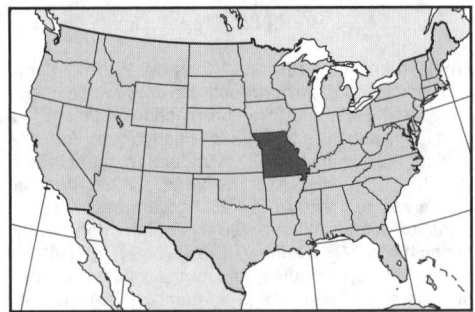

Jefferson City. **Rank:** population: 17th; area: 18th. **Motto:** *Salus Populi Suprema Lex Esto* (The Welfare of the People Shall Be the Supreme Law). **Song:** "Missouri Waltz," words by J.R. Shannon and music by John Valentine Eppel, arrangement by Frederick Knight Logan. **Aquatic animal:** paddlefish. **Bird:** bluebird. **Fish:** channel catfish. **Flower:** white hawthorn blossom. **Fossil:** crinoid. **Insect:** honeybee. **Mammal:** Missouri mule. **Mineral:** galena. **Rock:** mozarkite. **Tree:** flowering dogwood.

## Natural features

**Area:** 69,709 sq mi, 180,546 sq km. **Mountain ranges:** Ozark Plateau, St. Francois Mountains. **Highest point:** Taum Sauk Mountain, 1,772 ft (540 m). **Largest lake:** Truman Lake. **Major rivers:** Missouri, Mississippi, Des Plaines. **Natural regions:** the Central Lowland, northwestern, subdivided into the Dissected Till Plains to the north and the Osage Plains to the west; Ozark Plateaus, including the Springfield-Salem Plateaus, southeast; Coastal Plain, including the Mississippi Alluvial Plain, extreme southeast tip. **Location:** Midwest, bordering Iowa, Illinois, Kentucky, Tennessee, Arkansas, Oklahoma, Kansas, and Nebraska. **Climate:** continental, with hot, humid summers and cold winters; lies in "Tornado Alley," the zone of maximum tornado occurrence, and has an average of 27 tornadoes annually. **Land use:** agricultural, 45.4%; forest, 30.4%; pasture, 13.6%; other, 10.6%.

## People (2000 census)

**Population:** 5,595,211; 81.2 persons per sq mi (31.4 persons per sq km) (land area only). **Vital statistics** (1998; per 1,000 population): birth rate, 13.8 (1999); death rate, 10.1; marriage rate, 8.1; divorce rate, 4.7. **Major cities:** Kansas City, 441,545; St. Louis, 348,189; Springfield, 151,580; Independence, 113,288; Columbia, 84,531.

## Government

**Statehood:** entered the Union on 10 Aug 1821 as the 24th state. **State constitution:** adopted 1945. **Representation in US Congress:** 2 senators; 9 representatives. **Electoral college:** 11 votes. **Political divisions:** 114 counties.

## Economy

**Employment:** services, 29.3%; trade, 21.8%; government, 13.3%; manufacturing, 12.9%; finance, insurance, real estate, 6.8%; transportation, public utilities, 5.8%; construction, 5.5%; agriculture, forestry, fishing, 4.5%; mining, 0.2%. **Production:** services, 20.5%; manufacturing, 19.3%; trade, 17.1%; finance, insurance, real estate, 15.3%; government, 11.4%; transportation, utilities, 10.1%; construction, 4.9%; agriculture, 1.1%; mining, 0.3%. **Chief agricultural products:** *Crops:* soybeans, corn (maize), cotton, rice, grain sorghum, hay, wheat, fruits and vegetables, dairy products. *Livestock:* cattle, pigs, sheep, poultry. *Extractive industries:* timber. **Chief manufactured products:** industrial machinery, transportation equipment, food processing, malt beverages, soft drinks, meat and poultry products, preserved fruits and vegetables, soaps and detergents, agricultural chemicals, pharmaceuticals, printing and publishing, primary metals, nonelectrical machinery, fabricated metals, petroleum and coal products, electrical equipment, stone, clay and glass products.

**Internet resources:** <www.missouritourism.org>; <www.missouri.gov>.

# Montana

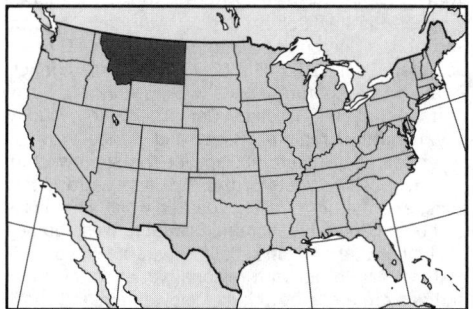

**Name:** Montana, from the Spanish word *montaña* ("mountain," or "mountainous region"). **Nickname:** Treasure State. **Capital:** Helena. **Rank:** population: 44th; area: 4th. **Motto:** *Oro y Plata* (Gold and Silver). **Song:** "Montana," words by Charles C. Cohan and music by Joseph E. Howard. **Bird:** western meadowlark. **Fish:** cutthroat trout. **Flower:** bitterroot. **Fossil:** *Maiasaura.* **Gemstones:** agate and sapphire. **Mammal:** grizzly bear. **Tree:** ponderosa pine.

## Natural features

**Area:** 147,046 sq mi, 380,849 sq km. **Mountain ranges:** Rocky Mountains, Grand Tetons. **Highest point:** Granite Peak, 12,799 ft (3,901 m). **Largest lake:** Flathead Lake. **Major rivers:** Kootenai, Clark Fork, Flathead, Missouri, Yellowstone. **Natural regions:** Northern Rocky Mountains, western two-fifths of the state; Middle Rocky Mountains, small area along the south-central border; Missouri Plateau region of the Great Plains Province, eastern three-fifths of the state. **Location:** Northwest, bordering North Dakota, South Dakota, Wyoming, and Idaho; international border with Canada. **Climate:** continental; most of Great Plains region is semiarid, with warm summers and cold winters; west of the Rocky Mountains the climate is milder. **Land use:** pasture, 49.4%; forest, 20.6%; agricultural, 19.9%; other, 10.1%.

## People (2000 census)

**Population:** 902,195; 6.2 persons per sq mi (2.4 persons per sq km) (land area only). **Vital statistics** (1998; per 1,000 population): birth rate, 12.2 (1999); death rate, 9.1; marriage rate, 7.2; divorce rate, 3.8. **Major cities:** Billings, 89,847; Missoula, 57,053; Great Falls, 56,690; Butte-Silver Bow, 34,606; Bozeman, 27,509; Helena, 25,780.

## Government

**Statehood:** entered the Union on 8 Nov 1889 as the 41st state. **State constitution:** adopted 1972. **Representation in US Congress:** 2 senators; 1 representative. **Electoral college:** 3 votes. **Political divisions:** 56 counties.

## Economy

**Employment:** services, 30.4%; trade, 23.4%; government, 15.5%; agriculture, forestry, fishing, 6.7%; finance, insurance, real estate, 6.1%; construction, 6.1%; manufacturing, 5.6%; transportation, public utilities, 5.0%; mining, 1.3%. **Production:** services, 20.3%; trade, 16.9%; government, 16.4%; finance, insurance, real estate, 13.7%; transportation, utilities, 11.9%; manufacturing, 7.5%; construction, 5.6%; agriculture, 4.0%; mining, 3.7%. **Chief agricultural products:** *Crops:* wheat, barley, hay, oats, safflowers, sunflowers, mustard, sugar beets, dry beans, grapes, garlic, oil seeds, corn (maize), potatoes, honey, cherries, dairy products. *Livestock:* beef and dairy cattle and calves, sheep and lambs, poultry, horses, llamas. *Extractive industries:* timber, Christmas trees. **Chief manufactured products:** food processing, lumber and wood products, metal processing, petroleum products, chemical manufacturing, cement and concrete products, fabricated metal products, machinery.

**Internet resources:** <www.visitmt.com>; <www.state.montana.gov>.

# Nebraska

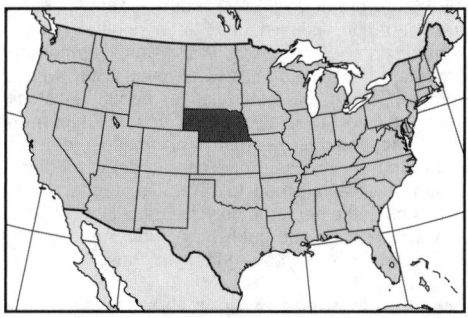

**Name:** Nebraska, from a Native American word meaning "flat water," a reference to the Platte River. **Nickname:** Cornhusker State. **Capital:** Lincoln. **Rank:** population: 38th; area: 15th. **Motto:** Equality Before the Law. **Song:** "Beautiful Nebraska," words and music by Jim Fras. **Bird:** western meadowlark. **Fish:** channel catfish. **Flower:** goldenrod. **Fossil:** mammoth. **Gemstone:** blue agate. **Insect:** honeybee. **Mammal:** white-tailed deer. **Rock:** prairie agate. **Tree:** cottonwood.

## Natural features

**Area:** 77,358 sq mi, 200,358 sq km. **Highest point:** 5,424 ft (1,653 m), in Johnson Township, southwestern part of Kimball County. **Largest lake:** Lake McConaughy. **Major rivers:** Missouri, Platte, Elkhorn, Loup, Republican, Big Blue, Niobrara. **Natural regions:** Great Plains Province, western three-quarters of the state; Missouri Plateau at the northern corners; High Plains, central and north central; Plains Border, south border; Central Lowland, including the Dissected Till Plains, eastern quarter of the state. **Location:** Central, bordering South Dakota, Iowa, Missouri, Kansas, Colorado, and Wyoming. **Climate:** continental, with hot summers and very cold winters; blizzards are not uncommon in winter; western half of state is semiarid. **Land use:** agricultural, 47.9%; pasture, 44.4%; forest, 1.6%; other, 6.1%.

## People (2000 census)

**Population:** 1,711,263; 22.5 persons per sq mi (8.7 persons per sq km) (land area only). **Vital statistics** (1998; per 1,000 population): birth rate, 14.3 (1999); death rate, 9.1; marriage rate, 7.4; divorce rate, 3.8. **Major cities:** Omaha, 390,007; Lincoln, 225,581; Bellevue, 44,382; Grand Island, 42,940; Kearney, 27,431.

## Government

**Statehood:** entered the Union on 1 Mar 1867 as the 37th state. **State constitution:** adopted 1875. **Representation in US Congress:** 2 senators; 3 representatives. **Electoral college:** 5 votes. **Political divisions:** 93 counties.

## Economy

**Employment:** services, 28.1%; trade, 22.2%; government, 14.1%; manufacturing, 10.4%; agriculture, forestry, fishing, 7.3%; finance, insurance, real estate, 7.2%; transportation, public utilities, 5.5%; construction, 5.0%; mining, 0.2%. **Production:** services, 19.1%; trade, 16.7%; finance, insurance, real estate, 15.5%; government, 14.1%; manufacturing, 14.0%; transportation, utilities, 10.8%; agriculture, 4.8%; construction, 4.8%; mining, 0.1%. **Chief agricultural products:** *Crops:* corn (maize), soybeans, hay, wheat, sorghum, dry edible beans, sugar beets. *Livestock:* beef and dairy cattle, pigs, sheep, poultry. **Chief manufactured products:** meatpacking, canned and frozen fruits and vegetables, flour, cereal, grain products, beverages, dairy products, livestock feeds, transportation equipment, motorcycles, small commercial vehicles, printing and publishing, rubber and plastic goods, fabricated metals, primary metals.

**Internet resources:** <www.visitnebraska.org>; <www.nebraska.gov>.

# Nevada

**Name:** Nevada, from the Spanish *nevada* ("snow clad"), a reference to the high mountain scenery of the Sierra Nevada on the southwestern border with California. **Nicknames:** Sagebrush State and Silver State. **Capital:** Carson City. **Rank:** population: 35th; area:

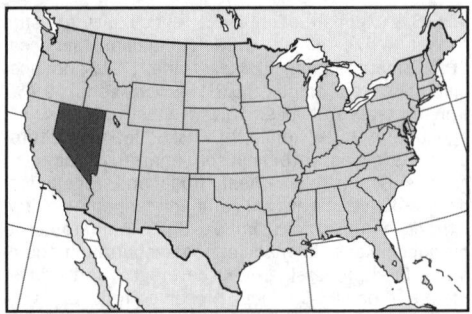

7th. **Motto:** All for Our Country. **Song:** "Home Means Nevada," words and music by Bertha Raffeto. **Bird:** mountain bluebird. **Fish:** Lahontan cutthroat trout. **Flower:** sagebrush. **Fossil:** ichthyosaur. **Gemstones:** fire opal, turquoise. **Mammal:** desert bighorn sheep. **Metal:** silver. **Reptile:** desert tortoise. **Rock:** sandstone. **Trees:** single-leaf piñon and bristlecone pine.

## Natural features

**Area:** 110,567 sq mi, 286,367 sq km. **Mountain ranges:** Snake, Schell Creek, Monitor, Toiyabe, Shoshone, Humboldt, Santa Rosa. **Highest point:** Boundary Peak, 13,140 ft (4,005 m). **Largest lakes:** Pyramid Lake (natural), Lake Mead (artificial). **Major rivers:** Humboldt, Truckee, Carson, Walker, Muddy, Virgin. **Natural regions:** Basin and Range Province covers all of the state, except for the southwestern corner, which consists of the Cascade-Sierra Mountains, and the northeastern corner, which comprises part of the Columbia Plateau. **Location:** West, bordering Idaho, Utah, Arizona, California, and Oregon. **Climate:** semiarid but with regional variation: northern and eastern areas have long, cold winters and short, relatively hot summers, whereas in southern Nevada the summers are long and hot and the winters brief and mild. **Land use:** pasture, 65.9%; forest, 11.7%; agricultural, 1.2%; other, 21.2%.

## People (2000 census)

**Population:** 1,998;257; 18.2 persons per sq mi (7.0 persons per sq km) (land area only). **Vital statistics** (1998; per 1,000 population): birth rate, 16.2 (1999); death rate, 8.3; marriage rate, 82.5; divorce rate, 8.5. **Major cities:** Las Vegas, 478,434; Reno, 180,480; Henderson, 175,381; North Las Vegas, 115,488; Sparks, 66,346.

## Government

**Statehood:** entered the Union on 31 Oct 1864 as the 36th state. **State constitution:** adopted 1864. **Representation in US Congress:** 2 senators; 2 representatives. **Electoral college:** 5 votes (in the 2004 general elections based on the 2000 census). **Political divisions:** 16 counties; 1 independent city.

## Economy

**Employment:** services, 42.2%; trade, 19.5%; government, 10.7%; construction, 8.9%; finance, insurance, real estate, 7.0%; transportation, public utilities, 4.7%; manufacturing, 4.1%; agriculture, forestry, fishing, 1.5%; mining, 1.5%. **Production:** services, 32.5%;

*For details about state governments, see pages 812–817; for energy data, see pages 840–842.*

finance, insurance, real estate, 16.9%; trade, 15.0%; government, 10.3%; construction, 10.2%; transportation, utilities, 8.0%; manufacturing, 4.1%; mining, 2.2%; agriculture, 0.7%. **Chief agricultural products:** *Crops:* hay, wheat, corn (maize), potatoes, rye, oats, alfalfa, barley, vegetables, dairy products, some fruits. *Livestock:* cattle, horses, sheep, hogs, poultry. **Chief manufactured products:** food processing, candy, frozen desserts, dairy products, soft drinks, paper products, chemical products, plastics, construction materials, industrial machinery, printing and publishing.

**Internet resources:** <www.travelnevada.com>; <www.nevada.gov>.

# New Hampshire

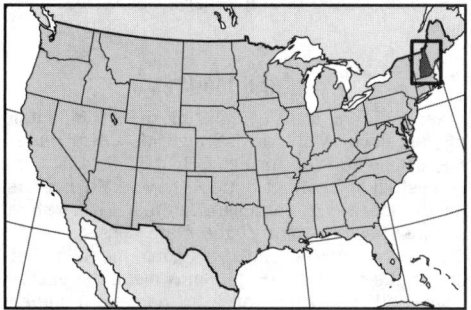

**Name:** New Hampshire, named for Hampshire, England by Captain John Mason. **Nickname:** Granite State. **Capital:** Concord. **Rank:** population: 41st; area: 44th. **Motto:** Live Free or Die. **Songs:** "Old New Hampshire," words by John F. Holmes and music by Maurice Hoffmann; "New Hampshire, My New Hampshire," words by Julius Richelson and music by Walter P. Smith. **Amphibian:** red-spotted newt. **Bird:** purple finch. **Fish:** brook trout (freshwater); striped bass (saltwater). **Flower:** purple lilac. **Gemstone:** smokey quartz. **Insect:** ladybug. **Mammal:** white-tailed deer. **Mineral:** beryl. **Rock:** granite. **Tree:** white birch.

## Natural features

**Area:** 9,283 sq mi, 24,044 sq km. **Mountain ranges:** White Mountains, Ossipee, Sandwich Range, Presidential Range. **Highest point:** Mount Washington, 6,288 ft (1,917 m). **Largest lake:** Lake Winnipesaukee. **Major rivers:** Merrimack, Salmon Falls, Connecticut, Saco, Piscataqua, Androscoggin. **Natural regions:** the New England Province covers the entire state, and is subdivided into the White Mountain Section occupying the northern third, the New England Upland Section in the south-central region, and the Seaboard Lowland Section in the southeast corner. **Location:** New England, bordering Maine, Massachusetts, and Vermont; international border with Canada. **Climate:** temperate, but highly varied: winter temperatures may drop below 0 °F (–18 °C) for days at a time; summers are relatively cool, and precipitation is rather evenly distributed over the four seasons. **Land use:** forest, 79.3%; agricultural, 2.0%; pasture, 0.7%; other, 18.1%.

## People (2000 census)

**Population:** 1,235,786; 137.8 persons per sq mi (53.2 persons per sq km) (land area only). **Vital statistics** (1998; per 1,000 population): birth rate, 11.7 (1999); death rate, 8.0; marriage rate, 6.2; divorce rate, 5.9. **Major cities:** Manchester, 107,006; Nashua, 86,605; Concord, 40,687; Derry, 34,021; Rochester, 28,461.

## Government

**Statehood:** entered the Union on 21 Jun 1788 as the 9th state. **State constitution:** adopted 1784. **Representation in US Congress:** 2 senators; 2 representatives. **Electoral college:** 4 votes. **Political divisions:** 10 counties.

## Economy

**Employment:** services, 31.5%; trade, 24.0%; manufacturing, 15.5%; government, 10.9%; finance, insurance, real estate, 6.9%; construction, 6.0%; transportation, public utilities, 3.5%; agriculture, forestry, fishing, 1.6%; mining, 0.1%. **Production:** finance, insurance, real estate, 23.2%; manufacturing, 22.1%; services, 19.6%; trade, 16.5%; government, 7.8%; transportation, utilities, 5.8%; construction, 4.1%; agriculture, 0.7%; mining, 0.1%. **Chief agricultural products:** *Crops:* apples, honey, fruits and vegetables, ornamental horticulture, Christmas trees, dairy products, eggs, herbs, maple syrup, wool. *Livestock:* horses, dairy cattle, sheep. *Fish catch:* marine fish, seafood. *Extractive products:* timber. **Chief manufactured products:** industrial machinery, computers and software, electrical equipment, semiconductors, processed foods, precision instruments, medical and surgical instruments, fabricated metal products, rubber and plastic products, printing and publishing, paper products.

**Internet resources:** <www.visitnh.gov>; <www.state.nh.us>.

# New Jersey

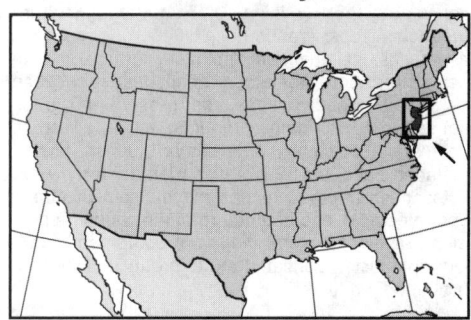

**Name:** New Jersey, named for the island of Jersey in the English Channel. **Nickname:** Garden State. **Capital:** Trenton. **Rank:** population: 9th; area: 46th. **Motto:** Liberty and Prosperity. **Bird:** eastern goldfinch. **Fish:** brook trout. **Flower:** violet. **Fossil:** *Hadrosaurus foulkii.* **Insect:** honeybee. **Mammal:** horse. **Tree:** red oak.

## Natural features

**Area:** 8,215 sq mi, 21,277 sq km. **Mountain range:** Appalachians. **Highest point:** Kittatinny Mountain,

1,803 ft (550 m). **Largest lake:** Lake Hopatcong. **Major rivers:** Delaware, Hudson, Passaic, Hackensack, Raritan. **Natural regions:** the Valley and Ridge Province, Middle Section, northwest corner; the New England Province, consisting of the New England Upland Section, located east of the Valley and Ridge area; Piedmont Province, including the Piedmont Lowlands, extending from the northeast corner to part of the border with Pennsylvania; the southern half of the state consists of the Coastal Plain, Embayed Section. **Location:** Northeast, bordering New York, Delaware, and Pennsylvania. **Climate:** continental; relatively colder winters in northwest, milder conditions in the south, and hot summers throughout the state. **Land use:** forest, 31.7%; agricultural, 13.4%; pasture, 0.6%; other, 54.3%.

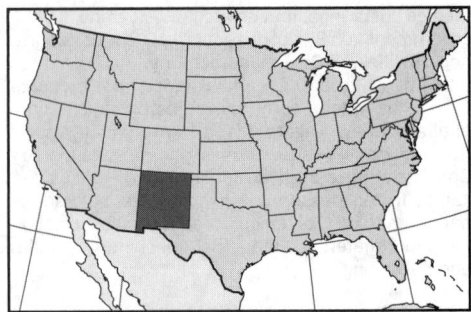

## People (2000 census)

**Population:** 8,414,350; 1,134.3 persons per sq mi (438.0 persons per sq km) (land area only). **Vital statistics** (1998; per 1,000 population): birth rate, 14.0 (1999); death rate, 8.8; marriage rate, 6.0; divorce rate, 3.1. **Major cities:** Newark, 273,546; Jersey City, 240,055; Paterson, 149,222; Elizabeth, 120,568; Trenton, 85,403.

## Government

**Statehood:** entered the Union on 18 Dec 1787 as the 3rd state. **State constitution:** adopted 1947. **Representation in US Congress:** 2 senators; 13 representatives. **Electoral college:** 15 votes. **Political divisions:** 21 counties.

## Economy

**Employment:** services, 32.8%; trade, 21.6%; government, 13.0%; manufacturing, 11.0%; finance, insurance, real estate, 9.7%; transportation, public utilities, 6.3%; construction, 4.3%; agriculture, forestry, fishing, 1.2%; mining, 0.1%. **Production:** finance, insurance, real estate, 23.7%; services, 23.5%; trade, 17.0%; manufacturing, 11.9%; government, 10.1%; transportation, utilities, 9.5%; construction, 3.8%; agriculture, 0.5%; mining, 0.1%. **Chief agricultural products:** *Crops:* cranberries, blueberries, peaches, asparagus, bell peppers, spinach, lettuce, cucumbers, sweet corn, tomatoes, snap beans, cabbage, escarole and endive, eggplants, nursery and greenhouse products, dairy products, eggs. *Livestock:* horses, cattle, poultry. *Fish catch:* bluefish, tilefish, flounder, hake, shellfish. **Chief manufactured products:** chemical products, pharmaceuticals, electronic and electrical equipment, communications equipment, semiconductors, industrial equipment, petroleum products, fabricated metal products, clay products, food products.

**Internet resources:** <www.visitnj.org>; <www.newjersey.gov>.

# New Mexico

**Name:** New Mexico, named for the country of Mexico. **Nickname:** Land of Enchantment. **Capital:** Santa Fe. **Rank:** population: 36th; area: 5th. **Motto:** *Crescit Eundo* (It Grows as It Goes). **Songs:** "O, Fair New Mexico," words and music by Elizabeth Garrett; *"Así es Nuevo Mexico,"* words and music by Amadeo Lucero. **Bird:** roadrunner. **Fish:** New Mexico cutthroat trout. **Flower:** yucca. **Fossil:** coelophysis. **Gemstone:** turquoise. **Insect:** tarantula hawk wasp. **Tree:** piñon pine.

## Natural features

**Area:** 121,598 sq mi, 314,939 sq km. **Mountain ranges:** Rocky Mountains, Sangre de Cristo Range. **Highest point:** Wheeler Peak, 13,160 ft (4,011 m). **Largest lake:** Elephant Butte Reservoir. **Major rivers:** Rio Grande, Pecos, Canadian, San Juan, Gila. **Natural regions:** eastern third of the state consists of the Great Plains Province, subdivided into the Raton Section to the north, the High Plains along the eastern edge, and the Pecos Valley to the west; Southern Rocky Mountains, north-central region; Colorado Plateau, including the Navajo Section and Datil Section, northwest corner; Basin and Range Province, central region and southwest corner, with the Sacramento Section to the east and the Mexican Highland to the south. **Location:** Southwest, bordering Colorado, Oklahoma, Texas, and Arizona; international border with Mexico. **Climate:** arid; moderate temperatures but great variation by altitude; temperatures drop dramatically after dark. **Land use:** Pasture, 67.2%; forest, 18.1%; agricultural, 3.1%; other, 11.6%.

## People (2000 census)

**Population:** 1,819,046; 15.0 persons per sq mi (5.8 persons per sq km). **Vital statistics** (1998; per 1,000 population). Birth rate, 15.6 (1999); death rate, 7.4; marriage rate, 7.7; divorce rate, 4.6. **Major cities:** Albuquerque, 448,607; Las Cruces, 74,267; Santa Fe, 62,203; Rio Rancho, 51,765; Roswell, 45,293.

## Government

**Statehood:** entered the Union on 6 Jan 1912 as the 47th state. **State constitution:** adopted 1911. **Representation in US Congress:** 2 senators; 3 representatives. **Electoral college:** 5 votes. **Political divisions:** 33 counties.

## Economy

**Employment:** services, 29.7%; trade, 21.9%; government, 20.4%; construction, 6.4%; finance, insurance, real estate, 6.0%; manufacturing, 5.7%; transportation, public utilities, 4.2%; agriculture, forestry, fishing, 3.6%; mining, 2.1%. **Production:** services, 18.0%;

*For details about state governments, see pages 812–817; for energy data, see pages 840–842.*

government, 16.8%; manufacturing, 16.7%; trade, 13.6%; finance, insurance, real estate, 13.1%; mining, 8.4%; transportation, utilities, 7.4%; construction, 4.0%; agriculture, 2.1%. **Chief agricultural products:** *Crops:* pecans, apples, potatoes, onions, dry beans, chile, peanuts (groundnuts), hay, sorghum, corn (maize), wheat, eggs, dairy products, wool. *Livestock:* dairy and beef cattle, poultry, sheep and lambs. *Extractive industries:* timber. **Chief manufactured products:** electronic equipment, semiconductors, printing and publishing, processed foods.

**Internet resources:** <www.newmexico.org>; <www.state.nm.us>.

# New York

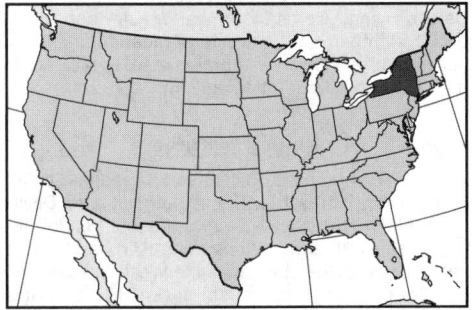

**Name:** New York, named in honor of the English Duke of York. **Nickname:** Empire State. **Capital:** Albany. **Rank:** population: 3rd; area: 30th. **Motto:** *Excelsior* (Ever Upward). **Song:** "I Love New York," words and music by Steve Karmen. **Bird:** bluebird. **Fish:** brook trout. **Flower:** rose. **Fossil:** *Eurypterus remipes.* **Gemstone:** garnet. **Mammal:** beaver. **Tree:** sugar maple.

## Natural features

**Area:** 53,989 sq mi, 139,833 sq km. **Mountain ranges:** Adirondack, Catskill, Shawangunk, Taconic. **Highest point:** Mount Marcy, 5,344 ft (1,629 m). **Largest lake:** Oneida Lake. **Major rivers:** Hudson, Mohawk, Genesee, Oswego, Delaware, Susquehanna, Allegheny. **Natural regions:** the Central Lowland, Eastern Lake Section, extends along the northern coast of Lake Ontario; St. Lawrence Valley, Northern Section, extends along the northern border with Canada; Adirondack Province, northeast; Appalachian Plateaus, including the Mohawks, Southern New York, and Catskill Sections, extend along southern border with Pennsylvania and up halfway through the state; Valley and Ridge Province, southeastern edge bordering Connecticut and Massachusetts; Coastal Plain, Embayed Section, covering the islands of Manhattan and Long Island. **Location:** Northeast, bordering Vermont, Massachusetts, Connecticut, New Jersey, and Pennsylvania; international border with Canada. **Climate:** temperate continental, with hot, humid summers and cold, dry, snowy winters. **Land use:** forest, 56.4%; agricultural, 17.4%; pasture, 8.7%; other, 17.5%.

## People (2000 census)

**Population:** 18,976,457; 401.8 persons per sq mi (155.2 persons per sq km) (land area only). **Vital statistics** (1999; per 1,000 population): birth rate, 14.0 (1999); death rate, 8.5; marriage rate, 7.0; divorce

rate, 3.2. **Major cities:** New York, 8,008,278; Buffalo, 292,648; Rochester, 219,773; Yonkers, 196,086; Syracuse, 147,306; Albany, 95,658.

## Government

**Statehood:** entered the Union on 26 Jul 1788 as the 11th state. **State constitution:** adopted 1894. **Representation in US Congress:** 2 senators; 31 representatives. **Electoral college:** 31 votes (in the 2004 general elections based on the 2000 census). **Political divisions:** 62 counties.

## Economy

**Employment:** services, 35.9%; trade, 19.0%; government, 14.1%; finance, insurance, real estate, 11.1%; manufacturing, 9.7%; transportation, public utilities, 4.9%; construction, 3.9%; agriculture, forestry, fishing, 1.3%; mining, 0.1%. **Production:** finance, insurance, real estate, 32.8%; services, 23.0%; trade, 12.9%; manufacturing, 10.3%; government, 10.2%; transportation, utilities, 7.3%; construction, 3.0%; agriculture, 0.4%; mining, 0.1%. **Chief agricultural products:** *Crops:* apples, cabbage, corn (maize), potatoes, onions, grapes, snap beans, dry beans, grain, hay, cherries, strawberries, maple syrup, horticulture products, milk, eggs, dairy products. *Livestock:* cattle and calves, chickens. **Chief manufactured products:** food processing, chemical products, apparel, primary metals, industrial machinery, computers and software, scientific and measuring instruments, transportation equipment, electric and electronic equipment, industrial machinery, printing and publishing, biotechnology.

**Internet resources:** <www.iloveny.com>; <www.state.ny.us>.

# North Carolina

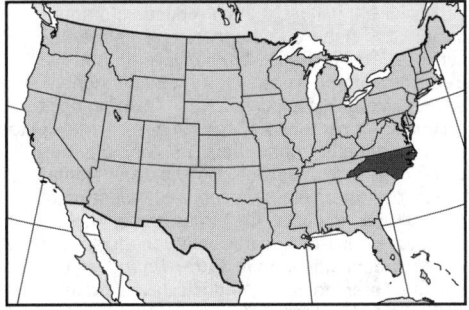

**Name:** North Carolina, named in honor of Charles I of England. **Nickname:** The Old North State. **Capital:** Raleigh. **Rank:** population: 11th; area: 29th. **Motto:** *Esse Quam Videri* (To Be Rather Than to Seem). **Song:** "The Old North State," words by William Gaston to a German tune. **Bird:** cardinal. **Fish:** channel bass. **Flower:** dogwood. **Gemstone:** emerald. **Insect:** honeybee. **Mammal:** gray squirrel. **Reptile:** eastern box turtle. **Rock:** granite. **Tree:** pine.

## Natural features

**Area:** 52,672 sq mi, 136,421 sq km. **Mountain ranges:** Appalachian, Great Smoky, Blue Ridge. **Highest point:** Mount Mitchell, 6,684 ft (2,037 m).

**Largest lake:** Lake Mattamuskeet. **Major rivers:** Roanoke, Yadkin, Pee Dee. **Natural regions:** Valley and Ridge Province, far western edge; Piedmont Province, consisting of the Piedmont Upland, extends in a southwest to northeast direction through the center of the state; Coastal Plain comprises the eastern third, divided into the Sea Island Section to the south and the Embayed Section to the north. **Location:** East coast, bordering Virginia, South Carolina, Georgia, and Tennessee. **Climate:** ranges from medium continental conditions in the mountain region (though summers are cooler and rainfall heavier) to the subtropical conditions of the state's southeastern corner; hurricanes occasionally occur along the coast, and there have been tornadoes inland. **Land use:** forest, 60%; agricultural, 19%; pasture, 3%; other, 19%.

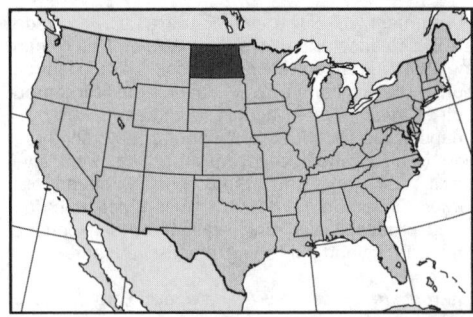

## People (2000 census)

**Population:** 8,049,313; 165.2 persons per sq mi (63.8 persons per sq km) (land area only). **Vital statistics** (1998; per 1,000 population): birth rate, 14.9 (1999); death rate, 9.0; marriage rate, 8.5; divorce rate, 4.9. **Major cities:** Charlotte, 540,828; Raleigh, 276,093; Greensboro, 223,891; Durham, 187,035; Winston-Salem, 185,776; Fayetteville, 121,015.

## Government

**Statehood:** entered the Union on 21 Nov 1789 as the 12th state. **State constitution:** adopted 1970. **Representation in US Congress:** 2 senators, 12 representatives. **Electoral college:** 15 votes (in the 2004 general elections based on the 2000 census). **Political divisions:** 100 counties.

## Economy

**Employment:** services, 25.1%; trade, 21.2%; manufacturing, 18.5%; government, 15.2%; construction, 6.6%; finance, insurance, real estate, 5.9%; transportation, public utilities, 4.3%; agriculture, forestry, fishing, 3.1%; mining, 0.1%. **Production:** manufacturing, 24.1%; finance, insurance, real estate, 18.3%; services, 16.4%; trade, 15.0%; government, 12.5%; transportation, utilities, 7.1%; construction, 4.9%; agriculture, 1.5%; mining, 0.2%. **Chief agricultural products:** *Crops:* tobacco, corn (maize), barley, potatoes, peanuts (groundnuts), apples, blueberries, grapes, peaches, pecans, strawberries, tomatoes, cabbages, watermelons, cucumbers, sweet potatoes, horticultural products, Christmas trees, dairy products, eggs. *Livestock:* cattle, chickens, pigs, horses. *Aquaculture:* catfish, trout. *Extractive industries:* timber. **Chief manufactured products:** textiles, cotton and synthetic fibers, yarns, threads, knitted goods, cigarettes and tobacco products, chemical products, pharmaceuticals, electronic and electrical equipment, furniture, lumber, paper products, processed foods.

**Internet resources:** <www.visitnc.com>; <www.northcarolina.gov>.

# North Dakota

**Name:** North Dakota, from the Dakota division of the Sioux, the Native American tribe who inhabited the plains before the arrival of Europeans; *dakota* is the Sioux word for "friend." **Nickname:** Peace Garden State. **Capital:** Bismarck. **Rank:** population: 47th; area: 17th. **Motto:** Liberty and Union Now and Forever, One and Inseparable. **Song:** "North Dakota Hymn," words by James W. Foley and music by C.S. Putnam. **Bird:** western meadowlark. **Fish:** northern pike. **Flower:** wild prairie rose. **Fossil:** teredo petrified wood. **Tree:** American elm.

## Natural features

**Area:** 70,704 sq mi, 183,123 sq km. **Highest point:** White Butte, 3,506 ft (1,069 m). **Largest lake:** Devils Lake. **Major rivers:** Red, Souris, Missouri, Little Missouri, James. **Natural regions:** central Lowland covers eastern half of the state, with the Western Lake Section lying in the east-central region; Great Plains Province, western half of the state, includes sections of the Missouri Plateau to the north and south. **Location:** North central, bordering Minnesota, South Dakota, and Montana; international border with Canada. **Climate:** continental, with hot summers and cold winters, warm days and cool nights in summer, low humidity and low precipitation, and much wind and sunshine. **Land use:** agricultural, 65.3%; pasture, 25.7%; forest, 1.0%; other, 8.1%.

## People (2000 census)

**Population:** 642,200; 9.3 persons per sq mi (3.6 persons per sq km) (land area only). **Vital statistics** (1998; per 1,000 population): birth rate, 12.1 (1999); death rate, 9.3; marriage rate, 6.6; divorce rate, 3.3. **Major cities:** Fargo, 90,599; Bismarck, 55,532; Grand Forks, 49,321; Minot, 36,567.

## Government

**Statehood:** entered the Union on 2 Nov 1889 as the 39th state. **State constitution:** adopted 1889. **Representation in US Congress:** 2 senators; 1 representative. **Electoral college:** 3 votes. **Political divisions:** 53 counties.

## Economy

**Employment:** services, 28.5%; trade, 22.5%; government, 16.4%; agriculture, forestry, fishing, 9.7%; manufacturing, 5.7%; finance, insurance, real estate, 5.6%; transportation, public utilities, 5.3%; construction, 5.2%; mining, 1.1%. **Production:** trade, 19.5%; services, 19.4%; government, 14.4%; finance, insurance, real estate, 14.1%; transportation, utilities, 10.3%; manufacturing, 9.0%; construction, 5.5%; agriculture, 4.1%; mining, 3.6%. **Chief agricultural**

*For details about state governments, see pages 812–817; for energy data, see pages 840–842.*

**products:** *Crops:* hard red spring wheat, durum wheat, flaxseed, canola, dry beans, sunflowers, barley, honey, potatoes, dairy products, wool. *Livestock:* cattle, sheep, pigs. *Extractive industries:* timber. **Chief manufactured products:** food processing, wood products, petroleum products, transportation equipment, machinery.

**Internet resources:** <www.ndtourism.com>; <www.northdakota.gov>.

# Ohio

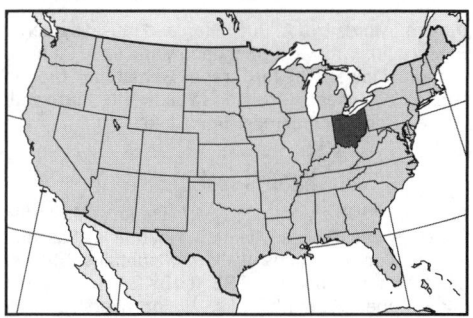

**Name:** Ohio, from an Iroquois word meaning "great river." **Nickname:** Buckeye State. **Capital:** Columbus. **Rank:** population: 7th; area: 35th. **Motto:** With God, All Things Are Possible. **Song:** "Beautiful Ohio," words by Ballad MacDonald and music by Mary Earl. **Bird:** cardinal. **Flower:** red carnation. **Fossil:** *Trilobite isotelus.* **Gemstone:** flint. **Insect:** ladybug. **Mammal:** white-tailed deer. **Reptile:** black racer snake. **Tree:** Ohio buckeye.

## Natural features

**Area:** 44,828 sq mi, 116,103 sq km. **Highest point:** Campbell Hill, 1,550 ft (472 m). **Largest lake:** Grand Lake St. Marys. **Major rivers:** Ohio, Maumee, Cuyahoga, Miami, Scioto, Muskingum. **Natural regions:** the Appalachian Plateau, eastern half of the state, includes the Southern New York Section to the north, and the Kanawha Section to the east; the Central Lowlands, western half of the state, includes the Eastern Lake Section in the northwest corner, the Till Plains in the central region, and the Lexington Plain in the southwest. **Location:** Midwest, bordering Michigan, Pennsylvania, West Virginia, Kentucky, and Indiana. **Climate:** continental, with hot, humid summers and cold, dry winters. **Land use:** agricultural, 45.9%; forest, 28.9%; pasture, 5.3%; other, 20.0%.

**Did you know?** Ohio is home to seven US presidents born after America gained its independence—more than any other state.

## People (2000 census)

**Population:** 11,353,140; 277.2 persons per sq mi (107.0 persons per sq km) (land area only). **Vital statistics** (1998; per 1,000 population): birth rate, 13.6 (1999); death rate, 9.4; marriage rate, 7.6; divorce rate, 4.1. **Major cities:** Columbus, 711,470; Cleveland, 478,403; Cincinnati, 331,285; Toledo, 313,619; Akron, 217,074; Dayton, 166,179.

## Government

**Statehood:** entered the Union on 1 Mar 1803 as the 17th state. **State constitution:** adopted 1851. **Representation in US Congress:** 2 senators; 19 representatives. **Electoral college:** 20 votes (in the 2004 general elections based on the 2000 census). **Political divisions:** 88 counties.

## Economy

**Employment:** services, 29.0%; trade, 22.8%; manufacturing, 17.0%; government, 12.1%; finance, insurance, real estate, 7.2%; construction, 5.1%; transportation, public utilities, 4.3%; agriculture, forestry, fishing, 2.3%; mining, 0.3%. **Production:** manufacturing, 25.8%; services, 18.2%; trade, 16.8%; finance, insurance, real estate, 15.5%; government, 10.7%; transportation, utilities, 7.4%; construction, 4.3%; agriculture, 0.8%; mining, 0.4%. **Chief agricultural products:** *Crops:* corn (maize), soybeans, grapes, apples, vegetables, tobacco, winter wheat, dairy products, eggs, greenhouse and nursery products. *Livestock:* cattle, hogs, poultry, goats. *Extractive industries:* timber. **Chief manufactured products:** industrial machinery, non-electrical machinery, food processing, transportation equipment, fabricated metals, iron and steel, chemical products and pharmaceuticals, rubber products.

**Internet resources:** <www.ohiotourism.com>; <www.ohio.gov>.

# Oklahoma

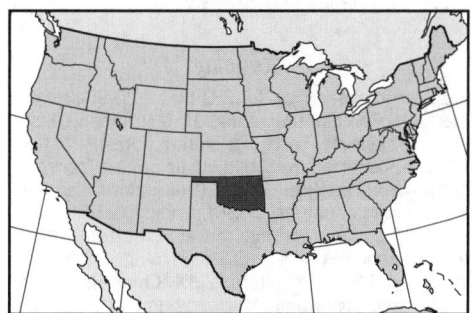

**Name:** Oklahoma, from two Choctaw words: *okla* meaning "people" and *humma* meaning "red." **Nickname:** Sooner State. **Capital:** Oklahoma City. **Rank:** population: 27th; area: 19th. **Motto:** *Labor Omnia Vincit* (Labor Conquers All Things). **Song:** "Oklahoma," words by Richard Rodgers and music by Oscar Hammerstein. **Bird:** scissor-tailed flycatcher. **Fish:** white, or sand, bass. **Flower:** mistletoe. **Insect:** honeybee. **Mammal:** bison. **Reptile:** collared lizard (also know as the mountain boomer). **Rock:** rose rock. **Tree:** redbud.

## Natural features

**Area:** 69,903 sq mi, 181,048 sq km. **Mountain ranges:** Ouachita, Arbuckle, Wichita, Sandstone Hills.

**Highest point:** Black Mesa, 4,978 ft (1,517 m). **Largest lake:** Lake Eufaula. **Major rivers:** Arkansas, Red, Canadian. **Natural regions:** Great Plains Province, panhandle region, includes the High Plains to the west and the Plains Border to the east; Central Lowland, covers most of the state, includes the Osage Plains in the central region; West Gulf Coastal Plain, southeastern corner; Ouachita Province, east-central region, includes the Arkansas Valley in the center and the Ouachita Mountains to the south; Ozark Plateaus, northeast corner, includes the Boston Mountains and Springfield-Salem Plateaus. **Location:** South central, bordering Kansas, Missouri, Arkansas, Texas, New Mexico, and Colorado. **Climate:** variable by region: the southern humid belt merges with a colder northern continental one and humid eastern and dry western zones that cut through the state; no region is free from heavy wind; typical sudden rises and falls in temperature cause many heavy thunderstorms, blizzards, and tornadoes. **Land use:** pasture, 39.4%; agricultural, 37.2%; forest, 14.2%; other, 9.3%.

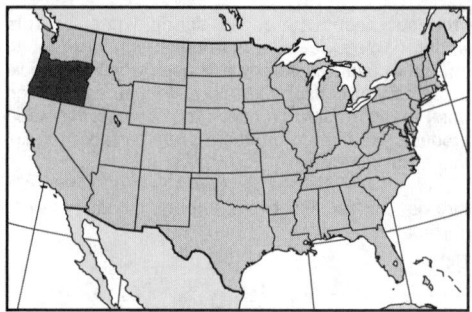

## People (2000 census)

**Population:** 3,450,654; 50.2 persons per sq mi (19.4 persons per sq km) (land area only). **Vital statistics** (1998; per 1,000 population): birth rate, 14.6 (1999); death rate, 10.1; marriage rate, 7.7; divorce rate, 6.0. **Major cities:** Oklahoma City, 506,132; Tulsa, 393,049; Norman, 95,694; Lawton, 92,757; Broken Arrow, 74,859.

## Government

**Statehood:** entered the Union on 16 Nov 1907 as the 46th state. **State constitution:** adopted 1907. **Representation in US Congress:** 2 senators; 6 representatives. **Electoral college:** 7 votes (in the 2004 general elections based on the 2000 census). **Political divisions:** 77 counties.

## Economy

**Employment:** services, 28.3%; trade, 20.9%; government, 16.6%; manufacturing, 10.0%; finance, insurance, real estate, 5.8%; agriculture, forestry, fishing, 5.6%; transportation, public utilities, 5.1%; construction, 4.8%; mining, 3.0%. **Production:** services, 18.2%; manufacturing, 16.9%; trade, 16.5%; government, 15.9%; finance, insurance, real estate, 12.2%; transportation, utilities, 9.2%; mining, 4.9%; construction, 3.8%; agriculture, 2.3%. **Chief agricultural products:** *Crops:* wheat, hay, sorghum, soybeans, cotton, dairy products. *Livestock:* cattle and calves, poultry, hogs and pigs. **Chief manufactured products:** electronics and electrical equipment, communications equipment, transportation equipment, food processing, petroleum products.

**Internet resources:** <www.travelok.com>; <www.state.ok.us>.

# Oregon

**Nickname:** Beaver State. **Capital:** Salem. **Rank:** population: 28th; area: 10th. **Motto:** *Alis Volat Propiis* (She Flies with Her Own Wings). **Song:** "Oregon, My Oregon," words by J.A. Buchanan and music by Henry B. Murtagh. **Bird:** western meadowlark. **Fish:** Chinook salmon. **Flower:** Oregon grape. **Gemstone:** Oregon sunstone. **Insect:** Oregon swallowtail. **Mammal:** beaver. **Rock:** thunderegg. **Tree:** Douglas fir.

## Natural features

**Area:** 97,132 sq mi, 251,517 sq km. **Mountain ranges:** Coast Range, Klamath Mountains, Cascade Range, Blue Mountains, Wallowa Mountains. **Highest point:** Mount Hood, 11,235 ft (3,424 m). **Largest lake:** Upper Klamath Lake. **Major rivers:** Snake, Owyhee, Columbia, Coquille. **Natural regions:** northern Rocky Mountains, northeastern corner, includes the Blue Mountain Section; Columbia Plateaus, north and north-central region, includes the Walla Walla Plateau in the central section, Harney Section to the south, and Payette Section to the southeast; Basin and Range Province, south-central border, includes the Great Basin; Cascade Sierra Mountains, includes the Middle and Southern Cascades, west central; Pacific Border Province, western coast, with the Klamath Mountains to the south, the Oregon Coast Range in the center and north, and the Puget Trough to the east. **Location:** Northwest, bordering Washington, Idaho, Nevada, and California. **Climate:** ranges from equable, mild, marine conditions on the coast to continental conditions of dryness and extreme temperature in the interior. **Land use:** forest, 43.4%; pasture, 36.4%; agricultural, 8.7%; other, 11.5%.

## People (2000 census)

**Population:** 3,421,399; 35.6 persons per sq mi (13.8 persons per sq km) (land area only). **Vital statistics** (1998; per 1,000 population): birth rate, 13.6 (1999); death rate, 9.0; marriage rate, 7.9; divorce rate, 4.6. **Major cities:** Portland, 529,121; Eugene, 137,893; Salem, 136,924; Gresham, 90,205; Beaverton, 76,129.

## Government

**Statehood:** entered the Union on 14 Feb 1859 as the 33rd state. **State constitution:** adopted 1857. **Representation in US Congress:** 2 senators; 5 representatives. **Electoral college:** 7 votes. **Political divisions:** 36 counties.

## Economy

**Employment:** services, 29.4%; trade, 22.8%; manufacturing, 13.1%; government, 12.6%; finance, insurance, real estate, 6.6%; construction, 5.7%; agricul-

*For details about state governments, see pages 812–817; for energy data, see pages 840–842.*

ture, forestry, fishing, 5.1%; transportation, public utilities, 4.5%; mining, 0.2%. **Production:** manufacturing, 24.8%; services, 17.6%; trade, 16.1%; finance, insurance, real estate, 14.4%; government, 11.8%; transportation, utilities, 7.1%; construction, 5.3%; agriculture, 2.8%; mining, 0.1%. **Chief agricultural products:** *Crops:* horticulture and nursery products, Christmas trees, berries, pears, cherries, apples, hazelnuts, snap beans, peas, onions, carrots, wheat, hay, potatoes, barley, dry beans, mint, hops, corn (maize), sugar beets, dairy products. *Livestock:* cattle and calves, horses, mink, poultry, sheep and lambs. *Fish catch:* marine fish, tuna, salmon, shellfish, crab, shrimp. *Extractive industries:* timber. **Chief manufactured products:** lumber and wood products, food processing, aircraft and spacecraft, electronics, semiconductors, computers.

**Internet resources:** <www.traveloregon.com>; <www.oregon.gov>.

# Pennsylvania

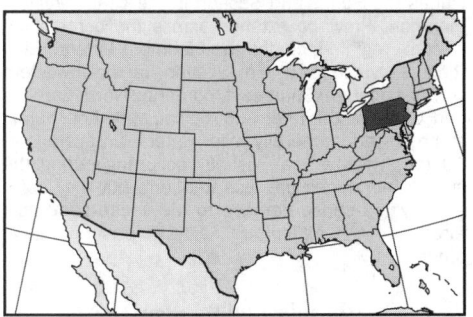

**Name:** Pennsylvania, named for Admiral Sir William Penn, father of the territory's founder, William Penn, and including also the term *sylvania* ("woodlands"). **Nickname:** Keystone State. **Capital:** Harrisburg. **Rank:** population: 6th; area: 32nd. **Motto:** Virtue, Liberty, and Independence. **Song:** "Pennsylvania," written and composed by Eddie Khoury and Ronnie Bonner. **Bird:** ruffled grouse. **Fish:** brook trout. **Flower:** mountain laurel. **Fossil:** *Phacops rana.* **Insect:** firefly. **Mammal:** white-tailed deer. **Tree:** hemlock.

## Natural features

**Area:** 46,058 sq mi, 119,291 sq km. **Mountain ranges:** Appalachian, Allegheny. **Highest point:** Mount Davis, 3,213 ft (979 m). **Largest lake:** Raystown Lake. **Major rivers:** Delaware, Lehigh, Schuylkill, Susquehanna, Ohio. **Natural regions:** central Lowland, Eastern Lake Section, extreme northwestern edge; Appalachian Plateaus, including the Southern New York, Allegheny Mountain, and Kanawha Sections, western half of state; Valley and Ridge Province, central region, includes portions of the Appalachian Mountains; Piedmont Province, comprising the Piedmont Lowlands and Upland, southeast corner; Coastal Plain, extreme southeast edge; New England Province, with the New England Upland Section, east-central border. **Location:** Northeast, bordering New York, New Jersey, Delaware, Maryland, West Virginia, Ohio. **Climate:** continental, with warm humid summers and cold snowy winters in general, but with wide fluctuations in seasonal temperatures. **Land use:** forest, 55.3%; agricultural, 18.1%; pasture, 3.2%; other, 23.5%.

## People (2000 census)

**Population:** 12,281,054; 274.0 persons per sq mi (105.8 persons per sq km) (land area only). **Vital statistics** (1998; per 1,000 population): birth rate, 12.1 (1999); death rate, 10.6; marriage rate, 6.2; divorce rate, 3.2. **Major cities:** Philadelphia, 1,517,550; Pittsburgh, 334,563; Allentown, 106,632; Erie, 103,717; Reading, 81,207.

## Government

**Statehood:** entered the Union on 12 Dec 1787 as the 2nd state. **State constitution:** adopted 1968. **Representation in US Congress:** 2 senators, 21 representatives. **Electoral college:** 21 votes (in the 2004 general elections based on the 2000 census). **Political divisions:** 67 counties.

## Economy

**Employment:** services, 32.7%; trade, 21.5%; manufacturing, 14.5%; government, 11.4%; finance, insurance, real estate, 7.7%; construction, 5.0%; transportation, public utilities, 4.9%; agriculture, forestry, fishing, 2.0%; mining, 0.4%. **Production:** services, 22.4%; manufacturing, 19.4%; finance, insurance, real estate, 18.4%; trade, 15.2%; government, 10.2%; transportation, utilities, 8.6%; construction, 4.2%; agriculture, 0.9%; mining, 0.7%. **Chief agricultural products:** *Crops:* mushrooms, apples, tobacco, grapes, peaches, cut flowers, dairy products. *Livestock:* cattle, poultry, pigs, horses. **Chief manufactured products:** electronic equipment, communications systems, semiconductors, chemical and pharmaceutical products, food processing, iron and steel, industrial machinery, transportation equipment, paper products, printing and publishing.

**Internet resources:** <www.experiencepa.com>; <www.state.pa.us>.

# Rhode Island

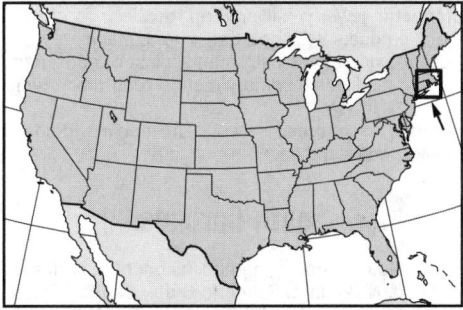

**Name:** Rhode Island, from the Greek island of Rhodes. **Nicknames:** Little Rhody and Ocean State. **Capital:** Providence. **Rank:** population: 43rd; area: 50th. **Motto:** Hope. **Song:** "Rhode Island," words and music by T. Clarke Brown. **Bird:** Rhode Island red. **Flower:** violet. **Mineral:** bowenite. **Rock:** cumberlandite.

## Natural features

**Area:** 1,231 sq mi, 3,189 sq km, including 168 sq mi, 435 sq km of water surface. **Highest point:** Jerimoth Hill, 812 ft (247 m). **Largest lake:** Scituate Reservoir.

Major rivers: Blackstone, Pawtuxet, Pawcatuck. **Natural regions:** the entire state is part of the New England Province, subdivided into the New England Upland (western two-thirds) and the Seaboard Lowland (eastern third). **Location:** New England, bordering Connecticut and Massachusetts. **Climate:** humid continental climate; marine influences are discernible in differences between coastal and inland location; extreme weather conditions including tropical storms, ice storms, and heavy snow. **Land use:** forest, 53.2%; agricultural, 4.5%; pasture, 0.4%; other, 41.9%.

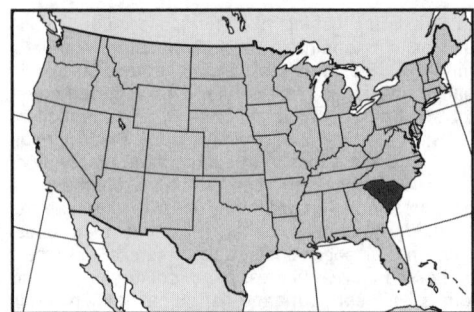

## People (2000 census)

**Population:** 1,048,319; 864.9 persons per sq mi (334.0 persons per sq km) (land area only). **Vital statistics** (1998; per 1,000 population): birth rate, 12.5 (1999); death rate, 9.7; marriage rate, 7.6; divorce rate, 3.2. **Major cities:** Providence, 173,618; Warwick, 85,808; Cranston, 79,269; Pawtucket, 72,958; East Providence, 48,688.

## Government

**Statehood:** entered the Union on 29 May 1790 as the 13th state. **State constitution:** adopted 1986. **Representation in US Congress:** 2 senators; 2 representatives. **Electoral college:** 4 votes. **Political divisions:** 5 counties.

## Economy

**Employment:** services, 34.7%; trade, 20.3%; manufacturing, 14.8%; government, 13.4%; finance, insurance, real estate, 7.6%; construction, 4.4%; transportation, public utilities, 3.4%; agriculture, forestry, fishing, 1.3%; mining, 0.1%. **Production:** finance, insurance, real estate, 26.7%; services, 21.7%; trade, 14.3%; manufacturing, 12.6%; government, 12.0%; transportation, utilities, 6.7%; construction, 5.3%; agriculture, 0.7%. **Chief agricultural products:** *Crops:* hay, corn (maize), apples, peaches, dairy products, eggs, potatoes. *Livestock:* poultry, cattle, sheep. *Fish catch:* marine fish, shellfish. **Chief manufactured products:** jewelry, silverware, textiles, fabricated metal products, electrical equipment, machinery, surgical and navigation instruments, plastic goods, printing and publishing, primary metals, food processing.

**Internet resources:** <www.visitrhodeisland.com>; <www.rhodeisland.gov>.

# South Carolina

**Name:** South Carolina, named in honor of Charles I of England. **Nickname:** Palmetto State. **Capital:** Columbia. **Rank:** population: 26th; area: 40th. **Mottoes:** *Animis Opibusque Parati* (Prepared in Mind and Resources); *Dum Spiro Spero* (While I Breathe, I Hope). **Songs:** "Carolina," words by Henry Timrod and music by Anne Custis Burgess; "South Carolina on My Mind," words and music by Hank Martin and Buzz Arledge. **Amphibian:** spotted salamander. **Bird:** Carolina wren. **Fish:** striped bass. **Flower:** Carolina jessamine. **Gemstone:** amethyst. **Insect:** Carolina mantid. **Mammal:** white-tailed deer. **Reptile:** loggerhead turtle. **Rock:** blue granite. **Tree:** palmetto.

## Natural features

**Area:** 31,189 sq mi, 80,779 sq km. **Mountain range:** Blue Ridge Mountains. **Highest point:** Sassafras Mountain, 3,560 ft (1,085 m). **Largest lake:** Lake Marion. **Major rivers:** Pee Dee, Savannah, Ashley, Combahee, Edisto. **Natural regions:** Coastal Plain covers the eastern two-thirds of the state and includes the Sea Island Section in the central region; Piedmont Province extends across the central and western region, includes the Piedmont Upland; Blue Ridge Province, Southern Section, far northwestern corner. **Location:** Southeast, bordering North Carolina and Georgia. **Climate:** subtropical, with hot, humid summers and generally mild winters; an average of 10 tornadoes a year, usually occurring during the spring; hurricanes are less frequent, but they do in some years cause damage to the coast. **Land use:** forest, 64.4%; agricultural, 13.1%; pasture, 2.4%; other, 20.0%.

## People (2000 census)

**Population:** 4,012,012; 133.2 persons per sq mi (51.4 persons per sq km) (land area only). **Vital statistics** (1998; per 1,000 population): birth rate, 14.1 (1999); death rate, 9.1; marriage rate, 10.8; divorce rate, 4.9. **Major cities:** Columbia, 116,278; Charleston, 96,650; North Charleston, 79,641; Greenville, 56,002; Rock Hill, 49,765.

## Government

**Statehood:** entered the Union on 23 May 1788 as the 8th state. **State constitution:** adopted 1895. **Representation in US Congress:** 2 senators; 6 representatives. **Electoral college:** 8 votes. **Political divisions:** 46 counties.

## Economy

**Employment:** services, 24.7%; trade, 22.4%; manufacturing, 17.3%; government, 16.7%; construction, 6.4%; finance, insurance, real estate, 5.9%; transportation, public utilities, 4.1%; agriculture, forestry, fishing, 2.4%; mining, 0.1%. **Production:** manufacturing, 21.4%; trade, 17.4%; services, 16.4%; government, 15.1%; finance, insurance, real estate, 13.7%; transportation, utilities, 8.9%; construction, 5.9%; agriculture, 1.1%; mining, 0.2%. **Chief agricultural products:** *Crops:* tobacco, cotton, barley, corn (maize), peanuts, oats, grains, peaches, apples, pecans, watermelons, sweet potatoes, tomatoes, snap beans, cucumbers, dairy products, eggs. *Livestock:* cattle

*For details about state governments, see pages 812–817; for energy data, see pages 840–842.*

and calves, chickens, pigs. **Chief extractive products:** timber, marine fish, oysters, clams, shrimp. **Chief manufactured products:** Chemical products, industrial chemicals, pharmaceuticals, and agricultural fertilizers, textiles, apparel, industrial machinery, plastic and rubber products, paper and paperboard, electronics and electrical equipment, motor vehicle parts and accessories, lumber.

**Internet resources:** <www.travelsc.com>; <www.state.sc.us>.

# South Dakota

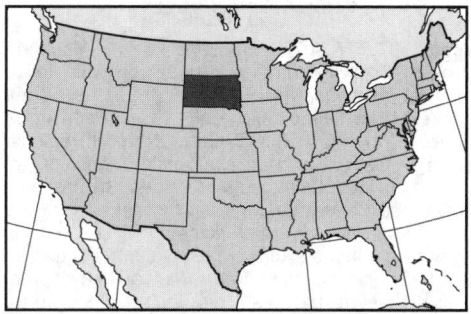

**Name:** South Dakota, from the Dakota division of the Sioux, the Native American tribe who inhabited the plains before the arrival of Europeans; *dakota* is the Sioux word for "friend." **Nickname:** Mount Rushmore State. **Capital:** Pierre. **Rank:** population: 46th; area: 16th. **Motto:** Under God the People Rule. **Song:** "Hail! South Dakota," words and music by Deecort Hammitt. **Bird:** Chinese ring-necked pheasant. **Fish:** walleye. **Flower:** pasque. **Fossil:** triceratops. **Gemstone:** Fairburn agate. **Insect:** honeybee. **Mammal:** coyote. **Mineral:** rose quartz. **Tree:** Black Hills spruce.

## Natural features

**Area:** 77,121 sq mi, 199,744 sq km. **Mountain range:** Black Hills. **Highest point:** Harney Peak, 7,242 ft (2,207 m). **Largest lake:** Lake Thompson. **Major rivers:** Big Sioux, Vermillion, James, Grand, Moreau, Cheyenne, Bad, White. **Natural regions:** the Central Lowland, eastern third of the state, includes the Dissected Till Plains along the eastern edge and the Western Lake Section at the center; the Great Plains Province, western two-thirds of the state; Black Hills, far west; High Plains, southern border; Missouri Plateau, west. **Location:** North central, bordering North Dakota, Minnesota, Iowa, Nebraska, Wyoming, and Montana. **Climate:** characterized by extremes in temperature, low precipitation, and relatively low humidity; cyclonic storms occur frequently in the east-river section during the spring and summer. **Land use:** pasture, 46.5%; agricultural, 44.8%; forest, 3.3%; other, 5.4%.

## People (2000 census)

**Population:** 754,844; 9.8 persons per sq mi (3.8 persons per sq km) (land area only). **Vital statistics** (1998; per 1,000 population): birth rate, 14.4 (1999); death rate, 9.3; marriage rate, 9.2; divorce rate, 3.5. **Major cities:** Sioux Falls, 123,975; Rapid City, 59,607; Aberdeen, 24,658.

## Government

**Statehood:** entered the Union on 2 Nov 1889 as the 40th state. **State constitution:** adopted 1889. **Representation in US Congress:** 2 senators; 1 representative. **Electoral college:** 3 votes. **Political divisions:** 66 counties.

## Economy

**Employment:** services, 27.5%; trade, 22.3%; government, 13.7%; manufacturing, 10.3%; agriculture, forestry, fishing, 9.1%; finance, insurance, real estate, 7.2%; construction, 5.0%; transportation, public utilities, 4.5%; mining, 0.5%. **Production:** finance, insurance, real estate, 18.1%; trade, 17.7%; services, 17.6%; manufacturing, 14.0%; government, 12.6%; transportation, utilities, 8.2%; agriculture, 6.9%; construction, 4.1%; mining, 0.6%. **Chief agricultural products:** *Crops:* corn (maize), hay, wheat, sunflowers, dairy products, eggs, flaxseed, barley, wool, rye, sorghum, soybeans. *Livestock:* cattle and calves, pigs, sheep. **Chief manufactured products:** industrial machinery, office machines, computers, food products, electronics, printing and publishing, lumber mills, fabricated metal products, medical instruments, truck-trailer manufactures, jewelry.

**Internet resources:** <www.travelsd.com>; <www.state.sd.us>.

# Tennessee

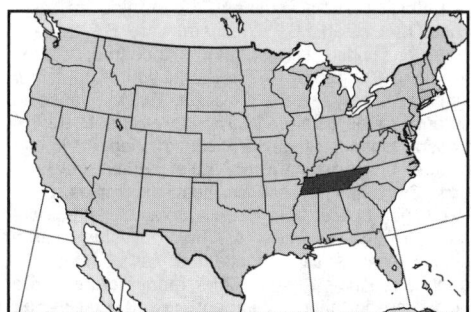

**Name:** Tennessee, from Cherokee village name. **Nickname:** Volunteer State. **Capital:** Nashville. **Rank:** population: 16th; area: 34th. **Motto:** Agriculture and Commerce. **Songs:** "My Homeland, Tennessee," by Nell Grayson Taylor and Roy Lamont Smith; "When It's Iris Time in Tennessee," by Willa Mae Waid; "My Tennessee," by Francis Hannah Tranum; "The Tennessee Waltz," by Redd Stewart and Pee Wee King; "Rocky Top," by Boudleaux and Felice Bryant. **Amphibian:** cave salamander. **Bird:** mockingbird. **Fish:** largemouth bass, channel catfish. **Flower:** iris. **Gemstone:** river pearl. **Insects:** firefly, ladybug. **Mammal:** raccoon. **Reptile:** box turtle. **Rocks:** limestone, agate. **Tree:** tulip poplar.

## Natural features

**Area:** 42,146 sq mi, 109,158 sq km. **Mountain ranges:** Unaka Mountains, Great Smoky Mountains. **Highest point:** Clingmans Dome, 6,642 ft (2,024 m). **Largest lake:** Reelfoot. **Major rivers:** Tennessee, Cumberland, Mississippi. **Natural regions:** Blue Ridge Province, eastern border; Valley and Ridge Province, extends from southwest to northeast; Appalachian

Plateau, central, running from south to north, includes the Cumberland Plateau Section in the center and the Cumberland Mountain Section at the northern end; Interior Low Plateau, west central, includes the Nashville Basin and Highland Rim Section. **Location:** South, bordering Kentucky, Virginia, North Carolina, Georgia, Alabama, Mississippi, Arkansas, and Missouri. **Climate:** moderate continental climate, with cool, but not cold, winters and warm summers. **Land use:** forest, 50.3%; agricultural, 28.4%; pasture, 4.3%; other, 17.1%.

## People (2000 census)

**Population:** 5,689,283; 138.0 persons per sq mi (53.3 persons per sq km) (land area only). **Vital statistics** (1998; per 1,000 population): birth rate, 14.2 (1999); death rate, 9.8; marriage rate, 14.9; divorce rate, 6.4. **Major cities:** Memphis, 650,100; Nashville-Davidson, 569,891; Knoxville, 173,890; Chattanooga, 155,554; Clarksville, 103,455.

## Government

**Statehood:** entered the Union on 1 Jun 1796 as the 16th state. **State constitution:** adopted 1870. **Representation in US Congress:** 2 senators; 9 representatives. **Electoral college:** 11 votes. **Political divisions:** 95 counties.

## Economy

**Employment:** services, 27.8%; trade, 21.8%; manufacturing, 16.2%; government, 12.1%; finance, insurance, real estate, 6.7%; construction, 5.9%; transportation, public utilities, 5.4%; agriculture, forestry, fishing, 3.8%; mining, 0.2%. **Production:** manufacturing, 20.8%; services, 20.6%; trade, 19.1%; finance, insurance, real estate, 14.1%; government, 11.5%; transportation, utilities, 8.3%; construction, 4.4%; agriculture, 0.9%; mining, 0.3%. **Chief agricultural products:** *Crops:* cotton, tobacco, peaches, apples, tomatoes, snap beans, honey, dairy products, eggs, wool, hay, corn (maize), wheat, sorghum. *Livestock:* cattle, poultry, hogs, sheep. *Aquaculture:* catfish, trout. *Extractive products:* timber. **Chief manufactured products:** transportation equipment, motor vehicles, aircraft parts, boats, chemical and pharmaceutical products, printing and publishing, electronics, lumber, paper, apparel, surgical appliances and supplies.

**Internet resources:** <www.tennessee.gov>.

## Texas

**Name:** Texas, from the Caddo Indian word *teysha*, or *tejas*, which means "hello friend." **Nickname:** Lone Star State. **Capital:** Austin. **Rank:** population: 2nd; area: 2nd. **Motto:** Friendship. **Song:** "Texas, Our Texas," by William J. Marsh and Gladys Yoakum Wright. **Bird:** mockingbird. **Fish:** Guadalupe bass. **Flower:** bluebonnet. **Fossil:** pleurocoelus. **Gemstone:** Texas blue topaz. **Insect:** monarch butterfly. **Mammal:** Mexican free-tailed bat (flying); longhorn (large); armadillo (small). **Reptile:** horned lizard. **Rock:** petrified palmwood. **Tree:** pecan.

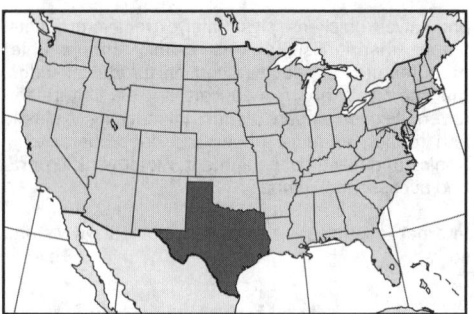

## Natural features

**Area:** 267,277 sq mi, 692,248 sq km. **Mountain ranges:** Rocky Mountains, Guadalupe Mountains. **Highest point:** Guadalupe Peak, 8,751 ft (2,667 m). **Largest lake:** Caddo Lake. **Major rivers:** Red, Trinity, Brazos, Colorado, Rio Grande. **Natural regions:** Coastal Plain, southern and eastern regions, includes the West Gulf Coastal Plain near the east-central coast; Central Lowland, north central, includes the Osage Plains; Great Plains Province, extends from the panhandle across most of central and western Texas, includes the Edwards Plateau to the south, Pecos Valley to the west, High Plains to the north, and Central Texas Section; Basin and Range Province, extreme western region, comprising the Mexican Highland to the south and the Sacramento Section to the north. **Location:** Southwest, bordering Oklahoma, Arkansas, Louisiana, and New Mexico; international border with Mexico. **Climate:** varies by region, though summers are generally very hot and winters are somewhat mild; East Texas is considerably wetter than the very dry West Texas region; tornadoes are a frequent threat between April and November. **Land use:** pasture, 58.5%; agricultural, 23.9%; forest, 7.0%; other, 10.6%.

## People (2000 census)

**Population:** 20,851,820; 79.6 persons per sq mi (30.7 persons per sq km) (land area only). **Vital statistics** (1998; per 1,000 population): birth rate, 17.4 (1999); death rate, 7.2; marriage rate, 9.6; divorce rate, NA. **Major cities:** Houston, 1,953,631; Dallas, 1,188,580; San Antonio, 1,144,646; Austin, 656,562; El Paso, 563,662; Fort Worth, 534,694; Arlington, 332,969; Corpus Christi, 277,454; Plano, 222,030; Garland, 215,768.

## Government

**Statehood:** entered the Union on 29 Dec 1845 as the 28th state. **State constitution:** adopted 1876. **Representation in US Congress:** 2 senators; 30 representatives. **Electoral college:** 34 votes (in the 2004 general elections based on the 2000 census). **Political divisions:** 254 counties.

## Economy

**Employment:** services, 29.1%; trade, 21.6%; government, 14.5%; manufacturing, 10.1%; finance, insurance, real estate, 7.5%; construction, 6.1%; transportation, public utilities, 5.4%; agriculture, forestry, fishing, 3.5%; mining, 2.2%. **Production:** services,

*For details about state governments, see pages 812–817; for energy data, see pages 840–842.*

19.9%; trade, 17.6%; finance, insurance, real estate, 14.7%; manufacturing, 14.0%; government, 11.2%; transportation, utilities, 10.9%; mining, 5.7%; construction, 4.7%; agriculture, 1.3%. **Chief agricultural products:** *Crops:* cotton, apples, greenhouse and nursery products, corn (maize), sorghum, wheat, dairy products, eggs, rice. *Livestock:* cattle, pigs, chickens. *Extractive products:* timber, shrimp. **Chief manufactured products:** Refined petroleum, petroleum products, food products, computers and electronics, chemicals and plastics, apparel, wood and paper products, nonelectrical machinery, fabricated metal products, aerospace products and parts, aircraft parts, motor vehicle parts.

**Internet resources:** <www.traveltex.com>; <www.texas.gov>.

# Utah

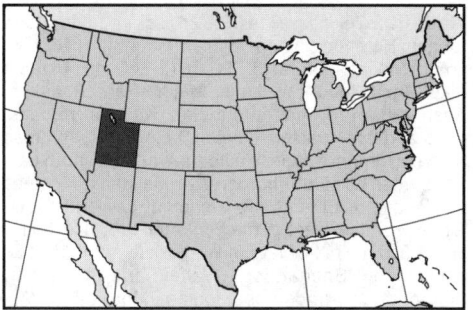

**Name:** Utah, named for the Ute tribe; the word *ute* means "people of the mountains." **Nickname:** Beehive State. **Capital:** Salt Lake City. **Rank:** population: 34th; area: 12th. **Motto:** Industry. **Song:** "Utah, We Love Thee," by Evan Stephens. **Bird:** California seagull. **Fish:** Bonneville cutthroat trout. **Flower:** sego lily. **Fossil:** allosaurus. **Gemstone:** topaz. **Insect:** honeybee. **Mammal:** Rocky Mountain elk. **Mineral:** copper. **Rock:** coal. **Tree:** blue spruce.

## Natural features

**Area:** 84,904 sq mi, 219,902 sq km. **Mountain ranges:** Uinta Mountains, Wasatch Range, Rocky Mountains. **Highest point:** Kings Peak, 13,528 ft (4,123 m). **Largest lake:** Great Salt Lake. **Major rivers:** Colorado, Green, Sevier. **Natural regions:** Basin and Range Province, western half of the state, includes the Great Salt Lake Desert and Bonneville Salt Flats to the north and the Great Basin to the south; Middle Rocky Mountains, northeast; Colorado Plateaus, east-central and southeast regions, includes the Grand Canyon Section to the south, the High Plateaus of Utah and Canyon Lands in the center, the Navajo Section in the extreme southeast corner, and the Uinta Basin to the north. **Location:** West, bordering Idaho, Wyoming, Colorado, Arizona, and Nevada. **Climate:** primarily arid; southwest has a warm, almost dry, subtropical climate, while the southern part of the Colorado Plateau has cool, dry winters and wet summers. **Land use:** pasture, 45.1%; forest, 26.3%; agricultural, 3.9%; other, 24.7%.

## People (2000 census)

**Population:** 2,233,169; 27.2 persons per sq mi (10.5 persons per sq km) (land area only). **Vital statistics** (1998; per 1,000 population): birth rate, 21.7 (1999); death rate, 5.6; marriage rate, 10.3; divorce rate, 4.2. **Major cities:** Salt Lake City, 181,743; West Valley City, 108,896; Provo, 105,166; Sandy, 88,418; Orem, 84,324.

## Government

**Statehood:** entered the Union on 4 Jan 1896 as the 45th state. **State constitution:** adopted 1895. **Representation in US Congress:** 2 senators; 3 representatives. **Electoral college:** 5 votes. **Political divisions:** 29 counties.

## Economy

**Employment:** services, 29.7%; trade, 22.0%; government, 14.6%; manufacturing, 10.9%; finance, insurance, real estate, 7.8%; construction, 7.0%; transportation, public utilities, 4.9%; agriculture, forestry, fishing, 2.4%; mining, 0.7%. **Production:** services, 20.6%; trade, 16.9%; finance, insurance, real estate, 16.4%; government, 14.4%; manufacturing, 13.3%; transportation, utilities, 8.8%; construction, 6.5%; mining, 1.8%; agriculture, 1.1%. **Chief agricultural products:** *Crops:* hay, grains, peaches, cherries, onions, dairy products. *Livestock:* cattle, sheep, mink, poultry. *Aquaculture:* trout. **Chief manufactured products:** industrial machinery, computers, office equipment, transportation equipment, aerospace products, missile parts, motor vehicle parts, surgical tools, electromedical equipment, food processing.

**Internet resources:** <www.utah.com>; <www.state.utah.gov>.

# Vermont

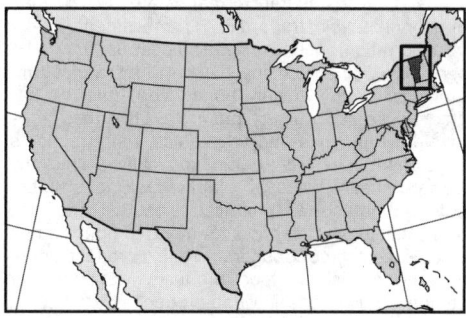

**Name:** Vermont, from the French *vert mont,* meaning "green mountain." **Nickname:** Green Mountain State. **Capital:** Montpelier. **Rank:** population: 49th; area: 43rd. **Motto:** Freedom and Unity. **Song:** "These Green Mountains," by Diane Martin and Rita Burgess Gluck. **Bird:** hermit thrush. **Flower:** red clover. **Insect:** honeybee. **Mammal:** Morgan horse. **Tree:** sugar maple.

## Natural features

**Area:** 9,615 sq mi, 24,903 sq km. **Mountain ranges:** Green Mountains, Appalachian Mountains, Hoosac Range, Taconic Range. **Highest point:** Mount Mansfield, 4,393 ft (1,339 m). **Largest lake:** Lake Champlain. **Major rivers:** Lamoille, Winooski, Otter Creek, Poultney, White, Missisquoi. **Natural regions:** the New England Province, eastern two-thirds of the state, includes the Taconic Section to the south, the Green Mountain Section in the center, New England Upland Section along the east-central edge, and the White Mountain Section in the far northeast corner; the St. Lawrence Valley, western edge of the state, with the Champlain Section in the central portion; the Valley and Ridge Province, with the Hudson Valley, small section along the west-central edge. **Location:** New England, bordering New Hampshire, Massachusetts, and New York; international border with Canada. **Climate:** cool continental, with very cold, snowy winters and warm, mild summers. **Land use:** forest, 75.4%; agricultural, 8.2%; pasture, 3.6%; other, 12.9%.

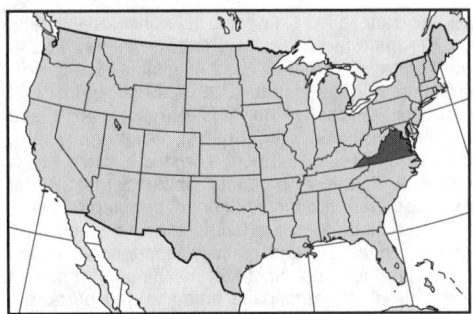

Virginia," words and music by James B. Bland. **Bird:** cardinal. **Fish:** brook trout. **Flower:** dogwood. **Fossil:** *Chesapecten jeffersonius.* **Insect:** tiger swallowtail butterfly. **Tree:** dogwood.

## People (2000 census)

**Population:** 608,827; 65.8 persons per sq mi (25.4 persons per sq km) (land area only). **Vital statistics** (1998; per 1,000 population): birth rate, 11.1 (1999); death rate, 8.4; marriage rate, 9.9; divorce rate, 4.3. **Major city:** Burlington, 38,889.

## Government

**Statehood:** entered the Union on 4 Mar 1791 as the 14th state. **State constitution:** adopted 1793. **Representation in US Congress:** 2 senators; 1 representative. **Electoral college:** 3 votes. **Political divisions:** 14 counties.

## Economy

**Employment:** services, 32.4%; trade, 21.0%; manufacturing, 13.7%; government, 12.8%; construction, 6.5%; finance, insurance, real estate, 5.7%; transportation, public utilities, 4.0%; agriculture, forestry, fishing, 3.7%; mining, 0.2%. **Production:** services, 22.3%; finance, insurance, real estate, 17.7%; manufacturing, 17.5%; trade, 15.7%; government, 12.4%; transportation, utilities, 7.6%; construction, 4.4%; agriculture, 2.2%; mining, 0.3%. **Chief agricultural products:** *Crops:* apples, honey, corn (maize), hay, greenhouse and nursery products, Christmas trees, maple syrup, fruits and vegetables, dairy products, eggs, wool. *Livestock:* cattle and calves, chickens, turkeys, sheep, horses. *Extractive products:* timber. **Chief manufactured products:** electrical and electronic equipment, fabricated metal products, nonelectrical machinery, paper and allied products, printing and publishing, food products, transportation equipment, lumber and wood products.

**Internet resources:** <www.travel-vermont.com>; <www.vermont.gov>.

# Virginia

**Name:** Virginia, named in honor of Elizabeth I of England, known as the "Virgin Queen." **Nickname:** Old Dominion. **Capital:** Richmond. **Rank:** population: 12th; area: 37th. **Motto:** *Sic Semper Tyrannis* (Thus Ever to Tyrants). **Song:** "Carry Me Back to Old

## Natural features

**Area:** 42,326 sq mi, 109,625 sq km. **Mountain ranges:** Blue Ridge, Appalachian Mountains. **Highest point:** Mount Rogers, 5,729 ft (1,746 m). **Largest lake:** Smith Mountain Lake. **Major rivers:** Potomac, Shenandoah, James, Roanoke. **Natural regions:** Coastal Plain, eastern region below the Potomac River; Piedmont Province extends from the south-central border up to the border with Maryland, includes the Piedmont Upland and Piedmont Lowlands; Blue Ridge Province, west of the Piedmont Province; Valley and Ridge region, covers most of western Virginia, includes the Shenandoah Valley and Allegheny, Shenandoah, and Appalachian Mountains; Appalachian Plateau, extreme western tip of the state, includes the Cumberland Mountain and Kanawha Sections. **Location:** East coast, bordering Maryland, North Carolina, Tennessee, Kentucky, and West Virginia. **Climate:** generally mild and equable but varies according to elevation and proximity to Chesapeake Bay and the Atlantic. **Land use:** forest, 60.5%; agricultural, 17.1%; pasture, 6.0%; other, 16.3%.

## People (2000 census)

**Population:** 7,078,515; 178.8 persons per sq mi (69.0 persons per sq km) (land area only). **Vital statistics** (1998; per 1,000 population): birth rate, 13.9 (1999); death rate, 8.0; marriage rate, 9.5; divorce rate, 4.4. **Major cities:** Virginia Beach, 425,257; Norfolk, 234,403; Chesapeake, 199,184; Richmond, 197,790; Newport News, 180,150; Hampton, 146,437; Alexandria, 128,283; Portsmouth, 100,565; Roanoke, 94,911.

## Government

**Statehood:** entered the Union on 26 Jun 1788 as the 10th state. **State constitution:** adopted 1970. **Representation in US Congress:** 2 senators; 11 representatives. **Electoral college:** 13 votes. **Political divisions:** 95 counties.

## Economy

**Employment:** services, 30.1%; trade, 20.1%; government, 18.9%; manufacturing, 10.2%; finance, insurance, real estate, 6.9%; construction, 6.2%; transportation, public utilities, 4.7%; agriculture, forestry,

*For details about state governments, see pages 812–817; for energy data, see pages 840–842.*

fishing, 2.5%; mining, 0.3%. **Production:** services, 22.6%; government, 17.8%; finance, insurance, real estate, 17.3%; trade, 14.4%; manufacturing, 13.1%; transportation, utilities, 9.0%; construction, 4.6%; agriculture, 0.8%; mining, 0.4%. **Chief agricultural products:** *Crops:* tobacco, soybeans, corn (maize), peanuts (groundnuts), cotton, apples, tomatoes, wheat, hay, potatoes, honey. *Livestock:* chickens, turkeys, pigs, cattle, sheep. *Aquaculture:* clams, soft-shell crabs, oysters, trout, catfish, hybrid striped bass. *Extractive products:* timber, blue crab. **Chief manufactured products:** electronics and electrical equipment, paper products, tobacco products, plastic materials, pharmaceutical and chemical products, food products, printing and publishing.

**Internet resources:** <www.virginia.org>; <www.virginia.gov>.

# Washington

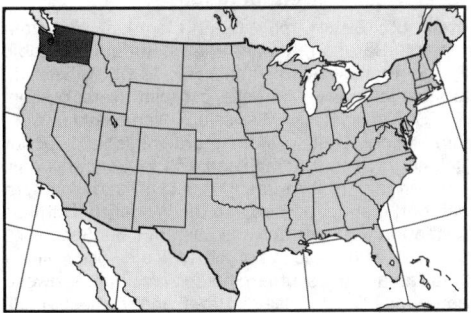

**Name:** Washington, named in honor of George Washington. **Nickname:** Evergreen State. **Capital:** Olympia. **Rank:** population: 15th; area: 20th. **Motto:** *Alki* (By and By). **Song:** "Washington My Home," words and music by Helen Davis. **Bird:** willow goldfinch. **Fish:** steelhead trout. **Flower:** coast rhododendron. **Fossil:** Columbian mammoth. **Gemstone:** petrified wood. **Insect:** green darner dragonfly. **Tree:** western hemlock.

## Natural features

**Area:** 70,637 sq mi, 182,949 sq km. **Mountain ranges:** Olympic Mountains, Cascade Range, Blue Mountains. **Highest point:** Mount Rainier, 14,410 ft (4,392 m). **Largest lake:** Moses Lake. **Major rivers:** Columbia, Pend Oreille, Snake, Yakima. **Natural regions:** Pacific Border Province, western quarter of the state, includes the Olympic Mountains to the west and the Puget Trough to the east; Cascade-Sierra Mountains, running north to south down center of state, include the Northern and Middle Cascades; Northern Rocky Mountains, northeast corner; Columbia Plateaus, eastern, central, and southern regions, include the Walla Walla Plateau in the center and the Blue Mountain Section in the southeast corner. **Location:** Northwest, bordering Idaho and Oregon; international border with Canada. **Climate:** moderate winters and cool summers west of the Cascades; east of the Cascade Range seasonal temperature variations are greater, with cold winters and warm, mild summers; throughout the state precipitation is greatest in the cooler months, with frequent cyclonic storms, some with gale-force winds. **Land use:** forest, 40.9%; agricultural, 19.7%; pasture, 17.4%; other, 22.0%.

## People (2000 census)

**Population:** 5,894,121; 88.5 persons per sq mi (34.2 persons per sq km) (land area only). **Vital statistics** (1998; per 1,000 population): birth rate, 13.8 (1999); death rate, 7.5; marriage rate, 7.2; divorce rate, 5.1. **Major cities:** Seattle, 563,374; Spokane, 195,629; Tacoma, 193,556; Vancouver, 143,560; Bellevue, 109,569; Everett, 91,488.

## Government

**Statehood:** entered the Union on 11 Nov 1889 as the 42nd state. **State constitution:** adopted 1889. **Representation in US Congress:** 2 senators; 9 representatives. **Electoral college:** 11 votes. **Political divisions:** 39 counties.

## Economy

**Employment:** services, 28.7%; trade, 21.9%; government, 15.7%; manufacturing, 11.8%; finance, insurance, real estate, 7.3%; construction, 5.6%; transportation, public utilities, 4.6%; agriculture, forestry, fishing, 4.2%; mining, 0.2%. **Production:** services, 25.0%; finance, insurance, real estate, 17.4%; trade, 16.8%; government, 13.2%; manufacturing, 12.6%; transportation, utilities, 7.9%; construction, 4.9%; agriculture, 2.1%; mining, 0.2%. **Chief agricultural products:** *Crops:* apples, peaches, pears, cherries, grapes, apricots, raspberries, dried peas, lentils, asparagus, carrots, sweet corn, green peas, potatoes, mint oil, hops, wheat, hay. *Livestock:* cattle and calves, poultry, horses. *Extractive products:* oysters, clams, mussels, crab, shrimp, geoduck, sea cucumbers, marine fish, salmon, timber. **Chief manufactured products:** aerospace equipment, food processing, forest products, advanced medical and technology products, aluminum products, fish processing.

**Internet resources:** <www.experiencewashington.com>; <www.wa.gov>.

# West Virginia

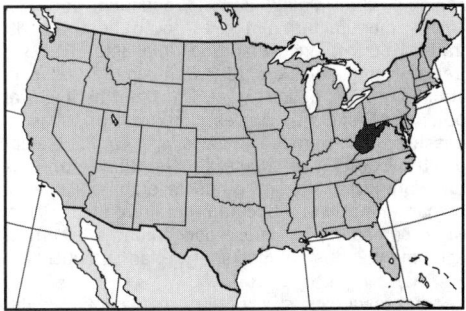

**Name:** West Virginia, named in honor of Elizabeth I of England, who was also known as the "Virgin Queen." **Nickname:** Mountain State. **Capital:** Charleston. **Rank:** population: 37th; area: 41st. **Motto:** *Montani Semper Liberi* (Mountaineers Are Always Free). **Song:** "This Is My West Virginia," words and music by Iris Bell; "West Virginia, My Home Sweet Home," words and music by Julian G. Hearne, Jr.; "The West Virginia Hills," words by David King and music by H.E. Engle. **Bird:** cardinal. **Fish:** brook trout. **Flower:** rhododendron.

Gemstone: West Virginia fossil coral. Insect: monarch butterfly. Mammal: black bear. Tree: sugar maple.

## Natural features

Area: 24,231 sq mi, 62,759 sq km. Mountain ranges: Appalachian Mountains, Allegheny Mountains. Highest point: Spruce Knob, 4,862 ft (1,482 m). Largest lake: Summersville Lake. Major rivers: Ohio, Big Sandy, Guyandotte, Great Kanawha, Little Kanawha, Monongahela, Potomac. Natural regions: Valley and Ridge Province, eastern edge of the state, includes portions of the Shenandoah Mountains; the remainder of the state consists of the Appalachian Plateaus and includes the Kanawha Section to the south, the Allegheny Mountains, and the Allegheny Mountains in the northeast. Location: East, bordering Pennsylvania, Maryland, Virginia, Kentucky, and Ohio. Climate: humid continental, except for a marine modification in the lower panhandle. Land use: forest, 77.2%; agricultural, 9.2%; pasture, 3.1%; other, 10.5%.

## People (2000 census)

Population: 1,808,344; 75.1 persons per sq mi (29.0 persons per sq km) (land area only). Vital statistics (1998; per 1,000 population): birth rate, 11.5 (1999); death rate, 11.5; marriage rate, 6.5; divorce rate, 5.1. Major cities: Charleston, 53,421; Huntington, 51,475; Parkersburg, 33,099; Wheeling, 31,419; Morgantown, 26,809.

## Government

Statehood: entered the Union on 20 Jun 1863 as the 35th state. State constitution: adopted 1872. Representation in US Congress: 2 senators; 3 representatives. Electoral college: 5 votes. Political divisions: 55 counties.

## Economy

Employment: services, 28.1%; trade, 22.2%; government, 17.1%; manufacturing, 9.9%; construction, 5.9%; transportation, public utilities, 5.2%; finance, insurance, real estate, 4.8%; agriculture, forestry, fishing, 3.3%; mining, 3.3%. Production: services, 17.9%; manufacturing, 16.0%; government, 15.5%; trade, 15.5%; finance, insurance, real estate, 11.3%; transportation, utilities, 11.3%; mining, 7.3%; construction, 4.6%; agriculture, 0.6%. Chief agricultural products: Crops: hay, apples, corn (maize), tobacco, peaches, dairy products. Livestock: cattle, sheep, poultry. Extractive products: timber. Chief manufactured products: chemical products, automobile parts, primary metal and fabricated metal products, glassware, computer software, wood products, electrical equipment, industrial machinery, pharmaceuticals.

Internet resources: <www.callwva.com>; <www.state.wv.us>.

# Wisconsin

Name: Wisconsin, an anglicized version of a French rendering of a Native American name said to mean "the place where we live." Nickname: Badger State. Capital: Madison. Rank: population: 18th; area: 25th.

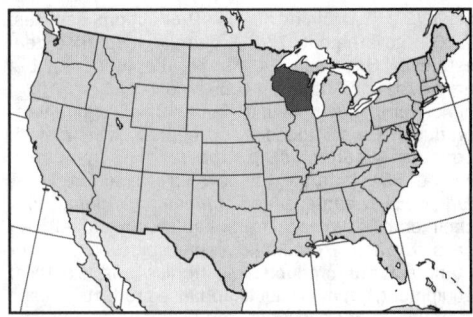

Motto: Forward. Song: "On, Wisconsin," words and music by William T. Purdy. Bird: robin. Fish: muskellunge (muskie). Flower: wood violet. Fossil: trilobite. Insect: honeybee. Mammal: badger. Mineral: galena. Rock: red granite. Tree: sugar maple.

## Natural features

Area: 65,499 sq mi, 169,643 sq km. Mountain ranges: Baraboo Range, Rib Mountain, Gogebic Range. Highest point: Timms Hill, 1,953 ft (595 m). Largest lake: Lake Winnebago. Major rivers: Wisconsin, St. Croix, Rock, Mississippi, Namekagon, Wolf, Pine-Popple, Brule, Pike. Natural regions: Superior Upland, divided into highland and lowland sections, northern half of the state; Central Lowland, southern half of the state, divided into the Wisconsin Driftless Section to the west and the Eastern Lake Section to the east, with a section of the Till Plains occupying a small area at the southern border. Location: Midwest, bordering Michigan, Illinois, Iowa, and Minnesota. Climate: continental, with long, cold winters and warm, but relatively short, summers. Land use: forest, 45.2%; agricultural, 27.5%; pasture, 5.3%; other, 22.0%.

## People (2000 census)

Population: 5,363,675; 98.8 persons per sq mi (38.1 persons per sq km). Vital statistics (1998; per 1,000 population): birth rate, 13.0 (1999); death rate, 8.8; marriage rate, 6.7; divorce rate, 3.4. Major cities: Milwaukee, 596,974; Madison, 208,054; Green Bay, 102,313; Kenosha, 90,352; Racine, 81,855.

## Government

Statehood: entered the Union on 29 May 1848 as the 30th state. State constitution: adopted 1848. Representation in US Congress: 2 senators; 9 representatives. Electoral college: 10 votes (in the 2004 general elections based on the 2000 census). Political divisions: 72 counties.

## Economy

Employment: services, 26.7%; trade, 21.8%; manufacturing, 19.2%; government, 11.9%; finance, insurance, real estate, 6.8%; construction, 4.8%; transportation, public utilities, 4.4%; agriculture, forestry, fishing, 4.2%; mining, 0.1%. Production: manufacturing, 26.3%; services, 17.8%; trade, 15.8%; finance, insurance, real estate, 15.6%; government, 10.6%; transportation, utilities, 7.1%; construction, 4.7%; agriculture, 1.9%; mining, 0.1%. Chief agricultural

*For details about state governments, see pages 812–817; for energy data, see pages 840–842.*

**products:** *Crops:* Dairy products, corn (maize), honey, maple syrup, oats, hay, snap and green beans, potatoes, strawberries, tart cherries, cranberries, Christmas trees, mint for oil, beets, cabbage, carrots, green peas, cucumbers. *Livestock:* cattle and calves, hogs, mink. *Extractive products:* freshwater fish. **Chief manufactured products:** processed foods, beer, industrial machinery, paper and paper products, fabricated metal products, transportation equipment, household appliances.

**Internet resources:** <www.travelwisconsin.com>; <www.wisconsin.gov>.

# Wyoming

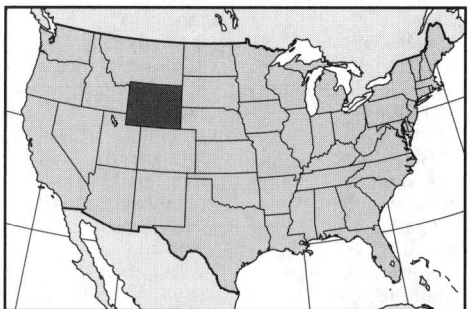

**Name:** Wyoming, from the Delaware Indian word, meaning "mountains and valleys alternating." **Nicknames:** Equality State and Cowboy State. **Capital:** Cheyenne. **Rank:** population: 50th; area: 9th. **Motto:** Equal Rights. **Song:** "Wyoming," words by Charles E. Winter and music by George E. Knapp. **Bird:** meadowlark. **Fish:** cutthroat trout. **Flower:** Indian paintbrush. **Fossil:** knightia. **Gemstone:** jade. **Mammal:** bison. **Reptile:** horned toad. **Tree:** plains cottonwood.

## Natural features

**Area:** 97,818 sq mi, 253,349 sq km. **Mountain ranges:** Rocky Mountains, Big Horn, Grand Tetons, Wind River Range, Continental Divide, Sierra Madre Range, Washakie Mountains. **Highest point:** Gannett Peak, 13,804 ft (4,207 m). **Largest lake:** Yellowstone Lake. **Major rivers:** Snake, Colorado, Green, Columbia. **Natural regions:** Great Plains Province, eastern third of the state, includes the Black Hills in the northeast corner, the High Plains in the southwest corner, and the Missouri Plateau in the center; Wyoming Basin, central and southern regions; Southern Rocky Mountains, southern border; the Middle Rocky Mountains, northwest third of the state, also cover a small area on the southern border; Northern Rocky Mountains, extreme northwest tip of the state. **Location:** West, bordering Montana, South Dakota, Nebraska, Colorado, Utah, and Idaho. **Climate:** semiarid continental, with long, cold winters and relatively short, warm summers. **Land use:** pasture, 72.2%; forest, 8.2%; agricultural, 5.0%; other, 14.7%.

## People (2000 census)

**Population:** 493,782; 5.1 persons per sq mi (2.0 persons per sq km) (land area only). **Vital statistics** (1998; per 1,000 population): birth rate, 12.8 (1999); death rate, 8.0; marriage rate, 9.7; divorce rate, 5.9. **Major cities:** Cheyenne, 53,011; Casper, 49,644; Laramie, 27,204.

## Government

**Statehood:** entered the Union on 10 Jul 1890 as the 44th state. **State constitution:** adopted 1889. **Representation in US Congress:** 2 senators; 1 representative. **Electoral college:** 3 votes. **Political divisions:** 23 counties.

## Economy

**Employment:** services, 25.0%; trade, 21.3%; government, 19.5%; construction, 6.9%; finance, insurance, real estate, 6.6%; mining, 5.9%; transportation, public utilities, 5.4%; agriculture, forestry, fishing, 5.3%; manufacturing, 4.1%. **Production:** mining, 22.0%; transportation, utilities, 14.8%; government, 14.1%; trade, 11.8%; services, 11.6%; finance, insurance, real estate, 11.3%; manufacturing, 6.6%; construction, 5.4%; agriculture, 2.5%. **Chief agricultural products:** *Crops:* hay, wheat, barley, sugar beets and sugar, corn (maize), wool. *Livestock:* cattle and calves, sheep and lambs. **Chief manufactured products:** refined petroleum, lumber and wood products, food products, fabricated metal products.

**Internet resources:** <www.wyomingtourism.com>; <www.state.wy.us>.

## Famous People from the 50 States, DC, and Puerto Rico

**Alabama**
Hank Aaron
Hugo Black
Helen Keller
Rosa Parks
**Alaska**
Charles E. Bunnell
William Egan
Jewel
Hillary Lindh
**Arizona**
Lynda Carter
Cesar Chavez
Barry Goldwater
Helen Hull Jacobs

**Arkansas**
Daisy Gatson Bates
Johnny Cash
Joycelyn Elders
Douglas MacArthur
**California**
Tom Hanks
Marilyn Monroe
Sally Ride
John Steinbeck
**Colorado**
Tim Allen
Ruth Handler
Florence Sabin
Paul Whiteman

**Connecticut**
Ethan Allen
Katharine Hepburn
Annie Leibovitz
Noah Webster
**Delaware**
Annie Jump Cannon
Pierre Samuel du Pont
Henry Heimlich
Elisabeth Shue
**District of Columbia**
Elgin Baylor
Katie Couric
Duke Ellington
Helen Hayes

**Florida**
Zora Neale Hurston
Jim Morrison
Sidney Poitier
Janet Reno
**Georgia**
Jimmy Carter
Otis Redding
Julia Roberts
Joanne Woodward
**Hawaii**
Hiram Bingham
King Kamehameha I
Queen Liliuokalani
Bette Midler

## Famous People from the 50 States, DC, and Puerto Rico (continued)

**Idaho**
Pappy Boyington
Ezra Pound
Sacagawea
Lana Turner

**Illinois**
Jane Addams
Hillary Rodham Clinton
Walt Disney
Wild Bill Hickok

**Indiana**
Anne Baxter
James Dean
David Letterman
Jane Pauley

**Iowa**
Johnny Carson
Ann Landers
Lillian Russell
John Wayne

**Kansas**
Annette Bening
Walter Chrysler
Amelia Earhart
Maurice Greene

**Kentucky**
Muhammad Ali
Kit Carson
bell hooks
Carry Nation

**Louisiana**
Louis Armstrong
Truman Capote
Ellen DeGeneres
Britney Spears

**Maine**
Dorothea Dix
Stephen King
Joan Benoit Samuelson
John Hay Whitney

**Maryland**
Goldie Hawn
Billie Holiday
Johns Hopkins
Babe Ruth

**Massachusetts**
Clara Barton
Cotton Mather
Dr. Seuss
Barbara Walters

**Michigan**
Ellen Burstyn
Magic Johnson
Charles Lindbergh
Madonna

**Minnesota**
Bob Dylan
Judy Garland
Garrison Keillor
Winona Ryder

**Mississippi**
Jim Henson
Elvis Presley
Eudora Welty
Oprah Winfrey

**Missouri**
Maya Angelou
Josephine Baker
Yogi Berra
Jesse James

**Montana**
Gary Cooper
Myrna Loy
David Lynch
Jeannette Rankin

**Nebraska**
Grace Abbott
Marlon Brando
Malcolm X
Mari Susette Sandoz

**Nevada**
Andre Agassi
Jack Kramer
Pat Nixon
Sarah Winnemucca

**New Hampshire**
Mary Baker Eddy
Sarah Josepha Hale
John Irving
Franklin Pierce

**New Jersey**
Amiri Baraka
Bruce Springsteen
Martha Stewart
Meryl Streep

**New Mexico**
Paula Allen
John Denver
William Hanna
Linda Wertheimer

**New York**
Woody Allen
Aaron Copland
Vera Wang
Edith Wharton

**North Carolina**
John Coltrane
Elizabeth Dole
Ava Gardner
Billy Graham

**North Dakota**
Angie Dickinson
Louis L'Amour
Peggy Lee
Lawrence Welk

**Ohio**
Thomas Edison
Toni Morrison
Sarah Jessica Parker
Ted Turner

**Oklahoma**
L. Gordon Cooper
Ron Howard
Reba McEntire
Maria Tallchief

**Oregon**
Beverly Cleary
Matt Groening
John Reed
Pat Schroeder

**Pennsylvania**
Marian Anderson
James Buchanan
Grace Kelly
Andy Warhol

**Puerto Rico**
Roberto Clemente
Sr. M. Isolina Ferré
Raul Julia
Rita Moreno

**Rhode Island**
Thomas Wilson Dorr
Gilbert Stuart
Mena Suvari
Jemima Wilkinson

**South Carolina**
Mary McLeod Bethune
John C. Calhoun
Althea Gibson
Jesse Jackson

**South Dakota**
Tom Brokaw
Tom Daschle
Mary Hart
Cheryl Ladd

**Tennessee**
Hattie Caraway
Davy Crockett
Aretha Franklin
Quentin Tarantino

**Texas**
Joan Crawford
Howard Hughes
Lyndon B. Johnson
Janis Joplin

**Utah**
Butch Cassidy
J. Willard Marriott
Marie Osmond
Roseanne

**Vermont**
John Deere
Stephen Douglas
Mary Jane Safford
Patty Sheehan

**Virginia**
Willa Cather
Ella Fitzgerald
John Marshall
Booker T. Washington

**Washington**
Gail Devers
Bill Gates
Robert Joffrey
Hilary Swank

**West Virginia**
Belle Boyd
Anna Jarvis
Cyrus Vance
Chuck Yeager

**Wisconsin**
Aldrich Ames
Carrie Chapman Catt
John Ringling
Laura Ingalls Wilder

**Wyoming**
Lynne Cheney
June Etta Downey
Curt Gowdy
Jackson Pollock

# State Government

## Governors of US States and Territories

*Governors of New Hampshire and Vermont serve two-year terms; all others serve four-year terms. Parties: Democrat (D); Republican (R); Popular Democrat (PD). Source: National Governors Association.*

| STATE | GOVERNOR | IN OFFICE SINCE | PRESENT TERM EXPIRES |
|---|---|---|---|
| Alabama | Bob Riley (R) | January 2003 | January 2007* |
| Alaska | Frank Murkowski (R) | January 2003 | January 2007* |
| Arizona | Janet Napolitano (D) | January 2003 | January 2007* |
| Arkansas | Mike Huckabee (R)[1] | July 1996 | January 2007 |
| California | Gray Davis (D) | January 1999 | January 2007 |
| Colorado | Bill Owens (R) | January 1999 | January 2007 |
| Connecticut | John G. Rowland (R) | January 1995 | January 2007* |
| Delaware[2] | Ruth Ann Minner (D) | January 2001 | January 2005* |

## Governors of US States and Territories (continued)

| STATE | GOVERNOR | IN OFFICE SINCE | PRESENT TERM EXPIRES |
|---|---|---|---|
| Florida | Jeb Bush (R) | January 1999 | January 2007 |
| Georgia | Sonny Perdue (R) | January 2003 | January 2007* |
| Hawaii | Linda Lingle (R) | December 2002 | December 2006* |
| Idaho | Dirk Kempthorne (R) | January 1999 | January 2007 |
| Illinois | Rod Blagojevich (D) | January 2003 | January 2007* |
| Indiana | Frank O'Bannon (D) | January 1997 | January 2005 |
| Iowa | Tom Vilsack (D) | January 1999 | January 2007* |
| Kansas | Kathleen Sebelius (D) | January 2003 | January 2007* |
| Kentucky | Paul E. Patton (D) | December 1995 | December 2003 |
| Louisiana | M.J. "Mike" Foster, Jr. (R) | January 1996 | January 2004 |
| Maine | John Baldacci (D) | January 2003 | January 2007* |
| Maryland | Robert Ehrlich (R) | January 2003 | January 2007* |
| Massachusetts | Mitt Romney (R) | January 2003 | January 2007* |
| Michigan | Jennifer Granholm (D) | January 2003 | January 2007* |
| Minnesota | Tim Pawlenty (R) | January 2003 | January 2007* |
| Mississippi | Ronnie Musgrove (D) | January 2000 | January 2004* |
| Missouri | Bob Holden (D) | January 2001 | January 2005* |
| Montana[3] | Judy Martz (R) | January 2001 | January 2005* |
| Nebraska[4] | Mike Johanns (R) | January 1999 | January 2007 |
| Nevada | Kenny C. Guinn (R) | January 1999 | January 2007 |
| New Hampshire | Craig Benson (R) | January 2003 | January 2005* |
| New Jersey | James E. McGreevey (D) | January 2002 | January 2006* |
| New Mexico | Bill Richardson (D) | January 2003 | January 2007* |
| New York | George E. Pataki (R) | January 1995 | January 2007* |
| North Carolina | Michael F. Easley (D) | January 2001 | January 2005* |
| North Dakota | John Hoeven (R) | January 2001 | January 2005* |
| Ohio | Bob Taft (R) | January 1999 | January 2007 |
| Oklahoma | Brad Henry (D) | January 2003 | January 2007* |
| Oregon | Ted Kulongoski (D) | January 2003 | January 2007* |
| Pennsylvania | Edward G. Rendell (D) | January 2003 | January 2007* |
| Rhode Island | Don Carcieri (R) | January 2003 | January 2007* |
| South Carolina | Mike Sanford (R) | January 2003 | January 2007* |
| South Dakota | Michael Rounds (R) | January 2003 | January 2007* |
| Tennessee | Phil Bredesen (D) | January 2003 | January 2007* |
| Texas | Rick Perry (R)[5] | December 2000 | January 2007* |
| Utah | Michael O. Leavitt (R)[6] | January 1993 | January 2005* |
| Vermont | Jim Douglas (R) | January 2003 | January 2005* |
| Virginia[7] | Mark R. Warner (D) | January 2002 | January 2006 |
| Washington | Gary Locke (D) | January 1997 | January 2005* |
| West Virginia | Bob Wise (D) | January 2001 | January 2005* |
| Wisconsin | Jim Doyle (D) | January 2003 | January 2007* |
| Wyoming | David Freudenthal (D) | January 2003 | January 2007* |

| TERRITORIES | GOVERNOR | IN OFFICE SINCE | PRESENT TERM EXPIRES |
|---|---|---|---|
| American Samoa | Togiola T.A. Tulafono (D)[8] | April 2003 | January 2005* |
| Guam | Felix Perez Camacho (R) | January 2003 | January 2007* |
| Northern Mariana Islands | Juan N. Babauta (R) | January 2002 | January 2006* |
| Puerto Rico | Sila M. Calderón (PD) | January 2001 | January 2005* |
| Virgin Islands | Charles W. Turnbull (D) | January 1999 | January 2007 |

*Present governor is eligible for reelection. [1]Lt. Gov. Mike Huckabee became governor in July 1996 following Jim Guy Tucker's resignation. He was elected to full four-year terms in November 1998 and November 2002. [2]Delaware allows two terms, but these need not be served consecutively. [3]Montana allows no more than 8 years of service every 16 years. [4]Nebraska allows the governor to serve two consecutive terms, but the candidate must wait four years before running for a third term. [5]Lt. Gov. Rick Perry became governor in December 2000 following George W. Bush's election as president of the United States. Gov. Perry was elected to a full term in November 2002. [6]During Michael Leavitt's term of service, Utah enacted a provision limiting the governor's term to three consecutive terms. Leavitt was grandfathered and may serve one more term upon completion of his present term. [7]In Virginia the governor cannot serve successive terms. [8]Lt. Gov. Togiola Tulafono became governor in April 2003 following the death of Gov. Tauese Sunia.

# State Officers and Legislatures

*N/A means not available. Sources: Web sites from the individual states,* The Book of the States, *vol. 35, and the* CSG State Directory, *published by The Council of State Governments.*

| STATE/OFFICE | OFFICEHOLDER | PAY[1] |
|---|---|---|
| **Alabama** | | |
| Governor | Bob Riley (R) | $101,432 |
| Lt. Gov. | Lucy Baxley (D) | $48,620 |
| Sec. of State | Nancy Worley (D) | $66,722 |
| Atty. Gen. | Bill Pryor (R) | $124,951 |
| Treasurer | Kay Ivey (R) | $66,722 |
| Legislature | | |
| Senate | Dem: 25; Rep: 10 | |
| House | Dem: 64; Rep: 41 | |
| **Alaska** | | |
| Governor | Frank H. Murkowski (R) | $83,280 |
| Lt. Gov. | Loren Leman (R) | $77,712 |
| Sec. of State[2] | | |
| Atty. Gen. | Gregg Renkes (R) | $88,548 |
| Treasurer | Tom Butin | $91,668 |
| Legislature | | |
| Senate | Dem: 8; Rep: 12 | |
| House | Dem: 13; Rep: 27 | |
| **Arizona** | | |
| Governor | Janet Napolitano (D) | $95,000 |
| Lt. Gov.[3] | | |
| Sec. of State | Jan Brewer (R) | $70,000 |
| Atty. Gen. | Terry Goddard (D) | $90,000 |
| Treasurer | David Petersen (R) | $70,000 |
| Legislature | | |
| Senate | Dem: 13; Rep: 17 | |
| House | Dem: 21; Rep: 39 | |
| **Arkansas** | | |
| Governor | Mike Huckabee (R) | $71,738 |
| Lt. Gov. | Win Rockefeller (R) | $34,673 |
| Sec. of State | Charlie Daniels (D) | $43,000 |
| Atty. Gen. | Mike Beebe (D) | $59,781 |
| Treasurer | Gus Wingfield (D) | $44,836 |
| Legislature | | |
| Senate | Dem: 27; Rep: 8 | |
| House | Dem: 72; Rep: 28 | |
| **California** | | |
| Governor | Gray Davis (D) | $175,000 |
| Lt. Gov. | Cruz M. Bustamante (D) | $131,250 |
| Sec. of State | Kevin Shelley (D) | $123,750 |
| Atty. Gen. | Bill Lockyer (D) | $148,750 |
| Treasurer | Philip Angelides (D) | $140,000 |
| Legislature | | |
| Senate | Dem: 25; Rep: 15 | |
| House | Dem: 48; Rep: 32 | |
| **Colorado** | | |
| Governor | Bill Owens (R) | $90,000 |
| Lt. Gov. | Jane Norton (R) | $68,500 |
| Sec. of State | Donetta Davidson (R) | $68,500 |
| Atty. Gen. | Ken Salazar (D) | $80,000 |
| Treasurer | Mike Coffman (R) | $68,500 |
| Legislature | | |
| Senate | Dem: 17; Rep: 18 | |
| House | Dem: 28; Rep: 37 | |
| **Connecticut** | | |
| Governor | John G. Rowland (R) | $150,000 |
| Lt. Gov. | M. Jodi Rell (R) | $77,756 |
| Sec. of State | Susan Bysiewicz (D) | $50,000 |
| Atty. Gen. | Richard Blumenthal (D) | $81,562 |
| Treasurer | Denise L. Nappier (D) | $76,125 |

| STATE/OFFICE | OFFICEHOLDER | PAY[1] |
|---|---|---|
| **Connecticut (continued)** | | |
| Legislature | | |
| Senate | Dem: 21; Rep: 15 | |
| House | Dem: 94; Rep: 57 | |
| **Delaware** | | |
| Governor | Ruth Ann Minner (D) | $114,000 |
| Lt. Gov. | John Carney (D) | $60,000 |
| Sec. of State | Harriet Smith Windsor (D) | $103,900 |
| Atty. Gen. | M. Jane Brady (R) | $114,400 |
| Treasurer | Jack Markell (D) | $92,200 |
| Legislature | | |
| Senate | Dem: 13; Rep: 8 | |
| House | Dem: 12; Rep: 29 | |
| **Florida** | | |
| Governor | Jeb Bush (R) | $120,171 |
| Lt. Gov. | Frank T. Brogan (R) | $115,112 |
| Sec. of State | Glenda Hood (R) | $116,056 |
| Atty. Gen. | Charlie Crist (R) | $118,957 |
| Treasurer | Tom Gallagher (R) | $118,957 |
| Legislature | | |
| Senate | Dem: 14; Rep: 25; Vacant: 1 | |
| House | Dem: 39; Rep: 81 | |
| **Georgia** | | |
| Governor | Sonny Perdue (R) | $127,303 |
| Lt. Gov. | Mark Taylor (D) | $83,148 |
| Sec. of State | Cathy Cox (D) | $112,776 |
| Atty. Gen. | Thurbert E. Baker (D) | $125,871 |
| Treasurer | W. Daniel Ebersole | $116,093 |
| Legislature | | |
| Senate | Dem: 26; Rep: 30 | |
| House | Dem: 107; Rep: 72; Ind: 1 | |
| **Hawaii** | | |
| Governor | Linda Lingle (R) | $94,780 |
| Lt. Gov. | James Aiona (R) | $90,041 |
| Sec. of State[2] | | |
| Atty. Gen. | Mark J. Bennett (R) | $85,302 |
| Treasurer[4] | Georgina K. Kawamura (Director of Finance) | $85,302 |
| Legislature | | |
| Senate | Dem: 20; Rep: 5 | |
| House | Dem: 36; Rep: 15 | |
| **Idaho** | | |
| Governor | Dirk Kempthorne (R) | $98,500 |
| Lt. Gov. | Jim Risch (R) | $26,000 |
| Sec. of State | Ben Ysursa (R) | $80,000 |
| Atty. Gen. | Lawrence Wasden (R) | $88,500 |
| Treasurer | Ron G. Crane (R) | $80,000 |
| Legislature | | |
| Senate | Dem: 7; Rep: 28 | |
| House | Dem: 16; Rep: 54 | |
| **Illinois** | | |
| Governor | Rod R. Blagojevich (D) | $150,691 |
| Lt. Gov. | Pat Quinn (D) | $115,235 |
| Sec. of State | Jesse White (D) | $123,700 |
| Atty. Gen. | Lisa Madigan (D) | $132,963 |
| Treasurer | Judy Baar Topinka (R) | $115,235 |
| Legislature | | |
| Senate | Dem: 26; Rep: 32; Ind: 1 | |
| House | Dem: 66; Rep: 52 | |

# State Officers and Legislatures (continued)

| STATE/OFFICE | OFFICEHOLDER | PAY[1] |
|---|---|---|
| **Indiana** | | |
| Governor | Frank O'Bannon (D) | $95,000 |
| Lt. Gov. | Joseph E. Kernan (D) | $76,000 |
| Sec. of State | Todd Rokita (R) | $66,000 |
| Atty. Gen. | Steve Carter (R) | $79,400 |
| Treasurer | Tim Berry (R) | $66,000 |
| Legislature | | |
| Senate | Dem: 18; Rep: 32 | |
| House | Dem: 51; Rep: 49 | |
| | | |
| **Iowa** | | |
| Governor | Tom Vilsack (D) | $107,482 |
| Lt. Gov. | Sally Pederson (D) | $76,698 |
| Sec. of State | Chet Culver (D) | $82,940 |
| Atty. Gen. | Tom Miller (D) | $105,430 |
| Treasurer | Michael L. Fitzgerald (D) | $87,990 |
| Legislature | | |
| Senate | Dem: 21; Rep: 29 | |
| House | Dem: 45; Rep: 54 | |
| | | |
| **Kansas** | | |
| Governor | Kathleen Sebelius (D) | $95,446 |
| Lt. Gov. | John Moore (D) | $26,967 |
| Sec. of State | Ron Thornburgh (R) | $74,148 |
| Atty. Gen. | Phill Kline (R) | $85,267 |
| Treasurer | Lynn Jenkins (R) | $74,148 |
| Legislature | | |
| Senate | Dem: 10; Rep: 30 | |
| House | Dem: 45; Rep: 80 | |
| | | |
| **Kentucky** | | |
| Governor | Paul Patton (D) | $103,018 |
| Lt. Gov. | Stephen L. Henry (D) | $87,580 |
| Sec. of State | John Y. Brown III (D) | $82,521 |
| Atty. Gen. | A. B. "Ben" Chandler III (D) | $87,580 |
| Treasurer | Jonathan Miller (D) | $87,580 |
| Legislature | | |
| Senate | Dem: 16; Rep: 22 | |
| House | Dem: 65; Rep: 35 | |
| | | |
| **Louisiana** | | |
| Governor | M.J. "Mike" Foster, Jr. (R) | $95,000 |
| Lt. Gov. | Kathleen Babineaux Blanco (D) | $85,008 |
| Sec. of State | Fox McKeithen (R) | $85,000 |
| Atty. Gen. | Richard P. Ieyoub (D) | $85,000 |
| Treasurer | John Neely Kennedy (D) | $85,000 |
| Legislature | | |
| Senate | Dem: 23; Rep: 15; Vacant: 1 | |
| House | Dem: 70; Rep: 34; Ind: 1 | |
| | | |
| **Maine** | | |
| Governor | John Baldacci (D) | $70,000 |
| Lt. Gov.[3] | | |
| Sec. of State | Dan A. Gwadosky (D) | N/A |
| Atty. Gen. | G. Steven Rowe (D) | $78,062 |
| Treasurer | Dale McCormick (D) | $71,032 |
| Legislature | | |
| Senate | Dem: 18; Rep: 17 | |
| House | Dem: 80; Rep: 67; Unenrolled: 3; Green Independent Party: 1 | |
| | | |
| **Maryland** | | |
| Governor | Robert L. Ehrlich, Jr. (R) | $120,000 |
| Lt. Gov. | Michael Steele (R) | $100,000 |
| Sec. of State | R. Karl Aumann (R) | $70,000 |
| Atty. Gen. | J. Joseph Curran, Jr. (D) | $100,000 |
| Treasurer | Nancy Kopp (D) | $100,000 |

| STATE/OFFICE | OFFICEHOLDER | PAY[1] |
|---|---|---|
| **Maryland (continued)** | | |
| Legislature | | |
| Senate | Dem: 33; Rep: 14 | |
| House | Dem: 98; Rep: 43 | |
| | | |
| **Massachusetts** | | |
| Governor | Mitt Romney (R)[5] | $135,000 |
| Lt. Gov. | Kerry Healey (R)[5] | $120,000 |
| Sec. of State | William Francis Galvin (D) | $120,000 |
| Atty. Gen. | Tom Reilly (D) | $122,500 |
| Treasurer | Tim Cahill (D) | $120,000 |
| Legislature | | |
| Senate | Dem: 34; Rep: 6 | |
| House | Dem: 135; Rep: 23; Unenrolled: 1 | |
| | | |
| **Michigan** | | |
| Governor | Jennifer Granholm (D) | $177,000 |
| Lt. Gov. | John Cherry (D) | $123,000 |
| Sec. of State | Terri Land (R) | $124,900 |
| Atty. Gen. | Mike Cox (R) | $124,900 |
| Treasurer | Jay Rising | $161,000 |
| Legislature | | |
| Senate | Dem: 16; Rep: 22 | |
| House | Dem: 62; Rep: 47 | |
| | | |
| **Minnesota** | | |
| Governor | Tim Pawlenty (R) | $120,303 |
| Lt. Gov. | Carol Molnau (R) | $62,980 |
| Sec. of State | Mary Kiffmeyer (R) | $66,169 |
| Atty. Gen. | Mike Hatch (D) | $93,000 |
| Treasurer[4] | Dan McElroy (Commissioner of Finance) | $71,129 |
| Legislature | | |
| Senate | Dem: 35; Rep: 31; Ind: 1 | |
| House | Dem: 53; Rep: 80 | |
| | | |
| **Mississippi** | | |
| Governor | Ronnie Musgrove (D) | $101,800 |
| Lt. Gov. | Amy Tuck (R) | $60,000 |
| Sec. of State | Eric Clark (D) | $75,000 |
| Atty. Gen. | Mike Moore (D) | $90,800 |
| Treasurer | Marshall Bennett (D) | $75,000 |
| Legislature | | |
| Senate | Dem: 31; Rep: 21 | |
| House | Dem: 81; Rep: 38; Ind: 3 | |
| | | |
| **Missouri** | | |
| Governor | Bob Holden (D) | $120,087 |
| Lt. Gov. | Joe Maxwell (D) | $77,184 |
| Sec. of State | Matt Blunt (R) | $90,471 |
| Atty. Gen. | Jeremiah W. Nixon (D) | $104,332 |
| Treasurer | Nancy Farmer (D) | $96,455 |
| Legislature | | |
| Senate | Dem: 14; Rep: 20 | |
| House | Dem: 73; Rep: 90 | |
| | | |
| **Montana** | | |
| Governor | Judy Martz (R) | $88,190 |
| Lt. Gov. | Karl Ohs (R) | $62,471 |
| Sec. of State | Bob Brown (R) | $67,512 |
| Atty. Gen. | Mike McGrath (D) | $75,550 |
| Treasurer[4] | Scott Darkenwald (Dept. of Administration) | $80,704 |
| Legislature | | |
| Senate | Dem: 21; Rep: 29 | |
| House | Dem: 47; Rep: 53 | |

## State Officers and Legislatures (continued)

| STATE/OFFICE | OFFICEHOLDER | PAY[1] |
|---|---|---|
| **Nebraska** | | |
| Governor | Mike Johanns (R) | $65,000 |
| Lt. Gov. | Dave Heineman (R) | $60,000 |
| Sec. of State | John A. Gale (R) | $65,000 |
| Atty. Gen. | Jon Bruning (R) | $64,500 |
| Treasurer | Lorelee Byrd (R) | $60,000 |
| Legislature (unicameral) | | |
| Senate | 49 nonpartisan members | |
| | | |
| **Nevada** | | |
| Governor | Kenny C. Guinn (R) | $117,000 |
| Lt. Gov. | Lorraine T. Hunt (R) | $50,000 |
| Sec. of State | Dean Heller (R) | $80,000 |
| Atty. Gen. | Brian Sandoval (R) | $110,000 |
| Treasurer | Brian K. Krolicki (R) | $80,000 |
| Legislature | | |
| Senate | Dem: 8; Rep: 13 | |
| House | Dem: 23; Rep: 19 | |
| | | |
| **New Hampshire** | | |
| Governor | Craig Benson (R) | $100,690 |
| Lt. Gov.[6] | | |
| Sec. of State | William M. Gardner (D) | $65,540 |
| Atty. Gen. | Peter W. Heed (R) | $85,753 |
| Treasurer | Michael Ablowich | $76,603 |
| Legislature | | |
| Senate | Dem: 6; Rep: 18 | |
| House | Dem: 117; Rep: 282; Vacant: 1 | |
| | | |
| **New Jersey** | | |
| Governor | James E. McGreevey (D) | $157,000 |
| Lt. Gov.[6] | | |
| Sec. of State | Regena L. Thomas (D) | $137,165 |
| Atty. Gen. | Peter C. Harvey | $137,165 |
| Treasurer | John E. McCormac | $137,165 |
| Legislature | | |
| Senate | Dem: 20; Rep: 20 | |
| House | Dem: 43; Rep: 35 | |
| | | |
| **New Mexico** | | |
| Governor | Bill Richardson (D) | $90,000 |
| Lt. Gov. | Diane Denish (D) | $65,000 |
| Sec. of State | Rebecca Vigil-Giron (D) | $65,000 |
| Atty. Gen. | Patricia A. Madrid (D) | $72,500 |
| Treasurer | Robert Vigil (D) | $65,000 |
| Legislature | | |
| Senate | Dem: 24; Rep: 18 | |
| House | Dem: 42; Rep: 28 | |
| | | |
| **New York** | | |
| Governor | George E. Pataki (R) | $179,000 |
| Lt. Gov. | Mary O. Donohue (R) | $151,500 |
| Sec. of State | Randy A. Daniels (D) | $120,800 |
| Atty. Gen. | Eliot Spitzer (D) | $151,500 |
| Treasurer | Aida Brewer | $108,510 |
| Legislature | | |
| Senate | Dem: 25; Rep: 37 | |
| House | Dem: 103; Rep: 47 | |
| | | |
| **North Carolina** | | |
| Governor | Michael F. Easley (D) | $118,430 |
| Lt. Gov. | Beverly Purdue (D) | $104,523 |
| Sec. of State | Elaine F. Marshall (D) | $94,552 |
| Atty. Gen. | Roy Cooper III (D) | $104,523 |
| Treasurer | Richard H. Moore (D) | $104,523 |
| Legislature | | |
| Senate | Dem: 28; Rep: 22 | |
| House | Dem: 60; Rep: 60 | |

| STATE/OFFICE | OFFICEHOLDER | PAY[1] |
|---|---|---|
| **North Dakota** | | |
| Governor | John Hoeven (R) | $83,013 |
| Lt. Gov. | Jack Dalrymple (R) | $64,452 |
| Sec. of State | Alvin A. Jaeger (R) | $68,000 |
| Atty. Gen. | Wayne Stenehjem (R) | $71,076 |
| Treasurer | Kathi Gilmore (D) | $62,976 |
| Legislature | | |
| Senate | Dem: 16; Rep: 31 | |
| House | Dem: 28; Rep: 66 | |
| | | |
| **Ohio** | | |
| Governor | Bob Taft (R) | $126,485 |
| Lt. Gov. | Jennette Bradley (R) | $73,715 |
| Sec. of State | J. Kenneth Blackwell (R) | $90,725 |
| Atty. Gen. | Jim Petro (R) | $93,434 |
| Treasurer | Joseph T. Deters (R) | $93,434 |
| Legislature | | |
| Senate | Dem: 11; Rep: 22 | |
| House | Dem: 38; Rep: 61 | |
| | | |
| **Oklahoma** | | |
| Governor | Brad Henry (D) | $101,040 |
| Lt. Gov. | Mary Fallin (R) | $75,530 |
| Sec. of State | M. Susan Savage (D) | $90,000 |
| Atty. Gen. | W.A. Drew Edmondson (D) | $94,349 |
| Treasurer | Robert Butkin (D) | $82,000 |
| Legislature | | |
| Senate | Dem: 27; Rep: 20; Vacant: 1 | |
| House | Dem: 53; Rep: 48 | |
| | | |
| **Oregon** | | |
| Governor | Ted Kulongoski (D) | $93,600 |
| Lt. Gov.[3] | | |
| Sec. of State | Bill Bradbury (D) | $72,000 |
| Atty. Gen. | Hardy Myers (D) | $77,200 |
| Treasurer | Randall Edwards (D) | $72,000 |
| Legislature | | |
| Senate | Dem: 15; Rep: 15 | |
| House | Dem: 25; Rep: 35 | |
| | | |
| **Pennsylvania** | | |
| Governor | Edward G. Rendell (D) | $144,416 |
| Lt. Gov. | Catherine Baker Knoll (D) | $119,399 |
| Sec. of State | Benjamin Ramos (D) | $102,343 |
| Atty. Gen. | Mike Fisher (R) | $118,262 |
| Treasurer | Barbara Hafer (R) | $118,262 |
| Legislature | | |
| Senate | Dem: 21; Rep: 28; Vacant: 1 | |
| House | Dem: 94; Rep: 108 | |
| | | |
| **Rhode Island** | | |
| Governor | Don Carcieri (R) | $95,000 |
| Lt. Gov. | Charles J. Fogarty (D) | $80,000 |
| Sec. of State | Matthew Brown (D) | $80,000 |
| Atty. Gen. | Patrick Lynch (D) | $85,000 |
| Treasurer | Paul J. Tavares (D) | $80,000 |
| Legislature | | |
| Senate | Dem: 32; Rep: 6 | |
| House | Dem: 63; Rep: 11; Ind: 1 | |
| | | |
| **South Carolina** | | |
| Governor | Mark Sanford (R) | $106,078 |
| Lt. Gov. | Andre Bauer (R) | $44,737 |
| Sec. of State | Mark Hammond (R) | $92,007 |
| Atty. Gen. | Henry McMaster (R) | $92,007 |
| Treasurer | Grady L. Patterson, Jr. (D) | $92,007 |

## State Officers and Legislatures (continued)

| STATE/OFFICE | OFFICEHOLDER | PAY[1] |
|---|---|---|
| **South Carolina** (continued) | | |
| Legislature | | |
|   Senate | Dem: 21; Rep: 24; Vacant: 1 | |
|   House | Dem: 50; Rep: 73; Vacant: 1 | |
| **South Dakota** | | |
| Governor | Mike Rounds (R) | $95,389 |
| Lt. Gov. | Dennis Daugaard (R) | $12,635 |
| Sec. of State | Chris Nelson (R) | $64,812 |
| Atty. Gen. | Larry Long (R) | $80,995 |
| Treasurer | Vern Larson (R) | $64,813 |
| Legislature | | |
|   Senate | Dem: 9; Rep: 26 | |
|   House | Dem: 21; Rep: 49 | |
| **Tennessee** | | |
| Governor | Phil Bredesen (D) | $85,000 |
| Lt. Gov. | John S. Wilder (D) | $49,500 |
| Sec. of State | Riley Darnell (D) | $127,308 |
| Atty. Gen. | Paul G. Summers (D) | $118,416 |
| Treasurer | Steve Adams (D) | $127,308 |
| Legislature | | |
|   Senate | Dem: 18; Rep: 15 | |
|   House | Dem: 54; Rep: 45 | |
| **Texas** | | |
| Governor | Rick Perry (R) | $115,345 |
| Lt. Gov. | David Dewhurst (R) | $99,122 |
| Sec. of State | Gwyn Shea (R) | $117,546 |
| Atty. Gen. | Greg Abbott (R) | $92,217 |
| Treasurer[4] | Carole Keeton Strayhorn (Comptroller) (R) | $92,217 |
| Legislature | | |
|   Senate | Dem: 12; Rep: 19 | |
|   House | Dem: 62; Rep: 88 | |
| **Utah** | | |
| Governor | Michael O. Leavitt (R) | $100,600 |
| Lt. Gov. | Olene S. Walker (R) | $78,200 |
| Sec. of State[2] | | |
| Atty. Gen. | Mark Shurtleff (R) | $84,600 |
| Treasurer | Edward T. Alter (R) | $80,700 |
| Legislature | | |
|   Senate | Dem: 7; Rep: 22 | |
|   House | Dem: 19; Rep: 56 | |
| **Vermont** | | |
| Governor | Jim Douglas (R) | $88,026 |
| Lt. Gov. | Brian Dubie (R) | $50,253 |
| Sec. of State | Deborah L. Markowitz (D) | $75,317 |
| Atty. Gen. | William H. Sorrell (D) | $90,272 |
| Treasurer | Jeb Spaulding (D) | $75,317 |

| STATE/OFFICE | OFFICEHOLDER | PAY[1] |
|---|---|---|
| **Vermont** (continued) | | |
| Legislature | | |
|   Senate | Dem: 19; Rep: 11 | |
|   House | Dem: 69; Rep: 74; Ind: 3 | |
| | Progressive: 4 | |
| **Virginia** | | |
| Governor | Mark R. Warner (D) | $124,855 |
| Lt. Gov. | Tim Kaine (D) | $36,321 |
| Sec. of State | Anita A. Rimler (D) | $128,479 |
| Atty. Gen. | Jerry Kilgore (R) | $110,667 |
| Treasurer | Jody M. Wagner | $112,653 |
| Legislature | | |
|   Senate | Dem: 17; Rep: 23 | |
|   House | Dem: 34; Rep: 64; Ind: 2 | |
| **Washington** | | |
| Governor | Gary Locke (D) | $139,087 |
| Lt. Gov. | Brad Owen (D) | $72,705 |
| Sec. of State | Sam Reed (R) | $89,004 |
| Atty. Gen. | Christine O. Gregoire (D) | $126,443 |
| Treasurer | Michael J. Murphy (D) | $97,446 |
| Legislature | | |
|   Senate | Dem: 24; Rep: 25 | |
|   House | Dem: 52; Rep: 46 | |
| **West Virginia** | | |
| Governor | Bob Wise (D) | $90,000 |
| Lt. Gov.[6] | Earl Ray Tomblin (D) | — |
| Sec. of State | Joe Manchin III (D) | $65,000 |
| Atty. Gen. | Darrell V. McGraw, Jr. (D) | $75,000 |
| Treasurer | John D. Perdue (D) | $70,000 |
| Legislature | | |
|   Senate | Dem: 24; Rep: 10 | |
|   House | Dem: 68; Rep: 32 | |
| **Wisconsin** | | |
| Governor | Jim Doyle (D) | $122,406 |
| Lt. Gov. | Barbara Lawton (D) | $69,579 |
| Sec. of State | Doug LaFollette (D) | $62,549 |
| Atty. Gen. | Peg Lautenschlager (D) | $127,868 |
| Treasurer | Jack C. Voight (R) | $62,549 |
| Legislature | | |
|   Senate | Dem: 13; Rep: 18; Vacant: 2 | |
|   House | Dem: 40; Rep: 58; Vacant: 1 | |
| **Wyoming** | | |
| Governor | Dave Freudenthal (D) | $130,000 |
| Lt. Gov.[3] | | |
| Sec. of State | Joseph B. Meyer (R) | $110,000 |
| Atty. Gen. | Pat Crank | $89,067 |
| Treasurer | Cynthia Lummis (R) | $110,000 |
| Legislature | | |
|   Senate | Dem: 10; Rep: 20 | |
|   House | Dem: 15; Rep: 45 | |

[1]In most cases, the salary rates are from January 2002. [2]Lieutenant governor serves as secretary of state. [3]Secretary of state assumes duties of lieutenant governor. [4]No official state treasurer—official in charge of general treasury performs duties. [5]Gov. Mitt Romney and Lt. Gov. Kerry Healey plan to forfeit their salaries for the next four years. [6]No official lieutenant governor—president of the senate succeeds the governor.

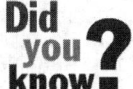

Thomas Jefferson was the first governor of a US state—Virginia—to go on to serve as president. Sixteen governors since have been elected president, including 4 of the last 5 executives. Andrew Jackson and William Henry Harrison served as territorial governors of Florida and Indiana, respectively, prior to their elections to the presidency.

## Area and Zip Codes Web Sites

US telephone area codes and postal codes change frequently to accommodate telecommunications user patterns and expansions and shifts in patterns of business and residential development. With regard to telephone area codes, in some cases, an area receives an entirely new area code; in others, a new area code "overlays" the preceding one. Check local listings to determine whether to dial "1" before dialing outside of the area code or whether to dial the area code as well as the telephone number when dialing within the area code.

**Area codes:**
<www.cs.ucsd.edu/users/bsy/area.html#872>.
**Zip codes:**
<www.usps.gov/ncsc/ziplookup/lookupmenu.htm>.

# Cities of the United States

## US Urban Growth, 1850–2000

*Source: US Census Bureau.*

| RANK | CITY | 1850 | 1900 | 1950 | 1980 | 1990 | 2000 |
|---|---|---|---|---|---|---|---|
| 1 | New York NY[1] | 515,547 | 3,437,202 | 7,891,957 | 7,071,639 | 7,322,564 | 8,008,278 |
| 2 | Los Angeles CA | 1,610 | 102,479 | 1,970,358 | 2,966,850 | 3,485,398 | 3,694,820 |
| 3 | Chicago IL | 29,963 | 1,698,575 | 3,620,962 | 3,005,072 | 2,783,726 | 2,896,016 |
| 4 | Houston TX | 2,396 | 44,633 | 596,163 | 1,595,138 | 1,630,553 | 1,953,631 |
| 5 | Philadelphia PA[1] | 121,376 | 1,293,697 | 2,071,605 | 1,688,210 | 1,585,577 | 1,517,550 |
| 6 | Phoenix AZ | | 5,544 | 106,818 | 789,704 | 983,403 | 1,321,045 |
| 7 | San Diego CA | | 17,700 | 334,387 | 875,538 | 1,110,549 | 1,223,400 |
| 8 | Dallas TX | | 42,638 | 434,462 | 904,078 | 1,006,877 | 1,188,580 |
| 9 | San Antonio TX | 3,488 | 53,321 | 408,442 | 785,880 | 935,933 | 1,144,646 |
| 10 | Detroit MI | 21,019 | 285,704 | 1,849,568 | 1,203,339 | 1,027,974 | 951,270 |
| 11 | San Jose CA | | 21,500 | 95,280 | 629,442 | 782,248 | 894,943 |
| 12 | Indianapolis IN | 8,091 | 169,164 | 427,173 | 700,807 | 741,952 | 791,926 |
| 13 | San Francisco CA[1] | 34,776 | 342,782 | 775,357 | 678,974 | 723,959 | 776,733 |
| 14 | Jacksonville FL | 1,045 | 28,429 | 204,517 | 540,920 | 635,230 | 735,617 |
| 15 | Columbus OH | 17,882 | 125,560 | 375,901 | 564,871 | 632,910 | 711,470 |
| 16 | Austin TX | 629 | 22,258 | 132,459 | 345,496 | 465,622 | 656,562 |
| 17 | Baltimore MD | 169,054 | 508,957 | 949,708 | 786,775 | 736,014 | 651,154 |
| 18 | Memphis TN | 8,841 | 102,320 | 396,000 | 646,356 | 610,337 | 650,100 |
| 19 | Milwaukee WI | 20,061 | 285,315 | 637,392 | 636,212 | 628,088 | 596,974 |
| 20 | Boston MA | 136,881 | 560,892 | 801,444 | 562,994 | 574,283 | 589,141 |
| 21 | Washington DC[1] | 40,001 | 278,718 | 802,178 | 638,333 | 606,900 | 572,059 |
| 22 | Nashville TN[1] | 10,165 | 80,865 | 174,307 | 455,651 | 510,784 | 569,891 |
| 23 | El Paso TX | | 15,906 | 130,485 | 425,259 | 515,342 | 563,662 |
| 24 | Seattle WA | | 80,671 | 467,591 | 493,846 | 516,259 | 563,374 |
| 25 | Denver CO[1] | | 133,859 | 415,786 | 492,365 | 467,610 | 554,636 |
| 26 | Charlotte NC | 1,065 | 18,091 | 134,042 | 314,447 | 395,934 | 540,828 |
| 27 | Fort Worth TX | | 26,688 | 278,778 | 385,164 | 447,619 | 534,694 |
| 28 | Portland OR | | 90,426 | 373,628 | 366,383 | 437,319 | 529,121 |
| 29 | Oklahoma City OK | | 10,037 | 243,504 | 403,213 | 444,719 | 506,132 |
| 30 | Tucson AZ | | 7,531 | 45,454 | 330,537 | 405,390 | 486,699 |
| 31 | New Orleans LA | 116,375 | 287,104 | 570,445 | 557,515 | 496,938 | 484,674 |
| 32 | Las Vegas NV | | | 24,624 | 164,674 | 258,295 | 478,434 |
| 33 | Cleveland OH | 17,034 | 381,768 | 914,808 | 573,822 | 505,616 | 478,403 |
| 34 | Long Beach CA | | 2,252 | 250,767 | 361,334 | 429,433 | 461,522 |
| 35 | Albuquerque NM | | 6,238 | 96,815 | 331,767 | 384,736 | 448,607 |
| 36 | Kansas City MO | | 163,752 | 456,622 | 448,159 | 435,146 | 441,545 |
| 37 | Fresno CA | | 12,470 | 91,669 | 218,202 | 354,202 | 427,652 |
| 38 | Virginia Beach VA | | | 5,390 | 262,199 | 393,069 | 425,257 |
| 39 | Atlanta GA | 2,572 | 89,872 | 331,314 | 425,022 | 394,017 | 416,474 |
| 40 | Sacramento CA | 6,820 | 29,282 | 137,572 | 275,741 | 369,365 | 407,018 |
| 41 | Oakland CA | | 66,960 | 384,575 | 339,337 | 372,242 | 399,484 |
| 42 | Mesa AZ | | 722 | 16,790 | 152,453 | 288,091 | 396,375 |
| 43 | Tulsa OK | | | 182,740 | 360,919 | 367,302 | 393,049 |
| 44 | Omaha NE | | 102,555 | 251,117 | 314,255 | 335,795 | 390,007 |
| 45 | Minneapolis MN | | 202,718 | 521,718 | 370,951 | 368,383 | 382,618 |
| 46 | Honolulu HI[1] | | 39,306 | 248,034 | 365,048 | 365,272 | 371,657 |
| 47 | Miami FL | | 1,681 | 249,276 | 346,865 | 358,548 | 362,470 |
| 48 | Colorado Springs CO | | 21,085 | 45,472 | 215,150 | 281,140 | 360,890 |
| 49 | St. Louis MO | 77,860 | 575,238 | 856,796 | 453,085 | 396,685 | 348,189 |
| 50 | Wichita KS | | 24,671 | 168,279 | 279,272 | 304,011 | 344,284 |
| 51 | Santa Ana CA | | 4,933 | 45,533 | 203,713 | 293,742 | 337,977 |
| 52 | Pittsburgh PA | 46,601 | 321,616 | 676,806 | 423,938 | 369,879 | 334,563 |

## US Urban Growth, 1850–2000 (continued)

| RANK | CITY | 1850 | 1900 | 1950 | 1980 | 1990 | 2000 |
|---|---|---|---|---|---|---|---|
| 53 | Arlington TX | | 1,079 | 7,692 | 160,113 | 261,721 | 332,969 |
| 54 | Cincinnati OH | 115,435 | 325,902 | 503,998 | 385,457 | 364,040 | 331,285 |
| 55 | Anaheim CA | | 1,456 | 14,556 | 219,311 | 266,406 | 328,014 |
| 56 | Toledo OH | 3,829 | 131,822 | 303,616 | 354,635 | 332,943 | 313,619 |
| 57 | Tampa FL | | 15,839 | 124,681 | 271,523 | 280,015 | 303,447 |
| 58 | Buffalo NY | 42,261 | 352,387 | 580,132 | 357,870 | 328,123 | 292,648 |
| 59 | St. Paul MN | 1,112 | 163,065 | 311,349 | 270,230 | 272,235 | 287,151 |
| 60 | Corpus Christi TX | | 4,703 | 108,287 | 231,999 | 257,453 | 277,454 |
| 61 | Aurora CO | | 202 | 11,421 | 158,588 | 222,103 | 276,393 |
| 62 | Raleigh NC | 4,518 | 13,643 | 65,679 | 150,255 | 207,951 | 276,093 |
| 63 | Newark NJ | 38,894 | 246,070 | 438,776 | 329,248 | 275,221 | 273,546 |
| 64 | Lexington KY | 8,159 | 26,369 | 55,534 | 204,165 | 225,366 | 260,512 |
| 65 | Anchorage AK[1] | | | 11,254 | 174,431 | 226,338 | 260,283 |
| 66 | Louisville KY | 43,194 | 204,731 | 369,129 | 298,451 | 269,063 | 256,231 |
| 67 | Riverside CA | | 7,973 | 46,764 | 170,876 | 226,505 | 255,166 |
| 68 | St. Petersburg FL | | 1,575 | 96,738 | 238,647 | 238,629 | 248,232 |
| 69 | Bakersfield CA | | 4,836 | 34,784 | 105,611 | 174,820 | 247,057 |
| 70 | Stockton CA | | 17,506 | 70,853 | 149,779 | 210,943 | 243,771 |
| 71 | Birmingham AL | | 38,415 | 326,037 | 284,413 | 265,968 | 242,820 |
| 72 | Jersey City NJ | 6,856 | 206,433 | 299,017 | 223,532 | 228,537 | 240,055 |
| 73 | Norfolk VA | 14,326 | 46,624 | 213,513 | 266,979 | 261,229 | 234,403 |
| 74 | Baton Rouge LA | 3,905 | 11,269 | 125,629 | 219,419 | 219,531 | 227,818 |
| 75 | Hialeah FL | | | 19,676 | 145,254 | 188,004 | 226,419 |
| 76 | Lincoln NE | | 40,169 | 98,884 | 171,932 | 191,972 | 225,581 |
| 77 | Greensboro NC | | 10,035 | 74,389 | 155,642 | 183,521 | 223,891 |
| 78 | Plano TX | | | | 72,331 | 128,713 | 222,030 |
| 79 | Rochester NY | 36,403 | 162,608 | 332,488 | 241,741 | 231,636 | 219,773 |
| 80 | Glendale AZ | | | | 97,172 | 148,134 | 218,812 |
| 81 | Akron OH | 3,266 | 42,728 | 274,605 | 237,177 | 223,019 | 217,074 |
| 82 | Garland TX | | 819 | 10,571 | 138,857 | 180,650 | 215,768 |
| 83 | Madison WI | 1,525 | 19,164 | 96,056 | 170,616 | 191,262 | 208,054 |
| 84 | Fort Wayne IN | 4,282 | 45,115 | 133,607 | 172,196 | 173,072 | 205,727 |
| 85 | Fremont CA | | | | 131,945 | 173,339 | 203,413 |
| 86 | Scottsdale AZ | | | | 88,412 | 130,069 | 202,705 |
| 87 | Montgomery AL | 8,728 | 30,346 | 106,525 | 177,857 | 187,106 | 201,568 |
| 88 | Shreveport LA | 1,728 | 16,013 | 127,206 | 205,820 | 198,525 | 200,145 |
| 89 | Augusta GA[1] | 9,448 | 39,441 | 71,508 | 47,532 | 44,639 | 199,775 |
| 90 | Lubbock TX | | | 71,747 | 173,979 | 186,206 | 199,564 |
| 91 | Chesapeake VA | | | | 114,486 | 151,976 | 199,184 |
| 92 | Mobile AL | 20,515 | 38,469 | 129,009 | 200,452 | 196,278 | 198,915 |
| 93 | Des Moines IA | | 62,139 | 177,965 | 191,003 | 193,187 | 198,682 |
| 94 | Grand Rapids MI | 2,686 | 87,565 | 176,515 | 181,843 | 189,126 | 197,800 |
| 95 | Richmond VA | 27,570 | 85,050 | 230,310 | 219,214 | 203,056 | 197,790 |
| 96 | Yonkers NY | | 47,931 | 152,798 | 195,351 | 188,082 | 196,086 |
| 97 | Spokane WA | | 36,848 | 161,721 | 171,300 | 177,196 | 195,629 |
| 98 | Glendale CA | | | 95,702 | 139,060 | 180,038 | 194,973 |
| 99 | Tacoma WA | | 37,714 | 143,673 | 158,501 | 176,664 | 193,556 |
| 100 | Irving TX | | | 2,621 | 109,943 | 155,037 | 191,615 |

[1]Cities with boundaries contiguous with their respective counties: New York, Philadelphia, San Francisco, Washington (District of Columbia), Nashville-Davidson (Davidson County), Denver, Honolulu, Anchorage, and Augusta (Augusta-Richmond County).

## Ten Fastest-Growing Cities in the US

Based on a population of 250,000 or more. Source: US Census Bureau.

| CITY | POPULATION | | CHANGE (%) |
|---|---|---|---|
| | 1 APR 1990 | 1 APR 2000 | |
| Las Vegas NV | 258,295 | 478,434 | +85.2 |
| Austin TX | 465,622 | 656,562 | +41.0 |
| Mesa AZ | 288,091 | 396,375 | +37.6 |
| Charlotte NC | 395,934 | 540,828 | +36.6 |
| Phoenix AZ | 983,403 | 1,321,045 | +34.3 |
| Raleigh NC | 207,951 | 276,093 | +32.8 |
| Colorado Springs CO | 281,140 | 360,890 | +28.4 |
| Arlington TX | 261,721 | 332,969 | +27.2 |
| Aurora CO | 222,103 | 276,393 | +24.4 |
| Anaheim CA | 266,406 | 328,014 | +23.1 |

## Ten Cities with the Greatest Population Losses in the US

*Based on a population of 250,000 or more. Source: US Census Bureau.*

| CITY | CHANGE (%) | POPULATION 1 APR 1990 | POPULATION 1 APR 2000 | CITY | CHANGE (%) | POPULATION 1 APR 1990 | POPULATION 1 APR 2000 |
|---|---|---|---|---|---|---|---|
| St. Louis MO | −12.2 | 396,685 | 348,189 | Detroit MI | −7.5 | 1,027,974 | 951,270 |
| Baltimore MD | −11.5 | 736,014 | 651,154 | Toledo OH | −5.8 | 332,943 | 313,619 |
| Buffalo NY | −10.8 | 328,123 | 292,648 | Washington DC | −5.7 | 606,900 | 572,059 |
| Pittsburgh PA | −9.5 | 369,879 | 334,563 | Cleveland OH | −5.4 | 505,616 | 478,403 |
| Cincinnati OH | −9.0 | 364,040 | 331,285 | Milwaukee WI | −5.0 | 628,088 | 596,974 |

## Racial Makeup of the Ten Largest US Cities

Information is given in percent of the total population. The Hispanic or Latino category is listed for comparative purposes even though Hispanic or Latino people may be of any race, thus the rows of racial percentages will not add up to 100 if the Hispanic or Latino entries are included. Source: US Census Bureau, census 2000.

| CITY | WHITE | BLACK OR AFRICAN AMERICAN | AMERICAN INDIAN AND ALASKA NATIVE | ASIAN | NATIVE HAWAIIAN AND OTHER PACIFIC ISLANDER | SOME OTHER RACE | TWO OR MORE RACES | HISPANIC OR LATINO | TOTAL POPULATION |
|---|---|---|---|---|---|---|---|---|---|
| New York NY | 44.7 | 26.6 | 0.5 | 9.8 | 0.1 | 13.4 | 4.9 | 27.0 | 8,008,278 |
| Los Angeles CA | 46.9 | 11.2 | 0.8 | 10.0 | 0.2 | 25.7 | 5.2 | 46.5 | 3,694,820 |
| Chicago IL | 42.0 | 36.8 | 0.4 | 4.3 | 0.1 | 13.6 | 2.9 | 26.0 | 2,896,016 |
| Houston TX | 49.3 | 25.3 | 0.4 | 5.3 | 0.1 | 16.5 | 3.1 | 37.4 | 1,953,631 |
| Philadelphia PA | 45.0 | 43.2 | 0.3 | 4.5 | − | 4.8 | 2.2 | 8.5 | 1,517,550 |
| Phoenix AZ | 71.1 | 5.1 | 2.0 | 2.0 | 0.1 | 16.4 | 3.3 | 34.1 | 1,321,045 |
| San Diego CA | 60.2 | 7.9 | 0.6 | 13.6 | 0.5 | 12.4 | 4.8 | 25.4 | 1,223,400 |
| Dallas TX | 50.8 | 25.9 | 0.5 | 2.7 | − | 17.2 | 2.7 | 35.6 | 1,188,580 |
| San Antonio TX | 67.7 | 6.8 | 0.8 | 1.6 | 0.1 | 19.3 | 3.7 | 58.7 | 1,144,646 |
| Detroit MI | 12.3 | 81.6 | 0.3 | 1.0 | − | 2.5 | 2.3 | 5.0 | 951,270 |

− Percent rounds to 0.0.

# Law and Crime

## US Crime Trends, 2002

The crime trends shown below represent the percent change in crimes reported to police for the first six months of 2002 as compared to the same time period in the year 2001. A negative number indicates that crime has declined. Source: Federal Bureau of Investigation, *Uniform Crime Reports*, January–June 2002.

| POPULATION GROUP AND AREA | NUMBER OF AGENCIES[1] | POPULATION ('000) | CRIME INDEX TOTAL | MODIFIED TOTAL[2] | VIOLENT CRIME[3] | PROPERTY CRIME[4] | MURDER |
|---|---|---|---|---|---|---|---|
| cities | | | | | | | |
| over 1,000,000 | 10 | 24,330 | +0.2 | +0.3 | −1.9 | +0.8 | +2.1 |
| 500,000 to 999,999 | 20 | 13,493 | +1.1 | +1.0 | −3.3 | +1.8 | +5.6 |
| 250,000 to 499,999 | 37 | 12,884 | +1.2 | +1.1 | −1.6 | +1.7 | +2.3 |
| 100,000 to 249,999 | 163 | 24,143 | +2.8 | +2.8 | −0.6 | +3.2 | −2.3 |
| 50,000 to 99,999 | 296 | 20,338 | +3.1 | +3.0 | −2.5 | +3.8 | +8.8 |
| 25,000 to 49,999 | 559 | 19,537 | +0.8 | +0.8 | +0.2 | +0.9 | +5.2 |
| 10,000 to 24,999 | 1,233 | 19,570 | −0.4 | −0.4 | −4.5 | <0.1 | −5.8 |
| under 10,000 | 4,334 | 14,804 | −1.9 | −1.9 | −5.0 | −1.6 | −16.0 |
| counties | | | | | | | |
| suburban[5] | 828 | 37,231 | +3.6 | +3.5 | +2.6 | +3.7 | +11.5 |
| rural[6] | 1,829 | 20,492 | −1.9 | −1.9 | −5.2 | −1.4 | −5.4 |
| areas | | | | | | | |
| suburban area[7] | 4,395 | 73,324 | +1.8 | +1.8 | −0.2 | +2.0 | +11.0 |
| cities outside metropolitan areas | 2,559 | 17,818 | −1.3 | −1.4 | −2.1 | −1.2 | −17.9 |
| total | 9,309 | 206,822 | +1.3 | +1.2 | −1.7 | +1.7 | +2.3 |

## US Crime Trends, 2002 (continued)

| POPULATION GROUP AND AREA | FORCIBLE RAPE | ROBBERY | AGGRAVATED ASSAULT | BURGLARY | LARCENY/ THEFT | CAR THEFT | ARSON |
|---|---|---|---|---|---|---|---|
| **cities** | | | | | | | |
| over 1,000,000 | -3.3 | -0.6 | -2.7 | +1.7 | -0.4 | +3.9 | +4.0 |
| 500,000 to 999,999 | -0.7 | -5.3 | -2.5 | +3.4 | +1.8 | +0.2 | -8.1 |
| 250,000 to 499,999 | +0.7 | +1.2 | -3.7 | +4.2 | -0.2 | +5.8 | -7.1 |
| 100,000 to 249,999 | +7.4 | -0.2 | -1.6 | +4.6 | +2.5 | +4.9 | +3.1 |
| 50,000 to 99,999 | +1.5 | -0.2 | -4.2 | +6.2 | +2.8 | +5.5 | -4.2 |
| 25,000 to 49,999 | +2.1 | -0.6 | +0.2 | +5.1 | -0.3 | +2.2 | -5.6 |
| 10,000 to 24,999 | +2.4 | +1.0 | -7.1 | +4.6 | -1.2 | +2.0 | -3.1 |
| under 10,000 | +6.7 | -0.7 | -6.9 | +3.2 | -2.7 | -0.2 | -3.6 |
| | | | | | | | |
| **counties** | | | | | | | |
| suburban[5] | +3.0 | +8.1 | +1.0 | +6.1 | +1.6 | +11.1 | -0.6 |
| rural[6] | -2.4 | -1.7 | -5.9 | +1.9 | -3.4 | +0.3 | -10.4 |
| | | | | | | | |
| **areas** | | | | | | | |
| suburban area[7] | +1.1 | +5.4 | -2.2 | +5.9 | +0.3 | +6.3 | -0.9 |
| cities outside metro-politan areas | +8.8 | -5.9 | -2.5 | -2.7 | -2.4 | +1.7 | -8.5 |
| | | | | | | | |
| **total** | **+1.8** | **-0.4** | **-2.8** | **+4.2** | **+0.5** | **+4.2** | **-2.6** |

[1]Law enforcement agencies.   [2]Modified total is sum of all offenses, including arson.   [3]Includes murder, forcible rape, robbery, and aggravated assault.   [4]Includes burglary, larceny/theft, and car theft, but excludes data for arson.   [5]Includes crimes reported to sheriffs' departments, county police departments, and state police within Metropolitan Statistical Areas.   [6]Includes crimes reported to sheriffs' departments, county police departments, and state police outside Metropolitan Statistical Areas.   [7]Includes crimes reported to city, county, and state law enforcement agencies within Metropolitan Statistical Areas, but outside the central cities.

**Did you know?** The 100-dollar bill is the highest denomination of currency in circulation in the US. One reason that bills of higher denominations were discontinued in 1969 was to make the illegal exchange of laundered money less convenient.

## State Crime Rates, 1999–2001

Crimes reported to the police per 100,000 population. Source: US Federal Bureau of Investigation.

| STATE | 1999 TOTAL | 2000 TOTAL | 2001[1] TOTAL | STATE | 1999 TOTAL | 2000 TOTAL | 2001[1] TOTAL |
|---|---|---|---|---|---|---|---|
| Alabama | 4,413 | 4,546 | 4,319 | Nebraska | 4,108 | 4,096 | 4,330 |
| Alaska | 4,360 | 4,249 | 4,236 | Nevada | 4,653 | 4,269 | 4,266 |
| Arizona | 5,896 | 5,830 | 6,077 | New Hampshire | 2,282 | 2,433 | 2,322 |
| Arkansas | 4,042 | 4,115 | 4,134 | New Jersey | 3,400 | 3,161 | 3,225 |
| California | 3,805 | 3,740 | 3,903 | New Mexico | 5,963 | 5,519 | 5,324 |
| Colorado | 4,063 | 3,983 | 4,219 | New York | 3,279 | 3,100 | 2,925 |
| Connecticut | 3,389 | 3,233 | 3,118 | North Carolina | 5,176 | 4,919 | 4,938 |
| Delaware[2] | 4,838 | 4,478 | 4,053 | North Dakota | 2,394 | 2,288 | 2,418 |
| District of Columbia[3] | 8,067 | 7,277 | 7,710 | Ohio | 3,997 | 4,042 | 4,178 |
| Florida | 6,205 | 5,695 | 5,570 | Oklahoma | 4,684 | 4,559 | 4,607 |
| Georgia | 5,148 | 4,751 | 4,646 | Oregon | 5,002 | 4,845 | 5,044 |
| Hawaii | 4,835 | 5,199 | 5,386 | Pennsylvania | 3,114 | 2,995 | 2,961 |
| Idaho | 3,150 | 3,186 | 3,133 | Rhode Island | 3,583 | 3,476 | 3,685 |
| Illinois[4] | 4,515 | 4,286 | 4,098 | South Carolina | 5,325 | 5,221 | 4,753 |
| Indiana | 3,766 | 3,752 | 3,831 | South Dakota | 2,644 | 2,320 | 2,332 |
| Iowa | 3,224 | 3,234 | 3,301 | Tennessee | 4,694 | 4,890 | 5,153 |
| Kansas[5] | 4,439 | 4,409 | 4,321 | Texas | 5,032 | 4,956 | 5,153 |
| Kentucky[4] | 2,953 | 2,960 | 2,938 | Utah | 4,977 | 4,476 | 4,243 |
| Louisiana | 5,747 | 5,423 | 5,338 | Vermont | 2,819 | 2,987 | 2,769 |
| Maine[6] | 2,875 | 2,620 | 2,688 | Virginia | 3,374 | 3,028 | 3,178 |
| Maryland | 4,920 | 4,816 | 4,867 | Washington | 5,255 | 5,106 | 5,152 |
| Massachusetts | 3,262 | 3,026 | 3,099 | West Virginia | 2,721 | 2,603 | 2,560 |
| Michigan | 4,325 | 4,110 | 4,082 | Wisconsin | 3,296 | 3,209 | 3,321 |
| Minnesota | 3,598 | 3,488 | 3,584 | Wyoming | 3,458 | 3,298 | 3,518 |
| Mississippi | 4,270 | 4,004 | 4,185 | | | | |
| Missouri | 4,578 | 4,528 | 4,776 | **Crime rate US** | **4,267** | **4,125** | **4,161** |
| Montana[5] | 3,534 | 3,533 | 3,689 | | | | |

## State Crime Rates, 1999–2001 (continued)

### 2001 CRIME RATES IN DETAIL

| STATE | MURDER[1] | VIOLENT CRIMES | | | | PROPERTY CRIMES | | | |
|---|---|---|---|---|---|---|---|---|---|
| | | FORCIBLE RAPE | AGGRAVATED ASSAULT | ROBBERY | TOTAL | BURGLARY | LARCENY/ THEFT | MOTOR VEHICLE THEFT | TOTAL |
| Alabama | 8.5 | 30.7 | 274 | 125 | 439 | 910 | 2,688 | 283 | 3,881 |
| Alaska | 6.1 | 78.9 | 422 | 81 | 588 | 606 | 2,630 | 412 | 3,648 |
| Arizona | 7.5 | 28.6 | 337 | 167 | 540 | 1,033 | 3,521 | 984 | 5,537 |
| Arkansas | 5.5 | 33.1 | 333 | 81 | 453 | 825 | 2,585 | 272 | 3,681 |
| California | 6.4 | 28.9 | 395 | 187 | 617 | 672 | 2,022 | 591 | 3,286 |
| Colorado | 3.6 | 43.7 | 223 | 81 | 351 | 646 | 2,747 | 475 | 3,868 |
| Connecticut | 3.1 | 18.7 | 192 | 122 | 336 | 501 | 1,920 | 361 | 2,782 |
| Delaware[2] | 2.9 | 52.8 | 411 | 145 | 611 | 646 | 2,446 | 349 | 3,441 |
| District of Columbia[3] | 40.6 | 32.9 | 974 | 690 | 1,737 | 876 | 3,755 | 1,341 | 5,973 |
| Florida | 5.3 | 40.5 | 551 | 201 | 797 | 1,074 | 3,150 | 548 | 4,773 |
| Georgia | 7.1 | 26.0 | 292 | 172 | 497 | 856 | 2,845 | 448 | 4,149 |
| Hawaii | 2.6 | 33.4 | 125 | 93 | 255 | 912 | 3,669 | 551 | 5,132 |
| Idaho | 2.3 | 32.2 | 190 | 19 | 243 | 568 | 2,141 | 181 | 2,890 |
| Illinois[4] | 7.9 | 31.5 | 398 | 199 | 637 | 632 | 2,438 | 391 | 3,461 |
| Indiana | 6.8 | 28.1 | 220 | 117 | 372 | 699 | 2,409 | 352 | 3,460 |
| Iowa | 1.7 | 22.2 | 206 | 40 | 269 | 578 | 2,266 | 188 | 3,032 |
| Kansas | 3.4 | 35.1 | 276 | 90 | 405 | 761 | 2,859 | 296 | 3,917 |
| Kentucky[4] | 4.7 | 27.8 | 144 | 81 | 257 | 652 | 1,799 | 230 | 2,681 |
| Louisiana | 11.2 | 31.4 | 468 | 176 | 687 | 1,040 | 3,125 | 486 | 4,651 |
| Maine | 1.4 | 25.3 | 64 | 21 | 112 | 536 | 1,911 | 130 | 2,577 |
| Maryland | 8.3 | 27.0 | 496 | 252 | 783 | 773 | 2,715 | 596 | 4,084 |
| Massachusetts | 2.3 | 29.1 | 347 | 102 | 480 | 508 | 1,675 | 436 | 2,619 |
| Michigan | 6.7 | 52.7 | 366 | 130 | 555 | 721 | 2,269 | 537 | 3,527 |
| Minnesota | 2.4 | 45.0 | 141 | 76 | 264 | 513 | 2,504 | 302 | 3,319 |
| Mississippi | 9.9 | 40.1 | 185 | 115 | 350 | 1,043 | 2,460 | 332 | 3,835 |
| Missouri | 6.6 | 24.6 | 372 | 138 | 541 | 763 | 2,974 | 498 | 4,235 |
| Montana | 3.8 | 20.8 | 302 | 25 | 352 | 406 | 2,729 | 201 | 3,336 |
| Nebraska | 2.5 | 25.2 | 211 | 66 | 304 | 570 | 3,077 | 379 | 4,025 |
| Nevada | 8.5 | 41.9 | 302 | 234 | 587 | 841 | 2,140 | 698 | 3,679 |
| New Hampshire | 1.4 | 36.4 | 97 | 35 | 170 | 388 | 1,593 | 170 | 2,151 |
| New Jersey | 4.0 | 15.1 | 205 | 166 | 390 | 552 | 1,839 | 444 | 2,835 |
| New Mexico | 5.4 | 46.5 | 582 | 147 | 781 | 1,069 | 3,084 | 390 | 4,543 |
| New York | 5.0 | 18.7 | 300 | 192 | 516 | 423 | 1,732 | 254 | 2,409 |
| North Carolina | 6.2 | 25.4 | 300 | 163 | 494 | 1,245 | 2,898 | 301 | 4,444 |
| North Dakota | 1.1 | 25.8 | 43 | 10 | 80 | 341 | 1,826 | 171 | 2,338 |
| Ohio | 4.0 | 39.3 | 157 | 151 | 352 | 852 | 2,602 | 371 | 3,826 |
| Oklahoma | 5.3 | 42.9 | 385 | 79 | 512 | 999 | 2,732 | 363 | 4,095 |
| Oregon | 2.4 | 33.8 | 191 | 79 | 307 | 767 | 3,543 | 427 | 4,737 |
| Pennsylvania | 5.3 | 28.2 | 235 | 142 | 410 | 442 | 1,818 | 291 | 2,551 |
| Rhode Island | 3.7 | 39.3 | 174 | 93 | 310 | 644 | 2,255 | 476 | 3,375 |
| South Carolina | 6.3 | 34.0 | 549 | 131 | 720 | 907 | 2,763 | 363 | 4,032 |
| South Dakota | 0.9 | 46.4 | 94 | 14 | 155 | 408 | 1,662 | 108 | 2,177 |
| Tennessee | 7.4 | 38.3 | 522 | 178 | 745 | 1,040 | 2,875 | 493 | 4,408 |
| Texas | 6.2 | 38.3 | 363 | 166 | 573 | 958 | 3,140 | 481 | 4,580 |
| Utah | 3.0 | 39.5 | 139 | 53 | 234 | 608 | 3,114 | 287 | 4,009 |
| Vermont | 1.1 | 17.5 | 69 | 18 | 105 | 514 | 2,027 | 124 | 2,664 |
| Virginia | 5.1 | 24.6 | 166 | 95 | 291 | 440 | 2,185 | 262 | 2,887 |
| Washington | 3.0 | 43.4 | 210 | 99 | 355 | 886 | 3,259 | 653 | 4,797 |
| West Virginia | 2.2 | 17.8 | 220 | 39 | 279 | 533 | 1,569 | 179 | 2,280 |
| Wisconsin | 3.6 | 21.1 | 124 | 82 | 231 | 499 | 2,319 | 273 | 3,090 |
| Wyoming | 1.8 | 30.9 | 208 | 17.0 | 257 | 502 | 2,618 | 141 | 3,260 |
| | | | | | | | | | |
| Total US | 5.6 | 31.8 | 319 | 149 | 504 | 741 | 2,485 | 431 | 3,656 |

[1]This table does not include the murder and nonnegligent homicides that occurred because of the terrorist attacks of 11 Sept 2001. [2]Forcible rape count estimated for 1999 and 2000. [3]Includes offenses at the National Zoo. [4]Crime counts estimated for all years shown. [5]Crime counts estimated for 1999 and 2000. [6]Crime counts estimated for 1999. [7]Includes nonnegligent manslaughter.

## Crime in the US, 1980–2002

This table presents the number of crimes reported in the seven categories that make up the FBI's Crime Index. Although the crime totals reported in 2002 were not available at press time, the Crime Index trends had been released. The FBI's Crime Index trends reflect the percent change in the offenses reported to law enforcement for the calendar years indicated. Source: Federal Bureau of Investigation.

| YEAR | CRIME INDEX TOTAL | VIOLENT CRIME MURDER[1] | FORCIBLE RAPE | ROBBERY | AGGRA- VATED ASSAULT | PROPERTY CRIME BURGLARY | LARCENY/ THEFT | MOTOR VEHICLE THEFT |
|---|---|---|---|---|---|---|---|---|
| 1980 | 13,408,300 | 23,040 | 82,990 | 565,840 | 672,650 | 3,795,200 | 7,136,900 | 1,131,700 |
| 1981 | 13,423,800 | 22,520 | 82,500 | 592,910 | 663,900 | 3,779,700 | 7,194,400 | 1,087,800 |
| 1982 | 12,974,400 | 21,010 | 78,770 | 553,130 | 669,480 | 3,447,100 | 7,142,500 | 1,062,400 |
| 1983 | 12,108,630 | 19,308 | 78,918 | 506,567 | 653,294 | 3,129,851 | 6,712,759 | 1,007,933 |
| 1984 | 11,881,755 | 18,692 | 84,233 | 485,008 | 685,349 | 2,984,434 | 6,591,874 | 1,032,165 |
| 1985 | 12,430,357 | 18,976 | 87,671 | 497,874 | 723,246 | 3,073,348 | 6,926,380 | 1,102,862 |
| 1986 | 13,211,869 | 20,613 | 91,459 | 542,775 | 834,322 | 3,241,410 | 7,257,153 | 1,224,137 |
| 1987 | 13,508,708 | 20,096 | 91,111 | 517,704 | 855,088 | 3,236,184 | 7,499,851 | 1,288,674 |
| 1988 | 13,923,086 | 20,675 | 92,486 | 542,968 | 910,092 | 3,218,077 | 7,705,872 | 1,432,916 |
| 1989 | 14,251,449 | 21,500 | 94,504 | 578,326 | 951,707 | 3,168,170 | 7,872,442 | 1,564,800 |
| 1990 | 14,475,613 | 23,438 | 102,555 | 639,271 | 1,054,863 | 3,073,909 | 7,945,670 | 1,635,907 |
| 1991 | 14,872,883 | 24,703 | 106,593 | 687,732 | 1,092,739 | 3,157,150 | 8,142,228 | 1,661,738 |
| 1992 | 14,438,191 | 23,760 | 109,062 | 672,478 | 1,126,974 | 2,979,884 | 7,915,199 | 1,610,834 |
| 1993 | 14,144,794 | 24,526 | 106,014 | 659,870 | 1,135,607 | 2,834,808 | 7,820,909 | 1,563,060 |
| 1994 | 13,989,543 | 23,326 | 102,216 | 618,949 | 1,113,179 | 2,712,774 | 7,879,812 | 1,539,287 |
| 1995 | 13,862,727 | 21,606 | 97,470 | 580,509 | 1,099,207 | 2,593,784 | 7,997,710 | 1,472,441 |
| 1996 | 13,493,863 | 19,645 | 96,252 | 535,594 | 1,037,049 | 2,506,400 | 7,904,685 | 1,394,238 |
| 1997 | 13,194,571 | 18,208 | 96,153 | 498,534 | 1,023,201 | 2,460,526 | 7,743,760 | 1,354,189 |
| 1998 | 12,485,714 | 16,974 | 93,144 | 447,186 | 976,583 | 2,332,735 | 7,376,311 | 1,242,781 |
| 1999 | 11,634,378 | 15,522 | 89,411 | 409,371 | 911,740 | 2,100,739 | 6,955,520 | 1,152,075 |
| 2000 | 11,608,070 | 15,586 | 90,178 | 408,016 | 911,706 | 2,050,992 | 6,971,590 | 1,160,002 |
| 2001 | 11,849,006 | 15,980 | 90,491 | 422,921 | 907,219 | 2,109,767 | 7,076,171 | 1,226,457 |

### Crime Index trends: percent change in number of offenses[2]

| YEARS COMPARED | CRIME INDEX TOTAL | VIOLENT CRIME MURDER[1] | FORCIBLE RAPE | ROBBERY | AGGRA- VATED ASSAULT | PROPERTY CRIME BURGLARY | LARCENY/ THEFT | MOTOR VEHICLE THEFT |
|---|---|---|---|---|---|---|---|---|
| 2001/1992 | -17.9 | -32.7 | -17.0 | -37.1 | -19.5 | -29.2 | -10.6 | -23.9 |
| 2001/1997 | -10.2 | -12.2 | -5.9 | -15.2 | -11.3 | -14.3 | -8.6 | -9.4 |
| 2001/2000 | +2.1 | +2.5 | +0.3 | +3.7 | -0.5 | +2.9 | +1.5 | +5.7 |
| 2002/2001[3] | +1.3 | +2.3 | +1.8 | -0.4 | -2.8 | +4.2 | +0.5 | +4.2 |

[1]*Includes the crime of nonnegligent manslaughter.*    [2]*A minus sign indicates a decrease in crime; a plus sign indicates an increase.*    [3]*Reported offenses for the first six months of the calendar years listed.*

## US Cities with Highest and Lowest Crime Rates

This table ranks cities by the number of violent and property crimes—the crime index total—reported during the first six months of 2002. All cities listed have a population of 100,000 or more. The information in the table is derived from preliminary data provided by the Federal Bureau of Investigation.

| CITIES | CRIME INDEX TOTAL[1] | MURDER | FORCIBLE RAPE | ROBBERY | AGGRAVATED ASSAULT | BURGLARY | LARCENY/ THEFT | CAR THEFT |
|---|---|---|---|---|---|---|---|---|
| **Highest Crime Rates** | | | | | | | | |
| New York NY | 118,346 | 270 | 762 | 11,887 | 15,703 | 14,140 | 62,619 | 12,965 |
| Los Angeles CA | 94,473 | 321 | 703 | 8,664 | 16,061 | 12,360 | 39,761 | 16,603 |
| Chicago IL[2] | 88,087 | 277 | N/A | 8,191 | 12,061 | 11,371 | 44,090 | 12,097 |
| Houston TX | 73,465 | 122 | 428 | 5,337 | 6,326 | 13,249 | 35,637 | 12,366 |
| Dallas TX | 53,530 | 78 | 309 | 3,603 | 4,054 | 9,798 | 26,897 | 8,791 |
| Phoenix AZ | 54,950 | 78 | 197 | 1,933 | 2,799 | 8,095 | 29,225 | 12,623 |
| San Antonio TX | 46,212 | 53 | 226 | 973 | 3,431 | 6,453 | 32,376 | 2,700 |
| Philadelphia PA | 41,050 | 138 | 502 | 4,138 | 5,007 | 5,520 | 19,228 | 6,517 |
| Detroit MI | 40,351 | 184 | 244 | 2,801 | 5,866 | 6,555 | 13,166 | 11,535 |
| Memphis TN | 31,654 | 65 | 235 | 1,953 | 2,784 | 7,687 | 14,521 | 4,409 |

## US Cities with Highest and Lowest Crime Rates (continued)

| CITIES | CRIME INDEX TOTAL[1] | MURDER | FORCIBLE RAPE | ROBBERY | AGGRAVATED ASSAULT | BURGLARY | LARCENY/ THEFT | CAR THEFT |
|---|---|---|---|---|---|---|---|---|
| **Lowest Crime Rates** | | | | | | | | |
| Simi Valley CA | 869 | 0 | 5 | 18 | 48 | 165 | 549 | 84 |
| Amherst Town NY | 924 | 0 | 2 | 25 | 23 | 96 | 735 | 43 |
| Thousand Oaks CA | 937 | 0 | 8 | 18 | 57 | 152 | 636 | 66 |
| Daly City CA | 1,051 | 1 | 13 | 48 | 73 | 115 | 596 | 205 |
| Stamford CT | 1,246 | 1 | 10 | 76 | 62 | 146 | 800 | 151 |
| Livonia MI | 1,299 | 0 | 16 | 33 | 54 | 170 | 917 | 109 |
| Sunnyvale CA | 1,359 | 1 | 12 | 37 | 56 | 177 | 955 | 121 |
| Santa Clarita CA | 1,552 | 2 | 16 | 33 | 84 | 292 | 906 | 219 |
| Erie PA | 1,569 | 3 | 29 | 95 | 88 | 296 | 979 | 79 |
| Manchester NH | 1,571 | 0 | 27 | 42 | 32 | 272 | 1,088 | 110 |

*N/A stands for not available.*   [1]*Includes murder, forcible rape, robbery, aggravated assault, burglary, larceny/theft, and car theft.*   [2]*Total excludes the crime of forcible rape.*

## US Crime Rates by Type of Victim

This table shows rates of violent crime, personal theft, and property crime for the year 2001. The crime rates are based on the reports of victims, thus the table does not include rates for murder and manslaughter. For violent crime and personal theft, each crime rate represents victimizations per 1,000 people of age 12 or older. Property crime rates are related in victimizations per 1,000 households. Source: US Bureau of Justice Statistics.

| | | VIOLENT CRIME RATES | | | | | |
|---|---|---|---|---|---|---|---|
| PROFILE OF VICTIM | ALL VIOLENT CRIME | RAPE/ SEXUAL ASSAULT | ROBBERY | ASSAULT AGGRAVATED | SIMPLE | PERSONAL THEFT RATES |
| **sex** | | | | | | |
| male | 27.3 | 0.2[1] | 3.8 | 6.5 | 16.7 | 0.8 |
| female | 23.0 | 1.9 | 1.7 | 4.2 | 15.1 | 0.9 |
| | | | | | | |
| **age** | | | | | | |
| 12–15 | 55.1 | 1.7[1] | 5.2 | 8.7 | 39.6 | 0.5[1] |
| 16–19 | 55.8 | 3.4 | 6.4 | 12.3 | 33.8 | 3.0 |
| 20–24 | 44.7 | 2.4 | 4.2 | 10.7 | 27.4 | 1.8 |
| 25–34 | 29.3 | 1.1 | 3.6 | 6.5 | 18.1 | 1.0 |
| 35–49 | 22.9 | 1.0 | 2.1 | 5.2 | 14.5 | 0.4[1] |
| 50–64 | 9.5 | 0.2[1] | 1.2 | 2.0 | 6.2 | 0.3[1] |
| 65 or older | 3.2 | 0.1[1] | 1.3[1] | 0.4[1] | 1.4 | 0.7[1] |
| | | | | | | |
| **race/ethnicity** | | | | | | |
| white | 24.5 | 1.0 | 2.6 | 5.1 | 15.7 | 0.8 |
| black | 31.2 | 1.1 | 3.6 | 8.1 | 18.3 | 0.8[1] |
| other[2] | 18.2 | 1.6[1] | 2.4[1] | 2.6[1] | 11.6 | 1.7[1] |
| Hispanic[3] | 29.5 | 1.1[1] | 5.3 | 6.6 | 16.6 | 0.7[1] |
| | | | | | | |
| **household income** | | | | | | |
| less than $7,500 | 46.6 | 3.7 | 4.7 | 16.1 | 22.1 | 1.0[1] |
| $7,500–$14,999 | 36.9 | 1.6[1] | 4.4 | 8.9 | 22.1 | 0.8[1] |
| $15,000–$24,999 | 31.8 | 2.0 | 4.3 | 7.8 | 17.6 | 0.9[1] |
| $25,000–$34,999 | 29.1 | 1.3 | 2.2 | 4.5 | 21.0 | 1.0[1] |
| $35,000–$49,999 | 26.3 | 1.1 | 2.4 | 6.0 | 16.8 | 0.6[1] |
| $50,000–$74,999 | 21.0 | 0.8 | 2.3 | 3.7 | 14.1 | 0.6[1] |
| $75,000 or more | 18.5 | 0.6[1] | 1.6 | 3.1 | 13.1 | 0.6 |

| PROFILE OF VICTIM | PROPERTY CRIME RATES ALL PROPERTY CRIME | BURGLARY | CAR THEFT | THEFT |
|---|---|---|---|---|
| **race/ethnicity** | | | | |
| white | 164.1 | 26.6 | 8.2 | 130.3 |
| black | 179.7 | 42.8 | 16.1 | 120.8 |
| other[2] | 163.6 | 27.6 | 8.4 | 127.6 |
| Hispanic[3] | 224.1 | 33.0 | 19.8 | 171.4 |

## US Crime Rates by Type of Victim (continued)

| PROFILE OF VICTIM | ALL PROPERTY CRIME | BURGLARY | CAR THEFT | THEFT |
|---|---|---|---|---|
| **PROPERTY CRIME RATES (CONTINUED)** | | | | |
| **household income** | | | | |
| less than $7,500 | 184.6 | 58.0 | 8.4 | 118.3 |
| $7,500-$14,999 | 181.6 | 37.1 | 11.5 | 133.0 |
| $15,000-$24,999 | 179.2 | 36.2 | 10.3 | 132.8 |
| $25,000-$34,999 | 170.4 | 33.3 | 9.8 | 127.4 |
| $35,000-$49,999 | 176.4 | 23.0 | 10.6 | 142.8 |
| $50,000-$74,999 | 178.8 | 20.2 | 7.8 | 150.8 |
| $75,000 or more | 180.0 | 22.7 | 7.4 | 149.9 |

[1]Based on 10 or fewer sample cases.   [2]Asians, Native Hawaiians, other Pacific Islanders, Alaska Natives, and American Indians.   [3]Hispanics may be of any race.

## Total Arrests in the US

Estimates for the year 2001. Numbers may not add up to totals because of rounding. Source: Federal Bureau of Investigation, Uniform Crime Reports 2001.

| TYPE OF CRIME | NUMBER OF ARRESTS | TYPE OF CRIME | NUMBER OF ARRESTS |
|---|---|---|---|
| **violent crime** | | **other crime types (continued)** | |
| aggravated assault | 477,809 | liquor laws | 610,591 |
| robbery | 108,400 | fraud | 323,308 |
| forcible rape | 27,270 | vandalism | 270,645 |
| murder and nonnegligent manslaughter | 13,653 | weapons (carrying, possessing, etc.) | 165,896 |
| **violent crime total** | **627,132** | offenses against the family and children | 143,683 |
| | | curfew and loitering law violations | 142,889 |
| **property crime** | | runaways | 133,259 |
| larceny/theft | 1,160,821 | stolen property (buying, receiving, possessing) | 121,972 |
| burglary | 291,444 | | |
| car theft | 147,451 | forgery and counterfeiting | 113,741 |
| arson | 18,749 | sex offenses (except forcible rape and prostitution) | 91,828 |
| **property crime total** | **1,618,465** | | |
| | | prostitution and commercialized vice | 80,854 |
| **other crime types** | | vagrancy | 27,935 |
| drug abuse violations | 1,586,902 | embezzlement | 20,157 |
| driving under the influence | 1,434,852 | gambling | 11,112 |
| other assaults | 1,315,807 | suspicion (not included in total) | 3,955 |
| disorderly conduct | 621,394 | all other offenses | 3,618,164 |
| drunkenness | 618,668 | **total arrests** | **13,699,254** |

## US State and Federal Prison Population

Source: US Bureau of Justice Statistics.

| STATE | 31 DEC 1980 | 31 DEC 1990 | 31 DEC 2001 | 30 JUNE 2002 | % CHANGE (31 DEC 2001 TO 30 JUNE 2002) |
|---|---|---|---|---|---|
| | **NUMBER OF PRISONERS** | | | | |
| Alabama | 6,543 | 15,665 | 26,741 | 27,495 | +2.8 |
| Alaska[1] | 822 | 2,622 | 4,571 | 4,205 | −8.0 |
| Arizona[2] | 4,372 | 14,261 | 27,710 | 29,103 | +5.0 |
| Arkansas | 2,911 | 7,322 | 12,594 | 12,655 | +0.5 |
| California | 24,569 | 97,309 | 159,444 | 160,315 | +0.5 |
| Colorado | 2,629 | 7,671 | 17,448 | 18,320 | +5.0 |
| Connecticut[1] | 4,308 | 10,500 | 19,196 | 20,243 | +5.5 |
| Delaware[1] | 1,474 | 3,471 | 7,003 | 6,957 | −0.7 |
| District of Columbia | 3,145 | 9,947 | 2,692 | 3,023 | +12.3 |
| Florida[2] | 20,735 | 44,387 | 72,404 | 73,553 | +1.6 |
| Georgia[2] | 12,178 | 22,411 | 45,937 | 46,417 | +1.0 |
| Hawaii[1] | 985 | 2,533 | 5,431 | 5,541 | +2.0 |
| Idaho | 817 | 1,961 | 6,006 | 5,802 | −4.4 |
| Illinois | 11,899 | 27,516 | 44,348 | 43,142 | −2.7 |
| Indiana | 6,683 | 12,736 | 20,966 | 21,425 | +2.2 |
| Iowa[2] | 2,481 | 3,967 | 7,962 | 8,172 | +2.6 |
| Kansas | 2,494 | 5,775 | 8,577 | 8,758 | +2.1 |
| Kentucky | 3,588 | 9,023 | 15,424 | 16,172 | +4.8 |

## US State and Federal Prison Population (continued)

| STATE | 31 DEC 1980 | 31 DEC 1990 | 31 DEC 2001 | 30 JUNE 2002 | % CHANGE (31 DEC 2001 TO 30 JUNE 2002) |
|---|---|---|---|---|---|
| | | NUMBER OF PRISONERS | | | |
| Louisiana | 8,889 | 18,599 | 35,810 | 36,171 | +1.0 |
| Maine | 814 | 1,523 | 1,704 | 1,841 | +8.0 |
| Maryland | 7,731 | 17,848 | 23,752 | 24,329 | +2.4 |
| Massachusetts | 3,185 | 8,345 | 10,588 | 10,620 | +0.3 |
| Michigan | 15,124 | 34,267 | 48,849 | 49,961 | +2.3 |
| Minnesota | 2,001 | 3,176 | 6,606 | 6,958 | +5.3 |
| Mississippi | 3,902 | 8,375 | 21,460 | 22,001 | +2.5 |
| Missouri | 5,726 | 14,943 | 28,757 | 30,034 | +4.4 |
| Montana | 739 | 1,425 | 3,328 | 3,515 | +5.6 |
| Nebraska | 1,446 | 2,403 | 3,937 | 4,031 | +2.4 |
| Nevada | 1,839 | 5,322 | 10,233 | 10,426 | +1.9 |
| New Hampshire | 326 | 1,342 | 2,392 | 2,476 | +3.5 |
| New Jersey | 5,884 | 21,128 | 28,142 | 28,054 | -0.3 |
| New Mexico | 1,279 | 3,187 | 5,668 | 5,875 | +3.7 |
| New York | 21,815 | 54,895 | 67,533 | 67,131 | -0.6 |
| North Carolina | 15,513 | 18,411 | 31,979 | 32,755 | +2.4 |
| North Dakota | 253 | 483 | 1,120 | 1,168 | +4.3 |
| Ohio | 13,489 | 31,822 | 45,281 | 45,349 | +0.2 |
| Oklahoma | 4,796 | 12,285 | 22,780 | 23,435 | +2.9 |
| Oregon | 3,177 | 6,492 | 11,410 | 11,812 | +3.5 |
| Pennsylvania | 8,171 | 22,290 | 38,062 | 39,275 | +3.2 |
| Rhode Island[1] | 813 | 2,392 | 3,241 | 3,694 | +14.0 |
| South Carolina | 7,862 | 17,319 | 22,576 | 23,017 | +2.0 |
| South Dakota | 635 | 1,341 | 2,790 | 2,900 | +3.9 |
| Tennessee | 7,022 | 10,388 | 23,671 | 24,277 | +2.6 |
| Texas | 29,892 | 50,042 | 162,070 | 158,131 | -2.4 |
| Utah | 932 | 2,496 | 5,339 | 5,353 | +0.3 |
| Vermont[1] | 480 | 1,049 | 1,741 | 1,784 | +2.5 |
| Virginia | 8,920 | 17,593 | 31,662 | 32,739 | +3.4 |
| Washington | 4,399 | 7,995 | 15,159 | 15,829 | +4.4 |
| West Virginia | 1,257 | 1,565 | 4,215 | 4,488 | +6.5 |
| Wisconsin | 3,980 | 7,465 | 21,533 | 21,978 | +2.1 |
| Wyoming | 534 | 1,110 | 1,684 | 1,732 | +2.9 |
| state | 305,458 | 708,393 | 1,249,526 | 1,264,437 | +1.2 |
| federal | 24,363 | 65,526 | 156,993 | 161,681 | +3.0 |
| US total | 329,821 | 773,919 | 1,406,519 | 1,426,118 | +1.4 |

[1]Jails and prisons are part of an integrated system. Data include total jail and prison population.    [2]Population figures are based on custody counts.

## Death Penalty Sentences in the US

*This table excludes military and federal sentences and executions. Sources: US Bureau of Justice Statistics; Death Penalty Information Center; NAACP Legal Defense and Educational Fund, Inc.*

| STATE | EXECUTIONS 1977–2001[1] | EXECUTIONS 2002 | PRISONERS UNDER DEATH SENTENCE (AS OF 1 APR 2003)[2] | SOME DEATH PENALTY CRIMES |
|---|---|---|---|---|
| Alabama | 23 | 2 | 193 | intentional murder[3] |
| Alaska | — | — | — | no death penalty |
| Arizona | 22 | 0 | 124 | 1st-degree murder[3] |
| Arkansas | 24 | 0 | 42 | capital murder[3]; treason |
| California | 9 | 1 | 624 | 1st-degree murder[3]; treason; train wrecking |
| Colorado | 1 | 0 | 6 | 1st-degree murder[3]; treason |
| Connecticut | 0 | 0 | 7 | capital felony (9 types of aggravated murder) |
| Delaware | 13 | 0 | 19 | 1st-degree murder[3] |
| District of Columbia | — | — | — | no death penalty |
| Florida | 51 | 3 | 381 | 1st-degree murder; felonious murder; capital drug trafficking; capital sexual battery |
| Georgia | 27 | 4 | 117 | murder; treason; aircraft hijacking; kidnapping[4] |
| Hawaii | — | — | — | no death penalty |
| Idaho | 1 | 0 | 21 | 1st-degree murder[3]; aggravated kidnapping |
| Illinois | 12 | 0 | 7 | 1st-degree murder[3] |
| Indiana | 9 | 0 | 41 | murder[3] |
| Iowa | — | — | — | no death penalty |
| Kansas | 0 | 0 | 7 | capital murder[3] |

## Death Penalty Sentences in the US (continued)

| STATE | EXECUTIONS 1977–2001[1] | 2002 | PRISONERS UNDER DEATH SENTENCE (AS OF 1 APR 2003)[2] | SOME DEATH PENALTY CRIMES |
|---|---|---|---|---|
| Kentucky | 2 | 0 | 38 | murder[3]; aggravated kidnapping |
| Louisiana | 26 | 1 | 96 | 1st-degree murder; treason; rape[5] |
| Maine | — | — | — | no death penalty |
| Maryland | 3 | 0 | 15 | 1st-degree murder[6] |
| Massachusetts | — | — | — | no death penalty |
| Michigan | — | — | — | no death penalty |
| Minnesota | — | — | — | no death penalty |
| Mississippi | 4 | 2 | 67 | capital murder; aircraft hijacking |
| Missouri | 53 | 6 | 70 | 1st-degree murder |
| Montana | 2 | 0 | 6 | capital murder[3]; capital sexual assault |
| Nebraska | 3 | 0 | 7 | 1st-degree murder[3] |
| Nevada | 9 | 0 | 86 | 1st-degree murder[3] |
| New Hampshire | 0 | 0 | 0 | capital murder (6 types) |
| New Jersey | 0 | 0 | 15 | murder by one's own conduct; contract murder; solicitation[7] |
| New Mexico | 0 | 0 | 3 | 1st-degree murder[3] |
| New York | 0 | 0 | 6 | 1st-degree murder[3] |
| North Carolina | 21 | 2 | 217 | 1st-degree murder |
| North Dakota | — | — | — | no death penalty |
| Ohio | 2 | 3 | 208 | murder[3] |
| Oklahoma | 48 | 7 | 114 | 1st-degree murder[3] |
| Oregon | 2 | 0 | 29 | murder[3] |
| Pennsylvania | 3 | 0 | 244 | 1st-degree murder[3] |
| Rhode Island | — | — | — | no death penalty |
| South Carolina | 25 | 3 | 77 | murder[3] |
| South Dakota | 0 | 0 | 4 | 1st-degree murder[3]; aggravated kidnapping |
| Tennessee | 1 | 0 | 105 | 1st-degree murder[3] |
| Texas | 256 | 33 | 454 | criminal homicide[3] |
| Utah | 6 | 0 | 11 | murder[3] |
| Vermont | — | — | — | no death penalty |
| Virginia | 83 | 4 | 26 | 1st-degree murder[3] |
| Washington | 4 | 0 | 12 | 1st-degree murder[3] |
| West Virginia | — | — | — | no death penalty |
| Wisconsin | — | — | — | no death penalty |
| Wyoming | 1 | 0 | 2 | 1st-degree murder |
| totals | 746 | 62 | 3,499 | |

[1]In 1976 the US Supreme Court ruled that capital punishment was not unconstitutional. [2]In mid-2002 the Supreme Court ruled that juries, not judges, must make decisions determining death penalty cases and that it was unconstitutional to execute mentally retarded offenders. These two decisions could reduce the number of people sentenced to death. [3]With aggravating factors or circumstances. [4]With bodily injury or ransom when the victim dies. [5]Aggravated rape of a victim under 12. [6]Premeditated or committed during the act of a felony and meeting certain death penalty requirements. [7]By command or threat in the act of a narcotics conspiracy.

## Directors of the Federal Bureau of Investigation (FBI)

The FBI evolved from an unnamed force appointed by Attorney General Charles J. Bonaparte on 26 Jul 1908. It is the unit of the Department of Justice responsible for investigating foreign intelligence and terrorist activities and violations of federal criminal law. The president appoints the director of the FBI with confirmation from the Senate. Since Hoover's tenure, a director's term may not exceed 10 years.

| NAME | DATES OF SERVICE |
|---|---|
| Stanley Finch | 26 Jul 1908–30 Apr 1912 |
| Alexander Bruce Bielaski | 30 Apr 1912–10 Feb 1919 |
| William E. Allen (acting) | 10 Feb 1919–30 Jun 1919 |
| William J. Flynn | 1 Jul 1919–21 Aug 1921 |
| William J. Burns | 22 Aug 1921–14 Jun 1924 |
| J. Edgar Hoover | 10 May 1924–2 May 1972 |
| L. Patrick Gray (acting) | 3 May 1972–27 Apr 1973 |
| William D. Ruckelshaus (acting) | 30 Apr 1973–9 Jul 1973 |
| Clarence M. Kelley | 9 Jul 1973–15 Feb 1978 |
| William H. Webster | 23 Feb 1978–25 May 1987 |
| John Otto (acting) | 26 May 1987–2 Nov 1987 |
| William S. Sessions | 2 Nov 1987–19 Jul 1993 |
| Floyd I. Clarke (acting) | 19 Jul 1993–1 Sep 1993 |
| Louis J. Freeh | 1 Sep 1993–25 Jun 2001 |
| Thomas J. Pickard (acting) | 25 Jun 2001–4 Sep 2001 |
| Robert S. Mueller, III | 4 Sep 2001– |

# Society

## Family

### Average Family Size, 1950–2002
Source: US Census Bureau.

| YEAR | NUMBER OF FAMILIES ('000) | PEOPLE PER FAMILY (AVERAGE) | YEAR | NUMBER OF FAMILIES ('000) | PEOPLE PER FAMILY (AVERAGE) | YEAR | NUMBER OF FAMILIES ('000) | PEOPLE PER FAMILY (AVERAGE) |
|---|---|---|---|---|---|---|---|---|
| 1950 | 39,303 | 3.54 | 1970 | 51,586 | 3.58 | 1990 | 66,090 | 3.17 |
| 1955 | 41,951 | 3.59 | 1975 | 55,712 | 3.42 | 1995 | 69,305 | 3.19 |
| 1960 | 45,111 | 3.67 | 1980 | 59,550 | 3.29 | 2000 | 72,025 | 3.17 |
| 1965 | 47,956 | 3.70 | 1985 | 62,706 | 3.23 | 2002 | 74,329 | 3.15 |

### US Population by Age
Numbers are in thousands ('000). Source: US Census Bureau estimate of 1 July 2001.

| AGE | POPULATION NUMBER | (%) | AGE | POPULATION NUMBER | (%) |
|---|---|---|---|---|---|
| under 5 years | 19,369 | 6.8 | 60 to 64 years | 11,118 | 3.9 |
| 5 to 9 years | 20,148 | 7.1 | 65 to 74 years | 18,313 | 6.4 |
| 10 to 14 years | 20,881 | 7.3 | 75 to 84 years | 12,574 | 4.4 |
| 15 to 19 years | 20,267 | 7.1 | 85 years and over | 4,404 | 1.5 |
| 20 to 24 years | 19,681 | 6.9 | total population | 284,797 | 100.0 |
| 25 to 34 years | 39,607 | 13.9 | | | |
| 35 to 44 years | 45,019 | 15.8 | under 18 years | 72,552 | 25.5 |
| 45 to 54 years | 39,188 | 13.8 | 18 years and over | 212,245 | 74.5 |
| 55 to 59 years | 14,190 | 5.0 | 65 years and over | 35,291 | 12.4 |

### Living Arrangements of Children Under 18 in the US
Children under 18 years of age, March 2000. Numbers in thousands ('000). Source: US Census Bureau.

| LIVING IN HOUSEHOLD WITH: | UNDER 6 | 6–11 | 12–17 | UNDER 18 |
|---|---|---|---|---|
| both parents | 16,590 | 17,024 | 16,181 | 49,795 |
| mother only | 5,118 | 5,774 | 5,270 | 16,162 |
| father only | 1,020 | 1,036 | 1,002 | 3,058 |
| neither parent | 846 | 922 | 1,214 | 2,981 |
| totals | 23,580 | 24,761 | 23,671 | 72,012 |

*(heading row: YEARS OF AGE)*

### Children Living Below the Poverty Level

This table covers children under the age of 18 (as of March of the following year). Hispanics may be of any race. All numbers are in thousands ('000). Statistics that are not available are noted N/A. Source: US Census Bureau. For the definition of the poverty level, see <www.census.gov/hhes/poverty/povdef.html>.

| YEAR | % ALL RACES | % WHITE | % BLACK | % ASIAN/ PACIFIC ISLANDER | % HISPANIC | NUMBER ALL RACES | NUMBER WHITE | NUMBER BLACK | NUMBER ASIAN/ PACIFIC ISLANDER | NUMBER HISPANIC |
|---|---|---|---|---|---|---|---|---|---|---|
| 1976 | 16.0 | 11.6 | 40.6 | N/A | 30.2 | 10,273 | 6,189 | 3,787 | N/A | 1,443 |
| 1977 | 16.2 | 11.6 | 41.8 | N/A | 28.3 | 10,288 | 6,097 | 3,888 | N/A | 1,422 |
| 1978 | 15.9 | 11.3 | 41.5 | N/A | 27.6 | 9,931 | 5,831 | 3,830 | N/A | 1,384 |
| 1979 | 16.4 | 11.8 | 41.2 | N/A | 28.0 | 10,377 | 6,193 | 3,833 | N/A | 1,535 |
| 1980 | 18.3 | 13.9 | 42.3 | N/A | 33.2 | 11,543 | 7,181 | 3,961 | N/A | 1,749 |
| 1981 | 20.0 | 15.2 | 45.2 | N/A | 35.9 | 12,505 | 7,785 | 4,237 | N/A | 1,925 |
| 1982 | 21.9 | 17.0 | 47.6 | N/A | 39.5 | 13,647 | 8,678 | 4,472 | N/A | 2,181 |
| 1983 | 22.3 | 17.5 | 46.7 | N/A | 38.1 | 13,911 | 8,862 | 4,398 | N/A | 2,312 |
| 1984 | 21.5 | 16.7 | 46.6 | N/A | 39.2 | 13,420 | 8,472 | 4,413 | N/A | 2,376 |
| 1985 | 20.7 | 16.2 | 43.6 | N/A | 40.3 | 13,010 | 8,253 | 4,157 | N/A | 2,606 |
| 1986 | 20.5 | 16.1 | 43.1 | N/A | 37.7 | 12,876 | 8,209 | 4,148 | N/A | 2,507 |
| 1987 | 20.3 | 15.3 | 45.1 | 23.5 | 39.3 | 12,843 | 7,788 | 4,385 | 455 | 2,670 |
| 1988 | 19.5 | 14.5 | 43.5 | 24.1 | 37.6 | 12,455 | 7,435 | 4,296 | 474 | 2,631 |
| 1989 | 19.6 | 14.8 | 43.7 | 19.8 | 36.2 | 12,590 | 7,599 | 4,375 | 392 | 2,603 |
| 1990 | 20.6 | 15.9 | 44.8 | 17.6 | 38.4 | 13,431 | 8,232 | 4,550 | 374 | 2,865 |

*(column group headers: % OF CHILDREN BELOW THE POVERTY LEVEL; NUMBER OF CHILDREN BELOW THE POVERTY LEVEL)*

## Children Living Below the Poverty Level (continued)

| | % OF CHILDREN BELOW THE POVERTY LEVEL | | | | | NUMBER OF CHILDREN BELOW THE POVERTY LEVEL | | | | |
|---|---|---|---|---|---|---|---|---|---|---|
| YEAR | ALL RACES | WHITE | BLACK | ASIAN/ PACIFIC ISLANDER | HISPANIC | ALL RACES | WHITE | BLACK | ASIAN/ PACIFIC ISLANDER | HISPANIC |
| 1991 | 21.8 | 16.8 | 45.9 | 17.5 | 40.4 | 14,341 | 8,848 | 4,755 | 360 | 3,094 |
| 1992 | 22.3 | 17.4 | 46.6 | 16.4 | 40.0 | 15,294 | 9,399 | 5,106 | 363 | 3,637 |
| 1993 | 22.7 | 17.8 | 46.1 | 18.2 | 40.9 | 15,727 | 9,752 | 5,125 | 375 | 3,873 |
| 1994 | 21.8 | 16.9 | 43.8 | 18.3 | 41.5 | 15,289 | 9,346 | 4,906 | 318 | 4,075 |
| 1995 | 20.8 | 16.2 | 41.9 | 19.5 | 40.0 | 14,665 | 8,981 | 4,761 | 564 | 4,080 |
| 1996 | 20.5 | 16.3 | 39.9 | 19.5 | 40.3 | 14,463 | 9,044 | 4,519 | 571 | 4,237 |
| 1997 | 19.9 | 16.1 | 37.2 | 20.3 | 36.8 | 14,113 | 8,990 | 4,225 | 628 | 3,972 |
| 1998 | 18.9 | 15.1 | 36.7 | 18.0 | 34.4 | 13,467 | 8,443 | 4,151 | 564 | 3,837 |
| 1999 | 16.9 | 13.5 | 33.1 | 11.8 | 30.3 | 12,109 | 7,568 | 3,759 | 361 | 3,506 |
| 2000 | 16.2 | 13.1 | 31.2 | 12.7 | 28.4 | 11,587 | 7,307 | 3,581 | 420 | 3,522 |
| 2001 | 16.3 | 13.4 | 30.2 | 11.5 | 28.0 | 11,733 | 7,527 | 3,492 | 369 | 3,570 |

## Child Care Arrangements in the US

This table is based on sample surveys of households with children 3–5 years old who were not yet in kindergarten. Day care centers, Head Start programs, preschools, prekindergarten, and nursery schools were included as center-based programs. The columns do not add to 100% because some children participated in more than one type of nonparental arrangement. Detail may not add to totals due to rounding. Although complete statistics from the 2001 survey were not available before press time, 56.4% of children ages 3–5 were enrolled in center-based programs in 2001, down 3.3% from 1999. Source: US National Center for Education Statistics.

| YEAR OF SURVEY | CHILDREN NUMBER | (%) | UNDER PARENTAL CARE (%) | UNDER A RELATIVE'S CARE (%) | UNDER A NONRELATIVE'S CARE (%) | IN A CENTER-BASED PROGRAM (%) |
|---|---|---|---|---|---|---|
| 1991 | 8,428,000 | 100.0 | 31.0 | 16.9 | 14.8 | 52.8 |
| 1995 | 9,232,000 | 100.0 | 25.9 | 19.4 | 16.9 | 55.1 |
| 1999 | 8,525,000 | 100.0 | 23.1 | 22.8 | 16.1 | 59.7 |

### details from the 1999 survey

| FEATURE | CHILDREN NUMBER | (%) | UNDER PARENTAL CARE (%) | UNDER A RELATIVE'S CARE (%) | UNDER A NONRELATIVE'S CARE (%) | IN A CENTER-BASED PROGRAM (%) |
|---|---|---|---|---|---|---|
| age | | | | | | |
| 3 years old | 3,814,000 | 44.7 | 30.8 | 24.4 | 16.2 | 45.7 |
| 4 years old | 3,705,000 | 43.5 | 17.7 | 22.0 | 15.9 | 69.6 |
| 5 years old | 1,006,000 | 11.8 | 13.5 | 20.2 | 16.1 | 76.5 |
| | | | | | | |
| race/ethnic group | | | | | | |
| white, non-Hispanic | 5,389,000 | 63.2 | 23.2 | 18.8 | 19.4 | 60.0 |
| black, non-Hispanic | 1,214,000 | 14.2 | 13.7 | 33.4 | 7.4 | 73.2 |
| Hispanic | 1,376,000 | 16.1 | 33.4 | 26.5 | 12.7 | 44.2 |
| other | 547,000 | 6.4 | 16.6 | 30.2 | 10.4 | 66.1 |
| | | | | | | |
| household income | | | | | | |
| less than $10,001 | 1,064,000 | 12.5 | 27.5 | 27.5 | 13.2 | 55.9 |
| $10,001–20,000 | 1,342,000 | 15.7 | 27.7 | 29.4 | 13.7 | 51.1 |
| $20,001–30,000 | 1,333,000 | 15.6 | 29.8 | 27.1 | 12.5 | 51.4 |
| $30,001–40,000 | 1,098,000 | 12.9 | 24.8 | 22.5 | 14.7 | 55.4 |
| $40,001–50,000 | 848,000 | 9.9 | 23.1 | 21.3 | 13.6 | 60.2 |
| $50,001–75,000 | 1,397,000 | 16.4 | 17.8 | 17.3 | 21.0 | 66.6 |
| more than $75,000 | 1,443,000 | 16.9 | 13.1 | 15.9 | 21.3 | 74.6 |

## Children in the US Living with Non-Parents

*Children under 18 years of age, March 2000. Numbers in thousands ('000). Source: US Census Bureau.*

| LIVING ARRANGEMENT | YEARS OF AGE UNDER 6 | 6–11 | 12–17 | UNDER 18 |
|---|---|---|---|---|
| with grandparent | 394 | 476 | 491 | 1,359 |
| with other relative | 228 | 222 | 350 | 799 |
| in foster home | 63 | 61 | 95 | 219 |
| with other nonrelative of householder | 162 | 162 | 278 | 603 |
| in group quarters | 6 | 4 | 4 | 15 |

## US Adoptions of Foreign-Born Children

*Adoptions of foreign children by US citizens are tracked by the number of immigrant visas issued to orphans entering the US. Source: US Department of State.*

| TOP 10 COUNTRIES OF ORIGIN | ADOPTIONS FISCAL YEAR 2002 | 2001 | TOP 10 COUNTRIES OF ORIGIN | ADOPTIONS FISCAL YEAR 2002 | 2001 | TOTAL FOREIGN ADOPTIONS CALENDAR YEAR | |
|---|---|---|---|---|---|---|---|
| 1. China | 5,053 | 4,681 | 6. Kazakhstan | 819 | 672 | 1996 | 10,641 |
| 2. Russia | 4,939 | 4,279 | 7. Vietnam | 766 | 737 | 1997 | 12,743 |
| 3. Guatemala | 2,219 | 1,609 | 8. India | 466 | 543 | 1998 | 15,774 |
| 4. South Korea | 1,779 | 1,870 | 9. Colombia | 334 | 407 | 1999 | 16,363 |
| 5. Ukraine | 1,106 | 1,246 | 10. Bulgaria | 260 | 297 | 2000 | 17,718 |
| | | | | | | 2001 | 19,237 |
| | | | | | | 2002 | 20,099 |

## US Nursing Home Population

The data in this table were gathered in 1999 through interviews conducted by the National Nursing Home Survey. Residents of more than one race were recorded in the "black and other" category. Numbers may not add to totals because of rounding. N/A indicates that reliable numbers were not available. Source: US National Center for Health Statistics.

| AGE AT INTERVIEW | TOTAL RESIDENTS | % | GENDER MALE | % | FEMALE | % |
|---|---|---|---|---|---|---|
| under 65 | 158,700 | 9.8 | 80,000 | 17.5 | 78,700 | 6.7 |
| 65–74 | 194,800 | 12.0 | 84,100 | 18.4 | 110,700 | 9.5 |
| 75–84 | 517,600 | 31.8 | 149,500 | 32.7 | 368,100 | 31.5 |
| 85 and older | 757,100 | 46.5 | 144,200 | 31.5 | 612,900 | 52.4 |
| total | 1,628,300 | 100.0 | 457,900 | 100.0 | 1,170,400 | 100.0 |

| | WHITE | % | RACE BLACK AND OTHER | % | BLACK | % | UNKNOWN |
|---|---|---|---|---|---|---|---|
| under 65 | 115,400 | 8.3 | 39,300 | 18.2 | 32,800 | 18.4 | N/A |
| 65–74 | 157,300 | 11.3 | 35,800 | 16.6 | 30,300 | 17.0 | N/A |
| 75–84 | 440,600 | 31.6 | 71,100 | 32.9 | 58,700 | 32.8 | N/A |
| 85 and older | 681,700 | 48.9 | 69,700 | 32.3 | 56,900 | 31.8 | N/A |
| total | 1,394,400 | 100.0 | 215,900 | 100.0 | 178,700 | 100.0 | 17,400 |

| | NORTHWEST | % | RESIDENT LOCATION MIDWEST | % | SOUTH | % | WEST | % |
|---|---|---|---|---|---|---|---|---|
| under 65 | 34,200 | 8.9 | 45,000 | 9.0 | 51,300 | 9.7 | 28,200 | 13.1 |
| 65–74 | 46,400 | 12.1 | 58,900 | 11.8 | 63,400 | 11.9 | 26,100 | 12.1 |
| 75–84 | 118,500 | 30.9 | 153,200 | 30.8 | 179,100 | 33.7 | 66,800 | 31.1 |
| 85 and older | 184,300 | 48.1 | 241,100 | 48.4 | 237,700 | 44.7 | 94,000 | 43.7 |
| total | 383,400 | 100.0 | 498,200 | 100.0 | 531,500 | 100.0 | 215,200 | 100.0 |

## Unmarried-Couple Households in the US

*Data based on Current Population Survey except for census years of 1960 and 1970. Census 2000 data shown separately. Numbers in thousands ('000). Source: US Census Bureau.*

| YEAR | TOTAL US HOUSEHOLDS | UNMARRIED-COUPLE HOUSEHOLDS (OPPOSITE SEX) | % OF TOTAL HOUSEHOLDS | NO CHILDREN UNDER 15 | WITH CHILDREN UNDER 15 |
|---|---|---|---|---|---|
| 1960 census | 52,799 | 439 | 0.8 | 242 | 197 |
| 1970 census | 63,401 | 523 | 0.8 | 327 | 196 |
| 1980 | 80,776 | 1,589 | 2.0 | 1,159 | 431 |
| 1985 | 86,789 | 1,983 | 2.3 | 1,380 | 603 |
| 1990 | 93,347 | 2,856 | 3.1 | 1,966 | 891 |
| 1995 | 98,990 | 3,668 | 3.7 | 2,349 | 1,319 |
| 1996 | 99,627 | 3,958 | 3.9 | 2,516 | 1,442 |
| 1997 | 101,018 | 4,130 | 4.0 | 2,660 | 1,470 |
| 1998 | 102,528 | 4,236 | 4.1 | 2,716 | 1,520 |
| 1999 | 103,874 | 4,486 | 4.3 | 2,981 | 1,505 |
| 2000 | 104,705 | 4,736 | 4.5 | 3,061 | 1,675 |

## Unmarried-Couple Households in the US (continued)

| UNMARRIED-COUPLE HOUSEHOLDS | 2000 CENSUS |
|---|---|
| male householder/female partner | 2,615 |
| male householder/male partner | 301 |
| female householder/female partner | 293 |
| female householder/male partner | 2,266 |
| **unmarried-couple households** | **5,475** |
| | |
| **total households** | **105,480** |

## Marriage Statistics, 1960–2001

Beginning in 1996, the collection of detailed data was suspended at the National Center for Health Statistics. Information that is not available is indicated with an N/A. Information is subject to monthly reporting variation and may differ from previously published statistics. Statistics for 1980 and later include nonlicensed marriages registered in California. Source: US National Center for Health Statistics.

| | | RATE PER 1,000 POPULATION | | | | |
|---|---|---|---|---|---|---|
| | | TOTAL | MEN, 15 | WOMEN, 15 | UNMARRIED WOMEN | |
| YEAR | NUMBER | POPULATION | AND OVER | AND OVER | 15 AND OVER | 15 TO 44 |
| 1960 | 1,523,000 | 8.5 | 25.4 | 24.0 | 73.5 | 148.0 |
| 1965 | 1,800,000 | 9.3 | 27.9 | 26.0 | 75.0 | 144.3 |
| 1970 | 2,158,802 | 10.6 | 31.1 | 28.4 | 76.5 | 140.2 |
| 1975 | 2,152,662 | 10.0 | 27.9 | 25.6 | 66.9 | 118.5 |
| 1980 | 2,390,252 | 10.6 | 28.5 | 26.1 | 61.4 | 102.6 |
| 1985 | 2,412,625 | 10.1 | 27.0 | 24.9 | 57.0 | 94.9 |
| 1990 | 2,443,489 | 9.8 | 26.0 | 24.1 | 54.5 | 91.3 |
| 1995 | 2,336,000 | 8.9 | N/A | N/A | 50.8 | 83.0 |
| 2000 | 2,398,000 | 8.7 | N/A | N/A | N/A | N/A |
| 2001 | 2,344,000 | 8.5 | N/A | N/A | N/A | N/A |

## Divorce Statistics, 1960–2001

Beginning in 1996, the collection of detailed data was suspended at the National Center for Health Statistics. Information that is not available is indicated with an N/A. Since 1998, divorce rates exclude data for California, Colorado, Indiana, and Louisiana. Information is subject to monthly reporting variation and may differ from previously published statistics. Source: US National Center for Health Statistics.

| | | RATE PER 1,000 POPULATION | | | | | RATE PER 1,000 POPULATION | |
|---|---|---|---|---|---|---|---|---|
| | DIVORCES | | MARRIED | | | DIVORCES | | MARRIED |
| | AND | TOTAL | WOMEN, 15 | | | AND | TOTAL | WOMEN, 15 |
| YEAR | ANNULMENTS | POPULATION | AND OVER | YEAR | ANNULMENTS | POPULATION | AND OVER |
| 1960 | 393,000 | 2.2 | 9.2 | 1985 | 1,190,000 | 5.0 | 21.7 |
| 1965 | 479,000 | 2.5 | 10.6 | 1990 | 1,182,000 | 4.7 | 20.9 |
| 1970 | 708,000 | 3.5 | 14.9 | 1995 | 1,169,000 | 4.4 | 19.8 |
| 1975 | 1,036,000 | 4.8 | 20.3 | 2000 | N/A | 4.1 | N/A |
| 1980 | 1,189,000 | 5.2 | 22.6 | 2001 | N/A | 4.0 | N/A |

# United States Education

## Educational Attainment by Gender and Race

For people 25 years old and older. Percentage rates for 1960, 1970, and 1980 are based on sample data from the decennial censuses. Rates for 1990, 2000, and 2002 are based on the Current Population Survey. Source: US Census Bureau.

### Percentage who had graduated from high school[1]

| | ALL RACES[2] | | WHITE | | BLACK | | HISPANIC[3] | | ASIAN/PACIFIC ISLANDER | |
|---|---|---|---|---|---|---|---|---|---|---|
| CENSUS | MALE | FEMALE | MALE | FEMALE | MALE | FEMALE | MALE | FEMALE | MALE | FEMALE |
| 1960 | 39.5 | 42.5 | 41.6 | 44.7 | 18.2 | 21.8 | N/A | N/A | N/A | N/A |
| 1970 | 51.9 | 52.8 | 54.0 | 55.0 | 30.1 | 32.5 | 37.9 | 34.2 | N/A | N/A |
| 1980 | 67.3 | 65.8 | 69.6 | 68.1 | 50.8 | 51.5 | 67.3 | 65.8 | N/A | N/A |
| 1990 | 77.7 | 77.5 | 79.1 | 79.0 | 65.8 | 66.5 | 50.3 | 51.3 | 84.0 | 77.2 |
| 2000 | 84.2 | 84.0 | 84.8 | 85.0 | 78.7 | 78.3 | 56.6 | 57.5 | 88.2 | 83.4 |
| 2002 | 83.8 | 84.4 | 84.3 | 85.2 | 78.5 | 78.9 | 56.1 | 57.9 | 89.5 | 85.5 |

## Educational Attainment by Gender and Race (continued)

### Percentage who had graduated from college[4]

| | ALL RACES[2] | | WHITE | | BLACK | | HISPANIC[3] | | ASIAN/PACIFIC ISLANDER | |
|---|---|---|---|---|---|---|---|---|---|---|
| CENSUS | MALE | FEMALE | MALE | FEMALE | MALE | FEMALE | MALE | FEMALE | MALE | FEMALE |
| 1960 | 9.7 | 5.8 | 10.3 | 6.0 | 2.8 | 3.3 | N/A | N/A | N/A | N/A |
| 1970 | 13.5 | 8.1 | 14.4 | 8.4 | 4.2 | 4.6 | 7.8 | 4.3 | N/A | N/A |
| 1980 | 20.1 | 12.8 | 21.3 | 13.3 | 8.4 | 8.3 | 9.4 | 6.0 | N/A | N/A |
| 1990 | 24.4 | 18.4 | 25.3 | 19.0 | 11.9 | 10.8 | 9.8 | 8.7 | 44.9 | 35.4 |
| 2000 | 27.8 | 23.6 | 28.5 | 23.9 | 16.3 | 16.7 | 10.7 | 10.6 | 47.6 | 40.7 |
| 2002 | 28.5 | 25.1 | 29.1 | 25.4 | 16.4 | 17.5 | 11.0 | 11.2 | 50.9 | 43.8 |

*N/A means not available. [1]Through 1990, finished four years or more of high school. [2]Includes races not shown separately in the table. [3]Hispanics may be of any race. [4]Through 1990, finished four years or more of college.*

---

**Did you know?** The first woman in the US to earn a Ph.D. degree was Helen Magill White. In 1877 she earned a doctorate in Greek from Boston University, with a dissertation on Greek drama. She received her doctorate 16 years after Yale conferred the first US Ph.D.'s on men.

---

# Libraries and Museums

## Public Libraries in the US

Information from public libraries reporting for fiscal year 2000. The number of libraries includes central and branch libraries. Data for operating income and the number of books and serial volumes are given in thousands ('000). The circulation percentages for children's materials are given as a percentage of total circulation. N/A means not available. The totals used at the bottom of the table were those provided by the source. Source: National Center for Education Statistics.

| STATE | NUMBER OF LIBRARIES | OPERATING INCOME ($) | TOTAL NUMBER OF BOOKS AND SERIAL VOLUMES | AVERAGE NUMBER OF INTERNET TERMINALS PER LIBRARY | CIRCULATION OF CHILDREN'S MATERIALS (%) |
|---|---|---|---|---|---|
| Alabama | 275 | 64,927 | 8,600 | 4.2 | 33.3 |
| Alaska | 104 | 24,458 | 2,224 | 5.7 | 35.7 |
| Arizona | 170 | 110,803 | 8,723 | 8.2 | 35.2 |
| Arkansas | 209 | 38,531 | 5,408 | 4.0 | 27.9 |
| California | 1,065 | 830,267 | 66,193 | 7.6 | 40.2 |
| Colorado | 243 | 158,704 | 10,863 | 5.9 | 37.2 |
| Connecticut | 242 | 137,326 | 14,238 | 4.8 | 37.6 |
| Delaware | 35 | 14,513 | 1,445 | 4.5 | 38.7 |
| District of Columbia | 27 | 25,669 | 2,385 | 6.2 | 32.6 |
| Florida | 466 | 355,388 | 29,222 | 10.0 | 28.8 |
| Georgia | 367 | 143,396 | 14,869 | 9.1 | 39.9 |
| Hawaii | 50 | 22,789 | 3,194 | 3.3 | 32.8 |
| Idaho | 142 | 23,811 | 3,506 | 4.1 | 41.2 |
| Illinois | 786 | 481,279 | 41,014 | 3.9 | 41.1 |
| Indiana | 426 | 224,581 | 21,730 | 6.6 | 36.3 |
| Iowa | 559 | 70,422 | 11,595 | 2.3 | 37.8 |
| Kansas | 370 | 70,936 | 10,207 | 4.3 | 40.8 |
| Kentucky | 190 | 72,818 | 7,856 | 6.2 | 30.5 |
| Louisiana | 327 | 112,091 | 10,608 | 5.1 | 28.7 |
| Maine | 278 | 26,059 | 5,683 | 2.4 | 36.8 |
| Maryland | 179 | 174,458 | 15,387 | 11.1 | 39.2 |
| Massachusetts | 489 | 205,569 | 30,238 | 5.5 | 39.1 |
| Michigan | 655 | 288,142 | 26,753 | 5.9 | 37.4 |
| Minnesota | 359 | 146,199 | 15,599 | 5.6 | 41.5 |
| Mississippi | 241 | 35,998 | 5,602 | 4.7 | 27.2 |
| Missouri | 359 | 146,528 | 22,697 | 4.8 | 37.5 |
| Montana | 107 | 16,021 | 2,638 | 3.4 | 34.1 |
| Nebraska | 255 | 34,635 | 5,605 | 2.9 | 43.1 |
| Nevada | 83 | 63,119 | 4,136 | 5.6 | 32.7 |
| New Hampshire | 237 | 33,217 | 5,506 | 2.0 | 40.5 |
| New Jersey | 452 | 299,426 | 30,593 | 6.6 | 38.0 |
| New Mexico | 99 | 29,416 | 4,108 | 5.3 | 35.2 |

## Public Libraries in the US (continued)

| STATE | NUMBER OF LIBRARIES | OPERATING INCOME ($) | TOTAL NUMBER OF BOOKS AND SERIAL VOLUMES | AVERAGE NUMBER OF INTERNET TERMINALS PER LIBRARY | CIRCULATION OF CHILDREN'S MATERIALS (%) |
|---|---|---|---|---|---|
| New York | 1,083 | 834,402 | 77,571 | 6.6 | 34.0 |
| North Carolina | 372 | 145,107 | 15,609 | 5.1 | 35.4 |
| North Dakota | 87 | 8,134 | 2,145 | 2.2 | 39.7 |
| Ohio | 716 | 680,401 | 47,122 | 7.1 | 33.6 |
| Oklahoma | 210 | 61,141 | 6,110 | 3.6 | 34.3 |
| Oregon | 206 | 108,554 | 8,346 | 4.8 | 31.8 |
| Pennsylvania | 631 | 235,416 | 26,351 | 6.7 | 36.8 |
| Rhode Island | 72 | 33,990 | 4,345 | 6.1 | 34.8 |
| South Carolina | 183 | 71,918 | 8,055 | 6.2 | 38.9 |
| South Dakota | 139 | 13,618 | 2,703 | 2.6 | 34.8 |
| Tennessee | 280 | 73,891 | 9,747 | 7.6 | 37.1 |
| Texas | 816 | 294,967 | 35,040 | 8.0 | 37.9 |
| Utah | 105 | 54,114 | 5,756 | 4.9 | 41.7 |
| Vermont | 193 | 12,640 | 2,772 | 1.7 | 42.7 |
| Virginia | 334 | 178,385 | 18,378 | 4.7 | 35.8 |
| Washington | 322 | 218,086 | 16,561 | 7.5 | 31.3 |
| West Virginia | 175 | N/A | 4,814 | 4.7 | 29.0 |
| Wisconsin | 454 | 156,649 | 18,294 | 5.4 | 38.1 |
| Wyoming | 74 | 14,539 | 2,375 | 2.7 | 34.7 |
| **total** | **16,298** | **7,702,768** | **760,513** | **5.8** | **36.4** |

## Selected Specialized Libraries in the United States

| NAME | LOCATION | TYPE OF COLLECTION | WEB SITE |
|---|---|---|---|
| American Antiquarian Society | Worcester MA | American history | <www.americanantiquarian.org/index.htm> |
| American Philosophical Society | Philadelphia PA | history of science, medicine, and technology | <www.amphilsoc.org> |
| The Athenaeum of Philadelphia | Philadelphia PA | architecture, interior design | <www.philaathenaeum.org> |
| Boston Athenaeum | Boston MA | history, art, literature | <www.bostonathenaeum.org> |
| Dumbarton Oaks Research Library | Washington DC | Byzantine and pre-Columbian art, gardening | <www.doaks.org> |
| Folger Shakespeare Library | Washington DC | Shakespeare | <www.folger.edu/Home_02B.html> |
| Frick Art Reference Library | New York NY | Western art | <www.frick.org> |
| Hagley Museum and Library | Wilmington DE | American business and technology history | <www.hagley.lib.de.us/index.html> |
| The Huntington Library, Art Collections, and Botanical Gardens | San Marino CA | history, literature, science | <www.huntington.org> |
| John Carter Brown Library | Providence RI | history, humanities | <www.brown.edu/Facilities/John_Carter_Brown_Library> |
| The Library Company of Philadelphia | Philadelphia PA | American history and culture through end of 19th century | <www.librarycompany.org> |
| Library of Congress | Washington DC | diverse knowledge | <www.loc.gov> |
| Linda Hall Library | Kansas City MO | science, engineering, technology | <www.lindahall.org> |
| The Morgan Library | New York NY | rare manuscripts, books, and prints | <www.morganlibrary.org/index.html> |
| National Agricultural Library | Beltsville MD | agriculture | <www.nal.usda.gov> |
| National Archives | College Park MD | American history | <www.archives.gov> |
| National Library of Education | Washington DC | education | <www.ed.gov/NLE> |
| National Library of Medicine | Bethesda MD | medical science | <www.nlm.nih.gov> |
| New York Academy of Medicine | New York NY | medical science | <www.nyam.org> |
| The Newberry Library | Chicago IL | humanities | <www.newberry.org/nl/newberryhome.html> |
| Smithsonian Institution Libraries | Washington DC | science, history, art, culture | <www.sil.si.edu> |
| Winterthur Museum, Garden, and Library | Winterthur DE | art, design, American material culture | <www.winterthur.org> |
| YIVO Institute for Jewish Research | New York NY | Jewish history and culture | <www.yivoinstitute.org> |

# National Spelling Bee

A spelling bee is a contest or game in which players attempt to spell correctly and aloud words assigned them by an impartial judge. Competition may be individual, with players eliminated when they misspell a word and the last remaining player being the winner, or between teams, the winner being the team with the most players remaining at the close of the contest. The spelling bee is an old custom that was revived in schools in the United States in the late 19th century and enjoyed a great vogue there and in Great Britain. In the US, local, regional, and national competitions continue to be held annually. The US National Spelling Bee was begun by the *Louisville Courier-Journal* newspaper in 1925, and it was taken over by Scripps Howard, Inc., in 1941. The National Spelling Bee was not held in 1943–45. To qualify, spellers must meet nine requirements, including that they have neither reached their 16th birthday nor passed beyond the eighth grade. National Spelling Bee Web site: <www.spellingbee.com>.

| YEAR | CHAMPION & SPONSOR | WINNING WORD |
|---|---|---|
| 1950 | Diana Reynard, *Cleveland Press* (Ohio) | |
| | Colquitt Dean, *Atlanta Journal* (Georgia) | meticulosity |
| 1951 | Irving Belz, *Memphis Press-Scimitar* (Tennessee) | insouciant |
| 1952 | Doris Ann Hall, *Winston-Salem Journal,* (North Carolina) | vignette |
| 1953 | Elizabeth Hess, *Arizona Republic* (Phoenix AZ) | soubrette |
| 1954 | William Cashore, *Norristown Times Herald* (Pennsylvania) | transept |
| 1955 | Sandra Sloss, *St. Louis Globe-Democrat* (Missouri) | crustaceology |
| 1956 | Melody Sachko, *The Pittsburgh Press* (Pennsylvania) | condominium |
| 1957 | Sandra Owen, *Canton Repository* (Ohio) | |
| | Dana Bennett, *Rocky Mountain News* (Denver CO) | schappe |
| 1958 | Jolitta Schlehuber, *Topeka Daily Capital* (Kansas) | syllepsis |
| 1959 | Joel Montgomery, *Rocky Mountain News* (Denver CO) | catamaran |
| 1960 | Henry Feldman, *Knoxville News-Sentinel* (Tennessee) | eudaemonic |
| 1961 | John Capehart, *Tulsa Tribune* (Oklahoma) | smaragdine |
| 1962 | Nettie Crawford, *El Paso Herald-Post* (Texas) | |
| | Michael Day, *St. Louis Democrat* (Missouri) | esquamulose |
| 1963 | Glen Van Slyke III, *The Knoxville News-Sentinel* (Tennessee) | equipage |
| 1964 | William Kerek, *Akron Beacon Journal* (Ohio) | sycophant |
| 1965 | Michael Kerpan, Jr., *Tulsa Tribune* (Oklahoma) | eczema |
| 1966 | Robert A. Wake, *Houston Chronicle* (Texas) | ratoon |
| 1967 | Jennifer Reinke, *The Omaha World-Herald* (Nebraska) | chihuahua |
| 1968 | Robert L. Walters, *The Topeka Daily Capital* (Kansas) | abalone |
| 1969 | Susan Yoachum, *Dallas Morning News* (Texas) | interlocutory |
| 1970 | Libby Childress, *Winston-Salem Journal & Sentinel* (North Carolina) | croissant |
| 1971 | Jonathan Knisely, *Phildelphia Bulletin* (Pennsylvania) | shalloon |
| 1972 | Robin Kral, *Lubbock Avalanche-Journal* (Texas) | macerate |
| 1973 | Barrie Trinkle, *Fort Worth Press* (Texas) | vouchsafe |
| 1974 | Julie Ann Junkin, *Birminghan Post-Herald* (Alabama) | hydrophyte |
| 1975 | Hugh Tosteson, *San Juan Star* (Puerto Rico) | incisor |
| 1976 | Tim Kneale, *Syracuse Herald Journal-American* (New York) | narcolepsy |
| 1977 | John Paola, *The Pittsburgh Press* (Pennsylvania) | cambist |
| 1978 | Peg McCarthy, *The Topeka Capital-Journal* (Kansas) | deification |
| 1979 | Katie Kerwin, *Rocky Mountain News* (Denver CO) | maculature |
| 1980 | Jacques Bailly, *Rocky Mountain News* (Denver CO) | elucubrate |
| 1981 | Paige Pipkin, *El Paso Herald-Post* (Texas) | sarcophagus |
| 1982 | Molly Dieveney, *Rocky Mountain News* (Denver CO) | psoriasis |
| 1983 | Blake Giddens, *El Paso Herald-Post* (Texas) | purim |
| 1984 | Daniel Greenblatt, *Loudoun Times-Mirror* (Virginia) | luge |
| 1985 | Balu Natarajan, *Chicago Tribune* (Illinois) | milieu |
| 1986 | Jon Pennington, *The Patriot News* (Harrisburg PA) | odontalgia |
| 1987 | Stephanie Petit, *The Pittsburgh Press* (Pennsylvania) | staphylococci |
| 1988 | Rageshree Ramachandran, *The Sacramento Bee* (California) | elegiacal |
| 1989 | Scott Isaacs, *Rocky Mountain News* (Denver CO) | spoliator |
| 1990 | Amy Marie Dimak, *The Seattle Times* (Washington) | fibranne |
| 1991 | Joanne Lagatta, *The Wisconsin State Journal* (Madison WI) | antipyretic |
| 1992 | Amanda Goad, *The Richmond News Leader* (Virginia) | lyceum |
| 1993 | Geoff Hooper, *The Commercial Appeal* (Memphis TN) | kamikaze |
| 1994 | Ned G. Andrews, *The Knoxville News-Sentinel* (Tennessee) | antediluvian |
| 1995 | Justin Tyler Carroll, *The Commercial Appeal* (Memphis TN) | xanthosis |
| 1996 | Wendy Guey, *The Palm Beach Post* (Florida) | vivisepulture |
| 1997 | Rebecca Sealfon, *Daily News* (New York NY) | euonym |
| 1998 | Jody-Anne Maxwell, Phillips & Phillips Stationery Suppliers, Ltd., (Kingston, Jamaica) | chiaroscurist |
| 1999 | Nupur Lala, *The Tampa Tribune* (Florida) | logorrhea |
| 2000 | George Abraham Thampy, *St. Louis Post-Dispatch* (Missouri) | demarche |
| 2001 | Sean Conley, *Aitkin Independent Age* (Minnesota) | succedaneum |
| 2002 | Pratyush Buddiga, *Rocky Mountain News* (Denver CO) | prospicience |
| 2003 | Sai Gunturi, *The Dallas Morning News* (Texas) | pococurante |

# Economics & Business

## World Economy
### Banking

The banking systems of the world share many similarities but have principal differences in the details of organization and technique. Banking systems may be classified in terms of their structure as unit banking, branch banking, or hybrids of the two. For example, unit banking prevails in the United States. In other countries, such as England and Wales, it is more usual to find a small number of large commercial banks, each operating a highly developed network of branches. Examples of hybrid systems include those of France, Germany, and India, where banks that are national in scope are supplemented by regional or local banks.

### Unit banking: the United States
In the years following World War II, bank organization in the US was still passing through a phase of structural development that many other countries had completed decades earlier. Because the US Constitution permits both national and state governments to regulate banking, there were particular state mandates against branch banking that contributed to the proliferation of unit banks.

From the 1970s there was an acceleration in the evolution of American banking patterns. New financial institutions moved into traditional banking activities; at the same time, depository institutions began offering a fuller range of financial services. Rapid changes in the industry resulted in legislation to improve monetary control, remove impediments to competition, and to expand the availability of financial services to the public.

### Branch banking: the United Kingdom
If the US banks can be taken as representative of a unit banking system, the British system is the prototype of branch banking. Its development was linked to the growth of transportation and communications, for otherwise banks cannot clear checks drawn on other banks and effect remittances speedily and efficiently. The Scots long favored branch banking (the Bank of Scotland was founded in 1695), though they were early hampered by poor communications and inadequate coinage.

As the Industrial Revolution progressed and as the size of businesses increased, the structure of English banking underwent a corresponding change. The growth in size of banks was also greatly encouraged by legislation that encouraged joint-stock ownership, beginning in 1826. The banking system in England and Wales evolved into its modern form before World War I, though there was to be a further degree of concentration in the years after World War II. By these means, British banks were able to attract deposits from all parts of the country and to spread the banking risk over a wide range of industries and areas.

### Hybrid systems
A third group of banking systems is characterized by the existence of a small number of banks with branches throughout the country, holding a signifi- cant part of total deposits, along with a relatively large number of smaller banks that are regional or local in emphasis. Such systems exist in France, Germany, and India. Japan has a small number of large city banks with branch networks but a larger number of local banks.

### France
In the years following World War II, banking activities in France were tightly controlled by the government through the Banque de France. However, deregulation in the last four decades of the century gradually reduced federal controls and led to a substantial increase in branch banking and bank account holders. The advent of the EU in the 1990s allowed the free movement of captial across country borders. In 1993 the Banque de France was granted independent staus, which freed it from state control.

### Germany
An even more direct conflict between the forces favoring concentration and those working against it may be seen in Germany, where modern banking developed in the latter part of the 19th century and eventually became concentrated in Berlin. The Berlin banks built up a widespread network of branch offices, which were also used to establish and maintain industrial contacts throughout the country. Each of the big Berlin banks came to be associated with a group of provincial banks more or less under its control. At the same time, all of the banks, Berlin and provincial alike, expanded their business by opening branches.

During World War I the degree of centralization increased and continued during the financial crisis of 1931, resulting in further consolidation until the German banking system was dominated by three giants. Among the countervailing forces were the establishment of publicly owned banking institutions, such as the communal savings banks and their central institutions, the Girozentralen, which became of increasing importance after World War II.

German savings banks offer a wide range of services, especially to lower income groups and smaller businesses, and now compete in wholesale banking as well. The large commercial banks have concerned themselves more with big business and with wealthy individuals. The Big Three (the Deutsche Bank, the Dresdner Bank, and the Commerzbank) remain unchallenged in stock exchange and foreign banking business. Regional and private banks are often within the sphere of influence of the Big Three. While banking in Germany remains a hybrid system, a trend toward greater concentration is evident.

### India
Until the 1950s, banking in India was carried on by a large number of banks, many of them quite small. India remains agricultural in parts, with an economic and social structure based on the village, and so banking and credit was handled by the so-called indigenous banker and the village moneylender. Al-

though their influence has been greatly reduced in recent years, the indigenous bankers offer genuine banking services: accepting deposits and remitting funds; making loans quickly and with a minimum of formality; and making use of the *hundi*, a credit instrument in the form of a bill of exchange.

Efforts to eliminate the local moneylender resulted in changes requiring banks to open branches in rural areas. This caused many smaller banks to close down, leaving a few dozen large national and commercial banks by the end of the 20th century. Banking services are also provided by chit funds, which accept and pay interest on monthly deposits against which it is possible to draw only by way of loan, and by Nidhis, mutual loan societies that have developed into semibanking institutions but deal only with their member shareholders.

The main path of banking development in India is the expansion of bank branches into the underbanked rural areas and to increase lending to weak areas of the economy. The ultimate objective is to encourage the mobilization of deposits on a massive scale throughout the country, a formidable challenge in a country of more than 500,000 villages.

### Japan

Banking business in Japan is largely concentrated in the hands of the big banks (some of which are specialized), though a number of small banks still survive. The principal classes of banks are city banks and regional banks, but it should be noted that the distinction has no legal basis, though they are separately supervised. Both belong to the Federation of Bankers' Associations of Japan.

Between World War II and the 1990s Japanese banking enjoyed notable stability. The decline in overall economic performance of the past decade, exacerbated by burdensome bad loans and a persistent lack of profitability, led to changes in the Japanese banking system including financial deregulation, increased competition, and greater governmental intervention.

### Islamic banking

In contrast to people in the West, many in the Islamic world look askance at some common practices of capitalism, notably giving or receiving interest payments and speculating on futures. The prohibition on collecting interest is based on the teachings of the Qur'an (Koran), the holy book of Islam, which prohibits the practice of *riba*, or usury. In Saudi Arabia, for example, banks charge service fees on loans but are disallowed from charging interest. Islamic alternatives to Western banking include interest-free loans, informal money-changers, and a form of profit-sharing known as *mudarabah*. Islamic banking expanded rapidly in the mid-1970s, fueled by the rise in oil industry revenues as well as growing Muslim conservatism. *Hawala*, like the *hundi* of India at times a facet of the black market economy, is the international movement of capital through a trust-based system of personal contacts, without governmental or institutional oversight.

# Economic Performance

## Real Gross Domestic Products of Selected Developed Countries

*% annual change*

| COUNTRY | 1998 | 1999 | 2000 | 2001 | 2002[1] |
|---|---|---|---|---|---|
| US | 4.3 | 4.1 | 3.8 | -0.3 | 2.2 |
| Japan | -1.2 | 0.8 | 2.4 | 0.3 | -0.5 |
| Germany | 2.0 | 2.0 | 2.9 | 0.6 | 0.5 |
| France | 3.5 | 3.2 | 4.2 | 1.8 | 1.2 |
| Italy | 1.8 | 1.6 | 2.9 | 1.8 | 0.7 |
| UK | 2.9 | 2.4 | 3.1 | 1.9 | 1.7 |
| Canada | 4.1 | 5.4 | 4.5 | 1.5 | 3.4 |
| European Union | 2.9 | 2.8 | 3.5 | 1.6 | 1.1 |
| Seven major countries above | 2.8 | 3.0 | 3.4 | 0.6 | 1.4 |
| All developed countries | 2.7 | 3.4 | 3.8 | 0.8 | 1.7 |

[1]*Estimated.   Note: Seasonally adjusted at annual rates.   Source: OECD; IMF World Economic Outlook, September 2002.*

## Standardized Unemployment Rates in Selected Developed Countries

*% of total labor force*

| COUNTRY | 1998 | 1999 | 2000 | 2001 | 2002 |
|---|---|---|---|---|---|
| US | 4.5 | 4.2 | 4.0 | 4.7 | 5.8 |
| Japan | 4.1 | 4.7 | 4.7 | 5.0 | 5.4 |
| Germany | 9.3 | 8.6 | 7.8 | 7.8 | 8.2 |
| France | 11.8 | 11.2 | 9.3 | 8.5 | 8.7 |
| Italy | 11.8 | 11.4 | 10.4 | 9.4 | 9.0 |
| UK | 6.3 | 6.1 | 5.4 | 5.0 | 5.1 |
| Canada | 8.3 | 7.6 | 6.8 | 7.2 | 7.7 |
| European Union | 9.9 | 9.1 | 7.8 | 7.4 | 7.6 |
| Seven major countries above | 6.4 | 6.1 | 5.6 | 5.9 | 6.5 |
| All developed countries | 7.1 | 6.8 | 6.3 | 6.5 | 6.9 |

*Source: OECD, Main Economic Indicators, May 2003.*

# Consumer Price Change in Selected Countries

Change of consumer prices from the year previous, expressed in percent. The change in consumer prices is used as an indicator of inflation. An increase in percent from one year to the next indicates an increase in the overall price of certain goods and services purchased by the average consumer. A negative number indicates a decrease in consumer prices. N/A means data were not available. Source: International Monetary Fund, *International Financial Statistics*, April 2003.

| COUNTRY | 2000 | 2001 | 2002 | COUNTRY | 2000 | 2001 | 2002 |
|---|---|---|---|---|---|---|---|
| Argentina | −0.9 | −1.1 | 25.9 | Malaysia | 1.5 | 1.4 | 1.8 |
| Australia | 4.5 | 4.4 | 3.0 | Mexico | 9.5 | 6.4 | 5.0 |
| Austria | 2.4 | 2.7 | 1.8 | Netherlands | 2.5 | 4.5 | 3.5 |
| Bangladesh | 3.9 | 1.7 | 2.2 | Nigeria | 14.5 | 13.0 | 12.9 |
| Belgium | 2.5 | 2.5 | 1.6 | Norway | 3.1 | 3.0 | 1.3 |
| Bolivia | 4.6 | 1.6 | 0.9 | Pakistan | 5.5 | 0.8 | −55.6 |
| Brazil | 7.0 | 6.9 | 8.4 | Peru | 3.8 | 2.0 | 0.2 |
| Canada | 2.7 | 2.5 | 2.2 | Philippines | 4.3 | 6.1 | 3.1 |
| Chile | 3.8 | 3.6 | 2.5 | Portugal | 2.9 | 4.4 | 3.6 |
| Colombia | 9.2 | 8.0 | 6.3 | Romania | 45.7 | 34.5 | 22.5 |
| Egypt | 2.7 | 2.3 | N/A | Russia | 20.8 | 21.5 | 15.8 |
| France | 1.7 | 1.6 | 1.9 | South Africa | 5.2 | 4.8 | 10.6 |
| Germany | 1.9 | 2.5 | 1.3 | South Korea | 2.2 | 4.1 | 2.8 |
| Ghana | 25.2 | 32.9 | 14.8 | Spain | 3.4 | 3.6 | 3.1 |
| Greece | 3.1 | 3.4 | 3.6 | Sri Lanka | 6.2 | 14.2 | 9.7 |
| Guatemala | 6.0 | 7.6 | 8.0 | Sweden | 1.0 | 2.4 | 2.2 |
| India | 4.0 | 3.7 | N/A | Switzerland | 1.6 | 1.0 | 0.6 |
| Indonesia | 3.7 | 11.5 | 11.9 | Thailand | 1.5 | 1.7 | 0.6 |
| Iran | 14.5 | 11.3 | 14.3 | Turkey | 54.9 | 54.4 | 45.0 |
| Israel | 1.1 | −5.0 | 5.7 | United Kingdom | 2.9 | 1.8 | 1.6 |
| Italy | 2.5 | 2.8 | 2.5 | United States | 3.4 | 2.8 | 1.6 |
| Japan | −0.7 | −0.7 | −0.9 | Venezuela | 16.2 | 12.5 | 22.4 |
| Kenya | 10.0 | 5.7 | N/A | | | | |

**Did you know?** Popcorn king Orville Redenbacher developed a hybrid popcorn with his partner, Charles Bowman. The hybrid produced plumper and more tender kernels, but no company would buy the product because it was so expensive to produce. Redenbacher and Bowman went into business for themselves, promoting Orville Redenbacher's Gourmet Popping Corn as "the world's most expensive," a marketing ploy that made their product an enormous success in the 1970s.

# Changes in Consumer Prices in Less-Developed Countries
*% change from preceding year*

| AREA | 1998 | 1999 | 2000 | 2001 | 2002[1] |
|---|---|---|---|---|---|
| All less-developed countries | 10.5 | 6.9 | 6.1 | 5.7 | 5.6 |
| Regional groups | | | | | |
| Africa | 10.9 | 12.3 | 14.3 | 13.1 | 9.6 |
| Asia | 7.7 | 2.5 | 1.9 | 2.6 | 2.1 |
| Middle East, Europe, Malta, & Turkey | 27.6 | 23.6 | 19.6 | 17.2 | 17.1 |
| Western Hemisphere | 9.8 | 8.9 | 8.1 | 6.4 | 8.6 |

[1]Projected.    Source: International Monetary Fund, *World Economic Outlook, September 2002.*

# Changes in Output in Less-Developed Countries
*% annual change in real gross domestic product*

| AREA | 1998 | 1999 | 2000 | 2001 | 2002[1] |
|---|---|---|---|---|---|
| All less-developed countries | 3.5 | 4.0 | 5.7 | 3.9 | 4.2 |
| Regional groups | | | | | |
| Africa | 3.4 | 2.8 | 3.0 | 3.5 | 3.1 |
| Asia | 4.0 | 6.1 | 6.7 | 5.6 | 6.1 |
| Middle East, Europe, Malta, & Turkey | 3.6 | 1.2 | 6.1 | 1.5 | 3.6 |
| Western Hemisphere | 2.3 | 0.2 | 4.0 | 0.6 | −0.6 |
| Countries in transition | −0.7 | 3.7 | 6.6 | 5.0 | 3.9 |

[1]Projected.    Source: International Monetary Fund, *World Economic Outlook, September 2002.*

# US Economy

## Banking

### The Federal Reserve System

The Federal Reserve System is the central banking authority of the United States. It acts as a fiscal agent for the US government, is custodian of the reserve accounts of commercial banks, makes loans to commercial banks, and issues paper currency. It protects the stability of the nation's financial system by regulating and supervising banking institutions and containing risk in financial markets. Created on 23 Dec 1913, it consists of the Board of Governors, the 12 Federal Reserve banks, and the Federal Open Market Committee. There are also several thousand member banks.

The Board of Governors determines the reserve requirements of the member banks, reviews and determines the discount rates established by the reserve banks, and reviews reserve bank budgets. It has seven members who each serve a single 14-year term (a member who finishes an incomplete term may be reappointed). The chairman and vice chairman are chosen for four-year terms. In mid-2002, the Federal Reserve Board consisted of Alan Greenspan (chairman), Roger W. Ferguson, Jr. (vice chairman), Edward M. Gramlich, Susan Schmidt Bies, and Mark W. Olson; two positions were vacant.

Each Federal Reserve bank is governed by nine directors. The banks are located in Boston, New York, Philadelphia, Chicago, San Francisco, Cleveland, Richmond, Atlanta, St. Louis, Minneapolis, Kansas City, and Dallas. The Federal Open Market Committee determines reserve bank policy for securities transactions on the open market. It consists of the Board of Governors, the president of the Federal Reserve Bank of New York, and four other bank presidents serving rotating one-year terms. All national banks are members of the Federal Reserve System, and state banks may qualify to become members. The Federal Advisory Council operates as a general advisory group. The Consumer Advisory Council addresses consumer finance and credit issues. The Thrift Institutions Advisory Council offers input on issues relating to banks, credit unions, and savings and loans.

The Federal Reserve System exercises its regulatory powers in several ways. One method is to adjust the legal reserve ratio (the proportion of deposits a member bank must hold in its reserve account), thus increasing or reducing the amount of new loans a bank can make. Because loans create new deposits, the money supply is expanded or reduced. The money supply is also influenced by manipulating the discount rate (the rate of interest charged by reserve banks on short-term secured loans to member banks). Since these loans are typically sought to maintain reserves at their required level, an increase in the cost of such loans has an effect similar to that of increasing the reserve requirement. Open-market operations may be employed to make small adjustments in the market. Reserve bank sales or purchases of securities on the open market tend to reduce or increase the size of commercial-bank reserves. The board can also change the margin requirements involved in the purchase of securities.

### The US Mint

The US Mint, the world's largest producer of coins and medals, was established by Congress on 2 Apr 1792. It is a bureau of the United States Department of the Treasury. The mint manufactures and distributes coins, protects the country's gold and silver assets, and creates medals, commemorative coins, and coin proof sets for purchase by the public. In 2001 it produced 19,401,459,500 pennies, nickels, dimes, quarters, half dollars, and Golden Dollars. The director of the mint is appointed by the president and serves a five-year term; in mid-2002 the director was Henrietta Holsman Fore.

From its Washington DC headquarters, the mint operates facilities in Philadelphia PA, Denver CO, San Francisco CA, and West Point NY. All designing and engraving of coins is done at the Philadelphia site (established 1792), where general circulation coins, medals, and coin dies are also produced. Denver (1863) manufactures general circulation coins and coin dies and provides storage for gold and silver bullion. San Francisco (1854) produces only commemorative coins and proof sets; West Point (1937) manufactures uncirculated and proof sets of gold, silver, and platinum coins and stores these metals. The mint is also responsible for the storage and protection of more than 145 million ounces of gold bullion at Fort Knox KY.

Although general circulation coins were once made from gold, silver, and copper, this is no longer the case. Gold coin production was discontinued in 1933, and in 1965 silver ceased to be used in dimes and quarters. Currently, pennies are composed of copper-plated zinc, golden dollar coins of manganese brass, and all other general circulation coins of cupronickel, an alloy of copper and nickel. In early 2000 the mint began circulating the Golden Dollar coin, intended to replace the older Susan B. Anthony dollar coin. The new coin featured the image of Sacagawea, the Shoshone Indian woman who traveled as a guide with the Lewis and Clark Expedition in 1804–06. In 1999 the mint began issuing a series of quarters featuring the 50 states. Over a 10-year period, five quarters were to be issued annually, about 10 weeks apart, each featuring one state's design. State quarters were released in order of the states' ratification of the US Constitution. Introduced in 2002 were Tennessee, Ohio, Louisiana, Indiana, and Mississippi; scheduled for 2003 were Illinois, Alabama, Maine, Missouri, and Arkansas.

# US Bureau of Engraving and Printing

The US Bureau of Engraving and Printing is responsible for the printing of paper money and is a part of the United States Department of the Treasury. In addition to Federal Reserve Notes (paper currency), the bureau produces other government security documents and creates postage stamps for the United States Postal Service. Each year it prints billions of bills at a rate of some 37 million per day (valued at nearly $700 million). The bureau operates facilities in Washington DC and Fort Worth TX. A director is appointed by the Secretary of the Treasury; in mid-2002, the director was Thomas A. Ferguson.

The vast majority of bills are printed to replace those already in circulation. Currency is printed on paper made of cotton and linen with red and blue fibers throughout and is produced in denominations of $1, $5, $10, $20, $50, $100, and, occasionally, $2. No currency has been printed in denominations of $500, $1,000, $5,000, or $10,000 since 1946. The greatest number of bills printed are the $1 denomination,

with more than five billion produced in fiscal year 2001.

The bureau was established in 1862 and by 1877 was the only producer of US paper money; previously, private companies had printed currency. In 1894 the bureau began producing postage stamps. By the mid-1980s it was recognized that a western office was needed, and the Fort Worth facility opened in April 1991. To protect against technologically advanced counterfeiting techniques, new currency designs began circulating in 1996 that incorporated enhanced deterrence measures. Since 1990 all paper money except $1 bills has included a security thread and microprinting, components that were improved for later print series. New anticounterfeiting features included watermarks, color-shifting inks, fine-line printing patterns, and enlarged, off-center portraits; elements were also added to help the blind and those with poor vision identify different denominations. Counterfeiting crimes are handled by the US Secret Service.

# Denominations of US Currency

A new $20 bill will appear in autumn 2003. In addition to the watermark, color-shifting ink, security thread, and microprinting that are present in the current $5–$100 bills, the new $20 bill will have multicolored printing, a blue eagle in the

background, a metallic green eagle and shield, and other anticounterfeiting features. Redesigns of the $50 and $100 bills are planned for 2004 and 2005, respectively.

### PAPER MONEY

| VALUE | PORTRAIT ON FRONT | DESIGN ON BACK | WHEN ISSUED |
|---|---|---|---|
| $1 | George Washington | Great Seal of US | 1929– |
| $2 | Thomas Jefferson | Monticello | 1929–75 |
| $2 | Thomas Jefferson | John Trumbull's *Signing of the Declaration of Independence* | 1976– |
| $5[1] | Abraham Lincoln | Lincoln Memorial | 2000– |
| $10[1] | Alexander Hamilton | US Treasury | 2000– |
| $20[1] | Andrew Jackson | White House | 1998– |
| $50[1] | Ulysses S. Grant | US Capitol | 1997– |
| $100[1] | Benjamin Franklin | Independence Hall | 1996– |
| $500[2] | William McKinley | ornate figure of value | 1929–69 |
| $1,000[2] | Grover Cleveland | ornate figure of value | 1929–69 |
| $5,000[2] | James Madison | ornate figure of value | 1929–69 |
| $10,000[2] | Salmon P. Chase | ornate figure of value | 1929–69 |
| $100,000[3] | Woodrow Wilson | ornate figure of value | — |

[1]*Earlier versions issued starting 1929 had same subjects front and back.*   [2]*Last printed in 1945.*   [3]*Printed 1934–35, but never issued to public.*

### COINS

| VALUE | PORTRAIT ON FRONT | DESIGN ON BACK | WHEN ISSUED |
|---|---|---|---|
| 1¢ | Abraham Lincoln | "one cent" and wheat | 1909–58 |
| 1¢ | Abraham Lincoln | Lincoln Memorial | 1959– |
| 5¢ | Thomas Jefferson | Monticello | 1938– |
| 10¢ | Franklin D. Roosevelt | torch | 1946– |
| 25¢ | George Washington | eagle | 1932–74; 1977–98 |
| 25¢ | George Washington | colonial drummer | 1975/76[1] |
| 25¢ | George Washington | 50 state designs | 1999–2008 |
| 50¢ | John F. Kennedy | presidential seal | 1964–74; 1977– |
| 50¢ | John F. Kennedy | Independence Hall | 1975/76[1] |
| $1 | Dwight D. Eisenhower | eagle | 1971–74 |
| $1 | Dwight D. Eisenhower | Liberty Bell and Moon | 1975/76[1] |
| $1 | Susan B. Anthony | eagle | 1979–81; 1999 |
| $1 | Sacagawea | eagle | 2000– |

[1]*All 25¢, 50¢, and $1 coins issued in 1975 and 1976 carried the double date 1776–1976.*

# Denominations of US Currency (continued)

## 50 STATE QUARTERS PROGRAM

| STATE | WHEN ISSUED | STATE | WHEN ISSUED | STATE | WHEN ISSUED |
|---|---|---|---|---|---|
| Alabama | March 2003 | Louisiana | May 2002 | Ohio | March 2002 |
| Alaska | 2008 | Maine | June 2003 | Oklahoma | 2008 |
| Arizona | 2008 | Maryland | March 2000 | Oregon | 2005 |
| Arkansas | 2003 | Massachusetts | January 2000 | Pennsylvania | March 1999 |
| California | 2005 | Michigan | 2004 | Rhode Island | May 2001 |
| Colorado | 2006 | Minnesota | 2005 | South Carolina | May 2000 |
| Connecticut | October 1999 | Mississippi | October 2002 | South Dakota | 2006 |
| Delaware | January 1999 | Missouri | 2003 | Tennessee | January 2002 |
| Florida | 2004 | Montana | 2007 | Texas | 2004 |
| Georgia | July 1999 | Nebraska | 2006 | Utah | 2007 |
| Hawaii | 2008 | Nevada | 2006 | Vermont | August 2001 |
| Idaho | 2007 | New Hampshire | August 2000 | Virginia | October 2000 |
| Illinois | January 2003 | New Jersey | May 1999 | Washington | 2007 |
| Indiana | August 2002 | New Mexico | 2008 | West Virginia | 2005 |
| Iowa | 2004 | New York | January 2001 | Wisconsin | 2004 |
| Kansas | 2005 | North Carolina | March 2001 | Wyoming | 2007 |
| Kentucky | October 2001 | North Dakota | 2006 | | |

# US Currency and Coins in Circulation

*Currency and coins outstanding, 21 Mar 2003, and currency in circulation by denomination, 31 Mar 2003. Source:* Treasury Bulletin, *June 2003.*

| | TOTAL CURRENCY AND COINS | CURRENCY | COINS[1] |
|---|---|---|---|
| amounts in circulation | $686,788,354,586 | $652,945,714,116 | $33,842,640,470 |
| plus amounts held by: | | | |
| US Treasury | 334,264,765 | 33,721,765 | 300,543,000 |
| Federal Reserve Banks | 115,295,688,715 | 114,189,348,327 | 1,106,340,388 |
| **total amounts outstanding** | **802,418,308,066** | **767,168,784,208** | **35,249,523,858** |

| DENOMINATION | TOTAL | FEDERAL RESERVE NOTES[2] | US NOTES | CURRENCY NO LONGER ISSUED |
|---|---|---|---|---|
| $1 | $ 7,653,468,440 | $ 7,507,775,030 | $ 143,481 | $145,549,929 |
| $2 | 1,312,310,036 | 1,179,976,394 | 132,321,066 | 12,576 |
| $5 | 8,934,659,030 | 8,795,705,815 | 109,563,110 | 29,390,105 |
| $10 | 14,063,602,720 | 14,041,879,430 | 5,950 | 21,717,340 |
| $20 | 97,726,858,540 | 97,706,753,340 | 3,380 | 20,101,820 |
| $50 | 57,025,572,350 | 57,014,076,950 | – | 11,495,400 |
| $100 | 465,915,241,400 | 465,874,148,500 | 19,102,500 | 21,990,400 |
| $500 | 142,745,000 | 142,557,000 | – | 188,000 |
| $1,000 | 166,061,000 | 165,855,000 | – | 206,000 |
| $5,000 | 1,755,000 | 1,700,000 | – | 55,000 |
| $10,000 | 3,440,000 | 3,340,000 | – | 100,000 |
| fractional parts | 485 | – | – | 485 |
| partial notes[3] | 115 | – | 90 | 25 |
| **total currency** | **$652,945,714,116** | **$652,433,767,459** | **$261,139,577** | **$250,807,080** |

[1]*Excludes coins sold to collectors at premium prices.* [2]*Issued on or after 1 Jul 1929.* [3]*Represents value of certain partial denominations not presented for redemption.*

# Energy

## Energy Consumption by State and Sector

*Figures represent '000,000,000,000 Btu. Source: Britannica World Data Annual 2003.*

| | TOTAL | RESIDENTIAL | COMMERCIAL | INDUSTRIAL | TRANS-PORTATION | PER CAPITA ('000,000 BTU) |
|---|---|---|---|---|---|---|
| Alabama | 2,005 | 341 | 226 | 977 | 461 | 459 |
| Alaska | 695 | 48 | 63 | 386 | 198 | 1,122 |
| Arizona | 1,220 | 279 | 267 | 222 | 453 | 255 |
| Arkansas | 1,204 | 193 | 124 | 589 | 297 | 472 |
| California | 8,375 | 1,416 | 1,237 | 2,824 | 2,899 | 253 |
| Colorado | 1,156 | 281 | 255 | 273 | 366 | 285 |
| Connecticut | 839 | 245 | 197 | 162 | 235 | 256 |
| Delaware | 279 | 56 | 45 | 107 | 71 | 370 |

## Energy Consumption by State and Sector (continued)

| | TOTAL | RESIDENTIAL | COMMERCIAL | INDUSTRIAL | TRANS-PORTATION | PER CAPITA ('000,000 BTU) |
|---|---|---|---|---|---|---|
| District of Columbia | 170 | 34 | 106 | 4 | 27 | 327 |
| Florida | 3,853 | 1,018 | 810 | 680 | 1,346 | 255 |
| Georgia | 2,798 | 553 | 416 | 957 | 871 | 359 |
| Hawaii | 241 | 23 | 25 | 71 | 122 | 204 |
| Idaho | 518 | 96 | 87 | 210 | 126 | 414 |
| Illinois | 3,883 | 897 | 722 | 1,273 | 991 | 320 |
| Indiana | 2,736 | 484 | 301 | 1,306 | 645 | 460 |
| Iowa | 1,122 | 223 | 159 | 463 | 278 | 391 |
| Kansas | 1,050 | 201 | 169 | 392 | 288 | 396 |
| Kentucky | 1,830 | 316 | 219 | 851 | 444 | 462 |
| Louisiana | 3,615 | 325 | 237 | 2,249 | 805 | 827 |
| Maine | 529 | 98 | 58 | 260 | 113 | 422 |
| Maryland | 1,378 | 359 | 337 | 277 | 405 | 267 |
| Massachusetts | 1,569 | 412 | 325 | 391 | 441 | 254 |
| Michigan | 3,240 | 744 | 568 | 1,083 | 845 | 328 |
| Minnesota | 1,675 | 340 | 218 | 618 | 500 | 351 |
| Mississippi | 1,209 | 203 | 146 | 451 | 409 | 437 |
| Missouri | 1,768 | 432 | 334 | 380 | 623 | 323 |
| Montana | 412 | 62 | 48 | 196 | 107 | 467 |
| Nebraska | 602 | 130 | 111 | 166 | 194 | 361 |
| Nevada | 615 | 122 | 97 | 198 | 198 | 340 |
| New Hampshire | 335 | 82 | 56 | 97 | 101 | 279 |
| New Jersey | 2,589 | 540 | 541 | 645 | 863 | 318 |
| New Mexico | 635 | 93 | 106 | 202 | 234 | 365 |
| New York | 4,283 | 1,092 | 1,216 | 995 | 980 | 235 |
| North Carolina | 2,447 | 563 | 440 | 754 | 491 | 320 |
| North Dakota | 366 | 54 | 43 | 186 | 82 | 577 |
| Ohio | 4,323 | 867 | 632 | 1,855 | 969 | 384 |
| Oklahoma | 1,378 | 259 | 198 | 518 | 403 | 410 |
| Oregon | 1,109 | 238 | 191 | 352 | 328 | 335 |
| Pennsylvania | 3,716 | 859 | 583 | 1,290 | 984 | 310 |
| Rhode Island | 261 | 66 | 52 | 77 | 66 | 264 |
| South Carolina | 1,493 | 288 | 210 | 618 | 376 | 384 |
| South Dakota | 239 | 53 | 39 | 62 | 84 | 326 |
| Tennessee | 2,071 | 442 | 328 | 711 | 590 | 378 |
| Texas | 11,501 | 1,323 | 1,147 | 6,482 | 2,549 | 574 |
| Utah | 694 | 128 | 120 | 235 | 211 | 326 |
| Vermont | 165 | 43 | 29 | 40 | 53 | 278 |
| Virginia | 2,227 | 494 | 463 | 614 | 656 | 324 |
| Washington | 2,241 | 436 | 332 | 856 | 617 | 389 |
| West Virginia | 735 | 142 | 101 | 311 | 182 | 407 |
| Wisconsin | 1,811 | 376 | 285 | 717 | 432 | 345 |
| Wyoming | 422 | 36 | 42 | 224 | 120 | 879 |
| total | 95,682 | 18,382 | 15,059 | 35,917 | 26,325 | 351 |

## Energy Consumption by Source

*Figures represent '000,000,000,000 Btu. Source: Britannica World Data 2003.*

| | PETROLEUM | NATURAL GAS | COAL | HYDROELECTRIC POWER | NUCLEAR ELECTRIC POWER |
|---|---|---|---|---|---|
| Alabama | 551 | 345 | 855 | 80 | 328 |
| Alaska | 253 | 420 | 11 | 9 | 0.0 |
| Arizona | 497 | 163 | 404 | 104 | 323 |
| Arkansas | 384 | 266 | 267 | 28 | 137 |
| California | 3,383 | 2,182 | 64 | 425 | 355 |
| Colorado | 426 | 318 | 355 | 17 | 0.0 |
| Connecticut | 440 | 135 | 0.0 | 14 | 135 |
| Delaware | 141 | 58 | 36 | 0.0 | 0.0 |
| District of Columbia | 34 | 33 | 0.6 | 0.0 | 0.0 |
| Florida | 1,912 | 542 | 672 | 2 | 335 |
| Georgia | 1,044 | 341 | 790 | 28 | 334 |
| Hawaii | 214 | 3 | 3 | 1 | 0.0 |
| Idaho | 170 | 72 | 8 | 140 | 0.0 |
| Illinois | 1,340 | 1,058 | 837 | 2 | 868 |
| Indiana | 899 | 577 | 1,451 | 4 | 0.0 |

## Energy Consumption by Source (continued)

| | PETROLEUM | NATURAL GAS | COAL | HYDROELECTRIC POWER | NUCLEAR ELECTRIC POWER |
|---|---|---|---|---|---|
| Iowa | 419 | 236 | 416 | 10 | 39 |
| Kansas | 437 | 302 | 329 | 0.0 | 97 |
| Kentucky | 726 | 220 | 885 | 27 | 0.0 |
| Louisiana | 1,452 | 1,558 | 228 | 8 | 139 |
| Maine | 250 | 6 | 3 | 81 | 0.0 |
| Maryland | 584 | 201 | 304 | 15 | 141 |
| Massachusetts | 639 | 356 | 13 | 15 | 48 |
| Michigan | 1,098 | 930 | 823 | 11 | 155 |
| Minnesota | 661 | 346 | 336 | 59 | 142 |
| Mississippi | 483 | 346 | 138 | 0.0 | 90 |
| Missouri | 781 | 270 | 686 | 18 | 91 |
| Montana | 174 | 64 | 174 | 143 | 0.0 |
| Nebraska | 246 | 121 | 196 | 18 | 107 |
| Nevada | 221 | 157 | 180 | 29 | 0.0 |
| New Hampshire | 188 | 21 | 35 | 25 | 92 |
| New Jersey | 1,236 | 641 | 68 | 0.0 | 308 |
| New Mexico | 257 | 225 | 298 | 3 | 0.0 |
| New York | 1,653 | 1,251 | 188 | 265 | 393 |
| North Carolina | 937 | 229 | 708 | 40 | 399 |
| North Dakota | 123 | 59 | 412 | 28 | 0.0 |
| Ohio | 1,340 | 878 | 1,379 | 4 | 175 |
| Oklahoma | 500 | 543 | 334 | 32 | 0.0 |
| Oregon | 392 | 219 | 39 | 475 | 0.0 |
| Pennsylvania | 1,385 | 696 | 1,143 | 16 | 756 |
| Rhode Island | 99 | 86 | 0.1 | 10 | 0.0 |
| South Carolina | 467 | 163 | 403 | 7 | 540 |
| South Dakota | 115 | 36 | 46 | 71 | 0.0 |
| Tennessee | 713 | 286 | 626 | 74 | 289 |
| Texas | 5,565 | 3,982 | 1,535 | 13 | 391 |
| Utah | 262 | 169 | 382 | 13 | 0.0 |
| Vermont | 85 | 8 | 2 | 61 | 43 |
| Virginia | 864 | 275 | 402 | 6 | 301 |
| Washington | 878 | 277 | 96 | 988 | 65 |
| West Virginia | 220 | 147 | 977 | 10 | 0.0 |
| Wisconsin | 668 | 379 | 472 | 23 | 122 |
| Wyoming | 156 | 102 | 495 | 12 | 0.0 |
| **total** | **37,960** | **22,295** | **20,498** | **3,449** | **7,736** |

# Travel and Tourism
## Passports, Visas, and Immunizations

With certain exceptions, a passport is required by law for all US citizens, including infants, to travel outside the United States and its territories. Exceptions include travel to Canada, Mexico, some Central American countries, and most Caribbean countries; these usually require a birth certificate or other proof of US citizenship for entry. Passports can be applied for at 5,000 passport acceptance facilities nationwide, including courts, post offices, libraries, and county and city offices. State Department passport agencies generally accept applications only by appointment, usually from those in need of expedited service (two weeks or less). Passport agencies are located in Boston MA, Chicago IL, Norwalk CT, Honolulu HI, Houston TX, Los Angeles CA, Miami FL, New Orleans LA, New York City NY, Philadelphia PA, San Francisco CA, Seattle WA, and Washington DC. Those age 14 and up must apply in person for new passports, but renewals may be done by mail. Applicants should submit the appropriate paperwork several months in advance of planned travel to allow for processing. New passport fees total $85 for persons age 16 and up ($55 passport fee, $30 execution

fee) and $70 for those under 16 ($40 passport fee, $30 execution fee); expedited service is an additional $60. Renewal fees are $55 for all ages. Passports are mailed to applicants in about six weeks, or about two weeks for rush service. The status of a passport application may be checked only by contacting the National Passport Information Center at 1-877-487-2778 (using a credit card; $5.50 per call) or 1-900-225-5674 (an operator-assisted call, required to check status, is $1.50 per minute; service is available weekdays from 8:30 am to 5:30 pm EST).

To apply in person for a passport requires submission of an application form; proof of US citizenship, such as a certified birth certificate; proof of identity, such as a driver's license; two identical recent 2×2-inch photographs; a social security number; and all applicable fees. Options for proving identity or citizenship are listed on the State Department Web site. A passport is valid for 10 years, or 5 years if issued to a person age 15 or younger. Passports can be renewed by mail if the applicant has received a passport within the past 15 years, was over age 16 when the passport was issued, and has legal documentation to verify any name changes (such as a marriage certificate or divorce decree). To renew by mail requires submission of an application form, the most recent passport, two identical photographs, and applicable fees. Frequent travelers may request a passport with extra pages. A passport that is lost or stolen in a foreign country must be immediately reported to local police and the nearest US embassy or consulate to allow for the citizen's reentry into the US. Replacing a lost or stolen passport requires completion of a form reporting the loss or theft and an application for a new passport, as well as the usual documentation, photographs, and fees.

**Visas.** A visa is usually a stamp placed on a US passport by a foreign country's officials allowing the passport owner to visit that country. It is the traveler's responsibility to check visa regulations and obtain visas where necessary before traveling to a foreign country. Visas may be acquired from the embassy or consulate of the intended destination, and can be applied for by mail. Processing fees vary among countries.

**Immunizations.** Under regulations adopted by the World Health Organization, some countries require International Certificates of Vaccination against yellow fever. Other immunizations, such as those for tetanus and polio, should also be up-to-date. Preventive measures for malaria are recommended for some destinations. There are no immunization requirements for returning to the United States. Many countries require HIV/AIDS testing for work, study, or residence permits or for long-term stays.

For passport information, forms, and office locations, access the State Department Web site at <http://travel.state.gov/passport_services.html>.

Entry requirements for foreign countries, including necessity of visas, immunizations, and HIV testing, are available at <http://travel.state.gov/foreignentry reqs.html>. Additional information on required or recommended health-care measures can be obtained from the Centers for Disease Control and Prevention at <www.cdc.gov/travel/> or by calling 1-877-FYI-TRIP; also helpful are local health departments and the Government Printing Office publication Health Information for International Travel, available for $20 at <http://travel.state.gov/foreignentry reqs.html>.

## Travelers to and from the US

Preliminary data for 2002 show that overseas travel to the US dropped significantly during 2002, primarily as a response to the terrorist attacks of 11 Sep 2001. Data for US resident travel to specific overseas countries are not yet available, but 2002 data for air travel to the various regions, as well as Mexico and Canada, are presented below. Source: US Department of Commerce, International Trade Administration.

TOP COUNTRIES OF ORIGIN FOR
VISITORS TO THE US (2002)

|  |  | % CHANGE FROM 2001 |
|---|---|---|
| UK | 3,816,736 | -7 |
| Japan | 3,627,264 | -11 |
| Germany | 1,189,856 | -9 |
| France | 734,260 | -16 |
| South Korea | 638,697 | +3 |
| Australia | 407,160 | -4 |
| Italy | 406,160 | -14 |
| Brazil | 405,094 | -27 |
| Venezuela | 395,913 | -29 |
| The Netherlands | 384,367 | -7 |
| **total overseas** | **19,116,707** | **-12** |
| Canada | 12,968,103 | -4 |
| Mexico | 9,807,000 | +3 |
| **total worldwide** | **41,891,810** | **-7** |

REGIONAL DESTINATION OF US TRAVELERS
ABROAD (2002)

|  |  | % CHANGE FROM 2001 |
|---|---|---|
| Europe | 10,677,881 | -12 |
| Caribbean | 4,324,345 | -2 |
| Asia | 3,918,842 | -3 |
| South America | 1,675,376 | -11 |
| Central America | 1,565,459 | -2 |
| Oceania | 746,464 | -9 |
| Middle East | 310,048 | -7 |
| Africa | 178,973 | -23 |
| **total overseas** | **23,397,388** | **-7** |
| Mexico | 4,175,927 | -9 |
| Canada | 3,792,550 | 0 |
| **total worldwide** | **31,365,865** | **-7** |

### Top 10 States and Cities Visited by Overseas Visitors in 2002[1]

| STATE | VISITORS/ IN THOUSANDS ('000) | % CHANGE FROM 2001 | CITY | VISITORS/ IN THOUSANDS ('000) | % CHANGE FROM 2001 |
|---|---|---|---|---|---|
| New York | 4,492 | -11 | New York NY | 4,244 | -12 |
| Florida | 4,416 | -16 | Los Angeles CA | 2,256 | -20 |
| California | 4,053 | -16 | Miami FL | 2,198 | -14 |
| Hawaii | 1,950 | -12 | Orlando FL | 1,873 | -24 |
| Nevada | 1,281 | -19 | San Francisco CA | 1,644 | -16 |
| Guam[2] | 1,071 | -4 | Oahu/Honolulu HI | 1,587 | -9 |
| Illinois | 1,071 | -4 | Las Vegas NV | 1,223 | -19 |
| Massachusetts | 937 | -21 | Washington DC | 1,023 | -14 |
| Texas | 822 | -12 | Chicago IL | 1,013 | -5 |
| New Jersey | 707 | -13 | Boston MA | 822 | -23 |

[1]Excludes Canadian and Mexican visitors to the US.  [2]Guam is a US territory. If Guam were excluded, Pennsylvania would rank 10th on the list with about 669,000 overseas visitors.

## Customs Exemptions

Upon returning to the US from a foreign country, travelers must pay duty on items purchased outside the US. If the value of the items is greater than the allowable exemption, duty must be paid on the excess amount. The general exemption is $800 per person, but it can also be $600 or $1,200 in certain situations. Exemptions apply if the items are in the traveler's possession, are for the traveler's own use, and are declared to Customs. The traveler must also have been out of the country for at least 48 hours (unless returning from Mexico or the US Virgin Islands) and must not have used any part of the exemption within the past 30 days; if one or both of these requirements does not apply, the allowable exemption drops to $200 per person and includes additional restrictions. The general exemption of $800 applies to travelers returning from any country except several in the Caribbean Sea region and from US island possessions. This exemption includes no more than 200 previously exported cigarettes, 100 cigars, and no more than one liter of alcoholic beverages. Cuban tobacco products purchased in any country other than Cuba are prohibited. Family members may combine their total exemptions in a joint declaration. A $600 exemption applies to travelers returning from any of 24 countries in the Caribbean region and may include two liters of alcoholic beverages, as long as one of the liters was produced in one of those countries. The 24 countries are Antigua and Barbuda, Aruba, The Bahamas, Barbados, Belize, the British Virgin Islands, Costa Rica, Dominica, the Dominican Republic, El Salvador, Grenada, Guatemala, Guyana, Haiti, Honduras, Jamaica, Montserrat, the Netherlands Antilles, Nicaragua, Panama, St. Kitts and Nevis, St. Lucia, St. Vincent and the Grenadines, and Trinidad and Tobago. A $1,200 exemption applies to travelers returning from a trip that included the US Virgin Islands, American Samoa, or Guam. This exemption includes 1,000 cigarettes and five liters of alcoholic beverages; of this amount, 800 cigarettes and one liter of alcohol must be from one of the US islands. The $1,200 exemption also applies to multi-country travel (such as a cruise) to a US possession and any of the 24 Caribbean region countries, as long as no more than $600 worth of goods was purchased in the Caribbean countries.

Gifts valued at $100 or less may be sent to the US without duty as long as no single person receives more than this value within a single day; the exempt value increases to $200 for gifts sent from American Samoa, Guam, or the US Virgin Islands. Alcoholic beverages may not be sent by mail; tobacco and alcohol-based perfumes worth more than $5 are not included in the exemption. Travelers may ship goods home for personal use without duty if the value of the goods is $200 or less and no single person receives more than this value within a single day. This personal exemption increases to $1,200 for goods purchased and shipped from American Samoa, Guam, or the US Virgin Islands.

Customs information is available from the Customs and Border Protection Web site at <www.cbp.gov/xp/cgov/home.xml>. The general-information brochure "Know Before You Go" and other Customs publications can be viewed or ordered online.

---

 **Did you know?** The Michelin guides were initiated by André Michelin, whose aim was to promote tourism by car and thus to support his tire industry. His first Red Guide (1900) listed French towns of interest that were large enough to contain hotels and garages. It included the prototypical rating symbols for which Michelin became famous. A select number of restaurants that provide "cooking worth a special journey" are indicated by the presence of three stars.

---

## US State Department Travel Warnings

The State Department issues Travel Warnings when it is believed best for Americans to avoid certain countries in the interests of safety. It also releases Public Announcements of more short-term hazards, such as terrorist threats or political coups, that may endanger American travelers; these include an expiration date when the announcement need no longer be heeded. The department also makes available Consular Information Sheets for all countries, which may discuss safety conditions in that country not severe enough to require a travel warning. Current information can be found at <http://travel.state.gov/travel_warnings.html> or by phone at 1-888-407-4747 (weekdays 8 AM to 8 PM Eastern Standard Time) or 1-202-647-5225 (all other times).

Travel Warnings were in effect on 10 June 2003 for the following: Afghanistan, Algeria, Angola, Bosnia and Herzegovina, Burundi, Central African Republic, China,[1] Colombia, the Democratic Republic of the Congo, Côte d'Ivoire, Hong Kong,[1] Indonesia, Iran, Iraq, Israel (including the West Bank and Gaza Strip), Kenya, Lebanon, Liberia, Libya, Macedonia, Nigeria, Pakistan, Saudi Arabia, Somalia, The Sudan, Taiwan,[1] Tajikistan, Venezuela, Yemen, and Zimbabwe.

Public Announcements in effect on the same day included advisories for the Republic of the Congo,[2] Djibouti, East Timor, Guatemala, Kyrgyzstan, Laos, Malaysia, Mauritania, Peru, the Philippines, Saudi Arabia, the Solomon Islands, and Uzbekistan.

[1]SARS (sudden acute respiratory syndrome).     [2]Ebola hemorrhagic fever.

# Employment

## US Employment by Gender and Occupation, 2002

*Numbers may not add up to totals due to rounding. Source: US Bureau of Labor Statistics.*

| OCCUPATION | 16 YEARS AND OLDER (NUMBERS IN '000) | | |
| --- | --- | --- | --- |
| | MEN | WOMEN | TOTAL |
| **managerial and professional specialty** | | | |
| officials and administrators, public administration | 405 | 403 | 808 |
| other executive, administrative, and managerial | 8,543 | 6,028 | 14,571 |
| management-related occupations | 2,167 | 3,015 | 5,182 |
| engineers | 1,809 | 219 | 2,028 |
| mathematical and computer scientists | 1,405 | 625 | 2,030 |
| natural scientists | 354 | 192 | 545 |
| health-diagnosing occupations | 832 | 344 | 1,176 |
| health-assessment and treating occupations | 446 | 2,822 | 3,267 |
| teachers, university and college level | 582 | 433 | 1,015 |
| teachers, except university and college | 1,411 | 4,242 | 5,652 |
| lawyers and judges | 681 | 282 | 963 |
| other professional specialty occupations | 2,403 | 2,842 | 5,245 |
| | **21,038** | **21,447** | **42,482** |
| **technical, sales, and administrative support** | | | |
| health technologists and technicians | 347 | 1,531 | 1,879 |
| engineering and science technicians | 931 | 341 | 1,272 |
| technicians, except health, engineering, and science | 790 | 569 | 1,359 |
| supervisors and proprietors | 2,916 | 1,912 | 4,828 |
| sales representatives, finance and business services | 1,626 | 1,318 | 2,944 |
| sales representatives, commodities, except retail | 1,170 | 393 | 1,563 |
| sales workers, retail and personal services | 2,542 | 4,270 | 6,811 |
| sales-related occupations | 31 | 76 | 107 |
| supervisors | 283 | 434 | 717 |
| computer-equipment operators | 163 | 145 | 308 |
| secretaries, stenographers, and typists | 73 | 2,947 | 3,020 |
| financial-records processing | 181 | 2,024 | 2,205 |
| mail and message distributing | 547 | 360 | 907 |
| other administrative support, including clerical | 2,666 | 8,361 | 11,027 |
| | **14,266** | **24,681** | **38,947** |
| **service occupations** | | | |
| private household | 40 | 706 | 746 |
| protective service | 2,081 | 516 | 2,596 |
| food service | 2,923 | 3,691 | 6,614 |
| health service | 305 | 2,511 | 2,817 |
| cleaning and building service | 1,717 | 1,445 | 3,162 |
| personal service | 635 | 2,649 | 3,284 |
| | **7,701** | **11,518** | **19,219** |
| **precision production, craft, and repair** | | | |
| mechanics and repairers | 4,545 | 215 | 4,760 |
| construction trades | 6,151 | 153 | 6,304 |
| other precision production, craft, and repair | 2,764 | 832 | 3,596 |
| | **13,460** | **1,200** | **14,660** |
| **operators, fabricators, and laborers** | | | |
| machine operators, assemblers, and inspectors | 4,198 | 2,290 | 6,488 |
| motor-vehicle operators | 3,940 | 541 | 4,482 |
| other transportation and material-moving occupations | 1,271 | 61 | 1,332 |
| construction laborers | 1,046 | 43 | 1,089 |
| other handlers, equipment cleaners, helpers, and laborers | 3,219 | 1,086 | 4,305 |
| | **13,674** | **4,021** | **17,696** |
| **farming, forestry, and fishing** | | | |
| farm operators and managers | 882 | 286 | 1,168 |
| other farming, forestry, and fishing occupations | 1,883 | 430 | 2,313 |
| | **2,765** | **716** | **3,481** |
| total | **72,903** | **63,382** | **136,485** |

# US Workers Earning the Minimum Wage

This table refers to wage and salary workers who are paid hourly rates. It excludes the incorporated self-employed. The prevailing federal minimum wage was $5.15/hour in 2001. Workers earning less than $5.15/hour may be working in jobs that are exempted from the minimum wage provision of the Fair Labor Standards Act. Numbers in thousands ('000). Source: US Bureau of Labor Statistics.

| WORKER CHARACTERISTICS | TOTAL NUMBER OF WORKERS | BELOW $5.15/HR | AT $5.15/HR | TOTAL NUMBER OF WORKERS AT OR BELOW $5.15/HR | |
|---|---|---|---|---|---|
| | | | | NUMBER | % |
| **age** | | | | | |
| 16–24 years | 16,602 | 830 | 376 | 1,206 | 7.3 |
| 25 years and over | 55,884 | 771 | 260 | 1,032 | 1.8 |
| **total (16 years and over)** | **72,486** | **1,602** | **636** | **2,238** | **3.1** |
| | | | | | |
| **men** | | | | | |
| 16–24 years | 8,491 | 296 | 177 | 473 | 5.6 |
| 25 years and over | 27,538 | 233 | 78 | 311 | 1.1 |
| 16 years and over | 36,029 | 529 | 255 | 784 | 2.2 |
| | | | | | |
| **women** | | | | | |
| 16–24 years | 8,111 | 534 | 199 | 733 | 9.0 |
| 25 years and over | 28,346 | 539 | 182 | 721 | 2.5 |
| 16 years and over | 36,457 | 1,073 | 381 | 1,454 | 4.0 |
| white (16 years and over) | 59,152 | 1,359 | 502 | 1,861 | 3.1 |
| black (16 years and over) | 10,014 | 183 | 114 | 297 | 3.0 |
| Hispanic (16 years and over) | 10,030 | 187 | 114 | 302 | 3.0 |
| | | | | | |
| **full- and part-time workers[2]** | | | | | |
| full-time | 55,232 | 662 | 191 | 853 | 1.5 |
| part-time | 17,124 | 937 | 441 | 1,378 | 8.0 |

[1]Data for racial groups other than the two listed are not included. Hispanics may be of any race and are included in both white and black population groups. For these reasons, data for the race/ethnic group category will not add up to total.    [2]Full- and part-time workers are distinguished by the number of hours worked. These data will not add up to total because of a small number of multiple jobholders whose full- or part-time status on the principal job is unknown.

# Comparative Hourly Compensation Costs

*The table shows private-industry employer compensation costs per hour worked by an employee in December 2002. Sums may not add to totals due to rounding. Source: US Bureau of Labor Statistics.*

| COMPENSATION | ALL WORKERS COST ($) | (%) | GOODS-PRODUCING WORKERS[1] COST ($) | (%) | SERVICE WORKERS[2] COST ($) | (%) |
|---|---|---|---|---|---|---|
| **wages and salaries** | 16.08 | 72.6 | 17.72 | 68.5 | 15.62 | 74.0 |
| | | | | | | |
| **paid leave** | 1.47 | 6.6 | 1.70 | 6.6 | 1.41 | 6.7 |
| vacation | 0.74 | 3.3 | 0.87 | 3.4 | 0.70 | 3.3 |
| holiday | 0.50 | 2.3 | 0.61 | 2.4 | 0.47 | 2.2 |
| sick | 0.17 | 0.8 | 0.13 | 0.5 | 0.18 | 0.9 |
| other | 0.06 | 0.3 | 0.08 | 0.3 | 0.06 | 0.3 |
| | | | | | | |
| **supplemental pay** | 0.61 | 2.8 | 1.09 | 4.2 | 0.48 | 2.3 |
| premium[3] | 0.24 | 1.1 | 0.55 | 2.1 | 0.16 | 0.8 |
| shift differentials | 0.06 | 0.3 | 0.08 | 0.3 | 0.05 | 0.2 |
| nonproduction bonuses | 0.31 | 1.4 | 0.46 | 1.8 | 0.27 | 1.3 |
| | | | | | | |
| **insurance** | 1.46 | 6.6 | 2.08 | 8.0 | 1.29 | 6.1 |
| life | 0.04 | 0.2 | 0.06 | 0.2 | 0.04 | 0.2 |
| health | 1.35 | 6.1 | 1.91 | 7.4 | 1.19 | 5.6 |
| short-term disability | 0.04 | 0.2 | 0.07 | 0.3 | 0.03 | 0.1 |
| long-term disability | 0.03 | 0.1 | 0.03 | 0.1 | 0.03 | 0.1 |
| | | | | | | |
| **retirement and savings** | 0.64 | 2.9 | 0.91 | 3.5 | 0.57 | 2.7 |
| defined benefit | 0.22 | 1.0 | 0.45 | 1.7 | 0.16 | 0.8 |
| defined contribution | 0.42 | 1.9 | 0.46 | 1.8 | 0.41 | 1.9 |

## Comparative Hourly Compensation Costs (continued)

| COMPENSATION | ALL WORKERS COST ($) | ALL WORKERS (%) | GOODS-PRODUCING WORKERS[1] COST ($) | GOODS-PRODUCING WORKERS[1] (%) | SERVICE WORKERS[2] COST ($) | SERVICE WORKERS[2] (%) |
|---|---|---|---|---|---|---|
| legally required benefits | 1.85 | 8.4 | 2.33 | 9.0 | 1.72 | 8.1 |
| Social Security[4] | 1.34 | 6.1 | 1.51 | 5.8 | 1.30 | 6.2 |
| Old-Age, Survivors, and Disability Insurance (OASDI) | 1.08 | 4.9 | 1.22 | 4.7 | 1.04 | 4.9 |
| Medicare | 0.26 | 1.2 | 0.29 | 1.1 | 0.26 | 1.2 |
| federal unemployment insurance | 0.03 | 0.1 | 0.03 | 0.1 | 0.03 | 0.1 |
| state unemployment insurance | 0.10 | 0.5 | 0.12 | 0.5 | 0.09 | 0.4 |
| workers' compensation | 0.38 | 1.7 | 0.67 | 2.6 | 0.30 | 1.4 |
| other benefits[5] | 0.03 | 0.1 | 0.07 | 0.3 | 0.02 | 0.1 |
| total benefits | 6.07 | 27.4 | 8.17 | 31.6 | 5.49 | 26.0 |
| total compensation | 22.14 | 100.0 | 25.88 | 100.0 | 21.11 | 100.0 |

[1]Includes mining, construction, and manufacturing. [2]Includes transportation, communication, and public utilities; wholesale and retail trade; finance, insurance, and real estate; and service industries. [3]Pay for over-time, weekends, and holidays. [4]The total employer cost for Social Security comprises an OASDI portion and a Medicare portion. [5]Includes severance pay and supplemental unemployment benefits.

## Median Income by Educational and Social Variables

Table refers to people who worked full time throughout the year and are 15 years and over as of March of the following year. Median income dollar amounts are not adjusted for inflation. N/A means not available. Source: US Census Bureau.

| | median income ($) males 1980 | 1990 | 2000 | 2001 | median income ($) females 1980 | 1990 | 2000 | 2001 |
|---|---|---|---|---|---|---|---|---|
| **educational level[1]** | | | | | | | | |
| less than 9th grade | 7,444 | 16,880 | 20,638 | 21,361 | 3,527 | 11,637 | 16,123 | 16,691 |
| 9th to 12th grade (no diploma) | 11,536 | 20,994 | 25,171 | 26,209 | 4,252 | 13,538 | 17,982 | 19,156 |
| high-school graduate | 16,211 | 26,218 | 34,035 | 34,723 | 5,903 | 18,042 | 24,675 | 25,303 |
| some college, no degree | 19,504 | 31,034 | 40,029 | 41,045 | 8,257 | 21,328 | 28,964 | 30,418 |
| associate degree | N/A | 32,221 | 41,822 | 42,776 | N/A | 23,862 | 31,789 | 32,153 |
| bachelor's degree | 21,838 | 42,367 | 56,117 | 55,929 | 9,607 | 30,393 | 40,408 | 40,994 |
| master's degree | N/A | 47,002 | 68,569 | 70,899 | N/A | 33,122 | 49,899 | 50,669 |
| professional degree | N/A | 70,284 | 100,000[2] | 100,000 | N/A | 42,604 | 62,235 | 61,748 |
| doctorate degree | N/A | 54,626 | 78,092 | 86,965 | N/A | 40,172 | 60,733 | 62,123 |
| **race and origin[3,4]** | | | | | | | | |
| white | 19,720 | 30,081 | 40,253 | 40,790 | 11,703 | 20,839 | 29,951 | 30,849 |
| white (non-Hispanic) | N/A | N/A | 42,327 | 43,194 | N/A | N/A | 30,987 | 31,794 |
| black | 13,875 | 21,481 | 30,489 | 31,921 | 10,915 | 18,544 | 25,750 | 27,297 |
| Hispanic origin | 13,790 | 19,358 | 24,175 | 25,271 | 9,887 | 16,181 | 21,196 | 21,973 |
| **age[3]** | | | | | | | | |
| 15 to 24 years | N/A | 15,462 | 20,776 | 21,120 | N/A | 13,994 | 18,375 | 19,859 |
| 25 to 34 years | 17,724 | 25,355 | 33,182 | 34,521 | 12,190 | 20,184 | 28,564 | 29,721 |
| 35 to 44 years | 21,777 | 32,607 | 41,668 | 42,404 | 12,239 | 22,505 | 30,800 | 31,323 |
| 45 to 54 years | 22,323 | 35,732 | 46,830 | 46,657 | 12,116 | 21,938 | 31,813 | 32,661 |
| 55 to 64 years | 21,053 | 33,169 | 45,925 | 46,751 | 11,931 | 20,755 | 29,968 | 31,679 |
| 65 years and over | 17,307 | 35,520 | 48,543 | 47,326 | 12,342 | 22,957 | 34,503 | 35,098 |
| **all males / all females** | 19,173 | 28,979 | 38,891 | 40,136 | 11,591 | 20,591 | 29,123 | 30,420 |

[1]The income figures for the various educational levels are for workers 25 years old and over. Before 1991, the level of education categories used by the US Census Bureau differed from the categories presented in this table. Because of this, the 1980 figures for the median income by educational level are not completely com-parable with the figures for later years. The figures for 1980 median income by educational levels are for both part-time and full-time workers. The figures presented in the 1990 column for educational levels are actually for 1991, the first year the educational categories listed in this table were used by the US Census Bureau. [2]Any entry of $100,000 means the median is greater than $100,000. [3]Figures for the 1980 sections cover-ing "race and origin" and "age" are for civilian workers only. [4]Hispanic people may be of any race.

## The 20 US Metropolitan Areas with the Highest Average Annual Salaries

*Includes workers covered by two programs, Unemployment Insurance and Unemployment Compensation for Federal Employees. A minus sign indicates a decrease in the average annual salary. Source: US Bureau of Labor Statistics.*

| METROPOLITAN AREA | ANNUAL SALARY ($) 2000 | 2001 | SALARY CHANGE (%) | METROPOLITAN AREA | ANNUAL SALARY ($) 2000 | 2001 | SALARY CHANGE (%) |
|---|---|---|---|---|---|---|---|
| San Jose CA | 76,252 | 65,926 | -13.5 | Trenton NJ | 44,657 | 45,746 | 2.4 |
| San Francisco CA | 59,288 | 59,761 | 0.8 | Seattle WA[5] | 45,344 | 45,326 | 0.0 |
| New York NY | 57,213 | 58,963 | 3.1 | Bergen-Passaic NJ | 43,879 | 44,667 | 1.8 |
| New Haven CT[1] | 50,596 | 52,177 | 3.1 | Boulder-Longmont CO | 45,564 | 44,313 | -2.7 |
| Middlesex NJ[2] | 48,987 | 49,830 | 1.7 | Hartford CT | 42,421 | 43,882 | 3.4 |
| Newark NJ | 48,656 | 47,713 | -1.9 | Houston TX | 40,996 | 42,782 | 4.4 |
| Jersey City NJ | 47,429 | 47,621 | 0.4 | Dallas TX | 42,095 | 42,692 | 1.4 |
| Washington DC[3] | 45,374 | 47,584 | 4.9 | Chicago IL | 41,527 | 42,646 | 2.7 |
| Oakland CA | 44,207 | 45,944 | 3.9 | Detroit MI | 42,321 | 42,613 | 0.7 |
| Boston MA[4] | 45,021 | 45,768 | 1.7 | Denver CO | 41,401 | 42,348 | 2.3 |

[1]New Haven area includes Bridgeport, Stamford, Waterbury, and Danbury.   [2]Middlesex area includes Somerset and Hunterdon.   [3]Washington DC entry includes areas in Maryland, Virginia, and West Virginia.   [4]Boston area includes Worcester, Lawrence, Lowell, and Brockton.   [5]Seattle area includes Bellevue and Everett.

## US Federal Minimum Wage Rates

*The table shows the actual minimum wage for the year in question (since 1950) and the value of that minimum wage adjusted for inflation in the year 2003. Source: US Bureau of Labor Statistics.*

| YEAR | minimum wage DOLLARS | 2003 DOLLARS | YEAR | minimum wage DOLLARS | 2003 DOLLARS | YEAR | minimum wage DOLLARS | 2003 DOLLARS |
|---|---|---|---|---|---|---|---|---|
| 1950 | 0.75 | 5.72 | 1968 | 1.60 | 8.45 | 1986 | 3.35 | 5.62 |
| 1951 | 0.75 | 5.30 | 1969 | 1.60 | 8.01 | 1987 | 3.35 | 5.42 |
| 1952 | 0.75 | 5.20 | 1970 | 1.60 | 7.58 | 1988 | 3.35 | 5.20 |
| 1953 | 0.75 | 5.16 | 1971 | 1.60 | 7.26 | 1989 | 3.35 | 4.97 |
| 1954 | 0.75 | 5.12 | 1972 | 1.60 | 7.04 | 1990 | 3.80 | 5.34 |
| 1955 | 0.75 | 5.14 | 1973 | 1.60 | 6.62 | 1991 | 4.25 | 5.74 |
| 1956 | 1.00 | 6.76 | 1974 | 2.00 | 7.46 | 1992 | 4.25 | 5.57 |
| 1957 | 1.00 | 6.54 | 1975 | 2.10 | 7.17 | 1993 | 4.25 | 5.41 |
| 1958 | 1.00 | 6.36 | 1976 | 2.30 | 7.43 | 1994 | 4.25 | 5.27 |
| 1959 | 1.00 | 6.32 | 1977 | 2.30 | 6.98 | 1995 | 4.25 | 5.13 |
| 1960 | 1.00 | 6.21 | 1978 | 2.65 | 7.47 | 1996 | 4.75 | 5.56 |
| 1961 | 1.15 | 7.07 | 1979 | 2.90 | 7.34 | 1997 | 5.15 | 5.90 |
| 1962 | 1.15 | 7.00 | 1980 | 3.10 | 6.91 | 1998 | 5.15 | 5.81 |
| 1963 | 1.25 | 7.51 | 1981 | 3.35 | 6.77 | 1999 | 5.15 | 5.68 |
| 1964 | 1.25 | 7.41 | 1982 | 3.35 | 6.38 | 2000 | 5.15 | 5.50 |
| 1965 | 1.25 | 7.29 | 1983 | 3.35 | 6.18 | 2001 | 5.15 | 5.34 |
| 1966 | 1.25 | 7.09 | 1984 | 3.35 | 5.93 | 2002 | 5.15 | 5.26 |
| 1967 | 1.40 | 7.70 | 1985 | 3.35 | 5.72 | 2003 | 5.15 | 5.15 |

## US Civilian Federal Employment

*Source: US Office of Personnel Management.*

| AGENCY[1] | 1970 | 1980 | 1990 | 2000 | 2001 |
|---|---|---|---|---|---|
| executive departments | 1,772,363 | 1,716,970 | 2,065,542 | 1,592,200 | 1,603,426 |
| State | 40,042 | 23,497 | 25,288 | 27,983 | 28,122 |
| Treasury | 90,683 | 124,663 | 158,655 | 143,508 | 148,186 |
| Defense | 1,169,173 | 960,116 | 1,034,152 | 676,268 | 671,591 |
| Justice | 40,075 | 56,327 | 83,932 | 125,970 | 127,783 |
| Interior | 71,671 | 77,357 | 77,679 | 73,818 | 75,846 |
| Agriculture | 114,309 | 129,139 | 122,594 | 104,466 | 108,540 |
| Commerce | 36,124 | 48,563 | 69,920 | 47,652 | 40,289 |
| Labor | 10,928 | 23,400 | 17,727 | 16,040 | 16,376 |
| Health & Human Services (HHS) | 110,186 | 155,662 | 123,959 | 62,605 | 64,343 |
| Housing & Urban Development | 15,046 | 16,964 | 13,596 | 10,319 | 10,178 |
| Transportation | 66,970 | 72,361 | 67,364 | 63,598 | 65,542 |
| Energy | 7,156 | 21,557 | 17,731 | 15,692 | 16,054 |
| Education | 0 | 7,364 | 4,771 | 4,734 | 4,683 |
| Veterans Affairs (formerly Veterans Administration) | 169,241 | 228,285 | 248,174 | 219,547 | 225,893 |

## US Civilian Federal Employment (continued)

| AGENCY[1] | 1970 | 1980 | 1990 | 2000 | 2001 |
|---|---|---|---|---|---|
| **independent agencies[2]** | | | | | |
| Board of Governors of the Federal Reserve System | N/A | N/A | 1,525 | 1,644 | 1,680 |
| Commodity Futures Trading Commission | N/A | N/A | 542 | 574 | 551 |
| Consumer Product Safety Commission | N/A | N/A | 520 | 479 | 479 |
| Environmental Protection Agency | 0 | 14,715 | 17,123 | 18,036 | 18,095 |
| Equal Employment Opportunity Commission | 797 | 3,515 | 2,880 | 2,780 | 2,910 |
| Federal Communications Commission | N/A | N/A | 1,778 | 1,965 | 2,004 |
| Federal Deposit Insurance Corporation | 2,462 | 3,520 | 17,641 | 6,958 | 6,402 |
| Federal Emergency Management Agency (FEMA) | 0 | 3,427 | 3,137 | 4,813 | 6,147 |
| Federal Trade Commission | N/A | N/A | 988 | 1,019 | 1,052 |
| General Services Administration[3] | 37,661 | 37,654 | 20,277 | 14,334 | 14,016 |
| National Archives & Records Administration | N/A | N/A | 3,120 | 2,702 | 2,878 |
| National Aeronautics & Space Administration | 30,674 | 23,714 | 24,872 | 18,819 | 18,918 |
| National Labor Relations Board | N/A | N/A | 2,263 | 2,054 | 2,110 |
| National Science Foundation | N/A | N/A | 1,318 | 1,247 | 1,287 |
| Nuclear Regulatory Commission | 0 | 3,283 | 3,353 | 2,858 | 2,871 |
| Office of Personnel Management | 5,513 | 8,280 | 6,636 | 3,780 | 3,349 |
| Peace Corps | N/A | N/A | 1,178 | 1,065 | 1,019 |
| Securities & Exchange Commission | N/A | N/A | 2,302 | 2,955 | 3,049 |
| Small Business Administration | 4,397 | 5,804 | 5,128 | 4,150 | 4,219 |
| Smithsonian Institution | 2,547 | 4,403 | 5,092 | 5,065 | 4,981 |
| Social Security Administration | N/A | N/A | N/A[4] | 64,474 | 65,351 |
| Tennessee Valley Authority | 23,785 | 51,714 | 28,392 | 13,145 | 13,430 |
| US Information Agency | 10,156 | 8,138 | 8,555 | 2,436 | 2,372 |
| US Postal Service | 721,183 | 660,014 | 816,886 | 860,726 | 847,821 |
| legislative branch total | 29,939 | 39,710 | 37,495 | 31,157 | 30,439 |
| judicial branch | 6,879 | 15,178 | 23,605 | 32,186 | 33,810 |
| executive branch total | 2,829,495 | 2,820,978 | 3,067,167 | 2,644,758 | 2,645,707 |
| **total, all agencies** | **2,866,313** | **2,875,866** | **3,128,267** | **2,798,101** | **2,709,956** |

*N/A means not available.* [1]*Includes other branches or agencies not shown separately. The Office of Homeland Security was created by an executive order of Pres. George W. Bush after the terrorist attacks of 11 Sep 2001. On 24 Jan 2003 the Department of Homeland Security, a cabinet-level agency within the executive branch of government, replaced the Office of Homeland Security. In the largest US governmental reorganization since World War II, the new department acquired 22 security-related agencies. Prior to this reorganization, the agencies had been administered by other governmental entities or, in FEMA's case, had been an independent agency.* [2]*The Defense Intelligence Agency was excluded as of November 1984, the National Imagery and Mapping Agency as of October 1996. Entries for 1990, 2000, and 2001 exclude the Central Intelligence Agency and the National Security Agency.* [3]*Entry for 1980 includes the National Archives and Records Administration, which became an independent agency in 1985.* [4]*Included with HHS.*

## Older Americans in the Workforce

*All numbers are in thousands ('000). Numbers may not add up to totals due to rounding.*
*Source: US Census Bureau.*

| | WORKFORCE BY AGE | | | | | | | |
|---|---|---|---|---|---|---|---|---|
| | 55 AND OVER | | 55–59 | | 60–64 | | 65 AND OLDER | |
| GENDER AND OCCUPATION TYPE | NUMBER | % | NUMBER | % | NUMBER | % | NUMBER | % |
| **men and women** | | | | | | | | |
| managerial and professional | 6,651 | 33.4 | 3,590 | 36.3 | 1,731 | 32 | 1,241 | 28.6 |
| technical, sales, and administrative support | 5,668 | 28.9 | 2,720 | 27.5 | 1,608 | 29.7 | 1,340 | 30.9 |
| service occupations | 2,525 | 12.9 | 1,130 | 11.4 | 733 | 13.6 | 662 | 15.3 |
| precision production, craft, and repair | 1,820 | 9.3 | 1,044 | 10.6 | 488 | 9 | 288 | 6.6 |
| operators, fabricators, and laborers | 2,344 | 11.9 | 1,163 | 11.8 | 680 | 12.6 | 501 | 11.6 |
| farming, forestry, and fishing | 700 | 3.6 | 233 | 2.4 | 169 | 3.1 | 299 | 6.9 |
| total | **19,708** | **100** | **9,880** | **100** | **5,409** | **100** | **4,331** | **100** |
| | | | | | | | | |
| **men** | | | | | | | | |
| managerial and professional | 3,701 | 34.9 | 1,868 | 35.7 | 1,025 | 35.8 | 808 | 32.3 |
| technical, sales, and administrative support | 2,072 | 19.5 | 984 | 18.8 | 541 | 18.9 | 546 | 21.9 |
| service occupations | 938 | 8.9 | 387 | 7.4 | 273 | 9.5 | 278 | 11.1 |

## Older Americans in the Workforce (continued)

| GENDER AND OCCUPATION TYPE | WORKFORCE BY AGE | | | | | | | |
|---|---|---|---|---|---|---|---|---|
| | 55 AND OVER | | 55–59 | | 60–64 | | 65 AND OLDER | |
| | NUMBER | % | NUMBER | % | NUMBER | % | NUMBER | % |
| men (continued) | | | | | | | | |
| precision production, craft, and repair | 1,633 | 15.4 | 956 | 18.3 | 427 | 14.9 | 250 | 10 |
| operators, fabricators, and laborers | 1,731 | 16.3 | 859 | 16.4 | 477 | 16.7 | 395 | 15.8 |
| farming, forestry, and fishing | 523 | 4.9 | 183 | 3.5 | 118 | 4.1 | 221 | 8.9 |
| total | 10,598 | 100 | 5,237 | 100 | 2,861 | 100 | 2,498 | 100 |
| | | | | | | | | |
| women | | | | | | | | |
| managerial and professional | 2,860 | 31.7 | 1,722 | 37.1 | 705 | 27.7 | 432 | 23.6 |
| technical, sales, and administrative support | 3,596 | 39.9 | 1,736 | 37.4 | 1,066 | 41.9 | 794 | 43.3 |
| service occupations | 1,587 | 17.6 | 743 | 16 | 461 | 18.1 | 384 | 20.9 |
| precision production, craft, and repair | 187 | 2.1 | 87 | 1.9 | 61 | 2.4 | 38 | 2.1 |
| operators, fabricators, and laborers | 613 | 6.8 | 304 | 6.5 | 203 | 8 | 107 | 5.8 |
| farming, forestry, and fishing | 177 | 2 | 49 | 1.1 | 51 | 2 | 78 | 4.2 |
| total | 9,020 | 100 | 4,641 | 100 | 2,547 | 100 | 1,833 | 100 |

## Strikes and Lockouts in the US

Strikes and lockouts are referred to as work stoppages by the Bureau of Labor Statistics. This table covers work stoppages since 1950 involving 1,000 workers or more. The number of workers and stoppages are for stoppages begun during that year. The number of days out from work pertains to all strikes or lockouts in effect during the year, whether they began in that year or not. The heading for estimated working time includes all workers except those employed in private households, forestry, or fisheries. Source: US Bureau of Labor Statistics.

| | strikes and lockouts | | work time lost | | | strikes and lockouts | | work time lost | |
|---|---|---|---|---|---|---|---|---|---|
| YEAR | NUMBER | WORKERS INVOLVED ('000) | DAYS LOST ('000) | % OF WORKING TIME | YEAR | NUMBER | WORKERS INVOLVED ('000) | DAYS LOST ('000) | % OF WORKING TIME |
| 1950 | 424 | 1,698 | 30,390 | 0.26 | 1977 | 298 | 1,212 | 21,258 | 0.10 |
| 1951 | 415 | 1,462 | 15,070 | 0.12 | 1978 | 219 | 1,006 | 23,774 | 0.11 |
| 1952 | 470 | 2,746 | 48,820 | 0.38 | 1979 | 235 | 1,021 | 20,409 | 0.09 |
| 1953 | 437 | 1,623 | 18,130 | 0.14 | 1980 | 187 | 795 | 20,844 | 0.09 |
| 1954 | 265 | 1,075 | 16,630 | 0.13 | 1981 | 145 | 729 | 16,908 | 0.07 |
| 1955 | 363 | 2,055 | 21,180 | 0.16 | 1982 | 96 | 656 | 9,061 | 0.04 |
| 1956 | 287 | 1,370 | 26,840 | 0.20 | 1983 | 81 | 909 | 17,461 | 0.08 |
| 1957 | 279 | 887 | 10,340 | 0.07 | 1984 | 62 | 376 | 8,499 | 0.04 |
| 1958 | 332 | 1,587 | 17,900 | 0.13 | 1985 | 54 | 324 | 7,079 | 0.03 |
| 1959 | 245 | 1,381 | 60,850 | 0.43 | 1986 | 69 | 533 | 11,861 | 0.05 |
| 1960 | 222 | 896 | 13,260 | 0.09 | 1987 | 46 | 174 | 4,481 | 0.02 |
| 1961 | 195 | 1,031 | 10,140 | 0.07 | 1988 | 40 | 118 | 4,381 | 0.02 |
| 1962 | 211 | 793 | 11,760 | 0.08 | 1989 | 51 | 452 | 16,996 | 0.07 |
| 1963 | 181 | 512 | 10,020 | 0.07 | 1990 | 44 | 185 | 5,926 | 0.02 |
| 1964 | 246 | 1,183 | 16,220 | 0.11 | 1991 | 40 | 392 | 4,584 | 0.02 |
| 1965 | 268 | 999 | 15,140 | 0.10 | 1992 | 35 | 364 | 3,989 | 0.01 |
| 1966 | 321 | 1,300 | 16,000 | 0.10 | 1993 | 35 | 182 | 3,981 | 0.01 |
| 1967 | 381 | 2,192 | 31,320 | 0.18 | 1994 | 45 | 322 | 5,021 | 0.02 |
| 1968 | 392 | 1,855 | 35,367 | 0.20 | 1995 | 31 | 192 | 5,771 | 0.02 |
| 1969 | 412 | 1,576 | 29,397 | 0.16 | 1996 | 37 | 273 | 4,889 | 0.02 |
| 1970 | 381 | 2,468 | 52,761 | 0.29 | 1997 | 29 | 339 | 4,497 | 0.01 |
| 1971 | 298 | 2,516 | 35,538 | 0.19 | 1998 | 34 | 387 | 5,116 | 0.02 |
| 1972 | 250 | 975 | 16,764 | 0.09 | 1999 | 17 | 73 | 1,996 | 0.01 |
| 1973 | 317 | 1,400 | 16,260 | 0.08 | 2000 | 39 | 394 | 20,419 | 0.06 |
| 1974 | 424 | 1,796 | 31,809 | 0.16 | 2001 | 29 | 99 | 1,151 | 0.00 |
| 1975 | 235 | 965 | 17,563 | 0.09 | 2002 | 19 | 46 | 6,596 | 0.00 |
| 1976 | 231 | 1,519 | 23,962 | 0.12 | | | | | |

**Did you know?** Even though Walt Disney himself sported a mustache, no Disney theme park employee was allowed to wear a mustache until 2000. Beards, goatees, tattoos, and body piercings are still prohibited in the theme-park grooming code.

## US Trade Union Membership

*Numbers are in thousands ('000). N/A means not available. Source: US Bureau of Labor Statistics.*

| YEAR | NUMBER OF UNION MEMBERS | % OF TOTAL LABOR FORCE | YEAR | NUMBER OF UNION MEMBERS | % OF TOTAL LABOR FORCE | YEAR | NUMBER OF UNION MEMBERS | % OF TOTAL LABOR FORCE |
|---|---|---|---|---|---|---|---|---|
| 1900[1] | 791 | N/A | 1940 | 8,717 | 26.9 | 1980 | 20,095 | 23.0 |
| 1905 | 1,918 | N/A | 1945 | 14,322 | 35.5 | 1985 | 16,996 | 18.0 |
| 1910 | 2,116 | N/A | 1950 | 14,300[3] | 31.5 | 1990 | 16,740 | 16.1 |
| 1915 | 2,560 | N/A | 1955 | 16,802 | 33.2 | 1995 | 16,360 | 14.9 |
| 1920 | 5,034 | N/A | 1960 | 17,049 | 31.4 | 2000 | 16,258 | 13.5 |
| 1925 | 3,566 | N/A | 1965 | 17,299 | 28.4 | 2001 | 16,387 | 13.4 |
| 1930[2] | 3,401 | 11.6 | 1970 | 19,381 | 27.4 | 2002 | 16,107 | 13.2 |
| 1935 | 3,584 | 13.2 | 1977[4] | 19,335 | 23.8 | | | |

[1]Data from 1900 to 1925 include Canadian members whose union headquarters were in the US.   [2]Agricultural workers were not included as part of the total labor force for the years from 1930 to 1970.   [3]Rounded to nearest hundred thousand.   [4]Data for 1975 were not available. Data for 1977 on include only employed union members.

## US Unemployment Rates

*Unemployment rates of the civilian labor force 16 years and older. Source: US Bureau of Labor Statistics.*

| YEAR | UNEMPLOYMENT RATE (%) | YEAR | UNEMPLOYMENT RATE (%) | YEAR | UNEMPLOYMENT RATE (%) | YEAR | UNEMPLOYMENT RATE (%) |
|---|---|---|---|---|---|---|---|
| 1947 | 3.9 | 1961 | 6.7 | 1975 | 8.5 | 1989 | 5.3 |
| 1948 | 3.8 | 1962 | 5.5 | 1976 | 7.7 | 1990 | 5.6 |
| 1949 | 5.9 | 1963 | 5.7 | 1977 | 7.1 | 1991 | 6.8 |
| 1950 | 5.3 | 1964 | 5.2 | 1978 | 6.1 | 1992 | 7.5 |
| 1951 | 3.3 | 1965 | 4.5 | 1979 | 5.8 | 1993 | 6.9 |
| 1952 | 3.0 | 1966 | 3.8 | 1980 | 7.1 | 1994 | 6.1 |
| 1953 | 2.9 | 1967 | 3.8 | 1981 | 7.6 | 1995 | 5.6 |
| 1954 | 5.5 | 1968 | 3.6 | 1982 | 9.7 | 1996 | 5.4 |
| 1955 | 4.4 | 1969 | 3.5 | 1983 | 9.6 | 1997 | 4.9 |
| 1956 | 4.1 | 1970 | 4.9 | 1984 | 7.5 | 1998 | 4.5 |
| 1957 | 4.3 | 1971 | 5.9 | 1985 | 7.2 | 1999 | 4.2 |
| 1958 | 6.8 | 1972 | 5.6 | 1986 | 7.0 | 2000 | 4.0 |
| 1959 | 5.5 | 1973 | 4.9 | 1987 | 6.2 | 2001 | 4.7 |
| 1960 | 5.5 | 1974 | 5.6 | 1988 | 5.5 | 2002 | 5.8 |

## Social Characteristics of the Unemployed in the US

*Unemployment as a percent of the civilian labor force. N/A means not available.*
*Source: US Bureau of Labor Statistics.*

| SOCIAL CHARACTERISTICS | UNEMPLOYMENT RATES BY YEAR (%) | | | | | | | |
|---|---|---|---|---|---|---|---|---|
| | 1975 | 1980 | 1985 | 1990 | 1995 | 2000 | 2001 | 2002 |
| age (both sexes) | | | | | | | | |
| 16–19 | 19.9 | 17.8 | 18.6 | 15.5 | 17.3 | 13.1 | 14.7 | 16.5 |
| 25 and over | 6.0 | 5.1 | 5.6 | 4.4 | 4.3 | 3.0 | 3.7 | N/A |
| sex (20 years and older) | | | | | | | | |
| men | 6.8 | 5.9 | 6.2 | 5.0 | 4.8 | 3.3 | 4.2 | 5.3 |
| women | 8.0 | 6.4 | 6.6 | 4.9 | 4.9 | 3.6 | 4.1 | 5.1 |
| race/ethnicity | | | | | | | | |
| white | 7.8 | 6.3 | 6.2 | 4.8 | 4.9 | 3.5 | 4.2 | 5.1 |
| black | 14.8 | 14.3 | 15.1 | 11.4 | 10.4 | 7.6 | 8.6 | 10.2 |
| Hispanic[1] | 12.2 | 10.1 | 10.5 | 8.2 | 9.3 | 5.7 | 6.6 | 7.5 |
| family | | | | | | | | |
| women who maintain families | 10.0 | 9.2 | 10.4 | 8.3 | 8.0 | 5.9 | 6.6 | N/A |
| married men, spouse present | 5.1 | 4.2 | 4.3 | 3.4 | 3.3 | 2.0 | 2.7 | N/A |
| overall unemployment | 8.5 | 7.1 | 7.2 | 5.6 | 5.6 | 4.0 | 4.7 | 5.8 |

[1]Hispanics may be of any race and are included in both the white and black racial categories in this table.

# US Unemployment Rates by Occupation

Unemployment rates are for the civilian noninstitutional population aged 16 years and older. Rates represent unemployment as a percent of the labor force for each occupational group. The unemployment rate totals include people without previous work experience and those whose last job was in the military. Data are not strictly comparable across the years. Source: US Bureau of Labor Statistics.

| | UNEMPLOYMENT RATES (%) | | | | |
|---|---|---|---|---|---|
| OCCUPATION | 1990 | 1995 | 2000 | 2001 | 2002 |
| **managerial and professional specialty** | 2.1 | 2.4 | 1.7 | 2.3 | 3.1 |
| executive, administrative, and managerial | 2.3 | 2.4 | 1.8 | 2.4 | 3.4 |
| professional specialty | 2.0 | 2.5 | 1.7 | 2.2 | 2.8 |
| **technical, sales, and administrative support** | 4.3 | 4.5 | 3.6 | 4.2 | 5.2 |
| technicians and related support | 2.9 | 2.8 | 2.2 | 2.9 | 3.7 |
| sales occupations | 4.8 | 5.0 | 4.0 | 4.7 | 5.8 |
| administrative support (including clerical) | 4.1 | 4.3 | 3.5 | 4.0 | 5.1 |
| **service occupations** | 6.6 | 7.5 | 5.3 | 5.9 | 6.7 |
| private household | 5.6 | 10.7 | 6.9 | 6.9 | 7.7 |
| protective service | 3.6 | 3.7 | 2.6 | 2.9 | 3.8 |
| service (except private household and protective) | 7.1 | 7.9 | 5.6 | 6.3 | 7.1 |
| **precision production, craft, and repair** | 5.9 | 6.0 | 3.6 | 4.6 | 6.1 |
| mechanics and repairers | 3.8 | 4.0 | 2.6 | 3.1 | 4.5 |
| construction trades | 8.5 | 9.0 | 4.9 | 5.9 | 7.5 |
| other precision production, craft, and repair | 4.7 | 4.2 | 2.8 | 4.2 | 5.8 |
| **operators, fabricators, and laborers** | 8.7 | 8.2 | 6.3 | 7.7 | 8.9 |
| machine operators, assemblers, inspectors | 8.1 | 7.4 | 5.9 | 7.8 | 8.8 |
| transportation and material moving occupations | 6.3 | 6.0 | 4.4 | 5.0 | 6.1 |
| handlers, equipment cleaners, helpers, and laborers | 11.6 | 11.7 | 8.7 | 10.3 | 11.8 |
| construction laborers | 18.1 | 18.7 | 11.6 | 13.1 | 14.1 |
| other handlers, equipment cleaners, helpers and laborers | N/A | N/A | N/A | 13.1 | 11.2 |
| **farming, forestry, and fishing** | 6.4 | 7.9 | 6.0 | 7.4 | 7.3 |
| **total** | 5.6 | 5.6 | 4.0 | 4.8 | 5.8 |

# Occupational Illnesses and Injuries in the US

This table displays the number of nonfatal work injuries and illnesses recorded in 2001. The injuries and illnesses resulted in days away from work in the private industries listed. Numbers may not add to totals because of rounding and nonclassifiable responses. Numbers are in thousands ('000). N/A means not available. Source: US Bureau of Labor Statistics.

| | | GOODS PRODUCING | | | |
|---|---|---|---|---|---|
| CHARACTERISTIC | PRIVATE INDUSTRY[1] | AGRICULTURE, FORESTRY, FISHING[1] | MINING[2] | CONSTRUCTION | MANU-FACTURING |
| **injury or illness** | | | | | |
| sprains, strains | 669.9 | 13.8 | 4.0 | 71.2 | 123.0 |
| bruises, contusions | 136.4 | 4.0 | 1.1 | 12.7 | 25.5 |
| cuts, lacerations | 114.8 | 4.0 | 0.7 | 21.8 | 27.9 |
| fractures | 108.1 | 3.3 | 1.5 | 19.8 | 22.5 |
| heat burns | 25.1 | 0.1 | 0.1 | 2.5 | 4.7 |
| carpal tunnel syndrome | 26.8 | 0.2 | 0.1 | 1.2 | 11.2 |
| tendinitis | 14.1 | 0.2 | —[3] | 1.2 | 5.6 |
| chemical burns | 9.5 | 0.2 | —[3] | 1.0 | 3.0 |
| amputations | 8.6 | 0.4 | 0.1 | 0.9 | 4.2 |
| multiple traumatic injuries | 53.2 | 1.8 | 0.6 | 6.3 | 10.2 |
| **body part affected by injury or illness** | | | | | |
| head | 99.5 | 3.4 | 0.6 | 13.8 | 22.8 |
| eye | 44.8 | 1.7 | 0.3 | 7.7 | 13.9 |
| neck | 27.1 | 0.4 | 0.2 | 2.3 | 4.6 |
| trunk | 561.6 | 13.6 | 3.5 | 60.9 | 108.3 |
| shoulder | 88.5 | 1.8 | 0.6 | 9.4 | 20.3 |
| back | 372.7 | 8.8 | 2.0 | 39.0 | 66.4 |
| upper extremities | 355.3 | 9.6 | 2.4 | 46.0 | 99.8 |
| wrist | 78.9 | 1.0 | 0.4 | 7.1 | 22.4 |
| hand, except finger | 63.7 | 2.5 | 0.5 | 9.9 | 15.2 |
| finger | 123.5 | 3.8 | 1.1 | 19.3 | 40.2 |

## Occupational Illnesses and Injuries in the US (continued)

| | | GOODS PRODUCING | | | |
| CHARACTERISTIC | PRIVATE INDUSTRY[1] | AGRICULTURE, FORESTRY, FISHING[1] | MINING[2] | CONSTRUCTION | MANU-FACTURING |
|---|---|---|---|---|---|
| **body part affected by injury or illness (continued)** | | | | | |
| lower extremities | 323.0 | 9.2 | 2.8 | 44.8 | 56.8 |
| knee | 119.7 | 2.5 | 1.1 | 15.6 | 21.2 |
| foot, except toe | 51.7 | 1.9 | 0.4 | 8.1 | 10.4 |
| toe | 16.4 | 0.5 | 0.1 | 2.2 | 3.6 |
| body systems | 21.7 | 0.4 | 0.1 | 2.3 | 3.8 |
| multiple parts | 139.7 | 3.2 | 0.9 | 14.6 | 20.0 |
| | | | | | |
| **source of injury or illness** | | | | | |
| chemicals and chemical products | 25.1 | 0.5 | 0.9 | 2.0 | 7.1 |
| containers | 209.1 | 3.3 | 0.5 | 8.1 | 41.7 |
| furniture and fixtures | 54.0 | 0.3 | 0.1 | 2.9 | 8.8 |
| machinery | 97.6 | 3.0 | 1.1 | 11.9 | 36.9 |
| parts and materials | 162.5 | 2.9 | 1.9 | 44.1 | 55.4 |
| worker motion or position | 245.9 | 5.6 | 0.6 | 25.8 | 64.5 |
| floors, walkways, ground surfaces | 264.7 | 5.8 | 1.8 | 34.3 | 34.6 |
| tools, instruments, and equipment | 96.6 | 3.7 | 0.7 | 20.9 | 19.5 |
| vehicles | 128.5 | 3.2 | 0.8 | 10.3 | 15.2 |
| health care patient | 67.6 | N/A | N/A | N/A | N/A |
| | | | | | |
| **exposure or event leading to injury or illness** | | | | | |
| contact with objects and equipment | 400.0 | 13.4 | 4.4 | 63.9 | 105.0 |
| struck by object | 199.9 | 7.0 | 2.5 | 35.6 | 45.8 |
| struck against object | 101.2 | 2.6 | 0.9 | 13.9 | 23.0 |
| caught in equipment or object | 67.3 | 2.2 | 1.0 | 7.9 | 27.4 |
| fall to lower level | 96.4 | 3.0 | 0.9 | 23.8 | 11.9 |
| fall on same level | 182.6 | 3.2 | 0.9 | 13.8 | 25.0 |
| slip, trip, loss of balance—without fall | 50.3 | 1.3 | 0.1 | 5.9 | 9.2 |
| overexertion | 409.0 | 7.1 | 2.8 | 38.5 | 80.6 |
| overexertion in lifting | 227.3 | 4.2 | 1.0 | 20.5 | 43.0 |
| repetitive motion | 65.2 | 0.7 | 0.1 | 3.7 | 28.6 |
| exposure to harmful substances | 68.3 | 1.5 | 0.4 | 6.2 | 16.1 |
| transportation accidents | 66.8 | 2.0 | 0.3 | 6.8 | 6.2 |
| fires and explosions | 3.7 | —[3] | —[3] | 0.8 | 0.5 |
| assaults and violent acts by person | 17.2 | N/A | —[3] | 0.2 | 0.4 |
| **Total cases** | **1,537.6** | **40.2** | **10.6** | **185.7** | **317.3** |

| | | SERVICE PRODUCING | | | |
| CHARACTERISTIC | TRANSPORTATION AND PUBLIC UTILITIES[2] | WHOLE-SALE TRADE | RETAIL TRADE | FINANCE, INSURANCE, REAL ESTATE | SERVICES |
|---|---|---|---|---|---|
| **injury or illness** | | | | | |
| sprains, strains | 96.8 | 52.3 | 113.7 | 14.9 | 180.2 |
| bruises, contusions | 18.7 | 11.5 | 27.7 | 2.8 | 32.4 |
| cuts, lacerations | 8.4 | 7.2 | 26.7 | 2.3 | 15.8 |
| fractures | 13.8 | 7.2 | 15.3 | 3.0 | 21.8 |
| heat burns | 1.1 | 0.9 | 10.1 | 0.2 | 5.3 |
| carpal tunnel syndrome | 1.7 | 1.7 | 3.4 | 2.2 | 5.1 |
| tendinitis | 1.1 | 1.0 | 2.0 | 0.6 | 2.4 |
| chemical burns | 0.8 | 0.4 | 1.7 | 0.1 | 2.0 |
| amputations | 0.3 | 0.6 | 1.3 | —[3] | 0.7 |
| multiple traumatic injuries | 7.9 | 4.0 | 7.8 | 1.6 | 13.0 |
| | | | | | |
| **body part affected by injury or illness** | | | | | |
| head | 11.7 | 6.0 | 16.4 | 2.7 | 22.0 |
| eye | 3.9 | 2.7 | 6.3 | 0.5 | 7.7 |
| neck | 3.9 | 2.0 | 4.1 | 0.5 | 9.1 |
| trunk | 78.2 | 46.4 | 93.6 | 11.2 | 146.0 |
| shoulder | 13.6 | 7.1 | 13.6 | 1.6 | 20.6 |
| back | 50.8 | 30.4 | 64.5 | 7.6 | 103.3 |
| upper extremities | 32.6 | 22.3 | 67.7 | 9.1 | 65.9 |
| wrist | 7.1 | 4.5 | 13.6 | 4.0 | 18.9 |
| hand, except finger | 5.4 | 3.9 | 14.7 | 1.2 | 10.6 |
| finger | 9.2 | 7.8 | 22.4 | 1.6 | 18.2 |

# Occupational Illnesses and Injuries in the US (continued)

| | SERVICE PRODUCING | | | | |
| CHARACTERISTIC | TRANSPORTATION AND PUBLIC UTILITIES[2] | WHOLE-SALE TRADE | RETAIL TRADE | FINANCE, INSURANCE, REAL ESTATE | SERVICES |
|---|---|---|---|---|---|
| **body part affected by injury or illness (continued)** | | | | | |
| lower extremities | 49.4 | 24.4 | 55.3 | 8.4 | 71.9 |
| knee | 17.9 | 8.4 | 20.9 | 2.9 | 29.2 |
| foot, except toe | 6.5 | 4.1 | 8.4 | 1.4 | 10.6 |
| toe | 1.7 | 1.9 | 3.4 | 0.2 | 2.8 |
| body systems | 2.7 | 0.8 | 3.0 | 1.3 | 7.1 |
| multiple parts | 20.4 | 9.3 | 23.0 | 4.4 | 43.8 |
| **source of injury or illness** | | | | | |
| chemicals and chemical products | 1.8 | 1.3 | 4.0 | 0.6 | 7.1 |
| containers | 41.8 | 26.0 | 55.5 | 3.4 | 28.7 |
| furniture and fixtures | 4.1 | 3.2 | 14.6 | 2.2 | 17.7 |
| machinery | 4.7 | 7.1 | 16.5 | 2.3 | 14.2 |
| parts and materials | 14.0 | 13.1 | 16.8 | 1.4 | 12.9 |
| worker motion or position | 32.2 | 16.4 | 36.5 | 8.7 | 55.6 |
| floors, walkways, ground surfaces | 34.0 | 15.2 | 53.4 | 11.1 | 74.4 |
| tools, instruments, and equipment | 8.2 | 3.9 | 18.8 | 1.7 | 19.2 |
| vehicles | 36.0 | 15.3 | 19.6 | 1.9 | 26.2 |
| health care patient | 1.9 | 0.1 | 0.2 | 0.4 | 64.9 |
| **exposure or event leading to injury or illness** | | | | | |
| contact with objects and equipment | 41.1 | 29.6 | 71.6 | 6.3 | 64.6 |
| struck by object | 19.5 | 14.6 | 39.5 | 3.1 | 32.2 |
| struck against object | 13.1 | 6.9 | 19.0 | 1.9 | 19.8 |
| caught in equipment or object | 5.5 | 5.7 | 9.1 | 0.8 | 7.7 |
| fall to lower level | 16.3 | 6.5 | 11.8 | 4.0 | 18.2 |
| fall on same level | 18.5 | 10.2 | 44.6 | 7.3 | 59.1 |
| slip, trip, loss of balance—without fall | 7.2 | 3.3 | 9.9 | 1.4 | 11.9 |
| overexertion | 57.5 | 34.7 | 67.8 | 7.3 | 112.7 |
| overexertion in lifting | 31.2 | 20.3 | 45.1 | 4.2 | 57.9 |
| repetitive motion | 5.1 | 3.7 | 7.6 | 4.2 | 11.5 |
| exposure to harmful substances | 6.9 | 2.4 | 15.3 | 1.4 | 18.0 |
| transportation accidents | 18.1 | 7.7 | 7.6 | 1.3 | 16.7 |
| fires and explosions | 0.4 | 0.7 | 0.8 | N/A | 0.4 |
| assaults and violent acts by person | 0.9 | 0.2 | 2.4 | 0.7 | 12.4 |
| **Total cases** | **199.9** | **111.9** | **265.7** | **38.0** | **368.3** |

[1]Excludes farms with fewer than 11 employees. [2]The Mine Safety and Health Administration provided data for mining; the Federal Railroad Administration provided railroad transportation data. The mining category excludes independent mining contractors. [3]Fewer than 50 cases.

# US Work-Related Fatalities by Cause

Totals for major categories may include some smaller categories not listed in the table. Percentages may not add up to totals because of rounding. Source: US Bureau of Labor Statistics.

| | 1996–2000 | 2001 | |
| CAUSE OF FATALITY | NUMBER (AVG.) | NUMBER | (%) |
|---|---|---|---|
| **transportation incidents** | **2,608** | **2,517** | **43** |
| highway | 1,408 | 1,404 | 24 |
| collision between vehicles, mobile equipment | 685 | 723 | 12 |
| moving in same direction | 117 | 142 | 2 |
| moving in opposite directions, oncoming | 247 | 256 | 4 |
| moving in intersection | 151 | 137 | 2 |
| vehicle struck stationary object or equipment | 289 | 295 | 5 |
| noncollision | 372 | 339 | 6 |
| jackknifed or overturned–no collision | 298 | 273 | 5 |
| nonhighway (farm, industrial premises) | 378 | 324 | 5 |
| overturned | 212 | 157 | 3 |
| aircraft | 263 | 247 | 4 |
| worker struck by a vehicle | 376 | 383 | 6 |
| water vehicle | 105 | 90 | 2 |
| rail vehicle | 71 | 62 | 1 |

## US Work-Related Fatalities by Cause (continued)

| CAUSE OF FATALITY | 1996-2000 NUMBER (AVG.) | 2001 NUMBER | (%) |
|---|---|---|---|
| assaults and violent acts | 1,015 | 902 | 15 |
| homicides | 766 | 639 | 11 |
| shooting | 617 | 505 | 9 |
| stabbing | 68 | 58 | 1 |
| other, including bombing | 80 | 76 | 1 |
| self-inflicted injuries | 216 | 228 | 4 |
| | | | |
| contact with objects and equipment | 1,005 | 962 | 16 |
| struck by object | 567 | 553 | 9 |
| struck by falling object | 364 | 343 | 6 |
| struck by flying object | 57 | 60 | 1 |
| caught in or compressed by equipment or objects | 293 | 266 | 5 |
| caught in running equipment or machinery | 157 | 144 | 2 |
| caught in or crushed in collapsing materials | 128 | 122 | 2 |
| | | | |
| falls | 714 | 808 | 14 |
| fall to lower level | 636 | 698 | 12 |
| fall from ladder | 106 | 122 | 2 |
| fall from roof | 153 | 159 | 3 |
| fall from scaffold | 90 | 91 | 2 |
| fall on same level | 55 | 84 | 1 |
| | | | |
| exposure to harmful substances or environments | 535 | 499 | 8 |
| contact with electric current | 290 | 285 | 5 |
| contact with overhead power lines | 132 | 124 | 2 |
| contact with temperature extremes | 40 | 35 | 1 |
| exposure to caustic, noxious, or allergenic substances | 112 | 96 | 2 |
| inhalation of substance | 57 | 49 | 1 |
| oxygen deficiency | 92 | 83 | 1 |
| drowning, submersion | 73 | 59 | 1 |
| | | | |
| fires and explosions | 196 | 188 | 3 |
| other causes of fatality | 20 | 24 | <0.5 |
| total, excluding fatalities from September 11th | 6,094 | 5,900 | 100 |
| total, including fatalities from September 11th | N/A | 8,786 | — |

# Consumer Prices

## US Consumer Price Index, 1913–2002

This table presents the annual change in the Consumer Price Index (CPI) since 1913. The CPI is used as an indicator of price changes in the goods and services purchased by US consumers. The information provided is based on the purchases of a specific group of urban consumers who serve as a sample population representing more than 80% of the total US population. Each annual CPI is compared with the average index level of 100, which is a base number that represents the average price level for the 36-month period covering the years 1982, 1983, and 1984. A minus sign indicates a decrease. Source: US Bureau of Labor Statistics.

| YEAR | ANNUAL CPI | % ANNUAL CHANGE IN CPI | YEAR | ANNUAL CPI | % ANNUAL CHANGE IN CPI | YEAR | ANNUAL CPI | % ANNUAL CHANGE IN CPI |
|---|---|---|---|---|---|---|---|---|
| 1913 | 9.9 | | 1926 | 17.7 | 1.1 | 1939 | 13.9 | -1.4 |
| 1914 | 10.0 | 1.0 | 1927 | 17.4 | -1.7 | 1940 | 14.0 | 0.7 |
| 1915 | 10.1 | 1.0 | 1928 | 17.1 | -1.7 | 1941 | 14.7 | 5.0 |
| 1916 | 10.9 | 7.9 | 1929 | 17.1 | 0.0 | 1942 | 16.3 | 10.9 |
| 1917 | 12.8 | 17.4 | 1930 | 16.7 | -2.3 | 1943 | 17.3 | 6.1 |
| 1918 | 15.1 | 18.0 | 1931 | 15.2 | -9.0 | 1944 | 17.6 | 1.7 |
| 1919 | 17.3 | 14.6 | 1932 | 13.7 | -9.9 | 1945 | 18.0 | 2.3 |
| 1920 | 20.0 | 15.6 | 1933 | 13.0 | -5.1 | 1946 | 19.5 | 8.3 |
| 1921 | 17.9 | -10.5 | 1934 | 13.4 | 3.1 | 1947 | 22.3 | 14.4 |
| 1922 | 16.8 | -6.1 | 1935 | 13.7 | 2.2 | 1948 | 24.1 | 8.1 |
| 1923 | 17.1 | 1.8 | 1936 | 13.9 | 1.5 | 1949 | 23.8 | -1.2 |
| 1924 | 17.1 | 0.0 | 1937 | 14.4 | 3.6 | 1950 | 24.1 | 1.3 |
| 1925 | 17.5 | 2.3 | 1938 | 14.1 | -2.1 | 1951 | 26.0 | 7.9 |

## US Consumer Price Index, 1913–2002 (continued)

| YEAR | ANNUAL CPI | % ANNUAL CHANGE IN CPI | YEAR | ANNUAL CPI | % ANNUAL CHANGE IN CPI | YEAR | ANNUAL CPI | % ANNUAL CHANGE IN CPI |
|---|---|---|---|---|---|---|---|---|
| 1952 | 26.5 | 1.9 | 1969 | 36.7 | 5.5 | 1986 | 109.6 | 1.9 |
| 1953 | 26.7 | 0.8 | 1970 | 38.8 | 5.7 | 1987 | 113.6 | 3.6 |
| 1954 | 26.9 | 0.7 | 1971 | 40.5 | 4.4 | 1988 | 118.3 | 4.1 |
| 1955 | 26.8 | -0.4 | 1972 | 41.8 | 3.2 | 1989 | 124.0 | 4.8 |
| 1956 | 27.2 | 1.5 | 1973 | 44.4 | 6.2 | 1990 | 130.7 | 5.4 |
| 1957 | 28.1 | 3.3 | 1974 | 49.3 | 11.0 | 1991 | 136.2 | 4.2 |
| 1958 | 28.9 | 2.8 | 1975 | 53.8 | 9.1 | 1992 | 140.3 | 3.0 |
| 1959 | 29.1 | 0.7 | 1976 | 56.9 | 5.8 | 1993 | 144.5 | 3.0 |
| 1960 | 29.6 | 1.7 | 1977 | 60.6 | 6.5 | 1994 | 148.2 | 2.6 |
| 1961 | 29.9 | 1.0 | 1978 | 65.2 | 7.6 | 1995 | 152.4 | 2.8 |
| 1962 | 30.2 | 1.0 | 1979 | 72.6 | 11.3 | 1996 | 156.9 | 3.0 |
| 1963 | 30.6 | 1.3 | 1980 | 82.4 | 13.5 | 1997 | 160.5 | 2.3 |
| 1964 | 31.0 | 1.3 | 1981 | 90.9 | 10.3 | 1998 | 163.0 | 1.6 |
| 1965 | 31.5 | 1.6 | 1982 | 96.5 | 6.2 | 1999 | 166.6 | 2.2 |
| 1966 | 32.4 | 2.9 | 1983 | 99.6 | 3.2 | 2000 | 172.2 | 3.4 |
| 1967 | 33.4 | 3.1 | 1984 | 103.9 | 4.3 | 2001 | 177.1 | 2.8 |
| 1968 | 34.8 | 4.2 | 1985 | 107.6 | 3.6 | 2002 | 179.9 | 1.6 |

## US Consumer Price Indexes by Item Group, 1975–2002

The information provided is based on the purchases of a specific group of urban consumers who serve as a sample population representing more than 80% of the total US population. Each annual CPI is compared with the average index level of 100, which is a base number that represents the average price level for the 36-month period covering the years 1982, 1983, and 1984. Source: US Bureau of Labor Statistics.

| | CONSUMER PRICE INDEX | | | | | | | |
|---|---|---|---|---|---|---|---|---|
| ITEM GROUP | 1975 | 1980 | 1985 | 1990 | 1995 | 2000 | 2001 | 2002 |
| all items | 53.8 | 82.4 | 107.6 | 130.7 | 152.4 | 172.2 | 177.1 | 179.9 |
| commodities | 58.2 | 86.0 | 105.4 | 122.8 | 136.4 | 149.2 | 150.7 | 149.7 |
| energy | 42.1 | 86.0 | 101.6 | 102.1 | 105.2 | 124.6 | 129.3 | 121.7 |
| food | 59.8 | 86.8 | 105.6 | 132.4 | 148.4 | 167.8 | 173.1 | 176.2 |
| shelter | 48.8 | 81.0 | 109.8 | 140.0 | 165.7 | 193.4 | 200.6 | 208.1 |
| transportation | 50.1 | 83.1 | 106.4 | 120.5 | 139.1 | 153.3 | 154.3 | 152.9 |
| medical care | 47.5 | 74.9 | 113.5 | 162.8 | 220.5 | 260.8 | 272.8 | 285.6 |
| apparel | 72.5 | 90.9 | 105.0 | 124.1 | 132.0 | 129.6 | 127.3 | 124.0 |

| | % CHANGE IN CPI[1] | | | | | | | |
|---|---|---|---|---|---|---|---|---|
| ITEM GROUP | 1975 | 1980 | 1985 | 1990 | 1995 | 2000 | 2001 | 2002 |
| all items | 9.1 | 13.5 | 3.6 | 5.4 | 2.8 | 3.4 | 2.8 | 1.6 |
| commodities | 8.8 | 12.3 | 2.1 | 5.2 | 1.9 | 3.3 | 1.0 | -.7 |
| energy | 10.5 | 30.9 | 0.7 | 8.3 | 0.6 | 16.9 | 3.8 | -5.9 |
| food | 8.5 | 8.6 | 2.3 | 5.8 | 2.8 | 2.3 | 3.2 | 1.8 |
| shelter | 9.9 | 17.6 | 5.6 | 5.4 | 3.2 | 3.3 | 3.7 | 3.7 |
| transportation | 9.4 | 17.9 | 2.6 | 5.6 | 3.6 | 6.2 | 0.7 | -.9 |
| medical care | 12.0 | 11.0 | 6.3 | 9.0 | 4.5 | 4.1 | 4.6 | 4.7 |
| apparel | 4.5 | 7.1 | 2.8 | 4.6 | -1.0 | -1.3 | -1.8 | -2.6 |

[1]Annual percent change from the preceding year.

## Sample US Consumer Price Indexes by Region, 2001–2002

This table presents the regional annual averages of the Consumer Price Index (CPI) for 2002 and the percent change of those averages from 2001 to 2002. The information provided is based on the purchases of a specific group of urban consumers who serve as a sample population representing more than 80% of the total US population. Each annual CPI is compared with the average index level of 100, which is a base number that represents the average price level for the 36-month period covering the years 1982, 1983, and 1984. A minus sign indicates a decrease in price from 2001. Source: US Bureau of Labor Statistics.

## Sample US Consumer Price Indexes by Region, 2001–2002 (continued)

| ITEM GROUP | NORTHEAST 2002 CPI | NORTHEAST % CHANGE FROM 2001 | MIDWEST 2002 CPI | MIDWEST % CHANGE FROM 2001 | SOUTH 2002 CPI | SOUTH % CHANGE FROM 2001 | WEST 2002 CPI | WEST % CHANGE FROM 2001 |
|---|---|---|---|---|---|---|---|---|
| all items | 188.2 | 2.1 | 174.9 | 1.2 | 173.3 | 1.3 | 184.7 | 1.9 |
| commodities | 150.9 | −.5 | 147.4 | −1.1 | 150.0 | −.4 | 150.6 | −.6 |
| energy | 118.8 | −6.9 | 119.0 | −7.1 | 116.6 | −6.0 | 137.9 | −3.1 |
| food | 177.9 | 1.7 | 172.1 | 1.4 | 173.9 | 1.7 | 181.4 | 2.5 |
| shelter | 233.8 | 5.1 | 201.0 | 3.4 | 184.1 | 2.9 | 213.5 | 3.7 |
| transportation | 153.0 | −.9 | 153.3 | −1.1 | 149.7 | −.7 | 156.1 | −1.0 |
| medical care | 304.4 | 5.2 | 280.3 | 4.6 | 277.1 | 4.3 | 285.7 | 5.0 |
| apparel | 122.9 | −1.8 | 118.3 | −3.7 | 136.9 | −2.2 | 114.4 | −2.7 |

# US Budget

## US Governmental Spending, 1800–2002

Entries for the years prior to 1933 are based on the administrative budget concept rather than on the unified budget concept. For a discussion of the unified budget concept see <www.whitehouse.gov/omb/budget/fy2004/histint.html>. The figures are in thousands ('000). A minus sign indicates a deficit. Source: US Office of Management and Budget.

| YEAR[1] | FEDERAL INCOME | FEDERAL SPENDING | SURPLUS OR DEFICIT | YEAR[1] | FEDERAL INCOME | FEDERAL SPENDING | SURPLUS OR DEFICIT |
|---|---|---|---|---|---|---|---|
| 1800 | 10,849 | 10,786 | 63 | 1842 | 19,976 | 25,206 | −5,230 |
| 1801 | 12,935 | 9,395 | 3,541 | 1843 | 8,303 | 11,858 | −3,555 |
| 1802 | 14,996 | 7,862 | 7,134 | 1844 | 29,321 | 22,338 | 6,984 |
| 1803 | 11,064 | 7,852 | 3,212 | 1845 | 29,970 | 22,937 | 7,033 |
| 1804 | 11,826 | 8,719 | 3,107 | 1846 | 29,700 | 27,767 | 1,933 |
| 1805 | 13,561 | 10,506 | 3,054 | 1847 | 26,496 | 57,281 | −30,786 |
| 1806 | 15,560 | 9,804 | 5,756 | 1848 | 35,736 | 45,377 | −9,641 |
| 1807 | 16,398 | 8,354 | 8,044 | 1849 | 31,208 | 45,052 | −13,844 |
| 1808 | 17,061 | 9,932 | 7,128 | 1850 | 43,603 | 39,543 | 4,060 |
| 1809 | 7,773 | 10,281 | −2,507 | 1851 | 52,559 | 47,709 | 4,850 |
| 1810 | 9,384 | 8,157 | 1,228 | 1852 | 49,847 | 44,195 | 5,652 |
| 1811 | 14,424 | 8,058 | 6,365 | 1853 | 61,587 | 48,184 | 13,403 |
| 1812 | 9,801 | 20,281 | −10,480 | 1854 | 73,800 | 58,045 | 15,755 |
| 1813 | 14,340 | 31,682 | −17,341 | 1855 | 65,351 | 59,743 | 5,608 |
| 1814 | 11,182 | 34,721 | −23,539 | 1856 | 74,057 | 69,571 | 4,486 |
| 1815 | 15,729 | 32,708 | −16,979 | 1857 | 68,965 | 67,796 | 1,170 |
| 1816 | 47,678 | 30,587 | 17,091 | 1858 | 46,655 | 74,185 | −27,530 |
| 1817 | 33,099 | 21,844 | 11,255 | 1859 | 53,486 | 69,071 | −15,585 |
| 1818 | 21,585 | 19,825 | 1,760 | 1860 | 56,065 | 63,131 | −7,066 |
| 1819 | 24,603 | 21,464 | 3,140 | 1861 | 41,510 | 66,547 | −25,037 |
| 1820 | 17,881 | 18,261 | −380 | 1862 | 51,987 | 474,762 | −422,774 |
| 1821 | 14,573 | 15,811 | −1,237 | 1863 | 112,697 | 714,741 | −602,043 |
| 1822 | 20,232 | 15,000 | 5,232 | 1864 | 264,627 | 865,323 | −600,696 |
| 1823 | 20,541 | 14,707 | 5,834 | 1865 | 333,715 | 1,297,555 | −963,841 |
| 1824 | 19,381 | 20,327 | −945 | 1866 | 558,033 | 520,809 | 37,223 |
| 1825 | 21,841 | 15,857 | 5,984 | 1867 | 490,634 | 357,543 | 133,091 |
| 1826 | 25,260 | 17,036 | 8,225 | 1868 | 405,638 | 377,340 | 28,298 |
| 1827 | 22,966 | 16,139 | 6,827 | 1869 | 370,944 | 322,865 | 48,078 |
| 1828 | 24,764 | 16,395 | 8,369 | 1870 | 411,255 | 309,654 | 101,602 |
| 1829 | 24,828 | 15,203 | 9,624 | 1871 | 383,324 | 292,177 | 91,147 |
| 1830 | 24,844 | 15,143 | 9,701 | 1872 | 374,107 | 277,518 | 96,589 |
| 1831 | 28,527 | 15,248 | 13,279 | 1873 | 333,738 | 290,345 | 43,393 |
| 1832 | 31,866 | 17,289 | 14,577 | 1874 | 304,979 | 302,634 | 2,345 |
| 1833 | 33,948 | 23,018 | 10,931 | 1875 | 288,000 | 274,623 | 13,377 |
| 1834 | 21,792 | 18,628 | 3,164 | 1876 | 294,096 | 265,101 | 28,995 |
| 1835 | 35,430 | 17,573 | 17,857 | 1877 | 281,406 | 241,334 | 40,072 |
| 1836 | 50,827 | 30,868 | 19,959 | 1878 | 257,764 | 236,964 | 20,800 |
| 1837 | 24,954 | 37,243 | −12,289 | 1879 | 273,827 | 266,948 | 6,879 |
| 1838 | 26,303 | 33,865 | −7,562 | 1880 | 333,527 | 267,643 | 65,884 |
| 1839 | 31,483 | 26,899 | 4,584 | 1881 | 360,782 | 260,713 | 100,069 |
| 1840 | 19,480 | 24,318 | −4,837 | 1882 | 403,525 | 257,981 | 145,544 |
| 1841 | 16,860 | 26,566 | −9,706 | 1883 | 398,288 | 265,408 | 132,879 |

## US Governmental Spending, 1800–2002 (continued)

| YEAR[1] | FEDERAL INCOME | FEDERAL SPENDING | SURPLUS OR DEFICIT | YEAR[1] | FEDERAL INCOME | FEDERAL SPENDING | SURPLUS OR DEFICIT |
|---|---|---|---|---|---|---|---|
| 1884 | 348,520 | 244,126 | 104,394 | 1944 | 43,747,000 | 91,304,000 | -47,557,000 |
| 1885 | 323,691 | 260,227 | 63,464 | 1945 | 45,159,000 | 92,712,000 | -47,553,000 |
| 1886 | 336,440 | 242,483 | 93,957 | 1946 | 39,296,000 | 55,232,000 | -15,936,000 |
| 1887 | 371,403 | 267,932 | 103,471 | 1947 | 38,514,000 | 34,496,000 | 4,018,000 |
| 1888 | 379,266 | 267,925 | 111,341 | 1948 | 41,560,000 | 29,764,000 | 11,796,000 |
| 1889 | 387,050 | 299,289 | 87,761 | 1949 | 39,415,000 | 38,835,000 | 580,000 |
| 1890 | 403,081 | 318,041 | 85,040 | 1950 | 39,443,000 | 42,562,000 | -3,119,000 |
| 1891 | 392,612 | 365,774 | 26,839 | 1951 | 51,616,000 | 45,514,000 | 6,102,000 |
| 1892 | 354,938 | 345,023 | 9,914 | 1952 | 66,167,000 | 67,686,000 | -1,519,000 |
| 1893 | 385,820 | 383,478 | 2,342 | 1953 | 69,608,000 | 76,101,000 | -6,493,000 |
| 1894 | 306,355 | 367,525 | -61,170 | 1954 | 69,701,000 | 70,855,000 | -1,154,000 |
| 1895 | 324,729 | 356,195 | -31,466 | 1955 | 65,451,000 | 68,444,000 | -2,993,000 |
| 1896 | 338,142 | 352,179 | -14,037 | 1956 | 74,587,000 | 70,640,000 | 3,947,000 |
| 1897 | 347,722 | 365,774 | -18,052 | 1957 | 79,990,000 | 76,578,000 | 3,412,000 |
| 1898 | 405,321 | 443,369 | -38,047 | 1958 | 79,636,000 | 82,405,000 | -2,769,000 |
| 1899 | 515,961 | 605,072 | -89,112 | 1959 | 79,249,000 | 92,098,000 | -12,849,000 |
| 1900 | 567,241 | 520,861 | 46,380 | 1960 | 92,492,000 | 92,191,000 | 301,000 |
| 1901 | 587,685 | 524,617 | 63,068 | 1961 | 94,388,000 | 97,723,000 | -3,335,000 |
| 1902 | 562,478 | 485,234 | 77,244 | 1962 | 99,676,000 | 106,821,000 | -7,146,000 |
| 1903 | 561,881 | 517,006 | 44,875 | 1963 | 106,560,000 | 111,316,000 | -4,756,000 |
| 1904 | 541,087 | 583,660 | -42,573 | 1964 | 112,613,000 | 118,528,000 | -5,915,000 |
| 1905 | 544,275 | 567,279 | -23,004 | 1965 | 116,817,000 | 118,228,000 | -1,411,000 |
| 1906 | 594,984 | 570,202 | 24,782 | 1966 | 130,835,000 | 134,532,000 | -3,698,000 |
| 1907 | 665,860 | 579,129 | 86,732 | 1967 | 148,822,000 | 157,464,000 | -8,643,000 |
| 1908 | 601,862 | 659,196 | -57,334 | 1968 | 152,973,000 | 178,134,000 | -25,161,000 |
| 1909 | 604,320 | 693,744 | -89,423 | 1969 | 186,882,000 | 183,640,000 | 3,242,000 |
| 1910 | 675,512 | 693,617 | -18,105 | 1970 | 192,807,000 | 195,649,000 | -2,842,000 |
| 1911 | 701,833 | 691,202 | 10,631 | 1971 | 187,139,000 | 210,172,000 | -23,033,000 |
| 1912 | 692,609 | 689,881 | 2,728 | 1972 | 207,309,000 | 230,681,000 | -23,373,000 |
| 1913 | 714,463 | 714,864 | -401 | 1973 | 230,799,000 | 245,707,000 | -14,908,000 |
| 1914 | 725,117 | 725,525 | -408 | 1974 | 263,224,000 | 269,359,000 | -6,135,000 |
| 1915 | 683,417 | 746,093 | -62,676 | 1975 | 279,090,000 | 332,332,000 | -53,242,000 |
| 1916 | 761,445 | 712,967 | 48,478 | 1976 | 298,060,000 | 371,792,000 | -73,732,000 |
| 1917 | 1,100,500 | 1,953,857 | -853,357 | TQ | 81,232,000 | 95,975,000 | -14,744,000 |
| 1918 | 3,645,240 | 12,677,359 | -9,032,120 | 1977 | 355,559,000 | 409,218,000 | -53,659,000 |
| 1919 | 5,130,042 | 18,492,665 | -13,362,623 | 1978 | 399,561,000 | 458,746,000 | -59,185,000 |
| 1920 | 6,648,898 | 6,357,677 | 291,222 | 1979 | 463,302,000 | 504,028,000 | -40,726,000 |
| 1921 | 5,570,790 | 5,061,785 | 509,005 | 1980 | 517,112,000 | 590,941,000 | -73,830,000 |
| 1922 | 4,025,901 | 3,289,404 | 736,496 | 1981 | 599,272,000 | 678,241,000 | -78,968,000 |
| 1923 | 3,852,795 | 3,140,287 | 712,508 | 1982 | 617,766,000 | 745,743,000 | -127,977,000 |
| 1924 | 3,871,214 | 2,907,847 | 963,367 | 1983 | 600,562,000 | 808,364,000 | -207,802,000 |
| 1925 | 3,640,805 | 2,923,762 | 717,043 | 1984 | 666,486,000 | 851,853,000 | -185,367,000 |
| 1926 | 3,795,108 | 2,929,964 | 865,144 | 1985 | 734,088,000 | 946,396,000 | -212,308,000 |
| 1927 | 4,012,794 | 2,857,429 | 1,155,365 | 1986 | 769,215,000 | 990,430,000 | -221,215,000 |
| 1928 | 3,900,329 | 2,961,245 | 939,083 | 1987 | 854,353,000 | 1,004,082,000 | -149,728,000 |
| 1929 | 3,861,589 | 3,127,199 | 734,391 | 1988 | 909,303,000 | 1,064,455,000 | -155,152,000 |
| 1930 | 4,057,884 | 3,320,211 | 737,673 | 1989 | 991,190,000 | 1,143,646,000 | -152,456,000 |
| 1931 | 3,115,557 | 3,577,434 | -461,877 | 1990 | 1,031,969,000 | 1,253,165,000 | -221,195,000 |
| 1932 | 1,923,892 | 4,659,182 | -2,735,290 | 1991 | 1,055,041,000 | 1,324,369,000 | -269,328,000 |
| 1933 | 1,996,844 | 4,598,496 | -2,601,652 | 1992 | 1,091,279,000 | 1,381,655,000 | -290,376,000 |
| 1934 | 2,955,000 | 6,541,000 | -3,586,000 | 1993 | 1,154,401,000 | 1,409,489,000 | -255,087,000 |
| 1935 | 3,609,000 | 6,412,000 | -2,803,000 | 1994 | 1,258,627,000 | 1,461,877,000 | -203,250,000 |
| 1936 | 3,923,000 | 8,228,000 | -4,304,000 | 1995 | 1,351,830,000 | 1,515,802,000 | -163,972,000 |
| 1937 | 5,387,000 | 7,580,000 | -2,193,000 | 1996 | 1,453,062,000 | 1,560,535,000 | -107,473,000 |
| 1938 | 6,751,000 | 6,840,000 | -89,000 | 1997 | 1,579,292,000 | 1,601,250,000 | -21,958,000 |
| 1939 | 6,295,000 | 9,141,000 | -2,846,000 | 1998 | 1,721,798,000 | 1,652,585,000 | 69,213,000 |
| 1940 | 6,548,000 | 9,468,000 | -2,920,000 | 1999 | 1,827,454,000 | 1,701,891,000 | 125,563,000 |
| 1941 | 8,712,000 | 13,653,000 | -4,941,000 | 2000 | 2,025,218,000 | 1,788,773,000 | 236,445,000 |
| 1942 | 14,634,000 | 35,137,000 | -20,503,000 | 2001 | 1,991,194,000 | 1,863,895,000 | 127,299,000 |
| 1943 | 24,001,000 | 78,555,000 | -54,554,000 | 2002 | 1,853,173,000 | 2,010,975,000 | -157,802,000 |

[1]The fiscal year ended on 31 December for the budgets from 1800 to 1842. It ended on 30 June for the budgets from 1844 through 1976 and on 30 September from fiscal year 1977. The budget figures for 1843 are for the period from 1 January to 30 June. The third quarter of 1976 was budgeted separately because of the change in the fiscal year calendar. It is referred to as the Transition Quarter (TQ).

## US Public Debt

In order to fund governmental operations while the federal budget is running at a deficit, the Department of the Treasury borrows money by selling Treasury bills, US savings bonds, and other securities to the public. The money borrowed by the Treasury is re-ferred to as the public debt. A broader measure of the federal debt is known as the gross federal debt. It consists of the public debt plus money borrowed by federal agencies. The GDP is the gross domestic prod-uct. Source: US Office of Management and Budget.

| END OF FISCAL YEAR | PUBLIC DEBT (IN $ MILLIONS) | % OF GDP | GROSS FEDERAL DEBT (IN $ MILLIONS) | % OF GDP | END OF FISCAL YEAR | PUBLIC DEBT (IN $ MILLIONS) | % OF GDP | GROSS FEDERAL DEBT (IN $ MILLIONS) | % OF GDP |
|---|---|---|---|---|---|---|---|---|---|
| 1940 | 42,772 | 44.2 | 50,696 | 52.4 | 1980 | 711,923 | 26.1 | 909,041 | 33.3 |
| 1945 | 235,182 | 106.3 | 260,123 | 117.5 | 1985 | 1,507,260 | 36.4 | 1,817,423 | 43.9 |
| 1950 | 219,023 | 80.1 | 256,853 | 93.9 | 1990 | 2,411,558 | 42.0 | 3,206,290 | 55.9 |
| 1955 | 226,616 | 57.3 | 274,366 | 69.4 | 1995 | 3,604,378 | 49.2 | 4,920,586 | 67.2 |
| 1960 | 236,840 | 45.6 | 290,525 | 56.0 | 2000 | 3,409,804 | 35.1 | 5,628,700 | 57.9 |
| 1965 | 260,778 | 37.9 | 322,318 | 46.9 | 2001 | 3,319,615 | 33.1 | 5,769,881 | 57.6 |
| 1970 | 283,198 | 28.0 | 380,921 | 37.6 | 2002 | 3,540,427 | 34.3 | 6,198,401 | 60.0 |
| 1975 | 394,700 | 25.3 | 541,925 | 34.7 | | | | | |

# US Taxes

## US Federal Taxation Structure

This table shows the range of income taxes for vari-ous types of households in each tax bracket. In 2003 the 10% bracket has expanded for all except for heads of households. The 15% bracket has expanded for those filing jointly and under status "married filing separately." The 27% rate has dropped to 25%; the 30% rate has dropped to 28%; the 35% rate has dropped to 33%; and the 38.6% rate has dropped to 35%. Standard deductions have increased for those filing jointly and under status "married filing sepa-rately."

| | SINGLE | JOINT | HEAD OF HOUSEHOLD | MARRIED FILING SEPARATELY |
|---|---|---|---|---|
| standard deduction | $ 4,750 | $ 9,500 | $ 7,000 | $ 4,750 |
| 10% tax bracket | 0–7,000 | 0–14,000 | 0–10,000 | 0–7,000 |
| 15% bracket | 7,001–28,400 | 14,001–56,800 | 10,001–38,050 | 7,001–28,400 |
| 25% bracket | 28,401–68,800 | 56,801–114,650 | 38,051–98,250 | 28,401–57,325 |
| 28% bracket | 68,801–143,500 | 114,651–174,700 | 98,251–159,100 | 57,326–87,350 |
| 33% bracket | 143,501–311,950 | 174,701–311,950 | 159,101–311,950 | 87,351–155,975 |
| 35% bracket | 311,951 and above | 311,951 and above | 311,951 and above | 155,976 and above |

## Individual Income Taxes by State

This table shows tax rates as of 1 Jan 2003 for tax year 2003. Source: The Federation of Tax Administrators from various sources. <www.taxadmin.org/fta/rate/ind_inc.html>.

| STATE | TAX RATES LOW | TAX RATES HIGH | NUMBER OF BRACKETS | INCOME BRACKETS LOW | INCOME BRACKETS HIGH | PERSONAL EXEMPTION SINGLE | PERSONAL EXEMPTION MARRIED | PERSONAL EXEMPTION CHILDREN | FEDERAL TAX DEDUCTIBLE |
|---|---|---|---|---|---|---|---|---|---|
| AL | 2 | 5 | 3 | 500[2] | 3,000[2] | 1,500 | 3,000 | 300 | Yes |
| AK | No state income tax | | | | | | | | |
| AZ | 2.87 | 5.04 | 5 | 10,000[2] | 150,000[2] | 2,100 | 4,200 | 2,300 | |
| AR[1] | 1 | 6.5[5] | 6 | 2,999 | 25,000 | 20[3] | 40[3] | 20[3] | |
| CA[1] | 1 | 9.3 | 6 | 5,834[2] | 38,291[2] | 80[3] | 160[3] | 251[3] | |
| CO | 4.63 | | 1 | ——Flat rate—— | | ——None—— | | | |
| CT | 3 | 4.5 | 2 | 10,000[2] | 10,000[2] | 12,500[6] | 24,000[6] | 0 | |
| DE | 2.2 | 5.95 | 7 | 5,000 | 60,000 | 110[3] | 220[3] | 110[3] | |
| DC | 4.5 | 8.7[7] | 3 | 10,000 | 40,000 | 1,370 | 2,740 | 1,370 | |
| FL | No state income tax | | | | | | | | |
| GA | 1 | 6 | 6 | 750[8] | 7,000[8] | 2,700 | 5,400 | 2,700 | |
| HI | 1.4 | 8.25 | 8 | 2,000[2] | 40,000[2] | 1,040 | 2,080 | 1,040 | |
| ID | 1.6 | 7.8 | 8 | 1,087[9] | 21,730[9] | 3,000[4] | 6,000[4] | 3,000[4] | |
| IL | 3 | | 1 | ——Flat rate—— | | 2,000 | 4,000 | 2,000 | |
| IN | 3.4 | | 1 | ——Flat rate—— | | 1,000 | 2,000 | 1,000 | |
| IA[1] | 0.36 | 8.98 | 9 | 1,211 | 54,495 | 40[3] | 80[3] | 40[3] | Yes |
| KS | 3.5 | 6.45 | 3 | 15,000[2] | 30,000[2] | 2,250 | 4,500 | 2,250 | |
| KY | 2 | 6 | 5 | 3,000 | 8,000 | 20[3] | 40[3] | 20[3] | |
| LA | 2 | 6 | 3 | 10,000[2] | 50,000[2] | 4,500[10] | 9,000[10] | 1,000[10] | Yes |
| ME[1] | 2 | 8.5 | 4 | 4,200[2] | 16,700[2] | 4,700 | 7,850 | 1,000 | |

## Individual Income Taxes by State (continued)

| STATE | TAX RATES LOW | TAX RATES HIGH | NUMBER OF BRACKETS | INCOME BRACKETS LOW | INCOME BRACKETS HIGH | PERSONAL EXEMPTION SINGLE | PERSONAL EXEMPTION MARRIED | PERSONAL EXEMPTION CHILDREN | FEDERAL TAX DEDUCTIBLE |
|---|---|---|---|---|---|---|---|---|---|
| MD | 2 | 4.75 | 4 | 1,000 | 3,000 | 2,400 | 4,800 | 2,400 | |
| MA | 5 | | 1 | —Flat rate— | | 4,400 | 8,800 | 1,000 | |
| MI[1] | 4[11] | | 1 | —Flat rate— | | 3,000 | 6,000 | 3,000 | |
| MN[1] | 5.35 | 7.85 | 3 | 18,710[12] | 61,461[12] | 3,000[4] | 6,000[4] | 3,000[4] | |
| MS | 3 | 5 | 3 | 5,000 | 10,000 | 6,000 | 12,000 | 1,500 | |
| MO | 1.5 | 6 | 10 | 1,000 | 9,000 | 2,100 | 4,200 | 2,100 | Yes[20] |
| MT[1] | 2 | 11 | 10 | 2,200 | 75,400 | 1,720 | 3,440 | 1,720 | Yes |
| NE[1] | 2.56 | 6.84 | 4 | 2,400[13] | 26,500[13] | 94[3] | 188[3] | 94[3] | |
| NV | No state income tax | | | | | | | | |
| NH | State income tax is limited to dividends and interest income only | | | | | | | | |
| NJ | 1.4 | 6.37 | 6 | 20,000[14] | 75,000[14] | 1,000 | 2,000 | 1,500 | |
| NM | 1.7 | 8.2 | 7 | 5,500[15] | 65,000[15] | 3,000[4] | 6,000[4] | 3,000[4] | |
| NY | 4 | 6.85 | 5 | 8,000[2] | 20,000[2] | 0 | 0 | 1,000 | |
| NC[15] | 6 | 8.25 | 4 | 12,750[16] | 120,000[16] | 3,000[4] | 6,000[4] | 3,000[4] | |
| ND | 2.1 | 5.54[17] | 5 | 27,050[16] | 297,350[17] | 3,000[4] | 6,000[4] | 3,000[4] | 17 |
| OH[1] | 0.743 | 7.5[18] | 9 | 5,000 | 200,000 | 1,200[18] | 2,400[18] | 1,200[18] | |
| OK | 0.5 | 7[19] | 8 | 1,000 | 10,000 | 1,000 | 2,000 | 1,000 | Yes[19] |
| OR[1] | 5 | 9 | 3 | 2,500[2] | 6,250[2] | 145[3] | 290[3] | 145[3] | Yes[20] |
| PA | 2.8 | | 1 | —Flat rate— | | —None— | | | |
| RI | 25.0% Federal tax liability[21] | | | | — | — | — | — | — |
| SC[1] | 2.5 | 7 | 6 | 2,400 | 12,000 | 3,000[4] | 6,000[4] | 3,000[4] | |
| SD | No state income tax | | | | | | | | |
| TN | State income tax is limited to dividends and interest income only | | | | | | | | |
| TX | No state income tax | | | | | | | | |
| UT[1] | 2.3 | 7 | 6 | 863[2] | 4,313[2] | 2,250[4] | 4,500[4] | 2,250[4] | Yes[22] |
| VT | 3.6 | 9.5 | 5 | 27,950[23] | 307,050[23] | 3,000[4] | 6,000[4] | 3,000[4] | |
| VA | 2 | 5.75 | 4 | 3,000 | 17,000 | 800 | 1,600 | 800 | |
| WA | No state income tax | | | | | | | | |
| WV | 3 | 6.5 | 5 | 10,000 | 60,000 | 2,000 | 4,000 | 2,000 | |
| WI | 4.6 | 6.75[24] | 4 | 8,280 | 124,200 | 700 | 1,400 | 400 | |
| WY | No state income tax | | | | | | | | |

[1]Eight states have statutory provision for automatic adjustment of tax brackets, personal exemption, or standard deductions to the rate of inflation. Arkansas, Michigan, Nebraska, and Ohio index the personal exemption amounts only. [2]For joint returns, the taxes are twice the tax imposed on half the income. [3]Tax credits. [4]These states allow personal exemption or standard deductions as provided in the Internal Revenue Code. Utah allows a personal exemption equal to three-fourths the federal exemptions. [5]A special tax table is available for low-income taxpayers reducing their tax payments. [6]Combined personal exemptions and standard deduction. An additional tax credit is allowed ranging from 75% to 0% based on state adjusted gross income. Exemption amounts are phased out for higher-income taxpayers until they are eliminated for households earning over $54,500. [7]Tax rate decreases are scheduled for tax years after 2003. [8]The tax brackets reported are for single individuals. For married households filing separately, the same rates apply to income brackets ranging from $500 to $5,000; and the income brackets range from $1,000 to $10,000 for joint filers. [9]For joint returns, the tax is twice the tax imposed on half the income. A $10 filing tax is charge for each return, and a $15 credit is allowed for each exemption. [10]Combined personal exemption and standard deduction. [11]Tax rate scheduled to decrease to 3.9% for tax years after 2003. [12]The tax brackets reported are for single individuals. For married couples filing jointly, the same rates apply for income under $27,350 to over $108,661. [13]The tax brackets reported are for single individuals. For married couples filing jointly, the same rates apply for income under $4,000 to over $46,750. [14]The tax brackets reported are for single individuals. For married couples filing jointly, the same rates apply for income under $20,000 to over $150,000. [15]The tax brackets reported are for single individuals. For married couples filing jointly, the same rates apply for income under $8,000 to over $100,000. Married households filing separately pay the tax imposed on half the income. [16]The tax brackets reported are for single individuals. For married taxpayers, the same rates apply to income brackets ranging from $21,250 to $200,000. Lower exemption amounts allowed for high-income taxpayers. Tax rate scheduled to decrease after tax year 2003. [17]Rates reported are for short-form filers. Long-form filers' rates range from 2.67% for income under $3,000 to 12% over $50,000. Long-form filers only can deduct federal income taxes. An additional $300 personal exemption is allowed for joint returns or unmarried head of households. [18]Plus an additional $20 per exemption tax credit. Rates reported are for tax year 2002; the 2003 rates will not be determined until July 2003. [19]The rate range reported is for single persons not deducting federal income tax. For married persons filing jointly, the same rates apply to income brackets ranging from $2,000 to $21,000. Separate schedules, with rates ranging from 0.5% to 10%, apply to taxpayers deducting federal income taxes. [20]Deduction is limited to $10,000 for joint returns, $5,000 for individuals in Missouri, and $5,000 in Oregon. [21]Federal tax liability prior to the enactment of Economic Growth and Tax Relief Act of 2001. [22]One-half of the federal income taxes are deductible. [23]The tax brackets reported are for single individuals. For married couples filing jointly, the same rates apply for income under $46,700 to over $307,050. [24]The tax brackets reported are for single individuals. For married taxpayers, the same rates apply to income brackets ranging from $11,040 to $165,600. An additional $250 exemption is provided for each taxpayer or spouse aged 65 or over.

# Arts, Entertainment, & Leisure

## Encyclopædia Britannica's 50 Great Museums of the World

*Listed alphabetically by country.*

**National Museum of Australia, Canberra, Australia:** The National Museum of Australia houses unique exhibitions that explore all aspects of Australian history and culture. Historical artifacts and interactive exhibits tell the story of the people, land, and symbols of the island nation.

**Kunsthistorisches Museum, Vienna, Austria:** The Museum of Art History's Picture Gallery was built around the collection of Archduke Leopold Wilhelm, who in the mid-17th century acquired some 1,400 paintings of the Venetian Renaissance (including works by Titian, Veronese, Tintoretto) and of Flemish masters from the 15th–17th century (van Eyck, Rubens, van Dyck). The museum's extensive collections also include ancient Egyptian and Near Eastern art and artifacts, Greek and Roman antiquities, more than 700,000 examples of historical currency, ancient musical instruments, arms and armor, and historical carriages and court uniforms.

**The Bahrain National Museum, Manama, Bahrain:** The museum houses a large collection of documents, artifacts, and craftwork relating to Arabic history and Islamic studies.

**Museum of Art, São Paulo, Brazil:** Known as "MASP" (Museu de Arte de São Paulo), the museum owns one of the world's most prestigious collections of works by European masters, including pieces from the 13th century through the present, with a strong emphasis on Impressionists.

**Museum of Art and History, Shanghai, China:** Also known as the Shanghai Museum, the institution is primarily devoted to ancient Chinese art. It has more than 120,000 relics on permanent display and is especially renowned for its collections of bronzes, ceramics, paintings, and calligraphy.

**Egyptian Museum, Cairo, Egypt:** Established by the Egyptian government in 1835, the Egyptian Museum houses more than 120,000 objects from prehistoric civilizations to the Greco-Roman period. Much of the museum is devoted to ancient Egyptian history; permanent exhibits explore the Pharaonic era.

**The British Museum, London, England:** The British Museum explores the histories of virtually all world cultures, from ancient to contemporary. Nations and their civilizations are represented by displays of art, sciences, cultural and historical artifacts, clothing, and currency.

**The National Gallery, London, England:** On permanent display at the National Gallery is one of the world's greatest collections of Western European painting, with more than 2,300 works from the 13th–20th century.

**Tate Britain (formerly the Tate Gallery), London, England:** One of the world's most prestigious art institutions, Tate Britain houses the world's most extensive collection of British art from the 16th century to the present. Branches of the Tate in Liverpool, St. Ives, and Bankside are devoted to modern British and world art.

**Victoria and Albert Museum, London, England:** Although it boasts a wide array of fine arts and cultural artifacts, the Victoria and Albert Museum is especially devoted to applied and decorative arts. Examples of fashion, sculpture, ceramics, glass, metalwork, jewelry, furniture, photography, and paintings from various nations are on permanent display.

**La Cité des Sciences et d'Industrie, Paris, France:** The museum is devoted primarily to popular science. It houses its own planetarium as well as permanent exhibits on space, information technology, medicine, mathematics, the ocean, and numerous other topics. Also on display is a French navy submarine.

**Musée d'Orsay, Paris, France:** The Musée d'Orsay acquired a reputation as a world-class museum soon after it opened in 1986. It is devoted to art of the Western world from 1848 to 1914, and its collection is drawn from three art institutions: the Louvre Museum, the Musée du Jeu de Paume, and France's National Museum of Modern Art.

**The Louvre Museum, Paris, France:** The Louvre is the most famous and revered museum in the world. The main building served as a medieval fortress and as a palace for the kings of France and has been used as a museum since 1793. The Louvre's collections are divided into seven departments: paintings; sculptures; prints and drawings; objets d'art; Oriental antiquities and Islamic art; Egyptian antiquities; and Greek, Etruscan, and Roman antiquities.

**Château de Versailles, Versailles, France:** The original château of the Palace of Versailles was built in 1623 as a hunting lodge and retreat for King Louis XIII. The palace was expanded throughout the 17th century, and in 1682 it became the official residence of the king and the Court of France. It is still used as an official national palace when both houses of parliament are convened, although much of the palace—including its many rooms of artistic and architectural masterpieces—is open to the public.

**Deutsches Historisches Museum, Berlin, Germany:** The German Historical Museum chronicles German history through its vast collection of artwork, historical documents, militaria, and artifacts of German culture.

**Gemäldegalerie Alte Meister, Dresden, Germany:** Located in historic Zwinger Castle, the Old Masters Picture Gallery houses a large collection of Italian Renaissance, Baroque, and 17th-century Flemish and Dutch paintings, including works by such masters as Rembrandt, Rubens, and Raphael.

**Alte Pinakothek, Munich, Germany:** The Old Pinakothek is home to one of the world's premier collections of European paintings from the 14th–18th century, including works by Rembrandt, da Vinci, and Raphael.

**The Acropolis Museum, Athens, Greece:** Located near the ruins of the Acropolis, the museum is the world's main repository of masterpieces of ancient Greek civilization, especially those of the Archaic period.

**National Archaeological Museum, Athens, Greece:** Considered the most important archaeological museum in Greece, the National Archaeological Museum is home to exhibits representative of all aspects of Greek cultural history. The museum houses one of the largest collections of ancient Greek art in the world.

**National Museum, New Delhi, India:** The National Museum houses a vast collection of art objects from India and the world. Its major holdings include archaeological objects, jewelry, paintings, decorative arts, and arms and armor.

**National Museum of Ireland, Dublin, Ireland:** The museum merged several major collections of Irish art and artifacts when it opened in 1890. Its archaeological and artistic exhibits include masterworks from 2000 BC to the 20th century.

**Galleria dell'Accademia, Florence, Italy:** The Gallery of the Academy houses a collection of 15th- and 16th-century paintings and many Tuscan paintings from the 13th–16th century. The museum is best known, however, for its sculptures by Michelangelo, notably his *David*.

**Galleria degli Uffizi, Florence, Italy:** The Uffizi is renowned for its world's finest collection of Italian Renaissance painting, particularly of the Florentine school. The gallery was established in the 16th century to house the many art treasures of the Medici family.

**Pinacoteca di Brera, Milan, Italy:** One of Italy's largest art galleries, founded in 1809 by Napoleon I, the Brera Picture Gallery is especially renowned for its paintings by the Venetian school.

**The Vatican Museums, Rome, Italy:** The Vatican Museums have housed the art collections of the popes since the beginning of the 15th century. The various galleries contain ancient sculptures and epigraphy, Etruscan and Egyptian artifacts, an outstanding collection of Italian religious paintings, and Russian and Byzantine paintings. A modern art collection was initiated in 1956, and the Vatican's first museum of contemporary art, housed in 65 galleries in the Vatican palace, opened in 1973.

**Gallerie dell'Accademia di Venezia, Venice, Italy:** The Galleries of the Academy of Venice house an unrivaled collection of paintings from the Venetian masters of the 13th–18th century, including outstanding works by Giovanni Bellini, Giorgione, Titian, Tintoretto, and Canaletto.

**Tokugawa Art Museum, Nagoya, Japan:** The Tokugawa Art Museum holds a vast collection of objects belonging to the descendants of the Tokugawa family, including weapons and furniture used by the family's feudal lords. One section of the museum is dedicated to the 12th-century picture scrolls of the Tale of Genji.

**Tokyo National Museum, Tokyo, Japan:** The TNM's collection includes major exhibits of Asian painting, sculpture, calligraphy, decorative art, rare books, photographs, metalwork, lacquerware, ceramics, textiles, and antiquities.

**Museo Nacional de Antropología, Mexico City, Mexico:** The collection of the National Museum of Anthropology includes anthropological, ethnological, and archaeological materials from Mexico's pre-Hispanic past, including treasures of the Aztecs, Mayas, Zapotecs, Mixtec, Purépechas, and Olmecs.

**Rijksmuseum, Amsterdam, The Netherlands:** With nearly one million objects, the Rijksmuseum is the largest museum of art and history in The Netherlands. It is perhaps best known for its collection of 17th-century Dutch paintings, including works by Rembrandt, Vermeer, and Jan Steen.

**Muzeum Narodowe w Warszawie, Warsaw, Poland:** The National Museum in Warsaw houses 780,000 items in its permanent galleries, including one of the richest and most diverse collections of European art in Poland. It is also home to the largest Polish scholarly library of books and documents related to art and world culture.

**The Catherine Palace, Moscow, Russia:** The immense Catherine Palace, with its extravagantly gilded interior, was originally built in the early 18th century for Catherine I. Visitors have access to several of the palace's suites, the Cameron Gallery, and the rooms of the Agate Pavilion.

**The State Hermitage Museum, St. Petersburg, Russia:** Occupying six buildings in the heart of St. Petersburg, the Hermitage was founded in 1764 as a private gallery for the art amassed by Empress Catherine the Great. In addition to its many Russian masterpieces, the museum houses works by Renaissance Italian and Baroque Dutch, Flemish, and French painters. Also noteworthy is its collection of Central Asian art.

**The State Russian Museum, St. Petersburg, Russia:** Housed in the buildings of the former Mikhailovsky Palace, the State Russian Museum is the central museum of Russian art and culture. The main building houses art from the 10th century through the revolution, including a comprehensive collection of painting and sculpture from the 18th and 19th centuries and an excellent collection of early Russian art, with fine icons from the 12th–14th century. In addition, there are collections of late 19th- and early 20th-century paintings, portraits, and applied arts and an ethnographic museum.

**Asian Civilisations Museum, Singapore:** The Asian Civilisations Museum traces the cultural history of China, Southeast Asia, India, and West Asia through its vast collection of ceramics, sculptures, and other artifacts.

**South African Museum, Cape Town, South Africa:** The South African Museum documents the natural history and anthropology of southern Africa. Objects dating to the origins of the region's indigenous populations are featured in the collection. The museum also houses a planetarium.

**Museo del Prado, Madrid, Spain:** The Prado Museum houses the world's richest and most comprehensive collection of Spanish painting, as well as masterpieces of other schools of European painting, especially Italian and Flemish art. The museum contains the world's most complete collections of the works of El Greco, Diego Velázquez, and Francisco de Goya.

**Swedish Museum of Natural History, Stockholm, Sweden:** Dedicated to the history of natural sciences, the Swedish Museum of Natural History houses millions of specimens within its four main divisions of botany, geology, paleontology, and zoology.

**National Palace Museum, Taipei, Taiwan:** The National Palace Museum houses several international art masterpieces but is especially known for its collections of porcelain, jade, silk paintings, calligraphy, and other arts of ancient China.

**The National Museum, Bangkok, Thailand:** In 1874 King Rama V established this first public museum in Bangkok to display the royal art collection. The museum today houses objects of art, archaeology, and culture from prehistoric to modern times. Among the major permanent exhibits are the Gallery of Thai History and the Gallery of Prehistory.

**Boston Museum of Fine Arts, Boston MA:** One of the world's most comprehensive art museums, the MFA was founded in 1870 with the art holdings of the Boston Athenaeum library as the nucleus of its collection. The museum has a major collection of Asian art from the 3rd millennium BC to modern times. It also has the largest collection outside France of paintings by Claude Monet, the world's foremost collection of 19th-century American art, and one of the world's finest collections of Egyptian Old Kingdom objects.

**The Art Institute of Chicago, Chicago IL:** The Art Institute's permanent exhibits include European, American, and Oriental sculpture, paintings, prints and drawings, and decorative arts, as well as photography and African and pre-Columbian American art. The museum is noted for its extensive collections of 19th-century French painting (Impressionist works in particular) and of 20th-century painting.

**Field Museum of Natural History, Chicago IL:** The Field Museum was established in 1893 to display the biological and anthropological artifacts gathered for the World's Columbian Exposition. Permanent exhibits explore the Earth's cultural history and biological and geologic development. A major addition to the museum in 2000 was "Sue," the largest, most complete, and best-preserved *Tyrannosaurus rex* fossil ever discovered.

**Los Angeles County Museum of Art, Los Angeles CA:** The museum's permanent collections emphasize Asian, Islamic, European, and American art from ancient times to the present. Also important are the exhibits of costumes and textiles, decorative arts, and photography that represent various world cultures.

**Guggenheim Museum, New York NY:** The museum's permanent collections emphasize modern art, including Impressionist, nonobjective, abstract, surrealist, minimalist, and avant-garde works.

**Metropolitan Museum of Art, New York NY:** The most prestigious art institution in the United States, the museum houses more than 3,000,000 objects representing virtually all nations and all periods of human history.

**Museum of Modern Art, New York NY:** The collection at "MoMA" includes more than 100,000 paintings, sculptures, drawings, prints, photographs, architectural models and drawings, and design objects. Also housed in the museum are more than 14,000 films, 4,000,000 film stills, and an extensive library of books and periodicals.

**The National Gallery of Art, Washington DC:** The National Gallery, founded by Andrew Mellon in the 1930s, houses many of the world's most renowned examples of European and American painting, sculpture, and graphic arts from the 14th century to the present.

**The Smithsonian Institution, Washington DC:** One of the world's leading museums and research institutions, the Smithsonian comprises 16 museums (which house more than 140 million artifacts) and several research facilities throughout the world. The museums include the National Museum of American History, the National Zoological Park, the National Air and Space Museum, the Anacostia Museum and Center for African American History and Culture, the National Museum of the American Indian, and the National Portrait Gallery.

**United States Holocaust Memorial Museum, Washington DC:** The United States' national institution for studying the Holocaust, the museum also serves as a memorial to the millions who died in the Holocaust. Located near the National Mall in Washington DC, the museum uses exhibitions, publications, and public programs to promote awareness of the issues related to the Holocaust.

---

**Did you know?** A museum dedicated to the history of cinema and the invention of film projection for mass audiences opened in 2003 in Lyon, France, at l'Institut Lumière. The institute is named for the the brothers Auguste and Louis Lumière, whose late 19th-century inventions led to the emergence of the motion picture industry.

---

# Motion Pictures

## Academy Awards (Oscars), 2002

The Academy of Motion Picture Arts and Sciences was formed in 1927 and first awarded the Academy Awards of Merit in May 1929. The honored categories have varied over the years, but best picture, actor, actress, and director have been awarded since the beginning. Awards for supporting actor and actress were added for the films of 1936 and best foreign-language film for 1947. The ceremony is generally held in the early spring of the year following the release of films under consideration; the latest Oscars were awarded 23 Mar 2003 in Los Angeles. Award: gold-plated statuette of a man with a sword.

Academy of Motion Picture Arts and Sciences Web site: <www.oscars.org>.

| CATEGORY | WINNER |
| --- | --- |
| Motion picture of the year | *Chicago* (US; Rob Marshall, director) |
| Director | Roman Polanski (*The Pianist,* UK/France/Germany/Netherlands/Poland) |
| Actor | Adrien Brody (*The Pianist,* UK/France/Germany/Netherlands/Poland) |
| Actress | Nicole Kidman (*The Hours,* US) |
| Supporting actor | Chris Cooper (*Adaptation,* US) |

## Academy Awards (Oscars), 2002 (continued)

| CATEGORY | WINNER |
|---|---|
| Supporting actress | Catherine Zeta-Jones (*Chicago*, US) |
| Foreign-language film | *Nowhere in Africa* (Germany; Caroline Link, director) |
| Animated feature | *Spirited Away* (US/Japan; Hayao Miyazaki, director) |
| Animated short | *The ChubbChubbs!* (US; Eric Armstrong, director) |
| Live-action short | *Der Er En Yndig Mand (This Charming Man)* (Denmark; Martin Strange-Hansen, director) |
| Documentary feature | *Bowling for Columbine* (US; Michael Moore, director) |
| Documentary short | *Twin Towers* (US; Bill Guttentag and Robert David Port, directors) |
| Art direction | John Myhre, art director, Gordon Sim, set decoration (*Chicago*, US) |
| Cinematography | Conrad L. Hall (*Road to Perdition*, US) |
| Costume design | Colleen Atwood (*Chicago*, US) |
| Film editing | Martin Walsh (*Chicago*, US) |
| Makeup | John Jackson, Beatrice De Alba (*Frida*, Canada/US) |
| Original score | Elliot Goldenthal (*Frida*, Canada/US) |
| Original song | "Lose Yourself," Eminem (*8 Mile*, US) |
| Sound | Michael Minkler, Dominick Tavella, David Lee (*Chicago*, US) |
| Sound editing | Ethan Van der Ryn and Michael Hopkins (*The Lord of the Rings: The Two Towers*, New Zealand/US) |
| Visual effects | Jim Rygiel, Joe Letteri, Randall William Cook, Alex Funke (*The Lord of the Rings: The Two Towers*, New Zealand/US) |
| Screenplay, adaptation | Ronald Harwood (*The Pianist*, UK/France/Germany/Netherlands/Poland) |
| Screenplay, original | Pedro Almodóvar (*Habla con ella [Talk to Her]*, Spain) |

## Academy Awards (Oscars), 1928–2002

*2003 awards ceremony scheduled to be held 29 Feb 2004 in Los Angeles.*

**BEST PICTURE**

| | |
|---|---|
| 1928 | *Wings* |
| 1929 | *The Broadway Melody* |
| 1930 | *All Quiet on the Western Front* |
| 1931 | *Cimarron* |
| 1932 | *Grand Hotel* |
| 1933 | *Cavalcade* |
| 1934 | *It Happened One Night* |
| 1935 | *Mutiny on the Bounty* |
| 1936 | *The Great Ziegfeld* |
| 1937 | *The Life of Emile Zola* |
| 1938 | *You Can't Take It with You* |
| 1939 | *Gone with the Wind* |
| 1940 | *Rebecca* |
| 1941 | *How Green Was My Valley* |
| 1942 | *Mrs. Miniver* |
| 1943 | *Casablanca* |
| 1944 | *Going My Way* |
| 1945 | *The Lost Weekend* |
| 1946 | *The Best Years of Our Lives* |
| 1947 | *Gentleman's Agreement* |
| 1948 | *Hamlet* |
| 1949 | *All the King's Men* |
| 1950 | *All About Eve* |
| 1951 | *An American in Paris* |
| 1952 | *The Greatest Show on Earth* |

**BEST PICTURE (CONTINUED)**

| | |
|---|---|
| 1953 | *From Here to Eternity* |
| 1954 | *On the Waterfront* |
| 1955 | *Marty* |
| 1956 | *Around the World in 80 Days* |
| 1957 | *The Bridge on the River Kwai* |
| 1958 | *Gigi* |
| 1959 | *Ben-Hur* |
| 1960 | *The Apartment* |
| 1961 | *West Side Story* |
| 1962 | *Lawrence of Arabia* |
| 1963 | *Tom Jones* |
| 1964 | *My Fair Lady* |
| 1965 | *The Sound of Music* |
| 1966 | *A Man for All Seasons* |
| 1967 | *In the Heat of the Night* |
| 1968 | *Oliver!* |
| 1969 | *Midnight Cowboy* |
| 1970 | *Patton* |
| 1971 | *The French Connection* |
| 1972 | *The Godfather* |
| 1973 | *The Sting* |
| 1974 | *The Godfather Part II* |
| 1975 | *One Flew Over the Cuckoo's Nest* |
| 1976 | *Rocky* |

**BEST PICTURE (CONTINUED)**

| | |
|---|---|
| 1977 | *Annie Hall* |
| 1978 | *The Deer Hunter* |
| 1979 | *Kramer vs. Kramer* |
| 1980 | *Ordinary People* |
| 1981 | *Chariots of Fire* |
| 1982 | *Gandhi* |
| 1983 | *Terms of Endearment* |
| 1984 | *Amadeus* |
| 1985 | *Out of Africa* |
| 1986 | *Platoon* |
| 1987 | *The Last Emperor* |
| 1988 | *Rain Man* |
| 1989 | *Driving Miss Daisy* |
| 1990 | *Dances with Wolves* |
| 1991 | *The Silence of the Lambs* |
| 1992 | *Unforgiven* |
| 1993 | *Schindler's List* |
| 1994 | *Forrest Gump* |
| 1995 | *Braveheart* |
| 1996 | *The English Patient* |
| 1997 | *Titanic* |
| 1998 | *Shakespeare in Love* |
| 1999 | *American Beauty* |
| 2000 | *Gladiator* |
| 2001 | *A Beautiful Mind* |
| 2002 | *Chicago* |

**BEST ACTOR**

| | |
|---|---|
| 1928 | Emil Jannings (*The Last Command; The Way of All Flesh*) |
| 1929 | Warner Baxter (*In Old Arizona*) |
| 1930 | George Arliss (*Disraeli*) |
| 1931 | Lionel Barrymore (*A Free Soul*) |
| 1932 | Wallace Beery (*The Champ*), Fredric March (*Dr. Jekyll and Mr. Hyde*) |
| 1933 | Charles Laughton (*The Private Life of Henry VIII*) |
| 1934 | Clark Gable (*It Happened One Night*) |
| 1935 | Victor McLaglen (*The Informer*) |

**BEST ACTOR (CONTINUED)**

| | |
|---|---|
| 1936 | Paul Muni (*The Story of Louis Pasteur*) |
| 1937 | Spencer Tracy (*Captains Courageous*) |
| 1938 | Spencer Tracy (*Boys Town*) |
| 1939 | Robert Donat (*Goodbye, Mr. Chips*) |
| 1940 | James Stewart (*The Philadelphia Story*) |
| 1941 | Gary Cooper (*Sergeant York*) |
| 1942 | James Cagney (*Yankee Doodle Dandy*) |
| 1943 | Paul Lukas (*Watch on the Rhine*) |
| 1944 | Bing Crosby (*Going My Way*) |
| 1945 | Ray Milland (*The Lost Weekend*) |
| 1946 | Fredric March (*The Best Years of Our Lives*) |

# Academy Awards (Oscars), 1928–2002 (continued)

## BEST ACTOR (CONTINUED)

1947  Ronald Colman *(A Double Life)*
1948  Laurence Olivier *(Hamlet)*
1949  Broderick Crawford *(All the King's Men)*
1950  José Ferrer *(Cyrano de Bergerac)*
1951  Humphrey Bogart *(The African Queen)*
1952  Gary Cooper *(High Noon)*
1953  William Holden *(Stalag 17)*
1954  Marlon Brando *(On the Waterfront)*
1955  Ernest Borgnine *(Marty)*
1956  Yul Brynner *(The King and I)*
1957  Alec Guinness *(The Bridge on the River Kwai)*
1958  David Niven *(Separate Tables)*
1959  Charlton Heston *(Ben-Hur)*
1960  Burt Lancaster *(Elmer Gantry)*
1961  Maximilian Schell *(Judgment at Nuremberg)*
1962  Gregory Peck *(To Kill a Mockingbird)*
1963  Sidney Poitier *(Lilies of the Field)*
1964  Rex Harrison *(My Fair Lady)*
1965  Lee Marvin *(Cat Ballou)*
1966  Paul Scofield *(A Man for All Seasons)*
1967  Rod Steiger *(In the Heat of the Night)*
1968  Cliff Robertson *(Charly)*
1969  John Wayne *(True Grit)*
1970  George C. Scott *(Patton)* (refused)
1971  Gene Hackman *(The French Connection)*
1972  Marlon Brando *(The Godfather)*
1973  Jack Lemmon *(Save the Tiger)*
1974  Art Carney *(Harry and Tonto)*
1975  Jack Nicholson *(One Flew Over the Cuckoo's Nest)*
1976  Peter Finch *(Network)* (posthumous)
1977  Richard Dreyfuss *(The Goodbye Girl)*
1978  Jon Voight *(Coming Home)*
1979  Dustin Hoffman *(Kramer vs. Kramer)*
1980  Robert De Niro *(Raging Bull)*
1981  Henry Fonda *(On Golden Pond)*
1982  Ben Kingsley *(Gandhi)*
1983  Robert Duvall *(Tender Mercies)*
1984  F. Murray Abraham *(Amadeus)*
1985  William Hurt *(Kiss of the Spider Woman)*
1986  Paul Newman *(The Color of Money)*
1987  Michael Douglas *(Wall Street)*
1988  Dustin Hoffman *(Rain Man)*
1989  Daniel Day-Lewis *(My Left Foot)*
1990  Jeremy Irons *(Reversal of Fortune)*
1991  Anthony Hopkins *(The Silence of the Lambs)*
1992  Al Pacino *(Scent of a Woman)*
1993  Tom Hanks *(Philadelphia)*
1994  Tom Hanks *(Forrest Gump)*
1995  Nicolas Cage *(Leaving Las Vegas)*
1996  Geoffrey Rush *(Shine)*
1997  Jack Nicholson *(As Good as It Gets)*
1998  Roberto Benigni *(Life Is Beautiful)*
1999  Kevin Spacey *(American Beauty)*
2000  Russell Crowe *(Gladiator)*
2001  Denzel Washington *(Training Day)*
2002  Adrien Brody *(The Pianist)*

## BEST ACTRESS

1928  Janet Gaynor *(7th Heaven; Street Angel; Sunrise)*
1929  Mary Pickford *(Coquette)*
1930  Norma Shearer *(The Divorcee)*
1931  Marie Dressler *(Min and Bill)*
1932  Helen Hayes *(The Sin of Madelon Claudet)*
1933  Katharine Hepburn *(Morning Glory)*
1934  Claudette Colbert *(It Happened One Night)*
1935  Bette Davis *(Dangerous)*

## BEST ACTRESS (CONTINUED)

1936  Luise Rainer *(The Great Ziegfeld)*
1937  Luise Rainer *(The Good Earth)*
1938  Bette Davis *(Jezebel)*
1939  Vivien Leigh *(Gone with the Wind)*
1940  Ginger Rogers *(Kitty Foyle)*
1941  Joan Fontaine *(Suspicion)*
1942  Greer Garson *(Mrs. Miniver)*
1943  Jennifer Jones *(The Song of Bernadette)*
1944  Ingrid Bergman *(Gaslight)*
1945  Joan Crawford *(Mildred Pierce)*
1946  Olivia de Havilland *(To Each His Own)*
1947  Loretta Young *(The Farmer's Daughter)*
1948  Jane Wyman *(Johnny Belinda)*
1949  Olivia de Havilland *(The Heiress)*
1950  Judy Holliday *(Born Yesterday)*
1951  Vivien Leigh *(A Streetcar Named Desire)*
1952  Shirley Booth *(Come Back, Little Sheba)*
1953  Audrey Hepburn *(Roman Holiday)*
1954  Grace Kelly *(The Country Girl)*
1955  Anna Magnani *(The Rose Tattoo)*
1956  Ingrid Bergman *(Anastasia)*
1957  Joanne Woodward *(The Three Faces of Eve)*
1958  Susan Hayward *(I Want to Live!)*
1959  Simone Signoret *(Room at the Top)*
1960  Elizabeth Taylor *(Butterfield 8)*
1961  Sophia Loren *(Two Women)*
1962  Anne Bancroft *(The Miracle Worker)*
1963  Patricia Neal *(Hud)*
1964  Julie Andrews *(Mary Poppins)*
1965  Julie Christie *(Darling)*
1966  Elizabeth Taylor *(Who's Afraid of Virginia Woolf?)*
1967  Katharine Hepburn *(Guess Who's Coming to Dinner)*
1968  Katharine Hepburn *(The Lion in Winter)*, Barbra Streisand *(Funny Girl)*
1969  Maggie Smith *(The Prime of Miss Jean Brodie)*
1970  Glenda Jackson *(Women in Love)*
1971  Jane Fonda *(Klute)*
1972  Liza Minnelli *(Cabaret)*
1973  Glenda Jackson *(A Touch of Class)*
1974  Ellen Burstyn *(Alice Doesn't Live Here Anymore)*
1975  Louise Fletcher *(One Flew Over the Cuckoo's Nest)*
1976  Faye Dunaway *(Network)*
1977  Diane Keaton *(Annie Hall)*
1978  Jane Fonda *(Coming Home)*
1979  Sally Field *(Norma Rae)*
1980  Sissy Spacek *(Coal Miner's Daughter)*
1981  Katharine Hepburn *(On Golden Pond)*
1982  Meryl Streep *(Sophie's Choice)*
1983  Shirley MacLaine *(Terms of Endearment)*
1984  Sally Field *(Places in the Heart)*
1985  Geraldine Page *(The Trip to Bountiful)*
1986  Marlee Matlin *(Children of a Lesser God)*
1987  Cher *(Moonstruck)*
1988  Jodie Foster *(The Accused)*
1989  Jessica Tandy *(Driving Miss Daisy)*
1990  Kathy Bates *(Misery)*
1991  Jodie Foster *(The Silence of the Lambs)*
1992  Emma Thompson *(Howards End)*
1993  Holly Hunter *(The Piano)*
1994  Jessica Lange *(Blue Sky)*
1995  Susan Sarandon *(Dead Man Walking)*
1996  Frances McDormand *(Fargo)*
1997  Helen Hunt *(As Good as It Gets)*

## Academy Awards (Oscars), 1928–2002 (continued)

**BEST ACTRESS (CONTINUED)**
1998 Gwyneth Paltrow (Shakespeare in Love)
1999 Hilary Swank (Boys Don't Cry)
2000 Julia Roberts (Erin Brockovich)
2001 Halle Berry (Monster's Ball)
2002 Nicole Kidman (The Hours)

**BEST SUPPORTING ACTOR**
1936 Walter Brennan (Come and Get It)
1937 Joseph Schildkraut (The Life of Emile Zola)
1938 Walter Brennan (Kentucky)
1939 Thomas Mitchell (Stagecoach)
1940 Walter Brennan (The Westerner)
1941 Donald Crisp (How Green Was My Valley)
1942 Van Heflin (Johnny Eager)
1943 Charles Coburn (The More the Merrier)
1944 Barry Fitzgerald (Going My Way)
1945 James Dunn (A Tree Grows in Brooklyn)
1946 Harold Russell (The Best Years of Our Lives)
1947 Edmund Gwenn (Miracle on 34th Street)
1948 Walter Huston (The Treasure of the Sierra Madre)
1949 Dean Jagger (Twelve O'Clock High)
1950 George Sanders (All About Eve)
1951 Karl Malden (A Streetcar Named Desire)
1952 Anthony Quinn (Viva Zapata!)
1953 Frank Sinatra (From Here to Eternity)
1954 Edmond O'Brien (The Barefoot Contessa)
1955 Jack Lemmon (Mister Roberts)
1956 Anthony Quinn (Lust for Life)
1957 Red Buttons (Sayonara)
1958 Burl Ives (The Big Country)
1959 Hugh Griffith (Ben-Hur)
1960 Peter Ustinov (Spartacus)
1961 George Chakiris (West Side Story)
1962 Ed Begley (Sweet Bird of Youth)
1963 Melvyn Douglas (Hud)
1964 Peter Ustinov (Topkapi)
1965 Martin Balsam (A Thousand Clowns)
1966 Walter Matthau (The Fortune Cookie)
1967 George Kennedy (Cool Hand Luke)
1968 Jack Albertson (The Subject Was Roses)
1969 Gig Young (They Shoot Horses, Don't They?)
1970 John Mills (Ryan's Daughter)
1971 Ben Johnson (The Last Picture Show)
1972 Joel Grey (Cabaret)
1973 John Houseman (The Paper Chase)
1974 Robert De Niro (The Godfather Part II)
1975 George Burns (The Sunshine Boys)
1976 Jason Robards (All the President's Men)
1977 Jason Robards (Julia)
1978 Christopher Walken (The Deer Hunter)
1979 Melvyn Douglas (Being There)
1980 Timothy Hutton (Ordinary People)
1981 John Gielgud (Arthur)
1982 Louis Gossett, Jr. (An Officer and a Gentleman)
1983 Jack Nicholson (Terms of Endearment)
1984 Haing S. Ngor (The Killing Fields)
1985 Don Ameche (Cocoon)
1986 Michael Caine (Hannah and Her Sisters)
1987 Sean Connery (The Untouchables)
1988 Kevin Kline (A Fish Called Wanda)
1989 Denzel Washington (Glory)
1990 Joe Pesci (Goodfellas)
1991 Jack Palance (City Slickers)
1992 Gene Hackman (Unforgiven)
1993 Tommy Lee Jones (The Fugitive)
1994 Martin Landau (Ed Wood)

**BEST SUPPORTING ACTOR (CONTINUED)**
1995 Kevin Spacey (The Usual Suspects)
1996 Cuba Gooding, Jr. (Jerry Maguire)
1997 Robin Williams (Good Will Hunting)
1998 James Coburn (Affliction)
1999 Michael Caine (The Cider House Rules)
2000 Benicio Del Toro (Traffic)
2001 Jim Broadbent (Iris)
2002 Chris Cooper (Adaptation)

**BEST SUPPORTING ACTRESS**
1936 Gale Sondergaard (Anthony Adverse)
1937 Alice Brady (In Old Chicago)
1938 Fay Bainter (Jezebel)
1939 Hattie McDaniel (Gone with the Wind)
1940 Jane Darwell (The Grapes of Wrath)
1941 Mary Astor (The Great Lie)
1942 Teresa Wright (Mrs. Miniver)
1943 Katina Paxinou (For Whom the Bell Tolls)
1944 Ethel Barrymore (None but the Lonely Heart)
1945 Anne Revere (National Velvet)
1946 Anne Baxter (The Razor's Edge)
1947 Celeste Holm (Gentleman's Agreement)
1948 Claire Trevor (Key Largo)
1949 Mercedes McCambridge (All the King's Men)
1950 Josephine Hull (Harvey)
1951 Kim Hunter (A Streetcar Named Desire)
1952 Gloria Grahame (The Bad and the Beautiful)
1953 Donna Reed (From Here to Eternity)
1954 Eva Marie Saint (On the Waterfront)
1955 Jo Van Fleet (East of Eden)
1956 Dorothy Malone (Written on the Wind)
1957 Miyoshi Umeki (Sayonara)
1958 Wendy Hiller (Separate Tables)
1959 Shelley Winters (The Diary of Anne Frank)
1960 Shirley Jones (Elmer Gantry)
1961 Rita Moreno (West Side Story)
1962 Patty Duke (The Miracle Worker)
1963 Margaret Rutherford (The V.I.P.s)
1964 Lila Kedrova (Zorba the Greek)
1965 Shelley Winters (A Patch of Blue)
1966 Sandy Dennis (Who's Afraid of Virginia Woolf?)
1967 Estelle Parsons (Bonnie and Clyde)
1968 Ruth Gordon (Rosemary's Baby)
1969 Goldie Hawn (Cactus Flower)
1970 Helen Hayes (Airport)
1971 Cloris Leachman (The Last Picture Show)
1972 Eileen Heckart (Butterflies Are Free)
1973 Tatum O'Neal (Paper Moon)
1974 Ingrid Bergman (Murder on the Orient Express)
1975 Lee Grant (Shampoo)
1976 Beatrice Straight (Network)
1977 Vanessa Redgrave (Julia)
1978 Maggie Smith (California Suite)
1979 Meryl Streep (Kramer vs. Kramer)
1980 Mary Steenburgen (Melvin and Howard)
1981 Maureen Stapleton (Reds)
1982 Jessica Lange (Tootsie)
1983 Linda Hunt (The Year of Living Dangerously)
1984 Peggy Ashcroft (A Passage to India)
1985 Anjelica Huston (Prizzi's Honor)
1986 Dianne Wiest (Hannah and Her Sisters)
1987 Olympia Dukakis (Moonstruck)
1988 Geena Davis (The Accidental Tourist)
1989 Brenda Fricker (My Left Foot)
1990 Whoopi Goldberg (Ghost)
1991 Mercedes Ruehl (The Fisher King)
1992 Marisa Tomei (My Cousin Vinny)

# Academy Awards (Oscars), 1928–2002 (continued)

**BEST SUPPORTING ACTRESS (CONTINUED)**
1993   Anna Paquin *(The Piano)*
1994   Dianne Wiest *(Bullets over Broadway)*
1995   Mira Sorvino *(Mighty Aphrodite)*
1996   Juliette Binoche *(The English Patient)*
1997   Kim Basinger *(L.A. Confidential)*
1998   Judi Dench *(Shakespeare in Love)*
1999   Angelina Jolie *(Girl, Interrupted)*
2000   Marcia Gay Harden *(Pollock)*
2001   Jennifer Connelly *(A Beautiful Mind)*
2002   Catherine Zeta-Jones *(Chicago)*

**FOREIGN LANGUAGE FILM (AMERICAN TITLES)**
1947   *Shoe-Shine* (Italy)
1948   *Monsieur Vincent* (France)
1949   *The Bicycle Thief* (Italy)
1950   *The Walls of Malapaga* (France/Italy)
1951   *Rashomon* (Japan)
1952   *Forbidden Games* (France)
1953   not awarded
1954   *Gate of Hell* (Japan)
1955   *Samurai, the Legend of Musashi* (Japan)
1956   *La Strada* (Italy)
1957   *The Nights of Cabiria* (Italy)
1958   *My Uncle* (France)
1959   *Black Orpheus* (France)
1960   *The Virgin Spring* (Sweden)
1961   *Through a Glass Darkly* (Sweden)
1962   *Sundays and Cybele* (France)
1963   *8½* (Italy)
1964   *Yesterday, Today and Tomorrow* (Italy)
1965   *The Shop on Main Street* (Czechoslovakia)
1966   *A Man and a Woman* (France)
1967   *Closely Watched Trains* (Czechoslovakia)
1968   *War and Peace* (USSR)
1969   *Z* (Algeria)
1970   *Investigation of a Citizen Above Suspicion* (Italy)
1971   *The Garden of the Finzi Continis* (Italy)
1972   *The Discreet Charm of the Bourgeoisie* (France)
1973   *Day for Night* (France)
1974   *Amarcord* (Italy)
1975   *Dersu Uzala* (USSR)
1976   *Black and White in Color* (Ivory Coast)
1977   *Madame Rosa* (France)
1978   *Get Out Your Handkerchiefs* (France)
1979   *The Tin Drum* (West Germany)
1980   *Moscow Does Not Believe in Tears* (USSR)
1981   *Mephisto* (Hungary)
1982   *To Begin Again* (Spain)
1983   *Fanny & Alexander* (Sweden)
1984   *Dangerous Moves* (Switzerland)
1985   *The Official Story* (Argentina)
1986   *The Assault* (The Netherlands)
1987   *Babette's Feast* (Denmark)
1988   *Pelle the Conqueror* (Denmark)
1989   *Cinema Paradiso* (Italy)
1990   *Journey of Hope* (Switzerland)
1991   *Mediterraneo* (Italy)
1992   *Indochine* (France)
1993   *Belle Epoque* (Spain)
1994   *Burnt by the Sun* (Russia)
1995   *Antonia's Line* (The Netherlands)
1996   *Kolya* (Czech Republic)
1997   *Character* (The Netherlands)
1998   *Life Is Beautiful* (Italy)
1999   *All About My Mother* (Spain)
2000   *Crouching Tiger, Hidden Dragon* (Taiwan)

**FOREIGN LANGUAGE FILM (AMERICAN TITLES) (CONTINUED)**
2001   *No Man's Land* (Belgium/Bosnia and Herzegovina/France/Italy/Slovenia/UK)
2002   *Nowhere in Africa* (Germany)

**DIRECTING**
1928   Lewis Milestone *(Two Arabian Knights)*, Frank Borzage *(7th Heaven)*
1929   Frank Lloyd *(The Divine Lady)*
1930   Lewis Milestone *(All Quiet on the Western Front)*
1931   Norman Taurog *(Skippy)*
1932   Frank Borzage *(Bad Girl)*
1933   Frank Lloyd *(Cavalcade)*
1934   Frank Capra *(It Happened One Night)*
1935   John Ford *(The Informer)*
1936   Frank Capra *(Mr. Deeds Goes to Town)*
1937   Leo McCarey *(The Awful Truth)*
1938   Frank Capra *(You Can't Take It with You)*
1939   Victor Fleming *(Gone with the Wind)*
1940   John Ford *(The Grapes of Wrath)*
1941   John Ford *(How Green Was My Valley)*
1942   William Wyler *(Mrs. Miniver)*
1943   Michael Curtiz *(Casablanca)*
1944   Leo McCarey *(Going My Way)*
1945   Billy Wilder *(The Lost Weekend)*
1946   William Wyler *(The Best Years of Our Lives)*
1947   Elia Kazan *(Gentleman's Agreement)*
1948   John Huston *(The Treasure of the Sierra Madre)*
1949   Joseph L. Mankiewicz *(A Letter to Three Wives)*
1950   Joseph L. Mankiewicz *(All About Eve)*
1951   George Stevens *(A Place in the Sun)*
1952   John Ford *(The Quiet Man)*
1953   Fred Zinnemann *(From Here to Eternity)*
1954   Elia Kazan *(On the Waterfront)*
1955   Delbert Mann *(Marty)*
1956   George Stevens *(Giant)*
1957   David Lean *(The Bridge on the River Kwai)*
1958   Vincente Minnelli *(Gigi)*
1959   William Wyler *(Ben-Hur)*
1960   Billy Wilder *(The Apartment)*
1961   Robert Wise, Jerome Robbins *(West Side Story)*
1962   David Lean *(Lawrence of Arabia)*
1963   Tony Richardson *(Tom Jones)*
1964   George Cukor *(My Fair Lady)*
1965   Robert Wise *(The Sound of Music)*
1966   Fred Zinnemann *(A Man for All Seasons)*
1967   Mike Nichols *(The Graduate)*
1968   Carol Reed *(Oliver!)*
1969   John Schlesinger *(Midnight Cowboy)*
1970   Franklin J. Schaffner *(Patton)*
1971   William Friedkin *(The French Connection)*
1972   Bob Fosse *(Cabaret)*
1973   George Roy Hill *(The Sting)*
1974   Francis Ford Coppola *(The Godfather Part II)*
1975   Milos Forman *(One Flew Over the Cuckoo's Nest)*
1976   John G. Avildsen *(Rocky)*
1977   Woody Allen *(Annie Hall)*
1978   Michael Cimino *(The Deer Hunter)*
1979   Robert Benton *(Kramer vs. Kramer)*
1980   Robert Redford *(Ordinary People)*
1981   Warren Beatty *(Reds)*
1982   Richard Attenborough *(Gandhi)*
1983   James L. Brooks *(Terms of Endearment)*

## Academy Awards (Oscars), 1928–2002 (continued)

**DIRECTING (CONTINUED)**

1984 Milos Forman (Amadeus)
1985 Sydney Pollack (Out of Africa)
1986 Oliver Stone (Platoon)
1987 Bernardo Bertolucci (The Last Emperor)
1988 Barry Levinson (Rain Man)
1989 Oliver Stone (Born on the Fourth of July)
1990 Kevin Costner (Dances with Wolves)
1991 Jonathan Demme (The Silence of the Lambs)
1992 Clint Eastwood (Unforgiven)
1993 Steven Spielberg (Schindler's List)
1994 Robert Zemeckis (Forrest Gump)
1995 Mel Gibson (Braveheart)
1996 Anthony Minghella (The English Patient)
1997 James Cameron (Titanic)
1998 Steven Spielberg (Saving Private Ryan)
1999 Sam Mendes (American Beauty)
2000 Steven Soderbergh (Traffic)
2001 Ron Howard (A Beautiful Mind)
2002 Roman Polanski (The Pianist)

**SCREENPLAY, ADAPTATION[1]**

1928 Benjamin Glazer (7th Heaven)
1931 Howard Estabrook (Cimarron)
1932 Edwin Burke (Bad Girl)
1933 Victor Heerman, Sarah Y. Mason (Little Women)
1934 Robert Riskin (It Happened One Night)
1935 Dudley Nichols (The Informer)[2]
1936 Pierre Collings, Sheridan Gibney (The Story of Louis Pasteur)[2]
1937 Norman Reilly Raine, Heinz Herald, Geza Herczeg (The Life of Emile Zola)[2]
1938 George Bernard Shaw, W.P. Lipscomb, Cecil Lewis, Ian Dalrymple (Pygmalion)[2]
1939 Sidney Howard (Gone with the Wind)[2]
1940 Donald Ogden Stewart (The Philadelphia Story)[2]
1941 Sidney Buchman, Seton I. Miller (Here Comes Mr. Jordan)[2]
1942 George Froeschel, James Hilton, Claudine West, Arthur Wimperis (Mrs. Miniver)[2]
1943 Julius J. Epstein, Philip G. Epstein, Howard Koch (Casablanca)[2]
1944 Frank Butler, Frank Cavett (Going My Way)[2]
1945 Charles Brackett, Billy Wilder (The Lost Weekend)[2]
1946 Robert E. Sherwood (The Best Years of Our Lives)[2]
1947 George Seaton (Miracle on 34th Street)[2]
1948 John Huston (The Treasure of the Sierra Madre)[2]
1949 Joseph L. Mankiewicz (A Letter to Three Wives)[2]
1950 Joseph L. Mankiewicz (All About Eve)[2]
1951 Michael Wilson, Harry Brown (A Place in the Sun)[2]
1952 Charles Schnee (The Bad and the Beautiful)[2]
1953 Daniel Taradash (From Here to Eternity)[2]
1954 George Seaton (The Country Girl)[2]
1955 Paddy Chayefsky (Marty)[2]
1956 James Poe, John Farrow, S.J. Perelman (Around the World in 80 Days)
1957 Pierre Boulle, Michael Wilson, Carl Foreman (The Bridge on the River Kwai)
1958 Alan Jay Lerner (Gigi)
1959 Neil Paterson (Room at the Top)
1960 Richard Brooks (Elmer Gantry)

**SCREENPLAY, ADAPTATION[1] (CONTINUED)**

1961 Abby Mann (Judgment at Nuremberg)
1962 Horton Foote (To Kill a Mockingbird)
1963 John Osborne (Tom Jones)
1964 Edward Anhalt (Becket)
1965 Robert Bolt (Doctor Zhivago)
1966 Robert Bolt (A Man for All Seasons)
1967 Stirling Silliphant (In the Heat of the Night)
1968 James Goldman (The Lion in Winter)
1969 Waldo Salt (Midnight Cowboy)
1970 Ring Lardner, Jr. (M*A*S*H)
1971 Ernest Tidyman (The French Connection)
1972 Mario Puzo, Francis Ford Coppola (The Godfather)
1973 William Peter Blatty (The Exorcist)
1974 Francis Ford Coppola, Mario Puzo (The Godfather Part II)
1975 Lawrence Hauben, Bo Goldman (One Flew Over the Cuckoo's Nest)
1976 William Goldman (All the President's Men)
1977 Alvin Sargent (Julia)
1978 Oliver Stone (Midnight Express)
1979 Robert Benton (Kramer vs. Kramer)
1980 Alvin Sargent (Ordinary People)
1981 Ernest Thompson (On Golden Pond)
1982 Costa-Gavras, Donald Stewart (Missing)
1983 James L. Brooks (Terms of Endearment)
1984 Peter Shaffer (Amadeus)
1985 Kurt Luedtke (Out of Africa)
1986 Ruth Prawer Jhabvala (A Room with a View)
1987 Mark Peploe, Bernardo Bertolucci (The Last Emperor)
1988 Christopher Hampton (Dangerous Liaisons)
1989 Alfred Uhry (Driving Miss Daisy)
1990 Michael Blake (Dances with Wolves)
1991 Ted Tally (The Silence of the Lambs)
1992 Ruth Prawer Jhabvala (Howards End)
1993 Steven Zaillian (Schindler's List)
1994 Eric Roth (Forrest Gump)
1995 Emma Thompson (Sense and Sensibility)
1996 Billy Bob Thornton (Sling Blade)
1997 Brian Helgeland, Curtis Hanson (L.A. Confidential)
1998 Bill Condon (Gods and Monsters)
1999 John Irving (The Cider House Rules)
2000 Stephen Gaghan (Traffic)
2001 Akiva Goldsman (A Beautiful Mind)
2002 Ronald Harwood (The Pianist)

**SCREENPLAY, ORIGINAL[1]**

1928 Ben Hecht (Underworld),[4] Joseph Farnham (The Fair Co-Ed; Laugh, Clown, Laugh; Telling the World [titles])
1929 Hans Kraly (The Patriot)
1930 Frances Marion (The Big House)
1931 John Monk Saunders (The Dawn Patrol)[4]
1932 Frances Marion (The Champ)[4]
1933 Robert Lord (One Way Passage)[4]
1934 Arthur Caesar (Manhattan Melodrama)[4]
1935 Ben Hecht, Charles MacArthur (The Scoundrel)[4]
1936 Pierre Collings, Sheridan Gibney (The Story of Louis Pasteur)[4]
1937 William A. Wellman, Robert Carson (A Star Is Born)[4]
1938 Eleanore Griffin, Dore Schary (Boys Town)[4]
1939 Lewis R. Foster (Mr. Smith Goes to Washington)[4]

# Academy Awards (Oscars), 1928–2002 (continued)

**SCREENPLAY, ORIGINAL[1] (CONTINUED)**

1940 Preston Sturges *(The Great McGinty)*,[3] Benjamin Glazer, John S. Toldy *(Arise, My Love)*[4]
1941 Herman J. Mankiewicz, Orson Welles *(Citizen Kane)*,[3] Harry Segall *(Here Comes Mr. Jordan)*[4]
1942 Michael Kanin, Ring Lardner, Jr. *(Woman of the Year)*,[3] Emeric Pressburger *(Forty-Ninth Parallel)*[4]
1943 Norman Krasna *(Princess O'Rourke)*,[3] William Saroyan *(The Human Comedy)*[4]
1944 Lamar Trotti *(Wilson)*,[3] Leo McCarey *(Going My Way)*[4]
1945 Richard Schweizer *(Marie-Louise)*,[3] Charles G. Booth *(The House on 92nd Street)*[4]
1946 Muriel Box, Sydney Box *(The Seventh Veil)*,[3] Clemence Dane *(Vacation from Marriage)*[4]
1947 Sidney Sheldon *(The Bachelor and the Bobby-Soxer)*,[3] Valentine Davies *(Miracle on 34th Street)*[4]
1948 Richard Schweizer, David Wechsler *(The Search)*[4]
1949 Robert Pirosh *(Battleground)*,[3] Douglas Morrow *(The Stratton Story)*[4]
1950 Charles Brackett, Billy Wilder, D.M. Marshman, Jr. *(Sunset Boulevard)*,[3] Edna Anhalt, Edward Anhalt *(Panic in the Streets)*[4]
1951 Alan Jay Lerner *(An American in Paris)*,[3] Paul Dehn, James Bernard *(Seven Days to Noon)*[4]
1952 T.E.B. Clarke *(The Lavender Hill Mob)*,[3] Fredric M. Frank, Theodore St. John, Frank Cavett *(The Greatest Show on Earth)*[4]
1953 Charles Brackett, Walter Reisch, Richard L. Breen *(Titanic)*,[3] Dalton Trumbo[5] (as Ian McLellan Hunter, *Roman Holiday)*[4]
1954 Budd Schulberg *(On the Waterfront)*,[3] Philip Yordan *(Broken Lance)*[4]
1955 William Ludwig, Sonya Levien *(Interrupted Melody)*,[3] Daniel Fuchs *(Love Me or Leave Me)*[4]
1956 Albert Lamorisse *(The Red Balloon)*,[3] Dalton Trumbo[5] (as Robert Rich, *The Brave One)*[4]
1957 George Wells *(Designing Woman)*
1958 Nedrick Young[5] (as Nathan E. Douglas), Harold Jacob Smith *(The Defiant Ones)*
1959 Russell Rouse, Clarence Greene, Stanley Shapiro, Maurice Richlin *(Pillow Talk)*
1960 Billy Wilder, I.A.L. Diamond *(The Apartment)*
1961 William Inge *(Splendor in the Grass)*
1962 Ennio de Concini, Alfredo Giannetti, Pietro Germi *(Divorce—Italian Style)*
1963 James R. Webb *(How the West Was Won)*
1964 S.H. Barnett, Peter Stone, Frank Tarloff *(Father Goose)*
1965 Frederic Raphael *(Darling)*
1966 Claude Lelouch, Pierre Uytterhoeven *(A Man and a Woman)*
1967 William Rose *(Guess Who's Coming to Dinner)*
1968 Mel Brooks *(The Producers)*
1969 William Goldman *(Butch Cassidy and the Sundance Kid)*
1970 Francis Ford Coppola, Edmund H. North *(Patton)*
1971 Paddy Chayefsky *(The Hospital)*
1972 Jeremy Larner *(The Candidate)*
1973 David S. Ward *(The Sting)*
1974 Robert Towne *(Chinatown)*

**SCREENPLAY, ORIGINAL[1] (CONTINUED)**

1975 Frank Pierson *(Dog Day Afternoon)*
1976 Paddy Chayefsky *(Network)*
1977 Woody Allen, Marshall Brickman *(Annie Hall)*
1978 Nancy Dowd, Waldo Salt, Robert C. Jones *(Coming Home)*
1979 Steve Tesich *(Breaking Away)*
1980 Bo Goldman *(Melvin and Howard)*
1981 Colin Welland *(Chariots of Fire)*
1982 John Briley *(Gandhi)*
1983 Horton Foote *(Tender Mercies)*
1984 Robert Benton *(Places in the Heart)*
1985 Earl W. Wallace, William Kelley, Pamela Wallace *(Witness)*
1986 Woody Allen *(Hannah and Her Sisters)*
1987 John Patrick Shanley *(Moonstruck)*
1988 Ronald Bass, Barry Morrow *(Rain Man)*
1989 Tom Schulman *(Dead Poets Society)*
1990 Bruce Joel Rubin *(Ghost)*
1991 Callie Khouri *(Thelma & Louise)*
1992 Neil Jordan *(The Crying Game)*
1993 Jane Campion *(The Piano)*
1994 Quentin Tarantino, Roger Avary *(Pulp Fiction)*
1995 Christopher McQuarrie *(The Usual Suspects)*
1996 Joel Coen, Ethan Coen *(Fargo)*
1997 Ben Affleck, Matt Damon *(Good Will Hunting)*
1998 Marc Norman, Tom Stoppard *(Shakespeare in Love)*
1999 Alan Ball *(American Beauty)*
2000 Cameron Crowe *(Almost Famous)*
2001 Julian Fellowes *(Gosford Park)*
2002 Pedro Almodóvar *(Talk to Her)*

**CINEMATOGRAPHY**

1928 Charles Rosher, Karl Struss *(Sunrise)*
1929 Clyde De Vinna *(White Shadows in the South Seas)*
1930 Joseph T. Rucker, Willard Van Der Veer *(With Byrd at the South Pole)*
1931 Floyd Crosby *(Tabu)*
1932 Lee Garmes *(Shanghai Express)*
1933 Charles Bryant Lang, Jr. *(A Farewell to Arms)*
1934 Victor Milner *(Cleopatra)*
1935 Hal Mohr *(A Midsummer Night's Dream)*
1936 Gaetano Gaudio *(Anthony Adverse)*
1937 Karl Freund *(The Good Earth)*
1938 Joseph Ruttenberg *(The Great Waltz)*
1939 Gregg Toland *(Wuthering Heights)*,[6] Ernest Haller, Ray Rennahan *(Gone with the Wind)*[7]
1940 George Barnes *(Rebecca)*,[6] Georges Perinal *(The Thief of Bagdad)*[7]
1941 Arthur Miller *(How Green Was My Valley)*,[6] Ernest Palmer, Ray Rennahan *(Blood and Sand)*[7]
1942 Joseph Ruttenberg *(Mrs. Miniver)*,[6] Leon Shamroy *(The Black Swan)*[7]
1943 Arthur Miller *(The Song of Bernadette)*,[6] Hal Mohr, W. Howard Greene *(The Phantom of the Opera)*[7]
1944 Joseph LaShelle *(Laura)*,[6] Leon Shamroy *(Wilson)*[7]
1945 Harry Stradling *(The Picture of Dorian Gray)*,[6] Leon Shamroy *(Leave Her to Heaven)*[7]
1946 Arthur Miller *(Anna and the King of Siam)*,[6] Charles Rosher, Leonard Smith, Arthur Arling *(The Yearling)*[7]
1947 Guy Green *(Great Expectations)*,[6] Jack Cardiff *(Black Narcissus)*[7]

# Academy Awards (Oscars), 1928–2002 (continued)

**CINEMATOGRAPHY (CONTINUED)**

1948 William Daniels (The Naked City),[6] Joseph Valentine, William V. Skall, Winton Hoch (Joan of Arc)[7]

1949 Paul C. Vogel (Battleground),[6] Winton Hoch (She Wore a Yellow Ribbon)[7]

1950 Robert Krasker (The Third Man),[6] Robert Surtees (King Solomon's Mines)[7]

1951 William C. Mellor (A Place in the Sun),[6] Alfred Gilks, John Alton (An American in Paris)[7]

1952 Robert Surtees (The Bad and the Beautiful),[6] Winton C. Hoch, Archie Stout (The Quiet Man)[7]

1953 Burnett Guffey (From Here to Eternity),[6] Loyal Griggs (Shane)[7]

1954 Boris Kaufman (On the Waterfront),[6] Milton Krasner (Three Coins in the Fountain)[7]

1955 James Wong Howe (The Rose Tattoo),[6] Robert Burks (To Catch a Thief)[7]

1956 Joseph Ruttenberg (Somebody Up There Likes Me),[6] Lionel Lindon (Around the World in 80 Days)[7]

1957 Jack Hildyard (The Bridge on the River Kwai)

1958 Sam Leavitt (The Defiant Ones),[6] Joseph Ruttenberg (Gigi)[7]

1959 William C. Mellor (The Diary of Anne Frank),[6] Robert L. Surtees (Ben-Hur)[7]

1960 Freddie Francis (Sons and Lovers),[6] Russell Metty (Spartacus)[7]

1961 Eugen Shuftan (The Hustler),[6] Daniel L. Fapp (West Side Story)[7]

1962 Jean Bourgoin, Walter Wottitz (The Longest Day),[6] Fred A. Young (Lawrence of Arabia)[7]

1963 James Wong Howe (Hud),[6] Leon Shamroy (Cleopatra)[7]

1964 Walter Lassally (Zorba the Greek),[6] Harry Stradling (My Fair Lady)[7]

1965 Ernest Laszlo (Ship of Fools),[6] Freddie Young (Doctor Zhivago)[7]

1966 Haskell Wexler (Who's Afraid of Virginia Woolf?),[6] Ted Moore (A Man for All Seasons)[7]

1967 Burnett Guffey (Bonnie and Clyde)

1968 Pasqualino De Santis (Romeo and Juliet)

1969 Conrad Hall (Butch Cassidy and the Sundance Kid)

1970 Freddie Young (Ryan's Daughter)

1971 Oswald Morris (Fiddler on the Roof)

1972 Geoffrey Unsworth (Cabaret)

1973 Sven Nykvist (Cries and Whispers)

1974 Fred Koenekamp, Joseph Biroc (The Towering Inferno)

1975 John Alcott (Barry Lyndon)

1976 Haskell Wexler (Bound for Glory)

1977 Vilmos Zsigmond (Close Encounters of the Third Kind)

1978 Nestor Almendros (Days of Heaven)

1979 Vittorio Storaro (Apocalypse Now)

1980 Geoffrey Unsworth, Ghislain Cloquet (Tess)

1981 Vittorio Storaro (Reds)

1982 Billy Williams, Ronnie Taylor (Gandhi)

1983 Sven Nykvist (Fanny & Alexander)

1984 Chris Menges (The Killing Fields)

1985 David Watkin (Out of Africa)

1986 Chris Menges (The Mission)

1987 Vittorio Storaro (The Last Emperor)

1988 Peter Biziou (Mississippi Burning)

1989 Freddie Francis (Glory)

1990 Dean Semler (Dances with Wolves)

**CINEMATOGRAPHY (CONTINUED)**

1991 Robert Richardson (JFK)

1992 Philippe Rousselot (A River Runs Through It)

1993 Janusz Kaminski (Schindler's List)

1994 John Toll (Legends of the Fall)

1995 John Toll (Braveheart)

1996 John Seale (The English Patient)

1997 Russell Carpenter (Titanic)

1998 Janusz Kaminski (Saving Private Ryan)

1999 Conrad L. Hall (American Beauty)

2000 Peter Pau (Crouching Tiger, Hidden Dragon)

2001 Andrew Lesnie (The Lord of the Rings: The Fellowship of the Ring)

2002 Conrad L. Hall (Road to Perdition)

**VISUAL EFFECTS[8]**

1939 E.H. Hansen (The Rains Came)

1940 Lawrence Butler (The Thief of Bagdad)

1941 Farciot Edouart, Gordon Jennings (I Wanted Wings)

1942 Farciot Edouart, Gordon Jennings, William L. Pereira (Reap the Wild Wind)

1943 Fred Sersen (Crash Dive)

1944 A. Arnold Gillespie, Donald Jahraus, Warren Newcombe (Thirty Seconds Over Tokyo)

1945 John P. Fulton (Wonder Man)

1946 Thomas Howard (Blithe Spirit)

1947 A. Arnold Gillespie, Warren Newcombe (Green Dolphin Street)

1948 Paul Eagler, J. McMillan Johnson, Russell Shearman, Clarence Slifer (Portrait of Jennie)

1949 Mighty Joe Young

1950 Destination Moon

1951 When Worlds Collide

1952 Plymouth Adventure

1953 The War of the Worlds

1954 20,000 Leagues Under the Sea

1955 The Bridges at Toko-Ri

1956 John Fulton (The Ten Commandments)

1958 Tom Howard (tom thumb)

1959 A. Arnold Gillespie, Robert MacDonald (Ben-Hur)

1960 Gene Warren, Tim Baar (The Time Machine)

1961 Bill Warrington (The Guns of Navarone)

1962 Robert MacDonald (The Longest Day)

1963 Emil Kosa, Jr. (Cleopatra)

1964 Peter Ellenshaw, Hamilton Luske, Eustace Lycett (Mary Poppins)

1965 John Stears (Thunderball)

1966 Art Cruickshank (Fantastic Voyage)

1967 L.B. Abbott (Doctor Dolittle)

1968 Stanley Kubrick (2001: A Space Odyssey)

1969 Robbie Robertson (Marooned)

1970 A.D. Flowers, L.B. Abbott (Tora! Tora! Tora!)

1971 Alan Maley, Eustace Lycett, Danny Lee (Bedknobs and Broomsticks)

1972 L.B. Abbott, A.D. Flowers (The Poseidon Adventure)

1974 Frank Brendel, Glen Robinson, Albert Whitlock (Earthquake)

1975 Albert Whitlock, Glen Robinson (The Hindenburg)

1976 Carlo Rambaldi, Glen Robinson, Frank Van der Veer (King Kong), L.B. Abbott, Glen Robinson, Matthew Yuricich (Logan's Run)

1977 John Stears, John Dykstra, Richard Edlund, Grant McCune, Robert Blalack (Star Wars)

## Academy Awards (Oscars), 1928–2002 (continued)

**VISUAL EFFECTS[8] (CONTINUED)**

1978  Les Bowie, Colin Chilvers, Denys Coop, Roy Field, Derek Meddings, Zoran Perisic *(Superman)*

1979  H.R. Giger, Carlo Rambaldi, Brian Johnson, Nick Allder, Denys Ayling *(Alien)*

1980  Brian Johnson, Richard Edlund, Dennis Muren, Bruce Nicholson *(The Empire Strikes Back)*

1981  Richard Edlund, Kit West, Bruce Nicholson, Joe Johnston *(Raiders of the Lost Ark)*

1982  Carlo Rambaldi, Dennis Muren, Kenneth F. Smith *(E.T. the Extra-Terrestrial)*

1983  Richard Edlund, Dennis Muren, Ken Ralston, Phil Tippet *(Return of the Jedi)*

1984  Dennis Muren, Michael McAlister, Lorne Peterson, George Gibbs *(Indiana Jones and the Temple of Doom)*

1985  Ken Ralston, Ralph McQuarrie, Scott Farrar, David Berry *(Cocoon)*

1986  Robert Skotak, Stan Winston, John Richardson, Suzanne Benson *(Aliens)*

1987  Dennis Muren, William George, Harley Jessup, Kenneth Smith *(Innerspace)*

1988  Ken Ralston, Richard Williams, Edward Jones, George Gibbs *(Who Framed Roger Rabbit)*

1989  John Bruno, Dennis Muren, Hoyt Yeatman, Dennis Skotak *(The Abyss)*

1990  Eric Brevig, Rob Bottin, Tim McGovern, Alex Funke *(Total Recall)*

1991  Robert Skotak *(Terminator 2: Judgment Day)*

1992  Ken Ralston, Doug Chiang, Doug Smythe, Tom Woodruff, Jr. *(Death Becomes Her)*

1993  Dennis Muren, Stan Winston, Phil Tippett, Michael Lantieri *(Jurassic Park)*

1994  Ken Ralston, George Murphy, Stephen Rosenbaum, Allen Hall *(Forrest Gump)*

1995  Scott E. Anderson, Charles Gibson, Neal Scanlan, John Cox *(Babe)*

1996  Volker Engel, Douglas Smith, Clay Pinney, Joseph Viskocil *(Independence Day)*

1997  Robert Legato, Mark Lasoff, Thomas L. Fisher, Michael Kanfer *(Titanic)*

1998  Joel Hynek, Nicholas Brooks, Stuart Robertson, Kevin Mack *(What Dreams May Come)*

**VISUAL EFFECTS[8] (CONTINUED)**

1999  John Gaeta, Janek Sirrs, Steve Courtley, Jon Thum *(The Matrix)*

2000  John Nelson, Neil Corbould, Tim Burke, Rob Harvey *(Gladiator)*

2001  Jim Rygiel, Randall William Cook, Richard Taylor, Mark Stetson *(The Lord of the Rings: The Fellowship of the Ring)*

2002  Jim Rygiel, Joe Letteri, Randall William Cook, Alex Funke *(The Lord of the Rings: The Two Towers)*

**MAKEUP**

1981  Rick Baker *(An American Werewolf in London)*

1982  Sarah Monzani, Michele Burke *(Quest for Fire)*

1984  Paul LeBlanc, Dick Smith *(Amadeus)*

1985  Michael Westmore, Zoltan Elek *(Mask)*

1986  Chris Walas, Stephan Dupuis *(The Fly)*

1987  Rick Baker *(Harry and the Hendersons)*

1988  Ve Neill, Steve La Porte, Robert Short *(Beetlejuice)*

1989  Manlio Rocchetti, Lynn Barber, Kevin Haney *(Driving Miss Daisy)*

1990  John Caglione, Jr., Doug Drexler *(Dick Tracy)*

1991  Stan Winston, Jeff Dawn *(Terminator 2: Judgment Day)*

1992  Greg Cannom, Michele Burke, Matthew W. Mungle *(Bram Stoker's Dracula)*

1993  Greg Cannom, Ve Neill, Yolanda Toussieng *(Mrs. Doubtfire)*

1994  Rick Baker, Ve Neill, Yolanda Toussieng *(Ed Wood)*

1995  Peter Frampton, Paul Pattison, Lois Burwell *(Braveheart)*

1996  Rick Baker, David LeRoy Anderson *(The Nutty Professor)*

1997  Rick Baker, David LeRoy Anderson *(Men in Black)*

1998  Jenny Shircore *(Elizabeth)*

1999  Christine Blundell, Trefor Proud *(Topsy-Turvy)*

2000  Rick Baker, Gail Ryan *(Dr. Seuss' How the Grinch Stole Christmas)*

2001  Peter Owen, Richard Taylor *(The Lord of the Rings: The Fellowship of the Ring)*

2002  John Jackson, Beatrice Alba *(Frida)*

---

[1]*The current screenplay categories were adopted for the 1957 awards. Until then, various separate writing awards were given for silent-film title writing, screenplay, story and screenplay, and motion picture story.* [2]*Screenplay (for script only).* [3]*Story and screenplay (for narrative and script; also called original screenplay).* [4]*Motion picture story (for narrative only; also called original story).* [5]*Actual winner was blacklisted at the time of the award and the honored work was attributed to another name or person; pseudonym or nominal winner listed in parentheses.* [6]*Black and white.* [7]*Color.* [8]*Until 1963, both visual and sound effects were honored as special effects. Only those awards for visual effects are listed here.*

---

**Did you know?**

Ava Gardner, who transformed herself from tomboyish farm girl into one of the most glamorous women in screen history, was given a screen test by MGM studios in 1941. Upon seeing it, studio chief Louis B. Mayer declared, "She can't act. She can't talk. She's terrific. Sign her."

## Golden Globes, 2003

The Hollywood Foreign Press Association, a group of non-US film critics working in Hollywood, began awarding prizes for outstanding American motion pictures and acting in 1944 and created the Golden Globe Award in 1945. Over the years the prizes have expanded from recognizing only motion pictures and actors and actresses to include direction (1946), screenwriting and film music (1947), foreign-language film (1950), and television (1955) as well as a number of other categories of achievement. Prize: globe encircled by a strip of motion picture film, in gold.

Golden Globes/Hollywood Foreign Press Association Web site: <www.hfpa.org>.

**Film**

| | |
|---|---|
| Drama | *The Hours* (director, Stephen Daldry) |
| Musical/comedy | *Chicago* (director, Rob Marshall) |
| Director | Martin Scorsese (*Gangs of New York*) |
| Actress, drama | Nicole Kidman (*The Hours*) |
| Actor, drama | Jack Nicholson (*About Schmidt*) |
| Actress, musical/comedy | Renée Zellweger (*Chicago*) |
| Actor, musical/comedy | Richard Gere (*Chicago*) |
| Foreign-language film | *Talk to Her* (Spain; director, Pedro Almodóvar) |
| Supporting actress | Meryl Streep (*Adaptation*) |
| Supporting actor | Chris Cooper (*Adaptation*) |
| Screenplay | Alexander Payne and Jim Taylor (*About Schmidt*) |
| Original score | Elliot Goldenthall (*Frida*) |
| Original song | "The Hands That Built America" (*Gangs of New York*) U2, music and lyrics |

**Television**

| | |
|---|---|
| Drama series | *The Shield*, Fox TV Studios and Sony Pictures TV |
| Actress, drama series | Edie Falco (*The Sopranos*) |
| Actor, drama series | Michael Chiklis (*The Shield*) |
| Musical/comedy series | *Curb Your Enthusiasm*, HBO |
| Actress, musical/comedy series | Jennifer Aniston (*Friends*) |
| Actor, musical/comedy series | Tony Shalhoub (*Monk*) |
| Miniseries/movie for TV | *The Gathering Storm*, HBO |
| Actress, miniseries/movie | Uma Thurman (*Hysterical Blindness*) |
| Actor, miniseries/movie | Albert Finney (*The Gathering Storm*) |
| Supporting actress, series/miniseries/movie | Kim Cattrall (*Sex and the City*) |
| Supporting Actor, series/miniseries/movie | Donald Sutherland (*Path to War*) |

## Sundance Film Festival, 2003

Founded as the Utah/US Film Festival in Salt Lake City in 1978, the exhibition has traditionally focused on documentary and dramatic works from outside the Hollywood mainstream. It came under the auspices of actor Robert Redford's Sundance Institute in 1985 and is held every January in Park City UT.

Sundance Institute Web site: <www.sundance.org>.

| | |
|---|---|
| Grand Jury Prize, drama | *American Splendor* (US; directors, Shari Springer Berman and Robert Pulcini) |
| Grand Jury Prize, documentary | *Capturing the Friedmans* (US; director, Andrew Jarecki) |
| Audience Award, drama | *The Station Agent* (US; director, Tom McCarthy) |
| Audience Award, documentary | *My Flesh and Blood* (US; director, Jonathan Karsh) |
| Audience Award, World Cinema | *Whale Rider* (NZ; director, Niki Caro) |
| Best director, drama | Catherine Hardwicke (*Thirteen*, US) |
| Best director, documentary | Jonathan Karsh (*My Flesh and Blood*, US) |
| Cinematography, drama | Derek Cianfrance (*Quattro Noza*, US) |
| Cinematography, documentary | Dana Kupper, Gordon Quinn, and Peter Gilbert (*Stevie*, US) |
| Freedom of Expression Award | *What I Want My Words to Do to You* (US; directors Judith Katz, Madelein Gavin, and Gary Sunshine |
| Waldo Scott Screenwriting Award | Tom McCarthy (*The Station Agent*, US) |
| Special Jury Prize, documentary | *The Murder of Emmett Till* (US; director, Stanley Nelson); *A Certain Kind of Death* (US; directors Grover Babcock and Blue Hadaegh) |
| Special Jury Prize for Outstanding Performance, drama | Patricia Clarkson (*The Station Agent*, *Pieces of April*, and *All the Real Girls*) and Charles Busch (*Die Mommie Die*) |
| Special Jury Prize for Emotional Truth, drama | *All the Real Girls* (US, director, David Gordon Green) and *What Alice Found* (US; director, A. Dean Bell) |
| Jury Prize, short filmmaking | *Terminal Bar*, US, Stefan Nadelman) |
| Sundance/NHK International Filmmakers Award | *Waiting for the Clouds* (Europe; director, Yesim Ustaoglu); *Whisky* (Latin America; directors, Juan Pablo Rebella and Pablo Stoll); *The Motel* (US; director, Michael Kang); *100% Pure Wool* (Japan; director, Mai Tominaga) |
| Alfred P. Sloan Feature Film Prize | *Dopamine* (US; director Mark Decena) |

# Cannes International Film Festival, 2003

Established in 1946, the Cannes International Film Festival is among the best known and most influential film exhibitions in the world. Some 50 feature films and 30 short films are chosen for several categories of the Official Selection each year, with a majority of those competing for the festival's various prizes. A nine-member feature film jury and a four-member short film and Cinéfondation jury give awards to the best film (Palme d'Or) and other outstanding films (special jury prizes) in their respective categories. The Grand Prix goes to the feature film judged the most original, and the feature jury also chooses the winners of the performance, direction, and screenplay awards. The Caméra d'Or, for best first film, draws on feature films from the Official Selection and from two parallel exhibitions, the Directors' Fortnight and the International Critics' Week, and is awarded by a jury comprising film industry professionals and members of the moviegoing public. The Cinéfondation awards are for works of one hour or less by film-school students.

Cannes International Film Festival Web site: <www.festival-cannes.com>.

## feature films
▶ **Palme d'Or:** *Elephant* (US; director, Gus Van Sant);  ▶ **Grand Prix:** *Uzak (Distant)* (Turkey; director Nuri Bilge Ceylan);  ▶ **Best actress:** Marie-Josée Croze (*Les Invasions barbares* [*The Barbarian Invasions*], Canada/France);  ▶ **Best actor:** Muzaffer Ozdemir and Mahmet Emin Toprak (*Uzak* [*Distant*], Turkey);  ▶ **Best direction:** Gus Van Sant (*Elephant*, US);  ▶ **Best screenplay:** Denys Arcand (*Les Invasions barbares* [*The Barbarian Invasions*], Canada/France) ;  ▶ **Special jury award:** *Panj é asr (At Five in the Afternoon)* (Iran/France; director Samira Makhmalbaf);  ▶ **Caméra d'Or:** *Reconstruction* (Denmark; director, Christoffer Boe)

## short films
▶ **Palme d'Or:** *Cracker Bag* (Australia; director, Glendyn Ivin);  ▶ **Special jury award:** *L'Homme sans tête (The Headless Man)* (France; director, Juan Solanas)

## Cinéfondation
▶ **1st prize:** *Bezi zeko bezi (Run Rabbit Run)* (Serbia and Montenegro; director, Pavle Vuckovic);  ▶ **2nd prize:** *Story of the Desert* (UK; director, Celia Galan Julve);  ▶ **3rd prize:** *Rebeca a esas alturas (At That Point...Rebeca)* (Mexico; director, Luciana Jauffred Gorostiza), *TV City* (Germany; directors, Alberto Couceiro and Alejandra Tomei)

# Berlin International Film Festival, 2003

The Berlin International Film Festival (Internationale Filmfestspiele Berlin), held annually since its founding in West Berlin in 1951, comprises some 20 separate competitions and juries emphasizing aspects of both worldwide and German cinema, each with their own prizes. The International Jury, made up of film-industry figures from across the globe, selects the winners of the Golden and Silver Berlin Bears, the festival's top awards.

Berlin International Film Festival Web site: <www.berlinale.de>.

| | |
|---|---|
| Golden Berlin Bear | *In This World* (UK; director, Michael Winterbottom) |
| Jury Grand Prize (Silver Bear) | *Adaptation* (US; director, Spike Jonze) |
| Silver Berlin Bear, director | Patrice Chéreau (*Son frère* [*His Brother*], France) |
| Silver Berlin Bear, actress | Meryl Streep, Nicole Kidman, and Julianne Moore (*The Hours*, US) |
| Silver Berlin Bear, actor | Sam Rockwell (*Confessions of a Dangerous Mind*, US) |
| Silver Berlin Bear, individual artistic contribution | Li Yang, writer and director (*Mang jing* [*Blind Shaft*], China/Germany/Hong Kong) |
| Silver Berlin Bear, film music | Majoly, Serge Fiori, and Mamadou Diabaté (*Madame Brouette*, Senegal/France/Canada) |
| Premiere First Movie Award | *not awarded* |
| Ecumenical Jury Prize | *In This World* (UK; director, Michael Winterbottom) |
| FIPRESCI Award | Competition: *Lichter* (*Distant Lights*, Germany; director, Hans-Christian Schmid); Panorama: *Wolfsburg* (Germany; director, Christian Petzold) |

# Toronto International Film Festival, 2002

Founded in 1976, the Toronto International Film Festival is one of North America's best-attended exhibitions and a frequent forum for the premiere of major feature films. The festival, held in September, awards six prizes, three of which are for Canadian films.

Toronto International Film Festival Web site: <www.e.bell.ca/filmfest>.

| | |
|---|---|
| Canadian feature | *Spider* (director David Cronenberg) |
| Canadian first feature | *Marion Bridge* (director Wiebke von Carolsfeld) |
| Canadian short | *Blue Skies* (director Ann Marie Fleming) |
| FIPRESCI Award | *Les Chemins de l'oued (Under Another Sky)* (France; director, Gaël Morel) |
| People's Choice Award | *Whale Rider* (New Zealand; director, Niki Caro) |
| Discovery Award | *The Magdalene Sisters* (Ireland/UK; director, Peter Mullan) |

# Encyclopædia Britannica's 100 Funniest Films

*Title, director, year of release.*

*Abbott and Costello Meet Frankenstein* (Charles Barton, 1948)

*Ace Ventura, Pet Detective* (Tom Shadyac, 1994)

*Airplane* (Jim Abrahams, David Zucker, and Jerry Zucker, 1980)

*Animal House* (John Landis, 1978)

*Annie Hall* (Woody Allen, 1977)

*Arsenic and Old Lace* (Frank Capra, 1944)

*Arthur* (Steve Gordon, 1981)

*Bagdad Café* (Percy Adlon, 1988)

*Bananas* (Woody Allen, 1971)

*The Bank Dick* (Edward F. Cline, 1940)

*Bedazzled* (Stanley Donen, 1967)

*Being John Malkovich* (Spike Jonze, 1999)

*Being There* (Hal Ashby, 1979)

*Big* (Penny Marshall, 1988)

*Blazing Saddles* (Mel Brooks, 1974)

*The Blues Brothers* (John Landis, 1980)

*Bringing Up Baby* (Howard Hawks, 1938)

*Caddyshack* (Harold Ramis, 1980)

*La Cage au folles* (Edouard Molinaro, 1978)

*Car Wash* (Michael Schultz, 1976)

*Chicken Run* (Peter Lord and Nick Park, 2000)

*Crocodile Dundee* (Peter Faiman, 1986)

*A Day at the Races* (Sam Wood, 1937)

*Dona Flor and Her Two Husbands (Dona Flor e seus dois maridos)* (Bruno Barreto, 1976)

*Dr. Strangelove, or How I Learned to Stop Worrying and Love the Bomb* (Stanley Kubrick, 1964)

*Drunken Master (Zui quan)* (Woo-ping Yuen, 1978)

*Duck Soup* (Leo McCarey, 1933)

*Fargo* (Joel Coen, 1996)

*Fast Times at Ridgemont High* (Amy Heckerling, 1982)

*Female Trouble* (John Waters, 1974)

*The Firemen's Ball (Horí má panenko)* (Milos Forman, 1967)

*A Fish Called Wanda* (Charles Crichton, 1988)

*Four Weddings and a Funeral* (Mike Newell, 1994)

*The Freshman* (Fred C. Newmeyer and Sam Taylor, 1925)

*The Full Monty* (Peter Cattaneo, 1997)

*The General* (Buster Keaton and Clyde Bruckman, 1927)

*The Gods Must Be Crazy* (Jamie Uys, 1980)

*The Gold Rush* (Charlie Chaplin, 1925)

*The Graduate* (Mike Nichols, 1967)

*Groundhog Day* (Harold Ramis, 1993)

*Hairspray* (John Waters, 1988)

*A Hard Day's Night* (Richard Lester, 1964)

*Harold and Maude* (Hal Ashby, 1971)

*The Heartbreak Kid* (Elaine May, 1972)

*High Hopes* (Mike Leigh, 1988)

*His Girl Friday* (Howard Hawks, 1940)

*Hollywood Shuffle* (Robert Townsend, 1987)

*The In-Laws* (Arthur Hiller, 1979)

*It Happened One Night* (Frank Capra, 1934)

*The Jerk* (Carl Reiner, 1979)

*Kind Hearts and Coronets* (Robert Hamer, 1949)

*The Lady Eve* (Preston Sturges, 1941)

*The Ladykillers* (Alexander Mackendrick, 1955)

*Life of Brian* (Terry Jones, 1979)

*Local Hero* (Bill Forsyth, 1983)

*Lost in America* (Albert Brooks, 1985)

*The Man in the White Suit* (Alexander Mackendrick, 1951)

*M*A*S*H* (Robert Altman, 1970)

*Men (Männer)* (Doris Dörrie, 1985)

*The Miracle of Morgan's Creek* (Preston Sturges, 1944)

*Modern Times* (Charlie Chaplin, 1936)

*Monsieur Hulot's Holiday (Les Vacances de M. Hulot* (Jacques Tati, 1953)

*Monty Python and the Holy Grail* (Terry Gilliam and Terry Jones, 1975)

*The Mouse That Roared* (Jack Arnold, 1959)

*My Life as a Dog (Mitt liv som hund)* (Lasse Hallström, 1985)

*Network* (Sidney Lumet, 1976)

*A Night at the Opera* (Sam Wood, 1935)

*Ninotchka* (Ernst Lubitsch, 1939)

*The Nutty Professor* (Jerry Lewis, 1963)

*The Odd Couple* (Gene Saks, 1968)

*The Philadelphia Story* (George Cukor, 1940)

*Pink Flamingos* (John Waters, 1972)

*The Pink Panther* (Blake Edwards, 1964)

*The Producers* (Mel Brooks, 1968)

*Rules of the Game (La Règle du jeu)* (Jean Renoir, 1939)

*The Ruling Class* (Peter Medak, 1972)

*Safety Last!* (Fred C. Newmeyer and Sam Taylor, 1923)

*The Search for Signs of Intelligent Life in the Universe* (John Bailey, 1991)

*The Seven Year Itch* (Billy Wilder, 1955)

*Shampoo* (Hal Ashby, 1975)

*She's Gotta Have It* (Spike Lee, 1986)

*Sleeper* (Woody Allen, 1973)

*Smiles of a Summer Night (Sommarnattens leende)* (Ingmar Bergman, 1955)

*Some Like It Hot* (Billy Wilder, 1959)

*Sons of the Desert* (William A. Seiter, 1933)

*South Park: Bigger, Longer & Uncut* (Trey Parker, 1999)

*Stranger Than Paradise* (Jim Jarmusch, 1983)

*Sullivan's Travels* (Preston Sturges, 1941)

*Take the Money and Run* (Woody Allen, 1969)

*Tampopo* (Juzo Itami, 1985)

*There's Something About Mary* (Bobby and Peter Farrelly, 1998)

*This Is Spinal Tap* (Rob Reiner, 1984)

*Three Men and a Cradle (3 Hommes et un couffin)* (Coline Serreau, 1985)

*To Be or Not to Be* (Ernst Lubitsch, 1942)

*Tootsie* (Sydney Pollack, 1982)

*Toy Story* (John Lasseter, 1995)

*Unfaithfully Yours* (Preston Sturges, 1948)

*Up in Smoke* (Lou Adler, 1978)

*Wayne's World* (Penelope Spheeris, 1992)

*What's Up, Doc?* (Peter Bogdanovich, 1972)

*What's Up, Tiger Lily?* (Woody Allen, 1966)

*Withnail and I* (Bruce Robinson, 1987)

*Women on the Verge of a Nervous Breakdown (Mujeres al borde de un ataque de nervios)* (Pedro Almodóvar, 1988)

*Young Frankenstein* (Mel Brooks, 1974)

## 100 Top-Grossing Films (Actual Dollars)

As of 10 Jun 2003. Source: The Internet Movie Database: <http://imdb.com>.

| | | | | | |
|---|---|---|---|---|---|
| 1 | Titanic | 1997 | 51 | Signs | 2002 |
| 2 | Harry Potter and the Sorcerer's Stone | 2001 | 52 | Gone with the Wind | 1939 |
| 3 | Star Wars: The Phantom Menace | 1999 | 53 | Robin Hood: Prince of Thieves | 1991 |
| 4 | Jurassic Park | 1993 | 54 | Raiders of the Lost Ark | 1981 |
| 5 | The Lord of the Rings: The Two Towers | 2002 | 55 | X2 | 2003 |
| 6 | Harry Potter and the Chamber of Secrets | 2002 | 56 | Grease | 1978 |
| 7 | The Lord of the Rings: The Fellowship of the Ring | 2001 | 57 | Ice Age | 2002 |
| | | | 58 | Beauty and the Beast | 1991 |
| 8 | Independence Day | 1996 | 59 | Godzilla | 1998 |
| 9 | Spider-Man | 2002 | 60 | What Women Want | 2000 |
| 10 | Star Wars | 1977 | 61 | The Fugitive | 1993 |
| 11 | The Lion King | 1994 | 62 | True Lies | 1994 |
| 12 | E.T. the Extraterrestrial | 1982 | 63 | Die Hard: With a Vengance | 1995 |
| 13 | Forrest Gump | 1994 | 64 | Notting Hill | 1999 |
| 14 | The Sixth Sense | 1999 | 65 | Jurassic Park III | 2001 |
| 15 | Star Wars: Attack of the Clones | 2002 | 66 | There's Something About Mary | 1998 |
| 16 | Jurassic Park: The Lost World | 1997 | 67 | Planet of the Apes | 2001 |
| 17 | Men in Black | 1997 | 68 | The Flintstones | 1994 |
| 18 | Star Wars: Return of the Jedi | 1983 | 69 | Toy Story | 1995 |
| 19 | Armageddon | 1998 | 70 | A Bug's Life | 1998 |
| 20 | The Matrix Reloaded | 2003 | 71 | The Exorcist | 1973 |
| 21 | Mission: Impossible 2 | 2000 | 72 | My Big Fat Greek Wedding | 2002 |
| 22 | Star Wars: The Empire Strikes Back | 1980 | 73 | Basic Instinct | 1992 |
| 23 | Home Alone | 1990 | 74 | The World Is Not Enough | 1999 |
| 24 | Monsters, Inc. | 2001 | 75 | GoldenEye | 1995 |
| 25 | Ghost | 1990 | 76 | Back to the Future | 1985 |
| 26 | Terminator 2: Judgment Day | 1991 | 77 | Se7en | 1995 |
| 27 | Aladdin | 1992 | 78 | Hannibal | 2001 |
| 28 | Indiana Jones and the Last Crusade | 1989 | 79 | Who Framed Roger Rabbit | 1988 |
| 29 | Twister | 1996 | 80 | Deep Impact | 1998 |
| 30 | Toy Story 2 | 1999 | 81 | Dinosaur | 2000 |
| 31 | Saving Private Ryan | 1998 | 82 | Pocahontas | 1995 |
| 32 | Jaws | 1975 | 83 | Tomorrow Never Dies | 1997 |
| 33 | The Matrix | 1999 | 84 | Top Gun | 1986 |
| 34 | Gladiator | 2000 | 85 | Minority Report | 2002 |
| 35 | Shrek | 2001 | 86 | How the Grinch Stole Christmas | 2000 |
| 36 | Mission: Impossible | 1996 | 87 | American Beauty | 1999 |
| 37 | Pearl Harbor | 2001 | 88 | Catch Me If You Can | 2002 |
| 38 | Ocean's Eleven | 2001 | 89 | Batman Forever | 1995 |
| 39 | Pretty Woman | 1990 | 90 | Apollo 13 | 1995 |
| 40 | Tarzan | 1999 | 91 | Indiana Jones and the Temple of Doom | 1984 |
| 41 | Men in Black II | 2002 | 92 | Back to the Future, Part II | 1989 |
| 42 | Die Another Day | 2002 | 93 | The Rock | 1996 |
| 43 | Dances with Wolves | 1990 | 94 | Rush Hour 2 | 2001 |
| 44 | Cast Away | 2000 | 95 | Crocodile Dundee | 1986 |
| 45 | Mrs. Doubtfire | 1993 | 96 | The Perfect Storm | 2000 |
| 46 | The Mummy Returns | 2001 | 97 | The Hunchback of Notre Dame | 1996 |
| 47 | The Mummy | 1999 | 98 | Schindler's List | 1993 |
| 48 | Batman | 1989 | 99 | The Mask | 1994 |
| 49 | Rain Man | 1988 | 100 | Fatal Attraction | 1987 |
| 50 | The Bodyguard | 1992 | | | |

## US Top-Grossing Films in Constant Dollars (Estimated)

Admissions—the number of tickets sold to a movie—tell a different story from the raw dollars earned. While recent films have made hundreds of millions of dollars, only seven of the top twenty films in terms of attendance were released after 1980. Source: Exhibitor Relations Co., Inc.

| | ADMISSIONS | 2002 DOLLARS | ACTUAL DOLLARS |
|---|---|---|---|
| 1 Gone with the Wind (1939) | 202,044,569 | $1,181,960,729 | $198,655,278 |
| 2 Star Wars (1977) | 178,119,595 | 1,041,999,631 | 460,998,007 |
| 3 E.T. The Extraterrestrial (1982) | 141,925,359 | 833,129,950 | 434,538,449 |
| 4 The Sound of Music (1965) | 142,415,376 | 830,263,350 | 158,671,368 |
| 5 The Ten Commandments (1956) | 131,000,000 | 766,350,000 | 65,500,000 |
| 6 Titanic (1997) | 129,201,761 | 755,830,301 | 600,788,188 |
| 7 Jaws (1975) | 128,078,818 | 749,261,084 | 260,000,000 |
| 8 Snow White (1937) | 109,000,000 | 637,650,000 | 184,925,486 |

## US Top-Grossing Films in Constant Dollars (Estimated) (continued)

| | | ADMISSIONS | 2002 DOLLARS | ACTUAL DOLLARS |
|---|---|---|---|---|
| 9 | *101 Dalmatians* (1961) | 99,917,251 | 584,515,919 | 144,880,014 |
| 10 | *The Empire Strikes Back* (1980) | 98,106,044 | 573,920,357 | 290,266,497 |
| 11 | *Ben-Hur* (1959) | 98,000,000 | 573,300,000 | 74,000,000 |
| 12 | *The Exorcist* (1973) | 94,285,714 | 551,571,429 | 165,000,000 |
| 13 | *Return of the Jedi* (1983) | 94,026,245 | 550,053,533 | 309,153,948 |
| 14 | *The Sting* (1973) | 89,142,857 | 521,485,714 | 156,000,000 |
| 15 | *Raiders of the Lost Ark* (1981) | 88,141,855 | 515,629,854 | 245,034,358 |
| 16 | *Jurassic Park* (1993) | 86,248,296 | 504,552,534 | 357,067,947 |
| 17 | *Star Wars: Episode I— The Phantom Menace* (1999) | 84,859,901 | 496,430,418 | 431,088,295 |
| 18 | *Fantasia* (1940) | 83,043,478 | 485,804,348 | 76,400,000 |
| 19 | *The Godfather* (1972) | 79,392,006 | 464,443,238 | 134,966,411 |
| 20 | *Forrest Gump* (1994) | 78,874,282 | 461,414,550 | 329,694,499 |

## Top US Video Rentals and Sales, 2002

*Data reflect combined VHS and DVD numbers.*
*Source: Video Business. Web site: <www.videobusiness.com>.*

| | RENTALS | SALES |
|---|---|---|
| 1 | *Don't Say a Word* | *Monsters, Inc.* |
| 2 | *Ocean's Eleven* | *The Lord of the Rings: The Fellowship of the Ring* |
| 3 | *Training Day* | *Spider-Man* |
| 4 | *The Fast and the Furious* | *Harry Potter and the Sorcerer's Stone* |
| 5 | *The Others* | *Ice Age* |
| 6 | *American Pie 2* | *Lilo & Stitch* |
| 7 | *Domestic Disturbance* | *Star Wars: Attack of the Clones* |
| 8 | *Shallow Hal* | *The Fast and the Furious* |
| 9 | *Black Hawk Down* | *Atlantis: The Lost Empire* |
| 10 | *Vanilla Sky* | *Austin Powers in Goldmember* |
| 11 | *Spy Game* | *Spirit: Stallion of the Cimarron* |
| 12 | *Rat Race* | *Scooby-Doo* |
| 13 | *Mr. Deeds* | *Beauty and the Beast* |
| 14 | *John Q.* | *Cinderella II* |
| 15 | *A Beautiful Mind* | *Ocean's Eleven* |
| 16 | *Panic Room* | *Men in Black II* |
| 17 | *Bandits* | *Band of Brothers* |
| 18 | *Changing Lanes* | *Training Day* |
| 19 | *The Lord of the Rings: The Fellowship of the Ring* | *The Rookie* |
| 20 | *The Sum of All Fears* | *Snow Dogs* |
| 21 | *Insomnia* | *Black Hawk Down* |
| 22 | *Behind Enemy Lines* | *American Pie 2* |
| 23 | *Spider-Man* | *A Beautiful Mind* |
| 24 | *High Crimes* | *The Scorpion King* |
| 25 | *We Were Soldiers* | *Blade II* |

 *Cleopatra* (1963) cost $44 million to make, and in constant dollars is still the most expensive film ever made by a Hollywood studio.

# Television

## Emmy Award-winning Television Series, 1948–2002

**1948**
Most popular program: *Pantomime Quiz,* KTLA
TV film: "The Necklace," *Your Show Time*

**1949**
Live show: *The Ed Wynn Show,* KTTV
Kinescope show: *The Texaco Star Theater,* KNBH (NBC)

## Emmy Award-winning Television Series, 1948–2002 (continued)

**1949 (continued)**
TV film: *The Life of Riley*, KNBH
Pub. svc./cultural/educ.: *Crusade in Europe*, KECA-TV/KTTV (ABC)
Children's: *Time for Beany*, KTLA

**1950**
Variety: *The Alan Young Show*, KTTV (CBS)
Drama: *Pulitzer Prize Playhouse*, KECA-TV (ABC)
Game/audience particip.: *Truth or Consequences*, KTTV (CBS)
Children's: *Time for Beany*, KTLA
Educational: *KFI-TV University*, KFI-TV
Cultural: *Campus Chorus and Orchestra*, KTSL

**1951**
Variety: *Your Show of Shows* (NBC)
Comedy: *The Red Skelton Show* (NBC)
Drama: *Studio One* (CBS)

**1952**
Variety: *Your Show of Shows* (NBC)
Comedy: *I Love Lucy* (CBS)
Drama: *Robert Montgomery Presents* (NBC)
Mystery/action/adventure: *Dragnet* (NBC)
Public affairs: *See It Now* (CBS)
Aud. particip./quiz/panel: *What's My Line?* (CBS)
Children's: *Time for Beany* (syndicated)

**1953**
Variety: *Omnibus* (CBS)
Comedy: *I Love Lucy* (CBS)
Drama: *The U.S. Steel Hour* (ABC)
Mystery/action/adventure: *Dragnet* (NBC)
Public affairs: *Victory at Sea* (NBC)
Aud. particip./quiz/panel: *This Is Your Life* (NBC); *What's My Line?* (CBS)
Children's: *Kukla, Fran and Ollie* (NBC)

**1954**
Variety: *Disneyland* (ABC)
Comedy: *Make Room for Daddy* (ABC)
Drama: *The United States Steel Hour* (ABC)
Mystery/intrigue: *Dragnet* (NBC)
Western/adventure: *Stories of the Century* (syndicated)
Cultural/relig./educ.: *Omnibus* (CBS)
Aud. particip./quiz/panel: *This Is Your Life* (NBC)
Children's: *Lassie* (CBS)

**1955**
Variety: *The Ed Sullivan Show* (CBS)
Comedy: *The Phil Silvers Show: You'll Never Get Rich* (CBS)
Drama: *Producers' Showcase* (NBC)
Action/adventure: *Disneyland* (ABC)
Music: *Your Hit Parade* (NBC)
Documentary: *Omnibus* (CBS)
Aud. particip. *The $64,000 Question* (CBS)
Children's: *Lassie* (CBS)

**1956**
Series (½ hr. or less): *The Phil Silvers Show: You'll Never Get Rich* (CBS)
Series (1 hr. or more): *Caesar's Hour* (NBC)
New series: *Playhouse 90* (CBS)

**1957**
Mus./var./aud.par./quiz: *The Dinah Shore Chevy Show* (NBC)
Comedy: *The Phil Silvers Show: You'll Never Get Rich* (CBS)
Drama, continuing: *Gunsmoke* (CBS)
Drama, anthology: *Playhouse 90* (CBS)
New series: *The Seven Lively Arts* (CBS)
Public service: *Omnibus* (ABC/NBC)

**1959[1]**
Musical/variety: *The Dinah Shore Chevy Show* (NBC)
Comedy: *The Jack Benny Show* (CBS)
Drama (<1 hr.): *Alcoa-Goodyear Playhouse* (NBC)
Drama (1 hr.+): *Playhouse 90* (CBS)
Western: *Maverick* (ABC)
News reporting: *The Huntley-Brinkley Report* (NBC)
Public service: *Omnibus* (NBC)
Panel/quiz/aud. particip.: *What's My Line?* (CBS)

**1960**
Variety: "The Fabulous Fifties" (CBS)
Humor: "Art Carney Special" (NBC)
Drama: *Playhouse 90* (CBS)
News: *The Huntley-Brinkley Report* (NBC)
Public affairs/education: *The Twentieth Century* (CBS)
Children's: *Huckleberry Hound* (syndicated)

**1961**
Variety: *Astaire Time* (NBC)
Humor: *The Jack Benny Show* (CBS)
Drama: "Macbeth," *Hallmark Hall of Fame* (NBC)
News: *The Huntley-Brinkley Report* (NBC)
Public affairs/education: *The Twentieth Century* (CBS)
Children's: "Aaron Copland's Birthday Party," *Young People's Concert* (CBS)
Program of the year: "Macbeth," *Hallmark Hall of Fame* (NBC)

**1962**
Variety: *The Garry Moore Show* (CBS)
Humor: *The Bob Newhart Show* (NBC)
Drama: *The Defenders* (CBS)
News: *The Huntley-Brinkley Report* (NBC)
Educational/public affairs: *David Brinkley's Journal* (NBC)
Children's: "New York Philharmonic Young People's Concert with Leonard Bernstein" (CBS)
Program of the year: "Victoria Regina," *Hallmark Hall of Fame* (NBC)

**1963**
Variety: *The Andy Williams Show* (NBC)
Humor: *The Dick Van Dyke Show* (CBS)
Drama: *The Defenders* (CBS)
News: *The Huntley-Brinkley Report* (NBC)
Commentary/public affairs: *David Brinkley's Journal* (NBC)
Documentary: "The Tunnel" (NBC)
Panel/quiz/aud. particip.: *G-E College Bowl* (CBS)
Children's: *Walt Disney's Wonderful World of Color* (NBC)
Program of the year: "The Tunnel" (NBC)

[1]*Because of a change in the eligibility period, no awards were given in 1958; the 1959 awards included all of calendar year 1958 and part of 1959.*

## Emmy Award-winning Television Series, 1948–2002 (continued)

**1964**
Variety: *The Danny Kaye Show* (CBS)
Comedy: *The Dick Van Dyke Show* (CBS)
Drama: *The Defenders* (CBS)
News reports: *The Huntley-Brinkley Report* (NBC)
Commentary/public affairs: "Cuba—Part I: The Bay of Pigs," "Cuba—Part II: The Missile Crisis," *NBC White Paper* (NBC)
Documentary: "The Making of the President 1960" (ABC)
Children's: *Discovery '63–'64* (ABC)
Program of the year: "The Making of the President 1960" (ABC)

**1965[2]**
Entertainment: *The Dick Van Dyke Show* (CBS); "The Magnificent Yankee," *Hallmark Hall of Fame* (NBC); "My Name Is Barbra" (CBS); "What Is Sonata Form?," *New York Philharmonic Young People's Concerts with Leonard Bernstein* (CBS)
News/docu./info./sports: "I, Leonardo da Vinci," *Saga of Western Man* (ABC); "The Louvre" (NBC)

**1966**
Variety: *The Andy Williams Show* (NBC)
Comedy: *The Dick Van Dyke Show* (CBS)
Drama: *The Fugitive* (ABC)

**1967**
Variety: *The Andy Williams Show* (NBC)
Comedy: *The Monkees* (NBC)
Drama: *Mission: Impossible* (CBS)

**1968**
Musical/variety: *Rowan and Martin's Laugh-In* (NBC)
Comedy: *Get Smart* (NBC)
Drama: *Mission: Impossible* (CBS)

**1969**
Musical/variety: *Rowan and Martin's Laugh-In* (NBC)
Comedy: *Get Smart* (NBC)
Drama: *NET Playhouse* (NET)

**1970**
Variety/musical: *The David Frost Show* (syndicated)
Comedy: *My World and Welcome to It* (NBC)
Drama: *Marcus Welby, M.D.* (ABC)

**1971**
Comedy: *All in the Family* (CBS)
Drama: *The Senator* (segment), *The Bold Ones* (NBC)
Variety, musical: *The Flip Wilson Show* (NBC)
Variety, talk: *The David Frost Show* (syndicated)
New series: *All in the Family* (CBS)

**1972**
Comedy: *All in the Family* (CBS)
Drama: "Elizabeth R," *Masterpiece Theatre* (PBS)
Variety, musical: *The Carol Burnett Show* (CBS)
Variety, talk: *The Dick Cavett Show* (ABC)
New series: "Elizabeth R," *Masterpiece Theatre* (PBS)

**1973**
Comedy: *All in the Family* (CBS)
Drama (continuing): *The Waltons* (CBS)

**1973 (continued)**
Drama/comedy (limited): "Tom Brown's Schooldays," *Masterpiece Theatre* (PBS)
Variety, musical: *The Julie Andrews Hour* (ABC)
New series: *America* (NBC)

**1974**
Comedy: *M*A*S*H* (CBS)
Drama: "Upstairs, Downstairs," *Masterpiece Theatre* (PBS)
Limited series: *Columbo* (NBC)
Music/variety: *The Carol Burnett Show* (CBS)

**1975**
Comedy: *The Mary Tyler Moore Show* (CBS)
Drama: "Upstairs, Downstairs," *Masterpiece Theatre* (PBS)
Limited series: "Benjamin Franklin" (CBS)
Comedy-variety/music: *The Carol Burnett Show* (CBS)

**1976**
Comedy: *The Mary Tyler Moore Show* (CBS)
Drama: *Police Story* (NBC)
Limited series: "Upstairs, Downstairs," *Masterpiece Theatre* (PBS)
Comedy-variety/music: *NBC's Saturday Night* (NBC)

**1977**
Comedy: *The Mary Tyler Moore Show* (CBS)
Drama: "Upstairs, Downstairs," *Masterpiece Theatre* (PBS)
Limited series: *Roots* (ABC)
Comedy-variety/music: *Van Dyke and Company* (NBC)

**1978**
Comedy: *All in the Family* (CBS)
Drama: *The Rockford Files* (NBC)
Limited series: *Holocaust* (NBC)
Comedy-variety/music: *The Muppet Show* (syndicated)
Informational: *The Body Human* (CBS)

**1979**
Comedy: *Taxi* (ABC)
Drama: *Lou Grant* (CBS)
Limited series: *Roots: The Next Generations* (ABC)
Comedy-variety/music: "Steve & Eydie Celebrate Irving Berlin" (NBC)

**1980**
Comedy: *Taxi* (ABC)
Drama: *Lou Grant* (CBS)
Limited series: *Edward & Mrs. Simpson* (syndicated)
Variety/music: *IBM Presents Baryshnikov on Broadway* (ABC)

**1981**
Comedy: *Taxi* (ABC)
Drama: *Hill Street Blues* (NBC)
Limited series: *Shogun* (NBC)
Informational: *Steve Allen's Meeting of Minds* (PBS)

**1982**
Comedy: *Barney Miller* (ABC)
Drama: *Hill Street Blues* (NBC)

[2]*Programs this year were classified only so far as "Entertainment" and "News, Documentaries, Information and Sports," with several winners in each classification.*

# Emmy Award-winning Television Series, 1948–2002 (continued)

**1982 (continued)**
Limited series: *Marco Polo* (NBC)
Informational: *Creativity with Bill Moyers* (PBS)

**1983**
Comedy: *Cheers* (NBC)
Drama: *Hill Street Blues* (NBC)
Limited series: *Nicholas Nickleby* (syndicated)
Informational: *The Barbara Walters Specials* (ABC)

**1984**
Comedy: *Cheers* (NBC)
Drama: *Hill Street Blues* (NBC)
Limited series: "Concealed Enemies," *American Playhouse* (PBS)
Informational: *A Walk Through the 20th Century with Bill Moyers* (PBS)

**1985**
Comedy: *The Cosby Show* (NBC)
Drama: *Cagney & Lacey* (CBS)
Limited series: "The Jewel in the Crown," *Masterpiece Theatre* (PBS)
Informational: *The Living Planet: A Portrait of the Earth* (PBS)

**1986**
Comedy: *The Golden Girls* (NBC)
Drama: *Cagney & Lacey* (CBS)
Miniseries: *Peter the Great* (NBC)
Informational: "Laurence Olivier—A Life," *Great Performances* (PBS); *Planet Earth* (PBS)

**1987**
Comedy: *The Golden Girls* (NBC)
Drama: *L.A. Law* (NBC)
Miniseries: *A Year in the Life* (NBC)
Informational: *Smithsonian World* (PBS); "Unknown Chaplin," *American Masters* (PBS)

**1988**
Comedy: *The Wonder Years* (ABC)
Drama: *thirtysomething* (ABC)
Miniseries: *The Murder of Mary Phagan* (NBC)
Informational: "Buster Keaton: A Hard Act to Follow," *American Masters* (PBS); *Nature* (PBS)

**1989**
Comedy: *Cheers* (NBC)
Drama: *L.A. Law* (NBC)
Miniseries: *War and Remembrance* (ABC)
Variety/music/comedy: *The Tracy Ullman Show* (Fox)
Informational: *Nature* (PBS)

**1990**
Comedy: *Murphy Brown* (CBS)
Drama: *L.A. Law* (NBC)
Miniseries: *Drug Wars: The Camarena Story* (NBC)
Variety/music/comedy: *In Living Color* (Fox)
Informational: *Smithsonian World* (PBS)

**1991**
Comedy: *Cheers* (NBC)
Drama: *L.A. Law* (NBC)
Miniseries: *Separate But Equal* (ABC)
Informational: *The Civil War* (PBS)

**1992**
Comedy: *Murphy Brown* (CBS)

**1992 (continued)**
Drama: *Northern Exposure* (CBS)
Miniseries: *A Woman Named Jackie* (NBC)
Variety/music/comedy: *The Tonight Show Starring Johnny Carson* (NBC)
Informational: *MGM: When the Lion Roars* (TNT)

**1993**
Comedy: *Seinfeld* (NBC)
Drama: *Picket Fences* (CBS)
Miniseries: *Prime Suspect 2* (PBS)
Variety/music/comedy: *Saturday Night Live* (NBC)
Informational: *Healing and the Mind with Bill Moyers* (PBS)

**1994**
Comedy: *Frasier* (NBC)
Drama: *Picket Fences* (CBS)
Miniseries: *Prime Suspect 3* (PBS)
Variety/music/comedy: *Late Show with David Letterman* (CBS)
Informational: *Later with Bob Costas* (NBC)

**1995**
Comedy: *Frasier* (NBC)
Drama: *NYPD Blue* (ABC)
Miniseries: *Joseph* (TNT)
Variety/music/comedy: *The Tonight Show with Jay Leno* (NBC)
Informational: *Baseball* (PBS); *TV Nation* (NBC)

**1996**
Comedy: *Frasier* (NBC)
Drama: *ER* (NBC)
Miniseries: *Gulliver's Travels* (NBC)
Variety/music/comedy: *Dennis Miller Live* (HBO)
Informational: *Lost Civilizations* (NBC)

**1997**
Comedy: *Frasier* (NBC)
Drama: *Law & Order* (NBC)
Miniseries: *Prime Suspect 5: Errors of Judgment* (PBS)
Variety/music/comedy: *Tracey Takes On . . .* (HBO)
Informational: *Biography* (A&E); *The Great War and the Shaping of the 20th Century* (PBS)

**1998**
Comedy: *Frasier* (NBC)
Drama: *The Practice* (ABC)
Miniseries: *From the Earth to the Moon* (HBO)
Variety/music/comedy: *Late Show with David Letterman* (CBS)
Non-fiction: *The American Experience* (PBS)

**1999**
Comedy: *Ally McBeal* (Fox)
Drama: *The Practice* (ABC)
Miniseries: *Horatio Hornblower: The Even Chance* (A&E)
Variety/music/comedy: *Late Show with David Letterman* (CBS)
Non-fiction: *The American Experience* (PBS); *American Masters* (PBS)

**2000**
Comedy: *Will & Grace* (NBC)
Drama: *The West Wing* (NBC)
Miniseries: *The Corner* (HBO)

## Emmy Award-winning Television Series, 1948–2002 (continued)

**2000 (continued)**
Variety/music/comedy: *Late Show with David Letterman* (CBS)
Non-fiction: "Hitchcock, Selznick and the End of Hollywood," *American Masters* (PBS)

**2001**
Comedy: *Sex and the City* (HBO)
Drama: *The West Wing* (NBC)
Miniseries: *Anne Frank* (ABC)
Variety/music/comedy: *Late Show with David Letterman* (CBS)

**2001 (continued)**
Non-fiction: "Lucille Ball: Finding Lucy," *American Masters* (PBS)

**2002**
Comedy: *Friends* (NBC)
Drama: *The West Wing* (NBC)
Miniseries: *Band of Brothers* (HBO)
Variety/music/comedy: *Late Show with David Letterman* (CBS)
Non-fiction: *9/11* (CBS)

# Theater

## Tony Award Winners, 2003

The American Theatre Wing, a philanthropic and educational organization established in 1939, created the Tony Awards in 1947 to recognize distinguished achievement in the theater arts as presented on Broadway. The award is named for Antoinette Perry, a former director of the American Theatre Wing; since 1967 it has been presented in conjunction with the League of American Theatres and Producers, a Broadway trade association. A 15–30-member nominating committee selects nominees each May from among the year's new or newly revived Broadway shows; a body of some 710 current and former theater professionals, critics, and agents votes for the winners. The awards are presented in New York City in early June. Prize: silver medallion, set in a base, depicting on one face the masks of tragedy and comedy and on the other the profile of Antoinette Perry.

Tony Awards Web site: <www.tonys.org>

**musical:** *Hairspray* (book, Mark O'Donnell and Thomas Meehan; music, Marc Shaiman; lyrics, Scott Wittman and Marc Shaiman); ▶ **play:** *Take Me Out* (playwright, Richard Greenberg); ▶ **special theatrical event**[1]: *Russell Simmons' Def Poetry Jam on Broadway*; ▶ **revival of a musical:** *Nine* (book, Arthur Kopit, adapted from the Italian by Mario Fratti; music and lyrics, Maury Yeston); ▶ **revival of a play:** *Long Day's Journey Into Night* (playwright, Eugene O'Neill); ▶ **book, musical:** Mark O'Donnell and Thomas Meehan (*Hairspray*); ▶ **score:** Marc Shaiman (music), Scott Wittman and Marc Shaiman (lyrics) (*Hairspray*); ▶ **leading actress, musical:** Marissa Jaret Winokur (*Hairspray*); ▶ **leading actor, musical:** Harvey Fierstein (*Hairspray*); ▶ **leading actress, play:** Vanessa Redgrave (*Long Day's Journey Into Night*); ▶ **leading actor, play:** Brain Dennehy (*Long Day's Journey Into Night*); ▶ **featured actress, musical:** Jane Krakowski (*Nine*); ▶ **featured actor, musical:** Dick Latessa (*Hairspray*); ▶ **featured actress, play:** Michele Pawk (*Hollywood Arms*); ▶ **featured actor, play:** Denis O'Hare (*Take Me Out*); ▶ **direction, musical:** Jack O'Brien (*Hairspray*); ▶ **direction, play:** Joe Mantello (*Take Me Out*); ▶ **costume design:** William Ivey Long (*Hairspray*); ▶ **lighting design:** Nigel Levings (*La Bohème*); ▶ **scenic design:** Catherine Martin (*La Bohème*); ▶ **orchestrations:** Billy Joel and Stuart Malina (*Movin' Out*); ▶ **choreography:** Twyla Tharp (*Movin' Out*); ▶ **special award for lifetime achievement in the theater:** Cy Feuer.

[1] Award for "productions that are considered neither plays nor musicals."

## Tony Awards, 1947–2003

Tony Awards Web site: <www.tonys.org>.

| YEAR | BEST MUSICAL | BEST PLAY |
|---|---|---|
| 1947 | *not awarded* | *All My Sons* (Arthur Miller)[1] |
| 1948 | *not awarded* | *Mister Roberts* (Thomas Heggen, Joshua Logan) |
| 1949 | *Kiss Me, Kate* (book, Bella and Samuel Spewack; music and lyrics, Cole Porter) | *Death of a Salesman* (Arthur Miller) |
| 1950 | *South Pacific* (book, Oscar Hammerstein II, Joshua Logan; music, Richard Rodgers; lyrics, Oscar Hammerstein II) | *The Cocktail Party* (T.S. Eliot) |
| 1951 | *Guys and Dolls* (book, Jo Swerling, Abe Burrows; music and lyrics, Frank Loesser) | *The Rose Tattoo* (Tennessee Williams) |
| 1952 | *The King and I* (book and lyrics, Oscar Hammerstein II; music, Richard Rodgers) | *The Fourposter* (Jan de Hartog) |
| 1953 | *Wonderful Town* (book, Joseph Fields, Jerome Chodorov; music, Leonard Bernstein; lyrics, Betty Comden, Adolph Green) | *The Crucible* (Arthur Miller) |
| 1954 | *Kismet* (book, Charles Lederer, Luther Davis; music, Alexander Borodin; adaptation and lyrics, Robert Wright, George Forrest) | *The Teahouse of the August Moon* (John Patrick) |
| 1955 | *The Pajama Game* (book, George Abbott, Richard Bissell; music and lyrics, Richard Adler, Jerry Ross) | *The Desperate Hours* (Joseph Hayes) |

# Tony Awards, 1947–2003 (continued)

| YEAR | BEST MUSICAL | BEST PLAY |
|---|---|---|
| 1956 | *Damn Yankees* (book and lyrics, George Abbott, Douglass Wallop; music, Richard Adler, Jerry Ross) | *The Diary of Anne Frank* (Frances Goodrich, Albert Hackett) |
| 1957 | *My Fair Lady* (book and lyrics, Alan Jay Lerner; music, Frederick Loewe) | *Long Day's Journey into Night* (Eugene O'Neill) |
| 1958 | *The Music Man* (book, Meredith Willson, Franklin Lacey; music and lyrics, Meredith Willson) | *Sunrise at Campobello* (Dore Schary) |
| 1959 | *Redhead* (book, Herbert and Dorothy Fields, Sidney Sheldon, David Shaw; music, Albert Hague; lyrics, Dorothy Fields) | *J.B.* (Archibald MacLeish) |
| 1960 (tie) | *The Sound of Music* (book, Howard Lindsay, Russel Crouse; music, Richard Rodgers; lyrics, Oscar Hammerstein II); *Fiorello!* (book, Jerome Weidman, George Abbott; music, Jerry Brock; lyrics, Sheldon Harnick) | *The Miracle Worker* (William Gibson) |
| 1961 | *Bye, Bye Birdie* (book, Michael Stewart; music, Charles Strouse; lyrics, Lee Adams) | *Beckett* (Jean Anouilh, translated by Lucienne Hill) |
| 1962 | *How to Succeed in Business Without Really Trying* (book, Abe Burrows, Jack Weinstock, Willie Gilbert; music and lyrics, Frank Loesser) | *A Man for All Seasons* (Robert Bolt) |
| 1963 | *A Funny Thing Happened on the Way to the Forum* (book, Burt Shevelove, Larry Gelbart; music and lyrics, Stephen Sondheim) | *Who's Afraid of Virginia Woolf?* (Edward Albee) |
| 1964 | *Hello, Dolly!* (book, Michael Stewart; music and lyrics, Jerry Herman) | *Luther* (John Osborne) |
| 1965 | *Fiddler on the Roof* (book, Joseph Stein; music, Jerry Bock; lyrics, Sheldon Harnick) | *The Subject Was Roses* (Frank Gilroy) |
| 1966 | *Man of La Mancha* (book, Dale Wasserman; music, Mitch Leigh; lyrics, Joe Darion) | *Marat/Sade* (Peter Weiss, translated by Geoffrey Skelton) |
| 1967 | *Cabaret* (book, Joe Masteroff; music, John Kander; lyrics, Fred Ebb) | *The Homecoming* (Harold Pinter) |
| 1968 | *Hallelujah, Baby!* (book, Arthur Laurents; music, Jule Styne; lyrics, Betty Comden, Adolph Green) | *Rosencrantz and Guildenstern Are Dead* (Tom Stoppard) |
| 1969 | *1776* (book, Peter Stone; music and lyrics, Sherman Edwards) | *The Great White Hope* (Howard Sackler) |
| 1970 | *Applause* (book, Betty Comden, Adolph Greene; music, Charles Strouse; lyrics, Lee Adams) | *Borstal Boy* (Frank McMahon) |
| 1971 | *Company* (book, George Furth; music and lyrics, Stephen Sondheim) | *Sleuth* (Anthony Shaffer) |
| 1972 | *Two Gentlemen of Verona* (book, John Guare, Mel Shapiro; music, Galt MacDermot; lyrics, John Guare) | *Sticks and Bones* (David Rabe) |
| 1973 | *A Little Night Music* (book, Hugh Wheeler; music and lyrics, Stephen Sondheim) | *That Championship Season* (Jason Miller) |
| 1974 | *Raisin* (book, Robert Nemiroff, Charlotte Zaltzberg; music, Judd Woldin; lyrics, Robert Brittan) | *The River Niger* (Joseph A. Walker) |
| 1975 | *The Wiz* (book, William F. Brown; music and lyrics, Charlie Smalls) | *Equus* (Peter Shaffer) |
| 1976 | *A Chorus Line* (book, James Kirkwood, Nicholas Dante; music, Marvin Hamlisch; lyrics, Edward Kleban) | *Travesties* (Tom Stoppard) |
| 1977 | *Annie* (book, Thomas Meehan; music, Charles Strouse; lyrics, Martin Charnin) | *The Shadow Box* (Michael Christofer) |
| 1978 | *Ain't Misbehavin'* (book, Murray Horwitz, Richard Maltby, Jr.; music, Fats Waller; lyrics, Fats Waller and many others) | *Da* (Hugh Leonard) |
| 1979 | *Sweeney Todd* (book, Hugh Wheeler; music and lyrics, Stephen Sondheim) | *The Elephant Man* (Bernard Pomerance) |
| 1980 | *Evita* (book and lyrics, Tim Rice; music, Andrew Lloyd Webber) | *Children of a Lesser God* (Mark Medoff) |
| 1981 | *42nd Street* (book, Michael Stewart, Mark Bramble; music, Harry Warren; lyrics, Al Dubin) | *Amadeus* (Peter Shaffer) |
| 1982 | *Nine* (book, Arthur Kopit; music and lyrics, Maury Yeston) | *The Life and Adventures of Nicholas Nickleby* (David Edgar) |
| 1983 | *Cats* (book and lyrics, T.S. Eliot; music, Andrew Lloyd Webber) | *Torch Song Trilogy* (Harvey Fierstein) |
| 1984 | *La Cage aux Folles* (book, Harvey Fierstein; music and lyrics, Jerry Herman) | *The Real Thing* (Tom Stoppard) |
| 1985 | *Big River* (book, William Hauptman; music and lyrics, Roger Miller) | *Biloxi Blues* (Neil Simon) |
| 1986 | *The Mystery of Edwin Drood* (book, music, lyrics, Rupert Holmes) | *I'm Not Rappaport* (Herb Gardner) |
| 1987 | *Les Misérables* (book, Alain Boublil, Claude-Michel Schönberg; music, Claude-Michel Schönberg; lyrics, Herbert Kretzmer, Alain Boublil) | *Fences* (August Wilson) |
| 1988 | *The Phantom of the Opera* (book, Richard Stilgoe, Andrew Lloyd Webber; music, Andrew Lloyd Webber; lyrics, Charles Hart, Richard Stilgoe) | *M. Butterfly* (David Henry Hwang) |

## Tony Awards, 1947–2003 (continued)

| YEAR | BEST MUSICAL | BEST PLAY |
|---|---|---|
| 1989 | *Jerome Robbins' Broadway* (compilation) | *The Heidi Chronicles* (Wendy Wasserstein) |
| 1990 | *City of Angels* (book, Larry Gelbart; music, Cy Coleman; lyrics, David Zippel) | *The Grapes of Wrath* (Frank Galati) |
| 1991 | *The Will Rogers Follies* (book, Peter Stone; music, Cy Coleman; lyrics, Betty Comden, Adolph Green) | *Lost in Yonkers* (Neil Simon) |
| 1992 | *Crazy for You* (book, Ken Ludwig; music and lyrics, George and Ira Gershwin) | *Dancing at Lughnasa* (Brian Friel) |
| 1993 | *Kiss of the Spider Woman—The Musical* (book, Terrence McNally; music, John Kander; lyrics, Fred Ebb) | *Angels in America: Millennium Approaches* (Tony Kushner) |
| 1994 | *Passion* (book, James Lapine; music and lyrics, Stephen Sondheim) | *Angels in America: Perestroika* (Tony Kushner) |
| 1995 | *Sunset Boulevard* (book and lyrics, Don Black, Christopher Hampton; music, Andrew Lloyd Webber) | *Love! Valour! Compassion!* (Terrence McNally) |
| 1996 | *Rent* (book, music, lyrics, Jonathan Larson) | *Master Class* (Terrence McNally) |
| 1997 | *Titanic* (book, Peter Stone; music and lyrics, Maury Yeston) | *The Last Night of Ballyhoo* (Alfred Uhry) |
| 1998 | *The Lion King* (book, Roger Allers, Irene Mecchi; music and lyrics, Elton John, Tim Rice, and others) | *Art* (Yasmina Reza) |
| 1999 | *Fosse* (compilation) | *Side Man* (Warren Leight) |
| 2000 | *Contact* (book, John Weidman; music and lyrics, various artists) | *Copenhagen* (Michael Frayn) |
| 2001 | *The Producers, the New Mel Brooks Musical* (book, Mel Brooks, Thomas Meehan; music and lyrics, Mel Brooks) | *Proof* (David Auburn) |
| 2002 | *Thoroughly Modern Millie* (book, Richard Morris, Dick Scanlan; music, Jeanine Tesori; lyrics, Dick Scanlan) | *The Goat or Who Is Sylvia?* (Edward Albee) |
| 2003 | *Hairspray* (book, Mark O'Donnell and Thomas Meehan; music, Marc Shaiman; lyrics, Scott Wittman and Marc Shaiman) | *Take Me Out* (Richard Greenberg) |

[1]*Awarded to author.*

## Longest-Running Broadway Shows

*As of 15 Jun 2003. Source: Internet Broadway Database <www.ibdb.com>.*

| | SHOW | RUN | TOTAL PERFORMANCES | | SHOW | RUN | TOTAL PERFORMANCES |
|---|---|---|---|---|---|---|---|
| 1 | *Cats* | 1982–2000 | 7,485 | 12 | *Tobacco Road* | 1933–1941 | 3,182 |
| 2 | *Les Misérables* | 1987–2003 | 6,680 | 13 | *Rent* | 1996– | 2,969 |
| 3 | *The Phantom of the Opera* | 1988– | 6,414 | 14 | *Hello, Dolly!* | 1964–1970 | 2,844 |
| | | | | 15 | *Chicago* [revival] | 1996– | 2,740 |
| 4 | *A Chorus Line* | 1975–1990 | 6,137 | 16 | *My Fair Lady* | 1956–1962 | 2,717 |
| 5 | *Oh! Calcutta!* [revival] | 1976–1989 | 5,959 | 17 | *Threepenny Opera* | 1955–1961 | 2,611 |
| | | | | 18 | *Annie* | 1977–1983 | 2,377 |
| 6 | *Miss Saigon* | 1991–2001 | 4,092 | 19 | *The Lion King* | 1997– | 2,332 |
| 7 | *Beauty and the Beast* | 1994– | 3,741 | 20 | *Man of La Mancha* | 1965–1971 | 2,328 |
| | | | | 21 | *Abie's Irish Rose* | 1922–1927 | 2,327 |
| 8 | *42nd Street* | 1980–1989 | 3,486 | 22 | *Oklahoma!* | 1943–1948 | 2,212 |
| 9 | *Grease* | 1972–1980 | 3,338 | 23 | *Cabaret* [revival] | 1998– | 2,146 |
| 10 | *Fiddler on the Roof* | 1964–1972 | 3,242 | 24 | *Smokey Joe's Cafe* | 1995–2000 | 2,037 |
| 11 | *Life with Father* | 1939–1947 | 3,224 | 25 | *Pippin* | 1972–1977 | 1,944 |

## Encyclopædia Britannica's Greatest Plays

*A Man for All Seasons*, by Robert Bolt
*Andromache*, by Jean Racine
*Angels in America*, by Tony Kushner
*Antigone*, by Sophocles
*Antony and Cleopatra*, by William Shakespeare
*Bacchants*, by Euripides
*The Bald Soprano*, by Eugène Ionesco
*The Birds*, by Aristophanes
*The Birthday Party*, by Harold Pinter
*Blood Wedding*, by Federico García Lorca
*The Caretaker*, by Harold Pinter
*Cat on a Hot Tin Roof*, by Tennessee Williams
*The Cherry Orchard*, by Anton Chekov
*The Children's Hour*, by Lillian Hellman

*Le Cid*, by Pierre Corneille
*Cinna*, by Pierre Corneille
*The Country-Wife*, by William Wycherley
*Death of a Salesman*, by Arthur Miller
*Doctor Faustus*, by Christopher Marlowe
*The Doll House*, by Henrik Ibsen
*The Dumb Waiter*, by Harold Pinter
*Electra*, by Sophocles
*Endgame*, by Samuel Beckett
*An Enemy of the People*, by Henrik Ibsen
*Entertaining Mr. Sloane*, by Joe Orton
*Faust*, by Goethe
*The Frogs*, by Aristophanes
*Ghosts*, by Henrik Ibsen

## Encyclopædia Britannica's Greatest Plays (continued)

The Ghost Sonata, by August Strindberg
The Glass Menagerie, by Tennessee Williams
Glengarry Glen Ross, by David Mamet
Gross Indecency, by Moisés Kaufman
Hamlet, by William Shakespeare
Hedda Gabler, by Henrik Ibsen
Horace, by Pierre Corneille
The House of Bernarda Alba, by Federico García Lorca
The Importance of Being Earnest, by Oscar Wilde
The Invention of Love, by Tom Stoppard
Iphigenia at Aulis, by Euripides
The Jew of Malta, by Christopher Marlowe
Julius Caesar, by William Shakespeare
Juno and the Paycock, by Sean O'Casey
King Lear, by William Shakespeare
Lady Windermere's Fan, by Oscar Wilde
Long Day's Journey into Night, by Eugene O'Neill
Look Back in Anger, by John Osborne
The "Lulu" dramas (Pandora's Box, Earthspirit), by Frank Wedekind
Lysistrata, by Aristophanes
Macbeth, by William Shakespeare
The Maids, by Jean Genet
Major Barbara, by George Bernard Shaw
Marriage A-la-Mode, by John Dryden
The Master Builder, by Henrik Ibsen
Medea, by Euripides
The Merchant of Venice, by William Shakespeare
A Midsummer Night's Dream, by William Shakespeare
The Misanthrope, by Molière
Miss Julie, by August Strindberg
Mother Courage and Her Children, by Bertolt Brecht
No Exit, by Jean-Paul Sartre
Noises Off, by Michael Frayn
Oedipus at Colonus, by Sophocles
Oedipus Rex, by Sophocles
Oresteia (Agamemnon, The Libation Bearers, and Eumenides), by Aeschylus
Othello, by William Shakespeare

Phèdre, by Jean Racine
The Physicists, by Friedrich Dürrenmatt
The Piano Lesson, by August Wilson
Plenty, by David Hare
The Plough and the Stars, by Sean O'Casey
Polyeucte, by Pierre Corneille
The Port Elizabeth plays, by Athol Fugard
Prometheus Bound, by Aeschylus
Pygmalion, by George Bernard Shaw
Raisin in the Sun, by Lorraine Hansberry
Richard III, by William Shakespeare
Romeo and Juliet, by William Shakespeare
Rosencrantz and Guildenstern are Dead, by Tom Stoppard
Saint Joan, by George Bernard Shaw
The School for Scandal, by Richard Brinsley Sheridan
The School for Wives, by Molière
The Seagull, by Anton Chekov
Seven Against Thebes, by Aeschylus
The Shadow of a Gunman, by Sean O'Casey
She Stoops to Conquer, by Oliver Goldsmith
Six Characters in Search of an Author, by Luigi Pirandello
A Streetcar Named Desire, by Tennessee Williams
Tartuffe, by Molière
The Tempest, by William Shakespeare
The Threepenny Opera, by Bertolt Brecht
Three Sisters, by Anton Chekov
Trojan Women, by Euripides
True West, by Sam Shepard
Twelfth Night, by William Shakespeare
Ubu Roi, by Alfred Jarry
Uncle Vanya, by Anton Chekov
Under Milk Wood, by Dylan Thomas
The Visit, by Friedrich Dürrenmatt
Waiting for Godot, by Samuel Beckett
Who's Afraid of Virginia Woolf?, by Edward Albee
The Wild Duck, by Henrik Ibsen
Yerma, by Federico García Lorca

## Encyclopædia Britannica's 25 Notable US Theater Companies

| COMPANY | LOCATION | ARTISTIC DIRECTOR (2003) |
|---|---|---|
| The Acting Company | New York NY | Margot Harley |
| Actors Theatre of Louisville | Louisville KY | Marc Masterson |
| Alley Theatre | Houston TX | Gregory Boyd |
| American Conservatory Theater | San Francisco CA | Carey Perloff |
| American Repertory Theatre | Cambridge MA | Robert Woodruff |
| Arena Stage | Washington DC | Molly Smith |
| Black Ensemble Theater | Chicago IL | Jackie Taylor |
| Center Theatre Group | Los Angeles CA | Gordon Davidson |
| Circle in the Square | New York NY | Theodore Mann |
| Cleveland Public Theatre | Cleveland OH | James A. Levin |
| Colony Theatre Company | Los Angeles CA | Barbara Beckley |
| El Teatro Campesino | San Juan Bautista CA | Luis Valdez |
| Ford's Theatre | Washington DC | Brian J. Laczko |
| Goodman Theatre | Chicago IL | Robert Falls |
| Guthrie Theater | Minneapolis MN | Joe Dowling |
| La Jolla Playhouse | La Jolla CA | Des McAnuff |
| Long Wharf Theatre | New Haven CT | Gordon Edelstein |
| National Actors Theatre | New York NY | Tony Randall |
| Pasadena Playhouse | Pasadena CA | Sheldon Epps |
| The Public Theater | New York NY | George C. Wolfe |
| Seattle Repertory Theatre | Seattle WA | Sharon Ott |
| Steppenwolf Theatre Company | Chicago IL | Martha Lavey |
| Studio Arena Theatre | Buffalo NY | Gavin Cameron-Webb |
| Victory Gardens Theater | Chicago IL | Dennis Zacek |
| Yale Repertory Theatre | New Haven CT | James Bundy |

# Music

## Grammy Awards 2003

The National Academy of Recording Arts and Sciences was established in 1957 as a professional organization for musicians, producers, technicians, and executives in the US recording industry. The Grammys, first awarded in 1958, recognize excellence in the recording industry without regard to record sales or chart position. Nominees and winners are selected by the Academy's individual members according to the members' areas of expertise. In addition to the four general categories (record, album, and song of the year, and best new artist) for which all members are eligible to vote, for 2001 there were 97 categories in 27 fields, of which Academy members were permitted to vote in no more than 8 fields. Prizes for works released 1 Oct 2001–30 Sep 2002 were awarded in New York on 23 Feb 2003; the ceremony for 2002–03 works is scheduled for 22 Feb 2004 in New York City. Prize: gold miniature phonograph.

Grammy Award Web site: <www.grammy.com>.

**category:** winner (performer in parentheses for songwriting/production awards)

**record (single) of the year:** "Don't Know Why," Norah Jones; ▶ **album of the year:** *Come Away with Me,* Norah Jones; ▶ **song of the year:** "Don't Know Why," Jesse Harris, songwriter (Norah Jones); ▶ **new artist:** Norah Jones; ▶ **pop vocal performance, female:** "Don't Know Why," Norah Jones; ▶ **pop vocal performance, male:** "Your Body is a Wonderland," John Mayer; ▶ **pop vocal performance, duo/group:** "Hey Baby," No Doubt; ▶ **pop vocal album:** *Come Away with Me,* Norah Jones; ▶ **pop vocal album, traditional:** *Playin' with My Friends: Bennett Sings the Blues,* Tony Bennett; ▶ **rock vocal performance, female:** "Steve McQueen," Sheryl Crow; ▶ **rock vocal performance, male:** "The Rising," Bruce Springsteen; ▶ **rock vocal performance, duo/group:** "In My Place," Coldplay; ▶ **hard rock performance:** "All My Life," Foo Fighters; ▶ **metal performance:** "Here to Stay," Korn; ▶ **rock song:** "The Rising," Bruce Springsteen, songwriter (Bruce Springsteen); ▶ **rock album:** *The Rising,* Bruce Springsteen; ▶ **alternative album:** *A Rush of Blood to the Head,* Coldplay; ▶ **R&B vocal performance, female:** "He Think I Don't Know," Mary J. Blige; ▶ **R&B vocal performance, male:** "U Don't Have to Call," Usher; ▶ **R&B vocal performance, duo/group:** "Love's in Need of Love Today," Stevie Wonder & Take 6; ▶ **R&B song:** "Love of My Life (An Ode to Hip Hop)," Erykah Badu, Madukwu Chinwah, Rashid Lonnie Lynn, Robert Ozuna, James Poyser, Raphael Saadiq & Glen Standridge, songwriters (Erykah Badu featuring Common); ▶ **R&B album:** *Voyage to India,* India.Arie; ▶ **contemporary R&B album:** *Ashanti,* Ashanti; ▶ **female rap performance, solo:** "Scream a.k.a. Itchin'," Missy Elliott; ▶ **male rap performance, solo:** "Hot in Herre," Nelly; ▶ **rap performance, duo/group:** "The Whole World," OutKast featuring Killer Mike; ▶ **rap album:** *The Eminem Show,* Eminem; ▶ **country vocal performance, female:** "Cry," Faith Hill; ▶ **country vocal performance, male:** "Give My Love to Rose," Johnny Cash; ▶ **country**

**vocal performance, duo/group:** "Long Time Gone," Dixie Chicks; ▶ **country song:** "Where Were You (When The World Stopped Turning)," Alan Jackson, songwriter (Alan Jackson); ▶ **country album:** *Home,* Dixie Chicks; ▶ **bluegrass album:** *Lost In The Lonesome Pines,* Jim Lauderdale, Ralph Stanley & The Clinch Mountain Boys; ▶ **new age album:** *Acoustic Garden,* Eric Tingstad & Nancy Rumbel; ▶ **jazz album, contemporary:** *Speaking of Now,* Pat Metheny Group; ▶ **jazz album, vocal:** *Live in Paris,* Diana Krall; ▶ **jazz album, instrumental:** *Directions in Music,* Herbie Hancock, Michael Brecker & Roy Hargrove; ▶ **jazz album, large ensemble:** *What Goes Around,* Dave Holland Big Band; ▶ **Latin jazz album:** *The Gathering,* Caribbean Jazz Project; ▶ **gospel album, rock:** *Come Together,* Third Day; ▶ **gospel album, pop/contemporary:** *The Eleventh Hour,* Jars of Clay; ▶ **gospel album, southern/country/bluegrass:** *We Called Him Mr. Gospel Music: The James Blackwood Tribute Album,* The Jordanaires, Larry Ford and the Light Crust Doughboys; ▶ **gospel album, soul, traditional:** *Higher Ground,* The Blind Boys of Alabama; ▶ **gospel album, soul, contemporary:** *Sidebars,* Eartha; ▶ **gospel album, choir/chorus:** *Be Glad,* Carol Cymbala, choir director; The Brooklyn Tabernacle Choir; ▶ **Latin album, pop:** *Caraluna,* Bacilos; ▶ **Latin album, rock/alternative:** *Revolución de amor,* Maná; ▶ **Latin album, traditional tropical:** *El Arte del sabor,* Bebo Valdés Trio with Israel López "Cachao" & Carlos "Patato" Valdés; ▶ **salsa album:** *La Negra tiene tumbao,* Celia Cruz; ▶ **merengue album:** *Latino,* Grupo Mania; ▶ **Mexican/Mexican-American album:** *Lo dijo el corazón,* Joan Sebastian; ▶ **Tejano album:** *Acuérdate,* Emilio Navaira; ▶ **blues album, traditional:** *A Christmas Celebration of Hope,* B.B. King; ▶ **blues album, contemporary:** *Don't Give Up on Me,* Solomon Burke; ▶ **folk album, traditional:** *Legacy,* Doc Watson & David Holt; ▶ **folk album, contemporary:** *This Side,* Nickel Creek; ▶ **Native American album:** *Beneath the Raven Moon,* Mary Youngblood; ▶ **reggae album:** *Jamaican E.T.,* Lee "Scratch" Perry; ▶ **world music album:** *Mundo,* Rubén Blades; ▶ **polka album:** *Top of the World,* Jimmy Sturr; ▶ **spoken word album:** *A Song Flung Up To Heaven,* Maya Angelou; ▶ **spoken comedy album:** *Robin Williams—Live 2002,* Robin Williams; ▶ **producer, non-classical:** Arif Mardin; ▶ **producer, classical:** Robert Woods; ▶ **classical album:** *Vaughan Williams: A Sea Symphony (Sym. No. 1);* Robert Spano, cond.; Norman Mackenzie, chorus dir.; Thomas C. Moore, producer (Christine Goerke, soprano & Brett Polegato, baritone; Atlanta Sym. Orch. Cho.; Atlanta Sym. Orch.); ▶ **orchestral performance:** *Mahler: Symphony No. 6,* Michael Tilson Thomas, cond. (San Francisco Sym.); ▶ **opera recording:** *Wagner: Tannhäuser,* Daniel Barenboim, cond.; Jane Eaglen, Thomas Hampson, Waltraud Meier, René Pape & Peter Seiffert; Christoph Classen, producer (Chor der Deutschen Staatsoper Berlin; Staatskapelle Berlin); ▶ **chamber music performance:** *Beethoven: String Quartets ("Razumovsky") Op. 59, 1–3; "Harp" Op. 74),* Takács Quartet; ▶ **classical vocal performance:** *Bel Canto,* Renée Fleming, soprano (Patrick Summers; Coro del Maggio Musicale Fiorentino; Orch. of St.*

## Grammy Awards 2003 (continued)

Luke's); ▶ **contemporary classical composition:** *Lamentations and Praises*, Sir John Tavener (Chanticleer; Joseph Jennings; Handel & Haydn Society of Boston); ▶ **music video, short form:** "Without Me," Joseph Kahn, dir.; Greg Tharp, prod. (Eminem)

## Grammy Awards Top Winners, 1958–2002

*The year denotes the period for which the winning work or artist was recognized; the prizes were generally awarded during the following year.*

| YEAR | RECORD (SINGLE) OF THE YEAR | ALBUM OF THE YEAR | BEST NEW ARTIST |
|------|------|------|------|
| 1958 | "Nel Blu Dipinto Di Blu (Volare)," Domenico Modugno | *The Music from Peter Gunn*, Henry Mancini | *not awarded* |
| 1959 | "Mack the Knife," Bobby Darin | *Come Dance with Me*, Frank Sinatra | Bobby Darin |
| 1960 | "Theme from A Summer Place," Percy Faith | *The Button-down Mind of Bob Newhart*, Bob Newhart | Bob Newhart |
| 1961 | "Moon River," Henry Mancini | *Judy at Carnegie Hall*, Judy Garland | Peter Nero |
| 1962 | "I Left My Heart in San Francisco," Tony Bennett | *The First Family*, Vaughn Meader | Robert Goulet |
| 1963 | "The Days of Wine and Roses," Henry Mancini | *The Barbra Streisand Album*, Barbra Streisand | Ward Swingle (The Swingle Singers) |
| 1964 | "The Girl from Ipanema," Stan Getz & Astrud Gilberto | *Getz/Gilberto*, Stan Getz & João Gilberto | The Beatles |
| 1965 | "A Taste of Honey," Herb Alpert | *September of My Years*, Frank Sinatra | Tom Jones |
| 1966 | "Strangers in the Night," Frank Sinatra | *A Man and His Music*, Frank Sinatra | *not awarded* |
| 1967 | "Up, Up and Away," The 5th Dimension | *Sgt. Pepper's Lonely Hearts Club Band*, The Beatles | Bobbie Gentry |
| 1968 | "Mrs. Robinson," Simon & Garfunkel | *By the Time I Get to Phoenix*, Glen Campbell | José Feliciano |
| 1969 | "Aquarius/Let the Sunshine In," The 5th Dimension | *Blood, Sweat & Tears*, Blood, Sweat & Tears | Crosby, Stills & Nash |
| 1970 | "Bridge over Troubled Water," Simon & Garfunkel | *Bridge over Troubled Water*, Simon & Garfunkel | Carpenters |
| 1971 | "It's Too Late," Carole King | *Tapestry*, Carole King | Carly Simon |
| 1972 | "The First Time Ever I Saw Your Face," Roberta Flack | *The Concert for Bangla Desh*, George Harrison & Friends | America |
| 1973 | "Killing Me Softly with His Song," Roberta Flack | *Innervisions*, Stevie Wonder | Bette Midler |
| 1974 | "I Honestly Love You," Olivia Newton-John | *Fulfillingness' First Finale*, Stevie Wonder | Marvin Hamlisch |
| 1975 | "Love Will Keep Us Together," Captain & Tennille | *Still Crazy After All These Years*, Paul Simon | Natalie Cole |
| 1976 | "This Masquerade," George Benson | *Songs in the Key of Life*, Stevie Wonder | Starland Vocal Band |
| 1977 | "Hotel California," The Eagles | *Rumours*, Fleetwood Mac | Debby Boone |
| 1978 | "Just the Way You Are," Billy Joel | *Saturday Night Fever*, The Bee Gees | A Taste of Honey |
| 1979 | "What a Fool Believes," The Doobie Brothers | *52nd Steet*, Billy Joel | Rickie Lee Jones |
| 1980 | "Sailing," Christopher Cross | *Christopher Cross*, Christopher Cross | Christopher Cross |
| 1981 | "Bette Davis Eyes," Kim Carnes | *Double Fantasy*, John Lennon & Yoko Ono | Sheena Easton |
| 1982 | "Rosanna," Toto | *Toto IV*, Toto | Men at Work |
| 1983 | "Beat It," Michael Jackson | *Thriller*, Michael Jackson | Culture Club |
| 1984 | "What's Love Got to Do with It," Tina Turner | *Can't Slow Down*, Lionel Richie | Cyndi Lauper |
| 1985 | "We Are the World," USA for Africa | *No Jacket Required*, Phil Collins | Sade |
| 1986 | "Higher Love," Steve Winwood | *Graceland*, Paul Simon | Bruce Hornsby and the Range |
| 1987 | "Graceland," Paul Simon | *The Joshua Tree*, U2 | Jody Watley |
| 1988 | "Don't Worry, Be Happy," Bobby McFerrin | *Faith*, George Michael | Tracy Chapman |
| 1989 | "Wind Beneath My Wings," Bette Midler | *Nick of Time*, Bonnie Raitt | Milli Vanilli [revoked] |

## Grammy Awards Top Winners, 1958–2002 (continued)

| YEAR | RECORD (SINGLE) OF THE YEAR | ALBUM OF THE YEAR | BEST NEW ARTIST |
|---|---|---|---|
| 1990 | "Another Day in Paradise," Phil Collins | *Back on the Block*, Quincy Jones | Mariah Carey |
| 1991 | "Unforgettable," Natalie Cole w/ Nat "King" Cole | *Unforgettable*, Natalie Cole w/ Nat "King" Cole | Marc Cohn |
| 1992 | "Tears in Heaven," Eric Clapton | *Unplugged*, Eric Clapton | Arrested Development |
| 1993 | "I Will Always Love You," Whitney Houston | *The Bodyguard*, Whitney Houston | Toni Braxton |
| 1994 | "All I Wanna Do," Sheryl Crow | *MTV Unplugged*, Tony Bennett | Sheryl Crow |
| 1995 | "Kiss from a Rose," Seal | *Jagged Little Pill*, Alanis Morissette | Hootie and the Blowfish |
| 1996 | "Change the World," Eric Clapton | *Falling into You*, Celine Dion | LeAnn Rimes |
| 1997 | "Sunny Came Home," Shawn Colvin | *Time Out of Mind*, Bob Dylan | Paula Cole |
| 1998 | "My Heart Will Go On," Celine Dion | *The Miseducation of Lauryn Hill*, Lauryn Hill | Lauryn Hill |
| 1999 | "Smooth," Santana feat. Rob Thomas | *Supernatural*, Santana | Christina Aguilera |
| 2000 | "Beautiful Day," U2 | *Two Against Nature*, Steely Dan | Shelby Lynne |
| 2001 | "Walk On," U2 | *O Brother, Where Art Thou?*, various artists | Alicia Keys |
| 2002 | "Don't Know Why," Norah Jones | *Come Away with Me*, Norah Jones | Norah Jones |
| 2003 | *to be held in February 2004* | | |

## Eurovision Song Contest, 1956–2003

The European Broadcasting Union (EBU), an association of national television and radio companies from Europe and the Mediterranean, began the Eurovision Song Contest in 1956 to promote European pop-music composers and performers. Each EBU member country, along with several provisional participants, can nominate one original song per year, in any language, with a maximum length of three minutes. The overall winner is selected through a point scheme based on call-in votes from viewers and juries in each participating country. Eurovision Song Contest Web site: <www.eurosong.net>.

| YEAR | SONG, SONGWRITER(S) (PERFORMER, COUNTRY) |
|---|---|
| 1956 | "Refrain," Emile Gardaz, Géo Voumard (Lys Assia, Switzerland) |
| 1957 | "Net als toen," Willy van Hemert, Guus Jansen (Corry Brokken, The Netherlands) |
| 1958 | "Dors mon amour," Pierre Delanoe, Hubert Giraud (André Clavaeu, France) |
| 1959 | "Een beetje," Willy van Hemert, Dick Schallies (Teddy Scholten, The Netherlands) |
| 1960 | "Tom Pillibi," Pierre Cour, André Popp (Jacqueline Boyer, France) |
| 1961 | "Nous les amoureux," Jacques Datin, Maurice Vidalin (Jean-Claude Pascal, Luxembourg) |
| 1962 | "Un Premier amour," Rolande Valade, Claude Henri Vic (Isabelle Aubret, France) |
| 1963 | "Dansevise," Sejr Volmer Sorensen, Otto Francker (Grethe and Jorgen Ingmann, Denmark) |
| 1964 | "Non ho l'étà," Nicola Salerno (Gigliola Cinquetti, Italy) |
| 1965 | "Poupée de cire, poupée de son," Serge Gainsbourg (France Gall, Luxembourg) |
| 1966 | "Merci chérie," Udo Jürgens, Thomas Horbiger (Udo Jürgens, Austria) |
| 1967 | "Puppet on a String," Bill Martin, Phil Coulter (Sandie Shaw, United Kingdom) |
| 1968 | "La, la, la . . ." Ramon Arcusa, Manuel de la Calva (Massiel, Spain) |
| 1969 | "Vivo cantando," A. Alcaide, Maria José de Cerato (Salomé, Spain); "Boom Bang-a-Bang," Peter Warne, Alan Moorhouse (Lulu, United Kingdom); "De Troubadour," Lennie Kuhr, David Hartsena (Lennie Kuhr, The Netherlands); "Un Jour, un enfant," Eddy Marnay, Emile Stern (Frida Boccara, France) (four-way tie) |
| 1970 | "All Kinds of Everything," Derry Lindsay, Jackie Smith (Dana, Ireland) |
| 1971 | "Un Banc, un arbre, une rue," Yves Dessca, Jean-Pierre Bourtayre (Séverine, Monaco) |
| 1972 | "Après toi," Klaus Munro, Yves Dessca, Mario Panas (Vicky Leandros, Luxembourg) |
| 1973 | "Tu te reconnaîtras," Vline Buggy, Claude Morgan (Anne-Marie David, Luxembourg) |
| 1974 | "Waterloo," Stikkan Anderson, Benny Andersson, Björn Ulvaeus (Abba, Sweden) |
| 1975 | "Ding dinge dong," Wil Luikinga, Eddy Owens, Dick Bakker (Teach-In, The Netherlands) |
| 1976 | "Save Your Kisses for Me," Tony Hiller, Lee Sheriden, Martin Lee (Brotherhood of Man, United Kingdom) |
| 1977 | "L'Oiseau et l'enfant," José Gracy, Jean-Paul Cara (Marie Myriam, France) |
| 1978 | "A-Ba-Ni-Bi," Ehud Manor, Nurit Hirsh (Izhar Cohen and the Alphabeta, Israel) |
| 1979 | "Hallelujah," Shimrit Orr, Kobi Oshrat (Gali Atari and Milk and Honey, Israel) |
| 1980 | "What's Another Year," Shay Healy (Johnny Logan, Ireland) |
| 1981 | "Making Your Mind Up," Andy Hill, John Danter (Bucks Fizz, United Kingdom) |
| 1982 | "Ein bisschen Frieden," Bernd Meinunger, Ralph Siegel (Nicole, West Germany) |
| 1983 | "Si la vie est cadeau," Alain Garcia, Jean-Pierre Millers (Corinne Hermes, Luxembourg) |
| 1984 | "Diggi-loo-diggi-ley," Britt Lindeborg, Torgny Soederberg (Herrey's, Sweden) |
| 1985 | "La det swinge," Rolg Loevland (Bobbysocks, Norway) |
| 1986 | "J'aime la vie," Marino Atria, J.P. Furnemont, A. Crisci (Sandra Kim, Belgium) |

## Eurovision Song Contest, 1956–2003 (continued)

| YEAR | SONG, SONGWRITER(S) (PERFORMER, COUNTRY) |
|------|------------------------------------------|
| 1987 | "Hold Me Now," Sean Sherrard (Johnny Logan, Ireland) |
| 1988 | "Ne partez pas sans moi," Nella Martinetti, Atilla Sereftug (Céline Dion, Switzerland) |
| 1989 | "Rock Me," Stevo Cvikich, Rajko Dujmich (Riva, Yugoslavia) |
| 1990 | "Insieme: 1992," Toto Cutugno (Toto Cutugno, Italy) |
| 1991 | "Fångad av en stormvind," Stephan Berg (Carola, Sweden) |
| 1992 | "Why Me," Sean Sherrard (Linda Martin, Ireland) |
| 1993 | "In Your Eyes," Jimmy Walsh (Niamh Kavanagh, Ireland) |
| 1994 | "Rock'n Roll Kids," Brendan Graham (Paul Harrington and Charlie McGettigan, Ireland) |
| 1995 | "Nocturne," Petter Skavlan, Rolf Lovland (Secret Garden, Norway) |
| 1996 | "The Voice," Brendan Graham (Eimear Quinn, Ireland) |
| 1997 | "Love Shine a Light," Kimberley Rew (Katrina and the Waves, United Kingdom) |
| 1998 | "Diva," Yoav Ginay (Dana International, Israel) |
| 1999 | "Take Me to Your Heaven," Gert Lengstrand (Charlotte Nilsson, Sweden) |
| 2000 | "Fly on the Wings of Love," Jørgen Olsen (Olsen Brothers, Denmark) |
| 2001 | "Everybody," Maian-Anna Käarmas, Ivar Must (Tanel Padar, Dave Benton, and 2XL, Estonia) |
| 2002 | "I Wanna," Marija Naumova, Marats Samauskis (Marie N, Latvia) |
| 2003 | "Every Way That I Can," Demir Demirkan, Sertab Erener (Sertab Erener, Turkey) |

## Brit Awards, 2003

The British Phonographic Industry, a trade association of British record companies, established the Brit Awards in 1977 to recognize pop acts from Great Britain and abroad. Prize: statuette. Brit Awards Web site: <www.brits.co.uk>.

**BRITISH CATEGORIES**
Male solo artist: Robbie Williams
Female solo artist: Ms Dynamite
Group: Coldplay
Album: *Rush of Blood to the Head*, Coldplay
Breakthrough artist: Will Young
Single: "Just a Little," Liberty X
Dance act: Sugababes

**INTERNATIONAL CATEGORIES**
Male solo artitst: Eminem
Female solo artist: Pink
Group: Red Hot Chili Peppers
Album: *The Eminem Show*, Eminem
Breakthrough artist: Norah Jones

**ADDITIONAL CATEGORIES**
Pop act: Blue
Outstanding contribution: Tom Jones

## Country Music Association Awards, 2002

The Country Music Association, founded in 1958 as a trade organization for the country and western music industry, began its annual awards ceremony in 1967 and made it the first nationally televised music awards show the following year. Ceremonies are held in November. Prize: hand-blown crystal statuette. Country Music Association Web site: <www.cmaworld.com>

▸ **entertainer of the year:** Alan Jackson; ▸ **female vocalist of the year:** Martina McBride; ▸ **male vocalist of the year:** Alan Jackson; ▸ **Horizon Award of the year:** Rascal Flatts; ▸ **vocal duo of the year:** Brooks & Dunn; ▸ **vocal group of the year:** Dixie Chicks; ▸ **album of the year:** *Drive*, Alan Jackson, Keith Stegall, prod.; ▸ **song of the year:** "Where Were You (When the World Stopped Turning)," Alan Jackson, songwriter; ▸ **single of the year:** "Where Were You (When the World Stopped Turning)," Alan Jackson, Keith Stegall, prod.; ▸ **music video of the year:** "I'm Gonna Miss Her (The Fishin' Song)," Peter Zavadil, dir. (Brad Paisley); ▸ **vocal event of the year:** "Mendocino County Line," Willie Nelson with Lee Ann Womack; ▸ **musician of the year:** Jerry Douglas (dobro)

## The All-Time Top 50 Best-Selling Albums

*As of November 2002. Source: Recording Industry Association of America (RIAA).*

| | ALBUM | ARTIST | YEAR | | ALBUM | ARTIST | YEAR |
|---|-------|--------|------|---|-------|--------|------|
| 1 | *Their Greatest Hits (1971–1975)* | The Eagles | 1976 | 8 | *Come on Over* | Shania Twain | 1997 |
| | | | | 9 | *Rumours* | Fleetwood Mac | 1977 |
| 2 | *Thriller* | Michael Jackson | 1982 | 10 | *The Bodyguard Soundtrack* | Whitney Houston & various artists | 1992 |
| 3 | *The Wall* | Pink Floyd | 1979 | | | | |
| 4 | *Untitled ("Led Zeppelin IV")* | Led Zeppelin | 1971 | 11 | *Boston* | Boston | 1976 |
| | | | | 12 | *Cracked Rear View* | Hootie & the Blowfish | 1994 |
| 5 | *Greatest Hits, Vols. 1 & 2 (1973–1985)* | Billy Joel | 1985 | | | | |
| | | | | 13 | *Hotel California* | The Eagles | 1976 |
| 6 | *Back in Black* | AC/DC | 1980 | 14 | *Jagged Little Pill* | Alanis Morissette | 1995 |
| 7 | *The Beatles ("The White Album")* | The Beatles | 1968 | 15 | *No Fences* | Garth Brooks | 1990 |
| | | | | 16 | *1967–70* | The Beatles | 1973 |

## The All-Time Top 50 Best-Selling Albums (continued)

| | ALBUM | ARTIST | YEAR | | ALBUM | ARTIST | YEAR |
|---|---|---|---|---|---|---|---|
| 17 | Appetite for Destruction | Guns 'n' Roses | 1987 | 33 | Simon & Garfunkel's Greatest Hits | Simon & Garfunkel | 1972 |
| 18 | Born in the U.S.A. | Bruce Springsteen | 1984 | 34 | Whitney Houston | Whitney Houston | 1985 |
| 19 | Dark Side of the Moon | Pink Floyd | 1973 | 35 | Abbey Road | The Beatles | 1969 |
| 20 | Greatest Hits | Elton John | 1974 | 36 | Breathless | Kenny G | 1992 |
| 21 | Physical Graffiti | Led Zeppelin | 1975 | 37 | Forrest Gump | various artists | 1994 |
| 22 | Saturday Night Fever Soundtrack | The Bee Gees & various artists | 1977 | 38 | Hysteria | Def Leppard | 1987 |
| 23 | 1962–66 | The Beatles | 1973 | 39 | II | Boyz II Men | 1994 |
| 24 | Double Live | Garth Brooks | 1998 | 40 | Greatest Hits | Kenny Rogers | 1980 |
| 25 | Backstreet Boys | Backstreet Boys | 1996 | 41 | Led Zeppelin II | Led Zeppelin | 1969 |
| 26 | Bat out of Hell | Meat Loaf | 1977 | 42 | Metallica | Metallica | 1991 |
| 27 | Ropin' the Wind | Garth Brooks | 1991 | 43 | No Jacket Required | Phil Collins | 1985 |
| 28 | Supernatural | Santana | 1999 | 44 | Slippery When Wet | Bon Jovi | 1986 |
| 29 | ...Baby One More Time | Britney Spears | 1999 | 45 | The Woman in Me | Shania Twain | 1995 |
| 30 | Live 1975–85 | Bruce Springsteen and the E Street Band | 1986 | 46 | Yourself or Someone Like You | matchbox twenty | 1996 |
| | | | | 47 | Hot Rocks, 1964–1971 | The Rolling Stones | 1972 |
| 31 | Millennium | Backstreet Boys | 1999 | 48 | Eagles Greatest Hits Volume 2 | The Eagles | 1982 |
| 32 | Purple Rain Soundtrack | Prince & the Revolution | 1984 | 49 | CrazySexyCool | TLC | 1994 |
| | | | | 50 | Dirty Dancing Soundtrack | various artists | 1987 |

## Rock and Roll Hall of Fame Inductees

Music-industry professionals established the Rock and Roll Hall of Fame Foundation in 1983 in order to "recognize the contributions of those who have had a significant impact on the evolution, development and perpetuation of rock and roll." Performers are eligible for induction 25 years after the release of their first record. The Foundation's nominating committee compiles an annual list of eligible artists and distributes this list to about 1,000 rock experts throughout the world. Those performers receiving the highest number of votes, as well as at least 50% of the vote, are inducted. Special committees select inductees in other categories. Those elected to membership receive a statuette depicting an abstract figure holding aloft a gold record.

**NAME (YEAR OF INDUCTION)**

AC/DC (2003)
Paul Ackerman[1] (1995)
Aerosmith (2001)
The Allman Brothers Band (1995)
The Animals (1994)
Louis Armstrong[2] (1990)
Chet Atkins[3] (2002)
LaVern Baker (1991)
Hank Ballard (1990)
The Band (1994)
Dave Bartholomew[1] (1991)
Ralph Bass[1] (1991)
The Beach Boys (1988)
The Beatles (1988)
The Bee Gees (1997)
Benny Benjamin[3] (2003)
Chuck Berry (1986)
Chris Blackwell[1] (2001)
Hal Blaine[3] (2000)
Bob Wills and His Texas Playboys[2] (1999)
Bobby "Blue" Bland (1992)
Booker T. and the M.G.'s (1992)
David Bowie (1996)
Charles Brown[2] (1999)
James Brown (1986)
Ruth Brown (1993)
Buffalo Springfield (1997)
Solomon Burke (2001)
James Burton[3] (2001)

**NAME (YEAR OF INDUCTION)**

The Byrds (1991)
Johnny Cash (1992)
Ray Charles (1986)
Leonard Chess[1] (1987)
Charlie Christian[2] (1990)
Eric Clapton (2000)
Dick Clark[1] (1993)
The Clash (2003)
The Coasters (1987)
Eddie Cochran (1987)
Nat "King" Cole[2] (2000)
Sam Cooke (1986)
Elvis Costello & the Attractions (2003)
Floyd Cramer[3] (2003)
Cream (1993)
Creedence Clearwater Revival (1993)
Crosby, Stills & Nash (1997)
King Curtis[3] (2000)
Bobby Darin (1990)
Clive Davis[1] (2000)
Bo Diddley (1987)
Dion (1989)
Willie Dixon[2] (1994)
Fats Domino (1986)
Tom Donahue[1] (1996)
The Doors (1993)
Steve Douglas[3] (2003)
The Drifters (1988)

**NAME (YEAR OF INDUCTION)**

Bob Dylan (1988)
The Eagles (1998)
Earth, Wind & Fire (2000)
Duane Eddy (1994)
Ahmet Ertegun[1] (1987)
Nesuhi Ertegun[4] (1991)
The Everly Brothers (1986)
Leo Fender[1] (1992)
The Flamingos (2001)
Fleetwood Mac (1998)
The Four Seasons (1990)
The Four Tops (1990)
Frankie Lymon and the Teenagers (1993)
Aretha Franklin (1987)
Alan Freed[1] (1986)
Milt Gabler[1] (1993)
Marvin Gaye (1987)
Gladys Knight and the Pips (1996)
Gerry Goffin and Carole King[1] (1990)
Berry Gordy, Jr.[1] (1988)
Bill Graham[1] (1992)
The Grateful Dead (1994)
Al Green (1995)
Woody Guthrie[2] (1988)
Bill Haley (1987)
John Hammond[4] (1986)
Isaac Hayes (2002)

## Rock and Roll Hall of Fame Inductees (continued)

NAME (YEAR OF INDUCTION)

Billie Holiday[2] (2000)
Holland, Dozier, and Holland[1] (1990)
Buddy Holly (1986)
John Lee Hooker (1991)
The Impressions (1991)
The Inkspots[2] (1989)
The Isley Brothers (1992)
The Jackson Five (1997)
Mahalia Jackson[2] (1997)
Michael Jackson (2001)
James Jamerson[3] (2000)
Elmore James[2] (1992)
Etta James (1993)
Jefferson Airplane (1996)
The Jimi Hendrix Experience (1992)
Billy Joel (1999)
Elton John (1994)
Little Willie John (1996)
Johnnie Johnson[3] (2001)
Robert Johnson[2] (1986)
Janis Joplin (1995)
Louis Jordan[2] (1987)
B.B. King (1987)
The Kinks (1990)
Leadbelly[2] (1988)
Led Zeppelin (1995)
Brenda Lee (2002)
Jerry Leiber and Mike Stoller[1] (1987)
John Lennon (1994)
Jerry Lee Lewis (1986)
Professor Longhair[2] (1992)
The Lovin' Spoonful (2000)
The Mamas and the Papas (1998)
Bob Marley (1994)
Martha and the Vandellas (1995)
George Martin[1] (1999)
Curtis Mayfield (1999)

NAME (YEAR OF INDUCTION)

Paul McCartney (1999)
Clyde McPhatter (1987)
Joni Mitchell (1997)
Bill Monroe[2] (1997)
The Moonglows (2000)
Scotty Moore[3] (2000)
Van Morrison (1993)
Jelly Roll Morton[2] (1998)
Syd Nathan[1] (1997)
Ricky Nelson (1987)
Roy Orbison (1987)
The Orioles[2] (1995)
Mo Ostin[1] (2003)
Johnny Otis[1] (1994)
Earl Palmer[3] (2000)
Parliament-Funkadelic (1997)
Les Paul[2] (1988)
Carl Perkins (1987)
Sam Phillips[1] (1986)
Wilson Pickett (1991)
Pink Floyd (1996)
Gene Pitney (2002)
The Platters (1990)
The Police (2003)
Doc Pomus[1] (1992)
Elvis Presley (1986)
Lloyd Price (1998)
Queen (2001)
Ma Rainey[2] (1990)
Bonnie Raitt (2000)
Ramones (2002)
Otis Redding (1989)
Jimmy Reed (1991)
Little Richard (1986)
The Righteous Brothers (2003)
Smokey Robinson (1987)
Jimmie Rodgers[2] (1986)
The Rolling Stones (1989)
Sam and Dave (1992)
Santana (1998)
Pete Seeger[2] (1996)

NAME (YEAR OF INDUCTION)

Del Shannon (1999)
The Shirelles (1996)
Simon and Garfunkel (1990)
Paul Simon (2001)
Sly and the Family Stone (1993)
Bessie Smith[2] (1989)
The Soul Stirrers[2] (1989)
Phil Spector[1] (1989)
Dusty Springfield (1999)
Bruce Springsteen (1999)
The Staple Singers (1999)
Steely Dan (2001)
Jim Stewart[1] (2002)
Rod Stewart (1994)
The Supremes (1988)
Talking Heads (2002)
James Taylor (2000)
The Temptations (1989)
Tom Petty and the Heartbreakers (2002)
Allen Toussaint[1] (1998)
Big Joe Turner (1987)
Ike and Tina Turner (1991)
Ritchie Valens (2001)
The Velvet Underground (1996)
Gene Vincent (1998)
T-Bone Walker[2] (1987)
Dinah Washington[2] (1993)
Muddy Waters (1987)
Jerry Wexler[1] (1987)
The Who (1990)
Hank Williams[2] (1987)
Jackie Wilson (1987)
Howlin' Wolf[2] (1991)
Stevie Wonder (1989)
Jimmy Yancey[2] (1986)
The Yardbirds (1992)
Neil Young (1995)
The (Young) Rascals (1997)
Frank Zappa (1995)

[1]Non-performer.   [2]Early Influence.   [3]Sidemen.   [4]Lifetime Achievement.

## Encyclopædia Britannica's Top 25 Opera Companies

| COMPANY | LOCATION | GENERAL OR ARTISTIC DIRECTOR (2003) | FOUNDED |
|---|---|---|---|
| Arena di Verona[1] | Verona, Italy | Claudio Orazi | 1913 |
| Bayerische Staatsoper (Bavarian State Opera) | Munich, Germany | Sir Peter Jonas | 1653 |
| Bolshoi Opera | Moscow, Russia | Anatoly Iksanov | 1776 |
| Boston Lyric Opera | Boston MA | Janice Mancini Del Sesto | 1976 |
| Canadian Opera Company | Toronto ON | Richard Bradshaw | 1950 |
| Cleveland Opera | Cleveland OH | David Bamberger | 1976 |
| Grand Théâtre de Genève | Geneva, Switzerland | Jean-Marie Blanchard | 1962 |
| Los Angeles Opera | Los Angeles CA | Plácido Domingo | 1986 |
| Lyric Opera of Chicago | Chicago IL | Matthew A. Epstein | 1954 |
| Magyar Állarmi Opera (Hungarian National Opera) | Budapest, Hungary | Miklós Szinetár | 1884 |
| Mariinsky Opera Company | St. Petersburg, Russia | Valery Gergiev | 1783 |
| Metropolitan Opera | New York NY | James Levine | 1883 |
| Opera Australia | Sydney and Melbourne, Australia | Richard Gill | 1956 |
| Opéra National de Paris | Paris, France | Hugues R. Gall | 1669 |
| Royal Opera | London, England | Elaine Padmore | 1732 |
| San Francisco Opera | San Francisco CA | Pamela Rosenberg | 1923 |

# Encyclopædia Britannica's Top 25 Opera Companies (continued)

| COMPANY | LOCATION | GENERAL OR ARTISTIC DIRECTOR (2003) | FOUNDED |
|---|---|---|---|
| Staatsoper Unter den Linden (Unter den Linden State Opera) | Berlin, Germany | Peter Mussbach | 1742 |
| Suomen Kansallisooppera (Finnish National Opera) | Helsinki, Finland | Erkki Korhonen | 1911 |
| Teatro alla Scala (La Scala) | Milan, Italy | Paolo Arcà | 1778 |
| Teatro dell'Opera di Roma | Rome, Italy | Gianni Tangucci | 1880 |
| Teatro di San Carlo | Naples, Italy | Marcello Panni | 1737 |
| Teatro Massimo | Palermo, Italy | Roberto Pagano | 1897 |
| Théâtre du Châtelet | Paris, France | Jean-Pierre Brossmann | 1862 |
| Vancouver Opera | Vancouver BC | James W. Wright | 1958 |
| Wiener Staatsoper (Vienna State Opera) | Vienna, Austria | Ioan Holender | 1869 |

[1]The Arena di Verona was built in the first century AD; it has been primarily an opera venue since 1913.

# Encyclopædia Britannica's 25 World-Class Orchestras

| ORCHESTRA | LOCATION | FOUNDED | CONDUCTOR (2003) |
|---|---|---|---|
| Berlin Philharmonic Orchestra | Berlin, Germany | 1882 | Simon Rattle |
| Boston Symphony Orchestra | Boston MA | 1881 | James Levine[1] |
| Chicago Symphony Orchestra | Chicago IL | 1891 | Daniel Barenboim |
| Cleveland Orchestra | Cleveland OH | 1918 | Franz Welser-Möst |
| Gewandhaus Orchestra | Leipzig, Germany | 1743 | Herbert Blomstedt |
| Israel Philharmonic Orchestra | Tel Aviv, Israel | 1936 | Zubin Mehta |
| London Philharmonic Orchestra | London, England | 1932 | Kurt Masur |
| London Symphony Orchestra | London, England | 1904 | Colin Davis |
| Los Angeles Philharmonic | Los Angeles CA | 1919 | Esa-Pekka Salonen |
| Montreal Symphony Orchestra | Montreal, Quebec | 1934 | Jacques Lacombe[2] |
| New York Philharmonic | New York NY | 1842 | Lorin Maazel |
| NHK Symphony Orchestra | Tokyo, Japan | 1926 | Charles Dutoit[3] |
| Orchestre de la Suisse Romande | Geneva, Switzerland | 1918 | Pinchas Steinberg |
| Orchestre de Paris | Paris, France | 1967 | Christoph Eschenbach |
| Orchestre National de France | Paris, France | 1934 | Kurt Masur |
| Oslo Philharmonic Orchestra | Oslo, Norway | 1919 | André Previn |
| Philadelphia Orchestra | Philadelphia PA | 1900 | Wolfgang Sawallisch |
| Philharmonia Orchestra | London, England | 1945 | Christoph von Dohnányi |
| Pittsburgh Symphony Orchestra | Pittsburgh PA | 1896 | Mariss Jansons |
| Royal Concertgebouw Orchestra | Amsterdam, The Netherlands | 1888 | Riccardo Chailly |
| Royal Philharmonic Orchestra | London, England | 1946 | Daniele Gatti |
| Saint Louis Symphony Orchestra | St. Louis MO | 1880 | David Amado |
| St. Petersburg State Symphony Orchestra | St. Petersburg, Russia | 1988 | Aleksandr Kantorov |
| San Francisco Symphony | San Francisco CA | 1911 | Michael Tilson Thomas |
| Vienna Philharmonic Orchestra | Vienna, Austria | 1842 | guest conductors |

[1]Levine will assume the full directorship of the Boston Symphony Orchestra in the fall of 2004. [2]Principal guest conductor. [3]Vladimir Ashkenazy will assume the directorship of the NHK Symphony Orchestra in the fall of 2004.

# Encyclopædia Britannica's 100 Greatest Dancers of All Time

This table includes figures who, in the opinion of the Britannica editors, have made the greatest contributions to the art of dance.

**Alvin Ailey, Jr.** (5 Jan 1931, Rogers TX—1 Dec 1989, New York NY) American dancer and choreographer; director of the Alvin Ailey American Dance Theater.

**Alicia Alonso** (Alicia Ernestina de la Caridad del Cobre Martínez Hoyo; 21 Dec 1921, Havana, Cuba) Cuban ballerina and ballet mistress; director of the National Ballet of Cuba.

**Carmen Amaya** (2 Nov 1913, Somorrostro, Barcelona, Spain—19 Nov 1963) Spanish Gypsy *bailaora,* or flamenco dancer, known as the "Queen of the Gypsies."

**Jacques d' Amboise** (Jacques Joseph Ahearn; 28 Jul 1934, Dedham MA) American dancer and choreographer of the New York City Ballet (1949–84) admired for his energetic, virile interpretations of both character and classical roles.

**La Argentina** (Antonia Mercé; 4 Sep 1890, Buenos Aires, Argentina—18 Jul 1936, Bayonne, France) Argentine dancer who originated the Neoclassical style of Spanish dancing and helped establish the Spanish dance as a theatrical art.

**La Argentinita** (Encarnación López Júlvez; 1895–1945) Spanish Gypsy flamenco dancer.

**Gerald Arpino** (14 Jan 1928, Staten Island NY) American ballet choreographer, a leader of the Joffrey Ballet from its founding in 1956.

**Sir Frederick William Mallandaine Ashton** (17 Sep 1904, Guayaquil, Ecuador–18 Aug 1988, Sussex, England) British principal choreographer and director of England's Royal Ballet, the repertoire of which includes about 30 of his ballets.

**Fred Astaire** (Frederick Austerlitz; 10 May 1899, Omaha NE–22 Jun 1987, Los Angeles CA) American dancer of stage and motion pictures; probably the most famous of American dancers and regarded by many as the greatest popular-music dancer of all time.

**Josephine Baker** (3 Jun 1906, St. Louis MO–12 Apr 1975, Paris, France) American dancer and singer who symbolized the beauty and vitality of black American culture, which took Paris by storm in the 1920s.

**George Balanchine** (Georgy Melitonovich Balanchivadze; 22 Jan 1904, St. Petersburg, Russia–30 Apr 1983, New York NY) Russian Georgian-born American choreographer of classical ballet, perhaps the most influential in the US in the 20th century.

**Mikhail (Nikolayevich) Baryshnikov** (28 Jan 1948, Riga, Latvian SSR, USSR [now in Latvia]) Soviet-born American ballet dancer who was the preeminent male classical dancer of the 1970s and '80s; he subsequently became a noted dance director.

**Maurice Béjart** (Maurice-Jean de Berger; 1 Jan 1927, Marseille, France) French-born dancer, choreographer, and opera director known for combining classical ballet and modern dance with jazz, acrobatics, and *musique concrète* (composition by tape recordings).

**August Bournonville** (21 Aug 1805, Copenhagen, [Denmark]–30 Nov 1879, Copenhagen, Denmark) Danish dancer and choreographer who directed the Royal Danish Ballet for nearly 50 years and established the Danish style based on bravura dancing and expressive mime.

**Erik Bruhn** (3 Oct 1928, Copenhagen, Denmark–1 Apr 1986, Toronto, ON, Canada) Danish ballet dancer noted for his outstanding classical technique.

**John Bubbles** (John William Sublett; "Bubber"; 19 Feb 1902, Louisville KY–18 May 1986, Louisville KY) American tap dancer and entertainer, who became known as the "Father of Rhythm Tap."

**Marie-Anne de Cupis de Camargo** (15 Apr 1710, Brussels, Spanish Netherlands [now in Belgium]–20 Apr 1770, Paris, France) Flemish ballerina of the Paris Opéra remembered for her numerous technical innovations.

**Tahia Carioca** (Badawiyya Muhammad Karim; 22 Feb 1919, Egypt–20 Sep 1999, Cairo, Egypt) Egyptian dancer and motion picture actress whose subtle sexuality and superb technique in the art of *raqs sharqi,* or belly dancing, made her a national figure and earned her the title "Queen of Oriental Dancing."

**Fanny Cerrito** (11 May 1817, Naples [Italy]–6 May 1909, Paris, France) Italian ballerina noted for the brilliance, strength, and vivacity of her dancing, and one of the few women in the 19th century to achieve distinction as a choreographer.

**Marge** (2 Sep 1923, Los Angeles CA) **and Gower Champion** (22 Jun 1921, Geneva IL–25 Aug 1980, New York NY) American dancers and choreographers who were one of the most famous dance teams in film history.

**Cyd Charisse** (Tula Ellice Finklea; 8 Mar 1923, Amarillo TX) American dancer and actress who attained fame in some of the leading film musicals of the 1950s.

**Charles ("Honi") Coles** (2 Apr 1911, Philadelphia PA–12 Nov 1992, New York NY) American tap dancer who attained fame in the 1930s at New York's Cotton Club and Apollo Theater.

**John Cranko** (15 Aug 1927, Rustenburg, South Africa–26 Jun 1973, Dublin, Ireland) South African dancer, choreographer, and ballet director best known for his work with the Stuttgart (Germany) Ballet.

**Merce Cunningham** (16 Apr 1919, Centralia WA) American modern dancer and choreographer who developed new forms of abstract dance movement.

**Alexandra Danilova** (Aleksandra Dionisyevna Danilova; 20 Nov 1903, Peterhof [now Petrodvorets], Russia–13 Jul 1997, New York NY) Russian prima ballerina who brought to American ballet the training and traditions of both the classical Russian and the modern Diaghilev repertoires.

**Agnes George de Mille** (18 Sep 1905, New York NY–7 Oct 1993, New York NY) American dancer and choreographer who developed the narrative aspect of dance and made innovative use of American themes, folk dances, and gestures in her choreography of musical plays and ballets.

**Dame Ninette de Valois** (Edris Stannus; 6 Jun 1898, Blessington, County Wicklow, Ireland–8 Mar 2001, London, England) Irish-born British dancer, choreographer, and founder of the company that in October 1956 became the Royal Ballet.

**Sir Anton Dolin** (27 Jul 1904, Slinfold, Sussex, England–25 Nov 1983, Paris, France) British ballet dancer, choreographer, and director who, with his frequent partner Alicia Markova, founded the Markova-Dolin companies and London's Festival ballet.

**William Henry Dollar** (20 Apr 1907, St. Louis MO–28 Feb 1986, Flourtown PA) American ballet dancer, choreographer, and ballet master.

**Isadora Duncan** (26 May 1877, San Francisco CA–14 Sep 1927, Nice, France) American dancer whose teaching and performances helped free ballet from its conservative restrictions and presaged the development of modern expressive dance.

**Katherine Dunham** (pseudonym Kaye Dunn; 22 Jun 1910, Joliet IL) American dancer, choreographer, and anthropologist noted for her innovative interpretations of primitive, ritualistic, and ethnic dances.

**Fanny Elssler** (23 Jun 1810, Vienna, Austria–27 Nov 1884, Vienna) Austrian ballerina who introduced theatricalized folk dance (character dance) into ballet. She was celebrated for her spirited, spectacular dancing and for her technique, especially her point work.

**Suzanne Farrell** (Roberta Sue Ficker; 16 Aug 1945, Cincinnati OH) American dancer especially known for her performances with the New York City Ballet.

**Eliot Feld** (5 Jul 1942, New York NY) American dancer, choreographer, and director who formed the Eliot Feld Ballet in 1973.

**Michel Fokine** (Mikhail Mikhaylovich Fokine; 23 Apr 1880, St. Petersburg, Russia—22 Aug 1942, New York NY) Russian dancer and choreographer who profoundly influenced the 20th-century classical ballet repertoire.

**Dame Margot Fonteyn** (Margaret Hookham; 18 May 1919, Reigate, Surrey, England—21 Feb 1991, Panama City, Panama) British ballerina of the English stage known especially for her partnership with Rudolf Nureyev.

**Nagwa Fouad** (c. 1943, Alexandria, Egypt) Egyptian dancer in the *raqs sharqi* (belly dancing) style; one of the top exponents of the style in Egypt from the mid-1970s.

**Samia Gamal** (Zainab Ibrahim Mahfuz; 1924, Wana, Egypt—1 Dec 1994, Cairo, Egypt) Egyptian belly dancer and film star of the 1940s and '50's; in 1949 Egypt's King Farouk proclaimed her the "National Dancer of Egypt."

**Mitzi Gaynor** (Francesca Mitzi Marlene de Czanyi von Gerber; 4 Sep 1931, Chicago IL) American singer, dancer, and film actress.

**Savion Glover** (19 Nov 1973, Newark NJ) American dancer and choreographer known for a style of dance called "hitting," a combination of the rhythms of hip-hop music and the pounding of tap dancing.

**Martha Graham** (11 May 1894, Allegheny county PA—1 Apr 1991, New York NY) American dancer, teacher, and choreographer of modern dance, whose ballets and other works were intended to "reveal the inner man."

**José Greco** (23 Dec 1918, Montorio nei Frentani, Italy—31 Dec 2000, Lancaster PA) Italian-born dancer who melded flamenco dancing with classical ballet and who came to be considered the world's greatest Spanish dancer.

**Melissa Hayden** (Mildred Herman; 25 Apr 1923, Toronto, ON, Canada) Canadian ballet dancer renowned for her technical and dramatic skills and her many performances with the New York City Ballet.

**Gregory Hines** (14 Feb 1946, New York NY) American dancer who came to prominence as a child performer and later became a successful film and television actor.

**Lev (Ivanovich) Ivanov** (18 Feb 1834, Moscow, Russia—24 Dec 1901, St. Petersburg, Russia) Russian ballet dancer who was choreographic assistant to Marius Petipa, the director and chief choreographer of the Imperial Russian Ballet.

**Judith Jamison** (10 May 1943, Philadelphia PA) American dancer and choreographer who became artistic director of the Alvin Ailey American Dance Theater in 1989.

**Robert Joffrey** (24 Dec 1930, Seattle WA—25 Mar 1988, New York NY) American dancer, choreographer, and director, founder of the Joffrey Ballet (1956); he was noted for his choreographic work on operatic productions.

**Tamara (Platonovna) Karsavina** (9 Mar 1885, St. Petersburg, Russia—26 May 1978, Beaconsfield, Buckinghamshire, England) Russian-born British ballerina whose partnership with Vaslav Nijinsky in Michel Fokine's avant-garde ballets helped to revive interest in ballet in Western Europe; she later coached Margot Fonteyn.

**Gene Kelly** (Eugene Curran Kelly; 23 Aug 1912, Pittsburgh PA—2 Feb 1996, Beverly Hills CA) American dancer, actor, choreographer, and film director; he was a film legend who popularized an assertive, masculine style of tap dancing.

**Serge Lifar** (2 Apr 1905, Kiev, Ukraine, Russian Empire—15 Dec 1986, Lausanne, Switzerland) Russian-born French dancer, choreographer, and ballet master.

**Sir Kenneth MacMillan** (11 Dec 1929, Dunfermline, Fife, Scotland—29 Oct 1992, London) British ballet choreographer who created more than 40 ballets during his career and helped revive the tradition of full-length ballets in Britain.

**Natalya (Romanovna) Makarova** (21 Oct 1940, Leningrad, USSR [now St. Petersburg, Russia]) Russian-born ballerina considered to be one of the greatest classical dancers.

**Dame Alicia Markova** (Lilian Alicia Marks; 1 Dec 1910, London, England) English ballerina noted for the ethereal lightness and poetic delicacy of her dancing.

**Peter Martins** (27 Oct 1946, Copenhagen, Denmark) Danish dancer and choreographer known for his work with the New York City Ballet as principal dancer (1969) choreographer (1977) ballet master-in-chief (from 1983).

**Léonide Massine** (Leonid Fyodorovich Miassin; 9 Aug 1896, Moscow, Russia—15 Mar 1979, Cologne, Germany) Russian dancer and innovative choreographer of more than 50 ballets; one of the most important figures in 20th-century dance, Massine brought the avant-garde into ballet and created the symphonic ballet.

**Patricia McBride** (23 Aug 1942, Teaneck NJ) American ballerina best known for her performances with the New York City Ballet; her radiant technique inspired roles in many works, perhaps most notably in George Balanchine's *Tarantella* (1964) and *Jewels* (1967).

**Arthur Mitchell** (27 Mar 1934, New York NY) American dancer, choreographer, and director of the Dance Theatre of Harlem.

**Igor (Aleksandrovich) Moiseyev** (21 Jan 1906, Kiev, Ukraine, Russian Empire [now Ukraine]) Russian choreographer and founder of the State Academic Folk Dance Ensemble of the USSR.

**Mark Morris** (29 Aug 1956, Seattle WA) American dancer and leading choreographer for several international dance companies; he founded the Mark Morris Dance Group in 1980.

**Fayard Nicholas** (20 Oct 1914, Mobile AL) American dancer who appeared with his brother Harold Lloyd Nicholas as the Nicholas Brothers dance team and attained fame on stage and in films for an energetic blend of jazz, tap, ballet, and acrobatics.

**Harold Lloyd Nicholas** (21/27 Mar 1921, Winston-Salem NC—3 Jul 2000, New York NY) American dancer, the other half of the Nicholas Brothers team.

**Vaslav Nijinsky** (Vatslav Fomich Nizhinsky; 12 Mar 1890, Kiev, Ukraine, Russian Empire—8 Apr 1950, London, England) Russian-born ballet dancer of almost legendary fame, celebrated for his spectacular leaps and sensitive interpretations.

**Alwin Nikolais** (25 Nov 1910/12(?) Southington CT—8 May 1993, New York NY) American choreographer, designer, and composer whose abstract dances combine motion with various technical effects and a complete freedom from technique and established patterns.

**Rudolf (Hametovich) Nureyev** (17 Mar 1938, Irkutsk, USSR—6 Jan 1993, Paris, France) Russian-born ballet dancer whose suspended leaps and fast turns were often compared to Vaslav Nijinsky's legendary feats.

**Anna (Pavlovna) Pavlova** (31 Jan 1881, St. Petersburg, Russia—23 Jan 1931, The Hague, The Netherlands) Russian ballerina who was the most celebrated dancer of her time; she was famed for dance creations such as *Le Cygne* (*The Swan*) *Papillons* (*Butterflies*) etc.

**Jules Joseph Perrot** (18 Aug 1810, Lyon, France—24 Aug 1892, Paramé, France) French virtuoso dancer and choreographer whose masterpieces of Romantic ballet include *Pas de Quatre* (1845) composed for four of the 19th century's leading ballerinas and frequently revived in the 20th century.

**Marius Petipa** (11 Mar 1818, Marseille, France—14 Jul 1910, Gurzuf, Crimea, Russian Empire) French dancer and choreographer who worked for nearly 60 years at the Mariinsky Theater in St. Petersburg and who had a profound influence on modern classical Russian ballet.

**Roland Petit** (13 Jan 1924, Villemomble, France) French dancer and choreographer whose dramatic ballets combined fantasy with elements of contemporary realism.

**Maya (Mikhaylovna) Plisetskaya** (20 Nov 1925, Moscow, USSR [now Russia]) Russian prima ballerina of the Bolshoi Ballet of Moscow, admired particularly for her technical virtuosity, expressive use of her arms, and ability to integrate acting with dancing.

**Eleanor Powell** (21 Nov 1912, Springfield MA—11 Feb 1982, Beverly Hills CA) American tap dancer and film performer known for her powerful and aggressive style of tap.

**Dame Peggy van Praagh** (1 Sep 1910, London, England—15 Jan 1990, Melbourne) British-born ballet dancer and director, and founder and artistic director (1963–74) of the Australian Ballet.

**Juliet Prowse** (25 Sep 1936, Bombay, India—14 Sep 1996, Los Angeles CA) South African–British dancer, choreographer, anthropologist, and teacher.

**Sally Rand** (Helen Gould Beck; 2 Jan 1904, Elkton MO—31 Aug 1979, Glendora CA) American actress and dancer who achieved fame as a fan dancer and bubble dancer.

**Jerome Robbins** (Jerome Wilson Rabinowitz; 11 Oct 1918, New York NY—29 Jul 1998, New York NY) American dancer and choreographer, first known for his skillful use of contemporary American themes in ballets and Broadway and Hollywood musicals.

**Bill ("Bojangles") Robinson** (25 May 1878, Richmond VA—25 Nov 1949, New York NY) American dancer of Broadway and Hollywood, a true legend whose "on the toes" style of tap dancing—with an emphasis on lightning-fast "nerve taps"—brought an end to the era of flat-footed hoofing.

**Ruth St. Denis** (20 Jan 1877, Newark NJ—21 Jul 1968, Los Angeles CA) American dancer and choreographer who influenced almost every phase of American dance, especially with her use of philosophical themes and Oriental dance forms and costumes; cofounder of the Denishawn school and company.

**Arthur Saint-Leon** (17 Sep 1821, Paris, France—2 Sep 1870, Paris, France) French dancer, choreographer, and violinist, acclaimed for the choreography of the ballet classic *Coppélia*.

**Malavika Sarukkai** (Bombay [now Mumbai], India) Indian dancer and choreographer, a leading exponent of the Bharata-natyam style.

**Konstantin (Mikhaylovich) Sergeyev** (5 Mar 1910, St. Petersburg, Russia—1 Apr 1992, St. Petersburg, Russia) Russian ballet dancer and director long associated with the Kirov ballet as a premier danseur (1930–61) and as both artistic director and chief choreographer (1951–55; 1960–70).

**Nicholas Sergeyev** (Nikolay Grigoryevich Sergeyev; 15 Sep 1876, St. Petersburg, Russia—23 Jun 1951, Nice, France) Russian dancer and company manager of the Imperial Russian Ballet in St. Petersburg who re-created for several Western European companies the many classical ballets that had been preserved in the Russian repertoire.

**Uday Shankar** (8 Dec 1900, Udaipur, India—26 Sep 1977, Calcutta, India) Indian dancer and choreographer whose adaptation of Western theatrical techniques to traditional Hindu dance popularized the ancient art form in India, Europe, and the US.

**Ted Shawn** (21 Oct 1891, Kansas City MO—9 Jan 1972, Orlando FL) American modern dancer and cofounder of the Denishawn school and company.

**Padma Subramaniam** 20th-century Indian dancer, scholar, and choreographer in the Bharata-natyam style, who expanded the expressiveness of the form by the use of her whole body and the reintroduction of *karanas* (unit dance movements).

**Swapnasundari** (Rao Pradesh; Madras, India) Indian dancer, choreographer, and vocalist in the Bharata-Natyam and Kuchipudi dance styles of southern India; she was the founding director of the Kuchipudi Dance Centre in New Delhi.

**Marie Taglioni** (23 Apr 1804, Stockholm, Sweden—24 Apr 1884, Marseille, France) Italian ballet dancer whose fragile, delicate dancing typified the early 19th-century Romantic style.

**Maria Tallchief** (24 Jan 1925, Fairfax OK) American national ballerina of Osage descent, noted for her fine technique and generally considered among the greatest of American ballerinas; she is remembered for the roles created for her by Balanchine.

**Paul Belville Taylor** (29 Jul 1930, Wilkinsburg PA) American modern dancer and choreographer noted for the inventive, frequently humorous, and sardonic dances that he choreographed for his company.

**Twyla Tharp** (1 Jul 1941, Portland IN) American dancer, director, and choreographer noted for her innovation and for the humor she brought to much of her work.

**Vasily (Dmitriyevich) Tikhomirov** (30 Mar 1876, Moscow, Russia—20 Jun 1956, Moscow, Russia) Russian ballet dancer and influential teacher who helped develop the vigorous style and technical virtuosity of the Bolshoi Ballet in Moscow.

**Antony Tudor** (William Cook; 4 Apr 1908, London, England–20 Apr 1987, New York NY) British-born American ballet dancer, teacher, and choreographer known for *Lilac Garden, Pillar of Fire, Romeo and Juliet,* and others.

**Galina (Sergeyevna) Ulanova** (8 Jan 1910, St. Petersburg, Russia–21 Mar 1998, Moscow, Russia) Russian dancer, first prima ballerina assoluta of the Soviet Union and one of the greatest ballet dancers of the 20th century.

**Agrippina (Yakovlevna) Vaganova** (6 Jul 1879, St. Petersburg, Russia–5 Nov 1951, Leningrad, USSR [now St. Petersburg, Russia]) Russian ballerina and teacher who developed a technique and system of instruction based on the classic style of the Imperial Russian Ballet but which also incorporated aspects of the more vigorous, acrobatic Soviet ballet developed after the Revolution.

**Alarmel Valli** (1957, Tamil Nadu state, India) Indian dancer considered the foremost exponent of the Pandanallur tradition in the Bharata-Natyam style of southern Indian dance.

**Martine Van Hamel** (16 Nov 1945, Brussels, Belgium) Belgian dancer and leading choreographer for the American Ballet Theatre.

**Gwen Verdon** (Gwyneth Evelyn Verdon; 13 Jan 1925, Culver City CA–18 Oct 2000, Woodstock VT) American dancer and actress best known for her performances in Broadway shows.

**Auguste Vestris** (27 Mar 1760, Paris, France–5 Dec 1842, Paris, France) French dancer, a leading performer of the Paris Opéra, whose unusually brilliant technique and prodigious leaps set a new style of ballet; he was the son of the great ballet dancer Gaetano Vestris and the ballerina Marie Allard.

**Gaetano Apolline Baldassare Vestris** (18 Apr 1729, Florence [Italy]–23 Sep 1808, Paris, France) French ballet dancer, considered the finest of his time.

**Edward Villella** (1 Oct 1936, New York NY) American ballet dancer and choreographer.

**Mary Wigman** (13 Nov 1886, Hanover, Germany–18 Sep 1973, West Berlin, Germany) German dancer, a pioneer of the modern expressive dance.

---

**Did you know?** The Ballets Russes, which Sergey Diaghilev ran between 1909 and 1929, included some of the greatest artists of the time: dancers Anna Pavlova and Vaslav Nijinsky; choreographer George Balanchine; composer Igor Stravinsky; and designers Pablo Picasso and Henri Matisse.

---

# Pageants

## Miss America Winners, 1921–2003

The Miss America Pageant was founded in 1921 as an Atlantic City NJ tourist attraction. Purely a beauty contest in its early years, the competition added a talent category in 1935 and began awarding scholarships a decade later. After 1989 the pageant required evidence of community service, and by 2001 contestants were judged on the basis of talent, community service, leadership, knowledge and understanding, and appearance in swimsuits and eveningwear. Prize: $50,000 college scholarship. Miss America Contest Web site: <www.missamerica.org>

| YEAR | WINNER (HOMETOWN) | YEAR | WINNER (HOMETOWN) |
|------|-------------------|------|-------------------|
| 1921 | Margaret Gorman (Washington DC) | 1948 | BeBe Shopp (Hopkins MN) |
| 1922 | Mary Katherine Campbell (Columbus OH) | 1949 | Jacque Mercer (Litchfield AZ) |
| 1923 | Mary Katherine Campbell (Columbus OH) | 1950[1] | |
| 1924 | Ruth Malcomson (Philadelphia PA) | 1951 | Yolande Betbeze (Mobile AL) |
| 1925 | Fay Lanphier (Oakland CA) | 1952 | Colleen Hutchins (Salt Lake City UT) |
| 1926 | Norma Smallwood (Tulsa OK) | 1953 | Neva Langley (Macon GA) |
| 1927 | Lois Delander (Joliet IL) | 1954 | Evelyn Ay (Ephrata PA) |
| 1928–32 | *not held* | 1955 | Lee Meriwether (San Francisco CA) |
| 1933 | Marian Bergeron (West Haven CT) | 1956 | Sharon Ritchie (Denver CO) |
| 1934 | *not held* | 1957 | Marian McKnight (Manning SC) |
| 1935 | Henrietta Leaver (Pittsburgh PA) | 1958 | Marilyn Van Derbur (Denver CO) |
| 1936 | Rose Coyle (Philadelphia PA) | 1959 | Mary Ann Mobley (Brandon MS) |
| 1937 | Bette Cooper (Bertrand Island NJ) | 1960 | Lynda Mead (Natchez MS) |
| 1938 | Marilyn Meseke (Marion OH) | 1961 | Nancy Fleming (Montague MI) |
| 1939 | Patricia Donnelly (Detroit MI) | 1962 | Maria Fletcher (Asheville NC) |
| 1940 | Frances Burke (Philadelphia PA) | 1963 | Jacquelyn Mayer (Sandusky OH) |
| 1941 | Rosemary LaPlanche (Los Angeles CA) | 1964 | Donna Axum (El Dorado AR) |
| 1942 | Jo-Carroll Dennison (Tyler TX) | 1965 | Vonda Van Dyke (Phoenix AZ) |
| 1943 | Jean Bartel (Los Angeles CA) | 1966 | Deborah Bryant (Overland Park KS) |
| 1944 | Venus Ramey (Washington DC) | 1967 | Jane Jayroe (Laverne OK) |
| 1945 | Bess Myerson (New York NY) | 1968 | Debra Barnes (Pittsburg KS) |
| 1946 | Marilyn Buferd (Los Angeles CA) | 1969 | Judith Ford (Belvidere IL) |
| 1947 | Barbara Walker (Memphis TN) | 1970 | Pam Eldred (Bloomfield MI) |

## Miss America Winners, 1921–2003 (continued)

| YEAR | WINNER (HOMETOWN) | YEAR | WINNER (HOMETOWN) |
|------|-------------------|------|-------------------|
| 1971 | Phyllis George (Denton TX) | 1988 | Kaye Lani Rae Rafko (Monroe MI) |
| 1972 | Laurel Schaefer (Bexley OH) | 1989 | Gretchen Carlson (Anoka MN) |
| 1973 | Terry Meeuwsen (De Pere WI) | 1990 | Debbye Turner (Columbia MO) |
| 1974 | Rebecca King (Denver CO) | 1991 | Marjorie Vincent (Oak Park IL) |
| 1975 | Shirley Cothran (Denton TX) | 1992 | Carolyn Sapp (Honolulu HI) |
| 1976 | Tawny Godin (Saratoga Springs NY) | 1993 | Leanza Cornett (Jacksonville FL) |
| 1977 | Dorothy Benham (Edina MN) | 1994 | Kimberly Aiken (Columbia SC) |
| 1978 | Susan Perkins (Columbus OH) | 1995 | Heather Whitestone (Birmingham AL) |
| 1979 | Kylene Barker (Roanoke VA) | 1996 | Shawntel Smith (Muldrow OK) |
| 1980 | Cheryl Prewitt (Ackerman MS) | 1997 | Tara Dawn Holland (Overland Park KS) |
| 1981 | Susan Powell (Elk City OK) | 1998 | Kate Shindle (Evanston IL) |
| 1982 | Elizabeth Ward (Russellville AR) | 1999 | Nicole Johnson (Virginia Beach VA) |
| 1983 | Debra Maffett (Anaheim CA) | 2000 | Heather French (Maysville KY) |
| 1984 | Suzette Charles (Mays Landing NJ)[2] | 2001 | Angela Perez Baraquio (Honolulu HI) |
| 1985 | Sharlene Wells (Salt Lake City UT) | 2002 | Katie Harman (Gresham OR) |
| 1986 | Susan Akin (Meridian MS) | 2003 | Erika Harold (Urbana IL) |
| 1987 | Kellye Cash (Memphis TN) | 2004 | *pageant to be held 20 Sep 2003* |

[1]*Until the 1950 competition, winners were given the title for the year in which they won; thereafter, they were given the title for the following year, during which most of their reign took place. As a result no Miss America 1950 was named.*  [2]*Runner-up, crowned after resignation of Vanessa Williams (Millwood NY).*

## Miss Universe Winners, 1952–2003

The Miss Universe contest originated in 1952 as a swimwear competition in Long Beach CA in conjunction with the Miss USA pageant. The two pageants were held concurrently until 1965. Women aged 18–27 from some 80 countries and dependencies participate in the competition annually, and the contest is broadcast across the globe. Judging is based on an interview and appearances in swimwear and evening wear. Though it remains primarily a beauty contest, the competition's organizers emphasize a message of cross-cultural harmony and opportunity for women, and winners work with the United Nations and other organizations to promote HIV/AIDS awareness and women's health and reproductive initiatives. Prize: one-year employment contract, cash, products, and services. Miss Universe Contest Web site: <www.missuniverse.com>

| YEAR | WINNER (COUNTRY) | YEAR | WINNER (COUNTRY) |
|------|------------------|------|------------------|
| 1952 | Armi Kuusela (Finland) | 1978 | Margaret Gardiner (South Africa) |
| 1953 | Christiane Martel (France) | 1979 | Maritza Sayalero (Venezuela) |
| 1954 | Miriam Stevenson (US) | 1980 | Shawn Nichols Weatherly (US) |
| 1955 | Hillevi Rombin (Sweden) | 1981 | Mona Irene Lailan Sáez Conde (Venezuela) |
| 1956 | Carol Morris (US) | 1982 | Karen Diane Baldwin (Canada) |
| 1957 | Gladys Zender (Peru) | 1983 | Lorraine Downes (New Zealand) |
| 1958 | Luz Marina Zuluaga (Colombia) | 1984 | Yvonne Ryding (Sweden) |
| 1959 | Akiko Kojima (Japan) | 1985 | Deborah Carthy-Deu (Puerto Rico) |
| 1960 | Linda Bement (US) | 1986 | Bárbara Palacios Teyde (Venezuela) |
| 1961 | Marlene Schmidt (West Germany) | 1987 | Cecilia Carolina Bolocco Fonck (Chile) |
| 1962 | Norma Nolan (Argentina) | 1988 | Porntip Nakhirunkanok (Thailand) |
| 1963 | Ieda Maria Vargas (Brazil) | 1989 | Angela Visser (The Netherlands) |
| 1964 | Kiriaki Corinna Tsopei (Greece) | 1990 | Mona Grudt (Norway) |
| 1965 | Apasra Hongsakula (Thailand) | 1991 | Lupita Jones (Mexico) |
| 1966 | Margareta Arvidsson (Sweden) | 1992 | Michelle McLean (Namibia) |
| 1967 | Sylvia Louise Hitchcock (US) | 1993 | Dayanara Torres (Puerto Rico) |
| 1968 | Martha Vasconcellos (Brazil) | 1994 | Sushmita Sen (India) |
| 1969 | Gloria Diaz (Philippines) | 1995 | Chelsi Smith (US) |
| 1970 | Marisol Malaret (Puerto Rico) | 1996 | Joseph Alicia Machado Fajardo (Venezuela) |
| 1971 | Georgina Rizk (Lebanon) | 1997 | Brook Antoinette Mahealani Lee (US) |
| 1972 | Kerry Anne Wells (Australia) | 1998 | Wendy Fitzwilliam (Trinidad and Tobago) |
| 1973 | Margarita Moran (Philippines) | 1999 | Mpule Kwelagobe (Botswana) |
| 1974 | Amparo Muñoz (Spain) | 2000 | Lara Dutta (India) |
| 1975 | Anne Marie Pohtamo (Finland) | 2001 | Denise M. Quiñones August (Puerto Rico) |
| 1976 | Rina Messinger (Israel) | 2002 | Justine Pasek (Panama)[1] |
| 1977 | Janelle Commissiong (Trinidad and Tobago) | 2003 | Amelia Vega (Dominican Republic) |

[1]*Oksana Fyodorova (Russia) was dismissed for breach of contract on 23 Sep 2002.*

# Arts and Letters Awards

## Pulitzer Prizes, 2003

The Pulitzer Prizes are awarded annually by Columbia University, New York City, based on recommendations from the Pulitzer Prize Board. The prizes, originally endowed by newspaper editor Joseph Pulitzer, were first awarded in 1917. Over the years categories have been added, and 21 prizes are now presented. All prizes include a $7,500 cash award; the exception is the prize for public service in journalism, which is a gold medal.

Pulitzer Prize Web site: <www.pulitzer.org>.

### Journalism

| CATEGORY AND DESCRIPTION | WINNER | PUBLICATION | SUBJECT |
| --- | --- | --- | --- |
| **Public Service:** awarded to a newspaper for notable public service. | | *Boston Globe* | coverage of sexual abuse by priests in the Roman Catholic church |
| **Breaking News Reporting:** awarded for local reporting of breaking news. | staff | *Eagle-Tribune,* Lawrence MA | coverage of the accidental drownings of four boys in the Merrimack River |
| **Investigative Reporting:** awarded to an individual or team for an investigative article or series. | Clifford J. Levy | *New York Times* | "Broken Homes," a series that revealed the abuse of mentally ill adults in state-regulated homes |
| **Explanatory Reporting:** awarded for clarification of a difficult subject through clear communication of in-depth knowledge. | staff | *Wall Street Journal* | corporate scandals in the US |
| **Beat Reporting:** awarded for consistent, intelligent coverage of a particular topic. | Diana K. Sugg | *Baltimore Sun* | discussion of complex medical issues through the lives of everyday people |
| **National Reporting:** awarded for coverage of national news. | Alan Miller, Kevin Sack | *Los Angeles Times* | examination of the military aircraft known as "The Widow Maker," which was linked to the deaths of 45 pilots |
| **International Reporting:** awarded for coverage of international news. | Kevin Sullivan, Mary Jordan | *Washington Post* | in-depth profile of Mexico's criminal justice system |
| **Feature Writing:** awarded for an original feature of high literary quality | Sonia Nazario | *Los Angeles Times* | "Enrique's Journey," an account of a Honduran boy's search for his mother, who had migrated to the US |
| **Commentary** | Colbert I. King | *Washington Post* | power and politics |
| **Criticism** | Stephen Hunter | *Washington Post* | film criticism |
| **Editorial Writing:** awarded for ability to sway public opinion through solid reasoning, clear style, and "moral purpose." | Cornelia Grumman | *Chicago Tribune* | reform of the death penalty |
| **Editorial Cartooning:** awarded for a cartoon or group of cartoons displaying creativity, superior drawing, and editorial effectiveness. | David Horsey | *Seattle Post-Intelligencer* | |
| **Breaking News Photography:** awarded for color or black-and-white photographs of breaking news, individually or as a group. | staff | *Rocky Mountain News* | coverage of Colorado's forest fires |
| **Feature Photography:** awarded for color or black-and-white feature photographs, individually or as a group | Don Bartletti | *Los Angeles Times* | record of undocumented Central American children as they travel to the US |

# Letters, Drama, and Music

## Fiction

*Awarded for a work of fiction, preferably about American life, by an American author.*

| YEAR | TITLE | AUTHOR | YEAR | TITLE | AUTHOR |
|---|---|---|---|---|---|
| 1917 | no award | | 1962 | *The Edge of Sadness* | Edwin O'Connor |
| 1918 | *His Family* | Ernest Poole | 1963 | *The Reivers* | William Faulkner |
| 1919 | *The Magnificent Ambersons* | Booth Tarkington | 1964 | no award | |
| | | | 1965 | *The Keepers Of The House* | Shirley Ann Grau |
| 1920 | no award | | | | |
| 1921 | *The Age of Innocence* | Edith Wharton | 1966 | *Collected Stories* | Katherine Anne Porter |
| 1922 | *Alice Adams* | Booth Tarkington | | | |
| 1923 | *One of Ours* | Willa Cather | 1967 | *The Fixer* | Bernard Malamud |
| 1924 | *The Able McLaughlins* | Margaret Wilson | 1968 | *The Confessions of Nat Turner* | William Styron |
| 1925 | *So Big* | Edna Ferber | | | |
| 1926 | *Arrowsmith* | Sinclair Lewis | 1969 | *House Made of Dawn* | N. Scott Momaday |
| 1927 | *Early Autumn* | Louis Bromfield | 1970 | *Collected Stories* | Jean Stafford |
| 1928 | *The Bridge of San Luis Rey* | Thornton Wilder | 1971 | no award | |
| | | | 1972 | *Angle of Repose* | Wallace Stegner |
| 1929 | *Scarlet Sister Mary* | Julia Peterkin | 1973 | *The Optimist's Daughter* | Eudora Welty |
| 1930 | *Laughing Boy* | Oliver Lafarge | 1974 | no award | |
| 1931 | *Years of Grace* | Margaret Ayer Barnes | 1975 | *The Killer Angels* | Michael Shaara |
| | | | 1976 | *Humboldt's Gift* | Saul Bellow |
| 1932 | *The Good Earth* | Pearl S. Buck | 1977 | no award | |
| 1933 | *The Store* | T.S. Stribling | 1978 | *Elbow Room* | James Alan McPherson |
| 1934 | *Lamb in His Bosom* | Caroline Miller | | | |
| 1935 | *Now in November* | Josephine Winslow Johnson | 1979 | *The Stories of John Cheever* | John Cheever |
| 1936 | *Honey in the Horn* | Harold L. Davis | 1980 | *The Executioner's Song* | Norman Mailer |
| 1937 | *Gone With the Wind* | Margaret Mitchell | 1981 | *A Confederacy of Dunces*[1] | John Kennedy Toole |
| 1938 | *The Late George Apley* | John Phillips Marquand | | | |
| 1939 | *The Yearling* | Marjorie Kinnan Rawlings | 1982 | *Rabbit Is Rich* | John Updike |
| | | | 1983 | *The Color Purple* | Alice Walker |
| | | | 1984 | *Ironweed* | William Kennedy |
| 1940 | *The Grapes of Wrath* | John Steinbeck | 1985 | *Foreign Affairs* | Alison Lurie |
| 1941 | no award | | 1986 | *Lonesome Dove* | Larry McMurtry |
| 1942 | *In This Our Life* | Ellen Glasgow | 1987 | *A Summons to Memphis* | Peter Taylor |
| 1943 | *Dragon's Teeth* | Upton Sinclair | | | |
| 1944 | *Journey in the Dark* | Martin Flavin | 1988 | *Beloved* | Toni Morrison |
| 1945 | *A Bell for Adano* | John Hersey | 1989 | *Breathing Lessons* | Anne Tyler |
| 1946 | no award | | 1990 | *The Mambo Kings Play Songs of Love* | Oscar Hijuelos |
| 1947 | *All the King's Men* | Robert Penn Warren | | | |
| | | | 1991 | *Rabbit At Rest* | John Updike |
| 1948 | *Tales of the South Pacific* | James A. Michener | 1992 | *A Thousand Acres* | Jane Smiley |
| | | | 1993 | *A Good Scent from a Strange Mountain* | Robert Olen Butler |
| 1949 | *Guard of Honor* | James Gould Cozzens | | | |
| | | | 1994 | *The Shipping News* | E. Annie Proulx |
| 1950 | *The Way West* | A.B. Guthrie, Jr. | 1995 | *The Stone Diaries* | Carol Shields |
| 1951 | *The Town* | Conrad Richter | 1996 | *Independence Day* | Richard Ford |
| 1952 | *The Caine Mutiny* | Herman Wouk | 1997 | *Martin Dressler: The Tale of an American Dreamer* | Steven Millhauser |
| 1953 | *The Old Man and the Sea* | Ernest Hemingway | | | |
| 1954 | no award | | 1998 | *American Pastoral* | Philip Roth |
| 1955 | *A Fable* | William Faulkner | 1999 | *The Hours* | Michael Cunningham |
| 1956 | *Andersonville* | MacKinlay Kantor | | | |
| 1957 | no award | | 2000 | *Interpreter of Maladies* | Jhumpa Lahiri |
| 1958 | *A Death In The Family*[1] | James Agee | 2001 | *The Amazing Adventures of Kavalier and Clay* | Michael Chabon |
| 1959 | *The Travels of Jaimie McPheeters* | Robert Lewis Taylor | | | |
| | | | 2002 | *Empire Falls* | Richard Russo |
| 1960 | *Advise and Consent* | Allen Drury | 2003 | *Middlesex* | Jeffrey Eugenides |
| 1961 | *To Kill A Mockingbird* | Harper Lee | | | |

[1]*Work published and prize awarded posthumously.*

# Letters, Drama, and Music (continued)

## Drama
*Awarded for a play, preferably about American life, by an American author.*

| YEAR | TITLE | AUTHOR | YEAR | TITLE | AUTHOR |
|---|---|---|---|---|---|
| 1917 | no award | | 1960 | *Fiorello!* | Jerome Weidman, |
| 1918 | *Why Marry?* | Jesse Lynch | | | George Abbott, |
| | | Williams | | | Jerry Bock, |
| 1919 | no award | | | | Sheldon Harnick |
| 1920 | *Beyond the Horizon* | Eugene O'Neill | 1961 | *All The Way Home* | Tad Mosel |
| 1921 | *Miss Lulu Bett* | Zona Gale | 1962 | *How To Succeed In* | Frank Loesser, Abe |
| 1922 | *Anna Christie* | Eugene O'Neill | | *Business Without* | Burrows |
| 1923 | *Icebound* | Owen Davis | | *Really Trying* | |
| 1924 | *Hell-Bent Fer Heaven* | Hatcher Hughes | 1963 | no award | |
| 1925 | *They Knew What They* | Sidney Howard | 1964 | no award | |
| | *Wanted* | | 1965 | *The Subject Was Roses* | Frank D. Gilroy |
| 1926 | *Craig's Wife* | George Kelly | 1966 | no award | |
| 1927 | *In Abraham's Bosom* | Paul Green | 1967 | *A Delicate Balance* | Edward Albee |
| 1928 | *Strange Interlude* | Eugene O'Neill | 1968 | no award | |
| 1929 | *Street Scene* | Elmer L. Rice | 1969 | *The Great White Hope* | Howard Sackler |
| 1930 | *The Green Pastures* | Marc Connelly | 1970 | *No Place To Be* | Charles Gordone |
| 1931 | *Alison's House* | Susan Glaspell | | *Somebody* | |
| 1932 | *Of Thee I Sing* | George S. Kaufman | 1971 | *The Effect of Gamma* | Paul Zindel |
| | | Morrie Ryskind, Ira | | *Rays on Man-in-the-* | |
| | | Gershwin | | *Moon Marigolds* | |
| 1933 | *Both Your Houses* | Maxwell Anderson | 1972 | no award | |
| 1934 | *Men in White* | Sidney Kingsley | 1973 | *That Championship* | Jason Miller |
| 1935 | *The Old Maid* | Zoe Akins | | *Season* | |
| 1936 | *Idiots Delight* | Robert E. | 1974 | no award | |
| | | Sherwood | 1975 | *Seascape* | Edward Albee |
| 1937 | *You Can't Take It With* | Moss Hart, George | 1976 | *A Chorus Line* | Michael Bennett, |
| | *You* | S. Kaufman | | | James Kirkwood, |
| 1938 | *Our Town* | Thornton Wilder | | | Nicholas Dante, |
| 1939 | *Abe Lincoln in Illinois* | Robert E. | | | Marvin Hamlisch, |
| | | Sherwood | | | Edward Kleban |
| 1940 | *The Time of Your Life* | William Saroyan | 1977 | *The Shadow Box* | Michael Cristofer |
| 1941 | *There Shall Be No Night* | Robert E. | 1978 | *The Gin Game* | Donald L. Coburn |
| | | Sherwood | 1979 | *Buried Child* | Sam Shepard |
| 1942 | no award | | 1980 | *Talley's Folly* | Lanford Wilson |
| 1943 | *The Skin of Our Teeth* | Thornton Wilder | 1981 | *Crimes of the Heart* | Beth Henley |
| 1944 | no award | | 1982 | *A Soldier's Play* | Charles Fuller |
| 1945 | *Harvey* | Mary Chase | 1983 | *'Night, Mother* | Marsha Norman |
| 1946 | *State of the Union* | Russel Crouse, | 1984 | *Glengarry Glen Ross* | David Mamet |
| | | Howard Lindsay | 1985 | *Sunday in the Park With* | Stephen |
| 1947 | no award | | | *George* | Sondheim, James |
| 1948 | *A Streetcar Named* | Tennessee | | | Lapine |
| | *Desire* | Williams | 1986 | no award | |
| 1949 | *Death of a Salesman* | Arthur Miller | 1987 | *Fences* | August Wilson |
| 1950 | *South Pacific* | Richard Rodgers, | 1988 | *Driving Miss Daisy* | Alfred Uhry |
| | | Oscar | 1989 | *The Heidi Chronicles* | Wendy |
| | | Hammerstein II, | | | Wasserstein |
| | | Joshua Logan | 1990 | *The Piano Lesson* | August Wilson |
| 1951 | no award | | 1991 | *Lost in Yonkers* | Neil Simon |
| 1952 | *The Shrike* | Joseph Kramm | 1992 | *The Kentucky Cycle* | Robert Schenkkan |
| 1953 | *Picnic* | William Inge | 1993 | *Angels in America:* | Tony Kushner |
| 1954 | *The Teahouse of the* | John Patrick | | *Millennium Approaches* | |
| | *August Moon* | | 1994 | *Three Tall Women* | Edward Albee |
| 1955 | *Cat on a Hot Tin Roof* | Tennessee | 1995 | *The Young Man From* | Horton Foote |
| | | Williams | | *Atlanta* | |
| 1956 | *Diary of Anne Frank* | Albert Hackett, | 1996 | *Rent* | Jonathan Larson[1] |
| | | Frances Goodrich | 1997 | no award | |
| 1957 | *Long Day's Journey Into* | Eugene O'Neill | 1998 | *How I Learned to Drive* | Paula Vogel |
| | *Night* | | 1999 | *Wit* | Margaret Edson |
| 1958 | *Look Homeward, Angel* | Ketti Frings | 2000 | *Dinner With Friends* | Donald Margulies |
| 1959 | *J.B.* | Archibald MacLeish | 2001 | *Proof* | David Auburn |
| | | | 2002 | *Topdog/Underdog* | Suzan-Lori Parks |
| | | | 2003 | *Anna in the Tropics* | Nilo Cruz |

[1]*Awarded posthumously.*

# Letters, Drama, and Music (continued)

## History
*Awarded for a work on the subject of American history.*

| YEAR | TITLE | AUTHOR |
|------|-------|--------|
| 1917 | With Americans of Past and Present Days | J.J. Jusserand |
| 1918 | A History of the Civil War, 1861–1865 | James Ford Rhodes |
| 1919 | no award | |
| 1920 | The War with Mexico, 2 vols. | Justin H. Smith |
| 1921 | The Victory at Sea | William Sowden Sims, Burton Jesse Hendrick |
| 1922 | The Founding of New England | James Truslow Adams |
| 1923 | The Supreme Court in United States History | Charles Warren |
| 1924 | The American Revolution: A Constitutional Interpretation | Charles Howard McIlwain |
| 1925 | History of the American Frontier | Frederic L. Paxson |
| 1926 | A History of the United States | Edward Channing |
| 1927 | Pinckney's Treaty | Samuel Flagg Bemis |
| 1928 | Main Currents in American Thought, 2 vols. | Vernon Louis Parrington |
| 1929 | The Organization and Administration of the Union Army, 1861–1865 | Fred Albert Shannon |
| 1930 | The War of Independence | Claude H. Van Tyne |
| 1931 | The Coming of the War, 1914 | Bernadotte E. Schmitt |
| 1932 | My Experiences in the World War | John J. Pershing |
| 1933 | The Significance of Sections in American History | Frederick J. Turner |
| 1934 | The People's Choice | Herbert Agar |
| 1935 | The Colonial Period of American History | Charles McLean Andrews |
| 1936 | A Constitutional History of the United States | Andrew C. McLaughlin |
| 1937 | The Flowering of New England, 1815–1865 | Van Wyck Brooks |
| 1938 | The Road to Reunion, 1865–1900 | Paul Herman Buck |
| 1939 | A History of American Magazines | Frank Luther Mott |
| 1940 | Abraham Lincoln: The War Years | Carl Sandburg |
| 1941 | The Atlantic Migration, 1607–1860 | Marcus Lee Hansen |
| 1942 | Reveille in Washington, 1860–1865 | Margaret Leech |
| 1943 | Paul Revere and the World He Lived In | Esther Forbes |
| 1944 | The Growth of American Thought | Merle Curti |
| 1945 | Unfinished Business | Stephen Bonsal |
| 1946 | The Age of Jackson | Arthur M. Schlesinger, Jr. |
| 1947 | Scientists Against Time | James Phinney Baxter III |
| 1948 | Across the Wide Missouri | Bernard De Voto |
| 1949 | The Disruption of American Democracy | Roy Franklin Nichols |
| 1950 | Art and Life in America | Oliver W. Larkin |
| 1951 | The Old Northwest: Pioneer Period, 1815–1840 | R. Carlyle Buley |
| 1952 | The Uprooted | Oscar Handlin |
| 1953 | The Era of Good Feelings | George Dangerfield |
| 1954 | A Stillness at Appomattox | Bruce Catton |
| 1955 | Great River: The Rio Grande in North American History | Paul Horgan |
| 1956 | The Age of Reform | Richard Hofstadter |
| 1957 | Russia Leaves the War: Soviet-American Relations, 1917–1920 | George F. Kennan |
| 1958 | Banks and Politics in America | Bray Hammond |
| 1959 | The Republican Era: 1869–1901 | Leonard D. White, Jean Schneider |
| 1960 | In the Days of McKinley | Margaret Leech |
| 1961 | Between War and Peace: The Potsdam Conference | Herbert Feis |
| 1962 | The Triumphant Empire: Thunder-Clouds Gather in the West, 1763–1766 | Lawrence H. Gipson |
| 1963 | Washington, Village and Capital, 1800–1878 | Constance McLaughlin Green |
| 1964 | Puritan Village: The Formation of a New England Town | Sumner Chilton Powell |
| 1965 | The Greenback Era | Irwin Unger |
| 1966 | The Life of the Mind in America | Perry Miller[1] |
| 1967 | Exploration and Empire: The Explorer and the Scientist in the Winning of the American West | William H. Goetzmann |
| 1968 | The Ideological Origins of the American Revolution | Bernard Bailyn |
| 1969 | Origins of the Fifth Amendment | Leonard W. Levy |
| 1970 | Present At The Creation: My Years In The State Department | Dean Acheson |
| 1971 | Roosevelt: The Soldier Of Freedom | James MacGregor Burns |
| 1972 | Neither Black Nor White | Carl N. Degler |
| 1973 | People of Paradox: An Inquiry Concerning the Origins of American Civilization | Michael Kammen |
| 1974 | The Americans: The Democratic Experience | Daniel J. Boorstin |
| 1975 | Jefferson and His Time, Vols. I–V | Dumas Malone |
| 1976 | Lamy of Santa Fe | Paul Horgan |

# Letters, Drama, and Music (continued)

## History (continued)

| YEAR | TITLE | AUTHOR | YEAR | TITLE | AUTHOR |
|---|---|---|---|---|---|
| 1977 | The Impending Crisis, 1841–1867 | David M. Potter, Don E. Fehrenbacher[2] | 1992 | The Fate of Liberty: Abraham Lincoln and Civil Liberties | Mark E. Neely, Jr. |
| 1978 | The Visible Hand: The Managerial Revolution in American Business | Alfred D. Chandler, Jr. | 1993 | The Radicalism of the American Revolution | Gordon S. Wood |
| 1979 | The Dred Scott Case | Don E. Fehrenbacher | 1994 | no award | |
| 1980 | Been in the Storm So Long | Leon F. Litwack | 1995 | No Ordinary Time: Franklin and Eleanor Roosevelt: The Home Front in World War II | Doris Kearns Goodwin |
| 1981 | American Education: The National Experience, 1783–1876 | Lawrence A. Cremin | 1996 | William Cooper's Town: Power and Persuasion on the Frontier of the Early American Republic | Alan Taylor |
| 1982 | Mary Chesnut's Civil War | C. Vann Woodward[3] | 1997 | Original Meanings: Politics and Ideas in the Making of the Constitution | Jack N. Rakove |
| 1983 | The Transformation of Virginia, 1740–1790 | Rhys L. Isaac | | | |
| 1984 | no award | | | | |
| 1985 | Prophets of Regulation | Thomas K. McCraw | 1998 | Summer for the Gods: The Scopes Trial and America's Continuing Debate Over Science and Religion | Edward J. Larson |
| 1986 | ...the Heavens and the Earth: A Political History of the Space Age | Walter A. McDougall | | | |
| 1987 | Voyagers to the West: A Passage in the Peopling of America on the Eve of the Revolution | Bernard Bailyn | 1999 | Gotham: A History of New York City to 1898 | Edwin G. Burrows, Mike Wallace |
| | | | 2000 | Freedom From Fear: The American People in Depression and War, 1929–1945 | David M. Kennedy |
| 1988 | The Launching of Modern American Science, 1846–1876 | Robert V. Bruce | | | |
| 1989 | Battle Cry of Freedom: The Civil War Era | James M. McPherson | 2001 | Founding Brothers: The Revolutionary Generation | Joseph J. Ellis |
| 1989 | Parting the Waters: America in the King Years, 1954–1963 | Taylor Branch | 2002 | The Metaphysical Club: A Story of Ideas in America | Louis Menand |
| 1990 | In Our Image: America's Empire in the Philippines | Stanley Karnow | 2003 | An Army at Dawn: The War in North Africa, 1942–1943 | Rick Atkinson |
| 1991 | A Midwife's Tale | Laurel Thatcher Ulrich | | | |

[1]Awarded posthumously.    [2]Potter died before completing the work; Fehrenbacher wrote the final chapters and edited it.    [3]Edited by Woodward.

## Biography or Autobiography
*Awarded for a biography or autobiography by an American author.*

| YEAR | TITLE | AUTHOR | YEAR | TITLE | AUTHOR |
|---|---|---|---|---|---|
| 1917 | Julia Ward Howe | Laura Elizabeth Howe Richards, Maude Howe Elliott; assisted by Florence Howe Hall | 1924 | From Immigrant to Inventor | Michael Idvorsky Pupin |
| | | | 1925 | Barrett Wendell and His Letters | M.A. De Wolfe Howe |
| | | | 1926 | The Life of Sir William Osler, 2 vols. | Harvey Cushing |
| 1918 | Benjamin Franklin, Self-Revealed | William Cabell Bruce | 1927 | Whitman | Emory Holloway |
| 1919 | The Education of Henry Adams | Henry Adams | 1928 | The American Orchestra and Theodore Thomas | Charles Edward Russell |
| 1920 | The Life of John Marshall, 4 vols. | Albert J. Beveridge | 1929 | The Training of an American: The Earlier Life and Letters of Walter H. Page | Burton J. Hendrick |
| 1921 | The Americanization of Edward Bok | Edward Bok | | | |
| 1922 | A Daughter of the Middle Border | Hamlin Garland | 1930 | The Raven | Marquis James |
| | | | 1931 | Charles W. Eliot | Henry James |
| | | | 1932 | Theodore Roosevelt | Henry F. Pringle |
| 1923 | The Life and Letters of Walter H. Page | Burton J. Hendrick | 1933 | Grover Cleveland | Allan Nevins |
| | | | 1934 | John Hay | Tyler Dennett |

# Letters, Drama, and Music (continued)

## Biography or Autobiography (continued)

| YEAR | TITLE | AUTHOR |
|------|-------|--------|
| 1935 | R.E. Lee | Douglas S. Freeman |
| 1936 | The Thought and Character of William James | Ralph Barton Perry |
| 1937 | Hamilton Fish | Allan Nevins |
| 1938 | Andrew Jackson, 2 vols. | Marquis James |
| 1938 | Pedlar's Progress | Odell Shepard |
| 1939 | Benjamin Franklin | Carl Van Doren |
| 1940 | Woodrow Wilson, Life and Letters, Vols. VII and VIII | Ray Stannard Baker |
| 1941 | Jonathan Edward | Ola Elizabeth Winslow |
| 1942 | Crusader in Crinoline | Forrest Wilson |
| 1943 | Admiral of the Ocean Sea | Samuel Eliot Morison |
| 1944 | The American Leonardo: The Life of Samuel F.B. Morse | Carleton Mabee |
| 1945 | George Bancroft: Brahmin Rebel | Russell Blaine Nye |
| 1946 | Son of the Wilderness | Linnie Marsh Wolfe |
| 1947 | The Autobiography of William Allen White | William Allen White |
| 1948 | Forgotten First Citizen: John Bigelow | Margaret Clapp |
| 1949 | Roosevelt and Hopkins | Robert E. Sherwood |
| 1950 | John Quincy Adams and the Foundations of American Foreign Policy | Samuel Flagg Bemis |
| 1951 | John C. Calhoun: American Portrait | Margaret Louise Coit |
| 1952 | Charles Evans Hughes | Merlo J. Pusey |
| 1953 | Edmund Pendleton, 1721–1803 | David J. Mays |
| 1954 | The Spirit of St. Louis | Charles A. Lindbergh |
| 1955 | The Taft Story | William S. White |
| 1956 | Benjamin Henry Latrobe | Talbot Faulkner Hamlin |
| 1957 | Profiles in Courage | John F. Kennedy |
| 1958 | George Washington, Volumes I–VI and Volume VII | Douglas Southall Freeman, John Alexander Carroll, Mary Wells Ashworth* |
| 1959 | Woodrow Wilson, American Prophet | Arthur Walworth |
| 1960 | John Paul Jones | Samuel Eliot Morison |
| 1961 | Charles Sumner and the Coming of the Civil War | David Donald |
| 1962 | no award | |
| 1963 | Henry James | Leon Edel |
| 1964 | John Keats | Walter Jackson Bate |
| 1965 | Henry Adams, three volumes | Ernest Samuels |
| 1966 | A Thousand Days | Arthur M. Schlesinger, Jr. |
| 1967 | Mr. Clemens and Mark Twain | Justin Kaplan |

| YEAR | TITLE | AUTHOR |
|------|-------|--------|
| 1968 | Memoirs | George E. Kennan |
| 1969 | The Man From New York: John Quinn and His Friends | Benjamin Lawrence Reid |
| 1970 | Huey Long | T. Harry Williams |
| 1971 | Robert Frost: The Years of Triumph, 1915–1938 | Lawrance Thompson |
| 1972 | Eleanor and Franklin | Joseph P. Lash |
| 1973 | Luce and His Empire | W.A. Swanberg |
| 1974 | O'Neill, Son and Artist | Louis Sheaffer |
| 1975 | The Power Broker: Robert Moses and the Fall of New York | Robert Caro |
| 1976 | Edith Wharton: A Biography | R.W.B. Lewis |
| 1977 | A Prince of Our Disorder: The Life of T.E. Lawrence | John E. Mack |
| 1978 | Samuel Johnson | Walter Jackson Bate |
| 1979 | Days of Sorrow and Pain: Leo Baeck and the Berlin Jews | Leonard Baker |
| 1980 | The Rise of Theodore Roosevelt | Edmund Morris |
| 1981 | Peter the Great: His Life and World | Robert K. Massie |
| 1982 | Grant: A Biography | William McFeely |
| 1983 | Growing Up | Russell Baker |
| 1984 | Booker T. Washington: The Wizard of Tuskegee, 1901–1915 | Louis R. Harlan |
| 1985 | The Life and Times of Cotton Mather | Kenneth Silverman |
| 1986 | Louise Bogan: A Portrait | Elizabeth Frank |
| 1987 | Bearing the Cross: Martin Luther King Jr. and the Southern Christian Leadership Conference | David J. Garrow |
| 1988 | Look Homeward: A Life of Thomas Wolfe | David Herbert Donald |
| 1989 | Oscar Wilde | Richard Ellmann† |
| 1990 | Machiavelli in Hell | Sebastian de Grazia |
| 1991 | Jackson Pollock | Steven Naifeh, Gregory White Smith |
| 1992 | Fortunate Son: The Healing of a Vietnam Vet | Lewis B. Puller, Jr. |
| 1993 | Truman | David McCullough |
| 1994 | W.E.B. Du Bois: Biography of a Race 1868–1919 | David Levering Lewis |
| 1995 | Harriet Beecher Stowe: A Life | Joan D. Hedrick |
| 1996 | God: A Biography | Jack Miles |
| 1997 | Angela's Ashes: A Memoir | Frank McCourt |
| 1998 | Personal History | Katharine Graham |
| 1999 | Lindbergh | A. Scott Berg |
| 2000 | Vera (Mrs. Vladimir Nabokov) | Stacy Schiff |

# Letters, Drama, and Music (continued)

## Biography and Autobiography (continued)

2001  *W.E.B. Du Bois: The Fight for Equality and the American Century, 1919–1963*  David Levering Lewis

2002  *John Adams*  David McCullough
2003  *Master of the Senate*  Robert A. Caro

*\*Freeman died in 1953 after completing Volumes I–VI; Carroll and Ashworth continued his work with Volume VII.   †Awarded posthumously.*

## Poetry
*Awarded for a collection of original verse by an American author.*

| YEAR | TITLE | AUTHOR | YEAR | TITLE | AUTHOR |
|---|---|---|---|---|---|
| 1922 | Collected Poems | Edwin Arlington Robinson | 1958 | Promises: Poems 1954–1956 | Robert Penn Warren |
| 1923 | The Ballad of the Harp-Weaver: A Few Figs from Thistles: Eight Sonnets in American Poetry, 1922. A Miscellany | Edna St. Vincent Millay | 1959 | Selected Poems 1928–1958 | Stanley Kunitz |
| | | | 1960 | Heart's Needle | W.D. Snodgrass |
| | | | 1961 | Times Three: Selected Verse From Three Decades | Phyllis McGinley |
| 1924 | New Hampshire: A Poem with Notes and Grace Notes | Robert Frost | 1962 | Poems | Alan Dugan |
| | | | 1963 | Pictures from Breughel | William Carlos Williams* |
| 1925 | The Man Who Died Twice | Edwin Arlington Robinson | 1964 | At The End Of The Open Road | Louis Simpson |
| 1926 | What's O'Clock | Amy Lowell* | 1965 | 77 Dream Songs | John Berryman |
| 1927 | Fiddler's Farewell | Leonora Speyer | 1966 | Selected Poems | Richard Eberhart |
| 1928 | Tristram | Edwin Arlington Robinson | 1967 | Live or Die | Anne Sexton |
| | | | 1968 | The Hard Hours | Anthony Hecht |
| 1929 | John Brown's Body | Stephen Vincent Benét | 1969 | Of Being Numerous | George Oppen |
| | | | 1970 | Untitled Subjects | Richard Howard |
| 1930 | Selected Poems | Conrad Aiken | 1971 | The Carrier of Ladders | William S. Merwin |
| 1931 | Collected Poems | Robert Frost | 1972 | Collected Poems | James Wright |
| 1932 | The Flowering Stone | George Dillon | 1973 | Up Country | Maxine Kumin |
| 1933 | Conquistador | Archibald MacLeish | 1974 | The Dolphin | Robert Lowell |
| | | | 1975 | Turtle Island | Gary Snyder |
| 1934 | Collected Verse | Robert Hillyer | 1976 | Self-Portrait in a Convex Mirror | John Ashbery |
| 1935 | Bright Ambush | Audrey Wurdemann | | | |
| | | | 1977 | Divine Comedies | James Merrill |
| 1936 | Strange Holiness | Robert P. Tristram Coffin | 1978 | Collected Poems | Howard Nemerov |
| | | | 1979 | Now and Then | Robert Penn Warren |
| 1937 | A Further Range | Robert Frost | | | |
| 1938 | Cold Morning Sky | Marya Zaturenska | 1980 | Selected Poems | Donald Justice |
| 1939 | Selected Poems | John Gould Fletcher | 1981 | The Morning of the Poem | James Schuyler |
| 1940 | Collected Poems | Mark Van Doren | 1982 | The Collected Poems | Sylvia Plath† |
| 1941 | Sunderland Capture | Leonard Bacon | 1983 | Selected Poems | Galway Kinnell |
| 1942 | The Dust Which Is God | William Rose Benét | 1984 | American Primitive | Mary Oliver |
| | | | 1985 | Yin | Carolyn Kizer |
| 1943 | A Witness Tree | Robert Frost | 1986 | The Flying Change | Henry Taylor |
| 1944 | Western Star | Stephen Vincent Benét* | 1987 | Thomas and Beulah | Rita Dove |
| | | | 1988 | Partial Accounts: New and Selected Poems | William Meredith |
| 1945 | V-Letter and Other Poems | Karl Shapiro | 1989 | New and Collected Poems | Richard Wilbur |
| 1946 | no award | | | | |
| 1947 | Lord Weary's Castle | Robert Lowell | 1990 | The World Doesn't End | Charles Simic |
| 1948 | The Age of Anxiety | W.H. Auden | 1991 | Near Changes | Mona Van Duyn |
| 1949 | Terror and Decorum | Peter Viereck | 1992 | Selected Poems | James Tate |
| 1950 | Annie Allen | Gwendolyn Brooks | 1993 | The Wild Iris | Louise Gluck |
| 1951 | Complete Poems | Carl Sandburg | 1994 | Neon Vernacular: New and Selected Poems | Yusef Komunyakaa |
| 1952 | Collected Poems | Marianne Moore | | | |
| 1953 | Collected Poems, 1917–1952 | Archibald MacLeish | 1995 | The Simple Truth | Philip Levine |
| | | | 1996 | The Dream of the Unified Field | Jorie Graham |
| 1954 | The Waking | Theodore Roethke | | | |
| 1955 | Collected Poems | Wallace Stevens | 1997 | Alive Together: New and Selected Poems | Lisel Mueller |
| 1956 | Poems: North & South | Elizabeth Bishop | | | |
| 1957 | Things of This World | Richard Wilbur | 1998 | Black Zodiac | Charles Wright |

## Letters, Drama, and Music (continued)

### Poetry (continued)

| YEAR | TITLE | AUTHOR | YEAR | TITLE | AUTHOR |
|------|-------|--------|------|-------|--------|
| 1999 | Blizzard of One | Mark Strand | 2002 | Practical Gods | Carl Dennis |
| 2000 | Repair | C.K. Williams | 2003 | Moy Sand and Gravel | Paul Muldoon |
| 2001 | Different Hours | Stephen Dunn | | | |

*Awarded posthumously.    †Work published and prize awarded posthumously.

### General Nonfiction
*Awarded for a work of nonfiction, ineligible for any other category, by an American author.*

| YEAR | TITLE | AUTHOR | YEAR | TITLE | AUTHOR |
|------|-------|--------|------|-------|--------|
| 1962 | The Making of the President, 1960 | Theodore H. White | 1982 | The Soul of a New Machine | Tracy Kidder |
| 1963 | The Guns of August | Barbara W. Tuchman | 1983 | Is There No Place On Earth For Me? | Susan Sheehan |
| 1964 | Anti-Intellectualism in American Life | Richard Hofstadter | 1984 | The Social Transformation Of American Medicine | Paul Starr |
| 1965 | O Strange New World | Howard Mumford Jones | 1985 | The Good War: An Oral History of World War Two | Studs Terkel |
| 1966 | Wandering Through Winter | Edwin Way Teale | 1986 | Common Ground: A Turbulent Decade in the Lives of Three American Families | J. Anthony Lukas |
| 1967 | The Problem of Slavery in Western Culture | David Brion Davis | | | |
| 1968 | Rousseau and Revolution: A History of Civilization in France, England, and Germany from 1756, and in the Remainder of Europe from 1715 to 1789 | Will and Ariel Durant | 1986 | Move Your Shadow: South Africa, Black and White | Joseph Lelyveld |
| | | | 1987 | Arab and Jew: Wounded Spirits in a Promised Land | David K. Shipler |
| 1969 | The Armies of the Night | Norman Mailer | 1988 | The Making of the Atomic Bomb | Richard Rhodes |
| 1969 | So Human An Animal | Rene Jules Dubos | 1989 | A Bright Shining Lie: John Paul Vann and America in Vietnam | Neil Sheehan |
| 1970 | Gandhi's Truth | Erik H. Erikson | | | |
| 1971 | The Rising Sun | John Toland | | | |
| 1972 | Stilwell and the American Experience in China, 1911–1945 | Barbara W. Tuchman | 1990 | And Their Children After Them | Dale Maharidge, Michael Williamson |
| 1973 | Fire in the Lake: The Vietnamese and the Americans in Vietnam | Frances Fitzgerald | 1991 | The Ants | Bert Holldobler, Edward O. Wilson |
| 1973 | Children of Crisis, Vols. II and III | Robert Coles | 1992 | The Prize: The Epic Quest For Oil, Money, and Power | Daniel Yergin |
| 1974 | The Denial of Death | Ernest Becker* | | | |
| 1975 | Pilgrim at Tinker Creek | Annie Dillard | 1993 | Lincoln at Gettysburg: The Words That Remade America | Garry Wills |
| 1976 | Why Survive? Being Old In America | Robert N. Butler | | | |
| 1977 | Beautiful Swimmers | William W. Warner | 1994 | Lenin's Tomb: The Last Days Of The Soviet Empire | David Remnick |
| 1978 | The Dragons of Eden | Carl Sagan | | | |
| 1979 | On Human Nature | Edward O. Wilson | 1995 | The Beak Of The Finch: A Story Of Evolution In Our Time | Jonathan Weiner |
| 1980 | Gödel, Escher, Bach: An Eternal Golden Braid | Douglas R. Hofstadter | | | |
| 1981 | Fin-de-Siècle Vienna: Politics and Culture | Carl E. Schorske | 1996 | The Haunted Land: Facing Europe's Ghosts After Communism | Tina Rosenberg |

**Did you know?** Robert Burns, the national poet of Scotland, wrote new words for old tunes and sometimes wrote several sets of words to the same melody. He described "Auld Lang Syne" as simply an old fragment he had discovered; the chorus and the first stanza are old, but most of the lyrics we have are almost certainly his. George Thomson set it to the tune to which it is now sung.

# Letters, Drama, and Music (continued)

## General Nonfiction (continued)

| YEAR | TITLE | AUTHOR | YEAR | TITLE | AUTHOR |
|---|---|---|---|---|---|
| 1997 | Ashes to Ashes: America's Hundred-Year Cigarette War, the Public Health, and the Unabashed Triumph of Philip Morris | Richard Kluger | 2001 | Hirohito and the Making of Modern Japan | Herbert P. Bix |
| | | | 2002 | Carry Me Home: Birmingham, Alabama, the Climactic Battle of the Civil Rights Revolution | Diane McWhorter |
| 1998 | Guns, Germs and Steel: The Fates of Human Societies | Jared Diamond | 2003 | "A Problem from Hell": America and the Age of Genocide | Samantha Power |
| 1999 | Annals of the Former World | John McPhee | | | |
| 2000 | Embracing Defeat: Japan in the Wake of World War II | John W. Dower | | | |

*Awarded posthumously.

## Music

*Awarded for a musical piece of "significant dimension" composed by an American and first performed in the United States during the year.*

| YEAR | TITLE | COMPOSER | YEAR | TITLE | COMPOSER |
|---|---|---|---|---|---|
| 1943 | Secular Cantata No. 2. A Free Song | William Schuman | 1977 | Visions of Terror and Wonder | Richard Wernick |
| 1944 | Symphony No. 4. Opus 34 | Howard Hanson | 1978 | Deja Vu for Percussion Quartet and Orchestra | Michael Colgrass |
| 1945 | Appalachian Spring | Aaron Copland | 1979 | Aftertones of Infinity | Joseph Schwantner |
| 1946 | The Canticle of the Sun | Leo Sowerby | 1980 | In Memory of a Summer Day | David Del Tredici |
| 1947 | Symphony No. 3 | Charles Ives | | | |
| 1948 | Symphony No. 3 | Walter Piston | 1981 | no award | |
| 1949 | Music for the film Louisiana Story | Virgil Thomson | 1982 | Concerto for Orchestra | Roger Sessions |
| 1950 | The Consul | Gian Carlo Menotti | 1983 | Symphony No. 1 (Three Movements for Orchestra) | Ellen Taaffe Zwilich |
| 1951 | Giants in the Earth | Douglas S. Moore | | | |
| 1952 | Symphony Concertante | Gail Kubik | 1984 | "Canti del Sole" for Tenor and Orchestra | Bernard Rands |
| 1953 | no award | | | | |
| 1954 | Concerto For Two Pianos and Orchestra | Quincy Porter | 1985 | Symphony, RiverRun | Stephen Albert |
| 1955 | The Saint of Bleecker Street | Gian Carlo Menotti | 1986 | Wind Quintet IV | George Perle |
| | | | 1987 | The Flight Into Egypt | John Harbison |
| 1956 | Symphony No. 3 | Ernst Toch | 1988 | 12 New Etudes for Piano | William Bolcom |
| 1957 | Meditation on Ecclesiastics | Norman Dello Joio | 1989 | Whispers Out of Time | Roger Reynolds |
| 1958 | Vanessa | Samuel Barber | 1990 | "Duplicates": A Concerto for Two Pianos and Orchestra | Mel Powell |
| 1959 | Concerto for Piano and Orchestra | John LaMontaine | | | |
| 1960 | Second String Quartet | Elliott Carter | 1991 | Symphony | Shulamit Ran |
| 1961 | Symphony No. 7 | Walter Piston | 1992 | The Face of the Night, The Heart of the Dark | Wayne Peterson |
| 1962 | The Crucible | Robert Ward | | | |
| 1963 | Piano Concerto No. 1 | Samuel Barber | 1993 | Trombone Concerto | Christopher Rouse |
| 1964 | no award | | | | |
| 1965 | no award | | 1994 | Of Reminiscences and Reflections | Gunther Schuller |
| 1966 | Variations for Orchestra | Leslie Bassett | | | |
| 1967 | Quartet No. 3 | Leon Kirchner | 1995 | Stringmusic | Morton Gould |
| 1968 | Echoes of Time and the River | George Crumb | 1996 | Lilacs, for voice and orchestra | George Walker |
| 1969 | String Quartet No. 3 | Karel Husa | | | |
| 1970 | Time's Encomium | Charles Wuorinen | 1997 | Blood on the Fields | Wynton Marsalis |
| 1971 | Synchronisms No. 6 for Piano and Electronic Sound (1970) | Mario Davidovsky | 1998 | String Quartet #2 (musica instrumentalis) | Aaron Jay Kernis |
| 1972 | Windows | Jacob Druckman | 1999 | Concerto for Flute, Strings and Percussion | Melinda Wagner |
| 1973 | String Quartet No. 3 | Elliott Carter | | | |
| 1974 | Notturno | Donald Martino | | | |
| 1975 | From the Diary of Virginia Woolf | Dominick Argento | 2000 | Life is a Dream, Opera in Three Acts: Act II, Concert Version | Lewis Spratlan |
| 1976 | Air Music | Ned Rorem | | | |

# Letters, Drama, and Music (continued)

## Music (continued)

| EAR | TITLE | COMPOSER | EAR | TITLE | COMPOSER |
|---|---|---|---|---|---|
| 2001 | Symphony No. 2 for String Orchestra | John Corigliano | 2003 | On the Transmigration of Souls | John Adams |
| 2002 | Ice Field | Henry Brant | | | |

## Special Awards

| YEAR | RECIPIENT | FOR | YEAR | RECIPIENT | FOR |
|---|---|---|---|---|---|
| 1944 | Richard Rodgers, Oscar Hammerstein II | theatrical musical Oklahoma! | 1978 | E.B. White | full body of his work |
| | | | 1982 | Milton Babbitt | life's work in music |
| 1957 | Kenneth Roberts | historical novels | 1984 | Theodor Seuss Geisel | Dr. Seuss children's books |
| 1960 | Garrett Mattingly | nonfiction work The Armada | 1985 | William Schuman | life's work in composition and music education |
| 1961 | American Heritage Picture History of the Civil War | "a distinguished example of American book publishing" | 1992 | Art Spiegelman | graphic novel Maus |
| | | | 1998 | George Gershwin* | centennial commemoration of his birth, celebrating his life's work in music |
| 1973 | James Thomas Flexner | nonfiction work George Washington, Vols. I–IV | | | |
| 1974 | Roger Sessions | life's work in music | 1999 | Duke Ellington* | centennial commemoration of his birth, celebrating his life's work in music |
| 1976 | Scott Joplin* | contributions to American music | | | |
| 1977 | Alex Haley | novel Roots | | | |

*Awarded posthumously.

# National Book Awards

In 1950 a consortium of publishing groups established the National Book Awards. The goals were to bring exceptional books written by Americans to the public's attention and to encourage reading in general. Award categories have varied from the inaugural 3 to as many as 28 in 1980. Today, the awards recognize achievements in 4 genres: fiction, nonfiction, poetry, and young people's literature. A five-member, independent judging panel chooses a winner for each genre. Award: $10,000 cash and a crystal sculpture.

## Fiction

| YEAR | TITLE | AUTHOR |
|---|---|---|
| 1950 | The Man with the Golden Arm | Nelson Algren |
| 1951 | The Collected Stories of William Faulkner | William Faulkner |
| 1952 | From Here to Eternity | James Jones |
| 1953 | Invisible Man | Ralph Ellison |
| 1954 | The Adventures of Augie March | Saul Bellow |
| 1955 | A Fable | William Faulkner |
| 1956 | Ten North Frederick | John O'Hara |
| 1957 | The Field of Vision | Wright Morris |
| 1958 | The Wapshot Chronicle | John Cheever |
| 1959 | The Magic Barrel | Bernard Malamud |
| 1960 | Goodbye, Columbus | Philip Roth |
| 1961 | The Waters of Kronos | Conrad Richter |
| 1962 | The Moviegoer | Walker Percy |
| 1963 | Morte d'Urban | J.F. Powers |
| 1964 | The Centaur | John Updike |
| 1965 | Herzog | Saul Bellow |
| 1966 | The Collected Stories of Katherine Anne Porter | Katherine Anne Porter |
| 1967 | The Fixer | Bernard Malamud |
| 1968 | The Eighth Day | Thornton Wilder |
| 1969 | Steps | Jerzy Kosinski |
| 1970 | Them | Joyce Carol Oates |
| 1971 | Mr. Sammler's Planet | Saul Bellow |
| 1972 | The Complete Stories | Flannery O'Connor |
| 1973 | Augustus | John Williams |

## Fiction (continued)

| YEAR | TITLE | AUTHOR |
|---|---|---|
| 1973 | Chimera | John Barth |
| 1974 | A Crown of Feathers and Other Stories | Isaac Bashevis Singer |
| 1974 | Gravity's Rainbow | Thomas Pynchon |
| 1975 | Dog Soldiers: A Novel | Robert Stone |
| 1975 | The Hair of Harold Roux | Thomas Williams |
| 1976 | J.R. | William Gaddis |
| 1977 | The Spectator Bird | Wallace Stegner |
| 1978 | Blood Tie | Mary Lee Settle |
| 1979 | Going After Cacciato | Tim O'Brien |
| 1980 | Sophie's Choice[1] | William Styron |
| 1981 | Plains Song[1] | Wright Morris |
| 1982 | Rabbit Is Rich[1] | John Updike |
| 1983 | The Color Purple[1] | Alice Walker |
| 1984 | Victory over Japan: A Book of Stories | Ellen Gilchrist |
| 1985 | White Noise | Don DeLillo |
| 1986 | World's Fair | E.L. Doctorow |
| 1987 | Paco's Story | Larry Heinemann |
| 1988 | Paris Trout | Pete Dexter |
| 1989 | Spartina | John Casey |
| 1990 | Middle Passage | Charles Johnson |
| 1991 | Mating | Norman Rush |
| 1992 | All the Pretty Horses | Cormac McCarthy |
| 1993 | The Shipping News | E. Annie Proulx |
| 1994 | A Frolic of His Own | William Gaddis |
| 1995 | Sabbath's Theater | Philip Roth |
| 1996 | Ship Fever | Andrea Barrett |
| 1997 | Cold Mountain | Charles Frazier |
| 1998 | Charming Billy | Alice McDermott |

# National Book Awards (continued)

## Fiction (continued)

| YEAR | TITLE | AUTHOR | YEAR | TITLE | AUTHOR |
|------|-------|--------|------|-------|--------|
| 1999 | *Waiting* | Ha Jin | 2001 | *The Corrections* | Jonathan Franzen |
| 2000 | *In America* | Susan Sontag | 2002 | *Three Junes* | Julia Glass |

## Nonfiction

| YEAR | TITLE | AUTHOR |
|------|-------|--------|
| 1950 | *The Life of Ralph Waldo Emerson* | Ralph L. Rusk |
| 1951 | *Herman Melville* | Newton Arvin |
| 1952 | *The Sea Around Us* | Rachel Carson |
| 1953 | *The Course of Empire* | Bernard A. De Voto |
| 1954 | *A Stillness at Appomattox* | Bruce Catton |
| 1955 | *The Measure of Man: On Freedom, Human Values, Survival, and the Modern Temper* | Joseph Wood Krutch |
| 1956 | *American in Italy* | Herbert Kubly |
| 1957 | *Russia Leaves the War* | George F. Kennan |
| 1958 | *The Lion and the Throne: The Life and Times of Sir Edward Coke (1552–1634)* | Catherine Drinker Bowen |
| 1959 | *Mistress to an Age: A Life of Madame de Staël* | J. Christopher Herold |
| 1960 | *James Joyce* | Richard Ellmann |
| 1961 | *The Rise and Fall of the Third Reich: A History of Nazi Germany* | William L. Shirer |
| 1962 | *The City in History: Its Origins, Its Transformations, and Its Prospects* | Lewis Mumford |
| 1963 | *Henry James, Vol. II: The Conquest of London (1870–1881); Vol. III: The Middle Years (1882–1895)* | Leon Edel |
| 1964 | *The Rise of the West: A History of the Human Community*[2] | William H. McNeill |
| 1965 | *The Life of Lenin*[2] | Louis Fischer |
| 1966 | *A Thousand Days: John F. Kennedy in the White House*[2] | Arthur M. Schlesinger, Jr. |
| 1967 | *The Enlightenment: An Interpretation, Vol. I*[2] | Peter Gay |
| 1968 | *Memoirs: 1925–1950*[2] | George F. Kennan |
| 1969 | *White over Black: American Attitudes Toward the Negro, 1550–1812*[2] | Winthrop D. Jordan |
| 1970 | *Huey Long*[2] | T. Harry Williams |
| 1971 | *Roosevelt: The Soldier of Freedom*[2] | James MacGregor Burns |
| 1972 | *Eleanor and Franklin: The Story of Their Relationship, Based on Eleanor Roosevelt's Private Papers*[3] | Joseph P. Lash |
| 1973 | *George Washington, Vol. IV: Anguish and Farewell, 1793–1799*[3] | James Thomas Flexner |
| 1974 | *Macaulay: The Shaping of the Historian*[4] | John Clive |
| 1975 | *The Life of Emily Dickinson*[3] | Richard B. Sewall |
| 1976 | *The Problem of Slavery in the Age of Revolution, 1770–1823*[2] | David Brion Davis |
| 1977 | *Norman Thomas: The Last Idealist*[5] | W.A. Swanberg |
| 1978 | *Samuel Johnson*[5] | W. Jackson Bate |
| 1979 | *Robert Kennedy and His Times*[5] | Arthur M. Schlesinger, Jr. |
| 1980 | *The Right Stuff*[6] | Tom Wolfe |
| 1981 | *China Men*[6] | Maxine Hong Kingston |
| 1982 | *The Soul of a New Machine*[6] | Tracy Kidder |
| 1983 | *China: Alive in the Bitter Sea*[6] | Fox Butterfield |
| 1984 | *Andrew Jackson and the Course of American Democracy, 1833–1845* | Robert V. Remini |
| 1985 | *Common Ground: A Turbulent Decade in the Lives of Three American Families* | J. Anthony Lukas |
| 1986 | *Arctic Dreams* | Barry Lopez |
| 1987 | *The Making of the Atomic Bomb* | Richard Rhodes |
| 1988 | *A Bright Shining Lie: John Paul Vann and America in Vietnam* | Neil Sheehan |
| 1989 | *From Beirut to Jerusalem* | Thomas L. Friedman |
| 1990 | *The House of Morgan: An American Banking Dynasty and the Rise of Modern Finance* | Ron Chernow |
| 1991 | *Freedom* | Orlando Patterson |
| 1992 | *Becoming a Man: Half a Life Story* | Paul Monette |
| 1993 | *United States: Essays, 1952–1992* | Gore Vidal |
| 1994 | *How We Die: Reflections on Life's Final Chapter* | Sherwin B. Nuland |
| 1995 | *The Haunted Land: Facing Europe's Ghosts After Communism* | Tina Rosenberg |
| 1996 | *An American Requiem: God, My Father, and the War That Came Between Us* | James Carroll |
| 1997 | *American Sphinx: The Character of Thomas Jefferson* | Joseph J. Ellis |
| 1998 | *Slaves in the Family* | Edward Ball |
| 1999 | *Embracing Defeat: Japan in the Wake of World War II* | John W. Dower |
| 2000 | *In the Heart of the Sea: The Tragedy of the Whaleship Essex* | Nathaniel Philbrick |
| 2001 | *The Noonday Demon: An Atlas of Depression* | Andrew Solomon |
| 2002 | *Master of the Senate: The Years of Lyndon Johnson* | Robert A. Caro |

# National Book Awards (continued)

## Poetry

| YEAR | TITLE | AUTHOR |
|------|-------|--------|
| 1950 | *Paterson: Book III and Selected Poems* | William Carlos Williams |
| 1951 | *The Auroras of Autumn* | Wallace Stevens |
| 1952 | *Collected Poems* | Marianne Moore |
| 1953 | *Collected Poems, 1917–1952* | Archibald MacLeish |
| 1954 | *Collected Poems* | Conrad Aiken |
| 1955 | *The Collected Poems of Wallace Stevens* | Wallace Stevens |
| 1956 | *The Shield of Achilles* | W.H. Auden |
| 1957 | *Things of This World: Poems* | Richard Wilbur |
| 1958 | *Promises: Poems, 1954–1956* | Robert Penn Warren |
| 1959 | *Words for the Wind: The Collected Verse of Theodore Roethke* | Theodore Roethke |
| 1960 | *Life Studies* | Robert Lowell |
| 1961 | *The Woman at the Washington Zoo* | Randall Jarrell |
| 1962 | *Poems* | Alan Dugan |
| 1963 | *Traveling Through the Dark* | William Stafford |
| 1964 | *Selected Poems* | John Crowe Ransom |
| 1965 | *The Far Field* | Theodore Roethke |
| 1966 | *Buckdancer's Choice: Poems* | James Dickey |
| 1967 | *Nights and Days* | James Merrill |
| 1968 | *The Light Around the Body: Poems* | Robert Bly |
| 1969 | *His Toy, His Dream, His Rest: 308 Dream Songs* | John Berryman |
| 1970 | *The Complete Poems* | Elizabeth Bishop |
| 1971 | *To See, To Take: Poems* | Mona Van Duyn |
| 1972 | *The Collected Poems of Frank O'Hara* | Frank O'Hara |
| 1972 | *Selected Poems* | Howard Moss |
| 1973 | *Collected Poems, 1951–1971* | A.R. Ammons |
| 1974 | *Diving into the Wreck: Poems, 1971–1972* | Adrienne Rich |
| 1974 | *The Fall of America: Poems of These States* | Allen Ginsberg |
| 1975 | *Presentation Piece* | Marilyn Hacker |
| 1976 | *Self-Portrait in a Convex Mirror: Poems* | John Ashbery |
| 1977 | *Collected Poems, 1930–1976* | Richard Eberhart |
| 1978 | *The Collected Poems of Howard Nemerov* | Howard Nemerov |
| 1979 | *Mirabell: Books of Number* | James Merrill |
| 1980 | *Ashes: Poems New & Old* | Philip Levine |
| 1981 | *The Need to Hold Still* | Lisel Mueller |
| 1982 | *Life Supports: New and Collected Poems* | William Bronk |
| 1983 | *Country Music: Selected Early Poems* | Charles Wright |
| 1984 | *Selected Poems* | Galway Kinnell |
| 1985 | *Yin* | Carolyn Kizer |
| 1986 | *The Flying Change* | Henry Taylor |
| 1987 | *Thomas and Beulah* | Rita Dove |
| 1988 | *Partial Accounts: New and Selected Poems* | William Meredith |
| 1989 | *New and Collected Poems* | Richard Wilbur |
| 1990 | *The World Doesn't End* | Charles Simic |
| 1991 | *What Work Is: Poems* | Philip Levine |
| 1992 | *New and Selected Poems* | Mary Oliver |
| 1993 | *Garbage* | A.R. Ammons |
| 1994 | *Worshipful Company of Fletchers: Poems* | James Tate |
| 1995 | *Passing Through: The Later Poems, New and Selected* | Stanley Kunitz |
| 1996 | *Scrambled Eggs & Whiskey: Poems, 1991–1995* | Hayden Carruth |
| 1997 | *Effort at Speech: New and Selected Poems* | William Meredith |
| 1998 | *This Time: New and Selected Poems* | Gerald Stern |
| 1999 | *Vice: New and Selected Poems* | Ai |
| 2000 | *Blessing the Boats: New and Selected Poems, 1988–2000* | Lucille Clifton |
| 2001 | *Poems Seven: New and Complete Poetry* | Alan Dugan |
| 2002 | *In the Next Galaxy* | Ruth Stone |

## Young People's Literature

| YEAR | TITLE | AUTHOR |
|------|-------|--------|
| 1969 | *Journey from Peppermint Street* | Meindert De Jong |
| 1970 | *A Day of Pleasure: Stories of a Boy Growing Up in Warsaw*[7] | Isaac Bashevis Singer |
| 1971 | *The Marvelous Misadventures of Sebastian*[7] | Lloyd Alexander |
| 1972 | *The Slightly Irregular Fire Engine; or, The Hithering Thithering Djinn*[7] | Donald Barthelme |
| 1973 | *The Farthest Shore*[7] | Ursula Le Guin |
| 1974 | *The Court of the Stone Children*[7] | Eleanor Cameron |
| 1975 | *M.C. Higgins, the Great*[7] | Virginia Hamilton |
| 1976 | *Bert Breen's Barn* | Walter D. Edmonds |

# National Book Awards (continued)

## Young People's Literature (continued)

| YEAR | TITLE | AUTHOR |
|------|-------|--------|
| 1977 | *The Master Puppeteer* | Katherine Paterson |
| 1978 | *The View from the Oak: The Private Worlds of Other Creatures* | Judith Kohl & Herbert Kohl |
| 1979 | *The Great Gilly Hopkins* | Katherine Paterson |
| 1980 | *A Gathering of Days: A New England Girl's Journal, 1830–32*[8] | Joan Blos |
| 1981 | *The Night Swimmers*[9] | Betsy Byars |
| 1982 | *Westmark*[9] | Lloyd Alexander |
| 1983 | *Homesick: My Own Story*[9] | Jean Fritz |
| 1996 | *Parrot in the Oven: Mi Vida*[10] | Victor Martinez |
| 1997 | *Dancing on the Edge*[10] | Han Nolan |
| 1998 | *Holes*[10] | Louis Sachar |
| 1999 | *When Zachary Beaver Came to Town*[10] | Kimberly Willis Holt |
| 2000 | *Homeless Bird*[10] | Gloria Whelan |
| 2001 | *True Believer*[10] | Virginia Euwer Wolff |
| 2002 | *The House of the Scorpion*[10] | Nancy Farmer |

[1]Fiction (Hardcover). [2]History and Biography (Nonfiction). [3]Biography. [4]History. [5]Biography and Autobiography. [6]General Nonfiction (Hardcover). [7]Children's Books. [8]Children's Books (Hardcover). [9]Children's Books, Fiction (Hardcover). [10]Young People's Literature.

# The PEN/Faulkner Award for Fiction

Named for William Faulkner and affiliated with the international writers' organization Poets, Playwrights, Editors, Essayists and Novelists (PEN), the PEN/Faulkner Award was founded by writers in 1980 to honor their peers. A panel of fiction writers selects a winning novel or short-story collection and four runners-up. The winning author receives $15,000, and each of the others receives $5,000. PEN/Faulkner Web site: <www.folger.edu/public/pfaulk/>.

| YEAR | TITLE | AUTHOR | YEAR | TITLE | AUTHOR |
|------|-------|--------|------|-------|--------|
| 1981 | *How German Is It?* | Walter Abish | 1992 | *Mao II* | Don Delillo |
| 1982 | *The Chaneysville Incident* | David Bradley | 1993 | *Postcards* | E. Annie Proulx |
| | | | 1994 | *Operation Shylock* | Philip Roth |
| 1983 | *Seaview* | Toby Olson | 1995 | *Snow Falling on Cedars* | David Guterson |
| 1984 | *Sent for You Yesterday* | John Edgar Wideman | 1996 | *Independence Day* | Richard Ford |
| 1985 | *The Barracks Thief* | Tobias Wolff | 1997 | *Women in Their Beds* | Gina Berriault |
| 1986 | *The Old Forest and Other Stories* | Peter Taylor | 1998 | *The Bear Comes Home* | Rafi Zabor |
| | | | 1999 | *The Hours* | Michael Cunningham |
| 1987 | *Soldiers in Hiding* | Richard Wiley | 2000 | *Waiting* | Ha Jin |
| 1988 | *World's End* | T. Coraghessan Boyle | 2001 | *The Human Stain* | Philip Roth |
| 1989 | *Dusk and Other Stories* | James Salter | 2002 | *Bel Canto* | Ann Patchett |
| 1990 | *Billy Bathgate* | E.L. Doctorow | 2003 | *The Caprices* | Sabina Murray |
| 1991 | *Philadelphia Fire* | John Edgar Wideman | 2004 | *scheduled to be announced in May* | |

**Did you know?** As the psychological novel developed in the 20th century, some writers attempted to capture the total flow of their characters' consciousness, rather than limit themselves to rational thoughts. These writers incorporated snatches of incoherent thought, ungrammatical constructions, and free associations of ideas, images, and words at the pre-speech level. The term for this technique is stream of consciousness.

# Coretta Scott King Award

Established in 1970, the Coretta Scott King Award honors outstanding African American authors and illustrators of books for young people. The books, which may be fiction or nonfiction, must be original works that portray some aspect of the black experience. In 1982 the award came under the aegis of the American Library Association. Prize: Citation, honorarium, and encyclopedia set.

Coretta Scott King Award Web site: <www.ala.org/srrt/csking>.

**2002**
author: Mildred D. Taylor, *The Land*
illustrator: Jerry Pinkney, *Goin' Someplace Special*

**2003**
author: Nikki Grimes, *Bronx Masquerade*
illustrator: E.B. Lewis, *Talkin' About Bessie: The Story of Aviator Elizabeth Coleman*
**2004** *prizes scheduled to be awarded in January*

# Newbery Medal Winners, 1922–2003

The American Library Association (ALA) began awarding the John Newbery Medal in 1922 to the author of the most distinguished American children's book of the previous year, as judged by the ALA's Children's Librarians' Section (now called the Association for Library Service to Children). Established at the suggestion of Frederic G. Melcher of the R.R. Bowker Publishing Company, the award is named for John Newbery, the 18th-century English publisher who was among the first to publish books exclusively for children. Prize: inscribed bronze medal.
ALA Newbery Medal Web site: <www.ala.org/alsc/newbery.html>.

| YEAR | TITLE | AUTHOR |
|---|---|---|
| 1922 | The Story of Mankind | Hendrik Willem van Loon |
| 1923 | The Voyages of Doctor Dolittle | Hugh Lofting |
| 1924 | The Dark Frigate | Charles Hawes |
| 1925 | Tales from Silver Lands | Charles Finger |
| 1926 | Shen of the Sea | Arthur Bowie Chrisman |
| 1927 | Smoky, the Cowhorse | Will James |
| 1928 | Gay Neck, the Story of a Pigeon | Dhan Gopal Mukerji |
| 1929 | The Trumpeter of Krakow | Eric P. Kelly |
| 1930 | Hitty, Her First Hundred Years | Rachel Field |
| 1931 | The Cat Who Went to Heaven | Elizabeth Coatsworth |
| 1932 | Waterless Mountain | Laura Adams Armer |
| 1933 | Young Fu of the Upper Yangtze | Elizabeth Lewis |
| 1934 | Invincible Louisa: The Story of the Author of Little Women | Cornelia Meigs |
| 1935 | Dobry | Monica Shannon |
| 1936 | Caddie Woodlawn | Carol Ryrie Brink |
| 1937 | Roller Skates | Ruth Sawyer |
| 1938 | The White Stag | Kate Seredy |
| 1939 | Thimble Summer | Elizabeth Enright |
| 1940 | Daniel Boone | James Daugherty |
| 1941 | Call It Courage | Armstrong Sperry |
| 1942 | The Matchlock Gun | Walter Edmonds |
| 1943 | Adam of the Road | Elizabeth Janet Gray |
| 1944 | Johnny Tremain | Esther Forbes |
| 1945 | Rabbit Hill | Robert Lawson |
| 1946 | Strawberry Girl | Lois Lenski |
| 1947 | Miss Hickory | Carolyn Sherwin Bailey |
| 1948 | The Twenty-One Balloons | William Pène du Bois |
| 1949 | King of the Wind | Marguerite Henry |
| 1950 | The Door in the Wall | Marguerite de Angeli |
| 1951 | Amos Fortune, Free Man | Elizabeth Yates |
| 1952 | Ginger Pye | Eleanor Estes |
| 1953 | Secret of the Andes | Ann Nolan Clark |
| 1954 | ...And Now Miguel | Joseph Krumgold |
| 1955 | The Wheel on the School | Meindert DeJong |
| 1956 | Carry On, Mr. Bowditch | Jean Lee Latham |
| 1957 | Miracles on Maple Hill | Virginia Sorenson |
| 1958 | Rifles for Watie | Harold Keith |
| 1959 | The Witch of Blackbird Pond | Elizabeth George Speare |
| 1960 | Onion John | Joseph Krumgold |
| 1961 | Island of the Blue Dolphins | Scott O'Dell |
| 1962 | The Bronze Bow | Elizabeth George Speare |
| 1963 | A Wrinkle in Time | Madeleine L'Engle |
| 1964 | It's Like This, Cat | Emily Neville |

| YEAR | TITLE | AUTHOR |
|---|---|---|
| 1965 | Shadow of a Bull | Maia Wojciechowska |
| 1966 | I, Juan de Pareja | Elizabeth Borton de Trevino |
| 1967 | Up a Road Slowly | Irene Hunt |
| 1968 | From the Mixed-Up Files of Mrs. Basil E. Frankweiler | E.L. Konigsburg |
| 1969 | The High King | Lloyd Alexander |
| 1970 | Sounder | William H. Armstrong |
| 1971 | Summer of the Swans | Betsy Byars |
| 1972 | Mrs. Frisby and the Rats of NIMH | Robert C. O'Brien |
| 1973 | Julie of the Wolves | Jean Craighead George |
| 1974 | The Slave Dancer | Paula Fox |
| 1975 | M. C. Higgins, the Great | Virginia Hamilton |
| 1976 | The Grey King | Susan Cooper |
| 1977 | Roll of Thunder, Hear My Cry | Mildred D. Taylor |
| 1978 | Bridge to Terabithia | Katherine Paterson |
| 1979 | The Westing Game | Ellen Raskin |
| 1980 | A Gathering of Days: A New England Girl's Journal, 1830–1832 | Joan W. Blos |
| 1981 | Jacob Have I Loved | Katherine Paterson |
| 1982 | A Visit to William Blake's Inn: Poems for Innocent and Experienced Travelers | Nancy Willard |
| 1983 | Dicey's Song | Cynthia Voigt |
| 1984 | Dear Mr. Henshaw | Beverly Cleary |
| 1985 | The Hero and the Crown | Robin McKinley |
| 1986 | Sarah, Plain and Tall | Patricia MacLachlan |
| 1987 | The Whipping Boy | Sid Fleischman |
| 1988 | Lincoln: A Photo-biography | Russell Freedman |
| 1989 | Joyful Noise: Poems for Two Voices | Paul Fleischman |
| 1990 | Number the Stars | Lois Lowry |
| 1991 | Maniac Magee | Jerry Spinelli |
| 1992 | Shiloh | Phyllis Reynolds Naylor |
| 1993 | Missing May | Cynthia Rylant |
| 1994 | The Giver | Lois Lowry |
| 1995 | Walk Two Moons | Sharon Creech |
| 1996 | The Midwife's Apprentice | Karen Cushman |
| 1997 | The View from Saturday | E.L. Konigsburg |
| 1998 | Out of the Dust | Karen Hesse |
| 1999 | Holes | Louis Sachar |
| 2000 | Bud, Not Buddy | Christopher Paul Curtis |
| 2001 | A Year Down Yonder | Richard Peck |
| 2002 | A Single Shard | Linda Sue Park |
| 2003 | Crispin: The Cross of Lead | Avi |

# Caldecott Medal Winners, 1938–2003

The American Library Association (ALA) awards the Caldecott Medal annually to "the artist of the most distinguished American picture book for children." It was established by the ALA in 1938 on the suggestion of Frederic G. Melcher, chairman of the board of the R.R. Bowker Publishing Company, and named for the 19th-century English illustrator Randolph Calde-cott. If the author/reteller/translator/editor is other than the illustrator, that person's name appears in parentheses after the illustrator. Prize: inscribed bronze medal.

ALA Caldecott Medal Web site: <www.ala.org/alsc/caldecott.html>.

| YEAR | TITLE | ILLUSTRATOR |
|---|---|---|
| 1938 | Animals of the Bible: A Picture Book | Dorothy P. Lathrop (Helen Dean Fish) |
| 1939 | Mei Li | Thomas Handforth |
| 1940 | Abraham Lincoln | Ingri and Edgar Parin d'Aulaire |
| 1941 | They Were Strong and Good | Robert Lawson |
| 1942 | Make Way for Ducklings | Robert McCloskey |
| 1943 | The Little House | Virginia Lee Burton |
| 1944 | Many Moons | Louis Slobodkin (James Thurber) |
| 1945 | Prayer for a Child | Elizabeth Orton Jones (Rachel Field) |
| 1946 | The Rooster Crows | Maude and Miska Petersham |
| 1947 | The Little Island | Leonard Weisgard (Golden MacDonald, pseud. [Margaret Wise Brown]) |
| 1948 | White Snow, Bright Snow | Roger Duvoisin (Alvin Tresselt) |
| 1949 | The Big Snow | Berta and Elmer Hader |
| 1950 | Song of the Swallows | Leo Politi |
| 1951 | The Egg Tree | Katherine Milhous |
| 1952 | Finders Keepers | Nicolas, pseud.; Nicholas Mordvinoff (Will, pseud. [William Lipkind]) |
| 1953 | The Biggest Bear | Lynd Ward |
| 1954 | Madeline's Rescue | Ludwig Bemelmans |
| 1955 | Cinderella, or the Little Glass Slipper | Marcia Brown (translated from Charles Perrault by Marcia Brown) |
| 1956 | Frog Went A-Courtin' | Feodor Rojankovsky (John Langstaff) |
| 1957 | A Tree Is Nice | Marc Simont (Janice Udry) |
| 1958 | Time of Wonder | Robert McCloskey |
| 1959 | Chanticleer and the Fox | Barbara Cooney (adapted from Chaucer's Canterbury Tales by Barbara Cooney) |
| 1960 | Nine Days to Christmas | Marie Hall Ets (Marie Hall Ets and Aurora Labastida) |
| 1961 | Baboushka and the Three Kings | Nicolas Sidjakov (Ruth Robbins) |
| 1962 | Once a Mouse | Marcia Brown |
| 1963 | The Snowy Day | Ezra Jack Keats |
| 1964 | Where the Wild Things Are | Maurice Sendak |
| 1965 | May I Bring a Friend? | Beni Montresor (Beatrice Schenk de Regniers) |
| 1966 | Always Room for One More | Nonny Hogrogian (Sorche Nic Leodhas, pseud. [Leclair Alger]) |
| 1967 | Sam, Bangs & Moonshine | Evaline Ness |
| 1968 | Drummer Hoff | Ed Emberley (Barbara Emberley) |
| 1969 | The Fool of the World and the Flying Ship | Uri Shulevitz (Arthur Ransome) |
| 1970 | Sylvester and the Magic Pebble | William Steig |
| 1971 | A Story A Story | Gail E. Haley |
| 1972 | One Fine Day | Nonny Hogrogian |
| 1973 | The Funny Little Woman | Blair Lent (Arlene Mosel) |
| 1974 | Duffy and the Devil | Margot Zemach (Harve Zemach) |
| 1975 | Arrow to the Sun | Gerald McDermott |
| 1976 | Why Mosquitoes Buzz in People's Ears | Leo and Diane Dillon (Verna Aardema) |
| 1977 | Ashanti to Zulu: African Traditions | Leo and Diane Dillon (Margaret Musgrove) |
| 1978 | Noah's Ark | Peter Spier |
| 1979 | The Girl Who Loved Wild Horses | Paul Goble |
| 1980 | Ox-Cart Man | Barbara Cooney (Donald Hall) |
| 1981 | Fables | Arnold Lobel |
| 1982 | Jumanji | Chris Van Allsburg |
| 1983 | Shadow | Marcia Brown (also translator of original French text by Blaise Cendrars) |
| 1984 | The Glorious Flight: Across the Channel with Louis Blériot | Alice and Martin Provensen |
| 1985 | Saint George and the Dragon | Trina Schart Hyman (Margaret Hodges) |
| 1986 | The Polar Express | Chris Van Allsburg |
| 1987 | Hey, Al | Richard Egielski (Arthur Yorinks) |
| 1988 | Owl Moon | John Schoenherr (Jane Yolen) |
| 1989 | Song and Dance Man | Stephen Gammell (Karen Ackerman) |

## Caldecott Medal Winners, 1938–2003 (continued)

| YEAR | TITLE | ILLUSTRATOR |
|------|-------|-------------|
| 1990 | Lon Po Po: A Red-Riding Hood Story from China | Ed Young |
| 1991 | Black and White | David Macaulay |
| 1992 | Tuesday | David Wiesner |
| 1993 | Mirette on the High Wire | Emily Arnold McCully |
| 1994 | Grandfather's Journey | Allen Say (Walter Lorraine) |
| 1995 | Smoky Night | David Diaz (Eve Bunting) |
| 1996 | Officer Buckle and Gloria | Peggy Rathmann |
| 1997 | Golem | David Wisniewski |
| 1998 | Rapunzel | Paul O. Zelinsky |
| 1999 | Snowflake Bentley | Mary Azarian (Jacqueline Briggs Martin) |
| 2000 | Joseph Had a Little Overcoat | Simms Taback |
| 2001 | So You Want to Be President? | David Small (Judith St. George) |
| 2002 | The Three Pigs | David Wiesner |
| 2003 | My Friend Rabbit | Eric Rohmann |

## The Man Booker Prize

Awarded to the best full-length novel of the year written by a citizen of the Commonwealth or the Republic of Ireland and published in the UK between 1 October and 30 September. Prize: £20,000 (about $28,000); each shortlisted author receives £1000 (about $1,400). In 1993, Salman Rushdie was awarded the Booker of Bookers, a special award to mark 25 years of the Booker Prize, for *Midnight's Children*.

Booker Prize Web site: <www.bookerprize.co.uk>.

| YEAR | TITLE | AUTHOR |
|------|-------|--------|
| 1969 | Something to Answer For | P. H. Newby |
| 1970 | The Elected Member | Bernice Rubens |
| 1971 | In a Free State | V. S. Naipaul |
| 1972 | G. | John Berger |
| 1973 | The Siege of Krishnapur | J. G. Farrell |
| 1974 | The Conservationist | Nadine Gordimer |
| 1974 | Holiday | Stanley Middleton |
| 1975 | Heat and Dust | Ruth Prawer Jhabvala |
| 1976 | Saville | David Storey |
| 1977 | Staying On | Paul Scott |
| 1978 | The Sea, The Sea | Iris Murdoch |
| 1979 | Offshore | Penelope Fitzgerald |
| 1980 | Rites of Passage | William Golding |
| 1981 | Midnight's Children | Salman Rushdie |
| 1982 | Schindler's Ark | Thomas Keneally |
| 1983 | Life and Times of Michael K | J. M. Coetzee |
| 1984 | Hotel du Lac | Anita Brookner |
| 1985 | The Bone People | Keri Hulme |
| 1986 | The Old Devils | Kingsley Amis |
| 1987 | Moon Tiger | Penelope Lively |
| 1988 | Oscar and Lucinda | Peter Carey |
| 1989 | The Remains of the Day | Kazuo Ishiguro |
| 1990 | Possession | A. S. Byatt |
| 1991 | The Famished Road | Ben Okri |
| 1992 | The English Patient | Michael Ondaatje |
| 1992 | Sacred Hunger | Barry Unsworth |
| 1993 | Paddy Clarke Ha Ha Ha | Roddy Doyle |
| 1994 | How Late It Was, How Late | James Kelman |
| 1995 | The Ghost Road | Pat Barker |
| 1996 | Last Orders | Graham Swift |
| 1997 | The God of Small Things | Arundhati Roy |
| 1998 | Amsterdam | Ian McEwan |
| 1999 | Disgrace | J. M. Coetzee |
| 2000 | The Blind Assassin | Margaret Atwood |
| 2001 | True History of the Kelly Gang | Peter Carey |
| 2002 | Life of Pi | Yann Martel |
| 2003 | scheduled to be awarded mid-October | |

## The Whitbread Book Awards

The Whitbread Book Awards were inaugurated in 1971. Since 1985, Whitbread Book Awards have been given in five categories: Novel, First Novel, Biography, Poetry, and Children's. From these a panel of judges chooses one overall winner—the Whitbread Book of the Year. The total prize fund is £50,000 (about $78,000): each of the category award winners receives £5,000 (about $7,800), and the Book of the Year winner receives an additional £25,000 (about $39,000).

This list includes Novel award winners from 1971 to 1984 and Book of the Year winners from 1985 to 2001.

Whitbread Book Awards Web site: <www.whitbread-bookawards.co.uk>.

| YEAR | TITLE | AUTHOR |
|------|-------|--------|
| 1971 | The Destiny Waltz | Gerda Charles |
| 1972 | The Bird of Night | Susan Hill |
| 1973 | The Chip-Chip Gatherers | Shiva Naipaul |
| 1974 | The Sacred and Profane Love Machine | Iris Murdoch |
| 1975 | Docherty | William McIlvanney |
| 1976 | The Children of Dynmouth | William Trevor |
| 1977 | Injury Time | Beryl Bainbridge |
| 1978 | Picture Palace | Paul Theroux |
| 1979 | The Old Jest | Jennifer Johnston |
| 1980 | How Far Can You Go? | David Lodge |
| 1981 | Silver's City | Maurice Leitch |

## The Whitbread Book Awards (continued)

| YEAR | TITLE | AUTHOR | YEAR | TITLE | AUTHOR |
|---|---|---|---|---|---|
| 1982 | Young Shoulders | John Wain | 1992 | Swing Hammer Swing! | Jeff Torrington |
| 1983 | Fools of Fortune | William Trevor | 1993 | Theory of War | Joan Brady |
| 1984 | Kruger's Alp | Christopher Hope | 1994 | Felicia's Journey | William Trevor |
| 1985 | Elegies | Douglas Dunn | 1995 | Behind the Scenes at the Museum | Kate Atkinson |
| 1986 | An Artist of the Floating World | Kazuo Ishiguro | 1996 | The Spirit Level | Seamus Heaney |
| 1987 | Under the Eye of the Clock | Christopher Nolan | 1997 | Tales from Ovid | Ted Hughes |
| 1988 | The Comforts of Madness | Paul Sayer | 1998 | Birthday Letters | Ted Hughes |
| 1989 | Coleridge: Early Visions | Richard Holmes | 1999 | Beowulf | Seamus Heaney |
| 1990 | Hopeful Monsters | Nicholas Mosley | 2000 | English Passengers | Matthew Kneale |
| 1991 | A Life of Picasso | John Richardson | 2001 | The Amber Spyglass | Philip Pullman |
| | | | 2002 | Samuel Pepys: The Unequalled Self | Claire Tomalin |

## The Orange Prize

Awarded to a work of published fiction written in English by a woman and published in the United Kingdom between 1 April and 31 March. Prize: £30,000 (about $42,500) and a bronze figurine called "The Bessie."

Orange Prize Web site: <www.orangeprize.co.uk>.

| YEAR | TITLE | AUTHOR | YEAR | TITLE | AUTHOR |
|---|---|---|---|---|---|
| 1996 | A Spell of Winter | Helen Dunmore | 2000 | When I Lived in Modern Times | Linda Grant |
| 1997 | Fugitive Pieces | Anne Michaels | 2001 | The Idea of Perfection | Kate Grenville |
| 1998 | Larry's Party | Carol Shields | 2002 | Bel Canto | Ann Patchett |
| 1999 | A Crime in the Neighborhood | Suzanne Berne | 2003 | Property | Valerie Martin |

## Prix Goncourt

The Prix de l'Académie Goncourt was first awarded in 1903 from the estate of the brothers and French literary figures Edmond Huot de Goncourt (1822–1896) and Jules Huot de Goncourt (1830–1870) for a work of contemporary prose in French. Prize: €10 (about $10.60). An additional prize is awarded for the best work of new fiction.

| YEAR | TITLE | AUTHOR | YEAR | TITLE | AUTHOR |
|---|---|---|---|---|---|
| 1903 | Force ennemie | John Antoine Nau | 1925 | Raboliot | Maurice Genevoix |
| 1904 | La Maternelle | Léon Frapié | 1926 | Le Supplice de Phèdre | Henry Deberly |
| 1905 | Les Civilisés | Claude Farrère | 1927 | Latitude nord | Maurice Bedel |
| 1906 | Dingley, l'illustre écrivain | Jérôme and Jean Tharaud | 1928 | Un Homme se penche sur son passé | Maurice Constantin Weyer |
| 1907 | Le Rouet d'ivoire | Emile Moselly | 1929 | L'Ordre | Marcel Arland |
| 1908 | Ecrit sur l'eau | Francis de Miomandre | 1930 | Malaisie | Henri Fauconnier |
| 1909 | En France | Marius & Ary Leblond | 1931 | Mal d'amour | Jean Fayard |
| | | | 1932 | Les Loups | Guy Mazeline |
| 1910 | De Goupil à Margot | Louis Pergaud | 1933 | La Condition humaine | André Malraux |
| 1911 | Monsieur des Lourdines | Alphonse de Chateaubriant | 1934 | Capitaine Conan | Roger Vercel |
| 1912 | Les Filles de la pluie | André Savignon | 1935 | Sang et lumières | Joseph Peyré |
| 1913 | Le Peuple de la mer | Marc Elder | 1936 | L'Empreinte de Dieu | Maxence Van Der Meersch |
| 1914 | L'Appel du sol | Adrien Bertrand | 1937 | Faux passeports | Charles Plisnier |
| 1915 | Gaspard | René Benjamin | 1938 | L'Araignée | Henri Troyat |
| 1916 | Le Feu | Henri Barbusse | 1939 | Les Enfants gâtés | Philippe Hériat |
| 1917 | La Flamme au poing | Henri Malherbe | 1940 | Les Grandes Vacances | Francis Ambrière |
| 1918 | Civilisation | Georges Duhamel | 1941 | Le Vent de mars | Henri Pourrat |
| 1919 | A l'ombre des jeunes filles en fleur | Marcel Proust | 1942 | Pareil à des enfants | Bernard Marc |
| | | | 1943 | Passage de l'homme | Marius Grout |
| 1920 | Nene | Ernest Perochon | 1944 | Le Premier accroc coûte 200 Francs | Elsa Triolet |
| 1921 | Batouala | René Maran | 1945 | Mon village à l'heure allemande | Jean-Louis Bory |
| 1922 | Le Vitriol de la lune | Henri Béraud | | | |
| 1922 | Le Martyre de l'obèse | Henri Béraud | 1946 | Histoire d'un fait divers | Jean-Jacques Gautier |
| 1923 | Rabevel; ou, le mal des ardents | Lucien Fabré | 1947 | Les Forêts de la nuit | Jean-Louis Curtis |
| 1924 | Le Chèvrefeuille, le Purgatoire, le Chapitre XIII | Thierry Sandre | 1948 | Les Grandes Familles | Maurice Druon |
| | | | 1949 | Week-end à Zuydcoote | Robert Merle |
| | | | 1950 | Les Jeux Sauvages | Paul Colin |

# Prix Goncourt (continued)

| YEAR | TITLE | AUTHOR |
|------|-------|--------|
| 1951 | *Le Rivage des Syrtes* | Julien Gracq |
| 1952 | *Léon Morin, prêtre* | Béatrice Beck |
| 1953 | *Les Bêtes* | Pierre Gascar |
| 1954 | *Mandarins* | Simone de Beauvoir |
| 1955 | *Les Eaux mêlées* | Roger Ikor |
| 1956 | *Les Racines du ciel* | Romain Gary |
| 1957 | *La Loi* | Roger Vailland |
| 1958 | *Saint Germain; ou, la négociation* | Francis Walder |
| 1959 | *Le Dernier des justes* | André Schwartz-Bart |
| 1960 | *Dieu est né en exil* | Vintila Horia |
| 1961 | *La Pitié de Dieu* | Jean Cau |
| 1962 | *Les Bagages de sable* | Anna Langfus |
| 1963 | *Quand la mer se retire* | Armand Lanoux |
| 1964 | *L'État sauvage* | Georges Conchon |
| 1965 | *L'Adoration* | Jacques Borel |
| 1966 | *Oublier Palerme* | Edmonde Charles-Roux |
| 1967 | *La Marge* | André-Pierre de Mandiargues |
| 1968 | *Les Fruits de l'hiver* | Bernard Clavel |
| 1969 | *Creezy* | Félicien Marceau |
| 1970 | *Le Roi des Aulnes* | Michel Tournier |
| 1971 | *Les Bêtises* | Jacques Laurent |
| 1972 | *L'Épervier de Maheux* | Jean Carrière |
| 1973 | *L'Ogre* | Jacques Chessex |
| 1974 | *La Dentellière* | Pascal Lainé |
| 1975 | *La Vie devant soi* | Emile Ajar |
| 1976 | *Les Flamboyants* | Patrick Grainville |
| 1977 | *John l'enfer* | Didier Decoin |
| 1978 | *Rue des boutiques obscures* | Patrick Modiano |
| 1979 | *Pélagie la charrette* | Antonine Maillet |

| YEAR | TITLE | AUTHOR |
|------|-------|--------|
| 1980 | *Le Jardin d'acclimatation* | Yves Navarre |
| 1981 | *Anne Marie* | Lucien Bodard |
| 1982 | *Dans la main de l'ange* | Dominique Fernandez |
| 1983 | *Les Égarés* | Frédérick Tristan |
| 1984 | *L'Amant* | Marguerite Duras |
| 1985 | *Les Noces barbares* | Yann Queffélec |
| 1986 | *Valet de nuit* | Michel Host |
| 1987 | *La Nuit sacrée* | Tahar Ben Jelloun |
| 1988 | *L'Exposition coloniale* | Erik Orsenna |
| 1989 | *Un Grand Pas vers le Bon Dieu* | Jean Vautrin |
| 1990 | *Les Champs d'honneur* | Jean Rouaud |
| 1991 | *Les Filles du calvaire* | Pierre Combescot |
| 1992 | *Texaco* | Patrick Chamoiseau |
| 1993 | *La Rocher de Tanios* | Amin Maalouf |
| 1994 | *Un Aller simple* | Didier Van Cauwelaert |
| 1995 | *Le Testament français* | Andreï Makine |
| 1996 | *Le Chasseur Zéro* | Pascale Roze |
| 1997 | *La Bataille* | Patrick Rambaud |
| 1998 | *Confidence pour confidence* | Paule Constant |
| 1999 | *Je m'en vais* | Jean Echenoz |
| 2000 | *Ingrid Caven* | Jean-Jacques Schuhl |
| 2001 | *Rouge Brésil* | Jean-Christophe Rufin |
| 2002 | *Les Ombres errantes* | Pascal Quignard |
| 2003 | scheduled to be announced in November | |

## Premio Cervantes, the Cervantes Prize for Hispanic Literature

The Spanish Ministry of Education, Culture and Sport sponsors the annual prize, which carries an award of €100,000 (about $110,000). Cervantes Prize Web site: <http://www.terra.es/cultura/premiocervantes>.

| YEAR | AUTHOR |
|------|--------|
| 1976 | Jorge Guillén |
| 1977 | Alejo Carpentier |
| 1978 | Dámaso Alonso |
| 1979 | Jorge Luis Borges and Gerardo Diego |
| 1980 | Juan Carlos Onetti |
| 1981 | Octavio Paz |
| 1982 | Luis Rosales |
| 1983 | Rafael Alberti |
| 1984 | Ernesto Sábato |
| 1985 | Juan Rulfo |
| 1986 | Antonio Buero Vallejo |
| 1987 | Carlos Fuentes |
| 1988 | María Zambrano |
| 1989 | Augusto Roa Bastos |

| YEAR | AUTHOR |
|------|--------|
| 1990 | Adolfo Bioy Casares |
| 1991 | Francisco Ayala |
| 1992 | Dulce María Loynaz |
| 1993 | Miguel Delibes |
| 1994 | Mario Vargas Llosa |
| 1995 | Camilo José Cela |
| 1996 | José García Nieto |
| 1997 | Guillermo Cabrera Infante |
| 1998 | José Hierro |
| 1999 | Jorge Edwards |
| 2000 | Francisco Umbral |
| 2001 | Álvaro Mutis |
| 2002 | José Jiménez Lozano |
| 2003 | scheduled to be awarded in April 2004 |

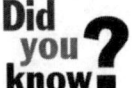

**Did you know?** It has been speculated that when King James I of England hired 54 of the best writers and scholars in the country for a new English version of the Bible in 1604, William Shakespeare might have been among them. Although there is no conclusive evidence for the Bard's participation in the project, it is nevertheless intriguing that the 46th word of the 46th Psalm is "shake," and the 46th word from the end of the Psalm is "spear." Shakespeare, who was fond of cryptograms, was 46 years old at the time the version was completed. This is probably pure coincidence, however, as earlier English translations of the Psalm are very similar.

## The Jerusalem Prize

The municipality of Jerusalem awards this prize at the biennial Jerusalem International Book Fair to a writer whose work explores the freedom of the individual in society. Prize: $10,000. Jerusalem Prize Web site: <www.jerusalembookfair.com>.

| YEAR | AUTHOR | COUNTRY | YEAR | AUTHOR | COUNTRY |
|------|--------|---------|------|--------|---------|
| 1963 | Bertrand Russell | United Kingdom | 1985 | Milan Kundera | France |
| 1965 | Max Frisch | Switzerland | 1987 | J.M. Coetzee | South Africa |
| 1967 | André Schwarz-Bart | France | 1989 | Ernesto Sábato | Argentina |
| 1969 | Ignazio Silone | Italy | 1991 | Zbigniew Herbert | France |
| 1971 | Jorge Luis Borges | Argentina | 1993 | Stefan Heym | Germany |
| 1973 | Eugène Ionesco | France | 1995 | Mario Vargas Llosa | Peru |
| 1975 | Simone de Beauvoir | France | 1997 | Jorge Semprun | Spain |
| 1977 | Octavio Paz | Mexico | 1999 | Don DeLillo | United States |
| 1979 | Sir Isaiah Berlin | United Kingdom | 2001 | Susan Sontag | United States |
| 1981 | Graham Greene | United Kingdom | 2003 | Arthur Miller | United States |
| 1983 | V.S. Naipaul | United Kingdom | | | |

## T.S. Eliot Prize

*Great Britain's Poetry Book Society awards the T.S. Eliot Prize to the best new collection of poetry published in the UK or the Republic of Ireland during the preceding year. The prize is £10,000 (about $15,000).*

| YEAR | WORK | AUTHOR | COUNTRY |
|------|------|--------|---------|
| 1993 | *First Language* | Ciaran Carson | Ireland |
| 1994 | *The Annals of Chile* | Paul Muldoon | Northern Ireland |
| 1995 | *My Alexandria* | Mark Doty | United States |
| 1996 | *Sub-Human Redneck Poems* | Les Murray | Australia |
| 1997 | *God's Gift to Women* | Don Paterson | United Kingdom |
| 1998 | *Birthday Letters* | Ted Hughes | United Kingdom |
| 1999 | *Billy's Rain* | Hugo Williams | United Kingdom |
| 2000 | *The Weather in Japan* | Michael Longley | Northern Ireland |
| 2001 | *The Beauty of the Husband* | Anne Carson | Canada |
| 2002 | *Dart* | Alice Oswald | United Kingdom |
| 2003 | *to be awarded in January 2004* | | |

## The Bollingen Prize in Poetry

The Bollingen Prize in Poetry is awarded biennially to "the American poet whose work, in the opinion of the Committee of Award, represents the highest achievement in the field of American poetry during the preceding two year period." The Committee considers published work, particularly work published during the preceding two year period, although the Committee may consider prior achievement. Former winners of the prize are not eligible. Award amount: $50,000.

| YEAR | POET | YEAR | POET |
|------|------|------|------|
| 1949 | Wallace Stevens | 1971 | Richard Wilbur |
| 1950 | John Crowe Ransom | | Mona Van Duyn |
| 1951 | Marianne Moore | 1973 | James Merrill |
| 1952 | Archibald MacLeish | 1975 | A.R. Ammons |
| | William Carlos Williams | 1977 | David Ignatow |
| 1953 | W.H. Auden | 1979 | W.S. Merwin |
| 1954 | Léonie Adams | 1981 | May Swenson |
| | Louise Bogan | | Howard Nemerov |
| 1955 | Conrad Aiken | 1983 | Anthony Hecht |
| 1956 | Allen Tate | | John Hollander |
| 1957 | E.E. Cummings | 1985 | John Ashbery |
| 1958 | Theodore Roethke | | Fred Chappell |
| 1959 | Delmore Schwartz | 1987 | Stanley Kunitz |
| 1960 | Yvor Winters | 1989 | Edgar Bowers |
| 1961 | Richard Eberhart | 1991 | Laura (Riding) Jackson |
| | John Hall Wheelock | | Donald Justice |
| 1963 | Robert Frost | 1993 | Mark Strand |
| 1965 | Horace Gregory | 1995 | Kenneth Koch |
| 1967 | Robert Penn Warren | 1997 | Gary Snyder |
| 1969 | John Berryman | 1999 | Robert Creeley |
| | Karl Shapiro | 2001 | Louise Glück |
| | | 2003 | Adrienne Rich |

## Bestselling Fiction (Hardcover), 2002

| | TITLE (PUBLISHER) | AUTHOR |
|---|---|---|
| 1 | *The Summons* (Doubleday) | John Grisham |
| 2 | *Red Rabbit* (Putnam) | Tom Clancy |
| 3 | *The Remnant (Left Behind #10)* (Tyndale House) | Tim LaHaye and Jerry B. Jenkins |
| 4 | *The Lovely Bones* (Little, Brown & Company) | Alice Sebold |
| 5 | *Prey* (HarperCollins) | Michael Crichton |
| 6 | *Skipping Christmas* (Doubleday) | John Grisham |
| 7 | *The Shelters of Stone* (Crown) | Jean M. Auel |
| 8 | *Four Blind Mice* (Little, Brown & Company) | James Patterson |
| 9 | *Everything's Eventual* (Scribner) | Stephen King |
| 10 | *The Nanny Diaries* (St. Martin's) | Nicola Kraus and Emma McLaughlin |

*Source:* Publisher's Weekly.

## Bestselling Nonfiction (Hardcover), 2002

| | TITLE (PUBLISHER) | AUTHOR |
|---|---|---|
| 1 | *Self Matters* (Simon & Schuster) | Phillip C. McGraw |
| 2 | *A Life God Rewards* (Multnomah) | Bruce Wilkinson with David Kopp |
| 3 | *Let's Roll!* (Tyndale House) | Lisa Beamer with Ken Abraham |
| 4 | *Guinness World Records 2003* (Guinness World Records Ltd.) | Claire Folkard (ed.) |
| 5 | *Who Moved My Cheese?* (Putnam) | Spencer Johnson |
| 6 | *Leadership* (Miramax) | Rudolph W. Giuliani with Ken Kurson |
| 7 | *The Prayer of Jabez for Women* (Multnomah) | Darlene Wilkinson |
| 8 | *Bush at War* (Simon & Schuster) | Bob Woodward |
| 9 | *Portrait of a Killer* (Putnam) | Patricia Cornwell |
| 10 | *Body for Life* (HarperCollins) | Bill Phillips and Michael D'Orso |

*Source:* Publisher's Weekly.

# Architecture

## Pritzker Architecture Prize

*The Pritzker Prize, awarded by the Hyatt Foundation since 1979, is given to an outstanding living architect for built work. Prize amount: $100,000. Web site: <www.pritzkerprize.com>.*

| YEAR | NAME | COUNTRY | YEAR | NAME | COUNTRY |
|---|---|---|---|---|---|
| 1979 | Philip Johnson | United States | 1992 | Alvaro Siza | Portugal |
| 1980 | Luis Barragan | Mexico | 1993 | Fumihiko Maki | Japan |
| 1981 | James Stirling | Great Britain | 1994 | Christian de | France |
| 1982 | Kevin Roche | United States | | Portzamparc | |
| 1983 | Ieoh Ming Pei | United States | 1995 | Tadao Ando | Japan |
| 1984 | Richard Meier | United States | 1996 | Rafael Moneo | Spain |
| 1985 | Hans Hollein | Austria | 1997 | Sverre Fehn | Norway |
| 1986 | Gottfried Boehm | West Germany | 1998 | Renzo Piano | Italy |
| 1987 | Kenzo Tange | Japan | 1999 | Sir Norman Foster | Great Britain |
| 1988 | Gordon Bunshaft | United States | 2000 | Rem Koolhaas | The Netherlands |
| | Oscar Niemeyer | Brazil | 2001 | Jacques Herzog | Switzerland |
| 1989 | Frank O. Gehry | United States | | Pierre de Meuron | Switzerland |
| 1990 | Aldo Rossi | Italy | 2002 | Glenn Murcutt | Australia |
| 1991 | Robert Venturi | United States | 2003 | Jørn Utzon | Denmark |

## AIA Gold Medal

*The American Institute of Architects awards the gold medal for an outstanding body of work.*

| YEAR | NAME | YEAR | NAME | YEAR | NAME |
|---|---|---|---|---|---|
| 1907 | Sir Aston Webb | 1925 | Sir Edwin L. Lutyens | 1944 | Louis Henry Sullivan* |
| 1909 | Charles Follen McKim | | Bertram Grosvenor | 1947 | Eliel Saarinen |
| 1911 | George Browne Post | | Goodhue* | 1948 | Charles Donagh Maginnis |
| 1914 | Jean Louis Pascal | 1927 | Howard Van Doren Shaw | 1949 | Frank Lloyd Wright |
| 1922 | Victor Laloux | 1929 | Milton Bennett Medary | 1950 | Sir Patrick Abercrombie |
| 1923 | Henry Bacon | 1933 | Ragnar Ostberg | 1951 | Bernard Ralph Maybeck |
| | | 1938 | Paul Philippe Cret | 1952 | Auguste Perret |

## AIA Gold Medal (continued)

| YEAR | NAME | YEAR | NAME | YEAR | NAME |
|------|------|------|------|------|------|
| 1953 | William Adams Delano | 1967 | Wallace K. Harrison | 1986 | Arthur Erickson |
| 1955 | Willem Marinus Dudok | 1968 | Marcel Breuer | 1989 | Joseph Esherick |
| 1956 | Clarence S. Stein | 1969 | William Wilson Wurster | 1990 | E. Fay Jones |
| 1957 | Ralph Walker | 1970 | Richard Buckminster | 1991 | Charles W. Moore |
|      | Louis Skidmore |      | Fuller | 1992 | Benjamin Thompson |
| 1958 | John Wellborn Root* | 1971 | Louis I. Kahn | 1993 | Thomas Jefferson* |
| 1959 | Walter Gropius | 1972 | Pietro Belluschi |      | Kevin Roche |
| 1960 | Ludwig Mies van der Rohe | 1977 | Richard Joseph Neutra* | 1994 | Sir Norman Foster |
| 1961 | Le Corbusier (Charles- | 1978 | Philip C. Johnson | 1995 | César Pelli |
|      | Édouard Jeanneret) | 1979 | Ieoh Ming Pei | 1997 | Richard Meier |
| 1962 | Eero Saarinen* | 1981 | José Luis Sert | 1999 | Frank O. Gehry |
| 1963 | Alvar Aalto | 1982 | Romaldo Giurgola | 2000 | Ricardo Legorreta |
| 1964 | Pier Luigi Nervi | 1983 | Nathaniel A. Owings | 2001 | Michael Graves |
| 1966 | Kenzo Tange | 1985 | William Wayne Caudill* | 2002 | Tadao Ando |

*Awarded posthumously.*

# Special Honors

## Hasty Pudding Theatricals Woman of the Year and Man of the Year

The Hasty Pudding Theatricals of Harvard University, an organization of undergraduates, has presented the Woman of the Year award since 1951 and the Man of the Year award since 1967 to performers who have made a "lasting and impressive contribution to the world of entertainment."

| YEAR | NAME | YEAR | NAME |
|------|------|------|------|
| 1951 | Gertrude Lawrence | 1978 | Beverly Sills and Richard Dreyfuss |
| 1952 | Barbara Bel Geddes | 1979 | Candice Bergen and Robert De Niro |
| 1953 | Mamie Eisenhower | 1980 | Meryl Streep and Alan Alda |
| 1954 | Shirley Booth | 1981 | Mary Tyler Moore and John Travolta |
| 1955 | Debbie Reynolds | 1982 | Ella Fitzgerald and James Cagney |
| 1956 | Peggy Ann Garner | 1983 | Julie Andrews and Steven Spielberg |
| 1957 | Carroll Baker | 1984 | Joan Rivers and Sean Connery |
| 1958 | Katharine Hepburn | 1985 | Cher and Bill Murray |
| 1959 | Joanne Woodward | 1986 | Sally Field and Sylvester Stallone |
| 1960 | Carol Lawrence | 1987 | Bernadette Peters and Mikhail Baryshnikov |
| 1961 | Jane Fonda | 1988 | Lucille Ball and Steve Martin |
| 1962 | Piper Laurie | 1989 | Kathleen Turner and Robin Williams |
| 1963 | Shirley MacLaine | 1990 | Glenn Close and Kevin Costner |
| 1964 | Rosalind Russell | 1991 | Diane Keaton and Clint Eastwood |
| 1965 | Lee Remick | 1992 | Jodie Foster and Michael Douglas |
| 1966 | Ethel Merman | 1993 | Whoopi Goldberg and Chevy Chase |
| 1967 | Lauren Bacall and Bob Hope | 1994 | Meg Ryan and Tom Cruise |
| 1968 | Angela Lansbury and Paul Newman | 1995 | Michelle Pfeiffer and Tom Hanks |
| 1969 | Carol Burnett and Bill Cosby | 1996 | Susan Sarandon and Harrison Ford |
| 1970 | Dionne Warwick and Robert Redford | 1997 | Julia Roberts and Mel Gibson |
| 1971 | Carol Channing and James Stewart | 1998 | Sigourney Weaver and Kevin Kline |
| 1972 | Ruby Keeler and Dustin Hoffman | 1999 | Goldie Hawn and Samuel L. Jackson |
| 1973 | Liza Minnelli and Jack Lemmon | 2000 | Jamie Lee Curtis and Billy Crystal |
| 1974 | Faye Dunaway and Peter Falk | 2001 | Drew Barrymore and Anthony Hopkins |
| 1975 | Valerie Harper and Warren Beatty | 2002 | Sarah Jessica Parker and Bruce Willis |
| 1976 | Bette Midler and Robert Blake | 2003 | Anjelica Huston and Martin Scorsese |
| 1977 | Elizabeth Taylor and Johnny Carson | 2004 | *scheduled to be awarded in February* |

# Sports

The tables that follow contain the significant information about the top contests of all the major sports that are international in character, as well as some professional and amateur sports that attract a huge national following—such as baseball in the United States and cricket in the United Kingdom, Australia, India, and the other Test Match countries—and some sports, such as rowing, in which national competition overshadows international events. In many sports the Olympic Games held every four years constitute the world championships; they are included in the listings below.

## Sporting Codes for Countries

*These codes are used to identify countries in the Sports section of the Britannica Almanac.*

### Codes of the International Olympic Committee (IOC)

| | | | | | |
|---|---|---|---|---|---|
| AFG | Afghanistan | CZE | Czech Rep. | KGZ | Kyrgyzstan |
| AHO | Netherlands Antilles | DEN | Denmark | KOR | Korea, Rep. of (South Korea) |
| ALB | Albania | DJI | Djibouti | KSA | Saudi Arabia |
| ALG | Algeria | DMA | Dominica | KUW | Kuwait |
| AND | Andorra | DOM | Dominican Rep. | LAO | Laos |
| ANG | Angola | ECU | Ecuador | LAT | Latvia |
| ANT | Antigua and Barbuda | EGY | Egypt | LBA | Libya |
| ARG | Argentina | ERI | Eritrea | LBR | Liberia |
| ARM | Armenia | ESA | El Salvador | LCA | St. Lucia |
| ARU | Aruba | ESP | Spain | LES | Lesotho |
| ASA | American Samoa | EST | Estonia | LIB | Lebanon |
| AUS | Australia | ETH | Ethiopia | LIE | Liechtenstein |
| AUT | Austria | FIJ | Fiji | LTU | Lithuania |
| AZE | Azerbaijan | FIN | Finland | LUX | Luxembourg |
| BAH | Bahamas | FRA | France | MAD | Madagascar |
| BAN | Bangladesh | FSM | Micronesia, Fed. States of | MAR | Morocco |
| BAR | Barbados | | | MAS | Malaysia |
| BDI | Burundi | GAB | Gabon | MAW | Malawi |
| BEL | Belgium | GAM | Gambia | MDA | Moldova |
| BEN | Benin | GBR | Great Britain | MDV | Maldives |
| BER | Bermuda | GBS | Guinea-Bissau | MEX | Mexico |
| BHU | Bhutan | GEO | Georgia | MGL | Mongolia |
| BIH | Bosnia and Herzegovina | GEQ | Equatorial Guinea | MKD | Macedonia |
| BIZ | Belize | GER | Germany | MLI | Mali |
| BLR | Belarus | GHA | Ghana | MLT | Malta |
| BOL | Bolivia | GRE | Greece | MON | Monaco |
| BOT | Botswana | GRN | Grenada | MOZ | Mozambique |
| BRA | Brazil | GUA | Guatemala | MRI | Mauritius |
| BRN | Bahrain | GUI | Guinea | MTN | Mauritania |
| BRU | Brunei Darussalam | GUM | Guam | MYA | Myanmar (Burma) |
| BUL | Bulgaria | GUY | Guyana | NAM | Namibia |
| BUR | Burkina Faso | HAI | Haiti | NCA | Nicaragua |
| CAF | Central African Rep. | HKG | Hong Kong | NED | Netherlands, The |
| CAM | Cambodia | HON | Honduras | NEP | Nepal |
| CAN | Canada | HUN | Hungary | NGR | Nigeria |
| CAY | Cayman Islands | INA | Indonesia | NIG | Niger |
| CGO | Congo | IND | India | NOR | Norway |
| CHA | Chad | IOA | International Olympic Athlete (East Timor) | NRU | Nauru |
| CHI | Chile | | | NZL | New Zealand |
| CHN | China, People's Rep. of | IRI | Iran | OMA | Oman |
| CIV | Côte d'Ivoire | IRL | Ireland | PAK | Pakistan |
| CMR | Cameroon | IRQ | Iraq | PAN | Panama |
| COD | Congo, Dem. Rep. of the | ISL | Iceland | PAR | Paraguay |
| COK | Cook Islands | ISR | Israel | PER | Peru |
| COL | Colombia | ISV | US Virgin Islands | PHI | Philippines |
| COM | Comoros | ITA | Italy | PLE | Palestine |
| CPV | Cape Verde | IVB | British Virgin Islands | PLW | Palau |
| CRC | Costa Rica | JAM | Jamaica | PNG | Papua New Guinea |
| CRO | Croatia | JOR | Jordan | POL | Poland |
| CUB | Cuba | JPN | Japan | POR | Portugal |
| CYP | Cyprus | KAZ | Kazakhstan | | |
| | | KEN | Kenya | | |

# Sporting Codes for Countries (continued)

## Codes of the International Olympic Committee (IOC) (continued)

| | | | | | |
|---|---|---|---|---|---|
| PRK | Korea, Dem. People's Rep. of (North Korea) | SRI | Sri Lanka | TUR | Turkey |
| | | STP | São Tomé and Príncipe | UAE | United Arab Emirates |
| PUR | Puerto Rico | SUD | Sudan | UGA | Uganda |
| QAT | Qatar | SUI | Switzerland | UKR | Ukraine |
| ROM | Romania | SUR | Suriname | URU | Uruguay |
| RSA | South Africa | SVK | Slovakia | USA | United States |
| RUS | Russia | SWE | Sweden | UZB | Uzbekistan |
| RWA | Rwanda | SWZ | Swaziland | VAN | Vanuatu |
| SAM | Samoa | SYR | Syria | VEN | Venezuela |
| SEN | Senegal | TAN | Tanzania | VIE | Vietnam |
| SEY | Seychelles | TGA | Tonga | VIN | St. Vincent and the Grenadines |
| SIN | Singapore | THA | Thailand | | |
| SKN | St. Kitts and Nevis | TJK | Tajikistan | YEM | Yemen |
| SLE | Sierra Leone | TKM | Turkmenistan | YUG | Yugoslavia |
| SLO | Slovenia | TOG | Togo | ZAM | Zambia |
| SMR | San Marino | TPE | Taiwan | ZIM | Zimbabwe |
| SOL | Solomon Islands | TRI | Trinidad and Tobago | | |
| SOM | Somalia | TUN | Tunisia | | |

## Continental, Historical, and Other Country Codes

| | | | | | | | |
|---|---|---|---|---|---|---|---|
| AFR | Africa | DMN | Dominica | MAC | Macao | SKR | Korea, Rep. of (South Korea) |
| AIA | Anguilla | ENG | England | MAU | Mauritius | | |
| AME | The Americas | EUR | Europe | MOL | Moldova | SPA | Spain |
| ARS | Saudi Arabia | FRG | Germany, Federal Rep. of (West Germany) | MOR | Morocco | SWZ | Switzerland |
| ASI | Asia | | | MSR | Montserrat | TAH | Tahiti |
| BIR | Burma (Myanmar) | | | NIC | Nicaragua | TAI | Taiwan |
| BLS | Belarus | FRO | Faroe Islands | NIR | Northern Ireland | TCA | Turks and Caicos Islands |
| BOH | Bohemia | GDR | German Demo-cratic Rep. (East Germany) | NKO | Korea, Dem. People's Rep. of (North Korea) | | |
| BOS | Bosnia and Herzegovina | | | | | TCH | Czechoslovakia |
| BUR | Burma | HBR | British Honduras | OCE | Oceania | UAR | United Arab Rep. |
| BWI | British West Indies | HEB | New Hebrides | PAL | Palestine | UCS | Union of the Czech Rep. and Slovakia |
| | | HOL | Holland/The Netherlands | PDR | Korea, Dem. People's Rep. of (North Korea) | | |
| CAM | Cameroon | | | | | UNT | Unified Team |
| CEY | Ceylon | ICE | Iceland | | | UPV | Upper Volta |
| CIS | Commonwealth of Indep. States | IHO | Netherlands India | PNG | Papua New Guinea | URS | USSR |
| | | IRE | Ireland | | | UVI | US Virgin Islands |
| CKN | Congo-Kinshasa | IVC | Côte d'Ivoire/Ivory Coast | RHO | Rhodesia | WAL | Wales |
| COB | Congo-Brazzaville | | | ROC | China, People's Rep. of | ZAI | Zaire |
| CSV | Czechoslovakia | JAP | Japan | | | | |
| CUR | Curaçao | KZK | Kazakhstan | SAA | Saarland | | |
| DAH | Dahomey | LIT | Lithuania | SCO | Scotland | | |

## The James E. Sullivan Memorial Trophy

Awarded by the Amateur Athletic Union (AAU) since 1930 to honor an athlete who, "by his or her performance, example and influence as an amateur, has done the most during the year to advance the cause of sportsmanship." The award, named for a past president of the AAU, is usually announced in April of the year after that for which the award is given. Winners receive a replica in bronze of the original trophy. **Web site:** <www.aausports.org>

| YEAR | WINNER | SPORT |
|---|---|---|
| 1930 | Bobby Jones | golf |
| 1931 | Barney Berlinger | track (decathlon) |
| 1932 | Jim Bausch | track (decathlon) |
| 1933 | Glenn Cunningham | track (distance running) |
| 1934 | Bill Bonthron | track (middle distance running) |
| 1935 | Lawson Little | golf |
| 1936 | Glenn Morris | track (decathlon) |
| 1937 | Don Budge | tennis |
| 1938 | Don Lash | track (distance running) |
| 1939 | Joe Burk | rowing |
| 1940 | Greg Rice | track (distance running) |
| 1941 | Leslie MacMitchell | track (middle distance running) |
| 1942 | Cornelius "Dutch" Warmerdam | track (pole vault) |
| 1943 | Gilbert Dodds | track (middle distance running) |
| 1944 | Ann Curtis | swimming |
| 1945 | Doc Blanchard | football |
| 1946 | Arnold Tucker | football |
| 1947 | John B. Kelly, Jr. | rowing |
| 1948 | Bob Mathias | track (decathlon) |

## The James E. Sullivan Memorial Trophy (continued)

| YEAR | WINNER | SPORT | YEAR | WINNER | SPORT |
|------|--------|-------|------|--------|-------|
| 1949 | Dick Button | figure skating | 1978 | Tracy Caulkins | swimming |
| 1950 | Fred Wilt | track (distance running) | 1979 | Kurt Thomas | gymnastics |
| 1951 | Bob Richards | track (pole vault/ decathlon) | 1980 | Eric Heiden | speed skating |
| | | | 1981 | Carl Lewis | track (sprints/long jump) |
| 1952 | Horace Ashenfelter | track (distance running) | | | |
| 1953 | Sammy Lee | diving | 1982 | Mary Decker | track (distance running) |
| 1954 | Mal Whitfield | track (middle distance running) | 1983 | Edwin Moses | track (hurdles) |
| | | | 1984 | Greg Louganis | diving |
| 1955 | Harrison Dillard | track (sprints/hurdles) | 1985 | Joan Benoit Samuelson | track (marathon) |
| 1956 | Pat McCormick | diving | 1986 | Jackie Joyner-Kersee | track (heptathlon) |
| 1957 | Bobby Morrow | track (sprints) | | | |
| 1958 | Glenn Davis | track (hurdles) | 1987 | Jim Abbott | baseball (pitcher) |
| 1959 | Parry O'Brien | track (shot put) | 1988 | Florence Griffith Joyner | track (sprints) |
| 1960 | Rafer Johnson | track (decathlon) | | | |
| 1961 | Wilma Rudolph | track (sprints) | 1989 | Janet Evans | swimming |
| 1962 | Jim Beatty | track (distance running) | 1990 | John Smith | freestyle wrestling |
| 1963 | John Pennel | track (pole vault) | 1991 | Mike Powell | track (long jump) |
| 1964 | Don Schollander | swimming | 1992 | Bonnie Blair | speed skating |
| 1965 | Bill Bradley | basketball | 1993 | Charlie Ward | football |
| 1966 | Jim Ryun | track (middle distance running) | 1994 | Dan Jansen | speed skating |
| | | | 1995 | Bruce Baumgartner | freestyle wrestling |
| 1967 | Randy Matson | track (shot put/discus) | 1996 | Michael Johnson | track (middle distance running) |
| 1968 | Debbie Meyer | swimming | | | |
| 1969 | Bill Toomey | track (decathlon) | 1997 | Peyton Manning | football |
| 1970 | John Kinsella | swimming | 1998 | Chamique Holdsclaw | basketball |
| 1971 | Mark Spitz | swimming | | | |
| 1972 | Frank Shorter | track (distance running) | 1999 | Coco and Kelly Miller | basketball |
| 1973 | Bill Walton | basketball | | | |
| 1974 | Rick Wohlhuter | track (middle distance running) | 2000 | Rulon Gardner | Greco-Roman wrestling |
| | | | 2001 | Michelle Kwan | figure skating |
| 1975 | Tim Shaw | swimming | 2002 | Sarah Hughes | figure skating |
| 1976 | Bruce Jenner | track (decathlon) | | | |
| 1977 | John Naber | swimming | | | |

# The Olympic Games

By the 6th century BC several sporting festivals had achieved cultural importance in the Greek world, the most prominent among them the Olympic Games at the city of Olympia, first recorded in 776 BC and held at four year intervals thereafter. Those games, comprising many of the sports now included in the Summer Games, were abolished in AD 393 by the Roman emperor Theodosius I.

In 1887 the 24-year-old French aristocrat and educator Pierre, baron de Coubertin, conceived the idea of reviving the Olympic Games and spent seven years gathering support for his plan. At a international congress in 1894, his plan was accepted and the International Olympic Committee (IOC) was founded. The first modern Olympic Games were held in Athens in April 1896, with some 300 representatives from 13 nations competing. The revival led to the formation of international amateur sports organizations and national Olympic committees throughout the world.

The IOC is responsible for maintaining the regular celebration of the games, seeing that the games are carried out in a spirit of peace and intercultural communication, and promoting amateur sport throughout the world. IOC members may not accept from the government of their country, or from any other entity, instructions that compromise their independence.

The Olympic Games have come to be regarded as the world's foremost sports competition. Before the 1970s the Games were officially limited to amateurs, but since that time many events have been opened to professional athletes. In 1924 the Winter Games were created, and in 1986 the IOC voted to alternate the Winter and Summer Games every two years, beginning in 1994.

The games were canceled during the two World Wars (1916, 1940, and 1944) and have frequently served as venues for the expression of political dissent. China refused to participate in the Summer Games from 1956 until 1984 because of Taiwan's participation; 26 nations boycotted in 1976 over the participation of New Zealand, some of whose athletes had competed in apartheid-era South Africa; the United States and some 60 other countries boycotted the 1980 games in Moscow to protest the Soviet invasion of Afghanistan, and the Communist bloc and Cuba in turn boycotted the 1984 Los Angeles games.

In light of the IOC's declared independence from political and financial interests, in 1998 the world was shocked by allegations of widespread corruption within the committee. Several committee members, it was found, had accepted bribes to approve the bid of Salt Lake City UT as the site for the 2002 Winter Games. Impropriety was also alleged for several previous bid committees. The IOC responded by expelling six members, and in 1999 announced a number of wide-ranging reforms.

# Sites of the Modern Olympic Games

## Summer Games

| YEAR | LOCATION | YEAR | LOCATION | YEAR | LOCATION |
|------|----------|------|----------|------|----------|
| 1896 | Athens, Greece | 1940–44 | *not held* | 1992 | Barcelona, Spain |
| 1900 | Paris, France | 1948 | London, England | 1996 | Atlanta GA |
| 1904 | St. Louis MO | 1952 | Helsinki, Finland | 2000 | Sydney, Australia |
| 1908 | London, England | 1956 | Melbourne, Australia | 2004 | *scheduled to be held* |
| 1912 | Stockholm, Sweden | 1960 | Rome, Italy | | *13–29 August, Athens,* |
| 1916 | *not held* | 1964 | Tokyo, Japan | | *Greece* |
| 1920 | Antwerp, Belgium | 1968 | Mexico City, Mexico | 2008 | *scheduled to be held 25* |
| 1924 | Paris, France | 1972 | Munich, West Germany | | *July–10 August, Beijing,* |
| 1928 | Amsterdam, The Nether- | 1976 | Montreal, Quebec | | *China* |
| | lands | 1980 | Moscow, USSR | | |
| 1932 | Los Angeles CA | 1984 | Los Angeles CA | | |
| 1936 | Berlin, Germany | 1988 | Seoul, South Korea | | |

## Winter Games

| YEAR | LOCATION | YEAR | LOCATION | YEAR | LOCATION |
|------|----------|------|----------|------|----------|
| 1924 | Chamonix, France | 1960 | Squaw Valley CA | 1994 | Lillehammer, Norway |
| 1928 | St. Moritz, Switzerland | 1964 | Innsbruck, Austria | 1998 | Nagano, Japan |
| 1932 | Lake Placid NY | 1968 | Grenoble, France | 2002 | Salt Lake City UT |
| 1936 | Garmisch-Partenkirchen, | 1972 | Sapporo, Japan | 2006 | *scheduled to be held* |
| | Germany | 1976 | Innsbruck, Austria | | *10–26 February, Torino,* |
| 1940–44 | *not held* | 1980 | Lake Placid NY | | *Italy* |
| 1948 | St. Moritz, Switzerland | 1984 | Sarajevo, Yugoslavia | 2010 | *scheduled to be held* |
| 1952 | Oslo, Norway | 1988 | Calgary, Alberta | | *12–28 February,* |
| 1956 | Cortina d'Ampezzo, Italy | 1992 | Albertville, France | | *Vancouver BC* |

# Summer Olympic Games Champions

Gold-medal winners in all Summer Olympic contests since 1896. Note: East and West Germany fielded a joint all-Germany team in 1956, 1960, and 1964, abbreviated here as GER. The Unified Team in 1992 consisted of the Commonwealth of Independent States plus Georgia, and is abbreviated here as UNT.

## Archery

**MEN'S INDIVIDUAL**
1972　John Williams (USA)
1976　Darrell Pace (USA)
1980　Tomi Poikolainen (FIN)
1984　Darrell Pace (USA)
1988　Jay Barrs (USA)
1992　Sebastien Flute (FRA)
1996　Justin Huish (USA)
2000　Simon Fairweather (AUS)

**AU CORDON DORÉ (50 METERS)**
1900　Henri Herouin (FRA)

**AU CORDON DORÉ (33 METERS)**
1900　Hubert van Innis (BEL)

**AU CHAPELET (50 METERS)**
1900　Eugène Mougin (FRA)

**SUR LA PERCHE À LA HERSE**
1900　Emmanuel Foulon (FRA)

**AU CHAPELET (33 METERS)**
1900　Hubert van Innis (BEL)

**SUR LA PERCHE À LA PYRAMIDE**
1900　Émile Grumiaux (FRA)

## Archery (continued)

**DOUBLE AMERICAN ROUND**
1904　George Philipp Bryant (USA)

**(DOUBLE) YORK ROUND**
1904　George Philipp Bryant (USA)
1908　William Dod (GBR)

**CONTINENTAL STYLE**
1908　Eugène G. Grizot (FRA)

**FIXED BIRD TARGET (SMALL)**
1920　Edmond van Moer (BEL)

**FIXED BIRD TARGET (LARGE)**
1920　Édouard Cloetens (BEL)

**MOVING BIRD TARGET (28 M)**
1920　Hubert van Innis (BEL)

**MOVING BIRD TARGET (33 M)**
1920　Hubert van Innis (BEL)

**MOVING BIRD TARGET (50 M)**
1920　Julien Brulé (FRA)

**WOMEN'S INDIVIDUAL**
1972　Doreen Wilber (USA)
1976　Luann Ryon (USA)
1980　Ketevan Losaberidze (URS)

# Summer Olympic Games Champions (continued)

## Archery (continued)

**WOMEN'S INDIVIDUAL**
1984 Seo Hyang Soon (KOR)
1988 Kim Soo Nyung (KOR)
1992 Cho Youn Jeong (KOR)
1996 Kim Kyung-Wook (KOR)
2000 Yun Mi-Jin (KOR)

**DOUBLE COLUMBIA ROUND**
1904 Matilda Scott Howell (USA)

**(DOUBLE) NATIONAL ROUND**
1904 Matilda Scott Howell (USA)
1908 Sybil Fenton "Queenie" Newall (GBR)

**MEN'S TEAM**
1904 United States
1988 South Korea
1992 Spain
1996 United States
2000 South Korea

**WOMEN'S TEAM**
1904 United States
1988 South Korea
1992 South Korea
1996 South Korea
2000 South Korea

**FIXED TARGET (2 EVENTS)**
1920 Belgium

**MOVING TARGET (28 M)**
1920 The Netherlands

**MOVING TARGET (33 M)**
1920 Belgium

**MOVING TARGET (50 M)**
1920 Belgium

## Association football (soccer)[1]

**MEN**
1900 Great Britain
1904 Canada
1908 Great Britain
1912 Great Britain
1920 Belgium
1924 Uruguay
1928 Uruguay
1936 Italy
1948 Sweden
1952 Hungary
1956 USSR
1960 Yugoslavia
1964 Hungary
1968 Hungary
1972 Poland
1976 East Germany
1980 Czechoslovakia
1984 France
1988 USSR
1992 Spain
1996 Nigeria
2000 Cameroon

**WOMEN**
1996 United States
2000 Norway

## Athletics (track-and-field) (men)

| 60 METERS | | SEC |
|---|---|---|
| 1900 | Alvin Kraenzlein (USA) | 7 |
| 1904 | Archie Hahn (USA) | 7 |

| 100 METERS | | SEC |
|---|---|---|
| 1896 | Thomas Burke (USA) | 12.0 |
| 1900 | Francis Jarvis (USA) | 11.0 |
| 1904 | Archie Hahn (USA) | 11.0 |
| 1908 | Reginald Walker (RSA) | 10.8 |
| 1912 | Ralph Craig (USA) | 10.8 |
| 1920 | Charles Paddock (USA) | 10.8 |
| 1924 | Harold Abrahams (GBR) | 10.6 |
| 1928 | Percy Williams (CAN) | 10.8 |
| 1932 | Eddie Tolan (USA) | 10.3 |
| 1936 | Jesse Owens (USA) | 10.3 |
| 1948 | Harrison Dillard (USA) | 10.3 |
| 1952 | Lindy Remigino (USA) | 10.4 |
| 1956 | Robert Morrow (USA) | 10.5 |
| 1960 | Armin Hary (GER) | 10.2 |
| 1964 | Robert Hayes (USA) | 10.0 |
| 1968 | James Hines (USA) | 9.9 |
| 1972 | Valery Borzov (URS) | 10.14 |
| 1976 | Hasely Crawford (TRI) | 10.06 |
| 1980 | Allan Wells (GBR) | 10.25 |
| 1984 | Carl Lewis (USA) | 9.99 |
| 1988 | Carl Lewis (USA) | 9.92 |
| 1992 | Linford Christie (GBR) | 9.96 |
| 1996 | Donovan Bailey (CAN) | 9.84 |
| 2000 | Maurice Greene (USA) | 9.87 |

| 200 METERS | | SEC |
|---|---|---|
| 1900 | Walter Tewksbury (USA) | 22.2 |
| 1904 | Archie Hahn (USA) | 21.6 |
| 1908 | Robert Kerr (CAN) | 22.6 |
| 1912 | Ralph Craig (USA) | 21.7 |
| 1920 | Allen Woodring (USA) | 22.0 |
| 1924 | Jackson Scholz (USA) | 21.6 |
| 1928 | Percy Williams (CAN) | 21.8 |
| 1932 | Eddie Tolan (USA) | 21.2 |
| 1936 | Jesse Owens (USA) | 20.7 |
| 1948 | Melvin Patton (USA) | 21.1 |
| 1952 | Andy Stanfield (USA) | 20.7 |
| 1956 | Robert Morrow (USA) | 20.6 |
| 1960 | Livio Berruti (ITA) | 20.5 |
| 1964 | Henry Carr (USA) | 20.3 |
| 1968 | Tommie Smith (USA) | 19.8 |
| 1972 | Valery Borzov (URS) | 20.00 |
| 1976 | Donald Quarrie (JAM) | 20.23 |
| 1980 | Pietro Mennea (ITA) | 20.19 |
| 1984 | Carl Lewis (USA) | 19.80 |
| 1988 | Joe DeLoach (USA) | 19.75 |
| 1992 | Mike Marsh (USA) | 20.01 |
| 1996 | Michael Johnson (USA) | 19.32 |
| 2000 | Konstantinos Kenteris (GRE) | 20.09 |

| 400 METERS | | SEC |
|---|---|---|
| 1896 | Thomas Burke (USA) | 54.2 |
| 1900 | Maxwell Long (USA) | 49.4 |
| 1904 | Harry Hillman (USA) | 49.2 |
| 1908 | Wyndham Halswelle (GBR) | 50.0 |
| 1912 | Charles Reidpath (USA) | 48.2 |
| 1920 | Bevil Rudd (RSA) | 49.6 |
| 1924 | Eric Liddell (GBR) | 47.6 |
| 1928 | Raymond Barbuti (USA) | 47.8 |
| 1932 | William Carr (USA) | 46.2 |
| 1936 | Archie Williams (USA) | 46.5 |
| 1948 | Arthur Wint (JAM) | 46.2 |
| 1952 | Vincent George Rhoden (JAM) | 45.9 |

# Summer Olympic Games Champions (continued)

## Athletics (track-and-field) (men) (continued)

### 400 METERS

| | | SEC |
|---|---|---|
| 1956 | Charles Jenkins (USA) | 46.7 |
| 1960 | Otis Davis (USA) | 44.9 |
| 1964 | Michael Larrabee (USA) | 45.1 |
| 1968 | Lee Evans (USA) | 43.8 |
| 1972 | Vincent Matthews (USA) | 44.66 |
| 1976 | Alberto Juantorena (CUB) | 44.26 |
| 1980 | Viktor Markin (URS) | 44.60 |
| 1984 | Alonzo Babers (USA) | 44.27 |
| 1988 | Steven Lewis (USA) | 43.87 |
| 1992 | Quincy Watts (USA) | 43.50 |
| 1996 | Michael Johnson (USA) | 43.49 |
| 2000 | Michael Johnson (USA) | 43.84 |

### 800 METERS

| | | MIN:SEC |
|---|---|---|
| 1896 | Edwin Flack (AUS) | 2:11.0 |
| 1900 | Alfred Tysoe (GBR) | 2:01.2 |
| 1904 | James Lightbody (USA) | 1:56.0 |
| 1908 | Melvin Sheppard (USA) | 1:52.8 |
| 1912 | James Edward Meredith (USA) | 1:51.9 |
| 1920 | Albert Hill (GBR) | 1:53.4 |
| 1924 | Douglas Lowe (GBR) | 1:52.4 |
| 1928 | Douglas Lowe (GBR) | 1:51.8 |
| 1932 | Thomas Hampson (GBR) | 1:49.7 |
| 1936 | John Woodruff (USA) | 1:52.9 |
| 1948 | Malvin Whitfield (USA) | 1:49.2 |
| 1952 | Malvin Whitfield (USA) | 1:49.2 |
| 1956 | Thomas Courtney (USA) | 1:47.7 |
| 1960 | Peter Snell (NZL) | 1:46.3 |
| 1964 | Peter Snell (NZL) | 1:45.1 |
| 1968 | Ralph Doubell (AUS) | 1:44.3 |
| 1972 | David Wottle (USA) | 1:45.9 |
| 1976 | Alberto Juantorena (CUB) | 1:43.50 |
| 1980 | Steven Ovett (GBR) | 1:45.40 |
| 1984 | Joaquim Cruz (BRA) | 1:43.00 |
| 1988 | Paul Ereng (KEN) | 1:43.45 |
| 1992 | William Tanui (KEN) | 1:43.66 |
| 1996 | Vebjoern Rodal (NOR) | 1:42.58 |
| 2000 | Nils Schumann (GER) | 1:45.08 |

### 1,500 METERS

| | | MIN:SEC |
|---|---|---|
| 1896 | Edwin Flack (AUS) | 4:33.2 |
| 1900 | Charles Bennett (GBR) | 4:06.2 |
| 1904 | James Lightbody (USA) | 4:05.4 |
| 1908 | Melvin Sheppard (USA) | 4:03.4 |
| 1912 | Arnold Jackson (GBR) | 3:56.8 |
| 1920 | Albert Hill (GBR) | 4:01.8 |
| 1924 | Paavo Nurmi (FIN) | 3:53.6 |
| 1928 | Harry Larva (FIN) | 3:53.2 |
| 1932 | Luigi Beccali (ITA) | 3:51.2 |
| 1936 | John Lovelock (NZL) | 3:47.8 |
| 1948 | Henry Eriksson (SWE) | 3:49.8 |
| 1952 | Joseph Barthel (LUX) | 3:45.1 |
| 1956 | Ronald Delany (IRE) | 3:41.2 |
| 1960 | Herbert Elliott (AUS) | 3:35.6 |
| 1964 | Peter Snell (NZL) | 3:38.1 |
| 1968 | Hezekiah Kipchoge ("Kip") Keino (KEN) | 3:34.9 |
| 1972 | Pekka Vasala (FIN) | 3:36.3 |
| 1976 | John Walker (NZL) | 3:39.17 |
| 1980 | Sebastian Coe (GBR) | 3:38.40 |
| 1984 | Sebastian Coe (GBR) | 3:32.53 |
| 1988 | Peter Rono (KEN) | 3:35.96 |
| 1992 | Fermin Cacho Ruiz (ESP) | 3:40.12 |
| 1996 | Noureddine Morceli (ALG) | 3:35.78 |
| 2000 | Noah Ngeny (KEN) | 3:32.07 |

## Athletics (track-and-field) (men) (continued)

### 5,000 METERS

| | | MIN:SEC |
|---|---|---|
| 1912 | Hannes Kolehmainen (FIN) | 14:36.6 |
| 1920 | Joseph Guillemot (FRA) | 14:55.6 |
| 1924 | Paavo Nurmi (FIN) | 14:31.2 |
| 1928 | Vilho Ritola (FIN) | 14:38.0 |
| 1932 | Lauri Lehtinen (FIN) | 14:30.0 |
| 1936 | Gunnar Höckert (FIN) | 14:22.2 |
| 1948 | Gaston Reiff (BEL) | 14:17.6 |
| 1952 | Emil Zatopek (TCH) | 14:06.6 |
| 1956 | Vladimir Kuts (URS) | 13:39.6 |
| 1960 | Murray Halberg (NZL) | 13:43.4 |
| 1964 | Robert Keyser Schul (USA) | 13:48.8 |
| 1968 | Mohamed Gammoudi (TUN) | 14:05.0 |
| 1972 | Lasse Viren (FIN) | 13:26.4 |
| 1976 | Lasse Viren (FIN) | 13:24.76 |
| 1980 | Miruts Yifter (ETH) | 13:21.00 |
| 1984 | Said Aouita (MAR) | 13:05.59 |
| 1988 | John Ngugi (KEN) | 13:11.70 |
| 1992 | Dieter Baumann (GER) | 13:12.52 |
| 1996 | Venuste Niyongabo (BDI) | 13:07.97 |
| 2000 | Millon Wolde (ETH) | 13:35.49 |

### 5 MILES

| | | MIN:SEC |
|---|---|---|
| 1908 | Emil Voigt (GBR) | 25:11.2 |

### 10,000 METERS

| | | MIN:SEC |
|---|---|---|
| 1912 | Hannes Kolehmainen (FIN) | 31:20.8 |
| 1920 | Paavo Nurmi (FIN) | 31:45.8 |
| 1924 | Vilho Ritola (FIN) | 30:23.2 |
| 1928 | Paavo Nurmi (FIN) | 30:18.8 |
| 1932 | Janusz Kusocinski (POL) | 30:11.4 |
| 1936 | Ilmari Salminen (FIN) | 30:15.4 |
| 1948 | Emil Zatopek (TCH) | 29:59.6 |
| 1952 | Emil Zatopek (TCH) | 29:17.0 |
| 1956 | Vladimir Kuts (URS) | 28:45.6 |
| 1960 | Pyotr Bolotnikov (URS) | 28:32.2 |
| 1964 | William Mills (USA) | 28:24.4 |
| 1968 | Nabiba Temu (KEN) | 29:27.4 |
| 1972 | Lasse Viren (FIN) | 27:38.4 |
| 1976 | Lasse Viren (FIN) | 27:40.38 |
| 1980 | Miruts Yifter (ETH) | 27:42.70 |
| 1984 | Alberto Cova (ITA) | 27:47.54 |
| 1988 | Brahim Boutaib (MAR) | 27:21.46 |
| 1992 | Khalid Skah (MAR) | 27:46.70 |
| 1996 | Haile Gebrselassie (ETH) | 27:07.34 |
| 2000 | Haile Gebrselassie (ETH) | 27:18.20 |

### MARATHON

| | | HR:MIN:SEC |
|---|---|---|
| 1896 | Spiridon Louis (GRE) | 2:58:50.0 |
| 1900 | Michel Theato (FRA) | 2:59:45.0 |
| 1904 | Thomas Hicks (USA) | 3:28:53.0 |
| 1908 | John Hayes (USA) | 2:55:18.4 |
| 1912 | Kenneth McArthur (RSA) | 2:36:54.8 |
| 1920 | Hannes Kolehmainen (FIN) | 2:32:35.8 |
| 1924 | Albin Stenroos (FIN) | 2:41:22.6 |
| 1928 | Boughèra El Ouafi (FRA) | 2:32:57.0 |
| 1932 | Juan Carlos Zabala (ARG) | 2:31:36.0 |
| 1936 | Kitei Son (JPN) | 2:29:19.2 |
| 1948 | Delfo Cabrera (ARG) | 2:34:51.6 |
| 1952 | Emil Zatopek (TCH) | 2:23:03.2 |
| 1956 | Alain Mimoun-O-Kacha (FRA) | 2:25:00.0 |
| 1960 | Abebe Bikila (ETH) | 2:15:16.2 |
| 1964 | Abebe Bikila (ETH) | 2:12:11.2 |
| 1968 | Mamo Wolde (ETH) | 2:20:26.4 |
| 1972 | Frank Shorter (USA) | 2:12:19.8 |
| 1976 | Waldemar Cierpinski (GDR) | 2:09:55.0 |
| 1980 | Waldemar Cierpinski (GDR) | 2:11:03.0 |
| 1984 | Carlos Lopes (POR) | 2:09:21.0 |

# Summer Olympic Games Champions (continued)

## Athletics (track-and-field) (men) (continued)

| MARATHON | | HR:MIN:SEC |
|---|---|---|
| 1988 | Gelindo Bordin (ITA) | 2:10:32.0 |
| 1992 | Hwang Young-Cho (KOR) | 2:13:23.0 |
| 1996 | Josia Thugwane (RSA) | 2:12:36.0 |
| 2000 | Gezahgne Abera (ETH) | 2:10:11.0 |

| 110-METER HURDLES | | SEC |
|---|---|---|
| 1896[2] | Thomas Curtis (USA) | 17.6 |
| 1900 | Alvin Kraenzlein (USA) | 15.4 |
| 1904 | Frederick Schule (USA) | 16.0 |
| 1908 | Forrest Smithson (USA) | 15.0 |
| 1912 | Frederick Kelly (USA) | 15.1 |
| 1920 | Earl Thomson (CAN) | 14.8 |
| 1924 | Daniel Kinsey (USA) | 15.0 |
| 1928 | Sydney Atkinson (RSA) | 14.8 |
| 1932 | George Saling (USA) | 14.6 |
| 1936 | Forrest Towns (USA) | 14.2 |
| 1948 | William Porter (USA) | 13.9 |
| 1952 | Harrison Dillard (USA) | 13.7 |
| 1956 | Lee Calhoun (USA) | 13.5 |
| 1960 | Lee Calhoun (USA) | 13.8 |
| 1964 | Hayes Wendell Jones (USA) | 13.6 |
| 1968 | Willie Davenport (USA) | 13.3 |
| 1972 | Rodney Milburn (USA) | 13.24 |
| 1976 | Guy Drut (FRA) | 13.30 |
| 1980 | Thomas Munkelt (GDR) | 13.39 |
| 1984 | Roger Kingdom (USA) | 13.20 |
| 1988 | Roger Kingdom (USA) | 12.98 |
| 1992 | Mark McKoy (CAN) | 13.12 |
| 1996 | Allen Johnson (USA) | 12.95 |
| 2000 | Anier Garcia (CUB) | 13.00 |

| 200-METER HURDLES | | SEC |
|---|---|---|
| 1900 | Alvin Kraenzlein (USA) | 25.4 |
| 1904 | Harry Hillman (USA) | 24.6 |

| 400-METER HURDLES | | SEC |
|---|---|---|
| 1900 | Walter Tewksbury (USA) | 57.6 |
| 1904[3] | Harry Hillman (USA) | 53.0 |
| 1908 | Charles Bacon (USA) | 55.0 |
| 1920 | Frank Loomis (USA) | 54.0 |
| 1924 | Frederick Morgan Taylor (USA) | 52.6 |
| 1928 | David George Burghley (GBR) | 53.4 |
| 1932 | Robert Tisdall (IRE) | 51.7 |
| 1936 | Glenn Hardin (USA) | 52.4 |
| 1948 | Roy Cochran (USA) | 51.1 |
| 1952 | Charles Moore (USA) | 50.8 |
| 1956 | Glenn Davis (USA) | 50.1 |
| 1960 | Glenn Davis (USA) | 49.3 |
| 1964 | Warren Cawley (USA) | 49.6 |
| 1968 | David Hemery (GBR) | 48.1 |
| 1972 | John Akii-Bua (UGA) | 47.82 |
| 1976 | Edwin Moses (USA) | 47.64 |
| 1980 | Volker Beck (GDR) | 48.70 |
| 1984 | Edwin Moses (USA) | 47.75 |
| 1988 | Andre Phillips (USA) | 47.19 |
| 1992 | Kevin Young (USA) | 46.78 |
| 1996 | Derrick Adkins (USA) | 47.54 |
| 2000 | Angelo Taylor (USA) | 47.50 |

| 2,500-METER STEEPLECHASE | | MIN:SEC |
|---|---|---|
| 1900 | George Orton (USA) | 7:34.4 |

| 2,590-METER STEEPLECHASE | | MIN:SEC |
|---|---|---|
| 1904 | James Lightbody (USA) | 7:39.6 |

| 3,000-METER STEEPLECHASE | | MIN:SEC |
|---|---|---|
| 1920 | Percy Hodge (GBR) | 10:00.4 |

## Athletics (track-and-field) (men) (continued)

| 3,000-METER STEEPLECHASE | | MIN:SEC |
|---|---|---|
| 1924 | Vilho Ritola (FIN) | 9:33.6 |
| 1928 | Toivo Loukola (FIN) | 9:21.8 |
| 1932 | Volmari Iso-Hollo (FIN) | 10:33.4[4] |
| 1936 | Volmari Iso-Hollo (FIN) | 9:03.8 |
| 1948 | Thore Sjöstrand (SWE) | 9:04.6 |
| 1952 | Horace Ashenfelter (USA) | 8:45.4 |
| 1956 | Christopher Brasher (GBR) | 8:41.2 |
| 1960 | Zdislaw Krzyszkowiak (POL) | 8:34.2 |
| 1964 | Gaston Roelants (BEL) | 8:30.8 |
| 1968 | Amos Biwott (KEN) | 8:51.0 |
| 1972 | Kipchoge Keino (KEN) | 8:23.6 |
| 1976 | Anders Gärderud (SWE) | 8:08.02 |
| 1980 | Bronislaw Malinowski (POL) | 8:09.70 |
| 1984 | Julius Korir (KEN) | 8:11.80 |
| 1988 | Julius Kariuki (KEN) | 8:05.51 |
| 1992 | Mathew Birir (KEN) | 8:08.84 |
| 1996 | Joseph Keter (KEN) | 8:07.12 |
| 2000 | Reuben Kosgei (KEN) | 8:21.43 |

| 3,200-METER STEEPLECHASE | | MIN:SEC |
|---|---|---|
| 1908 | Arthur Russell (GBR) | 10:47.8 |

| 3,000 METERS (TEAM) (TEAM/INDIVIDUAL WINNER) | | MIN:SEC |
|---|---|---|
| 1912 | United States/Tell Berna | 8:44.6 |
| 1920 | United States/Horace Brown | 8:45.4 |
| 1924 | Finland/Paavo Nurmi | 8:32 |

| 3 MILES (TEAM) (TEAM/INDIVIDUAL WINNER) | | MIN:SEC |
|---|---|---|
| 1908 | Great Britain/Joseph Deakin | 14:39.6 |

| 5,000 METERS (TEAM) (TEAM/INDIVIDUAL WINNER) | | MIN:SEC |
|---|---|---|
| 1900 | Great Britain-Australia/Charles Bennett | 15:20 |

| 4 MILES (TEAM) (TEAM/INDIVIDUAL WINNER) | | MIN:SEC |
|---|---|---|
| 1904 | United States/Arthur Newton (USA) | 21:17.8 |

| 4 × 100 METER RELAY | | SEC |
|---|---|---|
| 1912 | Great Britain | 42.4 |
| 1920 | United States | 42.2 |
| 1924 | United States | 41.0 |
| 1928 | United States | 41.0 |
| 1932 | United States | 40.0 |
| 1936 | United States | 39.8 |
| 1948 | United States | 40.6 |
| 1952 | United States | 40.1 |
| 1956 | United States | 39.5 |
| 1960 | Germany | 39.5 |
| 1964 | United States | 39.0 |
| 1968 | United States | 38.2 |
| 1972 | United States | 38.19 |
| 1976 | United States | 38.33 |
| 1980 | USSR | 38.26 |
| 1984 | United States | 37.83 |
| 1988 | USSR | 38.19 |
| 1992 | United States | 37.40 |
| 1996 | Canada | 37.69 |
| 2000 | United States | 37.61 |

| 4 × 400 METER RELAY | | MIN:SEC |
|---|---|---|
| 1912 | United States | 3:16.6 |
| 1920 | Great Britain | 3:22.2 |
| 1924 | United States | 3:16.0 |
| 1928 | United States | 3:14.2 |
| 1932 | United States | 3:08.2 |

# Summer Olympic Games Champions (continued)

### Athletics (track-and-field) (men) (continued)

#### 4 × 400 METER RELAY

| | | MIN:SEC |
|---|---|---|
| 1936 | Great Britain | 3:09.0 |
| 1948 | United States | 3:10.4 |
| 1952 | Jamaica | 3:03.9 |
| 1956 | United States | 3:04.8 |
| 1960 | United States | 3:02.2 |
| 1964 | United States | 3:00.7 |
| 1968 | United States | 2:56.1 |
| 1972 | Kenya | 2:59.8 |
| 1976 | United States | 2:58.65 |
| 1980 | USSR | 3:01.1 |
| 1984 | United States | 2:57.91 |
| 1988 | United States | 2:56.16 |
| 1992 | United States | 2:55.74 |
| 1996 | United States | 2:55.99 |
| 2000 | United States | 2:56.35 |

#### 1,600-METER RELAY (200 × 200 × 400 × 800 METERS)

| | | MIN:SEC |
|---|---|---|
| 1908 | United States | 3:29.4 |

#### 8,000 M CROSS-COUNTRY

| | | MIN:SEC |
|---|---|---|
| 1920 | Paavo Nurmi (FIN) | 27:15 |

#### 10,000 M CROSS-COUNTRY

| | | MIN:SEC |
|---|---|---|
| 1924 | Paavo Nurmi (FIN) | 32:54.8 |

#### 12,000 M CROSS-COUNTRY

| | | MIN:SEC |
|---|---|---|
| 1912 | Hannes Kolehmainen (FIN) | 45:11.6 |

#### 3,000-METER WALK

| | | MIN:SEC |
|---|---|---|
| 1920 | Ugo Frigerio (ITA) | 13:14.2 |

#### 3,500-METER WALK

| | | MIN:SEC |
|---|---|---|
| 1908 | George Larner (GBR) | 14:55 |

#### 10,000-METER WALK

| | | MIN:SEC |
|---|---|---|
| 1912 | George Goulding (CAN) | 46:28.4 |
| 1920 | Ugo Frigerio (ITA) | 48:06.2 |
| 1924 | Ugo Frigerio (ITA) | 47:49 |
| 1948 | John Mikaelsson (SWE) | 45:13.2 |
| 1952 | John Mikaelsson (SWE) | 45:02.8 |

#### 10-MILE WALK

| | | HR:MIN:SEC |
|---|---|---|
| 1908 | George Larner (GBR) | 1:15:57.4 |

#### 20,000-METER WALK

| | | HR:MIN:SEC |
|---|---|---|
| 1956 | Leonid Spirin (URS) | 1:31:27.4 |
| 1960 | Vladimir Golubnichy (URS) | 1:34:07.2 |
| 1964 | Kenneth Matthews (GBR) | 1:29:34.0 |
| 1968 | Vladimir Golubnichy (URS) | 1:33:58.4 |
| 1972 | Peter Frenkel (GDR) | 1:26:42.6 |
| 1976 | Daniel Bautista (MEX) | 1:24:40.6 |
| 1980 | Maurizio Damilano (ITA) | 1:23:35.5 |
| 1984 | Ernesto Canto (MEX) | 1:23:13.0 |
| 1988 | Jozef Pribilinec (TCH) | 1:19:57.0 |
| 1992 | Daniel Plaza Montero (ESP) | 1:21:45.0 |
| 1996 | Jefferson Pérez (ECU) | 1:20:07.0 |
| 2000 | Robert Korzeniowski (POL) | 1:18:59.0 |

#### 50,000-METER WALK

| | | HR:MIN:SEC |
|---|---|---|
| 1932 | Thomas Green (GBR) | 4:50:10.0 |
| 1936 | Harold Whitlock (GBR) | 4:30:41.4 |
| 1948 | John Ljunggren (SWE) | 4:41:52.0 |
| 1952 | Giuseppe Dordoni (ITA) | 4:28:07.8 |
| 1956 | Norman Read (NZL) | 4:30:42.8 |
| 1960 | Donald Thompson (GBR) | 4:25:30.0 |
| 1964 | Abdon Pamich (ITA) | 4:11:12.4 |

### Athletics (track-and-field) (men) (continued)

#### 50,000-METER WALK

| | | HR:MIN:SEC |
|---|---|---|
| 1968 | Christophe Höhne (GDR) | 4:20:13.6 |
| 1972 | Bernd Kannenberg (FRG) | 3:56:11.6 |
| 1980 | Hartwig Gauder (GDR) | 3:49:24.0 |
| 1984 | Raúl Gonzáles (MEX) | 3:47:26.0 |
| 1988 | Vyacheslav Ivanenko (URS) | 3:38:29.0 |
| 1992 | Andrey Perlov (UNT) | 3:50:13.0 |
| 1996 | Robert Korzeniowski (POL) | 3:43:03.0 |
| 2000 | Robert Korzeniowski (POL) | 3:42:22.0 |

#### HIGH JUMP

| | | METERS |
|---|---|---|
| 1896 | Ellery Clark (USA) | 1.81 |
| 1900 | Irving Baxter (USA) | 1.90 |
| 1904 | Samuel Jones (USA) | 1.80 |
| 1908 | Harry Porter (USA) | 1.90 |
| 1912 | Alma Richards (USA) | 1.93 |
| 1920 | Richmond Landon (USA) | 1.93 |
| 1924 | Harold Osborn (USA) | 1.98 |
| 1928 | Robert King (USA) | 1.94 |
| 1932 | Duncan McNaughton (CAN) | 1.97 |
| 1936 | Cornelius Johnson (USA) | 2.03 |
| 1948 | John Winter (AUS) | 1.98 |
| 1952 | Walter Davis (USA) | 2.04 |
| 1956 | Charles Dumas (USA) | 2.12 |
| 1960 | Robert Shavlakadze (URS) | 2.16 |
| 1964 | Valery Brumel (URS) | 2.18 |
| 1968 | Richard Fosbury (USA) | 2.24 |
| 1972 | Yury Tarmak (URS) | 2.23 |
| 1976 | Jacek Wszola (POL) | 2.25 |
| 1980 | Gerd Wessig (GDR) | 2.36 |
| 1984 | Dietmar Mögenburg (FRG) | 2.35 |
| 1988 | Gennady Avdeyenko (URS) | 2.38 |
| 1992 | Javier Sotomayor (CUB) | 2.34 |
| 1996 | Charles Austin (USA) | 2.39 |
| 2000 | Sergey Klyugin (RUS) | 2.35 |

#### STANDING HIGH JUMP

| | | METERS |
|---|---|---|
| 1900 | Ray Ewry (USA) | 1.65 |
| 1904 | Ray Ewry (USA) | 1.6 |
| 1908 | Ray Ewry (USA) | 1.57 |
| 1912 | Platt Adams (USA) | 1.63 |

#### POLE VAULT

| | | METERS |
|---|---|---|
| 1896 | William Welles Hoyt (USA) | 3.30 |
| 1900 | Irving Baxter (USA) | 3.30 |
| 1904 | Charles Dvorak (USA) | 3.50 |
| 1908 | Edward Cooke (USA); Alfred Gilbert (USA) (tied) | 3.71 |
| 1912 | Harry Babcock (USA) | 3.95 |
| 1920 | Frank Foss (USA) | 4.09 |
| 1924 | Lee Barnes (USA) | 3.95 |
| 1928 | Sabin Carr (USA) | 4.20 |
| 1932 | William Miller (USA) | 4.31 |
| 1936 | Earle Meadows (USA) | 4.35 |
| 1948 | Owen Guinn Smith (USA) | 4.30 |
| 1952 | Robert Richards (USA) | 4.55 |
| 1956 | Robert Richards (USA) | 4.56 |
| 1960 | Donald Bragg (USA) | 4.70 |
| 1964 | Fred Hansen (USA) | 5.10 |
| 1968 | Robert Seagren (USA) | 5.40 |
| 1972 | Wolfgang Nordwig (GDR) | 5.50 |
| 1976 | Tadeusz Slusarski (POL) | 5.50 |
| 1980 | Wladyslaw Kozakiewicz (POL) | 5.78 |
| 1984 | Pierre Quinon (FRA) | 5.75 |
| 1988 | Sergey Bubka (URS) | 5.90 |
| 1992 | Maksim Tarasov (UNT) | 5.80 |
| 1996 | Jean Galfione (FRA) | 5.92 |
| 2000 | Nick Hysong (USA) | 5.90 |

# Summer Olympic Games Champions (continued)

## Athletics (track-and-field) (men) (continued)

| LONG JUMP | | METERS |
|---|---|---|
| 1896 | Ellery Clark (USA) | 6.35 |
| 1900 | Alvin Kraenzlein (USA) | 7.18 |
| 1904 | Meyer Prinstein (USA) | 7.34 |
| 1908 | Francis Irons (USA) | 7.48 |
| 1912 | Albert Gutterson (USA) | 7.60 |
| 1920 | William Pettersson (SWE) | 7.15 |
| 1924 | William de Hart-Hubbard (USA) | 7.44 |
| 1928 | Edward Hamm (USA) | 7.73 |
| 1932 | Edward Gordon (USA) | 7.64 |
| 1936 | Jesse Owens (USA) | 8.06 |
| 1948 | Willie Steele (USA) | 7.82 |
| 1952 | Jerome Biffle (USA) | 7.57 |
| 1956 | Gregory Bell (USA) | 7.83 |
| 1960 | Ralph Boston (USA) | 8.12 |
| 1964 | Lynn Davies (GBR) | 8.07 |
| 1968 | Robert Beamon (USA) | 8.90 |
| 1972 | Randy Williams (USA) | 8.24 |
| 1976 | Arnie Robinson (USA) | 8.35 |
| 1980 | Lutz Dombrowski (GDR) | 8.54 |
| 1984 | Carl Lewis (USA) | 8.54 |
| 1988 | Carl Lewis (USA) | 8.72 |
| 1992 | Carl Lewis (USA) | 8.67 |
| 1996 | Carl Lewis (USA) | 8.50 |
| 2000 | Ivan Pedroso (CUB) | 8.55 |

| STANDING LONG JUMP | | METERS |
|---|---|---|
| 1900 | Ray Ewry (USA) | 3.21 |
| 1904 | Ray Ewry (USA) | 3.47 |
| 1908 | Ray Ewry (USA) | 3.33 |
| 1912 | Constantinos Tsiklitiras (GRE) | 3.37 |

| TRIPLE JUMP | | METERS |
|---|---|---|
| 1896 | James Connolly (USA) | 13.71 |
| 1900 | Myer Prinstein (USA) | 14.47 |
| 1904 | Myer Prinstein (USA) | 14.35 |
| 1908 | Timothy Ahearne (GBR) | 14.91 |
| 1912 | Gustaf Lindblom (SWE) | 14.76 |
| 1920 | Vilho Tuulos (FIN) | 14.50 |
| 1924 | Anthony Winter (AUS) | 15.53 |
| 1928 | Mikio Oda (JPN) | 15.21 |
| 1932 | Chuhei Nambu (JPN) | 15.72 |
| 1936 | Naoto Tajima (JPN) | 16.00 |
| 1948 | Arne Åhman (SWE) | 15.40 |
| 1952 | Adhemar Ferreira da Silva (BRA) | 16.22 |
| 1956 | Adhemar Ferreira da Silva (BRA) | 16.35 |
| 1960 | Josef Szmidt (POL) | 16.81 |
| 1964 | Josef Szmidt (POL) | 16.85 |
| 1968 | Viktor Saneyev (URS) | 17.39 |
| 1972 | Viktor Saneyev (URS) | 17.35 |
| 1976 | Viktor Saneyev (URS) | 17.29 |
| 1980 | Jaak Uudmae (URS) | 17.35 |
| 1984 | Al Joyner (USA) | 17.26 |
| 1988 | Khristo Markov (BUL) | 17.61 |
| 1992 | Michael Conley (USA) | 17.63 |
| 1996 | Kenny Harrison (USA) | 18.09 |
| 2000 | Jonathan Edwards (GBR) | 17.71 |

| STANDING TRIPLE JUMP | | METERS |
|---|---|---|
| 1900 | Ray Ewry (USA) | 10.58 |
| 1904 | Ray Ewry (USA) | 10.54 |

| SHOT PUT | | METERS |
|---|---|---|
| 1896 | Robert Garrett (USA) | 11.22 |
| 1900 | Richard Sheldon (USA) | 14.10 |
| 1904 | Ralph Rose (USA) | 14.81 |
| 1908 | Ralph Rose (USA) | 14.21 |
| 1912 | Patrick McDonald (USA) | 15.34 |

## Athletics (track-and-field) (men) (continued)

| SHOT PUT | | METERS |
|---|---|---|
| 1920 | Frans Pörhölä (FIN) | 14.81 |
| 1924 | Lemuel Clarence Houser (USA) | 14.99 |
| 1928 | John Kuck (USA) | 15.87 |
| 1932 | Leo Sexton (USA) | 16.00 |
| 1936 | Hans Woellke (GER) | 16.20 |
| 1948 | Wilbur Thompson (USA) | 17.12 |
| 1952 | William Parry O'Brien (USA) | 17.41 |
| 1956 | William Parry O'Brien (USA) | 18.57 |
| 1960 | William Nieder (USA) | 19.68 |
| 1964 | Dallas Long (USA) | 20.33 |
| 1968 | Randy Matson (USA) | 20.54 |
| 1972 | Wladislaw Komar (POL) | 21.18 |
| 1976 | Udo Beyer (GDR) | 21.05 |
| 1980 | Vladimir Kiselyov (URS) | 21.35 |
| 1984 | Alessandro Andrei (ITA) | 21.26 |
| 1988 | Ulf Timmermann (GDR) | 22.47 |
| 1992 | Michael Stulce (USA) | 21.70 |
| 1996 | Randy Barnes (USA) | 21.62 |
| 2000 | Arsi Harju (FIN) | 21.29 |

| SHOT PUT (TWO HANDS) | | METERS |
|---|---|---|
| 1912 | Ralph Rose (USA) | 27.7 |

| DISCUS THROW | | METERS |
|---|---|---|
| 1896 | Robert Garrett (USA) | 29.15 |
| 1900 | Rezso Bauer (HUN) | 36.04 |
| 1904 | Martin Sheridan (USA) | 39.28 |
| 1908 | Martin Sheridan (USA) | 40.89 |
| 1912 | Armas Taipale (FIN) | 45.21 |
| 1920 | Elmer Niklander (FIN) | 44.68 |
| 1924 | Lemuel Clarence Houser (USA) | 46.15 |
| 1928 | Lemuel Clarence Houser (USA) | 47.32 |
| 1932 | John Anderson (USA) | 49.49 |
| 1936 | Kenneth Carpenter (USA) | 50.48 |
| 1948 | Adolfo Consolini (ITA) | 52.78 |
| 1952 | Sim Iness (USA) | 55.03 |
| 1956 | Alfred Oerter (USA) | 56.36 |
| 1960 | Alfred Oerter (USA) | 59.18 |
| 1964 | Alfred Oerter (USA) | 61.00 |
| 1968 | Alfred Oerter (USA) | 64.78 |
| 1972 | Ludvig Danek (TCH) | 64.40 |
| 1976 | Mac Wilkins (USA) | 67.50 |
| 1980 | Viktor Rashchupkin (URS) | 66.64 |
| 1984 | Rolf Danneberg (FRG) | 66.60 |
| 1988 | Jürgen Schult (GDR) | 68.82 |
| 1992 | Romas Ubartas (LTU) | 65.12 |
| 1996 | Lars Riedel (GER) | 69.40 |
| 2000 | Virgilijus Alekna (LTU) | 69.30 |

| DISCUS (GREEK STYLE) | | METERS |
|---|---|---|
| 1908 | Martin Sheridan (USA) | 37.99 |

| DISCUS (TWO HANDS) | | METERS |
|---|---|---|
| 1912 | Armas Taipale (FIN) | 82.86 |

| HAMMER THROW | | METERS |
|---|---|---|
| 1900 | John Flanagan (USA) | 49.73 |
| 1904 | John Flanagan (USA) | 51.23 |
| 1908 | John Flanagan (USA) | 51.92 |
| 1912 | Matthew McGrath (USA) | 54.74 |
| 1920 | Patrick Ryan (USA) | 52.87 |
| 1924 | Frederick Tootell (USA) | 53.30 |
| 1928 | Patrick O'Callaghan (IRE) | 51.39 |
| 1932 | Patrick O'Callaghan (IRE) | 53.92 |
| 1936 | Karl Hein (GER) | 56.49 |
| 1948 | Imre Nemeth (HUN) | 56.07 |
| 1952 | Jozsef Csermak (HUN) | 60.34 |

# Summer Olympic Games Champions (continued)

## Athletics (track-and-field) (men) (continued)

### HAMMER THROW

| Year | Champion | METERS |
|---|---|---|
| 1956 | Harold Connolly (USA) | 63.19 |
| 1960 | Vasily Rudenkov (URS) | 67.10 |
| 1964 | Romuald Klim (URS) | 69.74 |
| 1968 | Gyula Zsivotzky (HUN) | 73.36 |
| 1972 | Anatoly Bondarchuk (URS) | 75.50 |
| 1976 | Yury Sedykh (URS) | 77.52 |
| 1980 | Yury Sedykh (URS) | 81.80 |
| 1984 | Juha Tiainen (FIN) | 78.08 |
| 1988 | Sergey Litvinov (URS) | 84.80 |
| 1992 | Andrey Abduvaliyev (UNT) | 82.53 |
| 1996 | Balazs Kiss (HUN) | 81.24 |
| 2000 | Szymon Ziolkowski (POL) | 80.02 |

### JAVELIN THROW

| Year | Champion | METERS |
|---|---|---|
| 1908 | Eric Lemming (SWE) | 54.83 |
| 1912 | Eric Lemming (SWE) | 60.64 |
| 1920 | Jonni Myyrä (FIN) | 65.78 |
| 1924 | Jonni Myyrä (FIN) | 62.96 |
| 1928 | Erik Lundkvist (SWE) | 66.60 |
| 1932 | Matti Järvinen (FIN) | 72.71 |
| 1936 | Gerhard Stöck (GER) | 71.84 |
| 1948 | Kai Rautavaara (FIN) | 69.77 |
| 1952 | Cy Young (USA) | 73.78 |
| 1956 | Egil Danielson (NOR) | 85.71 |
| 1960 | Viktor Tsybulenko (URS) | 84.64 |
| 1964 | Pauli Nevala (FIN) | 82.66 |
| 1968 | Janis Lusis (URS) | 90.10 |
| 1972 | Klaus Wolfermann (FRG) | 90.48 |
| 1976 | Miklos Nemeth (HUN) | 94.58 |
| 1980 | Dainis Kula (URS) | 91.20 |
| 1984 | Arto Härkönen (FIN) | 86.76 |
| 1988 | Tapio Korjus (FIN) | 84.28 |
| 1992 | Jan Zelezny (TCH) | 89.66 |
| 1996 | Jan Zelezny (CZE) | 88.16 |
| 2000 | Jan Zelezny (CZE) | 90.17 |

### JAVELIN (FREESTYLE)

| Year | Champion | METERS |
|---|---|---|
| 1908 | Eric Lemming (SWE) | 54.45 |

### JAVELIN (TWO HANDS)

| Year | Champion | METERS |
|---|---|---|
| 1912 | Juho Saaristo (FIN) | 109.42 |

### THROWING THE 56 LB WEIGHT

| Year | Champion | METERS |
|---|---|---|
| 1904 | Étienne Desmarteau (CAN) | 10.46 |
| 1920 | Patrick McDonald (USA) | 11.26 |

### TUG-OF-WAR

| Year | Champion |
|---|---|
| 1900 | Sweden-Denmark |
| 1904 | United States |
| 1908 | Great Britain |
| 1912 | Sweden |
| 1920 | Great Britain |

### TRIATHLON (LONG JUMP/SHOT PUT/100 YARDS)

| Year | Champion |
|---|---|
| 1904 | Max Emmerich (USA) |

### PENTATHLON

| Year | Champion |
|---|---|
| 1912 | Jim Thorpe (USA)[5]; Ferdinand Bie (NOR) (cowinners) |
| 1920 | Eero Lehtonen (FIN) |
| 1924 | Eero Lehtonen (FIN) |

### DECATHLON

| Year | Champion |
|---|---|
| 1904 | Thomas Kiely (IRL) |
| 1912 | Jim Thorpe (USA)[5]; Hugo Wieslander (SWE) (cowinners) |
| 1920 | Helge Lövland (NOR) |

## Athletics (track-and-field) (men) (continued)

### DECATHLON

| Year | Champion |
|---|---|
| 1924 | Harold Osborn (USA) |
| 1928 | Paavo Yrjölä (FIN) |
| 1932 | James Bausch (USA) |
| 1936 | Glenn Morris (USA) |
| 1948 | Robert Mathias (USA) |
| 1952 | Robert Mathias (USA) |
| 1956 | Milton Campbell (USA) |
| 1960 | Rafer Johnson (USA) |
| 1964 | Willi Holdorf (GER) |
| 1968 | William Toomey (USA) |
| 1972 | Nikolay Avilov (URS) |
| 1976 | Bruce Jenner (USA) |
| 1980 | Daley Thompson (GBR) |
| 1984 | Daley Thompson (GBR) |
| 1988 | Christian Schenk (GDR) |
| 1992 | Robert Zmelik (TCH) |
| 1996 | Dan O'Brien (USA) |
| 2000 | Erki Nool (EST) |

## Athletics (track-and-field) (women)

### 100 METERS

| Year | Champion | SEC |
|---|---|---|
| 1928 | Elizabeth Robinson (USA) | 12.2 |
| 1932 | Stanislawa Walasiewicz (POL) | 11.9 |
| 1936 | Helen Stephens (USA) | 11.5 |
| 1948 | Francina Blankers-Koen (NED) | 11.9 |
| 1952 | Marjorie Jackson (AUS) | 11.5 |
| 1956 | Elizabeth Cuthbert (AUS) | 11.5 |
| 1960 | Wilma Rudolph (USA) | 11.0 |
| 1964 | Wyomia Tyus (USA) | 11.4 |
| 1968 | Wyomia Tyus (USA) | 11.0 |
| 1972 | Renate Stecher (GDR) | 11.07 |
| 1976 | Annegret Richter (FRG) | 11.08 |
| 1980 | Lyudmila Kondratyeva (URS) | 11.06 |
| 1984 | Evelyn Ashford (USA) | 10.97 |
| 1988 | Florence Griffith Joyner (USA) | 10.54 |
| 1992 | Gail Devers (USA) | 10.82 |
| 1996 | Gail Devers (USA) | 10.94 |
| 2000 | Marion Jones (USA) | 10.75 |

### 200 METERS

| Year | Champion | SEC |
|---|---|---|
| 1948 | Francina Blankers-Koen (NED) | 24.4 |
| 1952 | Marjorie Jackson (AUS) | 23.7 |
| 1956 | Elizabeth Cuthbert (AUS) | 23.4 |
| 1960 | Wilma Rudolph (USA) | 24.0 |
| 1964 | Edith Marie McGuire (USA) | 23.0 |
| 1968 | Irena Szewinska (POL) | 22.5 |
| 1972 | Renate Stecher (GDR) | 22.40 |
| 1976 | Bärbel Eckert (GDR) | 22.37 |
| 1980 | Bärbel Eckert-Wöckel (GDR) | 22.03 |
| 1984 | Valerie Brisco-Hooks (USA) | 21.81 |
| 1988 | Florence Griffith Joyner (USA) | 21.34 |
| 1992 | Gwen Torrence (USA) | 21.81 |
| 1996 | Marie-Jose Perec (FRA) | 22.12 |
| 2000 | Marion Jones (USA) | 21.84 |

### 400 METERS

| Year | Champion | SEC |
|---|---|---|
| 1964 | Elizabeth Cuthbert (AUS) | 52.0 |
| 1968 | Colette Besson (FRA) | 52.0 |
| 1972 | Monika Zehrt (GDR) | 51.08 |
| 1976 | Irena Szewinska (POL) | 49.29 |
| 1980 | Marita Koch (GDR) | 48.88 |
| 1984 | Valerie Brisco-Hooks (USA) | 48.83 |
| 1988 | Olga Bryzgina (URS) | 48.65 |
| 1992 | Marie-Jose Perec (FRA) | 48.83 |
| 1996 | Marie-Jose Perec (FRA) | 48.25 |
| 2000 | Cathy Freeman (AUS) | 49.11 |

# Summer Olympic Games Champions (continued)

## Athletics (track-and-field) (women) (continued)

### 800 METERS

| | | MIN:SEC |
|---|---|---|
| 1928 | Lina Radke-Batschauer (GER) | 2:16.8 |
| 1960 | Lyudmila Lysenko-Shevtsova (URS) | 2:04.3 |
| 1964 | Ann Packer (GBR) | 2:01.1 |
| 1968 | Madeline Manning (USA) | 2:00.9 |
| 1972 | Hildegard Falck (FRG) | 1:58.6 |
| 1976 | Tatyana Kazankina (URS) | 1:54.94 |
| 1980 | Nadezhda Olizarenko (URS) | 1:53.50 |
| 1984 | Doina Melinte (ROM) | 1:57.6 |
| 1988 | Sigrun Wodars (GDR) | 1:56.10 |
| 1992 | Ellen van Langen (NED) | 1:55.54 |
| 1996 | Svetlana Masterkova (RUS) | 1:57.73 |
| 2000 | Maria Mutola (MOZ) | 1:56.15 |

### 1,500 METERS

| | | MIN:SEC |
|---|---|---|
| 1972 | Lyudmila Bragina (URS) | 4:01.4 |
| 1976 | Tatyana Kazankina (URS) | 4:05.48 |
| 1980 | Tatyana Kazankina (URS) | 3:56.6 |
| 1984 | Gabriella Dorio (ITA) | 4:03.25 |
| 1988 | Paula Ivan (ROM) | 3:53.96 |
| 1992 | Hassiba Boulmerka (ALG) | 3:55.30 |
| 1996 | Svetlana Masterkova (RUS) | 4:00.83 |
| 2000 | Nouria Merah-Benida (ALG) | 4:05.10 |

### 3,000 METERS

| | | MIN:SEC |
|---|---|---|
| 1984 | Maricica Puica (ROM) | 8:35.96 |
| 1988 | Tatyana Samolenko (URS) | 8:26.53 |
| 1992 | Yelena Romanova (UNT) | 8:46.04 |

### 5,000 METERS

| | | MIN:SEC |
|---|---|---|
| 1996 | Wang Jungxia (CHN) | 14:59.88 |
| 2000 | Gabriela Szabo (ROM) | 14:40.79 |

### 10,000 METERS

| | | MIN:SEC |
|---|---|---|
| 1988 | Olga Bondarenko (URS) | 31:05.21 |
| 1992 | Derartu Tulu (ETH) | 31:06.02 |
| 1996 | Fernanda Ribeiro (POR) | 31:01.63 |
| 2000 | Derartu Tulu (ETH) | 30:17.49 |

### MARATHON

| | | HR:MIN:SEC |
|---|---|---|
| 1984 | Joan Benoit (USA) | 2:24:52 |
| 1988 | Rosa Mota (POR) | 2:25:40 |
| 1992 | Valentina Yegorova (UNT) | 2:32:41 |
| 1996 | Fatuma Roba (ETH) | 2:26:05 |
| 2000 | Naoko Takahashi (JPN) | 2:23:14 |

### 80-METER HURDLES (100 METERS FROM 1972)

| | | SEC |
|---|---|---|
| 1932 | Mildred "Babe" Didrikson (USA) | 11.7 |
| 1936 | Trebisonda Valla (ITA) | 11.7 |
| 1948 | Francina Blankers-Koen (NED) | 11.2 |
| 1952 | Shirley Strickland de La Hunty (AUS) | 10.9 |
| 1956 | Shirley Strickland de La Hunty (AUS) | 10.7 |
| 1960 | Irina Press (URS) | 10.8 |
| 1964 | Karin Balzer (GER) | 10.5 |
| 1968 | Maureen Caird (AUS) | 10.3 |
| 1972 | Annelie Ehrhardt (GDR) | 12.59 |
| 1976 | Johanna Schaller (GDR) | 12.77 |
| 1980 | Vera Komisova (URS) | 12.56 |
| 1984 | Benita Fitzgerald-Brown (USA) | 12.84 |
| 1988 | Iordanka Donkova (BUL) | 12.38 |
| 1992 | Paraskevi Patoulidou (GRE) | 12.64 |
| 1996 | Ludmila Engquist (SWE) | 12.58 |
| 2000 | Olga Shishigina (KAZ) | 12.65 |

### 400-METER HURDLES

| | | SEC |
|---|---|---|
| 1984 | Nawal el Moutawakel (MAR) | 54.61 |
| 1988 | Debra Flintoff-King (AUS) | 53.17 |
| 1992 | Sally Gunnell (GBR) | 53.23 |
| 1996 | Deon Hemmings (JAM) | 52.82 |
| 2000 | Irina Privalova (RUS) | 53.02 |

### 4 × 100-METER RELAY

| | | SEC |
|---|---|---|
| 1928 | Canada | 48.4 |
| 1932 | United States | 47.0 |
| 1936 | United States | 46.9 |
| 1948 | The Netherlands | 47.5 |
| 1952 | United States | 45.9 |
| 1956 | Australia | 44.5 |
| 1960 | United States | 44.5 |
| 1964 | Poland | 43.6 |
| 1968 | United States | 42.8 |
| 1972 | West Germany | 42.81 |
| 1976 | East Germany | 42.55 |
| 1980 | East Germany | 41.60 |
| 1984 | United States | 41.65 |
| 1988 | United States | 41.98 |
| 1992 | United States | 42.11 |
| 1996 | United States | 41.95 |
| 2000 | The Bahamas | 41.95 |

### 4 × 400-METER RELAY

| | | MIN:SEC |
|---|---|---|
| 1972 | East Germany | 3:23.0 |
| 1976 | East Germany | 3:19.23 |
| 1980 | USSR | 3:20.2 |
| 1984 | United States | 3:18.29 |
| 1988 | USSR | 3:15.18 |
| 1992 | Unified Team | 3:20.20 |
| 1996 | United States | 3:20.91 |
| 2000 | United States | 3:22.62 |

### 10,000-METER WALK

| | | MIN:SEC |
|---|---|---|
| 1992 | Chen Yueling (CHN) | 44:32 |
| 1996 | Yelena Nikolayeva (RUS) | 41:49 |

### 20,000-METER WALK

| | | MIN:SEC |
|---|---|---|
| 2000 | Wang Liping (CHN) | 1:29.05 |

### HIGH JUMP

| | | METERS |
|---|---|---|
| 1928 | Ethel Catherwood (CAN) | 1.59 |
| 1932 | Jean Shiley (USA) | 1.66 |
| 1936 | Ibolya Csak (HUN) | 1.60 |
| 1948 | Alice Coachman (USA) | 1.68 |
| 1952 | Esther Brand (RSA) | 1.67 |
| 1956 | Mildred Louise McDaniel (USA) | 1.76 |
| 1960 | Iolanda Balas (ROM) | 1.85 |
| 1964 | Iolanda Balas (ROM) | 1.90 |
| 1968 | Miloslava Rezkova (TCH) | 1.82 |
| 1972 | Ulrike Meyfarth (FRG) | 1.92 |
| 1976 | Rosemarie Ackermann (GDR) | 1.93 |
| 1980 | Sara Simeoni (ITA) | 1.97 |
| 1984 | Ulrike Meyfarth (FRG) | 2.02 |
| 1988 | Louise Ritter (USA) | 2.03 |
| 1992 | Heike Henkel (GER) | 2.02 |
| 1996 | Stefka Kostadinova (BUL) | 2.05 |
| 2000 | Yelena Yelesina (RUS) | 2.01 |

### POLE VAULT

| | | METERS |
|---|---|---|
| 2000 | Stacy Dragila (USA) | 4.60 |

### LONG JUMP

| | | METERS |
|---|---|---|
| 1948 | Olga Gyarmati (HUN) | 5.69 |
| 1952 | Yvette Williams (NZL) | 6.24 |
| 1956 | Elzbieta Krzesinska (POL) | 6.35 |
| 1960 | Vera Krepkina (URS) | 6.37 |
| 1964 | Mary Rand (GBR) | 6.76 |

# Summer Olympic Games Champions (continued)

## Athletics (track-and-field) (women) (continued)

### LONG JUMP

| | | METERS |
|---|---|---|
| 1968 | Viorica Viscopoleanu (ROM) | 6.82 |
| 1972 | Heidemarie Rosendahl (FRG) | 6.78 |
| 1976 | Angela Voigt (GDR) | 6.72 |
| 1980 | Tatyana Kolpakova (URS) | 7.06 |
| 1984 | Anisoara Stanciu (ROM) | 6.96 |
| 1988 | Jackie Joyner-Kersee (USA) | 7.40 |
| 1992 | Heike Drechsler (GER) | 7.14 |
| 1996 | Chioma Ajunwa (NGR) | 7.12 |
| 2000 | Heike Drechsler (GER) | 6.99 |

### TRIPLE JUMP

| | | METERS |
|---|---|---|
| 1996 | Inessa Kravets (UKR) | 15.33 |
| 2000 | Tereza Marinova (BUL) | 15.20 |

### SHOT PUT

| | | METERS |
|---|---|---|
| 1948 | Micheline Ostermeyer (FRA) | 13.75 |
| 1952 | Galina Zybina (URS) | 15.28 |
| 1956 | Tamara Tyshkevich (URS) | 16.59 |
| 1960 | Tamara Press (URS) | 17.32 |
| 1964 | Tamara Press (URS) | 18.14 |
| 1968 | Margitta Gummel (GDR) | 19.61 |
| 1972 | Nadezhda Chizhova (URS) | 21.03 |
| 1976 | Ivanka Khristova (BUL) | 21.16 |
| 1980 | Ilona Slupianek (GDR) | 22.41 |
| 1984 | Claudia Losch (FRG) | 20.48 |
| 1988 | Natalya Lisovskaya (URS) | 22.24 |
| 1992 | Svetlana Krivalyova (UNT) | 21.06 |
| 1996 | Astrid Kumbernuss (GER) | 20.56 |
| 2000 | Yanina Korolchik (BLR) | 20.56 |

### DISCUS THROW

| | | METERS |
|---|---|---|
| 1928 | Halina Konopacka (POL) | 39.62 |
| 1932 | Lillian Copeland (USA) | 40.58 |
| 1936 | Gisela Mauermayer (GER) | 47.63 |
| 1948 | Micheline Ostermeyer (FRA) | 41.92 |
| 1952 | Nina Romashkova (URS) | 51.42 |
| 1956 | Olga Fikotova (TCH) | 53.69 |
| 1960 | Nina Ponomaryova-Romashkova (URS) | 55.10 |
| 1964 | Tamara Press (URS) | 57.27 |
| 1968 | Lia Manoliu (ROM) | 58.28 |
| 1972 | Faina Melnik (URS) | 66.62 |
| 1976 | Evelin Schlaak (GDR) | 69.00 |
| 1980 | Evelin Schlaak Jahl (GDR) | 69.96 |
| 1984 | Ria Stalman (NED) | 65.36 |
| 1988 | Martina Hellmann (GDR) | 72.30 |
| 1992 | Maritza Marten (CUB) | 70.06 |
| 1996 | Ilke Wyludda (GER) | 69.66 |
| 2000 | Ellina Zvereva (BLR) | 68.40 |

### HAMMER THROW

| | | METERS |
|---|---|---|
| 2000 | Kamila Skolimowska (POL) | 71.16 |

### JAVELIN THROW

| | | METERS |
|---|---|---|
| 1932 | Mildred "Babe" Didrikson (USA) | 43.68 |
| 1936 | Tilly Fleischer (GER) | 45.18 |
| 1948 | Hermine Bauma (AUT) | 45.57 |
| 1952 | Dana Zatopkova (TCH) | 50.47 |
| 1956 | Inese Jaunzeme (URS) | 53.86 |
| 1960 | Elvira Ozolina (URS) | 55.98 |
| 1964 | Mihaela Penes (ROM) | 60.54 |
| 1968 | Angela Nemeth (HUN) | 60.36 |
| 1972 | Ruth Fuchs (GDR) | 63.88 |
| 1976 | Ruth Fuchs (GDR) | 65.94 |
| 1980 | María Colón (CUB) | 68.40 |
| 1984 | Tessa Sanderson (GBR) | 69.56 |
| 1988 | Petra Felke (GDR) | 74.68 |
| 1992 | Silke Renk (GER) | 68.34 |

## Athletics (track-and-field) (women) (continued)

### JAVELIN THROW

| | | METERS |
|---|---|---|
| 1996 | Heli Rantanen (FIN) | 67.94 |
| 2000 | Trine Hattestad (NOR) | 68.91 |

### PENTATHLON (HEPTATHLON FROM 1984)

| | |
|---|---|
| 1964 | Irina Press (URS) |
| 1968 | Ingrid Becker (FRG) |
| 1972 | Mary Peters (GBR) |
| 1976 | Siegrun Siegl (GDR) |
| 1980 | Nadezhda Tkachenko (URS) |
| 1984 | Glynis Nunn (AUS) |
| 1988 | Jackie Joyner-Kersee (USA) |
| 1992 | Jackie Joyner-Kersee (USA) |
| 1996 | Ghada Shouaa (SYR) |
| 2000 | Denise Lewis (GBR) |

## Badminton

### MEN'S SINGLES

| | |
|---|---|
| 1992 | Allan Budi Kusuma (INA) |
| 1996 | Poul-Erik Hoyer-Larsen (DEN) |
| 2000 | Ji Xinpeng (CHN) |

### MEN'S DOUBLES

| | |
|---|---|
| 1992 | South Korea |
| 1996 | Indonesia |
| 2000 | Indonesia |

### WOMEN'S SINGLES

| | |
|---|---|
| 1992 | Susi Susanti (INA) |
| 1996 | Bang Soo-Hyun (KOR) |
| 2000 | Gong Zhichao (CHN) |

### WOMEN'S DOUBLES

| | |
|---|---|
| 1992 | South Korea |
| 1996 | China |
| 2000 | China |

### MIXED DOUBLES

| | |
|---|---|
| 1996 | South Korea |
| 2000 | China |

## Baseball

| | |
|---|---|
| 1992 | Cuba |
| 1996 | Cuba |
| 2000 | United States |

## Basketball

### MEN

| | |
|---|---|
| 1936 | United States |
| 1948 | United States |
| 1952 | United States |
| 1956 | United States |
| 1960 | United States |
| 1964 | United States |
| 1968 | United States |
| 1972 | USSR |
| 1976 | United States |
| 1980 | Yugoslavia |
| 1984 | United States |
| 1988 | USSR |
| 1992 | United States |
| 1996 | United States |
| 2000 | United States |

### WOMEN

| | |
|---|---|
| 1976 | USSR |
| 1980 | USSR |
| 1984 | United States |

# Summer Olympic Games Champions (continued)

## Basketball (continued)

**WOMEN**
- 1988 United States
- 1992 Unified Team
- 1996 United States
- 2000 United States

## Boxing

**LIGHT FLYWEIGHT (48 KG; 106 LB)**
- 1968 Francisco Rodríguez (VEN)
- 1972 Gyorgy Gedo (HUN)
- 1976 Jorge Hernández (CUB)
- 1980 Shamil Sabyrov (URS)
- 1984 Paul Gonzales (USA)
- 1988 Ivailo Khristov (BUL)
- 1992 Rogelio Marcelo (CUB)
- 1996 Daniel Petrov Bojilov (BUL)
- 2000 Brahim Asloum (FRA)

**FLYWEIGHT (51 KG; 112 LB)**
- 1904 George Finnegan (USA)
- 1920 Frank di Genaro (USA)
- 1924 Fidel La Barba (USA)
- 1928 Antal Kocsis (HUN)
- 1932 Istvan Enekes (HUN)
- 1936 Willi Kaiser (GER)
- 1948 Pascual Pérez (ARG)
- 1952 Nate Brooks (USA)
- 1956 Terence Spinks (GBR)
- 1960 Gyula Torok (HUN)
- 1964 Fernando Atzori (ITA)
- 1968 Ricardo Delgado (MEX)
- 1972 Georgi Kostadinov (BUL)
- 1976 Leo Randolph (USA)
- 1980 Petar Lesov (BUL)
- 1984 Steven McCrory (USA)
- 1988 Kim Kwang Sun (KOR)
- 1992 Chol Choi Su (PRK)
- 1996 Maikro Romero (CUB)
- 2000 Wijan Ponlid (THA)

**BANTAMWEIGHT (54 KG; 119 LB)**
- 1904 Oliver Kirk (USA)
- 1908 Henry Thomas (GBR)
- 1920 Clarence Walker (RSA)
- 1924 William Smith (RSA)
- 1928 Vittorio Tamagnini (ITA)
- 1932 Horace Gwynne (CAN)
- 1936 Ulderico Sergo (ITA)
- 1948 Tibor Csik (HUN)
- 1952 Pentti Hämäläinen (FIN)
- 1956 Wolfgang Behrendt (GER)
- 1960 Oleg Grigoryev (URS)
- 1964 Takao Sakurai (JPN)
- 1968 Valery Sokolov (URS)
- 1972 Orlando Martínez (CUB)
- 1976 Gu Yong Jo (PRK)
- 1980 Juan Hernández (CUB)
- 1984 Maurizio Stecca (ITA)
- 1988 Kennedy McKinney (USA)
- 1992 Joel Casamayor (CUB)
- 1996 Istvan Kovacs (HUN)
- 2000 Guillermo Rigondeaux (CUB)

**FEATHERWEIGHT (57 KG; 125 LB)**
- 1904 Oliver Kirk (USA)
- 1908 Richard Gunn (GBR)
- 1920 Paul Fritsch (FRA)
- 1924 John Fields (USA)

## Boxing (continued)

**FEATHERWEIGHT (57 KG; 125 LB)**
- 1928 Lambertus van Kleveren (NED)
- 1932 Carmelo Robledo (ARG)
- 1936 Oscar Casanovas (ARG)
- 1948 Ernesto Formenti (ITA)
- 1952 Jan Zachara (TCH)
- 1956 Vladimir Safronov (URS)
- 1960 Francesco Musso (ITA)
- 1964 Stanislav Stepashkin (URS)
- 1968 Antonio Roldan (MEX)
- 1972 Boris Kuznetsov (URS)
- 1976 Angel Herrera (CUB)
- 1980 Rudi Fink (GDR)
- 1984 Meldrick Taylor (USA)
- 1988 Giovanni Parisi (ITA)
- 1992 Andreas Tews (GER)
- 1996 Somluck Kamsing (THA)
- 2000 Bekzat Sattarkhanov (KAZ)

**LIGHTWEIGHT (60 KG; 132 LB)**
- 1904 Harry Spanger (USA)
- 1908 Frederick Grace (GBR)
- 1920 Samuel Mosberg (USA)
- 1924 Hans Nielsen (DEN)
- 1928 Carlo Orlandi (ITA)
- 1932 Lawrence Stevens (RSA)
- 1936 Imre Harangi (HUN)
- 1948 Gerald Dreyer (RSA)
- 1952 Aureliano Bolognesi (ITA)
- 1956 Richard McTaggart (GBR)
- 1960 Kazimierz Pazdzior (POL)
- 1964 Jozef Grudzien (POL)
- 1968 Ronnie Harris (USA)
- 1972 Jan Szczepanski (POL)
- 1976 Howard Davis (USA)
- 1980 Angel Herrera (CUB)
- 1984 Pernell Whitaker (USA)
- 1988 Andreas Zuelow (GDR)
- 1992 Oscar De La Hoya (USA)
- 1996 Hocine Soltani (ALG)
- 2000 Mario Kindelan (CUB)

**LIGHT WELTERWEIGHT (63.5 KG; 140 LB)**
- 1952 Charles Adkins (USA)
- 1956 Vladimir Engibaryan (URS)
- 1960 Bohumil Nemecek (TCH)
- 1964 Jerzy Kulej (POL)
- 1968 Jerzy Kulej (POL)
- 1972 Ray Seales (USA)
- 1976 Ray Leonard (USA)
- 1980 Patrizio Oliva (ITA)
- 1984 Jerry Page (USA)
- 1988 Vyacheslav Yanovsky (URS)
- 1992 Héctor Vinent (CUB)
- 1996 Héctor Vinent (CUB)
- 2000 Mahamadkadyz Abdullayev (UZB)

**WELTERWEIGHT (67 KG; 147 LB)**
- 1904 Albert Young (USA)
- 1920 Julius Schneider (CAN)
- 1924 Jean Delarge (BEL)
- 1928 Edward Morgan (NZL)
- 1932 Edward Flynn (USA)
- 1936 Sten Suvio (FIN)
- 1948 Julius Torma (TCH)
- 1952 Zygmunt Chychla (POL)
- 1956 Nicolae Linca (ROM)
- 1960 Giovanni Benvenuti (ITA)

# Summer Olympic Games Champions (continued)

## Boxing (continued)

**WELTERWEIGHT (67 KG; 147 LB)**

| | |
|---|---|
| 1964 | Marian Kasprzyk (POL) |
| 1968 | Manfred Wolke (GDR) |
| 1972 | Emilio Correa (CUB) |
| 1976 | Jochen Bachfeld (GDR) |
| 1980 | Andres Aldama (CUB) |
| 1984 | Mark Breland (USA) |
| 1988 | Robert Wangila (KEN) |
| 1992 | Michael Carruth (IRL) |
| 1996 | Oleg Saytov (RUS) |
| 2000 | Oleg Saytov (RUS) |

**LIGHT MIDDLEWEIGHT (71 KG; 156 LB)**

| | |
|---|---|
| 1952 | Laszlo Papp (HUN) |
| 1956 | Laszlo Papp (HUN) |
| 1960 | Wilbert McClure (USA) |
| 1964 | Boris Lagutin (URS) |
| 1968 | Boris Lagutin (URS) |
| 1972 | Dieter Kottysch (FRG) |
| 1976 | Jerzy Rybicki (POL) |
| 1980 | Armando Martínez (CUB) |
| 1984 | Frank Tate (USA) |
| 1988 | Park Si Hun (KOR) |
| 1992 | Juan Lemus (CUB) |
| 1996 | David Reid (USA) |
| 2000 | Yermakhan Ibraimov (KAZ) |

**MIDDLEWEIGHT (75 KG; 165 LB)**

| | |
|---|---|
| 1904 | Charles Mayer (USA) |
| 1908 | John Douglas (GBR) |
| 1920 | Harry Mallin (GBR) |
| 1924 | Harry Mallin (GBR) |
| 1928 | Piero Toscani (ITA) |
| 1932 | Carmen Barth (USA) |
| 1936 | Jean Despeaux (FRA) |
| 1948 | Laszlo Papp (HUN) |
| 1952 | Floyd Patterson (USA) |
| 1956 | Gennady Shatkov (URS) |
| 1960 | Edward Crook (USA) |
| 1964 | Valery Popenchenko (URS) |
| 1968 | Christopher Finnegan (GBR) |
| 1972 | Vyatcheslav Lemeshev (URS) |
| 1976 | Michael Spinks (USA) |
| 1980 | Jose Gómez (CUB) |
| 1984 | Shin Joon Sup (KOR) |
| 1988 | Henry Maske (GDR) |
| 1992 | Ariel Hernández (CUB) |
| 1996 | Ariel Hernández (CUB) |
| 2000 | Jorge Gutiérrez (CUB) |

**LIGHT HEAVYWEIGHT (81 KG; 178 LB)**

| | |
|---|---|
| 1920 | Edward Eagan (USA) |
| 1924 | Harry Mitchell (GBR) |
| 1928 | Viktor Avendano (ARG) |
| 1932 | David Carstens (RSA) |
| 1936 | Roger Michelot (FRA) |
| 1948 | George Hunter (RSA) |
| 1952 | Norvel Lee (USA) |
| 1956 | James Boyd (USA) |
| 1960 | Cassius Clay (USA) |
| 1964 | Cosimo Pinto (ITA) |
| 1968 | Dan Poznyak (URS) |
| 1972 | Mate Parlov (YUG) |
| 1976 | Leon Spinks (USA) |
| 1980 | Slobodan Kacar (YUG) |
| 1984 | Anton Josipovic (YUG) |
| 1988 | Andrew Maynard (USA) |
| 1992 | Torsten May (GER) |

## Boxing (continued)

**LIGHT HEAVYWEIGHT (81 KG; 178 LB)**

| | |
|---|---|
| 1996 | Vasily Zhirov (KAZ) |
| 2000 | Aleksandr Lebzyak (RUS) |

**HEAVYWEIGHT (OVER 81 KG; 179 LB) (91 KG; 200 LB FROM 1984)**

| | |
|---|---|
| 1904 | Samuel Berger (USA) |
| 1908 | Albert Oldman (GBR) |
| 1920 | Ronald Rawson (GBR) |
| 1924 | Otto Von Porat (NOR) |
| 1928 | Arturo Rodriguez (ARG) |
| 1932 | Alberto Santiago Lovell (ARG) |
| 1936 | Herbert Runge (GER) |
| 1948 | Rafael Iglesias (ARG) |
| 1952 | Edward Sanders (USA) |
| 1956 | Peter Rademacher (USA) |
| 1960 | Franco de Piccoli (ITA) |
| 1964 | Joseph Frazier (USA) |
| 1968 | George Foreman (USA) |
| 1972 | Teofilo Stevenson (CUB) |
| 1976 | Teofilo Stevenson (CUB) |
| 1980 | Teofilo Stevenson (CUB) |
| 1984 | Henry Tillman (USA) |
| 1988 | Ray Mercer (USA) |
| 1992 | Félix Savon (CUB) |
| 1996 | Félix Savon (CUB) |
| 2000 | Félix Savon (CUB) |

**SUPERHEAVYWEIGHT (OVER 91 KG; 200 LB)**

| | |
|---|---|
| 1984 | Tyrell Biggs (USA) |
| 1988 | Lennox Lewis (CAN) |
| 1992 | Roberto Balado (CUB) |
| 1996 | Vladimir Klichko (UKR) |
| 2000 | Audley Harrison (GBR) |

## Canoeing (men)

**KAYAK SINGLES (500 METERS)**

| | | MIN:SEC |
|---|---|---|
| 1976 | Vasile Diba (ROM) | 1:46.41 |
| 1980 | Vladimir Parfenovich (URS) | 1:43.43 |
| 1984 | Ian Ferguson (NZL) | 1:47.84 |
| 1988 | Zsolt Gyulay (HUN) | 1:44.82 |
| 1992 | Mikko Kolehmainen (FIN) | 1:40.34 |
| 1996 | Antonio Rossi (ITA) | 1:37.423 |
| 2000 | Knut Holmann (NOR) | 1:57.84 |

**KAYAK PAIRS (500 METERS)**

| | | MIN:SEC |
|---|---|---|
| 1976 | East Germany | 1:35.87 |
| 1980 | USSR | 1:32.38 |
| 1984 | New Zealand | 1:34.21 |
| 1988 | New Zealand | 1:33.98 |
| 1992 | Germany | 1:29.84 |
| 1996 | Germany | 1:28.697 |
| 2000 | Hungary | 1:47.05 |

**KAYAK SINGLES (1,000 METERS)**

| | | MIN:SEC |
|---|---|---|
| 1936 | Gregor Hradetzky (AUT) | 4:22.90 |
| 1948 | Gert Fredriksson (SWE) | 4:33.20 |
| 1952 | Gert Fredriksson (SWE) | 4:07.90 |
| 1956 | Gert Fredriksson (SWE) | 4:12.80 |
| 1960 | Erik Hansen (DEN) | 3:53.00 |
| 1964 | Rolf Peterson (SWE) | 3:57.13 |
| 1968 | Mihaly Hesz (HUN) | 4:03.58 |
| 1972 | Aleksandr Shaparenko (URS) | 3:48.06 |
| 1976 | Rüdiger Helm (GDR) | 3:48.20 |
| 1980 | Rüdiger Helm (GDR) | 3:48.77 |
| 1984 | Alan Thompson (NZL) | 3:45.73 |
| 1988 | Gregory Barton (USA) | 3:55.27 |
| 1992 | Clint Robinson (AUS) | 3:37.26 |

# Summer Olympic Games Champions (continued)

## Canoeing (men) (continued)

**KAYAK SINGLES (1,000 METERS)** — MIN:SEC
- 1996 Knut Holmann (NOR) — 3:25.785
- 2000 Knut Holmann (NOR) — 3:33.26

**KAYAK PAIRS (1,000 METERS)** — MIN:SEC
- 1936 Austria — 4:03.80
- 1948 Sweden — 4:07.30
- 1952 Finland — 3:51.10
- 1956 Germany — 3:49.60
- 1960 Sweden — 3:34.70
- 1964 Sweden — 3:38.54
- 1968 USSR — 3:37.54
- 1972 USSR — 3:31.23
- 1976 USSR — 3:29.01
- 1980 USSR — 3:26.72
- 1984 Canada — 3:24.22
- 1988 United States — 3:32.42
- 1992 Germany — 3:16.10
- 1996 Italy — 3:09.190
- 2000 Italy — 3:14.46

**KAYAK FOURS (1,000 METERS)** — MIN:SEC
- 1964 USSR — 3:14.67
- 1968 Norway — 3:14.38
- 1972 USSR — 3:14.02
- 1976 USSR — 3:08.69
- 1980 East Germany — 3:13.76
- 1984 New Zealand — 3:02.28
- 1988 Hungary — 3:00.20
- 1992 Germany — 2:54.18
- 1996 Germany — 2:51.528
- 2000 Hungary — 2:55.18

**KAYAK SINGLES (10,000 METERS)** — MIN:SEC
- 1936 Ernst Krebs (GER) — 46:01.6
- 1948 Gert Fredriksson (SWE) — 50:47.7
- 1952 Thorvald Strömberg (FIN) — 47:22.8
- 1956 Gert Fredriksson (SWE) — 47:43.4

**KAYAK PAIRS (10,000 METERS)** — MIN:SEC
- 1936 Germany — 41:45
- 1948 Sweden — 46:09.4
- 1952 Finland — 44:21.3
- 1956 Hungary — 43:37

**COLLAPSIBLE KAYAK SINGLES (10,000 METERS)** — MIN:SEC
- 1936 Gregor Hradetzky (AUT) — 50:01.2

**COLLAPSIBLE KAYAK PAIRS (10,000 METERS)** — MIN:SEC
- 1936 Sweden — 45:48.9

**KAYAK SINGLES RELAY (1,500 METERS)** — MIN:SEC
- 1960 Germany — 7:39.43

**SLALOM KAYAK SINGLES**
- 1972 Siegbert Horn (GDR)
- 1992 Pierpaolo Ferrazzi (ITA)
- 1996 Oliver Fix (GER)
- 2000 Thomas Schmidt (GER)

**CANADIAN SINGLES (500 METERS)** — MIN:SEC
- 1976 Aleksandr Rogov (URS) — 1:59.23
- 1980 Sergey Postrekin (URS) — 1:53.37
- 1984 Larry Cain (CAN) — 1:57.01
- 1988 Olaf Heukrodt (GDR) — 1:56.42
- 1992 Nikolay Bukhalov (BUL) — 1:51.15
- 1996 Martin Doktor (CZE) — 1:49.934
- 2000 Gyorgy Kolonics (HUN) — 2:24.81

## Canoeing (men) (continued)

**CANADIAN PAIRS (500 METERS)** — MIN:SEC
- 1976 USSR — 1:45.81
- 1980 Hungary — 1:43.39
- 1984 Yugoslavia — 1:43.67
- 1988 USSR — 1:41.77
- 1992 Unified Team — 1:41.54
- 1996 Hungary — 1:40.420
- 2000 Hungary — 1:51.28

**CANADIAN SINGLES (1,000 METERS)** — MIN:SEC
- 1936 Francis Amyot (CAN) — 5:32.10
- 1948 Josef Holecek (TCH) — 5:42.00
- 1952 Josef Holecek (TCH) — 4:56.30
- 1956 Leon Rottman (ROM) — 5:05.30
- 1960 Janos Parti (HUN) — 4:33.03
- 1964 Jürgen Eschert (GER) — 4:35.14
- 1968 Tibor Tatai (HUN) — 4:36.14
- 1972 Ivan Patzaichin (ROM) — 4:08.94
- 1976 Matija Ljubek (YUG) — 4:09.51
- 1980 Lyubomir Lyubenov (BUL) — 4:12.38
- 1984 Ulrich Eicke (FRG) — 4:06.32
- 1988 Ivans Klementyev (URS) — 4:12.78
- 1992 Nikolay Bukhalov (BUL) — 4:05.92
- 1996 Martin Doktor (CZE) — 3:54.418
- 2000 Andreas Dittmer (GER) — 3:54.37

**CANADIAN PAIRS (1,000 METERS)** — MIN:SEC
- 1936 Czechoslovakia — 4:50.10
- 1948 Czechoslovakia — 5:07.10
- 1952 Denmark — 4:38.30
- 1956 Romania — 4:47.40
- 1960 USSR — 4:17.04
- 1964 USSR — 4:04.65
- 1968 Romania — 4:07.18
- 1972 USSR — 3:52.60
- 1976 USSR — 3:52.76
- 1980 Romania — 3:47.65
- 1984 Romania — 3:40.60
- 1988 USSR — 3:48.36
- 1992 Germany — 3:37.42
- 1996 Germany — 3:31.870
- 2000 Romania — 3:37.35

**CANADIAN SINGLES (10,000 METERS)** — MIN:SEC
- 1948 Frantisek Capek (TCH) — 62:05.2
- 1952 Frank Havens (USA) — 57:41.1
- 1956 Leon Rottman (ROM) — 56:41.0

**CANADIAN PAIRS (10,000 METERS)** — MIN:SEC
- 1936 Czechoslovakia — 50:35.5
- 1948 United States — 55:55.4
- 1952 France — 54:08.3
- 1956 USSR — 54:02.4

**SLALOM CANADIAN SINGLES**
- 1972 Reinhard Eiben (GDR)
- 1992 Lukas Pollert (TCH)
- 1996 Michal Martikan (SVK)
- 2000 Tony Estanguet (FRA)

**SLALOM CANADIAN PAIRS**
- 1972 East Germany
- 1992 United States
- 1996 France
- 2000 Slovakia

# Summer Olympic Games Champions (continued)

## Canoeing (women)

### KAYAK SINGLES (500 METERS)

| | | MIN:SEC |
|---|---|---|
| 1948 | Karen Hoff (DEN) | 2:31.90 |
| 1952 | Sylvi Saimo (FIN) | 2:18.40 |
| 1956 | Yelizaveta Dementyeva (URS) | 2:18.90 |
| 1960 | Antonina Seredina (URS) | 2:08.08 |
| 1964 | Lyudmila Khvedosyuk (URS) | 2:12.87 |
| 1968 | Lyudmila Pinayeva-Khvedosyuk (URS) | 2:11.09 |
| 1972 | Yuliya Ryabchinskaya (URS) | 2:03.17 |
| 1976 | Carola Zirzow (GDR) | 2:01.05 |
| 1980 | Birgit Fischer (GDR) | 1:57.96 |
| 1984 | Agneta Andersson (SWE) | 1:58.72 |
| 1988 | Vanya Gecheva (BUL) | 1:55.19 |
| 1992 | Birgit Fischer Schmidt (GER) | 1:51.60 |
| 1996 | Rita Koban (HUN) | 1:47.655 |
| 2000 | Josefa Idem Guerrini (ITA) | 2:13.84 |

### KAYAK PAIRS (500 METERS)

| | | MIN:SEC |
|---|---|---|
| 1960 | USSR | 1:54.76 |
| 1964 | Germany | 1:56.95 |
| 1968 | West Germany | 1:56.44 |
| 1972 | USSR | 1:53.50 |
| 1976 | USSR | 1:51.15 |
| 1980 | East Germany | 1:43.88 |
| 1984 | Sweden | 1:45.25 |
| 1988 | East Germany | 1:43.46 |
| 1992 | Germany | 1:40.29 |
| 1996 | Sweden | 1:39.329 |
| 2000 | Germany | 1:56.99 |

### KAYAK FOURS (500 METERS)

| | | MIN:SEC |
|---|---|---|
| 1984 | Romania | 1:38.34 |
| 1988 | East Germany | 1:40.78 |
| 1992 | Hungary | 1:38.32 |
| 1996 | Germany | 1:31.077 |
| 2000 | Germany | 1:34.53 |

### SLALOM KAYAK SINGLES

| | |
|---|---|
| 1972 | Angelika Bahmann (GDR) |
| 1992 | Elisabeth Micheler (GER) |
| 1996 | Stepanka Hilgertova (CZE) |
| 2000 | Stepanka Hilgertova (CZE) |

## Cricket

| | |
|---|---|
| 1900 | Great Britain |

## Croquet

### SINGLES (ONE BALL)

| | |
|---|---|
| 1900 | Aumoitte (FRA) |

### SINGLES (TWO BALLS)

| | |
|---|---|
| 1900 | Waydelick (FRA) |

### DOUBLES

| | |
|---|---|
| 1900 | France |

## Cycling (men)

### 1,000-METER SPRINT

| | |
|---|---|
| 1896[6] | Paul Masson (FRA) |
| 1900[6] | Georges Taillandier (FRA) |
| 1920 | Mauritius Peeters (NED) |
| 1924 | Lucien Michard (FRA) |
| 1928 | Roger Beaufrand (FRA) |
| 1932 | Jacobus Van Egmond (NED) |
| 1936 | Toni Merkens (GER) |
| 1948 | Mario Ghella (ITA) |
| 1952 | Enzo Sacchi (ITA) |
| 1956 | Michel Rousseau (FRA) |

## Cycling (men) (continued)

### 1,000-METER SPRINT

| | |
|---|---|
| 1960 | Sante Gaiardoni (ITA) |
| 1964 | Giovanni Pettenella (ITA) |
| 1968 | Daniel Morelon (FRA) |
| 1972 | Daniel Morelon (FRA) |
| 1976 | Anton Tkac (TCH) |
| 1980 | Lutz Hesslich (GDR) |
| 1984 | Mark Gorski (USA) |
| 1988 | Lutz Hesslich (GDR) |
| 1992 | Jens Fiedler (GER) |
| 1996 | Jens Fiedler (GER) |
| 2000 | Marty Nothstein (USA) |

### 1,000-METER TIME TRIAL

| | | MIN:SEC |
|---|---|---|
| 1896[7] | Paul Masson (FRA) | 24.0 |
| 1928 | Willy Falck-Hansen (DEN) | 1:14.4 |
| 1932 | Edgar Gray (AUS) | 1:13.0 |
| 1936 | Arie van Vliet (NED) | 1:12.0 |
| 1948 | Jacques Dupont (FRA) | 1:13.5 |
| 1952 | Russell Mockridge (AUS) | 1:11.1 |
| 1956 | Leandro Faggin (ITA) | 1:09.8 |
| 1960 | Sante Gaiardoni (ITA) | 1:07.27 |
| 1964 | Patrick Sercu (BEL) | 1:09.59 |
| 1968 | Pierre Trentin (FRA) | 1:03.91 |
| 1972 | Niels Fredborg (DEN) | 1:06.44 |
| 1976 | Klaus-Jürgen Grünke (GDR) | 1:05.927 |
| 1980 | Lothar Thoms (GDR) | 1:02.955 |
| 1984 | Fredy Schmidtke (FRG) | 1:06.104 |
| 1988 | Aleksandr Kirichenko (URS) | 1:04.499 |
| 1992 | José Moreno (ESP) | 1:03.342 |
| 1996 | Florian Rousseau (FRA) | 1:02.712 |
| 2000 | Jason Queally (GBR) | 1:01.609 |

### 1,500-METER TEAM PURSUIT

| | |
|---|---|
| 1900 | United States |

### 2,000 METERS

| | |
|---|---|
| 1904 | Marcus Hurley (USA) |

### 2,000-METER TANDEM

| | |
|---|---|
| 1908 | France |
| 1920 | Great Britain |
| 1924 | France |
| 1928 | The Netherlands |
| 1932 | France |
| 1936 | Germany |
| 1948 | Italy |
| 1952 | Australia |
| 1956 | Australia |
| 1960 | Italy |
| 1964 | Italy |
| 1968 | France |
| 1972 | USSR |

### 4,000-METER INDIVIDUAL PURSUIT

| | |
|---|---|
| 1964 | Jiri Daler (TCH) |
| 1968 | Daniel Rebillard (FRA) |
| 1972 | Knut Knudsen (NOR) |
| 1976 | Gregor Braun (FRG) |
| 1980 | Robert Dill-Bondi (SUI) |
| 1984 | Steve Hegg (USA) |
| 1988 | Gintaoutas Umaras (URS) |
| 1992 | Christopher Boardman (GBR) |
| 1996 | Andrea Collinelli (ITA) |
| 2000 | Robert Bartko (GER) |

### 4,000-METER TEAM PURSUIT

| | |
|---|---|
| 1908 | Great Britain |

# Summer Olympic Games Champions (continued)

## Cycling (men) (continued)

**4,000-METER TEAM PURSUIT**
1920 Italy
1924 Italy
1928 Italy
1932 Italy
1936 France
1948 France
1952 Italy
1956 Italy
1960 Italy
1964 Germany
1968 Denmark
1972 West Germany
1976 West Germany
1980 USSR
1984 Australia
1988 USSR
1992 Germany
1996 France
2000 Germany

| **5,000 METERS** | MIN:SEC |
|---|---|
| 1908 Benjamin Jones (GBR) | 8:36.2 |

| **10,000 METERS** | MIN:SEC |
|---|---|
| 1896 Paul Masson (FRA) | 17:54.2 |

| **20,000 METERS** | MIN:SEC |
|---|---|
| 1908 Charles Kingsbury (GBR) | 34:13.6 |

| **50,000 METERS** | HR:MIN:SEC |
|---|---|
| 1920 Henry George (BEL) | 1:16:43.2 |
| 1924 Jacobus Willems (NED) | 1:18:24.0 |

| **100,000 METERS** | HR:MIN:SEC |
|---|---|
| 1896 Léon Flameng (FRA) | 3:08:19.2 |
| 1908 Charles Bartlett (GBR) | 2:41:48.6 |

| **ONE-QUARTER MILE (440 YARDS)** | SEC |
|---|---|
| 1904 Marcus Hurley (USA) | 31.8 |

| **ONE-THIRD MILE (586⅔ YARDS)** | SEC |
|---|---|
| 1904 Marcus Hurley (USA) | 43.8 |

| **ONE-LAP TIME TRIAL (660 YARDS)** | SEC |
|---|---|
| 1908 Victor Johnson (GBR) | 51.2 |

| **ONE-HALF MILE (880 YARDS)** | MIN:SEC |
|---|---|
| 1904 Marcus Hurley (USA) | 1:09.0 |

| **1 MILE** | MIN:SEC |
|---|---|
| 1904 Marcus Hurley (USA) | 2:41.6 |

**1 MILE 1 FURLONG (1,980 YARDS) TEAM PURSUIT**
1908 Great Britain

| **2 MILES** | MIN:SEC |
|---|---|
| 1904 Burton Downing (USA) | 4:58.0 |

| **5 MILES** | MIN:SEC |
|---|---|
| 1904 Charles Schlee (USA) | 13:08.2 |

**25 MILES**
1904 Burton Downing (USA)

**12 HOURS**
1896 Adolf Schmal (AUT)

## Cycling (men) (continued)

**POINTS RACE**
1984 Roger Ilegems (BEL)
1988 Dan Frost (DEN)
1992 Giovanni Lombardi (ITA)
1996 Silvio Martinello (ITA)
2000 Juan Llaneras (ESP)

| **KEIRIN** | SEC |
|---|---|
| 2000 Florian Rousseau (FRA) | 11.020 |

**MADISON**
2000 Australia

| **OLYMPIC SPRINT** | SEC |
|---|---|
| 2000 France | 44.233 |

| **ROAD RACE (INDIVIDUAL)**[8] | HR:MIN:SEC |
|---|---|
| 1896 Aristidis Konstantinidis (GRE) | 3:22:31.0 |
| 1912 Rudolph Lewis (RSA) | 10:42:39.0 |
| 1920 Harry Stenqvist (SWE) | 4:40:01.8 |
| 1924 Armand Blanchonnet (FRA) | 6:20:48.0 |
| 1928 Henry Hansen (DEN) | 4:47:18.0 |
| 1932 Attilio Pavesi (ITA) | 2:28:05.6 |
| 1936 Robert Charpentier (FRA) | 2:33:05.0 |
| 1948 Jose Beyaert (FRA) | 5:18:12.6 |
| 1952 Andre Noyelle (BEL) | 5:06:03.4 |
| 1956 Ercole Baldini (ITA) | 5:21:17.0 |
| 1960 Viktor Kapitonov (URS) | 4:20:37.0 |
| 1964 Mario Zanin (ITA) | 4:39:51.63 |
| 1968 Pierfranco Vianelli (ITA) | 4:41:25.24 |
| 1972 Hennie Kuiper (NED) | 4:14:37.0 |
| 1976 Bernt Johansson (SWE) | 4:46:52.0 |
| 1980 Sergey Sukhoruchenkov (URS) | 4:48:28.90 |
| 1984 Alexei Grewal (USA) | 4:59:57.0 |
| 1988 Olaf Ludwig (GDR) | 4:32:22.0 |
| 1992 Fabio Casartelli (ITA) | 4:35:21.0 |
| 1996 Pascal Richard (SUI) | 4:53:56.0 |
| 2000 Jan Ullrich (GER) | 5:29:08 |

| **ROAD RACE (TEAM)** | HR:MIN:SEC |
|---|---|
| 1912 Sweden | 44:35:33.6 |
| 1920 France | 19:16:43.2 |
| 1924 France | 19:30:14 |
| 1928 Denmark | 15:09:14 |
| 1932 Italy | 7:27:15.2 |
| 1936 France | 7:39:16.2 |
| 1948 Belgium | 15:58:17.4 |
| 1952 Belgium | 15:20:46.6 |
| 1956 France | 5:21:17 |

| **ROAD TIME TRIAL (INDIVIDUAL)** | HR:MIN:SEC |
|---|---|
| 1996 Miguel Indurain (ESP) | 1:04:05 |
| 2000 Vyacheslav Yekimov (RUS) | 57:40.420 |

| **ROAD TIME TRIAL (TEAM)** | HR:MIN:SEC |
|---|---|
| 1960 Italy | 2:14:33.53 |
| 1964 The Netherlands | 2:26:31.19 |
| 1968 The Netherlands | 2:07:49.06 |
| 1972 USSR | 2:11:17.8 |
| 1976 USSR | 2:08:53 |
| 1980 USSR | 2:01:21.7 |
| 1984 Italy | 1:58:28 |
| 1988 East Germany | 1:57:47.7 |
| 1992 Germany | 2:01:39 |

| **CROSS COUNTRY (MOUNTAIN BIKE)** | HR:MIN:SEC |
|---|---|
| 1996 Bart Jan Brentjens (NED) | 2:17:38 |
| 2000 Miguel Martinez (FRA) | 2:09:2.50 |

# Summer Olympic Games Champions (continued)

## Cycling (women)

**500-METER TIME TRIAL**

| | | HR:MIN:SEC |
|---|---|---|
| 2000 | Felicia Ballanger (FRA) | 34.140 |

**1,000-METER SPRINT**

| | |
|---|---|
| 1988 | Erika Salumae (URS) |
| 1992 | Erika Salumae (EST) |
| 1996 | Felicia Ballanger (FRA) |
| 2000 | Felicia Ballanger (FRA) |

**3,000-METER INDIVIDUAL PURSUIT**

| | |
|---|---|
| 1992 | Petra Rossner (GER) |
| 1996 | Antonella Bellutti (ITA) |
| 2000 | Leontien Zijlaard-van Moorsel (NED) |

**POINTS RACE**

| | |
|---|---|
| 1996 | Nathalie Lancien (FRA) |
| 2000 | Antonella Bellutti (ITA) |

**ROAD RACE (INDIVIDUAL)**

| | | HR:MIN:SEC |
|---|---|---|
| 1984 | Connie Carpenter-Phinney (USA) | 2:11:14.0 |
| 1988 | Monique Knol (NED) | 2:00:52.0 |
| 1992 | Kathryn Watt (AUS) | 2:04:42.0 |
| 1996 | Jeannie Longo-Ciprelli (FRA) | 2:36:13.0 |
| 2000 | Leontien Zijlaard-van Moorsel (NED) | 3:06:31 |

**ROAD TIME TRIAL (INDIVIDUAL)**

| | | MIN:SEC |
|---|---|---|
| 1996 | Zulfiya Zabirova (RUS) | 36:40 |
| 2000 | Leontien Zijlaard-van Moorsel (NED) | 42:00.781 |

**CROSS COUNTRY (MOUNTAIN BIKE)**

| | | HR:MIN:SEC |
|---|---|---|
| 1996 | Paola Pezzo (ITA) | 1:50:51 |
| 2000 | Paola Pezzo (ITA) | 1:49:24.38 |

## Diving (men)

**3-METER SPRINGBOARD**

| | |
|---|---|
| 1908 | Albert Zürner (GER) |
| 1912 | Paul Günther (GER) |
| 1920 | Louis Kuehn (USA) |
| 1924 | Albert White (USA) |
| 1928 | Peter Desjardins (USA) |
| 1932 | Michael Galitzen (USA) |
| 1936 | Richard Degener (USA) |
| 1948 | Bruce Harlan (USA) |
| 1952 | David Browning (USA) |
| 1956 | Robert Clotworthy (USA) |
| 1960 | Gary Tobian (USA) |
| 1964 | Kenneth Sitzberger (USA) |
| 1968 | Bernie Wrightson (USA) |
| 1972 | Vladimir Vasin (URS) |
| 1976 | Philip Boggs (USA) |
| 1980 | Aleksandr Portnov (URS) |
| 1984 | Gregory Louganis (USA) |
| 1988 | Gregory Louganis (USA) |
| 1992 | Mark Edward Lenzi (USA) |
| 1996 | Xiong Ni (CHN) |
| 2000 | Xiong Ni (CHN) |

**10-METER PLATFORM (HIGH) DIVING**

| | |
|---|---|
| 1904 | George Sheldon (USA) |
| 1908 | Hjalmar Johansson (SWE) |
| 1912 | Erik Adlerz (SWE) |
| 1920 | Clarence Pinkston (USA) |
| 1924 | Albert White (USA) |
| 1928 | Peter Desjardins (USA) |
| 1932 | Harold Smith (USA) |

## Diving (men) (continued)

**10-METER PLATFORM (HIGH) DIVING**

| | |
|---|---|
| 1936 | Marshall Wayne (USA) |
| 1948 | Samuel Lee (USA) |
| 1952 | Samuel Lee (USA) |
| 1956 | Joaquin Capilla Perez (MEX) |
| 1960 | Robert Webster (USA) |
| 1964 | Robert Webster (USA) |
| 1968 | Klaus DiBiasi (ITA) |
| 1972 | Klaus DiBiasi (ITA) |
| 1976 | Klaus DiBiasi (ITA) |
| 1980 | Falk Hoffman (GDR) |
| 1984 | Gregory Louganis (USA) |
| 1988 | Gregory Louganis (USA) |
| 1992 | Sun Shuwei (CHN) |
| 1996 | Dmitry Sautin (RUS) |
| 2000 | Tian Liang (CHN) |

**3-METER SYNCHRONIZED SPRINGBOARD DIVING**

| | |
|---|---|
| 2000 | China |

**10-METER SYNCHRONIZED PLATFORM (HIGH) DIVING**

| | |
|---|---|
| 2000 | Russia |

**PLUNGE FOR DISTANCE**

| | |
|---|---|
| 1904 | William Paul Dickey (USA) |

**PLAIN HIGH DIVING**

| | |
|---|---|
| 1912 | Erik Adlerz (SWE) |
| 1920 | Arvid Wallman (SWE) |
| 1924 | Richmond Eve (AUS) |

## Diving (women)

**3-METER SPRINGBOARD**

| | |
|---|---|
| 1920 | Aileen Riggin (USA) |
| 1924 | Elizabeth Becker-Pinkton (USA) |
| 1928 | Helen Meany (USA) |
| 1932 | Georgia Coleman (USA) |
| 1936 | Marjorie Gestring (USA) |
| 1948 | Victoria Draves (USA) |
| 1952 | Patricia McCormick (USA) |
| 1956 | Patricia McCormick (USA) |
| 1960 | Ingrid Krämer-Engel-Gulbin (GER) |
| 1964 | Ingrid Krämer-Engel-Gulbin (GER) |
| 1968 | Sue Gossick (USA) |
| 1972 | Micki King (USA) |
| 1976 | Jennifer Chandler (USA) |
| 1980 | Irina Kalinina (URS) |
| 1984 | Sylvie Bernier (CAN) |
| 1988 | Gao Min (CHN) |
| 1992 | Gao Min (CHN) |
| 1996 | Fu Mingxia (CHN) |
| 2000 | Fu Mingxia (CHN) |

**10-METER PLATFORM (HIGH) DIVING**

| | |
|---|---|
| 1912 | Greta Johansson (SWE) |
| 1920 | Stefani Fryland Clausen (DEN) |
| 1924 | Caroline Smith (USA) |
| 1928 | Elizabeth Anna Becker-Pinkston (USA) |
| 1932 | Dorothy Poynton (USA) |
| 1936 | Dorothy Poynton-Hill (USA) |
| 1948 | Victoria Draves (USA) |
| 1952 | Patricia McCormick (USA) |
| 1956 | Patricia McCormick (USA) |
| 1960 | Ingrid Krämer-Engel-Gulbin (GER) |
| 1964 | Lesley Leigh Bush (USA) |
| 1968 | Milena Duchkova (TCH) |
| 1972 | Ulrika Knape (SWE) |
| 1976 | Yelena Vaytsekhovskaya (URS) |

# Summer Olympic Games Champions (continued)

## Diving (women) (continued)

**10-METER PLATFORM (HIGH) DIVING**

| 1980 | Martina Jäschke (GDR) |
| 1984 | Zhou Ji-Hong (CHN) |
| 1988 | Xu Yan-Mei (CHN) |
| 1992 | Fu Mingxia (CHN) |
| 1996 | Fu Mingxia (CHN) |
| 2000 | Laura Wilkinson (USA) |

**3-METER SYNCHRONIZED SPRINGBOARD DIVING**

| 2000 | Russia |

**10-METER SYNCHRONIZED PLATFORM (HIGH) DIVING**

| 2000 | China |

## Equestrian sports

| GRAND PRIX (DRESSAGE) INDIVIDUAL | | MOUNT |
|---|---|---|
| 1912 | Carl Bonde (SWE) | Emperor |
| 1920 | Janne Lundblad (SWE) | Uno |
| 1924 | Ernst Linder (SWE) | Piccolomini |
| 1928 | Carl Friedrich Freiherr von | Draufgänger |
| | Langen-Parow (GER) | |
| 1932 | Xavier Lesage (FRA) | Taine |
| 1936 | Heinz Pollay (GER) | Kronos |
| 1948 | Hans Moser (SUI) | Hummer |
| 1952 | Henri St. Cyr (SWE) | Master Rufus |
| 1956 | Henri St. Cyr (SWE) | Juli |
| 1960 | Sergey Filatov (URS) | Absent |
| 1964 | Henri Chammartin (SUI) | Woermann |
| 1968 | Ivan Kizimov (URS) | Ikhor |
| 1972 | Liselott Linsenhoff (FRG) | Piaff |
| 1976 | Christine Stückelberger (SUI) | Granat |
| 1980 | Elisabeth Theurer (AUT) | Mon Cherie |
| 1984 | Reiner Klimke (FRG) | Ahlerich |
| 1988 | Nicole Uphoff (FRG) | Rembrandt 24 |
| 1992 | Nicole Uphoff (GER) | Rembrandt 24 |
| 1996 | Isabell Werth (GER) | Gigolo |
| 2000 | Anky van Grunsven (NED) | Bonfire |

**GRAND PRIX (DRESSAGE) TEAM**

| 1928 | Germany |
| 1932 | France |
| 1936 | Germany |
| 1948 | France |
| 1952 | Sweden |
| 1956 | Sweden |
| 1964 | Germany |
| 1968 | West Germany |
| 1972 | USSR |
| 1976 | West Germany |
| 1980 | USSR |
| 1984 | West Germany |
| 1988 | West Germany |
| 1992 | Germany |
| 1996 | Germany |
| 2000 | Germany |

| GRAND PRIX (JUMPING) INDIVIDUAL | | MOUNT |
|---|---|---|
| 1900 | Aimé Haegeman (BEL) | Benton II |
| 1912 | Jean Cariou (FRA) | Mignon |
| 1920 | Tommaso Lequio di Assaba (ITA) | Trebecco |
| 1924 | Alphonse Gemuseus (SUI) | Lucette |
| 1928 | Frantisek Ventura (TCH) | Eliot |
| 1932 | Takeichi Nishi (JPN) | Uranus |
| 1936 | Kurt Hasse (GER) | Tora |
| 1948 | Humberto Mariles Cortés (MEX) | Arete |
| 1952 | Pierre Jonquères d'Oriola (FRA) | Ali Baba |
| 1956 | Hans-Günter Winkler (GER) | Halla |
| 1960 | Raimondo d'Inzeo (ITA) | Posillipo |

## Equestrian sports (continued)

| GRAND PRIX (JUMPING) INDIVIDUAL | | MOUNT |
|---|---|---|
| 1964 | Pierre Jonquères d'Oriola (FRA) | Lutteur |
| 1968 | William Steinkraus (USA) | Snowbound |
| 1972 | Graziano Mancinelli (ITA) | Ambassador |
| 1976 | Alwin Schockemöhle (FRG) | Warwick Rex |
| 1980 | Jan Kowalczyk (POL) | Artemor |
| 1984 | Joe Fargis (USA) | Touch of Class |
| 1988 | Pierre Durand (FRA) | Jappeloup |
| 1992 | Ludger Beerbaum (GER) | Classic Touch |
| 1996 | Ulrich Kirchhoff (GER) | Jus des Pommes |
| 2000 | Jeroen Dubbeldam (NED) | Sjiem |

**GRAND PRIX (JUMPING) TEAM**

| 1912 | Sweden |
| 1920 | Sweden |
| 1924 | Sweden |
| 1928 | Spain |
| 1936 | Germany |
| 1948 | Mexico |
| 1952 | Great Britain |
| 1956 | Germany |
| 1960 | Germany |
| 1964 | Germany |
| 1968 | Canada |
| 1972 | West Germany |
| 1976 | France |
| 1980 | USSR |
| 1984 | United States |
| 1988 | West Germany |
| 1992 | The Netherlands |
| 1996 | Germany |
| 2000 | Germany |

| THREE-DAY EVENT (INDIVIDUAL) | | MOUNT |
|---|---|---|
| 1912 | Axel Nordlander (SWE) | Lady Artist |
| 1920 | Helmer Mörner (SWE) | Germania |
| 1924 | Adolph van der Voort van Zijp (NED) | Silver Piece |
| 1928 | Charles Pahud de Mortanges (NED) | Marcroix |
| 1932 | Charles Pahud de Mortanges (NED) | Marcroix |
| 1936 | Ludwig Stubbendorff (GER) | Nurmi |
| 1948 | Bernard Chevallier (FRA) | Aiglonne |
| 1952 | Hans von Blixen-Finecke, Jr. (SWE) | Jubal |
| 1956 | Petrus Kastenman (SWE) | Iluster |
| 1960 | Lawrence Morgan (AUS) | Salad Days |
| 1964 | Mauro Checcoli (ITA) | Surbean |
| 1968 | Jean-Jacques Goyon (FRA) | Pitou |
| 1972 | Richard Meade (GBR) | Laurieston |
| 1976 | Edmund Coffin (USA) | Bally-Cor |
| 1980 | Federico Euro Roman (ITA) | Rossinan |
| 1984 | Mark Todd (NZL) | Charisma |
| 1988 | Mark Todd (NZL) | Charisma |
| 1992 | Matthew Ryan (AUS) | Kibah Tic Toc |
| 1996 | Robert Blyth Tait (NZL) | Ready Teddy |
| 2000 | David O'Connor (USA) | Custom Made |

**THREE-DAY EVENT (TEAM)**

| 1912 | Sweden |
| 1920 | Sweden |
| 1924 | The Netherlands |
| 1928 | The Netherlands |
| 1932 | United States |
| 1936 | Germany |
| 1948 | United States |
| 1952 | Sweden |

# Summer Olympic Games Champions (continued)

## Equestrian sports (continued)

**THREE-DAY EVENT (TEAM)**
1956  Great Britain
1960  Australia
1964  Italy
1968  Great Britain
1972  Great Britain
1976  United States
1980  USSR
1984  United States
1988  West Germany
1992  Australia
1996  Australia
2000  Australia

**HIGH JUMP**                                     MOUNT
1900  Dominique Maximien      Canela; Oreste
       Gardéres (FRA); Gian
       Giorgio Trissino (ITA) (*tied*)

**LONG JUMP**                                     MOUNT
1900  Constant van Langhendonck      Extra Dry
       (BEL)

**FIGURE RIDING (INDIVIDUAL)**
1920  T. Bouckaert (BEL)

**FIGURE RIDING (TEAM)**
1920  Belgium

## Fencing (men)

**FOIL (INDIVIDUAL)**
1896  Eugène-Henri Gravelotte (FRA)
1900  Émile Coste (FRA)
1904  Ramón Fonst (CUB)
1912  Nedo Nadi (ITA)
1920  Nedo Nadi (ITA)
1924  Roger Ducret (FRA)
1928  Lucien Gaudin (FRA)
1932  Gustavo Marzi (ITA)
1936  Giulio Gaudini (ITA)
1948  Jehan Buhan (FRA)
1952  Christian d'Oriola (FRA)
1956  Christian d'Oriola (FRA)
1960  Viktor Zhdanovich (URS)
1964  Egon Franke (POL)
1968  Ion Drimba (ROM)
1972  Witold Woyda (POL)
1976  Fabio dal Zotto (ITA)
1980  Vladimir Smirnov (URS)
1984  Mauro Numa (ITA)
1988  Stefano Cerioni (ITA)
1992  Philippe Omnes (FRA)
1996  Alessandro Puccini (ITA)
2000  Kim Young Ho (KOR)

**FOIL (TEAM)**
1904  Cuba
1920  Italy
1924  France
1928  Italy
1932  France
1936  Italy
1948  France
1952  France
1956  Italy
1960  USSR
1964  USSR
1968  France

## Fencing (men) (continued)

**FOIL (TEAM)**
1972  Poland
1976  West Germany
1980  France
1984  Italy
1988  USSR
1992  Germany
1996  Russia
2000  France

**INDIVIDUAL FOIL, PROFESSIONAL (MASTERS)**
1896  Leon Pyrgos (GRE)
1900  Lucien Mérignac (FRA)

**INDIVIDUAL FOIL, JUNIOR**
1904  Arthur Fox (USA)

**ÉPÉE (INDIVIDUAL)**
1900  Ramón Fonst (CUB)
1904  Ramón Fonst (CUB)
1908  Gaston Alibert (FRA)
1912  Paul Anspach (BEL)
1920  Armand Massard (FRA)
1924  Charles Delporte (BEL)
1928  Lucien Gaudin (FRA)
1932  Giancarlo Cornaggia-Medici (ITA)
1936  Franco Riccardi (ITA)
1948  Luigi Cantone (ITA)
1952  Edoardo Mangiarotti (ITA)
1956  Carlo Pavesi (ITA)
1960  Giuseppe Delfino (ITA)
1964  Grigory Kriss (URS)
1968  Gyoso Kulcsar (HUN)
1972  Csaba Fenyvesi (HUN)
1976  Alexander Pusch (FRG)
1980  Johan Harmenberg (SWE)
1984  Philippe Boisse (FRA)
1988  Arnd Schmitt (FRG)
1992  Eric Srecki (FRA)
1996  Aleksandr Beketov (RUS)
2000  Pavel Kolobkov (RUS)

**ÉPÉE (TEAM)**
1908  France
1912  Belgium
1920  Italy
1924  France
1928  Italy
1932  France
1936  Italy
1948  France
1952  Italy
1956  Italy
1960  Italy
1964  Hungary
1968  Hungary
1972  Hungary
1976  Sweden
1980  France
1984  West Germany
1988  France
1992  Germany
1996  Italy
2000  Italy

**INDIVIDUAL ÉPÉE, PROFESSIONAL (MASTERS)**
1900  Albert Ayat (FRA)

# Summer Olympic Games Champions (continued)

## Fencing (men) (continued)

**INDIVIDUAL ÉPÉE, OPEN (AMATEUR AND MASTERS)**
1900 Albert Ayat (FRA)

**SABRE (INDIVIDUAL)**
1896 Ioannis Georgiadis (GRE)
1900 Georges de la Falaise (FRA)
1904 Manuel Díaz (CUB)
1908 Jeno Fuchs (HUN)
1912 Jeno Fuchs (HUN)
1920 Nedo Nadi (ITA)
1924 Sandor Posta (HUN)
1928 Odon Vitez Tersztyanszky (HUN)
1932 Gyorgy Piller (HUN)
1936 Endre Kabos (HUN)
1948 Aladar Gerevich (HUN)
1952 Pal Kovacs (HUN)
1956 Rudolph Karpati (HUN)
1960 Rudolph Karpati (HUN)
1964 Tibor Pezsa (HUN)
1968 Jerzy Pawlowski (POL)
1972 Viktor Sidyak (URS)
1976 Viktor Krovopuskov (URS)
1980 Viktor Krovopuskov (URS)
1984 Jean-François Lamour (FRA)
1988 Jean-François Lamour (FRA)
1992 Bence Szabo (HUN)
1996 Stanislav Pozdnyakov (RUS)
2000 Mihai Claudiu Covaliu (ROM)

**SABRE (TEAM)**
1908 Hungary
1912 Hungary
1920 Italy
1924 Italy
1928 Hungary
1932 Hungary
1936 Hungary
1948 Hungary
1952 Hungary
1956 Hungary
1960 Hungary
1964 USSR
1968 USSR
1972 Italy
1976 USSR
1980 USSR
1984 Italy
1988 Hungary
1992 Unified Team
1996 Russia
2000 Russia

**INDIVIDUAL SABRE, PROFESSIONAL (MASTERS)**
1900 Antonio Conte (ITA)

**THREE-CORNERED SABRE**
1906 Gustav Casmir (GER)

**SINGLE STICK**
1904 Albertson Van Zo Post (CUB)

## Fencing (women)

**FOIL (INDIVIDUAL)**
1924 Ellen Osiier (DEN)
1928 Helene Mayer (GER)
1932 Ellen Preis (AUT)
1936 Ilona Schacherer-Elek (HUN)
1948 Ilona Elek (HUN)

## Fencing (women) (continued)

**FOIL (INDIVIDUAL)**
1952 Irene Camber (ITA)
1956 Gillian Sheen (GBR)
1960 Adelheid Schmid (GER)
1964 Ildiko Ujlaki-Rejto (HUN)
1968 Yelena Novikova (URS)
1972 Antonella Ragno Lonzi (ITA)
1976 Ildiko Schwarczenberger (HUN)
1980 Pascale Trinquet (FRA)
1984 Jujie Luan (CHN)
1988 Anja Fichtel (FRG)
1992 Giovanna Trillini (ITA)
1996 Laura Gabriela Badea (ROM)
2000 Valentina Vezzali (ITA)

**FOIL (TEAM)**
1960 USSR
1964 Hungary
1968 USSR
1972 USSR
1976 USSR
1980 France
1984 West Germany
1988 West Germany
1992 Italy
1996 Italy
2000 Italy

**ÉPÉE (INDIVIDUAL)**
1996 Laura Flessel (FRA)
2000 Timea Nagy (HUN)

**ÉPÉE (TEAM)**
1996 France
2000 Russia

## Field hockey

**MEN**
1908 Great Britain
1920 Great Britain
1928 India
1932 India
1936 India
1948 India
1952 India
1956 India
1960 Pakistan
1964 India
1968 Pakistan
1972 West Germany
1976 New Zealand
1980 India
1984 Pakistan
1988 Great Britain
1992 Germany
1996 The Netherlands
2000 The Netherlands

**WOMEN**
1980 Zimbabwe
1984 The Netherlands
1988 Australia
1992 Spain
1996 Australia
2000 Australia

# Summer Olympic Games Champions (continued)

## Golf

**MEN, INDIVIDUAL**
1900   Charles Sands (USA)
1904   George Lyon (CAN)

**MEN, TEAM**
1904   United States

**WOMEN**
1900   Margaret Abbott (USA)

## Gymnastics (men)

**COMBINED, OR ALL-AROUND (INDIVIDUAL)**
1900   Gustave Sandras (FRA)
1904   Julius Lenhardt (USA)
1908   G. Alberto Braglia (ITA)
1912   G. Alberto Braglia (ITA)
1920   Giorgio Zampori (ITA)
1924   Leon Stukelj (YUG)
1928   Georges Miez (SUI)
1932   Romeo Neri (ITA)
1936   Karl-Alfred Schwarzmann (GER)
1948   Veikko Huhtanen (FIN)
1952   Viktor Chukarin (URS)
1956   Viktor Chukarin (URS)
1960   Boris Shakhlin (URS)
1964   Yukio Endo (JPN)
1968   Sawao Kato (JPN)
1972   Sawao Kato (JPN)
1976   Nikolay Andrianov (URS)
1980   Aleksandr Dityatin (URS)
1984   Koji Gushiken (JPN)
1988   Vladimir Artyomov (URS)
1992   Vitaly Shcherbo (UNT)
1996   Li Xiaosahuang (CHN)
2000   Aleksey Nemov (RUS)

**COMBINED, OR ALL-AROUND (TEAM)**
1920   Italy
1924   Italy
1928   Switzerland
1932   Italy
1936   Germany
1948   Finland
1952   USSR
1956   USSR
1960   Japan
1964   Japan
1968   Japan
1972   Japan
1976   Japan
1980   USSR
1984   United States
1988   USSR
1992   Unified Team
1996   Russia
2000   China

**FLOOR EXERCISE**
1932   Istvan Pelle (HUN)
1936   Georges Miez (SUI)
1948   Ferenc Pataki (HUN)
1952   William Thoresson (SWE)
1956   Valentin Muratov (URS)
1960   Nobuyuki Aihara (JPN)
1964   Franco Menichelli (ITA)
1968   Sawao Kato (JPN)
1972   Nikolay Andrianov (URS)
1976   Nikolay Andrianov (URS)

## Gymnastics (men) (continued)

**FLOOR EXERCISE**
1980   Roland Brückner (GDR)
1984   Li Ning (CHN)
1988   Sergey Kharikov (URS)
1992   Li Xiaosahuang (CHN)
1996   Ioannis Melissanidis (GRE)
2000   Igors Vihrovs (LAT)

**HORIZONTAL BAR**
1896   Hermann Weingärtner (GER)
1904   Anton Heida (USA); Edward Henning (USA)
      (tied)
1924   Leon Stukelj (YUG)
1928   Georges Miez (SUI)
1932   Dallas Bixler (USA)
1936   Aleksanteri Saarvala (FIN)
1948   Josef Stalder (SUI)
1952   Jack Günthard (SUI)
1956   Takashi Ono (JPN)
1960   Takashi Ono (JPN)
1964   Boris Shakhlin (URS)
1968   Mikhail Voronin (URS); Akinori Nakayama
      (JPN) (tied)
1972   Mitsuo Tsukahara (JPN)
1976   Mitsuo Tsukahara (JPN)
1980   Stoyan Delchev (BUL)
1984   Shinji Morisue (JPN)
1988   Vladimir Artyomov (URS); Valery Lyukin (URS)
      (tied)
1992   Trent Dimas (USA)
1996   Andreas Wecker (GER)
2000   Aleksey Nemov (RUS)

**PARALLEL BARS**
1896   Alfred Flatow (GER)
1904   George Eyser (USA)
1924   August Güttinger (SUI)
1928   Ladislav Vacha (TCH)
1932   Romeo Neri (ITA)
1936   Konrad Frey (GER)
1948   Michael Reusch (SUI)
1952   Hans Eugster (SUI)
1956   Viktor Chukarin (URS)
1960   Boris Shakhlin (URS)
1964   Yukio Endo (JPN)
1968   Akinori Nakayama (JPN)
1972   Sawao Kato (JPN)
1976   Sawao Kato (JPN)
1980   Aleksandr Tkachyov (URS)
1984   Bart Conner (USA)
1988   Vladimir Artyomov (URS)
1992   Vitaly Shcherbo (UNT)
1996   Rustam Sharipov (UKR)
2000   Li Xiaopeng (CHN)

**SIDE, OR POMMEL, HORSE**
1896   Louis Zutter (SUI)
1904   Anton Heida (USA)
1924   Josef Wilhelm (SUI)
1928   Hermann Hänggi (SUI)
1932   Istvan Pelle (HUN)
1936   Konrad Frey (GER)
1948   Paavo Aaltonen (FIN); Veikko Huhtanen (FIN);
      Heikki Savolainen (FIN) (tied)
1952   Viktor Chukarin (URS)
1956   Boris Shakhlin (URS)
1960   Boris Shakhlin (URS); Eugen Ekman (FIN)
      (tied)

# Summer Olympic Games Champions (continued)

## Gymnastics (men) (continued)

**SIDE, OR POMMEL, HORSE**

| | |
|---|---|
| 1964 | Miroslav Cerar (YUG) |
| 1968 | Miroslav Cerar (YUG) |
| 1972 | Viktor Klimenko (URS) |
| 1976 | Zoltan Magyar (HUN) |
| 1980 | Zoltan Magyar (HUN) |
| 1984 | Li Ning (CHN); Peter Vidmar (USA) (tied) |
| 1988 | Lyubomir Geraskov (BUL); Zsolt Borkai (HUN); Dmitry Bilozerchev (URS) (tied) |
| 1992 | Vitaly Shcherbo (UNT); Pae Gil-su (PRK) (tied) |
| 1996 | Li Donghua (SUI) |
| 2000 | Marius Urzica (ROM) |

**LONG, OR VAULTING, HORSE**

| | |
|---|---|
| 1896 | Karl Schuhmann (GER) |
| 1904 | Anton Heida (USA); George Eyser (USA) (tied) |
| 1924 | Frank Kriz (USA) |
| 1928 | Eugen Mack (SUI) |
| 1932 | Savino Guglielmetti (ITA) |
| 1936 | Karl-Alfred Schnorzmann (GER) |
| 1948 | Paavo Johannes Aaltonen (FIN) |
| 1952 | Viktor Chukarin (URS) |
| 1956 | Valentin Muratov (URS); Helmut Bantz (GER) (tied) |
| 1960 | Takashi Ono (JPN); Boris Shakhlin (URS) (tied) |
| 1964 | Haruhiro Yamashita (JPN) |
| 1968 | Mikhail Voronin (URS) |
| 1972 | Klaus Köste (GDR) |
| 1976 | Nikolay Andrianov (URS) |
| 1980 | Nikolay Andrianov (URS) |
| 1984 | Lou Yun (CHN) |
| 1988 | Lou Yun (CHN) |
| 1992 | Vitaly Shcherbo (UNT) |
| 1996 | Aleksey Nemov (RUS) |
| 2000 | Gervasio Deferr (ESP) |

**RINGS**

| | |
|---|---|
| 1896 | Ioannis Mitropoulos (GRE) |
| 1904 | Hermann Glass (USA) |
| 1924 | Francesco Martino (ITA) |
| 1928 | Leon Stukelj (YUG) |
| 1932 | George Gulack (USA) |
| 1936 | Alois Hudec (TCH) |
| 1948 | Karl Frei (SUI) |
| 1952 | Grant Shaginyan (URS) |
| 1956 | Albert Azaryan (URS) |
| 1960 | Albert Azaryan (URS) |
| 1964 | Takuji Hayata (JPN) |
| 1968 | Akinori Nakayama (JPN) |
| 1972 | Akinori Nakayama (JPN) |
| 1976 | Nikolay Andrianov (URS) |
| 1980 | Aleksandr Dityatin (URS) |
| 1984 | Li Ning (CHN); Koji Gushiken (JPN) (tied) |
| 1988 | Holger Behrendt (GDR); Dmitry Bilozerchev (URS) (tied) |
| 1992 | Vitaly Shcherbo (UNT) |
| 1996 | Yury Chechi (ITA) |
| 2000 | Szilveszter Csollany (HUN) |

**ROPE CLIMBING**

| | |
|---|---|
| 1896 | Nicolaos Andriakopoulos (GRE) |
| 1904 | George Eyser (USA) |
| 1924 | Bedrich Supcik (TCH) |
| 1932 | Raymond Bass (USA) |

**SWEDISH EXERCISES (TEAM)**

| | |
|---|---|
| 1912 | Sweden |

## Gymnastics (men) (continued)

**SWEDISH EXERCISES (TEAM)**

| | |
|---|---|
| 1920 | Sweden |

**OPTIONAL EXERCISES (TEAM)**

| | |
|---|---|
| 1912 | Norway |
| 1920 | Denmark |
| 1932 | United States |

**PARALLEL BARS (TEAM)**

| | |
|---|---|
| 1896 | Germany |

**HORIZONTAL BARS (TEAM)**

| | |
|---|---|
| 1896 | Germany |

**CLUB SWINGING**

| | |
|---|---|
| 1904 | Edward Hennig (USA) |
| 1932 | George Roth (USA) |

**TUMBLING**

| | |
|---|---|
| 1932 | Rowland Wolfe (USA) |

**COMBINED COMPETITION (7 APPARATUS)**

| | |
|---|---|
| 1904 | Anton Heida (USA) |

**COMBINED COMPETITION (9 EVENTS)**

| | |
|---|---|
| 1904 | Adolf Spinnler (SUI) |

**PRESCRIBED APPARATUS (TEAM)**

| | |
|---|---|
| 1904 | United States |
| 1908 | Sweden |
| 1912 | Italy |
| 1952 | Sweden |
| 1956 | Hungary |

**MASS EXERCISES (TEAM)**

| | |
|---|---|
| 1952 | Finland |

**SIDE HORSE (VAULTS)**

| | |
|---|---|
| 1924 | Albert Séguin (FRA) |

## Gymnastics (women)

**COMBINED, OR ALL-AROUND (INDIVIDUAL)**

| | |
|---|---|
| 1952 | Mariya Gorokhovskaya (URS) |
| 1956 | Larisa Latynina (URS) |
| 1960 | Larisa Latynina (URS) |
| 1964 | Vera Caslavska (TCH) |
| 1968 | Vera Caslavska (TCH) |
| 1972 | Lyudmila Turishcheva (URS) |
| 1976 | Nadia Comaneci (ROM) |
| 1980 | Yelena Davydova (URS) |
| 1984 | Mary-Lou Retton (USA) |
| 1988 | Yelena Shushunova (URS) |
| 1992 | Tatyana Gutsu (UNT) |
| 1996 | Liliya Podkopayeva (UKR) |
| 2000 | Simona Amanar (ROM) |

**COMBINED, OR ALL-AROUND (TEAM)**

| | |
|---|---|
| 1928 | The Netherlands |
| 1936 | Germany |
| 1948 | Czechoslovakia |
| 1952 | USSR |
| 1956 | USSR |
| 1960 | USSR |
| 1964 | USSR |
| 1968 | USSR |
| 1972 | USSR |
| 1976 | USSR |
| 1980 | USSR |

# Summer Olympic Games Champions (continued)

## Gymnastics (women) (continued)

### COMBINED, OR ALL-AROUND (TEAM)
1984 Romania
1988 USSR
1992 Unified Team
1996 United States
2000 Romania

### BALANCE BEAM
1952 Nina Bocharova (URS)
1956 Agnes Keleti (HUN)
1960 Eva Bosakova (TCH)
1964 Vera Caslavska (TCH)
1968 Natalya Kuchinskaya (URS)
1972 Olga Korbut (URS)
1976 Nadia Comaneci (ROM)
1980 Nadia Comaneci (ROM)
1984 Ecaterina Szabo (ROM); Simona Pauca
 (ROM) (tied)
1988 Daniela Silivas (ROM)
1992 Tatyana Lysenko (UNT)
1996 Shannon Miller (USA)
2000 Liu Xuan (CHN)

### UNEVEN PARALLEL BARS
1952 Margit Korondi (HUN)
1956 Agnes Keleti (HUN)
1960 Polina Astakhova (URS)
1964 Polina Astakhova (URS)
1968 Vera Caslavska (TCH)
1972 Karin Janz (GDR)
1976 Nadia Comaneci (ROM)
1980 Maxi Gnauck (GDR)
1984 Julianne McNamara (USA); Ma Yanhong
 (CHN) (tied)
1988 Daniela Silivas (ROM)
1992 Li Lu (CHN)
1996 Svetlana Khorkina (RUS)
2000 Svetlana Khorkina (RUS)

### VAULTING HORSE
1952 Yekaterina Kalinchuk (URS)
1956 Larisa Latynina (URS)
1960 Margarita Nikolayeva (URS)
1964 Vera Caslavska (TCH)
1968 Vera Caslavska (TCH)
1972 Karin Janz (GDR)
1976 Nelli Kim (URS)
1980 Natalya Shaposhnikova (URS)
1984 Ecaterina Szabo (ROM)
1988 Svetlana Boginskaya (URS)
1992 Henrietta Onodi (HUN); Lavinia Milosovici
 (ROM) (tied)
1996 Simona Amanar (ROM)
2000 Yelena Zamolodchikova (RUS)

### FLOOR EXERCISE
1952 Agnes Keleti (HUN)
1956 Larisa Latynina (URS); Agnes Keleti (HUN)
 (tied)
1960 Larisa Latynina (URS)
1964 Larisa Latynina (URS)
1968 Vera Caslavska (TCH); Larissa Petrik (URS)
 (tied)
1972 Olga Korbut (URS)
1976 Nelli Kim (URS)
1980 Nadia Comaneci (ROM); Nelli Kim (URS) (tied)
1984 Ecaterina Szabo (ROM)
1988 Daniela Silivas (ROM)

## Gymnastics (women) (continued)

### FLOOR EXERCISE
1992 Lavinia Milosovici (ROM)
1996 Liliya Podkopayeva (UKR)
2000 Yelena Zamolodchikova (RUS)

### RHYTHMIC GYMNASTICS (INDIVIDUAL)
1984 Lori Fung (CAN)
1988 Marina Lobatch (URS)
1992 Aleksandra Timoshenko (UNT)
1996 Yekaterina Serebryanskaya (UKR)
2000 Yuliya Barsukova (RUS)

### RHYTHMIC GYMNASTICS (TEAM)
1996 Spain
2000 Russia

### HAND APPARATUS (TEAM)
1952 Sweden
1956 Hungary

## Handball (team) (outdoors to 1972)

### MEN
1936 Germany
1952 Sweden (demonstration)
1972 Yugoslavia
1976 USSR
1980 East Germany
1984 Yugoslavia
1988 USSR
1992 Unified Team
1996 Croatia
2000 Russia

### WOMEN
1976 USSR
1980 USSR
1984 Yugoslavia
1988 South Korea
1992 South Korea
1996 Denmark
2000 Denmark

### JEU DE PAUME (ROYAL TENNIS)
1908 Jay Gould (USA)

## Judo (men)[9]

### 60 KG; 132.5 LB (EXTRA LIGHTWEIGHT)
1964 Takehide Nakatani (JPN)
1972 Takao Kawaguchi (JPN)
1976 Héctor Rodríguez (CUB)
1980 Thierry Rey (FRA)
1984 Shinji Hosokawa (JPN)
1988 Kim Jae-Yup (KOR)
1992 Nazim Guseynov (UNT)
1996 Tadahiro Nomura (JPN)
2000 Tadahiro Nomura (JPN)

### 66 KG; 145.5 LB (HALF-LIGHTWEIGHT)
1980 Nikolay Solodukhin (URS)
1984 Yoshiyuki Matsuoka (JPN)
1988 Lee Kyung Ken (KOR)
1992 Rogerio Sampaio Cardoso (BRA)
1996 Udo Quellmalz (GER)
2000 Huseyin Ozkan (TUR)

### 73 KG; 161 LB (LIGHTWEIGHT)
1972 Takao Kawaguchi (JPN)
1976 Héctor Rodríguez Torres (CUB)

# Summer Olympic Games Champions (continued)

## Judo (men)[9] (continued)

**73 KG; 161 LB (LIGHTWEIGHT)**

| | |
|---|---|
| 1980 | Ezio Gamba (ITA) |
| 1984 | Ahn Byeong Keun (KOR) |
| 1988 | Marc Alexandre (FRA) |
| 1992 | Toshihiko Koga (JPN) |
| 1996 | Kenzo Nakamura (JPN) |
| 2000 | Giuseppe Maddaloni (ITA) |

**81 KG; 178.5 LB (HALF-MIDDLEWEIGHT)**

| | |
|---|---|
| 1972 | Toyojazu Nomura (JPN) |
| 1976 | Vladimir Nevzorov (URS) |
| 1980 | Shota Khabareli (URS) |
| 1984 | Frank Wieneke (FRG) |
| 1988 | Waldemar Legien (POL) |
| 1992 | Hidehiko Yoshida (JPN) |
| 1996 | Djamel Bouras (FRA) |
| 2000 | Makoto Takimoto (JPN) |

**90 KG; 198 LB (MIDDLEWEIGHT)**

| | |
|---|---|
| 1964 | Isao Okano (JPN) |
| 1972 | Shinobu Sekine (JPN) |
| 1976 | Isamu Sonoda (JPN) |
| 1980 | Jürg Röthlisberger (SUI) |
| 1984 | Peter Seisenbacher (AUT) |
| 1988 | Peter Seisenbacher (AUT) |
| 1992 | Waldemar Legien (POL) |
| 1996 | Jeon Ki-Young (KOR) |
| 2000 | Mark Huizinga (NED) |

**100 KG; 220.5 LB (HALF-HEAVYWEIGHT)**

| | |
|---|---|
| 1972 | Shota Chochoshvili (URS) |
| 1976 | Kazuhiro Ninomiya (JPN) |
| 1980 | Robert van de Walle (BEL) |
| 1984 | Ha Young Zoo (KOR) |
| 1988 | Aurelio Miguel (BRA) |
| 1992 | Antal Kovacs (HUN) |
| 1996 | Pawel Nastula (POL) |
| 2000 | Kosei Inoue (JPN) |

**OVER 100 KG; 220.5 LB (HEAVYWEIGHT)**

| | |
|---|---|
| 1964 | Isao Inokuma (JPN) |
| 1972 | Willem Ruska (NED) |
| 1976 | Sergey Novikov (URS) |
| 1980 | Angelo Parisi (FRA) |
| 1984 | Hitoshi Saito (JPN) |
| 1988 | Hitoshi Saito (JPN) |
| 1992 | David Khakhaleishvili (UNT) |
| 1996 | David Douillet (FRA) |
| 2000 | David Douillet (FRA) |

**OPEN (NO WEIGHT LIMIT)**

| | |
|---|---|
| 1964 | Antonius Johannes Geesink (NED) |
| 1972 | Willem Ruska (NED) |
| 1976 | Haruki Uemura (JPN) |
| 1980 | Dietmar Lorenz (GDR) |
| 1984 | Yasuhiro Yamashita (JPN) |

## Judo (women)[10]

**48 KG; 106 LB (EXTRA LIGHTWEIGHT)**

| | |
|---|---|
| 1992 | Cecile Nowak (FRA) |
| 1996 | Kye Sun-Hi (PRK) |
| 2000 | Ryoko Tamura (JPN) |

**52 KG; 114.5 LB (HALF-LIGHTWEIGHT)**

| | |
|---|---|
| 1992 | Almudena Muñoz Martínez (ESP) |
| 1996 | Marie-Claire Restoux (FRA) |
| 2000 | Legna Verdecia (CUB) |

## Judo (women)[10] (continued)

**57 KG; 125.5 LB (LIGHTWEIGHT)**

| | |
|---|---|
| 1992 | Miriam Blasco Soto (ESP) |
| 1996 | Driulis González Morales (CUB) |
| 2000 | Isabel Fernández (ESP) |

**63 KG; 139 LB (HALF-MIDDLEWEIGHT)**

| | |
|---|---|
| 1992 | Catherine Fleury-Vachon (FRA) |
| 1996 | Yuko Emoto (JPN) |
| 2000 | Severine Vandenhende (FRA) |

**70 KG; 154.5 LB (MIDDLEWEIGHT)**

| | |
|---|---|
| 1992 | Odalis Reve Jiménez (CUB) |
| 1996 | Cho Min-Sun (KOR) |
| 2000 | Sibelis Veranes (CUB) |

**78 KG; 172 LB (HALF-HEAVYWEIGHT)**

| | |
|---|---|
| 1992 | Kim Mi-Jung (KOR) |
| 1996 | Ulla Werbrouck (BEL) |
| 2000 | Tang Lin (CHN) |

**OVER 78 KG; 172 LB (HEAVYWEIGHT)**

| | |
|---|---|
| 1992 | Zhuang Xiaoyan (CHN) |
| 1996 | Sun Fuming (CHN) |
| 2000 | Yuan Hua (CHN) |

## Lacrosse

| | |
|---|---|
| 1904 | Canada |
| 1908 | Canada |

## Modern pentathlon

**INDIVIDUAL (MEN)**

| | |
|---|---|
| 1912 | Gösta Lilliehöök (SWE) |
| 1920 | Gustaf Dyrssen (SWE) |
| 1924 | Bo Lindman (SWE) |
| 1928 | Sven Thofelt (SWE) |
| 1932 | Johan Oxenstierna (SWE) |
| 1936 | Gotthardt Handrick (GER) |
| 1948 | William Grut (SWE) |
| 1952 | Lars-Goran Hall (SWE) |
| 1956 | Lars-Goran Hall (SWE) |
| 1960 | Ferenc Nemeth (HUN) |
| 1964 | Ferenc Torok (HUN) |
| 1968 | Björn Ferm (SWE) |
| 1972 | Andras Balczo (HUN) |
| 1976 | Janusz Pyciak-Peciak (POL) |
| 1980 | Anatoly Starostin (URS) |
| 1984 | Daniele Masala (ITA) |
| 1988 | Janos Martinek (HUN) |
| 1992 | Arkadiusz Skrzypaszek (POL) |
| 1996 | Aleksandr Parygin (KAZ) |
| 2000 | Dmitry Svatkovsky (RUS) |

**INDIVIDUAL (WOMEN)**

| | |
|---|---|
| 2000 | Stephanie Cook (GBR) |

**TEAM (MEN)**

| | |
|---|---|
| 1952 | Hungary |
| 1956 | USSR |
| 1960 | Hungary |
| 1964 | USSR |
| 1968 | Hungary |
| 1972 | USSR |
| 1976 | Great Britain |
| 1980 | USSR |
| 1984 | Italy |
| 1988 | Hungary |
| 1992 | Poland |

# Summer Olympic Games Champions (continued)

## Motorboat racing

**OPEN CLASS, 40 NAUTICAL MILES**      BOAT
1908   Émile Thubron (FRA)     *Camille*

**8-METER CLASS, 40 NAUTICAL MILES**
1908   Thomas Thornycroft, Bernard    *Cyrinus*
       Redwood (GBR)

**UNDER 60-FOOT CLASS, 40 NAUTICAL MILES**
1908   Thomas Thornycroft, Bernard    *Cyrinus*
       Redwood (GBR)

## Polo

| | |
|---|---|
| 1900 | team comprising members from Great Britain and the United States |
| 1908 | Great Britain |
| 1920 | Great Britain |
| 1924 | Argentina |
| 1936 | Argentina |

## Rackets

**SINGLES**
1908   Evan Noel (GBR)

**DOUBLES**
1908   Vane Pennell, John Jacob Astor (GBR)

## Roque

1904   Charles Jacobus (USA)

## Rowing (men)[11]

| SINGLE SCULLS | | MIN:SEC |
|---|---|---|
| 1900 | Henri Barrelet (FRA) | 7:35.6 |
| 1904 | Frank Greer (USA) | 10:08.5 |
| 1908 | Harry Blackstaffe (GBR) | 9:26.0 |
| 1912 | William Kinnear (GBR) | 7:47.6 |
| 1920 | John Kelly, Sr. (USA) | 7:35.0 |
| 1924 | Jack Beresford (GBR) | 7:49.2 |
| 1928 | Henry Pearce (AUS) | 7:11.0 |
| 1932 | Henry Pearce (AUS) | 7:44.4 |
| 1936 | Gustav Schäfer (GER) | 8:21.5 |
| 1948 | Mervyn Wood (AUS) | 7:24.4 |
| 1952 | Yury Tyukalov (URS) | 8:12.8 |
| 1956 | Vyacheslav Ivanov (URS) | 8:02.5 |
| 1960 | Vyacheslav Ivanov (URS) | 7:13.96 |
| 1964 | Vyacheslav Ivanov (URS) | 8:22.51 |
| 1968 | Henri-Jan Wienese (NED) | 7:47.80 |
| 1972 | Yury Malyshev (URS) | 7:10.12 |
| 1976 | Pertti Karppinen (FIN) | 7:29.03 |
| 1980 | Pertti Karppinen (FIN) | 7:09.61 |
| 1984 | Pertti Karppinen (FIN) | 7:00.24 |
| 1988 | Thomas Lange (GDR) | 6:49.86 |
| 1992 | Thomas Lange (GER) | 6:51.40 |
| 1996 | Xeno Mueller (SUI) | 6:44.85 |
| 2000 | Robert Waddell (NZL) | 6:48.90 |

| DOUBLE SCULLS | | MIN:SEC |
|---|---|---|
| 1904 | United States | 10:03.2 |
| 1920 | United States | 7:09.0 |
| 1924 | United States | 6:34.0 |
| 1928 | United States | 6:41.4 |
| 1932 | United States | 7:17.4 |
| 1936 | Great Britain | 7:20.8 |
| 1948 | Great Britain | 6:51.3 |
| 1952 | Argentina | 7:32.2 |
| 1956 | USSR | 7:24.0 |
| 1960 | Czechoslovakia | 6:47.50 |
| 1964 | USSR | 7:10.66 |
| 1968 | USSR | 6:51.82 |

## Rowing (men)[11] (continued)

| DOUBLE SCULLS | | MIN:SEC |
|---|---|---|
| 1972 | USSR | 7:01.77 |
| 1976 | Norway | 7:13.20 |
| 1980 | East Germany | 6:24.33 |
| 1984 | United States | 6:36.87 |
| 1988 | The Netherlands | 6:21.13 |
| 1992 | Australia | 6:17.32 |
| 1996 | Italy | 6:16.98 |
| 2000 | Slovenia | 6:16.63 |

| FOUR SCULLS | | MIN:SEC |
|---|---|---|
| 1976 | East Germany | 6:18.65 |
| 1980 | East Germany | 5:49.81 |
| 1984 | West Germany | 5:57.55 |
| 1988 | Italy | 5:53.37 |
| 1992 | Germany | 5:45.17 |
| 1996 | Germany | 5:56.93 |
| 2000 | Italy | 5:45.56 |

| LIGHTWEIGHT DOUBLE SCULLS | | MIN:SEC |
|---|---|---|
| 1996 | Switzerland | 6:23.47 |
| 2000 | Poland | 6:21.75 |

| PAIRS (WITHOUT COXSWAIN) | | MIN:SEC |
|---|---|---|
| 1904 | United States | 10:57.0 |
| 1908 | Great Britain | 9:41.0 |
| 1924 | The Netherlands | 8:19.4 |
| 1928 | Germany | 7:06.4 |
| 1932 | Great Britain | 8:00.0 |
| 1936 | Germany | 8:16.1 |
| 1948 | Great Britain | 7:21.1 |
| 1952 | United States | 8:20.7 |
| 1956 | United States | 7:55.4 |
| 1960 | USSR | 7:02.01 |
| 1964 | Canada | 7:32.94 |
| 1968 | East Germany | 7:26.56 |
| 1972 | East Germany | 6:53.16 |
| 1976 | East Germany | 7:23.31 |
| 1980 | East Germany | 6:48.01 |
| 1984 | Romania | 6:45.39 |
| 1988 | Great Britain | 6:36.84 |
| 1992 | Great Britain | 6:27.72 |
| 1996 | Great Britain | 6:20.09 |
| 2000 | France | 6:32.97 |

| PAIRS (WITH COXSWAIN) | | MIN:SEC |
|---|---|---|
| 1900 | The Netherlands/France | 7:34.2 |
| 1920 | Italy | 7:56.0 |
| 1924 | Switzerland | 8:39.0 |
| 1928 | Switzerland | 7:42.6 |
| 1932 | United States | 8:25.8 |
| 1936 | Germany | 8:36.9 |
| 1948 | Denmark | 8:00.5 |
| 1952 | France | 8:28.6 |
| 1956 | United States | 8:26.1 |
| 1960 | Germany | 7:29.14 |
| 1964 | United States | 8:21.23 |
| 1968 | Italy | 8:04.81 |
| 1972 | East Germany | 7:17.25 |
| 1976 | East Germany | 7:58.99 |
| 1980 | East Germany | 7:02.54 |
| 1984 | Italy | 7:05.99 |
| 1988 | Italy | 6:58.79 |
| 1992 | Great Britain | 6:49.83 |

| LIGHTWEIGHT FOURS (WITHOUT COXSWAIN) | | MIN:SEC |
|---|---|---|
| 1996 | Denmark | 6:09.58 |
| 2000 | France | 6:01.68 |

## Summer Olympic Games Champions (continued)

### Rowing (men)[11] (continued)

| FOURS (WITHOUT COXSWAIN) | | MIN:SEC |
|---|---|---|
| 1900 | France | 7:11.0 |
| 1904 | United States | 9:53.8 |
| 1908 | Great Britain | 8:34.0 |
| 1920 | Great Britain | 7:08.6 |
| 1928 | Great Britain | 6:36.0 |
| 1932 | Great Britain | 6:58.2 |
| 1936 | Germany | 7:01.8 |
| 1948 | Italy | 6:39.0 |
| 1952 | Yugoslavia | 7:16.0 |
| 1956 | Canada | 7:08.8 |
| 1960 | United States | 6:26.26 |
| 1964 | Denmark | 6:59.30 |
| 1968 | East Germany | 6:39.18 |
| 1972 | East Germany | 6:24.27 |
| 1976 | East Germany | 6:37.42 |
| 1980 | East Germany | 6:08.17 |
| 1984 | New Zealand | 6:03.48 |
| 1988 | East Germany | 6:03.11 |
| 1992 | Australia | 5:55.04 |
| 1996 | Australia | 6:06.37 |
| 2000 | Great Britain | 5:56.24 |

| FOURS (WITH COXSWAIN) | | MIN:SEC |
|---|---|---|
| 1900 | Germany | 5:59.0 |
| 1912 | Germany | 6:59.4 |
| 1920 | Switzerland | 6:54.0 |
| 1924 | Switzerland | 7:18.4 |
| 1928 | Italy | 6:47.8 |
| 1932 | Germany | 7:19.0 |
| 1936 | Germany | 7:16.2 |
| 1948 | United States | 6:50.3 |
| 1952 | Czechoslovakia | 7:33.4 |
| 1956 | Italy | 7:19.4 |
| 1960 | Germany | 6:39.12 |
| 1964 | Germany | 7:00.44 |
| 1968 | New Zealand | 6:45.62 |
| 1972 | West Germany | 6:31.85 |
| 1976 | USSR | 6:40.22 |
| 1980 | East Germany | 6:14.51 |
| 1984 | Great Britain | 6:18.64 |
| 1988 | East Germany | 6:10.74 |
| 1992 | Romania | 5:59.37 |

| FOURS, INRIGGERS (WITH COXSWAIN) | | MIN:SEC |
|---|---|---|
| 1912 | Denmark | 7:47.0 |

| EIGHTS (WITH COXSWAIN) | | MIN:SEC |
|---|---|---|
| 1900 | United States | 6:09.8 |
| 1904 | United States | 7:50.0 |
| 1908 | Great Britain | 7:52.0 |
| 1912 | Great Britain | 6:15.0 |
| 1920 | United States | 6:02.6 |
| 1924 | United States | 6:33.4 |
| 1928 | United States | 6:03.2 |
| 1932 | United States | 6:37.6 |
| 1936 | United States | 6:25.4 |
| 1948 | United States | 5:56.7 |
| 1952 | United States | 6:25.9 |
| 1956 | United States | 6:35.2 |
| 1960 | Germany | 5:57.18 |
| 1964 | United States | 6:18.23 |
| 1968 | West Germany | 6:07.00 |
| 1972 | New Zealand | 6:08.94 |
| 1976 | East Germany | 5:58.29 |
| 1980 | East Germany | 5:49.05 |
| 1984 | Canada | 5:41.32 |
| 1988 | West Germany | 5:46.05 |

### Rowing (men)[11] (continued)

| EIGHTS (WITH COXSWAIN) | | MIN:SEC |
|---|---|---|
| 1992 | Canada | 5:29.53 |
| 1996 | The Netherlands | 5:42.74 |
| 2000 | Great Britain | 5:33.08 |

| SIX-MAN NAVAL ROWING BOATS (2,000 METERS) | | MIN:SEC |
|---|---|---|
| 1906 | Italy | 10:45.0 |

| SIXTEEN-MAN NAVAL ROWING BOATS (3,000 METERS) | | MIN:SEC |
|---|---|---|
| 1906 | Greece | 16:35.0 |

### Rowing (women)[12]

| SINGLE SCULLS | | MIN:SEC |
|---|---|---|
| 1976 | Christine Scheiblich (GDR) | 4:05.56 |
| 1980 | Sanda Toma (ROM) | 3:40.69 |
| 1984 | Valeria Racila (ROM) | 3:40.68 |
| 1988 | Jutta Behrendt (GDR) | 7:47.19 |
| 1992 | Elisabeta Lipa (ROM) | 7:25.54 |
| 1996 | Yekaterina Khodotovich (BLR) | 7:32.21 |
| 2000 | Yekaterina Khodotovich Karsten (BLR) | 7:28.14 |

| DOUBLE SCULLS | | MIN:SEC |
|---|---|---|
| 1976 | Bulgaria | 3:44.36 |
| 1980 | USSR | 3:16.27 |
| 1984 | Romania | 3:26.75 |
| 1988 | East Germany | 7:00.48 |
| 1992 | Germany | 6:49.00 |
| 1996 | Canada | 6:56.84 |
| 2000 | Germany | 6:55.44 |

| LIGHTWEIGHT DOUBLE SCULLS | | MIN:SEC |
|---|---|---|
| 1996 | Romania | 7:12.78 |
| 2000 | Romania | 7:02.64 |

| FOUR SCULLS | | MIN:SEC |
|---|---|---|
| 1976 | East Germany | 3:29.99 |
| 1980 | East Germany | 3:15.32 |
| 1984 | Romania | 3:14.11 |
| 1988 | East Germany | 6:21.06 |
| 1992 | Germany | 6:20.18 |
| 1996 | Germany | 6:27.44 |
| 2000 | Germany | 6:19.58 |

| PAIRS (WITHOUT COXSWAIN) | | MIN:SEC |
|---|---|---|
| 1976 | Bulgaria | 4:01.22 |
| 1980 | East Germany | 3:30.49 |
| 1984 | Romania | 3:32.60 |
| 1988 | Romania | 7:28.13 |
| 1992 | Canada | 7:06.22 |
| 1996 | Australia | 7:01.39 |
| 2000 | Romania | 7:11.00 |

| FOURS (WITH COXSWAIN [WITHOUT IN 1992]) | | MIN:SEC |
|---|---|---|
| 1976 | East Germany | 3:45.08 |
| 1980 | East Germany | 3:19.27 |
| 1984 | Romania | 3:19.3 |
| 1988 | East Germany | 6:56.0 |
| 1992 | Canada | 6:30.85 |

| EIGHTS (WITH COXSWAIN) | | MIN:SEC |
|---|---|---|
| 1976 | East Germany | 3:33.32 |
| 1980 | East Germany | 3:03.32 |
| 1984 | United States | 2:59.80 |
| 1988 | East Germany | 6:15.17 |
| 1992 | Canada | 6:02.62 |
| 1996 | Romania | 6:19.73 |

# Summer Olympic Games Champions (continued)

## Rowing (women)[12] (continued)

**EIGHTS (WITH COXSWAIN)**

| | | MIN:SEC |
|---|---|---|
| 2000 | Romania | 6:06.44 |

## Rugby football

| | |
|---|---|
| 1900 | France |
| 1908 | Australia |
| 1920 | United States |
| 1924 | United States |

## Sailing (yachting)

**BOARDSAILING (WINDGLIDER/DIVISION II) (OPEN)**

| | |
|---|---|
| 1984 | Stephan van den Berg (NED) |
| 1988 | Anthony Bruce Kendall (NZL) |

**BOARDSAILING (MISTRAL FROM 1996) (MEN)**

| | |
|---|---|
| 1992 | Franck David (FRA) |
| 1996 | Nikolaos Kaklamanakis (GRE) |
| 2000 | Christoph Sieber (AUT) |

**BOARDSAILING (MISTRAL FROM 1996) (WOMEN)**

| | |
|---|---|
| 1992 | Barbara Anne Kendall (NZL) |
| 1996 | Lee Lai Shan (HKG) |
| 2000 | Alessandra Sensini (ITA) |

**SINGLE-HANDED DINGHY (EUROPE) (WOMEN)**

| | |
|---|---|
| 1992 | Linda Andersen (NOR) |
| 1996 | Kristine Roug (DEN) |
| 2000 | Shirley Anne Robertson (GBR) |

**SINGLE-HANDED DINGHY (LASER) (OPEN)**

| | |
|---|---|
| 1996 | Robert Scheidt (BRA) |
| 2000 | Ben Ainslie (GBR) |

**SINGLE-HANDED DINGHY (FINN FROM 1952)**
**(MEN; OPEN UNTIL 1992)**

| | |
|---|---|
| 1924 | Léon Huybrechts (BEL) |
| 1928 | Sven Thorell (SWE) |
| 1932 | Jacques Lebrun (FRA) |
| 1936 | Daniel Kagchelland (NED) |
| 1948 | Paul Elvström (DEN) |
| 1952 | Paul Elvström (DEN) |
| 1956 | Paul Elvström (DEN) |
| 1960 | Paul Elvström (DEN) |
| 1964 | Wilhelm Kuhweide (GER) |
| 1968 | Valentin Mankin (URS) |
| 1972 | Serge Maury (FRA) |
| 1976 | Jochen Schümann (GDR) |
| 1980 | Esko Rechardt (FIN) |
| 1984 | Russell Coutts (NZL) |
| 1988 | José Luis Doreste (ESP) |
| 1992 | José van der Ploeg (ESP) |
| 1996 | Mateusz Kusznierewicz (POL) |
| 2000 | Iain Percy (GBR) |

**DOUBLE-HANDED DINGHY (470) (MEN)**

| | |
|---|---|
| 1976 | West Germany |
| 1980 | Brazil |
| 1984 | Spain |
| 1988 | France |
| 1992 | Spain |
| 1996 | Ukraine |
| 2000 | Australia |

**DOUBLE-HANDED DINGHY (470) (WOMEN)**

| | |
|---|---|
| 1988 | United States |
| 1992 | Spain |
| 1996 | Spain |
| 2000 | Australia |

## Sailing (yachting) (continued)

**HIGH-PERFORMANCE DINGHY (49ER) (OPEN)**

| | |
|---|---|
| 2000 | Finland |

**MULTIHULL (TORNADO) (OPEN)**

| | |
|---|---|
| 1976 | Great Britain |
| 1980 | Brazil |
| 1984 | New Zealand |
| 1988 | France |
| 1992 | France |
| 1996 | Spain |
| 2000 | Austria |

**FLEET/MATCH RACE KEELBOAT (SOLING) (OPEN)**

| | |
|---|---|
| 1972 | United States |
| 1976 | Denmark |
| 1980 | Denmark |
| 1984 | United States |
| 1988 | East Germany |
| 1992 | Denmark |
| 1996 | Germany |
| 2000 | Denmark |

**TWO-PERSON KEELBOAT (STAR) (OPEN)**

| | |
|---|---|
| 1932 | United States |
| 1936 | Germany |
| 1948 | United States |
| 1952 | Italy |
| 1956 | United States |
| 1960 | USSR |
| 1964 | The Bahamas |
| 1968 | United States |
| 1972 | Australia |
| 1980 | USSR |
| 1984 | United States |
| 1988 | Great Britain |
| 1992 | United States |
| 1996 | Brazil |
| 2000 | United States |

**40-METER CLASS**

| | |
|---|---|
| 1920 | Sweden |

**30-METER CLASS**

| | |
|---|---|
| 1920 | Sweden |

**12-METER CLASS**

| | |
|---|---|
| 1920 (old) | Norway |
| 1920 (new) | Norway |

**OVER-10-METER CLASS**

| | |
|---|---|
| 1900 | France |
| 1908 | Great Britain |
| 1912 | Norway |

**10-METER CLASS**

| | |
|---|---|
| 1900 | Germany |
| 1912 | Sweden |
| 1920 (old) | Norway |
| 1920 (new) | Norway |

**8-METER CLASS**

| | |
|---|---|
| 1900 | Great Britain |
| 1908 | Great Britain |
| 1912 | Norway |
| 1920 (old) | Norway |
| 1920 (new) | Norway |
| 1924 | Norway |
| 1928 | France |

# Summer Olympic Games Champions (continued)

## Sailing (yachting) (continued)

**8-METER CLASS**
1932 United States
1936 Italy

**7-METER CLASS**
1908 Great Britain
1920 (old) Great Britain

**6.5-METER CLASS**
1920 (new) The Netherlands

**6-METER CLASS**
1900 Switzerland
1908 Great Britain
1912 France
1920 (old) Belgium
1920 (new) Norway
1924 Norway
1928 Norway
1932 Sweden
1936 Great Britain
1948 United States
1952 United States

**5.5-METER CLASS**
1952 United States
1956 Sweden
1960 United States
1964 Australia
1968 Sweden

**18-FOOT CENTERBOARD BOAT**
1920 Great Britain

**12-FOOT CENTERBOARD BOAT**
1920 The Netherlands
1924 Belgium

**12-FOOT DINGHY**
1928 Sweden

**MONOTYPE CLASS**
1932 France

**MONOTYPE CLASS "NÜRNBERG"**
1936 The Netherlands

**SWALLOW**
1948 Great Britain

**FIREFLY**
1948 Denmark

**SHARPIE**
1956 New Zealand

**DRAGON**
1948 Norway
1952 Norway
1956 Sweden
1960 Greece
1964 Denmark
1968 United States
1972 Australia

**TEMPEST**
1972 USSR
1976 Sweden

## Sailing (yachting) (continued)

**FLYING DUTCHMAN**
1960 Norway
1964 New Zealand
1968 Great Britain
1972 Great Britain
1976 West Germany
1980 Spain
1984 United States
1988 Denmark
1992 Spain

## Shooting (men)

**individual**

**TRAP (CLAY PIGEON) (OPEN 1968–92)**
1900 Roger de Barbarin (FRA)
1908 Walter Ewing (CAN)
1912 James Graham (USA)
1920 Mark Arie (USA)
1924 Gyula Halasy (HUN)
1952 George Généreux (CAN)
1956 Galliano Rossini (ITA)
1960 Ion Dumitrescu (ROM)
1964 Ennio Mattarelli (ITA)
1968 John Braithwaite (GBR)
1972 Angelo Scalzone (ITA)
1976 Donald Haldeman (USA)
1980 Luciano Giovannetti (ITA)
1984 Luciano Giovannetti (ITA)
1988 Donald Monakov (URS)
1992 Petr Hrdlicka (TCH)
1996 Michael Constantine Diamond (AUS)
2000 Michael Constantine Diamond (AUS)

**DOUBLE TRAP**
1996 Russell Andrew Mark (AUS)
2000 Richard Faulds (GBR)

**SKEET (OPEN UNTIL 1996)**
1968 Yevgeny Petrov (URS)
1972 Konrad Wirnhier (FRG)
1976 Josef Panacek (TCH)
1980 Hans Kjeld Rasmussen (DEN)
1984 Matthew Dryke (USA)
1988 Axel Wegner (GDR)
1992 Zhang Shan (CHN)
1996 Ennio Falco (ITA)
2000 Mykola Milchev (UKR)

**FREE PISTOL**
1896 Sumner Paine (USA)
1900 Karl Konrad Röderer (SUI)
1912 Alfred Lane (USA)
1920 Carl Frederick (USA)
1936 Torsten Ullmann (SWE)
1948 Edwin Vásquez Cam (PER)
1952 Huelet Benner (USA)
1956 Pentti Tapio Linnosvuo (FIN)
1960 Aleksey Gushchin (URS)
1964 Väinö Johannes Markkanen (FIN)
1968 Grigory Kosykh (URS)
1976 Uwe Potteck (GDR)
1980 Aleksandr Melentev (URS)
1984 Xu Haifeng (CHN)
1988 Sorin Babii (ROM)
1992 Konstantin Lukachik (UNT)
1996 Boris Kokorev (RUS)
2000 Tanyu Kiryakov (BUL)

# Summer Olympic Games Champions (continued)

### Shooting (men) (continued)
**individual (continued)**

**RAPID-FIRE PISTOL**
1896  Joannis Phrangudis (GRE)
1900  Maurice Larrouy (FRA)
1908  Paul van Asbrock (BEL)
1912  Alfred Lane (USA)
1920  Guilherme Paraense (BRA)
1924  Henry Bailey (USA)
1932  Renzo Morigi (ITA)
1936  Cornelius van Oyen (GER)
1948  Karoly Takacs (HUN)
1952  Karoly Takacs (HUN)
1956  Stefan Petrescu (ROM)
1960  William McMillan (USA)
1964  Pentti Tapio Linnosvuo (FIN)
1968  Jozef Zapedzki (POL)
1972  Jozef Zapedzki (POL)
1976  Norbert Klaar (GDR)
1980  Corneliu Ion (ROM)
1984  Takeo Kamachi (JPN)
1988  Afanasy Kuzmin (URS)
1992  Ralf Schumann (GER)
1996  Ralf Schumann (GER)
2000  Sergey Alifirenko (RUS)

**SMALL-BORE RIFLE (PRONE)**
1908  Arthur Ashton Carnell (GBR)
1912  Frederick Hird (USA)
1920  Lawrence Nuesslein (USA)
1924  Pierre Coquelin de Lisle (FRA)
1932  Bertil Rönnmark (SWE)
1936  Willy Røgeberg (NOR)
1948  Arthur Cook (USA)
1952  Iosif Sarbu (ROM)
1956  Gerald Ouellette (CAN)
1960  Peter Kohnke (GER)
1964  Laszlo Hammerl (HUN)
1968  Jan Kurka (TCH)
1972  Ho Jun Li (PRK)
1976  Karlheinz Smieszek (FRG)
1980  Karoly Varga (HUN)
1984  Edward Etzel (USA)
1988  Miroslav Varga (TCH)
1992  Lee Eun Chul (KOR)
1996  Christian Klees (GER)
2000  Jonas Edman (SWE)

**SMALL-BORE RIFLE (3 POSITIONS)**
1952  Erling Kongshaug (NOR)
1956  Anatoly Bogdanov (URS)
1960  Viktor Shamburkin (URS)
1964  Lones Wesley Wigger (USA)
1968  Bernd Klingner (FRG)
1972  John Writer (USA)
1976  Lanny Bassham (USA)
1980  Viktor Vlasov (URS)
1984  Malcolm Cooper (GBR)
1988  Malcolm Cooper (GBR)
1992  Gratchia Petikian (UNT)
1996  Jean-Pierre Amat (FRA)
2000  Rajmond Debevec (SLO)

**MOVING TARGET (RUNNING BOAR)**
1900  Louis Debray (FRA)
1972  Yakov Zheleznyak (URS)
1976  Aleksandr Gazov (URS)
1980  Igor Sokolov (URS)
1984  Li Yuwei (CHN)

### Shooting (men) (continued)
**individual (continued)**

**MOVING TARGET (RUNNING BOAR)**
1988  Tor Heiestad (NOR)
1992  Michael Jakosits (GER)
1996  Yang Ling (CHN)
2000  Yang Ling (CHN)

**AIR RIFLE**
1984  Philippe Heberle (FRA)
1988  Goran Maksimovic (YUG)
1992  Yury Fedkin (UNT)
1996  Artyom Khadzhibekov (RUS)
2000  Cai Yalin (CHN)

**AIR PISTOL**
1988  Tanyu Kiryakov (BUL)
1992  Wang Yifu (CHN)
1996  Roberto di Donna (ITA)
2000  Franck Dumoulin (FRA)

**FREE RIFLE (300 M, 3 POSITIONS)**
1908  Albert Helgerud (NOR)
1912  Paul René Colas (FRA)
1920  Morris Fisher (USA)
1924  Morris Fisher (USA)
1948  Emil Grünig (SUI)
1952  Anatoly Bogdanov (URS)
1956  Vasily Borisov (URS)
1960  Hubert Hammerer (AUT)
1964  Gary Lee Anderson (USA)
1968  Gary Lee Anderson (USA)
1972  Lones Wesley Wigger (USA)

**ARMY RIFLE (300 M, 3 POSITIONS)**
1896  Georgios Orphanidis (GRE)
1900  Emil Kellenberger (SUI)
1912  Sandor Prokop (HUN)

**ARMY RIFLE (200 M)**
1896  Pantelis Karasevdas (GRE)

**FREE RIFLE (1,000 YD PRONE)**
1908  Joshua Millner (GBR)

**FULL-BORE RIFLE (300 M STANDING)**
1900  Lars Madsen (DEN)

**FULL-BORE RIFLE (300 M KNEELING)**
1900  Konrad Staeheli (SUI)

**FULL-BORE RIFLE (300 M PRONE)**
1900  Achille Paroche (FRA)

**FULL-BORE RIFLE (300 M)**
1900  Emil Kellenberger (SUI)

**RIFLE (300 M, 2 POSITIONS)**
1920  Morris Fisher (USA)

**RIFLE (300 M STANDING)**
1920  Carl Osburn (USA)

**RIFLE (300 M PRONE)**
1920  Otto Olsen (NOR)

**RIFLE (600 M PRONE)**
1920  Hugo Johansson (SWE)

# Summer Olympic Games Champions (continued)

## Shooting (men) (continued)

### individual (continued)

**6-MILLIMETER SMALL GUN (OPEN REAR SIGHT)**
1900   C. Grosett (FRA)

**SMALL-BORE RIFLE (VANISHING TARGET)**
1908   William Styles (GBR)
1912   Wilhelm Carlberg (SWE)

**SMALL-BORE RIFLE (MOVING TARGET)**
1908   John Francis Fleming (GBR)

**RUNNING DEER (100 M SINGLE SHOT)**
1908   Oscar Swahn (SWE)
1912   Alfred Swahn (SWE)
1920   Otto Olsen (NOR)
1924   John Boles (USA)

**RUNNING DEER (100 M DOUBLE SHOT)**
1908   Walter Winans (USA)
1912   Ake Lundeberg (SWE)
1920   Ole Andreas Lilloe-Olsen (NOR)
1924   Ole Andreas Lilloe-Olsen (NOR)

**RUNNING DEER (100 M SINGLE AND DOUBLE SHOT)**
1952   John Larsen (NOR)
1956   Vitaly Romanenko (URS)

**LIVE PIGEON**
1900   Léon de Lunden (BEL)

**GAME SHOOTING**
1900   Donald Mackintosh (AUS)

**MILITARY REVOLVER (25 M)**
1896   John Paine (USA)

**MILITARY REVOLVER (20 M)**
1906   Louis Richardet (SUI)
1906 (model 1873–74)   Jean Fouconnier (FRA)

**REVOLVER AND PISTOL**
1900   Paul van Asbrock (BEL)
1908   Paul van Asbrock (BEL)
1912   Alfred Lane (USA)

**DUELING PISTOL**
1906 (20 m)   Léon Moreaux (FRA)
1906 (25 m)   Konstantinos Skarlatos (GRE)
1912   Alfred Lane (USA)

### team

**FREE RIFLE (300 M)**
1908   Norway
1912   Sweden

**ARMY RIFLE (300 M)**
1900   Norway

**ARMY RIFLE (ALL-AROUND)**
1900   United States
1908   United States
1912   United States

**FULL-BORE RIFLE (300 M)**
1900   Switzerland

**SMALL-BORE RIFLE**
1900   Great Britain

## Shooting (men) (continued)

### team (continued)

**SMALL-BORE RIFLE**
1908   Great Britain
1920   United States
1924   France

**SMALL-BORE RIFLE (VANISHING TARGET)**
1912   Sweden

**RIFLE (600 M PRONE)**
1920   United States

**RIFLE (300 M, 2 POSITIONS)**
1920   United States

**RIFLE (300 M STANDING)**
1920   Denmark

**RIFLE (300 M PRONE)**
1920   United States

**RIFLE (ALL-AROUND)**
1920   United States
1924   United States

**RUNNING DEER (SINGLE SHOT)**
1908   Sweden
1912   Sweden
1920   Norway
1924   Norway

**RUNNING DEER (DOUBLE SHOT)**
1920   Norway
1924   Great Britain

**CLAY PIGEON**
1900   Great Britain
1908   Great Britain
1912   United States
1920   United States
1924   United States

**REVOLVER**
1900   Switzerland

**PISTOL**
1920   United States
1924   United States

**REVOLVER AND PISTOL**
1900   United States
1908   United States
1912   United States
1920   United States

**DUELING PISTOL**
1912   Sweden

## Shooting (women)

**TRAP (CLAY PIGEON)**
2000   Daina Gudzineviciute (LTU)

**DOUBLE TRAP**
1996   Kim Rhode (USA)
2000   Pia Hansen (SWE)

**SKEET**
2000   Zemfira Meftakhetdinova (AZE)

# Summer Olympic Games Champions (continued)

## Shooting (women) (continued)

**SPORT PISTOL**
| | | |
|---|---|---|
| 1984 | Linda Thom (CAN) | |
| 1988 | Nino Salukvadze (URS) | |
| 1992 | Marina Logvinenko (UNT) | |
| 1996 | Li Duihong (CHN) | |
| 2000 | Maria Zdravkova Grozdeva (BUL) | |

**SMALL-BORE RIFLE (3 POSITIONS)**
| | |
|---|---|
| 1984 | Wu Xiao-Xuan (CHN) |
| 1988 | Silvia Sperber (FRG) |
| 1992 | Launi Meili (USA) |
| 1996 | Aleksandra Ivosev (YUG) |
| 2000 | Renata Mauer (POL) |

**AIR RIFLE**
| | |
|---|---|
| 1984 | Pat Spurgin (USA) |
| 1988 | Irina Chilova (URS) |
| 1992 | Yeo Kab Soon (KOR) |
| 1996 | Renata Mauer (POL) |
| 2000 | Nancy Johnson (USA) |

**AIR PISTOL**
| | |
|---|---|
| 1988 | Jasna Sekaric (YUG) |
| 1992 | Marina Logvinenko (UNT) |
| 1996 | Olga Klochneva (RUS) |
| 2000 | Tao Luna (CHN) |

## Softball
| | |
|---|---|
| 1996 | United States |
| 2000 | United States |

## Swimming (men)

**50-METER FREESTYLE** — SEC
| | | |
|---|---|---|
| 1988 | Matthew Biondi (USA) | 22.14 |
| 1992 | Aleksandr Popov (UNT) | 21.91 |
| 1996 | Aleksandr Popov (RUS) | 22.13 |
| 2000 | Anthony Ervin (USA); Gary Hall, Jr. (USA) (*tied*) | 21.98 |

**100-METER FREESTYLE** — MIN:SEC
| | | |
|---|---|---|
| 1896 | Alfred Hajos (HUN) | 1:22.2 |
| 1904 | Zoltan Halmay (HUN) | 1:02.8[13] |
| 1908 | Charles Daniels (USA) | 1:05.6 |
| 1912 | Duke Paoa Kahanamoku (USA) | 1:03.4 |
| 1920 | Duke Paoa Kahanamoku (USA) | 1:00.4 |
| 1924 | Johnny Weissmuller (USA) | 59.0 |
| 1928 | Johnny Weissmuller (USA) | 58.6 |
| 1932 | Yasuji Miyazaki (JPN) | 58.2 |
| 1936 | Ferenc Csik (HUN) | 57.6 |
| 1948 | Walter Ris (USA) | 57.3 |
| 1952 | Clark Scholes (USA) | 57.4 |
| 1956 | Jon Henricks (AUS) | 55.4 |
| 1960 | John Devitt (AUS) | 55.2 |
| 1964 | Donald Schollander (USA) | 53.4 |
| 1968 | Michael Wenden (AUS) | 52.2 |
| 1972 | Mark Spitz (USA) | 51.22 |
| 1976 | Jim Montgomery (USA) | 49.99 |
| 1980 | Jörg Wöithe (GDR) | 50.40 |
| 1984 | Ambrose Gaines (USA) | 49.80 |
| 1988 | Matthew Biondi (USA) | 48.63 |
| 1992 | Aleksandr Popov (UNT) | 49.02 |
| 1996 | Aleksandr Popov (RUS) | 48.74 |
| 2000 | Pieter Van den Hoogenband (NED) | 48.30 |

**100 METER FREESTYLE FOR SAILORS** — MIN:SEC
| | | |
|---|---|---|
| 1896 | Ioannis Malokinis (GRE) | 2:20.4 |

## Swimming (men) (continued)

**200-METER FREESTYLE** — MIN:SEC
| | | |
|---|---|---|
| 1900 | Fred Lane (AUS) | 2:25.2 |
| 1904 | Charles Daniels (USA) | 2:44.2[14] |
| 1968 | Michael Wenden (AUS) | 1:55.2 |
| 1972 | Mark Spitz (USA) | 1:52.78 |
| 1976 | Bruce Furniss (USA) | 1:50.29 |
| 1980 | Sergey Koplyakov (URS) | 1:49.81 |
| 1984 | Michael Gross (FRG) | 1:47.44 |
| 1988 | Duncan Armstrong (AUS) | 1:47.25 |
| 1992 | Yevgeny Sadovy (UNT) | 1:46.70 |
| 1996 | Danyon Loader (NZL) | 1:47.63 |
| 2000 | Pieter Van den Hoogenband (NED) | 1:45.35 |

**400-METER FREESTYLE** — MIN:SEC
| | | |
|---|---|---|
| 1896 | Paul Neumann (AUT) | 8:12.6[15] |
| 1904 | Charles Daniels (USA) | 6:16.2[16] |
| 1908 | Henry Taylor (GBR) | 5:36.8 |
| 1912 | George Hodgson (CAN) | 5:24.4 |
| 1920 | Norman Ross (USA) | 5:26.8 |
| 1924 | Johnny Weissmuller (USA) | 5:04.2 |
| 1928 | Victoriano Zorilla (ARG) | 5:01.6 |
| 1932 | Clarence Crabbe (USA) | 4:48.4 |
| 1936 | Jack Medica (USA) | 4:44.5 |
| 1948 | William Smith (USA) | 4:41.0 |
| 1952 | Jean Boiteux (FRA) | 4:30.7 |
| 1956 | Murray Rose (AUS) | 4:27.3 |
| 1960 | Murray Rose (AUS) | 4:18.3 |
| 1964 | Donald Schollander (USA) | 4:12.2 |
| 1968 | Michael Burton (USA) | 4:09.0 |
| 1972 | Bradford Cooper (AUS) | 4:00.27 |
| 1976 | Brian Goodell (USA) | 3:51.93 |
| 1980 | Vladimir Salnikov (URS) | 3:51.31 |
| 1984 | George DiCarlo (USA) | 3:51.23 |
| 1988 | Uwe Dassler (GDR) | 3:46.95 |
| 1992 | Yevgeny Sadovy (UNT) | 3:45.00 |
| 1996 | Danyon Loader (NZL) | 3:47.97 |
| 2000 | Ian Thorpe (AUS) | 3:40.59 |

**1,500-METER FREESTYLE** — MIN:SEC
| | | |
|---|---|---|
| 1896 | Alfred Hajos (HUN) | 18:22.2[17] |
| 1900 | Johnny Arthur Jarvis (GBR) | 13:40.2[18] |
| 1904 | Emil Rausch (GER) | 27:18.2[19] |
| 1908 | Henry Taylor (GBR) | 22:48.4 |
| 1912 | George Hodgson (CAN) | 22:00.0 |
| 1920 | Norman Ross (USA) | 22:23.2 |
| 1924 | Andrew Charlton (AUS) | 20:06.6 |
| 1928 | Arne Borg (SWE) | 19:51.8 |
| 1932 | Kusuo Kitamura (JPN) | 19:12.4 |
| 1936 | Noburu Terada (JPN) | 19:13.7 |
| 1948 | James McLane (USA) | 19:18.5 |
| 1952 | Ford Konno (USA) | 18:30.0 |
| 1956 | Murray Rose (AUS) | 17:58.9 |
| 1960 | John Konrads (AUS) | 17:19.6 |
| 1964 | Robert Windle (AUS) | 17:01.7 |
| 1968 | Michael Burton (USA) | 16:38.9 |
| 1972 | Michael Burton (USA) | 15:52.58 |
| 1976 | Brian Goodell (USA) | 15:02.40 |
| 1980 | Vladimir Salnikov (URS) | 14:58.27 |
| 1984 | Michael O'Brien (USA) | 15:05.20 |
| 1988 | Vladimir Salnikov (URS) | 15:00.40 |
| 1992 | Kieren Perkins (AUS) | 14:43.48 |
| 1996 | Kieren Perkins (AUS) | 14:56.40 |
| 2000 | Grant Hackett (AUS) | 14:48.33 |

**4,000-METER FREESTYLE** — MIN:SEC
| | | |
|---|---|---|
| 1900 | Johnny Arthur Jarvis (GBR) | 58:24 |

# Summer Olympic Games Champions (continued)

## Swimming (men) (continued)

| 880-YARD FREESTYLE | MIN:SEC |
|---|---|
| 1904 Emil Rausch (GER) | 13:11.4 |

| 1-MILE FREESTYLE | MIN:SEC |
|---|---|
| 1904 Emil Rausch (GER) | 27:18.2 |

| 100-METER BUTTERFLY | SEC |
|---|---|
| 1968 Douglas Russell (USA) | 55.9 |
| 1972 Mark Spitz (USA) | 54.27 |
| 1976 Matt Vogel (USA) | 54.35 |
| 1980 Pär Arvidsson (SWE) | 54.92 |
| 1984 Michael Gross (FRG) | 53.08 |
| 1988 Anthony Nesty (SUR) | 53.00 |
| 1992 Pablo Morales (USA) | 53.32 |
| 1996 Denis Pankratov (RUS) | 52.27 |
| 2000 Lars Frölander (SWE) | 52.00 |

| 200-METER BUTTERFLY | MIN |
|---|---|
| 1956 William Yorzyk (USA) | 2:19.3 |
| 1960 Michael Troy (USA) | 2:12.8 |
| 1964 Kevin Berry (AUS) | 2:06.6 |
| 1968 Carl Robie (USA) | 2:08.7 |
| 1972 Mark Spitz (USA) | 2:00.70 |
| 1976 Mike Bruner (USA) | 1:59.23 |
| 1980 Sergey Fesenko (URS) | 1:59.76 |
| 1984 Jonathan Sieben (AUS) | 1:57.04 |
| 1988 Michael Gross (FRG) | 1:56.94 |
| 1992 Mel Stewart (USA) | 1:56.26 |
| 1996 Denis Pankratov (RUS) | 1:56.51 |
| 2000 Tom Malchow (USA) | 1:55.35 |

| 100-METER BACKSTROKE | MIN:SEC |
|---|---|
| 1904 Walter Brack (GER) | 1:16.8[20] |
| 1908 Arno Bieberstein (GER) | 1:24.6 |
| 1912 Harry Hebner (USA) | 1:21.2 |
| 1920 Warren Paoa Kealoha (USA) | 1:15.2 |
| 1924 Warren Paoa Kealoha (USA) | 1:13.2 |
| 1928 George Kojac (USA) | 1:08.2 |
| 1932 Masaji Kiyokawa (JPN) | 1:08.6 |
| 1936 Adolph Kiefer (USA) | 1:05.9 |
| 1948 Allen Stack (USA) | 1:06.4 |
| 1952 Yoshinobu Oyakawa (JPN) | 1:05.4 |
| 1956 David Theile (AUS) | 1:02.2 |
| 1960 David Theile (AUS) | 1:01.9 |
| 1968 Roland Matthes (GDR) | 58.7 |
| 1972 Roland Matthes (GDR) | 56.58 |
| 1976 John Naber (USA) | 55.49 |
| 1980 Bengt Baron (SWE) | 56.53 |
| 1984 Richard Carey (USA) | 55.79 |
| 1988 Daichi Suzuki (JPN) | 55.05 |
| 1992 Mark Tewksbury (CAN) | 53.98 |
| 1996 Jeff Rouse (USA) | 54.10 |
| 2000 Lenny Krayzelburg (USA) | 53.72 |

| 200-METER BACKSTROKE | MIN:SEC |
|---|---|
| 1900 Ernst Hoppenberg (GER) | 2:47.0 |
| 1964 Jed Graef (USA) | 2:10.3 |
| 1968 Roland Matthes (GDR) | 2:09.6 |
| 1972 Roland Matthes (GDR) | 2:02.82 |
| 1976 John Naber (USA) | 1:59.19 |
| 1980 Sandor Wladar (HUN) | 2:01.93 |
| 1984 Richard Carey (USA) | 2:00.23 |
| 1988 Igor Polyansky (URS) | 1:59.37 |
| 1992 Martin López-Zubero (ESP) | 1:58.47 |
| 1996 Brad Bridgewater (USA) | 1:58.54 |
| 2000 Lenny Krayzelburg (USA) | 1:56.76 |

## Swimming (men) (continued)

| 100-METER BREASTSTROKE | MIN:SEC |
|---|---|
| 1968 Donald McKenzie (USA) | 1:07.7 |
| 1972 Nobutaka Tagushi (JPN) | 1:04.94 |
| 1976 John Hencken (USA) | 1:03.11 |
| 1980 Duncan Goodhew (GBR) | 1:03.34 |
| 1984 Steve Lundquist (USA) | 1:01.65 |
| 1988 Adrian Moorhouse (GBR) | 1:02.04 |
| 1992 Nelson Diebel (USA) | 1:01.50 |
| 1996 Frederick Deburghgraeve (BEL) | 1:00.65 |
| 2000 Domenico Fioravanti (ITA) | 1:00.46 |

| 200-METER BREASTSTROKE | MIN:SEC |
|---|---|
| 1908 Frederick Holman (GBR) | 3:09.2 |
| 1912 Walter Bathe (GER) | 3:01.8 |
| 1920 Hakan Malmroth (SWE) | 3:04.4 |
| 1924 Robert Skelton (USA) | 2:56.6 |
| 1928 Yoshiyuki Tsuruta (JPN) | 2:48.8 |
| 1932 Yoshiyuki Tsuruta (JPN) | 2:45.4 |
| 1936 Tetsuo Hamuro (JPN) | 2:42.5 |
| 1948 Joseph Verdeur (USA) | 2:39.3 |
| 1952 John Davies (AUS) | 2:34.4 |
| 1956 Masaru Furukawa (JPN) | 2:34.7 |
| 1960 William Mulliken (USA) | 2:37.4 |
| 1964 Ian O'Brien (AUS) | 2:27.8 |
| 1968 Felipe Muñoz (MEX) | 2:28.7 |
| 1972 John Hencken (USA) | 2:21.55 |
| 1976 David Wilkie (GBR) | 2:15.11 |
| 1980 Robertas Zulpa (URS) | 2:15.85 |
| 1984 Victor Davis (CAN) | 2:13.34 |
| 1988 Jozsef Szabo (HUN) | 2:13.52 |
| 1992 Mike Barrowman (USA) | 2:10.16 |
| 1996 Norbert Rozsa (HUN) | 2:12.57 |
| 2000 Domenico Fioravanti (ITA) | 2:10.87 |

| 400-METER BREASTSTROKE | MIN:SEC |
|---|---|
| 1904 Georg Zacharias (GER) | 7:23.6[21] |
| 1912 Walter Bathe (GER) | 6:29.6 |
| 1920 Hakan Malmroth (SWE) | 6:31.8 |

| 200-YARD RELAY | MIN:SEC |
|---|---|
| 1904 United States | 2:04.6 |

| 200-METER MEDLEY | MIN:SEC |
|---|---|
| 1968 Charles Hickcox (USA) | 2:12.0 |
| 1972 Gunnar Larsson (SWE) | 2:07.17 |
| 1984 Alex Baumann (CAN) | 2:01.42 |
| 1988 Tamas Darnyi (HUN) | 2:00.17 |
| 1992 Tamas Darnyi (HUN) | 2:00.76 |
| 1996 Attila Czene (HUN) | 1:59.91 |
| 2000 Massimiliano Rosolino (ITA) | 1:58.98 |

| 400-METER MEDLEY | MIN:SEC |
|---|---|
| 1964 Richard William Roth (USA) | 4:45.4 |
| 1968 Charles Hickcox (USA) | 4:48.4 |
| 1972 Gunnar Larsson (SWE) | 4:31.98 |
| 1976 Rod Strachan (USA) | 4:23.68 |
| 1980 Aleksandr Sidorenko (URS) | 4:22.89 |
| 1984 Alex Baumann (CAN) | 4:17.41 |
| 1988 Tamas Darnyi (HUN) | 4:14.75 |
| 1992 Tamas Darnyi (HUN) | 4:14.23 |
| 1996 Tom Dolan (USA) | 4:14.90 |
| 2000 Tom Dolan (USA) | 4:11.76 |

| 4 × 100-METER MEDLEY RELAY | MIN:SEC |
|---|---|
| 1960 United States | 4:05.4 |
| 1964 United States | 3:58.4 |
| 1968 United States | 3:54.9 |
| 1972 United States | 3:48.16 |

# Summer Olympic Games Champions (continued)

## Swimming (men) (continued)

### 4 × 100-METER MEDLEY RELAY

| | | MIN:SEC |
|---|---|---|
| 1976 | United States | 3:42.22 |
| 1980 | Australia | 3:45.70 |
| 1984 | United States | 3:39.30 |
| 1988 | United States | 3:36.93 |
| 1992 | United States | 3:36.93 |
| 1996 | United States | 3:34.84 |
| 2000 | United States | 3:33.73 |

### 4 × 100-METER FREESTYLE RELAY

| | | MIN:SEC |
|---|---|---|
| 1964 | United States | 3:33.2 |
| 1968 | United States | 3:31.7 |
| 1972 | United States | 3:26.42 |
| 1984 | United States | 3:19.03 |
| 1988 | United States | 3:16.53 |
| 1992 | United States | 3:16.74 |
| 1996 | United States | 3:15.41 |
| 2000 | Australia | 3:13.67 |

### 4 × 200-METER FREESTYLE RELAY

| | | MIN:SEC |
|---|---|---|
| 1908 | Great Britain | 10:55.6 |
| 1912 | Australia | 10:11.2 |
| 1920 | United States | 10:04.4 |
| 1924 | United States | 9:53.4 |
| 1928 | United States | 9:36.2 |
| 1932 | Japan | 8:58.4 |
| 1936 | Japan | 8:51.5 |
| 1948 | United States | 8:46.0 |
| 1952 | United States | 8:31.1 |
| 1956 | Australia | 8:23.6 |
| 1960 | United States | 8:10.2 |
| 1964 | United States | 7:52.1 |
| 1968 | United States | 7:52.3 |
| 1972 | United States | 7:35.78 |
| 1976 | United States | 7:23.22 |
| 1980 | USSR | 7:23.50 |
| 1984 | United States | 7:15.69 |
| 1988 | United States | 7:12.51 |
| 1992 | Unified Team | 7:11.95 |
| 1996 | United States | 7:14.84 |
| 2000 | Australia | 7:07.05 |

### 60-METER UNDERWATER

| | | MIN:SEC (UNDERWATER) |
|---|---|---|
| 1900 | Charles de Vendeville (FRA) | 1:08.4 |

### 200-METER OBSTACLE

| | | MIN:SEC |
|---|---|---|
| 1900 | Frederick Lane (AUS) | 2:38.4 |

## Swimming (women)

### 50-METER FREESTYLE

| | | SEC |
|---|---|---|
| 1988 | Kristin Otto (GDR) | 25.49 |
| 1992 | Yang Wenyi (CHN) | 24.79 |
| 1996 | Amy Van Dyken (USA) | 24.87 |
| 2000 | Inge de Bruijn (NED) | 24.32 |

### 100-METER FREESTYLE

| | | MIN:SEC |
|---|---|---|
| 1912 | Fanny Durack (AUS) | 1:22.2 |
| 1920 | Ethelda Bleibtrey (USA) | 1:13.6 |
| 1924 | Ethel Lackie (USA) | 1:12.4 |
| 1928 | Albina Osipowich (USA) | 1:11.0 |
| 1932 | Helene Madison (USA) | 1:06.8 |
| 1936 | Hendrika Mastenbroek (NED) | 1:05.9 |
| 1948 | Greta Andersen (DEN) | 1:06.3 |
| 1952 | Katalin Szoke (HUN) | 1:06.8 |
| 1956 | Dawn Fraser (AUS) | 1:02.0 |
| 1960 | Dawn Fraser (AUS) | 1:01.2 |
| 1964 | Dawn Fraser (AUS) | 59.5 |

## Swimming (women) (continued)

### 100-METER FREESTYLE

| | | MIN:SEC |
|---|---|---|
| 1968 | Jan Henne (USA) | 1:00.0 |
| 1972 | Sandra Neilson (USA) | 58.59 |
| 1976 | Kornelia Ender (GDR) | 55.65 |
| 1980 | Barbara Krause (GDR) | 54.79 |
| 1984 | Carrie Steinseifer (USA); Nancy Hogshead (USA) (tied) | 55.92 |
| 1988 | Kristin Otto (GDR) | 54.93 |
| 1992 | Zhuang Yong (CHN) | 54.64 |
| 1996 | Le Jingyi (CHN) | 54.50 |
| 2000 | Inge de Bruijn (NED) | 53.83 |

### 200-METER FREESTYLE

| | | MIN:SEC |
|---|---|---|
| 1968 | Debbie Meyer (USA) | 2:10.5 |
| 1972 | Shane Gould (AUS) | 2:03.56 |
| 1976 | Kornelia Ender (GDR) | 1:59.26 |
| 1980 | Barbara Krause (GDR) | 1:58.33 |
| 1984 | Mary Wayte (USA) | 1:59.23 |
| 1988 | Heike Friedrich (GDR) | 1:57.65 |
| 1992 | Nicole Haislett (USA) | 1:57.90 |
| 1996 | Claudia Poll (CRC) | 1:58.16 |
| 2000 | Susie O'Neill (AUS) | 1:58.24 |

### 400-METER FREESTYLE

| | | MIN:SEC |
|---|---|---|
| 1920 | Ethelda Bleibtrey (USA) | 4:34.0[22] |
| 1924 | Martha Norelius (USA) | 6:02.2 |
| 1928 | Martha Norelius (USA) | 5:42.8 |
| 1932 | Helene Madison (USA) | 5:28.5 |
| 1936 | Hendrika Mastenbroek (NED) | 5:26.4 |
| 1948 | Ann Curtis (USA) | 5:17.8 |
| 1952 | Valeria Gyenge (HUN) | 5:12.1 |
| 1956 | Lorraine Crapp (AUS) | 4:54.6 |
| 1960 | Susan Christina von Saltza (USA) | 4:50.6 |
| 1964 | Virginia Duenkel (USA) | 4:43.3 |
| 1968 | Debbie Meyer (USA) | 4:31.8 |
| 1972 | Shane Gould (AUS) | 4:19.04 |
| 1976 | Petra Thümer (GDR) | 4:09.89 |
| 1980 | Ines Diers (GDR) | 4:08.76 |
| 1984 | Tiffany Cohen (USA) | 4:07.10 |
| 1988 | Janet Evans (USA) | 4:03.85 |
| 1992 | Dagmar Hase (GER) | 4:07.18 |
| 1996 | Michelle Smith (IRE) | 4:07.25 |
| 2000 | Brooke Bennett (USA) | 4:05.80 |

### 800-METER FREESTYLE

| | | MIN:SEC |
|---|---|---|
| 1968 | Debbie Meyer (USA) | 9:24.0 |
| 1972 | Keena Rothhammer (USA) | 8:53.68 |
| 1976 | Petra Thümer (GDR) | 8:37.14 |
| 1980 | Michelle Ford (AUS) | 8:28.90 |
| 1984 | Tiffany Cohen (USA) | 8:24.95 |
| 1988 | Janet Evans (USA) | 8:20.20 |
| 1992 | Janet Evans (USA) | 8:25.52 |
| 1996 | Brooke Bennett (USA) | 8:27.89 |
| 2000 | Brooke Bennett (USA) | 8:19.67 |

### 100-METER BUTTERFLY

| | | MIN:SEC |
|---|---|---|
| 1956 | Shelley Mann (USA) | 1:11.0 |
| 1960 | Carolyn Schuler (USA) | 1:09.5 |
| 1964 | Sharon Stouder (USA) | 1:04.7 |
| 1968 | Lynette McClements (AUS) | 1:05.5 |
| 1972 | Mayumi Aoki (JPN) | 1:03.34 |
| 1976 | Kornelia Ender (GDR) | 1:00.13 |
| 1980 | Caren Metschuck (GDR) | 1:00.42 |
| 1984 | Mary Meagher (USA) | 59.26 |
| 1988 | Kristin Otto (GDR) | 59.00 |
| 1992 | Qian Hong (CHN) | 58.62 |
| 1996 | Amy Van Dyken (USA) | 59.13 |
| 2000 | Inge de Bruijn (NED) | 56.61 |

# Summer Olympic Games Champions (continued)

## Swimming (women) (continued)

### 200-METER BUTTERFLY

| Year | Champion | MIN:SEC |
|---|---|---|
| 1968 | Aagje Kok (NED) | 2:24.7 |
| 1972 | Karen Moe (USA) | 2:15.57 |
| 1976 | Andrea Pollack (GDR) | 2:11.41 |
| 1980 | Ines Geissler (GDR) | 2:10.44 |
| 1984 | Mary Meagher (USA) | 2:06.90 |
| 1988 | Kathleen Nord (GDR) | 2:09.51 |
| 1992 | Summer Sanders (USA) | 2:08.67 |
| 1996 | Susie O'Neill (AUS) | 2:07.76 |
| 2000 | Misty Hyman (USA) | 2:05.88 |

### 100-METER BACKSTROKE

| Year | Champion | MIN:SEC |
|---|---|---|
| 1924 | Sybil Bauer (USA) | 1:23.2 |
| 1928 | Maria Braun (NED) | 1:22.0 |
| 1932 | Eleanor Holm (USA) | 1:19.4 |
| 1936 | Dina Senff (NED) | 1:18.9 |
| 1948 | Karen-Margrete Harup (DEN) | 1:14.4 |
| 1952 | Joan Harrison (RSA) | 1:14.3 |
| 1956 | Judith Grinham (GBR) | 1:12.9 |
| 1960 | Lynn Burke (USA) | 1:09.3 |
| 1964 | Cathy Ferguson (USA) | 1:07.7 |
| 1968 | Kaye Hall (USA) | 1:06.2 |
| 1972 | Melissa Belote (USA) | 1:05.78 |
| 1976 | Urike Richter (GDR) | 1:01.83 |
| 1980 | Rica Reinisch (GDR) | 1:00.86 |
| 1984 | Theresa Andrews (USA) | 1:02.55 |
| 1988 | Kristin Otto (GDR) | 1:00.89 |
| 1992 | Krisztina Egerszegi (HUN) | 1:00.68 |
| 1996 | Beth Botsford (USA) | 1:01.19 |
| 2000 | Diana Mocanu (ROM) | 1:00.21 |

### 200-METER BACKSTROKE

| Year | Champion | MIN:SEC |
|---|---|---|
| 1968 | Pokey Watson (USA) | 2:24.8 |
| 1972 | Melissa Belote (USA) | 2:19.19 |
| 1976 | Ulrike Richter (GDR) | 2:13.43 |
| 1980 | Rica Reinisch (GDR) | 2:11.77 |
| 1984 | Jolanda De Rover (NED) | 2:12.38 |
| 1988 | Krisztina Egerszegi (HUN) | 2:09.29 |
| 1992 | Krisztina Egerszegi (HUN) | 2:07.06 |
| 1996 | Krisztina Egerszegi (HUN) | 2:07.83 |
| 2000 | Diana Mocanu (ROM) | 2:08.16 |

### 100-METER BREASTSTROKE

| Year | Champion | MIN:SEC |
|---|---|---|
| 1968 | Djurdjica Bjedov (YUG) | 1:15.8 |
| 1972 | Cathy Carr (USA) | 1:13.58 |
| 1976 | Hannelore Anke (GDR) | 1:11.16 |
| 1980 | Ute Geveniger (GDR) | 1:10.22 |
| 1984 | Petra van Staveren (NED) | 1:09.88 |
| 1988 | Tanya Dangalakova (BUL) | 1:07.95 |
| 1992 | Yelena Rudkovskaya (UNT) | 1:08.00 |
| 1996 | Penelope Heyns (RSA) | 1:07.73 |
| 2000 | Megan Quann (USA) | 1:07.05 |

### 200-METER BREASTSTROKE

| Year | Champion | MIN:SEC |
|---|---|---|
| 1924 | Lucy Morton (GBR) | 3:33.2 |
| 1928 | Hilde Schrader (GER) | 3:12.6 |
| 1932 | Claire Dennis (AUS) | 3:06.3 |
| 1936 | Hideko Maehata (JPN) | 3:03.6 |
| 1948 | Petronella van Vliet (NED) | 2:57.2 |
| 1952 | Eva Szekely (HUN) | 2:51.7 |
| 1956 | Ursula Happe (GER) | 2:53.1 |
| 1960 | Anita Lonsbrough (GBR) | 2:49.5 |
| 1964 | Galina Prozumenshchikova-Stepanova (URS) | 2:46.4 |
| 1968 | Sharon Wichman (USA) | 2:44.4 |
| 1972 | Beverley Whitfield (AUS) | 2:41.71 |
| 1976 | Marina Koshevaya (URS) | 2:33.35 |
| 1980 | Lina Kachushite (URS) | 2:29.54 |

## Swimming (women) (continued)

### 200-METER BREASTSTROKE

| Year | Champion | MIN:SEC |
|---|---|---|
| 1984 | Anne Ottenbrite (CAN) | 2:30.38 |
| 1988 | Silke Hörner (GDR) | 2:26.71 |
| 1992 | Kyoko Iwasaki (JPN) | 2:26.65 |
| 1996 | Penelope Heyns (RSA) | 2:25.41 |
| 2000 | Agnes Kovacs (HUN) | 2:24.35 |

### 200-METER MEDLEY

| Year | Champion | MIN:SEC |
|---|---|---|
| 1968 | Claudia Kolb (USA) | 2:24.7 |
| 1972 | Shane Gould (AUS) | 2:23.07 |
| 1984 | Tracy Caulkins (USA) | 2:12.64 |
| 1988 | Daniela Hunger (GDR) | 2:12.59 |
| 1992 | Li Lin (CHN) | 2:11.65 |
| 1996 | Michelle Smith (IRE) | 2:13.93 |
| 2000 | Yana Klochkova (UKR) | 2:10.68 |

### 400-METER MEDLEY

| Year | Champion | MIN:SEC |
|---|---|---|
| 1964 | Donna De Varona (USA) | 5:18.7 |
| 1968 | Claudia Kolb (USA) | 5:08.5 |
| 1972 | Gail Neall (AUS) | 5:02.97 |
| 1976 | Ulrike Tauber (GDR) | 4:42.77 |
| 1980 | Petra Schneider (GDR) | 4:36.29 |
| 1984 | Tracy Caulkins (USA) | 4:39.24 |
| 1988 | Janet Evans (USA) | 4:37.76 |
| 1992 | Krisztina Egerszegi (HUN) | 4:36.54 |
| 1996 | Michelle Smith (IRE) | 4:39.18 |
| 2000 | Yana Klochkova (UKR) | 4:33.59 |

### 4 × 100-METER MEDLEY RELAY

| Year | Champion | MIN:SEC |
|---|---|---|
| 1960 | United States | 4:41.1 |
| 1964 | United States | 4:33.9 |
| 1968 | United States | 4:28.3 |
| 1972 | United States | 4:20.75 |
| 1976 | East Germany | 4:07.95 |
| 1980 | East Germany | 4:06.67 |
| 1984 | United States | 4:08.34 |
| 1988 | East Germany | 4:03.74 |
| 1992 | United States | 4:02.54 |
| 1996 | United States | 4:02.88 |
| 2000 | United States | 3:58.30 |

### 4 × 100-METER FREESTYLE RELAY

| Year | Champion | MIN:SEC |
|---|---|---|
| 1912 | Great Britain | 5:52.8 |
| 1920 | United States | 5:11.6 |
| 1924 | United States | 4:58.8 |
| 1928 | United States | 4:47.6 |
| 1932 | United States | 4:38.0 |
| 1936 | The Netherlands | 4:36.0 |
| 1948 | United States | 4:29.2 |
| 1952 | Hungary | 4:24.4 |
| 1956 | Australia | 4:17.1 |
| 1960 | United States | 4:08.9 |
| 1964 | United States | 4:03.8 |
| 1968 | United States | 4:02.5 |
| 1972 | United States | 3:55.19 |
| 1976 | United States | 3:44.82 |
| 1980 | East Germany | 3:42.71 |
| 1984 | United States | 3:43.43 |
| 1988 | East Germany | 3:40.63 |
| 1992 | United States | 3:39.46 |
| 1996 | United States | 3:39.29 |
| 2000 | United States | 3:36.61 |

### 4 × 200-METER FREESTYLE RELAY

| Year | Champion | MIN:SEC |
|---|---|---|
| 1996 | United States | 7:59.87 |
| 2000 | United States | 7:57.80 |

# Summer Olympic Games Champions (continued)

## Swimming (women) (continued)

**SYNCHRONIZED SWIMMING (INDIVIDUAL)**
1984   Tracie Ruiz (USA)
1988   Carolyn Waldo (CAN)
1992   Kristen Babb-Sprague (USA);
     Sylvie Fréchette (CAN)[23]

**SYNCHRONIZED SWIMMING (DUET)**
1984   United States
1988   Canada
1992   United States
2000   Russia

**SYNCHRONIZED SWIMMING (TEAM)**
1996   United States
2000   Russia

## Table tennis (men)

**SINGLES**
1988   Yoo Nam Kyu (KOR)
1992   Jan-Ove Waldner (SWE)
1996   Liu Guoliang (CHN)
2000   Kong Linghui (CHN)

**DOUBLES**
1988   China
1992   China
1996   China
2000   China

## Table tennis (women)

**SINGLES**
1988   Chen Jing (CHN)
1992   Deng Yaping (CHN)
1996   Deng Yaping (CHN)
2000   Wang Nan (CHN)

**DOUBLES**
1988   South Korea
1992   China
1996   China
2000   China

## Taekwondo (men)

**58 KG (128 LBS)**
2000   Michail Mouroutsos (GRE)

**68 KG (150 LBS)**
2000   Steven Lopez (USA)

**80 KG (176.5 LBS)**
2000   Angel Valodia Matos (CUB)

**OVER 80 KG (176.5 LBS)**
2000   Kim Kyong-Hun (KOR)

## Taekwondo (women)

**49 KG (108 LBS)**
2000   Lauren Burns (AUS)

**57 KG (125.5 LBS)**
2000   Jung Jae-Eun (KOR)

**67 KG (147.5 LBS)**
2000   Lee Sun-Hee (KOR)

**OVER 67 KG (147.5 LBS)**
2000   Chen Zhong (CHN)

## Tennis (men)

**SINGLES**
1896   John Pius Boland (GBR)
1900   Hugh (Laurie) Doherty (GBR)
1904   Beals Wright (USA)
1908   Josiah Ritchie (GBR)
1912   Charles Winslow (RSA)
1920   Louis Raymond (RSA)
1924   Vincent Richards (USA)
1988   Miloslav Mecir (TCH)
1992   Marc Rosset (SUI)
1996   Andre Agassi (USA)
2000   Yevgeny Kafelnikov (RUS)

**DOUBLES**
1896   John Pius Boland (GBR), Friedrich Thraun (GER)
1900   Hugh (Laurie) Doherty, Reginald Doherty (GBR)
1904   Edgar Leonard, Beals Wright (USA)
1908   George Hillyard, Reginald Doherty (GBR)
1912   Harold Kitson, Charles Winslow (RSA)
1920   Oswald Noel Turnbull, Maxwell Woosnam (GBR)
1924   Francis Hunter, Vincent Richards (USA)
1988   Kenneth Flach, Robert Seguso (USA)
1992   Boris Becker, Michael Stich (GER)
1996   Todd Woodbridge, Mark Woodforde (AUS)
2000   Sebastien Lareau, Daniel Nestor (CAN)

**MIXED DOUBLES**
1900   Charlotte Cooper, Reginald Doherty (GBR)
1912   Dora Köring, Heinrich Schomburgk (GER)
1920   Suzanne Lenglen, Max Décugis (FRA)
1924   Hazel Wightman, R. Norris Williams (USA)

## Tennis (women)

**SINGLES**
1900   Charlotte Cooper (GBR)
1908   Dorothy Chambers-Lambert (GBR)
1912   Marguerite Broquedis (FRA)
1920   Suzanne Lenglen (FRA)
1924   Helen Wills-Moody (USA)
1988   Steffi Graf (FRG)
1992   Jennifer Capriati (USA)
1996   Lindsay Davenport (USA)
2000   Venus Williams (USA)

**DOUBLES**
1920   Winifred Margaret McNair, Kathleen McKane (GBR)
1924   Helen Wills-Moody, Hazel Wightman (USA)
1988   Zina Garrison, Pamela Shriver (USA)
1992   Gigi Fernandez, Mary Joe Fernandez (USA)
1996   Gigi Fernandez, Mary Joe Fernandez (USA)
2000   Serena Williams, Venus Williams (USA)

## Tennis—Covered Courts (indoor tennis)

**MEN'S SINGLES**
1908   Arthur Gore (GBR)
1912   André Gobert (FRA)

**MEN'S DOUBLES**
1908   Arthur Gore, Herbert Roper-Barrett (GBR)
1912   Maurice Germot, André Gobert (FRA)

**WOMEN'S SINGLES**
1908   Gladys Eastlake-Smith (GBR)
1912   Edith Hannam (GBR)

# Summer Olympic Games Champions (continued)

## Tennis—Covered Courts (indoor tennis)
### (continued)

**MIXED DOUBLES**
1912 Edith Hannam, Charles Dixon (GBR)

## Triathlon (swim/bike/run) (men)
2000 Simon Whitfield (CAN)

## Triathlon (swim/bike/run) (women)
2000 Brigitte McMahon (SUI)

## Volleyball (men)
**INDOOR**
1964 USSR
1968 USSR
1972 Japan
1976 Poland
1980 USSR
1984 United States
1988 United States
1992 Brazil
1996 The Netherlands
2000 Yugoslavia

**BEACH**
1996 United States
2000 United States

## Volleyball (women)
**INDOOR**
1964 Japan
1968 USSR
1972 USSR
1976 Japan
1980 USSR
1984 China
1988 USSR
1992 Cuba
1996 Cuba
2000 Cuba

**BEACH**
1996 Brazil
2000 Australia

## Water polo (men)
1900 Great Britain
1904 United States
1908 Great Britain
1912 Great Britain
1920 Great Britain
1924 France
1928 Germany
1932 Hungary
1936 Hungary
1948 Italy
1952 Hungary
1956 Hungary
1960 Italy
1964 Hungary
1968 Yugoslavia
1972 USSR
1976 Hungary
1980 USSR
1984 Yugoslavia
1988 Yugoslavia
1992 Italy
1996 Spain
2000 Hungary

## Water polo (women)
2000 Australia

## Weight lifting (men)[24, 25]

| 56 KG (123.5 LB) | | KG |
|---|---|---|
| 1972 | Zygmunt Smalcerz (POL) | 337.5 |
| 1976 | Aleksandr Voronin (URS) | 242.5 |
| 1980 | Kanybek Osmanaliyev (URS) | 245.0 |
| 1984 | Zeng Guoqiang (CHN) | 235.0 |
| 1988 | Sevdalin Marinov (BUL) | 270.0 |
| 1992 | Ivan Ivanov (BUL) | 265.0 |
| 1996 | Halil Mutlu (TUR) | 287.5 |
| 2000 | Halil Mutlu (TUR) | 305.0 |

| 62 KG (136.5 LB) | | KG |
|---|---|---|
| 1948 | Joseph de Pietro (USA) | 307.5 |
| 1952 | Ivan Udodov (URS) | 315.0 |
| 1956 | Charles Vinci (USA) | 342.5 |
| 1960 | Charles Vinci (USA) | 345.0 |
| 1964 | Aleksey Vakhonin (URS) | 357.5 |
| 1968 | Mohammad Nassiri (IRI) | 367.5 |
| 1972 | Imre Foldi (HUN) | 377.5 |
| 1976 | Norair Nurikian (BUL) | 262.5 |
| 1980 | Daniel Núñez (CUB) | 275.0 |
| 1984 | Wu Shude (CHN) | 267.5 |
| 1988 | Oksen Mirzoyan (URS) | 292.5 |
| 1992 | Chun Byung Kwan (KOR) | 287.5 |
| 1996 | Tang Ningsheng (CHN) | 307.5 |
| 2000 | Nikolay Pechalov (CRO) | 325.0 |

| 69 KG (152 LB) | | KG |
|---|---|---|
| 1920 | Frans de Haes (BEL) | 220.0 |
| 1924 | Pierino Gabetti (ITA) | 402.5[26] |
| 1928 | Franz Andrysek (AUT) | 287.5 |
| 1932 | Raymond Suvigny (FRA) | 287.5 |
| 1936 | Anthony Terlazzo (USA) | 312.5 |
| 1948 | Mahmoud Fayad (EGY) | 332.5 |
| 1952 | Rafael Chimishkyan (URS) | 337.5 |
| 1956 | Isaac Berger (USA) | 352.5 |
| 1960 | Yevgeny Minayev (URS) | 372.5 |
| 1964 | Yoshinobu Miyake (JPN) | 397.5 |
| 1968 | Yoshinobu Miyake (JPN) | 392.5 |
| 1972 | Norair Nurikian (BUL) | 402.5 |
| 1976 | Nikolay Kolesnikov (URS) | 285.0 |
| 1980 | Viktor Mazin (URS) | 290.0 |
| 1984 | Chen Weiqiang (CHN) | 282.5 |
| 1988 | Naim Suleymanoglu (TUR) | 342.5 |
| 1992 | Naim Suleymanoglu (TUR) | 320.0 |
| 1996 | Naim Suleymanoglu (TUR) | 335.0 |
| 2000 | Galabin Boevski (BUL) | 357.5 |

| 70 KG (154.5 LB) | | KG |
|---|---|---|
| 1920 | Alfred Neyland (EST) | 257.5 |
| 1924 | Edmond Décottignies (FRA) | 440.0[26] |
| 1928 | Kurt Helbig (GER); Hans Haas (AUT) (tied) | 322.5 |
| 1932 | René Duverger (FRA) | 325.0 |
| 1936 | Mohamed Ahmed Mesbah (EGY); Robert Fein (AUT) (tied) | 342.5 |
| 1948 | Ibrahim Shams (EGY) | 360.0 |
| 1952 | Tommy Kono (USA) | 362.5 |
| 1956 | Igor Rybak (URS) | 380.0 |
| 1960 | Viktor Bushuyev (URS) | 397.5 |
| 1964 | Waldemar Baszanowski (POL) | 432.5 |
| 1968 | Waldemar Baszanowski (POL) | 437.5 |
| 1972 | Mukharbi Kirzhinov (URS) | 460.0 |
| 1976 | Pyotr Korol (URS) | 305.0 |
| 1980 | Yanko Rusev (BUL) | 342.5 |
| 1984 | Yao Jingyuan (CHN) | 320.0 |

## Summer Olympic Games Champions (continued)

### Weight lifting (men)[24, 25] (continued)

| 70 KG (154.5 LB) | | KG |
|---|---|---|
| 1988 | Joachim Kunz (GDR) | 340.0 |
| 1992 | Israil Militosyan (UNT) | 337.5 |
| 1996 | Zhan Xugang (CHN) | 357.5 |

| 77 KG (170 LB) | | KG |
|---|---|---|
| 1920 | Henri Gance (FRA) | 245.0 |
| 1924 | Carlo Galimberti (ITA) | 492.5[26] |
| 1928 | François Roger (FRA) | 335.0 |
| 1932 | Rudolf Ismayr (GER) | 345.0 |
| 1936 | Khadr el Thouni (EGY) | 387.5 |
| 1948 | Frank Spellman (USA) | 390.0 |
| 1952 | Peter George (USA) | 400.0 |
| 1956 | Fyodor Bogdanovsky (URS) | 420.0 |
| 1960 | Aleksandr Kurynov (URS) | 437.5 |
| 1964 | Hans Zdrazila (TCH) | 445.0 |
| 1968 | Viktor Kurentsov (URS) | 475.0 |
| 1972 | Iordan Bikov (BUL) | 485.0 |
| 1976 | Iordan Mitkov (BUL) | 335.0 |
| 1980 | Asen Zlatev (BUL) | 360.0 |
| 1984 | Karl-Heinz Radschinsky (FRG) | 340.0 |
| 1988 | Borislav Gidikov (BUL) | 375.0 |
| 1992 | Fyodor Kassapu (UNT) | 357.5 |
| 1996 | Pablo Lara (CUB) | 367.5 |
| 2000 | Zhan Xugang (CHN) | 367.5 |

| 85 KG (187.5 LB) | | KG |
|---|---|---|
| 1920 | Ernest Cadine (FRA) | 290.0 |
| 1924 | Charles Rigoulot (FRA) | 502.5[26] |
| 1928 | El Sayed Nosseir (EGY) | 355.0 |
| 1932 | Louis Hostin (FRA) | 365.0 |
| 1936 | Louis Hostin (FRA) | 372.5 |
| 1948 | Stanley Stanczyk (USA) | 417.5 |
| 1952 | Trofim Lomakin (URS) | 417.5 |
| 1956 | Tommy Kono (USA) | 447.5 |
| 1960 | Ireneusz Palinski (POL) | 442.5 |
| 1964 | Rudolph Plyukfelder (URS) | 475.0 |
| 1968 | Boris Selitsky (URS) | 485.0 |
| 1972 | Leif Jenssen (NOR) | 507.5 |
| 1976 | Valery Shary (URS) | 365.0 |
| 1980 | Yury Vardanyan (URS) | 400.0 |
| 1984 | Petre Becheru (ROM) | 355.0 |
| 1988 | Israil Arsamakov (URS) | 377.5 |
| 1992 | Pyrros Dimas (GRE) | 370.0 |
| 1996 | Pyrros Dimas (GRE) | 392.5 |
| 2000 | Pyrros Dimas (GRE) | 390.0 |

| 94 KG (207 LB) | | KG |
|---|---|---|
| 1952 | Norbert Schemansky (USA) | 445.0 |
| 1956 | Arkady Vorobyev (URS) | 462.5 |
| 1960 | Arkady Vorobyev (URS) | 472.5 |
| 1964 | Vladimir Golovanov (URS) | 487.5 |
| 1968 | Kaarlo Kangasniemi (FIN) | 517.5 |
| 1972 | Andon Nikolov (BUL) | 525.0 |
| 1976 | David Rigert (URS) | 382.5 |
| 1980 | Peter Baczako (HUN) | 377.5 |
| 1984 | Nicu Vlad (ROM) | 392.5 |
| 1988 | Anatoly Khrapaty (URS) | 412.5 |
| 1992 | Kakhi Kakhiashvili (UNT) | 412.5 |
| 1996 | Aleksey Petrov (RUS) | 402.5 |
| 2000 | Akakios Kakhiashvilis (GRE) | 405.0 |

| 99 KG (218.5 LB) | | KG |
|---|---|---|
| 1980 | Ota Zaremba (TCH) | 395.0 |
| 1984 | Rolf Milser (FRG) | 385.0 |
| 1988 | Pavel Kuznetsov (URS) | 425.0 |
| 1992 | Viktor Tregubov (UNT) | 410.0 |
| 1996 | Akakios Kakhiashvilis (GRE) | 420.0 |

### Weight lifting (men)[24, 25] (continued)

| 105 KG (231.5 LB) | | KG |
|---|---|---|
| 1972 | Jan Talts (URS) | 580.0 |
| 1976 | Yury Zaytsev (URS) | 385.0 |
| 1980 | Leonid Taranenko (URS) | 422.5 |
| 1984 | Norberto Oberburger (ITA) | 390.0 |
| 1988 | Yury Zakharevitch (URS) | 455.0 |
| 1992 | Ronny Weller (GER) | 432.5 |
| 1996 | Timur Taymazov (UKR) | 430.0 |
| 2000 | Hossein Tavakoli (IRI) | 425.0 |

| OVER 105 KG (231.5 LB) | | KG |
|---|---|---|
| 1920 | Filippo Bottino (ITA) | 265.5 |
| 1924 | Giuseppe Tonani (ITA) | 517.5[26] |
| 1928 | Josef Strassberger (GER) | 372.5 |
| 1932 | Jaroslav Skobia (TCH) | 380.0 |
| 1936 | Josef Manger (GER) | 410.0 |
| 1948 | John Davis (USA) | 452.5 |
| 1952 | John Davis (USA) | 460.0 |
| 1956 | Paul Anderson (USA) | 500.0 |
| 1960 | Yury Vlasov (URS) | 537.5 |
| 1964 | Leonid Zhabotinsky (URS) | 572.5 |
| 1968 | Leonid Zhabotinsky (URS) | 572.5 |
| 1972 | Vasily Alekseyev (URS) | 640.0 |
| 1976 | Vasily Alekseyev (URS) | 440.0 |
| 1980 | Sultan Rakhmanov (URS) | 440.0 |
| 1984 | Dinko Lukin (AUS) | 412.5 |
| 1988 | Aleksandr Kurlovich (URS) | 462.5 |
| 1992 | Aleksandr Kurlovich (UNT) | 450.0 |
| 1996 | Andrey Chemerkin (RUS) | 457.5 |
| 2000 | Hossein Rezazadeh (IRI) | 472.5 |

| ONE-HAND LIFT (UNLIMITED CLASS) | | KG |
|---|---|---|
| 1896 | Launceston Elliot (GBR) | 71.0 |
| 1906 | Josef Steinbach (AUT) | 76.55 |

| TWO-HAND LIFT (UNLIMITED CLASS) | | KG |
|---|---|---|
| 1896 | Viggo Jensen (DEN) | 111.5 |
| 1904 | Perikles Kakousis (GRE) | 111.7 |
| 1906 | Dimitrios Tofalos (GRE) | 142.4 |

| ALL-AROUND DUMBBELLS (UNLIMITED CLASS) | |
|---|---|
| 1904 | Oscar Osthoff (USA) |

### Weight lifting (women)

| 48 KG (106 LB) | | KG |
|---|---|---|
| 2000 | Tara Nott (USA) | 185.0 |

| 53 KG (117 LB) | | KG |
|---|---|---|
| 2000 | Yang Xia (CHN) | 225.0 |

| 58 KG (128 LB) | | KG |
|---|---|---|
| 2000 | Soraya Jiménez Mendívil (MEX) | 222.5 |

| 63 KG (139 LB) | | KG |
|---|---|---|
| 2000 | Chen Xiaomin (CHN) | 242.5 |

| 69 KG (152 LB) | | KG |
|---|---|---|
| 2000 | Lin Weining (CHN) | 242.5 |

| 75 KG (165.5 LB) | | KG |
|---|---|---|
| 2000 | Maria Isabel Urrutia (COL) | 245.0 |

| OVER 75 KG (165.5 LB) | | KG |
|---|---|---|
| 2000 | Ding Meiyuan (CHN) | 300.0 |

### Wrestling—Freestyle[24]

| 48 KG (106 LB) | |
|---|---|
| 1904 | Robert Curry (USA) |

# Summer Olympic Games Champions (continued)

### Wrestling—Freestyle[24] (continued)

**48 KG (106 LB)**
1972 Roman Dmitriyev (URS)
1976 Khassan Issaev (BUL)
1980 Claudio Pollio (ITA)
1984 Robert Weaver (USA)
1988 Takashi Kobayashi (JPN)
1992 Kim Il (PRK)
1996 Kim Il (PRK)

**54 KG (119 LB)**
1904 George Mehnert (USA)
1948 Lennart Viitala (FIN)
1952 Hasan Gemici (TUR)
1956 Mirian Tsalkalamanidze (URS)
1960 Ahmet Bilek (TUR)
1964 Yoshikatsu Yoshida (JPN)
1968 Shigeo Nakata (JPN)
1972 Kiyomi Kato (JPN)
1976 Yuji Takada (JPN)
1980 Anatoly Beloglazov (URS)
1984 Saban Trstena (YUG)
1988 Mitsuru Sato (JPN)
1992 Li Hak-son (PRK)
1996 Valentin Iordanov (BUL)
2000 Namig Amdullayev (AZE)

**58 KG (128 LB)**
1904 Isidor "Jack" Niflot (USA)
1908 George Mehnert (USA)
1924 Kustaa Pihlajamäki (FIN)
1928 Kaarlo Maakinen (FIN)
1932 Robert Pearce (USA)
1936 Odon Zombory (HUN)
1948 Nasuh Akar (TUR)
1952 Shohachi Ishii (JPN)
1956 Mustafa Dagistanli (TUR)
1960 Terence McCann (USA)
1964 Yojiro Uetake (JPN)
1968 Yojiro Uetake (JPN)
1972 Hideaki Yanagida (JPN)
1976 Vladimir Yumin (URS)
1980 Sergey Beloglazov (URS)
1984 Hideaki Tomiyama (JPN)
1988 Sergey Beloglazov (URS)
1992 Alejandro Puerto Diaz (CUB)
1996 Kendall Cross (USA)
2000 Alireza Dabir (IRI)

**63 KG (139 LB)**
1904 Benjamin Bradshaw (USA)
1908 George Dole (USA)
1920 Charles Ackerly (USA)
1924 Robin Reed (USA)
1928 Allie Morrison (USA)
1932 Hermanni Pihlajamäki (FIN)
1936 Kustaa Pihlajamäki (FIN)
1948 Gazanfer Bilge (TUR)
1952 Bayram Sit (TUR)
1956 Shozo Sasahara (JPN)
1960 Mustafa Dagistanli (TUR)
1964 Osamu Watanabe (JPN)
1968 Masaaki Kaneko (JPN)
1972 Zagalav Abdulbekov (URS)
1976 Yang Jung Mo (KOR)
1980 Magomedgasan Abushev (URS)
1984 Randy Lewis (USA)
1988 John Smith (USA)
1992 John Smith (USA)

### Wrestling—Freestyle[24] (continued)

**63 KG (139 LB)**
1996 Tom Brands (USA)
2000 Murad Umakhanov (RUS)

**69 KG (152 LB)**
1904 Otto Roehm (USA)
1908 George de Relwyskow (GBR)
1920 Kaarlo "Kalle" Anttila (FIN)
1924 Russell Vis (USA)
1928 Osvald Käpp (EST)
1932 Charles Pacome (FRA)
1936 Karoly Karpati (HUN)
1948 Celal Atik (TUR)
1952 Olle Anderberg (SWE)
1956 Emamali Habibi (IRI)
1960 Shelby Wilson (USA)
1964 Enio Valchev Dimov (BUL)
1968 Abdollah Movahed (IRI)
1972 Dan Gable (USA)
1976 Pavel Pinigin (URS)
1980 Saipulla Absaldov (URS)
1984 You In Tak (KOR)
1988 Arsen Fadzayev (URS)
1992 Arsen Fadzayev (UNT)
1996 Vadim Bogiyev (RUS)
2000 Daniel Igali (CAN)

**76 KG (167.5 LB)**
1904 Charles Eriksen (USA)
1924 Hermann Gehri (SUI)
1928 Arvo Haavisto (FIN)
1932 Jack van Bebber (USA)
1936 Frank Lewis (USA)
1948 Yasar Dogu (TUR)
1952 William Smith (USA)
1956 Mitsuo Ikeda (JPN)
1960 Douglas Blubaugh (USA)
1964 Ismail Ogan (TUR)
1968 Mahmut Atalay (TUR)
1972 Wayne Wells (USA)
1976 Jiichiro Date (JPN)
1980 Valentin Raychev (BUL)
1984 David Schultz (USA)
1988 Kenneth Monday (USA)
1992 Park Jang Soon (KOR)
1996 Buvaisa Saytyev (RUS)
2000 Brandon Slay (USA)

**85 KG (187.5 LB)**
1908 Stanley Bacon (GBR)
1920 Eino Leino (FIN)
1924 Fritz Haggmann (SUI)
1928 Ernst Kyburz (SUI)
1932 Ivar Johansson (SWE)
1936 Émile Poilvé (FRA)
1948 Glen Brand (USA)
1952 David Tsimakurdze (URS)
1956 Nikola Stanchev (BUL)
1960 Hasan Gungor (TUR)
1964 Prodan Stoyanov Gardchev (BUL)
1968 Boris Gurevich (URS)
1972 Levan Tediashvili (URS)
1976 John Peterson (USA)
1980 Ismail Abilov (BUL)
1984 Mark Schultz (USA)
1988 Han Myung Woo (KOR)
1992 Kevin Jackson (USA)
1996 Khadshimurad Magomedov (RUS)

# Summer Olympic Games Champions (continued)

### Wrestling—Freestyle[24] (continued)

**85 KG (187.5 LB)**
2000   Adam Saytev (RUS)

**90 KG (198.5 LB)**
1920   Anders Larsson (SWE)
1924   John Franklin Spellman (USA)
1928   Thure Sjöstedt (SWE)
1932   Peter Mehringer (USA)
1936   Knut Fridell (SWE)
1948   Henry Wittenberg (USA)
1952   Bror Wiking Palm (SWE)
1956   Gholam-Reza Takhti (IRI)
1960   Ismet Atli (TUR)
1964   Aleksandr Medved (URS)
1968   Ahmet Ayuk (TUR)
1972   Ben Peterson (USA)
1976   Levan Tediashvili (URS)
1980   Sanasar Oganesyan (URS)
1984   Ed Banach (USA)
1988   Macharbek Khadartsev (URS)
1992   Macharbek Khadartsev (UNT)
1996   Rasul Khadem Azghadi (IRI)

**97 KG (214 LB)**
1896   Karl Schumann (GER)
1904   Bernhuff Hansen (USA)
1908   George O'Kelly (GBR)
1920   Robert Rothe (SUI)
1924   Harry Steele (USA)
1928   Johan Richthoff (SWE)
1932   Johan Richthoff (SWE)
1936   Kristjan Palusalu (EST)
1948   Gyula Bobis (HUN)
1952   Arsen Mekokishvili (URS)
1956   Hamit Kaplan (TUR)
1960   Wilfried Dietrich (GER)
1964   Aleksandr Ivanitsky (URS)
1968   Aleksandr Medved (URS)
1972   Ivan Yarygin (URS)
1976   Ivan Yarygin (URS)
1980   Ilya Mate (URS)
1984   Lou Banach (USA)
1988   Vasile Puscasu (ROM)
1992   Leri Khabelov (UNT)
1996   Kurt Angle (USA)
2000   Sagid Murtasaliyev (RUS)

**OVER 130 KG (286.5 LB)**
1972   Aleksandr Medved (URS)
1976   Soslan Andiyev (URS)
1980   Soslan Andiyev (URS)
1984   Bruce Baumgartner (USA)
1988   David Gobedishvili (URS)
1992   Bruce Baumgartner (USA)
1996   Mahmut Demir (TUR)
2000   David Musulbes (RUS)

### Wrestling—Greco-Roman[24]

**48 KG (106 LB)**
1972   Gheorghe Berceanu (ROM)
1976   Aleksey Shumakov (URS)
1980   Zhaksylyk Ushkempirov (URS)
1984   Vincenzo Maenza (ITA)
1988   Vincenzo Maenza (ITA)
1992   Oleg Kucherenko (UNT)
1996   Sim Kwon-Ho (KOR)

### Wrestling—Greco-Roman[24] (continued)

**54 KG (119 LB)**
1948   Pietro Lombardi (ITA)
1952   Boris Gurevich (URS)
1956   Nikolay Solovyev (URS)
1960   Dumitru Pirvulescu (ROM)
1964   Tsutomu Hanahara (JPN)
1968   Petar Kirov (BUL)
1972   Petar Kirov (BUL)
1976   Vitaly Konstantinov (URS)
1980   Vakhtang Blagidze (URS)
1984   Atsuji Miyahara (JPN)
1988   Jon Ronningen (NOR)
1992   Jon Ronningen (NOR)
1996   Armen Nazaryan (ARM)
2000   Sim Kwon-Ho (KOR)

**58 KG (128 LB)**
1924   Eduard Pütsep (EST)
1928   Kurt Leucht (GER)
1932   Jakob Brendel (GER)
1936   Marton Lorincz (HUN)
1948   Kurt Pettersen (SWE)
1952   Imre Hodos (HUN)
1956   Konstantin Vyrupayev (URS)
1960   Oleg Karavayev (URS)
1964   Masamitsu Ichiguchi (JPN)
1968   Janos Varga (HUN)
1972   Rustem Kazakov (URS)
1976   Pertti Ukkola (FIN)
1980   Shamil Serikov (URS)
1984   Pasquale Passarelli (FRG)
1988   Andras Sike (HUN)
1992   An Han Bong (KOR)
1996   Yury Melnichenko (KAZ)
2000   Armen Nazarian (BUL)

**63 KG (139 LB)**
1912   Kaarlo Koskelo (FIN)
1920   Oskar Friman (FIN)
1924   Kalle Anttila (FIN)
1928   Voldemar Väli (EST)
1932   Giovanni Gozzi (ITA)
1936   Yasar Erkan (TUR)
1948   Mehmet Oktav (TUR)
1952   Yakov Punkin (URS)
1956   Rauno Leonard Mäkinen (FIN)
1960   Muzahir Sille (TUR)
1964   Imre Polyak (HUN)
1968   Roman Rurua (URS)
1972   Georgi Markov (BUL)
1976   Kazimierz Lipien (POL)
1980   Stilianos Migiakis (GRE)
1984   Kim Weon Kee (KOR)
1988   Kamandar Madzhidov (URS)
1992   Akif Pirim (TUR)
1996   Wlodzimierz Zawadzki (POL)
2000   Varteres Samurgashev (RUS)

**69 KG (152 LB)**
1908   Enrico Porro (ITA)
1912   Eemil Väre (FIN)
1920   Eemil Väre (FIN)
1924   Oskar Friman (FIN)
1928   Lajos Keresztes (HUN)
1932   Erik Malmberg (SWE)
1936   Lauri Koskela (FIN)
1948   Karl Freij (SWE)
1952   Shazam Safin (URS)

# Summer Olympic Games Champions (continued)

## Wrestling—Greco-Roman[24] (continued)

### 69 KG (152 LB)
1956 Kyösti Emil Lehtonen (FIN)
1960 Avtandil Koridze (URS)
1964 Kazim Ayvaz (TUR)
1968 Munji Mumemura (JPN)
1972 Shamil Khisamutdinov (URS)
1976 Suren Nalbandyan (URS)
1980 Stefan Rusu (ROM)
1984 Vlado Lisjak (YUG)
1988 Levon Dzhulfalakyan (URS)
1992 Attila Repka (HUN)
1996 Ryszard Wolny (POL)
2000 Filiberto Ascuy Aguilera (CUB)

### 76 KG (167.5 LB)
1932 Ivar Johansson (SWE)
1936 Rudolf Svedberg (SWE)
1948 Erik Gösta Andersson (SWE)
1952 Miklos Szilvasi (HUN)
1956 Mithat Bayrak (TUR)
1960 Mithat Bayrak (TUR)
1964 Anatoly Kolesov (URS)
1968 Rudolf Vesper (GDR)
1972 Viteslav Macha (TCH)
1976 Anatoly Bykov (URS)
1980 Ferenc Kocsis (HUN)
1984 Jouko Salomaki (FIN)
1988 Kim Young Nam (KOR)
1992 Mnatsakan Iskandaryan (UNT)
1996 Filiberto Ascuy Aguilera (CUB)
2000 Murat Kardanov (URS)

### 85 KG (187.5 LB)
1908 Frithiof Martenson (SWE)
1912 Claes Johansson (SWE)
1920 Carl Westergren (SWE)
1924 Edward Westerlund (FIN)
1928 Väinö Kokkinen (FIN)
1932 Väinö Kokkinen (FIN)
1936 Ivar Johansson (SWE)
1948 Axel Grönberg (SWE)
1952 Axel Grönberg (SWE)
1956 Givi Kartoziya (URS)
1960 Dimitar Dobrev (BUL)
1964 Branislav Simic (YUG)
1968 Lothar Metz (GDR)
1972 Csaba Hegedus (HUN)
1976 Momir Petkovic (YUG)
1980 Gennady Korban (URS)
1984 Ion Draica (ROM)
1988 Mikhail Mamiashvili (URS)
1992 Peter Farkas (HUN)
2000 Hamza Yerlikaya (TUR)

## Wrestling—Greco-Roman[24] (continued)

### 90 KG (198.5 LB)
1908 Verner Weckman (FIN)
1912 Anders Ahlgren (SWE)
1920 Claes Johansson (SWE)
1924 Carl Westergren (SWE)
1928 Ibrahim Moustafa (EGY)
1932 Rudolf Svensson (SWE)
1936 Axel Cadier (SWE)
1948 Karl-Erik Nilsson (SWE)
1952 Kelpo Olavi Gröndahl (FIN)
1956 Valentin Nikolayev (URS)
1960 Tevfik Kis (TUR)
1964 Boyan Radev (BUL)
1968 Boyan Radev (BUL)
1972 Valery Rezantsev (URS)
1976 Valery Rezantsev (URS)
1980 Norbert Nottny (HUN)
1984 Steven Fraser (USA)
1988 Atanas Komchev (BUL)
1992 Maik Bullmann (GER)
1996 Vyatsheslav Oleynyk (UKR)

### 97 KG (214 LB)
1896 Karl Schumann (GER)
1908 Richard Weisz (HUN)
1912 Yrjö Saarela (FIN)
1920 Adolf Lindfors (FIN)
1924 Henri Deglane (FRA)
1928 Rudolf Svensson (SWE)
1932 Carl Westergren (SWE)
1936 Kristjan Palusalu (EST)
1948 Ahmet Kirecci (TUR)
1952 Johannes Kotkas (URS)
1956 Anatoly Parfenov (URS)
1960 Ivan Bogdan (URS)
1964 Istvan Kozma (HUN)
1968 Istvan Kozma (HUN)
1972 Nicolae Martinescu (ROM)
1976 Nikolay Balboshin (URS)
1980 Georgi Raikov-Petkov (BUL)
1984 Vasile Andrei (ROM)
1988 Andrzej Wronski (POL)
1992 Héctor Milian (CUB)
1996 Andrzej Wronski (POL)
2000 Mikael Ljungberg (SWE)

### 130 KG (286.5 LB)
1972 Anatoly Roshchin (URS)
1976 Aleksandr Kolchinsky (URS)
1980 Aleksandr Kolchinsky (URS)
1984 Jeffrey Blatnick (USA)
1988 Aleksandr Karelin (URS)
1992 Aleksandr Karelin (UNT)
1996 Aleksandr Karelin (RUS)
2000 Rulon Gardner (USA)

[1]The competitions in 1900 and 1904 are said to be unofficial.  [2]100-meter event.  [3]Hurdles were 2' 6" high, not 3'.  [4]An extra lap of 460 meters was run in error.  [5]Jim Thorpe was stripped of his gold medals in 1913 when it was discovered he had briefly competed as a professional athlete; in 1982 his gold medals were restored, and he was declared "cowinner" of the events.  [6]2,000-meter event.  [7]333.3-meter event.  [8]Distance varied from 87 to 320 km.  [9]Weight classifications were changed in 1980 and 1996.  [10]Weight classifications were changed in 2000.  [11]The distances in men's rowing events have varied from time to time. In 1904 it was 2 miles; in 1908, 1.5 miles; from 1912 to 1936, 2,000 m; in 1948, 1 mile 350 yards; and since 1952, 2,000 m (1 mile 427 yards).  [12]The distance in women's rowing events was 1,000 m until 1988, at which time it became 2,000 m.  [13]100 yards.  [14]220 yards.  [15]500 meters.  [16]440 yards.  [17]1,200 meters.  [18]1,000 meters.  [19]One mile.  [20]100 yards.  [21]440 yards.  [22]300 meters.  [23]Fréchette's gold medal awarded in 1993 on basis of error in scoring.  [24]Weight classifications have been revised numerous times, most recently after the 1996 Games.  [25]In 1976 the press lift was removed, weights given thereafter being the total for the clean and jerk and the snatch.  [26]Total of five lifts.

# Winter Olympic Games Champions

*Gold medalists in all events, 1908–2002 (separate Winter Games were not held until 1924).*

## Biathlon

**MEN**

**10 KILOMETER** — MIN:SEC

| | | |
|---|---|---|
| 1980 | Frank Ullrich (GDR) | 32:10.69 |
| 1984 | Eirik Kvalfoss (NOR) | 30:53.8 |
| 1988 | Frank-Peter Rötsch (GDR) | 25:08.1 |
| 1992 | Mark Kirchner (GER) | 26:02.3 |
| 1994 | Sergey Chepikov (RUS) | 28:07.0 |
| 1998 | Ole Einar Bjørndalen (NOR) | 27:16.2 |
| 2002 | Ole Einar Bjørndalen (NOR) | 24:51.3 |

**12.5 KILOMETER PURSUIT** — MIN:SEC

| | | |
|---|---|---|
| 2002 | Ole Einar Bjørndalen (NOR) | 32:34.6 |

**20 KILOMETER** — HR:MIN:SEC

| | | |
|---|---|---|
| 1960 | Klas Lestander (SWE) | 1:33:21.6 |
| 1964 | Vladimir Melanin (URS) | 1:20:26.8 |
| 1968 | Magnar Solberg (NOR) | 1:13:45.9 |
| 1972 | Magnar Solberg (NOR) | 1:15:55.50[1] |
| 1976 | Nikolay Kruglov (URS) | 1:14:12.26 |
| 1980 | Anatoly Alyabyev (URS) | 1:08:16.31 |
| 1984 | Peter Angerer (FRG) | 1:11:52.70 |
| 1988 | Frank-Peter Rötsch (GDR) | 56:33.3 |
| 1992 | Yevgeny Redkin (UNT)[2] | 57:34.4 |
| 1994 | Sergey Tarasov (RUS) | 57:25.3 |
| 1998 | Halvard Hanevold (NOR) | 56:16.4 |
| 2002 | Ole Einar Bjørndalen (NOR) | 51:03.3 |

**4 × 7.5-KILOMETER RELAY** — HR:MIN:SEC

| | | |
|---|---|---|
| 1968 | USSR | 2:13:02.4 |
| 1972 | USSR | 1:51:44.92[1] |
| 1976 | USSR | 1:57:55.64 |
| 1980 | USSR | 1:34:03.27 |
| 1984 | USSR | 1:38:51.70 |
| 1988 | USSR | 1:22:30.00 |
| 1992 | Germany | 1:24:43.5 |
| 1994 | Germany | 1:30:22.1 |
| 1998 | Germany | 1:19:43.3 |
| 2002 | Norway | 1:23:42.3 |

**MILITARY SKI PATROL**

| | |
|---|---|
| 1924 | Switzerland |
| 1928 | Norway |
| 1936 | Italy |
| 1948 | Switzerland |

**DISTANCE SHOOTING**

| | |
|---|---|
| 1936 | Georg Edenhauser (AUT) |

**ICE SHOOTING (TEAM)**

| | |
|---|---|
| 1936 | Austria |

**TARGET SHOOTING**

| | |
|---|---|
| 1936 | Ignaz Reiterer (AUT) |

**WOMEN**

**7.5 KILOMETER** — MIN:SEC

| | | |
|---|---|---|
| 1992 | Anfisa Restsova (UNT)[2] | 24:29.2 |
| 1994 | Myriam Bédard (CAN) | 26:08.8 |
| 1998 | Galina Kukleva (RUS) | 23:08.0 |
| 2002 | Kati Wilhelm (GER) | 20:41.4 |

**10 KILOMETER PURSUIT** — MIN:SEC

| | | |
|---|---|---|
| 2002 | Olga Pyleva (RUS) | 31:07.7 |

**15 KILOMETER** — MIN:SEC

| | | |
|---|---|---|
| 1992 | Antje Misersky (GER) | 51:47.2 |

## Biathlon (continued)

**15 KILOMETER** — MIN:SEC

| | | |
|---|---|---|
| 1994 | Myriam Bédard (CAN) | 52:06.6 |
| 1998 | Ekaterina Dafovska (BUL) | 54:52.0 |
| 2002 | Andrea Henkel (GER) | 47:29.1 |

**4 × 7.5-KILOMETER RELAY** — HR:MIN:SEC

| | | |
|---|---|---|
| 1992 | France (3 × 7.5-meter event) | 1:15:55.6 |
| 1994 | Russia | 1:47:19.5 |
| 1998 | Germany | 1:40:13.6 |
| 2002 | Germany | 1:27:55.0 |

## Bobsled

**TWO-MAN BOBSLED** — MIN:SEC

| | | |
|---|---|---|
| 1932 | United States | 8:14.74 |
| 1936 | United States | 5:29.29 |
| 1948 | Switzerland | 5:29.2 |
| 1952 | West Germany | 5:24.54 |
| 1956 | Italy | 5:30.14 |
| 1964 | Great Britain | 4:21.90 |
| 1968 | Italy | 4:41.54 |
| 1972 | West Germany | 4:57.07 |
| 1976 | East Germany | 3:44.42 |
| 1980 | Switzerland | 4:09.36 |
| 1984 | East Germany | 3:25.56 |
| 1988 | USSR | 3:53.48 |
| 1992 | Switzerland | 4:03.26 |
| 1994 | Switzerland | 3:30.81 |
| 1998 | Canada, Italy (tied) | 3:37.24 |
| 2002 | Germany | 3:10.11 |

**FOUR-MAN BOBSLED** — MIN:SEC

| | | |
|---|---|---|
| 1924 | Switzerland | 5:45.54 |
| 1928 | United States | 3:20.5[3] |
| 1932 | United States | 7:53.68 |
| 1936 | Switzerland | 5:19.85 |
| 1948 | United States | 5:20.1 |
| 1952 | West Germany | 5:07.84 |
| 1956 | Switzerland | 5:10.44 |
| 1964 | Canada | 4:14.46 |
| 1968 | Italy | 2:17.39 |
| 1972 | Switzerland | 4:43.07 |
| 1976 | East Germany | 3:40.43 |
| 1980 | East Germany | 3:59.92 |
| 1984 | East Germany | 3:20.22 |
| 1988 | Switzerland | 3:47.51 |
| 1992 | Austria | 3:53.90 |
| 1994 | Germany | 3:27.78 |
| 1998 | Germany | 2:39.41 |
| 2002 | Germany | 3:07.51 |

**TWO-WOMAN BOBSLED** — MIN:SEC

| | | |
|---|---|---|
| 2002 | United States | 1:37.76 |

## Curling

**MEN**

| | |
|---|---|
| 1924 | Great Britain |
| 1998 | Switzerland |
| 2002 | Norway |

**WOMEN**

| | |
|---|---|
| 1998 | Canada |
| 2002 | Great Britain |

## Figure Skating

**MEN'S SINGLES**

| | |
|---|---|
| 1908 | Ulrich Salchow (SWE) |

# Winter Olympic Games Champions (continued)

## Figure Skating (continued)

**MEN'S SINGLES**

| | |
|---|---|
| 1920 | Gillis Gräfström (SWE) |
| 1924 | Gillis Gräfström (SWE) |
| 1928 | Gillis Gräfström (SWE) |
| 1932 | Karl Schäfer (AUT) |
| 1936 | Karl Schäfer (AUT) |
| 1948 | Richard Button (USA) |
| 1952 | Richard Button (USA) |
| 1956 | Hayes Alan Jenkins (USA) |
| 1960 | David Jenkins (USA) |
| 1964 | Manfred Schnelldorfer (GER)[4] |
| 1968 | Wolfgang Schwarz (AUT) |
| 1972 | Ondrej Nepela (TCH) |
| 1976 | John Curry (GBR) |
| 1980 | Robin Cousins (GBR) |
| 1984 | Scott Hamilton (USA) |
| 1988 | Brian Boitano (USA) |
| 1992 | Viktor Petrenko (UNT)[2] |
| 1994 | Aleksey Urmanov (RUS) |
| 1998 | Ilia Kulik (RUS) |
| 2002 | Aleksey Yagudin (RUS) |

**WOMEN'S SINGLES**

| | |
|---|---|
| 1908 | Madge Syers (GBR) |
| 1920 | Magda Julin-Mauroy (SWE) |
| 1924 | Herma Planck-Szabo (AUT) |
| 1928 | Sonja Henie (NOR) |
| 1932 | Sonja Henie (NOR) |
| 1936 | Sonja Henie (NOR) |
| 1948 | Barbara Ann Scott (CAN) |
| 1952 | Jeanette Altwegg (GBR) |
| 1956 | Tenley Albright (USA) |
| 1964 | Sjoukje Dijkstra (NED) |
| 1968 | Peggy Fleming (USA) |
| 1972 | Beatrix Schuba (AUT) |
| 1976 | Dorothy Hamill (USA) |
| 1980 | Annett Potzsch (GDR) |
| 1984 | Katarina Witt (GDR) |
| 1988 | Katarina Witt (GDR) |
| 1992 | Kristi Yamaguchi (USA) |
| 1994 | Oksana Bayul (UKR) |
| 1998 | Tara Lipinski (USA) |
| 2002 | Sarah Hughes (USA) |

**PAIRS**

| | |
|---|---|
| 1908 | Anna Hübler, Heinrich Burger (GER) |
| 1920 | Ludoviga Jakobsson-Eilers, Walter Jakobsson (FIN) |
| 1924 | Helene Engelmann, Alfred Berger (AUT) |
| 1928 | Andrée Joly, Pierre Brunet (FRA) |
| 1932 | Andrée Brunet-Joly, Pierre Brunet (FRA) |
| 1936 | Maxi Herber, Ernst Baier (GER) |
| 1948 | Micheline Lannoy, Pierre Baugniet (BEL) |
| 1952 | Ria Falk, Paul Falk (FRG) |
| 1956 | Elisabeth Schwarz, Kurt Oppelt (AUT) |
| 1960 | Barbara Wagner, Robert Paul (CAN) |
| 1964 | Lyudmila Belousova, Oleg Protopopov (URS) |
| 1968 | Lyudmila Belousova, Oleg Protopopov (URS) |
| 1972 | Irina Rodnina, Aleksey Ulanov (URS) |
| 1976 | Irina Rodnina, Aleksandr Zaytsev (URS) |
| 1980 | Irina Rodnina, Aleksandr Zaytsev (URS) |
| 1984 | Yelena Valova, Oleg Vasilyev (URS) |

**PAIRS**

| | |
|---|---|
| 1988 | Yekaterina Gordeyeva, Sergey Grinkov (URS) |
| 1992 | Natalya Mishkutyonok, Artur Dmitriyev (UNT)[2] |
| 1994 | Yekaterina Gordeyeva, Sergey Grinkov (RUS) |

## Figure Skating (continued)

**PAIRS**

| | |
|---|---|
| 1998 | Oksana Kazakova, Artur Dmitriyev (RUS) |
| 2002 | Yelena Berezhnaya, Anton Sikharulidze (RUS); Jamie Sale, David Pelletier (CAN) (shared) |

**ICE DANCING**

| | |
|---|---|
| 1976 | Lyudmila Pakhomova, Aleksandr Gorshkov (URS) |
| 1980 | Natalya Linichuk, Gennady Karponosov (URS) |
| 1984 | Jayne Torvill, Christopher Dean (GBR) |
| 1988 | Natalya Bestemyanova, Andrey Bukin (URS) |
| 1992 | Marina Klimova, Sergey Ponomarenko (UNT)[2] |
| 1994 | Oksana Grishchuk, Yevgeny Platov (RUS) |
| 1998 | Oksana Grishchuk, Yevgeny Platov (RUS) |
| 2002 | Marina Anissina, Gwendal Peizerat (FRA) |

## Ice Hockey

**MEN**

| | |
|---|---|
| 1920 | Canada |
| 1924 | Canada |
| 1928 | Canada |
| 1932 | Canada |
| 1936 | Great Britain |
| 1948 | Canada |
| 1952 | Canada |
| 1956 | USSR |
| 1960 | United States |
| 1964 | USSR |
| 1968 | USSR |
| 1972 | USSR |
| 1976 | USSR |
| 1980 | United States |
| 1984 | USSR |
| 1988 | USSR |
| 1992 | Unified Team[2] |
| 1994 | Sweden |
| 1998 | Czech Republic |
| 2002 | Canada |

**WOMEN**

| | |
|---|---|
| 1998 | United States |
| 2002 | Canada |

## Luge

| **MEN'S SINGLES** | | **MIN:SEC** |
|---|---|---|
| 1964 | Thomas Köhler (GER)[4] | 3:26.77 |
| 1968 | Manfred Schmid (AUT) | 2:52.48 |
| 1972 | Wolfgang Schneidel (GDR) | 3:27.58 |
| 1976 | Detlef Guenther (GDR) | 3:27.688[5] |
| 1980 | Bernhard Glass (GDR) | 2:54.796 |
| 1984 | Paul Hildgartner (ITA) | 3:04.258 |
| 1988 | Jens Müller (GDR) | 3:05.548 |
| 1992 | Georg Hackl (GER) | 3:02.363 |
| 1994 | Georg Hackl (GER) | 3:21.571 |
| 1998 | Georg Hackl (GER) | 3:18.436 |
| 2002 | Armin Zöggeler (ITA) | 2:57.941 |

| **MEN'S PAIRS** | | **MIN:SEC** |
|---|---|---|
| 1964 | Austria | 1:41.62 |
| 1968 | East Germany | 1:35.85 |
| 1972 | Italy; East Germany (tied) | 1:28.35 |
| 1976 | East Germany | 1:25.604[5] |
| 1980 | East Germany | 1:19.331 |
| 1984 | West Germany | 1:23.620 |
| 1988 | East Germany | 1:31.940 |

# Winter Olympic Games Champions (continued)

## Luge (continued)

### MEN'S PAIRS

| | | MIN:SEC |
|---|---|---|
| 1992 | Germany | 1:32.053 |
| 1994 | Italy | 1:36.720 |
| 1998 | Germany | 1:41.105 |
| 2002 | Germany | 1:26.082 |

### WOMEN'S SINGLES

| | | MIN:SEC |
|---|---|---|
| 1964 | Ortrun Enderlein (GER)[4] | 3:24.67 |
| 1968 | Erica Lechner (ITA) | 2:29.37 |
| 1972 | Anna-Maria Müller (GDR) | 2:59.18 |
| 1976 | Margit Schumann (GDR) | 2:50.621[5] |
| 1980 | Vera Zozulya (URS) | 2:36.537 |
| 1984 | Steffi Martin (GDR) | 2:46.570 |
| 1988 | Steffi Walter-Martin (GDR) | 3:03.973 |
| 1992 | Doris Neuner (AUT) | 3:06.696 |
| 1994 | Gerda Weissensteiner (ITA) | 3:15.517 |
| 1998 | Silke Kraushaar (GER) | 3:23.779 |
| 2002 | Sylke Otto (GER) | 2:52.464 |

## Skeleton

### MEN

| | | MIN:SEC |
|---|---|---|
| 1928 | Jennison Heaton (USA) | 3:01.8 |
| 1948 | Nino Bibbia (ITA) | 5:23.2 |
| 2002 | Jim Shea (USA) | 1:41.96 |

### WOMEN

| | | MIN:SEC |
|---|---|---|
| 2002 | Tristan Gale (USA) | 1:45.11 |

## Alpine Skiing (men)

### DOWNHILL

| | | MIN:SEC |
|---|---|---|
| 1948 | Henri Oreiller (FRA) | 2:55.0 |
| 1952 | Zeno Colò (ITA) | 2:30.8 |
| 1956 | Toni Sailer (AUT) | 2:52.2 |
| 1960 | Jean Vuarnet (FRA) | 2:06.0 |
| 1964 | Egon Zimmermann (AUT) | 2:18.16[1] |
| 1968 | Jean-Claude Killy (FRA) | 1:59.85 |
| 1972 | Bernhard Russi (SUI) | 1:51.43 |
| 1976 | Franz Klammer (AUT) | 1:45.73 |
| 1980 | Leonhard Stock (AUT) | 1:45.50 |
| 1984 | Bill Johnson (USA) | 1:45.59 |
| 1988 | Pirmin Zurbriggen (SUI) | 1:59.63 |
| 1992 | Patrick Ortlieb (AUT) | 1:50.37 |
| 1994 | Tommy Moe (USA) | 1:45.75 |
| 1998 | Jean-Luc Cretier (FRA) | 1:50.11 |
| 2002 | Fritz Strobl (AUT) | 1:39.13 |

### SLALOM

| | | MIN:SEC |
|---|---|---|
| 1948 | Edy Reinalter (SUI) | 2:10.3 |
| 1952 | Othmar Schneider (AUT) | 2:00.0 |
| 1956 | Toni Sailer (AUT) | 3:14.7 |
| 1960 | Ernst Hinterseer (AUT) | 2:08.9 |
| 1964 | Josef Stiegler (AUT) | 2:21.13[1] |
| 1968 | Jean-Claude Killy (FRA) | 1:39.73 |
| 1972 | Francisco Ochoa (ESP) | 1:49.27 |
| 1976 | Piero Gros (ITA) | 2:03.29 |
| 1980 | Ingemar Stenmark (SWE) | 1:44.26 |
| 1984 | Phil Mahre (USA) | 1:39.41 |
| 1988 | Alberto Tomba (ITA) | 1:39.47 |
| 1992 | Finn Christian Jagge (NOR) | 1:44.39 |
| 1994 | Thomas Stangassinger (AUT) | 2:02.02 |
| 1998 | Hans-Petter Buraas (NOR) | 1:49.31 |
| 2002 | Jean-Pierre Vidal (FRA) | 1:41.06 |

### GIANT SLALOM

| | | MIN:SEC |
|---|---|---|
| 1952 | Stein Eriksen (NOR) | 2:25.0 |
| 1956 | Toni Sailer (AUT) | 3:00.1 |
| 1960 | Roger Staub (SUI) | 1:48.3 |
| 1964 | François Bonlieu (FRA) | 1:46.71[1] |

## Alpine Skiing (men) (continued)

### GIANT SLALOM

| | | MIN:SEC |
|---|---|---|
| 1968 | Jean-Claude Killy (FRA) | 3:29.28 |
| 1972 | Gustavo Thöni (ITA) | 3:09.62 |
| 1976 | Heini Hemmi (SUI) | 3:26.97 |
| 1980 | Ingemar Stenmark (SWE) | 2:40.74 |
| 1984 | Max Julen (SUI) | 2:41.18 |
| 1988 | Alberto Tomba (ITA) | 2:06.37 |
| 1992 | Alberto Tomba (ITA) | 2:06.98 |
| 1994 | Markus Wasmeier (GER) | 2:52.46 |
| 1998 | Hermann Maier (AUT) | 2:38.51 |
| 2002 | Stephan Eberharter (AUT) | 2:23.28 |

### SUPERGIANT SLALOM

| | | MIN:SEC |
|---|---|---|
| 1988 | Franck Piccard (FRA) | 1:39.66 |
| 1992 | Kjetil-Andre Aamodt (NOR) | 1:13.04 |
| 1994 | Markus Wasmeier (GER) | 1:32.53 |
| 1998 | Hermann Maier (AUT) | 1:34.82 |
| 2002 | Kjetil Andre Aamodt (NOR) | 1:21.58 |

### ALPINE COMBINED

| | | MIN:SEC |
|---|---|---|
| 1936 | Franz Pfnür (GER) | |
| 1948 | Henri Oreiller (FRA) | |
| 1972 | Gustavo Thoeni (ITA) | |
| 1976 | Gustavo Thoeni (ITA) | |
| 1988 | Hubert Strolz (AUT) | |
| 1992 | Josef Polig (ITA) | |
| 1994 | Lasse Kjus (NOR) | 3:17.53[6] |
| 1998 | Mario Reiter (AUT) | 3:08.06 |
| 2002 | Kjetil-Andre Aamodt (NOR) | 3:17.56 |

## Alpine Skiing (women)

### DOWNHILL

| | | MIN:SEC |
|---|---|---|
| 1948 | Hedy Schlunegger (SUI) | 2:28.3 |
| 1952 | Trude Jochom-Beiser (AUT) | 1:47.1 |
| 1956 | Madeleine Berthod (SUI) | 1:40.7 |
| 1960 | Heidi Beibl (GER)[4] | 1:37.6 |
| 1964 | Christl Haas (AUT) | 1:55.39[1] |
| 1968 | Olga Pall (AUT) | 1:40.87 |
| 1972 | Marie-Thérèse Nadig (SUI) | 1:36.68 |
| 1976 | Rosi Mittermaier (FRG) | 1:46.16 |
| 1980 | Annemarie Moser-Pröll (AUT) | 1:37.52 |
| 1984 | Michael Figini (SUI) | 1:13.36 |
| 1988 | Marina Kiehl (FRG) | 1:25.86 |
| 1992 | Kerrin Lee-Gartner (CAN) | 1:52.55 |
| 1994 | Katja Seizinger (GER) | 1:35.93 |
| 1998 | Katja Seizinger (GER) | 1:28.29 |
| 2002 | Carole Montillet (FRA) | 1:39.56 |

### SLALOM

| | | MIN:SEC |
|---|---|---|
| 1948 | Gretchen Fraser (USA) | 1:57.2 |
| 1952 | Andrea Lawrence-Mead (USA) | 2:10.6 |
| 1956 | Renée Colliard (SUI) | 1:52.3 |
| 1960 | Anne Heggtveit (CAN) | 1:49.6 |
| 1964 | Christine Goitschel (FRA) | 1:29.86[1] |
| 1968 | Marielle Goitschel (FRA) | 1:59.85 |
| 1972 | Barbara Cochran (USA) | 1:31.24 |
| 1976 | Rosi Mittermaier (FRG) | 1:30.54 |
| 1980 | Hanni Wenzel (LIE) | 1:25.09 |
| 1984 | Paoletta Magoni (ITA) | 1:36.47 |
| 1988 | Vreni Schneider (SUI) | 1:36.69 |
| 1992 | Petra Kronberger (AUT) | 1:32.68 |
| 1994 | Vreni Schneider (SUI) | 1:56.01 |
| 1998 | Hilde Gerg (GER) | 1:32.40 |
| 2002 | Janica Kostelic (CRO) | 1:46.10 |

### GIANT SLALOM

| | | MIN:SEC |
|---|---|---|
| 1952 | Andrea Lawrence-Mead (USA) | 2:06.8 |
| 1956 | Ossi Reichert (GER)[4] | 1:56.5 |

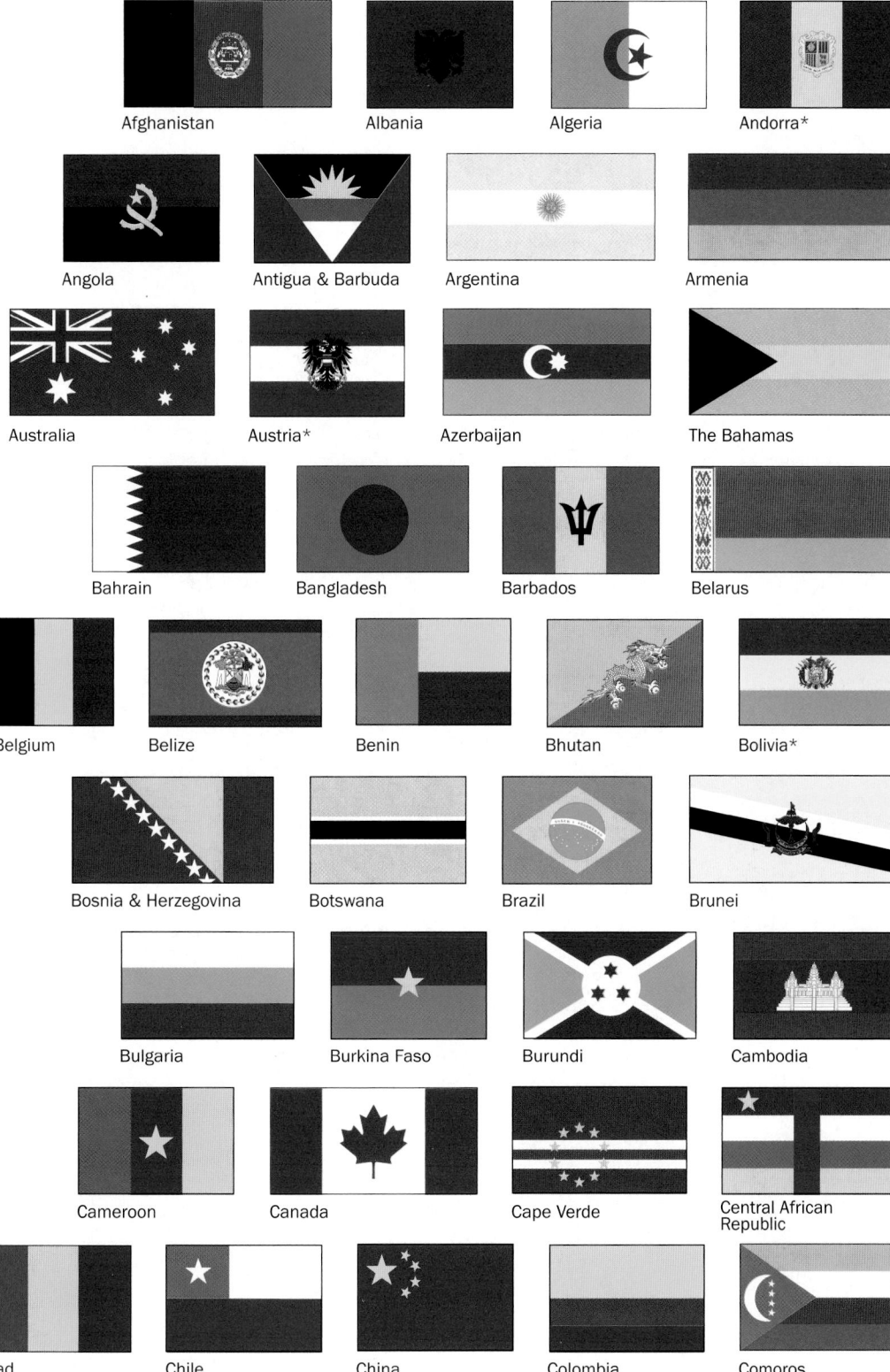

Afghanistan

Albania

Algeria

Andorra*

Angola

Antigua & Barbuda

Argentina

Armenia

Australia

Austria*

Azerbaijan

The Bahamas

Bahrain

Bangladesh

Barbados

Belarus

Belgium

Belize

Benin

Bhutan

Bolivia*

Bosnia & Herzegovina

Botswana

Brazil

Brunei

Bulgaria

Burkina Faso

Burundi

Cambodia

Cameroon

Canada

Cape Verde

Central African Republic

Chad

Chile

China

Colombia

Comoros

Civil flags are shown except where marked thus (*); in these cases, government flags are shown in order to illustrate emblems. Both styles are official national flags.

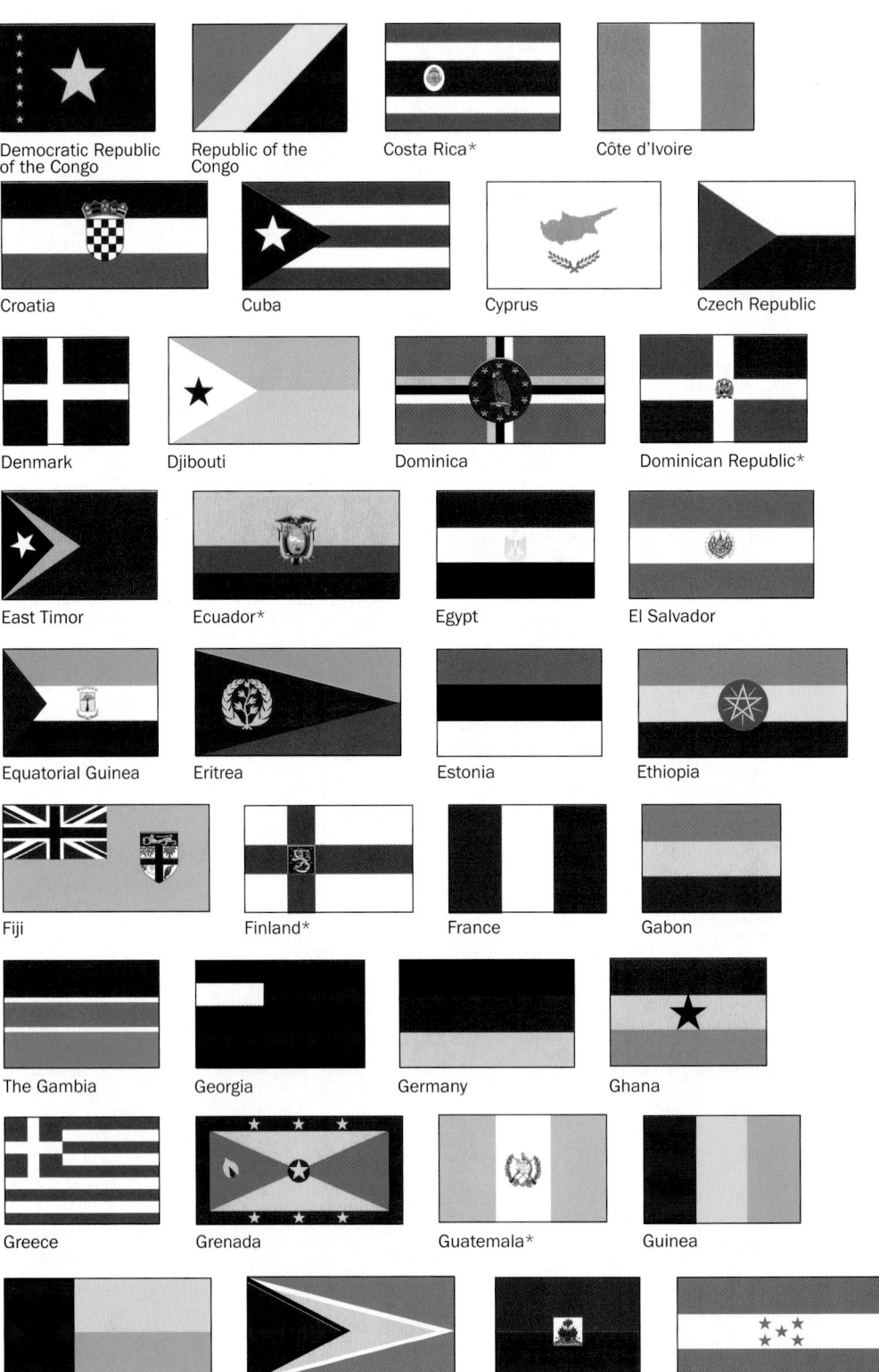

Democratic Republic of the Congo

Republic of the Congo

Costa Rica*

Côte d'Ivoire

Croatia

Cuba

Cyprus

Czech Republic

Denmark

Djibouti

Dominica

Dominican Republic*

East Timor

Ecuador*

Egypt

El Salvador

Equatorial Guinea

Eritrea

Estonia

Ethiopia

Fiji

Finland*

France

Gabon

The Gambia

Georgia

Germany

Ghana

Greece

Grenada

Guatemala*

Guinea

Guinea-Bissau

Guyana

Haiti*

Honduras

Civil flags are shown except where marked thus (*); in these cases, government flags are shown in order to illustrate emblems. Both styles are official national flags.

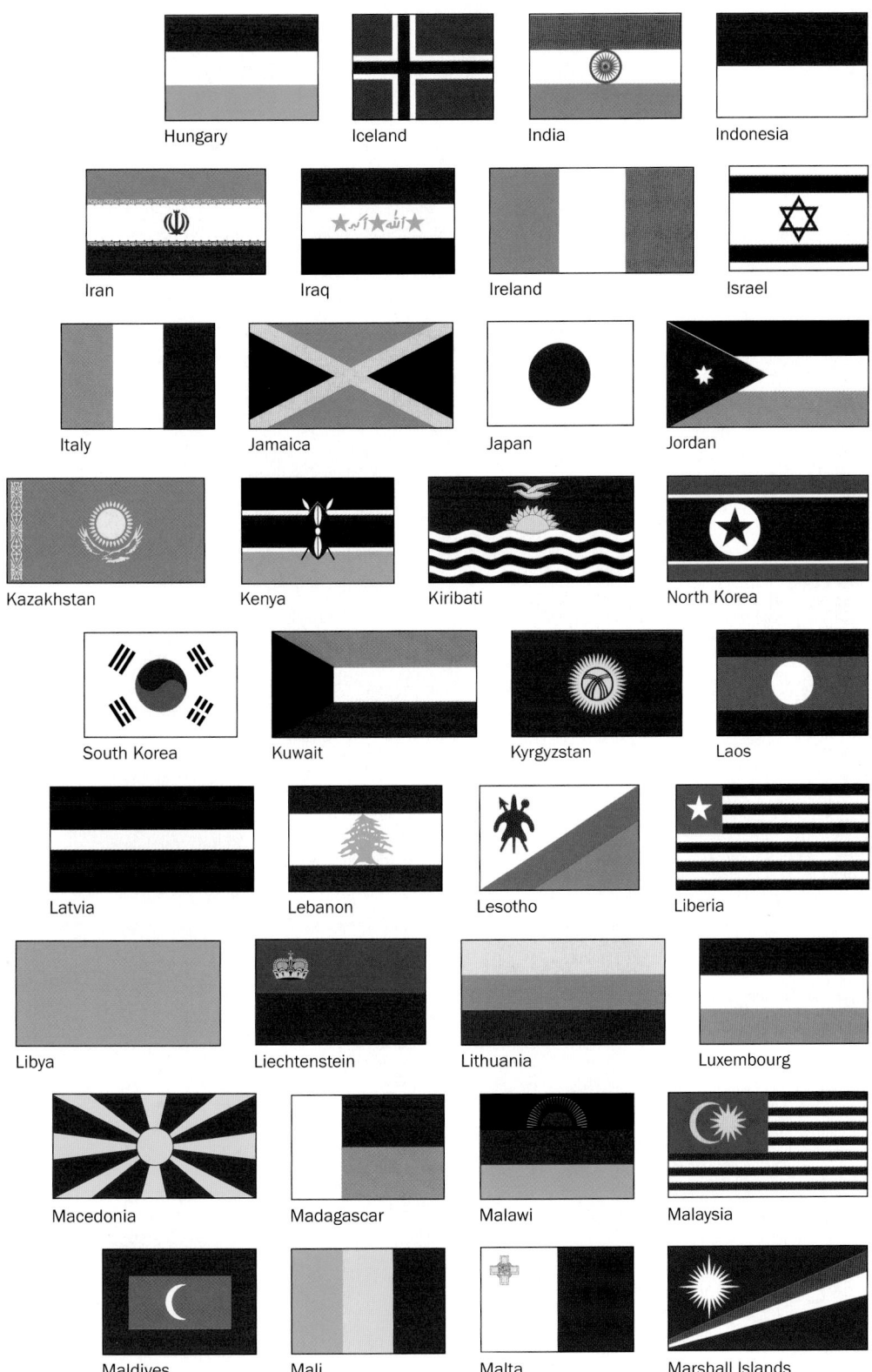

Hungary     Iceland     India     Indonesia

Iran     Iraq     Ireland     Israel

Italy     Jamaica     Japan     Jordan

Kazakhstan     Kenya     Kiribati     North Korea

South Korea     Kuwait     Kyrgyzstan     Laos

Latvia     Lebanon     Lesotho     Liberia

Libya     Liechtenstein     Lithuania     Luxembourg

Macedonia     Madagascar     Malawi     Malaysia

Maldives     Mali     Malta     Marshall Islands

Civil flags are shown except where marked thus (*); in these cases, government flags are shown in order to illustrate emblems. Both styles are official national flags.

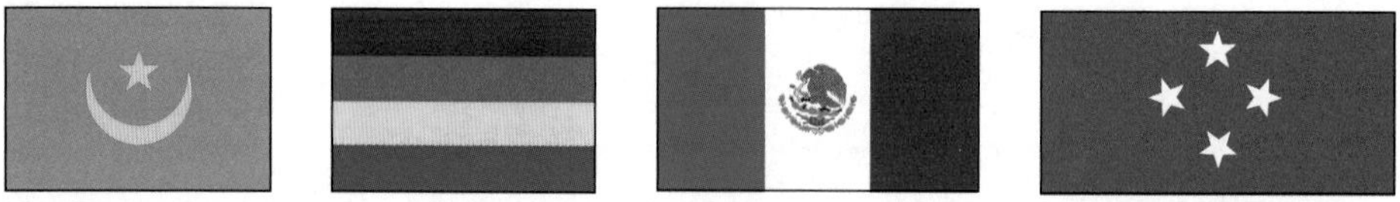

Mauritania

Mauritius

Mexico

Micronesia,
Federated States of

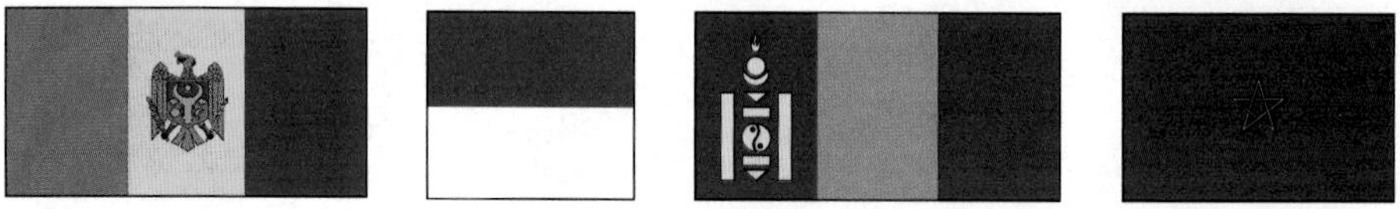

Moldova

Monaco

Mongolia

Morocco

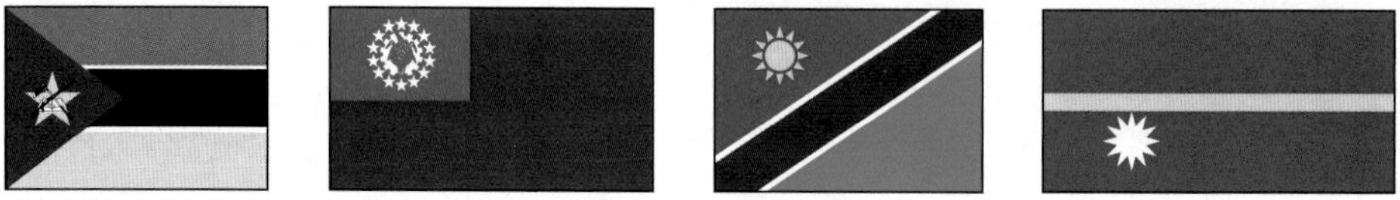

Mozambique

Myanmar

Namibia

Nauru

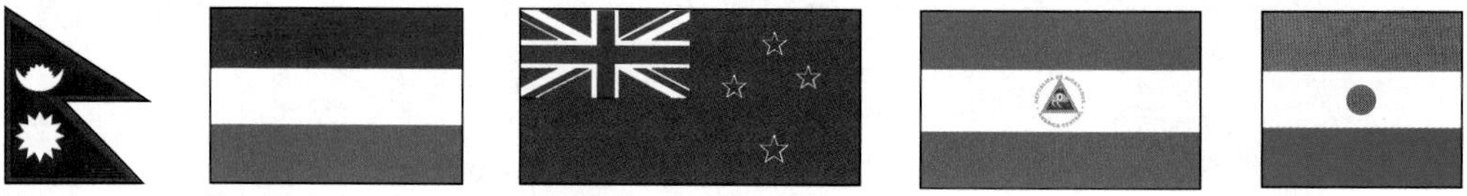

Nepal

The Netherlands

New Zealand

Nicaragua*

Niger

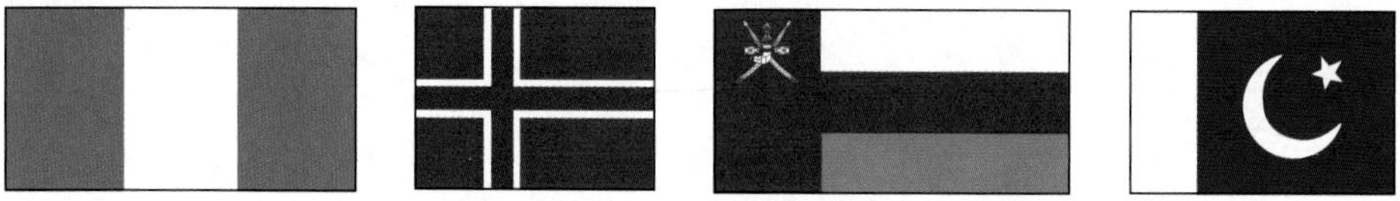

Nigeria

Norway

Oman

Pakistan

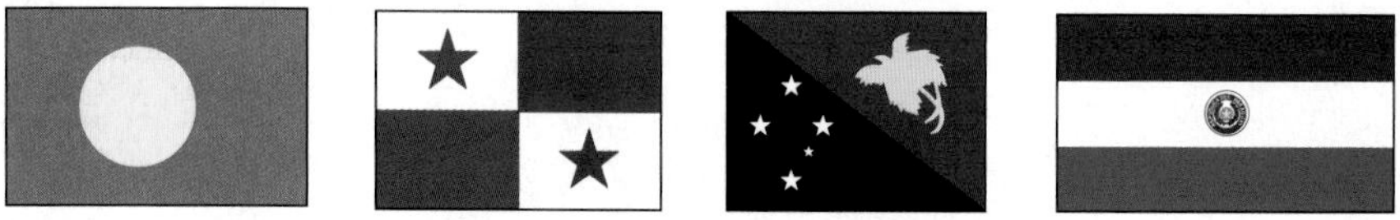

Palau

Panama

Papua New Guinea

Paraguay

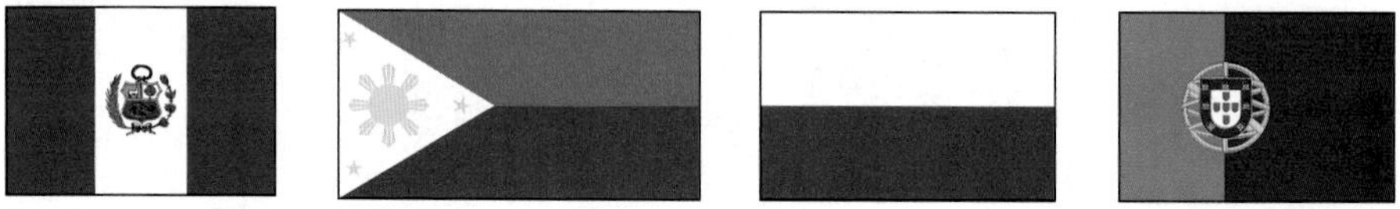

Peru*

Philippines

Poland

Portugal

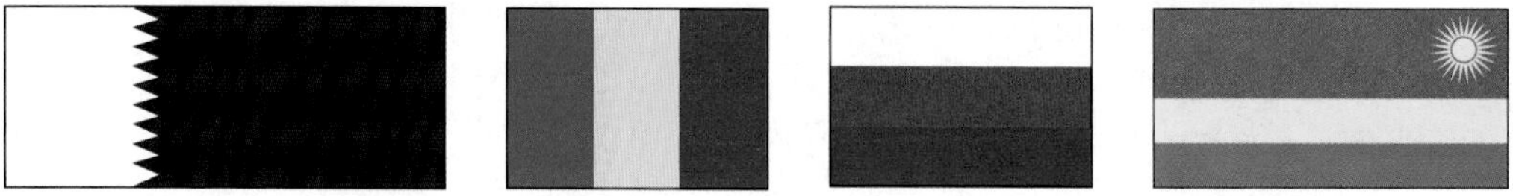

Qatar

Romania

Russia

Rwanda

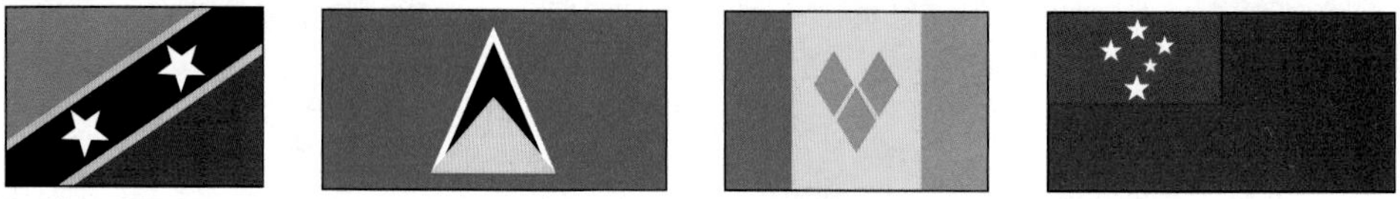

St. Kitts & Nevis

St. Lucia

St. Vincent & the
Grenadines

Samoa

Civil flags are shown except where marked thus (*); in these cases, government flags are shown in order to illustrate emblems. Both styles are official national flags.

San Marino*

São Tomé and Príncipe

Saudi Arabia

Senegal

Serbia and Montenegro

Seychelles

Sierra Leone

Singapore

Slovakia

Slovenia

Solomon Islands

Somalia

South Africa

Spain

Sri Lanka

Sudan

Suriname

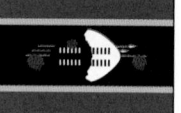
Swaziland

Sweden

Switzerland

Syria

Taiwan

Tajikistan

Tanzania

Thailand

Togo

Tonga

Trinidad & Tobago

Tunisia

Turkey

Turkmenistan

Tuvalu

Uganda

Ukraine

United Arab Emirates

United Kingdom

United States

Civil flags are shown except where marked thus (*); in these cases, government flags are shown in order to illustrate emblems. Both styles are official national flags.

PLATE 6      FLAGS OF THE WORLD

Uruguay

Uzbekistan

Vanuatu

Vatican City

Venezuela*

Vietnam

Yemen

Zambia

Zimbabwe

Civil flags are shown except where marked thus (*); in these cases, government flags are shown in order to illustrate emblems. Both styles are official national flags.

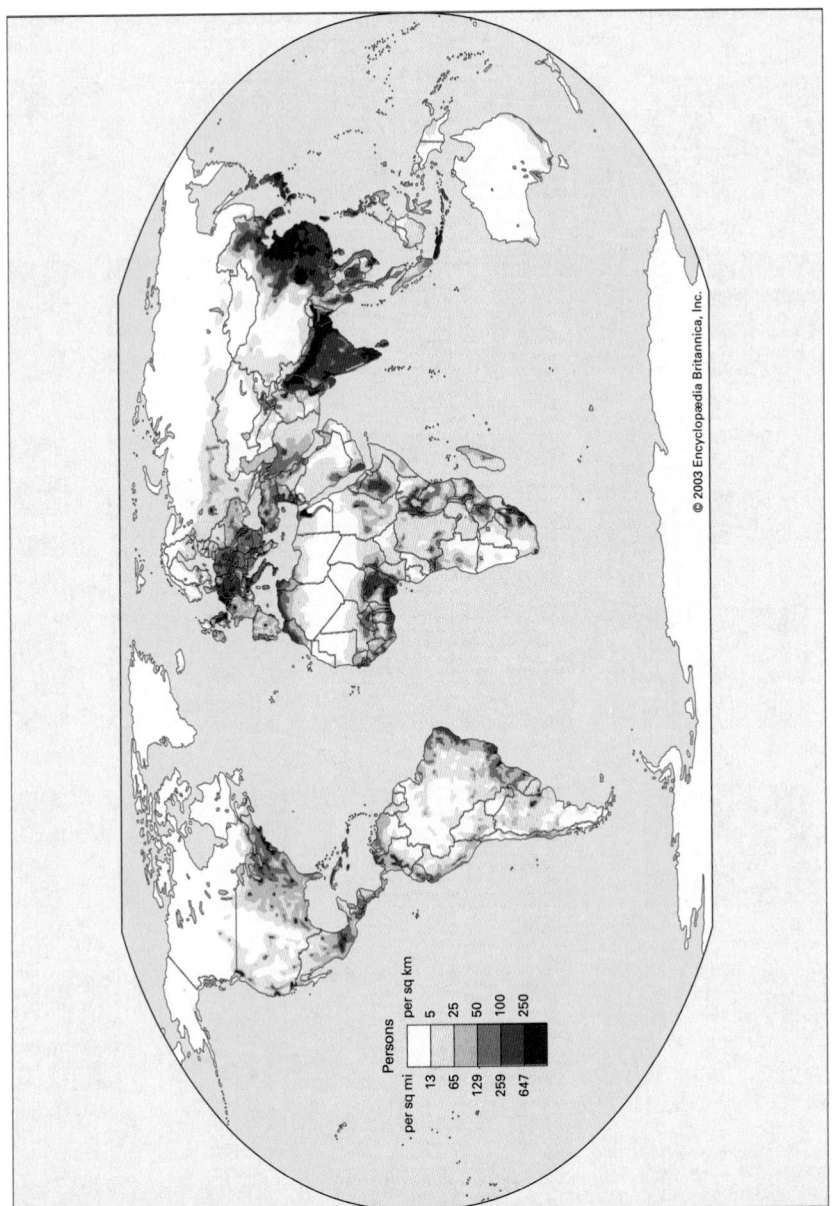

© 2003 Encyclopædia Britannica, Inc.

World Population Density

Persons

per sq mi    per sq km

13    5
65    25
129    50
259    100
647    250

# World Religions

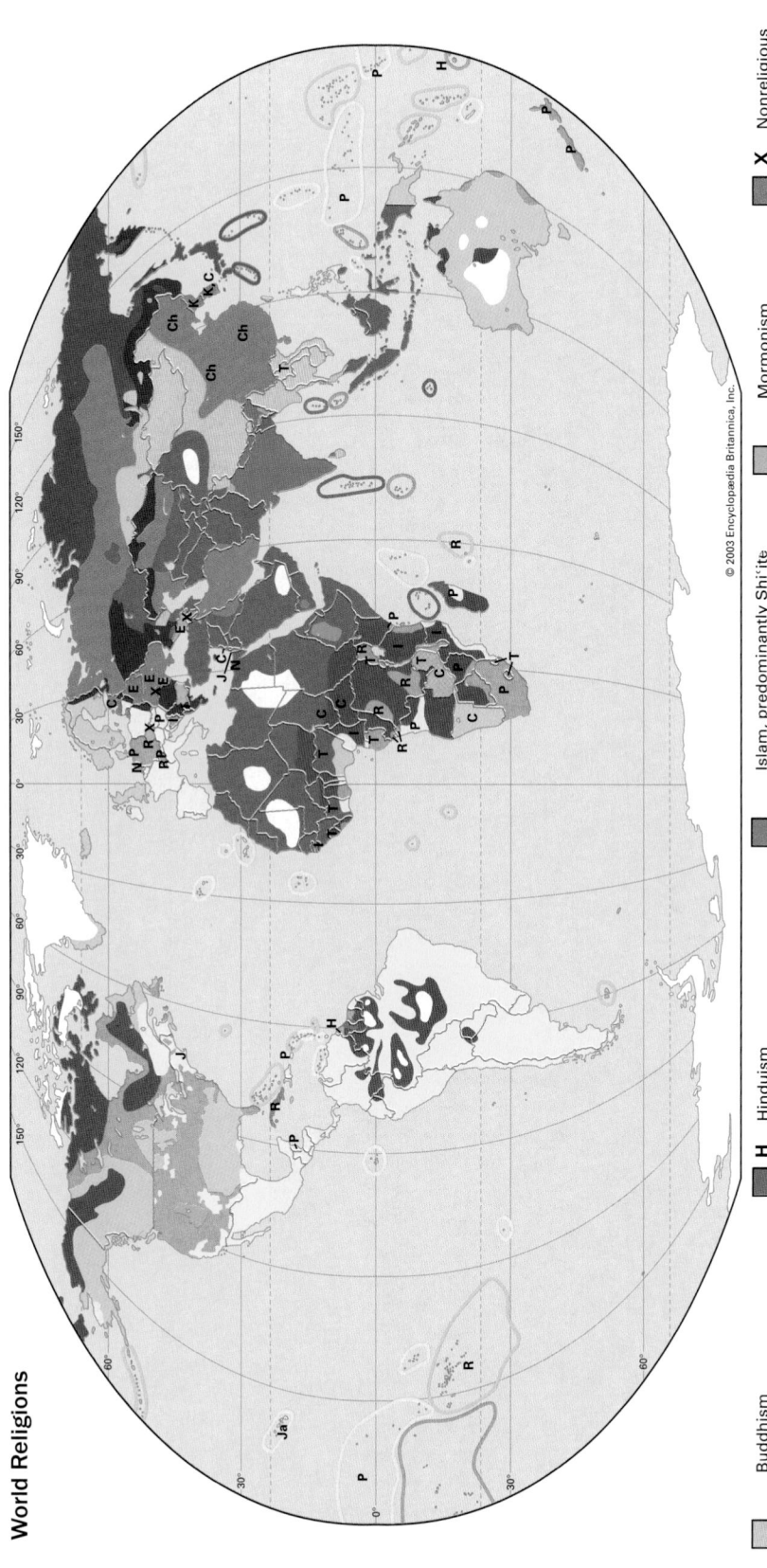

© 2003 Encyclopaedia Britannica, Inc.

Buddhism

**Ch** Chinese religions[1]

**C** Christianity, undifferentiated by branch[2]

**E** Eastern Orthodoxy[3]

**H** Hinduism

**N** Independent churches of Eastern Christianity[4]

**T** Indigenous (tribal) religions

**I** Islam, predominantly Sunni

Islam, predominantly Shi'ite

**Ja** Japanese religions[1]

**J** Judaism

**K** Korean religions[1]

Mormonism

Sikhism

**P** Protestantism

**R** Roman Catholicism

**X** Nonreligious

No dominant religion

Uninhabited

Note:
The majority of the inhabitants in each of the areas colored on the map share the religious tradition indicated. Letter symbols show religious traditions shared by at least 25 percent of the inhabitants within areas no smaller than 1,000 square miles. Therefore minority religions of city dwellers have generally not been represented.

Footnotes:
[1] In certain eastern Asian areas, many of the people have plural religious affiliations. Religions in China and Korea include Buddhism, Taoism, Confucianism, and folk cults. The Japanese religions include Shintō and Buddhism.
[2] Chiefly mingled Protestantism and Roman Catholicism, neither predominant.
[3] Including Greek and Russian Orthodox Christianity.
[4] Including Armenian, Coptic, Ethiopian, East and West Syrian.

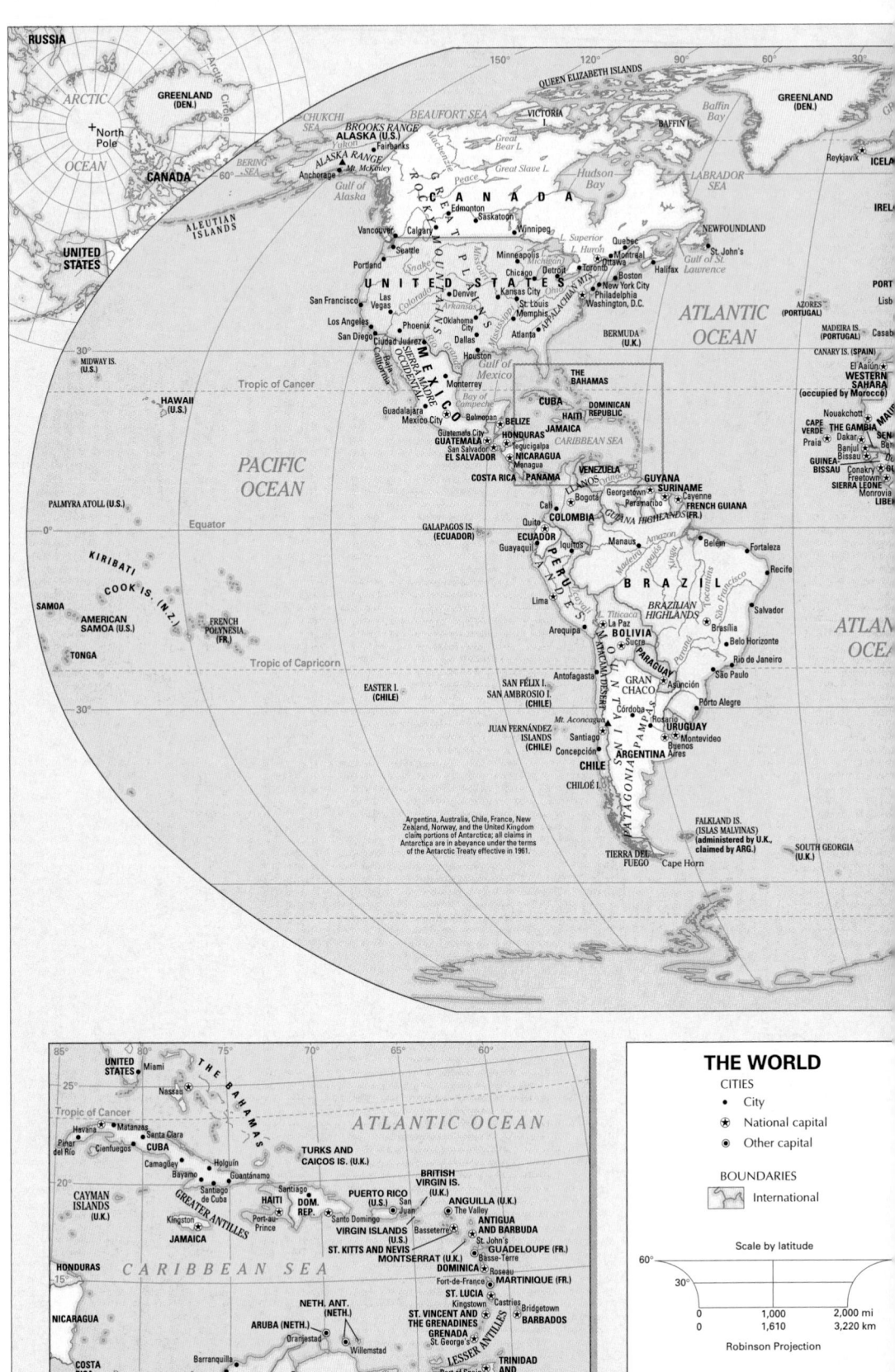

RUSSIA

ARCTIC
OCEAN

GREENLAND
(DEN.)

North Pole

CANADA

UNITED
STATES

QUEEN ELIZABETH ISLANDS

BEAUFORT SEA

VICTORIA I.

BAFFIN I.

Baffin Bay

GREENLAND (DEN.)

Reykjavík  ICELA

CHUKCHI SEA

BROOKS RANGE

ALASKA (U.S.)

Fairbanks

Yukon

Great Bear L.

Mackenzie

Hudson Bay

LABRADOR SEA

IREL

BERING SEA

ALASKA RANGE

Mt. McKinley

Anchorage

Gulf of Alaska

Peace

Great Slave L.

ALEUTIAN ISLANDS

Vancouver  Calgary

Saskatoon

Edmonton

Winnipeg

CANADA

Quebec

NEWFOUNDLAND

St. John's

PORT

Seattle

Portland

GREAT PLAINS

Minneapolis

L. Superior

L. Huron

Montréal

Toronto

Ottawa

Halifax

Gulf of St. Lawrence

AZORES (PORTUGAL)

Lisb

San Francisco

Las Vegas

Denver

Chicago

Detroit

Boston

New York City

Philadelphia

Washington, D.C.

ATLANTIC OCEAN

BERMUDA (U.K.)

MADEIRA IS. (PORTUGAL)

Casab

Los Angeles

Phoenix

Oklahoma City

Kansas City

St. Louis

Memphis

APPALACHIAN MTS.

CANARY IS. (SPAIN)

El Aaiún

San Diego

Ciudad Juárez

Dallas

Atlanta

WESTERN SAHARA (occupied by Morocco)

MIDWAY IS. (U.S.)

Tropic of Cancer

Houston

Gulf of Mexico

THE BAHAMAS

Nouakchott

HAWAII (U.S.)

Guadalajara

Mexico City

Bay of Campeche

CUBA

DOMINICAN REPUBLIC

HAITI

CAPE VERDE

Praia

Dakar

THE GAMBIA

SEN

MAU

Banjul

PACIFIC OCEAN

Belmopan

BELIZE

JAMAICA

GUINEA BISSAU

Bissau

Conakry

Freetown

Guatemala City

San Salvador

GUATEMALA

HONDURAS

Tegucigalpa

CARIBBEAN SEA

SIERRA LEONE

Monrovia

LIBER

EL SALVADOR

NICARAGUA

Managua

VENEZUELA

GUYANA

SURINAME

PALMYRA ATOLL (U.S.)

COSTA RICA

PANAMA

Cali

Bogotá

Georgetown

Paramaribo

Cayenne

FRENCH GUIANA (FR.)

KIRIBATI

Equator

GALAPAGOS IS. (ECUADOR)

Quito

COLOMBIA

LLANOS

GUIANA HIGHLANDS

COOK IS. (N.Z.)

ECUADOR

Iquitos

Manaus

Amazon

Belém

Fortaleza

SAMOA

AMERICAN SAMOA (U.S.)

FRENCH POLYNESIA (FR.)

Guayaquil

Lima

PERU

BRAZIL

Recife

TONGA

Tropic of Capricorn

La Paz

BOLIVIA

Sucre

BRAZILIAN HIGHLANDS

Brasília

Salvador

Belo Horizonte

EASTER I. (CHILE)

SAN FÉLIX I. SAN AMBROSIO I. (CHILE)

Arequipa

Antofagasta

PARAGUAY

GRAN CHACO

Asunción

Rio de Janeiro

São Paulo

Pôrto Alegre

Córdoba

JUAN FERNÁNDEZ ISLANDS (CHILE)

Mt. Aconcagua

Santiago

Concepción

ARGENTINA

Rosario

URUGUAY

Montevideo

Buenos Aires

CHILE

CHILOÉ I.

Argentina, Australia, Chile, France, New Zealand, Norway, and the United Kingdom claim portions of Antarctica; all claims in Antarctica are in abeyance under the terms of the Antarctic Treaty effective in 1961.

PAMPAS

PATAGONIA

FALKLAND IS. (ISLAS MALVINAS) (administered by U.K., claimed by ARG.)

SOUTH GEORGIA (U.K.)

TIERRA DEL FUEGO

Cape Horn

ATLANTIC OCEA

---

UNITED STATES

Miami

THE BAHAMAS

Tropic of Cancer

Nassau

ATLANTIC OCEAN

Havana  Matanzas

Santa Clara

Pinar del Río

Cienfuegos

CUBA

CAYMAN ISLANDS (U.K.)

Camagüey

Bayamo

Holguín

Guantánamo

TURKS AND CAICOS IS. (U.K.)

BRITISH VIRGIN IS. (U.K.)

ANGUILLA (U.K.)

The Valley

Santiago de Cuba

PUERTO RICO (U.S.)

San Juan

HAITI

DOM. REP.

ANTIGUA AND BARBUDA

St. John's

Kingston

Port-au-Prince

Santo Domingo

VIRGIN ISLANDS (U.S.)

Basseterre

GUADELOUPE (FR.)

Basse-Terre

JAMAICA

ST. KITTS AND NEVIS

MONTSERRAT (U.K.)

DOMINICA

Roseau

GREATER ANTILLES

Fort-de-France

MARTINIQUE (FR.)

CARIBBEAN SEA

ST. LUCIA

Castries

HONDURAS

Kingstown

Bridgetown

NETH. ANT. (NETH.)

ST. VINCENT AND THE GRENADINES

BARBADOS

NICARAGUA

ARUBA (NETH.)

Oranjestad

Willemstad

GRENADA

St. George's

LESSER ANTILLES

TRINIDAD AND TOBAGO

COSTA RICA

San José

Barranquilla

Maracaibo

Barquisimeto

Port of Spain

PANAMA

Cartagena

Panama Canal

Panama City

Lake Maracaibo

Caracas

COLOMBIA

VENEZUELA

Orinoco

Ciudad Guayana

---

# THE WORLD

## CITIES

• City

✪ National capital

◉ Other capital

## BOUNDARIES

International

Scale by latitude

60°

30°

0    1,000    2,000 mi

0    1,610    3,220 km

Robinson Projection

© 2003 Encyclopædia Britannica, Inc.

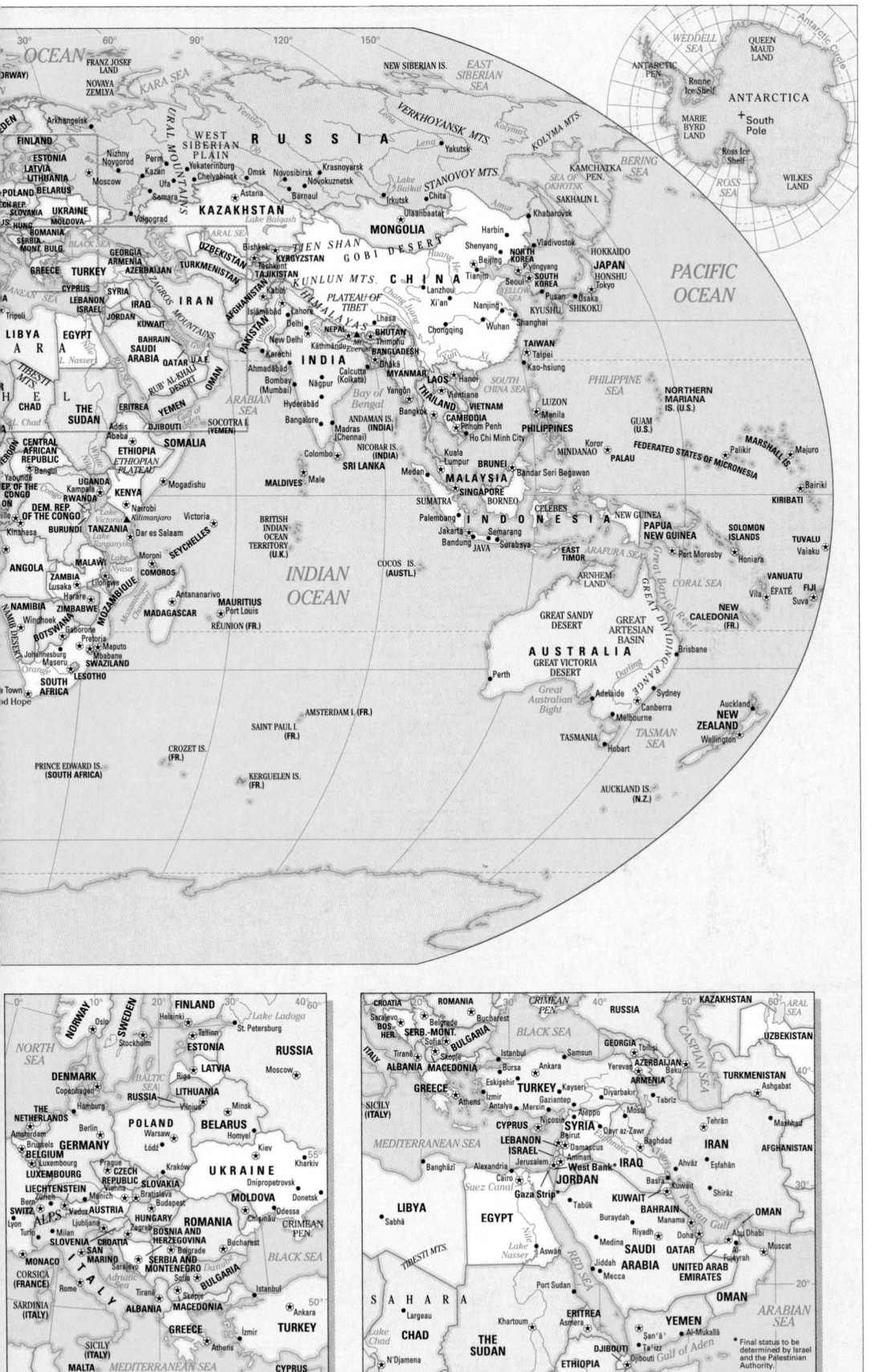

PLATE 10 WORLD MAPS

# Africa

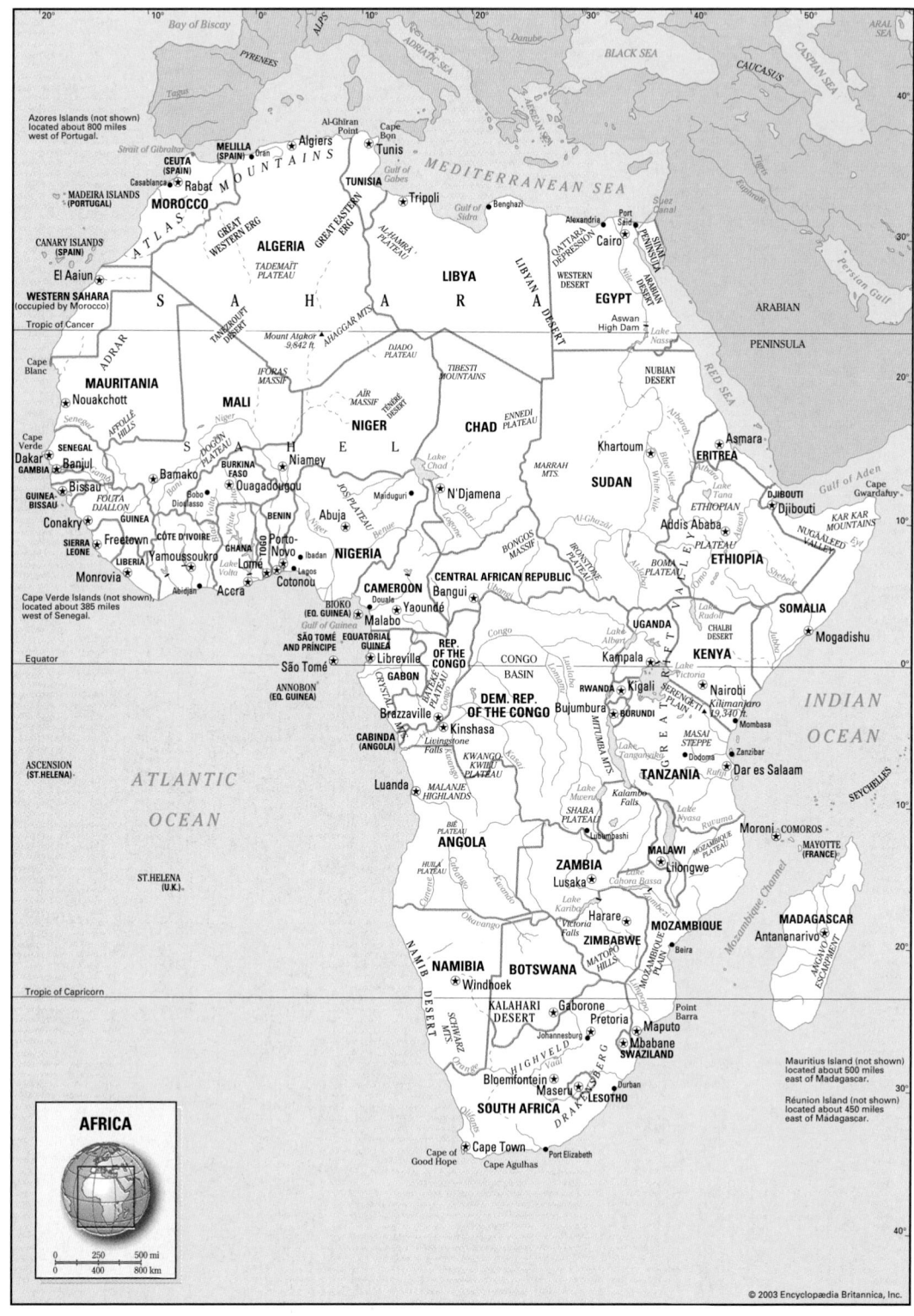

Azores Islands (not shown) located about 800 miles west of Portugal.

MADEIRA ISLANDS (PORTUGAL)

CANARY ISLANDS (SPAIN)

El Aaiun

WESTERN SAHARA (occupied by Morocco)

Tropic of Cancer

Cape Blanc

MAURITANIA
Nouakchott

Cape Verde

SENEGAL
Dakar
GAMBIA Banjul
GUINEA-BISSAU Bissau
Conakry
SIERRA LEONE Freetown
LIBERIA
Monrovia

Cape Verde Islands (not shown), located about 385 miles west of Senegal.

ASCENSION (ST.HELENA)

ATLANTIC

OCEAN

ST.HELENA (U.K.)

Bay of Biscay
PYRENEES
ALPS
ADRIATIC SEA
Danube
BLACK SEA
CAUCASUS
CASPIAN SEA
ARAL SEA

Strait of Gibraltar
MELILLA (SPAIN)
CEUTA (SPAIN)
Casablanca Rabat
MOROCCO
ATLAS MOUNTAINS
Oran
Al-Ghiran Point
Algiers
Cape Bon
Tunis
TUNISIA
Gulf of Gabes
Tripoli

GREAT WESTERN ERG
ALGERIA
GREAT EASTERN ERG
AL-HAMRA PLATEAU

MEDITERRANEAN SEA
Gulf of Sidra
Benghazi
Alexandria
Port Said
Suez Canal
Cairo
QATTARA DEPRESSION
SINAI PENINSULA

ADRAR
TADEMAÏT PLATEAU
S A H A R A
TANEZROUFT DESERT
Mount Atakor 9,842 ft.
AHAGGAR MTS.
IFORAS MASSIF
DJADO PLATEAU

LIBYA
WESTERN DESERT
EGYPT
Aswan High Dam
LIBYAN DESERT
ARABIAN DESERT
Lake Nasser

ARABIAN

PENINSULA

S A H E L
DOGON PLATEAU
AFFOLLÉ HILLS
Senegal
MALI
Niger
AÏR MASSIF
TÉNÉRÉ DESERT
TIBESTI MOUNTAINS
NUBIAN DESERT
RED SEA

MAURITANIA
Bamako
Niamey
NIGER
ENNEDI PLATEAU
CHAD
Khartoum
Asmara
ERITREA

BURKINA FASO
Bobo Dioulasso
Ouagadougou
JOS PLATEAU
Maiduguri
N'Djamena
MARRAH MTS.
SUDAN
Lake Tana
Blue Nile
White Nile
DJIBOUTI Djibouti
Gulf of Aden
Cape Gwardafuy

GUINEA
FOUTA DJALLON
CÔTE D'IVOIRE
GHANA
BENIN
Abuja
Benue
NIGERIA
Al-Ghazal
BONGOS MASSIF
BOUNSTONE PLATEAU
Addis Ababa
ETHIOPIAN PLATEAU
KAR KAR MOUNTAINS
NUGAALEED VALLEY

Yamoussoukro
TOGO Porto-Novo
Ibadan
Lagos
CAMEROON
Douala
Yaoundé
CENTRAL AFRICAN REPUBLIC
Bangui
Ubangi
BOMA PLATEAU
ETHIOPIA

Abidjan Accra
Cotonou
BIOKO (EQ. GUINEA)
Malabo
SÃO TOMÉ AND PRÍNCIPE
EQUATORIAL GUINEA
REP. OF THE CONGO
UGANDA
Lake Albert
CHALBI DESERT
SOMALIA
Mogadishu

Gulf of Guinea
São Tomé
ANNOBON (EQ. GUINEA)
GABON
CRYSTAL
Libreville
Congo
CONGO BASIN
Lake Rudolf
Lake Victoria
KENYA
Kampala

Equator

DEM. REP. OF THE CONGO
Kinshasa
Brazzaville
RWANDA Kigali
Bujumbura
BURUNDI
SERENGETI PLAIN
Nairobi
Kilimanjaro 19,340 ft.
Mombasa

INDIAN

OCEAN

CABINDA (ANGOLA)
Livingstone Falls
KWANGO KWILU PLATEAU
Kasai
MITUMBA MTS.
MASAI STEPPE
Dodoma
Zanzibar
Dar es Salaam
SEYCHELLES

Luanda
MALANJE HIGHLANDS
Lake Mweru
Lake Tanganyika
TANZANIA
Rufiji

BIÉ PLATEAU
SHABA PLATEAU
Kalambo Falls
Moroni COMOROS
MAYOTTE (FRANCE)

ANGOLA
HUÍLA PLATEAU
Cubango
Lubumbashi
Lake Nyasa
MALAWI
Lilongwe
MOZAMBIQUE PLATEAU
MADAGASCAR
Antananarivo

ZAMBIA
Lusaka
Cahora Bassa
MOZAMBIQUE

NAMIB DESERT
Okavango
Lake Kariba
Harare
Victoria Falls
ZIMBABWE
Beira
MOZAMBIQUE PLAIN
Mozambique Channel

Cunene
NAMIBIA
BOTSWANA
Windhoek
MATOPO HILLS
ANGANO ESCARPMENT

Tropic of Capricorn

SCHWARZ MTS.
KALAHARI DESERT
Gaborone
Point Barra
Mauritius Island (not shown) located about 500 miles east of Madagascar.

Orange
Johannesburg
Pretoria
Maputo
Mbabane
SWAZILAND
Réunion Island (not shown) located about 450 miles east of Madagascar.

HIGHVELD
Vaal
Bloemfontein
Maseru LESOTHO
Durban
DRAKENSBERG

SOUTH AFRICA
Cape of Good Hope
Cape Town
Cape Agulhas
Port Elizabeth

AFRICA

0   250   500 mi
0   400   800 km

© 2003 Encyclopædia Britannica, Inc.

# Asia

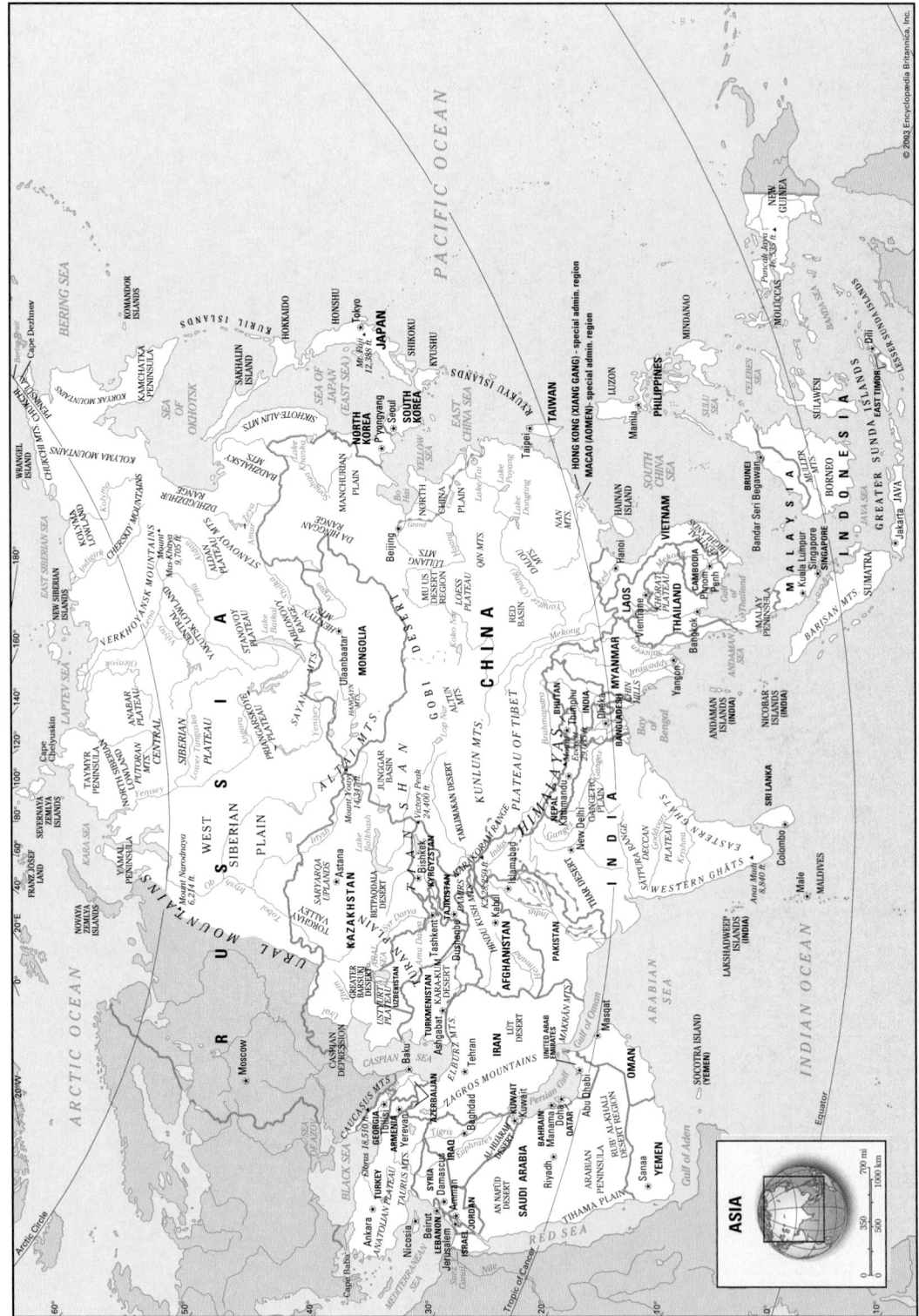

PLATE 12

# WORLD MAPS

## Europe

© 2003 Encyclopædia Britannica, Inc.

EUROPE

## North America

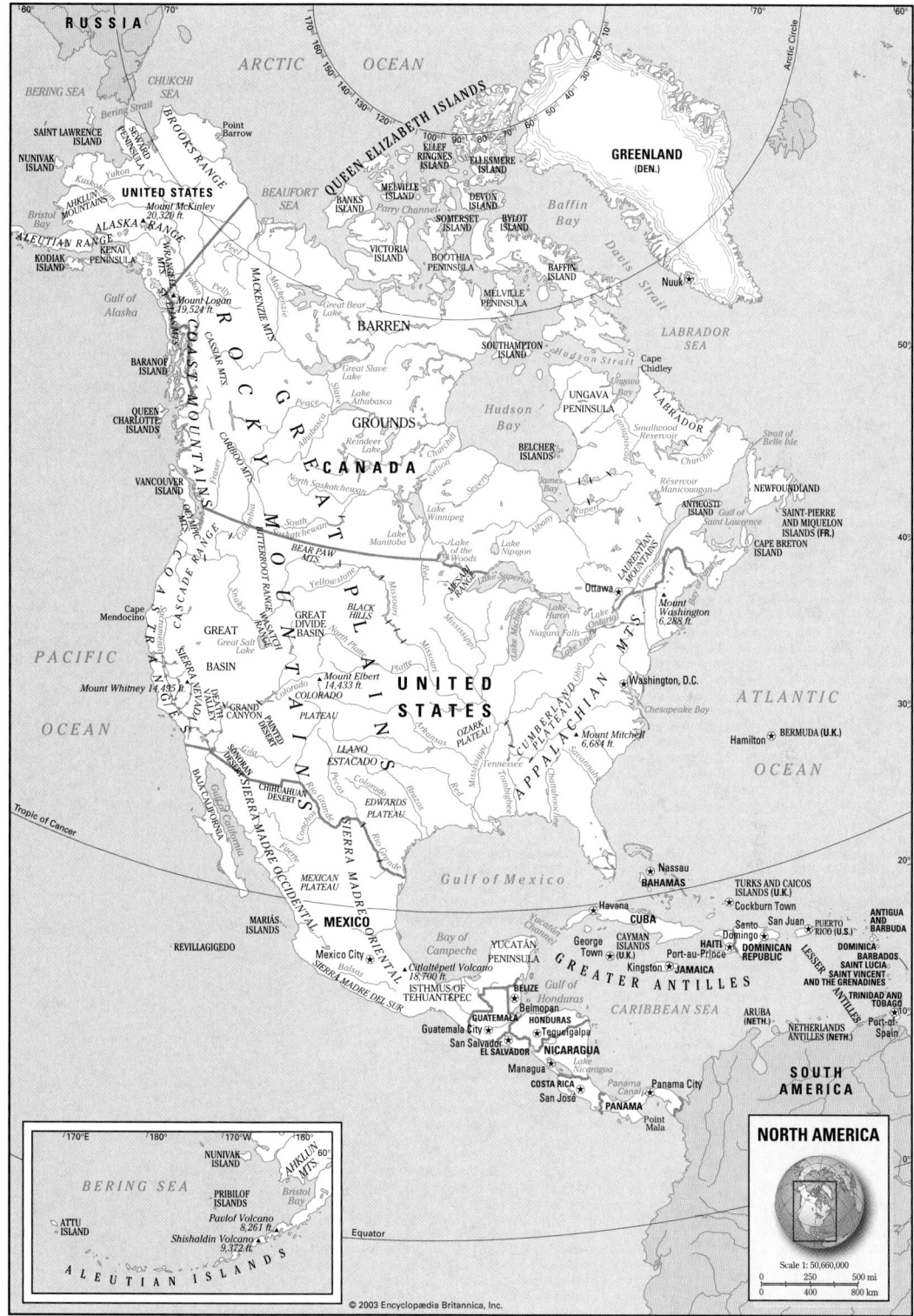

NORTH AMERICA

Scale 1: 50,660,000

0     250     500 mi
0     400     800 km

PLATE 14                    WORLD MAPS

## South America

## Australia

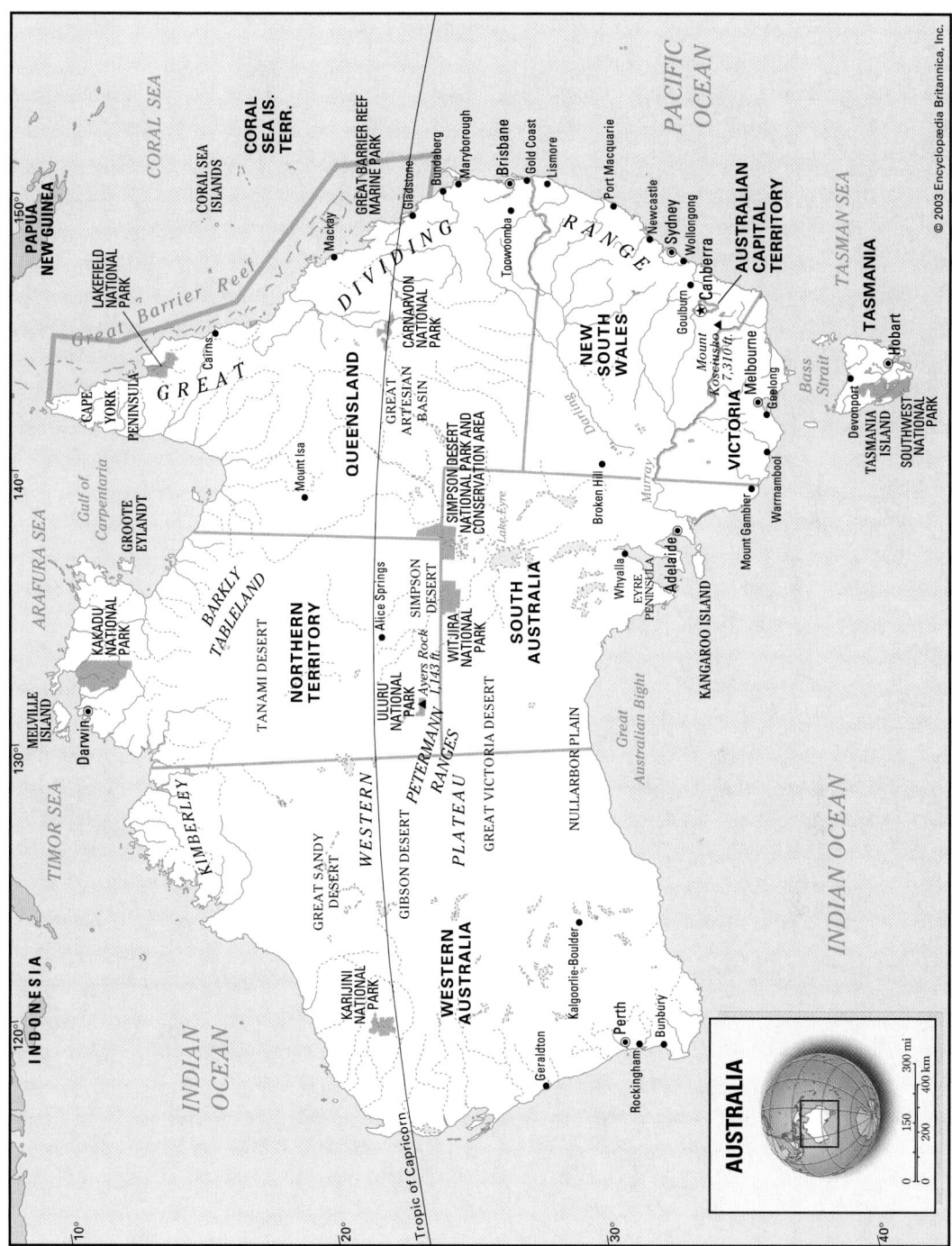

PLATE 16

# WORLD MAPS

## Oceania/Pacific Islands

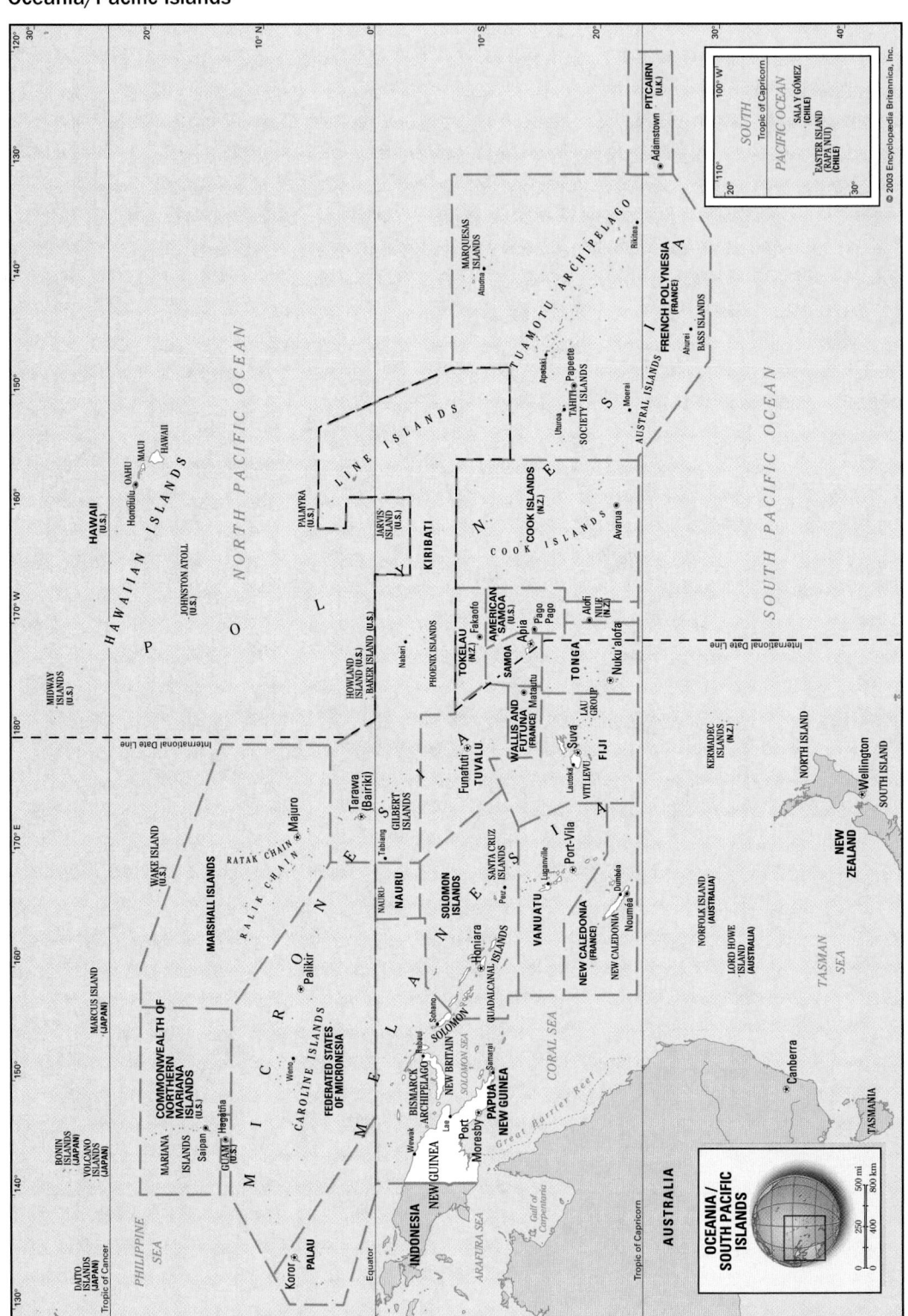

# Winter Olympic Games Champions (continued)

## Alpine Skiing (women) (continued)

**GIANT SLALOM** — MIN:SEC

| | | |
|---|---|---|
| 1960 | Yvonne Rüegg (SUI) | 1:39.9 |
| 1964 | Marielle Goitschel (FRA) | 1:52.24[1] |
| 1968 | Nancy Greene (CAN) | 1:51.97 |
| 1972 | Marie-Thérèse Nadig (SUI) | 1:29.90 |
| 1976 | Kathy Kreiner (CAN) | 1:29.13 |
| 1980 | Hanni Wenzel (LIE) | 2:41.66 |
| 1984 | Debbie Armstrong (USA) | 2:20.98 |
| 1988 | Vreni Schneider (SUI) | 2:06.49 |
| 1992 | Pernilla Wiberg (SWE) | 2:12.74 |
| 1994 | Deborah Compagnoni (ITA) | 2:30.97 |
| 1998 | Deborah Compagnoni (ITA) | 2:50.59 |
| 2002 | Janica Kostelic (CRO) | 2:30.01 |

**SUPERGIANT SLALOM** — MIN:SEC

| | | |
|---|---|---|
| 1988 | Sigrid Wolf (AUT) | 1:19.03 |
| 1992 | Deborah Compagnoni (ITA) | 1:21.22 |
| 1994 | Diann Roffe-Steinrotter (USA) | 1:22.15 |
| 1998 | Picabo Street (USA) | 1:18.02 |
| 2002 | Daniela Ceccarelli (ITA) | 1:13.59 |

**ALPINE COMBINED** — MIN:SEC

| | | |
|---|---|---|
| 1936 | Chrislt Cranz (GER) | |
| 1948 | Trude Beiser (AUT) | |
| 1972 | Annemarie Pröll (AUT) | |
| 1976 | Rosi Mittermaier (FRG) | |
| 1988 | Anita Wachter (AUT) | |
| 1992 | Petra Kronberger (AUT) | |
| 1994 | Pernilla Wiberg (SWE) | 3:05.16[6] |
| 1998 | Katja Seizinger (GER) | 2:40.74 |
| 2002 | Janica Kostelic (CRO) | 2:43.28 |

### Freestyle Skiing

**MEN'S MOGULS**

| | |
|---|---|
| 1992 | Edgar Grospiron (FRA) |
| 1994 | Jean-Luc Brassard (CAN) |
| 1998 | Jonny Moseley (USA) |
| 2002 | Janne Lahtela (FIN) |

**MEN'S AERIALS**

| | |
|---|---|
| 1994 | Andreas Schönbächler (SUI) |
| 1998 | Eric Bergoust (USA) |
| 2002 | Ales Valenta (CZE) |

**WOMEN'S MOGULS**

| | |
|---|---|
| 1992 | Donna Weinbrecht (USA) |
| 1994 | Stine Lise Hattestad (NOR) |
| 1998 | Tae Satoya (JPN) |
| 2002 | Kari Traa (NOR) |

**WOMEN'S AERIALS**

| | |
|---|---|
| 1994 | Lina Cheryazova (UZB) |
| 1998 | Nikki Stone (USA) |
| 2002 | Alisa Camplin (AUS) |

### Nordic Skiing (men)

**1.5-KILOMETER CROSS-COUNTRY SPRINT** — MIN:SEC

| | | |
|---|---|---|
| 2002 | Tor Arne Hetland (NOR) | 2:56.9 |

**10-KILOMETER CROSS-COUNTRY** — MIN:SEC

| | | |
|---|---|---|
| 1992 | Vegard Ulvang (NOR) | 27:36.0 |
| 1994 | Bjørn Daehlie (NOR) | 24:20.1 |
| 1998 | Bjørn Daehlie (NOR) | 27:24.5 |

**15-KILOMETER CROSS-COUNTRY[7]** — HR:MIN:SEC

| | | |
|---|---|---|
| 1924 | Thorleif Haug (NOR) | 1:14:31.0 |
| 1928 | Johan Gröttumsbraaten (NOR) | 1:37:01.0 |
| 1932 | Sven Utterström (SWE) | 1:23:07.0 |

## Nordic Skiing (men) (continued)

**15-KILOMETER CROSS-COUNTRY[7]** — HR:MIN:SEC

| | | |
|---|---|---|
| 1936 | Erik-August Larsson (SWE) | 1:14:38.0 |
| 1948 | Martin Lundström (SWE) | 1:13:50.0 |
| 1952 | Hallgeir Brenden (NOR) | 1:01:34.0 |
| 1956 | Hallgeir Brenden (NOR) | 49:39.0 |
| 1960 | Hakkon Brusveen (NOR) | 51:55.5 |
| 1964 | Eero Mäntyranta (FIN) | 50:54.1 |
| 1968 | Harald Grönningen (NOR) | 47:54.2 |
| 1972 | Sven-Ake Lundbäck (SWE) | 45:28.24[1] |
| 1976 | Nikolay Bazhukov (URS) | 43:58.47 |
| 1980 | Thomas Wassberg (SWE) | 41:57.63 |
| 1984 | Gunde Svan (SWE) | 41:25.60 |
| 1988 | Mikhail Devyatyarov (URS) | 41:18.9 |
| 1998 | Thomas Alsgaard (NOR) | 39:13.7 |
| 2002 | Andrus Veerpalu (EST) | 37:07.4 |

**COMBINED PURSUIT[8]** — HR:MIN:SEC

| | | |
|---|---|---|
| 1992 | Bjørn Daehlie (NOR) | 1:05:37.9 |
| 1994 | Bjørn Daehlie (NOR) | 1:00:08.8 |
| 1998 | Thomas Alsgaard (NOR) | 1:07:01.7 |
| 2002 | Johann Mühlegg (ESP) | 49:20.4 |

**30-KILOMETER CROSS-COUNTRY** — HR:MIN:SEC

| | | |
|---|---|---|
| 1956 | Veikko Hakulinen (FIN) | 1:44:06.0 |
| 1960 | Sixten Jernberg (SWE) | 1:51:03.9 |
| 1964 | Eero Mäntyranta (FIN) | 1:30:50.7 |
| 1968 | Franco Nones (ITA) | 1:35:39.2 |
| 1972 | Vyacheslav Vedenin (URS) | 1:36:31.15[1] |
| 1976 | Sergey Savelyev (URS) | 1:30:29.38 |
| 1980 | Nikolay Zimyatov (URS) | 1:27:02.80 |
| 1984 | Nikolay Zimyatov (URS) | 1:28:56.30 |
| 1988 | Aleksey Prokourorov (URS) | 1:24:26.3 |
| 1992 | Vegard Ulvang (NOR) | 1:22:27.8 |
| 1994 | Thomas Alsgaard (NOR) | 1:12:26.4 |
| 1998 | Mika Myllylä (FIN) | 1:33:56.0 |
| 2002 | Johann Mühlegg (ESP) | 1:09:28.9 |

**50-KILOMETER CROSS-COUNTRY** — HR:MIN:SEC

| | | |
|---|---|---|
| 1924 | Thorleif Haug (NOR) | 3:44:32.0 |
| 1928 | Per Erik Hedlund (SWE) | 4:52:03.3 |
| 1932 | Veli Saarinen (FIN) | 4:28:00.0 |
| 1936 | Elis Viklund (SWE) | 3:30:11.0 |
| 1948 | Nils Karlsson (SWE) | 3:47:48.0 |
| 1952 | Veikko Hakulinen (FIN) | 3:33:33.0 |
| 1956 | Sixten Jernberg (SWE) | 2:50:27.0 |
| 1960 | Kalevi Hämäläinen (FIN) | 2:59:06.3 |
| 1964 | Sixten Jernberg (SWE) | 2:43:52.6 |
| 1968 | Olle Ellefsäter (NOR) | 2:28:45.8 |
| 1972 | Pål Tyldum (NOR) | 2:43:14.75[1] |
| 1976 | Ivar Formo (NOR) | 2:37:30.05 |
| 1980 | Nikolay Zimyatov (URS) | 2:27:24.60 |
| 1984 | Thomas Wassberg (SWE) | 2:15:55.80 |
| 1988 | Gunde Svan (SWE) | 2:04:30.9 |
| 1992 | Bjørn Daehlie (NOR) | 2:03:41.5 |
| 1994 | Vladimir Smirnov (KAZ) | 2:07:20.3 |
| 1998 | Bjørn Daehlie (NOR) | 2:05:08.2 |
| 2002 | Mikhail Ivanov (RUS)[9] | 2:06:20.8 |

**4 × 10-KILOMETER RELAY** — HR:MIN:SEC

| | | |
|---|---|---|
| 1936 | Finland | 2:41:33.0 |
| 1948 | Sweden | 2:32:08.0 |
| 1952 | Finland | 2:20:16.0 |
| 1956 | USSR | 2:15:30.0 |
| 1960 | Finland | 2:18:45.6 |
| 1964 | Sweden | 2:18:34.6 |
| 1968 | Norway | 2:08:33.5 |
| 1972 | USSR | 2:04:47.94[1] |
| 1976 | Finland | 2:07:59.72 |

# Winter Olympic Games Champions (continued)

## Nordic Skiing (men) (continued)

### 4 × 10-KILOMETER RELAY

| | | HR:MIN:SEC |
|---|---|---|
| 1980 | USSR | 1:57:03.46 |
| 1984 | Sweden | 1:55:06.30 |
| 1988 | Sweden | 1:43:58.6 |
| 1992 | Norway | 1:39:26.0 |
| 1994 | Italy | 1:41:15.0 |
| 1998 | Norway | 1:40:55.7 |
| 2002 | Norway | 1:32:45.5 |

### SKI JUMPING (70 M)[10]

| | |
|---|---|
| 1924 | Jacob Tullin Thams (NOR) |
| 1928 | Alf Andersen (NOR) |
| 1932 | Birger Ruud (NOR) |
| 1936 | Birger Ruud (NOR) |
| 1948 | Petter Hugsted (NOR) |
| 1952 | Arnfinn Bergmann (NOR) |
| 1956 | Antti Hyvärinen (FIN) |
| 1960 | Helmut Recknagel (GER)[4] |
| 1964 | Veikko Kankkonen (FIN) |
| 1968 | Jiri Raska (TCH) |
| 1972 | Yukio Kasaya (JPN) |
| 1976 | Hans-Georg Aschenbach (GDR) |
| 1980 | Toni Innauer (AUT) |
| 1984 | Jens Weissflog (GDR) |
| 1988 | Matti Nykänen (FIN) |

### SKI JUMPING (90 M)[10]

| | |
|---|---|
| 1964 | Toralf Engan (NOR) |
| 1968 | Vladimir Belousov (URS) |
| 1972 | Wojciech Fortuna (POL) |
| 1976 | Karl Schnabl (AUT) |
| 1980 | Jens Tormanen (FIN) |
| 1984 | Matti Nykänen (FIN) |
| 1988 | Matti Nykänen (FIN) |
| 1992 | Ernst Vettori (AUT) |
| 1994 | Espen Bredesen (NOR) |
| 1998 | Jani Soininen (FIN) |
| 2002 | Simon Ammann (SUI) |

### SKI JUMPING (120 M)[10]

| | |
|---|---|
| 1992 | Toni Nieminen (FIN) |
| 1994 | Jens Weissflog (GER) |
| 1998 | Kazuyoshi Funaki (JPN) |
| 2002 | Simon Ammann (SUI) |

### NORDIC COMBINED SPRINT (7.5 KILOMETERS) AND JUMPING

| | |
|---|---|
| 2002 | Samppa Lajunen (FIN) |

### NORDIC COMBINED 15 KILOMETERS AND JUMPING

| | |
|---|---|
| 1924 | Thorleif Haug (NOR) |
| 1928 | Johan Gröttumsbraaten (NOR) |
| 1932 | Johan Gröttumsbraaten (NOR) |
| 1936 | Oddbjörn Hagen (NOR) |
| 1948 | Heikki Hasu (NOR) |
| 1952 | Simon Slåttvik (NOR) |
| 1956 | Sverre Stenersen (NOR) |
| 1960 | Georg Thoma (GER)[4] |
| 1964 | Tormod Knutsen (NOR) |
| 1968 | Franz Keller (FRG) |
| 1972 | Ulrich Wehling (GDR) |
| 1976 | Ulrich Wehling (GDR) |
| 1980 | Ulrich Wehling (GDR) |
| 1984 | Tom Sandberg (NOR) |
| 1988 | Hippolyt Kempf (SUI) |
| 1992 | Fabrice Guy (FRA) |
| 1994 | Fred Börre Lundberg (NOR) |
| 1998 | Bjarte Engen Vik (NOR) |
| 2002 | Samppa Lajunen (FIN) |

## Nordic Skiing (men) (continued)

### TEAM SKI JUMPING (120 M)

| | |
|---|---|
| 1988 | Finland (90-m event) |
| 1992 | Finland |
| 1994 | Germany |
| 1998 | Japan |
| 2002 | Germany |

### NORDIC COMBINED 30-KILOMETER RELAY AND JUMPING (TEAM)

| | |
|---|---|
| 1988 | West Germany |
| 1992 | Japan |
| 1994 | Japan |
| 1998 | Norway |
| 2002 | Finland |

## Nordic Skiing (women)

### 1.5-KILOMETER CROSS-COUNTRY SPRINT

| | | MIN:SEC |
|---|---|---|
| 2002 | Yuliya Chepalova (RUS) | 3:10.6 |

### 5-KILOMETER CROSS-COUNTRY

| | | MIN:SEC |
|---|---|---|
| 1964 | Klavdia Boyarskikh (URS) | 17:50.5 |
| 1968 | Toini Gustafsson (SWE) | 16:45.2 |
| 1972 | Galina Kulakova (URS) | 17:00.50[1] |
| 1976 | Helena Takalo (FIN) | 15:48.69 |
| 1980 | Raisa Smetanina (URS) | 15:06.92 |
| 1984 | Marja-Liisa Hämäläinen (FIN) | 17:04.00 |
| 1988 | Marjo Matikainen (FIN) | 15:04.00 |
| 1992 | Marjut Lukkarinen (FIN) | 14:13.8 |
| 1994 | Lyubov Yegorova (RUS) | 14:08.8 |
| 1998 | Larisa Lazutina (RUS) | 17:39.9 |

### 10-KILOMETER CROSS-COUNTRY

| | | MIN:SEC |
|---|---|---|
| 1952 | Lydia Wideman (FIN) | 41:40.0 |
| 1956 | Lyubov Kozyreva (URS) | 38:11.0 |
| 1960 | Mariya Gusakova (URS) | 39:46.6 |
| 1964 | Klavdia Boyarskikh (URS) | 40:24.3 |
| 1968 | Toini Gustafsson (SWE) | 36:46.5 |
| 1972 | Galina Kulakova (URS) | 34:17.82[1] |
| 1976 | Raisa Smetanina (URS) | 30:13.41 |
| 1980 | Barbara Petzold (GDR) | 30:31.54 |
| 1984 | Marja-Liisa Hämäläinen (FIN) | 31:44.20 |
| 1988 | Vida Ventsene (URS) | 30:08.30 |
| 1998 | Larisa Lazutina (RUS) | 46:06.9 |
| 2002 | Bente Skari (NOR) | 28:05.6 |

### COMBINED PURSUIT[11]

| | | MIN:SEC |
|---|---|---|
| 1992 | Lyubov Yegorova (UNT)[2] | 40:08.4 |
| 1994 | Lyubov Yegorova (RUS) | 41:38.1 |
| 1998 | Larisa Lazutina (RUS) | 46:06.9 |
| 2002 | Olga Danilova (RUS) | 24:52.1 |

### 15-KILOMETER CROSS-COUNTRY

| | | MIN:SEC |
|---|---|---|
| 1992 | Lyubov Yegorova (UNT)[2] | 42:20.8 |
| 1994 | Manuela di Centa (ITA) | 39:44.5 |
| 1998 | Olga Danilova (RUS) | 46:55.40 |
| 2002 | Stefania Belmondo (ITA) | 39:54.4 |

### 20-KILOMETER CROSS-COUNTRY

| | | HR:MIN:SEC |
|---|---|---|
| 1984 | Marja-Liisa Hämäläinen (FIN) | 1:01:45.0 |
| 1988 | Tamara Tikhonova (URS) | 55:53.6 |

### 30-KILOMETER CROSS-COUNTRY

| | | HR:MIN:SEC |
|---|---|---|
| 1992 | Stefania Belmondo (ITA) | 1:22:30.1 |
| 1994 | Manuela di Centa (ITA) | 1:25:41.6 |
| 1998 | Yuliya Chepalova (RUS) | 1:22:01.5 |
| 2002 | Gabriella Paruzzi (ITA)[9] | 1:30:57.1 |

# Winter Olympic Games Champions (continued)

## Nordic Skiing (women) (continued)

| 4 × 5-KILOMETER RELAY | | HR:MIN:SEC |
|---|---|---|
| 2002 | Germany | 49:30.6 |

## Sled-dog Race

| | | |
|---|---|---|
| 1932 | Emile St.Goddard (CAN) | |

## Snowboarding

### GIANT SLALOM—MEN

| | |
|---|---|
| 1998 | Ross Rebagliati (CAN) |
| 2002 | Philipp Schoch (SUI) |

### GIANT SLALOM—WOMEN

| | |
|---|---|
| 1998 | Karine Ruby (FRA) |
| 2002 | Isabelle Blanc (FRA) |

### HALFPIPE—MEN

| | |
|---|---|
| 1998 | Gian Simmen (SUI) |
| 2002 | Ross Powers (USA) |

### HALFPIPE—WOMEN

| | |
|---|---|
| 1998 | Nicola Thost (GER) |
| 2002 | Kelly Clark (USA) |

## Speed Skating (men)

| 4 × 5-KILOMETER RELAY[12] | | HR:MIN:SEC |
|---|---|---|
| 1956 | Finland | 1:09:01.0 |
| 1960 | Sweden | 1:04:21.4 |
| 1964 | USSR | 59:20.2 |
| 1968 | Norway | 57:30.0 |
| 1972 | USSR | 48:46.15[1] |
| 1976 | USSR | 1:07:49.75 |
| 1980 | East Germany | 1:02:11.10 |
| 1984 | Norway | 1:06:49.70 |
| 1988 | USSR | 59:51.10 |
| 1992 | Unified Team[2] | 59:34.8 |
| 1994 | Russia | 57:12.5 |

| 500 METERS | | SEC |
|---|---|---|
| 1924 | Charles Jewtraw (USA) | 44.0 |
| 1928 | Clas Thunberg; Bernt Evensen (tied) (FIN; NOR) | 43.4 |
| 1932 | John Shea (USA) | 43.4 |
| 1936 | Ivar Ballangrud (NOR) | 43.4 |
| 1948 | Finn Helgesen (NOR) | 43.1 |
| 1952 | Kenneth Henry (USA) | 43.2 |
| 1956 | Yevgeny Grishin (URS) | 40.2 |
| 1960 | Yevgeny Grishin (URS) | 40.2 |
| 1964 | Richard McDermott (USA) | 40.1 |
| 1968 | Erhard Keller (FRG) | 40.3 |
| 1972 | Erhard Keller (FRG) | 39.44[1] |
| 1976 | Yevgeny Kulikov (URS) | 39.17 |
| 1980 | Eric Heiden (USA) | 38.03 |
| 1984 | Sergey Fokichev (URS) | 38.19 |
| 1988 | Uew-Jens Mey (GDR) | 36.45 |
| 1992 | Uew-Jens Mey (GER) | 37.14 |
| 1994 | Aleksandr Golubyov (RUS) | 36.33 |
| 1998 | Hiroyasu Shimizu (JPN) | 71.35[13] |
| 2002 | Casey Fitzrandolph (USA) | 69.23[13] |

| 1,000 METERS | | MIN:SEC |
|---|---|---|
| 1976 | Peter Mueller (USA) | 1:19.32[1] |
| 1980 | Eric Heiden (USA) | 1:15.18 |
| 1984 | Gaetan Boucher (CAN) | 1:15.80 |
| 1988 | Nikolay Gulyayev (URS) | 1:13.03 |
| 1992 | Olaf Zinke (GER) | 1:14.85 |
| 1994 | Dan Jansen (USA) | 1:12.43 |
| 1998 | Ids Postma (NED) | 1:10.71 |
| 2002 | Gerard van Velde (NED) | 1:07.18 |

## Speed Skating (men) (continued)

| 1,500 METERS | | MIN:SEC |
|---|---|---|
| 1924 | Clas Thunberg (FIN) | 2:20.8 |
| 1928 | Clas Thunberg (FIN) | 2:21.1 |
| 1932 | John Shea (USA) | 2:57.5 |
| 1936 | Charles Mathisen (NOR) | 2:19.2 |
| 1948 | Sverre Farstad (NOR) | 2:17.6 |
| 1952 | Hjalmar Andersen (NOR) | 2:20.4 |
| 1956 | Yury Mikhaylov; Yevgeny Grishin (tied) (URS; URS) | 2:08.6 |
| 1960 | Yevegeny Grishin; Roald Aas (tied) (URS; NOR) | 2:10.4 |
| 1964 | Ants Antson (URS) | 2:10.3 |
| 1968 | Cornelis Verkerk (NED) | 2:03.4 |
| 1972 | Ard Schenk (NED) | 2:02.96[1] |
| 1976 | Jan Egil Storholt (NOR) | 1:59.38 |
| 1980 | Eric Heiden (USA) | 1:55.44 |
| 1984 | Gaetan Boucher (CAN) | 1:58.36 |
| 1988 | André Hoffmann (GDR) | 1:52.06 |
| 1992 | Johann Olav Koss (NOR) | 1:54.81 |
| 1994 | Johann Olav Koss (NOR) | 1:51.29 |
| 1998 | Aadne Sondral (NOR) | 1:47.87 |
| 2002 | Derek Parra (USA) | 1:43.95 |

| 5,000 METERS | | MIN:SEC |
|---|---|---|
| 1924 | Clas Thunberg (FIN) | 8:39.0 |
| 1928 | Ivar Ballangrud (NOR) | 8:50.5 |
| 1932 | Irving Jaffee (USA) | 9:40.8 |
| 1936 | Ivar Ballangrud (NOR) | 8:19.6 |
| 1948 | Reidar Liaklev (NOR) | 8:29.4 |
| 1952 | Hjalmar Andersen (NOR) | 8:10.6 |
| 1956 | Boris Shilkov (URS) | 7:48.7 |
| 1960 | Viktor Kosichkin (URS) | 7:51.3 |
| 1964 | Knut Johannesen (NOR) | 7:38.4 |
| 1968 | Fred Anton Maier (NOR) | 7:22.4 |
| 1972 | Ard Schenk (NED) | 7:23.61[1] |
| 1976 | Sten Stensen (NOR) | 7:24.48 |
| 1980 | Eric Heiden (USA) | 7:02.29 |
| 1984 | Thomas Gustafson (SWE) | 7:12.28 |
| 1988 | Thomas Gustafson (SWE) | 6:44.63 |
| 1992 | Geir Karlstad (NOR) | 6:59.97 |
| 1994 | Johann Olav Koss (NOR) | 6:34.96 |
| 1998 | Gianni Romme (NED) | 6:22.20 |
| 2002 | Jochem Uytdehaage (NED) | 6:14.66 |

| 10,000 METERS | | MIN:SEC |
|---|---|---|
| 1924 | Julius Skutnabb (FIN) | 18:04.8 |
| 1932 | Irving Jaffee (USA) | 19:13.6 |
| 1936 | Ivar Ballangrud (NOR) | 17:24.3 |
| 1948 | Ake Seyffarth (SWE) | 17:26.3 |
| 1952 | Hjalmar Andersen (NOR) | 16:45.8 |
| 1956 | Sigvard Ericsson (SWE) | 16:35.9 |
| 1960 | Knut Johannesen (NOR) | 15:46.6 |
| 1964 | Jonny Nilsson (SWE) | 15:50.1 |
| 1968 | Johnny Höglin (SWE) | 15:23.6 |
| 1972 | Ard Schenk (NED) | 15:01.35[1] |
| 1976 | Piet Kleine (NED) | 14:50.59 |
| 1980 | Eric Heiden (USA) | 14:28.13 |
| 1984 | Igor Malkov (URS) | 14:39.90 |
| 1988 | Thomas Gustafson (SWE) | 13:48.20 |
| 1992 | Bart Veldkamp (NED) | 14:12.12 |
| 1994 | Johann Olav Koss (NOR) | 13:30.55 |
| 1998 | Gianni Romme (NED) | 13:15.33 |
| 2002 | Jochem Uytdehaage (NED) | 12:58.92 |

### COMBINED SPEED SKATING (MEN)

| | | |
|---|---|---|
| 1922 | Clas Thunberg (FIN) | |

# Winter Olympic Games Champions (continued)

## Speed Skating (women)

**500 METERS** — SEC

| | | SEC |
|---|---|---|
| 1960 | Helga Haase (GER)[4] | 45.9 |
| 1964 | Lidiya Skoblikova (URS) | 45.0 |
| 1968 | Lyudmila Titova (URS) | 46.1 |
| 1972 | Anne Henning (USA) | 43.33[1] |
| 1976 | Sheila Young (USA) | 42.76 |
| 1980 | Karin Enke (GDR) | 41.78 |
| 1984 | Christa Rothenburger (GDR) | 41.02 |
| 1988 | Bonnie Blair (USA) | 39.10 |
| 1992 | Bonnie Blair (USA) | 40.33 |
| 1994 | Bonnie Blair (USA) | 39.25 |
| 1998 | Catriona LeMay Doan (CAN) | 76.60[13] |
| 2002 | Catriona LeMay Doan (CAN) | 74.75[13] |

**1,000 METERS** — MIN:SEC

| | | MIN:SEC |
|---|---|---|
| 1960 | Klara Guseva (URS) | 1:34.1 |
| 1964 | Lidiya Skoblikova (URS) | 1:32.6 |
| 1968 | Carolina Geijssen (NED) | 1:32.6 |
| 1972 | Monika Pflug (FRG) | 1:31.40[1] |
| 1976 | Tatyana Averina (URS) | 1:28.43 |
| 1980 | Natalya Petruseva (URS) | 1:24.10 |
| 1984 | Karin Enke (GDR) | 1:21.61 |
| 1988 | Christa Rothenburger (GDR) | 1:17.65 |
| 1992 | Bonnie Blair (USA) | 1:21.90 |
| 1994 | Bonnie Blair (USA) | 1:18.74 |
| 1998 | Marianne Timmer (NED) | 1:16.51 |
| 2002 | Chris Witty (USA) | 1:13.83 |

**1,500 METERS** — MIN:SEC

| | | MIN:SEC |
|---|---|---|
| 1960 | Lidiya Skoblikova (URS) | 2:25.2 |
| 1964 | Lidiya Skoblikova (URS) | 2:22.6 |
| 1968 | Kaija Mustonen (FIN) | 2:22.4 |
| 1972 | Dianne Holum (USA) | 2:20.85[1] |
| 1976 | Galina Stepanskaya (URS) | 2:16.58 |
| 1980 | Annie Borckink (NED) | 2:10.95 |
| 1984 | Karin Enke (GDR) | 2:03.42 |
| 1988 | Yvonne van Gennip (NED) | 2:00.68 |
| 1992 | Jacqueline Börner (GER) | 2:05.87 |
| 1994 | Emese Hunyady (AUT) | 2:02.19 |
| 1998 | Marianne Timmer (NED) | 1:57.58 |
| 2002 | Anni Friesinger (GER) | 1:54.02 |

**3,000 METERS** — MIN:SEC

| | | MIN:SEC |
|---|---|---|
| 1960 | Lidiya Skoblikova (URS) | 5:14.3 |
| 1964 | Lidiya Skoblikova (URS) | 5:14.9 |
| 1968 | Johanna Schut (NED) | 4:56.2 |
| 1972 | Christina Baas-Kaiser (NED) | 4:52.14[1] |
| 1976 | Tatyana Averina (URS) | 4:45.19 |
| 1980 | Björg Eva Jensen (NOR) | 4:32.13 |
| 1984 | Andrea Schöne (GDR) | 4:24.79 |
| 1988 | Yvonne van Gennip (NED) | 4:11.94 |
| 1992 | Gunda Niemann (GER) | 4:19.90 |
| 1994 | Svetlana Bazhanova (RUS) | 4:17.43 |
| 1998 | Gunda Niemann-Stirnemann (GER) | 4:07.29 |
| 2002 | Claudia Pechstein (GER) | 3:57.70 |

## Speed Skating (women) (continued)

**5,000 METERS** — MIN:SEC

| | | MIN:SEC |
|---|---|---|
| 1988 | Yvonne van Gennip (NED) | 7:14.13 |
| 1992 | Gunda Niemann (GER) | 7:31.57 |
| 1994 | Claudia Pechstein (GER) | 7:14.37 |
| 1998 | Claudia Pechstein (GER) | 6:59.61 |
| 2002 | Claudia Pechstein (GER) | 6:46.91 |

## Short-track Speed Skating (men)

**500 METERS** — SEC

| | | SEC |
|---|---|---|
| 1994 | Chae Ji-Hoon (KOR) | 43.45 |
| 1998 | Takafumi Nishitani (JPN) | 42.862[5] |
| 2002 | Marc Gagnon (CAN) | 41.802 |

**1,000 METERS** — MIN:SEC

| | | MIN:SEC |
|---|---|---|
| 1992 | Kim Ki-Hoon (KOR) | 1:30.76 |
| 1994 | Kim Ki-Hoon (KOR) | 1:34.57 |
| 1998 | Kim Dong Sung (KOR) | 1:32.428[5] |
| 2002 | Steven Bradbury (AUS) | 1:29.109 |

**1,500 METERS** — MIN:SEC

| | | MIN:SEC |
|---|---|---|
| 2002 | Apolo Anton Ohno (USA) | 2:18.541 |

**5000-METER RELAY** — MIN:SEC

| | | MIN:SEC |
|---|---|---|
| 1992 | South Korea | 7:14.02 |
| 1994 | Italy | 7:11.74 |
| 1998 | Canada | 7:06.075[5] |
| 2002 | Canada | 6:51.579 |

## Short-track Speed Skating (women)

**500 METERS** — SEC

| | | SEC |
|---|---|---|
| 1992 | Cathy Turner (USA) | 47.04 |
| 1994 | Cathy Turner (USA) | 45.98 |
| 1998 | Annie Perreault (CAN) | 46.568[5] |
| 2002 | Yang Yang (A) (CHN) | 44.187 |

**1,000 METERS** — MIN:SEC

| | | MIN:SEC |
|---|---|---|
| 1994 | Chun Lee-Kyung (KOR) | 1:36.87 |
| 1998 | Chun Lee-Kyung (KOR) | 1:42.776[5] |
| 2002 | Yang Yang (A) (CHN) | 1:36.391 |

**1,500 METERS** — MIN:SEC

| | | MIN:SEC |
|---|---|---|
| 2002 | Ko Gi-Hyun (KOR) | 2:31.581 |

**3000-METER RELAY** — MIN:SEC

| | | MIN:SEC |
|---|---|---|
| 1992 | Canada | 4:36.62 |
| 1994 | South Korea | 4:26.64 |
| 1998 | South Korea | 4:16.260[5] |
| 2002 | South Korea | 4:12.793 |

## Winter Pentathlon[14]

| | |
|---|---|
| 1948 | Gustav Lindh (SWE) |

[1]Race first timed in hundredths of a second.   [2]Unified Team, consisting of athletes from the Commonwealth of Independent States plus Georgia.   [3]Five men.   [4]Joint East-West German team.   [5]Race first timed in thousandths of a second.   [6]Competition scored on points until 1994.   [7]1924–52, 18 km.   [8]Results of a 10-km classical leg determine the starting order of a 10- or 15-km freestyle leg, the first finisher of which is the overall winner; the freestyle leg was shortened from 15 to 10 km in the 2002 games.   [9]Winner after disqualification of top finisher for drug use.   [10]From 1924 to 1960 the jumping was held on one hill. In 1964 there were two events, one on a 70-m and the other on an 80-m hill; from 1968 to 1988 there were 70-m and 90-m events. From 1992 there were 90-m and 120-m events.   [11]Results of a 5-km classical leg determine the starting order of a 5- or 10-km freestyle leg, the first finisher of which is the overall winner; the freestyle leg was shortened from 10 to 5 km in the 2002 games.   [12]3 × 5-km relay until 1976.   [13]Combined time for two runs.   [14]Includes elements of cross-country skiing, downhill skiing, shooting, fencing, and horse riding.

# Olympic Medal Winners—XXVII Summer Games

*The XXVII Summer Games were held in Sydney, Australia, 15 Sep–1 Oct 2000.*

| EVENT | GOLD MEDALIST | PERFORMANCE | SILVER MEDALIST | BRONZE MEDALIST |
|---|---|---|---|---|
| **Archery** | | | | |
| Men's individual | Simon Fairweather (AUS) | 113–106 | Victor Wunderle (USA) | Wietse van Alten (NED) |
| Men's team | Korea | 255–247 | Italy | United States |
| Women's individual | Yun Mi-Jin (KOR) | 107–106 | Kim Nam–Soon (KOR) | Kim Soo-Nyung (KOR) |
| Women's team | Korea | 251–239 | Ukraine | Germany |
| **Badminton** | | | | |
| Men's singles | Ji Xinpeng (CHN) | 15–4, 15–13 | Hendrawan (INA) | Xia Xuanze (CHN) |
| Men's doubles | Indonesia | 15–10, 9–15, 15–7 | Korea | Korea |
| Women's singles | Gong Zhichao (CHN) | 13–10 11–3 | Camilla Martin (DEN) | Ye Zhaoying (CHN) |
| Women's doubles | China | 15–5, 15–5 | China | China |
| Mixed doubles | China | 1–15, 15–13, 15–11 | Indonesia | Great Britain |
| **Baseball** | United States | 4–0 | Cuba | Korea |
| **Basketball** | | | | |
| Men | United States | 85–75 | France | Lithuania |
| Women | United States | 76–54 | Australia | Brazil |
| **Boxing\*** | | | | |
| 48 kg (light flyweight) | Brahim Asloum (FRA) | | Rafael Lozano Muñoz (ESP) | Kim Un Chol (PRK); Maikro Romero Esquirol (CUB) |
| 51 kg (flyweight) | Wijan Ponlid (THA) | | Bulat Jumadilov (KAZ) | Vladimir Sidorenko (UKR); Jerome Thomas (FRA) |
| 54 kg (bantamweight) | Guillermo Ortiz (CUB) | | Raimkul Malakh-bekov (RUS) | Clarence Vinson (USA); Sergy Danylchenko (UKR) |
| 57 kg (featherweight) | Bekzat Sattarkhanov (KAZ) | | Ricardo Juárez (USA) | Kamil Dzamalut-dinov (RUS); Tahar Tamsamani (MAR) |
| 60 kg (lightweight) | Mario Kindelan (CUB) | | Andry Kotelnyk (UKR) | Aleksandr Maletin (RUS); Cristian Benitez (MEX) |
| 63.5 kg (light welter-weight) | Mahamadkadyz Abdullayev (UZB) | | Ricardo Williams (USA) | Mohamed Allalou (ALG); Diogenes Luna Martínez (CUB) |
| 67 kg (welterweight) | Oleg Saytov (RUS) | | Sergy Dotsenko (UKR) | Dorel Simion (ROM); Vitalii Grusac (MDA) |
| 71 kg (light middle-weight) | Yermakhan Ibraimov (KAZ) | | Marin Simion (ROM) | Jermaine Taylor (USA); Pornchai Thongburan (THA) |
| 75 kg (middleweight) | Jorge Gutiérrez (CUB) | | Gaidarbek Gaidar-bekov (RUS) | Vugar Alekperov (AZE); Zsolt Erdei (HUN) |
| 81 kg (light heavy-weight) | Aleksandr Lebzyak (RUS) | | Rudolf Kraj (CZE) | Sergey Mikhaylov (UZB); Andry Fedchuk (UKR) |
| 91 kg (heavyweight) | Félix Savon Fabré (CUB) | | Sultanahmed Ibzagi-mov (RUS) | Sebastian Kober (GER); Vladimir Chanturia (GEO) |
| 91+ kg (super heavy-weight) | Audley Harrison (GBR) | | Mukhatarkhan Dilda-bekov (KAZ) | Rustam Saidov (UZB); Paolo Vidoz (ITA) |
| **Canoeing** | | | | |
| **Men** | | | | |
| 500-m kayak singles | Knut Holman (NOR) | 1 min 57.84 sec | Petar Merkov (BUL) | Michael Kolganov (ISR) |
| 1,000-m kayak singles | Knut Holman (NOR) | 3 min 33.26 sec | Petar Merkov (BUL) | Tim Brabants (GBR) |
| 500-m kayak pairs | Hungary | 1 min 47.05 sec | Australia | Germany |
| 1,000-m kayak pairs | Italy | 3 min 14.46 sec | Sweden | Hungary |
| 1,000-m kayak fours | Hungary | 2 min 55.18 sec | Germany | Poland |

# Olympic Medal Winners—XXVII Summer Games (continued)

| EVENT | GOLD MEDALIST | PERFORMANCE | SILVER MEDALIST | BRONZE MEDALIST |
|---|---|---|---|---|
| **Canoeing (continued)** | | | | |
| **Men** | | | | |
| Slalom kayak singles | Thomas Schmidt (GER) | 217.25 pt | Paul Ratcliffe (GBR) | Pierpaolo Ferrazzi (ITA) |
| 500-m Canadian singles | Gyorgy Kolonics (HUN) | 2 min 24.81 sec | Maksim Opalev (RUS) | Andreas Dittmer (GER) |
| 1,000-m Canadian singles | Andreas Dittmer (GER) | 3 min 54.37 sec | Ledys Frank Balceiro (CUB) | Steve Giles (CAN) |
| 500-m Canadian pairs | Hungary | 1 min 51.28 sec | Poland | Romania |
| 1,000-m Canadian pairs | Romania | 3 min 37.35 sec | Cuba | Germany |
| Slalom Canadian singles | Tony Estanguet (FRA) | 231.87 pt | Michal Martikan (SVK) | Juraj Mincik (SVK) |
| Slalom Canadian pairs | Slovakia | 237.74 pt | Poland | Czech Rep. |
| **Women** | | | | |
| 500-m kayak singles | Josefa Idem Guerrini (ITA) | 2 min 13.84 sec | Caroline Brunet (CAN) | Katrin Borchert (AUS) |
| 500-m kayak pairs | Germany | 1 min 56.99 sec | Hungary | Poland |
| 500-m kayak fours | Germany | 1 min 34.53 sec | Hungary | Romania |
| Slalom kayak singles | Stepanka Hilgertova (CZE) | 247.04 pt | Brigitte Guibal (FRA) | Anne-Lise Bardet (FRA) |
| **Cycling** | | | | |
| **Men** | | | | |
| Road race | Jan Ullrich (GER) | 5 hr 29 min 08 sec | Aleksandr Vinokourov (KAZ) | Andreas Kloeden (GER) |
| Individual road time trial | Vyacheslav Yekimov (RUS) | 57 min 40.420 sec | Jan Ullrich (GER) | Lance Armstrong (USA) |
| 1-km time trial | Jason Queally (GBR) | 1 min 1.609 sec | Stefan Nimke (GER) | Shane Kelly (AUS) |
| 4,000-m individual pursuit | Robert Bartko (GER) | 4 min 18.515 sec† | Jens Lehmann (GER) | Brad McGee (AUS) |
| 4,000-m team pursuit | Germany | 3 min 59.710 sec‡ | Ukraine | Great Britain |
| Individual match sprint | Marty Nothstein (USA) | | Florian Rousseau (FRA) | Jens Fiedler (GER) |
| Olympic sprint | France | 44.233 sec | Great Britain | Australia |
| Individual points race | Juan Llaneras (ESP) | | Milton Wynants (URU) | Aleksey Markov (RUS) |
| Madison | Australia | | Belgium | Italy |
| Keirin | Florian Rousseau (FRA) | 11.020 sec | Gary Neiwand (AUS) | Jens Fiedler (GER) |
| Mountain bike | Miguel Martinez (FRA) | 2 hr 9 min 2.50 sec | Filip Meirhaeghe (BEL) | Christoph Sauser (SUI) |
| **Women** | | | | |
| Road race | Leontien Zijlaard–van Moorsel (NED) | 3 hr 6 min 31 sec | Hanka Kupfernagel (GER) | Diana Ziliute (LTU) |
| Individual road time trial | Leontien Zijlaard–van Moorsel (NED) | 42 min 0.781 sec | Mari Holden (USA) | Jeannie Longo-Ciprelli (FRA) |
| 500-m time trial | Felicia Ballanger (FRA) | 34.140 sec | Michelle Ferris (AUS) | Jiang Cuihua (CHN) |
| Individual pursuit | Leontien Zijlaard–van Moorsel (NED) | 3 min 33.360 sec | Marion Clignet (FRA) | Yvonne McGregor (GBR) |
| Individual sprint | Felicia Ballanger (FRA) | | Oksana Grishina (RUS) | Iryna Yanovych (UKR) |
| Individual points race | Antonella Bellutti (ITA) | | Leontin Zijlaard–van Moorsel (NED) | Olga Slyusareva (RUS) |
| Mountain bike | Paola Pezzo (ITA) | 1 hr 49 min 24.38 sec | Barbara Blatter (SUI) | Margarita Fullana (ESP) |
| **Diving** | | | | |
| **Men** | | | | |
| 3-m springboard | Xiong Ni (CHN) | 708.72 pt | Fernando Platas (MEX) | Dmitry Sautin (RUS) |
| 10-m platform | Tian Liang (CHN) | 724.53 pt | Hu Jia (CHN) | Dmitry Sautin (RUS) |
| 3-m synchronized springboard | China | 365.58 pt | Russia | Australia |

## Olympic Medal Winners—XXVII Summer Games (continued)

| EVENT | GOLD MEDALIST | PERFORMANCE | SILVER MEDALIST | BRONZE MEDALIST |
|---|---|---|---|---|
| **Diving (continued)** | | | | |
| **Men** | | | | |
| 10-m synchronized platform | Russia | 365.04 pt | China | Germany |
| | | | | |
| **Women** | | | | |
| 3-m springboard | Fu Mingxia (CHN) | 609.42 pt | Guo Jingjing (CHN) | Doerte Lindner (GER) |
| 10-m platform | Laura Wilkinson (USA) | 543.75 pt | Li Na (CHN) | Anne Montminy (CAN) |
| 3-m synchronized springboard | Russia | 332.64 pt | China | Ukraine |
| 10-m synchronized platform | China | 345.12 pt | Canada | Australia |
| | | | | |
| **Equestrian** | | | | |
| Individual 3-day event | David O'Connor (USA) | | Andrew Hoy (AUS) | Mark Todd (NZL) |
| Team 3-day event | Australia | | Great Britain | United States |
| Individual dressage | Anky van Grunsven (NED) | | Isabell Werth (GER) | Ulla Salzgeber (GER) |
| Team dressage | Germany | | The Netherlands | United States |
| Individual show jumping | Jeroen Dubbeldam (NED) | | Albert Voorn (NED) | Khaled al Eid (SAU) |
| Team show jumping | Germany | | Switzerland | Brazil |
| | | | | |
| **Fencing** | | | | |
| **Men** | | | | |
| Individual foil | Kim Young Ho (KOR) | | Ralf Bissdorf (GER) | Dmitry Shevchenko (RUS) |
| Team foil | France | | China | Italy |
| Individual épée | Pavel Kolobkov (RUS) | | Hugues Obry (FRA) | Lee Sang-Ki (KOR) |
| Team épée | Italy | | France | Cuba |
| Individual sabre | Mihai Claudiu Covaliu (ROM) | | Mathieu Gourdain (FRA) | Wiradech Kothny (GER) |
| Team sabre | Russia | | France | Germany |
| | | | | |
| **Women** | | | | |
| Individual foil | Valentina Vezzali (ITA) | | Rita Koenig (GER) | Giovanna Trillini (ITA) |
| Team foil | Italy | | Poland | Germany |
| Individual épée | Timea Nagy (HUN) | | Gianna Buerki (SUI) | Laura Flessel-Colovic (FRA) |
| Team épée | Russia | | Switzerland | China |
| | | | | |
| **Field Hockey** | | | | |
| Men | The Netherlands | 8–7 | Korea | Australia |
| Women | Australia | 3–1 | Argentina | The Netherlands |
| | | | | |
| **Gymnastics** | | | | |
| **Men** | | | | |
| Team | China | 231.919 pt | Ukraine | Russia |
| All-around | Aleksey Nemov (RUS) | 58.474 pt | Yang Wei (CHN) | Oleksandr Beresh (UKR) |
| Floor exercise | Igors Vihrovs (LAT) | 9.812 pt | Aleksey Nemov (RUS) | Iordan Iovchev (BUL) |
| Vault | Gervasio Deferr (ESP) | 9.712 pt | Aleksey Bondarenko (RUS) | Leszek Blanik (POL) |
| Pommel horse | Marius Urzica (ROM) | 9.862 pt | Eric Poujade (FRA) | Aleksey Nemov (RUS) |
| Rings | Szilveszter Csollany (HUN) | 9.850 pt | Dimosthenis Tampakos (GRE) | Iordan Iovchev (BUL) |
| Parallel bars | Li Xiaopeng (CHN) | 9.825 pt | Lee Joo Hyung (KOR) | Aleksey Nemov (RUS) |
| Horizontal bar | Aleksey Nemov (RUS) | 9.787 pt | Benjamin Varonian (FRA) | Lee Joo Hyung (KOR) |
| Trampoline | Aleksandr Moskalenko (RUS) | 41.70 pt | Ji Wallace (AUS) | Mathieu Turgeon (CAN) |
| **Women** | | | | |
| Team | Romania | 154.608 pt | Russia | China |
| All-around | Simona Amanar (ROM) | 38.642 pt | Maria Olaru (ROM) | Liu Xuan (CHN) |

# Olympic Medal Winners—XXVII Summer Games (continued)

| EVENT | GOLD MEDALIST | PERFORMANCE | SILVER MEDALIST | BRONZE MEDALIST |
|---|---|---|---|---|
| **Gymnastics (continued)** | | | | |
| **Women** | | | | |
| Floor exercise | Yelena Zamolodchikova (RUS) | 9.850 pt | Svetlana Khorkina (RUS) | Simona Amanar (ROM) |
| Vault | Yelena Zamolodchikova (RUS) | 9.731 pt | Andreea Raducan (ROM) | Yekaterina Lobaznyuk (RUS) |
| Uneven bars | Svetlana Khorkina (RUS) | 9.862 pt | Ling Jie (CHN) | Yang Yun (CHN) |
| Balance beam | Liu Xuan (CHN) | 9.825 pt | Yekaterina Lobaznyuk (RUS) | Yelena Produnova (RUS) |
| Trampoline | Irina Karavayeva (RUS) | 38.90 pt | Oksana Tsyhuleva (UKR) | Karen Cockburn (CAN) |
| Individual rhythmic | Yuliya Barsukova (RUS) | 39.632 pt | Yuliya Raskina (BLR) | Alina Kabayeva (RUS) |
| Team rhythmic | Russia | 39.500 pt | Belarus | Greece |
| | | | | |
| **Handball (Team)** | | | | |
| Men | Russia | 28–26 | Sweden | Spain |
| Women | Denmark | 31–27 | Hungary | Norway |
| | | | | |
| **Judo*§** | | | | |
| **Men** | | | | |
| 60 kg (extra light-weight) | Tadahiro Nomura (JPN) | | Jung Bu-Kyung (KOR) | Manolo Poulot (CUB); Aidyn Smagulov (KGZ) |
| 66 kg (half light-weight) | Huseyein Ozkan (TUR) | | Larbi Benboudaoud (FRA) | Girolamo Giovinazzo (ITA); Giorgi Vazagasvili (GEO) |
| 73 kg (lightweight) | Giuseppe Maddaloni (ITA) | | Tiago Camilo (BRA) | Vsevolods Zelonijs (LAT); Anatoly Laryukov (BLR) |
| 81 kg (half middle-weight) | Makoto Takimoto (JPN) | | Cho In-Chul (KOR) | Nuno Delgado (POR); Aleksy Budolin (EST) |
| 90 kg (middleweight) | Mark Huizinga (NED) | | Carlos Honorato (BRA) | Ruslan Mashurenko (UKR); Frederic Demontfaucon (FRA) |
| 100 kg (half heavy-weight) | Kosei Inoue (JPN) | | Nicolas Gill (CAN) | Yury Stepkin (RUS); Stephane Traineau (FRA) |
| 100+ kg (heavy-weight) | David Douillet (FRA) | | Shinichi Shinohara (JPN) | Tamerlan Tmenov (RUS); Indrek Pertelson (EST) |
| | | | | |
| **Women** | | | | |
| 48 kg (extra light-weight) | Ryoko Tamura (JPN) | | Lyubov Bruletova (RUS) | Anna-Maria Gradante (GER); Ann Simons (BEL) |
| 52 kg (half light-weight) | Legna Verdecia (CUB) | | Noriko Narazaki (JPN) | Kye Sun Hui (PRK); Liu Yuxiang (CHN) |
| 57 kg (lightweight) | Isabel Fernández (ESP) | | Driulys González (CUB) | Kie Kusakabe (JPN); Maria Pekli (AUS) |
| 63 kg (half middle-weight) | Severine Vandenhende (FRA) | | Li Shufang (CHN) | Jung Sung-Sook (KOR); Gella Vandecaveye (BEL) |
| 70 kg (middleweight) | Sibelis Veranes (CUB) | | Kate Howey (GBR) | Cho Min-Sun (KOR); Ylenia Scapin (ITA) |
| 78 kg (half heavy-weight) | Tang Lin (CHN) | | Celine Lebrun (FRA) | Simona Marcela Richter (ROM); Emanuela Pierantozzi (ITA) |
| 78+ kg (heavyweight) | Yuan Hua (CHN) | | Daima Mayelis Beltran (CUB) | Kim Seon-Young (KOR); Mayumi Yamashita (JPN) |
| | | | | |
| **Modern Pentathlon** | | | | |
| Men | Dmitry Svatkovsky (RUS) | | Gabor Balogh (HUN) | Pavel Dovgal (BLR) |
| Women | Stephanie Cook (GBR) | | Emily de Riel (USA) | Kate Allenby (GBR) |

## Olympic Medal Winners—XXVII Summer Games (continued)

| EVENT | GOLD MEDALIST | PERFORMANCE | SILVER MEDALIST | BRONZE MEDALIST |
|---|---|---|---|---|
| **Rowing** | | | | |
| **Men** | | | | |
| Single sculls | Rob Waddell (NZL) | 6 min 48.90 sec | Xeno Mueller (SUI) | Marcel Hacker (GER) |
| Double sculls | Slovenia | 6 min 16.63 sec | Norway | Italy |
| Quadruple sculls | Italy | 5 min 45.56 sec | The Netherlands | Germany |
| Coxless pairs (oars) | France | 6 min 32.97 sec | United States | Australia |
| Coxless fours (oars) | Great Britain | 5 min 56.24 sec | Italy | Australia |
| Eights | Great Britain | 5 min 33.08 sec | Australia | Croatia |
| Lightweight double sculls | Poland | 6 min 21.75 sec | Italy | France |
| Lightweight fours | France | 6 min 1.68 sec | Australia | Denmark |
| | | | | |
| **Women** | | | | |
| Single sculls | Yekaterina Karsten (BLR) | 7 min 28.14 sec | Rumyana Neykova (BUL) | Katrin Rutschow (GER) |
| Double sculls | Germany | 6 min 55.44 sec | The Netherlands | Lithuania |
| Quadruple sculls | Germany | 6 min 19.58 sec | Great Britain | Russia |
| Coxless pairs (oars) | Romania | 7 min 11.00 sec | Australia | United States |
| Eights | Romania | 6 min 6.44 sec | The Netherlands | Canada |
| Lightweight double sculls | Romania | 7 min 2.64 sec | Germany | United States |
| **Sailing** | | | | |
| Men's 470 | Australia | | United States | Argentina |
| Women's 470 | Australia | | United States | Ukraine |
| Men's Mistral | Christoph Sieber (AUT) | | Carlos Espiñola (ARG) | Aaron McIntosh (NZL) |
| Women's Mistral | Alessandra Sensini (ITA) | | Amelie Lux (GER) | Barbara Kendall (NZL) |
| Men's Finn | Iain Percy (GBR) | | Luca Devoti (ITA) | Fredrik Loof (SWE) |
| Women's Europe | Shirley Robertson (GBR) | | Margriet Matthysse (NED) | Serena Amato (ARG) |
| Mixed 49er | Finland | | Great Britain | United States |
| Mixed Laser | Ben Ainslie (GBR) | | Robert Scheidt (BRA) | Michael Blackburn (AUS) |
| Mixed Soling | Denmark | | Germany | Norway |
| Mixed Star | United States | | Great Britain | Brazil |
| Mixed Tornado | Austria | | Australia | Germany |
| **Shooting** | | | | |
| **Men** | | | | |
| Rapid-fire pistol | Sergey Alifirenko (RUS) | 687.6 pt | Michal Ansermet (SUI) | Iulian Raicea (ROM) |
| Free pistol | Tanyu Kiriakov (BUL) | 666.0 pt | Igor Basinsky (BLR) | Martin Tenk (CZE) |
| Air pistol | Franck Dumoulin (FRA) | 688.9 pt† | Wang Yifu (CHN) | Igor Basinsky (BLR) |
| 10-m running (game) target | Yang Ling (CHN) | 681.1 pt | Oleg Moldovan (MDA) | Niu Zhiyuan (CHN) |
| Small-bore (sport) rifle, 3 positions | Rajmond Debevec (SLO) | 1,275.1 pt† | Juha Hirvi (FIN) | Harald Stenvaag (NOR) |
| Small-bore (sport) rifle, prone | Jonas Edman (SWE) | 701.3 pt | Torben Grimmel (DEN) | Sergey Martynov (BLR) |
| Air rifle | Cai Yalin (CHN) | 696.4 pt† | Artyom Khadjibekov (RUS) | Yevgeny Aleynikov (RUS) |
| Trap | Michael Diamond (AUS) | 147.0 pt | Ian Peel (GBR) | Giovani Pellielo (ITA) |
| Double trap | Richard Faulds (GBR) | 187.0 pt | Russell Mark (AUS) | Fehaid al Deehani (KUW) |
| Skeet | Mykola Milchev (UKR) | 150.0 pt‡ | Petr Malek (CZE) | James Graves (USA) |
| **Women** | | | | |
| Sport pistol | Maria Grozdeva (BUL) | 690.3 pt† | Tao Luna (CHN) | Lolita Yevglevskaya (BLR) |
| Air pistol | Tao Luna (CHN) | 488.2 pt | Jasna Sekaric (YUG) | Annemarie Forder (AUS) |
| Small-bore (sport) rifle | Renata Mauer–Rozanska (POL) | 684.6 pt | Tatyana Goldobina (RUS) | Mariya Feklisova (RUS) |
| Air rifle | Nancy Johnson (USA) | 497.7 pt | Kang Cho-Hyun (KOR) | Gao Jing (CHN) |

# Olympic Medal Winners—XXVII Summer Games (continued)

| EVENT | GOLD MEDALIST | PERFORMANCE | SILVER MEDALIST | BRONZE MEDALIST |
|---|---|---|---|---|
| **Shooting (continued)** | | | | |
| **Women** | | | | |
| Trap | Daina Gudzineviciute (LTU) | 93.0 pt | Delphine Racinet (FRA) | Gao E (CHN) |
| Double trap | Pia Hansen (SWE) | 148.0 pt† | Deborah Gelisio (ITA) | Kimberly Rhode (USA) |
| Skeet | Zemfira Meftakhetdinova (AZE) | 98.0 pt† | Svetlana Demina (RUS) | Diana Igaly (HUN) |
| | | | | |
| **Soccer (Association Football)** | | | | |
| Men | Cameroon | 2–2 (5–3 on PKs) | Spain | Chile |
| Women | Norway | 3–2 (overtime) | United States | Germany |
| | | | | |
| **Softball** | United States | 2–1 | Japan | Australia |
| | | | | |
| **Swimming** | | | | |
| **Men** | | | | |
| 50-m freestyle | Gary Hall, Jr. (USA); Anthony Ervin (USA)¶ | 21.98 sec | N/A | Pieter Van den Hoogenband (NED) |
| 100-m freestyle | Pieter Van den Hoogenband (NED) | 48.30 sec | Aleksandr Popov (RUS) | Gary Hall, Jr. (USA) |
| 200-m freestyle | Pieter Van den Hoogenband (NED) | 1 min 45.35 sec‡ | Ian Thorpe (AUS) | Massimiliano Rosolino (ITA) |
| 400-m freestyle | Ian Thorpe (AUS) | 3 min 40.59 sec‡ | Massimiliano Rosolino (ITA) | Klete Keller (USA) |
| 1,500-m freestyle | Grant Hackett (AUS) | 14 min 48.33 sec | Kieren Perkins (AUS) | Chris Thompson (USA) |
| 100-m backstroke | Lenny Krayzelburg (USA) | 53.72 sec† | Matthew Welsh (AUS) | Stev Theloke (GER) |
| 200-m backstroke | Lenny Krayzelburg (USA) | 1 min 56.76 sec† | Aaron Peirsol (USA) | Matthew Welsh (AUS) |
| 100-m breaststroke | Domenico Fioravanti (ITA) | 1 min 0.46 sec† | Ed Moses (USA) | Roman Sludnov (RUS) |
| 200-m breaststroke | Domenico Fioravanti (ITA) | 2 min 10.87 sec | Terence Parkin (RSA) | Davide Rummolo (ITA) |
| 100-m butterfly | Lars Froelander (SWE) | 52.00 sec | Michael Klim (AUS) | Geoff Huegill (AUS) |
| 200-m butterfly | Tom Malchow (USA) | 1 min 55.35 sec† | Denys Sylantyev (UKR) | Justin Norris (AUS) |
| 200-m individual medley | Massimiliano Rosolino (ITA) | 1 min 58.98 sec† | Tom Dolan (USA) | Tom Wilkens (USA) |
| 400-m individual medley | Tom Dolan (USA) | 4 min 11.76 sec‡ | Erik Vendt (USA) | Curtis Myden (CAN) |
| 4 x 100-m freestyle relay | Australia | 3 min 13.67 sec‡ | United States | Brazil |
| 4 x 200-m freestyle relay | Australia | 7 min 7.05 sec‡ | United States | The Netherlands |
| 4 x 100-m medley relay | United States | 3 min 33.73 sec‡ | Australia | Germany |
| | | | | |
| **Women** | | | | |
| 50-m freestyle | Inge de Bruijn (NED) | 24.32 sec | Therese Alshammar (SWE) | Dara Torres (USA) |
| 100-m freestyle | Inge de Bruijn (NED) | 53.83 sec | Therese Alshammar (SWE) | Jenny Thomspon (USA); Dara Torres (USA)¶ |
| 200-m freestyle | Susie O'Neill (AUS) | 1 min 58.24 sec | Martina Moravcova (SVK) | Claudia Poll (CRC) |
| 400-m freestyle | Brooke Bennett (USA) | 4 min 5.80 sec | Diana Munz (USA) | Claudia Poll (CRC) |
| 800-m freestyle | Brooke Bennett (USA) | 8 min 19.67 sec† | Yana Klochkova (UKR) | Kaitlin Sandeno (USA) |
| 100-m backstroke | Diana Mocanu (ROM) | 1 min 0.21 sec† | Mai Nakamura (JPN) | Nina Zhivanevskaya (ESP) |
| 200-m backstroke | Diana Mocanu (ROM) | 2 min 8.16 sec | Roxana Maracineanu (FRA) | Miki Nakao (JPN) |
| 100-m breaststroke | Megan Quann (USA) | 1 min 7.05 sec | Leisel Jones (AUS) | Penny Heyns (RSA) |
| 200-m breaststroke | Agnes Kovacs (HUN) | 2 min 24.35 sec | Kristy Kowal (USA) | Amanda Beard (USA) |
| 100-m butterfly | Inge de Bruijn (NED) | 56.61 sec‡ | Martina Moravcova (SVK) | Dara Torres (USA) |

# Olympic Medal Winners—XXVII Summer Games (continued)

| EVENT | GOLD MEDALIST | PERFORMANCE | SILVER MEDALIST | BRONZE MEDALIST |
|---|---|---|---|---|
| **Swimming (continued)** | | | | |
| **Women** | | | | |
| 200-m butterfly | Misty Hyman (USA) | 2 min 5.88 sec† | Susie O'Neill (AUS) | Petria Thomas (AUS) |
| 200-m individual medley | Yana Klochkova (UKR) | 2 min 10.68 sec† | Beatrice Caslaru (ROM) | Cristina Teuscher (USA) |
| 400-m individual medley | Yana Klochkova (UKR) | 4 min 33.59 sec‡ | Yasuko Tajima (JPN) | Beatrice Caslaru (ROM) |
| 4 x 100-m freestyle relay | United States | 3 min 36.61 sec‡ | The Netherlands | Sweden |
| 4 x 200-m freestyle relay | United States | 7 min 57.80 sec† | Australia | Germany |
| 4 x 100-m medley relay | United States | 3 min 58.30 sec‡ | Australia | Japan |
| **Synchronized Swimming** | | | | |
| Duet | Russia | 99.580 pt | Japan | France |
| Team | Russia | 99.146 pt | Japan | Canada |
| **Table Tennis** | | | | |
| Men's singles | Kong Linghui (CHN) | 21–16, 21–19, 17–21, 14–21, 21–13 | Jan-Ove Waldner (SWE) | Liu Guoliang (CHN) |
| Men's doubles | China | 22–20, 17–21, 21–19, 21–18 | China | France |
| Women's singles | Wang Nan (CHN) | 21–12, 12–21, 19–21, 21–17, 21–18 | Li Ju (CHN) | Chen Jing (TPE) |
| Women's doubles | China | 21–18, 21–11, 21–11 | China | Korea |
| **Taekwondo** | | | | |
| **Men** | | | | |
| 58 kg (flyweight) | Michail Mouroutsis (GRE) | | Gabriel Esparaza (ESP) | Huang Chih-Hsiung (TPE) |
| 68 kg (featherweight) | Steven Lopez (USA) | | Sin Joon-Sik (KOR) | Hadi Saeiboneh-kohal (IRI) |
| 80 kg (welterweight) | Angel Matos Fuentes (CUB) | | Faissal Ebnoutalib (GER) | Victor Estrada-Garibay (MEX) |
| 80+ kg (heavyweight) | Kim Kyong-Hun (KOR) | | Daniel Trenton (AUS) | Pascal Gentil (FRA) |
| **Women** | | | | |
| 49 kg (flyweight) | Lauren Burns (AUS) | | Urbia Rodríguez (CUB) | Chi Shu-Ji (TPE) |
| 57 kg (featherweight) | Jung Jae-Eun (KOR) | | Hieu Ngan Tran (VIE) | Hamide Bikcin (TUR) |
| 67 kg (welterweight) | Lee Sun-Hee (KOR) | | Trude Gundersen (NOR) | Yoriko Okamoto (JPN) |
| 67+ kg (heavyweight) | Chen Zhong (CHN) | | Natalya Ivanova (RUS) | Dominique Bosshart (CAN) |
| **Tennis** | | | | |
| Men's singles | Yevgeny Kafelnikov (RUS) | 7–6 (7–4), 3–6, 6–2, 4–6, 6–3 | Tommy Haas (GER) | Arnaud Di Pasquale (FRA) |
| Men's doubles | Canada | 5–7, 6–3, 6–4, 7–6 (7–2) | Australia | Spain |
| Women's singles | Venus Williams (USA) | 6–2, 6–4 | Yelena Dementyeva (RUS) | Monica Seles (USA) |
| Women's doubles | United States | 6–1, 6–1 | The Netherlands | Belgium |
| **Track and Field (Athletics)** | | | | |
| **Men** | | | | |
| 100 m | Maurice Greene (USA) | 9.87 sec | Ato Boldon (TRI) | Obadele Thompson (BAR) |
| 200 m | Konstantinos Kenteris (GRE) | 20.09 sec | Darren Campbell (GBR) | Ato Boldon (TRI) |
| 400 m | Michael Johnson (USA) | 43.84 sec | Alvin Harrison (USA) | Gregory Haughton (JAM) |
| 4 x 100-m relay | United States | 37.61 sec | Brazil | Cuba |
| 4 x 400-m relay | United States | 2 min 56.35 sec | Nigeria | Jamaica |
| 800 m | Nils Schumann (GER) | 1 min 45.08 sec | Wilson Kipketer (DEN) | Aissa Said Guerni (ALG) |
| 1,500 m | Noah Ngeny (KEN) | 3 min 32.07 sec† | Hicham El Guerrouj (MAR) | Bernard Lagat (KEN) |

## Olympic Medal Winners—XXVII Summer Games (continued)

| EVENT | GOLD MEDALIST | PERFORMANCE | SILVER MEDALIST | BRONZE MEDALIST |
|---|---|---|---|---|
| **Track and Field (Athletics) (continued)** | | | | |
| **Men** | | | | |
| 5,000 m | Millon Wolde (ETH) | 13 min 35.49 sec | Ali Saidi-Sief (ALG) | Brahim Lahlafi (MAR) |
| 10,000 m | Haile Gebrselassie (ETH) | 27 min 18.20 sec | Paul Tergat (KEN) | Assefa Mezgebu (ETH) |
| Marathon | Gezahgne Abera (ETH) | 2 hr 10 min 11 sec | Eric Wainaina (KEN) | Tesfaye Tola (ETH) |
| 110-m hurdles | Anier Garcia (CUB) | 13.00 sec | Terrence Trammell (USA) | Mark Crear (USA) |
| 400-m hurdles | Angelo Taylor (USA) | 47.50 sec | Hadi Souan Somayli (SAU) | Llewellyn Herbert (RSA) |
| 3,000-m steeple-chase | Reuben Kosgei (KEN) | 8 min 21.43 sec | Wilson Bolt Kipketer (KEN) | Ali Ezzine (MAR) |
| 20-km walk | Robert Korzeniow-ski (POL) | 1 hr 18 min 59 sec† | Noe Hernández (MEX) | Vladimir Andreyev (RUS) |
| 50-km walk | Robert Korzeniow-ski (POL) | 3 hr 42 min 22 sec | Aigars Fadejevs (LAT) | Joel Sánchez (MEX) |
| High jump | Sergey Klyugin (RUS) | 2.35 m | Javier Sotomayor (CUB) | Abderrahmane Hammad (ALG) |
| Long jump | Ivan Pedroso (CUB) | 8.55 m | Jai Taurima (AUS) | Roman Shchurenko (UKR) |
| Triple jump | Jonathan Edwards (GBR) | 17.71 m | Yoel Garcia (CUB) | Denis Kapustin (RUS) |
| Pole vault | Nick Hysong (USA) | 5.90 m | Lawrence Johnson (USA) | Maksim Tarasov (RUS) |
| Shot put | Arsi Harju (FIN) | 21.29 m | Adam Nelson (USA) | John Godina (USA) |
| Discus throw | Virgilijus Alekna (LTU) | 69.30 m | Lars Riedel (GER) | Frantz Kruger (RSA) |
| Javelin throw | Jan Zelezny (CZE) | 90.17 m† | Steve Backley (GBR) | Sergey Makarov (RUS) |
| Hammer throw | Szymon Ziolkowski (POL) | 80.02 m | Nicola Vizzoni (ITA) | Igor Astapkovich (BLR) |
| Decathlon | Erki Nool (EST) | 8,641 pt | Roman Sebrle (CZE) | Chris Huffins (USA) |
| **Women** | | | | |
| 100 m | Marion Jones (USA) | 10.75 sec | Ekaterini Thanou (GRE) | Tanya Lawrence (JAM) |
| 200 m | Marion Jones (USA) | 21.84 sec | Pauline Davis-Thompson (BAH) | Susanthika Jayasinghe (SRI) |
| 400 m | Cathy Freeman (AUS) | 49.11 sec | Lorraine Graham (JAM) | Katharine Merry (GBR) |
| 4 x 100-m relay | The Bahamas | 41.95 sec | Jamaica | United States |
| 4 x 400-m relay | United States | 3 min 22.62 sec | Jamaica | Russia |
| 800 m | Maria Mutola (MOZ) | 1 min 56.15 sec | Stephanie Graf (AUT) | Kelly Holmes (GBR) |
| 1,500 m | Nouria Mérah-Benida (ALG) | 4 min 5.10 sec | Violeta Szekely (ROM) | Gabriela Szabo (ROM) |
| 5,000 m | Gabriela Szabo (ROM) | 14 min 40.79 sec† | Sonia O'Sullivan (IRL) | Gete Wami (ETH) |
| 10,000 m | Derartu Tulu (ETH) | 30 min 17.49 sec† | Gete Wami (ETH) | Fernanda Ribeiro (POR) |
| Marathon | Naoko Takahashi (JPN) | 2 hr 23 min 14 sec† | Lidia Simon (ROM) | Joyce Chepchumba (KEN) |
| 100-m hurdles | Olga Shishigina (KAZ) | 12.65 sec | Glory Alozie (NGR) | Melissa Morrison (USA) |
| 400-m hurdles | Irina Privalova (RUS) | 53.02 sec | Deon Hemmings (JAM) | Nouzha Bidouane (MAR) |
| 20-km walk | Wang Liping (CHN) | 1 hr 29 min 5 sec | Kjersti Plätzer (NOR) | Maria Vasco (ESP) |
| High jump | Yelena Yelesina (RUS) | 2.01 m | Hestrie Cloete (RSA) | Kajsa Bergqvist (SWE) |
| Long jump | Heike Drechsler (GER) | 6.99 m | Fiona May (ITA) | Marion Jones (USA) |
| Triple jump | Tereza Marinova (BUL) | 15.20 m | Tatyana Lebedeva (RUS) | Olena Hovorova (UKR) |
| Pole vault | Stacy Dragila (USA) | 4.60 m | Tatyana Grigoryeva (AUS) | Vala Flosadottir (ISL) |
| Shot put | Yanina Korolchik (BLR) | 20.56 m | Larisa Peleshenko (RUS) | Astrid Kumbernuss (GER) |
| Discus throw | Ellina Zvereva (BLR) | 68.40 m | Anastasia Kelesidou (GRE) | Irina Yachenko (BLR) |

## Olympic Medal Winners—XXVII Summer Games (continued)

| EVENT | GOLD MEDALIST | PERFORMANCE | SILVER MEDALIST | BRONZE MEDALIST |
|---|---|---|---|---|
| **Track and Field (Athletics) (continued)** | | | | |
| **Women** | | | | |
| Javelin throw | Trine Hattestad (NOR) | 68.91 m | Mirella Maniani-Tzelli (GRE) | Osleidys Menéndez (CUB) |
| Hammer throw | Kamila Skolimowska (POL) | 71.16 m | Olga Kuzenkova (RUS) | Kirsten Muenchow (GER) |
| Heptathlon | Denise Lewis (GBR) | 6,584 pt | Yelena Prokhorova (RUS) | Natalya Sazanovich (BLR) |
| **Triathlon** | | | | |
| Men | Simon Whitfield (CAN) | 1 hr 48 min 24 sec | Stefan Vuckovic (GER) | Jan Rehula (CZE) |
| Women | Brigitte McMahon (SUI) | 2 hr 40 sec | Michellie Jones (AUS) | Magali Messmer (SUI) |
| **Volleyball** | | | | |
| Men's 12-team tournament | Yugoslavia | 25–22, 25–22, 25–20 | Russia | Italy |
| Women's 12-team tournament | Cuba | 25–27, 32–34, 25–19, 25–18, 15–7 | Russia | Brazil |
| Men's beach | United States | 12–11, 12–9 | Brazil | Germany |
| Women's beach | Australia | 12–11, 12–10 | Brazil | Brazil |
| **Water Polo** | | | | |
| Men | Hungary | 13–6 | Russia | Yugoslavia |
| Women | Australia | 4–3 | United States | Russia |
| **Weightlifting§** | | | | |
| **Men** | | | | |
| 56 kg (bantamweight) | Halil Mutlu (TUR) | 305.0 kg‡ | Wu Wenxiong (CHN) | Zhang Xiangxiang (CHN) |
| 62 kg (featherweight) | Nikolay Pechalov (CRO) | 325.0 kg† | Leonidas Sabanis (GRE) | Gennady Oleschchuk (BLR) |
| 69 kg (lightweight) | Galabin Boevski (BUL) | 357.5 kg† | Georgi Markov (BUL) | Sergey Lavrenov (BLR) |
| 77 kg (middleweight) | Zhan Xugang (CHN) | 367.5 kg | Viktor Mitrou (GRE) | Arsen Melikyan (ARM) |
| 85 kg (light heavyweight) | Pyrros Dimas (GRE) | 390.0 kg | Marc Huster (GER) | George Asanidze (GEO) |
| 94 kg (middle heavyweight) | Akakios Kakiasvilis (GRE) | 405.0 kg | Szymon Kolecki (POL) | Aleksey Petrov (RUS) |
| 105 kg (heavyweight) | Hossein Tavakoli (IRI) | 425.0 kg | Alan Tsagayev (BUL) | Said Saif Asaad (QAT) |
| 105+ kg (super heavyweight) | Hossein Rezazadeh (IRI) | 472.5 kg‡ | Ronny Weller (GER) | Andrey Chemerkin (RUS) |
| **Women** | | | | |
| 48 kg (flyweight) | Tara Nott (USA) | 185.0 kg | Raema Lisa Rumbewas (INA) | Sri Indriyani (INA) |
| 53 kg (featherweight) | Yang Xia (CHN) | 225.0 kg‡ | Li Feng-Ying (TPE) | Winarni Binti Slamet (INA) |
| 58 kg (lightweight) | Soraya Mendivil (MEX) | 222.5 kg | Ri Song Hui (PRK) | Khassaraporn Suta (THA) |
| 63 kg (middleweight) | Chen Xiaomin (CHN) | 242.5 kg‡ | Valentina Popova (RUS) | Ioanna Chatziioannou (GRE) |
| 69 kg (light heavyweight) | Lin Weining (CHN) | 242.5 kg | Erzsebet Markus (HUN) | Karnam Malleswari (IND) |
| 75 kg (heavyweight) | Maria Isabel Urrutia (COL) | 245.0 kg | Ruth Ogbeifo (NGR) | Kuo Yi Hang (TPE) |
| 75+ kg (super heavyweight) | Ding Meiyuan (CHN) | 300.0 kg‡ | Agata Wrobel (POL) | Cheryl Haworth (USA) |
| **Wrestling§** | | | | |
| **Freestyle** | | | | |
| 54 kg (flyweight) | Namig Abdullayev (AZE) | | Samuel Henson (USA) | Amiran Karntanov (GRE) |
| 58 kg (bantamweight) | Alireza Dabir (IRI) | | Yevgen Buslovych (UKR) | Terry Brands (USA) |

## Olympic Medal Winners—XXVII Summer Games (continued)

| EVENT | GOLD MEDALIST | PERFORMANCE | SILVER MEDALIST | BRONZE MEDALIST |
|---|---|---|---|---|
| **Wrestling (continued)** | | | | |
| **Freestyle** | | | | |
| 63 kg (featherweight) | Murad Umakhanov (RUS) | | Serafim Barzakov (BUL) | Jang Jae Sung (KOR) |
| 69 kg (lightweight) | Daniel Igali (CAN) | | Arsen Gitinov (RUS) | Lincoln McIlravy (USA) |
| 76 kg (welterweight) | Brandon Slay (USA) | | Moon Eui Jae (KOR) | Adem Bereket (TUR) |
| 85 kg (middleweight) | Adam Saytyev (RUS) | | Yoel Romero (CUB) | Mogamed Ibragimov (MKD) |
| 97 kg (light heavy-weight) | Saghid Murtasaliyev (RUS) | | Islam Bayramukov (KAZ) | Eldar Kurtanidze (GEO) |
| 130+ kg (super heavyweight) | David Musulbes (RUS) | | Artur Taymazov (UZB) | Alexis Rodriguez (CUB) |
| | | | | |
| **Greco-Roman** | | | | |
| 54 kg (flyweight) | Sim Kwon Ho (KOR) | | Lazaro Rivas (CUB) | Kang Young Gyun (PRK) |
| 58 kg (bantamweight) | Armen Nazaryan (BUL) | | Kim In Sub (KOR) | Sheng Zetian (CHN) |
| 63 kg (featherweight) | Varteres Samurgashev (RUS) | | Juan Luis Maren (CUB) | Akaki Chachua (GEO) |
| 69 kg (lightweight) | Filiberto Azcuy (CUB) | | Katsuhiko Nagata (JPN) | Aleksey Glushkov (RUS) |
| 76 kg (welterweight) | Murat Kardanov (RUS) | | Matt James Lindland (USA) | Marko Yli-Hannuksela (FIN) |
| 85 kg (middleweight) | Hamza Yerlikaya (TUR) | | Sandor Istvan Bar-dosi (HUN) | Mukran Vaktang-adze (GEO) |
| 97 kg (light heavy-weight) | Mikael Ljungberg (SWE) | | Davyd Saldadze (UKR) | Garrett Lowney (USA) |
| 130+ kg (super heavyweight) | Rulon Gardner (USA) | | Aleksandr Karelin (RUS) | Dmitry Debelka (BLR) |

*Two bronze medals awarded in each weight division.　†Olympic record.　‡World record.　§New weight classes introduced for 2000 games.　¶Tie.*

Although the first Olympic champion listed in the records was one Coroebus of Elis, a cook, who won the sprint race in 776 BC, it is generally accepted that the Games were probably at least 500 years old at that time.

## Olympic Medal Winners—XIX Winter Games (2002)

*The XIX Winter Games were held in Salt Lake City UT, 8–24 Feb 2002.*

| EVENT | GOLD MEDALIST | PERFORMANCE | SILVER MEDALIST | BRONZE MEDALIST |
|---|---|---|---|---|
| **Alpine Skiing** | | | | |
| **Men** | | | | |
| Downhill | Fritz Strobl (AUT) | 1 min 39.13 sec | Lasse Kjus (NOR) | Stephan Eberharter (AUT) |
| Slalom | Jean-Pierre Vidal (FRA) | 1 min 41.06 sec | Sebastien Amiez (FRA) | Benjamin Raich (AUT) |
| Giant slalom | Stephan Eberharter (AUT) | 2 min 23.28 sec | Bode Miller (USA) | Lasse Kjus (NOR) |
| Super G | Kjetil Andre Aamodt (NOR) | 1 min 21.58 sec | Stephan Eberharter (AUT) | Andreas Schifferer (AUT) |
| Combined event | Kjetil Andre Aamodt (NOR) | 3 min 17.56 sec | Bode Miller (USA) | Benjamin Raich (AUT) |
| | | | | |
| **Women** | | | | |
| Downhill | Carole Montillet (FRA) | 1 min 39.56 sec | Isolde Kostner (ITA) | Renate Götschl (AUT) |
| Slalom | Janica Kostelic (CRO) | 1 min 46.10 sec | Laure Pequegnot (FRA) | Anja Pärson (SWE) |
| Giant slalom | Janica Kostelic (CRO) | 2 min 30.01 sec | Anja Pärson (SWE) | Sonja Nef (SUI) |
| Super G | Daniela Ceccarelli (ITA) | 1 min 13.59 sec | Janica Kostelic (CRO) | Karen Putzer (ITA) |
| Combined event | Janica Kostelic (CRO) | 2 min 43.28 sec | Renate Götschl (AUT) | Martina Ertl (GER) |

## Olympic Medal Winners—XIX Winter Games (2002) (continued)

| EVENT | GOLD MEDALIST | PERFORMANCE | SILVER MEDALIST | BRONZE MEDALIST |
|---|---|---|---|---|
| **Nordic Skiing** | | | | |
| **Men** | | | | |
| 1.5-km sprint | Tor Arne Hetland (NOR) | 2 min 56.9 sec | Peter Schlickenrieder (GER) | Cristian Zorzi (ITA) |
| 10-km freestyle pursuit | Johann Mühlegg (ESP) | 49 min 20.4 sec | Thomas Alsgaard (NOR)*; Frode Estil (NOR)* | |
| 15-km classical | Andrus Veerpalu (EST) | 37 min 7.4 sec | Frode Estil (NOR) | Jaak Mae (EST) |
| 30-km freestyle mass start | Johann Mühlegg (ESP) | 1 hr 9 min 28.9 sec | Christian Hoffmann (AUT) | Mikhail Botvinov (AUT) |
| 50-km classical | Mikhail Ivanov (RUS) | 2 hr 6 min 20.8 sec | Andrus Veerpalu (EST) | Odd-Björn Hjelmeset (NOR) |
| 4 x 10-km relay | Norway | 1 hr 32 min 45.5 sec | Italy | Germany |
| 90-m ski jump | Simon Ammann (SUI) | 269.0 pt | Sven Hannawald (GER) | Adam Malysz (POL) |
| 120-m ski jump | Simon Ammann (SUI) | 281.4 pt | Adam Malysz (POL) | Matti Hautamäki (FIN) |
| 120-m team ski jump | Germany | 974.1 pt | Finland | Slovenia |
| Nordic combined sprint (7.5-km) | Samppa Lajunen (FIN) | 16 min 40.1 sec | Ronny Ackermann (GER) | Felix Gottwald (AUT) |
| Nordic combined 15-km | Samppa Lajunen (FIN) | 39 min 11.7sec | Jaakko Tallus (FIN) | Felix Gottwald (AUT) |
| Nordic combined team relay | Finland | 48 min 42.2 sec | Germany | Austria |
| **Women** | | | | |
| 1.5-km sprint | Yuliya Chepalova (RUS) | 3 min 10.6 sec | Evi Sachenbacher (GER) | Anita Moen (NOR) |
| 5-km freestyle pursuit | Olga Danilova (RUS) | 24 min 52.1 sec | Larisa Lazutina (RUS) | Beckie Scott (CAN) |
| 10-km classical | Bente Skari (NOR) | 28 min 5.6 sec | Olga Danilova (RUS) | Yuliya Chepalova (RUS) |
| 15-km freestyle mass start | Stefania Belmondo (ITA) | 39 min 54.4 sec | Larisa Lazutina (RUS) | Katerina Neumannova (CZE) |
| 30-km classical | Gabriella Paruzzi (ITA) | 1 hr 30 min 57.1 sec | Stefania Belmondo (ITA) | Bente Skari (NOR) |
| 4 x 5-km relay | Germany | 49 min 30.6 sec | Norway | Switzerland |
| **Biathlon** | | | | |
| **Men** | | | | |
| 10-km sprint | Ole Einar Björndalen (NOR) | 24 min 51.3 sec | Sven Fischer (GER) | Wolfgang Perner (AUT) |
| 12.5-km pursuit | Ole Einar Björndalen (NOR) | 32 min 34.6 sec | Raphael Poiree (FRA) | Ricco Gross (GER) |
| 20 km | Ole Einar Björndalen (NOR) | 51 min 3.3 sec | Frank Luck (GER) | Viktor Maygourov (RUS) |
| 4 x 7.5-km relay | Norway | 1 hr 23 min 42.3 sec | Germany | France |
| **Women** | | | | |
| 7.5-km sprint | Kati Wilhelm (GER) | 20 min 41.4 sec | Uschi Disl (GER) | Magdalena Forsberg (SWE) |
| 10-km pursuit | Olga Pyleva (RUS) | 31 min 7.7 sec | Kati Wilhelm (GER) | Irina Nikulchina (RUS) |
| 15 km | Andrea Henkel (GER) | 47 min 29.1 sec | Liv Grete Poiree (NOR) | Magdalena Forsberg (SWE) |
| 4 x 7.5-km relay | Germany | 1 hr 27 min 55.0 sec | Norway | Russia |
| **Freestyle Skiing** | | | | |
| **Men** | | | | |
| Moguls | Janne Lahtela (FIN) | 27.97 pt | Travis Mayer (USA) | Richard Gay (FRA) |
| Aerials | Ales Valenta (CZE) | 257.02 pt | Joe Pack (USA) | Aleksey Grishin (BLR) |
| **Women** | | | | |
| Moguls | Kari Traa (NOR) | 25.94 pt | Shannon Bahrke (USA) | Tae Satoya (JPN) |
| Aerials | Alisa Camplin (AUS) | 193.47 pt | Veronica Brenner (CAN) | Deidra Dionne (CAN) |

## Olympic Medal Winners—XIX Winter Games (2002) (continued)

| EVENT | GOLD MEDALIST | PERFORMANCE | SILVER MEDALIST | BRONZE MEDALIST |
|---|---|---|---|---|
| **Snowboarding** | | | | |
| **Men** | | | | |
| Parallel giant slalom | Philipp Schoch (SUI) | | Richard Richardsson (SWE) | Chris Klug (USA) |
| Halfpipe | Ross Powers (USA) | 46.1 pt | Danny Kass (USA) | Jarret Thomas (USA) |
| **Women** | | | | |
| Parallel giant slalom | Isabelle Blanc (FRA) | | Karine Ruby (FRA) | Lidia Trettel (ITA) |
| Halfpipe | Kelly Clark (USA) | 47.9 pt | Doriane Vidal (FRA) | Fabienne Reuteler (SUI) |
| **Figure skating** | | | | |
| Men | Aleksey Yagudin (RUS) | 1.5 pt | Yevgeny Plushchenko (RUS) | Timothy Goebel (USA) |
| Women | Sarah Hughes (USA) | 3.0 pt | Irina Slutskaya (RUS) | Michelle Kwan (USA) |
| Pairs | Yelena Berezhnaya, Anton Sikharulidze (RUS)*; Jamie Salé, David Pelletier (CAN)* | | | Shen Xue, Zhao Hongbo (CHN) |
| Ice dancing | Marina Anissina, Gwendal Peizerat (FRA) | 2.0 pt | Irina Lobacheva, Ilya Averbukh (RUS) | Barbara Fusar Poli, Maurizio Margaglio (ITA) |
| **Speed Skating** | | | | |
| **Men** | | | | |
| 500 m | Casey FitzRandolph (USA) | 1 min 9.23 sec | Hiroyasu Shimizu (JPN) | Kip Carpenter (USA) |
| 1,000 m | Gerard van Velde (NED) | 1 min 7.18 sec† | Jan Bos (NED) | Joey Cheek (USA) |
| 1,500 m | Derek Parra (USA) | 1 min 43.95 sec† | Jochem Uytdehaage (NED) | Adne Sondral (NOR) |
| 5,000 m | Jochem Uytdehaage (NED) | 6 min 14.66 sec† | Derek Parra (USA) | Jens Boden (GER) |
| 10,000 m | Jochem Uytdehaage (NED) | 12 min 58.92 sec† | Gianni Romme (NED) | Lasse Saetre (NOR) |
| **Women** | | | | |
| 500 m | Catriona LeMay Doan (CAN) | 1 min 14.75 sec | Monique Garbrecht-Enfeldt (GER) | Sabine Völker (GER) |
| 1,000 m | Chris Witty (USA) | 1 min 13.83 sec† | Sabine Völker (GER) | Jennifer Rodriguez (USA) |
| 1,500 m | Anni Friesinger (GER) | 1 min 54.02 sec† | Sabine Völker (GER) | Jennifer Rodriguez (USA) |
| 3,000 m | Claudia Pechstein (GER) | 3 min 57.70 sec† | Renate Groenewold (NED) | Cindy Klassen (CAN) |
| 5,000 m | Claudia Pechstein (GER) | 6 min 46.91 sec† | Gretha Smit (NED) | Clara Hughes (CAN) |
| **Short-Track Speed Skating** | | | | |
| **Men** | | | | |
| 500 m | Marc Gagnon (CAN) | 41.802 sec‡ | Jonathan Guilmette (CAN) | Rusty Smith (USA) |
| 1,000 m | Steven Bradbury (AUS) | 1 min 29.109 sec | Apolo Anton Ohno (USA) | Mathieu Turcotte (CAN) |
| 1,500 m | Apolo Anton Ohno (USA) | 2 min 18.541 sec | Li Jiajun (CHN) | Marc Gagnon (CAN) |
| 5,000-m relay | Canada | 6 min 51.579 sec | Italy | China |
| **Women** | | | | |
| 500 m | Yang Yang (A) (CHN) | 44.187 sec | Evgeniya Radanova (BUL) | Wang Chunlu (CHN) |
| 1,000 m | Yang Yang (A) (CHN) | 1 min 36.391 sec | Ko Gi Hyun (KOR) | Yang Yang (S) (CHN) |
| 1,500 m | Ko Gi Hyun (KOR) | 2 min 31.581 sec | Choi Eun Kyung (KOR) | Evgeniya Radanova (BUL) |
| 3,000-m relay | South Korea | 4 min 12.793 sec† | China | Canada |
| **Ice Hockey** | | | | |
| Men (winning team) | Canada | 4–1–1 | United States | Russia |
| Women (winning team) | Canada | 5–0–0 | United States | Sweden |

## Olympic Medal Winners—XIX Winter Games (2002) (continued)

| EVENT | GOLD MEDALIST | PERFORMANCE | SILVER MEDALIST | BRONZE MEDALIST |
|---|---|---|---|---|
| **Curling** | | | | |
| Men (winning team) | Norway | 9-2-0 | Canada | Switzerland |
| Women (winning team) | Great Britain | 9-4-0 | Switzerland | Canada |
| **Bobsleigh (Bobsled)** | | | | |
| Two man | Christoph Langen, Markus Zimmermann (GER 1) | 3 min 10.11 sec | Steve Anderhub, Christian Reich (SUI 1) | Martin Annen, Beat Hefti (SUI 2) |
| Four man | Germany 2 | 3 min 7.51 sec | United States 1 | United States 2 |
| Women | Jill Bakken, Vonetta Flowers (USA 2) | 1 min 37.76 sec | Sandra Prokoff, Ulrike Holzner (GER 1) | Susi-Lisa Erdmann, Nicole Hersch-mann (GER 2) |
| **Luge** | | | | |
| Men (singles) | Armin Zöggeler (ITA) | 2 min 57.941 sec | Georg Hackl (GER) | Markus Prock (AUT) |
| Men (doubles) | Patric-Fritz Leitner, Alexander Resch (GER) | 1 min 26.082 sec | Brian Martin, Mark Grimmette (USA) | Chris Thorpe, Clay Ives (USA) |
| Women (singles) | Sylke Otto (GER) | 2 min 52.464 sec | Barbara Niedern-huber (GER) | Silke Kraushaar (GER) |
| **Skeleton** | | | | |
| Men | Jim Shea (USA) | 1 min 41.96 sec | Martin Rettl (AUT) | Gregor Staehli (SUI) |
| Women | Tristan Gale (USA) | 1 min 45.11 sec | Lea Ann Parsley (USA) | Alex Coomber (GBR) |

*Two medals awarded.   †World record.   ‡Olympic record.*

# Special Olympics

The Special Olympics is an international program to provide retarded persons (8 years of age or older) with year-round sports training and athletic competition in a variety of Olympic-type summer and winter sports. Inaugurated in 1968, the Special Olympics was officially recognized by the International Olympic Committee on 15 Feb 1988. **International headquarters** are in Washington DC.

In June 1963, with support from the Joseph P. Kennedy, Jr., Foundation, **Eunice Kennedy Shriver** (sister of Pres. John F. Kennedy) started a summer day-camp for retarded children at her home in Rockville MD. Between 1963 and 1968, the Kennedy Foundation promoted the creation of dozens of similar camps in the United States and Canada. Special awards were developed for physical achievements, and by 1968 Shriver had persuaded the Chicago Park District to join with the Kennedy Foundation in sponsoring a "Special Olympics," held at Soldier Field on 19–20 July. About 1,000 athletes from 26 US states and Canada participated. The games were such a success that, in December, Special Olympics, Inc. (now **Special Olympics International**), was founded, with chapters in the United States, Canada, and France. The first International Winter Special Olympics Games were held on **5–11 Feb 1977** (in Steamboat Springs CO). The number of participating countries proliferated so that by the 1990s there were chapters in some 90 countries. Over 15,000 meets and tournaments are held worldwide each year, culminating in the International Special Olympics Games every two years, alternating between winter and summer sports and each lasting for nine days.

**Special Olympics Web site:** <www.specialolympics.org>

**Did you know?** Soviet gymnast Larisa Latynina holds the record for number of Olympic medals won, having won 18 medals in Olympic competitions between 1956 and 1964.

# Archery

The international governing body for archery, the **Fédération Internationale de Tir à l'Arc (FITA)**, instituted world championships in 1931. Between 1931 and 1957 a variety of scoring rounds were used. In 1957, however, FITA established its own competition standard—two FITA rounds shot over four days. A single FITA **round** consists of 36 arrows shot from each of four distances; different distances are used for men's and women's competition. From 1987 to 1991 the grand FITA round was used. The Olympic round was used for the 1992 Olympic Games and the 1993 world championships; under this system the highest possible individual score in the finals round was 120. Since 1959 championships have been held biennially. Olympic competition is held with the **recurve style** of bow in which the limbs of the bow curve in one direction, then "recurve" in the other.

**FITA Web site:** <www.archery.org>

## FITA Outdoor World Target Archery Championships

Competition dates from 1931. Table includes data from 1985 in the Olympic (recurve) division only.

| | men's | | | | women's | | | |
|---|---|---|---|---|---|---|---|---|
| YEAR | INDIVIDUAL | POINTS | TEAM | POINTS | INDIVIDUAL | POINTS | TEAM | POINTS |
| 1985 | Rick McKinney (USA) | 2,601 | KOR | 7,660 | Irina Soldatova (URS) | 2,595 | URS | 7,721 |
| 1987 | Vladimir Yesheyev (URS) | 329 | FRG | 891 | Ma Xiangjun (CHN) | 330 | URS | 884 |
| 1989 | Stanislav Zabrodsky (URS) | 332 | URS | 985 | Kim Soo Nyung (KOR) | 338 | KOR | 995 |
| 1991 | Simon Fairweather (AUS) | 334 | KOR | 998 | Kim Soo Nyung (KOR) | 333 | KOR | 1,030 |
| 1993 | Park Kyung Mo (KOR) | 113 | FRA | 249 | Kim Soo Nyung (KOR) | 104 | KOR | 236 |
| 1995 | Lee Kyung Chul (KOR) | 109 | KOR | 255 | Natalya Valeyeva (MDA) | 113 | KOR | 247 |
| 1997 | Kim Kyung Ho (KOR) | 108 | KOR | 254 | Kim Du Ri (KOR) | 105 | KOR | 242 |
| 1999 | Hong Sung Chil (KOR) | 115 | ITA | 252 | Lee Eun Kyung (KOR) | 115 | ITA | 240 |
| 2001 | Yeon Jung Ki (KOR) | 115 | KOR | 247 | Park Sung Hyun (KOR) | 111 | CHN | 232 |
| 2003 | Michele Frangilli (ITA) | 113 | KOR | 238 | Mi-Jin Yun (KOR) | 116 | KOR | 252 |

**Did you know?** Sportswriter Grantland Rice's syndicated column, "The Sportlight," was the most influential of its day. It was Rice who in 1924 gave the backfield of the University of Notre Dame's football team its enduring nickname, the "Four Horsemen," and his annual selections of All-American football teams for Collier's magazine were considered to be authoritative. He coined the famous phrase that it was not important whether you "won or lost, but how you played the game."

# Automobile Racing

Of the various types of automobile races, the closed-circuit, or speedway, course was largely developed in the United States. The Indianapolis 500—now the premier Indy car event—was first run in 1911. A low-slung, fenderless, open-wheel car—called an Indy car—is essential for this race; its suspension (i.e., its ability to hold the track) is as important to a car's performance as its turbocharged engine. Often the chassis manufacturer is different from the engine manufacturer, resulting in cars identified, for example, as a Brabham/Repco. In such cases the chassis-maker is listed first, and the chassis-maker receives any money or awards that the car may win.

Indy car racing began in 1909, when the American Automobile Association (AAA) began sponsoring a 24-race championship series, including three races at the newly opened Indianapolis Motor Speedway (IMS). In 1956 the AAA gave up its involvement with auto racing, and the United States Auto Club (**USAC**) was organized as the sport's governing body. In 1978 two race-car owners broke away from USAC to form a new organization, Championship Auto Racing Teams, Inc. (**CART**), which sponsored its own series of races. In 1980 CART and USAC joined to form the Championship Racing League, which dissolved after five races. In 1994 the IMS announced a new Indy Racing League (IRL) to oversee the Indianapolis 500 beginning in 1996 and a new series of IRL races (leading to an annual drivers' championship) separate from those sponsored by CART.

The standard cars used for Grand Prix road (i.e., closed highway) racing are known as Formula One (or F-1) cars because they are built according to an evolving formula that was established after World War I by the Fédération Internationale de l'Automobile (**FIA**). Like the Indy car, the Formula One racer is open-wheeled and low-slung, but the F-1 is slightly smaller and more maneuverable.

There are approximately 17 Grand Prix events held worldwide throughout the year. Drivers compete for the **World Championship of Drivers** (inaugurated in 1950), receiving a total number of points based on their placement in each of the official Grand Prix events.

Many Grand Prix drivers participate in various endurance races, the most famous of which is the **Le Mans Grand Prix d'Endurance**, held on the 13.4-km (8.3-mi) Sarthe circuit, Le Mans, France.

Another type of popular racing event is the rally, which was established in 1907. More than 35 such competitions, raced over a specified route on public roads, take place yearly throughout the world. The classic occasion for rally racing is the **Rallye Automobile Monte-Carlo**, now started in various European cities with Monaco as its terminal point.

Stock car racing, which began in the United States in the first half of the 20th century, involves the racing of commercial cars that have been altered to increase their speed and maneuverability. The National Association for Stock Car Auto Racing (**NASCAR**) was founded in 1947 and awards the Winston Cup to the driver who has achieved the greatest number of points earned in a series of official NASCAR Winston Cup events over the stock car racing season. The **Daytona 500** is the premiere stock car event.

**Related Internet sites:** CART: <www.cart.com>; USAC: <www.usacracing.com>; IRL: <www.indyracingleague.com>; FIA (English and French): <www.fia.com>; Automobile Club de Monaco (rallye—English and French) <www.acm.mc/acm/acm-intro.php>; NASCAR: <www.nascar.com>

## Formula One Grand Prix Race Results, 2002–03

*The following 17 races constitute the Formula One circuit. The season is March–October.*
*The United States Grand Prix, held at the Indianapolis Motor Speedway, was added in 2000.*

| RACE | DATE | LOCALE | DRIVER (COUNTRY) | WINNER'S TIME (HR:MIN:SEC) |
|---|---|---|---|---|
| Hungarian Grand Prix | 18 Aug 2002 | Budapest | Rubens Barrichello (BRA) | 1:41:49.001 |
| Belgian Grand Prix | 1 Sep 2002 | Spa-Francorchamps | Michael Schumacher (GER) | 1:21:20.634 |
| Italian Grand Prix | 15 Sep 2002 | Monza | Rubens Barrichello (BRA) | 1:16:19.982 |
| United States Grand Prix | 29 Sep 2002 | Indianapolis | Rubens Barrichello (BRA) | 1:31:07.934 |
| Japanese Grand Prix | 13 Oct 2002 | Suzuka | Michael Schumacher (GER) | 1:26:59.698 |
| Australian Grand Prix | 9 Mar 2003 | Albert Park, Melbourne | David Coulthard (GBR) | 1:34:42.124 |
| Malaysian Grand Prix | 23 Mar 2003 | Kuala Lumpur | Kimi Raikkonen (FIN) | 1:32:22.195 |
| Brazilian Grand Prix | 6 Apr 2003 | São Paulo | Giancarlo Fisichella (ITA) | 1:31:17.748 |
| San Marino Grand Prix | 20 Apr 2003 | Imola | Michael Schumacher (GER) | 1:28:12.058 |
| Spanish Grand Prix | 4 May 2003 | Catalunya | Michael Schumacher (GER) | 1:33:46.933 |
| Austrian Grand Prix | 18 May 2003 | Spielberg | Michael Schumacher (GER) | 1:24:04.888 |
| Monaco Grand Prix | 1 Jun 2003 | Monaco | Juan Pablo Montoya (COL) | 1:42:19.010 |
| Canadian Grand Prix | 15 Jun 2003 | Montreal | Michael Schumacher (GER) | 1:31:13.591 |
| European Grand Prix | 29 Jun 2003 | Nurburgring, Germany | Ralf Schumacher (GER) | 1:34:43.622 |
| French Grand Prix | 6 Jul 2003 | Magny-Cours | Ralf Schumacher (GER) | 1:30:49.213 |
| British Grand Prix | 20 Jul 2003 | Silverstone | Rubens Barrichello (BRA) | 1:28:37.554 |
| German Grand Prix | 3 Aug 2003 | Hockenheim | Juan Pablo Montoya (COL) | 1:28:48.769 |

## World Championship of Drivers

Points are awarded to the top-finishing drivers in each race on the Grand Prix circuit and totaled at the end of the season to determine the championship. In 2002 the top three were: Michael Schumacher (GER) 144 points, Rubens Barrichello (BRA) 77 points, Juan Pablo Montoya (COL) 50 points. Where chassis and engine are made by different manufacturers, the chassis is given first and separated from the engine name by a slash.

| YEAR | DRIVER (NATIONALITY) | CONSTRUCTOR |
|---|---|---|
| 1950 | Giuseppe Farina (ITA) | Alfa Romeo |
| 1951 | Juan Manuel Fangio (ARG) | Alfa Romeo |
| 1952 | Alberto Ascari (ITA) | Ferrari |
| 1953 | Alberto Ascari (ITA) | Ferrari |
| 1954 | Juan Manuel Fangio (ARG) | Mercedes & Maserati |
| 1955 | Juan Manuel Fangio (ARG) | Mercedes |
| 1956 | Juan Manuel Fangio (ARG) | Lancia/Ferrari |
| 1957 | Juan Manuel Fangio (ARG) | Maserati |
| 1958 | Mike Hawthorn (GBR) | Ferrari |
| 1959 | Jack Brabham (AUS) | Cooper/Climax |
| 1960 | Jack Brabham (AUS) | Cooper/Climax |
| 1961 | Phil Hill (USA) | Ferrari |
| 1962 | Graham Hill (GBR) | BRM |
| 1963 | Jim Clark (GBR) | Lotus/Climax |
| 1964 | John Surtees (GBR) | Ferrari |
| 1965 | Jim Clark (GBR) | Lotus/Climax |
| 1966 | Jack Brabham (AUS) | Brabham/Repco |
| 1967 | Denny Hulme (NZL) | Brabham/Repco |
| 1968 | Graham Hill (GBR) | Lotus/Ford |
| 1969 | Jackie Stewart (GBR) | Matra/Ford |
| 1970 | Jochen Rindt (AUT) | Lotus/Ford |
| 1971 | Jackie Stewart (GBR) | Tyrrell/Ford |
| 1972 | Emerson Fittipaldi (BRA) | John Player Special/Ford |
| 1973 | Jackie Stewart (GBR) | Tyrrell/Ford |
| 1974 | Emerson Fittipaldi (BRA) | McLaren/Ford |
| 1975 | Niki Lauda (AUT) | Ferrari |
| 1976 | James Hunt (GBR) | McLaren/Ford |
| 1977 | Niki Lauda (AUT) | Ferrari |
| 1978 | Mario Andretti (USA) | Lotus |
| 1979 | Jody Scheckter (RSA) | Ferrari |
| 1980 | Alan Jones (AUS) | Williams |
| 1981 | Nelson Piquet (BRA) | Brabham |
| 1982 | Keke Rosberg (FIN) | Williams |
| 1983 | Nelson Piquet (BRA) | Brabham |
| 1984 | Niki Lauda (AUT) | McLaren/Porsche-TAG |
| 1985 | Alain Prost (FRA) | McLaren/Porsche-TAG |
| 1986 | Alain Prost (FRA) | McLaren/Porsche-TAG |
| 1987 | Nelson Piquet (BRA) | Williams/Honda |
| 1988 | Ayrton Senna (BRA) | McLaren/Honda |
| 1989 | Alain Prost (FRA) | McLaren/Honda |
| 1990 | Ayrton Senna (BRA) | McLaren/Honda |
| 1991 | Ayrton Senna (BRA) | McLaren/Honda |
| 1992 | Nigel Mansell (GBR) | Williams/Renault |
| 1993 | Alain Prost (FRA) | Williams/Renault |
| 1994 | Michael Schumacher (GER) | Benetton/Ford |
| 1995 | Michael Schumacher (GER) | Benetton/Renault |
| 1996 | Damon Hill (GBR) | Williams/Renault |
| 1997 | Jacques Villeneuve (CAN) | Williams/Renault |
| 1998 | Mika Häkkinen (FIN) | McLaren/Mercedes |
| 1999 | Mika Häkkinen (FIN) | McLaren/Mercedes |
| 2000 | Michael Schumacher (GER) | Ferrari |
| 2001 | Michael Schumacher (GER) | Ferrari |
| 2002 | Michael Schumacher (GER) | Ferrari |

**Did you know?** The average speed clocked at the Indianapolis 500 has more than doubled over the 92 years since the race began.

## Constructors' Championship

Points are awarded to the constructors of the top-finishing autos in each race on the Grand Prix circuit and are totaled at the end of the season to determine the Constructors' Championship. In 2002 the top three were: Ferrari 221 points, Williams/BMW 92 points, McLaren/Mercedes 65 points.

| YEAR | CONSTRUCTOR | YEAR | CONSTRUCTOR | YEAR | CONSTRUCTOR | YEAR | CONSTRUCTOR |
|---|---|---|---|---|---|---|---|
| 1958 | Vanwall | 1970 | Lotus | 1982 | Ferrari | 1993 | Williams/Renault |
| 1959 | Cooper | 1971 | Tyrrell | 1983 | Ferrari | 1994 | Williams/Renault |
| 1960 | Cooper | 1972 | Lotus | 1984 | McLaren | 1995 | Benetton/Renault |
| 1961 | Ferrari | 1973 | Lotus | 1985 | McLaren | 1996 | Williams/Renault |
| 1962 | BRM | 1974 | McLaren | 1986 | Williams/Honda | 1997 | Williams/Renault |
| 1963 | Lotus | 1975 | Ferrari | 1987 | Williams/Honda | 1998 | McLaren/Mercedes |
| 1964 | Ferrari | 1976 | Ferrari | 1988 | McLaren/Honda | 1999 | Ferrari |
| 1965 | Lotus | 1977 | Ferrari | 1989 | McLaren/Honda | 2000 | Ferrari |
| 1966 | Brabham | 1978 | Lotus | 1990 | McLaren/Honda | 2001 | Ferrari |
| 1967 | Brabham | 1979 | Ferrari | 1991 | McLaren/Honda | 2002 | Ferrari |
| 1968 | Lotus | 1980 | Williams | 1992 | Williams/Renault | | |
| 1969 | Matra | 1981 | Williams | | | | |

## Indy Car Champions

Between 1909 and 1955 called the AAA National Champions; called the USAC National Champions from 1956 to 1978. There was no competition 1942–45. The title was won by an American racer except as indicated. Indianapolis Motor Speedway Web site: <www.cart.com>.

| YEAR | DRIVER | YEAR | DRIVER | YEAR | DRIVER |
|---|---|---|---|---|---|
| 1909 | George Robertson | 1940 | Rex Mays | 1975 | A.J. Foyt, Jr. |
| 1910 | Ray Harroun | 1941 | Rex Mays | 1976 | Gordon Johncock |
| 1911 | Ralph Mulford | 1946 | Ted Horn | 1977 | Tom Sneva |
| 1912 | Ralph DePalma | 1947 | Ted Horn | 1978 | Tom Sneva |
| 1913 | Earl Cooper | 1948 | Ted Horn | 1979 | A.J. Foyt, Jr.*; Rick Mears† |
| 1914 | Ralph DePalma | 1949 | Johnnie Parsons | | |
| 1915 | Earl Cooper | 1950 | Henry Banks | 1980 | Johnny Rutherford |
| 1916 | Dario Resta (FRA) | 1951 | Tony Bettenhausen, Sr. | 1981 | Rick Mears |
| 1917 | Earl Cooper | 1952 | Chuck Stevenson | 1982 | Rick Mears |
| 1918 | Ralph Mulford | 1953 | Sam Hanks | 1983 | Al Unser |
| 1919 | Howard ("Howdy") Wilcox | 1954 | Jimmy Bryan | 1984 | Mario Andretti |
| 1920 | Tommy Milton | 1955 | Robert Sweikert | 1985 | Al Unser |
| 1921 | Tommy Milton | 1956 | Jimmy Bryan | 1986 | Bobby Rahal |
| 1922 | Jimmy Murphy | 1957 | Jimmy Bryan | 1987 | Bobby Rahal |
| 1923 | Eddie Hearne | 1958 | Tony Bettenhausen, Sr. | 1988 | Danny Sullivan |
| 1924 | Jimmy Murphy | 1959 | Rodger Ward | 1989 | Emerson Fittipaldi (BRA) |
| 1925 | Peter DePaolo | 1960 | A.J. Foyt, Jr. | 1990 | Al Unser, Jr. |
| 1926 | Harry Hartz | 1961 | A.J. Foyt, Jr. | 1991 | Michael Andretti |
| 1927 | Peter DePaolo | 1962 | Rodger Ward | 1992 | Bobby Rahal |
| 1928 | Louie Meyer | 1963 | A.J. Foyt, Jr. | 1993 | Nigel Mansell (GBR) |
| 1929 | Louie Meyer | 1964 | A.J. Foyt, Jr. | 1994 | Al Unser, Jr. |
| 1930 | Billy Arnold | 1965 | Mario Andretti | 1995 | Jacques Villeneuve (CAN) |
| 1931 | Louis Schneider | 1966 | Mario Andretti | 1996 | Jimmy Vasser |
| 1932 | Bob Carey | 1967 | A.J. Foyt, Jr. | 1997 | Alessandro (Alex) Zanardi (ITA) |
| 1933 | Louie Meyer | 1968 | Bobby Unser | | |
| 1934 | Bill Cummings | 1969 | Mario Andretti | 1998 | Alessandro (Alex) Zanardi (ITA) |
| 1935 | Kelly Petillo | 1970 | Al Unser | | |
| 1936 | Mauri Rose | 1971 | Joe Leonard | 1999 | Juan Montoya (COL) |
| 1937 | Wilbur Shaw | 1972 | Joe Leonard | 2000 | Gil de Ferran (BRA) |
| 1938 | Floyd Roberts | 1973 | Roger McCluskey | 2001 | Gil de Ferran (BRA) |
| 1939 | Wilbur Shaw | 1974 | Bobby Unser | 2002 | Cristiano da Matta (BRA) |

*USAC champion.     †CART champion from 1980.

## Indianapolis 500

*There was no competition in 1917–18 and 1942–45.*
*The race was won by an American racer unless otherwise noted.*

| YEAR | WINNER | AVG. SPEED (MPH) | YEAR | WINNER | AVG. SPEED (MPH) | YEAR | WINNER | AVG. SPEED (MPH) |
|---|---|---|---|---|---|---|---|---|
| 1911 | Ray Harroun | 74.602 | 1913 | Jules Goux (FRA) | 75.933 | 1915 | Ralph DePalma | 89.840 |
| 1912 | Joe Dawson | 78.719 | 1914 | René Thomas (FRA) | 82.474 | 1916[1] | Dario Resta (FRA) | 84.001 |

# Indianapolis 500 (continued)

| YEAR | WINNER | AVG. SPEED (MPH) | YEAR | WINNER | AVG. SPEED (MPH) | YEAR | WINNER | AVG. SPEED (MPH) |
|------|--------|------------------|------|--------|------------------|------|--------|------------------|
| 1919 | Howdy Wilcox | 88.050 | 1956 | Pat Flaherty | 128.490 | 1985 | Danny Sullivan | 152.982 |
| 1920 | Gaston Chevrolet | 88.618 | 1957 | Sam Hanks | 135.601 | 1986 | Bobby Rahal | 170.722 |
| 1921 | Tommy Milton | 89.621 | 1958 | Jimmy Bryan | 133.791 | 1987 | Al Unser | 162.175 |
| 1922 | Jimmy Murphy | 94.484 | 1959 | Rodger Ward | 135.857 | 1988 | Rick Mears | 144.809 |
| 1923 | Tommy Milton | 90.954 | 1960 | Jim Rathmann | 138.767 | 1989 | Emerson Fitti-paldi (BRA) | 167.581 |
| 1924 | L.L. Corum, Joe Boyer | 98.234 | 1961 | A.J. Foyt, Jr. | 139.131 | | | |
| | | | 1962 | Rodger Ward | 140.293 | 1990 | Arie Luyendyk (NED) | 185.984 |
| 1925 | Peter DePaolo | 101.127 | 1963 | Parnelli Jones | 143.137 | | | |
| 1926[2] | Frank Lockhart | 95.904 | 1964 | A.J. Foyt, Jr. | 147.350 | 1991 | Rick Mears | 176.457 |
| 1927 | George Souders | 97.545 | 1965 | Jim Clark (GBR) | 150.686 | 1992 | Al Unser, Jr. | 134.479 |
| 1928 | Louie Meyer | 99.482 | 1966 | Graham Hill (GBR) | 144.317 | 1993 | Emerson Fitti-paldi (BRA) | 157.207 |
| 1929 | Ray Keech | 97.585 | | | | | | |
| 1930 | Billy Arnold | 100.448 | 1967 | A.J. Foyt, Jr. | 151.207 | 1994 | Al Unser, Jr. | 160.872 |
| 1931 | Louis Schneider | 96.629 | 1968 | Bobby Unser | 152.882 | 1995 | Jacques Ville-neuve (CAN) | 153.616 |
| 1932 | Fred Frame | 104.144 | 1969 | Mario Andretti | 156.867 | | | |
| 1933 | Louie Meyer | 104.162 | 1970 | Al Unser | 155.749 | 1996 | Buddy Lazier | 147.956 |
| 1934 | Bill Cummings | 104.863 | 1971 | Al Unser | 157.735 | 1997 | Arie Luyendyk (NED) | 145.827 |
| 1935 | Kelly Petillo | 106.240 | 1972 | Mark Donohue | 162.962 | | | |
| 1936 | Louie Meyer | 109.069 | 1973[2] | Gordon John-cock | 159.036 | 1998 | Eddie Cheever, Jr. | 145.155 |
| 1937 | Wilbur Shaw | 113.580 | | | | | | |
| 1938 | Floyd Roberts | 117.200 | 1974 | Johnny Ruther-ford | 158.589 | 1999 | Kenny Brack (SWE) | 153.176 |
| 1939 | Wilbur Shaw | 115.035 | | | | | | |
| 1940 | Wilbur Shaw | 114.277 | 1975[2] | Bobby Unser | 149.213 | 2000 | Juan Montoya (COL) | 167.607 |
| 1941 | Floyd Davis, Mauri Rose | 115.117 | 1976[2] | Johnny Ruther-ford | 148.725 | 2001 | Helio Castro-neves (BRA) | 153.601 |
| 1946 | George Robson | 114.820 | 1977 | A.J. Foyt, Jr. | 161.331 | | | |
| 1947 | Mauri Rose | 116.338 | 1978 | Al Unser | 161.363 | 2002 | Helio Castro-neves (BRA) | 166.499 |
| 1948 | Mauri Rose | 119.814 | 1979 | Rick Mears | 158.899 | | | |
| 1949 | Bill Holland | 121.327 | 1980 | Johnny Ruther-ford | 142.862 | 2003 | Gil de Ferran (BRA) | 156.291 |
| 1950[2] | Johnnie Parsons | 124.002 | | | | | | |
| 1951 | Lee Wallard | 126.244 | 1981 | Bobby Unser | 139.084 | | | |
| 1952 | Troy Ruttman | 128.922 | 1982 | Gordon John-cock | 162.029 | | | |
| 1953 | Bill Vukovich | 128.740 | | | | | | |
| 1954 | Bill Vukovich | 130.840 | 1983 | Tom Sneva | 162.117 | | | |
| 1955 | Robert Sweikert | 128.209 | 1984 | Rick Mears | 163.612 | | | |

[1]Scheduled 300-mile race.  [2]Race stopped because of rain (in 1926 after 400 miles, in 1950 after 345 miles, in 1973 after 332.5 miles, in 1975 after 435 miles, in 1976 after 255 miles).

# Le Mans Grand Prix d'Endurance

*Also called Le Mans 24-hour Race.*

| YEAR | CAR | DRIVERS |
|------|-----|---------|
| 1923 | Chenard & Walcker | André Lagache, René Léonard |
| 1924 | Bentley | John Duff, Frank Clément |
| 1925 | Lorraine-Dietrich | Gérard de Courcelles, André Rossignol |
| 1926 | Lorraine-Dietrich | Robert Bloch, André Rossignol |
| 1927 | Bentley | John Benjafield, Sammy Davis |
| 1928 | Bentley | Woolf Barnato, Bernard Rubin |
| 1929 | Bentley | Woolf Barnato, Henry Birkin |
| 1930 | Bentley | Woolf Barnato, Glen Kidston |
| 1931 | Alfa Romeo | Lord Howe, Henry Birkin |
| 1932 | Alfa Romeo | Raymond Sommer, Luigi Chinetti |
| 1933 | Alfa Romeo | Raymond Sommer, Tazio Nuvolari |
| 1934 | Alfa Romeo | Luigi Chinetti, Philippe Etancelin |
| 1935 | Lagonda | John Hindmarsh, Luis Fontés |
| 1936 | *no competition* | |
| 1937 | Bugatti | Jean-Pierre Wimille, Robert Benoist |
| 1938 | Delahaye | Eugene Chaboud, Jean Tremoulet |
| 1939 | Bugatti | Jean-Pierre Wimille, Pierre Veyron |
| 1940–48 | *no competition* | |
| 1949 | Ferrari | Luigi Chinetti, Lord Selsdon |
| 1950 | Talbot | Louis Rosier, Jean-Louis Rosier |
| 1951 | Jaguar | Peter Walker, Peter Whitehead |
| 1952 | Mercedes-Benz | Hermann Lang, Fritz Riess |
| 1953 | Jaguar C-type | Tony Rolt, Duncan Hamilton |

## Le Mans Grand Prix d'Endurance (continued)

| YEAR | CAR | DRIVERS |
|------|-----|---------|
| 1954 | Ferrari 375 | Froilan Gonzalez, Maurice Trintignant |
| 1955 | Jaguar D-type | Mike Hawthorn, Ivor Bueb |
| 1956 | Jaguar D-type | Ron Flockhart, Ninian Sanderson |
| 1957 | Jaguar D-type | Ivor Bueb, Ron Flockhart |
| 1958 | Ferrari | Phil Hill, Olivier Gendebien |
| 1959 | Aston Martin | Roy Salvadori, Carroll Shelby |
| 1960 | Ferrari | Paul Frère, Olivier Gendebien |
| 1961 | Ferrari | Phil Hill, Olivier Gendebien |
| 1962 | Ferrari | Phil Hill, Olivier Gendebien |
| 1963 | Ferrari | Lodovico Scarfiotti, Lorenzo Bandini |
| 1964 | Ferrari | Jean Guichet, Nino Vaccarella |
| 1965 | Ferrari | Masten Gregory, Jochen Rindt |
| 1966 | Ford Mk II | Bruce McLaren, Chris Amon |
| 1967 | Ford Mk IV | A.J. Foyt, Dan Gurney |
| 1968 | Ford G.T. 40 | Pedro Rodriguez, Lucien Bianchi |
| 1969 | Ford G.T. 40 | Jacky Ickx, Jackie Oliver |
| 1970 | Porsche | Richard Attwood, Hans Hermann |
| 1971 | Porsche | Helmut Marko, Gijs van Lennep |
| 1972 | Matra-Simca | Henri Pescarolo, Graham Hill |
| 1973 | Matra-Simca | Henri Pescarolo, Gérard Larrousse |
| 1974 | Matra-Simca | Henri Pescarolo, Gérard Larrousse |
| 1975 | Gulf-Ford | Jacky Ickx, Derek Bell |
| 1976 | Porsche | Jacky Ickx, Gijs van Lennep |
| 1977 | Porsche | Jacky Ickx, Jurgen Barth, Hurley Haywood |
| 1978 | Renault-Alpine | Jean-Pierre Jaussaud, Didier Pironi |
| 1979 | Porsche | Klaus Ludwig, Don Whittington, Bill Whittington |
| 1980 | Porsche | Jean Rondeau, Jean-Pierre Jaussaud |
| 1981 | Porsche | Derek Bell, Jacky Ickx |
| 1982 | Porsche 956 | Derek Bell, Jacky Ickx |
| 1983 | Porsche 956 | Al Holbert, Hurley Hayward, Vern Schuppan |
| 1984 | Porsche 956 | Henri Pescarolo, Klaus Ludwig |
| 1985 | Porsche 956 | Klaus Ludwig, John Winter, Paulo Barilla |
| 1986 | Porsche 962 C | Derek Bell, Hans Stuck, Al Holbert |
| 1987 | Porsche 962 C | Hans Stuck, Derek Bell, Al Holbert |
| 1988 | Jaguar XJR 9 LM | Jan Lammers, Johnny Dumfries, Andy Wallace |
| 1989 | Sauber Mercedes-Benz C9 | Jochen Mass, Manuel Reuter, Stanley Dickens |
| 1990 | Jaguar XJR 12 | John Nielsen, Price Cobb, Martin Brundle |
| 1991 | Mazda 787 B | Volker Weidler, Johnny Herbert, Bertrand Gachot |
| 1992 | Peugeot 905 | Yannick Dalmas, Mark Blundell, Derek Warwick |
| 1993 | Peugeot 905 | Geoff Brabham, Christophe Bouchut, Eric Helary |
| 1994 | Dauer Porsche 962 LM | Yannick Dalmas, Hurley Haywood, Mauro Baldi |
| 1995 | McLaren F1 GTR | Yannick Dalmas, J.J. Lehto, Masanori Sekiya |
| 1996 | TWR-Porsche WSC 95 | Manuel Reuter, Davy Jones, Alex Wurz |
| 1997 | TWR-Porsche WSC 95 | Michele Alboreto, Stefan Johansson, Tom Kristensen |
| 1998 | Porsche 911 GT1 | Alan McNish, Laurent Aiello, Stephane Ortelli |
| 1999 | BMW V12 LMR | Yannick Dalmas, Pierluigi Martini, Joachim Winkelhock |
| 2000 | Audi R8 | Frank Biela, Tom Kristensen, Emanuele Pirro |
| 2001 | Audi 3596 T | Frank Biela, Tom Kristensen, Emanuele Pirro |
| 2002 | Audi R8 2002 | Frank Biela, Tom Kristensen, Emanuele Pirro |
| 2003 | Bentley | Tom Kristensen, Rinaldo Capello, Guy Smith |

## Monte-Carlo Rally

| YEAR | CAR | DRIVER, CODRIVER |
|------|-----|------------------|
| 1911 | Turcat Méry | Henri Rougier (FRA) |
| 1912 | Berliet | Julius Beutler (GER) |
| 1913–23 | *no competition* | |
| 1924 | Bignan | Jean Ledure (FRA) |
| 1925 | Renault 40CV | François Repusseau (FRA) |
| 1926 | A.C. Bristol | Victor Bruce (GBR) |
| 1927 | Amilcar | Lefèbvre (FRA), Despeaux (FRA) |
| 1928 | Fiat | Jacques Bignan (FRA) |
| 1929 | Graham-Paige | Dr. Sprenger van Eijk (NED) |
| 1930 | Licorne | Hector Petit (FRA) |
| 1931 | Invicta | Donald Healey (GBR) |
| 1932 | Hotchkiss | M. Vasselle (FRA) |
| | Peugeot | G. de Lavelette, C. de Cortanze |

# Monte-Carlo Rally (continued)

| YEAR | CAR | DRIVER, CODRIVER |
|---|---|---|
| 1933 | Hotchkiss | M. Vasselle (FRA) |
| 1934 | Hotchkiss | Gas (FRA), Jean Trevoux (FRA) |
| 1935 | Renault Nervasport | Christian Lahaye (FRA), R. Quatresous (FRA) |
| 1936 | Ford | Lionel Samfirescu (ROM), Petre Cristea (ROM) |
| 1937 | Delahaye | Rene Le Begue (FRA), J. Quinlin (FRA) |
| 1938 | Ford | G. Baker Schut (NED), Karelton (NED) |
| 1939 | Hotchkiss | Jean Trevoux (FRA), Marcel Lesurque (FRA) |
|  | Delahaye | Joseph Paul, Marcel Contet (FRA) |
| 1940–48 | *no competition* | |
| 1949 | Hotchkiss | Jean Trevoux (FRA), Marcel Lesurque (FRA) |
| 1950 | Hotchkiss | Marcel Becquart (FRA), H. Secret (FRA) |
| 1951 | Delahaye | Jean Trevoux (FRA), Roger Crovetto (FRA) |
| 1952 | Allard P-1 | Sydney Allard (GBR), Guy Warburton (GBR), Tom Lush (GBR) |
| 1953 | Ford Zephyr | Maurice Gatsonides (NED), P. Worledge (GBR) |
| 1954 | Lancia Aurelia | Louis Chiron (FRA), Giro Basadonna (SPA) |
| 1955 | Sunbeam Talbot | Per Malling (NOR), Gunnar Fadum (NOR) |
| 1956 | Jaguar Mk VII | Ronnie Adams (GBR), Frank Bigger (GBR) |
| 1957 | *no competition* | |
| 1958 | Renault Dauphine | Guy Monraisse (FRA), Jacques Feret (FRA) |
| 1959 | Citroën ID19 | Paul Coltelloni (FRA), Pierre Alexandre (FRA) |
| 1960 | Mercedes 220SE | Walter Schock (FRG), Rolf Moll (FRG) |
| 1961 | Panhard PL17 | M. Martin (FRA), Roger Bateau (FRA) |
| 1962 | Saab 96 | Erik Carlsson (SWE), Gunnar Häggbom (SWE) |
| 1963 | Saab 96 | Erik Carlsson (SWE), Gunnar Palm (SWE) |
| 1964 | Mini-Cooper S | Paddy Hopkirk (GBR), Henry Liddon (GBR) |
| 1965 | Mini-Cooper S | Timo Makinen (FIN), Paul Easter (GBR) |
| 1966 | Citroën ID19 | Pauli Toivonen (FIN), Ensio Mikkander (FIN) |
| 1967 | Mini-Cooper S | Rauno Aaltonen (FIN), Henry Liddon (GBR) |
| 1968 | Porsche 911T | Vic Elford (GBR), David Stone (GBR) |
| 1969 | Porsche 911S | Bjorn Waldegaard (SWE), Lars Helmer (SWE) |
| 1970 | Porsche 911S | Bjorn Waldegaard (SWE), Lars Helmer (SWE) |
| 1971 | Alpine-Renault A110 | Ove Andersson (SWE), David Stone (GBR) |
| 1972 | Lancia Fulvia 1.6HF | Sandro Munari (ITA), Mario Mannucci (ITA) |
| 1973 | Alpine-Renault A110 | Jean-Claude Andruet (FRA), Michèle "Biche" Petit (FRA) |
| 1974 | *no competition* | |
| 1975 | Lancia Stratos HF | Sandro Munari (ITA), Mario Mannucci (ITA) |
| 1976 | Lancia Stratos HF | Sandro Munari (ITA), Mario Mannucci (ITA) |
| 1977 | Lancia Stratos HF | Sandro Munari (ITA), Silvio Maiga (ITA) |
| 1978 | Porsche 911 Carrera | Jean-Pierre Nicolas (FRA), Vincent Laverne (FRA) |
| 1979 | Lancia Stratos HF | Bernard Darniche (FRA), Alain Mahé (FRA) |
| 1980 | Fiat 131 Abarth | Walter Röhrl (FRG), Christian Geistdorfer (FRG) |
| 1981 | Renault 5 Turbo | Jean Ragnotti (FRA), Jean-Marc Andrie (FRA) |
| 1982 | Opel Ascona 400 | Walter Röhrl (FRG), Christian Geistdorfer (FRG) |
| 1983 | Lancia Rally 037 | Walter Röhrl (FRG), Christian Geistdorfer (FRG) |
| 1984 | Audi Quattro | Walter Röhrl (FRG), Christian Geistdorfer (FRG) |
| 1985 | Peugeot 205 Turbo | Ari Vatanen (FIN), Terry Harryman (GBR) |
| 1986 | Lancia Delta S4 | Henri Toivonen (FIN), Sergio Cresto (USA) |
| 1987 | Lancia Delta HF 4WD | Mickey Biasion (ITA), Tiziano Siviero (ITA) |
| 1988 | Lancia Delta HF 4WD | Bruno Saby (FRA), Jean-François Fauchille (FRA) |
| 1989 | Lancia Delta HF Integrale | Mickey Biasion (ITA), Tiziano Siviero (ITA) |
| 1990 | Lancia Delta HF Integrale | Didier Auriol (FRA), Bernard Occelli (FRA) |
| 1991 | Toyota Celica GT4 | Carlos Sainz (ESP), Luis Moya (ESP) |
| 1992 | Lancia Delta HF Integrale | Didier Auriol (FRA), Bernard Occelli (FRA) |
| 1993 | Toyota Celica Turbo 4WD | Didier Auriol (FRA), Bernard Occelli (FRA) |
| 1994 | Ford Escort RS Cosworth | François Delecour (FRA), Daniel Grataloup (FRA) |
| 1995 | Subaru Impreza 555 | Carlos Sainz (ESP), Luis Moya (ESP) |
| 1996 | Ford Escort RS Cosworth | Patrick Bernardini (FRA), Bernard Occelli (FRA) |
| 1997 | Subaru Impreza WRC97 | Piero Liatti (ITA), Fabrizia Pons (ITA) |
| 1998 | Toyota Corolla WRC | Carlos Sainz (ESP), Luis Moya (ESP) |
| 1999 | Mitsubishi Lancer Evo VI | Tommi Mäkinen (FIN), Risto Mannisenmaki (FIN) |
| 2000 | Mitsubishi Lancer Evo VI | Tommi Mäkinen (FIN), Risto Mannisenmaki (FIN) |
| 2001 | Mitsubishi Lancer Evo VI | Tommi Mäkinen (FIN), Risto Mannisenmaki (FIN) |
| 2002 | Subaru Impreza | Tommi Mäkinen (FIN), Kaj Lindstrom (FIN) |
| 2003 | Citroën | Sébastien Loeb (FRA), Daniel Elena (MON) |
| 2004 | *to be held in January* | |

## NASCAR Winston Cup Champions

| YEAR | WINNER | YEAR | WINNER | YEAR | WINNER | YEAR | WINNER |
|------|--------|------|--------|------|--------|------|--------|
| 1949 | Red Byron | 1964 | Richard Petty | 1978 | Cale Yarborough | 1992 | Alan Kulwicki |
| 1950 | Bill Rexford | 1965 | Ned Jarrett | 1979 | Richard Petty | 1993 | Dale Earnhardt |
| 1951 | Herb Thomas | 1966 | David Pearson | 1980 | Dale Earnhardt | 1994 | Dale Earnhardt |
| 1952 | Tim Flock | 1967 | Richard Petty | 1981 | Darrell Waltrip | 1995 | Jeff Gordon |
| 1953 | Herb Thomas | 1968 | David Pearson | 1982 | Darrell Waltrip | 1996 | Terry Labonte |
| 1954 | Lee Petty | 1969 | David Pearson | 1983 | Bobby Allison | 1997 | Jeff Gordon |
| 1955 | Tim Flock | 1970 | Bobby Isaac | 1984 | Terry Labonte | 1998 | Jeff Gordon |
| 1956 | Buck Baker | 1971 | Richard Petty | 1985 | Darrell Waltrip | 1999 | Dale Jarrett |
| 1957 | Buck Baker | 1972 | Richard Petty | 1986 | Dale Earnhardt | 2000 | Bobby Labonte |
| 1958 | Lee Petty | 1973 | Benny Parsons | 1987 | Dale Earnhardt | 2001 | Jeff Gordon |
| 1959 | Lee Petty | 1974 | Richard Petty | 1988 | Bill Elliott | 2002 | Tony Stewart |
| 1960 | Rex White | 1975 | Richard Petty | 1989 | Rusty Wallace | 2003 | *season ends* |
| 1961 | Ned Jarrett | 1976 | Cale Yarborough | 1990 | Dale Earnhardt | | *16 November in* |
| 1962 | Joe Weatherly | 1977 | Cale Yarborough | 1991 | Dale Earnhardt | | *Homestead FL* |
| 1963 | Joe Weatherly | | | | | | |

## Daytona 500 Winners, 1959–2003

*The most recent race was held at Daytona International Speedway, Daytona Beach FL, 22 Feb 2003. Daytona 500 Web site: <www.daytona500.com>.*

| YEAR | WINNER | YEAR | WINNER | YEAR | WINNER |
|------|--------|------|--------|------|--------|
| 1959 | Lee Petty | 1973 | Richard Petty | 1990 | Derrike Cope |
| 1960 | Junior Johnson | 1974 | Richard Petty | 1991 | Ernie Irvan |
| 1961 | Marvin Panch | 1975 | Benny Parsons | 1992 | David Carl ("Davey") Allison |
| 1962 | Edward Glen ("Fireball") Roberts | 1976 | David Pearson | | |
| 1963 | DeWayne Louis ("Tiny") Lund | 1977 | Cale Yarborough | 1993 | Dale Jarrett |
| | | 1978 | Bobby Allison | 1994 | Sterling Marlin |
| | | 1979 | Richard Petty | 1995 | Sterling Marlin |
| 1964 | Richard Petty | 1980 | Wylie ("Buddy") Baker, Jr. | 1996 | Dale Jarrett |
| 1965 | Fred Lorenzen | 1981 | Richard Petty | 1997 | Jeff Gordon |
| 1966 | Richard Petty | 1982 | Bobby Allison | 1998 | Dale Earnhardt, Sr. |
| 1967 | Mario Andretti | 1983 | Cale Yarborough | 1999 | Jeff Gordon |
| 1968 | William Caleb ("Cale") Yarborough | 1984 | Cale Yarborough | 2000 | Dale Jarrett |
| | | 1985 | Bill Elliott | 2001 | Michael Waltrip |
| 1969 | Lee Roy Yarbrough | 1986 | Geoff Bodine | 2002 | Ward Burton |
| 1970 | Pete Hamilton | 1987 | Bill Elliott | 2003 | Michael Waltrip |
| 1971 | Richard Petty | 1988 | Bobby Allison | | |
| 1972 | A.J. Foyt | 1989 | Darrell Waltrip | | |

# Badminton

The oldest, and still the classic, tournament for badminton is the All-England Badminton Championships, which have been held annually since 1900. A governing body, the International Badminton Federation (**IBF**), was established in 1934. It first proposed international team badminton for men in 1939, but actual tournament play for the **Thomas Cup** did not begin until 1948–49. A similar contest for women's teams, the **Uber Cup**, was inaugurated in 1956–57. Competition for the biennial team championships (held in even years since 1982) consists of three singles matches and two doubles matches.

Official **world badminton championships** were first held in 1977. The program for this biennial event (held in odd years) includes mixed doubles and individual and doubles competition for men and for women.

**International Badminton Federation Web site:** <www.intbadfed.org>

## Uber Cup

| YEAR | WINNER | RUNNER-UP | YEAR | WINNER | RUNNER-UP |
|------|--------|-----------|------|--------|-----------|
| 1956–57 | United States | Denmark | 1985–86 | China | Indonesia |
| 1959–60 | United States | Denmark | 1987–88 | China | South Korea |
| 1962–63 | United States | England | 1989–90 | China | South Korea |
| 1965–66 | Japan | United States | 1991–92 | China | South Korea |
| 1968–69 | Japan | Indonesia | 1993–94 | Indonesia | China |
| 1971–72 | Japan | Indonesia | 1995–96 | Indonesia | China |
| 1974–75 | Indonesia | Japan | 1997–98 | China | Indonesia |
| 1977–78 | Japan | Indonesia | 1999–2000 | China | Denmark |
| 1980–81 | Japan | Indonesia | 2001–02 | China | South Korea |
| 1983–84 | China | England | | | |

## All-England Championships—Singles

*Held since 1900. No competition 1915–19; 1940–46. Table shows results for past 20 years.*

| YEAR | MEN | WOMEN | YEAR | MEN | WOMEN |
|---|---|---|---|---|---|
| 1984 | Morten Frost (DEN) | Li Lingwei (CHN) | 1996 | Poul-Erik Hoyer-Larsen (DEN) | Bang Soo Hyun (KOR) |
| 1985 | Zhao Jianhua (CHN) | Han Aiping (CHN) | 1997 | Dong Jiong (CHN) | Ye Zhaoying (CHN) |
| 1986 | Morten Frost (DEN) | Kim Yun Ja (KOR) | 1998 | Sun Jun (CHN) | Ye Zhaoying (CHN) |
| 1987 | Morten Frost (DEN) | Kirsten Larsen (DEN) | 1999 | Peter Gade Christen-sen (DEN) | Ye Zhaoying (CHN) |
| 1988 | Ib Frederiksen (DEN) | Gu Jiaming (CHN) | | | |
| 1989 | Yang Yang (CHN) | Li Lingwei (CHN) | 2000 | Xia Xuanze (CHN) | Gong Zhichao (CHN) |
| 1990 | Zhao Jianhua (CHN) | Susi Susanti (INA) | 2001 | Pulella Gopichand (IND) | Gong Zhichao (CHN) |
| 1991 | Ardy Wiranata (INA) | Susi Susanti (INA) | | | |
| 1992 | Liu Jun (CHN) | Tang Jiuhong (CHN) | 2002 | Chen Hong (CHN) | Camilla Martin (DEN) |
| 1993 | Heryanto Arbi (INA) | Susi Susanti (INA) | 2003 | Muhammad Hafiz Hashim (MAS) | Zhou Mi (CHN) |
| 1994 | Heryanto Arbi (INA) | Susi Susanti (INA) | | | |
| 1995 | Poul-Erik Hoyer-Larsen (DEN) | Lim Xiao Qing (SWE) | 2004 | TBA | |

## Thomas Cup

| YEAR | WINNER | RUNNER-UP | YEAR | WINNER | RUNNER-UP |
|---|---|---|---|---|---|
| 1948–49 | Malaya | Denmark | 1981–82 | China | Indonesia |
| 1951–52 | Malaya | United States | 1983–84 | Indonesia | China |
| 1954–55 | Malaya | Denmark | 1985–86 | China | Indonesia |
| 1957–58 | Indonesia | Malaya | 1987–88 | China | Malaysia |
| 1960–61 | Indonesia | Thailand | 1989–90 | China | Malaysia |
| 1963–64 | Indonesia | Denmark | 1991–92 | Malaysia | Indonesia |
| 1966–67 | Malaysia (by default) | Indonesia | 1993–94 | Indonesia | Malaysia |
| | | | 1995–96 | Indonesia | Denmark |
| 1969–70 | Indonesia | Malaysia | 1997–98 | Indonesia | Malaysia |
| 1972–73 | Indonesia | Denmark | 1999–2000 | Indonesia | China |
| 1975–76 | Indonesia | Malaysia | 2001–02 | Indonesia | Malaysia |
| 1978–79 | Indonesia | Denmark | | | |

## World Badminton Championships

| YEAR | MEN'S SINGLES | WOMEN'S SINGLES | MEN'S DOUBLES |
|---|---|---|---|
| 1977 | Flemming Delfs (DEN) | Lene Köppen (DEN) | Tjun Tjun, Johan Wahjudi (INA) |
| 1980 | Rudy Hartono (INA) | Verawaty Wiharjo (INA) | Ade Chandra, Christian Hadinata (INA) |
| 1983 | Icuk Sugiarto (INA) | Li Lingwei (CHN) | Steen Fladberg, Jasper Helledie (DEN) |
| 1985 | Han Jian (CHN) | Han Aiping (CHN) | Park Joo Bong, Kim Moon Soo (KOR) |
| 1987 | Yang Yang (CHN) | Han Aiping (CHN) | Li Yongbo, Tian Bingyi (CHN) |
| 1989 | Yang Yang (CHN) | Li Lingwei (CHN) | Li Yongbo, Tian Bingyi (CHN) |
| 1991 | Zhao Jianhua (CHN) | Tang Jiuhong (CHN) | Park Joo Bong, Kim Moon Soo (KOR) |
| 1993 | Joko Suprianto (INA) | Susi Susanti (INA) | Ricky Subagja, Rudy Gunawan (INA) |
| 1995 | Heryanto Arbi (INA) | Ye Zhaoying (CHN) | Ricky Subagja, Rexy Mainaky (INA) |
| 1997 | Peter Rasmussen (DEN) | Ye Zhaoying (CHN) | Budiarto Sigit, Candra Wijaya (INA) |
| 1999 | Sun Jun (CHN) | Camilla Martin (DEN) | Kim Dong Moon, Ha Tae Kwon (KOR) |
| 2001 | Hendrawan (INA) | Gong Ruina (CHN) | Tony Gunawan, Halim Haryanto (INA) |
| 2003 | Xia Huanze (CHN | Zhang Ning (CHN) | Lars Paaske, Jonas Rasmussen (DEN) |

| YEAR | WOMEN'S DOUBLES | MIXED DOUBLES |
|---|---|---|
| 1977 | Etsuko Toganu, Erniko Ueno (JPN) | Steen Skovgaard, Lene Köppen (DEN) |
| 1980 | Nora Perry, Jane Webster (ENG) | Christian Hadinata, Imelda Wiguno (INA) |
| 1983 | Lin Ying, Wu Dixi (CHN) | Thomas Kihlström, Nora Perry (SWE, ENG) |
| 1985 | Han Aiping, Li Lingwei (CHN) | Park Joo Bong, Yoo Sang Hee (KOR) |
| 1987 | Lin Ying, Guan Weizhen (CHN) | Wang Pengren, Shi Fangjing (CHN) |
| 1989 | Lin Ying, Guan Weizhen (CHN) | Park Joo Bong, Chung Myung Hee (KOR) |
| 1991 | Guan Weizhen, Nong Qunhua (CHN) | Park Joo Bong, Chung Myung Hee (KOR) |
| 1993 | Nong Qunhua, Zhou Lei (CHN) | Thomas Lund, Catrine Bengtsson (DEN, SWE) |
| 1995 | Gil Young Ah, Jang Hye Ock (KOR) | Thomas Lund, Marlene Thomsen (DEN) |
| 1997 | Ge Fei, Gu Jun (CHN) | Liu Yong, Ge Fei (CHN) |
| 1999 | Ge Fei, Gu Jun (CHN) | Kim Dong Moon, Ra Kyung Min (KOR) |
| 2001 | Gao Ling, Huang Sui (CHN) | Zhang Jun, Gao Ling (CHN) |
| 2003 | Gao Ling, Huang Sui (CHN) | Kim Dong Moon, Ra Kyung Min (KOR) |

# Baseball

The sport of baseball—given its definitive form in the United States in the late 19th century—is popular throughout the world, though it is not organized internationally except at the **Little League** (for children ages 5–18) level. Little League Baseball was founded in Pennsylvania in 1939. The first Little League World Series was in 1947, and the first Little League outside the US was organized in British Columbia in 1951. Baseball is especially popular in Japan and Latin America; it is also one of the national sports of the US.

On a **professional** level, the premier event of baseball in the US is the **World Series** of **Major League Baseball**, in which the first team to win four games wins the Series. In fact, the Series is not contested on an international level, but rather it is played between the leading team of the **National League** (NL; formed 1876 and including, from 1969, one Canadian team) and the leading team of the **American League** (AL; formed 1900 and also including, from 1977, one Canadian team).

Professional baseball began in Japan in 1936. Teams are organized into two leagues of six teams each. The seven-game **Japan Series**, first played in 1950, is contested between the leading team of the Central League (CL) and the leading team of the Pacific League (PL). The modern **Caribbean Series** began in 1970 with the winning team from each league in the Dominican Republic, Mexico, Puerto Rico, and Venezuela.

**Related Web sites:** Major League: <mlb.mlb.com>; Little League: <www.littleleague.org>

## Final Major League Standings, 2002

### American League

| East Division | | | | Central Division | | | | West Division | | | |
|---|---|---|---|---|---|---|---|---|---|---|---|
| CLUB | WON | LOST | GAMES BACK | CLUB | WON | LOST | GAMES BACK | CLUB | WON | LOST | GAMES BACK |
| New York* | 103 | 58 | — | Minnesota* | 94 | 67 | — | Oakland* | 103 | 59 | — |
| Boston | 93 | 69 | 10½ | Chicago | 81 | 81 | 13½ | Anaheim* | 99 | 63 | 4 |
| Toronto | 78 | 84 | 25½ | Cleveland | 74 | 88 | 20½ | Seattle | 93 | 69 | 10 |
| Baltimore | 67 | 95 | 36½ | Kansas City | 62 | 100 | 32½ | Texas | 72 | 90 | 31 |
| Tampa Bay | 55 | 106 | 48 | Detroit | 55 | 106 | 39 | | | | |

### National League

| East Division | | | | Central Division | | | | West Division | | | |
|---|---|---|---|---|---|---|---|---|---|---|---|
| CLUB | WON | LOST | GAMES BACK | CLUB | WON | LOST | GAMES BACK | CLUB | WON | LOST | GAMES BACK |
| Atlanta* | 101 | 59 | — | St. Louis* | 97 | 65 | — | Arizona* | 98 | 64 | — |
| Montreal | 83 | 79 | 19 | Houston | 84 | 78 | 13 | San Francisco* | 95 | 66 | 2½ |
| Philadephia | 80 | 81 | 21½ | Cincinnati | 78 | 84 | 19 | Los Angeles | 92 | 70 | 6 |
| Florida | 79 | 83 | 23 | Pittsburgh | 72 | 89 | 24½ | Colorado | 73 | 89 | 25 |
| New York | 75 | 86 | 26½ | Chicago | 67 | 95 | 30 | San Diego | 66 | 96 | 32 |
| | | | | Milwaukee | 56 | 106 | 41 | | | | |

*Gained play-off berth.

---

 **Did you know?** Barry Bonds's 73 home runs in 2001 broke the major-league record of 70 hit by the St. Louis Cardinals' Mark McGwire only three years earlier. But the previous record for home runs by a professional ballplayer was 72, hit by Joe Bauman for the minor-league Roswell Rockets in 1954. Bauman also hit .400 with 224 RBIs that season, yet he never made it to the major leagues.

---

## World Series

*AL—American League; NL—National League.*

| YEAR | WINNING TEAM | LOSING TEAM | RESULTS |
|---|---|---|---|
| 1903 | Boston Pilgrims (AL) | Pittsburgh Pirates (NL) | 5–3 |
| 1904 | *not held* | | |
| 1905 | New York Giants (NL) | Philadelphia Athletics (AL) | 4–1 |
| 1906 | Chicago White Sox (AL) | Chicago Cubs (NL) | 4–2 |
| 1907* | Chicago Cubs (NL) | Detroit Tigers (AL) | 4–0 |
| 1908 | Chicago Cubs (NL) | Detroit Tigers (AL) | 4–1 |
| 1909 | Pittsburgh Pirates (NL) | Detroit Tigers (AL) | 4–3 |
| 1910 | Philadelphia Athletics (AL) | Chicago Cubs (NL) | 4–1 |
| 1911 | Philadelphia Athletics (AL) | New York Giants (NL) | 4–2 |
| 1912* | Boston Red Sox (AL) | New York Giants (NL) | 4–3 |
| 1913 | Philadelphia Athletics (AL) | New York Giants (NL) | 4–1 |
| 1914 | Boston Braves (NL) | Philadelphia Athletics (AL) | 4–0 |
| 1915 | Boston Red Sox (AL) | Philadelphia Phillies (NL) | 4–1 |

# World Series (continued)

| YEAR | WINNING TEAM | LOSING TEAM | RESULTS |
|---|---|---|---|
| 1916 | Boston Red Sox (AL) | Brooklyn Robins (NL) | 4–1 |
| 1917 | Chicago White Sox (AL) | New York Giants (NL) | 4–2 |
| 1918 | Boston Red Sox (AL) | Chicago Cubs (NL) | 4–2 |
| 1919 | Cincinnati Reds (NL) | Chicago White Sox (AL) | 5–3 |
| 1920 | Cleveland Indians (AL) | Brooklyn Robins (NL) | 5–2 |
| 1921 | New York Giants (NL) | New York Yankees (AL) | 5–3 |
| 1922* | New York Giants (NL) | New York Yankees (AL) | 4–0 |
| 1923 | New York Yankees (AL) | New York Giants (NL) | 4–2 |
| 1924 | Washington Senators (AL) | New York Giants (NL) | 4–3 |
| 1925 | Pittsburgh Pirates (NL) | Washington Senators (AL) | 4–3 |
| 1926 | St. Louis Cardinals (NL) | New York Yankees (AL) | 4–3 |
| 1927 | New York Yankees (AL) | Pittsburgh Pirates (NL) | 4–0 |
| 1928 | New York Yankees (AL) | St. Louis Cardinals (NL) | 4–0 |
| 1929 | Philadelphia Athletics (AL) | Chicago Cubs (NL) | 4–1 |
| 1930 | Philadelphia Athletics (AL) | St. Louis Cardinals (NL) | 4–2 |
| 1931 | St. Louis Cardinals (NL) | Philadelphia Athletics (AL) | 4–3 |
| 1932 | New York Yankees (AL) | Chicago Cubs (NL) | 4–0 |
| 1933 | New York Giants (NL) | Washington Senators (AL) | 4–1 |
| 1934 | St. Louis Cardinals (NL) | Detroit Tigers (AL) | 4–3 |
| 1935 | Detroit Tigers (AL) | Chicago Cubs (NL) | 4–2 |
| 1936 | New York Yankees (AL) | New York Giants (NL) | 4–2 |
| 1937 | New York Yankees (AL) | New York Giants (NL) | 4–1 |
| 1938 | New York Yankees (AL) | Chicago Cubs (NL) | 4–0 |
| 1939 | New York Yankees (AL) | Cincinnati Reds (NL) | 4–0 |
| 1940 | Cincinnati Reds (NL) | Detroit Tigers (AL) | 4–3 |
| 1941 | New York Yankees (AL) | Brooklyn Dodgers (NL) | 4–1 |
| 1942 | St. Louis Cardinals (NL) | New York Yankees (AL) | 4–1 |
| 1943 | New York Yankees (AL) | St. Louis Cardinals (NL) | 4–1 |
| 1944 | St. Louis Cardinals (NL) | St. Louis Browns (AL) | 4–2 |
| 1945 | Detroit Tigers (AL) | Chicago Cubs (NL) | 4–3 |
| 1946 | St. Louis Cardinals (NL) | Boston Red Sox (AL) | 4–3 |
| 1947 | New York Yankees (AL) | Brooklyn Dodgers (NL) | 4–3 |
| 1948 | Cleveland Indians (AL) | Boston Braves (NL) | 4–2 |
| 1949 | New York Yankees (AL) | Brooklyn Dodgers (NL) | 4–1 |
| 1950 | New York Yankees (AL) | Philadelphia Phillies (NL) | 4–0 |
| 1951 | New York Yankees (AL) | New York Giants (NL) | 4–2 |
| 1952 | New York Yankees (AL) | Brooklyn Dodgers (NL) | 4–3 |
| 1953 | New York Yankees (AL) | Brooklyn Dodgers (NL) | 4–2 |
| 1954 | New York Giants (NL) | Cleveland Indians (AL) | 4–0 |
| 1955 | Brooklyn Dodgers (NL) | New York Yankees (AL) | 4–3 |
| 1956 | New York Yankees (AL) | Brooklyn Dodgers (NL) | 4–3 |
| 1957 | Milwaukee Braves (NL) | New York Yankees (AL) | 4–3 |
| 1958 | New York Yankees (AL) | Milwaukee Braves (NL) | 4–3 |
| 1959 | Los Angeles Dodgers (NL) | Chicago White Sox (AL) | 4–2 |
| 1960 | Pittsburgh Pirates (NL) | New York Yankees (AL) | 4–3 |
| 1961 | New York Yankees (AL) | Cincinnati Reds (NL) | 4–1 |
| 1962 | New York Yankees (AL) | San Francisco Giants (NL) | 4–3 |
| 1963 | Los Angeles Dodgers (NL) | New York Yankees (AL) | 4–0 |
| 1964 | St. Louis Cardinals (NL) | New York Yankees (AL) | 4–3 |
| 1965 | Los Angeles Dodgers (NL) | Minnesota Twins (AL) | 4–3 |
| 1966 | Baltimore Orioles (AL) | Los Angeles Dodgers (NL) | 4–0 |
| 1967 | St. Louis Cardinals (NL) | Boston Red Sox (AL) | 4–3 |
| 1968 | Detroit Tigers (AL) | St. Louis Cardinals (NL) | 4–3 |
| 1969 | New York Mets (NL) | Baltimore Orioles (AL) | 4–1 |
| 1970 | Baltimore Orioles (AL) | Cincinnati Reds (NL) | 4–1 |
| 1971 | Pittsburgh Pirates (NL) | Baltimore Orioles (AL) | 4–3 |
| 1972 | Oakland Athletics (AL) | Cincinnati Reds (NL) | 4–3 |
| 1973 | Oakland Athletics (AL) | New York Mets (NL) | 4–3 |
| 1974 | Oakland Athletics (AL) | Los Angeles Dodgers (NL) | 4–1 |
| 1975 | Cincinnati Reds (NL) | Boston Red Sox (AL) | 4–3 |
| 1976 | Cincinnati Reds (NL) | New York Yankees (AL) | 4–0 |
| 1977 | New York Yankees (AL) | Los Angeles Dodgers (NL) | 4–2 |
| 1978 | New York Yankees (AL) | Los Angeles Dodgers (NL) | 4–2 |
| 1979 | Pittsburgh Pirates (NL) | Baltimore Orioles (AL) | 4–3 |
| 1980 | Philadelphia Phillies (NL) | Kansas City Royals (AL) | 4–2 |
| 1981 | Los Angeles Dodgers (NL) | New York Yankees (AL) | 4–2 |
| 1982 | St. Louis Cardinals (NL) | Milwaukee Brewers (AL) | 4–3 |
| 1983 | Baltimore Orioles (AL) | Philadelphia Phillies (NL) | 4–1 |

## World Series (continued)

| YEAR | WINNING TEAM | LOSING TEAM | RESULTS |
|---|---|---|---|
| 1984 | Detroit Tigers (AL) | San Diego Padres (NL) | 4–1 |
| 1985 | Kansas City Royals (AL) | St. Louis Cardinals (NL) | 4–3 |
| 1986 | New York Mets (NL) | Boston Red Sox (AL) | 4–3 |
| 1987 | Minnesota Twins (AL) | St. Louis Cardinals (NL) | 4–3 |
| 1988 | Los Angeles Dodgers (NL) | Oakland Athletics (AL) | 4–1 |
| 1989 | Oakland Athletics (AL) | San Francisco Giants (NL) | 4–0 |
| 1990 | Cincinnati Reds (NL) | Oakland Athletics (AL) | 4–0 |
| 1991 | Minnesota Twins (AL) | Atlanta Braves (NL) | 4–3 |
| 1992 | Toronto Blue Jays (AL) | Atlanta Braves (NL) | 4–2 |
| 1993 | Toronto Blue Jays (AL) | Philadelphia Phillies (NL) | 4–2 |
| 1994 | not held | | |
| 1995 | Atlanta Braves (NL) | Cleveland Indians (AL) | 4–2 |
| 1996 | New York Yankees (AL) | Atlanta Braves (NL) | 4–2 |
| 1997 | Florida Marlins (NL) | Cleveland Indians (AL) | 4–3 |
| 1998 | New York Yankees (AL) | San Diego Padres (NL) | 4–0 |
| 1999 | New York Yankees (AL) | Atlanta Braves (NL) | 4–0 |
| 2000 | New York Yankees (AL) | New York Mets (NL) | 4–1 |
| 2001 | Arizona Diamondbacks (NL) | New York Yankees (AL) | 4–3 |
| 2002 | Anaheim Angels (AL) | San Francisco Giants (NL) | 4–3 |

*One tied game.

## Major League Baseball All-Time Records[1]

| | PLAYERS/TEAMS | NUMBER | SEASON/DATE |
|---|---|---|---|
| **Individual career records** | | | |
| Games played | Pete Rose | 3,562 | 1963–1986 |
| World Series games played | Yogi Berra | 75 | 14 series 1947–1963 |
| At bats | Pete Rose | 14,053 | 1963–1986 |
| Batting average[2] | Ty Cobb | .366 | 1905–1928 |
| Earned run average[3] | Ed Walsh | 1.82 | 1904–1917 |
| Home runs | Hank Aaron | 755 | 1954–1976 |
| Runs | Rickey Henderson[4] | 2,288 | 1979–2002 |
| Runs batted in | Hank Aaron | 2,297 | 1954–1976 |
| Doubles | Tris Speaker | 792 | 1907–1928 |
| Triples | Sam Crawford | 309 | 1899–1917 |
| Walks (batting) | Rickey Henderson[4] | 2,179 | 1979–2002 |
| Stolen bases (batting) | Rickey Henderson[4] | 1,403 | 1979–2002 |
| Strikeouts (pitching) | Nolan Ryan | 5,714 | 1966–1993 |
| Wins | Cy Young | 511 | 1890–1911 |
| Saves | Lee Smith | 478 | 1980–1997 |
| No-hitters | Nolan Ryan | 7 | 1966–1993 |
| Shutouts | Walter Johnson | 110 | 1907–1927 |
| Losses | Cy Young | 316 | 1890–1911 |
| **Individual season records** | | | |
| At bats | Willie Wilson | 705 | 1980 |
| Batting average[5] | Hugh Duffy | .440 | 1894 |
| Earned run average[6] | Dutch Leonard | 0.96 | 1914 |
| Home runs | Barry Bonds[4] | 73 | 2001 |
| Runs | Billy Hamilton | 192 | 1894 |
| Runs batted in | Hack Wilson | 191 | 1930 |
| Doubles | Earl Webb | 67 | 1931 |
| Triples | Chief Wilson | 36 | 1912 |
| Walks (batting) | Barry Bonds[4] | 198 | 2002 |
| Stolen bases (batting) | Hugh Nicol | 138 | 1887 |
| Strikeouts (pitching) | Charlie Buffinton | 417 | 1884 |
| Wins | Al Spalding | 54 | 1875 |
| Saves | Bobby Thigpen | 57 | 1990 |
| Shutouts | Grover Alexander | 16 | 1916 |
| Losses | John Coleman | 48 | 1883 |
| **Individual game records[7]** | | | |
| Home runs | 11 players hold record | 4 | N/A |
| Runs | 14 players hold record | 6 | N/A |
| Runs batted in | Jim Bottomley; Mark Whiten | 12 | 16 Sep 1924; 7 Sep 1993 |

# Major League Baseball All-Time Records[1] (continued)

| | PLAYERS/TEAMS | NUMBER | SEASON/DATE |
|---|---|---|---|
| **Individual game records[7] (continued)** | | | |
| Doubles | *too numerous to list* | 4 | N/A |
| Triples | George Strief; Bill Joyce | 4 | 25 Jun 1885; 18 May 1897 |
| Walks (batting) | Jimmie Fox; Walt Wilmot | 6 | 16 Jun 1938; 22 Aug 1891 |
| Stolen bases (batting) | George Gore; Billy Hamilton | 7 | 25 Jun 1881; 31 Aug 1894 |
| Strikeouts (pitching) | Roger Clemens (twice); Kerry Wood | 20 | 29 Apr 1986 and 18 Sep 1996; 6 May 1998 |
| | | | |
| **Team season records** | | | |
| Games won (percentage) | Chicago Cubs | 116–36 (.763) | 1906 |
| Home runs | Seattle Mariners | 264 | 1997 |
| Runs | Boston Braves | 1,220 | 1894 |
| Runs batted in | Boston Braves | 1,043 | 1894 |
| Doubles | Boston Red Sox; St. Louis Cardinals | 373 | 1997; 1930 |
| Triples | Philadelphia Phillies | 131 | 1894 |
| Walks (batting) | Boston Red Sox | 835 | 1949 |
| Stolen bases (batting) | St. Louis Cardinals | 581 | 1887 |
| Strikeouts (pitching) | Chicago Cubs | 1,344 | 2001 |
| | | | |
| **Game records** | | | |
| Highest total score | Chicago Cubs v. Philadelphia Phillies | 26 to 23 (total 49) | 25 Aug 1922 |
| Longest nine-inning game | Los Angeles Dodgers v. San Francisco Giants | 4 hr 27 min | 5 Oct 2001 |
| Longest extra-innings game (time) | Chicago White Sox v. Milwaukee Brewers | 8 hr 6 min | 9 May 1984 |
| Longest extra-innings game (innings) | Brooklyn Dodgers v. Boston Braves | 26 innings | 1 May 1920 |

[1]*Through the 2002 season.* [2]*Minimum of 5,000 at-bats.* [3]*Minimum of 2,000 innings pitched.* [4]*Active in 2003.* [5]*Minimum of 3.1 plate appearances per game played.* [6]*Minimum of one inning pitched per game played.* [7]*Nine-inning games only.*

## Caribbean Series

| YEAR | WINNING TEAM | COUNTRY | YEAR | WINNING TEAM | COUNTRY |
|---|---|---|---|---|---|
| 1970 | Magallanes Navigators | VEN | 1987 | Caguas Creoles | PUR |
| 1971 | Licey Tigers | DOM | 1988 | Escogido Lions | DOM |
| 1972 | Ponce Lions | PUR | 1989 | Zulia Eagles | VEN |
| 1973 | Licey Tigers | DOM | 1990 | Escogido Lions | DOM |
| 1974 | Caguas Creoles | PUR | 1991 | Licey Tigers | DOM |
| 1975 | Bayamon Cowboys | PUR | 1992 | Mayagüez Indians | PUR |
| 1976 | Hermosillo Orange Growers | MEX | 1993 | Santurce Crabbers | PUR |
| 1977 | Licey Tigers | DOM | 1994 | Licey Tigers | DOM |
| 1978 | Mayagüez Indians | PUR | 1995 | San Juan Senators | PUR |
| 1979 | Magallanes Navigators | VEN | 1996 | Culiacán Tomato Growers | MEX |
| 1980 | Licey Tigers | DOM | 1997 | Northern Eagles | DOM |
| 1981 | *not held* | | 1998 | Northern Eagles | DOM |
| 1982 | Caracas Lions | VEN | 1999 | Licey Tigers | DOM |
| 1983 | Arecibo Wolves | PUR | 2000 | Santurce Crabbers | PUR |
| 1984 | Zulia Eagles | VEN | 2001 | Cibao Eagles | DOM |
| 1985 | Licey Tigers | DOM | 2002 | Culiacán Tomato Growers | MEX |
| 1986 | Mexicali Eagles | MEX | 2003 | Cibao Eagles | DOM |

## Japan Series

*CL—Central League; PL—Pacific League.*

| YEAR | WINNING TEAM | LOSING TEAM | RESULTS |
|---|---|---|---|
| 1992 | Seibu Lions (PL) | Yakult Swallows (CL) | 4–3 |
| 1993 | Yakult Swallows (CL) | Seibu Lions (PL) | 4–3 |
| 1994 | Yomiuri Giants (CL) | Seibu Lions (PL) | 4–2 |
| 1995 | Yakult Swallows (CL) | Orix BlueWave (PL) | 4–1 |
| 1996 | Orix BlueWave (PL) | Yomiuri Giants (CL) | 4–1 |
| 1997 | Yakult Swallows (CL) | Seibu Lions (PL) | 4–1 |

## Japan Series (continued)

*CL—Central League; PL—Pacific League.*

| YEAR | WINNING TEAM | LOSING TEAM | RESULTS |
|------|-------------|-------------|---------|
| 1998 | Yokohama BayStars (CL) | Seibu Lions (PL) | 4–2 |
| 1999 | Fukuoka Daiei Hawks (PL) | Chunichi Dragons (CL) | 4–1 |
| 2000 | Yomiuri Giants (CL) | Fukuoka Daiei Hawks (PL) | 4–2 |
| 2001 | Yakult Swallows (CL) | Osaka Kintetsu Buffaloes (PL) | 4–1 |
| 2002 | Yomiuri Giants (CL) | Seibu Lions (PL) | 4–0 |
| 2003 | *series begins on 18 October* | | |

## Little League World Series

*The Little League World Series, first called the National Little League Tournament, was established in 1947. The table shows the Series winners for the past 10 years.*

| YEAR | WINNING TEAM/HOME | RUNNER-UP | SCORE |
|------|-------------------|-----------|-------|
| 1993 | Long Beach/Long Beach CA | David Doleguita/Chiriquí (PAN) | 3–2 |
| 1994 | Coquivacoa/Maracaibo (VEN) | Northridge City/Northridge CA | 4–3 |
| 1995 | Shan-Hua/Tainan county (TAI) | Northwest 45/Spring TX | 17–3 |
| 1996 | Fu-Hsing/Kao-Hsuing (TAI) | Cranston/Cranston RI | 13–3 |
| 1997 | Linda Vista/Guadalupe (MEX) | South Mission Viejo/Mission Viejo CA | 5–4 |
| 1998 | Toms River/Toms River NJ | Kashima/Ibaraki (JPN) | 12–9 |
| 1999 | Hirakata/Osaka (JPN) | Phenix City National/Phenix City AL | 5–0 |
| 2000 | Sierra Maestra/Maracaibo (VEN) | Bellaire/Bellaire TX | 3–2 |
| 2001 | Kitasuna/Tokyo (JPN) | Apopka National/Apopka FL | 2–1 |
| 2002 | Valley Sports American/Louisville KY | Sendai Higashi/Sendai (JPN) | 1–0 |
| 2003 | *to be held 15–24 August* | | |

**Did you know?** World War II depleted the ranks of many professional sports teams, thereby allowing players into the game who otherwise would not have qualified. Perhaps the two best-known examples of this were Pete Gray, a one-armed outfielder for the St. Louis Browns; and Joe Nuxhall, a 15-year-old pitcher for the Cincinnati Reds.

# Basketball

American professional basketball is directed by the **National Basketball Association** (NBA; formed 1949). The NBA is divided into two conferences, the top-ranking teams of which compete yearly for the championship. The NBA began a **women's professional league,** known as the WNBA, in 1997.

As an **amateur** sport, basketball is organized on an international level. Since the inclusion of basketball as an **Olympic sport** in 1936, the winners of the Olympic tournament have been considered the world champions. The **Fédération Internationale de Basketball Amateur** (FIBA; founded 1932) instituted separate world championships in 1950 for men and in 1953 for women. (Women's basketball was not admitted to the Olympics until 1976.) Amateur basketball in the United States is most closely followed at the **collegiate** level, where the most important event of the season is the **National Collegiate Athletic Association (NCAA) Championship.** The NCAA tournament was first contested in 1939 (by men's teams only). Women's college basketball was first played on a national level in 1972, under the auspices of the Association for Intercollegiate Athletics for Women (AIAW), which gave way in 1982 to the NCAA's first tournament for women.

**Related Web sites:** NBA: <www.nba.com>; WNBA: <www.wnba.com>; NCAA: <www.ncaa.org>; FIBA: <www.fiba.com>

## National Basketball Association Final Standings, 2002–03

### EASTERN CONFERENCE

| Atlantic Division | | | | Central Division | | | |
|-------------------|-----|------|----------------|------------------|-----|------|----------------|
| TEAM | WON | LOST | GAMES BACK | TEAM | WON | LOST | GAMES BACK |
| *New Jersey Nets | 49 | 33 | — | *Detroit Pistons | 50 | 32 | — |
| *Philadelphia 76ers | 48 | 34 | 1 | *Indiana Pacers | 48 | 34 | 2 |
| *Boston Celtics | 44 | 38 | 5 | *New Orleans Hornets | 47 | 35 | 3 |
| *Orlando Magic | 42 | 40 | 7 | *Milwaukee Bucks | 42 | 40 | 8 |
| Washington Wizards | 37 | 45 | 12 | Atlanta Hawks | 35 | 47 | 15 |
| New York Knicks | 37 | 45 | 12 | Chicago Bulls | 30 | 52 | 20 |
| Miami Heat | 25 | 57 | 24 | Toronto Raptors | 24 | 58 | 26 |
| | | | | Cleveland Cavaliers | 17 | 65 | 33 |

## National Basketball Association Final Standings, 2002–03 (continued)

### WESTERN CONFERENCE

| Midwest Division | | | | Pacific Division | | | |
|---|---|---|---|---|---|---|---|
| TEAM | WON | LOST | GAMES BACK | TEAM | WON | LOST | GAMES BACK |
| *San Antonio Spurs | 60 | 22 | — | *Sacramento Kings | 59 | 23 | — |
| *Dallas Mavericks | 60 | 22 | — | *Los Angeles Lakers | 50 | 32 | 9 |
| *Minnesota Timberwolves | 51 | 31 | 9 | *Portland Trail Blazers | 50 | 32 | 9 |
| *Utah Jazz | 47 | 35 | 13 | *Phoenix Suns | 44 | 38 | 15 |
| Houston Rockets | 43 | 39 | 17 | Seattle SuperSonics | 40 | 42 | 19 |
| Memphis Grizzlies | 28 | 54 | 32 | Golden State Warriors | 38 | 44 | 21 |
| Denver Nuggets | 17 | 65 | 43 | Los Angeles Clippers | 27 | 55 | 32 |

*Gained play-off berth.

## National Basketball Association All-Time Records

| | PLAYERS/TEAMS | NUMBER | SEASON/DATE |
|---|---|---|---|
| **Individual career records** | | | |
| Games played | Robert Parish | 1,611 | 1976-77—1996-97 |
| Points scored | Kareem Abdul-Jabbar | 38,387 | 1969-70—1988-89 |
| Field goals attempted | Kareem Abdul-Jabbar | 28,307 | 1969-70—1988-89 |
| Field goals made | Kareem Abdul-Jabbar | 15,837 | 1969-70—1988-89 |
| Field-goal percentage[1] | Artis Gilmore | .599 | 1976-77—1987-88 |
| Three-point field goals attempted | Reggie Miller[3] | 5,854 | 1987-88—2002-03 |
| Three-point field goals made | Reggie Miller[3] | 2,330 | 1987-88—2002-03 |
| Three-point field-goal percentage[2] | Steve Kerr[3] | .454 | 1988-89—2002-03 |
| Free throws attempted | Karl Malone[3] | 12,963 | 1985-86—2002-03 |
| Free throws made | Karl Malone[3] | 9,619 | 1985-86—2002-03 |
| Free-throw percentage[4] | Mark Price | .904 | 1986-87—1997-98 |
| Assists | John Stockton | 15,806 | 1984-85—2002-03 |
| Rebounds | Wilt Chamberlain | 23,924 | 1959-60—1972-73 |
| Coaching total wins (losses) | Lenny Wilkens[3] | 1,292 (1,114) | 1969-70—2002-03 |
| Coaching winning percentage[5] | Phil Jackson[3] | .728 | 1989-90—2002-03 |
| **Individual season records** | | | |
| Points scored | Wilt Chamberlain (Philadelphia Warriors) | 4,029 | 1961-62 |
| Field goals attempted | Wilt Chamberlain (Philadelphia Warriors) | 3,159 | 1961-62 |
| Field goals made | Wilt Chamberlain (Philadelphia Warriors) | 1,597 | 1961-62 |
| Field-goal percentage | Wilt Chamberlain (Los Angeles Lakers) | .727 | 1972-73 |
| Three-point field goals attempted | George McCloud (Dallas Mavericks) | 678 | 1995-96 |
| Three-point field goals made | Dennis Scott (Orlando Magic) | 267 | 1995-96 |
| Three-point field-goal percentage | Steve Kerr (Chicago Bulls) | .524 | 1994-95 |
| Free throws attempted | Wilt Chamberlain (Philadelphia Warriors) | 1,363 | 1961-62 |
| Free throws made | Jerry West (Los Angeles Lakers) | 840 | 1965-66 |
| Free-throw percentage | Calvin Murphy (Houston Rockets) | .958 | 1980-81 |
| Assists | John Stockton (Utah Jazz) | 1,164 | 1990-91 |
| Rebounds | Wilt Chamberlain (Philadelphia Warriors) | 2,149 | 1960-61 |
| **Individual game records** | | | |
| Points scored | Wilt Chamberlain (Philadelphia Warriors) | 100 | 2 Mar 1962 |
| Field goals attempted | Wilt Chamberlain (Philadelphia Warriors) | 63 | 2 Mar 1962 |
| Field goals made | Wilt Chamberlain (Philadelphia Warriors) | 36 | 2 Mar 1962 |
| Field goals, none missed | Wilt Chamberlain (Philadelphia 76ers) | 18 | 24 Feb 1967 |
| Three-point field goals attempted | Michael Adams (Denver Nuggets); George McCloud (Dallas Mavericks) | 20 | 12 Apr 1991; 5 Mar 1996 |
| Three-point field goals made | Dennis Scott (Orlando Magic) | 11 | 18 Apr 1996 |
| Three-point field goals, none missed | Jeff Hornacek (Utah Jazz); Sam Perkins (Seattle Supersonics) Steve Smith (San Antonio Spurs) | 8 | 23 Nov 1994; 15 Jan 1997; 3 Nov 2001 |
| Free throws attempted | Wilt Chamberlain (Philadelphia Warriors) | 34 | 22 Feb 1962 |
| Free throws made | Wilt Chamberlain (Philadelphia Warriors); Adrian Dantley (Utah Jazz) | 28 | 2 Mar 1962; 4 Jan 1984 |
| Free throws made, none missed | Dominique Wilkins (Atlanta Hawks) | 23 | 8 Dec 1992 |
| Assists | Scott Skiles (Orlando Magic) | 30 | 30 Dec 1990 |
| Rebounds | Wilt Chamberlain (Philadelphia Warriors) | 55 | 24 Nov 1960 |

## National Basketball Association All-Time Records (continued)

| | PLAYERS/TEAMS | NUMBER | SEASON/DATE |
|---|---|---|---|
| **Team records** | | | |
| Highest winning pct., one season | Chicago Bulls | .878 (72–10) | 1995–96 |
| Highest winning pct., all time | Los Angeles Lakers (Minneapolis Lakers to 1960–61) | .618 (2,621–1,616) | 1948–49–2002–03 |
| Highest winning pct., one playoff series | Los Angeles Lakers | .938 (15–1) | 2000–01 |
| Most championships won | Boston Celtics | 16 | |
| Most championships won consecutively | Boston Celtics | 8 | 1959–66 |
| Most consecutive wins, one season | Los Angeles Lakers | 33 | 5 Nov 1971–7 Jan 1972 |
| Most consecutive losses, one season | Vancouver Grizzlies; Denver Nuggets | 23 | 16 Feb–2 Apr 1996; 9 Dec 1997–23 Jan 1998 |
| | | | |
| **Game records** | | | |
| Highest combined score | Detroit Pistons v. Denver Nuggets | 370 (186–184) | 13 Dec 1983 |
| Largest margin of victory | Cleveland Cavaliers v. Miami Heat | 68 (148–80) | 17 Dec 1991 |
| Longest game (overtime periods) | Indianapolis Olympians v. Rochester Royals | 6 | 6 Jan 1951 |

[1]Minimum 2,000 made.  [2]Minimum 250 made.  [3]Active in 2002–03.  [4]Minimum 1,200 made.
[5]Minimum 400 games.

 Steve Kerr is the only player to play for four consecutive NBA championship teams: the Chicago Bulls 1996-98, and the San Antonio Spurs in 1999.

## National Basketball Association (NBA) Championship

| SEASON | WINNER | RUNNER-UP | RESULTS |
|---|---|---|---|
| 1946–47 | Philadelphia Warriors | Chicago Stags | 4–1 |
| 1947–48 | Baltimore Bullets | Philadelphia Warriors | 4–2 |
| 1948–49 | Minneapolis Lakers | Washington Capitols | 4–2 |
| 1949–50 | Minneapolis Lakers | Syracuse Nationals | 4–2 |
| 1950–51 | Rochester Royals | New York Knickerbockers | 4–3 |
| 1951–52 | Minneapolis Lakers | New York Knickerbockers | 4–3 |
| 1952–53 | Minneapolis Lakers | New York Knickerbockers | 4–1 |
| 1953–54 | Minneapolis Lakers | Syracuse Nationals | 4–3 |
| 1954–55 | Syracuse Nationals | Fort Wayne Pistons | 4–3 |
| 1955–56 | Philadelphia Warriors | Fort Wayne Pistons | 4–1 |
| 1956–57 | Boston Celtics | St. Louis Hawks | 4–3 |
| 1957–58 | St. Louis Hawks | Boston Celtics | 4–2 |
| 1958–59 | Boston Celtics | Minneapolis Lakers | 4–0 |
| 1959–60 | Boston Celtics | St. Louis Hawks | 4–3 |
| 1960–61 | Boston Celtics | St. Louis Hawks | 4–1 |
| 1961–62 | Boston Celtics | Los Angeles Lakers | 4–3 |
| 1962–63 | Boston Celtics | Los Angeles Lakers | 4–2 |
| 1963–64 | Boston Celtics | San Francisco Warriors | 4–1 |
| 1964–65 | Boston Celtics | Los Angeles Lakers | 4–1 |
| 1965–66 | Boston Celtics | Los Angeles Lakers | 4–3 |
| 1966–67 | Philadelphia 76ers | San Francisco Warriors | 4–2 |
| 1967–68 | Boston Celtics | Los Angeles Lakers | 4–2 |
| 1968–69 | Boston Celtics | Los Angeles Lakers | 4–3 |
| 1969–70 | New York Knickerbockers | Los Angeles Lakers | 4–3 |
| 1970–71 | Milwaukee Bucks | Baltimore Bullets | 4–0 |
| 1971–72 | Los Angeles Lakers | New York Knickerbockers | 4–1 |
| 1972–73 | New York Knickerbockers | Los Angeles Lakers | 4–1 |
| 1973–74 | Boston Celtics | Milwaukee Bucks | 4–3 |
| 1974–75 | Golden State Warriors | Washington Bullets | 4–0 |
| 1975–76 | Boston Celtics | Phoenix Suns | 4–2 |
| 1976–77 | Portland Trail Blazers | Philadelphia 76ers | 4–2 |

## National Basketball Association (NBA) Championship (continued)

| SEASON | WINNER | RUNNER-UP | RESULTS |
|--------|--------|-----------|---------|
| 1977–78 | Washington Bullets | Seattle SuperSonics | 4–3 |
| 1978–79 | Seattle SuperSonics | Washington Bullets | 4–1 |
| 1979–80 | Los Angeles Lakers | Philadelphia 76ers | 4–2 |
| 1980–81 | Boston Celtics | Houston Rockets | 4–2 |
| 1981–82 | Los Angeles Lakers | Philadelphia 76ers | 4–2 |
| 1982–83 | Philadelphia 76ers | Los Angeles Lakers | 4–0 |
| 1983–84 | Boston Celtics | Los Angeles Lakers | 4–3 |
| 1984–85 | Los Angeles Lakers | Boston Celtics | 4–2 |
| 1985–86 | Boston Celtics | Houston Rockets | 4–2 |
| 1986–87 | Los Angeles Lakers | Boston Celtics | 4–2 |
| 1987–88 | Los Angeles Lakers | Detroit Pistons | 4–3 |
| 1988–89 | Detroit Pistons | Los Angeles Lakers | 4–0 |
| 1989–90 | Detroit Pistons | Portland Trail Blazers | 4–1 |
| 1990–91 | Chicago Bulls | Los Angeles Lakers | 4–1 |
| 1991–92 | Chicago Bulls | Portland Trail Blazers | 4–2 |
| 1992–93 | Chicago Bulls | Phoenix Suns | 4–2 |
| 1993–94 | Houston Rockets | New York Knickerbockers | 4–3 |
| 1994–95 | Houston Rockets | Orlando Magic | 4–0 |
| 1995–96 | Chicago Bulls | Seattle SuperSonics | 4–2 |
| 1996–97 | Chicago Bulls | Utah Jazz | 4–2 |
| 1997–98 | Chicago Bulls | Utah Jazz | 4–2 |
| 1998–99 | San Antonio Spurs | New York Knickerbockers | 4–1 |
| 1999–2000 | Los Angeles Lakers | Indiana Pacers | 4–2 |
| 2000–01 | Los Angeles Lakers | Philadelphia 76ers | 4–1 |
| 2001–02 | Los Angeles Lakers | New Jersey Nets | 4–0 |
| 2002–03 | San Antonio Spurs | New Jersey Nets | 4–2 |

## Women's National Basketball Association (WNBA) Championship

| SEASON | WINNER | RUNNER-UP | RESULTS |
|--------|--------|-----------|---------|
| 1996–97 | Houston Comets | New York Liberty | 1–0 |
| 1997–98 | Houston Comets | Phoenix Mercury | 2–1 |
| 1998–99 | Houston Comets | New York Liberty | 2–1 |
| 1999–2000 | Houston Comets | New York Liberty | 2–0 |
| 2000–01 | Los Angeles Sparks | Charlotte Sting | 2–0 |
| 2001–02 | Los Angeles Sparks | New York Liberty | 2–0 |
| 2002–03 | *to be held September 2003* | | |

## Division I National Collegiate Athletic Association (NCAA) Championship—Men

| YEAR | WINNER | RUNNER-UP | SCORE | YEAR | WINNER | RUNNER-UP | SCORE |
|------|--------|-----------|-------|------|--------|-----------|-------|
| 1939 | Oregon | Ohio State | 46–43 | 1962 | Cincinnati | Ohio State | 71–59 |
| 1940 | Indiana | Kansas | 60–42 | 1963 | Loyola (IL) | Cincinnati | 60–58 |
| 1941 | Wisconsin | Washington State | 39–34 | 1964 | UCLA | Duke | 98–83 |
| 1942 | Stanford | Dartmouth | 53–38 | 1965 | UCLA | Michigan | 91–80 |
| 1943 | Wyoming | Georgetown | 46–34 | 1966 | Texas Western | Kentucky | 72–65 |
| 1944 | Utah | Dartmouth | 42–40 | 1967 | UCLA | Dayton | 79–64 |
| 1945 | Oklahoma A & M | New York | 49–45 | 1968 | UCLA | North Carolina | 78–55 |
| 1946 | Oklahoma A & M | North Carolina | 43–40 | 1969 | UCLA | Purdue | 92–72 |
| 1947 | Holy Cross | Oklahoma | 58–47 | 1970 | UCLA | Jacksonville | 80–69 |
| 1948 | Kentucky | Baylor | 58–42 | 1971 | UCLA | Villanova | 68–62 |
| 1949 | Kentucky | Oklahoma State | 46–36 | 1972 | UCLA | Florida State | 81–76 |
| 1950 | CCNY | Bradley | 71–68 | 1973 | UCLA | Memphis State | 87–66 |
| 1951 | Kentucky | Kansas State | 68–58 | 1974 | North Carolina State | Marquette | 76–64 |
| 1952 | Kansas | St. John's (NY) | 80–63 | | | | |
| 1953 | Indiana | Kansas | 69–68 | 1975 | UCLA | Kentucky | 92–85 |
| 1954 | La Salle | Bradley | 92–76 | 1976 | Indiana | Michigan | 86–68 |
| 1955 | San Francisco | La Salle | 77–63 | 1977 | Marquette | North Carolina | 67–59 |
| 1956 | San Francisco | Iowa | 83–71 | 1978 | Kentucky | Duke | 94–88 |
| 1957 | North Carolina | Kansas | 54–53 | 1979 | Michigan State | Indiana State | 75–64 |
| 1958 | Kentucky | Seattle | 84–72 | 1980 | Louisville | UCLA | 59–54 |
| 1959 | California (Berkeley) | West Virginia | 71–70 | 1981 | Indiana | North Carolina | 63–50 |
| | | | | 1982 | North Carolina | Georgetown | 63–62 |
| 1960 | Ohio State | California (Berkeley) | 75–55 | 1983 | North Carolina State | Houston | 54–52 |
| 1961 | Cincinnati | Ohio State | 70–65 | 1984 | Georgetown | Houston | 84–75 |

## Division I National Collegiate Athletic Association (NCAA) Championship—Men (continued)

| YEAR | WINNER | RUNNER-UP | SCORE | YEAR | WINNER | RUNNER-UP | SCORE |
|------|--------|-----------|-------|------|--------|-----------|-------|
| 1985 | Villanova | Georgetown | 66–64 | 1995 | UCLA | Arkansas | 89–78 |
| 1986 | Louisville | Duke | 72–69 | 1996 | Kentucky | Syracuse | 76–67 |
| 1987 | Indiana | Syracuse | 74–73 | 1997 | Arizona | Kentucky | 84–79 |
| 1988 | Kansas | Oklahoma | 83–79 | 1998 | Kentucky | Utah | 78–69 |
| 1989 | Michigan | Seton Hall | 80–79 | 1999 | Connecticut | Duke | 77–74 |
| 1990 | UNLV | Duke | 103–73 | 2000 | Michigan State | Florida | 89–76 |
| 1991 | Duke | Kansas | 72–65 | 2001 | Duke | Arizona | 82–72 |
| 1992 | Duke | Michigan | 71–51 | 2002 | Maryland | Indiana | 64–52 |
| 1993 | North Carolina | Michigan | 77–71 | 2003 | Syracuse | Kansas | 81–78 |
| 1994 | Arkansas | Duke | 76–72 | | | | |

## Division I National Collegiate Athletic Association (NCAA) Championship—Women

| YEAR | WINNER | RUNNER-UP | SCORE | YEAR | WINNER | RUNNER-UP | SCORE |
|------|--------|-----------|-------|------|--------|-----------|-------|
| 1982 | Louisiana Tech | Cheney (PA) | 76–62 | 1993 | Texas Tech | Ohio State | 84–82 |
| 1983 | Southern California | Louisiana Tech | 69–67 | 1994 | North Carolina | Louisiana Tech | 60–59 |
| 1984 | Southern California | Tennessee | 72–61 | 1995 | Connecticut | Tennessee | 70–64 |
| 1985 | Old Dominion | Georgia | 70–65 | 1996 | Tennessee | Georgia | 83–65 |
| 1986 | Texas | Southern California | 97–81 | 1997 | Tennessee | Old Dominion | 68–59 |
| 1987 | Tennessee | Louisiana Tech | 67–44 | 1998 | Tennessee | Louisiana Tech | 93–75 |
| 1988 | Louisiana Tech | Auburn | 56–54 | 1999 | Purdue | Duke | 62–45 |
| 1989 | Tennessee | Auburn | 76–60 | 2000 | Connecticut | Tennessee | 71–52 |
| 1990 | Stanford | Auburn | 88–81 | 2001 | Notre Dame | Purdue | 68–66 |
| 1991 | Tennessee | Virginia | 70–67 | 2002 | Connecticut | Oklahoma | 82–70 |
| 1992 | Stanford | Western Kentucky | 78–62 | 2003 | Connecticut | Tennessee | 73–68 |

## World Amateur Basketball Championship—Men

| YEAR | WINNER | RUNNER-UP | YEAR | WINNER | RUNNER-UP |
|------|--------|-----------|------|--------|-----------|
| 1936* | United States | Canada | 1976* | United States | Yugoslavia |
| 1948* | United States | France | 1978 | Yugoslavia | USSR |
| 1950 | Argentina | United States | 1980* | Yugoslavia | Italy |
| 1952* | United States | USSR | 1982 | USSR | United States |
| 1954 | United States | Brazil | 1984* | United States | Spain |
| 1956* | United States | USSR | 1986 | United States | USSR |
| 1959 | Brazil† | United States | 1988* | USSR | Yugoslavia |
| 1960* | United States | USSR | 1990 | Yugoslavia | USSR |
| 1963 | Brazil | Yugoslavia | 1992* | United States | Croatia |
| 1964* | United States | USSR | 1994 | United States | Russia |
| 1967 | USSR | Yugoslavia | 1996* | United States | Yugoslavia |
| 1968* | United States | Yugoslavia | 1998 | Yugoslavia | Russia |
| 1970 | Yugoslavia | Brazil | 2000* | United States | France |
| 1972* | USSR | United States | 2002 | Yugoslavia | Argentina |
| 1974 | USSR | Yugoslavia | 2004 | to be held in Athens, 13–29 August | |

*Olympic championships, recognized as world championships.    †By default.

## World Amateur Basketball Championship—Women

| YEAR | WINNER | RUNNER-UP | YEAR | WINNER | RUNNER-UP |
|------|--------|-----------|------|--------|-----------|
| 1953 | United States | Chile | 1984* | United States | South Korea |
| 1957 | United States | USSR | 1986 | United States | USSR |
| 1959 | USSR | Bulgaria | 1988* | United States | Yugoslavia |
| 1964 | USSR | Czechoslovakia | 1990 | United States | Yugoslavia |
| 1967 | USSR | South Korea | 1992* | Unified Team† | China |
| 1971 | USSR | Czechoslovakia | 1994 | Brazil | China |
| 1975 | USSR | Japan | 1996* | United States | Brazil |
| 1976* | USSR | United States | 1998 | United States | Russia |
| 1979 | United States | South Korea | 2000* | United States | Australia |
| 1980* | USSR | Bulgaria | 2002 | United States | Russia |
| 1983 | USSR | United States | 2004 | to be held in Athens, 13–29 August | |

*Olympic championships, recognized as world championships.    †Athletes from the Commonwealth of Independent States plus Georgia.

# Billiard Games

The game of billiards has a surprising number of varieties throughout the world. Factors in that variety include the number and appearance of the billiard balls, the size of the table, the existence of side and corner pockets, and the object of play. The classic form of the game—three-cushion billiards—is played on a pocketless table with one red ball and two white balls, one of which is marked with a spot; it is often known as French billiards, carom, or (simply) billiards.

**Pocket billiards,** which embraces both **snooker** and the game sometimes known (for the sake of clarity) as **English billiards,** is the prevalent form of billiards in the United Kingdom. The world professional snooker championship was first held in 1927; until 1947 it was won each year by Joe Davis (championships were not held during World War II). The championship was discontinued during the 1950s; it was revived during the 1960s, and in 1969 it became a knockout event. The results that are given in the table below begin with that year. Competition is open to both men and women.

The American form of pocket billiards, usually known as **pool,** differs markedly from the British game. Its most popular variations are **eight-ball, nine-ball,** and **straight (or 14.1) pool.** Though earlier straight pool tournaments were held with regularity, the game has largely fallen into abeyance for national competition, and few national tournaments are held. Since the 1970s nine-ball and eight-ball pool have surpassed straight pool in popularity in the United States, and **nine-ball** has gained some prominence internationally. In 1990 the **World Pool-Billiard Association** (WPA; founded 1987) inaugurated the nine-ball world championship.

**WPA Web site:** <www.wpa-pool.com>

## World Three-Cushion Championship

*Competition has been held since 1928; table shows champions for the past 20 years.*

| YEAR | WINNER | YEAR | WINNER | YEAR | WINNER |
|---|---|---|---|---|---|
| 1983 | Raymond Ceulemans (BEL) | 1991 | Torbjörn Blomdahl (SWE) | 1999 | Dick Jaspers (NED) |
| 1984 | Kobayashi Nobuaki (JAP) | 1992 | Torbjörn Blomdahl (SWE) | 2000 | Dick Jaspers (NED) |
| 1985 | Raymond Ceulemans (BEL) | 1993 | Sang Chun Lee (USA) | 2001 | Raymond Ceulemans (BEL) |
| 1986 | Avelino Rico (SPA) | 1994 | Torbjörn Blomdahl (SWE) | 2002 | Marco Zanetti (ITA) |
| 1987 | Torbjörn Blomdahl (SWE) | 1995 | Torbjörn Blomdahl (SWE) | 2003 | *to be held 6–9 November,* |
| 1988 | Torbjörn Blomdahl (SWE) | 1996 | Torbjörn Blomdahl (SWE) | | *Valladolid, Spain* |
| 1989 | Ludo Dielis (BEL) | 1997 | Dick Jaspers (NED) | | |
| 1990 | Raymond Ceulemans (BEL) | 1998 | Torbjörn Blomdahl (SWE) | | |

## World Professional Snooker Championship

*Won by a British player unless otherwise noted.*

| YEAR | WINNER | YEAR | WINNER | YEAR | WINNER | YEAR | WINNER |
|---|---|---|---|---|---|---|---|
| 1969 | John Spencer | 1978 | Ray Reardon | 1987 | Steve Davis | 1996 | Stephen Hendry |
| 1970 | Ray Reardon | 1979 | Terry Griffiths | 1988 | Steve Davis | 1997 | Ken Doherty (IRE) |
| 1971 | John Spencer | 1980 | Cliff Thorburn (CAN) | 1989 | Steve Davis | 1998 | John Higgins |
| 1972 | Alex Higgins | 1981 | Steve Davis | 1990 | Stephen Hendry | 1999 | Stephen Hendry |
| 1973 | Ray Reardon | 1982 | Alex Higgins | 1991 | John Parrott | 2000 | Mark Williams |
| 1974 | Ray Reardon | 1983 | Steve Davis | 1992 | Stephen Hendry | 2001 | Ronnie O'Sullivan |
| 1975 | Ray Reardon | 1984 | Steve Davis | 1993 | Stephen Hendry | 2002 | Peter Ebdon |
| 1976 | Ray Reardon | 1985 | Dennis Taylor | 1994 | Stephen Hendry | 2003 | Mark Williams |
| 1977 | John Spencer | 1986 | Joe Johnson | 1995 | Stephen Hendry | | |

## WPA World Nine-Ball Championships

| YEAR | MEN'S CHAMPION | WOMEN'S CHAMPION | YEAR | MEN'S CHAMPION | WOMEN'S CHAMPION |
|---|---|---|---|---|---|
| 1990 | Earl Strickland (USA) | Robin Bell (USA) | 1996 | Ralf Souquet (GER) | Allison Fisher (GBR) |
| 1991 | Earl Strickland (USA) | Robin Bell (USA) | 1997 | Johnny Archer (USA) | Allison Fisher (GBR) |
| 1992 | Johnny Archer (USA) | Franziska Stark (FRG) | 1998 | Kunihiko Takahashi (JPN) | Allison Fisher (GBR) |
| 1993 | Chao Fong-Pang (TPE) | Loree Jon Jones (USA) | 1999 | Nick Varner (USA) | Liu Shin-Mei (TPE) |
| 1994 | Takeshi Okumura (JPN) | Ewa Mataya-Laurance (USA) | 2000 | Chao Fong-Pang (TPE) | Julie Kelly (IRE) |
| 1995 | Oliver Ortmann (GER) | Gerda Hofstatter (AUT) | 2001 | Mika Immonen (FIN) | Allison Fisher (GBR) |
| | | | 2002 | Earl Strickland (USA) | Liu Shin-Mei (TPE) |
| | | | 2003 | Thorsten Hohmann (GER) | *canceled* |

# Bowling

The world governing body for bowling is the **Fédération Internationale des Quilleurs (FIQ)**. Since 1954 it has sponsored world bowling championships, with seven countries participating. In 1979 the FIQ discontinued the eights for men and fours for women and introduced the triples competition for men and for women.

In the **United States** men's bowling is governed by the **American Bowling Congress (ABC)**, which was founded in 1895. Six years later the first national championship was organized; in 1961 the yearly competition was split into two divisions—regular (for those with a combined average score of 851 or higher) and classic for professionals. The classic division was discontinued in 1980. The **Women's International Bowling Congress (WIBC)** was organized in 1916 and has since sponsored an annual women's championship. The women's open division is for those with a combined average score of 851 or higher, but the highest score in the tournament wins, regardless of division. In both the ABC tournament and the WIBC tournament, competition takes place between teams, doubles, and singles. The all-events category is won by the individual who has the best score of nine games—three team, three doubles, and three singles scores. The **Professional Bowlers Association (PBA)** was established in 1958. One of its major tournaments is the annual Tournament of Champions.

**Related Web sites:** FIQ: <www.fiq.org>; WBC: <www.bowl.com>; WIBC: <www.bowl.com/bowl/wibc>; PBA: <www.pba.com>

## Professional Bowlers Association (PBA) Tournament of Champions

| YEAR | CHAMPION | YEAR | CHAMPION | YEAR | CHAMPION |
|---|---|---|---|---|---|
| 1965 | Billy Hardwick | 1978 | Earl Anthony | 1991 | David Ozio |
| 1966 | Wayne Zahn | 1979 | George Pappas | 1992 | Marc McDowell |
| 1967 | Jim Stefanich | 1980 | Wayne Webb | 1993 | George Branham III |
| 1968 | Dave Davis | 1981 | Steve Cook | 1994 | Norm Duke |
| 1969 | Jim Godman | 1982 | Mike Durbin | 1995 | Mike Aulby |
| 1970 | Don Johnson | 1983 | Joe Berardi | 1996 | Dave D'Entremont |
| 1971 | Johnny Petraglia | 1984 | Mike Durbin | 1997 | John Gant |
| 1972 | Mike Durbin | 1985 | Mark Williams | 1998 | Bryan Goebel |
| 1973 | Jim Godman | 1986 | Marshall Holman | 1999 | Jason Couch |
| 1974 | Earl Anthony | 1987 | Pete Weber | 2000 | Jason Couch |
| 1975 | Dave Davis | 1988 | Mark Williams | 2001 | *not held* |
| 1976 | Marshall Holman | 1989 | Del Ballard, Jr. | 2002 | Jason Couch |
| 1977 | Mike Berlin | 1990 | Dave Ferraro | | |

## American Bowling Congress (ABC) Bowling Championships—Regular Division

*The championships have been held since 1901. This table shows results for the past 20 years.*

| YEAR | SINGLES | SCORE | ALL-EVENTS | SCORE |
|---|---|---|---|---|
| 1984 | Bob Antczak & Neal Young (tied) | 764 | Bob Goike | 2,142 |
| 1985 | Glenn Harbison | 774 | Barry Asher | 2,033 |
| 1986 | Jeff Mackey | 774 | Ed Marzka | 2,116 |
| 1987 | Terry Taylor | 749 | Ryan Shafer | 2,044 |
| 1988 | Steve Hutkowski | 774 | Rick Steelsmith | 2,053 |
| 1989 | Paul Tetreault | 813 | George Hall | 2,227 |
| 1990 | Robert Hochrein | 791 | Mike Neumann | 2,168 |
| 1991 | Ed Deines | 826 | Tom Howery | 2,216 |
| 1992 | Gary Blatchford & Bob Youker, Jr. (tied) | 801 | Mike Tucker | 2,158 |
| 1993 | Dan Bock | 798 | Jeff Nimke | 2,254 |
| 1994 | John Weltzien | 810 | Thomas Holt | 2,190 |
| 1995 | Matt Surina | 826 | Jeff Kwiatkowski | 2,191 |
| 1996 | Don Scudder, Jr. | 823 | Scott Kurtz | 2,224 |
| 1997 | John Socha | 847 | Jeff Richgels | 2,241 |
| 1998 | John Gaines | 814 | Chris Barnes | 2,151 |
| 1999 | Dan Winter | 825 | Thomas Jones | 2,158 |
| 2000 | Garran Hein | 811 | Roy Daniels | 2,181 |
| 2001 | Nicholas Hoagland | 798 | D.J. Archer | 2,219 |
| 2002 | Mark Millsap | 823 | Stephen A. Hardy | 2,279 |
| 2003 | Ron Bahr | 837 | Steve Kloempken | 2,215 |

## Women's International Bowling Congress (WIBC) Bowling Championships—Open Division

*The championships have been held since 1916. The table shows results for the past 20 years.*

| YEAR | SINGLES | SCORE | ALL-EVENTS | SCORE |
|---|---|---|---|---|
| 1984 | Frieda Gate | 712 | Shigeo Saito (JPN) | 1,921 |
| 1985 | Polly Schwarzel | 694 | Aleta (Rzepecki) Sill | 1,900 |
| 1986 | Dana Stewart | 698 | Robin Romeo & Maria Lewis (tied) | 1,877 |

## Women's International Bowling Congress (WIBC) Bowling Championships—Open Division (continued)

*The championships have been held since 1916. The table shows results for the past 20 years.*

| YEAR | SINGLES | SCORE | ALL-EVENTS | SCORE |
|---|---|---|---|---|
| 1987 | Regi Jonak | 728 | Leanne Barrette | 1,972 |
| 1988 | Michelle Meyer-Welty | 690 | Lisa Wagner | 1,988 |
| 1989 | Laura Anderson | 683 | Nancy Fehr | 1,911 |
| 1990 | Paula Carter & Dana Miller-Mackie (tied) | 705 | Carol Norman | 1,984 |
| 1991 | Debbie Kuhn | 773 | Debbie Kuhn | 2,036 |
| 1992 | Patty Ann | 680 | Mitsuko Tokimoto (JPN) | 1,928 |
| 1993 | Karen Collura (CAN) & Kari Murph (tied) | 747 | Anne Marie Duggan | 1,990 |
| 1994 | Vicki Fifield | 716 | Wendy Macpherson-Papanos | 1,940 |
| 1995 | Beth Owen | 749 | Beth Owen | 1,983 |
| 1996 | Cindy Berlanga | 723 | Lorrie Nichols | 1,985 |
| 1997 | Jan Schmidt | 765 | Kendra Cameron | 2,039 |
| 1998 | Nellie Glandon | 714 | Liz Johnson | 1,989 |
| 1999 | Nikki Gianulias | 746 | Hidemi Mizobuchi | 2,065 |
| 2000 | Cathy Krasner | 729 | Carolyn Dorin-Ballard | 2,147 |
| 2001 | Lisa Wagner | 756 | Jonquay Armon | 2,044 |
| 2002 | Theresa Smith | 752 | Cara Honeychurch | 2,150 |
| 2003 | Michelle Feldman | 764 | Michelle Feldman | 2,048 |

## FIQ World Bowling Championships—Men

*In 1979 the singles category was added; previously, the masters had been the only individual event. Also in that year, eights were discontinued and triples were introduced.*

| YEAR | SINGLES | MASTERS | PAIRS | TRIPLES | FIVES | EIGHTS |
|---|---|---|---|---|---|---|
| 1954 | | Gösta Algeskog (SWE) | FIN | | SWE | SWE |
| 1955 | | Nisse Backstrom (SWE) | SWE | | FRG | FIN |
| 1958 | | Kalle Asukas (FIN) | SWE | | FIN | SWE |
| 1960 | | Tito Reynolds (MEX) | MEX | | VEN | MEX |
| 1963 | | Les Zikes (USA) | USA | | USA | USA |
| 1967 | | David Pond (GBR) | GBR | | FIN | USA |
| 1971 | | Ed Luther (USA) | PUR | | USA | USA |
| 1975 | | Bud Stoudt (USA) | GBR | | FIN | FRG |
| 1979 | Ollie Ongtawco (PHI) | Gary Bugden (GBR) | AUS | MAS | AUS | |
| 1983 | Armando Marino (COL) | Tony Cariello (USA) | AUS | SWE | FIN | |
| 1987 | Patrick Rolland (FRA) | Roger Pieters (BEL) | SWE | USA | SWE | |
| 1991 | Ying Chieh Ma (TAI) | Mika Koivuniemi (FIN) | USA | USA | TAI | |
| 1995 | Marc Doi (CAN) | Chen-Min Yang (TPE) | SWE | NED | NED | |
| 1999 | Gery Verbruggen (BEL) | Ahmed Shaheen (QAT) | SWE | FIN | SWE | |
| 2003 | *to be held 9–20 September in Kuala Lumpur, Malaysia* | | | | | |

## FIQ World Bowling Championships—Women

*In 1963 fives was played as a four-woman team, European style (either the entire game on one lane or half of game on one lane, balance on accompanying lane). In 1979 fours were discontinued altogether and triples were introduced. Also in that year, the singles category was added; previously, the masters had been the only individual event.*

| YEAR | MASTERS | SINGLES | PAIRS | TRIPLES | FOURS | FIVES |
|---|---|---|---|---|---|---|
| 1963 | Helen Shablis (USA) | | USA | | MEX | USA |
| 1967 | Helen Weston (USA) | | MEX | | FIN | FIN |
| 1971 | Ashie Gonzalez (PUR) | | JPN | | USA | USA |
| 1975 | Anne Haefker (FRG) | | SWE | | JPN | JPN |
| 1979 | Lita de la Rosa (PHI) | Lita de la Rosa (PHI) | PHI | USA | | USA |
| 1983 | Lena Sulkanen (SWE) | Lena Sulkanen (SWE) | DEN | FRG | | SWE |
| 1987 | Annette Hägre (SWE) | Edda Piccini (MEX) | USA | USA | | USA |
| 1991 | Catherine Willis (CAN) | Martina Beckel (GER) | JPN | CAN | | KOR |
| 1995 | Celia Flores (MEX) | Debby Ship (CAN) | THA | AUS | | FIN |
| 1999 | Ann-Maree Putney (AUS) | Kelly Kulick (USA) | AUS | KOR | | KOR |
| 2003 | *to be held 9–20 September in Kuala Lumpur, Malaysia* | | | | | |

**Did you know?** Yogi Berra's Words of Wisdom about a hotel stay: "The towels were so thick there, I could hardly close my suitcase."

# Boxing

**M**odern boxing is dated to about the 1880s, when the **Marquess of Queensberry**'s rules (or rules derived from them) became more or less standard. John L. Sullivan (USA) was the last of the **bare-knuckles** heavyweight champions and one of the first recognized champions to fight by the "new" rules. Despite an early trend toward some kind of organization, there is no single recognized world governing body in professional boxing. Europe, the Commonwealth, and Great Britain—not to mention a number of Asian boxing federations—all have championships. The **World Boxing Association (WBA)**, formed under a different name in 1920, is basically an American organization, though its headquarters are currently situated in Venezuela. It was once the largely undisputed governing body for the Americas. Since 1963 it has had some competition from the **World Boxing Council (WBC)**, which includes British and European countries as well as Latin American and Asian countries. In 1983 another organization, the **International Boxing Federation** (IBF; called the United States Boxing Association International from 1983 to 1984) was born of dissatisfaction with the WBA and the WBC. Other federations, such as the World Boxing Organization (WBO; formed in 1988), have not received international recognition.

The tables below contain the names of the **undisputed champions** in each weight class, their nationalities, and the dates of title bouts when titles changed hands, followed by the champions recognized by the three sanctioning bodies. Each organization (or sanctioning body) ranks boxers according to its own criteria and sanctions fights according to its own rules. Only a ranked boxer who wins a sanctioned fight is recognized as champion. Unless otherwise indicated, a champion retains his title until he is defeated. In the early 1990s the WBA, WBC, and IBF all recognized 17 weight divisions. In the tables below the primary name given for each division is that used by the WBA. If a different name is used by the WBC or the IBF, or by both, that name is given as an alternate.

**Related Web sites:** WBA: <www.wbaonline.com>; WBC: <www.wbcboxing.com>; IBF-USBA: <www.ibf-usba-boxing.com>.

## World Heavyweight Champions
*No weight limit.*

| CHAMPION (NATIONALITY) | DATE OF TITLE | CHAMPION (NATIONALITY) | DATE OF TITLE |
|---|---|---|---|
| **Undisputed champions** | | **WBA (continued)** | |
| John L. Sullivan (USA) | 29 Aug 1885 | George Foreman (USA) | 22 Jan 1973 |
| James J. Corbett (USA) | 7 Sep 1892 | Muhammad Ali (USA) | 30 Oct 1974 |
| Bob Fitzsimmons (USA—formerly a | 17 Mar 1897 | Leon Spinks (USA) | 15 Feb 1978 |
| British subject) | | Muhammad Ali (USA) | 15 Sep 1978 |
| James J. Jeffries (USA) | 9 Jun 1899 | retired in 1979 | |
| retired in 1905 | | John Tate (USA) | 20 Oct 1979 |
| Marvin Hart (USA) | 3 Jul 1905 | Mike Weaver (USA) | 21 Mar 1980 |
| Tommy Burns (CAN) | 23 Feb 1906 | Michael Dokes (USA) | 10 Dec 1982 |
| Jack Johnson (USA) | 26 Dec 1908 | Gerrie Coetzee (RSA) | 23 Sep 1983 |
| Jess Willard (USA) | 5 Apr 1915 | Greg Page (USA) | 1 Dec 1984 |
| Jack Dempsey (USA) | 4 Jul 1919 | Tony Tubbs (USA) | 29 Apr 1985 |
| Gene Tunney (USA) | 23 Sep 1926 | Tim Witherspoon (USA) | 17 Jan 1986 |
| retired in 1928 | | James Smith (USA) | 12 Dec 1986 |
| Max Schmeling (GER) | 12 Jun 1930 | Mike Tyson (USA) | 7 Mar 1987 |
| Jack Sharkey (USA) | 21 Jun 1932 | James Douglas (USA) | 11 Feb 1990 |
| Primo Carnera (ITA) | 29 Jun 1933 | Evander Holyfield (USA) | 26 Oct 1990 |
| Max Baer (USA) | 14 Jun 1934 | Riddick Bowe (USA) | 13 Nov 1992 |
| James J. Braddock (USA) | 13 Jun 1935 | Evander Holyfield (USA) | 6 Nov 1993 |
| Joe Louis (USA) | 22 Jun 1937 | Michael Moorer (USA) | 22 Apr 1994 |
| retired in 1949 | | George Foreman (USA) | 5 Nov 1994 |
| Ezzard Charles (USA) | 27 Sep 1950 | stripped of title in 1995 | |
| Jersey Joe Walcott (USA) | 18 Jul 1951 | Bruce Seldon (USA) | 8 Apr 1995 |
| Rocky Marciano (USA) | 23 Sep 1952 | Mike Tyson (USA) | 7 Sep 1996 |
| Floyd Patterson (USA) | 30 Nov 1956 | Evander Holyfield (USA) | 9 Nov 1996 |
| Ingemar Johansson (SWE) | 26 Jun 1959 | Lennox Lewis (GBR) | 13 Nov 1999 |
| Floyd Patterson (USA) | 20 Jun 1960 | stripped of title in 2000 | |
| Sonny Liston (USA) | 25 Sep 1962 | Evander Holyfield (USA) | 12 Aug 2000 |
| Cassius Clay (later Muhammad Ali) | 25 Feb 1964 | John Ruiz (PUR) | 3 Mar 2001 |
| (USA) | | Roy Jones, Jr. (USA) | 1 Mar 2003 |
| stripped of WBA title in 1965; | | | |
| stripped of WBC title in 1967; | | **WBC** | |
| title in dispute | | Joe Frazier (USA) | 16 Feb 1970 |
| | | George Foreman (USA) | 22 Jan 1973 |
| | | Muhammad Ali (USA) | 30 Oct 1974 |
| **WBA** | | stripped of title in 1978 | |
| Ernest Terrell (USA) | 5 Mar 1965 | Ken Norton (USA) | 18 Mar 1978 |
| defeated by Ali 6 Feb 1967; | | Larry Holmes (USA) | 9 Jun 1978 |
| gave up title | | gave up title in 1983 | |
| Jimmy Ellis (USA) | 27 Apr 1968 | Tim Witherspoon (USA) | 9 Mar 1984 |
| Joe Frazier (USA) | 16 Feb 1970 | | |

## World Heavyweight Champions (continued)

| CHAMPION (NATIONALITY) | DATE OF TITLE | CHAMPION (NATIONALITY) | DATE OF TITLE |
|---|---|---|---|
| **WBC (continued)** | | **IBF (continued)** | |
| Pinklon Thomas (USA) | 31 Aug 1984 | Michael Spinks (USA) | 21 Sep 1985 |
| Trevor Berbick (CAN) | 22 Mar 1986 | stripped of title in 1987 | |
| Mike Tyson (USA) | 22 Nov 1986 | Tony Tucker (USA) | 30 May 1987 |
| James Douglas (USA) | 11 Feb 1990 | Mike Tyson (USA) | 1 Aug 1987 |
| Evander Holyfield (USA) | 26 Oct 1990 | James Douglas (USA) | 11 Feb 1990 |
| Riddick Bowe (USA) | 13 Nov 1992 | Evander Holyfield (USA) | 25 Oct 1990 |
| stripped of title in 1992 | | Riddick Bowe (USA) | 13 Nov 1992 |
| Lennox Lewis (GBR) | 14 Dec 1992 | Evander Holyfield (USA) | 6 Nov 1993 |
| Oliver McCall (USA) | 24 Sep 1994 | Michael Moorer (USA) | 22 Apr 1994 |
| Frank Bruno (GBR) | 2 Sep 1995 | George Foreman (USA) | 5 Nov 1994 |
| Mike Tyson (USA) | 16 Mar 1996 | gave up title in 1995 | |
| gave up title in 1996 | | François Botha (RSA) | 9 Dec 1995 |
| Lennox Lewis (GBR) | 7 Feb 1997 | stripped of title in 1996 | |
| Hasim Rahman (USA) | 22 Apr 2001 | Michael Moorer (USA) | 22 Jun 1996 |
| Lennox Lewis (GBR) | 17 Nov 2001 | Evander Holyfield (USA) | 8 Nov 1997 |
| | | Lennox Lewis (GBR) | 13 Nov 1999 |
| **IBF** | | Hasim Rahman (USA) | 22 Apr 2001 |
| Larry Holmes (USA) | 25 Nov 1983 | Lennox Lewis (GBR) | 17 Nov 2001 |
| recognized as champion in | | gave up title in 2002 | |
| November 1983 | | Chris Byrd (USA) | 14 Dec 2002 |

## World Cruiserweight Champions
*Top weight 195 pounds; until 1982 not over 182 pounds. Division first recognized by WBA in 1982.*

| CHAMPION (NATIONALITY) | DATE OF TITLE | CHAMPION (NATIONALITY) | DATE OF TITLE |
|---|---|---|---|
| **WBA** | | **WBC (continued)** | |
| Ossie Ocasio (PUR) | 13 Feb 1982 | Carlos de León (PUR) | 17 May 1989 |
| Piet Crous (RSA) | 1 Dec 1984 | Massimiliano Duran (ITA) | 27 Jul 1990 |
| Dwight Muhammad Qawi (USA) | 27 Jul 1985 | Anaclet Wamba (FRA) | 20 Jul 1991 |
| Evander Holyfield (USA) | 12 Jul 1986 | Marcelo Domínguez (ARG) | 19 Apr 1996 |
| gave up title in 1988 | | Juan Carlos Gómez (GER—formerly | 21 Feb 1998 |
| Taoufik Belbouli (FRA) | 25 Mar 1989 | a Cuban citizen) | |
| declared vacant in 1989 | | gave up title in 2000 | |
| Robert Daniels (USA) | 28 Nov 1989 | Wayne Braithwaite (GUY) | 12 Oct 2002 |
| Bobby Czyz (USA) | 8 Mar 1991 | | |
| vacant | | **IBF** | |
| Orlin Norris (USA) | 6 Nov 1993 | Marvin Camel (USA) | 13 Dec 1983 |
| Nate Miller (USA) | 22 Jul 1995 | Lee Roy Murphy (USA) | 6 Oct 1984 |
| Fabrice Tiozzo (FRA) | 8 Nov 1997 | Rickey Parkey (USA) | 25 Oct 1986 |
| Virgil Hill (USA) | 9 Dec 2000 | Evander Holyfield (USA) | 15 May 1987 |
| Jean-Marc Mormeck (FRA) | 22 Feb 2002 | Glenn McCrory (GBR) | 3 Jun 1989 |
| | | Jeff Lampkin (USA) | 22 Mar 1990 |
| **WBC** | | gave up title in 1991 | |
| Marvin Camel (USA) | 31 Mar 1980 | James Warring (USA) | 7 Sep 1991 |
| Carlos de León (PUR) | 25 Nov 1980 | Alfred Cole (USA) | 30 Jul 1992 |
| S.T. Gordon (USA) | 27 Jun 1982 | gave up title in 1996 | |
| Carlos de León (PUR) | 17 Jul 1983 | Adolpho Washington (USA) | 31 Aug 1996 |
| Alfonso Ratliff (USA) | 6 Jun 1985 | Uriah Grant (USA) | 21 Jun 1997 |
| Bernard Benton (USA) | 21 Sep 1985 | Imamu Mayfield (USA) | 8 Nov 1997 |
| Carlos de León (PUR) | 22 Mar 1986 | Arthur Williams (USA) | 30 Oct 1998 |
| Evander Holyfield (USA) | 9 Apr 1988 | Vassily Jirov (KAZ) | 5 Jun 1999 |
| gave up title in 1988 | | James Toney (USA) | 26 Apr 2003 |

## World Light Heavyweight Champions
*Top weight 175 pounds.*

| CHAMPION (NATIONALITY) | DATE OF TITLE | CHAMPION (NATIONALITY) | DATE OF TITLE |
|---|---|---|---|
| **Undisputed champions** | | **Undisputed champions (continued)** | |
| Jack Root (AUT) | 22 Apr 1903 | Jack Dillon (USA) | 28 Apr 1914 |
| George Gardner (IRE) | 4 Jul 1903 | Battling Levinsky (USA) | 24 Oct 1916 |
| Bob Fitzsimmons (USA—formerly a | 25 Nov 1903 | Georges Carpentier (FRA) | 12 Oct 1920 |
| British subject) | | Battling Siki (Louis Phal) (SEN) | 24 Sep 1922 |
| Philadelphia Jack O'Brien (USA) | 20 Dec 1905 | Mike McTigue (IRE) | 17 Mar 1923 |
| retired in 1912 | | Paul Berlenbach (USA) | 30 May 1925 |

# World Light Heavyweight Champions (continued)

| CHAMPION (NATIONALITY) | DATE OF TITLE |
| --- | --- |
| **Undisputed champions (continued)** | |
| Jack Delaney (CAN) | 16 Jul 1926 |
| gave up title in 1927 | |
| Tommy Loughran (USA) | 12 Dec 1927 |
| gave up title in 1929 | |
| Maxie Rosenbloom (USA) | 14 Jul 1932 |
| Bob Olin (USA) | 16 Nov 1934 |
| John Henry Lewis (USA) | 31 Oct 1935 |
| retired in 1939 | |
| Melio Bettina (USA) | 3 Feb 1939 |
| Billy Conn (USA) | 13 Jul 1939 |
| gave up title in 1941 | |
| Gus Lesnevich (USA) | 14 May 1946 |
| Freddie Mills (GBR) | 26 Jul 1948 |
| Joey Maxim (USA) | 24 Jan 1950 |
| Archie Moore (USA) | 17 Dec 1952 |
| stripped of title in 1962 | |
| Harold Johnson (USA) | 12 May 1962 |
| Willie Pastrano (USA) | 1 Jun 1963 |
| José Torres (PUR) | 30 Mar 1965 |
| Dick Tiger (NGR) | 16 Dec 1966 |
| Bob Foster (USA) | 24 May 1968 |
| stripped of WBA title in 1970 | |
| | |
| **WBA** | |
| Vicente Rondon (VEN) | 27 Feb 1971 |
| Bob Foster (USA) | 7 Apr 1972 |
| retired in 1974 | |
| Víctor Galíndez (ARG) | 7 Dec 1974 |
| Mike Rossman (USA) | 15 Sep 1978 |
| Víctor Galíndez (ARG) | 14 Apr 1979 |
| Marvin Johnson (USA) | 30 Nov 1979 |
| Eddie Gregory (later Eddie | 31 Mar 1980 |
| Mustafa Muhammad) (USA) | |
| Michael Spinks (USA) | 18 Jul 1981 |
| gave up title in 1985 | |
| Marvin Johnson (USA) | 9 Feb 1986 |
| Leslie Stewart (TRI) | 23 May 1987 |
| Virgil Hill (USA) | 5 Sep 1987 |
| Thomas Hearns (USA) | 3 Jun 1991 |
| Iran Barkley (USA) | 21 Mar 1992 |
| gave up title in 1992 | |
| Virgil Hill (USA) | 29 Sep 1992 |
| Dariusz Michalczewski (GER) | 13 Jun 1997 |
| stripped of title in 1997 | |
| Lou Del Valle (USA) | 20 Sep 1997 |
| Roy Jones, Jr. (USA) | 18 Jul 1998 |
| gave up title in 2002 | |
| Mehdi Sahnoune (FRA) | 8 Mar 2003 |

| CHAMPION (NATIONALITY) | DATE OF TITLE |
| --- | --- |
| **WBC** | |
| Bob Foster (USA) | 24 May 1968 |
| retired in 1974 | |
| John Conteh (GBR) | 1 Oct 1974 |
| stripped of title in 1977 | |
| Miguel Cuello (ARG) | 21 May 1977 |
| Mate Parlov (YUG) | 7 Jan 1978 |
| Marvin Johnson (USA) | 2 Dec 1978 |
| Matthew Franklin (later Matthew | 22 Apr 1979 |
| Saad Muhammad) (USA) | |
| Dwight Braxton (later Dwight | 19 Dec 1981 |
| Muhammad Qawi) (USA) | |
| Michael Spinks (USA) | 18 Mar 1983 |
| gave up title in 1985 | |
| J.B. Williamson (USA) | 10 Dec 1985 |
| Dennis Andries (GBR) | 30 Apr 1986 |
| Thomas Hearns (USA) | 7 Mar 1987 |
| gave up title in 1987 | |
| Don Lalonde (CAN) | 27 Nov 1987 |
| Sugar Ray Leonard (USA) | 7 Nov 1988 |
| gave up title in 1988 | |
| Dennis Andries (GBR) | 2 Feb 1989 |
| Jeff Harding (AUS) | 24 Jun 1989 |
| Dennis Andries (GBR) | 28 Jul 1990 |
| Jeff Harding (AUS) | 11 Sep 1991 |
| Mike McCallum (JAM) | 23 Jul 1994 |
| Fabrice Tiozzo (FRA) | 16 Jun 1995 |
| Roy Jones, Jr. (USA) | 23 Nov 1996 |
| Montell Griffin (USA) | 21 Mar 1997 |
| Roy Jones, Jr. (USA) | 7 Aug 1997 |
| gave up title in 2003 | |
| Antonio Tarver (USA) | 26 Apr 2003 |
| | |
| **IBF** | |
| Slobodan Kacar (YUG) | 21 Dec 1985 |
| Bobby Czyz (USA) | 6 Sep 1986 |
| Charles Williams (USA) | 29 Oct 1987 |
| Henry Maske (GER) | 20 Mar 1993 |
| Virgil Hill (USA) | 23 Nov 1996 |
| Dariusz Michalczewski (GER) | 13 Jun 1997 |
| gave up title in 1997 | |
| William Guthrie (USA) | 19 Jul 1997 |
| Reggie Johnson (USA) | 6 Feb 1998 |
| Roy Jones, Jr. (USA) | 5 Jun 1999 |
| gave up title in 2003 | |
| Antonio Tarver (USA) | 26 Apr 2003 |

# World Super Middleweight Champions

*Top weight 168 pounds. Super middleweight division first recognized by WBA in 1987 and by WBC in 1988.*

| CHAMPION (NATIONALITY) | DATE OF TITLE |
| --- | --- |
| **WBA** | |
| Park Chong-Pal (KOR) | 6 Dec 1987 |
| Fulgencio Obelmejias (VEN) | 23 May 1988 |
| Baek In-chul (KOR) | 27 May 1989 |
| Christophe Tiozzo (FRA) | 30 Mar 1990 |
| Víctor Cordoba (PAN) | 5 Apr 1991 |
| Michael Nunn (USA) | 12 Sep 1992 |
| Steve Little (USA) | 26 Feb 1994 |
| Frank Liles (USA) | 12 Aug 1994 |
| Byron Mitchell (USA) | 12 Jun 1999 |
| Bruno Girard (FRA) | 8 Apr 2000 |
| stripped of title in 2001 | |

| CHAMPION (NATIONALITY) | DATE OF TITLE |
| --- | --- |
| **WBA (continued)** | |
| Byron Mitchell (USA) | 3 Mar 2001 |
| Sven Ottke (GER) | 15 Mar 2003 |
| | |
| **WBC** | |
| Sugar Ray Leonard (USA) | 7 Nov 1988 |
| gave up title in 1990 | |
| Mauro Galvano (ITA) | 15 Dec 1990 |
| Nigel Benn (GBR) | 3 Oct 1992 |
| Thulane Malinga (RSA) | 2 Mar 1996 |
| Vincenzo Nardiello (ITA) | 6 Jul 1996 |
| Robin Reid (GBR) | 12 Oct 1996 |

## World Super Middleweight Champions (continued)

| CHAMPION (NATIONALITY) | DATE OF TITLE | CHAMPION (NATIONALITY) | DATE OF TITLE |
|---|---|---|---|
| **WBC (continued)** | | **IBF (continued)** | |
| Thulane Malinga (RSA) | 19 Dec 1997 | Graciano Rocchigiani (GER) | 12 Mar 1988 |
| Richie Woodhall (GBR) | 27 Mar 1998 | gave up title in 1989 | |
| Markus Beyer (GER) | 23 Oct 1999 | Lindell Holmes (USA) | 27 Jan 1990 |
| Glenn Catley (GBR) | 6 May 2000 | Darrin Van Horn (USA) | 18 May 1991 |
| Dingaan Thobela (RSA) | 1 Sep 2000 | Iran Barkley (USA) | 10 Jan 1992 |
| Davey Hilton (CAN) | 15 Dec 2000 | James Toney (USA) | 13 Feb 1993 |
| stripped of title in 2001 | | Roy Jones, Jr. (USA) | 18 Nov 1994 |
| Eric Lucas (CAN) | 10 Jul 2001 | gave up title in 1997 | |
| Markus Beyer (GER) | 5 Apr 2003 | Charles Brewer (USA) | 21 Jun 1997 |
| | | Sven Ottke (GER) | 24 Oct 1998 |
| **IBF** | | | |
| Murray Sutherland (GBR) | 28 Mar 1984 | | |
| Park Chong-Pal (KOR) | 22 Jul 1984 | | |
| gave up title in 1987 | | | |

## World Middleweight Champions

*Top weight 160 pounds; until 1915 not over 158 pounds.*

| CHAMPION (NATIONALITY) | DATE OF TITLE | CHAMPION (NATIONALITY) | DATE OF TITLE |
|---|---|---|---|
| **Undisputed champions** | | **WBA** | |
| Jack ("the Nonpareil") Dempsey (USA) | 30 Jul 1884 | Carlos Monzón (ARG) | 5 Oct 1974 |
| Bob Fitzsimmons (GBR—later | 14 Jan 1891 | gave up title in 1977 | |
| became US citizen) | | Rodrigo Valdés (COL) | 5 Nov 1977 |
| gave up title in 1895 | | Hugo Corro (ARG) | 22 Apr 1978 |
| Tommy Ryan (USA) | 24 Oct 1898 | Vito Antuofermo (ITA) | 30 Jun 1979 |
| retired in 1907 | | Alan Minter (GBR) | 16 Mar 1980 |
| Stanley Ketchel (USA) | 9 May 1908 | Marvin Hagler (USA) | 27 Sep 1980 |
| Billy Papke (USA) | 7 Sep 1908 | stripped of title in 1987 | |
| Stanley Ketchel (USA) | 26 Nov 1908 | Sumbu Kalambay (ITA) | 23 Oct 1987 |
| died in 1910 | | stripped of title in 1989 | |
| George Chip (USA) | 11 Oct 1913 | Mike McCallum (JAM) | 13 May 1989 |
| Al McCoy (USA) | 6 Apr 1914 | stripped of title in 1991 | |
| Mike O'Dowd (USA) | 14 Nov 1917 | Reggie Johnson (USA) | 22 Apr 1992 |
| Johnny Wilson (USA) | 6 May 1920 | John David Jackson (USA) | 2 Oct 1993 |
| Harry Greb (USA) | 31 Aug 1923 | stripped of title in 1994 | |
| Tiger Flowers (USA) | 26 Feb 1926 | Jorge Castro (ARG) | 12 Aug 1994 |
| Mickey Walker (USA) | 3 Dec 1926 | Shinji Takehara (JPN) | 19 Dec 1995 |
| gave up title in 1931; | | William Joppy (USA) | 24 Jun 1996 |
| title in dispute | | Julio César Green (DOM) | 23 Aug 1997 |
| Tony Zale (USA) | 28 Nov 1941 | William Joppy (USA) | 31 Jan 1998 |
| Rocky Graziano (USA) | 16 Jul 1947 | Félix Trinidad (PUR) | 12 May 2001 |
| Tony Zale (USA) | 10 Jun 1948 | Bernard Hopkins (USA) | 29 Sep 2001 |
| Marcel Cerdan (FRA) | 21 Sep 1948 | | |
| Jake La Motta (USA) | 16 Jun 1949 | **WBC** | |
| Sugar Ray Robinson (USA) | 14 Feb 1951 | Rodrigo Valdés (COL) | 24 May 1974 |
| Randy Turpin (GBR) | 10 Jul 1951 | Carlos Monzón (ARG) | 26 Jun 1976 |
| Sugar Ray Robinson (USA) | 12 Sep 1951 | gave up title in 1977 | |
| retired 1952–54 | | Rodrigo Valdés (COL) | 5 Nov 1977 |
| Carl Olson (USA) | 21 Oct 1953 | Hugo Corro (ARG) | 22 Apr 1978 |
| Sugar Ray Robinson (USA) | 9 Dec 1955 | Vito Antuofermo (ITA) | 30 Jun 1979 |
| Gene Fullmer (USA) | 2 Jan 1957 | Alan Minter (GBR) | 16 Mar 1980 |
| Sugar Ray Robinson (USA) | 1 May 1957 | Marvin Hagler (USA) | 27 Sep 1980 |
| Carmen Basilio (USA) | 23 Sep 1957 | Sugar Ray Leonard (USA) | 6 Apr 1987 |
| Sugar Ray Robinson (USA) | 25 Mar 1958 | gave up title in 1987 | |
| stripped of National Boxing Association | | Thomas Hearns (USA) | 29 Oct 1987 |
| (later WBA) title in 1959 | | Iran Barkley (USA) | 6 Jun 1988 |
| Dick Tiger (Richard Ihetu) (NGR) | 10 Aug 1963 | Roberto Durán (PAN) | 24 Feb 1989 |
| Joey Giardello (USA) | 7 Dec 1963 | stripped of title in 1990 | |
| Dick Tiger (NGR) | 21 Oct 1965 | Julian Jackson (USA) | 24 Nov 1990 |
| Emile Griffith (USA) | 25 Apr 1966 | Gerald McClellan (USA) | 8 May 1993 |
| Nino Benvenuti (ITA) | 17 Apr 1967 | vacant | |
| Emile Griffith (USA) | 29 Sep 1967 | Julian Jackson (USA) | 17 Mar 1995 |
| Nino Benvenuti (ITA) | 4 Mar 1968 | Quincy Taylor (USA) | 19 Aug 1995 |
| Carlos Monzón (ARG) | 7 Nov 1970 | Keith Holmes (USA) | 16 Mar 1996 |
| stripped of WBC title in 1974 | | Hassine Cherifi (FRA) | 2 May 1998 |

# World Middleweight Champions (continued)

| CHAMPION (NATIONALITY) | DATE OF TITLE | CHAMPION (NATIONALITY) | DATE OF TITLE |
|---|---|---|---|
| **WBC (continued)** | | **IBF (continued)** | |
| Keith Holmes (USA) | 24 Apr 1999 | Michael Nunn (USA) | 28 Jul 1988 |
| Bernard Hopkins (USA) | 14 Apr 2001 | James Toney (USA) | 10 May 1991 |
| | |   gave up title in 1993 | |
| **IBF** | | Roy Jones, Jr. (USA) | 22 May 1993 |
| Marvin Hagler (USA) | 27 May 1983 |   gave up title in 1994 | |
|   relinquished title in 1987 | | Bernard Hopkins (USA) | 29 Apr 1995 |
| Frank Tate (USA) | 10 Oct 1987 | | |

# World Super Welterweight Champions

*Top weight 154 pounds. Also called junior middleweight.*

| CHAMPION (NATIONALITY) | DATE OF TITLE | CHAMPION (NATIONALITY) | DATE OF TITLE |
|---|---|---|---|
| **WBA** | | **WBC** | |
| Dennis Moyer (USA) | 20 Oct 1962 | Miguel de Oliveira (BRA) | 7 May 1975 |
| Ralph Dupas (USA) | 29 Apr 1963 | Elisha Obed (BAH) | 13 Nov 1975 |
| Sandro Mazzinghi (ITA) | 7 Sep 1963 | Eckhard Dagge (FRG) | 18 Jun 1976 |
| Nino Benvenuti (ITA) | 18 Jun 1965 | Rocco Mattioli (ITA) | 6 Aug 1977 |
| Kim Ki Soo (KOR) | 25 Jun 1966 | Maurice Hope (GBR) | 4 Mar 1979 |
| Sandro Mazzinghi (ITA) | 25 May 1968 | Wilfred Benítez (PUR) | 3 May 1981 |
|   stripped of title in 1969 | | Thomas Hearns (USA) | 3 Dec 1982 |
| Freddie Little (USA) | 17 Mar 1969 |   gave up title in 1986 | |
| Carmelo Bossi (ITA) | 9 Jul 1970 | Duane Thomas (USA) | 5 Dec 1986 |
| Koichi Wajima (JPN) | 31 Oct 1971 | Lupe Aquino (MEX) | 12 Jul 1987 |
| Oscar Albarado (USA) | 3 Jun 1974 | Gianfranco Rosi (ITA) | 2 Oct 1987 |
| Koichi Wajima (JPN) | 21 Jan 1975 | Donald Curry (USA) | 8 Jul 1988 |
| Yuh Jae Do (KOR) | 7 Jun 1975 | René Jacquot (FRA) | 11 Feb 1989 |
| Koichi Wajima (JPN) | 17 Feb 1976 | John Mugabi (UGA) | 8 Jul 1989 |
| José Durán (ESP) | 18 May 1976 | Terry Norris (USA) | 31 Mar 1990 |
| Miguel Castellini (ARG) | 8 Oct 1976 | Simon Brown (USA) | 18 Dec 1993 |
| Eddie Gazo (NCA) | 5 Mar 1977 | Terry Norris (USA) | 7 May 1994 |
| Kudo Masashi (JPN) | 9 Aug 1978 | Luis Santana (DOM) | 12 Nov 1994 |
| Ayub Kalule (DEN) | 24 Oct 1979 | Terry Norris (USA) | 19 Aug 1995 |
| Sugar Ray Leonard (USA) | 25 Jun 1981 | Keith Mullings (USA) | 6 Dec 1997 |
|   gave up title in 1981 | | Javier Castillejo (ESP) | 29 Jan 1999 |
| Tadashi Mihara (JPN) | 7 Nov 1981 | Oscar de la Hoya (USA) | 23 Jun 2001 |
| Davey Moore (USA) | 2 Feb 1982 | Mark Medal (USA) | 11 Mar 1984 |
| Roberto Durán (PAN) | 16 Jun 1983 | Carlos Santos (PUR) | 2 Nov 1984 |
|   gave up title in 1984 | | Buster Drayton (USA) | 4 Jun 1986 |
| Mike McCallum (JAM) | 19 Oct 1984 | Matthew Hilton (CAN) | 27 Jun 1987 |
|   gave up title in 1987 | | Robert Hines (USA) | 4 Nov 1988 |
| Julian Jackson (USA) | 21 Nov 1987 | Darrin Van Horn (USA) | 4 Feb 1989 |
|   gave up title in 1990 | | Gianfranco Rosi (ITA) | 16 Jul 1989 |
| Gilbert Dele (FRA) | 23 Feb 1991 | Vincent Pettway (USA) | 17 Sep 1994 |
| Vinny Pazienza (USA) | 11 Oct 1991 | Paul Vaden (USA) | 12 Aug 1995 |
|   gave up title in 1992 | | Terry Norris (USA) | 16 Dec 1995 |
| Julio César Vásquez (ARG) | 22 Dec 1992 |   gave up title in 1997 | |
| Pernell Whitaker (USA) | 4 Mar 1995 | Raul Marquez (USA) | 12 Apr 1997 |
|   gave up title in 1995 | | Yory Boy Campas (MEX) | 6 Dec 1997 |
| Carl Daniels (USA) | 16 Jun 1995 | Fernando Vargas (USA) | 12 Dec 1998 |
| Julio César Vásquez (ARG) | 16 Dec 1995 | Félix Trinidad (PUR) | 2 Dec 2000 |
| Laurent Boudouani (FRA) | 21 Aug 1996 |   gave up title in 2001 | |
| David Reid (USA) | 6 Mar 1999 | Ronald Wright (USA) | 12 Oct 2001 |
| Félix Trinidad (PUR) | 3 Mar 2000 | | |
|   gave up title in 2001 | | | |
| Fernando Vargas (USA) | 22 Sep 2001 | | |
| Oscar de la Hoya (USA) | 14 Sep 2002 | | |

Gatorade was named for the Gators football team of the University of Florida, where the sport drink was first developed in 1965.

# World Welterweight Champions
*Top weight 147 pounds; until about 1909 not over 145 pounds.*

| CHAMPION (NATIONALITY) | DATE OF TITLE | CHAMPION (NATIONALITY) | DATE OF TITLE |
|---|---|---|---|
| **Undisputed champions** | | **WBA (continued)** | |
| Paddy Duffy (USA) | 30 Oct 1888 | Thomas Hearns (USA) | 2 Aug 1980 |
| died in 1890 | | Sugar Ray Leonard (USA) | 16 Sep 1981 |
| Mysterious Billy Smith (USA) | 14 Dec 1892 | retired in 1982 | |
| Tommy Ryan (USA) | 26 Jul 1894 | Donald Curry (USA) | 13 Feb 1983 |
| gave up title in 1898 | | Lloyd Honeyghan (GBR) | 27 Sep 1986 |
| Mysterious Billy Smith (USA) | 25 Aug 1898 | gave up title in 1986 | |
| Jim ("Rube") Ferns (USA) | 15 Jan 1900 | Mark Breland (USA) | 6 Feb 1987 |
| Matty Matthews (USA) | 16 Oct 1900 | Marlon Starling (USA) | 22 Aug 1987 |
| Jim ("Rube") Ferns (USA) | 24 May 1901 | Tomás Molinares (COL) | 29 Jul 1988 |
| Joe Walcott (BAR) | 18 Dec 1901 | gave up title in 1988 | |
| title in dispute from 1904 | | Mark Breland (USA) | 4 Feb 1989 |
| Ted ("Kid") Lewis (GBR) | 31 Aug 1915 | Aaron Davis (USA) | 8 Jul 1990 |
| Jack Britton (USA) | 24 Apr 1916 | Meldrick Taylor (USA) | 19 Jan 1991 |
| Ted ("Kid") Lewis (GBR) | 25 Jun 1917 | Crisanto España (VEN) | 31 Oct 1992 |
| Jack Britton (USA) | 17 Mar 1919 | Ike Quartey (GHA) | 4 Jun 1994 |
| Mickey Walker (USA) | 1 Nov 1922 | stripped of title in 1998 | |
| Pete Latzo (USA) | 20 May 1926 | James Page (USA) | 10 Oct 1998 |
| Joe Dundee (USA) | 3 Jun 1927 | stripped of title in 2000 | |
| stripped of National Boxing Association | | Andrew Lewis (GUY) | 17 Feb 2001 |
| (later WBA) title in 1928 | | Ricardo Mayorga (NCA) | 28 Jul 2001 |
| Jackie Fields (USA) | 25 Jul 1929 | | |
| Young Jack Thompson (USA) | 9 May 1930 | **WBC** | |
| Tommy Freeman (USA) | 5 Sep 1930 | John Stracey (GBR) | 6 Dec 1975 |
| Young Jack Thompson (USA) | 14 Apr 1931 | Carlos Palomino (USA) | 22 Jun 1976 |
| Lou Brouillard (CAN) | 23 Oct 1931 | Wilfred Benítez (PUR) | 14 Jan 1979 |
| Jackie Fields (USA) | 28 Jan 1932 | Sugar Ray Leonard (USA) | 30 Nov 1979 |
| Young Corbett III (Rafelle Giordano) | 22 Feb 1933 | Roberto Durán (PAN) | 20 Jun 1980 |
| (USA) | | Sugar Ray Leonard (USA) | 25 Nov 1980 |
| Jimmy McLarnin (CAN) | 29 May 1933 | retired in 1982 | |
| Barney Ross (USA) | 28 May 1934 | Milton McCrory (USA) | 13 Aug 1983 |
| Jimmy McLarnin (CAN) | 17 Sep 1934 | Donald Curry (USA) | 6 Dec 1985 |
| Barney Ross (USA) | 28 May 1935 | Lloyd Honeyghan (GBR) | 27 Sep 1986 |
| Henry Armstrong (USA) | 31 May 1938 | Jorge Vaca (MEX) | 28 Oct 1987 |
| Fritzie Zivic (USA) | 4 Oct 1940 | Lloyd Honeyghan (GBR) | 29 Mar 1988 |
| Freddie ("Red") Cochrane (USA) | 29 Jul 1941 | Marlon Starling (USA) | 4 Feb 1989 |
| Marty Servo (USA) | 1 Feb 1946 | Maurice Blocker (USA) | 19 Aug 1990 |
| retired in 1946 | | Simon Brown (JAM) | 18 Mar 1991 |
| Sugar Ray Robinson (USA) | 20 Dec 1946 | James McGirt (USA) | 29 Nov 1991 |
| gave up title in 1951 | | Pernell Whitaker (USA) | 6 Mar 1993 |
| Kid Gavilan (CUB) | 18 May 1951 | Oscar de la Hoya (USA) | 12 Apr 1997 |
| Johnny Saxton (USA) | 20 Oct 1954 | Félix Trinidad (PUR) | 18 Sep 1999 |
| Tony DeMarco (USA) | 1 Apr 1955 | gave up title in 2000 | |
| Carmen Basilio (USA) | 10 Jun 1955 | Oscar de la Hoya (USA) | 20 Mar 2000 |
| Johnny Saxton (USA) | 14 Mar 1956 | Shane Mosley (USA) | 17 Jun 2000 |
| Carmen Basilio (USA) | 12 Sep 1956 | Ricardo Mayorga (NCA) | 25 Jan 2003 |
| gave up title in 1957 | | | |
| Virgil Akins (USA) | 6 Jun 1958 | **IBF** | |
| Don Jordan (USA) | 5 Dec 1958 | Donald Curry (USA) | 4 Feb 1984 |
| Benny ("Kid") Paret (CUB) | 27 May 1960 | Lloyd Honeyghan (GBR) | 27 Sep 1986 |
| Emile Griffith (USA) | 1 Apr 1961 | stripped of title in 1987 | |
| Benny ("Kid") Paret (CUB) | 3 Sep 1961 | Simon Brown (JAM) | 23 Apr 1988 |
| Emile Griffith (USA) | 24 Mar 1962 | gave up title in 1991 | |
| Luis Rodríguez (CUB) | 21 Mar 1963 | Maurice Blocker (USA) | 4 Oct 1991 |
| Emile Griffith (USA) | 8 Jun 1963 | Félix Trinidad (PUR) | 19 Jun 1993 |
| gave up title in 1966 | | gave up title in 2000 | |
| Curtis Cokes (USA) | 28 Nov 1966 | Vernon Forrest (USA) | 12 May 2001 |
| José Nápoles (MEX) | 18 Apr 1969 | stripped of title in 2001 | |
| Billy Backus (USA) | 3 Dec 1970 | Michele Piccirillo (ITA) | 13 Apr 2002 |
| José Nápoles (MEX) | 4 Jun 1971 | Cory Spinks (USA) | 22 Mar 2003 |
| stripped of WBA title in 1975 | | | |
| | | | |
| **WBA** | | | |
| Ángel Espada (PUR) | 28 Jun 1975 | | |
| Pipino Cuevas (MEX) | 17 Jul 1976 | | |

## World Super Lightweight Champions
*Top weight 140 pounds. Also called junior welterweight.*

| CHAMPION (NATIONALITY) | DATE OF TITLE | CHAMPION (NATIONALITY) | DATE OF TITLE |
|---|---|---|---|
| **Undisputed champions** | | **WBC** | |
| Myron Mitchell (USA) | 15 Nov 1922 | Pedro Adigue (PHI) | 14 Dec 1968 |
| proclaimed champion as the result | | Bruno Arcari (ITA) | 31 Jan 1970 |
| of a poll taken by *The Boxing Blade* | | gave up title in 1974 | |
| Mushy Callahan (USA) | 21 Sep 1926 | Perico Fernández (ESP) | 21 Sep 1974 |
| Jack ("Kid") Berg (GBR) | 18 Feb 1930 | Saensak Muangsurin (THA) | 15 Jul 1975 |
| Tony Canzoneri (USA) | 24 Apr 1931 | Miguel Velásquez (ESP) | 30 Jun 1976 |
| Johnny Jadick (USA) | 18 Jan 1932 | Saensak Muangsurin (THA) | 29 Oct 1976 |
| Battling Shaw (MEX) | 20 Feb 1933 | Kim Sang Hyun (KOR) | 30 Dec 1978 |
| Tony Canzoneri (USA) | 21 May 1933 | Saoul Mamby (USA) | 23 Feb 1980 |
| Barney Ross (USA) | 23 Jun 1933 | Leroy Haley (USA) | 26 Jun 1982 |
| gave up title in 1935; title vacant | | Bruce Curry (USA) | 18 May 1983 |
| Tippy Larkin (USA) | 29 Apr 1946 | Bill Costello (USA) | 29 Jan 1984 |
| title vacant from 1946 | | Lonnie Smith (USA) | 21 Aug 1985 |
| Carlos Ortíz (PUR) | 12 Jun 1959 | René Arredondo (MEX) | 6 May 1986 |
| Duilio Loi (ITA) | 1 Sep 1960 | Tsuyoshi Hamada (JPN) | 24 Jul 1986 |
| Eddie Perkins (USA) | 14 Sep 1962 | René Arredondo (MEX) | 22 Jul 1987 |
| Duilio Loi (ITA) | 15 Dec 1962 | Roger Mayweather (USA) | 12 Nov 1987 |
| retired in 1963 | | Julio César Chávez (MEX) | 13 May 1989 |
| Eddie Perkins (USA) | 15 Jun 1963 | Frankie Randall (USA) | 29 Jan 1994 |
| Carlos Hernández (VEN) | 18 Jan 1965 | Julio César Chávez (MEX) | 7 May 1994 |
| Sandro Lopopolo (ITA) | 29 Apr 1966 | Oscar de la Hoya (USA) | 7 Jun 1996 |
| Paul Takeshi Fujii (USA) | 30 Apr 1967 | gave up title in 1997 | |
| | | Kostya Tszyu (AUS) | 21 Aug 1999 |
| **WBA** | | | |
| Nicolino Loche (ARG) | 12 Dec 1968 | **IBF** | |
| Alfonso Frazer (PAN) | 10 Mar 1972 | Aaron Pryor (USA) | December 1984 |
| Antonio Cervantes (COL) | 28 Oct 1972 | recognized as champion by | |
| Wilfred Benítez (PUR) | 6 Mar 1976 | the IBF; stripped of title in 1985 | |
| stripped of title in 1976 | | Gary Hinton (USA) | 26 Apr 1986 |
| Antonio Cervantes (COL) | 25 Jun 1977 | Joe Louis Manley (USA) | 30 Oct 1986 |
| Aaron Pryor (USA) | 2 Aug 1980 | Terry Marsh (GBR) | 4 Mar 1987 |
| retired in 1983 | | gave up title in 1987 | |
| Johnny Bumphus (USA) | 22 Jan 1984 | James McGirt (USA) | 14 Feb 1988 |
| Gene Hatcher (USA) | 1 Jun 1984 | Meldrick Taylor (USA) | 3 Sep 1988 |
| Ubaldo Sacco (ARG) | 21 Jul 1985 | Julio César Chávez (MEX) | 17 Mar 1990 |
| Patrizio Oliva (ITA) | 15 Mar 1986 | gave up title in 1991 | |
| Juan Martín Coggi (ARG) | 4 Jul 1987 | Rafael Pineda (COL) | 7 Dec 1991 |
| Loreto Garza (USA) | 17 Aug 1990 | Pernell Whitaker (USA) | 18 Jul 1992 |
| Edwin Rosario (PUR) | 15 Jun 1991 | gave up title in 1993 | |
| Akinobu Hiranaka (JPN) | 10 Apr 1992 | Charles Murray (USA) | 15 May 1993 |
| Morris East (PHI) | 9 Sep 1992 | Jake Rodriguez (PUR) | 13 Feb 1994 |
| Juan Martín Coggi (ARG) | 12 Jan 1993 | Kostya Tszyu (AUS) | 28 Jan 1995 |
| Frankie Randall (USA) | 17 Sep 1994 | Vince Phillips (USA) | 31 May 1997 |
| Juan Martín Coggi (ARG) | 13 Jan 1996 | Terronn Millett (USA) | 20 Feb 1999 |
| Frankie Randall (USA) | 16 Aug 1996 | stripped of title in 2000 | |
| Khalid Rahilou (FRA) | 11 Jan 1997 | Zab Judah (USA) | 12 Feb 2000 |
| Sharmba Mitchell (USA) | 10 Oct 1998 | Kostya Tszyu (AUS) | 3 Nov 2001 |
| Kostya Tszyu (AUS) | 3 Feb 2001 | | |

## World Lightweight Champions
*Top weight 135 pounds; until 1912 usually 133 pounds, but sometimes as high as 140 pounds.*

| CHAMPION (NATIONALITY) | DATE OF TITLE | CHAMPION (NATIONALITY) | DATE OF TITLE |
|---|---|---|---|
| **Undisputed champions** | | **Undisputed champions (continued)** | |
| George ("Kid") Lavigne (USA) | 1 Jun 1896 | Rocky Kansas (USA) | 7 Dec 1925 |
| Frank Erne (USA) | 3 Jul 1899 | Sammy Mandell (USA) | 3 Jul 1926 |
| Joe Gans (USA) | 12 May 1902 | Al Singer (USA) | 17 Jul 1930 |
| Battling Nelson (USA) | 4 Jul 1908 | Tony Canzoneri (USA) | 14 Nov 1930 |
| Ad Wolgast (USA) | 22 Feb 1910 | Barney Ross (USA) | 23 Jun 1933 |
| Willie Ritchie (USA) | 28 Nov 1912 | gave up title in 1933 | |
| Freddie Welsh (GBR) | 7 Jul 1914 | Tony Canzoneri (USA) | 10 May 1935 |
| Benny Leonard (USA) | 28 May 1917 | Lou Ambers (USA) | 3 Sep 1936 |
| retired in 1925 | | Henry Armstrong (USA) | 17 Aug 1938 |
| Jimmy Goodrich (USA) | 13 Jul 1925 | Lou Ambers (USA) | 22 Aug 1939 |

# World Lightweight Champions (continued)

| CHAMPION (NATIONALITY) | DATE OF TITLE | CHAMPION (NATIONALITY) | DATE OF TITLE |
|---|---|---|---|
| **Undisputed champions (continued)** | | **WBA (continued)** | |
| Lew Jenkins (USA) | 10 May 1940 | Raul Balbi (ARG) | 8 Oct 2001 |
| Sammy Angott (USA) | 19 Dec 1941 | Leonard Dorin (ROM) | 5 Jan 2002 |
| retired in 1942 | | | |
| Ike Williams (USA) | 4 Aug 1947 | **WBC** | |
| Jimmy Carter (USA) | 25 May 1951 | Rodolfo Gonzáles (MEX) | 10 Nov 1972 |
| Lauro Salas (MEX) | 14 May 1952 | Ishimatsu Suzuki (JPN) | 11 Apr 1974 |
| Jimmy Carter (USA) | 15 Oct 1952 | Esteban de Jesus (PUR) | 8 May 1976 |
| Paddy DeMarco (USA) | 5 Mar 1954 | Roberto Durán (PAN) | 21 Jan 1978 |
| Jimmy Carter (USA) | 17 Nov 1954 | gave up title in 1979 | |
| Wallace ("Bud") Smith (USA) | 29 Jun 1955 | Jim Watt (GBR) | 17 Apr 1979 |
| Joe Brown (USA) | 24 Aug 1956 | Alexis Argüello (NCA) | 20 Jun 1981 |
| Carlos Ortíz (PUR) | 21 Apr 1962 | gave up title in 1983 | |
| Ismael Laguna (PAN) | 10 Apr 1965 | Edwin Rosario (PUR) | 1 May 1983 |
| Carlos Ortíz (PUR) | 13 Nov 1965 | José Luis Ramírez (MEX) | 3 Nov 1984 |
| Carlos Teo Cruz (DOM) | 29 Jun 1968 | Hector Camacho (PUR) | 10 Aug 1985 |
| Armando Ramos (USA) | 18 Feb 1969 | stripped of title in 1987 | |
| Ismael Laguna (PAN) | 3 Mar 1970 | José Luis Ramírez (MEX) | 19 Jul 1987 |
| stripped of WBC title in 1970 | | Julio César Chávez (MEX) | 29 Oct 1988 |
| | | gave up title in 1989 | |
| **WBA** | | Pernell Whitaker (USA) | 20 Aug 1989 |
| Ken Buchanan (GBR) | 26 Sep 1970 | gave up title in 1992 | |
| Roberto Durán (PAN) | 26 Jun 1972 | Miguel González (MEX) | 24 Aug 1992 |
| gave up title in 1979 | | gave up title in 1996 | |
| Ernesto España (VEN) | 16 Jun 1979 | Jean-Baptiste Mendy (FRA) | 20 Apr 1996 |
| Hilmer Kenty (USA) | 2 Mar 1980 | Steve Johnston (USA) | 1 Mar 1997 |
| Sean O'Grady (USA) | 12 Apr 1981 | César Bazan (MEX) | 13 Jun 1998 |
| stripped of title in 1981 | | Steve Johnston (USA) | 27 Feb 1999 |
| Claude Noel (TRI) | 12 Sep 1981 | José Luis Castillo (MEX) | 17 Jun 2000 |
| Arturo Frias (USA) | 5 Dec 1981 | Floyd Mayweather, Jr. (USA) | 20 Apr 2002 |
| Ray Mancini (USA) | 8 May 1982 | | |
| Livingstone Bramble (ISV) | 1 Jun 1984 | **IBF** | |
| Edwin Rosario (PUR) | 26 Sep 1986 | Charlie Brown (USA) | 30 Jan 1984 |
| Julio César Chávez (MEX) | 21 Nov 1987 | Harry Arroyo (USA) | 15 Apr 1984 |
| gave up title in 1989 | | Jimmy Paul (USA) | 6 Apr 1985 |
| Edwin Rosario (PUR) | 9 Jul 1989 | Greg Haugen (USA) | 6 Dec 1986 |
| Juan Nazario (PUR) | 4 Apr 1990 | Vinny Pazienza (USA) | 7 Jun 1987 |
| Pernell Whitaker (USA) | 11 Aug 1990 | Greg Haugen (USA) | 6 Feb 1988 |
| gave up title in 1992 | | Pernell Whitaker (USA) | 20 Feb 1989 |
| Joey Gamache (USA) | 13 Jun 1992 | gave up title in 1992 | |
| Tony Lopez (USA) | 24 Oct 1992 | Fred Pendleton (USA) | 10 Jan 1993 |
| Dingaan Thobela (RSA) | 26 Jun 1993 | Rafael Ruelas (USA) | 19 Feb 1994 |
| Olzubek Nazarov (RUS) | 30 Oct 1993 | Oscar de la Hoya (USA) | 6 May 1995 |
| Jean-Baptiste Mendy (FRA) | 16 May 1998 | gave up title in 1995 | |
| Julien Lorcy (FRA) | 10 Apr 1999 | Philip Holiday (RSA) | 19 Aug 1995 |
| Stefano Zoff (ITA) | 7 Aug 1999 | Shane Mosley (USA) | 2 Aug 1997 |
| Gilberto Serrano (VEN) | 13 Nov 1999 | gave up title in 1999 | |
| Takanori Hatakeyama (JPN) | 11 Jun 2000 | Paul Spadafora (USA) | 20 Aug 1999 |
| Julien Lorcy (FRA) | 1 Jul 2001 | | |

# World Super Featherweight Champions

*Top weight 130 pounds. Also called junior lightweight.*

| CHAMPION (NATIONALITY) | DATE OF TITLE | CHAMPION (NATIONALITY) | DATE OF TITLE |
|---|---|---|---|
| **Undisputed champions** | | **Undisputed champions** | |
| Johnny Dundee (USA) | 18 Nov 1921 | Sandy Saddler (USA) | 6 Dec 1949 |
| Jack Bernstein (USA) | 30 May 1923 | title vacant from 1951 | |
| Johnny Dundee (USA) | 17 Dec 1923 | Harold Gomes (USA) | 20 Jul 1959 |
| Steve ("Kid") Sullivan (USA) | 20 Jun 1924 | Gabriel ("Flash") Elorde (PHI) | 16 Mar 1960 |
| Mike Ballerino (USA) | 1 Apr 1925 | Yoshiaki Numata (JPN) | 15 Jun 1967 |
| Tod Morgan (USA) | 2 Dec 1925 | Hiroshi Kobayashi (JPN) | 14 Dec 1967 |
| Benny Bass (USA) | 20 Dec 1929 | stripped of WBC title in 1969 | |
| Kid Chocolate (Eligio Sardinias) (CUB) | 15 Jul 1931 | | |
| | | **WBA** | |
| Frankie Klick (USA) | 25 Dec 1933 | Alfredo Marcano (VEN) | 29 Jul 1971 |
| title vacant from 1934 | | Ben Villaflor (PHI) | 25 Apr 1972 |

## World Super Featherweight Champions (continued)

| CHAMPION (NATIONALITY) | DATE OF TITLE | CHAMPION (NATIONALITY) | DATE OF TITLE |
|---|---|---|---|
| **WBA (continued)** | | **WBC (continued)** | |
| Kuniaki Shibata (JPN) | 12 Mar 1973 | Hector Camacho (USA) | 7 Aug 1983 |
| Ben Villaflor (PHI) | 17 Oct 1973 | gave up title in 1984 | |
| Samuel Serrano (PUR) | 16 Oct 1976 | Julio César Chávez (MEX) | 13 Sep 1984 |
| Yasutsune Uehara (JPN) | 2 Aug 1980 | vacant | |
| Samuel Serrano (PUR) | 9 Apr 1981 | Azumah Nelson (GHA) | 29 Feb 1988 |
| Roger Mayweather (USA) | 19 Jan 1983 | Jesse James Leija (USA) | 7 May 1994 |
| Rocky Lockridge (USA) | 26 Feb 1984 | Gabriel Ruelas (USA) | 17 Sep 1994 |
| Wilfredo Gómez (PUR) | 19 May 1985 | Azumah Nelson (GHA) | 1 Dec 1995 |
| Alfredo Layne (PAN) | 24 May 1986 | Genaro Hernandez (USA) | 22 Mar 1997 |
| Brian Mitchell (RSA) | 27 Sep 1986 | Floyd Mayweather, Jr. (USA) | 3 Oct 1998 |
| gave up title in 1991 | | gave up title in 2002 | |
| Joey Gamache (USA) | 28 Jun 1991 | Sirimongkol Singmanassuk (THA) | 24 Aug 2002 |
| gave up title in 1991 | | | |
| Genaro Hernandez (USA) | 22 Nov 1991 | **IBF** | |
| gave up title in 1995 | | Yuh Hwan-Kil (KOR) | 2 Apr 1984 |
| Choi Yong Soo (KOR) | 21 Oct 1995 | Lester Ellis (AUS) | 15 Feb 1985 |
| Takanori Hatakeyama (JPN) | 5 Sep 1998 | Barry Michael (AUS) | 12 Jul 1985 |
| Lakva Sim (MGL) | 27 Jun 1999 | Rocky Lockridge (USA) | 9 Aug 1987 |
| Jong Kwon Baek (KOR) | 31 Oct 1999 | Tony Lopez (USA) | 27 Jul 1988 |
| Joel Casamayor (CUB) | 21 May 2000 | Juan Molina (PUR) | 7 Oct 1989 |
| Acelino Freitas (BRA) | 12 Jan 2002 | Tony Lopez (USA) | 20 May 1990 |
| | | Brian Mitchell (RSA) | 13 Sep 1991 |
| **WBC** | | gave up title in 1992 | |
| Rene Barrientos (PHI) | 15 Feb 1969 | Juan Molina (PUR) | 22 Feb 1992 |
| Yoshiaki Numata (JPN) | 5 Apr 1970 | vacant | |
| Ricardo Arredondo (MEX) | 10 Oct 1971 | Eddie Hopson (USA) | 22 Apr 1995 |
| Kuniaki Shibata (JPN) | 28 Feb 1974 | Tracy Patterson (USA) | 9 Jul 1995 |
| Alfredo Escalera (PUR) | 5 Jul 1975 | Arturo Gatti (USA) | 15 Dec 1995 |
| Alexis Argüello (NCA) | 28 Jan 1978 | gave up title in 1998 | |
| gave up title in 1980 | | Roberto Garcia (USA) | 13 Mar 1998 |
| Rafael Limón (MEX) | 11 Dec 1980 | Diego Corrales (USA) | 23 Oct 1999 |
| Cornelius Boza-Edwards (UGA) | 8 Mar 1981 | gave up title in 2000 | |
| Rolando Navarette (PHI) | 29 Aug 1981 | Steve Forbes (USA) | 3 Dec 2000 |
| Rafael Limón (MEX) | 29 May 1982 | stripped of title in 2002 | |
| Bobby Chacon (USA) | 11 Dec 1982 | Carlos Hernandez (ESA) | 1 Feb 2003 |
| stripped of title in 1983 | | | |

## World Featherweight Champions

*Top weight 126 pounds; until 1901 weight varied between 115 and 122 pounds.*

| CHAMPION (NATIONALITY) | DATE OF TITLE | CHAMPION (NATIONALITY) | DATE OF TITLE |
|---|---|---|---|
| **Undisputed champions** | | **Undisputed champions (continued)** | |
| Billy Murphy (NZL) | 13 Jan 1890 | Henry Armstrong (USA) | 29 Oct 1937 |
| Young Griffo (AUS) | 2 Feb 1890 | gave up title in 1938 | |
| vacant | | Joey Archibald (USA) | 18 Apr 1939 |
| George Dixon (CAN) | 27 Jun 1892 | Harry Jeffra (USA) | 20 May 1940 |
| Solly Smith (USA) | 4 Oct 1897 | Joey Archibald (USA) | 12 May 1941 |
| Dave Sullivan (GBR) | 26 Sep 1898 | Chalky Wright (USA) | 11 Sep 1941 |
| George Dixon (CAN) | 11 Nov 1898 | Willie Pep (USA) | 20 Nov 1942 |
| Terry McGovern (USA) | 19 Jan 1900 | Sandy Saddler (USA) | 29 Oct 1948 |
| Young Corbett (USA) | 28 Nov 1901 | Willie Pep (USA) | 11 Feb 1949 |
| Jimmy Britt (USA) | 25 Mar 1904 | Sandy Saddler (USA) | 8 Sep 1950 |
| title vacant in 1904 | | retired in 1957 | |
| Tommy Sullivan (USA) | 13 Oct 1904 | Hogan Bassey (NGR) | 24 Jun 1957 |
| title vacant from 1905 | | Davey Moore (USA) | 18 Mar 1959 |
| Abe Atell (USA) | 22 Feb 1906 | Sugar Ramos (CUB) | 21 Mar 1963 |
| Johnny Kilbane (USA) | 22 Feb 1912 | Vicente Saldivar (MEX) | 26 Sep 1964 |
| Eugène Criqui (FRA) | 2 Jun 1923 | retired 1967–70 | |
| Johnny Dundee (USA) | 26 Jul 1923 | | |
| gave up title in 1924 | | **WBA** | |
| Louis ("Kid") Kaplan (USA) | 2 Jan 1925 | Raoul Rojas (USA) | 28 Mar 1968 |
| gave up title in 1926 | | Shozo Saijo (JPN) | 28 Sep 1968 |
| Tony Canzoneri (USA) | 24 Oct 1927 | Antonio Gómez (VEN) | 2 Sep 1971 |
| André Routis (FRA) | 28 Sep 1928 | Ernesto Marcel (PAN) | 19 Aug 1972 |
| Battling Battalino (USA) | 23 Sep 1929 | retired in 1974 | |
| gave up title in 1932 | | Rubén Olivares (MEX) | 9 Jul 1974 |

## World Featherweight Champions (continued)

| CHAMPION (NATIONALITY) | DATE OF TITLE |
|---|---|
| WBA (continued) | |
| Alexis Argüello (NCA) | 23 Nov 1974 |
| gave up title in 1976 | |
| Rafael Ortega (PAN) | 15 Jan 1977 |
| Cecilio Lastra (ESP) | 17 Dec 1977 |
| Eusebio Pedroza (PAN) | 15 Apr 1978 |
| Barry McGuigan (NIR) | 8 Jun 1985 |
| Steve Cruz (USA) | 23 Jun 1986 |
| Antonio Esparragoza (VEN) | 6 Mar 1987 |
| Park Yung Kyun (KOR) | 30 Mar 1991 |
| Eloy Rojas (VEN) | 4 Dec 1993 |
| Wilfredo Vásquez (PUR) | 18 May 1996 |
| gave up title in 1998 | |
| Freddie Norwood (USA) | 3 Apr 1998 |
| stripped of title in 1998 | |
| Antonio Cermeño (VEN) | 3 Oct 1998 |
| Freddie Norwood (USA) | 29 May 1999 |
| Derrick Gainer (USA) | 9 Sep 2000 |
| | |
| WBC | |
| José Legra (CUB) | 24 Jul 1968 |
| Johnny Famechon (AUS) | 21 Jan 1969 |
| Vicente Saldivar (MEX) | 9 May 1970 |
| Kuniaki Shibata (JPN) | 11 Dec 1970 |
| Clemente Sánchez (MEX) | 19 May 1972 |
| José Legra (ESP) | 16 Dec 1972 |
| Eder Jofre (BRA) | 5 May 1973 |
| stripped of title in 1974 | |
| Bobby Chacon (USA) | 7 Sep 1974 |
| Rubén Olivares (MEX) | 20 Jun 1975 |
| David Kotey (GHA) | 20 Sep 1975 |
| Danny López (USA) | 5 Nov 1976 |
| Salvador Sánchez (MEX) | 2 Feb 1980 |
| died in 1982 | |
| Juan LaPorte (PUR) | 15 Sep 1982 |
| Wilfredo Gómez (PUR) | 31 Mar 1984 |
| Azumah Nelson (GHA) | 8 Dec 1984 |
| gave up title in 1988 | |

| CHAMPION (NATIONALITY) | DATE OF TITLE |
|---|---|
| WBC (continued) | |
| Jeff Fenech (AUS) | 7 Mar 1988 |
| gave up title in 1990 | |
| Marcos Villasana (MEX) | 2 Jun 1990 |
| Paul Hodkinson (GBR) | 13 Nov 1991 |
| Gregorio Vargas (MEX) | 28 Apr 1993 |
| Kevin Kelley (USA) | 4 Dec 1993 |
| Alejandro González (MEX) | 7 Jan 1995 |
| Manuel Medina (MEX) | 23 Sep 1995 |
| Luisito Espinosa (PHI) | 11 Dec 1995 |
| César Soto (MEX) | 15 May 1999 |
| Naseem Hamed (GBR) | 22 Oct 1999 |
| stripped of title in 1999 | |
| Gustavo Espadas (MEX) | 14 Apr 2000 |
| Erik Morales (MEX) | 17 Feb 2001 |
| | |
| IBF | |
| Oh Min-kuem (KOR) | 4 Mar 1984 |
| Chung Ki-yung (KOR) | 29 Nov 1985 |
| Antonio Rivera (PUR) | 30 Aug 1986 |
| Calvin Grove (USA) | 23 Jan 1988 |
| Jorge Paez (MEX) | 4 Aug 1988 |
| gave up title in 1991 | |
| Troy Dorsey (USA) | 3 Jun 1991 |
| Manuel Medina (MEX) | 12 Aug 1991 |
| Tom Johnson (USA) | 26 Feb 1993 |
| Naseem Hamed (GBR) | 8 Feb 1997 |
| gave up title in 1997 | |
| Hector Lizarraga (USA) | 13 Dec 1997 |
| Manuel Medina (MEX) | 24 Apr 1998 |
| Paul Ingle (GBR) | 13 Nov 1999 |
| Mbulelo Botile (RSA) | 16 Dec 2000 |
| Frankie Toledo (USA) | 6 Apr 2001 |
| Manuel Medina (MEX) | 16 Nov 2001 |
| Juan Manuel Marquez (MEX) | 1 Feb 2003 |

## World Super Bantamweight Champions

*Top weight 122 pounds. Also called junior featherweight. Weight division at first recognized only by WBC.*

| CHAMPION (NATIONALITY) | DATE OF TITLE |
|---|---|
| WBA | |
| Hong Soo Hwan (KOR) | 26 Nov 1977 |
| Ricardo Cardona (COL) | 7 May 1978 |
| Leo Randolph (USA) | 4 May 1980 |
| Sergio Palma (ARG) | 9 Aug 1980 |
| Leonardo Cruz (DOM) | 12 Jun 1982 |
| Loris Stecca (ITA) | 22 Feb 1984 |
| Víctor Callejas (PUR) | 26 May 1984 |
| stripped of title in 1986 | |
| Louie Espinoza (USA) | 16 Jan 1987 |
| Julio Gervacio (DOM) | 28 Nov 1987 |
| Bernardo Pinango (VEN) | 5 Mar 1988 |
| Juan José Estrada (MEX) | 28 May 1988 |
| Jesus Salud (USA) | 11 Dec 1989 |
| stripped of title in 1990 | |
| Luís Mendoza (COL) | 11 Sep 1990 |
| Raul Pérez (MEX) | 7 Oct 1991 |
| Wilfredo Vásquez (PUR) | 27 Mar 1992 |
| Antonio Cermeño (VEN) | 13 May 1995 |
| gave up title in 1997 | |
| Enrique Sanchez (MEX) | 8 Feb 1998 |
| vacant | |
| Néstor Garza (MEX) | 12 Dec 1998 |

| CHAMPION (NATIONALITY) | DATE OF TITLE |
|---|---|
| WBA (continued) | |
| Clarence Adams (USA) | 4 Mar 2000 |
| stripped of title in 2001 | |
| Yober Ortega (VEN) | 17 Nov 2001 |
| Yoddamrong Sithyodthong (THA) | 21 Feb 2002 |
| Osamu Sato (JPN) | 18 May 2002 |
| Salim Medjkoune (FRA) | 9 Oct 2002 |
| | |
| WBC | |
| Rigoberto Riasco (PAN) | 3 Apr 1976 |
| Kazuo Kobayashi (JPN) | 10 Oct 1976 |
| Yum Dong Kyun (KOR) | 24 Nov 1976 |
| Wilfredo Gómez (PUR) | 21 May 1977 |
| gave up title in 1983 | |
| Jaime Garza (USA) | 15 Jun 1983 |
| Juan Meza (MEX) | 3 Nov 1984 |
| Guadalupe Pintor (MEX) | 18 Aug 1985 |
| Samart Payakaroon (THA) | 18 Jan 1986 |
| Jeff Fenech (AUS) | 8 May 1987 |
| gave up title in 1990 | |
| Daniel Zaragoza (MEX) | 29 Feb 1988 |
| Paul Banke (USA) | 23 Apr 1990 |
| Pedro Decima (ARG) | 5 Nov 1990 |

## World Super Bantamweight Champions (continued)

| CHAMPION (NATIONALITY) | DATE OF TITLE | CHAMPION (NATIONALITY) | DATE OF TITLE |
|---|---|---|---|
| **WBC (continued)** | | **IBF (continued)** | |
| Kiyoshi Hatanaka (JPN) | 3 Feb 1991 | Kim Ji-won (KOR) | 3 Jan 1985 |
| Daniel Zaragoza (MEX) | 14 Jun 1991 | vacant | |
| Thierry Jacob (FRA) | 20 Mar 1992 | Lee Seung-hoon (KOR) | 18 Jan 1987 |
| Tracy Patterson (USA) | 23 Jun 1992 | gave up title in 1988 | |
| Hector Acero-Sánchez (USA) | 26 Aug 1994 | José Sanabria (VEN) | 21 May 1988 |
| Daniel Zaragoza (MEX) | 6 Nov 1995 | Fabrice Benichou (FRA) | 10 Mar 1989 |
| Erik Morales (MEX) | 6 Sep 1997 | Welcome Ncita (RSA) | 10 Mar 1990 |
| gave up title in 2000 | | Kennedy McKinney (USA) | 2 Dec 1992 |
| Willie Jorrin (USA) | 9 Sep 2000 | Vuyani Bungu (RSA) | 20 Aug 1994 |
| Oscar Larios (MEX) | 1 Nov 2002 | gave up title in 1999 | |
| | | Lehlohonolo Ledwaba (RSA) | 29 May 1999 |
| **IBF** | | Manny Pacquiao (PHI) | 23 Jun 2001 |
| Bobby Berna (PHI) | 4 Dec 1983 | | |
| Suh Seung-il (KOR) | 15 Apr 1984 | | |

## World Bantamweight Champions

*Top weight 118 pounds; until 1920 weight limits varied between 105 and 116 pounds.*

| CHAMPION (NATIONALITY) | DATE OF TITLE | CHAMPION (NATIONALITY) | DATE OF TITLE |
|---|---|---|---|
| **Undisputed champions** | | **Undisputed champions (continued)** | |
| Terry McGovern (USA) | 12 Sep 1899 | Enrique Pinder (PAN) | 30 Jul 1972 |
| gave up title in 1900 | | stripped of WBC title in 1972 | |
| Harry Harris (USA) | 18 Mar 1901 | | |
| gave up title in 1901 | | **WBA** | |
| Harry Forbes (USA) | 2 Apr 1901 | Romeo Anaya (MEX) | 20 Jan 1973 |
| Frankie Neil (USA) | 13 Aug 1903 | Arnold Taylor (RSA) | 3 Nov 1973 |
| Joe Bowker (GBR) | 17 Oct 1904 | Hong Soo Hwan (KOR) | 3 Jul 1974 |
| gave up title in 1905; | | Alfonso Zamora (MEX) | 14 Mar 1975 |
| title in dispute | | Jorge Luján (PAN) | 19 Nov 1977 |
| Kid Williams (USA) | 9 Jun 1914 | Julian Solís (PUR) | 29 Aug 1980 |
| Pete Herman (USA) | 9 Jan 1917 | Jeff Chandler (USA) | 14 Nov 1980 |
| Joe Lynch (USA) | 22 Dec 1920 | Richie Sandoval (USA) | 7 Apr 1984 |
| Pete Herman (USA) | 25 Jul 1921 | Gaby Canizales (USA) | 10 Mar 1986 |
| Johnny Buff (USA) | 23 Sep 1921 | Bernardo Pinango (VEN) | 4 Jun 1986 |
| Joe Lynch (USA) | 10 Jul 1922 | gave up title in 1987 | |
| Abe Goldstein (USA) | 21 Mar 1924 | Takuyama Muguruma (JPN) | 29 Mar 1987 |
| Eddie Martin (USA) | 19 Dec 1924 | Park Chang Young (KOR) | 24 May 1987 |
| Charlie Rosenberg (USA) | 20 Mar 1925 | Wilfredo Vásquez (PUR) | 4 Oct 1987 |
| stripped of title in 1927; | | Khaokor Galaxy (THA) | 9 May 1988 |
| title in dispute | | Moon Sung Kil (KOR) | 14 Aug 1988 |
| Panama Al Brown (PAN) | 18 Jun 1929 | Khaokor Galaxy (THA) | 9 Jul 1989 |
| stripped of NBA (later WBA) title | | Luisito Espinosa (PHI) | 18 Oct 1989 |
| in 1934; title in dispute | | Israel Contreras (VEN) | 19 Oct 1991 |
| Sixto Escobar (PUR) | 31 Aug 1936 | Eddie Cook (USA) | 15 Mar 1992 |
| Harry Jeffra (USA) | 23 Sep 1937 | Eliecer Julio (COL) | 10 Oct 1992 |
| Sixto Escobar (PUR) | 20 Feb 1938 | Junior Jones (USA) | 23 Oct 1993 |
| gave up title in 1939 | | John Michael Johnson (USA) | 22 Apr 1994 |
| Lou Salica (USA) | 13 Jan 1941 | Daorung Chuvatana Siriwat (THA) | 16 Jul 1994 |
| Manuel Ortiz (USA) | 7 Aug 1942 | Veeraphol Sahaprom (THA) | 17 Sep 1995 |
| Harold Dade (USA) | 6 Jan 1947 | Nana Konadu (GHA) | 28 Jan 1996 |
| Manuel Ortiz (USA) | 11 Mar 1947 | Daorung Chuvatana Siriwat (THA) | 26 Oct 1996 |
| Vic Toweel (RSA) | 31 May 1950 | Nana Konadu (GHA) | 21 Jun 1997 |
| Jimmy Carruthers (AUS) | 15 Nov 1952 | Johnny Tapia (USA) | 6 Dec 1998 |
| retired in 1954; title in dispute | | Paulie Ayala (USA) | 26 Jun 1999 |
| Alphonse Halimi (ALG) | 6 Nov 1957 | stripped of title in 2001 | |
| José Becerra (MEX) | 8 Jul 1959 | Eidy Moya (VEN) | 14 Oct 2001 |
| retired in 1961 | | Johnny Bredahl (DEN) | 19 Apr 2002 |
| Eder Jofre (BRA) | 18 Jan 1962 | | |
| Masahiko Harada (JPN) | 17 May 1965 | **WBC** | |
| Lionel Rose (AUS) | 26 Feb 1968 | Rafael Herrera (MEX) | 15 Apr 1973 |
| Rubén Olivares (MEX) | 22 Aug 1969 | Rodolfo Martínez (MEX) | 7 Dec 1974 |
| Chucho Castillo (MEX) | 16 Oct 1970 | Carlos Zárate (MEX) | 8 May 1976 |
| Rubén Olivares (MEX) | 3 Apr 1971 | Guadalupe Pintor (MEX) | 3 Jun 1979 |
| Rafael Herrera (MEX) | 19 Mar 1972 | stripped of title in 1983 | |

## World Bantamweight Champions (continued)

| CHAMPION (NATIONALITY) | DATE OF TITLE | CHAMPION (NATIONALITY) | DATE OF TITLE |
|---|---|---|---|
| **WBC (continued)** | | **IBF** | |
| Alberto Davila (USA) | 1 Sep 1983 | Satoshi Shingaki (JPN) | 15 Apr 1984 |
| stripped of title in 1985 | | Jeff Fenech (AUS) | 26 Apr 1985 |
| Daniel Zaragoza (MEX) | 4 May 1985 | vacant | |
| Miguel Lora (COL) | 9 Aug 1985 | Kelvin Seabrooks (USA) | 16 May 1987 |
| Raul Pérez (MEX) | 29 Oct 1988 | Orlando Canizales (USA) | 9 Jul 1988 |
| Greg Richardson (USA) | 25 Feb 1991 | gave up title in 1994 | |
| Joichiro Tatsuyoshi (JPN) | 19 Sep 1991 | Harold Mestre (COL) | 21 Jan 1995 |
| vacant | | Mbulelo Botile (RSA) | 29 Apr 1995 |
| Victor Rabañales (MEX) | 30 Mar 1992 | Tim Austin (USA) | 19 Jul 1997 |
| Byun Jong-il (KOR) | 28 Mar 1993 | Rafael Marquez (MEX) | 15 Feb 2003 |
| Yasuei Yakushiji (JPN) | 22 Dec 1993 | | |
| Wayne McCullough (NIR) | 30 Jul 1995 | | |
| Sirimongkol Singmanassuk (THA) | 10 Aug 1996 | | |
| Joichiro Tatsuyoshi (JPN) | 22 Nov 1997 | | |
| Veeraphol Sahaprom (THA) | 29 Dec 1998 | | |

## World Super Flyweight Champions
*Top weight 115 pounds. Also called junior bantamweight.*

| CHAMPION (NATIONALITY) | DATE OF TITLE | CHAMPION (NATIONALITY) | DATE OF TITLE |
|---|---|---|---|
| **WBA** | | **WBC (continued)** | |
| Gustavo Ballas (ARG) | 12 Sep 1981 | Moon Sung Kil (KOR) | 20 Jan 1990 |
| Rafael Pedroza (PAN) | 5 Dec 1981 | José Luis Bueno (MEX) | 13 Nov 1993 |
| Watanabe Jiro (JPN) | 8 Apr 1982 | Hiroshi Kawashima (JPN) | 4 May 1994 |
| stripped of title in 1984 | | Gerry Peñalosa (PHI) | 20 Feb 1997 |
| Khaosai Galaxy (THA) | 21 Nov 1984 | Cho In Joo (KOR) | 29 Aug 1998 |
| gave up title in 1991 | | Masanori Tokuyama (JPN) | 27 Aug 2000 |
| Katsuya Onizuka (JPN) | 10 Apr 1992 | | |
| Lee Hyung Chul (KOR) | 18 Sep 1994 | **IBF** | |
| Alima Goitia (VEN) | 22 Jul 1995 | Chun Joo-do (KOR) | 10 Dec 1983 |
| Yokthai Sithoar (THA) | 24 Aug 1996 | Ellyas Pical (INA) | 3 May 1985 |
| Satoshi Iida (JPN) | 23 Dec 1997 | César Polanco (DOM) | 15 Feb 1986 |
| Jesús Rojas (VEN) | 23 Dec 1998 | Ellyas Pical (INA) | 6 Jul 1986 |
| Hideki Todaka (JPN) | 31 Jul 1999 | vacant | |
| Leo Gámez (VEN) | 9 Oct 2000 | Chang Tae-il (KOR) | 17 May 1987 |
| Shoji Kobayashi (JPN) | 11 Mar 2001 | Ellyas Pical (INA) | 17 Oct 1987 |
| Alexander Muñoz (VEN) | 9 Mar 2002 | Juan Polo Pérez (COL) | 14 Oct 1989 |
| | | Robert Quiroga (USA) | 21 Apr 1990 |
| **WBC** | | Julio Borboa (MEX) | 16 Jan 1993 |
| Rafael Oroño (VEN) | 1 Feb 1980 | Harold Grey (COL) | 29 Aug 1994 |
| Kim Chul Ho (KOR) | 24 Jan 1981 | Carlos Salazar (ARG) | 7 Oct 1995 |
| Rafael Oroño (VEN) | 28 Nov 1982 | Harold Grey (COL) | 27 Apr 1996 |
| Payao Poontarat (THA) | 27 Nov 1983 | Danny Romero (USA) | 24 Aug 1996 |
| Watanabe Jiro (JPN) | 5 Jul 1984 | Johnny Tapia (USA) | 18 Jul 1997 |
| Gilberto Román (MEX) | 30 Mar 1986 | gave up title in 1998 | |
| Santos Laciar (ARG) | 16 May 1987 | Mark Johnson (USA) | 24 Apr 1999 |
| Jesús Rojas (COL) | 9 Aug 1987 | stripped of title in 2000 | |
| Gilberto Román (MEX) | 8 Apr 1988 | Félix Machado (VEN) | 22 Jul 2000 |
| Nana Konadu (GHA) | 7 Nov 1989 | Luis Perez (NCA) | 4 Jan 2003 |

## World Flyweight Champions
*Top weight 112 pounds.*

| CHAMPION (NATIONALITY) | DATE OF TITLE | CHAMPION (NATIONALITY) | DATE OF TITLE |
|---|---|---|---|
| **Undisputed champions** | | **Undisputed champions (continued)** | |
| Jimmy Wilde (GBR) | 18 Dec 1916 | Rinty Monaghan (IRE) | 23 Mar 1948 |
| Pancho Villa (Francisco Guilledo) (PHI) | 18 Jun 1923 | retired in 1950 | |
| died in 1925 | | Terry Allen (GBR) | 25 Apr 1950 |
| Fidel La Barba (USA) | 21 Jan 1927 | Dado Marino (Hawaii) | 1 Aug 1950 |
| retired in 1927; title in dispute | | Yoshio Shirai (JPN) | 19 May 1952 |
| Benny Lynch (GBR) | 19 Jan 1937 | Pascual Pérez (ARG) | 26 Nov 1954 |
| gave up title in 1938 | | Pone Kingpetch (THA) | 16 Apr 1960 |
| Peter Kane (GBR) | 22 Sep 1938 | Masahiko Harada (JPN) | 10 Oct 1962 |
| Jackie Paterson (GBR) | 19 Jun 1943 | Pone Kingpetch (THA) | 12 Jan 1963 |
| title in dispute from 1947 | | Hiroyuki Ebihara (JPN) | 18 Sep 1963 |

## World Flyweight Champions (continued)

| CHAMPION (NATIONALITY) | DATE OF TITLE | CHAMPION (NATIONALITY) | DATE OF TITLE |
|---|---|---|---|
| **Undisputed champions (continued)** | | **WBC (continued)** | |
| Pone Kingpetch (THA) | 23 Jan 1964 | Venice Borkorsor (THA) | 29 Sep 1972 |
| Salvatore Burruni (ITA) | 23 Apr 1965 | gave up title in 1973 | |
| title in dispute from 1965 | | Betulio González (VEN) | 4 Aug 1973 |
| | | Shoji Oguma (JPN) | 1 Oct 1974 |
| **WBA** | | Miguel Canto (MEX) | 8 Jan 1975 |
| Horacio Accavallo (ARG) | 1 Mar 1966 | Park Chan Hee (KOR) | 18 Mar 1979 |
| retired in 1968 | | Shoji Oguma (JPN) | 18 May 1980 |
| Hiroyuki Ebihara (JPN) | 30 Mar 1969 | Antonio Avelar (MEX) | 12 May 1981 |
| Bernabe Villacampo (PHI) | 19 Oct 1969 | Prudencio Cardona (COL) | 20 Mar 1982 |
| Berkrerk Chartvanchai (THA) | 14 Apr 1970 | Freddie Castillo (MEX) | 24 Jul 1982 |
| Ohba Masao (JPN) | 22 Oct 1970 | Eleoncio Mercedes (DOM) | 6 Nov 1982 |
| died in 1973 | | Charlie Magri (GBR) | 15 Mar 1983 |
| Chartchai Chionoi (THA) | 17 May 1973 | Frank Cedeno (PHI) | 27 Sep 1983 |
| Susumu Hanagata (JPN) | 18 Oct 1974 | Koji Kobayashi (JPN) | 18 Jan 1984 |
| Erbito Salavarria (PHI) | 1 Apr 1975 | Gabriel Bernal (MEX) | 9 Apr 1984 |
| Alfonso López (PAN) | 27 Feb 1976 | Sot Chitalada (THA) | 8 Oct 1984 |
| Gustavo Espadas (MEX) | 2 Oct 1976 | Kim Yong Kang (KOR) | 24 Jul 1988 |
| Betulio González (VEN) | 12 Aug 1978 | Sot Chitalada (THA) | 3 Jun 1989 |
| Luis Ibarra (PAN) | 17 Nov 1979 | Muangchai Kittikasem (THA) | 15 Feb 1991 |
| Kim Tae Shik (KOR) | 16 Feb 1980 | Yury Arbachakov (RUS) | 23 Jun 1992 |
| Peter Mathebula (RSA) | 13 Dec 1980 | Chatchai Dutchboygym (Sasakul) (THA) | 9 May 1997 |
| Santos Laciar (ARG) | 28 Mar 1981 | Manny Pacquiao (PHI) | 4 Dec 1998 |
| Luis Ibarra (PAN) | 6 Jun 1981 | stripped of title in 1999 | |
| Juan Herrera (MEX) | 26 Sep 1981 | Medgeon Singsurat (THA) | 17 Sep 1999 |
| Santos Laciar (ARG) | 1 May 1982 | Malcolm Tunacao (PHI) | 19 May 2000 |
| gave up title in 1985 | | Pongsaklek Wongjongkam (THA) | 2 Mar 2001 |
| Hilario Zapata (PAN) | 5 Oct 1985 | | |
| Fidel Bassa (COL) | 13 Feb 1987 | **IBF** | |
| Jesús Rojas (VEN) | 30 Sep 1989 | Kwon Soon Chun (KOR) | 24 Dec 1983 |
| Lee Yul Woo (KOR) | 10 Mar 1990 | Chung Chong Kwan (KOR) | 20 Dec 1985 |
| Leopard Tamakuma (JPN) | 29 Jul 1990 | Chung Bi Won (KOR) | 27 Apr 1986 |
| Elvis Álvarez (COL) | 14 Mar 1991 | Shin Hi Sup (KOR) | 2 Aug 1986 |
| Kim Yong Kang (KOR) | 1 Jun 1991 | Dodie Penalosa (PHI) | 22 Feb 1987 |
| Aquiles Guzmán (VEN) | 26 Sep 1992 | Choi Chang Ho (KOR) | 5 Sep 1987 |
| David Griman (VEN) | 15 Dec 1992 | Rolando Bohol (PHI) | 16 Jan 1988 |
| San Sow Ploenchit (THA) | 13 Feb 1994 | Duke McKenzie (GBR) | 5 Oct 1988 |
| José Bonilla (VEN) | 14 Nov 1996 | Dave McAuley (GBR) | 7 Jun 1989 |
| Hugo Soto (ARG) | 29 May 1998 | Rodolfo Blanco (COL) | 11 Jun 1992 |
| Leo Gámez (VEN) | 13 Mar 1999 | Phichit Sithbangprachan (THA) | 29 Nov 1992 |
| Sornpichai Kratchingdaeng (THA) | 3 Sep 1999 | vacant | |
| Eric Morel (USA) | 5 Aug 2000 | Francisco Tejedor (COL) | 18 Feb 1995 |
| | | Danny Romero (USA) | 22 Apr 1995 |
| **WBC** | | gave up title in 1996 | |
| Walter McGowan (GBR) | 14 Jun 1966 | Mark Johnson (USA) | 4 May 1996 |
| Chartchai Chionoi (THA) | 30 Dec 1966 | gave up title in 1999 | |
| Efren Torres (MEX) | 23 Feb 1969 | Irene Pacheco (COL) | 10 Apr 1999 |
| Chartchai Chionoi (THA) | 20 Mar 1970 | | |
| Erbito Salavarria (PHI) | 7 Dec 1970 | | |
| stripped of title in 1971 | | | |
| Betulio González (VEN) | 20 Nov 1971 | | |

## World Light Flyweight Champions

*Top weight 108 pounds. Also called junior flyweight.*

| CHAMPION (NATIONALITY) | DATE OF TITLE | CHAMPION (NATIONALITY) | DATE OF TITLE |
|---|---|---|---|
| **WBA** | | **WBA (continued)** | |
| Jaime Ríos (PAN) | 23 Aug 1975 | Joey Olivo (USA) | 29 Mar 1985 |
| Juan Guzmán (DOM) | 1 Jul 1976 | Yuh Myung Woo (KOR) | 8 Dec 1985 |
| Yoko Gushiken (JPN) | 10 Oct 1976 | Hiroki Ioka (JPN) | 17 Dec 1991 |
| Pedro Flores (MEX) | 8 Mar 1981 | Yuh Myung Woo (KOR) | 18 Nov 1992 |
| Kim Hwan Jin (KOR) | 19 Jul 1981 | gave up title in 1993 | |
| Katsuo Tokashiki (JPN) | 16 Dec 1981 | Leo Gámez (VEN) | 21 Oct 1993 |
| Lupe Madera (MEX) | 10 Jul 1983 | Choi Hi Yong (KOR) | 4 Feb 1995 |
| Francisco Quiroz (DOM) | 19 May 1984 | Carlos Murillo (PAN) | 13 Jan 1996 |

## World Light Flyweight Champions (continued)

| CHAMPION (NATIONALITY) | DATE OF TITLE | CHAMPION (NATIONALITY) | DATE OF TITLE |
|---|---|---|---|
| **WBA (continued)** | | **WBC (continued)** | |
| Keiji Yamaguchi (JPN) | 21 May 1996 | Chiquita González (MEX) | 19 Feb 1994 |
| Pichitnoi Siriwat (THA) | 3 Dec 1996 | Saman Sorjaturong (THA) | 15 Jul 1995 |
| vacant | | Choi Yo Sam (KOR) | 17 Oct 1999 |
| Bebis Mendoza (COL) | 12 Aug 2000 | Jorge Arce (MEX) | 6 Jul 2002 |
| Rosendo Álvarez (NCA) | 3 Mar 2001 | | |
| | | **IBF** | |
| **WBC** | | Dodie Penalosa (PHI) | 10 Dec 1983 |
| Franco Udella (ITA) | 4 Apr 1975 | stripped of title in 1986 | |
| stripped of title in 1975 | | Choi Chong Hwon (KOR) | 7 Dec 1986 |
| Luis Alberto Estaba (VEN) | 13 Sep 1975 | Tacy Macalos (PHI) | 6 Nov 1988 |
| Freddie Castillo (MEX) | 19 Feb 1978 | Muangchai Kittikasem (THA) | 2 May 1989 |
| Netrnoi Sor Vorasingh (THA) | 6 May 1978 | Michael Carbajal (USA) | 29 Jul 1990 |
| Kim Sung Jun (KOR) | 30 Sep 1978 | Chiquita González (MEX) | 19 Feb 1994 |
| Shigeo Nakajima (JPN) | 3 Jan 1980 | Saman Sorjaturong (THA) | 15 Jul 1995 |
| Hilario Zapata (PAN) | 24 Mar 1980 | vacant | |
| Amado Ursua (MEX) | 6 Feb 1982 | Michael Carbajal (USA) | 16 Mar 1996 |
| Tadashi Tomori (JPN) | 13 Apr 1982 | Mauricio Pastrana (COL) | 18 Jan 1997 |
| Hilario Zapata (PAN) | 20 Jul 1982 | stripped of title in 1997 | |
| Chang Jung Koo (KOR) | 26 Mar 1983 | Mauricio Pastrana (COL) | 13 Dec 1997 |
| gave up title in 1988 | | stripped of title in 1998 | |
| German Torres (MEX) | 11 Dec 1988 | Will Grigsby (USA) | 18 Dec 1998 |
| Lee Yul Woo (KOR) | 19 Mar 1989 | Ricardo López (MEX) | 2 Oct 1999 |
| Humberto González (MEX) | 25 Jun 1989 | retired in 2002 | |
| Rolando Pascua (PHI) | 19 Dec 1990 | Victor Burgos (MEX) | 15 Feb 2003 |
| Melchor Cob Castro (MEX) | 25 Mar 1991 | | |
| Humberto González (MEX) | 4 Jun 1991 | | |
| Michael Carbajal (USA) | 13 Mar 1993 | | |

## World Minimumweight Champions

*Top weight 105 pounds. Also called strawweight. Division first recognized by WBA in 1988 and by WBC and IBF in 1987.*

| CHAMPION (NATIONALITY) | DATE OF TITLE | CHAMPION (NATIONALITY) | DATE OF TITLE |
|---|---|---|---|
| **WBA** | | **WBC (continued)** | |
| Leo Gámez (VEN) | 10 Jan 1988 | Ricardo López (MEX) | 25 Oct 1990 |
| vacant | | gave up title in 1999 | |
| Kim Bong Jun (KOR) | 16 Apr 1989 | Wande Chareon (THA) | 4 May 1999 |
| Choi Hi Yong (KOR) | 2 Feb 1991 | José Antonio Aguirre (MEX) | 11 Feb 2000 |
| Hideyuki Ohashi (JPN) | 14 Oct 1992 | | |
| Chana Porpaoin (THA) | 10 Feb 1993 | **IBF** | |
| Rosendo Álvarez (NCA) | 2 Dec 1995 | Lee Kyung Yun (KOR) | 14 Jun 1987 |
| Ricardo López (MEX) | 13 Nov 1998 | vacant | |
| gave up title in 1999 | | Samuth Sithnaruepol (THA) | 24 Mar 1988 |
| Noel Arambulet (VEN) | 9 Oct 1999 | Nico Thomas (INA) | 17 Jun 1989 |
| stripped of title in 2000 | | Eric Chávez (PHI) | 21 Sep 1989 |
| Joma Gamboa (PHI) | 20 Aug 2000 | Falan Lookmingkwan (THA) | 21 Feb 1990 |
| Hoshino Keitaro (JPN) | 6 Dec 2000 | Manny Melchor (PHI) | 6 Sep 1992 |
| Chana Porpaoin (THA) | 16 Apr 2001 | Ratanapol Vorapin (THA) | 10 Dec 1992 |
| Yutaka Niida (JPN) | 25 Aug 2001 | stripped of title in 1996 | |
| gave up title in 2001 | | Ratanapol Vorapin (THA) | 16 May 1996 |
| Hoshino Keitaro (JPN) | 29 Jan 2002 | Zolani Petelo (RSA) | 27 Dec 1997 |
| Noel Arambulet (VEN) | 29 Jul 2002 | gave up title in 2000 | |
| | | Roberto Leyva (MEX) | 29 Apr 2001 |
| **WBC** | | Miguel Barrera (COL) | 9 Aug 2002 |
| Ioka Hiroki (JPN) | 18 Oct 1987 | Edgar Cardenas (MEX) | 31 May 2003 |
| Napa Kiatwanchai (THA) | 13 Nov 1988 | | |
| Choi Jum Hwan (KOR) | 12 Nov 1989 | | |
| Hideyuki Ohashi (JPN) | 7 Feb 1990 | | |

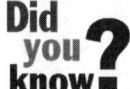

**Did you know?** Pittsburgh PA is the only city in the US where all uniforms of professional sports teams are the same colors: black and gold.

# Chess

**W**illiam Steinitz is generally recognized as the first official chess world champion, although dates for his 19th-century reign vary. With a few notable exceptions, each successive champion defeated his predecessor in match play. The first exception followed the death of the incumbent **Alexander Alekhine** in 1946. The **Fédération Internationale des Échecs** (FIDE; founded 1924) stepped into the vacancy and arranged a tournament among leading contenders to determine a new champion in 1948. FIDE continued to oversee regular tournaments and matches to determine challengers—although another exception occurred in 1975, when **Robert (Bobby) Fischer** refused to defend his crown and retired. In 1993 **Garry Kasparov** pulled out of FIDE to defend his title under rival organizations (Professional Chess Association and later Braingames). Without a universally recognized champion, FIDE struggled to obtain funding for its multiyear system of tournaments and matches leading to a title match. So, in 1999 FIDE began to hold annual **"knockout" tournaments**, with very fast game play, to determine their champion. Few chess players recognize the FIDE champion as legitimate, however.

FIDE began organizing the **women's chess championship** in 1953. Controversy also has afflicted this title, with **Zsuzsa Polgar** refusing to accept FIDE's terms for her title defense in 1999. In 2000, FIDE adopted a knockout tournament format for the women's championship, similar to the open tournament.

The **Olympiads** are held biennially. Competition is open to both men and women, but since 1957 there has been a separate Olympiad that is restricted to women.

**FIDE Web site:** <www.fide.com>

## World Chess Champions—Men
*Generally recognized (see head note)*

| REIGN | NAME | NATIONALITY | REIGN | NAME | NATIONALITY |
|---|---|---|---|---|---|
| 1866–94 | Wilhelm Steinitz | Austrian American | 1961–63 | Mikhail Botvinnik | Soviet Russian |
| 1894–1921 | Emanuel Lasker | German | 1963–69 | Tigran Petrosyan | Soviet Georgian-born Armenian |
| 1921–27 | José Raúl Capablanca | Cuban | 1969–72 | Boris Spassky | Soviet Russian |
| 1927–35 | Alexander Alekhine | Russian-born French | 1972–75 | Robert (Bobby) Fischer | American |
| 1935–37 | Max Euwe | Dutch | 1975–85 | Anatoly Karpov | Soviet Russian |
| 1937–46 | Alexander Alekhine | Russian-born French | 1985–2000 | Garry Kasparov | Azerbaijani-born Russian |
| 1948–57 | Mikhail Botvinnik | Soviet Russian | 2000– | Vladimir Kramnik | Russian |
| 1957–58 | Vasily Smyslov | Soviet Russian | | | |
| 1958–60 | Mikhail Botvinnik | Soviet Russian | | | |
| 1960–61 | Mikhail Tal | Soviet Russian | | | |

## World Chess Champions—Women

| REIGN | NAME | NATIONALITY | REIGN | NAME | NATIONALITY |
|---|---|---|---|---|---|
| 1927–44 | Vera Menchik* | Soviet Russian | 1991–96 | Xie Jun | Chinese |
| 1949–53 | Lyudmila Rudenko | Soviet Russian | 1996–99 | Zsuzsa Polgar† | Hungarian |
| 1953–56 | Yelizaveta Bykova | Soviet Russian | 1999–2001 | Xie Jun | Chinese |
| 1956–58 | Olga Rubtsova | Soviet Russian | 2001– | Zhu Chen | Chinese |
| 1958–62 | Yelizaveta Bykova | Soviet Russian | | | |
| 1962–78 | Nona Gaprindashvili | Soviet Georgian | | | |
| 1978–91 | Maya Chiburdanidze | Soviet Georgian | | | |

*Killed in an air raid on London in 1944; title left vacant.   †Rejected conditions for title defense; title regained by Xie.

## Chess Olympiads
*The table lists the competitions for the past 20 years only.*
*The 2004 Olympiads will take place in Menorca, Spain.*

| | Open | | Women | | | Open | | Women | |
|---|---|---|---|---|---|---|---|---|---|
| YEAR | WINNER | RUNNER-UP | WINNER | RUNNER-UP | YEAR | WINNER | RUNNER-UP | WINNER | RUNNER-UP |
| 1984 | USSR | Great Britain | USSR | Bulgaria | 1994 | Russia | Bosnia | Georgia | Hungary |
| 1986 | USSR | Great Britain | USSR | Hungary | 1996 | Russia | Ukraine | Georgia | China |
| 1988 | USSR | Great Britain | Hungary | USSR | 1998 | Russia | United States | China | Russia |
| 1990 | USSR | United States | Hungary | USSR | 2000 | Russia | Germany | China | Georgia |
| 1992 | Russia | Uzbekistan | Georgia | Ukraine | 2002 | Russia | Hungary | China | Russia |

Chess first appeared in India about the 6th century AD and by the 10th century had spread from Asia to the Middle East and Europe. Since at least the 15th century, chess has been known as the "royal game" because of its popularity among the nobility.

# Contract Bridge

The world team contract bridge championships were instituted in 1950 with what was then an annual and zonal competition called the **Bermuda Bowl.** When the **World Team Olympiad,** held quadrennially, was instituted in 1960, it represented the world team championship. The only exception to this rule occurred in 1976, when both events were held. The Bermuda Bowl is organized by the **World Bridge Federation** (WBF; founded 1958), and since 1977 it has been held in odd-numbered years (the 1999 competition took place in January 2000). Among women's teams the major competition is the World Team Olympiad, although another team competition, the **Venice Trophy,** was inaugurated in 1974. In pairs competition the quadrennial **World Bridge Championships** (inaugurated in 1962, it features open and women's sections) is the premiere international event.

**WBF Web site:** <www.worldbridge.org>

## Bermuda Bowl

| YEAR | WINNER | RUNNER-UP | YEAR | WINNER | RUNNER-UP |
|------|--------|-----------|------|--------|-----------|
| 1950 | United States | United Kingdom | 1972 | *not held\** | |
| 1951 | United States | Italy | 1973 | Italy | United States |
| 1952 | *postponed* | | 1974 | Italy | North America |
| 1953 | United States | Sweden | 1975 | Italy | North America |
| 1954 | United States | France | 1976 | North America | Italy |
| 1955 | United Kingdom | United States | 1977 | North American | North American |
| 1956 | France | United States | | Defenders | Challengers |
| 1957 | Italy | United States | 1979 | North America | Italy |
| 1958 | Italy | United States | 1981 | United States | Pakistan |
| 1959 | Italy | United States | 1983 | United States | Italy |
| 1960 | *not held\** | | 1985 | United States | Austria |
| 1961 | Italy | North America | 1987 | United States | United Kingdom |
| 1962 | Italy | North America | 1989 | Brazil | United States |
| 1963 | Italy | North America | 1991 | Iceland | Poland |
| 1964 | *not held\** | | 1993 | The Netherlands | Norway |
| 1965 | Italy | United States | 1995 | United States | Canada |
| 1966 | Italy | North America | 1997 | France | United States |
| 1967 | Italy | North America | 2000 | United States | Brazil |
| 1968 | *not held\** | | 2001 | United States II | Norway |
| 1969 | Italy | Taiwan | 2003 | *tentatively scheduled for October* | |
| 1970 | North America | Taiwan | | | |
| 1971 | United States | France | | | |

*\*not held because of World Team Olympiad*

## World Contract Bridge Team Olympiad

| | open | | women's | |
|------|--------|-----------|--------|-----------|
| YEAR | WINNER | RUNNER-UP | WINNER | RUNNER-UP |
| 1960 | France | United Kingdom | United Arab Republic | France |
| 1964 | Italy | United States | Great Britain | United States |
| 1968 | Italy | United States | Sweden | South Africa |
| 1972 | Italy | United States | Italy | South Africa |
| 1976 | Brazil | Italy | Italy | United Kingdom |
| 1980 | France | United States | United States | Italy |
| 1984 | Poland | France | United States | United Kingdom |
| 1988 | United States | Austria | Denmark | United Kingdom |
| 1992 | France | United States | Austria | United Kingdom |
| 1996 | France | Indonesia | United States | China |
| 2000 | Italy | Poland | United States | Canada |
| 2004 | *will possibly be held in Istanbul, Turkey* | | | |

Playing cards are thought to have originated in China in about the 10th century. An Indian origin has been suggested by the resemblance of symbols on some early European decks to the ring, sword, cup, and baton classically depicted in the four hands of Hindu statues. Yet another theory is that cards derived from ancient divinatory procedures used by primitive peoples.

## World Contract Bridge Pair Championships

| YEAR | OPEN WINNERS | WOMEN'S WINNERS | MIXED WINNERS |
|---|---|---|---|
| 1962 | Pierre Jais, Roger Trézel (FRA) | Rixi Markus, Fritzi Gordon (GBR) | * |
| 1966 | Bob Slavenburg, Hans Kreyns (NED) | Joan Durran, Jane Juan (GBR) | Mary Jane Ferell, Ivan Erdos (USA) |
| 1970 | Fritz Babsch, Peter Manhardt (AUT) | Mary Jane Farell, Marilyn Johnson (USA) | Barbara Brier, Waldemar von Zedtwitz (USA) |
| 1974 | Robert Hamman, Bobby Wolff (USA) | Fritzi Gordon, Rixi Markus (GBR) | Loula Gordon, Tony Trad (SUI) |
| 1978 | Marcelo Branco, Gabino Cintra (BRA) | Kathie Wei, Judi Radin (USA) | Barry Crane, Kerri Shuman (USA) |
| 1982 | Chip Martel, Lew Stansby (USA) | Carol Saders, Betty Ann Kennedy (USA) | Dianna Gordon, George Mittelman (CAN) |
| 1986 | Jeff Mecksroth, Eric Rodwell (USA) | Jacqui Mitchell, Amalya Kearse (USA) | Pam Wittes, John Wittes (USA) |
| 1990 | Marcelo Branco, Gabriel Chagas (BRA) | Kerri Shuman, Karen McCallum (USA) | Peter Wechsel, Juanita Chambers (USA) |
| 1994 | Martin Lesniewski, Marek Szymanowski (POL) | Carla Arnolds, Bep Vriend (NED) | Danuta Hocheker, Apolinare Kowalski (POL) |
| 1998 | Michal Kwiecien, Jacek Pszczola (POL) | Jill Meyers, Shawn Quinn (USA) | Enza Rossano, Antonio Vivaldi (ITA) |
| 2002 | Fulvio Fantoni, Claudio Nunes (ITA) | Karen McCallum, Debbie Rosenberg (USA) | Becky Rogers, Jeff Meckstroth (USA) |

*A mixed team competition, won by a team from the United Kingdom, was held in 1962.

# Cricket

Cricket is one of the **national sports** of England, and consequently it is played in nearly all the countries with which England has been associated. The world governing body is the **International Cricket Council** (ICC; founded as the Imperial Cricket Conference in 1909). The most important international cricket matches are the **Test matches**, which have been played since 1877. The Test-playing countries are England, Australia, South Africa (banned from international competition between about 1970 and 1992), West Indies (representing Barbados, Guyana, Jamaica, Trinidad and Tobago, and the Leeward and Windward islands), New Zealand, India, Pakistan, Sri Lanka, Zimbabwe (since 1992), and Bangladesh (since 2001).

The Test table is designed to be read from left to right across the columns. This will indicate, for example, that in Test match play against England, South Africa has won 23 games, has had 47 drawn matches, and has lost 50 games.

The **World Cup** is a quadrennial one-day, limited-overs competition. It was first held in 1975.

**Related Web sites:** CricInfo: <www.cricket.org>; John Wisden & Co Ltd: <www.wisden.com>

## All-Time First-Class Test Cricket Standings (as of 30 Sep 2002)

| | England | | | Australia | | | South Africa | | | West Indies | | | New Zealand | | |
|---|---|---|---|---|---|---|---|---|---|---|---|---|---|---|---|
| | WINS | DRAWS | LOSSES | W | D | L | W | D | L | W | D | L | W | D | L |
| England v. | — | — | — | 94 | 86 | 121 | 50 | 47 | 23 | 31 | 43* | 52 | 38 | 40 | 7 |
| Australia v. | 121 | 86 | 94 | — | — | — | 39 | 17 | 15 | 42 | 22† | 31 | 18 | 15 | 7 |
| South Africa v. | 23 | 47 | 50 | 15 | 17 | 39 | — | — | — | 7 | 2 | 2 | 15 | 9 | 3 |
| West Indies v. | 52 | 43* | 31 | 31 | 22† | 42 | 2 | 2 | 7 | — | — | — | 10 | 15 | 7 |
| New Zealand v. | 7 | 40 | 38 | 7 | 15 | 18 | 3 | 9 | 15 | 7 | 15 | 10 | — | — | — |
| India v. | 16 | 42 | 33 | 13 | 18† | 29 | 2 | 5 | 7 | 8 | 37 | 30 | 14 | 20* | 7 |
| Pakistan v. | 10 | 34 | 16 | 11 | 17 | 18 | 1 | 1 | 2 | 12 | 14 | 13 | 20 | 17 | 6 |
| Sri Lanka v. | 3 | 2 | 7 | 1 | 5 | 7 | 1 | 4 | 6 | 3 | 2 | 1 | 4 | 7 | 7 |
| Zimbabwe v. | 0 | 3 | 1 | 0 | 0 | 1 | 0 | 1 | 4 | 0 | 1 | 3 | 0 | 6 | 5 |
| Bangladesh v. | ‡ | ‡ | ‡ | ‡ | ‡ | ‡ | ‡ | ‡ | ‡ | ‡ | ‡ | ‡ | 0 | 0 | 2 |

## All-Time First-Class Test Cricket Standings (as of 30 Sep 2002) (continued)

| | India | | | Pakistan | | | Sri Lanka | | | Zimbabwe | | | Bangladesh | | |
|---|---|---|---|---|---|---|---|---|---|---|---|---|---|---|---|
| | WINS | DRAWS | LOSSES | W | D | L | W | D | L | W | D | L | W | D | L |
| England v. | 33 | 42 | 16 | 16 | 34 | 10 | 7 | 2 | 3 | 1 | 3 | 0 | ‡ | ‡ | ‡ |
| Australia v. | 29 | 18† | 13 | 18 | 17 | 11 | 7 | 5 | 1 | 1 | 0 | 0 | ‡ | ‡ | ‡ |
| South Africa v. | 7 | 5 | 2 | 2 | 1 | 1 | 6 | 4 | 1 | 4 | 1 | 0 | ‡ | ‡ | ‡ |
| West Indies v. | 30 | 37 | 8 | 13 | 14 | 12 | 1 | 2 | 3 | 3 | 1 | 0 | ‡ | ‡ | ‡ |
| New Zealand v. | 7 | 20* | 14 | 6 | 17 | 20 | 7 | 7 | 4 | 5 | 6 | 0 | 2 | 0 | 0 |
| India v. | — | — | — | 5 | 33 | 9 | 8 | 12 | 3 | 5 | 2 | 2 | 1 | 0 | 0 |
| Pakistan v. | 9 | 33 | 5 | — | — | — | 13 | 9* | 6 | 6 | 5* | 2 | 3 | 0 | 0 |
| Sri Lanka v. | 3 | 12 | 8 | 6 | 9* | 13 | — | — | — | 8 | 5 | 0 | 3 | 0 | 0 |
| Zimbabwe v. | 2 | 2 | 5 | 2 | 5* | 6 | 0 | 5 | 8 | — | — | — | 3 | 1 | 0 |
| Bangladesh v. | 0 | 0 | 1 | 0 | 0 | 3 | 0 | 0 | 3 | 0 | 1 | 3 | — | — | — |

*Including one match abandoned.    †Including one tie.    ‡No matches.

## Cricket World Cup

| YEAR | RESULT | | | | | YEAR | RESULT | | | | |
|---|---|---|---|---|---|---|---|---|---|---|---|
| 1975 | West Indies | 291–8 | Australia | 274 | | 1992 | Pakistan | 249–6 | England | 227 |
| 1979 | West Indies | 286–9 | England | 194 | | 1996 | Sri Lanka | 245–3 | Australia | 241 |
| 1983 | India | 183 | West Indies | 140 | | 1999 | Australia | 133–2 | Pakistan | 132 |
| 1987 | Australia | 253–5 | England | 246–8 | | 2003 | Australia | 359–2 | India | 234 |

 **Did you know?** The earliest reference to an 11-a-side cricket match, played in Sussex for a stake of 50 guineas, dates from 1697.

# Curling

The game of curling, played on ice and somewhat akin to bowls or shuffleboard, varies little from country to country. The maximum permitted weight of the curling stones is 44 lb (19.9 kg). The top international **men's competition** was instituted in 1959 (called the Scotch Whisky Cup from 1959 to 1967; the Silver Broom from 1968 to 1985; and the World Curling Championship since 1986). Although curling has been played among women of many countries since at least the mid-20th century, the first **women's world curling championship** was not held until 1979.

**World Curling Federation Web site:**
<www.worldcurlingfederation.org>

## World Curling Championships—Men

| YEAR | WINNER | RUNNER-UP | YEAR | WINNER | RUNNER-UP |
|---|---|---|---|---|---|
| 1959 | Canada | Scotland | 1978 | United States | Canada |
| 1960 | Canada | Scotland | 1979 | Norway | Switzerland |
| 1961 | Canada | Scotland | 1980 | Canada | Norway |
| 1962 | Canada | Scotland | 1981 | Switzerland | United States |
| 1963 | Canada | Scotland | 1982 | Canada | Switzerland |
| 1964 | Canada | Scotland | 1983 | Canada | West Germany |
| 1965 | United States | Canada | 1984 | Norway | Switzerland |
| 1966 | Canada | Scotland | 1985 | Canada | Sweden |
| 1967 | Scotland | Canada | 1986 | Canada | Scotland |
| 1968 | Canada | Scotland | 1987 | Canada | West Germany |
| 1969 | Canada | Scotland | 1988 | Norway | Canada |
| 1970 | Canada | Scotland | 1989 | Canada | Switzerland |
| 1971 | Canada | Scotland | 1990 | Canada | Scotland |
| 1972 | Canada | United States | 1991 | Scotland | Canada |
| 1973 | Sweden | Canada | 1992 | Switzerland | Scotland |
| 1974 | United States | Canada | 1993 | Canada | Scotland |
| 1975 | Switzerland | Canada | 1994 | Canada | Sweden |
| 1976 | United States | Scotland | 1995 | Canada | Scotland |
| 1977 | Sweden | Canada | 1996 | Canada | Scotland |

## World Curling Championships—Men (continued)

| YEAR | WINNER | RUNNER-UP | YEAR | WINNER | RUNNER-UP |
|------|--------|-----------|------|--------|-----------|
| 1997 | Sweden | Germany | 2002 | Canada | Norway |
| 1998 | Canada | Sweden | 2003 | Canada | Switzerland |
| 1999 | Scotland | Canada | 2004 | *to be held Gävle, Sweden,* | |
| 2000 | Canada | Sweden | | *17–25 April* | |
| 2001 | Sweden | Switzerland | | | |

## World Curling Championships—Women

| YEAR | WINNER | RUNNER-UP | YEAR | WINNER | RUNNER-UP |
|------|--------|-----------|------|--------|-----------|
| 1979 | Switzerland | Sweden | 1995 | Sweden | Canada |
| 1980 | Canada | Sweden | 1996 | Canada | United States |
| 1981 | Sweden | Canada | 1997 | Canada | Norway |
| 1982 | Denmark | Sweden | 1998 | Sweden | Denmark |
| 1983 | Switzerland | Norway | 1999 | Sweden | United States |
| 1984 | Canada | Switzerland | 2000 | Canada | Switzerland |
| 1985 | Canada | Scotland | 2001 | Canada | Sweden |
| 1986 | Canada | West Germany | 2002 | Scotland | Sweden |
| 1987 | Canada | West Germany | 2003 | United States | Canada |
| 1988 | West Germany | Canada | 2004 | *to be held Gävle, Sweden,* | |
| 1989 | Canada | Norway | | *17–25 April* | |
| 1990 | Norway | Scotland | | | |
| 1991 | Norway | Canada | | | |
| 1992 | Sweden | United States | | | |
| 1993 | Canada | Germany | | | |
| 1994 | Canada | Scotland | | | |

**Did you know?** Curling is particularly associated with Scotland, where the game dates to the early 16th century. Paintings by Pieter Bruegel the Elder in The Netherlands dating from about the same time are evidence that the game was also played there, but it was Scotland that promoted the game worldwide.

# Cycling

By all accounts, the greatest cycling event of all is the annual **Tour de France** road race (founded 1903). It is raced in several stages over distances exceeding 3,500 km (2,175 mi). From 1911 to 1929 distances exceeded 5,300 km. A Tour de France for women was first held in 1984, over an 18-stage course of 991 km. In addition to this and a great number of other road races held yearly, there are yearly **road racing world championships.**

**Track racing** championships are also held. The oldest events of track racing are the **sprint** (in which only the last part of the race can actually be considered sprinting) and the **pursuit** (both a team and an individual event in which contestants start the race on opposite sides of the track and attempt to catch each other). **Mountain bike racing** and **cyclo-cross,** a cross-country bicycle race that requires cyclists to carry their bikes over parts of the course, developed in the latter part of the 20th century. World championships were established for these sports in 1997.

**International Cycling Union (Union Cycliste Internationale—UCI) Web site:** <www.uci.ch>

## Cycling Champions, 2002–03

*In the case of multiday events, the concluding date is given.*

| EVENT | WINNER (COUNTRY) | DATE |
|-------|------------------|------|
| **world champions—mountain bikes** | | **1 Sep 2002** |
| **men** | | |
| Cross-country | Roland Green (CAN) | |
| Downhill | Nicolas Vouilloz (FRA) | |
| **women** | | |
| Cross-country | Gunn-Rita Dahle (NOR) | |
| Downhill | Anne-Caroline Chausson (FRA) | |

# Cycling Champions, 2002–03 (continued)

| EVENT | WINNER (COUNTRY) | DATE |
|---|---|---|
| world champions—track | | 29 Sep 2002 |
| **men** | | |
| Sprint | Sean Eadie (AUS) | |
| Individual pursuit | Brad McGee (AUS) | |
| Kilometre time trial | Chris Hoy (GBR) | |
| 40-km points | Chris Newton (GBR) | |
| Team pursuit | Peter Dawson, Brett Lancaster, Stephen Wooldridge, Luke Roberts (AUS) | |
| Keirin | Jobie Dajka (AUS) | |
| Olympic sprint | Chris Hoy, Craig MacLean, Jamie Staff (GBR) | |
| 60-km Madison | Jérôme Neuville, Franck Perque (FRA) | |
| **women** | | |
| Sprint | Natalya Tsylinskaya (BLR) | |
| Individual pursuit | Leontien Zijlaard-Van Moorsel (NED) | |
| 500-m time trial | Natalya Tsylinskaya (BLR) | |
| 24-km points | Olga Slyusareva (RUS) | |
| world champions—road | | 13 Oct 2002 |
| **men** | | |
| Individual road race | Mario Cipollini (ITA) | |
| Individual time trial | Santiago Botero (COL) | |
| **women** | | |
| Individual road race | Susanne Ljungskog (SWE) | |
| Individual time trial | Zulfiya Zabirova (RUS) | |
| world champions—cyclo-cross | | 2 Feb 2003 |
| Men | Bart Wellens (BEL) | |
| Women | Daphny Van den Brand (NED) | |

**major elite road-race winners (starred races comprise the World Cup)**

| EVENT | WINNER (COUNTRY) | DATE |
|---|---|---|
| *HEW–Cyclassics Cup | Johan Museeuw (BEL) | 4 Aug 2002 |
| *San Sebastian Classic (Klasika Ciclista San Sebastian) | Laurent Jalabert (FRA) | 10 Aug 2002 |
| *Zürich Championship (Meisterschaft von Zürich) | Dario Frigo (ITA) | 18 Aug 2002 |
| Tour of Spain (Vuelta a España) | Aitor González (ESP) | 29 Sep 2002 |
| *Paris–Tours | Jakob Piil (DEN) | 6 Oct 2002 |
| *Tour of Lombardy (Giro di Lombardia) | Michele Bartoli (ITA) | 19 Oct 2002 |
| Paris–Nice | Aleksandr Vinokurov (KAZ) | 6 Mar 2003 |
| Tirreno–Adriatico | Filippo Pozzato (ITA) | 19 Mar 2003 |
| *Milan–San Remo | Paolo Bettini (ITA) | 22 Mar 2003 |
| *Tour of Flanders (Ronde van Vlaanderen) | Peter Van Petegem (BEL) | 6 Apr 2003 |
| Ghent–Wevelgem | Andreas Klier (GER) | 9 Apr 2003 |
| *Paris–Roubaix | Peter Van Petegem (BEL) | 13 Apr 2003 |
| *Amstel Gold | Aleksandr Vinokurov (KAZ) | 20 Apr 2003 |
| La Flèche Wallonne | Igor Astarloa (ESP) | 23 Apr 2003 |
| *Liège–Bastogne–Liège | Tyler Hamilton (USA) | 27 Apr 2003 |
| Tour of Romandie (Tour de Romandie) | Tyler Hamilton (USA) | 4 May 2003 |
| Tour of Italy (Giro d'Italia) | Gilberto Simoni (ITA) | 1 Jun 2003 |
| Critérium de Dauphiné Libéré | Cédric Vasseur (FRA) | 15 Jun 2003 |
| Tour of Switzerland (Tour de Suisse) | Aleksandr Vinokurov (KAZ) | 25 Jun 2003 |
| Tour de France | Lance Armstrong (USA) | 27 Jul 2003 |

**Did you know?** Cycling as a sport officially began on May 31, 1868, with a 1,200-metre (1,312-yard) race between the fountains and the entrance of Saint-Cloud Park (near Paris). The winner was James Moore, an 18-year-old expatriate Englishman from Paris. On November 7, 1869, the first city-to-city race was held between Paris and Rouen; again Moore was the winner, covering the 135 km (84 miles) in 10 hours 25 minutes, including time spent walking his bicycle up the steeper hills.

## Tour de France

| YEAR | WINNER (COUNTRY) | LENGTH OF ROUTE (KM) | YEAR | WINNER (COUNTRY) | LENGTH OF ROUTE (KM) |
|---|---|---|---|---|---|
| 1903 | Maurice Garin (FRA) | 2,428 | 1959 | Federico Bahamontes (ESP) | 4,355 |
| 1904 | Henri Cornet (FRA) | 2,388 | 1960 | Gastone Nencini (ITA) | 4,173 |
| 1905 | Louis Trousselier (FRA) | 2,975 | 1961 | Jacques Anquetil (FRA) | 4,397 |
| 1906 | René Pottier (FRA) | 4,637 | 1962 | Jacques Anquetil (FRA) | 4,274 |
| 1907 | Lucien Petit-Breton (FRA) | 4,488 | 1963 | Jacques Anquetil (FRA) | 4,137 |
| 1908 | Lucien Petit-Breton (FRA) | 4,487 | 1964 | Jacques Anquetil (FRA) | 4,504 |
| 1909 | François Faber (LUX) | 4,507 | 1965 | Felice Gimondi (ITA) | 4,183 |
| 1910 | Octave Lapize (FRA) | 4,474 | 1966 | Lucien Aimar (FRA) | 4,303 |
| 1911 | Gustave Garrigou (FRA) | 5,344 | 1967 | Roger Pingeon (FRA) | 4,780 |
| 1912 | Odile Defraye (BEL) | 5,319 | 1968 | Jan Janssen (NED) | 4,662 |
| 1913 | Philippe Thys (BEL) | 5,387 | 1969 | Eddy Merckx (BEL) | 4,110 |
| 1914 | Philippe Thys (BEL) | 5,405 | 1970 | Eddy Merckx (BEL) | 4,366 |
| 1915–18 | *not held* | | 1971 | Eddy Merckx (BEL) | 3,689 |
| 1919 | Firmin Lambot (BEL) | 5,560 | 1972 | Eddy Merckx (BEL) | 3,846 |
| 1920 | Philippe Thys (BEL) | 5,519 | 1973 | Luis Ocaña (ESP) | 4,140 |
| 1921 | Léon Scieur (BEL) | 5,484 | 1974 | Eddy Merckx (BEL) | 4,098 |
| 1922 | Firmin Lambot (BEL) | 5,375 | 1975 | Bernard Thévenet (FRA) | 4,000 |
| 1923 | Henri Pélissier (FRA) | 5,386 | 1976 | Lucien Van Impe (BEL) | 4,050 |
| 1924 | Ottavio Bottecchia (ITA) | 5,425 | 1977 | Bernard Thévenet (FRA) | 4,098 |
| 1925 | Ottavio Bottecchia (ITA) | 5,430 | 1978 | Bernard Hinault (FRA) | 3,920 |
| 1926 | Lucien Buysse (BEL) | 5,745 | 1979 | Bernard Hinault (FRA) | 3,719 |
| 1927 | Nicolas Frantz (LUX) | 5,341 | 1980 | Joop Zoetemelk (NED) | 3,948 |
| 1928 | Nicolas Frantz (LUX) | 5,377 | 1981 | Bernard Hinault (FRA) | 3,765 |
| 1929 | Maurice De Waele (BEL) | 5,286 | 1982 | Bernard Hinault (FRA) | 3,489 |
| 1930 | André Leducq (FRA) | 4,818 | 1983 | Laurent Fignon (FRA) | 3,568 |
| 1931 | Antonin Magne (FRA) | 5,095 | 1984 | Laurent Fignon (FRA) | 3,880 |
| 1932 | André Leducq (FRA) | 4,520 | 1985 | Bernard Hinault (FRA) | 4,100 |
| 1933 | Georges Speicher (FRA) | 4,395 | 1986 | Greg LeMond (USA) | 4,091 |
| 1934 | Antonin Magne (FRA) | 4,363 | 1987 | Stephen Roche (IRL) | 4,100 |
| 1935 | Romain Maes (BEL) | 4,338 | 1988 | Pedro Delgado (ESP) | 3,300 |
| 1936 | Romain Maes (BEL) | 4,442 | 1989 | Greg LeMond (USA) | 3,215 |
| 1937 | Roger Lapébie (FRA) | 4,415 | 1990 | Greg LeMond (USA) | 3,399 |
| 1938 | Gino Bartali (ITA) | 4,694 | 1991 | Miguel Indurain (ESP) | 3,935 |
| 1939 | Sylvere Maes (BEL) | 4,224 | 1992 | Miguel Indurain (ESP) | 3,983 |
| 1940–46 | *not held* | | 1993 | Miguel Indurain (ESP) | 3,700 |
| 1947 | Jean Robic (FRA) | 4,640 | 1994 | Miguel Indurain (ESP) | 3,978 |
| 1948 | Gino Bartali (ITA) | 4,922 | 1995 | Miguel Indurain (ESP) | 3,635 |
| 1949 | Fausto Coppi (ITA) | 4,808 | 1996 | Bjarne Riis (DEN) | 3,764 |
| 1950 | Ferdi Kubler (SUI) | 4,775 | 1997 | Jan Ullrich (GER) | 3,944 |
| 1951 | Hugo Koblet (SUI) | 4,697 | 1998 | Marco Pantani (ITA) | 3,831 |
| 1952 | Fausto Coppi (ITA) | 4,807 | 1999 | Lance Armstrong (USA) | 3,687 |
| 1953 | Louison Bobet (FRA) | 4,479 | 2000 | Lance Armstrong (USA) | 3,663 |
| 1954 | Louison Bobet (FRA) | 4,469 | 2001 | Lance Armstrong (USA) | 3,454 |
| 1955 | Louison Bobet (FRA) | 4,855 | 2002 | Lance Armstrong (USA) | 3,272 |
| 1956 | Roger Walkowiak (FRA) | 4,496 | 2003 | Lance Armstrong (USA) | 3,428 |
| 1957 | Jacques Anquetil (FRA) | 4,686 | | | |
| 1958 | Charly Gaul (LUX) | 4,319 | | | |

# Fencing

What had been the European fencing championship from 1921 to 1935 was officially recognized as the **world fencing** championship at the Olympic Games of 1936. The only event that does not reflect Olympics winners in the designated years is the women's team foil competition, which was not an Olympic event until 1960. Traditionally **women** competed only in the foil; women's épée competition has been part of the world championships since 1989 and sabre since 1999.

**Men's fencing** bouts last about six minutes, and the first man to score five hits with the designated portion of the weapon (for foil and épée, only hits made with the point of the weapon are scored) is the winner. Women's bouts last about five minutes, and only four hits must be scored.

Each **weapon** has a different target area: for the **foil**, it is the torso; for the **épée**, the entire body; and for the **sabre**, roughly the upper half of the body (including the head and arms).

**Related Web sites:** Fédération Internationale d'Escrime (FIE): <www.fie.ch>; US Fencing Association (USFA): <www.usfencing.org>

# World Fencing Championships—Men

*Competition has been held since 1936. Table shows results for the past 20 years.*
*The 2003 championships are scheduled to be concluded 11 October in Havana, Cuba.*

### Foil

| YEAR | INDIVIDUAL | TEAM |
|------|------------|------|
| 1983 | Aleksandr Romankov (URS) | West Germany |
| 1984* | Mauro Numa (ITA) | Italy |
| 1985 | Mauro Numa (ITA) | Italy |
| 1986 | Andrea Borella (ITA) | Italy |
| 1987 | Mathias Gey (FRG) | West Germany |
| 1988* | Stefano Cerioni (ITA) | USSR |
| 1989 | Alexander Koch (FRG) | USSR |
| 1990 | Philippe Omnès (FRA) | Italy |
| 1991 | Ingo Weissenborn (GER) | Cuba |
| 1992* | Philippe Omnès (FRA) | Germany |
| 1993 | Alexander Koch (GER) | Germany |
| 1994 | Rolando Tucker (CUB) | Germany |
| 1995 | Dmitry Shevchenko (RUS) | Cuba |
| 1996 | Alessandro Puccini (ITA) | Russia |
| 1997 | Sergey Golubitsky (UKR) | France |
| 1998 | Sergey Golubitsky (UKR) | Poland |
| 1999 | Sergey Golubitsky (UKR) | France |
| 2000 | Kim Young Ho (KOR) | France |
| 2001 | Salvatore Sanzo (ITA) | France |
| 2002 | Simone Vanni (ITA) | Germany |

### Épée

| YEAR | INDIVIDUAL | TEAM |
|------|------------|------|
| 1983 | Elmar Bormann (FRG) | France |
| 1984* | Philippe Boisse (FRA) | West Germany |
| 1985 | Philippe Boisse (FRA) | West Germany |
| 1986 | Philippe Riboud (FRA) | West Germany |
| 1987 | Volker Fischer (FRG) | USSR |
| 1988* | Arnd Schmitt (FRG) | France |
| 1989 | Manuel Pereira (SPA) | Italy |
| 1990 | Thomas Gerull (FRG) | Italy |
| 1991 | Andrey Shuvalov (URS) | USSR |
| 1992* | Eric Srecki (FRA) | Germany |
| 1993 | Pavel Kolobkov (RUS) | Italy |
| 1994 | Pavel Kolobkov (RUS) | France |
| 1995 | Eric Srecki (FRA) | Germany |
| 1996 | Aleksandr Beketov (RUS) | Italy |
| 1997 | Eric Srecki (FRA) | Cuba |
| 1998 | Hugues Obry (FRA) | Hungary |
| 1999 | Arnd Schmitt (GER) | France |
| 2000 | Pavel Kolobkov (RUS) | Italy |
| 2001 | Paolo Milanoli (ITA) | Hungary |
| 2002 | Pavel Kolobkov (RUS) | France |

### Sabre

| YEAR | INDIVIDUAL | TEAM |
|------|------------|------|
| 1983 | Vassil Etropolski (BUL) | USSR |
| 1984* | Jean-François Lamour (FRA) | Italy |
| 1985 | Gyorgy Nebald (HUN) | USSR |
| 1986 | Sergey Mindirgasov (URS) | USSR |
| 1987 | Jean-François Lamour (FRA) | USSR |
| 1988* | Jean-François Lamour (FRA) | Hungary |
| 1989 | Grigory Kiriyenko (URS) | USSR |
| 1990 | Gyorgy Nebald (HUN) | USSR |
| 1991 | Grigory Kiriyenko (URS) | Hungary |
| 1992* | Bence Szabo (HUN) | Unified Team† |

### Sabre

| YEAR | INDIVIDUAL | TEAM |
|------|------------|------|
| 1993 | Grigory Kiriyenko (URS) | Hungary |
| 1994 | Felix Becker (GER) | Russia |
| 1995 | Grigory Kiriyenko (URS) | Italy |
| 1996 | Stanislav Pozdnyakov (RUS) | Russia |
| 1997 | Stanislav Pozdnyakov (RUS) | France |
| 1998 | Luigi Tarantino (ITA) | Hungary |
| 1999 | Damien Touya (FRA) | France |
| 2000 | Mihai Claudiu Covaliu (ROM) | Russia |
| 2001 | Stanislav Pozdnyakov (RUS) | Russia |
| 2002 | Stanislav Pozdnyakov (RUS) | Russia |

*Olympic titles are recognized as world championships. †Consisting of athletes from the Commonwealth of Independent States and Georgia.

**Did you know?** Although the use of swords dates to prehistoric times and swordplay to ancient civilizations, the organized sport of fencing began only at the end of the 19th century.

# World Fencing Championships—Women

*Foil competition has been held since 1936. Table shows results for the past 20 years.*
*The 2003 championships are scheduled to be concluded 11 October in Havana, Cuba.*

### Foil

| YEAR | INDIVIDUAL | TEAM |
|------|------------|------|
| 1983 | Dorina Vaccaroni (ITA) | Italy |
| 1984* | Luan Jujie (CHN) | West Germany |
| 1985 | Cornelia Hanisch (FRG) | West Germany |
| 1986 | Anja Fichtel (FRG) | USSR |
| 1987 | Elisabeta Tufan (ROM) | Hungary |
| 1988* | Anja Fichtel (FRG) | West Germany |
| 1989 | Olga Velichko (URS) | West Germany |
| 1990 | Anja Fichtel (FRG) | Italy |
| 1991 | Giovanna Trillini (ITA) | Italy |
| 1992* | Giovanna Trillini (ITA) | Italy |
| 1993 | Francesca Bortolozzi (ITA) | Germany |
| 1994 | Reka Szabo (ROM) | Romania |

### Foil (continued)

| YEAR | INDIVIDUAL | TEAM |
|------|------------|------|
| 1995 | Laura Badea (ROM) | Italy |
| 1996 | Laura Badea (ROM) | Italy |
| 1997 | Giovanna Trillini (ITA) | Italy |
| 1998 | Sabine Bau (GER) | Italy |
| 1999 | Valentina Vezzali (ITA) | Germany |
| 2000 | Valentina Vezzali (ITA) | Italy |
| 2001 | Valentina Vezzali (ITA) | Italy |
| 2002 | Svetlana Boyko (RUS) | Russia |

### Epée

| YEAR | INDIVIDUAL | TEAM |
|------|------------|------|
| 1989 | Anja Straub (SUI) | Hungary |
| 1990 | Taymi Chappe (CUB) | West Germany |

## World Fencing Championships—Women (continued)

| | Epée (continued) | | | Sabre | |
|---|---|---|---|---|---|
| YEAR | INDIVIDUAL | TEAM | YEAR | INDIVIDUAL | TEAM |
| 1991 | Mariann Horvath (HUN) | Hungary | 1999 | Yelena Yemayeva (AZE) | Italy |
| 1992 | *not held* | | 2000 | Yelena Yemayeva (AZE) | United States |
| 1993 | Oksana Jermakova (EST) | Hungary | 2001 | Anne-Lise Touya (FRA) | Russia |
| 1994 | Laura Chiesa (ITA) | Spain | 2002 | Tan Xue (CHN) | Russia |
| 1995 | Joanna Jakimiuk (POL) | Hungary | | | |
| 1996 | Laura Flessel (FRA) | France | | | |
| 1997 | Mirayda Garcia-Soto (CUB) | Hungary | | | |
| 1998 | Laura Flessel (FRA) | France | | | |
| 1999 | Laura Flessel-Colovic (FRA) | Hungary | | | |
| 2000 | Timea Nagy (HUN) | Russia | | | |
| 2001 | Claudia Bokel (GER) | Russia | | | |
| 2002 | Hyun Hee (KOR) | Hungary | | | |

*Olympic titles are recognized as world championships.*

# Field Hockey

The sport of **field hockey** is quite popular in the United Kingdom, India, Pakistan, and much of Europe. Curiously, the sport was not seriously promoted among American men, and, in the United States, field hockey has been largely regarded as a sport for women. Despite its recognizable origins in the mid-19th century the game was not organized on an **international** level until the mid-20th century. One of a number of international tournaments is the **World Cup,** which is organized by the **International Hockey Federation** (Fédération Internationale de Hockey, FIH; founded 1924).

**FIH Web site:** <www.fihockey.org>

## World Cup Field Hockey Championship

| | men | | | women | |
|---|---|---|---|---|---|
| YEAR | WINNER | RUNNER-UP | YEAR | WINNER | RUNNER-UP |
| 1971 | Pakistan | India | 1974 | The Netherlands | Argentina |
| 1973 | The Netherlands | India | 1976 | West Germany | Argentina |
| 1975 | India | Pakistan | 1978 | The Netherlands | West Germany |
| 1978 | Pakistan | The Netherlands | 1981 | West Germany | The Netherlands |
| 1982 | Pakistan | West Germany | 1983 | The Netherlands | Canada |
| 1986 | Australia | England | 1986 | The Netherlands | West Germany |
| 1990 | The Netherlands | Pakistan | 1990 | The Netherlands | Australia |
| 1994 | Pakistan | The Netherlands | 1994 | Australia | Argentina |
| 1998 | The Netherlands | Spain | 1998 | Australia | The Netherlands |
| 2002 | Germany | Australia | 2002 | Argentina | The Netherlands |

**Did you know?** The first professional football game was played in 1895 in Latrobe, Pennsylvania, when Latrobe beat Jeannette 12-0. Soon professional teams were organized in Pittsburgh, upstate New York, Ohio, and many other parts of the country. In 1920 the American Professional Football Association was formed with 11 teams. It became the National Football League in 1922.

# Football

Many types of games are known as football, among them association football (also called soccer), gridiron football (also called American football and known in the United States as, simply, football), Canadian football (also called rugby football), Australian Rules Football (also called footy), and Rugby Union and Rugby League football (also known as rugby, or rugger). Each of these games is unique, although some—such as US football and Canadian football—bear more than a little resemblance, and each has its own distinct following.

**American Football—professional.** The National Football League (NFL) championship play-offs were organized in 1933. The American Football League (founded 1959) was a rival organization until 1970, when it merged with the NFL. The resulting reorganization added a few new teams (1976) and divided the reconstituted NFL into two conferences, the

American Football Conference and the National Football Conference. The play-off winner in each conference becomes that conference's representative in the Super Bowl, the final game of the professional football season.

**American Football—college.** Historically the national champion of college football has been informally selected by two rival opinion polls—one based on a survey of collegiate football coaches (currently conducted by *USA Today*/ESPN) and the other by sports writers (conducted by the Associated Press [AP]). The AP sports writers' poll began in 1936. The coaches' poll was begun in 1950 by the United Press (now United Press International [UPI]). Where polls designated different teams, both are listed. Desire for a clear-cut national champion led to the creation of the Bowl Championship Series (BCS) in 1999. The BCS uses a formula involving team records, strength of schedule, and rankings to determine the top two teams, who then meet in a national championship game. The site of the game annually shifts between the four major Bowls—Fiesta, Orange, Rose, and Sugar. The first of the Bowl games, the Rose Bowl, was played in 1902 during the 12th annual Tournament of Roses festival in Pasadena CA. In 1935 the Sugar Bowl (played in New Orleans) and the Orange Bowl (played in Miami) were inaugurated. The Fiesta Bowl (played in Phoenix) began play in 1971.

**Canadian football—professional.** The rules and organization of professional football in Canada have evolved gradually for well over 100 years based on the Canadian Rugby Union (formed in 1891). Until 1936 the game included intercollegiate teams. Since 1959, the Canadian Football League has been divided into two conferences, Eastern and Western. The two teams that win the division championships meet for the championship of the League, the Grey Cup (instituted in 1909). The intercollegiate teams withdrew from the Grey Cup competition in 1936, but the league did not become strictly professional until the mid-1950s.

**Australian football.** Australian Rules Football, originally called Melbourne Rules Football, emerged in the state of Victoria in the late 1850s as a sporting alternative during the southern winter when cricket was not played. The Victorian Football Association (formed in 1877) was supplanted by the Victorian Football League (formed in 1896), which was renamed the Australian Football League (AFL) in 1990 after two teams from outside Victoria were admitted in 1987. Currently, the eight AFL teams with the best records at the end of a 22-week season qualify for the play-offs. The first premiership Grand Final was played in 1886.

**Association football.** The game of association football is governed by the Fédération Internationale de Football Association (FIFA; founded 1904). The quadrennial FIFA World Cup (organized as the World Cup in 1930) was the first official internationally contested association football match. The popularity of the World Cup and the even earlier Copa América (1916) in South America led to the development of several regional cup competitions, including the European Champion Clubs' Cup (1955; discontinued after the 1992–93 season and superseded by the UEFA Champions League), the Asian Cup (1956), the African Cup of Nations (1957), and the Libertadores de América Cup (1960). Competition for the FIFA Women's World Cup began in 1991. The Major League Soccer Cup in the US was launched in 1996.

**Rugby Union football.** Rugby Union football was open to amateurs only until 1995. The Six Nations Championship was first played in 1882 (as the Four Nations) and is now contested by England, Scotland, Wales, Ireland, France (since 1910), and Italy (since 2000). The international Test matches further include South Africa, New Zealand, and Australia. The International Rugby Football League (FIRA; now FIRA-AER) oversees rugby in 39 other (i.e., non-Test) countries. The chief international competition between Rugby Union clubs in the southern hemisphere is the tri-nation Super 12 (Super 10 from 1993 until 1996). Teams from Australia (three), South Africa (four), and New Zealand (five) play in a round-robin tournament; the four teams with the best records qualify for the semifinals. The World Cup, sponsored by the International Rugby Board (IRB; founded 1886), was inaugurated in 1987. The competition is held every four years.

**Rugby League football.** Rugby League World Cup competition began in 1954 between professionals from Australia, France, Great Britain, and New Zealand. In 1975 it was renamed the International Championship. Competition was discontinued after 1977 but revived during the 1980s. The match has been held irregularly every few years.

**Related Web sites:** National Football League (NFL): <www.nfl.com>; Canadian Football League (CFL): <www.cfl.ca>; Australian Football League (AFL): <www.afl.com.au>; Fédération Internationale de Football Association (FIFA): <www.fifa.com>; Union des Associations Européennes de Football (UEFA): <www.uefa.com>; Major League Soccer (MLS): <www.majorleaguesoccer.com>; International Rugby Board (Rugby Union): <www.irb.org> or <www.irfb.com>; International Rugby League: <www.world.rleague.com>, (Super 12) <www.super12.rugby.com.au>

## National Football League (NFL) Final Standings, 2002–03

### American Conference

| TEAM | WON | LOST | TIED | TEAM | WON | LOST | TIED |
|---|---|---|---|---|---|---|---|
| **East Division** | | | | **South Division** | | | |
| New York Jets[1] | 9 | 7 | 0 | Tennessee[1] | 11 | 5 | 0 |
| New England | 9 | 7 | 0 | Indianapolis[1] | 10 | 6 | 0 |
| Miami | 9 | 7 | 0 | Jacksonville | 6 | 10 | 0 |
| Buffalo | 8 | 8 | 0 | Houston | 4 | 12 | 0 |
| | | | | | | | |
| **North Division** | | | | **West Division** | | | |
| Pittsburgh[1] | 10 | 5 | 1 | Oakland[1] | 11 | 5 | 0 |
| Cleveland[1] | 9 | 7 | 0 | Denver | 9 | 7 | 0 |
| Baltimore | 7 | 9 | 0 | San Diego | 8 | 8 | 0 |
| Cincinnati | 2 | 14 | 0 | Kansas City | 8 | 8 | 0 |

## National Football League (NFL) Final Standings, 2002–03 (continued)

### National Conference

| TEAM | WON | LOST | TIED | TEAM | WON | LOST | TIED |
|---|---|---|---|---|---|---|---|
| **East Division** | | | | **South Division** | | | |
| Philadelphia[1] | 12 | 4 | 0 | Tampa Bay[1] | 12 | 4 | 0 |
| New York Giants[1] | 10 | 6 | 0 | Atlanta[1] | 9 | 6 | 1 |
| Washington | 7 | 9 | 0 | New Orleans | 9 | 7 | 0 |
| Dallas | 5 | 11 | 0 | Carolina | 7 | 9 | 0 |
| | | | | | | | |
| **North Division** | | | | **West Division** | | | |
| Green Bay[1] | 12 | 4 | 0 | San Francisco[1] | 10 | 6 | 0 |
| Minnesota | 6 | 10 | 0 | St. Louis | 7 | 9 | 0 |
| Chicago | 4 | 12 | 0 | Seattle | 7 | 9 | 0 |
| Detroit | 3 | 13 | 0 | Arizona | 5 | 11 | 0 |

[1]*Gained play-off berth.*

## American Pro Football All-Time Records

| PLAYERS/TEAMS | | NUMBER | SEASON/DATE |
|---|---|---|---|
| **Individual career records** | | | |
| Total appearances | George Blanda | 340 | 1949–1975, except 1959 |
| Total Super Bowl appearances | Mike Lodish | 6 | 1991, '92, '93, '94, '98, '99 |
| Total points | Morten Andersen[1] | 2,153 | 1982–2002 |
| Touchdowns, total | Jerry Rice[1] | 202 | 1985–2001 |
| Touchdowns, passing | Dan Marino | 420 | 1983–1999 |
| Touchdowns, receiving | Jerry Rice[1] | 192 | 1985–2002 |
| Touchdowns, rushing | Emmitt Smith[1] | 153 | 1990–2002 |
| Field goals made | Morten Andersen[1] | 486 | 1982–2002 |
| Extra points made (kicked) | George Blanda | 943 | 1949–1975, except 1959 |
| Passing yardage | Dan Marino | 61,361 | 1983–1999 |
| Passing completions (attempts) | Dan Marino | 4,967 (8,358) | 1983–1999 |
| Receiving yardage | Jerry Rice[1] | 21,597 | 1985–2002 |
| Rushing yardage | Emmitt Smith[1] | 17,162 | 1990–2002 |
| Interceptions (defense) | Paul Krause | 81 | 1964–1979 |
| Sacks (defense)[2] | Reggie White | 198 | 1985–2000, except 1999 |
| Coaching total wins | Don Shula | 328-156-6 | 1963–1995 |
| Coaching winning percentage | Vince Lombardi | .740 | 1959–1969 |
| | | | |
| **Individual season records** | | | |
| Total points | Paul Hornung (Green Bay Packers) | 176 | 1960 |
| Touchdowns, total | Marshall Faulk[1] (St. Louis Rams) | 26 | 2000 |
| Touchdowns, passing | Dan Marino (Miami Dolphins) | 48 | 1984 |
| Touchdowns, receiving | Jerry Rice (San Francisco 49ers) | 22 | 1987 |
| Touchdowns, rushing | Emmit Smith (Dallas Cowboys) | 25 | 1995 |
| Field goals made | Olindo Mare (Miami Dolphins) | 39 | 1999 |
| Extra points made (kicked) | Uwe von Schamann (Miami Dolphins) | 66 | 1984 |
| Passing yardage | Dan Marino (Miami Dolphins) | 5,084 | 1984 |
| Passing completions (attempts) | Rich Gannon (Oakland Raiders) | 418 (618) | 2002 |
| Receiving yardage | Jerry Rice (San Francisco 49ers) | 1,848 | 1995 |
| Rushing yardage | Eric Dickerson (Los Angeles Rams) | 2,105 | 1984 |
| Interceptions (defense) | Dick "Night Train" Lane (Los Angeles Rams) | 14 | 1952 |
| Sacks (defense)[2] | Michael Strahan (New York Giants) | 22.5 | 2001 |
| | | | |
| **Individual game records** | | | |
| Total points | Ernie Nevers (Chicago Cardinals v. Chicago Bears) | 40 | 28 Nov 1929 |
| Touchdowns, total | Ernie Nevers (Chicago Cardinals v. Chicago Bears); Dub Jones (Cleveland Browns v. Chicago Bears); Gale Sayers (Chicago Bears v. San Francisco 49ers) | 6 | 28 Nov 1929; 25 Nov 1951; 12 Dec 1965 |

## American Pro Football All-Time Records (continued)

| PLAYERS/TEAMS | | NUMBER | SEASON/DATE |
|---|---|---|---|

**Individual game records (continued)**

| | | | |
|---|---|---|---|
| Touchdowns, passing | Sid Luckman (Chicago Bears v. New York Giants); Adrian Burk (Philadelphia Eagles v. Washington Redskins); George Blanda (Houston Oilers v. New York Titans); Y.A. Tittle (New York Giants v. Washington Redskins); Joe Kapp (Minnesota Vikings v. Baltimore Colts) (tied) | 7 | 14 Nov 1943; 17 Oct 1954; 19 Nov 1961; 28 Oct 1962; 28 Sept 1969 |
| Touchdowns, receiving | Bob Shaw (Chicago Cardinals v. Baltimore Colts); Kellen Winslow (San Diego Chargers v. Oakland Raiders); Jerry Rice (San Francisco 49ers v. Atlanta Falcons) | 5 | 2 Oct 1950; 22 Nov 1981; 14 Oct 1990 |
| Touchdowns, rushing | Ernie Nevers (Chicago Cardinals v. Chicago Bears) | 6 | 28 Nov 1929 |
| Field goals made | Jim Bakken (St. Louis Cardinals v. Pittsburgh Steelers); Rich Karlis (Minnesota Vikings v. Los Angeles Rams); Chris Boniol (Dallas Cowboys v. Green Bay Packers) | 7 | 24 Sep 1967; 5 Nov 1989 (OT); 18 Nov 1996 |
| Longest field goal | Tom Dempsey (New Orleans Saints); Jason Elam (Denver Broncos) | 63 yd | 8 Nov 1970; 25 Oct 1998 |
| Extra points scored (kicked) | Pat Harder (Chicago Cardinals v. New York Giants); Bob Waterfield (Los Angeles Rams v. Baltimore Colts); Charlie Gogolack (Washington Redskins v. New York Giants) | 9 | 17 Oct 1948; 22 Oct 1950; 27 Nov 1966 |
| Passing yardage | Norm Van Brocklin (Los Angeles Rams v. New York Yanks) | 554 | 28 Sep 1951 |
| Passing completions (non-overtime game) | Richard Todd (New York Jets v. San Francisco 49ers) | 42 | 21 Sep 1980 |
| Receiving yardage (non-overtime game) | Stephone Paige (Kansas City Chiefs v. San Diego Chargers) | 309 | 22 Dec 1985 |
| Rushing yardage | Corey Dillon (Cincinnati Bengals v. Denver Broncos) | 278 | 22 Oct 2000 |
| Longest run from scrimmage | Tony Dorsett (Dallas Cowboys v. Minnesota Vikings) | 99 yd | 3 Jan 1983 |
| Interceptions (defense) | *too numerous to list* | 4 | |
| Sacks (defense)[2] | Derrick Thomas (Kansas City Chiefs v. Seattle Seahawks) | 7 | 11 Nov 1990 |

**Team season records**

| | | | |
|---|---|---|---|
| Total points scored | Minnesota Vikings | 556 | 1998 |
| Touchdowns, total | Miami Dolphins | 70 | 1984 |
| Touchdowns, passing | Miami Dolphins | 49 | 1984 |
| Touchdowns, rushing | Green Bay Packers | 36 | 1962 |
| Field goals made | Miami Dolphins | 39 | 1999 |
| Passing yardage | St. Louis Rams | 5,232 | 2000 |
| Passing completions (attempts) | San Francisco 49ers | 432 (644) | 1995 |
| Rushing yardage | New England Patriots | 3,165 | 1978 |

**Game records**

| | | | |
|---|---|---|---|
| Highest total score | Washington Redskins v. New York Giants | 113 (72–41) | 27 Nov 1966 |
| Widest margin of victory in a shutout | Philadelphia Eagles v. Cincinnati Reds | 64–0 | 6 Nov 1934 |
| Longest game | Miami Dolphins v. Kansas City Chiefs | 82:40 (two overtimes) | 25 Dec 1971 |

[1]*Active in 2003.* [2]*Since 1982; before that year sacks were not officially recorded by the NFL.*

## Super Bowl

*NFL-AFL championship 1966–70; NFL championship from 1971–72 season.*

| | SEASON | WINNER | RUNNER-UP | SCORE |
|---|---|---|---|---|
| I | 1966–67 | Green Bay Packers (NFL) | Kansas City Chiefs (AFL) | 35–10 |
| II | 1967–68 | Green Bay Packers (NFL) | Oakland Raiders (AFL) | 33–14 |
| III | 1968–69 | New York Jets (AFL) | Baltimore Colts (NFL) | 16–7 |
| IV | 1969–70 | Kansas City Chiefs (AFL) | Minnesota Vikings (NFL) | 23–7 |
| V | 1970–71 | Baltimore Colts (AFC) | Dallas Cowboys (NFC) | 16–13 |
| VI | 1971–72 | Dallas Cowboys (NFC) | Miami Dolphins (AFC) | 24–3 |
| VII | 1972–73 | Miami Dolphins (AFC) | Washington Redskins (NFC) | 14–7 |
| VIII | 1973–74 | Miami Dolphins (AFC) | Minnesota Vikings (NFC) | 24–7 |
| IX | 1974–75 | Pittsburgh Steelers (AFC) | Minnesota Vikings (NFC) | 16–6 |
| X | 1975–76 | Pittsburgh Steelers (AFC) | Dallas Cowboys (NFC) | 21–17 |
| XI | 1976–77 | Oakland Raiders (AFC) | Minnesota Vikings (NFC) | 32–14 |
| XII | 1977–78 | Dallas Cowboys (NFC) | Denver Broncos (AFC) | 27–10 |
| XIII | 1978–79 | Pittsburgh Steelers (AFC) | Dallas Cowboys (NFC) | 35–31 |

## Super Bowl (continued)

| | SEASON | WINNER | RUNNER-UP | SCORE |
|---|---|---|---|---|
| XIV | 1979–80 | Pittsburgh Steelers (AFC) | Los Angeles Rams (NFC) | 31–19 |
| XV | 1980–81 | Oakland Raiders (AFC) | Philadelphia Eagles (NFC) | 27–10 |
| XVI | 1981–82 | San Francisco 49ers (NFC) | Cincinnati Bengals (AFC) | 26–21 |
| XVII | 1982–83 | Washington Redskins (NFC) | Miami Dolphins (AFC) | 27–17 |
| XVIII | 1983–84 | Los Angeles Raiders (AFC) | Washington Redskins (NFC) | 38–9 |
| XIX | 1984–85 | San Francisco 49ers (NFC) | Miami Dolphins (AFC) | 38–16 |
| XX | 1985–86 | Chicago Bears (NFC) | New England Patriots (AFC) | 46–10 |
| XXI | 1986–87 | New York Giants (NFC) | Denver Broncos (AFC) | 39–20 |
| XXII | 1987–88 | Washington Redskins (NFC) | Denver Broncos (AFC) | 42–10 |
| XXIII | 1988–89 | San Francisco 49ers (NFC) | Cincinnati Bengals (AFC) | 20–16 |
| XXIV | 1989–90 | San Francisco 49ers (NFC) | Denver Broncos (AFC) | 55–10 |
| XXV | 1990–91 | New York Giants (NFC) | Buffalo Bills (AFC) | 20–19 |
| XXVI | 1991–92 | Washington Redskins (NFC) | Buffalo Bills (AFC) | 37–24 |
| XXVII | 1992–93 | Dallas Cowboys (NFC) | Buffalo Bills (AFC) | 52–17 |
| XXVIII | 1993–94 | Dallas Cowboys (NFC) | Buffalo Bills (AFC) | 30–13 |
| XXIX | 1994–95 | San Francisco 49ers (NFC) | San Diego Chargers (AFC) | 49–26 |
| XXX | 1995–96 | Dallas Cowboys (NFC) | Pittsburgh Steelers (AFC) | 27–17 |
| XXXI | 1996–97 | Green Bay Packers (NFC) | New England Patriots (AFC) | 35–21 |
| XXXII | 1997–98 | Denver Broncos (AFC) | Green Bay Packers (NFC) | 31–24 |
| XXXIII | 1998–99 | Denver Broncos (AFC) | Atlanta Falcons (NFC) | 34–19 |
| XXXIV | 1999–2000 | St. Louis Rams (NFC) | Tennessee Titans (AFC) | 23–16 |
| XXXV | 2000–01 | Baltimore Ravens (AFC) | New York Giants (NFC) | 34–7 |
| XXXVI | 2001–02 | New England Patriots (AFC) | St. Louis Rams (NFC) | 20–17 |
| XXXVII | 2002–03 | Tampa Bay Buccaneers (NFC) | Oakland Raiders (AFC) | 48–21 |

## College Football National Champions

| SEASON | CHAMPION | SEASON | CHAMPION | SEASON | CHAMPION |
|---|---|---|---|---|---|
| 1924 | Notre Dame | 1953 | Maryland | 1978 | Alabama (AP), Southern California (UPI) |
| 1925 | Dartmouth | 1954 | Ohio State (AP), UCLA (UP) | | |
| 1926 | Stanford | 1955 | Oklahoma | 1979 | Alabama |
| 1927 | Illinois | 1956 | Oklahoma | 1980 | Georgia |
| 1928 | Southern California | 1957 | Auburn (AP), Ohio State (UP) | 1981 | Clemson |
| 1929 | Notre Dame | 1958 | Louisiana State | 1982 | Penn State |
| 1930 | Notre Dame | 1959 | Syracuse | 1983 | Miami (FL) |
| 1931 | Southern California | 1960 | Minnesota | 1984 | Brigham Young |
| 1932 | Michigan | 1961 | Alabama | 1985 | Oklahoma |
| 1933 | Michigan | 1962 | Southern California | 1986 | Penn State |
| 1934 | Minnesota | 1963 | Texas | 1987 | Miami (FL) |
| 1935 | Southern Methodist | 1964 | Alabama | 1988 | Notre Dame |
| 1936 | Minnesota | 1965 | Alabama (AP), Michigan State (UPI) | 1989 | Miami (FL) |
| 1937 | Pittsburgh | | | 1990 | Colorado (AP), Georgia Tech (UPI) |
| 1938 | Texas Christian | 1966 | Notre Dame | | |
| 1939 | Texas A&M | 1967 | Southern California | 1991 | Miami (FL; AP), Washington (UPI) |
| 1940 | Minnesota | 1968 | Ohio State | | |
| 1941 | Minnesota | 1969 | Texas | 1992 | Alabama |
| 1942 | Ohio State | 1970 | Nebraska (AP), Texas (UPI) | 1993–94 | Florida State |
| 1943 | Notre Dame | 1971 | Nebraska | 1994–95 | Nebraska |
| 1944 | Army | 1972 | Southern California | 1995–96 | Nebraska |
| 1945 | Army | 1973 | Notre Dame (AP), Alabama (UPI) | 1996–97 | Florida |
| 1946 | Notre Dame | | | 1997–98 | Michigan/Nebraska (tied) |
| 1947 | Notre Dame | 1974 | Oklahoma (AP), Southern California (UPI) | | |
| 1948 | Michigan | | | 1998–99 | Tennessee |
| 1949 | Notre Dame | 1975 | Oklahoma | 1999–2000 | Florida State |
| 1950 | Oklahoma | 1976 | Pittsburgh | 2000–01 | Oklahoma |
| 1951 | Tennessee | 1977 | Notre Dame | 2001–02 | Miami (FL) |
| 1952 | Michigan State | | | 2002–03 | Ohio State |

**Did you know?** The CBS television network's broadcast of the Army vs. Navy football game on 7 Dec 1963 was the first to use instant replay.

# Rose Bowl

| SEASON | WINNER | RUNNER-UP | SCORE | SEASON | WINNER | RUNNER-UP | SCORE |
|--------|--------|-----------|-------|--------|--------|-----------|-------|
| 1901–02 | Michigan | Stanford | 49–0 | 1961–62 | Minnesota | UCLA | 21–3 |
| 1915–16 | Washington State | Brown | 14–0 | 1962–63 | Southern California | Wisconsin | 42–37 |
| 1916–17 | Oregon | Pennsylvania | 14–0 | 1963–64 | Illinois | Washington | 17–7 |
| 1917–18 | Mare Island | Camp Lewis | 19–7 | 1964–65 | Michigan | Oregon State | 34–7 |
| 1918–19 | Great Lakes | Mare Island | 17–0 | 1965–66 | UCLA | Michigan State | 14–12 |
| 1919–20 | Harvard | Oregon | 7–6 | | | | |
| 1920–21 | California | Ohio State | 28–0 | 1966–67 | Purdue | Southern California | 14–13 |
| 1921–22 | California | Washington & Jefferson | 0–0 | 1967–68 | Southern California | Indiana | 14–3 |
| 1922–23 | Southern California | Penn State | 14–3 | 1967–68 | Southern California | Indiana | 14–3 |
| 1923–24 | Washington | Navy | 14–14 | 1968–69 | Ohio State | Southern California | 27–16 |
| 1924–25 | Notre Dame | Stanford | 27–10 | | | | |
| 1925–26 | Alabama | Washington | 20–19 | 1969–70 | Southern California | Michigan | 10–3 |
| 1926–27 | Alabama | Stanford | 7–7 | | | | |
| 1927–28 | Stanford | Pittsburgh | 7–6 | 1970–71 | Stanford | Ohio State | 27–17 |
| 1928–29 | Georgia Tech | California | 8–7 | 1971–72 | Stanford | Michigan | 13–12 |
| 1929–30 | Southern California | Pittsburgh | 47–14 | 1972–73 | Southern California | Ohio State | 42–17 |
| 1930–31 | Alabama | Washington State | 24–0 | 1973–74 | Ohio State | Southern California | 42–21 |
| 1931–32 | Southern California | Tulane | 21–12 | 1974–75 | Southern California | Ohio State | 18–17 |
| 1932–33 | Southern California | Pittsburgh | 35–0 | 1975–76 | UCLA | Ohio State | 23–10 |
| 1933–34 | Columbia | Stanford | 7–0 | 1976–77 | Southern California | Michigan | 14–6 |
| 1934–35 | Alabama | Stanford | 29–13 | | | | |
| 1935–36 | Stanford | Southern Methodist | 7–0 | 1977–78 | Washington | Michigan | 27–20 |
| | | | | 1978–79 | Southern California | Michigan | 17–10 |
| 1936–37 | Pittsburgh | Washington | 21–0 | | | | |
| 1937–38 | California | Alabama | 13–0 | 1979–80 | Southern California | Ohio State | 17–16 |
| 1938–39 | Southern California | Duke | 7–3 | | | | |
| | | | | 1980–81 | Michigan | Washington | 23–6 |
| 1939–40 | Southern California | Tennessee | 14–0 | 1981–82 | Washington | Iowa | 28–0 |
| | | | | 1982–83 | UCLA | Michigan | 24–14 |
| 1940–41 | Stanford | Nebraska | 21–13 | 1983–84 | UCLA | Illinois | 45–9 |
| 1941–42 | Oregon State | Duke | 20–16 | 1984–85 | Southern California | Ohio State | 20–17 |
| 1942–43 | Georgia | UCLA | 9–0 | | | | |
| 1943–44 | Southern California | Washington | 29–0 | 1985–86 | UCLA | Iowa | 45–28 |
| | | | | 1986–87 | Arizona State | Michigan | 22–15 |
| 1944–45 | Southern California | Tennessee | 25–0 | 1987–88 | Michigan State | Southern California | 20–17 |
| 1945–46 | Alabama | Southern California | 34–14 | 1988–89 | Michigan | Southern California | 22–14 |
| 1946–47 | Illinois | UCLA | 45–14 | 1989–90 | Southern California | Michigan | 17–10 |
| 1947–48 | Michigan | Southern California | 49–0 | 1990–91 | Washington | Iowa | 46–34 |
| 1948–49 | Northwestern | California | 20–14 | 1991–92 | Washington | Michigan | 34–14 |
| 1949–50 | Ohio State | California | 17–14 | 1992–93 | Michigan | Washington | 38–31 |
| 1950–51 | Michigan | California | 14–6 | 1993–94 | Wisconsin | UCLA | 21–16 |
| 1951–52 | Illinois | Stanford | 40–7 | 1994–95 | Penn State | Oregon | 38–20 |
| 1952–53 | Southern California | Wisconsin | 7–0 | 1995–96 | Southern California | Northwestern | 41–32 |
| 1953–54 | Michigan State | UCLA | 28–20 | 1996–97 | Ohio State | Arizona State | 20–17 |
| 1954–55 | Ohio State | Southern California | 20–7 | 1997–98 | Michigan | Washington State | 21–16 |
| 1955–56 | Michigan State | UCLA | 17–14 | 1998–99 | Wisconsin | UCLA | 38–31 |
| 1956–57 | Iowa | Oregon State | 35–19 | 1999–2000 | Wisconsin | Stanford | 17–9 |
| 1957–58 | Ohio State | Oregon | 10–7 | 2000–01 | Washington | Purdue | 34–24 |
| 1958–59 | Iowa | California | 38–12 | 2001–02 | Miami (FL) | Nebraska | 37–14 |
| 1959–60 | Washington | Wisconsin | 44–8 | 2002–03 | Oklahoma | Washington State | 34–14 |
| 1960–61 | Washington | Minnesota | 17–7 | | | | |

## Orange Bowl

| SEASON | WINNER | RUNNER-UP | SCORE | SEASON | WINNER | RUNNER-UP | SCORE |
|--------|--------|-----------|-------|--------|--------|-----------|-------|
| 1934–35 | Bucknell | Miami (FL) | 26–0 | 1968–69 | Penn State | Kansas | 15–14 |
| 1935–36 | Catholic | Mississippi | 20–19 | 1969–70 | Penn State | Missouri | 10–3 |
| 1936–37 | Duquesne | Mississippi State | 13–12 | 1970–71 | Nebraska | Louisiana State | 17–12 |
| | | | | 1971–72 | Nebraska | Alabama | 38–6 |
| 1937–38 | Auburn | Michigan State | 6–0 | 1972–73 | Nebraska | Notre Dame | 40–6 |
| 1938–39 | Tennessee | Oklahoma | 17–0 | 1973–74 | Penn State | Louisiana State | 16–9 |
| 1939–40 | Georgia Tech | Missouri | 21–7 | 1974–75 | Notre Dame | Alabama | 13–11 |
| 1940–41 | Mississippi State | Georgetown | 14–7 | 1975–76 | Oklahoma | Michigan | 14–6 |
| | | | | 1976–77 | Ohio State | Colorado | 27–10 |
| 1941–42 | Georgia | Texas Christian | 40–26 | 1977–78 | Arkansas | Oklahoma | 31–6 |
| 1942–43 | Alabama | Boston College | 37–21 | 1978–79 | Oklahoma | Nebraska | 31–24 |
| 1943–44 | Louisiana State | Texas A&M | 19–14 | 1979–80 | Oklahoma | Florida State | 24–7 |
| 1944–45 | Tulsa | Georgia Tech | 26–12 | 1980–81 | Oklahoma | Florida State | 18–17 |
| 1945–46 | Miami (FL) | Holy Cross | 13–6 | 1981–82 | Clemson | Nebraska | 22–15 |
| 1946–47 | Rice | Tennessee | 8–0 | 1982–83 | Nebraska | Louisiana State | 21–20 |
| 1947–48 | Georgia Tech | Kansas | 20–14 | 1983–84 | Miami (FL) | Nebraska | 31–30 |
| 1948–49 | Texas | Georgia | 41–28 | 1984–85 | Washington | Oklahoma | 28–17 |
| 1949–50 | Santa Clara | Kentucky | 21–13 | 1985–86 | Oklahoma | Penn State | 25–10 |
| 1950–51 | Clemson | Miami (FL) | 15–14 | 1986–87 | Oklahoma | Arkansas | 42–8 |
| 1951–52 | Georgia Tech | Baylor | 17–14 | 1987–88 | Miami (FL) | Oklahoma | 20–14 |
| 1952–53 | Alabama | Syracuse | 61–6 | 1988–89 | Miami (FL) | Nebraska | 23–3 |
| 1953–54 | Oklahoma | Maryland | 7–0 | 1989–90 | Notre Dame | Colorado | 21–6 |
| 1954–55 | Duke | Nebraska | 34–7 | 1990–91 | Colorado | Notre Dame | 10–9 |
| 1955–56 | Oklahoma | Maryland | 20–6 | 1991–92 | Miami (FL) | Nebraska | 22–0 |
| 1956–57 | Colorado | Clemson | 27–21 | 1992–93 | Florida State | Nebraska | 27–14 |
| 1957–58 | Oklahoma | Duke | 48–21 | 1993–94 | Florida State | Nebraska | 18–16 |
| 1958–59 | Oklahoma | Syracuse | 21–6 | 1994–95 | Nebraska | Miami | 24–17 |
| 1959–60 | Georgia | Missouri | 14–0 | 1995–96 | Florida State | Notre Dame | 31–26 |
| 1960–61 | Missouri | Navy | 21–14 | 1996–97 | Nebraska | Virginia Tech | 41–21 |
| 1961–62 | Louisiana State | Colorado | 25–7 | 1997–98 | Nebraska | Tennessee | 42–17 |
| 1962–63 | Alabama | Oklahoma | 17–0 | 1998–99 | Florida | Syracuse | 31–10 |
| 1963–64 | Nebraska | Auburn | 13–7 | 1999–2000 | Michigan | Alabama | 35–34 |
| 1964–65 | Texas | Alabama | 21–17 | 2000–01 | Oklahoma | Florida State | 13–2 |
| 1965–66 | Alabama | Nebraska | 39–28 | 2001–02 | Florida | Maryland | 56–23 |
| 1966–67 | Florida | Georgia Tech | 27–12 | 2002–03 | Southern California | Iowa | 38–17 |
| 1967–68 | Oklahoma | Tennessee | 26–24 | | | | |

## Sugar Bowl

| SEASON | WINNER | RUNNER-UP | SCORE | SEASON | WINNER | RUNNER-UP | SCORE |
|--------|--------|-----------|-------|--------|--------|-----------|-------|
| 1934–35 | Tulane | Temple | 20–14 | 1961–62 | Alabama | Arkansas | 10–3 |
| 1935–36 | Texas Christian | Louisiana State | 3–2 | 1962–63 | Mississippi | Arkansas | 17–13 |
| 1936–37 | Santa Clara | Louisiana State | 21–14 | 1963–64 | Alabama | Mississippi | 12–7 |
| 1937–38 | Santa Clara | Louisiana State | 6–0 | 1964–65 | Louisiana State | Syracuse | 13–10 |
| 1938–39 | Texas Christian | Carnegie Tech | 15–7 | | | | |
| 1939–40 | Texas A&M | Tulane | 14–13 | 1965–66 | Missouri | Florida | 20–18 |
| 1940–41 | Boston College | Tennessee | 19–13 | 1966–67 | Alabama | Nebraska | 34–7 |
| 1941–42 | Fordham | Missouri | 2–0 | 1967–68 | Louisiana State | Wyoming | 20–13 |
| 1942–43 | Tennessee | Tulsa | 14–7 | | | | |
| 1943–44 | Georgia Tech | Tulsa | 20–18 | 1968–69 | Arkansas | Georgia | 16–2 |
| 1944–45 | Duke | Alabama | 29–26 | 1969–70 | Mississippi | Arkansas | 27–22 |
| 1945–46 | Oklahoma A&M | St. Mary's | 33–13 | 1970–71 | Tennessee | Air Force | 34–13 |
| 1946–47 | Georgia | North Carolina | 20–10 | 1971–72 | Oklahoma | Auburn | 40–22 |
| 1947–48 | Texas | Alabama | 27–7 | 1972–73 | Oklahoma | Penn State | 14–0 |
| 1948–49 | Oklahoma | North Carolina | 14–6 | 1973–74 | Notre Dame | Alabama | 24–23 |
| 1949–50 | Oklahoma | Louisiana State | 35–0 | 1974–75 | Nebraska | Florida | 13–10 |
| 1950–51 | Kentucky | Oklahoma | 13–7 | 1975–76 | Alabama | Penn State | 13–6 |
| 1951–52 | Maryland | Tennessee | 28–13 | 1976–77 | Pittsburgh | Georgia | 27–3 |
| 1952–53 | Georgia Tech | Mississippi | 24–7 | 1977–78 | Alabama | Ohio State | 35–6 |
| 1953–54 | Georgia Tech | West Virginia | 42–19 | 1978–79 | Alabama | Penn State | 14–7 |
| 1954–55 | Navy | Mississippi | 21–0 | 1979–80 | Alabama | Arkansas | 24–9 |
| 1955–56 | Georgia Tech | Pittsburgh | 7–0 | 1980–81 | Georgia | Notre Dame | 17–10 |
| 1956–57 | Baylor | Tennessee | 13–7 | 1981–82 | Pittsburgh | Georgia | 24–20 |
| 1957–58 | Mississippi | Texas | 39–7 | 1982–83 | Penn State | Georgia | 27–23 |
| 1958–59 | Louisiana State | Clemson | 7–0 | 1983–84 | Auburn | Michigan | 9–7 |
| 1959–60 | Mississippi | Louisiana State | 21–0 | 1984–85 | Nebraska | Louisiana State | 28–10 |
| 1960–61 | Mississippi | Rice | 14–6 | 1985–86 | Tennessee | Miami (FL) | 35–7 |

## Sugar Bowl (continued)

| SEASON | WINNER | RUNNER-UP | SCORE | SEASON | WINNER | RUNNER-UP | SCORE |
|---|---|---|---|---|---|---|---|
| 1986–87 | Nebraska | Louisiana State | 30–15 | 1995–96 | Virginia Tech | Texas | 28–10 |
| 1987–88 | Auburn | Syracuse | 16–16 | 1996–97 | Florida | Florida State | 52–20 |
| 1988–89 | Florida State | Auburn | 13–7 | 1997–98 | Florida State | Ohio State | 31–14 |
| 1989–90 | Miami (FL) | Alabama | 33–25 | 1998–99 | Ohio State | Texas A&M | 24–14 |
| 1990–91 | Tennessee | Virginia | 23–22 | 1999–2000 | Florida State | Virginia Tech | 46–29 |
| 1991–92 | Notre Dame | Florida | 39–28 | 2000–01 | Miami (FL) | Florida | 37–20 |
| 1992–93 | Alabama | Miami (FL) | 34–13 | 2001–02 | Louisiana | Illinois | 47–34 |
| 1993–94 | Florida | West Virginia | 41–7 | | | State | |
| 1994–95 | Florida State | Florida | 23–17 | 2002–03 | Georgia | Florida State | 26–13 |

## Fiesta Bowl

| SEASON | WINNER | RUNNER-UP | SCORE | SEASON | WINNER | RUNNER-UP | SCORE |
|---|---|---|---|---|---|---|---|
| 1971–72 | Arizona State | Florida State | 45–38 | 1987–88 | Florida State | Nebraska | 31–28 |
| 1972–73 | Arizona State | Missouri | 49–35 | 1988–89 | Notre Dame | West Virginia | 34–21 |
| 1973–74 | Arizona State | Pittsburgh | 28–7 | 1989–90 | Florida State | Nebraska | 41–17 |
| 1974–75 | Oklahoma State | Brigham Young | 16–6 | 1990–91 | Louisville | Alabama | 34–7 |
| 1975–76 | Arizona State | Nebraska | 17–14 | 1991–92 | Penn State | Tennessee | 42–17 |
| 1976–77 | Oklahoma | Wyoming | 41–7 | 1992–93 | Syracuse | Colorado | 26–22 |
| 1977–78 | Penn State | Arizona State | 42–30 | 1993–94 | Arizona | Miami (FL) | 29–0 |
| 1978–79 | Arkansas | UCLA | 10–10 | 1994–95 | Colorado | Notre Dame | 41–24 |
| 1979–80 | Pittsburgh | Arizona | 16–10 | 1995–96 | Nebraska | Florida | 62–24 |
| 1980–81 | Penn State | Ohio State | 31–19 | 1996–97 | Penn State | Texas | 38–15 |
| 1981–82 | Penn State | Southern | 26–10 | 1997–98 | Kansas State | Syracuse | 35–18 |
| | | California | | 1998–99 | Tennessee | Florida State | 23–16 |
| 1982–83 | Arizona State | Oklahoma | 32–21 | 1999–2000 | Nebraska | Tennessee | 31–21 |
| 1983–84 | Ohio State | Pittsburgh | 28–23 | 2000–01 | Oregon State | Notre Dame | 41–9 |
| 1984–85 | UCLA | Miami (FL) | 39–37 | 2001–02 | Oregon | Colorado | 38–16 |
| 1985–86 | Michigan | Nebraska | 27–23 | 2002–03 | Ohio State | Miami (FL) | 31–24 |
| 1986–87 | Penn State | Miami (FL) | 14–10 | | | | |

## Heisman Trophy Winners

The Heisman Trophy is named for John Heisman, a director of the Downtown Athletic Club (DAC) in New York City who died in 1936. The trophy goes to an outstanding college football player at the end of the football season each year. A committee comprised of DAC members, members of the media, and representatives from each of the 50 states cast ballots to determine the winner. Web site: <www.heisman.com>.

| YEAR | WINNER | COLLEGE | POSITION | YEAR | WINNER | COLLEGE | POSITION |
|---|---|---|---|---|---|---|---|
| 1935 | Jay Berwanger | University of Chicago | HB | 1960 | Joe Bellino | Navy | HB |
| | | | | 1961 | Ernie Davis | Syracuse | HB |
| 1936 | Larry Kelley | Yale | E | 1962 | Terry Baker | Oregon State | QB |
| 1937 | Clint Frank | Yale | HB | 1963 | Roger Staubach | Navy | QB |
| 1938 | Davey O'Brien | TCU | QB | 1964 | John Huarte | Notre Dame | QB |
| 1939 | Nile Kinnick | Iowa | HB | 1965 | Mike Garrett | USC | HB |
| 1940 | Tom Harmon | Michigan | HB | 1966 | Steve Spurrier | Florida | QB |
| 1941 | Bruce Smith | Minnesota | HB | 1967 | Gary Beban | UCLA | QB |
| 1942 | Frank Sinkwich | Georgia | HB | 1968 | O.J. Simpson | USC | HB |
| 1943 | Angelo Bertelli | Notre Dame | HB | 1969 | Steve Owens | Oklahoma | HB |
| 1944 | Les Horvath | Ohio State | QB | 1970 | Jim Plunkett | Stanford | QB |
| 1945 | Felix Blanchard | Army | FB | 1971 | Pat Sullivan | Auburn | QB |
| 1946 | Glenn Davis | Army | HB | 1972 | Johnny Rodgers | Nebraska | WR |
| 1947 | John Lujack | Notre Dame | QB | 1973 | John Cappelletti | Penn State | HB |
| 1948 | Doak Walker | SMU | HB | 1974 | Archie Griffin | Ohio State | HB |
| 1949 | Leon Hart | Notre Dame | DE | 1975 | Archie Griffin | Ohio State | HB |
| 1950 | Vic Janowicz | Ohio State | HB | 1976 | Tony Dorsett | Pittsburgh | HB |
| 1951 | Dick Kazmaier | Princeton | HB | 1977 | Earl Campbell | Texas | HB |
| 1952 | Billy Vessels | Oklahoma | HB | 1978 | Billy Sims | Oklahoma | HB |
| 1953 | John Lattner | Notre Dame | HB | 1979 | Charles White | USC | HB |
| 1954 | Alan Ameche | Wisconsin | FB | 1980 | George Rogers | South Carolina | HB |
| 1955 | Howard Cassady | Ohio State | HB | 1981 | Marcus Allen | USC | HB |
| 1956 | Paul Hornung | Notre Dame | QB | 1982 | Herschel Walker | Georgia | HB |
| 1957 | John David Crow | Texas A&M | HB | 1983 | Mike Rozier | Nebraska | HB |
| 1958 | Pete Dawkins | Army | HB | 1984 | Doug Flutie | Boston College | QB |
| 1959 | Billy Cannon | LSU | HB | 1985 | Bo Jackson | Auburn | HB |

## Heisman Trophy Winners (continued)

| YEAR | WINNER | COLLEGE | POSITION | YEAR | WINNER | COLLEGE | POSITION |
|---|---|---|---|---|---|---|---|
| 1986 | Vinny Testaverde | Miami | QB | 1995 | Eddie George | Ohio State | RB |
| 1987 | Tim Brown | Notre Dame | WR | 1996 | Danny Wuerffel | Florida | QB |
| 1988 | Barry Sanders | Oklahoma State | RB | 1997 | Charles Woodson | Michigan | DB |
| 1989 | Andre Ware | Houston | QB | 1998 | Ricky Williams | Texas | RB |
| 1990 | Ty Detmer | BYU | QB | 1999 | Ron Dayne | Wisconsin | RB |
| 1991 | Desmond Howard | Michigan | WR | 2000 | Chris Weinke | Florida State | QB |
| 1992 | Gino Torretta | Miami | QB | 2001 | Eric Crouch | Nebraska | QB |
| 1993 | Charlie Ward | Florida State | QB | 2003 | Carson Palmer | USC | QB |
| 1994 | Rashaan Salaam | Colorado | TB | | | | |

## Canadian Football League Grey Cup

| YEAR | WINNER | RUNNER-UP | SCORE |
|---|---|---|---|
| 1983 | Toronto Argonauts (EFC) | British Columbia Lions (WFC) | 18–17 |
| 1984 | Winnipeg Blue Bombers (WFC) | Hamilton Tiger-Cats (EFC) | 47–17 |
| 1985 | British Columbia Lions (WFC) | Hamilton Tiger-Cats (EFC) | 37–24 |
| 1986 | Hamilton Tiger-Cats (EFC) | Edmonton Eskimos (WFC) | 39–15 |
| 1987 | Edmonton Eskimos (WFC) | Toronto Argonauts (EFC) | 38–36 |
| 1988 | Winnipeg Blue Bombers (EFC) | British Columbia Lions (WFC) | 22–21 |
| 1989 | Saskatchewan Roughriders (WFC) | Hamilton Tiger-Cats (EFC) | 43–40 |
| 1990 | Winnipeg Blue Bombers (EFC) | Edmonton Eskimos (WFC) | 50–11 |
| 1991 | Toronto Argonauts (EFC) | Calgary Stampeders (WFC) | 36–21 |
| 1992 | Calgary Stampeders (WFC) | Winnipeg Blue Bombers (EFC) | 24–10 |
| 1993 | Edmonton Eskimos (WFC) | Winnipeg Blue Bombers (EFC) | 33–23 |
| 1994 | British Columbia Lions (WFC) | Baltimore Stallions (EFC) | 26–23 |
| 1995 | Baltimore Stallions (SD) | Calgary Stampeders (ND) | 37–20 |
| 1996 | Toronto Argonauts (ED) | Edmonton Eskimos (WD) | 43–37 |
| 1997 | Toronto Argonauts (ED) | Saskatchewan Roughriders (WD) | 47–23 |
| 1998 | Calgary Stampeders (WD) | Hamilton Tiger-Cats (ED) | 26–24 |
| 1999 | Hamilton Tiger-Cats (ED) | Calgary Stampeders (WD) | 32–21 |
| 2000 | British Columbia Lions (WD) | Montreal Alouettes (ED) | 28–26 |
| 2001 | Calgary Stampeders (WD) | Winnipeg Blue Bombers (EFC) | 27–19 |
| 2002 | Montreal Alouettes (ED) | Edmonton Eskimos (WD) | 25–16 |

## Australian Football League Final Standings, 2002

*League ladder after round 22; teams that qualified for play-offs only.*

| TEAM | WON | LOST | TIED | POINTS | TEAM | WON | LOST | TIED | POINTS |
|---|---|---|---|---|---|---|---|---|---|
| Port Adelaide Power | 18 | 4 | 0 | 72 | Melbourne Demons | 12 | 10 | 0 | 48 |
| Brisbane Lions | 17 | 5 | 0 | 68 | (North Melbourne) Kangaroos | 12 | 10 | 0 | 48 |
| Adelaide Crows | 15 | 7 | 0 | 60 | | | | | |
| Collingwood Magpies | 13 | 9 | 0 | 52 | West Coast Eagles | 11 | 11 | 0 | 44 |
| Essendon Bombers | 12 | 9 | 1 | 50 | | | | | |

## Super 12 Rugby Championship

*Four points are awarded for a win and two for a draw; one bonus point is given for a loss by seven points or fewer and one for a team that scores four or more tries. Final match held 24 May 2003, Auckland, New Zealand.*

| TEAMS (COUNTRY) | POINTS | W | L | D | BONUS | TEAMS (COUNTRY) | POINTS | W | L | D | BONUS |
|---|---|---|---|---|---|---|---|---|---|---|---|
| Auckland Blues (NZL) | 49 | 10 | 1 | 0 | 9 | Otago Highlanders (NZL) | 29 | 6 | 5 | 0 | 5 |
| Canterbury Crusaders (NZL) | 40 | 8 | 3 | 0 | 8 | QLD Reds (AUS) | 26 | 5 | 6 | 0 | 6 |
| Wellington Hurricanes (NZL) | 34 | 7 | 4 | 0 | 6 | Stormers (RSA) | 23 | 5 | 6 | 0 | 3 |
| ACT Brumbies (AUS) | 31 | 6 | 5 | 0 | 7 | Waikato Chiefs (NZL) | 18 | 2 | 9 | 0 | 10 |
| NSW Waratahs (AUS) | 31 | 6 | 5 | 0 | 7 | Sharks (RSA) | 16 | 3 | 8 | 0 | 4 |
| Northern Bulls (RSA) | 30 | 6 | 5 | 0 | 6 | Cats (RSA) | 13 | 2 | 9 | 0 | 5 |

## Six Nations Championship

*Five Nations until 2000. Round-robin tournament, usually ending in April.*

| YEAR | WINNER | YEAR | WINNER | YEAR | WINNER |
|---|---|---|---|---|---|
| 1947 | England, Wales* | 1950 | Wales† | 1953 | England |
| 1948 | Ireland† | 1951 | Ireland | 1954 | England‡, France, Wales* |
| 1949 | Ireland‡ | 1952 | Wales† | 1955 | France, Wales* |

## Six Nations Championship (continued)

| YEAR | WINNER | YEAR | WINNER | YEAR | WINNER |
|------|--------|------|--------|------|--------|
| 1956 | Wales | 1972 | not completed | 1988 | Wales† |
| 1957 | England† | 1973 | quintuple tie | 1989 | France |
| 1958 | England | 1974 | Ireland | 1990 | Scotland§ |
| 1959 | France | 1975 | Wales | 1991 | England§ |
| 1960 | England‡, France* | 1976 | Wales† | 1992 | England§ |
| 1961 | France | 1977 | France§‖ | 1993 | France |
| 1962 | France | 1978 | Wales† | 1994 | Wales |
| 1963 | England | 1979 | Wales‡ | 1995 | England§ |
| 1964 | Scotland, Wales* | 1980 | England† | 1996 | England |
| 1965 | Wales‡ | 1981 | France§ | 1997 | France§ |
| 1966 | Wales | 1982 | Ireland‡ | 1998 | France§ |
| 1967 | France | 1983 | France, Ireland* | 1999 | Scotland |
| 1968 | France§ | 1984 | Scotland† | 2000 | England |
| 1969 | Wales‡ | 1985 | Ireland† | 2001 | England |
| 1970 | France, Wales* | 1986 | France, Scotland* | 2002 | France§ |
| 1971 | Wales† | 1987 | France§ | 2003 | England§ |

*Tied.   †Triple Crown (all three matches, excluding France) and Grand Slam (all four matches) winner.
‡Triple Crown winner.   §Grand Slam winner.   ‖Triple Crown won by Wales.

## Rugby Union World Cup

| YEAR | WINNER | RUNNER-UP | SCORE | YEAR | WINNER | RUNNER-UP | SCORE |
|------|--------|-----------|-------|------|--------|-----------|-------|
| 1987 | New Zealand | France | 29–9 | 1999 | Australia | France | 35–12 |
| 1991 | Australia | England | 12–6 | 2003 | scheduled to be held in November 2003 in Australia | | |
| 1995 | South Africa | New Zealand | 15–12 | | | | |

## Rugby League World Cup

| YEAR | WINNER | RUNNER-UP | SCORE | YEAR | WINNER | RUNNER-UP | SCORE |
|------|--------|-----------|-------|------|--------|-----------|-------|
| 1954 | Great Britain | France | 16–12 | 1977† | Australia | Great Britain | 13–12 |
| 1957 | Australia | Great Britain | 29–21 | 1988 | Australia | New Zealand | 25–12 |
| 1960 | Great Britain | Australia | 66–37 | 1992 | Australia | Great Britain | 10–6 |
| 1968 | Australia | France | 20–2 | 1995 | Australia | England | 16–8 |
| 1970 | Australia | Great Britain | 12–7 | 2000 | Australia | New Zealand | 40–12 |
| 1972 | Great Britain | Australia | 10–10* | 2005 | scheduled to be held in England | | |
| 1975† | Australia‡ | | | | | | |

*Great Britain won on match points.   †Called International Championship from 1975 to 1977.   ‡Championships played without a grand final match; England was the runner-up.

## FIFA World Cup—Men

| YEAR | WINNER | RUNNER-UP | SCORE | YEAR | WINNER | RUNNER-UP | SCORE |
|------|--------|-----------|-------|------|--------|-----------|-------|
| 1930 | Uruguay | Argentina | 4–2 | 1974 | West Germany | The Netherlands | 2–1 |
| 1934 | Italy | Czechoslovakia | 2–1 | 1978 | Argentina | The Netherlands | 3–1 |
| 1938 | Italy | Hungary | 4–2 | 1982 | Italy | West Germany | 3–1 |
| 1950 | Uruguay | Brazil | 2–1 | 1986 | Argentina | West Germany | 3–2 |
| 1954 | West Germany | Hungary | 3–2 | 1990 | West Germany | Argentina | 1–0 |
| 1958 | Brazil | Sweden | 5–2 | 1994 | Brazil | Italy | 0–0 (3–2*) |
| 1962 | Brazil | Czechoslovakia | 3–1 | 1998 | France | Brazil | 3–0 |
| 1966 | England | West Germany | 4–2 | 2002 | Brazil | Germany | 2–0 |
| 1970 | Brazil | Italy | 4–1 | | | | |

*Penalty kick shoot-out.

## FIFA World Cup—Women

| YEAR | WINNER | RUNNER-UP | SCORE | YEAR | WINNER | RUNNER-UP | SCORE |
|------|--------|-----------|-------|------|--------|-----------|-------|
| 1991 | United States | Norway | 2–1 | 2003 | to be held September–October 2003 in the US | | |
| 1995 | Norway | Germany | 2–0 | | | | |
| 1999 | United States* | China | 0–0 | | | | |

*Won on penalty kicks.

# Association Football (Soccer) National Champions

*List reflects the reigning champions of selected countries as of 2 Jul 2003.*

| COUNTRY | LEAGUE CHAMPION | CUP WINNER | COUNTRY | LEAGUE CHAMPION | CUP WINNER |
|---|---|---|---|---|---|
| Albania | Sportklub Tiranë | Dinamo Tiranë | Luxembourg | Grevenmacher | Grevenmacher |
| Andorra | Santa Coloma | | Mexico | Morelia | Monterrey (playoffs) |
| Argentina | Independiente (opening) | | Morocco | Hassania | Raja Casablanca |
| | River Plate (closing) | | Netherlands | PSV Eindhoven | Utrecht |
| Australia | Perth Glory | | Nigeria | Enyimba | Julius Berger |
| Austria | Wein | Wein | Northern Ireland | Glentoran | Coleraine |
| Belgium | FC Brugge | La Louviere | Norway | Rosenborg | Vålerenga |
| Bolivia | The Strongest | | Peru | Alianza (opening) | |
| Bosnia and Herzegovina | Leotar | NK Zeljeznicar | | Sporting Cristal (closing) | |
| Brazil | São Paulo | Cruzeiro | Poland | Wisla | Wisla |
| Bulgaria | CSKA | Levski | Portugal | FC Porto | FC Porto |
| Cameroon | Canon | Mt. Cameroon | Romania | Rapid | Dinamo |
| Chile | Cobreloa | | Russia | Locomotiv | Spartak Moscow |
| China | Dalian Shide | Qingdao Hademen | Saudi Arabia | Al-Ittihad | Al-Hilal |
| Colombia | Deportivo Cali | | Scotland | Rangers | Rangers |
| Costa Rica | Alajuelense | | Senegal | Jeanne d'Arc | AS Douanes |
| Croatia | Dynamo Zagreb | Hajduk | Serbia & Montenegro | Partizan Belgrade | Sartid |
| Cyprus | Omonia | Anorthosis Famagusta | Slovakia | Zilina | Matador Puchov |
| Czech Rep. | Sparta | Teplice | Slovenia | Maribor | Olimpija |
| Denmark | FC Copenhagen | Brondby | South Africa | Orlando Pirates | |
| Ecuador | Emelec | | South Korea | Seongnam | Samsung Bluewings |
| England | Manchester United | Arsenal | Spain | Real Madrid | Mallorca |
| Finland | HJK | Haka | Sweden | Djurgärdens | Djurgärdens |
| France | Lyon | Monaco | Switzerland | Grasshopper | Basle |
| Georgia | Dynamo Tbilisi | Dynamo Tbilisi | Tunisia | Esperance | Stade Tunisien |
| Germany | Bayern Munich | Bayern Munich | Turkey | Besiktas | Trabzonspor |
| Greece | Olympiakos | PAOK | Ukraine | Dinamo Kiev | Dinamo Kiev |
| Hungary | Ferencvaros | Ferencvaros | United States (MLS) | Los Angeles Galaxy | Los Angeles Galaxy |
| Ireland | Bohemians | Derry City | Uruguay | Penarol | |
| Israel | Maccabi Tel Aviv | Hapoel Ramat-Gan | Wales | Barry Town | Barry Town |
| Italy | Juventus | AC Milan | | | |
| Japan | Jubilo Iwata | Kyoto Purple Sanga | | | |

# UEFA Champions League

*Known until 1992–93 as the European Champion Clubs' Cup; played on a knockout basis until 1992–93 and a combination of group, knockout, and quarterfinals, semifinals, and finals since then.*

| SEASON | WINNING TEAM (COUNTRY) | RUNNER-UP (COUNTRY) | SCORE |
|---|---|---|---|
| 1955–56 | Real Madrid CF (ESP) | Stade de Reims (FRA) | 4–3 |
| 1956–57 | Real Madrid CF (ESP) | AC Fiorentina (ITA) | 2–0 |
| 1957–58 | Real Madrid CF (ESP) | AC Milano (ITA) | 3–2 |
| 1958–59 | Real Madrid CF (ESP) | Stade de Reims (FRA) | 2–0 |
| 1959–60 | Real Madrid CF (ESP) | Eintracht Frankfurt (FRG) | 7–3 |
| 1960–61 | SL Benfica (POR) | FC Barcelona (ESP) | 3–2 |
| 1961–62 | SL Benfica (POR) | Real Madrid CF (ESP) | 5–3 |
| 1962–63 | AC Milano (ITA) | SL Benfica (POR) | 2–1 |
| 1963–64 | Internazionale FC (ITA) | Real Madrid CF (ESP) | 3–1 |
| 1964–65 | Internazionale FC (ITA) | SL Benfica (POR) | 1–0 |
| 1965–66 | Real Madrid CF (ESP) | FK Partizan (YUG) | 2–1 |
| 1966–67 | Celtic FC (SCO) | Internazionale FC (ITA) | 2–1 |
| 1967–68 | Manchester United (ENG) | SL Benfica (POR) | 4–1 |
| 1968–69 | AC Milano (ITA) | AFC Ajax (NED) | 4–1 |
| 1969–70 | Feyenoord (NED) | Celtic FC (SCO) | 2–1 |
| 1970–71 | AFC Ajax (NED) | Panathinaikos FC (GRE) | 2–0 |
| 1971–72 | AFC Ajax (NED) | Internazionale FC (ITA) | 2–0 |
| 1972–73 | AFC Ajax (NED) | Juventus FC (ITA) | 1–0 |
| 1973–74 | Bayern München (FRG) | Club Atlético de Madrid (ESP) | 1–1, 4–0† |
| 1974–75 | Bayern München (FRG) | Leeds United AFC (ENG) | 2–0 |

## UEFA Champions League (continued)

| SEASON | WINNING TEAM (COUNTRY) | RUNNER-UP (COUNTRY) | SCORE |
|---|---|---|---|
| 1975–76 | Bayern München (FRG) | AS Saint-Etienne (FRA) | 1–0 |
| 1976–77 | Liverpool FC (ENG) | VfL Borussia Mönchengladbach (FRG) | 3–1 |
| 1977–78 | Liverpool FC (ENG) | Club Brugge KV (BEL) | 1–0 |
| 1978–79 | Nottingham Forest FC (ENG) | Malmö FF (SWE) | 1–0 |
| 1979–80 | Nottingham Forest FC (ENG) | Hamburger SV (FRG) | 1–0 |
| 1980–81 | Liverpool FC (ENG) | Real Madrid CF (ESP) | 1–0 |
| 1981–82 | Aston Villa FC (ENG) | Bayern München (FRG) | 1–0 |
| 1982–83 | Hamburger SV (FRG) | Juventus FC (ITA) | 1–0 |
| 1983–84 | Liverpool FC (ENG) | AS Roma (ITA) | 1–1* |
| 1984–85 | Juventus FC (ITA) | Liverpool FC (ENG) | 1–0 |
| 1985–86 | FC Steaua Bucuresti (ROM) | FC Barcelona (ESP) | 0–0* |
| 1986–87 | FC Porto (POR) | Bayern München (FRG) | 2–1 |
| 1987–88 | PSV Eindhoven (NED) | SL Benfica (POR) | 0–0* |
| 1988–89 | AC Milan (ITA) | FC Steaua Bucuresti (ROM) | 4–0 |
| 1989–90 | AC Milan (ITA) | SL Benfica (POR) | 1–0 |
| 1990–91 | FK Crvena Zvezda Beograd (YUG) | Olympique de Marseille (FRA) | 0–0* |
| 1991–92 | FC Barcelona (ESP) | Sampdoria UC (ITA) | 1–0 |
| 1992–93 | Olympique de Marseille (FRA) | AC Milan (ITA) | 1–0 |
| 1993–94 | AC Milan (ITA) | FC Barcelona (ESP) | 4–0 |
| 1994–95 | AFC Ajax (NED) | AC Milan (ITA) | 1–0 |
| 1995–96 | Juventus FC (ITA) | AFC Ajax (NED) | 1–1* |
| 1996–97 | BV Borussia Dortmund (GER) | Juventus FC (ITA) | 3–1 |
| 1997–98 | Real Madrid CF (ESP) | Juventus FC (ITA) | 1–0 |
| 1998–99 | Manchester United (ENG) | Bayern München (GER) | 2–1 |
| 1999–2000 | Real Madrid CF (ESP) | Valencia CF (ESP) | 3–0 |
| 2000–01 | Bayern München (GER) | Valencia CF (ESP) | 1–1* |
| 2001–02 | Real Madrid CF (ESP) | Bayer 04 Leverkusen (GER) | 2–1 |
| 2002–03 | AC Milan (ITA) | Juventus FC (ITA) | 0–0* |

*Won on penalty kicks.    †Match replayed.

## UEFA Cup

The UEFA Cup is considered Europe's second most important football competition. Established in the 1971–72 season, the Cup was restructured after the UEFA Cup Winners' Cup was abolished in 1998–99. Originally played on a knockout basis, since 1998 the competition has concluded with a single match. The Cup competition is open to top- and second-ranked teams in each country's league as well as winners of domestic cups.

| SEASON | WINNING TEAM (COUNTRY) | RUNNER-UP (COUNTRY) | SCORE |
|---|---|---|---|
| 1971–72 | Tottenham Hotspur FC (ENG) | Wolverhampton Wanderers FC (ENG) | 2–1; 1–1 |
| 1972–73 | Liverpool FC (ENG) | VfL Borussia Mönchengladbach (FRG) | 3–0; 0–2 |
| 1973–74 | Feyenoord (NED) | Tottenham Hotspur FC (ENG) | 2–2; 2–0 |
| 1974–75 | VfL Borussia Mönchengladbach (FRG) | FC Twente (NED) | 0–0; 5–1 |
| 1975–76 | Liverpool FC (ENG) | Club Brugge KV (BEL) | 3–2; 1–1 |
| 1976–77 | Juventus FC (ITA) | Athletic Club Bilbao (ESP) | 1–0; 1–2 |
| 1977–78 | PSV Eindhoven (NED) | SC Bastia (FRA) | 0–0; 3–0 |
| 1978–79 | VfL Borussia Mönchengladbach (FRG) | FK Crvena Zvezda Beograd (YUG) | 1–1; 1–0 |
| 1979–80 | Eintracht Frankfurt (FRG) | VfL Borussia Mönchengladbach (FRG) | 2–3; 1–0 |
| 1980–81 | Ipswich Town FC (ENG) | AZ Alkmaar (NED) | 3–0; 2–4 |
| 1981–82 | IFK Göteborg (SWE) | Hamburger SV (FRG) | 1–0; 3–0 |
| 1982–83 | RSC Anderlecht (BEL) | SL Benfica (POR) | 1–0; 1–1 |
| 1983–84 | Tottenham Hotspur FC (ENG)* | RSC Anderlecht (BEL) | 1–1; 1–1 |
| 1984–85 | Real Madrid CF (ESP) | Videoton FCF (HUN) | 3–0; 0–1 |
| 1985–86 | Real Madrid CF (ESP) | 1. FC Köln (FRG) | 5–1; 0–2 |
| 1986–87 | IFK Göteborg (SWE) | Dundee United FC (SCO) | 1–0; 1–1 |
| 1987–88 | Bayer 04 Leverkusen (FRG)* | RCD Espanyol (ESP) | 0–3; 3–0 |
| 1988–89 | SSC Napoli (ITA) | VfB Stuttgart (FRG) | 2–1; 3–3 |
| 1989–90 | Juventus FC (ITA) | AC Fiorentina (ITA) | 3–1; 0–0 |
| 1990–91 | Internazionale FC (ITA) | AS Roma (ITA) | 2–0; 0–1 |
| 1991–92 | AFC Ajax (NED) | Torino Calcio (ITA) | 2–2; 0–0 |
| 1992–93 | Juventus FC (ITA) | BV Borussia Dortmund (FRG) | 3–1; 3–0 |
| 1993–94 | Internazionale FC (ITA) | SV Austria Salzburg (AUT) | 1–0; 1–0 |
| 1994–95 | Parma AC (ITA) | Juventus FC (ITA) | 1–0; 1–1 |
| 1995–96 | FC Bayern München (GER) | FC Girondins de Bordeaux (FRA) | 2–0; 3–1 |
| 1996–97 | FC Schalke 04 (GER)* | Internazionale FC (ITA) | 1–0; 0–1 |
| 1997–98 | Internazionale FC (ITA) | S.S. Lazio (ITA) | 3–0 |

## UEFA Cup (continued)

| SEASON | WINNING TEAM (COUNTRY) | RUNNER-UP (COUNTRY) | SCORE |
|---|---|---|---|
| 1998–99 | Parma AC (ITA) | Olympique de Marseille (FRA) | 3–0 |
| 1999–2000 | Galatasaray SK (TUR)* | Arsenal FC (ENG) | 0–0 |
| 2000–01 | Liverpool FC (ENG) | Deportivo Alavés (ESP) | 5–4 |
| 2001–02 | Feyenoord (NED) | BV Borussia Dortmund (GER) | 3–2 |
| 2002–03 | FC Porto (POR)† | Celtic FC (SCO) | 3–2 |

*Won on penalty kicks.  †Won on "Silver Goal" in overtime.*

## Libertadores de América Cup

*Contested since 1960. Table shows results for the past 20 years.*

| YEAR | WINNER (COUNTRY) | RUNNER-UP (COUNTRY) | SCORES |
|---|---|---|---|
| 1984 | Independiente (ARG) | Grêmio (BRA) | 1–0, 0–0 |
| 1985 | Argentinos Juniors (ARG) | América de Cali (COL) | 1–0, 0–1, 1–1* |
| 1986 | River Plate (ARG) | América de Cali (COL) | 2–1, 1–0 |
| 1987 | Peñarol (URU) | América de Cali (COL) | 0–2, 2–1, 1–0* |
| 1988 | Nacional (URU) | Newell's Old Boys (ARG) | 0–1, 3–0 |
| 1989 | Atlético Nacional (COL) | Olímpia (PAR) | 0–2, 2–0, 5–4* |
| 1990 | Olímpia (PAR) | Barcelona (ECU) | 2–0, 1–1 |
| 1991 | Colo Colo (CHI) | Olímpia (PAR) | 0–0, 3–0 |
| 1992 | São Paulo (BRA) | Newell's Old Boys (ARG) | 0–1, 1–0, 3–2* |
| 1993 | São Paulo (BRA) | Universidad Católica (CHI) | 5–1, 0–2 |
| 1994 | Vélez Sarsfield (ARG) | São Paulo (BRA) | 1–0, 0–1, 5–4* |
| 1995 | Grêmio (BRA) | Atlético Nacional (COL) | 3–1, 1–1 |
| 1996 | River Plate (ARG) | América de Cali (COL) | 1–0, 2–0 |
| 1997 | Cruzeiro (BRA) | Sporting Cristal (PER) | 0–0, 1–0 |
| 1998 | Vasco da Gama (BRA) | Barcelona (ECU) | 2–0, 2–1 |
| 1999 | Palmeiras (BRA) | Deportiva Cali (COL) | 0–1, 2–1, 4–3* |
| 2000 | Boca Juniors (ARG) | Palmeiras (BRA) | 2–2, 0–4, 4–2* |
| 2001 | Boca Juniors (ARG) | Cruz Azul (MEX) | 1–0, 0–1, 3–1* |
| 2002 | Olímpia (PAR) | São Caetano (BRA) | 0–1, 2–1, 4–2* |
| 2003 | Boca Juniors (ARG) | Santos (BRA) | 2–0, 3–1 |

*Winner determined in penalty shoot-out after tiebreaking game.*

## Copa América

Held since 1916. Table shows results for past 20 years. The cup was contested by a best-of-series in 1983, by rounds in 1989 and 1991 (scores are shown here as winner's wins/losses/draws in final round), and by a final championship match in 1987 and from 1993.

| YEAR | WINNER | RUNNER-UP | SCORE | YEAR | WINNER | RUNNER-UP | SCORE |
|---|---|---|---|---|---|---|---|
| 1983 | Uruguay | Brazil | 1/0/1 | 1997 | Brazil | Bolivia | 3–1 |
| 1987 | Uruguay | Chile | 1–0 | 1999 | Brazil | Uruguay | 3–0 |
| 1989 | Brazil | Uruguay | 3/0/0 | 2001 | Colombia | Mexico | 1–0 |
| 1991 | Argentina | Brazil | 4/0/0 | 2003 | postponed until 2004 | | |
| 1993 | Argentina | Mexico | 2–1 | 2004 | to be held in June or | | |
| 1995 | Uruguay* | Brazil | 1–1 | | July in Peru | | |

*Uruguay won penalty shoot-out 5–3.*

## Asian Cup

*Scored on a points (percentage of wins) system until 1972.*

| YEAR | WINNER | RUNNER-UP | SCORE | YEAR | WINNER | RUNNER-UP | SCORE |
|---|---|---|---|---|---|---|---|
| 1956 | South Korea | Israel | 83.3 | 1984 | Saudi Arabia | China | 2–0 |
| 1960 | South Korea | Israel | 100 | 1988 | Saudi Arabia | South Korea | 0–0 (4–3*) |
| 1964 | Israel | India | 100 | 1992 | Japan | Saudi Arabia | 1–0 |
| 1968 | Iran | Burma | 100 | 1996 | Saudi Arabia | United Arab Emirates | 0–0 (4–2*) |
| 1972 | Iran | South Korea | 2–1 | 2000 | Japan | Saudi Arabia | 1–0 |
| 1976 | Iran | Kuwait | 1–0 | 2004 | to be held in China | | |
| 1980 | Kuwait | South Korea | 3–0 | | | | |

*Penalty kick shoot-out.*

## African Cup of Nations

| YEAR | WINNER | RUNNER-UP | SCORE | YEAR | WINNER | RUNNER-UP | SCORE |
|------|--------|-----------|-------|------|--------|-----------|-------|
| 1957 | Egypt | Ethiopia | 4–0 | 1982 | Ghana | Libya | 1–1 (7–6‡) |
| 1959 | Egypt | The Sudan | 2–1 | 1984 | Cameroon | Nigeria | 3–1 |
| 1962 | Ethiopia | Egypt | 4–2 | 1986 | Egypt | Cameroon | 0–0 (5–4‡) |
| 1963 | Ghana | The Sudan | 3–0 | 1988 | Cameroon | Nigeria | 1–0 |
| 1965 | Ghana | Tunisia | 3–2 | 1990 | Algeria | Nigeria | 1–0 |
| 1968 | Congo (Kinshasa) | Ghana | 1–0 | 1992 | Côte d'Ivoire | Ghana | 0–0 (11-10‡) |
| 1970 | The Sudan | Ghana | 1–0 | 1994 | Nigeria | Zambia | 2–1 |
| 1972 | Congo (Brazzaville) | Mali | 3–2 | 1996 | South Africa | Tunisia | 2–0 |
| 1974 | Zaire | Zambia | 2–2, 2–0* | 1998 | Egypt | South Africa | 2–0 |
| 1976 | Morocco | Guinea | 1–1† | 2000 | Cameroon | Nigeria | 2–2 (4–3‡) |
| 1978 | Ghana | Uganda | 2–0 | 2002 | Cameroon | Senegal | 0–0 (3–2‡) |
| 1980 | Nigeria | Algeria | 3–0 | 2004 | *final game to be played in Tunisia* | | |

*Game replayed.　†Group format.　‡Penalty kick shoot-out.

## Major League Soccer Cup

| YEAR | WINNER | RUNNER-UP | SCORE | YEAR | WINNER | RUNNER-UP | SCORE |
|------|--------|-----------|-------|------|--------|-----------|-------|
| 1996 | DC United | Los Angeles Galaxy | 3–2 (OT) | 2001 | San Jose Earthquakes | Los Angeles Galaxy | 2–1 (OT) |
| 1997 | DC United | Colorado Rapids | 2–1 | | | | |
| 1998 | Chicago Fire | DC United | 2–0 | 2002 | Los Angeles Galaxy | New England Revolution | 1–0 |
| 1999 | DC United | Los Angeles Galaxy | 2–0 | | | | |
| 2000 | Kansas City Wizards | Chicago Fire | 1–0 | 2003 | *final match to be held 26 October, Columbus OH* | | |

# Golf

**I**ndividual events. Two of the major men's golf championships, the **British and US Open tournaments**, are played annually at a variety of golf courses in their respective countries. Each is played over 72 holes, and each is preceded by qualifying rounds. The **Professional Golfers' Association championship** and the invitational **Masters Tournament** (which is held annually at the Augusta [GA] National Golf Course) are also top tournaments. Events for amateurs include the **US and British Amateur championships.**

Women's golf has been around nearly as long as men's golf, but until the late 1940s, it was limited to amateurs. Thus, for women, the **British and US Amateur championships** were the major tournaments. The **US Women's Open Championship** was started in 1946, and the **Ladies Professional Golf Association** (LPGA) was formed in 1950. Since that time, women's professional golf has flourished. In 1976 the **Women's British Open Championship** was added to the golf calendar.

**Team events.** The **Ryder Cup** was originally a biennial match between the United States and Great Britain, but beginning in 1979, it was expanded into a biennial match between the United States and Europe. The **World Cup**, formerly known as the Canada Cup, is a men's tournament for two-man professional teams. Teams of British and US women golfers compete every two years for the **Curtis Cup**, which since 1964 has involved two days' play of three 18-hole foursomes and six 18-hole singles. The **Solheim Cup**, the women's professional team tournament, had been played in even-numbered years since 1990 but was moved to odd-numbered years (beginning in 2003) following the rescheduling of the Ryder Cup because of the events of 11 Sep 2001. **Related Web sites:** United States Golf Association: <www.usga.org>; Professional Golf Association: <www.pgatour.com>; Ladies Professional Golf Association:<www.lpga.com>

## Masters Tournament
*Won by an American golfer except as indicated.*

| YEAR | WINNER | YEAR | WINNER | YEAR | WINNER |
|------|--------|------|--------|------|--------|
| 1934 | Horton Smith | 1948 | Claude Harmon | 1960 | Arnold Palmer |
| 1935 | Gene Sarazen | 1949 | Sam Snead | 1961 | Gary Player (RSA) |
| 1936 | Horton Smith | 1950 | Jimmy Demaret | 1962 | Arnold Palmer |
| 1937 | Byron Nelson | 1951 | Ben Hogan | 1963 | Jack Nicklaus |
| 1938 | Henry Picard | 1952 | Sam Snead | 1964 | Arnold Palmer |
| 1939 | Ralph Guldahl | 1953 | Ben Hogan | 1965 | Jack Nicklaus |
| 1940 | Jimmy Demaret | 1954 | Sam Snead | 1966 | Jack Nicklaus |
| 1941 | Craig Wood | 1955 | Cary Middlecoff | 1967 | Gay Brewer |
| 1942 | Byron Nelson | 1956 | Jack Burke | 1968 | Bob Goalby* |
| 1943–45 | *not held* | 1957 | Doug Ford | 1969 | George Archer |
| 1946 | Herman Keiser | 1958 | Arnold Palmer | 1970 | Billy Casper |
| 1947 | Jimmy Demaret | 1959 | Art Wall | 1971 | Charles Coody |

## Masters Tournament (continued)

| YEAR | WINNER | YEAR | WINNER | YEAR | WINNER |
|------|--------|------|--------|------|--------|
| 1972 | Jack Nicklaus | 1984 | Ben Crenshaw | 1996 | Nick Faldo (GBR) |
| 1973 | Tommy Aaron | 1985 | Bernhard Langer (FRG) | 1997 | Tiger Woods |
| 1974 | Gary Player (RSA) | 1986 | Jack Nicklaus | 1998 | Mark O'Meara |
| 1975 | Jack Nicklaus | 1987 | Larry Mize | 1999 | José María Olazábal (ESP) |
| 1976 | Raymond Floyd | 1988 | Sandy Lyle (SCO) | 2000 | Vijay Singh (FIJ) |
| 1977 | Tom Watson | 1989 | Nick Faldo (GBR) | 2001 | Tiger Woods |
| 1978 | Gary Player (RSA) | 1990 | Nick Faldo (GBR) | 2002 | Tiger Woods |
| 1979 | Fuzzy Zoeller† | 1991 | Ian Woosnam (GBR) | 2003 | Mike Weir (CAN) |
| 1980 | Seve Ballesteros (ESP) | 1992 | Fred Couples | 2004 | *scheduled to be held* |
| 1981 | Tom Watson | 1993 | Bernhard Langer (GER) | | *5–11 April,* |
| 1982 | Craig Stadler‡ | 1994 | José María Olazábal (ESP) | | *Augusta GA* |
| 1983 | Seve Ballesteros (ESP) | 1995 | Ben Crenshaw | | |

*\*Play-off averted when R. de Vicenzo was penalized for signing an incorrect scorecard.    †Sudden-death play-off against T. Watson and E. Sneed.    ‡Won on the first hole of a play-off against D. Pohl.*

## United States Open Championship—Men

*Won by an American golfer except as indicated.*

| YEAR | WINNER | YEAR | WINNER | YEAR | WINNER |
|------|--------|------|--------|------|--------|
| 1895 | Horace Rawlins | 1932 | Gene Sarazen | 1971 | Lee Trevino |
| 1896 | James Foulis | 1933 | John Goodman | 1972 | Jack Nicklaus |
| 1897 | Joe Lloyd | 1934 | Olin Dutra | 1973 | Johnny Miller |
| 1898 | Fred Herd | 1935 | Sam Parks, Jr. | 1974 | Hale Irwin |
| 1899 | Willie Smith | 1936 | Tony Manero | 1975 | Lou Graham |
| 1900 | Harry Vardon (GBR) | 1937 | Ralph Guldahl | 1976 | Jerry Pate |
| 1901 | Willie Anderson | 1938 | Ralph Guldahl | 1977 | Hubert Green |
| 1902 | Laurence Auchterlonie | 1939 | Byron Nelson | 1978 | Andy North |
| 1903 | Willie Anderson | 1940 | Lawson Little | 1979 | Hale Irwin |
| 1904 | Willie Anderson | 1941 | Craig Wood | 1980 | Jack Nicklaus |
| 1905 | Willie Anderson | 1942–45 *not held* | | 1981 | David Graham (AUS) |
| 1906 | Alex Smith | 1946 | Lloyd Mangrum | 1982 | Tom Watson |
| 1907 | Alex Ross | 1947 | Lew Worsham | 1983 | Larry Nelson |
| 1908 | Fred McLeod | 1948 | Ben Hogan | 1984 | Fuzzy Zoeller |
| 1909 | George Sargent | 1949 | Cary Middlecoff | 1985 | Andy North |
| 1910 | Alex Smith | 1950 | Ben Hogan | 1986 | Raymond Floyd |
| 1911 | John J. McDermott | 1951 | Ben Hogan | 1987 | Scott Simpson |
| 1912 | John J. McDermott | 1952 | Julius Boros | 1988 | Curtis Strange |
| 1913 | Francis Ouimet | 1953 | Ben Hogan | 1989 | Curtis Strange |
| 1914 | Walter Hagen | 1954 | Ed Furgol | 1990 | Hale Irwin |
| 1915 | Jerome D. Travers | 1955 | Jack Fleck | 1991 | Payne Stewart |
| 1916 | Chick Evans | 1956 | Cary Middlecoff | 1992 | Tom Kite |
| 1917–18 *not held* | | 1957 | Dick Mayer | 1993 | Lee Janzen |
| 1919 | Walter Hagen | 1958 | Tommy Bolt | 1994 | Ernie Els (RSA) |
| 1920 | Edward Ray (GBR) | 1959 | Billy Casper | 1995 | Corey Pavin |
| 1921 | James M. Barnes | 1960 | Arnold Palmer | 1996 | Steve Jones |
| 1922 | Gene Sarazen | 1961 | Gene Littler | 1997 | Ernie Els (RSA) |
| 1923 | Bobby Jones | 1962 | Jack Nicklaus | 1998 | Lee Janzen |
| 1924 | Cyril Walker | 1963 | Julius Boros | 1999 | Payne Stewart |
| 1925 | Willie MacFarlane, Jr. | 1964 | Ken Venturi | 2000 | Tiger Woods |
| 1926 | Bobby Jones | 1965 | Gary Player (RSA) | 2001 | Retief Goosen (RSA) |
| 1927 | Tommy Armour | 1966 | Billy Casper | 2002 | Tiger Woods |
| 1928 | Johnny Farrell | 1967 | Jack Nicklaus | 2003 | Jim Furyk |
| 1929 | Bobby Jones | 1968 | Lee Trevino | 2004 | *to be held 17–20 June,* |
| 1930 | Bobby Jones | 1969 | Orville Moody | | *Shinnecock Hills Golf* |
| 1931 | Billy Burke | 1970 | Tony Jacklin (GBR) | | *Club, Southampton NY* |

## British Open Tournament—Men

*Won by a British golfer unless otherwise indicated.*

| YEAR | WINNER | YEAR | WINNER | YEAR | WINNER |
|------|--------|------|--------|------|--------|
| 1860 | Willie Park, Sr. | 1865 | Andrew Strath | 1870 | Tom Morris, Jr. |
| 1861 | Tom Morris, Sr. | 1866 | Willie Park, Sr. | 1871 | *not held* |
| 1862 | Tom Morris, Sr. | 1867 | Tom Morris, Sr. | 1872 | Tom Morris, Jr. |
| 1863 | Willie Park, Sr. | 1868 | Tom Morris, Jr. | 1873 | Tom Kidd |
| 1864 | Tom Morris, Sr. | 1869 | Tom Morris, Jr. | 1874 | Mungo Park |

# British Open Tournament—Men (continued)

| YEAR | WINNER | YEAR | WINNER | YEAR | WINNER |
|------|--------|------|--------|------|--------|
| 1875 | Willie Park, Jr. | 1920 | George Duncan | 1966 | Jack Nicklaus (USA) |
| 1876 | Bob Martin | 1921 | Jock Hutchison (USA) | 1967 | Roberto de Vicenzo (ARG) |
| 1877 | Jamie Anderson | 1922 | Walter Hagen (USA) | 1968 | Gary Player (RSA) |
| 1878 | Jamie Anderson | 1923 | Arthur Havers | 1969 | Tony Jacklin |
| 1879 | Jamie Anderson | 1924 | Walter Hagen (USA) | 1970 | Jack Nicklaus (USA) |
| 1880 | Robert Ferguson | 1925 | James Barnes (USA) | 1971 | Lee Trevino (USA) |
| 1881 | Robert Ferguson | 1926 | Bobby Jones (USA) | 1972 | Lee Trevino (USA) |
| 1882 | Robert Ferguson | 1927 | Bobby Jones (USA) | 1973 | Tom Weiskopf (USA) |
| 1883 | Willie Fernie | 1928 | Walter Hagen (USA) | 1974 | Gary Player (RSA) |
| 1884 | Jack Simpson | 1929 | Walter Hagen (USA) | 1975 | Tom Watson (USA) |
| 1885 | Bob Martin | 1930 | Bobby Jones (USA) | 1976 | Johnny Miller (USA) |
| 1886 | David Brown | 1931 | Tommy Armour (USA) | 1977 | Tom Watson (USA) |
| 1887 | Willie Park, Jr. | 1932 | Gene Sarazen (USA) | 1978 | Jack Nicklaus (USA) |
| 1888 | Jack Burns | 1933 | Denny Shute (USA) | 1979 | Seve Ballesteros (ESP) |
| 1889 | Willie Park, Jr. | 1934 | Henry Cotton | 1980 | Tom Watson (USA) |
| 1890 | John Ball | 1935 | Alfred Perry | 1981 | Bill Rogers (USA) |
| 1891 | Hugh Kirkaldy | 1936 | Alfred Padgham | 1982 | Tom Watson (USA) |
| 1892 | Harold Hilton | 1937 | Henry Cotton | 1983 | Tom Watson (USA) |
| 1893 | William Auchterlonie | 1938 | Reg A. Whitcombe | 1984 | Seve Ballesteros (ESP) |
| 1894 | John H. Taylor | 1939 | Richard Burton | 1985 | Sandy Lyle (SCO) |
| 1895 | John H. Taylor | 1940–45 not held | | 1986 | Greg Norman (AUS) |
| 1896 | Harry Vardon | 1946 | Sam Snead (USA) | 1987 | Nick Faldo |
| 1897 | Harold Hilton | 1947 | Fred Daly (IRE) | 1988 | Seve Ballesteros (ESP) |
| 1898 | Harry Vardon | 1948 | Henry Cotton | 1989 | Mark Calcavecchia (USA) |
| 1899 | Harry Vardon | 1949 | Bobby Locke (RSA) | 1990 | Nick Faldo |
| 1900 | John H. Taylor | 1950 | Bobby Locke (RSA) | 1991 | Ian Baker-Finch (AUS) |
| 1901 | James Braid | 1951 | Max Faulkner | 1992 | Nick Faldo |
| 1902 | Sandy Herd | 1952 | Bobby Locke (RSA) | 1993 | Greg Norman (AUS) |
| 1903 | Harry Vardon | 1953 | Ben Hogan (USA) | 1994 | Nick Price (ZIM) |
| 1904 | Jack White | 1954 | Peter Thomson (AUS) | 1995 | John Daly (USA) |
| 1905 | James Braid | 1955 | Peter Thomson (AUS) | 1996 | Tom Lehman (USA) |
| 1906 | James Braid | 1956 | Peter Thomson (AUS) | 1997 | Justin Leonard (USA) |
| 1907 | Arnaud Massy (FRA) | 1957 | Bobby Locke (RSA) | 1998 | Mark O'Meara (USA) |
| 1908 | James Braid | 1958 | Peter Thomson (AUS) | 1999 | Paul Lawrie (SCO) |
| 1909 | John H. Taylor | 1959 | Gary Player (RSA) | 2000 | Tiger Woods (USA) |
| 1910 | James Braid | 1960 | Kel Nagle (AUS) | 2001 | David Duval (USA) |
| 1911 | Harry Vardon | 1961 | Arnold Palmer (USA) | 2002 | Ernie Els (RSA) |
| 1912 | Ted Ray | 1962 | Arnold Palmer (USA) | 2003 | Ben Curtis (USA) |
| 1913 | John H. Taylor | 1963 | Bob Charles (NZL) | 2004 | to be held 15–18 July, |
| 1914 | Harry Vardon | 1964 | Tony Lema (USA) | | Royal Troon, South |
| 1915–19 not held | | 1965 | Peter Thomson (AUS) | | Ayrshire, Scotland |

# US Professional Golfers' Association (PGA) Championship

*Won by an American golfer except as indicated.*

| YEAR | WINNER | YEAR | WINNER | YEAR | WINNER |
|------|--------|------|--------|------|--------|
| 1916 | James M. Barnes | 1938 | Paul Runyan | 1959 | Bob Rosburg |
| 1917–18 not held | | 1939 | Henry Picard | 1960 | Jay Hebert |
| 1919 | James M. Barnes | 1940 | Byron Nelson | 1961 | Jerry Barber* |
| 1920 | Jock Hutchison | 1941 | Vic Ghezzi | 1962 | Gary Player (RSA) |
| 1921 | Walter Hagen | 1942 | Sam Snead | 1963 | Jack Nicklaus |
| 1922 | Gene Sarazen | 1943 | not held | 1964 | Bobby Nichols |
| 1923 | Gene Sarazen | 1944 | Bob Hamilton | 1965 | Dave Marr |
| 1924 | Walter Hagen | 1945 | Byron Nelson | 1966 | Al Geiberger |
| 1925 | Walter Hagen | 1946 | Ben Hogan | 1967 | Don January* |
| 1926 | Walter Hagen | 1947 | Jim Ferrier | 1968 | Julius Boros |
| 1927 | Walter Hagen | 1948 | Ben Hogan | 1969 | Raymond Floyd |
| 1928 | Leo Diegel | 1949 | Sam Snead | 1970 | Dave Stockton |
| 1929 | Leo Diegel | 1950 | Chandler Harper | 1971 | Jack Nicklaus |
| 1930 | Tommy Armour | 1951 | Sam Snead | 1972 | Gary Player (RSA) |
| 1931 | Tom Creavy | 1952 | Jim Turnesa | 1973 | Jack Nicklaus |
| 1932 | Olin Dutra | 1953 | Walter Burkemo | 1974 | Lee Trevino |
| 1933 | Gene Sarazen | 1954 | Chick Harbert | 1975 | Jack Nicklaus |
| 1934 | Paul Runyan | 1955 | Doug Ford | 1976 | Dave Stockton |
| 1935 | Johnny Revolta | 1956 | Jack Burke | 1977 | Lanny Wadkins |
| 1936 | Denny Shute | 1957 | Lionel Hebert | 1978 | John Mahaffey* |
| 1937 | Denny Shute | 1958 | Dow Finsterwald | 1979 | David Graham (AUS)* |

# US Professional Golfers' Association (PGA) Championship (continued)

| YEAR | WINNER | YEAR | WINNER | YEAR | WINNER |
|------|--------|------|--------|------|--------|
| 1980 | Jack Nicklaus | 1990 | Wayne Grady (AUS) | 2000 | Tiger Woods |
| 1981 | Larry Nelson | 1991 | John Daly | 2001 | David Toms |
| 1982 | Raymond Floyd | 1992 | Nick Price (ZIM) | 2002 | Rich Beems |
| 1983 | Hal Sutton | 1993 | Paul Azinger | 2003 | *to be held 14–17 August* |
| 1984 | Lee Trevino | 1994 | Nick Price (ZIM) | | *Oak Hill Country Club,* |
| 1985 | Hubert Green | 1995 | Steve Elkington (AUS) | | *Rochester NY* |
| 1986 | Bob Tway | 1996 | Mark Brooks | 2004 | *to be held 9–15 August* |
| 1987 | Larry Nelson | 1997 | Davis Love III | | *Whistling Straits,* |
| 1988 | Jeff Sluman | 1998 | Vijay Singh (FIJ) | | *Kohler WI* |
| 1989 | Payne Stewart | 1999 | Tiger Woods | | |

*\*Winner by play-off.*

# Ladies Professional Golf Association (LPGA) Champions
*Won by an American golfer except as indicated.*

| YEAR | WINNER | YEAR | WINNER | YEAR | WINNER |
|------|--------|------|--------|------|--------|
| 1955 | Beverly Hanson | 1972 | Kathy Ahern | 1989 | Nancy Lopez |
| 1956 | Marlene Hagge | 1973 | Mary Mills | 1990 | Beth Daniel |
| 1957 | Louise Suggs | 1974 | Sandra Haynie | 1991 | Meg Mallon |
| 1958 | Mickey Wright | 1975 | Kathy Whitworth | 1992 | Betsy King |
| 1959 | Betsy Rawls | 1976 | Betty Burfeindt | 1993 | Patty Sheehan |
| 1960 | Mickey Wright | 1977 | Chako Higuchi | 1994 | Laura Davies (GBR) |
| 1961 | Mickey Wright | 1978 | Nancy Lopez | 1995 | Kelly Robbins |
| 1962 | Judy Kimball | 1979 | Donna Caponi | 1996 | Laura Davies (GBR) |
| 1963 | Mickey Wright | 1980 | Sally Little | 1997 | Chris Johnson |
| 1964 | Mary Mills | 1981 | Donna Caponi | 1998 | Se Ri Pak (KOR) |
| 1965 | Sandra Haynie | 1982 | Jan Stephenson (AUS) | 1999 | Juli Inkster |
| 1966 | Gloria Ehret | 1983 | Patty Sheehan | 2000 | Juli Inkster |
| 1967 | Kathy Whitworth | 1984 | Patty Sheehan | 2001 | Karrie Webb (AUS) |
| 1968 | Sandra Post | 1985 | Nancy Lopez | 2002 | Se Ri Pak (KOR) |
| 1969 | Betsy Rawls | 1986 | Pat Bradley | 2003 | Annika Sörenstam (SWE) |
| 1970 | Shirley Englehorn | 1987 | Jane Geddes | | |
| 1971 | Kathy Whitworth | 1988 | Sherri Turner | | |

# United States Women's Open Champions
*Won by an American golfer except as indicated.*

| YEAR | WINNER | YEAR | WINNER | YEAR | WINNER |
|------|--------|------|--------|------|--------|
| 1946 | Patty Berg | 1967 | Catherine Lacoste (FRA)* | 1988 | Liselotte Neumann (SWE) |
| 1947 | Betty Jameson | 1968 | Susie Berning | 1989 | Betsy King |
| 1948 | Babe Didrikson Zaharias | 1969 | Donna Caponi | 1990 | Betsy King |
| 1949 | Louise Suggs | 1970 | Donna Caponi | 1991 | Meg Mallon |
| 1950 | Babe Didrikson Zaharias | 1971 | JoAnne Carner | 1992 | Patty Sheehan |
| 1951 | Betsy Rawls | 1972 | Susie Berning | 1993 | Lauri Merten |
| 1952 | Louise Suggs | 1973 | Susie Berning | 1994 | Patty Sheehan |
| 1953 | Betsy Rawls | 1974 | Sandra Haynie | 1995 | Annika Sörenstam (SWE) |
| 1954 | Babe Didrikson Zaharias | 1975 | Sandra Palmer | 1996 | Annika Sörenstam (SWE) |
| 1955 | Fay Crocker | 1976 | JoAnne Carner | 1997 | Alison Nicholas (GBR) |
| 1956 | Kathy Cornelius | 1977 | Hollis Stacy | 1998 | Se Ri Pak (KOR) |
| 1957 | Betsy Rawls | 1978 | Hollis Stacy | 1999 | Juli Inkster |
| 1958 | Mickey Wright | 1979 | Jerilyn Britz | 2000 | Karrie Webb (AUS) |
| 1959 | Mickey Wright | 1980 | Amy Alcott | 2001 | Karrie Webb (AUS) |
| 1960 | Betsy Rawls | 1981 | Pat Bradley | 2002 | Juli Inkster |
| 1961 | Mickey Wright | 1982 | Janet Anderson | 2003 | Hilary Lunke |
| 1962 | Murle Breer | 1983 | Jan Stephenson (AUS) | 2004 | *to be held 1–4* |
| 1963 | Mary Mills | 1984 | Hollis Stacy | | *July at the Orchards* |
| 1964 | Mickey Wright | 1985 | Kathy Baker | | *Golf Club, South* |
| 1965 | Carol Mann | 1986 | Jane Geddes | | *Hadley MA* |
| 1966 | Sandra Spuzich | 1987 | Laura Davies (GBR) | | |

*\*Amateur.*

## Ryder Cup

| YEAR | RESULT | YEAR | RESULT |
|------|--------|------|--------|
| 1927 | United States 9½, Great Britain 2½ | 1973 | United States 19, Great Britain 13 |
| 1929 | Great Britain 7, United States 5 | 1975 | United States 21, Great Britain 11 |
| 1931 | United States 9, Great Britain 3 | 1977 | United States 12½, Great Britain 7½ |
| 1933 | Great Britain 6½, United States 5½ | 1979 | United States 17, Europe 11 |
| 1935 | United States 9, Great Britain 3 | 1981 | United States 18½, Europe 9½ |
| 1937 | United States 8, Great Britain 4 | 1983 | United States 14½, Europe 13½ |
| 1939–45 | *not held* | 1985 | Europe 16½, United States 11½ |
| 1947 | United States 11, Great Britain 1 | 1987 | Europe 15, United States 13 |
| 1949 | United States 7, Great Britain 5 | 1989 | Europe 14, United States 14 |
| 1951 | United States 9½, Great Britain 2½ | 1991 | United States 14½, Europe 13½ |
| 1953 | United States 6½, Great Britain 5½ | 1993 | United States 15, Europe 13 |
| 1955 | United States 8, Great Britain 4 | 1995 | Europe 14½, United States 13½ |
| 1957 | Great Britain 7½, United States 4½ | 1997 | Europe 14½, United States 13½ |
| 1959 | United States 8½, Great Britain 3½ | 1999 | United States 14½, Europe 13½ |
| 1961 | United States 14½, Great Britain 9½ | 2001 | *postponed until 2002* |
| 1963 | United States 23, Great Britain 9 | 2002 | Europe 15½, United States 12½ |
| 1965 | United States 19½, Great Britain 12½ | 2004 | *to be held 17–19 September,* |
| 1967 | United States 23½, Great Britain 8½ | | *Oakland Hills Country Club,* |
| 1969 | United States 16, Great Britain 16 | | *Bloomfield Hills MI* |
| 1971 | United States 18½, Great Britain 13½ | | |

## British Amateur Championship—Men
*Won by a British golfer except as indicated.*

| YEAR | WINNER | YEAR | WINNER | YEAR | WINNER |
|------|--------|------|--------|------|--------|
| 1885 | Allen MacFie | 1927 | William Tweddell | 1970 | Michael Bonallack |
| 1886 | Horace Hutchinson | 1928 | Thomas Perkins | 1971 | Steve Melnyk (USA) |
| 1887 | Horace Hutchinson | 1929 | Cyril Tolley | 1972 | Trevor Homer |
| 1888 | John Ball | 1930 | Bobby Jones (USA) | 1973 | Richard Siderowf (USA) |
| 1889 | Johnny Laidlay | 1931 | Eric Smith | 1974 | Trevor Homer |
| 1890 | John Ball | 1932 | John de Forest | 1975 | Vinny Giles (USA) |
| 1891 | Johnny Laidlay | 1933 | Michael Scott | 1976 | Richard Siderowf (USA) |
| 1892 | John Ball | 1934 | Lawson Little (USA) | 1977 | Peter McEvoy |
| 1893 | Peter Anderson | 1935 | Lawson Little (USA) | 1978 | Peter McEvoy |
| 1894 | John Ball | 1936 | Hector Thomson | 1979 | Jay Sigel (USA) |
| 1895 | Leslie Balfour-Melville | 1937 | Robert Sweeny, Jr. (USA) | 1980 | Duncan Evans |
| 1896 | Freddie Tait | 1938 | Charles Yates (USA) | 1981 | Phillipe Ploujoux (FRA) |
| 1897 | Jack Allan | 1939 | Alexander Kyle | 1982 | Martin Thompson |
| 1898 | Freddie Tait | 1940–45 | *not held* | 1983 | Philip Parkin |
| 1899 | John Ball | 1946 | James Bruen | 1984 | José María Olazábal |
| 1900 | Harold Hilton | 1947 | William Turnesa | | (ESP) |
| 1901 | Harold Hilton | 1948 | Frank Stranahan (USA) | 1985 | Garth McGimpsey (IRL) |
| 1902 | Charles Hutchings | 1949 | Samuel McCready | 1986 | David Curry |
| 1903 | Robert Maxwell | 1950 | Frank Stranahan (USA) | 1987 | Paul Mayo |
| 1904 | Walter Travis (USA) | 1951 | Richard Chapman (USA) | 1988 | Christian Hardin (SWE) |
| 1905 | Arthur Barry | 1952 | Harvie Ward (USA) | 1989 | Stephen Dodd |
| 1906 | James Robb | 1953 | Joe Carr (IRL) | 1990 | Rolf Muntz (NED) |
| 1907 | John Ball | 1954 | Douglas Bachli | 1991 | Gary Wolstenholme |
| 1908 | E.A. Lassen | 1955 | Joe Conrad (USA) | 1992 | Stephen Dundas |
| 1909 | Robert Maxwell | 1956 | John Beharrell | 1993 | Ian Pyman |
| 1910 | John Ball | 1957 | Reid Jack | 1994 | Lee James |
| 1911 | Harold Hilton | 1958 | Joe Carr (IRL) | 1995 | Gordon Sherry |
| 1912 | John Ball | 1959 | Deane Beman (USA) | 1996 | Warren Bledon |
| 1913 | Harold Hilton | 1960 | Joe Carr (IRL) | 1997 | Craig Watson |
| 1914 | J.L.C. Jenkins | 1961 | Michael Bonallack | 1998 | Sergio Garcia (ESP) |
| 1915–19 | *not held* | 1962 | Richard Davies (USA) | 1999 | Graeme Storm |
| 1920 | Cyril Tolley | 1963 | Michael Lunt | 2000 | Mikko Ilonen (FIN) |
| 1921 | William Hunter | 1964 | Gordon Clark | 2001 | Michael Hoey (IRL) |
| 1922 | Ernest Holderness | 1965 | Michael Bonallack | 2002 | Alejandro Larrazabal |
| 1923 | Roger Wethered | 1966 | Bobby Cole (RSA) | | (ESP) |
| 1924 | Ernest Holderness | 1967 | Bob Dickson (USA) | 2003 | Gary Wolstenholme |
| 1925 | Robert Harris | 1968 | Michael Bonallack | | |
| 1926 | Jesse Sweetser (USA) | 1969 | Michael Bonallack | | |

## United States Amateur Championship—Men

*Won by an American golfer except as indicated.*

| YEAR | WINNER | YEAR | WINNER | YEAR | WINNER |
|------|--------|------|--------|------|--------|
| 1895 | Charles Macdonald | 1932 | Ross Somerville | 1971 | Gary Cowan (CAN) |
| 1896 | H.J. Whigham | 1933 | George Dunlap | 1972 | Vinny Giles |
| 1897 | H.J. Whigham | 1934 | Lawson Little | 1973 | Craig Stadler |
| 1898 | Findlay Douglas | 1935 | Lawson Little | 1974 | Jerry Pate |
| 1899 | H.M. Harriman | 1936 | John Fischer | 1975 | Fred Ridley |
| 1900 | Walter Travis | 1937 | John Goodman | 1976 | Bill Sander |
| 1901 | Walter Travis | 1938 | William Turnesa | 1977 | John Fought |
| 1902 | Louis James | 1939 | Bud Ward | 1978 | John Cook |
| 1903 | Walter Travis | 1940 | Richard Chapman | 1979 | Mark O'Meara |
| 1904 | H.Chandler Egan | 1941 | Bud Ward | 1980 | Hal Sutton |
| 1905 | H.Chandler Egan | 1942–45 | *not held* | 1981 | Nathaniel Crosby |
| 1906 | Eben Byers | 1946 | Ted Bishop | 1982 | Jay Sigel |
| 1907 | Jerry Travers | 1947 | Skee Riegel | 1983 | Jay Sigel |
| 1908 | Jerry Travers | 1948 | William Turnesa | 1984 | Scott Verplank |
| 1909 | Robert Gardner | 1949 | Charles Coe | 1985 | Sam Randolph |
| 1910 | W.C. Fownes, Jr. | 1950 | Sam Urzetta | 1986 | Buddy Alexander |
| 1911 | Harold Hilton | 1951 | Billy Maxwell | 1987 | Billy Mayfair |
| 1912 | Jerry Travers | 1952 | Jack Westland | 1988 | Eric Meeks |
| 1913 | Jerry Travers | 1953 | Gene Littler | 1989 | Chris Patton |
| 1914 | Francis Ouimet | 1954 | Arnold Palmer | 1990 | Phil Mickelson |
| 1915 | Robert Gardner | 1955 | Harvie Ward | 1991 | Mitch Voges |
| 1916 | Chick Evans | 1956 | Harvie Ward | 1992 | Justin Leonard |
| 1917–18 | *not held* | 1957 | Hillman Robbins | 1993 | John Harris |
| 1919 | Davidson Herron | 1958 | Charles Coe | 1994 | Tiger Woods |
| 1920 | Chick Evans | 1959 | Jack Nicklaus | 1995 | Tiger Woods |
| 1921 | Jesse Guildford | 1960 | Deane Beman | 1996 | Tiger Woods |
| 1922 | Jess Sweetser | 1961 | Jack Nicklaus | 1997 | Matt Kuchar |
| 1923 | Max Marston | 1962 | Labron Harris, Jr. | 1998 | Hank Kuehne |
| 1924 | Bobby Jones | 1963 | Deane Beman | 1999 | David Gossett |
| 1925 | Bobby Jones | 1964 | Bill Campbell | 2000 | Jeff Quinney |
| 1926 | George von Elm | 1965 | Bob Murphy | 2001 | Ben Dickerson |
| 1927 | Bobby Jones | 1966 | Gary Cowan (CAN) | 2002 | Ricky Barnes |
| 1928 | Bobby Jones | 1967 | Bob Dickson | 2003 | *to be held 18–24 August, Oakmont Country Club, Oakmont PA* |
| 1929 | Harrison Johnston | 1968 | Bruce Fleisher | | |
| 1930 | Bobby Jones | 1969 | Steve Melnyk | | |
| 1931 | Francis Ouimet | 1970 | Lanny Wadkins | | |

## Women's British Open Championship

| YEAR | WINNER | YEAR | WINNER | YEAR | WINNER |
|------|--------|------|--------|------|--------|
| 1976 | J. Lee Smith (GBR) | 1986 | Laura Davies (GBR) | 1995 | Karrie Webb (AUS) |
| 1977 | Vivien Saunders (GBR) | 1987 | Alison Nicholas (GBR) | 1996 | Emilee Klein (USA) |
| 1978 | Janet Melville (GBR) | 1988 | Corinne Dibnah (AUS) | 1997 | Karrie Webb (AUS) |
| 1979 | Alison Sheard (RSA) | 1989 | Jane Geddes (USA) | 1998 | Sherri Steinhauer (USA) |
| 1980 | Debbie Massey (USA) | 1990 | Helen Alfredsson (SWE) | 1999 | Sherri Steinhauer (USA) |
| 1981 | Debbie Massey (USA) | 1991 | Penny Grice-Whittaker (GBR) | 2000 | Sophie Gustafson (SWE) |
| 1982 | Marta Figueras-Dotti (SPA) | | | 2001 | Se Ri Pak (KOR) |
| 1983 | *not held* | 1992 | Patty Sheehan (USA) | 2002 | Karrie Webb (AUS) |
| 1984 | Okamoto Ayako (JAP) | 1993 | Mardi Lunn (AUS) | 2003 | Annika Sörenstam (SWE) |
| 1985 | Betsy King (USA) | 1994 | Liselotte Neumann (SWE) | | |

## Ladies' British Amateur Championship

*Won by a British golfer except as indicated.*

| YEAR | WINNER | YEAR | WINNER | YEAR | WINNER |
|------|--------|------|--------|------|--------|
| 1893 | Lady Margaret Scott | 1903 | Rhona Adair | 1913 | Muriel Dodd |
| 1894 | Lady Margaret Scott | 1904 | Lottie Dod | 1914 | Cecil Leitch |
| 1895 | Lady Margaret Scott | 1905 | Bertha Thompson | 1915–19 | *not held* |
| 1896 | Amy Pascoe | 1906 | Mrs. W. Kennion | 1920 | Cecil Leitch |
| 1897 | Edith Orr | 1907 | May Hezlet | 1921 | Cecil Leitch |
| 1898 | Lena Thomson | 1908 | Maud Titterton | 1922 | Joyce Wethered |
| 1899 | May Hezlet | 1909 | Dorothy Campbell | 1923 | Doris Chambers |
| 1900 | Rhona Adair | 1910 | Elsie Grant-Suttie | 1924 | Joyce Wethered |
| 1901 | Mary Graham | 1911 | Dorothy Campbell | 1925 | Joyce Wethered |
| 1902 | May Hezlet | 1912 | Gladys Ravenscroft | 1926 | Cecil Leitch |

## Ladies' British Amateur Championship (continued)

| YEAR | WINNER | YEAR | WINNER | YEAR | WINNER |
|------|--------|------|--------|------|--------|
| 1927 | Simone de la Chaume (FRA) | 1956 | Wiffi Smith (USA) | 1981 | Belle Robertson |
| 1928 | Nanette le Blan (FRA) | 1957 | Philomena Garvey | 1982 | Kitrina Douglas |
| 1929 | Joyce Wethered | 1958 | Jessie Valentine | 1983 | Jill Thornhill |
| 1930 | Diana Fishwick | 1959 | Elizabeth Price | 1984 | Jody Rosenthal (USA) |
| 1931 | Enid Wilson | 1960 | Barbara McIntire (USA) | 1985 | Lillian Behan (IRE) |
| 1932 | Enid Wilson | 1961 | Marley Spearman | 1986 | Marnie McGuire |
| 1933 | Enid Wilson | 1962 | Marley Spearman | 1987 | Janet Collingham |
| 1934 | Helen Holm | 1963 | Brigitte Varangot (FRA) | 1988 | Joanne Furby |
| 1935 | Wanda Morgan | 1964 | Carol Sorenson (USA) | 1989 | Helen Dobson |
| 1936 | Pam Barton | 1965 | Brigitte Varangot (FRA) | 1990 | Julie Wade Hall |
| 1937 | Jessie Anderson | 1966 | Elizabeth Chadwick | 1991 | Valerie Michaud |
| 1938 | Helen Holm | 1967 | Elizabeth Chadwick | 1992 | Bernille Pedersen (DEN) |
| 1939 | Pam Barton | 1968 | Brigitte Varangot (FRA) | 1993 | Catriona Lambert |
| 1940–45 | not held | 1969 | Catherine Lacoste (FRA) | 1994 | Emma Duggleby |
| 1946 | Jean Hetherington | 1970 | Dinah Oxley | 1995 | Julie Wade Hall |
| 1947 | Babe Didrikson Zaharias (USA) | 1971 | Michelle Walker | 1996 | Kelli Kuehne (USA) |
| | | 1972 | Michelle Walker | 1997 | Alison Rose |
| 1948 | Louise Suggs (USA) | 1973 | Ann Irvin | 1998 | Kim Rostron |
| 1949 | Frances Stephens | 1974 | Carol Semple (USA) | 1999 | Marine Monnet (FRA) |
| 1950 | Lally de Saint Sauveur (FRA) | 1975 | Nancy Roth Syms (USA) | 2000 | Rebecca Hudson |
| 1951 | Catherine MacCann | 1976 | Cathy Panton | 2001 | Marta Prieto (ESP) |
| 1952 | Moira Paterson | 1977 | Angela Uzielli | 2002 | Rebecca Hudson |
| 1953 | Marlene Stewart (CAN) | 1978 | Edwina Kennedy (AUS) | 2003 | Elisa Serramia (ESP) |
| 1954 | Frances Stephens | 1979 | Maureen Madill | | |
| 1955 | Jessie Valentine | 1980 | Anne Quast Sander (USA) | | |

## United States Women's Amateur Championship

*Won by an American golfer except as indicated.*

| YEAR | WINNER | YEAR | WINNER | YEAR | WINNER |
|------|--------|------|--------|------|--------|
| 1895 | Mrs. C.S. Brown | 1933 | Virginia Van Wie | 1973 | Carol Semple |
| 1896 | Beatrix Hoyt | 1934 | Virginia Van Wie | 1974 | Cynthia Hill |
| 1897 | Beatrix Hoyt | 1935 | Glenna Collett Vare | 1975 | Beth Daniel |
| 1898 | Beatrix Hoyt | 1936 | Pamela Barton (GBR) | 1976 | Donna Horton |
| 1899 | Ruth Underhill | 1937 | Estelle Lawson Page | 1977 | Beth Daniel |
| 1900 | Frances C. Griscom | 1938 | Patty Berg | 1978 | Cathy Sherk (CAN) |
| 1901 | Genevieve Hecker | 1939 | Betty Jameson | 1979 | Cynthia Hill |
| 1902 | Genevieve Hecker | 1940 | Betty Jameson | 1980 | Juli Inkster |
| 1903 | Bessie Anthony | 1941 | Elizabeth Hicks | 1981 | Juli Inkster |
| 1904 | Georgianna M. Bishop | 1942–45 | not held | 1982 | Juli Inkster |
| 1905 | Pauline Mackay | 1946 | Babe Didrikson Zaharias | 1983 | Joanne Pacillo |
| 1906 | Harriot S. Curtis | 1947 | Louise Suggs | 1984 | Deb Richard |
| 1907 | Margaret Curtis | 1948 | Grace Lenczyk | 1985 | Michiko Hattori (JPN) |
| 1908 | Katherine Harley | 1949 | Dorothy Porter | 1986 | Kay Cockerill |
| 1909 | Dorothy I. Campbell | 1950 | Beverly Hanson | 1987 | Kay Cockerill |
| 1910 | Dorothy I. Campbell | 1951 | Dorothy Kirby | 1988 | Pearl Sinn |
| 1911 | Margaret Curtis | 1952 | Jacqueline Pung | 1989 | Vicki Goetze |
| 1912 | Margaret Curtis | 1953 | Mary Lena Faulk | 1990 | Pat Hurst |
| 1913 | Gladys Ravenscroft | 1954 | Barbara Romack | 1991 | Amy Fruhwirth |
| 1914 | Katherine Harley Jackson | 1955 | Patricia Lesser | 1992 | Vicki Goetze |
| 1915 | Florence Vanderbeck | 1956 | Marlene Stewart (CAN) | 1993 | Jill McGill |
| 1916 | Alexa Stirling | 1957 | JoAnne Gunderson | 1994 | Wendy Ward |
| 1917–18 | not held | 1958 | Anne Quast | 1995 | Kelli Kuehne |
| 1919 | Alexa Stirling | 1959 | Barbara McIntire | 1996 | Kelli Kuehne |
| 1920 | Alexa Stirling | 1960 | JoAnne Gunderson | 1997 | Silvia Cavalleri (ITA) |
| 1921 | Marion Hollins | 1961 | Anne Quast Sander | 1998 | Grace Park |
| 1922 | Glenna Collett | 1962 | JoAnne Gunderson | 1999 | Dorothy Delasin |
| 1923 | Edith Cummings | 1963 | Anne Quast Sander | 2000 | Marcy Newton |
| 1924 | Dorothy Campbell Hurd | 1964 | Barbara McIntire | 2001 | Meredith Duncan |
| 1925 | Glenna Collett | 1965 | Jean Ashley | 2002 | Becky Lucidi |
| 1926 | Helen Stetson | 1966 | JoAnne Gunderson Carner | 2003 | *to be held 4–10 August, Philadelphia Country Club, Gladwyne PA* |
| 1927 | Miriam Burns Horn | 1967 | Mary Lou Dill | | |
| 1928 | Glenna Collett | 1968 | JoAnne Gunderson Carner | | |
| 1929 | Glenna Collett | 1969 | Catherine Lacoste (FRA) | | |
| 1930 | Glenna Collett | 1970 | Martha Wilkinson | | |
| 1931 | Helen Hicks | 1971 | Laura Baugh | | |
| 1932 | Virginia Van Wie | 1972 | Mary Budke | | |

# World Cup

| YEAR | WINNER |
|---|---|
| 1953 | Argentina (Antonio Cerda and Roberto de Vicenzo) |
| 1954 | Australia (Peter Thomson and Kel Nagle) |
| 1955 | United States (Chick Harbert and Ed Furgol) |
| 1956 | United States (Ben Hogan and Sam Snead) |
| 1957 | Japan (Torakichi Nakamura and Koichi Ono) |
| 1958 | Ireland (Harry Bradshaw and Christy O'Connor) |
| 1959 | Australia (Peter Thomson and Kel Nagle) |
| 1960 | United States (Sam Snead and Arnold Palmer) |
| 1961 | United States (Sam Snead and Jimmy Demaret) |
| 1962 | United States (Sam Snead and Arnold Palmer) |
| 1963 | United States (Arnold Palmer and Jack Nicklaus) |
| 1964 | United States (Arnold Palmer and Jack Nicklaus) |
| 1965 | South Africa (Gary Player and Harold Henning) |
| 1966 | United States (Arnold Palmer and Jack Nicklaus) |
| 1967 | United States (Arnold Palmer and Jack Nicklaus) |
| 1968 | Canada (Al Balding and George Knudson) |
| 1969 | United States (Orville Moody and Lee Trevino) |
| 1970 | Australia (David Graham and Bruce Devlin) |
| 1971 | United States (Jack Nicklaus and Lee Trevino) |
| 1972 | Taiwan (Hsieh Min-nan and Lu Liang-huan) |
| 1973 | United States (Johnny Miller and Jack Nicklaus) |

| YEAR | WINNER |
|---|---|
| 1974 | South Africa (Bobby Cole and Dale Hayes) |
| 1975 | United States (Johnny Miller and Lou Graham) |
| 1976 | Spain (Seve Ballesteros and Manuel Piñero) |
| 1977 | Spain (Seve Ballesteros and Antonio Garrido) |
| 1978 | United States (John Mahaffey and Andy North) |
| 1979 | United States (Hale Irwin and John Mahaffey) |
| 1980 | Canada (Dan Halldorson and Jim Nelford) |
| 1981 | *not held* |
| 1982 | Spain (Manuel Piñero and Jose-Maria Cañizares) |
| 1983 | United States (Rex Caldwell and John Cook) |
| 1984 | Spain (Jose-Maria Cañizares and Jose Rivero) |
| 1985 | Canada (Dan Halldorson and Dave Barr) |
| 1986 | *not held* |
| 1987 | Wales (Ian Woosnam and David Llewellyn) |
| 1988 | United States (Ben Crenshaw and Mark McCumber) |
| 1989 | Australia (Peter Fowler and Wayne Grady) |
| 1990 | Germany (Bernhard Langer and Torsten Giedeon) |
| 1991 | Sweden (Anders Forsbrand and Per-Ulrik Johansson) |
| 1992 | United States (Fred Couples and Davis Love III) |
| 1993 | United States (Fred Couples and Davis Love III) |
| 1994 | United States (Fred Couples and Davis Love III) |
| 1995 | United States (Fred Couples and Davis Love III) |
| 1996 | South Africa (Ernie Els and Wayne Westner) |
| 1997 | Ireland (Padraig Harrington and Paul McGinley) |
| 1998 | England (Nick Faldo and David Carter) |
| 1999 | United States (Tiger Woods and Mark O'Meara) |
| 2000 | United States (Tiger Woods and David Duval) |
| 2001 | South Africa (Ernie Els and Retief Goosen) |
| 2002 | Japan (Shigeki Maruyama and Toshi Izawa) |
| 2003 | *to be held 11–16 November, Kiawah Island SC* |

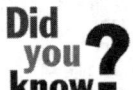

**Did you know?** In golf parlance, the "yips" describe the nervous twitching that golfers sometimes experience when putting. Golfer Tommy Armour coined the term in the 1930s.

# Curtis Cup

| YEAR | RESULT |
|---|---|
| 1932 | United States 5½, Britain 3½ |
| 1934 | United States 6½, Britain and Ireland 2½ |
| 1936 | United States* 4½, Britain and Ireland 4½ |
| 1938 | United States 5½, Britain and Ireland 3½ |
| 1940–46 | not held |
| 1948 | United States 6½, Britain and Ireland 2½ |
| 1950 | United States 7½, Britain and Ireland 2½ |
| 1952 | Britain and Ireland 5, United States 4 |
| 1954 | United States 6, Britain and Ireland 3 |
| 1956 | Britain and Ireland 5, United States 4 |
| 1958 | Britain and Ireland* 4½, United States 4½ |
| 1960 | United States 6½, Britain and Ireland 2½ |
| 1962 | United States 8, Britain and Ireland 1 |
| 1964 | United States 10½, Britain and Ireland 7½ |
| 1966 | United States 13, Britain and Ireland 5 |
| 1968 | United States 10½, Britain and Ireland 7½ |
| 1970 | United States 11½, Britain and Ireland 6½ |

| YEAR | RESULT |
|---|---|
| 1972 | United States 10, Britain and Ireland 8 |
| 1974 | United States 13, Britain and Ireland 5 |
| 1976 | United States 11½, Britain and Ireland 6½ |
| 1978 | United States 12, Britain and Ireland 6 |
| 1980 | United States 13, Britain and Ireland 5 |
| 1982 | United States 14½, Britain and Ireland 3½ |
| 1984 | United States 9½, Britain and Ireland 8½ |
| 1986 | Britain and Ireland 13, United States 5 |
| 1988 | Britain and Ireland 11, United States 7 |
| 1990 | United States 14, Britain and Ireland 4 |
| 1992 | Britain and Ireland 10, United States 8 |
| 1994 | Britain and Ireland 9, United States 9 |
| 1996 | Britain and Ireland 11½, United States 6½ |
| 1998 | United States 10, Britain and Ireland 8 |
| 2000 | United States 10, Britain and Ireland 8 |
| 2002 | United States 11, Britain and Ireland 7 |
| 2004 | *to be held 12-13 June, Formby Golf Club, Merseyside, England* |

*In case of a tie the defenders retain the cup.

# Gymnastics

Aside from the gymnastics events in **Olympic Games,** the most popular venue for gymnastics competition is the **world championship games.** Men's events are six in number with all-around individual and all-around team awards in addition. The latter two awards are given on a cumulative points basis. Women also have all-around team and individual awards, determined by their performance in four individual events.

**International Gymnastics Federation Web site:** <www.fig-gymnastics.com>

## World Gymnastics Championships—Men

| YEAR | ALL-AROUND TEAM | ALL-AROUND INDIVIDUAL | HORIZONTAL BAR | PARALLEL BARS |
|---|---|---|---|---|
| 1950 | Switzerland | Walter Lehmann (SUI) | Paavo Aaltonen (FIN) | Hans Eugster (SUI) |
| 1952* | USSR | Viktor Chukarin (URS) | Jack Günthard (SUI) | Hans Eugster (SUI) |
| 1954 | USSR | Valentin Muratov (URS) | Valentin Muratov (URS) | Viktor Chukarin (URS) |
| 1956* | USSR | Viktor Chukarin (URS) | Takashi Ono (JPN) | Viktor Chukarin (URS) |
| 1958 | USSR | Boris Shakhlin (URS) | Boris Shakhlin (URS) | Boris Shakhlin (URS) |
| 1960* | Japan | Boris Shakhlin (URS) | Takashi Ono (JPN) | Boris Shakhlin (URS) |
| 1962 | Japan | Yury Titov (URS) | Takashi Ono (JPN) | Miroslav Cerar (YUG) |
| 1964* | Japan | Yukio Endo (JPN) | Boris Shakhlin (URS) | Yukio Endo (JPN) |
| 1966 | Japan | Mikhail Voronin (URS) | Akinori Nakayama (JPN) | Sergey Diomidov (URS) |
| 1968* | Japan | Sawao Kato (JPN) | Mikhail Voronin (URS), Akinori Nakayama (JPN)† | Akinori Nakayama (JPN) |
| 1970 | Japan | Eizo Kenmotsu (JPN) | Eizo Kenmotsu (JPN) | Akinori Nakayama (JPN) |
| 1972* | Japan | Sawao Kato (JPN) | Mitsuo Tsukahara (JPN) | Sawao Kato (JPN) |
| 1974 | Japan | Shigeru Kasamatsu (JPN) | Eberhard Gienger (FRG) | Eizo Kenmotsu (JPN) |
| 1976* | Japan | Nikolay Andrianov (URS) | Mitsuo Tsukahara (JPN) | Sawao Kato (JPN) |
| 1978 | Japan | Nikolay Andrianov (URS) | Shigeru Kasamatsu (JPN) | Eizo Kenmotsu (JPN) |
| 1979 | USSR | Aleksandr Dityatin (URS) | Kurt Thomas (USA) | Bart Conner (USA) |
| 1980* | USSR | Aleksandr Dityatin (URS) | Stoyan Delchev (BUL) | Aleksandr Tkachyov (URS) |
| 1981 | USSR | Yury Korolyov (URS) | Aleksandr Tkachyov (URS) | Aleksandr Dityatin (URS), Koji Gushiken (JPN)† |
| 1983 | China | Dmitry Bilozerchev (URS) | Dmitry Bilozerchev (URS) | Lou Yun (CHN), Vladimir Artyomov (URS)† |
| 1984* | United States | Koji Gushiken (JPN) | Shinji Morisue (JPN) | Bart Conner (USA) |
| 1985 | USSR | Yury Korolyov (URS) | Tong Fei (CHN) | Sylvio Kroll (GDR), Valentin Mogilny (URS)† |
| 1987 | USSR | Dmitry Bilozerchev (URS) | Dmitry Bilozerchev (URS) | Vladimir Artyomov (URS) |
| 1988* | USSR | Vladimir Artyomov (URS) | Vladimir Artyomov (URS), Valery Lyukin (URS)† | Vladimir Artyomov (URS) |
| 1989 | USSR | Igor Korobchinsky (URS) | Li Chunyang (CHN) | Vladimir Artyomov (URS), Li Jing (CHN)† |
| 1991 | USSR | Grigory Misutin (URS) | Ralf Buechner (GER), Li Chunyang (CHN)† | Li Jing (CHN) |
| 1992 | ‡ | ‡ | Grigory Misutin (CIS) | Li Jing (CHN), Aleksey Voropayev (CIS)† |
| 1993 | ‡ | Vitaly Sherbo (BLR) | Sergey Charkov (RUS) | Vitaly Sherbo (BLR) |
| 1994 | China | Ivan Ivankov (BLR) | Vitaly Sherbo (BLR) | Liping Huang (CHN) |
| 1995 | China | Li Xiaoshuang (CHN) | Andreas Wecker (GER) | Vitaly Sherbo (BLR) |
| 1996 | ‡ | ‡ | Jesús Carballo (ESP) | Rustam Charipov (UKR) |
| 1997 | China | Ivan Ivankov (BLR) | Jani Tanskanen (FIN) | Zhang Jinjing (CHN) |
| 1999 | China | Nikolay Krukov (RUS) | Jesús Carballo (ESP) | Lee Joo Hyung (KOR) |
| 2000* | China | Aleksey Nemov (RUS) | Aleksey Nemov (RUS) | Li Xiaopeng (CHN) |
| 2001 | Belarus | Feng Jing (CHN) | Vlasios Maras (GRE) | Sean Townsend (USA) |
| 2003 | *The competition is scheduled to be held 16–24 Aug 2003, Anaheim CA.* | | | |

| YEAR | POMMEL HORSE | RINGS | VAULT | FLOOR EXERCISE |
|---|---|---|---|---|
| 1950 | Josef Stalder (SUI) | Walter Lehmann (SUI) | Ernst Gebendinger (SUI) | Josef Stalder (SUI) |
| 1952* | Viktor Chukarin (URS) | Grant Shaginyan (URS) | Viktor Chukarin (URS) | Karl Thoresson (SWE) |
| 1954 | Grant Shaginyan (URS) | Albert Azaryan (URS) | Leo Sotornik (TCH) | Valetin Muratov (URS), Masao Takemoto (JPN)† |
| 1956* | Boris Shakhlin (URS) | Albert Azaryan (URS) | Valentin Muratov (URS), Helmut Bantz (FRG)† | Valentin Muratov (URS) |
| 1958 | Boris Shakhlin (URS) | Albert Azaryan (URS) | Yury Titov (URS) | Masao Takemoto (JPN) |
| 1960* | Boris Shakhlin (URS), Eugen Ekman (FIN)† | Albert Azaryan (URS) | Takashi Ono (JPN), Boris Shakhlin (URS)† | Nobuyuki Aihara (JPN) |
| 1962 | Miroslav Cerar (YUG) | Yury Titov (URS) | Premysel Krbec (TCH) | Nobuyuki Aihara (JPN), Yukio Endo (JPN)† |
| 1964* | Miroslav Cerar (YUG) | Takuji Hayata (JPN) | Haruhiro Yamasita (JPN) | Franco Menichelli (ITA) |

# World Gymnastics Championships—Men (continued)

| YEAR | POMMEL HORSE | RINGS | VAULT | FLOOR EXERCISE |
|---|---|---|---|---|
| 1966 | Miroslav Cerar (YUG) | Mikhail Voronin (URS) | Haruhiro Matsuda (JPN) | Akinori Nakayama (JPN) |
| 1968* | Miroslav Cerar (YUG) | Akinori Nakayama (JPN) | Mikhail Voronin (URS) | Sawao Kato (JPN) |
| 1970 | Miroslav Cerar (YUG) | Akinori Nakayama (JPN) | Mitsuo Tsukahara (JPN) | Akinori Nakayama (JPN) |
| 1972* | Viktor Klimenko (URS) | Akinori Nakayama (JPN) | Klaus Koeste (GDR) | Nikolay Andrianov (URS) |
| 1974 | Zoltan Magyar (HUN) | Danut Grecu (ROM), Nikolay Andrianov (URS)† | Shigeru Kasamatsu (JPN) | Shigeru Kasamatsu (JPN) |
| 1976* | Zoltan Magyar (HUN) | Nikolay Andrianov (URS) | Nikolay Andrianov (URS) | Nikolay Andrianov (URS) |
| 1978 | Zoltan Magyar (HUN) | Nikolay Andrianov (URS) | Junichi Shimizu (JPN) | Kurt Thomas (USA) |
| 1979 | Zoltan Magyar (HUN) | Aleksandr Dityatin (URS) | Alexandr Dityatin (URS) | Kurt Thomas (USA), Roland Bruckner (GDR)† |
| 1980* | Zoltan Magyar (HUN) | Aleksandr Dityatin (URS) | Nikolay Andrianov (URS) | Roland Bruckner (GDR) |
| 1981 | Li Xiaoping (CHN), Michael Nikolay (GDR)† | Aleksandr Dityatin (URS) | Ralf-Peter Hemmann (GDR) | Li Yuijiu (CHN), Yury Korolyov (URS)† |
| 1983 | Dmitry Bilozerchev (URS) | Dmitry Bilozerchev (URS), Koji Gushiken (JPN)† | Arthur Akopyan (URS) | Tong Fei (CHN) |
| 1984* | Li Ning (CHN), Peter Vidmar (USA)† | Koji Gushiken (JPN), Li Ning (CHN)† | Lou Yun (CHN) | Li Ning (CHN) |
| 1985 | Valentin Mogilny (URS) | Li Ning (CHN), Yury Korolyov (URS)† | Yury Korolyov (URS) | Tong Fei (CHN) |
| 1987 | Dmitry Bilozerchev (URS), Zsolt Borkai (HUN)† | Yury Korolyov (URS) | Sylvio Kroll (GDR), Lou Yun (CHN)† | Lou Yun (CHN) |
| 1988* | Dmitry Bilozerchev (URS), Zsolt Borkai (HUN), Lyubomir Geraskov (BUL)† | Holger Behrendt (GDR), Dmitri Bilozerchev (URS)† | Lou Yun (CHN) | Sergey Kharkov (URS) |
| 1989 | Valentin Mogilny (URS) | Andreas Aguilar (FRG) | Joerg Behrend (GDR) | Igor Korobchinsky (URS) |
| 1991 | Valery Belenky (URS) | Grigory Misutin (URS) | You Ok Youl (KOR) | Igor Korobchinsky (URS) |
| 1992 | Pae Gil Su (PRK), Vitaly Sherbo (CIS), Li Jing (CHN)† | Vitaly Sherbo (CIS) | You Ok Youl (KOR) | Igor Korobchinsky (CIS) |
| 1993 | Pae Gil Su (PRK) | Yury Chechi (ITA) | Vitaly Sherbo (BLR) | Grigory Misutin (UKR) |
| 1994 | Marius Urzica (ROM) | Yury Chechi (ITA) | Vitaly Sherbo (BLR) | Vitaly Sherbo (BLR) |
| 1995 | Li Donghua (SUI) | Yury Chechi (ITA) | Aleksey Nemov (RUS), Grigory Misutin (UKR)† | Vitaly Sherbo (BLR) |
| 1996 | Pae Gil Su (PRK) | Yury Chechi (ITA) | Aleksey Nemov (RUS) | Vitaly Sherbo (BLR) |
| 1997 | Valery Belenki (GER) | Yury Chechi (ITA) | Sergey Fedorchenko (KAZ) | Aleksey Nemov (RUS) |
| 1999 | Aleksey Nemov (RUS) | Dong Zhen (CHN) | Li Xiaopeng (CHN) | Aleksey Nemov (RUS) |
| 2000* | Marius Urzica (ROM) | Szilveszter Csollany (HUN) | Gervasio Deferr (ESP) | Igor Vihrons (LAT) |
| 2001 | Marius Urzica (ROM) | Jordan Jovtchev (BUL) | Marian Dragulescu (ROM) | Jordan Jovtchev (BUL), Marian Dragulescu (ROM)† |

2003     *The competition is scheduled to be held 16–24 Aug 2003, Anaheim CA.*

*\*Olympic championships, recognized as world championships (for Olympic results 1896–1948, and from 1992, see Olympic Games).  †Tied.  ‡Not held.*

# World Gymnastics Championships—Women

| YEAR | ALL-AROUND TEAM | ALL-AROUND INDIVIDUAL | BALANCE BEAM | UNEVEN PARALLEL BARS |
|---|---|---|---|---|
| 1950 | Sweden | Helena Rakoczy (POL) | Helena Rakoczy (POL) | Gertchen Kolar (AUT), Anna Pettersson (SWE)* |
| 1952† | USSR | Mariya Gorokhovskaya (URS) | Nina Bocharova (URS) | Margit Korondi (HUN) |
| 1954 | USSR | Galina Rudiko (URS) | Keiko Tanaka (JPN) | Agnes Keleti (HUN) |
| 1956† | USSR | Larisa Latynina (URS) | Agnes Keleti (HUN) | Agnes Keleti (HUN) |
| 1958 | USSR | Larisa Latynina (URS) | Larisa Latynina (URS) | Larisa Latynina (URS) |
| 1960† | USSR | Larisa Latynina (URS) | Eva Bosakova (TCH) | Polina Astakhova (URS) |

# World Gymnastics Championships—Women (continued)

| YEAR | ALL-AROUND TEAM | ALL-AROUND INDIVIDUAL | BALANCE BEAM | UNEVEN PARALLEL BARS |
|------|-----------------|-----------------------|--------------|----------------------|
| 1962 | USSR | Larisa Latynina (URS) | Eva Bosakova (TCH) | Irina Pervushina (URS) |
| 1964† | USSR | Vera Caslavska (TCH) | Vera Caslavska (TCH) | Polina Astakhova (URS) |
| 1966 | Czechoslovakia | Vera Caslavska (TCH) | Natalya Kuchinskaya (URS) | Natalya Kuchinskaya (URS) |
| 1968† | USSR | Vera Caslavska (TCH) | Natalya Kuchinskaya (URS) | Vera Caslavska (TCH) |
| 1970 | USSR | Lyudmila Turishcheva (URS) | Erika Zuchold (GDR) | Karin Janz (GDR) |
| 1972† | USSR | Lyudmila Turishcheva (URS) | Olga Korbut (URS) | Karin Janz (GDR) |
| 1974 | USSR | Lyudmila Turishcheva (URS) | Lyudmila Turishcheva (URS) | Annelore Zinke (GDR) |
| 1976† | USSR | Nadia Comaneci (ROM) | Nadia Comaneci (ROM) | Nadia Comaneci (ROM) |
| 1978 | USSR | Yelena Mukhina (URS) | Nadia Comaneci (ROM) | Marcia Frederick (USA) |
| 1979 | Romania | Nelli Kim (URS) | Vera Cerna (TCH) | Ma Yanhong (CHN), Maxi Gnauck (GDR)* |
| 1980† | USSR | Yelena Davydova (URS) | Nadia Comaneci (ROM) | Maxi Gnauck (GDR) |
| 1981 | USSR | Olga Bicherova (URS) | Maxi Gnauck (GDR) | Maxi Gnauck (GDR) |
| 1983 | USSR | Natalya Yurchenko (URS) | Olga Mostepanova (URS) | Maxi Gnauck (GDR) |
| 1984† | Romania | Mary Lou Retton (USA) | Ecaterina Szabo (ROM), Simona Pauca (ROM)* | Julianne McNamara (USA), Ma Yanhong (CHN)* |
| 1985 | USSR | Yelena Shushunova (URS), Oksana Omelyanchik (URS)* | Daniela Silivas (ROM) | Gabriele Fahnrich (GDR) |
| 1987 | Romania | Aurelia Dobre (ROM) | Aurelia Dobre (ROM) | Daniela Silivas (ROM), Doerte Thuemmler (GDR)* |
| 1988† | USSR | Yelena Shushunova (URS) | Daniela Silivas (ROM) | Daniela Silivas (ROM) |
| 1989 | USSR | Svetlana Boginskaya (URS) | Daniela Silivas (ROM) | Fan Di (CHN), Daniela Silivas (ROM)* |
| 1991 | USSR | Kim Zmeskal (USA) | Svetlana Boginskaya (URS) | Kim Gwang Suk (PRK) |
| 1992 | ‡ | ‡ | Kim Zmeskal (USA) | Lavinia Milosovici (ROM) |
| 1993 | ‡ | Shannon Miller (USA) | Lavinia Milosovici (ROM) | Shannon Miller (USA) |
| 1994 | Romania | Shannon Miller (USA) | Shannon Miller (USA) | Li Luo (CHN) |
| 1995 | Romania | Liliya Podkopayeva (UKR) | Mo Huilan (CHN) | Svetlana Khorkina (RUS) |
| 1996 | ‡ | ‡ | Dina Kochetkova (RUS) | Svetlana Khorkina (RUS), Yelena Piskun (BLR)* |
| 1997 | Romania | Svetlana Khorkina (RUS) | Gina Gogean (ROM) | Svetlana Khorkina (RUS) |
| 1999 | Romania | Maria Olaru (ROM) | Ling Jie (CHN) | Svetlana Khorkina (RUS) |
| 2000† | Romania | Simona Amanar (ROM) | Liu Xuan (CHN) | Svetlana Khorkina (RUS) |
| 2001 | Romania | Svetlana Khorkina (RUS) | Andreea Raducan (ROM) | Svetlana Khorkina (RUS) |
| 2003 | *The competition is scheduled to be held 16–24 Aug 2003, Anaheim CA.* | | | |

| YEAR | VAULT | FLOOR EXERCISE |
|------|-------|----------------|
| 1950 | Helena Rakoczy (POL) | Helena Rakoczy (POL) |
| 1952† | Yekaterina Kalinchuk (URS) | Agnes Keleti (HUN) |
| 1954 | Anna Pettersson (SWE), Tamara Manina (URS)† | Tamara Manina (URS) |
| 1956† | Larisa Latynina (URS) | Larissa Latynina (URS), Agnes Keleti (HUN)* |
| 1958 | Larisa Latynina (URS) | Eva Bosakova (TCH) |
| 1960† | Margarita Nikolayeva (URS) | Larisa Latynina (URS) |
| 1962 | Vera Caslavska (TCH) | Larisa Latynina (URS) |
| 1964† | Vera Caslavska (TCH) | Larisa Latynina (URS) |
| 1966 | Vera Caslavska (TCH) | Natalya Kuchinskaya (URS) |
| 1968† | Vera Caslavska (TCH) | Vera Caslavska (TCH), Larisa Petrik (URS)* |
| 1970 | Erika Zuchold (GDR) | Lyudmila Turishcheva (URS) |
| 1972† | Karin Janz (GDR) | Olga Korbut (URS) |
| 1974 | Olga Korbut (URS) | Lyudmila Turishcheva (URS) |
| 1976† | Nelli Kim (URS) | Nelli Kim (URS) |
| 1978 | Nelli Kim (URS) | Yelena Mukhina (URS), Nelli Kim (URS)* |
| 1979 | Dumitrita Turner (ROM) | Emilia Eberle (ROM) |
| 1980† | Natalya Shaposhnikova (URS) | Nadia Comaneci (ROM), Nelli Kim (URS)* |
| 1981 | Maxi Gnauck (GDR) | Natalya Ilenko (URS) |
| 1983 | Boriana Stoyanova (BUL) | Ecaterina Szabo (ROM) |
| 1984† | Ecaterina Szabo (ROM) | Ecaterina Szabo (ROM) |
| 1985 | Yelena Shushunova (URS) | Oksana Omelyanchik (URS) |

## World Gymnastics Championships—Women (continued)

| YEAR | VAULT | FLOOR EXERCISE |
|---|---|---|
| 1987 | Yelena Shushunova (URS) | Yelena Shushunova (URS), Daniela Silivas (ROM)* |
| 1988† | Svetlana Boginskaya (URS) | Daniela Silivas (ROM) |
| 1989 | Olesia Dudnik (URS) | Svetlana Boginskaya (URS), Daniela Silivas (ROM)* |
| 1991 | Lavinia Milosovici (ROM) | Cristina Bontas (ROM), Oksana Chusovitina (URS)* |
| 1992 | Henrietta Onodi (HUN) | Kim Zmeskal (USA) |
| 1993 | Yelena Piskun (BLR) | Shannon Miller (USA) |
| 1994 | Gina Gogean (ROM) | Dina Kochetkova (RUS) |
| 1995 | Simona Amanar (ROM), Liliya Podkopayeva (UKR)* | Gina Gogean (ROM) |
| 1996 | Gina Gogean (ROM) | Gina Gogean (ROM), Kui Yuanyuan (CHN)* |
| 1997 | Simona Amanar (ROM) | Gina Gogean (ROM) |
| 1999 | Yelena Zamolodchikova (RUS) | Andreea Raducan (ROM) |
| 2000† | Yelena Zamolodchikova (RUS) | Yelena Zamolodchikova (RUS) |
| 2001 | Svetlana Khorkina (RUS) | Andreea Raducan (ROM) |
| 2003 | *The competition is scheduled to be held 16–24 Aug 2003, Anaheim CA.* | |

*Tied.　†Olympic championships, recognized as world championships (for 1896–1952 Olympics, see Olympic Games).　‡Not held.

# Horse Racing

In the **oldest type** of horse racing, the rider sits astride the horse; in the other type of race, best known as **harness racing**, the driver sits in a sulky—a two-wheeled vehicle attached by shafts and traces to the horse. In the former type, a **Thoroughbred** horse is raced over either a track or over a course of jumps and turns (**steeplechase**). Harness horses can be trotters or pacers and are Standardbred horses raced on a track.

**The English Thoroughbred classics.** The races are run by 3-year-old colts and fillies. **The Derby,** first run in 1780, is run at Epsom Downs, Surrey, over 1½ miles. **The Oaks** (for fillies only), also run at Epsom Downs, was first run in 1779; the oldest of the English races, however, is the **St. Leger** (1776). It is run over 1 mile 6½ furlongs at Doncaster, South Yorkshire. The **2,000 Guineas** (1809) is run over 1 mile at Newmarket, Suffolk. A horse that wins the 2,000 Guineas, the Derby, and the St. Leger all in one year is said to have won the **British Triple Crown.**

**The American Thoroughbred classics.** The **Kentucky Derby,** a **Triple Crown** event first run in 1875 and perhaps the best known of American horse races, is raced at Churchill Downs in Louisville KY, over a 10-furlong (1¼-mile) track. Another of the Triple Crown classics, the **Preakness Stakes,** was instituted in 1873; it is run over 9½ furlongs (1³⁄₁₆ miles) at Pimlico Race Track in Baltimore MD. The third Triple Crown event is the 12-furlong (1½-mile) **Belmont Stakes,** established in 1867. It is run at Belmont Park Race Track, Long Island NY. All three events are for 3-year-old horses.

**Australian Thoroughbred racing.** The Victoria Racing Club's **Melbourne Cup,** first run in 1861, is one of the world's great handicap races. The day on which it is held (the first Tuesday in November) is a public holiday in Melbourne.

**Dubai World Cup,** first run in 1996, is the world's richest horse race ($6 million in 2002). The 2,000-m (about 1¼-mi) race is held on the dirt track at the Nad Al Sheba Racecourse in Dubai, United Arab Emirates, and is open to four-year-old and older Thoroughbred horses.

The **Grand National,** the world's most significant and widely followed **steeplechase** race, has been run annually at Aintree Racecourse near Liverpool, England, since 1839. The race includes 30 jumps over a traditional distance of 4 miles 4 furlongs.

**Harness racing.** In the United States, the **Hambletonian Trot** is probably the most prestigious of harness races. It was established in 1926, was raced in New York, Kentucky, and Illinois, and is now run at The Meadowlands in New Jersey.

**Related Web sites:** US National Thoroughbred Racing Association: <www.ntra.com>; Fédération Equestre Internationale: <www.horsesport.org>; the magazine *Thoroughbred Times:* <www.thoroughbred times.com>; and <www.racingpost.co.uk>.

## Major Thoroughbred Race Winners 2002–03

### United States

| DATE | RACE | WINNER | JOCKEY |
|---|---|---|---|
| 14 Jul 2002 | Hollywood Gold Cup | Sky Jack | Laffit Pincay, Jr. |
| 14 Jul 2002 | Swaps Stakes | Came Home | Mike Smith |
| 20 Jul 2002 | Coaching Club American Oaks | Jilbab | Mike Luzzi |
| 27 Jul 2002 | Test Stakes | You | Jerry Bailey |
| 28 Jul 2002 | Eddie Read Handicap | Sarafan | Corey Nakatani |
| 28 Jul 2002 | Go for Wand Handicap | Dancethruthedawn | Jerry Bailey |
| 3 Aug 2002 | Whitney Handicap | Left Bank | John Velazquez |
| 4 Aug 2002 | Jim Dandy Stakes | Medaglia d'Oro | Jerry Bailey |
| 4 Aug 2002 | Haskell Invitational | War Emblem | Victor Espinoza |

# Major Thoroughbred Race Winners (continued)

### United States (continued)

| DATE | RACE | WINNER | JOCKEY |
|------|------|--------|--------|
| 10 Aug 2002 | Sword Dancer Invitational Handicap | With Anticipation | Pat Day |
| 17 Aug 2002 | Secretariat Stakes | Chiselling | Kent Desormeaux |
| 17 Aug 2002 | Arlington Million[1] | Beat Hollow | Jerry Bailey |
| 17 Aug 2002 | Beverly D. Stakes | Golden Apples | Pat Valenzuela |
| 17 Aug 2002 | Alabama Stakes | Farda Amiga | Pat Day |
| 23 Aug 2002 | Personal Ensign Handicap | Summer Colony | John Velazquez |
| 24 Aug 2002 | King's Bishop Stakes | Gygistar | John Velazquez |
| 24 Aug 2002 | Travers Stakes | Medaglia d'Oro | Jerry Bailey |
| 25 Aug 2002 | Pacific Classic | Came Home | Mike Smith |
| 25 Aug 2002 | Ballerina Handicap | Shine Again | Jean-Luc Samyn |
| 30 Aug 2002 | Spinaway Stakes | Awesome Humor | Pat Day |
| 31 Aug 2002 | Del Mar Debutante Stakes | Miss Houdini | Gary Stevens |
| 31 Aug 2002 | Hopeful Stakes | Sky Mesa | Edgar Prado |
| 1 Sep 2002 | Forego Handicap | Orientate | Jerry Bailey |
| 7 Sep 2002 | Gazelle Handicap | Imperial Gesture | José Santos |
| 7 Sep 2002 | Man o' War Stakes | With Anticipation | Pat Day |
| 7 Sep 2002 | Woodward Stakes | Lido Palace | Jorge Chávez |
| 14 Sep 2002 | Ruffian Handicap | Mandy's Gold | José Santos |
| 14 Sep 2002 | Kentucky Cup Classic | Pure Prize | Mike Smith |
| 15 Sep 2002 | Futurity Stakes | Whywhywhy | Edgar Prado |
| 15 Sep 2002 | Matron Stakes | Storm Flag Flying | John Velazquez |
| 21 Sep 2002 | Vosburgh Stakes | Bonapaw | Gerard Melancon |
| 21 Sep 2002 | Super Derby XXIII | Essence of Dubai | Jorge Chávez |
| 28 Sep 2002 | Jockey Club Gold Cup | Evening Attire | Shaun Bridgmohan |
| 28 Sep 2002 | Flower Bowl Invitational | Kazzia | Jorge Chávez |
| 29 Sep 2002 | Turf Classic Invitational | Denon | Edgar Prado |
| 5 Oct 2002 | Ancient Title Breeders' Cup Handicap | Kalookan Queen | Alex Solis |
| 5 Oct 2002 | Frizette Stakes | Storm Flag Flying | John Velazquez |
| 5 Oct 2002 | Champagne Stakes | Toccet | Jorge Chávez |
| 5 Oct 2002 | Beldame Stakes | Imperial Gesture | Jerry Bailey |
| 5 Oct 2002 | Yellow Ribbon Stakes | Golden Apples | Patrick Valenzuela |
| 6 Oct 2002 | Oak Leaf Stakes | Composure | Mike Smith |
| 6 Oct 2002 | Clement L. Hirsch Memorial Turf Championship | The Tin Man | Mike Smith |
| 6 Oct 2002 | Overbrook Spinster Stakes | Take Charge Lady | Edgar Prado |
| 12 Oct 2002 | Queen Elizabeth II Challenge Cup | Riskaverse | Mark Guidry |
| 26 Oct 2002 | Breeders' Cup Juvenile Fillies | Storm Flag Flying | John Velazquez |
| 26 Oct 2002 | Breeders' Cup Sprint | Orientate | Jerry Bailey |
| 26 Oct 2002 | Breeders' Cup Juvenile | Vindication | Mike Smith |
| 26 Oct 2002 | Breeders' Cup Mile | Domedriver | Thierry Thulliez |
| 26 Oct 2002 | Breeders' Cup Filly and Mare Turf | Starine | John Velazquez |
| 26 Oct 2002 | Breeders' Cup Turf[1] | High Chaparral | Michael Kinane |
| 26 Oct 2002 | Breeders' Cup Distaff | Azeri | Mike Smith |
| 26 Oct 2002 | Breeders' Cup Classic[1] | Volponi | José Santos |
| 16 Nov 2002 | Frank J. DeFrancis Memorial | D'Wildcat | Jorge Chávez |
| 23 Nov 2002 | Hollywood Turf Cup | Sligo Bay | Laffit Pincay, Jr. |
| 30 Nov 2002 | Cigar Mile Handicap | Congaree | Jerry Bailey |
| 1 Dec 2002 | Hollywood Derby | Johar | Alex Solis |
| 1 Dec 2002 | Matriarch Stakes | Dress to Thrill | Patrick Smullen |
| 21 Dec 2002 | Hollywood Futurity | Toccet | Jorge Chávez |
| 1 Feb 2003 | Charles H. Strub Stakes | Medaglia d'Oro | Jerry Bailey |
| 15 Feb 2003 | Fountain of Youth Stakes | Trust N Luck | Cornelio Velasquez |
| 22 Feb 2003 | Donn Handicap | Harlan's Holiday | John Velazquez |
| 1 Mar 2003 | Santa Anita Handicap | Milwaukee Brew | Edgar Prado |
| 8 Mar 2003 | Santa Anita Oaks | Composure | Jerry Bailey |
| 9 Mar 2003 | Louisiana Derby | Peace Rules | Edgar Prado |
| 15 Mar 2003 | Florida Derby | Empire Maker | Jerry Bailey |
| 22 Mar 2003 | Lane's End Spiral Stakes | New York Hero | Norberto Arroyo, Jr. |
| 29 Mar 2003 | Gulfstream Park Handicap | Hero's Tribute | Edgar Prado |
| 5 Apr 2003 | Ashland Stakes | Elloluv | Robby Albarado |
| 5 Apr 2003 | Santa Anita Derby | Buddy Gil | Gary Stevens |
| 5 Apr 2003 | Illinois Derby | Ten Most Wanted | Pat Day |
| 5 Apr 2003 | Oaklawn Handicap | Medaglia d'Oro | Jerry Bailey |
| 5 Apr 2003 | Apple Blossom Handicap | Azeri | Mike Smith |
| 12 Apr 2003 | Blue Grass Stakes | Peace Rules | Edgar Prado |
| 12 Apr 2003 | Arkansas Derby | Sir Cherokee | Terry Thompson |
| 12 Apr 2003 | Wood Memorial Stakes | Empire Maker | Jerry Bailey |

# Major Thoroughbred Race Winners (continued)

## United States (continued)

| DATE | RACE | WINNER | JOCKEY |
|------|------|--------|--------|
| 20 Apr 2003 | San Juan Capistrano Invitational Handicap | Passinetti | Brice Blanc |
| 2 May 2003 | Kentucky Oaks | Bird Town | Edgar Prado |
| 3 May 2003 | Kentucky Derby[2] | Funny Cide | José Santos |
| 10 May 2003 | Lone Star Derby | Dynever | Edgar Prado |
| 17 May 2003 | Preakness Stakes[2] | Funny Cide | José Santos |
| 26 May 2003 | Gamely Breeders' Cup Handicap | Tates Creek | Pat Valenzuela |
| 26 May 2003 | Metropolitan Mile Handicap | Aldebaran | Jerry Bailey |
| 26 May 2003 | Shoemaker Breeders' Cup Mile Stakes | Redattore | Alex Solis |
| 6 Jun 2003 | Acorn Stakes | Bird Town | Edgar Prado |
| 7 Jun 2003 | Belmont Stakes[2] | Empire Maker | Jerry Bailey |
| 14 Jun 2003 | Charles Whittingham Memorial Handicap | Storming Home | Gary Stevens |
| 14 Jun 2003 | Californian Stakes | Kudos | Alex Solis |
| 28 Jun 2003 | Mother Goose Stakes | Spoken Fur | Jerry Bailey |
| 5 Jul 2003 | United Nations Handicap | Balto Star | José Velez, Jr. |
| 5 Jul 2003 | Suburban Handicap | Mineshaft | Robby Albarado |
| 13 Jul 2003 | Hollywood Gold Cup | Congaree | Jerry Bailey |
| 19 Jul 2003 | Coaching Club American Oaks | Spoken Fur | Jerry Bailey |
| 26 Jul 2003 | Test Stakes | Lady Tak | Jerry Bailey |
| 26 Jul 2003 | Diana Handicap | Voodoo Dancer | Corey Nakatani |
| 27 Jul 2003 | Eddie Read Handicap | Special Ring | David Flores |
| 3 Aug 2003 | Jim Dandy Stakes | Strong Hope | John Velazquez |

## Canada

| DATE | RACE | WINNER | JOCKEY |
|------|------|--------|--------|
| 21 Jul 2002 | Prince of Wales Stakes[3] | Le Cinquieme Essai | Brian Bochinski |
| 10 Aug 2002 | Breeders' Stakes[3] | Portcullis | Slade Callaghan |
| 8 Sep 2002 | Atto Mile Stakes | Good Journey | Pat Day |
| 21 Sep 2002 | Mazarine Breeders' Cup Stakes | Brusque | Emile Ramsammy |
| 29 Sep 2002 | Canadian International Stakes[1] | Ballingarry | Michael Kinane |
| 22 Jun 2003 | Queen's Plate Stakes[3] | Wando | Patrick Husbands |
| 20 Jul 2003 | Prince of Wales Stakes[3] | Wando | Patrick Husbands |

## England

| DATE | RACE | WINNER | JOCKEY |
|------|------|--------|--------|
| 6 Jul 2002 | Coral-Eclipse Stakes | Hawk Wing | Michael Kinane |
| 11 Jul 2002 | Darley July Cup | Continent | Darryll Holland |
| 27 Jul 2002 | King George VI and Queen Elizabeth Diamond Stakes[1] | Golan | Kieren Fallon |
| 31 Jul 2002 | Sussex Stakes | Rock of Gibraltar | Michael Kinane |
| 20 Aug 2002 | Juddmonte International Stakes | Nayef | Richard Hills |
| 22 Aug 2002 | Nunthorpe Stakes | Kyllachy | Jamie Spencer |
| 14 Sep 2002 | St. Leger | Bollin Eric | Kevin Darley |
| 28 Sep 2002 | Queen Elizabeth II Stakes | Where or When | Kevin Darley |
| 19 Oct 2002 | Dubai Champion Stakes | Storming Home | Michael Hills |
| 3 May 2003 | Two Thousand Guineas | Refuse to Bend | Pat Smullen |
| 4 May 2003 | One Thousand Guineas | Russian Rhythm | Kieren Fallon |
| 6 Jun 2003 | Epsom Oaks | Casual Look | Martin Dwyer |
| 19 Jun 2003 | Ascot Gold Cup | Mr Dinos | Kieren Fallon |
| 5 Jul 2003 | Coral-Eclipse Stakes | Falbrav | Darryll Holland |
| 26 Jul 2003 | King George VI and Queen Elizabeth Diamond Stakes[1] | Alamshar | Johnny Murtagh |
| 30 Jul 2003 | Sussex Stakes | Reel Buddy | Pat Eddery |

## Ireland

| DATE | RACE | WINNER | JOCKEY |
|------|------|--------|--------|
| 30 Jun 2002 | Irish Derby | High Chaparral | Michael Kinane |
| 14 Jul 2002 | Irish Oaks | Margarula | Kevin Manning |
| 7 Sep 2002 | Irish Champion Stakes[1] | Grandera | Frankie Dettori |
| 14 Sep 2002 | Irish St. Leger | Vinnie Roe | Pat Smullen |
| 24 May 2003 | Irish Two Thousand Guineas | Indian Haven | John Egan |
| 25 May 2003 | Irish One Thousand Guineas | Yesterday | Michael Kinane |
| 29 Jun 2003 | Irish Derby | Alamshar | Johnny Murtagh |

## France

| DATE | RACE | WINNER | JOCKEY |
|------|------|--------|--------|
| 23 Jun 2002 | Grand Prix de Paris | Khalkevi | Christophe Soumillon |
| 30 Jun 2002 | Grand Prix de Saint-Cloud | Ange Gabriel | Thierry Jarnet |
| 18 Aug 2002 | Prix du Haras de Fresnay-le-Buffard | Banks Hill | Olivier Peslier |
| 15 Sep 2002 | Prix Niel | Sulamani | Thierry Thulliez |
| 6 Oct 2002 | Prix de l'Arc de Triomphe[1] | Marienbard | Frankie Dettori |

## Major Thoroughbred Race Winners (continued)

### France (continued)

| DATE | RACE | WINNER | JOCKEY |
|---|---|---|---|
| 6 Oct 2002 | Grand Criterium | Hold That Tiger | Kieren Fallon |
| 27 Oct 2002 | Prix Royal-Oak | Mr Dinos | Dominique Boeuf |
| 27 Apr 2003 | Prix Ganay | Fair Mix | Olivier Peslier |
| 11 May 2003 | Poule d'Essai des Poulains | Clodovil | Christophe Soumillon |
| 11 May 2003 | Poule d'Essai des Pouliches | Musical Chimes | Christophe Soumillon |
| 1 Jun 2003 | Prix du Jockey-Club | Dalakhani | Christophe Soumillon |
| 8 Jun 2003 | Prix de Diane | Nebraska Tornado | Richard Hughes |
| 22 Jun 2003 | Grand Prix de Paris | Vespone | Christophe Lemaire |
| 29 Jun 2003 | Grand Prix de Saint-Cloud | Ange Gabriel | Thierry Jarnet |

### Germany

| DATE | RACE | WINNER | JOCKEY |
|---|---|---|---|
| 7 Jul 2002 | Deutsches Derby | Next Desert | Andrasch Starke |
| 1 Sep 2002 | Grosser Preis von Baden[1] | Marienbard | Frankie Dettori |
| 22 Sep 2002 | Preis von Europa | Well Made | Terrence Hellier |
| 6 Jul 2003 | Deutsches Derby | Dai Jin | Olivier Peslier |

### Italy

| DATE | RACE | WINNER | JOCKEY |
|---|---|---|---|
| 20 Oct 2002 | Gran Premio del Jockey Club | Black Sam Bellamy | Michael Kinane |
| 25 May 2003 | Derby Italiano | Osorio | Mario Esposito |

### Australia

| DATE | RACE | WINNER | JOCKEY |
|---|---|---|---|
| 19 Oct 2002 | Caulfield Cup | Northerly | Greg Childs |
| 26 Oct 2002 | Cox Plate[1] | Northerly | Patrick Payne |
| 5 Nov 2002 | Melbourne Cup | Media Puzzle | Damien Oliver |

### United Arab Emirates

| DATE | RACE | WINNER | JOCKEY |
|---|---|---|---|
| 29 Mar 2003 | Godolphin Mile | Firebreak | Frankie Dettori |
| 29 Mar 2003 | UAE Derby | Victory Moon | Wayne Smith |
| 29 Mar 2003 | Dubai Sheema Classic | Sulamani | Frankie Dettori |
| 29 Mar 2003 | Dubai Golden Shaheen | State City | Michael Hills |
| 29 Mar 2003 | Dubai Duty Free | Ipi Tombe | Kevin Shea |
| 29 Mar 2003 | Dubai World Cup[1] | Moon Ballad | Frankie Dettori |

### Japan

| DATE | RACE | WINNER | JOCKEY |
|---|---|---|---|
| 24 Nov 2002 | Japan Cup[1] | Falbrav | Frankie Dettori |

### Hong Kong

| DATE | RACE | WINNER | JOCKEY |
|---|---|---|---|
| 15 Dec 2002 | Hong Kong Cup[1] | Precision | Michael Kinane |
| 27 Apr 2003 | Queen Elizabeth II Cup[1] | Eishin Preston | Yuichi Fukunaga |

### Singapore

| DATE | RACE | WINNER | JOCKEY |
|---|---|---|---|
| 17 May 2003 | International Cup[1] | *canceled due to SARS* | |

[1]*World Series race (14 races in 11 countries).*   [2]*American Triple Crown race.*   [3]*Canadian Triple Crown race.*

---

**Did you know?** Charles II (reigned 1660–85) became known as "the father of the English turf" and inaugurated the King's Plates, races for which prizes were awarded the winners. The horses raced were six years old and carried 168 pounds (76 kg), and the winner was the first to win two 4-mi (6.4-km) heats.

---

## Triple Crown Champions—United States

| YEAR | HORSE | YEAR | HORSE | YEAR | HORSE | YEAR | HORSE |
|---|---|---|---|---|---|---|---|
| 1919 | Sir Barton | 1937 | War Admiral | 1946 | Assault | 1977 | Seattle Slew |
| 1930 | Gallant Fox | 1941 | Whirlaway | 1948 | Citation | 1978 | Affirmed |
| 1935 | Omaha | 1943 | Count Fleet | 1973 | Secretariat | | |

# The Kentucky Derby

| YEAR | HORSE | JOCKEY | YEAR | HORSE | JOCKEY |
|---|---|---|---|---|---|
| 1875 | Aristides | Oliver Lewis | 1940 | Gallahadion | Carroll Bierman |
| 1876 | Vagrant | Bobby Swim | 1941 | Whirlaway | Eddie Arcaro |
| 1877 | Baden-Baden | William Walker | 1942 | Shut Out | Wayne D. Wright |
| 1878 | Day Star | Jimmy Carter | 1943 | Count Fleet | John Longden |
| 1879 | Lord Murphy | Charlie Shauer | 1944 | Pensive | Conn McCreary |
| 1880 | Fonso | George Garret Lewis | 1945 | Hoop Jr. | Eddie Arcaro |
| 1881 | Hindoo | James McLaughlin | 1946 | Assault | Warren Mehrtens |
| 1882 | Apollo | Babe Hurd | 1947 | Jet Pilot | Eric Guerin |
| 1883 | Leonatus | William Donohue | 1948 | Citation | Eddie Arcaro |
| 1884 | Buchanan | Isaac Murphy | 1949 | Ponder | Steve Brooks |
| 1885 | Joe Cotton | Erskine Henderson | 1950 | Middleground | William Boland |
| 1886 | Ben Ali | Paul Duffy | 1951 | Count Turf | Conn McCreary |
| 1887 | Montrose | Isaac Lewis | 1952 | Hill Gail | Eddie Arcaro |
| 1888 | Macbeth II | George Covington | 1953 | Dark Star | Henry Moreno |
| 1889 | Spokane | Thomas Kiley | 1954 | Determine | Raymond York |
| 1890 | Riley | Isaac Murphy | 1955 | Swaps | William Shoemaker |
| 1891 | Kingman | Isaac Murphy | 1956 | Needles | David Erb |
| 1892 | Azra | Alonzo Clayton | 1957 | Iron Liege | William Hartack |
| 1893 | Lookout | Eddie Kunze | 1958 | Tim Tam | Ismael Valenzuela |
| 1894 | Chant | Frank Goodale | 1959 | Tomy Lee | William Shoemaker |
| 1895 | Halma | James Perkins | 1960 | Venetian Way | William Hartack |
| 1896 | Ben Brush | Willie Simms | 1961 | Carry Back | John Sellers |
| 1897 | Typhoon II | Fred Garner | 1962 | Decidedly | William Hartack |
| 1898 | Plaudit | Willie Simms | 1963 | Chateaugay | Braulio Baeza |
| 1899 | Manuel | Fred Taral | 1964 | Northern Dancer | William Hartack |
| 1900 | Lieut. Gibson | Jimmy Boland | 1965 | Lucky Debonair | William Shoemaker |
| 1901 | His Eminence | James Winkfield | 1966 | Kauai King | Don Brumfield |
| 1902 | Alan-a-Dale | James Winkfield | 1967 | Proud Clarion | Robert Ussery |
| 1903 | Judge Himes | Harold Booker | 1968 | Forward Pass | Ismael Valenzuela |
| 1904 | Elwood | Frank Prior | 1969 | Majestic Prince | William Hartack |
| 1905 | Agile | Jack Martin | 1970 | Dust Commander | Mike Manganello |
| 1906 | Sir Huon | Roscoe Troxler | 1971 | Canonero II | Gustavo Avila |
| 1907 | Pink Star | Andy Minder | 1972 | Riva Ridge | Ron Turcotte |
| 1908 | Stone Street | Arthur Pickens | 1973* | Secretariat | Ron Turcotte |
| 1909 | Wintergreen | Vincent Powers | 1974 | Cannonade | Angel Cordero, Jr. |
| 1910 | Donau | Fred Herbert | 1975 | Foolish Pleasure | Jacinto Vasquez |
| 1911 | Meridian | George Archibald | 1976 | Bold Forbes | Angel Cordero, Jr. |
| 1912 | Worth | Carroll Hugh Shilling | 1977 | Seattle Slew | Jean Cruguet |
| 1913 | Donerail | Roscoe Goose | 1978 | Affirmed | Steve Cauthen |
| 1914 | Old Rosebud | John McCabe | 1979 | Spectacular Bid | Ronnie Franklin |
| 1915 | Regret | Joe Notter | 1980 | Genuine Risk | Jacinto Vasquez |
| 1916 | George Smith | John Loftus | 1981 | Pleasant Colony | Jorge Velasquez |
| 1917 | Omar Khayyam | Charles Borel | 1982 | Gato del Sol | Eddie Delahoussaye |
| 1918 | Exterminator | William Knapp | 1983 | Sunny's Halo | Eddie Delahoussaye |
| 1919 | Sir Barton | John Loftus | 1984 | Swale | Laffit Pincay, Jr. |
| 1920 | Paul Jones | Ted Rice | 1985 | Spend a Buck | Angel Cordero, Jr. |
| 1921 | Behave Yourself | Charles Thompson | 1986 | Ferdinand | William Shoemaker |
| 1922 | Morvich | Albert Johnson | 1987 | Alysheba | Chris McCarron |
| 1923 | Zev | Earl Sande | 1988 | Winning Colors | Gary Stevens |
| 1924 | Black Gold | John D. Mooney | 1989 | Sunday Silence | Patrick Valenzuela |
| 1925 | Flying Ebony | Earl Sande | 1990 | Unbridled | Craig Perret |
| 1926 | Bubbling Over | Albert Johnson | 1991 | Strike the Gold | Chris Antley |
| 1927 | Whiskery | Linus McAtee | 1992 | Lil E. Tee | Pat Day |
| 1928 | Reigh Count | Charles Lang | 1993 | Sea Hero | Jerry Bailey |
| 1929 | Clyde Van Dusen | Linus McAtee | 1994 | Go for Gin | Chris McCarron |
| 1930 | Gallant Fox | Earl Sande | 1995 | Thunder Gulch | Gary Stevens |
| 1931 | Twenty Grand | Charles Kurtsinger | 1996 | Grindstone | Jerry Bailey |
| 1932 | Burgoo King | Eugene James | 1997 | Silver Charm | Gary Stevens |
| 1933 | Brokers Tip | Don Meade | 1998 | Real Quiet | Kent Desormeaux |
| 1934 | Cavalcade | Mack Garner | 1999 | Charismatic | Chris Antley |
| 1935 | Omaha | William Saunders | 2000 | Fusaichi Pegasus | Kent Desormeaux |
| 1936 | Bold Venture | Ira Hanford | 2001 | Monarchos | Jorge Chávez |
| 1937 | War Admiral | Charles Kurtsinger | 2002 | War Emblem | Victor Espinoza |
| 1938 | Lawrin | Eddie Arcaro | 2003 | Funny Cide | José Santos |
| 1939 | Johnstown | James Stout | | | |

*Fastest time—1 min 59⅖ sec. No other horse has raced the Derby in less than 2 min.*

# The Preakness Stakes

| YEAR | HORSE | JOCKEY | YEAR | HORSE | JOCKEY |
|------|-------|--------|------|-------|--------|
| 1873 | Survivor | George Barbee | 1940 | Bimelech | Fred A. Smith |
| 1874 | Culpepper | William Donohue | 1941 | Whirlaway | Eddie Arcaro |
| 1875 | Tom Ochiltree | Lloyd Hughes | 1942 | Alsab | Basil James |
| 1876 | Shirley | George Barbee | 1943 | Count Fleet | John Longden |
| 1877 | Cloverbrook | Cyrus Holloway | 1944 | Pensive | Conn McCreary |
| 1878 | Duke of Magenta | Cyrus Holloway | 1945 | Polynesian | Wayne D. Wright |
| 1879 | Harold | Lloyd Hughes | 1946 | Assault | Warren Mehrtens |
| 1880 | Grenada | Lloyd Hughes | 1947 | Faultless | Doug Dodson |
| 1881 | Saunterer | T. Costello | 1948 | Citation | Eddie Arcaro |
| 1882 | Vanguard | T. Costello | 1949 | Capot | Ted Atkinson |
| 1883 | Jacobus | George Barbee | 1950 | Hill Prince | Eddie Arcaro |
| 1884 | Knight of Ellerslie | S. Fisher | 1951 | Bold | Eddie Arcaro |
| 1885 | Tecumseh | James McLaughlin | 1952 | Blue Man | Conn McCreary |
| 1886 | The Bard | S. Fisher | 1953 | Native Dancer | Eric Guerin |
| 1887 | Dunboyne | William Donohue | 1954 | Hasty Road | Johnny Adams |
| 1888 | Refund | F. Littlefield | 1955 | Nashua | Eddie Arcaro |
| 1889 | Buddhist | George Anderson | 1956 | Fabius | William Hartack |
| 1890 | Montague | W. Martin | 1957 | Bold Ruler | Eddie Arcaro |
| 1894[1] | Assignee | Fred Taral | 1958 | Tim Tam | Ismael Valenzuela |
| 1895 | Belmar | Fred Taral | 1959 | Royal Orbit | William Harmatz |
| 1896 | Margrave | Henry Griffin | 1960 | Bally Ache | Robert Ussery |
| 1897 | Paul Kauvar | T. Thorpe | 1961 | Carry Back | John Sellers |
| 1898 | Sly Fox | Willie Simms | 1962 | Greek Money | John L. Rotz |
| 1899 | Half Time | R. Clawson | 1963 | Candy Spots | William Shoemaker |
| 1900 | Hindus | H. Spencer | 1964 | Northern Dancer | William Hartack |
| 1901 | The Parader | Fred Landry | 1965 | Tom Rolfe | Ron Turcotte |
| 1902 | Old England | L. Jackson | 1966 | Kauai King | Don Brumfield |
| 1903 | Flocarline | W. Gannon | 1967 | Damascus | William Shoemaker |
| 1904 | Bryn Mawr | Eugene Hildebrand | 1968 | Forward Pass | Ismael Valenzuela |
| 1905 | Cairngorm | W. Davis | 1969 | Majestic Prince | William Hartack |
| 1906 | Whimsical | Walter Miller | 1970 | Personality | Eddie Belmonte |
| 1907 | Don Enrique | G. Mountain | 1971 | Canonero II | Gustavo Avila |
| 1908 | Royal Tourist | Eddie Dugan | 1972 | Bee Bee Bee | Eldon Nelson |
| 1909 | Effendi | Willie Doyle | 1973 | Secretariat | Ron Turcotte |
| 1910 | Layminster | R. Estep | 1974 | Little Current | Miguel Rivera |
| 1911 | Watervale | Eddie Dugan | 1975 | Master Derby | Darrel McHargue |
| 1912 | Colonel Holloway | C. Turner | 1976 | Elocutionist | John Lively |
| 1913 | Buskin | James Butwell | 1977 | Seattle Slew | Jean Cruguet |
| 1914 | Holiday | Andy Schuttinger | 1978 | Affirmed | Steve Cauthen |
| 1915 | Rhine Maiden | Douglas Hoffman | 1979 | Spectacular Bid | Ron Franklin |
| 1916 | Damrosch | Linus McAtee | 1980 | Codex | Angel Cordero, Jr. |
| 1917 | Kalitan | E. Haynes | 1981 | Pleasant Colony | Jorge Velasquez |
| 1918[2] | War Cloud | John Loftus | 1982 | Aloma's Ruler | Jack Kaenel |
|  | Jack Hare, Jr. | Charles Peak | 1983 | Deputed Testamony | Donald Miller |
| 1919 | Sir Barton | John Loftus | 1984 | Gate Dancer | Angel Cordero, Jr. |
| 1920 | Man o' War | Clarence Kummer | 1985[3] | Tank's Prospect | Pat Day |
| 1921 | Broomspun | Frank Coltiletti | 1986 | Snow Chief | Alex Solis |
| 1922 | Pillory | L. Morris | 1987 | Alysheba | Chris McCarron |
| 1923 | Vigil | Benny Marinelli | 1988 | Risen Star | Eddie Delahoussaye |
| 1924 | Nellie Morse | John Merimee | 1989 | Sunday Silence | Patrick Valenzuela |
| 1925 | Coventry | Clarence Kummer | 1990 | Summer Squall | Pat Day |
| 1926 | Display | John Maiben | 1991 | Hansel | Jerry Bailey |
| 1927 | Bostonian | A. Abel | 1992 | Pine Bluff | Chris McCarron |
| 1928 | Victorian | Raymond Workman | 1993 | Prairie Bayou | Mike Smith |
| 1929 | Dr. Freeland | Louis Schaefer | 1994 | Tabasco Cat | Pat Day |
| 1930 | Gallant Fox | Earl Sande | 1995 | Timber Country | Pat Day |
| 1931 | Mate | George Ellis | 1996 | Louis Quatorze | Pat Day |
| 1932 | Burgoo King | Eugene James | 1997 | Silver Charm | Gary Stevens |
| 1933 | Head Play | Charles Kurtsinger | 1998 | Real Quiet | Kent Desormeaux |
| 1934 | High Quest | Robert Jones | 1999 | Charismatic | Chris Antley |
| 1935 | Omaha | Willie Saunders | 2000 | Red Bullet | Jerry Bailey |
| 1936 | Bold Venture | George Woolf | 2001 | Point Given | Gary Stevens |
| 1937 | War Admiral | Charles Kurtsinger | 2002 | War Emblem | Victor Espinoza |
| 1938 | Dauber | Maurice Peters | 2003 | Funny Cide | José Santos |
| 1939 | Challedon | George Seabo |  |  |  |

[1]No competition 1891–93.    [2]Run in two divisions in 1918 because of the large number of starters.
[3]Fastest time—1 min 53⅖ sec.

# The Belmont Stakes

| YEAR | HORSE | JOCKEY | YEAR | HORSE | JOCKEY |
|------|-------|--------|------|-------|--------|
| 1867 | Ruthless | Gilbert Patrick | 1935 | Omaha | Willie Saunders |
| 1868 | General Duke | Bobby Swim | 1936 | Granville | James Stout |
| 1869 | Fenian | Charley Miller | 1937 | War Admiral | Charles Kurtsinger |
| 1870 | Kingfisher | Edward Brown | 1938 | Pasteurized | James Stout |
| 1871 | Harry Bassett | W. Miller | 1939 | Johnstown | James Stout |
| 1872 | Joe Daniels | James Rowe | 1940 | Bimelech | Fred A. Smith |
| 1873 | Springbok | James Rowe | 1941 | Whirlaway | Eddie Arcaro |
| 1874 | Saxon | George Barbee | 1942 | Shut Out | Eddie Arcaro |
| 1875 | Calvin | Bobby Swim | 1943 | Count Fleet | John Longden |
| 1876 | Algerine | Billy Donohue | 1944 | Bounding Home | Gayle L. Smith |
| 1877 | Cloverbrook | Cyrus Holloway | 1945 | Pavot | Eddie Arcaro |
| 1878 | Duke of Magenta | Lloyd Hughes | 1946 | Assault | Warren Mehrtens |
| 1879 | Spendthrift | George Evans | 1947 | Phalanx | Ruperto Donoso |
| 1880 | Grenada | Lloyd Hughes | 1948 | Citation | Eddie Arcaro |
| 1881 | Saunterer | T. Costello | 1949 | Capot | Ted Atkinson |
| 1882 | Forester | James McLaughlin | 1950 | Middleground | William Boland |
| 1883 | George Kinney | James McLaughlin | 1951 | Counterpoint | David Gorman |
| 1884 | Panique | James McLaughlin | 1952 | One Count | Eddie Arcaro |
| 1885 | Tyrant | Paul Duffy | 1953 | Native Dancer | Eric Guerin |
| 1886 | Inspector B | James McLaughlin | 1954 | High Gun | Eric Guerin |
| 1887 | Hanover | James McLaughlin | 1955 | Nashua | Eddie Arcaro |
| 1888 | Sir Dixon | James McLaughlin | 1956 | Needles | David Erb |
| 1889 | Eric | W. Hayward | 1957 | Gallant Man | William Shoemaker |
| 1890 | Burlington | Shelby Barnes | 1958 | Cavan | Pete Anderson |
| 1891 | Foxford | Edward Garrison | 1959 | Sword Dancer | William Shoemaker |
| 1892 | Patron | W. Hayward | 1960 | Celtic Ash | William Hartack |
| 1893 | Comanche | Willie Simms | 1961 | Sherluck | Braulio Baeza |
| 1894 | Henry of Navarre | Willie Simms | 1962 | Jaipur | William Shoemaker |
| 1895 | Belmar | Fred Taral | 1963 | Chateaugay | Braulio Baeza |
| 1896 | Hastings | Henry Griffin | 1964 | Quadrangle | Manuel Ycaza |
| 1897 | Scottish Chieftain | J. Scherrer | 1965 | Hail to All | John Sellers |
| 1898 | Bowling Brook | F. Littlefield | 1966 | Amberoid | William Boland |
| 1899 | Jean Bereaud | R. Clawson | 1967 | Damascus | William Shoemaker |
| 1900 | Ildrim | Nash Turner | 1968 | Stage Door Johnny | Heliodoro Gustines |
| 1901 | Commando | H. Spencer | 1969 | Arts and Letters | Braulio Baeza |
| 1902 | Masterman | John Bullman | 1970 | High Echelon | John Rotz |
| 1903 | Africander | John Bullman | 1971 | Pass Catcher | Walter Blum |
| 1904 | Delhi | George Odom | 1972 | Riva Ridge | Ron Turcotte |
| 1905 | Tanya | Eugene Hildebrand | 1973[2] | Secretariat | Ron Turcotte |
| 1906 | Burgomaster | Lucien Lyne | 1974 | Little Current | Miguel Rivera |
| 1907 | Peter Pan | G. Mountain | 1975 | Avatar | William Shoemaker |
| 1908 | Colin | Joe Notter | 1976 | Bold Forbes | Angel Cordero, Jr. |
| 1909 | Joe Madden | Eddie Dugan | 1977 | Seattle Slew | Jean Cruguet |
| 1910 | Sweep | James Butwell | 1978 | Affirmed | Steve Cauthen |
| 1913[1] | Prince Eugene | Roscoe Troxler | 1979 | Coastal | Ruben Hernandez |
| 1914 | Luke McLuke | Merritt Buxton | 1980 | Temperence Hill | Eddie Maple |
| 1915 | The Finn | George Byrne | 1981 | Summing | George Martens |
| 1916 | Friar Rock | E. Haynes | 1982 | Conquistador Cielo | Laffit Pincay, Jr. |
| 1917 | Hourless | James Butwell | 1983 | Caveat | Laffit Pincay, Jr. |
| 1918 | Johren | Frank Robinson | 1984 | Swale | Laffit Pincay, Jr. |
| 1919 | Sir Barton | John Loftus | 1985 | Creme Fraiche | Eddie Maple |
| 1920 | Man o' War | Clarence Kummer | 1986 | Danzig Connection | Chris McCarron |
| 1921 | Grey Lag | Earl Sande | 1987 | Bet Twice | Craig Perret |
| 1922 | Pillory | C.H. Miller | 1988 | Risen Star | Eddie Delahoussaye |
| 1923 | Zev | Earl Sande | 1989 | Easy Goer | Pat Day |
| 1924 | Mad Play | Earl Sande | 1990 | Go and Go | Michael Kinane |
| 1925 | American Flag | Albert Johnson | 1991 | Hansel | Jerry Bailey |
| 1926 | Crusader | Albert Johnson | 1992 | A.P. Indy | Eddie Delahoussaye |
| 1927 | Chance Shot | Earl Sande | 1993 | Colonial Affair | Julie Krone |
| 1928 | Vito | Clarence Kummer | 1994 | Tabasco Cat | Pat Day |
| 1929 | Blue Larkspur | Mack Garner | 1995 | Thunder Gulch | Gary Stevens |
| 1930 | Gallant Fox | Earl Sande | 1996 | Editor's Note | Rene Douglas |
| 1931 | Twenty Grand | Charles Kurtsinger | 1997 | Touch Gold | Chris McCarron |
| 1932 | Faireno | Tom Malley | 1998 | Victory Gallop | Gary Stevens |
| 1933 | Hurryoff | Mack Garner | 1999 | Lemon Drop Kid | José Santos |
| 1934 | Peace Chance | Wayne D. Wright | 2000 | Commendable | Pat Day |

## The Belmont Stakes (continued)

| 2001 | Point Given | Gary Stevens | 2003 | Empire Maker | Jerry Bailey |
| 2002 | Sarava | Edgar S. Prado | | | |

[1]No competition 1911–1912.    [2]Fastest time—2 min 24 sec.

## Horse of the Year

A Horse of the Year was selected by the *Daily Racing Form* from 1936 to 1970 and independently by the Thoroughbred Racing Association beginning in 1950. From 1971 these two organizations, plus the National Turf Writers Association, founded the Eclipse Awards, of which the Horse of the Year is the top among the 22 American prizes.

| YEAR | HORSE | YEAR | HORSE | YEAR | HORSE | YEAR | HORSE |
|------|-------|------|-------|------|-------|------|-------|
| 1936 | Granville | 1953 | Tom Fool | 1970 | Fort Marcy;* | 1987 | Ferdinand |
| 1937 | War Admiral | 1954 | Native Dancer | | Personality† | 1988 | Alysheba |
| 1938 | Seabiscuit | 1955 | Nashua | 1971 | Ack Ack | 1989 | Sunday Silence |
| 1939 | Challedon | 1956 | Swaps | 1972 | Secretariat | 1990 | Criminal Type |
| 1940 | Challedon | 1957 | Bold Ruler;* | 1973 | Secretariat | 1991 | Black Tie Affair |
| 1941 | Whirlaway | | Dedicate† | 1974 | Forego | 1992 | A.P. Indy |
| 1942 | Whirlaway | 1958 | Round Table | 1975 | Forego | 1993 | Kotashaan |
| 1943 | Count Fleet | 1959 | Sword Dancer | 1976 | Forego | 1994 | Holy Bull |
| 1944 | Twilight Tear | 1960 | Kelso | 1977 | Seattle Slew | 1995 | Cigar |
| 1945 | Busher | 1961 | Kelso | 1978 | Affirmed | 1996 | Cigar |
| 1946 | Assault | 1962 | Kelso | 1979 | Affirmed | 1997 | Favorite Trick |
| 1947 | Armed | 1963 | Kelso | 1980 | Spectacular Bid | 1998 | Skip Away |
| 1948 | Citation | 1964 | Kelso | 1981 | John Henry | 1999 | Charismatic |
| 1949 | Capot;* Coal-town† | 1965 | Roman Brother;* Moccasin† | 1982 | Conquistador Cielo | 2000 | Tiznow |
| 1950 | Hill Prince | 1966 | Buckpasser | 1983 | All Along | 2001 | Point Given |
| 1951 | Counterpoint | 1967 | Damascus | 1984 | John Henry | 2002 | Azeri |
| 1952 | One Count;* Native Dancer† | 1968 | Dr. Fager | 1985 | Spend a Buck | | |
| | | 1969 | Arts and Letters | 1986 | Lady's Secret | | |

*Daily Racing Form.    †Thoroughbred Racing Association.

## 2,000 Guineas

England's 2,000 Guineas race has been run since 1809. The table shows the winners for the past 20 years.

| YEAR | HORSE | JOCKEY | YEAR | HORSE | JOCKEY |
|------|-------|--------|------|-------|--------|
| 1984 | El Gran Señor | Pat Eddery | 1994 | Mister Baileys | Jason Weaver |
| 1985 | Shadeed | Lester Piggott | 1995 | Pennekamp | Thierry Jarnet |
| 1986 | Dancing Brave | Greville Starkey | 1996 | Mark of Esteem | Frankie Dettori |
| 1987 | Don't Forget Me | Willie Carson | 1997 | Entrepreneur | Michael Kinane |
| 1988 | Doyoun | Walter R. Swinburn | 1998 | King of Kings | Michael Kinane |
| 1989 | Nashwan | Willie Carson | 1999 | Island Sands | Frankie Dettori |
| 1990 | Tirol | Michael Kinane | 2000 | King's Best | Kieren Fallon |
| 1991 | Mystiko | Michael Roberts | 2001 | Golan | Kieren Fallon |
| 1992 | Rodrigo de Triano | Lester Piggot | 2002 | Rock of Gibraltar | Johnny Murtagh |
| 1993 | Zafonic | Pat Eddery | 2003 | Refuse To Bend | Pat Smullen |

## The Derby

The Derby has been run since 1780. The table shows the winners for the past 20 years.

| YEAR | HORSE | JOCKEY | YEAR | HORSE | JOCKEY |
|------|-------|--------|------|-------|--------|
| 1984* | Secreto | Christy Roche | 1994 | Erhaab | Willie Carson |
| 1985 | Slip Anchor | Steve Cauthen | 1995 | Lammtarra | Walter R. Swinburn |
| 1986 | Shahrastani | Walter R. Swinburn | 1996 | Shaamit | Michael Hills |
| 1987 | Reference Point | Steve Cauthen | 1997 | Benny the Dip | Willie Ryan |
| 1988 | Kahyasi | Ray Cochrane | 1998 | High Rise | Olivier Peslier |
| 1989 | Nashwan | Willie Carson | 1999 | Oath | Kieren Fallon |
| 1990 | Quest for Fame | Pat Eddery | 2000 | Sinndar | Johnny Murtagh |
| 1991 | Generous | Alan Munro | 2001 | Galileo | Michael Kinane |
| 1992 | Dr Devious | John Reid | 2002 | High Chaparral | Johnny Murtagh |
| 1993 | Commander in Chief | Michael Kinane | 2003 | Kris Kin | Kieren Fallon |

*Record time—2 min 12 sec.

## The St. Leger

*The St. Leger has been run since 1776. The table shows the winners for the past 20 years.*

| YEAR | HORSE | JOCKEY | YEAR | HORSE | JOCKEY |
|------|-------|--------|------|-------|--------|
| 1983 | Sun Princess | Willie Carson | 1994 | Moonax | Pat Eddery |
| 1984 | Comanche Run | Lester Piggott | 1995 | Classic Cliché | Frankie Dettori |
| 1985 | Oh So Sharp | Steve Cauthen | 1996 | Shantou | Frankie Dettori |
| 1986 | Moon Madness | Pat Eddery | 1997 | Silver Patriarch | Pat Eddery |
| 1987 | Reference Point | Steve Cauthen | 1998 | Nedawi | John Reid |
| 1988 | Minster Son | Willie Carson | 1999 | Mutafaweq | Richard Hills |
| 1989 | Michelozzo | Steve Cauthen | 2000 | Millenary | Richard Quinn |
| 1990 | Snurge | Richard Quinn | 2001 | Milan | Michael Kinane |
| 1991 | Toulon | Pat Eddery | 2002 | Bollin Eric | Kevin Darley |
| 1992 | User Friendly | George Duffield | 2003 | *to be held 13 September, Doncaster, England* | |
| 1993 | Bob's Return | Philip Robinson | | | |

## Triple Crown Champions—British

| YEAR | WINNER | YEAR | WINNER | YEAR | WINNER | YEAR | WINNER |
|------|--------|------|--------|------|--------|------|--------|
| 1853 | West Australian | 1891 | Common | 1900 | Diamond Jubilee | 1918 | Gainsborough |
| 1865 | Gladiateur | 1893 | Isinglass | 1903 | Rock Sand | 1935 | Bahram |
| 1866 | Lord Lyon | 1897 | Galtee More | 1915 | Pommern | 1970 | Nijinsky |
| 1886 | Ormonde | 1899 | Flying Fox | 1917 | Gay Crusader | | |

## Melbourne Cup

*The Melbourne Cup race has been run since 1861. The table shows the winners for the past 20 years.*

| YEAR | HORSE | JOCKEY | YEAR | HORSE | JOCKEY |
|------|-------|--------|------|-------|--------|
| 1983 | Kiwi | Jim Cassidy | 1994 | Jeune | Wayne Harris |
| 1984 | Black Knight | Peter Cook | 1995 | Doriemus | Damien Oliver |
| 1985 | What a Nuisance | Pat Hyland | 1996 | Saintly | Darren Beadman |
| 1986 | At Talaq | Michael Clarke | 1997 | Might and Power | Jim Cassidy |
| 1987 | Kensei | Larry Olsen | 1998 | Jezabeel | Chris Munce |
| 1988 | Empire Rose | Tony Allan | 1999 | Rogan Josh | John Marshall |
| 1989 | Tawrrific | Shane Dye | 2000 | Brew | Kerrin McEvoy |
| 1990 | Kingston Rule | Darren Beadman | 2001 | Ethereal | Scott Seamer |
| 1991 | Let's Elope | Steven King | 2002 | Media Puzzle | Damien Oliver |
| 1992 | Subzero | Greg Hall | 2003 | *to be held 4 November, Flemington, Australia* | |
| 1993 | Vintage Crop | Michael Kinane | | | |

## The Hambletonian Trot

| YEAR | HORSE | DRIVER | YEAR | HORSE | DRIVER |
|------|-------|--------|------|-------|--------|
| 1926 | Guy McKinney | Nat Ray | 1949 | Miss Tilly | Fred Egan |
| 1927 | Iosola's Worthy | Marvin Childs | 1950 | Lusty Song | Delvin Miller |
| 1928 | Spencer | William H. Leese | 1951 | Mainliner | Guy Crippen |
| 1929 | Walter Dear | Walter Cox | 1952 | Sharp Note | Bion Shively |
| 1930 | Hanover's Bertha | Thomas Berry | 1953 | Helicopter | Harry Harvey |
| 1931 | Calumet Butler | Richard D. McMahon | 1954 | Newport Dream | Adelbert Cameron |
| 1932 | The Marchioness | William Caton | 1955 | Scott Frost | Joseph O'Brien |
| 1933 | Mary Reynolds | Ben White | 1956 | The Intruder | Ned Bower |
| 1934 | Lord Jim | Hugh M. Parshall | 1957 | Hickory Smoke | John Simpson, Sr. |
| 1935 | Greyhound | Scepter F. Palin | 1958 | Emily's Pride | Flave Nipe |
| 1936 | Rosalind | Ben White | 1959 | Diller Hanover | Frank Ervin |
| 1937 | Shirley Hanover | Henry Thomas | 1960 | Blaze Hanover | Joseph O'Brien |
| 1938 | McLin Hanover | Henry Thomas | 1961 | Harlan Dean | James Arthur |
| 1939 | Peter Astra | Hugh M. Parshall | 1962 | A.C.'s Viking | Sanders Russell |
| 1940 | Spencer Scott | Fred Egan | 1963 | Speedy Scot | Ralph Baldwin |
| 1941 | Bill Gallon | Lee Smith | 1964 | Ayres | John Simpson, Sr. |
| 1942 | The Ambassador | Ben White | 1965 | Egyptian Candor | Adelbert Cameron |
| 1943 | Volo Song | Ben White | 1966 | Kerry Way | Frank Ervin |
| 1944 | Yankee Maid | Henry Thomas | 1967 | Speedy Streak | Adelbert Cameron |
| 1945 | Titan Hanover | Harry Pownall, Sr. | 1968 | Nevele Pride | Stanley Dancer |
| 1946 | Chestertown | Thomas Berry | 1969 | Lindy's Pride | Howard Beissinger |
| 1947 | Hoot Mon | Scepter F. Palin | 1970 | Timothy T. | John Simpson, Sr. |
| 1948 | Demon Hanover | Harrison Hoyt | 1971 | Speedy Crown | Howard Beissinger |

## The Hambletonian Trot (continued)

| YEAR | HORSE | DRIVER | YEAR | HORSE | DRIVER |
|------|-------|--------|------|-------|--------|
| 1972 | Super Bowl | Stanley Dancer | 1989* | Park Avenue Joe | Ronald Waples |
| 1973 | Flirth | Ralph Baldwin | | Probe | William Fahy |
| 1974 | Christopher T. | William Haughton | 1990 | Harmonious | John Campbell |
| 1975 | Bonefish | Stanley Dancer | 1991 | Giant Victory | Jack Moiseyev |
| 1976 | Steve Lobell | William Haughton | 1992 | Alf Palema | Mickey McNichol |
| 1977 | Green Speed | William Haughton | 1993 | American Winner | Ron Pierce |
| 1978 | Speedy Somolli | Howard Beissinger | 1994 | Victory Dream | Michel Lachance |
| 1979 | Legend Hanover | George Sholty | 1995 | Tagliabue | John Campbell |
| 1980 | Burgomeister | William Haughton | 1996 | Continentalvictory | Michel Lachance |
| 1981 | Shiaway St. Pat | Ray Remmen | 1997 | Malabar Man | Malvern Burroughs |
| 1982 | Speed Bowl | Tom Haughton | 1998 | Muscles Yankee | John Campbell |
| 1983 | Duenna | Stanley Dancer | 1999 | Self Possessed | Michel Lachance |
| 1984 | Historic Freight | Ben Webster | 2000 | Yankee Paco | Trevor Ritchie |
| 1985 | Prakas | William O'Donnell | 2001 | Scarlet Knight | Stefan Melander |
| 1986 | Nuclear Kosmos | Ulf Thoresen | 2002 | Chip Chip Hooray | Eric Ledford |
| 1987 | Mack Lobell | John Campbell | 2003 | Amigo Hall | Michel Lachance |
| 1988 | Armbro Goal | John Campbell | | | |

*Tied.

## The Dubai World Cup

| YEAR | HORSE | JOCKEY | YEAR | HORSE | JOCKEY |
|------|-------|--------|------|-------|--------|
| 1996 | Cigar | Jerry Bailey | 2001 | Captain Steve | Jerry Bailey |
| 1997 | Singspiel | Jerry Bailey | 2002 | Street Cry | Jerry Bailey |
| 1998 | Silver Charm | Gary Stevens | 2003 | Moon Ballad | Lanfranco Dettori |
| 1999 | Almutawakel | Richard Hills | 2004 | to be held 27 March, Dubai, UAE | |
| 2000 | Dubai Millennium | Lanfranco Dettori | | | |

# Ice Hockey

The **National Hockey League** (NHL), which was organized in Canada in 1917 with five professional teams, welcomed the first US team, the Boston Bruins, in 1924. Since 1926 the symbol of supremacy in professional hockey has been the **Stanley Cup**, which is awarded to the winner of a play-off that concludes the season of the National Hockey League. The Stanley Cup was presented to amateur champions from 1893 to 1925. The **World Hockey Championships**, contested by national teams and sponsored by the **International Ice Hockey Federation** (IIHF; founded 1908), has been held since 1930 for men and 1990 for women.

**Related Web sites:** National Hockey League: <www.nhl.com>; International Ice Hockey Federation: <www.iihf.com>

## World Hockey Championship—Men

| YEAR | WINNER | YEAR | WINNER | YEAR | WINNER | YEAR | WINNER |
|------|--------|------|--------|------|--------|------|--------|
| 1930 | Canada | 1954 | USSR | 1972† | Czechoslovakia | 1990 | Sweden |
| 1931 | Canada | 1955 | Canada | 1973 | USSR | 1991 | Sweden |
| 1932* | Canada | 1956* | USSR | 1974 | USSR | 1992 | Sweden |
| 1933 | United States | 1957 | Sweden | 1975 | USSR | 1993 | Russia |
| 1934 | Canada | 1958 | Canada | 1976 | Czechoslovakia | 1994 | Canada |
| 1935 | Canada | 1959 | Canada | 1977 | Czechoslovakia | 1995 | Finland |
| 1936* | Great Britain | 1960* | United States | 1978 | USSR | 1996 | Czech Republic |
| 1937 | Canada | 1961 | Canada | 1979 | USSR | 1997 | Canada |
| 1938 | Canada | 1962 | Sweden | 1980* | United States | 1998 | Sweden |
| 1939 | Canada | 1963 | USSR | 1981 | USSR | 1999 | Czech Republic |
| 1940–46 | not held | 1964* | USSR | 1982 | USSR | 2000 | Czech Republic |
| 1947 | Czechoslovakia | 1965 | USSR | 1983 | USSR | 2001 | Czech Republic |
| 1948* | Canada | 1966 | USSR | 1984* | USSR | 2002 | Slovakia |
| 1949 | Czechoslovakia | 1967 | USSR | 1985 | Czechoslovakia | 2003 | Canada |
| 1950 | Canada | 1968* | USSR | 1986 | USSR | 2004 | to be held 24 |
| 1951 | Canada | 1969 | USSR | 1987 | Sweden | | April–9 May |
| 1952* | Canada | 1970 | USSR | 1988 | USSR | | in the Czech |
| 1953 | Sweden | 1971 | USSR | 1989 | USSR | | Rep. |

*Olympic champions, recognized as world champions (for earlier Olympics, see Olympic Games).
†In 1972 a separate world championship was held for the first time.

## World Hockey Championship—Women

| YEAR | WINNER | YEAR | WINNER | YEAR | WINNER |
|------|--------|------|--------|------|--------|
| 1990 | Canada | 1998* | United States | 2002* | Canada |
| 1992 | Canada | 1999 | Canada | 2003 | canceled |
| 1994 | Canada | 2000 | Canada | 2004 | to be held 30 March–6 April |
| 1997 | Canada | 2001 | Canada | | in Halifax NS |

*Olympic champion; separate world championships have not been held in Olympic years. Olympic gold medalists are sometimes considered world champions.*

## National Hockey League (NHL) Final Standings, 2003

### EASTERN CONFERENCE

| Northeast Division | W | L | T | OTL* | Atlantic Division | W | L | T | OTL* | Southeast Division | W | L | T | OTL* |
|---|---|---|---|---|---|---|---|---|---|---|---|---|---|---|
| †Ottawa Senators | 52 | 21 | 8 | 1 | †New Jersey Devils | 46 | 20 | 10 | 6 | †Tampa Bay Lightning | 36 | 25 | 16 | 5 |
| †Toronto Maple Leafs | 44 | 28 | 7 | 3 | †Philadelphia Flyers | 45 | 20 | 13 | 4 | †Washington Capitals | 39 | 29 | 8 | 6 |
| †Boston Bruins | 36 | 31 | 11 | 4 | †New York Islanders | 35 | 34 | 11 | 2 | Atlanta Thrashers | 31 | 39 | 7 | 5 |
| †Montreal Canadiens | 30 | 35 | 8 | 9 | New York Rangers | 32 | 36 | 10 | 4 | Florida Panthers | 24 | 36 | 13 | 9 |
| Buffalo Sabres | 27 | 37 | 10 | 8 | Pittsburgh Penguins | 27 | 44 | 6 | 5 | Carolina Hurricanes | 22 | 43 | 11 | 6 |

### WESTERN CONFERENCE

| Central Division | W | L | T | OTL* | Northwest Division | W | L | T | OTL* | Pacific Division | W | L | T | OTL* |
|---|---|---|---|---|---|---|---|---|---|---|---|---|---|---|
| †Detroit Red Wings | 48 | 20 | 10 | 4 | †Colorado Avalanche | 42 | 19 | 13 | 8 | †Dallas Stars | 46 | 17 | 15 | 4 |
| †St. Louis Blues | 41 | 24 | 11 | 6 | †Vancouver Canucks | 45 | 23 | 13 | 1 | †Anaheim Mighty Ducks | 40 | 27 | 9 | 6 |
| †Chicago Blackhawks | 30 | 33 | 13 | 6 | Minnesota Wild | 42 | 29 | 10 | 1 | Los Angeles Kings | 33 | 37 | 6 | 6 |
| Nashville Predators | 27 | 35 | 13 | 7 | Edmonton Oilers | 36 | 26 | 11 | 9 | Phoenix Coyotes | 31 | 35 | 11 | 5 |
| Columbus Blue Jackets | 29 | 42 | 8 | 3 | Calgary Flames | 29 | 36 | 13 | 4 | San Jose Sharks | 28 | 37 | 9 | 8 |

*Overtime losses, worth one point. †Qualified for play-offs.*

## The Stanley Cup

| SEASON | WINNER | RUNNER-UP | GAMES |
|--------|--------|-----------|-------|
| 1892–93 | Montreal Amateur Athletic Association | no challengers | |
| 1893–94 | Montreal Amateur Athletic Association | Ottawa Generals | 2–0 |
| 1894–95 | Montreal Victorias | no challengers | |
| 1895–96 | Winnipeg Victorias (Feb.), Montreal Victorias (Dec.) | Montreal Victorias (Feb.), Winnipeg Victorias (Dec.) | 1–0, 1–0 |
| 1896–97 | Montreal Victorias | Ottawa Capitals | 1–0 |
| 1897–98 | Montreal Victorias | no challengers | |
| 1898–99 | Montreal Victorias (Feb.), Montreal Shamrocks (March) | Winnipeg Victorias (Feb.), Queen's University (March) | 2–0, 1–0 |
| 1899–1900 | Montreal Shamrocks | Winnipeg Victorias, Halifax Crescents | 2–1, 2–0 |
| 1900–01 | Winnipeg Victorias | Montreal Shamrocks | 2–0 |
| 1901–02 | Winnipeg Victorias (Jan.), Montreal Amateur Athletic Association (March) | Toronto Wellingtons (Jan.), Winnipeg Victorias (March) | 2–0, 2–1 |
| 1902–03 | Montreal Amateur Athletic Association (Feb.), Ottawa Silver Seven (March) | Winnipeg Victorias (Feb.), Montreal Victorias (March), Rat Portage Thistles (March) | 2–1, 1–0, 2–0 |
| 1903–04 | Ottawa Silver Seven | Winnipeg Rowing Club, Toronto Marlboros, Montreal Wanderers, Brandon Wheat Kings | 2–1, 2–0, tie, 2–0 |
| 1904–05 | Ottawa Silver Seven | Dawson City Nuggets, Rat Portage Thistles | 2–0, 2–1 |

# The Stanley Cup (continued)

| SEASON | WINNER | RUNNER-UP | GAMES |
|---|---|---|---|
| 1905–06 | Ottawa Silver Seven (Feb.), Montreal Wanderers (March, Dec.) | Queen's University (Feb.), Smiths Falls (Feb.), Ottawa Silver Seven (March), New Glasgow Cubs (Dec.) | 2–0, 2–0, 1–1, 2–0 |
| 1906–07 | Kenora Thistles (Jan.), Montreal Wanderers (March) | Montreal Wanderers (Jan.), Kenora Thistles (March) | 2–0, 1–1 |
| 1907–08 | Montreal Wanderers | Ottawa Victorias, Winnipeg Maple Leafs, Toronto Trolley Leaguers, Edmonton Eskimos | 2–0, 2–0, 1–0, 1–1 |
| 1908–09 | Ottawa Senators | *no challengers* | |
| 1909–10 | Montreal Wanderers, Ottawa Senators | Berlin Union Jacks, Edmonton Eskimos, Galt | 1–0, 2–0, 2–0 |
| 1910–11 | Ottawa Senators | Port Arthur Bearcats, Galt | 1–0, 1–0 |
| 1911–12 | Quebec Bulldogs | Moncton Victories | 2–0 |
| 1912–13[1] | Quebec Bulldogs | Sydney Miners | 2–0 |
| 1913–14 | Toronto Blueshirts | Victoria Cougars, Montreal Canadiens | 3–0, 1–1 |
| 1914–15 | Vancouver Millionaires | Ottawa Senators | 3–0 |
| 1915–16 | Montreal Canadiens | Portland Rosebuds | 3–2 |
| 1916–17 | Seattle Metropolitans | Montreal Canadiens | 3–1 |
| 1917–18 | Toronto Arenas | Vancouver Millionaires | 3–2 |
| 1918–19 | no decision[2] | | |
| 1919–20 | Ottawa Senators | Seattle Metropolitans | 3–2 |
| 1920–21 | Ottawa Senators | Vancouver Millionaires | 3–2 |
| 1921–22 | Toronto St. Pats | Vancouver Millionaires | 3–2 |
| 1922–23 | Ottawa Senators | Edmonton Eskimos, Vancouver Maroons | 2–0, 3–1 |
| 1923–24 | Montreal Canadiens | Calgary Tigers, Vancouver Maroons | 2–0, 2–0 |
| 1924–25 | Victoria Cougars | Montreal Canadiens | 3–1 |
| 1925–26 | Montreal Maroons | Victoria Cougars | 3–1 |
| 1926–27 | Ottawa Senators | Boston Bruins | 2–0 |
| 1927–28 | New York Rangers | Montreal Maroons | 3–2 |
| 1928–29 | Boston Bruins | New York Rangers | 2–0 |
| 1929–30 | Montreal Canadiens | Boston Bruins | 2–0 |
| 1930–31 | Montreal Canadiens | Chicago Black Hawks | 3–2 |
| 1931–32 | Toronto Maple Leafs | New York Rangers | 3–0 |
| 1932–33 | New York Rangers | Toronto Maple Leafs | 3–1 |
| 1933–34 | Chicago Black Hawks | Detroit Red Wings | 3–1 |
| 1934–35 | Montreal Maroons | Toronto Maple Leafs | 3–0 |
| 1935–36 | Detroit Red Wings | Toronto Maple Leafs | 3–1 |
| 1936–37 | Detroit Red Wings | New York Rangers | 3–2 |
| 1937–38 | Chicago Black Hawks | Toronto Maple Leafs | 3–1 |
| 1938–39 | Boston Bruins | Toronto Maple Leafs | 4–1 |
| 1939–40 | New York Rangers | Toronto Maple Leafs | 4–2 |
| 1940–41 | Boston Bruins | Detroit Red Wings | 4–0 |
| 1941–42 | Toronto Maple Leafs | Detroit Red Wings | 4–3 |
| 1942–43 | Detroit Red Wings | Boston Bruins | 4–0 |
| 1943–44 | Montreal Canadiens | Chicago Black Hawks | 4–0 |
| 1944–45 | Toronto Maple Leafs | Detroit Red Wings | 4–3 |
| 1945–46 | Montreal Canadiens | Boston Bruins | 4–1 |
| 1946–47 | Toronto Maple Leafs | Montreal Canadiens | 4–2 |
| 1947–48 | Toronto Maple Leafs | Detroit Red Wings | 4–0 |
| 1948–49 | Toronto Maple Leafs | Detroit Red Wings | 4–0 |
| 1949–50 | Detroit Red Wings | New York Rangers | 4–3 |
| 1950–51 | Toronto Maple Leafs | Montreal Canadiens | 4–1 |
| 1951–52 | Detroit Red Wings | Montreal Canadiens | 4–0 |
| 1952–53 | Montreal Canadiens | Boston Bruins | 4–1 |
| 1953–54 | Detroit Red Wings | Montreal Canadiens | 4–3 |
| 1954–55 | Detroit Red Wings | Montreal Canadiens | 4–3 |
| 1955–56 | Montreal Canadiens | Detroit Red Wings | 4–1 |
| 1956–57 | Montreal Canadiens | Boston Bruins | 4–1 |
| 1957–58 | Montreal Canadiens | Boston Bruins | 4–2 |
| 1958–59 | Montreal Canadiens | Toronto Maple Leafs | 4–1 |
| 1959–60 | Montreal Canadiens | Toronto Maple Leafs | 4–0 |
| 1960–61 | Chicago Black Hawks | Detroit Red Wings | 4–2 |
| 1961–62 | Toronto Maple Leafs | Chicago Black Hawks | 4–2 |
| 1962–63 | Toronto Maple Leafs | Detroit Red Wings | 4–1 |
| 1963–64 | Toronto Maple Leafs | Detroit Red Wings | 4–3 |
| 1964–65 | Montreal Canadiens | Chicago Black Hawks | 4–3 |
| 1965–66 | Montreal Canadiens | Detroit Red Wings | 4–2 |

## The Stanley Cup (continued)

| SEASON | WINNER | RUNNER-UP | GAMES |
|---|---|---|---|
| 1966–67 | Toronto Maple Leafs | Montreal Canadiens | 4–2 |
| 1967–68 | Montreal Canadiens | St. Louis Blues | 4–0 |
| 1968–69 | Montreal Canadiens | St. Louis Blues | 4–0 |
| 1969–70 | Boston Bruins | St. Louis Blues | 4–0 |
| 1970–71 | Montreal Canadiens | Chicago Black Hawks | 4–3 |
| 1971–72 | Boston Bruins | New York Rangers | 4–2 |
| 1972–73 | Montreal Canadiens | Chicago Black Hawks | 4–2 |
| 1973–74 | Philadelphia Flyers | Boston Bruins | 4–2 |
| 1974–75 | Philadelphia Flyers | Buffalo Sabres | 4–2 |
| 1975–76 | Montreal Canadiens | Philadelphia Flyers | 4–0 |
| 1976–77 | Montreal Canadiens | Boston Bruins | 4–0 |
| 1977–78 | Montreal Canadiens | Boston Bruins | 4–2 |
| 1978–79 | Montreal Canadiens | New York Rangers | 4–1 |
| 1979–80 | New York Islanders | Philadelphia Flyers | 4–2 |
| 1980–81 | New York Islanders | Minnesota North Stars | 4–1 |
| 1981–82 | New York Islanders | Vancouver Canucks | 4–0 |
| 1982–83 | New York Islanders | Edmonton Oilers | 4–0 |
| 1983–84 | Edmonton Oilers | New York Islanders | 4–1 |
| 1984–85 | Edmonton Oilers | Philadelphia Flyers | 4–1 |
| 1985–86 | Montreal Canadiens | Calgary Flames | 4–1 |
| 1986–87 | Edmonton Oilers | Philadelphia Flyers | 4–3 |
| 1987–88 | Edmonton Oilers | Boston Bruins | 4–0 |
| 1988–89 | Calgary Flames | Montreal Canadiens | 4–2 |
| 1989–90 | Edmonton Oilers | Boston Bruins | 4–1 |
| 1990–91 | Pittsburgh Penguins | Minnesota North Stars | 4–2 |
| 1991–92 | Pittsburgh Penguins | Chicago Black Hawks | 4–0 |
| 1992–93 | Montreal Canadiens | Los Angeles Kings | 4–1 |
| 1993–94 | New York Rangers | Vancouver Canucks | 4–3 |
| 1994–95 | New Jersey Devils | Detroit Red Wings | 4–0 |
| 1995–96 | Colorado Avalanche | Florida Panthers | 4–0 |
| 1996–97 | Detroit Red Wings | Philadelphia Flyers | 4–0 |
| 1997–98 | Detroit Red Wings | Washington Capitals | 4–0 |
| 1998–99 | Dallas Stars | Buffalo Sabres | 4–2 |
| 1999–2000 | New Jersey Devils | Dallas Stars | 4–2 |
| 2000–01 | Colorado Avalanche | New Jersey Devils | 4–3 |
| 2001–02 | Detroit Red Wings | Carolina Hurricanes | 4–1 |
| 2002–03 | New Jersey Devils | Mighty Ducks of Anaheim | 4–3 |
| 2003–04 | *will be held in May or June 2004* | | |

[1]*Though Victoria defeated Quebec in challenge games, Victoria's win was not officially recognized.*
[2]*Series called because of flu epidemic.*

---

**Did you know?** In the mid-1980s, research turned up mention of a hockeylike game played in the early 1800s in Nova Scotia by the Micmac Indians. The game appears to have been heavily influenced by the Irish game of hurling; it included the use of a "hurley" (stick) and a square wooden block instead of a ball.

---

# Ice Skating

The world governing body for ice skating, the **International Skating Union** (ISU; founded 1892), held the first world **figure skating competition** in 1896. Women's figure skating was not a separate event until 1906, and pairs championships were first held in 1908. Until 1991, individual competitors were judged on a set of **compulsory figures** as well as programs of **freestyle** moves. In 1991 the compulsory figures portion of the competition was eliminated, and judging was based on a short technical program and a long freestyle program. **Ice dancing**, officially introduced in 1950, is based on compulsory and freestyle movements—in this case, dances.

In contrast to figure skating and ice dancing, **speed skating** involves only two factors—speed and endurance. **Men** compete over distances of 500 m, 1,000 m, 1,500 m, 5,000 m, and 10,000 m. **Women,** who entered the sport several decades after men, compete over 500 m, 1,000 m, 1,500 m, 3,000 m, and 5,000 m. **World speed-skating sprint** championships for both men and women were inaugurated in 1972. **Short-track speed skating**—very different from distance skating in strategy and skill—is held indoors over distances of 500 m, 1,000 m, 1,500 m, and 3,000 m. The skater having the best combined results is the overall winner. Championships were held annually from 1978 to 1980 before being recognized by the ISU in 1981.

**International Skating Union Web site:** <www.isu.org>

## World Figure Skating Championship—Men

| YEAR | WINNER | YEAR | WINNER | YEAR | WINNER |
|------|--------|------|--------|------|--------|
| 1896 | Gilbert Fuchs (GER) | 1935 | Karl Schäfer (AUT) | 1975 | Sergey Volkov (URS) |
| 1897 | Gustav Hügel (AUT) | 1936 | Karl Schäfer (AUT) | 1976 | John Curry (GBR) |
| 1898 | Henning Grenander | 1937 | Felix Kaspar (AUT) | 1977 | Vladimir Kovalyov (URS) |
|      | (SWE) | 1938 | Felix Kaspar (AUT) | 1978 | Charles Tickner (USA) |
| 1899 | Gustav Hügel (AUT) | 1939 | Graham Sharp (GBR) | 1979 | Vladimir Kovalyov (URS) |
| 1900 | Gustav Hügel (AUT) | 1940–46 | not held | 1980 | Jan Hoffmann (GDR) |
| 1901 | Ulrich Salchow (SWE) | 1947 | Hans Gerschwiler (SUI) | 1981 | Scott Hamilton (USA) |
| 1902 | Ulrich Salchow (SWE) | 1948 | Richard Button (USA) | 1982 | Scott Hamilton (USA) |
| 1903 | Ulrich Salchow (SWE) | 1949 | Richard Button (USA) | 1983 | Scott Hamilton (USA) |
| 1904 | Ulrich Salchow (SWE) | 1950 | Richard Button (USA) | 1984 | Scott Hamilton (USA) |
| 1905 | Ulrich Salchow (SWE) | 1951 | Richard Button (USA) | 1985 | Aleksandr Fadeyev (URS) |
| 1906 | Gilbert Fuchs (GER) | 1952 | Richard Button (USA) | 1986 | Brian Boitano (USA) |
| 1907 | Ulrich Salchow (SWE) | 1953 | Hayes Alan Jenkins (USA) | 1987 | Brian Orser (CAN) |
| 1908 | Ulrich Salchow (SWE) | 1954 | Hayes Alan Jenkins (USA) | 1988 | Brian Boitano (USA) |
| 1909 | Ulrich Salchow (SWE) | 1955 | Hayes Alan Jenkins (USA) | 1989 | Kurt Browning (CAN) |
| 1910 | Ulrich Salchow (SWE) | 1956 | Hayes Alan Jenkins (USA) | 1990 | Kurt Browning (CAN) |
| 1911 | Ulrich Salchow (SWE) | 1957 | David Jenkins (USA) | 1991 | Kurt Browning (CAN) |
| 1912 | Fritz Kachler (AUT) | 1958 | David Jenkins (USA) | 1992 | Viktor Petrenko (UNT†) |
| 1913 | Fritz Kachler (AUT) | 1959 | David Jenkins (USA) | 1993 | Kurt Browning (CAN) |
| 1914 | Gösta Sandahl (SWE) | 1960 | Alain Giletti (FRA) | 1994 | Elvis Stojko (CAN) |
| 1915–21 | not held | 1961 | not held* | 1995 | Elvis Stojko (CAN) |
| 1922 | Gillis Grafström (SWE) | 1962 | Donald Jackson (CAN) | 1996 | Todd Eldredge (USA) |
| 1923 | Fritz Kachler (AUT) | 1963 | Donald McPherson (CAN) | 1997 | Elvis Stojko (CAN) |
| 1924 | Gillis Grafström (SWE) | 1964 | Manfred Schnelldorfer (FRG) | 1998 | Aleksey Yagudin (RUS) |
| 1925 | Willy Böckl (AUT) | 1965 | Alain Calmat (FRA) | 1999 | Aleksey Yagudin (RUS) |
| 1926 | Willy Böckl (AUT) | 1966 | Emmerich Danzer (AUT) | 2000 | Aleksey Yagudin (RUS) |
| 1927 | Willy Böckl (AUT) | 1967 | Emmerich Danzer (AUT) | 2001 | Yevgeny Plushchenko |
| 1928 | Willy Böckl (AUT) | 1968 | Emmerich Danzer (AUT) |      | (RUS) |
| 1929 | Gillis Grafström (SWE) | 1969 | Tim Wood (USA) | 2002 | Aleksey Yagudin (RUS) |
| 1930 | Karl Schäfer (AUT) | 1970 | Tim Wood (USA) | 2003 | Yevgeny Plushchenko |
| 1931 | Karl Schäfer (AUT) | 1971 | Ondrej Nepela (TCH) |      | (RUS) |
| 1932 | Karl Schäfer (AUT) | 1972 | Ondrej Nepela (TCH) | 2004 | to be held 22–28 |
| 1933 | Karl Schäfer (AUT) | 1973 | Ondrej Nepela (TCH) |      | March, Dortmund, |
| 1934 | Karl Schäfer (AUT) | 1974 | Jan Hoffmann (GDR) |      | Germany |

*The entire US team died in an airplane crash, and the championships were canceled.
†Unified Team, consisting of athletes from the Commonwealth of Independent States plus Georgia.

## World Figure Skating Championship—Women

| YEAR | WINNER | YEAR | WINNER | YEAR | WINNER |
|------|--------|------|--------|------|--------|
| 1906 | Madge Syers (GBR) | 1937 | Cecilia Colledge (GBR) | 1969 | Gabriele Seyfert (GDR) |
| 1907 | Madge Syers (GBR) | 1938 | Megan Taylor (GBR) | 1970 | Gabriele Seyfert (GDR) |
| 1908 | Lily Kronberger (HUN) | 1939 | Megan Taylor (GBR) | 1971 | Beatrix Schuba (AUT) |
| 1909 | Lily Kronberger (HUN) | 1940–46 | not held | 1972 | Beatrix Schuba (AUT) |
| 1910 | Lily Kronberger (HUN) | 1947 | Barbara Ann Scott (CAN) | 1973 | Karen Magnussen (CAN) |
| 1911 | Lily Kronberger (HUN) | 1948 | Barbara Ann Scott (CAN) | 1974 | Christine Errath (GDR) |
| 1912 | Opika von Meray Horvath | 1949 | Alena Vrzanova (TCH) | 1975 | Dianne de Leeuw (NED) |
|      | (HUN) | 1950 | Alena Vrzanova (TCH) | 1976 | Dorothy Hamill (USA) |
| 1913 | Opika von M. Horvath (HUN) | 1951 | Jeannette Altwegg (GBR) | 1977 | Linda Fratianne (USA) |
| 1914 | Opika von M. Horvath (HUN) | 1952 | Jacqueline du Bief (FRA) | 1978 | Anett Pötzsch (GDR) |
| 1915–21 | not held | 1953 | Tenley Albright (USA) | 1979 | Linda Fratianne (USA) |
| 1922 | Herma Planck-Szabo (AUT) | 1954 | Gundi Busch (GER) | 1980 | Anett Pötzsch (GDR) |
| 1923 | Herma Planck-Szabo (AUT) | 1955 | Tenley Albright (USA) | 1981 | Denise Biellmann (SUI) |
| 1924 | Herma Planck-Szabo (AUT) | 1956 | Carol Heiss (USA) | 1982 | Elaine Zayak (USA) |
| 1925 | Herma Planck-Szabo (AUT) | 1957 | Carol Heiss (USA) | 1983 | Rosalynn Sumners (USA) |
| 1926 | Herma Planck-Szabo (AUT) | 1958 | Carol Heiss (USA) | 1984 | Katarina Witt (GDR) |
| 1927 | Sonja Henie (NOR) | 1959 | Carol Heiss (USA) | 1985 | Katarina Witt (GDR) |
| 1928 | Sonja Henie (NOR) | 1960 | Carol Heiss (USA) | 1986 | Debi Thomas (USA) |
| 1929 | Sonja Henie (NOR) | 1961 | not held* | 1987 | Katarina Witt (GDR) |
| 1930 | Sonja Henie (NOR) | 1962 | Sjoukje Dijkstra (NED) | 1988 | Katarina Witt (GDR) |
| 1931 | Sonja Henie (NOR) | 1963 | Sjoukje Dijkstra (NED) | 1989 | Midori Ito (JPN) |
| 1932 | Sonja Henie (NOR) | 1964 | Sjoukje Dijkstra (NED) | 1990 | Jill Trenary (USA) |
| 1933 | Sonja Henie (NOR) | 1965 | Petra Burka (CAN) | 1991 | Kristi Yamaguchi (USA) |
| 1934 | Sonja Henie (NOR) | 1966 | Peggy Fleming (USA) | 1992 | Kristi Yamaguchi (USA) |
| 1935 | Sonja Henie (NOR) | 1967 | Peggy Fleming (USA) | 1993 | Oksana Baiul (UKR) |
| 1936 | Sonja Henie (NOR) | 1968 | Peggy Fleming (USA) | 1994 | Yuka Sato (JPN) |

## World Figure Skating Championship—Women (continued)

| YEAR | WINNER | YEAR | WINNER | YEAR | WINNER |
|------|--------|------|--------|------|--------|
| 1995 | Chen Lu (CHN) | 1999 | Maria Butyrskaya (RUS) | 2003 | Michelle Kwan (USA) |
| 1996 | Michelle Kwan (USA) | 2000 | Michelle Kwan (USA) | 2004 | *to be held 22–28* |
| 1997 | Tara Lipinski (USA) | 2001 | Michelle Kwan (USA) | | *March, Dortmund,* |
| 1998 | Michelle Kwan (USA) | 2002 | Irina Slutskaya (RUS) | | *Germany* |

*\*The entire US team died in an airplane crash, and the championships were canceled.*

## World Figure Skating Championship—Pairs

| YEAR | WINNERS | YEAR | WINNERS |
|------|---------|------|---------|
| 1908 | Anna Hübler, Heinrich Burger (GER) | 1964 | Marika Kilius, Hans-Jürgen Bäumler (FRG) |
| 1909 | Phyllis Johnson, James Johnson (GBR) | 1965 | Lyudmila Belousova, Oleg Protopopov (URS) |
| 1910 | Anna Hübler, Heinrich Burger (GER) | 1966 | Lyudmila Belousova, Oleg Protopopov (URS) |
| 1911 | Ludowika Eilers, Walter Jakobsson (FIN) | 1967 | Lyudmila Belousova, Oleg Protopopov (URS) |
| 1912 | Phyllis Johnson, James Johnson (GBR) | 1968 | Lyudmila Belousova, Oleg Protopopov (URS) |
| 1913 | Helene Engelmann, Karl Mejstrik (AUT) | 1969 | Irina Rodnina, Aleksey Ulanov (URS) |
| 1914 | Ludowika Jakobsson, Walter Jakobsson (FIN) | 1970 | Irina Rodnina, Aleksey Ulanov (URS) |
| 1915–21 | *not held* | 1971 | Irina Rodnina, Aleksey Ulanov (URS) |
| 1922 | Helene Engelmann, Alfred Berger (AUT) | 1972 | Irina Rodnina, Aleksey Ulanov (URS) |
| 1923 | Ludowika Jakobsson, Walter Jakobsson (FIN) | 1973 | Irina Rodnina, Aleksandr Zaytsev (URS) |
| 1924 | Helene Engelmann, Alfred Berger (AUT) | 1974 | Irina Rodnina, Aleksandr Zaytsev (URS) |
| 1925 | Herma Planck-Szabo, Ludwig Wrede (AUT) | 1975 | Irina Rodnina, Aleksandr Zaytsev (URS) |
| 1926 | Andrée Joly, Pierre Brunet (FRA) | 1976 | Irina Rodnina, Aleksandr Zaytsev (URS) |
| 1927 | Herma Planck-Szabo, Ludwig Wrede (AUT) | 1977 | Irina Rodnina, Aleksandr Zaytsev (URS) |
| 1928 | Andrée Joly, Pierre Brunet (FRA) | 1978 | Irina Rodnina, Aleksandr Zaytsev (URS) |
| 1929 | Lily Scholz, Otto Kaiser (AUT) | 1979 | Tai Babilonia, Randy Gardner (USA) |
| 1930 | Andrée Brunet, Pierre Brunet (FRA) | 1980 | Marina Cherkasova, Sergey Shakhray (URS) |
| 1931 | Emilia Rotter, Laszlo Szollas (HUN) | 1981 | Irina Vorobyova, Igor Lisovsky (URS) |
| 1932 | Andrée Brunet, Pierre Brunet (FRA) | 1982 | Sabine Baess, Tassilo Thierbach (GDR) |
| 1933 | Emilia Rotter, Laszlo Szollas (HUN) | 1983 | Yelena Valova, Oleg Vasilyev (URS) |
| 1934 | Emilia Rotter, Laszlo Szollas (HUN) | 1984 | Barbara Underhill, Paul Martini (CAN) |
| 1935 | Emilia Rotter, Laszlo Szollas (HUN) | 1985 | Yelena Valova, Oleg Vasilyev (URS) |
| 1936 | Maxi Herber, Ernst Baier (GER) | 1986 | Yekaterina Gordeyeva, Sergey Grinkov (URS) |
| 1937 | Maxi Herber, Ernst Baier (GER) | 1987 | Yekaterina Gordeyeva, Sergey Grinkov (URS) |
| 1938 | Maxi Herber, Ernst Baier (GER) | 1988 | Yelena Valova, Oleg Vasilyev (URS) |
| 1939 | Maxi Herber, Ernst Baier (GER) | 1989 | Yekaterina Gordeyeva, Sergey Grinkov (URS) |
| 1940–46 | *not held* | 1990 | Yekaterina Gordeyeva, Sergey Grinkov (URS) |
| 1947 | Micheline Lannoy, Pierre Baugniet (BEL) | 1991 | Natalya Mishkutyonok, Artur Dmitriyev (URS) |
| 1948 | Micheline Lannoy, Pierre Baugniet (BEL) | 1992 | Natalya Mishkutyonok, Artur Dmitriyev (UNT†) |
| 1949 | Andrea Kekessy, Ede Kiraly (HUN) | 1993 | Isabelle Brasseur, Lloyd Eisler (CAN) |
| 1950 | Karol Kennedy, Peter Kennedy (USA) | 1994 | Yevgeniya Shishkova, Vadim Naumov (RUS) |
| 1951 | Ria Baran, Paul Falk (FRG) | 1995 | Radka Kovarikova, René Novotny (CZE) |
| 1952 | Ria Falk, Paul Falk (FRG) | 1996 | Marina Yeltsova, Andrey Bushkov (RUS) |
| 1953 | Jennifer Nicks, John Nicks (GBR) | 1997 | Mandy Wötzel, Ingo Steur (GER) |
| 1954 | Frances Dafoe, Norris Bowden (CAN) | 1998 | Yelena Berezhnaya, Anton Sikharulidze (RUS) |
| 1955 | Frances Dafoe, Norris Bowden (CAN) | 1999 | Yelena Berezhnaya, Anton Sikharulidze (RUS) |
| 1956 | Elisabeth Schwarz, Kurt Oppelt (AUT) | 2000 | Mariya Petrova, Aleksey Tikhonov (RUS) |
| 1957 | Barbara Wagner, Robert Paul (CAN) | 2001 | Jamie Sale, David Pelletier (CAN) |
| 1958 | Barbara Wagner, Robert Paul (CAN) | 2002 | Xue Shen, Hongbo Zhao (CHN) |
| 1959 | Barbara Wagner, Robert Paul (CAN) | 2003 | Xue Shen, Hongbo Zhao (CHN) |
| 1960 | Barbara Wagner, Robert Paul (CAN) | 2004 | *to be held 22–28 March, Dortmund, Germany* |
| 1961 | *not held\** | | |
| 1962 | Maria Jelinek, Otto Jelinek (CAN) | | |
| 1963 | Marika Kilius, Hans-Jürgen Bäumler (FRG) | | |

*\*The entire US team died in an airplane crash, and the championships were canceled.    †Unified Team, consisting of athletes from the Commonwealth of Independent States plus Georgia.*

## World Ice Dancing Championships

| YEAR | WINNERS | YEAR | WINNERS |
|------|---------|------|---------|
| 1950 | Lois Waring, Michael McGean (USA) | 1953 | Jean Westwood, Lawrence Demmy (GBR) |
| 1951 | Jean Westwood, Lawrence Demmy (GBR) | 1954 | Jean Westwood, Lawrence Demmy (GBR) |
| 1952 | Jean Westwood, Lawrence Demmy (GBR) | 1955 | Jean Westwood, Lawrence Demmy (GBR) |

# World Ice Dancing Championships (continued)

| YEAR | WINNERS | YEAR | WINNERS |
|---|---|---|---|
| 1956 | Pamela Weight, Paul Thomas (GBR) | 1981 | Jayne Torvill, Christopher Dean (GBR) |
| 1957 | June Markham, Courtney Jones (GBR) | 1982 | Jayne Torvill, Christopher Dean (GBR) |
| 1958 | June Markham, Courtney Jones (GBR) | 1983 | Jayne Torvill, Christopher Dean (GBR) |
| 1959 | Doreen Denny, Courtney Jones (GBR) | 1984 | Jayne Torvill, Christopher Dean (GBR) |
| 1960 | Doreen Denny, Courtney Jones (GBR) | 1985 | Natalya Bestemyanova, Andrey Bukin (URS) |
| 1961 | *not held** | 1986 | Natalya Bestemyanova, Andrey Bukin (URS) |
| 1962 | Eve Romanova, Pavel Roman (TCH) | 1987 | Natalya Bestemyanova, Andrey Bukin (URS) |
| 1963 | Eve Romanova, Pavel Roman (TCH) | 1988 | Natalya Bestemyanova, Andrey Bukin (URS) |
| 1964 | Eve Romanova, Pavel Roman (TCH) | 1989 | Marina Klimova, Sergey Ponomarenko (URS) |
| 1965 | Eve Romanova, Pavel Roman (TCH) | 1990 | Marina Klimova, Sergey Ponomarenko (URS) |
| 1966 | Diane Towler, Bernard Ford (GBR) | 1991 | Isabelle Duchesnay, Paul Duchesnay (FRA) |
| 1967 | Diane Towler, Bernard Ford (GBR) | 1992 | Marina Klimova, Sergey Ponomarenko |
| 1968 | Diane Towler, Bernard Ford (GBR) | | (UNT†) |
| 1969 | Diane Towler, Bernard Ford (GBR) | 1993 | Maya Usova, Aleksandr Zhulin (RUS) |
| 1970 | Lyudmila Pakhomova, Aleksandr Gorshkov (URS) | 1994 | Oksana Grichuk, Yevgeny Platov (RUS) |
| | | 1995 | Oksana Grichuk, Yevgeny Platov (RUS) |
| 1971 | L. Pakhomova, A. Gorshkov (URS) | 1996 | Oksana Grichuk, Yevgeny Platov (RUS) |
| 1972 | L. Pakhomova, A. Gorshkov (URS) | 1997 | Oksana Grichuk, Yevgeny Platov (RUS) |
| 1973 | L. Pakhomova, A. Gorshkov (URS) | 1998 | Angelika Krylova, Oleg Ovsyannikov (RUS) |
| 1974 | L. Pakhomova, A. Gorshkov (URS) | 1999 | Angelika Krylova, Oleg Ovsyannikov (RUS) |
| 1975 | Irina Moiseyeva, Andrey Minenkov (URS) | 2000 | Marina Anissina, Gwendal Peizarat (FRA) |
| 1976 | L. Pakhomova, A. Gorshkov (URS) | 2001 | Barbara Fusar-Poli, Maurizio Margaglio (ITA) |
| 1977 | Irina Moiseyeva, Andrey Minenkov (URS) | 2002 | Irina Lobachyova, Ilya Averbukh (RUS) |
| 1978 | Natalya Linichuk, Gennady Karponosov (URS) | 2003 | Shae-Lynn Bourne, Victor Kraatz (CAN) |
| | | 2004 | *to be held 22–28 March, Dortmund,* |
| 1979 | N. Linichuk, G. Karponosov (URS) | | *Germany* |
| 1980 | Krisztina Regoczy, Andras Sallay (HUN) | | |

*The entire US team died in an airplane crash, and the championships were canceled.*
*†Unified Team, consisting of athletes from the Commonwealth of Independent States plus Georgia.*

# Speed Skating World Records (Major Tracks)

## men

| EVENT | RECORD HOLDER (NATIONALITY) | PERFORMANCE | DATE |
|---|---|---|---|
| 500 m | Hiroyasu Shimizu (JPN) | 34.32 sec | 10 Mar 2001 |
| 1,000 m | Gerard van Velde (NED) | 1 min 7.18 sec | 16 Feb 2002 |
| 1,500 m | Derek Parra (USA) | 1 min 43.95 sec | 19 Feb 2002 |
| 3,000 m | Gianni Romme (NED) | 3 min 42.75 sec | 11 Aug 2000 |
| 5,000 m | Jochem Uytdehaage (NED) | 6 min 14.66 sec | 9 Feb 2002 |
| 10,000 m | Jochem Uytdehaage (NED) | 12 min 58.92 sec | 22 Feb 2002 |

## women

| EVENT | RECORD HOLDER (NATIONALITY) | PERFORMANCE | DATE |
|---|---|---|---|
| 500 m | Catriona LeMay Doan (CAN) | 37.22 sec | 9 Dec 2001 |
| 1,000 m | Christine Witty (USA) | 1 min 13.83 sec | 17 Feb 2002 |
| 1,500 m | Anni Friesinger (GER) | 1 min 54.02 sec | 20 Feb 2002 |
| 3,000 m | Claudia Pechstein (GER) | 3 min 57.70 sec | 10 Feb 2002 |
| 5,000 m | Claudia Pechstein (GER) | 6 min 46.91 sec | 23 Feb 2002 |

# Speed Skating World Records (Short Tracks)

## men

| EVENT | RECORD HOLDER (NATIONALITY) | PERFORMANCE | DATE |
|---|---|---|---|
| 500 m | Jeff Scholten (CAN) | 41.289 sec | 8 Mar 2003 |
| 1,000 m | Jean-François Monette (CAN) | 1 min 25.662 sec | 9 Mar 2003 |
| 1,500 m | Steve Robillard (CAN) | 2 min 12.234 sec | 17 Oct 2002 |
| 3,000 m | Steve Robillard (CAN) | 4 min 38.061 sec | 17 Oct 2002 |
| 5,000-m relay | Canada National Team | 6 min 43.730 sec | 14 Oct 2001 |

## women

| EVENT | RECORD HOLDER (NATIONALITY) | PERFORMANCE | DATE |
|---|---|---|---|
| 500 m | Evgeniya Radanova (BUL) | 43.671 sec | 19 Oct 2001 |
| 1,000 m | Chun-Sa Byun (KOR) | 1 min 30.483 sec | 12 Jan 2003 |
| 1,500 m | Choi Eun Kyung (KOR) | 2 min 21.069 sec | 13 Feb 2002 |
| 3,000 m | Choi Eun Kyung (KOR) | 5 min 01.976 sec | 22 Oct 2000 |
| 3,000-m relay | South Korea National Team | 4 min 12.793 sec | 20 Feb 2002 |

## World All-Around Speed-Skating Championship—Men

*There was no winner in 1894, 1902, 1903, 1906, and 1907. Before the points system was established, only a contestant who had won at least three of the four events was considered the all-around champion.*

| YEAR | WINNER | YEAR | WINNER | YEAR | WINNER |
|------|--------|------|--------|------|--------|
| 1893 | Jaap Eden (NED) | 1936 | Ivar Ballangrud (NOR) | 1975 | Harm Kuipers (NED) |
| 1895 | Jaap Eden (NED) | 1937 | Michael Staksrud (NOR) | 1976 | Piet Kleine (NED) |
| 1896 | Jaap Eden (NED) | 1938 | Ivar Ballangrud (NOR) | 1977 | Eric Heiden (USA) |
| 1897 | Jack K. McCullock (CAN) | 1939 | Birger Wasenius (FIN) | 1978 | Eric Heiden (USA) |
| 1898 | Peder Østlund (NOR) | 1940– | *no competition* | 1979 | Eric Heiden (USA) |
| 1899 | Peder Østlund (NOR) | 46 | | 1980 | Hilbert van der Duim |
| 1900 | Edvard Engelsaas (NOR) | 1947 | Lassi Parkkinnen (FIN) | | (NED) |
| 1901 | Franz Wathen (FIN) | 1948 | Odd Lundberg (NOR) | 1981 | Amund Sjøbrend (NOR) |
| 1904 | Sigurd Mathisen (NOR) | 1949 | Kornel Pajor (HUN) | 1982 | Hilbert van der Duim |
| 1905 | C. Coen de Koning (NED) | 1950 | Hjalmar Andersen (NOR) | | (NED) |
| 1908 | Oscar Mathisen (NOR) | 1951 | Hjalmar Andersen (NOR) | 1983 | Rolf Falk-Larssen (NOR) |
| 1909 | Oscar Mathisen (NOR) | 1952 | Hjalmar Andersen (NOR) | 1984 | Oleg Bozhyev (URS) |
| 1910 | Nikolay Strunnikov (RUS) | 1953 | Oleg Goncharenko (URS) | 1985 | Hein Vergeer (NED) |
| 1911 | Nikolay Strunnikov (RUS) | 1954 | Boris Shilkov (URS) | 1986 | Hein Vergeer (NED) |
| 1912 | Oscar Mathisen (NOR) | 1955 | Sigvard Ericsson (SWE) | 1987 | Nikolai Gulyaev (URS) |
| 1913 | Oscar Mathisen (NOR) | 1956 | Oleg Goncharenko (URS) | 1988 | Eric Flaim (USA) |
| 1914 | Oscar Mathisen (NOR) | 1957 | Knut Johannesen (NOR) | 1989 | Leo Visser (NED) |
| 1915– | *no competition* | 1958 | Oleg Goncharenko (URS) | 1990 | Johann Olav Koss (NOR) |
| 21 | | 1959 | Juhani Jäevinen (FIN) | 1991 | Johann Olav Koss (NOR) |
| 1922 | Harald Strom (NOR) | 1960 | Boris Stenin (URS) | 1992 | Roberto Sighel (ITA) |
| 1923 | Clas Thunberg (FIN) | 1961 | Henk van der Grift (NED) | 1993 | Falko Zandstra (NED) |
| 1924 | Roald Larsen (NOR) | 1962 | Viktor Kosichkin (URS) | 1994 | Johann Olav Koss (NOR) |
| 1925 | Clas Thunberg (FIN) | 1963 | Jonny Nilsson (SWE) | 1995 | Rintje Ritsma (NED) |
| 1926 | Ivar Ballangrud (NOR) | 1964 | Knut Johannesen (NOR) | 1996 | Rintje Ritsma (NED) |
| 1927 | Bernt Evensen (NOR) | 1965 | Per Ivar Moe (NOR) | 1997 | Ids Postma (NED) |
| 1928 | Clas Thunberg (FIN) | 1966 | Kees Verkerk (NED) | 1998 | Ids Postma (NED) |
| 1929 | Clas Thunberg (FIN) | 1967 | Kees Verkerk (NED) | 1999 | Rintje Ritsma (NED) |
| 1930 | Michael Staksrud (NOR) | 1968 | Fred Anton Maier (NOR) | 2000 | Gianni Romme (NED) |
| 1931 | Clas Thunberg (FIN) | 1969 | Dag Fornaess (NOR) | 2001 | Rintje Ritsma (NED) |
| 1932 | Ivar Ballangrud (NOR) | 1970 | Ard Schenk (NED) | 2002 | Jochem Uytdehaage (NED) |
| 1933 | Hans Engnestangen | 1971 | Ard Schenk (NED) | 2003 | Gianni Romme (NED) |
| | (NOR) | 1972 | Ard Schenk (NED) | 2004 | *to be held 6–8 February,* |
| 1934 | Bernt Evensen (NOR) | 1973 | Göran Claeson (SWE) | | *Hamar, Norway* |
| 1935 | Michael Staksrud (NOR) | 1974 | Sten Stensen (NOR) | | |

## World All-Around Speed-Skating Championship—Women

| YEAR | WINNER | YEAR | WINNER | YEAR | WINNER |
|------|--------|------|--------|------|--------|
| 1936 | Kit Klein (USA) | 1965 | Inga Artamonova (URS) | 1985 | Andrea Schöne (GDR) |
| 1937 | Laila Schou Nilsen (NOR) | 1966 | Valentina Stenina (URS) | 1986 | Karin Kania (GDR) |
| 1938 | Laila Schou Nilsen (NOR) | 1967 | Stien Kaiser (NED) | 1987 | Karin Kania (GDR) |
| 1939 | Verné Lesche (FIN) | 1968 | Stien Kaiser (NED) | 1988 | Karin Kania (GDR) |
| 1940–46 | *not held* | 1969 | Lasma Kauniste (URS) | 1989 | Constanze Moser (GDR) |
| 1947 | Verné Lesche (FIN) | 1970 | Atje Keulen-Deelstra | 1990 | Jacqueline Börner (GDR) |
| 1948 | Mariya Isakova (URS) | | (NED) | 1991 | Gunda Kleeman (GER) |
| 1949 | Mariya Isakova (URS) | 1971 | Nina Statkevich (URS) | 1992 | Gunda Kleeman (GER) |
| 1950 | Mariya Isakova (URS) | 1972 | Atje Keulen-Deelstra | 1993 | Gunda Kleeman (GER) |
| 1951 | Eevi Huttunen (FIN) | | (NED) | 1994 | Emese Hunyady (AUT) |
| 1952 | Lidiya Selikhova (URS) | 1973 | Atje Keulen-Deelstra | 1995 | Gunda Niemann (GER) |
| 1953 | Khalida Shchegoleva | | (NED) | 1996 | Gunda Niemann (GER) |
| | (URS) | 1974 | Atje Keulen-Deelstra | 1997 | Gunda Niemann (GER) |
| 1954 | Lidiya Selikhova (URS) | | (NED) | 1998 | Gunda Niemann- |
| 1955 | Rimma Zhukova (URS) | 1975 | Karin Kessow (GDR) | | Stirnemann (GER) |
| 1956 | Sofiya Kondakova (URS) | 1976 | Sylvia Burka (CAN) | 1999 | Gunda Niemann- |
| 1957 | Inga Artamonova (URS) | 1977 | Vera Bryndzey (URS) | | Stirnemann (GER) |
| 1958 | Inga Artamonova (URS) | 1978 | Tatyana Averina (URS) | 2000 | Claudia Pechstein (GER) |
| 1959 | Tamara Rylova (URS) | 1979 | Beth Heiden (USA) | 2001 | Anni Friesinger (GER) |
| 1960 | Valentina Stenina (URS) | 1980 | Natalya Petruseva (URS) | 2002 | Anni Friesinger (GER) |
| 1961 | Valentina Stenina (URS) | 1981 | Natalya Petruseva (URS) | 2003 | Cindy Klassen (CAN) |
| 1962 | Inga Artamonova (URS) | 1982 | Karin Busch (GDR) | 2004 | *to be held 6–8 February,* |
| 1963 | Lidiya Skoblikova (URS) | 1983 | Andrea Schöne (GDR) | | *Hamar, Norway* |
| 1964 | Lidiya Skoblikova (URS) | 1984 | Karin Enke (GDR) | | |

## World Speed-Skating Sprint Championships

| YEAR | MEN | WOMEN | YEAR | MEN | WOMEN |
|---|---|---|---|---|---|
| 1970 | Valery Muratov (URS) | Lyudmila Titova (URS) | 1989 | Igor Zhelezovsky (URS) | Bonnie Blair (USA) |
| 1971 | Erhard Keller (FRG) | Ruth Schleiermacher (GDR) | 1990 | Ki-Tae Bae (KOR) | Angela Hauck (GDR) |
| 1972 | Leo Linkovesi (FIN) | Monica Pflug (FRG) | 1991 | Igor Zhelezovsky (URS) | Monique Garbrecht (GER) |
| 1973 | Valery Muratov (URS) | Sheila Young (USA) | 1992 | Igor Zhelezovsky (UNT*) | Ye Qiaobo (CHN) |
| 1974 | Per Bjørang (NOR) | Leah Poulos (USA) | 1993 | Igor Zhelezovsky (URS) | Ye Qiaobo (CHN) |
| 1975 | Aleksandr Safronov (URS) | Sheila Young (USA) | 1994 | Dan Jansen (USA) | Bonnie Blair (USA) |
| 1976 | Johan Granath (SWE) | Sheila Young (USA) | 1995 | Kim Yoon Man (KOR) | Bonnie Blair (USA) |
| 1977 | Eric Heiden (USA) | Sylvia Burka (CAN) | 1996 | Sergey Klevchenya (RUS) | Christine Witty (USA) |
| 1978 | Eric Heiden (USA) | Lyubov Sadchikova (URS) | 1997 | Sergey Klevchenya (RUS) | Franziska Schenk (GER) |
| 1979 | Eric Heiden (USA) | Leah Poulos-Mueller (USA) | 1998 | Jan Bos (NED) | Catriona LeMay Doan (CAN) |
| 1980 | Eric Heiden (USA) | Karin Enke (GDR) | 1999 | Jeremy Wotherspoon (CAN) | Monique Garbrecht (GER) |
| 1981 | Frode Ronning (NOR) | Karin Enke (GDR) | 2000 | Jeremy Wotherspoon (CAN) | Monique Garbrecht (GER) |
| 1982 | Sergey Khlebnikov (URS) | Natalya Petruseva (URS) | 2001 | Michael Ireland (CAN) | Monique Garbrecht-Enfeldt (GER) |
| 1983 | Akira Kuroiwa (JPN) | Karin Enke (GDR) | 2002 | Jeremy Wotherspoon (CAN) | Catriona LeMay Doan (CAN) |
| 1984 | Gaetan Boucher (CAN) | Karin Enke (GDR) | 2003 | Jeremy Wotherspoon (CAN) | Monique Garbrecht-Enfeldt (GER) |
| 1985 | Igor Zhelezovsky (URS) | Christa Rothenburger (GDR) | 2004 | to be held 9–11 January, Nagano, Japan | |
| 1986 | Igor Zhelezovsky (URS) | Karin Kania (GDR) | | | |
| 1987 | Akira Kuroiwa (JPN) | Karin Kania (GDR) | | | |
| 1988 | Dan Jansen (USA) | Christa Rothenburger (GDR) | | | |

*Unified Team, consisting of athletes from the Commonwealth of Independent States plus Georgia.

## World Short-Track Speed-Skating Championships—Overall Winners

| YEAR | MEN | WOMEN | YEAR | MEN | WOMEN |
|---|---|---|---|---|---|
| 1976 | Alan Rattray (USA) | Celeste Chlapaty (USA) | 1989 | Michel Daignault (CAN) | Sylvie Daigle (CAN) |
| 1977 | Gaetan Boucher (CAN) | Brenda Webster (CAN) | 1990 | Joon-ho Lee (KOR) | Sylvie Daigle (CAN) |
| 1978 | James Lynch (AUS) | Sarah Docter (CAN) | 1991 | Wilfred O'Reilly (GBR) | Nathalie Lambert (CAN) |
| 1979 | Hiroshi Toda (JPN) | Sylvie Daigle (CAN) | 1992 | Ki Hoon Kim (KOR) | So He Kim (KOR) |
| 1980 | Gaetan Boucher (CAN) | Miyoshi Kato (JPN) | 1993 | Marc Gagnon (CAN) | Nathalie Lambert (CAN) |
| 1981 | Benoît Baril (CAN) | Miyoshi Kato (JPN) | 1994 | Marc Gagnon (CAN) | Nathalie Lambert (CAN) |
| 1982 | Guy Daigneault (CAN) | Maryse Perreault (CAN) | 1995 | Chae Ji Hoon (KOR) | Chun Lee Kyung (KOR) |
| 1983 | Louis Grenier (CAN) | Sylvie Daigle (CAN) | 1996 | Marc Gagnon (CAN) | Chun Lee Kyung (KOR) |
| 1984 | Guy Daigneault (CAN) | Mariko Kinoshita (JPN) | 1997 | Kim Dong Sung (KOR) | Chun Lee Kyung (KOR), Yang Yang (A) (CHN)* |
| 1985 | Toshinobu Kawai (JPN) | Eiko Shishii (JPN) | 1998 | Marc Gagnon (CAN) | Yang Yang (A) (CHN) |
| 1986 | Tatsuyoshi Isihara (JPN) | Bonnie Blair (USA) | 1999 | Li Jianjun (CHN) | Yang Yang (A) (CHN) |
| 1987 | Michel Daignault (CAN), Toshinobu Kawai (JPN)* | Eiko Shishii (JPN) | 2000 | Min Ryung (KOR) | Yang Yang (A) (CHN) |
| | | | 2001 | Li Jianjun (CHN) | Yang Yang (A) (CHN) |
| 1988 | Peter van der Velde (NED) | Sylvie Daigle (CAN) | 2002 | Kim Dong Sung (KOR) | Yang Yang (A) (CHN) |
| | | | 2003 | Ahn Hyun Soo (KOR) | Choi Eun Kyung (KOR) |
| | | | 2004 | to be held 19–21 March, Gothenburg, Sweden | |

*Tied.

**Did you know?** Ice skating probably developed in Scandinavia as early as 1000 BC, the first skates being made from shank or rib bones of elk, oxen, reindeer, and other animals.

# Judo

**W**orld championships for judo were first held in 1956 under the auspices of the International Judo Federation (IJF; founded 1951). At that time all contestants participated on an equal basis. At the fourth world championship match, 65 kg, 78 kg, and 95 kg classes were added to the open weight division; at the next championship match, two more weight classes were added, and in 1979 two of the classes were divided once more and assigned weight values. World championships for **women** were first held in 1980; they are contested biennially in eight weight classes. New weight classes were established in 1999.

**International Judo Federation Web site: <www.ijf.org>.**

## World Judo Championships—Men

*Figures in parentheses represent weight classes before 1999. The 2003 championship is scheduled to be held in Osaka, Japan, on 11–14 September.*

| YEAR | OPEN WEIGHTS |
|---|---|
| 1956[1] | Shokichi Natsui (JPN) |
| 1958[1] | Koji Sone (JPN) |
| 1961[1] | Anton Geesink (NED) |
| 1965[2] | Isao Inokuma (JPN) |
| 1967[3] | Mitsuo Matsunaga (JPN) |
| 1969[3] | Masatoshi Shinomaki (JPN) |
| 1971[3] | Masatoshi Shinomaki (JPN) |
| 1973[3] | Kasuhiro Ninomiya (JPN) |
| 1975[3] | Haruki Uemura (JPN) |
| 1979 | Sumio Endo (JPN) |
| 1981 | Yasuhiro Yamashita (JPN) |
| 1983 | Hitoshi Saito (JPN) |
| 1985 | Y. Masaki (JPN) |
| 1987 | Naoya Ogawa (JPN) |
| 1989 | Naoya Ogawa (JPN) |
| 1991 | Naoya Ogawa (JPN) |
| 1993 | Rafael Kubacki (POL) |
| 1995 | David Douillet (FRA) |
| 1997 | Rafael Kubacki (POL) |
| 1999 | Shinichi Shinohara (JPN) |
| 2001 | Aleksandr Mikhaylin (RUS) |

| YEAR | 60 KG |
|---|---|
| 1979 | Thierry Rey (FRA) |
| 1981 | Yasuhiro Moriwaki (JPN) |
| 1983 | Khazret Tletseri (URS) |
| 1985 | Shinji Hosokawa (JPN) |
| 1987 | Kim Jae Yup (KOR) |
| 1989 | Amiran Totikashvili (URS) |
| 1991 | Tadanori Koshino (JPN) |
| 1993 | Ryoji Sonada (JPN) |
| 1995 | Nikolay Ozhegin (RUS) |
| 1997 | Tadahiro Nomura (JPN) |
| 1999 | Manuelo Poulot (CUB) |
| 2001 | Anis Lounifi (TUN) |

| YEAR | 66 KG (65 KG) |
|---|---|
| 1965[2] | Hirofumi Matsuda (JPN) |
| 1967[3] | Takafumi Shigeoka (JPN) |
| 1969[3] | Yoshio Sonoda (JPN) |
| 1971[3] | Takao Kawaguchi (JPN) |
| 1973[3] | Yoshiharu Minami (JPN) |
| 1975[3] | Yoshiharu Minami (JPN) |
| 1979 | Nikolay Solodukhin (URS) |
| 1981 | Katsuhito Kashiwazaki (JPN) |
| 1983 | Nicolai Solodukhin (URS) |
| 1985 | Yuri Sokolov (URS) |
| 1987 | Yosuke Yamamoto (JPN) |

| YEAR | 66 KG (65 KG) (CONTINUED) |
|---|---|
| 1989 | Dragomir Becanovic (YUG) |
| 1991 | Udo Quellmalz (GER) |
| 1993 | Yukimasa Nakamura (JPN) |
| 1995 | Udo Quellmalz (GER) |
| 1997 | Kim Hyuk (KOR) |
| 1999 | Larbi Benboudaoud (FRA) |
| 2001 | Arash Miresmaeili (IRI) |

| YEAR | 73 KG (71 KG) |
|---|---|
| 1967[3] | Hiroshi Minatoya (JPN) |
| 1969[3] | Hiroshi Minatoya (JPN) |
| 1971[3] | Hisashi Tsuzawa (JPN) |
| 1973[3] | Toyokazu Nomura (JPN) |
| 1975[3] | Vladimir Nevzorov (URS) |
| 1979 | Kyoto Katsuki (JPN) |
| 1981 | Park Chong Hak (KOR) |
| 1983 | Hidetoshi Nakanishi (JPN) |
| 1985 | Keun Ahn Byung (KOR) |
| 1987 | Mike Swain (USA) |
| 1989 | Toshihigo Koga (JPN) |
| 1991 | Toshihigo Koga (JPN) |
| 1993 | Yung Chung Hoon (KOR) |
| 1995 | Daisuke Hideshima (JPN) |
| 1997 | Kenzo Nakamura (JPN) |
| 1999 | Jimmy Pedro (USA) |
| 2001 | Vitaly Makarov (RUS) |

| YEAR | 81 KG (78 KG) |
|---|---|
| 1965[2] | Isao Okano (JPN) |
| 1967[3] | Eijii Maruki (JPN) |
| 1969[3] | Isamu Sonoda (JPN) |
| 1971[3] | Shozo Fujii (JPN) |
| 1973[3] | Shozo Fujii (JPN) |
| 1975[3] | Shozo Fujii (JPN) |
| 1979 | Shozo Fujii (JPN) |
| 1981 | Neil Adams (GBR) |
| 1983 | Nobutoshi Hikage (JPN) |
| 1985 | Nobutoshi Hikage (JPN) |
| 1987 | Hirotaka Okada (JPN) |
| 1989 | Kim Bying Ju (KOR) |
| 1991 | Daniel Lascau (GER) |
| 1993 | Chun Ki Young (KOR) |
| 1995 | Toshihigo Koga (JPN) |
| 1997 | Cho In Chul (KOR) |
| 1999 | Graeme Randall (GBR) |
| 2001 | Cho In Chul (KOR) |

| YEAR | 90 KG (86 KG) |
|---|---|
| 1967[3] | Nobuyuki Sato (JPN) |
| 1969[3] | Fumio Sasahara (JPN) |

| YEAR | 90 KG (86 KG) (CONTINUED) |
|---|---|
| 1971[3] | Fumio Sasahara (JPN) |
| 1973[3] | Nobuyuki Sato (JPN) |
| 1975[3] | Jean-Louc Rouge (FRA) |
| 1979 | Detlef Ultsch (GDR) |
| 1981 | Bernard Tchoullouyan (FRA) |
| 1983 | Detlef Ultsch (GDR) |
| 1985 | Peter Seisenbacher (AUT) |
| 1987 | Fabien Canu (FRA) |
| 1989 | Fabien Canu (FRA) |
| 1991 | Hirotaka Okada (JPN) |
| 1993 | Yoshio Nakamura (JPN) |
| 1995 | Chun Ki Young (KOR) |
| 1997 | Jeon Ki Young (KOR) |
| 1999 | Hidehiko Yoshida (JPN) |
| 2001 | Frédéric Demontfaucon (FRA) |

| YEAR | 100 KG (95 KG) |
|---|---|
| 1965[2] | Anton Geesink (NED) |
| 1967[3] | Wilhem Ruska (NED) |
| 1969[3] | Shuji Suma (JPN) |
| 1971[3] | Wilhem Ruska (NED) |
| 1973[3] | Chonosuke Takagi (JPN) |
| 1975[3] | Sumio Endo (JPN) |
| 1979 | Tengiz Khubuluri (URS) |
| 1981 | Tengiz Khubuluri (URS) |
| 1983 | Andreas Preschel (GDR) |
| 1985 | Hitoshi Sugai (JPN) |
| 1987 | Hitoshi Sugai (JPN) |
| 1989 | Koba Kurtanidze (URS) |
| 1991 | Stéphane Traineau (FRA) |
| 1993 | Antal Kovacs (HUN) |
| 1995 | Pawel Nastula (POL) |
| 1997 | Pawel Nastula (POL) |
| 1999 | Kosei Inoue (JPN) |
| 2001 | Kosei Inoue (JPN) |

| YEAR | +100 KG (+95 KG) |
|---|---|
| 1979 | Yasuhiro Yamashita (JPN) |
| 1981 | Yasuhiro Yamashita (JPN) |
| 1983 | Yasuhiro Yamashita (JPN) |
| 1985 | Chul Cho Yong (KOR) |
| 1987 | Grigory Verichev (URS) |
| 1989 | Naoya Ogawa (JPN) |
| 1991 | Sergey Kosorotov (URS) |
| 1993 | David Douillet (FRA) |
| 1995 | David Douillet (FRA) |
| 1997 | David Douillet (FRA) |
| 1999 | Shinichi Shinohara (JPN) |
| 2001 | Aleksandr Mikhaylin (RUS) |

[1]*Weight classes not held—open weight division only.* [2]*Divisions called lightweight, middleweight, heavyweight.* [3]*Divisions called lightweight, light-middleweight, middleweight, light-heavyweight, and heavyweight.*

# World Judo Championships—Women

*Figures in parentheses represent weight classes before 1999. The 2003 championship is scheduled to be held in Osaka, Japan, on 11–14 September.*

| YEAR | OPEN WEIGHTS | YEAR | 52 KG (CONTINUED) | YEAR | 70 KG (66 KG) (CONTINUED) |
|---|---|---|---|---|---|
| 1980 | Ingrid Berghmans (BEL) | 1997 | Marie-Claire Restoux (FRA) | 1989 | Emanuela Pierantozzi (ITA) |
| 1982 | Ingrid Berghmans (BEL) | 1999 | Noriko Narasaki (JPN) | 1991 | Emanuela Pierantozzi (ITA) |
| 1984 | Ingrid Berghmans (BEL) | 2001 | Kye Sun Hui (PRK) | 1993 | Cho Min Sun (KOR) |
| 1986 | Ingrid Berghmans (BEL) | | | 1995 | Cho Min Sun (KOR) |
| 1987 | Fengliang Gao (CHN) | YEAR | 57 KG (56 KG) | 1997 | Kate Howey (GBR) |
| 1989 | Estela Rodriguez (CUB) | 1980 | Gerda Winklbauer (AUT) | 1999 | Sibelis Veranes (CUB) |
| 1991 | Zhuang Xiaoyan (CHN) | 1982 | Béatrice Rodriguez (FRA) | 2001 | Masae Ueno (JPN) |
| 1993 | Beata Maksymow (POL) | 1984 | Anne-Marie Burns (USA) | | |
| 1995 | Monique van der Lee (NED) | 1986 | Ann Hughes (GBR) | YEAR | 78 KG (72 KG) |
| 1997 | Daina Beltran (CUB) | 1987 | Catherine Arnaud (FRA) | 1980 | Jocelyne Triadou (FRA) |
| 1999 | Daina Beltran (CUB) | 1989 | Catherine Arnaud (FRA) | 1982 | Barbara Classen (FRG) |
| 2001 | Celine Lebrun (FRA) | 1991 | Miriam Blasco (ESP) | 1984 | Ingrid Berghmans (BEL) |
| | | 1993 | Nicola Fairbrother (GBR) | 1986 | Irene de Kok (NED) |
| YEAR | 48 KG | 1995 | Driulis González (CUB) | 1987 | Irene de Kok (NED) |
| 1980 | Jane Bridge (GBR) | 1997 | Isabel Fernández (ESP) | 1989 | Ingrid Berghmans (BEL) |
| 1982 | Karen Briggs (GBR) | 1999 | Driulis González (CUB) | 1991 | Kim Mi Jong (KOR) |
| 1984 | Karen Briggs (GBR) | 2001 | Yurisleidis Lupetey (CUB) | 1993 | Leng Chin Hui (CHN) |
| 1986 | Karen Briggs (GBR) | | | 1995 | Castellano Diaz Luna (CUB) |
| 1987 | Zhang Yun Li (CHN) | YEAR | 63 KG (61 KG) | 1997 | Noriko Anno (JPN) |
| 1989 | Karen Briggs (GBR) | 1980 | Anita Staps (NED) | 1999 | Noriko Anno (JPN) |
| 1991 | Cecile Nowak (FRA) | 1982 | Martine Rottier (FRA) | 2001 | Noriko Anno (JPN) |
| 1993 | Ryoko Tamura (JPN) | 1984 | Natasha Hernández (VEN) | | |
| 1995 | Ryoko Tamura (JPN) | 1986 | Diane Bell (GBR) | YEAR | +78 KG (+72 KG) |
| 1997 | Ryoko Tamura (JPN) | 1987 | Diane Bell (GBR) | 1980 | Margerita de Cal (ITA) |
| 1999 | Ryoko Tamura (JPN) | 1989 | Catherine Fleury (FRA) | 1982 | Natalina Lupino (FRA) |
| 2001 | Ryoko Tamura (JPN) | 1991 | Frauke Eickoff (GER) | 1984 | Maria-Theresa Motta (ITA) |
| | | 1993 | Gella van de Cavaye (BEL) | 1986 | Fengliang Gao (CHN) |
| YEAR | 52 KG | 1995 | Jung Sung Sook (KOR) | 1987 | Fengliang Gao (CHN) |
| 1980 | Edith Hrovat (AUT) | 1997 | Serverin Vandenhende (FRA) | 1989 | Fengliang Gao (CHN) |
| 1982 | Loretta Doyle (GBR) | 1999 | Keiko Maeda (JPN) | 1991 | Moon Ji Yoon (KOR) |
| 1984 | Kaori Yamaguchi (JPN) | 2001 | Gella van de Cavaye (BEL) | 1993 | Johanna Hagn (GER) |
| 1986 | Dominique Brun (FRA) | | | 1995 | Angelique Seriese (NED) |
| 1987 | Sharon Rendle (GBR) | YEAR | 70 KG (66 KG) | 1997 | Christine Cicot (FRA) |
| 1989 | Sharon Rendle (GBR) | 1980 | Edith Simon (AUT) | 1999 | Beata Maksymow (POL) |
| 1991 | Alessandra Giungi (ITA) | 1982 | Brigitte Deydier (FRA) | 2001 | Yuan Hua (CHN) |
| 1993 | Legna Verdecia Rodríguez (CUB) | 1984 | Brigitte Deydier (FRA) | | |
| 1995 | Marie-Claire Restoux (FRA) | 1986 | Brigitte Deydier (FRA) | | |
| | | 1987 | Alexandra Schreiber (FRG) | | |

**Did you know?** Kano Jigoro (1860–1938) combined the knowledge of the old jujitsu schools of the Japanese samurai with the sporting ideology of the "muscular Christianity" movement and in 1882 founded his Kodokan School of judo (from the Chinese *jou-tao*, or *roudao*, meaning "gentle way"), the beginning of the sport in its modern form.

# Marathon

The marathon is a long-distance footrace first held at the revival of the Olympic Games at Athens, Greece, in 1896. It commemorates the legendary feat of a Greek soldier who, in 490 BC, is supposed to have run from Marathon to Athens, a distance of about 40 km (25 mi), to bring news of the Athenian victory over the Persians. Appropriately, the first modern marathon winner in 1896 was a Greek, Spyridon Louis. In 1924 the **Olympic marathon distance** was standardized at 42,195 m, or 26 mi 385 yd. This was based on a decision of the British Olympic Committee to start the 1908 Olympic race from Windsor Castle and finish it in front of the royal box in the stadium at London. The marathon was added to the **women's Olympic program** in 1984. Because marathon courses are not of equal difficulty, the International Amateur Athletic Federation does not list a world record for the event. After the Olympic Games championship, one of the most coveted honors in marathon running is victory in the **Boston Marathon**, held annually since 1897. It draws athletes from all parts of the world and in 1972 became the first marathon to officially allow women to compete. The **New York Marathon** also attracts participants from many countries. Other popular marathons are held in London, Berlin, Rotterdam (Neth.), and Chicago.

## Boston Marathon

*Won by an American runner except as indicated.*
*Times are given in hours:minutes:seconds.*

### men

| YEAR | WINNER | TIME | YEAR | WINNER | TIME |
|------|--------|------|------|--------|------|
| 1897 | John J. McDermott | 2:55:10 | 1952 | Doroteo Flores (GUA) | 2:31:53 |
| 1898 | Ronald J. McDonald (CAN) | 2:42:00 | 1953 | Yamada Keizo (JPN) | 2:18:51 |
| 1899 | Lawrence J. Brignoli | 2:54:38 | 1954 | Veikko L. Karanen (FIN) | 2:20:39 |
| 1900 | John J. Caffrey (CAN) | 2:39:44 | 1955 | Hamamura Hideo (JPN) | 2:18:22 |
| 1901 | John J. Caffrey (CAN) | 2:29:23 | 1956 | Antti Viskari (FIN) | 2:14:14 |
| 1902 | Sammy A. Mellor | 2:43:12 | 1957 | John J. Kelley | 2:20:05 |
| 1903 | John C. Lorden | 2:41:29 | 1958 | Franjo Mihalic (YUG) | 2:25:54 |
| 1904 | Michael Spring | 2:39:04 | 1959 | Eino Oksanen (FIN) | 2:22:42 |
| 1905 | Frederick Lorz | 2:38:25 | 1960 | Paavo Kotila (FIN) | 2:20:54 |
| 1906 | Tim Ford | 2:45:45 | 1961 | Eino Oksanen (FIN) | 2:23:39 |
| 1907 | Thomas Longboat (CAN) | 2:24:24 | 1962 | Eino Oksanen (FIN) | 2:23:48 |
| 1908 | Thomas P. Morrissey | 2:25:43 | 1963 | Aurele Vandendriessche (BEL) | 2:18:58 |
| 1909 | Henri Renaud | 2:53:36 | 1964 | Aurele Vandendriessche (BEL) | 2:19:59 |
| 1910 | Fred L. Cameron (CAN) | 2:28:52 | 1965 | Shigematsu Morio (JPN) | 2:16:33 |
| 1911 | Clarence H. DeMar | 2:21:39 | 1966 | Kimihara Kenji (JPN) | 2:17:11 |
| 1912 | Michael J. Ryan | 2:21:18 | 1967 | David McKenzie (NZL) | 2:15:45 |
| 1913 | Fritz Carlson | 2:25:14 | 1968 | Amby Burfoot | 2:22:17 |
| 1914 | James Duffy (CAN) | 2:25:01 | 1969 | Unetani Yoshiaki (JPN) | 2:13:49 |
| 1915 | Edouard Fabre (CAN) | 2:31:41 | 1970 | Ron Hill (ENG) | 2:10:30 |
| 1916 | Arthur V. Roth | 2:27:16 | 1971 | Alvaro Mejia (COL) | 2:18:45 |
| 1917 | William K. Kennedy | 2:28:37 | 1972 | Olavi Suomalainen (FIN) | 2:15:30 |
| 1918 | *no regular competition* | | 1973 | Jon Anderson | 2:16:03 |
| 1919 | Carl W.A. Linder | 2:29:13 | 1974 | Neil Cusack | 2:13:39 |
| 1920 | Peter Trivoulides (GRE) | 2:29:31 | 1975 | Bill Rodgers | 2:09:55 |
| 1921 | Frank Zuna | 2:18:57 | 1976 | Jack Fultz | 2:20:19 |
| 1922 | Clarence H. DeMar | 2:18:10 | 1977 | Jerome Drayton (CAN) | 2:14:46 |
| 1923 | Clarence H. DeMar | 2:23:47 | 1978 | Bill Rodgers | 2:10:13 |
| 1924 | Clarence H. DeMar | 2:29:40 | 1979 | Bill Rodgers | 2:09:27 |
| 1925 | Charles L. Mellor | 2:33:06 | 1980 | Bill Rodgers | 2:12:11 |
| 1926 | John C. Miles (CAN) | 2:25:40 | 1981 | Seko Toshihiko (JPN) | 2:09:26 |
| 1927 | Clarence H. DeMar | 2:40:22 | 1982 | Alberto Salazar | 2:08:51 |
| 1928 | Clarence H. DeMar | 2:37:07 | 1983 | Greg A. Meyer | 2:09:00 |
| 1929 | John C. Miles (CAN) | 2:33:08 | 1984 | Geoff Smith (ENG) | 2:10:34 |
| 1930 | Clarence H. DeMar | 2:34:48 | 1985 | Geoff Smith (ENG) | 2:14:05 |
| 1931 | James P. Hennigan | 2:46:45 | 1986 | Robert de Castella (AUS) | 2:07:51 |
| 1932 | Paul deBruyn | 2:33:36 | 1987 | Seko Toshihiko (JPN) | 2:11:50 |
| 1933 | Leslie S. Pawson | 2:31:01 | 1988 | Ibrahim Hussein (KEN) | 2:08:43 |
| 1934 | Dave Komonen (CAN) | 2:32:53 | 1989 | Abebe Mekonnen (ETH) | 2:09:06 |
| 1935 | John A. Kelley | 2:32:07 | 1990 | Gelindo Bordin (ITA) | 2:08:19 |
| 1936 | Ellison M. Brown | 2:33:40 | 1991 | Ibrahim Hussein (KEN) | 2:11:06 |
| 1937 | Walter Young (CAN) | 2:33:20 | 1992 | Ibrahim Hussein (KEN) | 2:08:14 |
| 1938 | Leslie S. Pawson | 2:35:34 | 1993 | Cosmas N'Deti (KEN) | 2:09:33 |
| 1939 | Ellison M. Brown | 2:28:51 | 1994 | Cosmas N'Deti (KEN) | 2:07:15 |
| 1940 | Gerard Cote (CAN) | 2:28:28 | 1995 | Cosmas N'Deti (KEN) | 2:09:22 |
| 1941 | Leslie S. Pawson | 2:30:38 | 1996 | Moses Tanui (KEN) | 2:09:16 |
| 1942 | Joe Smith | 2:26:51 | 1997 | Lameck Aguta (KEN) | 2:10:34 |
| 1943 | Gerard Cote (CAN) | 2:28:25 | 1998 | Moses Tanui (KEN) | 2:07:34 |
| 1944 | Gerard Cote (CAN) | 2:31:50 | 1999 | Joseph Chebet (KEN) | 2:09:52 |
| 1945 | John A. Kelley | 2:30:40 | 2000 | Elijah Lagat (KEN) | 2:09:47 |
| 1946 | Stylianos Kyriakides (GRE) | 2:29:27 | 2001 | Bong-Ju Lee (KOR) | 2:09:43 |
| 1947 | Suh Yun Bok (KOR) | 2:25:39 | 2002 | Rodgers Rop (KEN) | 2:09:02 |
| 1948 | Gerard Cote (CAN) | 2:31:02 | 2003 | Robert Kipkoech | 2:10:11 |
| 1949 | Karl G. Leandersson (SWE) | 2:31:50 | | Cheruiyot (KEN) | |
| 1950 | Ham Kee Yong (KOR) | 2:32:39 | 2004 | *to be run 22 April* | |
| 1951 | Tanaka Shigeki (JPN) | 2:27:45 | | | |

### women

| YEAR | WINNER | TIME | YEAR | WINNER | TIME |
|------|--------|------|------|--------|------|
| 1972 | Nina Kuscsik | 3:10:26 | 1979 | Joan Benoit | 2:35:15 |
| 1973 | Jacqueline Hansen | 3:05:59 | 1980 | Jacqueline Gareau (CAN) | 2:34:28 |
| 1974 | Michiko Gorman | 2:47:11 | 1981 | Allison Roe (NZL) | 2:26:46 |
| 1975 | Liane Winter (FRG) | 2:42:24 | 1982 | Charlotte Teske (FRG) | 2:29:33 |
| 1976 | Kim Merritt | 2:47:10 | 1983 | Joan Benoit | 2:22:42 |
| 1977 | Michiko Gorman | 2:46:22 | 1984 | Lorraine Moller (NZL) | 2:29:28 |
| 1978 | Gayle S. Barron | 2:44:52 | 1985 | Lisa Larsen | 2:34:06 |

## Boston Marathon (continued)

### women (continued)

| YEAR | WINNER | TIME | YEAR | WINNER | TIME |
|------|--------|------|------|--------|------|
| 1986 | Ingrid Kristiansen (NOR) | 2:24:55 | 1996 | Uta Pippig (GER) | 2:27:12 |
| 1987 | Rosa Mota (POR) | 2:25:21 | 1997 | Fatuma Roba (ETH) | 2:26:23 |
| 1988 | Rosa Mota (POR) | 2:24:30 | 1998 | Fatuma Roba (ETH) | 2:23:21 |
| 1989 | Ingrid Kristiansen (NOR) | 2:24:33 | 1999 | Fatuma Roba (ETH) | 2:23:25 |
| 1990 | Rosa Mota (POR) | 2:25:23 | 2000 | Catherine Ndereba (KEN) | 2:26:11 |
| 1991 | Wanda Panfil (POL) | 2:24:18 | 2001 | Catherine Ndereba (KEN) | 2:23:53 |
| 1992 | Olga Markova (RUS) | 2:23:43 | 2002 | Margaret Okayo (KEN) | 2:20:43 |
| 1993 | Olga Markova (RUS) | 2:25:27 | 2003 | Svetlana Zakharova (RUS) | 2:25:20 |
| 1994 | Uta Pippig (GER) | 2:21:45 | 2004 | to be run 22 April | |
| 1995 | Uta Pippig (GER) | 2:25:11 | | | |

## New York City Marathon

*Won by an American runner except as indicated.*
*Times are given in hours:minutes:seconds.*

| YEAR | MEN | TIME | WOMEN | TIME |
|------|-----|------|-------|------|
| 1970 | Gary Muhrcke | 2:31:38 | no finisher | |
| 1971 | Norm Higgins | 2:22:54 | Beth Bonner | 2:55:22 |
| 1972 | Robert Karlin | 2:27:52 | Nina Kuscsik | 3:08:41 |
| 1973 | Tom Fleming | 2:21:54 | Nina Kuscsik | 2:57:07 |
| 1974 | Norbert Sander | 2:26:30 | Katherine Switzer | 3:07:29 |
| 1975 | Tom Fleming | 2:19:27 | Kim Merritt | 2:46:14 |
| 1976 | Bill Rodgers | 2:10:09 | Michiko Gorman | 2:39:11 |
| 1977 | Bill Rodgers | 2:11:28 | Michiko Gorman | 2:43:10 |
| 1978 | Bill Rodgers | 2:12:12 | Grete Waitz (NOR) | 2:32:30 |
| 1979 | Bill Rodgers | 2:11:42 | Grete Waitz (NOR) | 2:27:33 |
| 1980 | Alberto Salazar | 2:09:41 | Grete Waitz (NOR) | 2:25:41 |
| 1981 | Alberto Salazar | 2:08:13 | Allison Roe (NZL) | 2:25:29 |
| 1982 | Alberto Salazar | 2:09:29 | Grete Waitz (NOR) | 2:27:14 |
| 1983 | Rod Dixon | 2:08:59 | Grete Waitz (NOR) | 2:27:00 |
| 1984 | Orlando Pizzolato | 2:14:53 | Grete Waitz (NOR) | 2:29:30 |
| 1985 | Orlando Pizzolato | 2:11:34 | Grete Waitz (NOR) | 2:28:34 |
| 1986 | Gianni Poli (ITA) | 2:11:06 | Grete Waitz (NOR) | 2:28:06 |
| 1987 | Ibrahim Hussein (KEN) | 2:11:01 | Priscilla Welch (GBR) | 2:30:17 |
| 1988 | Steve Jones (WAL) | 2:08:20 | Grete Waitz (NOR) | 2:28:07 |
| 1989 | Juma Ikangaa (TAN) | 2:08:01 | Ingrid Kristiansen (NOR) | 2:25:30 |
| 1990 | Douglas Wakiihuri (KEN) | 2:12:39 | Wanda Panfil (POL) | 2:30:45 |
| 1991 | Salvador Garcia (MEX) | 2:09:28 | Liz McColgan (SCO) | 2:27:23 |
| 1992 | Willie Mtolo (RSA) | 2:09:29 | Lisa Ondieki (AUS) | 2:24:40 |
| 1993 | Andres Espinosa (MEX) | 2:10:04 | Uta Pippig (GER) | 2:26:24 |
| 1994 | German Silva (MEX) | 2:11:21 | Tegla Loroupe (KEN) | 2:27:37 |
| 1995 | German Silva (MEX) | 2:11:00 | Tegla Loroupe (KEN) | 2:28:06 |
| 1996 | Giacomo Leone (ITA) | 2:09:54 | Anuta Catuna (ROM) | 2:28:18 |
| 1997 | John Kagwe (KEN) | 2:08:12 | Franziska Rochat-Moser (SUI) | 2:28:43 |
| 1998 | John Kagwe (KEN) | 2:08:45 | Franca Fiacconi (ITA) | 2:25:17 |
| 1999 | Joseph Chebet (KEN) | 2:09:14 | Adriana Fernández (MEX) | 2:25:06 |
| 2000 | Abdelkhader El Mouaziz (MAR) | 2:10:09 | Lyudmila Petrova (RUS) | 2:25:45 |
| 2001 | Tesfaye Jifar (ETH) | 2:07:43 | Margaret Okayo (KEN) | 2:24:21 |
| 2002 | Rodgers Rop (KEN) | 2:08:07 | Joyce Chepchumba (KEN) | 2:25:56 |
| 2003 | to be run 2 November | | | |

# Rodeo

A uniquely **North American** competition, the rodeo has been held on a more-or-less formal basis since the late 1920s. From 1929 to 1944 the **men's world all-around rodeo champion** was named by the **Rodeo Association of America**. Since 1944 the all-around champion has been the leading money-winner of the year—with the exception of the years 1976–78, when the champion was the cowboy who won the most money at the National Finals Rodeo. The Rodeo Association of America changed its name several times, but has been known as the **Professional Rodeo Cowboys Association** (PRCA) since 1975. Among other rodeo sanctioning activities, the PRCA qualifies cowboys for the **National Finals Rodeo**, a contest held in early December in Las Vegas NV among the top competitors in each of several events including bronc riding (bareback and saddle), bull riding, calf roping, and steer wrestling (individual and team). Women compete in one event only, barrel racing.

**Professional Rodeo Cowboys Association Web site:** <www.prorodeo.com>.

## Men's World All-Around Rodeo Champions

*Awarded since 1929. Table shows champions for the past 20 years.*

| YEAR | WINNER | YEAR | WINNER | YEAR | WINNER | YEAR | WINNER |
|------|--------|------|--------|------|--------|------|--------|
| 1983 | Roy Cooper | 1988 | Dave Appleton | 1993 | Ty Murray | 1998 | Ty Murray |
| 1984 | Dee Pickett | 1989 | Ty Murray | 1994 | Ty Murray | 1999 | Fred Whitfield |
| 1985 | Lewis Feild | 1990 | Ty Murray | 1995 | Joe Beaver | 2000 | Joe Beaver |
| 1986 | Lewis Feild | 1991 | Ty Murray | 1996 | Joe Beaver | 2001 | Cody Ohl |
| 1987 | Lewis Feild | 1992 | Ty Murray | 1997 | Dan Mortensen | 2002 | Trevor Brazile |

# Rowing

World championship rowing was established in 1962 by the **Fédération Internationale des Sociétés d'Aviron** (FISA; International Federation of Rowing Associations; founded 1892). Events are contested over a 2,000-m (6,560-ft) course and include single, double, and quadruple sculls; pairs (with and without coxswain); fours (with and without coxswain); and eights (with coxswain). **Women's world championships**, held since 1974, include single, double, and coxed quadruple sculls; coxless pairs; fours; and eights, raced over a 1,000-m (3,280-ft) course until 1985 (2,000-m course thereafter).

The most famous and historic of rowing courses is the 2,112-m (1 mi-550 yd) course at Henley-on-Thames, Oxfordshire, England. Two events of the Henley Regatta are open to the world, the **Diamond Challenge Sculls** for single sculls and the **Grand Challenge Cup** for eights. Unless otherwise mentioned, the clubs listed in the Henley Regatta events are English.

Another historic event is the annual University Boat Race between Eights from Oxford and Cambridge universities, which was instituted on 10 Jun 1829. The record time for the course of 6,779 m (4 mi 374 yd) from Putney to Mortlake on the River Thames is 16 min 19 sec by Cambridge in 1998.

**International Federation of Rowing Associations Web site:** <www.fisa.org>.

## World Rowing Championships—Men

*The competition has been held since 1962. The table shows only the past 20 years.*
*Results are for heavyweight events only. Times are given in minutes:seconds.*
*The next championship is scheduled to be held in August 2003.*

| YEAR | SINGLE SCULLS | TIME | DOUBLE SCULLS | TIME |
|------|---------------|------|---------------|------|
| 1983 | Peter-Michael Kolbe (FRG) | 6:49.88 | Tom Lange, Uwe Heppner (GDR) | 6:20.17 |
| 1984[1] | Pertti Karppinen (FIN) | 7:00.24 | Bradley Lewis, Paul Enquist (USA) | 6:36.87 |
| 1985 | Pertti Karppinen (FIN) | 6:48.08 | Uwe Heppner, Thomas Lange (GDR) | 6:15.49 |
| 1986 | Peter-Michael Kolbe (FRG) | 6:54.09 | Alberto Belgeri, Igor Pescialli (ITA) | 6:33.64 |
| 1987 | Thomas Lange (GDR) | 7:36.41 | D. Iordanov, V. Dadev (BUL) | 7:03.33 |
| 1988[1] | Thomas Lange (GDR) | 6:49.86 | Ronald Florijan, Nicolaas Rienks (NED) | 6:21.13 |
| 1989 | Thomas Lange (GDR) | 6:58.14 | Rolf Thorsen, Lars Bjoenness (NOR) | 6:23.40 |
| 1990 | Yury Jensen (URS) | 7:22.15 | Christoph Zerbst, Arnold Jonke (AUT) | 6:56.37 |
| 1991 | Thomas Lange (GDR) | 6:41.29 | Henk-Jan Zwolle, Nicolaas Rienks (NED) | 6:06.14 |
| 1992[1] | Thomas Lange (GDR) | 6:51.40 | Stephen Hawkins, Peter Antonie (AUT) | 6:17.32 |
| 1993 | Derek Porter (CAN) | 6:59.03 | Yves Lamarque, Samuel Barathay (FRA) | 6:24.69 |
| 1994 | André Willims (GER) | 6:46.33 | Rolf Thorsen, Lars Bjoenness (NOR) | 6:08.33 |
| 1995 | Iztok Cop (SLO) | 6:52.93 | Lars Christensen, Martin Haldbo-Hansen (DEN) | 6:17.01 |
| 1996 | Xeno Müller (SUI) | 6:44.85 | Davide Tizzano, Agostino Abbagnale (ITA) | 6:16.90 |
| 1997 | James Koven (USA) | 6:44.86 | Stephan Volkert, Andreas Hajek (GER) | 6:13.35 |
| 1998 | Robert Waddell (NZL) | 6:39.65 | Stephan Volkert, Andreas Hajek (GER) | 6:13.20 |
| 1999 | Robert Waddell (NZL) | 6:36.68 | Luka Spik, Iztok Cop (SLO) | 6:04.37 |
| 2000 | Robert Waddell (NZL) | 6:48.90 | Luka Spik, Iztok Cop (SLO) | 6:16.63 |
| 2001 | Olaf Tufte (NOR) | 6:43.04 | Akos Haller, Tibor Peto (HUN) | 6:14.16 |
| 2002 | Marcel Hacker (GER) | 6:36.33 | Akos Haller, Tibor Peto (HUN) | 6:05.74 |

| YEAR | COXED PAIRS | TIME | COXLESS PAIRS | TIME |
|------|-------------|------|---------------|------|
| 1983 | Thoman Greiner, Ullrich Diessner (GDR) | 6:49.75 | C. Ertel, Ulf Sauerbrey (GDR) | 6:35.85 |
| 1984[1] | G. Abbagnale, C. Abbagnale (ITA) | 7:05.99 | Petru Iosub, Valer Toma (ROM) | 6:45.39 |
| 1985 | G. Abbagnale, C. Abbagnale (ITA) | 6:53.40 | Nikolay Pimenov, Yury Pimenov (URS) | 6:38.39 |
| 1986 | Andy Holmes, Steve Redgrave (GBR) | 6:51.66 | Nikolay Pimenov, Yury Pimenov (URS) | 6:42.37 |
| 1987 | G. Abbagnale, C. Abbagnale (ITA) | 7:40.81 | Steve Redgrave, Andrew Holmes (GBR) | 7:11.20 |
| 1988[1] | G. Abbagnale, C. Abbagnale (ITA) | 6:58.79 | Steve Redgrave, Andrew Holmes (GBR) | 6:36.84 |
| 1989 | G. Abbagnale, C. Abbagnale (ITA) | 6:54.81 | Thomas Jung, Uwe Kellner (GDR) | 6:39.95 |
| 1990 | G. Abbagnale, C. Abbagnale (ITA) | 6:48.30 | Thomas Jung, Uwe Kellner (GDR) | 7:07.91 |
| 1991 | G. Abbagnale, C. Abbagnale (ITA) | 7:34.49 | Steve Redgrave, Matthew Pinsent (GBR) | 6:21.35 |
| 1992[1] | Jonny Searle, Greg Searle (GBR) | 6:49.83 | Steve Redgrave, Matthew Pinsent (GBR) | 6:27.72 |
| 1993 | Jonny Searle, Greg Searle (GBR) | 7:01.50 | Steve Redgrave, Matthew Pinsent (GBR) | 6:37.11 |
| 1994 | Tihomir Frankovic, Igor Boraska (CRO) | 6:42.16 | Steve Redgrave, Matthew Pinsent (GBR) | 6:18.65 |

## World Rowing Championships—Men (continued)

| YEAR | COXED PAIRS | TIME | COXLESS PAIRS | TIME |
|------|-------------|------|---------------|------|
| 1995 | Luca Sartori, Giuliano DeStabile (ITA) | 7:35.11 | Steve Redgrave, Matthew Pinsent (GBR) | 6:28.11 |
| 1996 | Yannick Schulte, Luc Prevot (FRA) | 7:18.26 | Steve Redgrave, Matthew Pinsent (GBR) | 6:20.09 |
| 1997 | Scott Fentress, Jordan Irving (USA) | 6:56.30 | Michel Andrieux, Jean-Christophe Rolland (FRA) | 6:27.69 |
| 1998 | Nick Green, James Tomkins (AUS) | 6:45.01 | Robert Sens, Detlef Kirchhoff (GER) | 6:22.32 |
| 1999 | James Neil, Phil Henry (USA) | 6:48.56 | Drew Ginn, James Tomkins (AUS) | 6:19.00 |
| 2000 | Kurt Borcherding, Matt Guerrieri (USA) | 7:07.15 | Michel Andrieux, Jean-Christophe Rolland (FRA) | 6:32.97 |
| 2001 | James Cracknell, Matthew Pinsent (GBR) | 6:49.33 | James Cracknell, Matthew Pinsent (GBR) | 6:27.57 |
| 2002 | Lars Krisch, Andreas Werner (GER) | 6:47.93 | James Cracknell, Matthew Pinsent (GBR) | 6:14.27 |

| YEAR | COXED FOURS | TIME | YEAR | COXLESS FOURS | TIME | YEAR | EIGHTS | TIME |
|------|-------------|------|------|---------------|------|------|--------|------|
| 1983 | New Zealand | 6:13.89 | 1983 | West Germany | 5:57.02 | 1983 | New Zealand | 5:34.39 |
| 1984[1] | Great Britain | 6:18.64 | 1984[1] | New Zealand | 6:03.48 | 1984[1] | Canada | 5:41.32 |
| 1985 | USSR | 6:07.23 | 1985 | West Germany | 6:00.19 | 1985 | USSR | 5:33.71 |
| 1986 | East Germany | 6:03.81 | 1986 | United States | 6:03.53 | 1986 | Australia | 5:33.54 |
| 1987 | East Germany | 6:41.74 | 1987 | East Germany | 6:39.70 | 1987 | United States | 5:58.83 |
| 1988[1] | East Germany | 6:10.74 | 1988[1] | East Germany | 6:03.11 | 1988[1] | West Germany | 5:46.05 |
| 1989 | Romania | 6:14.90 | 1989 | East Germany | 6:06.94 | 1989 | West Germany | 5:43.88 |
| 1990 | East Germany | 6:46.73 | 1990 | Australia | 5:52.20 | 1990 | West Germany | 5:26.62 |
| 1991 | Germany | 5:58.96 | 1991 | Australia | 6:29.69 | 1991 | Germany | 5:50.98 |
| 1992[1] | Romania | 5:59.37 | 1992[1] | Australia | 5:55.04 | 1992[1] | Canada | 5:29.53 |
| 1993 | Romania | 6:14.64 | 1993 | France | 6:04.54 | 1993 | Germany | 5:37.08 |
| 1994 | Romania | 6:06.69 | 1994 | Italy | 5:48.44 | 1994 | United States | 5:24.50 |
| 1995 | United States | 6:37.50 | 1995 | Italy | 5:58.28 | 1995 | Germany | 5:53.40 |
| 1996 | Romania | 6:25.74 | 1996 | Australia | 6:06.37 | 1996 | Netherlands | 5:42.74 |
| 1997 | France | 6:04.17 | 1997 | Great Britain | 5:52.40 | 1997 | United States | 5:27.20 |
| 1998 | Australia | 6:09.43 | 1998 | Great Britain | 5:48.06 | 1998 | United States | 5:38.78 |
| 1999 | United States | 6:38.31 | 1999 | Great Britain | 5:48.57 | 1999 | United States | 6:01.58 |
| 2000 | Great Britain | 6:16.82 | 2000 | Great Britain | 5:56.24 | 2000 | Great Britain | 5:33.08 |
| 2001 | France | 6:08.25 | 2001 | Great Britain | 5:48.98 | 2001 | Romania | 5:27.48 |
| 2002 | Great Britain | 6:06.70 | 2002 | Germany | 5:41.35 | 2002 | Canada | 5:26.92 |

[1]Olympic champions, recognized as world champions.

## World Rowing Championships—Women

*The competition has been held since 1974. The table shows only the past 20 years. Results are for heavyweight events only. Times are given in minutes:seconds.*

| YEAR | SINGLE SCULLS | TIME | DOUBLE SCULLS | TIME |
|------|---------------|------|---------------|------|
| 1983 | Jutta Behrendt-Hampe (GDR) | 3:36.51 | J. Schenk, Martina Schröter (GDR) | 3:13.44 |
| 1984[1] | Valeria Racila (ROM) | 3:40.68 | Marioara Popescu, Elisabeta Oleniuc (ROM) | 3:26.75 |
| 1985 | Cornelia Linse (GDR) | 7:40.37 | Sylvia Schwabe, Martina Schröter (GDR) | 6:58.80 |
| 1986 | Jutta Behrendt-Hampe (GDR) | 7:29.60 | Sylvia Schwabe, Martina Schröter (GDR) | 6:57.71 |
| 1987 | Magdalena Georgieva (BUL) | 8:59.26 | Stefka Madina, Violeta Ninova (BUL) | 7:47.89 |
| 1988[1] | Jutta Behrendt-Hampe (GDR) | 7:47.19 | Birgit Peter, Martina Schröter (GDR) | 7:00.48 |
| 1989 | Elisabeth Lipa (ROM) | 7:27.96 | Jana Sorges, Beate Schramm (GDR) | 7:01.71 |
| 1990 | Birgit Peter (GDR) | 7:24.10 | Kathrin Boron, Beate Schramm (GDR) | 8:18.63 |
| 1991 | Silken Laumann (CAN) | 8:17.58 | Kathrin Boron, Beate Schramm (GER) | 6:44.71 |
| 1992[1] | Elisabeth Lipa (ROM) | 7:25.54 | Kathrin Boron, Kerstin Köppen (GER) | 6:49.00 |
| 1993 | Jana Thieme (GER) | 7:26.00 | Philippa Baker, Brenda Lawson (NZL) | 7:03.42 |
| 1994 | Trine Hansen (DEN) | 7:23.96 | Philippa Baker, Brenda Lawson (NZL) | 6:45.30 |
| 1995 | Maria Brandin (SWE) | 7:26.00 | Marnie McBean, Kathleen Heddle (CAN) | 6:55.76 |
| 1996 | Yekaterina Khodotovich (BLR) | 7:32.21 | Marnie McBean, Kathleen Heddle (CAN) | 6:56.84 |
| 1997 | Yekaterina Khodotovich (BLR) | 7:29.30 | Meike Evers, Kathrin Boron (GER) | 6:51.07 |
| 1998 | Irina Fedotova (RUS) | 7:25.09 | Miriam Batten, Gillian Lindsay (GBR) | 6:48.85 |
| 1999 | Yekaterina Khodotovich-Karsten (BLR) | 7:11.68 | Jana Thieme, Kathrin Boron (GER) | 6:41.98 |
| 2000 | Yekaterina Khodotovich-Karsten (BLR) | 7:28.14 | Jana Thieme, Kathrin Boron (GER) | 6:55.44 |
| 2001 | Katrin Rutschow-Stomporowski (GER) | 7:19.25 | Kathrin Boron, Kerstin Kowalski (GER) | 6:50.20 |
| 2002 | Rumyana Neykova (BUL) | 7:07.71 | Georgina Evers-Swindell, Caroline Evers-Swindell (NZL) | 6:38.78 |
| 2003 | *to be held 24–31 August, Milan, Italy* | | | |

# World Rowing Championships—Women (continued)

| YEAR | QUADRUPLE SCULLS | TIME | YEAR | QUADRUPLE SCULLS | TIME |
|---|---|---|---|---|---|
| 1983 | USSR | 3:02.48 | 1994 | Germany | 6:11.73 |
| 1984[1] | Romania | 3:14.11 | 1995 | Germany | 6:40.80 |
| 1985 | East Germany | 6:22.47 | 1996 | Germany | 6:27.44 |
| 1986 | East Germany | 6:13.91 | 1997 | Germany | 6:16.15 |
| 1987 | East Germany | 6:58.42 | 1998 | Germany | 6:24.38 |
| 1988[1] | East Germany | 6:21.06 | 1999 | Germany | 7:06.53 |
| 1989 | East Germany | 6:16.62 | 2000 | Germany | 6:19.58 |
| 1990 | East Germany | 6:14.08 | 2001 | Germany | 6:12.95 |
| 1991 | Germany | 6:55.85 | 2002 | Germany | 6:15.66 |
| 1992[1] | Germany | 6:20.18 | 2003 | to be held 24–31 | |
| 1993 | China | 6:21.07 | | August, Milan, Italy | |

| YEAR | COXLESS PAIRS | TIME | YEAR | COXLESS PAIRS | TIME |
|---|---|---|---|---|---|
| 1983 | Marita Gasch, S. Fruhlich (GDR) | 3:26.7 | 1993 | Christine Gosse, Helene Cortin (FRA) | 7:24.7 |
| 1984[1] | Rodica Arba, Elena Horvat (ROM) | 3:32.6 | 1994 | Christine Gosse, Helene Cortin (FRA) | 7:01.8 |
| 1985 | Rodica Arba, Elena Horvat-Florea (ROM) | 7:25.1 | 1995 | Megan Still, Kate Slatter (AUS) | 7:12.7 |
| | | | 1996 | Megan Still, Kate Slatter (AUS) | 7:01.4 |
| 1986 | Rodica Arba, Olga Homeghi (ROM) | 7:12.2 | 1997 | Emma Robinson, Alison Korn (CAN) | 7:08.1 |
| 1987 | Rodica Arba, Olga Homeghi (ROM) | 8:00.7 | 1998 | Emma Robinson, Alison Korn (CAN) | 7:05.2 |
| 1988[1] | Rodica Arba, Olga Homeghi (ROM) | 7:28.1 | 1999 | Emma Robinson, Theresa Luke (CAN) | 7:00.9 |
| 1989 | K. Haaker, Judith Zeidler (GDR) | 7:27.0 | 2000 | Georgeta Damian, Doina Ignat (ROM) | 7:11.0 |
| 1990 | Stefani Werremeier, Ingeburg Althoff (FRG) | 8:28.4 | 2001 | Georgeta Damian, Vlorica Susanu (ROM) | 7:01.2 |
| 1991 | Marnie McBean, Kathleen Heddle (CAN) | 6:57.4 | 2002 | Georgeta Andrunache, Vlorica Susanu (ROM) | 6:53.8 |
| 1992[1] | Marnie McBean, K. Heddle (CAN) | 7:06.2 | 2003 | to be held 24–31 August, Milan, Italy | |

| YEAR | FOURS[2] | TIME | YEAR | FOURS[2] | TIME | YEAR | EIGHTS | TIME |
|---|---|---|---|---|---|---|---|---|
| 1983 | East Germany | 3:11.18 | 1999 | Belarus | 6:26.25 | 1991 | Canada | 6:28.20 |
| 1984[1] | Romania | 3:19.30 | 2000 | Belarus | 6:44.90 | 1992[1] | Canada | 6:02.62 |
| 1985 | East Germany | 6:50.08 | 2001 | Australia | 6:27.23 | 1993 | Romania | 6:18.88 |
| 1986 | Romania | 6:43.86 | 2002 | Australia | 6:26.11 | 1994 | Germany | 6:07.42 |
| 1987 | Romania | 7:30.12 | 2003 | to be held 24–31 | | 1995 | United States | 6:50.73 |
| 1988[1] | East Germany | 6:56.00 | | August, Milan, Italy | | 1996 | Romania | 6:19.73 |
| 1989 | East Germany | 6:45.81 | | | | 1997 | Romania | 6:02.40 |
| 1990 | Romania | 7:51.68 | YEAR | EIGHTS | TIME | 1998 | Romania | 6:14.62 |
| 1991 | Canada | 6:25.43 | 1983 | USSR | 2:56.22 | 1999 | Romania | 6:47.66 |
| 1992[1] | Canada | 6:30.85 | 1984[1] | United States | 2:59.80 | 2000 | Romania | 6:44.00 |
| 1993 | China | 6:42.06 | 1985 | USSR | 6:14.00 | 2001 | Australia | 6:03.66 |
| 1994 | Netherlands | 6:30.76 | 1986 | USSR | 6:08.76 | 2002 | United States | 6:04.25 |
| 1995 | United States | 7:03.53 | 1987 | Romania | 6:55.61 | 2003 | to be held 24–31 | |
| 1996 | United States | 6:49.48 | 1988[1] | East Germany | 6:15.17 | | August, Milan, Italy | |
| 1997 | Great Britain | 6:40.30 | 1989 | Romania | 6:07.92 | | | |
| 1998 | Ukraine | 6:30.63 | 1990 | Romania | 5:59.26 | | | |

[1]Olympic champions, recognized as world champions.　[2]With coxswain until 1989; coxless since then.

# Grand Challenge Cup

Cup has been contested since 1839. Table shows results for the past 20 years. Winners are British except as indicated. Times are given in minutes:seconds.

| YEAR | WINNER | TIME | YEAR | WINNER | TIME |
|---|---|---|---|---|---|
| 1984 | Leander Club and London R.C.[1] | 6:22 | 1995 | San Diego Training Center (USA) | 5:59 |
| 1985 | Harvard University (USA) | 6:27 | 1996 | Imperial College and Queens Tower | 6:11 |
| 1986 | Nautilus R.C.[1] | 6:18 | 1997 | Institutes of Sport (AUS) | 6:03 |
| 1987 | Soviet Army (URS) | 6:11 | 1998 | Hansa Dortmund and Berlin (GER) | 6:18 |
| 1988 | Leander-University of London | 6:17 | 1999 | Hansa Dortmund and Berlin (GER) | 6:15 |
| 1989 | Hansa Dortmund (FRG) | 5:58 | 2000 | Institutes of Sport (AUS) | 6:19 |
| 1990 | Hansa Dortmund (FRG) | 6:36 | 2001 | H.A.V.K. Mladost and V.K. Croatia (CRO) | 6:29 |
| 1991 | Leander and Star R.C.[1] | 6:22 | | | |
| 1992 | University of London | 6:04 | 2002 | Victoria City R.C.[1] and University of Victoria (CAN) | |
| 1993 | Dortmund (GER) | 6:11 | | | |
| 1994 | Charles River and San Diego (USA) | 6:13 | 2003 | Victoria City R.C.[1] (CAN) | 6:12 |
| | | | 2004 | to be held in July | |

[1]R.C.—Rowing Club.

## The Diamond Challenge Sculls

*The race has been rowed since 1844. The table shows the winners for the past 20 years. Winners are British except as indicated. Times are given in minutes:seconds.*

| YEAR | WINNER (CLUB, COUNTRY) | TIME | YEAR | WINNER (CLUB, COUNTRY) | TIME |
|------|------------------------|------|------|------------------------|------|
| 1984 | Chris Baillieu (Leander Club) | 7:57 | 1994 | Xeno Müller (Grasshopper, SUI) | 7:35 |
| 1985 | Steve Redgrave (Marlow Rowing Club) | 8:28 | 1995 | Juri Jaanson (Parnu, EST) | 7:24 |
| 1986 | B. Eltang (DEN) | 8:08[1] | 1996 | Merlin Vervoorn (Delft, NED) | 7:42 |
| 1987 | Peter-Michael Kolbe (Ruder-Club Hamburg) | 7:52 | 1997 | Greg Searle (Molesey Boating Club) | 7:38 |
| | | | 1998 | James Koven (USA) | 7:56 |
| 1988 | Hamish McGlashan (Melbourne Univ.) | 7:43 | 1999 | Marcel Hacker (GER) | 7:59 |
| | | | 2000 | Aquil Abdullah (USA) | 8:12 |
| 1989 | Vaclav Chalupa (Dukla Praha, TCH) | 7:23[2] | 2001 | Duncan Free (AUS) | 8:18 |
| 1990 | Eric Verdonk (Koru, NZL) | 8:21 | 2002 | P.J.C. Wells (Univ. of London) | 8:30 |
| 1991 | W. Van Belleghem (BEL) | 8:14[1] | 2003 | Alan Campbell (The Tideway Scullers' School) | 8:03 |
| 1992 | R.G.F. Henderson (Leander Club) | 7:44 | | | |
| 1993 | Tomas Lange (GER) | 7:39 | 2004 | *to be held in July* | |

[1]*Not rowed out.*   [2]*Record.*

# Sailing (Yachting)

One of the classic sailing events is the race that was first proposed by the Royal Yacht Squadron (RYS), best known as the **America's Cup**. This cup, open to challenge since 1870, was originally the Hundred-Guinea Cup, presented by the RYS for a race around the Isle of Wight, UK, and won handily by the American yacht *America*. The most graceful of the yachts entered for the America's Cup are generally considered to have been the J-class yachts raced between 1930 and 1937. The cost of maintenance, however, was prohibitive, and since 1958, both winning and challenging vessels have been 12-m (39-ft).

The **Transpacific Race** was inaugurated in 1906 and usually was raced over 3,580 km (2,225 mi) between San Pedro CA, and Diamond Head Light, Oahu, HI. It was made biennial in 1939, alternating with the Bermuda Race.

The **Bermuda Race**, from 1906 to 1910, was an annual race between Gravesend Bay NY (in 1908 the starting point was Marblehead MA), and Bermuda. Six races from New London CT, and one from Montauk Point NY (1932), were held in 1923–34. Since 1936 it has been raced biennially from Newport RI over a 1,022-km (635-mi) course. In 1982 it was divided into two classes—one for cruiser/racers and one for grand prix racers—with the craft winning its race by the greatest margin as overall winner. Since 1986 two equal awards have been offered.

The Admiral's Cup is awarded biennially to the national team accumulating the most total points in a series of six races (five until 1987) held off the southern coast of England.

**Related Internet resources:** America's Cup: <www.americascupnews.com>; Transpacific Race: <www.transpacificyc.org>; Bermuda Race: <www.bermuda-race.com>; Admiral's Cup (Royal Ocean Racing Club Web site): <www.rorc.org>.

## World-Class Boat Champions, 2002

| CLASS | WINNER | CLASS | WINNER |
|-------|--------|-------|--------|
| Europe | Sarah Blanck (AUS) | Mistral (men) | Gal Fridman (ISR) |
| Finn | John Greenwood (GBR) | Mistral (women) | Barbara Kendall (NZL) |
| 470 (men) | Simon Cooke/Peter Nicholas (NZL) | Star | Iain Percy/Steven Mitchell (GBR) |
| 470 (women) | Sofia Bekatorou/ Emilia Tsoulfa (GRE) | Tornado | Darren Bundock/John Forbes (AUS) |
| 49er | Iker Martínez/Xabi Fernández (ESP) | Yngling | Monica Azon/Laia Tutzo/ Sandra Azon (ESP) |
| Laser | Robert Scheidt (BRA) | | |

**Did you know?** The "Bermuda Triangle," an area of the North Atlantic Ocean between Bermuda, the US, and the Greater Antilles, is notorious for the large number of airplanes and ships that have disappeared there without a trace, but scientific substantiation for the peril of the region does not exist.

## America's Cup

| YEAR | WINNING YACHT | OWNER | SKIPPER | LOSING YACHT | OWNER |
|---|---|---|---|---|---|
| 1851 | America (USA) | John Cox Stevens | Richard Brown | Aurora (GBR) | Thomas Le Marchant |
| 1870 | Magic (USA) | Franklin Osgood | Andrew Comstock | Cambria (GBR) | James Ashbury |
| 1871 | Columbia (USA) | Franklin Osgood | Nelson Comstock | Livonia (GBR) | James Ashbury |
| | Sappho (USA) | William P. Douglas | Sam Greenwood | | |
| 1876 | Madeleine (USA) | John S. Dickerson | Josephus Williams | Countess of Dufferin (CAN) | Charles Gifford and syndicate |
| 1881 | Mischief (USA) | Joseph R. Busk | Nathaniel Clock | Atalanta (CAN) | Alexander Cuthbert |
| 1885 | Puritan (USA) | J. Malcolm Forbes, Charles J. Paine and syndicate | Aubrey Crocker | Genesta (GBR) | Sir Richard Sutton |
| 1886 | Mayflower (USA) | Charles J. Paine | Martin V.B. Stone | Galatea (GBR) | William Henn |
| 1887 | Volunteer (USA) | Charles J. Paine | Henry C. Haff | Thistle (GBR) | James Bell and syndicate |
| 1893 | Vigilant (USA) | C. Oliver Iselin and syndicate | William Hansen | Valkyrie II (GBR) | Lord Dunraven |
| 1895 | Defender (USA) | William K. Vanderbilt, C. Oliver Iselin, Edwin D. Morgan | Henry C. Haff | Valkyrie III (GBR) | Lord Dunraven, Lord Lonsdale, Lord Wolverton, H. McCalmont |
| 1899 | Columbia (USA) | J.P. Morgan, C. Oliver Iselin, Edwin D. Morgan | Charles Barr | Shamrock (GBR) | Sir Thomas Lipton |
| 1901 | Columbia (USA) | J.P. Morgan, Edwin D. Morgan | Charles Barr | Shamrock II (GBR) | Sir Thomas Lipton |
| 1903 | Reliance (USA) | C. Oliver Iselin and syndicate | Charles Barr | Shamrock III (GBR) | Sir Thomas Lipton |
| 1920 | Resolute (USA) | Henry Walters and syndicate | Charles Francis Adams II | Shamrock IV (GBR) | Sir Thomas Lipton |
| 1930 | Enterprise (USA) | Winthrop Aldrich and syndicate | Harold S. Vanderbilt | Shamrock V (GBR) | Sir Thomas Lipton |
| 1934 | Rainbow (USA) | Harold S. Vanderbilt and syndicate | Harold S. Vanderbilt | Endeavour (GBR) | Thomas Octave Murdoch Sopwith |
| 1937 | Ranger (USA) | Harold S. Vanderbilt | Harold S. Vanderbilt | Endeavour II (GBR) | Thomas Octave Murdoch Sopwith |
| 1958 | Columbia (USA) | Henry Sears and syndicate | Briggs S. Cunningham | Sceptre (GBR) | Hugh L. Goodson and syndicate |
| 1962 | Weatherly (USA) | Henry D. Mercer, Arnold D. Frese, Cornelius S. Walsh | Emil Mosbacher, Jr. | Gretel (AUS) | Sir Frank Packer and syndicate |
| 1964 | Constellation (USA) | Walter S. Gubelmann, Eric Ridder and syndicate | Robert N. Bavier, Jr., Eric Ridder | Sovereign (GBR) | J. Anthony Boyden |
| 1967 | Intrepid (USA) | Intrepid syndicate | Emil Mosbacher, Jr. | Dame Pattie (GBR) | Emil Christensen and 15 commercial firms |
| 1970 | Intrepid (USA) | Intrepid syndicate | William Ficker | Gretel II (AUS) | Sir Frank Packer and syndicate |
| 1974 | Courageous (USA) | Courageous syndicate | Ted Hood | Southern Cross (AUS) | Alan Bond |
| 1977 | Courageous (USA) | Courageous syndicate | Ted Turner | Australia (AUS) | Alan Bond and syndicate |
| 1980 | Freedom (USA) | Maritime College at Ft. Schuyler Foundation, Inc. | Dennis Conner | Australia (AUS) | Alan Bond and syndicate |
| 1983 | Australia II (AUS) | Alan Bond and syndicate | John Bertrand | Liberty (USA) | Maritime Col. at Ft. Schuyler Foundation, Inc. |
| 1987 | Stars & Stripes (USA) | Sail America syndicate | Dennis Conner | Kookaburra III (AUS) | Kevin Parry and syndicate |
| 1988 | Stars & Stripes (USA) | Sail America syndicate | Dennis Conner | New Zealand (NZL) | Michael Fay |
| 1992 | America³ (USA) | America³ Foundation | William Koch | Il Moro di Venezia (ITA) | Compagnia della Vela di Venezia |
| 1995 | Black Magic (NZL) | Peter Blake and Team New Zealand | Russell Coutts | Young America (USA) | Pact 95 syndicate |
| 2000 | Black Magic (NZL) | Team New Zealand | Russell Coutts | Luna Rossa (ITA) | Prada Challenge |
| 2003 | Alinghi (SUI) | Alinghi Swiss Challenge | Russell Coutts | New Zealand (NZL) | Team New Zealand |

## Transpacific Race

| YEAR | WINNING YACHT | OWNER | YEAR | WINNING YACHT | OWNER |
|------|---------------|-------|------|---------------|-------|
| 1906 | Lurline | Harold H. Sinclair | 1963 | Islander | Earl Corkett |
| 1908 | Lurline | Harold H. Sinclair | 1965 | Psyche | Don Salisbury |
| 1910 | Hawaii | Honolulu Yachting Club | 1967 | Holiday Too | Robert Allan |
| 1912 | Lurline | A.E. Davis | 1969 | Argonaut | Jon Andron |
| 1923 | Diablo | A.R. Pedder | 1971 | Windward Passage | Robert Johnson |
| 1925 | Mariner | L.A. Norris | 1973 | Chutzpah | Stuart Cowan |
| 1926 | Invader | Don M. Lee | 1975 | Chutzpah | Stuart Cowan |
| 1928 | Teva | Clem W. Stose | 1977 | Merlin | Bill Lee |
| 1930 | Enchantress | Morgan Adams | 1979 | Arriba | Dennis Choate |
| 1932 | Fayth | William S. McNutt | 1981 | Sweet Okole | Dean Treadway |
| 1934 | Manulwa | Harold Dillingham | 1983 | Bravura | Irving Loube |
| 1936 | Dorade | James Flood | 1985 | Montgomery Street | James Denning |
| 1939 | Blitzen | T.J. Reynolds | 1987 | Merlin | Don Campion |
| 1941 | Escapade | D.W. Elliott | 1989 | Silver Bullet | John DeLaura |
| 1943-45 | not held | | 1991 | Chance | Robert McNulty |
| 1947 | Dolphin | Frank Morgan | 1993 | Silver Bullet | John DeLaura |
| 1949 | Kitten | Fred W. Lyon | 1995 | Merlin | Dan Sinclair |
| 1951 | Sea Witch | A.L. McCormick | 1997 | Ralphie | Jerry Montgomery |
| 1953 | Staghound | Ira P. Fulmor | 1999 | Grand Illusion | James McDowell |
| 1955 | Staghound | Ira P. Fulmor | 2001 | Bull | Seth Radow |
| 1957 | Legend | Charles Ullman | 2003 | Alta Vita | Bill Turpin |
| 1959 | Nalu II | Peter Grant | 2005 | to be held in July, Los Angeles to Hawaii | |
| 1961 | Nam Sang | A.B. Robbs, Jr. | | | |

## Bermuda Race

| YEAR | WINNING YACHT | OWNER | YEAR | WINNING YACHT | OWNER |
|------|---------------|-------|------|---------------|-------|
| 1906 | Tamerlane | Frank Maier | 1962 | Nina | DeCoursey Fales |
| 1907 | Dervish | Henry A. Morss | 1964 | Burgoo | Milton Ernstof |
| 1908 | Venona | Elmer J. Bliss | 1966 | Thunderbird | T.V. Learson |
| 1909 | Margaret | George S. Runk | 1968 | Robin | Ted Hood |
| 1910 | Vagrant | Harold S. Vanderbilt | 1970 | Carina | Richard S. Nye |
| 1923[1] | Malabar IV | John G. Alden | 1972 | Noryema | Ron Amey |
| 1924 | Memory | Robert N. Bavier | 1974 | Scaramouche | Charles Kirsch |
| 1926 | Malabar VII | John G. Alden | 1976 | Running Tide | Al Van Metre |
| 1928 | Rugosa II | Russell Grinnell | 1978 | Babe | Arnie Gay |
| 1930 | Malay | Raymond W. Ferris | 1980 | Holger Danske | Rich Wilson |
| 1932 | Malabar X | John G. Alden and R.I. Gale | 1982[2] | Brigadoon III | Robert Morton |
| 1934 | Edlu | Rudolph J. Schaefer | 1984 | Pamir | Francis H. Curren, Jr. |
| 1936 | Kirawan | Robert P. Baruch | 1986[3] | Silver Star | David H. Clarke |
| 1938 | Baruna | Henry C. Taylor | | Puritan | Donald P. Robinson |
| 1946[1] | Gesture | Howard Fuller | 1988 | Congere | Bevin Koeppel |
| 1948 | Baruna | Henry C. Taylor | 1990 | Denali | Lawrence S. Huntington |
| 1950 | Argyll | William T. Moore | 1992 | Constellation | US Naval Academy |
| 1952 | Carina | Richard S. Nye | 1994 | Gaylark | Kaighn Smith |
| 1954 | Malay | D.D. Strohmeier | 1996 | Boomerang | George Coumantaros |
| 1956 | Finisterre | Carleton Mitchell | 1998 | Kodiak | Llwyd Ecclestone |
| 1958 | Finisterre | Carleton Mitchell | 2000 | Restless | Eric Crawford |
| 1960 | Finisterre | Carleton Mitchell | 2002 | Zaraffa | Huntington Sheldon, M.D. |

[1]No competition 1911–22; 1940–44.    [2]Overall winner under new measurement rules.    [3]First listed is IOR (International Offshore Rule) winner; second is IMS (International Measurement System) winner.

## Admiral's Cup

| YEAR | WINNING TEAM | YEAR | WINNING TEAM | YEAR | WINNING TEAM | YEAR | WINNING TEAM |
|------|--------------|------|--------------|------|--------------|------|--------------|
| 1957 | United Kingdom | 1969 | United States | 1981 | United Kingdom | 1993 | Germany |
| 1959 | United Kingdom | 1971 | United Kingdom | 1983 | West Germany | 1995 | Italy |
| 1961 | United States | 1973 | West Germany | 1985 | West Germany | 1997 | United States |
| 1963 | United Kingdom | 1975 | United Kingdom | 1987 | New Zealand | 1999 | The Netherlands |
| 1965 | United Kingdom | 1977 | United Kingdom | 1989 | United Kingdom | 2001 | canceled |
| 1967 | Australia | 1979 | Australia | 1991 | France | 2003 | Australia |

# Skiing

Although most of the events had been contested at the regional level since the mid-19th century, the first internationally organized **skiing championships** did not take place until 1924. From 1924 to 1931 only **Nordic** competition was involved; **Alpine** championship events were added to world competition in 1931 and to the Olympics in 1936. Except for Olympic years, the Nordic and Alpine championships are held separately and at different locations. **Events** include cross-country races, ski-jumping, biathlon, and relay races (Nordic) and downhill and slalom skiing (Alpine). Since 1967, an **Alpine World Cup** has been presented to the competitor with the best combined downhill, slalom, supergiant slalom (super-G), and giant slalom performance over a series of major contests. A **Nordic World Cup** for cross-country events has been awarded since 1979.

**International Ski Federation Web site:** <www.fis-ski.com>

## Alpine Skiing World Championships—Men

*The next championships are scheduled to be held in January 2004, in Austria and the Czech Rep.*

**DOWNHILL**
| | |
|---|---|
| 1931 | Walter Prager (SUI) |
| 1932 | *not held* |
| 1933 | Walter Prager (SUI), Hans Hauser (AUT)[1] |
| 1934 | David Zogg (SUI) |
| 1935 | Franz Zingerle (AUT) |
| 1936[2] | *not held* |
| 1937 | Emile Allais (FRA) |
| 1938 | James Couttet (FRA) |
| 1939 | Hermuth Lantschner (GER) |
| 1940–47 | *not held* |
| 1948[2] | Henri Oreiller (FRA) |
| 1950 | Zeno Colo (ITA) |
| 1952[2] | Zeno Colo (ITA) |
| 1954 | Christian Pravda (AUT) |
| 1956[2] | Anton (Toni) Sailer (AUT) |
| 1958 | Anton (Toni) Sailer (AUT) |
| 1960[2] | Jean Vuarnet (FRA) |
| 1962 | Karl Schranz (AUT) |
| 1964[2] | Egon Zimmermann (AUT) |
| 1966 | Jean-Claude Killy (FRA) |
| 1968[2] | Jean-Claude Killy (FRA) |
| 1970 | Bernhard Russi (SUI) |
| 1972[2] | Bernhard Russi (SUI) |
| 1974 | David Zwilling (AUT) |
| 1976[2] | Franz Klammer (AUT) |
| 1978 | Josef Walcher (AUT) |
| 1980[2] | Leonhard Stock (AUT) |
| 1982 | Harti Weirather (AUT) |
| 1984[2] | Bill Johnson (USA) |
| 1985 | Permin Zurbriggen (SUI) |
| 1987 | Peter Müller (SUI) |
| 1988[2] | Permin Zurbriggen (SUI) |
| 1989 | Hansjorg Tauscher (FRG) |
| 1991 | Franz Heinzer (SUI) |
| 1992[2] | Patrick Ortlieb (AUS) |
| 1993 | Urs Lehmann (SUI) |
| 1994[2] | Tommy Moe (USA) |
| 1995 | *not held* |
| 1996 | Patrick Ortlieb (AUS) |
| 1997 | Bruno Kernen (SUI) |
| 1998[2] | Jean-Luc Cretier (FRA) |
| 1999 | Hermann Maier (AUT) |
| 2000 | *not held* |
| 2001 | Hannes Trinkl (AUT) |
| 2002[2] | Fritz Strobl (AUT) |
| 2003 | Michael Walchhofer (AUT) |

**COMBINED**
| | |
|---|---|
| 1933 | Anton Seelos (AUT) |
| 1934 | David Zogg (SUI) |
| 1935 | Anton Seelos (AUT) |

**COMBINED (CONTINUED)**
| | |
|---|---|
| 1936[2] | Franz Pfnür (GER) |
| 1937 | Emile Allais (FRA) |
| 1938 | Emile Allais (FRA) |
| 1939 | Josef Jennewein (GER) |
| 1940–47 | *not held* |
| 1948[2] | Henri Oreiller (FRA) |
| 1950 | *not held* |
| 1952[2] | *not held* |
| 1954 | Stein Eriksen (NOR) |
| 1956[2] | *not held* |
| 1958 | Anton (Toni) Sailer (AUT) |
| 1960[2] | *not held* |
| 1962 | Karl Schranz (AUT) |
| 1964[2] | *not held* |
| 1966 | Jean-Claude Killy (FRA) |
| 1968[2] | *not held* |
| 1970 | Bill Kidd (USA) |
| 1972[2] | Gustavo Thoeni (ITA) |
| 1974 | Franz Klammer (AUT) |
| 1976[2] | Gustavo Thoeni (ITA) |
| 1978 | Andreas Wenzel (LIE) |
| 1980[2] | *not held* |
| 1982 | Michel Vion (FRA) |
| 1984[2] | *not held* |
| 1985 | Pirmin Zurbriggen (SUI) |
| 1986 | *not held* |
| 1987 | Marc Girardelli (LUX) |
| 1988[2] | Hubert Strolz (AUT) |
| 1989 | Marc Girardelli (LUX) |
| 1991 | Stefan Eberharter (AUT) |
| 1992[2] | Josef Polig (ITA) |
| 1993 | Lasse Kjus (NOR) |
| 1994[2] | Lasse Kjus (NOR) |
| 1995 | *not held* |
| 1996 | Marc Girardelli (LUX) |
| 1997 | Kjetil Andre Aamodt (NOR) |
| 1998[2] | Mario Reiter (AUT) |
| 1999 | Kjetil Andre Aamodt (NOR) |
| 2000 | *not held* |
| 2001 | Kjetil Andre Aamodt (NOR) |
| 2002[2] | Kjetil Andre Aamodt (NOR) |
| 2003 | Bode Miller (USA) |

**SLALOM**
| | |
|---|---|
| 1931 | David Zogg (SUI) |
| 1932 | *not held* |
| 1933 | Anton Seelos (AUT) |
| 1934 | Franz Pfnür (GER) |
| 1935 | Anton Seelos (AUT) |

**SLALOM (CONTINUED)**
| | |
|---|---|
| 1936[2] | *not held* |
| 1937 | Emile Allais (FRA) |
| 1938 | Rudi Rominger (SUI) |
| 1939 | Rudi Rominger (SUI) |
| 1940–47 | *not held* |
| 1948[2] | Edi Reinalter (SUI) |
| 1950 | Georges Schneider (SUI) |
| 1952[2] | Othmar Schneider (AUT) |
| 1954 | Stein Eriksen (NOR) |
| 1956[2] | Anton (Toni) Sailer (AUT) |
| 1958 | Josi Rieder (AUT) |
| 1960[2] | Ernst Hinterseer (AUT) |
| 1962 | Charles Bozon (FRA)[3] |
| 1964[2] | Josef Stiegler (AUT) |
| 1966 | Carlo Senoner (ITA)[3] |
| 1968[2] | Jean-Claude Killy (FRA) |
| 1970 | Jean-Noël Augert (FRA) |
| 1972[2] | Francisco Ochoa (ESP) |
| 1974 | Gustavo Thoeni (ITA) |
| 1976[2] | Piero Gros (ITA) |
| 1978 | Ingemar Stenmark (SWE) |
| 1980[2] | Ingemar Stenmark (SWE) |
| 1982 | Ingemar Stenmark (SWE) |
| 1984[2] | Phil Mahre (USA) |
| 1985 | Jonas Nilsson (SWE) |
| 1987 | Frank Woerndl (FRG) |
| 1988[2] | Alberto Tomba (ITA) |
| 1989 | Rudolf Nierlich (AUT) |
| 1991 | Marc Girardelli (LUX) |
| 1992[2] | Finn Christian Jagge (NOR) |
| 1993 | Kjetil Andre Aamodt (NOR) |
| 1994[2] | Thomas Stangassinger (AUT) |
| 1995 | *not held* |
| 1996 | Alberto Tomba (ITA) |
| 1997 | Tom Stiansen (NOR) |
| 1998[2] | Hans-Petter Buraas (NOR) |
| 1999 | Kalle Palander (FIN) |
| 2000 | *not held* |
| 2001 | Mario Matt (AUT) |
| 2002[2] | Jean-Pierre Vidal (FRA) |
| 2003 | Ivica Kostelic (CRO) |

**GIANT SLALOM**
| | |
|---|---|
| 1950 | Zeno Colo (ITA) |
| 1952[2] | Stein Eriksen (NOR) |
| 1954 | Stein Eriksen (NOR) |
| 1956[2] | Anton (Toni) Sailer (AUT) |
| 1958 | Anton (Toni) Sailer (AUT) |
| 1960[2] | Roger Staub (SUI) |

## Alpine Skiing World Championships—Men (continued)

**GIANT SLALOM (CONTINUED)**

| | |
|---|---|
| 1962 | Egon Zimmermann (AUT) |
| 1964[2] | François Bonlieu (FRA) |
| 1966 | Guy Perillat (FRA) |
| 1968[2] | Jean-Claude Killy (FRA) |
| 1970 | Karl Schranz (AUT) |
| 1972[2] | Gustavo Thoeni (ITA) |
| 1974 | Gustavo Thoeni (ITA) |
| 1976[2] | Heini Hemmi (SUI) |
| 1978 | Ingemar Stenmark (SWE) |
| 1980[2] | Ingemar Stenmark (SWE) |
| 1982 | Steve Mahre (USA) |
| 1984[2] | Max Julen (SUI) |
| 1985 | Markus Wasmeier (FRG) |
| 1987 | Pirmin Zurbriggen (SUI) |
| 1988[2] | Alberto Tomba (ITA) |
| 1989 | Rudolf Nierlich (AUT) |
| 1991 | Rudolf Nierlich (AUT) |

**GIANT SLALOM (CONTINUED)**

| | |
|---|---|
| 1992[2] | Alberto Tomba (ITA) |
| 1993 | Kjetil Andre Aamodt (NOR) |
| 1994[2] | Markus Wasmeier (GER) |
| 1995 | not held |
| 1996 | Alberto Tomba (ITA) |
| 1997 | Michael von Grünigen (SUI) |
| 1998[2] | Hermann Maier (AUT) |
| 1999 | Lasse Kjus (NOR) |
| 2000 | not held |
| 2001 | Michael von Grünigen (SUI) |
| 2002[2] | Stephan Eberharter (AUT) |
| 2003 | Bode Miller (USA) |

**SUPERGIANT SLALOM**

| | |
|---|---|
| 1987 | Pirmin Zurbriggen (SUI) |

**SUPERGIANT SLALOM (CONTINUED)**

| | |
|---|---|
| 1988[2] | Franck Piccard (FRA) |
| 1989 | Martin Hangl (SUI) |
| 1991 | Stephan Eberharter (AUT) |
| 1992[2] | Kjetil Andre Aamodt (NOR) |
| 1993 | not held |
| 1994[2] | Markus Wasmeier (GER) |
| 1995 | not held |
| 1996 | Atle Skaardal (NOR) |
| 1997 | Atle Skaardal (NOR) |
| 1998[2] | Hermann Maier (AUT) |
| 1999 | Lasse Kjus (NOR), Hermann Maier (AUT)[4] |
| 2000 | not held |
| 2001 | Daron Rahlves (USA) |
| 2002[2] | Kjetil Andre Aamodt (NOR) |
| 2003 | Stephan Eberharter (AUT) |

[1]Special downhill champion. [2]Olympic champions, recognized as world champions. [3]Special slalom. [4]Tie.

## Alpine Skiing World Championships—Women

*The next championships are scheduled to be held in January 2004, in Austria and the Czech Rep.*

**DOWNHILL**

| | |
|---|---|
| 1931 | Esme Mackinnon (GBR) |
| 1932 | Paula Wiesinger (ITA) |
| 1933 | Inge Wersin-Lantschner (AUT) |
| 1934 | Anny Rüegg (SUI) |
| 1935 | Christl Cranz (GER) |
| 1936 | Evelyn Pinching (GBR) |
| 1937 | Christl Cranz (GER) |
| 1938 | Lisa Resch (GER) |
| 1939 | Christl Cranz (GER) |
| 1940–47 | not held |
| 1948[1] | Hedy Schlunegger (SUI) |
| 1950 | Trude Jochum-Beiser (AUT) |
| 1952[1] | Trude Jochum-Beiser (AUT) |
| 1954 | Ida Schöpfer (SUI) |
| 1956[1] | Madeleine Berthod (SUI) |
| 1958 | Lucille Wheeler (CAN) |
| 1960[1] | Heidi Beibl (GER[2]) |
| 1962 | Christl Hass (AUT) |
| 1964[1] | Christl Hass (AUT) |
| 1966 | Marielle Goitschel (FRA)[3] |
| 1968[1] | Olga Pall (AUT) |
| 1970 | Annerösli Zryd (SUI) |
| 1972[1] | Marie-Thérèse Nadig (SUI) |
| 1974 | Annemarie Moser-Pröll (AUT) |
| 1976[1] | Rosi Mittermaier (FRG) |
| 1978 | Annemarie Moser-Pröll (AUT) |
| 1980[1] | Annemarie Moser-Pröll (AUT) |
| 1982 | Gerry Sorensen (CAN) |
| 1984[1] | Michela Figini (SUI) |
| 1985 | Michela Figini (SUI) |
| 1987 | Maria Walliser (SUI) |
| 1988[1] | Marina Kiehl (FRG) |
| 1989 | Maria Walliser (SUI) |
| 1991 | Petra Kronberger (AUT) |
| 1992[1] | Kerrin Lee-Gartner (CAN) |

**DOWNHILL (CONTINUED)**

| | |
|---|---|
| 1993 | Kate Pace (CAN) |
| 1994[1] | Katja Seizinger (GER) |
| 1995 | not held |
| 1996 | Picabo Street (USA) |
| 1997 | Hilary Lindh (USA) |
| 1998[1] | Katja Seizinger (GER) |
| 1999 | Renate Götschl (AUT) |
| 2000 | not held |
| 2001 | Michaela Dorfmeister (AUT) |
| 2002[1] | Carole Montillet (FRA) |
| 2003 | Mélanie Turgeon (CAN) |

**COMBINED**

| | |
|---|---|
| 1932 | Rösli Streiff (SUI) |
| 1933 | Inge Wersin-Lantschner (AUT) |
| 1934 | Christl Cranz (GER) |
| 1935 | Christl Cranz (GER) |
| 1936 | Evelyn Pinching (GBR) |
| 1937 | Christl Cranz (GER) |
| 1938 | Christl Cranz (GER) |
| 1939 | Christl Cranz (GER) |
| 1940–47 | not held |
| 1948[1] | Trude Beiser (AUT) |
| 1950 | not held |
| 1952 | not held |
| 1954 | Ida Schöpfer (SUI) |
| 1956 | Madeleine Berthod (SUI) |
| 1958 | Frida Dänzer (SUI) |
| 1960 | Anne Heggveit (CAN) |
| 1962 | Marielle Goitschel (FRA) |
| 1964 | Marielle Goitschel (FRA) |
| 1966 | Marielle Goitschel (FRA) |
| 1968 | Nancy Greene (CAN) |
| 1970 | Michèle Jacot (FRA) |
| 1972 | Toril Forland (NOR) |
| 1974 | Fabienne Serrat (FRA) |
| 1976 | Rosi Mittermaier (FRG) |
| 1978 | Annemarie Moser-Pröll (AUT) |
| 1980 | Hanni Wenzel (LIE) |

**COMBINED (CONTINUED)**

| | |
|---|---|
| 1982 | Erika Hess (SUI) |
| 1984[1] | not held |
| 1985 | Erika Hess (SUI) |
| 1987 | Erika Hess (SUI) |
| 1988[1] | Anita Wachter (AUT) |
| 1989 | Tamara McKinney (USA) |
| 1991 | Chantal Bournissen (SUI) |
| 1992[1] | Petra Kronberger (AUT) |
| 1993 | Miriam Vogt (GER) |
| 1994[1] | Pernilla Wiberg (SWE) |
| 1995 | not held |
| 1996 | Pernilla Wiberg (SWE) |
| 1997 | Renate Götschl (AUT) |
| 1998[1] | Katja Seizinger (GER) |
| 1999 | Pernilla Wiberg (SWE) |
| 2000 | not held |
| 2001 | Martina Ertl (GER) |
| 2002[1] | Janica Kostelic (CRO) |
| 2003 | Janica Kostelic (CRO) |

**SLALOM**

| | |
|---|---|
| 1931 | Esme Mackinnon (GBR) |
| 1932 | Rösli Streiff (SUI) |
| 1933 | Inge Wersin-Lantschner (AUT) |
| 1934 | Christl Cranz (GER) |
| 1935 | Anny Rüegg (SUI) |
| 1936 | Gerda Paumgarten (AUT) |
| 1937 | Christl Cranz (GER) |
| 1938 | Christl Cranz (GER) |
| 1939 | Christl Cranz (GER) |
| 1940–47 | not held |
| 1948[1] | Gretchen Fraser (USA) |
| 1950 | Dagmar Rom (AUT) |
| 1952[1] | Andrea Mead Lawrence (USA) |
| 1954 | Trude Klecker (AUT) |
| 1956[1] | Renée Colliard (SUI) |
| 1958 | Inge Björnbakken (NOR) |
| 1960[1] | Anne Heggtveit (CAN) |
| 1962 | Marianne Jahn (Austria)[4] |
| 1964[1] | Christine Goitschel (FRA) |

## Alpine Skiing World Championships—Women (continued)

**SLALOM** (CONTINUED)

| | |
|---|---|
| 1966 | Annie Famose (FRA)[3] |
| 1968[1] | Marielle Goitschel (FRA) |
| 1970 | Ingrid Lafforgue (FRA) |
| 1972[1] | Barbara Cochran (USA) |
| 1974 | Hanni Wenzel (LIE) |
| 1976[1] | Rosi Mittermaier (FRG) |
| 1978 | Lea Sölkner (AUT) |
| 1980[1] | Hanni Wenzel (LIE) |
| 1982 | Erika Hess (SUI) |
| 1984[1] | Paoletta Magoni (ITA) |
| 1985 | Perrine Pelen (FRA) |
| 1987 | Erika Hess (SUI) |
| 1988[1] | Vreni Schneider (SUI) |
| 1989 | Mateja Svet (YUG) |
| 1991 | Vreni Schneider (SUI) |
| 1992[1] | Petra Kronberger (AUT) |
| 1993 | Karin Buder (AUT) |
| 1994[1] | Vreni Schneider (SUI) |
| 1995 | *not held* |
| 1996 | Pernilla Wiberg (SWE) |
| 1997 | Deborah Compagnoni (ITA) |
| 1998[1] | Hilde Gerg (GER) |
| 1999 | Zali Steggall (AUS) |
| 2000 | *not held* |
| 2001 | Anja Paerson (SWE) |
| 2002[1] | Janica Kostelic (CRO) |
| 2003 | Janica Kostelic (CRO) |

**GIANT SLALOM**

| | |
|---|---|
| 1950 | Dagmar Rom (AUT) |
| 1952[1] | Andrea M. Lawrence (USA) |

**GIANT SLALOM** (CONTINUED)

| | |
|---|---|
| 1954 | Lucienne Schmidt-Couttet (FRA) |
| 1956[1] | Ossi Reichert (FRG) |
| 1958 | Lucille Wheeler (CAN) |
| 1960[1] | Yvonne Rüegg (SUI) |
| 1962 | Marianne Jahn (AUT) |
| 1964[1] | Marielle Goitschel (FRA) |
| 1966 | Marielle Goitschel (FRA) |
| 1968[1] | Nancy Greene (CAN) |
| 1970 | Betsy Clifford (CAN) |
| 1972[1] | Marie-Therese Nadig (SUI) |
| 1974 | Fabienne Serrat (FRA) |
| 1976[1] | Kathy Kreiner (CAN) |
| 1978 | Maria Epple (FRG) |
| 1980[1] | Hanni Wenzel (LIE) |
| 1982 | Erika Hess (SUI) |
| 1984[1] | Debbie Armstrong (USA) |
| 1985 | Diann Roffe (USA) |
| 1987 | Vreni Schneider (SUI) |
| 1988[1] | Vreni Schneider (SUI) |
| 1989 | Vreni Schneider (SUI) |
| 1991 | Pernilla Wiberg (SWE) |
| 1992[1] | Pernilla Wiberg (SWE) |
| 1993 | Carole Merle (FRA) |
| 1994[1] | Deborah Compagnoni (ITA) |
| 1995 | *not held* |
| 1996 | Deborah Compagnoni (ITA) |
| 1997 | Deborah Compagnoni (ITA) |

**GIANT SLALOM** (CONTINUED)

| | |
|---|---|
| 1998[1] | Deborah Compagnoni (ITA) |
| 1999 | Alexandra Meissnitzer (AUT) |
| 2000 | *not held* |
| 2001 | Sonja Nef (SUI) |
| 2002[1] | Janica Kostelic (CRO) |
| 2003 | Anja Pärson (SWE) |

**SUPERGIANT SLALOM**

| | |
|---|---|
| 1987 | Maria Walliser (SUI) |
| 1988[1] | Sigrid Wolf (AUT) |
| 1989 | Ulrike Maier (AUT) |
| 1991 | Ulrike Maier (AUT) |
| 1992[1] | Deborah Compagnoni (ITA) |
| 1993 | Katja Seizinger (GER) |
| 1994[1] | Diann Roffe-Steinrotter (USA) |
| 1995 | *not held* |
| 1996 | Isolde Kostner (ITA) |
| 1997 | Isolde Kostner (ITA) |
| 1998[1] | Picabo Street (USA) |
| 1999 | Alexandra Meissnitzer (AUT) |
| 2000 | *not held* |
| 2001 | Régine Cavagnoud (FRA) |
| 2002[1] | Daniela Ceccarelli (ITA) |
| 2003 | Michaela Dorfmeister (AUT) |

[1]*Olympic champions, recognized as world champions.*    [2]*Joint East-West German team.*    [3]*Originally won by Erika Schinegger (AUT), who renounced the medal after a sex test performed for a later Olympic game determined she was actually a man.*    [4]*Special slalom.*

## Alpine World Cup

*The winner is determined by the number of points awarded for various wins during the season.*

| YEAR | MEN | WOMEN | YEAR | MEN | WOMEN |
|---|---|---|---|---|---|
| 1967 | Jean-Claude Killy (FRA) | Nancy Greene (CAN) | 1986 | Marc Girardelli (LUX) | Maria Walliser (SUI) |
| 1968 | Jean-Claude Killy (FRA) | Nancy Greene (CAN) | 1987 | Pirmin Zurbriggen (SUI) | Maria Walliser (SUI) |
| 1969 | Karl Schranz (AUT) | Gertrude Gabl (AUT) | | | |
| 1970 | Karl Schranz (AUT) | Michele Jacot (FRA) | 1988 | Pirmin Zurbriggen (SUI) | Michela Figini (SUI) |
| 1971 | Gustavo Thoeni (ITA) | Annemarie Pröll (AUT) | | | |
| 1972 | Gustavo Thoeni (ITA) | Annemarie Pröll (AUT) | 1989 | Marc Girardelli (LUX) | Vreni Schneider (SUI) |
| 1973 | Gustavo Thoeni (ITA) | Annemarie Pröll (AUT) | 1990 | Pirmin Zurbriggen (SUI) | Petra Kronberger (AUT) |
| 1974 | Piero Gros (ITA) | Annemarie Moser-Pröll (AUT) | | | |
| | | | 1991 | Marc Girardelli (LUX) | Petra Kronberger (AUT) |
| 1975 | Gustavo Thoeni (ITA) | Annemarie Moser-Pröll (AUT) | | | |
| | | | 1992 | Paul Accola (SUI) | Petra Kronberger (AUT) |
| 1976 | Ingemar Stenmark (SWE) | Rosi Mittermaier (FRG) | 1993 | Marc Girardelli (LUX) | Anita Wachter (AUT) |
| 1977 | Ingemar Stenmark (SWE) | Lise-Marie Morerod (SUI) | 1994 | Kjetil Andre Aamodt (NOR) | Vreni Schneider (SUI) |
| 1978 | Ingemar Stenmark (SWE) | Hanni Wenzel (LIE) | 1995 | Alberto Tomba (ITA) | Vreni Schneider (SUI) |
| 1979 | Peter Luescher (SUI) | Annemarie Moser-Pröll (AUT) | 1996 | Lasse Kjus (NOR) | Katja Seizinger (GER) |
| | | | 1997 | Luc Alphand (FRA) | Pernilla Wiberg (SWE) |
| 1980 | Andreas Wenzel (LIE) | Hanni Wenzel (LIE) | 1998 | Hermann Maier (AUT) | Katja Seizinger (GER) |
| 1981 | Phil Mahre (USA) | Marie-Therese Nadig (SUI) | 1999 | Lasse Kjus (NOR) | Alexandra Meissnitzer (AUT) |
| 1982 | Phil Mahre (USA) | Erika Hess (SUI) | 2000 | Hermann Maier (AUT) | Renate Götschl (AUT) |
| 1983 | Phil Mahre (USA) | Tamara McKinney (USA) | 2001 | Hermann Maier (AUT) | Janica Kostelic (CRO) |
| 1984 | Pirmin Zurbriggen (SUI) | Erika Hess (SUI) | 2002 | Stephan Eberharter (AUT) | Michaela Dorfmeister (AUT) |
| 1985 | Marc Girardelli (LUX) | Michela Figini (SUI) | 2003 | Stephan Eberharter (AUT) | Janica Kostelic (CRO) |

## Nordic Skiing World Championships—Men

*Championships in some events have been held since 1924. The table shows results for the past 20 years. The next championships are scheduled to be held in February 2004.*

**SPRINT**
2001 Tor Arne Hetland (NOR)
2002[1] Samppa Lajunen (FIN)
2003 Thobias Fredriksson (SWE)

**10-KM CROSS-COUNTRY**
1991 Terje Langli (NOR)
1992[1] Vegard Ulvang (NOR)
1993 Sture Sivertsen (NOR)
1994[1] Bjørn Daehlie (NOR)
1995 Vladimir Smirnov (KAZ)
1996 *not held*
1997 Bjørn Daehlie (NOR)
1998[1] Bjørn Daehlie (NOR)
1999 Mika Myllyla (FIN)
2000 *not held*
2001[2] Per Elofsson (SWE)
2002[1,2] Johann Mühlegg (ESP)
2003 *discontinued*

**15-KM CROSS-COUNTRY[3]**
1984[1] Gunde Svan (SWE)
1985 Kari Härkönen (FIN)
1987 Marco Albarello (ITA)
1988[1] Mikhail Devyatyarov (URS)
1989 Gunde Svan (SWE)
1991 Bjørn Daehlie (NOR)
1992[1] Bjørn Daehlie (NOR)
1993 Bjørn Daehlie (NOR)
1994[1] Bjørn Daehlie (NOR)
1995 Vladimir Smirnov (KAZ)
1996 *not held*
1997 Bjørn Daehlie (NOR)

**15-KM CROSS-COUNTRY[3] (CONTINUED)**
1998[1] Thomas Alsgaard (NOR)
1999 Thomas Alsgaard (NOR)
2000 *not held*
2001[2] Per Elofsson (SWE)
2002[1,2] Andrus Veerpalu (EST)
2003 Axel Teichmann (GER)

**30-KM CROSS-COUNTRY**
1984[1] Nikolay Zimyatov (URS)
1985 Gunde Svan (SWE)
1987 Thomas Wassberg (SWE)
1988[1] Aleksey Prokurorov (URS)
1989 Vladimir Smirnov (URS)
1991 Gunde Svan (SWE)
1992[1] Vegard Ulvang (NOR)
1993 Bjørn Daehlie (NOR)
1994[1] Thomas Alsgaard (NOR)
1995 Vladimir Smirnov (KAZ)
1996 *not held*
1997 Aleksey Prokurorov (RUS)
1998[1] Mika Myllyla (FIN)
1999 Mika Myllyla (FIN)
2000 *not held*
2001 Andrus Veerpalu (EST)
2002[1] Johann Mühlegg (ESP)
2003 Thomas Alsgaard (NOR)

**50-KM CROSS-COUNTRY**
1984[1] Thomas Wassberg (SWE)
1985 Gunde Svan (SWE)
1987 Maurilio DeZolt (ITA)
1988[1] Gunde Svan (SWE)
1989 Gunde Svan (SWE)
1991 Torgny Mogren (SWE)

**50-KM CROSS-COUNTRY (CONTINUED)**
1992[1] Bjørn Daehlie (NOR)
1993 Torgny Mogren (SWE)
1994 Vladimir Smirnov (KAZ)
1995 Silvio Fauner (ITA)
1996 *not held*
1997 Mika Myllyla (FIN)
1998[1] Bjørn Daehlie (NOR)
1999 Mika Myllyla (FIN)
2000 *not held*
2001 Johann Mühlegg (ESP)
2002[1] Mikhail Ivanov (RUS)
2003 Martin Koukal (CZE)

**RELAY[4]**
1984[1] Sweden
1985 Norway
1987 Sweden
1988[1] Sweden
1989 Sweden
1991 Norway
1992[1] Norway
1993 Norway
1994[1] Italy
1995 Norway
1996 *not held*
1997 Norway
1998[1] Norway
1999 Austria
2001 Norway
2002[1] Norway
2003 Norway

[1]*Olympic champions, recognized as world champions.* [2]*From 1991 to 2000, the 10-km event was held in tandem with the 15-km event; one event featured classical and the other freestyle technique. Medals were awarded for both races. Beginning in 2001 this pursuit race (skiers competing directly against each other rather than against the clock) led to one medal being awarded upon winning. In 2002 the pursuit race featured two 10-km races and the 15-km was a stand-alone event featuring classical technique.* [3]*18-km cross-country until 1952; 15-km in 1954 and thereafter.* [4]*Military relay until 1939; 40-km relay in 1948 and thereafter.*

## Nordic Skiing World Championships—Nordic Combined

*The Nordic combined involves a 15-km cross-country race and ski jumping; the sprint is a 7.5-km race plus ski jumping. The next championships are scheduled to be held in February 2004.*

| YEAR | COMBINED | YEAR | COMBINED (CONTINUED) | YEAR | COMBINED (CONTINUED) |
|---|---|---|---|---|---|
| 1924[1] | Thorleif Haug (NOR) | 1934 | Oddbjørn Hagen (NOR) | 1960[1] | Georg Thoma (GER[2]) |
| 1925 | Ottokar Nemecky (TCH) | 1935 | Oddbjørn Hagen (NOR) | 1962 | Arne Larsen (NOR) |
| 1926 | Johan Gröttumsbraaten (NOR) | 1936[1] | Oddbjørn Hagen (NOR) | 1964[1] | Tormod Knutsen (NOR) |
| | | 1937 | Sigurd Røen (NOR) | 1966 | Georg Thoma (FRG) |
| 1927 | Rudolf Purkert (TCH) | 1938 | Olaf Hoffsbakken (NOR) | 1968[1] | Franz Keller (FRG) |
| 1928[1] | Johan Gröttumsbraaten (NOR) | | | 1970 | Ladislav Rygl (TCH) |
| 1929 | Hans Vinjarengen (NOR) | 1939 | Gustl Berauer (TCH) | 1972[1] | Ulrich Wehling (GDR) |
| 1930 | Hans Vinjarengen (NOR) | 1940–47 *not held* | | 1974 | Ulrich Wehling (GDR) |
| 1931 | Johan Gröttumsbraaten (NOR) | 1948[1] | Heikki Hasu (FIN) | 1976[1] | Ulrich Wehling (GDR) |
| | | 1950 | Heikki Hasu (FIN) | 1978 | Konrad Winkler (GDR) |
| 1932[1] | Johan Gröttumsbraaten (NOR) | 1952[1] | Simon Slåttvik (NOR) | 1980[1] | Ulrich Wehling (GDR) |
| | | 1954 | Sverre Stenersen (NOR) | 1982 | Tom Sandberg (NOR) |
| 1933 | Sven Eriksson (SWE) | 1956[1] | Sverre Stenersen (NOR) | 1984[1] | Tom Sandberg (NOR) |
| | | 1958 | Paavo Korhonen (FIN) | 1985 | Herman Weinbach (FRG) |

## Nordic Skiing World Championships—Nordic Combined (continued)

| YEAR | COMBINED (CONTINUED) |
|---|---|
| 1987 | Torbjørn Løkken (NOR) |
| 1988[1] | Hippolyt Kempf (SUI) |
| 1989 | Trond Einar Elden (NOR) |
| 1991 | Fred Børre Lundberg (NOR) |
| 1992[1] | Fabrice Guy (FRA) |
| 1993 | Kenji Ogiwara (JPN) |
| 1994[1] | Fred Børre Lundberg (NOR) |
| 1995 | Fred Børre Lundberg (NOR) |
| 1996 | *not held* |
| 1997 | Kenji Ogiwara (JPN) |
| 1998[1] | Bjarte Engen Vik (NOR) |
| 1999 | Bjarte Engen Vik (NOR) |

| YEAR | |
|---|---|
| 2001 | Bjarte Engen Vik (NOR) |
| 2002[1] | Samppa Lajunen (FIN) |
| 2003 | Ronny Ackermann (GER) |

| YEAR | SPRINT |
|---|---|
| 1999 | Bjarte Engen Vik (NOR) |
| 2001 | Marco Baacke (GER) |
| 2002[1] | Samppa Lajunen (FIN) |
| 2003 | Johnny Spillane (USA) |

| | TEAM |
|---|---|
| 1982 | East Germany |
| 1984[1] | Norway |
| 1985 | West Germany |
| 1987 | West Germany |
| 1988[1] | West Germany |

| YEAR | TEAM (CONTINUED) |
|---|---|
| 1989 | Norway |
| 1991 | Austria |
| 1992[1] | Japan |
| 1993 | Japan |
| 1994[1] | Japan |
| 1995 | Japan |
| 1996 | *not held* |
| 1997 | Norway |
| 1998[1] | Norway |
| 1999 | Finland |
| 2001 | Norway |
| 2002[1] | Finland |
| 2003 | Austria |

[1]Olympic champions, recognized as world champions.    [2]Combined East-West German team.

## Nordic Skiing World Championships—Ski Jump

The next championships are scheduled to be held in February 2005 in Oberstdorf, Germany.

| YEAR | NORMAL HILL[1] |
|---|---|
| 1924[2] | Jacob Tullin-Thams (NOR) |
| 1925 | Willen Dick (TCH) |
| 1926 | Jacob Tullin-Thams (NOR) |
| 1927 | Tore Edman (SWE) |
| 1928[2] | Alf Gunnar Andersen (NOR) |
| 1929 | Sigmund Ruud (NOR) |
| 1930 | Gunnar Andersen (NOR) |
| 1931 | Birger Ruud (NOR) |
| 1932[2] | Birger Ruud (NOR) |
| 1933 | Marcel Reymond (SUI) |
| 1934 | Kristian Johansson (NOR) |
| 1935 | Birger Ruud (NOR) |
| 1936[2] | Birger Ruud (NOR) |
| 1937 | Birger Ruud (NOR) |
| 1938 | Asbjørn Ruud (NOR) |
| 1939 | Josef Bradl (AUS) |
| 1940–47 | *not held* |
| 1948[2] | Petter Hugsted (NOR) |
| 1950 | Hans Bjørnstad (NOR) |
| 1952[2] | Arnfinn Bergmann (NOR) |
| 1954 | Matti Pietikäinen (FIN) |
| 1956[2] | Antti Hyvärinen (FIN) |
| 1958 | Juhani Kärkinen (FIN) |
| 1960[2] | Helmut Recknagel (GER[3]) |
| 1962 | Toralf Engan (NOR) |
| 1964[2] | Veikko Kankkonen (FIN) |
| 1966 | Bjørn Wirkola (NOR) |
| 1968[2] | Jiri Raška (TCH) |
| 1970 | Gary Napalkov (URS) |
| 1972[2] | Yukio Kasaya (JPN) |
| 1974 | Hans-Georg Aschenbach (GDR) |
| 1976[2] | Hans-Georg Aschenbach (GDR) |
| 1978 | Mathias Buse (GDR) |
| 1980[2] | Toni Innauer (AUT) |
| 1982 | Armin Kogler (AUT) |
| 1984[2] | Jens Weissflog (GDR) |
| 1985 | Jens Weissflog (GDR) |

| YEAR | NORMAL HILL[1] (CONTINUED) |
|---|---|
| 1987 | Jiri Parma (TCH) |
| 1988[2] | Matti Nykänen (FIN) |
| 1989 | Jens Weissflog (GDR) |
| 1991 | Heinz Kuttin (AUT) |
| 1992[2] | Ernst Vettori (AUT) |
| 1993 | Masahiko Harada (JPN) |
| 1994[2] | Espen Bredesen (NOR) |
| 1995 | Takanobu Okabe (JPN) |
| 1996 | *not held* |
| 1997 | Janne Ahonen (FIN) |
| 1998[2] | Jani Soininen (FIN) |
| 1999 | Kazuyoshi Funaki (JPN) |
| 2001 | Adam Malysz (POL) |
| 2002[2] | Simon Ammann (SUI) |
| 2003 | Adam Malysz (POL) |

| YEAR | LARGE HILL[4] |
|---|---|
| 1962 | Helmut Recknagel (GDR) |
| 1964[2] | Toralf Engan (NOR) |
| 1966 | Bjørn Wirkola (NOR) |
| 1968[2] | Vladimir Belousov (URS) |
| 1970 | Gary Napalkov (URS) |
| 1972[2] | Wojciech Fortuna (POL) |
| 1974 | Hans-Georg Aschenbach (GDR) |
| 1976[2] | Karl Schnabl (AUT) |
| 1978 | Tapio Räisänen (FIN) |
| 1980[2] | Jouko Törmänen (FIN) |
| 1982 | Matti Nykänen (FIN) |
| 1984[2] | Matti Nykänen (FIN) |
| 1985 | Per Bergerud (NOR) |
| 1987 | Andreas Felder (AUT) |
| 1988[2] | Matti Nykänen (FIN) |
| 1989 | Jari Puikkonen (FIN) |
| 1991 | Franci Petek (YUG) |
| 1992[2] | Toni Nieminen (FIN) |
| 1993 | Espen Bredesen (NOR) |
| 1994[2] | Jens Weissflog (GER) |

| YEAR | LARGE HILL[4] (CONTINUED) |
|---|---|
| 1995 | Tommy Ingebrigtsen (NOR) |
| 1996 | *not held* |
| 1997 | Masahiko Harada (JPN) |
| 1998[2] | Kazuyoshi Funaki (JPN) |
| 1999 | Martin Schmitt (GER) |
| 2001 | Martin Schmitt (GER) |
| 2002[2] | Simon Ammann (SUI) |
| 2003 | Adam Malysz (POL) |

| | TEAM JUMP (NORMAL HILL) |
|---|---|
| 2001 | Austria |
| 2002[2] | *not held* |
| 2003 | *not held* |

| | TEAM JUMP (LARGE HILL) |
|---|---|
| 1982 | Norway |
| 1984[2] | *not held* |
| 1985 | Finland |
| 1987 | Finland |
| 1988[2] | Finland |
| 1989 | Finland |
| 1991 | Austria |
| 1992[2] | Finland |
| 1993 | Norway |
| 1994[2] | Germany |
| 1995 | Finland |
| 1996 | *not held* |
| 1997 | Finland |
| 1998[2] | Japan |
| 1999 | Germany |
| 2001 | Germany |
| 2002[2] | Germany |
| 2003 | Finland |

[1]The distance of the jump in the normal hill competition has varied over time; as of 1992 it was set at 90 meters.    [2]Olympic champions, recognized as world champions.    [3]Combined East-West German team.    [4]The distance of the jump in the large hill competition has varied over time; it was set at 120 meters in 1992.

## Nordic Skiing World Championships—Women

*Championships in some events have been held since 1952. The table shows results for the past 20 years. The next championships are scheduled to be held in February 2005 in Oberstdorf, Germany.*

**SPRINT**
2001  Pirjo Manninen (FIN)
2002[1]  Yuliya Chepalova (RUS)
2003  Marit Bjoergen (NOR)

**5-KM CROSS-COUNTRY[2]**
1984[1]  Marja-Liisa Hämälainen
      (FIN)
1985  *not held*
1987  Marjo Matikainen (FIN)
1988[1]  Marjo Matikainen (FIN)
1989  *not held*
1991  Trude Dybendahl (NOR)
1992[1]  Marjut Lukkarinen (FIN)
1993  Larisa Lazutina (RUS)
1994[1]  Lyubov Yegorova (RUS)
1995  Larisa Lazutina (RUS)
1997  Yelena Vyalbe (RUS)
1998[1]  Larisa Lazutina (RUS)
1999  Bente Martinsen (NOR)
2001  Virpi Kuitunen (FIN)
2002[1]  Olga Danilova (RUS)
2003  *not held*

**10-KM CROSS-COUNTRY[2]**
1984[1]  Marja-Liisa Hämälainen
      (FIN)
1985  Anette Böe (NOR)
1987  Anne Jahren (NOR)
1988[1]  Vida Ventsene (URS)
1989  Marja-Liisa Kirvesniemi
      (FIN–classical); Yelena
      Vyalbe (URS–freestyle)
1991  Yelena Vyalbe (URS)

**10-KM CROSS-COUNTRY[2] (CONT.)**
1992[1]  Lyubov Yegorova (UNT[3])
1993  Stefania Belmondo (ITA)
1994[1]  Lyubov Yegorova (RUS)
1995  Larisa Lazutina (RUS)
1997  Stefania Belmondo (ITA)
1998[1]  Larisa Lazutina (RUS)
1999  Stefania Belmondo (ITA)
2001  Bente Skari-Martinsen
      (NOR)
2002[1]  Bente Skari (NOR)
2003  Bente Skari (NOR)

**15-KM CROSS-COUNTRY**
1989  Marjo Matikainen (FIN)
1991  Yelena Vyalbe (URS)
1992[1]  Lyubov Egorova (URS)
1993  Yelena Vyalbe (URS)
1994[1]  Manuela Di Centa (ITA)
1995  Larissa Lazutina (RUS)
1997  Yelena Vyalbe (RUS)
1998[1]  Olga Danilova (RUS)
1999  Stefania Belmondo (ITA)
2001  Bente Skari-Martinsen
      (NOR)
2002[1]  Stefania Belmondo (ITA)
2003  Bente Skari (NOR)

**20-KM CROSS-COUNTRY**
1984[1]  Marja-Liisa Hämälainen
      (FIN)
1985  Grete Nykelmo (NOR)
1987  Marie H. Oestlund (SWE)
1988[1]  Tamara Tikhonova (URS)
1989  *discontinued*

**30-KM CROSS-COUNTRY**
1989  Yelena Vyalbe (URS)
1991  Lyubov Yegorova (URS)
1992[1]  Stefania Belmondo (ITA)
1993  Stefania Belmondo (ITA)
1994[1]  Manuela Di Centa (ITA)
1995  Yelena Vyalbe (RUS)
1997  Yelena Vyalbe (RUS)
1998[1]  Yulia Chepalova (RUS)
1999  Larisa Lazutina (RUS)
2001  *canceled*
2002[1]  Gabriella Paruzzi (ITA)
2003  Olga Savyalova (RUS)

**RELAY[4]**
1984[1]  Norway
1985  USSR
1987  USSR
1988[1]  USSR
1989  Finland
1991  USSR
1992[1]  Unified Team
1993  Russia
1994[1]  Russia
1995  Russia
1997  Russia
1998[1]  Russia
1999  Russia
2001  Russia
2002[1]  Germany
2003  Germany

[1]*Olympic champions, recognized as world champions.* [2]*From 1991–2001, the 5-km event was held in tandem with the 10-km event; one event would feature classical and the other freestyle technique. Medals were awarded for both races. Beginning in 2001 this pursuit race instead led to one medal being awarded upon winning. In 2001 and 2002 the pursuit race featured two 5-km races and the 10-km was a stand-alone event featuring classical technique.* [3]*Unified Team, consisting of athletes from the Commonwealth of Independent States plus Georgia.* [4]*15-km relay until 1974; 20-km in 1976 and thereafter.*

The oldest skis, found in bogs in Sweden and Finland, are believed to be 4,000 to 5,000 years old.

## Nordic World Cup

| YEAR | MEN | WOMEN | YEAR | MEN | WOMEN |
|------|-----|-------|------|-----|-------|
| 1979 | Oddvar Braa (NOR) | Galina Kulakova (URS) | 1987 | Torgny Mogren (SWE) | Marjo Matikainen (FIN) |
| 1981 | Aleksandr Zavyalov (URS) | Raisa Smetanina (URS) | 1988 | Gunde Svan (SWE) | Marjo Matikainen (FIN) |
| 1982 | Bill Koch (USA) | Berit Aunli (NOR) | 1989 | Gunde Svan (SWE) | Yelena Vyalbe (URS) |
| 1983 | Aleksandr Zavyalov (URS) | Marja-Liisa Hämä-lainen (FIN) | 1990 | Vegard Ulvang (NOR) | Larisa Lazutina (URS) |
| 1984 | Gunde Svan (SWE) | Marja-Liisa Hämä-lainen (FIN) | 1991 | Vladimir Smirnov (URS) | Yelena Vyalbe (URS) |
| 1985 | Gunde Svan (SWE) | Anette Boe (NOR) | 1992 | Bjørn Daehlie (NOR) | Yelena Vyalbe (URS) |
| 1986 | Gunde Svan (SWE) | Marjo Matikainen (FIN) | 1993 | Bjørn Daehlie (NOR) | Lyudmila Yegorova (RUS) |

## Nordic World Cup (continued)

| YEAR | MEN | WOMEN | YEAR | MEN | WOMEN |
|---|---|---|---|---|---|
| 1994 | Vladimir Smirnov (KAZ) | Manuela Di Centa (ITA) | 1999 | Bjørn Daehlie (NOR) | Bente Martinsen (NOR) |
| 1995 | Bjørn Daehlie (NOR) | Yelena Vyalbe (RUS) | 2000 | Johann Mühlegg (ESP) | Bente Skari-Martinsen (NOR) |
| 1996 | Bjørn Daehlie (NOR) | Manuela Di Centa (ITA) | 2001 | Per Elofsson (SWE) | Yuliya Chepalova (RUS) |
| 1997 | Bjørn Daehlie (NOR) | Yelena Vyalbe (RUS) | 2002 | Per Elofsson (SWE) | Bente Skari (NOR) |
| 1998 | Thomas Alsgaard (NOR) | Larisa Lazutina (RUS) | 2003 | Mathias Fredriksson (SWE) | Bente Skari (NOR) |

# Sled Dog Racing

Sled Dog racing (or dogsled racing) is the sport of racing sleds pulled by sled dogs over snow-covered cross-country courses; it was developed from a principal **Eskimo** method of transportation. Dogsleds are still used for transportation and working purposes in some northern areas, although they largely have been replaced by aircraft and snowmobiles. The modern, lightweight **racing sled** weighs about 30 lb (13.5 kg). Its ash frame is lashed together with leather and its runners sheathed with steel or aluminum. **Dogs** usually are especially bred and trained Eskimo dogs, Siberian huskies, Samoyeds, or Alaskan Malamutes. The **teams** typically consist of 4–10 dogs, with more being used for longer races. They are driven in pairs in a gang hitch.

Control of the team is by voice, although drivers may carry whips of limited length. In open country, point-to-point races are held. In more populated areas, back roads form the course, with races usually varying in **length** from 12–30 mi (19–48 km). A team of 6–8 dogs can pull the sled and its driver, called a **musher**, at speeds of more than 20 mph (32 km/hr). Teams start at intervals and race for time. Usually, all dogs must finish in the order they start, and an injured dog must be carried on the sled.

A dogsled-racing event was included in the 1932 **Winter Olympics** program. The sport is popular in Norway, Canada, Alaska, and the northern states of the contiguous United States. The **Iditarod Trail Sled Dog Race** has been held in Alaska since 1973.

## Iditarod Trail Sled Dog Race

Men and women compete together in this annual race held in March between Anchorage and Nome AK. A short race of 56 mi (90 km) organized in 1967 evolved in 1973 into the current race. The course, roughly 1,100 mi (1,770 km) long, partially follows the old Iditarod Trail dogsled mail route blazed from Knik to Nome in 1910. The course length and route vary slightly from year to year, and the middle third takes alternate routes in odd and even years. In 1976 the US Congress designated the original Iditarod Trail as a National Historic Trail. **Iditarod Web site:** <www.iditarod.com>.

| YEAR | WINNER | TIME | YEAR | WINNER | TIME |
|---|---|---|---|---|---|
| 1973 | Dick Wilmarth | 20 days 49 min 41 sec | 1989 | Joe Runyan | 11 days 5 hr 24 min 34 sec |
| 1974 | Carl Huntington | 20 days 15 hr 2 min 7 sec | 1990 | Susan Butcher | 11 days 1 hr 53 min 23 sec |
| 1975 | Emmitt Peters | 14 days 14 hr 43 min 45 sec | 1991 | Rick Swenson | 12 days 16 hr 34 min 39 sec |
| 1976 | Gerald Riley | 18 days 22 hr 58 min 17 sec | 1992 | Martin Buser | 10 days 19 hr 17 min 15 sec |
| 1977 | Rick Swenson | 16 days 16 hr 27 min 13 sec | 1993 | Jeff King | 10 days 15 hr 38 min 15 sec |
| 1978 | Dick Mackey | 14 days 18 hr 52 min 24 sec | 1994 | Martin Buser | 10 days 13 hr 5 min 39 sec |
| 1979 | Rick Swenson | 15 days 10 hr 37 min 47 sec | 1995 | Doug Swingley | 10 days 13 hr 2 min 39 sec |
| 1980 | Joe May | 14 days 7 hr 11 min 51 sec | 1996 | Jeff King | 9 days 5 hr 43 min 13 sec |
| 1981 | Rick Swenson | 12 days 8 hr 45 min 2 sec | 1997 | Martin Buser | 9 days 8 hr 30 min 45 sec |
| 1982 | Rick Swenson | 16 days 4 hr 40 min 10 sec | 1998 | Jeff King | 9 days 5 hr 52 min 26 sec |
| 1983 | Rick Mackey | 12 days 14 hr 10 min 44 sec | 1999 | Doug Swingley | 9 days 14 hr 31 min 7 sec |
| 1984 | Dean Osmar | 12 days 15 hr 7 min 33 sec | 2000 | Doug Swingley | 9 days 58 min 6 sec |
| 1985 | Libby Riddles | 18 days 20 min 17 sec | 2001 | Doug Swingley | 9 days 19 hr 55 min 50 sec |
| 1986 | Susan Butcher | 11 days 15 hr 6 min 0 sec | 2002 | Martin Buser | 8 days 22 hr 46 min 2 sec |
| 1987 | Susan Butcher | 11 days 2 hr 5 min 13 sec | 2003 | Robert Sørlie | 9 days 15 hr 47 min 36 sec |
| 1988 | Susan Butcher | 11 days 11 hr 41 min 40 sec | | | |

# Squash

The oldest professional squash rackets tournament recognized as such is the **British Open**, inaugurated in 1930. Both men's amateur and women's squash rackets championships had been held since 1922. The International **Squash Rackets Federation** (ISRF; founded 1967) instituted **world open championships** in 1974 (men) and 1976 (women). The game as played in Great Britain and the rest of the world is quite different in a number of ways from that played in the United States, Canada, and Mexico. **World Squash Federation Web site:** <www.worldsquash.org>

# World Open Championship

## men

| YEAR | WINNER (NATIONALITY) | YEAR | WINNER (NATIONALITY) | YEAR | WINNER (NATIONALITY) |
|---|---|---|---|---|---|
| 1975 | Geoff B. Hunt (AUS) | 1987 | Jansher Khan (PAK) | 1997 | Rodney Eyles (AUS) |
| 1977 | Geoff B. Hunt (AUS) | 1988 | Jahangir Khan (PAK) | 1998 | Jonathon Power (CAN) |
| 1979 | Geoff B. Hunt (AUS) | 1989 | Jansher Khan (PAK) | 1999 | Peter Nicol (SCO) |
| 1980 | Geoff B. Hunt (AUS) | 1990 | Jansher Khan (PAK) | 2000 | *not held* |
| 1981 | Jahangir Khan (PAK) | 1991 | Rodney Martin (AUS) | 2001 | *canceled* |
| 1982 | Jahangir Khan (PAK) | 1992 | Jansher Khan (PAK) | 2002 | David Palmer (AUS) |
| 1983 | Jahangir Khan (PAK) | 1993 | Jansher Khan (PAK) | 2003 | *TBA* |
| 1984 | Jahangir Khan (PAK) | 1994 | Jansher Khan (PAK) | | |
| 1985 | Jahangir Khan (PAK) | 1995 | Jansher Khan (PAK) | | |
| 1986 | Ross Norman (NZL) | 1996 | Jansher Khan (PAK) | | |

## women

| YEAR | WINNER (NATIONALITY) | YEAR | WINNER (NATIONALITY) | YEAR | WINNER (NATIONALITY) |
|---|---|---|---|---|---|
| 1976 | Heather P. Blundell McKay (AUS) | 1989 | Martine LeMoignan (GBR) | 1996 | Sarah Fitz-Gerald (AUS) |
| | | | | 1997 | Sarah Fitz-Gerald (AUS) |
| 1979 | Heather McKay (AUS) | 1990 | Susan Devoy (NZL) | 1998 | Sarah Fitz-Gerald (AUS) |
| 1981 | Rhonda Thorne (AUS) | 1991 | *not held* | 1999 | Cassie Campion (ENG) |
| 1983 | Vicki Hoffman Cardwell (AUS) | 1992 | Susan Devoy (NZL) | 2000 | Carol Owens (AUS) |
| | | 1993 | Michelle Martin (AUS) | 2001 | Sarah Fitz-Gerald (AUS) |
| 1985 | Susan Devoy (NZL) | 1994 | Michelle Martin (AUS) | 2002 | Sarah Fitz-Gerald (AUS) |
| 1987 | Susan Devoy (NZL) | 1995 | Michelle Martin (AUS) | 2003 | *TBA* |

# British Open Championship

*The championships have been held since 1921–22 (women's) and 1930–31 (men's). The table shows the results for the past 20 years.*

| | men | | women |
|---|---|---|---|
| YEAR | WINNER (NATIONALITY) | YEAR | WINNER (NATIONALITY) |
| 1983–84 | Jahangir Khan (PAK) | 1983–84 | Susan Devoy (NZL) |
| 1984–85 | Jahangir Khan (PAK) | 1984–85 | Susan Devoy (NZL) |
| 1985–86 | Jahangir Khan (PAK) | 1985–86 | Susan Devoy (NZL) |
| 1986–87 | Jahangir Khan (PAK) | 1986–87 | Susan Devoy (NZL) |
| 1987–88 | Jahangir Khan (PAK) | 1987–88 | Susan Devoy (NZL) |
| 1988–89 | Jahangir Khan (PAK) | 1988–89 | Susan Devoy (NZL) |
| 1989–90 | Jahangir Khan (PAK) | 1989–90 | Susan Devoy (NZL) |
| 1990–91 | Jahangir Khan (PAK) | 1990–91 | Liz Opie (GBR) |
| 1991–92 | Jansher Khan (PAK) | 1991–92 | Susan Devoy (NZL) |
| 1992–93 | Jansher Khan (PAK) | 1992–93 | Michelle Martin (AUS) |
| 1993–94 | Jansher Khan (PAK) | 1993–94 | Michelle Martin (AUS) |
| 1994–95 | Jansher Khan (PAK) | 1994–95 | Michelle Martin (AUS) |
| 1995–96 | Jansher Khan (PAK) | 1995–96 | Michelle Martin (AUS) |
| 1996–97 | Jansher Khan (PAK) | 1996–97 | Michelle Martin (AUS) |
| 1997–98 | Peter Nicol (SCO) | 1997–98 | Michelle Martin (AUS) |
| 1998–99 | Jonathon Power (CAN) | 1998–99 | Leilani Joyce (NZL) |
| 1999–2000 | David Evans (WAL) | 1999–2000 | Leilani Joyce (NZL) |
| 2000–01 | David Palmer (AUS) | 2000–01 | Sarah Fitz-Gerald (AUS) |
| 2001–02 | Peter Nicol (GBR) | 2001–02 | Sarah Fitz-Gerald (AUS) |
| 2002–03 | *postponed until fall 2003* | 2002–03 | *postponed until fall 2003* |

# Swimming

The **Fédération Internationale de Natation** (International Swimming Federation, still known by its French acronym that includes an "a" for "Amateur," FINA; founded 1908) is the world governing body for amateur swimming. It held the first world swimming championships in 1973. After 1975 the FINA championships were held in non-Olympic, even-numbered years. (An exception was the championship held in Australia, which took place during the summer month of January 1991.) Diving, synchronized (or synchro) swimming, and water polo events are included in the competition.

A distinction is made between **long-course** (50-m) and **short-course** (25-m) pools for purposes of record-setting; world championships and other major contests were long held in 50-m pools, but there is now a separate World Championship and World Cup for 25-m pools.

**International Swimming Federation Web site:** <www.fina.org>

# World Swimming & Diving Championships—Men
*The next competition is scheduled to be held in 2005 in Montreal.*

## swimming

**50 M FREESTYLE**
| | |
|---|---|
| 1986 | Tom Jager (USA) |
| 1991 | Tom Jager (USA) |
| 1994 | Aleksandr Popov (RUS) |
| 1998 | Bill Pilczuk (USA) |
| 2001 | Anthony Ervin (USA) |
| 2003 | Aleksandr Popov (RUS) |

**100 M FREESTYLE**
| | |
|---|---|
| 1973 | Jim Montgomery (USA) |
| 1975 | Andy Coan (USA) |
| 1978 | David McCagg (USA) |
| 1982 | Jorg Woithe (GDR) |
| 1986 | Matt Biondi (USA) |
| 1991 | Matt Biondi (USA) |
| 1994 | Aleksandr Popov (RUS) |
| 1998 | Aleksandr Popov (RUS) |
| 2001 | Anthony Ervin (USA) |
| 2003 | Aleksandr Popov (RUS) |

**200 M FREESTYLE**
| | |
|---|---|
| 1973 | Jim Montgomery (USA) |
| 1975 | Tim Shaw (USA) |
| 1978 | Bill Forrester (USA) |
| 1982 | Michael Gross (FRG) |
| 1986 | Michael Gross (FRG) |
| 1991 | Giorgio Lamberti (ITA) |
| 1994 | Antti Kasvio (FIN) |
| 1998 | Michael Klim (AUS) |
| 2001 | Ian Thorpe (AUS) |
| 2003 | Ian Thorpe (AUS) |

**400 M FREESTYLE**
| | |
|---|---|
| 1973 | Rick DeMont (USA) |
| 1975 | Tim Shaw (USA) |
| 1978 | Vladimir Salnikov (URS) |
| 1982 | Vladimir Salnikov (URS) |
| 1986 | Rainer Henkel (FRG) |
| 1991 | Jörg Hoffmann (GER) |
| 1994 | Kieren Perkins (AUS) |
| 1998 | Ian Thorpe (AUS) |
| 2001 | Ian Thorpe (AUS) |
| 2003 | Ian Thorpe (AUS) |

**800 M FREESTYLE**
| | |
|---|---|
| 2001 | Ian Thorpe (AUS) |
| 2003 | Grant Hackett (AUS) |

**1,500 M FREESTYLE**
| | |
|---|---|
| 1973 | Steve Holland (AUS) |
| 1975 | Tim Shaw (USA) |
| 1978 | Vladimir Salnikov (URS) |
| 1982 | Vladimir Salnikov (URS) |
| 1986 | Rainer Henkel (FRG) |
| 1991 | Jörg Hoffmann (GER) |
| 1994 | Kieren Perkins (AUS) |
| 1998 | Grant Hackett (AUS) |
| 2001 | Grant Hackett (AUS) |
| 2003 | Grant Hackett (AUS) |

**50 M BACKSTROKE**
| | |
|---|---|
| 2001 | Randall Bal (USA) |
| 2003 | Thomas Rupprath (GER) |

**100 M BACKSTROKE**
| | |
|---|---|
| 1973 | Roland Matthes (GDR) |
| 1975 | Roland Matthes (GDR) |
| 1978 | Bob Jackson (USA) |
| 1982 | Dirk Richter (GDR) |
| 1986 | Igor Polyansky (URS) |
| 1991 | Jeff Rouse (USA) |
| 1994 | Martín Lopez-Zubero (ESP) |
| 1998 | Lenny Krayzelburg (USA) |
| 2001 | Matt Welsh (AUS) |
| 2003 | Aaron Peirsol (USA) |

**200 M BACKSTROKE**
| | |
|---|---|
| 1973 | Roland Matthes (GDR) |
| 1975 | Zoltan Verraszto (HUN) |
| 1978 | Jesse Vassallo (USA) |
| 1982 | Rick Carey (USA) |
| 1986 | Igor Polyansky (URS) |
| 1991 | Martín Lopez-Zubero (ESP) |
| 1994 | Vladimir Selkov (RUS) |
| 1998 | Lenny Krayzelburg (USA) |
| 2001 | Aaron Peirsol (USA) |
| 2003 | Aaron Peirsol (USA) |

**50 M BREASTSTROKE**
| | |
|---|---|
| 2001 | Oleg Lisogor (UKR) |
| 2003 | James Gibson (GBR) |

**100 M BREASTSTROKE**
| | |
|---|---|
| 1973 | John Hencken (USA) |
| 1975 | David Wilkie (GBR) |
| 1978 | Walter Kusch (FRG) |
| 1982 | Steve Lundquist (USA) |
| 1986 | Victor Davis (CAN) |
| 1991 | Norbert Rozsa (HUN) |
| 1994 | Norbert Rozsa (HUN) |
| 1998 | Fred De Burghgraeve (BEL) |
| 2001 | Roman Sloudnov (RUS) |
| 2003 | Kosuke Kitajima (JPN) |

**200 M BREASTSTROKE**
| | |
|---|---|
| 1973 | David Wilkie (GBR) |
| 1975 | David Wilkie (GBR) |
| 1978 | Nick Nevid (USA) |
| 1982 | Victor Davis (CAN) |
| 1986 | Joszef Szabo (HUN) |
| 1991 | Mike Barrowman (USA) |
| 1994 | Norbert Rozsa (HUN) |
| 1998 | Kurt Grote (USA) |
| 2001 | Brendan Hansen (USA) |
| 2003 | Kosuke Kitajima (JPN) |

**50 M BUTTERFLY**
| | |
|---|---|
| 2001 | Geoff Huegill (AUS) |
| 2003 | Matt Welsh (AUS) |

**100 M BUTTERFLY**
| | |
|---|---|
| 1973 | Bruce Robertson (CAN) |
| 1975 | Greg Jagenburg (USA) |
| 1978 | Joseph Bottom (USA) |
| 1982 | Matt Gribble (USA) |
| 1986 | Pablo Morales (USA) |
| 1991 | Anthony Nesty (SUR) |

**100 M BUTTERFLY (CONTINUED)**
| | |
|---|---|
| 1994 | Rafal Szukala (POL) |
| 1998 | Michael Klim (AUS) |
| 2001 | Lars Frolander (SWE) |
| 2003 | Ian Crocker (USA) |

**200 M BUTTERFLY**
| | |
|---|---|
| 1973 | Robin Backhaus (USA) |
| 1975 | Bill Forrester (USA) |
| 1978 | Mike Bruner (USA) |
| 1982 | Michael Gross (FRG) |
| 1986 | Michael Gross (FRG) |
| 1991 | Melvin Stewart (USA) |
| 1994 | Denis Pankratov (RUS) |
| 1998 | Denys Silantyev (UKR) |
| 2001 | Michael Phelps (USA) |
| 2003 | Michael Phelps (USA) |

**200 M INDIVIDUAL MEDLEY**
| | |
|---|---|
| 1973 | Gunnar Larsson (SWE) |
| 1975 | Andras Hargitay (HUN) |
| 1978 | Graham Smith (CAN) |
| 1982 | Aleksandr Sidorenko (URS) |
| 1986 | Tamas Darnyi (HUN) |
| 1991 | Tamas Darnyi (HUN) |
| 1994 | Jani Sievinen (FIN) |
| 1998 | Marcel Wouda (NED) |
| 2001 | Massimiliano Rosolino (ITA) |
| 2003 | Michael Phelps (USA) |

**400 M INDIVIDUAL MEDLEY**
| | |
|---|---|
| 1973 | Andras Hargitay (HUN) |
| 1975 | Andras Hargitay (HUN) |
| 1978 | Jesse Vassallo (USA) |
| 1982 | Ricardo Prado (BRA) |
| 1986 | Tamas Darnyi (HUN) |
| 1991 | Tamas Darnyi (HUN) |
| 1994 | Tom Dolan (USA) |
| 1998 | Tom Dolan (USA) |
| 2001 | Alessio Boggiatto (ITA) |
| 2003 | Michael Phelps (USA) |

**4 X 100-M FREESTYLE RELAY**
| | |
|---|---|
| 1973 | United States |
| 1975 | United States |
| 1978 | United States |
| 1982 | United States |
| 1986 | United States |
| 1991 | United States |
| 1994 | United States |
| 1998 | United States |
| 2001 | Australia |
| 2003 | Russia |

**4 X 200-M FREESTYLE RELAY**
| | |
|---|---|
| 1973 | United States |
| 1975 | West Germany |
| 1978 | United States |
| 1982 | United States |
| 1986 | East Germany |
| 1991 | Germany |

## World Swimming & Diving Championships—Men (continued)

**4 X 200-M FREESTYLE RELAY**
**(CONTINUED)**
1994 Sweden
1998 Australia
2001 Australia
2003 Australia

**4 X 100-M MEDLEY RELAY**
1973 United States
1975 United States
1978 United States
1982 United States
1986 United States

**X 100-M MEDLEY RELAY**
**(CONTINUED)**
1991 United States
1994 United States
1998 Australia
2001 Australia
2003 United States

### diving

**1-M SPRINGBOARD**
1991 Edwin Jongejans (NED)
1994 Evan Stewart (ZIM)
1998 Yu Zhuocheng (CHN)
2001 Wang Feng (CHN)
2003 Xu Xiang (CHN)

**3-M SPRINGBOARD**
1973 Phil Boggs (USA)
1975 Phil Boggs (USA)

**3-M SPRINGBOARD (CONTINUED)**
1978 Phil Boggs (USA)
1982 Greg Louganis (USA)
1986 Greg Louganis (USA)
1991 Kent Ferguson (USA)
1994 Yu Zhuocheng (CHN)
1998 Dmitry Sautin (RUS)
2001 Dmitry Sautin (RUS)
2003 Aleksandr Dobrosok (RUS)

**PLATFORM**
1973 Klaus Dibiasi (ITA)
1975 Klaus Dibiasi (ITA)
1978 Greg Louganis (USA)
1982 Greg Louganis (USA)
1986 Greg Louganis (USA)
1991 Sun Shuwei (CHN)
1994 Dmitry Sautin (RUS)
1998 Dmitry Sautin (RUS)
2001 Tian Liang (CHN)
2003 Alexandre Despatie (CAN)

## World Swimming & Diving Championships—Women

*The next competition is scheduled to be held in 2005 in Montreal.*

### swimming

**50 M FREESTYLE**
1986 Tamara Costache (ROM)
1991 Zhuang Yong (CHN)
1994 Le Jingyi (CHN)
1998 Amy Van Dyken (USA)
2001 Inge De Bruijn (NED)
2003 Inge De Bruijn (NED)

**100 M FREESTYLE**
1973 Kornelia Ender (GDR)
1975 Kornelia Ender (GDR)
1978 Barbara Krause (GDR)
1982 Birgit Meineke (GDR)
1986 Kristin Otto (GDR)
1991 Nicole Haislett (USA)
1994 Le Jingyi (CHN)
1998 Jenny Thompson (USA)
2001 Inge De Bruijn (NED)
2003 Hanna-Maria Seppälä
     (FIN)

**200 M FREESTYLE**
1973 Keena Rothhammer
     (USA)
1975 Shirley Babashoff (USA)
1978 Cynthia Woodhead (USA)
1982 Annemarie Verstappen
     (NED)
1986 Heike Friedrich (GDR)
1991 Hayley Lewis (AUS)
1994 Franziska van Almsick
     (GER)
1998 Claudia Poll (CRC)
2001 Giaan Rooney (AUS)
2003 Alena Popchanka (BLR)

**400 M FREESTYLE**
1973 Heather Greenwood (USA)
1975 Shirley Babashoff (USA)
1978 Tracey Wickham (AUS)
1982 Carmela Schmidt (GDR)
1986 Heike Friedrich (GDR)

**400 M FREESTYLE (CONTINUED)**
1991 Janet Evans (USA)
1994 Yang Aihua (CHN)
1998 Chen Yan (CHN)
2001 Yana Klochkova (UKR)
2003 Hannah Stockbauer (GER)

**800 M FREESTYLE**
1973 Novella Calligaris (ITA)
1975 Jenny Turrall (AUS)
1978 Tracey Wickham (AUS)
1982 Kim Linehan (USA)
1986 Astrid Strauss (GDR)
1991 Janet Evans (USA)
1994 Janet Evans (USA)
1998 Brooke Bennett (USA)
2001 Hannah Stockbauer (GER)
2003 Hannah Stockbauer (GER)

**1,500 M FREESTYLE**
2001 Hannah Stockbauer (GER)
2003 Hannah Stockbauer (GER)

**50 M BREASTSTROKE**
2001 Luo Xuejuan (CHN)
2003 Luo Xuejuan (CHN)

**100 M BREASTSTROKE**
1973 Renate Vogel (GDR)
1975 Hannelore Anke (GDR)
1978 Yuliya Bogdanova (URS)
1982 Ute Geweniger (GDR)
1986 Sylvia Gerasch (GDR)
1991 Linley Frame (AUS)
1994 Samantha Riley (AUS)
1998 Kristy Kowal (USA)
2001 Luo Xuejuan (CHN)
2003 Luo Xuejuan (CHN)

**200 M BREASTSTROKE**
1973 Renate Vogel (GDR)
1975 Hannelore Anke (GDR)

**200 M BREASTSTROKE (CONTINUED)**
1978 Lina Kachushite (URS)
1982 Svetlana Varganova (URS)
1986 Silke Hörner (GDR)
1991 Yelena Volkova (URS)
1994 Samantha Riley (AUS)
1998 Agnes Kovacs (HUN)
2001 Agnes Kovacs (HUN)
2003 Amanda Beard (USA)

**50 M BUTTERFLY**
2001 Inge De Bruijn (NED)
2003 Inge De Bruijn (NED)

**100 M BUTTERFLY**
1973 Kornelia Ender (GDR)
1975 Kornelia Ender (GDR)
1978 Joan Pennington (USA)
1982 Mary T. Meagher (USA)
1986 Kornelia Gressler (GDR)
1991 Qian Hong (CHN)
1994 Liu Limin (CHN)
1998 Jenny Thompson (USA)
2001 Petria Thomas (AUS)
2003 Jenny Thompson (USA)

**200 M BUTTERFLY**
1973 Rosemarie Kother (GDR)
1975 Rosemarie Kother (GDR)
1978 Tracy Caulkins (USA)
1982 Ines Geissler (GDR)
1986 Mary T. Meagher (USA)
1991 Summer Sanders (USA)
1994 Liu Limin (CHN)
1998 Susie O'Neill (AUS)
2001 Petria Thomas (AUS)
2003 Otylia Jedrzejczak (POL)

**50 M BACKSTROKE**
2001 Haley Cope (USA)
2003 Nina Zhivanevskaya (ESP)

# World Swimming & Diving Championships—Women (continued)

**100 M BACKSTROKE**
| | |
|---|---|
| 1973 | Ulrike Richter (GDR) |
| 1975 | Ulrike Richter (GDR) |
| 1978 | Linda Jezek (USA) |
| 1982 | Kristin Otto (GDR) |
| 1986 | Betsy Mitchell (USA) |
| 1991 | Krisztina Egerszegi (HUN) |
| 1994 | He Cihong (CHN) |
| 1998 | Lea Maurer (USA) |
| 2001 | Natalie Coughlin (USA) |
| 2003 | Antje Buschschulte (GER) |

**200 M BACKSTROKE**
| | |
|---|---|
| 1973 | Melissa Belote (USA) |
| 1975 | Birgit Treiber (GDR) |
| 1978 | Linda Jezek (USA) |
| 1982 | Cornelia Sirch (GDR) |
| 1986 | Cornelia Sirch (GDR) |
| 1991 | Krisztina Egerszegi (HUN) |
| 1994 | He Cihong (CHN) |
| 1998 | Roxanna Maracineanu (FRA) |
| 2001 | Diana Mocanu (ROM) |
| 2003 | Katy Sexton (GBR) |

**200 M INDIVIDUAL MEDLEY**
| | |
|---|---|
| 1973 | Andrea Hubner (GDR) |
| 1975 | Kathy Heddy (USA) |
| 1978 | Tracy Caulkins (USA) |
| 1982 | Petra Schneider (GDR) |
| 1986 | Kristin Otto (GDR) |

**200 M INDIVIDUAL MEDLEY (CONTINUED)**
| | |
|---|---|
| 1991 | Lin Li (CHN) |
| 1994 | Lu Bin (CHN) |
| 1998 | Wu Yanyan (CHN) |
| 2001 | Martha Bowen (USA) |
| 2003 | Yana Klochkova (UKR) |

**400 M INDIVIDUAL MEDLEY**
| | |
|---|---|
| 1973 | Gudrun Wegner (GDR) |
| 1975 | Ulrika Tauber (GDR) |
| 1978 | Tracy Caulkins (USA) |
| 1982 | Petra Schneider (GDR) |
| 1986 | Kathleen Nord (GDR) |
| 1991 | Lin Li (CHN) |
| 1994 | Dai Guohong (CHN) |
| 1998 | Chen Yan (CHN) |
| 2001 | Yana Klochkova (UKR) |
| 2003 | Yana Klochkova (UKR) |

**4 X 100-M FREESTYLE RELAY**
| | |
|---|---|
| 1973 | East Germany |
| 1975 | East Germany |
| 1978 | United States |
| 1982 | East Germany |
| 1986 | East Germany |
| 1991 | United States |

**4 X 100-M FREESTYLE RELAY (CONTINUED)**
| | |
|---|---|
| 1994 | China |
| 1998 | United States |
| 2001 | Germany |
| 2003 | United States |

**4 X 200-M FREESTYLE RELAY**
| | |
|---|---|
| 1986 | East Germany |
| 1991 | Germany |
| 1994 | China |
| 1998 | Germany |
| 2001 | Great Britain |
| 2003 | United States |

**4 X 100-M MEDLEY RELAY**
| | |
|---|---|
| 1973 | East Germany |
| 1975 | East Germany |
| 1978 | United States |
| 1982 | East Germany |
| 1986 | East Germany |
| 1991 | United States |
| 1994 | China |
| 1998 | United States |
| 2001 | Australia |
| 2003 | China |

## diving

**1-M SPRINGBOARD**
| | |
|---|---|
| 1991 | Gao Min (CHN) |
| 1994 | Chen Lixia (CHN) |
| 1998 | Irina Lashko (RUS) |
| 2001 | Blythe Hartley (CAN) |
| 2003 | Irina Lashko (AUS) |

**3-M SPRINGBOARD**
| | |
|---|---|
| 1973 | Christa Kohler (GDR) |
| 1975 | Irina Kalinina (URS) |
| 1978 | Irina Kalinina (URS) |
| 1982 | Megan Neyer (USA) |
| 1986 | Gao Min (CHN) |
| 1991 | Gao Min (CHN) |
| 1994 | Tan Shuping (CHN) |
| 1998 | Yulia Pakhalina (RUS) |
| 2001 | Guo Jingjing (CHN) |
| 2003 | Guo Jingjing (CHN) |

**PLATFORM**
| | |
|---|---|
| 1973 | Ulrika Knape (SWE) |
| 1975 | Janet Ely (USA) |
| 1978 | Irina Kalinina (URS) |
| 1982 | Wendy Wyland (USA) |
| 1986 | Chen Lin (CHN) |
| 1991 | Fu Mingxia (CHN) |
| 1994 | Fu Mingxia (CHN) |
| 1998 | Olena Zhupina (UKR) |
| 2001 | Xu Mian (CHN) |
| 2003 | Emilie Heymans (CAN) |

# Swimming World Records—Long Course (50-m)

## men

| EVENT | RECORD HOLDER (NATIONALITY) | PERFORMANCE | DATE |
|---|---|---|---|
| 50-m freestyle | Aleksandr Popov (RUS) | 21.64 sec | 16 Jun 2000 |
| 100-m freestyle | Pieter van den Hoogenband (NED) | 47.84 sec | 19 Sep 2000 |
| 200-m freestyle | Ian Thorpe (AUS) | 1 min 44.06 sec | 25 Jul 2001 |
| 400-m freestyle | Ian Thorpe (AUS) | 3 min 40.17 sec | 22 Jul 2001 |
| 800-m freestyle | Ian Thorpe (AUS) | 7 min 39.16 sec | 24 Jul 2001 |
| 1,500-m freestyle | Grant Hackett (AUS) | 14 min 34.56 sec | 29 Jul 2001 |
| 50-m backstroke | Lenny Krayzelburg (USA) | 24.99 sec | 28 Aug 1999 |
| 100-m backstroke | Lenny Krayzelburg (USA) | 53.60 sec | 24 Aug 1999 |
| 200-m backstroke | Aaron Peirsol (USA) | 1 min 55.15 sec | 20 Mar 2002 |
| 50-m breaststroke | Oleg Lisogor (UKR) | 27.18 sec | 2 Aug 2002 |
| 100-m breaststroke | Kosuke Kitajima (JPN) | 59.78 sec | 21 Jul 2003 |
| 200-m breaststroke | Kosuke Kitajima (JPN) | 2 min 9.42 sec | 24 Jul 2003 |
| 50-m butterfly | Matt Welsh (AUS) | 23.43 sec | 21 Jul 2003 |
| 100-m butterfly | Michael Phelps (USA) | 51.47 sec | 25 Jul 2003 |
| 200-m butterfly | Michael Phelps (USA) | 1 min 53.93 sec | 22 Jul 2003 |

# Swimming World Records—Long Course (50-m) (continued)

## men

| EVENT | RECORD HOLDER (NATIONALITY) | PERFORMANCE | DATE |
|---|---|---|---|
| 200-m individual medley | Michael Phelps (USA) | 1 min 56.04 sec | 25 Jul 2003 |
| 400-m individual medley | Michael Phelps (USA) | 4 min 11.09 sec | 15 Aug 2002 |
| 4 × 100 free relay | Australia (Michael Klim, Chris Fydler, Ashley Callus, Ian Thorpe) | 3 min 13.67 sec | 16 Sep 2000 |
| 4 × 200 free relay | Australia (Grant Hackett, Michael Klim, William Kirby, Ian Thorpe) | 7 min 4.66 sec | 27 Jul 2001 |
| 4 × 100 medley relay | United States (Aaron Peirsol, Brendon Hansen, Michael Phelps, Jason Lezak) | 3 min 33.48 sec | 29 Aug 2002 |

## women

| EVENT | RECORD HOLDER (NATIONALITY) | PERFORMANCE | DATE |
|---|---|---|---|
| 50-m freestyle | Inge de Bruijn (NED) | 24.13 sec | 22 Sep 2000 |
| 100-m freestyle | Inge de Bruijn (NED) | 53.77 sec | 20 Sep 2000 |
| 200-m freestyle | Franziska Van Almsick (GER) | 1 min 56.64 sec | 3 Aug 2002 |
| 400-m freestyle | Janet Evans (USA) | 4 min 3.85 sec | 22 Sep 1988 |
| 800-m freestyle | Janet Evans (USA) | 8 min 16.22 sec | 20 Aug 1989 |
| 1,500-m freestyle | Janet Evans (USA) | 15 min 52.10 sec | 26 Mar 1988 |
| 50-m backstroke | Sandra Völker (GER) | 28.25 sec | 17 Jun 2000 |
| 100-m backstroke | Natalie Coughlin (USA) | 59.58 sec | 13 Aug 2002 |
| 200-m backstroke | Kristina Egerszergi (HUN) | 2 min 6.62 sec | 25 Aug 1991 |
| 50-m breaststroke | Zoe Baker (GBR) | 30.57 sec | 30 Jul 2002 |
| 100-m breaststroke | Jones Leisel (AUS) | 1 min 6.37 sec | 21 Jul 2003 |
| 200-m breaststroke | Hui Qui (CHN) | 2 min 22.99 sec | 13 Apr 2001 |
| 50-m butterfly | Inge de Bruijn (NED) | 25.64 sec | 26 May 2000 |
| 100-m butterfly | Inge de Bruijn (NED) | 56.61 sec | 17 Sep 2000 |
| 200-m butterfly | Otylia Jedrzejczak (POL) | 2 min 5.78 sec | 4 Aug 2002 |
| 200-m individual medley | Wu Yanyan (CHN) | 2 min 9.72 sec | 17 Oct 1997 |
| 400-m individual medley | Yana Klochkova (UKR) | 4 min 33.59 sec | 16 Sep 2000 |
| 4 × 100 free relay | Germany (Kathrin Meissner, Petra Dallmann, Sandra Volker, Franziska Van Almsick) | 3 min 36.00 sec | 29 Jul 2002 |
| 4 × 200 free relay | East Germany (Manuela Stellmach, Astrid Strauss, Anke Möhring, Heike Friedrich) | 7 min 55.47 sec | 18 Aug 1987 |
| 4 × 100 medley relay | United States (B.J. Bedford, Megan Quann, Jenny Thompson, Dara Torres) | 3 min 58.30 sec | 23 Sep 2000 |

# Swimming World Records—Short Course (25-m)

## men

| EVENT | RECORD HOLDER (NATIONALITY) | PERFORMANCE | DATE |
|---|---|---|---|
| 50-m freestyle | Mark Foster (GBR) | 21.13 sec | 28 Jan 2001 |
| 100-m freestyle | Aleksandr Popov (RUS) | 46.74 sec | 19 Mar 1994 |
| 200-m freestyle | Ian Thorpe (AUS) | 1 min 41.10 sec | 6 Feb 2000 |
| 400-m freestyle | Grant Hackett (AUS) | 3 min 34.58 sec | 18 Jul 2002 |
| 800-m freestyle | Grant Hackett (AUS) | 7 min 25.28 sec | 3 Aug 2001 |
| 1,500-m freestyle | Grant Hackett (AUS) | 14 min 10.10 sec | 7 Aug 2001 |
| 50-m backstroke | Matt Welsh (AUS) | 23.31 sec | 2 Sep 2002 |
| 100-m backstroke | Thomas Rupprath (GER) | 50.58 sec | 8 Dec 2002 |
| 200-m backstroke | Aaron Peirsol (USA) | 1 min 51.17 sec | 7 Apr 2002 |
| 50-m breaststroke | Oleg Lisogor (UKR) | 26.20 sec | 26 Jan 2002 |
| 100-m breaststroke | Ed Moses (USA) | 57.47 sec | 23 Jan 2002 |
| 200-m breaststroke | Ed Moses (USA) | 2 min 3.17 sec | 26 Jan 2002 |
| 50-m butterfly | Geoffrey Huegill (AUS) | 22.74 sec | 26 Jan 2002 |
| 100-m butterfly | Thomas Rupprath (GER) | 50.10 sec | 27 Jan 2002 |
| 200-m butterfly | Frank Esposito (FRA) | 1 min 50.73 sec | 8 Dec 2002 |
| 100-m individual medley | Peter Mankoc (SLO) | 52.65 sec | 15 Dec 2001 |
| 200-m individual medley | Jani Sievinen (FIN) | 1 min 54.65 sec | 21 Apr 1994 |
| | Atilla Czene (HUN) | tied record | 23 Mar 2000 |
| 400-m individual medley | Brian Johns (CAN) | 4 min 2.72 sec | 21 Feb 2003 |
| 4 × 100 free relay | Sweden (Johan Nystrom, Lars Frölander, Mattias Ohlin, Stefan Nystrand) | 3 min 9.57 sec | 16 Mar 2002 |
| 4 × 200 free relay | Australia (William Kirby, Ian Thorpe, Michael Kim, Grant Hackett) | 6 min 56.41 sec | 7 Aug 2001 |
| 4 × 100 medley relay | Australia (Matt Welsh, Jim Pipes, Geoff Huegill, Ashley Callus) | 3 min 28.12 sec | 4 Sep 2002 |

## Swimming World Records—Short Course (25-m) (continued)

### women

| EVENT | RECORD HOLDER (NATIONALITY) | PERFORMANCE | DATE |
|---|---|---|---|
| 50-m freestyle | Therese Alshammar (SWE) | 23.59 sec | 18 Mar 2000 |
| 100-m freestyle | Therese Alshammar (SWE) | 52.17 sec | 17 Mar 2000 |
| 200-m freestyle | Lindsay Benko (USA) | 1 min 54.04 sec | 7 Apr 2002 |
| 400-m freestyle | Lindsay Benko (USA) | 3 min 59.53 sec | 26 Jan 2003 |
| 800-m freestyle | Sachiko Yamada (JPN) | 8 min 14.35 sec | 2 Apr 2002 |
| 50-m backstroke | Li Hui (CHN) | 26.83 sec | 2 Dec 2001 |
| 100-m backstroke | Natalie Coughlin (USA) | 56.71 sec | 23 Nov 2002 |
| 200-m backstroke | Natalie Coughlin (USA) | 2 min 3.62 sec | 27 Nov 2001 |
| 50-m breaststroke | Emma Igelström (SWE) | 29.96 sec | 4 Apr 2002 |
| 100-m breaststroke | Emma Igelstrom (SWE) | 1 min 5.11 sec | 16 Mar 2003 |
| 200-m breaststroke | Qi Hui (CHN) | 2 min 19.25 sec | 28 Jan 2001 |
| 50-m butterfly | Anna-Karin Kammerling (SWE) | 25.36 sec | 25 Jan 2001 |
| 100-m butterfly | Natalie Coughlin (USA) | 56.34 sec | 22 Nov 2002 |
| 200-m butterfly | Susan O'Neill (AUS) | 2 min 4.16 sec | 18 Jan 2000 |
| 100-m individual medley | Natalie Coughlin (USA) | 58.80 sec | 23 Nov 2002 |
| 200-m individual medley | Allison Wagner (USA) | 2 min 7.79 sec | 5 Dec 1993 |
| 400-m individual medley | Yana Klochkova (UKR) | 4 min 27.83 sec | 19 Jan 2002 |
| 4 × 100 free relay | China (Le Jingyi, Na Chao, Shang Ying, Nian Yin) | 3 min 34.55 sec | 19 Apr 1997 |
| 4 × 200 free relay | China (Xu Yanvei, Zhu Yingven, Tang Jingzhi, Yang Yu) | 7 min 46.30 sec | 3 Apr 2002 |
| 4 × 100 medley relay | Sweden (Therese Alshammar, Emma Igelström, Anna-Karin Kammerling, Johanna Sjöberg) | 3 min 55.78 sec | 5 Apr 2002 |

# Table Tennis

Official **world table tennis championships** were first held in 1927 under the auspices of the **International** Table **Tennis Federation** (ITTF; founded 1926). **Women's doubles** competition was added in 1928 and women's team competition in 1934. In 1980 the ITTF first sponsored a men's **World Cup** competition for the top 16 ranking players; it has been held annually since then.

At world championships, held biennially since 1957, players compete for: the **Swaythling Cup** (men's team event; best of nine singles matches); the **Marcel Corbillon Cup** (women's team event; best of four singles and one doubles matches); the **St. Bride's Vase** (men's singles); the **G. Geist Prize** (women's singles); the **Iran Cup** (men's doubles championships); the **W.J. Pope Trophy** (women's doubles championships); and the **Heydusek Prize** (mixed doubles championships).

International Table Tennis Federation Web site: <www.ittf.com>

## Table Tennis World Rankings

*ITTF rankings as of 1 Aug 2003.*

| | MEN (NATIONALITY) | | WOMEN (NATIONALITY) |
|---|---|---|---|
| 1 | Timo Boll (GER) | 1 | Zhang Yining (CHN) |
| 2 | Werner Schlager (AUT) | 2 | Wang Nan (CHN) |
| 3 | Ma Lin (CHN) | 3 | Niu Jianfeng (CHN) |
| 4 | Vladimir Samsonov (BLR) | 4 | Tamara Boros (HRV) |
| 5 | Chuan Chih-Yuan (TPE) | 5 | Lin Ling (HKG) |

## World Table Tennis Championships—Men

*Competition was held annually beginning in 1927 and usually every other year since 1957.*
*Table shows results for the past 20 years.*

| YEAR | ST. BRIDE'S VASE | IRAN CUP | YEAR | SWAYTHLING CUP |
|---|---|---|---|---|
| 1983 | Guo Yuehua (CHN) | Dragutin Surbek, Zoran Kalinic (YUG) | 1983 | China |
| 1985 | Jiang Jialiang (CHN) | Mikael Appelgren, Ulf Carlsson (SWE) | 1985 | China |
| 1987 | Jiang Jialiang (CHN) | Chen Longcan, Wei Qingguang (CHN) | 1987 | China |
| 1989 | Jan-Ove Waldner (SWE) | Jorg Rosskopf, Steffen Fetzner (FRG) | 1989 | Sweden |
| 1991 | Jorgen Persson (SWE) | Peter Karlsson, Thomas Von Scheele (SWE) | 1991 | Sweden |
| 1993 | Jean-Philippe Gatien (FRA) | Wang Tao, Lu Lin (CHN) | 1993 | Sweden |
| 1995 | Kong Linghui (CHN) | Wang Tao, Lu Lin (CHN) | 1995 | China |
| 1997 | Jan-Ove Waldner (SWE) | Kong Linghui, Liu Guoliang (CHN) | 1997 | China |
| 1999 | Liu Guoliang (CHN) | Kong Linghui, Liu Guoliang (CHN) | 2000 | Sweden |
| 2001 | Wang Liqin (CHN) | Wang Liqin, Yan Sen (CHN) | 2001 | China |
| 2003 | Werner Schlager (AUT) | Wang Liqin, Yan Sen (CHN) | 2004 | *to be held 1–7 March, Doha, Qatar* |

## World Table Tennis Championships—Women

*Competition was held annually beginning in 1927 (Geist Prize), 1928 (Pope Trophy), and 1934 (Corbillon Cup) and usually every other year since 1957. Table shows the results for the past 20 years.*

| YEAR | G. GEIST PRIZE | W.J. POPE TROPHY | YEAR | CORBILLON CUP |
|------|----------------|------------------|------|---------------|
| 1983 | Cao Yanhua (CHN) | Shen Jianping, Dai Lili (CHN) | 1983 | China |
| 1985 | Cao Yanhua (CHN) | Dai Lili, Geng Lijuan (CHN) | 1985 | China |
| 1987 | He Zhili (CHN) | Hyun Jung Hwa, Yang Young Ja (KOR) | 1987 | China |
| 1989 | Qiao Hong (CHN) | Qiao Hong, Deng Yaping (CHN) | 1989 | China |
| 1991 | Deng Yaping (CHN) | Gao Jun, Chen Zihe (CHN) | 1991 | Korea |
| 1993 | Hyun Jung Hwa (KOR) | Liu Wei, Qiao Yunping (CHN) | 1993 | China |
| 1995 | Deng Yaping (CHN) | Deng Yaping, Qiao Hong (CHN) | 1995 | China |
| 1997 | Deng Yaping (CHN) | Deng Yaping, Yang Ying (CHN) | 1997 | China |
| 1999 | Wang Nan (CHN) | Wang Nan, Li Ju (CHN) | 2000 | China |
| 2001 | Wang Nan (CHN) | Wang Nan, Li Ju (CHN) | 2001 | China |
| 2003 | Wang Nan (CHN) | Wang Nan, Zhang Yining (CHN) | 2004 | to be held 1–7 March, Doha, Qatar |

## World Table Tennis Championships—Mixed

*Competition has been held since 1927–28. Table shows results for the past 20 years.*

| YEAR | HEYDUSEK PRIZE | YEAR | HEYDUSEK PRIZE |
|------|----------------|------|----------------|
| 1983 | Guo Yuehua, Ni Xialian (CHN) | 1995 | Wang Tao, Liu Wei (CHN) |
| 1985 | Cai Zhenhua, Cao Yanhua (CHN) | 1997 | Liu Guoliang, Wu Na (CHN) |
| 1987 | Hui Jun, Geng Lijuan (CHN) | 1999 | Ma Lin, Zhang Yingying (CHN) |
| 1989 | Yoo Nam Kyu, Hyung Jung Hwa (KOR) | 2001 | Qin Zhijian, Yang Ying (CHN) |
| 1991 | Wang Tao, Liu Wei (CHN) | 2003 | Ma Lin, Wang Nan (CHN) |
| 1993 | Wang Tao, Liu Wei (CHN) | | |

## Table Tennis World Cup

| | men | | | | women | |
|------|-----------------------|------|----------------------------|------|----------------------|
| YEAR | WINNER | YEAR | WINNER | YEAR | WINNER |
| 1980 | Guo Yuehua (CHN) | 1992 | Ma Wenge (CHN) | 1996 | Deng Yaping (CHN) |
| 1981 | Tibor Klampar (HUN) | 1993 | Zoran Primorac (CRO) | 1997 | Wang Nan (CHN) |
| 1982 | Guo Yuehua (CHN) | 1994 | Jean-Philippe Gatien (FRA) | 1998 | Wang Nan (CHN) |
| 1983 | Mikael Appelgren (SWE) | 1995 | Kong Linghui (CHN) | 1999 | Wang Nan (CHN) |
| 1984 | Jiang Jialiang (CHN) | 1996 | Liu Guoliang (CHN) | 2000 | Li Ju (CHN) |
| 1985 | Chen Xinhua (CHN) | 1997 | Zoran Primorac (CRO) | 2001 | Zhang Yining (CHN) |
| 1986 | Chen Longcan (CHN) | 1998 | Jorg Rosskopf (GER) | 2002 | Zhang Yining (CHN) |
| 1987 | Teng Yi (CHN) | 1999 | Vladimir Samsonov (BLR) | 2003 | to be held in October |
| 1988 | Andrzej Grubba (POL) | 2000 | Ma Lin (CHN) | | |
| 1989 | Ma Wenge (CHN) | 2001 | Vladimir Samsonov (BLR) | | |
| 1990 | Jan-Ove Waldner (SWE) | 2002 | Timo Boll (GER) | | |
| 1991 | Jörgen Persson (SWE) | 2003 | to be held in October | | |
| 1992 | Ma Wenge (CHN) | | | | |

# Tennis

Four events dominate world championship tennis. The first of the traditional "Big Four," or "Grand Slam," events was the **All-England Lawn Tennis Championships** (better known as the **Wimbledon** Championships), founded in 1877. Its only event the first year was the men's singles championships; women first competed in 1884. Major tennis tournaments also sprang up in the **United States** (1881 for men; women's singles competition first contested 1887, added officially 1889), **France** (1891 for men; women's singles competition added 1897), and **Australia** (1905 for men; women's singles competition added 1922). Open tennis (open, that is, both to professionals and to amateurs) became the rule in the Big Four tournaments in 1968.

International team tennis was organized in 1900 with the institution of the **Davis Cup**. Competing men's teams play four singles matches and one doubles match for the trophy. The **Wightman Cup** was contested yearly between British and American women's teams from 1923 to 1989. The **International Tennis Federation** (ITF, formerly the International Lawn Tennis Federation; founded 1913) established the **Federation Cup** in 1963 (called the Fed Cup since 1994) for international women's team competition. It is decided by elimination rounds of two singles and one doubles contest.

**Related Web sites:** International Tennis Federation: <www.itftennis.com>; Association of Tennis Professionals: <www.atptour.com>; Women's Tennis Association: <www.wtatour.com>

# Australian Open Tennis Championships—Singles

| YEAR | MEN | WOMEN |
|---|---|---|
| 1905 | Rodney Heath (AUS) | |
| 1906 | Tony Wilding (NZL) | |
| 1907 | Horace Rice (AUS) | |
| 1908 | Fred Alexander (USA) | |
| 1909 | Tony Wilding (NZL) | |
| 1910 | Rodney Heath (AUS) | |
| 1911 | Norman Brookes (AUS) | |
| 1912 | J. Cecil Parke (GBR) | |
| 1913 | E.F. Parker (AUS) | |
| 1914 | Pat O'Hara Wood (AUS) | |
| 1915 | Francis Lowe (GBR) | |
| 1916–18 | *not held* | |
| 1919 | A.R.F. Kingscote (GBR) | |
| 1920 | Pat O'Hara Wood (AUS) | |
| 1921 | Rhys Gemmell (AUS) | |
| 1922 | James Anderson (AUS) | Margaret Molesworth (AUS) |
| 1923 | Pat O'Hara Wood (AUS) | Margaret Molesworth (AUS) |
| 1924 | James Anderson (AUS) | Sylvia Lance (AUS) |
| 1925 | James Anderson (AUS) | Daphne Akhurst (AUS) |
| 1926 | John Hawkes (AUS) | Daphne Akhurst (AUS) |
| 1927 | Gerald Patterson (AUS) | Esna Boyd (AUS) |
| 1928 | Jean Borotra (FRA) | Daphne Akhurst (AUS) |
| 1929 | John Gregory (GBR) | Daphne Akhurst (AUS) |
| 1930 | Gar Moon (AUS) | Daphne Akhurst (AUS) |
| 1931 | Jack Crawford (AUS) | Coral Buttsworth (AUS) |
| 1932 | Jack Crawford (AUS) | Coral Buttsworth (AUS) |
| 1933 | Jack Crawford (AUS) | Joan Hartigan (AUS) |
| 1934 | Fred Perry (GBR) | Joan Hartigan (AUS) |
| 1935 | Jack Crawford (AUS) | Dorothy Round (GBR) |
| 1936 | Adrian Quist (AUS) | Joan Hartigan (AUS) |
| 1937 | Vivian McGrath (AUS) | Nancye Wynne (AUS) |
| 1938 | Don Budge (USA) | Dorothy Bundy (USA) |
| 1939 | John Bromwich (AUS) | Emily Westacott (AUS) |
| 1940 | Adrian Quist (AUS) | Nancye Wynne (AUS) |
| 1941–45 | *not held* | |
| 1946 | John Bromwich (AUS) | Nancye Wynne Bolton (AUS) |
| 1947 | Dinny Pails (AUS) | Nancye Wynne Bolton (AUS) |
| 1948 | Adrian Quist (AUS) | Nancye Wynne Bolton (AUS) |
| 1949 | Frank Sedgman (AUS) | Doris Hart (USA) |
| 1950 | Frank Sedgman (AUS) | Louise Brough (USA) |
| 1951 | Dick Savitt (USA) | Nancye Wynne Bolton (AUS) |
| 1952 | Ken McGregor (AUS) | Thelma Long (AUS) |
| 1953 | Ken Rosewall (AUS) | Maureen Connolly (USA) |
| 1954 | Mervyn Rose (AUS) | Thelma Long (AUS) |
| 1955 | Ken Rosewall (AUS) | Beryl Penrose (AUS) |
| 1956 | Lew Hoad (AUS) | Mary Carter (AUS) |
| 1957 | Ashley Cooper (AUS) | Shirley Fry (USA) |
| 1958 | Ashley Cooper (AUS) | Angela Mortimer (GBR) |
| 1959 | Alex Olmedo (PER) | Mary Carter-Reitano (AUS) |
| 1960 | Rod Laver (AUS) | Margaret Smith (AUS) |
| 1961 | Roy Emerson (AUS) | Margaret Smith (AUS) |
| 1962 | Rod Laver (AUS) | Margaret Smith (AUS) |
| 1963 | Roy Emerson (AUS) | Margaret Smith (AUS) |
| 1964 | Roy Emerson (AUS) | Margaret Smith (AUS) |
| 1965 | Roy Emerson (AUS) | Margaret Smith (AUS) |
| 1966 | Roy Emerson (AUS) | Margaret Smith (AUS) |
| 1967 | Roy Emerson (AUS) | Nancy Richey (USA) |
| 1968 | Bill Bowrey (AUS) | Billie Jean King (USA) |
| 1969 | Rod Laver (AUS) | Margaret Smith Court (AUS) |
| 1970 | Arthur Ashe (USA) | Margaret Smith Court (AUS) |
| 1971 | Ken Rosewall (AUS) | Margaret Smith Court (AUS) |
| 1972 | Ken Rosewall (AUS) | Virginia Wade (GBR) |
| 1973 | John Newcombe (AUS) | Margaret Smith Court (AUS) |
| 1974 | Jimmy Connors (USA) | Evonne Goolagong (AUS) |
| 1975 | John Newcombe (AUS) | Evonne Goolagong (AUS) |

# Australian Open Tennis Championships—Singles (continued)

| YEAR | MEN | WOMEN |
|------|-----|-------|
| 1976 | Mark Edmondson (AUS) | Evonne Goolagong Cawley (AUS) |
| 1977 | Roscoe Tanner (USA) | Kerry Reid (AUS) |
| 1978* | Vitas Gerulaitis (USA) | Evonne Goolagong Cawley (AUS) |
| 1979 | Guillermo Vilas (ARG) | Chris O'Neill (AUS) |
| 1980 | Guillermo Vilas (ARG) | Barbara Jordan (USA) |
| 1981 | Brian Teacher (USA) | Hana Mandlikova (TCH) |
| 1982 | Johan Kriek (RSA) | Martina Navratilova (USA) |
| 1983 | Johan Kriek (RSA) | Chris Evert Lloyd (USA) |
| 1984 | Mats Wilander (SWE) | Martina Navratilova (USA) |
| 1985 | Mats Wilander (SWE) | Chris Evert Lloyd (USA) |
| 1986 | Stefan Edberg (SWE) | Martina Navratilova (USA) |
| 1987 | Stefan Edberg (SWE) | Hana Mandlikova (TCH) |
| 1988 | Mats Wilander (SWE) | Steffi Graf (FRG) |
| 1989 | Ivan Lendl (TCH) | Steffi Graf (FRG) |
| 1990 | Ivan Lendl (TCH) | Steffi Graf (FRG) |
| 1991 | Boris Becker (GER) | Monica Seles (YUG) |
| 1992 | Jim Courier (USA) | Monica Seles (YUG) |
| 1993 | Jim Courier (USA) | Monica Seles (YUG) |
| 1994 | Pete Sampras (USA) | Steffi Graf (GER) |
| 1995 | Andre Agassi (USA) | Mary Pierce (FRA) |
| 1996 | Boris Becker (GER) | Monica Seles (YUG) |
| 1997 | Pete Sampras (USA) | Martina Hingis (SUI) |
| 1998 | Petr Korda (TCH) | Martina Hingis (SUI) |
| 1999 | Yevgeny Kafelnikov (RUS) | Martina Hingis (SUI) |
| 2000 | Andre Agassi (USA) | Lindsay Davenport (USA) |
| 2001 | Andre Agassi (USA) | Jennifer Capriati (USA) |
| 2002 | Thomas Johansson (SWE) | Jennifer Capriati (USA) |
| 2003 | Andre Agassi (USA) | Serena Williams (USA) |
| 2004 | *Scheduled to be held 19 Jan–1 Feb 2004* | |

*Tournaments (since December 1977) held in December rather than January.*

# Australian Open Tennis Championships—Doubles

| YEAR | MEN | WOMEN |
|------|-----|-------|
| 1905 | Tom Tachell, Randolph Lycett | |
| 1906 | Tony Wilding, Rodney Heath | |
| 1907 | Harry Parker, William Gregg | |
| 1908 | Fred Alexander, Alfred Dunlop | |
| 1909 | Ernie F. Parker, J.P. Keane | |
| 1910 | Horace Rice, Ashley Campbell | |
| 1911 | Rodney Heath, Randolph Lycett | |
| 1912 | J. Cecil Parke, Charles Dixon | |
| 1913 | Ernie F. Parker, Alf Hedemann | |
| 1914 | Ashley Campbell, Gerald Patterson | |
| 1915 | Horace Rice, Clarrie Todd | |
| 1916–18 | *not held* | |
| 1919 | Pat O'Hara Wood, Ron Thomas | |
| 1920 | Pat O'Hara Wood, Ron Thomas | |
| 1921 | S.H. Eaton-Rice, Rhys Gemmell | |
| 1922 | Gerald Patterson, John Hawkes | Esne Boyd, Marjorie Mountain |
| 1923 | Pat O'Hara Wood, Bert St. John | Esne Boyd, Sylvia Lance |
| 1924 | Norman Brookes, James Anderson | Daphne Akhurst, Sylvia Lance |
| 1925 | Gerald Patterson, Pat O'Hara Wood | Daphne Akhurst, Sylvia Lance Harper |
| 1926 | Gerald Patterson, John Hawkes | Meryl O'Hara Wood, Esne Boyd |
| 1927 | Gerald Patterson, John Hawkes | Meryl O'Hara Wood, Louise Bickerton |
| 1928 | Jean Borotra, Jacques Brugnon | Daphne Akhurst, Esne Boyd |
| 1929 | Jack Crawford, Harry Hopman | Daphne Akhurst, Louise Bickerton |
| 1930 | Jack Crawford, Harry Hopman | Margaret Molesworth, Emily Hood |
| 1931 | Charles Donohoe, Ray Dunlop | Daphne Akhurst Cozens, Louise Bickerton |
| 1932 | Jack Crawford, Gar Moon | Coral Buttsworth, Marjorie Cox Crawford |
| 1933 | Ellsworth Vines, Keith Gledhill | Margaret Molesworth, Emily Hood Westacott |
| 1934 | Fred Perry, George Hughes | Margaret Molesworth, Emily Hood Westacott |
| 1935 | Jack Crawford, Vivian McGrath | Evelyn Dearman, Nancye Wynne Lyle |
| 1936 | Adrian Quist, D.P. Turnbull | Thelma Coyne, Nancye Wynne |

# Australian Open Tennis Championships—Doubles (continued)

| YEAR | MEN | WOMEN |
|------|-----|-------|
| 1937 | Adrian Quist, D.P. Turnbull | Thelma Coyne, Nancye Wynne |
| 1938 | Adrian Quist, John Bromwich | Thelma Coyne, Nancye Wynne |
| 1939 | Adrian Quist, John Bromwich | Thelma Coyne, Nancye Wynne |
| 1940 | Adrian Quist, John Bromwich | Thelma Coyne, Nancye Wynne Bolton |
| 1941–45 | *not held* | |
| 1946 | Adrian Quist, John Bromwich | Joyce Fitch, Mary Bevis |
| 1947 | Adrian Quist, John Bromwich | Thelma Coyne Long, Nancye Wynne Bolton |
| 1948 | Adrian Quist, John Bromwich | Thelma Coyne Long, Nancye Wynne Bolton |
| 1949 | Adrian Quist, John Bromwich | Thelma Coyne Long, Nancye Wynne Bolton |
| 1950 | Adrian Quist, John Bromwich | Louise Brough, Doris Hart |
| 1951 | Frank Sedgman, Ken McGregor | Thelma Coyne Long, Nancye Wynne Bolton |
| 1952 | Frank Sedgman, Ken McGregor | Thelma Coyne Long, Nancye Wynne Bolton |
| 1953 | Lew Hoad, Ken Rosewall | Marueen Connolly, Julia Sampson |
| 1954 | Rex Hartwig, Mervyn Rose | Mary Bevis Hawton, Beryl Penrose |
| 1955 | Vic Seixas, Tony Trabert | Mary Bevis Hawton, Beryl Penrose |
| 1956 | Lew Hoad, Ken Rosewall | Mary Bevis Hawton, Thelma Coyne Long |
| 1957 | Lew Hoad, Neale Fraser | Althea Gibson, Shirley Fry |
| 1958 | Ashley Cooper, Neale Fraser | Mary Bevis Hawton, Thelma Coyne Long |
| 1959 | Rod Laver, Robert Mark | Renee Schuurman, Sandra Reynolds |
| 1960 | Rod Laver, Robert Mark | Maria Bueno, Christine Truman |
| 1961 | Rod Laver, Robert Mark | Mary Reitano, Margaret Smith |
| 1962 | Roy Emerson, Neale Fraser | Margaret Smith, Robyn Ebbern |
| 1963 | Bob Hewitt, Fred Stolle | Margaret Smith, Robyn Ebbern |
| 1964 | Bob Hewitt, Fred Stolle | Judy Tegart, Lesley Turner |
| 1965 | John Newcombe, Tony Roche | Margaret Smith, Lesley Turner |
| 1966 | Roy Emerson, Fred Stolle | Carole Graebner, Nancy Richey |
| 1967 | John Newcombe, Tony Roche | Judy Tegart, Lesley Turner |
| 1968 | Dick Crealy, Allan Stone | Karen Krantzcke, Karrie Melville |
| 1969 | Roy Emerson, Rod Laver | Margaret Smith Court, Judy Tegart |
| 1970 | Bob Lutz, Stan Smith | Margaret Smith Court, Judy Tegart Dalton |
| 1971 | John Newcombe, Tony Roche | Margaret Smith Court, Evonne Goolagong |
| 1972 | Owen Davidson, Ken Rosewall | Kerry Harris, Helen Gourlay |
| 1973 | Mal Anderson, John Newcombe | Margaret Smith Court, Virginia Wade |
| 1974 | Ross Case, Geoff Masters | Evonne Goolagong, Peggy Michel |
| 1975 | John Alexander, Phil Dent | Evonne Goolagong, Peggy Michel |
| 1976 | John Newcombe, Tony Roche | Evonne Goolagong Cawley, Helen Gourlay |
| 1977 | Arthur Ashe, Tony Roche | Dianne Fromholtz, Helen Gourlay |
| 1978* | Allan Stone, Ray Ruffels | Evonne Goolagong Cawley, Helen Gourlay Cawley; Mona Guerrant, Kerry Reid† |
| 1979 | Wojtek Fibak, Kim Warwick | Renata Tomanova, Betsy Nagelsen |
| 1980 | Peter McNamara, Paul McNamee | Judy Chaloner, Dianne Evers |
| 1981 | Kim Warwick, Mark Edmondson | Martina Navratilova, Betsy Nagelsen |
| 1982 | Kim Warwick, Mark Edmondson | Kathy Jordan, Anne Smith |
| 1983 | J. Alexander, J. Fitzgerald | Martina Navratilova, Pam Shriver |
| 1984 | Mark Edmondson, Paul McNamee | Martina Navratilova, Pam Shriver |
| 1985 | Mark Edmondson, Sherwood Stewart | Martina Navratilova, Pam Shriver |
| 1986 | Paul Annacone, Christo van Rensburg | Martina Navratilova, Pam Shriver |
| 1987 | Stefan Edberg, Anders Jarryd | Martina Navratilova, Pam Shriver |
| 1988 | Rick Leach, Jim Pugh | Martina Navratilova, Pam Shriver |
| 1989 | Rick Leach, Jim Pugh | Martina Navratilova, Pam Shriver |
| 1990 | Pieter Aldrich, Danie Visser | Jana Novotna, Helena Sukova |
| 1991 | Scott Davis, David Pate | Patty Fendick, Mary Joe Fernandez |
| 1992 | Todd Woodbridge, Mark Woodforde | Arantxa Sánchez Vicario, Helena Sukova |
| 1993 | Danie Visser, Laurie Warder | Gigi Fernandez, Natasha Zvereva |
| 1994 | Paul Haarhuis, Jacco Eltingh | Gigi Fernandez, Natasha Zvereva |
| 1995 | Jared Palmer, Richey Reneberg | Arantxa Sánchez Vicario, Jana Novotna |
| 1996 | Stefan Edberg, Petr Korda | Arantxa Sánchez Vicario, Chanda Rubin |
| 1997 | Todd Woodbridge, Mark Woodforde | Martina Hingis, Natasha Zvereva |
| 1998 | Jonas Bjorkman, Jacco Eltingh | Martina Hingis, Mirjana Lucic |
| 1999 | Jonas Bjorkman, Patrick Rafter | Martina Hingis, Anna Kournikova |
| 2000 | Ellis Ferreira, Rick Leach | Lisa Raymond, Rennae Stubbs |
| 2001 | Jonas Bjorkman, Todd Woodbridge | Serena Williams, Venus Williams |
| 2002 | Mark Knowles, Daniel Nestor | Martina Hingis, Anna Kournikova |
| 2003 | Michael Llodra, Fabrice Santoro | Serena Williams, Venus Williams |
| 2004 | *to be held 19 Jan–1 Feb 2004* | |

*Tournaments (since December 1977) held in December rather than January.*     †Tie; finals rained out.

# French Open Tennis Championships—Singles

*From 1891 to 1924, only members of French tennis clubs were eligible to play in the French Open. The table shows the winners only since 1925, when the tournament was opened to international competition.*

| YEAR | MEN | WOMEN |
|------|-----|-------|
| 1925 | René Lacoste (FRA) | Suzanne Lenglen (FRA) |
| 1926 | Henri Cochet (FRA) | Suzanne Lenglen (FRA) |
| 1927 | René Lacoste (FRA) | Kornelia Bouman (NED) |
| 1928 | Henri Cochet (FRA) | Helen Wills (USA) |
| 1929 | René Lacoste (FRA) | Helen Wills (USA) |
| 1930 | Henri Cochet (FRA) | Helen Wills Moody (USA) |
| 1931 | Jean Borotra (FRA) | Cilly Aussem (GER) |
| 1932 | Henri Cochet (FRA) | Helen Wills Moody (USA) |
| 1933 | John Crawford (AUS) | Margaret Scriven (GBR) |
| 1934 | Gottfried von Cramm (GER) | Margaret Scriven (GBR) |
| 1935 | Fred Perry (GBR) | Hilde Sperling (DEN) |
| 1936 | Gottfried von Cramm (GER) | Hilde Sperling (DEN) |
| 1937 | Henner Henkel (GER) | Hilde Sperling (DEN) |
| 1938 | Don Budge (USA) | Simone Mathieu (FRA) |
| 1939 | Don McNeill (USA) | Simone Mathieu (FRA) |
| 1940 | *not held* | *not held* |
| 1941 | Bernard Destremau (FRA) | *not held* |
| 1942 | Bernard Destremau (FRA) | *not held* |
| 1943 | Yvon Petra (FRA) | *not held* |
| 1944 | Yvon Petra (FRA) | *not held* |
| 1945 | Yvon Petra (FRA) | *not held* |
| 1946 | Marcel Bernard (FRA) | Margaret Osborne (USA) |
| 1947 | Joseph Asboth (HUN) | Patricia Todd (USA) |
| 1948 | Frank Parker (USA) | Nelly Landry (BEL) |
| 1949 | Frank Parker (USA) | Margaret Osborne du Pont (USA) |
| 1950 | Budge Patty (USA) | Doris Hart (USA) |
| 1951 | Jaroslav Drobny (TCH) | Shirley Fry (USA) |
| 1952 | Jaroslav Drobny (TCH) | Doris Hart (USA) |
| 1953 | Ken Rosewall (AUS) | Maureen Connolly (USA) |
| 1954 | Tony Trabert (USA) | Maureen Connolly (USA) |
| 1955 | Tony Trabert (USA) | Angela Mortimer (GBR) |
| 1956 | Lew Hoad (AUS) | Althea Gibson (USA) |
| 1957 | Sven Davidson (SWE) | Shirley Bloomer (GBR) |
| 1958 | Mervyn Rose (AUS) | Zsuzsi Kormoczi (HUN) |
| 1959 | Nicola Pietrangeli (ITA) | Christine Truman (GBR) |
| 1960 | Nicola Pietrangeli (ITA) | Darlene Hard (USA) |
| 1961 | Manuel Santana (ESP) | Ann Haydon (GBR) |
| 1962 | Rod Laver (AUS) | Margaret Smith (AUS) |
| 1963 | Roy Emerson (AUS) | Lesley Turner (AUS) |
| 1964 | Manuel Santana (ESP) | Margaret Smith (AUS) |
| 1965 | Fred Stolle (AUS) | Lesley Turner (AUS) |
| 1966 | Tony Roche (AUS) | Ann Haydon Jones (GBR) |
| 1967 | Roy Emerson (AUS) | Françoise Durr (FRA) |
| 1968 | Ken Rosewall (AUS) | Nancy Richey (USA) |
| 1969 | Rod Laver (AUS) | Margaret Smith Court (AUS) |
| 1970 | Jan Kodes (TCH) | Margaret Smith Court (AUS) |
| 1971 | Jan Kodes (TCH) | Evonne Goolagong (AUS) |
| 1972 | Andres Gimeno (ESP) | Billie Jean King (USA) |
| 1973 | Ilie Nastase (ROM) | Margaret Smith Court (AUS) |
| 1974 | Bjorn Borg (SWE) | Chris Evert (USA) |
| 1975 | Bjorn Borg (SWE) | Chris Evert (USA) |
| 1976 | Adriano Panatta (ITA) | Sue Barker (USA) |
| 1977 | Guillermo Vilas (ARG) | Mima Jausovec (YUG) |
| 1978 | Bjorn Borg (SWE) | Virginia Ruzici (ROM) |
| 1979 | Bjorn Borg (SWE) | Chris Evert Lloyd (USA) |
| 1980 | Bjorn Borg (SWE) | Chris Evert Lloyd (USA) |
| 1981 | Bjorn Borg (SWE) | Hana Mandlikova (TCH) |
| 1982 | Mats Wilander (SWE) | Martina Navratilova (USA) |
| 1983 | Yannick Noah (FRA) | Chris Evert Lloyd (USA) |
| 1984 | Ivan Lendl (TCH) | Martina Navratilova (USA) |
| 1985 | Mats Wilander (SWE) | Chris Evert Lloyd (USA) |
| 1986 | Ivan Lendl (TCH) | Chris Evert Lloyd (USA) |
| 1987 | Ivan Lendl (TCH) | Steffi Graf (FRG) |
| 1988 | Mats Wilander (SWE) | Steffi Graf (FRG) |

# French Open Tennis Championships—Singles (continued)

| YEAR | MEN | WOMEN |
|------|-----|-------|
| 1989 | Michael Chang (USA) | Arantxa Sánchez Vicario (ESP) |
| 1990 | Andres Gomez (ECU) | Monica Seles (YUG) |
| 1991 | Jim Courier (USA) | Monica Seles (YUG) |
| 1992 | Jim Courier (USA) | Monica Seles (YUG) |
| 1993 | Sergi Bruguera (ESP) | Steffi Graf (GER) |
| 1994 | Sergi Bruguera (ESP) | Arantxa Sánchez Vicario (ESP) |
| 1995 | Thomas Muster (AUT) | Steffi Graf (GER) |
| 1996 | Yevgeny Kafelnikov (RUS) | Steffi Graf (GER) |
| 1997 | Gustavo Kuerten (BRA) | Iva Majoli (CRO) |
| 1998 | Carlos Moya (ESP) | Arantxa Sánchez Vicario (ESP) |
| 1999 | Andre Agassi (USA) | Steffi Graf (GER) |
| 2000 | Gustavo Kuerten (BRA) | Mary Pierce (FRA) |
| 2001 | Gustavo Kuerten (BRA) | Jennifer Capriati (USA) |
| 2002 | Albert Costa (ESP) | Serena Williams (USA) |
| 2003 | Juan Carlos Ferrero (ESP) | Justine Henin-Hardenne (BEL) |

# French Open Tennis Championships—Doubles

| YEAR | MEN | WOMEN |
|------|-----|-------|
| 1925 | Jean Borotra, René Lacoste | Suzanne Lenglen, Didi Vlasto |
| 1926 | Vinnie Richards, Howard Kinsey | Suzanne Lenglen, Didi Vlasto |
| 1927 | Henri Cochet, Jacques Brugnon | Irene Peacock, Bobby Heine |
| 1928 | Jean Borotra, Jacques Brugnon | Phoebe Watson, Eileen Bennett |
| 1929 | Jean Borotra, René Lacoste | Lili de Alvarez, Kea Bouman |
| 1930 | Henri Cochet, Jacques Brugnon | Helen Wills Moody, Elizabeth Ryan |
| 1931 | George Lott, John Van Ryn | Eileen Whittingstall, Betty Nuthall |
| 1932 | Henri Cochet, Jacques Brugnon | Helen Wills Moody, Elizabeth Ryan |
| 1933 | Pat Hughes, Fred Perry | Simone Mathieu, Elizabeth Ryan |
| 1934 | Jean Borotra, Jacques Brugnon | Simone Mathieu, Elizabeth Ryan |
| 1935 | Jack Crawford, Adrian Quist | Margaret Scriven, Kay Stammers |
| 1936 | Jean Borotra, Marcel Bernard | Simone Mathieu, Billy Yorke |
| 1937 | Gottfried von Cramm, Henner Henkel | Simone Mathieu, Billy Yorke |
| 1938 | Bernard Destremau, Yvon Petra | Simone Mathieu, Billy Yorke |
| 1939 | Don McNeill, Charles Harris | Simone Mathieu, Jadwiga Jedrzejowska |
| 1940–45 | *not held* | |
| 1946 | Marcel Bernard, Yvon Petra | Louise Brough, Margaret Osborne |
| 1947 | Eustace Fannin, Eric Sturgess | Louise Brough, Margaret Osborne |
| 1948 | Lennart Bergelin, Jaroslav Drobny | Doris Hart, Patricia Todd |
| 1949 | Pancho Gonzales, Frank Parker | Louise Brough, Margaret Osborne du Pont |
| 1950 | Billy Talbert, Tony Trabert | Doris Hart, Shirley Fry |
| 1951 | Ken McGregor, Frank Sedgman | Doris Hart, Shirley Fry |
| 1952 | Ken McGregor, Frank Sedgman | Doris Hart, Shirley Fry |
| 1953 | Lew Hoad, Ken Rosewall | Doris Hart, Shirley Fry |
| 1954 | Vic Seixas, Tony Trabert | Maureen Connolly, Nell Hopman |
| 1955 | Vic Seixas, Tony Trabert | Beverly Fleitz, Darlene Hard |
| 1956 | Don Candy, Robert Perry | Angela Buxton, Althea Gibson |
| 1957 | Mal Anderson, Ashley Cooper | Shirley Bloomer, Darlene Hard |
| 1958 | Ashley Cooper, Neale Fraser | Rosie Reyes, Yola Ramirez |
| 1959 | Nicola Pietrangeli, Orlando Sirola | Sandra Reynolds, Renee Schuurman |
| 1960 | Roy Emerson, Neale Fraser | Maria Bueno, Darlene Hard |
| 1961 | Roy Emerson, Rod Laver | Sandra Reynolds, Renee Schuurman |
| 1962 | Roy Emerson, Neale Fraser | Sandra Reynolds Price, Renee Schuurman |
| 1963 | Roy Emerson, Manuel Santana | Ann Haydon Jones, Renee Schuurman |
| 1964 | Roy Emerson, Ken Fletcher | Margaret Smith, Leslie Turner |
| 1965 | Roy Emerson, Fred Stolle | Margaret Smith, Leslie Turner |
| 1966 | Clark Graebner, Dennis Ralston | Margaret Smith, Judy Tegart |
| 1967 | John Newcombe, Tony Roche | Françoise Durr, Gail Sheriff |
| 1968 | Ken Rosewall, Fred Stolle | Françoise Durr, Ann Haydon Jones |
| 1969 | John Newcombe, Tony Roche | Françoise Durr, Ann Haydon Jones |
| 1970 | Ilie Nastase, Ion Tiriac | Françoise Durr, Gail Chanfreau |
| 1971 | Arthur Ashe, Marty Riessen | Françoise Durr, Gail Chanfreau |
| 1972 | Bob Hewitt, Frew McMillan | Billie Jean King, Betty Stove |
| 1973 | John Newcombe, Tom Okker | Margaret Smith Court, Virginia Wade |
| 1974 | Dick Crealy, Onny Parun | Chris Evert, Olga Morozova |

## French Open Tennis Championships—Doubles (continued)

| YEAR | MEN | WOMEN |
| --- | --- | --- |
| 1975 | Brian Gottfried, Raul Ramirez | Chris Evert, Martina Navratilova |
| 1976 | Fred McNair, Sherwood Stewart | Fiorella Bonicelli, Gail Chanfreau Lovera |
| 1977 | Brian Gottfried, Raul Ramirez | Regina Marsikova, Pam Teeguarden |
| 1978 | Hank Pfister, Gene Mayer | Mimi Jausovec, Virginia Ruzici |
| 1979 | Sandy Mayer, Gene Mayer | Betty Stove, Wendy Turnbull |
| 1980 | Victor Amaya, Hank Pfister | Kathy Jordan, Anne Smith |
| 1981 | Heinz Gunthardt, Balazs Taroczy | Rosalyn Fairbank, Tanya Harford |
| 1982 | Sherwood Stewart, Ferdi Taygan | Martina Navratilova, Anne Smith |
| 1983 | Anders Jarryd, Hans Simonsson | Rosalyn Fairbank, Candy Reynolds |
| 1984 | Henri Leconte, Yannick Noah | Martina Navratilova, Pam Shriver |
| 1985 | Mark Edmondson, Kim Warwick | Martina Navratilova, Pam Shriver |
| 1986 | John Fitzgerald, Tomas Smid | Martina Navratilova, Andrea Temesvari |
| 1987 | Robert Seguso, Anders Jarryd | Martina Navratilova, Pam Shriver |
| 1988 | Emilio Sánchez, Andres Gomez | Martina Navratilova, Pam Shriver |
| 1989 | Jim Grabb, Patrick McEnroe | Larisa Savchenko, Natasha Zvereva |
| 1990 | Sergio Casal, Emilio Sánchez | Jana Novotna, Helena Sukova |
| 1991 | John Fitzgerald, Anders Jarryd | Gigi Fernandez, Jana Novotna |
| 1992 | Jacob Hlasek, Marc Rosset | Gigi Fernandez, Natasha Zvereva |
| 1993 | Luke Jensen, Murphy Jensen | Gigi Fernandez, Natasha Zvereva |
| 1994 | Byron Black, Jonathan Stark | Gigi Fernandez, Natasha Zvereva |
| 1995 | Jacco Eltingh, Paul Haarhuis | Gigi Fernandez, Natasha Zvereva |
| 1996 | Yevgeny Kafelnikov, Daniel Vacek | Lindsay Davenport, Mary Joe Fernandez |
| 1997 | Yevgeny Kafelnikov, Daniel Vacek | Gigi Fernandez, Natasha Zvereva |
| 1998 | Jacco Eltingh, Paul Haarhuis | Martina Hingis, Jana Novotna |
| 1999 | Mahesh Bhupathi, Leander Paes | Serena Williams, Venus Williams |
| 2000 | Todd Woodbridge, Mark Woodforde | Martina Hingis, Mary Pierce |
| 2001 | Mahesh Bhupathi, Leander Paes | Virginia Ruano Pascal, Paola Suarez |
| 2002 | Yevgeny Kafelnikov, Paul Haarhuis | Virginia Ruano Pascal, Paola Suarez |
| 2003 | Bob Bryan, Mike Bryan | Kim Clijsters, Ai Sugiyama |

 The origins of tennis can be traced to a 12th–13th-century French handball game called *jeu de paume* ("game of the palm").

## All-England (Wimbledon) Tennis Championships—Singles

| YEAR | MEN | WOMEN |
| --- | --- | --- |
| 1877 | Spencer Gore (GBR) | |
| 1878 | Frank Hadow (GBR) | |
| 1879 | John Hartley (GBR) | |
| 1880 | John Hartley (GBR) | |
| 1881 | Willie Renshaw (GBR) | |
| 1882 | Willie Renshaw (GBR) | |
| 1883 | Willie Renshaw (GBR) | |
| 1884 | Willie Renshaw (GBR) | Maud Watson (GBR) |
| 1885 | Willie Renshaw (GBR) | Maud Watson (GBR) |
| 1886 | Willie Renshaw (GBR) | Blanche Bingley (GBR) |
| 1887 | Herbert Lawford (GBR) | Lottie Dod (GBR) |
| 1888 | Ernest Renshaw (GBR) | Lottie Dod (GBR) |
| 1889 | Willie Renshaw (GBR) | Blanche Bingley Hillyard (GBR) |
| 1890 | William Hamilton (GBR) | Lena Rice (GBR) |
| 1891 | Wilfred Baddeley (GBR) | Lottie Dod (GBR) |
| 1892 | Wilfred Baddeley (GBR) | Lottie Dod (GBR) |
| 1893 | Joshua Pim (GBR) | Lottie Dod (GBR) |
| 1894 | Joshua Pim (GBR) | Blanche Bingley Hillyard (GBR) |
| 1895 | Wilfred Baddeley (GBR) | Charlotte Cooper (GBR) |
| 1896 | Harold Mahony (GBR) | Charlotte Cooper (GBR) |
| 1897 | Reggie Doherty (GBR) | Blanche Bingley Hillyard (GBR) |
| 1898 | Reggie Doherty (GBR) | Charlotte Cooper (GBR) |
| 1899 | Reggie Doherty (GBR) | Blanche Bingley Hillyard (GBR) |
| 1900 | Reggie Doherty (GBR) | Blanche Bingley Hillyard (GBR) |
| 1901 | Arthur Gore (GBR) | Charlotte Cooper Sterry (GBR) |

# All-England (Wimbledon) Tennis Championships—Singles (continued)

| YEAR | MEN | WOMEN |
|---|---|---|
| 1902 | Laurie Doherty (GBR) | Muriel Robb (GBR) |
| 1903 | Laurie Doherty (GBR) | Dorothea Douglass (GBR) |
| 1904 | Laurie Doherty (GBR) | Dorothea Douglass (GBR) |
| 1905 | Laurie Doherty (GBR) | May Sutton (USA) |
| 1906 | Laurie Doherty (GBR) | Dorothea Douglass (GBR) |
| 1907 | Norman Brookes (AUS) | May Sutton (USA) |
| 1908 | Arthur Gore (GBR) | Charlotte Cooper Sterry (GBR) |
| 1909 | Arthur Gore (GBR) | Dora Boothby (GBR) |
| 1910 | Tony Wilding (NZL) | Dorothea Douglass Lambert Chambers (GBR) |
| 1911 | Tony Wilding (NZL) | Dorothea Douglass Lambert Chambers (GBR) |
| 1912 | Tony Wilding (NZL) | Ethel Larcombe (GBR) |
| 1913 | Tony Wilding (NZL) | Dorothea Douglass Lambert Chambers (GBR) |
| 1914 | Norman Brookes (AUS) | Dorothea Douglass Lambert Chambers (GBR) |
| 1915–18 | not held | |
| 1919 | Gerald Patterson (AUS) | Suzanne Lenglen (FRA) |
| 1920 | Bill Tilden (USA) | Suzanne Lenglen (FRA) |
| 1921 | Bill Tilden (USA) | Suzanne Lenglen (FRA) |
| 1922 | Gerald Patterson (AUS) | Suzanne Lenglen (FRA) |
| 1923 | Bill Johnston (USA) | Suzanne Lenglen (FRA) |
| 1924 | Jean Borotra (FRA) | Kathleen McKane (GBR) |
| 1925 | René Lacoste (FRA) | Suzanne Lenglen (FRA) |
| 1926 | Jean Borotra (FRA) | Kathleen McKane Godfree (GBR) |
| 1927 | Henri Cochet (FRA) | Helen Wills (USA) |
| 1928 | René Lacoste (FRA) | Helen Wills (USA) |
| 1929 | Henri Cochet (FRA) | Helen Wills (USA) |
| 1930 | Bill Tilden (USA) | Helen Wills Moody (USA) |
| 1931 | Sidney Wood (USA) | Cilly Aussem (GER) |
| 1932 | Ellsworth Vines (USA) | Helen Wills Moody (USA) |
| 1933 | Jack Crawford (AUS) | Helen Wills Moody (USA) |
| 1934 | Fred Perry (GBR) | Dorothy Round (GBR) |
| 1935 | Fred Perry (GBR) | Helen Wills Moody (USA) |
| 1936 | Fred Perry (GBR) | Helen Jacobs (USA) |
| 1937 | Don Budge (USA) | Dorothy Round (GBR) |
| 1938 | Don Budge (USA) | Helen Wills Moody (USA) |
| 1939 | Bobby Riggs (USA) | Alice Marble (USA) |
| 1940–45 | not held | |
| 1946 | Yvon Petra (FRA) | Pauline Betz (USA) |
| 1947 | Jack Kramer (USA) | Margaret Osborne (USA) |
| 1948 | Bob Falkenburg (USA) | Louise Brough (USA) |
| 1949 | Ted Schroeder (USA) | Louise Brough (USA) |
| 1950 | Budge Patty (USA) | Louise Brough (USA) |
| 1951 | Dick Savitt (USA) | Doris Hart (USA) |
| 1952 | Frank Sedgman (AUS) | Maureen Connolly (USA) |
| 1953 | Vic Seixas (USA) | Maureen Connolly (USA) |
| 1954 | Jaroslav Drobny (TCH) | Maureen Connolly (USA) |
| 1955 | Tony Trabert (USA) | Louise Brough (USA) |
| 1956 | Lew Hoad (AUS) | Shirley Fry (USA) |
| 1957 | Lew Hoad (AUS) | Althea Gibson (USA) |
| 1958 | Ashley Cooper (AUS) | Althea Gibson (USA) |
| 1959 | Alex Olmedo (PER) | Maria Bueno (BRA) |
| 1960 | Neale Fraser (AUS) | Maria Bueno (BRA) |
| 1961 | Rod Laver (AUS) | Angela Mortimer (GBR) |
| 1962 | Rod Laver (AUS) | Karen Susman (USA) |
| 1963 | Chuck McKinley (USA) | Margaret Smith (AUS) |
| 1964 | Roy Emerson (AUS) | Maria Bueno (BRA) |
| 1965 | Roy Emerson (AUS) | Margaret Smith (AUS) |
| 1966 | Manuel Santana (ESP) | Billie Jean King (USA) |
| 1967 | John Newcombe (AUS) | Billie Jean King (USA) |
| 1968* | Rod Laver (AUS) | Billie Jean King (USA) |
| 1969 | Rod Laver (AUS) | Ann Jones (GBR) |
| 1970 | John Newcombe (AUS) | Margaret Smith Court (AUS) |
| 1971 | John Newcombe (AUS) | Evonne Goolagong (AUS) |
| 1972 | Stan Smith (USA) | Billie Jean King (USA) |
| 1973 | Jan Kodes (TCH) | Billie Jean King (USA) |
| 1974 | Jimmy Connors (USA) | Chris Evert (USA) |
| 1975 | Arthur Ashe (USA) | Billie Jean King (USA) |
| 1976 | Björn Borg (SWE) | Chris Evert (USA) |
| 1977 | Björn Borg (SWE) | Virginia Wade (GBR) |

## All-England (Wimbledon) Tennis Championships—Singles (continued)

| YEAR | MEN | WOMEN |
|---|---|---|
| 1978 | Björn Borg (SWE) | Martina Navratilova (TCH) |
| 1979 | Björn Borg (SWE) | Martina Navratilova (USA) |
| 1980 | Björn Borg (SWE) | Evonne Goolagong Cawley (AUS) |
| 1981 | John McEnroe (USA) | Chris Evert Lloyd (USA) |
| 1982 | Jimmy Connors (USA) | Martina Navratilova (USA) |
| 1983 | John McEnroe (USA) | Martina Navratilova (USA) |
| 1984 | John McEnroe (USA) | Martina Navratilova (USA) |
| 1985 | Boris Becker (FRG) | Martina Navratilova (USA) |
| 1986 | Boris Becker (FRG) | Martina Navratilova (USA) |
| 1987 | Pat Cash (AUS) | Martina Navratilova (USA) |
| 1988 | Stefan Edberg (SWE) | Steffi Graf (GDR) |
| 1989 | Boris Becker (FRG) | Steffi Graf (GDR) |
| 1990 | Stefan Edberg (SWE) | Martina Navratilova (USA) |
| 1991 | Michael Stich (GER) | Steffi Graf (GER) |
| 1992 | Andre Agassi (USA) | Steffi Graf (GER) |
| 1993 | Pete Sampras (USA) | Steffi Graf (GER) |
| 1994 | Pete Sampras (USA) | Conchita Martínez (ESP) |
| 1995 | Pete Sampras (USA) | Steffi Graf (GER) |
| 1996 | Richard Krajicek (NED) | Steffi Graf (GER) |
| 1997 | Pete Sampras (USA) | Martina Hingis (SUI) |
| 1998 | Pete Sampras (USA) | Jana Novotna (CZE) |
| 1999 | Pete Sampras (USA) | Lindsay Davenport (USA) |
| 2000 | Pete Sampras (USA) | Venus Williams (USA) |
| 2001 | Goran Ivanisevic (CRO) | Venus Williams (USA) |
| 2002 | Lleyton Hewitt (AUS) | Serena Williams (USA) |
| 2003 | Roger Federer (SUI) | Serena Williams (USA) |

*Open since 1968.

## All-England (Wimbledon) Tennis Championships—Doubles

| YEAR | MEN | WOMEN |
|---|---|---|
| 1879 | L.R. Erskine, H. Lawford | |
| 1880 | William Renshaw, Ernest Renshaw | |
| 1881 | William Renshaw, Ernest Renshaw | |
| 1882 | J.T. Hartley, R.T. Richardson | |
| 1883 | C.W. Grinstead, C.E. Welldon | |
| 1884 | William Renshaw, Ernest Renshaw | |
| 1885 | William Renshaw, Ernest Renshaw | |
| 1886 | William Renshaw, Ernest Renshaw | |
| 1887 | Herbert Wilberforce, P.B. Lyon | |
| 1888 | William Renshaw, Ernest Renshaw | |
| 1889 | William Renshaw, Ernest Renshaw | |
| 1890 | Joshua Pim, F.O. Stoker | |
| 1891 | Wilfred Baddeley, Herbert Baddeley | |
| 1892 | E.W. Lewis, H.S. Barlow | |
| 1893 | Joshua Pim, F.O. Stoker | |
| 1894 | Wilfred Baddeley, Herbert Baddeley | |
| 1895 | Wilfred Baddeley, Herbert Baddeley | |
| 1896 | Wilfred Baddeley, Herbert Baddeley | |
| 1897 | Reggie Doherty, Laurie Doherty | |
| 1898 | Reggie Doherty, Laurie Doherty | |
| 1899 | Reggie Doherty, Laurie Doherty | |
| 1900 | Reggie Doherty, Laurie Doherty | |
| 1901 | Reggie Doherty, Laurie Doherty | |
| 1902 | Sidney Smith, Frank Riseley | |
| 1903 | Reggie Doherty, Laurie Doherty | |
| 1904 | Reggie Doherty, Laurie Doherty | |
| 1905 | Reggie Doherty, Laurie Doherty | |
| 1906 | Sidney Smith, Frank Riseley | |
| 1907 | Norman Brookes, Anthony Wilding | |
| 1908 | Anthony Wilding, M.J.G. Ritchie | |
| 1909 | Arthur Gore, H. Roper Barrett | |
| 1910 | Anthony Wilding, M.J.G. Ritchie | |
| 1911 | Andre Gobert, Max Decugis | |
| 1912 | H. Roper Barrett, Charles Dixon | |
| 1913 | H. Roper Barrett, Charles Dixon | Winifred McNair, Dora Boothby |

## All-England (Wimbledon) Tennis Championships—Doubles (continued)

| YEAR | MEN | WOMEN |
|------|-----|-------|
| 1914 | Norman Brookes, Anthony Wilding | Elizabeth Ryan, Agatha Morton |
| 1915–18 | *not held* | |
| 1919 | R.V. Thomas, Pat O'Hara Wood | Suzanne Lenglen, Elizabeth Ryan |
| 1920 | Richard Williams, Chuck Garland | Suzanne Lenglen, Elizabeth Ryan |
| 1921 | Randolph Lycett, Max Woosnam | Suzanne Lenglen, Elizabeth Ryan |
| 1922 | James Anderson, Randolph Lycett | Suzanne Lenglen, Elizabeth Ryan |
| 1923 | Leslie Godfree, Randolph Lycett | Suzanne Lenglen, Elizabeth Ryan |
| 1924 | Frank Hunter, Vincent Richards | Hazel Wightman, Helen Wills |
| 1925 | Jean Borotra, René Lacoste | Suzanne Lenglen, Elizabeth Ryan |
| 1926 | Jacques Brugnon, Henri Cochet | Mary Browne, Elizabeth Ryan |
| 1927 | Bill Tilden, Frank Hunter | Helen Wills, Elizabeth Ryan |
| 1928 | Jacques Brugnon, Henri Cochet | Peggy Saunders, Phoebe Watson |
| 1929 | Wilmer Allison, John Van Ryn | Peggy Saunders Michell, Phoebe Watson |
| 1930 | Wilmer Allison, John Van Ryn | Helen Wills Moody, Elizabeth Ryan |
| 1931 | George Lott, John Van Ryn | Phyllis Mudford, Dorothy Barron |
| 1932 | Jean Borotra, Jacques Brugnon | Doris Metaxa, Josane Sigart |
| 1933 | Jean Borotra, Jacques Brugnon | Elizabeth Ryan, Simone Mathieu |
| 1934 | George Lott, Lester Stoefen | Elizabeth Ryan, Simone Mathieu |
| 1935 | Jack Crawford, Adrian Quist | Freda James, Kay Stammers |
| 1936 | Pat Hughes, Raymond Tuckey | Freda James, Kay Stammers |
| 1937 | Don Budge, Gene Mako | Simone Mathieu, Billie Yorke |
| 1938 | Don Budge, Gene Mako | Sarah Palfrey Fabyan, Alice Marble |
| 1939 | Bobby Riggs, Elwood Cooke | Sarah Palfrey Fabyan, Alice Marble |
| 1940–45 | *not held* | |
| 1946 | Jack Kramer, Tom Brown | Louise Brough, Margaret Osborne |
| 1947 | Jack Kramer, Bob Falkenburg | Patricia Todd, Doris Hart |
| 1948 | John Bromwich, Frank Sedgman | Louise Brough, Margaret Osborne du Pont |
| 1949 | Pancho Gonzales, Frank Parker | Louise Brough, Margaret Osborne du Pont |
| 1950 | John Bromwich, Adrian Quist | Louise Brough, Margaret Osborne du Pont |
| 1951 | Ken McGregor, Frank Sedgman | Doris Hart, Shirley Fry |
| 1952 | Ken McGregor, Frank Sedgman | Doris Hart, Shirley Fry |
| 1953 | Ken Rosewall, Lew Hoad | Doris Hart, Shirley Fry |
| 1954 | Rex Hartwig, Mervyn Rose | Louise Brough, Margaret Osborne du Pont |
| 1955 | Rex Hartwig, Lew Hoad | Angela Mortimer, Anne Shilcock |
| 1956 | Ken Rosewall, Lew Hoad | Angela Buxton, Althea Gibson |
| 1957 | Budge Patty, Gardnar Mulloy | Althea Gibson, Darlene Hard |
| 1958 | Sven Davidson, Ulf Schmidt | Maria Bueno, Althea Gibson |
| 1959 | Roy Emerson, Neale Fraser | Jeanne Arth, Darlene Hard |
| 1960 | Rafael Osuna, Dennis Ralston | Maria Bueno, Darlene Hard |
| 1961 | Roy Emerson, Neale Fraser | Karen Hantze, Billie Jean Moffitt |
| 1962 | Bob Hewitt, Fred Stolle | Karen Hantze Susman, Billie Jean Moffitt |
| 1963 | Rafael Osuna, Antonio Palafox | Maria Bueno, Darlene Hard |
| 1964 | Bob Hewitt, Fred Stolle | Margaret Smith, Leslie Turner |
| 1965 | John Newcombe, Tony Roche | Maria Bueno, Billie Jean Moffitt |
| 1966 | John Newcombe, Ken Fletcher | Maria Bueno, Nancy Richey |
| 1967 | Bob Hewitt, Frew McMillan | Rosemary Casals, Billie Jean Moffitt King |
| 1968 | John Newcombe, Tony Roche | Rosemary Casals, Billie Jean King |
| 1969 | John Newcombe, Tony Roche | Margaret Smith Court, Judy Tegart |
| 1970 | John Newcombe, Tony Roche | Rosemary Casals, Billie Jean King |
| 1971 | Rod Laver, Roy Emerson | Rosemary Casals, Billie Jean King |
| 1972 | Bob Hewitt, Frew McMillan | Billie Jean King, Betty Stove |
| 1973 | Jimmy Connors, Ilie Nastase | Rosemary Casals, Billie Jean King |
| 1974 | John Newcombe, Tony Roche | Evonne Goolagong, Peggy Michel |
| 1975 | Vitas Gerulaitis, Sandy Mayer | Ann Kiyomura, Kazuko Sawamatsu |
| 1976 | Brian Gottfried, Raul Ramirez | Chris Evert, Martina Navratilova |
| 1977 | Ross Case, Geoff Masters | Helen Gourlay Cawley, Joanne Russell |
| 1978 | Bob Hewitt, Frew McMillan | Kerry Reid, Wendy Turnbull |
| 1979 | John McEnroe, Peter Fleming | Billie Jean King, Martina Navratilova |
| 1980 | Peter McNamara, Paul McNamee | Kathy Jordan, Anne Smith |
| 1981 | John McEnroe, Peter Fleming | Martina Navratilova, Pam Shriver |
| 1982 | Peter McNamara, Paul McNamee | Martina Navratilova, Pam Shriver |
| 1983 | John McEnroe, Peter Fleming | Martina Navratilova, Pam Shriver |
| 1984 | John McEnroe, Peter Fleming | Martina Navratilova, Pam Shriver |
| 1985 | Heinz Gunthardt, Balazs Taroczy | Kathy Jordan, Elizabeth Smylie |
| 1986 | Joakim Nystrom, Mats Wilander | Martina Navratilova, Pam Shriver |
| 1987 | Robert Seguso, Ken Flach | Claudia Kohde-Kilsche, Helena Sukova |
| 1988 | Robert Seguso, Ken Flach | Steffi Graf, Gabriela Sabatini |

## All-England (Wimbledon) Tennis Championships—Doubles (continued)

| YEAR | MEN | WOMEN |
|---|---|---|
| 1989 | John Fitzgerald, Anders Jarryd | Jana Novotna, Helena Sukova |
| 1990 | Rick Leach, Jim Pugh | Jana Novotna, Helena Sukova |
| 1991 | John Fitzgerald, Anders Jarryd | Larisa Savchenko, Natasha Zvereva |
| 1992 | John McEnroe, Michael Stich | Gigi Fernandez, Natasha Zvereva |
| 1993 | Todd Woodbridge, Mark Woodforde | Gigi Fernandez, Natasha Zvereva |
| 1994 | Todd Woodbridge, Mark Woodforde | Gigi Fernandez, Natasha Zvereva |
| 1995 | Todd Woodbridge, Mark Woodforde | Arantxa Sánchez Vicario, Jana Novotna |
| 1996 | Todd Woodbridge, Mark Woodforde | Helena Sukova, Martina Hingis |
| 1997 | Todd Woodbridge, Mark Woodforde | Gigi Fernandez, Natasha Zvereva |
| 1998 | Jacco Eltingh, Paul Haarhuis | Martina Hingis, Jana Novotna |
| 1999 | Mahesh Bhupathi, Leander Paes | Lindsay Davenport, Corina Morariu |
| 2000 | Todd Woodbridge, Mark Woodforde | Venus Williams, Serena Williams |
| 2001 | Donald Johnson, Jared Palmer | Lisa Raymond, Rennae Stubbs |
| 2002 | Todd Woodbridge, Jonas Bjorkman | Venus Williams, Serena Williams |
| 2003 | Todd Woodbridge, Jonas Bjorkman | Kim Clijsters, Ai Sugiyama |

**Did you know?** In 1988 tennis was restored to medal-sport status in the Olympic Games, the first time since 1924.

## United States Open Tennis Championships—Singles

| YEAR | MEN | WOMEN |
|---|---|---|
| 1881 | Richard Sears (USA) | |
| 1882 | Richard Sears (USA) | |
| 1883 | Richard Sears (USA) | |
| 1884 | Richard Sears (USA) | |
| 1885 | Richard Sears (USA) | |
| 1886 | Richard Sears (USA) | |
| 1887 | Richard Sears (USA) | Ellen Hansell (USA) |
| 1888 | Henry Slocum, Jr. (USA) | Bertha Townsend (USA) |
| 1889 | Henry Slocum, Jr. (USA) | Bertha Townsend (USA) |
| 1890 | Oliver Campbell (USA) | Ellen Roosevelt (USA) |
| 1891 | Oliver Campbell (USA) | Mabel Cahill (USA) |
| 1892 | Oliver Campbell (USA) | Mabel Cahill (USA) |
| 1893 | Robert Wrenn (USA) | Aline Terry (USA) |
| 1894 | Robert Wrenn (USA) | Helen Helwig (USA) |
| 1895 | Fred Hovey (USA) | Juliette Atkinson (USA) |
| 1896 | Robert Wrenn (USA) | Elisabeth Moore (USA) |
| 1897 | Robert Wrenn (USA) | Juliette Atkinson (USA) |
| 1898 | Malcom Whitman (USA) | Juliette Atkinson (USA) |
| 1899 | Malcom Whitman (USA) | Marion Jones (USA) |
| 1900 | Malcom Whitman (USA) | Myrtle McAteer (USA) |
| 1901 | William Larned (USA) | Elisabeth Moore (USA) |
| 1902 | William Larned (USA) | Marion Jones (USA) |
| 1903 | Laurie Doherty (GBR) | Elisabeth Moore (USA) |
| 1904 | Holcombe Ward (USA) | May Sutton (USA) |
| 1905 | Beals Wright (USA) | Elisabeth Moore (USA) |
| 1906 | Bill Clothier (USA) | Helen Homans (USA) |
| 1907 | William Larned (USA) | Evelyn Sears (USA) |
| 1908 | William Larned (USA) | Maud Barger-Wallach (USA) |
| 1909 | William Larned (USA) | Hazel Hotchkiss (USA) |
| 1910 | William Larned (USA) | Hazel Hotchkiss (USA) |
| 1911 | William Larned (USA) | Hazel Hotchkiss (USA) |
| 1912 | Maurice McLoughlin (USA) | Mary Browne (USA) |
| 1913 | Maurice McLoughlin (USA) | Mary Browne (USA) |
| 1914 | R. Norris Williams (USA) | Mary Browne (USA) |
| 1915 | Bill Johnston (USA) | Molla Bjurstedt (NOR) |
| 1916 | R. Norris Williams (USA) | Molla Bjurstedt (NOR) |
| 1917 | Lindley Murray (USA) | Molla Bjurstedt (NOR) |
| 1918 | Lindley Murray (USA) | Molla Bjurstedt (NOR) |

# United States Open Tennis Championships—Singles (continued)

| YEAR | MEN | WOMEN |
|------|-----|-------|
| 1919 | Bill Johnston (USA) | Hazel Hotchkiss Wightman (USA) |
| 1920 | Bill Tilden (USA) | Molla Bjurstedt Mallory (USA) |
| 1921 | Bill Tilden (USA) | Molla Bjurstedt Mallory (USA) |
| 1922 | Bill Tilden (USA) | Molla Bjurstedt Mallory (USA) |
| 1923 | Bill Tilden (USA) | Helen Wills (USA) |
| 1924 | Bill Tilden (USA) | Helen Wills (USA) |
| 1925 | Bill Tilden (USA) | Helen Wills (USA) |
| 1926 | René Lacoste (FRA) | Molla Bjurstedt Mallory (USA) |
| 1927 | René Lacoste (FRA) | Helen Wills (USA) |
| 1928 | Henri Cochet (FRA) | Helen Wills (USA) |
| 1929 | Bill Tilden (USA) | Helen Wills (USA) |
| 1930 | John Doeg (USA) | Betty Nuthall (GBR) |
| 1931 | Ellsworth Vines (USA) | Helen Wills Moody (USA) |
| 1932 | Ellsworth Vines (USA) | Helen Jacobs (USA) |
| 1933 | Fred Perry (GBR) | Helen Jacobs (USA) |
| 1934 | Fred Perry (GBR) | Helen Jacobs (USA) |
| 1935 | Wilmer Allison (USA) | Helen Jacobs (USA) |
| 1936 | Fred Perry (GBR) | Alice Marble (USA) |
| 1937 | Don Budge (USA) | Anita Lizana (CHI) |
| 1938 | Don Budge (USA) | Alice Marble (USA) |
| 1939 | Bobby Riggs (USA) | Alice Marble (USA) |
| 1940 | Don McNeill (USA) | Alice Marble (USA) |
| 1941 | Bobby Riggs (USA) | Sarah Palfrey Cooke (USA) |
| 1942 | Ted Schroeder (USA) | Pauline Betz (USA) |
| 1943 | Joe Hunt (USA) | Pauline Betz (USA) |
| 1944 | Frank Parker (USA) | Pauline Betz (USA) |
| 1945 | Frank Parker (USA) | Sarah Palfrey Cooke (USA) |
| 1946 | Jack Kramer (USA) | Pauline Betz (USA) |
| 1947 | Jack Kramer (USA) | Louise Brough (USA) |
| 1948 | Pancho Gonzales (USA) | Margaret du Pont (USA) |
| 1949 | Pancho Gonzales (USA) | Margaret du Pont (USA) |
| 1950 | Arthur Larsen (USA) | Margaret du Pont (USA) |
| 1951 | Frank Sedgman (AUS) | Maureen Connolly (USA) |
| 1952 | Frank Sedgman (AUS) | Maureen Connolly (USA) |
| 1953 | Tony Trabert (USA) | Maureen Connolly (USA) |
| 1954 | Vic Seixas (USA) | Doris Hart (USA) |
| 1955 | Tony Trabert (USA) | Doris Hart (USA) |
| 1956 | Ken Rosewall (AUS) | Shirley Fry (USA) |
| 1957 | Mal Anderson (AUS) | Althea Gibson (USA) |
| 1958 | Ashley Cooper (AUS) | Althea Gibson (USA) |
| 1959 | Neale Fraser (AUS) | Maria Bueno (BRA) |
| 1960 | Neale Fraser (AUS) | Darlene Hard (USA) |
| 1961 | Roy Emerson (AUS) | Darlene Hard (USA) |
| 1962 | Rod Laver (AUS) | Margaret Smith (AUS) |
| 1963 | Rafael Osuna (MEX) | Maria Bueno (BRA) |
| 1964 | Roy Emerson (AUS) | Maria Bueno (BRA) |
| 1965 | Manuel Santana (SPA) | Margaret Smith (AUS) |
| 1966 | Fred Stolle (AUS) | Maria Bueno (BRA) |
| 1967 | John Newcombe (AUS) | Billie Jean King (USA) |
| 1968* | Arthur Ashe (USA) | Virginia Wade (GBR); Margaret Smith Court (AUS) |
| 1969* | Rod Laver (AUS); Stan Smith (USA) | Margaret Smith Court (AUS) |
| 1970 | Ken Rosewall (AUS) | Margaret Smith Court (AUS) |
| 1971 | Stan Smith (USA) | Billie Jean King (USA) |
| 1972 | Ilie Nastase (ROM) | Billie Jean King (USA) |
| 1973 | John Newcombe (AUS) | Margaret Smith Court (AUS) |
| 1974 | Jimmy Connors (USA) | Billie Jean King (USA) |
| 1975 | Manuel Orantes (SPA) | Chris Evert (USA) |
| 1976 | Jimmy Connors (USA) | Chris Evert (USA) |
| 1977 | Guillermo Vilas (ARG) | Chris Evert (USA) |
| 1978 | Jimmy Connors (USA) | Chris Evert (USA) |
| 1979 | John McEnroe (USA) | Tracy Austin (USA) |
| 1980 | John McEnroe (USA) | Chris Evert Lloyd (USA) |
| 1981 | John McEnroe (USA) | Tracy Austin (USA) |
| 1982 | Jimmy Connors (USA) | Chris Evert Lloyd (USA) |
| 1983 | Jimmy Connors (USA) | Martina Navratilova (USA) |
| 1984 | John McEnroe (USA) | Martina Navratilova (USA) |

## United States Open Tennis Championships—Singles (continued)

| YEAR | MEN | WOMEN |
|---|---|---|
| 1985 | Ivan Lendl (TCH) | Hana Mandlikova (TCH) |
| 1986 | Ivan Lendl (TCH) | Martina Navratilova (USA) |
| 1987 | Ivan Lendl (TCH) | Martina Navratilova (USA) |
| 1988 | Mats Wilander (SWE) | Steffi Graf (FRG) |
| 1989 | Boris Becker (FRG) | Steffi Graf (FRG) |
| 1990 | Pete Sampras (USA) | Gabriela Sabatini (ARG) |
| 1991 | Stefan Edberg (SWE) | Monica Seles (YUG) |
| 1992 | Stefan Edberg (SWE) | Monica Seles (YUG) |
| 1993 | Pete Sampras (USA) | Steffi Graf (GER) |
| 1994 | Andre Agassi (USA) | Arantxa Sánchez Vicario (SPA) |
| 1995 | Pete Sampras (USA) | Steffi Graf (GER) |
| 1996 | Pete Sampras (USA) | Steffi Graf (GER) |
| 1997 | Patrick Rafter (AUS) | Martina Hingis (SUI) |
| 1998 | Patrick Rafter (AUS) | Lindsay Davenport (USA) |
| 1999 | Andre Agassi (USA) | Serena Williams (USA) |
| 2000 | Marat Safin (RUS) | Venus Williams (USA) |
| 2001 | Lleyton Hewitt (AUS) | Venus Williams (USA) |
| 2002 | Pete Sampras (USA) | Serena Williams (USA) |
| 2003 | *to be held in August and September* | |

*In 1968 and 1969 both amateur and open championships were held. Ashe won both men's competitions in 1968; Smith won the amateur championship in 1969. Court won the women's amateur competition in 1968 and both championships in 1969. Thereafter the championships were open.*

## United States Open Tennis Championships—Doubles

| YEAR | MEN | WOMEN |
|---|---|---|
| 1881 | Clarence Clark, Fred Taylor | |
| 1882 | Richard Sears, James Dwight | |
| 1883 | Richard Sears, James Dwight | |
| 1884 | Richard Sears, James Dwight | |
| 1885 | Richard Sears, Joseph Clark | |
| 1886 | Richard Sears, James Dwight | |
| 1887 | Richard Sears, James Dwight | |
| 1888 | Oliver Campbell, Valentine Hall | |
| 1889 | Henry Slocum, Howard Taylor | Bertha Townsend, Margarette Ballard |
| 1890 | Valentine Hall, Clarence Hobart | Ellen Roosevelt, Grace Roosevelt |
| 1891 | Oliver Campbell, Robert Huntington | Mabel Cahill, Mrs. W. Fellowes Morgan |
| 1892 | Oliver Campbell, Robert Huntington | Mabel Cahill, Adeline McKinley |
| 1893 | Clarence Hobart, Fred Hovey | Aline Terry, Hattie Butler |
| 1894 | Clarence Hobart, Fred Hovey | Helen Helwig, Juliette Atkinson |
| 1895 | Malcom Chace, Robert Wrenn | Helen Helwig, Juliette Atkinson |
| 1896 | Carr Neel, Samuel Neel | Elisabeth Moore, Juliette Atkinson |
| 1897 | Leo Ware, George Sheldon | Juliette Atkinson, Kathleen Atkinson |
| 1898 | Leo Ware, George Sheldon | Juliette Atkinson, Kathleen Atkinson |
| 1899 | Holcombe Ward, Dwight Davis | Jane Craven, Myrtle McAteer |
| 1900 | Holcombe Ward, Dwight Davis | Edith Parker, Hallie Champlin |
| 1901 | Holcombe Ward, Dwight Davis | Juliette Atkinson, Myrtle McAteer |
| 1902 | Reginald Doherty, Hugh Doherty | Juliette Atkinson, Marion Jones |
| 1903 | Reginald Doherty, Hugh Doherty | Elisabeth Moore, Carrie Neely |
| 1904 | Holcombe Ward, Beals Wright | Mary Sutton, Miriam Hall |
| 1905 | Holcombe Ward, Beals Wright | Helen Homans, Carrie Neely |
| 1906 | Holcombe Ward, Beals Wright | Mrs. L.S. Coe, Mrs. D.S. Platt |
| 1907 | Fred Alexander, Harold Hackett | Marie Weimer, Carrie Neely |
| 1908 | Fred Alexander, Harold Hackett | Evelyn Sears, Margaret Curtis |
| 1909 | Fred Alexander, Harold Hackett | Hazel Hotchkiss, Edith Rotch |
| 1910 | Fred Alexander, Harold Hackett | Hazel Hotchkiss, Edith Rotch |
| 1911 | Raymond Little, Gustave Touchard | Hazel Hotchkiss, Eleanora Sears |
| 1912 | Maurice McLoughlin, Thomas Bundy | Dorothy Green, Mary Browne |
| 1913 | Maurice McLoughlin, Thomas Bundy | Mary Browne, Mrs. R.H. Williams |
| 1914 | Maurice McLoughlin, Thomas Bundy | Mary Browne, Mrs. R.H. Williams |
| 1915 | William Johnston, Clarence Griffin | Hazel Hotchkiss Wightman, Eleanora Sears |
| 1916 | William Johnston, Clarence Griffin | Molla Bjurstedt, Eleanora Sears |
| 1917 | Fred Alexander, Harold Throckmorton | Molla Bjurstedt, Eleanora Sears |
| 1918 | Bill Tilden, Vincent Richards | Marion Zinderstein, Eleanor Goss |
| 1919 | Norman Brookes, Gerald Patterson | Marion Zinderstein, Eleanor Goss |

# United States Open Tennis Championships—Doubles (continued)

| YEAR | MEN | WOMEN |
|------|-----|-------|
| 1920 | William Johnston, Clarence Griffin | Marion Zinderstein, Eleanor Goss |
| 1921 | Bill Tilden, Vincent Richards | Mary Browne, Mrs. R.H. Williams |
| 1922 | Bill Tilden, Vincent Richards | Marion Zinderstein Jessup, Helen Wills |
| 1923 | Bill Tilden, Brian Norton | Kathleen McKane, Phyllis Covell |
| 1924 | Howard Kinsey, Robert Kinsey | Hazel Hotchkiss Wightman, Helen Wills |
| 1925 | Richard Williams, Vincent Richards | Mary Browne, Helen Wills |
| 1926 | Richard Williams, Vincent Richards | Elizabeth Ryan, Eleanor Goss |
| 1927 | Bill Tilden, Frank Hunter | Kathleen McKane Godfree, Ermyntrude Harvey |
| 1928 | George Lott, John Hennessey | Hazel Hotchkiss Wightman, Helen Wills |
| 1929 | George Lott, John Doeg | Phoebe Watson, Peggy Michell |
| 1930 | George Lott, John Doeg | Betty Nuthall, Sarah Palfrey |
| 1931 | Wilmer Allison, John Van Ryn | Betty Nuthall, Eileen Whittingstall |
| 1932 | Elsworth Vines, Keith Gledhill | Helen Jacobs, Sarah Palfrey |
| 1933 | George Lott, Lester Stoefen | Betty Nuthall, Freda James |
| 1934 | George Lott, Lester Stoefen | Helen Jacobs, Sarah Palfrey |
| 1935 | Wilmer Allison, John Van Ryn | Helen Jacobs, Sarah Palfrey Fabyan |
| 1936 | Don Budge, Gene Mako | Marjorie Van Ryn, Carolin Babcock |
| 1937 | Gottfried von Cramm, Henner Henkel | Sarah Palfrey Fabyan, Alice Marble |
| 1938 | Don Budge, Gene Mako | Sarah Palfrey Fabyan, Alice Marble |
| 1939 | Adrian Quist, John Bromwich | Sarah Palfrey Fabyan, Alice Marble |
| 1940 | Jack Kramer, Ted Schroeder | Sarah Palfrey Fabyan, Alice Marble |
| 1941 | Jack Kramer, Ted Schroeder | Sarah Palfrey Fabyan, Margaret Osborne |
| 1942 | Gardnar Mulloy, Billy Talbert | Louise Brough, Margaret Osborne |
| 1943 | Jack Kramer, Frank Parker | Louise Brough, Margaret Osborne |
| 1944 | Don McNeill, Bob Falkenburg | Louise Brough, Margaret Osborne |
| 1945 | Gardnar Mulloy, Billy Talbert | Louise Brough, Margaret Osborne |
| 1946 | Gardnar Mulloy, Billy Talbert | Louise Brough, Margaret Osborne |
| 1947 | Jack Kramer, Ted Schroeder | Louise Brough, Margaret Osborne |
| 1948 | Gardnar Mulloy, Billy Talbert | Louise Brough, Margaret Osborne du Pont |
| 1949 | John Bromwich, Billy Sidwell | Louise Brough, Margaret Osborne du Pont |
| 1950 | John Bromwich, Frank Sedgman | Louise Brough, Margaret Osborne du Pont |
| 1951 | Ken McGregor, Frank Sedgman | Shirley Fry, Doris Hart |
| 1952 | Mervyn Rose, Vic Seixas | Shirley Fry, Doris Hart |
| 1953 | Mervyn Rose, Rex Hartwig | Shirley Fry, Doris Hart |
| 1954 | Vic Seixas, Tony Trabert | Shirley Fry, Doris Hart |
| 1955 | Kosei Kamo, Atushi Miyagi | Louise Brough, Margaret Osborne du Pont |
| 1956 | Lew Hoad, Ken Rosewall | Louise Brough, Margaret Osborne du Pont |
| 1957 | Ashley Cooper, Neale Fraser | Louise Brough, Margaret Osborne du Pont |
| 1958 | Alex Olmedo, Hamilton Richardson | Jeanne Arth, Darlene Hard |
| 1959 | Neale Fraser, Roy Emerson | Jeanne Arth, Darlene Hard |
| 1960 | Neale Fraser, Roy Emerson | Darlene Hard, Maria Bueno |
| 1961 | Charles McKinley, Dennis Ralston | Darlene Hard, Lesley Turner |
| 1962 | Rafael Osuna, Antonio Palafox | Darlene Hard, Maria Bueno |
| 1963 | Charles McKinley, Dennis Ralston | Robyn Ebbern, Margaret Smith |
| 1964 | Charles McKinley, Dennis Ralston | Billie Jean Moffitt, Karen Susman |
| 1965 | Roy Emerson, Fred Stolle | Carole Caldwell Graebner, Nancy Richey |
| 1966 | Roy Emerson, Fred Stolle | Maria Bueno, Nancy Richey |
| 1967 | John Newcombe, Tony Roche | Billie Jean Moffitt King, Rosemary Casals |
| 1968* | Robert Lutz, Stan Smith | Maria Bueno, Margaret Smith Court |
| 1969* | Ken Rosewall, Fred Stolle; Dick Crealy, Allan Stone | Françoise Durr, Darlene Hard; Margaret Smith Court, Virginia Wade |
| 1970 | Pierre Barthes, Nikki Pilic | Margaret Smith Court, Judy Dalton |
| 1971 | John Newcombe, Roger Taylor | Rosemary Casals, Judy Dalton |
| 1972 | Cliff Drysdale, Roger Taylor | Françoise Durr, Betty Stove |
| 1973 | Owen Davidson, John Newcombe | Margaret Smith Court, Virginia Wade |
| 1974 | Robert Lutz, Stan Smith | Billie Jean King, Rosemary Casals |
| 1975 | Jimmy Connors, Ilie Nastase | Margaret Smith Court, Virginia Wade |
| 1976 | Tom Okker, Marty Riessen | Delina Boshoff, Ilana Kloss |
| 1977 | Bob Hewitt, Frew McMillan | Martina Navratilova, Betty Stove |
| 1978 | Robert Lutz, Stan Smith | Martina Navratilova, Billie Jean King |
| 1979 | John McEnroe, Peter Fleming | Wendy Turnbull, Betty Stove |
| 1980 | Robert Lutz, Stan Smith | Martina Navratilova, Billie Jean King |
| 1981 | John McEnroe, Peter Fleming | Kathy Jordan, Anne Smith |
| 1982 | Kevin Curren, Steve Denton | Rosemary Casals, Wendy Turnbull |
| 1983 | John McEnroe, Peter Fleming | Martina Navratilova, Pam Shriver |
| 1984 | John Fitzgerald, Tomas Smid | Martina Navratilova, Pam Shriver |
| 1985 | Ken Flach, Robert Seguso | Claudia Kohde-Kilsch, Helena Sukova |
| 1986 | Andres Gómez, Slobodan Zivojinovic | Martina Navratilova, Pam Shriver |

## United States Open Tennis Championships—Doubles (continued)

| YEAR | MEN | WOMEN |
|------|-----|-------|
| 1987 | Stefan Edberg, Anders Jarryd | Martina Navratilova, Pam Shriver |
| 1988 | Sergio Casal, Emilio Sánchez | Gigi Fernandez, Robin White |
| 1989 | John McEnroe, Mark Woodforde | Martina Navratilova, Hana Mandlikova |
| 1990 | Pieter Aldrich, Danie Visser | Martina Navratilova, Gigi Fernandez |
| 1991 | John Fitzgerald, Anders Jarryd | Pam Shriver, Natasha Zvereva |
| 1992 | Jim Grabb, Richey Reneberg | Gigi Fernandez, Natasha Zvereva |
| 1993 | Ken Flach, Rick Leach | Arantxa Sánchez Vicario, Helena Sukova |
| 1994 | Paul Haarhuis, Jacco Eltingh | Arantxa Sánchez Vicario, Jana Novotna |
| 1995 | Todd Woodbridge, Mark Woodforde | Gigi Fernandez, Natasha Zvereva |
| 1996 | Todd Woodbridge, Mark Woodforde | Gigi Fernandez, Natasha Zvereva |
| 1997 | Yevgeny Kafelnikov, Daniel Vacek | Lindsay Davenport, Jana Novotna |
| 1998 | Sandon Stolle, Cyril Suk | Martina Hingis, Jana Novotna |
| 1999 | Sebastian Lareau, Alex O'Brien | Venus Williams, Serena Williams |
| 2000 | Lleyton Hewitt, Max Mirnyi | Julie Halard-Decugis, Ai Sugiyama |
| 2001 | Wayne Black, Kevin Ullyet | Lisa Raymond, Rennae Stubbs |
| 2002 | Mahesh Bhupathi, Max Mirnyi | Virginia Ruano Pascual, Paola Suarez |
| 2003 | *to be held in August and September* | |

*In 1968 and 1969 both amateur and open championships were held. Lutz and Smith won both men's competitions in 1968; Crealy and Stone took the men's amateur championships in 1969. Bueno and Court won both women's competitions in 1968; Court and Wade took the women's amateur championships in 1969. Thereafter the championships were open.*

## Davis Cup

| YEAR | WINNER | RUNNER-UP | RESULTS | YEAR | WINNER | RUNNER-UP | RESULTS |
|------|--------|-----------|---------|------|--------|-----------|---------|
| 1900 | United States | British Isles | 3-0 | 1949 | United States | Australia | 4-1 |
| 1901 | *not held* | | | 1950 | Australia | United States | 4-1 |
| 1902 | United States | British Isles | 3-2 | 1951 | Australia | United States | 3-2 |
| 1903 | British Isles* | United States | 4-1 | 1952 | Australia | United States | 4-1 |
| 1904 | British Isles | Belgium | 5-0 | 1953 | Australia | United States | 3-2 |
| 1905 | British Isles | United States | 5-0 | 1954 | United States | Australia | 3-2 |
| 1906 | British Isles | United States | 5-0 | 1955 | Australia | United States | 5-0 |
| 1907 | Australasia† | British Isles | 3-2 | 1956 | Australia | United States | 5-0 |
| 1908 | Australasia | United States | 3-2 | 1957 | Australia | United States | 3-2 |
| 1909 | Australasia | United States | 5-0 | 1958 | United States | Australia | 3-2 |
| 1910 | *not held* | | | 1959 | Australia | United States | 3-2 |
| 1911 | Australasia | United States | 5-0 | 1960 | Australia | Italy | 4-1 |
| 1912 | British Isles | Australia | 3-2 | 1961 | Australia | Italy | 5-0 |
| 1913 | United States | British Isles | 3-2 | 1962 | Australia | Mexico | 5-0 |
| 1914 | Australasia | United States | 3-2 | 1963 | United States | Australia | 3-2 |
| 1915-18 | *not held* | | | 1964 | Australia | United States | 3-2 |
| 1919 | Australasia | British Isles | 4-1 | 1965 | Australia | Spain | 4-1 |
| 1920 | United States | Australasia | 5-0 | 1966 | Australia | India | 4-1 |
| 1921 | United States | Japan | 5-0 | 1967 | Australia | Spain | 4-1 |
| 1922 | United States | Australasia | 4-1 | 1968 | United States | Australia | 4-1 |
| 1923 | United States | Australasia | 4-1 | 1969 | United States | Romania | 5-0 |
| 1924 | United States | Australasia | 5-0 | 1970 | United States | West Germany | 5-0 |
| 1925 | United States | France | 5-0 | 1971 | United States | Romania | 3-2 |
| 1926 | United States | France | 4-1 | 1972 | United States | Romania | 3-2 |
| 1927 | France | United States | 3-2 | 1973 | Australia | United States | 5-0 |
| 1928 | France | United States | 4-1 | 1974 | South Africa‡ | India | |
| 1929 | France | United States | 3-2 | 1975 | Sweden | Czechoslovakia | 3-2 |
| 1930 | France | United States | 4-1 | 1976 | Italy | Chile | 4-1 |
| 1931 | France | United Kingdom | 3-2 | 1977 | Australia | Italy | 3-1 |
| 1932 | France | United States | 3-2 | 1978 | United States | United Kingdom | 4-1 |
| 1933 | United Kingdom | France | 3-2 | 1979 | United States | Italy | 5-0 |
| 1934 | United Kingdom | United States | 4-1 | 1980 | Czechoslovakia | Italy | 4-1 |
| 1935 | United Kingdom | United States | 5-0 | 1981 | United States | Argentina | 3-1 |
| 1936 | United Kingdom | Australia | 3-2 | 1982 | United States | France | 4-1 |
| 1937 | United States | United Kingdom | 4-1 | 1983 | Australia | Sweden | 3-2 |
| 1938 | United States | Australia | 3-2 | 1984 | Sweden | United States | 4-1 |
| 1939 | Australia | United States | 3-2 | 1985 | Sweden | West Germany | 3-2 |
| 1940-45 | *not held* | | | 1986 | Australia | Sweden | 3-2 |
| 1946 | United States | Australia | 5-0 | 1987 | Sweden | India | 5-0 |
| 1947 | United States | Australia | 4-1 | 1988 | West Germany | Sweden | 4-1 |
| 1948 | United States | Australia | 5-0 | 1989 | West Germany | Sweden | 3-2 |

## Davis Cup (continued)

| YEAR | WINNER | RUNNER-UP | RESULTS | YEAR | WINNER | RUNNER-UP | RESULTS |
|------|--------|-----------|---------|------|--------|-----------|---------|
| 1990 | United States | Australia | 3–2 | 1997 | Sweden | United States | 5–0 |
| 1991 | France | United States | 3–1 | 1998 | Sweden | Italy | 4–1 |
| 1992 | United States | Switzerland | 3–1 | 1999 | Australia | France | 3–2 |
| 1993 | Germany | Australia | 4–1 | 2000 | Spain | Australia | 3–1 |
| 1994 | Sweden | Russia | 4–1 | 2001 | France | Australia | 3–2 |
| 1995 | United States | Russia | 3–2 | 2002 | Russia | France | 3–2 |
| 1996 | France | Sweden | 3–2 | 2003 | *to be played in November* | | |

*Included Ireland up to 1922.     †Included New Zealand up to 1923.     ‡Forfeit; India withdrew from final.*

## Federation Cup

| YEAR | WINNER | RUNNER-UP | RESULTS | YEAR | WINNER | RUNNER-UP | RESULTS |
|------|--------|-----------|---------|------|--------|-----------|---------|
| 1963 | United States | Australia | 2–1 | 1984 | Czechoslovakia | Australia | 2–1 |
| 1964 | Australia | United States | 2–1 | 1985 | Czechoslovakia | United States | 2–1 |
| 1965 | Australia | United States | 2–1 | 1986 | United States | Czechoslovakia | 3–0 |
| 1966 | United States | West Germany | 3–0 | 1987 | West Germany | United States | 2–1 |
| 1967 | United States | United Kingdom | 2–0 | 1988 | Czechoslovakia | USSR | 2–1 |
| 1968 | Australia | The Netherlands | 3–0 | 1989 | United States | Spain | 3–0 |
| 1969 | United States | Australia | 2–1 | 1990 | United States | USSR | 2–1 |
| 1970 | Australia | West Germany | 3–0 | 1991 | Spain | United States | 2–1 |
| 1971 | Australia | United Kingdom | 3–0 | 1992 | Germany | Spain | 2–1 |
| 1972 | South Africa | United Kingdom | 2–1 | 1993 | Spain | Australia | 3–0 |
| 1973 | Australia | South Africa | 3–0 | 1994 | Spain | United States | 3–0 |
| 1974 | Australia | United States | 2–1 | 1995 | Spain | United States | 3–2 |
| 1975 | Czechoslovakia | Australia | 3–0 | 1996 | United States | Spain | 5–0 |
| 1976 | United States | Australia | 2–1 | 1997 | France | The Netherlands | 4–1 |
| 1977 | United States | Australia | 2–1 | 1998 | Spain | Switzerland | 3–2 |
| 1978 | United States | Australia | 2–1 | 1999 | United States | Russia | 4–1 |
| 1979 | United States | Australia | 3–0 | 2000 | United States | Spain | 5–0 |
| 1980 | United States | Australia | 3–0 | 2001 | Belgium | Russia | 2–1 |
| 1981 | United States | United Kingdom | 3–0 | 2002 | Slovakia | Spain | 3–1 |
| 1982 | United States | West Germany | 3–0 | 2003 | *to be played in November* | | |
| 1983 | Czechoslovakia | West Germany | 2–1 | | | | |

# Track & Field

The world governing body for track and field, or athletics, is the **International Association of Athletics Federations** (IAAF), founded in 1912. The sport includes relay running, a number of individual running, jumping, and throwing events, and one event (the decathlon for men and the heptathlon for women) that includes all three activities. The best-known occasion for most track-and-field athletics is the **Olympic Games** held every four years. The **World Cup** (inaugurated 1977) is a finals-only competition for national, hemispheric, and continental teams. In 1983, however, the first officially recognized non-Olympic world athletics championships were held.

A long-distance event that has special status is the **marathon race.** The standard distance for marathons is 42,195 m (26 mi 385 yd), but they are run over routes of varying severity and under a wide array of weather conditions. One of the most renowned marathon races is held in **Boston.** Except for 1918, it has been held every year since 1897; women's competition officially began in 1972. The **New York City Marathon** began in 1970.

Related Web sites: IAAF: <www.iaaf.org>; Boston Marathon: <www.bostonmarathon.org>; New York City Marathon <www.nyrrc.org>

## Outdoor Track & Field World Records

### men

| EVENT | RECORD HOLDER (NATIONALITY) | PERFORMANCE | DATE |
|-------|------------------------------|-------------|------|
| 100 m | Tim Montgomery (USA) | 9.78 sec | 14 Sep 2002 |
| 200 m | Michael Johnson (USA) | 19.32 sec | 1 Aug 1996 |
| 400 m | Michael Johnson (USA) | 43.18 sec | 26 Aug 1999 |
| 800 m | Wilson Kipketer (DEN) | 1 min 41.11 sec | 24 Aug 1997 |
| 1,000 m | Noah Ngeny (KEN) | 2 min 11.96 sec | 5 Sep 1999 |
| 1,500 m | Hicham El Guerrouj (MAR) | 3 min 26.00 sec | 14 Jul 1998 |
| 1 mile | Hicham El Guerrouj (MAR) | 3 min 43.13 sec | 7 Jul 1999 |
| steeplechase | Brahim Boulami (MAR) | 7 min 53.17 sec | 16 Aug 2002 |
| 3,000 m | Daniel Komen (KEN) | 7 min 20.67 sec | 1 Sep 1996 |
| 5,000 m | Haile Gebrselassie (ETH) | 12 min 39.36 sec | 13 Jun 1998 |

# Outdoor Track & Field World Records (continued)

## men (continued)

| EVENT | RECORD HOLDER (NATIONALITY) | PERFORMANCE | DATE |
|---|---|---|---|
| 10,000 m | Haile Gebrselassie (ETH) | 26 min 22.75 sec | 1 Jun 1998 |
| marathon* | Khalid Khannouchi (USA) | 2 h 5 min 38 sec | 14 Apr 2002 |
| 110-m hurdles | Colin Jackson (GBR) | 12.91 sec | 20 Aug 1993 |
| 400-m hurdles | Kevin Young (USA) | 46.78 sec | 6 Aug 1992 |
| 20-km walk | Bernardo Segura (MEX) | 1 h 17 min 25.6 sec | 7 May 1994 |
| 50-km walk | Thierry Toutain (FRA) | 3 h 40 min 57.9 sec | 29 Sep 1996 |
| 4 × 100-m relay | United States | 37.40 sec | 8 Aug 1992 |
| 4 × 400-m relay | United States | 2 min 54.20 sec | 22 Jul 1998 |
| high jump | Javier Sotomayor (CUB) | 2.45 m (8 ft ½ in) | 27 Jul 1993 |
| long jump | Mike Powell (USA) | 8.95 m (29 ft 4½ in) | 30 Aug 1991 |
| triple jump | Jonathan Edwards (GBR) | 18.29 m (60 ft ¼ in) | 7 Aug 1995 |
| pole vault | Sergey Bubka (UKR) | 6.14 m (20 ft 1¾ in) | 31 Jul 1994 |
| shot put | Randy Barnes (USA) | 23.12 m (75 ft 10¼ in) | 20 May 1990 |
| discus throw | Jürgen Schult (GDR) | 74.08 m (243 ft) | 6 Jun 1986 |
| hammer throw | Yury Sedykh (URS) | 86.74 m (284 ft 7 in) | 30 Aug 1986 |
| javelin throw | Jan Zelezny (CZE) | 98.48 m (323 ft 1 in) | 25 May 1996 |
| decathlon | Roman Sebrle (CZE) | 9,026 pt | 27 May 2001 |

## women

| EVENT | RECORD HOLDER (NATIONALITY) | PERFORMANCE | DATE |
|---|---|---|---|
| 100 m | Florence Griffith-Joyner (USA) | 10.49 sec | 16 Jul 1988 |
| 200 m | Florence Griffith-Joyner (USA) | 21.34 sec | 29 Sep 1988 |
| 400 m | Marita Koch (GDR) | 47.60 sec | 6 Oct 1985 |
| 800 m | Jarmila Kratochvilova (TCH) | 1 min 53.28 sec | 26 Jul 1983 |
| 1,000 m | Svetlana Masterkova (RUS) | 2 min 28.98 sec | 23 Aug 1996 |
| 1,500 m | Qu Yunxia (CHN) | 3 min 50.46 sec | 11 Sep 1993 |
| 1 mile | Svetlana Masterkova (RUS) | 4 min 12.56 sec | 14 Aug 1996 |
| steeplechase | Alesya Turova (BLR) | 9 min 16.51 sec | 27 Jul 2002 |
| 3,000 m | Wang Junxia (CHN) | 8 min 6.11 sec | 13 Sep 1993 |
| 5,000 m | Jiang Bo (CHN) | 14 min 28.09 sec | 23 Oct 1997 |
| 10,000 m | Wang Junxia (CHN) | 29 min 31.78 sec | 8 Sep 1993 |
| marathon* | Paula Radcliffe (GBR) | 2 h 15 min 25 sec | 13 Apr 2003 |
| 100-m hurdles | Yordanka Donkova (BUL) | 12.21 sec | 20 Aug 1988 |
| 400-m hurdles | Kim Batten (USA) | 52.61 sec | 11 Aug 1995 |
| 20-km walk | Olimpiada Ivanova (RUS) | 1 h 26 min 52.3 sec | 6 Sep 2001 |
| 4 × 100-m relay | East Germany | 41.37 sec | 6 Oct 1985 |
| 4 × 400-m relay | USSR | 3 min 15.17 sec | 1 Oct 1988 |
| high jump | Stefka Kostadinova (BUL) | 2.09 m (6 ft 10¼ in) | 30 Aug 1987 |
| long jump | Galina Chistyakova (URS) | 7.52 m (24 ft 8¼ in) | 11 Jun 1988 |
| triple jump | Inessa Kravets (UKR) | 15.50 m (50 ft 10¼ in) | 10 Aug 1995 |
| pole vault | Stacy Dragila (USA) | 4.81 m (15 ft 9¼ in) | 9 Jun 2001 |
| shot put | Natalya Lisovskaya (URS) | 22.63 m (74 ft 3 in) | 7 Jun 1987 |
| discus throw | Gabriele Reinsch (GDR) | 76.80 m (252 ft) | 9 Jul 1988 |
| hammer throw | Mihaela Melinte (ROM) | 76.07 m (249 ft 7 in) | 29 Aug 1999 |
| javelin throw | Osleidys Menéndez (CUB) | 71.54 m (234 ft 8 in) | 1 Jul 2001 |
| heptathlon | Jackie Joyner-Kersee (USA) | 7,291 pt | 24 Sep 1988 |

*Not an officially ratified event; best performance on record.

# Indoor Track & Field World Records

## men

| EVENT | RECORD HOLDER (NATIONALITY) | PERFORMANCE | DATE |
|---|---|---|---|
| 50 m | Donovan Bailey (CAN) | 5.56 sec | 9 Feb 1996 |
| 60 m | Maurice Greene (USA) | 6.39 sec | 3 Feb 1998 |
| 200 m | Frank Fredericks (NAM) | 19.92 sec | 18 Feb 1996 |
| 400 m | Michael Johnson (USA) | 44.63 sec | 4 Mar 1995 |
| 800 m | Wilson Kipketer (DEN) | 1 min 42.67 sec | 9 Mar 1997 |
| 1,000 m | Wilson Kipketer (DEN) | 2 min 14.96 sec | 20 Feb 2000 |
| 1,500 m | Hicham El Guerrouj (MAR) | 3 min 31.18 sec | 2 Feb 1997 |
| 1 mile | Hicham El Guerrouj (MAR) | 3 min 48.45 sec | 12 Feb 1997 |
| 3,000 m | Daniel Komen (KEN) | 7 min 24.90 sec | 6 Feb 1998 |
| 5,000 m | Haile Gebrselassie (ETH) | 12 min 50.38 sec | 14 Feb 1999 |
| 50-m hurdles | Mark McKoy (CAN) | 6.25 sec | 5 Mar 1986 |
| 60-m hurdles | Colin Jackson (GBR) | 7.30 sec | 6 Mar 1994 |
| 5-km walk | Mikhail Shchennikov (RUS) | 18 min 7.08 sec | 14 Feb 1995 |

## Indoor Track & Field World Records (continued)

### men (continued)

| EVENT | RECORD HOLDER (NATIONALITY) | PERFORMANCE | DATE |
|---|---|---|---|
| 4 × 200-m relay | Great Britain | 1 min 22.11 sec | 3 Mar 1991 |
| 4 × 400-m relay | United States | 3 min 2.83 sec | 7 Mar 1999 |
| 4 × 800-m relay | United States | 7 min 13.94 sec | 6 Feb 2000 |
| high jump | Javier Sotomayor (CUB) | 2.43 m (7 ft 11½ in) | 4 Mar 1989 |
| long jump | Carl Lewis (USA) | 8.79 m (28 ft 10¼ in) | 27 Jan 1984 |
| triple jump | Aliecer Urrutia (CUB) | 17.83 m (58 ft 6 in) | 1 Mar 1997 |
| pole vault | Sergey Bubka (UKR) | 6.15 m (20 ft 2 in) | 21 Feb 1993 |
| shot put | Randy Barnes (USA) | 22.66 m (74 ft 4¼ in) | 20 Jan 1989 |
| heptathlon | Dan O'Brien (USA) | 6,476 pt | 14 Mar 1993 |

### women

| EVENT | RECORD HOLDER (NATIONALITY) | PERFORMANCE | DATE |
|---|---|---|---|
| 50 m | Irina Privalova (RUS) | 5.96 sec | 9 Feb 1995 |
| 60 m | Irina Privalova (RUS) | 6.92 sec | 11 Feb 1993 |
| 200 m | Merlene Ottey (JAM) | 21.87 sec | 13 Feb 1993 |
| 400 m | Jarmila Kratochvilova (TCH) | 49.59 sec | 7 Mar 1982 |
| 800 m | Jolanda Ceplak (SLO) | 1 min 55.82 sec | 3 Mar 2002 |
| 1,000 m | Maria Mutola (MOZ) | 2 min 30.94 sec | 25 Feb 1999 |
| 1,500 m | Regina Jacobs (USA) | 3 min 59.98 sec | 1 Feb 2003 |
| 1 mile | Doina Melinte (ROM) | 4 min 17.14 sec | 9 Feb 1990 |
| 3,000 m | Berhane Adere (ETH) | 8 min 29.15 sec | 3 Feb 2002 |
| 5,000 m | Gabriela Szabo (ROM) | 14 min 47.35 sec | 13 Feb 1999 |
| 50-m hurdles | Cornelia Oschkenat (GDR) | 6.58 sec | 20 Feb 1988 |
| 60-m hurdles | Lyudmila Engquist (URS) | 7.69 sec | 4 Feb 1990 |
| 3-km walk | Gillian O'Sullivan (IRL) | 11 min 35.34 sec | 15 Feb 2003 |
| 4 × 200-m relay | West Germany | 1 min 32.55 sec | 20 Feb 1988 |
| 4 × 400-m relay | Russia | 3 min 24.25 sec | 7 Mar 1999 |
| 4 × 800-m relay | Russia | 8 min 18.71 sec | 4 Feb 1994 |
| high jump | Heike Henkel (GER) | 2.07 m (6 ft 9½ in) | 8 Feb 1992 |
| long jump | Heike Drechsler (GDR) | 7.37 m (24 ft 2¼ in) | 13 Feb 1988 |
| triple jump | Ashia Hansen (GBR) | 15.16 m (49 ft 9 in) | 28 Feb 1998 |
| pole vault | Svetlana Feofanova (RUS) | 4.80 m (15 ft 9 in) | 16 Mar 2003 |
| shot put | Helena Fibingerova (TCH) | 22.50 m (73 ft 10 in) | 19 Feb 1977 |
| pentathlon | Irina Belova (EUN) | 4,991 pt | 15 Feb 1992 |

## World Track & Field Championships—Men

*The next championships are scheduled to be held 22–31 Aug 2003, Paris.*

**100 M**
1983 Carl Lewis (USA)
1987 Carl Lewis (USA)
1991 Carl Lewis (USA)
1993 Linford Christie (GBR)
1995 Donovan Bailey (CAN)
1997 Maurice Greene (USA)
1999 Maurice Greene (USA)
2001 Maurice Greene (USA)

**200 M**
1983 Calvin Smith (USA)
1987 Calvin Smith (USA)
1991 Michael Johnson (USA)
1993 Frank Fredericks (NAM)
1995 Michael Johnson (USA)
1997 Ato Boldon (TRI)
1999 Maurice Greene (USA)
2001 Konstadinos Kederis (GRE)

**400 M**
1983 Bert Cameron (JAM)
1987 Thomas Schoenlebe (GDR)
1991 Antonio Pettigrew (USA)
1993 Michael Johnson (USA)
1995 Michael Johnson (USA)

**400 M (CONTINUED)**
1997 Michael Johnson (USA)
1999 Michael Johnson (USA)
2001 Avard Moncur (BAH)

**800 M**
1983 Willi Wülbeck (FRG)
1987 Billy Konchellah (KEN)
1991 Billy Konchellah (KEN)
1993 Paul Ruto (KEN)
1995 Wilson Kipketer (DEN)
1997 Wilson Kipketer (DEN)
1999 Wilson Kipketer (DEN)
2001 André Bucher (SUI)

**1,500 M**
1983 Steve Cram (GBR)
1987 Abdi Bile (SOM)
1991 Noureddine Morceli (ALG)
1993 Noureddine Morceli (ALG)
1995 Noureddine Morceli (ALG)
1997 Hicham El Guerrouj (MAR)
1999 Hicham El Guerrouj (MAR)
2001 Hicham El Guerrouj (MAR)

**5,000 M**
1983 Eamonn Coghlan (IRL)
1987 Said Aouita (MAR)

**5,000 M (CONTINUED)**
1991 Yobes Ondieki (KEN)
1993 Ismael Kirui (KEN)
1995 Ismael Kirui (KEN)
1997 Daniel Komen (KEN)
1999 Salah Hissou (MAR)
2001 Richard Limo (KEN)

**10,000 M**
1983 Alberto Cova (ITA)
1987 Paul Kipkoech (KEN)
1991 Moses Tanui (KEN)
1993 Haile Gebrselassie (ETH)
1995 Haile Gebrselassie (ETH)
1997 Haile Gebrselassie (ETH)
1999 Haile Gebrselassie (ETH)
2001 Charles Kamathi (KEN)

**STEEPLECHASE**
1983 Patriz Ilg (FRG)
1987 Francesco Panetta (ITA)
1991 Moses Kiptanui (KEN)
1993 Moses Kiptanui (KEN)
1995 Moses Kiptanui (KEN)
1997 Wilson Boit Kipketer (KEN)
1999 Christopher Koskei (KEN)
2001 Reuben Kosgei (KEN)

# World Track & Field Championships—Men (continued)

## 110-M HURDLES
1983 Greg Foster (USA)
1987 Greg Foster (USA)
1991 Greg Foster (USA)
1993 Colin Jackson (GBR)
1995 Allen Johnson (USA)
1997 Allen Johnson (USA)
1999 Colin Jackson (GBR)
2001 Allen Johnson (USA)

## 400-M HURDLES
1983 Edwin Moses (USA)
1987 Edwin Moses (USA)
1991 Samuel Matete (ZAM)
1993 Kevin Young (USA)
1995 Derrick Adkins (USA)
1997 Stéphane Diagana (FRA)
1999 Fabrizio Mori (ITA)
2001 Felix Sánchez (DOM)

## MARATHON
1983 Robert de Castella (AUS)
1987 Douglas Wakiihuri (KEN)
1991 Hiromi Taniguchi (JPN)
1993 Mark Plaatjes (USA)
1995 Martín Fiz (ESP)
1997 Abel Antón (ESP)
1999 Abel Antón (ESP)
2001 Gezahegne Abera (ETH)

## 20-KM WALK
1983 Ernesto Canto (MEX)
1987 Maurizio Damilano (ITA)
1991 Maurizio Damilano (ITA)
1993 Valentí Massana (ESP)
1995 Michele Didoni (ITA)
1997 Daniel García (MEX)
1999 Ilya Markov (RUS)
2001 Roman Rasskazov (RUS)

## 50-KM WALK
1983 Ronald Weigel (GDR)
1987 Hartwig Gauder (GDR)
1991 Aleksandr Potashov (URS)
1993 Jesús Angel García (ESP)
1995 Valentin Kononen (FIN)
1997 Robert Korzeniowski (POL)
1999 Ivano Brugnetti (ITA)
2001 Robert Korzeniowski (POL)

## 4 X 100-M RELAY
1983 United States
1987 United States
1991 United States

## 4 X 100-M RELAY (CONTINUED)
1993 United States
1995 Canada
1997 Canada
1999 United States
2001 United States

## 4 X 400-M RELAY
1983 USSR
1987 United States
1991 United Kingdom
1993 United States
1995 United States
1997 United States
1999 United States
2001 United States

## HIGH JUMP
1983 Gennady Avdeyenko (URS)
1987 Patrik Sjöberg (SWE)
1991 Charles Austin (USA)
1993 Javier Sotomayor (CUB)
1995 Troy Kemp (BAH)
1997 Javier Sotomayor (CUB)
1999 Vyacheslav Voronin (RUS)
2001 Martin Buss (GER)

## POLE VAULT
1983 Sergey Bubka (URS)
1987 Sergey Bubka (URS)
1991 Sergey Bubka (URS)
1993 Sergey Bubka (UKR)
1995 Sergey Bubka (UKR)
1997 Sergey Bubka (UKR)
1999 Maksim Tarasov (RUS)
2001 Dmitri Markov (AUS)

## LONG JUMP
1983 Carl Lewis (USA)
1987 Carl Lewis (USA)
1991 Mike Powell (USA)
1993 Mike Powell (USA)
1995 Iván Pedroso (CUB)
1997 Iván Pedroso (CUB)
1999 Iván Pedroso (CUB)
2001 Iván Pedroso (CUB)

## TRIPLE JUMP
1983 Zdzislaw Hoffman (POL)
1987 Khristo Markov (BUL)
1991 Kenny Harrison (USA)
1993 Mike Conley (USA)
1995 Jonathan Edwards (GBR)
1997 Yoelbi Quesada (CUB)

## TRIPLE JUMP (CONTINUED)
1999 Charles Michael Friedek (GER)
2001 Jonathan Edwards (GBR)

## SHOT PUT
1983 Edward Sarul (POL)
1987 Werner Günthör (SUI)
1991 Werner Günthör (SUI)
1993 Werner Günthör (SUI)
1995 John Godina (USA)
1997 John Godina (USA)
1999 C.J. Hunter (USA)
2001 John Godina (USA)

## DISCUS THROW
1983 Imrich Bugar (TCH)
1987 Jürgen Schult (GDR)
1991 Lars Riedel (GER)
1993 Lars Riedel (GER)
1995 Lars Riedel (GER)
1997 Lars Riedel (GER)
1999 Anthony Washington (USA)
2001 Lars Riedel (GER)

## HAMMER THROW
1983 Sergey Litvinov (URS)
1987 Sergey Litvinov (URS)
1991 Yury Sedykh (URS)
1993 Andrey Abduvaliyev (TJK)
1995 Andrey Abduvaliyev (TJK)
1997 Heinz Weis (GER)
1999 Karsten Kobs (GER)
2001 Szymon Ziolkowski (POL)

## JAVELIN THROW
1983 Detlef Michel (GDR)
1987 Seppo Räty (FIN)
1991 Kimmo Kinnunen (FIN)
1993 Jan Zelezny (CZE)
1995 Jan Zelezny (CZE)
1997 Marius Corbett (RSA)
1999 Aki Parviainen (FIN)
2001 Jan Zelezny (CZE)

## DECATHLON
1983 Daley Thompson (GBR)
1987 Torsten Voss (GDR)
1991 Dan O'Brien (USA)
1993 Dan O'Brien (USA)
1995 Dan O'Brien (USA)
1997 Tomas Dvorak (CZE)
1999 Tomas Dvorak (CZE)
2001 Tomas Dvorak (CZE)

# World Track & Field Championships—Women

*The next championships are scheduled for 22–31 Aug 2003, Paris.*

## 100 M
1983 Marlies Göhr (GDR)
1987 Silke Gladisch (GDR)
1991 Katrin Krabbe (GER)
1993 Gail Devers (USA)
1995 Gwen Torrence (USA)
1997 Marion Jones (USA)
1999 Marion Jones (USA)
2001 Zhanna Pintusevich (UKR)

## 200 M
1983 Marita Koch (GDR)
1987 Silke Gladisch (GDR)
1991 Katrin Krabbe (GER)
1993 Merlene Ottey (JAM)
1995 Merlene Ottey (JAM)
1997 Zhanna Pintusevich (UKR)
1999 Inger Miller (USA)
2001 Marion Jones (USA)

## 400 M
1983 Jarmila Kratochvilova (TCH)
1987 Olga Bryzgina (URS)
1991 Marie-José Pérec (FRA)
1993 Jearl Miles (USA)
1995 Marie-José Pérec (FRA)
1997 Cathy Freeman (AUS)
1999 Cathy Freeman (AUS)
2001 Amy Mbacke Thiam (SEN)

# World Track & Field Championships—Women (continued)

**800 M**
1983 Jarmila Kratochvilova (TCH)
1987 Sigrun Wodars (GDR)
1991 Liliya Nurutdinova (URS)
1993 Maria Mutola (MOZ)
1995 Ana Quirot (CUB)
1997 Ana Quirot (CUB)
1999 Ludmila Formanova (CZE)
2001 Maria Mutola (MOZ)

**1,500 M**
1983 Mary Decker (USA)
1987 Tatyana Samolenko (URS)
1991 Hassiba Boulmerka (ALG)
1993 Liu Dong (CHN)
1995 Hassiba Boulmerka (ALG)
1997 Carla Sacramento (POR)
1999 Svetlana Masterkova (RUS)
2001 Gabriela Szabo (ROM)

**3,000 M§**
1983 Mary Decker (USA)
1987 Tatyana Samolenko (URS)
1991 Tatyana Dorovskikh (URS)
1993 Qu Yunxia (CHN)
1995 Sonia O'Sullivan (IRL)
1997 Gabriela Szabo (ROM)
1999 Gabriela Szabo (ROM)
2001 Olga Yegorova (RUS)

**10,000 M\***
1987 Ingrid Kristiansen (NOR)
1991 Liz McColgan (GBR)
1993 Wang Junxia (CHN)
1995 Fernanda Ribeiro (POR)
1997 Sally Barsosio (KEN)
1999 Gete Wami (ETH)
2001 Derartu Tulu (ETH)

**100-M HURDLES**
1983 Bettine Jahn (GDR)
1987 Ginka Zagorcheva (BUL)
1991 Ludmila Narozhilenko (URS)
1993 Gail Devers (USA)
1995 Gail Devers (USA)
1997 Ludmila Engquist (SWE)
1999 Gail Devers (USA)
2001 Anjanette Kirkland (USA)

**400-M HURDLES**
1983 Yekaterina Fesenko (URS)
1987 Sabine Busch (GDR)
1991 Tatyana Ledovskaya (URS)
1993 Sally Gunnell (GBR)
1995 Kim Batten (USA)
1997 Nezha Bidouane (MAR)
1999 Daimí Pernía (CUB)
2001 Nezha Bidouane (MAR)

**MARATHON**
1983 Grete Waitz (NOR)
1987 Rosa Mota (POR)
1991 Wanda Panfil (POL)
1993 Asari Junko (JPN)
1995 Maria Machado (POR)
1997 Hiromi Suzuki (JPN)
1999 Jong Song Ok (PRK)
2001 Lidia Simon (ROM)

**10-KM WALK\***
1987 Irina Strakhova (URS)
1991 Alina Ivanova (URS)
1993 Sari Essayeh (FIN)
1995 Irina Stankina (RUS)
1997 Annarita Sidoti (ITA)

**20-KM WALK‡**
1999 Liu Hongyu (CHN)
2001 Olimpiada Ivanova (RUS)

**4 X 100-M RELAY**
1983 East Germany
1987 United States
1991 Jamaica
1993 Russia
1995 United States
1997 United States
1999 Bahamas
2001 United States

**4 X 400-M RELAY**
1983 East Germany
1987 East Germany
1991 USSR
1993 United States
1995 United States
1997 Germany
1999 Russia
2001 Jamaica

**HIGH JUMP**
1983 Tamara Bykova (URS)
1987 Stefka Kostadinova (BUL)
1991 Heike Henkel (GER)
1993 Ioamnet Quintero (CUB)
1995 Stefka Kostadinova (BUL)
1997 Hanne Haugland (NOR)
1999 Inga Babakova (UKR)
2001 Hestrie Cloete (RSA)

**POLE VAULT‡**
1999 Stacy Dragila (USA)
2001 Stacy Dragila (USA)

**LONG JUMP**
1983 Heike Daute (GDR)
1987 Jackie Joyner-Kersee (USA)
1991 Jackie Joyner-Kersee (USA)

**LONG JUMP (CONTINUED)**
1993 Heike Drechsler (GER)
1995 Fiona May (ITA)
1997 Ludmila Galkina (RUS)
1999 Niurka Montalvo (ESP)
2001 Fiona May (ITA)

**TRIPLE JUMP†**
1993 Anna Biryukova (RUS)
1995 Inessa Kravets (UKR)
1997 Sarka Kasparkova (CZE)
1999 Paraskevi Tsiamita (GRE)
2001 Tatyana Lebedeva (RUS)

**SHOT PUT**
1983 Helena Fibingerova (TCH)
1987 Natalya Lisovskaya (URS)
1991 Huang Zhihong (CHN)
1993 Huang Zhihong (CHN)
1995 Astrid Kumbernuss (GER)
1997 Astrid Kumbernuss (GER)
1999 Astrid Kumbernuss (GER)
2001 Yanina Korolchik (BLR)

**DISCUS THROW**
1983 Martina Opitz (GDR)
1987 Martina Hellmann (GDR)
1991 Tsvetanka Khristova (BUL)
1993 Olga Burova (RUS)
1995 Ellina Zvereva (BLR)
1997 Beatrice Faumuina (NZL)
1999 Franka Dietzsch (GER)
2001 Natalya Sadova (RUS)

**HAMMER THROW‡**
1999 Mihaela Melinte (ROM)
2001 Yipsi Moreno (CUB)

**JAVELIN THROW**
1983 Tiina Lillak (FIN)
1987 Fatima Whitbread (GBR)
1991 Xu Demei (CHN)
1993 Trine Hattestad (NOR)
1995 Natalya Shikolenko (BLR)
1997 Trine Hattestad (NOR)
1999 Mirela Tzelili (GRE)
2001 Osleidys Menéndez (CUB)

**HEPTATHLON**
1983 Ramona Neubert (GDR)
1987 Jackie Joyner-Kersee (USA)
1991 Sabine Braun (GER)
1993 Jackie Joyner-Kersee (USA)
1995 Ghada Shouaa (SYR)
1997 Sabine Braun (GER)
1999 Eunice Barber (FRA)
2001 Yelena Prokhorova (RUS)

*Event added in 1987.   †Event added in 1993.   ‡Event added in 1999.   §Became 5,000 m in 1995.*

# IAAF World Cup—Men

## 100 m
| YEAR | WINNER |
| --- | --- |
| 1977 | Steve Williams (USA) |
| 1979 | James Sanford (USA) |
| 1981 | Allan Wells (EUR) |
| 1985 | Ben Johnson (AME) |
| 1989 | Linford Christie (GBR) |
| 1992 | Linford Christie (GBR) |
| 1994 | Linford Christie (GBR) |
| 1998 | Obadele Thompson (AME) |
| 2002 | Uchenna Emedolu (AFR) |

## 200 m
| YEAR | WINNER |
| --- | --- |
| 1977 | Clancy Edwards (USA) |
| 1979 | Silvio Leonard (AME) |
| 1981 | Melvin Lattany (USA) |
| 1985 | Robson Caetano da Silva (AME) |
| 1989 | Robson Caetano da Silva (AME) |
| 1992 | Robson Caetano da Silva (AME) |
| 1994 | John Regis (GBR) |
| 1998 | Frank Fredericks (AFR) |
| 2002 | Francis Obikwelu (EUR) |

## 400 m
| YEAR | WINNER |
| --- | --- |
| 1977 | Alberto Juantorena (AME) |
| 1979 | Kashief Hassan (AFR) |
| 1981 | Cliff Wiley (USA) |
| 1985 | Mike Franks (USA) |
| 1989 | Roberto Hernández (AME) |
| 1992 | Sunday Bada (AFR) |
| 1994 | Antonio Pettigrew (USA) |
| 1998 | Iwan Thomas (GBR) |
| 2002 | Michael Blackwood (AME) |

## 800 m
| YEAR | WINNER |
| --- | --- |
| 1977 | Alberto Juantorena (AME) |
| 1979 | James Maina (AFR) |
| 1981 | Sebastian Coe (EUR) |
| 1985 | Sammy Koskei (AFR) |
| 1989 | Tom McKean (GBR) |
| 1992 | David Sharpe (GBR) |
| 1994 | Mark Everett (USA) |
| 1998 | Nils Schumann (GER) |
| 2002 | Antonio Manuel Reina (ESP) |

## 1,500 m
| YEAR | WINNER |
| --- | --- |
| 1977 | Steve Ovett (EUR) |
| 1979 | Thomas Wessinghage (EUR) |
| 1981 | Steve Ovett (EUR) |
| 1985 | Omer Khalifa (AFR) |
| 1989 | Abdi Bile (AFR) |
| 1992 | Mohammed Suleiman (ASI) |
| 1994 | Noureddine Morceli (AFR) |
| 1998 | Laban Rotich (AFR) |
| 2002 | Bernard Lagat (AFR) |

## 3,000 m
| YEAR | WINNER |
| --- | --- |
| 1998 | Dieter Baumann (GER) |
| 2002 | Craig Mottram (OCE) |

## 5,000 m
| YEAR | WINNER |
| --- | --- |
| 1977 | Miruts Yifter (AFR) |
| 1979 | Miruts Yifter (AFR) |
| 1981 | Eamonn Coghlan (EUR) |
| 1985 | Doug Padilla (USA) |
| 1989 | Said Aouita (AFR) |
| 1992 | Fita Bayesa (AFR) |
| 1994 | Brahim Lahlafi (AFR) |
| 1998 | Daniel Komen (AFR) |
| 2002 | Alberto García (ESP) |

## 10,000 m
| YEAR | WINNER |
| --- | --- |
| 1977 | Miruts Yifter (AFR) |
| 1979 | Miruts Yifter (AFR) |
| 1981 | Werner Schildhauer (GDR) |
| 1985 | Wodajo Bulti (AFR) |
| 1989 | Salvatore Antibo (EUR) |
| 1992 | Addis Abebe (AFR) |
| 1994 | Khalid Skah (AFR) |

## Steeplechase
| YEAR | WINNER |
| --- | --- |
| 1977 | Michael Karst (FRG) |
| 1979 | Henry Rono (AFR) |
| 1981 | Boguslaw Maminski (EUR) |
| 1985 | Julius Kariuki (AFR) |
| 1989 | Julius Kariuki (AFR) |
| 1992 | Philip Barkutwo (AFR) |
| 1994 | Moses Kiptanui (AFR) |
| 1998 | Damian Kallabis (GER) |
| 2002 | Wilson Boit Kipketer (AFR) |

## 110-m hurdles
| YEAR | WINNER |
| --- | --- |
| 1977 | Thomas Munkelt (GDR) |
| 1979 | Reynaldo Nehemiah (USA) |
| 1981 | Greg Foster (USA) |
| 1985 | Tony Campbell (USA) |
| 1989 | Roger Kingdom (USA) |
| 1992 | Colin Jackson (GBR) |
| 1994 | Tony Jarrett (GBR) |
| 1998 | Falk Balzer (GER) |
| 2002 | Anier García (AME) |

## 400-m hurdles
| YEAR | WINNER |
| --- | --- |
| 1977 | Edwin Moses (USA) |
| 1979 | Edwin Moses (USA) |
| 1981 | Edwin Moses (USA) |
| 1985 | Andre Phillips (USA) |
| 1989 | David Patrick (USA) |
| 1992 | Samuel Matete (AFR) |
| 1994 | Samuel Matete (AFR) |
| 1998 | Samuel Matete (AFR) |
| 2002 | James Carter (USA) |

## 4 x 100-m relays
| YEAR | WINNER |
| --- | --- |
| 1977 | United States |
| 1979 | Americas |
| 1981 | Europe |
| 1985 | United States |
| 1989 | United States |
| 1992 | United States |
| 1994 | Great Britain |
| 1998 | Great Britain |
| 2002 | United States |

## 4 x 400-m relays
| YEAR | WINNER |
| --- | --- |
| 1977 | West Germany |
| 1979 | United States |
| 1981 | United States |
| 1985 | United States |
| 1989 | Americas |
| 1992 | Africa |
| 1994 | Great Britain |
| 1998 | United States |
| 2002 | Americas |

## Triple jump
| YEAR | WINNER |
| --- | --- |
| 1977 | João de Oliveira (AME) |
| 1979 | João de Oliveira (AME) |
| 1981 | João de Oliveira (AME) |
| 1985 | Willie Banks (USA) |
| 1989 | Mike Conley (USA) |
| 1992 | Jonathan Edwards (GBR) |
| 1994 | Yoelbi Quesada (AME) |
| 1998 | Charles Friedek (GER) |
| 2002 | Jonathan Edwards (GBR) |

## High jump
| YEAR | WINNER |
| --- | --- |
| 1977 | Rolf Beilschmidt (GDR) |
| 1979 | Franklin Jacobs (USA) |
| 1981 | Tyke Peacock (USA) |
| 1985 | Patrik Sjöberg (EUR) |
| 1989 | Patrik Sjöberg (EUR) |
| 1992 | Yury Sergeyenko (UNT*) |
| 1994 | Javier Sotomayor (AME) |
| 1998 | Charles Austin (USA) |
| 2002 | Yaroslav Rybakov (EUR) |

## Pole vault
| YEAR | WINNER |
| --- | --- |
| 1977 | Mike Tully (USA) |
| 1979 | Mike Tully (USA) |
| 1981 | Konstantin Volkov (URS) |
| 1985 | Sergey Bubka (URS) |
| 1989 | Philippe Collet (EUR) |
| 1992 | Igor Potapovich (UNT*) |
| 1994 | Okkert Brits (AFR) |
| 1998 | Maksim Tarasov (EUR) |
| 2002 | Okkert Brits (AFR) |

## Long jump
| YEAR | WINNER |
| --- | --- |
| 1977 | Arnie Robinson (USA) |
| 1979 | Larry Myricks (USA) |
| 1981 | Carl Lewis (USA) |
| 1985 | Mike Conley (USA) |
| 1989 | Larry Myricks (USA) |
| 1992 | Iván Pedroso (AME) |
| 1994 | Fred Salle (GBR) |
| 1998 | Iván Pedroso (AME) |
| 2002 | Savanté Stringfellow (USA) |

## Shot put
| YEAR | WINNER |
| --- | --- |
| 1977 | Udo Beyer (GDR) |
| 1979 | Udo Beyer (GDR) |
| 1981 | Udo Beyer (GDR) |
| 1985 | Ulf Timmermann (GDR) |
| 1989 | Ulf Timmermann (GDR) |
| 1992 | Mike Stulce (USA) |
| 1994 | C.J. Hunter (USA) |
| 1998 | John Godina (USA) |
| 2002 | Adam Nelson (USA) |

## Discus throw
| YEAR | WINNER |
| --- | --- |
| 1977 | Wolfgang Schmidt (GDR) |
| 1979 | Wolfgang Schmidt (GDR) |
| 1981 | Armin Lemme (GDR) |
| 1985 | Gennady Kolnootchenko (URS) |

## IAAF World Cup—Men (continued)

| YEAR | WINNER |
|---|---|
| **Discus throw (continued)** | |
| 1989 | Jürgen Schult (GDR) |
| 1992 | Anthony Washington (USA) |
| 1994 | Vladimir Dubrovshchik (EUR) |
| 1998 | Virgilijus Alekna (EUR) |
| 2002 | Róbert Fazekas (EUR) |
| **Javelin throw** | |
| 1977 | Michael Wessing (FRG) |

| YEAR | WINNER |
|---|---|
| **Javelin throw (continued)** | |
| 1979 | Wolfgang Hanisch (FRG) |
| 1981 | Dainis Kula (URS) |
| 1985 | Uwe Hohn (GDR) |
| 1989 | Steve Backley (GBR) |
| 1992 | Jan Zelezny (EUR) |
| 1994 | Steve Backley (GBR) |
| 1998 | Steve Backley (GBR) |
| 2002 | Sergey Makarov (EUR) |

| YEAR | WINNER |
|---|---|
| **Team** | |
| 1977 | East Germany |
| 1979 | United States |
| 1981 | Europe |
| 1985 | United States |
| 1989 | United States |
| 1992 | Africa |
| 1994 | Africa |
| 1998 | Africa |
| 2002 | Africa |

*Unified Team, consisting of athletes from the Commonwealth of Independent States plus Georgia.*

## IAAF World Cup—Women

| YEAR | WINNER |
|---|---|
| **100 m** | |
| 1977 | Marlies Oelsner (GDR) |
| 1979 | Evelyn Ashford (USA) |
| 1981 | Evelyn Ashford (USA) |
| 1985 | Marlies Göhr (GDR) |
| 1989 | Sheila Echols (USA) |
| 1992 | Natalya Voronova (UNT*) |
| 1994 | Irina Privalova (EUR) |
| 1998 | Marion Jones (USA) |
| 2002 | Marion Jones (USA) |
| **200 m** | |
| 1977 | Irina Szewinska (EUR) |
| 1979 | Evelyn Ashford (USA) |
| 1981 | Evelyn Ashford (USA) |
| 1985 | Marita Koch (GDR) |
| 1989 | Silke Möller (GDR) |
| 1992 | Marie-José Pérec (EUR) |
| 1994 | Merlene Ottey (AME) |
| 1998 | Marion Jones (USA) |
| 2002 | Debbie Ferguson (AME) |
| **400 m** | |
| 1977 | Irina Szewinska (EUR) |
| 1979 | Marita Koch (GDR) |
| 1981 | Jarmila Kratochvilova (EUR) |
| 1985 | Marita Koch (GDR) |
| 1989 | Ana Quirot (AME) |
| 1992 | Jearl Miles (USA) |
| 1994 | Irina Privalova (EUR) |
| 1998 | Falilat Ogunkoya (AFR) |
| 2002 | Ana Guevara (AME) |
| **800 m** | |
| 1977 | Totka Petrova (EUR) |
| 1979 | Nikolina Shtereva (EUR) |
| 1981 | Lyudmila Veselkova (URS) |
| 1985 | Christine Wachtel (GDR) |
| 1989 | Ana Quirot (AME) |
| 1992 | Maria Mutola (AFR) |
| 1994 | Maria Mutola (AFR) |
| 1998 | Maria Mutola (AFR) |
| 2002 | Maria Mutola (AFR) |
| **1,500 m** | |
| 1977 | Tatyana Kazankina (URS) |
| 1979 | Christiane Wartenburg (GDR) |
| 1981 | Tamara Sorokina (URS) |

| YEAR | WINNER |
|---|---|
| **1,500 m** | |
| 1985 | Hildegard Körner (GDR) |
| 1989 | Paula Ivan (EUR) |
| 1992 | Yekaterina Podkopayeva (UNT*) |
| 1994 | Hassiba Boulmerka (AFR) |
| 1998 | Svetlana Masterkova (RUS) |
| 2002 | Süreyya Ayhan (EUR) |
| **3,000 m** | |
| 1977 | Grete Waitz (EUR) |
| 1979 | Svetlana Ulmasova (URS) |
| 1981 | Angelika Zauber (GDR) |
| 1985 | Ulrike Bruns (GDR) |
| 1989 | Yvonne Murray (EUR) |
| 1992 | Derartu Tulu (AFR) |
| 1994 | Yvonne Murray (GBR) |
| 1998 | Gabriela Szabo (EUR) |
| 2002 | Berhane Adere (AFR) |
| **5,000 m** | |
| 1998 | Sonia O'Sullivan (EUR) |
| 2002 | Olga Yegorova (RUS) |
| **10,000 m** | |
| 1985 | Aurora Cunha (EUR) |
| 1989 | Kathrin Ullrich (GDR) |
| 1992 | Derartu Tulu (AFR) |
| 1994 | Elana Meyer (AFR) |
| **100-m hurdles** | |
| 1977 | Grazyna Rabsztyn (EUR) |
| 1979 | Grazyna Rabsztyn (EUR) |
| 1981 | Tatyana Anisimova (URS) |
| 1985 | Cornelia Oschkenat (GDR) |
| 1989 | Cornelia Oschkenat (GDR) |
| 1992 | Aliuska López (AME) |
| 1994 | Aliuska López (AME) |
| 1998 | Glory Alozie (AFR) |
| 2002 | Gail Devers (USA) |
| **400-m hurdles** | |
| 1979 | Bärbel Klepp (GDR) |
| 1981 | Ellen Neumann (GDR) |
| 1985 | Sabine Busch (GDR) |
| 1989 | Sandra Farmer-Patrick (USA) |
| 1992 | Sandra Farmer-Patrick (USA) |

| YEAR | WINNER |
|---|---|
| **400-m hurdles** | |
| 1994 | Sally Gunnell (GBR) |
| 1998 | Nezha Bidouane (AFR) |
| 2002 | Yuliya Pechonkina (RUS) |
| **4 x 100-m relays** | |
| 1977 | Europe Select |
| 1979 | Europe Select |
| 1981 | East Germany |
| 1985 | East Germany |
| 1989 | East Germany |
| 1992 | Asia |
| 1994 | Africa |
| 1998 | United States |
| 2002 | Americas |
| **4 x 400-m relays** | |
| 1977 | East Germany |
| 1979 | East Germany |
| 1981 | East Germany |
| 1985 | East Germany |
| 1989 | Americas |
| 1992 | Americas |
| 1994 | Great Britain |
| 1998 | Germany |
| 2002 | Americas |
| **Triple jump** | |
| 1994 | Anna Biryukova (EUR) |
| 1998 | Olga Vasdeki (EUR) |
| 2002 | Françoise Mbango Etone (AFR ) |
| **High jump** | |
| 1977 | Rosemarie Ackermann (GDR) |
| 1979 | Debbie Brill (AME) |
| 1981 | Ulrike Meyfarth (EUR) |
| 1985 | Stefka Kostadinova (URS) |
| 1989 | Silvia Costa (AME) |
| 1992 | Ioamnet Quintero (AME) |
| 1994 | Britta Bilac (EUR) |
| 1998 | Monica Iagar-Dinescu (EUR) |
| 2002 | Hestrie Cloete (AFR) |
| **Long jump** | |
| 1977 | Lyn Jacenko (OCE) |
| 1979 | Anita Stukane (URS) |

## IAAF World Cup—Women (continued)

| YEAR | WINNER |
|------|--------|
| **Long jump (continued)** | |
| 1981 | Sigrid Ulbricht (GDR) |
| 1985 | Heike Daute Drechsler (GDR) |
| 1989 | Galina Chistyakova (URS) |
| 1992 | Heike Drechsler (GER) |
| 1994 | Inessa Kravets (EUR) |
| 1998 | Heike Drechsler (GER) |
| 2002 | Tatyana Kotova (RUS) |
| **Shot put** | |
| 1977 | Helena Fibingerova (EUR) |
| 1979 | Ilona Slupianek (GDR) |
| 1981 | Ilona Slupianek (GDR) |
| 1985 | Natalya Lisovskaya (URS) |
| 1989 | Zhihong Huang (ASI) |
| 1992 | Belsis Laza (AME) |
| 1994 | Zhihong Huang (ASI) |
| 1998 | Vita Pavlysh (EUR) |
| 2002 | Irina Korzhanenko (RUS) |

| YEAR | WINNER |
|------|--------|
| **Discus throw** | |
| 1977 | Faina Melnik (URS) |
| 1979 | Evelin Jahl (GDR) |
| 1981 | Evelin Jahl (GDR) |
| 1985 | Martina Optiz (GDR) |
| 1989 | Ilke Wyludda (GDR) |
| 1992 | Maritza Marten (AME) |
| 1994 | Ilke Wyludda (EUR) |
| 1998 | Franka Dietzsch (GER) |
| 2002 | Beatrice Faumuina (OCE) |
| **Javelin throw** | |
| 1977 | Ruth Fuchs (GDR) |
| 1979 | Ruth Fuchs (GDR) |
| 1981 | Antoaneta Todorova (EUR) |
| 1985 | Olga Gavrilova (URS) |
| 1989 | Petra Felke (GDR) |
| 1992 | Tessa Sanderson (GBR) |
| 1994 | Trine Hattestad (EUR) |
| 1998 | Joanna Stone (OCE) |
| 2002 | Osleidys Menéndez (AME) |

| YEAR | WINNER |
|------|--------|
| **Team** | |
| 1977 | Europe Select |
| 1979 | East Germany |
| 1981 | East Germany |
| 1985 | East Germany |
| 1989 | East Germany |
| 1992 | Unified Team* |
| 1994 | Europe |
| 1998 | United States |
| 2002 | Russia |

*Unified Team, consisting of athletes from the Commonwealth of Independent States plus Georgia.

## World Cross Country Championships

Men's competition held since 1903, women's since 1967. Table shows results from the past 20 years.

### men (12,000 meters)

| YEAR | INDIVIDUAL (NATIONALITY) | TEAM |
|------|--------------------------|------|
| 1984 | Carlos Lopes (POR) | Ethiopia |
| 1985 | Carlos Lopes (POR) | Ethiopia |
| 1986 | John Ngugi (KEN) | Kenya |
| 1987 | John Ngugi (KEN) | Kenya |
| 1988 | John Ngugi (KEN) | Kenya |
| 1989 | John Ngugi (KEN) | Kenya |
| 1990 | Khalid Skah (MAR) | Kenya |
| 1991 | Khalid Skah (MAR) | Kenya |
| 1992 | John Ngugi (KEN) | Kenya |
| 1993 | William Sigei (KEN) | Kenya |
| 1994 | William Sigei (KEN) | Kenya |
| 1995 | Paul Tergat (KEN) | Kenya |
| 1996 | Paul Tergat (KEN) | Kenya |
| 1997 | Paul Tergat (KEN) | Kenya |
| 1998 | Paul Tergat (KEN) | Kenya |
| 1999 | Paul Tergat (KEN) | Kenya |
| 2000 | Mohammed Mourhit (BEL) | Kenya |
| 2001 | Mohammed Mourhit (BEL) | Kenya |
| 2002 | Kenenisa Bekele (ETH) | Kenya |
| 2003 | Kenenisa Bekele (ETH) | Kenya |

### women (8,000 meters)

| YEAR | INDIVIDUAL (NATIONALITY) | TEAM |
|------|--------------------------|------|
| 1984 | Maricica Puica (ROM) | United States |
| 1985 | Zola Budd (GBR) | United States |
| 1986 | Zola Budd (GBR) | England |
| 1987 | Annette Sargent (FRA) | United States |
| 1988 | Ingrid Kristiansen (NOR) | USSR |
| 1989 | Annette Sargent (FRA) | USSR |
| 1990 | Lynn Jennings (USA) | USSR |
| 1991 | Lynn Jennings (USA) | Kenya |
| 1992 | Lynn Jennings (USA) | Kenya |
| 1993 | Albertina Dias (POR) | Kenya |
| 1994 | Hellen Chepngeno (KEN) | Portugal |
| 1995 | Derartu Tulu (ETH) | Kenya |
| 1996 | Gete Wami (ETH) | Kenya |
| 1997 | Derartu Tulu (ETH) | Ethiopia |
| 1998 | Sonia O'Sullivan (IRE) | Kenya |
| 1999 | Gete Wami (ETH) | Ethiopia |
| 2000 | Derartu Tulu (ETH) | Ethiopia |
| 2001 | Paula Radcliffe (GBR) | Kenya |
| 2002 | Paula Radcliffe (GBR) | Ethiopia |
| 2003 | Werknesh Kidane (ETH) | Ethiopia |

**Did you know?** Eddie Eagen, boxer and bobsledder, was the only athlete to win gold medals at both the Summer and Winter Olympics.

# Volleyball

**W**orld volleyball championships for men were inaugurated in 1949. **Women's** competition began in 1952. These biennial championships are organized by the **Fédération Internationale de Volleyball** (FIVB; founded 1947). Indoor volleyball has been included in the Olympic Games from 1964, and beach volleyball from 1996.

FIVB Web site: <www.fivb.ch>

## World Volleyball Championships

| YEAR | MEN | WOMEN | YEAR | MEN | WOMEN |
|---|---|---|---|---|---|
| 1949 | USSR | | 1980* | USSR | USSR |
| 1952 | USSR | USSR | 1982 | USSR | China |
| 1956 | Czechoslovakia | USSR | 1984* | United States | China |
| 1960 | USSR | USSR | 1986 | United States | China |
| 1962 | USSR | Japan | 1988* | United States | USSR |
| 1964* | USSR | Japan | 1990 | Italy | USSR |
| 1966 | Czechoslovakia | Japan | 1992* | Brazil | Cuba |
| 1967 | not held | Japan | 1994 | Italy | Cuba |
| 1968* | USSR | USSR | 1996* | The Netherlands | Cuba |
| 1970 | East Germany | USSR | 1998 | Italy | Cuba |
| 1972* | Japan | USSR | 2000* | Yugoslavia | Cuba |
| 1974 | Poland | Japan | 2002 | Brazil | Italy |
| 1976* | Poland | Japan | 2004 | to be held in Athens in August | |
| 1978 | USSR | Cuba | | | |

*Olympic champions, considered world champions.*

# Weight Lifting

**W**orld weight lifting is overseen by the **International Weightlifting Federation** (IWF; founded 1905). The first **men's international weight lifting competition** was held in London in 1891; the sport was also included in the first modern Olympic Games in 1896. By the 1930s championship events consisted of the snatch, clean and jerk, and press, which was eliminated in 1972. **Women's world** championships have been held since 1987, and women's competition was added to the Olympics in 2000. In 1998 the IWF established **new weight classes** (eight for men and seven for women) as well as a new world standard for each class in determining world records.

IWF Web site: <www.iwf.net>

## Weight Lifting World Records

*Total weight for snatch and clean & jerk. World standards were reset on 1 Jan 1998 and have not been achieved in some men's events.*

### men

| WEIGHT CLASS | WINNER (NATIONALITY) | PERFORMANCE | DATE |
|---|---|---|---|
| 56 kg (123 lb) | Halil Mutlu (TUR) | 305 kg (671 lb) | 16 Sep 2000 |
| 62 kg (136.5 lb) | world standard | 325 kg (715 lb) | 1 Jan 1998 |
| 69 kg (152 lb) | Galabin Boevski (BUL) | 357.5 kg (786.5 lb) | 24 Nov 1999 |
| 77 kg (169.5 lb) | Plamen Zhelyazkov (BUL) | 377.5 kg (830.5 lb) | 27 Mar 2002 |
| 85 kg (187 lb) | world standard | 395 kg (869 lb) | 1 Jan 1998 |
| 94 kg (207 lb) | world standard | 417.5 kg (918.5 lb) | 1 Jan 1998 |
| 105 kg (231 lb) | world standard | 440 kg (968 lb) | 1 Jan 1998 |
| +105 kg (+231 lb) | Hossein Rezazadeh (IRI) | 472.5 kg (1039.5 lb) | 26 Sep 2000 |

### women

| WEIGHT CLASS | WINNER (NATIONALITY) | PERFORMANCE | DATE |
|---|---|---|---|
| 48kg (105.5 lb) | Wang Mingjuan (CHN) | 207.5 kg (457.5 lb) | 19 Nov 2002 |
| 53 kg (116.5 lb) | Yang Xia (CHN) | 225 kg (496 lb) | 18 Sep 2000 |
| 58 kg (127.5 lb) | Sun Caiyan (CHN) | 237.5 kg (523.5 lb) | 28 Jun 2002 |
| 63 kg (138.5 lb) | Chen Xiaomin (CHN) | 242.5 kg (534.5 lb) | 19 Sep 2000 |
| 69 kg (152 lb) | Liu Chunhong (CHN) | 262.5 kg (578.5 lb) | 3 Oct 2002 |
| 75 kg (165 lb) | Sun Ruiping (CHN) | 270 kg (595 lb) | 7 Oct 2002 |
| +75 kg (+165 lb) | Ding Meiyuan (CHN) | 300 kg (661 lb) | 22 Sep 2000 |

## World Weight Lifting Champions, 2002

*Next competition scheduled to be held 14-24 Nov 2003 in Vancouver BC.*

### men

| WEIGHT CLASS | WINNER (NATIONALITY) | PERFORMANCE |
|---|---|---|
| 56 kg (123 lb) | Wu Meijin (CHN) | 287.5 kg (633.5 lb) |
| 62 kg (136.5 lb) | Im Yong Su (PRK) | 315 kg (694 lb) |
| 69 kg (152 lb) | Zhang Gouzheng (CHN) | 347.5 kg (766 lb) |
| 77 kg (169.5 lb) | Georgi Markov (BUL) | 370 kg (815.5 lb) |
| 85 kg (187 lb) | Zlatan Vasilev (BUL) | 385 kg (848.5 lb) |
| 94 kg (207 lb) | Nizami Pashayev (AZE) | 392.5 kg (865 lb) |
| 105 kg (231 lb) | Denys Gotfrid (UKR) | 420 kg (925.5 lb) |
| +105 kg (+231 lb) | Hossein Rezazadeh (IRI) | 472.5 kg (1041.5 lb) |

### women

| WEIGHT CLASS | WINNER (NATIONALITY) | PERFORMANCE |
|---|---|---|
| 48 kg (105.5 lb) | Wang Mingjuan (CHN) | 207.5 kg (457.5 lb) |
| 53 kg (116.5 lb) | Ri Song Hui (PRK) | 225 kg (496 lb) |
| 58 kg (127.5 lb) | Song Zhijuan (CHN) | 230 kg (507 lb) |
| 63 kg (138.5 lb) | Liu Xia (CHN) | 242.5 kg (534.5 lb) |
| 69 kg (152 lb) | Pawina Thongsuk (THA) | 260 kg (573 lb) |
| 75 kg (165 lb) | Svetlana Khabirova (RUS) | 262.5 kg (578.5 lb) |
| +75 kg (+165 lb) | Agata Wrobel (POL) | 287.5 kg (633.5 lb) |

## Wrestling

**G**reco-Roman wrestling involves holds made only above the waist and forbids wrapping the legs about an opponent when the wrestlers go down. **Freestyle (catch-as-catch-can)**, permits holds above the waist and leg grips and is won by a pin-fall (the opponent must be held down for a measurable length of time). In Japanese **sumo** the object is to propel the opponent out of a ring about 4.6 m (15 ft) in diameter or to force him to touch the ground with any part of his body other than the soles of his feet. The wrestlers wear only loincloths and grip each other by the belt.

The first official amateur wrestling **world championship** was organized by the Fédération Internationale des Lutte Amateur (FILA; founded 1913, reconstituted 1921; and now called the **International Federation of Associated Wrestling Styles**). Although Greco-Roman style wrestling championships were held in 1910 and 1920–22, they were in effect (like the championships of 1923–49 in fact) open European championships, and the first actual world Greco-Roman wrestling championships were not held until 1950. World amateur **freestyle wrestling championships** were first held in 1951.

**Related Web sites:** International Federation of Associated Wrestling Styles <www.fila-wrestling.org>; sumo <www.sumoweb.com>.

## World Wrestling Championships—Greco-Roman Style

*The maximum weight in some classes was revised in 1962, 1969, 1985, 1997, and 2002. The 2003 competition is scheduled to be held 2–5 Oct 2003 in Créteil, France.*

| YEAR | WINNER (NATIONALITY) | YEAR | WINNER (NATIONALITY) | YEAR | WINNER (NATIONALITY) |
|---|---|---|---|---|---|
| **48 kg** | | **48 kg (continued)** | | **55 kg** | |
| 1969 | Gheorghe Berceanu (ROM) | 1983 | Bratan Tsenov (BUL) | 1950 | Bengt Johansson (SWE) |
| 1970 | Gheorghe Berceanu (ROM) | 1984[1] | Vincenzo Maenza (ITA) | 1952[1] | Boris Gurevich (URS) |
| 1971 | Vladimir Zubkov (URS) | 1985 | Magyatdin Allakhverdiyev (URS) | 1953 | Boris Gurevich (URS) |
| 1972[1] | Gheorghe Berceanu (ROM) | 1986 | Magyatdin Allakhverdiyev (URS) | 1955 | Ignazio Fabra (ITA) |
| 1973 | Vladimir Zubkov (URS) | 1987 | Magyatdin Allakhverdiyev (URS) | 1956[1] | Nikolay Solovyov (URS) |
| 1974 | Vladimir Zubkov (URS) | | | 1958 | Boris Gurevich (URS) |
| 1975 | Vladimir Zubkov (URS) | 1988[1] | Vincenzo Maenza (ITA) | 1960[1] | Dumitru Pirvulescu (ROM) |
| 1976[1] | Aleksey Shumakov (URS) | 1989 | Oleg Kucherenko (URS) | 1961 | Armais Sayadov (URS) |
| 1977 | Aleksey Shumakov (URS) | 1990 | Oleg Kucherenko (URS) | 1962 | Sergey Rybalko (URS) |
| 1978 | Constantin Alexandru (ROM) | 1991 | Gooun Duk-Yong (KOR) | 1963 | Borivoje Vukov (YUG) |
| | | 1992[1] | Oleg Kucherenko (UNT)[2] | 1964[1] | Tsutomu Hanahara (JPN) |
| 1979 | Constantin Alexandru (ROM) | 1993 | Wilber Sánchez (CUB) | 1965 | Sergey Rybalko (URS) |
| | | 1994 | Wilber Sánchez (CUB) | 1966 | Angel Keresov (BUL) |
| 1980[1] | Saksylik Ushkempirov (URS) | 1995 | Sim Kwon Ho (KOR) | 1967 | Vladimir Bakulin (URS) |
| | | 1996[1] | Sim Kwon Ho (KOR) | 1968[1] | Petar Kirov (BUL) |
| 1981 | Saksylik Ushkempirov (URS) | 1997 | *discontinued* | 1969 | Feerooz Aluzadeh (IRI) |
| | | | | 1970 | Petar Kirov (BUL) |
| 1982 | Temo Kazarashvili (URS) | | | 1971 | Petar Kirov (BUL) |
| | | | | 1972[1] | Petar Kirov (BUL) |
| | | | | 1973 | Nicu Ginga (ROM) |

## World Wrestling Championships—Greco-Roman Style (continued)

| YEAR | WINNER (NATIONALITY) |
|------|----------------------|
| **55 kg (continued)** | |
| 1974 | Petar Kirov (BUL) |
| 1975 | Vitaly Konstantinov (URS) |
| 1976[1] | Vitaly Konstantinov (URS) |
| 1977 | Nicu Ginga (ROM) |
| 1978 | Vakhtang Blagidze (URS) |
| 1979 | Lajos Racz (HUN) |
| 1980[1] | Vakhtang Blagidze (URS) |
| 1981 | Vakhtang Blagidze (URS) |
| 1982 | Benur Pashayan (URS) |
| 1983 | Benur Pashayan (URS) |
| 1984[1] | Atsuji Miyahara (JPN) |
| 1985 | Jon Ronningen (NOR) |
| 1986 | Sergey Dudayev (URS) |
| 1987 | Pedro Favier Roque (CUB) |
| 1988[1] | Jon Ronningen (NOR) |
| 1989 | Aleksandr Ignatenko (URS) |
| 1990 | Aleksandr Ignatenko (URS) |
| 1991 | Raul Martínez (CUB) |
| 1992[1] | Jon Ronningen (NOR) |
| 1993 | Raul Martínez (CUB) |
| 1994 | Alfred Ter-Mkrtchyan (GER) |
| 1995 | Samvel Danielane (RUS) |
| 1996[1] | Armen Nazaryan (ARM) |
| 1997 | Ercan Yildiz (TUR) |
| 1998 | Sim Kwon Ho (KOR) |
| 1999 | Lazaro Rivas (CUB) |
| 2000[1] | Sim Kwon Ho (KOR) |
| 2001 | Hassan Rangraz (IRI) |
| 2002 | Gaidar Mamedaliev (RUS) |
| **60 kg** | |
| 1950 | Ali Mahmoud Hassan (EGY) |
| 1952[1] | Imre Hodos (HUN) |
| 1953 | Artyom Teryan (URS) |
| 1955 | Vladimir Stashkevich (URS) |
| 1956[1] | Konstantin Vyrupayev (URS) |
| 1958 | Oleg Karavayev (URS) |
| 1960[1] | Oleg Karavayev (URS) |
| 1961 | Oleg Karavayev (URS) |
| 1962 | Masamitsu Ichiguchi (JPN) |
| 1963 | Janos Varga (HUN) |
| 1964[1] | Masamitsu Ichiguchi (JPN) |
| 1965 | Ion Chernya (ROM) |
| 1966 | Fritz Stange (FRG) |
| 1967 | Ion Baciu (ROM) |
| 1968[1] | Janos Varga (HUN) |
| 1969 | Rustam Kazakov (URS) |
| 1970 | Janos Varga (HUN) |
| 1971 | Rustam Kazakov (URS) |
| 1972[1] | Rustam Kazakov (URS) |
| 1973 | Jozef Lipien (POL) |
| 1974 | Farhat Mustafin (URS) |
| 1975 | Farhat Mustafin (URS) |
| 1976[1] | Pertti Olavi Ukkola (FIN) |
| 1977 | Pertti Olavi Ukkola (FIN) |
| 1978 | Shamil Serikov (URS) |
| 1979 | Shamil Serikov (URS) |
| 1980[1] | Shamil Serikov (URS) |

| YEAR | WINNER (NATIONALITY) |
|------|----------------------|
| **60 kg (continued)** | |
| 1981 | Pasquale Passarelli (FRG) |
| 1982 | Piotr Michalik (POL) |
| 1983 | Masaki Ito (JPN) |
| 1984[1] | Pasquale Passarelli (FRG) |
| 1985 | Stoyan Balov (BUL) |
| 1986 | Emil Ivanov (BUL) |
| 1987 | Patrice Mourier (FRA) |
| 1988[1] | Andras Sike (HUN) |
| 1989 | Emil Ivanov (BUL) |
| 1990 | Rifat Yildiz (GER) |
| 1991 | Rifat Yildiz (GER) |
| 1992[1] | An Han-Bong (KOR) |
| 1993 | Agazi Manukyan (ARM) |
| 1994 | Yury Melnichenko (KAZ) |
| 1995 | Dennis Hall (USA) |
| 1996[1] | Yury Melnichenko (KAZ) |
| 1997 | Yury Melnichenko (KAZ) |
| 1998 | Kim In Sub (KOR) |
| 1999 | Kim In Sub (KOR) |
| 2000[1] | Armen Nazaryan (BUL) |
| 2001 | Dilshod Aripov (UZB) |
| 2002 | Armen Nazarian (BUL) |
| **66 kg** | |
| 1950 | Olle Anderberg (SWE) |
| 1952[1] | Yakov Punkin (URS) |
| 1953 | Olle Anderberg (SWE) |
| 1955 | Imre Polyak (HUN) |
| 1956[1] | Rauno Leonhard Mäki-nen (FIN) |
| 1958 | Imre Polyak (HUN) |
| 1960[1] | Muzahir Sille (TUR) |
| 1961 | Hamid Mansour Mustafa (EGY) |
| 1962 | Imre Polyak (HUN) |
| 1963 | Gennady Sapunov (URS) |
| 1964[1] | Imre Polyak (HUN) |
| 1965 | Yury Grigoryev (URS) |
| 1966 | Roman Rurua (URS) |
| 1967 | Roman Rurua (URS) |
| 1968[1] | Roman Rurua (URS) |
| 1969 | Roman Rurua (URS) |
| 1970 | Hideo Fujimoto (JPN) |
| 1971 | Georgi Markov (BUL) |
| 1972[1] | Georgi Markov (BUL) |
| 1973 | Kazimierz Lipien (POL) |
| 1974 | Kazimierz Lipien (POL) |
| 1975 | Nelson Davidyan (URS) |
| 1976[1] | Kazimierz Lipien (POL) |
| 1977 | Laszlo Reczi (HUN) |
| 1978 | Boris Kramarenko (URS) |
| 1979 | Istvan Toth (HUN) |
| 1980[1] | Stylianos Migiakis (GRE) |
| 1981 | Istvan Toth (HUN) |
| 1982 | Ryszard Swierad (POL) |
| 1983 | Hannu Lahtinen (FIN) |
| 1984[1] | Kim Weon-Kee (KOR) |
| 1985 | Zhivko Vangelov Atanasov (BUL) |
| 1986 | Komandar Madshidov (URS) |
| 1987 | Zhivko Vangelov Atanasov (BUL) |
| 1988[1] | Komandar Madshidov (URS) |

| YEAR | WINNER (NATIONALITY) |
|------|----------------------|
| **66 kg (continued)** | |
| 1989 | Komandar Madshidov (URS) |
| 1990 | Mario Olivera (CUB) |
| 1991 | Sergey Martinov (URS) |
| 1992[1] | Akif Mehmet Pirim (TUR) |
| 1993 | Sergey Martinov (RUS) |
| 1994 | Sergey Martinov (RUS) |
| 1995 | Sergey Martinov (RUS) |
| 1996[1] | Wlodzimierz Zawadzki (POL) |
| 1997 | Seref Eroglu (TUR) |
| 1998 | Makhidar Manukyan (KAZ) |
| 1999 | Makhidar Manukyan (KAZ) |
| 2000[1] | Varteres Samurgashev (RUS) |
| 2001 | Vaghinak Galustyan (ARM) |
| 2002 | Jimmy Samuelsson (SWE) |
| **69 kg** | |
| 1950 | Jozsef Gal (HUN) |
| 1952[1] | Shazam Safin (URS) |
| 1953 | Gustav Freij (SWE) |
| 1955 | Grigory Gamarnik (URS) |
| 1956[1] | Kyösti Emil Lehtonen (FIN) |
| 1958 | Riza Dogan (TUR) |
| 1960[1] | Avtandil Koridze (URS) |
| 1961 | Avtandil Koridze (URS) |
| 1962 | Kazim Ayvaz (TUR) |
| 1963 | Stevan Horvat (YUG) |
| 1964[1] | Kazim Ayvaz (TUR) |
| 1965 | Gennady Sapunov (URS) |
| 1966 | Stevan Horvat (YUG) |
| 1967 | Eero Tapio (FIN) |
| 1968[1] | Muneji Mumemura (JPN) |
| 1969 | Simion Popescu (ROM) |
| 1970 | Roman Rurua (URS) |
| 1971 | Sreten Damjanovic (YUG) |
| 1972[1] | Shamil Khisamutdinov (URS) |
| 1973 | Shamil Khisamutdinov (URS) |
| 1974 | Nelson Davidyan (URS) |
| 1975 | Shamil Khisamutdinov (URS) |
| 1976[1] | Suren Nalbandyan (URS) |
| 1977 | Heinz-Helmut Wehling (GDR) |
| 1978 | Stefan Rusu (ROM) |
| 1979 | Andrzej Supron (POL) |
| 1980[1] | Stefan Rusu (ROM) |
| 1981 | Gennady Yermilov (URS) |
| 1982 | Gennady Yermilov (URS) |
| 1983 | Tapio Sipila (FIN) |
| 1984[1] | Vlado Lisjak (YUG) |
| 1985 | Stefan Negrisan (ROM) |
| 1986 | Levon Dzulfalakyan (URS) |
| 1987 | Aslaudin Abayev (URS) |
| 1988[1] | Levon Dzulfalakyan (URS) |
| 1989 | Claudio Passarelli (FRG) |
| 1990 | Islam Doguchiyev (RUS) |
| 1991 | Islam Doguchiyev (RUS) |

# World Wrestling Championships—Greco-Roman Style (continued)

| YEAR | WINNER (NATIONALITY) | YEAR | WINNER (NATIONALITY) | YEAR | WINNER (NATIONALITY) |
|---|---|---|---|---|---|
| **69 kg (continued)** | | **74 kg (continued)** | | **84 kg (continued)** | |
| 1992[1] | Attila Repka (HUN) | 1993 | Nestor Alamanza (CUB) | 1998 | Aleksandr Menshikov |
| 1993 | Islam Doguchiyev (RUS) | 1994 | Mnazakan Iskandaryan | | (RUS) |
| 1994 | Islam Doguchiyev (RUS) | | (RUS) | 1999 | Luiz Enrique Mendez |
| 1995 | Rustam Adzhy (UKR) | 1995 | Yvon Riemer (FRA) | | Lazo (CUB) |
| 1996[1] | Ryszard Wolny (POL) | 1996[1] | Filiberto Ascuy Aguilera | 2000[1] | Hamza Yerlikaya (TUR) |
| 1997 | Son Sang-Pil (KOR) | | (CUB) | 2001 | Muhran Vakhtangadze |
| 1998 | Aleksandr Tretyakov | 1997 | Marko Yli-Hannuksela | | (GEO) |
| | (RUS) | | (FIN) | 2002 | Ara Abrahamian (SWE) |
| 1999 | Son Sang-Pil (KOR) | 1998 | Bakhtiar Bayseytov (KAZ) | | |
| 2000[1] | Filiberto Ascuy Aguilera | 1999 | Nazmi Avluca (TUR) | **90 kg** | |
| | (CUB) | 2000[1] | Murat Kardanov (RUS) | 1950 | Muharrem Candas (TUR) |
| 2001 | Filiberto Ascuy Aguilera | 2001 | Ara Abrahamian (SWE) | 1952[1] | Kelpo Olavi Gröndahl |
| | (CUB) | 2002 | Varteres Samourgashev | | (FIN) |
| 2002 | *discontinued* | | (RUS) | 1953 | August Englas (URS) |
| | | | | 1955 | Valentin Nikolayev (URS) |
| **74 kg** | | **84 kg** | | 1956[1] | Valentin Nikolayev (URS) |
| 1950 | Matti Siimanainen (FIN) | 1950 | Axel Grönberg (SWE) | 1958 | Rostom Abashidze (URS) |
| 1952[1] | Miklos Szilvasi (HUN) | 1952[1] | Axel Grönberg (SWE) | 1960[1] | Tevfik Kis (TUR) |
| 1953 | Georgy Chatvorgian (URS) | 1953 | Givi Kartoziya (URS) | 1961 | Gyorgy Gurics (HUN) |
| 1955 | Vladimir Maneyev (URS) | 1955 | Givi Kartoziya (URS) | 1962 | Rostom Abashidze (URS) |
| 1956[1] | Mithat Bayrak (TUR) | 1956[1] | Givi Kartoziya (URS) | 1963 | Rostom Abashidze (URS) |
| 1958 | Kazim Ayvaz (TUR) | 1958 | Givi Kartoziya (URS) | 1964[1] | Boyan Radev (BUL) |
| 1960[1] | Mithat Bayrak (TUR) | 1960[1] | Dimitar Dobrev (BUL) | 1965 | Valery Anisimov (URS) |
| 1961 | Valeriu Bularca (ROM) | 1961 | Vasily Zenin (URS) | 1966 | Boyan Radev (BUL) |
| 1962 | Anatoly Kolesov (URS) | 1962 | Tevfik Kis (TUR) | 1967 | Nikolay Yakovenko (URS) |
| 1963 | Anatoly Kolesov (URS) | 1963 | Tevfik Kis (TUR) | 1968[1] | Boyan Radev (BUL) |
| 1964[1] | Anatoly Kolesov (URS) | 1964[1] | Branislav Simic (YUG) | 1969 | Aleksandr Yurkevich |
| 1965 | Anatoly Kolesov (URS) | 1965 | Rimantes Bogdanas | | (URS) |
| 1966 | Viktor Igumenov (URS) | | (URS) | 1970 | Valery Rezantsev (URS) |
| 1967 | Viktor Igumenov (URS) | 1966 | Valentin Olenik (URS) | 1971 | Valery Rezantsev (URS) |
| 1968[1] | Rudolph Vesper (GDR) | 1967 | Laszlo Sillai (HUN) | 1972[1] | Valery Rezantsev (URS) |
| 1969 | Viktor Igumenov (URS) | 1968[1] | Lothar Metz (GDR) | 1973 | Valery Rezantsev (URS) |
| 1970 | Viktor Igumenov (URS) | 1969 | Petar Krumov (BUL) | 1974 | Valery Rezantsev (URS) |
| 1971 | Viktor Igumenov (URS) | 1970 | Anatoly Nazarenko (URS) | 1975 | Valery Rezantsev (URS) |
| 1972[1] | Viteslav Macha (TCH) | 1971 | Csaba Hegedus (HUN) | 1976[1] | Valery Rezantsev (URS) |
| 1973 | Ivan Kolev (BUL) | 1972[1] | Csaba Hegedus (HUN) | 1977 | Frank Andersson (SWE) |
| 1974 | Viteslav Macha (TCH) | 1973 | Leonid Liberman (URS) | 1978 | Stoyan Nikolov Ivanov |
| 1975 | Anatoly Bykov (URS) | 1974 | Anatoly Nazarenko (URS) | | (BUL) |
| 1976[1] | Anatoly Bykov (URS) | 1975 | Anatoly Nazarenko (URS) | 1979 | Frank Andersson (SWE) |
| 1977 | Viteslav Macha (TCH) | 1976[1] | Momir Petkovic (YUG) | 1980[1] | Norbert Nottny (HUN) |
| 1978 | Arif Niftulayev (URS) | 1977 | Vladimir Cheboksarov | 1981 | Igor Kanygin (URS) |
| 1979 | Ferenc Kocsis (HUN), | | (URS) | 1982 | Frank Andersson (SWE) |
| | Iyanko Chopov (BUL)[3] | 1978 | Ion Draica (ROM) | 1983 | Igor Kanygin (URS) |
| 1980[1] | Ferenc Kocsis (HUN) | 1979 | Gennady Korban (URS) | 1984[1] | Steven Fraser (USA) |
| 1981 | Aleksandr Kudryavtsev | 1980[1] | Gennady Korban (URS) | 1985 | Michael Houck (USA) |
| | (URS) | 1981 | Gennady Korban (URS) | 1986 | Andrzej Malina (POL) |
| 1982 | Stefan Rusa (ROM) | 1982 | Taymuraz Abkhasava | 1987 | Vladimir Popov (URS) |
| 1983 | Mikhail Mamiashvili | | (URS) | 1988[1] | Atanas Komchev (BUL) |
| | (URS) | 1983 | Taymuraz Abkhasava | 1989 | Maik Bullmann (GDR) |
| 1984[1] | Jouko Johann Salomaki | | (URS) | 1990 | Maik Bullmann (GER) |
| | (FIN) | 1984[1] | Ion Draica (ROM) | 1991 | Maik Bullmann (GER) |
| 1985 | Mikhail Mamiashvili | 1985 | Bogdan Daras (POL) | 1992[1] | Maik Bullmann (GER) |
| | (URS) | 1986 | no award | 1993 | Georgy Koguchavilli (RUS) |
| 1986 | Mikhail Mamiashvili | 1987 | Tibor Komaromi (HUN) | 1994 | Georgy Koguchavilli (RUS) |
| | (URS) | 1988[1] | Mikhail Mamiashvili | 1995 | Hakki Basar (TUR) |
| 1987 | Jouko Johann Salomaki | | (URS) | 1996[1] | Vyatsheslav Oleynyk |
| | (FIN) | 1989 | Tibor Komaromi (HUN) | | (UKR) |
| 1988[1] | Kim Young-Nam (KOR) | 1990 | Peter Farkas (HUN) | 1997 | *discontinued* |
| 1989 | Daulet Turlykhanov (URS) | 1991 | Peter Farkas (HUN) | | |
| 1990 | Mnazakan Iskandaryan | 1992[1] | Peter Farkas (HUN) | **96 kg** | |
| | (RUS) | 1993 | Hamza Yerlikaya (TUR) | 1950 | Bertil Antonsson (SWE) |
| 1991 | Mnazakan Iskandaryan | 1994 | Thomas Zander (GER) | 1952[1] | Johannes Kotkas (URS) |
| | (RUS) | 1995 | Hamza Yerlikaya (TUR) | 1953 | Bertil Antonsson (SWE) |
| 1992[1] | Mnazakan Iskandaryan | 1996[1] | Hamza Yerlikaya (TUR) | 1955 | Aleksandr Mazur (URS) |
| | (UNT)[2] | 1997 | Sergey Tsvir (RUS) | 1956[1] | Anatoly Parfenov (URS) |

# World Wrestling Championships—Greco-Roman Style (continued)

| YEAR | WINNER (NATIONALITY) | YEAR | WINNER (NATIONALITY) | YEAR | WINNER (NATIONALITY) |
|---|---|---|---|---|---|
| **96 kg (continued)** | | **96 kg (continued)** | | **120 kg (continued)** | |
| 1958 | Ivan Bogdan (URS) | 1986 | Tamas Gaspar (HUN) | 1977 | Nikola Dinev (BUL) |
| 1960[1] | Ivan Bogdan (URS) | 1987 | Guram Guedekhaorui | 1978 | Aleksandr Kolchinsky |
| 1961 | Ivan Bogdan (URS) | | (URS) | | (URS) |
| 1962 | Istvan Kozma (HUN) | 1988[1] | Andrzej Wronski (POL) | 1979 | Aleksandr Tomov (BUL) |
| 1963 | Anatoly Roshchin (URS) | 1989 | Gerhard Himmel (FRG) | 1980[1] | Aleksandr Kolchinsky |
| 1964[1] | Istvan Kozma (HUN) | 1990 | Sergey Demyashkevich | | (URS) |
| 1965 | Nikolay Shmakov (URS) | | (URS) | 1981 | Refik Memisevic (YUG) |
| 1966 | Istvan Kozma (HUN) | 1991 | Hector Milian (CUB) | 1982 | Nikola Dinev (BUL) |
| 1967 | Istvan Kozma (HUN) | 1992[1] | Hector Milian (CUB) | 1983 | Yevgeny Artyukhin (URS) |
| 1968[1] | Istvan Kozma (HUN) | 1993 | Mikael Ljungberg (SWE) | 1984[1] | Jeffrey Blatnick (USA) |
| 1969 | Nikolay Yakovenko (URS) | 1994 | Andrzej Wronski (POL) | 1985 | Igor Rostorotsky (URS) |
| 1970 | Per Oskar Svensson | 1995 | Mikael Ljungberg (SWE) | 1986 | Tomas Johansson (SWE) |
| | (SWE) | 1996[1] | Andrzej Wronski (POL) | 1987 | Igor Rostorotsky (URS) |
| 1971 | Per Oskar Svensson | 1997 | Georgy Koguchavilli (RUS) | 1988[1] | Aleksandr Karelin (URS) |
| | (SWE) | 1998 | Georgy Koguchavilli (RUS) | 1989 | Aleksandr Karelin (URS) |
| 1972[1] | Nicolae Martinescu | 1999 | Georgy Koguchavilli (RUS) | 1990 | Aleksandr Karelin (URS) |
| | (ROM) | 2000[1] | Mikael Ljungberg (SWE) | 1991 | Aleksandr Karelin (URS) |
| 1973 | Nikolay Balboshin (URS) | 2001 | Aleksandr Bezruchkin | 1992[1] | Aleksandr Karelin (UNT)[2] |
| 1974 | Nikolay Balboshin (URS) | | (RUS) | 1993 | Aleksandr Karelin (RUS) |
| 1975 | Kamen Losanov (BUL) | 2002 | Mehmet Oezal (TUR) | 1994 | Aleksandr Karelin (RUS) |
| 1976[1] | Nikolay Balboshin (URS) | | | 1995 | Aleksandr Karelin (RUS) |
| 1977 | Nikolay Balboshin (URS) | **120 kg** | | 1996[1] | Aleksandr Karelin (RUS) |
| 1978 | Nikolay Balboshin (URS) | 1969 | Anatoly Roshchin (URS) | 1997 | Aleksandr Karelin (RUS) |
| 1979 | Nikolay Balboshin (URS) | 1970 | Anatoly Roshchin (URS) | 1998 | Aleksandr Karelin (RUS) |
| 1980[1] | Georgi Raykov-Petkov | 1971 | Aleksandar Tomov (BUL) | 1999 | Aleksandr Karelin (RUS) |
| | (BUL) | 1972[1] | Anatoly Roshchin (URS) | 2000[1] | Rulon Gardner (USA) |
| 1981 | Michail Saladze (URS) | 1973 | Aleksandar Tomov (BUL) | 2001 | Rulon Gardner (USA) |
| 1982 | Roman Wroclawski (POL) | 1974 | Aleksandar Tomov (BUL) | 2002 | Dremiel D. Byers (USA) |
| 1983 | Andrey Dimitrov (BUL) | 1975 | Aleksandar Tomov (BUL) | | |
| 1984[1] | Vasile Andrei (ROM) | 1976[1] | Aleksandr Kolchinsky | | |
| 1985 | Andrey Dimitrov (BUL) | | (URS) | | |

[1]*Olympic champions, recognized as world champions (for earlier Olympic champions, see Olympic Games).* [2]*Unified Team, consisting of athletes from the Commonwealth of Independent States plus Georgia.* [3]*Tied.*

# World Wrestling Championships—Freestyle

*The maximum weight in some classes was revised in 1962, 1969, 1985, 1997, and 2002. The 2003 competition is scheduled for 12–14 Sep 2003, New York City.*

| YEAR | WINNER (NATIONALITY) | YEAR | WINNER (NATIONALITY) | YEAR | WINNER (NATIONALITY) |
|---|---|---|---|---|---|
| **48 kg** | | **48 kg (continued)** | | **55 kg (continued)** | |
| 1969 | Ibrahim Javadi (IRI) | 1988[1] | Takashi Kobayashi (JPN) | 1961 | Ali Aliyev (URS) |
| 1970 | Ibrahim Javadi (IRI) | 1989 | Kim Jong-shin (KOR) | 1962 | Ali Aliyev (URS) |
| 1971 | Ibrahim Javadi (IRI) | 1990 | Aldo Martínez (CUB) | 1963 | Cemal Yanilmaz (TUR) |
| 1972[1] | Roman Dmitriyev (URS) | 1991 | Vugar Orudzhev (URS) | 1964[1] | Yoshikatsu Yoshida (JPN) |
| 1973 | Roman Dmitriyev (URS) | 1992[1] | Kim II (PRK) | 1965 | Yoshikatsu Yoshida (JPN) |
| 1974 | Hassan Issaev (Murselov) | 1993 | Alexis Vila (CUB) | 1966 | Chang-Sun Chang (KOR) |
| | (BUL) | 1994 | Alexis Vila (CUB) | 1967 | Shigeo Nakata (JPN) |
| 1975 | Hassan Issaev (BUL) | 1995 | Vugar Orudzhev (RUS) | 1968[1] | Shigeo Nakata (JPN) |
| 1976[1] | Hassan Issaev (BUL) | 1996[1] | Kim II (PRK) | 1969 | Richard Joseph Sanders |
| 1977 | Anatoly Beloglazov (URS) | 1997 | *discontinued* | | (USA) |
| 1978 | Sergey Kornilayev (URS) | | | 1970 | Ali Riza Alan (TUR) |
| 1979 | Sergey Kornilayev (URS) | **55 kg** | | 1971 | Mohammad Ghorbani |
| 1980[1] | Claudio Pollio (ITA) | 1951 | Ali Yucel (TUR) | | (IRI) |
| 1981 | Sergey Kornilayev (URS) | 1952[1] | Hasan Gemici (TUR) | 1972[1] | Kiyomi Kato (JPN) |
| 1982 | Sergey Kornilayev (URS) | 1954 | Huseyin Akbas (TUR) | 1973 | Ibrahim Javadi (IRI) |
| 1983 | Kim Hwan Cher (PRK) | 1956[1] | Mirian Tsalkalamanidze | 1974 | Yuji Takada (JPN) |
| 1984[1] | Robert Weaver (USA) | | (URS) | 1975 | Yuji Takada (JPN) |
| 1985 | Kim Chol Hwan (PRK) | 1957 | Mehmet Kartal (TUR) | 1976[1] | Yuji Takada (JPN) |
| 1986 | Li Yae-sik (PRK) | 1959 | Ali Aliyev (URS) | 1977 | Yuji Takada (JPN) |
| 1987 | Li Yae-sik (PRK) | 1960[1] | Ahmet Bilek (TUR) | 1978 | Anatoly Beloglazov (URS) |

# World Wrestling Championships—Freestyle (continued)

| YEAR | WINNER (NATIONALITY) |
|---|---|
| **55 kg (continued)** | |
| 1979 | Yuji Takada (JPN) |
| 1980[1] | Anatoly Beloglazov (URS) |
| 1981 | Toshio Asakura (JPN) |
| 1982 | Hartmut Reich (GDR) |
| 1983 | Valentin Iordanov (BUL) |
| 1984[1] | Saban Trstena (YUG) |
| 1985 | Valentin Iordanov (BUL) |
| 1986 | Kim Yong-sik (PRK) |
| 1987 | Valentin Iordanov (BUL) |
| 1988[1] | Mitsuru Sato (JPN) |
| 1989 | Valentin Iordanov (BUL) |
| 1990 | Majid Torkan (IRI) |
| 1991 | Larry Zeke Jones (USA) |
| 1992[1] | Li Hak-Son (PRK) |
| 1993 | Valentin Iordanov (BUL) |
| 1994 | Valentin Iordanov (BUL) |
| 1995 | Valentin Iordanov (BUL) |
| 1996[1] | Valentin Iordanov (BUL) |
| 1997 | Wilfredo Garcia Quintana (CUB) |
| 1998 | Samuel Henson (USA) |
| 1999 | Kim Woo Yong (KOR) |
| 2000[1] | Namik Abdullayev (AZE) |
| 2001 | Herman Kontoyev (BLR) |
| 2002 | Rene Montero Rosales (CUB) |
| **60 kg** | |
| 1951 | Nasuh Akar (TUR) |
| 1952[1] | Shohachi Ishii (JPN) |
| 1954 | Mustafa Dagistanli (TUR) |
| 1956[1] | Mustafa Dagistanli (TUR) |
| 1957 | Huseyin Akbas (TUR) |
| 1959 | Huseyin Akbas (TUR) |
| 1960[1] | Terrence McCann (USA) |
| 1961 | Mohamad Ebrahim Saif-pour Saidabadi (IRI) |
| 1962 | Huseyin Akbas (TUR) |
| 1963 | Aydyn Ibragimov (URS) |
| 1964[1] | Yojiro Uetake (JPN) |
| 1965 | Tomiaki Fukuda (JPN) |
| 1966 | Ali Aliyev (URS) |
| 1967 | Ali Aliyev (URS) |
| 1968[1] | Yojiro Uetake (JPN) |
| 1969 | Tadamichi Tanaka (JPN) |
| 1970 | Hideaki Yanagida (JPN) |
| 1971 | Hideaki Yanagida (JPN) |
| 1972[1] | Hideaki Yanagida (JPN) |
| 1973 | Moshen Faravashi (IRI) |
| 1974 | Vladimir Yumin (URS) |
| 1975 | Masao Arai (JPN) |
| 1976[1] | Vladmir Yumin (URS) |
| 1977 | Tadashi Sasaki (JPN) |
| 1978 | Hideaki Tomiyama (JPN) |
| 1979 | Hideaki Tomiyama (JPN) |
| 1980[1] | Sergey Beloglazov (URS) |
| 1981 | Sergey Beloglazov (URS) |
| 1982 | Anatoly Beloglazov (URS) |
| 1983 | Sergey Beloglazov (URS) |
| 1984[1] | Hideaki Tomiyama (JPN) |
| 1985 | Sergey Beloglazov (URS) |
| 1986 | Sergey Beloglazov (URS) |
| 1987 | Sergey Beloglazov (URS) |
| 1988[1] | Sergey Beloglazov (URS) |
| 1989 | Kim Sik-seung (PRK) |
| 1990 | Alejandro Puerto (CUB) |
| 1991 | Sergey Smal (URS) |

| YEAR | WINNER (NATIONALITY) |
|---|---|
| **60 kg (continued)** | |
| 1992[1] | Alejandro Puerto (CUB) |
| 1993 | Terry Brands (USA) |
| 1994 | Alejandro Puerto (CUB) |
| 1995 | Terry Brands (USA) |
| 1996[1] | Kendall Cross (USA) |
| 1997 | Mohammad Talaee (IRI) |
| 1998 | Ali Reza Dabir (IRI) |
| 1999 | Harun Dogan (TUR) |
| 2000[1] | Ali Reza Dabir (IRI) |
| 2001 | Guivi Sissaouri (CAN) |
| 2002 | Aram Markaryan (ARM) |
| **66 kg** | |
| 1951 | Nurettin Zafer (TUR) |
| 1952[1] | Bayram Sit (TUR) |
| 1954 | Shozo Sasahara (JPN) |
| 1956[1] | Shozo Sasahara (JPN) |
| 1957 | Mustafa Dagistanli (TUR) |
| 1959 | Mustafa Dagistanli (TUR) |
| 1960[1] | Mustafa Dagistanli (TUR) |
| 1961 | Vladimir Rubashvili (URS) |
| 1962 | Osamu Watanabe (JPN) |
| 1963 | Osamu Watanabe (JPN) |
| 1964[1] | Osamu Watanabe (JPN) |
| 1965 | Mohamad Ebrahim Saif-pour Saidabadi (IRI) |
| 1966 | Masaaki Kaneko (JPN) |
| 1967 | Masaaki Kaneko (JPN) |
| 1968[1] | Masaaki Kaneko (JPN) |
| 1969 | Takeo Morita (JPN) |
| 1970 | Shamseddin Seyed-Abbassi (IRI) |
| 1971 | Sagalav Abdulbekov (URS) |
| 1972[1] | Sagalav Abdulbekov (URS) |
| 1973 | Sagalav Abdulbekov (URS) |
| 1974 | Zeveg Oydov (MGL) |
| 1975 | Zeveg Oydov (MGL) |
| 1976[1] | Yang Jung-Mo (KOR) |
| 1977 | Vladimir Yumin (URS) |
| 1978 | Vladimir Yumin (URS) |
| 1979 | Vladimir Yumin (URS) |
| 1980[1] | Magomedgasan Abushev (URS) |
| 1981 | Simeon Sterev (BUL) |
| 1982 | Sergey Beloglazov (URS) |
| 1983 | Viktor Alekseyev (URS) |
| 1984[1] | Randy Lewis (USA) |
| 1985 | Viktor Alekseyev (URS) |
| 1986 | Hassar Issayev (URS) |
| 1987 | John Smith (USA) |
| 1988[1] | John Smith (USA) |
| 1989 | John Smith (USA) |
| 1990 | John Smith (USA) |
| 1991 | John Smith (USA) |
| 1992[1] | John Smith (USA) |
| 1993 | Thomas Brands (USA) |
| 1994 | Magomed Azizov (RUS) |
| 1995 | Elbrus Tedeyev (UKR) |
| 1996[1] | Thomas Brands (USA) |
| 1997 | Abbas Hajd Kenari (IRI) |
| 1998 | Serafim Barzakov (BUL) |
| 1999 | Elbrus Tedeyev (UKR) |
| 2000[1] | Murad Umakhanov (RUS) |
| 2001 | Serafim Barzakov (BUL) |
| 2002 | Elbrus Tedeev (UKR) |

| YEAR | WINNER (NATIONALITY) |
|---|---|
| **69 kg** | |
| 1951 | Olle Anderberg (SWE) |
| 1952[1] | Olle Anderberg (SWE) |
| 1954 | Djahanbakte Tovfighe (IRI) |
| 1956[1] | Emam Goudarzi Habibi (IRI) |
| 1957 | Alimbeg Bestayev (URS) |
| 1959 | Vladimir Sinyavsky (URS) |
| 1960[1] | Shelby Wilson (USA) |
| 1961 | Mohammad Sanatkaran (IRI) |
| 1962 | Eniu Valchev-Dimov (BUL) |
| 1963 | Iwao Horiuchi (JPN) |
| 1964[1] | Eniu Valchev-Dimov (BUL) |
| 1965 | Abdullah Movahed Ardabili (IRI) |
| 1966 | Abdullah Movahed Ardabili (IRI) |
| 1967 | Abdullah Movahed Ardabili (IRI) |
| 1968[1] | Abdullah Movahed Ardabili (IRI) |
| 1969 | Abdullah Movahed Ardabili (IRI) |
| 1970 | Abdullah Movahed Ardabili (IRI) |
| 1971 | Danny Mack Gable (USA) |
| 1972[1] | Danny Mack Gable (USA) |
| 1973 | Lloyd Keaser (USA) |
| 1974 | Nasrula Nasrullayev (URS) |
| 1975 | Pavel Pinigin (URS) |
| 1976[1] | Pavel Pinigin (URS) |
| 1977 | Pavel Pinigin (URS) |
| 1978 | Pavel Pinigin (URS) |
| 1979 | Mikhail Kharachura (URS) |
| 1980[1] | Saipulla Absaidov (URS) |
| 1981 | Saipulla Absaidov (URS) |
| 1982 | Mikhail Kharachura (URS) |
| 1983 | Arsen Fadzayev (URS) |
| 1984[1] | You In-Tak (KOR) |
| 1985 | Arsen Fadzayev (URS) |
| 1986 | Arsen Fadzayev (URS) |
| 1987 | Arsen Fadzayev (URS) |
| 1988[1] | Arsen Fadzayev (URS) |
| 1989 | Boris Bovdayev (URS) |
| 1990 | Arsen Fadzayev (URS) |
| 1991 | Arsen Fadzayev (URS) |
| 1992[1] | Arsen Fadzayev (UNT)[2] |
| 1993 | Akbar Fallah (IRI) |
| 1994 | Alexander Leipold (GER) |
| 1995 | Araik Gevorkian (ARM) |
| 1996[1] | Vadim Bogiyev (RUS) |
| 1997 | Araik Gevorkian (ARM) |
| 1998 | Araik Gevorkian (ARM) |
| 1999 | Daniel Igali (CAN) |
| 2000[1] | Daniel Igali (CAN) |
| 2001 | Nikolay Paslari (BUL) |
| 2002 | *discontinued* |
| **74 kg** | |
| 1951 | Celal Atik (TUR) |
| 1952[1] | William Thomas Smith (USA) |
| 1954 | Vakhtang Balavadze (URS) |
| 1956[1] | Mitsuo Ikeda (JPN) |
| 1957 | Vakhtang Balavadze (URS) |

# World Wrestling Championships—Freestyle (continued)

| YEAR | WINNER (NATIONALITY) |
|------|----------------------|
| **74 kg (continued)** | |
| 1959 | Emam Goudarzi Habibi (IRI) |
| 1960[1] | Douglas Blubaugh (USA) |
| 1961 | Emam Goudarzi Habibi (IRI) |
| 1962 | Emam Goudarzi Habibi (IRI) |
| 1963 | Guliko Sagaradze (URS) |
| 1964[1] | Ismail Ogan (TUR) |
| 1965 | Guliko Sagaradze (URS) |
| 1966 | Mahmut Atalay (TUR) |
| 1967 | Daniel Sauton-Robin (FRA) |
| 1968[1] | Mahmut Atalay (TUR) |
| 1969 | Zarbeg Beriashvili (URS) |
| 1970 | Wayne Wells (USA) |
| 1971 | Yury Gusov (URS) |
| 1972[1] | Wayne Turner Wells (USA) |
| 1973 | Mansoor Barzegar (IRI) |
| 1974 | Ruslan Ashuraliyev (URS) |
| 1975 | Ruslan Ashuraliyev (URS) |
| 1976[1] | Jiichiro Date (JPN) |
| 1977 | Stanley Dziedzic (USA) |
| 1978 | Leroy Kemp (USA) |
| 1979 | Leroy Kemp (USA) |
| 1980[1] | Valentin Raychev (BUL) |
| 1981 | Martin Knosp (FRG) |
| 1982 | Leroy Kemp (USA) |
| 1983 | David Schultz (USA) |
| 1984[1] | David Schultz (USA) |
| 1985 | Raul Cascaret Fonseca (CUB) |
| 1986 | Raul Cascaret Fonseca (CUB) |
| 1987 | Adlan Varayev (URS) |
| 1988[1] | Kenneth Monday (USA) |
| 1989 | Kenneth Monday (USA) |
| 1990 | Rahmat Sukra (BUL) |
| 1991 | Amir Reza Khadem Azghadi (IRI) |
| 1992[1] | Park Jang-Soon (KOR) |
| 1993 | Park Jang-Soon (KOR) |
| 1994 | Turan Ceylan (TUR) |
| 1995 | Buvaysa Saytev (RUS) |
| 1996[1] | Buvaysa Saytev (RUS) |
| 1997 | Buvaysa Saytev (RUS) |
| 1998 | Buvaysa Saytev (RUS) |
| 1999 | Adam Saytev (RUS) |
| 2000[1] | Brandon Slay (USA) |
| 2001 | Buvaysa Saytev (RUS) |
| 2002 | Mehdi Hajizadeh Jouibari (IRI) |
| **84 kg** | |
| 1951 | Haydar Zafer (TUR) |
| 1952[1] | David Tsimakurdze (URS) |
| 1954 | Abbas Zandi (IRI) |
| 1956[1] | Nikola Stanchev (BUL) |
| 1957 | Nabi Soruri (IRI) |
| 1959 | Georgy Skhirtladze (URS) |
| 1960[1] | Hassan Gungor (TUR) |
| 1961 | Mansoor Mehdizadeh (IRI) |
| 1962 | Mansoor Mehdizadeh (IRI) |
| 1963 | Prodan Gardzhev (BUL) |
| 1964[1] | Prodan Gardzhev (BUL) |

| YEAR | WINNER (NATIONALITY) |
|------|----------------------|
| **84 kg (continued)** | |
| 1965 | Mansoor Mehdizadeh (IRI) |
| 1966 | Prodan Gardzhev (BUL) |
| 1967 | Boris Gurevich (URS) |
| 1968[1] | Boris Gurevich (URS) |
| 1969 | Fred Fozzard (USA) |
| 1970 | Yury Shakhmuradov (URS) |
| 1971 | Levan Tediashvili (URS) |
| 1972[1] | Levan Tediashvili (URS) |
| 1973 | Vasily Syulzhin (URS) |
| 1974 | Viktor Novozhilov (URS) |
| 1975 | Adolf Seger (FRG) |
| 1976[1] | John Allan Peterson (USA) |
| 1977 | Adolf Seger (FRG) |
| 1978 | Magomed Aratsilov (URS) |
| 1979 | Istvan Kovacs (HUN) |
| 1980[1] | Ismail Abilov (BUL) |
| 1981 | Christopher Campbell (USA) |
| 1982 | Tajmuraz Dzgoyev (URS) |
| 1983 | Tajmuraz Dzgoyev (URS) |
| 1984[1] | Mark Schultz (USA) |
| 1985 | Mark Schultz (USA) |
| 1986 | Vladimir Modozyan (URS) |
| 1987 | Mark Schultz (USA) |
| 1988[1] | Han Myung-Woo (KOR) |
| 1989 | Elmadi Jabrailov (URS) |
| 1990 | Jozef Lohyna (TCH) |
| 1991 | Kevin Jackson (USA) |
| 1992[1] | Kevin Jackson (USA) |
| 1993 | Sabahattin Ozturk (TUR) |
| 1994 | Lukman Jabrailov (MDA) |
| 1995 | Kevin Jackson (USA) |
| 1996[1] | Khadshimurad Magomedov (RUS) |
| 1997 | Leslie Gutches (USA) |
| 1998 | Ali Reza Heydari (IRI) |
| 1999 | Yoel Romero Palacio (CUB) |
| 2000[1] | Adam Saitiev (RUS) |
| 2001 | Khadshimurad Magomedov (RUS) |
| 2002 | Adam Saitiev (RUS) |
| **90 kg** | |
| 1951 | Yasar Dogu (TUR) |
| 1952[1] | Viking Palm (SWE) |
| 1954 | Arsen Englas (URS) |
| 1956[1] | Gholamreza Takhti (IRI) |
| 1957 | Petko Sirakov Atanasov (BUL) |
| 1959 | Gholamreza Takhti (IRI) |
| 1960[1] | Ismet Atli (TUR) |
| 1961 | Gholamreza Takhti (IRI) |
| 1962 | Aleksandr Medved (URS) |
| 1963 | Aleksandr Medved (URS) |
| 1964[1] | Aleksandr Medved (URS) |
| 1965 | Ahmet Ayik (TUR) |
| 1966 | Aleksandr Medved (URS) |
| 1967 | Ahmet Ayik (TUR) |
| 1968[1] | Ahmet Ayik (TUR) |
| 1969 | Boris Gurevich (URS) |
| 1970 | Gennady Strakhov (URS) |
| 1971 | Rusi Petrov (BUL) |

| YEAR | WINNER (NATIONALITY) |
|------|----------------------|
| **90 kg (continued)** | |
| 1972[1] | Benjamin Lee Peterson (USA) |
| 1973 | Levan Tediashvili (URS) |
| 1974 | Levan Tediashvili (URS) |
| 1975 | Levan Tediashvili (URS) |
| 1976[1] | Levan Tediashvili (URS) |
| 1977 | Anatoly Prokopchuk (URS) |
| 1978 | Uwe Neupert (GDR) |
| 1979 | Khasan Ortsuyev (URS) |
| 1980[1] | Sanasar Oganisyan (URS) |
| 1981 | Sanasar Oganisyan (URS) |
| 1982 | Uwe Neupert (GDR) |
| 1983 | Pyotr Naniyev (URS) |
| 1984[1] | Edward Banach (USA) |
| 1985 | William Scherr (USA) |
| 1986 | Macharbek Khadartsev (URS) |
| 1987 | Macharbek Khadartsev (URS) |
| 1988[1] | Macharbek Khadartsev (URS) |
| 1989 | Macharbek Khadartsev (URS) |
| 1990 | Macharbek Khadartsev (URS) |
| 1991 | Macharbek Khadartsev (URS) |
| 1992[1] | Macharbek Khadartsev (UNT)[2] |
| 1993 | Melvin Douglas (USA) |
| 1994 | Rasul Khadem Azghadi (IRI) |
| 1995 | Rasul Khadem Azghadi (IRI) |
| 1996[1] | Rasul Khadem Azghadi (IRI) |
| 1997 | *discontinued* |
| **96 kg** | |
| 1951 | Bertil Antonsson (SWE) |
| 1952[1] | Arsen Mekokishvili (URS) |
| 1954 | Arsen Mekokishvili (URS) |
| 1956[1] | Hamit Kaplan (TUR) |
| 1957 | Hamit Kaplan (TUR) |
| 1959 | Lyutvi Akhmedov (BUL) |
| 1960[1] | Wilfried Dietrich (FRG) |
| 1961 | Wilfried Dietrich (FRG) |
| 1962 | Aleksandr Ivanitsky (URS) |
| 1963 | Aleksandr Ivanitsky (URS) |
| 1964[1] | Aleksandr Ivanitsky (URS) |
| 1965 | Aleksandr Ivanitsky (URS) |
| 1966 | Aleksandr Ivanitsky (URS) |
| 1967 | Aleksandr Medved (URS) |
| 1968[1] | Aleksandr Medved (URS) |
| 1969 | Shota Lomidze (URS) |
| 1970 | Vladimir Gulyutkin (URS) |
| 1971 | Shota Lomidze (URS) |
| 1972[1] | Ivan Yarygin (URS) |
| 1973 | Ivan Yarygin (URS) |
| 1974 | Vladimir Gulyutkin (URS) |
| 1975 | Khorloo Bayanmunkh (MGL) |
| 1976[1] | Ivan Yarygin (URS) |

# World Wrestling Championships—Freestyle (continued)

| YEAR | WINNER (NATIONALITY) |
|---|---|
| **96 kg (continued)** | |
| 1977 | Aslanbek Bisultanov (URS) |
| 1978 | Harald Buettner (GDR) |
| 1979 | Ilya Mate (URS) |
| 1980[1] | Ilya Mate (URS) |
| 1981 | Roland Gehrke (GDR) |
| 1982 | Ilya Mate (URS) |
| 1983 | Aslan Khadartzev (URS) |
| 1984[1] | Louis Banach (USA) |
| 1985 | Leri Khabelov (URS) |
| 1986 | Aslan Khadartzev (URS) |
| 1987 | Leri Khabelov (URS) |
| 1988[1] | Vasile Puscasu (ROM) |
| 1989 | Ahmed Atavov (URS) |
| 1990 | Leri Khabelov (URS) |
| 1991 | Leri Khabelov (URS) |
| 1992[1] | Leri Khabelov (UNT)[2] |
| 1993 | Leri Khabelov (RUS) |
| 1994 | Arawat Sabejew (GER) |
| 1995 | Kurt Angle (USA) |
| 1996[1] | Kurt Angle (USA) |
| 1997 | Kuramagomed Kuramagomedov (RUS) |
| 1998 | Abbas Jadidi (IRI) |
| 1999 | Sagid Murtasaliyev (RUS) |
| 2000[1] | Sagid Murtasaliyev (RUS) |
| 2001 | Georgy Gogchelidze (RUS) |
| 2002 | Eldari Kurtanidze (GEO) |

| YEAR | WINNER (NATIONALITY) |
|---|---|
| **120 kg** | |
| 1969 | Aleksandr Medved (URS) |
| 1970 | Aleksandr Medved (URS) |
| 1971 | Aleksandr Medved (URS) |
| 1972[1] | Aleksandr Medved (URS) |
| 1973 | Soslan Andiyev (URS) |
| 1974 | Simon Ladislav (ROM) |
| 1975 | Soslan Andiyev (URS) |
| 1976[1] | Soslan Andiyev (URS) |
| 1977 | Soslan Andiyev (URS) |
| 1978 | Soslan Andiyev (URS) |
| 1979 | Salman Khasimikov (URS) |
| 1980[1] | Soslan Andiyev (URS) |
| 1981 | Salman Khasimikov (URS) |
| 1982 | Salman Khasimikov (URS) |
| 1983 | Salman Khasimikov (URS) |
| 1984[1] | Bruce Baumgartner (USA) |
| 1985 | David Gobedzhishvili (URS) |
| 1986 | Bruce Baumgartner (USA) |
| 1987 | Aslan Khadartzev (URS) |
| 1988[1] | David Gobedzhishvili (URS) |
| 1989 | Ali Reza Soleimani (IRI) |
| 1990 | David Gobedzhishvili (URS) |

| YEAR | WINNER (NATIONALITY) |
|---|---|
| **120 kg (continued)** | |
| 1991 | Andreas Schröder (GER) |
| 1992[1] | Bruce Baumgartner (USA) |
| 1993 | Bruce Baumgartner (USA) |
| 1994 | Mahmut Demir (TUR) |
| 1995 | Bruce Baumgartner (USA) |
| 1996[1] | Mahmut Demir (TUR) |
| 1997 | Zekeriya Guclu (TUR) |
| 1998 | Alexis Rodríguez Valera (CUB) |
| 1999 | Stephen Neal (USA) |
| 2000[1] | David Musulbes (RUS) |
| 2001 | David Musulbes (RUS) |
| 2002 | David Musulbes (RUS) |

[1]Olympic champions, recognized as world champions (for earlier Olympic champions, see Olympic Games). [2]Unified Team, consisting of athletes from the Commonwealth of Independent States plus Georgia.

# 2002–03 Sumo Tournament Champions

| TOURNAMENT | LOCATION | DATE | WINNER | WINNER'S RECORD |
|---|---|---|---|---|
| Nagoya Basho (Nagoya tournament) | Nagoya | 7–21 Jul 2002 | Chiyotaikai | 14–1 |
| Aki Basho (autumn tournament) | Tokyo | 8–22 Sep 2002 | Asashoryu | 10–5 |
| Kyushu Basho (Kyushu tournament) | Fukuoka | 10–24 Nov 2002 | Asashoryu | 14–1 |
| Hatsu Basho (New Year's tournament) | Tokyo | 12–26 Jan 2003 | Asashoryu | 14–1 |
| Haru Basho (spring tournament) | Osaka | 9–23 Mar 2003 | Chiyotaikai | 12–3 |
| Natsu Basho (summer tournament) | Tokyo | 11–25 May 2003 | Asashoryu | 13–2 |
| Nagoya Basho (Nagoya tournament) | Nagoya | 6–20 Jul 2003 | Kaio | 12–3 |
| Aki Basho (autumn tournament) | Tokyo | 7–21 Sep 2003 | | |
| Kyushu Basho (Kyushu tournament) | Fukuoka | 9–23 Nov 2003 | | |
| Hatsu Basho (New Year's tournament) | Tokyo | 11–25 Jan 2004 | | |
| Haru Basho (spring tournament) | Osaka | 14–28 Mar 2004 | | |
| Natsu Basho (summer tournament) | Tokyo | 9–23 May 2004 | | |

# Index

Page numbers in **boldface** indicate the main references; references in *italics* indicate illustrations.
Photographs are on the plates after page 192; flags and maps of the world are on the plates after page 960.

Nevada Department of Human
   Resources v. Hibbs 759
Neves, Lucas Moreira Cardinal
   132
New Brunswick
   universities of the world 680
New Caledonia 528
   universities of the world 668
New Hampshire 797
   chronology 45
   congressional apportionment
      754
   crime rates 821
   death penalty sentences 827
   electoral votes 756
   energy consumption 841
   governors of US states and
      territories 813
   immigration 776
   income taxes 860
   libraries 832
   poverty level 777
   prison population 826
   signers of the Declaration of
      Independence 704
   state officers and legislatures
      816
   state population 772
   US House 751
   US Senate 747
   universities of the world 675
New Jersey 797
   congressional apportionment
      754
   crime rates 821
   death penalty sentences 827
   electoral votes 756
   energy consumption 841
   governors of US states and
      territories 813
   immigration 776
   income taxes 860
   libraries 832
   poverty level 777
   prison population 826
   signers of the Declaration of
      Independence 704
   state officers and legislatures
      816
   state population 772
   US House 751
   US Senate 747
   universities of the world 675
New Mexico 798
   congressional apportionment
      754
   crime rates 821
   death penalty sentences 827
   electoral votes 756
   energy consumption 841
   governors of US states and
      territories 813
   immigration 776
   income taxes 860
   libraries 832
   poverty level 777
   prison population 826
   state officers and legislatures
      816
   state population 772
   US House 751

US Senate 747
universities of the world 676
new-religionist 685
   religious adherents 682, 684
New York 799
   congressional apportionment
      754
   crime rates 821
   death penalty sentences 827
   electoral votes 756
   energy consumption 841
   governors of US states and
      territories 813
   immigration 776
   income taxes 860
   libraries 833
   poverty level 777
   prison population 826
   signers of the Declaration of
      Independence 704
   state officers and legislatures
      816
   state population 772
   US House 751
   US Senate 747
   universities of the world 676
New York City (NY) 36, 42
New York City Marathon 1065
New York Times 19, 45, 48
New York Times Co. v. Sullivan
   758
New York Times Co. v. United
   States 758
New Zealand 529
   flags of the world Plate 4
   universities of the world 668
Newbery Medal 909
Newbury, Mickey 132
Newfoundland and Labrador
   (Canada)
   universities of the world 680
news, or current events
   chronology 15
   Web sites 230
NFL: see National Football
   League
Nguyen Van Thuan, François
   Xavier Cardinal 132
niacin 309
   nutritional values 312
Nicaragua 531
   flags of the world Plate 4
   universities of the world 668
Nicholas, Fayard 892
Nicholas, Harold Lloyd 892
Nicholson, Max 132
Niger 532
   flags of the world Plate 4
   universities of the world 668
Nigeria 534
   chronology 18, 29, 41, 44, 45
   disasters 54, 56
   flags of the world Plate 4
   photographs Plate 8
   universities of the world 668
NIH: see National Institutes of
   Health
Nijinsky, Vaslav 892
Nikolais, Alwin 893
nine-ball pool 995
9/11: see September 11 attack

Nixon, Richard M. 723
   presidential cabinets 738
   presidential libraries 741
   presidents' wives and children
      728
   Supreme Court appointments
      757
   US presidents 715
   US vice presidents 730
Nobel Prize 141
nonfiction
   bestselling nonfiction 915
   National Book Award 906
   Pulitzer Prize
      general nonfiction 903
      history 899
Nordic Council of Ministers 643
Nordic skiing
   Nordic World Cup 1077
   Olympic Games
      champions 961
      2002 medal winners 975
   world championships 1075,
      1076, 1077
North America
   causes of death 291
   caves 281
   continents 274
   deserts 282
   forests 273
   mountains 279
   religions 683
   rivers 286
   temperature extremes 240
   universities of the world 670
   volcanoes 283
   world maps Plate 13
   worldwide health indicators
      289
   see also individual nations by
      name
North Atlantic Treaty
   Organization, or NATO
   Bush, Iraq, and the World 6
   chronology 29
   international commands 760
   international organizations
      643
North Carolina 799
   Confederate states and
      secession dates 713
   congressional apportionment
      754
   crime rates 821
   death penalty sentences 827
   disasters 53
   electoral votes 756
   energy consumption 841
   governors of US states and
      territories 813
   immigration 776
   income taxes 860
   libraries 833
   poverty level 777
   prison population 826
   signers of the Declaration of
      Independence 704
   state officers and legislatures
      816
   state population 772
   US House 751